CW01543457

Important disclaimer

This publication is sold on the understanding that the information provided within it is for guidance only, and that the publisher is not in business to provide legal or accounting advice or other professional services. Readers entering into transactions on the basis of, or otherwise relying on, such information should seek the services of a competent professional adviser.

Whilst every care has been taken to ensure the accuracy of the contents, the editors and the publishers cannot accept responsibility for any loss occasioned to any person acting or refraining to act as a result of any statement in it.

FL Memo Limited

ISBN: 978-0-9568162-1-4

FL MEMO LIMITED
185 Park Street
Bankside
London SE1 9DY
Telephone 020 7803 4666, Fax 020 7803 4699
Email: flm@flmemo.co.uk
Website: www.flmemo.co.uk

Written by the editors at FL Memo.

British Library Cataloguing in Publication Data.
A catalogue record for this book is available from the British Library.

FL MEMO

Tax

2011-2012

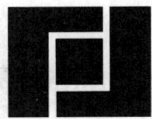

Abbreviations

The following abbreviations are used in *Tax Memo*:

ACT	Advance Corporation Tax
AGM	Annual General Meeting
AIM	Alternative Investment Market
Art	Article
ARTG	Appeals, Reviews and Tribunals Guidance
BERR	Department for Business, Enterprise and Regulatory Reform
BIM	Business Income Manual
C&E	Customs and Excise
CAA 2001	Capital Allowances Act 2001
CG Group	Capital Gains Group
CG	Capital Gains Manual
CGT	Capital Gains Tax
CH	Compliance Handbook
CISR	Construction Industry Scheme Reform Manual
CJEU	Court of Justice of the European Union (formerly ECJ)
CPI	Consumer Prices Index
CTA 2009	Corporation Tax Act 2009
CTA 2010	Corporation Tax Act 2010
DMB	Debt Management and Banking Manual
DOTAS	Disclosure of Tax Avoidance Schemes
DVLA	Driver and Vehicle Licensing Authority
DWP	Department for Work and Pensions
EBT	Employee Benefit Trust
EC	European Community
ECGD	Export Credits Guarantee Department
ECJ	European Court of Justice
EEA	European Economic Area
EIM	Employment Income Manual
EIS	Enterprise Investment Scheme
EMI	Enterprise Management Initiative
EPM	Employment Procedures Manual
ERSM	Employment Related Securities Manual
ESC	Extra Statutory Concession
ESM	Employment Status Manual
EU	European Union
FA	Finance Act
FIFO	First in First out
FII	Franked Investment Income
FSA	Financial Services Authority
FURBS	Funded Unapproved Retirement Benefit Schemes
GAAP	Generally Accepted Accounting Principles
HMRC	H.M. Revenue and Customs
ICTA 1988	Income And Corporation Taxes Act 1988
IHT	Inheritance Tax
IHTA 1984	Inheritance Tax Act 1984
IHTM	Inheritance Tax Manual
INTM	International Manual (HMRC)
IRC	Inland Revenue Commissioners
ITA 2007	Income Tax Act 2007
ITEPA 2003	Income Tax (Earnings and Pensions) Act 2003
ITTOIA 2005	Income Tax (Trading and Other Income) Act 2005
LIFFE	London International Financial Futures and Options Exchange
LIFO	Last in First out
LLM	Lloyd's Manual
LLP	Limited Liability Partnership
Ltd	Limited
MSR	Member state of refund
NIC	National Insurance Contributions
OECD	Organisation for Economic Co-operation and Development
OEIC	Open Ended Investment Company
Para	Paragraph
PAYE	Pay As You Earn
PEM	Partial Exemption Manual
PET	Potentially exempt transfer
PIM	Property Income Manual
PR	Press Release
QCB	Qualifying Corporate Bond
RBC	Remittance Basis Charge
RD	Revenue Decision
RDRM	Residence, Domicile and Remittance Basis Manual
Reg	Regulation
RI	Revenue Interpretation
RPI	Retail Prices Index
RPSM	Registered Pension Schemes Manual
s	Section
SA 1891	Stamp Act 1891
SACM	Self Assessment Claims Manual
Sch	Schedule
SDLT	Stamp Duty Land Tax
SDMA 1891	Stamp Duties Management Act 1891
SDRT	Stamp Duty Reserve Tax

SI	Statutory Instrument
SIPP	Self Invested Personal Pension
SP	Statement of Practice
SRF	(Lloyd's) Special Reserve Fund
SSAS	Small Self Administered (Pension) Scheme
SVM	Shares and Assets Valuation Manual
TCGA 1992	Taxation of Chargeable Gains Act 1992
TIOPA 2010	Taxation (International and Other Provisions) Act 2010
TMA 1970	Taxes Management Act 1970
TNRB	Transferable Nil Rate Band
TSEM	Trusts, Settlements and Estates Manual
UITF	Urgent Issues Task Force
VAT	Value Added Tax
VATA 1994	Value Added Tax Act 1994
VATTOS	VAT Time of Supply Manual
VCM	Venture Capital Schemes Manual
VCT	Venture Capital Trust
VTOGC	VAT Transfer of a Going Concern Manual

Contents

Part 1: Corporation tax

Part 2: Income tax

Part 3: PAYE and NIC

Part 4: Capital gains tax

Part 5: Inheritance tax

Part 6: Trusts, settlements and estates

Part 7: Value added tax

Part 8: Stamp taxes

Part 9: Harmonisation of tax administration

General information

Preface

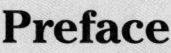

Finance Act 2011 has introduced a number of significant changes across a range of different taxes.

Tax Memo 2011-2012 has been updated to reflect law and practice at the date of Royal Assent to FA 2011, including commentary on:
- changes to capital allowances rates;
- new rules relating to pensions; and
- changes to the VAT Capital Goods Scheme.

Tax Memo 2011-2012 provides up-to-date commentary on the major UK taxes. In addition to the handbook the service includes:
- a full **online service**, with integrated updates;
- **fortnightly emails** detailing developments or points of interest; and
- newsletters providing a full analysis of the **Budget** report and other significant developments.

Tax Memo 2011-2012 is unique in its style, with the full complexities of tax law explained in a language you can understand, reliably written by our experienced in-house tax professionals. The **precise text** is founded on statute, case law and other official material, with legislative references given throughout. The book is also packed with **worked examples** and practical tips to enhance the expert commentary.

Tax Memo 2011-2012 is **easy to navigate**, progressing from section plan through chapter outline to specific paragraph, which means you can easily find the answer to your particular query. Each section is devoted to a specific topic, comprehensively indexed and fully cross-referenced to related issues. The appendix contains many useful tables of numerical and factual data.

FL Memo Ltd
September 2011

PART 1

Corporation tax

Corporation tax
Summary

The numbers cross-refer to paragraphs.

CHAPTER 9 **Special situations**

CHAPTER 10 **Overseas issues**

CHAPTER 11 **Administration**

CHAPTER 1

General principles

OUTLINE ¶¶

A. Scope

1. When is corporation tax due?

A company is within the scope of corporation tax if it carries out a business activity (¶40) which produces income or chargeable gains, and it is either: **10** s 2 CTA 2009
- UK resident; or
- non-UK resident, but carrying on a UK trade through a permanent establishment.

MEMO POINTS This section provides a **broad overview** of the main principles underpinning the corporation tax regime. The detailed concepts are examined in the relevant parts of *Tax Memo*.

2. Definition of a company

A company includes any: **14** s 1121 CTA 2010

a. body corporate. This is a legal term encompassing any body which has legal status conferred upon it by law. This includes not only companies registered under the various Companies Acts (whether limited by share or by guarantee), but also building societies registered under the Building Societies Acts and societies registered under the Industrial and Provident Societies Acts; and

b. unincorporated association. This is a term that is not defined by statute. However, the following quote illustrates the accepted definition.

"Two or more persons bound together for one or more common undertakings, each having mutual duties and obligations, in an organisation which has rules which identify in whom control of it and its funds rest and on what terms, and which can be joined or left at will." *Conservative & Unionist Central Office v Burrell* [1982]

This definition encompasses a variety of organisations, for example, friendly societies and members' clubs. Due to the mutuality principle (¶68), which simply says that a person cannot trade with himself, any excess of members' subscriptions to such organisations over expenses will not be chargeable to corporation tax. Investment income of mutual organisations does, however, remain within the charge to corporation tax.

Unless otherwise stated, the term "company" throughout *Tax Memo* refers to all entities described in this section.

MEMO POINTS A **partnership** is specifically excluded from the definition of a company, although it is possible for a company to be a partner. The special rules applying to partnerships are at ¶2526 onwards.

3. Residence

Why is residence important?

16 A company's residence status determines the scope of its liability to UK tax and the type of tax chargeable.

ss 13 - 18 CTA 2009 The residence of a company is **generally** determined by where the company is incorporated. However, these **rules are modified** for a Societas Europaea (¶2193), as its residence is determined by the location of its registered office (i.e. if the registered office is in the UK, the Societas Europaea is regarded as UK resident).

Incorporated in the UK

18 ss 14, 18 CTA 2009 A company incorporated in the UK will be resident in the UK, unless a tie-breaker clause in a double taxation treaty applies.

MEMO POINTS Prior to the introduction of the current legislation, a small number of companies became **non-UK resident with Treasury consent**. In most cases, these companies retain their non-resident status despite being incorporated in the UK.

Incorporated outside the UK

19 Companies incorporated outside the UK will still be considered resident in the UK if the **central management and control** of the company is carried out in the UK. Even where a company is not resident in the UK it may still be subject to tax in the UK if it has a **permanent establishment** in the UK.

20 The test for **central management and control** (referred to as control throughout) is not set down by statute but is based on case law and HMRC practice. There is no single test and each case is judged upon its facts. The question is where the high level control of the business is exercised, not the day to day control of business activities. It should not be assumed that HMRC will accept the location of board meetings as the place where control is exercised, if it is clear that the directors are acting on instructions from elsewhere which are simply rubber-stamped at the formal board meeting. It is the location where those key decisions are actually made that matters.

MEMO POINTS When determining the central management and control of a company the Court of Appeal highlighted an important issue that must be considered where **third parties are involved** (for example, a parent company, direct or indirect shareholders etc):
- if they only propose, advise and influence decisions, which are nevertheless subsequently taken independently by the Board, then they cannot be said to alter where the central management and control is;
- if, however, they exercise so much influence that they essentially usurp the function of the Board then they will alter where the central management and control is. *Wood v Holden* [2006]

22 Subject to the terms of any double tax treaty, a company will be deemed to have a UK **permanent establishment** if:
- it has a fixed place of business in the UK; or
- an agent acting on behalf of the non-resident company has authority (and habitually exercises the authority) to conduct business on behalf of the non-UK resident company.

MEMO POINTS **Excluded** from the scope of these provisions are activities that are:
- carried on by an independent agent acting in the ordinary course of his business in the UK;
- preparatory or auxiliary (e.g. facilities for storage, display, delivery).

B. Liability to tax

1. What type of tax is due?

The type of tax due on a company's chargeable profits **differs depending upon** whether the company is: 24
– resident in the UK (when it will be liable to corporation tax on its worldwide profits); or s 5 CTA 2009
– resident outside the UK (when it will be liable to either corporation tax, or income tax depending on the nature of the profits, on profits arising in the UK). s 19 CTA 2009
The following table summarises the rules.

Residence Status	Non-UK income and gains	UK income	UK gains
UK resident	Corporation tax	Corporation tax	Corporation tax
Non-UK resident but trading through UK permanent establishment (PE)	Not taxed	UK PE profits[1] are subject to corporation tax Other profits are subject to income tax[2]	Assets used in UK PE are subject to corporation tax Other assets are not taxed
Other non-UK residents	Not taxed	Income tax[2]	Not taxed

Note:
1. Trading profits and any income derived from property used by the UK permanent establishment.
2. At basic rate.

MEMO POINTS Non-resident companies liable to corporation tax are still subject to the **administrative obligations** of UK resident companies (¶2210).

2. Chargeable profits

The company's tax liability for each accounting period (¶30) is based on its chargeable profits (¶80), from whatever source, after relief is given for allowable losses. 25

MEMO POINTS Companies with an **investment business** (¶2118), are subject to special rules for determining the chargeable profits and may, in some circumstances, not be able to take advantage of certain reliefs.

The extent to which **losses** are allowable depends on the source of the loss (¶1260). Although tax is chargeable on the aggregated profits, different calculation rules apply to income from different sources, which can be classed as follows: 26

Income	¶¶
Trading income	¶119, ¶780
Non-trading loan relationship gains	¶870
Income from land and property	¶780
Overseas income	¶2173
Miscellaneous income	¶922
Distributions and income received under deduction of tax	¶940
Chargeable gains	¶1110

27 The company must prepare a computation of its profit chargeable to corporation tax (PCTCT) for each accounting period, and calculate the corporation tax payable (¶1250). The rate at which corporation tax is payable will depend on the profits of the accounting period. The basic format of the tax computation is as follows:

	£
Trading income	x
Loan relationship gains	x
Overseas income	x
Miscellaneous income	x
Income from land and property	x
Income received under deduction of tax	x
Chargeable gains	x
	x
Less: charitable donations relief (¶958)	(x)
Profit chargeable to corporation tax	x
Corporation tax thereon @ x %	x.xx
Less: Income tax suffered at source	(x.xx)
Net corporation tax payable	x.xx

3. Accounting periods

Basis on which tax is charged

30 Tax is charged for an accounting period, although the rates and thresholds are set for **financial years**. A financial year (FY) runs from 1 April through to 31 March and is denoted by the year in which it starts, for example, FY11 runs from 1 April 2011 to 31 March 2012.

In the **normal course of events**, a company's accounting period will be the same as the 12 month period for which it makes up its statutory accounts (the accounting reference date). Accounting periods run consecutively and a new one starts as soon as the previous one ends.

EXAMPLE If a company prepares its statutory accounts regularly for the 12 months to 31 December each year, the accounting period will be the same, i.e. from 1 January to 31 December.

32
ss 9 - 10 CTA 2009

In **general**, an accounting period can never exceed 12 months and will end at the company's accounting reference date. However, this rule is **modified** in the following situations:

a. the first accounting period of a newly incorporated company will begin when the company first becomes chargeable to corporation tax and will end at the earlier of:
– the accounting reference date; or
– 12 months from the start of the accounting period;

b. an accounting period will end (regardless of the accounting reference date) if there is a change in the company's status as a result of one of the following:
– change of residence (¶16); or
– a liquidation/administration;

c. if the company decides to change its accounting reference date (for example, to align the accounting reference date of a newly acquired group company), the accounting period will depend on the length of the new period of account. If it is:
– 12 months or less, the accounting period will still be the same as the period of account; or
– greater than 12 months (i.e. a long period of account), the rules at ¶34 will apply; and

d. when a company ceases to be chargeable to corporation tax, the final accounting period will end on the date of cessation.

EXAMPLE A Ltd was incorporated on 5 March 2008 and opened a bank account on 1 April 2008. It began trading on 28 May 2008 and prepared its first accounts to 30 June 2009. The next accounts were for the 12 months to 30 June 2010 and, after poor trading results, a set of accounts were prepared to 31 March 2011. The company subsequently ceased trading on 4 June 2011 with final accounts being drawn up to 30 June 2011. The accounting periods would be as follows:

Accounts	**Accounting period**	**Reason**
05/03/08 – 30/06/09	01/04/08 – 27/05/08	Coming within the charge to corporation tax
	28/05/08 – 27/05/09	Start at commencement of trade and end after 12 months
	28/05/09 – 30/06/09	Start at end of previous accounting period and end at accounting reference date
01/07/09 – 30/06/10	01/07/09 – 30/06/10	Basic rule
01/07/10 – 31/03/11	01/07/10 – 31/03/11	Basic rule
01/04/11 – 30/06/11	01/04/11 – 04/06/11	End at cessation of trade

Long period of account

Apportionment Where a company prepares its accounts for a period in **excess of 12 months** (a long period of account), this will generally be split into two periods: 34
- one for the first 12 months; and
- the second for the remainder of the period.

A separate corporation tax computation and return will be required for each of the periods. It is necessary to apportion the profits (and losses) between these two periods. The rules for apportioning the various sources of income to each period are dependent upon the nature of the income.

Trading income For most companies, it would be very difficult to establish at what point during an accounting period its trading profits arose. For this reason, the computation of trading profits is initially prepared for the long period of account, and the adjusted profit, before deduction of capital allowances, is then allocated between the periods on a simple time apportionment basis. Apportionment must be made based on the number of days in each period. 36 s 52 CTA 2009

EXAMPLE A Ltd prepares its accounts for the 18 months to 31 December 2010. The trading result for the period, adjusted for tax purposes but before capital allowances, shows a profit of £36,000. The period will be split into two and the trading profit apportioned as follows:

Period 1:		
01/07/09 to 30/06/10	365/549 × 36,000	£23,934
Period 2:		
01/07/10 to 31/12/10	184/549 × 36,000	£12,066

It should be noted that HMRC may seek to use an alternative method of apportionment if it appears that time apportionment would produce an unreasonable result. This would apply, for example, where a company has a relatively constant level of profit but at the start of a long period of account entered into a transaction which produced a significant profit, out of proportion with the rest of the results. HMRC may seek to ensure that the profit from such a transaction is assessed wholly within the accounting period in which it arose.

Other income and deductions The following table summarises how other items are allocated. Where items are time-apportioned, this must be calculated on a daily basis, as for trading income. 38

Type of income/deductions	Basis of allocation
Non-trading loan relationship credits and debits	Not specified by legislation Where possible, allocate to accounting period in which item accrues, otherwise time apportion
Overseas income	Overseas trades: time apportion Other sources: allocate to accounting period in which income arises
Miscellaneous income	Time apportion
Income from land and property	Time apportion
Chargeable gains	Accounting period in which disposal occurs
Payments qualifying for charitable donations relief	Accounting period in which paid
Capital allowances	Calculate separately for each accounting period

CHAPTER 2

What is a business activity?

OUTLINE ¶¶

A. Basis of chargeable profits

Chargeable business profits are based on the profits arising from business activities. Therefore, before calculating the profits arising from a transaction, it is necessary to decide whether the activity in question constitutes a business activity, and only then can the taxable profits be calculated. 40

MEMO POINTS This section deals with the general principles necessary to establish whether a business is being carried on and it **applies equally** to companies and to individuals carrying on a trade.

Businesses have a common feature in that a supplier provides goods or services to a customer in return for payment. Business activities generally fall into one of three **categories**: 50
- trading;
- provision of the services of professionals; or
- undertaking a vocation.

The tax position of all three is identical and therefore the distinction between them is of no practical importance. However, it is important to identify that an activity falls under one of these headings.

MEMO POINTS A company will be deemed to be carrying on a trade as opposed to a profession or vocation. s 34 CTA 2009

B. Professions and vocations

The term **profession** indicates an occupation requiring intellectual skill, for example an accountant, or a controlled manual skill, such as sculpture or surgery. A **vocation** is analogous to a calling (although not limited to religious calling), for example playwrights and professional singers. 52

When considering the professions and vocations of individuals, the distinction between employment and self-employment (¶2986) must also be taken into account.

EXAMPLE An accountant working for an accountancy firm is unlikely to be operating a business whereas a lawyer operating as a sole practitioner will be operating a business.

C. Trades

1. Definition

54 s 1119 CTA 2010 s 989 ITA 2007 A trade is defined by statute as including "any venture in the nature of trade". Inevitably, this, and previous, vague definitions led to a volume of **case law** and, in 1955, a Royal Commission was set up to review the existing case law. The Commission sought to clarify the position and set out its six badges of trade. There are also a number of other factors which must be taken into account (¶66).

MEMO POINTS **In practice**, it will often be obvious that a trade is being carried on (for example, it is clear that a company set up to manufacture and distribute tools is trading). However, not all trading activities are so easily identifiable. When considering a trade, it will be necessary to look not only at the whole structure of the operation, but also at individual transactions undertaken. Some transactions undertaken by a trading operation may not be trading transactions, they may simply be the realisation of investments.

2. Badges of trade

What are these?

56 The badges are simply **indicators** of whether a trade is being carried on and cannot be used as a checklist. No one badge has overriding importance. Instead, the badges should be used as guidance and each case should be considered on its merits. *Marson v Morton* [1986]

Subject matter

58 Some assets can be purchased either as an investment or for trading purposes. It is generally accepted that for an asset to be an **investment** it must either:
- yield income;
- provide the owner with personal enjoyment simply by virtue of his ownership; or
- be a fixed asset (for example plant and machinery).

However, for some assets the only logical conclusion is that they have been purchased with a view to resale and are therefore part of a **trading transaction**. This is illustrated in a number of cases, where vast quantities of a particular asset were purchased and subsequently sold. The sheer volume of the asset in question indicated that they could only have been acquired with a view to resale, and the transaction was therefore of a trading nature.

Period of ownership

60 As a **guideline**, the longer an asset is held, the more likely it is to constitute an investment. Conversely, where assets are purchased and sold within a short space of time this may be indicative of trading activity. However, this test must not be viewed in isolation and, in particular, the circumstances surrounding the sale must be taken into account.

Frequency and number of transactions

61 In general, **single transactions** and those which are repeated after a long interval are indicative of investment activity.

In contrast, where a **large number of similar transactions** occur or where the interval between transactions is short, this may indicate that a trade is being carried on. However, this badge does not imply that a one-off transaction cannot be a trading activity. *Rutledge v CIR* [1929]

EXAMPLE A company purchasing a new car every 2 or 3 years for the use of a member of staff, and selling the previous car at the same time is not likely to be trading in cars. Even if a car was purchased and sold within only a few months, this would not be a strong indication of trading. However, if the company regularly bought and sold cars, the frequency of transactions may indicate a trading activity.

Supplementary work

If an asset is subjected to **work during the period of ownership** to make it more marketable, or the owner takes active steps to create a market for its sale, this may be indicative of a trading activity. However, supplementary work which does not change the asset is generally ignored. 62

EXAMPLE If a company reconditioned cars prior to sale, that would be a strong indication of a trading activity. However, if the cars were simply washed and waxed prior to sale that may not be relevant when considering whether there was a trading activity.

Efforts made to **promote the sale** are also considered. Simply placing an advert in a local paper or taking a painting to an auction house would not be indicative one way or the other. However, setting up an organisation to advertise and sell the asset would indicate trading. Similarly, repackaging the asset, or breaking it down into smaller lots to facilitate sale may indicate trading.

The **absence** of any supplementary work is not indicative of investment activity, but merely neutral.

Circumstances of sale

The circumstances surrounding the sale are important. Assets may be sold as an emergency source of funds obscuring the fact that the intention was to hold the asset for a long time and derive personal pleasure from it. Similarly, an asset acquired with a view to immediate resale may prove unsaleable due to market conditions, such that it is retained for a period far longer than planned. 64

Motive

The taxpayer's intention is **unlikely to be the main factor** in determining whether a transaction is a trading activity. However, if, after considering the other badges of trade, the position is balanced, motive may be the deciding factor. Investments are generally held for personal enjoyment or the income they produce, although a profit may be expected on their eventual sale as they appreciate. In contrast, trading assets are acquired with a view to making money simply through their purchase and resale, without taking any enjoyment or income from the asset during the period of ownership. 65

A distinction must also be drawn between **fiscal and commercial motive**. There must be an element of commercial motive for a transaction to be trading. Where the motive behind a transaction is to gain a tax advantage, this is not a trading transaction (although it may be a supply for VAT purposes. See *VAT Memo* for details).

3. Other factors

What else is indicative of trading?

In **addition** to the badges of trade set out by the Royal Commission, the following factors should also be taken into consideration: 66

– circumstances of acquisition; and
– mutual trading activities.

Circumstances of acquisition

67 The **method of financing** purchases can be a critical factor. A purchase is likely to be seen as a trading activity if its acquisition is funded by, for example:
- short-term borrowing which can only be repaid by sale of the asset; or
- a trade being carried on by the taxpayer.

In contrast, if the taxpayer realises some investments to finance the acquisition, it is likely that he is merely updating his investment portfolio and no trading activity is intended.

It is generally accepted that the sale of an **asset acquired by way of gift or inheritance** is unlikely to be a trading transaction. However, this is not a cast-iron rule. For example, if a car was inherited by an individual who was a car dealer, any disposal of that car through his business would probably be considered a trading transaction (and the asset will be treated as having been appropriated to trading stock prior to the sale (¶92)).

Mutual trading

68
BIM 24001

A fundamental rule is that a person cannot derive a taxable profit from trading with himself. This applies not only to companies, but also to individuals and groups of people. Where the customers are the same group of people as the traders, no taxable profit will derive. However, this principle does not extend to a trader removing goods from a business for their own use (¶2422).

A key feature of mutual trading is the presence of a common fund belonging to the members used entirely for their benefit and with profits capable of being returned to the members. Any profit is therefore simply treated as a surplus of members' contributions and can be returned to the contributors without charge. The mutuality principle applies only to trading profits of the organisation.

It is not essential for the activities to be exclusively mutual. It is possible for a mutual organisation to carry on investment activities or other taxable activities with non-members.

EXAMPLE A surplus arising in respect of members' contributions at a golf club was exempt from tax, but income from non-members, such as green fees and bar receipts, was taxable. *Carlisle and Silloth Golf Club v Smith* [1913]

MEMO POINTS 1. Any **distributions made on the liquidation** of a mutual company to contributors who previously had a trading deduction for their contributions are taxed as trading profits.
2. It should also be noted that a **company trading with its shareholders** does not necessarily satisfy the conditions for the mutuality principle to apply. *Liverpool Corn Trade Association Ltd v Monks* [1926]

4. Specified activities

Property rental

72
s 44 CTA 2009
s 21 ITTOIA 2005

Property rental income is generally **assessable as** property income (¶780, ¶2735). However, certain receipts may be treated as trading income where they are ancillary to an existing trade and arise from temporarily **surplus business accommodation**. This does not apply to property which is exclusively let as a portion of the property must continue to be used for trading purposes. In addition, the rental received must be comparatively small (¶2785).

Commission income

74
SP 4/97

Commission income can be received following the introduction of a customer to a supplier of goods or services.

Where the person making the introduction is **in trade**, and regularly receives such commission income, this will be taxed as trading income. Even where the person arranges for the customer to receive the commission direct (by a reduction in insurance or pension policy premiums for example), it will remain taxable trading income on him if he has an enforceable legal right to the commission which he forgoes in favour of the customer. However, where the person does not receive the commission, and never had any entitlement to it, there will be no taxable receipt.

Where the person making the introduction is **not in trade**, the commission will be taxable as miscellaneous income if it arises under an enforceable contract. Where the commission is passed on to the customer, a deduction will be available if the customer required the commission to be passed on to him as a condition of entering into the transaction. However, where an ordinary retail customer receives a sum for purchasing goods or services, this will not be taxable on him. Employees are taxable on commission received on goods, investments and services sold to third parties during the course of their employment. Where the employee is obliged to pass on the commission to another party, wholly, exclusively and necessarily to perform his employment duties, he will be able to claim a deduction for the amount paid.

Illegal or immoral activities

Illegal or immoral activities may still constitute a taxable trade. This covers items such as prostitution and profits from illegal gaming machines. *IRC v Aken* [1990] 76

Gambling

Gambling does not constitute a trade for the person gambling. Gambling winnings are therefore not taxable, and conversely tax relief is not available for any losses. *Graham v Green* [1925] 78

However, profits from running a gambling establishment (including any winnings of the owner from within the establishment) are assessable as a trade. *Burdge v Pyne* [1968]

CHAPTER 3

Chargeable profits

OUTLINE ¶¶

SECTION 1

Establishing chargeable profits

80 Having established that an activity is a business, the **next step** is to determine the chargeable profits arising. This section deals with the general rules for the adjustment of profits and **applies equally to** companies, sole traders and partnerships.

For rules specific to companies see ¶780 onwards and for individuals ¶2420 onwards.

81 The **starting point** is the accounting profit/loss before tax as shown in the accounts. (Note it is important to review the accounting principles adopted when preparing this figure to ensure that all valuation methods are acceptable and consistent, and that income is recognised at the appropriate time).

The accounting profit/loss figure (¶82) may then need to be **adjusted** for tax purposes so that the following items are excluded:
- non-trading income (¶106);
- capital expenditure (¶108); and
- other expenses that are not deductible for tax purposes (¶120 onwards).

A **pro-forma computation** is included at ¶194 to illustrate the operation of these rules.

SECTION 2

Accounting profit/loss

1. Calculation

82 s 46 CTA 2009 s 25 ITTOIA 2005 The starting point when calculating chargeable profits is the accounting profit/loss, which is generally prepared in accordance with strict accounting principles. The main requirements are compliance with Generally Accepted Accounting Principles (GAAP), International Accounting Standards (IAS), Financial Reporting Standards (FRS) and Statements of Standard Accounting Practice (SSAP), which are continually updated. These principles are also regularly adopted in the preparation of accounts for sole traders and partnerships.

In recent years, the courts have placed considerable emphasis on the accounting treatment of items when considering the taxable profit, and the tax treatment generally tends to follow the accounting treatment unless there is a specific requirement to the contrary.

There are a number of **key areas** which must be considered when adjusting accounts profits for tax purposes in relation to:
- trading stock and work in progress;
- provisions; and
- income recognition.

2. Trading stock and work in progress

Accounts treatment

84 The value of trading stock (and work in progress) held at the end of the accounts period is brought into the profit and loss account as a trading receipt. Similarly, the value of the opening stock and any purchases are deducted as an expense. The valuation of stock can therefore have a significant impact on the trading profit. Adjustments may also be required for stock items on:
- the cessation of a trade; or
- the transfer of assets from fixed assets to stock (and vice versa).

Valuation

The value included in the accounts should represent, for each individual item of stock, the **lower of**: 86
- cost; or
- net realisable value (market value).

In many cases it is impractical, if not impossible, to value each item individually. HMRC will generally accept any method of valuing stock which meets the requirements of an accepted accounting practice.

Provisions can be made against slow moving stock and mark-downs which may also be deductible for tax purposes (¶98).

Appropriations

Where assets are appropriated **from trading stock** for any purpose (or retained by the trader on cessation of trade), the market value of the stock is included as a receipt for tax purposes and the trader will be treated as having acquired the asset at market value. 90 s 158 CTA 2009; ss 172A - 172F ITTOIA 2005

A similar provision applies where fixed assets are appropriated **to trading stock** (for example, a car dealer decides to sell a car originally used as the showroom manager's car). In this case, the asset is deemed to be sold at market value and stock acquired at that same price. However, where this would result in either a chargeable gain or allowable capital loss, the trader may make an election which, in effect, treats the gain (or loss) as part of the trading profit. This is achieved by reducing the market value included in stock by the amount of the gain (or increasing it if the result is a loss). The election must be made: 92 s 161 TCGA 1992
- for corporation tax purposes, within 2 years of the end of the accounting period in which the asset was appropriated; and
- for income tax purposes, within 12 months of 31 January following the end of the tax year in which the chargeable period in which the asset is appropriated ends.

EXAMPLE In Year 1, A purchased assets for his personal use at a cost of £25,000. In Year 3 he decided to sell the assets through his business, when their market value was £45,000.
Ignoring taper relief and indexation the capital gain would be £20,000 (45,000 – 25,000).
If A elects to treat this gain as part of his trading profits, no chargeable gain will accrue. Instead the cost of the assets for the purposes of establishing his trading profits will be reduced to £25,000 (the original cost).

MEMO POINTS Special rules apply to appropriations to/from stock between members of a **group of companies** (¶1625).

Cessation of trade

On the cessation of a trade, any **stock remaining unsold** must be treated as being sold at its market value. Where the stock is sold to a person who is trading or intending to trade, the actual proceeds are used and there is no scope for HMRC to insist on a substitution of market value. Where stock is transferred along with other assets, the valuation of stock should be determined by making a just and reasonable apportionment of the total consideration. 94 s 162 CTA 2009; ss 173 - 181 ITTOIA 2005

MEMO POINTS Where stock is **transferred to a connected party** who is trading or intending to trade in the UK, an arm's length price is substituted for the actual sale proceeds. Where this price is more than the acquisition value of the stock and the price actually received for it, the transferor and transferee may jointly elect, within 2 years, to substitute the greater of the actual price and the acquisition value.

Similar provisions apply to **work in progress** at the date of cessation. However, the taxpayer may elect that work in progress is sold at its cost price, with any proceeds subsequently received in excess of cost being treated as a post-cessation receipt (¶140). The time limit for such an election is as above for appropriations to stock. 96 s 163(2) CTA 2009; ss 182 - 185 ITTOIA 2005

3. Provisions

98 Provisions which have been properly calculated and can be justified are usually deductible. However, provisions which are simply estimates without foundation are not deductible. Provisions are **properly calculated if** they have some reasonable basis and are either:
- specific to a particular item (for example, a provision against a particular debt); or
- as a result of a general formula applied to particular items (for example stock items).

Provided the formulae used are specific to the items concerned, and are adopted consistently, they should be acceptable for tax purposes, whereas a general calculation method applied to all stock (for example a global 5% mark-down) will not.

MEMO POINTS Where provisions are made, the **tax treatment** should be noted such that any future changes in the provisions can be dealt with correctly.

4. Recognition of income

Special rules

100 In accordance with accepted accounting practice, accounts should be prepared on the accruals basis. Special rules apply for:
- income recognised as a result of Application Note G; and
- deposits.

Application Note G

102 s 102, Sch 15 FA 2006 Application Note G (ANG), as interpreted by **UITF 40**, is an accounting standard that applies to all accounting periods ending on or after 22 June 2005. ANG **requires traders** to recognise income once they have established a "right to consideration" from their performance of the contract. In other words, revenue is to be recognised for accounting purposes (and therefore tax purposes) as the contract activity progresses, to reflect the partial performance of the contractual obligations.

This change will result in a one-off adjustment in the accounts, but to ease the transition it is possible to **spread this adjustment income** over a maximum of 6 years as follows:

Year	Charged to tax
1 – 3	Lower of: – 1/3 of the original adjustment income; or – 1/6 of the business profits for that year
4 – 5	Lower of: – the amount remaining untaxed (if any); – 1/3 of the original adjustment income; or – 1/6 of the business profits for that year
6	Any balance outstanding

EXAMPLE A is a sole trader who, in Year 1, changed to comply with ANG for the first time. His profit adjustment to comply with the accounting standard was an increase of £120,000. His adjustment income is calculated as follows:

Year	Profits	Adjustment income	
	£	£	Calculation method
1	180,000	30,000	1/6 of the business profits for that year
2	300,000	40,000	1/3 of the original adjustment income
3	120,000	20,000	1/6 of the business profits for that year
4	96,000	16,000	1/6 of the business profits for that year
5	60,000	10,000	1/6 of the business profits for that year
6	60,000	4,000	Balance

An election can be made to **bring forward the adjustment income** so that more of it is taxed in one year than would otherwise be required. Such an election must be made before the first anniversary of the normal self-assessment filing date for the tax year in question and must show how much adjustment income is to be taxed. In future years, the original adjustment income is treated as being reduced by the amount charged early.

EXAMPLE In Year 1, Mr A has adjustment income of £6,000. He makes an election to charge £1,000 early in Year 1. For subsequent years, when comparing 1/3 of the adjustment income with 1/6 of the business profits, the amount of adjustment income is £5,000.

MEMO POINTS 1. This **spreading is only available for** adjustment income arising in a period of account ending on or after 22 June 2005 (if therefore Application Note G was adopted in a period of account ending before this date any one-off income arising as a consequence cannot be spread).
2. If the **business ceases** before the adjustment income has been fully charged to tax, the usual spreading limit of 1/6 of the business profits or 1/3 of the adjustment income continues to apply in the year of cessation. Thereafter, only the 1/3 alternative applies.
3. The **business profits** are the profits as computed for tax purposes, excluding any capital allowances.
4. For **companies** the following rules also apply:
– if the accounting period ends by reason of the company ceasing to be within the charge to corporation tax or the commencement of winding up proceedings, the whole of the remaining untaxed adjustment income will be taxed; and
– the 1/3 limit is proportionately reduced for short periods of account, but the whole adjustment income can still be spread over 6 years, irrespective of how many accounting periods are included in the 6 year period.
5. For **partnerships**, the following rules also apply:
– on the cessation of a partnership, any untaxed adjustment income is allocated to the partners based on the profit sharing ratios from the date of the change of accounting practice (or if later, an anniversary of this date) to the date of cessation. If the cessation occurs on the date of the change of accounting practice, the allocation is based on the profit sharing ratio for the immediately preceding 12 months.
– if an election is made to bring forward the adjustment income, it must be made by all the partners concerned; and
– the adjustment income is allocated to the partners based on the profit sharing arrangement for the previous 12 months (with the first 12 month period being the period that immediately precedes the date on which the change of accounting practice took place). For corporate partnerships, the adjustment income is allocated according to the profit sharing arrangements of the previous accounting periods.

EXAMPLE

1. A partnership draws up accounts to 30 June. A partner who retires on 30 June 2005 will be taxed on his share of the adjustment income arising for the period ended 30 June 2006, as the allocation is based on the profit sharing arrangement for the previous 12 months (i.e. the period to 30 June 2005).

2. A partnership draws up accounts to 30 June and a new partner joins the partnership on 1 July 2006. He will be assessed in 2008/09 on his share of the adjustment income, allocated to him on the basis of his profit sharing arrangements for the period ended 30 June 2007.

Deposits

The time at which a deposit should be recognised as income depends on the nature of the payment. Where a deposit is a **payment in advance**, for example a deposit on an item of made to order furniture, the amount should be recognised at the date of receipt. 104

Where, however, the deposit is a **form of guarantee**, returnable at a set point in the future, for example a deposit on hired machinery refundable when the machinery is returned, this is not recognised as trading income. However, should the deposit cease to be refundable, it should be recognised as a trading receipt at that time.

MEMO POINTS In certain circumstances, **unclaimed deposits** cannot legally be appropriated by the trader and must remain the property of the customer. In this situation, the deposit will never form part of the trading profits. However, this should not be confused with payments received in error that are appropriated to the profit and loss account following a period of time, even where the sums would be repayable if claimed at a later date. *Pertemps Recrtuiment Partnership Ltd v HMRC* [2011]

SECTION 3

Non-trading income

106 Non-trading income must be excluded from the computation of trading profits and will include, for **example**:
– receipts from mutual trading (¶68);
– profit or loss arising on the disposal of fixed assets or investments;
– income taxable under another category (e.g. investment income, property income);
– income which is specifically exempted from tax (e.g. gambling);
– refunds in respect of a pension scheme surplus. Instead the scheme administrator is required to deduct 35% tax at source; and
– items which represent the reversal of items not originally allowed for tax purposes (e.g. the reversal of a general provision which was previously disallowed). Reversals of specific provisions are taxable as relief would have been given at the time the provision was set up.

s 130 CTA 2009

MEMO POINTS 1. Where the trade consists of dealing in shares and investments, **dividends** (¶940) are treated as trading income. For dividends generally see ¶952.
2. Rental income derived from **surplus business accommodation** (¶2785) may be included in trading profits in certain circumstances.

SECTION 4

Capital expenditure

Why distinguish?

108 s 53 CTA 2009; s 33 ITTOIA 2005

Taxable business profits are computed solely by reference to revenue items. No deduction is allowed for capital expenditure. It is therefore essential to identify whether receipts and expenses are capital or revenue in nature.

MEMO POINTS 1. Capital items generally fall within the **chargeable gains regime**, and capital allowances (¶200) may also be available.
2. **Abortive expenditure** incurred on a capital asset will still constitute capital expenditure. For example, expenditure incurred by a brewer in trying to obtain new licences was capital, even though the attempt was unsuccessful. *Southwell v Savill Bros Ltd* [1901]
3. Items that are taken into account when calculating income cannot also be taken into account when computing a chargeable gain. This ensures that **no receipt can be subject to tax more than once** and, correspondingly, relief can only be given for an item of expenditure once.

What is capital expenditure?

110 A common metaphor used to distinguish between revenue and capital is that capital items are like a tree whereas revenue items are the fruit that it bears. Taking this a stage further, capital items tend to be **singular in nature**, whilst revenue items are **recurrent**.

112 A distinction must also be made between **fixed and circulating capital** of a business. Expenditure on fixed capital will usually be capital expenditure and will consist of assets which are acquired and retained by the business and either:
– produce income without further activity (e.g. investments); or
– are used to generate profits (e.g. machinery).

Expenditure on circulating capital will usually be revenue expenditure consisting of assets which are acquired in the course of a business and either sold or consumed in the production of other articles for sale.

MEMO POINTS It is possible for an asset to be **fixed capital for one business and circulating for another**. For example, a company carrying on a business will have debtors, which are part of circulating capital. If those debts are sold to another business (other than a debt collection firm), then any recovery of those debts will be in respect of fixed capital and therefore a capital receipt. *Crompton v Reynolds and Gibson* [1952]

Although the distinction between capital and revenue will in general be fairly easy to draw there will always be a number of cases where the **distinction is not so clear**. 114

In these situations it is necessary to consider both the nature of the item and the benefit to the business.

When considering the **nature of the item** the fact that it is likely to recur is the key factor in distinguishing revenue expenditure (not whether it actually does recur). For example, a business may incur legal expenses one year for suing for recovery of bad debts. If, in the following year, no such expense is incurred, that would not prevent the initial expense being revenue expenditure as it is of a type that would be likely to recur. 116

Similarly, capital items, although singular in nature, may actually recur.

EXAMPLE A shipbuilding company incurred expenditure on dredging a channel for a deep water berth. This activity may have had to be repeated after a number of years, but that did not change the fact that it was a capital expense. *Ounsworth v Vickers Ltd* [1915]

Where a single lump sum payment is made as an alternative to regular annual payments, it will not change a revenue item into a capital expenditure.

EXAMPLE

1. A firm received a lump sum in return for cancelling an agreement under which commission was received. This was held to be a revenue receipt. *Shove v Dura Manufacturing Co Ltd* [1941]

2. A company decided to commute its regular annual payment to an existing pension fund into a single payment. This was held to be a revenue payment. *Green v Craven's Railway Carriage and Wagon Co Ltd* [1951]

Capital items tend to provide an **enduring benefit to the business** as a whole (in contrast to revenue items which tend to focus on the creation of profit). However it is possible that an item of capital expenditure will prove to have a short life span. Similarly, an item of revenue expenditure may prove to be long lasting. There is no set time limit for an item of expenditure to be considered enduring and each case should be considered on its merits. (For example a 3 year licence to undertake a specific trade was held to be a capital item. *Henriksen v Grafton Hotel Ltd* [1942]) 117

MEMO POINTS An **enduring benefit often entails** the creation of an asset or advantage for the business. (For example, a lump sum payment to establish a pension fund for staff was held to be capital as the payment created an asset for the business. *Atherton v British Insulated and Helsby Cables Ltd* [1926])
Similarly, payments to extract a company from a lease with onerous terms were held to be capital, as renegotiating the lease secured a long-term advantage for the company. *Tucker v Granada Motorway Services Ltd* [1979]

SECTION 5

Trading income and expenses

1. Trading income

Trading income is essentially any revenue receipt from the trading activity (that has not been excluded as non-trading income or capital expenditure), and **includes** the following: 119

- payments received for goods and services which derive from the trading activity; and

– other receipts, including gratuitous receipts deriving from the trading activity (if they are in recognition of past, present or future services).

2. Trading expenses

Purpose of the trade

120 s 54 CTA 2009; s 34 ITTOIA 2005 Revenue expenditure is **only deductible** in computing a chargeable profit/loss if it is incurred wholly and exclusively for the purposes of the trade.

MEMO POINTS **Capital expenditure** is not deductible, although capital allowances (¶200) may be available.

122 Expenditure is incurred for the purposes of the trade if it enables a person to carry on that trade and earn revenue. Therefore, expenditure is only allowable if it relates to the trade being carried on by the taxpayer incurring the expense.

EXAMPLE Mr A, a sole trader, incurs expenditure on stationery for his wife's business.
No deduction would be available for the costs of the stationery in computing the profits of Mr A's trade, as it provides no benefit to his trade. Nor would a deduction be available in calculating his wife's trading profits, as she did not incur the expenditure.

Wholly and exclusively

124 Expenditure will be deductible if it is incurred wholly and exclusively for the purposes of the trade. There can be no duality of purpose. The only reason for incurring the expenditure must be to benefit the trade.

The question of whether expenditure is exclusively for the purposes of the trade is by its very nature subjective and has led to a volume of **case law**, with each case being decided on its own particular facts. What is key for every decision is the taxpayer's intention at the time the expense was incurred.

The following cases are **examples** of the treatment of common expenses:

Expenditure	Deductible?	Reasoning
Overnight accommodation and reasonable cost of meals	y	Provided they are incurred on a business trip that necessarily involves this expense
Donations and subscriptions	y	If incurred for the purposes of the trade and no other reason
Uniforms and protective clothing	y	Necessary for the work in question
Clothes to meet a specific dress code	n	People must wear some sort of clothing regardless of the specific requirements of certain professions
Meals eaten away from the place of business	n	Everyone must eat to live

126 s 34 ITTOIA 2005 Strictly, where there is any **ancillary benefit**, there can be no deduction of the whole expense. However, where part of the expense can be identified as relating wholly to the trade, a deduction will be allowed for the trade element.

EXAMPLE If Mr A incurs costs in going abroad for a week which comprised both holiday and business, none of the expenditure would be deductible.
If whilst on holiday abroad, he was required to cancel his return flight and book an extra night's accommodation to allow a business meeting to take place, the cost relating to the extension of the trip would be a deductible expense.

Where the ancillary benefit is **purely incidental** to the trade purpose, expenditure may be deductible. This was examined in a case where a self-employed stockbroker fell foul of Stock Exchange requirements and was suspended. To preserve his business, he incurred legal costs in appealing against the suspension. It was decided that the restoration of his personal reputation was merely incidental to the preservation of the business and therefore did not prevent the legal expenses from being deductible. *McKnight v Sheppard* [1999]

SECTION 6

Specific income and expense items

1. Income items

Common items

The following paragraphs detail the treatment of a number of certain income items. 128

Type of income	¶¶
Compensation payments	¶129
Exclusivity agreements	¶134
Leased assets (other than land)[1]	¶136
Revenue receipts on cessation of trade	¶140
Reverse premiums	¶141

Note:
1. For details on income from land for companies and individuals, see ¶780 and ¶2735 respectively.

MEMO POINTS For details of the treatment of certain **other income items** that apply only to companies, see ¶780 onwards.

Compensation payments

When considering the status of compensation payments, the **most important factors** are the underlying asset and the reason why payment was made. Compensation is often expressed as being in lieu of profits. Although this is not the only factor to consider, it is generally a good indication that the item is a trading receipt. 129 BIM 40101

However, a number of **other factors** must also be considered, which are best illustrated by reference to decided cases which primarily focus on assets and contracts. 130

Compensation in respect of **fixed assets** usually arises where the asset is out of use for a time. In this case, it is the length of time which is covered by the compensation which is important. 131

The rationale behind this is that **temporary disuse** of the asset affects profits for the period of disuse, whereas **permanent disuse** has a more fundamental impact on the business as a whole.

EXAMPLE A payment made in respect of an asset which was temporarily unavailable was held to be revenue. *Burmah Steamship Co Ltd v CIR* [1931]
In contrast, compensation paid to a company to permanently cease working on an asset was capital. *Glenboig Union Fireclay Ltd v CIR* [1921]

A distinction has been drawn between **contracts** which are fundamental to the overall structure of the business and those which are ordinary commercial contracts undertaken in the course of a business. 132

EXAMPLE Compensation received by a toy seller following the termination of an agency agreement with a specific manufacturer was a revenue receipt as similar agreements with other manufacturers continued. *Elson v Johnston (James G) Ltd* [1965]
This contrasts with the case of a car dealership which had chief distributor rights for a certain manufacturer in a specified area and was precluded from selling any other make of vehicle. When the contract was re-written, including revisions to renewal clauses and changing the specified area, compensation was received. As the contract was fundamental to the trade, the receipt was held to be capital. *Sabine v Lookers Ltd* [1958]

133 Compensation from **utility companies** (for example, for interruption of supply) is **generally** treated as a trading receipt. This applies regardless of the fact that compensation may exceed any profits lost due to the disruption.

However, by **exception**, compensation received for damage or destruction to the trader's property is treated as a capital receipt.

Exclusivity agreements

134 BIM 35550 - 35560

The **general rule** is that payments are treated as trading receipts spread over the life of the agreement (in accordance with accepted accounting practice). The only **exception** is where the agreement specifically designates the payment for a capital purpose, and the recipient uses it accordingly.

MEMO POINTS The position of payments received under an exclusivity agreement is an area covered by HMRC practice rather than case law.

Leased assets

136 ss 870 - 879 CTA 2010

Non-long funding leases In general, income accruing **to the lessor** from leased assets (other than land) will be taxed either as income of a trade, or as miscellaneous income (if the lessor's main trade is not leasing).

However if the lessee subsequently leases out the asset concerned the receipts received **by the lessee** will be taxable as miscellaneous income. The amount so taxable is the lower of:
– the capital sum received; or
– the amount on which the trader has received tax relief (by way of a trading deduction, management expense etc).

EXAMPLE Mr A, a trader, leases an asset from B Ltd (a leasing company) for 23 years at a rent of £4,000 a year for 3 years and £1 a year thereafter. After 3 years, Mr A assigns his lease to C Ltd (a financial dealing company entitled to write off, over the remaining 20 years, the price it pays for the assignment) for £5,000. The amount assessable on Mr A is £5,000 being the lower of:
– £5,000 (capital receipt); or
– £12,000 (£4,000 annual rental paid by Mr A over 3 years).

MEMO POINTS 1. Allowable lease **deductions** by the lessee are restricted to a commercial rent if the lessee previously owned the asset concerned.

Sch 25 FA 2009

2. Where a **rent factoring agreement** (¶2787) is entered into in connection with plant and machinery, the capital sum so received will be taxed as rental income of the trade, unless the agreement represents a structured finance arrangement (¶4064), in which case the structured finance arrangements apply.

138 ss 360 - 370, 890 CTA 2010; ss 148A, 148B, 148F, 148H, 809ZA ITTOIA 2005; Sch 8 paras 18 - 26 FA 2006

Long funding leases A long funding lease can be loosely **defined as** a lease of over five years in duration of plant and machinery. See ¶483 for the full definition.

The tax treatment of any **income** received from long funding leases differs depending upon whether the lease is a long funding finance lease or long funding operating lease as follows:

Type of lease	Lessor	Lessee
Long funding finance lease	Taxed on amount of rental earnings as recognised in the trader's accounts [1,2,3]	Any termination payment received from the lessor is not taxable income, but is still brought into account in the capital allowances pool in the usual manner
Long funding operating lease	A complicated formula [4] is prescribed to determine whether the lessor has made a profit over the term of the lease. If he has, the profit is treated as taxable income (if a loss is made it is an allowable loss)	

Note:
1. Where the lease is accounted for as a loan, the interest is to be treated as if it were rental earnings.
2. This also includes any profit or loss on the lease that accrues to the trader and falls to be recognised under GAAP but would not otherwise be taxed.
3. For leases granted on or after 13 December 2007 capital payments made by the lessee will also be included unless:
– the payment is accounted for by way of an adjustment to the capital allowances due; or
– the payment is compensation for loss caused by damage to or by the leased asset.
The capital payment will be taxed as income in the period in which it is received or when the obligation to pay it became unconditional.
4. To determine the profit (or loss) the following steps are taken:
a. find the termination value (i.e. the value of the plant and machinery at or about the time when the lease terminates);
b. find the relevant value (¶172);
c. find the total deductions allowed to the lessor (¶171);
d. find the amount by which **b.** exceeds **c.** (if any);
e. if the termination value (plus any other sums paid to the lessee) exceeds step **d.** then the excess is treated as a taxable profit (if the figure is a loss, it is an allowable trading loss).

These rules **apply to** all long funding leases where the lease was finalised (i.e. agreed with a contract in place) or commenced:
– on or after 1 April 2006 and the lease is not an excepted lease; or
– before 1 April 2006 but the plant and machinery was not brought into use until on or after 1 April 2006.

MEMO POINTS 1. An **excepted lease** is one where all of the following are met:
a. the principal terms had been agreed before 21 July 2005;
b. the construction of the plant or machinery had begun before 1 April 2006;
c. the lease was finalised and commenced before 1 April 2007. This can be extended to 1 April 2009 if the lease is not finalised or does not commence because the plant and machinery is not constructed, provided:
– the lease is finalised and commences as soon as is reasonably practicable after the construction is substantially complete; and
– the construction has proceeded continuously from 1 April 2006 at a pace that is normal for an asset of its type (ignoring any delays due to events beyond the control of the parties);
d. the lessee is the same person identified in the pre-existing heads of agreement; and
e. the principal finalised terms are not materially different to the pre-existing heads of agreement.
2. A long funding lease is more akin to loan financing and therefore these **provisions have been introduced to** ensure that the tax treatment of loan financing and this type of leasing financing are the same. Previous differences in the regimes meant that commercial decisions were often affected by the tax treatment of the transaction.
3. For details of trading **deductions** and the **capital allowances** regime for such assets see ¶171 and ¶483 respectively. The **capital gains** implications are at ¶6032.
4. A lessor can **elect to opt into** the long funding lease regime. Such an election can be made for any date on or after 1 April 2006. SI 2007/304
5. For expenditure **after 9 October 2007** the long funding leasing rules cannot be used where the lessor is able to claim a revenue deduction for purchase of an asset as it is held as trading stock or where the rules are used to generate a tax loss without a commercial loss arising. ss 370, 371 CTA 2010

Revenue receipts on cessation of trade

Revenue receipts arising after the cessation of a trade are taxed as sundry income in the year in which they are received. However, **for income tax purposes**, if any sums are received within 6 years of the date of cessation, an **election** may be made to treat the sums as being received on the last day of trading. See ¶2466 for details of the provisions. **140** ss 188 – 191 CTA 2009; s 243 ITTOIA 2005

Reverse premiums

141 s 98 CTA 2009; ss 99 - 101 ITTOIA 2005; BIM 41050 +

Where reverse premiums (¶2760) are received by a:
- **trader**, they are taxed as revenue income in the computation of trading profits; or
- **non-trader**, they are taxed as income from land and property.

MEMO POINTS Where they are **paid by**:
- a builder or developer in the course of his trade, they will normally be treated as an allowable revenue deduction; or
- a landlord as part of his property letting business, they will be treated as a capital payment.

2. Expense items

Common items

142 The following paragraphs detail the treatment of a number of common expenses.

Expense	¶¶
Computer software	¶175
Depreciation	¶157
Donations	¶176
Enterprise contributions	¶192
Entertaining	¶158
ECGD payments	¶190
Fines and illegal payments	¶180
Gifts	¶178
Impairment losses (previously bad debts)	¶156
Interest payments	¶179
Leased assets	¶165
Leased land	¶161
Legal and professional fees	¶143
Management charges and income	¶144
Patent expenses	¶188
Pension contributions	¶159
Pre-trading expenditure	¶160
Repairs and renewals	¶146
Research and development	¶152
Reverse premiums	¶155
Staff costs	¶181
Withdrawal of capital	¶193

MEMO POINTS For details of the treatment of certain **other expense items** that apply only to companies, see ¶780 onwards.

Legal and professional fees

143 Legal and professional fees in respect of **capital assets** are not allowable as a trading deduction. Relief for such items may be available as incidental costs for chargeable gains purposes, or the expense may qualify for capital allowances.

One exception is legal fees in respect of a **short lease** (one with a duration of less than 50 years). Although a lease is, strictly speaking, a capital asset, and fees relating to its acquisition will not be allowable, fees in connection with the renewal of a short lease are allowable.

Fees in respect of **revenue items** are deductible. This includes, for example, debt collection expenses, and fees for the preparation of trade agreements and employment contracts. Audit and accountancy fees will generally be allowable, although relief is not available for costs in connection with tax appeals or tax investigations. However, fees in connection with a **tax investigation** will be deductible where the investigation exonerates the taxpayer completely and there is neither:
- an adjustment of profits; nor
- a liability for interest and penalties.

Insurance premiums paid to protect against professional fees in the event of an HMRC enquiry are only allowable if all the costs insured against would themselves have been allowable. It is not possible to apportion the premiums between allowable and non-allowable purposes. Consequently if the premiums cover any non-allowable purposes (for example fees for negotiating tax settlements arising out of fraudulent or negligent conduct) all of the premiums will be non-deductible for corporation tax purposes. Should the company make no claim, or only claim for allowable expenses under the policy, the premiums will still be non-deductible as they cover some risks that are not allowable for tax purposes.

Registered companies must comply with the Companies Act and in doing so may incur fees, for example, **Companies House filing fees**, audit costs, and expenses in respect of the Annual General Meeting. Such expenses are deductible in computing the profits of the trade. Costs relating to the formation of a company are not deductible.

Similarly, costs of maintaining a **Stock Exchange listing** are deductible, although the costs of obtaining the listing are not.

A trading deduction may be available for **property revaluation fees** where the revaluation is undertaken for accounts purposes, despite the fact that the property is a capital asset. Revaluation fees in connection with the acquisition or disposal of a property are capital and therefore disallowed.

Management charges and income

Charges paid to group companies for management services provided will generally be allowed as a trading expense. However, where there is no commercial justification for the management charge, and it is simply being used to manipulate profits, HMRC will seek to disallow the payment. If any disallowed payments are made to a shareholder, the rules for distributions (¶940) may apply. **144**

Conversely, **management fee income** is included in trading profits. The full amount of income received will be included in profits, regardless of any disallowance in the paying company's computation.

Repairs and renewals

Expenditure on repairs is a deductible trading expense. However, this refers simply to expenditure incurred in **restoring** an asset to its original state. Any element of **improvement** in the asset means the expenditure is capital and therefore not deductible. If the work constitutes an improvement or addition, the expenditure is disallowed in full. There is no scope for apportioning expenditure between the notional repair and the improvement element of the work. **146**

This principle extends to expenditure on **newly acquired assets**. Where the expenditure remedies ordinary wear and tear on the asset which occurred prior to the acquisition it is deductible. However, where it is necessary to incur expenditure to put a newly acquired asset in a useable condition, or where the purchase price of the asset is reduced to reflect the work required, this is capital and therefore disallowed.

EXAMPLE 1. The costs of work performed on a ship shortly after it was purchased were deemed to be capital as the original cost reflected the fact that the ship was not seaworthy. *Law Shipping Co Ltd v CIR* [1923]

2. Where a company performed substantial work over a period of years on a cinema it purchased the costs were considered to be on repairs as the cinema was in a useable state prior to the repairs being carried out. *Odeon Associated Theatres Ltd v Jones* [1971]

MEMO POINTS 1. The use of modern materials to **replace outdated materials** when carrying out repairs does not in itself constitute an improvement. For example, replacing single glazed units with double glazed units is not a capital item.
2. The **timing of the expenditure** (i.e. whether the work is carried out as it becomes necessary, or at some future date, perhaps due to lack of funds) is irrelevant for determining whether the work is a repair or not. Expenditure on repairs is generally only deductible when it is actually incurred.
3. Whether work constitutes repairs or improvements is a matter of degree and each case will be considered on its facts.

148 When considering **structural work** to a building, HMRC will look at the external size of the building and if it has increased, for example by adding extra floors, it is likely that any work undertaken would constitute an improvement. If, however, the cost of repairing a dilapidated wall includes, for example, increasing the number of windows, this may be treated as a revenue expense.

150 Where an asset is **replaced in its entirety**, this is a capital expense. This has been examined in the courts, and the key fact to consider is whether the expenditure incurred relates to an asset in its own right, or a part of a larger asset.

EXAMPLE A stand at a football ground is a separate asset and its replacement is therefore a capital expense. *Brown v Burnley Football and Athletic Co Ltd* [1980]
A chimney which is integral to a factory is merely a part of the factory, and its replacement is therefore a revenue expense. *Samuel Jones and Co (Devonvale) Ltd v CIR* [1951]

MEMO POINTS For the rules relating to the replacement of items classified as integral features see ¶306.

Research and development

152
ss 87, 88 CTA 2009; ss 87, 88 ITTOIA 2005

Revenue expenditure on qualifying research and development (R & D) will be deductible as an expense of the trade **provided** the expenditure:
– is related to the trade and is undertaken directly by or on behalf of the trader; or
– consists of contributions to an approved UK scientific research organisation, university, college, or other such similar institution provided the research undertaken relates to a trade carried on by the trader.
Qualifying R & D is as detailed in ¶686.

MEMO POINTS Certain companies qualify for **enhanced allowances** for R & D expenditure as detailed in ¶794.

Reverse premiums

155
s 96 CTA 2009; ss 99 – 101 ITTOIA 2005; BIM 41050 +

Where a reverse premium (¶2760) is **paid by** a:
– builder or developer in the course of his trade, it will normally be treated as an allowable revenue deduction; or
– landlord as part of his property letting business, it will be treated as a capital payment.

MEMO POINTS Where a reverse premium is **received by** a:
– trader, it is taxed as revenue income in the computation of trading profits; or
– non-trader, it is taxed as income from land and property.

Impairment losses

156
s 55 CTA 2009; s 35 ITTOIA 2005

To be deductible, an impairment loss (previously known as a **bad debt**) must be incurred in the course of the business. This means that an irrecoverable trading debt will be deductible, whereas an irrecoverable loan to a member of staff will not, unless the trade in question is one of making loans.

A **general bad debt provision** (for example, a fixed percentage of all outstanding debts) is not deductible. However, where individual debts have been specifically reviewed and a decision taken as to the likelihood of them being recovered, a **specific provision** will be allowed.

MEMO POINTS The term "impairment loss" was introduced to reflect the terminology of IAS (¶82).

Depreciation

As depreciation is a notional expense and is not actually incurred, no deduction is generally available for tax purposes. Depreciation may be allowed in respect of finance leased assets (¶166). **157**

MEMO POINTS The House of Lords ruled that, provided accounts are prepared on a true and fair basis (in accordance with GAAP etc), then only depreciation that has actually been deducted when computing the accounting profit/loss need be added back for tax purposes. *HMRC v William Grant and Sons Distillers Ltd* [2007]

Entertaining

No deduction is available for **business entertaining** costs. Entertaining includes all forms of hospitality. The only exception is **staff entertaining** which may be deducted but may also be a taxable benefit in kind as discussed in ¶3224. **158** ss 1298, 1299 CTA 2009; ss 45, 46 ITTOIA 2005

Pension contributions

The **general rule** is that contributions to registered pension schemes are allowed in the period in which they are made, regardless of when they are deducted in the accounts, where they are paid wholly and exclusively for the purposes of the business. **159** ss 197, 198 FA 2004

Where **special payments** are made (for example lump sum payments to make up a shortfall in the fund), relief for the payment will be spread where the excess payment amounts to:
– more than 210% of the previous year's contribution; and
– £500,000 or more.

The **excess payment** is the amount by which the special payment exceeds 110% of the previous year's contribution and it is spread as follows:

Amount	Spread over
< £500,000	n/a
£500,000 – £1,000,000	2 years
£1,000,000 – £2,000,000	3 years
> £2,000,000	4 years

Payments are deducted evenly over the periods. If a period is less than 12 months, the deduction is restricted accordingly.

EXAMPLE

1. A Ltd makes the following contributions into its pension scheme:
Year 1 – £100,000
Year 2 – £600,000

The excess payment exceeds 210% of the prior year's contribution but is only £490,000 (£600,000 – (110 % x £100,000) therefore the spreading rules do not apply and relief will be obtained in full in the year of payment, giving the following deductions:
Year 1 – £100,000
Year 2 – £600,000

2. B Ltd makes the following contributions into its pension scheme:
Year 1 – £100,000
Year 2 – £620,000

The excess is £510,000 (£620,000 – (110 % × £100,000)) therefore the excess contribution is spread forward over 2 years, giving the following deductions:
Year 1 – £100,000
Year 2 – £365,000 (£110,000 + (50 % × £510,000))
Year 3 – £255,000 (50 % × £510,000)

Comment It can be seen from these examples that careful consideration needs to be given to the size and timing of special payments to avoid unnecessarily pushing a tax deduction into a later period.

Pre-trading expenditure

160
s 61 CTA 2009; s 57 ITTOIA 2005

Pre-trading expenditure can be **treated as** a trading expense incurred on the first day of trade, where it is incurred by the trader in the 7 years prior to the commencement of trade and it would be a deductible trading expense if incurred after the commencement of trade.

Leased land

161
ss 62, 63 CTA 2009; s 277 ITTOIA 2005

The **general rule** is that a lease is a capital asset, and therefore payments in respect of a lease are usually disallowed as capital.

However, where a premium is paid for the **grant of a short lease** of land (one lasting less than 50 years), part of the premium will be treated as income in the hands of the landlord, calculated as follows:

$$P - ((P \times (Y - 1)) \times 2\%)$$

where:
- P is the premium received; and
- Y is the number of complete years of the lease.

The lessee will be entitled to a deduction equal to this amount, spread over the life of the lease.

EXAMPLE Mr A occupies a property under a 40-year lease for which he paid a premium of £16,000. The proportion of the premium deductible as a trading expense is £3,520, calculated as follows:
16,000 – (16,000 × (40 – 1) × 2%) = £3,520
The deduction will be given over the life of the lease, i.e. £88 p.a.

For further details in respect of lease premiums, see ¶2742.

MEMO POINTS See ¶4052 onwards for **anti-avoidance** provisions.

Leased cars

162
s 56 CTA 2009; s 48 ITTOIA 2005

Agreements commencing before 1 April 2009 For agreements commencing before 1 April 2009 (6 April 2009 for income tax), where a **car costing over £12,000** is leased for trade purposes, the amount available as a deduction in computing profits for tax purposes is restricted. (Note this restriction does not apply to cars acquired under hire purchase as it is restricted under the capital allowances code (¶427)).

No restriction is required for vehicles with a cost of £12,000 or less.

The amount available as a deduction is restricted to the amount produced by the following formula:

$$\frac{12{,}000 + P}{2P} \times L$$

where:
- P is the retail price of the car when new; and
- L is the amount paid for the hire.

EXAMPLE A Ltd leases a car with an original cost of £18,650. The annual leasing costs are £3,350. The allowable element of the leasing cost is calculated as follows:

$$\frac{12{,}000 + 18{,}650}{37{,}300} \times 3{,}350 = £2{,}753$$

Therefore, £597 (i.e. 3,350 – 2,753) must be added back in the trading computation.

Where the leasing charge includes an identifiable element in respect of **maintenance**, that amount is allowable in full.

MEMO POINTS This restriction does not apply to cars with low carbon dioxide emissions (¶406). Where a lease commenced prior to the reduction in the qualifying level of CO_2 for a car that now exceeds the limit the restriction will continue to be disapplied for the length of the lease.

Agreements commencing on or after 1 April 2009 For agreements commencing on or after 1 April 2009 (6 April 2009 for income tax), where a car is leased for trade purposes and: 163
- is registered on or after 1 March 2001;
- has a CO_2 emission level of over 160g/km; and
- is not a qualifying hire car,

there will be a flat rate disallowance of 15% of the expense incurred.

MEMO POINTS 1. An agreement commences on the first day that the vehicle is to be made available.
2. A qualifying hire car is one that:
– is hired under a hire-purchase contract with no option to purchase or where there is such an option the cost is less than 1% of the price of the vehicle when new; or
– is made available under a long funding lease.

Where the taxpayer leases a car for 45 days or less, or where the taxpayer leases the car to someone else for more than 45 days, then the lease restriction **will not apply**. In calculating the period of the lease any periods not separated by more than 14 days will be amalgamated. These provisions are intended to ensure that only one lease in a chain will be subject to the restriction. 164 s 58A CTA 2009; s 50A ITTOIA 2005

EXAMPLE A Ltd leases a car to a trader from 11 April 2011 to 30 April 2011. On 12 May 2011 it again leases a car to the same trader until 23 June 2011. While neither period exceeds 45 days the two periods fall less than 14 days apart and as such should be amalgamated. This will result in a period of over 45 days.

MEMO POINTS These exceptions do not apply where the lessee is an employee of the company.

Other leased assets

Assets other than land Payments for the lease of an asset (other than land) that will be used for the purposes of the trade are allowable trading deductions under general principles. (Note the payments must be for the use of the asset. If they are, for example, instalment payments for an outright purchase, then they will be treated as capital expenditure). 165

MEMO POINTS 1. **Anti-avoidance provisions** apply in certain situations when capital sums are received in respect of leased assets, other than land (¶136). ss 871 - 874 CTA 2010
2. For details on **capital allowances** on leased assets see ¶482.
3. Special provisions apply for **long funding leases** of plant and machinery (¶171).

Finance leases Where assets are acquired under a finance lease, the tax treatment differs depending upon how the lease is **accounted for**: 166 SP 3/91
- if it is accounted for in accordance with SSAP 21, HMRC practice is to allow both the finance charge in the profit and loss account and the depreciation in respect of the finance leased asset;
- if it is not accounted for in accordance with SSAP 21, the finance element is deductible when it is paid and any rental payments are spread evenly over the life of the asset (They cannot be front loaded for tax purposes.).

In either situation, the lessee does not qualify for **capital allowances**, as the assets remain the property of the lessor.

s 60A CTA 2010; s 55B ITTOIA 2005 Where a **refund** is made on a lease by the lessor the sum is allowable as a deduction but this is limited to the amounts that have been charged to tax previously (excluding any finance element, payments for services and taxes). Where the total rebate exceeds the cost of the asset the disallowed proportion of the refund will be an allowable loss but it can only be used against any gain arising on that asset in the future.

MEMO POINTS A **finance lease is** a lease which transfers substantially all the risks and rewards of ownership of an asset to the lessee while maintaining the lessor's legal ownership of the asset.

167 s 228C CAA 2001 **Sale and finance leaseback** Where S sells plant or machinery to B, who then grants a finance leaseback to S, there is a restriction on the revenue deduction available to the **lessee** (S). Under these provisions, the deduction available is the sum of the:
– total finance charge shown in the accounts; and
– depreciation which would have been charged based on the disposal proceeds brought into account for capital allowances purposes (¶295).

s 228C CAA 2001 On the **termination or assignment** of a finance leaseback agreement the following adjustments are made to S in the accounting period of the termination:

a. there is a deemed income receipt, calculated as follows:

$$NC \times \frac{CV}{OV}$$

where:
– NC is the original consideration paid to S less the restricted disposal value (¶295);
– CV is the net book value of the asset immediately before termination etc; and
– OV is the net book value of the asset at the beginning of the leaseback; and

s 228B CAA 2001 **b.** the revenue deduction is increased using the following formula:

$$CV \times \frac{OC}{BV}$$

where:
– CV is the net book value of the asset immediately before termination etc; and
– OC is the original consideration paid to the vendor for the disposal; and
– BV is the net book value of the asset at the beginning of the leaseback.

s 228D CAA 2001 MEMO POINTS **Lessors** will be taxed on the total of the:
a. gross earnings (as shown in their accounts in respect of the leaseback); and
b. allowable proportion of the capital repayment, calculated as follows:

$$RDV \times \frac{IRP}{NI}$$

where:
– RDV is the restricted disposal value (¶295);
– IRP is the amount shown in the lessor's accounts in respect of the reduction in the net investment in the leaseback; and
– NI is the amount shown in the lessor's accounts as his net investment in the leaseback at the beginning of its term.

168 The tax treatment for **lease and finance leaseback** arrangements are as for a sale and finance leaseback with the following exceptions:
– lessees can only claim a revenue deduction for the finance charge element; and
– lessors are taxed on the full amount of the rent receivable (not just the finance charge element of the rent).

MEMO POINTS See ¶295 for details of the **capital allowances** restrictions.

Long funding leases A long funding lease can be **defined as** a lease of over 5 years duration of plant and machinery. See ¶483 for the full definition. **171** ss 363, 377 – 380 CTA 2010; ss 148C, 148D, 148E, 148G, 148I ITTOIA 2005; Sch 8 paras 18 – 26 FA 2006

The **deductible expenses** for such leases differ depending upon whether the lease is a long funding finance lease or long funding operating lease as follows:

Type of lease	Lessor	Lessee
Long funding finance lease	Any rental rebate paid by the lessor may be deductible[1]	Payments made under the terms of the lease[2]
Long funding operating lease	A deduction is available to essentially compensate lessors for the fact that they can no longer claim capital allowances (¶172)	A deduction is allowed as computed at ¶174

Note:
1. It is common, on the termination of the lease, for the lessor to pay an amount to the lessee based on the value of the asset (often called a rebate of rentals). Such a payment is only deductible if it had previously been brought into account in determining the company's taxable rental income (¶138).
2. To the extent that they do not exceed the finance charges shown in the company's accounts. (In cases where the long funding lease is accounted for as a loan, the loan is to be treated as a finance lease.)

These provisions **apply to** all long funding leases where either the lease was finalised (i.e. agreed with a contract in place) or commenced:
– on or after 1 April 2006 and the lease is not an excepted lease; or
– before 1 April 2006 but the plant and machinery was not brought into use until on or after 1 April 2006.

MEMO POINTS 1. An **excepted lease** is one where all of the following are met:
a. the principal terms had been agreed before 21 July 2005;
b. the construction of the plant or machinery had begun before 1 April 2006;
c. the lease was finalised and commenced before 1 April 2007. This can be extended to 1 April 2009 if the lease is not finalised or does not commence because the plant and machinery is not constructed, provided:
– the lease is finalised and commences as soon as is reasonably practicable after the construction is substantially complete; and
– the construction has proceeded continuously from 1 April 2006 at a pace that is normal for an asset of its type (ignoring any delays due to events beyond the control of the parties);
d. the lessee is a particular person identified in the pre-existing heads of agreement; and
e. the principal finalised terms are not materially different to the pre-existing heads of agreement.
2. For details of the treatment of **income** from these arrangements and the **capital allowances** regime for such assets see ¶138 and ¶483 respectively. The **capital gains** implications are at ¶6032.
3. A lessor can **elect to opt into** the long funding lease regime. Such an election can be made for any date on or after 1 April 2006. SI 2007/304

172 For a **long funding operating lease, the lessor's deduction** is calculated as follows:
a. find the relevant value of the assets, which varies depending upon the use of the asset by the lessor, as follows:

Use by lessor	Relevant value
Only used for leasing under a long funding operating lease	Cost
Last previous use was for leasing under a long funding operating lease	Market value
Last previous use was for leasing under a long funding finance lease	Recognised value
Last previous use was for a qualifying activity (¶214) other than leasing under a long funding lease	Lower of: – cost; and – market value
Previously owned for a non-qualifying purpose, but brought into use on or after 1 April 2006, for a qualifying activity which consists of leasing under a long funding operating lease	Lower of: – first use market value; and – first used amortised value

b. deduct from the relevant value the amount which, at the start of the lease, is the expected market value of the plant and machinery at the end of the lease (less any estimated costs of disposing of it);
c. the figure arrived at in **b**. is an allowable deduction, spread equally over the life of the lease.

MEMO POINTS This calculation is further complicated if the lessor incurs **additional capital expenditure** on the leased plant and machinery during the course of the lease. To calculate the deductible costs the following steps need to be taken:
a. establish, at the time of incurring the additional capital expenditure, the anticipated market value of the plant and machinery at the end of the lease (less any estimated costs of disposing of it);
b. find the figure used at the start of the lease that was estimated to be the expected market value of the plant and machinery at the end of the lease (less any estimated costs of disposing of it);
c. if **a**. exceeds **b**. the excess is deducted from the additional expenditure and the figure arrived at is an allowable deduction, spread equally over the remaining life of the lease. (If **a**. does not exceed **b**., the total additional expenditure is treated as an allowable deduction, spread equally over the remaining life of the lease.)

174 For a **long funding operating lease, the lessee's deduction** is calculated as follows:
a. find the relevant value of the assets which varies depending upon the use of the asset by the lessor, as follows:

Use by lessee	Relevant value
For a qualifying activity (¶214)	Market value
Previously had use of the assets for a non-qualifying purpose, but brought into use on or after 1 April 2006, for a qualifying activity	Lower of: – first use market value; and – first use amortised value

b. deduct from the relevant value the amount which, at the start of the lease, is the expected market value of the plant and machinery at the end of the lease and spread this equally over the term of the lease;
c. the figure arrived at in **b**. is the disallowable element of the expenditure charged in the accounts. As such this should be added back in tax computation.

Computer software

175 Where computer **software and hardware are acquired at the same time**, then normally the whole expenditure will qualify for capital allowances (¶200).

However, where computer software is **acquired separately** and it is expected to have a useful life of less than 2 years, it will be treated as an allowable revenue expense. This includes not only licences for third party software but also costs of developing software in-house and outright purchases of software.

Where software is **acquired under licence** and regular payments are made for its use, these will always be allowable as a trading expense for tax purposes, regardless of the estimated life of the software. Relief will be given for the expenditure as it is charged to the accounts (provided the accounts are prepared in accordance with acceptable accounting practice).

MEMO POINTS Although not conclusive, where there is any **uncertainty** over whether such expenditure is a revenue item, the accounting treatment will be taken into consideration. Therefore, if expenditure is treated as a balance sheet item, this may reduce the chances of HMRC agreeing to a trading deduction. Capital allowances (¶200) may be available in respect of any capital expenditure.

Donations

176 **Political donations** are not generally deductible as a trading expense unless the payments are made solely to preserve the trade.

ss 1298, 1300 CTA 2009; s 47(5) ITTOIA 2005

Charitable donations (or donations to registered community amateur sports clubs) paid under the gift aid scheme (¶4420) are not deductible as a trading expense but should be allowed under the provisions relating to the charitable donations relief (¶958), or as a deduction from income for individuals (¶4382).

Other charitable donations will only be deductible if they meet the normal requirements, i.e. they are wholly and exclusively for business purposes. This is likely to limit relief to small payments to local charities which result in a conspicuous advert for the business.

Gifts

Subject to the **overriding provision** that gifts of food, drink or tobacco to customers, suppliers and contacts are not deductible, the tax treatment of various gifts is as follows: **178** ss 105 - 108 CTA 2009; ss 108, 109 ITTOIA 2005

Type of gift	Recipient	Qualifying conditions	Tax treatment
Items that are manufactured or sold by the donor	Charities; or registered community amateur sports clubs	Donor (or any person connected with him) must not be entitled to a benefit in any form as a result of the gift [1]	Deductible
	Designated educational establishment [2]	Gift must qualify as plant or machinery in the hands of the recipient	
Qualifying investment	Charity	See ¶958 and ¶4382 onwards	Relief claimed as a charge on income (or as a deduction from income for individuals)
All other types of gifts	Non-employees	Must carry a conspicuous advert for the business and cost no more than £50 per donee per accounting period or year of assessment	Deductible
	Employees		Deductible, but may be taxed as a benefit in kind (¶3196)

Note:
1. If they do obtain such a benefit, the market value of the benefit is added to the trading profits for the accounting period in which it is received.
2. To obtain this relief a claim must be made by the donor within 2 years of the end of the accounting period in which the gift was made.

MEMO POINTS This does not mean that expenditure in **providing samples** of a trader's own product (including food, drink or tobacco) must be disallowed.

Interest payments

Any interest payments on **late paid tax** are not deductible, although note that interest paid by a company on unpaid/late paid corporation tax is allowable under the loan relationship rules (¶870). **179** s 54 ITTOIA 2005

This specifically **includes** interest on late paid:
- income tax deducted under PAYE;
- National Insurance Contributions;
- tax under the Construction Industry Scheme; and
- student loan repayments.

Fines and illegal payments

Such payments are not incurred for the purposes of a trade but in breaking the law, and therefore **no deduction** is available. **180** s 1304 CTA 2009; s 55 ITTOIA 2005

This general disallowance extends to payments which may be argued as being wholly and necessarily incurred. For example, bribes are a common feature of trade in many countries, and a business is unlikely to be successful if payments are not made. However, no deduction would be available for such payments for UK tax purposes.

In addition to fines, a deduction is specifically prohibited for any payments (made inside or outside the UK) which constitute the commission of a **criminal offence**. This includes protection fees and blackmail payments.

Staff costs

181 s 1288 CTA 2009; ss 36, 37 ITTOIA 2005

Staff remuneration Costs of employing staff are generally an **allowable deduction provided**:
– the remuneration is not excessive. If HMRC consider that the remuneration is excessive for the work done, they may seek to disallow part of the expense. This is most likely to be an issue where members of the family are employed in the business; and
– it is paid within 9 months of the end of the period of account for which the accounts are prepared. If payment is not made within that period, the expenditure must be disallowed, and claimed as a deduction for the period in which it is actually paid.

Remuneration is **treated as being paid** on the earliest of the following dates:
a. when a payment of (or on account of) the remuneration is made;
b. when the employee becomes entitled to the payment;
c. if the employee is a **director** of the company and the earnings are from employment with the company (whether or not as director), the earliest of:
– the time the payments are credited in the company accounts or records (regardless of whether he has the right to draw the money);
– the date on which the period of account ends (where the amount of the remuneration for a period has already been determined); or
– the date on which the amount of the remuneration for a period is determined (where the period of account has already ended).

If any **remuneration is unpaid at the date the tax computation is prepared**, the computation must be prepared on the assumption that the remuneration will not be paid within the 9 month period. If this subsequently proves to be incorrect, a claim may be made to adjust the computation accordingly. Such a claim must be made within 2 years of the end of the period of account for which a deduction is due.

MEMO POINTS 1. It is common for a **general accrual to be made for directors' bonuses** in the draft accounts, which is then approved at the AGM. For the accrual to be recognised for accounting purposes (and therefore for tax), it is important that the business has at least a constructive obligation at the balance sheet date to pay extra remuneration to the directors, and this should be appropriately minuted as a board resolution.
2. Payments to directors for **compensation for loss of office** are deductible where it is felt that the departure of the director is in the interests of the company.
However, to prevent any sale price being manipulated, payments made in connection with the **sale of the company** are disallowable unless it can be demonstrated that the sale price of the shares was full market value and that the compensation payment was negotiated separately. Any mention of compensation payments in an agreement for the sale of shares is likely to prevent a trading deduction.

EXAMPLE Mr A is a director of B Ltd and also owns 22% of the shares. When the company is sold to C Ltd for £2m, Mr A receives £410,000 for his shares (which had a market value of £425,000) and a compensation payment for his loss of office of £30,000.
The company will not be able to claim a deduction in respect of the compensation payment as Mr A's shares were sold for less than market value.
If Mr A had sold his shares for £425,000 and received a separately negotiated payment in respect of the loss of office, the compensation payment would be deductible in full.

s 70 CTA 2009

3. Where an employer sends a member of **staff on secondment** to work for a charity or educational establishment the costs of employment are deductible, provided they are paid within 9 months of the end of the relevant accounting period.

4. Costs incurred by a company on **staff training** will be deductible provided it can be demonstrated that the training is incurred wholly and exclusively for the purposes of the trade. Specifically for **self-employed** traders, HMRC take the view that training expenditure will only be deductible if it merely updates expertise etc. If it provides such traders with new expertise, knowledge or skills then the expenditure will be treated as capital. BIM 35660

Staff welfare Such costs are usually allowable and may include any costs such as subsidised or free lunch facilities (provided they are available to all staff), entertaining and training. **182**

Redundancy payments Statutory redundancy payments are automatically deductible in computing profits. Additional payments will generally be deductible unless they relate to the sale of the business. Payments arising on the cessation of trade may be deducted, up to a maximum of three times the statutory limit. **183** ss 76-79 CTA 2009; s 76 ITTOIA 2005

MEMO POINTS Expenditure incurred by an employer on **retraining courses** for employees (or past employees) are deductible, where certain conditions are met (¶3210).

Employee benefit contributions Contributions to a scheme manager (i.e. a person who administers an employee benefit scheme) are **deductible if**, within 9 months of the end of the period for which the accounts are prepared, the third party is entitled or required to pay qualifying benefits or expenses to employees out of the contributions. The deductions are limited to the amount charged to income tax on the recipient. **184** ss 1290-1296 CTA 2009; s 38 ITTOIA 2005

These rules **do not apply** to:
- contributions to employer financed retirement benefits scheme (¶3900); or
- the statutory deductions in connection with employee share schemes (¶785).

MEMO POINTS 1. A **qualifying benefit** is a payment of money or transfer of assets (other than by way of loan) that gives rise to both a charge to tax on employment income and a charge to NICs (or would do so but for available exemptions for duties performed outside the UK or in connection with termination of employment).
2. **Qualifying expenses** are those expenses of the third party in operating the scheme that would have been deductible if they had been incurred by the employer.
3. These rules also apply to **self-declared trusts** made by employers over assets which they already own. Previously employers had been able to declare a trust over assets which they already owned (for example, a bank account) and then claim a deduction equal to the value of the declaration. From 21 March 2007 such declarations of trust (and further contributions) are only deductible if the assets are required to be paid over within 9 months from the end of the period for which the accounts are prepared in a form which gives rise to an income tax and national insurance charge.

Key staff insurance Many businesses take out life and critical illness insurance policies for important members of staff. The payment of the premiums is deductible provided that the purpose of taking out the policy is wholly and exclusively for the purposes of the trade. This is generally satisfied where the policy is taken out to replace lost profits from the absence of that member of staff. Where the policy is intended to protect the capital value of the business the premiums will not be allowable, and consequently the proceeds will not be taxable. *Greycon Ltd v Klaentschi* [2003] **186** BIM 45525, 45530

Likewise premiums paid for policies that have no trade purpose will also be disallowed. *Beauty Consultants v HMIT* [2002]

Where the premiums are not deductible the proceeds from the policy will not be taxable. However in strict theory the two are unrelated and as such it is believed that where the premiums are allowable but not claimed the proceeds may still be taxable.

Patent expenses

Sundry expenditure (for example patent office fees) incurred in connection with **obtaining a grant of** a patent for trade purposes is specifically allowed as a deduction for: **188** ss 89, 90 CTA 2009; s 89 ITTOIA 2005
- sole traders and partnerships; and

– companies if the expense relates to patents that were in existence before 1 April 2002. (Expenditure after this date on post-1 April 2002 patents will fall within the intangible asset regime (¶824).)

This includes costs in respect of:
– obtaining a grant of a patent (i.e. the right to use a patent for trade purposes);
– extending the term of an existing patent;
– registration of a design or trademark;
– renewal of trademark registration;
– extension of the term for which trademark rights subsist; and
– abortive expenditure on rejected or abandoned applications.

MEMO POINTS 1. The **payment of patent royalties** is not deductible in computing trading profits but is relieved as an expense of management (¶2120) for companies, or as a deduction in calculating net income for individuals (¶4387).
2. Where the **expenditure is capital** (for example the cost of purchasing an existing patent), no deduction is available, but capital allowances may be due (¶698). Capital allowances do not apply if the intangible asset regime applies to the patent rights.
3. See ¶934 and ¶3956 for details on the taxation of **patent receipts**.

ECGD payments

190 s 91 CTA 2009; s 91 ITTOIA 2005

Payments to the Export Credit Guarantee Department are specifically allowable as a trading deduction.

Enterprise contributions

192 s 82 CTA 2009; s 82 ITTOIA 2005

Expenditure incurred by a person in making a contribution, in cash or in kind, to the following organisations is specifically **deductible** as a trading expense:
– local enterprise agency/company;
– training and enterprise council; and
– urban regeneration companies.

Relief will be **denied** where the contribution entitles the contributor (or any person connected with him) to a benefit in any form.

MEMO POINTS It is the expenditure that is incurred that is allowed as a deduction. Therefore in the case of a **gift** it may be that the allowable deduction will be the original cost to the donor, although HMRC guidance on this point is not clear.

Withdrawal of capital

193 The withdrawal of capital, for example by way of **drawings or dividend**, is not an allowable deduction. This includes salaries paid to sole traders or partners, and any personal expenses borne by the business in respect of the proprietors.

SECTION 7

Adjustments required

194 Having identified any capital items and expenses which are not deductible for tax purposes, a statement should be prepared showing the adjustments required to arrive at the taxable trading profit.

Any expenses included in the profit and loss account which are not deductible for tax purposes must be disallowed when calculating the adjusted profit for tax purposes. This is achieved by adding the amount back to the profit before tax shown in the accounts. Similarly, any taxable income which is not included in the profit and loss account must also be added to the accounts profit.

Expenses which are deductible for tax purposes, but which are not included in the profit and loss account should be deducted from the accounts profit. This may arise where items are capitalised for accounts purposes, but are specifically allowable for tax purposes, or where a deduction is given in a different period (for example pension contributions). Any capital receipts, or other income items which do not form part of trading profit should also be deducted along with any capital allowances (¶200).

	£	£
Profit before tax per accounts		x
Add:		
Depreciation	x	
Capital expenses	x	
Increase in general provisions	x	
Other non-deductible expenses	x	
Revenue receipts not credited to P and L	x	
		x
Deduct:		
Capital allowances	x	
Capital receipts	x	
Reduction in general provisions	x	
Other non-taxable receipts	x	
Revenue expenditure not charged to P and L	x	
		(x)
Adjusted profit for tax purposes		x

CHAPTER 4

Capital allowances

OUTLINE ¶¶

SECTION 1

General principles

200 Expenditure incurred on the acquisition of capital assets is not allowable as a deduction in the calculation of the adjusted profits of a business. Similarly, any depreciation given in the accounts must be added back for tax purposes. Instead, capital allowances are given as a relief to businesses that purchase capital assets in the course of their trading activities. Relief may also be available for employed individuals in appropriate cases.

The capital allowances rules generally apply equally to companies, sole traders and partnerships.

MEMO POINTS 1. Capital **allowances are given in the form of** a writing down allowance at different rates for different types of capital expenditure. Also, in some circumstances, first year allowances or initial allowances may be available, giving a higher rate of relief in the year of acquisition to encourage investment.
On the **disposal of an asset**, a balancing adjustment may be required to ensure that allowances given equate to the actual cost incurred.
2. An item of expenditure **cannot qualify for more than one category of allowance**. Where an allowance would appear to be due under more than one heading, the claimant must choose which rules to apply. Once a decision has been made in respect of an item of expenditure, it cannot be changed. However, a subsequent purchaser of such an asset is not bound by the previous owner's decision when he comes to claim allowances.

202 The **purpose of this section** is to set out the general rules relating to all of the different types of asset which are eligible for capital allowances, in particular:
– what constitutes qualifying capital expenditure, when it is incurred and the timing and nature of disposals;
– the basis of relief including the methods of calculating allowances and of giving relief (¶239); and
– the processes involved in claiming relief for allowances (¶247).

MEMO POINTS Capital allowances cannot be claimed on assets that fall within the **intangible asset regime** (¶824).

A. Capital expenditure

Basic rule

204 s 4 CAA 2001 Capital expenditure is not defined by the legislation, other than to say that it **does not include** expenditure which is allowed as a deduction in the calculation of the profits of the trade.

The **basic rule** is that expenditure must be capital in nature (¶110). It follows that the same person cannot treat expenditure as revenue for one purpose and capital for another. Therefore, expenditure on assets which, if sold, would produce a revenue receipt, cannot be treated as capital expenditure.

MEMO POINTS Where assets previously treated as trading stock are **appropriated to fixed assets**, the original expenditure on acquiring the assets is treated as capital expenditure. Adjustments are also required to the trading computation in these circumstances (¶90).

207 Allowances are given where:
– capital expenditure is incurred on the provision of assets used wholly and exclusively for the purposes of the trade; and
– the asset belongs to the person claiming the allowances.

ss 175, 176 CAA 2001 MEMO POINTS 1. Whether an asset **belongs** to a person is a question of fact, and has its ordinary meaning. In simple terms, an asset belongs to a person if they can give it away. This definition is extended to allow tenants to claim allowances for assets they are required to provide under the terms of a lease for as long as the assets are used in the tenant's trade. Once such assets cease to be used in the tenant's trade, the allowances are available to the landlord in place of the tenant, if the assets legally become the landlord's.

2. It is possible for someone making a **contribution** to another person's acquisition to be able to claim allowances as if they had purchased the asset themselves. The amount of the contribution can be claimed as allowable expenditure if the asset would have qualified for the contributor had they purchased it and the two parties are not connected. s 537 CAA 2001

Notably, the **general rule is modified** for: 209

a. capital allowances claimed in respect of assets used for the **purposes of employment**. Here the test is more stringent, and additionally requires that the asset is used necessarily for the purposes of the employment. This broadly requires that the taxpayer would be unable to perform the duties of his employment without the asset, and thus a claim will be unlikely to succeed where an employee's predecessor had not found it necessary to acquire a similar asset. No capital allowances are available for private cars used for business purposes, instead a separate claim for mileage allowance can be made (¶3168); s 20 CAA 2001

b. capital allowances claimed by the lessee of an asset leased under a **long funding lease** (¶483 onwards); and

c. companies providing energy management services who can claim capital allowances for plant and machinery installed on a client's land even where they do not have an interest in that land. s 175A CAA 2001

MEMO POINTS **Energy management companies** are companies that provide a range of energy management services (including the provision, operation and maintenance of plant and machinery), aimed towards reducing their clients' energy bills.

In order for the energy management company to claim the allowances:
– both parties must submit an election within the usual time limits (¶2255 for companies and ¶4496 for individuals);
– the energy management company, or another connected person, must carry out all (or substantially all) of the operation and maintenance of the plant and machinery;
– the client must have an interest in the land; and
– the plant and machinery must not be for use in a dwelling house.

In order for an energy management company to claim 100% FYA on such expenditure, the assets must also satisfy the conditions in ¶390.

Ascertaining amount of expenditure

Expenditure includes **payment** in the form of money and the exchange of assets (in which case the market value of the asset will be used). 211

In order to qualify for allowances, expenditure **must be incurred** on the provision of an asset for the purposes of a **qualifying activity**, being any of the following (to the extent that any profits arising would be chargeable to tax): 214 s 15 CAA 2001
– a trade, profession or vocation;
– a UK or overseas property business;
– a furnished holiday letting business;
– the management of companies with investment business;
– a special leasing business; or
– an employment or office.

HMRC will generally allow **professional fees** (such as fees of architects, consultants and surveyors) to be included in capital expenditure where separate fee notes are issued, or where costs are separately identified in respect of work done in connection with the building and with the provision of plant. Where **preliminary costs**, for instance labour costs for overrun on projects, insurance and site costs, are incurred and these cannot be allocated specifically, a just and reasonable apportionment across the relevant development costs can be made. *J D Wetherspoon plc v HMRC* [2007]

Incidental costs (other than those connected with the provision of money) may not be included in the acquisition cost of an asset.

EXAMPLE Commitment fees and interest on money borrowed which were correctly charged to capital were held not to be eligible for allowances. *Ben-Odeco Ltd v Powlson* [1978]
In contrast, additional expenses incurred in order to make a payment by instalments in a foreign currency were held to be eligible for allowances. *Van Arkadie v Sterling Coated Materials Ltd* [1983]

MEMO POINTS There are further particular rules in relation to plant and machinery (¶290).

216 s 532 CAA 2001 Where expenditure is funded by a **subsidy or grant** then the amount of that subsidy will not qualify for allowances. Where a grant is subsequently repaid, the amount repaid then becomes eligible for capital allowances.

MEMO POINTS 1. There is an exception in the case of **grants which are taxable as income**, in which case the expenditure will be considered to be eligible expenditure.
2. The rules for grants and subsidies **apply not only to** payments made by public bodies, but also to contributions by others who would be able to claim tax relief in respect of that expenditure.

218 Where **VAT** is incurred in connection with the acquisition of assets, and the VAT is not recoverable, either in part or in full, the irrecoverable element is treated as capital expenditure. Where an adjustment is made under the VAT capital goods scheme (¶8250), any additional VAT liability is treated as capital expenditure. Similarly, any VAT rebates must also be adjusted for.

Timing of expenditure

221 s 5 CAA 2001 **General rule** The timing of expenditure is important because it will determine the period in which relief will be given and, where there is a change in regime, the rules that apply. The general rule is that capital expenditure is deemed to be incurred on the date when the obligation to pay becomes unconditional. This rule applies whether or not payment is actually made on a later date.

The terms of the contract will generally determine the relevant date, but where payment is required on or within a specified period from delivery, the obligation is deemed to become unconditional when the asset is delivered.

The **exception** to the general rule is where the **credit period** for payment after delivery exceeds 4 months. In this case, the expenditure is incurred when payment is actually made.

Where payment is made in **instalments**, some of which are more than 4 months after delivery, each instalment is considered separately. Payments incurred within 4 months of delivery are treated as incurred on the date of delivery, with any amounts payable more than 4 months after delivery being incurred on the actual date of payment.

MEMO POINTS 1. If the date on which the obligation to pay becomes unconditional is **earlier** than it would be under normal commercial usage (so that the expenditure falls into an earlier period), then that date is ignored and the date on which the expenditure was actually incurred will be taken.
s 12 CAA 2001 2. Expenditure on plant and machinery which is incurred **before the commencement of trade** is deemed to be incurred on the first day of trading. However, the actual date is relevant for the purposes of the annual investment and first year allowances.
3. Adjustments arising as a result of the **VAT capital goods scheme** (¶8250) are generally deemed to have been incurred in the chargeable period in which the rebate is received or payment made unless:
– an earlier assessment has been raised by HMRC, in which case the date of the assessment will be taken; or
– the trade has permanently discontinued before the liability has been accounted for (and before an assessment has been raised), in which case the last day of the period of discontinuance is taken.

223 ss 67 – 69 CAA 2001 **Hire purchase contracts** Capital allowances can be claimed by the lessee of a hire purchase contract that is finalised (i.e. agreed with a contract in place) on or after 1 April 2006, provided:
– the hire purchase contract is accounted for as a finance lease by the lessee (or would be so if accounts were prepared); and
– the assets are used for a qualifying activity (¶214).

If the above conditions are not met, neither the lessor nor the lessee can claim capital allowances.

MEMO POINTS 1. Even if the lessee is carrying out a qualifying activity **outside the UK**, he will be able to claim capital allowances if the above conditions are met.
2. These provisions were introduced to stop abuse of the **previous regime** that had allowed lessees of all hire purchase contracts to claim capital allowances.

225 Capital expenditure on a hire purchase contract that is **incurred before the asset is brought into use** for the purposes of the trade is deemed to be incurred as soon as there is an

unconditional obligation to pay for the goods. All other capital expenditure is deemed to be incurred when the asset is brought into use for trade purposes.

EXAMPLE A Ltd prepares its accounts to 30 June 200X. On 1 June 200X, it entered into a hire purchase contract to acquire printing equipment. The cash price was £100,000 but, under the terms of the hire purchase agreement, A Ltd had to pay a total price of £125,000 (a deposit of £20,000 to be paid on 1 June 200X, with the balance of £105,000 to be paid in 25 monthly instalments, representing monthly payments of £1,000 hire charge and £3,200 capital).
The printing equipment was delivered on 1 July, and brought into use by 31 July 200X.
The deposit of £20,000 will qualify for capital allowances for the period ended 30 June 200X, with the balance of capital expenditure (£80,000) qualifying for capital allowances in the accounting period ending 30 June 200X + 1.
The £25,000 (£125,000 – £100,000) that represents hire charges will be allowed as a trading deduction in the period they are incurred.

Milestone contracts Large scale construction projects are often undertaken under a milestone contract. This is a contract where the asset under construction becomes the property of the purchaser as it is being constructed, and payment is made in stages as work is completed. **228** s 5(4) CAA 2001

The obligation for payment generally becomes due when a certificate is issued that a specific stage of work has been satisfactorily completed. The **general rule** is that the expenditure is incurred on the date the certificate is issued.

By **exception**, where the work completed becomes the property of the purchaser in one accounting period and the certificate is issued within a month of the end of the period, the expenditure will be treated as incurred on the final day of the accounting period in which ownership was transferred.

B. Common concepts

Capital allowance calculations follow a similar structure regardless of the nature of the asset. **232**
All assets that qualify are given a writing down allowance (WDA) on an annual basis (although some assets may qualify for a first year allowance (FYA) or initial allowances (IA) in the year of acquisition). Since 1 April 2008 (6 April 2008 for income tax) the majority of assets may attract the annual investment allowance (AIA) in the year they are acquired.

There are **two methods for calculating WDA**, the reducing balance basis and the straight line basis. The method used is dependent upon the nature of the asset, but the general rule is that the straight line basis is reserved for buildings whilst all other allowances are calculated using the reducing balance basis. The asset or pool is then reduced by the amount claimed and then carried forward for future periods.

Chargeable periods

Capital allowances are given for a chargeable period which: **239** s 6 CAA 2001
- for **corporation tax** purposes will be the same as the accounting period; or
- for **income tax** purposes will be the same as the period for which the accounts are drawn up.

The rates for WDA are based on a **12 month period**. Where a chargeable period is longer or shorter than 12 months, the allowance is increased or reduced accordingly. Calculations should strictly be made to the nearest day, but calculations to the nearest month are generally accepted.

MEMO POINTS 1. Except for successions to trade (¶272), the chargeable period for a **company** can never exceed 12 months.
2. Where accounts for **income tax purposes** are drawn up for a period in excess of 18 months, this will be split for capital allowances into a period of 12 months, and the remainder. (For periods of up to 18 months, allowances can simply be proportionately increased.) s 56 CAA 2001

EXAMPLE Mr A purchases an asset for £10,000, which qualifies for allowances at a rate of 20% p.a. Assuming Mr A has a regular 12 month chargeable period, a writing down allowance of £2,000 will be available.
If Mr A has a 9 month chargeable period, the allowance would be £1,500 (£2,000 x 9/12).
If Mr A has a 16 month chargeable period, the allowance would be £2,667 (£2,000 x 16/12).

Disposals

243 The **most frequent way** of disposing of an asset will be by sale which is deemed to occur when ownership of the asset passes or, if later, at the time of completion of the contract.

However, any event which results in the cessation of ownership constitutes a disposal for capital allowance purposes (for example, the loss, destruction or gift of an asset). The disposal of an asset requires an adjustment to be made to the pool (where the asset was accounted for in a pool) or a balancing calculation performed for single assets. This may result in a **balancing charge or allowance**. The proceeds will generally be the amount received for the asset, although specific rules apply in certain circumstances. This figure is always restricted to the original cost of the asset.

Method of relief

245 In **general** capital allowances are deducted as a trading expense. This means that allowances can create or augment a loss. A balancing charge will arise when the disposal proceeds exceed the written down value (WDV) of the asset or pool. Balancing charges will be treated as trading receipts for the chargeable period in which they arise.
However, this principle **does not apply to** assets leased other than in the course of the trade (¶518). Instead any capital allowances on such assets can only be relieved against income from leasing, with any unrelieved allowances being carried forward.

Claim

247
s 3 CAA 2001
Capital allowances must be claimed, and all claims should be made on the tax return although it is common practice for the claim to be made in the form of a computation. For details of the company tax return and income tax return requirements see ¶2240 and ¶4476 respectively.

MEMO POINTS 1. **Provisional claims** will not be acceptable but a claim can be **amended or withdrawn** once it has been submitted, again via a tax return.
2. Claims can be made for any amount of the allowance up to the total amount due for a period. It may be beneficial to **claim a reduced amount** of allowance where loss relief is available, or for individuals, where personal allowances would be wasted.

250 This rule **does not apply** for the following claims (i.e. the claim need not be made on the tax return):
- allowances on assets leased other than in the course of a trade (¶518);
- carry back of balancing allowances arising on industrial buildings used for mineral extractions; and
- allowances on non-trade patent expenditure (¶701).

C. Successions to trade

252 Special rules apply to the calculation of capital allowances on successions to trade, where there is either:
ss 939 - 950 CTA 2010
- a transfer of a trade (or part of a trade) **between two companies** in common ownership; or
s 265 CAA 2001
- a change in the **person(s)** carrying on the trade without a sale of the assets.

1. Companies in common ownership

Transfer of trade

Where there is a transfer of a trade between two companies in common ownership, there is no disposal of the fixed assets and the successor company simply takes over the capital allowances and effectively stands in the shoes of the predecessor. WDA are calculated for the chargeable period of transfer and apportioned between the two companies, on a time basis. FYA and balancing charges are allocated to the company carrying on the trade at the time of the acquisition or disposal of the relevant asset. 254 s 948 CTA 2010

MEMO POINTS Companies are in **common ownership** if the same person (or persons) has an interest in at least 75% in the ordinary share capital (¶1508) for the:
– year preceding the transfer; and
– 2 years after the transfer of trade.

Where the two companies in question have **different accounting periods**, WDA are calculated for a notional chargeable period: 257
– starting with the first day of the accounting period of the predecessor company in which the transfer occurs; and
– ending with the last day of the accounting period of the successor company in which the transfer occurs.

This period may exceed 12 months, in which case, WDA will be increased and the calculated allowances apportioned between the companies, on a time basis.

EXAMPLE A Ltd and B Ltd are both wholly owned subsidiaries of C Ltd. A Ltd prepares its accounts annually to 30 June, and B Ltd to 31 October. On 1 May 2011, A Ltd's trade was transferred to B Ltd. Assuming A Ltd had a general pool WDV of £40,000 on 1 July 2010 and there were no acquisitions or disposals, capital allowances would be due as follows:

Notional chargeable period:	1 July 2010 – 31 October 2011 i.e. 16 months
Capital allowances due:	(40,000 × 25%) × 16/12 = £13,333
Allocated:	A Ltd: 1 July 2010 – 30 April 2011 i.e. 10/16 × £13,333 = £8,333 B Ltd: 1 May 2011 – 31 October 2011 i.e. 6/16 × £13,333 = £5,000

MEMO POINTS 1. **Trading losses** transferred on a succession to a trade or part of a trade can be carried forward and set against profits arising on the trade transferred, in the usual manner (¶1264).
2. These provisions are extended for trades transferred **on or after 12 March 2008** where a trade is transferred from A to B under these provisions where a further sale to C, who is not under common control, takes place. Where the transfer from A to B is effected to secure a balancing allowance for B this will now be denied by C taking over the assets at WDV from B. ss 954 - 957 CTA 2010

Transfer of leasing trade

Where a trade of leasing plant and machinery, i.e. a **lessor company**, is transferred on or after 22 November 2006 (¶1810), then the transfer of trade provisions only apply if the principal company (¶1815) of the predecessor trade is also the principal company of the successor trade. 260 s 950 CTA 2010

If the company is carrying on a trade in partnership the old trade must cease entirely on the transfer.

MEMO POINTS In addition, if the principal company is a **consortium company** the percentage of ordinary shares held or the entitlement to profits/assets available for distribution within the consortium relationship must be the same for the predecessor and the successor.

If the above **conditions are not met** there is instead a deemed disposal and reacquisition at market value, and capital allowances will be available to the successor on the market value. 262

2. Changes in person carrying on the trade

264
s 265 CAA 2001

Special provisions apply where:
– a person succeeds to a trade that was carried on by another person; and
– the succession causes the old trade to be treated as discontinued.
In this situation, the **assets of the trade are deemed to be transferred** at the date of succession for their market value, and acquired by the new business at that price. The successor can claim WDA in respect of the asset, but is not entitled to FYA or AIA.

MEMO POINTS Special rules apply when there is a **change in the composition of a partnership**. The trade of the partner that leaves the partnership is deemed to have discontinued, but the remaining partners are not affected. (See ¶2526 onwards for details).

267
ss 266 - 268 CAA 2001

The **rules are modified** where the transfer is of plant and machinery and either:
a. the predecessor and successor are connected (¶5570). In this situation, a joint election may be made to transfer the assets at WDV, which means that no allowances are due to the predecessor for the final period of trade. Such an election must be made within 2 years of the date of the succession; or
b. the succession occurs by virtue of the death of an individual. In this situation the successor may make an election for the deemed plant and machinery proceeds to be their tax written down value (if that is less than the market value). The WDV to be used is the WDV before any allowances are given for the final year of the deceased individual's trade.

MEMO POINTS The provisions at **a**. above **do not apply if** the predecessor and successor are companies:
– in **common ownership**. In this situation the rules at ¶254 apply; or
– carrying on a **business of leasing** plant and machinery. In this situation, no election is permitted and the capital allowances on disposal will be calculated using the consideration actually received.

Restrictions

268
ss 212A - 212S CAA 2001

From 21 July 2009 new provisions were introduced to **counteract the "buying"** of allowances where:
1. either:
– there is a change in ownership of the company, either by virtue of it being transferred or the interests of consortium companies changing;
– **a non-corporate owns the company** and transfers it to corporate ownership (for transactions after 9 December 2009);
– the trade ceases to be carried on by the company but is commenced by a partnership, which the original company is not a member of; or
– the company carries on the trade in partnership and it **reduces its interest in the partnership**, including leaving it;
2. the **motive** behind the change was to secure a tax advantage; and
3. there is an **excess of allowances**. This is defined as where the tax written down value of the plant and machinery exceeds the net book value shown on the balance sheet.
Where the provisions apply, the accounting period ends on the date of the change, with a new one starting the following day. At the beginning of the new period the pools where there are excess allowances are reduced by that amount, but where there is a shortfall of allowances in another pool this can be allowed against the potential reduction. Any excess left in relation to a particular pool is then placed in a secondary pool of the same type. The use of allowances from these secondary pools is limited. The limitations effectively mean that the allowances arising from these pools will only be available against the profits of that trade.

MEMO POINTS 1. In looking at the **potential excess** of allowances, the tax written down value of any class pool, any single asset pool and the main pool are added together and compared against the net balance sheet value of the assets, or net investment for finance leased assets.
2. If an asset on which allowances have been claimed has been **classified as land** in the balance sheet a just and reasonable apportionment is made.
3. In looking at the separate pools a just and reasonable apportionment is made of the balance sheet values where the **assets cannot be identified separately**.

SECTION 2

Types of asset

270 Principally there are three type of assets:
- plant and machinery;
- buildings; and
- intangible assets.

Each of these categories are further split but the categorisation between buildings and plant and machinery has been problematic. Furthermore, some items which might appear to be buildings are deemed to be plant and vice versa.

Plant and machinery or buildings

272 In order to clarify whether certain items were plant or part of a building, **statutory lists** detailing buildings and structures which qualify for capital allowances were introduced. The lists are not exhaustive and attention should still be given to relevant case law.

In the event that the statutory lists are unclear on any point the following **definitions** (based on decided case law) should be used:

a. machinery can be broadly defined as any asset with moving parts, and qualification for allowances is generally a question of fact;

b. plant is a more complex area, and from the large number of cases the following criteria will apply when determining whether an asset qualifies as plant (in any particular case, some or all may be relevant):
- is it actively used in the business?
- does it serve a purpose peculiar to the business?
- is it part of the function as opposed to the setting of the business? and
- does it perform the function of providing an atmosphere?

1. Statutory lists

279 The **first column** of each table shows assets that are specifically included within the definition of plant and machinery even though they would normally fall within the definition of buildings or structures.

The **second column** of each table shows assets that are excluded from the definition of plant and machinery (i.e. they are specifically included within the definition of buildings or structures).

281

LIST A – BUILDINGS	
Assets specifically included within the definition of plant and machinery [1]	**Assets specifically excluded from the definition of plant and machinery**
1. Any machinery (including devices for providing motive power) not within any other item in this column.	Walls, floors, ceilings, doors, gates, shutters, windows and stairs.
2. Gas and sewerage systems provided mainly to: [2] – meet the particular requirements of the trade; or – serve particular machinery or plant used for the purposes of the trade.	Mains services, and systems, of water, electricity and gas. Waste disposal systems; sewerage and drainage systems.
3. Manufacturing or processing equipment; storage equipment, including cold rooms; display equipment; counters, check-outs and similar equipment [3, 4].	
4. Cookers, washing machines, dishwashers, refrigerators and similar equipment; washbasins, sinks, baths, showers, sanitaryware and similar equipment; furniture and furnishings.	

LIST A – BUILDINGS	
Assets specifically included within the definition of plant and machinery [1]	**Assets specifically excluded from the definition of plant and machinery**
5. Hoists (including wiring and any alterations to an existing building necessary to operate it) [5, 6].	Shafts or other structures in which hoists are installed.
6. Sound insulation provided mainly to meet the particular requirements of the qualifying activity.	
7. Computer, telecommunication and surveillance systems (including their wiring or other links).	
8. Refrigeration or cooling equipment.	
9. Sprinkler equipment and other equipment for extinguishing or containing fire; fire alarm systems.	Fire safety systems generally.
10. Burglar alarm systems.	
11. Strong rooms in bank or building society premises; safes.	
12. Partition walls, where moveable and intended to be moved in the course of the qualifying activity [7].	
13. Decorative assets provided for the enjoyment of the public in a hotel, restaurant or similar trade.	
14. Advertising hoardings; signs, displays and similar assets.	
15. Swimming pools (including diving boards, slides and structures on which such boards or slides are mounted) [8].	

Note:

1. An asset does not fall within the second column if its **principal purpose is to insulate or enclose** the interior of the building or provide an interior wall, a floor or a ceiling which (in each case) is intended to remain permanently in place.
2. Prior to the introduction of the integral features class of expenditure (¶304), this description included electrical systems (including lighting) and cold water systems. Further included was space or water heating systems; powered systems of ventilation, air cooling or purification; any ceiling or floor comprised in such systems. However, false ceilings in a restaurant were not considered to perform a function (even though they were installed to cover pipes and wiring) and were therefore not allowed as plant. *Hampton v Fortes Autogrill Ltd* [1980]
3. Mezzanine floors incorporated into warehouses were held to be plant on the basis that they were **used to provide additional storage** and could be removed to leave the warehouses in their original state. The view was taken that the mezzanine floors in question were no different to other storage racking. *Hunt v Henry Quick* [1992], *King v Brindisco* [1992]
4. Free-standing decorative screens used in the windows of a building society branch were held to be plant on the basis that they were **not part of the setting** but rather were part of the apparatus by which the building society carried on its business. *Leeds Permanent Building Society v Proctor* [1982]

If a trade involves the creation of an attractive setting etc, pictures and removable wall decorations chosen to help create that setting will generally qualify for capital allowances.

It was agreed that money spent on brightening and modernising hotel facilities offered to the public (including the cost of rewiring, new light fittings, tapestries and pictures) was plant because it performed the function of **creating an atmosphere**. *IRC v Scottish and Newcastle Breweries* [1982]

This principle was considered in two further cases in which the taxpayers contended that items of expenditure incurred for restaurants were plant. It was held, however, that the question was one of fact, so for example a door is part of the fabric of the building whether or not it adds to the atmosphere of the restaurant. *Wimpey International Ltd v Warland* [1988] *Associated Restaurants Ltd v Warland* [1988]

On the basis of this test, suspended ceilings (over eating areas), light fittings, decorative brickwork, wall panels and mirrors were all considered to be plant whereas shop fronts, floor and wall tiles, suspended ceilings (over stairwell), raised floor area and stairs were all deemed not to be plant.

However this has to be contrasted with the case of *J D Wetherspoon plc v HMRC* [2007]. Wall panelling that could easily be removed without damage to the building was installed to create the correct atmosphere. However as it was an unexceptional component of the building it was deemed to be part of the building and as such not available for allowances.

5. Prior to the introduction of the integral features class of expenditure (¶304), this description included lifts, escalators and moving walkways.
6. Expenditure on the installation of a lift shaft in an existing building will qualify for capital allowances on the basis that it is incidental to the installation of qualifying plant and machinery. (Such expenditure in a new building will not qualify for capital allowances.)
7. It was held that moveable partitions provided **flexibility of accommodation** for the taxpayer and as such were plant and not part of the setting. Subsequent cases have shown that partitions that remain in the same place for an indefinite period are likely to be considered to be part of the building and not plant. *Jarrold v John Good & Sons Ltd* [1962]
8. Two swimming pools at a caravan site were held to be plant on the basis that they were provided to **attract custom** to the site and the water which the pools were designed to contain could not be divorced from the structure of the pools and their apparatus. A distinction was drawn between this type of pool and one purely for ornamental purposes which would not qualify as plant. *Cooke v Beach Station Caravans Ltd* [1974]

283

LIST B STRUCTURES	
Assets specifically included within the definition of plant and machinery [1]	**Assets specifically excluded from the definition of plant and machinery**
1. Glasshouses constructed so that the proper environment for the growing of plants is provided automatically by means of devices forming an integral part of the structure.	Any structure not within any other item in this column.
2. Cold stores.	
3. Caravans provided mainly for holiday lettings.	
4. Buildings provided for testing aircraft engines run within the buildings.	
5. Moveable buildings intended to be moved in the course of the qualifying activity [1].	
6. Expenditure on the alteration of land for the purpose only of installing machinery or plant [2].	
7. Expenditure on the provision of dry docks [3].	Any dock including: – any harbour, wharf, pier, marina or jetty; – any other structure in or at which vessels may be kept, or merchandise or passengers may be shipped or unshipped.
8. Any jetty or similar structure provided mainly to carry machinery or plant.	
9. Pipelines or underground ducts or tunnels with a primary purpose of carrying utility conduits.	Any tunnel, bridge, viaduct, aqueduct, embankment or cutting.
10. Towers provided to support floodlights.	
11. Any reservoir incorporated into a water treatment works or the provision of any service reservoir of treated water for supply within any housing estate or other particular locality.	Any dam, reservoir or barrage (including any sluices, gates, generators and other equipment associated with it). Any dike, sea wall, weir or drainage ditch.
12. Silos provided for temporary storage or the provision of storage tanks [4].	
13. Slurry pits or silage clamps.	
14. Fish tanks or fish ponds.	
15. Rails, sleepers and ballast for a railway or tramway.	Any way or hard standing, such as a pavement, road, railway or tramway, a park for vehicles or containers, or an airstrip or runway. Any inland navigation, including a canal or basin or a navigable river.
16. Structures and other assets for providing the setting for any ride at an amusement park or exhibition.	
17. Fixed zoo cages.	

Note:

1. Plant is sometimes moved from one site to another. If the costs of removal and re-erection are not allowable as a revenue deduction, capital allowances should be available.

2. The creation of three new putting greens was not considered to be the alteration of land to install plant but was deemed to be part of the premises on which the trade was carried on. *Family Golf Centres Ltd v Thorne* [1998]
However expenditure incurred on the excavation, infilling and draining of land prior to the installation of sand filled synthetic grass turf was plant on the basis it was altering the land to accept the plant. *IRC v Anchor International Ltd* [2004]

3. An item may still be plant even where it is providing an **additional function**, such as being the place in which the business is carried on. For example, the construction of a dry dock (including excavation, lining the site with concrete and installing machinery) was considered to be plant because it provided an active function of removing ships from the water and holding them upright while repairs were carried out. *CIR v Barclay, Curle & Co Ltd* [1969]

4. Allowances were claimed on silos used at the dockside for storage and distribution of grain. It was held that the silos were plant because the silos themselves and their external walls were part of a complex unit in which every piece was essential for the efficient operation of the whole. The silos were determined to be more than a **general setting of the trade** and instead were in the nature of a tool of the company's trade. *Schofield v R & H Hall Ltd* [1974]

2. Other specific items

285 Although not qualifying as plant under the general rules, the legislation identifies certain items that qualify for capital allowances provided the relevant conditions have been satisfied and the expenditure is not deductible in computing profits.

Asset	Conditions	Reference
Computer software	Capital expenditure on the acquisition of software or the right to use software will qualify for allowances, unless a revenue deduction is available (¶175). Where a right or licence is later granted to another person a disposal will arise (¶304)	s 71 CAA 2001
Safety at sports grounds	Expenditure must be incurred to comply with a safety certificate issued under the Safety of Sports Grounds Act 1975 or as certified by a local authority	ss 30 – 32 CAA 2001
Personal security expenditure	Expenditure must be incurred by an individual or partnership to improve the security of the trader or a partner where the threat arises wholly or mainly as a result of that trade and it is a special threat to that individual's personal security	s 33 CAA 2001

MEMO POINTS The allowance for expenditure on safety at sports grounds is to be removed at some point after April 2012.

SECTION 3

Plant and machinery

290 Once an item has been classed as being plant or machinery its treatment will differ based on what sub-class it is allocated to. This may result in the asset being held in a pool of expenditure or being noted separately in order for adjustments to be made on an asset-by-asset basis. Those assets that do not fall into the main pool are detailed below.

Asset	Treatment	¶¶
Car – CO_2 emission level over 160g/km	Special rate pool	¶308
Car costing over £12,000[1]	Held separately	¶420
Assets with private use[2]	Held separately	¶447
Assets expected to be held less than 4 years	Short life asset	¶430
Assets with an expected useful life of over 25 years	Special rate pool	¶315
Integral features in a building	Special rate pool	¶304
Thermal insulation	Special rate pool	¶301
Ships[3]	Special regime	
Assets for leasing	Special regime	¶482

Note:
1. This only applies to cars purchased prior to 1 April 2009 (6 April 2009 for income tax purposes) that are still held.
2. This only applies to traders subject to income tax as companies cannot have private use of an asset.
3. For details of the regime applying to ships see *Corporation Tax Memo*.

I. Quantifying the expenditure

291 As well as the basic rules (¶214) there are additional rules that apply for the purposes of quantifying the amount of qualifying expenditure incurred on plant and machinery.

Additional costs

292 ss 25 - 26 CAA 2001

Capital expenditure **includes** the cost of:
- acquisition of the plant or machinery;
- altering buildings incidental to the installation of plant and machinery for the purposes of the trade;
- demolition of existing plant and machinery that is being replaced (if the plant is not replaced, the net cost of the demolition is treated as qualifying expenditure in its own right); and
- moving plant from one site to another and re-erecting it (providing the costs are not deductible from profits).

Also, where an additional VAT liability arises under the VAT **capital goods scheme** (¶8250), this is treated as qualifying expenditure for the chargeable period in which the adjustment occurs.

Transactions between connected persons

294 ss 213 - 224 CAA 2001

The amount of capital expenditure on which allowances can be claimed is **restricted** when:
- ownership of the plant and machinery is transferred between connected persons (¶5570) via a sale, hire purchase or a sale and leaseback agreement; and
- the **main purpose of the transaction** is the obtaining of a writing down allowance.

In this situation the capital expenditure deemed to be incurred by the **new purchaser** is either:
- the disposal value that the vendor is required to bring into account on the transaction (¶402); or
- if there is no such amount, the lower of the current market value of the plant or machinery or the amount originally incurred by the vendor.

MEMO POINTS In addition, the purchaser is not entitled to claim FYA (¶325) nor is the expenditure eligible for the annual investment allowance (¶360).

Sale and leaseback

295 ss 225 - 228 CAA 2001

Where S sells plant or machinery to B, who then grants a leaseback (or finance leaseback) to S, an **election can be made** such that the capital expenditure on which B can claim capital allowances is the lower of:
- the cost to the lessor (B); and
- the original cost to the lessee (S).

The following **conditions** must be satisfied before the election can be made:
- S must have incurred expenditure on the provision of the plant or machinery;
- the plant or machinery must be new when originally acquired by S;
- the sale must occur not more than 4 months after the assets were brought into use by any person for any purpose
- S must not have claimed capital allowances on the asset nor included the asset in a capital allowances pool;
- S and B must not be connected; and
- the election must be made by both parties.

The election must be **submitted within** 2 years of the date of sale and, once made, is irrevocable. Where an election has been made, the lessee may not claim capital allowances on the assets sold.

MEMO POINTS 1. If **no election is made and there is a sale and finance leaseback**, B's capital expenditure on which capital allowances can be claimed is the lower of the: s 222 CAA 2001
- consideration for the disposal;
- market value of the asset transferred to him; or
- notional written down value of the asset (i.e. the capital expenditure less any allowances that could have been claimed if the expenditure was qualifying expenditure).

2. If **no election is made and there is a sale and leaseback**, B's capital expenditure on which capital allowances can be claimed will be the net proceeds of sale, in accordance with the general rules (¶402).

3. These provisions also extend to cover a sale of an asset which is on **hire purchase**.
4. See ¶166 for details of the **restriction on the revenue deduction** for S on a sale and finance leaseback.

II. Pools

A. Allocation of expenditure

296
ss 53, 54 CAA 2001
There are two main pools for plant and machinery allowances: the main pool and the special rate pool. If a company carries on **more than one activity** it should calculate its allowances separately for each trade so it is possible for a company to have more than one of each type of pool.

1. Main pool

298
s 54(6) CAA 2001
The statutory **definition** for the main rate pool is by exclusion, in that any plant that is not to be held separately or allocated to the special rate pool should be allocated here. As such it is a "catch-all" pool for those items that would not receive allowances under the other headings.

2. Special rate pool

300
s 104A CAA 2001
On 1 April 2008 (6 April 2008 for income tax purposes) this new class of expenditure was created. The list of assets contained in it are **defined by statute**. The assets contained in this pool are expected to have a longer life span than those assets allocated to the main pool and as such attract a lower rate of allowances (see ¶413 for details). The one **exception** to this is the addition of cars with high emission levels where the lower rate of allowances is intended to penalise those purchasing such cars.

Thermal insulation

301
s 28 CAA 2001
Where a building used for a qualifying activity is insulated against heat loss the costs incurred will enter the pool. Prior to 1 April 2008 (6 April 2008 for income tax purposes) only expenditure incurred on **industrial buildings** qualified.

CA 22220
MEMO POINTS Roof lining, double glazing, draught exclusion and cavity wall filling are all considered to be methods of thermal insulation.

Integral features

304
s 33A CAA 2001
As well as the new special rate pool a **sub-class of plant** was introduced for expenditure on or after 1 April 2008 (6 April 2008 for income tax purposes) for the following items:
a. electrical systems (including lighting systems);
b. cold water systems;
c. space or water heating systems;
d. powered systems of ventilation, air cooling or purification;
e. any floor or ceiling comprised in the systems described in **c**. or **d**.;
f. lifts, escalators or moving walkways; and
g. external solar shading.

MEMO POINTS Nothing in this section will include an asset where its primary purpose is to insulate or enclose the interior of a building, or provide means of permanent internal divisions within a building.

Replacement costs Typically replacement costs would be considered to be revenue in nature and allowed as a deduction against profits when incurred. However, where, in a 12 month period, **expenditure in excess of 50%** of the total estimated replacement cost is incurred on such expenditure then it will be considered capital. As such it is entered into the special rate pool and obtains allowances in the normal way. Where a series of works are carried out in a 12 month period the total cost must be aggregated. 306 CA 22340

EXAMPLE

1. ABC Ltd obtain a quote to replace the electrical system in their factory and office unit. The quote given is £100,000. A further quote was given for the elements of the system in the office areas at £48,000. On the proviso that the original quote was *bona fide* then the fact that the quote for the whole factory could have been obtained for less with another contractor is irrelevant. The cost will be treated as a repair.

2. Z Ltd incur the following expenditure on their air conditioning system.

Date	Cost (£)	12 months total (£)	Replacement cost (£)	% age of replacement	50% exceeded?
April 10	10,000	10,000	60,000	16.66	n
September 10	20,000	30,000	65,000	50[2]	n
December 10	5,000	35,000	65,000	58.33[2]	y
July 11	10,000	35,000[1]	65,000	53.28[2]	y

Note:
1. The 12 month cumulative total for July 2011 covers the period from August 2010 to July 2011.
2. In looking at the percentage of the total replacement cost, it is the earliest total replacement cost within the 12 month window. So for the expenditure to December 2010 the relevant cost is £60,000. However with regard to the expenditure in July 2011 it is the estimate in September 2010 that becomes relevant.

While the expenditure in April and September 2010 is less than 50% of the replacement cost the further expenditure in December 2010 takes the total expenditure over the limit. This results in all of the expenditure being classed as replacement expenditure.

Cars with emissions of over 160g/km

For purchases on or after 1 April 2009 the division of cars depending on the cost (¶422) was replaced by one relating to emission levels. 308

Where a car registered on or after 1 March 2001 has an EC certificate of conformity (or UK approval certificate) showing a CO_2 emission level of over 160g/km, it is termed a "special rate car" and will enter the special rate pool.

Where **more than one CO_2 emissions figure** is given the one specified as the "CO_2 emissions (combined)" will be used.

As such the car will attract the lower rate of allowance and no balancing allowances will be given on disposal.

MEMO POINTS 1. A special rate car will not enter the special rate pool if there is private use of it. It will then be held separately but will receive allowances based on the same rate.
2. A car is defined as a mechanically propelled road vehicle, except one: s 268C CAA 2001
– primarily suited for the conveyance of goods or burden of any description; or
– of a type not commonly used as a private vehicle and unsuitable for such use.
3. In the case of a bi-fuel car the lowest combined figure is taken. If there is no combined figure the lowest shown will apply.
4. Cars already treated under the old rules will remain so.

Cessation of hire trades Where a trade ceases, any residue left in the special rate pool, after taking account of disposals made, is available as a balancing allowance. However, 311 s 104F CAA 2001 where a trade of hiring or leasing cars ceases and a group company (¶1260) commences a similar trade within 6 months of the termination of the original trade, the balancing allowance arising may be restricted.

The restriction only applies in cases where the allowance from the special rate pool exceeds the total of any charges to be levied, after allowing for allowances, in other pools. The provisions ensure the allowance will be restricted so that the effect of all charges and allowances from the pools will be nil.

The new company will be deemed to have incurred expenditure equating to the amount of the restriction, irrespective or whether or not the actual cars involved were transferred from the group company ceasing the trade.

EXAMPLE A Ltd ceased the trade of car hiring on 2 June 2011. In October 2011 B Ltd, a company within the same group as A Ltd commences a similar trade. A Ltd made disposals of its assets to third parties, receiving £25,000 in total. B Ltd purchased vehicles amounting to £100,000.

A Ltd's main pool shows a balancing charge of £5,000. The special rate pool calculation at cessation would be:

Written down value brought forward	80,000
Disposal proceeds	(25,000)
Balancing allowance	55,000
Restricted to total pool charges	10,000
Restriction applied	45,000

So A Ltd will only be entitled to £10,000 of allowances from the special rate pool.

On commencing its trade B Ltd will be entitled to allowances on the £100,000 of actual expenditure it incurs and also on the £45,000 deemed expenditure arising from the restriction on A Ltd's pool.

313 s 208A CAA 2001 **Disposal value** While the disposal value will generally be the proceeds received for the transfer of the car, where the transaction is entered into for the **purposes of the avoidance of tax** the disposal value will be the lower of the market value of the car and the amount of expenditure deemed to have been incurred on the acquisition of the car by the person selling it.

Long life assets

315 **Pooling** Prior to the introduction of the special rate pool all such assets were added to one pool and attracted allowances at the rate of 6%. From the relevant date (¶300) they fall into the special rate pool.

318 ss 90, 91, 97 - 100 CAA 2001 **Definition** Assets are considered to be long life assets if:
– they have a **useful economic life** in excess of 25 years; and
– the trader has **spent more than** £100,000 on such long life assets in the particular accounting period. (This limit is reduced proportionately where the chargeable period is less than a year and where there are associated companies (¶1360).)

MEMO POINTS 1. For the purposes of the **useful economic life test**, an asset's life runs from the date when it is first used for any purpose to the time when it ceases to be used as a fixed asset of any business. The life of the asset is determined in relation to the whole asset, and will not be affected by the fact that parts of it have to be replaced or repaired within the 25 year period.

2. Expenditure on the following is **not affected by the £100,000 limit** and will always be within the scope of the long life asset regime:
– a share in plant and machinery;
– contributions to expenditure on plant and machinery; and
– plant for leasing.

320 ss 93 - 96 CAA 2001 Specifically **excluded** from long life asset treatment are:
a. cars;
b. plant and machinery used wholly or mainly in a building used as an office, showroom, hotel, retail shop or dwelling house;
c. ships and railway assets (until 1 January 2011).

B. Allowances available

There are a number of allowances that apply to both pools. It is important that in looking at the total allowances for a year that the allowance types are followed in order. 322

1. First year allowances

Over a number of years various first year allowances (FYA) have been available at different rates depending on the asset purchased or size of the taxpayer. They are only available in the chargeable period that an asset is acquired. However this rule is modified for payments made under the **VAT capital goods scheme** (¶8250). If the original asset qualified for an FYA then the further payment will also qualify in the period it is made provided the asset is still owned. 325

At present the only first year allowances available are those relating to expenditure on assets categorised as being environmentally friendly.

Environmentally beneficial plant and machinery

Where expenditure is incurred on **new, unused assets** (not second-hand) that are not considered to be long life assets (¶315), FYA will be available if the asset is within one of the water technology classes defined as: 329 s 45H CAA 2001 SI 2003/2076

- flow controllers;
- meters and monitoring equipment;
- leakage detection;
- efficient toilets and taps;
- rainwater harvesting equipment;
- efficient membrane filtration systems for the treatment of wastewater for recovery and re-use;
- cleaning in place equipment;
- efficient showers and washing machines;
- small scale slurry and sludge dewatering equipment;
- vehicle wash waste reclaim units;
- efficient industrial cleaning equipment; and
- water management for mechanical seals.

Where a **company makes a loss** due to these allowances it may be able to claim first year tax credits (¶339).

MEMO POINTS Expenditure on environmentally beneficial plant and machinery that is purchased for **leasing** can also qualify for FYA provided the plant and machinery is background plant and machinery (¶487).

Energy-saving plant and machinery

Expenditure qualifies for FYA if it is incurred on new, unused plant and machinery and meets the **following conditions**: 332 s 45A CAA 2001

- it is of a description specified by Treasury Order; and
- it meets the energy-saving criteria specified in the Energy Technology List.

A certificate of compliance is required from the supplier in order for the expenditure to be eligible for allowances. Associated costs such as transport and installation can also be included.

Where a **company makes a loss** due to these allowances it may be able to claim first year tax credits (¶339).

MEMO POINTS 1. The technologies that qualify for FYA are largely derived from the **Energy Technology List** which is produced by the government. Currently the technologies that qualify comprise:
- combined heat and power;
- motors;
- boilers;
- lighting;
- variable speed drives;
- refrigeration equipment;
- pipe insulation;
- automatic monitoring and targeting equipment;
- compressed air equipment;
- heat pumps for space heating;
- solar thermal systems;
- warm air and radiant heaters;
- air to air recovery equipment;
- heating, ventilation and air conditioning equipment;
- uninterruptible power supplies; and
- high speed hand air driers.

2. Expenditure on energy-saving plant or machinery that is purchased for **leasing** can also qualify for FYAs provided the plant and machinery is background plant and machinery (¶487).
3. The person responsible for issuing the **certificate** depends on where the plant is used:
- England: the Secretary of State;
- Wales: the National Assembly;
- Scotland: the Scottish Ministers; or
- Northern Ireland: the Department of Enterprise, Trade and Investment.

Cars with low carbon dioxide emissions

334
s 45D CAA 2001

Unused (not second-hand) cars, including Hackney carriages, with low carbon dioxide (CO_2) emissions and electrically propelled cars qualify for FYA.

To **qualify** as having low CO_2 emissions, the car must be registered with an EC certificate of conformity or a UK approval certificate, and must have an applicable CO_2 emissions figure of 110g/km driven or less. Where **more than one CO_2 emissions figure** is given, the one specified as the "CO_2 emissions (combined)" will be used.

When the full **FYA is not claimed** for a car that qualifies under these provisions, the balance of the expenditure is placed into the main rate pool (¶300) and, as such, no balancing allowances or charges will arise on disposal.

MEMO POINTS 1. For **bi-fuel cars**, where separate figures are given for different fuels, the lowest figure will be used.
2. **Electrically propelled cars** must be propelled solely by electrical power.
3. **Motorcycles** are specifically excluded under this provision.
4. Expenditure on cars with low CO_2 emissions that are purchased for **leasing** can also qualify for FYA.

Gas refuelling stations

336
s 45E CAA 2001

Plant and machinery installed solely for use to refuel vehicles with natural gas or hydrogen will qualify for FYA. This **includes** any:
- storage tank for natural gas or hydrogen fuel;
- compressor, pump, control or meter used in connection with the refuelling of vehicles with natural gas or hydrogen;
- equipment for dispensing the natural gas or hydrogen to the vehicle; and
- expenditure on biogas refuelling equipment.

Associated costs such as transport and installation are also eligible for allowances.

Zero-emission goods vehicles

337

Where a **new, unused** vehicle, designed for the carriage of goods, is purchased on or after 1 April 2010 (6 April 2010 for income tax purposes) it will qualify for 100% FYA in the period it is purchased where it cannot produce any CO_2 emissions.

However, the following businesses are excluded from claiming the FYA:
- those that are considered to be in **difficulty**;
- those **yet to repay State Aid** that has been deemed illegal;
- those involved in the **fisheries or aquaculture** sectors; and
- those that **manage the waste** of others.

In order to stay within the State Aid rules there will be an overall cap on eligible expenditure of €85 million, which will cover all companies in a group.

MEMO POINTS This incentive will remain open for 5 years under current proposals. s 45DA CAA 2001

First year tax credits

339 Sch A1 CAA 2001

Where a **company makes a loss** due to claiming the allowances available on environmentally beneficial plant and machinery (¶329) or energy-saving plant and machinery (¶332) on expenditure incurred on or after 1 April 2008, they may be entitled to a repayable tax credit.

The amount of loss that can be surrendered is the amount of the loss arising from the FYA claimed on the qualifying expenditure less any amounts that:
- **could have been** utilised to set off against other profits arising in the same year;
- have been utilised to offset against profits from an earlier period;
- **could have been surrendered** as group (¶1540) or consortium relief (¶1575);
- have been surrendered for another form of credit; and
- reduce the loss a company incurs by virtue of a government investment in the company being written off.

EXAMPLE A Ltd incurs £100,000 on qualifying plant and makes a claim for 100% FYA. As a result it makes a loss for the year of £30,000. Its surrenderable loss will be £30,000.
If the loss incurred had been £130,000 the surrenderable loss would have been £100,000.

MEMO POINTS 1. The credit system is only available to those companies within the charge to corporation tax.
2. The credit system is currently in place for expenditure incurred on these types of assets until 31 March 2013.
3. Any sums that become due as a result of an additional VAT liability arising will not be eligible for the credit system.
4. The deeming provisions that treat pre-trading expenditure as occurring on the first day of trade do not apply for this purpose.

Amount of credit The total amount of the repayable credit is 19% of the loss that is surrendered up to a maximum of the greater of: 341 Sch A1 para 2 CAA 2001
- the company's total PAYE and NIC liability for payment periods ending during that year (¶812); and
- £250,000.

The entire surrenderable loss does not have to be surrendered in favour of a repayable credit. As with most allowances the company has the choice of how much it wishes to surrender.

Clawback of credit Where a company claims a credit and, within the period ending 4 years from the end of the period in relation to which the credit was paid, disposes of an asset that attracted the FYA, there may be a clawback of the credits paid with a corresponding increase in the loss carried forward from that period. This will occur where the remaining expenditure on which the claim was made falls to below the amount of expenditure claimed upon. The amount of the loss that is added back is the difference between the original loss surrendered and the amount of capital expenditure that is still left after the disposal. This amount is reduced by any deficit on the sale of the asset and also any losses that have previously been added back. This loss is then multiplied by the percentage that applied in the year the credit was due for, not the percentage applying at the time of the clawback. This sum is then repaid by the company. 343 Sch A1 para 24 CAA 2001

EXAMPLE

1. A Ltd invested £100,000 in qualifying expenditure, claiming 100% FYA. This resulted in a loss of £150,000 for the year, with the £100,000 being surrendered for the credit. Two years later the company sold one of those assets, originally costing £50,000, for £40,000. In this case the amount of loss that will be required to be added back will be:

Original loss surrendered		100,000
Amount of expenditure remaining		(50,000)
		50,000
Cost of asset sold	50,000	
Disposal proceeds	(40,000)	
		(10,000)
Loss to be added back		40,000

The credit to be repaid will be £40,000 × 19% = 7,600. The loss treated as being carried forward from the original accounting period will be £90,000.

2. Using the same facts as above but the loss created by the claim is £40,000, all of which was surrendered for a repayable credit. In this case there will be no clawback as the amount of original expenditure remaining (£50,000) exceeds the amount of loss surrendered (£40,000).

MEMO POINTS For these purposes, the term disposal is extended to include a transfer of an asset where the purchaser is deemed to stand in the shoes of the vendor.

346 s 3(2B), Sch A1 para 18 CAA 2001

Procedure The tax credit has to be **claimed**, and must be shown separately, in the corporation tax return. Where a valid claim is made the payment will be made to the company with the following restrictions:
- any outstanding corporation tax liabilities will be settled first by the credit;
- where there are any PAYE or Class 1 NIC liabilities outstanding for the payment periods covered by the accounting period there is no requirement for HMRC to make the payment; and
- HMRC may withhold a payment where the period for which the credit is due is under enquiry. However they may make a partial payment at their own discretion.

2. Annual investment allowance

360 The annual investment allowance (AIA) was introduced as a means of modernising and simplifying the capital allowances system. It is relevant for expenditure incurred on or after 1 April 2008 (or 6 April 2008 for income tax purposes). It complements the continuing first year allowances on "green" expenditure (¶327).

a. Who can claim?

362 s 38A CAA 2001

The AIA is **available to**:
- sole traders;
- companies; and
- partnerships, where all the partners are individuals.

As such, trusts, limited liability partnerships and partnerships involving a corporate partner are **excluded** from claiming the allowance.

Businesses under common control, while entitled to an allowance, may find that they are required to share the allowance (¶371).

b. Qualifying expenditure

364 s 38B CAA 2001

The allowance can cover capital expenditure (¶204) incurred during a chargeable period provided that it is **owned** at some point during that period. While the asset has to be **acquired** for use in the trade it does not have to have come **into use** for the allowance to be available.

Also excluded from the allowance is:
1. expenditure on **cars**;
2. expenditure in the **final period** of the business;
3. **notional expenditure** on bringing into trade use an asset that:
– was previously owned by the trader and not used for trade purposes;
– ceased to be used for the purposes of a long funding lease; or
– is received by way of gift;
4. expenditure incurred by someone in connection with a change in the nature of another's business and one of the main benefits of the expenditure was to secure an allowance that would **not reasonably have arisen** otherwise;
5. expenditure incurred under **arrangements** to enable a claim to be made that would not otherwise have been possible; and s 218A CAA 2001
6. assets acquired from connected persons.

MEMO POINTS Where a VAT payment is made under the capital goods scheme (¶8250) where the asset it relates to qualified for the AIA in an earlier period, then the payment is eligible for the allowance in the period in which it is made.

Where an **additional VAT liability** is incurred, provided the original expenditure to which it relates was eligible for the allowance and the asset is still held, then this can also attract the allowance. **367**

c. Amount of the allowance

The allowance is given at the **rate** of 100% up to a maximum amount of expenditure. The maximum level of expenditure covered has changed a number of times since the allowance's introduction. **369** s 51A CAA 2001

Expenditure between	Amount
1 April 2008 to 31 March 2010	£50,000
1 April 2010 to 31 March 2012	£100,000
From 1 April 2012	£25,000

Note:
For income tax purposes the periods run from 6 April to 5 April.

Where a period straddles one of these dates a calculation has to be performed to ascertain the maximum amount.

EXAMPLE A Ltd has a year ending 31 December 2010. Its total AIA is calculated as follows:

3/12 x £50,000	£12,500
9/12 x £100,000	£75,000
Total AIA available for the year	£87,500

While the total available allowance is £87,500, for expenditure incurred prior to 1 April 2010 the maximum will be £50,000. So if the company incurred expenditure of £90,000 prior to 1 April 2010 only £50,000 of this would qualify for the allowance, even where there is no further qualifying expenditure in the year.

Where the chargeable period (¶257) is not 12 months in length this limit is prorated. The **allocation** of the allowance against qualifying assets purchased during the year is a matter of choice for the taxpayer.

d. Businesses under common control

Where businesses are under common control and, with the exception of group companies, related, they will only receive one AIA between them. How this is shared among the various businesses is then a matter of choice for the taxpayer. When testing businesses under common control there is no provision to connect a company and a business subject to **371** income tax. As such a company and its sole shareholder, who runs a sole trade, would each be entitled to a full allowance.

Companies

374
s 51B CAA 2001

A company will only receive one AIA regardless of the number of trades it carries on. The method of allocation between the trades is a matter of choice for the company.

376
s 1162 Companies Act 2006
s 51C CAA 2001

Companies in a group Companies in a **group** (using the *Companies Act* definition, see *Company Law Memo*) will only receive one AIA. A subsidiary company will be considered to be in a group for a financial year where, at the end of its chargeable period ending in that financial year, it is under the control of the parent.

378
ss 51E, 51F CAA 2001

Other companies under common control For other companies under common control at the end of any of their chargeable periods, they will be required to share an allowance where they are **related**.

MEMO POINTS Control is defined as being able to secure that the affairs of the company are carried out in accordance with someone's wishes, either by way of shareholding or the possession of voting rights in that or another company, or by way of some agreement including the articles of association. However, in looking at this no account is to be taken of the rights of connected parties.

381
s 51G CAA 2001

Two companies are **related** where they either:
– **share premises** at the end of the chargeable period for either of them. In the absence of any statutory definition the ordinary meaning of premises will apply; or

EC Regulation 1893/2006

– are engaged in **similar activities** using the first level of the European Nace classification (http://eur-lex.europa.eu/LexUriServ/LexUriServ.do? uri = OJ:L:2006:393:0001:01:EN:HTML).
Companies can either be related **directly**, as above, or **indirectly** by virtue of two companies being related to a third.

EXAMPLE Companies A Ltd, B Ltd and C Ltd are all owned by Mr Z. Companies A and B share premises and as such are related. Companies B and C are engaged in similar activities. Without any further provisions A and C would not be related as they neither share premises nor engage in similar activities. However they are indirectly related as they are both directly related to B. In this case A, B and C will share one allowance.

MEMO POINTS Two companies will be considered to be engaging in similar activities where 50% or more of their turnover for the chargeable period comes from the same classification.

383

Groups under common control of someone other than a company Without specific legislation groups would be able to claim more than one allowance where they were controlled by anyone other than a company. As such, groups under common control, where at least one company in each group is related, will be entitled to only one AIA.

EXAMPLE Mr A controls two groups of companies – the M group containing M, N and O Ltd, and the X group containing X, Y and Z Ltd. Each group would be entitled to an AIA to divide among the three companies in each group. However where any company in one group is related to a company in the other group all of the companies will have to share one allowance.

Businesses other than companies

385
s 51H CAA 2001

An individual can receive more than one AIA where they carry on more than one trade in a year. However where an individual or number of individuals **control** more than one trade they will be only be entitled to one AIA where the businesses are also **related**.

388
s 51I CAA 2001

Control Where a trade is controlled by one or more persons at the end of its chargeable period it is considered to be controlled by them for the tax year that the chargeable period ends in.

EXAMPLE A, B and C operate partnership Y on an equal profit share basis. A and B also operate partnership Z. As A and B are entitled to more than 50% of both businesses Y and Z are under common control.

MEMO POINTS A **sole trader** controls the trade that he operates. A **partnership** is controlled by the person or persons who have the right to more than half of the income or assets of the partnership. In looking at this no account is taken of the rights of connected persons.

Related Two trades can be related either by sharing premises or by carrying out similar activities (¶381). Both tests are applied at the end of the chargeable periods for the businesses and if either is satisfied at any of these points then they will be related. Where one business, A, is related to another, B, it will also be treated as related to any other businesses that B is related to. 390 s 51J CAA 2001

EXAMPLE Trader A operates from premises for a period of time. At the end of his accounting period, 30 April 2010, this is the only trade operating from the premises. In November a partnership that he controls moved in. The partnership's accounting period ends on 31 March 2011. As at the end of the partnership's year the shared premises test is met, only one AIA will be available to the businesses for the tax year 2010/11.

MEMO POINTS The Nace classification (¶381) is used to ascertain if the individual trades are similar. This is the same as for companies but as the test applies to each trade there is no need to apply a 50% of turnover test.

Long periods of account Where someone controls two or more related businesses and one of these has a long period of account, further provisions may allow additional amounts of allowance to be claimed. However any additional allowance will still have to remain within the overall cap adjusted for the length of the period (¶369). Without these provisions a long period of account ending in one tax year with a second business would result in only £50,000 of allowance being available across both businesses. 392 s 51M CAA 2001

EXAMPLE M has carried on business as a hotelier for many years making up his accounts to 31 March each year. In November 2008 he opens a public house and his first set of accounts run until 30 April 2010. These two businesses fall within the same Nace classification and therefore are related.
In renovating the public house M incurred qualifying expenditure of £100,000 in the 18 month period. Meanwhile the allowances used by the hotel business have been as follows:
Year ended 31 March 2009 – £20,000
Year ended 31 March 2010 – £10,000
In the year to 31 March 2011 £40,000 of expenditure that potentially qualified was incurred.
Without these provisions only a maximum allowance of £50,000 could be utilised in 2010/11 even though one business period is 18 months in length. In order to ascertain the amount of allowance that can be utilised in 2010/2011 you have to look back at the tax years in which M carried on the business with the long period and ascertain what amount of allowances had not been utilised in those years.
In this case £40,000 of the allowances in 2009/10 were unused and will be available for the new business.
The unused allowances of £30,000 in 2008/09 will only be partly available as the new business was only carried on for 5 months in that tax year. As such only 5/12 × 30,000 = £12,500 will be available.
The total given over these 2 years that could then be used against the expenditure in the new business would appear to be £52,500, leaving the maximum for the year 2010/2011 as £102,500. However the maximum cannot exceed the maximum for 18 months (being the longer period of account) and as such is capped at £75,000. This would result in the new business being able to use £52,500 of the earlier year's allowances and up to £22,500 of the 2010/11 allowance. This would leave £27,500 available for the hotel business.
If M decides to allocate £40,000 of the allowance to the hotel business to cover all its expenditure then the remaining £10,000 could be added to the £52,500 for use in the public house business.

3. Allowances given through pool

The remaining allowances are given via the operation of the pool mechanics allowing annual writing down allowances (WDA). Balancing allowances are only given on cessation of the trade even if no assets remain in the trader's ownership. Balancing charges may also 395 arise as a result of the operation of the pool. Since 1 April 2008 there has also been a small pools allowance available for all traders.

EXAMPLE A Ltd ceases trading on 31 March and prepares accounts for a 10 month period up to that date. During this final period an asset was sold for £2,350 but all the other assets remained in the pool to the date of cessation. WDV brought forward on the general pool is £15,775.

	General pool £	Allowances given £
Period ended 31 March:		
WDV b/fwd	15,775	
Less: disposal	(2,350)	
	13,425	
Balancing allowance	(13,425)	13,425
WDV c/fwd	–	

Operation of the pools

397 In order to understand the scheme of allowances it is necessary to understand how the pools themselves function. The following pro forma computation shows the structure of the allowances in pools.

Written down value brought forward		x
Expenditure qualifying for AIA	x	
Less AIA allocated	(x)	
		x
Add expenditure not qualifying for FYA		x
Disposal proceeds		(x)
		x[1]
Writing down allowance[2]		(x)
		x
Add residue of qualifying expenditure after FYA not previously added to the pool[3, 4]		x
Written down value carried forward (WDV c/fwd)		x

Notes:
1. The small pool test is applied at this stage.
2. The writing down allowance depends on the pool. See ¶413 for details.
3. It is not necessary to allocate expenditure immediately to either pool. However it must be allocated prior to its disposal. In practice it will always be allocated to enable writing down allowances to be given in future years.
4. Where an asset receives a 100% first year allowance there is no residue to allocate to the pool. However it is still deemed to be added to one of the pools so that any balancing adjustment due to a sale is accounted for in the correct pool.

Disposals from the pool

399 On disposals from the pool the disposal proceeds are deducted from the pool. If the proceeds exceed the original cost of the asset disposed of then the disposal value brought into account is generally **restricted to the original expenditure** incurred. Where the disposal value exceeds the expenditure, the balance may be dealt with via the chargeable gains regime (¶5924).

402 **Disposal proceeds** There are also specific circumstances where the disposal proceeds are not the amount received for the sale of an asset.

s 61 CAA 2001

The legislation sets out a table of all **disposal events and their associated disposal values**, as follows:

Disposal event	Disposal value[1]
1. Sale of machinery or plant except where item 2 applies	The net proceeds of sale together with: – any insurance money received as a result of an event affecting the price on sale; and – any other compensation of any description which consists of a capital sum
2. Sale of plant and machinery where: – the sale is at less than market value; – there is no charge to tax under the employment income provisions; and – the buyer's expenditure does not qualify for research and development capital allowances	The market value of the machinery or plant at the time of sale, unless the purchaser is either: – entitled to capital allowances on the asset; or – an employee who will be subject to tax on the receipt of the asset as a benefit in kind (¶3276), in which case actual disposal proceeds will be used
3. Demolition or destruction of the plant and machinery	The net amount received for the remains of the plant and machinery together with: – any insurance money received for the demolition or destruction; and – any other compensation of any description which consists of a capital sum
4. Permanent loss of the machinery or plant otherwise than as a result of its demolition or destruction	Any insurance money received and any other compensation of any description which consists of a capital sum
5. Abandonment of any machinery or plant that has been in use for mineral exploration and access to the site where it was in use for that purpose	Any insurance money received and any other compensation of any description which consists of a capital sum
6. Commencement of a long funding finance lease of plant and machinery (¶483)	An amount equal to the lessor's net investment in the lease (on the assumption that the accounts are prepared in accordance with accepted accountancy principles)
7. Commencement of a long funding operating lease of plant and machinery (¶483)	An amount equal to the market value of the plant and machinery at the commencement of the term of the lease
8. Permanent cessation of the qualifying activity followed by any of the events listed above	The disposal value for the item in question
9. Any event not listed above	The market value of the machinery or plant at the time of the event

Note:
1. The disposal value is generally restricted to the original expenditure incurred. Where the disposal value exceeds the expenditure, the balance may be dealt with via the chargeable gains regime (¶5924).

Special rate pool: sales below market value The special rate pool has anti-avoidance provisions for circumstances where an asset is sold for less than its notional written down value and this forms part of a scheme to secure a tax advantage. Where this applies, the seller's disposal proceeds will be deemed to be the notional written down value and the purchaser will still only be able to claim allowances based on their acquisition value. 404 s 104E CAA 2001

MEMO POINTS The **notional written down value** is calculated as being the amount of qualifying expenditure incurred on the asset less the maximum allowances that could have been claimed in respect of the asset.

Special rate pool: connected party disposals Where **connected parties** (¶5570) transfer an asset in order to obtain allowances on assets that did not qualify prior to the special rate pool's introduction, the party acquiring the asset will not be entitled to allowances on the expenditure. 406 Sch 26 paras 15 – 17 FA 2008

However, within a **group situation** (¶1524), a joint election can be made where the asset qualified for allowances in the general pool before the transfer but would enter the special rate pool in the buyer's hands. Where the election is made, the notional written down value of the asset is quantified (¶404) and this figure is used as both the disposal and acquisition cost, with the buyer entering the asset into its general pool. If the buyer sells the asset the proceeds are not capped at the transfer value but at the original acquisition price. This election has to be made within the normal time limits (¶2255).

Acquisition and disposal in same period

409 Where expenditure is incurred on an asset and it is then disposed of in the same chargeable period, WDA will still be available. For example an asset **bought and sold in the same period** will still be eligible for allowances, as will enhancement expenditure incurred on an asset which is then sold during the period.

a. Small pools allowance

411
s 56A CAA 2001

Where the residue in either pool is less than or equal to £1,000, after accounting for disposals and acquisitions as above, then the company can claim the full amount of the residue as an allowance for the year.

The limit is prorated where the chargeable period is **more or less than 12 months**. The limit is also prorated where the activity has not been carried out for an entire 12 months. A claim must be made for this although the company may claim a lower amount.

The allowance applies to both types of pool and, if there is more than one activity being carried on, it will apply to all such pools in isolation.

b. Writing down allowances

413
ss 56, 104D CAA 2001

This allowance is available year on year in both pools and is based on a percentage of the remaining expenditure in the pool at the time the allowance is applied (¶397). The current rates are:

- 20% for the main rate pool; and
- 10% for the special rate pool.

The amount claimed as an allowance reduces the pool for future periods. It is not necessary to claim the full amount available. Any allowance that is not claimed will result in a larger residue being carried forward.

Where the chargeable period is **more or less than a year** the amount of the allowance will be prorated. Although the apportionment should be made on the basis of the number of days in the chargeable period, typically it can be calculated based on the number of months.

EXAMPLE A Limited has a residue of expenditure of £10,000 brought forward in the main pool and makes no additions or disposals of assets in its accounting period of only 6 months. The allowances the company claim will be £1,000 (10,000 x 20% x 6/12).

MEMO POINTS 1. These rates also apply to items that would enter either pool but for the fact that an asset has private use (¶447).

2. For **individuals**, allowances may be proportionately increased for chargeable periods in excess of 12 months although periods of more than 18 months will be split into two periods, one of 12 months and one of the remainder (see ¶239).

3. These rates are to be reduced for accounting periods ending **on or after 1 April 2012** (6 April 2012 for income tax purposes) to 18% and 8%.

c. Balancing allowances and charges

418
ss 55, 65 CAA 2001

In the context of the pools, a balancing allowance will only occur at the end of the final chargeable period in which a qualifying activity is carried on. At that point the balance of the pools can then be claimed as an allowance.

A balancing charge will be imposed where the disposal proceeds of an asset exceed the amount of expenditure left in the pool. The balancing charge will be the amount of the excess.

III. Separately identified assets

1. Expensive cars

The provisions for expensive cars are still applicable for cars that were purchased prior to 1 April 2009 (6 April 2009 for income tax purposes) and will continue to apply until periods ending on or after 31 March 2014 (5 April 2014 for income tax purposes). For cars purchased on or after this date see ¶290. 420

Pooling

Cars that cost more than £12,000 (expensive cars) were excluded from the main pool and treated individually. Cars that cost £12,000 or less were simply placed in the main pool, unless there was private use. 422

MEMO POINTS Cars with **low carbon dioxide emissions** (¶334) are eligible for FYA and, regardless of the original cost of the car, any remaining expenditure is placed in the general pool.

Definition

For these purposes a car is defined as any mechanically propelled road vehicle **except for**: 425 s 268A CAA 2001
a. commercial vehicles; and
b. vehicles provided in the ordinary course of a trade wholly or mainly for:
- the transportation of (or short-term hire to) members of the public; or
- hire to disabled persons.

This definition therefore includes **motorcycles**.

A vehicle which came under one of the exceptions fell into the main pool providing the plant and machinery conditions were met (¶272).

MEMO POINTS **Commercial vehicles** are those primarily suited for the conveyance of goods which are not commonly used as a private vehicle and are unsuitable for private use.

Writing down allowance

Each expensive car was placed in a separate capital allowances pool and WDA continues to be **given at a rate of** 20% per annum. The allowance for each car may not exceed £3,000 per year and this restriction is reduced or increased proportionately where the chargeable period is more or less than a year. 427 ss 74, 75 CAA 2001

A **balancing adjustment** will arise where the car is disposed of either through sale, permanent loss or destruction, or where it begins to be used wholly or partly for non-business purposes. To calculate the adjustment, the disposal value (¶402) is deducted from the brought forward balance before WDA are given. If the result is a negative figure then a balancing charge arises and if it is positive then a balancing allowance arises.

EXAMPLE During the 8 month period ending 31 March 2008 A Ltd purchases car A, costing £20,000. In the year ending 31 March 2009 car B is purchased for £13,950. Car A is then sold in the year ended 31 March 2010 for £12,950.

	Car A	Car B	Allowances given
	£	£	£
Period ended 31 March 2008:			
Addition	20,000		
WDA restricted to £3,000 × 8/12	(2,000)		2,000
Year ended 31 March 2009:			
WDV b/fwd	18,000		
Addition		13,950	
WDA restricted to £3,000	(3,000)	(3,000)	6,000

Year ended 31 March 2010:			
WDV b/fwd	15,000	10,950	
Disposal	(12,950)		
	2,050		
WDA @ 20%		(2,190)	2,190
Balancing allowance	(2,050)		2,050
WDV c/fwd	Nil	8,760	4,240

Transactions between connected persons

429
s 79 CAA 2001

Special provisions aim to **prevent the manipulation of balancing adjustments** when either:
- a car (of any value) is disposed of to a connected person (¶5570); or
- a car hire purchase contract is assigned to a connected person.

Consequently, in such situations the disposal value of the car (and the corresponding acquisition cost for the purchaser) will be the lesser of its:
- market value; or
- original cost.

These anti-avoidance rules **do not apply** if an election has been made to continue the trade on a change of ownership or on a company reconstruction (¶264).

2. Short life assets

Pooling

430 An asset which is not likely to remain in use for the whole of the period over which it would be written off in the general pool may **optionally** be treated as a short life asset for capital allowances purposes. Short life assets are identified separately and as a result balancing adjustments are available on disposal providing the assets are still in the short life asset pool.

Definition

432
s 83 CAA 2001

A short life asset can essentially be defined as any asset that is expected to have a working life of less than 8 years from the end of the chargeable period in which the expenditure occurred, unless specifically excluded.

s 84 CAA 2001

Assets which are excluded from the main pool under other capital allowances provisions are **excluded** from the definition of short life assets, as follows:

Excluded assets	¶¶
Cars (other than those hired out to persons receiving disability allowance)	¶422
Assets leased other than in the course of a trade	¶518
Assets which have previously been used for long funding leasing	¶483
Assets used only partly for trade purposes	¶447
Plant and machinery in respect of which a subsidy is received	¶216
Ships	¶290

MEMO POINTS For expenditure incurred before 1 April 2011 (6 April 2011 for income tax purposes) the period was 4 years.

434
s 85 CAA 2001

A short life asset **election must be made** in writing and must specify the assets concerned, the expenditure incurred and the date on which it was incurred. The election, once made, is irrevocable. The normal time limits apply (¶2255 for companies and ¶4496 for individuals).

Writing down allowance

Every short life asset is treated as being in a pool of its own which is separate from the general pool, and allowances are given at the same rate as those in the main pool. WDA are reduced or increased proportionately for chargeable periods of less or more than a year. 437 s 86 CAA 2001

If the asset **is disposed of** within 8 years from the end of the chargeable period in which the expenditure was incurred, then the disposal proceeds are deducted from the brought forward balance on the pool and a balancing adjustment will arise. If the asset has **not been disposed of** by the end of the 8 year period the WDV is transferred to the general pool at the beginning of the next chargeable period.

Where assets are held in large numbers that would make separate identification impossible, or impractical a modified computation with assets shown in **batches** will be accepted. Each batch will form a separate pool. 440 SP 1/86

MEMO POINTS Where separate identification would be impossible, the **assets in the batch must** be shown to have a broadly similar average working life. Where separate identification is merely impractical the number of assets from each batch bought and sold in a period must be identifiable.

If, during the initial 8 year period, a short life asset begins to be used **partly for non-trade** purposes it will cease to be a short life asset and will be treated as any other partly non-trade asset (¶447). The change will be deemed to take place at the beginning of the chargeable period in which the non-qualifying use begins. 442

Transactions between connected persons

If, during the initial 8 year period, a short life asset is disposed of to a connected person (¶5570) then a joint **election may be made** for the asset to be transferred at tax written down value (and no balancing adjustment will arise). The connected person is deemed to have made the short life asset election himself, and the original date of acquisition is used to determine when the asset should be transferred to the general pool. 444 ss 88, 89 CAA 2001

MEMO POINTS 1. The **election must be made within** 2 years from the end of the chargeable period in which the disposal occurs.
2. If such an **election is not made**, the purchaser is still deemed to have acquired the asset at the original date of acquisition, but the asset will be transferred at the greater of market value or the price actually paid Therefore a balancing adjustment will normally arise to the vendor.

---

3. Private use assets

Definition

A private use asset is essentially **any asset** that is used partly for the purposes of the trade and partly for private use. 447 ss 54, 206 - 207 CAA 2001

Writing down allowance

The amount of WDA that can be claimed will be restricted to the proportion relating to the trade use. Consequently a **separate pool** is used for each private use asset. Available allowances are still restricted where the chargeable period is less than 12 months and the remaining balance will be reduced in the normal way. 449

Where the asset is eligible for the AIA, only that part of the expenditure that is considered to be business is allowable.

If the asset **qualified for FYA**, the allowance will be apportioned in the same way as for WDA. The remaining balance available will not be affected, but will be transferred to a separate private use asset pool instead of the general pool.

EXAMPLE During the 9 month period ended 30 September a sole trader purchases a van costing £10,000. He uses the van 80% for the purposes of the trade and 20% for private use. WDV brought forward on the general pool is £6,775.

	Private use asset pool	Private use (20 %)	Main pool	Allowances given
	£	£	£	£
WDV b/fwd			6,775	
Addition	10,000			
WDA 6,775 x 20% x 9/12			(1,016)	1,016
WDA 10,000 x 20% x9/12	(1,500)	300		1,200
				2,216
WDV c/fwd	8,500		5,759	

MEMO POINTS 1. The rate of allowance that is applied depends on whether the asset would be allocated to the main or special rate pool except for these rules.
2. If the asset had **previously been included in the main pool**, the start of private use is treated as a disposal, with the disposal value being the market value of the asset at the date when it ceased to be used wholly for trade purposes.
3. If the asset is **subsequently used for only business purposes**, it is transferred back to the pool it would have been allocated to under the normal rules.
4. Any additional VAT liability or rebate under the VAT **capital goods scheme** (¶8250) has to be reduced in the same proportion.

451 s 208 CAA 2001

A **balancing adjustment arises where**:
– there is a reduction in the proportion of qualifying use due to a change in circumstances; and
– the open market value of the asset at the end of the chargeable period exceeds the tax written down value by more than £1 million.

In this case a disposal value (equal to the market value) is brought into the private asset pool for the chargeable period in which the reduction takes place. An equivalent amount may be allocated to a new private use asset pool in the next chargeable period, as if new qualifying expenditure has been incurred.

IV. Assets for leasing

482 Where expenditure is incurred on the provision of capital assets which are then used for leasing, the capital allowance rules **differ depending upon** whether the lease is a long funding lease (LFL) or not. The most significant difference is that if the lease is an LFL it is the lessee who can claim allowances, whereas if it is not, it is the lessor who can claim allowances.

1. Long funding leases

Definition

483 s 70G CAA 2001

A long funding lease is defined as a long lease (usually more than five years (¶486)) of plant and machinery which:
a. is for use in a qualifying activity (¶214); and

ss 70J, 70N–70P CAA 2001

b. meets one or more of the following tests:
– the lease is accounted for as a finance lease under GAAP (or loan, as in the case of a sale and leaseback arrangement);

– the present value of the minimum lease payments (excluding charges for services) is 80% or more of the market value of the leased plant and machinery, less any grants received towards the purchase or use of the plant and machinery; or
– the term of the lease exceeds 65% of the remaining useful economic life of the leased plant and machinery.

The LFL regime **applies to** all such leases that:
– were finalised (i.e. agreed with a contract in place) or commenced on or after 1 April 2006 and are not an excepted lease; or
– commenced before 1 April 2006 but the plant and machinery was not brought into use until on or after 1 April 2006.

MEMO POINTS 1. If an asset is **not initially used for a qualifying activity**, but subsequently is, then it will be treated as an LFL if (apart from the qualifying activity condition) it would have been an LFL at the outset. This provision may apply where, for example, plant and machinery is leased to a non-resident, under a lease which would have been an LFL if the lessee had been resident, and the lessee subsequently becomes resident.
2. An **excepted lease** is one where all of the following are met: Sch 8 para 17 FA 2006
a. the principal terms had been agreed before 21 July 2005;
b. the construction of the plant or machinery had begun before 1 April 2006;
c. the lease was finalised and commenced before 1 April 2007. (This could be extended to 1 April 2009 if the lease was not finalised or did not commence because the plant and machinery was not yet constructed, provided:
– the lease was finalised and commenced as soon as was reasonably practicable after the construction was substantially complete; and
– the construction proceeded continuously from 1 April 2006 at a pace that was normal for an asset of its type (ignoring any delays due to events beyond the control of the parties));
d. the lessee is a particular person identified in the pre-existing heads of agreement; and
e. the principal finalised terms are not materially different to the pre-existing heads of agreement.
3. The **rationale** behind the LFL leasing rules is to align the tax treatment of long leases of plant and machinery with other forms of asset finance (such as borrowing to purchase an asset). Previously, finance leases were attractive to traders that did not have sufficient capacity to use capital allowances, as a finance lease would allow the trader the use of the capital asset, while passing the capital allowances to the taxable lessor, the benefit of this being reflected in the lease rentals charged to the lessee.
4. For details of the **taxable income** and **trading deductions** available to lessors and lessees see ¶138 and ¶171 respectively. The **capital gains** implications are at ¶6032.

484 The following are specifically **excluded** from the LFL provisions (and are taxed under the non-LFL provisions (¶500)):
– leases that fall within the de minimis limits (¶485);
– short leases (¶486);
– leases of background plant and machinery (¶487);
– hire purchase contracts;
– leases finalised before 21 July 2005 (provided the lessor was also within the charge to tax on 17 May 2006);
– assets that have been leased out for at least 10 years prior to 1 April 2006; and
– assets that have been previously leased out (as a non-LFL), provided the total term of the previous leases exceeds 65% of the remaining useful economic life of the asset when it was first subject to a lease.

EXAMPLE An asset with a life expectancy of 15 years was leased out as follows:

Lessee	Term of lease
Mr A	4 years
Mr B	3 years
Mr C	3 years

The asset was then leased out to Mr D on a 5 year term.
This will not be an LFL as:
– it has been previously leased out as a non-LFL; and
– the total term of the previous leases (10 years) is more than 65% of the remaining useful economic life of the asset at the start of the lease (9.75 years (i.e. 65% x 15 years)).

485
s 70U CAA 2001

De minimis provisions Plant and machinery leased with land will not be an LFL if its value does not exceed both:
- 10% of the value of any background plant and machinery; and
- 5% of the market value of the land (including buildings).

MEMO POINTS **Anti-avoidance** provisions apply to prevent such leases being excluded if:
- the rentals vary according to the value of the capital allowances available to the lessor; or
- the main purpose of the transaction is to ensure that the lessor obtains capital allowances.

486
s 70I CAA 2001

Short lease Short leases are excluded from the LFL rules as any timing advantage in utilising the capital allowances is generally not significant. A short lease is **generally** a lease of plant and machinery for five years or less.

However the **general rule is modified** to allow leases of no longer than seven years to be treated as short leases if the following conditions are met:
- the lease is treated as a finance lease under GAAP;
- the residual value (i.e. the fair value of plant and machinery that cannot reasonably be expected to be recovered by the lessor from the lease payments) implied in the lease is not more than 5% of the market value of the plant and machinery at the commencement of lease;
- if the rent due in the first year is less than that due in the second year, it is not more than 10% less; and
- if the rent due in any year after the second year is more than that due in the second year, it is not more than 10% more.

MEMO POINTS See ¶503 for details of the **restriction of capital allowances** on assets leased for more than 4 years but no more than 5 years.

487
s 70R CAA 2001

Background plant and machinery Where a lease is of land that incorporates a building, any plant and machinery that would reasonably be expected to be installed on such land, and that is there primarily to contribute to the functionality of the building or its site, will not be an LFL.

MEMO POINTS **Anti-avoidance** provisions apply to prevent such leases being excluded if:
- the rentals vary according to the value of the capital allowances available to the lessor; or
- the main purpose of the transaction is to ensure that the lessor obtains capital allowances.

488
SI 2007/303

The following guidance has been issued detailing what constitutes background plant and machinery:

Background plant and machinery	Not background plant and machinery
Lighting installations (fixed and emergency)	If used for moving or displaying goods to be sold as part of the trade
Telephone, audio-visual installations, data installations and computer networking facilities incidental to the occupation of the building	If used either for manufacturing goods or materials or subjecting goods to a process, in the course of the trade
Sanitary and other bathroom fittings	If used to store goods or materials: – on their arrival to the UK from a place outside the UK; – pending delivery/sale to a customer (after having been manufactured or subjected to a process in the course of the trade); or – that are to be used in the manufacture of other goods or materials, or subjected to a process (in the course of the trade)
Kitchen and catering facilities for the occupants of the building	
Fixed seating, signs and public address systems	
Intruder alarm systems and other security equipment	

In addition, the following specific **examples** are given of plant and machinery that would fall within the definition of background plant and machinery:
– heating, hot water and air-conditioning installations (including ceilings with integral air-conditioning);
– electrical installations that provide power to a building (for example, high and low voltage switchgear, standby generators etc);
– mechanisms for opening and closing doors, windows and vents;
– escalators and passenger lifts;
– window cleaning installations;
– fittings (for example, fitted cupboards, blinds, curtains etc);
– demountable partitions;
– protective installations (for example, sprinklers, lightning protection etc); and
– building management systems.

Writing down allowance

The lessee can claim capital allowances on the leased plant and machinery, provided the: 492 ss 34A, 70A – 70C CAA 2001
a. plant and machinery is used for a qualifying activity (¶214) by the lessee; and
b. lease is either:
– an LFL (as defined (¶483); or
– not an LFL, but one which the lessor has elected to be treated as an LFL.

Essentially in this situation the lessee is **treated** as if he owned the asset and incurred expenditure on its acquisition

MEMO POINTS 1. Lessors can **elect to opt into** the LFL regime for plant and machinery leases (other than cars) which are not an LFL, provided: SI 2007/304
a. the lease is for a term of 12 months or more, finalised on or after 1 April 2006; and
b. the asset:
– does not exceed £10 million in value;
– is not background plant and machinery (¶487) or within the de minimis limits (¶485); and
– at the start of the lease was either new, previously only leased as an LFL or subject to a sale and leaseback election (¶295), before the lessor made a return for the period in which the lease commenced.
2. A lessee is under **no obligation to treat a lease as an LFL** (and therefore claim capital allowances). However once a return has been made (and become final) the treatment of the lease as an LFL, or otherwise, must be followed and it is not possible to make an error or mistake claim on the basis that the lease should have (or should not have) been taxed as an LFL. s 70H CAA 2001

The lessee can claim capital allowances in the usual manner, as if he had incurred the expenditure on the acquisition of the asset concerned. 493

The amount of **capital expenditure upon which the claim is based** differs depending upon whether the lease is a long funding operating or finance lease, as follows:

Type of lease	Eligible capital expenditure
Long funding operating lease	Market value of the plant and machinery at the later of the: – commencement of the lease; – date the asset is first brought into use for the qualifying activity
Long funding finance lease	Total of the present value of the minimum lease payments plus the amount (if any) of rentals paid, before the lease commenced but for which relief is not otherwise available

MEMO POINTS 1. **Anti-avoidance provisions** attack arrangements that are intended to artificially inflate the amount on which capital allowances can be claimed. If a lease is entered into in order to obtain capital allowances in excess of the market value of the asset, the amount on which capital allowances can be claimed will be restricted to the market value of the asset.
2. Where the lease is a long funding finance lease and the **lessor incurs additional capital expenditure** on the leased assets and as a result the lease payments increase, the lessee can be treated as incurring additional expenditure for capital allowances purposes when the additional expenditure is first recognised. s 70D CAA 2001

s 70Q CAA 2001 3. It is only possible to **claim capital allowances once** on any plant and machinery, therefore if the lessor or any superior lessor is, or would be, entitled to claim capital allowances then the lessee cannot make a claim.

4. Amounts may be available for relief via other methods where the residual amount is guaranteed by the lessee, that amount is included within the minimum lease payments due to the arrangement, and it is reasonable to assume that if this sum were paid relief would be available for it.

Disposals

494 s 70E CAA 2001 The **termination** of an LFL is treated as a disposal event for capital allowances purposes and the lessee brings in a disposal value in the period of the termination.

The **disposal value** differs depending upon whether the lease was a long funding operating or finance lease, as follows:

Type of lease	Disposal value
Long funding operating lease	Amount by which the market value of the plant and machinery at the start of the lease (or date first bought into use, if later) exceeds the total of the: – trading deductions allowed (¶171); and – payments made to the lessee when the lease terminates
Long funding finance lease	Total of the amounts payable on termination plus the present value of the balance of the minimum lease rentals[1] (less any payments made to the lessor as a result of the termination)

Note:
1. This is the difference between the minimum lease payments at the start of the lease and the amount that would have been the minimum lease payment if the lease had been intended to expire on the date of termination.

MEMO POINTS The **commencement** of a long funding lease is treated as a disposal by the lessor. The disposal value to be brought into account is as detailed at ¶402.

Sundry provisions

495 ss 70W, 70X CAA 2001 **Transfer/assignment** An LFL is **treated as** coming to an end and a new lease will commence if either the:
– lessor transfers or assigns an LFL; or
– lessee transfers plant and machinery (that is leased under an LFL) to another person, who continues to lease the asset.

As long as the term and the amounts receivable under the new lease are equivalent to the old terms then the new lease will remain to be treated as an LFL.

MEMO POINTS On an **assignment of a non-LFL lease**, the assignee can elect to opt into the LFL regime, provided the conditions at ¶492 are met and:
– the assignment occurs within 4 months of the commencement of the original lease; and
– the original lessor has not claimed capital allowances on the assets.

496 s 70Y CAA 2001 **Sale and leaseback** Where an LFL asset is subject to a sale and leaseback or **lease and leaseback**, the new lease is treated as an LFL. (This ensures that the head lessor cannot claim capital allowances.)

EXAMPLE An existing long funding lessor, B, sells plant and machinery to A and leases it back from him. The leaseback is treated as an LFL, thereby ensuring that the new head lessor cannot claim capital allowances and the existing lease becomes a sub-lease.

497 s 70YA CAA 2001 **Change in accounting treatment** If there is a change in the accounting treatment of an LFL (i.e. from a finance lease to an operating lease or vice versa) then the old lease is treated as coming to an end and a new lease will commence.

498 ss 70YB, 70YC CAA 2001 **Extension of lease term** Where the term of a long funding operating lease is extended, the old lease is treated as coming to an end and a new lease will commence for a term equal to the remainder of the term of the lease. This new lease is to be taken to be an LFL.

MEMO POINTS Where an operating **lease that is not an LFL is extended** the new lease may be treated as an LFL if it would otherwise qualify, from the date of the extension.

Cessation A lessor can obtain capital allowances when an asset ceases to be used for long funding leases but is retained for use in a qualifying activity. The amount on which capital allowances can be obtained is the termination amount (i.e. the value of the plant and machinery at or about the time when the lease terminates). However it is not possible to claim first year allowances or short life asset treatment on such assets, except for: **499** ss 13A, 70YG CAA 2001
- cars with low CO_2 emissions; or
- plant and machinery which was leased with a building as background plant and machinery (¶487).

2. Non-long funding leases

Broadly speaking the capital allowances treatment can be divided into assets that are leased in the course of a trade and those that are not. **500**

MEMO POINTS The general question of **whether a trade exists** is covered in detail in ¶54 and the factors discussed there, such as the numbers of transactions, should also be considered in determining whether a leasing activity constitutes a trade.

a. Assets leased in the course of a trade

UK leases and overseas leases finalised on or after 1 April 2006

General rules Where a trade consists of or includes the leasing of plant and machinery, capital expenditure incurred on the provision of assets for leasing either within the UK or overseas (where the lease is finalised on or after 1 April 2006) is included in the general pool and the following rules apply: **501**

a. writing down allowances are given in accordance with the general rules outlined for plant and machinery (¶413);

b. first year allowances are generally not available on assets that are purchased for leasing, although expenditure incurred on the following assets on or after 1 April 2006 will qualify: s 46 CAA 2001
- energy saving or environmentally beneficial plant and machinery that is purchased as background plant and machinery (¶487); and
- cars with low CO_2 emissions; and

c. the following provisions detailing assets that must be **separately identified** apply equally to leased assets:
- cars costing more than £12,000 (¶422);
- short life assets (¶430);
- long life assets and integral features (¶315); and
- assets used only partly for trade use (¶447).

MEMO POINTS 1. From 9 December 2009 the amount of allowances that are available will be restricted where arrangements are entered into where the **expected economic value** of the asset, being total rentals plus the residual value of the asset (for an operating lease), is **less than the capital expenditure** incurred at acquisition. Where the restriction applies the allowances will be capped at the expected economic return. ss 228MA - 228MC CAA 2001
2. See ¶505 for details of the treatment of **overseas leases** that were finalised before 1 April 2006.

Acquisitions by group companies Allowances available on assets acquired by a company, for leasing on or after 1 April 2006, will be **restricted** if: **503** s 220 CAA 2001
- the leasing company buying the plant and machinery is a member of a group (¶1524) and it does not have the same accounting date as the principal company in the group; and
- the lease is either a finance lease or an operating lease (i.e. a funding lease) that is more than 4 years, but no more than 5 years long.

The restriction (which it must be stressed only applies to companies) is **calculated as follows**:

$$\text{Capital expenditure} \times \frac{\text{Days from acquisition of asset to end of chargeable period}}{\text{Days in chargeable period}}$$

The balance of any expenditure not relieved in the period of acquisition is added to the pool for the next chargeable period.

EXAMPLE A Ltd is a member of the ABC group and it prepares accounts to 31 December each year, although the other group companies prepare their accounts to 31 March. On 1 October 2009 it acquires an asset to lease, under a finance lease to B Ltd, for £20,000. Assuming A Ltd has a brought forward balance of £100,000 in the general pool as at 1 January 2009 the capital allowances computation will be as follows:

	General pool £	Allowances claimed £
Year ended 31 December 2009:		
WDV b/fwd	100,000	
Addition (92/365 x 20,000)	5,041	
	105,041	
WDA @ 20%	(21,008)	21,008
WDV c/fwd	84,033	
Year ended 31 December 2010:		
WDV b/fwd	84,033	
Addition (20,000 – 5,041)	14,959	
	98,992	
WDA @ 20%	(19,798)	19,798
WDV c/fwd	79,194	

MEMO POINTS For expenditure incurred **before 1 April 2006**, this restriction applied to all traders.

504 s 229 CAA 2001 Where an asset acquired for leasing under a finance lease is acquired under a **hire purchase agreement**, the restriction of the capital expenditure described above applies to any initial payment and, in addition, each instalment payment is also restricted on the same principle.

EXAMPLE A Ltd is a member of the ABC group and it prepares accounts to 31 December each year, although the other group companies prepare their accounts to 31 March. It has a trade involving the leasing of business assets and on 1 May 2009 acquires (under a hire purchase agreement) machinery which is going to be leased under a finance lease. A Ltd made an initial payment of £15,000 and quarterly payments of £1,500 (of which £500 represents the hire charge) payable on 1 January, 1 April, 1 July and 1 October.

Assuming the brought forward balance on the general pool is nil, capital allowances will be calculated as follows:

	General pool £	Allowances claimed £
Year ended 31 December 2009:		
WDV b/fwd	Nil	
Initial payment (245/365 × 15,000)	10,068	
Instalments:		
1 July 2006 (184/365 × 1,000)	504	
1 October 2006 (92/365 × 1,000)	252	
	10,824	
WDA @ 20%	(2,165)	2,165
WDV c/fwd	8,659	
Year ended 31 December 2010:		
WDV b/fwd	8,659	
Balance of initial payment (15,000 – 10,068)	4,932	
Balance of quarterly instalments (2,000 – 756)	1,244	

Instalments:		
1 January 2007 (No restriction)	1,000	
1 April 2007 (275/365 × 1,000)	753	
1 July 2007 (184/365 × 1,000)	504	
1 October 2007 (92/365 × 1,000)	252	
	17,344	
WDA @ 20%	(3,469)	3,469
	13,875	

Overseas lease to non EU/EEA resident finalised before 1 April 2006

Writing down allowances Where assets are leased overseas to a non-EU/EEA resident and the lease was finalised before 1 April 2006, allowances are either: 505 ss 105, 109, 110 CAA 2001
- restricted to 10% per annum, if the assets are, within the designated period, leased overseas (provided the lease is not a protected lease (¶509)); or
- not allowed at all (¶507).

MEMO POINTS The **designated period** is a period of 10 years beginning with the date when the asset is first brought into use by the person who incurred the expenditure. If the person ceases to own the asset within the 10 year period, the designated period ends when he ceases to own the asset. s 106(1) CAA 2001

Calculation of allowances Where assets are placed into the separate "overseas leasing" pool a WDA of 10% per annum is applied (provided the allowances are not prohibited under the provisions at ¶507). 506

Where there is no separate pooling because the assets are:
- **long life assets**, the assets will attract the special rate (¶304); or
- otherwise **separately pooled** (¶420), the 10% WDA are applied within the existing pool.

EXAMPLE A Ltd has a trade involving the leasing of business assets. It has a brought forward balance in the general pool of £6,000 and acquires the following assets for leasing overseas during the year ended 30 September:

Assets for leasing:

Machinery	£10,000
Car 1	£25,000

	General pool	Assets for leasing overseas	Expensive cars	Allowances given
	£	£	£	£
Year ended 30 September				
WDV b/fwd	6,000			
Addition		10,000	25,000	
WDA @ 20%	(1,200)			1,200
WDA @ 10%		(1,000)	(2,500)	3,500
WDV c/fwd	4,800	9,000	22,500	
Total allowances for year				4,700

MEMO POINTS Where the restriction applies, it also includes assets **leased through a chain**, if any lease in the chain is an overseas lease.

However, **allowances will not be given** if the plant and machinery is not used for a qualifying purpose, and either: 507 s 110 CAA 2001
- there is more than one year between consecutive payments due under the lease;
- any payments other than periodical payments are due under the lease;
- the payment terms under the lease are non-standard;
- the rates under the lease change;

– the lease is for a period in excess of 13 years or through agreement can be extended or renewed to be in excess of 13 years; or
– at any time, the lessor or a connected person could be entitled to receive a payment of an amount determined before expiry of the lease and referable to the value of the plant or machinery at or after that expiry (whether or not the payment relates to a disposal of the plant or machinery).

MEMO POINTS 1. A **qualifying purpose** is where:
– the lessee or the original buyer uses it for the purposes of a qualifying activity (¶214) without leasing it;
– the buyer uses it for short-term leasing; or
– the lessee uses it for short-term leasing and is either UK resident or uses it in the course of a qualifying activity carried on in the UK.
For the purposes of the above provisions, where the plant or machinery is disposed of to a connected person, or on a change in the members of a partnership where there is no discontinuance of the trade, the new owner is treated as the buyer.

s 121 CAA 2001
2. A **short-term lease** is a lease to the same person of either:
– not more than 30 consecutive days and not more than 90 days in any 12 month period; or
– not more than 365 consecutive days and, during any 4 year period in the designated period (¶505), the total period for which it is leased directly to a person carrying on a qualifying activity does not exceed 2 years.

509
s 105 CAA 2001
Protected lease A lease of plant and machinery is a protected lease if it is for:
a. assets that are used for short-term leasing (¶507); or
b. a ship, aircraft or transport container that is used in the course of a qualifying activity (¶214). For this purpose the following are also qualifying activities:
– ships/aircraft which are let on charter by a person who is UK resident and carries on a trade of operating ships/aircraft in the UK; and
– transport containers that are let in the course of a UK trade of operating ships or aircraft and the container is at other times used by the lessor for the operation of ships or aircraft.

MEMO POINTS Where there is a **chain of leases** which contains at least one non-protected lease, capital allowances will be restricted.

510
ss 111, 112, 114 CAA 2001
Clawback of allowances Capital allowances will be clawed back via a **balancing charge** in the following situations:

Allowances given	Calculation of balancing charge
10% WDA given but within the designated period an event occurs such that no allowances should have been given	Aggregate of allowances given [1, 2]
Normal plant and machinery WDA given (¶290) but within the designated period the asset is used for non-protected overseas leasing	The sum of the: – allowances given in the periods up to and including the period in which the asset is first used for leasing overseas; less – maximum allowances that could have been given if the 10% rate had been used instead [2, 3, 4]

Note:
1. The balancing charge is made in the period in which the event occurs.
2. In the same period, an amount equal to the unused expenditure (i.e. expenditure incurred less WDA actually given) is also brought into the pool as a disposal value.
3. The balancing charge is made in the period in which the asset is first used for leasing overseas.
4. In the following period an amount equal to the balancing charge, together with the disposal value, is treated as an addition to the overseas leasing pool. (The purpose of this provision is to ensure that the WDV in the overseas leasing pool is the same as it would have been if the expenditure had been in the overseas leasing pool from the start.)

MEMO POINTS A similar clawback of allowances occurs where the owner acquired machinery or plant from a **connected person** who claimed FYA, WDA or balancing allowance on the asset. The allowances given to the owner and the connected party are used to calculate the clawback. The exception to this rule is where the qualifying activity is treated as continuing (for example, where there has been a company reconstruction without a change of ownership (¶252)).

Overseas lease to EU/EEA resident finalised before 1 April 2006

512 HMRC Brief 40/07

Where assets are leased overseas to an EU/EEA resident and the lease was finalised before 1 April 2006, HMRC will adopt the following approach:
- where the EU/EEA country gives the lessee a relief that is broadly equivalent to capital allowances, WDA of 10% will continue to be available in the UK as above (although the rules at ¶507 will not apply); and
- where the relevant EU/EEA country does not give the lessee a relief broadly equivalent to capital allowances the lessor will be entitled to the normal rate of WDA applicable (¶290).

b. Assets leased other than in the course of a trade

518 ss 19, 258 - 260 CAA 2001

Each asset (with the exception of a dwelling house) acquired for leasing other than in the course of a qualifying activity (¶214) is placed in an **individual pool**. Where the asset is used only partly for leasing the allowances will be restricted accordingly (¶447).

Allowances given for assets leased other than in the course of a qualifying activity may either be:
- relieved against income from leasing. Any allowances that remain unrelieved are carried forward to the next accounting period (or year of assessment for individuals); or
- deducted from profits generally for the immediately preceding accounting period.

MEMO POINTS A claim to **deduct allowances from profits** generally must be made within two years of the end of the accounting period in which the loss arose. Such a claim can only be made if the lessee does not use the assets concerned for the purposes of a trade.

SECTION 4

Buildings

520

Allowances for qualifying buildings were usually given at a rate of 4% per annum on a straight line basis, meaning the same amount is written off every year. In addition 100% initial allowances may be available in certain situations. In recent years the rates of allowances for **industrial** (¶523) and **agricultural** (¶631) buildings have been reduced so that from 1 April 2011 (6 April 2011 for income tax purposes) neither will attract allowances. The same is true of expenditure on **hotels** (¶597). The allowances available for expenditure incurred in **enterprise zones** were not phased out gradually but have also been removed in their entirety from 1 April 2011 (6 April 2011 for income tax purposes). This section contains the specific regulations for buildings. For the general principles of capital allowances, see ¶200 onwards.

A. Industrial buildings

1. Rate of allowance

523

Capital expenditure on the construction of industrial buildings and structures (referred to in this chapter as industrial buildings) may qualify for industrial buildings **allowances** (IBA) in the form of a writing down allowance (WDA) usually at a rate of 4% per annum.

On the **disposal** of an industrial building there will be no balancing adjustment provided the balancing event (i.e. the disposal) is on or after 21 March 2007. Instead the new owner's allowances will simply be based on the original owner's expenditure. Allowances for the period of the transfer are apportioned.

MEMO POINTS 1. For disposals **before 21 March 2007** (or before 1 April 2011 under a pre-commencement contract made before 21 March 2007) a balancing charge or allowance may arise and the allowances available to a new purchaser will be recalculated. See ¶583 onwards for details.

2. The abolition of balancing adjustments was introduced to lay the foundations for the phasing out and **eventual abolition** of industrial buildings allowances by 2011/12. The rate of IBA has been progressively reduced by 1% each financial year since in 2008/09. Consequently, from 2011/12 onwards no allowances are available.

2. Definition

What is an industrial building?

526 ss 271, 274, 275 CAA 2001

The **broad** definition of a qualifying industrial building is that is should be used in the course of production (e.g. a factory) as opposed to distribution (e.g. a retail shop).

An industrial building will qualify for allowances if it is:
– used for a qualifying trade (¶530). This includes buildings provided by the person carrying on the qualifying trade that are used for the welfare of his staff; or
– occupied as part of a trade and used as a sports pavilion for the welfare of the workers employed in that trade.

MEMO POINTS 1. If a **building is let**, the nature of the lessee's activity will determine whether the building qualifies as an industrial building.
2. The legislation gives a detailed explanation of what constitutes an industrial building but the **definition is still the subject of some debate**. The courts have indicated that each case should be addressed on its own merits, and in particular they will ignore what a building is called and will look at its actual use in deciding whether or not it is an industrial building.

528 s 277 CAA 2001

Specifically **excluded** from the definition of an industrial building is any building in use as, or as part of, a:
– dwelling house;
– retail shop;
– showroom;
– hotel (although see ¶597); or
– office.

Qualifying trade

530 s 274 CAA 2001

A qualifying trade is defined in the legislation by the use of two tables. Table A sets out the qualifying trades, and Table B sets out undertakings which are treated as qualifying trades if they are carried on as a trade.

532

The qualifying trades listed in **Table A** are:

Qualifying trade	Detail
Manufacturing	Any trade consisting of manufacturing goods or materials
Processing	Any trade consisting of subjecting goods or materials to a process[1] (this includes repair or maintenance of goods or materials)
Storage	Any trade consisting of storing goods or materials: – which are to be used in the manufacture of other goods or materials; – which are to be subjected, in the course of the trade, to any process; – which have been manufactured, produced or subjected to a process in the course of a trade and have not yet been delivered to the purchaser; or – on their arrival in any part of the UK from a place outside the UK
Agricultural	Any trade consisting of: – ploughing or cultivation of land occupied by another; – carrying out any other agricultural operation on land occupied by another, or – threshing another's crops
Working foreign plantations	Any trade consisting of working land outside the UK used for: – growing and harvesting crops; – husbandry; or – forestry

Qualifying trade	Detail
Fishing	Any trade consisting of catching or taking fish or shellfish
Mineral extraction	Any trade consisting of working a source of mineral deposits

Note:
1. The definition of the word process has been widely discussed and decisions are made on the particular facts of each case. For example, neither a freezer room attached to a supermarket nor a building used for the preparation of wage packets were considered to have been used for the subjection of goods to a process. Conversely, a warehouse used to store tyres before they were sold for remoulding qualified for allowances even though the remoulding process was to be carried out by somebody else.

The undertakings listed in **Table B** consist of activities involving: 535
- the generation, transformation, conversion, transmission or distribution of electrical energy;
- the supply of water or hydraulic power;
- the provision of sewerage services;
- the design, building, financing or operation of highways; or
- a transport, tunnel, bridge, inland navigation or a dock undertaking.

Partial use

Allowances will **be restricted** pro rata where only part of a building is used for qualifying industrial purposes, for example where the building contains offices, or the trader carries on two trades in one building and only one of them qualifies. 537 ss 276, 283 CAA 2001

However, where the expenditure on the non-industrial part is less than 25% of the total expenditure, allowances will be available on the whole building. Where premises consist of a collection of buildings, the test must be applied to each building individually.

EXAMPLE

1. A Ltd is building a factory at a cost of £375,000. They wish to include an office and the architect has suggested that they can simply increase the overall size of the proposed building and section off part for use as the office. This would increase the cost of the building by £15,000. This represents less than 25% of the total cost of the building and allowances can be claimed on the full cost of the building (£390,000).
An alternative is to add a separate office attached by a covered walkway, which would cost £30,000. Although this is still less than 25% of the overall cost, the office would be treated as a separate building, and allowances would not be available for this expenditure.

2. A warehouse is used by a company that carries on two trades, one manufacturing watch parts for assembly and sale by a third party, and one retailing watches. If the building is used equally by the two trades, allowances will only be available on the proportion of the building used for manufacturing. However, if the expenditure on the part of the building used by the retail trade is less than 25% of the cost of the whole building, allowances will be available for the full cost.

3. Qualifying expenditure

The following expenditure on an industrial building will qualify for IBA (where certain **conditions** are met): 550

Building type	Expenditure	Conditions
New	Construction cost (¶552)	Where the person claiming the allowances actually constructed the building
	Purchase price	Purchased from a developer
	Lower of: – purchase price paid before the property is brought into use; – first sale price paid to the developer	Purchased from a developer and there have been one or more previous sales before the property is brought into use
	Lower of: – purchase price; – construction cost	Purchased from a builder who is not a developer

Building type	Expenditure	Conditions
Second-hand	Lower of: – purchase price; – residue after sale (¶588)	Has previously been the subject of a claim to IBA and the contract is concluded either before: – 21 March 2007; or – 1 April 2011 under a written contract made before 21 March 2007
	Vendor's original expenditure	Has previously been the subject of a claim to IBA and the contract is concluded on or after 21 March 2007
New or second-hand	Repairs to a qualifying building	

ss 272 - 273 CAA 2001

MEMO POINTS 1. The cost of the **land** does not qualify for allowances in any circumstances. However, the cost of preparatory work done on-site prior to laying foundations will qualify, as will the costs of **preparing the land** for the installation of plant and machinery.
2. Where expenditure is not eligible for allowances as **plant and machinery**, because the asset is deemed to be part of the building (¶281), that expenditure is qualifying expenditure for IBA purposes.

552 The **cost of construction** includes:
– demolition costs for a previous building (whether an industrial building or not) on the same site, where the demolition costs have not previously been taken into account for IBA purposes; and
– professional fees relating to the design and construction of a building (that is eventually built).

Certain expenditure is not considered by HMRC to form part of the costs of construction and is therefore **non-qualifying**. This includes costs for:
– obtaining planning permission, although, if this has been included in a builder's quotation for construction, it is not necessary to apportion the total cost;
– capitalised interest;
– a public enquiry;
– landscaping; and
– legal expenses.

s 282 CAA 2001 MEMO POINTS The construction cost of an industrial building **overseas** may still qualify for allowances if the business is taxed in the UK as a UK trade.

559 Where the building falls within the **VAT capital goods scheme** (¶8250), changes to the VAT paid will be added to or deducted from the unrelieved expenditure on the building (¶577).

4. Calculation of allowance

When are allowances available?

565 s 309 CAA 2001 WDA are **available for** any chargeable period if at the end of that period the claimant both:
– holds the relevant interest in the building; and
– the building is in qualifying use.

568 s 286 CAA 2001 A **relevant interest** is defined as the interest a person has at the time he incurs the expenditure on a building.

The grant of a **lease** does not cause the relevant interest in a building to cease, providing the lessee continues to use the building for qualifying purposes. A lessee can create an additional relevant interest by extending or improving the building and is able to claim allowances on that element of the property. It is possible for more than one person to have a relevant interest at one time. For example, a tenant has an interest in a building but so does the landlord who may have an interest in the freehold.

EXAMPLE A Ltd purchased land and built a factory on it at a cost of £300,000. It subsequently let the building to B Ltd for 10 years. B Ltd then built a qualifying extension to the factory at a cost of £50,000.
A Ltd has a relevant interest in its expenditure of £300,000 and B Ltd will have a relevant interest in its expenditure of £50,000.
On the subsequent reversion of B's interest to A Ltd, A Ltd's relevant interest will be the full £350,000.

MEMO POINTS Where a **long lease** (one that is over 50 years) is granted and both the lessor and lessee elect (within 2 years from the date the lease takes effect), the lessee can claim allowances even if the expenditure is made by the lessor. This may be of benefit where the landlord cannot benefit from the allowances, for example if it is a pension scheme with no tax liability. Any capital sum paid in consideration for the lease is taken as the purchase price. This claim is not available if the lessor and lessee are connected persons (¶5570) or if the election is undertaken with a view to generating a balancing allowance. s 290 CAA 2001

For an industrial building to be in **qualifying use**, it must be used for one of the trades in ¶530 to ¶535 above. It is the use of a building on the **final day** of the period which is important. An industrial building in non-qualifying use throughout a period which is brought into qualifying use on the final day of that period will still get the full allowance due for the period. 571

WDA continue to be available for a qualifying building which is **temporarily disused**, immediately following a period of qualifying use. (In practice, all periods of disuse following a period of qualifying use will be regarded as temporary, except for that preceding demolition). s 285 CAA 2001

A distinction must be made between temporary periods of disuse, and those where a building is subject to non-qualifying use, such as office space. Where an industrial building is in non-qualifying use the owner does not receive allowances, but **notional allowances** are taken into account when calculating the residue after sale (¶588).

Amount of WDA

WDA are given at a **rate of** 4% per annum (2 % per annum for pre 6-November 1962 buildings) in the chargeable period in which the tax life commences on the qualifying expenditure (¶550). Once the tax life of a building has expired, no further allowances can be claimed. 574 s 310 CAA 2001

The **tax life** is 25 years from the date the building is first used for any purpose (50 years for buildings first used prior to 6 November 1962) and is not affected by periods of disuse or non-qualifying use.

(Allowances are being **progressively reduced** by 1% each financial year, which started in 2008/09. Consequently from 2011/12 onwards no allowances will be available.)

MEMO POINTS Allowances are given for a chargeable period (¶239). Where a **chargeable period is greater than or less than 12 months**, the allowance is increased or reduced correspondingly. Calculations should strictly be made to the nearest day but calculations to the nearest month are generally accepted. This will be relevant where, for example, a company has a short accounting period. s 310(2) CAA 2001

EXAMPLE A Ltd constructed a factory at a cost of £950,000. Assuming the building remains in qualifying use throughout its tax life, and the company has regular 12 month accounting periods, a writing down allowance of £38,000 (£950,000 @ 4%) will be available.
If the company had a 9 month accounting period, the allowance would be £28,500 (£950,000 @ 4% × 9/12).
If A Ltd had purchased the building from the builder for £950,000 and the builder's costs had been £900,000, allowances would be £36,000 (£900,000 @ 4%) in a 12 month period.

Where an additional VAT liability or rebate arises under the VAT **capital goods scheme** (¶8250) the writing down allowance will be revised for the chargeable period in which the adjustment occurs and for subsequent periods. Allowances given in earlier periods remain unaffected. 577

ss 347 - 350 CAA 2001

The revised writing down allowance is calculated with reference to the residue of expenditure (¶588) at the date of the VAT adjustment, which is deemed to be increased or reduced by the VAT liability or rebate. The revised figure is then distributed evenly over the remaining tax life of the building.

EXAMPLE A Ltd prepares accounts to 31 December but has a VAT year end of 31 March. A factory is built on 1 October 2003 at a cost of £100,000 (inc. VAT) and is immediately brought into a qualifying industrial use. A capital goods scheme liability of £10,000 arises in the VAT year ended 31 March 2007. The VAT is treated as accruing on 30 September 2007.
Allowances will be available as follows:

Year	IBA available £	Cumulative balance £
Cost		100,000
Year ended 31 December 2003	4,000	(4,000)
Year ended 31 December 2004	4,000	(4,000)
Year ended 31 December 2005	4,000	(4,000)
Year ended 31 December 2006	4,000	(4,000)
Residue of expenditure at 1 January 2007		84,000
Additional expenditure at 30 September 2007		10,000
Residue of expenditure at 30 September 2007		94,000

Remaining tax life = 21 years

$$\text{WDA for year ended 31 December 2007} = \frac{94{,}000}{21 \text{ years}} = £4{,}476$$

The allowances in subsequent years will be progressively reduced to take account of the abolition of the IBA regime, as follows:
- 2008/09: £3,357 (75 % of £4,476);
- 2009/10: £2,238 (50 % of £4,476);
- 2010/11: £1,119 (25 % of £4,476);
- 2011/12: Nil.

5. Disposal during tax life

a. Overview

580 ss 314, 359 CAA 2001

The treatment differs **depending upon** whether the disposal is before or after 21 March 2007, as follows:

Date of disposal	Treatment	
	Vendor	Purchaser
On or after 21 March 2007	No balancing adjustment on disposal	Entitled to WDA on the same basis as the vendor
Before 21 March 2007 (or 1 April 2011 under a pre-commencement contract (¶583) made before 21 March 2007)	Balancing adjustment (¶583) may arise based on the difference between the disposal proceeds and the residue of expenditure before sale	Entitled to WDA based on the lower of: – residue of expenditure after sale; and – purchase price

MEMO POINTS A **disposal occurs if** the relevant interest in a qualifying building is sold, or the building is demolished, destroyed, or falls into permanent disuse.
Where the relevant interest is a lease, the **assignment of a lease** is a disposal. However, the **expiry of a lease** is not a disposal if the lessee remains in the property after its expiry either with or without a further lease being granted. In both these circumstances the lessee will continue to be entitled to WDA and there will be no balancing allowance or charge until he ceases to occupy the building.

Where a leaseholder acquires the freehold (or some other superior interest in the building), this will not constitute a disposal of the leasehold interest and it will simply merge with the superior interest.

b. Disposal on or after 21 March 2007

Vendor

Where a disposal is made on or after 21 March 2007, there will **no longer** be any balancing adjustment to the vendor's IBA pool. **581** s 36 FA 2007

In effect **this means** that disposal proceeds will be dealt with via the capital gains regime in the usual manner and vendors will be able to keep any allowances they have had up to the date of disposal. (In the past, such allowances were clawed back via balancing adjustments (¶583)).

MEMO POINTS This regime applies until 2010/11, after which **IBAs are to be abolished**.

Purchaser

When a **second-hand building** is purchased which has previously been the subject of a claim to IBA, the purchaser will be entitled to WDA on the same basis as the vendor. **582**

EXAMPLE A factory is built by A Ltd and brought into qualifying industrial use on 1 January 2003 at a cost of £250,000. A Ltd had annual WDA of £10,000 on this expenditure (4 % of £250,000). The building was sold on 1 January 2008 for £275,000.

The purchaser will receive the same allowances that the vendor received, reducing progressively by 1% p.a. from 2008/09 as follows:
- 2007/08: £10,000 (4 %)
- 2008/09: £7,500 (3 %)
- 2009/10: £5,000 (2 %)
- 2010/11: £2,500 (1 %)
- 2011/12: Nil.

c. Disposal or binding sale contract before 21 March 2007

Vendor

Balancing adjustment Where a building was sold before 21 March 2007 (or 1 April 2011 under a pre-commencement contract made before 21 March 2007) the vendor would be entitled to a balancing adjustment, which was **calculated by** comparing any disposal proceeds to the residue of expenditure before sale. This will then result in either a: **583** s 318 CAA 2001
- balancing allowance, if the building was sold at less than the residue of expenditure; or
- balancing charge, if the building was sold for more than the residue of expenditure. (Note though that the balancing charge may not exceed the allowances made. Any excess of proceeds over cost may be subject to a chargeable gain.)

MEMO POINTS A **pre-commencement contract** is one that is:
- made in writing with no significant terms left to be agreed before 21 March 2007;
- unconditional (or any conditions were satisfied before 21 March 2007); and
- not varied in a significant way on or after 21 March 2007.

Disposal proceeds In general, when an asset is sold, the net **sale proceeds** will be the disposal proceeds. However, a **market value** figure will be substituted where either: **587** ss 316, 568, 569 CAA 2001

a. the control test is met. That is where:
- the buyer has control (¶1729) over the seller (or vice versa);
- a third party has control over both the buyer and the seller; or
- the buyer and seller are connected (¶5570);

b. the sale has been artificially arranged in order to obtain a tax advantage by all or any of the parties concerned.

For **other types of disposal**, such as gift, demolition, destruction or the permanent cessation of the use of the building, the disposal value will be the total of any capital compensation, insurance or salvage money received. Any receipts chargeable as income are excluded from the disposal value.

MEMO POINTS 1. Where the **control test only is met** it is possible for the parties to jointly elect that the sale be treated as being for an alternative amount (rather than market value). The alternative amount is the lower of market value and the unrelieved qualifying expenditure immediately before sale.
The election, which does not apply to agricultural building, business premises renovation or flat conversion allowances, must be made within 2 years of the sale.
2. These **provisions also apply** to disposals of eligible hotels (¶597), buildings in enterprise zones (¶601), premises that qualify for business premises renovation allowances (¶612), flat conversions (¶620), agricultural buildings (¶631), and assets that qualify either for R & D allowances (¶683) or mineral extraction allowances.

588 **Residue of expenditure** The residue of expenditure **before sale** is the original cost minus any allowances given (including notional allowances).

The residue of expenditure **after sale** is simply the residue of expenditure before sale plus or minus any balancing adjustments arising on sale.

EXAMPLE A factory is built by A Ltd in Year 1 at a cost of £250,000 and is immediately brought into a qualifying industrial use. The building is sold in Year 5.

	£
Cost	250,000
£250,000 @ 4% × 4 years	(40,000)
Residue of expenditure before sale	210,000

If the building is **sold** for:
– £200,000 then a balancing allowance of £10,000 (i.e. £210,000 less £200,000) will arise;
– £225,000 then a balancing charge of £15,000 (i.e. £210,000 less £225,000) will arise; or
– £260,000 then the balancing charge will be restricted to the amount of the allowances given i.e. £40,000. Any excess over the allowances given may be treated as a chargeable gain.

ss 325, 357, 570A CAA 2001

MEMO POINTS 1. If a relevant interest is sold, and is subject to a **subordinate interest**, any balancing allowance on sale is denied to the vendor if:
– any of the vendor, purchaser or grantee of the subordinate interest are connected; and
– the sole or main benefit of the transaction was to obtain a balancing allowance.
The residue of expenditure upon which the subsequent purchaser can claim allowances is computed as though the balancing allowance had been given in full.
2. If **artificial pricing arrangements** exist which seek to enhance the value of the interest disposed of, anti-avoidance provisions ensure that such arrangements are ignored when calculating any balancing allowance or balancing charge, and sale proceeds are reduced to the market value that would apply if the arrangements had not been in place.
3. If, as a result of a **tax avoidance scheme** (i.e. a scheme or arrangement where the taxpayer's main purpose included the obtaining of a tax advantage), proceeds on the sale of a building are less than they would be on the open market, a balancing allowance will be denied to the vendor. (However, the residue after sale for both the purchaser and the vendor is still computed as if the balancing allowances had been given in full.)
These **provisions also apply** to disposals of eligible hotels (¶597), buildings in enterprise zones (¶601), premises that qualify for business premises renovation allowances (¶612), flat conversions (¶620), agricultural buildings (¶631), and assets that qualify either for R & D allowances (¶683) or mineral extraction allowances.

590
s 319 CAA 2001

If there are **periods of non-industrial use**, and a balancing allowance or charge is due, it must be adjusted to reflect periods of non-industrial use. This is done by calculating the adjusted net cost.

$$\text{Adjusted net cost} = (\text{Capital expenditure} - \text{Proceeds}) \times \frac{\text{Period of qualifying use}}{\text{Whole period of use}}$$

The adjusted net cost is then compared to allowances given (both WDA and IA) to generate a balancing allowance or charge.

EXAMPLE A factory is built by A Ltd in Year 1 at a cost of £250,000 and is immediately brought into qualifying use. The building is used for industrial purposes for the first year, non-industrial use for the next 2 years and then industrial use from then on. The building is sold in Year 5.

	£	Allowances given £
Year 1:		
Cost	250,000	
IBAs @ 4%	(10,000)	10,000
	240,000	
Year 2:		
Notional IBAs (non-industrial use)	(10,000)	
	230,000	
Year 3:		
Notional IBAs (non-industrial use)	(10,000)	
	220,000	
Year 4:		
IBAs @ 4%	(10,000)	10,000
Residue of expenditure (before sale)	210,000	20,000

The balancing adjustment will be calculated as follows, if the building is sold in Year 5 for:

Sold for	Adjusted net cost	Allowances given	Balancing adjustment
£200,000	$250{,}000 - 200{,}000 \times \frac{2\text{ years}}{4\text{ years}} = 25{,}000$	£20,000	£5,000 (allowance)
£225,000	$250{,}000 - 225{,}000 \times \frac{2\text{ years}}{4\text{ years}} = 12{,}500$	£20,000	£7,500 (charge)
£500,000	$250{,}000 - 500{,}000 \times \frac{2\text{ years}}{4\text{ years}} = \text{nil}$ (no actual cost as profit made on sale)	£20,000	£20,000 [1](charge)

Note:
1. Restricted to allowances already given.

Purchaser

When a **second-hand building** is purchased which has previously been the subject of a claim to IBA, the purchaser is entitled to WDA for the remainder of the tax life of the building (or until 2010/11, if earlier), based on the residue of expenditure after sale (¶588). **595** s 311 CAA 2001

Strictly, the tax life of a building should be calculated on a daily basis although HMRC generally accept calculations to the nearest month. If the tax life has expired, no allowances are due.

EXAMPLE A factory is built by A Ltd and brought into qualifying industrial use on 1 January 2002 at a cost of £250,000. For 2002, 2003, 2004, and 2006 the building was used as an industrial building (2005 was a period of temporary disuse so only notional allowances were given).
The building is sold on 1 January 2007 for £275,000.
The purchaser's allowances are based on the residue of expenditure after sale, calculated as follows:

		£
Cost to A Ltd		250,000
Less:		
Actual WDA (250,000 @ 4% x 3 years)	30,000	
Notional WDA (250,000 @ 4% x 1 year)	10,000	
		(40,000)
Residue of expenditure before sale		210,000
Add: Balancing charge restricted to allowances given)		30,000
Residue of expenditure after sale		240,000

The purchaser is entitled to allowances on £240,000 divided over the remaining tax life of the building

His allowances will be calculated as follows:

Annual allowance: $\frac{240,000}{20 \text{ years}}$ = £12,000 p.a.

In light of the phase out of IBAs this allowance will be reduced year on year by 25% as follows:
- 2008/09: 25% effective reduction of allowance to £9,000;
- 2009/10: 50% effective reduction of allowance to £6,000;
- 2010/11: 75% effective reduction of allowance to £3,000;
- 2011/12: No allowances will be given.

MEMO POINTS The provisions at ¶577 to ¶590 apply equally to purchasers of second-hand buildings.

B. Hotels

597 In certain circumstances, expenditure on a building used as a hotel may qualify for:
s 279 CAA 2001
a. industrial buildings allowances (IBA) if the hotel is located outside an enterprise zone, and it:
– is of a permanent nature;
– is open for at least 4 months between April and October;
– has at least 10 bedrooms offering sleeping accommodation (which should not normally be in the same occupation for more than 1 month); and
– provides services such as breakfast, evening meal, and general housekeeping.
b. enterprise zone allowances, which are available for any hotel located within a designated zone.

598 In addition to the general IBA rules (¶523 onwards), the following **specific rules apply** to expenditure incurred on hotels:
– where the property includes accommodation for the owner or his family, during the months between April and October a proportion of the expenditure will not qualify for allowances. This is not the case if the owner is a company and the accommodation is provided to a director or employee of the company (in which case allowances will be permitted, and the director/employee will be assessed to tax under the benefit in kind rules (¶3196 onwards));
– a hotel that is temporarily disused will only qualify for IBAs for 2 years from the end of the period in which it became disused; and
– a balancing event will be triggered 2 years after a hotel ceases to be a qualifying hotel (if no other balancing events have occurred).

In line with the allowances for industrial buildings, expenditure on hotels does not qualify for allowances from 1 April 2011 (6 April 2011 for income tax purposes).

600 As with other buildings, the hotel may be **located outside the UK** as long as the trade is taxed as a UK trade.

MEMO POINTS The **anti-avoidance provisions** at ¶587 and ¶588 apply equally to qualifying hotels.

C. Enterprise zones

1. Available allowances

601 In an enterprise zone, expenditure on an industrial or commercial building may qualify for allowances, with the exception of dwellings (although if the dwelling comprises 25% or less of a building, the whole of the expenditure still qualifies).

An **initial allowance** of up to 100% of the qualifying expenditure is available. However, if this is not claimed (or only partly claimed) the balance of expenditure will be subject to 25% **writing down allowances** (WDA) on a straight line basis.

The phased changes to the IBA regime, including the removal of balancing adjustments on 21 March 2007 (¶523), did not apply to expenditure in enterprise zones. However, the allowances given to expenditure incurred in enterprise zones have also been withdrawn from 1 April 2011 (6 April 2011 for income tax purposes).

2. Definition

An enterprise zone is an area designated by the Secretary of State, which qualifies for special tax breaks and grants designed to attract investment to an area and stimulate development. 602

Each enterprise zone has a life of 10 years, from the date it was designated as a zone.

3. Qualifying expenditure

Expenditure on the construction of an industrial or commercial building during the life of an enterprise zone qualifies for this allowance. This includes expenditure actually **incurred or contracted for** within the 10 year life. 604 s 298 CAA 2001

Where expenditure is contracted for within the life of the enterprise zone, but incurred more than 20 years after the creation of the zone, no enterprise zone allowances are available, and only normal IBA are available. (Note that the **new IBA regime** for disposals on or after 21 March 2007 does not apply to buildings in enterprise zones; instead the old rules continue to apply.)

4. Calculation of allowance

a. First claimant

The first claimant for these purposes is taken to mean the person constructing the building, or where a building was purchased unused from a builder, the first purchaser. 605 ss 295-300 CAA 2001

The allowance available to a **purchaser of an unused building** from a builder depends upon whether the builder is a developer (i.e. carries on a trade of constructing buildings for resale) or not and is identical to the IBA rules (¶550).

EXAMPLE A qualifying building is constructed by A Ltd for its own use, in an enterprise zone, at a total qualifying cost of £1,500,000. However, for cash flow reasons, the building is sold before being brought into use for £1,750,000 to B Ltd.
B Ltd will be entitled to claim allowances on £1,500,000 (being the lower of cost and purchase price paid).

MEMO POINTS If an initial allowance is given for a building under construction that is **never completed**, the allowance is withdrawn. This is not the case where work is temporarily suspended, perhaps due to recession.

If the **initial allowance is not claimed** in full (for example to leave sufficient profits in charge to absorb losses), the balance of expenditure is written off at 25% of cost on a straight line basis. 606

EXAMPLE Expenditure of £1,250,000 is incurred on a qualifying building in an enterprise zone. An initial allowance of £850,000 is claimed, leaving the balance of £400,000 to be used as WDA.
WDA of £312,500 (£1,250,000 @ 25%) would be given in the year the expenditure is incurred, with the balance of £87,500 available for the next year.

Where **part of the expenditure qualifies** because it is incurred or contracted for within the life of the enterprise zone and part is not, it is necessary to apportion the expenditure qualifying for allowances using the following formula: 608

$$A \times \frac{B}{C}$$

where:
– A is the lower of actual cost and purchase price;
– B is the expenditure incurred or contracted for within the life of the enterprise zone; and
– C is the actual expenditure.

EXAMPLE A Ltd contracts to build a factory in an enterprise zone for £1,000,000, of which £900,000 was incurred within the life of the enterprise zone. For cash flow reasons, the factory was sold to B Ltd for £800,000, after the life of the enterprise zone had expired, but before the factory was first used.

B Ltd is entitled to claim allowances on the following amounts:

Enterprise zone element: $800{,}000 \times \frac{900{,}000}{1{,}000{,}000}$ = £720,000

Non-enterprise zone element: = £80,000

Enterprise zone allowances may be claimed on £720,000. The non-enterprise zone element may qualify for IBA.

Disposal during tax life

609 s 314 CAA 2001 Although the availability of initial allowances may mean that expenditure is written off over a short period, the tax life of an industrial building located in an enterprise zone is still 25 years. The pre-21 March 2007 rules apply for calculating **balancing adjustments** on a sale of a building (¶583) and therefore, in the early years, a substantial balancing charge is likely to arise on the sale of a building within an enterprise zone.

MEMO POINTS **Anti-avoidance provisions** apply in connection with:
– sales where the control test is met, or the sale has been artificially arranged in order to obtain a tax advantage (¶587); and
– sales where, as part of a tax avoidance scheme, the proceeds are less than they would be on the open market (¶588).

EXAMPLE Taking the facts from the example at ¶606, the building is sold halfway through Year 4 for £950,000. A balancing charge of £950,000 will be made.

	£
Original cost	1,250,000
Allowances given	(1,250,000)
Net cost	nil
Proceeds	(950,000)
Balancing charge	(950,000)

b. Subsequent claimant

610 s 301 CAA 2001 If a qualifying building in an enterprise zone is **purchased within 2 years** of first being used, enterprise zone allowances (IA and WDA) are available to the purchaser on the lower of the:
– costs of construction; or
– purchase price paid.

For expenditure **after the first 2 years** of a building's tax life, WDA are available on the lower of the:
– price paid; and
– construction cost,

spread over the remaining tax life of the building.

MEMO POINTS 1. Any balancing adjustment arising to the vendor is calculated in the normal way.
2. The provisions at ¶606 to ¶609 apply equally to purchasers of second-hand buildings.

D. Business premises renovation allowances

1. Available allowances

Business premises renovation allowances (in the form of a 100% **initial allowance**) are available to the person who both: 612 ss 360A - Z4 CAA 2001; SI 2007/107; SI 2007/945
- incurs qualifying expenditure on or after 11 April 2007; and
- has a relevant interest (¶568) in the property.

However, if this is not claimed (or only partly claimed) the balance of expenditure will be subject to 25% **writing down allowances** (WDA) on a straight line basis.

2. Qualifying expenditure

Expenditure is qualifying if: 613

a. it is incurred on the **conversion, renovation or repair** of a building into premises suitable for the purposes of a trade, profession etc or an office (or for letting as such);

b. the **building**:
- is situated in either Northern Ireland or a designated "development area" (as listed in SI 2007/107);
- was unused for at least 12 months before the date the renovation etc began; and
- was previously used for the purposes of a trade, profession etc or as an office.

MEMO POINTS The renovation etc of **part of a building** will only qualify for the allowance if it was not used in common with any other part of the building unless that other part:
- was a dwelling; or
- had also been unused for at least 12 months.

Specifically **excluded** from the scheme is expenditure on: 614

a. the acquisition of, or of rights in or over, land;

b. the development of adjoining or adjacent land;

c. the extension of a qualifying building (except if necessary to provide access to qualifying business premises);

d. the provision of plant and machinery, unless it is, or it becomes, a fixture; and

e. premises that are used by businesses engaged in the following trades:
- fisheries and aquaculture;
- shipbuilding;
- coal and steel;
- synthetic fibres;
- primary production of certain agricultural products; or
- manufacture of products which imitate or substitute milk or milk products.

3. Calculation of allowance

If the full 100% **allowance is not claimed**, any remaining expenditure will be eligible for WDA at 25% on a straight line basis, provided at the end of the period for which the claim is made: 616
- the person still has a relevant interest in the property;
- a long lease (more than 50 years) has not been granted on the property; and
- the building is still a qualifying business premises.

The expenditure will not qualify for relief (or any allowances given will be withdrawn) if it is **funded by a relevant grant** or other payment (¶216).

MEMO POINTS 1. Although this allowance was only intended to be available for 5 years it has been extended by Treasury Order for a further 5 years.

2. **Anti-avoidance provisions** apply in connection with:
– sales where the control test is met, or the sale has been artificially arranged in order to obtain a tax advantage. (Note here though that it is not possible for the parties to elect that the sale be treated as for an alternative amount. (See ¶587));
– sales where as part of a tax avoidance scheme, the proceeds are less than they would be on the open market (¶588).

618 There will be a balancing adjustment if, within 7 years of the premises being made available for letting, one of the following events happens:

Balancing event [1]	Deemed proceeds
Sale	Net sale proceeds
Grant of a long lease (more than 50 years)	The capital sum involved, or if greater the premium that would have been paid in an arm's length transaction
The end of a lease, where a person entitled to the lease and a person entitled to any superior interest are connected persons	The market value of the relevant interest in the property
Death of person incurring the qualifying expenditure	Residue of qualifying expenditure (i.e. tax written down value) (¶588)
Demolition or destruction of the property	Net amount received, plus any insurance or compensation monies
Property ceases to be qualifying business premises	Market value of the property

Note:
1. If the proceeds exceed the residue of qualifying expenditure (i.e. the tax written down value) there will be a **balancing charge** normally equal to the excess but limited to the total initial allowances and WDA previously given to the person.
If the proceeds are less than the residue of qualifying expenditure there will be a **balancing allowance** normally equal to the excess but subject to the anti-avoidance rules at ¶588.

MEMO POINTS Where, as a result of the **capital goods scheme** (¶8250), an additional VAT liability is incurred in respect of qualifying expenditure, the amount of the VAT liability is also treated as qualifying expenditure and an allowance is available.
Where a **VAT rebate** is received it:
– will not give rise to a balancing allowance; and
– will give rise to a balancing charge if it exceeds the residue of qualifying expenditure at the time the rebate accrues (if it does not, then the rebate is simply deducted from the residue at the time it accrues).

E. Flat conversions

1. Available allowances

620 ss 393A - 393W CAA 2001 In order to encourage investment in the conversion and renovation of unused space above shops for short-term lets, an **initial allowance** is available if a person incurs qualifying expenditure.

However, if this is not claimed (or only partly claimed) the balance of expenditure will be subject to 25% **writing down allowances** (WDA) on a straight line basis.

MEMO POINTS 1. Flat conversion allowances are **very like IBA** (in that the allowance goes to the person that holds the relevant interest and there is a balancing adjustment if the relevant interest is sold or the flat ceases to be held for letting out). However the notable **differences** are that:
– on a transfer of an interest in the property, allowances are clawed back, and the transferee cannot claim allowances; and
– allowances are not clawed back if a transfer takes place more than 7 years from the time the flat is suitable for letting.
2. This relief will be **abolished** at some stage after April 2012 as part of the government's ongoing simplification of tax reliefs project.

2. Qualifying expenditure

Eligible flat

Certain capital expenditure (¶626) will qualify for allowances if it is incurred on an eligible flat (that was unused (or used only for storage) for at least 1 year preceding the commencement of the expenditure). **621** s 393B CAA 2001

An eligible flat is **defined** as a separate set of premises which must: **622**
- form part of a qualifying building (¶624);
- be divided horizontally from another part of the building;
- be suitable for letting as a dwelling; and
- be held for the purposes of short term-letting (i.e. not more than 5 years).

It must **also not be**:
- let to a person connected with the person who incurred the expenditure on the conversion etc;
- a high value flat (¶625) or be part of a scheme for creating or renovating one or more high value flats; and
- more than four rooms (**excluding** the kitchen and bathroom, and any cloakroom, closet or hallway of less than five square metres).

A **qualifying building** is one that was built before 1 January 1980 where: **624** s 393C CAA 2001
- all or most of the ground floor is authorised for business use;
- it appears that when the building was constructed all storeys above the ground floor were primarily for use as one or more dwellings; and
- there are no more than four storeys above the ground floor (other than the attic unless it has been used as a dwelling).

A flat is defined as a **high value flat** if the notional rent exceeds the following limits: **625** s 393E CAA 2001

Number of rooms in flat	Flats in Greater London	Flats elsewhere
1 or 2 rooms	£350 per week	£150 per week
3 rooms	£425 per week	£225 per week
4 rooms	£480 per week	£300 per week

MEMO POINTS The **notional rent** is the rent which could reasonably be expected to be paid (on the date when the qualifying expenditure is first incurred), assuming that:
- the conversion or renovation has been completed;
- the flat is let furnished on a shorthold tenancy;
- the tenant is not required to pay a premium to the landlord or any person connected with him; and
- the tenant is not connected with the person incurring the qualifying expenditure.

Capital expenditure

Expenditure on flat conversions will **qualify if** the capital expenditure relates to: **626** s 393B CAA 2001
- the conversion of part of a qualifying building into a qualifying flat;
- the renovation of a flat in a qualifying building if the flat is, or will be, a qualifying flat; or
- repairs to a qualifying building, to the extent that the repairs are incidental.

MEMO POINTS Expenditure is **not qualifying** if it is incurred in connection with the:
- acquisition of land or rights over land;
- extension of the building other than to provide access to the flat;
- development of land adjoining or adjacent to the building; or
- provision of furnishings or chattels.

3. Calculation of allowance

628 s 393H CAA 2001

Expenditure on an eligible flat qualifies for an **initial allowance** (IA) of 100%. The allowance may be reduced by the claimant to a specific amount. Where the initial allowance claimed is not the full amount, the qualifying expenditure is available for 25% **writing down allowances** (WDA) on a straight line basis in the same and subsequent periods until it is written off.

The **allowance is not available** (and any initial allowances already given will be withdrawn) if, when the flat is first suitable for letting, it:
- is not an eligible flat; or
- the person who incurred the expenditure has sold his interest.

EXAMPLE During the 12 month period to 31 December A Ltd incurred expenditure on a qualifying flat of £250,000.

1. **Full IA claimed:**

	IA assets £	Allowances £
Year ended 31 December		
Additions	250,000	250,000
WDV c/fwd	Nil	

2. **IA partially claimed:**

		IA assets £	WDA assets £	Allowances £
Year ended 31 December				
Additions		250,000		
FYA	250,000			
Less: unclaimed FYA	(100,000)			
		(150,000)		150,000
Transfer from FYA assets		(100,000)	100,000	
WDA @ 25% of £250,000 (restricted to balance)[1]			(62,500)	62,500
Total allowances for the year				212,500
WDV c/fwd		Nil	37,500	

Note:
1. The balance of the WDA will be claimed in the next year. There is no requirement to claim it all.

629 ss 393M - 393P CAA 2001

A **balancing adjustment** will be made in the chargeable period in which a balancing event occurs. Where more than one balancing event occurs, only the first will give rise to a balancing adjustment. No balancing adjustment is made if the balancing event occurs more than 7 years after the time when the flat was first suitable for letting as a dwelling.

The **balancing events** and the respective relevant proceeds for these purposes are as detailed at ¶618.

MEMO POINTS **Anti-avoidance provisions** apply in connection with:
- sales where the control test is met, or the sale has been artificially arranged in order to obtain a tax advantage. (Note here though that it is not possible for the parties to elect that the sale be treated as for an alternative amount. (See ¶587));
- sales where as part of a tax avoidance scheme, the proceeds are less than they would be on the open market (¶588).

F. Agricultural land and buildings

1. Available allowances

Capital expenditure incurred by the owner or tenant of agricultural land on agricultural buildings and structures (referred to here as buildings) may qualify for allowances. Agricultural buildings allowance (ABA) is given in the form of a **writing down allowance** (WDA), usually at a rate of 4% per annum on a straight line basis. 631

On the **disposal** of a building, allowances continue to be available to the purchaser on the same basis as the vendor was entitled. Allowances for the period of the transfer are apportioned.

MEMO POINTS 1. Parties to a transaction can elect for a **balancing adjustment** to arise on a disposal that is made before 21 March 2007 (or 1 April 2011 under a pre-commencement contract made before 21 March 2007 (¶583)). In practice it is unlikely that parties will so elect as it will usually be to the detriment of one of the parties.
2. The abolition of balancing adjustments for disposals on or after 21 March 2007 was introduced to lay the foundations of the phasing out and **abolition** of agricultural buildings allowances by the end of 2010/11. The rate of ABA was progressively reduced by 1% each financial year, starting with 2008/09. Consequently, from 2011/12 onwards no allowances will be available.

2. Definition

ABA are given to a person incurring qualifying expenditure on his freehold or leasehold interest in agricultural land. 634 s 361 CAA 2001

Agricultural land is defined as land in the UK occupied for the purposes of husbandry, which includes the following: 637 s 362 CAA 2001
- farming and market gardening;
- intensive rearing of fish or livestock for human consumption;
- manuring land for crop production;
- laying of grass;
- short rotation coppice (i.e. trees planted at high density and harvested at intervals of less than 10 years); and
- arranging for seasonal eating of grass by cattle.

3. Qualifying expenditure

The following expenditure on agricultural buildings will qualify for allowances: 652 s 369 CAA 2001

a. for new buildings, the costs of **construction** on:
- buildings (such as farmhouses, cottages, farm buildings etc); and
- fences and other works provided they are built by the claimant and the interest has not been sold;

b. where the building is **purchased second-hand** from a builder, the relevant provisions at ¶550 apply.

The cost of the **land** does not qualify for allowances in any circumstances.

MEMO POINTS Where only **part of a building** is used for agricultural purposes, for example where a farm cottage has rooms which are used for bed and breakfast, allowances will generally be restricted, by agreement with HMRC, based on the facts of the particular case. s 369(5) CAA 2001

Construction costs

Capital expenditure on construction **includes** not only building costs but also: 654
- expenditure on repairs which are not deductible elsewhere, capital improvements or reconstruction;

- demolition costs prior to constructing a replacement building; and
- architects' fees.

655 **Buildings** A **farmhouse** is, broadly speaking, a house on the farm which is occupied by the person running the farm. Where the farm is run in partnership, it is possible for there to be more than one farmhouse. Where the expenditure relates to a farmhouse, qualifying expenditure is restricted to 1/3 of the cost, unless the farmhouse is considered out of proportion to the nature of the farm, in which case a greater restriction may apply.

A **cottage** is a building occupied by an agricultural worker. Neither the size of the property nor the status of the occupier affects this. The property does not need to be located on agricultural land but must be used for the purposes of husbandry on the agricultural land in question. Cottages occupied by retired farm-workers also qualify.

Farm buildings include not only, for example, barns and cowsheds, but also welfare facilities and buildings used as retail shops for the produce of the farm.

MEMO POINTS Where the building is constructed using materials (e.g. stone or gravel) from an **on-site quarry**, a proportion of the working costs of the quarry may also be treated as qualifying expenditure unless relief is otherwise available.

656 **Other works** Other works **include** the following:
- drainage and sewerage facilities;
- shelter belts;
- gas, water and electricity installations;
- silos;
- farm roads;
- glasshouses (for market gardens);
- demolition of hedges; and
- reclamation of agricultural land.

4. Calculation of allowance

a. Amount of WDA

658 WDA are available at 4% on a straight line basis, for any chargeable period starting with the period in which the expenditure is incurred. Allowances may therefore be available before the building is used. A claim can be made to reduce the WDA to a specified amount.

Once a building is first used for husbandry, it will qualify for ABA for the full 25 year period, regardless of any subsequent **changes of use**.

MEMO POINTS 1. Where allowances are claimed **before the building is used**, and the building is subsequently not used for the purposes of husbandry, allowances will be withdrawn.
2. As WDA are being phased out on agricultural buildings in a similar way to industrial buildings, the percentages of allowance will drop as in ¶574.

b. First claimant

661 ss 370 - 372 CAA 2001 The first claimant for these purposes **means** the person constructing the building etc, or where a building was purchased unused from the builder, the first purchaser.

WDA are given from the first day of the chargeable period in which the expenditure is incurred and are available for a period of 25 years from that date. The qualifying expenditure is written off equally over the 25 year life, which effectively gives a WDA of 4% per annum. Once the 25 year life has expired, no further allowances can be claimed.

Note, however that the rate of ABA was **progressively reduced** by 1% each financial year starting with 2008/09. Consequently from 2011/12 onwards no allowances will be available.

EXAMPLE A Ltd, which prepares its accounts to 31 December, constructed a barn on 1 June 2007, at a cost of £95,000. Assuming the company has regular 12 month accounting periods, a writing down allowance of £3,800 will be available for the year to 31 December 2007.
If the company had a 9 month accounting period, the allowance would be £2,850 (£3,800 × 9/12).
If A Ltd had purchased the building from the builder for £95,000 and the builder's costs had been £90,000, allowances would be £3,600 (£90,000 × 4%).

c. Subsequent claimants

General treatment

In **general**, when a second-hand building is purchased which has previously been the subject of a claim to ABA, the purchaser is entitled to WDA on the same basis as the vendor. Where the sale takes place part way through a chargeable period, the allowances due for that period are apportioned between the two parties. 664 s 375 CAA 2001

EXAMPLE A Ltd (whose year end is 31 December) constructed a barn in 2004 at a cost of £68,000 and sells the barn to B Ltd (whose year end is 30 September) on 30 June 2007 for £59,000. Allowances would be available as follows:

		£
A Ltd		
	Cost	68,000
	Year ended 31 December 2004	2,720
	Year ended 31 December 2005	2,720
	Year ended 31 December 2006	2,720
	Year ended 31 December 2007 (6/12 × 2,720)	1,360
B Ltd		
	Year ended 30 September 2007 (3/12 × 2,720)	680
	Year ended 30 September 2008 (75 % of £2,720)[1]	2,040
	Year ended 30 September 2009 (50 % of £2,720)[1]	1,360
	Year ended 30 September 2010 (25 % of £2,720)[1]	680
	Year ended 30 September 2011 (allowances abolished)[1]	Nil

Note
1. The rate of ABA is to be progressively reduced by 1% each financial year starting in 2008/09. Consequently the effective rate for purchasers of second-hand buildings is also correspondingly reduced.

MEMO POINTS Where a **lease merges with a superior interest** (for example, because the lease term has expired and the lessee has vacated the property), this is treated as an acquisition by the holder of the superior interest.

Alternative treatment

For disposals **before 21 March 2007** (or 1 April 2011 under a pre-commencement contract made before 21 March 2007 (¶583)), the parties can **jointly elect** that a transfer be treated as giving rise to a balancing adjustment. 667 ss 376, 377, 382 CAA 2001

The disposal events, relevant proceeds and calculation of balancing adjustments and WDA for the purchaser are as for industrial buildings (¶587 onwards). The election must be made in writing within 2 years of the end of the chargeable period (or 22 months after the end of the relevant tax year for income tax purposes) and is only available if both parties are subject to UK tax. An election cannot be made where the main reason for making the election would be to gain a balancing allowance.

MEMO POINTS 1. **Anti-avoidance provisions** apply in connection with:
– sales where the control test is met, or the sale has been artificially arranged in order to obtain a tax advantage (¶587); and
– sales where as part of a tax avoidance scheme, the proceeds are less than they would be on the open market (¶588).

2. Where the disposal is as a result of the **demolition, destruction** etc of the agricultural building, the election need only be made by the owner of the relevant interest at the time.
3. This alternative treatment is not available for disposals made **on or after 21 March 2007** (unless they are made before 1 April 2011 under a pre-commencement contract made before 21 March 2007).

SECTION 5

Sundry capital allowances

680 This section deals with capital allowances of a more specialist nature. Unless otherwise indicated, the general rules for calculating and giving relief for allowances apply (¶200).

MEMO POINTS For information about allowances available for dredging or mineral extraction see *Corporation Tax Memo*.

A. Research and development

683 s 437 CAA 2001 Any **capital expenditure** incurred on research and development (R & D) may qualify for 100% R & D allowances with the **exception of** expenditure on land and dwellings. It is not necessary for the R & D to be carried on by the trader, but it must be carried out on behalf of the trader.

Balancing charges may arise on the disposal of assets representing R & D expenditure, but there are no balancing allowances.

MEMO POINTS 1. **Expenditure on dwellings** will qualify for R & D allowances, if they constitute no more than 25% of the total expenditure.
2. Where expenditure is **carried out on behalf of the trader**, a relationship akin to an agency must exist before it will be eligible for R & D allowances.
3. Any **revenue expenditure** may be deducted as an expense of the trade (¶152) and additional relief is available for certain companies (¶794).

1. Qualifying expenditure

686 To qualify for allowances, the expenditure **must be incurred on** R & D for the trade carried on. (It does not include expenditure to acquire rights in, or arising out of, R & D.) For capital allowances purposes only (i.e. not for the purposes of the enhanced trade deduction (¶794)) this **also includes** expenditure on oil and gas exploration and appraisal.

MEMO POINTS **R & D is broadly defined as** activities which are involved in the fields of natural or applied science for the extension of knowledge. This may involve research which leads to an extension of the trade, or research of a medical nature which has a special significance for employees in the trade, for example, research on the implications of coal dust for the health of miners. For a **full definition**, see ¶794.

2. Calculation of allowance

Available allowances

689 s 441 CAA 2001 Allowances are only available **for the chargeable period** in which the qualifying expenditure was incurred. No writing down or balancing allowances are available. This means that if the trader decides not to take the allowance in full, the balance is lost.

No allowances are available when an asset is acquired for ordinary business use and is later used for R & D.

MEMO POINTS Where expenditure may qualify for **more than one type** of allowance (for example R & D and industrial buildings allowance), the trader may choose which scheme of allowances to take. Once the decision has been made, it is not possible to change to the other scheme.

Disposals

Where an R & D asset is disposed of, a **balancing charge** arises equal either to the: 692 s 442 CAA 2001
– disposal value (¶587), if 100% R & D allowances were claimed (although note that any such charge cannot exceed the allowances already given); or
– the excess, if any, of the disposal value over the unrelieved expenditure, if partial R & D allowances were claimed.
This charge is treated as a trading receipt.

MEMO POINTS 1. An asset is **treated as disposed of** if:
– the trader ceases to own it; or
– it is demolished or destroyed before the trader ceases to own it.
2. Any **demolition costs** incurred by the trader will reduce the disposal value. If the demolition costs exceed the disposal value the excess is treated as qualifying R & D expenditure, incurred at the time of demolition.
3. **Anti-avoidance provisions** apply in connection with:
– sales where the control test is met, or the sale has been artificially arranged in order to obtain a tax advantage (¶587); and
– sales where as part of a tax avoidance scheme, the proceeds are less than they would be on the open market (¶588).

If an **acquisition and disposal is made in the same chargeable period**, the person incurring the expenditure is only entitled to an allowance equal to the amount by which the original expenditure exceeds the disposal value. 693

EXAMPLE A Ltd incurs £5,000 on an asset qualifying for R & D allowances. In the same accounting period, the asset is sold for £4,000. A Ltd will be entitled only to an allowance of £1,000.

VAT capital goods scheme

Where, as a result of the capital goods scheme (¶8250), an additional **VAT liability** is incurred in respect of any R & D expenditure, the amount of the VAT liability is also treated as R & D expenditure and an allowance is available. Where a **VAT rebate** is made while the person still owns the research asset, this is taxable as a trading receipt for the period in which the rebate is made. 695 ss 446-449 CAA 2001

B. Patent rights

1. Available allowances

The following provisions **apply to** qualifying expenditure on patents and patent royalties incurred by: 698 s 464 CAA 2001
– individual traders (i.e. sole traders, partnerships); or
– companies before 1 April 2002 (expenditure by companies on or after 1 April 2002 is governed by the intangible assets regime (¶824)).

Qualifying expenditure incurred to purchase patent rights will qualify for **writing down allowances** (WDA) at a rate of 25% per annum on a reducing balance basis. No initial allowances are available. 699

Balancing adjustments may arise on the **disposal** of patent rights or on the permanent cessation of a trade.

MEMO POINTS 1. **Patent rights are defined as** the right to do, or authorise the doing of, anything which would be, but for that right, the infringement of a patent.
2. Where the **expenditure is revenue** (for example the cost of obtaining a grant of a patent), a revenue deduction may be allowable (¶188).

2. Qualifying expenditure

701 ss 467 - 469 CAA 2001

Two types of capital expenditure are eligible for allowances:
a. qualifying trade expenditure on the purchase of patent rights for the purposes of the trade carried on by the purchaser; and
b. qualifying non-trade expenditure on the purchase of patent rights if:
– any of the income receivable in respect of the rights would be chargeable to tax; and
– the expenditure is not qualifying trade expenditure.

Essentially this means that to qualify for allowances the expenditure must either be incurred for existing patent rights or in order to acquire patent rights in the future for inventions for which patents have not yet been granted.

3. Calculation of allowance

Rate of WDA

704 ss 470 - 472 CAA 2001

WDA are first given in the chargeable period in which the qualifying expenditure is incurred. To calculate the allowances, the expenditure is separately pooled between trade and non-trade expenditure.

The rate of WDA is 25% of the pool balance at the end of the period in question, calculated in accordance with the general rules (¶290), unless the patent rights are fully disposed of.

EXAMPLE A Ltd, who prepares accounts to 31 December, acquires two new patent rights for trading purposes as follows:

Patent	Date of acquisition	Cost
1	Year 1	£10,000
2	Year 2	£25,000

In Year 3, part of the rights of patent 2 were sold for £10,000.

Capital allowances are calculated as follows:

	Pool £	Allowances £
Year 1:		
Addition	10,000	
WDA	(2,500)	2,500
WDV c/fwd	7,500	
Year 2:		
WDV b/fwd	7,500	
Addition	25,000	
	32,500	
WDA	(8,125)	8,125
WDV c/fwd	24,375	
Year 3:		
WDV b/fwd	24,375	
Disposal	(10,000)	
	14,375	
WDA	(3,594)	3,594
WDV c/fwd	10,781	

MEMO POINTS 1. Allowances on **trade expenditure** are treated as trade expenses in the usual manner.
2. Allowances on **non-trade patent expenditure** are set against the company's non-trade patent income for the same accounting period, with any excess being carried forward without time limit against such income for subsequent accounting periods.

Disposals

The general rules for **balancing adjustments** (¶399) apply on the disposal of patent rights. **However**, where disposal proceeds exceed the original capital expenditure, the excess is taxed as income of the vendor. This contrasts with other forms of capital expenditure where the excess is subject to the chargeable gains provisions. 707 ss 476-477 CAA 2001

MEMO POINTS Where the disposal proceeds exceed the original capital expenditure, the **purchaser** only brings into account the amount which is brought into account by the vendor as disposal proceeds for capital allowances purposes.

Where the disposal is to a **connected person** (¶5570) or where the main benefit is to obtain writing down allowances, the purchaser's qualifying expenditure will be either: 708 ss 477, 481 CAA 2001
a. the disposal value (or capital receipt) brought into account by the vendor; or
b. the lesser of the:
- market value of the rights;
- amount of capital expenditure, if any, incurred by the seller (or any person connected with the seller) on acquiring the rights.

Where the trade (and associated patent right) is **transferred without significant change in ownership**, allowances continue to be available to the successor on the same basis as the transferor. 710

MEMO POINTS There is **no significant change of ownership** where there is a change in the membership of a partnership, or a company reconstruction without change of ownership. Similarly, a transfer of trade between either of the following is not a significant change:
- companies which are under common ownership (¶254); or
- connected persons (¶5570).

C. Know-how

1. Available allowances

The following provisions **apply to** qualifying expenditure on know-how incurred by: 716 s 452 CAA 2001
- individual traders (i.e. sole traders, partnerships); or
- companies before 1 April 2002 (expenditure by companies on or after 1 April 2002 is governed by the intangible assets regime (¶824)).

Qualifying expenditure incurred to purchase know-how will qualify for **writing down allowances** (WDA) at a rate of 25% per annum on a reducing balance basis. No initial allowances are available. 718

Balancing adjustments may arise on the **disposal** of know-how or on the permanent cessation of a trade.

MEMO POINTS **Know-how is defined** as any industrial information and technique likely to assist in the manufacture or processing of goods or materials. HMRC take the view that this does not include any commercial know-how (e.g. marketing or distribution techniques), for which no allowances are available.

2. Qualifying expenditure

719 s 454 CAA 2001 To qualify for allowances, the expenditure must be incurred for industrial information and techniques for one of the following:
- the manufacture or processing of goods or materials;
- working mines or oil wells; or
- undertaking agriculture, fishing or forestry operations.

3. Calculation of allowance

Rate of WDA

722 s 456 CAA 2001 WDA are first given in the chargeable period in which the expenditure is incurred. Expenditure on know-how is pooled, with a separate pool for each trade in respect of which the taxpayer has qualifying expenditure. WDA are given at 25% of the pool balance at the end of the period in question, calculated in accordance with the general rules (¶290).

Disposals

725 s 462 CAA 2001 Disposal proceeds will **either be**:
- brought into the pool, although the proceeds are not restricted to the cost incurred, unlike plant and machinery; or
- treated as a payment for goodwill and subject to the capital gains regime. For this treatment to apply, the disposal of the know-how must arise as an integral part of a disposal of the trade. (These proceeds are therefore not taken into account in the pool balance, and no balancing adjustment will arise.)

MEMO POINTS As regards the **goodwill treatment**:
- it is possible for both parties to the transaction to **elect** for the payment not to be treated as goodwill, in which case the proceeds will be brought into the pool calculation. This election cannot be made if the parties are under common control; and
- the purchaser will not be subject to the goodwill treatment if the **trade is carried on overseas**, and may be able to claim allowances in respect of his expenditure on know-how.

728 Where the trade (and know-how) is transferred **without significant change in ownership**, allowances continue to be available to the successor on the same basis as the transferor.

MEMO POINTS There is **no significant change of ownership** where there is a change in the membership of a partnership, or a company reconstruction without change of ownership. Similarly, a transfer of trade between either of the following is not a significant change:
- companies which are under common ownership (¶254); or
- connected persons (¶5570).

D. Land remediation relief

1. Overview

Available claims

757 ss 1143 - 1158 CTA 2009 Companies that acquire contaminated land (or a major interest in it) for the purposes of their trade, including a UK property business, can claim an enhanced deduction for certain expenditure incurred on their relevant clean up work. For expenditure incurred on or after 1 April 2009 this relief is extended for qualifying expenditure on **derelict land** where the

land has been derelict from the earlier of 1 April 1998 and the date it was acquired. This deduction can be treated either as:
- a trading deduction when computing taxable profits/losses; or
- the amount on which a "land remediation credit" is calculated (¶766).

MEMO POINTS 1. For these purposes a major interest is either the ownership of the land or a lease lasting at least 7 years. s 1178A CTA 2009
2. This relief is **only available to companies**.
3. Companies **that do not qualify for this enhanced relief** may still be able to claim a revenue deduction (¶152) or capital allowances depending on the nature of the expenditure.
4. If the expenditure is incurred **before the trade commenced**, it is treated as being incurred on the first day of trading.
5. Relief cannot be claimed for any expenditure that is attributable to **disqualifying arrangements**. Arrangements are disqualifying where the sole or main object, or one of them, is to obtain or increase the amount of a claim.
6. The requirement that land must be contaminated when acquired has been relaxed for Japanese Knotweed. SI 2009/2037 reg 7
7. This relief will be **abolished** at some stage after April 2012 as part of the government's ongoing simplification of tax reliefs project.

2. Contaminated or derelict land

Contaminated land

Land is contaminated if something in, on, or under the land is causing harm, or there is a serious possibility that harm, will be caused. 758

However, the land in the following situations is not considered to be contaminated:
- where there is a presence of living organisms, or the decaying matter deriving from such organisms, or from air or water. However, from 1 April 2009, this does not apply to arsenic (or compounds based on it), Japanese Knotweed or radon; s 1145(2) CTA 2009; SI 2009/2037
- any substance is present other than as a result of an industrial activity; or s 1145(2) CTA 2009
- where the land is subject to a nuclear site licence or where it has expired, the licensee is still responsible for the land. s 1145B CTA 2009

MEMO POINTS Harm is defined as any of:
- the death or significant injury or damage to living organisms;
- significant pollution of controlled waters;
- a significant adverse consequence on the ecosystem; or
- structural damage to, or significant interference with the use of, a building or structure.

Derelict land

Land is derelict where it is not in productive use and cannot be used productively without the removal of buildings or other structures. 759 s 1145A CTA 2009

3. Qualifying work

Definition

Qualifying activities include the doing of any works or operations undertaken directly by or on behalf of the company in order to: 760 s 1146 CTA 2009
- prevent, minimise, remedy or mitigate the effects of any harm or pollution of territorial waters;
- restore the land or waters to their former state; or
- in the case of derelict land, to undertake work on the land that is specified by Treasury order. s 1146A CTA 2009

Qualifying activities include any preparatory activities provided they are for the purposes of assessing the condition of the land or waters concerned for the works, and that the work itself qualifies for the relief.

The removal of Japanese Knotweed to a landfill site is not included, nor are any works that are required by other enactments specified by Treasury order.

SI 2009/2037

MEMO POINTS The removal of the following items have been stated to qualify for relief:
– post-tensioned concrete heavyweight construction;
– building foundations and machinery bases;
– reinforced concrete pilecaps and basements;
– redundant services that are located below ground including all piping, wiring, cabling, equipment, infrastructure or similar. These include those relating to gas and water supplies, drainage, sewerage, electricity supply and telecommunications.

4. What expenditure is eligible?

Qualifying expenditure

761 ss 1144, 1170, 1171 CTA 2009

Expenditure will qualify for land remediation relief if:

a. it **relates to** either:
– materials employed directly in the relevant remediation work;
– salary costs of directors and employees directly and actively engaged in the relevant remediation work (prorated if only part of their time relates to such activities); or
– sub-contracted costs; and

b. the following **conditions** are met:
– the land is contaminated or derelict;
– the expenditure is incurred purely because of the contamination or dereliction;
– the expenditure is not subsidised; and
– the expenditure does not relate to landfill tax.

Salary **costs will not be prorated** if the director/employee spends:
– less than 20% of his time on such activities (in this case none of the costs will be eligible for the relief); or
– more than 80% of his time on such activities (in this case all of the costs will be eligible for relief).

MEMO POINTS **Salary costs** exclude benefits in kind, but include secondary Class 1 NIC and pension contributions.

Sub-contracted expenditure

762 ss 1174 - 1176 CTA 2009

If all or part of the relevant remediation works are sub-contracted out by a company (A), to another person (B), the payment to B will qualify in full. However, if the parties are **connected** (¶5570) the payment will only qualify in full if, in accordance with normal UK accounting practice, the:
– whole of the payment to B; and
– qualifying expenditure incurred by B in carrying out the works;
have been brought into account when determining B's profit/loss for a period which ends not more than 12 months after A's.

5. Relief

Amount of relief

763 ss 1147 - 1149 CTA 2009

A company can claim relief for 150% of the qualifying expenditure. This relief can be claimed in the accounting period in which the expenditure is, under normal accountancy principles, recognised in the accounts.

MEMO POINTS 1. Any capital expenditure allowed as relief in computing profits is not treated as an allowable deduction for **capital gains tax** purposes.
2. Relief is **not available** for clean up costs if the company (or anyone connected with the company) has contaminated the land in the first place.

Utilisation of relief

The relief can either be treated as: 764
- an increased deduction; or
- the amount on which a "land remediation credit" is calculated.

Increased deduction The original qualifying expenditure plus an additional 50% is allowed as a trading deduction when computing the taxable profits of the trade. 765

EXAMPLE A Ltd acquires contaminated land as part of its trading stock. It incurs £200,000 qualifying clean up costs in the accounting period of acquisition.
A deduction of £300,000 (150 % of £200,000) can be claimed when calculating its profits chargeable to corporation tax.

Land remediation credit If a company has a "qualifying land remediation loss", it may claim a credit of 16% of that loss. A **qualifying land remediation loss** is the lower of: 766 s 1151 CTA 2009

a. 150% of the qualifying remediation expenditure; and

b. the unrelieved trading loss for the accounting period, calculated in the normal manner but:
- ignoring any losses brought forward or carried back;
- assuming the maximum loss has been set against other income of the accounting period (¶1273); and
- taking into account any actual claims to carry back the loss against profits of earlier accounting periods (¶1274) or to surrender the loss as group/consortium relief (¶1540).

Where a land remediation credit is claimed, the **company is deemed to have** surrendered the loss such that it is not available for carry forward against future profits. 767

The tax credit itself may be applied to any corporation tax liability of the company.

EXAMPLE A Ltd incurs qualifying land remediation expenditure of £50,000 in an accounting period (and claims a further 50% of this expenditure as land remediation relief).
After taking other expenses into account, the company has an overall trading loss for the accounting period of £70,000.
It makes a claim to surrender the full amount of its qualifying land remediation loss in exchange for a payment of land remediation tax credit. No other loss relief or group relief claims for the period were made.
A Ltd's qualifying land remediation loss is £70,000, being the lower of:
- £75,000: 150% of the qualifying land remediation expenditure (£50,000 x 150%); and
- £70,000: the company's unrelieved trading loss for the accounting period.

The tax credit payable is £11,200 (£70,000 x 16%) and no losses can be carried forward to later periods.

MEMO POINTS 1. Land remediation credits paid to a company carry **interest** from the filing date (¶2275) for the return for the accounting period in which they are claimed (or the actual date on which the return was submitted, if later) to the date they are paid to the company. The tax credit payment is not treated as income for any tax purposes.
2. A company is liable to a **penalty** if it fraudulently or negligently makes an incorrect claim for tax credits. The penalty cannot exceed the excess tax credit claimed. A similar penalty may be charged where a company realises that a tax credit claim is incorrect, but fails to correct the claim without unreasonable delay.

Claiming the relief

A claim for land remediation relief must be made on the tax return for the accounting period to which it is attributable. (Note that claims for land remediation credit must be quantified at the time of the claim.) 768

The claim can be varied or withdrawn within 12 months of the filing date for the relevant tax return.

CHAPTER 5

Other income and expenses

OUTLINE ¶¶

SECTION 1

Property income

780
s 209 CTA 2009
Income arising to a company from land or property is **assessable** as income from a property business if it consists of income arising from the **exploitation of any estate**, interest or right in or over land (including buildings, structures and land covered with water). There are two types of business:
– a UK property business, which includes all income from the exploitation of land in the UK; and,
– an overseas property business, which includes all income generated from property abroad.
For these purposes, the UK excludes the Isle of Man and the Channel Islands. Income arising from the following sources is specifically included:
– licences to occupy or use land;
– ground rents; and
– the granting of a right to an individual to use a caravan or houseboat in one particular location.

MEMO POINTS For accounting periods commencing on or after 1 January 2007, companies that carry out a **property rental trade can elect** to join a special regime, known as the real estate investment trust regime. For full details of this see *Corporation Tax Memo*.

781 Property receipts are **outside the scope** of the charge to tax as property income if they are:
a. exempt from tax (such as income from the occupation of commercially managed woodlands); or
b. taxed as trading income, such as:
– farming or market gardening;
– profits or rent charged in connection with mining, quarrying, fishing etc;
– rental receipts in respect of tied property;
– rent in connection with easements; and
– profits from running hotels and guest houses.

782 When calculating **the taxable income** for a property business, the income and expenses from all UK sources (including furnished holiday lettings) arising in an accounting period are pooled and treated as a UK property business. A similar calculation is performed for an overseas property business.

783
s 210 CTA 2009
The rules for determining the taxable profits of a property business are essentially the same for companies and individuals (¶2739 onwards), with the following **differences**:
– interest relief for companies is dealt with under the loan relationship provisions (¶870);
– any profit is not trading or earned income, but property income; and
– the rules regarding the manner in which property business losses can be utilised (¶1280).

MEMO POINTS Note also that the following special rules for property **apply equally to companies** and individuals:
– furnished holiday lettings (¶2777);
– surplus business accommodation (¶2785); and
– rent factoring (¶2787).

SECTION 2

Specific trading expenses

A. Employee share ownership

1. Employee share schemes

General rules

Some employers **reward their staff** with shares in the company they work for. The employer may choose to set up an employee share scheme trust which creates an artificial trading market, as well as being a vehicle in which to store shares. **784**

MEMO POINTS **Alternatively**, the employer may simply award the shares or options direct to the employees.

Costs incurred in **setting up** the following approved employee share schemes (¶3416) are deductible as a trading expense, provided that no options are granted before the scheme is given approval by HMRC: **785** ss 987, 999, 1000 CTA 2009
- approved company share option plans (ACSOPs);
- SAYE option schemes and
- share incentive plans (SIPs).

Relief is generally given in the period in which the expense is incurred. If the trust deed is executed, or the scheme approved, more than 9 months after the end of the period of account, relief will be given for the period in which the execution or approval occurs.

Share incentive plans (SIP)

In addition the **following costs** incurred in connection with a SIP (¶3510) are deductible: **786** s 983-998 CTA 2009
- running costs;
- payments to the trustees of a SIP to acquire shares; and
- cost of the shares awarded to employees.

However, **no deduction is available** for:
- shares awarded to non-PAYE individuals;
- shares awarded to employees which have previously been awarded but forfeited, and for which the company has previously claimed a deduction;
- shares for which a deduction has previously been given for their provision to this or another trust (for example shares originally acquired by an approved profit sharing scheme);
- expenses in providing dividend shares;
- shares which are liable to depreciate substantially for reasons that do not generally apply to the company's shares; or
- where the main purpose of making the payments to the scheme is the avoidance of tax.

MEMO POINTS When claiming a deduction for the **cost of the shares**, only the market value of the shares at the time they were acquired by the trustees can be claimed. This deduction can only be made in the period of account in which the shares are awarded to the employees. A deduction is also available for partnership shares (¶3512), equal to the excess of the market value of the shares over the amount paid by the employee.

2. Employee share acquisitions

Direct supply to employees

787 ss 1014 - 1013 CTA 2009 A corporation tax deduction for the **costs of** providing shares directly to employees (rather than through a share scheme trust) can be claimed. Under these provisions there is no requirement for complex and expensive arrangements using trusts in order to gain a corporation tax deduction.

MEMO POINTS Any deduction available under the **share incentive plan** is given in priority to this statutory corporation tax deduction.

Qualifying conditions

788 To qualify the following conditions must be met at the time the shares are awarded (or the options to acquire the shares are exercised):

1. The **shares** (or an option to acquire shares) must be:

a. granted by reason of an individual's (or another person's) employment with the employing company;

b. granted in respect of:

– the employing company;

– the parent of the employing company;

– a member of a consortium that owns the employing company;

– a member of the same consortium as the employing company or its parent which is a member of the same commercial association as another company owned by the consortium; or

– a qualifying successor company (where the original grant was an option);

c. ordinary, fully paid up non-redeemable shares and either;

– listed on a recognised stock exchange (¶9995) or under the control of a company whose shares are listed on a recognised stock exchange; or

– unlisted in a company that is not under the control of any other company.

2. The **company** granting the shares (or options) must be one whose business is within the charge to UK corporation tax. (Note, for a grant of an option to acquire shares, this condition needs to be satisfied at the time the option is granted, whereas the other conditions need to be satisfied at the time the option is exercised); and

3. The **employee** must be subject to UK tax for the award of the shares or options.

MEMO POINTS 1. A company is a **parent company** if it owns 51% of the share capital of the subsidiary.

2. A **commercial association** of companies is a number of companies carrying on businesses of such a nature that they may be reasonably considered to make up a single composite undertaking.

3. Following a **company takeover**, any qualifying options can be transferred to the new company, which will then be eligible for the corporation tax deduction (assuming all the other conditions are met by the new company).

Relief

789 s 1010 CTA 2009 **General rules** A tax deduction is given to the company in the accounting period in which the employee acquires a beneficial interest in the shares, **equal to**:

– the difference between the market value of the shares at the time of acquisition and the amount paid or payable by the employee (or another) for the shares. This deduction is therefore equal to the amount that is subject to income tax on the employee; and

– other expenses relating directly to the provision of the shares.

MEMO POINTS Costs incurred in relation to the **establishment and administration of the share scheme**, as well as any financing costs (interest, fees, commission, stamp duty), are not deductible under these provisions. They continue to be deductible under existing law and practice. See ¶785.

Convertible/restricted shares The corporation tax deduction for convertible (¶3376) and restricted shares (¶3382) is similar in each case and is available as follows: 790 s 1011 CTA 2009

Event	Amount of relief	When is relief given
Award of the shares	Amount that constitutes employment income[1, 2]	In the accounting period in which the recipient acquires a beneficial interest in the shares
Acquisition as a result of the exercise of an option	Amount that constitutes employment income (¶3394) plus any National Insurance contributions of the employer which were relieved in arriving at that income. If the option is granted under the EMI scheme (¶3450) the corporation tax relief is equal to the market value of the share when the option is exercised less any amounts paid by the employee, ignoring any discount given to the employee (¶3498)[3]	
Chargeable event[1]	Amount that constitutes employment income[1]. Any income tax relief for secondary Class 1 contributions met by the employee and any increase in market value under the rules relating to restricted securities with artificially depressed market value are ignored when calculating the relief (¶3368)	
Death of employee	Amount that constitutes employment income[1] on the assumption that there was a deemed chargeable event[1] at the date of death	In the accounting period in which the employee dies

Note:
1. For convertible shares see ¶3378. For restricted shares see ¶3386.
2. Where the shares are both convertible and restricted shares the corporation tax relief is the greater amount that is assessable as employment income.
3. For this purpose, the market value would depend on whether the employee had made a restricted value election (¶3388).

B. Donations for humanitarian purposes

Where a company donates **medical supplies or equipment** for human use from its trading stock the cost is an allowable trading deduction. This relief also covers the costs of transportation, delivery or distribution. 792 s 107 CTA 2009

C. Research and development expenditure

1. Overview

Available claims

Companies incurring certain revenue expenditure on qualifying research and development (R & D) or vaccine research can claim a **deduction** of an amount greater than the actual expenditure. 794 ss 1039 - 1142 CTA 2009

Alternatively, a small or medium sized enterprise (SME) that has a trading loss may claim a **payment** (known as an R & D tax credit) from HMRC (¶810) instead.

MEMO POINTS 1. Traders that **do not qualify for this enhanced relief** may be able to claim a standard revenue deduction (¶152) depending on the nature of the expenditure.
2. **Capital expenditure** incurred on qualifying R & D may qualify for capital allowances (¶683).
3. Relief cannot be claimed for any expenditure attributable to **disqualifying arrangements**. Arrangements are disqualifying where the main object, or one of them, is to obtain, or to increase the amount of, a claim to tax relief or tax credit.

Large company or SME?

795 ss 1119, 1120 CTA 2009

The qualifying expenditure and deduction available differs slightly depending upon whether the company is a small or medium sized enterprise (SME) or a large company, which are **defined as** follows:

a. large companies are all companies which are not SMEs; and

b. small or medium sized enterprises are ones which have fewer than 500 employees, and which have either:
- turnover of not more than €100m; or
- balance sheet assets of not more than €86m.

When establishing whether a company is an SME, the results of any related enterprise must be taken into account when determining the thresholds.

A company is **specifically excluded** from the SME definition if more than 25% of its share capital or voting rights are owned by enterprises that are not themselves SMEs (unless the enterprises are investment corporations, venture capital companies or institutional investors that do not exercise control over the company).

MEMO POINTS 1. If a company that **was previously an SME** breaches the thresholds, it will only cease to be an SME if the thresholds are breached for two consecutive periods. Similarly, a company that **was not previously an SME** must satisfy the conditions for two consecutive periods to become an SME. (However this condition does not apply in a period where it is only the related enterprise that exceeds the limit, but the company in isolation does not).

HMRC Brief 55/08 CIRD 92000

2. Where an SME joins a group, or is taken over in some other way, resulting in it becoming large it will be considered to be large for the entire period in which it joins the group.
3. A **related enterprise** is essentially a:
- linked enterprise where one enterprise is able to exercise control, either directly or indirectly, over the affairs of the other; or
- a partner enterprise where one of them holds (either on its own or in combination with other enterprises with which it is linked), 25% or more of the capital or voting rights in the other.

2. Qualifying R & D activities

796 ss 1041, 1042 CTA 2009; s 1138 CTA 2010

Research and development takes its definition from normal accounting practice, specifically Statement of Standard Accounting Practice (SSAP) 13. Under SSAP 13, R & D may **take the form of**:

a. pure research (i.e. experimental or theoretical work undertaken primarily to acquire new scientific or technical knowledge for its own sake, rather than directed towards any specific aim or application);

b. applied research (i.e. original or critical investigation undertaken in order to gain new scientific or technical knowledge which is directed towards a specific practical aim or objective); or

c. development (i.e. the use of scientific or technical knowledge to:
- produce new or substantially improved materials, devices, products or services;
- install new processes or systems prior to the commencement of commercial production or commercial application; or
- substantially improve those already produced or installed).

There are two **key factors** which can be identified from the above definitions. Firstly, the research or development must be in a scientific or technical field, and secondly there must be advancement of knowledge. The aim must be to acquire new information or knowledge or to produce something new or improved.

SSAP 13 provides a list of **examples** of activities which would generally be considered as R & D and a corresponding list of activities which would be excluded from the definition. 797

Activities normally included	Activities normally excluded
Experimental, theoretical or other work aimed at the discovery of new knowledge, or the advancement of existing knowledge	Testing analysis either of equipment or products for the purposes of quality or quantity control
Searching for applications of that knowledge	Periodic alterations to existing products, services or processes even though these may represent some improvement
Formulation and design of possible applications for such work	Optional research not tied to specific research and development activity
Testing in search for, or evaluation of, product, service or process alternatives	Cost of corrective action in connection with breakdowns during commercial production
Design, construction and testing of pre-production prototypes and models and development batches	Legal and administrative work in connection with patent applications, records and litigation and the sale or licensing of patents
Design of products, processes, services or systems involving new technology or substantially improving those already installed	Activity, including design and construction engineering, relating to the construction, relocation, rearrangement or start up of facilities or equipment other than facilities or equipment whose sole use is for a particular research and development project
Construction and operation of prototypes and pilot plants	Market research

3. Qualifying expenditure

Conditions

Expenditure will qualify for R & D relief if: 798 ss 1051, s 1065 CTA 2009

a. it is incurred on qualifying R & D activities, for one or more of the following:
- staffing costs;
- software or consumable items;
- payments to volunteers for participating in clinical trials; or
- qualifying subcontracted R & D;

b. it is at least £10,000 in a 12 month accounting period (proportionately reduced for periods of less than 12 months), and

c. the R & D is for a trade carried on by the company, or which the company will carry on. This includes R & D which is expected to result in an extension to an existing trade, or research of a medical nature which has special significance for employees in the trade, for example, research into the implications of coal dust for the health of miners.

MEMO POINTS 1. For accounting periods ending before 9 December 2009 where the company was an SME it also had to own, either alone or with others, any intellectual property that was created.
2. R & D expenditure will be qualifying even if it is **subsidised**. Expenditure is subsidised to the extent that:
- a grant or subsidy is received;
- a person other than the company meets the expense; or;
- state aid (as approved by the European Commission) is received for the R & D or any other expenditure attributable to the project.
3. It is **proposed** to abolish the minimum expenditure requirement for periods after 1 April 2012.

Staffing costs

799 ss 1123, 1124 CTA 2009

The costs which can be attributable to R & D differ depending upon the nature of the payments, as follows:

a. 100% of the payments made for **directors and employees** directly and actively engaged in R & D will be attributable to R & D if they are for:
- emoluments, excluding benefits;
- secondary (i.e. employer's) Class 1 National Insurance Contributions; or
- pension contributions.

Where the director or employee is not wholly engaged in R & D, the proportion of expenditure allowable will be apportioned on a just and reasonable basis.

Staffing costs incurred for support services (for example secretaries) are not attributable to R & D;

b. 65% of the qualifying payments made to another person (a 'staff provider') for the supply of **external workers** will be attributable to R & D if the external workers are directly engaged in qualifying R & D activities of the company. (If they are only partly so engaged, the costs are split on a just and reasonable basis).

s 1128 CTA 2009

MEMO POINTS 1. **External workers** are individuals who are not directors or employees of the company, but who, as a result of their contract with the staff provider, are required personally to provide services to the company, subject to the usual supervision and direction as to how these services are performed.

2. The provision of the externally provided worker must not be as part of a **subcontractor relationship** (¶803).

800 ss 1129 - 1131 CTA 2009

Where a company and the staff provider supplying external workers are **connected** the 65% restriction on qualifying payments does not apply. Instead the payments attributable to R & D are the lower of:
- the whole of the payment to the staff provider; or
- the whole of the expenditure incurred by the staff provider on staffing costs.

This treatment is **only available where** the full amount of the payment to the staff provider and the expenditure of the staff provider has, in accordance with normal accountancy practice, been brought into account in computing the staff provider's profit or loss. The amount must be brought into account in an accounting period which ends no later than 12 months after the period of account in which the company deducts the payments to the staff provider.

MEMO POINTS It is possible for **unconnected parties to make a joint election** for the connected party rule to apply. This election must be made in writing within 2 years of the end of the accounting period in which the contract is entered into. The election is irrevocable and applies to all staff provision payments paid under the same contract.

Software or consumable items

801 ss 1125, 1126 CTA 2009

Expenditure on software or consumable items is attributable to R & D if the items are directly employed in R & D. If the items are only partly so employed, an appropriate apportionment of the expenditure can be made.

Software or consumable items specifically include:
- consumable or transformable materials;
- utility costs; and
- software licences where the software is used directly and actively in the R & D.

Clinical trial volunteers

802 s 1140 CTA 2009

Payments to volunteers participating in clinical trials is qualifying R & D expenditure where it is incurred by a large company on or after 1 April 2006, or on or after 1 August 2008 by an SME.

MEMO POINTS A **clinical trial is defined as** an investigation in human subjects undertaken in connection with the development of a healthcare treatment or procedure.

Subcontracted R & D

Where payment is made to a subcontractor, 65% of it will be qualifying R & D expenditure (even if the subcontracted work is not R & D in its own right, provided it is part of a larger project that is R & D). This category includes expenditure on qualifying R & D activities that are subcontracted out by **803** s 1133 - 1136 CTA 2009

a. an SME to another person, that is not an SME itself; or

b. a large company (or a person whose trading activities are not within the scope of UK tax), to an SME.

As a result of these rules, relief is denied where work is subcontracted to an SME by another SME, as this would effectively result in a double credit.

Relief will be given if the SME has incurred the minimum expenditure on its aggregate R & D (i.e. its subcontracted and own R & D expenditure).

MEMO POINTS 1. To qualify for relief under **b**. above, the subcontracted work must be either:
- carried out by the SME; or
- further subcontracted out by the SME to a qualifying body, individual or partnership with no corporate members.

2. A **qualifying body** is a charity, higher educational institution, scientific research organisation or health service body.

3. There are **proposals** to reform the relief available to large companies where they subcontract R & D work from 1 April 2012.

Where the company and the subcontractor are **connected**, the 65% restriction on qualifying payments does not apply. Instead the qualifying payments are the lower of: **804** s 1135 CTA 2009
- the subcontractor payment; or
- the relevant R & D expenditure incurred by the subcontractor (i.e. the unsubsidised revenue expenditure on staffing costs (including externally provided workers), software or consumable items and payments to clinical trial volunteers).

This treatment is **only available where** the full amount of the subcontractor payment and the relevant expenditure has, in accordance with normal accounting practice, been brought into account in computing the subcontractor's profit or loss for a relevant period. A relevant period is a period for which the subcontractor makes up accounts and which ends no later than 12 months after the end of the period of account in which the company deducts the payment in its accounts.

MEMO POINTS It is possible for **unconnected parties to make a joint election** for the connected party rule to apply. This election must be made in writing within 2 years of the end of the accounting period in which the contract is entered into. The election is irrevocable and applies to all subcontractor payments made between the two parties.

4. Relief

Amount of relief

The following trading deductions can be claimed: **806** ss 1044(8), 1063(7), 1068(8), 1074(7) CTA 2009

a. SMEs may claim a deduction for 200% of the qualifying expenditure, provided the company is a **going concern**, unless the work is:
- subcontracted to an SME when the deduction is 130% for the sub-contractor SME; or
- subsidised R & D (¶798) undertaken by an SME when the deduction is again 130%.

b. large companies may claim a deduction for 130% of the qualifying expenditure.

MEMO POINTS 1. For expenditure incurred **between 1 August 2008 and 1 April 2011** the higher rate of relief was 175%. For expenditure **prior to 1 August 2008** the rates were 150% and 125% respectively. It is **proposed** to increase the higher rate to 225% for expenditure incurred on or after 1 April 2012. ss 1046, 1057 CTA 2009

2. A company is considered a going concern where its last published accounts were prepared on a going concern basis and nothing in those accounts indicated that the availability of R & D relief or tax credits (¶810) was the only reason the accounts were prepared on that basis.

3. From 1 August 2008 the amount of expenditure on which relief can be claimed is capped at €7.5m per qualifying project. Prior to this date the relief was uncapped. s 1113 CTA 2009

Utilisation of relief

808 **Trading deduction** The R & D relief can be set against current year taxable profits as a trading deduction.

MEMO POINTS Alternatively (and for SMEs only) an **R & D credit** can be claimed if the R & D relief results in the company having a surrenderable loss.

810 s 1054 - 1057 CTA 2009 **R & D credit** An R & D tax credit can be claimed by an SME if it has a surrenderable loss, provided it is a going concern (¶806). A **surrenderable loss** is the lower of:
a. 200% of the qualifying payments; or
b. the unrelieved trading loss for the accounting period calculated in the normal way but:
– ignoring any losses brought forward or carried back (¶1278);
– assuming the maximum loss has been set against other income of the accounting period (¶1273); and
– taking into account any actual claims to carry back the loss against profits of earlier accounting periods (¶1274) or to surrender the loss as group/consortium relief (¶1540).

MEMO POINTS 1. If an SME company is **owned by a consortium** (at least one of which is a non-SME company), losses cannot be surrendered as group relief to the non-SME consortium members.
2. For expenditure incurred **between 1 August 2008 and 1 April 2011** the rate was 175%. For expenditure **prior to 1 August 2008** the rate was 150%. It is **proposed** to increase the rate to 225% for expenditure incurred on or after April 2012.

812 s 1058 CTA 2009 The **amount that may be claimed** as a tax free R & D credit is the lower of:
– 12.5% of the surrenderable loss; and
– the total PAYE and NIC payable by the company for payment periods ending during the accounting period. A payment period is a period which ends on the fifth day of a month, and in respect of which the company is liable to account for income tax and NIC to HMRC.

MEMO POINTS 1. When computing the **total PAYE and NIC payable**, any deductions the company is authorised to make for the following are ignored:
– statutory parental pay; and
– statutory sick pay.
2. For expenditure incurred **between 1 August 2008 and 1 April 2011** the rate of the credit was 14%. For expenditure **prior to 1 August 2008** the rate of the credit was 16%. It is likely this rate will be amended for expenditure incurred on or after 1 April 2012 when the rate of additional relief is enhanced.
3. It is **proposed** to abolish the limit to the amount of credit that can be claimed for expenditure incurred on or after 1 April 2012.

813 Where an R & D **tax credit is claimed**, the company is deemed to have surrendered the loss such that it is not available for carry forward against future profits of the trade. Where the tax credit is restricted due to the total PAYE and NIC liability, the amount of the loss deemed to be surrendered is calculated on a pro rata basis.

EXAMPLE A Ltd (an SME) incurs a £2,500,000 loss for the accounting period ended 31 March 2011, of which £2,000,000 is attributable to R & D tax relief. Its total PAYE and NIC liability is £230,000. The amount of tax credit the company may claim is £230,000, being the lower of:

14% of loss attributable to R & D tax relief	£280,000
PAYE/ NIC liability	£230,000

The amount of the loss which is deemed to be surrendered is therefore: £1,642,857 (i.e. 230,000/280,000 × 2,000,000).

MEMO POINTS 1. R & D tax credits paid to a company carry **interest** from the due filing date (¶2275) for the return for the accounting period in which they are claimed (or the actual date on which the return was submitted, if later) to the date they are paid to the company. The tax credit payment received is not treated as income for any tax purposes.
2. A company is liable to a **penalty** if it fraudulently or negligently makes an incorrect claim for tax credits. The penalty cannot exceed the excess tax credit claimed. A similar penalty may be charged where a company realises that a tax credit claim is incorrect, but fails to correct the claim without unreasonable delay.

Claiming relief

R & D relief must be claimed on the tax return for the accounting period to which it is attributable. The time limit for making, amending or withdrawing a claim is 12 months after the filing date for the relevant tax return. 814

MEMO POINTS There are now seven **specialist R & D tax credit units** around the country to deal with R & D tax credit claims and vaccine research relief claims (¶817). From 1 November 2006, corporation tax returns with R & D tax credit or vaccine research relief claims should be sent to the allocated unit. Units are allocated according to the postcode of the main R & D activity of the company, and a full list can be found on the HMRC website. This is a departure from the traditional practice where companies are normally allocated to tax offices on the basis of the address of the company's Registered Office. Note that this approach does **not apply to** companies whose tax affairs are dealt with by: Tax Bulletin 85
- the large business service;
- the specialist pharmaceutical units in Manchester, Cambridge and Croydon;
- the Small Company Enterprise Centres in Maidstone and Cardiff; or
- HMRC charities in Bootle.

Such companies should continue with their current existing arrangements for claiming R & D tax credit relief.

Pre-trading expenditure

Qualifying R & D expenditure incurred prior to the commencement of trade **by an SME** may be treated as a trading loss for the accounting period in which the expenditure was incurred, using the same rates of relief (¶806). 815 ss 1045, 1047 CTA 2009

The company must **elect** for this treatment to apply. An election in this respect must be made in writing, specifying the accounting period to which it relates, and must be made within 2 years of the end of that accounting period.

Loss relief is available in the normal ways (¶1260) although the loss cannot be carried back against profits of an earlier accounting period unless the company was also entitled to R & D tax relief in that accounting period. If any part of the loss remains unrelieved at the time the company starts the relevant trade, the loss is treated as a loss brought forward and is available to be set against future profits of the relevant trade (i.e. the trade derived from the R & D undertaken).

MEMO POINTS Where this treatment is adopted, the expense cannot also be claimed as **pre-trading expenditure** (¶160).

---

5. Vaccine research relief

Qualifying activities

Relief can be claimed for expenditure on research for the: 817 s 1086 CTA 2009
- prevention or treatment of tuberculosis or malaria;
- prevention of infection by HIV; or
- prevention of the onset of, or the treatment of, AIDS.

MEMO POINTS Vaccine research relief (VRR) operates in a similar way to R & D relief but is an **additional relief** available to both SMEs and large companies.

Qualifying expenditure

Expenditure will qualify for VRR if: 818

a. it is **incurred on qualifying R & D activities**, for one or more of the following:
- staffing costs (¶799);
- software or consumable items (¶801);
- payments to volunteers for participating in clinical trials (¶802); or
- qualifying subcontracted R & D (¶803);

b. it is **unsubsidised** (¶798) and at least £10,000 in a 12 month accounting period (proportionately reduced for periods of less than 12 months);

c. the R & D is **in respect of a trade** carried on by the company, or which the company will carry on. This includes R & D which is expected to result in an extension to an existing trade; and

s 1088 CTA 2009 **d.** if the **company is large**, it submits a declaration regarding the effect of the relief on their activities.

Relief

822 ss 1089 - 1091 CTA 2009 **Amount of relief** Where a company qualifies for VRR a trading deduction can be claimed as follows:

For **SMEs**:

- a further 20% of qualifying expenditure if the expenditure also qualifies for SME R & D relief; and
- 140% of any balance of qualifying expenditure that only qualifies for VRR.

EXAMPLE A Ltd, an SME, incurs £4m of qualifying expenditure on research into a treatment for malaria in its accounts for the year ended 31 March 2011.
In addition to its normal deduction of £4m, it can deduct a further £3m (75 % × £4m) as SME R & D relief, and a further £1.6m (40 % × £4m) as VRR relief, giving a total deduction of £8.6m.

For **large companies** the deduction is a further 40% of qualifying expenditure if the expenditure is deductible in computing the company's trading profits (this is in addition to any deduction that may be available as R & D relief).

EXAMPLE Assume the facts as above but A Ltd is a large company. In this situation A would be entitled to further deductions under the R & D scheme of £1.2m (30 % × £4m) and under the VRR scheme of £1.6m (40 % × £4m), giving a total deduction of £6.8m.

MEMO POINTS For expenditure incurred **before 1 April 2011** the SME rate where the expenditure also qualified for R & D relief was 40%. It is **proposed** that for expenditure incurred on or after 1 April 2012 that this rate will be reduced to nil.

823 **Utilisation of relief** For **SMEs** the relief can be utilised as for the R & D relief. However, when establishing a surrenderable loss (¶810), for the purposes of the vaccine credit, any losses surrendered for R & D tax credit relief are to be ignored.

For **large companies** the relief can be set against current year taxable profits as a trading deduction. Any loss unrelieved will be carried forward for offset against future profits in the usual manner

The relief must be **claimed** as detailed in ¶814

MEMO POINTS **Pre-trading expenditure** can be treated as a trading loss of the accounting period in which it was incurred as detailed in ¶815.

SECTION 3

Intangible assets

1. Corporation tax code

824 Intangible assets (including goodwill, intellectual property and payments for the use of intangible assets) created or acquired on or after 1 April 2002, are, for corporation tax purposes only, taxed under a self contained intangible asset code.

MEMO POINTS 1. Intangible assets **created or acquired before 1 April 2002** continue to be taxed under the general piecemeal provisions which are discussed in the relevant sections of *Tax Memo*.
2. For a business that was carried on at any time before 1 April 2002, any **goodwill** that relates to that business will be treated as being created before 1 April 2002 (and therefore subject to the capital gains regime).

The regime is, in practice, fairly straightforward as certain debits (expenses), credits (income) and gains recognised in the company accounts for qualifying intangible assets are also allowed for tax purposes. The main distinction being whether they arise on trading or non-trading items, as follows: **825**

a. trading items: credits and debits arising on assets held for the purposes of the trade are taxed as trading income (or as property income if the trade is a property business); and

b. non-trading items:

– credits arising on assets held for a non-trade purpose are aggregated and taxed as miscellaneous income and,

– debits arising on assets held for a non-trade purpose may be set against the company's total profits or surrendered by way of group relief (¶1540). Unused non-trading debits are automatically carried forward and can be set against the company's profits of later accounting periods. They may not be surrendered by way of group relief in later accounting periods. The company must make a claim to set the non-trading debits against its total profits within 2 years of the end of the accounting period in which the profits arose.

MEMO POINTS In general, the taxable credits and debits will be the same as the accounting income/expense, but certain **items specifically need to be adjusted** for:

a. the following non-deductible trading expenses:

– business entertaining

– crime related expenditure;

– expensive leased cars;

– delayed payments of earnings/pension contributions;

– bad debts;

– transactions of royalties between related parties;

b. assets with nil accounting value;

c. finance lease assets which are specifically treated as intangible assets in the hands of the lessor; and

d. any transfer pricing adjustments.

2. Qualifying intangible fixed assets

The **definition** of qualifying intangible fixed assets is contained in statute and the accounting standards (FRS 10). **826** ss 712 - 714 CTA 2009

The **statutory** definition is:

a. intellectual property:

– any patent, trademark, registered design, copyright, design right, or plant breeders right registered in the UK or overseas;

– any information having industrial, commercial or economic value (e.g. know-how); or

– any licence or right in respect of any of the items above;

b. goodwill; and

c. options to acquire/dispose of intangible fixed assets.

Assets not within the statutory definition may still be within the regime if they fall within the **FRS 10** definition of goodwill and intangible assets.

Finance leases of intangible assets (including hire purchase and conditional sale contracts) are specifically treated as intangible assets in the hands of the lessor. (Without this provision such finance leases would be treated as financial assets in the hands of the lessor, and therefore outside the scope of the intangible asset regime (¶830)). SI 2002/1967

3. Excluded assets

Types of assets

828 s 800 CTA 2009 There are **three** classes of intangible assets which are specifically excluded from this regime, as follows:
- those that are excluded entirely;
- those that are partially excluded; and
- those that are excluded except to the extent that it represents expenditure/income on royalties.

Assets entirely excluded

830 ss 803 - 809 CTA 2009 These include expenditure/income on:
- rights over tangible assets;
- oil licences;
- financial assets (defined in accordance with FRS 13, but also specifically including loan relationships, derivative contracts and insurance contracts);
- shares and other rights in companies, trusts and partnerships; and
- assets held either for non-commercial purposes or for purposes outside the charge to corporation tax.

MEMO POINTS If the assets of a **trust or partnership** (not companies) are themselves intangible assets, then the right/interest in the trust or partnership will be treated as an intangible fixed asset.

Assets partially excluded

831 ss 814 - 816 CTA 2009 These include the following intangible fixed assets:
- assets that represent expenditure on R & D (¶686), but not proceeds derived from R & D; and
- expenditure and receipts from computer software.

Assets excluded except as regards royalties

832 ss 810 - 813 CTA 2009 Expenditure/income on the following is excluded unless it represents expenditure/income on royalties:
- assets that represent expenditure on computer software that, under accepted accounting practice, would properly fall to be treated as computer hardware;
- assets that represent expenditure on the production of films and sound recording;
- assets held for the purpose of any life assurance business (although computer software held by a life assurance business is within the regime); and
- assets held for the purposes of any mutual trade (this does not apply to mutual life assurance business).

MEMO POINTS The **result of this exclusion** is that all royalty income and expenditure falls within the intangible asset regime (whether or not they relate to pre 1 April 2002 assets).

4. Income and expenditure

Debits

838 s 726 CTA 2009 **Eligible expenditure** The following debits are brought into account:
- revenue items charged to the company's profit and loss account, as adjusted (¶839);
- amortisation/ depreciation charged to the profit and loss account (¶840); and
- a debit reversing in whole or in part, a previous accounting credit (¶841).

839 s 727 CTA 2009 **Revenue items** Expenditure charged to the profit and loss account (as adjusted (¶825)) will be brought into account. In particular:

a. immediate R & D relief is also available to companies and other entities which add **research and development expenditure** to the cost of an intangible asset in accordance with accepted accounting practice. (Previously, relief for such expenditure could only be given as the cost of the asset was amortised through the profit and loss account);
b. royalties are brought within the regime at the time when they are recognised for accounting purposes. This therefore means that royalty receipts in respect of existing assets (i.e. pre 1 April 2002 assets) will also be within the regime.

MEMO POINTS See ¶861 for **royalty payments between related parties**.

Amortisation/depreciation In **general**, amortisation/depreciation charged to the profit and loss account is an allowable debit. The allowable amortisation/depreciation charged for tax purposes will usually be the same as the amount charged to the profit and loss account but in some cases the profit and loss charge will need to be adjusted using the following formula: **840** ss 729 - 731 CTA 2009

$$\text{Accounting loss} \times \frac{\text{Tax cost}}{\text{Accounting cost}}$$

where:
- accounting loss is the amount charged to the profit and loss account as amortisation;
- tax cost is expenditure on the asset that is recognised for tax purpose (or tax written down value for subsequent periods); and
- accounting cost is expenditure on the asset capitalised for accounting purposes.

The tax cost and accounting cost may be different because, for example, of reinvestment or rollover relief.

EXAMPLE An asset is acquired at a capitalised cost of £1,000.
It is amortised over 10 years on a straight line basis.
For tax purposes, the acquisition cost is reduced to £800 following a reinvestment relief claim.
The charge in the accounts in Year 1 would be changed for tax purposes to become:

$$100 \times \frac{800}{1{,}000} = 80$$

In Year 2 the company incurs enhancement expenditure of £300, so the revised book value of the asset is £900 + £300 = £1,200
The tax written down value of the asset is £720 + £300 = £1,020.
The debit for Year 2 will become:

$$120 \times \frac{1{,}020}{1{,}200} = 102$$

Alternatively, a company may elect for an annual fixed rate deduction equal to a 4% straight line writing down allowance of the tax cost of the asset (or the remaining tax written down value of the asset if less). The deduction is proportionately reduced for accounting periods of less than 12 months. The tax cost of the asset is proportionately reduced after a part disposal.

This election once made is irrevocable, and must be made within 2 years of the end of the accounting period in which the asset was acquired or created.

EXAMPLE A company buys an asset for £100,000 and elects for fixed rate treatment. In Year 5, the company makes a part disposal of the asset for £60,000, setting £50,000 of the acquisition cost against this disposal. The tax written down value is £84,000.
The accounting profit is therefore £10,000, the revised book value £50,000. The amount of the remaining tax written down value attributable to the disposal is £42,000 (84,000 × 50,000/100,000).
Therefore the taxable profit on sale is £18,000.
The fixed rate deductions now relate to the remaining book value expenditure of £50,000 and are therefore reduced to £2,000 p.a.. These deductions will be set against the tax written down value until the amount has expired.

MEMO POINTS This fixed 4% deduction is not available to **finance leased assets** that are treated as intangible assets (¶326).

841 s 732 CTA 2009 **Reversal of a previous credit** A debit reversing in whole or in part a previous accounting credit is an allowable debit.

If the previous accounting credit was different from the previous taxable credit, the allowable debit will be adjusted using the following formula:

$$\text{Accounting loss} \times \frac{\text{Previous credit}}{\text{Accounting gain}}$$

where:
- accounting loss is the debit recognised for accounting purposes;
- accounting gain is the credit that is in whole or part reversed; and
- previous credit is the credit previously brought into account for tax purposes.

EXAMPLE A company realises an accounting gain of £100, of which £80 was taxable. Half that gain is reversed so the allowable debit is:

$$50 \times \frac{80}{100} = 40$$

Credits

842 ss 720-725 CTA 2009 The credits that can be brought into account for tax purposes are:

a. receipts charged to the profit and loss account when they accrue (subject to any adjustments for tax purposes (¶825));
b. royalty receipts for intangible assets held by companies prior to 1 April 2002;
c. revaluations. If this results in an increase of the accounting value of an asset, a credit is brought into charge (limited to the amount of previous debits (¶841) given). Revaluations of assets where the company has elected for the annual fixed rate deduction are not taxable. When the tax value of an asset and the accounting value differed before revaluation (due, for example, to a reinvestment relief claim), the increase for accounting purposes is adjusted by the ratio of the tax written down value before the revaluation to the accounting value at the same time;
d. negative goodwill recognised in a company's profit and loss account;
e. catch up adjustments as a result of a company changing its accounting policies from one valid basis to another. The catch up adjustment is adjusted by the ratio of the tax written value at the end of the earlier period to the accounting value at the end of the same period; and
f. reversal of a previous accounting debit. The provisions in ¶841 in relation to the reversal of a previous accounting credit apply here in reverse.

5. Disposals of qualifying intangible assets

What is a disposal?

843 s 734 CTA 2009 A disposal (referred to in the legislation as a realisation) is **defined as** any transaction whereby:
- the asset ceases to be recognised on the company balance sheet; or
- there is a reduction in the accounting value of the asset (following, for example, a part sale of the asset concerned).

On the disposal of a qualifying intangible asset, a taxable credit/allowable debit will arise based on the difference between the proceeds received for the asset and its tax written down value.

MEMO POINTS **Abortive expenditure** in connection with a sale is an allowable debit (subject to adjustments for tax purposes).

Proceeds

The proceeds received for the asset are the amounts recognised for accounting purposes, less any incidental costs of disposal subject to any tax adjustments (for example, reinvestment relief). 844 s 739 CTA 2009

Tax written down value

This is calculated using the following formula: 845 s 742 CTA 2009

Tax cost – Debits + Credits

where:
- tax cost is the cost of the asset recognised for tax purposes;
- debits are the total debits brought into account by way of amortisation (¶840); and
- credits are the total credits brought into account by way of revaluation or as a result of a change in accounting policy (¶842).

For assets written down at a **fixed rate deduction**, the calculation is: 846 s 743 CTA 2009

Tax costs – Debits

where:
- tax cost is as above; and
- debits are the total debits previously brought into account under the fixed rate basis (¶840).

MEMO POINTS The tax written down value may be the same as the tax cost if the asset had not been written down for tax purposes, for example, if it was bought and sold in the same accounting period.

For **part disposals**, the calculations of tax cost and tax written down value are proportionately reduced. 847 s 744 CTA 2009

Rollover relief

Taxable credits on the disposal of a qualifying intangible asset can be deferred by claiming rollover relief. A claim must specify the old assets and identify the replacement assets and the amount of relief claimed. A company can make a provisional claim. 848 ss 754 - 763 CTA 2009

The following **conditions** need to be satisfied to make a claim:

a. conditions relating to the **old asset**:
- the asset must have been a qualifying intangible asset of the company throughout the company's period of ownership; and
- the sale proceeds of the old asset must exceed its tax cost; and

b. conditions relating to the **replacement asset**:
- expenditure must be incurred in the period from 1 year before to 3 years after the disposal of the old asset;
- expenditure must be capitalised in the company accounts. (An asset that is unexpectedly sold after acquisition and is not therefore capitalised in the accounts may nonetheless still qualify); and
- the replacement asset must be a qualifying intangible asset in the company's hands immediately after acquisition.

MEMO POINTS If the **old asset was not a qualifying intangible asset throughout the company's period of ownership**, it may still qualify for rollover providing it was a qualifying intangible asset when it was sold, and for a substantial part of the company's period of ownership it was a qualifying intangible asset (in which case a just and reasonable apportionment is made).

A rollover claim has the effect of reducing the disposal proceeds of the old asset and the acquisition cost of the new asset by the amount of the claim. 849

The **relief is the amount** by which the lower of the:
- disposal proceeds of the old asset; and
- acquisition cost of the replacement asset,

exceeds the cost of the old asset.

EXAMPLE A Ltd buys an asset for £75 and sells it for £125, when its tax and book value is £40. The sale triggers a taxable credit of £85 (£125 – £40).
If a replacement asset was purchased for £150, the amount eligible for relief would be £50 (£125 – £75). Proceeds are therefore reduced by £50, and the taxable credit would become £35 (£75 – £40).
If a replacement asset was purchased for £100, the amount eligible for relief would be £25 (£100 – £75). Proceeds are therefore reduced by £25, and the taxable credit would become £60 (£100 – £40).

MEMO POINTS In the case of a **part disposal**, the proceeds are compared to the appropriate portion of the tax cost of the old asset.

Transfers between groups of companies

850
s 775 CTA 2009

Tax neutral transfers Transfers between members of a 75% chargeable gains group (¶1524) are on a tax neutral basis, so that the transferee inherits the transferor's tax history of the asset.

The asset being transferred must be an intangible asset of the transferor company immediately before the transfer and the transferee company immediately after the transfer.

MEMO POINTS This provision **takes priority over** company reconstructions (¶857) or related party transfers (¶860).

852
s 777 CTA 2009

Rollover relief **Gains** realised by one member of a 75% group can be rolled into acquisitions by other group members provided that:
- the disposing company (Co A) is a member of the group at the time of disposal;
- the replacement expenditure is by a company that is a member of the same group as Co A (and is not a dual resident investing company);
- the replacement asset is a qualifying intangible asset immediately after acquisition; and
- both companies make the claim.

MEMO POINTS 1. The two companies do not have to be **members of the group at the same time**.
ss 778 - 779 CTA 2009
2. Gains can also be **rolled into an acquisition of a controlling interest in a company**, provided that the company which is acquired (or an existing subsidiary of that company) has qualifying intangible assets. A controlling interest is a 75% capital gains interest (¶1524).
In this situation the acquisition cost of the replacement asset will be the lower of:
- the tax written down value of the underlying intangible asset; or
- the purchase price of the shares.
The claim must be made jointly by both companies and will reduce the tax cost of the underlying asset by the amount of the relief claimed.

854
s 780 CTA 2009

Degrouping charges The provisions relating to degrouping charges (¶1606) apply equally to intangible assets.

EXAMPLE Group company A Ltd acquires an intangible asset for £10,000, which has an estimated life of 10 years. The annual accounts show a deduction of £1,000 p.a. which is allowable for tax purposes.
At the beginning of the fourth accounting period company A Ltd transfers the asset to group company B Ltd. The transfer is at a book value of £7,000 when the market value is £9,000.
B Ltd continues to write down the asset at £1,000 p.a. for the fourth and fifth years following the transfer by A Ltd.
B Ltd leaves the group at the end of the fifth year.
B Ltd is deemed to have disposed of the asset for £9,000 which gives a taxable credit of £2,000 (£9,000 – £7,000).
B Ltd's amortisation charge for the fourth period is recomputed, based on an acquisition value of £9,000. The charge should have been £1,286 ($1{,}000 \times \frac{9{,}000}{7{,}000}$)

Therefore in the fifth period, the tax treatment is:
- credit £1,714 (£2,000 – £286); and
- debit of £1,286 ($1{,}000 \times \frac{(6{,}000 + 1{,}174)}{6{,}000}$)

The transferee company can jointly elect with another group company (Company Y) for all or part of the degrouping charge to be **reallocated** to Company Y and treated as if it accrued to Company Y. 855 s 792 CTA 2009

To be eligible to make the election:
– Y must have been a member of the same group as the transferee company immediately before the transferee company left the group. (Where the degrouping charge has arisen as a result of the transferee leaving an enlarged group, Y must be a member of the enlarged group immediately before the transferee company leaves that group); and
– Company Y must be within the charge to corporation tax.

The election must be made in writing no later than 2 years after the end of the accounting period in which the transferee leaves the group.

Rollover relief can be claimed on a degrouping charge but: 856
– the old asset must be a qualifying intangible asset in the hands of the transferor company (not the company subject to the degrouping charge); and
– the time limits for reinvestment (¶848) apply to the date of the event triggering the degrouping charge (not the date of the original transfer).

On a degrouping charge, the disposal proceeds are taken to be the market value used to compute the degrouping charge.

MEMO POINTS 1. Rollover relief can also be claimed on a **reallocated degrouping charge**. The company to which the charge is reallocated will qualify for rollover if the original transferee company (i.e. the company leaving the group) would have qualified under the provisions above. s 794 CTA 2009
2. **Payments** between group members for rollover relief or the reallocation of a degrouping charge are ignored for tax purposes provided the payment does not exceed the amount of relief.

Transfer of a business or trade

Tax neutral transfers The transfer of a qualifying intangible asset can be done on a tax neutral basis in the following situations: 857 ss 818, 819, 821 CTA 2009
– on a company **reconstruction** or amalgamation (¶1166);
– on a **transfer of a UK trade** (i.e. a trade carried on by a UK permanent establishment owned by an EU company) to another EU resident company (¶1171); or
– on a **formation of a Societas Europaea** by the merger of a UK trade (¶2195).

MEMO POINTS In all of the above situations the following **conditions must be met**:
– the asset must be a qualifying intangible asset in the hands of the transferor company immediately prior to the transaction, and in the hands of the transferee company immediately after the transaction; and
– the transaction must be for bona fide commercial reasons, and not form part of a scheme or arrangement the main purpose of which is to avoid tax. (Advance clearance can be requested for these provisions to apply).

Taxable transfers The transfer of an intangible asset is taxable when a UK resident company **transfers an EU trade** (i.e. a trade of the UK company carried on through an EU permanent establishment) to another non-EU resident company. However a claim can be made to **defer** the tax arising. 858 ss 827 - 830 CTA 2009

MEMO POINTS The tax charge so deferred is **brought into charge** as detailed at ¶1183.

Related party transactions

Transfers between Transfers of qualifying intangible assets between related parties are **deemed to be done** at market value **unless**: 860 ss 845 - 849 CTA 2009
a. the transfer pricing regulations apply (¶1721), in which case the asset is deemed to be transferred at the price determined under the transfer pricing regulations;
b. the transfer is a tax neutral transfer (e.g. intra-group transfer);
c. the asset is transferred to a company by a related party on or after 16 March 2005, and gift holdover relief (¶6095) is claimed on the transfer. In this case the transfer will be deemed to take place at market value less the amount of the heldover gain; or

d. the asset is transferred on or after 16 March 2005, either:
– from a company at less than market value; or
– to a company at more than market value,
by a related party (which must not be a company or if it is, the asset so transferred must not be a qualifying intangible asset in its hands), and the amount for which it is transferred is taken into account as a distribution or as earnings.
In this situation, the value at which the asset is transferred will apply.

EXAMPLE A controlling shareholder transfers an intangible asset to a company for £10,000 (when it is worth £1,000). The transfer will be deemed to take place at £1,000, and the consideration received in excess of its market value will be taxed as a distribution on the transferee.

ss 835 - 843 CTA 2009

MEMO POINTS **Parties are related** in the following situations:
a. where both parties are companies and:
– one person controls them both;
– one controls or has a major interest in the other; or
– they are members of the same 75% group;
b. where the company is a close company, it is related to a participator (or associate of a participator) of the close company; or
c. where a person is a participator (or associate of a participator) of a close company it is related to any company that the close company has a major interest in. (This provision applies to assets transferred or debits/credits bought into account on or after 16 March 2005).
Control is the power of a person to secure that the affairs of the company are carried out in accordance with his wishes. As of 12 March 2008 this is not affected by one of the parties entering administration or similar.
A **major interest** is when a person and one other together have control of the company, and each person controls at least 40% of the relevant rights and powers.
The rights and powers of an individual include the current and future rights of him and any person he is connected with (¶5570), plus the rights and powers of a person connected with the connected person.

861 Where assets transferred have a **nil accounting value** (e.g. internally generated goodwill), but are transferred for tax purposes at market value, the transferee can claim deductions based on the market value.

Rollover relief cannot be claimed on a part disposal of an intangible fixed asset, where a related party acquires any interest in that asset, or in an asset whose value is derived from that asset.

Royalties payable to a related party are only deducted when they are paid if:
– the related party is not within the charge to corporation tax for the royalty receivable; and
– the royalty is not actually paid in full within 12 months of the end of accounting period of the paying company.

862 **Excluded income and expenditure** Debits and credits brought into account on or after 5 December 2005 are not within the scope of the intangible asset regime if an asset is transferred between related parties and either:

ss 893 - 895 CTA 2009

a. the asset:
– was created on or after 1 April 2002; and
– derives its value from an asset that was an existing asset (i.e. a pre 1 April 2002 asset), in the hands of the related party; or

EXAMPLE A Ltd (a group company) owns a trademark which it had acquired before 1 April 2002. It grants a licence out of this trademark to another group company. This is an "asset derived from an existing asset" so the licence will not be within the intangible asset regime.

b. the transaction involves the:
– disposal of an existing intangible asset; and
– acquisition of an intangible fixed asset (directly or indirectly as a consequence of the disposal).
In this situation, the newly acquired asset remains to be treated as an existing asset for the acquiring company.

6. Sundry provisions

Grants

Grants intended to meet the cost of an intangible asset are netted off against relevant expenditure or recognised as a separate source of income. Regional development grants and grants made under Northern Ireland legislation are, however, ignored. **863** s 852 CTA 2009

Assets ceasing to be qualifying intangible assets

Assets will cease to be qualifying intangible assets when: **864** s 859 CTA 2009
- a company ceases to be UK resident;
- an asset owned by a non-UK resident company ceases to be used for the purposes of a UK trade through a permanent establishment; or
- an asset begins to be used for the purposes of a mutual trade.

The company will be deemed to have made a disposal and subsequent reacquisition at market value and any gain or loss will taxed under this regime.

MEMO POINTS Where a **company ceases to be UK resident, the resultant charge can be postponed** if the: ss 860 - 862 CTA 2009
- asset is held for the purpose of a non-UK trade carried on through a permanent establishment;
- company remains a 75% subsidiary of its UK resident parent company; and
- deemed disposal proceeds of the asset exceed the original cost of the asset recognised for tax purposes.

The deferred gain is brought back into charge (in the UK parent company) if:
- within 6 years of its becoming non-resident, the non-UK company disposes of the intangible fixed asset;
- the non-resident company ceases to be a 75% subsidiary of the UK parent company; or
- the parent company leaves the UK.

Assets becoming qualifying intangible assets

An asset will become a qualifying intangible asset when: **866** s 863 CTA 2009
- a company, holding an intangible asset, becomes resident in the UK;
- a non-resident company begins to use an intangible asset for the purposes of a trade in the UK through a permanent establishment; or
- an asset ceases to be held for the purposes of a mutual trade.

The company will be treated as acquiring the asset at its book value at the time of change, although if the asset was originally created/acquired before 1 April 2002, it will not be within the scope of the intangible asset regime.

SECTION 4

Loan relationships

1. Scope

When establishing whether transactions are within the loan relationship provisions the following questions need to be considered: **870**
- does the transaction fall within the **definition** of a loan relationship;
- have the figures in the accounts been computed in accordance with an **acceptable accounting method**; and
- what amounts can be **brought into account for tax purposes**. This issue is essentially straightforward in that it is usually the accounts figures, but it can become more complicated when exchange movements are matched. For interest paid in periods **commencing on or after 1 January 2010** the situation also becomes potentially more complex for groups of companies.

In addition **special rules** apply:
– on the termination of loan relationship contracts (¶902);
– for impairment losses (previously known as bad debts (¶904)); and
– for transactions between connected parties (¶908).

The loan relationship regime **can be complex** and this section covers the basic principles. For a more detailed analysis of the rules see *Corporation Tax Memo*.

2. Definition

876
ss 302, 477, 486A, 521A CTA 2009

Put **simply**, a loan relationship can be defined as any form of financing, including alternative finance arrangements (¶2832) that a company undertakes to fund business operations (for example a bank loan).

More specifically, the **following transactions** fall within the loan relationships regime:

Transaction	Detail	Examples
Where the company stands as a debtor or creditor on a money debt [1] arising from a money lending transaction	This is extended to include the issue of an instrument representing security for a money debt	Overdrafts, bank loans, debentures, mortgages, gilts, loan stock
Interest on money debts that do not arise from the lending of money [2] Profits from the disposal of interest and from all discounts [3]		Interest arising due to late payment for goods or services, interest payable to HMRC
Certain income from shares [4,5,6]	For the times in an accounting period when the company holds shares in the issuing company and: – the share is subject to outstanding third party obligations [7,8]; and – it receives an interest like return on its capital investment (i.e. where the return equates in substance to a reasonable return on an investment of money at a commercial rate of interest)	

Note:
1. A money debt is defined as any debt falling to be satisfied by the:
– payment of money (even if other forms of repayment may be acceptable, it will be a money debt if there is any possibility that the debt will be settled by the payment of money);
– transfer of a right to settlement under a debt which is itself a money debt; or
– issue or transfer of any shares in any company.
2. Such transactions are not loan relationships, but any interest or exchange movements arising on them will be included within the loan relationship regime.
3. To be within the loan relationship regime, the following conditions must be met:
– the company must be the creditor on the debt giving rise to the discount;
– the discount must not be within the alternative finance arrangement provisions (¶2832); and
– the discount must not be a trading receipt.
4. In general shares are not within the loan relationship provisions (they fall within the capital gains regime), but specific interest and distributions will fall within the regime.
5. Shares transferred intra-group cannot be transferred under the no-gain/no-loss provisions (¶1600) if the share so transferred was a loan relationship share in the hands of the transferor or the transferee (after the intra-group disposal).
6. Shares falling within these loan relationship provisions are, for capital gains tax purposes, deemed to be disposed of and reacquired for fair value. Similarly, when shares fall out of these provisions (because, for example, the company's interest in the shares changes), there is a deemed disposal for loan relationship provisions and a deemed reacquisition for capital gains tax purposes.
7. Outstanding third party obligations are where shares are subject (or could under any relevant arrangements become subject) to an obligation to:
– meet unpaid calls on the share; or
– contribute capital to the issuing company that could affect the value of the shares.
8. Other types of schemes that are designed to generate interest like return on shares are also within the loan relationship regime irrespective of whether the share is subject to outstanding third party obligations.

For accounting periods commencing on or after 1 January 2010, new restrictions were introduced to ensure that the deduction for interest costs in a UK company does not exceed the total interest cost of the group to which it belongs. These are often referred to as the **worldwide debt cap rules**. These restrictions **will only apply** where the total of the UK companies' net debt exceeds 75% of the group's worldwide gross debt. In looking at the net debt: 877 Part 7 TIOPA 2010
- any long-term relationships similar to a loan, including an interest-like return, will be counted in the calculation;
- a company with net assets will not be counted, and as such an intra-group loan will be a liability for one company without a corresponding credit for the other; and
- a single company with net debt below £3 million is deemed to have no net debt.

Where the rules apply the interest deduction shown in the accounts is reduced by any amount by which the tested expense amount exceeds the available amount. The **tested expense amount** is the total of any loan relationship debit (excluding impairment losses and exchange losses), less any loan relationship credits (excluding the reversal of an impairment loss or exchange gain). If the result of this calculation is less than £500,000 then the result is deemed to be zero and no addback will be required.

The **available amount** is the total of the group's:
- interest payable on amounts borrowed;
- amortisation of discounts or premiums on amounts borrowed;
- amortisation of ancillary costs relating to borrowings;
- finance cost in finance lease payments; and
- any finance costs relating to debt factoring.

MEMO POINTS **a.** The net debt is calculated as the average of the opening and closing net debt of each company, being the debt liabilities (loans and finance leases) less the liquid assets shown on the company's balance sheet.
b. The gross debt is the average of the opening and closing debt shown in the group's consolidated balance sheet.

Relief for debits can also be **denied**, on a just and reasonable basis: 878
a. where the **loan is for an unallowable purpose**. Any loan relationship debits (and exchange rate credits) are simply excluded from the loan relationship computation;
b. where a **transfer pricing adjustment** would disregard all or part of the interest paid on a loan relationship between group companies. A similar proportion of any exchange gains and losses arising on the loan are excluded from the loan relationship computation. Similarly, if a transfer pricing adjustment imputes an interest charge on a loan, exchange gains and losses arising on the loan will be taxed/relieved in full; or
c. when interest under a loan relationship falls to be **treated as a distribution** (in whole or in part). The amount of the interest and the corresponding exchange gains and losses, are excluded from the loan relationship computation.

MEMO POINTS 1. A **purpose is unallowable** if:
- it is not for the commercial or other purposes of the business;
- it is for activities of the company that are outside the scope of corporation tax; or
- the main purpose for entering into the loan relationship was to obtain a tax advantage.

HMRC have issued only limited guidance on these matters, presumably in an attempt to prevent companies and their advisers devising schemes to manipulate the rule. However, where a loan relationship is for a bona fide commercial purpose, relief should be available.
2. HMRC will treat interest **payments as distributions** if:
- the borrowing company is a 75% subsidiary of the lender, or both companies are 75% subsidiaries of a third company; and
- all or part of the interest would not have been paid if the companies did not have a special relationship.

3. Acceptable accounting methods

The gains and losses that are included in a corporation tax computation essentially mirror those that are computed for accounts purposes, providing an acceptable method has been adopted. (This covers accounts prepared under UK GAAP and IAS). 880 s 1127 CTA 2010

MEMO POINTS 1. Since 1 January 2005, listed companies are required to use **international accounting standards** (IAS), for the preparation of consolidated accounts (other companies can choose to adopt IAS). To ensure that companies are not unfairly discriminated against when they adopt IAS, special provisions apply to ensure that companies moving to IAS will be treated in a similar manner as those preparing accounts under UK GAAP for the purposes of the loan relationship provisions. The differences are detailed where appropriate.
In the rest of this section, references to companies adopting IAS will also include those companies that prepare their accounts under UK GAAP, but adopt FRS 26 (This is because FRS 26 requires adoption of FRS 23, which in turn incorporates IAS 21).
2. As accounting standards change the application of these rules are affected. Legislation is to be introduced to allow changes to be made by regulation to respond more quickly than the current position.

882 Companies will account for loan relationships using one of the following methods:
a. fair value accounting. This is where assets or liabilities are shown in the company's balance sheet at their fair value (i.e. the amount that an independent third party would pay for a debt asset, or the amount that the company would have to pay to a third party to release the debt liability in the profit and loss account); or
b. amortised cost base accounting. This is where the loan asset or liability is shown in the balance sheet at cost as adjusted for:
- amortisation of any discount or premium, fees for borrowing/lending etc; and
- any impairment (bad debt), releases or repayments.

s 349 CTA 2009 MEMO POINTS If companies are **connected** (¶908), both parties must account for the loan relationship using the amortised cost basis.

884 Where one of these methods **has been adopted**, the gain or loss shown in the accounts will be accepted for tax purposes.

s 309 CTA 2009 Where one of these methods **has not been adopted**, the taxable profit or loss must be recomputed using an acceptable basis. Any brought forward amounts are also similarly recomputed if they were not prepared on an acceptable basis.

SI 2004/3271 reg 3A MEMO POINTS Where a company **changes from GAAP to IAS** any difference in the carrying value of an asset or liability between the period of change and the previous period can be spread over 10 years, commencing in 2006.

4. Taxable amounts

General rules

886 s 307 CTA 2009 **Debits and credits** The treatment of credits and debits (i.e. income and expenditure) arising on loan relationship contracts depends upon whether the items arise in respect of trading or non-trading transactions.

Trading items are included in the computation of profits either as income or expenses. Where the accounts have been prepared on an acceptable basis, no adjustment is required to the accounts figures. (If an unacceptable method has been used, the profits/losses must be recomputed).

Non-trading items are pooled. If the net figure is a credit (income), it is assessable as a non-trading loan relationship credit. If the net position is a debit this is known as a non-trading loan relationship deficit. The rules for obtaining relief are set out in ¶1295.

s 482(1) CTA 2009 MEMO POINTS **Interest paid to, or by, HMRC** is specifically treated as a non-trading item.

888 **Eligible income and expenditure** The following items are **brought into account** under the loan relationship provisions:
- all profits, gains and losses (including those of a capital nature) arising to the company from the loan relationship;
- all interest under the loan relationships (including any interest imputed under the transfer pricing regulations (¶1721));

– exchange movements on loan relationship assets (unless they are recognised in the company's statement of recognised gains and losses or statement of changes in equity or matched (¶892)); and
– all charges and expenses incurred under, or for the purposes of, the company's loan relationships or related transactions.

MEMO POINTS 1. The above items are **brought into account when they are recognised** in a company's:
– profit and loss account;
– statement of recognised gains and losses, or statement of changes in equity; or
– any other statement of items brought into account when computing the company's profit and loss for the period. (This will include a company's income statement).
2. **Anti-avoidance** provisions apply to bring into the loan relationship regime, the full amount of any profits and losses arising on a transaction if the accounting treatment has not fully recorded the profit or loss. (These provisions prevent a company arguing, for example, that an interest receipt that is, for GAAP purposes, offset against a dividend payment, leaves no net liability to tax). ss 311, 312 CTA 2009

Only **charges and expenses** incurred in respect of the following are allowed: 890 s 307 CTA 2009
– bringing a loan relationship into existence;
– entering into, or giving effect to, a related transaction;
– making payments under a loan relationship or related transaction; or
– taking steps to ensure receipt of payments due under a loan relationship or related transaction.

MEMO POINTS A **related transaction** is the acquisition or disposal of rights or liabilities under the loan relationship.

HMRC have given guidance on the types of expenses it considers eligible for relief as follows: 891
– **abortive expenditure** is allowed if it would have been allowed if the loan had actually come into existence; and, s 329 CTA 2009; CFM 30170
– **guarantee fees** will only be allowed if the loan would not have been advanced without the provision of the guarantee. If this is not the case, relief may be available under the normal trading expense rules, if the expenditure is incurred wholly and exclusively for the purposes of the trade (¶120). CTM 53550

Pre-trading expenditure incurred during the 7 years prior to commencement of trade may be treated as a trading debit for the first trading period if it would have been a trading debit if incurred post-commencement. The company must elect for this treatment to apply within 2 years from the end of the first accounting period. s 330 CTA 2009

Matching

General rules **Foreign exchange movements** arising on loan relationships can be taken to reserves and matched. Companies can elect, for matching purposes, for the shares against which a debt/currency contract is matched to be valued at the higher of net asset value or book value. A restriction was introduced from 22 April 2009 so that only genuine movements, as opposed to those entered into for tax avoidance purposes, can be matched. 892 SI 2004/3256 reg 4

The **effect of the matching regulations** is that the taxation of any exchange movements on a loan relationship on a relevant asset will be deferred, and brought into account at a later date (¶900).

MEMO POINTS Strictly speaking, **companies using IAS** are not permitted to take exchange movements to reserves for matching so special rules ensure companies using IAS will be treated in a similar manner as those preparing accounts under UK GAAP.

Taxing matched amounts Exchange movements which have been matched (and therefore not taxed) are brought into account when the company disposes of the matched asset. The treatment of the amount brought into account depends upon which asset it was matched against. This means in some cases, such as where it is matched against a shareholding that qualifies for the substantial sharheoldings exemption on disposal, the matched amount will fall outside the corporation tax net. 900

5. Special situations

Termination of a loan relationship

902 s 331 CTA 2009 Where a company ceases to be party to a loan relationship but circumstances are such that the full amount of the **consideration for the disposal cannot be ascertained** in the accounting period of disposal, any gains or losses arising in a subsequent accounting period in relation to the loan relationship so disposed of are recognised in the later accounting period as if the company were still a party to the loan relationship.

ss 333 - 334 CTA 2009 Where a company or UK resident permanent establishment **ceases to be UK resident** it will be treated as having disposed of and reacquired any loan relationship assets at fair value and any gains will be taxed accordingly.

Impairment losses (bad debts)

904 Where a company prepares its accounts in accordance with an acceptable accounting method (¶880), it is required to assess its financial assets at each balance sheet date and to see whether there is **objective evidence** that an asset or group of assets can be said to be impaired. Any profit or loss so arising as a result is recognised in the company's profit and loss account.

Impairment losses, under these provisions, are not restricted to cases where the creditor feels default is probable (or has in fact occurred), but can **extend to** situations where there is data indicating that the estimated future cash flows from a group of assets will decrease.

EXAMPLE A Ltd has statistical evidence that a rise in mortgage rates correlates with an increase in credit default by its customers. In Year 1, mortgage rates increase and A Ltd recognises an impairment loss. This loss will be allowable for tax purposes, even though it cannot be attributed to individual customers.

906 ss 358, 359 CTA 2009 On the **release of a debt**, the amount released is normally included as a credit in the tax computation, unless:
- the parties are connected (¶914);
- the amount is released as part of a relevant arrangement or compromise under the Insolvency Act or Companies Act; or
- the company releasing the debt is in insolvent liquidation/administrative receivership etc.

907 ss 364 - 371 CTA 2009 There is a restriction on relief for impairment losses when there is a loan to a **consortium company** which is also claiming consortium relief. This restriction will apply where a consortium member recognises a debit for a bad debt in connection with a loan between it (or another member of its group) and the consortium company.

The provisions apply such that if, in an accounting period, there is a debit in respect of a bad debt, it will be reduced (but not below nil) by the amount of consortium relief surrendered by the consortium company to the consortium member (or a member of its group). Any subsequent recovery of the debt will be set off against the disallowed bad debt.

EXAMPLE
1. In Year 1, A Ltd (a consortium member) claims £500 as a bad debt from B Ltd (a consortium company). In the same year, consortium relief of £550 is surrendered from B Ltd to A Ltd.
In Year 2, £400 of the bad debt is recovered from B Ltd.

The tax treatment will be as follows:
Year 1: the bad debt will be reduced to nil and consortium relief given on the full amount of the £550.
Year 2: the £400 will be set against the previously disallowed debt and consequently will not be a taxable receipt. The balance of the disallowed bad debt can be carried forward for offset against future recoveries.

2. Using the above situation, but assume that this time the debit recognised by A Ltd in respect of a bad debt from B Ltd for Year 1 is £200, and consortium relief of £150 is surrendered from B Ltd to A Ltd.

In Year 2, A Ltd claims that a further £200 of the debt is bad and consortium relief of £250 is surrendered from B Ltd to A Ltd.

The tax treatment will be as follows:
Year 1: the bad debt is reduced to £50 and consortium relief given on the £150.
Year 2: the bad debt is reduced to nil by set off against the consortium relief. The consortium relief is reduced to £200 by set off against the bad debt relief of the prior year.

Connected parties

Definition Companies are defined as connected if, during the accounting period, one has control of the other, or both are under the control of the same person. **908** s 348 CTA 2009

This **applies not only to** direct loans between the connected parties, but also to loans where the connected party stands in the position of creditor or debtor by way of a series of loan relationships.

MEMO POINTS 1. For this purpose **control** of a company means:
– the power of a person to secure that the affairs of the company are conducted in accordance with his wishes by means of holding shares or the possession of voting power (in the company or any other company); or
– by virtue of powers conferred by the Articles of Association or any other document.
2. The relationship between a **consortium** owned company and a consortium member does not constitute a connected party relationship.
3. In a **group** situation there are rules to target schemes using a mismatch between the accounting and taxation treatments of certain instruments to create a tax advantage.

Acceptable accounting methods The **basic rule** is that all debits and credits for connected party loans must be calculated using the amortised cost basis. When a **company becomes connected** with another party (and it had previously accounted for the bad debt on a fair value basis), the debt must be recomputed on an amortised cost basis and the difference accounted for in the period in which it becomes connected. **910** ss 349 - 351 CTA 2009

When a **company ceases to be connected**, and it reverts to accounting for the debt on a fair value basis, any difference between the fair value and amortised cost basis must be brought into account in the accounting period in which the connection ceases.

Late paid interest In certain circumstances interest paid late, that is **more than 12 months** after the end of the accounting period it is accrued in, will only be allowed on a paid basis. This is only the case for connected companies where the creditor company does not account for the full amount of the interest due in their return. For accounting periods beginning on or after 1 April 2009 the rules have been amended so that it will only be the case if the creditor company is in a "non-qualifying territory". However it is possible to claim to use the paid basis. **912** ss 373, 374 CTA 2009

The rules on late paid interest **also apply** when: ss 375 - 377 CTA 2009
a. the debtor is a close company (¶2100) and the creditor is a participator or an associate of a participator, or a company in which such a participator has control or a major interest;
b. one of the parties has a major interest in the other.

MEMO POINTS A company (A) has a **major interest** in another company (B) if:
– company A and another person controls company B; and
– both A and the other person each own at least 40% of the rights in respect of which they are treated as owning company B. In determining this the rights of A include companies with which it is connected. (Similarly, if the other person is a company, its rights include those of any companies it is connected with).

Impairment losses (bad debts) There is no relief for impairment losses on connected party loans. Taking this a step further, no relief is available for a loan waived and, correspondingly, the borrower is not taxed on the amount waived. The appointment of an administrator or liquidator does not break any connected party status. **914**

MEMO POINTS For **parties becoming connected** any impairment loss relief previously given before connection will not be clawed back, although no relief will be given for subsequent impairment loss claims. Similarly, where **connection ceases** the company gets no relief for impairment losses previously disallowed and any amounts recovered in relation to these losses are not taxed.

916 ss 335-341 CTA 2009 **Group transfers** Where one company replaces another group company (¶1524) as a party to a loan relationship contract (i.e. the **contract is assigned or novated**) the following rules apply depending upon which accounting method the transferor company adopted:
– amortised cost basis of accounting: the transferor will account for the "notional carrying value" of the loan relationship contract. The transferee will bring the same amount into account. (The notional carrying value is the deemed accounting value of the contract calculated as if a period of account had ended immediately before ceasing to be a party to the contract); and
– fair value basis of accounting: the transferor company will account for the fair value of the contract at the date of transfer and the transferee company will account for the "notional carrying value" of the contract.

ss 344-346 CTA 2009 MEMO POINTS Where a company **ceases to be a member of a group**, a degrouping charge will apply if a loan relationship asset was transferred to it by way of an intra-group transfer.
The degrouping charge is calculated by deeming a disposal and reacquisition immediately before the company leaves the group and will only apply if:
– a credit arises in the company; or
– a debit arises in the company, but a corresponding credit is brought into account by the company on a hedging derivative contract.

918 s 453 CTA 2009 **Benefits received by connected persons** Where a company (C) enters into a loan relationship, on terms such that it receives a non-commercial return on its investment, but its connected company (P) receives a benefit, specific **anti-avoidance** provisions apply. These provisions ensure that the credits to be brought into account by C will be determined on the basis of fair value accounting and must include the fair value of the benefit received by P.

MEMO POINTS These provisions **apply to** loan relationships that a company is a party to on or after 22 March 2006, in respect of income arising after that date.

Interaction with capital gains tax

920 s 117(A1) TCGA 1992 A loan relationship is treated as a **qualifying corporate bond** (¶5234). This means that gains and losses arising on a loan relationship do not fall within the capital gains regime. Instead, such amounts are included as a loan relationship debit or credit. Special rules apply when shares are exchanged for a QCB (¶5848). Where a QCB acquired in this way is exchanged for a non-QCB, there is a disposal of the QCB and any credit or debit must be brought into account. Any gain heldover in respect of the QCB also becomes chargeable at that time.

SECTION 5

Other activities

A. Miscellaneous income

1. General rules

922 s 979 CTA 2009 In addition to the main income sources, a number of types of income are assessable to tax as **miscellaneous income**.

This is a residual heading of income used to catch items that are not otherwise caught by the legislation. However, income will only fall **within the scope** of it if the receipts have the quality of income and are comparable to receipts which would otherwise be assessable as trading income or similar.

EXAMPLE A manufacturing company owned a yacht which was not used for the purposes of the trade. Any receipts for chartering that yacht would not form part of the company's trading profit, but would be taxable as miscellaneous income.

MEMO POINTS 1. If an item is gratuitous, such as a receipt by way of a gift or gambling winnings, it will **not fall within the scope** of sundry income. Income which derives from a hobby is also not taxable.
2. **In addition**, legislation has been enacted which specifically includes certain income sources within miscellaneous income.

The general rule is that miscellaneous income is **assessed** on the profits received during an accounting period. Where accounts are prepared for a period in excess of 12 months, the accounts figures should be apportioned on a daily basis to arrive at the income for each accounting period. **924**

The amount included in the tax computation is the gross amount, regardless of whether income tax has been deducted at source. Relief will be available for any income tax suffered on miscellaneous income in accordance with the general rules (¶1380).

MEMO POINTS **Special rules** apply to patent income (¶934).

Relief for **losses** incurred on transactions which would be assessable under the term miscellaneous income (if profitable) can be obtained by setting the loss against other miscellaneous income for the same period, or, if this is not possible, by carrying forward the loss and setting it against future profits of any miscellaneous income. **926** s 152 ITA 2007

2. Specific sources of income

Special rules

Certain amounts are specifically taxed as miscellaneous income, including: **932**
a. proceeds from the sale of patent rights;
b. assessments to recover tax repaid in error (¶2342);
c. certain commission income (¶74); and
d. income arising after the cessation of the trade (¶140);
e. the following income charged under anti-avoidance provisions:
- tax advantages from transactions in securities (¶4040);
- charges in respect of certain property transactions (¶4052);
- gains from life policies (¶4066); and
- gains from offshore income funds (¶4110).

MEMO POINTS 1. By their very nature, **anti-avoidance rules** are complex, and expert advice should be sought if in doubt.
2. **Disclosure** of tax saving schemes to HMRC is also required within a very strict time limit (¶2215).

Patent receipts

Scope The following provisions **apply to** income from patents received by companies before 1 April 2002 (receipts by companies for patents created or acquired on or after 1 April 2002 are governed by the intangible assets regime (¶824)). **934**

Under these provisions there are two sets of rules, depending on whether the receipt is capital or income in nature.

MEMO POINTS These rules **apply equally to individuals**, but income will be assessed as sundry income (¶3956).

936
ss 912 - 920 CTA 2009

Capital receipt The **sale of future patent rights** for a capital sum is charged to tax as patent income. Receipts are automatically spread over a period of 6 years beginning on the first day of the chargeable period in which payment is received.

EXAMPLE A Ltd prepares its accounts regularly for the 12 months to 31 December and receives capital proceeds of £12,000 on the disposal of patent rights in the period ending 31 December 2006. £2,000 (i.e. £12,000 ÷ 6) will be assessable for each accounting period starting with the period ending 31 December 2006 and ending with the period ending 31 December 2011.

Where a **chargeable period is less than 12 months**, the amount assessable is reduced proportionately on a daily basis, with the assessable amount for the final period being proportionately reduced for the remainder of the 6 years.

EXAMPLE Taking the facts from the previous example, if A Ltd prepared accounts for the 6 months to 30 June 2008 before resuming regular 12 month accounts, the receipt would be spread as follows:

Period ended		**Assessable £**
31/12/06	12 months	2,000
31/12/07	12 months	2,000
30/06/08	01/01/08 – 30/06/08 (181/365 × 2,000)	992
30/06/09	12 months	2,000
30/06/10	12 months	2,000
30/06/11	12 months	2,000
30/06/12	01/07/11 – 31/12/11 184/365 × 2,000	1,008

An election can be made to **disapply the spreading provisions** and treat the full amount as taxable in the year of receipt if appropriate. This may be beneficial where, for example, there are expenses incurred on patents in the year of receipt which can be set against the patent receipt, or where spreading the payment would result in a company being liable to tax at the marginal rate (¶1350).

This election must be made within 2 years of the end of the accounting period in which payment is actually received.

MEMO POINTS If a **non-UK resident** company sells a UK patent right for a capital sum it is taxed under the miscellaneous income provisions and the payer must deduct tax at the basic rate (¶1372).

938
s 527 ICTA 1988

Income receipt The receipt of a royalty (or other such payment) **for the prior use of a patented invention** is either:
- treated as an income receipt, taxable in the year of receipt; or
- spread over a number of years (if an appropriate claim is made).

A **spreading claim** may only be made where the receipts are receivable for a period in excess of 2 years, in which case they may be spread over a period of between 2 and 6 years, depending on the number of complete years for which they are receivable. (Fractions of a year are ignored.) Where receipts are due for a period in excess of 6 years, they are spread over the maximum 6 year period. For example, receipts under a 3 year agreement can be spread over 3 years, whereas receipts under a 9 year agreement can only be spread over 6 years.

When spreading income receipts, the income is deemed to be received in equal annual instalments on the same date in each year as the actual receipt, with the final instalment being the date of the actual receipt. For example, a payment of £20,000 under a 4 year agreement which was received on 1 July 2011 would be deemed to be received in £5,000 instalments on 1 July 2008, 2009, 2010 and 2011. The length of each individual chargeable period is therefore irrelevant when spreading income receipts.

EXAMPLE A Ltd receives income in respect of a patent it owns under a 3 year agreement as follows:

Period ended	**31/12/07**	**31/12/08**	**31/12/09**	**31/12/10**	**31/12/11**
Other profits	40,000	45,000	50,000	55,000	60,000
Patent income	0	0	24,000	21,000	15,000
PCTCT	40,000	45,000	74,000	76,000	75,000

If a claim is made for the patent income to be spread, PCTCT will be as follows:

Period ended	31/12/07	31/12/08	31/12/09	31/12/10	31/12/11
Other profits	40,000	45,000	50,000	55,000	60,000
Patent income 1	8,000	8,000	8,000	-	-
Patent income 2	-	7,000	7,000	7,000	-
Patent income 3	-	-	5,000	5,000	5,000
PCTCT	48,000	60,000	70,000	67,000	65,000

A claim to spread income receipts must be **made within** 4 years of the end of the accounting period in which a payment is received. Any other relief or allowance that becomes due as a result of the claim can also be given. Sch 18 para 55 FA 1998

B. Distributions

1. Definition

General rules

Broadly, a distribution is any payment made by a company which reduces its assets, i.e. a return of profits to the shareholders. Such payments are not deductible for corporation tax purposes. 940 s 1000 CTA 2010

The following items are **specifically** defined as distributions:
- dividends (¶944);
- transfer of assets (¶945); and
- interest on certain securities (¶948).

For additional items treated as distributions in respect of close companies, see ¶2108.

MEMO POINTS The following payments are **specifically excluded** from the definition of a distribution:
- distributions made by a liquidator, in respect of share capital during the course of a liquidation; s 1030 CTA 2010
- stock dividends (¶944); s 1033 CTA 2010
- payments for group relief (provided the payment does not exceed the group relief surrendered); and
- certain purchases by a company of its own shares (¶2080). s 1049 CTA 2010

The distribution legislation is designed to prevent companies giving assets to its shareholders free of tax. Where assets are transferred to shareholders who are also employees or directors, these are likely to be subject to tax as benefits in kind (¶3278) and would not therefore be covered by the distribution rules.

Also, by **concession**, the following items may be excluded from the definition of a distribution, providing certain conditions are met and assurances are given: ESC C15, C16
- distributions of assets prior to dissolution under s 652 or s 652A Companies Act 1985; and
- distributions to members of an unincorporated association prior to dissolution.

Distributions fall into **two categories**: qualifying and non-qualifying distributions. The distinction for the paying company is largely immaterial. However, for the recipient, the amount of qualifying distributions received may affect the rate of corporation tax payable. The tax treatment of distributions received by individual shareholders is also different (¶2817). 942

MEMO POINTS 1. Broadly speaking, **qualifying distributions** are any distributions other than bonus issues of redeemable share capital. Bonus issues are non-qualifying because they do not give rise to an immediate reduction in the company's assets. Where the shares are redeemed, a qualifying distribution may arise.

2. Historically, a company was required to deduct advance corporation tax (ACT) from any qualifying distributions it paid. This system was abolished with effect from 6 April 1999, and replaced by a system of **shadow ACT** (¶1405) to allow companies ongoing relief for any surplus ACT they had at that date.

Dividends

944 With the exception of stock dividends, all dividends are treated as distributions. This **includes**:
- cash dividends;
- dividends in specie; and
- capital dividends (i.e. distributions paid out of the surplus arising on the realisation of a capital asset).

MEMO POINTS 1. A **stock dividend** is:
- share capital issued by a UK resident company to a shareholder as a result of the shareholder exercising his option to receive a dividend in cash or additional share capital; or
- bonus share capital issued by a UK resident company in respect of shares which carry the right to receive bonus shares.

2. Legislation is to be enacted in *Finance (N° 2) Act* to include a return of capital made as a result of a reduction in share capital.

Transfer of assets

946 A transfer of assets **or liabilities** from a company to its members is treated as a distribution if the market value of the benefit received by the member exceeds the consideration received by the company for the transfer.

However these rules do not apply (i.e. there will be no distribution) if the transfer is:
- in cash or kind between UK resident companies under common control or where one is a 51% subsidiary of the other;
- of assets (other than cash) or liabilities between unconnected UK resident companies, neither of which is a 51% subsidiary of a non-resident company; and
- to employees or directors who are taxed under the benefits in kind legislation (¶3278).

MEMO POINTS In the majority of cases, where a **company purchases its own shares** from the shareholders, this will be a distribution. However, in limited circumstances, an unquoted trading company will be treated as making a capital payment and not a distribution (¶2080).

Interest on securities

948 Payments of interest by a company at a rate **in excess of a normal commercial rate** (determined by reference to the amount invested) may be treated as a distribution.

949 Payments of interest **in respect of the following securities** (including secured and unsecured loan stock) may also be treated as a distribution:
- bonus issues of securities;
- securities convertible into shares;
- securities carrying a right to receive shares or securities;
- securities carrying interest at a rate dependent upon the level of profits;
- securities connected with shares in the company; and
- equity notes held by a company which is associated with, or funded by, the issuing company.

MEMO POINTS 1. Where the shares received on **conversion** are listed on a recognised stock exchange (¶9995), or issued on terms comparable with listed securities, no distribution arises.

2. Securities are **connected with shares** in a company where the rights attaching to the shares or securities are such that it is necessary or advantageous to own both.

3. **Equity notes** are, broadly, those where the likely redemption date is more than 50 years after the date of issue.

4. **Companies are associated** if one owns 75% of the other, or both are 75% subsidiaries of a third company.

2. Tax treatment

Paying company

950 When a **company makes a distribution**, the value of the distribution is not deductible in computing the profit chargeable to corporation tax.

Recipient company

For dividends received on or after 1 July 2009 the rules for the taxation treatment of dividends received changed significantly. These changes apply to both dividends received from UK companies and from overseas companies. There are two regimes, one for small companies and one for other companies. However, both share similar provisions. Where a **dividend meets the conditions** listed it will be exempt from tax and will not form part of the profits chargeable to tax. 952

MEMO POINTS 1. A **small company** for these purposes is one with fewer than 50 employees and either a turnover not exceeding €10 million or gross balance sheet total not exceeding €10 million. The company will only be considered not small once these conditions have not been satisfied for two consecutive periods.
2. Where the company is part of a group the group is tested against the limits.
3. It is possible to elect to have a dividend that would be exempt treated as taxable. This may be beneficial in order to gain benefits under certain foreign tax treaties.
4. For the rules relating to dividends received prior to 1 July 2009 see earlier editions of *Tax Memo*.

For **all companies** the distribution cannot: 953
- be a deemed distribution that is interest in nature; nor s 931B CTA 2009
- entitle the paying company to a foreign deduction for the payment.

For **small companies** there are only two further conditions. Firstly that the payer of the dividend is either resident in the UK or a qualifying territory. Secondly that the payment is not part of a scheme designed to secure a tax advantage.

MEMO POINTS 1. Prior to 1 July 2009 a capital dividend would not be able to benefit from the exemption. The extension of the exemption to capital dividends does not affect their treatment for capital gains purposes.
2. A **qualifying territory** is essentially a country with which the UK has a double tax treaty with a standard non-discrimination provision.

Other companies For companies that are not small the dividend must also fall into one of five exempt classes. s 931D CTA 2009

General disqualified situations

As well as restrictions placed individually on each of the exempt classes there are four situations where, if a scheme is entered into, the exemption is denied: 954 s 931N - 931Q CTA 2009
- where the dividend is part of a scheme that is designed to **obtain a deduction** for an amount that is calculated by reference to the dividend. This extends the general condition to ensure that schemes involving chains of transactions, one of which receives a deduction, will be covered;
- where a tax deduction is obtained or taxable income is given up in order to receive the distribution;
- where taxable profits are reduced (or loss increased) by virtue of the dividend forming part of a scheme involving the acquisition of goods or services for an amount less than would have been payable if the dividend had not been paid. This will not apply where the transfer pricing rules (¶1721) already eliminate the benefit of the transaction; or
- where a company, in whose hands the dividend would be taxable, diverts the receipt to a connected company where it is not.

Exempt classes

There are five exempt classes available. Each of these also carry specific disqualifying scenarios. 955

Distributions from controlled companies For these purposes control is defined in the same way as it is for the controlled foreign companies legislation (¶2148) but having no regard to the rights of parties connected to the company. As such only the company's rights will count towards the control test. s 931E, 931J CTA 2009

However, a dividend will not qualify for exemption where there is a scheme in place that involves either a manipulation of the CFC rules or those regarding loan relationships.

s 931F, 931K CTA 2009 **Distributions paid on non-redeemable, ordinary shares** To qualify the share should contain no preferential rights compared to any other share issued in the company. However, undertaking a scheme involving quasi-redeemable or quasi-preferential shares will disqualify the dividend from exemption.

MEMO POINTS Some companies do not issue shares. Where a company that does not issue shares pays dividends these may be exempt if the certificates issued in lieu of shares equate to shares based on the facts of the situation and meet the criteria above.

s 931G, 931L CTA 2009 **Distributions received on portfolio holdings** Where the dividend is paid on a shareholding representing less than 10% of that particular class of shares of the company the dividend will be exempt. This ensures that dividends received on small preference or redeemable shares will be exempted from tax. Where there is a scheme in place to utilise this exemption and the total aggregate holdings of all connected companies is at least 10% this exemption cannot apply.

s 931H CTA 2009 **Dividends from transaction not designed to reduce tax** Unlike the other exemptions **this can only apply to dividends** and not other distributions made by a company. In order to ascertain whether a dividend will be exempt under this category it is necessary to look at the underlying profits it is paid from. If the profits arise from transactions entered into to secure a UK tax deduction and that was one of the transaction's main purposes then any dividend arising from these profits will not be exempt. However any dividend being paid from other profits will be exempt. In looking at this exemption it is presumed that the dividend in question will be taken from non-eligible profits first. However, dividends exempt via another class reduce the pool of eligible profits first.

s 931I CTA 2009 **Distributions from shares accounted for as liabilities** In some cases shares can be dealt with under the loan relationship rules (¶876). However where the shares do not fall into the loan relationship rules only by virtue of not being held for an unallowable purpose any distributions paid in respect of them will be exempt.

3. Reporting requirements

956 s 1101 CTA 2010 There is no obligation to notify HMRC of any **qualifying distributions** made.

However, HMRC must be provided with the following information with regard to **non-qualifying distributions**:
- details of the transaction;
- name and address of recipient(s); and
- value of distribution received by each recipient.

This information must be provided within 14 days of the end of the accounting period in which the distribution is made.

C. Charitable donations relief

958 Donations to charity by a company are not **deductible** from a particular source of income, but may be deducted from total profits. These can reduce a company's profits to nil, but cannot create a loss. A company can make a qualifying donation in cash or in kind.

1. Monetary donations

960 ss 191 - 202 CTA 2010 Monetary payments by a non-charitable company to a charity (including any payments under covenant) may be made under the **gift aid** scheme, unless the payment is a distribution or otherwise deductible in computing profits chargeable to corporation tax.

There is no requirement for the company to deduct income tax at source and the charity is not taxed on the payment it receives.

See ¶4420 onwards for details.

MEMO POINTS Subsidiaries that are **wholly owned by one or more charities** can donate their profits to those charities under the gift aid scheme.

For a donation to qualify for relief it must meet the **following criteria**: **964** ss 197, 939C CTA 2010
– there must be no conditions as to repayment of the sum;
– it must not be connected in any way with the acquisition of property by the charity from the company (or a person connected to the company), other than by way of gift;
the donation must not be considered to have been tainted; and
– the value of any benefit received by the company (or a person connected to the company) as a result of the payment must not exceed the following prescribed limits:

Amount of the gift	Prescribed limit [1]
Up to £100	25% of gift
£100 to £1,000	£25
Over £1,000	5% of gift, up to £500 [2]

Note:
1. Where **more than one donation** is made to the same charity in an accounting period, each donation is considered separately, and only the donation resulting in a breach of the limit is ineligible for relief. Subsequent donations will only be eligible for relief if no further benefit is received.
2. In any accounting period there is also an overriding annual limit of benefits that can be received which is set at £500.

Where the **benefit is for a period of less than 12 months**, the annual value of the benefit must be calculated when determining whether the limit has been breached.

EXAMPLE A Ltd makes an annual gift aid payment to a charity of £10,000. As a result of the payment, the managing director of the company is entitled to use the gym at the charity headquarters for a period of 6 months, and this benefit is valued at £350.
The value of the benefit for a full year is calculated as follows:

$$\frac{\text{Benefit}}{\text{Number of days in the period}} \times 365 = \frac{350}{182} \times 365 = £702$$

The maximum permitted benefit for a donation of £10,000 is £500 (i.e. 5%) and therefore the payment does not qualify for relief, as it exceeds the limit.

Similarly, where a **payment is made at intervals of less than 12 months**, the annual equivalent is calculated.

EXAMPLE A Ltd makes regular payments to a charity of £60 at 8 months intervals. As a result of the payments, the company is entitled to a benefit which has an annual value of £20.
The value of the payment for a full year is calculated as follows:

$$\frac{\text{Payment}}{\text{Average number of days in the period}} \times 365 = \frac{60}{243} \times 365 = £90$$

The maximum permitted benefit for a donation of £90 is £22.50 (i.e. 25%) and therefore the payments qualify for relief.

MEMO POINTS For the definition of **tainted donation** see ¶7334

2. Gift of qualifying investments

A gift (or transfer at an undervalue) of a qualifying investment to a charity may also be deductible as a donation for the accounting period in which the disposal takes place, **provided** the donation is not deemed to be tainted ¶7334. **966** ss 203-216 CTA 2010

Qualifying investments are **defined as**:
– shares and securities listed or dealt in on a recognised stock exchange (¶9995);

– units in an authorised unit trust;
– shares in an open-ended investment company;
– interests in offshore funds; and
– freehold or leasehold land.

The **allowable charge** that can be deducted from total profits is:

a. for a gift, equal to the lower of the:
– market value on the date of the gift; or
– net benefit to the charity;

b. for a transfer at undervalue, equal to the lower of the:
– difference between the market value and the proceeds received; and
– excess of the net benefit to the charity, over the market value of the consideration.

In either case, the charge is increased for any expenses incurred on the transfer, but reduced for any benefit received by the company as a result of the transfer.

Relief must be **claimed** within 2 years of the end of the accounting period in which the transfer occurs.

MEMO POINTS Where the gift is of **land**, no relief is available unless the company has received a certificate from the charity. Such a certificate must specify the date of the gift, give a description of the land, and contain a statement to the effect that the charity has acquired the land.

3. Method of giving relief

968 Donations are deducted from total profits after all other reliefs, with the exception of group relief. As donations are not an allowable trading expense, any items charged to the profit and loss account should be disallowed in the computation of trading profits.

In **general** relief is only available for charges actually paid during an accounting period. However, payments to a charity by its **subsidiaries** are deductible if paid within 9 months of the end of the accounting period in which they are charged to the accounts. In this case the repayment condition is relaxed so that the charity may refund any payment to the subsidiary where the amount refunded is simply the excess of that required to reduce its profit to nil.

MEMO POINTS No relief is available for any donations made **prior to the commencement of trade**.

D. Transactions in securities

975 Transactions involving securities may require a clearance from HMRC in order to be sure of the tax treatment, because anti-avoidance legislation may treat profits (including gains) from securities as income.

Comment These rules are subject to ongoing consultation and may be completely repealed in future.

1. General principles

977
s 733 CTA 2010
Whenever a company is party to a transaction in securities, there is always a risk that HMRC will counteract any corporation tax advantage obtained which falls within any of the following circumstances:
– a taxpayer receives an abnormal dividend (i.e. substantially exceeding a normal return on the amount paid for the security) and as a consequence of that transaction, the company receives non-taxable consideration;

– company receives consideration in connection with the distribution of profits, or realisation of assets, of a close company; or
– non-taxable consideration, in the form of securities issued by a close company, received as part of a transaction involving the transfer of an asset between two close companies, or a transaction in securities involving at least two close companies

MEMO POINTS 1. **Corporation tax advantage** means: s 732 CTA 2010
– obtaining relief or increased relief from corporation tax;
– becoming entitled to a repayment or increased repayment of corporation tax; or
– avoiding an assessment (or a possible assessment) to tax, or obtaining a reduced assessment.
An advantage may be obtained as a result of a single or multiple transactions in securities.
2. **Securities** include unsecured loan notes, debentures, and shares. Where a company is not limited by shares (e.g. limited by guarantee), securities also include any interests in the company held by its members. s 751 CTA 2010
3. **Transactions** in securities include:
– sale, purchase, redemption or transfer of securities;
– issuing or securing the issue of new securities;
– applying or subscribing for new securities; and
– altering the rights attached to securities.
A transaction could also possibly involve the liquidation of a company.
4. For this purpose, a **close company** is all unquoted companies (unless controlled by a quoted company) and any company under the control of 5 persons or less.

Exception

To **avoid a counteraction**, the company must convince HMRC (i.e. the onus proof is on the company) that the main object of the transaction is not to obtain a tax advantage, and also that the transaction is being carried out either: **979** s 734 CTA 2010
– for bona fide commercial reasons; or
– in the ordinary course of making or managing investments.

2. HMRC counteraction

If HMRC intend to counteract a tax advantage, a set procedure is followed whereby the company is informed how the transaction will be taxed, and given the opportunity to appeal. **981** ss 743 - 746, 750 CTA 2010

Counteraction **may include** disallowing a loss, taxing a capital receipt as income, or refusing a repayment of tax.

Obtaining clearances

In order to obtain **certainty** on how a transaction will be taxed, it is advisable to apply for clearance in advance that HMRC will not counteract any tax advantage. **983** ss 748, 749 CTA 2010

Once the written application is received, HMRC have 30 days in which to give clearance or request further information (to which the taxpayer must respond within 30 days, or the application will lapse).

When **refusing** an application, HMRC will usually state their reasons. There is no right of appeal against a refusal.

CHAPTER 6

Chargeable gains

OUTLINE

SECTION 1

General principles

The basic principles involved in calculating chargeable gains are **common to both individuals and companies**, for details of which see ¶5220 onwards. There are a number of further provisions relating to companies only. This chapter details these provisions. **1110** ss 1, 2, 8 TCGA 1992

MEMO POINTS For details of the treatment of corporate **capital losses**, see ¶1310 onwards.

Gains are deemed to arise in the accounting period in which the date of disposal falls (¶5502) and are **chargeable to** corporation tax (not capital gains tax). The extent of the charge differs depending upon whether the company is UK resident or not, as follows: **1111**

a. UK resident companies are subject to corporation tax on all gains arising, regardless of where the assets are located;

b. non-UK resident companies trading:

– in the UK through a permanent establishment are only taxable on gains accruing on assets situated in the UK and used for the purposes of the trade;

– outside the UK through a permanent establishment are not taxable in the UK, regardless of where the assets are situated.

1113 The amount of gain included in the tax computation is **calculated** as follows:

	£
Total chargeable gains of the accounting period	x
Allowable capital losses of the accounting period	(x)
Capital losses brought forward from an earlier accounting period	(x)
Assessable gains	x

MEMO POINTS 1. **Losses** for an accounting period are set against gains arising in the same accounting period. Any surplus losses not absorbed in this way may be carried forward indefinitely and set against chargeable gains arising for subsequent periods. See ¶1310.
2. Restrictions apply to the use of losses arising on transactions between **connected persons** (¶5462).

1115 **Special rules** apply to:
– the disposal of assets that have been subject to capital allowances (¶5924); and
– transfers of capital assets between 75% group companies (¶1600).

1116 Simply deducting cost from proceeds produces an unindexed gain. This may be reduced by an allowance for inflation, known as **indexation**.

SECTION 2

Indexation allowance

1. Purpose

1118 s 53 TCGA 1992 Indexation allowance **aims** to take account of inflation between the dates of purchase and sale of an asset and is effectively used to increase the original cost of an asset.

The **two elements** to an indexation allowance calculation are identification of:
– expenditure qualifying for indexation allowance; and
– dates of acquisition and disposal.

2. Qualifying expenditure

1120 s 38 TCGA 1992 Indexation allowance is available for expenditure incurred wholly and exclusively:
– on the **acquisition** of an asset (including any incidental associated costs);
– for the purpose of **enhancing** the value of an asset (if reflected in the nature of the asset when it is sold); or
– in establishing or defending **title** or right to an asset.

MEMO POINTS **Incidental costs** (¶5330) incurred on the acquisition of an asset qualify for indexation allowance while those connected to a disposal do not.

1121 Where an asset is **acquired before 31 March 1982** the qualifying expenditure for indexation allowance will be the higher of:
– actual expenditure; or
– market value at 31 March 1982. (See ¶1133 for full details of assets acquired before 31 March 1982.)

1123 Qualifying expenditure must be adjusted to take account of **restrictions or reductions made to the cost of the asset**; for example, where an asset is a wasting asset or has any estimated scrap value. See ¶5922 for details.

3. Timing of expenditure

In order to calculate indexation allowance, it is necessary to determine the dates of expenditure for each asset, summarised as follows: 1125

Transaction	Deemed date for indexation purposes
Acquisition	Date the asset itself is acquired or provided
Enhancement [1, 2]	Date it becomes due and payable
Disposal	Date when contracts are made, unless one of the exceptions applies [3]

Note:
1. Where an asset is enhanced (e.g. where a building is extended) between the date of acquisition and the date of disposal, the indexation allowance on the original cost and the enhancement expenditure will be calculated separately, based on the dates that each item of expenditure was incurred.
2. Where the enhancement took place before 31 March 1982 and market value has been used (¶1135) for the calculation of the gain, the enhancement expenditure is effectively ignored as it will be reflected in the market value at 31 March 1982.
3. The following exceptions to this rule apply:
a. where an asset is gifted, it is treated as disposed of on the date the donor has done everything possible to transfer the asset;
b. where an asset is disposed of under a:
– conditional contract, it is treated as disposed of on the date the condition is fulfilled;
– hire purchase contract, it is treated as disposed of on the date the use or enjoyment of the asset passes;
– compulsory purchase order, it is treated as disposed of on the date the compensation is agreed;
c. where a negligible value claim is made, the asset is treated as disposed of on the date of the claim unless an earlier date is specified; and
d. where there is an insurance payout, the asset is treated as disposed of on the date the insurance money is received.

MEMO POINTS Special rules apply to the timing of transactions relating to **shares** (see ¶5755).

4. Calculation of indexation allowance

Indexation factor

Indexation allowance is calculated by applying the indexation factor to the qualifying expenditure. The indexation factor is based on the **retail price index** (RPI) (see ¶9979) and is calculated using the following formula: 1126

$$\frac{RD - RI}{RI}$$

where:
- RD is the RPI for the month of disposal; and
- RI is the RPI for the month in which the expenditure was incurred (or, if later, March 1982).

The indexation factor is generally expressed as a decimal rounded to three decimal places (unless the disposal relates to shares in which case no rounding takes place (¶1205)). If RD does not exceed RI the indexation factor will be nil. 1128

EXAMPLE A Ltd buys an asset in October 1987 for £18,000 and sells it for £45,000 in March 2011. The indexed gain is:

	£	£
Disposal proceeds		45,000
Less: Cost	18,000	
Indexation Oct 87 to March 2011		
$(\frac{232.5 - 102.9}{102.9} = 1.259) \times 18,000$	22,662	
		(40,662)
Indexed gain		4,338

1130 Indexation allowance can never be used to **create or increase a loss** and is therefore restricted to the amount of the unindexed gain.

EXAMPLE B Ltd buys an asset in August 1983 at a cost of £13,000. It sells the asset for £25,000 in August 2010.

	Cost £
Disposal proceeds	25,000
Cost	(13,000)
Unindexed gain	12,000
Indexation Aug 83 to Aug 10	
$(\frac{224.5 - 85.68}{85.68}) = 1.620 \times 13{,}000 = 21{,}060$	
Restricted to unindexed gain	(12,000)
Indexed gain	Nil

5. Small part disposals and compensation payments

1131 s 56 TCGA 1992

Where:
- compensation or insurance policy payouts for lost or destroyed assets are received (¶5518+);
- a small part disposal of land is made (¶5682);
- a small part disposal of land occurs due to a compulsory purchase order (¶5737); or
- a small cash receipt arises in respect of shares (¶5830),

indexation allowance will be calculated on the whole cost (or 31 March 1982 value, if applicable) from the date of acquisition to the date of disposal. A notional reduction is then made to take account of the indexation on the part disposal. The notional indexation will run from the date of the part disposal to the date of the subsequent disposal of the remainder and will be based on the disposal proceeds of that part disposal.

EXAMPLE A Ltd owns land which it acquired in August 1995 for £75,000. In June 1997 it sold part of the land for £16,000. This was the only land transaction made in the year. The value of the entire holding immediately prior to the disposal was £100,000. Assuming that A Ltd submits the appropriate claim, proceeds are less than:
- £20,000; and
- 20% of the value of the whole immediately before the disposal.

The transaction will therefore qualify as a small part disposal and the allowable expenditure of the remaining land will be reduced as follows:

	£
Allowable expenditure	75,000
Less proceeds from small part disposal	(16,000)
Adjusted expenditure	59,000

If the remaining land was disposed of in June 2010 for £95,000 the resulting gain would be calculated as follows:

	£	£
Disposal proceeds		95,000
Adjusted expenditure	59,000	
Indexation allowance Aug 1995 to Jun 2010		
$\frac{224.1 - 149.9}{149.9} = 0.495 \times 75{,}000$	37,125	
Less notional indexation allowance Jun 1997 to Jun 2010		
$\frac{224.1 - 157.5}{157.5} = 0.423 \times 16{,}000$	(6,768)	
		(89,357)
Gain		5,643

6. Options

Where the asset being disposed of was acquired by way of an option, indexation allowance is calculated separately on the cost of: **1132** s 145 TCGA 1992
- the option (deemed to occur when the option was granted); and
- acquiring the asset (deemed to occur on the exercise of the option).

See ¶5600 onwards for details.

SECTION 3

Rebasing

1. General rebasing rules

Rebasing is the term used to describe the treatment of assets held on 31 March 1982. **1133** s 35 TCGA 1992

Essentially, it **means** that when calculating a gain or loss on a disposal of an asset that was held on 31 March 1982 it is possible to use the value of the asset on 31 March 1982 as the allowable expenditure (i.e. the value is rebased).

Rebasing may **either be** carried out on the disposal of each single relevant asset (¶1135), or an irrevocable election may be made for all assets held on 31 March 1982 to be re-valued at that date (¶1138).

MEMO POINTS Special rules also apply for **assets held on 6 April 1965** (¶1146).

2. Single asset treatment

On the disposal of an asset that was held on 31 March 1982, two computations are prepared: one based on the original cost of the asset, and the other on the assumption that the asset was sold and immediately reacquired on 31 March 1982, at the market value at that date. **1135** s 35(1), (2) TCGA 1992
Indexation allowance is calculated on the higher of the:
- original cost; and
- value on 31 March 1982.

The computation that results in the smaller gain or loss will prevail. Where one computation results in a gain, and another in a loss, the disposal is treated as giving rise to neither a gain nor a loss. **1136** s 35(3) TCGA 1992

EXAMPLE

1. A Ltd acquired an asset on 1 December 1978 for £100,000 and sold it on 1 May 2010. Indexation allowance is given at the rate of 1.815.
A Ltd sold the asset for £800,000, and the March 1982 value was £150,000.

	Cost	March 1982
	£	£
Disposal proceeds	800,000	800,000
Less: Cost/March 1982 value	(100,000)	(150,000)
Indexation allowance (150,000 × 1.815)	(272,250)	(272,250)
Indexed gain	427,750	377,750

In this case the value on March 1982 will apply because it gives rise to the smaller gain.

2. Assume the facts are as for 1. above, but A Ltd sold the asset for £380,000.

	Cost	March 1982
	£	£
Disposal proceeds	380,000	380,000
Less: Cost/March 1982 value	(100,000)	(150,000)
Indexation allowance (150,000 × 1.815)[1]	(272,250)	(230,000)
Indexed gain	7,750	Nil

Note:
1. Restricted for the March 1982 disposal as indexation cannot create or augment a loss.

In this case the disposal will be treated as giving rise to neither a gain nor a loss.

3. Assume the facts are as in 1. above, but A Ltd sold the asset for £75,000.

	Cost	March 1982
	£	£
Disposal proceeds	75,000	75,000
Less: Cost/March 1982 value	(100,000)	(150,000)
Allowable loss	(25,000)	(75,000)

In this case the original cost will apply because it gives rise to a smaller loss.

3. Global rebasing election

1138 s 35(5) TCGA 1992 A company **may elect** for the gains on all disposals of assets held on 31 March 1982 to be calculated only by reference to the 31 March 1982 value.

The election, which is **irrevocable**, must be made in writing before 2 years after the end of the relevant accounting period.

Sch 3 para 2 TCGA 1992 MEMO POINTS The **election does not apply** to the disposal of machinery and plant qualifying for capital allowances.

1140 **Once the election has been made**, all gains will be calculated using the 31 March 1982 value even if the original cost is higher. Similarly, indexation allowance will always be based on the 31 March 1982 value.

4. Special situations

Shares and securities

1141 Sch 3 para 1A TCGA 1992 Where a company disposes of shares that:
- were transferred to it from a group company after 31 March 1982; and
- formed part of a larger holding when held by the group company at 31 March 1982,

the valuation of the smaller holding can be based on a proportion of the value of the larger holding. Depending on the level of the original holding this may increase the value of each share.

Rolled over gains

1143 Sch 4 para 2 TCGA 1992 If a gain on the disposal of an asset was rolled over (¶6050) into another asset **before 31 March 1982**, the gain will effectively be eliminated because the 31 March 1982 value will be the full value rather than the original cost reduced by the rolled over gain.

Alternatively, a claim can be made for the rolled over gain to be reduced by half if: 1145
- the rolled over gain was made before 31 March 1982;
- the asset into which the gain was rolled was acquired between 1 April 1982 and 5 April 1988; and
- that asset was disposed of after 6 April 1988.

MEMO POINTS A claim for this relief must be **submitted by** 2 years after the end of the relevant accounting period.

SECTION 4

Assets held on 6 April 1965

1. General principles

Apportionment

As capital gains tax did not exist before 6 April 1965, gains arising on assets held on this date are **deemed** to accrue equally over the period of ownership and only the part of the gain that arises after 6 April 1965 is chargeable. The element of the gain arising before 6 April 1965 is excluded from the charge. 1146 Sch 2 para 16 TCGA 1992

MEMO POINTS 1. Special rules apply for **land** with development value (¶1158) and **quoted shares** (¶1211).
2. These provisions only apply if a **global rebasing election** (¶1138) is not in force.

The apportionment is **calculated** using the following formula: 1148

$$\frac{\text{Period after 6 April 1965}}{\text{Period of ownership}} \times \text{Indexed gain}$$

MEMO POINTS For the purposes of the above formula, assets **acquired before 6 April 1945** will be deemed to have been acquired on 6 April 1945.

Indexation allowance

Indexation allowance will **always be calculated using** the higher of the: 1150
- original cost; or
- value on 31 March 1982.

The resulting gain is then used to determine whether rebasing should apply. Special rules apply where a loss arises (¶1156).

EXAMPLE A Ltd acquired an asset on 1 October 1954 for £25,000 and sold it on 1 October 2010 for £230,000. The value at 31 March 1982 was £75,000. Indexation allowance is given at the rate of 1.842.

	Original cost	March 1982 value
	£	£
Disposal proceeds	230,000	230,000
Less: Cost/31 March 1982 value	(25,000)	(75,000)
Indexation allowance on higher of cost and March 82		
1.842 × 75,000	(138,150)	(138,150)
Indexed gain	66,850	16,850

Time apportioned gain:

$$66{,}850 \times \frac{45.5\text{ years}}{56\text{ years}} = £54{,}316$$

The gain using the 31 March 1982 value is less than the time apportioned gain and will therefore be the chargeable gain.

Enhancement expenditure

1151 Sch 2 para 16(4) TCGA 1992

Where enhancement expenditure was incurred, the chargeable **gain will be apportioned** between the original cost and the enhancement expenditure, and each part is then separately time apportioned based on the dates on which the expenditure was incurred.

EXAMPLE A Ltd acquired an asset on 1 April 1954 for £50,000. On 1 April 1964 it spent £45,000 enhancing the asset. The asset was sold on 1 April 2010 for £350,000. The value at 31 March 1982 was £100,000. Indexation allowance is given at the rate of 1.805.

	Original cost	March 1982 value
	£	£
Disposal proceeds	350,000	350,000
Less: Cost/March 1982 value	(50,000)	(100,000)
Enhancement expenditure	(45,000)	
Indexation allowance on higher of cost and March 82		
1.805 × 100,000	(180,500)	(180,500)
Indexed gain	74,500	69,500
Allocated:	£	
Original cost (50,000/95,000 × 74,500)	39,211	
Enhancement expenditure (45,000/95,000 × 74,500)	35,289	
Time apportioned gain:		
Original cost		
$39{,}211 \times \frac{45 \text{ years}}{56 \text{ years}}$	30,809	
Enhancement expenditure		
$35{,}289 \times \frac{45 \text{ years}}{46 \text{ years}}$	34,522	
	65,331	

The time apportioned gain is compared to the gain using the 31 March 1982 value (£69,500). In this case the time apportioned gain will be the chargeable gain as it is lower.

1153 Sch 2 para 16(5) TCGA 1992

Where the **initial expenditure is disproportionately small** compared with the value of the asset immediately before the enhancement expenditure is incurred, apportionment of the gain may be made on the basis of fact if this gives a more realistic result. In this case the actual gain attributable to the enhancement expenditure will be used, and the balance will be deemed to apply to the initial expenditure.

2. Market value 6 April 1965 election

1155 Sch 2 para 17 TCGA 1992

A company **may elect** for the gain to be calculated using the market value at 6 April 1965. The election, which is irrevocable, must be **submitted** within 2 years of the end of the relevant accounting period.

Indexation allowance in this case will be calculated using the higher of the value on:
- 6 April 1965; and
- 31 March 1982.

EXAMPLE A Ltd acquired an asset on 6 April 1953 for £20,000. The asset was sold on 6 April 2010 for £225,000. The value on 6 April 1965 was £70,000 and on 31 March 1982 it was £80,000. Indexation allowance is given at the rate of 1.826.

	Original cost £	6 April 1965 value £
Disposal proceeds	225,000	225,000
Less: Cost/April 1965 value	(20,000)	(70,000)
Indexation allowance on higher of April 65 and March 82 (1.826 × 80,000)	(146,080)	(146,080)
	58,920	8,920
Time apportioned gain: $58,920 \times \frac{45 \text{ years}}{57 \text{ years}}$	46,516	

A Ltd should make an election to use the 6 April 1965 value for this asset as that gives rise to a smaller gain than under time apportionment. The resulting gain of £8,980 is then compared to the gain under the rebasing rules.

3. Losses

Because the election to use the 6 April 1965 value is voluntary, a company is not obliged to apply the 6 April 1965 value when that gives rise to a smaller loss than with the original cost. The following table **summarises** the position with respect to losses. The final column indicates whether the company should then go on to apply the rebasing provisions (¶1133). 1156

Gain/loss under time apportionment	Gain/loss using 6 April 1965 value	Treatment	Rebasing?
Loss	Gain	No election	Rebasing applies
Loss	Smaller loss	No election	Rebasing applies
Loss	Larger loss	Loss restricted[1]	Rebasing applies
Gain	Loss	No gain/no loss	No rebasing

Note:
1. Where the 6 April 1965 value gives rise to a larger loss than under time apportionment, the allowable loss is restricted to the actual loss incurred before time apportionment was applied.

EXAMPLE A Ltd acquired an asset on 6 April 1958 for £30,000. The asset was sold on 6 April 2010 for £10,000. The value on 6 April 1965 was £35,000 and on 31 March 1982 it was £40,000.

	Original cost £	6 April 1965 value £
Disposal proceeds	10,000	10,000
Less: Cost/April 1965 value	(30,000)	(35,000)
	(20,000)	(25,000)

Time apportionment:

$$20,000 \times \frac{45 \text{ years}}{52 \text{ years}} = £17,308$$

In this case the 6 April 1965 value gives rise to a larger loss so an election should be made. The loss will, however, be restricted to the actual loss before time apportionment i.e. £20,000. This amount will then be compared to the result of the rebasing exercise:

	£
Disposal proceeds	10,000
Less: 31 March 1982 value	(40,000)
	(30,000)

The restricted loss (£20,000) arising from the 6 April 1965 election will be used in this case as it gives rise to a smaller loss than the 31 March 1982 value.

4. Land with development value

1158 Sch 2 paras 9 - 15 TCGA 1992 Special rules apply where land in the UK was held at 6 April 1965 and is **disposed of** either:
- at a price exceeding the value of the land if the valuation had been made on the basis that development would be unlawful; or
- where any material development has been carried out by the transferor after 17 December 1973.

Where this provision applies, the **computation** of the chargeable gain or allowable loss is made by reference to:
- the original cost; or
- the market value at 6 April 1965.

The computation that results in the **smaller gain or loss** will prevail.

Where one computation results in a **gain and the other a loss**, the disposal is treated as giving rise to neither a gain nor a loss. The chargeable gain/allowable loss will then be compared to the 31 March 1982 value in accordance with the **rebasing** provisions (¶1133).

SECTION 5

Specific transactions

A. No gain/no loss disposals

1165 In a number of situations, a disposal is deemed to be a no gain/no loss disposal (¶5550). For companies this will also specifically include:
- transfers within a 75% CG group of companies (¶1600);
- certain transfers as part of a company scheme of reconstruction; and
- certain transfers of UK trades.

Scheme of reconstruction

1166 s 139 TCGA 1992 As part of a scheme of reconstruction, a company may **transfer the whole, or part, of its trade** to another company for no consideration, other than the assumption of liabilities.

Such a transfer is a no gain/no loss disposal, providing that:
- the reconstruction is carried out for bona fide commercial reasons;
- the avoidance of tax is not the main purpose of the transaction; and
- the asset is a chargeable asset. This means that one or both of the parties may be non-UK resident companies, provided that the asset is chargeable for capital gains tax purposes in the UK. Consequently, the trade and assets of a UK permanent establishment of a non-resident company may be covered by these provisions.

1168 s 138 TCGA 1992 The provisions for transfer of a trade are linked to those for share exchanges for individuals (¶5854), as typically the transfer of a trade will be coupled with an issue of shares to the shareholders in the company. As such, the clearance provisions can apply to those circumstances.

1170 s 136 TCGA 1992 Strictly, the acquiring company should carry on substantially the same business and have substantially the same members as the disposing company. In practice, the requirement for **mirrored shareholdings** is waived where the transfer is for bona fide commercial reasons, or where there is a separation of trades or business into identifiable parts.

EXAMPLE A Ltd is owned equally by two family groups, the B family and the C family, and carries on two trades. Following a disagreement over the future of one of the trades, it is agreed to undertake a scheme of reconstruction, under which:
- a new company, D Ltd, is created;

– shares in D Ltd are issued to members of the C family, whose A Ltd shares are cancelled; and
– one of the trades is hived off to D Ltd.
Although the members of A Ltd and D Ltd are not the same, HMRC would be likely to consider this to be a no gain/no loss scheme of reconstruction.

MEMO POINTS 1. These provisions do not apply to any **preliminary reorganisation** of share capital prior to a reconstruction.
2. A no gain/no loss transfer must not be confused with a **disposal giving rise to neither a gain nor a loss** (for example the deemed disposal on March 1982 rebasing). In a disposal giving rise to neither a gain nor a loss, the transferor's allowable expenditure is deemed to be that which results in neither a gain nor a loss. The transferee is therefore not affected and the acquisition cost is the actual consideration.

Transfer of UK trade

The transfer of a UK trade (i.e. a trade carried on by a UK permanent establishment owned by an EU company) **to another EU resident company** will be treated as a no gain/no loss disposal providing the assets so transferred remain within the charge to UK corporation tax and: **1171** s 140A TCGA 1992
– the consideration for the transfer is wholly in the form of shares (or other securities) issued by the transferee company;
– the two companies concerned are resident in different member states;
– the transaction is carried out for bona fide commercial reasons, and the avoidance of tax is not the main purpose of the transaction; and
– both companies concerned make a claim for the relief.

MEMO POINTS 1. The **shares** acquired by the transferor company will be treated as being acquired at their market value at the time of the transaction.
2. Where this relief is claimed, no balancing allowance or charge is deemed to accrue for **capital allowance** purposes.

The transfer of a UK trade (i.e. a trade carried on by a UK permanent establishment owned by an EU company) **to a UK company** will be treated as a no gain/no loss disposal providing the assets transferred are chargeable assets both before and after the transfer. **1173** s 171 TCGA 1992

B. Appropriations to or from trading stock

General rule

Where an **asset is transferred between members of a 75% CG group** of companies (¶1524) and one of the companies holds the asset as stock and the other company as a fixed asset, the asset is always transferred as a fixed asset. **1175**

Asset held as fixed asset

Where the **transferor holds** the asset as a fixed asset (and the transferee will hold it as stock), the transferee acquires a fixed asset, as part of a no gain/no loss transfer, and then appropriates the asset to stock, giving rise to a disposal at market value. The transferee may make an election to treat the resulting gain or loss as an income transaction in the normal way (¶90). **1176** s 173(1) TCGA 1992

EXAMPLE A Ltd holds a plot of development land with a view to building a new office block, purchased for £50,000 and currently valued at £125,000. Following a slump in the office market, it transfers the land to its 80% subsidiary, B Ltd, a land dealing company, with a view to selling the land.
The land will be transferred from A Ltd to B Ltd as a fixed asset, at the no gain/no loss price (i.e. £50,000 plus indexation of, say, £5,000).

B Ltd will then appropriate the asset to stock at market value (£125,000), realising an indexed gain of £70,000.
If B Ltd makes the appropriate election, the gain will not be charged and the stock will be included at £55,000 (i.e. market value of the stock, as reduced by the amount of the gain (£125,000- £70,000)).

Asset held as stock

1178 s 173(2) TCGA 1992

Where the **transferor holds** the asset as stock (and the transferee will hold it as a fixed asset), the transferor is deemed to appropriate it to fixed assets immediately before the transfer. The market value of the asset is therefore included as a trading receipt. The transfer takes place at no gain/no loss, and the transferee acquires a fixed asset, with an allowable cost equal to the market value on the date of transfer.

EXAMPLE A Ltd holds a piece of land as trading stock. The land cost £200,000 and now has a market value of £300,000. It is decided to redevelop the land as the group's new headquarters building. The land is therefore transferred to B Ltd, the group holding company.
A Ltd is deemed to appropriate the asset to fixed assets immediately before the transfer and must therefore bring into its trading account a disposal at market value. The asset is then transferred at this market value to B Ltd and the allowable cost for B Ltd in relation to a subsequent disposal of the land will be £300,000.

C. Change of residence

Definition

1180 s 185 TCGA 1992

There is a deemed change of residence when:
a. a company:
– **ceases to be resident** in the UK (Where the company continues to carry on a trade in the UK via a permanent establishment, the assets which are used for the purposes of the permanent establishment will not be chargeable.); or
– trading in the UK through a permanent establishment **ceases to trade**. (Note there will be no deemed disposal in this case if the trade is transferred to another company as part of a scheme of reconstruction (¶1166)); or
b. a chargeable asset becomes **located outside the UK** (for example, where a UK permanent establishment transfers an asset offshore).
As a result of a residence change, a chargeable gain may arise. The **gain is calculated** by assuming a deemed disposal of all the chargeable assets held at the relevant date and an immediate reacquisition at market value.

ss 185(3), 187 TCGA 1992

MEMO POINTS 1. A company cannot make a claim to **roll over the gain on a business asset** (¶6050) into the acquisition of an asset which occurs after the cessation of residence, unless the new assets are purchased for use in a trade carried on in the UK via a permanent establishment.
2. If a gain accrues to a company that is a 75% subsidiary of a UK resident company, it is possible to make an election to **postpone this gain**. The gain will, however, become chargeable if:
– within 6 years of its departure, the company that left the UK disposes of the assets;
– the subsidiary ceases to be a 75% subsidiary of the principal company; or
– the principal company changes its residence.

Transfer of non-UK trade

1181 s 140C TCGA 1992

Where a UK resident company transfers a trade (carried on through an EU permanent establishment) **to another EU resident company**, EU regulations prohibit the member state where the trade is carried on from charging any capital gains tax.

However, in the UK the transfer will be treated as a chargeable event and taxed accordingly, but credit will be given, in the form of **double tax relief** (¶2173), for the deemed local member state tax that would have been charged had the EU regulations not prohibited it.

A claim can only be made for double tax relief by the UK resident company if:
- all the assets of the trade are transferred; and
- the transaction was carried out for bona fide commercial reasons (i.e. the avoidance of tax was not the main purpose of the transaction).

However, a claim can be made to **defer** the tax on the transfer, if the following conditions are met: **1183** s 140 TCGA 1992
- all the assets of the trade are transferred;
- the consideration for the transfer is wholly in the form of shares (or other securities) issued by the transferee company. (If the consideration is only partly in the form of shares or securities, the amount of corporation tax on the chargeable gain that can be deferred is proportionately reduced); and
- as a result of the share issue, the UK company holds at least 25% of the ordinary issued share capital of the overseas company.

The **deferred gain is brought back into charge** on a disposal either by the:
- UK company of any of the shares in the overseas company (pro-rated if only part are so disposed); or
- overseas company of any of the assets transferred within 6 years of the transfer (pro-rated if only part are so disposed).

MEMO POINTS A **claim under this provision cannot be made** if a claim has been made for relief on the transfer of a trade to an EU company (¶1171).

D. Liquidation

When a company enters into liquidation it is, for chargeable gains purposes, a non-event. **1185**

Although the assets become vested in the liquidator, there is no chargeable disposal. The actions of the liquidator are deemed to be actions of the company, and any disposals during the liquidation are therefore taxed in accordance with the normal rules.

If a company receives a **distribution** during the course of a liquidation from a company in which it holds shares, the distribution is always treated as capital and therefore a part disposal of the underlying shares. This includes both cash distributions and the distribution of assets in specie.

The distribution is treated in the same way as a sale of rights nil paid (¶5821), so that the general part disposal rules will apply using the following formula:

$$\frac{\text{Amount of capital distribution}}{\text{Amount of capital distribution + market value of remaining holding}} \times \text{acquisition cost}$$

If the cash element is small, relief for small capital receipts will apply where relevant (¶5830).

MEMO POINTS 1. Where the company is a member of a 75% CG **group of companies** (¶1524), the liquidation does not affect that position and therefore assets continue to be eligible for transfer between members of the group on a no gain/no loss basis.
2. When a company enters liquidation, this will bring its accounting period to an end. **Capital losses** from the pre-liquidation period can still be carried forward and offset against chargeable gains accruing in the liquidation period.

E. Disposals of assets with heldover gains

In some cases a company may receive, and then dispose of, an asset where a gain has been subject to gift relief (¶6095) or rollover relief (¶6050). **1186**

The heldover or rolled over gain will be **reduced by half** where the:
- original asset was disposed of before 31 March 1982; and
- replacement asset was acquired between 1 April 1982 and 5 April 1988 and disposed of after 6 April 1988.

For this relief to apply, a claim must be made 2 years after the end of the accounting period in which the final disposal occurred.

MEMO POINTS 1. If **holdover relief was originally claimed**, but before the charge was triggered, the claim was withdrawn and the gain rolled over into a replacement asset (acquired after 18 March 1991), then the 50% reduction is only available if it would have been available on the original asset into which the gain was heldover.
2. Rebasing is where assets held before 31 March 1982 are treated as if they were sold and immediately reacquired on that date, so that the element of the gain arising before 31 March 1982 is not generally charged to tax. For details see ¶1133.

SECTION 6

Shares and securities

A. Overview

1188 Shares and securities are subject to a number of special rules due to the very nature of the assets.

For companies only, certain disposals of shares are exempt from tax. Shares that do not fall within this exemption are chargeable disposals.

MEMO POINTS The word **securities** encompasses, for example, shares and debentures. Securities which are also qualifying corporate bonds (¶5234) do not give rise to a chargeable gain, and are subject to the loan relationship regime (¶870). Throughout this section, the word **share** will be used to refer to shares and securities, other than qualifying corporate bonds.

B. Exempt disposals

Disposal of substantial shareholding

1190 Sch 7AC TCGA 1992 A substantial shareholding is **defined as** a holding of not less than 10% of the ordinary share capital of a company, which carries an entitlement to not less than 10% of the:
- profits available for distribution; and
- assets on a winding up.

MEMO POINTS In looking at the level of shareholding, other group company (¶1524) holdings can be aggregated. In looking at group companies for this purpose the percentage is reduced from 75% to 51%. The companies may also be located anywhere in the world.

1191 A gain on a disposal of such a shareholding by a company is exempt (and a loss is not allowable) if the **following conditions** are satisfied at the time of disposal, or would have been satisfied had the disposal taken place up to 2 years earlier (the "2 year look back" exemption):

a. the investing company holds a substantial shareholding in the company whose shares are disposed of (the "target" company), both at the time of disposal and for a continuous 12 month period beginning not more than 2 years prior to the disposal; and

b. throughout the 12 month period (and immediately after the date of disposal), the investing company and the target company were carrying on qualifying trading activities either as:
- stand-alone companies; or
- members of a 51% group (¶1520).

If the investing company cannot satisfy the above requirements but another **group member** can, then the disposal will be treated as if made by the other group company and will therefore qualify for exemption.

EXAMPLE A Ltd held a 14% shareholding in B Ltd from 1 January 2009 until 1 May 2010, when the holding was sold. A Ltd then reacquired a 6% shareholding in B Ltd on 1 September 2010 which it sold on 1 April 2011.
The sale on 1 May 2010 will be an exempt disposal as a 10% holding has been held for a continuous 12 month period.
The sale on 1 April 2011 will also qualify as an exempt disposal as a 10% holding has been held for a continuous 12 month period in the 2 years prior to disposal.

MEMO POINTS 1. The **2 year look back exemption is not available** if the investing company was not a trading company after the disposal, unless the reason it was not a trading company after the disposal was that it was being, or was about to be, wound up.
2. If the **target company was not trading** immediately after the date of disposal, the 2 year look back exemption is only available if at some time during the 2 year period the target company was controlled by the:
- investing company (plus any connected persons); or
- a group company of the investing company.
3. Where the investing company had acquired the shares by means of a **no gain/no loss transfer** (¶1600), its period of ownership is treated as including that of the transferor company. If during the transferor company's period of ownership there is a degrouping charge (¶1606), any period of ownership prior to the degrouping charge is ignored.

A company or group will be said to be carrying on **qualifying trading activities** if the activities substantially relate to carrying on, preparing to carry on or acquiring a trade or a 51% interest in a trading company/group. Intra-group activities are ignored when deciding if a company is trading for the purpose of these provisions. 1193

Disposal of assets relating to shares

A gain on a disposal of assets relating to shares (i.e. options over shares, or a security with rights to convert into or acquire shares) by a company is also exempt (and a loss is not allowable) if the **following conditions** are satisfied: 1195
- immediately before the disposal of the assets relating to shares the investing company held shares in the target company which, if sold, would qualify as an exempt disposal of a substantial shareholding; or
- a 51% group company (¶1520) held such shares.

Interaction with other reliefs

The substantial shareholding exemption is ignored for the purposes of determining whether an asset is a chargeable asset for the purposes of any other reliefs etc. In particular: 1196
- on an **appropriation to trading stock** there is normally a deemed disposal and reacquisition of the assets concerned at market value (¶1176). An appropriation of assets that would qualify as exempt under these provisions is still an exempt disposal and the acquisition cost of the assets concerned on an appropriation will be market value;
- a **negligible value claim** cannot be backdated (¶6025) for claims made where the substantial shareholding exemption applies; and
- **heldover gains** (e.g. gift relief etc) do not fall within this exemption. On a disposal of exempt assets any gains heldover will be charged to capital gains tax.

C. Chargeable disposals

1. When is a disposal chargeable?

1198 Disposals of shares that do not fall within the substantial shareholding exemption will be chargeable disposals subject to specific rules.

2. Identification rules

1200 Where a company acquires a single holding of shares on one day which is subsequently sold in its entirety, it is easy to see which shares have been sold.

However, where a holding of shares has been built up over time, and has been subject to a number of acquisitions and disposals, identification rules are used to match a disposal with various acquisitions.

To identify shares, they are split into **three main groups**:
– shares acquired on or after 1 April 1982 (the section 104 holding (¶1203));
– shares acquired on or after 6 April 1965 and on or before 31 March 1982 (the 1982 pool (¶1208)); and
– shares acquired on or before 5 April 1965 (known as 1965 shares (¶1210)).

1201 On a disposal, **shares are matched** in the following order:
s 107 TCGA 1992
– shares acquired on the same day as the disposal;
– shares acquired in the 9 days prior to the date of disposal;
– shares forming part of the section 104 holding;
– shares from the 1982 pool;
– 1965 shares on a last in first out (LIFO) basis; and
– shares acquired after the disposal on a first in first out (FIFO) basis.

MEMO POINTS 1. No indexation is available for disposals of shares acquired within the **9 days prior to the date of sale**, although the date of acquisition and date of disposal may be in different months.
2. A company could make a **pooling election** (¶1213), for shares acquired on or before 5 April 1965. In this case, the pooled shares are included in the 1982 pool.

3. Section 104 pool

1203 Any shares acquired after 31 March 1982 are put in the section 104 pool and thereafter treated as a single asset.

The section 104 pool is treated as coming into existence at 6 April 1985 and all shares acquired before that date are indexed before they are added to the pool. The **addition of shares** after 6 April 1985 is known as an operative event.

Other **operative events** are:
– disposals;
– scrip issues in lieu of dividends; and
– rights issues.

1205 Immediately before each operative event, **indexation** is added to the pool. To calculate the indexation, the total value of the indexed pool of expenditure to date is multiplied by the indexation formula. The indexation formula for these purposes is:

$$\frac{RE - RL}{RL}$$

where:
- RE is the RPI for the month in which the operative event occurs; and
- RL is the RPI for the month of the previous operative event (or, if this is the first operative event, the month in which the pool commenced).

MEMO POINTS 1. For the purposes of the section 104 pool, there is no requirement for the indexation allowance formula to be **rounded to three decimal places**.
2. **Strictly**, each acquisition in the period from 1 April 1982 to 5 April 1985 inclusive should be **indexed separately** to 5 April 1985 and then aggregated on that date. In practice, however, this requirement is overlooked.

On a disposal from the section 104 pool, the acquisition cost is the proportion of the indexed pool of expenditure, based on the number of shares disposed of against the total number of shares in the pool. Where the indexed cost exceeds the disposal proceeds the indexation will be restricted to eliminate the gain as indexation cannot create or augment a loss. **1206**

EXAMPLE A Ltd made the following acquisitions and disposals of ordinary shares in B Ltd, an unquoted company:

Date	Holding	Acquisition cost £
October 1984	1,000	10,000
April 1990	2,000	25,000
June 1992 (disposal)	(500)	
August 1995	3,000	45,000

On 10 February 2007 A Ltd sold 4,000 shares for £100,000. On 29 March 2011 it sold a further 1,000 shares. The resulting chargeable gain/allowable loss will be calculated as follows:

Section 104 pool:

	Holding	Cost £	Indexed cost £
Indexed pool at 6 April 1985[1]	1,000	10,000	10,450
Indexation to Apr 1990			
$\frac{125.1 - 94.78}{94.78} \times 10,450$			3,343
			13,793
Addition Apr 1990	2,000	25,000	25,000
	3,000	35,000	38,793
Indexation to Jun 1992			
$\frac{139.3 - 125.1}{125.1} \times 38,793$			4,403
			43,196
Disposal Jun 1992	(500)		
500/3,000 × 35,000		(5,833)	
500/3,000 × 43,196			(7,199)
	2,500	29,167	35,997
Indexation to Aug 1995			
$\frac{149.9 - 139.3}{139.3} \times 35,997$			2,739
			38,736
Addition Aug 1995	3,000	45,000	45,000
	5,500	74,167	83,736
Indexation to Feb 2007			
$\frac{203.1 - 149.9}{149.9} \times 83,736$			29,718
			113,454
Disposal Feb 2007	(4,000)		
4,000/5,500 × 74,167		(53,940)	
4,000/5,500 × 113,454			(82,512)
Balance of pool c/fwd at Feb 2007	1,500	20,227	30,942

	£
Chargeable gain February 2007:	
Disposal proceeds	100,000
Indexed cost	(82,512)
Gain	17,488

Section 104 pool:

	Holding	Cost	Indexed cost
Balance of pool b/fwd	1,500	20,227	30,942
Indexation to Mar 11 $\frac{232.5-203.1}{203.1} \times 30,942$			4,479
			35,421
Disposal March 2011	(1,000)		
1,000/1,500 x 20,227		(13,485)	
1,000/1,500 x 35,421			(23,641)
	500	6,742	11,807

	£
Chargeable gain March 2011:	
Disposal proceeds	30,000
Indexed cost	(23,614)
Gain	6,386

Note:
1. Pool at 6 April 1985

	£
Cost	10,000
Add: Indexation Oct 1984 to Apr 1985: $\frac{94.78-90.67}{90.67} = 0.045 \times 10,000$	450
Value of pool at 6 April 1985	10,450

4. The 1982 pool

1208 Shares of the same class acquired between 6 April 1965 and 31 March 1982 are placed in the 1982 pool (also known as the frozen 1982 pool). The pool is not indexed but the number of shares at 5 April 1982, the original cost and the March 1982 value should be recorded.

On disposal, the cost and March 1982 value are apportioned between the number of shares in the pool.

EXAMPLE A Ltd made the following acquisitions of ordinary shares in B Ltd, an unquoted company:

Date	Holding	Acquisition cost £
September 1976	1,500	9,000
May 1978	3,000	30,000
June 1980	2,000	25,000

At March 1982 the value per share was £14.

A Ltd sold 2,700 of the shares on 8 May 2010 for £120,000. The resulting chargeable gain/allowable loss is calculated as follows:

1982 pool:	**Holding**	**Cost**	**March 1982 value**
		£	£
Value of pool b/fwd	6,500	64,000	91,000
Disposal	(2,700)		
2,700/6,500 × 64,000		(26,585)	
2,700/6,500 × 91,000			(37,800)
Value of pool c/fwd	3,800	37,415	53,200

Chargeable gain May 2010:	**Cost**	**March 1982 value**
	£	£
Disposal proceeds	120,000	120,000
Less: Cost/March 1982 value	(26,585)	(37,800)
Less: Indexation Mar 1982 to May 2010		
$\frac{223.6 - 79.44}{79.44} = 1.815 \times 37{,}800$	(68,607)	(68,607)
Gain	24,808	13,953
The smaller gain will be taken	13,953	

5. Shares acquired before 6 April 1965

Unquoted shares

Provided **no rebasing election** for March 1982 value (¶1138) has been submitted, unquoted shares acquired before 6 April 1965 are treated as being disposed of on a last in first out (LIFO) basis rather than being pooled. The calculation of the chargeable gain or allowable loss for each separate acquisition is subject to time apportionment (¶1148) in order to ensure that only the post-1965 proportion of the gain is brought into charge. 1210

EXAMPLE A Ltd made the following acquisitions of ordinary shares in B Ltd, an unquoted company:

Date	**Holding**	**Acquisition cost**
		£
1 May 1951	5,000	50,000
1 November 1953	4,000	45,000

The market value at 31 March 1982 was £14 per share.
On 31 December 2010 A Ltd sold 6,000 shares for £300,000. Using the LIFO, method all of the shares acquired on 1 November 1953 and 2,000 of the shares acquired on 1 May 1951 will be treated as disposed of. The resulting chargeable gain/allowable loss is calculated as follows:

1 November 1953 holding:	**Cost**	**March 1982**
	£	£
Disposal proceeds (4,000/6,000 × 300,000)	200,000	200,000
Less: Cost	(45,000)	(56,000)
Less: Indexation Mar 1982 to Dec 2010		
$\frac{228.4 - 79.44}{79.44} = 1.875 \times$ higher of cost/March 1982 value	(105,000)	(105,000)
Gain before time apportionment	50,000	39,000
Time apportionment:		
$\frac{45\ 9/12}{57\ 2/12} \times 50{,}000$	40,014	
Gain (the smaller gain will be taken)	39,000	

1 May 1951 holding;	Cost	March 1982
	£	£
Disposal proceeds (2,000/6,000 × 300,000)	100,000	100,000
Less: Cost	(20,000)	(28,000)
Less: Indexation Mar 1982 to Dec 2010		
$\frac{228.4 - 79.44}{79.44}$ = 1.875 × higher of cost/March 1982 value	(52,500)	(52,500)
Gain before time apportionment	27,500	19,500
Time apportionment:		
$\frac{45\ 9/12}{59\ 8/12}$ × 27,500	21,086	
Gain (the smaller gain will be taken)	19,500	

Sch 2 para 17 TCGA 1992

MEMO POINTS Like other assets acquired before 6 April 1965, an election may be made for the **original cost of unquoted shares to be replaced with the market value** at that date (¶1155).

Quoted shares

1211 Sch 2 para 2 TCGA 1992

Provided **no rebasing election** for March 1982 value (¶1133) has been submitted, three calculations are carried out for quoted shares acquired before 6 April 1965 using:
- actual cost;
- market value at 6 April 1965; and
- market value at 31 March 1982.

Time apportionment (¶1148) does not apply to quoted securities.

Indexation will be based on the higher of cost or March 1982 value.

If all of the calculations give rise to either a gain or a loss then the smallest gain or loss will be the chargeable gain or allowable loss. If one computation gives rise to a gain while the others give rise to a loss or vice versa, the disposal will be deemed to give rise to neither a chargeable gain nor an allowable loss.

Identification of quoted shares acquired before 6 April 1965 is on a LIFO basis.

EXAMPLE A Ltd made the following acquisitions of ordinary shares in B Plc, a quoted company:

Date	Holding	Acquisition cost
		£
1 January 1958	10,000	60,000
1 July 1960	5,000	40,000

The market value at 6 April 1965 was £10 per share and at 31 March 1982 it was £14 per share. On 30 June 2010 A Ltd sold 9,000 shares for £300,000. All of the shares acquired on 1 July 1960 and 4,000 of the shares acquired on 1 January 1958 will be treated as disposed of. The resulting chargeable gain/allowable loss is calculated as follows:

1 July 1960 holding:	Cost	April 1965	March 1982
	£	£	£
Disposal proceeds (5,000/9,000 × 360,000)	200,000	200,000	200,000
Less: Cost/April 1965/March 1982 value	(40,000)	(50,000)	(70,000)
Less: Indexation Mar 1982 to June 2010			
$\frac{224.1 - 79.44}{79.44}$ = 1.821[1]	(127,470)	(127,470)	(127,470)
	32,531	22,530	2,530
Gain (the smallest gain will be taken)			2,530

1 January 1958 holding	Cost	April 1965	March 1982
	£	£	£
Disposal proceeds (4,000/9,000 × 360,000)	160,000	160,000	160,000
Less: Cost (4,000/10,000 × 60,000)	(24,000)		
(April 1965/March 1982 value)		(40,000)	(56,000)
Less: Indexation Mar 1982 to June 2010			
$\frac{224.1 - 79.44}{79.44} = 1.821$ [1]	(101,976)	(101,976)	(101,976)
	34,024	18,024	2,024
Gain (the smaller gain will be taken)			2,024

Note:
1. Indexation is applied to the higher of cost or March 1982 value.

MEMO POINTS Quoted shares are **defined** as those that had a quoted market price on a recognised stock exchange (¶9995) either on 6 April 1965 or at any time in the 6 year period ending on that date.

As an **alternative** to the above treatment, a company may elect to value all disposals of quoted shares acquired before 6 April 1965 at the market value at that date. The election may be made in respect of: **1213** Sch 2 para 4 TCGA 1992
- quoted shares;
- fixed interest securities; or
- preference shares.

The election must be submitted within 2 years of the end of the accounting period in which the first disposal is made. Once made, the election is irrevocable.

The result of the election is that the shares are included in the 1982 pool (¶1208) for calculation purposes.

6. Re-organisations

A company may receive new shares in a method other than purchasing shares on the open market. Typically, this will be by way of a bonus issue, rights issue or scrip issue. In each case the shares may be issued in the same class as those held or in a different class. Some of the rules applying to individuals also apply to companies (¶5803+), but with the added complication of multiple pools and indexation. **1215**

Bonus issue of shares of the same class

Where shares of the same class are issued without any payment from the shareholder, the bonus shares are deemed to have been acquired on the same date as the original holding. **1216** s 127 TCGA 1992

Where the original holding is in the **section 104 pool**, the effect of a bonus issue is to increase the number of shares in the pool. The acquisition does not constitute an operative event (¶1203) for indexation allowance.

Where shares are added to the **1982 pool**, following a bonus issue, it is important to ensure that the March 1982 value is correctly calculated. The share value at March 1982 may be based on either:
- the actual shares in issue on 31 March 1982; or
- the shares as adjusted for the bonus issue.

The value must therefore be applied to the correct number of shares.

EXAMPLE A Ltd made the following acquisitions of ordinary shares in B Ltd, an unquoted company.

Date	Holding	Acquisition cost £
January 1982	2,000	10,000
June 1995	4,000	30,000
October 1998	6,000	60,000

The March 1982 value of the shares was £6 per share (£4 as adjusted for the bonus issue).
In September 1999 B Ltd made a 1 for 2 bonus issue of ordinary shares and in October 2010 A Ltd sold 16,000 shares for £200,000.
The disposal is matched to the acquisitions as follows:

	1982 pool		s104 pool	
	Holding	**£**	**Holding**	**£**
Original	2,000	10,000	10,000	90,000
Bonus 1: 2	1,000		5,000	
	3,000	10,000	15,000	90,000
Disposal	(1,000)	(3,333)	(15,000)	(90,000)
	2,000	6,667	-	-

Section 104 pool:

	Holding	Cost £	Indexed cost £
Jun 1995 purchase	4,000	30,000	30,000
Indexation to Oct 1998 $\frac{164.5 - 149.8}{149.8} \times 30{,}000$			2,943
			32,943
Oct 1998 purchase	6,000	60,000	60,000
	10,000	90,000	92,943
Sept 1999 bonus issue[1]	5,000		
	15,000		
Indexation to Oct 2010 $\frac{225.8 - 164.5}{164.5} \times 92{,}943$			34,635
			127,578
Disposal Oct 2010	(15,000)	(90,000)	(127,578)
	-	-	-

Proceeds (15,000/16,000 x 200,000)	187,500
Indexed cost	(127,578)
Gain	59,922

	Cost £	March 1982 £	
1982 pool: 1,000 shares:			
Disposal proceeds (1,000/16,000 × 200,000)	12,500	12,500	
Less: Cost (1,000/3,000 × 10,000)	(3,333)		
March 1982 value (1,000 × 4)		(4,000)	
Less: Indexation Mar 1982 to Oct 2010 $\frac{225.8 - 79.44}{79.44} = 1.842 \times 4{,}000$	(7,368)	(7,368)	
	1,799	1,132	
Gain (smaller gain taken)			1,132

The total gain on the disposal will be £67,083

Note:
1. As a bonus issue is not an operative event no indexation allowance is added at this point.

Rights issue of shares of the same class

1218 Where a rights issue of the same class of shares as the original holding is taken up, the shares are deemed to have been acquired on the same date as the original holding for matching purposes.

Where the original holding is in the **section 104 pool**, a rights issue is an operative event (¶1203), and will increase the cost as well as the number of shares in the pool. Indexation allowance must be added to the pool, where applicable, before adding the cost of the rights issue.

Where the original holding is in the **1982 pool**, the cost of the rights issue shares is included in the pool value. On a subsequent disposal from the 1982 pool the shares must be separated into two parts for the purposes of calculating indexation allowance, if applicable. Indexation allowance on the rights issue shares will only be available from the date of the issue. Indexation allowance on the original shares in the pool will run from March 1982.

The share value at March 1982 may be based on either:
- the actual shares in issue on 31 March 1982; or
- the shares as adjusted for the rights issue.

MEMO POINTS Where there is a rights issue but a **shareholder does not take up any new shares**, the rights issue is disregarded in calculating his capital gains liability on subsequent disposals. Consequently, where the market value at 6 April 1965 or 31 March 1982 is quoted at an adjusted figure which assumes that shareholders have taken up all rights issues, that quotation does not apply to the shareholder.

SECTION 7

Anti-avoidance

A. Specific provisions

To prevent companies undertaking artificial transactions to avoid tax, the following anti-avoidance provisions apply: 1220
- depreciatory transactions (¶1221);
- dividend stripping (¶1228); and
- manipulation of capital losses (¶1232).

By their very nature, anti-avoidance provisions are complex and only an overview is given here.

MEMO POINTS For details of the **value shifting** anti-avoidance provisions see ¶5650.

B. Depreciatory transactions

The depreciatory transactions provisions apply to transactions within a 75% CG **group of companies** (¶1524). 1221
s 176 TCGA 1992

A depreciatory transaction can be **defined** as a transfer of assets between group members which materially reduces the value of shares or securities in a company, and there is subsequently a sale of those shares (or securities).

EXAMPLE X Ltd owns 100% of the share capital of Y Ltd. The two companies therefore form a group of companies.
A number of investments owned by Y Ltd are transferred to X Ltd for nominal consideration.
This will be a depreciatory transaction if the shares in Y Ltd are subsequently sold.

MEMO POINTS There is no statutory definition of **material reduction** although HMRC take the view that any reduction is material unless it is negligible.

1223 A transaction is **not a depreciatory transaction** where it consists of:
– a payment which is brought into account in computing the chargeable gain arising on the ultimate disposal; or
– a transfer between group members at market value.

1225 The **effect of the provisions** is to reduce the allowable loss accruing on the disposal of the shares on a just and reasonable basis, to the extent that it is attributable to the depreciatory transaction.

EXAMPLE A Ltd owns the entire issued share capital (10,000 Ordinary £1 shares which were subscribed for at par) of B Ltd, which owns a property valued at £275,000.
B Ltd transfers the property to A Ltd for £1,000 and A Ltd then sells the shares in B Ltd for £1,000.
A Ltd would realise a loss on the disposal of B Ltd of £9,000.
However, the transfer of the property out of B Ltd was a depreciatory transaction. The loss would therefore be allowable only so far as it was just and reasonable. In this situation, HMRC would probably argue that no allowable loss arose.

1226
s 176(6) TCGA 1992

Where a company was party to a depreciatory transaction and its **shares are sold within 6 years** of the transaction, any gain arising may be correspondingly reduced, on a just and reasonable basis, to reflect the effect of the depreciatory transaction.

The reduction cannot, however, exceed the amount by which the allowable loss was restricted.

EXAMPLE Continuing the previous example, if the shares in A Ltd were sold within 6 years of the transfer of the property, and the property was still held at that date, any gain arising could be reduced by up to £9,000.

C. Dividend stripping

1228
s 177 TCGA 1992

The depreciatory transaction provisions above are extended to include **distributions** paid between companies where:
– one company owns 10% or more of a class of shares in another company; and
– the distribution materially reduces the value of the shareholding.

MEMO POINTS 1. In deciding whether a company owns **10% or more of a class of shares**, the following rules apply:
– shares held by connected persons (¶5570) must be taken into account;
– shares of different classes are treated as separate holdings; and
– shares of the same class but carrying different rights or entitlements are treated as separate holdings.
2. There is no statutory definition of **material reduction** although HMRC take the view that any reduction is material unless it is negligible.
3. These provisions do not apply where the company receiving the distribution holds the shares in its capacity as a **share dealing company**.

1230 In these circumstances, the **distribution is treated as** a depreciatory transaction in relation to a subsequent disposal of those shares and, for these purposes, the companies are deemed to be members of the same CG group (¶1524).

EXAMPLE A Ltd acquires 12% of the ordinary share capital of B Ltd, and the following week B Ltd pays a distribution equal to the full amount of its distributable reserves. Shortly thereafter, A Ltd sells the shares for significantly less than the acquisition cost.
This will be caught by the dividend stripping provisions and therefore treated as a depreciatory transaction.

1231 In practice, **dividends paid out of post-acquisition profits** are not subject to the dividend stripping provisions, although this is not statutory. However, this reflects the substance of the transaction in that pre-acquisition profits retained by a company are reflected in the acquisition price of the shares. Any reduction in those retained profits therefore reduces the value of the shares. Profits earned post-acquisition are not reflected in the acquisition price of the share.

Where a company has both pre and post-acquisition reserves, any distribution is matched with post-acquisition profits as far as possible.

D. Manipulation of capital losses

The use of existing capital losses is restricted where an arrangement has been entered into by a company to: **1232**
ss 184G - 184I TCGA 1992
- **convert an income profit into a capital gain** (and avoid tax on the gain through the use of capital losses); or
- realise a capital gain, against which it already has losses available to offset, and it (or a connected company) also incurs **expenses which can be deducted** against its trading profits, as opposed to its chargeable gains.

In such situations, HMRC can **issue a notice** to prevent the use of the capital losses. On receipt of the notice a company then has a further 90 days in which to amend its return. **1234**

The following restrictions apply as to **when** a notice can be issued:

a. if a company has already submitted a return, a notice can only be issued if a notice of enquiry has been given to the company within the usual time limits; and

b. if enquiries have already been completed, a notice can only be issued if:
- at the time the enquiries were completed HMRC could not have been reasonably expected to have been aware of the circumstances; or
- information that might have prompted HMRC to issue a notice was requested, but not provided, during an enquiry.

MEMO POINTS 1. The **HMRC notice** must:
- specify the arrangements;
- specify the accounting period in which the relevant gain accrues; and
- inform the company of the effect of the notice.

One notice is sufficient where affected gains arise in more than one accounting period.

2. HMRC can only make a **discovery assessment** after the end of the 90 day period (or the date the company amends its tax return, if earlier).

CHAPTER 7

Computation

OUTLINE

SECTION 1

Basic computation

1250 Once the amount of chargeable income or allowable loss for each source has been calculated for the accounting period, it is necessary to pull all the figures together to arrive at the profit chargeable to corporation tax (PCTCT). This calculation is known as the tax computation.

1252 In the tax computation, all taxable profits are aggregated and any allowable deductions made. Any amounts paid or received under deduction of tax are included in the computation gross. Any non-taxable items, for example dividends from other companies, are left out of the computation. Where a loss has been incurred from a particular source, the profit should be shown as '0' rather than as a negative. The extent to which any available losses may be utilised will depend on the nature of the loss (¶1260).

Once PCTCT has been calculated, the corporation tax liability can be determined. Income tax suffered at source (¶1370) and any double tax relief may reduce this figure to give the net corporation tax payable. The tax computation, including the calculation of the tax liability, will form the main supporting document for the company tax return (¶2240).

MEMO POINTS The **currency** used in a tax computation is generally sterling, although in certain circumstances another currency may be used.

1254 The basic format of the computation is as follows:

	£
Trading income	x
Income from other sources	x
Income received under deduction of tax	x
Chargeable gains	x
	x
Less: charitable donations relief (¶958+)	(x)
Profit chargeable to corporation tax	x
Corporation tax thereon @ x %	x.xx
Less: Income tax suffered at source	(x.xx)
Net corporation tax payable	x.xx

MEMO POINTS In a tax computation, **numbers are generally** rounded to the nearest pound, except for the tax figures below the PCTCT line, for example income tax suffered at source, where figures are always given in pence (i.e. two decimal places).

SECTION 2

Losses

A. Method of relief

1260 The method in which a company obtains relief for any losses it incurs will **depend upon** whether the loss is a trading or capital loss.

The **pro forma computation** at ¶1335 illustrates the order in which the different types of losses are used.

MEMO POINTS For modifications to these rules when applied to **companies with investment business**, see ¶2118.

In general, losses must be claimed and the normal **time limit** for claiming losses is 2 years from the end of the accounting period in which the loss arises. 1262

B. Trading losses

1. Overview

Where a company incurs a loss on its trading activities, the loss may be relieved in one or all of the **following methods**: 1264
- set against general profits of the current period;
- carried back against earlier profits; or
- carried forward against future profits.

The method by which relief may be obtained differs depending upon the source of the loss, as follows:

Source of loss	Relief available			¶¶
	Set against general profits of current year	Carried back	Carried forward	
Trade	y	y	y	¶1270
UK property business	y	n	y	¶1280
Overseas property business	n	n	y	¶1285
Miscellaneous transactions	n	n	y	¶1290
Non-trading loan relationship deficits	y	y	y	¶1295

It is possible to **utilise part** of a loss in one way and the balance another way. However, the relief given cannot exceed the amount of the loss actually incurred. 1266

EXAMPLE A Ltd incurs a loss of £15,000 in respect of trading activities for the period ended 30 October. Assuming A Ltd made a claim to set £5,000 against general profits, the balance of the loss (£10,000) is available for use by carry back and/or carry forward. The maximum total loss which can be claimed in all three ways is the loss incurred i.e. £15,000.

When utilising trading losses, it is important to remember that losses are **used chronologically**. This means that losses are used in the order in which they arise and set against the first available profits, whether being carried forward or back.

MEMO POINTS 1. Where a **trade ceases**, a further form of loss relief, known as terminal loss relief, may be available (¶1330).
2. Companies which are members of a 75% **group** may also be eligible to surrender losses to members of the same group (¶1540).

2. Options for relief

Method of relief

Where a company incurs a trading loss, in an accounting period, the loss may be: 1270
- set against general profits of the current period;
- carried back against earlier profits; or
- carried forward against future profits.

The first two options must be **claimed**, whereas the third is automatic and will apply if no other claim is made.

MEMO POINTS Companies which are members of a 75% **group** may also be eligible to surrender losses to members of the same group (¶1540).

Set against general profits

1273
s 37(3)(a) CTA 2010

A company may make a claim to set a trading loss against general profits of the accounting period in which the loss arises. General profits means profits from any source, including chargeable gains.

Relief is generally only available for losses incurred in trades which are carried out on a commercial basis and with a view to realising a profit. Where trades are considered non-commercial, loss relief may be denied.

EXAMPLE A Ltd incurs a loss of £31,000 in respect of trading activities for the period ended 31 December 2010, and had profits from a UK property business of £15,000 and net loan relationship credits of £3,750 for the same period. The loss which can be offset against current year profits is as follows:

	£
UK property business profits	15,000
Profits from loan relationships	3,750
	18,750
Less: Trading losses of current period	(18,750)
Profit chargeable to corporation tax	Nil
Loss remaining unrelieved (31,000 – 18,750)	12,250

Loss relief must be claimed within the normal **time limit** (¶1262). HMRC have the power to extend this time limit in exceptional circumstances.

Set against profits of earlier periods

1274
s 37(3)(b) CTA 2010

Where a company claims to set a loss against general profits of the accounting period and part of that loss **remains unrelieved**, it may also make a claim to carry back the surplus against general profits of other accounting periods ending within a specified period.

The **specified period** is the 12 months immediately preceding the accounting period in which the loss arose. Losses can only be carried back against profits of accounting periods during which the same trade was being carried on.

EXAMPLE Continuing the previous example, A Ltd had profits chargeable to corporation tax for the 12 month period ended 31 December 2009 of £28,050. If the appropriate claim is made, the balance of the unrelieved loss (£12,250) may be carried back and set against these profits.

MEMO POINTS 1. Losses **can only be carried back** to the extent that they cannot be utilised against profits of the same period.
2. An **extended carry back period** was available for losses incurred in accounting periods ending between 24 November 2008 and 23 November 2010. For further details of this see earlier editions of *Tax Memo*.

1276 Where an accounting period falls **partly within the specified period**, the loss can only be set against profits attributable to the specified period and therefore the profits of such a period must be apportioned on a time basis. Losses cannot be carried back to an accounting period ending before the specified period.

EXAMPLE A Ltd has the following trading results:

12 months to 30 June 2009	Profit £12,000
6 months to 31 December 2009	Profit £28,000
12 months to 31 December 2010	Loss (£35,000)

The company had no profits from any other source.

Assuming the appropriate claims are made, the loss for the period ended 31 December 2010 may be offset as follows:

	£	Loss memo £
Year ended 31/12/10	0	35,000
6 mths ended 31/12/09		
Trading profit	28,000	
Less: Trading losses of subsequent period	(28,000)	(28,000)
	Nil	7,000
Year ended 30/06/09		
Trading profit	12,000	
Less: Trading losses of subsequent period [1]	(6,000)	(6,000)
Assessable profit	6,000	
Unrelieved loss		1,000

Note:
1. As the period ended 30 June 2009 falls only partly within the specified period (1 January 2009 to 31 December 2009), the amount of the loss which can be relieved is £6,000 being the lower of:
– the unrelieved loss (£7,000); and
– the profits of the 6 months falling within the specified period (6/12 × 12,000 = £6,000).
The balance (£1,000) will automatically be carried forward against future trading income.

Loss relief must be claimed within the normal **time limit** (¶1262). HMRC have the power to extend this time limit in exceptional circumstances.

Carry forward against future income

Losses may also be carried forward **indefinitely** and set against the first available future **profit from that trade**. 1278 s 45 CTA 2010

The amount of a loss which may be carried forward in this way is the total loss incurred for any period, less any amounts which have been used for relief in another manner, i.e. against general profits or used for group relief purposes (¶1540).

When the **trade ceases**, relief is lost. It is therefore important to correctly identify the point at which a trade is considered to have ceased.

EXAMPLE A Ltd has the following results:

	Year 1	Year 2	Year 3
Trading result	(27,500)	13,875	19,965
UK property business	1,175	3,250	
Chargeable gain	12,000	3,000	2,250

Assuming a claim is made to offset the loss against general profits of the period, the loss for Year 1 may be offset as follows:

	Year 1	Year 2	Year 3
Trading profit	–	13,875	19,965
Less: Trading losses b/fwd	–	(13,875)	(450)
	–	–	19,515
UK property business	1,175	3,250	–
Chargeable gain	12,000	3,000	2,250
Less: Trading losses of current period	(13,175)	–	–
Profit chargeable to corporation tax	Nil	6,250	21,765

No **claim** is required to utilise losses in this way. Any trading losses that are not otherwise utilised are **automatically carried forward** and set against future trading income.

MEMO POINTS The **definition of trading income** in this case is extended to include income such as interest and dividends which would be trading income if not subject to tax under other provisions. In practice, this extension will only apply to banks and investment dealing companies.

3. UK property business

1280 s 62 CTA 2010 Losses incurred in a UK property rental business (¶780) are **automatically** set against any other chargeable profits or gains in the year they arise. Any excess is carried forward and treated as a loss of the later period so that they can be offset against any income or gains arising. The loss will only cease to be carried forward once it is fully utilised or the trade giving rise to it ceases. HMRC may seek to **deny relief** for losses where the business is not carried out on a commercial basis.

MEMO POINTS Companies which are members of a 75% **group** may also be eligible to surrender losses to members of the same group (¶1540).

1282 There are no rules covering the **interaction of UK property business losses and trading losses** carried forward (¶1278). The order of offset will therefore be decided by the company and based on its individual circumstances.

It should be remembered that trading losses can only be set off against profits of the same trade, whereas UK property business losses can be set against general profits. However, losses from either source can only be utilised whilst the same business is being carried on. Therefore, if there is a proposal to cease the property business, it may be beneficial to utilise any property business losses in priority to trading losses.

4. Overseas property business

1285 s 66 CTA 2010 Losses from an **overseas property business** may only be carried forward and set against future profits of the overseas property business.

Similarly, losses from **overseas trades** can only be carried forward and set against future profits of the same trade.

Relief is not available for losses arising on **other overseas sources**.

5. Losses from miscellaneous transactions

1290 s 91 CTA 2010 Losses arising from transactions which would (if profitable) be subject to tax as miscellaneous income, are set against any income in the same or subsequent accounting periods that would also be chargeable to tax the same provisions.

Losses must be set against the first arising profits. No claims are required in this respect.

6. Non-trading loan relationship deficits

1295 ss 457 – 459 CTA 2009 Where a company incurs a net deficit on non-trading loan relationships (¶870), in an accounting period, the loss can either be:
- set against general profits of the deficit period;
- carried back against earlier loan relationship and derivative contract profits; or
- carried forward against non-trading profits for succeeding accounting periods.

The first two options must be **claimed**, whereas the third is automatic and will apply if no other claim is made.

Part of a deficit may be used in one way and the balance another way, although the total relief given cannot exceed the amount of the actual deficit.

MEMO POINTS 1. Claims to utilise the deficit must be made within the normal **time limit** (¶1262). The claim must specify the amount of the deficit to be utilised, which may be any amount up to the amount of the deficit not otherwise relieved (i.e. set off against general income or by carry forward).
2. Companies which are members of a 75% **group** may also be eligible to surrender deficits to members of the same group (¶1546).

Where a claim is made to **carry back** the deficit it can only be set against loan relationship and derivative contract profits of accounting periods ending within the specified period (¶1274). The profits against which relief is given are the profits after deducting: **1296**
- brought forward loan relationship deficits;
- trade charges of the same accounting period;
- trading losses of the same or subsequent accounting periods; and
- for companies with investment business, capital allowances, management expenses and business charges.

Unlike trading losses, there is no requirement to set the deficit against current year general profits in priority to carrying it back.

In the absence of a claim to relieve the deficit in any of the above ways, the net deficit will be **carried forward** and treated as a deficit of the subsequent accounting period but it is not aggregated with any other debits or credits of that period. It can then only be relieved if a claim is made to set it against non-trading profits of that accounting period. **1298**

A company may claim to utilise a specified amount of the deficit carried forward against non-trading profits of the following period. This claim must be made within the usual time limits (¶1262). Where a company wishes to preserve entitlement to double tax relief, for example, it may be beneficial to make this claim, thus leaving further profits in charge to tax.

C. Capital losses

Where a company has incurred capital losses in an accounting period, the losses are automatically set against chargeable gains of the same period. Any excess is then **carried forward** and set against future chargeable gains. No claims are required in this respect. However, any losses arising during an accounting period must be reported to HMRC on the appropriate corporation tax return before any relief can be given. **1310** s 8 TCGA 1992

MEMO POINTS 1. For details as to when an allowable **loss arises** see ¶5452 onwards.
2. For **restrictions on the utilisation of capital losses** see ¶1232.
3. For details of capital losses in a group situation see ¶1620.

D. Losses following a merger of trades

If there has been a transfer of trade (¶252) between two companies in common ownership, losses brought forward from the trade transferred can be carried forward and set against future profits of the trade transferred. **1312** ss 938 - 943 CTA 2010

Losses of the trade transferred arising in subsequent periods cannot be carried back to a period before the transfer of the trade.

E. Losses following a change of ownership

1. Restriction of relief

1314 ss 673 - 675 CTA 2010 Special rules apply to restrict the offset of losses where:
- there has been (in any order) both a **major change** in the nature or conduct of a trade and a change of ownership within a 3 year period; or
- the scale of a company's activities has become **small or negligible** and subsequently, following a change of ownership, there is a considerable revival of the trade.

1316 Where these provisions apply, the accounting period in which the change in ownership occurs is deemed to be **split into two notional periods** at the date of the change. Profits and losses are apportioned between the two notional periods on a just and reasonable basis. In practice, time apportionment will apply unless another method is considered more appropriate.

Losses arising before the change of ownership (including non-trading loan relationship deficits) cannot be carried forward against profits after that date. Similarly, trading **losses arising after the change** of ownership cannot be carried back to a period before that date. There is no facility to carry back UK property business losses at any time.

MEMO POINTS When computing a **balancing charge** that is triggered after a change in ownership, any capital allowances made before the change that could not be relieved against profits before the change are ignored.

2. Change in ownership

1318 A change in ownership of a company **occurs if** either:
- a single person acquires a holding of more than half the ordinary share capital (¶1508);
- two or more persons each acquire a holding of at least 5% and jointly more than half of the ordinary share capital; or
- two or more persons each increase their holdings such that they each hold at least 5% and jointly more than half of the ordinary share capital.

MEMO POINTS 1. When considering the **change in holdings**, any two points in time within a 3 year period may be considered.
2. HMRC may consider that the ordinary share capital test is not appropriate where persons have **extraordinary rights**. In this situation, an alternative basis for quantifying ownership may be proposed.
3. When considering a person's holding, shares held and acquisitions by **connected persons** (¶5570) are also taken into account.
4. Where an individual acquires shares through an unsolicited **bequest or gift**, such an acquisition may be ignored.

1320 There is **no change in ownership** of a company where it remains a 75% subsidiary (¶1522) of one company, regardless of changes to intermediate direct shareholdings. This is to allow the situation where a company is a member of a group and its direct ownership is passed between members of the group whilst still being a subsidiary of the ultimate group holding company.

3. Major change in nature or conduct of a trade

Statutory definition

1322 s 674(4) CTA 2010 The legislation includes a **list of factors** which may be relevant when considering whether a major change has occurred. This includes the following:
- the type of property dealt in;

– the services or facilities provided; and
– the customers, outlets and markets.

Revenue guidance

To clarify the position, HMRC have published guidance on what they consider to be a major change and provide a number of examples to illustrate their view. In general, changes resulting from technological advances, efficiency measures or product rationalisation will not be considered a major change, although each case will be considered on its own facts. 1324 SP 10/91

The following **would not constitute a major change**:
– moving production from a number of outdated factories to a single modern production plant;
– replacing a product component with a different material without changing the overall nature of the product;
– changing the brand of product which is dealt with but not the actual product type; or
– withdrawing an unprofitable product line and increasing production of another existing and similar product.

The following **would constitute a major change**: 1326
– ceasing to deal in one product and beginning to deal in a product with a totally different use;
– changing from being a service company to a production company; or
– changing from investments in stocks and shares to investment in property.

F. Losses on cessation of trade

The rules for **carrying back losses** against general profits of an earlier period are modified in relation to losses incurred during the 12 months immediately before a company ceases to trade. In this case, the **specified period** (¶1274) is extended to 36 months. 1330 s 39 CTA 2010

EXAMPLE A Ltd prepares its accounts annually to 30 June and ceased to trade on 30 June 2010. The specified period is the 36 months from 1 July 2006 to 30 June 2009.

MEMO POINTS For cessations of trade occurring on or after 21 May 2009 the terminal loss rules extending the period of carry back **will not apply** where: s 41 CTA 2010
– upon the cessation of trade someone not in the charge to corporation tax begins to undertake any of the activities previously carried on; and,
– the cessation of trade was designed as part of a scheme to secure the terminal loss relief.

The accounting period in which a company ceases to trade is often shorter than 12 months. A proportion of any losses incurred in the penultimate accounting period are therefore eligible for this enhanced relief, and the loss must be apportioned on a time basis to establish the losses of the last 12 months. When apportioning a loss to determine the amount which can form part of the terminal loss, the total loss for the accounting period is used. However, relief will be restricted where the loss has been utilised against general profits of the same or the previous periods. Relief can never be given for losses in excess of those actually incurred. 1332

Where an accounting **period falls partly within the specified period**, the loss can only be set against profits attributable to the specified period, and therefore the profits of such a period must also be apportioned on a time basis.

Terminal loss relief must be claimed within the normal **time limit** (¶1262). HMRC have the power to extend this time limit in exceptional circumstances. 1333

G. Interaction of loss reliefs

1335 The following pro forma computation illustrates the order in which the various loss reliefs operate.

		£	£	£
Trading profits			x	
Less: Trade losses b/fwd	¶1278		(x)	
				x
Non-trade credits[1]		x		
Less: Loan relationship deficits of subsequent period	¶1296	(x)		
			x	
Overseas property business		x		
Less: Overseas property business losses b/fwd	¶1285	(x)		
			x	
Profits from miscellaneous transactions		x		
Less: Losses arising from miscellaneous transactions b/fwd	¶1290	(x)		
			x	
UK property business profits			x	
Chargeable gains		x		
Less: Capital losses b/fwd	¶1310	(x)		
			x	
Non-trading income			x	
Less: Loan relationship deficits b/fwd[2]	¶1298		(x)	
				x
				x
Less:				
Non-trading loan relationship deficits of current period	¶1295			(x)
UK property business loss – current period and brought forward	¶1280			(x)
Trading losses of current period	¶1273			(x)
Trading losses of subsequent periods carried back	¶1274			(x)
Payments in the period qualifying for charitable donations relief	¶958			(x)
Profit chargeable to corporation tax				x

Note:
1. As restricted (¶1296) and net of deficits brought forward for which no specific claim has been made (¶1298).
2. Deficits set against non-trading income of the subsequent period.

SECTION 3

Calculation of the corporation tax liability

A. Tax rates and thresholds

1340 Corporation tax is chargeable on a company's profits for an accounting period. Having calculated the profit chargeable to corporation tax (PCTCT), the next step is to determine the corporation tax liability by reference to the current tax rates and thresholds.

MEMO POINTS This figure may be **further reduced by** double tax relief (¶2173), ACT (¶1400) or income tax (¶1370) to arrive at the mainstream corporation tax liability. For the rules governing the payment of corporation tax, see ¶2259.

The rates of corporation tax are set annually and **apply for** financial years. A financial year (FY) runs from 1 April through to 31 March and is denoted by the year in which it starts, for example, FY11 runs from 1 April 2011 to 31 March 2012. **1342**

There are two rates of corporation tax for FY11, each of which applies to a specific band of profits as follows:

Tax rate	PCTCT	CT rate
Small profits rate	£0 – £300,000	20%
Main rate	Over £1,500,000	26%

Special rules apply where:
- PCTCT falls between these bands (¶1350); and
- a company has one or more associated companies (¶1360).

MEMO POINTS 1. For details of rates applicable to **earlier financial years** see ¶9962.
2. **Close investment holding companies** (¶2117) and non-resident companies trading in the UK through a **permanent establishment** pay tax at the main rate regardless of the level of their profits.
3. A club that is registered as a **community amateur sports club** will be exempt from corporation tax on interest, income received under the gift aid scheme, trading income (up to £30,000), property income (up to £20,000), and capital gains on disposal of assets. ss 658 - 671 CTA 2010

B. Calculating the tax

1. Basic calculation

Accounting period coinciding with financial year

Where the company's **accounting period coincides with the FY** (i.e. runs from 1 April through to 31 March) and PCTCT falls within one of the bands above, corporation tax is calculated simply by multiplying the PCTCT by the appropriate rate of tax. **1344**

EXAMPLE A Ltd has PCTCT of £59,000 for the year to 31 March 2011. This falls within the small profits rate band and the corporation tax due is therefore £11,800 (£59,000 × 20%).

Accounting period straddling two financial years

Where the accounting period straddles two FYs and there is **no change in the rate of tax**, there is no requirement to apportion the profit between the FYs. **1346**

However, where the accounting period straddles two FYs and there is a **change in the rate of tax**, it is necessary to apportion the profit and apply the rates for each FY separately. The apportionment should be made on a daily basis and reflect the number of days falling into each FY.

EXAMPLE A Ltd has PCTCT of £1,575,000 for the year to 31 December and is therefore subject to tax at the main rate. Assuming a main rate of 28% for the first FY and 26% for the subsequent FY, corporation tax is due as follows:

		£
First FY:		
90/365 × 1,575,000 =	388,356 @ 28%	108,739.68
Subsequent FY:		
275/365 × 1,575,000 =	1,186,644 @ 26%	308,527.44
Total corporation tax due		417,267.12

Accounting period of less than 12 months

1348 Where the accounting period is less than 12 months, the profit thresholds must be correspondingly reduced to determine the rate of tax payable. In addition, any apportionment between FYs should reflect the overall length of the accounting period.

EXAMPLE A Ltd has PCTCT of £150,000 for the 9 months to 30 September. Tax will be due at the small profits rate, as profits do not exceed £224,384 (273/365 × 300,000). Assuming a rate of 21% for the first FY and 20% for the second FY, corporation tax is due as follows:

		£
First FY:		
90/273 × 150,000 =	49,451 @ 21%	10,384.71
Subsequent FY:		
183/273 × 150,000 =	100,549 @ 20%	20,109.80
Total corporation tax due		30,494.51

2. Marginal relief

General rule

1350 s 19 CTA 2010 Where PCTCT falls in the margin between the taxable profit bands (¶1342), marginal relief may be claimed. Marginal relief **aims to** smooth the transition from one rate to another and the effect is to charge any profits falling into the margin at a slightly higher rate. For FY11, the effective rate on profits in the margin between the small profits and the main rate is 27.5%.

Where marginal relief applies, corporation tax is calculated using the rate for the higher profit band. For example, if a company had PCTCT of £320,000, the tax would be calculated using the main rate. Marginal relief, calculated using the following formula, is then deducted from the calculated tax:

$$(U - P) \times \frac{I}{P} \times F$$

where:
- I is PCTCT;
- F is the prescribed fraction (3/200);
- U is the upper limit of the margin (£1,500,000); and
- P is notional profit (i.e. PCTCT together with any franked investment income (¶954) received during the period, other than receipts from 51% subsidiaries. Franked investment income consists of qualifying distributions received by the company together with the appropriate tax credit at 1/9).

EXAMPLE A Ltd has PCTCT of £425,000 for the year to 31 March 2011 and received franked investment income of £20,000 (a dividend of £18,000 plus the credit). With a main rate of 28% for FY10 and a fraction of 7/400, corporation tax is due as follows:

		£
Tax at main rate	425,000 @ 28%	119,000.00
Less: Marginal relief	(1,500,000 – 445,000) × 425,000/ 445,000 × 7/400	(17,632.72)
Total corporation tax due		101,367.28

1352 The operation of both the small profits rate and marginal relief is automatic, no claim being required to be made.

Accounting period straddling two financial years

1354 Where the company's accounting period straddles two FYs, it is necessary to calculate the marginal relief separately for each FY if there has been a change in the fraction and/or the thresholds.

EXAMPLE A Ltd has PCTCT of £360,000 for the year to 31 December. Assuming a main tax rate of 30% for FY 1 and FY 2, but a marginal relief fraction of 1/40 for FY 1 and 7/400 for FY 2 (due to a change in the lower rate), corporation tax is due as follows:

		£	£	£
First FY:				
Profit	90/365 × 360,000	88,767		
Upper limit of margin	90/365 × 1,500,000	369,863		
Tax at 30%	88,767 @ 30%		26,630.10	
Less: Marginal relief	369,863 – 88,767 × 1/40		(7,027.40)	
				19,602.70
Second FY:				
Profit	275/365 × 360,000	271,232		
Upper limit of margin	275/365 × 1,500,000	1,130,137		
Tax at 30%	271,232 @ 30%		81,369.60	
Less: Marginal relief	1,130,137 – 271,232 × 7/400		(15,030.84)	
				66,338.76
Total corporation tax due				85,941.46

Accounting period of less than 12 months

Where the accounting period is less than 12 months, the profit thresholds must be correspondingly reduced when calculating the marginal relief due. In addition, any apportionment between FYs should reflect the overall length of the accounting period. 1356

EXAMPLE A Ltd has PCTCT of £325,000 for the 8 months to 30 November 200x. With a main rate of 28% for FY0x and a fraction of 7/400 corporation tax is due as follows:

		£	£
Profit		325,000	
Upper limit of margin	244/365 × 1,500,000	1,002,740	
Tax at 28%	325,000 @ 28%		91,000.00
Less: Marginal relief	1,002,740 – 325,000 × 7/400		(11,860.45)
Total corporation tax due			79,139.55

3. Associated companies

General rule

To prevent profitable companies from splitting into several smaller companies to take advantage of the lower tax rates, special rules apply where a company has one or more associated companies resident in the UK or overseas. 1360 s 25 CTA 2010

These rules **ensure that** the bands for determining the rate of tax are divided equally between all the associated companies. Therefore if a company is associated with three other companies, the bands are divided by four (three plus the company itself) to determine the rate applicable.

EXAMPLE A Ltd has PCTCT of £520,000 for the year to 31 March 2011. It has two associated companies. The thresholds must be divided by three (i.e. 2 + 1) to determine the rate, as follows:

	PCTCT	Threshold ÷ 3
Small profits rate: 21%	£0 – £300,000	£0 – £100,000
Main rate: 28%	Over £1,500,000	Over £500,000

A Ltd's profits are therefore taxable at the main rate.

1364 A company is associated with another company if **one controls the other**, or both are controlled by a third party.

It is usually fairly obvious if two companies are under the control of the same (singular) person. However the position can become complicated when determining whether a **group of persons** controls two companies. HMRC treat a group of persons as controlling two companies if the same irreducible group of persons controls each company.

An irreducible group is any number of persons who together have control but who, if any one of those persons were removed, would no longer have control.

EXAMPLE Mr A, Mr B and Mr C each own 33% of A Ltd. Mr D holds the remaining 1%. In determining control, there are 3 irreducible groups:
- Mr A and Mr B;
- Mr A and Mr C; and
- Mr B and Mr C.

Companies are only under common control if the same irreducible group controls both companies.

EXAMPLE Mr A and Mr B control 2 companies as follows:

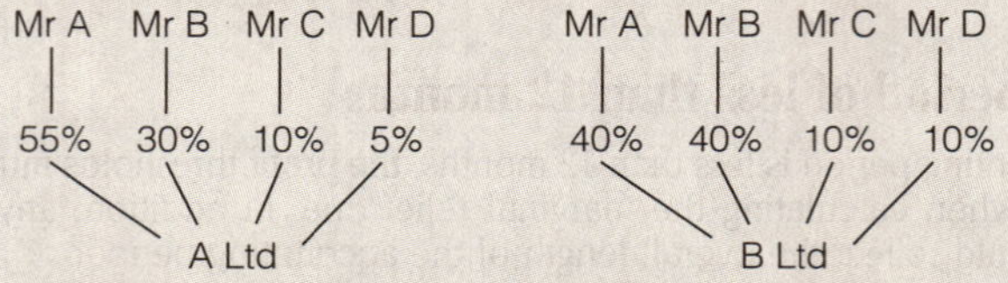

Mr A can control A Ltd on his own and is therefore an irreducible group. Mr A can only control B Ltd as part of an irreducible group with Mr B. As no single irreducible group can control both companies, the companies are not associated.

MEMO POINTS **Inactive companies** (i.e. companies that have not carried on any trade or business throughout the accounting period) are specifically excluded from the definition of an associated company. This includes dormant companies, and holding companies that receive no income other than dividends which are paid out to the shareholders and own no assets other than shares in its 51% subsidiaries (¶1520).

Control and associates

1366 s 27 CTA2010 The definition of control is given at ¶1902. However, in certain circumstances the rights that have to be attributed under these rules to an individual will be restricted for the purposes of ascertaining the existence, and number of, associated companies. Where two companies have **no substantial commercial interdependence** then they will not be connected by virtue of the rights of associates of the individual.

EXAMPLE Mr A owns all of the shares in X Limited. Mrs A, his wife, owns the entire shareholding of Z Limited. Provided they have no substantial commercial interdependence then they will not be treated as associated.

If there is **evidence of substantial commercial independence** then the rights of associates will be attributed in looking at the number of associated companies.

EXAMPLE If in the previous example the two companies were interdependent then in looking at X Limited, Mr A would have been deemed to have controlled Y Limited by virtue of the holding of an associate (his wife), and as such the two would have been associated.

MEMO POINTS These rules came into affect for accounting periods ending on or after 1 April 2011. An election can be made by a company for these provisions to only apply for periods commencing on or after 1 April 2011 provided it is made within 12 months of the end of the period it relates to. For the rules prior to this date see earlier editions of *Tax Memo*.

Substantial commercial interdependence Whether two companies are substantially commercial interdependent or not will be judged based on the **degree** of: 1367
- **financial** interdependence, in that one gives the other financial assistance or both are financially interested in the affairs of the same business;
- **economic** interdependence, in that they share the same economic goals, the activities of one benefits the other or they share common customers; and
- **organisational** interdependence, where they share employees, premises, management or equipment.

Accounting period of less than 12 months

Where a company's accounting period is less than 12 months, the thresholds for determining the rate of tax are reduced correspondingly. 1368

EXAMPLE A Ltd has PCTCT of £105,000 for the 9 months to 31 March 2011. It has one associated company. The thresholds must be divided by two (i.e. 1 + 1) and reduced for the short accounting period, as follows:

	PCTCT	Threshold ÷ 2	Threshold × 274/365
Small companies' rate: 21%	£0 – £300,000	£0 – £150,000	£0 – £112,603
Main rate: 28%	Over £1,500,000	Over £750,000	Over £563,014

A Ltd's profits are therefore taxable at the small companies' rate.

Variable number of associated companies

In **general**, where the number of associated companies varies throughout the accounting period, the total number of associated companies at any time during the accounting period is used. 1369

EXAMPLE A Ltd prepares its accounts to 31 December each year. It had three associated companies (B, C and D) at 1 January. On 1 June, C Ltd ceased to be an associate, and on 1 July, A Ltd became associated with E Ltd.
When determining the rate of tax, the thresholds should be divided by five (A, B, C, D and E) for the whole of the period. The fact that C and E were not associated at the same time is irrelevant.

The only **exception** is where all the following requirements are met:
- the accounting period straddles two FYs;
- the number of associated companies has changed for the two FYs; and
- the thresholds for determining the rate of tax have also changed for the two FYs.

In this situation, the accounting period is effectively split in two (before and after 31 March) and each part is treated as a separate notional period, and the maximum number of associated companies for each notional period is used.

SECTION 4

Income tax

1. Deduction of tax

Although companies are not generally subject to income tax, they are required to deduct income tax from certain payments they make. Similarly, some forms of income they receive may already have had income tax deducted at source. 1370

The income tax suffered at source can be set against the income tax deductible from payments. Where the net position at the end of an accounting period is that income tax has been suffered, this can be set against the corporation tax liability. If the income tax suffered exceeds the corporation tax due, a refund may be obtained. ss 952, 968 ITA 2007

MEMO POINTS Companies are required to **account quarterly** for any income tax they deduct, and a return (form CT61) must be completed for this. For further details on the administrative requirements, see ¶2250.

2. Compulsory deduction

1372 ss 901, 903 ITA 2007 There are four common types of payment which must **generally** be paid net of income tax, as follows:
- annual payments;
- annual interest;
- patent royalties. (See ¶2190 and ¶2192 for patent royalties paid overseas); and
- a sale of a UK patent right by a non-UK resident.

MEMO POINTS 1. **Annual payments** include items such as annuities. They are characterised by a legal obligation to pay, and by being treated as income in the hands of the recipient. If a payment forms part of the recipient's trading receipts it is not an annual payment. The word annual in this respect does not imply a payment once per year, but denotes a quality of recurrence. However, the obligation must cover a period of more than 1 year to be considered an annual payment.
2. **Annual interest** is interest paid by a company for a loan capable of lasting more than 1 year. Loans from banks carrying on business in the UK (and from persons whose business consists wholly or mainly of dealing, as principal, in financial instruments) are excluded from this definition.
3. Where a **royalty** relates to copyright royalties, income tax must be deducted if the recipient usually lives outside the UK.

1374 ss 930, 933-937 ITA 2007 However, the **general rule is modified** to allow such payments to be made gross if they are made by a company (or local authority) to one of the following recipients:
- UK resident company or permanent establishment (PE);
- partnership in which all the partners are either UK resident companies/PE or approved bodies;
- an approved body;
- a manager of a PEP or ISA; or
- a TESSA provider.

The onus is on the payer to satisfy himself that the recipient falls within one of the above categories. An initial penalty of up to £3,000 (and a continuing daily penalty of £600 a day thereafter) can be imposed if HMRC believe that the payer could not reasonably have believed the payments could be made gross.

MEMO POINTS An **approved body** is:
- a local authority;
- a health service body;
- a public office, crown department or charity;
- a scientific research organisation;
- the UK Atomic Energy Authority;
- the National Radiological Protection Board;
- an exempt approved superannuation scheme;
- a parliamentary pension fund;
- certain exempt colonial pension funds;
- an exempt retirement annuity trust scheme; and
- a registered pension scheme.

1376 The **rate of tax** which must be deducted depends on the nature of the payment. Prior to 6 April 2008 the general rule was that income tax at the basic rate (22 %) should be deducted. However, where the payment was annual interest, the lower rate of income tax applies (20 %). From that date both rates are now the same and as such the distinction for these purposes is irrelevant, the deduction always being made at 20%.

s 975 ITA 2007 MEMO POINTS 1. A **tax deduction certificate** providing the following information must be provided to the recipient of a payment made under deduction of tax, if requested:
- the gross amount of the payment;
- the rate and the amount of income tax deducted;

– the net payment actually made; and
– the date the payment was made.

2. Any tax deducted from payments must be **paid to HMRC** unless offset by tax suffered at source. For payment requirements see ¶2259.

3. Receipt of income taxed at source

Available relief

Where a company has received income from which income tax has been deducted at source, relief for the tax suffered **may be obtained** in the following order: **1380**
- offset against payments made in the same quarter;
- carried forward to the next quarter within the same accounting period and offset;
- deduction from mainstream corporation tax liability;
- repayment from HMRC.

Offset against payments made

Companies need to account for income tax on form CT61 on a quarterly basis (¶2250). In any one quarter, receipts can be set against payments made by the company under deduction of tax (¶1372). Only the net amount of tax needs to be paid to HMRC with any **unrelieved amounts** being carried forward until the next quarter. **1382** ss 952, 953 ITA 2007

EXAMPLE A Ltd pays annual interest of £10,000 (gross) during the period ended 30 June 2010, and receives income under deduction of tax of £12,000 (net). The income tax position is as follows:

		£
Tax deducted from annual interest	10,000 @ 20%	2,000.00
Tax suffered	12,000 × 20/80	(3,000.00)
Net income tax suffered		(1,000.00)

To the extent that **income tax suffered is less than income tax deducted** by the company, the company must pay the difference to HMRC.

EXAMPLE A Ltd makes annual payments of £1,000 (gross) during the period ended 30 June 2010, and receives income under deduction of tax of £600 (net). The income tax position is as follows:

		£
Tax deducted from annual payments	1,000 @ 20%	200.00
Tax suffered	600 × 20/80	(150.00)
Net income tax payable to HMRC		50.00

Deduction from mainstream corporation tax liability

If any amounts have not been relieved via form CT61 at the end of the accounting period, the **balance** may be deducted from the corporation tax payable. **1384** s 967 CTA 2010

EXAMPLE A Ltd has one associated company, and has trading profits of £50,000 and received income under deduction of tax of £30,000 (net) for the period ended 31 March 2011. The tax position is as follows:

		£	£
Trading profit		50,000	
Income received under deduction of tax (gross) 30,000 × 100/80		37,500	
Profit chargeable to corporation tax			87,500
Tax thereon @ 21%			18,375.00
Income tax suffered at source	37,500 @ 20%		(7,500.00)
Net corporation tax payable			10,875.00

Repayment from HMRC

1386 If any **income tax remains unrelieved** (i.e. it exceeds the corporation tax liability), a repayment may be obtained from HMRC. Evidence will need to be submitted in support of any repayment, in the form of tax deduction certificates.

EXAMPLE During the period ended 31 March 2010, A Ltd (which has three associated companies), incurred a trading loss of £5,000 and received annual payments of £15,000 (net). The tax position is as follows:

		£	£
Income received under deduction of tax (gross)			
15,000 × 100/80		18,750	
Trading loss set against general income		(5,000)	
Profit chargeable to corporation tax			13,750
Tax thereon @ 21%			2,887.50
Income tax suffered at source	18,750 @ 20%		(3,750.00)
Net income tax repayable			(862.50)

1388 **Repayments** of income tax in this way should be claimed by completing the appropriate section of the corporation tax return. HMRC are not required to make a repayment until the corporation tax liability has been finally agreed. Interest may be due on any repayments made late (¶2275).

1390 A **provisional repayment** may be made where it is clear that a repayment will be due, for example where evidence of substantial losses is available. If a provisional repayment is made which subsequently proves to be excessive, it must be repaid to HMRC and interest will be charged.

SECTION 5

ACT

1. Background

1400 Historically, companies making qualifying distributions had to deduct tax from the dividend at source. This was known as advance corporation tax (ACT) and the net dividend was known as a franked payment. (Any such payments received by a company were known as franked investment income (FII.)

If, during an accounting period, a company's franked payments had exceeded its FII, ACT would have to be paid to HMRC as, essentially, an advance on the company's mainstream corporation tax liability, as it could (up to a certain limit) either be:
– offset against the final tax liability; or
– surrendered to a subsidiary for offset against its corporation tax liability.

The restriction on the amount of offset meant that many companies had surplus ACT, which could be used in a number of ways, including carry forward for offset against future corporation tax liabilities.

MEMO POINTS **Surplus ACT** carried forward could not be surrendered to a subsidiary. However, the amount of current year ACT which could be surrendered to a subsidiary was not limited to the amount the subsidiary could use. In addition, an election for surrender had a time limit of 6 years from the end of the accounting period in which the ACT arose, so an election could be made subsequently if it became apparent that the subsidiary could utilise that ACT.

When ACT was abolished in 1999, a number of companies still had surplus ACT which they had not been able to use. This surplus ACT can still be carried forward and set against future tax liabilities of the company holding that surplus at 5 April 1999. **1402**

However, the system of shadow ACT (¶1405) limits the amount of surplus ACT which can be used, in a way similar to the old ACT rules.

MEMO POINTS 1. If a company feels that it is unlikely to be able to recover its surplus ACT, it may **opt out of the shadow ACT scheme**. Where a company is a member of a 51% group of companies (¶1520), such an election may only be made by the parent company for the whole group. Individual members of the group cannot be excluded.
2. For modifications to these rules when applied to members of a 51% **group of companies**, see ¶1714.

2. Shadow ACT

Calculation

The shadow ACT regime is simply a method to calculate how much of the surplus ACT brought forward from dividends paid before 6 April 1999 can be utilised. It is calculated **as follows**: **1405** SI 1999/358

a. calculate the shadow ACT (distributions paid × 25% (¶1410));
b. calculate the maximum ACT capacity (taxable profits × 20%); and
c. deduct **a**. from **b**. to give the ACT available for offset against the company's tax liability (¶1415).

Shadow ACT capacity

When calculating shadow ACT the 25% is applied to all distributions (whether qualifying or not) made by a company during an accounting period, with the exception of: **1410**

– intra-group dividends; and
– manufactured dividends.

The **calculation is modified** where a company has also received franked investment income during the accounting period, as follows:

FD		
(FI)		
Net FD	× 25%	= shadow ACT

Where:

FD is franked distributions calculated as distributions made × 125%; and

FI is franked income calculated as:
– franked investment income × 9/8; plus
– any surplus FII brought forward from earlier periods.

EXAMPLE A Ltd makes a distribution of £100,000 on 1 September, and receives a distribution of £25,000. A Ltd has surplus FII brought forward of £22,000. Shadow ACT is calculated as follows:

		£
Franked distributions	100,000 × 125%	125,000
Franked income	25,000 × 9/8	(28,125)
	Surplus FII b/fwd	(22,000)
Net distributions		74,875
Shadow ACT	74,875 × 25%	18,718.75

MEMO POINTS 1. ACT is always stated to 2 decimal places.
2. If the franked income for a period exceeds the franked distributions, this is surplus franked investment income and must be carried forward and included in the computation for the subsequent period.

ACT available for offset

1415 The **maximum surplus ACT** which can be offset in an accounting period is calculated as follows:

A – B

where:
- A is the company's ACT capacity (i.e. 20% of the company's PCTCT); and
- B the shadow ACT attributed to that period.

Assuming a company has capacity to offset surplus ACT, the corporation tax liability for the period is reduced. The figure after deduction of ACT is known as the mainstream corporation tax payable. No reduction is made for shadow ACT. If the capacity is less than the full amount of surplus ACT, the balance is carried forward to the subsequent period.

MEMO POINTS If a company is liable to tax on an apportionment of profits from a **controlled foreign company** (¶2145), the apportionment is included in PCTCT for these purposes.

EXAMPLE A Ltd has surplus ACT of £125,000. During its accounting period ended 31 March, it made a distribution of £50,000 and received franked investment income of £13,000. Assuming profits of £350,000 and a corporation tax liability (before ACT) of £105,000, the ACT position is as follows:

		£
Profit chargeable to corporation tax		350,000
Maximum ACT capacity	350,000 × 20%	70,000
Distributions	50,000 × 125%	62,500
Franked income	13,000 × 9/8	(14,625)
Net distributions		47,875
Shadow ACT	47,875 × 25%	11,968.75
Maximum ACT capacity		70,000.00
Less: Shadow ACT		(11,968.75)
Surplus ACT offset against corporation tax liability		58,031.25
Corporation tax liability		105,000.00
Less: Surplus ACT		(58,031.25)
Mainstream corporation tax payable		46,968.75
Surplus ACT c/fwd	125,000 – 58,031.25	66,968.75

Interaction with income tax and double tax relief

1420 Surplus ACT is deducted from the company's corporation tax liability in priority to any income tax suffered (¶1370). Double tax relief is however allocated against any tax due on overseas profits in priority to surplus ACT.

These rules are generally to the company's advantage. If a company cannot fully recover income tax by deduction from the corporation tax liability, it can simply claim a refund from HMRC (¶1386), whereas unrelieved ACT is simply carried forward. The order of offset therefore restricts the amount of relief which may be lost.

3. Surplus shadow ACT

1425 It is possible that a company will have surplus shadow ACT for an accounting period. This is where the shadow ACT exceeds the maximum which can be utilised against the current year corporation tax liability.

Surplus shadow ACT is carried back and **treated as** shadow ACT of the previous 6 years, set against later years first. This rule is of limited importance for companies who are not a member of a group, as a company with surplus ACT would not have capacity to absorb surplus shadow ACT during this period.

However, shadow ACT carried back **displaces surplus ACT** offset during a certain period:
a. for companies with regular 12 month accounting periods, the period is the accounting period immediately prior to the one in which the surplus shadow ACT arises;
b. for companies with irregular accounting periods, the period is determined as follows:
– the period begins 24 months before the end of the accounting period in which the surplus shadow ACT arises; and
– the period ends the day before the start of the accounting period in which the surplus shadow ACT arises.
A simple way to calculate the period is to deduct the length of the accounting period giving rise to surplus shadow ACT (in months) from 24. The number remaining is the number of months for which the surplus is carried back. Surplus shadow ACT carried back is used in the latest period first. Where an accounting period falls partly within the period, the surplus shadow ACT is apportioned on a time basis.

Any **displaced surplus ACT** continues to be carried forward, unless the company has opted out of the shadow ACT regime, in which case it is lost.

EXAMPLE A Ltd prepares its accounts to 31 December regularly until 2007, when a set of accounts are prepared for the 8 months to 31 August. Surplus shadow ACT of £27,500 arose in the period to 31 August 2007. Surplus ACT had been used as follows:
P/e 31/12/05 £16,000
P/e 31/12/06 £15,000
Balancing remaining unused £18,000.
The surplus shadow ACT will be carried back as follows:

Maximum period for carry back (in months)	24
Months in period in which surplus arose	(8)
Remaining period for carry back	16

i.e. the 12 month period ended 31/12/06, and the 4 months 01/09/05 – 31/12/05

Surplus ACT position:		£
Balance of surplus ACT		18,000
P/e 31/12/06		
Surplus ACT displaced		15,000
P/e 31/12/05		
Surplus ACT displaced	4/12 × 16,000	5,333
Total surplus ACT remaining at 31/08/07		38,333

4. Opting out of the shadow ACT regime

Once a company has **fully utilised its surplus ACT**, it no longer has to worry about the shadow ACT regulations. 1430

If, whilst **surplus ACT remains unused**, the company decides that it no longer wants to try and utilise the surplus ACT, it can notify HMRC that it wishes to opt out of the regime. In this case, its final accounting period for these purposes is the period in which the notification is made. No surplus ACT can be utilised after the end of the final accounting period. However, the company may still be affected by the shadow ACT regulations. Shadow ACT continues to be calculated for any accounting period beginning in the 12 months immediately following the accounting period in which the notification is given, and the normal rules for the carry back of surplus shadow ACT apply. If these rules result in the displacement of surplus ACT, that surplus ACT is no longer recoverable.

CHAPTER 8

Groups of companies

OUTLINE ¶¶

SECTION 1

Group companies

1500 Various areas of tax legislation include specific provisions for groups of companies. All groups include a parent and one or more subsidiaries. The definition of a group (and extent of ownership of the subsidiary required) varies according to the area of legislation concerned and the aim of this section is to define the terms **group** and **consortium**, and highlight the areas of legislation which are affected.

1505 The following table shows the **key areas** of the legislation which concern groups.

Topics	General rules	Relevant definition			
		51%	75%	75% CG	Consortium
ACT	¶1400	✓			
Appropriations to/from stock	¶90			✓	
Capital losses	¶1310			✓	
Income tax	¶1370	✓			
Loan relationships	¶870			✓	
Loss relief	¶1260		✓		✓
Rollover relief (replacement of business assets)	¶6050			✓	
Ships (capital allowances)	¶456		✓		
Tax payments	¶2259	✓			
Tax refunds	¶2290		✓		
Transfer of chargeable assets	¶1600			✓	

The relevant definitions can be found as follows:

51%	¶1520
75%	¶1522
75% CG	¶1524
90%	¶1528
Consortium	¶1530

For a definition of a group for VAT purposes see ¶7807.

A. Types of group

1. Factors of ownership

1506 In determining ownership, three things may be considered (either together or individually): share capital, entitlement to distributable profits and entitlement to assets on winding up.

Share capital

1508 s 160 CTA 2010 In determining whether companies form part of a group, the main consideration is ownership of ordinary share capital.

Ordinary share capital is defined by exclusion and includes all shares other than those termed "restricted preference" shares. A restricted preference share is a share that has no right of conversion to a share other than a further relevant preference share (or shares in a quoted parent company) and has no right to a premium on redemption other than one that a similar listed share may have. It should also carry no right to a dividend.

However, it can carry a right to a dividend where the dividend is no more than a reasonable commercial return on the shares, and either is a:
- fixed amount or fixed percentage of the nominal value of the shares; or
- percentage of nominal value based on RPI or similar index.

Further, there can be no option for the company to reduce or not pay the dividend attaching to the shares except where:
- paying the dividend in full would put the company in severe financial difficulty; or
- reducing or eliminating the payment is necessary due to regulatory advice or constraints.

Ownership of share capital in this situation means beneficial ownership. This means that where a company cannot actually take the benefit of the shares it owns, it ceases to have beneficial ownership. Beneficial ownership does not cease where the company has granted an option over shares which may or may not be taken up. Where, however, another person has a specifically enforceable right to acquire the shares, ownership ceases to be beneficial.

MEMO POINTS 1. With the exception of 75% CG groups, the passing of a resolution or making an order for the **winding up** of a company will bring a group relationship to an end.
2. Shares held as **trading stock** are not included when determining a company's shareholding; neither are shares held indirectly via a company whose shares are held as trading stock.

Distributable profits

The entitlement of equity holders to distributable profits is often a factor determining corporate ownership. **1510** s 165 CTA 2010

Equity holders include owners of ordinary shares and loan creditors (with the exception of loan creditors holding normal commercial loans). A normal commercial loan is one which:
a. is not convertible into shares or securities; and
b. does not charge interest at a rate which:
- depends on the company's results;
- depends on the value of the company's assets; or
- exceeds a normal commercial return on the loan.

It is, however, acceptable for the interest rate to reduce as the company's results improve and it becomes less of a risk.

Distributable profits are the commercial profits (i.e. accounts figure), not the profit calculated for corporation tax purposes. The amount is before equity distributions but after fixed rate preference dividends and commercial loan interest. Prior year adjustments are also excluded. If there is no commercial profit, a notional profit of £100 is used.

When determining the distributable profits for any company that is not resident in the UK, the profits for the accounting period are computed as though the company were UK resident throughout the period.

Assets on winding up

The entitlement to assets on a winding up is **calculated as if**, on a notional winding up, the value of assets available for distribution is equal to the excess of those assets over the balance sheet liabilities shown at the end of the accounting period. **1512** s 166 CTA 2010

If there is no excess, a notional value of £100 is used.

MEMO POINTS Any amounts distributable to equity holders which are equivalent to new consideration for shares are **left out** when calculating the total asset value.

2. Calculation of holdings

1514 ss 1154 - 1157 CTA 2010 There are **two methods of holding shares**, direct or indirect. For example, if company A owns 100% of company B which in turn owns 100% of company C, company A directly owns company B and indirectly owns company C. Any company, whatever its country of **residence**, can be a member of a group.

1516 With the exception of holdings for chargeable gains purposes (¶1524), where the holdings are less than 100%, the ownership is determined by multiplying the fraction of ownership throughout the series.

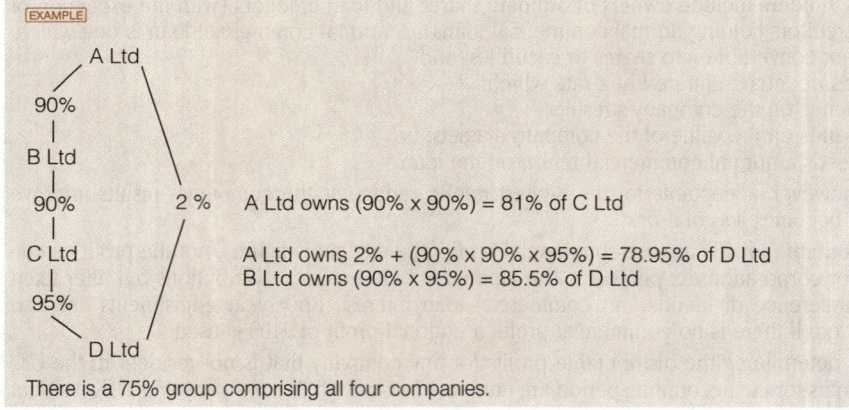

EXAMPLE

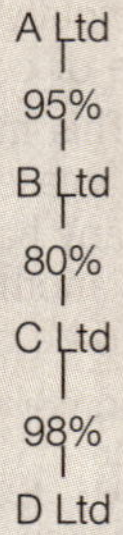

A Ltd owns (95 % x 80%) = 76 % of C Ltd

A Ltd owns (95 % x 80% x 98%) = 74.5 % of D Ltd
B Ltd owns (80 % x 98%) = 78.4 % of D Ltd

There are two 75% groups in this situation: A Ltd, B Ltd and C Ltd form one group, and B Ltd, C Ltd and D form another.

1518 A series may also include the situation where a company owns shares in another company both directly and indirectly.

EXAMPLE

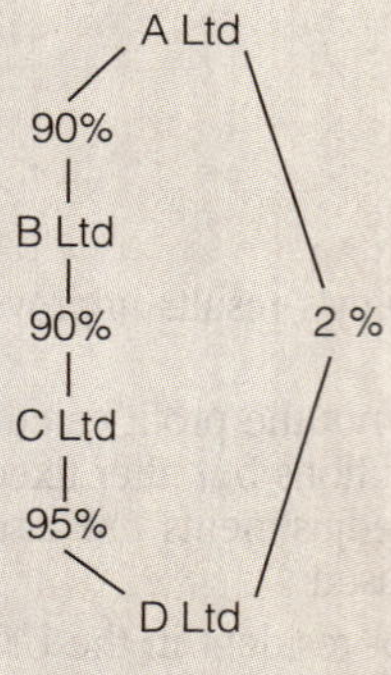

A Ltd owns (90% x 90%) = 81% of C Ltd

A Ltd owns 2% + (90% x 90% x 95%) = 78.95% of D Ltd
B Ltd owns (90% x 95%) = 85.5% of D Ltd

There is a 75% group comprising all four companies.

3. Rules for specific groups

51% group

1520 s 1154(2) CTA 2010 In determining whether a 51% group is in existence, the factor to consider is ownership of share capital. Despite its name, a 51% group exists where a company owns more than 50% of the share capital of another company (a 51% subsidiary).

75% group

1522 s 1154(3) CTA 2010 When considering a 75% group, all three factors (share capital, distributable profits and entitlement to assets on winding up) must be considered. The parent company must be beneficially entitled to not less than 75% of the share capital, distributable profits and assets on a winding up. Holdings may be direct or indirect and must be at least 75% in each case.

75% CG group

When considering a 75% CG group, which is generally only relevant for chargeable gains purposes, all three factors (share capital, distributable profits and entitlement to assets on winding up) must again be considered. The ownership of share capital must be at least 75%, and each subsidiary must be an effective 51% subsidiary (i.e. the parent must be beneficially entitled to more than 50% of the distributable profits and assets on winding up). **1524** s 170(6), (7) TCGA 1992

When calculating the 75% capital ownership, there is no requirement to multiply the fractional holdings, as in ¶1516, although this calculation will be relevant for determining whether the company has a minimum 50% interest.

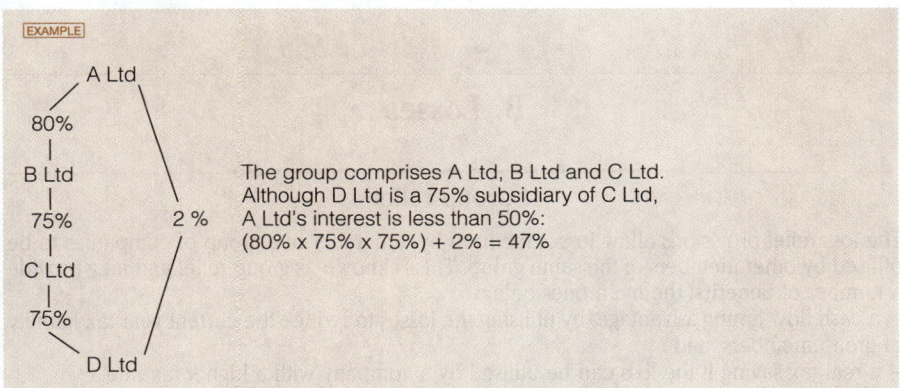

EXAMPLE

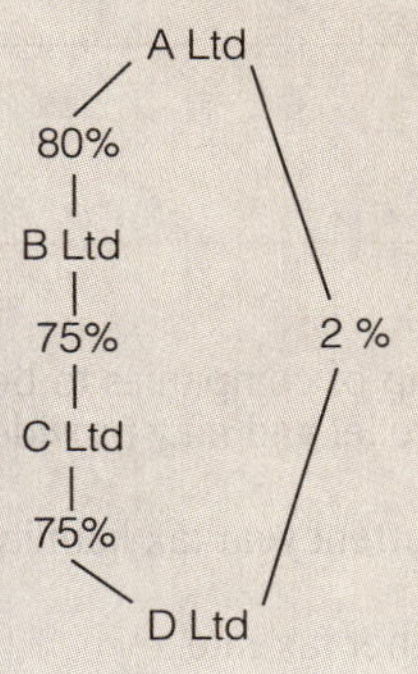

The group comprises A Ltd, B Ltd and C Ltd.
Although D Ltd is a 75% subsidiary of C Ltd,
A Ltd's interest is less than 50%:
(80% x 75% x 75%) + 2% = 47%

If a company is not UK **resident**, it can be looked through. This means that although the non-resident company cannot be part of the group, its 75% subsidiaries can be, providing the other tests are met. In these circumstances, the effective interest must be 75% (using the multiplication of interests) and not at least 50% as above.

A 75% CG group comprises a **principal member** and its 75% subsidiaries, and a company may only be a member of one 75% CG group. A company cannot be a principal member if it is itself a 75% subsidiary of another company.

EXAMPLE Taking the facts from the previous example, A Ltd is the principal member of the group, and the other members are B Ltd and C Ltd.
Although D Ltd is a 75% subsidiary of C Ltd, C Ltd cannot be a principal member of a group as it is already a member of A Ltd's group.
If, however, D Ltd had its own 75% subsidiaries, D Ltd could be the principal member of a separate group.

90% group

When considering a 90% group, all three factors (share capital, distributable profits and entitlement to assets on winding up) must be considered. The parent company must be beneficially entitled to not less than 90% of the share capital, distributable profits and assets on a winding up. Holdings may only be direct in each case. (Contrast this to the position for a 75% group.) **1528** s 1154(4) CTA 2010

Consortium

A consortium exists where 20 or fewer companies (the consortium members) each own at least 5% and jointly at least 75% of the ordinary share capital of another company (the consortium company). A company cannot be a consortium company if it is a 75% subsidiary **1530** s 153 CTA 2010 of another company. The consortium company must also be a trading company (or a holding company directly owning a minimum of 90% of another trading company).

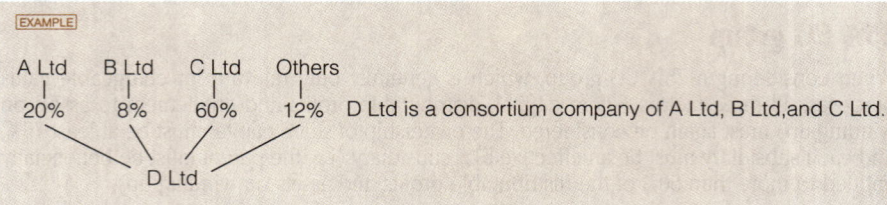

EXAMPLE

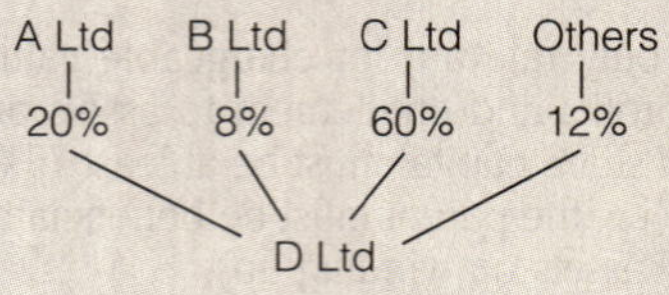

D Ltd is a consortium company of A Ltd, B Ltd,and C Ltd.

MEMO POINTS The **ownership of the remaining 25%** or less of the shares does not affect consortium status and therefore the shares may be held by individuals.

B. Losses

1. Group relief

1540 The loss relief provisions allow losses incurred by a member of a group of companies to be utilised by other members of the same group. This is known as group relief and may provide a number of **benefits**, the main ones being:
– a cash flow timing advantage, by utilising the losses to reduce the current year tax liability of group members; and
– a real tax saving if the loss can be utilised by a company with a higher tax rate.

s 130 CTA 2010 Group relief must be claimed by the company utilising the losses, and the company incurring the loss must formally consent to surrender its loss.

MEMO POINTS 1. **Capital losses** may not be group relieved, although an alternative form of relief may be available (¶1620).
2. Similar provisions, with slight modifications, apply to **consortia** (¶1575).

2. Conditions for group relief

1542 Group relief can be **claimed from** a group member that is:
– resident either in the UK or an EU member state. (Note though, that if the surrendering company is resident in an EU member state it must also be within the charge to tax in the relevant EU member state (either as a resident company or permanent establishment)); and
– a member of the same 75% group (¶1522) as the claimant.

MEMO POINTS 1. There are **special rules** for the calculation of the relief where the surrendering company is:
– a UK permanent establishment (¶1562);
– an overseas permanent establishment (¶1564); or
– an EU resident company (¶1566).
2. **Consortium relief claims** can only be made between UK resident companies (or permanent establishments).

1544 Losses may be **surrendered by** a:
– parent company to one or more of its subsidiaries;
– subsidiary to its parent;
– subsidiary to its fellow subsidiaries.

Group relief is available in full where the companies form part of the same group throughout the accounting period. See ¶1573 for modifications to the rules where companies join or leave a group partway through an accounting period.

MEMO POINTS In certain circumstances, losses may be surrendered between companies which have no direct relationship, but where a **consortium company acts as a link**. See ¶1587 for further details.

3. Calculation of the relief

Eligible losses

Losses **eligible for group relief** are: 1546 s 99 CTA 2010
- trading losses (¶1264), including capital allowances (¶200);
- non-trading loan relationship deficits (¶1295);
- non-trading loss on an intangible fixed asset;
- payments qualifying for charitable donations relief (¶958); and
- excess UK property business losses (¶1280).

MEMO POINTS Companies with **investment business** may also surrender excess management expenses (¶2125).

UK resident company

The **amount of losses** that can be surrendered differs depending on the type of income, as follows: 1548
- trading losses (including capital allowances) and non-trading loan relationship deficits can be surrendered as group relief in their entirety. There is no requirement for the surrendering company to first set them against its own profits of the accounting period; and
- donations, non-trading losses on intangible fixed assets and UK property business losses can only be surrendered to the extent that they cannot be used by the company i.e. only the excess is eligible for group relief. The excess is calculated by totalling these for the accounting period and deducting the total profits of the accounting period before relief for any losses of the same or other accounting periods. Where a company has 2 or more of these they are treated as surrendered in the following order: s 105 CTA 2010
  - donations;
  - UK property business losses; then
  - non-trading losses on intangible fixed assets.

MEMO POINTS Where a company has **excess management charges** these are treated as surrendered after property losses but before losses on intangible assets.

Group relieved **losses may be set against** the total profits of the claimant company that arise in the overlap period. 1550

A claimant company's **total profits** are its profits chargeable to corporation tax. Where the company incurs a trading loss, its total profits are calculated on the basis that a claim has been made to set that loss against its general income of the accounting period (¶1273) whether or not such a claim has actually been made. Group relief is given after any reliefs of the same or an earlier accounting period, but in priority to any losses carried back from a subsequent accounting period. 1552

EXAMPLE A Ltd incurs a trading loss of £5,000 in the 12 month period ended 31 May, and has Schedule A business profits of £17,000. Its total profits for group relief purposes are calculated as £12,000 (i.e. actual profits of £17,000 less the amount of the trading loss which is eligible to be set against general income). It is irrelevant whether a claim for this loss relief is actually made or whether the loss is utilised in another way.

The **overlap period** is the part of the surrendering company's accounting period which corresponds with the claimant company's accounting period for which both companies were members of the same group. 1554 ss 138 - 142 CTA 2010

Where the companies have **identical accounting periods**, there is no problem as the complete accounting period will be the overlap period.

However, where the surrendering and claimant companies have **different accounting periods**, or one of the companies ceases to be a member of the group, losses can only be set against profits of the period which is common to both the surrendering and claimant companies. To calculate the maximum group relief, it is necessary to calculate the loss of the overlap period and the profit of the overlap period. The maximum amount that can be surrendered is the lower of these two figures.

EXAMPLE A Ltd prepares its accounts for the 12 months to 31 December 2010 and incurs a loss eligible for group relief of £30,000. B Ltd prepares its accounts for the 10 months to 31 March 2011 and has total profits of £24,000. The maximum group relief is calculated as follows:

	Start	**End**	
A Ltd	01/01/10	31/12/10	
B Ltd	01/06/10	31/03/11	
Overlap period	01/06/10	31/12/10	i.e. 7 months
Eligible loss	7/12 × £30,000	£17,500	
Eligible profit	7/10 × £24,000	£16,800	

Therefore the maximum group relief is £16,800.

As companies have consecutive accounting periods, the whole loss incurred during an accounting period will generally be available, although it may be split between two different accounting periods of the claimant company.

EXAMPLE A Ltd prepares accounts annually to 31 December and has a loss available for group relief of £16,000 for the period ended 31 December 2010. (A Ltd makes profits in its other periods.) B Ltd prepares accounts annually to 30 June and has profits for the period ended 30 June 2010 of £15,000 and 30 June 2011 of £20,000. The maximum group relief is calculated as follows:

	Start	**End**	
A Ltd	01/01/10	31/12/10	
B Ltd	01/07/09	30/06/10	
Overlap period 1	01/01/10	30/06/10	i.e. 6 months
B Ltd	01/07/10	30/06/11	
Overlap period 2	01/07/10	31/12/10	i.e. 6 months
A Ltd – eligible loss:			
Overlap period 1	6/12 × £16,000	£8,000	
Overlap period 2	6/12 × £16,000	£8,000	
B Ltd – eligible profit:			
Overlap period 1	6/12 × £15,000	£7,500	
Overlap period 2	6/12 × £20,000	£10,000	

Therefore the maximum group relief A Ltd can surrender to B Ltd is:
- £7,500 for the period ended 30/06/10; and
- £8,000 for the period ended 30/06/11.

1556 s 183 CTA 2010 There is no further restriction on the amount of the loss which can be group relieved simply because the relationship between the companies is less than 100%. A minority shareholder might therefore feel disadvantaged if losses are surrendered. To compensate, it is common practice for the claimant company to make a **payment for group relief** surrendered. Payments of up to £1 for every £1 loss surrendered are ignored for tax purposes.

Comment Payments on a £ for £ basis are actually advantageous to the surrendering company, as the benefit of losses is restricted to the amount of tax which would otherwise be payable. For a company paying tax at the main rate, losses of £1,000 therefore have a tax effect of £260 (i.e. £1,000 @ 26%).

1560 Where a **group consists of more than two companies**, the group may allocate losses eligible for group relief, up to the maximum group relief available for each claimant company, to whichever group company it chooses. Maximum benefit is generally obtained by allocating losses to companies in the following order:

- companies falling in the margin (¶1350) between the small companies' rate and the main rate (to reduce their profits to the small companies' rate threshold);
- companies paying tax at the main rate; and
- companies paying tax at the small companies' rate.

However, the immediate cash flow advantage of surrendering losses against current year profits must be weighed against the merits of setting the loss against future trading profits which might be taxed at a higher rate. Similarly, group relief should be structured such that reliefs are not wasted.

UK permanent establishment

Where a company is trading in the UK via a permanent establishment, losses can only be: **1562** s 107 CTA 2010
- **surrendered** from a permanent establishment if they are attributable to activities which, if profitable, would be subject to UK corporation tax. (Losses that can be offset against non-UK profits of a third person for the purposes of any foreign taxes are not available for group relief); and
- **claimed** by a permanent establishment if they are to be offset against profits which are subject to UK corporation tax and are not excluded, for example, under a double tax agreement.

MEMO POINTS Losses surrendered under this provision are **in addition** to any losses that may be available for surrender from an EU resident company (¶1566).

Overseas permanent establishment

Where a company is UK resident but has an overseas permanent establishment, losses of the permanent establishment **can only be surrendered if** they are attributable to activities which, if profitable, would be subject to UK corporation tax. **1564** s 106 CTA 2010

Losses that can be offset against non-UK profits of a third person for the purposes of any foreign taxes are not available for group relief.

EEA resident company

Where a non-UK company is resident in the EEA (or carries on a trade via a permanent establishment in the EEA) the EU losses **can be surrendered** to a UK claimant company if they meet certain conditions. Where these conditions are met the loss is recomputed for UK group relief purposes. **1566** ss 112, 113 CTA 2010

The UK **claimant company will be responsible** for demonstrating that the loss meets the following conditions: **1569** ss 114-128 CTA 2010

a. equivalence condition: i.e. it corresponds to an amount of a kind that could be available for group relief by a UK resident company (¶1546); and

b. EEA tax loss condition: i.e. there is a tax loss in the EEA member state, as computed under local laws. In addition if the surrendering company is:
- resident in the EEA, the loss must not be attributable to a UK permanent establishment of the EEA company; or
- trading in the EEA via a permanent establishment, the loss must not be attributable to activities of the permanent establishment which are exempt from tax under a double tax treaty.

It is important to note that the loss cannot be relieved in the UK if it **can be relieved overseas** for any period (current, previous or future). The EEA company must take all possible steps to obtain such relief.

MEMO POINTS When considering whether a company has **taken all possible steps** to relieve the loss overseas, the Court of Appeal has held that the test must be applied at the date when a final group relief claim is made in the UK. Losses can only be surrendered to the UK at this time if there is no possibility that they can be relieved overseas. *Marks & Spencer plc v HMRC* [2007]

To calculate the amount of the EEA tax loss that can be relieved in the UK, the EEA loss must be **recomputed in accordance with UK tax rules**. (If the recalculation produces a **1570** loss, that amount is available for surrender. If it produces a profit, no group relief can be surrendered.)

MEMO POINTS 1. If only a **proportion of the EEA loss is available for relief** in the UK (because, for example, some part of it is relievable elsewhere), then only that proportion should be compared with the UK recalculated amount.

s 127 CTA 2010 2. **Anti-avoidance provisions** prohibit such loss relief where companies have entered into artificial arrangements in order to create overseas unrelievable losses against which to obtain UK group relief.

3. It is likely that the rules will be amended as the European Commission has stated that the rules as implemented are too restrictive.

4. Companies leaving the group

1573 ss 154 - 156 CTA 2010 Where **arrangements** exist for the sale of a group company to a third party, no group relief is available. This restriction applies from the date the arrangements exist and the accounting period is split into two notional periods for this purpose. Group relief is available up to the date of the arrangements (calculated on a time apportioned basis).

SP 3/93 The legislation does not **define** arrangements other than to say they may take any form. There is no requirement for the arrangements to be either in writing or enforceable. However, HMRC have stated that simple negotiations for the sale of the company do not constitute arrangements until an offer is accepted subject to contract, or on similar terms. Similarly, where the disposal requires shareholder approval, arrangements do not exist until approval is given or before the directors become aware that approval will be given. The issue of written heads of agreement will however generally constitute arrangements. Arrangements can exist even where the sale proves abortive.

ESC C10 MEMO POINTS 1. A **mortgage** using shares in a group company as security is not considered an arrangement for these purposes, until the mortgagee can exercise his rights.

2. A **joint venture agreement** which provides for shares belonging to one of the joint venture companies to be transferred to the others on specific events, such as the company going into liquidation, is not an arrangement until that event actually occurs.

3. **Options** granted over shares affect the ownership of the company for group relief purposes, and may therefore result in the holding falling below the required level.

5. Consortia

1575 ss 132 - 134 CTA 2010 A modified form of group relief is available to consortia (¶1530). This relief is known as **consortium relief** and losses may be surrendered by a:
- consortium member to the consortium company; and
- consortium company to the consortium members.

In addition, where the consortium company is a **holding company**, losses may be group relieved in either direction between the consortium members and the 90% trading subsidiaries of the consortium company.

Consortium relief is only available between companies that are resident in the UK or trading in the UK via a permanent establishment. The relief for losses incurred by an EU resident group company (¶1566) does not apply to consortia.

MEMO POINTS A **consortium member** is one of 20 or fewer companies that owns at least 5% of the ordinary share capital of another company (the **consortium company**). See ¶1530 for details.

1577 The **basic calculation** of consortium relief is the same as group relief, with equivalent restrictions for companies joining or leaving the consortium during an accounting period, or where arrangements are in force.

ss 143 - 145 CTA 2010 However, the **calculation is modified** to take account of the holding of each consortium member in the consortium company. The restriction depends on whether it is the consortium company or the consortium member which has incurred the loss, as follows:

– where the consortium company (or its 90% trading subsidiary) incurs the loss, the loss may be surrendered in proportion to the consortium member's interest in that company; or
– where the consortium member incurs the loss, the loss can be surrendered in proportion to its interest in the profits of the consortium company.

EXAMPLE A Ltd is a consortium company and B Ltd a consortium member with a 30% interest. Both companies prepare accounts annually to 31 December. During the 12 months to 31 December, one of the companies makes a profit of £15,000 and one a loss of £12,000.
If A Ltd incurs the loss, the maximum eligible for consortium relief would be:

Interest × consortium company loss	30% × £12,000	£3,600

If B Ltd incurs the loss, the maximum eligible for consortium relief would be:

Interest × consortium company profit	30% × £15,000	£4,500

It is therefore important to identify the correct **level of the consortium member's interest**. **1580**
In most cases, this will simply be the percentage of the owned share capital. However, there are two situations in which the consortium member's holding may not be immediately obvious:
– if the consortium member's interest in the consortium company has varied throughout the accounting period; or
– where there is more than one class of shares in issue.

MEMO POINTS 1. Where the **interest has varied**, the appropriate percentage is simply the average holding over the course of the accounting period.
2. Where there is **more than one class of shares** in issue, the member's interest for the accounting period is taken to be the lowest of the following percentages:
– ordinary share capital held;
– entitlement to distributable assets on a winding up; or
– entitlement to distributable profits.
From a future date a fourth percentage will be added to this based on the level of control via voting rights.

6. Interaction of group relief and consortium relief

Both group relief and consortium relief may be available, where: **1585** ss 147 - 149 CTA 2010
– the consortium company has 75% subsidiaries; or
– a consortium member has 75% subsidiaries.

The **general rule** is that group relief takes precedence over consortium relief. When a loss making company is a 75% subsidiary of a consortium company, it is assumed that any losses which could be group relieved are group relieved (taking into account any actual group relief claims by group members), when calculating the balance of the loss available for consortium relief. **1586**

Similarly, if the consortium company has profits, it can only claim consortium relief to the extent that its profits exceed losses which it could claim from its subsidiaries under the group relief provisions (again, taking into account any group relief claims actually made by members of the group).

The **exception** is where the loss making company is both a group member and a consortium member. In this case, the company may surrender its loss in whichever order it chooses. There is no requirement for the loss to be utilised by group companies in priority to the consortium company.

Where a company is both a group member and a consortium member, it may act as a **link company**. This means that any losses which are available to be surrendered to it as consortium relief may be used either by the company itself or by its fellow group members. Similarly, any loss it incurs which is eligible for group relief may be surrendered to its consortium company. This may be of benefit where, for example, the link company has insufficient profits to absorb the loss or pays tax at a lower rate than the other company. **1587**

EXAMPLE

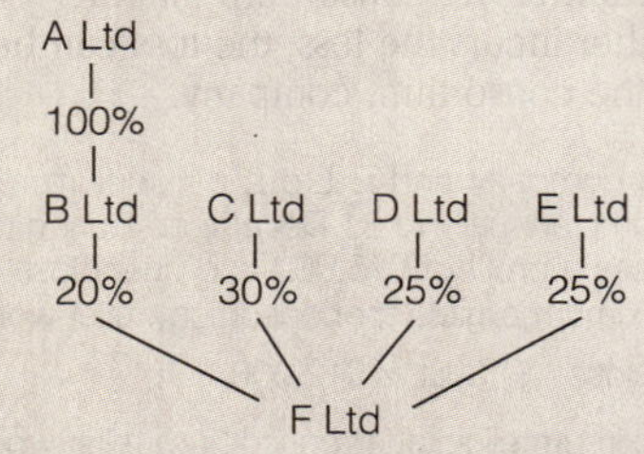

If F Ltd incurs a loss, 20% thereof is available for B Ltd. B Ltd is the link company and therefore the loss can be used by either A Ltd or B Ltd in any combination (up to the maximum of their profits).
Similarly, any loss incurred by A Ltd that is eligible for group relief to B Ltd can be surrendered to F Ltd.

7. Claims for group relief and consortium relief

1590 Sch 18 paras 67, 74 FA 1998

All claims must be made on the corporation tax return (or amended return), **usually** within 12 months of the filing date for the accounting period to which the claim relates.

If there has been an **enquiry** into a return (¶2330), the time limit is extended to 30 days after whichever of the following applies to the particular enquiry:
- the issue of a closure notice;
- the amendment of the return by HMRC; or
- the determination of an appeal against an amended return.

HMRC have the power to extend these time limits in exceptional circumstances.

MEMO POINTS Claims may be made after the claimant or surrendering company has **left the group**, providing the group membership conditions were satisfied for the accounting period specified in the claim.

1592 Sch 18 paras 68, 69 FA 1998

To be valid, a **claim must specify** the:
- surrendering company;
- amount claimed (claims will be invalid if the amount claimed is greater than the actual loss available, although claims may be made for less than the maximum available); and
- residence of the claimant and surrendering company.

1593 Sch 18 paras 70, 71 FA 1998

The surrendering company must notify HMRC of its **consent to the surrender**, no later than the date the claim is made. (If the surrendering company is resident in the EU (¶1566), such notice of consent must be given by the claimant company.)

A copy of the consent notice must accompany the corresponding claim. The consent notice should provide the following information in respect of the claimant:
- company name;
- tax district reference (although if the surrendering company is not within the charge to corporation tax, obviously this information cannot be provided);
- amount of relief surrendered. (In the case of EU resident companies (¶1566), the EEA tax loss amount must also be specified (¶1569)); and
- the accounting period to which the surrender relates.

MEMO POINTS 1. Once made, a consent cannot be amended but, within the time limits, **may be withdrawn** and a revised consent submitted. Notice of the withdrawal must generally be given by the surrendering company, unless it is resident in an EU member state (¶1566), in which case the notice of withdrawal is given by the claimant company.
2. If a company has given consent to a surrender for an **amount which subsequently proves to exceed** the total loss available, it must withdraw its consent within 30 days, submit a consent to a reduced claim, and notify the affected companies of the reduction. (If the surrendering company is resident in an EU member state (¶1566), the requisite notices must be completed by the claimant company.)
The affected companies must then amend their corporation tax returns if possible (¶2247).

In certain circumstances, HMRC may enter into **special arrangements** with a group such that the parent company (or another specified company) may act on behalf of the group members, amending returns as appropriate. The requirement for claims to be accompanied by a copy of the surrender notice is waived in this situation. This has considerable administrative advantages for both the companies and HMRC. **1594**

If it becomes apparent that the **group relief claimed is excessive**, for example where an amendment to the surrendering company's return has reduced the amount available and the claimant company cannot amend its return, HMRC will issue an assessment to recover the tax lost. Such an assessment affects the time limit for making certain claims (¶2257). **1596** Sch 18 para 76 FA 1998

C. Transfers of chargeable assets

1. No gain/no loss transfer

Transfers of chargeable assets within a 75% CG group (intra-group transfers) **must be** treated as no gain/no loss disposals (¶1165). **1600** s 171 TCGA 1992
This means that the disposing company is deemed to sell the asset at a price which gives rise to neither a gain nor a loss i.e. the original cost plus indexation.

A transfer is only an intra-group transfer if one of the following **conditions** is met: **1602**
- both companies are resident in the UK; or
- the asset is a chargeable asset both before and after the transfer. An asset is a chargeable asset if any gain arising on its disposal would be a chargeable gain. This means that a transfer may be an intra-group transfer if one party to the transfer (or both) is a non-resident company trading in the UK via a permanent establishment.

EXAMPLE A Ltd owned an investment property which cost £295,000 in April 1997. The property was transferred to B Ltd its 100% subsidiary, in March 2009 at book value, £295,000. The disposal is deemed to be a no gain/no loss disposal, and therefore the consideration for the disposal is calculated as follows:

	£
Cost	295,000
Indexation allowance (Apr 97 to Mar 10) $\frac{220.70 - 156.3}{156.3} = 0.412 \times £295,000$	121,540
Deemed consideration	173,460

The no gain/no loss provisions **do not apply to** the following transactions: **1604**
a. the redemption of shares;
b. the repayment of debt;
c. capital distributions;
d. disposals to a dual resident investing company;
e. transfers under the group reorganisation provisions; and
f. disposals to or by:
- venture capital trusts;
- qualifying friendly societies; and
- investment trusts.

In addition, the no gain/no loss rules do not apply if a disposal is made from one group company to another as a result of the **exercise of an option**, if the option was granted when the companies were not grouped. This provision applies to all options exercised on or after 6 March 2007 and will ensure that a charge to tax will arise where consideration is paid between two unconnected companies for the grant of an option to acquire an asset and that option is then exercised after the company owning the asset is sold to the purchaser group.

EXAMPLE A Ltd granted an option to B Ltd that enabled B Ltd to acquire an asset from A Ltd for £40,000. A Ltd subsequently joined the B Ltd group and B Ltd then exercised its option.
The no gain/no loss provisions will not apply on the transfer of the asset to B Ltd. Instead, A Ltd will be treated as if it had sold an asset for £40,000 to B Ltd and capital gains will be computed accordingly.

2. Degrouping charges

Scope

1606 s 179 TCGA 1992 A **chargeable gain** (known as a degrouping charge) will arise when a company ceases to be a member of a 75% CG group after receiving an asset:
– which was acquired via an intra-group transfer within the 6 years prior to leaving the group; or
– into which a gain has been rolled over (¶6050) and the gain arose on an asset acquired via an intra-group transfer in the previous 6 years.

No charge will arise if the company ceases to be a member of the group as the result of:
– another company ceasing to exist;
– an approved merger, where an original group becomes part of a larger group (i.e. the parent company of the original group becomes a subsidiary of another company); or
– the disposal of a sub-group where the asset in question was acquired as a result of an intra-group transfer between members of that sub-group.

EXAMPLE A Ltd owns 100% of B Ltd which in turn owns 100% of C Ltd. A Ltd is therefore the principal member of the group with B Ltd and C Ltd as members.
B Ltd transfers an asset to C Ltd on 1 January 2008. In July 2010, A Ltd sells its entire shareholding in B Ltd.
Although C Ltd is no longer in the same chargeable gains group as A Ltd, the gain in respect of the asset transferred from B Ltd does not crystallise, as the subgroup consisting of B Ltd and C Ltd is sold, and the transfer was between members of that subgroup.
If C Ltd had been sold separately, a degrouping charge would have arisen.

Calculating the charge

1607 The charge is calculated by **deeming the departing company** to have sold, and immediately reacquired, the asset at its market value on the date of the intra-group transfer. This will effectively be a calculation of that gain that would have arisen at the date of the original transfer but for the provisions allowing transfers between group companies on a no gain no loss basis.

Applying the charge

1608 For charges triggered on or after 19 July 2011, **where shares are disposed of** by a group company the charge will fall to the disposing company as an adjustment to the gain or loss that would arise on the share disposal itself, provided that the share sale would be subject to tax, ignoring reliefs such as the substantial shareholding exemption. The **ability to elect to reallocate** the gain (¶1609) and to **roll over** the gain (¶1612) arising are both removed where this situation occurs.

Where the charge is triggered **before** that date the degrouping charge will **accrue to** the company leaving the group (in the absence of any election to reallocate or roll over the charge). The gain is **chargeable on** the later of:
– the date of the intra-group transfer; and
– the start of the accounting period in which the company leaves the group.

Reallocation of charge

Where the charge is triggered by a company **leaving a group before 19 July 2011** an **election** can be made to reallocate a degrouping charge to another company that is a member of the relevant group at the time of the degrouping charge, provided: **1609**
– the party to which the charge is reallocated is UK resident (or trading in the UK through a permanent establishment such that the asset would be a chargeable asset);
– neither party to the election is a qualifying friendly society; and
– the party to which the charge is reallocated is not an investment trust, venture capital trust or a dual resident investing company.

MEMO POINTS The **relevant group** is:
– the group which the transferee company has just left; or
– in the case when an original group becomes part of a larger group (i.e. the parent company of the original group becomes a subsidiary of another company), the new enlarged group.

The **election must be made in writing** no later than 2 years after the end of the accounting period in which the deemed sale fell. **1610**

Payment may be made between the two parties of an amount not exceeding the chargeable gain or allowable loss reallocated. Such a payment is ignored for tax purposes.

Rollover of charges

Where the charge is triggered by a company **leaving a group before 19 July 2011**, a **claim** can be made to roll over a gain arising on a degrouping charge. The provisions as detailed in ¶6050 apply, with the exception that the replacement asset must be acquired within 1 year before and 3 years after the date the degrouping charge is deemed to accrue. **1612** s 179B TCGA 1992

MEMO POINTS If an election is made to **reallocate the degrouping charge**, any claim for rollover must be made by the company to which the charge has been reallocated.

Recovery of tax

If tax arising from a degrouping charge **remains unpaid** more than 6 months after it becomes payable (¶2259), HMRC may recover the tax from: **1614** s 190 TCGA 1992
– the principal member of the group at the date the gain accrued; or
– any other company which had an interest in the asset and was a member of the group during the 12 months preceding the date on which the gain accrued.

3. Notional intra-group transfers

Strictly, **capital losses** realised by a company can only be set against its own gains. They cannot be group relieved. **1620**

However, depending on the date of the disposal, mechanisms exist to effectively group relieve losses made.

For assets disposed of **prior** to 21 July 2009 it is possible for group companies to **elect** for an asset to be treated as if it were transferred intra-group immediately before sale (i.e. a notional intra-group transfer). Such an election enables assets that will realise a loss to be treated as if they were sold by a company that will, for example, also realise a capital gain on other assets. The loss can therefore be set against the realised gains. **1621**

This election essentially mirrors the effect of actually making a transfer but removes the actual transfer requirement.

The **election may be made** where a company, A, which is a member of a 75% CG group, disposes of an asset to a third party, C, outside the group. The election specifies that the asset (or any part of it) was transferred to another member of the group, B, immediately prior to the disposal to C. The transfer from A to B is an intra-group transfer and therefore the gain (or loss) arising on the disposal to C is made by B. Any incidental costs incurred by A in making the actual disposal to C are treated as incidental costs of B in making the deemed disposal to C.

An election may only be made where an actual transfer of the asset between the two companies would have been an intra-group transfer. There is no requirement that the two parties to the transfer are UK **resident**, provided the asset is a chargeable UK asset at all times. This therefore means that a UK permanent establishment of an overseas group company can be a party to the election.

Payment may be made between A and B (in either direction) of an amount not exceeding the amount of the chargeable gain or allowable loss accruing to B on the disposal. Such a payment is ignored for tax purposes.

1622 ss 171A, 171B TCGA 1992

For assets disposed of **on or after** 21 July 2009 it is possible to elect that either a **gain or loss** be transferred between A and B provided both were members of the same group at the time the gain or loss accrued and any transfer between them would have been under the no gain/no loss provisions for intra-group transfers. In this case it is not a prerequisite that the asset has to be disposed of. As such it will cover claims for negligible values which would not have been available for transfer under the previous rules. However, it is **not available** to cover degrouping charges (¶1606).

The **effect of the election** is to treat the gain or loss as arising to company B at the time it accrued to A.

Where the election is made, or a number of elections are made, they will be invalid if they exceed the total amount of loss or gain that is available for reallocation.

1624 In **either case** a joint election for this treatment must be made **in writing no later than** 2 years after the end of the accounting period of the company realising the gain or loss.

D. Transfers of trading stock

1625 s 173 TCGA 1992

Where an asset is transferred between two members of the same 75% CG group, and the asset is a capital asset in the hands of one of the companies, but trading stock for the other company, the asset is always transferred as a capital asset.

MEMO POINTS These **provisions apply to** transfers where the trade is carried on by a UK resident company or by a non-resident company trading in the UK via a permanent establishment.

1627 Where the **transferor company held the asset as stock**, it is deemed to appropriate the asset to capital immediately before the transfer and the market value of the asset is brought into the trading computation. The capital asset is then transferred at the no gain/no loss price (¶1165) i.e. market value.

EXAMPLE A Ltd holds trading stock with a value of £12,000. The asset is transferred to B Ltd when its market value is £19,750 and B Ltd holds the asset on its capital account.

A Ltd is deemed to appropriate the asset to capital giving rise to a trading profit of £7,750 (£19,750 – £12,000).

B Ltd acquires a capital asset with a base cost of £19,750.

1629 Where the **transferor company holds the asset as capital**, the transferee acquires a capital asset at the no gain/no loss price (¶1165) and immediately appropriates it to stock. The transferee therefore has a chargeable gain (or allowable loss) equivalent to the excess of the market value of the asset over the no gain/no loss price.

s 161(3) TCGA 1992

The **transferee may elect** to substitute the no gain/no loss price for the market value in the trading account, effectively converting the chargeable gain (or allowable loss) into a trading profit (or loss). Such an election must be made within 2 years of the end of the accounting period in which the asset is appropriated to trading stock.

EXAMPLE A Ltd holds a capital asset with an indexed cost of £29,500. The asset is transferred to B Ltd when its market value is £33,050. B Ltd holds the asset as trading stock and sells it for £36,175.

The tax position is as follows:
- A Ltd transfers the asset at the no gain/no loss price i.e. £29,500.
- B Ltd acquires the capital asset with a base cost of £29,500 and appropriates it to trading stock. This is a deemed disposal at market value giving rise to a chargeable gain of £3,550 (£33,050 – £29,500).
- B Ltd then sells the asset giving rise to a chargeable profit of £3,125 (£36,175 – £33,050).

Alternatively, B Ltd could make an election to appropriate the asset to stock at the no gain/no loss price (£29,500). The subsequent sale of the asset would then give rise to a trading profit of £6,675 (£36,175 – £29,500).

E. Reliefs on replacement of business assets

The provisions for rollover and holdover reliefs (¶6050) are modified when applied to a 75% CG group of companies in that: **1630** s 175 TCGA 1992
- the group is treated as carrying on a **single trade**; and
- there is no requirement for both companies to be UK **resident**. Provided the asset remains within the scope of UK taxation, the reliefs will be available. This therefore extends the provisions to include non-resident companies trading in the UK via a permanent establishment.

MEMO POINTS The reliefs cannot be claimed for an **intra-group transfer** as the mandatory no gain/no loss rules apply instead.

Providing all other conditions are fulfilled, any gain arising on the disposal of a qualifying asset may be rolled (or held) over into a qualifying replacement asset acquired by **another group member**. **1632** s 175(2A) TCGA 1992

There is no requirement for both companies to be members of the group at the same time. The disposing company must be a member of the group at the time of disposal, and the acquiring company must be a member at the time at which the replacement asset is acquired.

For the reliefs to apply, a **joint election** must be made by both companies.

In addition, assets acquired or disposed of by a **non-trading member of the group** are eligible for the reliefs (providing all the other conditions are satisfied) where they are used for the purposes of a trade carried on by a trading member of the group. **1634** s 175(2B) TCGA 1992

F. Pre-entry capital losses and gains

1. Anti-avoidance rules

As the legislation allows groups flexibility when transferring assets, special anti-avoidance provisions exist which **aim to** prevent groups of companies avoiding tax by buying a company with capital losses or gains. These provisions are particularly complex, and this section covers the basic principles. **1635**

From 19 July 2011 these provisions changed significantly. For the rules prior to this date see earlier editions of *Tax Memo*.

2. Pre-entry losses

Restriction of capital loss

1636 s 177A, Sch 7A TCGA 1992 A pre-entry capital loss, defined as a loss that has been realised by a company but as yet unutilised, can **generally** only be set against gains arising on the disposal of assets held by the company before the change of ownership (pre-change assets).

However, such losses can also be relieved against gains arising on assets:
– acquired by the company, or another member of the group, after the date of entry into the group from a party that was not a member of the group at that time; and
– that asset has not been used or held for any purpose other than the trade or business of the company that was carried on at the entry date and continued until disposal of the asset, either by the company itself or another group company.

MEMO POINTS Where a **subgroup** of two or more companies (which were previously members of another 75% CG group) join a new group at the same time, there is no restriction on the offset of losses against assets held by that subgroup at the date of joining.

1639 The restriction **operates for**:
– ordinary merger and acquisition activity with groups of companies; and
– transactions undertaken with the intention of obtaining a tax advantage.

MEMO POINTS Where the rules restricting the use of pre-entry capital losses for ordinary merger and acquisition activity and tax advantage transactions **could both apply** the tax advantage rules at ¶1655 take priority.

Tax advantage transactions

1655 s 184A TCGA 1992 The loss buying rules above are overridden if the following specific **anti-avoidance provisions** apply.

These provisions essentially **prohibit the offset** of losses on pre-change assets against any gains of the company where:
– a transaction is entered into with the aim of securing a tax advantage;
– the ownership of a company has changed hands;
– a capital loss is realised by that company on an asset that was owned by it before the change in ownership (note the capital loss can be realised before or after the change); and
– the tax avoidance arrangements involve an intention to deduct this loss in the calculation of gains chargeable to corporation tax either for that company or another company.

s 184D TCGA 1992 MEMO POINTS A **tax advantage** is defined as:
– relief or increased relief from corporation tax;
– repayment or increased repayment of corporation tax;
– the avoidance or reduction of a charge to corporation tax or an assessment to corporation tax; or
– the avoidance of a possible assessment to corporation tax.

1657 s 184C TCGA 1992 There is a **change of ownership** if a company either:
a. joins or leaves a capital gains group. Where an original group becomes part of a larger group (i.e. the parent company of the original group becomes a subsidiary of another company) the original group members are deemed to have joined a new group. (Contrast this to the general position for capital gains groups (¶1606).) However, there will be no deemed change in ownership if, as a result of a group reconstruction, a new holding company is simply inserted as the top company of an existing group and:
– the new top company is not the top company of another group and owns nothing (or almost nothing) other than the shares in the old top company; and
– the shareholders of the old group and the new group are the same; or
b. becomes subject to different control (¶2104). There will, however, be no deemed change in ownership under this provision if the only relevant change is the:
– insertion of a new top company above an existing capital gains group; or
– reconstruction of company ownership within an existing capital gains group.

MEMO POINTS 1. Where a pre-change asset is sold, but due to specific relieving provisions the **gain or loss is deferred**, it will be tracked until it falls to be recognised and then it will be taxed as a gain or loss on a pre-change asset.
The specific deferral reliefs mentioned in the legislation are:
– replacement of business assets (¶6050);
– reconstruction involving the transfer of a business (¶1166);
– transfer of a UK trade (¶1171);
– transfer of a non-UK trade to another non-UK resident company (¶1183);
– postponement of the charge that would otherwise arise on the deemed disposal of a company's assets when it ceases to be resident in the UK (¶1180); and
– formation of a Societas Europaea via a merger of a UK trade (¶2195).
2. These provisions apply equally when a loss is allocated to a company under the **notional intra-group transfer** rules (¶1620).
3. Assets that were owned before the change of ownership that are **subsequently transferred intra-group** under the no gain/no loss provisions remain "pre-change" assets until they are disposed of to a third party.
4. Assets that did not exist at the time of the change of ownership, but are **derived from pre-change assets**, are also treated as pre-change assets (for example, a new licence to exploit intellectual property where the intellectual property was a pre-change asset).
5. **Pooled assets** (e.g. shares) are essentially split into separate pools before and after the change in ownership. On the disposal of such assets they are matched firstly with the non-pre-change assets. (This order of matching takes priority over the standard share matching rules (¶1201).) s 184F TCGA 1992

3. Pre-entry gains

1662 s 184B TCGA 1992

Similar **anti-avoidance provisions** also prohibit the offset of gains on pre-change assets against any losses of the company where:
– the transaction is entered into with the aim of securing a tax advantage (¶1655);
– the ownership of a company has changed hands (¶1657);
– a capital gain is realised by that company on an asset that it owned before the change in ownership (note the capital gain can be realised before or after the change); and
– the tax avoidance arrangements involve an intention to deduct a loss from the gain in the calculation of gains chargeable to corporation tax either for that company or another company.

MEMO POINTS 1. The same provisions as those detailed in ¶1659 apply to track any **deferred gain** following the disposal of a pre-change asset.
2. These provisions apply equally when a gain is allocated to a company under the **notional intra-group transfer** rules (¶1620).
3. Assets that were owned before the change of ownership that are **subsequently transferred intra-group** under the no gain/no loss provisions remain "pre-change" assets until they are disposed of to a third party.
4. Assets that did not exist at the time of the change of ownership, but are **derived from pre-change assets** are also treated as pre-change assets (for example, a new licence to exploit intellectual property where the intellectual property was a pre-change asset).
5. **Pooled assets** (e.g. shares) are essentially split into separate pools before and after the change in ownership. On the disposal of such assets they are matched firstly with the non-pre-change assets. (This order of matching takes priority over the standard share matching rules (¶1201.) s 184F TCGA 1992

G. Tax payments

Interest on corporation tax paid late is charged at a higher rate than interest paid by HMRC in respect of overpayments of tax. In order to mitigate the effect of this difference and ease administrative burdens, groups of companies may: **1665**
– claim to **offset refunds** of tax due for one company against tax payable by another member of the group; and

– enter into arrangements with HMRC to make corporation **tax payments on a group-wide basis**.

Members of a group of companies **may also be** liable for any unpaid tax liabilities of a fellow group member (¶1700).

MEMO POINTS 1. The **tax payment facility** is a formal arrangement with HMRC which must be set up in advance.
2. The **surrender of tax refunds** can be done on an ad hoc basis, simply by giving the appropriate notice to HMRC.

1. Surrender of tax refunds

When may a surrender be made?

1667 ss 963 - 966 CTA 2010 Where one member of a 75% group of companies (¶1522) has overpaid tax for an accounting period and another member of the group has underpaid its liability, it is possible to give a joint notice to HMRC that the refund is to be surrendered between the companies.

The **effect of the surrender** is to treat the underpaying company as having made a payment on the later of the:
– due date for payment; or
– actual date the payment was made.

This will minimise interest charges arising to the group as a whole.

MEMO POINTS The surrender is effective only for interest purposes. It will not be taken into account when considering any **tax geared late filing penalties** (¶2316). In this case the tax will be treated as being paid on the day the notice is given.

1670 There are certain **conditions to be satisfied** for the surrender to be valid:
– both companies must have the same accounting period;
– both companies must be members of the same 75% group throughout the relevant period; and
– a joint notice must be given to HMRC before a refund of the overpayment is made.

MEMO POINTS 1. The **relevant period** starts on the first day of the accounting period for which a surrender is required and ends on the date the notice is given. This means that companies joining or leaving a group during the relevant period cannot participate in the surrender. Similarly, companies commencing or ceasing to trade during the period are excluded.
2. Once a refund has actually been made, it is too late to seek for the refund to be **reallocated**.

Refunds which may be surrendered

1672 A surrender may be made for the following:
– a refund of corporation tax (including corporation tax paid in instalments (¶2262));
– a repayment of income tax deducted at source (¶1370); or
– a payment of a tax credit for franked investment income received in the period (¶954).

2. Group payment arrangements

When may arrangements be made?

1675 ss 59F TMA 1970 To facilitate the administration of the **quarterly instalment regime** (¶2262), groups of companies may enter into a formal arrangement with HMRC for a nominated member of the group to make payments in respect of the group's corporation tax liability.

The payments can be allocated to different members as required, once the tax liability of individual companies has been established. This will help minimise the impact of the differing rates of interest payable in respect of over and underpayments of tax.

MEMO POINTS 1. The arrangement may cover any **members of a 51% group** (¶1520) and their 51% subsidiaries. It is not necessary for all members of a group to be covered by the arrangements. Different arrangements may be made for different subsets within the group, if required.
2. A company can only **participate in** any one group payment arrangement.

There are certain **conditions to be satisfied** for companies to participate in the arrangement: 1677
- at least one participating company must be a large company and therefore required to pay its tax in instalments;
- all companies must prepare accounts for the same period (the group accounting period), subject to ¶1682;
- the 51% relationship must exist on the date the arrangement document is signed;
- the group tax liability must be paid either by electronic transfer or by bank giro credit (cheque payments are not accepted); and
- each company must be up to date with their filing and payment obligations for prior accounting periods.

MEMO POINTS 1. The arrangements are not restricted to **UK resident companies** (i.e. UK permanent establishments can participate in the arrangements), although the nominated company must be UK resident.
2. Once an arrangement has been made, it will **roll forward automatically** and the nominated company should advise HMRC of any change to the companies covered by the arrangement.
3. See ¶2261 onwards for details of the payment requirements for **large companies**.

For the arrangements to apply, a **standardised formal document** providing details of the companies covered by the arrangements must be completed and signed by the nominated company. The arrangement document must be signed and submitted at least 2 months prior to the date of the first instalment payable. 1680

EXAMPLE For a group with an accounting date of 31 December 2007, the first instalment under the quarterly payments regime would be due on 14 July 2007 and therefore the group payment arrangement must be in place by 14 May 2007.

Companies joining or leaving a group

Where a company **joins a group**, for example on acquisition, it may be included in the arrangements for a period which starts after it joins, provided its accounts are prepared for a period ending on the same date as the group accounting period. 1682

Where a participating company **leaves the group**, the nominated company must remove the company from the arrangements.

MEMO POINTS Where a participating company's **accounting period ends during the group accounting period**, for example on the cessation of trade, it may remain part of the group arrangement, providing its accounts continue to be prepared for the same period.

Effect of the arrangement

Once an arrangement is in place, the **nominated company is responsible** for making payments covering the corporation tax liability of all participating companies. This includes not only the mainstream corporation tax liability, but also any payments required in respect of loans to participators (¶2111) or apportioned profits of controlled foreign companies (¶2145). 1685

Once the returns of all participating companies have been filed, or the liability has been otherwise determined by HMRC, a period is considered closed. **Once the period is closed**, HMRC will issue the nominated company with a notice setting out the total liability of all participating companies, and the total payments made. If insufficient tax has been paid, the nominated company is required to make a further payment. Alternatively, where it is believed that the liability of a company may be reduced, for example as a result of losses carried back from a subsequent period, the shortfall can be allocated to a specific company. 1690

MEMO POINTS If a shortfall is allocated in this way and not subsequently recovered, HMRC can seek payment from the nominated company.

1695 The nominated company should then notify HMRC of its proposed **allocation** of the tax payment between the participating companies.

Once the allocation has been made, and accepted by HMRC, any interest liabilities for individual companies will be calculated. Each participating company is responsible for its own interest and penalty position.

MEMO POINTS HMRC will not accept an allocation to a company which would otherwise be liable to a **tax geared penalty** for late filing of a return (¶2316) if the tax could be allocated to other companies.

3. Group liability for tax of group members

1700 Members of a group of companies are responsible for unpaid tax of fellow members in certain circumstances. A **liability may arise where** tax is unpaid:
– by a non-resident company; or
– in respect of chargeable gains.

Non-resident company

1704 ss 974 - 980 CTA 2010 If a non-resident company fails to pay its UK corporation tax liability within 6 months of the date on which it becomes payable, HMRC may seek to recover the money from a company which, during the relevant period, is a member of:
a. the same group of companies;
b. a consortium which owns the non-resident company; or
c. the same group of companies as a company which is a member of a consortium which owns the non-resident company.

The **definition of group** for these purposes depends on the relationship to the non-resident company. Two companies are members of the same group for **a**. above if one is a 51% subsidiary of the other, or both are 51% subsidiaries of a third company. However, for **c**. above, companies are members of the same group of companies using the group relief definition i.e. requiring a 75% relationship.

MEMO POINTS The **relevant period** is the period:
– beginning 12 months before the start of the accounting period for which the liability is due; and
– ending at the date on which the tax became payable.

1706 s 979 CTA 2010 Where the liability arises through a **consortium relationship**, the amount of the tax which the company can be required to pay is restricted to the relevant percentage of the non-resident company's liability.

Where the liability arises by virtue of being a member of a consortium which owns the non-resident company, the percentage is determined by the company's interest in the non-resident company during the relevant period. Where the liability arises due to a group of companies having an interest in the consortium, it is the total interest the group members have in the consortium. Where the liability arises for both these reasons, the higher percentage is taken.

MEMO POINTS The rules for **determining the level of a company's interest** in a consortium company are set out in ¶1580.

Chargeable gains

1708 s 190 TCGA 1992 If a member of a group of companies fails to pay any corporation tax in respect of chargeable gains within 6 months of the date on which it becomes payable, HMRC may recover that amount from the company which was the principal member of the group at the date the gain accrued.

The **liability** in this situation **is restricted to** the lower of:
– the tax outstanding; and
– the tax on the chargeable gain at the rate in force when the gain accrued.

The **definition of a group** is, for this provision, as defined in ¶1524, except that references to 75% subsidiaries are replaced with references to 51% subsidiaries.

MEMO POINTS 1. If the company realising the gain was a **non-resident company trading in the UK** via a permanent establishment, the controlling director (of the company or a company having control of the company) is also liable. This extends to any person who was a controlling director during the 12 months prior to the disposal.
2. If the gain is the result of a **degrouping charge** (¶1606), any member of the group which had an interest in the asset in the 12 months prior to disposal is liable for the tax.

Method of collection

In order to recover the tax, HMRC must issue the company with **a notice** specifying: 1710 s 977 CTA 2010
- the amount of tax assessed which remains unpaid;
- the date on which the tax became payable; and
- the amount the company is required to pay within 30 days of the issue of the notice.

The notice acts as an assessment and the company may appeal against it if it believes it to be incorrect.

The **time limit for issuing a notice** is 3 years after the liability for the accounting period is finally determined as follows: 1712 s 978 CTA 2010
a. if the liability is agreed following a **self-assessment return** without an enquiry being launched, the liability is finally determined on the last date on which an enquiry could be launched (¶2330);
b. if an **enquiry** is launched, the liability is determined 30 days after whichever of the following applies to the particular enquiry:
- the issue of a closure notice;
- the amendment of the return by HMRC; or
- the determination of an appeal against an amended return;

c. if no tax return is submitted, or the return is incomplete, HMRC may issue **a notice of determination** (¶2317) setting out the amount of the liability, in which case the relevant date is the date on which the determination is issued; and
d. if the tax relates to a **discovery assessment** (¶2342) against which no appeal is made, the relevant date is the date on which the tax becomes due and payable. If an appeal is issued, the liability is determined on the date on which the appeal is determined.

MEMO POINTS A **payment made as a result of a notice** is not deductible for tax purposes, but the paying company may recover the amount paid from the company that was originally liable.

H. Shadow ACT

1. Aim of provisions

The shadow ACT system (¶1400) is modified when applied to companies which are members of a 51% group (¶1520) The legislation is designed to prevent one company utilising surplus ACT whilst other members of the group have shadow ACT. 1714 SI 1999/358

2. Utilisation of shadow ACT

Where a company has surplus shadow ACT for an accounting period after the automatic 6 year carry back (¶1425), the balance is compulsorily surrendered to other companies within the same 51% group up to the limit of their capacity. The parent company can allocate the surplus shadow ACT to group members as it sees fit. However, if such an allocation is not made, HMRC can determine the allocation. If the surplus shadow ACT exceeds the capacity for the whole group, the balance is carried forward by the company which actually gave rise to the surplus. 1716

Surplus shadow ACT is surrendered to group companies for any accounting period starting within the 24 months ending on the last day of the surrendering company's accounting period. Where there is more than one accounting period falling within this period for a specific group company, the shadow ACT is allocated in the following order:
- accounting periods beginning and ending on the same dates as, or falling wholly within, the surrendering company's accounting period;
- accounting periods beginning before but ending in the surrendering company's accounting period;
- accounting periods beginning in but ending after the surrendering company's accounting period; and
- any other accounting period falling within the 24 month period.

3. Intra-group dividends

1718 Intra-group dividends (i.e. distributions made by a 51% subsidiary company to its parent) are **generally** outside the shadow ACT regime. Such dividends are excluded from the calculation of shadow ACT and are not treated as franked investment income in the hands of the parent.

However, **in some circumstances** it may be preferable to include these distributions. Where the subsidiary has sufficient franked investment income (including surplus franked investment income brought forward) to cover the distribution, it **may elect to** treat that distribution as subject to shadow ACT. The election must be made on the tax return and must be made within 2 years of the end of the accounting period in which the distribution is made. Such an election is irrevocable. Where the election is made, the distribution becomes franked investment income in the hands of the parent and therefore reduces the shadow ACT payable by the parent.

The election is made for a specified amount of franked investment income. Therefore, where the distribution to the parent exceeds the available franked investment income, the election only relates to that amount which would be covered by the franked investment income.

1720 The question of whether it is beneficial to make such an election will depend upon the capacity of each company to absorb shadow ACT, the extent to which surplus ACT may be displaced, and also the level of proposed future distributions.

SECTION 2

Transfer pricing

1. Aim of provisions

1721 Part 4 TIOPA 2010 To prevent the manipulation of internal pricing structures, provisions exist whereby transactions between organisations (¶1728) must be computed on an arm's length basis. This is known as transfer pricing.

The transfer pricing regulations apply to **UK and international groups**. The provisions can be complex and this section covers the basic principles.

2. Exemption from transfer pricing rules

1722 The **following companies** are exempt from the transfer pricing regulations:
- companies that were dormant immediately before 1 April 2004 and continue to be so;
- companies that have become dormant after 1 April 2004; and
- small and medium-sized enterprises.

Dormant companies

Companies that have assets in them that the group wishes to use will not qualify for exemption as the transfer pricing rules will impute an arm's length charge for the asset. In this situation the assets will need to be moved out of the company if it is to become dormant. 1723

Small and medium-sized enterprises

Small and medium-sized enterprises (SMEs) are defined differently to SMEs for the purposes of capital allowances. For the purposes of transfer pricing, SMEs are defined firstly by the number of employees, and then by the level of turnover or assets (which are defined in euros). 1725

Condition	Small-sized enterprise	Medium-sized enterprise
Max no. of employees	less than 50	less than 250
And then either:		
Max turnover	€10m	€50m
Or		
Max balance sheet assets	€10m	€43m

MEMO POINTS These thresholds are applied on an annualised basis, to the worldwide consolidated group, and will include any **linked enterprises** (broadly any enterprises that the SME controls (¶1729)).

The **exemption will not apply** if: 1726
a. the enterprise is an SME and:
– an election is made by the company for the exemption not to apply. Such an election once made is irrevocable; or
– the other party to the transaction(s) is resident and liable to tax in a non-qualifying territory (i.e. any country with which the UK does not have a suitable double tax treaty (unless the territory is specified as qualifying in a regulation)); or
b. the enterprise is a **medium-sized enterprise** and HMRC consider that a transfer pricing misstatement will give rise to a significant loss of tax and they issue a transfer pricing notice to that effect. s 168 TIOPA 2010

MEMO POINTS 1. A party to the transaction will be **resident in a non-qualifying territory** if it is liable to tax in the territory by reason of domicile, residence or place of management. (This therefore does not include a person who is liable to tax in the territory simply by virtue of income from sources in that territory).
2. HMRC have issued a **list of qualifying territories** (available on their website).
3. A **transfer pricing notice** cannot be issued unless the return is the subject of an enquiry. The recipient of the notice can appeal (within 30 days) against the notice, but only on the grounds that it is not a medium-sized enterprise for the purposes of the transfer pricing regulations. Following receipt of the notice the enterprise has 90 days to amend its return. (The 90-day limit is extended where an appeal has been made.) HMRC will not be able to issue a closure notice to the enquiry until the 90 day period has elapsed or the return has been amended.

3. Scope of transfer pricing rules

When do the rules apply?

The transfer pricing regime applies to transactions of **goods and services and financing arrangements** (e.g. inter-company loans) where: 1728 s 147 TIOPA 2010
– one organisation directly or indirectly participates in the management, control or capital of the other organisation; or
– another party directly or indirectly participates in the management, control or capital of both organisations.

The **controlled organisation** must be a body corporate or a partnership for transfer pricing to apply. Although aimed primarily at transactions between companies, the legislation applies equally to transactions between individuals and the companies they control.

MEMO POINTS **HMRC's guidance** as to the exact scope of the transfer pricing regulations is unclear, but states that it will apply to any form of trading activities undertaken in a business or commercial manner. Consequently individuals, charities etc will not always be within the scope of the regime as it depends largely on the capacity of the parties in the transaction. For example, HMRC state that they would not expect transfer pricing to apply to a salary paid to a director of a company where he also controlled the company (as the director would not be undertaking trading activities in his capacity as director), but they would expect an arm's length price to be charged for property rented to a company by an individual who also controlled the company.

Direct participation

1729 s 157 TIOPA 2010; s 1124 CTA 2010

Direct participation **means that** a person has control over the organisation. A person has **control**:

a. over a company if he can secure that the affairs of the company are conducted in accordance with his wishes either by possession of votes or shares, or by powers conferred under the Articles of Association or other binding legal document. In addition to the rights owned by a person, the following rights will be attributed to him:
– the rights of persons connected with him;
– rights which he is entitled to acquire in the future; and
– the rights which persons connected with him are entitled to acquire in the future; and

b. over a partnership if he has the right to more than half of the assets or income of the partnership.

Indirect participation

1730 ss 158, 160 TIOPA 2010

Indirect participation is **where a person**:

a. is one of a number of major participants in the organisation. A major participant is a person who, with another person, controls the organisation and each has a minimum 40% interest in the organisation;

s 159 TIOPA 2010 **b.** would have been treated as directly participating if the following various rights and powers were attributed to him:
– rights and powers which he is (or will become) entitled to acquire in the future;
– rights and powers of any person which are, or may be, required to be exercised on behalf of, under the direction of, or for the benefit of, the potential participant;
– rights and powers of persons connected with him; and
– rights and powers which would be attributable to a person connected with the potential participant if he were the potential participant; or

ss 161, 162 TIOPA 2010 **c.** has acted together with others in relation to financing arrangements of the business and collectively they could control the business. (This condition is still satisfied for up to 6 months after they ceased to act together.) In determining whether a party could collectively control the business all the rights and powers detailed in **b**. above in respect of one party should be attributed to all the other parties at the time they are acting together and for up to 6 months after they cease to so act together.

HMRC's guidance detailing when parties can be said to be acting together to collectively control an organisation stipulates that:
– generally, financial transactions between two parties where neither controls the other will constitute an arm's length transaction between independent parties and they will not be treated as acting together to collectively control the business;
– there does not need to be any discussion or direct agreement between the parties for them to be acting together; and
– it is not necessary for both persons to have an ownership interest in the business (for example a 100% shareholder may act together with a lender holding 100% of the company debt). Conversely, a simple ownership interest will not in itself constitute acting together (where, for example, shares are held as an investment, with no other involvement in the shareholders of the company).

EXAMPLE

1. A company agrees with its three shareholders that they will all make separate loans to the company to provide additional investment and three separate loan agreements are drawn up. The three shareholders will be deemed to be acting together.

2. The commercial lending team of a bank makes loans to a company and the bank happens to hold shares in the company (with no other involvement with the other shareholders). The bank will not be treated as acting together with the other shareholders.

MEMO POINTS 1. **Financing arrangements** refer not only to the simple provision of finance. They apply to all financing transactions for a company or partnership and can include leasing or hire purchase.
2. For these purposes, **a person is connected with** his spouse/civil partner, his (and his spouse's/-civil partner's) relatives and their spouses/civil partners. A relative is a sibling, ancestor or lineal descendant. Persons who are trustees of a settlement are also connected with the settlor and persons connected with the settlor.

4. Application of transfer pricing rules

Transfer pricing adjustment

Transactions that are not made on an arm's length basis will need to be recalculated on an arm's length basis and profits adjusted accordingly. This is known as a transfer pricing adjustment. 1731

A transfer pricing adjustment is **not required** in respect of:
- capital allowances;
- chargeable gains;
- loan relationship debits and credits; or
- foreign exchange gains and losses.

Cross-border transfer pricing adjustments (as opposed to adjustments between UK residents) apply unilaterally which means that where the profits of a UK organisation are increased, there is no corresponding reduction in profits of an overseas organisation. However, relief may be available if the overseas organisation is located in a country with which the UK has a double taxation agreement (¶4227).

Compensating adjustments

Basic rules Where both parties to the transfer pricing adjustment are **UK taxpayers** a compensating adjustment may be available. This means that where the profits of one organisation (the advantaged company) have been increased due to a transfer pricing adjustment, the other organisation (the disadvantaged company) may claim an equivalent reduction in its profits. The returns of both parties will therefore be prepared using the arm's length terms. 1732 ss 174, 177 TIOPA 2010

A **claim** for a compensating adjustment must generally be made within 2 years of the date on which the advantaged company files its return. If the advantaged company originally prepared its return using the actual terms of the transaction and then submitted an amended return incorporating the arm's length terms, the time limit for a claim is 2 years from the date on which the advantaged company filed the amended return. If the adjustment is the result of an HMRC enquiry into the advantaged company's affairs, the time limit is 2 years from the date the closure notice (¶2337) is issued.

A **balancing payment** can be made between the affected companies up to the amount of the compensating adjustment with no tax implications. ss 195, 196 TIOPA 2010

Specific provisions provide details as to how the compensating adjustment will work for transactions involving:
- trading stock;
- CFCs (¶1734);
- interest; and
- group share incentive plans.

MEMO POINTS Guidance has been issued by HMRC concerning the **interaction of VAT with transfer pricing adjustments** and balancing payments.

In general, a transfer pricing adjustment (whether or not accompanied by a balancing payment) is outside the scope of VAT, but it may be indicative that the value of the relevant transaction was understated and consequently the transaction may need to be revisited to see if a correction for VAT is required.

Any VAT adjustment depends upon the nature of the balancing payment:

– if the balancing payment is made as further consideration for the earlier supply, any necessary correction to the VAT return must be made in the usual manner (¶9222); and

– if there is an arrangement linking the payment to the supply of further goods or services, then a further supply of goods or services will be treated as being made for non-monetary consideration (i.e. the consideration being the agreement to pay the balancing payment).

If a partial monetary charge is made for such further supplies of goods or services (i.e. a charge that does not represent full consideration), then the value of the non-monetary consideration is determined accordingly and VAT would be due on the aggregate of the monetary and the non-monetary consideration.

EXAMPLE Company A agrees to provide Company B with management services if Company B agrees to make a balancing payment to Company A. Company A has therefore agreed to perform certain services in return for non-monetary consideration (i.e. Company B's agreement to make a balancing payment) and the management services would have to be valued to determine the amount of VAT due.

Where both parties to the balancing payment are within the same VAT group (¶7807), no liability to VAT would normally arise.

1733
s 180 TIOPA 2010

Trading stock When trading stock (or work in progress) is transferred from one company to an associated person at less than arm's length price, a transfer pricing adjustment may be made in respect of the transfer. In this situation, the transferee can deduct a compensating adjustment in the accounting period in which the transfer pricing adjustment is made.

MEMO POINTS **Without these provisions** the transferor would be taxed on the additional profit immediately but the transferee would not be entitled to deduct the compensating adjustment until they sold the relevant stock or work in progress.

1734
s 179 TIOPA 2010

CFCs When the advantaged company is a CFC (¶2145), and a transfer pricing adjustment is made, a compensating adjustment can be made by the UK disadvantaged company, provided the profits (as adjusted for transfer pricing) are wholly apportioned to UK corporate interest holders.

1735
s 181 TIOPA 2010

Interest A compensating adjustment can be made in respect of a transfer pricing adjustment arising from interest payments on securities.

Similarly, where a transfer pricing adjustment arises from the **provision of a guarantee** on a security, a compensating adjustment can be made to effectively treat the sponsor as if he had paid the interest that was denied as a tax deduction for the borrower. However, the compensating adjustment is limited to the amount that an independent third party lender would take the guarantee into account when determining the borrower's debt capacity.

Interest paid to a **non-resident lender** in respect of an uncommercial loan can be paid gross (i.e. with no withholding tax deducted) where the borrower has been denied an interest deduction under the transfer pricing rules.

MEMO POINTS A compensating **adjustment cannot be made** in respect of a provision relating to a security if the guarantor directly or indirectly participates in the management, control or capital of the business.

1736

Group share incentive plans HMRC have issued guidance on the interaction between share incentive plans and the transfer pricing regime. (The term "share incentive plan" in this context includes schemes for the provision of shares and share options.)

The guidance covers the situation where a group company (which will often be the parent company) provides employee share plans to its own, and its subsidiaries', employees. Typically there are two elements to the facility being provided:

– the **provision of the shares** or share options; and
– the **provision of the administration services** for the operation of the share plan.

The arm's length value that must be paid for these facilities and the tax treatment of the payments is as follows:

Arm's length payment to be made to parent company	Value of the arm's length payment to be made[1]	Tax treatment	
		Recipient (parent company)	Payer (subsidiary)
For the provision of shares/options	Market value of the shares/options	Taken to reserves and not recognised for tax purposes[2]	Disallowed as the payer will obtain a statutory corporation tax deduction (¶787)
For the administration of the scheme	An arm's length market value (i.e. cost plus an arm's length mark up)	Taxable	Deductible under normal principles[3]

Note:
1. A transfer pricing adjustment may be made if no charge is made, or the charge that is made is not a market value charge.
2. If, however, the parent company obtains a tax deduction for this payment anywhere in the world and all the other arbitrage conditions are satisfied (¶2207), then HMRC may issue a notice on the recipient requiring it to recompute its tax liability (¶2197).
3. If the total charge for the facility cannot be split into identifiable parts for the share award and the administration charge, then the whole amount will be disallowed.

EXAMPLE A Ltd has a subsidiary, B Ltd, and, on 1 January, all the employees of B Ltd are granted options over shares in A Ltd exercisable in 3 years at the current market value of £1. A transfer pricing adjustment is made on both A Ltd's and B Ltd's tax computations representing the administrative costs of the scheme. In A Ltd, a deduction for the costs of providing the administrative services will be allowed. B Ltd will be able to claim a deduction equal to the administrative charge and, in 3 years' time, will obtain a statutory deduction for the options that are exercised by its employees.

Arm's length terms

The OECD also produced guidelines on a number of possible methods of determining the arm's length price. The most frequently used are detailed below. 1737

a. comparable uncontrolled price method: Where there is adequate third-party information for the same goods, the price charged to third parties may be used;

b. cost-plus method: The cost incurred by the supplier of goods or services is increased by a margin for profit calculated to take into account the supplier's role, the market conditions and the risk involved. This is most commonly used for part-finished goods and for services;

c. resale price method: The final selling price is reduced by a margin to reflect the vendor's costs, and an element of profit. This is most commonly used for distribution, marketing and sales activities; and

d. profit-split method: The overall profit earned from a transaction is calculated and split between the organisations involved on an economically valid basis. This may be used where there are complex transactions which cannot easily be broken down into the constituent parts.

Whichever method is used, the company must be able to justify and explain the method of calculation.

As regards payments of **interest on loans**, the following factors will be considered to determine whether a loan is made on an arm's length basis:
– amount of the loan;
– rate of interest; and
– whether the loan would have been made at all in the absence of a special relationship.

The borrowing company and its subsidiaries are looked at in isolation from the parent group when considering the amount of the loan that it would receive from an unconnected lender.

Any guarantees etc provided by connected companies are disregarded when determining whether the loan is on an arm's length basis.

Advance pricing agreements

1738 s 218 TIOPA 2010 Where a company has substantial complex business arrangements which are subject to transfer pricing, it may be preferable to get an Advance Pricing Agreement (APA). An APA is an agreement between the company and HMRC regarding the method for resolving transfer pricing issues before the tax return is filed.

Any **company may request an APA** from HMRC. However, APAs may be time consuming to prepare and are intended only for situations where there are complex transfer pricing issues. Therefore, HMRC will not enter into an APA with a company where it appears that the issues are straightforward. HMRC are unlikely to consider a company's transfer pricing issues to be complex where reliable market comparables are readily available.

There are **two sorts of APA**, unilateral and bilateral. A unilateral APA is binding only on the UK tax authorities, whereas a bilateral APA is binding on the tax authorities of both countries. HMRC will seek to negotiate a bilateral APA where the associated company is based in a country with which the UK has a double tax agreement (¶4227) which includes a Mutual Agreement Procedure article.

1740 SP 2/07 Similar rules apply for advance thin capitalisation agreements (ATCAs). HMRC will enter discussions to agree an ATCA where:
- a UK tax paying business is receiving finance from an overseas company;
- one company controls the other, or both are under common control (¶1728); and
- the transaction is not a normal arm's length commercial agreement e.g. where an overseas company is providing funding by way of loan rather than equity.

Applications for agreements should be made on the model ATCA application provided in HMRC's guidance. Typically such agreements will require the company to maintain a specific level of debt: equity ratio or interest cover, and are generally made for periods of 5 years.

1742 Where the **terms of an ATCA are breached** the company may choose to disallow a proportion of the interest charged in the accounts for that period. They should also notify HMRC of this and the steps they are taking to remedy the breach. The company may choose not to disallow any of the interest charged and enter into discussions with HMRC. However, this is only expected if there have been "unusual, unexpected or catastrophic" circumstances that result in the breach. An example of such circumstances is given as the closing of a UK production plant for a considerable period of time.

5. Record-keeping

Documentation

1743 Sch 18 para 21 FA 1998 Under the self-assessment regime, companies are required to prepare and retain documentation in support of the tax return. This requirement extends to their transfer pricing policies. The transfer pricing documentation **must exist**, at the latest, by the time the tax return for the accounting period is filed. Documentation prepared for one accounting period may be retained for subsequent accounting periods where there is no change in circumstances.

In any event, the documentation applicable to an accounting period **must be retained** for 6 years after the end of that accounting period. If an enquiry is launched into a return, the documentation must be retained until the conclusion of the enquiry, if later.

Tax Bulletin 37 MEMO POINTS 1. HMRC accept that the documentation prepared by a company may take into account the size and complexity of the company's affairs. However, the documentation must be sufficient to allow HMRC to be satisfied that the correct basis has been used. Therefore, the **documentation must identify**:
- the commercial or financial relationships to which transfer pricing applies;
- the nature, terms (including price) and amounts involved in relevant transactions;

– the method adopted in arriving at the terms of those transactions;
– that the method has resulted in arm's length terms or, if not, what adjustment is required and how it is to be calculated; and
– the terms of relevant commercial arrangements with third parties and affiliated customers.
2. It is possible to agree a shorter period of retention of records with HMRC. See ¶9892 for details.

Penalties

The following penalties may be imposed: 1744

Sch 18 para 23 FA 1998; s 86(8) FA 1999

Offence	Penalty
Documentation is not prepared or retained for the required period	£3,000
Submission of an incorrect tax return [1, 2]	See ¶9780
Supply of false or misleading information in connection with an application for an APA [3]	£10,000

Note:
1. This includes the situation where a company has an APA but has not prepared the return in accordance with the terms of the agreement.
2. A penalty will not be charged where a company has made a genuine attempt to use a third party valuation but HMRC are not happy with the basis of that valuation.
3. This also nullifies the APA and therefore the company may also be exposed to penalties for submitting an incorrect return.

CHAPTER 9

Special situations

OUTLINE ¶¶

SECTION 1

Sale of lessor companies

A. Scope of rules

When do the rules apply?

1800 ss 382 - 437 CTA 2010

Special rules apply to a "lessor" company (¶1810) that carries on a trade on its own or in partnership if there is a change of:
- ownership of the company; or
- the partnership profit sharing arrangements.

1802 These **rules impose** on the company a:
- **charge** on the day of the change, that is essentially the difference between the balance sheet value and the tax written down value of the leased assets at the date of the change. If this results in a negative figure, the charge is nil; and
- **corresponding deduction** on the day after the change, equal to the earlier charge. If this results in a loss, it cannot be carried back. Also if the obtaining of the deduction was the main object of the transaction, any loss arising cannot be group relieved or set against other income.

1805 The **aim of these provisions** is to claw back the capital allowances that have already been given to the old owner and effectively reallocate them to the new owner.

> EXAMPLE A Ltd bought an asset for £100,000, leasing it out on a 20 year finance lease. Capital allowances meant that in the first 6 years, A Ltd would be loss making and able to group relieve these losses accordingly and from Year 7 onwards it would be profitable.
> Assuming A Ltd was sold in Year 7 to B Ltd (another loss making group) then on the date of sale there will be a charge in A Ltd equal to the difference between the balance sheet value and tax written down value of the leased asset. A corresponding deduction equal to this charge will then be available in A Ltd on the day after the change in ownership.

Electing out of the regime

1807 ss 398A - G CTA 2010

Where the change took place on or after 9 December 2009 but **before 23 March 2011**, it was possible for the lessor company to elect not to come within the regime. Where this election was made no charge nor corresponding deduction was made and the trade was ring-fenced so that the deferred profits could not be extinguished by the use of losses from other businesses in the future.

What is a lessor company?

1810 s 387 CTA 2010

A lessor company is **defined as** any company where either:
- half the accounting value of the plant or machinery owned by the company relates to qualifying leased plant or machinery; or

– half of the company's income in the pervious 12 month period (ending with the day of change) is from qualifying leased plant or machinery.

Qualifying leased plant or machinery is any plant or machinery which in the past 12 months is or has been subject to a lease, which is not an excluded lease of background plant and machinery (¶487).

MEMO POINTS 1. The **accounting value** is the balance sheet value of plant and machinery, plus the value of any plant and machinery transferred to it by associated companies. Where plant and machinery is subject to a finance lease, the lease figure is to be treated as part of the balance sheet value.
Any **liabilities** that would otherwise increase or reduce the accounting value of qualifying leased plant or machinery are ignored. s 436 CTA 2010
2. **Prior to 23 March 2011** the assets also had to qualify for capital allowances.

Change of ownership

There is a change in ownership when the lessor company ceases to be a 75% subsidiary (¶1522) of its principal company. To establish the principal company the legislation describes a series of relationships traced up from the lessor company until this "chain" of relationships can go no further because the company at the top of the chain is not a 75% subsidiary of another company. This top company therefore becomes the principal company and a change of ownership occurs whenever any of the links in the 75% chain from the principal company are broken. **1815** ss 392, 393 CTA 2010

MEMO POINTS If the lessor company is a **consortium company** (or a 90% subsidiary of a consortium company) the chain is traced upwards through any 75% relationships above the consortium company. There is a change in ownership if there is either a: s 394 CTA 2010
– break in the 75% relationship if the consortium member is a 75% subsidiary of another company; or
– fall in the percentage of ordinary shares held or the entitlement to profits/assets available for distribution within the consortium relationship.

B. Charge and deduction

Calculation of the charge

Where there is a change in ownership (or partnership profit share arrangements) of a lessor company the company is treated as receiving income on the day of the change and its accounting period then ends. **1820** ss 394 - 406 CTA 2010

The **income** (referred to as the basic amount) is calculated using the formula:

$$PM - TWDV$$

where:

– PM is the total of the balance sheet value of all the company's plant and machinery, the net investment in any finance leased assets and the market value of any plant and machinery transferred to it from associated companies. (Specifically excluded is plant and machinery that does not qualify for capital allowances because the asset is a long funding lease (¶483) or hire purchase or similar contract); and

– TWDV is the tax written down value of all assets at the start of the new accounting period (excluding any expenditure on the acquisition of plant and machinery on this day, other than plant and machinery acquired from associated parties).

If the calculation results in a negative figure, the charge is nil.

MEMO POINTS 1. A company is an **associated company** when: s 408 CTA 2010
– one has control (¶1902) of the other; or
– both are under the control of the same person(s).

In addition any company that is owned by a consortium (or is a 90% subsidiary of a company owned by a consortium) is associated with:
– its consortium members; and
– any associates of the consortium members.
2. See ¶1830 for modifications to these provisions where there is a change in **partnership profit share arrangements**.

Calculation of the deduction

1825 On the day after the change of ownership of the company (or partnership profit share arrangements) and resultant charge:
– a new accounting period starts; and
– a deductible expense accrues to the company, equal to the basic amount. Any loss that arises as a result of this expense cannot be carried back to an earlier accounting period and can only be carried forward to subsequent accounting periods starting within 12 months of the change in ownership.

MEMO POINTS 1. See ¶1830 for modifications to this rule where there is a change in **partnership profit share arrangements**.

ss 432, 433 CTA 2010 2. If a company enters into **arrangements purely in order to obtain the deduction**, any loss derived from the deduction can only be carried forward against leasing income from a lease in place at the time the company obtained the deduction.

Leasing business carried on by a company in partnership

1830 ss 409 - 431 CTA 2010 Where a company carries on a leasing business in partnership and there is a change in the company's interest in the business then the above provisions apply (¶1800 to ¶1825), with the **following modifications**:
a. the charge (basic amount (¶1820)) is triggered when there is a change in the company's interest in the business (i.e. when there is a fall in the percentage share of a partner's profits or losses of the business);
b. the basic amount is levied on the partner who has reduced his interest (based on the amount by which its percentage interest has been reduced);
c. the corresponding deduction is available to the company increasing its interest (if there are several partners, the deduction is allocated between them based on their percentage partnership interests); and
d. the definition of an associate company of the lessor company is extended to include:
– the partner company;
– any company associated (¶1820) with that partner.

MEMO POINTS In addition if there is a qualifying change of:
– interest by a partner company and that partner company is a **consortium** company, associated companies will include any member of the consortium and any company associated with that partner; and
– ownership of the consortium company, but no change in that company's interest in the partnership interest, associated companies will include a company that is an associate of the other consortium members.

C. Anti-avoidance rules

When do the rules apply?

1835 Specific anti-avoidance provisions apply to certain structures which may be set up to **counter the sale of lessor company provisions**, whereby:
– partnership structures artificially allocate profits and losses to ensure profits go to a loss making partner and losses to a profitable partner;

– there is a sale of a leased asset, but a retention of the income stream;
– there is a change in the person carrying on the trade; or
– the balance sheet values of leased assets are manipulated.

Artificial partnership structures

There is a restriction on the **utilisation of losses** where: **1840** ss 887 - 889 CTA 2010
– a company carries on a business of leasing plant and machinery in partnership;
– the leasing business makes a loss; and
– the company's profit sharing and capital allowance arrangements in the leasing business are not determined by using the same single set percentage.

Where these conditions are met, the losses can only be relieved against income from leases entered into by the partnership before the end of the period in which the loss arose.

Sale and retention of income

Special rules apply to **determine the disposal value** of leased plant and machinery where: **1845** s 228K CTA 2010
– a company carries on a business of leasing plant and machinery (alone or in partnership);
– an asset subject to a lease is sold; and
– some or all of the income from the leased asset is retained.

In this situation, the disposal **value varies** as follows: **1850** s 228L CAA 2001

a. if the **consideration received exceeds the original cost** of the asset the whole of the consideration received for capital allowances purposes is taken as the disposal consideration (there is no restriction based on the original cost of the asset); and

b. if the **consideration received does not exceed the original cost** of the asset the disposal value to be brought into account for capital allowances purposes is the total of:
– the consideration received; plus
– the net present value of future rentals, calculated as follows:

$$RI/(1 + T)^{i}$$

where:
– RI is the rental payment to which the seller is entitled to immediately after the disposal;
– T is the temporal discount rate (currently 3.5%); and
– i is the number of days in the period beginning with the day of the sale and ending with the payment day, divided by 365.

Change in person carrying on the trade

On a change in the person carrying on the trade, the **disposal value**, for capital allowances purposes, is the consideration actually received. **1855** s 267A CAA 2001

MEMO POINTS The rules allowing a connected transferee and transferor to elect that plant and machinery can be **transferred at written down value** for capital allowances purposes (¶267) do not apply where the transferor and transferee are lessor companies.

Manipulation of balance sheet values

Special rules apply when a company enters into arrangements that both: **1860** ss 434 - 436 CTA 2010
– increase or decrease the balance sheet value of an asset; and
– have as their main purpose, or one of their main purposes, that of securing a tax advantage.

In **such circumstances** the increase or decrease is ignored for the purposes of determining whether a company is a lessor company.

MEMO POINTS A company will be treated as securing a **tax advantage** if, by reason of the arrangements:
– it is not considered to be a lessor company; or
– the amount of the charge (¶1820) would be reduced, or the deduction (¶1825) increased.

SECTION 2

Corporate venturing scheme

A. Aim of scheme

1890 Sch 15 FA 2000

The corporate venturing scheme (CVS) is **intended to** facilitate smaller companies raising finance by offering tax relief to potential corporate investors. It operates in a similar way to the enterprise investment scheme for individual investors (¶2861).

Under the CVS, the investing company is able to:
– claim tax relief (known as investment relief) for investments made in qualifying unquoted trading companies (¶1928);
– defer gains on eligible CVS shares by rolling over the gain into other CVS shares (known as deferral relief (¶2004)); and
– claim relief against income for any loss suffered in respect of the shares (CVS loss relief (¶2007)).

MEMO POINTS The scheme **is available for** shares issued on or after 1 April 2000 and before 1 April 2010.

B. Investment relief

1. Conditions for relief

1892 A company qualifying for investment relief is **entitled to claim** a deduction against its corporation tax liability based on the amount of its investment. To qualify for investment relief, numerous conditions must be satisfied. Once relief has been obtained, it may be withdrawn if any of the conditions are subsequently breached.

Sch 15 para 3 FA 2000

Many of the conditions must be satisfied throughout the **qualification period**, which is the period beginning with the issue of the shares and ending immediately before the third anniversary of:
– the issue of the shares; or
– the commencement of the qualifying trade, if later.

1894 In order to qualify for CVS relief, a qualifying investing company must subscribe for relevant shares in a qualifying issuing company. A breach of any of the conditions may lead to relief being withdrawn.

a. Qualifying investing company

Definition

1896 Sch 15 paras 4, 13 FA 2000

Any company is a qualifying investing company **provided** that it subscribes for relevant shares (¶1910) in a qualifying issuing company (¶1912) and throughout the qualification period (¶1892), it does not:
– have a material interest (¶1900) in the issuing company;
– control (¶1902) the issuing company; or
– exist wholly for the purposes of carrying on a financial trade (¶1906).

Immediately after issue, the shares must be a **chargeable asset** in the hands of the investing company. This means that if the shares were sold, any gain would be a chargeable gain and subject to corporation tax.

MEMO POINTS Shares will be chargeable assets for these provisions even if they fall within the **substantial shareholding exemption** (¶1160).

There must be no reciprocal arrangements in connection with the subscription, and the subscription itself must be made for commercial purposes and not as part of any scheme or arrangement for the avoidance of tax. **1898** Sch 15 paras 6, 14 FA 2000

MEMO POINTS There are **reciprocal arrangements** if an arrangement exists whereby:
- the investing company subscribes for shares in a company with which it is not connected; and
- another individual or company subscribes for shares in a related company (i.e. a company in which the investing company, or any other party to the arrangement, has a material interest).

Material interest

A company has a material interest if it has **direct or indirect ownership of** (¶1514), or is entitled to acquire, more than 30% of the ordinary share capital or voting rights in the issuing company (or a 51% subsidiary of the issuing company). **1900** Sch 15 para 7 FA 2000

Ordinary share capital means all shares issued by the company and any loan capital which carries the right of conversion into, or to acquisition of, shares, but excludes relevant preference shares (¶1904).

MEMO POINTS **Loan capital** does not include debts incurred in the ordinary course of business or by overdrawing a bank account.

Control

A company has control of the issuing company where it exercises, is able to exercise, or is entitled to acquire, **direct or indirect** control over the affairs of the company. **1902** ss 450, 451 CTA 2010

For these purposes a company is entitled to acquire anything it:
- has a right to acquire at a future date; and
- will, at a future date, have a right to acquire.

Control **includes**, but is not limited to, the possession of, or right to acquire, more than 50% of the issuing company's: s 450 CTA 2010
- share capital (¶1508);
- voting power;
- distributable profits (¶1510); or
- net assets on a winding-up (¶1512).

MEMO POINTS When considering control, the following person's **rights are attributed** to the investing company:
- the company's nominee;
- any company controlled by the investing company;
- any person connected (¶5570) with the investing company; and
- any director or employee of the investing company (or a connected company) and his relatives. A person's relatives are his spouse/civil partner and his lineal ascendants and descendants (i.e. parents, grandparents, children and grandchildren).

The following are **excluded** when determining control: **1904** Sch 15 para 9 FA 2000

a. any rights as a loan creditor; and

b. any relevant preference shares that:
- are issued for wholly new consideration;
- do not carry voting rights;
- have no right of conversion into, or to the acquisition of, other shares; and
- are only entitled to preference dividends.

MEMO POINTS 1. **Preference dividends** are dividends which are not dependent on the results of the company or the value of its assets and which represent no more than a reasonable commercial return, including any redemption premium. The amount of a preference dividend must be either:

a. a fixed amount or percentage of nominal value; or

b. a percentage of nominal value which fluctuates according to:
– a standard published rate of interest;
– the rate of tax;
– the retail prices index (or a similar index); or
– a published share index for a recognised stock exchange (¶9995).
2. Shares which are not **entitled to dividends** for a period may still be relevant preference shares provided the other conditions are satisfied.
3. Dividends are not considered to be **dependent on results** or assets where there is an inverse relationship, i.e. where the profits or the value of the assets increase, the return on the dividends decreases, and vice versa.

Financial trade

1906 Sch 15 paras 10, 11 FA 2000

A financial trade is **defined** by exclusion as any trade which is not a non-financial trade.

A non-financial trade is one carried out on a commercial basis with the view to the realisation of profits and which does not consist wholly, or substantially, of carrying on financial activities.

MEMO POINTS The following are specifically defined as **financial activities** but the list is not exhaustive:
– banking or money-lending;
– debt factoring;
– finance leasing;
– hire purchase financing;
– insurance;
– dealing in shares, securities, currency, debts or other financial assets; and
– dealing in commodity or financial futures or options.

1907 A **single company** is treated as carrying on a non-financial trade if, excluding incidental purposes, it exists wholly for the purpose of carrying on one or more non-financial trades. Holding and managing property used for the purpose of that trade is ignored, as is the holding of the CVS shares, unless this forms a major part of the company's business.

MEMO POINTS **Incidental purposes** are purposes which have no significant effect on the extent of the company's other activities.

1908 Sch 15 para 12 FA 2000

If the investing company is a member of a 51% **group of companies** (¶1520), the following conditions must both be satisfied:
a. the group must be a non-financial trading group; and
b. the company must either:
– exist wholly for the purpose of carrying on one or more non-financial trades or businesses other than trades; or
– be the parent company.

MEMO POINTS 1. Any group will be treated as a **non-financial trading group** unless, taking the group as a whole, its trade consists wholly or substantially of carrying on:
– one or more trades which are financial trades; or
– businesses which are not trades.
2. The following are **ignored for the purposes of the above tests**:
– holding and managing property used by a group company for the purposes of one or more non-financial trades carried on by a group company;
– holding shares of, securities in, or making loans to, another group company;
– holding the CVS shares, unless this forms a major part of the company's business; and
– activities which are for incidental purposes (i.e. which have no significant effect on the activities of the company as a whole).

Relevant shares

1910 Sch 15 paras 35, 35A FA 2000

The shares **must be**:
– acquired by way of subscription in cash;
– new, ordinary shares that are fully paid up at the time of issue; and
– issued for commercial reasons and not as part of any scheme or arrangement for the avoidance of tax.

Shares which carry the following rights at any point during the qualification period (¶1892), are **not relevant shares**:
- present or future preferential rights to dividends;
- present or future preferential rights to assets on a winding-up; or
- present or future rights to redemption.

MEMO POINTS The **total funding** a company can raise under the CVS, EIS and VCT schemes combined, in any year (ending with the date of issue of the relevant shares), is £2 million. This limit includes amounts raised by any companies that are, or have been, within that year a subsidiary of the issuing company.

b. Qualifying issuing company

Definition

To be eligible for relief, the investment must be in a qualifying issuing company, which is defined as one that: **1912** Sch 15 paras 15 - 23 FA 2000
- is unquoted;
- satisfies the independence tests;
- has no non-qualifying subsidiaries;
- satisfies the gross assets requirements;
- does not exceed the number of employees limit; and
- meets the trading activities requirement.

In addition, at least 80% of the **money raised by the share issue must be used** to finance a qualifying trade within 12 months of the date of the share issue or, if later, within 12 months from the commencement of the trade. A further 12 month period is available for the remaining 20% to be so used. The trade which benefits from the finance is known as the funded trade. Sch 15 para 36 FA 2000

For **investments made on or after 22 April 2009** the time limit for the investment is relaxed, requiring only that all of the money raised must be invested within 24 months.

Unquoted

A company is unquoted if, at the time the **shares are issued**, it is not listed on a recognised stock exchange (¶9995) and there are no arrangements for the company to become listed, or to become the subsidiary of a listed company. **1913** Sch 15 para 16 FA 2000

Independence

A company is independent if, **throughout the qualification period** (¶1892): **1914** Sch 15 paras 17 - 19 FA 2000
a. it is not a 51% subsidiary of another company nor controlled (¶1729) by another company;
b. independent individuals own at least 20% of the ordinary share capital of the company; and
c. the company, or its qualifying subsidiary, is not carrying on the qualifying trade through the medium of a non-qualifying partnership or joint venture.

MEMO POINTS 1. Any person is an **independent individual** unless he is a director or employee of the issuing company, or a connected company, or the relative of a director or employee. A person's relatives are his spouse/civil partner and his lineal ascendants and descendants (i.e. parents, grandparents, children and grandchildren).
2. A **non-qualifying partnership/joint venture** is one that carries on the qualifying trade where:
- another member of the partnership or joint venture is a company; and
- another person(s) owns more than 75% of the issued share capital of both the issuing company and at least one other party to the partnership/joint venture.

Qualifying subsidiary

A qualifying subsidiary is **a company in which** the issuing company has an interest of at least 51% in: **1915** Sch 15 paras 20 - 21A FA 2000
- the issued share capital;
- voting rights;

– distributable profits; and
– rights of equity holders in a winding-up.

However, the following will only be qualifying subsidiaries if they are 90% subsidiaries:
– a property management subsidiary;
– a subsidiary which carries on the trade for which the CVS funds were raised; and
– a subsidiary which carries on research and development for which the CVS funds were raised.

MEMO POINTS 1. A **90% subsidiary** is a company which only the issuing company controls (¶1729), and in which it has an interest of at least 90% in the:
– issued share capital;
– voting rights;
– distributable profits; and
– rights of equity holders in a winding up.

Sch 15 para 23A FA 2000 2. For shares issued on or after 6 April 2007, a company is **also a 90% subsidiary if** it is:
– a 90% subsidiary of a 100% subsidiary of the issuing company; or
– a 100% subsidiary of a 90% subsidiary of the issuing company.

1916 A company is **not a qualifying subsidiary** if any other person has control of the subsidiary, or there are arrangements in force which would result in the company ceasing to be a qualifying subsidiary. The sale of a subsidiary for commercial reasons, which are not part of an arrangement for the avoidance of tax, does not result in a subsidiary ceasing to be qualifying.

Gross assets

1917 Sch 15 para 22 FA 2000 A company satisfies the gross assets requirements if immediately:
– **before the share issue**, its gross assets do not exceed £7 million; and
– **after the share issue** they do not exceed £8 million.

SP 2/06 MEMO POINTS **Gross assets** are the assets of the company (or group where appropriate) calculated as the aggregate of the assets which would be shown on a balance sheet prepared to that date, without any deduction for liabilities.

Employee limit

1918 Sch 15 para 22A FA 2000 From 19 July 2007 an issuing company **must have** less than 50 full time equivalent employees at the time it issues the relevant shares.

MEMO POINTS 1. If the issuing company is a **parent company of a group of companies**, this 50 employee limit is found by aggregating the number of full time equivalent employees employed by the parent company and each of its qualifying subsidiaries at the time of issue.
2. An **employee includes** a director, but excludes those on maternity or paternity leave and students on vocational training.

Trading activities

1919 Sch 15 paras 25 – 33 FA 2000 Throughout the qualification period (¶1892), a **qualifying trade** must be carried on. This consists of any trade that is carried out:
– wholly or mainly in the UK; and
– on a commercial basis with a view to the realisation of profits.

The **following are ignored** when considering whether a company exists wholly for the purposes of a qualifying trade:
– holding or managing property for the purposes of the trade; and
– holding the CVS shares, unless this forms a major part of the company's business.

Undertaking research and development (¶683) (but not preparing to do so) with a view to deriving a qualifying trade is treated as a qualifying trade for these purposes.

SP 3/00 MEMO POINTS 1. In considering whether a trade is carried on **wholly or mainly in the UK**, HMRC will look at the totality of the activities of the trade, and each case will depend on its own facts and circumstances.

2. Where a company is **preparing to carry on the qualifying trade**, the trading activities requirement is met only if that trade begins within 2 years of the issue of the shares.
3. If the issuing company is the **parent company of a group of companies**, the trading activities requirement is satisfied if:
– taking the business of the group as a whole, it does not consist wholly or substantially of non-qualifying activities; and
– the issuing company or a qualifying 90% subsidiary (¶1915) exists wholly for the purpose of carrying on one or more qualifying trades and is either carrying on that trade or preparing to do so.
The **following activities are ignored** when determining whether a group company exists wholly for the purposes of the qualifying trade:
– holding and managing property used by a group company for the purposes of one or more qualifying trades carried on by a group company;
– holding shares of, securities in, or making loans to, another group company;
– holding the CVS shares, unless this forms a major part of the company's business; and
– activities which are for incidental purposes (i.e. which have no significant effect on the activities of the company as a whole).

A trade will be **non-qualifying** if the company carries on any excluded activities, and they comprise more than 20% of the trade. These include: 1920
– dealing in goods other than as part of a wholesale or retail distribution trade;
– property dealing and development;
– financial activities, including, for example, debt factoring, dealing in commodities, futures and shares, and insurance;
– leasing, including chartering ships (other than short term) or hiring goods;
– receiving royalties and licence fees (for example green fees at a golf course), excluding those attributable to relevant intangible assets;
– farming, market gardening, occupying and managing woodlands;
– operating or managing hotels, nursing homes and residential care homes;
– providing legal or accountancy services; or
– from 6 April 2008, shipbuilding, coal or steel production.

MEMO POINTS 1. **Relevant intangible assets** are where the whole or greater part of the value of the asset was created by the share issuing company (or by a company that was a qualifying subsidiary of the issuing company at all times during which it created the asset). For intellectual property, creation means creation in circumstances such that the exploitation rights vest in the company.
2. Special restrictions apply if the activities of the business consist of the **provision of services or facilities to another business**, where the same person has a controlling interest in both businesses. The provision of services in this case will be an excluded activity if the other business consists substantially of excluded activities.
3. A person has a **controlling interest in a company** if:
– he has control of the company (¶1902);
– at least 50% of the business belongs to him; or
– in the case of a close company, he, or an associate of his (¶2105), is a director of the company and has beneficial ownership or control over more than 30% of the ordinary share capital.
4. A person has a controlling interest in an **unincorporated business** if he is entitled to at least 50% of the assets or profits of the business.

2. Obtaining relief

When can relief be claimed?

Where all the conditions are met, the investing company is **entitled to claim** a corporation tax deduction of the lower of: 1928 Sch 15 paras 39, 40 FA 2000
– tax at 20% on the amount invested; and
– the corporation tax payable for the accounting period in which the shares are issued.

EXAMPLE A Ltd subscribed for 12,500 shares in B Ltd at a cost of £500,000. The shares were issued on 1 March 2010. A Ltd's corporation tax liability for the accounting period ended 30 June 2010 is £106,015.

CVS investment relief would be given as follows:

		£
Corporation tax due		106,015
Less: CVS investment relief:		
Lower of: Amount invested i.e. £500,000 @ 20%; and	100,000	
Corporation tax liability for the period	106,015	
		(100,000)
Corporation tax payable		6,015

Note:
Investment relief is given after any marginal relief but before any reduction in respect of community investment tax relief (¶2927) or double tax relief (¶2173).

1929 Relief may only be **claimed** after:
a. the investing company has received a compliance certificate (¶1988) from the issuing company; and
b. the funded trade has been carried on for a minimum of 4 months by the issuing company or a qualifying 90% subsidiary. The 4 month minimum trading period is waived if, within the 4 month period, the company is:
- wound up;
- dissolved; or
- put into administration or receivership.

This only applies if the action is taken for commercial reasons and does not form part of an arrangement for the avoidance of tax.

However, **relief will be denied where** pre-arranged exit arrangements exist. This is not restricted to arrangements for the sale of the shares, but encompasses plans for the discontinuance of the trade, the sale of the assets, or where the investor has insurance, indemnities or guarantees against the risks of making the investment.

Sch 18 para 9(4) FA 1998

MEMO POINTS A claim for relief must be **made within** 4 years of the end of the accounting period in which the shares are issued. Prior to 1 April 2010 this limit was 6 years.

Attribution of relief to shares

1930 Sch 15 para 45 FA 2000

The investment relief given (i.e. the amount by which the corporation tax liability is reduced) for an accounting period is allocated to the CVS shares issued in that period. A proportion of the investment relief is attributed to each underlying share.

EXAMPLE Continuing the previous example, if the shares in B Ltd were the only CVS shares acquired by A Ltd during the period ended 30 June 2010, the corporation tax reduction (£100,000) is allocated to each share comprised in the issue. The relief per share is therefore £8 (i.e. £100,000 ÷ 12,500).

Where **more than one issue** of shares qualifies for relief in a year, the relief is apportioned equally between each issue. This is of importance only where the subscriptions in an accounting period exceed the maximum for which relief is available.

EXAMPLE Continuing the example at ¶1928, if A Ltd had subscribed a further £50,000 for 5,000 shares in C Ltd for which CVS relief was due, the total investment relief due for the accounting period would be:

		£
Corporation tax due		106,015
Less: CVS investment relief:		
Lower of: Amount invested i.e. £550,000 @ 20%; and	110,000	
Corporation tax liability for the period	106,015	
		(106,015)
Corporation tax payable		Nil

The corporation tax relief is attributed proportionately to each issue:

B Ltd	$\frac{500,000}{550,000} \times 106,015 =$	£96,377
C Ltd	$\frac{50,000}{550,000} \times 106,015 =$	£9,638

The relief is then attributed to the underlying shares:

B Ltd	96,377 ÷ 12,500 shares = £7.71016 per share
C Ltd	9,638 ÷ 5,000 shares = £1.9276 per share

If **bonus shares** are issued in respect of original CVS shares, the relief attributed to the original shares is apportioned between the original shares and the bonus shares. The bonus shares are deemed to have been issued at the same time as the original shares and to have been held throughout the period from the issue of the original shares. **1932** Sch 15 para 81 FA 2000

This only applies if the bonus shares:
- are in the same company;
- are of the same class; and
- have the same rights as the original shares.

The original shares must have been held by the company throughout the period from the date of issue to the date of the bonus issue.

EXAMPLE Continuing the example at ¶1930, if C Ltd made a bonus issue of 1 new share for every 5 original shares, A Ltd would acquire a further 1,000 shares. The relief attributable to the original shares (£9,638) is apportioned between the original and bonus shares and the relief per share is therefore £1.6063 (i.e. £9,638 ÷ 6,000).

MEMO POINTS 1. New shares issued as a result of a **rights issue** are treated as a separate holding acquired by the investing company. They will not qualify for CVS relief simply because the original holding so qualified.
2. When an investing company exchanges shares for **qualifying corporate bonds** (¶5234) on a company reorganisation, they are treated as disposing of the original shares, giving rise to a chargeable gain or allowable loss.

3. Withdrawal of relief

a. Occasions of withdrawal

Relief will be withdrawn in the event of: **1936**
- the disposal of the shares (¶1938) before the end of the qualification period (¶1892);
- a breach of conditions by the investing company, the issuing company or the shares (¶1942);
- the investing company receiving a return of value (¶1946);
- the issuing company making certain payments to other investors (¶1962); or
- an option being granted over CVS shares (¶1972).

The amount of relief withdrawn is dependent upon the reason for the withdrawal.

MEMO POINTS Where relief is to be withdrawn, the amount is treated as income arising from a miscellaneous transaction.

Share disposal

Relief will be withdrawn if the investing company disposes of the shares **within the qualification period** (¶1892). **1938** Sch 15 para 46 FA 2000

1939 **Amount of relief withdrawn** The amount of relief withdrawn depends on the nature of the disposal as follows:

Type of disposal	Amount of relief withdrawn
Bargain at arm's length for full consideration; Distribution in the course of dissolving or winding up the issuing company; Deemed disposal following a negligible value claim (¶6025); or Disposal arising from the loss, destruction or extinction of the asset	Lower of: – 20% of the disposal proceeds; and – the relief originally given
All other types of disposals	The relief originally given

EXAMPLE A Ltd subscribed for 10,000 shares in B Ltd under the CVS scheme in Year 1 at a cost of £150,000. Investment relief of £30,000 (£150,000 @ 20%) was claimed. In Year 2, the shares were disposed of by way of a bargain at arm's length for £110,000. The amount of investment relief withdrawn is calculated as the lower of:

	£	£
Proceeds × 20% (110,000 × 20%)	22,000	
Relief originally given (150,000 × 20%)	30,000	
Therefore relief withdrawn		22,000

MEMO POINTS For the **chargeable gains implications** of a sale of CVS shares, see ¶2000.

1940 Where the initial **investment relief was restricted** (i.e. the company's corporation tax liability was insufficient to absorb the full amount of relief available), the relief withdrawn is calculated by applying the fraction A/B, where:
– A is the CVS relief given (in terms of the reduction in the tax liability); and
– B is 20% of the amount subscribed for the shares.

EXAMPLE Taking the facts from the previous example, if A Ltd's relief in respect of the B Ltd shares had been restricted because the corporation tax liability for the accounting period was £19,625, the relief withdrawn on the disposal of B Ltd shares would be:

	£	£
Proceeds × 20% ((110,000 × 20%) × 19,625/30,000)	14,392	
Relief originally given	19,625	
Therefore relief withdrawn		14,392

Breach of conditions

1942 Relief will be **withdrawn in full** where:
– either the investing company or the issuing company breaches the conditions during the qualification period (¶1892); or
– the shares cease to be relevant shares.

This means, for example, that if the company ceases to carry on a qualifying trade, all relief originally given will be withdrawn.

1944 Sch 15 paras 83 – 85 FA 2000

A company **will not breach conditions if** it:
a. ceases to trade due to a winding-up for bona fide commercial reasons and not as part of an arrangement to avoid tax; or
b. is taken over by a new holding company in a share for share exchange.

MEMO POINTS 1. For **a**. above, the **trade must cease** as a result of the winding up, rather than the other way round. If the cessation of trade occurs first, the conditions are breached and relief will be withdrawn.
2. For **b**. above, the **exchange** must be for bona fide commercial reasons and not part of an arrangement to avoid a liability to tax. This provision only applies where a new company (Newco), in which only subscriber shares have previously been issued, acquires the entire issued capital of the CVS company (CVSco) for consideration consisting entirely of shares in Newco. The Newco shares must be of the same class and have the same rights as the existing CVSco shares, and the Newco shares must be issued to the holders of CVSco shares in proportion to their holdings in CVSco.

Approval must be obtained from HMRC before the exchange takes place. Assuming approval is granted, Newco simply stands in the shoes of CVSco, there is no disposal of the shares and the investors will not lose their relief. Newco must therefore continue to satisfy all the conditions for the remainder of the qualification period (¶1892).
3. Following a **company reconstruction** (¶5854), the rules allowing new shares to stand in the shoes of old shares do not apply. Instead, the investing company is treated as having disposed of the original shares and acquired a new holding at the time of the reconstruction.

Return of value

A return of value, within what is referred to as the **restriction period** (i.e. the period beginning 1 year before the issue of the shares and ending at the end of the qualification period (¶1892)), will lead to a withdrawal of investment relief, unless the return of value is matched with replacement value (¶1956). **1946** Sch 15 para 47 FA 2000

A return of value is essentially a payment by the issuing company, or a person connected with the company, to the investing company or to a connected person, directly or indirectly, for its benefit.

The following table summarises the **items treated as a return of value**, and how the value returned is quantified. **1948** Sch 15 para 49 FA 2000

Event	Value returned[1]
Repayment, redemption or repurchase of shares or securities	Greater of amount received or market value of shares or securities
Payment for giving up rights to share capital or securities on its redemption	
Repayment of a debt to the investing company incurred before the subscription for CVS shares	Greater of amount of loan repaid or market value of debt
Payment to the investing company for giving up rights to repayment of any debt (except an ordinary trade debt)	Greater of amount received or market value of debt
Issuing company waives or releases any liability of the investing company to the company[2]	Amount of liability
Issuing company discharges the investing company's liability to a third party	
Issuing company makes a loan to the investing company which is not fully repaid before share issue	Amount of loan outstanding, less any repayment made before issue of shares
Issuing company provides any benefit or facility to a director or employee (or their associates) of the investing company	Cost of providing benefit, reduced by any contribution from recipient (or his associate)
Issuing company transfers an asset to the investing company at less than market value	Excess of market value over consideration given
Issuing company acquires an asset from the investing company at more than market value	Excess of consideration given over market value
Issuing company makes any payment, other than a qualifying payment, to the investing company[3]	Amount of the payment

Note:
1. **Insignificant payments** during the restriction period may be ignored. An insignificant payment is a payment not exceeding £1,000, or a payment which is considered insignificant in relation to the amount subscribed for the shares. At the time of receiving an insignificant payment, it must be aggregated with any other insignificant payments previously received which have not been treated as a return of value, to determine whether the limits have been breached. There is no exception for insignificant payments if, during the 12 months prior to the issue of the shares, there were arrangements in force for the investing company to receive any value from the issuing company during the restriction period.
2. A liability is treated as being **waived or released** if it is not discharged within 12 months of the date on which it ought to have been discharged.
3. The following are treated as **qualifying payments**:
- payments for goods, services or facilities supplied by the investing company which are reasonable in relation to the market value of the supply;
- interest payments which represent no more than a reasonable commercial return;
- dividends or distributions which are no more than a normal return on investments in that company;
- payments to acquire assets which do not exceed the market value of the assets;
- payments of rent at commercial rates for the use of property; and
- payments to discharge ordinary trade debts.

1951 Sch 15 para 47 FA 2000

Amount of relief withdrawn The amount of relief withdrawn is equal to 20% of the value returned, but cannot exceed the relief originally given and not previously withdrawn.

EXAMPLE A Ltd subscribed for shares in B Ltd at a cost of £275,000 and obtained investment relief of £55,000 (£275,000 @ 20%). 2 years after the subscription, B Ltd purchased a building from A Ltd for £600,000 at a time when its market value was £500,000. A Ltd has received a return of value as follows:

	£
Market value of asset transferred	500,000
Consideration paid by B Ltd	(600,000)
Value returned	100,000

The amount of investment relief withdrawn is therefore £20,000 (i.e. £100,000 @ 20%).

1952 Sch 15 para 52 FA 2000

Where the **investment relief was restricted** (i.e. the company's corporation tax liability was insufficient to absorb the full amount of relief available), the value returned is restricted by applying the fraction A/B, where:
- A is the CVS relief given (in terms of the reduction in the tax liability); and
- B is 20% of the amount subscribed for the shares.

EXAMPLE Taking the facts from the previous example, if A Ltd's relief in respect of the B Ltd shares was restricted as the corporation tax liability for the accounting period had been £48,000, the relief withdrawn on the disposal of B Ltd shares would be:

	£
Value returned as originally calculated	100,000
Restricted: £100,000 × 48,000/55,000	87,273

The amount of investment relief withdrawn is therefore £17,454.60 (i.e. £87,273 @ 20%).

1954 Sch 15 para 51 FA 2000

The value returned must be apportioned where:
- the investing company **made more than one subscription** for shares qualifying for investment relief; and
- it falls in the restriction period (¶1946), for two or more of those issues (the relevant issues).

The value returned in respect of each issue is calculated by applying the fraction A/B, where:
- A is the amount subscribed for the particular issue; and
- B is the aggregate amount subscribed for the relevant issues.

EXAMPLE A Ltd subscribed for shares in B Ltd, a company which commenced trading on 1 July 2003. A Ltd prepares its accounts annually to 31 December and received investment relief as follows:

Issue	Date	Shares	Cost	Relief	Note
1	01/06/04	50,000	£50,000	£9,344	Restricted by CT liability
2	01/12/04	25,000	£30,000	£5,606	Restricted by CT liability
3	01/06/05	30,000	£18,000	£3,600	

On 25 July 2007, A Ltd receives a return of value and the value returned is calculated at £8,000. Issue 1 is not a relevant issue in respect of this payment as the restriction period (¶1946) has ended.
The **return of value** is therefore attributed to issues 2 and 3 as follows:

Issue 2	$\frac{30,000}{48,000} \times 8,000 =$	£5,000
Issue 3	$\frac{18,000}{48,000} \times 8,000 =$	£3,000

The **amount of relief withdrawn** is calculated as follows:

Issue 2	£4,671.66 x 20% [1]	£934.33
Issue 3	£3,000 × 20% =	£600.00

Note:
1. The amount on which relief is withdrawn for issue 2 is restricted as full relief was not originally given. The restriction is calculated as follows:

$$\frac{\text{Relief actually given}}{\text{20\% of subscription}} \qquad \frac{5,606}{6,000} \times 5,000 = \qquad £4,671.66$$

Replacement value A replacement value payment may be matched against the return of value and **relief will not be withdrawn** provided: **1956** Sch 15 para 54 FA 2000

a. the amount of the replacement value is not less than the original value returned; and
b. the payment is a qualifying receipt. In other words it is either:
- not an excepted payment;
- intended to reverse the release or waiver of a liability of the investing company or the discharge of the investing company's liability to a third party;
- a transfer of an asset at an overvalue to reverse the transfer of an asset to the investing company at less than market value; or
- a transfer of an asset at an undervalue to reverse the transfer of an asset at more than market value to the issuing company.

Replacement value received can only be **matched once** with a return of value.

EXAMPLE A Ltd holds shares in B Ltd for which investment relief was claimed. A Ltd purchased an asset from B Ltd for £5,000 when its market value was £8,000. A Ltd then gave an asset valued at £3,000 to B Ltd.
The gift of the asset constitutes replacement value as it reverses the effect of A Ltd acquiring an asset at undervalue.

MEMO POINTS An **excepted payment** is essentially a payment which is reasonable in relation to market value, or in relation to a commercial rate of return, in respect of the following:
- goods, supplies or facilities provided (whether in the course of a trade or otherwise);
- interest;
- rent;
- a dividend or other distribution;
- the acquisition of an asset;
- the discharge of an ordinary trade debt; or
- shares or securities in any company.

The receipt of **replacement value is ignored** if it occurs: **1958** Sch 15 para 55 FA 2000
- before the restriction period (¶1946);
- after a period of unreasonable delay; or
- more than 60 days after the amount of relief to be withdrawn is determined following the issue of an appeal against an assessment to withdraw relief.

MEMO POINTS It is possible for the replacement value to be **received before the return of value** is made.

Payments to other investors

Relief is withdrawn from CVS investors where the issuing company (or its 51% subsidiary): **1962** Sch 15 para 56 FA 2000
- repays, redeems or repurchases any share capital belonging to any member (other than those listed below) during the restriction period (¶1946); or
- makes a payment (that is not insignificant) to any member in return for cancellation or extinguishment of his interest in the share capital of the company or its subsidiary.

Payments made to the following investors are **ignored**:
- the investing company where the transaction results in the withdrawal of investment relief (either as a disposal of the shares or as a return of value);
- a person who suffers a withdrawal of EIS income tax relief (¶2883), either as a disposal of the shares or as a return of value; or
- a person who crystallises a deferred gain under EIS deferral relief (¶6221) as a result of the payment.

Sch 15 para 57 FA 2000

MEMO POINTS 1. A payment is **insignificant** if, when compared to the market value of the remaining issued share capital immediately after the payment, the greater of the following is insignificant (¶1948):
- market value of the shares to which the payment relates (before the payment); and
- the amount received by the member.

Payments are not ignored if, during the 12 months prior to the issue of the shares, there were arrangements in existence for the issuing company to make any payments, or for any person to be entitled to a payment, during the restriction period (¶1946).

Sch 15 para 58(5) FA 2000

2. If the company issues share capital simply to **comply with the Companies Act** requirements for a minimum share capital, the redemption of such shares within 12 months of issue does not cause a withdrawal of relief.

1964 **Amount of relief withdrawn** If CVS relief was given to only **one company**, that company's relief will be withdrawn by the lower of:
- 20% of the amount of value returned to investors; or
- the investment relief originally given.

If **more than one company** received CVS relief, the relief withdrawn is apportioned between them in proportion to their shareholdings.

EXAMPLE A Ltd subscribed for shares in B Ltd at a cost of £135,000 and obtained investment relief of £27,000 (£135,000 @ 20%). 2 years after the subscription, the company redeemed shares for £42,000.
CVS relief will be withdrawn from A Ltd as follows:

1. Assuming A Ltd was the only CVS investor:

	£	£
20% of the value returned (42,000 @ 20%)	8,400	
Relief initially given	27,000	
Relief withdrawn		8,400

2. Assuming there were other investors and the total amount subscribed for CVS shares was £945,000:

	£	£
Value returned allocated to A Ltd's CVS investment in proportion to total CVS subscriptions: 42,000 × 135,000/945,000 = 6,000		
20% of value returned attributable to A Ltd (6,000 @ 20%)	1,200	
Relief initially given	27,000	
Relief withdrawn		1,200

1966 Sch 15 para 56(6) FA 2000

Where the **investment relief was restricted** (i.e. the company's corporation tax liability was insufficient to absorb the full amount of relief available), the value returned is restricted by applying the fraction A/B, where:
- A is the CVS relief given (in terms of the reduction in the tax liability); and
- B is 20% of the amount subscribed for the shares.

EXAMPLE Continuing part 2 of the previous example, if A Ltd's relief had originally been restricted to £21,750, the relief withdrawn on the return of value would be:

	£
Value returned as originally calculated	6,000
Restricted: 6,000 × 21,750/27,000	4,833

The amount of investment relief withdrawn is therefore £966.60 (£4,833 @ 20%).

1970 Sch 15 para 58(2) – (4) FA 2000

Any withdrawal of relief must be apportioned where the investing company made **more than one subscription** for shares in the issuing company and the payment to the member falls within the restriction period (¶1946), for 2 or more of the issues. The calculation is the same as for returns of value to the investing company (¶1954).

Options

If, during the qualification period (¶1892), an option is **granted** in respect of shares on which investment relief has been given, any relief attributable to those shares will be withdrawn. This applies to options granted by the investing company which bind the: **1972** Sch 15 para 59 FA 2000
- investing company to sell shares; or
- grantor to buy shares.

The withdrawal of relief occurs when the option is granted. It is irrelevant whether the option is exercised.

b. Consequences of withdrawal

In **general** where relief is withdrawn, an assessment will be issued for the accounting period in which relief was obtained. **1974** Sch 15 paras 60 – 63 FA 2000

Where the withdrawal follows a **breach of conditions**, an assessment may only be issued where:
- the issuing company has given the appropriate notification to HMRC (¶1992); or
- HMRC have notified the issuing company that investment relief was not due in respect of a specified issue of shares.

If relief is withdrawn following the **return of value** to the investing company or other member, HMRC must also give the investing company notice of that fact, specifying the reason for withdrawal of relief.

MEMO POINTS 1. An **assessment can be issued** no later than 6 years after the end of the relevant accounting period, which is the later of:
- the accounting period in which the latest date for employing the funds raised by the issue falls (¶1912); or
- the accounting period in which the event triggering the withdrawal of relief falls.

2. Any amounts assessed carry **interest** from the date of the event triggering the withdrawal.

4. Information requirements

a. Investing company

Once investment relief has been obtained, the investing company is **obliged to notify** HMRC if the relief must be withdrawn as a result of: **1978** Sch 15 para 64 FA 2000
- the company not being a qualifying investing company;
- a receipt of value (even if it can be matched with replacement value); or
- the grant of options.

Notice must be **given within** 60 days of the event or, if the receipt of value occurs before the issue of the shares, 60 days after the issue of the shares. Where the withdrawal is caused by the receipt of value by a person connected with the company, the notification deadline is extended to 60 days after the investing company becomes aware of the event.

MEMO POINTS A **penalty** of £300 may be charged for failing to give the required notification, and a further daily penalty of up to £60 may be charged for continuing failure. The daily penalty cannot be imposed once the failure has been remedied. If a company gives notice fraudulently or negligently, a penalty of £3,000 may be imposed. s 98 TMA 1970

b. Issuing company

Statutory obligations

Investment relief is only available for subscriptions for shares in qualifying issuing companies. HMRC therefore need to be provided with information: **1982** Sch 15 para 65 FA 2000
- following the issue of the shares; and
- on an ongoing basis.

In addition, it is possible for the issuing company to apply for clearance from HMRC that the conditions are satisfied, prior to the issue of shares. This clearance process is voluntary.

1986 Sch 15 paras 41, 42 FA 2000

Information requirements following share issue Before the investing company is entitled to relief, the issuing company is required to provide HMRC with sufficient information to establish that the qualifying conditions are satisfied. This is achieved by submitting a **compliance statement** which confirms that the conditions for investment relief are satisfied, and have been satisfied since the issue of the shares. HMRC may also require further information concerning the issue of the shares, in particular they may require details of the investing companies and the cash subscriptions.

The issuing company must submit a compliance statement:
– no earlier than 4 months after the qualifying trading activity commences; and
– no later than 2 years after the end of the accounting period in which the shares are issued (or, if later, 2 years and 4 months from the commencement of the qualifying activity).

1988 Sch 15 para 43 FA 2000

Where HMRC are satisfied that the conditions are met, authority will be given to the company to issue a **compliance certificate** to the investors. If HMRC refuse permission to issue compliance certificates, the issuing company may appeal against the decision.

1990 Sch 15 para 44 FA 2000

A **penalty** of up to £3,000 may be charged if the company:
– fraudulently or negligently provides a compliance statement or issues a compliance certificate; or
– issues a compliance certificate without authority from HMRC.

1992 Sch 15 para 65 FA 2000

Ongoing information requirements After issuing a compliance statement, the issuing company is obliged to notify HMRC if the **qualifying conditions cease to be satisfied** as a result of:
– the company not being a qualifying issuing company;
– a return of value (even if it can be matched with replacement value); or
– the shares ceasing to be relevant shares.

Notice must be **given within** 60 days of the event or, if the receipt of value occurs before the issue of the shares, 60 days after the issue of the shares. Where the withdrawal is caused by the return of value by a person connected with the company, or a breach of the individual owner's requirement (¶1914), the notification deadline is extended to 60 days after the issuing company becomes aware of the event.

s 98 TMA 1970

MEMO POINTS 1. A **penalty** of £300 may be charged for failing to give the required notification, and a further daily penalty of up to £60 may be charged for continuing failure. The daily penalty cannot be imposed once the failure has been remedied. If a company gives notice fraudulently or negligently, a penalty of £3,000 may be imposed.
2. Any person **connected with the issuing company** who is aware of the matters set out in this paragraph is subject to the same notification requirements.

1993 Sch 15 paras 89 – 92 FA 2000

Advance clearance In addition, prior to the issue of shares, a company **may apply** to HMRC for clearance that the conditions for relief are satisfied by the company and the shares. Clearance cannot be granted after the shares are issued.

SP 1/00

When a company has applied for clearance, HMRC have 30 days in which they must either refuse clearance or request further information from the issuing company before making a decision.

If further information is requested, the issuing company must provide it within 30 days (or such longer period as the notice specifies) if it wishes to proceed with the clearance application. Having received the requested information, HMRC have a further 30 days in which to respond.

If clearance is given, HMRC will issue an advance clearance notice. An advance clearance notice is only valid if the application fully and accurately discloses the facts and circumstances, and the issuing company (and its subsidiaries) act in accordance with the disclosures.

If clearance is refused, HMRC must notify the company accordingly and the company has the right to appeal against the decision.

Moral obligations

The company may feel it has a moral obligation not to do anything which would result in a withdrawal of CVS relief from investing companies. It is therefore important that the company continues to satisfy all the qualifying conditions and makes no returns of value. Some of the key points to consider are: **1994**

– relevant shares must have no **preferential rights**. This means that any non-CVS shares must not have restrictions imposed on them, which would result in the CVS shares having preferential rights;

– the **trade must be carried on wholly or mainly in the UK**. Therefore, any overseas expansion should be reviewed to ensure it does not breach the conditions;

– the company must have no subsidiaries other than **qualifying subsidiaries** (¶1915). This may be of particular concern when acquiring new subsidiaries; and

– **funds raised** through the issue of CVS shares must be used for the purposes of the qualifying activity within a set period. Therefore the relevant monies should be identified and retained separately, in order to establish that the requirements are met.

c. HMRC

HMRC may issue a **notice** to any person or company **requiring the production of information** where they believe that a person or company: **1998** Sch 15 para 66 FA 2000

– has not given any required notification; or

– has made or received a return of value.

The notice must specify the information required and the deadline for its production, which must be at least 60 days from the issue of the notice.

MEMO POINTS Failure to comply with a notice may result in a **penalty** of up to £300 being charged. Where a company or person provides fraudulent or negligent information in response to a notice, a penalty of up to £3,000 may be charged. s 98 TMA 1970

C. Chargeable gains implications

1. Modification of general rules

Shares on which investment relief has been claimed are subject to the usual chargeable gains regime, with minor modifications to the rules: **2000**

– relating to share identification on a disposal; and

– on a share reorganisation.

The normal **share identification rules** do not apply to CVS shares. CVS shares are not pooled in a section 104 pool. Instead such shares that are sold are deemed to be disposed of on a first in first out basis. **2002** Sch 15 para 93 FA 2000

Where more than one batch of shares is purchased on the same day, shares to which no investment relief is attributable are deemed to be sold in priority to those with investment relief.

On a **reorganisation of share capital** (the most common being the issue of bonus shares and rights issues) the following rules apply: **2003** Sch 15 paras 80 – 88 FA 2000

– shares issued on a rights issue are treated as a separate acquisition (i.e. the share reorganisation rules (¶5812) are disapplied where investment relief is attributable to the original holding or the new shares); and

– where there is a bonus issue of shares (¶5797), any CVS relief attributable to the original holding is also attributable to the bonus shares (i.e. the share reorganisation rules are not disapplied).

MEMO POINTS When an investing company exchanges shares for **qualifying corporate bonds** (¶5234) on a company reorganisation, they are treated as disposing of the original shares, giving rise to a chargeable gain or allowable loss.

2. Chargeable gains deferral relief

2004 Sch 15 paras 73, 74 FA 2000

A gain realised on a disposal of shares which qualified for investment relief (the original gain) may be deferred if some or all of the gain (not the proceeds) is reinvested in replacement shares.

A gain **can only be deferred in this way if** the:
- original shares have been held continuously by the company from the date of issue to the date of disposal; and
- investing company makes a further qualifying investment in the 4 year period beginning 1 year before the disposal of the original shares.

MEMO POINTS 1. A **qualifying investment** is a further subscription for shares to which investment relief is attributable in a company which is not a prohibited company. The company in which the original shares were held is a prohibited company, as is any company which is a member of the same 51% group of companies.
2. If the **replacement shares were acquired before the disposal**, the shares must still be held, and still be attributed with investment relief, at the date of the disposal.

2005 Sch 15 para 76 FA 2000

The **maximum gain which can be deferred** is the amount of the subscription for the replacement shares. However, the company may claim any amount of deferral relief up to the maximum. It may be beneficial, for example, to leave part of the gain in charge if there are capital losses during the accounting period which can be set against the gain.

MEMO POINTS Deferral **relief must be claimed within** 4 years of the end of the accounting period in which the replacement investment is made. The claim should specify the amount of the gain to be deferred and the details of the replacement shares. Before 1 April 2010 the time limit was 6 years.

2006 Sch 15 para 79 FA 2000

The **original gain is deferred until** a chargeable event occurs. A chargeable event is the disposal of the replacement shares or the withdrawal of investment relief from those shares. The deferred gain crystallises at the time of the chargeable event, and must be included in the tax computation for the accounting period in which the event occurs. The deferred gain is apportioned equally between all the shares in the replacement holding.

EXAMPLE A Ltd realised the following gains in respect of CVS investments:
- £27,000 in respect of B Ltd; and
- £117,000 in respect of C Ltd.

A Ltd made a claim to defer the full amount of both gains, having acquired 60,000 shares in D Ltd at a cost of £180,000.

If A Ltd sold 20,000 shares in D Ltd, the following gains would crystallise:
- B Ltd: £9,000 (20,000/60,000 × £27,000); and
- C Ltd: £39,000 (20,000/60,000 × £117,000).

3. Relief for losses

Type of loss relief

2007 Where the disposal of CVS shares gives rise to a loss, that loss can either be set against:
- other chargeable gains; or
- income (if specifically claimed).

Offset against chargeable gains

A loss on the disposal of CVS shares may be set against other chargeable gains. 2008 Sch 15 para 94 FA 2000

When **calculating the loss**, the allowable expenditure must be reduced to take account of any investment relief given and not withdrawn. This only applies where investment relief is not fully withdrawn as a result of the disposal. This reduction can reduce a loss to nil, but it cannot turn an allowable loss into a chargeable gain.

EXAMPLE A Ltd invested £100,000 in qualifying CVS shares and obtained investment relief of £20,000 (£100,000 @ 20%). The shares were sold 8 months later for £38,000, consequently investment relief is withdrawn. The amount of relief withdrawn is restricted to the value received for the shares at 20% (£38,000 @ 20% = £7,600).
The allowable loss on disposal is calculated as follows:

	£	£
Proceeds		38,000
Less: Cost	100,000	
Investment relief given (20,000 – 7,600)	(12,400)	
		(87,600)
Capital loss		(49,600)

If the disposal had taken place after the end of the qualification period (¶1892), no investment relief would be withdrawn and the loss would be calculated as follows.

	£	£
Proceeds		38,000
Less: Cost	100,000	
Investment relief given	(20,000)	
		(80,000)
Capital loss		(42,000)

Offset against income

If, on a disposal of CVS shares, the investing company incurs a loss, it may claim relief for the loss against income rather than against chargeable gains. 2012 Sch 15 paras 67 – 70 FA 2000

This loss relief is only **available if**:

a. the shares have been held continuously by the company since the date of issue and investment relief has not been fully withdrawn; and

b. the disposal is either:

- by way of a bargain at arm's length for full consideration;
- by way of a distribution in the course of dissolving or winding up the issuing company;
- a deemed disposal following a negligible value claim (¶6025); or
- a disposal arising from the loss, destruction or extinction of the asset.

CVS loss relief must be **claimed within** 2 years of the end of the accounting period in which the loss arises. The loss is calculated in accordance with the rules set out in ¶2008. If the loss cannot be absorbed by the income for the accounting period in which the loss arises, it may be carried back and set against income of the previous 12 months. 2014

Where an accounting period falls partly within the previous 12 months, the loss can only be set against income attributable to the specified period (¶1274) and therefore profits of the accounting period must be apportioned on a time basis.

There is no facility to carry forward a CVS loss so if the loss cannot be fully utilised within the specified period, a claim may not be beneficial.

MEMO POINTS 1. CVS **loss relief is given in priority to** charges on income (¶958) and losses on unquoted shares for investment companies (¶2132). If CVS loss relief is claimed, relief cannot also be given as a capital loss (¶1310) or as a loss on unquoted shares.
2. If CVS loss **relief is not claimed**, or the requirements for such a claim are not satisfied, relief may be given as a capital loss, in the normal way.
3. If the disposal giving rise to the loss is part of a **scheme involving tax avoidance**, the value shifting provisions (¶5650) will apply with the modification that any benefit arising from the Sch 15 para 71 FA 2000

transaction is not required to be tax free. This means that the disposal proceeds will be increased by the amount of the benefit (i.e. the loss), with the effect that the loss is cancelled out.

SECTION 3

Purchase of own shares

2080 In the majority of cases, where a company purchases its own shares from the shareholders, this will be treated as a distribution (¶940). However, special provisions apply for certain share buy backs by both unquoted and listed companies.

A. Unquoted companies

2081 A company purchase of own shares is **usually** treated as a distribution **unless** certain conditions are met to enable it to be treated as a capital payment and subject to the capital gains tax legislation.
s 1033 CTA 2010

Capital treatment

2082 Where the following criteria are satisfied, capital treatment will **automatically apply**:
a. the company is a UK resident unquoted trading company (or the holding company of a trading group);
b. the purchase is either:
– for the benefit of the trade (¶2084); or
– to enable inheritance tax to be paid on the death of a shareholder (where undue hardship would otherwise arise); and
c. the vendor:
– is UK resident (¶4154) and ordinarily resident (¶4160) in the year of sale;
– has held the shares for 5 years (3 years if the shares were inherited); and
– is not connected with the company immediately after the repurchase.
Capital treatment **will not apply** where the transaction is carried on either:
– for the avoidance of tax; or
– to enable the vendor to share in the profits of the company without receiving a dividend.

MEMO POINTS A person is **connected with the company** if, immediately following the purchase of own shares, he:
a. controls the company (¶1729); or
b. owns, or is entitled to acquire (together with his associates), more than 30% of the:
– voting power;
– issued share capital;
– issued share and loan capital combined HMRC v Taylor & Haimendorf [2010]; or
– assets on a winding up.

2084 HMRC have published guidance on the situations in which they consider a purchase of own shares would be for the **benefit of the trade**. These primarily relate to the existence of an unwilling shareholder who could disrupt the operation of the business, including:
SP 2/82
– outside shareholders who wish to withdraw their equity finance;
– a controlling shareholder retiring to make way for new management;
– personal representatives of a deceased shareholder wishing to realise the value of the shares; and
– a legatee of a deceased shareholder who does not want to hold shares in the company.

MEMO POINTS HMRC generally require the **entire shareholding** of an unwilling shareholder to be purchased by the company, although they may accept a lower amount in the following situations:

– insufficient funds are available to purchase the full holding in one tranche; or
– for sentimental reasons, a retiring controlling shareholder wishes to retain a small stake in the business.
In this situation, the vendor's holding (including shares held by his associates) must be substantially reduced. This means that his interest in the company (after the purchase of own shares) must be less than 75% of his interest immediately before the purchase.

Where a company wishes to buy out a shareholder but has insufficient funds, it is not unusual for the departing shareholder to loan part of the proceeds back to the company. Where the issued share capital of the company is low in relation to market value, this may result in the former shareholder being connected with the company. To avoid this, it is acceptable for the company to make a bonus issue to shareholders prior to the purchase of own shares, thus increasing the issued share capital. 2088

Clearance may be obtained from HMRC confirming whether or not capital treatment applies to a particular transaction. 2090 ss 1044, 1045 CTA 2010

Distribution treatment

In certain circumstances, it may be less beneficial for the shareholder to receive a capital payment. For a purchase of own shares to be treated as a distribution, it will be necessary to breach one of the conditions for capital treatment. In such a case, it may be possible to manipulate the loan and share capital such that an individual remains connected with the company following the purchase. 2092

B. Listed companies

UK companies listed on the stock exchange or AIM are permitted to purchase their own shares and hold them in "Treasury" and subsequently either cancel or sell them. Other public company shares, and shares in private companies, will not fall within these regulations. 2094 s 195 FA 2003

For tax purposes, Treasury shares will be treated as if they do not exist. They will be treated as cancelled when they are purchased into Treasury. Any subsequent disposal of Treasury shares by the company to a third party investor is treated as a new share issue, but no venture capital trust (VCT) investment relief (¶2909) is available to the investor. The company must notify the investor at the time of such a subscription that he is not eligible for VCT investment relief. A copy of this notice must also be sent to HMRC no later than 3 months after the subscription. 2096

SECTION 4
Close companies

A. Why are there special rules?

Where a small number of shareholders and directors control a company, it is thought that the company's affairs may be manipulated to the benefit of those people. Special rules therefore apply to certain companies termed close companies. Further restrictions also apply to those close companies which are also close investment holding companies (¶2117). 2100

B. Close company definitions

Company

2101 s 439 CTA 2010 A close company is defined as any UK resident company which is controlled by five or fewer participators, or any number of participators who are directors.

Participator

2102 ss 454, 1068, 1069 CTA 2010 A participator is defined as any person having a share or interest in the capital or income of the company. In addition to the share capital and voting rights this includes the right to:
- secure that income and/or assets are applied for his benefit; or
- participate in any distributions.

Loan creditors with a beneficial interest in the debt (excluding commercial and business loans) also have an interest in the company for these purposes.

MEMO POINTS 1. An interest includes not only present entitlement but also the right to acquire an interest at some time in the future.
2. Any participator in a company that controls another company is treated as a participator in that other company.

EXAMPLE The issued share capital of A Ltd, an unquoted company, is held as follows:

		%
A	Director	11
B	Director	10
C	Director	9
D	Director	8
E	Director	8
F	Director	7
G		5
Others	(each less than 5%)	42
		100

The top 5 participators (A to E) own 46% of the company. However, the directors own 53% and therefore the company is a close company.

Director

2103 s 452 CTA 2010 The term director is quite widely drawn and is not limited to individuals with the title of director but includes people who act as directors, (i.e. people on whose wishes the directors are accustomed to act). In addition, any person involved in the management of the business who, together with associates, controls more than 20% of the ordinary share capital is a director for these purposes.

Control

2104 ss 450, 451 CTA 2010 Control is defined as the ownership of (or entitlement to acquire) more than 50% of either the:
- share capital (¶1508);
- voting power;
- distributable profits (¶1510); or
- net assets on winding-up (¶1512).

EXAMPLE Four friends each own 25% of the ordinary shares of a company. A fifth friend, Mr E, owns 2,500 £1 preference shares which are entitled to a fixed dividend of 10%. At first glance, it would appear that none of the friends has control of the company.

However, if the company has distributable profit of £450, Mr E will control the company, as he is entitled to £250, which is more than 50% of the total distributable profit. If the company had distributable profit of over £500, no-one would have control.

MEMO POINTS An interest includes **not only present entitlement** but also the right to acquire an interest at some time in the future.

When considering a person's interest, the rights of the person's nominee and of certain associates are also included. **2105** s 448 CTA 2010

Associates include relatives, business partners and trustees of settlements established by the individual or his relative. (Associates of associates, for example the director's brother's business partner, are not included.)

Relatives include:
- spouse/civil partner;
- parent;
- grandparent;
- children;
- grandchildren; and
- brother or sister.

Aunts, uncles and in-laws are not included, neither are step relatives.

EXAMPLE The issued share capital of A Ltd, an unquoted company, is held as follows:

		%
A	Director	8
B	Director	6
C	Director	6
D	Director	6
E	Director	5
F	General manager	1
G	F's wife	22
Others	(each less than 5%)	46
		100

When considering G's interest as a participator, the 1% owned by her husband, F, brings her holding to 23%, in which case, the top 5 participators (A, B, C, D and G) own 49% of the company. However, F will be considered a director as, with his wife's interest, he owns more than 20% of the company. The company is therefore under the control of its directors (who control 54%) and is a close company.

Where a person could be treated as an associate of more than one other shareholder, the interests of that person can only be included once, usually in whichever combination produces the greatest overall holdings.

EXAMPLE The issued share capital of A Ltd, an unquoted company is held as follows:

		%
A	Director	8
B	Director	6
C	Director	6
D	Director	5
E	Director	5
F		4
G	F's wife and A's sister	17
Others	(each less than 5%)	49
		100

When considering the top 5 participators, A's interest could include G's 17% as she is his sister, but not F's 4%. In this situation, the directors, or top 5 participators, control only 47%. However, G's interest can include the 4% owned by her husband, F, and the 8% owned by her brother, A. This brings her holding to 29%, in which case, the top 5 participators (B, C, D, E and G) own 51% of the company, and it is therefore a close company.

C. Exceptions from close company status

2106 ss 442 – 447 CTA 2010 The following companies are specifically excluded from the definition of a close company:
- certain quoted companies;
- companies controlled by non-close companies (and which could only be a close company by treating a non-close company as one of the five participators controlling it);
- companies controlled by or on behalf of the Crown;
- non-UK resident companies; and
- industrial and provident societies and building societies.

2107 A **quoted company** is not a close company if 35% or more of the share capital is in the hands of the general public, unless 85% of the voting power is possessed by the principal members.

The **principal members** are the top five participators each having an interest of 5% or more. (Where more than one participator is eligible for the fifth principal member position because of equal shareholdings, they may all be treated as principal members, with the result that there may be more than five principal members in total).

The **general public** excludes:
- directors and their associates;
- companies controlled by the directors or their associates;
- associated companies (¶1360) of the quoted company;
- funds for the benefit of past, present and future directors or employees, or their dependants;
- the principal members (with the exception of non-close companies); and
- nominees of any of the above.

EXAMPLE The issued share capital of A plc, a quoted company is held as follows:

		%
A Ltd	Non-close company	30
B	Director	12
C	Director	10
D	B's nominee	5
E	C's son	2
F		8
G		7
H		7
Others	(each less than 5%)	19
		100

Test 1: Is A plc under the control of its directors or five or fewer participators?

		%	%
A Ltd			30
B		12	
D	Associate of B	5	
			17
C		10	
E	Associate of C	2	
			12
			59

Five or fewer participators therefore control the company, and it would be close subject to tests 2 and 3.

Test 2: Is at least 35% of the ordinary share capital held by the public?

	%
A Ltd	30
Others	19
	49

The public therefore controls at least 35% and the company could be treated as not close, subject to test 3.
Test 3: Do the principal members own more than 85% of the ordinary share capital?

		%
A Ltd		30
B	(Incl. D's interest)	17
C	(Incl. E's interest)	12
F		8
G		7
H		7
		81

The principal members own less than 85% of the ordinary share capital and the company is therefore not close.

D. Implications of close company status

1. Affected transactions

The main implications of being a close company are that: 2108
- certain benefits are treated as though they are distributions; and
- special rules apply where loans have been made to participators in a close company.

2. Benefits

Where a company provides a benefit to a participator which would be treated as a benefit in kind (¶3196) if provided to an employee or director, it is treated as a **distribution**. 2109 s 1064 CTA 2010

MEMO POINTS This rule **does not apply** where the participator has already been taxed under the benefit in kind provisions.

For the **company**, this means that any expenses incurred in providing the benefit cannot be deducted in the corporation tax computation. 2110

The **participator** is deemed to have received a distribution which is calculated by determining the value of an equivalent benefit in kind under the normal provisions, and then grossing this amount up at the lower dividend rate, currently 10%. The gross figure is treated as income in the hands of the recipient with a tax credit attached and is subject to tax in the normal way.

EXAMPLE A Ltd provided medical insurance costing £360 to Mr A (a participator) on 1 June 2011. Mr A is not an employee or director of the company.
A Ltd cannot deduct the expense in computing its corporation tax, as it will be treated as a distribution.
Mr A will be treated as having received income of £400 (£360 × 100/90) for the tax year 2011/12.
If Mr A is taxable at the higher or additional rate, further tax will be payable.

3. Loans to participators

What is a loan?

To discourage companies from making loans to participators rather than paying salary or dividends, a special tax charge is made on the company. 2111 s 455 CTA 2010

For these purposes, a loan **includes** any form of indebtedness to the company including, for example, overdrawn director's current accounts.

s 456 CTA 2010 The following loans are **excluded** from these provisions:
- loans made in the ordinary course of the company's business. This includes not only loans made by banking businesses but also credit terms on a sale of goods to a participator which are the same as the credit facilities offered to members of the general public, providing the credit period does not exceed 6 months; and
- loans not exceeding £15,000 in total made to directors or employees working full time for the company (or an associated company (¶1360)) who do not have a material interest in the company.

MEMO POINTS A **material interest** is defined as control of more than 5% of the ordinary share capital or an entitlement to more than 5% of the assets which could be distributed on a notional winding up.

Implications for company

2112 Where a company makes a loan or advance to a participator, it must account for tax at 25% on the amount of the loan. The tax paid is known as **section 455 tax** (previously this was known as section 419 tax).

MEMO POINTS In addition to the close company provisions, the normal **beneficial loan** rules (¶3322) may apply where the loan is made to a director or employee and therefore a benefit in kind may arise.

2113 Any section 455 tax is **payable** at the same time as the company's mainstream corporation tax liability for the accounting period in which the loan is made. This is 9 months and 1 day from the end of the accounting period, or in quarterly instalments if the close company is also a large company (¶2261). Interest will be charged on any late paid section 455 tax on the same basis as interest on late paid corporation tax (¶2275).

MEMO POINTS Although payable at the same time, the section 455 tax is not corporation tax.

EXAMPLE A Ltd makes a loan on 1 April 2010 of £20,000 to Mr A, a participator. A Ltd prepares its accounts annually to 31 December. At 1 October 2011 the whole amount of the loan remains outstanding. A Ltd must account for tax of £5,000 (£20,000 x 25%) to HMRC with its mainstream corporation tax liability for the accounting period ended 31 December 2010.

Loan repayments

2114 s 458 CTA 2010 When the loan is repaid, the company **can make a claim** for the section 455 tax to be repaid. The claim must be made within 4 years of the end of the financial year in which repayment of the loan is made. Where the loan is partially repaid, a claim may be made for recovery of the section 455 tax on the proportion repaid.

EXAMPLE A Ltd made a loan on 1 April 2008 of £5,000 to Mr A, a participator, and accounted for section 455 tax of £1,250. On 1 July 2010, Mr A repaid £3,000. A Ltd can therefore make a claim to recover £750 (3,000/5,000 × £1,250). A claim must be made by 31 March 2015.

A repayment of section 455 tax will not generally be made earlier than 9 months and 1 day from the end of the accounting period in which the event giving rise to the repayment occurred. A repayment of section 455 tax after this date will carry interest from this date (or the date the section 455 tax was actually paid if later) until the date the repayment is made.

MEMO POINTS 1. There is no liability to section 455 tax where the loan is **repaid within 9 months** of the end of the accounting period in which it is made. In this situation the loan must still be reported on the supplementary pages to the company's tax return but there is no actual requirement to pay the tax.
2. Prior to 1 April 2010 the time limit for claiming relief was 6 years.

Loan waivers

2115 Where a loan is waived, the **company** may make a claim to recover the section 455 tax. The claim must be made within 4 years of the end of the financial year in which the loan is written off. The company cannot claim a deduction for the amount of the loan written off in its corporation tax computation.

In addition the **participator** will be taxable on the amount of the loan waived, grossed up at the lower dividend rate which is currently 10%. There will only be a further liability if the participator is liable to tax at a higher rate, in which case the income will be taxed at the upper dividend rate, currently 32.5%, with relief for the tax credit. s 463 CTA 2010

EXAMPLE On 31 January 2006 A Ltd advanced £36,000 to Mr B, a participator in the company. The loan was written off on 31 March 2011, this also being the end of the company's financial year.
The company should have paid section 455 tax of £9,000 for its year ended 31 March 2006. Following the waiver of the loan the company has up to 31 March 2015 to claim repayment of this amount.
Mr A will be treated as having received income of £40,000 (£36,000 × 100/90) for the tax year 2010/2011. If Mr A is taxable at either of the higher rates, further tax will be payable.

MEMO POINTS Prior to 1 April 2010 the time limit for claiming relief was 6 years.

E. Close investment holding companies

Certain close companies are subject to the further requirement that they must **pay tax at the main rate** (¶1342) on their profits regardless of the level of these profits. These companies are termed close investment holding companies (CIHCs). **2117** s 34 CTA 2010

CIHCs are **defined** by exclusion. This means that all close companies are CIHCs unless the main purpose/activity of the company is as a:
- trading company;
- property investment company (which lets property to persons who are not connected (¶5570) with the company); or
- holding company or service company of either of the above two companies.

In simple terms this means that the only companies which will be a CIHC are:
- companies dealing purely with investments; and
- companies letting property to connected persons (¶5570).

SECTION 5

Companies with investment business

Companies with investment business can obtain relief for the expenses of managing their investments. (Note that expenses of a capital nature are not expenses of management and therefore do not qualify for relief.) **2118**

MEMO POINTS 1. In addition to relief for management expenses, companies that are **investment companies** (¶2132) can claim that capital losses on shares are set against income rather than gains. (Note this relief is only available to investment companies as specifically defined.)
2. If a company is a **close investment holding company** (¶2117), it is subject to the further restriction that it must pay tax at the main rate.

An **essential factor of an investment business** is that the company must be carrying on a business; the passive receipt of investment income without the business element of managing the investments will not qualify for relief. **2119** s 1218 CTA 2009

A number of cases have considered whether **property management** constitutes investment income. The conclusion has been that although property management might produce a profit and therefore rank as an investment activity, the business in question is the management of property not the making of investments.

Where the main purpose of the company is **dealing in investments**, it will not be an investment company, but a trading company.

A. Management expenses

1. When can a deduction be claimed?

2120 s 1219 CTA 2009 Companies with investment business may claim a deduction from profits for their expenses so long as the investment activities are within the charge to corporation tax and:
a. the expenses are:
– incurred in connection with the company's investment business; and
– referable to the accounting period in question (¶2121); and
b. the investments are held for a business/commercial purpose of the company (and not, for example, for recreational or social purposes).

Any apportionment of these expenses (where, for example, some of the company's investments are held for recreational purposes and therefore do not qualify for relief) is to be made on a just and reasonable basis.

MEMO POINTS The requirement that a company's investment activities are within the charge to corporation tax would **exclude**:
– a non-resident company with a permanent establishment in the UK, where the investment activities are not part of the permanent establishment's activities; and
– mutual trades and members' clubs.

However it would **not exclude** a company whose investment income is exempt from tax under other provisions (for example, the substantial shareholding exemption.)

2121 Expenses charged to a company's accounts in accordance with accepted accounting practice will be **referable to the accounting period** (¶2120) that coincides with the company's accounting reference date.

In the normal course of events the relevant accounting period will be the same as the period for which the company prepares its statutory accounts. If, however, the company has prepared its accounts for a period which is not an accounting period, the relevant expenses are time apportioned between any accounting periods which fall in the accounts period.

2. Disallowable expenses

2122 Any expenses which are deductible under any other provisions (for example, expenses deductible in computing profits from land and property) are not allowable as management expenses.

In addition, many expenses are **disallowed** in accordance with general principles, for example:
– business entertaining (¶158);
– depreciation (¶157);
– illegal payments (¶180);
– deficits on non-trading loan relationships (¶870), where relief is given by deduction from total profits of the same accounting period, in the normal way; and
– annual payments made in consideration for the right to receive dividends.

Relief for the following types of expenses are subject to the same **restrictions** as for trading companies:
– pension contributions (¶159);
– car leasing (¶163); and
– charitable donations (¶176).

MEMO POINTS In addition, no deduction is available for management expenses incurred on or after 20 June 2007 if they are incurred in connection with any arrangements, the main purpose of which was to secure a **tax advantage**.

3. Allowable expenses

The following **types of expenses** are deductible: **2123** s 1221 CTA 2009
- capital allowances on plant and machinery (¶270 onwards) used for business purposes are given by deduction from profits of the accounting period. To the extent that capital allowances cannot be used in this way, the excess is treated as an expense of the company's investment business;
- certain payments in connection with employees (¶2124);
- annuities or other annual payments (excluding annual or short interest payments where relief is given under the loan relationship provisions) paid on or after 16 March 2005. (Such payments made before this date were deducted as a charge on income (¶958));
- contributions to approved local enterprise agencies, training and enterprise councils, local enterprise companies and urban regeneration companies; and
- statutory costs (for example costs of valuations to comply with the Companies Act regulations).

The following types of **employee payments** are deductible as expenses of management: **2124**
- statutory redundancy payments;
- ordinary annual contributions to a registered pension scheme;
- salary costs (including expenses in connection with seconding an employee to work for a charity, retraining courses, counselling services etc);
- reasonable relocation costs;
- payments to an employee for entering into a restrictive undertaking; and
- awards of shares under a share incentive plan (¶786), or as an employee share acquisition (¶787).

MEMO POINTS As regards **employee remuneration**, a deduction may only be made for amounts charged to the profit and loss account, if it is paid within 9 months of the end of the period for which the accounts are prepared. If payment is not made within that period, the expenditure must be disallowed, and claimed as a deduction for the period in which it is actually paid. See ¶181 for details as to when remuneration is treated as being paid. ss 1249 - 1250 CTA 2009

4. Relief for management expenses

Current year relief

As with a trading company, the tax computation aggregates the income of the company's investment business from all sources. Expenses of managing the company's investment business are deducted from profits after capital allowances but before all other reliefs. For an illustration of the interaction of management expenses with other reliefs, see ¶2135. **2125**

MEMO POINTS If a company's **expenses of managing its investment business exceed its profit** for an accounting period, relief is available for the excess in one of two ways:
- by carry forward against profits of future accounting periods; or
- by surrender as group relief.

Unlike trading losses, there is no provision to allow excess management expenses to be carried back to earlier accounting periods.

Carry forward against future profits

A company with investment business may carry forward any excess management expenses (including capital allowances) against its investment business profits of subsequent accounting periods. Management expenses carried forward in this way are set against total profits (including chargeable gains) of subsequent accounting periods and must be set against the first available profits. **2127** s 1223 CTA 2009

MEMO POINTS If a company with investment business becomes, for example, a pure trading company, any excess management expenses carried forward are lost.

Group relief

2128 s 99 CTA 2010 The group relief provisions (¶1540) are extended to allow companies with investment business to surrender excess management expenses. Only the excess of current year management expenses may be surrendered as group relief. This means that the company must utilise the maximum amount of management expenses against its own profits in priority, and that management expenses brought forward from an earlier period cannot be surrendered.

5. Restrictions on change of ownership

Offset of excess expenses

2129 ss 677 - 682 CTA 2010 In certain circumstances, special rules apply to **restrict** the offset of excess:
- management expenses carried forward; and
- non-trading loan relationship deficits.

The provisions are similar to those that apply to trading companies, where there has been both a **change in ownership** (¶1318) of the company and one of the following trigger events:
- a major change in the nature or conduct of the company's business during the 6 year period beginning 3 years before the change in ownership;
- a significant increase in the capital of the company after the change in ownership; or
- a considerable revival of the business following a change of ownership (provided that, prior to the change, the scale of a company's activities had become small or negligible).

Where these provisions apply, the accounting period in which the change in ownership occurs is deemed to be **split into two notional periods**, at the date of the change. Management expenses and non-trading loan relationship deficits are then apportioned between the two notional periods.

Management expenses and non-trading loan relationship deficits arising **before the change** of ownership cannot be carried forward against income after that date.

Where it appears that a company has deferred the payment of interest to minimise the impact of these rules, that interest may be disallowed.

ss 692 - 699 CTA 2010 MEMO POINTS In addition, separate anti-avoidance rules restrict the offset of **chargeable gains** realised on an asset transferred intra-group within 3 years of the initial change in ownership. Such realised gains cannot be offset against management expenses arising before the change in ownership. These rules apply whether or not there is a "trigger event" after the change of ownership.

Major change of business

2130 SP 10/91 HMRC have published **guidance** on what they consider to be a major change in the nature or conduct of a business for a company with investment business. The main criteria is the nature of the investments held (even if the change is the result of a gradual process which began before the 6 year period).

For example, a change in the company's portfolio of quoted shares and securities would not be a major change, but a change from holding quoted shares to investing in rental property would be.

Significant capital increase

2131 ss 688 - 691 CTA 2010 To **determine whether** there has been a significant increase in the capital of the company, two figures must be established:

a. the first figure, A, which is the lower of:
- the capital immediately before the change in ownership; and
- the highest 60 day minimum amount during the year before the change; and

b. the second figure, B, which is the highest 60 day minimum amount during the 3 years following the change in ownership.
There has been a significant increase if either:
- B exceeds A by more than £1 million; or
- B is more than twice A.

MEMO POINTS The **60 day minimum** is determined by finding the highest amount of the company's capital for each day during the relevant period, and then finding the highest of those amounts which existed for a period of 60 days or more.

B. Losses on unquoted shares

1. Relief available to investment company

An investment company that sustains a loss on the disposal of ordinary unquoted shares in a qualifying trading company **may claim relief** for the loss by setting it against its income (as opposed to its chargeable gains) of the same or preceding year. A claim must be submitted within 2 years of the end of the accounting period in which the loss arose. 2132

MEMO POINTS 1. An **investment company** is one:
- whose business consists wholly or mainly of making investments; and
- the main part of whose income is derived from those investments.

For the purpose of these provisions a holding company of a trading group is not treated as an investment company.
2. The **capital loss must arise in one of the following circumstances**:
- on an arm's length sale for full consideration;
- as a result of a negligible value claim (¶6025);
- as a capital distribution on a winding-up; or
- following the loss, dissolution or extinction of the asset.

3. See ¶5486 for details of a **similar relief available to individuals**.

2. Qualifying conditions

There are several conditions that need to be satisfied before this relief can be claimed: 2133
a. the investment company must:
- have been an investment company throughout the 6 years preceding the disposal (or for a shorter period provided it has never been a trading company or an excluded company); and
- not be associated with, or in the same group as, the unquoted trading company in question;

b. the shares acquired by the investment company must be in a company that, from the date of incorporation (or, if later, 1 year before the shares were subscribed for) to the date of disposal:
- is unquoted (this includes shares listed on AIM); and
- carries on its activities wholly or mainly in the UK; and

c. at the date of disposal of the shares, the company invested in must:
- be a trading company; or
- have ceased to trade not more than 3 years before that time and not subsequently been an excluded company or an investment company.

MEMO POINTS 1. A **trading company** is a company:
- whose business consists wholly or mainly of carrying on one or more trades; or
- which is the holding company of a trading group.

A **trading group** is made up of a company with one or more 51% subsidiaries, where the business of the companies combined consists wholly or mainly of carrying on a trade (or trades).

For the purpose of this definition, if the subsidiary is an excluded company or is not resident in the UK, the activity is not treated as a trade.

2. An **excluded company** is one whose trade consists wholly or mainly of dealing in shares, securities, land, or commodity futures, or where the trade is not carried out on a commercial basis and in such a way that profits can be reasonably be expected to be realised. The holding company of a non-trading group, building society or registered industrial and provident society is also an excluded company.

3. Utilisation of losses

2134 The loss is calculated in accordance with the chargeable gains rules but is excluded from the total chargeable gains for the period, and deducted from the total income of the accounting period in which the loss arises in priority to expenses such as management expenses and charges on income, but after any CVS loss relief claim (¶2012).

If the loss **cannot be fully utilised** in this way, the excess may be carried back and set against income of the previous 12 months. Where an accounting period falls partly within the 12 month period, the loss can only be set against income attributable to the specified period (¶1274) and therefore the profits of such an accounting period must be apportioned on a time basis. There is no facility to carry forward any element of the loss, and therefore if the loss cannot be utilised within the specified period, a claim should not be made.

C. Interaction of reliefs

2135 The following pro forma computation illustrates the order in which reliefs are given against the income of a company with investment business, which may of course not have all the sources shown.

	£	£
Trading income	x	
UK property business income	x	
Non-trading loan relationship credits	x	
Income from other sources	x	
Income received under deduction of tax	x	
		x
Losses on unquoted shares		(x)
		x
Chargeable gains	x	
Capital losses b/fwd	(x)	
		x
Less:		
Capital allowances	(x)	
Management expenses of the period	(x)	
Management expenses b/fwd	(x)	
NTLR deficit of the period	(x)	
Charitable donations relief	(x)	
		(x)
		x
Group relief claimed		(x)
Profit chargeable to corporation tax		x

SECTION 6

Enterprise investment scheme: corporate implications

A. Statutory obligations

When a company seeks to raise funds through the issue of shares qualifying for Enterprise Investment Scheme relief (¶2861), it has certain statutory requirements. 2136

MEMO POINTS In addition, it is arguable that the company has a **moral obligation** not to do anything which would result in the withdrawal of relief from those investors.

EIS relief is only available in respect of subscriptions for shares in qualifying trading companies (or groups). HMRC therefore need to be provided with information both at the time of issue of shares and on an ongoing basis. 2137

Initial requirements

Before the investor is entitled to relief, the **company is required to provide** HMRC with sufficient information to establish that the qualifying conditions are satisfied. This is achieved by completing form EIS 1 which requires details of: 2138 s 204 ITA 2007
- the capital structure of the company;
- the activities; and
- the subscribers.

The company must submit the EIS 1:
a. no earlier than 4 months after the qualifying activity commences; and
b. no later than 2 years from the end of the year of assessment in which the shares are issued (or, if later, 2 years and 4 months from the commencement of the qualifying activity).

Assuming HMRC are satisfied that the conditions are met, authority will be given to the company to **issue certificates of eligibility** (EIS 3) to the investors. 2139

Form EIS 3 can be issued to any eligible investor, regardless of whether relief is actually claimed.

A **penalty** of up to £3,000 may be charged if the company: 2140 s 98 TMA 1970
- fraudulently or negligently completes form EIS 1, or issues form EIS 3; or
- issues form EIS 3 without authority from HMRC.

Ongoing requirements

If the company becomes aware of any event resulting in a **breach of the qualifying conditions** (for example, it acquires a non-qualifying subsidiary), it must notify HMRC. 2141 ss 240-244 ITA 2007

Similarly, if the company makes a return of value or issues replacement capital which results in the withdrawal of relief, it must notify HMRC.

Notification must be made in writing and, in all cases, the time limit for giving notification is 60 days from the date of the event, or, if later, 60 days from the date on which the company became aware of the relevant event.

A **penalty** of up to £300 may be imposed for failure to notify. Once the initial penalty has been imposed, a further penalty of up to £60 per day may be charged for continuing failure. If a company gives notice fraudulently or negligently, a penalty of up to £3,000 may be imposed. s 98 TMA 1970

B. Moral obligations

2142 The company may feel it has a moral obligation not to do anything which would result in a withdrawal of EIS relief from investors. It is therefore important that the company continues to satisfy all the qualifying conditions and makes no returns of value.

Some of the key points to consider are outlined below:
– **eligible shares** must have no preferential rights. This means that any non-EIS shares must not have restrictions imposed on them, which would result in the EIS shares having preferential rights;
– the trade must be carried on **wholly or mainly in the UK**. Therefore, any overseas expansion should be reviewed to ensure it does not breach the conditions;
– the company must have no subsidiaries other than **qualifying subsidiaries** (¶2873). This may be of particular concern when acquiring new subsidiaries; and
– **funds raised** through the issue of EIS shares must be used for the purposes of the qualifying activity within a set period. Therefore the relevant monies should be identified and retained separately in order to establish that the requirements are met.

CHAPTER 10

Overseas issues

OUTLINE ¶¶

SECTION 1

Controlled foreign companies

A. Why have special rules?

2145 s 747, Sch 24 ICTA 1988 To prevent international groups of companies generating and retaining profits in low tax jurisdictions, legislation exists to apportion profits of controlled foreign companies (CFCs) back to the UK and charge tax at the main UK corporation tax rate (although the tax charged is not corporation tax as such).

MEMO POINTS 1. Any apportionment is restricted to income of the CFC; no apportionment can be made in respect of **chargeable gains**.
2. An apportionment may be made to **anyone holding an interest** in a CFC, whether an individual or a company, UK resident or not. However, tax will only be charged on profits apportioned to UK resident companies, and therefore companies owned entirely by UK resident individuals and overseas residents, although possibly CFCs, will not give rise to a tax charge. The rules for determining the residence status of individuals and companies are set out at ¶4152 onwards and ¶16 respectively.
3. The rules as outlined here apply for accounting periods beginning on or after 1 January 2011. For earlier periods see earlier editions of *Tax Memo*.
4. The rules relating to CFCs are complex, and this section only seeks to give an **overview of the provisions**. For a more detailed analysis see *Corporation Tax Memo*.

B. Scope of provisions

1. Definition

2146 A CFC is a company resident outside the UK that is:
– controlled (¶2148) by UK residents (whether individuals or companies); and
– subject to a lower level of taxation (¶2149) in its country of residence than would be the case in the UK.

2. Residence

2147 The **basic rule** for the determination of residence for the CFC provisions is that a company is deemed to be resident in a territory in an accounting period if, throughout the period, it was liable to tax there by reason of domicile, residence or place of management. It is not necessary for tax to have actually been paid by the company, only that it was potentially payable.

If there are **two or more territories** in which the company could be deemed to be resident, the company will be deemed to be resident in the territory:
– where effective management takes place; or if that is not conclusive
– where the greater amount of its assets (as determined by the market value) are situated immediately before the end of the accounting period; or if that is not conclusive
– as directed by HMRC.

Where a company does not have a territory of residence a right of election arises which is available to the holders of the majority UK assessable interest.

s 90 FA 2002

MEMO POINTS UK resident companies that are deemed to be non-resident as a result of a **double tax treaty** from 1 April 2002 remain subject to the CFC legislation. Where such companies became non-resident as the result of a double tax treaty before 1 April 2002, they are outside the scope of the CFC regime, unless either of the **following conditions** are met at any time on or after 22 March 2006:
– the non-UK resident company (with no current subsidiaries) acquires, directly or indirectly, any UK subsidiary; or
– the non-UK resident company (with existing subsidiaries) acquires, directly or indirectly, any UK subsidiary and there is a qualifying change in activities (i.e. a major change in the nature, conduct or size) of the non-resident company or of the group of which it is a member at the time the subsidiary is acquired or later.

3. Control

2148 Control **means** the power of a person to ensure that the affairs of the company are conducted in accordance with his wishes:
s 755D ICTA 1988
– by holding shares or possessing voting power in that or any other company;
– as a result of any powers conferred by the Articles of Association or other document regulating that or any other company.

Further, control also includes those who:
- if the company distributed all of its profits, would be entitled to receive the greater part;
- if the whole of the company's share capital was disposed of, would be entitled to receive the greater part of the proceeds; and
- if the company was wound up, would receive the greater part of the surplus of assets.

If **two or more persons**, when considered together, have such power, then they control the company. For this purpose each person is also deemed to hold:
- rights and powers which he is entitled to acquire in the future (or will in the future be entitled to acquire);
- rights and powers which (whether now or in the future) may be exercised by other persons on his behalf, under his direction, or for his benefit; and
- (if UK resident) rights and powers of any person connected with him who is also UK resident.

A company which would not otherwise be regarded as being controlled by UK residents is treated for the purposes of the CFC legislation as being so controlled if:
- two persons (A and B) together control the company;
- one of them (A) is UK resident, and holds at least 40% of the interests, rights and powers held by A and B together; and
- the other person (B) is not UK resident and also holds at least 40% (but not more than 55%) of the interests, rights and powers held by A and B together.

4. Lower level of taxation

What is a lower level?

A company is considered to be subject to a lower level of taxation if the local taxes payable on its profits are less than 75% of the corresponding liability that would be incurred in the UK. Local taxes are those imposed by the country of residence on income. Any taxes imposed, for example, on capital profits or turnover, are excluded. Other foreign taxes are not included in the local tax, but any double tax relief is also deducted when calculating the notional UK liability. **2149** s 750 ICTA 1988

Hypothetical UK chargeable profit

In calculating the hypothetical UK chargeable profit and hence the UK tax liability, the following **assumptions must be made**: **2150**
- the overseas company is UK resident and therefore foreign profits are included in the company's taxable profit;
- the overseas company is not close (¶2100);
- all appropriate claims and elections are made (including capital allowances);
- group relief (¶1540) is not available;
- unremittable foreign income is subject to relief (¶2177); and
- losses incurred may be utilised if incurred in the previous 6 years.

B. Apportionment

1. Relevant accounting period

An apportionment is made for each relevant accounting period of the CFC. For these purposes, the normal rules for determining the accounting period apply (¶30) subject to the following modifications: **2152**

a. an accounting period will start when the company comes under the control of UK residents;
b. an accounting period will end:
– when it ceases to be controlled by UK residents; or
– if the country of residence changes.

The apportioned profit will be taxable in the hands of the UK company for its accounting period in which the CFC's accounting period ends.

EXAMPLE A Inc is a CFC wholly owned by B Ltd. A Inc prepares its accounts to 31 December, and B Ltd to 31 March. An apportionment of £127,500 is made for A Inc's accounting period ended 31 December 2010. This will be included on B Ltd's corporation tax return for the accounting period to 31 March 2011.

2. Exemptions from apportionment

Conditions

2154 ss 747, 748 ICTA 1988

An apportionment will not be made where one of the **following conditions** is met:
– the overseas company is resident in an excluded country;
– the accounting profit (not taxable profit) of the CFC does not exceed £200,000 (reduced correspondingly for accounting periods of less than 12 months);
– the UK resident company is entitled to less than 25% of the apportioned profit;
– there is intra-group trading with no significant connection to the UK;
– the main business of the company is the exploitation of intellectual property where the CFC or the intellectual property have only a minimal connection with the UK;
– for a three year period companies which find themselves caught within the rules due to a reorganisation or change of ownership;
– the overseas company is engaged in exempt activities; or
– the motive test is satisfied.

MEMO POINTS **Advance clearance** is available from HMRC where it is believed that the last three items above apply.

Excluded countries

2156 SI 1998/3081

HMRC maintain a list of excluded countries. The list is actually two lists:
a. list one being a **list of countries which are excluded provided** that income and gains derived outside that country do not exceed the greater of:
– 10% of the company's income and gains; or
– £50,000; and
b. list two contains countries which can be regarded as **excluded subject** to the additional requirement that none of the specified exemptions or reliefs is available to the overseas company.

Where an overseas company is located in an excluded country, there is no requirement to include its financial details on the UK company tax return.

Significant connection to the UK

2158 Sch 25 para 12E ICTA 1988

A company will have a significant connection to the UK where:
a. more than 10% of its **gross income** is UK connected and the following do not apply:
– it maintains sufficient staff outside the UK to run the CFC;
– its profits do not exceed 10% of its relevant operating expenses; and
– its UK-connected income for the period does not exceed 50% of its gross income; or
b. expenditure in the UK exceeds 50% of its total expenditure and the company is involved in a scheme which has the main purpose of securing a tax advantage.

Exempt activities

An overseas **trading company** is engaged in exempt activities if each of the following requirements is met: 2159 Sch 25 paras 5 - 8 ICTA 1988

1. The overseas company has real presence in the country of residence (i.e. a business establishment, not simply a postal address) and is effectively managed there.
2. The main activity of the overseas company does not consist of:

a. investment business;
b. dealing in goods for delivery to or from the UK or connected persons;
c. wholesale, distributive, financial or service business where at least 50% of its gross trading income derives from:

- connected persons (¶5570);
- persons connected with persons who control the CFC by virtue of the 40% test (¶2148);
- persons holding a stake of at least 25% in the overseas company; or
- UK resident individuals, companies or permanent establishments.

MEMO POINTS The definition of **effective management** differs slightly depending upon whether the CFC is resident in an EU/EEA member state or not, as follows:
- if the company is **EU/EEA resident**, it will be seen as effectively managed in its country of residence if there are sufficient individuals working for the company with the competence and authority to undertake all, or substantially all of the company's business; and
- if the company is **non EU/EEA resident**, it will be seen as effectively managed in its country of residence if there are enough individuals employed by the company to deal with the volume of the company's business (and any services provided by the company for persons resident outside that territory must not be performed in the United Kingdom).

An overseas **holding company** will be exempt if: 2160
a. it has real presence in its country of residence and it is managed there;
b. at least 90% of its gross income is derived from companies which it controls (¶2148), which are either:
- local holding companies; or
- companies engaged in exempt activities.

In addition, if the holding company is a **superior holding company**, it will be exempt if 90% of its income derives from companies which it controls which are resident in the same territory as the superior holding company, and which themselves are:
- holding companies, local holding companies or engaged in an exempt activity; or
- superior holding companies with such qualifying exempt income from their subsidiaries.

MEMO POINTS 1. A **holding company** is a company whose business consists of holding shares in:
- 90% owned local holding companies; or
- 51% owned trading companies.

2. A **local holding company** is a holding company where 90% of its income derives from subsidiaries that it controls that are:
- resident in the same territory as the local holding company; and
- not themselves holding companies but are otherwise engaged in exempt activities.

3. A **superior holding company** is a company whose business consists wholly or mainly in the holding of shares in companies which are holding companies or local holding companies or are themselves superior holding companies.
4. The exemptions for **non-local holding** companies and **superior holding** companies were removed for accounting periods beginning on or after 1 July 2009. Where a company qualified under these provisions in its last period ending before 1 July 2009 the exemption will continue until 1 July 2012. If an accounting period **straddles** this date an apportionment will be necessary.

Motive test

The motive test has **two parts**, both of which must be satisfied: 2162 Sch 25 paras 16 - 18 ICTA 1988; s 748(3) ICTA 1988
- any reduction in UK tax must be minimal or not the main purpose of the transactions; and
- the reduction of UK tax by the diversion of UK profits must not be a main reason for the overseas company's existence during the period.

The **aim of this test** is to exempt companies which were established for genuine commercial purposes from the CFC legislation.

MEMO POINTS HMRC apply special rules to **holding companies** when considering the motive test. A holding company will be considered to satisfy the motive test where the main purpose of the company is either:
– receiving interest and dividends from overseas subsidiaries as a staging post before reinvestment into the trading operations of the subsidiaries concerned; or
– holding funds outside the source country for the purposes of reinvestment in that country due to exchange controls, inflation concerns, or political instability and the risk of expropriation.

3. Calculating the apportionment

Basic rule

2163 Where the CFC provisions apply, the net chargeable profit will be apportioned among all the persons having an interest in the CFC. This apportionment is generally **based on** share ownership. If the share ownership has changed during the accounting period, an average should be used.

The UK company must calculate the amount itself and include details on its tax return. If this requirement is not met, interest and penalties may be charged.

EXAMPLE The ordinary share capital of A Inc, a CFC, is owned as follows:

Mr B	UK resident	20%
C SA	French resident	40%
D Ltd	UK resident	30%
E Ltd	UK resident	10%

No other shares are in issue.
If A Inc has profits of £325,000 including a chargeable gain of £50,000, the apportionment to D Ltd will be:

Net chargeable profit:	£275,000	(325,000 – 50,000)
Apportionment:	£82,500	(30 % × £275,000)

No apportionment is made to E Ltd as its interest is less than 25%. An apportionment of £110,000 is made to C SA, but this is outside the scope of UK corporation tax.

2164 The basic rule **can be modified** if HMRC feel it would not be appropriate. In these situations, apportionments can be made on a just and reasonable basis. This may be necessary where, for example, a UK company has only a small interest in the ordinary share capital but has control of the company by some other means.

EXAMPLE A Ltd owns 100% of the preference shares in B Inc (a CFC), and is therefore entitled to all the assets on winding up, but no votes. In addition, A Ltd owns 10% of the ordinary voting shares, with the remainder being owned by C Ltd.
Based on the ordinary shares, A Ltd might avoid an apportionment as its interest is less than 25%. However, it is likely that HMRC would seek to apply a just and reasonable basis, and apportion a greater percentage to A Ltd.

MEMO POINTS **Loan creditors** are not considered to have an interest in the CFC for these purposes.

Indirect holdings

2165 Profits of the CFC may be apportioned to indirect owners, subject to the rules below:
– a UK resident company which holds the interest directly must be treated as the sole holder of the shares;
– if the direct holder is not UK resident and the only indirect holder is a UK resident company, the latter must be treated as the holder; and

– if the direct holder is resident outside the UK and there is more than one UK resident indirect shareholder, the lowest UK resident company in the chain of ownership is deemed to be the holder.

Income arising to trustees of a settlement where the company is a settlor or beneficiary will be included in the apportionment of profit. Where more than one beneficiary exists a just and reasonable apportionment is required.

EXAMPLE A Inc (a CFC) is owned 50% by B Inc (not UK resident) which is itself 100% owned by C Ltd (UK resident). C Ltd also owns 20% of A Inc directly. The remaining 30% of A Inc is owned by D Inc (not UK resident) which is 100% owned by D Ltd (UK resident) which itself is 100% owned by E Ltd (UK resident).
C Ltd will be deemed to hold 70% of A Inc (20 % + 50%) with the remaining 30% attributable to D Ltd.

MEMO POINTS Under no circumstances can the total apportionments exceed 100% of the profit.

Creditable tax

When apportioning profits, creditable tax is also apportioned. Creditable tax is the **aggregate of**: 2166
– any income tax deducted at source from income received by the CFC;
– any double tax relief available in the UK in respect of foreign tax due against chargeable profits; and
– any corporation tax payable in the UK on CFC income taxable in the UK.

Claim to reduce apportionment

A company can apply for profits from a CFC to be reduced or disregarded entirely for the purposes of calculating the apportionment **where the**: 2167 s 751A ICTA 1988
– CFC has a business establishment in an EU/EEA member state; and
– profits to be reduced/disregarded represent the net economic value (before tax) accruing to the CFC from the activities of individuals working for the CFC in at least one EU/EEA member state.

If an application is successful, the CFC's **creditable tax** is also reduced by an amount that represents the reduction in the attributable profits.

EXAMPLE
1. A UK company sets up a CFC in another EEA state to operate a call centre. The CFC opens the office, appoints a local management team and recruits local staff. In a situation such as this it can be seen that the:
– CFC has a business establishment in an EEA state; and
– the profits from the services provided by the call centre are part of the group's real business.
Consequently an application to disregard the profits of the call centre will be likely to be granted.

2. A UK company sets up a CFC in another EEA state to route funds through it. The CFC rents an office and pays two employees of a group company in the same member state to carry out the administration. The funds are sent to the CFC, which then, on the instructions of the UK company, passes them on to other group companies as interest bearing loans. In this situation, although the CFC has a business establishment in an EEA state, the profits are not part of the group's real business. Consequently an application to disregard the profits of the call centre will be unlikely to be granted.

MEMO POINTS 1. The **net economic value** is equal to the amount that the company/group would be prepared to pay to a third party for the work in question.
2. An application can be **made at any time** on or before the UK company's usual filing date (and can be amended or withdrawn at any time before the application is determined by HMRC). If an application is determined after the company has filed its tax return, it then has 30 days from the date it was determined in which to amend its return. Any refusal of an application can be appealed in the usual manner.

C. Taxation of apportioned profits

1. Liability

2168 The apportioned profit is taxed at the **main corporation tax** rate in the hands of a UK resident company, regardless of the rate applicable to that company's own taxable profits. Details of the apportionment calculation must be included with the company's tax return for the accounting period in which the CFC's accounting period ends. Tax is payable at the same date as the company's mainstream tax liability, either in quarterly instalments (¶2262) or 9 months and 1 day from the end of the accounting period (¶2260), and is subject to the usual rules for interest (¶2275) and penalties (¶2304).

2. Reliefs for apportioned profits

Offset

2169 Sch 26 para 1 ICTA 1988

Apportioned profits can be relieved by offset against the following:
- trading losses (including a UK property business loss);
- charitable donations relief;
- group relief;
- non-trading loan relationship deficits;
- capital allowances given by discharge or repayment of tax; and
- management expenses.

Relief is given in terms of tax at the rate the apportioned profits are taxed. Full or partial claims are accepted.

EXAMPLE In the year to 31 March 2010, A Ltd made a trading loss of £100,000 and was charged to tax in respect of apportioned profits of £120,000.
In the absence of a claim, A Ltd will be liable to pay tax of £33,600 (£120,000 x 28%). However, A Ltd can make a claim to offset the trading losses against the apportioned profits. This relief will be expressed in terms of a tax reduction (i.e. the reduction in tax as a result of the claim will be £28,000 (£100,000 @ 28%) and the trading losses will be deemed to have been fully utilised).

Comment It should be noted that losses may be relieved at a relatively low tax rate where creditable tax is also available.

Surplus ACT

2170 SI 1999/358 reg 20

Where a company has surplus ACT (¶1402), this may be offset against the tax due on any apportioned profits. In broad terms, the ACT which can be offset is restricted to the amount of shadow ACT which would have been due if a dividend equal to the net chargeable profits was paid. Relief cannot be given for the same amounts twice, which means that surplus shadow ACT relieved in this way cannot be relieved in any other way.

Gains on disposals of CFC shares

2171 Sch 26 para 3 ICTA 1988

Any chargeable gain arising on a disposal of shares in the CFC **may be reduced** where tax has previously been paid on the apportionment of profits. To obtain relief, a claim must be made within 3 months of the end of the accounting period in which the share disposal takes place.

The amount by which the gain can be reduced is calculated using the following formula:

$$\frac{\text{Average market value of shares disposed of in accounting period}}{\text{Average market value of entire holding in accounting period}} \times \text{Tax paid on apportioned profits in accounting period}$$

This calculation is performed for each accounting period in which an apportionment occurs.

EXAMPLE A Ltd holds 3,000 shares in CFC Co. In Year 1, A Ltd pays tax of £7,200 in respect of apportioned profits. In Year 2, A Ltd sells 1,000 of its shares in CFC Co, when each share is worth £20. A Ltd realises a chargeable gain of £8,000, which can be reduced as follows:

$$\frac{20{,}000\ (1{,}000 \times £20)}{60{,}000\ (3{,}000 \times £20)} \times 7{,}200 = £2{,}400$$

Dividends from CFCs

Where a UK company receives a dividend from a CFC, out of profits which have previously been subject to apportionment, **underlying tax** (¶2180) will be deemed to have been paid. The underlying tax can be set against the UK company's corporation tax liability in the accounting period in which the dividend is paid. The usual double tax relief rules apply subject to the following **modifications**: **2172** Sch 26 para 4 ICTA 1988

- there is no restriction of relief if the company's interest is less than 10% of the voting control of the CFC; and
- the amount of the dividend is not grossed up by reference to the deemed underlying tax.

The underlying tax is calculated by working out the UK tax on the proportion of apportioned profits subsequently paid out as a dividend.

Comment It is likely that this will be of significantly less importance following the exemptions introduced for dividends received (¶952).

EXAMPLE A Inc pays a dividend to B Ltd of £50,000 (gross) out of profits of £375,000. B Ltd had paid tax at 30% on apportioned profits of £125,000.

UK tax on apportioned profit 125,000 × 30%	£37,500
Effective rate of tax: $\frac{37{,}500}{375{,}000} = 10\ \%$	
Underlying tax credit on dividend 50,000 × 10%	£5,000

The credit of £5,000 can be set against the tax liability of B Ltd.

SECTION 2

Overseas payments and receipts

A. General rules

Basis of taxation

UK resident companies are **taxable** on their overseas income regardless of its country of origin, although where tax has been suffered in the overseas country **double taxation relief** may be available. **2173**

To claim relief a company must first look to the double tax treaty (¶4227), but if there is no treaty or the terms are not favourable, then unilateral relief can be claimed, usually as a credit (¶4231) against the UK corporation tax liability. This credit cannot reduce the corporation tax liability below nil, so therefore no relief will be available for foreign tax suffered in excess of the corporation tax liability. (It may therefore be beneficial for a company in a loss making position to claim any overseas tax as an expense (¶4235) arising in the accounting period.)

Special rules apply for:
- calculation of double tax relief on overseas dividends (¶2178); and
- withholding tax on payment/receipt of overseas interest and royalties (¶2190).

Liability

2174 The **general rule** is that overseas income from whatever source is assessable including, for example, income from overseas property letting, foreign dividends and profits of trades carried on wholly overseas. These profits are treated separately from their UK counterparts mainly for the purposes of loss reliefs.

The **exception** to this is profits or losses arising from loan relationships, which are treated in the same way as UK source loan relationships (¶870).

MEMO POINTS 1. The deciding factor when considering the source of **foreign dividends** is the location of the central management and control (¶20) of the paying company, not simply the country of incorporation.
2. Overseas income is assessable on the basis of the profits arising during an accounting period. Profits from overseas trades and overseas rental properties are calculated using the same rules as UK trades and income from UK property respectively.

Exemption for foreign branches

2175 ss 18A-18S CTA 2009

From 19 July 2011 an **election** is available to companies that have a foreign permanent establishment (¶22). This election, which applies for that period and any subsequent periods, means that a foreign permanent establishment's profits will not be subjected to UK tax. In a similar manner its **gains** will also be exempted.

The corresponding position is that no losses arising can be utilised nor can any foreign tax deducted be claimed.

Credit relief restriction

2176 s 44 TIOPA 2010

Where credit relief is claimed by a company for foreign tax paid, the amount of credit relief is restricted if the overseas income arises from a **trade or property business**. In this situation, double tax relief will be the lower of the:
- overseas tax paid; or
- UK tax liability on the net foreign profits (i.e. the gross foreign income less any direct expenses attributable to the earning of that income and a reasonable proportion of all indirect expenses (e.g. overheads etc)).

In other words, credit for overseas tax is not allowed against unrelated UK profits and is restricted to the corporation tax liability on the net foreign profits.

This provision **will not apply** to foreign income where there are no attributable expenses (e.g. dividend income received otherwise than in the course of a trade).

EXAMPLE During Year 1, a **financial trader** acquires a shareholding at a cost of £1,000. A dividend of £85 is received after deduction of tax at source of £15, and subsequently the shareholding is sold for £950. Other expenses attributable to the whole period of the shareholding were £30. The overall result is calculated as follows:

	£	£
Sale of shares	950	
Gross dividend	100	
		1,050
Purchase of shares	1,000	
Other overheads	30	
		(1,030)
Net profit		20
Tax @ 28%		6
Less double tax relief		(6)
UK tax liability		Nil

The remaining overseas tax suffered of £9 (£15 – £6) cannot be relieved against any other income the trader may have.

MEMO POINTS 1. There is a **similar restriction for individuals** for overseas trading or property income (¶4237).
2. **Royalty income** arising from the same asset is treated as one single source of income for these provisions.
3. **Anti-avoidance provisions** deny relief for foreign and/or UK tax if certain specified schemes or arrangements are entered into with the aim of obtaining a foreign tax credit. These provisions are aimed at attacking highly contrived transactions. s 45 TIOPA 2010

Income that cannot be remitted to the UK

In certain circumstances, relief may be available for amounts which cannot be remitted to the UK. This relief is **only available for** amounts which cannot be remitted, despite the company's best endeavours, because either: **2177** ss 1274 - 1278 CTA 2009
– remittance is prevented by the laws or the government of the overseas country; or
– it is impossible to obtain foreign currency in that country.

Relief is not available for any amounts which the company has managed to convert into another currency outside the country.

Relief is given by reducing the assessable income for an accounting period by the amount which is unremittable. If the income subsequently becomes capable of remittance, the income is deemed to arise in the accounting period in which the restriction is lifted.

Claims for relief must be made within 2 years of the end of the accounting period in which the income arises.

B. Overseas dividends

1. Double tax relief

Where an overseas dividend is not exempt from tax (¶942), the dividend (grossed up to include withholding and underlying tax) is taxed. Where relief is not claimed under a double tax treaty, **unilateral relief** is available in the UK for: **2178** ss 9 - 14 TIOPA 2010
– withholding tax on dividends paid to the UK; and
– underlying tax if the UK company, directly or indirectly, owns not less than 10% of the ordinary share capital of the paying company.

MEMO POINTS Where the company now holds less than 10% and the cause of this was unforeseeable or could not have reasonably been avoided the exemption will still apply. s 15 TIOPA 2010

2. Withholding tax

This can essentially be **defined** as tax withheld as a direct result of the payment of the dividend to the recipient. To claim double tax relief for this tax, evidence will usually need to be provided to HMRC at the time of the claim, usually in the form of a foreign notice of assessment, together with foreign tax receipts/payments. **2179** s 13 TIOPA 2010

MEMO POINTS HMRC have indicated that **evidence will not need to be provided** if the total amount of credit relief claimed for an accounting period does not exceed £2,000 or if the claim is in respect of a continuing source of income and satisfactory evidence has been provided in the past. However, under self-assessment, the onus is on the taxpayer to provide, if requested, supporting documentation for all entries on a tax return, and so companies should continue to obtain documentation for their files.

3. Underlying tax

Calculation

2180 s 59 TIOPA 2010 This is calculated using the following formula:

$$\frac{\text{Actual tax paid} \times 100}{\text{Actual tax paid} + \text{Relevant profits}}$$

where:
– actual tax paid is the tax paid by the overseas company in the accounting period to which the dividend relates. Companies cannot specify particular profits out of which a dividend can be paid, but can specify which accounting period a dividend is paid from; and
– relevant profits are a company's profits available for distribution as shown in the company accounts. Relevant profits will also include capital profits credited to capital reserves. If the company has accumulated losses, relevant profits for these purposes are the undistributed profits of the most recent period at the time of payment. For dividends received on or after 1 July 2009 this definition is amended slightly for companies that are not considered small (¶942). Where the dividend is considered to be paid from profits other than those arising from transactions not designed to reduce tax then it is the amount of that profit that forms the relevant profits.

EXAMPLE A Inc, a non-UK resident company, has the following results for its accounting period ended 31 December:

	£
Accounting profit before tax	100,000
Foreign tax paid	20,000
Accounting profit after tax	80,000

The underlying tax attributable to a dividend paid out of these profits is 20%, calculated as follows:

$$\frac{(\text{Actual tax paid} \times 100)}{(\text{Actual tax paid} + \text{relevant profits})} = \frac{(20{,}000 \times 100)}{(20{,}000 + 80{,}000)} = 20\ \%.$$

If A Inc were to pay a dividend to its UK parent in circumstances where the dividend was not exempt, the UK company will be able to claim double tax relief for 20% underlying tax attributable to the dividend received.

Mixer cap

2182 s 58 TIOPA 2010 If the underlying tax exceeds the mainstream tax rate in force when the dividend is received it is then **further restricted** by the following formula (known as the mixer cap) to arrive at the underlying tax available for double tax relief in the UK:

$$(D + PA) \times M\ \%$$

where:
– D is the dividend received (inclusive of any withholding tax);
– PA is the amount of tax attributable to the dividend; and
– M % is the UK corporation tax rate in force at the time the dividend was paid.

The mixer cap only **applies to** underlying tax. If a withholding tax has been imposed it is not restricted. However, if the dividend passes through an intermediate company, any withholding tax becomes underlying tax for the purpose of this restriction and is included in the calculation.

EXAMPLE A and B are non-UK subsidiaries of a French holding company (C SA). A pays a dividend of 60 (with an underlying tax rate of 40%) and B pays a dividend of 80 (with an underlying tax rate of 20%). C SA then pays a dividend of 140 to the ultimate UK parent company. The mixer cap will apply as follows:

Dividend	Tax attributable	Mixer cap	Credit allowable to UK parent
A to C SA	40	(60 + 40) × 28% = 28	28
B to C SA	20	(80 + 20) × 28% = 28	20

The total underlying tax available to the UK parent company is therefore restricted to 48 and the excess underlying tax of 12 is lost.

In general, the mixer cap will **not apply to** companies resident in the same country if they are taxed in the foreign county on a consolidated basis. Instead, such companies are treated as a single entity, with the relevant profits, losses and taxes paid being aggregated for the purposes of the calculation of double tax relief. **2183** s 71 TIOPA 2010

EXAMPLE A consolidated group of companies, resident overseas has the following results:

	A Ltd	B Ltd	Total
Accounting profits/losses before tax	50,000	125,000	175,000
Foreign tax (30 %)	15,000	37,500	52,500
Local tax	3,000	5,000	8,000
Accounting profit after tax	32,000	82,500	114,500

If a full dividend was paid to its UK parent, the underlying tax would be calculated as follows:

	A Ltd	B Ltd	Total
Relevant profits	32,000	82,500	114,500
Tax paid (allocated pro rata)	16,908	43,592	60,500
Underlying tax rate: (60,500 x 100)/(114,500 + 60,500)			34.57%

As the underlying rate is more than 30%, the mixer cap will apply to restrict the amount of underlying tax relief in the UK.

MEMO POINTS No underlying tax relief is available if a **tax deduction** in respect of the dividend **has been given in another territory**. This provision is aimed at blocking schemes whereby certain payments are characterised as interest in one country but a dividend in the UK, enabling a company to claim a deduction for the interest payment, whilst in the UK credit would otherwise be given for the underlying tax. s 57(3) TIOPA 2010

4. Method of giving relief

Credit or expense

Relief for withholding and underlying tax is usually given as a **credit** against the UK corporation tax liability in the accounting period in which the dividend is received. **2184** s 18 TIOPA 2010

Where a credit is claimed, any double tax relief given is restricted to the UK corporation tax rate in force at the time the relief is claimed.

EXAMPLE Company A (UK resident) receives a dividend from its 100% foreign subsidiary Company B of 100, net of 50% underlying tax.
On the assumption that credit relief is claimed, Company A's tax computation would be:

Net dividend	100
Underlying tax	50
Foreign profits	150
UK tax @ 28%	42
Less DTR (restricted)	(42)
UK tax payable	Nil

However, companies can instead claim for the foreign tax to be treated as a trading **expense** (¶4235) of the period. This claim would only be beneficial to companies not liable to UK corporation tax in the accounting period in which the dividend is received.

C. Interest and royalties

Inside the EU

2190 ss 757 - 767 ITTOIA 2005

Interest or patent royalty payments between EU companies are exempt from income tax, if the following conditions are satisfied:
– the recipient and paying company are 25% associates;
– the paying company is either a UK company or a UK permanent establishment of an EU company. (Payments of interest or royalties by a permanent establishment will only qualify for exemption if the payment is directly connected with the business of the permanent establishment); and
– the recipient company is an EU company (and not a UK or non-EU permanent establishment of an EU company).

If the payment is of **interest**, tax free payments cannot be made before an exemption notice is issued after an appropriate application has been made on Form EU Interest and Royalties.

If the payment is a **royalty**, tax free payments can be made immediately providing the paying company believes the recipient will be entitled to exemption. There is no requirement to obtain advance approval from HMRC, but if the belief of the taxpayer turns out to be mistaken, HMRC can recover the tax that should have been deducted.

MEMO POINTS These provisions regarding royalty payments between EU companies **closely mirror** the rules for royalty payments outside the EU (¶2192).

2191 Companies are **25% associates** if:
– one holds directly 25% or more of the share capital or voting rights of the other; or
– a third company holds directly 25% or more of the share capital or voting rights of the other companies.

A **repayment** of tax can be claimed if any interest or royalty payments are made under deduction of tax that should have qualified for the exemption.

MEMO POINTS **Anti-avoidance provisions** prevent the exemption from applying if financing arrangements appear to have been structured where the main benefit was to obtain a tax advantage.

Outside the EU

2192 ss 930, 934 ITA 2007

When a company pays **interest** overseas, income tax (at the basic rate) must be deducted from the payments. An application can be made to HMRC to pay this interest gross or at a reduced rate in line with the terms of a relevant treaty, but, until clearance is given, income tax must be withheld.

When a company pays a patent **royalty** overseas, and believes that the non-resident recipient is entitled to relief from UK tax on the royalty under the terms of a double tax treaty, the company may pay the royalty gross, or at a reduced rate of deduction, in line with the terms of the relevant treaty. No prior clearance is required from HMRC, but if the belief of the taxpayer turns out to be mistaken, HMRC can recover the tax that should have been deducted.

SECTION 3

European company statute

2193 A special type of company, known as a **Societas Europaea** (SE), can be formed to essentially enable groups to operate throughout the EU using a single corporate entity, which is subject to the tax law of the country of residence.

Specific provisions apply to the **formation** of an SE. Where such an entity is formed by way of a merger of two or more companies, which are all resident in member states (but not the same member state), the following provisions apply, provided the merger is carried out for bona fide commercial reasons: **2195** s 140E TCGA 1992; s 561A CAA 2001
– if the merger is of **a UK trade** (i.e. the transferor and the resultant SE are UK resident (or non-UK resident but carrying on a trade through a PE in the UK)), then any qualifying assets are transferred on a no gain/no loss basis and no balancing allowances or charges for capital allowance purposes will be triggered;
– if the merger is of **a non-UK trade** (i.e. the transferor is a UK resident company trading in another member state via a PE) and the transfer involves the transfer of all the assets and liabilities of the PE to a non-UK resident transferee then the transfer will give rise to a chargeable gain (with credit for any local tax that should have been deducted were it not for the EU merger regulations (¶1181)).

MEMO POINTS 1. If a merger involves the transfer of **intangible assets**, they are treated as being transferred on a no gain/no loss basis provided the asset concerned was a qualifying intangible asset in the hands of the transferor before the merger and the transferee after the merger. If, however, these conditions are not met because the transferor is trading in another member state through a PE, then the transferor can claim double tax relief for the tax which would have arisen if the EU merger regulations did not apply. Broadly, these regulations prohibit member states from charging tax on such transactions.
2. If the merger involves the transfer of **loan relationships** and, immediately after the merger, the SE is either a UK resident company or PE, then the loan relationship is to be disregarded.
3. Any of the above mergers are treated as a **scheme of reconstruction** and, consequently, the new SE shares stand in the shoes of the old company shares.
4. In a **group situation**, where the principal member of any group becomes an SE (or a subsidiary of an SE) the original group and the "new" group are to be treated as the same group for the purposes of the following provisions:
– transfers of chargeable assets (¶1600) including intangible fixed assets (¶826);
– transfers of trading stock (¶1625);
– reliefs on replacement of business assets (¶1630);
– pre-entry capital gains and losses (¶1636);
– depreciatory transactions (¶1190); and
– dividend stripping (¶1196).

SECTION 4

Arbitrage

Aim of provisions

Provisions apply to prevent companies avoiding tax through the **exploitation of differences between or within different tax codes**. The provisions apply to companies using contrived schemes involving certain types of hybrid entities or instruments for UK tax avoidance purposes, but only if HMRC issue a notice to the company directing that the legislation applies. If such a notice is issued, the company must re-compute its tax liability in accordance with the notice. There are separate rules dealing with deductions and receipts. **2197** s 231 TIOPA 2010

Deductions

In order for HMRC to issue a notice (which must identify the payment and accounting period concerned), the following **conditions must be satisfied**: **2199** s 233 TIOPA 2010
– the transaction must be part of a qualifying scheme;
– as a result of the transaction there is or will be a double deduction of tax or a deduction not matched by a taxable receipt;
– the main purpose of the transaction is to achieve a UK tax advantage; and
– the amount of UK tax advantage must be more than minimal (i.e. more than £50,000).

2201 ss 236 - 242 TIOPA 2010 A scheme is a **qualifying scheme** if it:

a. involves hybrid entities (i.e. entities that are recognisable as a person for one tax code, whilst its profits, gains and losses are within the scope of another person(s)). This will include, for example, a limited partnership. The UK does not recognise a limited partnership as existing independently of its partners, but many other tax codes treat limited partnerships as separate taxable entities. (CFCs (¶2145) are specifically excluded from the scope of these provisions);

b. contains a hybrid instrument that:

– has an alterable characteristic (i.e. one of the parties to the transaction can, by way of an election, alter the instrument such that the tax treatment of it will change);

– contains shares that can be converted to debt, or securities that can be converted to shares on the occurrence of some event and there was a reasonable expectation that they would be so converted at the time of issue (or when the conversion right was created); or

– contains debt instruments treated as equity under GAAP;

c. includes the issue of shares to a connected party (¶5570) that does not confer on the holder a relevant proportion of profits and assets on a winding-up; or

d. includes the transfer of the right to receive income or gains from a security to a connected party (¶5570).

2205 s 243 TIOPA 2010 If HMRC issue a notice, the company has 90 days in which to **amend its tax return** to disallow deductions in relation to the scheme which:

– have been deducted more than once. This includes corporation tax, income tax and similar overseas tax deductions. It does not include indirect taxes. (This rule applies even if the non-UK territory has a similar rule to the UK arbitrage provisions. Consequently a deduction may be disallowed twice); or

– are not taxed in the recipient company. If the recipient company is only exempt from tax on a proportion of the receipt, the same proportion will be disallowed for the payer. (The legislation specifically excludes from these provisions entities that are statutorily exempt from tax (for example, charities)). The exempt receipt need not be in respect of the same payment that gave rise to the UK tax deduction, but it must arise out of the same transaction.

EXAMPLE A UK resident company A makes a tax deductible payment to overseas company B which is taxed on the receipt. B makes a matching payment to overseas company C which is not taxed on receipt. In this example A is the payer and C is the recipient and the UK arbitrage provisions will apply.

MEMO POINTS The UK company can, after receipt of a notice, **voluntarily choose to disclaim** an amount of the expenses in order to cancel out the effect of the UK tax advantage in relation to the scheme.

Receipts

2207 ss 249, 250 TIOPA 2010 This part of the legislation applies more narrowly than the provisions relating to deductions. In order for HMRC to issue a notice (which must identify the payment and accounting period concerned), all of the following **conditions** must be satisfied:

– a company has entered into a scheme under which it receives an amount that is not taxable in the UK;

– that amount is deductible in the hands of the payer;

– the mismatch in the tax treatment is a reasonable expectation of the parties to the transaction; and

– the payment constitutes a contribution to the capital of the recipient company.

s 254 TIOPA 2010 If HMRC issue a notice the company has 90 days in which to **amend its tax return** to treat the receipts identified as taxable income.

Administration

2209 ss 255, 256 TIOPA 2010 Notices can be issued before a return is made (or after, in the form of an enquiry (¶2330)). Exceptionally, notices may also be made on a discovery basis if the time limit in which to raise an enquiry has expired.

If a company disagrees with a notice, any dispute with HMRC should be settled through the usual self-assessment enquiry procedures. A company has 90 days from the receipt of a notice in which to amend its tax return.

MEMO POINTS A company can apply for **informal clearance** from HMRC as to whether a transaction will be caught by these provisions. Where possible HMRC will give a decision as to whether any notice will be issued in respect of the proposed transaction.

CHAPTER 11

Administration

OUTLINE ¶¶

SECTION 1

Self-assessment

2210 The administration of the corporation tax regime is through a system of self-assessment where companies are **responsible for**:
- notifying HMRC of their chargeability to tax;
- completing and filing tax returns;
- calculating and paying their tax liabilities; and
- maintaining detailed records to support the entries on the tax return.

The various requirements and deadlines of the self-assessment regime are discussed below, together with the implications of failing to meet specific obligations.

SECTION 2

Notification

Notification by the company

2211 s 55 FA 2004 Each company must give notice to HMRC when it has come within the **charge to corporation tax**. Notification must be given within 3 months of the beginning of its first accounting period.

HMRC are notified when a **new company** is formed by Companies House and will usually send a form CT41G, which can be used by the company to notify coming within the charge.

The information does not have to be provided on a form CT41G and can be supplied in any other reasonable form.

If a **dormant company** becomes active and comes within the charge to corporation tax, it must notify HMRC within 3 months of the date it became active.

MEMO POINTS 1. For notification purposes the **first accounting period** is deemed to commence when the company first comes within the charge to corporation tax. This will generally be when the company commences its trading activity. However, an accounting period will also be deemed to have commenced as soon as the company acquires a source of income. This could be as simple as the company setting up an interest-bearing bank account, so companies should be aware that the 3-month time limit may begin earlier than they expect.
2. As the system is computerised, it is important to let HMRC know of any changes to the company's details, including the accounting reference date (that is, the date to which accounts are prepared), as early as possible. This is to ensure that any forms reflect the correct details and are issued for the appropriate accounting period.

Notification by HMRC

2212 Once notice has been given, HMRC will issue a **notice to file a return**. The self-assessment return form (CT600) is no longer generally issued to companies, because they now have to file **online**. If a company requires a hard copy of the return, this can be downloaded from HMRC's website.

Sch 18 para 2 FA 1998 If a company is due to file a tax return for an accounting period but has **not received a notice** to file a return from HMRC, the company must notify an officer of HMRC within 12 months of the end of the chargeable period that it is liable to submit a return.

2213 Once a notice to file a return has been issued, the company must **identify the period** for which a return is required. Each notice to file specifies a notice period of up to 12 months and this is used to determine the action required.

In most cases, the notice period **coincides with an accounting period** of the company and a return is then submitted for a period matching the accounting period.

EXAMPLE A Ltd prepares accounts for the 12 months to 31 December 2011. The notice period in the notice to file is 1 January 2011 to 31 December 2011.
A return will be required for the period 1 January 2011 to 31 December 2011.

If the notice period **does not coincide with an accounting period** of the company the following rules will determine the return or returns required: 2214

a. if an **accounting period ends** during the notice period, a return is required for that accounting period. If more than one accounting period ends within the notice period, returns are required for both;

EXAMPLE A Ltd prepares accounts for the 12 months to 31 December 2011. The specified period in the notice to file is 1 January 2011 to 31 December 2011. The return period is therefore 1 January 2011 to 31 December 2011.
If the company ceased to trade on 30 June 2011 but continued to receive investment income, two returns would be required: 1 January 2011 to 30 June 2011, and 1 July 2011 to 31 December 2011.

b. if the company is **outside the scope of corporation tax** (for example dormant) throughout the notice period, a nil return is required for the notice period, although in many cases HMRC will agree not to issue a notice in these circumstances;
c. if an **accounting period begins** during the notice period (for example, where a company starts to trade), a return is required for the period before the start of the accounting period;

EXAMPLE A Ltd is incorporated on 1 January 2011 but did not acquire a source of income until 8 July 2011. It prepares its first accounts to 30 June 2012. The notice to file specifies a period of 1 January 2011 to 31 December 2011. A return is required for the period 1 January 2011 to 7 July 2011.

d. if **none of the above** apply, no return is required. In this case it is best practice to notify HMRC that a return will not be filed, otherwise a penalty will be automatically charged and will need to be appealed.

EXAMPLE A Ltd is incorporated on 1 March 2010 but does not commence trading until 1 May 2010. Accounts are prepared for the year to 30 April 2011. The notice to file specifies a period of 1 June 2010 to 28 February 2011. No return will be required.

SECTION 3

Disclosure rules

A. When is disclosure required?

Disclosure rules require details of certain tax schemes to be provided to HMRC. **Responsibility** for disclosure lies principally with scheme promoters (¶2231) and occasionally users (¶2236). 2215 s 306 FA 2004

Schemes are notifiable if they satisfy the following **conditions**:

a. they will, or might be expected to, give rise to an income tax, corporation tax, capital gains tax or National Insurance contributions advantage (which includes avoidance or reduction of a charge to tax, relief or increased relief from tax, deferral of payment or advancement of repayment);

b. the obtaining of a tax advantage is the main benefit, or one of the main benefits, of the scheme; and
c. the scheme falls within one or more of the applicable hallmarks (¶2216) and is either:
– marketed, etc, by a promoter; or
– designed for use in-house by a large business (note, small and medium-sized enterprises (¶795) that design in-house products are not therefore caught by the disclosure rules).

In addition HMRC can apply to the tribunal for disclosure to be made for schemes even if they do not fall within one of the applicable hallmarks (¶2229).

MEMO POINTS 1. HMRC have stated that **everyday advice** and arrangements are not caught by the disclosure rules. In particular where an individual merely provides advice as to how the tax system operates, this does not create a requirement to disclose. They also go on to specify that advice on the following simple transactions is exempt from disclosure:
– flexible benefits packages, such as the opportunity to forgo salary in return for a car;
– salary sacrifice arrangements, such as those involving pension contributions, computers and childcare vouchers;
– simple incorporations;
– dividend payments to employees;
– standard dual contract arrangements; and
– deferral of bonus payments until after the termination of employment.
2. For the disclosure rules relating to **VAT, SDLT and inheritance tax**, see ¶9240, ¶9422 and ¶7130, respectively.

B. Hallmarked schemes

1. Overview

2216 Disclosure will need to be made if a scheme falls within one or more of the hallmarks listed below. All of the hallmarks apply to schemes where a promoter is involved, but only three apply to schemes designed in-house where there is no promoter, as follows:

Hallmark	Applicable to
Confidentiality from competitors and HMRC	Applicable both to schemes where a promoter is involved and those designed in-house
Premium fee	
Leasing arrangements	
Standardised tax products	Applicable only to schemes where a promoter is involved
Loss schemes	
Pension arrangements	

MEMO POINTS The hallmarks are currently in the process of being updated.

2. Confidentiality

Scope

2217 SI 2006/1543 regs 6, 7 This hallmark applies to both promoted and in-house schemes, although there are slightly different rules depending upon whether there is a promoter for the scheme or not.

Schemes with a promoter

2218 Schemes will fall within this hallmark if:
a. any element of the arrangements gives rise to the expected tax advantage; and

b. it might reasonably be expected that a promoter would want to keep the element that secures the tax advantage confidential from other promoters; or
c. but for the disclosure rules the promoter would wish to keep that element confidential from HMRC.

The **confidentiality from other promoters** test is a hypothetical test (i.e. would a typical promoter want to keep the product confidential). Products with tax avoidance elements that are well known to other tax advisers will not fall within this hallmark, even if the promoter has chosen to keep the arrangements confidential. 2219
In their guidance, HMRC state that the use of an explicit confidentiality agreement before revealing full details of the scheme to a client by advisers who do not normally use such agreements may indicate that the test is met.

The **confidentiality from HMRC** test is not a hypothetical test. The key issue is not what another promoter would do, but what the individual promoter is doing. 2220
Disclosure will have to be made if the promoter wants to keep an element of the scheme confidential from HMRC in order to facilitate repeated or continued use of that element in the future. In other words, would the element that secures the tax advantage otherwise be kept confidential in order to insert it into further schemes?

MEMO POINTS If the person with a duty to disclose is the **user** (¶2236), he will need to disclose if he would otherwise want to keep the scheme confidential from HMRC for any reason (not just if he wants to use it repeatedly).

Schemes without a promoter

A scheme that is designed in-house, to be used by a **large enterprise**, will need to be disclosed if it gives rise to a tax advantage and was originally intended to be kept confidential from HMRC: 2221
a. in order to facilitate repeated or continued use in the future; or
b. to reduce the risk that HMRC might open an enquiry into a return made by the enterprise; or
c. to reduce the risk that HMRC might withhold repayment for certain losses.
This test is not a hypothetical test. The key issue is not what another enterprise would do, but what the enterprise actually did.

MEMO POINTS 1. A **large enterprise** is any enterprise that is not a small or medium-sized enterprise (¶795).
2. The **losses** mentioned at **c.** above are those relating to the use of trading losses by an individual or partner against income and gains. s 261B TCGA 1992 part 4 ITA 2007

3. Premium fee

This hallmark applies to both promoted and in-house schemes (although for in-house schemes the person intended to obtain the tax advantage must be a large enterprise). 2222 SI 2006/1543 reg 8
A scheme will fall within this hallmark if a person could reasonably expect to receive a premium and/or contingent fee dependent upon, or linked to, the obtaining of a tax advantage from the arrangements in question.
This test is a hypothetical test focusing on whether a fee could be reasonably charged or not. If it could, the fact that it might not is not in itself sufficient to nullify this hallmark.

4. Leasing arrangements

This hallmark applies to both promoted and in-house schemes (although for in-house schemes, the person intended to obtain the tax advantage must be a large enterprise). The hallmark is met when there is a **high value, long lease** of plant or machinery and at least one of the following conditions is met: 2223 SI 2006/1543 regs 13 - 17

a. the lease involves a party that is not within the charge to corporation tax;
b. the lease is structured so that the risk usually taken by the lessor that rental payments will not be made is removed (by the provision of money); or
c. the lease is a finance leaseback, although specifically excluded from this are finance leasebacks of:
– new plant and machinery that was acquired or created by the seller not more than 4 months before the sale; and
– plant and machinery typically within a building where it is the building that is subject to a finance leaseback, provided that the rent payable under the lease is not dependent on the availability of capital allowances and the plant and machinery is a fixture of the leased land and its value does not exceed half the value of the leased building.

MEMO POINTS 1. A **long lease** for these purposes is one of more than 2 years. This **includes** leases where there:
– is an option to extend beyond the 2-year limit;
– are arrangements in place at the start of the lease that contemplate an extension beyond the 2 years.
2. A lease is a **high value lease** if the cost (or market value, whichever is lower) to the lessor is either:
– at least £10 million for any one asset; or
– at least £25 million for all the assets.
3. Leases involving plant and machinery used for storage or production do not fall within the exemption of plant and machinery that is **leased within a building**.

5. Standardised tax products

2225 SI 2006/1543 regs 10, 11

This hallmark applies only to promoted schemes and is intended to capture **mass-marketed schemes**, where the fundamental characteristic of the scheme is its ease of replication. All the client will need to do is purchase a prepared tax product that requires little, if any, modification to suit his circumstances. To fall within this hallmark, the following **conditions** must be met:
a. the scheme must be a product (as opposed to a package of proposed arrangements and additional services), in that it must:
– have standardised documentation, which does not require any material alteration to suit client circumstances and which enables the client to implement the arrangements;
– commit the client to enter into a standardised, or substantially standardised, transaction (for example, the client may be required to join a specific partnership, take out a specific loan, etc); and
b. the arrangements must be tax-driven and made available to two or more potential clients, with little or no tailoring to meet individual client requirements.

MEMO POINTS Specifically **excluded** from this hallmark are:
a. schemes that were made available before 1 August 2006;
b. any tax product that falls within the following:
– arrangements that consist solely of plant and machinery leases;
– EIS schemes;
– arrangements that use VCT, CVS or qualify for community investment tax relief;
– accounts which are ISAs;
– approved share incentive plans, share option schemes or CSOP schemes;
– grant of EMI options;
– registered pension schemes; and
– schemes for paying out periodical personal injury damages.

6. Loss schemes

2226 SI 2006/1543 reg 12

This hallmark applies only to promoted schemes and is intended to capture various loss creation schemes which are essentially aimed at **generating trading losses** for individuals that can then be set against income tax and capital gains tax liabilities or used to generate a repayment. To fall within this hallmark:

– the promoter must expect that more than one individual will implement the same (or substantially the same) tax arrangements; and
– an informed individual would reasonably conclude that the main benefit of the arrangements is to provide the individual participants with losses that will be used to reduce their income tax liabilities, or capital gains tax liabilities, or generate a repayment.

MEMO POINTS In their guidance, HMRC state that this test is **not intended to catch** genuine business start-ups where any losses are an unintended, albeit possibly predictable, outcome.

7. Pension arrangements

From 1 September 2009 a hallmark was added in relation to the introduction of the special annual allowance (¶3777). **2228** SI 2006/1543 reg 18

Where a scheme is entered into involving the accrual, expected or actual, of benefits in a pension scheme and the main benefit is either to avoid or reduce the special annual allowance charge, this hallmark will apply.

C. Other schemes

HMRC can apply to the tribunal for an **order requiring disclosure** to be made for a scheme that does not otherwise fall within one of the specific hallmarks. **2229** s 306A FA 2004

An order will **only be made if** HMRC have:
– taken all reasonable steps to establish whether the proposal or arrangements are notifiable; and,
– reasonable grounds to suspect that the scheme should be disclosed.

MEMO POINTS 1. **Reasonable grounds** to suspect that a scheme should be disclosed may include the fact that:
– the scheme is within one of the hallmarks; or
– there is or has in the past been an attempt to avoid or delay providing information to HMRC when requested.
2. Where such an order is granted the time limit for **notification** is 10 working days, starting with the day after the order is made. SI 2004/1864 reg 4(1A)

D. Notification

1. Who is responsible?

A scheme that is a notifiable scheme must be disclosed to HMRC. Responsibility for this lies principally with scheme promoters and occasionally scheme users. **2230**

2. Promoters

Definition

A promoter is a person who, in the course of providing services relating to taxation (or, where applicable, National Insurance contributions), or a bank or securities house which: **2231** s 307 FA 2004
– is to any extent responsible for the design of a scheme;

– makes a firm approach to another person with a view to making a scheme available for implementation by that person or others;
– makes a scheme available for implementation by others; or
– organises or manages the implementation of a scheme.

Both UK- and non-UK-based promoters are subject to the rules but only insofar as the scheme relates to a UK tax advantage.

A notifiable scheme **also includes** any scheme that must be disclosed by order (¶2229).

HMRC have specifically stated that merely documenting or pricing a product to someone else's design will not fall within the definition of promoter, but development of a solution to a problem will.

MEMO POINTS An **introducer** is someone who makes a marketing contact in relation to a scheme. An introducer is not necessarily a promoter but is subject to HMRC's information-gathering powers.

2232 s 308 FA 2004 If **more than one person is a promoter** in relation to the same scheme, only one person need notify HMRC. Any other promoter will be deemed to have its liability to notify discharged if it holds the scheme reference number, or HMRC have been provided with its identity and address. In addition, the other promoters must hold copies of the information provided to HMRC.

s 314A FA 2004 MEMO POINTS HMRC can apply to the tribunal for an **order** that a scheme is to be disclosed. Such an order will only be given if it falls within the hallmarked schemes. If it does not, HMRC can apply for a scheme to be treated as if it should be disclosed (¶2229). This measure was introduced simply to enable HMRC to better police the disclosure rules and ensure that all promoters comply with their responsibilities.

2233 The following person(s) are **specifically excluded** from the definition of a promoter:
– a company which provides tax services to another company from the same 51% group (¶1520);
– an employee of an employer who is a promoter or a user;
– a person who is responsible for the design of the scheme but does not provide tax advice in relation to the scheme;
– a person who, in the course of providing tax advice, is not responsible for the design of the scheme;
– a person who is not responsible for the design of the scheme and could not reasonably be expected to know whether the scheme is notifiable; and
– a person who is prevented from being able to make full disclosure, by virtue of legal professional privilege.

MEMO POINTS A user can inform his lawyer that he does not wish the transaction to remain subject to **legal professional privilege**. If the user does this, the duty for notification will fall on the lawyer, as the promoter, and he will be required to disclose information in the usual manner.

Time limits for disclosure

2234 SI 2004/1864 reg 4 Notification must be made to HMRC within a strict timescale of 5 working days from the earliest of the date on which the promoter:
– makes a firm approach to another person with a view to making the scheme available for implementation by that person or others;
– makes a scheme available for implementation by another person; or
– becomes aware of a transaction forming part of the scheme.

SI 2004/1864 reg 5 If a promoter is expecting to make a **pre-transaction clearance application** to HMRC for any of the following transactions:
– an exempt distribution;
– a purchase of own shares;
– a transaction in securities; or
– a company reconstruction,

he must notify HMRC of the scheme with the clearance application, or 5 working days from the day he no longer has a reasonable expectation of making such a clearance application.

If HMRC suspect that a person is promoting a scheme that should be disclosed they can issue a **pre-disclosure enquiry**. This will essentially ask the promoter whether he thinks he will be required to disclose in future, and if not, why not. Any reasons for not disclosing must be by reference to the hallmarks – in other words, simple reliance on a professional opinion that disclosure need not be made is insufficient. HMRC can apply to the tax tribunal for an order requesting that further specified information be provided in relation to the reasons given. ss 313A, 313B FA 2004

MEMO POINTS 1. **When a scheme has been disclosed**, HMRC will, within 30 days of receipt, allocate a reference number to the scheme.
2. A promoter must notify any person it has provided services to of the: SI 2004/1864 regs 7, 8
– name and address of the promoter;
– name and brief description of the proposal;
– scheme reference number; and
– date the number was sent to the promoter to the client, or client to end-user.
The client must provide the same to any end-user of the scheme.
3. Where a reference number has to be given by the promoter to a user the details of the user are reported to HMRC on a quarterly return, due 30 days after the quarter end.
4. An employer does not have to provide the scheme reference number to an employee in the case of employment schemes.

Penalties

There are three categories of penalty: 2235
– for failure to disclose; s 98C TMA 1970
– for failure to comply with information requirements; and
– for failure by users (see ¶2238).

If there is a failure to **disclose** a notifiable scheme, the tribunal can set a penalty at up to a maximum of £600 per day (unless this would be insufficient deterrent, when the maximum penalty may be £1 million).

However, if HMRC have successfully applied to the tribunal for a declaration that the scheme is disclosable (see ¶2229 and ¶2232), but the 10-day time limit is not met, a daily penalty of up to £5,000 may be imposed.

If there is a failure to comply with **information** requirements (such as failure to respond to a pre-disclosure enquiry, or to provide a user with a scheme reference number), the tribunal can set an initial penalty of up to £5,000 and a daily penalty of up to £600 thereafter.

3. Users

Definition

A user is simply defined as a person who implements the scheme for his own benefit. 2236

Users are required to provide full disclosure where: ss 309, 310 FA 2004
– a scheme is **purchased from an overseas promoter** (with no UK presence) who has not notified HMRC of the scheme; SI 2004/1864 reg 4
– there is no external promoter (for example, where a scheme is developed and implemented **in-house**) – in practice, it is unusual for a scheme to be devised totally in-house, as most users would seek professional advice before implementing a scheme and any changes made by an adviser, however small, would render him liable to make a disclosure as a promoter; or
– the promoter is protected by **legal professional privilege** from making disclosure (¶2233).

MEMO POINTS **Where there is no duty to disclose**, users of schemes are only required to inform HMRC that they have used/intend to use a registered scheme, normally on the relevant return. Users should provide the scheme reference number in the return(s) covering the earlier of the accounting period in which the:
– tax advantage arises; or
– scheme reference number is received.

Where the tax advantage covers more than one accounting period, the information must be provided on the return for each year affected.

Time limits for disclosure

2237 Information/notification must be disclosed to HMRC by users within the following timescales:

Type of scheme	Timescale
Users of products from overseas promoters	Within 5 working days of entering into the first transaction forming part of the scheme
User where promoter is protected by legal professional privilege	
All other users	Within 30 working days of entering into the first transaction forming part of the scheme

Penalties

2238 s 98C TMA 1970 The following penalties can be imposed on users who fail to comply with their disclosure requirements:

a. users that are required to make full disclosure (that is, users of in-house products, products from overseas promoters and users required to disclose due to legal professional privilege):
- £5,000 maximum initial penalty; and
- £600 daily penalty for ongoing failure;

b. users that are required to disclose the scheme reference number:
- £100 for the first failure to notify;
- £500 for the second failure to notify within 3 years; and
- £1,000 for the third and all subsequent failures to notify.

4. Disclosure notice

2239 s 316 FA 2004 The following **information** will need to be included in a notification disclosure:
- sufficient details to enable HMRC to understand the operation of the scheme;
- name and address of the promoter or, if different, the person giving notification;
- details of the disclosure rules under which the scheme is notifiable;
- name of scheme (if any);
- summary of the scheme; and
- details of the significance of each step and the legal provisions relied upon.

s 308A FA 2004 MEMO POINTS HMRC may apply to the tax tribunal for an order that **further specified information be provided** if they have reasonable grounds for believing that the information originally supplied is not complete.

SECTION 4

Returns

1. Format of a return

Required documentation

2240 For the majority of companies, a return **comprises**:
- a tax return (CT600);
- any required supplementary pages;

– a set of signed accounts; and
– a tax computation (¶1250).

Companies which carry on a business in **partnership** must include details of their share of the partnership results with their tax return. Where the partnership accounts do not correspond with the period covered by the company's return, the partnership results should be apportioned, usually on a time basis. Sch 18 para 12 FA 1998

Where a return is filed on or after 1 April 2011 for an accounting period ending on or after 1 April 2010 the required documentation must be filed electronically. If it is filed by paper it will be deemed not to have been filed. Amendments to returns will still be able to be made by paper. SI 2003/282 reg 3(2A)

Such returns not only have to be **filed electronically** but those entities which prepare accounts under the Companies Act 2006 also have to submit accounts and computations in a special format, known as iXBRL. This attaches a tag to each item in the accounts or computation, describing what that item is. The accounts or computation can then be analysed electronically by HMRC.

MEMO POINTS 1. Returns are **also required** where a company has made any of the following:
– payments under deduction of income tax (¶1370);
– non-qualifying distributions (¶942); and
– stock dividends (¶944).
For details of these returns see ¶2250.
2. Following the abolition of the nil starting rate of corporation tax from 1 April 2006, some clubs and unincorporated associations may be liable to tax on very small amounts of income. HMRC have therefore formally stated that where the annual corporation tax liability is **not expected to exceed £100**, returns will not be required from:
a. clubs and unincorporated associations run exclusively for the benefit of their own members; or
b. property management companies if:
– their business consists of the management, on a non-profit-making basis, of a block(s) of flats or apartments for the owners, lessees or tenants of the flats or apartments;
– their Articles of Association contain rules to ensure that only the persons having an interest in the property under management own the shares in the company;
– they are not entitled to receive any income from an interest in land; and
– they do not pay a dividend or make any other distribution of profit.
HMRC will treat the organisation as dormant and review the position every 5 years. For each year of dormancy there must be no anticipated allowable trading losses, disposals of chargeable assets or payments from which tax is deductible and payable to HMRC.
If a company receives **interest on service charges** held in trust on behalf of tenants, it will be required to submit an income tax self-assessment return unless the annual interest is less than £1,000 and taxed at source.

Composition of the CT600

There are two versions of Form CT600, the short and standard returns. 2241

The standard Form CT600 is divided into a number of sections, which can be found on the following pages of the form:

Page	Details
1	Summary of company information
2 – 3	Summary of turnover, and profits from various sources, including deductions and reliefs
4 – 5	Detailed tax calculation, including reliefs in the form of tax and payment reconciliation
6	Information regarding capital allowances and research and development expenditure
7	Losses, deficits and excess amounts
7 – 8	Repayments of tax
8	Declaration that the return is correct and complete

The short Form CT600 can be used by companies with simpler affairs, primarily those with limited types of income or losses

Many figures used on the form are the result of other calculations and therefore the form must be accompanied by a supporting tax computation (¶1250) and by the company accounts (¶2243).

2242 In addition to the above information, the following **supplementary pages** may also need to be completed:
- close company loans to participators (¶2111);
- controlled foreign companies (¶2145);
- group and consortium relief (¶1540);
- insurance companies;
- charities and community amateur sports clubs;
- tonnage tax;
- the corporate venturing scheme (¶1890);
- cross-border royalties;
- supplementary tax on ring-fenced profits; and
- disclosure of tax avoidance schemes.

Accounts

2243 Sch 18 para 11 FA 1998

The **general rule** is that if a company is obliged to file accounts at Companies House, the full statutory accounts are required for tax purposes. The abbreviated accounts for the Registrar are not acceptable.

The **general rule is modified** in the following situations:

Entity	Requirement
Group holding company	Both group consolidation and individual company accounts
Non-resident companies trading via a permanent establishment	Profit and loss account and balance sheet for both company and UK permanent establishment (balance sheet for company may be omitted if none has been prepared)
Unincorporated associations and societies	Any accounts (including balance sheet) required under law or by the company's constitution
Companies outside the scope of corporation tax	Any accounts prepared for a period falling partly within the return period, or if none, accounts for the most recent previous period

MEMO POINTS Whilst it was possible already to file the return and supporting documents online, via either HMRC's own service or through a third-party software supplier, this became mandatory from 1 April 2011 for accounting periods ending after 31 March 2010.

2. Filing date

2244 Sch 18 para 14 FA 1998

The **basic rule** is that the filing date for a return is the later of:
- 12 months from the end of the period to which the return relates; or
- 3 months after the date the notice to file is received.

EXAMPLE A Ltd prepares accounts for the 12 months to 31 August 2010 and receives a notice to make a return for this period.
The notice was issued on 22 September 2010, therefore the filing date is 31 August 2011.

MEMO POINTS 1. As a general rule, **12 months** from the end of the return period is taken to be the same day of the same month in the following year. The exception to this rule is where the last day of the return period is 29 February, in which case the filing date is 1 March in the following year.

2. For the purposes of the **3-month** rule, HMRC assume that a notice which is served by post will be received 4 working days after it is issued. CTSA Guide para 3.7

EXAMPLE A Ltd prepares accounts for the 12 months to 31 August 2010 and receives a notice to make a return for this period.
If the notice was issued on Monday, 25 June 2011, it would be deemed to be received on Friday, 29 June 2011 and the filing date would be 30 September 2011.

Where a return relates to an **accounting period which ends other than at the accounting reference date**, the filing date will be the later of: 2245
- 12 months from the last day of the period of account; or
- 3 months after the date the notice is received.

This will be the case, for example, where the accounts are prepared for an 18-month period, when the accounting period will be split into two.

EXAMPLE A Ltd prepares its accounts for the 18 months to 31 December 2011 and receives a notice for both periods within 3 months of the end of the period of account.
A return is prepared for each of the accounting periods: 1 July 2010 to 30 June 2011, and 1 July 2011 to 31 December 2011. The filing date for both returns is 12 months from the accounting reference date – that is, 31 December 2012.

MEMO POINTS 1. Where the accounts are prepared for a period **in excess of 18 months**, the filing date is restricted to 30 months from the start of the period for which the accounts are prepared, or 3 months from the date the notice is received, if later.
2. If a **company fails to file** its return by the appropriate date, in addition to issuing a fixed penalty, HMRC may issue a determination of the tax payable (¶2306).
3. The table at ¶2272 illustrates the filing date and payment date for a number of scenarios.

3. Complete and correct return

Each return must include a declaration, signed by the person making the return, that to the best of his or her knowledge the return is complete and correct. For these purposes, a complete and correct return is one that contains **accurate figures** and all of the other information that the company is required to include. 2246 Sch 18 paras 3, 4 FA 1998

Where the company can show that all reasonable steps have been taken to establish a final figure but that it has not been possible to do so, it will be acceptable to file a return containing a **best estimate**. A return submitted in this way will not be regarded as incomplete. However, where the company subsequently becomes aware that an estimated figure is no longer the "best estimate" or where an accurate figure becomes available, HMRC should be advised as soon as possible.

MEMO POINTS HMRC have yet to provide any guidance on the application of the new penalties regime (see ¶9780+) to estimated figures. It is likely that provided reasonable care is taken a penalty will be avoided. However, HMRC may take the view that the inability to be able to quantify a figure is significant enough for a penalty to be levied.

4. Amendments

After a return has been filed, it may be amended either by the company or HMRC. 2247 Sch 18 paras 15, 16 FA 1998

The **company** may amend a return where it becomes aware that an entry on the return is incorrect, or that the return has been made for the wrong period. Further, HMRC can amend a return where they have information that an entry is incorrect. The **time limit** for amending returns is 12 months from the filing date. The 12-month period also runs from this date in the case of returns submitted for the wrong period.

HMRC may only amend a return for obvious mistakes, such as arithmetical errors, or errors of principle by issuing a notice of correction. The **time limit** for such amendments is 9 months from the filing date, or 9 months from the date on which a company amends its own return. The company may reject an amendment by HMRC by further amending its own return. Alternatively, if the time limit for the company to amend its return has expired, it may reject HMRC's amendment in writing, within 3 months of the date of issue of the notice of correction.

The only way HMRC can **enforce their amendment** is to open an enquiry into the return (¶2330).

2248 Sch 18 para 88 FA 1998 In general, figures included on a corporation tax return **become final** 12 months after the filing date for the return, unless HMRC open an enquiry into the return. In the event of an **enquiry**, the figures become final 30 days after whichever of the following applies to the particular enquiry:
- the issue of a closure notice;
- the amendment of the return by HMRC; or
- the determination of an appeal against an amended return.

2249 Exceptionally, claims for **group relief or capital allowances** may result in amendments to the figures at a later date, in which case, the figures cease to be final until the latest of the following:
- the date on which HMRC can no longer open an enquiry;
- the date on which the company can no longer appeal against an amendment to the return; or
- if an enquiry is opened, the latest of the three dates in ¶2248.

5. Sundry returns

2250 Returns must be filed if a company has made any of the following payments during a return period:
- payments under deduction of income tax (¶1370);
- non-qualifying distributions (¶942); and
- stock dividends (¶944).

A **return period** will end on each of the following dates:
- 31 March;
- 30 June;
- 30 September; and
- 31 December.

In addition, if the company's accounting period ends on a date other than those above, a return period ends on the final day of the accounting period.

EXAMPLE A Ltd prepares its accounts annually to 31 October. Its return periods for the period to 31 October 2011 will therefore be:
01/11/10 – 31/12/10
01/01/11 – 31/03/11
01/04/11 – 30/06/11
01/07/11 – 30/09/11
01/10/11 – 31/10/11

MEMO POINTS If any of these returns are filed after the filing deadline, a **penalty** of £300 may be imposed, increasing by £60 for each subsequent day. A penalty cannot be imposed after the position has been rectified. For further details of the penalty procedure, see ¶2306.

Income tax

2251 s 951 ITA 2007 When a company makes a payment under deduction of income tax (¶1370), it must provide details to HMRC by completing form CT61. The return should also include details of any income tax deducted from income received by the company (¶1382) which the company wishes to offset against its income tax liability.

Returns of income received are not required for any return period in which no payments are made. It is possible to carry forward credit for tax deducted from income received, but the receipt must be included on a CT61 for a later return period in the same accounting period.

MEMO POINTS 1. Returns should be accompanied by **payment** in respect of any income tax due for the return period.
2. The **filing deadline** for form CT61 is 14 days after the end of the return period.

Non-qualifying distributions

No specific return exists for reporting non-qualifying distributions (¶942). However, HMRC must be provided with the following information with regard to non-qualifying distributions: 2252 s 1101 CTA 2010
- details of the transaction;
- name and address of recipient(s); and
- value of distribution received by each recipient.

MEMO POINTS The **filing deadline** for this information is 14 days after the end of the accounting period in which the distribution is made. If the distribution is made on a date not falling within an accounting period the return of information should be submitted 14 days after the date of the distribution.

Stock dividends

A company issuing a stock dividend (¶944) must provide HMRC with the following information: 2253 ss 1052, 1053 CTA 2010
- the date of issue of the share capital;
- the date on which the company was first required to issue the share capital, if different;
- the terms of issue; and
- the appropriate amount in cash.

MEMO POINTS The **filing deadline** for this information is 30 days after the end of the return period.

SECTION 5

Claims and elections

Normal claims

Under the self-assessment regime, the procedures for making claims and elections (hereafter referred to as claims) are identical. 2254

MEMO POINTS **Special rules** apply to claims or elections following an HMRC amendment or assessment (known as consequential claims (¶2257)).

Wherever possible, claims must be **made on the corporation tax return**. Claims for capital allowances (¶200) and group relief (¶1540) can only be made by inclusion on a corporation tax return. 2255

It is not possible to include a claim on the return where the claim is made before the notice to file a return has been issued (¶2212), or the time limit for amending the return has expired (¶2247).

In these situations, claims should be made in writing and must include a declaration that the particulars of the claim are correct to the best of the company's knowledge.

At the time they are made, claims for allowances, reliefs or repayment of tax must **quantify the amount** claimed. This means that an actual figure must be provided; a formula for calculating the relief is not acceptable. Sch 18 para 54 FA 1998

Unless otherwise specified, the **time limit** for making claims is 4 years from the end of the accounting period to which they relate. Sch 18 para 55 FA 1998

MEMO POINTS As with tax returns, the company is required to maintain and **preserve any records** (¶2300) in respect of the claim.

2256 If the company discovers an **error in a claim**, it may amend the claim by making a supplementary claim at any time within the time limit. Once the time limit for making a claim has expired, no further amendments can be made.

Where a claim is amended via the tax return, the normal rules for amendments to tax returns apply (¶2247). Similar rules apply for amendments to claims which are not made on the tax return, with the time limits running from the day on which the claim is submitted.

Consequential claims

2257
Sch 18 paras 61 – 65 FA 1998

Claims can be made or amended **outside the normal time limit** as a result of the:
– amendment of a corporation tax return following an HMRC enquiry;
– issue of a discovery assessment; or
– issue of an assessment to recover excessive group relief.

Such claims must be made within 12 months of the end of the accounting period in which the amendment or assessment is made. The claim must result in a reduction in:
– the company's increased liability arising from the amendment or assessment made by HMRC; or
– any other tax liability of the company for the accounting period in question or a subsequent accounting period ending in the following 12 months.

MEMO POINTS 1. The **reduction in the tax liability** as a result of a consequential claim cannot exceed the increase in the liability resulting from the assessment or amendment.
2. If the **claim would affect the liability of any other person**, written consent must be obtained from that person before effect can be given to the claim.

2258 These provisions do not apply where the increased liability is a result of an assessment to recover tax due to **careless or deliberate conduct**. In this situation, the company may, however, claim that in calculating the increased liability, relief is given for any relief or allowance to which the company would have been entitled for the accounting period. Such a claim must be made before the assessment is raised, or within the time limit for an appeal to be made against the assessment.

MEMO POINTS See ¶9780+ for further details of the penalties regime.

SECTION 6

Payment requirements

A. Tax liability

When is payment due?

2259 There are **two systems** which are used to determine when a company must pay its corporation tax liability for an accounting period. Most companies will pay according to the normal rules outlined below. However, if a company is a large company (¶2261), the corporation tax liability will be due in instalments.

Interest and penalties may be charged if tax is not paid by the required date.

MEMO POINTS 1. To minimise exposure to interest charges on tax paid late, **overpayments can be surrendered** between companies which are members of 75% groups (¶1667).

2. All corporation tax payments must be made electronically, by:
- direct debit;
- BACS direct credit, Internet or telephone banking services;
- credit card (subject to a 1.4% fee) or debit card (no fee) over the Internet via the BillPay service;
- CHAPS;
- Bank Giro; or
- at any participating Post Office.

The normal rule

The normal rule is that a company must pay the whole of its corporation tax liability for an accounting period 9 months and 1 day after the end of the accounting period. 2260 s 59D TMA 1970

Where the accounting period ends on the last day of a calendar month the due date will be the first day of the tenth month following the end of the accounting period.

Where the accounting period ends on another day the due date will be the day after the same day in the ninth month following the end of the accounting period.

Where the ninth following month does not have a day that corresponds to the end of the accounting period the normal due date is the first day of the tenth month following the end of the accounting period.

EXAMPLE

Accounting period ended	Due date
28 May 2010	1 March 2011
30 May 2010	1 March 2011
31 May 2010	1 March 2011
1 August 2010	2 May 2011
31 December 2010	1 October 2011

MEMO POINTS As the date of payment under the normal rule is based on the chargeable accounting period rather than the period of account, it is unaffected by a company having a **long period of account**. A company will therefore have a due date of payment for each tax accounting period within a long period of account. It should be noted that this is different from the rules for filing of returns.

EXAMPLE If a company had an 18-month period of account ending on 31 December 2010, this would be split into 2 accounting periods ending on 30 June 2010 and 31 December 2010 and the liability for each accounting period would be due on 1 April 2011 and 1 October 2011, respectively.

Large companies

Definition The basic definition of a large company is one where the taxable profits (including non-group franked investment income (¶951)) for an accounting period exceed the main rate threshold (¶1342). This threshold is reduced proportionately for accounting periods of less than 12 months. 2261 SI 1998/3175 reg 3

For large companies, corporation tax is payable in **quarterly instalments** based on an estimate of the current-year corporation tax liability. Tax due as a result of loans to participators (¶2111) and under the controlled foreign company provisions (¶2145) is included in the calculation. 2262

However, a company is **outside the scope** of the quarterly instalment regime if:
- the tax liability is less than £10,000; or
- the taxable profits for the accounting period are less than £10 million and the company was not within the instalment regime in the 12 months immediately prior to the accounting period.

These limits are reduced proportionately for periods of less than 12 months.

MEMO POINTS A company cannot take advantage of the second exception for two consecutive periods.

EXAMPLE

1. A Ltd has profits as follows for the following 12-month accounting periods:

Period ended	Profits
31/12/09	£50,000
31/12/10	£8,000,000
31/12/11	£7,500,000

A Ltd is not a large company for the accounting period ended 31 December 2009, as profits are below the main rate threshold.

For the accounting period ended 31 December 2010 A Ltd can take advantage of the exception, as although profits are in excess of the main rate threshold, they do not exceed £10m and A Ltd was not within the quarterly instalment regime in the previous 12 months.

For the accounting period ended 31 December 2011 A Ltd is a large company and subject to the instalment regime. Although its profits are still less than £10m, it would have been within the quarterly instalment regime in the previous 12 months apart from the exception. It cannot take advantage of that exception in two consecutive periods and must therefore be regarded as a large company.

2. B Ltd has profits as follows for its first 12-month accounting period:

Period ended	Profits
31/12/10	£7,500,000

B Ltd is not a large company for the accounting period ended 31 December 2010, since although profits are in excess of the main rate threshold, they do not exceed £10m and it was not within the quarterly instalment regime in the previous 12 months.

2263 Where a company has **associated companies** (¶1360), the upper threshold and the £10 million limit will be reduced proportionately by the number of associated companies in existence:
– at any point during the accounting period for the upper threshold test; and
– at the end of the immediately preceding accounting period for the £10 million limit.

2264 SI 1998/3175 reg 5 **Instalment dates** A company with a **12-month accounting period** will pay tax in four instalments starting in the seventh month of the accounting period. The instalment dates are calculated as follows:

Instalment	Payable	Month
1	6 months and 13 days from the start of the accounting period	7
2	3 months after instalment 1	10
3	3 months after instalment 2	13
4	3 months and 14 days after the end of the accounting period	16

EXAMPLE A Ltd has a 12-month accounting period starting on 1 January 2011 and ending on 31 December 2011. Instalments will be due as follows.

Instalment		Payment date
1	6 months and 13 days from the start of the accounting period	14 July 2011
2	3 months after instalment 1	14 October 2011
3	3 months after instalment 2	14 January 2012
4	3 months and 14 days after the end of the accounting period	14 April 2012

2265 Where the accounting period is **shorter than 12 months**, the instalment dates (there will be between one and four, depending on the length of the accounting period) are calculated in the following order:
a. the final instalment is 3 months and 14 days after the end of the accounting period;
b. the first instalment is 6 months and 13 days after the start of the accounting period (unless this is later than the date in **a**. above, in which case the final instalment is also the first and only instalment);

c. subsequent instalments are due at intervals of 3 months after the first instalment (provided that such dates are before the date in **a**. above).

EXAMPLE A Ltd has an 8-month accounting period starting on 1 March 2011 and ending on 31 October 2011. Instalments will be due as follows.

Instalment		Payment date
1	6 months and 13 days from the start of the accounting period	14 September 2011
2	3 months after instalment 1	14 December 2011
3	3 months and 14 days after the end of the accounting period	14 February 2012

Calculation of instalments Quarterly instalments are based on an estimate of the current-year corporation tax liability of the company. Each instalment is calculated separately, based on the following formula: 2266

$$3 \times \frac{\text{CTI}}{\text{n}}$$

where:
- CTI is the best estimate of the corporation tax liability for the accounting period; and
- n is the number of complete months in the accounting period.

MEMO POINTS If the **accounting period does not contain a whole number of months**, the excess number of days (as a fraction of 30) is turned into a decimal. If, for example, an accounting period lasts for 6 months and 19 days, n will be 6.63.

For the **first instalment** the amount to be paid is the amount resulting from the formula. The only exception is for accounting periods of 3 months or less, where the first (and only) instalment will be equal to CTI. 2267

For **subsequent instalments**, the amount to be paid is generally the amount resulting from the formula, unless the balance of CTI remaining unpaid is less.

The **final instalment** should always be the difference between CTI and the amounts previously paid.

As some of the instalments are due to be paid before the end of the accounting period, it is likely that the value used for CTI will be an estimate, and the value of CTI is likely to vary from instalment to instalment. It may therefore be necessary to make additional payments to HMRC where the liability has been underestimated, in order to minimise any interest exposure. This situation may arise where a large increase in profitability or a large chargeable gain has occurred towards the end of the accounting period. 2268

EXAMPLE A Ltd has a 10-month accounting period ending on 30 September 2011. The tax liability is initially estimated at £275,000. When calculating the third instalment, the estimated liability is reduced to £205,000. The liability is agreed in January 2012 as £260,000. Instalments are due as follows:

	Due date	Calculation	£
Instalment 1	14/06/11	3 × £275,000/10	82,500
Instalment 2	14/09/11	As above	82,500
Instalment 3	14/12/11	Lower of: 3 × £205,000/10 or £205,000 – £165,000	40,000
Final instalment	14/01/12	£260,000 – £205,000	55,000

A **group payment facility** (¶1675) is available allowing companies which are members of 51% groups to make payments on a group-wide basis. 2269

Interest charges will arise if instalments are insufficient or paid late. Similarly, if too much tax is paid, interest will be paid to the company. **Penalties** may arise if a company deliberately fails to make instalment payments or makes instalment payments of insufficient size. Such penalties will only be levied in extreme cases and can be up to twice the amount of the interest payable. 2270

Summary

2272 The following table illustrates the payment and filing dates for some example periods. All examples assume the notice was issued shortly after the end of the accounting period.

Accounts prepared	Accounting period	Payment dates		Filing date
		Normal rules	Large companies	
Year to 31 March 2011	01/04/10 – 31/03/11	01/01/12	14/10/10 14/01/11 14/04/11 14/07/11	31/03/12
Year to 30 September 2011	01/10/10 – 30/09/11	01/07/12	14/04/11 14/07/11 14/10/11 14/01/12	30/09/12
Year to 31 December 2011	01/01/11 – 31/12/11	01/10/12	14/07/11 14/10/11 14/01/12 14/04/12	31/12/12
Nine months to 30 April 2011	01/08/10 – 30/04/11	01/02/12	14/02/11 14/05/11 14/08/11	30/04/12
Eighteen months to 31 May 2011	01/12/09 – 30/11/10	01/09/11	14/06/10 14/09/10 14/12/10 14/03/11	31/05/12
	01/12/10 – 31/05/11	01/03/12	14/06/11 14/09/11	31/05/12

B. Interest

1. When will it arise?

2275 Unless a company pays exactly the right amount of corporation tax on the correct day, interest will arise. HMRC **charge interest** on underpayments and late payments, and **pay interest** to the company for any overpayments.

s 87A TMA 1970
s 826 ICTA 1988

Any interest paid to HMRC is deductible in the company's corporation tax computation, whereas any interest received is taxable. Interest paid or received is treated as a debit or credit under the loan relationship rules (¶870).

2277 The **rate of interest** charged on late-paid tax exceeds the rate payable on repayments of tax and companies therefore need to balance the risk of underpaying the liability against the low rate of interest on repayments (¶9964). Different rates apply for payments under the quarterly instalments regime. The rates of interest are determined by reference to an average of the base lending rate of six clearing banks and are reviewed monthly, with the exception of interest for quarterly instalments, which is reviewed twice a month.

2280 To **calculate** interest, it is necessary to know the exact date of any payments made, the due date for payment and the interest rates in force. For interest on repayments of tax, it is also necessary to establish the date on which HMRC made any repayments. Special rules apply where any repayment of tax is as a result of the carry back of losses (either trading losses or loan relationship deficits) to an earlier period.

FA 2008 added provisions which allow the Treasury to order that, in certain circumstances, HMRC are permitted to agree to defer payments to them without charge to interest or surcharges. FA 2009 further added to these provisions in relation to managed payment plans (¶9857). **2281** s 135 FA 2008 s 111 FA 2009

2. Underpayments

Calculation of interest

Interest is charged on any tax paid late. Interest **runs from** the due date for payment until the date that payment is actually made. The calculation is based on the final tax liability and not the estimated liability at the time payment was made. **2282** s 87A TMA 1970

EXAMPLE A Ltd is not within the instalment regime and has a tax liability for the period to 31 December 2008 of £78,000. Owing to cash flow problems, the company paid £50,000 on the due date (1 October 2010) and the balance on 1 January 2011. Interest will be charged on the late paid tax (£28,000) from 1 October 2010 to 1 January 2011.

Interaction with losses carried back

If losses are carried back to an accounting period that: **2284**
- **falls entirely within the 12-month period** preceding the loss period, the interest on unpaid tax for the earlier period is calculated on the net amount after deducting the loss carry-back;
- does **not fall wholly within the 12 months** preceding the loss period, interest on any unpaid tax for the earlier period will be chargeable until the normal payment date (¶2260) for the loss-making period.

EXAMPLE A Ltd has a tax liability for the period to 30 June 2008 of £23,000 and pays only £10,000 on the due date, 1 April 2009. Losses are incurred in the following period, which are carried back and reduce the liability to £15,000. The company made a further tax payment of £2,000 on 12 May 2010. The company ceases trading on 30 June 2011 and further losses are carried back which reduce the liability to £12,000.
Interest is charged as follows:

Period	Notional liability	Paid	Interest due on
01/04/09 – 12/05/10	15,000	10,000	5,000
13/05/10 – 01/04/12*	15,000	12,000	3,000

* normal payment date for period to 30 June 2011.

Quarterly instalments

Where a company pays an instalment **late, or underestimates** an instalment, interest is charged. Interest for any period prior to the normal payment date is calculated at a lower rate. Interest cannot run for a period before the due date for the first instalment. The interest position will not be calculated until the company has filed a return and the normal payment date (¶2260) has passed. **2286** SI 1998/3175 reg 7

EXAMPLE A Ltd has a 12-month accounting period ending 31 December and has a tax liability for the period of £88m. Throughout the accounting period, it reviewed its tax position and made quarterly payments (and a top-up payment) as follows (all payments were made on the correct date, with the exception of the second payment, which was made on 21 October):

Payment date	Estimated total liability	Actual payments made	Correct payments	Cumulative difference
14 July	60,000,000	15,000,000	22,000,000	(7,000,000)
21 October	80,000,000	25,000,000	22,000,000	(4,000,000)
7 November	100,000,000	10,000,000	n/a	6,000,000
14 January	95,000,000	21,250,000	22,000,000	5,250,000
14 April	88,000,000	16,750,000	22,000,000	-

From 14/07 to 13/10 the company has underpaid £7m and debit interest will run.
From 14/10 to 20/10 the company has underpaid £29m and debit interest will run.

From 21/10 to 06/11 the company has underpaid £4m and debit interest will run.
From 07/11 to 13/01 the company has overpaid £6m and credit interest will run.
From 14/01 to 13/04 the company has overpaid £5.25m and credit interest will run.
From 14/04 the company has paid the correct liability and no further interest is due.

Tax on loans to participators

2288
s 109 TMA 1970

Where tax is charged on a close company loan to a participator (¶2111), interest is only due for the period until the loan is repaid, released or written off. Payments of tax are allocated to mainstream corporation tax liabilities in preference to this for the purposes of this rule, which is in the taxpayer's favour.

3. Overpayments

Calculation of interest

2290
s 826 ICTA 1988

Interest on overpayments of corporation tax **runs from** the later of:
- the normal due date for payment; and
- the actual date of payment.

Special rules apply where the overpayment arises through losses being carried back from a later accounting period.

Where a company has made more than one payment in respect of its liability, a later payment is deemed to be repaid in priority to an earlier one.

Interaction with losses carried back

2292
s 826(7A), (7C) ICTA 1988

If losses carried back generate an overpayment and are carried back to an accounting period that:
- **falls entirely within the 12-month period** preceding the loss period, the interest on overpaid tax for the earlier period is calculated on the net amount overpaid after deducting the loss carry-back;
- does **not fall wholly within the 12 months** preceding the loss period, interest on any overpaid tax for the earlier period will be payable from the normal payment date (¶2260) for the loss-making period.

EXAMPLE A Ltd has a tax liability for the period to 30 June 2008 of £18,000, which is paid in full on the due date, 1 April 2009. Losses are incurred in the following accounting period, which are carried back and reduce the liability to £15,000. The repayment is made on 1 November 2009. The company ceases trading on 30 June 2011 and further losses are carried back which reduce the liability to £6,000. This repayment is made on 12 May 2012.
Interest is due as follows:

Period	Notional liability	Paid	Interest due on
01/04/09 – 01/11/09	15,000	18,000	3,000
01/04/12* – 12/05/12	6,000	15,000	9,000

* normal payment date for period to 30 June 2011.

Quarterly instalments

2294
SI 1998/3175 reg 8

All companies are entitled to receive interest for corporation tax overpaid. Interest for any period prior to the normal payment date is calculated at a higher rate. Interest cannot run for a period before the due date for the first instalment. The interest position will not be calculated until the company has filed its corporation tax return and the normal payment date (¶2260) has passed.

EXAMPLE A Ltd has a 12-month accounting period ending 31 December and has a tax liability for the period of £90m. It reviewed its tax position throughout the accounting period, and made quarterly payments (and a top-up payment) as follows (all payments were made on the correct date):

Payment date	Estimated total liability	Actual payments made	Correct payments	Cumulative difference
14 July	100,000,000	25,000,000	22,500,000	2,500,000
14 October	90,000,000	20,000,000	22,500,000	-
7 November	110,000,000	10,000,000	n/a	10,000,000
14 January	95,000,000	16,250,000	22,500,000	3,750,000
14 April	90,000,000	18,750,000	22,500,000	-

From 14/07 to 13/10 the company has overpaid £2.5m and credit interest will run.
From 14/10 to 06/11 the company has paid the correct liability.
From 07/11 to 13/01 the company has overpaid £10m and credit interest will run.
From 14/01 to 13/04 the company has overpaid £3.75m and credit interest will run.
From 14/04 the company has paid the correct liability and no further interest is due.

Tax on loans to participators

Where tax is charged on a close company loan to a participator (¶2111) which is subsequently repaid, released or written off, repayment interest is only due from the normal payment date of the accounting period in which the loan is repaid, released or written off. **2296** s 826(4) ICTA 1988

SECTION 7

Record-keeping

Under self-assessment, companies are **required to maintain** detailed records and supporting documentation to enable them to complete a correct return and to preserve these records for future inspection. The records to be maintained are not specified but include records of all receipts and expenses, and all sales and purchases of goods, together with supporting documentation. Supporting documentation specifically includes: **2300** Sch 18 para 21 FA 1998
- accounts;
- books;
- deeds;
- contracts;
- vouchers; and
- receipts.

With the exception of tax vouchers, there is no requirement for records to be maintained in the **original format** (for example till receipts) but the information must be retained (for example, in a cash book). Information may also be preserved in computerised form or using techniques such as digital imaging.

If a company satisfies the Companies Act requirements for maintaining records, this will generally be sufficient for tax purposes, although the period of retention may be longer for tax purposes.

MEMO POINTS Additional records in excess of the Companies Act requirements must be maintained for **transfer pricing** (¶1743) purposes.

Records must be **preserved for a specified period** following the end of the accounting period to which they relate. This period ends on the latest of the following: **2302**
- 6 years from the end of the accounting period to which they relate;
- the date on which HMRC no longer have the power to enquire into the return; or
- the date on which an enquiry into the return is completed.

HMRC may specify an earlier date in a particular case that will supersede any of these dates.

SECTION 8

Penalties

Harmonised penalties

2304 As self-assessment relies heavily on timely compliance with the regime, there is a **range of penalties** which aims to encourage companies to deal promptly with their affairs. As part of the **harmonisation** of HMRC's powers, the penalties regime is being aligned across all taxes. The first set of penalties to change relate to incorrect returns for periods commencing on or after 1 April 2008 when the return was due to be submitted on or after 1 April 2009. Details of these can be found at ¶9780. Penalties for failures in relation to information notices have also been enacted (¶9852).

There is also legislation in place relating to the late filing of returns (¶9855) and late payment of tax (¶9857) but as yet no commencement date has been announced in relation to corporation tax. The following paragraphs outline the existing regime.

Penalty procedure

2306 HMRC may impose a penalty by issuing a **notice of determination**, which must specify the date of issue and the time within which an appeal may be made. A penalty is payable 30 days after the issue of a notice of determination and is treated as an amount of tax payable. As such, interest is due if the penalty is paid late.

Once a notice of determination has been issued, **the penalty charged can be reduced** only if an appeal is made, or if the penalty is due to the late submission of the tax return and the amount of the tax liability changes (¶2317).

HMRC may **mitigate penalties** either before the issue of the notice of determination, or as part of the appeals process.

Sch 18 para 90 FA 1998 A company may be liable for **multiple tax-geared penalties** in respect of the same accounting period – for example, a penalty for late filing and a penalty for negligence. Only one such penalty may be levied for an accounting period and the amount charged will be the highest of the penalties applicable.

2308 If a company believes the penalty determination is incorrect, it may issue a formal notice of **appeal** in writing, specifying the grounds for appeal. If agreement cannot be reached between HMRC and the company, the matter will be put before the tax tribunal.

MEMO POINTS If a **tribunal hearing** is necessitated to settle any tax liability, a penalty determination should, in practice, be issued so that both appeals (against the tax liability and the penalty determination) can be heard at the same hearing. For details of the existing appeals procedure see ¶4580.

Late filing of return

2312 Sch 18 paras 17 – 19 FA 1998 If a company fails to file a corporation tax return within the appropriate time limits it will become liable to one or more penalties, which may be **calculated** as a fixed sum, or as a percentage of the amount of tax outstanding.

2314 A **fixed penalty** of £100 applies if the return is delivered within 3 months after the filing date. If the return is delivered more than 3 months after the filing date, the fixed penalty becomes £200.

Where a company within the charge to corporation tax persistently (that is, in 3 successive accounting periods) fails to file a return on time, these penalties are increased to £500 and £1,000, respectively.

MEMO POINTS Fixed penalties are **not charged where**:
– the company has obtained a concessionary extension to its filing date from HMRC; or
– the Registrar of Companies has allowed a filing extension for submission of accounts to Companies House and the company files its tax return within this revised time limit.

In addition to the fixed penalties, a company will be liable to the following **tax-geared penalties** in certain circumstances: 2316

Return filed	Amount of penalty
More than 18 months after the end of the accounting period	10% of any outstanding corporation tax for that period
More than 2 years after the end of the accounting period	20% of corporation tax that was outstanding at the date the 10% penalty arose

MEMO POINTS When computing the amount of any tax-geared penalty, the liability of **close companies** (¶2100) includes any tax payable on loans to participators (including tax which would have been payable on loans repaid within 9 months).

HMRC may issue a **determination** of the amount of tax they believe to be payable if a company fails to file its corporation tax return by the filing date, or if this date cannot be established by the later of: 2317 Sch 18 paras 36 - 40 FA 1998
- 18 months from the end of the period specified in the return notice; or
- 3 months from the date of issue of the return notice.

The determination is HMRC's best estimate of the company's tax liability based on the information available to them at that time.

The determination **has effect** as though it was the company's self-assessment of its liability, which means HMRC have the ability to charge interest and penalties, and to enforce payment of the liability.

Once a determination has been issued, the company cannot appeal against the figures and the tax must be paid.

The determination can only be **superseded** by the company submitting a return for the period and this must be made by the later of:
- 12 months from the date of the determination; and
- 3 years from the date on which the determination could be made.

MEMO POINTS 1. A **determination cannot be issued** more than 3 years after the date on which HMRC first have the power to issue one.
2. For periods ending prior to 1 April 2010 the time limit for making an assessment was 5 years.

Failure to maintain records

If records are not maintained or preserved, a penalty of up to £3,000 may be charged. A penalty may not be charged if the records not preserved relate solely to a claim or election which did not form part of the tax return for the accounting period in question. 2320 Sch 18 para 23 FA 1998

SECTION 9

Enquiries

When can these be made?

An enquiry may be made by HMRC into any tax return, either selected at random or specifically chosen because they believe the return to be inaccurate. 2330 Sch 18 paras 24-35 FA 1998

Commencement of an enquiry

HMRC must **notify** the company of their intention to make the enquiry by issuing an enquiry notice, the scope of which may extend to anything which is, or should have been, contained in the return (including claims). An enquiry must be started within a set **timescale**. The general rule is that HMRC have 12 months from the date of filing of the return in which to 2331 commence an enquiry. However, this deadline is extended to the quarter end following the anniversary of the date the return (or amendment) was filed if the return is either filed late, or amended (including the making of a claim after the tax return has been filed).

MEMO POINTS 1. If the **enquiry** is raised after the date which would have been the deadline had there been no amendments to the return, the scope of the enquiry is restricted to the amendments.
2. The **quarter ends** are 31 January, 30 April, 31 July and 31 October.
3. For accounting periods ending before 31 March 2008 the time limit for the opening of an enquiry was 12 months from the due filing date rather than the actual filing date. Where a return was late the quarter ends were still applicable. These rules still continue for returns filed by large groups of companies. HMRC have stated that they intend to open any enquiry in such a situation within 12 months of the last company's return being filed.

During an enquiry

2332 During the course of the enquiry:
a. the **company** may:
– amend its tax return, although any such amendment will not take effect until the closure of the enquiry, at which point the closure notice will incorporate the amendment, or will show that it was considered by HMRC to be incorrect;
– apply to the tribunal to direct a closure notice if it believes an enquiry is continuing unnecessarily (the tribunal must give the direction unless HMRC can show that they have reasonable grounds for continuing the enquiry beyond the specified period);
b. HMRC may:
– give notice to the company requiring production of documents or information in connection with the enquiry – further details of HMRC's ability to request documents are detailed at ¶9864;
– amend the company's self-assessment and issue a notice of amendment if they believe there has been an underpayment of tax and that tax may be lost without immediate action (where the enquiry relates solely to an amendment of the return, only the loss of tax attributable to that amendment may be charged; the company may appeal against an amendment within 30 days but such an appeal will not be heard until after the enquiry is concluded).

MEMO POINTS The ability to request documents is no longer limited to the duration of an enquiry. HMRC can now request documents at any time.

2334 Questions in connection with the subject matter of the enquiry may be referred to the tribunal for determination. A decision by the tribunal is binding on the parties and HMRC must take the decision into account when ending the enquiry. An enquiry cannot be closed if a tribunal decision is still pending.

End of an enquiry

2337 Once HMRC have concluded the investigation, they will issue a **closure notice** to the company setting out their conclusions and stating any adjustments they believe are required to the tax return or any affected claims.

If HMRC conclude that a **return has been submitted for the wrong period**, the closure notice will set out the correct accounting period start and end dates. Where this means that more than one return was due for the notice period (¶2214), the closure notice conclusions apply to the first of those accounting periods. The company has 30 days from the issue of the closure notice to file a return for the second period. This may be the case where, for example, HMRC conclude that a company changed its status during the period in question.

The company has 30 days from the issue of the closure notice to **amend its return** in accordance with HMRC's conclusions. The company may also amend any other returns which are affected, even where the time limit for such amendment would otherwise have expired.

If the **company fails to amend its return**, or HMRC are not happy with the amendments made, HMRC have an additional 30 days to make any further amendments they believe are required. The company may appeal against such amendments within 30 days. If the matter cannot be agreed between HMRC and the company, it may be put into the hands of the tribunal.

SECTION 10

Late amendments to returns

When permitted

If there is no enquiry into a return within 12 months from the filing deadline, the figures generally cannot be amended. However, provisions exist to allow late amendments in the following circumstances: 2340
- if a loss of tax is discovered (discovery assessment);
- if an amount of tax has been repaid to a company or overpaid by a company in error (overpayment relief claim); or
- if a company believes it has been assessed to tax more than once on the same profits (double assessment claim).

Discovery assessment

Since 1 April 2010 the **time limit** for raising a discovery assessment is 4 years from the end of the accounting period to which it relates **unless**: 2342 Sch 18 paras 41-49 FA 1998
- the loss of tax was brought about **carelessly** by the taxpayer, in which case an assessment may be made at any time not more than 6 years from the end of accounting period to which it relates; or
- the loss of tax was brought about **deliberately** by the company, or a person acting on behalf of the company, or the company has not complied with the rules relating to disclosure of information relating to **tax avoidance schemes**. In these cases HMRC may raise an assessment not more than 20 years after the end of the accounting period in which the error arose.

MEMO POINTS 1. For the definition of careless and deliberate see ¶9795+.
2. Prior to 1 April 2010 the normal **time limit** for raising a discovery assessment was 6 years from the end of the accounting period to which it relates. This was **extended** to 21 years in respect of fraudulent or negligent conduct. **Fraudulent or negligent** conduct includes conduct on the part of the company, a person acting on its behalf (its agent) or a person who was a partner of the company at the time when HMRC could launch an enquiry into the return. FA 2008 includes provisions to change the definition from fraudulent and negligent to carelessly or deliberately.

Discovery assessments **can only be made** if: 2344
a. there is a loss of tax (or an amount over-repaid) due to careless or deliberate conduct; or
b. HMRC could not have been expected to be aware of the facts giving rise to an underpayment (or over-repayment), based on the information available at either the:
- date of completion of an enquiry into a return; or
- latest date an enquiry could have commenced.

A discovery assessment **cannot be made** if the return was correctly prepared in accordance with prevailing practice.

MEMO POINTS 1. Information is deemed to be **available to HMRC** if it is contained in:
- the company's return for the current and two preceding years (or supporting documentation for these returns);
- a claim for the current year (or supporting documentation for the claim); or
- documents provided in the course of an enquiry.

2. There is an **underpayment** of tax when it becomes apparent that an amount of tax has not been assessed because of one of the following:
- profits which ought to have been assessed to tax have not been so assessed;
- an assessment has become insufficient; or
- a relief given has become excessive.

3. Where there has been an **over-repayment** of tax an assessment can be made to recover tax which HMRC discover has been repaid to the company in error. Such an assessment treats the amount repaid as miscellaneous income and carries interest from the date on which it was repaid until such time as the company pays the tax.

4. HMRC have **published guidance** so that taxpayers can be more certain that if no enquiry is raised within the normal time limits their tax affairs will be settled. They specify that information should be entered in the additional information space as follows:

a. where a **valuation** is used in the tax return, the following information should be disclosed:
– the fact that a valuation has been used; and
– who carried it out, stating whether the valuer was independent and suitably qualified;
b. where an **unusual item** appears in the accounts, such as a large item in repairs, the background to it and the method of accounting (such as the allocation between revenue and capital items) should be disclosed; and
c. where a company has **adopted a different view** of the law from that published by HMRC, and this has impacted on the tax return entries, this should be disclosed.

2346 If the **company does not agree** with the amount of the assessment, it must issue a formal notice of appeal, in writing, within 30 days of the date of issue of the assessment. If the position cannot be agreed with HMRC, the appeal may be heard by the tax tribunal.

2351 **Interest** will be included in a discovery assessment, calculated from the date the tax should have been paid.

Overpayment relief claim

2352 Sch 18 paras 51-51G FA 1998 This relief was introduced for claims after 1 April 2010 and replaces the previous error or mistake claim provisions. For details of these please see earlier editions of *Tax Memo*.

A company is able to claim this relief where it believes it has either paid too much tax or an assessment raised against it is excessive. It must **apply in writing** to HMRC within 4 years of the end of the period to which the overpayment relates and must contain the following:
SACM12150
– a statement that the company is making a claim under the overpayment relief provisions;
– details of the period it relates to;
– the grounds on which the assessment or payment is considered excessive;
– whether the matter has been the subject of an appeal previously;
– if a claim for repayment is made, proof that the tax has been suffered in some way; and
– a declaration signed on the company's behalf stating that the details given are correct to the best of the company's knowledge and belief.

The relief cannot be used where:
– an overpayment arises due to an error in a capital allowances claim;
– the matter has already been the subject of a tribunal decision or court hearing;
– the return was prepared based on the generally prevailing practice at that time; or
– the company ought to have known of the mistake and been able to correct it within the normal time limits.

2353 **Interest** will be payable by HMRC to the company, in addition to any repayment of tax made following a successful claim.

Double assessment claim

2354 Sch 18 para 50 FA 1998 If a company believes it has been **assessed to tax more than once** on the same profits for the same accounting period (known as double assessment), it may make a claim for relief in writing. HMRC will then review the position and, if appropriate, adjust the assessment concerned or make a repayment to the company.

SECTION 11

Senior accounting officers

Application

2360 Sch 46 para 15 FA 2009 For accounting periods commencing on or after 21 July 2009 a new burden has been imposed on qualifying companies and their senior accounting officers.

This burden will only apply for a year where, in the previous financial year, the company (or the group if applicable) has either (or both):
– turnover in excess of £200 million; or
– balance sheet assets in excess of £2 billion (this is applied before any deductions for liabilities).

MEMO POINTS A financial year is defined in terms of the Companies Act definition. This is typically the same as the accounting period used for tax. For further details see *Company Law Memo*.

Responsibilities

The **senior accounting officer** is required to take reasonable steps to: 2362 Sch 46 para 1 FA 2009

a. ensure the company has **appropriate tax accounting arrangements** in place, which includes arrangements for keeping records. The arrangements must enable the company to accurately calculate its tax liabilities in all material respects. The taxes covered are:
– corporation tax;
– VAT;
– PAYE and NIC;
– insurance premium tax;
– stamp duty land tax and stamp duty reserve tax; and
– customs and excise duties;

b. monitor the accounting arrangements of the company;

c. identify any areas where the arrangements would not be considered to be appropriate tax accounting arrangements; and

d. provide an **annual certificate** to HMRC in respect of each financial year.

The **company** must inform HMRC of the identity of the senior accounting officers of the company or group annually. This person (or persons) should be those that in the company's opinion have overall responsibility for the accounting arrangements of the company or group. It is possible for a group to have only one such officer, or it may have several. This notification must be made by the date that the company is obliged to file its annual accounts.

MEMO POINTS For public companies the filing deadline will typically be 6 months after the end of the financial year concerned. For private companies this will be 9 months. For further details see *Company Law Memo*.

Annual certificate

The annual certificate must be provided by the same date as the deadline for filing accounts with Companies House (see *Company Law Memo* for details). 2364 Sch 46 para 2 FA 2009

The certificate must contain a statement that the accounting arrangements were appropriate throughout the year. If this is not the case an explanation must be given of the areas in which the arrangements failed to meet the requirement. It is possible for a certificate to cover more than one company.

Penalties

The following failures attract penalties. 2366 Sch 46 paras 4-12 FA 2009

Party responsible	Failure
Senior accounting officer	Not ensuring that appropriate tax accounting arrangements are in place
	Not providing a certificate or providing one that is carelessly or deliberate inaccurate.
	Not advising HMRC of an error later discovered in a certificate
Company	Not advising HMRC of identity of senior accounting officer(s)

The penalty for any failure is £5,000. All penalties are subject to appeal to HMRC and also the tribunal. This must be done within 30 days of receiving the penalty in writing, stating the grounds of appeal. There are provisions to remove penalties where there is a reasonable excuse.

Where the **identity** of a senior accounting officer **changes** during a financial year, only the last appointed officer during the period will be liable to a penalty. However, where an officer ceases to be such before the due filing date for the certificate, he or she will not be liable to a penalty. Further, if someone who has been, or is, the nominated officer files a certificate, correct or otherwise, no other party will be liable for a penalty for that company for that year.

MEMO POINTS 1. An inaccuracy is deemed to be careless if the officer failed to take reasonable care.
2. Reasonable excuse does not include:
– insufficiency of funds, unless attributable to an event not within the person's control; or,
– reliance on another person, unless reasonable care was taken to avoid the failure of another.
If a reasonable excuse exists and then ceases it is deemed to continue, provided that the position is rectified without unreasonable delay.

2368 **Restrictions on penalties** A penalty **cannot be levied more than**:
– 6 months after the failure or inaccuracy comes to HMRC's attention; or
– 6 years after the end of the filing date for the company's accounts for that financial year.

Where a person is the senior accounting officer for more than one company in a group, he or she will only be liable to one penalty for a financial year, regardless of the number of companies in the group in respect of which there are failures. The same is true where the company has failed to meet its obligations and forms part of a group at its year end. Where the companies involved do not share the same year end, a company cannot be penalised where another company in the same group has already been penalised during a period that ends in the company's financial year in question.

EXAMPLE Company A and B are in a group. A Ltd's year end is 31 March 2011, B Ltd's is 31 December 2010. If Company B is subject to a penalty for the year to 31 December 2010, A Ltd cannot be penalised for a failure in the year to 31 March 2011, as a group company has been assessed for a penalty in a period that ends during A's financial year.

PART 2

Income tax

Income tax
Summary

The numbers cross-refer to paragraphs.

CHAPTER 1 General principles

CHAPTER 2 Trading income

CHAPTER 3 Income from UK land and property

CHAPTER 4 Savings and investments

CHAPTER 5 Employment income

CHAPTER 6 State benefits and pensions

CHAPTER 7 **Sundry income and anti-avoidance**

CHAPTER 8 **Overseas issues**

CHAPTER 9 **Computation**

CHAPTER 10 **Administration**

CHAPTER 1

General principles

OUTLINE ¶¶

A. Taxable persons

Income tax is payable in respect of **taxable income** arising during a **tax year** (year ending 5 April: so 2011/12 is the year ending 5 April 2012). **2400**

An **individual's** taxable income is calculated as his total income, reduced by any deductions and allowances available. **2402** ss 4, 23ITA 2007

A **deceased individual** is liable to income tax on any income arising before his death. The personal allowance (and any other allowance to which the individual was entitled) is available in full for the year of death.

A **minor child** (one under the age of 18 years) is liable to income tax on any income he receives, and is entitled to the personal allowance (¶4392).

MEMO POINTS 1. **Married couples** are taxed independently of each other, but special rules apply for the computation of income which derives from jointly held property (¶4354). In particular, arrangements may be challenged under the settlements provisions (¶7352).
2. **Same sex couples** registered under a statutory **civil partnership** are treated as married couples for tax purposes. In this part, unless stated otherwise, references to:
- marriage and married couples include civil partnership ceremonies and civil partners;
- a spouse, husband or wife include a civil partner;
- divorce include the dissolution of a civil partnership; and
- a widow or widower include a surviving civil partner.
3. **Partnerships** are not charged directly to tax. The partnership profits are computed and allocated to the individual partners in accordance with their profit sharing ratios (¶2540). Each share is taxed on the individual partner.
4. **Personal representatives** are responsible for paying the tax on income received after the date of the individual's death, and during the period of administration. Once administration is complete, the income belongs to the **beneficiaries**, and they are responsible for paying the tax. See ¶7220 onwards for further details.
5. For a foreign domiciled and resident minor, see ¶4150+.
A child's income derived from a parent is taxed on the parent if it exceeds £100 in the tax year. The parent cannot claim the child's personal allowance. s 629 ITA 2007

EXAMPLE Mr A set up a savings account for his daughter on the day she was born. During the first year the account earned £95 interest and during the second, £105.
The income for the first year will belong to the child and (assuming she has no further income in the year) will be covered by her personal allowance and therefore not taxable.
The whole of the income for the second year will be subject to tax on Mr A.

2404 **UK and foreign sources of income** An individual's liability to UK income tax depends on his UK residence and domicile status:

UK domiciled?	UK resident?	Liable to UK income tax on:
Yes	Yes	Worldwide income
No	Yes, but not for more than 7 of the last 9 tax years	Income arising in or remitted to the UK
No	Yes, for more than 7 of the last 9 tax years	Worldwide income, unless electing for the remittance basis (¶4200)
Either	No	UK source income only

Broadly, income will be from a **UK source** if it is derived from the UK, but **double tax relief** is available where income is taxed both overseas and in the UK.
See ¶4147 onwards for further details.

B. Assessable income

2406 Income is taxable if it is of an **income nature** (i.e. not capital), falling within specified categories and not specifically exempted from tax.

s 3 ITA 2007 **Categories** Each income item must be classified under one of the following categories, which are mutually exclusive (income can only be taxed once), and taxed accordingly:

Category	¶¶
Trading income	¶2420
Income for UK land and property	¶2735
Income from savings and investments	¶2795
Employment income	¶2975
State benefits and pensions	¶3650
Sundry income	¶3945

2408 **Exempt income** Certain types of income are specifically exempt from tax, whilst other sources of income will be exempt provided certain conditions are met:

Type of income	Includes	¶¶
Specifically exempted	Adoption allowances, paid under the Adoption Allowances Regulations	
	Payments to special guardians or kinship carers	
	Small annual withdrawals from certain life assurance policies and guaranteed income bonds	¶4080
	Premium bond prizes	
	Savings certificates income	
	Miners' free coal, or cash received in lieu of it	
	Repayment supplement received in respect of overpaid income tax, capital gains tax or, in some cases, VAT	
	Disability or injury pensions following service in the armed forces	
	Pensions or annuities payable under Austrian or German law to victims of Nazi persecution	

Type of income	Includes	¶¶
Exempted provided certain conditions met	Income of foster carers and providers of local authority shared lives placements	¶2608
	Income from individual savings accounts	¶2797
	Certain annual payments received from insurance policies	¶2842
	Compensation for loss of employment	¶3078
	Long service awards to employees	¶3230
	Certain state benefits	¶3680
	Income of child trust funds	¶3695
	Compensation for mis-sold pensions	¶3964
	Income from domestic microgeneration	¶3966
	Interest on certain government securities held by non-residents	¶4290
	Income of care providers under an adult placement scheme	
	Foreign service allowance to an employee of the Crown, to the extent that it represents compensation for the extra cost of living abroad	
	Compensation under the Equitable Life Payment Scheme (ELPS) for loss due to government maladministration	

Computation Once the taxable income from each category has been calculated, the **amount chargeable to tax may be reduced** by any reliefs and allowances to which the taxpayer is entitled. The eventual rate at which tax will be charged will vary according to the source of the income and the individual's total income and allowances. (See ¶4345 onwards for details of computational matters.) 2410

Self-assessment

The UK operates a system of self-assessment, which means that each individual is responsible for assessing (i.e. calculating and paying) their own tax liabilities. If a taxpayer fails to self-assess, Revenue and Customs can raise assessments to collect any tax they believe is due. Interest and penalties may be charged if the system is not operated correctly. (See ¶4470 onwards for full details.) 2412

CHAPTER 2

Trading income

OUTLINE

¶¶

SECTION 1

Sole traders

I. Profits

A. Computation of trading income

General rules

2420 Trading income comprises profits from a trade, profession or vocation. Tax is charged for each tax year on the profits of the basis period for that year (¶2426). The profits of sole traders (individuals) are computed in the same manner as the trading profits of companies (see ¶80 onwards), except that for sole traders, special rules apply to:
- disposals of trading stock other than in the course of the trade (¶2422); and
- home working arrangements (¶2423).

Non-trade disposals of stock

2422 ss 172A, 172D ITTOIA 2005 If a self-employed person disposes of trading stock other than in the course of the trade, the stock is treated as having been **sold at market value**. The value is thus effectively treated as a trading receipt.

This applies in particular when the individual takes stock for his own use or that of his family. *Sharkey v Wernher* [1955]

BIM 33630 MEMO POINTS HMRC take a broad view of the application of this principle, but accept that it does not apply to:
- services received by the individual if the cost is disallowable for trading purposes;
- services rendered in the course of the trade (for example, meals provided to the proprietor of a hotel or restaurant); or
expenditure on the construction of an asset which is to be used in the trade.

Home working arrangements

2423 BIM 47800 Where a self-employed person uses his home for the purpose of his business, a proportion of the **household expenses** may be treated as **deductible expenditure** when computing his trading profit. To be deductible they must relate to a part of the house that is used solely for business purposes. (If part of the house is used for business and non-business purposes at the same time, no deduction is due.)

This exercise will inevitably involve **apportioning** such expenses between the period of sole business use and non-business use. Such an apportionment can be done on any fair and reasonable basis, which HMRC suggest could be on:
- area (i.e. the proportion in terms of area of the home that is used for business purposes);
- usage (i.e. how much of the supply is consumed for business purposes). This is appropriate where there is a metered or measurable supply such as electricity, gas or water; or
- time (i.e. how long the supply is used for business purposes, as compared to any other use).

If another method of allocation is more suitable to the particular activity in question then that should be accepted by HMRC provided the result is fair and reasonable.

2424 The following expenses are provided as **examples** of what type of expenses may be allowable and how they should be apportioned. The list is **not intended to be exhaustive** and different expenses may be allowable based on the particular facts of each case.

Type of cost	Expense	Detail
Fixed costs	Insurance	Either: – apportion the domestic policy; or – if business use is covered by a separate policy, then the cost of that policy is allowed in full, with no deduction for the domestic policy
	Council tax	Straight apportionment
	Mortgage interest	Apportion interest payments only (not capital repayments)
	Rent	Straight apportionment where the whole house is rented[1]
	Repairs and maintenance	Either: – if the repair etc relates to the whole of the house, apportion the cost; – if the repair etc relates solely to the part of the house that is used for the business it is allowed in full; or – if the repair etc relates solely to the part of the house that is not used for the business it is not deductible
Running costs	Cleaning	Straight apportionment if the whole house is cleaned. If, for example, the office is not touched then none of the costs will be allowable
	Heat, light and power	Straight apportionment that reflects the facts of usage[2] (taking into account the number and nature of any power consuming items involved)
	Telephone	The cost of business calls and a proportion[3] of the line rental costs are allowable
	Broadband	If the connection is for mixed personal and business use, a proportion[3] of the line rental costs are allowable
	Metered water charges	Either: – in the case of heavy usage, the business part of the house may be separately charged, and therefore fully allowable[4]; or – in the case of minor business use none of the water charge is allowable

Note:
1. An individual cannot charge rent to his own business (because individuals are prevented from letting property to themselves).
2. Where the usage is minor, such as the occasional writing up of records, any reasonable estimate consistent with usage should be accepted.
3. Based on the ratio of business use to total use. This will obviously vary with each bill.
4. There is no guidance on what happens if there is heavy usage and no separate billing of the business part of the house. Presumably apportionment will apply.

HMRC also provide the following examples as to how these provisions **operate in practice**.

EXAMPLE

1. Angela writes up her business records at home. She uses a room solely for business use for a short period each week. She estimates that £104 covers the cost of the proportion of the establishment costs, plus the electricity for heating and lighting. Although the claim for £104 is obviously an estimate of £2 per week, the claim is small and reflects the facts of the case. It is a reasonable estimate of the expense incurred and should be allowed.

2. Bill runs a small business. He uses one small room at home as an office, exclusively for the purposes of his trade. The room represents 5% of the floor area of the house. His expenses are:

Expense	Total	Claimed	
	£	£	
Council tax, insurance and mortgage interest	4,500	225	(5 % of total)
Electricity bill for heating & lighting	300	15	(5 % of total)
Total claim		240	

Although Bill has apportioned his electricity bill by floor area rather than usage, the amount claimed is small and there is nothing to suggest that his business use is significantly greater or lesser than his private use. It can be accepted as a reasonable estimate.

3. Bert runs a small business. He uses the spare bedroom at home as his office except for a week at Easter and a week at Christmas. All he does is to write up his records, once a week. The house has 10 rooms. Bert calculates that his business expense, based on 1/10 of the total costs, would be £450. Bert recognises that this is far too much for what he actually does at home and estimates that £104 covers the cost of the proportion of the establishment costs, plus the electricity for heating and lighting.
Although the claim for £104 is obviously an estimate of £2 per week, the claim is small and reflects the facts of the case. It is a reasonable estimate of the expense incurred and should be allowed.

Comment The claims made in the examples above are in line with the expenses allowance for employees working from home (¶3186). Since 6 April 2008, this allowance has remained fixed at £3 per week. It is possible that HMRC would allow a reasonable rise for claims by sole traders to reflect the increased cost of fuel.

4. Chris is an author working from home. She uses her living room from 8am to 12am. During the evening, from 6pm until 10pm, it is used by her family. The room used represents 10% of the area of the house. The costs shown in the table are apportioned by the 10% floor area and the time which she devotes to the business:

Type of exepense	Amount	Allocation by area	Allocation by time	Amount claimed
	£	£		£
Cleaning, insurance, council tax and mortgage interest etc	6,600	660[1]	110[2]	110
Electricity	1,500	150[1]	75[3]	75
Total				185

Note:
1. 10% of the floor space of the house.
2. One sixth of use by time is for business.
3. One half of use by time is for business.

She also uses the telephone to connect to the internet for research purposes. Her itemised telephone bill shows that a third of the calls made are business calls. She can claim the cost of those calls plus a third of the standing charge.

5. The facts are as in example 4. above. Chris has the exterior of the house painted and at the same time has the dining room re-decorated.
The exterior painting is a general household cost and a proportion can be claimed based on business use. However, Chris does not use her dining room for business purposes, so the cost of redecorating the dining room is not an allowable expense.

6. Gordon, an architect, dedicates a room solely for use as his office between 9am and 5pm daily. The room contains a workstation, office furniture and storage for his drawings. He uses the room for an average of 4 hours each day, though often this is spread over his working 8 hour day as he has a number of regular site visits to make. In addition it is not uncommon for Gordon to accommodate clients in his office to discuss plans, outside normal hours. The room is available for domestic use outside business hours and his family regularly make use of the room for around 2 hours each evening.
Gordon calculates the apportionment in two ways:
– based on the number of rooms in the house, the room uses £300 of running costs (electric and oil) and £600 of fixed costs (council tax, mortgage interest, insurance);
– based on simple time apportionment, the room uses £200 of running costs (4/6ths) and £480 of fixed costs (8/10ths).
The latter claim is equal to 75% of the £900 total costs attributable to the room.
Going forward, Gordon views the 75% claim as a more straightforward but equally reasonable basis for future claims, should his circumstances remain unchanged.

7. Bill entertains a number of customers at his home. Each time he hires caterers and also a firm of cleaners. Although Bill has used his home for business purposes, he cannot claim any of the costs as they relate to entertaining costs, which are not allowable (¶158).

MEMO POINTS For details of the tax treatment of **homeworking expenses for employees**, see ¶3187.

B. Taxation of trading profits

1. General principles

For each tax year, a **basis period must be identified**. Tax is charged on the profits of the basis period. The basis period will differ depending upon whether the business is: 2426
- a continuing business;
- changing its accounting date; or
- commencing or ceasing to trade.

On the commencement or cessation of trade or on the change of an accounting date, the same profits may be assessed to tax more than once. These are known as **overlap profits**, and may be relieved in certain circumstances. 2428

MEMO POINTS 1. Overlap profits can also arise for businesses that commenced trading before 6 April 1994 as a result of the **transitional rules** when the basis of taxation for business profits changed from the prior year basis to the current year basis. The profits would be those in the basis period for 1997/98 that arose before 6 April 1997 but after the basis period for 1996/97, apportioned without accounting for capital allowances.

EXAMPLE Mr A has been in business since 1985 and his accounting period ends on 30 April. For the year ended 30 April 1997, he made profits of £60,000 before capital allowances.
The related overlap profits are those that arose before 6 April 1997 but after the basis period for 1996/97. In this case it will be £55,000 (11/12 x £60,000), relating to the period from 1 May 1996 to 5 April 1997.

2. Where overseas tax has been paid on trading profits, **double taxation relief** (¶4229) will be given on the basis period for each tax year. This means that relief will be given twice for profits in an overlap period. Excess relief given in this manner will be clawed back on the cessation of trade.

2. The continuing business

Basis periods

A continuing business is one which has been in existence for more than 3 tax years and which has not been the subject of a change of accounting date during the current tax year. 2430 s 198 ITTOIA 2005

For each such trade, the **taxable profits** is the adjusted profit for the period of 12 months ending with the accounting date in the tax year.

EXAMPLE A has been trading as a carpenter for many years. He prepares his accounts for each year to 31 December. For the tax year 2011/12 A will be taxed on his adjusted profits for the year ended 31 December 2011.

MEMO POINTS If accounts are regularly prepared to a **particular day in the year** (as opposed to a fixed date), they will be treated as if prepared to a fixed date (and the change of accounting date provisions will therefore not be triggered), provided the "day" can only fall within a set of seven consecutive days (8 in February). This covers the situation where it is more convenient to prepare accounts to, for example, the last Friday in September or the last day of the summer term. s 211 ITTOIA 2005

Change of accounting date

On the change of an accounting date, profits may be taxed more than once (overlap profits). To ensure relief is given for these profits the following steps need to be taken: 2432 s 214 ITTOIA 2005

a. Identify the tax **year of change**. This will be the first year of assessment in which accounts are drawn up to the new date, or (if earlier) the first tax year in which accounts are not drawn up to the old date.

b. Identify the **relevant period**. This is the period from the end of the basis period for the previous year, to the new accounting date. Different rules apply depending on whether the relevant period is more or less than 12 months.

2434
s 216 ITTOIA 2005

If the **relevant period is less than 12 months**, then the basis period will be the 12 months to the new accounting date. In this case, overlap profits will arise because profits from an earlier period will have been taxed more than once.

EXAMPLE A has been trading for many years and has been drawing up accounts for the year ended 31 January. He decides to change the accounting date and draws up accounts to 30 September 2011.

Adjusted profits were as follows:

Year ended 31 January 2011	£100,000
Period ended 30 September 2011	£ 55,000
Year ended 30 September 2012	£120,000

The **tax year of change** is the first tax year in which accounts are not made up to the old date i.e. 2011/12.

The **relevant period** begins 1 February 2011 and ends 30 September 2011 (8 months).

The relevant period is less than 12 months so the basis period for the year of change will be the 12 months to 30 September 2011 (the new accounting date).

Assessments will be as follows:

2010/11	Year ended 31January 2011	£100,000
2011/12	1 October 2010 to 30 September 2011 123/365 × 100,000 = 33,699 242/242 × 55,000 = 55,000	
		£88,699
2012/13	Year ended 30 September 2012	£120,000

Overlap profits will arise for the period 1 October 2010 to 31 January 2011 (i.e. 123/365 x 100,000 = £33,699).

2436

If the **relevant period is more than 12 months**, then the basis period will be the same as the relevant period.

s 220 ITTOIA 2005

In this case, any overlap profits brought forward from earlier tax years must be deducted. The proportion of overlap profits that can be deducted relates to the number of days that the basis period is in excess of 365. This is calculated using the following formula:

$$\text{Total unused overlap profits} \times \frac{\text{(Days in the basis period} - 365)}{\text{Days in the overlap period}}$$

MEMO POINTS If the period used in calculating the deduction contains 29 February, this can be ignored when calculating the deduction if the accounting date in the tax year is either 5 April or treated as though it were 5 April, because it ends in the period 31 March to 4 April.

EXAMPLE B has been trading for many years and has been drawing up accounts for the year ended 30 September. He decides to change the accounting date and draws up accounts for the 15 months to 31 December 2011. B had the following overlap profits brought forward:

Overlap period		Profits
1 October 1996 to 5 April 1997	187 days	£15,775

Adjusted profits were as follows:

Year ended 30 September 2010	£100,000
Period ended 31 December 2011	£135,000
Year ended 31 December 2012	£120,000

The **tax year of change** is the first tax year in which accounts are first made up to the new date (2011/12).

The **relevant period** begins 1 October 2010 and ends 31 December 2011 (15 months).

The relevant period (457 days) is more than 12 months so that becomes the **basis period**.

Assessments will be as follows:

2010/11	Year ended 30 September 2010		£100,000
2011/12	Period ended 31 December 2011	135,000	
	Overlap profits that can be relieved:		
	$15,775 \times \frac{(457 - 365)}{187} =$	(7,761)	
			£127,239
2012/13	Year ended 31 December 2012		£120,000

Overlap relief carried forward will be £8,014 (= 15,775 – 7,761).

MEMO POINTS A trader is **free to change the accounting date of a continuing business** provided the following conditions are satisfied: s 217 ITTOIA 2005
– the accounting date was not changed in any of the 5 tax years immediately preceding the year of change;
– the accounting period to the new accounting date does not exceed 18 months; and
– notice of the change of accounting date is given to HMRC on a tax return by 31 January following the tax year of the change.

Where the first condition is the only one that is not satisfied, the change may still be accepted if there is a bona fide commercial reason for the change. Otherwise the trader will continue to be assessed on the basis of his old accounting date and apportionment will be necessary.
Following a failure to correctly change an accounting date, the situation will be reviewed in the subsequent tax year and, if the conditions are satisfied at that time, the change of accounting date will take effect from that tax year onwards.

3. Commencement of trade (first 3 years)

Basis periods

Why are there special rules? The basis period rules on the commencement of a trade attempt to ensure that profits are taxed evenly over the first 3 years. The results of one accounting period may be spread across more than one tax year and **apportionment** may be necessary. Similarly, more than one set of accounts may relate to each tax year and the results may need to be **aggregated**. **2438** s 199 ITTOIA 2005

MEMO POINTS 1. Strictly speaking, the **apportionment** should be made on the basis of the number of days in the respective periods. In practice HMRC may accept another reasonable time-based apportionment (such as weeks or months) provided that the approach is applied consistently across different periods. s 203 ITTOIA 2005
2. **Accounts prepared for the year to 31 March** (or 1, 2, 3 or 4 April) are treated as if they relate to the actual tax year of 6 April to 5 April.
3. Where **more than one accounting period ends in the same tax year**, only the latest is considered in establishing the basis period.
4. **Business start up payments** (previously known as enterprise allowances) received in a period which falls within two basis periods will be brought into account for tax purposes in the first basis period only. s 207 ITTOIA 2005

The **date** on which a trade commences is a question of fact and each case will be taken on its own merits. It is important to clarify the date of commencement so that the basis periods can be identified. **2440**

MEMO POINTS 1. As a general rule, **preparing** for the commencement of trade is not the same as actually trading, so that, for example, arranging for the installation of machinery and the purchase of raw materials will not constitute commencement whereas processing raw materials will. *Birmingham and District Cattle By-Products Ltd v CIR* [1919]
2. **Pre-trading expenditure** incurred by the trader is treated as if it were incurred on the date trade commenced provided it was actually incurred by the trader within 7 years before the commencement of the trade and it would be a deductible trading expense if incurred after the commencement of the trade.
3. Where a trader already has a trade and **commences a new trade**, the two will generally be treated separately and the new trade will be subject to the commencement rules. If the trader can establish that the new activity is merely the development of the existing one then the commencement rules will

not apply. It is important to note however that where two trades are amalgamated a possible outcome could be the cessation of both and the commencement of a new trade.

2442
s 199 ITTOIA 2005
First tax year The basis period runs from the date of commencement to the next 5 April.

EXAMPLE
1. A commences trading on 1 June 2011 and prepares his first accounts for the 16 months to 30 September 2012. A has adjusted profits of £75,000. For the tax year 2011/12 A will be taxed on the proportion of his adjusted profits relating to the period 1 June 2011 to 5 April 2012.

i.e. 309/487 × 75,000	£47,587

2. B commences trading on 1 May 2011 and prepares accounts for the 8 months to 31 December 2011 and the 12 months to 31 December 2012. Adjusted profits were £30,000 and £45,000 respectively. For the tax year 2011/12 B will be taxed on the proportion of his adjusted profits relating to the period 1 May 2011 to 5 April 2012.

i.e.1 May 2011 to 31 December 2011 (245/245 × 30,000)	30,000
1 January 2012 to 5 April 2012 (95/365 × 45,000)	11,712
	£41,712

2444
ss 200, 201 ITTOIA 2005
Second tax year The basis period for the second tax year is always 12 months in length. Which 12 months are used depends on whether an accounting period ends in the tax year:

a. if an **accounting period ends in the second tax year** then:
– if that accounting period is 12 months or more, the basis period will be the 12 months to the accounting date;
– otherwise, the basis period will be the 12 months from the date of commencement.

EXAMPLE Continuing on from the previous example 1. above, for the second tax year (2012/13) A has an accounting period of more than 12 months that ends in the tax year (the 16 months to 30 September 2012). A will be taxed on the adjusted profits relating to the period of 12 months ending 30 September 2012.

i.e. 365/487 × 75,000	£56,211

(The overlap period will be 1 October 2011 to 5 April 2012, giving overlap profits of £28,799 (187/487 × 75,000)).

If the first set of accounts had been prepared for the 11 month period from 1 June 2011 to 30 April 2012, then the basis period for 2012/13 (the second year of trading) would be the first 12 months of trading. This would include one month's profits from the next accounting period. The overlap period arising in this second tax year would be 1 June 2011 to 5 April 2012. The overlap period arising in the third tax year would be 1 May 2012 to 31 May 2012 (¶2448).

b. where an **accounting period does not end in the second tax year** the basis period will be the 12 months from 6 April to 5 April (the "actual basis").

EXAMPLE C commences trading on 1 March 2011 and prepares his first set of accounts for the 18 month period to 31 August 2012 with adjusted profits of £60,000. There is no accounting period ending in the second tax year (2011/12), so C will be assessed using the following basis periods:

2010/11	1 March 2011 to 5 April 2011 (36/549 × 60,000)	£3,934
2011/12	6 April 2011 to 5 April 2012 (365/549 × 60,000)	£39,891

In this case there is no overlap period between the first and second tax years.

2446
s 201 ITTOIA 2005
Third tax year For the third tax year the **general rule** (assuming there is no change of accounting date) is that the basis period is the 12 months starting immediately after the end of the basis period for the second tax year.

EXAMPLE D commences trading on 1 August 2010. She prepares her first set of accounts for the 6 month period to 31 January 2011 and annually thereafter. Adjusted profits for the first three periods are as follows:

Period ended 31 January 2011		£25,000
Year ended 31 January 2012		£100,000
Year ended 31 January 2013		£150,000

Basis periods and assessments for the first and second tax years are as follows:

2010/11	1 August 2010 to 5 April 2011 (183/183 × 25,000 = £25,000) (65/366 × 100,000 = £17,759)	£42,534
2011/12	12 months to 31 January 2012 (Overlap period 1 February 2011 to 5 April 2011 i.e. 65/366 × 100,000 = 17,759)	£100,000

The basis period for the third tax year will begin immediately after the end of the previous one:

2012/13	Next 12 months to 31 January 2013	£150,000

The **general rule is modified** where the third tax year is the first one in which an accounting period ends at least 12 months from the date of commencement of the trade. In this case the basis period for the third tax year will be the 12 months ending with the accounting date. **2448** s 198 ITTOIA 2005

This rule will be relevant where the accounting period ending in the second tax year ends less than 12 months from the date of commencement or where there is no accounting period ending in the second tax year.

EXAMPLE E commences trading on 1 January 2011 and prepares his first set of accounts for the 18 month period to 30 June 2012 with adjusted profits of £90,000. The basis periods for the first, second and third tax years are as follows:

2010/11	1 January 2011 to 5 April 2011 (96/547 × 90,000)	£15,795
2011/12	6 April 2011 to 5 April 2012 (365/547 × 90,000)	£60,055
2012/13	12 months to 30 June 2012 (365/547 × 90,000 – i.e. the 12 months ended with the accounting date in the 3rd year)	£ 60,055

The overlap period and profits will be 1 July 2011 to 5 April 2012 (279/547 × 90,000 = 45,905).

Change of accounting date

The calculation of the basis periods for a change in the **third year** of trading are as detailed in ¶2432 onwards. **2450** s 215 ITTOIA 2005

A change in the **second year** will follow the commencement rules (¶2444), in that if the new accounting date is:
– less than 12 months from the date of commencement, the basis period for the second year will be 12 months from the date of commencement; and
– more than 12 months from the date of commencement, the basis period for the second year will be the 12 months to the new accounting date.

EXAMPLE A commenced trading on 1 July 2011 and had the following results:

1 July 2011 – 30 November 2011	£20,000
1 December 2011 – 31 May 2012	£15,000
1 June 2012 – 31 May 2013	£40,000

The accounting date in the second tax year (2012/13) is less than 12 months from the date of commencement, so A will be assessed using the following basis periods:

2011/12	1 July 2011 to 5 April 2012		
	(153/153 × 20,000)	20,000	
	(127/183 × 15,000)	10,410	
			£30,410
2012/13	1 July 2011 to 30 June 2012		
	(153/153 × 20,000)	20,000	
	(183/183 × 15,000)	15,000	
	(30/365 × 40,000)	3,288	
			£38,288
2013/14	Year ended 31 May 2013		£40,000

The total overlap period will be:
- 1 July 2011 to 30 November 2011 (£20,000);
- 1 December 2011 to 5 April 2012 (£10,410 (i.e. 127/183 × 15,000)); and
- 1 June 2012 to 30 June 2012 (£3,288 (i.e. 30/365 × 40,000)).

MEMO POINTS A trader is **free to change** the accounting date in the first 3 years of assessment as he wishes. Changes made after this period need to meet specific conditions (¶2436).

4. Cessation of trade

What is a cessation?

2452 A cessation of trade is when a **permanent discontinuance** of the trade occurs, either because:
- the trader ceases to carry on his trade;
- there is a significant change in the way that the trade is carried on;
- the trade is transferred to another person; or
- a trader ceases to be resident in the UK.

An interruption in production will not constitute discontinuance unless production ceases permanently. Like the commencement of trade each case will be addressed on its own merits.

Basis periods

2454 s 202 ITTOIA 2005 **General rule** When a trade is permanently discontinued, the assessment of the tax year of cessation is adjusted. For this final tax year the basis period will begin on the day after the previous basis period ended, and will end on the date of cessation. This applies irrespective of whether one or more accounting periods end in the final tax year.

EXAMPLE A, who has been trading for many years, ceases to trade on 31 December 2012. His adjusted profits for the years up to cessation have been:

Year ended 30 June 2011	£50,000
Year ended 30 June 2012	£45,000
Period ended 31 December 2012	£15,000

The basis periods and assessments will be:

2011/12	Year ended 30 June 2011	£50,000
2012/13	1 July 2011 to 31 December 2012 (45,000 + 15,000)	£60,000

2456 **Exceptions** There are **two** exceptions to the general rule on cessation as follows:
- where there is no accounting period ending in the penultimate year; or
- where the trade ceases in the second tax year.

2458 s 201 ITTOIA 2005 **No accounting period ending in the penultimate year** If there is no accounting period in the year before the final tax year, the basis period will depend on whether the reason for the change of accounting date in the penultimate year was valid or not (¶2436):

	Basis period: penultimate year	Basis period: final year
Not a valid change	12 months immediately following the basis period for the previous year	From the end of the basis period for the penultimate year, to the date of cessation
Valid change	12 months to the new accounting date	From the end of the basis period for the penultimate year, to the date of cessation

EXAMPLE B has drawn up accounts for the year ended 31 March for many years. He ceases trading on 31 July 2011 and prepares his last set of accounts for the 16 months to that date. Adjusted profits are as follows:

Year ended 31 March 2009	£50,000
Year ended 31 March 2010	£60,000
Period ended 31 July 2011	£70,000

Assessments to cessation will be as follows:

Scenario 1:
Not a valid change of accounting date

2010/11	12 months from 1 April 2010 to 31 March 2011 365/487 × 70,000		£52,464
2011/12	1 April 2011 to 31 July 2011 122/487 × 70,000		£17,536

Scenario 2:
Valid change of accounting date

2010/11	12 months from 1 August 2009 to 31 July 2010		
	244/366 × 60,000	40,000	
	121/487 × 70,000	17,392	
			£57,392
2011/12	1 August 2010 to 31 July 2011		
	365/487 × 70,000	52,464	
	Overlap profits from 1 August 2009 to 31 March 2010	(40,000)	
			£12,464

Note:
The same amount (£70,000) is taxed over the 2 tax years but the timing is different.

Trade ceases in the second tax year If the trade ceases in the second tax year of the trade, the basis period will run from the 6 April (i.e. the day after the end of the first basis period) to the date of cessation. **2462** s 202 ITTOIA 2005

EXAMPLE C commenced trading on 1 June 2010 and ceased on 31 December 2011. Adjusted profits are as follows:

1 June 2010 to 31 May 2011	£35,000
1 June 2011 to 31 December 2011	£20,000

Assessments will be as follows:

2010/11	1 June 2010 to 5 April 2011 309/365 × 35,000	£29,630
2011/12	6 April 2011 to 31 December 2011 56/365 × 35,000 = 5,370 214/214 x 20,000 = 20,000	
		£25,370

Overlap relief

On cessation, overlap profits are brought forward from earlier years and, to the extent that they have not already been utilised on the change of an accounting date, are deducted from the assessment for the year. **2464** s 205 ITTOIA 2005

EXAMPLE Mr A commenced trading on 1 October 2006 and prepares his first set of accounts for the 15 months to 31 December 2007. He carries on drawing up accounts to 31 December until he decides to change his accounting date and draws up accounts for the 15 months to 31 March 2010. He carries on drawing up accounts to 31 March until he ceases trading on 30 September 2011.

Adjusted profits are as follows:

Period ended 31 December 2007	£30,000
Year ended 31 December 2008	£40,000
Period ended 31 March 2010	£50,000
Year ended 31 March 2011	£60,000
Period ended 30 September 2011	£20,000

Assessments will be as follows:

2006/07	1 October 2006 to 5 April 2007 (187/457 × 30,000)		£12,276
2007/08	12 months to 31 December 2007 (365/457 × 30,000) Overlap period 1 January 2007 to 5 April 2007 (95 days) 95/457 × 30,000 = 6,236		£23,961
2008/09	Year ended 31 December 2008		£40,000
2009/10	15 months to 31 March 2010 Less overlap relief $\frac{(455 - 365)}{95} \times 6{,}236$	50,000 (5,908)	 £44,092
2010/11	Year ended 31 March 2011		£60,000
2011/12	1 April 2011 to 30 September 2011 Less overlap relief (6,236 – 5,908)	20,000 (328)	 £19,672

Post-cessation receipts and expenses

2466 s 243 ITTOIA 2005 Any **receipts** arising from the activity of a trade after it has ceased are usually assessed in the tax year in which they are received.

s 257 ITTOIA 2005 **However**, the taxpayer can elect for them to be treated as being received on the last day of trading if they are received in a tax year beginning no later than 6 years after the date of cessation.

An election must be made within 12 months of 31 January following the tax year in which the income was received.

MEMO POINTS Receipts arising from the **transfer of stock or work in progress** held at the date of cessation are not taxed, as these will be included in the adjustment of profits on cessation. See ¶90 for the usual treatment of appropriation of stock.

2467 ss 248, 254 ITTOIA 2005 In addition, the following types of **post-trading expenditure** incurred during the 7 years following the date of cessation of trade may be relieved against post-cessation receipts or other income and gains of the year as follows:

Relieved against	Expense
Post-cessation receipts[1]	Items which would have been deductible if the trade had been continuing (for example, any unrelieved capital allowances etc)
Other income and capital gains of the year[1]	Debts which are written off as being irrecoverable[2]
	Payments made wholly and exclusively for defective work done, goods supplied or services rendered if they are payments for: – remedial work; – damages; – legal and professional expenses for a claim against the business; or – insurance against liabilities arising from a claim

Note:
1. A claim must be made within 12 months of 31 January following the tax year in which the expense is incurred.
2. The costs of collecting debts after the cessation of trade also qualify. Relief is only available where the debt had been taken into account in computing the profits of the trade. Any amount subsequently recovered is then taxable.

MEMO POINTS If there is insufficient income or capital gains to cover post-trading expenditure of a particular year, the **expenditure can be carried forward** to be set against post-cessation receipts only.

II. Losses

1. Relief

A loss incurred in the course of a trade may be relieved in a number of ways as summarised in the table below. **2468**

Type of loss	Available relief	Timing	Exclusions or restrictions	¶¶
Losses of a continuing trade	Set against general income of the same year and/or the preceding year	Claim by first anniversary of 31 January following tax year of loss. Example: loss arising in 2011/12: claim by 31 January 2014	Restrictions if not active in the business[1] or loss artificially created[2]	¶2478
	Set against capital gains of the same year (whether arising from trading or personal assets)	Claim by first anniversary of 31 January following tax year of loss. Example: loss arising in 2011/12: claim by 31 January 2014	Restrictions if not active in the business[1] or loss artificially created[2]. Must be set against income first	¶2484
	Carried forward against subsequent profits of the same trade	4 years from end of tax year of loss. Example: loss in 2011/12: claim by 5 April 2016	None	¶2492
Losses in the first 4 years of a trade	Carried back against general income of earlier years	Claim by first anniversary of 31 January following tax year of loss. Example: loss arising in 2011/12: claim by 31 January 2014	Restrictions if not active in the business[1] or loss artificially created[2]. Must be trading with a view of profits	¶2500
Losses on cessation of trade	Carried back against earlier profits of the same trade	4 years from end of tax year of loss. Example: loss in 2011/12: claim by 5 April 2016	Must be set against later years first	¶2512

Note:
1. The annual maximum relief against general income or capital gains is £25,000 for an individual carrying on a business in a non-active capacity (¶2476). This does not apply to an individual trading as a Lloyd's underwriter (¶2688) or to losses arising from a qualifying film partnership (¶4368).
2. No relief is given against general income or capital gains if the loss arises directly or indirectly because of tax avoidance arrangements entered into on or after 21 October 2009 (¶2477) or from furnished holiday lettings (¶2780).
3. It is common for a loss to be relieved in more than one way. For example, part might be set against general income of the same year, and the rest carried forward against future profits of the trade.

As a general rule trading losses will only be available for relief if it can be shown that during the year in which the loss was made the trade was carried out on a **commercial basis with a view to realising profits**. For these purposes, where the manner in which the trade was operated changed during the year, the situation at the end of the year will be deemed to have applied for the whole period. Similarly, where a trade commenced or ceased during **2470** s 66 ITA 2007 the year the situation at the end of the period will be examined. Where the trade in question is part of a larger undertaking, the whole undertaking must satisfy this test.

Where the trader can show that the trade was carried on so as to afford a reasonable expectation of profit, this will generally be acceptable evidence of trading with a view to realising profit. In particular, where unforeseen or unpredictable events occurred to prevent a profit arising, loss relief may still be available. The test is subjective: that is, it depends on the taxpayer's purpose. *Walls v Livesey* [1995]

2. The continuing business

a. Losses available for relief

2472 Losses available for relief in a year of assessment are **calculated** in the same way as profits. The profit or loss figure from the accounts is adjusted in the normal way and in accordance with the normal basis periods (¶2430). In the general course of events the basis period for a year of assessment will be the accounting period ending in that year and if the accounting period results in a loss then relief will be available.

EXAMPLE A trader who has been in business for many years prepares accounts for the year ending 31 December. His accounts for the current year of assessment show a loss before tax of £15,000. The following expenses were included in the accounts:

Depreciation	£1,775
Entertaining	£400

The adjusted loss available for relief in respect of the current year of assessment will be:

	£	£
Loss before tax		(15,000)
Add: Depreciation	1,775	
Entertaining	400	
		2,175
Adjusted loss		(12,825)

2473 Capital allowances are deducted as an **expense** of the trade and therefore automatically create or augment a loss. Balancing charges are treated as a trading receipt and consequently reduce the amount of loss relief available. See ¶200 for full details of capital allowances.

MEMO POINTS In addition, **payments of qualifying interest** (¶4363) which have not been allowed because the individual had insufficient income can be treated as trading losses available for loss relief providing they were made wholly and exclusively for the purposes of the trade.

2474 Interest and dividends will be treated as trading **income** and relief will be given accordingly where a trader has:

s 85 ITA 2007

- unrelieved losses carried forward; and
- interest or dividends arising in the year that would have formed part of the trading profit but for the fact that they are taxed as savings income.

b. Claiming relief

2475 A person who makes a trading loss in a year of assessment can claim relief for the loss by:

s 64 ITTOIA 2005

- setting it against the general income and capital gains of the same or the preceding year (the claim must be made within 12 months from 31 January following the year of assessment in which the loss arises); or
- carrying it forward against the trading profits of later years (the claim must be made within 4 years from the end of the tax year in which the loss arises).

MEMO POINTS 1. The claim for **relief against capital gains** should strictly be submitted with the claim for losses to be set against general income. In practice, providing both claims are submitted within the time limit, a later claim for relief against capital gains will be accepted.

2. A **late claim** may be accepted where the claimant is able to show that he had:
- been unable to submit a claim on time for reasons beyond his control;
- made an informal claim within the time limit and had not been advised that a written claim was required; or
- been misled by some relevant and uncorrected error made by HMRC.

Restrictions on utilisation

There are **restrictions** on relief for losses by individuals who carry on a business in a **non-active capacity**. The maximum amount of losses which can be set against general income of the tax year or against capital gains is £25,000. **2476** s 74A ITA 2007

Non-active capacity is defined as working less than 10 hours a week, on average, over the basis period for tax purposes (or, if that is less than 6 months, from the date of commencement or to the date of cessation).

MEMO POINTS 1. This restriction does not apply to losses from trading as an underwriter at Lloyd's, or from qualifying film expenditure.

Tax-generated losses

If a loss arises directly or indirectly because of relevant **tax avoidance arrangements** entered into on or after 21 October 2009, relief will not be given against other income or capital gains. The loss is still available for relief against profits from the same trade in other periods. **2477** s 74ZA ITA 2007

Relevant tax avoidance arrangements are any arrangements of which one of the purposes is to obtain a reduction in a tax liability by means of a loss claim against general income of the tax year or against capital gains.

Losses set off against general income

Loss relief may be claimed against general income: **2478** s 65 ITA 2007
- in the year of loss; and/or
- the preceding year.

If a claim is made for a loss to be **offset against both years**, the losses can be set against either year first, providing the available income for the first year claimed is exhausted before any loss is set against the other year. This rule applies even where the effect is that personal allowances will be wasted.

EXAMPLE Mr A has the following income:

Tax year	Trading income	Other income
2011/12	(£6,500)	£10,000
2010/11	Nil	£6,000

Mr A may choose which year to set the losses against, but he must use as much of the loss as possible in the year he chooses, before using them in the other year. If he chose to set the losses against 2010/11 first, the result would be:

	2010/11 £	2011/12 £
Income	6,000	10,000
Less		
Losses	(6,000)	(500)
Personal allowance	n/a	(6475)
Taxable income	Nil	3,025

MEMO POINTS As a temporary measure, losses arising in 2008/09 or 2009/10 could be carried back up to two years, subject to a maximum claim for each year. For details, see *Tax Memo 2010-2011*. Sch 6 FA 2009

If a claim is made for a loss to be **offset against one year only**, any remaining losses can be carried forward (¶2492) or set against capital gains (¶2484). **2479**

Relief is given by deducting the loss from the net income of the trader before personal allowances are deducted.

EXAMPLE Mr B has been trading for many years and has the following adjusted results:

Year 1	£20,000
Year 2	£14,000
Year 3	£ (12,000)

His other income for the years in question was as follows:

	Rental income	Savings (gross)
Year 1	£2,000	£1,250
Year 2	£2,500	£1,100
Year 3	£3,000	£750

Mr B has the following options:

1. Offset against income of current year (Year 3) first:

	Year 1 £	Year 2 £	Year 3 £
Trading income	20,000	14,000	-
Rental income	2,000	2,500	3,000
Savings income	1,250	1,100	750
	23,250	17,600	3,750
Loss relief	-	(8,250)	(3,750)
	23,250	9,350	Nil

2. Offset against income of preceding year (Year 2) first:

	Year 1 £	Year 2 £	Year 3 £
Trading income	20,000	14,000	-
Rental income	2,000	2,500	3,000
Savings income	1,250	1,100	750
	23,250	17,600	3,750
Loss relief	-	(12,000)	-
	23,250	5,600	3,750

In this example setting the losses against the preceding year first allows the taxpayer to preserve income in the year of the loss to prevent personal allowances being wasted.

2480 Where income for a year could be relieved as a result of **two separate losses**, one for the current year and one for the following year, the current year loss will be utilised first.

EXAMPLE Mr C has been trading for many years and has the following adjusted results:

Year 1	£1,000
Year 2	£ (2,000)
Year 3	£ (8,000)

His other income for the years in question was as follows:

	Salary	Savings (gross)
Year 1	-	£250
Year 2	£9,000	£100
Year 3	£2,800	£75

Assuming loss relief for both periods is claimed against Year 2 first, the order of offset will be as follows:

	Year 1 £	Year 2 £	Year 3 £
Trading income	1,000	-	-
Salary	-	9,000	2,800
Savings income	250	100	75
	1,250	9,100	2,875
Loss for Year 2	-	(2,000)	-
Loss for Year 3	-	(7,100)	(900)
	1,250	Nil	1,975

2482 Where a trade is charged to tax on its **income from overseas**, current year losses arising from that trade may be set against general income in the same way as for trades carried on in the UK.

Set off against capital gains

Trading losses may be set against capital gains for the same year of assessment and the preceding year. This rule applies whether the capital gain arises from trade or personal assets. 2484 s 261B TCGA 1992

A claim must be made within 12 months from 31 January following the tax year in which the loss arises.

MEMO POINTS Losses available for offset against capital gains are calculated in the same way as for offset against general income (¶2472).

Before a claim can be made to relieve trading losses against capital gains, the losses must first be set against general income of the same period. Only after general income has been exhausted (even if the result is that personal allowances are wasted) can losses be utilised against capital gains. 2486

Similarly, if the taxpayer wishes to utilise trading losses against the capital gains of the preceding year of assessment, the losses must first be set against the general income of the preceding year.

MEMO POINTS The taxpayer can choose whether the trading loss will be set firstly against the current year income and gains or the preceding year. The taxpayer is not obliged to claim for both years and may relieve the loss against the income and gains of one year and just the income of the other.

Relief against capital gains is restricted to the "total net capital gain" for the year. The total net capital gain is the current year's gains, after deduction of current year losses and capital losses brought forward from earlier years. 2488

The result of this restriction is that the annual exempt amount (¶6326) may be wasted.

2490

EXAMPLE Mr A has been trading for many years and has the following adjusted results:

Year ended 31 December 2010	£3,000
Year ended 31 December 2011	£ (20,000)

Mr A also had the following income and gains	2010/11	2011/12
Rent	£3,750	£4,000
Chargeable gains	£12,000	£15,000
Capital loss brought forward:	£ (5,000)	

The tax position will be as follows:

		2010/11 £		2011/12 £
Income from trade		3,000		-
Rent		3,750		4,000
		6,750		4,000
Loss relief		(6,750)		(4,000)
		Nil		Nil
Chargeable gains		12,000		15,000
Trading loss available for relief against gains:				
Gain	12,000		15,000	
Capital loss b/fwd	(5,000)		(5,000)	
Maximum trading loss offset	7,000		10,000	
Trading loss claimed: 2010/11		(7,000)		
Trading loss claimed 2011/12[1]				(2,250)
		5,000		12,750
Less: Capital loss brought forward from 2010/11[2]				(2,150)
Less: Exempt amount		(10,100)		(10,600)
		Nil		Nil

Note:
1. Restricted to balance of loss.
2. Claim restricted to preserve annual exemption.

Summary of losses

Trading losses:			**Capital losses:**	
Year ended 31 December 2011		20,000	B/fwd at 2010/11	5,000
Set off 2010/11	Income	(6,750)	Set off 2011/12	(2,150)
	Gains	(7,000)	(Restricted to preserve exempt amount)	
		6,250	Carried forward	2,850
Set off 2011/12	Income	(4,000)		
	Gains	(2,250)		
		Nil		

Carry forward of losses

2492 s 83 ITA 2007 The general rule is that an unused loss is carried forward and set against the first available profits arising from the same trade.

There is **no time limit for relief** of the loss carried forward. It will be carried forward indefinitely until it has been extinguished or the trade ceases. If profits arise, the loss must be used as far as possible, even if the result is that personal allowances are wasted.

MEMO POINTS 1. A loss is deemed to have been **used** by aggregation (¶2510), or if a claim has been submitted under the current year loss rules (¶2478), or on a carry back claim for 2008/09 or 2009/10 (¶2478), or on commencement (¶2500) or cessation (¶2512).
2. Where a **trade ceases** to be carried out on a commercial basis with a view to realising profits, the carry forward of losses will stop because the trade will be deemed to have ceased.

2494 It is important to note that trading losses can only be carried forward against profits of the **same trade**. Two conditions must be fulfilled:
- the trade must be carried on by the same person; and
- the trade must be the same as when the loss was made.

A material change in the nature of the trade will cause the trade to cease and the losses to be forfeited. Any unused losses arising in this way may be set against post-cessation receipts (¶2466).

EXAMPLE Mr A has been trading for many years. Adjusted results are as follows:

Year ended:	
31 December 2008	£ (45,000)
31 December 2009	£35,000
31 December 2010	£ (12,000)
31 December 2011	£50,000

Assessments will be as follows:		**£**	**Assessment**
2008/09	Year ended 31 December 2008		Nil
2009/10	Year ended 31 December 2009	35,000	
	Less: Losses brought forward	(35,000)	
			Nil
2010/11	Year ended 31 December 2010		Nil
2011/12	Year ended 31 December 2011	50,000	
	Less: Losses brought forward	(22,000)	
			28,000

Summary of losses

Year ended 31 December 2008	45,000
Less: relieved against year ended 31 December 2009	(35,000)
	10,000
Add: Year ended 31 December 2010	12,000
	22,000
Less: relieved for year ended 31 December 2011	(22,000)
Loss carried forward	Nil

3. Losses on commencement of trade

a. Losses available for relief

Losses arising in a year of assessment are **calculated** on the same basis periods as profits (¶2438). 2500

The commerciality test is extended, so that a trade must be carried on with a view to realising profits either in the period of the loss, or within a reasonable time. HMRC interpretations have stated that a reasonable time will depend on the activity in question, but that furnished holiday letting, for example, would be expected to be profitable within 5 years of commencement.

b. Claiming relief

A trading loss arising in the **first 4 years of assessment** of a trade can be carried back and set against total income for the 3 years preceding the year of loss, taking earlier years first. 2504 s 72 ITA 2007

Any unutilised losses must be carried forward and set against the first available profits of the same trade (¶2492).

A **claim** for relief must be submitted to HMRC by the first anniversary of the 31 January following the year of assessment. 2506

MEMO POINTS **Partial claims** for relief are not accepted, so if the loss for a particular year of assessment is relieved under this rule it must be relieved in full against the available income for the 3 years preceding it, even if personal allowances are wasted as a result.

There is an element of overlap between loss relief in the early years of trade and the offset of current year losses (¶2478). This is because in the early years a loss can be carried back 3 years, and under the current year loss rules a loss can be set off against the current or preceding year. The immediately preceding year is therefore common to both rules. Providing he has sufficient income, a trader can use both types of loss relief in the same period. 2508 s 73 ITA 2007

EXAMPLE A trader commences trading on 1 January 2011. He prepares accounts for the year to 31 December 2011 and annually thereafter. Adjusted results are as follows:

Year ended:	
31 December 2011	£ (25,000)
31 December 2012	£5,000
31 December 2013	£ (8,000)

He also had other income, as follows:

	Salary	Savings (gross)
2007/08	£11,500	£1,500
2008/09	£12,500	£2,000
2009/10	£15,000	£2,500
2010/11	£8,150	£1,750

Losses available for offset will be as follows:		Loss	Assessment
2010/11	1 January 2011 to 5 April 2011 95/365 × (25,000)	6,507	Nil
2011/12	12 months to 31 December 2011 25,000 – 6,507	18,493	Nil
2012/13	12 months to 31 December 2012		5,000
2013/14	12 months to 31 December 2013	8,000	Nil

Loss relief will be given as follows:

		2007/08	2008/09	2009/10	2010/11
		£	£	£	£
Salary		11,500	12,500	15,000	8,150
Savings		1,500	2,000	2,500	1,750
		13,000	14,500	17,500	9,900
Less: Losses from:	2010/11	(6,557)			
	2011/12		(14,500)	(3,943)	
	2012/13				(8,000)
Income before allowances		6,443	–	13,557	1,900

Note:
The claim for the losses for 2011/12 to be carried back must be made in full, even though personal allowances for 2008/09 will be wasted.

2510 Where a loss arises in the first 3 years of a new business (or on the change of an accounting date), the **losses in aggregation** rule must be applied. This states that where the results of one accounting period are used as part of the basis period for more than one year of assessment, any losses arising can only be used once. See ¶2438 for the detailed basis period rules.

EXAMPLE

1. A trader commences trading on 1 June 2010. He prepares accounts for the 8 month period to 31 January 2011 and annually thereafter. Adjusted results are as follows:

Period ended 31 January 2011	£12,000
Year ended 31 January 2012	£ (20,000)

Assessments will be calculated as follows:

		£	Assessment
2010/11	1 June 2010 to 5 April 2011		
	8 months of period ended 31 January 2011	12,000	
	2 months of year ended 31 January 2012 (64/365 × 20,000)	(3,507)	
			8,493
2011/12	12 months to 31 January 2012	(20,000)	
	Less: Losses already used in aggregation	3,507	
	Loss available for relief	(16,493)	
			Nil

2. A trader commences trading on 1 September 2010. He prepares accounts for the 16 month period to 31 December 2011 with adjusted losses of £50,000. The following losses will be available:

		Losses available	Assessment
2010/11	1 September 2010 to 5 April 2011 (217/487 × 50,000)	(22,279)	Nil
2011/12	12 months to 31 December 2011 Lower of: 365/487 × 50,000 = 37,474 50,000 – 22,279 = 27,721	(27,721)	Nil

3. A trader commences trading on 1 January 2011. He prepares accounts for the 9 month period to 30 September 2011 and annually thereafter. Adjusted results are as follows:

Period ended 30 September 2011	£ (15,000)
Year ended 30 September 2012	£25,000

			Losses available	Assessment
2010/11	1 January 2011 to 5 April 2011 (95/273 × 15,000)		(5,220)	Nil
2011/12	12 months to 31 December 2011 Period ended 30 September 2011	(15,000)		
	Less: Losses already used in aggregation	5,220		
		(9,780)		
	3 months of year ended 30 September 2011 92/365 × 25,000	6,301		
			(3,479)	Nil

4. Cessation of trade

a. Losses available for relief

Calculation of loss

Losses available for relief in a year of assessment are calculated in the same way as profits. To then calculate the losses available for terminal loss relief, the period to cessation must be split into two parts: 2512 s 90 ITA 2007

a. the period from 12 months before the date of cessation to 5 April; and

b. the period from 6 April to the date of cessation.

The terminal loss relief available will be the total of the adjusted losses in each period. In addition, unutilised overlap relief brought forward (¶2428) will be added to the loss for the final period.

If either of the two periods results in a profit it will be disregarded for terminal loss relief purposes.

MEMO POINTS Losses relieved under any other provisions are not included in the terminal loss.

EXAMPLE

1. Mr B had the following adjusted results for the period to the cessation of his trade on 31 December 2010:

Year ended 31 January 2008	£15,000
Year ended 31 January 2009	£18,000
Year ended 31 January 2010	£12,000
Year ended 31 January 2011	£5,000
Period ended 31 December 2011	£ (25,000)

Terminal loss relief will be available as follows:

		£	£
1 January 2011 to 5 April 2011	31/365 × 5,000	425	
	64/334 × (25,000)	(4,790)	
			4,365
6 April 2011 to 31 December 2011	270/334 × (25,000)		20,210
	Terminal loss		24,575

Relief will be offset as follows:

	2008/09	2009/10	2010/11
	£	£	£
Original trading assessment	18,000	12,000	5,000
Less: Terminal loss			(5,000)
		(12,000)	
	(7,575)		
Revised trading assessment	10,425	Nil	Nil

Summary of losses:		£
Terminal loss		24,575
Utilised:	2010/11	(5,000)
	2009/10	(12,000)
	2008/09	(7,575)
		Nil

2. Mr A permanently ceased trading on 30 September 2011 and had the following adjusted results for the period to cessation:

Year ended 31 December 2010	£22,000
Period ended 30 September 2011	£ (12,000)

Mr A has overlap relief brought forward of £3,775.
The two periods will be:
- 1 October 2010 to 5 April 2011
- 6 April 2011 to 30 September 2011

Terminal losses will be calculated as follows:

		£	£
1 October 2010 to 5 April 2011	92/366 × 22,000	5,530	
	95/273 × (12,000)	(4,176)	
			Nil
6 April 2010 to 30 September 2010	178/273 × (12,000)	(7,824)	
	Overlap relief	(3,775)	
	Terminal loss available		(11,599)

Annual payments

2516 s 448 ITA 2007 The profits for earlier years against which terminal losses can be set must be reduced to take account of any annual payments (e.g. annuity, patent royalties) made in the 3 years prior to cessation which were made out of profits charged to income tax. The reason for this is that the individual has already received relief in the form of tax deducted at source, and to claim terminal loss relief on that income would give relief twice.

If an annual payment is made during the 12 months prior to cessation:
- other than wholly and exclusively for the purposes of the trade; or
- out of profits chargeable to income tax,

the terminal loss available for relief will be **reduced** by the amount of that annual payment.

b. Claiming relief

2518 s 89 ITA 2007 On the permanent cessation of a trade, losses of the **last 12 months of trading** can be set against assessable profits of the trade for the year of discontinuance and the preceding 3 years of assessment.

MEMO POINTS The following events will also be **treated as a permanent cessation** for the purposes of loss relief:
- incorporation of a business; and
- the taxpayer changing his residence and commencing to trade wholly or partly outside the UK.

A **temporary suspension** of trading activities will not constitute permanent cessation, and each case must therefore be addressed on its own merits.

2520 The **time limit** for a claim is 4 years from the end of the year of assessment.

Relief is given as far as possible against the profits of later years before earlier years, even if the result is that personal allowances are wasted. Relief may be given by repayment of tax or reduction of outstanding self-assessments. 2522

III. Administration

Once the net trading income is calculated, the figures are entered in the sole trader's personal **tax return** for the relevant year of assessment, to form part of the taxable income computation. The computation and sole trader accounts may be submitted to HMRC, together with the tax return, to support the trade income. 2524

See ¶4470 onwards for full details of the self-assessment regime.

MEMO POINTS If trading accounts are not available when the income tax is paid, tax must be paid on the basis of estimated figures. Interest will be charged from the original due of payment should it turn out that tax was underpaid. See ¶4504 for full details of payment requirements.

SECTION 2

Partnerships

A. Basic principles

Definition

A partnership is defined in general law as "the relationship that subsists between persons carrying on a business in common with a view to profit". There is, however, **no statutory definition for tax purposes** of a partnership. 2525 s 1 Partnership Act 1890

A partnership does not include a company or incorporated association. Unlike a company, a partnership is not a separate legal entity (except in Scotland), and partners are therefore liable for their own actions and those of their partners.

Non-resident partners are taxed on the profits of the UK trade in the same way as residents: see ¶4328.

A **limited liability partnership (LLP)** is treated as a separate legal entity, which must file annual accounts and returns with Companies House. Despite this treatment, an LLP is taxed in the same way as other partnerships, except for minor differences in the treatment of losses (¶2556). 2526

HMRC will consider many factors in order to decide whether a partnership exists. The presence or absence of a particular factor will not be conclusive (although it may be persuasive) evidence. The main factors that indicate the existence of a partnership are: 2527
- a partnership agreement;
- all of the partners having the power to bind the firm in transactions and authorize payments;
- the business being registered as a partnership for VAT;
- the presence of partners' names on letter headings; and
- the partners sharing losses as well as profits.

Partners' liability to taxation

A partnership is not liable to tax, because it has no separate legal identity. Instead, **each partner is liable to tax** on his share of the partnership income (¶2532). The partnership is, however, obliged to submit a separate tax return (¶2598). 2528

2529 A partner's liability to tax depends on his legal status as a person, which may be that of:
- an individual;
- a body corporate (typically, a company);
- a trust.

Liability may also depend on the partner's function within the partnership.

2530 BIM 72060, 72115 **Individual partners** Whether a partner's share of profit is treated as earned income depends on the type of partnership position held. This is important in determining the individual's earnings for the purposes of pension contributions, and the extent to which partnership losses can be offset against other sources of income.

The different types of individual partner are summarized in the following table:

Type	Definition	Profit share taxed as	Restrictions on losses
Full or equity	Shares in both profits and losses and has an active role in running the business.	Self-employed trading income	No
Non-active (or "sleeping")	Shares in both profits and losses but has a restricted role[1] in running the business.	Self-employed unearned income[2]	Yes: see ¶2556
Salaried	Interest in the partnership is primarily through a fixed salary. Does not share losses.	Employment income[3]	Not applicable.
Limited	Not entitled to take any part in the management of the business and cannot bind the partnership. Commercial liability is limited to the capital contributed by him to the partnership	Self-employed unearned income[2]	Yes: see ¶2556
Limited Liability	A partner in an LLP. Commercial liability is limited to the capital contributed by him to the partnership	Self-employed earned income	Yes: see ¶2556

Notes
1. A non-active partner is an individual who does not personally spend an average of at least 10 hours a week on activities connected with the partnership's trade, which are conducted on a commercial basis and with a view to realizing a profit.
2. Does not count as earned income for pension contributions or NIC.
3. May be treated as self-employed if HMRC consider him to be in fact a full partner (for example, if he is held out to third parties as a partner and/or has power to commit the partnership to expenditure).

2531 **Corporate and trust partners** The different types of non-individual partner are summarized in the following table:

Type	Definition	Profit share taxed as	Restrictions on losses
Body corporate	Shares in both profits and losses and has an active role in running the business.	Profits, losses, capital allowances and charges on income are subject to corporation tax	No
Body corporate and limited	Normally means a partner in an LLP. Commercial liability is limited to the capital contributed to the partnership.	As above	Yes: see ¶2556

Type	Definition	Profit share taxed as	Restrictions on losses
Trust: direct	Trustees carry on a trade directly	Non-earned income of the trust	No
Trust: indirect, active[1]	Trustees carry on a trade through a beneficiary and/or beneficiary's spouse	Earned income of the trust	No
Trust: indirect, inactive[1]	Trustees carry on a trade through a beneficiary and/or beneficiary's spouse	Non-earned income of the trust	Yes: see ¶2556

Notes
1. The distinction between active and non-active (¶2530) applies only to individuals. In the case of a trust, it is the beneficiary who is or is not active in the trade.

B. Partnership profits

1. Computation of trading income

A partnership which includes one or more non-corporate partners must prepare a **computation of its trading profits** for income tax purposes. 2532

In a **mixed partnership** (one with at least one corporate and at least one non-corporate partner), two profit computations are required, one using income tax principles and one using corporation tax principles. Each partner's share is determined using the appropriate computation.

Computation for income tax

For income tax purposes, partnership trading profits are computed according to the standard rules used for all trading persons (¶80 – ¶194), with a few exceptions as follows: 2533

Item	Standard treatment	Partnership treatment
Salary/bonus or commission	¶181	The partnership agreement may provide for one or more partners to draw a specified salary/bonus or commission. In reality these payments are not earnings from employment, but a share of partnership profits and consequently are not deductible when computing the partnership profits.
Interest on partners' capital	¶179	Not allowable as a deduction when computing partnership profits. As for salary/bonus or commission payments, they are treated as a share of partnership profits.
Deductions from income	¶194	Allocated to each partner in accordance with the profit sharing ratio. The deductions so allocated are then treated as personal deductions from income (¶4387).
Any financial benefit given to a partner	¶181–¶184	Not an allowable deduction. However, bona fide rent paid to a partner who owns business premises occupied by the partnership will be deductible.

Computation for corporate partners

2534 ss 1259, 1260 CTA 2009 CTM 36510, 36520 If one of the partners is a UK resident body corporate, a **separate computation** of taxable profits or losses must be prepared for the partnership using corporation tax (rather than income tax) principles. This computation forms the basis of the corporate partner's share of profits, capital allowances, charges on income, and losses. If the mixed partnership includes at least one non-resident corporate partner, a separate computation must be prepared for the non-resident.

Interest paid to partners, and other prior allocations of profit, are not treated as distributions for corporation tax, and are therefore deductible from the taxable profits. Qualifying charitable donations (¶958) made by the partnership are apportioned to the corporate partner by reference to the accounting period in which they are paid, and become known as charges on income.

Changes of partner are ignored by the body corporate provided it remains a partner both before and after the change.

2535 The share of profit, capital allowances, charges on income, and losses allocated to a corporate partner are subject to corporation tax as though the share were derived from a trade carried on by the company on its own.

This means that the trade will be **separate from other trades** carried on by the company, and losses from one will not be allowed against the other. If the accounting periods of the partnership and the company do not correspond, the partnership profits are apportioned between the company's own accounting periods.

2536 Sch 24 CTA 2009 Corporation tax is charged on a company which realises capital from the untaxed profits of a partnership of which the company is a partner. The profit is treated as though it arose from a loan relationship (see ¶870+).

Partners' assets used and expenditure incurred for partnership purposes

2538 BIM 72075 A partner may:
- incur partnership expenses personally (such as motor expenses or rental costs), which are not directly reimbursed from partnership funds; or
- claim capital allowances on personal assets used by the partnership.

These amounts cannot be claimed as a deduction in the tax return of the partner but (providing they were incurred **wholly and exclusively** for the purposes of the partnership business) can be included in the partnership accounts or as an adjustment in the partnership's taxable profit computation. The partner receives a deduction for the expenditure as a specific allocation in the profit-sharing arrangement.

2. Taxation of partnership profits

Apportionment between the partners

2540 s 849 ITTOIA 2005 Partnership profits (or losses) for an accounting period are **allocated among the partners** in accordance with their interests in the partnership during that period. Each partner is then treated as if the profits were derived from a separate business carried on by him as a sole trader, using the same basis periods as for sole traders (¶2430, ¶2438 and ¶2454).

When a partner **leaves** or **joins** a continuing partnership (one in which there is at least one common partner before and after a change), the opening and closing year rules and overlap provisions apply to his share of the partnership profits, without affecting the other partners.

2541 Salaries and interest on capital paid to partners are treated as **a prior allocation of profit** made before the main division between the partners.

EXAMPLE

1. Mr A and Mr B have been in partnership for many years and share profits 60: 40. Adjusted partnership profits for the current tax year are £500,000. Mr A receives interest on capital of £18,000 and Mr B receives interest on capital of £10,000 and a salary of £15,000.

	Total £	Mr A £	Mr B £
Interest on capital	28,000	18,000	10,000
Salary	15,000		15,000
Balance (60: 40)	457,000	274,200	182,800
Adjusted partnership profit	500,000	292,200	207,800

2. Mr A, Mr B and Mr C have been in partnership for many years. The profit sharing ratios for 2010/11 and 2011/12 are as follows:

	2010/11	2011/12
Mr A	45%	40%
Mr B	40%	35%
Mr C	15%	25%

The adjusted partnership profits for the accounting period 31 December 2011 are £200,000. The profits are allocated between the partners as follows:

	Mr A £	Mr B £	Mr C £
Period ended 5 April 2011: 200,000 × 95/365 = 52,055 @ 45: 40: 15	23,425	20,822	7,808
Period ended 31 December 2011 200,000 × 270/365 = 147,945 @ 40: 35: 25	59,178	51,781	36,986
	82,603	72,603	44,794

If the partnership as a whole makes a profit, but as a result of the allocation **an individual partner receives a loss**, his loss figure must be reallocated between the profit-making partners, in proportion to the profit originally allocated to them. Similarly, if an individual partner is allocated a profit while the partnership as a whole makes a loss, his profit figure is reallocated between the loss-making partners. **2542** s 850 ITTOIA 2005

EXAMPLE Mr A, Mr B and Mr C have been in partnership for many years and share profits in the ratio 50: 30: 20. During the current tax year the adjusted profits of the partnership are £25,000. The partners receive the following salaries:

Mr A	£30,000
Mr B	£25,000
Mr C	£5,000

	Total £	Mr A £	Mr B £	Mr C £
Salary	60,000	30,000	25,000	5,000
Balance (50: 30: 20)	(35,000)	(17,500)	(10,500)	(7,000)
Adjusted partnership profits	25,000	12,500	14,500	(2,000)
Re-allocation of Mr C's loss				
12,500/(12,500 + 14,500) x 2,000		(926)		926
14,500/(12,500 + 14,500) x 2,000			(1,074)	1,074
Final allocation		11,574	13,426	–

Change of partnership accounting date

If the partnership changes its accounting date, then providing the change is valid for tax purposes (¶2436), the new date will be applied to the notional trade of each individual partner. One nominated partner may give notification to HMRC of the change of accounting date on behalf of the whole firm. **2548** s 853 ITTOIA 2005

C. Use of partnership losses

2550 Each partner can claim loss relief in the way that is most beneficial to him: there is no obligation for all the partners to claim relief in the same way. The reliefs available are the same as those for trading persons generally, except that there are some restrictions on limited and non-active partners (¶2530-¶2531).

1. Available reliefs

2552 **Individuals and trustees** Once a loss has been allocated to an individual partner or a trust, all of the loss relief claims available to a sole trader will be available. The following table summarises the claims that are available and where further information can be found.

Type of loss	Available relief	¶¶
Losses of an ongoing trade	Set against general income of the same year and/or the preceding year	¶2478
	Set against capital gains of the same year	¶2484
	Carried forward against subsequent profits of the same trade	¶2492
Losses in the first 4 years of a trade	Treated as losses of on ongoing trade, or carried back against general income of earlier years	¶2500
Losses on cessation of trade	Carried back against earlier profits of the same trade	¶2512

MEMO POINTS Where a partnership business is **transferred to a company** in return for a consideration which consists wholly or mainly of the allotment to the partners of shares in the company, the partners may set any partnership losses which were unused at the date of the transfer against income from the company (e.g. dividend income).

2554 **Bodies corporate** The following table summarises the claims that are available to a corporate partner and where further information can be found:

Available relief	¶¶
Set against general profits of the same year	¶1273
Set against general profits of previous 12 months	¶1274
Carried forward against future income	¶1278

2. Restrictions on relief

Limited and non-active partners

2556 ss 104 – 106 ITA 2007 Loss relief claims by limited or non-active partners (¶2530-¶2531) of a **trading partnership or LLP** (but not of a professional or vocational partnership or LLP) may be restricted.

The restrictions apply only to claims for **relief against other income or gains** of the partner (including for losses on commencement of a trade). There are no restrictions on the relief of losses against profits of the partnership's trade.

	Trading partnership		Trading LLP		
	Limited (individual) or non-active	**Limited (corporate)**	**Active individual partner**	**Non-active partner**	**Corporate partner**
Maximum loss that can be claimed [1]	Capital contribution [2,7] *less* Relief given in earlier years	Capital contribution [3,7] *less* Relief given in earlier years	Capital contribution [4,7] *less* Relief given in earlier years	Capital contribution [5,7] *less* Relief given in earlier years	Capital contribution [6,7] *less* Relief given in earlier years
£25,000 limit applies [8]	Yes [8]	No	No	Yes [8]	No

Notes
1. This is effectively the amount that the partner has at risk in the partnership.
2. Capital contribution means the net capital contributed by the partner as at the end of the tax year, plus any undrawn profits (accounting profits, not taxable profits) to which he is entitled.
3. Capital contribution means the net capital contributed by the company to the partnership at the end of the company's year, excluding any amounts it can withdraw if it wishes, plus any accounting profits (rather than taxable profits) to which the company is entitled but has not received.
4. Capital contribution is as note 3, plus the partner's liability on a winding-up of the LLP.
5. Capital contribution is as note 3, plus any actual amounts contributed on a winding-up of the LLP.
6. Capital contribution is the greater of (a) the amount in note 4 and (b) the company's liability on a winding-up of the LLP.
7. Contributions are excluded if their main purpose was to enable the partner to have access to partnership losses, or if:
– the contribution is financed by a loan which is either on less than arm's length terms or is to be repaid by another person (or by the partnership); or
– the contribution is to be reimbursed to the individual by another person (or by the partnership).
8. A single £25,000 limit applies to the total of all trading losses from all partnerships in which the individual was a partner of this type.

Where loss relief has been restricted, any excess can be **carried forward** against the partner's future share of partnership profits. **2557** s 83 ITA 2007

EXAMPLE Mr A contributes £15,000 to the ABC partnership but is not involved in the trade. The maximum loss he can claim in respect of the partnership's trade is £15,000. If a loss of £20,000 is allocated to him by virtue of the partnership profit share agreement, he must carry forward £5,000 of the loss until he contributes further capital to the partnership, or the partnership makes a profit against which the loss can be relieved.

3. Exit charge on disposal of a licence

A partnership trade may involve the use of a licence to exploit intellectual property (such as a patent or trademark). **2560** ss 805, 806 ITA 2007

If a partner has claimed loss relief against general income or gains for a loss related in any way to that licence which arose in the first four years of trading, there may be an **income tax charge** on the disposal of the licence by the partner, if he was a non-active partner (¶2530) in the year when the loss arose.

MEMO POINTS The **disposal of a licence** would include the following:
– revocation of a licence;
– disposal or giving up of a licence by the individual or partnership;
– disposal or giving up of a right to any income under an agreement that is related to a licence, by the partner or the partnership;

– any default in the payment of income to the partner or the partnership under the licence;
– change in the partner's entitlement to profits or losses; and
– dissolution of the partnership holding the licence.

2562 A tax charge arises if:
– the total losses claimed by the partner exceed the total profits charged to him in the period from the date he commenced trading to the end of the tax year when the charge arises; and
– any part of the consideration for the disposal would otherwise not be liable to income tax.
The charge arises when the claim is made or the consideration is received, whichever is earlier.

2564 The **taxable amount** is the lesser of:
– any disposal proceeds not already liable to income tax; and
– the amount by which the claimed losses exceed the cumulative profits.

EXAMPLE Mr X sets up the XYZ partnership which acquires the distribution rights to a new product. Mr X spends only 2 hours per week on average actively working in the trade. In Year 3, Mr X disposes of his rights under the distribution agreement for £70,000. The profits and losses attributable to Mr X are as follows:

	Profit/ (loss)
Year 1	(£80,000)
Year 2	£10,000
Year 3	£10,000

Mr X claims £80,000 of loss relief against other income in Year 1.
An income tax charge will be levied in Year 3 on £60,000, which is the lower of the:
– disposal proceeds not already liable to income tax (£70,000); and
– amount by which the losses exceed the cumulative profits (£60,000).
The balance of £10,000 will be taxable under the capital gains tax rules.

D. Special partnership situations

1. Spouses or civil partners in partnership

2578 Taking a spouse or civil partner into a partnership ensures the efficient use of personal allowances and basic rate bands, but the spouse's share of profits must be a genuine reflection of his contribution to the partnership. If not, HMRC may try to attack the arrangements under the settlement provisions (see ¶7353).

2. Non-trading income of a partnership

2580 s 854 ITTOIA 2005 The taxation of non-trading income from a partnership will depend on whether it is taxed income (that is, income which is received after deduction of income tax by the payer, or which carries a tax credit) or untaxed income (such as interest on government securities):
a. Taxed income The amount taxed is the actual amount received by the partnership during the tax year. This amount is apportioned between the partners according to their shares for the period of account in which the income arose.
b. Untaxed income is taxed using the same basis periods as trading income, and the profits will be allocated to the partners according to their interests during the basis period. This is done by treating untaxed partnership income as a second (notional) trade or profession which is deemed to commence when the individual becomes a partner and cease when he ceases to be a partner. All sources of untaxed income are therefore taxed together, and each

individual source is not separately subject to the usual commencement and cessation rules. Any overlap relief (¶2428) arising from this notional trade will be pooled.

EXAMPLE Mr A and Mr B have been in partnership for many years, preparing accounts to 30 September annually. Mr C joins the partnership on 1 January 2010. The profit sharing ratios are as follows:

	01/10/10 to 31/12/10	01/01/11 to 30/09/11
Mr A	55%	50%
Mr B	45%	40%
Mr C		10%

They received the following taxed and untaxed income:

	2010/11	2011/12
Taxed income (received 31 October)	£12,000	£13,000
Untaxed income	£18,000	£20,000

The income will be allocated as follows:

	Mr A £	Mr B £	Mr C £
Taxed income:			
2010/11			
12,000 @ 55: 45	6,600	5,400	
2011/12			
13,000 @ 50: 40: 10	6,500	5,200	1,300
Untaxed income:			
The income received during the year ended 30 September 2011 is calculated as follows:			
	£	£	£
01/10/10 to 31/12/10			
92/365 × 18,000 = 4,537 @ 55: 45	2,495	2,042	
01/01/11 to 05/04/11			
95/365 × 18,000 = 4,685 @ 50: 40: 10	2,342	1,874	469
06/04/11 to 30/09/11			
178/365 × 20,000 = 9,753 @ 50: 40: 10	4,877	3,901	975
	9,714	7,817	1,444
The income will be assessed in 2011/12 as follows:			
Current year basis	£9,714	£7,817	
Commencement rules for Mr C (2010/11):			
01/01/10 to 05/04/10			
95/365 × 1,444			£376

3. Reconstructions

Mergers

The result of a partnership merger will depend on whether the businesses carried on before the merger were similar in nature. 2590 s 860 ITTOIA 2005

If the new business is of a **similar nature** to both of the old businesses, there are three possible scenarios for the taxation of each of the partners:

– those **partners who remain with the new partnership** will be treated as continuing to trade, in which case the accounting dates will need to be brought into line. This will generally result in a change of accounting date for the partners of at least one of the partnerships;

– the **cessation rules** will apply to any **partners who are not part of the new partnership**; and

– the **commencement rules** will apply in the normal way to any **partners who join the new partnership**.

Whether one business is of a similar nature to another will depend on the facts of each case, but HMRC have indicated that disparity of size will not be a significant issue. In the merger of two accountancy firms into one new firm, for example, the new business will clearly be a succession of the old one. If two accountancy partnerships merged with a view to setting up a firm to develop software, the cessation and commencement rules would apply.

EXAMPLE Mr B and Mr C are partners of Partnership A, a long-established firm of solicitors, which prepares accounts for the year ended 30 September. Mr E and Mr F are partners of Partnership D which is also a long-established firm of solicitors, and which prepares accounts to 31 December. On 1 January 2011 the partners agree to merge the two partnerships and set up a new firm of solicitors called Partnership G which will prepare accounts to 30 September 2011.
Both partnerships prepare accounts to 31 December 2010.
Because the businesses of the old and new partnerships are similar in nature the cessation and commencement rules will not be applied. The assessments for the partners will therefore cover the following periods:

Mr B and Mr C (Partnership A)

2009/10	Year ended 30 September 2009
2010/11	Year ended 30 September 2010
2011/12	Year ended 30 September 2011

Mr E and Mr F (Partnership D)

2009/10	Year ended 31 December 2009
2010/11	Year ended 31 December 2010
2011/12	Change of accounting date – 12 months to 30 September 2011 (Gives rise to overlap relief from 1 October 2010 to 31 December 2010)

For the purposes of allocating profits in 2011/12, the profits of Partnership A from 1 October 2010 to 31 December 2010 are allocated to Mr B and Mr C, and the profits of Partnership D from 1 October 2010 to 31 December 2010 are allocated to Mr E and Mr F. Thereafter, the profits of Partnership G will be allocated between the four partners.

2592 Where the new business is **different in nature** to the old businesses, the cessation rules apply to all of the partners, and the commencement rules apply to all those who join the new partnership.

Demergers

2594 When an existing partnership divides into two or more partnerships, the main issue is **whether any of the new partnerships have succeeded to the business** of the old partnership. As a general rule, a succession will only be deemed to have taken place when one of the new partnerships is so large in relation to the other(s) that it is recognisably still the same business. In this case, that partnership will be deemed to continue. The partners in the other new partnerships will be subject to the cessation and commencement rules.

In **most demerger cases** the old partnership ceases and the cessation rules apply to the partners. The partners of the new partnerships are subject to the commencement rules.

There are no circumstances in which a partnership can be divided, and the business treated as continuing in both of the new partnerships.

MEMO POINTS If it is apparent that the demerger has taken place **solely for tax reasons**, HMRC are likely to suggest that the same trade is carried on after the demerger as before and the business will therefore be deemed to continue.

E. Administration of partnership tax

Partnership tax returns

When a business is carried on by two or more persons in partnership, HMRC may serve a notice requiring the submission of a **partnership tax return**. The notice may be served on the partnership as a whole or on one or more of the partners, but as a general rule one of the partners (the **nominated partner**) will be made responsible for the delivery of the partnership return to HMRC. **2598**

The notice requires a return to be made for a **relevant period**. This and the **filing date** depend on the composition of the partnership, as follows: s 12AA(4), (5) TMA 1970

Partnership make-up	Relevant period	Filing date
Entirely of individuals and/or trusts	The tax year	As for individuals (¶4484)
Entirely of bodies corporate	Partnership accounting period ending in the tax year	As for companies (¶2244)
At least one of each	Partnership accounting period ending in the tax year	Whichever of the above is later

A **partnership tax return** provides HMRC with enough information to determine the amount on which each of the individual partners will be taxable and includes the following: **2600**
- the names, addresses and tax references of anyone who has been a partner for all or part of the relevant period;
- details of each source of income received by the partnership;
- details of disposals and acquisitions of partnership property; and
- a declaration that the return is complete and correct to the best of the knowledge of the person signing it.

In addition to a partnership return, a **partnership statement** is required. This shows the income or losses from each source of income arising during the accounting period for business income, and during the tax year for other income. The amounts of income or losses declared should take account of any reliefs or allowances claimed and of any tax credits or income tax deducted. Deductions from income should also be included. **2602**

The statement must also show how the income, losses, tax deducted, tax credits and deductions from income are allocated between the partners. These figures are then used to determine the individual partners' taxable income.

Enforcement

The fixed penalty for **failure to submit a tax return** is the same as for individuals (¶4542) and is levied on each of the partners. Unlike the penalty for individuals there is no provision for the partnership return penalty to be reduced. **2604** s 93A TMA 1970

Appeals against penalties for late submission must be made by the nominated partner (¶2598) or his successor.

The tax-related penalties for submission of an **incorrect return or accounts** (¶4546) are tax related, and levied on the partners rather than the partnership. **2606** s 95A TMA 1970 Sch 24 FA 2007

A penalty will apply if a return or accounts have been submitted with **careless or deliberate errors**.

The **amount of the penalty** is calculated by applying a percentage to the potential amount of tax lost. If more than one partner wishes to **appeal** against the penalty, the partner responsible for submitting the partnership return must submit the appeal.

SECTION 3

Special trades

A. Qualifying carers

2608 ss 803 - 819 ITTOIA 2005 Sch 1 F(N° 3)A 2010 SI 2011/712

Profits from qualifying caring activities are **assessable** either as:
- trading income, if caring is the individual's trade or profession; or
- sundry income.

These rules apply to:
- foster carers; and
- shared lives carers.

The **computation of carers' income** is as for sole traders (¶2420), with the exception that where annual gross receipts of the foster carer do not exceed the individual limit, the profit for the year is deemed to be nil (no profit, no loss).

The **individual limit** is applied on a per-household basis and consists of a fixed amount of £10,000 plus:
- £200 per week for each child under 11 years of age; or
- £250 per week for each child aged 11 years or more.

Where total receipts **exceed the individual limit**, profits will be calculated on total receipts, less actual expenses and capital allowances. **Alternatively**, an election can be made to tax only those receipts in excess of the individual limit (with no relief for expenses or capital allowances). The election must be made by the 31 January following the tax year to which it relates (i.e. for the year 2011/12 the deadline will be 31 January 2014).

MEMO POINTS 1. If the income period for care receipts is less than a year, the £10,000 figure is reduced according to the number of days in the income period.
2. **Shared lives carers** are persons who:
- provide accommodation, care and support for up to 3 individuals who have been placed with them under a local authority shared lives scheme; and
- share their home and family life with such individuals.
3. For the income tax exemption for special guardians and kinship carers, available from 6 April 2010, see ¶2408.

B. Farmers

2609 The profits of farmers (and market gardeners) are calculated under the normal trading rules, with additional refinement due to the unique nature of the trade. The rules are designed to take account of the hardships affecting farmers, such as the problems caused by severe weather. In addition, the benefit of loss relief is limited to those carrying on the trade of farming on a commercial basis, rather than those for whom it is considered to be merely a hobby.

1. General principles

Activities

Farming is defined as the **occupation** of agricultural land in the UK wholly or mainly for the purposes of "husbandry", which also includes the following: 2610 s 996(1) ITA 2007
- hop growing;
- manuring land for crop production;
- cultivation of short rotation coppice;
- laying of grass;
- arranging for seasonal eating of grass by cattle; and
- operating stud farms.

Market gardening is defined as the occupation of land as a nursery, or a garden for growing sale produce. Market gardening is not farming, but most of the same rules apply. For the remainder of this section, farming will be taken to include market gardening unless stated otherwise.

All farming activities carried on by the same person **are treated as the same trade**. This is regardless of the fact that a farmer may own, for example, a dairy farm in Sussex and a sheep farm in Scotland which are managed separately. For tax purposes, they will be treated as a single trade. This means that profits and losses from all farm sources are aggregated. 2612 s 9 ITTOIA 2005

This rule **does not apply to market gardening**. Note also that farming carried on by a partnership is treated as a separate trade from any farming carried on by individual partners.

As a consequence, when **one farm is sold** and another subsequently purchased, there is no cessation of trade unless the interval between sale and acquisition is substantial. HMRC will consider each case on its merits, but a general guideline is that intervals in excess of 12 months will be considered substantial and therefore one trade will cease and another commence.

MEMO POINTS 1. In **share farming**, where the landowner contracts with a farmer to farm his land, both parties are treated as carrying on a farming business.
2. Farming within Europe is regulated by the imposition of **quotas**. Some quotas are designed to prevent overproduction of certain products (milk, potatoes) by charging levies whilst others encourage farmers to keep certain animals (ewes, suckler cows) by paying subsidies. All such quotas are capital assets and therefore subject to capital gains tax.

Overview of taxable profits

Farmers receive a large number of **grants**, subsidies and compensation payments, which are subject to the normal rules for computing trading profits. 2614 Tax Bulletin 14

The tax treatment depends on the terms of the particular agreement. Receipts which are intended to replace income are usually taxable.

Generally, animals (excluding those working on the farm) are accounted for as trading **stock**, at the lower of cost and net realisable value. The basis of valuation should be consistent, and should include direct costs. Although each animal should be valued separately, in practice, a valuation can include animals of similar type and age. 2616 BIM 55410

For stock which has been **bred or acquired before maturity**, an estimate of the actual production cost can be made by taking the following percentages of open market value:
- 60% for cattle; and
- 75% for sheep and pigs.

Alternatively, HMRC will sometimes accept another reasonable basis if this is more appropriate.

MEMO POINTS 1. **Direct costs** would include veterinary fees, feed and relevant labour.
2. **Open market value** should include the future anticipated income stream of the animal.
3. Where a farmer is accounting for his animals as trading stock, and his herd has been **compulsorily slaughtered** he can spread the compensation proceeds over the next 3 years, starting in the year of assessment after the year the slaughter took place. ESC B11 BIM 55180

2618 s 67 ITA 2007 As with all trades, **relief for losses** (¶2468) is only available where the trade is carried out on a commercial basis, with a view to realising a profit. However, the legislation for farming takes this one step further. If a farmer incurs losses (before relief for capital allowances) in 6 consecutive years, relief for the loss of the 6th year will not be available against general income of that year or the preceding year. The loss can however be carried forward against future profits of the same trade.

This **restriction does not apply** if the trade is being carried on with a reasonable expectation of realising a profit, and if circumstances are such that a profit could not have been expected to arise in the 6 years. This is designed to ensure that people who simply undertake farming as a hobby are not given relief, whereas genuine farmers trying to make a living are not penalised.

Summary of special reliefs

2620 There are special reliefs for farmers concerning both trading profits and capital assets.

Type of relief	Provision	¶¶
Trading profits	Herd basis [1]	¶2622
	Farmers' averaging relief [2]	¶2650
Capital items	Agricultural buildings allowance [3]	¶631
	Rollover relief for business assets [4]	¶6050
	Agricultural property relief [5]	¶6750

Note:
1. An election treats production herds as capital assets rather than stock.
2. Fluctuations in profits of consecutive years may be smoothed out.
3. Capital allowances are available in respect of expenditure on agricultural buildings and structures.
4. Rollover relief may be available in respect of chargeable gains accruing on the disposal of farm assets such as milk quota.
5. Relief is available to allow a family farm to be passed on with a reduced charge to inheritance tax.

2. Herd basis

2622 ss 111 - 129 ITTOIA 2005 ss 109 - 127 CTA 2009 As a **general rule**, farm animals are treated as stock, so any related expenditure or receipts will have a direct effect on the trading profits for each period. In addition stock must be revalued at the end of each accounting period.

Where a herd of animals has an enduring benefit to the farm, for example a production milk herd, it may be possible to make a herd basis election for it to be treated as a single capital asset, with the following implications:
- any profit on the eventual disposal of the herd is not taxable; and
- the set up costs and additions to the herd are not a deductible expense.

The **election** must be made early in the life of the herd (although no election can be made for the first year of trade) and once made is irrevocable. A sole trader, partnership or company may elect.

The herd basis election is also available to companies. Except as noted, all the same rules apply.

MEMO POINTS This election may be of particular benefit where the herd consists of **pedigree stock** which is expected to appreciate in value. However, animals kept mainly for show, racing, other competitive purposes or for working on the farm, cannot be included in a herd for these purposes.

Qualifying herds

2624 s 112 ITTOIA 2005 A production herd is one kept for produce, which includes the live young and other products such as wool, eggs and milk. Items that can only be obtained by slaughtering the animal are not produce for these purposes.

A herd can **consist** of any number of animals, including just one, or even a share in an animal. An election applies to all animals of the same species kept for the same produce, otherwise known as a herd of the same class.

MEMO POINTS Herd in this context is a **generic term**, encompassing the terms flock, gaggle and any other collection of animals.

In general, only **mature animals** can be part of the herd. The exception to this is animals such as acclimatised hill sheep, where immature animals which are bred and reared can only be kept with the herd, with the sole intention of replacing mature animals. 2626 ss 112-113 ITTOIA 2005

MEMO POINTS 1. Female animals are deemed to be **mature** when they produce their first offspring.
2. Where mature animals are acquired whilst **in calf**, the herd value is the acquisition cost reduced by the value of the unborn calf, and the value of the unborn calf is a trading expense.

An election **applies to** all herds of the same class owned by the farmer, whether past, present or future, and wherever maintained. For example, an election in respect of egg-laying hens applies not only to the flock owned at the time the election is made, but also to any previous or subsequent flocks of egg-laying hens. 2628

The only **exception** is where a herd is fully disposed of and an interval of at least 5 years elapses before a subsequent herd of the same class is acquired. In this case, the original election lapses and the farmer may decide whether to make a new election in respect of the new herd. s 125 ITTOIA 2005

EXAMPLE If a farmer has both a Friesian dairy herd and a Jersey dairy herd, these are the same class. Consequently, he cannot make the election solely in respect of the Jerseys; any election must relate to all his dairy cattle.
However, where a farmer keeps angora goats for their wool, and another herd of goats is kept for their milk which is made into cheese, these are different classes and a separate election can be made in respect of each herd.

Capital treatment of herds

General rule The tax treatment of expenditure on, or proceeds from, any specific animal will depend upon when, and why, it is acquired or sold. 2630

MEMO POINTS 1. Any references to animals being **sold** include animals which die (or are slaughtered), whether or not any monies are received on the death of the animal.
2. No **capital allowances** are available for herds.
3. Herds are exempt from **capital gains tax**.

Initial costs of the herd, and the cost of any subsequent additions, are not deductible expenses. 2632 s 114 ITTOIA 2005

Sale of individual animals Where an animal is a **replacement** for one in the herd which has been sold, the replacement cost is a deductible trading expense. Any proceeds for the departing animal are a taxable receipt. 2634 s 116 ITTOIA 2005

MEMO POINTS 1. To **identify** whether an animal has been replaced, it is customary to look at the overall size of the herd at the start and the end of the period of account. HMRC accept that an animal will be treated as a replacement if it is brought into the herd within 12 months of the related disposal.
2. Where the replacement animal is of a **higher quality** than the original animal, the deductible trading expense is restricted to the amount which would have been incurred on an animal of the same quality (i.e. the cost of replacement is allowable but not the cost of improvement). s 116(5) ITTOIA 2005
3. Where the replacement animal is of a **lower quality** than the original animal, and the original was **compulsorily slaughtered** under a disease control order, the trading receipt is limited to the deductible cost of the replacement. s 117 ITTOIA 2005

Where individual animals are sold and **not replaced**, a taxable receipt arises equivalent to any proceeds less the actual cost of the animals disposed. 2636 s 118 ITTOIA 2005

MEMO POINTS The **cost** of animals is the purchase price plus any costs incurred by the farmer in maturing the animal. If a farmer does not have **records** enabling him to identify the actual cost of the animals disposed, HMRC will accept the actual cost as a percentage of the sale proceeds (¶2616).

EXAMPLE Mr A started his herd in 1962 with an initial purchase of 60 cows costing £100 each. Over the years he maintained his herd by regularly replacing his stock with animals of the same quality. This year he decides to sell 10 of his cattle (without replacement), 5 of which were recently bought for £450 a head. The sale proceeds were £5,500.
The profit is calculated as follows:

	£
Proceeds	5,500
Cost of cattle recently purchased: 5 x 450	(2,250)
Net decrease in herd: 5 x 100	(500)
Profit	2,750

2638 s 115 ITTOIA 2005 **Increasing the herd** An increase is treated as an addition to the herd and is not a deductible expense.

Where animals are **transferred from trading stock** to a production herd (other than as a replacement), a trading receipt must be included in the accounts. This is to adjust for the fact that costs previously incurred in respect of the animal will have been deducted in the accounts, and the receipt should therefore be equivalent to the cost of breeding and rearing the animal.

MEMO POINTS To **simplify matters**, HMRC will generally accept a receipt equivalent to a percentage of the open market value (¶2616) at the time of transfer. However, if a farmer believes this to be inappropriate, HMRC will usually accept an alternative basis of valuation, such as actual cost, as long as it is consistently applied.

EXAMPLE Year 1: Mr A acquires a dairy herd of 30 mature cattle at a cost of £400 per head. He also acquires 15 calves at £300 per head. A valid herd basis election is made. The entries in the accounts in respect of the herd are as follows:

Trading account	No		£	**Capital account**	No		£
Calves	15	15 × 300	4,500	Cows	30	30 × 400	12,000
Allowable trading expense			4,500			C/fwd	12,000

Year 2: Mr A receives proceeds of £60 as a result of the death of 3 of his cows. He purchases replacements of same quality at a cost of £450 and decides also to purchase an additional 7 cows at the same price. 8 of the calves have reached maturity and are transferred into the herd. Mr A cannot identify the cost of the calves and decides to adopt the accepted percentage of market value of £350.

Trading account	No		£	**Capital account**	No		£
				B/fwd	30	30 × 400	12,000
Deaths	(3)		(60)				
Replacements	3	3 × 450	1,350				
				Additions	7	7 × 450	3,150
Transfers from stock	(8)	8 × (350 × 60%)	(1,680)		8	8 × (350 × 60%)	1,680
Trading receipt			(390)		45	C/fwd	16,830

2640 ss 119 - 123 ITTOIA 2005 **Reducing the herd** The tax treatment depends on the size of the decrease, so where the number of animals in the herd is reduced by:
- less than 20%, this is treated as a sale without replacement, which is taxable; and
- at least 20%, this is treated as a disposal of part of the herd, and the treatment depends on whether there is a further replacement within 5 years.

If at least 20% of the herd is sold within a year and **not replaced** within the next 5 years, no taxable profit or loss occurs.

Where at least 20% of the herd is sold within a year, and a **replacement occurs** within 5 years, the proceeds for the original animals will be brought into the trading account in the year in which the replacement is acquired.

2642

EXAMPLE Continuing the example at ¶2638:
Year 3: Mr A sells 5 cattle at a price of £600 per head. He also sells 3 calves at £500 and transfers the remaining 4 to the herd on reaching maturity, when the market value is £525 per head.

Trading account	**No**		**£**	**Capital account**	**No**		**£**
				B/fwd	30	30 × 400	12,000
					7	7 × 450	3,150
					8	8 × 350 × 60%	1,680
					45		16,830
Sales – cattle	(5)	5 × (600 – 400)	(1,000)	Reduction	(5)	(5 × 400)	(2,000)
– calves	(3)	3 × 500	(1,500)				
Transfers from stock	(4)	4 × (525 x 60%)	(1,260)	Additions	4	4 × (525 x 60%)	1,260
Trading receipt			(3,760)		44	C/fwd	16,090

Year 4: Mr A is forced to slaughter his entire herd due to disease. He receives compensation, but decides to quit farming rather than acquire a replacement herd. There is no trading entry, and his capital account is reduced to nil.

Capital account	**No**		**£**
B/fwd	25	25 × 400	10,000
	7	7 × 450	3,150
	8	8 × 350 × 60%	1,680
	4	4 × 525 × 60%	1,260
	44		16,090
Disposal	(44)		(16,090)
	Nil		Nil

Note:
1. An entry in the trading account would be required in respect of compensation for any **calves slaughtered**, but compensation for the herd is a capital receipt and therefore not taxable.
2. If, however, Mr A did decide to acquire a **replacement herd within 5 years**, the trading account would include a trading receipt equivalent to the proceeds for the slaughtered cattle less their original cost, and a trading deduction for the cost of the replacement herd.

Administration For **individuals** (including partnerships), the time limit for submitting a herd basis election is 12 months from 31 January following the end of the year of assessment in which the qualifying relevant period of account ends. 2644 s 124 ITTOIA 2005 s 122 CTA 2009

For **companies**, the time limit is 2 years after the end of the accounting period in which the herd is acquired.

MEMO POINTS 1. The **qualifying period of account** is the first period when the herd was kept.
2. A farmer who acquires a herd in his **commencement year** and is not in partnership, can only elect for the herd basis to apply in respect of his second year of trade onwards.
3. Where a farmer receives **compensation for the compulsory slaughter** of his animals due to disease, the time limit is extended as follows: s 126 ITTOIA 2005
– for individuals and partnerships, 12 months from 31 January following the end of the year of assessment in which the period of account in which the compensation is received, ends; and
– for companies, 2 years after the end of the accounting period in which the compensation is received.
The election is deemed to come into force at the beginning of the period in which the compensation is received. An adjustment will therefore be required to transfer those animals from stock to the production herd, although the accounts for earlier years will not be affected.

Once an election is made, it **applies from** the date the herd is acquired. Where the trade is transferred to a new owner, the new farmer will need to make a fresh election if he wants to continue the herd basis. This includes the situation where there is a **change of partners** in a farming partnership. 2648

The farmer is required to maintain adequate **records** such that any movement in the herd can be readily identified. Indeed it is recommended that a herd account be maintained and submitted to HMRC with the tax computation and accounts.

s 125 ITTOIA 2005 MEMO POINTS If a farmer previously made a herd election, but disposed of that herd **over 5 years ago**, and then subsequently acquires a new herd, the period of account in which the acquisition occurs is treated afresh, and any previous election ceases to have effect. Therefore the farmer can choose whether to make a herd election in respect of his new herd.

3. Averaging of farming profits

Purpose

2650 s 221 ITTOIA 2005 Under self-assessment there is a time lag between the making of profits and the payment of tax. A farmer, whose profits can fluctuate due to natural conditions, may be obliged to pay tax on high levels of profit at a time when his income (and hence his cash flow) is low. Averaging is designed to smooth out the tax payments for consecutive tax years.

Averaging relief is only available to individuals and partners, and not to companies.

MEMO POINTS Averaging also applies to the **intensive rearing** of livestock and fish.

Conditions for averaging

2652 s 222 ITTOIA 2005 Averaging is **available when**, looking at two consecutive tax years:
- the profits of one year are less than 75% of the profits of the other year; or
- a loss is sustained in one of those years.

The operation of the relief depends on the extent of the difference.

MEMO POINTS **Profits** for these purposes are the adjusted trading profits after deduction of capital allowances, but before any loss relief.

2654 s 222(4) ITTOIA 2005 Averaging **is not available for**:
- companies;
- the year of commencement of a trade;
- the year of cessation; or
- a year which precedes a year for which an averaging claim has already been made (i.e. if a claim has been made to average the profits of years 4 and 5, a claim cannot subsequently be made to average the profits of years 3 and 4).

MEMO POINTS 1. Averaging claims can be made for a pair of years where the **earlier** of those years has already been the subject of an averaging claim.
2. For **partners**, no averaging claim can be made in the year in which they start or cease to carry on a qualifying trade in partnership.

Calculation of averaged profits

2656 s 223 ITTOIA 2005 **Full averaging** is available where:
- the profits of one year do not exceed 70% of the profits of the other year; or
- a loss is incurred in one of the years in question.

Where full averaging applies, the profits for both years are simply added together and divided by two.

Where the result for one year is a **loss**, a nil profit is used in the calculation. Relief for the loss is given in accordance with the normal rules (¶2472 and ¶2618).

EXAMPLE Mr A is a farmer and has the following results:

Year	£
4	15,000
5	35,000
6	(2,750)

As the profits for Year 4 are less than 70% of the profits of Year 5 (i.e. 70% × 35,000 = 24,500), full averaging is available. If a claim to average the profits was made, the assessable profit for both Years 4 and 5 would be:

Year	£
4	15,000
5	35,000
Total profits	50,000
Average, assessable Years 4 and 5	25,000

For Years 5 and 6, full averaging is also available as a loss is sustained in one of the years. If a claim to average the profits was made (taking into account the revised profit for Year 5), the assessable profit for both Years 5 and 6 would be:

Year	£
5	25,000
6	–
Total profits	25,000
Average, assessable in Years 5 and 6	12,500

Relief for the loss of £2,750 would be available in accordance with the normal rules.

The calculation for **partial averaging** is slightly more complicated, and uses the following formula: 2658 s 223(4) ITTOIA 2005

$$3(H - L) - 0.75H$$

where:
- H is the higher profit; and
- L is the lower profit.

The amount found by the formula is then:
- deducted from the higher profit; and
- added to the lower profit,

to find the assessable profits for each year.

EXAMPLE Mr B is a farmer and has the following results:

Year	£
4	15,000
5	10,750

As the profits for Year 5 are more than 70% of the profits of Year 4 (70 % x 15,000 = 10,500) but less than 75% (75 % x 15,000 = 11,250), partial averaging is available.

If a claim to average the profits was made, the assessable profits for Years 4 and 5 would be calculated as follows:
Applying the formula:
3 × (15,000 – 10,750) – 11,250 = 1,500

This amount is then deducted from the profit of Year 4:

	£
Year 4	15,000
Deduct	(1,500)
Averaged profits, assessable for Year 4	13,500

The amount of £1,500 is added to the profit of Year 5.

	£
Year 5	10,750
Add	1,500
Averaged profits, assessable for Year 5	12,250

Subsequent years

2660 s 224 ITTOIA 2005 Once an averaging claim has been made in respect of a tax year, the averaged profits **are used** for all income tax purposes.

In particular, this means that when considering the subsequent year's profits, the averaged profit is used in determining whether an averaging claim can be made. The example at ¶2656 shows how this operates.

Claims

2662 s 224(5) ITTOIA 2005 Averaging relief must be claimed in writing within 12 months from 31 January following the end of the second tax year in question, on the tax return (or amended tax return) for that year.

s 225 ITTOIA 2005 If, after an averaging claim has been made, an **adjustment** is required to the profits of either year involved, the averaging claim is invalid. A further claim can be made, using the newly adjusted profits, and the time limit for such a claim is 12 months from 31 January following the tax year in which the adjustment was made.

2664 Claims are **voluntary**, and although a farmer meets the criteria for a claim, he may prefer not to make a claim in respect of a specific pair of years. This does not affect the right to make claims for any subsequent years.

EXAMPLE Taking the facts from example in ¶2656, ignoring loss relief, Mr A's averaged profits assessable were:

Year	£
4	25,000
5	12,500
6	12,500

If Mr A chose not to make an averaging claim for Years 4 and 5, the calculation for Years 5 and 6 would be:

Year	£
5	35,000
6	–
Total profits	35,000
Average, assessable in Years 5 and 6	17,500

This would give the following assessable profits, which may be preferable:

Year	£
4	15,000
5	17,500
6	17,500

2666 Sch 1B para 3 TMA 1970 An averaging claim does not result in a **revision** of the self-assessment for the earlier of the 2 years in question. When a claim is made, the claimant should recalculate the tax liability for the earlier year as though the profits had been increased or reduced as a result of averaging. The amount by which the tax liability would increase or reduce is then added to, or deducted from, the tax liability for the second year, which can result in a repayment.

Interest on any further payment or repayment runs from the due date of the second year.

EXAMPLE Mr C is a farmer, who is a higher rate taxpayer, and he made the following profits from his farming trade:

Year	£
4	50,000
5	10,000

If an averaging claim is made, profits of £30,000 will be assessed in each year.

Mr C's self-assessment for Year 5 would be:

	£
Taxable farming trade profits	30,000
Tax payable (say)	12,000
Reduction in tax for Year 4 (50,000 – 30,000) @ 40%	(8,000)
Tax liability for Year 5	4,000

C. Literary and artistic income

1. General principles

Where an author or artist is carrying on a trade, any profits will be assessed as trading income, and an averaging claim may be available. Where the activities do not amount to a trade (for example, writing occasional magazine articles as a hobby), any profits will be assessed as sundry income. 2668

Throughout this section, unless otherwise specified, references to literary works and authors can be read as applying to:
- works of art and artists;
- designs and designers;
- musical works and composers; and
- dramatic works and playwrights.

MEMO POINTS The work must be created personally, or by a person who is in partnership.

If the author of a literary or artistic work disposes of it by way of **gift**, whether complete or incomplete, the consideration to be brought into account is the market value of the asset, irrespective of the amount of the consideration received (if any): see ¶2422. 2670 s 172A ITTOIA 2005

2. Averaging of literary and artistic profits

Averaging is **available** where, looking at two consecutive tax years: 2672 ss 221 - s 223 ITTOIA 2005
- the trading profits of one year are less than 75% of the trading profits of the other year; or
- a loss is sustained in one of those years.

The legislation is the same as that which applies to farmers (¶2650), and the rules of computation are identical.

Averaging is **not available** for: 2674 s 222 ITTOIA 2005
- companies;
- the year of commencement of the activity;
- the year of cessation; or
- a year which precedes a year for which an averaging claim has already been made (e.g. if a claim has been made to average the profits of years 4 and 5, a claim cannot subsequently be made to average the profits of years 3 and 4).

3. Copyright income

Amounts received for the exploitation of copyright, whether by way of a licence fee or a fee for the assignment, are taxable as income from the trade, even where the amount is a lump 2678 sum. The income is **assessed** as income of the accounts year in which it is received, subject to an averaging claim (¶2672).

MEMO POINTS If the **trade has already ceased**, any payments subsequently received are taxable as sundry income (¶2466).

2680 Under the Copyright, Designs and Patents Act 1988, various **categories of work can be protected** by copyright. The copyright generally protects the author for a specified period and the author can grant licences to other persons to use the copyright or assign the copyright during the period of its validity.

The **author** is generally the person creating the material in question.

The **period** for which copyright endures depends on the nature of the material to which it applies.

ss 12 – 15 CDPA 1988 SI 1995/3297

The following table sets out the various categories of copyright.

Material	Duration
Original literary, dramatic, musical and artistic works	Author's lifetime plus 70 years or 50 years from creation if computer generated [1, 2]
Sound recordings, broadcasts and cable programmes	50 years from first release or transmission
Films	70 years from the death of the last of the principal director, screenplay or dialogue author, or the composer of music specially created for and used in the film [1, 2]
Typographical arrangement of a published edition [3]	25 years from publication [4]

Note:
1. For **films and broadcasts**, the author is generally the person with overall control of the project and not the individual technicians.
2. If the **identity** of the individuals involved in the creation of a literary, dramatic, musical or artistic work, or a film is unknown, the duration of any copyright is 70 years from first publication.
3. For the **typographical arrangement** of published works, it is the publisher who is protected and not the author.
4. **Publication** means the first occasion on which a work is published, performed, exhibited, released or transmitted as the case may be.

4. Literary awards

2684 BIM 50710 Numerous **competition** prizes and awards are open to authors and it is generally accepted that entering competitions is a normal part of such trades. Therefore, where an author has in any way solicited the prize, the prize will form part of the income from the trade.

However, in certain circumstances, a prize will not be taxable and each case must therefore be considered on its facts. In particular, a literary prize which is unexpected and perhaps awarded as a matter of professional distinction is not taxable.

MEMO POINTS Where the competition **entry is made by the publisher** rather than the author, the author is generally considered to have solicited the prize if his permission was sought before a competition entry was made.

2686 BIM 50715 Awards may be made to authors by one of the **Arts Councils**, which provide financial support in a number of ways. The Arts Council should advise the author whether the award is taxable. As a general rule, awards which allow for a period of training or development of talents will not be taxable, whereas awards to supplement income or meet specific expenses will be taxable.

D. Lloyd's underwriters

1. General principles

Individual Lloyd's underwriters are known as Names. Each individual Name is a trader operating in his own right, but he will be a member of a number of syndicates through which underwriting activities are carried out. 2688

MEMO POINTS 1. There are many detailed provisions which relate to acting as a Lloyd's underwriter, but only the main income tax provisions are dealt with here.
2. A Name accepts a share of the risk which the syndicate underwrites. The syndicate is actually run by the managing agent who appoints a professional underwriter. The Name himself appoints a member's agent who advises on which syndicates to join.
3. An individual can only become a Name if he is over 21, and has sufficient financial backing. He is required to maintain a minimum level of personal funds at Lloyds. A Central Fund is also maintained which requires a certain amount to be paid by the Name annually, and payments can be made out of the Fund on behalf of the Name in certain situations.

The **accounting year at Lloyd's** is the calendar year, so the accounting year ending on 31 December 2011 is known as "the 2011 underwriting account". Each account is normally kept open for 2 more years, so the 2008 account closed on 31 December 2010. 2690

An account may, however, be left open for a further year (or more), because the liabilities remaining at the end of the period cannot be estimated with any certainty. This is known as a **run-off account**.

MEMO POINTS 1. Because underwriting accounts are kept open, the **time limits** for claims and elections are generally longer for underwriters than for other taxpayers.
2. In the case of a run-off account, **provisional accounts** will be available when the account should have normally closed, and further annual accounts will be completed when the year is closed or outstanding claims re-insured. A Name **cannot resign** while any syndicates of which he is a member are in run-off.

2. Taxation of Lloyd's income

Income and gains from Lloyd's underwriting may come from various sources, and these can be divided into those derived from membership of syndicates and those arising from investments which the Name has used to create his fund at Lloyd's. All Lloyd's income and expenses should be entered on the special Lloyd's pages of the tax return. 2692

a. Syndicate profits

Income and gains from membership of syndicates

Underwriting profits are charged to tax as **earned income** under the income from trade provisions. Essentially, profits represent the excess premium income, compared to the cost of claims and expenses. 2694

Profits are **assessed** on a "distribution" basis. This means that an assessment is issued in the year in which the profits are declared. Profits are declared in the year following that in which the account is closed, so the profits for the 2008 account were closed on 31 December 2010, will be declared in 2011, and assessed in 2011/12.

MEMO POINTS 1. Underwriting profits are classified as earnings for **pension contribution** purposes.
2. Names are liable to **National Insurance** as self-employed persons.

2696
ss 171 - 176 FA 1993

Each Name is treated as carrying on a **single trade of underwriting**, rather than a trade for each syndicate in which he participates. The various types of income are summarised in the following table.

Element	Detail	Recognised for tax purposes	Reference
Syndicate trading profit	Premiums received less costs	Underwriting year basis	s 172 FA 1993
Syndicate investment income	Arising on syndicate investments in the premium trust fund (¶2716)	Underwriting year basis [1]	s 172 FA 1993
Gains and losses from premium trust funds (¶2716)	Arising on the disposal of fund assets, and also on the annual revaluation of fund assets at 31 December	Underwriting year basis [2]	ss 171, 174 FA 1993
Payments from the Central Fund [3]	Payment made on behalf of Name	Cash basis [4]	s 172 FA 1993
Net withdrawals or releases from the Special Reserve Fund (SRF)	The SRF is made up of sums set aside each year by a Name out of profits to meet future losses (¶2704)	Underwriting year to which they relate [5]	s 175 FA 1993 Sch 20 FA 1993
Compensation receipts [6]	Including the following: – amounts awarded as damages as a result of court action; – recoveries of legal costs arising from litigation; and – any sums paid in out of court settlements	Cash basis [4]	s 172 FA 1993
Stop-loss recoveries	Where a payment is made out of an insurance policy as a result of losses	Distribution basis [7]	BIM4150

Note:
1. For every calendar year, the investment income is spread over the 3 open years. Gains and losses are combined, and are also spread over the 3 open years. For example, income received in 2011 will be spread over 2009, 2010 and 2011.
2. For every calendar year, the gains and losses are combined, and spread over the 3 open years.
3. HMRC can agree that all Central Fund payments and repayments can be ignored for tax purposes.
4. This means that income is recognised in the tax year in which the calendar year ends. For example, income received in January 2011 is taxed in 2011/12.
5. There are special rules for amounts received on ceasing to be a Name (¶2706).
6. Where the compensation is received by a member who has resigned and who is no longer a member of a syndicate, it will be assessed as sundry income in the year of receipt. The member may elect for the receipt to be treated as having been received on the date that trading ceased, providing the compensation is received within 6 years of that date.
7. That is, in the same accounting period as the profits of the syndicate year to which the recovery relates.

2698 Income directly relating to the syndicate (comprising the first three entries in the table), must be **reported** in the syndicate's self-assessment return.

Deductions from underwriting profits

2700
ss 172, 178 FA 1993
SI 2001/1757

When calculating the trading profits, in addition to the usual deductions (¶120), the following expenses are also relieved:

Element	Detail
Annual subscription [1]	Usually included in the syndicate profits provided by the underwriting agent
Stop-loss premiums	Relief is given on a distribution basis [2]
Reinsurance premiums	Where premiums are paid for the purposes of closing the account for the underwriting year [3]. The relief is restricted to an amount that is sufficient to meet the anticipated liabilities and a percentage of any excess is clawed back

Element	Detail
Bank guarantees and letter of credit fees[4]	The annual cost of maintaining such a facility is allowed as a deduction, as are any costs associated with increasing it, on a cash basis[5]
Expenses associated with Lloyd's members associations	Subscriptions to the Association of Lloyd's members and the cost of the League Tables and Syndicate Results are an allowable deduction from underwriting profits[6]
Personal quota share premiums	Where one Name makes an arrangement for another Name to take over some or all of his rights or liabilities for any syndicate of which he is a member. Relief is given on a cash basis[5]
Estate Protection Plan payments[7]	Intended to provide immediate unlimited cover against underwriting losses arising after death. Premiums are allowed as a deduction in the year in which they are paid rather than the year which is covered under the policy
Interest on loans to fund underwriting	Interest paid personally by a Name is allowed as a deduction on a cash basis where it relates to borrowing to fund: – losses; – cash calls; – accounts at Lloyd's; or – stop loss premiums or other Lloyd's personal expenses
Net transfers to the SRF	Not obligatory and relief is limited (¶2704)
Other expenses associated with Lloyd's[8]	Allowed as a deduction from underwriting profits on a cash basis: – member's agent commission and salary; – accountancy fees relating to Lloyd's profits but not for other work such as other business interests or inheritance tax planning; and – litigation fees in connection with actions for compensation or damages in respect of underwriting losses and subscriptions to action groups

Note:
1. When a new Name joins Lloyd's, a separate deduction may be made for the annual subscription, where it is paid personally. The entrance fee payable by a new Name is not allowable.
2. That is, in the same accounting period as the profits of the syndicate year to which the recovery relates.
3. The reinsurer must be a member of the syndicate to which the premium is payable, and entitled to receive the premium.
4. The initial cost of setting up a bank guarantee or letter of credit to provide the deposit at Lloyd's is not allowed as a deduction.
5. This means that income is recognised in the tax year in which the calendar year ends. For example, income received in January 2011 is taxed in 2011/12.
6. Subscriptions to other associations may be allowable, and the organiser of the relevant association should be contacted for further information. In addition subscription to Names action groups may also be deductible.
7. This allows the Lloyd's deposit to be released as early as possible to allow the Name's estate to be distributed.
8. Other expenses relating specifically to Lloyd's underwriting may be allowed, but will be judged on individual circumstances.

Where expenses are incurred personally by the Name, they are deductible in the tax year in which the calendar year of payment ends (this is known as the **cash basis**). For example, an expense incurred in 2011 is given relief in 2011/12. 2702

EXAMPLE Mr A is a Lloyd's Name. His 2011/12 tax return will include the following:
- distributions from the 2008 accounts of the syndicates;
- compensation receipts from the 2011 calendar year; and
- expenses which he incurred personally in the 2011 calendar year.

Special Reserve Fund (SRF)

Where a Name makes a **payment into** the SRF it is treated as an expense in calculating underwriting profits for the year. 2704 Sch 20 FA 1993

The payment must be made by the earlier of:
- 31 October of the year of distribution; and
- the date on which the Name receives the balance of profits.

Payments made into the SRF are **limited** to the lower of:
– 50% of the syndicate profit for the year; and
– the amount necessary to bring the value of the fund up to 50% of the overall premium limit.

MEMO POINTS **Syndicate profit** for these purposes is the amount by which aggregate profits exceed aggregate losses for the year. Tax adjusted profits are not relevant.

2706 The normal rule is that **withdrawals** are taxed as trading receipts in the underwriting year to which they relate. Exceptionally, any balance paid over on cessation (whether as a result of death or otherwise) will be treated as received after the end of the relevant underwriting year.

MEMO POINTS 1. Where the cessation occurred as a result of the death of the member, the **relevant underwriting year** is the year immediately preceding the tax year in which the Name died. In all other cases the relevant underwriting year is the underwriting year immediately preceding the final year of assessment.
2. Withdrawals must be made out of the SRF:
– to cover cash calls;
– to cover syndicate losses;
– to eliminate excess amounts (the value of the fund may not exceed 50% of the overall premium limit); and
– on cessation.

b. Income from personal investments held at Lloyd's

2708 s 176 FA 1993 Funds which must be maintained at Lloyd's (other than the SRF) are called **ancillary trust funds**, comprising the personal reserve fund, and Lloyd's deposit.

Income is assessed on a cash basis, in the calendar year of receipt. For example, interest received on 31 January 2011 arose in the calendar year 2011, and will be taxed in 2011/12.

2710 Income, such as interest and dividends, from personal investments used to create funds at Lloyd's, will be taxed as **earned trading income** and will therefore be taxed at the same rate as other underwriting profits.

2712 A distinction will be drawn however, between income from personal funds and other underwriting profits for the purposes of **calculating the income tax liability** for the year. This is necessary to identify those investments that carry non-refundable notional tax (in particular, dividend income received after 6 April 1999 and stock (or scrip) dividends received at any time).

EXAMPLE In 2011/12 Mr A had the following income:

	£	
Employment	28,000	(PAYE – £6,500)
Interest (net)	4,000	
Dividends (net)	1,800	
Lloyd's income	6,000	

The Lloyd's income was made up of the following:

	£
Underwriting profits	
Syndicate profits	5,550
Stop loss premiums	(550)
Income from personal funds	
Interest (net)	100
Dividends (net)	900

The income tax calculation will be as follows:

	Non-savings £	Savings £	Tax £
Earned income:			
Employment	28,000		6,500
Lloyd's underwriting (5,550 – 550)	5,000		0
Income from personal funds (100 x 100/80 + 900 x 100/90)	1,125		125
Savings income:			
Interest (4,000 x 100/80)		5,000	1,000
Dividends (1,800 x 100/90)		2,000	200
	34,125		
Less: Personal allowance	(7,475)		
Net taxable income	26,650	7,000	7,825
Tax thereon:			
Non-savings income:			
26,650 @ 20%		5,330	
Savings income			
5,000 @ 20%		1,000	
Dividend income			
2,000 @ 10%		200	
		6,530	
Tax deducted at source:			
PAYE	6,500		
Lloyd's underwriting (interest only)	25		
Interest	1,000		
Dividends	200		
		(7,725)	
Tax repayable		(1,195)	

1. The income from non-savings is in excess of £2,440 and therefore the 10% savings band does not apply.
2. The £100 tax credit attached to the dividend from personal funds at Lloyd's is not refundable although it could have been utilised against a tax liability, if one had remained, after credit had been given for the other tax deducted at source.

3. Taxation of Lloyd's gains

A Name at Lloyd's may become liable in respect of chargeable gains arising from either: **2714**
- capital appreciation of investments acquired with the syndicate's premium income;
- actual disposal of syndicate assets; or
- capital gains on the disposal of personal investments used to provide the deposit or create other funds at Lloyd's.

Type of gain/(loss)	Tax treatment	¶¶
Change in value of syndicate's assets in premium trust fund	Trading income	¶2716
Disposal of syndicate's assets in premium trust fund	Trading income	¶2716
Disposal of personal investments held as Lloyd's funds	Capital gain	¶2718

Each Name holds a **premium trust fund** into which premiums received by the member (or by the member's agent on behalf of the member) are paid. The fund is then available for **2716** s 174 FA 1993

the payment of re-insurance premiums, claims and other syndicate expenses. Each premiums trust fund is made up of the following:
- a sterling fund;
- a US dollar fund; and
- a Canadian dollar fund.

All of the investments held in the fund are **revalued** on 31 December each year and any resulting capital appreciation will be chargeable to tax as earned trading income in the same way as syndicate profits. Where the investments depreciate, loss relief will be available.

Similarly **actual disposals** of assets will be taxed in the same way.

2718 s 176 FA 1993 Where gains arise from the disposal of **personal investment** assets held in an ancillary trust fund, a Name may be liable to capital gains tax.

The Name is treated as absolutely entitled to the assets forming part of his ancillary trust fund, so any gains or losses will therefore be amalgamated with non-Lloyd's gains for the purpose of computing the Name's capital gains tax liability for a particular tax year. Any transfers of assets between a Name's personal portfolio and an ancillary fund at Lloyd's is not chargeable to capital gains tax.

MEMO POINTS 1. Gains and losses are calculated in accordance with the normal rules (¶5220) but the assets held in an underwriter's ancillary trust funds or special reserve funds are treated as held separately, and not pooled with any assets held in a personal capacity.
2. **Rollover relief** (¶6050) is available in relation to the sale of syndicate interests.
Sch 20A FA 1993, SI 2006/112 3. Where a Name **transfers his underwriting business** to a company (or a limited liability partnership) in exchange for an issue of shares (¶6179), he can postpone the capital gain (net of losses) arising. The chargeable gain held over is deducted from the acquisition cost of the shares issued to the Name. The Name must own over 50% of the company's ordinary share capital and also control it.

4. Underwriting losses

Calculation

2720 A syndicate will make a loss where the expenses and claims which it settles exceed its premium and investment income. In order to calculate his underwriting loss, a Name will need to aggregate the:
- results from all the syndicates of which he is a member (including the change in value of syndicate assets, and any capital gains on disposals);
- personal investment income from funds at Lloyd's (other than the SRF); and deduct
- any expenses personally incurred.

Use of losses

2722 s 172, s 174 FA 1993 Underwriting losses are first of all **mitigated** by a withdrawal from the SRF. Any loss then remaining is a trading loss and may therefore be relieved in the usual ways as outlined below:

a. underwriting losses may be offset against the **total income and gains** of the same and/or the preceding year in the same way as for other trades (¶2476);

b. an underwriting **loss sustained in the first 4 years** of assessment may be set against the total income of the 3 years immediately prior to the year in which the loss arose, taking the earliest year first (¶2504);

c. unused underwriting losses may be **carried forward** indefinitely against future underwriting profits (¶2492); and

d. terminal loss relief (¶2518) may be claimed when a member dies or resigns from Lloyd's and a loss arises in the final 12 months. The loss may be carried back against underwriting profits of the 3 years prior to cessation. The exception is where the member is in run-off syndicates, in which case he is still deemed to be trading.

MEMO POINTS 1. Losses **carried forward** can be set against income from investments in funds at Lloyd's, as this is treated as trading income.
2. In the case of a **run-off account**, the loss is treated as relating to the year in which the account would normally have closed. For example, if a 2005 syndicate is running-off and sustains a loss in 2010, this is relieved in 2011/12, because it is treated as if it were a 2008 account.
3. If a Lloyd's Name **transfers his underwriting business** to a company (or a limited liability partnership), he can set his underwriting losses carried forward against remuneration, dividends or other income derived from the company. The Name must own over 50% of the company's ordinary share capital and also control it. Sch 20A FA 1993 SI 2006/112

CHAPTER 3

Income from UK land and property

OUTLINE ¶¶

SECTION 1

Types of property income

Property business income

Income generated from UK land and property (hereafter referred to as property) is charged to tax as income of a **property business** if it consists of income arising from the exploitation of any estate, interest or rights in or over land (including buildings, structures and land covered with water). **2735** ss 264, 266 ITTOIA 2005 s 205 CTA 2009

An individual has only one property business, which includes all his activities for generating income from land in the UK. For these purposes, the UK excludes the Isle of Man and the Channel Islands.

Income arising from the following sources is **specifically included**:
– licences to occupy or use land;
– ground rents; and
– the granting of a right to an individual to use a caravan or houseboat in one particular location.

Income from property is, with the exception of furnished holiday letting (¶2777), treated as an **investment income** profit or loss, rather than trading income. This means that:

- different rules apply to the relief of losses (¶2472); and
- individuals cannot treat the income as eligible for pension contributions.

For details of the tax treatment of property situated in the UK but owned by a non-UK resident, see ¶4318. For overseas furnished holiday lettings, see ¶2777+; for other overseas land or property, see ¶4312.

ss 548-549, CTA 2010

MEMO POINTS Dividends received by shareholders from a **Real Estate Investment Trust** (REIT) are treated for income tax purposes as profits from a UK property business. There is no tax credit (¶2821), although basic rate tax may have been deducted at source (¶2846). This notional property business is separate from other businesses, so that losses from other rental activities cannot be set off against REIT distributions..

2736
s 267 ITTOIA 2005

Property receipts are **outside the scope** of property business income if they are:
a. exempt from tax (income from the occupation of commercially managed woodlands); or
b. taxed as trading income:
- farming or market gardening;
- profits or rent charged in connection with mining, quarrying, fishing etc;
- rental receipts in respect of tied property;
- rent in connection with easements; and
- profits from running hotels and guest houses.

SECTION 2

Basis of assessment

Individuals and sole traders

2737
s 275 ITTOIA 2005

Profits arising in a tax year form the basis of assessment for property income.

Generally, where an individual prepares **accounts which do not coincide with the tax year**, the results from one or more sets of accounts are apportioned to arrive at a result for the tax year in question. Strictly, apportionment should be made on the basis of the number of days in the respective periods. In practice, HMRC may accept another reasonable time based apportionment (such as weeks or months) provided that the approach is applied consistently across the different periods.

PIM 1101

MEMO POINTS All accounts prepared for property income must be prepared in accordance with accepted accounting principles, which means that the accruals basis must be adopted. By concession, individuals whose gross rental receipts in the tax year do not exceed £15,000 may prepare accounts on the cash basis. If adopted, the cash basis must be used consistently year on year.

EXAMPLE Mr A has a property business, and prepares accounts to 31 December each year. Recent accounts have shown the following results:
31 December 2010 – £8,000
31 December 2011 – £6,500
31 December 2012 – £7,500

The profits will be allocated to tax years as follows:

		£	£
2010/11			
6 April – 31 December 2010 (270 days)	270/365 × 8,000	5,918	
1 January – 5 April 2011 (96 days)	96/366 × 6,500	1,705	
			7,623
2011/12			
6 April – 31 December 2011 (270 days)	270/366 × 6,500	4,795	
1 January – 5 April 2012 (95 days)	95/365 × 7,500	1,952	
			6,747

Partnerships

Partnerships are assessed on property income arising in the accounting period ending in the tax year in question. This is the same as the basis for trading income (¶2528). 2738

MEMO POINTS The ownership and letting of property jointly by two or more individuals does not itself create a partnership for tax purposes. Unless a partnership exists for other business purposes, there is no need to register as a partnership, and each joint owner's share of rental income is reported in the land and property section of his self-assessment return. PIM 1030

SECTION 3

Taxable profits

To determine taxable profits, all taxable income from property is pooled and a deduction made for any allowable expenses. Assessable property income is **calculated** in the same way as trading income (¶2420), with the exception of the following specific rules: 2739 s 272 ITTOIA 2005

Subject	Details	¶¶
Taxable income	Dilapidation receipts	¶2741
	Lease premiums	¶2743
	Reverse premiums	¶2760
Deductible expenses	Specified revenue expenditure	¶2765
	Capital allowances for dwelling houses	¶2767
	Interest paid	¶2767

MEMO POINTS The rules in the remainder of this chapter also apply for **corporation tax** purposes, except for those relating to interest and loss relief, references to capital gains tax, and matters specifically stated to relate to individuals. s 210 CTA 2009

A. Dilapidations

Payments by a tenant to the landlord in respect of dilapidations (repairs) will be taxable as either a capital receipt or rental income. 2741 PIM 2020

If, following the tenant's payment, the **landlord sells the property**, or occupies it himself, the receipt will be treated as capital.

If the **landlord does not occupy or sell** the property (e.g. re-lets the property) the payment may be regarded either as:
– compensation to the landlord based on a deemed reduction in the rental income the property can now command; or
– a contribution for the cost of actually carrying out the repairs.

Such contributions are assessable in the year they are received and the corresponding expenses are allowed when they are incurred. *Raja's Commercial College v Gian Singh* [1976]

Alternatively, the tenant can pay a sum to the landlord towards the cost of carrying out the repairs. This will not be treated as income, but the landlord can only get a deduction for the net expenditure (i.e. cost of repairs less tenant contribution).

B. Lease premiums

2742 Lease premiums are payments made by incoming tenants in consideration for the grant of the lease. The tax treatment of both the grantor and the incoming tenant will depend on the nature of the payment.

1. The grantor of the lease

2743 Premiums (including deemed premiums) received on the grant of a lease are taxed in one of two ways, depending on the term of the lease:
- if the lease is for a term of 50 years or more, a **long lease**, the premium is treated as a capital receipt and subject to capital gains tax (¶5690); or
- if the lease is for a term of less than 50 years, a **short lease**, part of the premium is taxed as rental income, with the balance subject to capital gains tax.

Premiums for short leases

2745 s 277 ITTOIA 2005 s 217 CTA 2009

To calculate the amount of premium that will be treated as rental income, the following formula is used:

$$P - ((P \times (Y\text{-}1) \times 2\%))$$

where:
- P is the premium received; and
- Y is the number of complete years of the lease.

EXAMPLE Mr A lets a property on a 40 year lease and receives a premium of £16,000. The proportion of the premium taxed as rent is £3,520, calculated as follows:
16,000 – ((16,000 × (40 – 1) × 2%)) = £3,520

MEMO POINTS If a premium is payable in **instalments**, a landlord can elect to pay the tax in instalments, spread over the shorter of 8 years or the period over which the premium is payable.

2746 ss 303 - 305 ITTOIA 2005 ss 243 - 245 CTA 2009

Special provisions exist to prevent landlords **manipulating the length of the lease** term so as to gain a tax advantage. HMRC will look to the terms of the lease, and if there is a clause in the lease or other agreement by which the lease:
- is likely to **terminate before** the expiry of the lease, the lease term will deem to end at that earlier date. For example, if a 60 year lease at a commercial rent includes a clause whereby the rent can be doubled after 10 years have expired, it would be likely that the lease term will end after the 10 years have expired;
- is likely to **continue beyond** the expiry of the lease, the lease will be deemed to end at the later date. For example, a 20 year lease with an excessive rent charged, containing a clause permitting the lease to continue for a further 20 years at a reduced rent, would be likely to be deemed to end after the 40 years have expired; or
- of the **same premises** is likely to be granted to the tenant or person connected with him on the expiry of the original lease, the lease term will be deemed to end at the expiry of the further lease. For example, a 10 year lease, granted to Mr B, containing a clause that on expiry a further lease will be granted to Mrs B will be likely to be deemed to end on the expiry of Mrs B's lease.

Deemed premiums

2747 In some specific situations, a landlord will be deemed to have received a premium, and the normal calculation will be required.

These rules may apply in the following situations:
- tenant improvement obligations;
- lump sum payments;

- sale with a right to reconveyance or leaseback; and
- assignment of a lease granted at an undervalue.

Tenant improvement obligations

Where a landlord imposes an obligation on the tenant to undertake improvement work, and forgoes income in return, the landlord will be assessed on a deemed premium. The deemed premium will be valued as the amount by which the requirement to undertake the improvement work increases the value of the landlord's reversionary interest (valued at the date of the commencement of the lease). **2749** s 278 ITTOIA 2005 s 218 CTA 2009

EXAMPLE Mr A granted a 10 year lease, with a requirement that, in the first year, the tenant would undertake specific improvement works, in return for which the tenant was charged no rent for that year. The improvement works increased the value of the landlord's reversionary interest by £100,000 from the value at the date the lease commenced.

Mr A is therefore assessable on the deemed premium as follows:
100,000 – ((100,000 × (10-1) × 2%)) = 82,000
Therefore £82,000 will be taxed as rental income in the year the lease is granted.

Lump sum payments

The following lump sum payments will be taxable as premiums in the usual manner in the year in which the sum is paid: **2751** ss 279-281 ITTOIA 2005 ss 219-221A CTA 2009
- payments in lieu of rent;
- payments for the surrender of the lease; and
- payments for the variation or waiver of the lease terms.

For the purposes of calculating the deemed premium, the **duration of the lease** is the period from the year the payment was made to the end of the original lease term or, where applicable, the period for which the variation/waiver is effective.

EXAMPLE Mr B granted a 10 year lease, containing a clause whereby the tenant could pay £20,000 in Year 5 in lieu of rent for the remaining term of the lease.

Mr B will be assessed on the deemed premium as follows in the year of receipt:
20,000 – ((20,000 × (5-1) × 2%)) = 18,400

Sale with right to reconveyance or leaseback

A vendor will be taxed on a deemed premium if he sells a property with a clause giving him (or a person connected with him (¶5570)) the right within 50 years to re-acquire the freehold, or to be granted a leasehold interest in the property, unless the leaseback is granted within 1 month of the sale. **2753** ss 284-286 ITTOIA 2005 ss 224-226 CTA 2009

The deemed premium is calculated as follows:

a. if the **reconveyance** takes place:
- less than 2 years after the sale, the assessable amount is the excess of the original sale price over the repurchase price; or
- two years or more after the sale, the assessable amount is the excess of the original sale price over the repurchase price, reduced by 2% for each year in the intervening period (except the first);

EXAMPLE Mr C sold his property in Year 1 for £500,000, with a right that he could repurchase it in Year 3 for £475,000. Mr C will be assessed on the deemed premium in Year 1 as follows:
Amount of deemed premium:
(500,000 – 475,000) = £25,000
Assessable amount:
(25,000 – (25,000 × (3-1) × 2%)) = £24,000

b. leaseback – the assessable amount is the excess of the original sale price over the sum of any lease premium and the value at the date of the sale of the freehold of the reversionary interest immediately after the lease has begun to run. It will usually be necessary to agree a value with the District Valuer.

EXAMPLE The facts are as above, but Mr C sold the property with a clause giving him a right to be granted a lease of the property in Year 3 for a premium of £100,000. After liaising with the District Valuer it was agreed that the value of the reversionary interest was £300,000. Mr C will be assessed on the deemed premium as follows:
Amount of deemed premium:
(500,000 – (100,000 + 300,000) = £100,000
Assessable amount:
(100,000 – (100,000 × (3-1) × 2%)) = £96,000

MEMO POINTS 1. Where the sale contract **does not fix the date** of reconveyance or leaseback, and the price varies with the date, the calculation is first performed using the lowest possible contractual price. When the reconveyance or leaseback takes place, the calculation can be recomputed and a repayment claimed. HMRC cannot increase the original charge.
2. Any agreement for a leaseback would have to be **in writing** – if not, and the purchaser later granted a lease to the vendor under bona fide commercial terms, there would be no charge.
3. See ¶4060 and ¶4062 for **anti-avoidance provisions** in connection with sale and leaseback transactions.
4. See ¶5744 for details of the **capital gain implications** on a subsequent disposal.

Assignment of a lease at an undervalue

2755
ss 282 - 283 ITTOIA 2005
ss 222 - 223 CTA 2009

Where a short lease is granted at an undervalue and a profit is made on a **subsequent assignment** of the lease, the assignor will be treated as having received a premium, calculated in the usual manner, on the smaller of:
– the amount forgone by the landlord (i.e. the additional amount which the original grantor of the lease could have charged but did not); and
– the profit made on the assignment of the lease (i.e. any profit made in excess of the amount paid for the original lease or, where applicable, the amount paid for the last assignment).

For the purposes of calculating the deemed premium, the **duration** of the original lease is used.

EXAMPLE Mr D granted a 10 year lease in Year 1 to Mr E. A premium of £50,000 would have represented a market rate, but in fact only £10,000 was charged. The amount forgone by the landlord is therefore £40,000. (£50,000 – £10,000)

In Year 3 Mr E assigns the lease to Mr F for £35,000. Mr E would be chargeable as follows:

	£	£
Consideration received		
Smaller of:		
Mr E's profit: amount received	35,000	
Less: premium paid	(10,000)	
Profit on assignment to Mr F	25,000	
Amount forgone	40,000	
Lower of profit and amount forgone		25,000
Assessable as property income:		
25,000 – (25,000 × (10-1) × 2%)		20,500

In Year 5, Mr F assigns the lease to Mr G for £50,000. Mr F would be chargeable as follows:

	£	£
Smaller of:		
Mr F's profit: amount received	50,000	
Less: premium paid to Mr E	(35,000)	
Profit on assignment to Mr G	15,000	
Balance of amount forgone (£40,000 – £35,000)	5,000	
Lower of profit and amount forgone		5,000
Assessable as property income:		
5,000 – (5,000 × (10-1) × 2%)		4,100

2. The tenant

The lessee may be entitled to **relief** for the premium paid in the following situations on the grant of a subsequent sublease of the property, or where the property is used for business purposes. 2756

Grant of sublease

Relief may be available for the premium paid under the head lease if the **tenant sublets the property**. The calculation of the relief, which depends on whether the tenant charges a premium for the sublease, is as follows: 2757 ss 287 - 289 ITTOIA 2005 ss 227 - 229 CTA 2009

a. where **no premium is charged**, an annual deduction is available to the tenant subletting the property in computing his taxable profits. The deduction is the part of the premium on which the landlord is assessed to income tax, divided by the length of the head lease in years.

EXAMPLE Mr A grants a 25 year lease on a property to Mr B for rent of £10,000 p.a. and a premium of £5,000. After 2 years Mr B sublets the property to Mr C at a rent of £15,000 p.a.
Mr A is taxable on the premium as follows:
(5,000 – (5,000 × (25-1) × 2%)) = £2,600
On granting the sublease, Mr B is entitled to an annual deduction of £104 (2,600/25) from the rental income. The rent of £10,000 paid by Mr B to Mr A is also deductible from the rental income received.

b. where a **premium is charged**, a deduction is available to the tenant subletting the property in computing his income tax liability on the premium. The deduction is the amount of the premium assessable to income tax on the landlord under the superior interest (i.e. the head lease), multiplied by the number of years in the sublease over the number of years in the head lease.

EXAMPLE The facts are as above, but Mr B sublets the property to Mr C for 10 years at a premium of £4,000, and annual rent of £12,000.
Mr B is taxable as follows:

		£
Premium 4,000 – (4,000 × (10 – 1) × 2%)		3,280
Less:		
$\left(\frac{\text{Years of sublease}}{\text{Years of head lease}}\right)$ × taxable element of head lease premium (amount assessed on Mr A in the above example)	$\left(\frac{10}{25}\right)$ × 2,600	(1,040)
Premium assessable on Mr B		2,240

MEMO POINTS 1. The deduction **cannot create a loss** in the hands of the tenant subletting the property and will be restricted accordingly. If the deduction exceeds the assessable amount of a premium, the unrelieved balance is deducted from rental income over the period of the sublease. If the sublease is granted part way through a tax year the deduction available against rental income should be pro-rated.
2. The deduction will be **apportioned** on a just and reasonable basis if, for example, only a proportion of the property is sublet.
3. This calculation applies equally to a **deemed premium** arising on payments made for the variation or waiver of a lease (¶2751) or an assignment of a lease at an undervalue (¶2755).

Property used for business purposes

Where the lessee uses the leased premises as part of a property business, for example offices from which a property business is run, he will be entitled to a deduction from his trading profits equal to the amount of the chargeable premium, spread over the length of the lease. 2758 ss 291 - 295 ITTOIA 2005 ss 231 - 235 CTA 2009

EXAMPLE Mr A grants a 40 year lease to Mr B for a premium of £16,000. The chargeable amount of this premium on Mr A is £3,520 (16,000 – (16,000 × 40 – 1) × 2%). Mr B (who uses the premises for his property business) will be allowed a deduction of £88 a year (3,520/40) in computing the assessable profits of his property business.

MEMO POINTS 1. Where only **part** of the leased premises is used for a property business, a just and reasonable apportionment will be made.
2. The lessee is also entitled to an **annual deduction** against profits for any rent paid under the lease. Again, if only part of the premises is used for business purposes a just and reasonable apportionment is required.
3. The above rules also apply for any **trade, profession or vocation** (¶2423).
s 71 FA 2009 4. If accommodation is provided for **use by an employee** in a property held on a lease of 10 years or less, which was entered into (or extended) on or after 22 April 2009, the value of the lease premium must be taken into account when working out the benefit in kind charge (see ¶3261).

Interaction with capital allowances

2759 s 4 CAA 2001 If relief is given for part of a premium in the profit and loss account, that element must be excluded from any capital allowances computation.

MEMO POINTS 1. This applies to the **incoming tenant** if the property has fixtures attached, and the landlord and tenant have jointly elected that the lessee is entitled to any plant and machinery allowances.
2. It will apply if the **landlord was not entitled to the allowances**, and the assets have not previously been used for the purposes of the lessor's trade, because the lessee may be entitled to claim capital allowance on the fixtures.

C. Reverse premiums

2760 In certain circumstances, a landlord (or person connected with him (¶5570)) may make a payment (known as a **reverse premium**) to a tenant in order to persuade them to take a lease on a property. This may arise where, for example, a new retail development is being constructed, in which case a reverse premium may be paid to a major department store in the expectation that its presence would attract shoppers to the centre and encourage other retailers to rent property within the development.

1. Recipient

2761 ss 99 - 101 ITTOIA 2005 s 98 CTA 2009 Reverse premiums are **taxed as revenue receipts** in the hands of the recipient. They will generally be assessed as property income, unless the payment is to a trader, in which case it will be included as a trading receipt.

The reverse premium provisions **do not apply** to:

a. payments to an individual, in relation to premises occupied or to be occupied as his only or main residence;

b. inducements which do not represent an outlay of money, such as reduced rent for a set period or an initial rent-free period;

c. payments which form part of the sale consideration in a sale and leaseback arrangement; and

d. payments which reduce the recipient's qualifying expenditure for capital allowances purposes.

2762 BIM 41075 Only payments that actually represent an **outlay of money** are taxed as a reverse premium. These include:
- lump sum cash payments;
- contribution towards tenant's costs (e.g. start-up costs or fit-out costs);
- assumption by the landlord of a tenant's existing obligations (e.g. under an existing lease); and
- payment of cash by indirect means (e.g. writing off a loan).

MEMO POINTS 1. Generally, if the works are for the **benefit of the lessee**, such as the installation of fixtures and chattels to allow the lessee to properly use the property, then any contribution by the landlord is likely to be a reverse premium.
2. If **costs are incurred by the landlord** in preparing the property to be let, or a tenant takes on a partially completed building and finishes it with a contribution from the landlord, there is no reverse premium because the landlord is benefiting from the expenditure, either by an increase in the value of the reversion, or an increase in rental generating potential.

Reverse premiums are generally taxed in the period or periods in which they are **recognised in the accounts**, in accordance with accepted accountancy principles. **2763** s 102 ITTOIA 2005 s 99 CTA 2009

However, the whole of a reverse premium will be taxed in the period in which the transaction is entered into, if the parties to the transaction are connected (¶5570), and the terms of the transaction are **not on an arm's length basis**.

If the transaction is not at arm's length and the **trade has not yet commenced**, the reverse premium will be brought into charge in the period in which the trade commences.

MEMO POINTS In accordance with accepted accountancy principles (UITF 28), a reverse premium receipt is spread on a straight line basis, usually over the term of the lease.

2. Payer

If a reverse premium is paid by: **2764** BIM 41060
- the **landlord** of a property which is part of a property letting business, the payment is treated as a capital payment; or
- a **builder or developer** in the course of his trade, it will normally be treated as an allowable revenue deduction.

D. Revenue expenditure

The principles discussed at ¶120 – ¶193 also apply to property businesses. In addition, where a rental property is **temporarily empty** (for example, between tenancies), expenditure incurred during a void period may still be deducted provided it relates wholly and exclusively to the rental business. **2765** ss 272, 315 ITTOIA 2005 SI 2007/3278

MEMO POINTS 1. The rules relating to **pre-trading and post-cessation expenditure** (¶140 and ¶160) apply equally to the operation of a property business, except that pre-trading expenditure is only deductible if incurred not more than 6 months before the commencement of the business.
2. Capital expenditure on the construction of a **sea wall or embankment** to protect the premises against flooding is deductible as a revenue expense spread over 21 years. This deduction is subject to the condition that the same person is carrying on the property trade and incurring the expense.

Energy saving allowances

An energy saving allowance of up to £1,500 per let dwelling per tax year is available until 5 April 2015 to landlords who install any of the following items in any part of a building containing a dwelling house: **2766** s 312 ITTOIA 2005 SI 2007/3278
- loft or cavity wall insulation;
- solid wall insulation;
- draught proofing or insulation for hot water systems; and
- floor insulation.

The allowance is **not available** in respect of:
- a property in the course of construction;
- furnished holiday lettings or Rent a Room properties; or
- where the person incurring the expenditure does not have an interest in the property, even if they are in the course of acquiring an interest.

If expenditure is **incurred by two or more persons**, or if a property is **jointly or separately owned** or subject to differing estates or interests, a just and reasonable apportionment of the expenditure will be made between the persons concerned.

Any **contribution** from any other person towards the expenditure is to be deducted from the amount that may be claimed, whether or not the contributor will be making a claim.

s 251 CTA 2009 MEMO POINTS 1. The energy saving allowance is available to **corporate landlords**.
2. If expenditure is incurred on a building which includes both residential and commercial units, a deduction is available to the extent that the expenditure relates to the residential units. Any apportionment of expenditure should be on a just and reasonable basis. The maximum available deduction is £1,500 per dwelling.
3. If expenditure is incurred on a building containing **more than one dwelling**, the cost should be apportioned. The relief is only available on the portion of the cost allocated to each dwelling, up to the limit of £1,500 per dwelling. If, for example, dwelling 1 has been allocated costs of £2,000, and dwelling 2 has been allocated costs of £1,000, the deductions available are £1,500 for dwelling 1, and £1,000 for dwelling 2. The excess over the £1,500 limit cannot be transferred from dwelling 1 to dwelling 2.

E. Capital allowances

2767
s 15(3) CAA 2001
ESC B47
PIM 3200

No allowance is available for plant and machinery used in a **dwelling house**. Instead, the landlord of a property which is **let furnished** can claim one of the following:
– wear and tear allowance (an annual allowance of 10% of the gross rents received less any council tax and water rates paid); or
– renewals allowance (the entire initial cost of an asset is non-deductible, but the cost of any replacement asset is deductible, less any scrap value or sale proceeds of the items replaced).

MEMO POINTS 1. Whichever **basis** is adopted should be applied consistently to all furnished properties which are let.
2. Capital allowances for plant and machinery used **other than in a dwelling house** are available as for trading income (¶270). This includes furnished holiday lettings.
3. From a date to be announced, the **wear and tear allowance** is to be reformed so that it becomes conditional upon the energy efficiency of the let property.

F. Interest

2769
s 272 ITTOIA 2005
BIM 45690

A revenue deduction is permitted for interest paid in respect of a loan incurred **wholly and exclusively** for the purposes of the property business (including interest paid to non-residents). It is not necessary to match a loan with a particular property so, for example, interest on a loan taken out to purchase property A would continue to be deductible even after property A was sold, provided the property business continued.

Interest on any loan up to the value of the property when it first entered the property business is regarded as incurred wholly and exclusively for the purposes of the business.

EXAMPLE Mr A bought a private residence 10 years ago for £125,000 with a mortgage of £80,000. He decides to move overseas to live and work, and to let the property (now worth £375,000) whilst he is absent from the UK. He may take out an additional mortgage of up to £295,000 for any purpose, and interest paid on the total mortgage will be an allowable expense of the property business.

SECTION 4

Loss relief

There are **two methods** of loss relief available: 2771
- carry forward for offset against future income from the property business; or
- offset against total income for the current and/or following year.

Where a loss is incurred, the **general rule** is that the loss (after deduction of capital allowances) is carried forward and set against income from the property business for the following year. Any excess which cannot be offset in that year is carried forward to subsequent years until it is fully utilised. 2773 ss 118, 119 ITA 2007

MEMO POINTS When the **property business ceases**, any unrelieved losses brought forward will be lost. It is therefore important to correctly identify the point at which the business has ceased. As a rule of thumb, a property business will be deemed to have ceased when the last let property is disposed of or starts to be used for some other purpose.

EXAMPLE Mr A has a property business and results for recent years are as follows:
Year 1 – loss – £22,000
Year 2 – profit – £5,000
Year 3 – profit – £11,000
Year 4 – profit – £12,000
The assessable profit is as follows:

		£	Loss memo (£)
Year 1	Loss	0	22,000
Year 2	Profit	5,000	
	Less: loss b/fwd	(5,000)	(5,000)
	Assessable profit	Nil	
			17,000
Year 3	Profit	11,000	
	Less: loss b/fwd	(11,000)	(11,000)
	Assessable profit	Nil	
			6,000
Year 4	Profit	12,000	
	Less: loss b/fwd	(6,000)	(6,000)
	Assessable profit	6,000	
	Loss c/fwd		Nil

A claim may be made to set all or part of the **loss against the total income** of the year or the following year only where a loss includes capital allowances and/or allowable agricultural expenses (e.g. deductible maintenance, repair, insurance or management expenses attributable to an agricultural estate). 2775 ss 120, 121 ITA 2007

The maximum loss which can be offset in this way is the lowest of:
- the property trade loss for the year;
- the net capital allowances of the property business for the year (i.e. capital allowances less any balancing charges); or
- if the business has incurred relevant agricultural expenditure, the amount of allowable expenditure; and
- the total income for the year, after deducting any property trade losses brought forward and any relief under this provision in respect of the previous year.

MEMO POINTS A loss attributable to the annual investment allowance (¶360) cannot be offset against general income if it arises from or in connection with tax avoidance arrangements entered into on or after 24 March 2010. s 127A ITA 2007

EXAMPLE Mr B incurs a loss in his property business of £10,000, which includes capital allowances of £3,000. His total other income of the year is £21,000. The amount of loss which can be offset against general income for the year is the lowest of:

	£
The loss	10,000
Net capital allowances	3,000
Total income	21,000

Therefore £3,000 can be offset in the year, with the balance carried forward to the next year.

SECTION 5

Furnished holiday lettings

Treatment as a trade

2777 ss 322, 327 ITTOIA 2005 ss 264, 269 CTA 2009 ss 241 - 241A TCGA 1992 s 189 FA 2004

When a rental business consists of the letting on a commercial basis of furnished holiday accommodation (including caravans) in the UK, the activity is generally **treated as trading**. All of a person's furnished holiday letting activities constitute a single trade, which is separate from any other property business activities.

Furnished holiday letting treatment also applies to properties within the **European Economic Area** (EEA). This treatment has been accepted informally by HMRC for some years, and becomes statutory:
- for individuals, from 2011/12 onwards; and
- for companies, for accounting periods beginning on or after 1 April 2011.

Treatment as a trade has the following consequences:
1. The **computation** of assessable profits or relievable losses is as for other property income, except that a separate capital allowances pool must be maintained for plant and machinery used for furnished holiday lettings.
2. The taxable profits or losses are **treated as** trading profit and losses. The consequences of this treatment are that:
a. profits are treated as earnings and are therefore eligible for pension contributions; and
b. the following capital gains tax reliefs are available:
- rollover relief (¶6050);
- gift relief (¶6095);
- relief for loans to traders (¶6008); and
- entrepreneurs' relief (¶6035).

Qualifying conditions

2778 ss 323 - 326 ITTOIA 2005 ss 265 - 268 CTA 2009

The following conditions must be satisfied:
- the property must be let on a commercial basis with a view of profit;
- the tenant must be entitled to the use of the furniture;
- the property must satisfy minimum periods of availability for letting and actual letting (see below); and
- periods of longer-term occupation (see below) do not total more than 155 days..

These conditions must all be satisfied for a **fixed period of 12 months**, which is usually the tax year, unless the accommodation was first let or ceased to be let part way through the tax year, in which case the 12 month period is either:
- the 12 months from the date the letting commenced; or
- the 12 months ending with the date the letting ceased.

The **minimum periods** of availability and actual letting are as follows:

Period	Availability condition[1]	Letting condition[2]
2011/12 and earlier (individuals)[3] Accounting periods beginning before 1 April 2012 (companies)	140 days	70 days
2012/13 and later (individuals) Accounting periods beginning on or after 1 April 2012 (companies)	210 days	105 days

Notes
1. The minimum period for which the property must be available for commercial letting to the general public.
2. The minimum period for which the property was commercially let to the general public.
3. These limits also apply to a basis period which straddles 6 April 2011.

A period of **longer-term occupation** is one in which the same person occupies the property for more than 31 consecutive days. Such periods do not count towards the required minimum period for the letting condition. Occupation by the owner himself outside the holiday season is ignored for this purpose. PIM 4110

MEMO POINTS 1. As a result of the rules, it is possible to let the property for just under 7 months to the same person, and for the property to still qualify as a furnished holiday letting. This would not be uncommon in areas which have defined holiday seasons, and where a reduced rent is charged over the winter to ensure occupation.
2. Where the owner has **more than one property** which would be treated as furnished holiday lettings but for the actual letting period rule, the number of days actually let can be averaged. UK lettings must be averaged separately from EEA lettings. Claims for averaging must be made in accordance with the usual self-assessment procedures.

EXAMPLE Mr A let the following properties in 2011/12:

Property	Days available	Days let	Eligible as furnished holiday let?
1 (existing property)	210	195	Y
2 (existing property)	110	95	N
3 (existing property)	150	65	N (but see below)
4 (acquired 1 June)	150	60 (plus 30 days to 31 May)	Y (see below)
5 (sold 30 June)	30 (plus 175 days in the previous tax year from 1 July)	5 (plus 55 days in the previous tax year from 1 July)	N (but see below)

Property 1 – qualifies as it meets both the 140 day and 70 day tests.
Property 2 – does not qualify as it does not meet the 140 day test (averaging is only possible where the 70 day test is not met).
Property 3 – does not qualify as it does not meet the 70 day test, but it may be included in an averaging claim.
Property 4 – the 12 month period commences on 1 June and, as the property was let for a further 30 days after the end of the tax year, this equates to total days let in the 12 month period of 90 days, therefore satisfying both the 70 and 140 day tests.
Property 5 – the 12 month period ends on 30 June, and taking into account the days let and days available in this 12 month period, it would not qualify as it did not meet the 70 day test, but it may be included in an averaging claim.

Averaging claim:
It is possible to include all four or fewer properties in an averaging claim in order to achieve the desired result. If all four properties are included, the average days let for each property would be:
(195 + 65 + 90 + 60)/4 = 102.5
meaning that all four properties would qualify as furnished holiday lettings.

Period of grace

2779
s 326A ITTOIA 2005
s 268A CTA 2009

Once a property has qualified as a furnished holiday letting in one period, the owner may **elect** to treat it as continuing to qualify for up to two subsequent periods even if it no longer meets the letting condition (¶2778), provided that:
- there is still a genuine intention to continue the letting activity in those periods; and
- the other qualifying conditions continue to be fulfilled.

This election:
- cannot be made if an averaging election (¶2778) has been made for the same period; and
- must be made in the first period for which the letting condition is not met.

The period referred to is the tax year for individuals, and the accounting period for companies. Although this legislation was introduced by the Finance Act 2011, it applies to individuals for tax years from 2010/11 onwards, and to company accounting periods beginning on or after 1 April 2010.

Losses

2780
ss 117, 127, 127ZA ITA 2007
ss 65, 67A CTA 2009

A loss arising from a furnished holiday business can **only be relieved by carrying it forward** against future income from the same furnished holiday lettings business. This restriction applies:
- for **income tax**(¶2492), to 2011/12 and subsequent tax years; and
- for **corporation tax** (¶1278), to accounting periods beginning on or after 1 April 2011.

For this purpose, UK and EEA furnished holiday letting activities are treated as separate businesses.

MEMO POINTS 1. For tax years up to and including 2010/11, an individual could claim relief for losses from furnished holiday lettings against general income and gains (¶2475), and make a claim for terminal loss relief (¶2512) in appropriate circumstances.
2. For accounting periods beginning before 1 April 2011, a company could claim relief for losses from furnished holiday lettings against total profits (¶1273).

SECTION 6

Other special situations

Rent a Room relief

2781
ss 784 - 802 ITTOIA 2005

Rent a Room relief is available where an individual lets furnished accommodation in his own main UK residence. How the relief applies depends on the level of letting income and/or profit arising, as follows:

a. if the **gross letting income is below £4,250** (before any deduction for expenses etc), the profits or losses are treated as nil. Any unrelieved losses brought forward are simply carried forward to later years, but any current year losses would be lost. An election for the exemption not to apply can be made (for example, an individual may wish to utilise losses brought forward, or current year losses);

b. if the **gross letting income is in excess of £4,250** (before any deductions for expenses etc), the net income will be taxed in the normal way. However, an election can be made for only the gross income in excess of £4,250 to be taxed. If the income is from two or more sources, the taxable excess amount is apportioned between the properties on the basis of the rental income received from each property.

MEMO POINTS 1. **Elections** either to apply or disapply the relief or to be taxed on the profits in excess of £4,250 must be made in writing by the first anniversary of 31 January following the end of the tax year. For example, claims for Rent a Room relief for the tax year ended 5 April 2012 must be made by 31 January 2014.

2. Taxpayers who are **living abroad** or are **occupying job related accommodation** will not normally be entitled to Rent a Room relief.
3. Any income an individual receives in respect of letting a room in an **overseas residence** will not prevent the individual being eligible for Rent a Room relief in respect of letting a room in his UK residence. This provision covers the scenario where an individual's main residence changes in a tax year.
4. HMRC do not accept that letting a room as **office accommodation** qualifies for relief; the accommodation must be residential.
5. The individual limit of £4,250 is halved if **more than one person** lets rooms in the same house or there is third party letting of any kind in the premises.
6. If the letting is a **trade**, balancing charges are added to the letting income to determine whether the £4,250 limit has been reached.

EXAMPLE Mr A and Mr B share a house, taking in lodgers on a regular basis. The annual rental income is as follows:

	Year 1		Year 2		Year 3	
	Mr A	Mr B	Mr A	Mr B	Mr A	Mr B
	£	£	£	£	£	£
Gross rental income	3,800	1,900	2,400	1,200	4,400	2,200
Allowable expenses	(550)	(550)	(2,200)	(2,200)	(1,100)	(1,100)
Net rent	3,250	1,350	200	(1,000)	3,300	1,100

The tax treatment will be as follows:

Year 1:
Mr A's share of gross rent is more than one half of £4,250 (£2,125). He can either be taxed on £3,250 or he can elect to be taxed on the gross rents which exceed £2,125 (i.e. £1,125). It would be beneficial to make an election for this year.
Mr B's share of gross rent is less than one half of £4,250 (£2,125), consequently his share of profits can be treated as nil.

Year 2:
Mr A's share of gross rent continues to exceed £2,125. He can either be taxed on £200 or he can elect to be taxed on the gross rents which exceed £2,125 (i.e. £275). It would be beneficial for him to withdraw the election in force from Year 1, so that he is taxed on the lower amount in Year 2.
Mr B's share of gross rent continues to be less that £2,125, consequently his share of profits can be treated as nil, but he would not get any relief for the current year loss. It would therefore be beneficial for him to make an election for the exemption not to apply – the election having effect for Year 2 only.

Year 3:
Mr A's share of gross rent exceeds £2,125. He can either be taxed on £3,300 or he can elect to be taxed on the gross rents which exceed £2,125 (i.e. £2,275). It would be beneficial to make an election for this year.
Mr B's share of gross rent now exceeds £2,125. He will therefore either be taxed on £1,100 or he can elect to be taxed on the gross rents which exceed £2,125 (i.e. £75). This would be further reduced to nil by the utilisation of brought forward losses from Year 2. It would be beneficial to make an election for this year.

Surplus business accommodation

Where a trader receives rental income from the letting of surplus business accommodation, this may be **included in the trading profit** calculation. This is only possible where the: **2785** s 21 ITTOIA 2005 s 44 CTA 2009
- premises are partly used for the trade and partly let;
- let accommodation is temporarily surplus to requirements; and
- rental income is comparatively small.

MEMO POINTS For **income tax** purposes, accommodation is temporarily surplus to requirements if:
- it has either been used for the purposes of the trade, or acquired, within the last 3 years;
- it is intended to use the premises for the purposes of the trade at a later date; and
- the accommodation is let, or a licence to occupy is granted, for less than 3 years.

Rent factoring

2787 ss 43A-43G, ss 758-776 CTA 2010

Rent factoring is an arrangement whereby a person obtains a lump sum payment (the finance amount) in return for selling a rental income stream. The finance amount is, in effect, a loan which is repaid by the regular rental payments and is calculated to take into account an interest charge over the term of the agreement.

Arrangements **entered into on or after 6 June 2006** are covered by the rules for structured finance arrangements (¶4064). Arrangements **entered into before 6 June 2006** are dealt with by the former rent factoring provisions, which treat the finance amount as property business income for the chargeable period in which the agreement is made.

The following arrangements are **excluded** from the rent factoring provisions, as the amount received is taxed under other provisions:
- arrangements under which a lease is granted (but see ¶2789 for anti-avoidance provisions);
- where the finance amount is taken into account in determining trading profits;
- sale and reconveyance or sale and leaseback arrangements; and
- where the pricing of the arrangement depended on the anticipated availability of capital allowances on the land.

2789

As an **anti-avoidance provision**, where a lease is artificially interposed over property in what is essentially a rent factoring arrangement in order to sidestep the provisions, any premium charged for the lease will be taxed under the rent factoring provisions (i.e. the premium is effectively a loan against the future income stream).

An arrangement that depends on capital allowances being available to an unconnected third party is **excluded** from the scope of these provisions.

MEMO POINTS 1. See ¶136 for anti-avoidance rules in relation to leasing of **plant and machinery**.
2. If the rent factoring provisions apply, the **lease premium** provisions do not apply (¶2743).

CHAPTER 4

Savings and investments

OUTLINE ¶¶

The tax treatment of **UK source** financial savings and investments can be broadly divided into income that is taxable on the recipient and income that is exempt, as follows: 2795

Product	Exempt (y/n)	¶¶
Individual savings accounts	y	¶2797
National savings investments	y (specified investments)	¶2815
Certified contractual savings (SAYE)	y	¶3554
Dividend income	n	¶2817
Interest	n	¶2829
Annuities	n	¶2835
Annual payments	n	¶2840
Deeply discounted securities	n	¶2849

For the tax treatment of **non-UK source** savings and investment income, see ¶4286, and for details of specific anti-avoidance provisions, see ¶4010 onwards.

Additionally there are specific investment schemes which offer **tax incentives** to encourage investment in particular sectors, details of which can be found at ¶2861 onwards.

SECTION 1

Tax exempt income from savings and investments

A. Individual Savings Accounts (ISAs)

2797 ss 694 - 701 ITTOIA 2005 SI 1998/1870

Interest from an ISA is **exempt** from income tax and capital gains tax. Only qualifying individuals (¶2799) may subscribe for ISAs. The account must be managed by a fund manager, who invests the subscriptions in cash or securities (stocks and shares) in accordance with detailed regulations.

An individual is permitted to maintain two ISAs (one investing in cash, the other in stocks and shares) each year. Each ISA must be designated as one type or the other at the time of the subscription.

The **annual maximum subscription** is as follows:

	2011/12 £	2010/11 £
Cash value of limit	10,680	10,200
Maximum investment in cash ISA	5,340	5,100

There is no minimum subscription limit. Except for transfers of employee shares (¶2811), all subscriptions must be in cash.

Previous years' subscriptions may be transferred at will from the cash ISA to the stocks and shares ISA.

Amounts withdrawn from the ISA during the tax year are ignored when applying the annual limits.

EXAMPLE Mr A subscribes £5,000 to an ISA on 1 May 2011. In October, he withdraws £500, and in November he wishes to make a further subscription to the ISA. The maximum further subscription he can make is £5,680 (£10,680 – £5,000). The amount withdrawn is not taken into account.

SI 2006/3194

MEMO POINTS Building society bonuses paid on accounts held in an ISA are exempt from income tax and capital gains tax, and do not count towards the annual investment limit. For these purposes, a building society bonus is defined as a payment under a building society bonus scheme, excluding any payment or entitlement to shares on the demutualisation of a society.

Qualifying individual

2799 SI 1998/1870 regs 10, 11

To qualify for an ISA (other than a Junior ISA: see ¶2812), an individual must be resident and ordinarily resident in the UK and either:
- aged 18 or over; or
- aged 16 or over, provided that he invests only in a cash ISA.

MEMO POINTS 1. Where the individual is **aged under 18**, the maximum subscription is £5,200 in a tax year, which must be invested in a cash ISA. In the tax year in which the individual reaches the age of 18, only this lower amount may be subscribed prior to his birthday. After the birthday, the individual may make further subscriptions up to the £10,200 limit.

2811 SI 1998/1870 reg 7

Employee share schemes An employee who receives shares from an approved, all employee savings-related scheme (¶3554) or share incentive plan (¶3510) may transfer those shares into a stocks and shares ISA within the following timescales:
- savings-related schemes – within 90 days of the exercise of the option; and
- share incentive plan – within 90 days of the shares ceasing to be subject to the plan.

The market value of the shares at the date of the transfer counts against the annual maximum subscription limit.

Junior ISAs (JISAs)

To replace the now-abolished Child Trust Fund (¶3695), a new type of tax-free savings account for minor children, referred to as a Junior ISA, will be introduced by regulations to be issued in autumn 2011. Any child born on or after 1 January 2011 will be eligible to own one cash and one shares JISA. There will be no Government contributions. **2812** s 40 FA 2011 s 695A ITTOIA 2005 SI 2011/1780

The main features of the JISA are expected to be similar to those for ISAs, with the following specific differences:
- the JISA will be the property of the child, and cannot be alienated or used as security by another person;
- any person can contribute funds, but contributions by a parent will not make the income of the JISA taxable on him;
- funds cannot be withdrawn until the holder's 18th birthday, except in cases of terminal illness; and
- the fund manager will be instructed by the child's parent, but the child himself may take this duty over from his 16th birthday.

B. National Savings investments

Interest from the following National Savings products are exempt from tax: **2815** ss 692, 693 ITTOIA 2005
- premium savings bonds;
- children's bonus bonds; and
- national savings certificates.

MEMO POINTS The National Savings Bank used to have **ordinary accounts**, of which the first £70 of interest was tax free. Any interest earned over that amount was paid gross and was taxable. Ordinary accounts were, from 31 July 2004, made dormant and savers can only access them either to close them or transfer the balances to an "easy access savings account". Interest on the easy access account is paid gross and is taxable – there is no exempt slice of interest income.

SECTION 2

Taxable income from savings and investments

A. Dividends and other corporate distributions

Taxable dividends and other distributions **include**: **2817** s 383 ITTOIA 2005
- dividends paid by UK companies;
- stock or scrip dividends issued by UK companies;
- other qualifying distributions, such as the transfer of value by a company to a shareholder by selling an asset at less than market value, or paying interest on a loan at more than a commercial rate;
- distributions consisting of the purchase by a company of its own shares;
- dividend distributions from UK unit trusts and open-ended investment companies; and
- non-qualifying distributions and loans written off.

The treatment of distributions depends upon whether a qualifying or a non-qualifying distribution is paid.

s 372 ITTOIA 2005

MEMO POINTS So-called "dividends" paid by a building society are taxed as interest in the hands of the recipient.

1. Qualifying distributions

2819
s 1136 CTA 2010

A qualifying distribution is defined as **any distribution except**:
– a bonus issue of securities or redeemable shares by a UK company;
– the redemption of bonus shares on a winding up (a redemption in any other situation is a qualifying distribution); or
– a distribution by a company in the form of shares or securities which it received as a distribution from another company.

Tax treatment

2821
s 397 ITTOIA 2005
ss 8 – 14 ITA 2007

Dividend income is taxed as the top slice of an individual's savings income. **Tax is payable** on the amount of the distribution, plus the tax credit, **at the following rates**:

Taxable amount 2011/12 (£)	Rate	Known as
0 – 35,000 (basic rate band)	10%	the "dividend ordinary rate"
35,000 – 150,000 (higher rate band)	32.5%	the "dividend upper rate"
Over 150,000 (additional rate band)	42.5%	the "dividend additional rate"

A notional **tax credit** is calculated as 1/9th of the net dividend (i.e. 10% of the gross dividend). Tax is charged on the gross amount. UK residents and certain eligible non-residents can deduct tax credits from their income tax liability. A tax credit cannot give rise to a refund (if a distribution is, for example, partly covered by the personal allowance).

See ¶4404 + for details of how these rules are applied.

MEMO POINTS The following non-residents **can claim a tax credit** for qualifying distributions:
– citizens of the Republic of Ireland, Commonwealth citizens and nationals of EEA states, who are entitled to, and actually have claimed, personal allowances (¶4390); and
– residents of an overseas territory with which the UK has a double taxation treaty (¶4226), which provides for tax credits.

2. Non-qualifying distributions

Tax treatment

2825
s 400 ITTOIA 2005

Non-qualifying distributions (any distributions other than those defined in ¶2819) are taxed like qualifying distributions except that there is **no tax credit**. Tax is therefore charged on the actual distribution received. Income tax is still treated as having been paid at the 10% dividend rate. This reduces the tax liability, but cannot give rise to a refund.

Where the redemption of bonus shares other than on a winding up gives rise to a higher rate liability, the liability will be reduced by the amount of any higher rate tax paid on the original issue of bonus shares (i.e. the non-qualifying distribution).

EXAMPLE In Year 1, Mr A, a higher rate taxpayer, received a non-qualifying distribution of bonus shares of £2,500 from B Ltd. His income tax liability in respect of the distribution was:

	£
Non-qualifying distribution	2,500
Tax thereon:	
2,500 @ 32.5%	812
Less: Tax treated as paid at the dividend rate	
(2,500 @ 10%)	(250)
Tax liability	562

In Year 2, the shares were redeemed (other than on a winding up) for £2,500, which represents a qualifying distribution. The liability in this respect is:

	£
Qualifying distribution (2,500 x 100/90)	2,778
Tax thereon:	
2,778 @ 32.5%	902
Less: Tax credit	(277)
	625
Less: Excess liability paid in Year 1	(562)
Tax liability	63

B. Interest

Deduction of tax at source

Normally, **basic rate tax** (20%) is deducted by the payer from interest and, from 9 January 2006, from alternative finance returns and profit share returns under alternative finance arrangements (¶2832). Non-taxpayers, or those liable to tax at the starting rate for savings income, can reclaim the tax deducted, and parents or guardians can reclaim tax on behalf of a child. If the amount deducted exceeds the individual's tax liability, a repayment of tax can be claimed in the usual manner (¶4522). **2829** ss 851 - 862 ITA 2007 SI 2008/2682

MEMO POINTS Income is deemed to have been received by the recipient in the year in which it was due, and any repayment of tax deducted will relate to that year.

By exception, income will be paid **gross** if it is: **2830**

a. bank or building society interest paid to:

– a non-ordinarily resident individual who has completed a not ordinarily resident (NOR) declaration either in writing or electronically; or

– an ordinarily resident individual who has submitted a certificate to the effect that he is unlikely to become liable to income tax for the year of assessment in which the payment is made; or

b. income from the following sources:

– non-exempt national savings accounts;
– government stocks (gilts);
– overseas branches of UK and foreign banks; or
– qualifying certificates of deposit.

MEMO POINTS 1. **Non-exempt national savings accounts** consist of:
– ordinary accounts;
– capital bonds;
– income bonds;
– pensioner bonds;
– treasurer accounts; and
– guaranteed equity bonds.

2. A **qualifying certificate of deposit** is a non-transferable deposit of £50,000 or more which is repayable within 5 years. From 6 April 2012, interest on certain of these certificates (known as qualifying time deposits) will no longer be paid gross.

3. **Statutorily exempt** forms of interest (e.g. compensation on mis-sold personal pensions, interest on damages for personal injury) will be paid tax free.

4. **Children** are entitled to the same personal allowances as adults. They can therefore have income up to this amount before they start paying tax. If however savings income due to a child is derived from funds provided by parents, the whole of the gross income arising will be assessed on the parents in any tax year where the gross income exceeds £100 p.a. A child, in this context, is an unmarried person aged less than 18 years.

5. Compensation paid by UK and foreign banks on unclaimed accounts opened by **Holocaust victims** is exempt from income tax and capital gains tax. The exemption covers amounts repre- s 756A ITTOIA 2005

senting interest which should have been credited to accounts and also a revaluation element to take account of inflation. For the inheritance tax position, see ¶6462.

Tax treatment

2831 s 370 ITTOIA 2005 ss 7, 12,16, 18 ITA 2007

Interest is assessed **in the tax year in which it arises**. Tax is charged at the following rates:

Taxable amount 2011/12 (£)	Rate
0 – 2,440 (starting rate band)[1]	10%
2,441 – 35,000 (basic rate band)	20%
35,000 – 150,000 (higher rate band)	40%
Over 150,000 (higher rate band)	50%

1. Only savings income is taxable at 10%, and only to the extent that it does not exceed this band. If savings income does exceed the band, the 10% rate does not apply and all income received is taxable at basic, higher or additional rates.

Alternative finance arrangements

2832 ss 564A – 564Y ITA 2007

Alternative financial arrangements are those which the financial services industry has developed to cater for those who want to avoid the receipt or payment of interest (because, for example, such payments are prohibited by Shari'a law). For tax purposes, any profit element attributable to the following financial arrangements entered into on or after the stated dates is treated as interest by both the payer and the recipient (although for financing purposes, the profit element continues to be treated as a finance return, not interest):

a. Purchase and resale arrangements, by which a person buys an asset for onward sale at a profit to another person and all or part of the sale price is deferred. At least one party to the arrangements must be a financial institution for these provisions to apply.

b. Profit share return arrangements, by which a person deposits money with a financial institution, which then invests it as it sees fit and shares any profit it makes with the depositor.

c. Profit share agency contracts which are equivalent to savings accounts.

d. Diminishing share ownership arrangements, used to finance the purchase of property or other assets.

e. Alternative finance investment bonds, which are similar to debt securities and are used by companies to raise funds. The following detailed rules apply:

– any part of a payment which equates to a discount will be taxed as a discount and not as a finance return, and if the arrangements constitute deeply discounted securities (¶2849), the relevant special rules will apply;

– bonds that are convertible into, or exchangeable for, shares will be treated in the same way as conventional convertible or exchangeable securities; and

– a gain on disposal of a bond by a non-corporate bondholder will be dealt with under the capital gains tax rules.

MEMO POINTS 1. Where parties to an alternative financing arrangement are **connected**, and the recipient of the finance return is not subject to tax, then the arrangement is not treated as an alternative financing arrangement and the payer is not entitled to any deduction for the payment.

2. For **capital gains tax purposes**, any finance return taxed or relieved as interest cannot be taken into account in computing any chargeable gain on the eventual disposal of the asset.

3. If any party to the arrangements is a **company**, payments made or received by the company will be taxed under the loan relationship provisions (¶870).

C. Annuities and annual payments

2835 Most annuities, and certain other annual payments, constitute taxable income in the hands of the recipient.

MEMO POINTS 1. An annuity payment can be **described** as an exchange of a capital amount for income. *Lady Foley v Fletcher* [1858]
2. An annual payment is not defined but, based on decided case law, the **characteristics** of an annual payment are that it will be:
– of an income nature;
– payable under some legal obligation;
– recurrent (or capable of being recurrent); and
– a "pure income profit".

Exempt annuities

The following types of annuity are exempt: **2838** ss 717, 725, 731, 732 ITTOIA 2005
– the **capital element** of a purchased life annuity. Only the amount that represents income is taxable;
– **immediate needs** annuities, provided they are paid to a care provider for the benefit of the person in care;
– a purchased life annuity which settles a **personal injury claim**; and
– an annuity purchased or provided under an award of **compensation** made under the Criminal Injuries Compensation Scheme.

MEMO POINTS A **purchased life annuity** is a policy in which an individual invests capital to purchase future income. For tax purposes, the annuity is divided into capital and income elements. The following annuities are not purchased life annuities for tax purposes: s 423 ITTOIA 2005
– those that are treated by other tax provisions as being the payment or repayment of a capital sum;
– those purchased as the result of a pension arrangement; and
– those purchased or provided for under the directions of a will or settlement.

Annual payments

As a **general rule** only annual payments that fall within the following categories will be taxable: **2840** ss 728, 729 ITTOIA 2005
– payments of interest;
– payments made for bona fide commercial reasons in connection with a trade, profession or vocation; and
– payments made for non-taxable consideration.

The types of annual payment which are **specifically exempt** are: **2842** ss 734, 735, 744 – 748, 776 ITTOIA 2005
a. payments arising in the UK made by an individual which do not fall within ¶2840 above;
b. income from the following types of insurance policy when paid to the insured (or, on his death, to his spouse or estate):
– mortgage payment protection insurance;
– permanent health insurance;
– creditor insurance; and
– long term care insurance taken out before the need for care becomes apparent.
To **qualify** for exemption, the annual payment must be made under a policy insuring against a qualifying risk (i.e. a risk for the insured or spouse of a physical or mental illness, disability etc or loss of employment). The provisions of the policy must:
– be self-contained, in that they should not provide benefits other than those relating to the qualifying risk;
– exclude payments relating to the risk in periods where the relevant conditions for payment are not satisfied; and
– at all times have been such that the insurer runs a genuine risk of loss, in that the proceeds payable may exceed the amount of the premium received together with an investment return on those premiums.
Annual payments under insurance policies will however **be taxable** if:
– the income is included in business profits; and
– tax relief has been obtained for the contributions to the policy (e.g. as a deduction from business profits).

c. payments to adopters;
d. scholarship income;
e. payments from trusts for injured persons; and
f. payments by persons liable to pool betting duty.

EXAMPLE An employer takes out a group policy to meet the costs of sick pay for the employees. Any income received by the employee in respect of employer contributions will be taxable on the recipient. However, the proportion of income relating to contributions by the employee will be exempt.

Tax treatment

2844
ss 10, 18 ITA 2007
s 424 ITTOIA 2005

Taxable annuities and annual payments are charged to tax in the year of assessment in which the payment is due, at the following rates:

Taxable income 2011/12 (£)	Rate (%)	
	Purchased life annuities	Other annuities and annual payments
0 – 35,000 (basic rate band)	20	20
Over 35,000 (higher rate band)	40	40

Deduction of tax at source

2846
ss 900, 901, 902 ITA 2007

Income tax must be **deducted at the basic rate** (20%) by the payer from qualifying annual payments which are paid by:
a. an **individual**, in the course of his trade, profession or vocation, for genuine commercial reasons.; or
b. other persons, excluding payments made by an individual's personal representatives where the payments would have been made for genuine commercial reasons if made by the individual before his death.
If the amount deducted exceeds the individual's tax liability, a repayment of tax can be claimed in the usual manner (¶4522).

s 899 ITA 2007

MEMO POINTS A **qualifying annual payment** is any annuity or annual payment which arises in the UK, other than:
– interest;
– annuities charged to tax as pension income, consequently subject to PAYE;
– exempt annuities (¶2838) and annual payments (¶2842);
– payments for the right to receive dividends;
– payments under a maintenance agreement to a spouse or a former spouse;
– any payment, made in relation to the surrender, assignment or release in an interest in settled property, to (or in favour of) a person with a subsequent interest;
– donations which obtain tax relief under gift aid (¶4420) or as a charitable donation by a company (¶960); or
– payments in respect of which a settlor or beneficiary of a discretionary trust is treated as having paid tax, or would have been so treated but for the fact that the trustees are non-UK resident.

D. Deeply discounted securities

2849
s 430 ITTOIA 2005

A **discounted security** is one on which the return to the investor consists of a **discount or premium** payable on redemption, rather than interest payable during its lifetime. The amount of the discount or premium is the difference between the price at which the security was issued and the amount payable on redemption or transfer.

A **deeply discounted security** is one for which the discount or premium is or can be more than the lower of:
- 15% of the redemption amount; or
- 0.5% of the redemption price for every year between the date of issue and the date of redemption. (Where this period is not a complete number of years, each complete month and part of a month is treated as 1/12th of a year.)

The **comparison** between the issue price and the amount received on redemption is made **at the time the security is issued**. The comparison is made on the assumption that redemption will be made on maturity or any other contractually permitted earlier occasion (in accordance with the terms of the issue). A security will be considered to be a deeply discounted security if the qualifying conditions are met on at least one of these occasions.

MEMO POINTS 1. Securities issued with rights to convert into shares or other securities are said to be **redeemed** when the conversion takes place. The amount payable on the deemed redemption is taken to be the market value of the replacement shares or other securities.
2. A **transfer** of a security means a transfer by way of sale, gift, exchange or otherwise. Where the holder dies, there is a deemed transfer to the personal representatives at market value at the date of death.

A **charge to tax** arises on a deeply discounted security for the tax year in which it is redeemed or transferred. The discount or premium received will be taxed at the same rates as interest income (¶2831). **2851** s 427 ITTOIA 2005

MEMO POINTS 1. **Redemptions other than final** are ignored if the redemption:
- is not at the option of the holder (unless the security is issued to a person connected with the issuer, or the main benefit from the redemption provision is the obtaining of a tax advantage by any person); or
- can only occur on the exercise of an option following a particular event(s) or set of circumstances which (when judged at the time of issue) are unlikely to arise.
2. **Costs** in connection with the acquisition and redemption or transfer can be deducted in arriving at profits chargeable to tax if they were incurred:
a. before 27 March 2003; or
b. on or after 27 March 2003, if:
- the redemption or transfer is by a person who held the security continuously since before 27 March 2003, and
- the security was listed on a recognised stock exchange (¶9995) at any time before that date.

The following are **excluded** from the definition of deeply discounted securities: **2855** ss 432, 436 ITTOIA 2005
- shares in a company;
- gilt edged securities (other than gilt strips);
- life assurance policies;
- capital redemption policies;
- excluded indexed securities; and
- securities issued under the same prospectus as other previously issued securities that were not deeply discounted securities.

MEMO POINTS 1. **Gilt strips** are always treated as deeply discounted securities regardless of their issue terms. A gilt strip involves the separation of the interest coupon from the underlying security on which the interest is payable. Corporate stripped bonds created out of an interest bearing security that are acquired on or after 2 December 2004 are included within the definition of relevant discounted securities. Consequently any premium (paid on redemption of the bond) is subject to income tax as if it were interest. (Prior to this date, the capital element of such bonds avoided both income and capital gains tax.)
2. An **excluded indexed security** is one where the amount payable on redemption is determined by taking the amount for which the security was issued, and applying to it a percentage based on the change in the value of chargeable assets of any particular description over a specified period.

SECTION 3

Tax incentive investment schemes

A. Enterprise Investment Scheme (EIS)

2861 This scheme is intended to help small unquoted trading companies to raise finance, by encouraging individuals to subscribe for shares. Its main features are as follows:

Relief	¶¶
Income tax relief at 30% [1] on amounts subscribed for qualifying EIS shares	¶2863
No chargeable gain arises on disposal of the shares	¶6200
Amounts invested may be used to defer tax on other chargeable gains	¶6221
Note: 1. Income tax relief was given at 20% for shares issued before 6 April 2011	

1. Conditions for relief

2863 The requirements for EIS income tax relief are that:
– a **qualifying investor** (¶2865)
– must subscribe for **eligible shares** (¶2869)
– in a **qualifying company** (¶2871).

A breach of any of the conditions may lead to relief being withdrawn. Special provisions apply to subscriptions through an EIS fund (¶2875).

The maximum amount subscribed in a tax year may not exceed £500,000 (¶2877).

MEMO POINTS For 2012/13, the maximum investment in one tax year will increase to £1 million.

Qualifying investor

2865 ss 157, 163 – 165 ITA 2007 The requirements for a qualifying investor are shown in the following table. The investor must:

Requirement	Qualifying period [1]	¶¶
Be an individual	(None)	
Have subscribed for the shares for genuine commercial reasons, and not as part of a tax avoidance scheme.	(None)	
Not be connected with the issuing company	Beginning 2 years before the issue of the shares and ending immediately before the termination date [2].	¶2867
not received a **linked loan**	Beginning 2 years before the issue of the shares (or on the incorporation of the company, if later) and ending immediately before the termination date [2]	¶2868
Notes: 1. The condition must be satisfied throughout the period indicated. 2. The **termination date** is the later of: – the third anniversary of the issue of the shares; and – the third anniversary of the commencement of the trade.		

MEMO POINTS 1. Any subscription etc by a **nominee** is treated as that of the individual. Shares held in a bare trust (¶7176) for two or more individuals are deemed to belong in full to all the beneficiaries (i.e. no particular shares are deemed to belong to a particular individual) and each beneficiary is deemed to have contributed an equal amount. s 250 ITA 2007

2. EIS relief is not available where the investment is made as part of a **reciprocal arrangement** in order to meet the conditions of the scheme. For example, EIS relief will not be available for an individual who is connected with company B but subscribes for shares in a company with which he is not connected (company A) on the condition that another person, who is connected with company A, will subscribe for shares in company B. s 171 ITA 2007

Connected persons A person is connected with the issuing company if he or his associate: **2867** ss 166 - 170 ITA 2007

a. is an employee, director or partner of the company, or a subsidiary or partner of the company;

b. has control of the company; or

c. has a substantial interest in the company.

MEMO POINTS 1. For the purposes of EIS relief, a person is **associated** with:
- his relatives or partners (a relative is as detailed in ¶2105, with the exclusion of brothers and sisters);
- the trustees of a settlement of which the investor or his relative was the settlor; and
- the trustees or personal representatives of any trust or estate holding shares in which the investor has an interest.

2. For the purposes of point **a**. above, **directorships** may be ignored where the director is either unpaid or a "business angel".

A director will be deemed to be **unpaid** where the only payments received comprise:
- payment or reimbursement of expenses allowable for employment income purposes (¶3128);
- normal commercial payments in respect of interest on loans, rent for property, supplies of goods and dividends; or
- reasonable remuneration provided to the director (directly or indirectly) for services in the course of a trade or profession.

It is HMRC's view that a company secretary who receives no payment, has no benefits in kind or employment contract and carries out only company secretarial duties is not an employee for EIS purposes.

A **business angel** is the term commonly used to describe a person, unconnected with the company, who is prepared to provide finance and expertise to the company. A subscription by a business angel will qualify for relief if, at the time of the subscription for the EIS shares, the business angel was never:
- connected with the issuing company; or
- involved in the trade of the issuing company (either on his own, in partnership or as a director or employee).

A business angel will continue to qualify for relief even if he subsequently becomes a paid director of the company, or a subsidiary or partner of the company, provided any remuneration he receives is reasonable in relation to services performed. Any further subscription after he becomes a paid director will qualify for EIS relief if the shares are issued within 3 years of the last issue to him before he became a paid director (and provided he is not otherwise connected with the company – e.g by holding a 30% interest).

3. For the purposes of point **b**. above, a person has **control** of the issuing company where, by virtue of his (or his associates') shareholding or voting rights, or under the Articles of Association or other regulatory document, he can secure that the company's affairs are conducted in accordance with his wishes.

4. For the purposes of point **c**. above a person has a **substantial interest** in a company if he (together with his associates) has possession of, or is entitled to acquire, over 30% of the company's or any 51% (¶1520) subsidiary's:
- issued ordinary share capital;
- voting rights;
- loan and issued share capital; or
- net assets on a winding up (directly or indirectly).

In this context, a subsidiary company means a company which at any time in the period beginning on the incorporation of the company (or, if later, 2 years before the share issue) and ending on the termination date (¶2865) is a 51% subsidiary.

The 30% limit must be applied to the total of a person's issued share capital and loans made to the company, rather than being applied to each category separately. In addition, for this purpose "issued share capital" refers to the nominal value rather than the subscribed value of the shares. *HMRC v Taylor & Haimendorf* [2010]

2868 s 164 ITA 2007 **Linked loan** A linked loan is any loan made to the investor or an associate which would not have been made, or would not have been made on the same terms, if the investor had not subscribed or proposed to subscribe for the shares in question.

MEMO POINTS A loan **includes** the giving of any credit, or the assignment of a debt.

Eligible shares

2869 ss 172 - 179 ITA 2007 The shares must be newly-issued ordinary shares acquired by subscription.

The purpose of the share issue must be to raise money for a **qualifying business activity**. There is also a general requirement that shares must be issued for genuine commercial purposes and not as part of a tax avoidance scheme.

Shares are **not eligible** if, prior to the termination date (¶2865), they carry present or future:
- preferential rights to dividends;
- preferential rights to assets on a winding up; or
- rights to redemption.

2870 s 175(3) ITA 2007 All of the money raised by the issue of shares must be used for the purposes of a qualifying trade by the later of:
- 2 years from the date of the share issue; or
- 2 years from the commencement of the trade.

Qualifying company

2871 ss 180 - 199 ITA 2007 The company. must satisy two sets of conditions:
- one set at the date the shares are issued; and
- a further set throughout the period from that date until the termination date (¶2865).

Conditions to be satisfied at the date of issue The company must:

Requirement	¶¶
Be unquoted (and there must be no arrangements in place for it to cease being so)	
Not exceed a maximum permitted level of gross assets	¶2872
Not exceed a maximum permitted number of employees	¶2872
Not be in financial difficulty[1]	

Note:
1. Financial difficulty is defined by the EC Guidelines on State Aid for Rescuing and Restructuring Firms in Difficulty: see http://europa.eu/legislation_summaries/other/l26079_en.htm. This requirement did not apply to shares issued before 6 April 2011.

Conditions to be satisfied throughout the period The company must:

Requirement	¶¶
Have a permanent establishment in the UK[1].	¶2874
Exist wholly for the purposes of carrying on one or more qualifying trades, or be the parent company of a trading group	¶2875
Control no non-qualifying subsidiaries.	¶2876
Be neither the 51% subsidiary of another company nor controlled by another company.	¶2876

Note:
1. This requirement did not apply to shares issued before 6 April 2011.

Maximum size The company must not exceed the following size limits: 2872 ss 186–186A ITA 2007

Requirement	2011/12	2012/13[1]
Maximum number of employees	50	250
Maximum gross relevant assets[3] immediately before the investment is made	£7 million	£15 million
Maximum gross relevant assets[3] immediately after the investment is made	£8 million	£16 million[4]
Maximum annual investment[5]	£2 million	£10 million

Notes:
1. Measures announced in the Budget 2011.
2. Employee includes a director, but does not include an employee on maternity or paternity leave, or a student on vocational training.
3. Relevant assets are the assets of the company (or group, where appropriate, ignoring intra-group holdings and obligations) calculated as the aggregate of the assets which would be shown on a balance sheet prepared to that date, without any deduction for liabilities.
4. Assumed.
5. This is the maximum amount that may be raised by the company through CVS, EIS and VCT schemes in the 12 months ending on the date of the investment in question.

Permanent establishment 2874 s 191A ITA 2007

A company has a permanent establishment in the UK if (and only if):
– it has a fixed place of business in the UK through which the business of the company is wholly or partly carried on; or
– an agent acting on behalf of the company has the authority to enter into contracts on behalf of the company and habitually exercises that authority in the UK.

The activities carried on at the fixed place of business or by the agent must, when considered in relation to the company's business as a whole, have more than a simply preparatory or auxiliary character (such as mere storage of goods).

MEMO POINTS 1. A company does **not** have a permanent establishment in the UK simply because:
– it carries on business in the UK through an independent agent or a broker; or
– it controls a UK resident company or a company carrying on business in the UK (whether through a permanent establishment or not).
2. **Prior to 6 April 2011**, the analogous requirement was that the company conducted a qualifying trade wholly or mainly in the UK

Qualifying trades A qualifying trade means the carrying on (or preparing to carry on) of a trade on a commercial basis with a view to making a profit. This can include the carrying on of research and development, either to benefit an existing trade or to develop a new trade. 2875 ss 181–183, 189, 192–199 ITA 2007

A company is the parent company of a **trading group** when it has only qualifying subsidiaries. A qualifying subsidiary is:
– a qualifying 51% subsidiary (¶1520); or
– a qualifying 90% subsidiary (¶1528); or
– a qualifying 90% subsidiary of a 100% subsidiary; or
– a qualifying 100% subsidiary of a 90% subsidiary.

To qualify, the subsidiary must either carry on the EIS trade or research and development during the period beginning on the date of issue of the shares and ending on the termination date (¶2865), or be a property management subsidiary.

If the company carries on certain excluded activities, and they comprise more than 20% of its trade, the trade is non-qualifying.

MEMO POINTS 1. If the share issue takes place **before the trade commences**, the company must be preparing to trade and intend to begin trading within 2 years of the date of issue. HMRC do not consider that preliminary activities, such as raising capital or market research to establish whether a trade would be successful, constitute "preparing to trade".
2. **Excluded activities include**:
– dealing in goods other than as part of a wholesale or retail distribution trade;
– property dealing and development;
– financial activities including, for example, debt factoring, dealing in commodities, futures and shares and insurance;
– leasing or hiring goods, including chartering ships (other than short term hiring or chartering);

– receiving royalties and licence fees (for example green fees at a golf course) but excluding those attributable to film production, research and development and relevant intangible assets where the whole or greater part of the value of the asset was created by the company (or by a company that was a qualifying subsidiary at all times during which it created the asset);
– farming, market gardening, occupying and managing woodlands;
– the production of coal or steel;
– operating or managing hotels, nursing homes and residential care homes;
– providing legal or accountancy services; and
– providing services for a trade carried on by another person (which consists substantially of non-qualifying activities) if the person has a controlling interest in both.
From April 2012, the generation of electricity by solar or wind power will be an excluded activity.

2876 ss 185, 190-191 ITA 2007

Control requirements The company:
– must not control any non-qualifying subsidiaries (control being defined as in ¶1902); and
– must not be the 51% subsidiary of another company;
– must not be controlled by another company (control being defined as in ¶2867).

2. Using the relief

2877 ss 157, 158, 176, 177 ITA 2007

Provided at least £500 is subscribed in a single qualifying company and all the other conditions are met, the individual **may claim** relief either on the self-assessment tax return, or by submitting a claim accompanied by form EIS 3 which will be issued by the company.

There is no maximum investment limit, but the maximum amount on which relief will be given is £500,000, whether the shares are issued in that year or a subsequent year (but see ¶2879 for details of carrying back relief to the previous year).

A claim for relief cannot be made until the trade has been carried on for 4 months, and must be made within 4 years from the end of the tax year in which the shares were issued.

MEMO POINTS 1. Relief will be denied where **pre-arranged exit arrangements** exist. This is not restricted to arrangements for the sale of shares, but encompasses plans for the discontinuance of the trade, the sale of the assets, or where the investor has insurance, indemnities or guarantees against the risk of making the investment.
2. To spread the risk, an individual may make investments through an approved **EIS fund** (a pool of monies from qualifying individuals). The differences of such an investment from an individual subscription are as follows:
– the minimum subscription limit of £500 for an individual investor does not apply to subscriptions made through an approved fund; and
– relief is given to the contributors as if the shares were issued on the date the fund closed.

EXAMPLE Mr A made the following subscriptions:
– £400 in B Ltd on 1 March; and
– £450 in C Ltd on 7 April.

The shares were both issued on 15 April. No relief is available as in each case the amount subscribed for is less than £500.
If the subscriptions had both been for B Ltd, relief would have been available as the total amount subscribed for shares was more than £500, even though the subscriptions made in each tax year were less than £500.

2878 s 158 ITA 2007

EIS relief is given as a tax reduction (¶4440).

A **restricted claim** may be made where, for example, the personal allowance would otherwise be wasted.

EXAMPLE Mr B subscribes for shares in A Ltd at a cost of £200,000. His tax liability for the year (before double tax relief and the married couple's allowance) is £38,250. EIS income tax relief would normally be £60,000 (£200,000 @ 30%), but is restricted to the income tax liability for the year. Mr B will therefore not get any double tax relief or married couple's allowance for the year.

Carry back of relief

2879 s 158(4) ITA 2007

The full amount subscribed in a tax year may be carried back and treated as invested in the previous year. As with any claim for relief, the relief cannot exceed the income tax due for the year – therefore it may not be beneficial to carry back relief if there is insufficient income tax liability to absorb the relief.

MEMO POINTS If the total subscribed exceeds the permitted maximum contribution for the year, no part of the excess can be carried back.

Attribution of relief to shares

The relief given for a tax year is allocated to the shares issued in that year. If there is **more than one issue** of shares which qualifies for relief, the relief is apportioned equally between them. This is of importance only when the subscription in a year exceeds the maximum for which relief is available. 2881 s 201 ITA 2007

Where a claim is made to carry back part of the relief, there is deemed to be a separate issue of shares in the earlier year.

MEMO POINTS If a company makes a bonus issue of shares, the relief given to the shares in the original holding is amended to attribute the relief to all of the shares in the new holding (i.e. the original holding plus the bonus issue).

3. Withdrawal of relief

Income tax relief may be withdrawn in the following circumstances: 2883 ss 235, 256A ITA 2007

Circumstance	¶¶
A breach of conditions by the investor, the company or the shares	¶2885
A receipt of replacement capital	¶2887
A disposal of the shares	¶2889
A return of value to the investor	¶2893
The making of payments to non-EIS investors	¶2899

Assessments to withdraw relief are made for the year in which the relief was originally given. In some circumstances the amount to be withdrawn is computed using the rate at which the relief was originally calculated, which is known as the **EIS original rate**.

Breach of conditions

Relief will be withdrawn in full where: 2885 ss 177, 247 ITA 2007 Sch 8 FA 2009
- the company or investor breaches the conditions for relief; or
- the shares cease to be eligible shares.

MEMO POINTS The following will **not be treated** as a breach of conditions:

a. share exchange – special rules exist to prevent the withdrawal of relief where an EIS company is taken over by a new company (Newco), in a share for share exchange. The exchange must be for bona fide commercial reasons and not form part of an arrangement to avoid a liability to tax.

This provision only applies if all of the following conditions are satisfied:
- Newco must have only previously issued subscriber-only shares;
- Newco must acquire the entire issued capital of the EIS company (EISco) for consideration consisting entirely of shares in Newco;
- the Newco shares must be of the same class and have the same rights as the existing EISco shares; and
- the Newco shares must be issued to the holders of EISco shares in proportion to their holdings in EISco.

Advance clearance must be obtained from HMRC before the exchange takes place. Assuming clearance is given, the effect of the provisions are:
- Newco stands in the shoes of EISco – therefore the investor is deemed to have acquired the Newco shares at the time the EISco shares were issued and for the same consideration;
- there is no deemed disposal of the EISco shares by the investors; and
- investors will not lose their EIS income tax or capital gains tax relief; or

b. winding up – a company will not cease to be a qualifying company or 90% subsidiary company simply because the company, subsidiary or any other company is wound up, or is in receivership/administration, provided the winding up etc is for bona fide commercial reasons and does not form part of an arrangement to avoid a liability to tax.
Similarly, a company will not cease to be a qualifying 90% subsidiary company, if there are arrangements in place by the parent company for the disposal of its interest in the subsidiary, providing the arrangements are for bona fide commercial reasons and do not form part of an arrangement to avoid tax.

Replacement capital

2887 s 232 ITA 2007 EIS relief will be withdrawn in full if the EIS company (or one of its subsidiaries) **during the period** beginning on the incorporation of the company (or, if later, 2 years before the share issue) and ending on the termination date (¶2865) either:
a. acquires the entire issued share capital of another company, and the investor (or group of persons including the investor), at any time in the period, controlled the EIS company and the company whose shares were acquired; or
b. acquires the trade, or most of the assets of a trade, and the investor (or a group of persons including the investor), at any time in the period, either:
- owned more than a half share in that trade; or
- controlled the EIS company and another company which carried on the trade.

Share disposal

2889 ss 209, 245 ITA 2007 Relief will be withdrawn if the investor disposes (or makes a deemed disposal) of the shares **in the period** beginning on the incorporation of the company (or, if later, 2 years before the share issue) and ending on the termination date (¶2865).

MEMO POINTS 1. The following transactions will give rise to a **deemed disposal**:
- the grant of a put option on the EIS shares requiring the grantor of the option to purchase the EIS shares. (Any shares acquired by the investor after the granting of the put option are ignored and are not deemed to be disposed of); or
- the grant of a call option on the EIS shares requiring the investor to sell the shares.
2. The following transactions **do not constitute a disposal**:
- transfers of shares between spouses – the receiving spouse stands in the shoes of the original investor;
- standard provisions in a company's Articles of Association requiring a shareholder to sell his shares if the majority of the shareholders accept an offer from a third party to purchase the company's entire issued share capital.

2891 The **amount of relief withdrawn** is calculated using the EIS original rate (¶2883), and depends on whether the disposal was at arm's length, as follows:
a. disposal not at arm's length – the relief is withdrawn in full; or
b. disposal at arm's length – the amount of relief withdrawn is the lower of:
- the proceeds from the disposal, multiplied by the EIS original rate; and
- the relief originally given.

MEMO POINTS Where the **initial relief** given on the subscription was **restricted** (i.e. it was less than the tax at the EIS original rate on the amount invested because, for example, the individual had insufficient income tax liability to utilise the relief), the relief withdrawn is calculated by applying the fraction A/B where:
- A is the EIS relief given (in terms of the reduction in the tax liability); and
- B is the notional tax at the EIS original rate on the amount subscribed.

EXAMPLE Mr A acquired 1,000 shares in B Ltd under the EIS scheme in 2010/11. He paid £150,000 and benefited from EIS relief of £30,000 (£150,000 @ 20%). The shares were sold at arm's length in 2011/12, for £125,000. The amount of income tax relief withdrawn is calculated as the lower of:

	£
Proceeds x EIS original rate (£125,000 @ 20%)	25,000
Relief originally given (£150,000 @ 20%)	30,000
Therefore, relief withdrawn	25,000

EXAMPLE Taking the facts from the previous example, if Mr A's relief in respect of the shares was restricted as his tax liability for 2010/11 was only £22,500, the relief withdrawn on the disposal of B Ltd shares would be £18,750 ((125, 000 @ 20%) x (22,500/30,000)).

Return of value

Relief will be withdrawn if the company, or a person connected with the company, makes a payment (which is not insignificant) to the investor, directly or indirectly, **in the period** commencing 1 year before the issue of the shares and ending on the termination date (¶2865). **2893** ss 213 - 231 ITA 2007

MEMO POINTS For these purposes, **insignificant** means a sum which does not exceed £1,000, or, if it does, an amount which is insignificant in relation to the whole amount subscribed for the shares by the individual. If the individual receives a return of value (whether or not insignificant), and before that time had received an insignificant return of value, the amounts are aggregated to calculate the reduction or withdrawal of relief.

The following table **summarises** the items which are treated as a return of value, and how the value is quantified: **2895** ss 213 - 230 ITA 2007

Event	Value returned
Repayment, redemption or repurchase of shares or securities. Payment for giving up rights to share capital or securities on its redemption.	Greater of: – amount received; or – market value of shares.
Repayment of a debt to the investor incurred before the subscription for EIS shares, if made in connection with any arrangement for their acquisition. Payment to individual for giving up rights to repayment of debt (except an ordinary trade debt).	Greater of: – amount received; or – market value of debt.
Company releases or waives any liability of the individual to the company. Company discharges the individual's liability to a third party.	Amount of liability.
Company transfers an asset to the individual at less than market value. Company acquires an asset from the individual at more than market value.	Excess of market value over consideration given.
Company makes a loan to the individual which is not fully repaid before share issue.	Amount of loan outstanding, less any repayment made before issue of shares.
Company provides any benefit or facility to the individual.	Cost of providing benefit, reduced by any contribution from the individual.
Company makes any other payment to the individual.	Amount of the payment.
Individual receives a payment/asset in the course of winding up the company.	Amount of payment or market value of asset as appropriate.

MEMO POINTS There will be **no reduction or withdrawal** of EIS relief if the company receives **replacement value** from the individual during the period which is at least as much as the original return of value to individual. The replacement value can be received before or after the original receipt of value, but it will be ignored if it takes place outside **the period** commencing 1 year before the issue of shares and ending on the termination date (¶2865).
The following payments constitute replacement value:
– a payment to the company (other than an excepted payment) to acquire an asset at more than market value;
– a sale of an asset to the company at less than market value;
– the reversal of an initial waiver by the company of a subscriber's liability; and
– the reversal of an initial discharge by the company of a subscriber's liability.

An **excepted payment** is broadly any payment for goods, services, interest etc at a commercial market rate.

2897 The **amount of relief withdrawn** is equal to the amount of value received, at the EIS original rate of tax (¶2883). The relief withdrawn cannot exceed the relief originally given.

EXAMPLE In 2010/11 Mr A subscribed for shares in B Ltd at a cost of £30,000. He obtained income tax relief of £6,000 (£30,000 @ 20%). In 2011/12, the company transferred a car valued at £6,500 to Mr H for £4,000. Income tax relief will be withdrawn as follows:

	£
Market value of asset transferred	6,500
Consideration paid	(4,000)
Excess	2,500
Income tax relief withdrawn (2,500 @ 20%)	500

Payments to non-EIS investors

2899 ss 224–231 ITA 2007 Relief is withdrawn if the company repays, redeems or repurchases any share capital belonging to non-EIS investors **during the period** commencing 1 year before the issue of shares and ending on the termination date (¶2865), providing such a payment is not insignificant (¶2893).

MEMO POINTS **Redemption of shares** within 12 months of their issue to enable the company to comply with Companies Act provisions will not give rise to a withdrawal of relief.

2901 The **amount of relief withdrawn** depends on how many investors claimed the relief as follows:

a. only one investor – that person's relief will be reduced by the lower of:
– tax at the EIS original rate (¶2883) on the amount received by the non-EIS investor; or
– the total relief initially given; or

b. more than one investor – the relief withdrawn is apportioned amongst the investors in proportion to their shareholdings.

EXAMPLE In 2010/11 Mr A subscribed for shares in B Ltd at a cost of £20,000. He obtained income tax relief of £4,000 (20,000 @ 20%). In 2011/12 the company redeemed shares belonging to one of the directors for £18,000. EIS relief will be withdrawn as follows:

1. Assuming Mr A was the only EIS investor:

	£	£
Tax at EIS original rate on value returned (£18,000 @ 20%)	3,600	
Relief initially given	4,000	
Relief withdrawn		3,600

2. Assuming there were several investors and the total amount subscribed for EIS shares was £250,000:

	£	£
Tax at EIS original rate on value returned (£3,600) apportioned in relation to Mr A's investment to total EIS subscriptions:		
3,600 × 20,000/250,000	288	
Relief initially given	4,000	
Relief withdrawn		288

4. Administration

2903 ss 240 – 243 ITA 2007 The investor and the company both have a **duty to notify** HMRC within 60 days of any change in circumstances that means that the investor is no longer a qualifying individual or the company is no longer a qualifying company.

If the inspector believes that the individual or company has not given him the required information, he may issue a notice requesting the details.

MEMO POINTS Information may also be requested in connection with:
– the winding up, dissolution, administration or receivership of the company or a subsidiary; or
– arrangements that are in place for a company to cease to be a qualifying 90% or 50% subsidiary.

The following **penalties** apply in relation to the EIS: **2905** s 98 TMA 1970

Action	Penalty
Failure to give notice of a change in circumstances/failure to comply with inspector's notice for information.	Initial penalty of £300, and £60 a day thereafter if the failure continues.
Careless or deliberate supply of incorrect information.	Not exceeding £3,000.
Careless or deliberate claim by an investor for EIS relief.	Not exceeding the difference between the tax paid and the amount that would have been paid if a correct claim made.

B. Venture Capital Trusts (VCTs)

A Venture Capital Trust (VCT) is a **quoted investment vehicle**, intended to encourage investment in unquoted trading companies. An individual can make tax-efficient investments in the VCT, which in turn invests in trading companies. **2907** ss 258 – 332 ITA 2007 s 709 ITTOIA 2005

Provided the VCT shares are acquired for **bona fide commercial reasons** and not as part of an arrangement to avoid tax, an individual may obtain the following reliefs:

Relief	¶¶
Income tax relief at 30% on amounts subscribed for VCT shares	¶2909
Distributions from VCT shares are exempt from income tax	¶2925
No chargeable gain arises on disposal of the shares	¶6250

1. Investment relief

a. Conditions for relief

In order to qualify for VCT relief, an individual must make a **qualifying subscription** for shares in a **qualifying VCT company**. A breach of any of the conditions may lead to relief being withdrawn. **2909**

Qualifying subscription

This is a subscription for shares in a qualifying company by an individual aged 18 or over, up to an **annual maximum value of £200,000**. **2911** ss 261, 262 ITA 2007

Shares must be newly-issued ordinary shares acquired by way of subscription. They must not carry any of the following present or future rights for the 5 years after issue:
– preferential rights to dividends;
– preferential rights to assets on a winding up; or
– rights to redemption.

Loan-linked investments An individual is **not entitled** to VCT relief if, in the relevant period, he or his associate receives a loan which is linked to the VCT share subscription. **2912** s 264 ITA 2007

MEMO POINTS 1. A loan is **linked** to a VCT subscription if it would not have been made, or made on the same terms, if the individual had not subscribed for the shares.

2. The **relevant period** for these purposes begins 2 years before the date of issue of the shares (or on the date of incorporation of the company, if that is later) and ends immediately before the fifth anniversary of the date of issue of the shares.
3. For the purposes of VCT relief, a person is **associated** with:
- his relatives or partners (a relative is as detailed in ¶2105, with the exclusion of brothers and sisters);
- the trustees of a settlement of which the investor or his relative was the settlor; and
- the trustees or personal representatives of any trust or estate holding shares in which the investor has an interest.
4. A **loan** includes the giving of credit or assignment of a debt.

Qualifying VCT company

2913 ss 274-282 ITA 2007 To be eligible for relief, the VCT must be a quoted, non-close company, **approved by HMRC** as a VCT.

Conditions for approval fall into two classes:
- conditions which must be satisfied by the VCT itself; and
- conditions which must be satisfied by companies in which the VCT invests ("qualifying holdings").

MEMO POINTS 1. A **close company** is, broadly speaking, one that is controlled by five or fewer persons (¶2100).
2. HMRC may **grant provisional approval** to a VCT if it is satisfied that the conditions will be met by the end of the following accounting period (or within 3 years in the case of conditions relating to the VCT's investments). If provisional approval is granted, but the company does not satisfy the conditions within the required time, the company is deemed never to have been a VCT and any relief given is withdrawn.

2914 **Conditions upon the VCT** HMRC will only grant approval if the VCT company meets **all** of the following conditions:
a. each class of the VCT's ordinary share capital is quoted on the official list of any EEA stock market;
b. its income derives wholly or mainly from shares or securities;
c. at least 85% of its income from shares and securities is distributed;
d. no more than 15% of its investments are in one single company (other than another VCT);
e. at least 70% of its investments are in the form of shares or securities which are qualifying holdings (¶2915);
f. at least 70% of the value of qualifying holdings is in the form of eligible shares

Eligible shares are ordinary shares which throughout the five years following the date of issue carry none of the following present or future rights:
- preferential rights to dividends;
- preferential rights to assets on a winding up; or
- to redemption.

MEMO POINTS 1. In accounting periods ending before 6 April 2011, VCTs were required to be **quoted** on the UK Stock Exchange.
2. When determining the VCT's **income** (conditions **b** and **c**), the sums to be included in respect of loan relationships (¶870) are exclusive of interest and other amounts in respect of money borrowed by the VCT.
3. For the purposes of conditions **e**. and **f**., **investments** include all money held by a company (or owed to it, where the company has account-holder's rights). A period of 6 months is however allowed for the reinvestment or distribution of monetary or non-monetary proceeds of investment disposals.
4. In accounting periods ending before 6 April 2011, the **minimum holding** of eligible shares was 30%. HMRC have indicated that the definition may be amended to include shares that may carry certain preferential rights to dividends, but no date has been set for this change.

2915 **Qualifying holdings** For an investment by a VCT to be a qualifying holding, the target company must meet all the same qualifying conditions as those for an **EIS company**: see ¶2871+.

The following **additional conditions** must also be satisfied:
a. The **maximum investment in the company** by the VCT does not exceed £1 million in the period ending with the issue of the shares and beginning on the earlier of:
- 6 months before the issue of the shares; or
- the start of the tax year in which the shares were issued.

b. At least 10% of the company's shares are eligible shares (¶2914).
c. The securities held by the VCT are not related to a guaranteed loan.

MEMO POINTS Securities are related to a **guaranteed loan** if there are arrangements for the VCT to receive anything from a third party in the event of the failure by any person to comply with the terms of a loan to which the security relates, or the terms of the security itself.

b. Using the relief

Where all the conditions are met, the individual may make a **claim** for relief within 4 years from the end of the tax year in which the shares are issued. Partial claims are allowed. 2917 s 43 TMA 1970
VCT relief is given as a tax reduction (¶4440).

c. Withdrawal of relief

VCT income tax relief may be withdrawn in the following circumstances: 2919
– a breach of conditions; or
– the disposal of some or all of the shares by the investor.
Assessments to withdraw relief are made for the year in which the relief was originally given.

Breach of conditions

Relief will be withdrawn in full where: 2921
– the VCT company or investor breaches the conditions; or
– the shares cease to be eligible shares.
HMRC have the power not to withdraw approval from a VCT which breaches its approval conditions as a result of events outside its control.

MEMO POINTS VCTs can retain approval: s 314 ITA 2007
– when they merge, provided the merger is for bona fide commercial reasons; and
– whilst being wound up, provided the winding up is for bona fide commercial reasons.

Share disposal

Relief will be withdrawn if the investor disposes of the shares **within the period** of 5 years from the date of acquisition. 2923
The **amount of relief withdrawn** is calculated in the same way as for EIS shares (¶2891).

2. VCT distribution relief

Dividends (including capital distributions) paid in respect of VCT shares (whether acquired by subscription or purchase), are exempt from tax in the hands of the recipient, provided that: 2925 ss 709, 712 ITTOIA 2005
– the individual has not acquired more than his permitted maximum value of shares in the tax year (¶2911); and
– the company was a VCT at the time the distributions were paid.

MEMO POINTS 1. If shares are acquired in **excess of the maximum value**, dividend income on the excess shares will be taxed in the usual manner (¶2817). The excess shares are identified as those acquired later in the tax year. If two or more classes of shares are acquired on the same day, which together take the total over the permitted maximum, the excess is apportioned between the various classes based on the respective values of each class.

EXAMPLE Mr A made the following subscription to a VCT in the current tax year:
May – £190,000 for 190,000 shares
August – £50,000 for 30,000 shares

A dividend of £11,000 (5 pence per share) is paid in September.

As the acquisitions exceed the permitted maximum by £40,000, the dividend will be pro-rated using the following formula on the subscription which contains the excess shares:
Amount in excess of permitted maximumCash subscription for the shares that include the excess shares × Number of shares acquired in the single subscription that include excess shares
Therefore shares representing the excess are:
40,000/50,000 × 30,000 = 24,000
Consequently £1,200 (24,000 × 0.05) of the dividend received will be taxed in the usual manner, with the balance being exempt from tax.

2. If an individual acquires shares within the permitted maximum which are then subject to a **reorganisation**, giving rise to new shares which are treated as part of the original holding, the new shares are ignored when calculating whether the permitted maximum has been exceeded. Where the new shares are attributed to shares within the permitted maximum, the new shares will also be treated as within the permitted maximum.

C. Community Investment Tax Relief (CITR)

2927 ss 333 - 382 ITA 2007 ss 218 - 269 CTA 2010

The Community Investment Tax Relief (CITR) scheme was set up to fund business, social and community enterprises in disadvantaged areas.
An individual (or company) investor may **claim** tax relief equivalent to 25% of the amount invested, spread over 5 years. Relief is available at no more than 5% for each of the 5 years (or accounting periods in the case of companies).

MEMO POINTS CITR is an EU-notifiable State Aid, with clearance from the European Commission until October 2012. HMRC have said that the scheme will be re-notified to the Commission to ensure that it continues to operate after that time.

1. Conditions for relief

2929 Relief is available to a **qualifying investor**, making a **qualifying investment** in an accredited Community Development Finance Institution (CDFI).

Qualifying investors

2931 ss 334, 350, 351 ITA 2007 ss 219, 231, 232 CTA 2010

An investor will qualify if the investment is not made for the purpose of avoiding tax, and he:
a. or any person connected (¶5570) with him does not control the CDFI during the 5 year period from the date of investment;
b. is the sole beneficial owner of the investment when it is made;
c. is not an accredited CDFI; and
d. has received a tax certificate from the CDFI.

MEMO POINTS 1. An **investor controls** the CDFI if he has power to ensure that the CDFI's affairs are conducted in accordance with his wishes through his possession of voting power in the CDFI, or by any powers conferred on him by the constitution of, or other document regulating, the CDFI.
2. If the **CDFI is a partnership**, the investment must not be a capital contribution by the partner on becoming a partner.
3. If the **investment is a loan**, the person beneficially entitled to the repayment is treated as the beneficial owner of the loan.
4. A CDFI must issue a **tax certificate** to the investor or his nominee within 30 days from the receipt of the investment (or, if later, 30 days from the date of accreditation).

Qualifying investment

2933 s 344 ITA 2007 s 225 CTA 2010

An investment in a CDFI must be either:
a. a loan to the CDFI (secured or unsecured); or
b. a subscription for CDFI shares or securities.

Loans The following conditions must be satisfied before a loan can be a qualifying investment: 2935 s 345 ITA 2007 s 226 CTA 2010
a. the full amount of the loan must be received by the CDFI (or, if a draw-down facility exists, the full amount must be drawn down within 18 months of the investment date);
b. the loan must not have any present or future right to be converted into any right which can be redeemed within 5 years from the date of the investment; and
c. the maximum amount of the initial loan that can be repaid during the 5-year period must not exceed the following:
– first 2 years from the date of investment – nil;
– third year – 25% of the initial loan;
– fourth year – 50% of the initial loan; and
– fifth year – 75% of the initial loan.

MEMO POINTS 1. The **initial loan** for any tax year is as follows:
a. Year 1 – the average capital balance for Year 1;
b. Year 2 – the average capital balance for Year 2; and
c. Years 3 – 5 – the smaller of the average capital balance for:
– the year (beginning with the anniversary of the investment that falls in the tax year in question); or
– the 6 months beginning 18 months after the investment date.
2. Usual commercial clauses requiring **repayment** in the event of a default will be disregarded for these purposes.

EXAMPLE Mr A makes a loan to a CDFI of £75,000 that provides for £7,000 to be repaid at the beginning of Year 3, and every year thereafter until the loan is repaid. In Year 5 the loan is increased to £90,000. Tax relief is available as follows:

	Average capital balance (£)	**Tax relief** (£)
Year 1	75,000	3,750 (5 % of 75,000)
Year 2	75,000	3,750 (5 % of 75,000)
Year 3	68,000	3,400 (5 % of 68,000)
Year 4	61,000	3,050 (5 % of 61,000)
Year 5	Lower of average capital balance for: – the year that falls in this tax year –£90,000; or – the 6 months beginning 18 months after the investment date – £75,000	3,750 (5 % of 75,000)

Shares and securities The following conditions must be satisfied before a subscription for shares and/or securities can be a qualifying investment: 2937 ss 346, 347 ITA 2007 ss 227, 228 CTA 2010
a. the subscription must be wholly in cash, fully paid for on the investment date; and
b. the shares and securities must carry no present or future preferential rights to be redeemed or converted into any right which can be redeemed within 5 years from the date of the investment.

2. Obtaining relief

Where all the conditions are met, the investor **must claim** relief on the amount invested after the end of the tax year to which it relates (usually via the self-assessment tax return or corporation tax return, as appropriate). A separate claim must be made for each of the 5 relevant tax years that relief is available. 2939 ss 335, 349 ITA 2007 ss 220, 230 CTA 2010

MEMO POINTS 1. If individual investors wish to obtain **relief during the current tax year**, then providing they have received a tax certificate, they can either:
– request a change to their PAYE coding (¶4618); or
– claim a reduction in their self-assessment payments on account.
2. Relief will be denied if the **investment was made under any arrangements** designed to provide complete or partial protection for the investor against the risks attached to the investment (e.g. protection by way of insurance, indemnity or guarantee).

For **individual** investors CITR is given as a tax reduction (¶4440). 2941 s 335 ITA 2007 s 220 CTA 2010

For **corporate** investors, CITR is given as a deduction against the corporation tax liability (after marginal relief (¶1350), or relief under the corporate venturing scheme (¶1890), but before any double tax relief (¶2173) or relief for ACT (¶1400).

3. Withdrawal of relief

2943 ss 354 - 372 ITA 2007 ss 231 - 255 CTA 2010

Tax relief will be withdrawn in the following circumstances:

The CDFI has its accreditation status withdrawn	¶2945
A disposal of the loan, shares or securities	¶2947
A repayment of loan capital	¶2951
A return of value to an investor	¶2953

Assessments to withdraw tax relief are made for the year in which the relief was originally given.

MEMO POINTS Tax relief already given is not withdrawn or reduced because of an event that occurred after the **investor's death**.

Loss of accreditation

2945 s 356 ITA 2007 s 238 CTA 2010

If a CDFI ceases to be accredited during the period of **5 years from the date of investment**, a claim cannot be made for the tax year in which accreditation ceases (or for any subsequent tax years).

EXAMPLE A CDFI obtains accreditation in October of Year 1. This accreditation ceases in March of Year 3 (i.e. during the 3rd of the five 12-month periods).
The last anniversary of the investment before accreditation was lost was October in Year 2. This falls part way through a tax year, so no claim can be made for that tax year or any subsequent years.

Disposals

2947 s 360 ITA 2007 s 243 CTA 2010

Loans Any full or part disposal (but not repayment) of the loan during the period of **5 years** from the date of investment by the investor will result in the withdrawal of any CITR, unless the disposal is a permitted disposal.

A **permitted disposal** is:
– a disposal by way of a distribution in the course of a winding up or dissolution;
– a disposal arising from the entire loss, destruction or extinction of the asset;
– a deemed disposal, following a negligible value claim (¶6025); and
– a disposal made after the CDFI has ceased to be accredited.

2949 s 361 ITA 2007 s 244 CTA 2010

Shares or securities Relief will be withdrawn if the investor disposes of shares or securities **during the period** of 5 years from the date of investment, unless the disposal arose because of a repayment, redemption or repurchase of the shares or securities.

The **amount of relief withdrawn** depends on whether the disposal was at arm's length, as follows:
a. disposal not at arm's length – relief is withdrawn in full; and
b. disposal at arm's length (or a permitted disposal – ¶2947) – amount of relief withdrawn is the lower of:
– 5% of the disposal proceeds; or
– the relief originally given.

EXAMPLE Mr A subscribes £15,000 for shares in a CDFI on 6 April in Year 1. He sells all the shares at arm's length for £5,000 on 30 October in Year 5. Tax relief is claimed and withdrawn as follows:

	Tax relief claimed	Tax relief withdrawn
Years 1 – 4	£750 (£15,000 @ 5%)	£250 (£5,000 @ 5%)
Year 5	Nil	Nil

If, for example, the investor's liability to income tax in Year 2 was only £400, he would only have obtained tax relief for 80% of the relief available (400/500). The withdrawal of relief for that year would be restricted by the same proportion i.e. 80% x 250 = £200.

Repayment of loan capital

Any repayments of loan capital in excess of the permitted balances (¶2935) will result in a withdrawal of relief in full, unless the repayment is insignificant (¶2893). **2951** ss 356, 362 ITA 2007 ss 238, 245 CTA 2010

MEMO POINTS Usual commercial clauses requiring **repayment** in the event of a default will be disregarded for these purposes.

Return of value

Relief will be withdrawn if the CDFI makes a payment (which is not insignificant (¶2893)) to the investor, or any person connected (¶5570) with him, **in the period** commencing 1 year before and ending 5 years after the date of investment. **2953** ss 363, 364 ITA 2007 ss 246, 247 CTA 2010

This provision **does not apply** if the payments are qualifying payments, as follows:
– payments for goods, services, facilities or interest at a market rate;
– dividends that represent a normal commercial return on the investment; and
– a payment discharging an ordinary trade debt (i.e. a debt for goods or services, supplied in the ordinary course of business with no more than 6 months' credit).

Any return of value is deemed to be a repayment equal to the amount of value received. The following table **summarises** the items which are treated as a return of value, and how the value is quantified. **2955** s 367 ITA 2007 s 250 CTA 2010

Event	Value returned
Repayment, redemption or repurchase of an investment in shares or securities CDFI releases or waives any liability of the individual investor to the company CDFI discharges the investor's liability to a third party	The amount received
CDFI makes a loan to the investor which is not fully repaid before the investment is made	Amount of loan outstanding less any repayment made before the investment is made
CDFI provides any benefit or facility to the investor or his associates	Cost of providing benefit reduced by any contributions from the investor or his associate
CDFI transfers an asset to the investor at less than market value	Excess of market value over consideration given
CDFI acquires an asset from the investor at more than market value	Excess of consideration given over market value
CDFI makes any other payment to the investor (provided it is not a qualifying payment)	Amount of the payment

MEMO POINTS A **liability is treated as released or waived** if it is not discharged within 12 months of when it should have been.

The calculation of the **amount of relief withdrawn** depends upon whether the investment was a loan or shares and securities. Special rules apply where the investor holds more than one CDFI investment. **2957** ss 363, 364 ITA 2007 ss 246, 247 CTA 2010

Loans The position depends upon whether the permitted repayment restrictions (¶2935) have been exceeded. **2958**

MEMO POINTS If the **return of value is received in the first or second year** of restriction, it is deemed to have been received at the beginning of the second year. Thereafter any return of value is deemed to have been received at the beginning of the year in which it is received. The period of restriction commences 1 year before the date of investment and ends 5 years after the date of investment.

EXAMPLE Mr A loans £50,000 to a CDFI in Year 1, with no repayments until the beginning of Year 3, when £5,000 is to be repaid and every year thereafter until the loan is repaid. In Year 4, Mr A receives a return of value of £20,000 from the CDFI. Tax relief is withdrawn as follows:

	Average capital balance (£)	Permitted balance (£)
Year 1	50,000	50,000
Year 2	50,000	50,000
Year 3	45,000	37,500 (75 % × 50,000)
Year 4	20,000 (45,000- 5,000 – 20,000)	25,000 (50 % × 50,000)

The capital balance in Year 4 exceeds the repayment restrictions, so all the relief given under the CITR scheme will be withdrawn.

2959 **Shares or securities** Any relief must be withdrawn where the return of value exceeds the permitted levels of receipts. If the return of value is within the permitted levels, any relief given is reduced rather than withdrawn.

Permitted levels of receipts are as follows:

Year	Value of receipt
Year 1 (i.e. the year before the date of investment)	Nil
Years 2-3	Nil
Year 4	25% or less of invested capital
Year 5	50% or less of invested capital
Year 6	75% or less of invested capital

EXAMPLE Mr B subscribed £100,000 for shares in a CDFI. After 4 years, he received a loan of £20,000 from the CDFI. This return of value is within the permitted level of receipts so he will be eligible for tax relief as follows:

Year	Tax relief (£)
1	5,000 (5 % × 100,000)
2	5,000 (5 % × 100,000)
3	5,000 (5 % × 100,000)
4	4,000 (5 % × (100,000 – 20,000))
5	4,000 (5 % × (100,000 – 20,000))

2961
s 368 ITA 2007
s 251 CTA 2010

Return of value involving more than one investment A return of value is pro-rated between the investments made in the tax year in which it is received, using the formula A/B, where:

– A is the appropriate amount for the investment in question; and
– B is the total of A plus the appropriate amounts for the other investments.

The appropriate amount for the investment in question depends upon:

– when the return of value is received and
– whether the investment is a **loan** or a subscription for **shares or securities**.

Year in which return of value made	Loan	Shares or securities
Year 1 (i.e. the year before the date of investment)	Average capital balance of loan for year 2	Amount subscribed for shares or securities
Year 2	Average capital balance of loan for year 2	Amount subscribed for shares or securities that are still held by the investor
Years 3-6	Average capital balance of loan for year of receipt	Amount subscribed for shares or securities that are still held by the investor

EXAMPLE Mr C makes the following investments to a CDFI in Year 2:
- £20,000 loan
- £25,000 share subscription

In Year 4 he receives a return of value of £5,000 – this is allocated across the two investments as follows:
Loan – £5,000 × £20,000/(£20,000 + £25,000) = £2,222
Shares – £5,000 × £25,000/(£20,000 + £25,000) = £2,778

4. Administration

If an investor who has obtained tax relief for an investment in a CDFI becomes aware of an event causing relief to be reduced or withdrawn, he must **notify** HMRC. Notification must be given not later than 31 January following the tax year in which the event occurred (or, for companies, within 12 months of the end of the accounting period in which the event occurred). **2963** s 373 ITA 2007 s 260 CTA 2010

MEMO POINTS When value is received by a person connected (¶5570) with the investor, the **time limit for notification** is extended to 60 days from the date the investor became aware of the receipt.

CHAPTER 5

Employment income

OUTLINE

¶¶

2975 In addition to a regular monetary payment, employees may be remunerated in a variety of ways, including one-off payments and flexible benefits packages. Such income may arise from either an office or an employment.

The tax treatment of employment income must be considered in light of the close interaction with NIC (see Part 3).

The legal aspects of employment, including the rules relating to the minimum wage, working time, unfair dismissal and redundancy, can be found in the latest edition of *Employment Memo*.

SECTION 1

Employment status

2978 The status of a worker is of primary importance in determining the tax treatment of any amounts paid to him. Status is often clear cut, but areas of uncertainty remain, and there have been attempts by HMRC to prescribe the tax treatment in specific situations. If a worker is deemed to be employed, there are important consequences both for the employee and employer.

A. Office or employment

Office

2980 ss 5, 564 ITEPA 2003

Office is widely **defined** in the legislation as any position which has an existence, independent of the person who holds it, and may be filled by successive holders.

The interpretation of office has historically relied on the element of permanence. *Great Western Rly Co v Bater* [1920] However, the position does not need to be particularly long term.

In a case involving a civil engineer, who was sometimes invited to act as an inspector in local environmental enquiries, it was held that no office existed because the engagement was ad hoc and personal to the individual. If he had been unable to complete the enquiry, no successor would have been appointed. *Edwards v Clinch* [1981]

Common examples of an office would include positions held by a coroner, company secretary, or company director.

2982 ESC A37

Remuneration from an office is treated as earnings from employment.

As an **exception**, where director's fees are received by a partner of a professional firm and divided among the partners, modest amounts can be included in the trading income of the partnership.

Non-executive directors who invoice a company will be treated as self-employed by HMRC. In this case, any expenses incurred should be included on the invoice to prevent tax or NIC problems.

Employment

Employment is a **broader category** than office. An individual will be an employee where he is engaged: 2984 s 4 ITEPA 2003
- by a contract of service;
- by a contract of apprenticeship; or
- in the service of the Crown.

There is no prescribed definition of employment, and so each case must be considered on its merits in the light of the following paragraphs.

For the remainder of this chapter, the term "employment" includes the holding of an office.

B. Employed or self-employed

For tax purposes, the terms employed and self-employed are **not defined by statute**, and it is therefore not possible to say that one type of work represents employment and another, self-employment. For example, an electrician could be employed by a company providing building services, or he could trade in his own name. It is not uncommon for the same individual to be in both positions at the same time. For example, a doctor could be self-employed as a private consultant, while also being employed by a hospital. 2986

HMRC will often take the position that an employment exists, and it is then up to the individual to prove that he is self-employed.

1. Criteria

Summary of factors

The main conclusion that can be drawn from case law is that **no single factor** will give a definitive answer. The following table summarises some of the elements (in approximate order of importance) that commonly occur in decided cases. The list is not exhaustive and other factors may be relevant, depending on the particular case. 2988

It must also be understood that deciding the employment status of an individual "is not a mechanical exercise of running through items on a checklist", but requires a qualitative judgement of the overall position. *Hall v Lorimer* [1994]

	Factors indicating that a taxpayer is:	
	Employed	**Self-employed**
Mutuality of obligation	Individual required to accept work Other party required to provide work	Individual not obliged to accept work Other party not obliged to provide work
Control	Individual is supervised, and must obtain permission for absence etc	Individual has autonomy and can decide how work will be performed
Substitution/subcontracting	Individual is unable to subcontract his work to another without permission of other party	Individual can genuinely engage a substitute without permission of the other party
Integration	Central part of the other party's business	Peripheral to other party's business

	Factors indicating that a taxpayer is:	
	Employed	**Self-employed**
Risk	Individual does not risk any of his own money in performing the work Other party responsible for professional liability insurance	Individual can profit from good work, but risks his own money in performing the work Individual responsible for professional liability insurance
Length of engagement	Usually long term	Usually short term
Equipment	Other party provides equipment	Individual provides own equipment
Location	Work is performed in premises provided or controlled by the other party	Individual decides where work will be performed
Hours of work	Hours of work are regular and defined by the other party	Individual determines when work will be performed
Payment	Paid regularly, usually on a weekly or monthly basis	Paid subject to the performance of the work

2989 MEMO POINTS 1. It is useful to consider **HMRC's** own interpretation. Their employment status manual gives detailed guidance to this for many occupations
2. An **employment status indicator** (ESI) is also available from www.hmrc.gov.uk/calcs/esi.htm, which bases its interpretation on the terms of the worker's engagement. It is mandatory for HMRC staff to use it as a first point of reference.
In a **dispute with HMRC**, a result obtained from the ESI tool can be relied upon as evidence of a worker's status if both of the following are true:
– answers to the ESI questions accurately reflect the terms and conditions under which the worker provides his services; and
– the ESI has been completed by the person engaging the worker or his authorised representative (if a worker completes the ESI tool, the result is only indicative).
When using the ESI, a 14-digit number is generated as a reference. Copies of the "Enquiry Details" screen and the "ESI Result screen", bearing the 14-digit reference, should be printed or saved. If the worker's employment status is questioned in the future, HMRC will only be bound by the ESI outcome if these copies can be produced.
There has been much professional criticism of the tool. Users should bear in mind that it cannot cover all possible circumstances, and the status it gives is not legally binding on the taxpayer.

Discussion of case law

2990 A number of tests are customarily applied in unclear situations involving worker status. The **contractual position** is often taken as the starting point, with the following important distinction:
– a contract **of service** is an employment relationship; but
– a contract **for services** is a self-employment relationship.

In a case involving a professional dancer working under a standard Equity contract, it was held that an employment relationship existed because the contract was one of service, even though he was encouraged to find other work when not attending for rehearsal or performance. During the engagement, which lasted a number of months, the taxpayer was:
– required to work full time for a periodic payment;
– provided with costumes; and
– the contract could be terminated with a fortnight's notice by either party. *Fall v Hitchin* [1972]

ESM 4121 Note that nowadays most entertainers' contracts are such that they are not usually treated as employees.

2991 In a case involving a lorry driver who owned his delivery vehicle, it was held that the contract was one of carriage rather than a contract of service. The crucial element to this case was that the driver had to bear the risk of purchasing the lorry without the guarantee of future work.

The following **three components** were identified which had to be present for an employment relationship to exist:
– mutuality of obligation;
– control; and
– personal service (i.e. no substitution possible).
Ready Mixed Concrete (South East) Ltd v Minister of Pensions and National Insurance [1968]

In a more recent case concerning a construction company, heard by the then Special Commissioners, it was held that the bricklayers and scaffolders were self-employed, as they provided their own tools and protective clothing, worked flexible hours (coming and leaving of their own accord, including sudden absence to look after a sick child), and were not subject to much control by the contractor. It was stated, however, that the substitution clause within each contract was a "fiction".

It was also held that the fork-lift truck drivers and one lorry driver were employed, as they operated expensive plant made available by the contractor, who exercised more control as a consequence. *Castle Construction (Chesterfield) Ltd v HMRC* [2008]

The **terms** of the **agreement** between the parties will never be the sole factor in determining employment status, but it has been held that the agreement can be decisive if all of the other factors are consistent with its terms. In an exceptional case, a taxpayer who worked as a technician purely for his father's firm, and never raised any invoices, argued that he was an employee but it was held that he was in fact self-employed because: **2992**
– he could control his hours of work and absences;
– he had already accepted assessments for being self-employed; and
– the terms of agreement indicated as such. *Barnett v Brabyn* [1996]

Whether an individual is in **business on his own account** has been used as a test, requiring a review of the whole situation and not just one single factor. In a case involving a market research interviewer (who was found to be employed), the following criteria were examined: **2993**
– terms of the contract;
– extent of control by the organisation;
– level of financial risk faced;
– degree of integration into the organisation;
– ownership of the equipment used;
– responsibility for investment and management; and
– opportunity for profiting from sound management of tasks. *Market Investigations Ltd v Minister of Social Security* [1969]

These **criteria** were **extended** in a case involving a vision mixer, where it was held that the following were influential factors in determining him to be self-employed: **2995**
– the number of people who engaged the taxpayer during the course of a year;
– the risk of bad debts;
– the nature of expenses incurred;
– the short duration of each of the engagements; and
– the fact that he had on occasion provided a substitute worker.

This was despite the fact that the taxpayer did not use his own equipment or premises to perform his role. Again the court stressed that the overall effect of the various factors should be considered. *Hall v Lorimer* [1994]

In a more recent case involving an individual working for a client through his company, the following **factors** were indicative of a **non-employment relationship** with the company's clients: **2996**
– there was no obligation on the individual to work a set number of hours, whether per day or throughout the entire period of the engagement;
– similarly there was no obligation on the client to provide the individual with work during the period of the engagement;
– the client could terminate the contract with minimal notice, and there was no obligation on the client to engage the individual in the future;

– the individual could take time off without obtaining permission from the client's management;
– the contract included a genuine substitution clause which would allow the individual to suggest an alternative person to fulfil his role; and
– there was no provision of sick pay, holiday pay or social club membership.

The **factors** indicating **employment** (which were of limited application because the individual worked in an area requiring security clearance) were:
– the limited financial risk faced by the individual;
– the main equipment used for the task was provided by the client; and
– the individual could not manage his tasks autonomously. *Ansell Computer Services Ltd v Richardson* [2004]

Main consequences

2998 The following table highlights some of the **differences between employment and self-employment** in their tax treatment. These may be significant when arguing a worker's status. The relative importance of different factors will depend on the circumstances of the individual.

Factor	Employment	Self-employment
Expenses	A deduction can only be claimed for: – travel expenses incurred necessarily in the performance of employment duties (¶3148); and – other expenses incurred wholly, exclusively and necessarily in the performance of employment duties (¶3135 and following)	A deduction can be claimed for expenses incurred wholly and exclusively for the purposes of the trade (see ¶120, ¶142 and ¶2423)
Capital allowances	Claims are very restricted (¶3191)	Claim on any capital assets used in the trade
Income tax and NIC	Collected via PAYE on a weekly or monthly basis (¶4608) Employees Class 1 NIC payable (¶4974)	Collected under self-assessment by two instalments and a final balancing payment (¶4504). Class 2 and 4 NIC payable (See part 3)
	Employer liable to employer's Class 1 NIC (¶4974)	Other party has no NIC obligations
VAT	As outside scope of VAT, no facility to register	May be required to charge VAT in respect of the services supplied, but can then usually recover VAT suffered
Termination	Compensation paid on the termination of an employment can in some circumstances be tax-free	Compensation paid on the termination of a contract will be taxed as a trading receipt (¶129)
Residence of taxpayer[2]	Income from an overseas source may be taxed preferentially depending on the residence status of the taxpayer (¶4190)	UK resident individuals with trading income will be taxed in the UK wherever the source (¶4270)

Notes
1. An individual is likely to be able to claim a greater proportion of his expenses as a deduction if he is self-employed than if he is employed. For example, the costs of acquiring the position (e.g. advertising) will be a deductible expense for a self-employed person but not for an employee. Similarly the rules for claiming travel expenses are more generous for self-employed taxpayers.
2. For overseas source employment income see ¶4250; for UK employment income of a foreign individual, see ¶4324

3000 **Recategorisation** If HMRC successfully argue that a worker has been incorrectly treated as self-employed, the individual will be **recategorised** as an employee.

In a recategorisation it is likely that the **consequences will fall on the employer**, who is liable to account for the income tax and NIC that should have been deducted under PAYE. In addition, penalties and interest may be charged.

There is no automatic recognition of the **tax and NIC paid by the individual** as a self-employed person.

However, HMRC may transfer all or part of the PAYE liability from the employer to the employee. When assessing the employer for PAYE, any tax paid by the employee under self-assessment or under the construction industry scheme will be taken into account. For further details, see www.hmrc.gov.uk/employers/demibourne-case.pdf.

For the NIC treatment of recategorisation, see ¶4960.

The status of freelance workers should be reviewed regularly. If a worker who was previously self-employed **becomes employed**, the employer must immediately start deducting tax and NIC through the payroll. 3002

2. Agency workers

Agency workers are often hired by employers (referred to in this section as end-users) from agencies, who supply them on assignments where they will work under the end-user's instructions and control. Such workers are often temporary or casual workers of the agency, and they may sign on with several agencies to increase their chances of a regular supply of work. 3004

There is no **obligation** on the part of an agency worker to accept an assignment, though once he does he is bound by various obligations according to that agency's written statement of terms and conditions. Likewise, in return the agency will be obliged to pay the worker for work done in accordance with the assignment. Usually, the end-user pays the agency for the services of the worker and the agency pays the worker directly according to its agreement with him.

For details of the legal rights of agency workers, and further discussion of their status, see *Employment Memo*.

Status of agency workers

Where a worker is supplied to a client through an agency (or similar organisation), the employment status is usually determined by considering the **relationship between the worker and the agency**. Even if the general relationship between the worker and the agency is only a contract for services, there may be a contract of service (i.e. of employment) in relation to a specific assignment, which will last for the duration of that assignment. *McMeechan v Secretary of State for Employment* [1997] 3005

A worker will be an **employee of the agent**, and all related remuneration will therefore be employment income, where all of the following conditions are met by the worker: 3006 s 44 ITEPA 2003
- he provides personal services, other than excluded services, to a third party;
- he is subject to supervision, management and control in carrying out those services;
- he is not treated as employed under the normal rules; and
- his services are supplied under the terms of an agency contract.

MEMO POINTS 1. **Excluded services** are those: s 47 ITEPA 2003
- of an actor, musician, singer, other entertainer or model; or
- which are carried out at home, or at other premises which are neither controlled by the end-user nor prescribed by the nature of the work).

2. For the deductibility of **travel expenses**, see ¶3153 and following.

Case law indicates that there may be an implied contract of employment between the agency and the agency worker in a **long-term assignment** (over a period of years, as distinct from weeks or months typical of temporary or casual work), if: 3008
- an end-user has exclusive day-to-day control of the agency worker; and
- it is the end-user who tells the agency when it no longer requires the worker.

Dacas v Brook Street Bureau (UK) Ltd [2004]

3. Personal service companies

3010 s 49 ITEPA 2003 The personal service company rules attack arrangements which aim to convert employment income into investment income (which is taxed at a lower rate and avoids NIC). They are commonly known as **IR35** rules, from the name of the HMRC document which first introduced them.

IR35 **applies** to anyone who provides his services to a client through an intermediary (usually a company), in circumstances such that he would be treated as an employee of the client but for the existence of the intermediary. The factors outlined in at ¶2988 above are used to decide whether such a worker would be an employee (if a hypothetical contract existed between client and worker).

If the worker is held to be an employee, a certain amount of employment income is taxed on the worker, irrespective of the actual income (in any form) received from the intermediary.

s 51 ITEPA 2003, s 966 ITA 2007 These rules will **not apply** where the worker:
– receives sufficient actual employment income from the intermediary; or
– controls both the intermediary and the client, taking into account any interests of his associates (i.e. relatives (¶2105), business partners, and trustees of settlements established by the individual or his relative); or
– is a non-resident entertainer or sportsman (¶4330).

Case law shows that the issues surrounding these rules are complex, and it is good practice for a potentially affected business to **review** its position regularly.

The intermediary

3014 s 51 ITEPA 2003 Where the intermediary is a **company**, an individual may be caught by the IR35 provisions if the worker (and/or his associates):
– controls more than 5% of ordinary share capital; or
– is entitled to receive more than 5% of any company dividends; or
– could receive payments or benefits from the company in recognition of his services rendered to clients.

MEMO POINTS If the intermediary is a **partnership**, an individual may be caught by these provisions if any of the following apply:
s 52 ITEPA 2003 – the individual is entitled to at least 60% of the partnership's profits; or
– all or most of the partnership's profits relate to a single client; or
– the profit sharing agreement allows the individual to receive an amount which reflects the client's payments in respect of his services.

3016 s 50(4) ITEPA 2003 **Relevant engagement** The "relevant engagement" is the **relationship between the intermediary and the client**, in a case where an employment is held to exist between the client and individual.

Tax Bulletin 74 MEMO POINTS For **NIC purposes**, the test is whether the worker would be regarded as employed in an employed earner's employment (¶4958) by the client. This means that the following could be deemed to be an employee for NIC purposes (but not necessarily for income tax purposes):
– non-executive directors without a service contract;
– cleaners;
– lecturers, teachers and instructors; and
– entertainers.

> EXAMPLE Mr Smith provides services to C plc via his personal company, B Ltd.
> If, in the absence of B Ltd, Mr Smith would effectively be an employee of C plc, then the relationship between B Ltd and C plc is known as a relevant engagement.
> Mr Smith would be taxed as if he had received employment income from C plc.

3017 **Case law** In a case which found that a worker was caught by these provisions, an **agent** was involved in finding work for the intermediary company. In the contract between these two parties, there was a **substitution clause** so that another individual could carry out the work instead of the taxpayer. However, there was no similar substitution clause in the contract between the intermediary company and the client, and this counted against the worker being self-employed. The taxpayer also **worked for a period** of 17 months for the client, with average weekly hours of 58 hours per week, which suggested that the client was obliged to find work for the taxpayer. *Usetech Ltd v Young* [2004]

In another case, it was held that despite the existence of a **service company**, an individual remained employed by his original employer. The individual had been forced into using a service company which was engaged by an agency, but continued to provide the same services to his previous employer. Although there was a contract of employment between the individual and the service company, and there was an intervening agency agreement, this did not preclude the existence of an **implied and enforceable contract** of employment between the individual and the employer. In addition, the employer supplied a mobile phone and laptop to the individual, and paid his phone bills. Internally, the individual still had an employee number. *Cable & Wireless v Muscat* [2006]

A software engineer's company contracted with an agency to provide his services almost exclusively to the Automobile Association (AA) for a period of 3 years. It was held that the engineer should be regarded as an employee of the AA because he was:
– integrated into the business, working mainly at the AA's premises or at home with an internet connection to the office server;
– working as part of a highly skilled team; and
– subject to control by the AA, as his work allocation was decreed by the team leader.

Whilst there was an effective substitution clause in the contract between the company and the agency, this was not the case in the contract between the agency and the AA. The **paperwork retrospectively put in place** to confirm that the AA would indeed accept a substitute, if the need arose, did not reflect the reality of the relationship. *Dragonfly Consulting Ltd v HMRC* [2008]

Implications for the worker

An individual will be taxed on the **gross income of the intermediary** from all relevant engagements, less certain prescribed **expenses**. **3018** s 54 ITEPA 2003

This **pro-forma** shows the calculation of the taxable amount.

MEMO POINTS

		£	£
1.	Gross income received by the intermediary on relevant contracts	X	
	Flat rate deduction of 5%:	(X)	
			X
2.	Add other payments or benefits received by the worker, in respect of the relevant contracts, but not received by the intermediary		X
			X
3.	Deduct the following:		
	Expenses incurred that would be deductible by an employee (¶3135)	X	
	Capital allowances deductible by employee	X	
	Pension contributions paid by the intermediary to a registered scheme	X	
	Employer's NIC paid in respect of the worker (see note)	X	
	Amounts paid to the worker already assessed as employment income	X	
			(X)
	Deemed earnings inclusive of employer's NIC		A
4.	Deduct notional employer's NIC: Employer's rate /(Employer's rate + 100) x A		(B)
	Deemed earnings payment		C

Note: the deduction for employer's NIC paid (step 3) includes Class 1 and Class 1A actually paid during the year.

3020 s 50 ITEPA 2003 The **taxable amount** (otherwise known as the deemed earnings payment) is then reduced by any employment income actually received (and taxed under PAYE) in the tax year. PAYE and NIC are due on the balance as if it were salary paid on 5 April (even though it may never actually be paid to the employee).

Entries are required on the year end PAYE returns (¶4704). Provisional figures are normally used when the forms are first submitted because few workers will have done their accounts by May, so long as subsequent amendments are made by the filing date (¶4484) to reflect the actual position. The related tax and NIC must be paid by 19 April immediately following the tax year to avoid interest charges.

s 57 ITEPA 2003 MEMO POINTS 1. If the individual **stops working** for the intermediary during the tax year, the deemed earnings payment will be assessed at the date of cessation.
2. The **deemed earnings** payment is taken into account for the following:
– the classification of the employee) for the purposes of expenses and benefits (¶3116); and
– earnings for the purposes of registered pension schemes.

EXAMPLE In 2011/12, D Ltd receives gross income of £100,000 from relevant contracts involving Mr E. Mr E also receives vouchers worth £500 as a Christmas present from D Ltd's clients. Mr E receives an annual salary of £40,000 (employer's NIC thereon £4,500) from D Ltd. Travel expenses of £4,000 are incurred, and D Ltd pays a pension contribution of £5,000 to Mr E's pension scheme. D Ltd's year end is 31 March.
The deemed earnings payment is calculated as follows:

Step		£	£
1.	Gross income	100,000	
	Less: 5%	(5,000)	
			95,000
2.	Amounts received from clients		500
			95,500
3.	Less: Expenses		
	Travel expenses	4,000	
	Pension contributions	5,000	
	Employer's NIC paid	4,500	
	Salary paid	40,000	
			(53,500)
			42,000
4.	Employer's NIC: 13.8/113.8 × 42,000		(5,093)
	Deemed earnings payment		36,907

So Mr E is taxed as if he received extra salary of £36,907 on 5 April 2012, and the income tax and NIC must be paid by 19 April 2012 to avoid interest.

3022 s 58 ITEPA 2003 To avoid taxing the same income twice, **dividends** paid out of the amount that has been taxed as a deemed earnings payment will not be taxed again if an appropriate claim is made by the intermediary (within 5 years of 31 January following the tax year in which the dividend is paid).

s 58(5) ITEPA 2003 The deemed earnings payment should be set against dividends of:
a. the same year before those of other years; then
b. paid to him before those paid to others (such as a spouse or civil partner); and then
c. earlier years before those of later years.

MEMO POINTS 1. In the less common situation of a **partnership**, the amount of deemed earnings will be excluded from the individual's taxable trading income.
2. Where a claim is made, the **associated tax credit** will also be ignored in the income tax computation (¶4462).
3. There is no relief in the situation where **further salary is paid** to the individual after the deemed earnings payment crystallises, so further remuneration should preferably be taken in the form of dividends.

Implications for the worker

3026 The deemed earnings payment and related NIC is **deductible** against the intermediary's taxable profits as if it was incurred on 5 April. This can create a trading loss.

MEMO POINTS 1. If the intermediary has a **31 March year end**, relief for the deemed earnings payment will be delayed by almost a year.
2. If a company is also subject to the **construction industry scheme**, any repayments due under that scheme may be set against the PAYE on the deemed earnings payment.

EXAMPLE Continuing the example at ¶3020, D Ltd only obtains relief for the extra salary in the year ended on 31 March 2013. So if D Ltd receives £105,000 of income, incurs other costs of £20,000, and all the same expenses are repeated in that year, the taxable result of D Ltd will be: **3028**

	£	£
Turnover		105,000
Less: Expenses		
Salary	40,000	
Employer's NIC paid	4,500	
Pension contributions	5,000	
Travel expenses	4,000	
Other costs	20,000	
		(73,500)
Taxable profits before adjusting for deemed earnings		31,500
Less: Deemed earnings payment	36,907	
Employer's NIC thereon	5,093	
		(42,000)
Trading loss		(10,500)

Managed service companies (MSCs)

MSCs also allow individuals to save tax and NIC, without the administrative burden of setting up a company themselves, by using a packaged deal supplied by an MSC provider. HMRC view their use as an **avoidance device**, intended to circumvent the IR35 rules. **3029**

Scope A managed service company is **defined** as a company: **3030** s 61B ITEPA 2003
a. whose business consists wholly or mainly of providing (directly or indirectly) the services of an individual to other persons;
b. which pays the majority (if not all) of the consideration it receives for the individual's services to him (including his associates) in a way which saves tax and NIC, so that the remuneration exceeds that which would be received if the payment for the services were employment income of the individual; and,
c. which is involved with an MSC provider (i.e. a person who is in the business of promoting or facilitating the use of companies to provide the services of individuals) or his associate.

MEMO POINTS For this purpose, an **MSC provider** does not include someone who is merely providing normal accounting or legal services to small businesses in a professional capacity i.e. professionally qualified (or training for a professional qualification) and regulated by a regulatory body.

Consequences All **income received** from an MSC is taxed as employment income and liable to PAYE and Class 1 NIC when received. The normal relief for employment expenses (¶3135) operates, treating the client as the employer (so travel to clients' premises is not deductible because it is deemed to be commuting). **3031** s 61D ITEPA 2003

When calculating its **taxable profits**, the MSC can deduct the deemed employment income and employer's NIC in the accounting period when the payments to the individual are taxable. s 164A ITTOIA 2005

Any **debt owed to HMRC** by an MSC (which may have no assets) is recoverable from certain other persons, including: s 688A ITEPA 2003
– the MSC's director, any other officeholders and associates;
– the MSC provider and associates; and
– anyone else who encourages the use of or is actively involved with MSCs, but excluding:

– a person who merely provides accountancy and legal services in a professional capacity; and
– an employment agency which merely places individuals with clients.

MEMO POINTS 1. **Further guidance** can be found on the HMRC website at www.hmrc.gov.uk/employment-status/msc.htm.
2. **Umbrella companies** are not affected by the MSC rules above. These companies make employment income payments to employees who undertake short-term contracts for clients. Their only advantage is enabling the deduction of related expenses when travelling to clients.

SECTION 2

Earnings

A. Regular payments

3032 Generally, once employment status has been established, **remuneration** derived from the employment, including in return for the services of an employee, will be taxed as earnings.

Earnings is **defined** as:

s 62 ITEPA 2003 – any salary, wages or fee;
– any gratuity or other profit or incidental benefit of any kind obtained by the employee if it is in money's worth; or
– anything else that constitutes an emolument of employment.

The **factors** which must be taken into account are:
– whether there is a direct link between the payment and the employment;
– its monetary value; and
– the time when the remuneration is assessed.

s 62(3) ITEPA 2003 MEMO POINTS 1. **Money's worth** is defined as something that is:
– of direct monetary value to the employee; or
– capable of being converted into money or something of direct monetary value to the employee.
2. **Overseas** employments and individuals who are not UK resident or domiciled are considered at ¶4250.
SP 4/97 3. Employees are taxable on **commission** received in respect of goods, investments and services sold to third parties during the course of their employment. Where the employee is obliged to pass on the commission to another party, wholly, exclusively and necessarily to perform his employment duties, he will be able to claim a deduction for the amount paid.

Payment derived from an employment

3034 Earnings can essentially be **summarised** as a payment in return for acting as or being, an employee. In a case involving GCHQ employees, payments made in return for waiving trade union membership rights were held to be earnings, because they were paid in return for the individuals acting as employees, and there was a direct link between the payment and the employment. *Hamblett v Godfrey* [1987]

Providing the earnings arise from the office or employment, they are assessable for tax whether or not they are received from the employer. *Hochstrasser v Mayes* [1960], *Shilton v Wilmshurst* [1991]

3036 Not all payments made by employers to employees constitute earnings, however. Conversely, some payments made by persons other than the employer will constitute earnings.

The crucial test is whether the payment is **derived from the employment**, which essentially means a reward for service, rendered either in the past, currently, or in the future, or to encourage the employee generally.

Each case will be addressed on its merits, but as with employment status, a body of case law exists from which the **following treatments** have evolved: 3038

Type of payment	Details	Reference
Gifts	Recognition of the person, such as gifts on marriage, does not constitute earnings. However, gift vouchers given to employees at Christmas were held to be earnings because the primary reason for the gift was the position of the individuals as employees, with a secondary reason of encouraging future productivity. (The fact that the employees were not contractually entitled to the payment was ignored.)	*Laidler v Perry* [1966]
Prizes	A payment relating to exceptional examination performance was held not to be earnings, as it was paid for personal reasons. However, employees earning more than £8,500 p.a. are still assessed under statute (¶3244).	*Ball v Johnson* [1971]
Compensation	May not be earnings. In the case of a payment made to an employee on the withdrawal of a savings-related share option scheme, it was held that the payment was a recognition of the loss of the right to benefit from the scheme, and not made as a result of employment.	*Wilcock v Eve* [1995]
	However, a payment to an employee in return for giving up a benefit was held to be taxable as earnings.	*Bird v Martland* [1982]
	Where an employer reimburses an employee in respect of bank charges, which have arisen due to a failing of the employer, this will not be earnings.	EIM 01010
Inducement	May be earnings if it can be shown that there is link between the payment and future service. A payment may be taxable even where the old employer, or an unrelated third party, makes a payment to induce an individual to take up employment with another employer.	¶3054
	In a case involving a football player, a sum paid by his old club when he had already joined his new club was still earnings, even though there was no link between the old club and his future service.	*Shilton v Wilmshurst* [1991]
Reasonable expenses	Paid to a teacher attending a course voluntarily has been held not to be earnings.	*Donnelly v Williamson* [1982]
Payments from someone other than the employer	Generally earnings, including tips to waiters or taxi drivers. For the PAYE treatment of tips see ¶4600, and for the NIC treatment see ¶4982.	*Calvert v Wainwright* [1947]
Payments to a third party	By the employer on behalf of the employee are earnings taxable on the employee. So payment of the employee's tailoring bill is taxable as earnings.	*Wilkins v Rogerson* [1960]
Payments made in exceptional circumstances	May not be taxable. Testimonial payments made by the FA to the victorious 1966 England football team captain were held not to be earnings.	*Moore v Griffiths* [1972]
Payment anticipated by employee	It is likely that such a payment will be earnings, as in the case of a cricketer who was assessed on the proceeds from a benefit match.	*Moorhouse v Dooland* [1954]

Disguised earnings provided through third parties

New legislation came into force on 6 April 2011 to discourage the use of a number of methods for rewarding employees by using trusts and other vehicles to hold assets (which may include shares or cash) on their behalf. This strategy relies on the argument that because of the way the arrangements are structured, the employee has no legal right to the assets, and hence is not taxable on their value. 3039 s 554A - s 554Z14 ITEPA 2003

Arrangements of this kind include:
– Employee Benefit Trusts (EBTs);

– trusts used by quoted companies to hold employee shares; and
– Employer Funded Retirement Benefit Schemes (EFRBS).

The legislation **treats as earnings** benefits or sums derived from certain forms of arrangement involving an employer, an employee and a third party to provide rewards or recognition in connection with the employment, in circumstances such that the benefit or sum would not otherwise be taxed as earnings. To fall within this treatment, the arrangements must include:
– a loan of money or assets to the employee; or
– the earmarking (however informally) of money or assets for the subsequent benefit of the employee; or
– a payment of money or transfer of assets to the employee.

HMRC will apply a series of subjective tests to decide whether a particular set of arrangements gives rise to a tax charge.

The **taxable amount** is the higher of:
– the sum of money made available to the employee; and
– the market value of any asset or other benefit provided.

The rules also apply to retirement benefit arrangements other than those made through registered schemes (¶3745), but not to payments that are taxable as pension income.

MEMO POINTS 1. The provisions are very **widely drawn**, embracing employees and employers irrespective of whether the employment relationship is past, present or future, and includes transactions with persons linked to either the employee or the employer.
2. There are a number of **conditional exclusions** for arrangements involving the provision of taxable benefits such as car schemes and share schemes, and for normal commercial transactions or terms.
3. **Earmarking** can also give rise to a tax charge if it involves action by the employer rather than a third party.
4. **Anti-forestalling provisions** apply from 9 December 2010, to ensure that arrangements made before the legislation was finalised still come within its scope.

Value of remuneration

3040 **Monetary** payments made in the form of cash, cheque or bank transfer are the most common forms of earnings, and are easy to value. By its very nature, **non-monetary** remuneration, such as benefits in kind (¶3196) or shares (¶3342), does not have an immediate cash value, so special valuation rules exist.

3042 If an employee **accepts a reduction** in his pay in return for a benefit in kind, the unreduced pay will still be liable to tax. *Heaton v Bell* [1969]

As an **exception**, this rule no longer applies when an employer provides a car as a benefit in kind in return for an agreed reduction in pay, as the employee will almost always be taxed on the benefit in kind.

For salary sacrifices, see ¶3219.

Time of assessment

3044 s 16 ITEPA 2003 **Monetary** earnings are assessed on a receipts basis, irrespective of when the services which relate to the earnings were actually performed. There are special rules for **non-monetary** earnings such as benefits in kind (¶3240 onwards), including vouchers.

In most cases it is straightforward to ascertain when the earnings are assessable. However, the following rules apply if earnings are paid:

s 17 ITEPA 2003 – in a tax year **before commencement** of the employment, when the earnings will be assessed as occurring in the tax year when the employment commences;
– **after cessation** of the employment, such as in the case of continuing medical benefit, when the earnings are assessed on a receipts basis; or

s 13 ITEPA 2003 – **after death**, when it is likely that the employee's personal representatives will be assessed to income tax on a receipts basis.

Earnings for **employees other than directors** are treated as received on the earlier of the following dates: **3046** s 18(1) ITEPA 2003
– when the payment of earnings is made; or
– when the employee becomes entitled to the payment.

EXAMPLE Mr A is entitled to receive a bonus of £10,000 on 28 February 2012. Payment is actually made in June 2012, once the accounts for the year ended 28 February 2012 have been approved.
For income tax purposes, the bonus is received in 2011/12, when the entitlement arose.
If Mr A's entitlement only arose in June, the bonus would be taxed in 2012/13.

For **directors**, the rules are extended so that earnings (whether arising from the directorship or a different role) are treated as received on the earliest of the following dates: **3048** s 18(2) ITEPA 2003
– when the payment of earnings is made;
– when the director becomes entitled to the payment;
– when sums on account of earnings are credited in the company accounts or records (regardless of whether the director has the right to draw the money);
– where the amount of earnings for a period has already been determined, the date on which the period of account ends; or
– where the period of account has already ended, the date when the amount of earnings for a period is determined.

EXAMPLE Mr B is a director of C Ltd. The company year end is 31 October 2010. The amount of each director's bonus is decided at a board meeting in the following March. The accounts are approved at the company's AGM in May 2011, and the bonuses are paid in July 2011.
Mr B's bonus is assessed in 2011/12 because it is determined at the board meeting, and the financial year to which it relates has already ended.

MEMO POINTS 1. For these purposes, a director is **defined** as: s 18(3) ITEPA 2003
– a member of the board of directors which manages the company;
– a single director who manages the company;
– a member of the company where the company is managed by its members; or
– any person in accordance with whose directions or instructions (other than in a professional capacity) the company directors are accustomed to act.
2. It is common for a **general accrual** to be made for directors' bonuses in the draft accounts, which is then approved at the AGM. For the accrual to be recognised for accounting purposes (and therefore for corporation tax), it is important that the company has at least a constructive obligation at the balance sheet date to pay extra remuneration to the directors, and this should be appropriately minuted as a board resolution. If so, the date of the AGM will be the key date for the directors' receipt of remuneration, unless the directors are also shareholders, when the date of the decision regarding the amount of bonuses will be the operative date.

Employment losses

An employee can claim for an employment loss to be set against his **taxable general income** for the loss-making year and/or the previous tax year (¶2478). **3050** s 128 ITA 2007

No relief is given if the main purpose, or one of the main purposes, is to avoid tax.

If the loss is still unrelieved, it is possible to set it against capital gains in the current year. s 130 ITA 2007

B. Lump sum payments

Payments may be made to an employee in the form of a lump sum on the commencement, termination or variation of an employment. Such payments are often made as compensation for the loss or surrender of rights, or for failure to give notice of the termination of an employment. Alternatively, a lump sum payment may simply be made to reward an employee for past or future service. **3052**

1. Inducement payments

3054 The **crucial question** with respect to payments made on the commencement of employment, is whether the payment is a reward for becoming an employee, in anticipation of future service. If this is the case, the payment will be taxed as earnings. In contrast, payments that are shown to be compensation for giving up an advantage relating to a previous employment will be free from income tax.

Each case must be addressed on its own merits. However, the very fact that a payment will be tax-free if it is not earnings means that HMRC will generally argue that a payment constitutes earnings.

3056 The distinction can be **illustrated** by two cases. In the first, the controlling shareholder of a company transferred shares to the senior partner of a firm of chartered accountants. The transfer was made as consideration for an agreement that the partner would leave his position with the practice and take up the role of joint managing director of the company. The transfer of shares was held not to be taxable earnings. *Pritchard v Arundale* [1971]

In the second case, a cash payment was made to induce an accountant to give up the security, status and prospects of his position with an international firm of chartered accountants and take up employment as the financial director of a company. This payment was held to be earnings because it constituted protection against the risks involved in moving employment, rather than compensation for the loss of advantage. *Glantre Engineering v Goodhand* [1983]

Comment The two cases above can be **distinguished** by the following factors:
– in the first case the payment was in the form of a transfer of shares by someone other than the employer, whereas in the second case the payment originated from the employer;
– the taxpayer in the first case changed his professional status from senior partner to that of managing director, whereas in the second case the taxpayer continued to work as an accountant; and
– the transfer of shares in the first case occurred 3 months before the employment commenced.

2. Payments on cessation of employment

General principles

3060 EIM12800 There are **many factors** which influence the tax treatment of a lump sum received such as:
– the intention behind the award (e.g. a bonus for past service, dismissal, redundancy, ill-health, retirement);
– the various elements of the package itself;
– whether it is customary for the employer to pay a lump sum at the end of an employment;
– the terms of the employment contract (which should include notice periods, holiday entitlement, and may include a payment in lieu of notice (PILON) clause and restrictive covenants); and
– other documentation such as board minutes, and correspondence relating to the termination.

3062 Depending on the circumstances, either part or all of the payment may be exempt from tax if it is a valid termination payment (¶3078).

EIM 12810 To decide on the tax treatment, HMRC apply the following **four tests** to each element of a package. The tests are applied strictly in the order shown. If a payment is caught by more than one test, it will be taxed under the earliest (for example, a payment which is both earnings and a termination payment is taxed as earnings).

Test	Criteria	Tax treatment	¶¶
1	Earnings from the employment	Taxable	¶3064
2	Restrictive covenant	Taxable	¶3068
3	Benefits from an employer financed retirement benefit scheme	Taxable	¶3072
4	Termination payment	Possibly exempt	¶3078

a. Earnings from employment

Contractual payments

If the elements of a package are **contractual**, and paid **in return for services**, they will be taxable as earnings on general principles. Such payments may include salary up to the termination date, a bonus, benefits while employed and holiday pay. **3064** s 6 ITEPA 2003 EIM12976

If the employee is on **gardening leave**, any payments made during the period will be taxable as earnings and liable to NIC, because the employee is still employed until the end of the notice period, even though he is not attending his place of work.

MEMO POINTS 1. Evidence of a **contractual** commitment may be found in the staff handbook or the letter offering employment.
2. If the employee **disposes** of shares in the employer company on cessation of employment, any excess consideration received over market value is likely to be taxed as earnings.
3. **Loan** write offs (¶3336) are always taxable, except on death.

Unfair dismissal

Where damages for unfair dismissal are awarded by an employment tribunal, the tax treatment will depend on whether the employee is reinstated. **3065** EIM12960

If the employee is **reinstated or re-engaged**, there is no termination, and any arrears of pay are usually taxable as earnings.

Otherwise, any compensatory award is a valid termination payment.

MEMO POINTS 1. Compensation awarded in relation to the employer's failure to provide a **written statement** detailing the reasons for dismissal is also a termination payment for tax purposes.
2. In a recent case, an individual was employed by a city council, and received an allowance for using his car on council business. The council **terminated this contract** so that it could vary the employment and remove the allowance. On appeal to an employment tribunal, it was held that the termination of the previous contract was unfair, and the council was ordered to pay compensation and reinstate the car allowance. The parties agreed a compromise and a compensation payment was made voluntarily. HMRC argued that this was taxable, but it was held that the payment was made to compensate the taxpayer for unfair dismissal, and so it was a valid termination payment. *Wilson v Clayton* [2004]

Payments in lieu of notice (PILONs)

A PILON can **include** the following: **3066** EIM12975
- a contractual payment to avoid giving adequate notice;
- a discretionary payment made by the employer instead of giving notice; and
- a payment agreed between the employer and employee at the time of termination with no prior contractual commitment or understanding.

An employer who has **established a practice** of making non-contractual PILONs may be deemed to have created an implied term in the employment contract, and subsequent payments to other employees in the same situation are likely to be taxable. HMRC distinguish between the case where an employer automatically makes a payment, and an employer who undertakes a genuine critical assessment of each individual employee's circumstances. Tax Bulletin 63

3067 The tax treatment of PILONs has been subject to much interpretative case law.

If a contractual PILON is subject to the **employer's discretion**, the payment will constitute earnings, because it is paid in lieu of salary that the employee should otherwise have received, and the contract is not breached. *EMI Group Electronics Ltd v Coldicott* [1999]

In a similar case involving a compromise agreement on termination, a lump sum was paid, and as there was **no identifiable breach** of the contract, the discretionary PILON was taxable (even though the payment did not follow the amount or form specified in the contract). *Richardson v Delaney* [2001]

Where the **employer ignores the contract** by failing to give notice, and fails to make payment, any compensation payable to the employee for breach of contract is not a discretionary PILON and is not therefore earnings from employment. *Cerberus Software Ltd v Rowley* [2001]

If a PILON is made **in circumstances contemplated in the employment contract**, the payment must be taxable as earnings. Although the contract itself did not give the employer the right to dismiss employees on the payment of a PILON, there was a reference to a memorandum of understanding agreed between the employer and trade union. It was this document which contained provisions relating to redundancy, notice periods and PILONS. *SCA Packaging Ltd v HMRC* [2007]

EXAMPLE Mr C earns £60,000 p.a. and his employment is to be terminated. In his contract, there are provisions relating to a notice period of 6 months, with a discretionary PILON clause. Mr C works 2 months of his notice period. The employer pays Mr C £40,000, and it is likely that the following treatment will result:

a. £20,000 will be taxed as a contractual payment in lieu of the 4 months' salary which Mr C would have received if he had worked out his notice period; and
b. £20,000 will be treated as a termination payment.

b. Restrictive covenants

3068 s 225 ITEPA 2003

A restrictive covenant payment is **defined** as a payment which is made to the employee in return for restricting their future activities (whether legally valid or not), and is taxable as earnings. The payment will be taxed on the employee in the year of assessment in which it is made.

If the restrictive covenant payment is made after the **death** of the employee, it is deemed to have been made immediately before the date of death.

Comment It is **common practice** to include a nominal amount in a termination package which is easily identifiable as a restrictive covenant, and this will be taxed accordingly. It is necessary to attribute some monetary value to the covenant, as without any consideration, the covenant is not legally binding.

Contained within compromise agreements

3070 SP 3/96

HMRC will not seek to tax a payment, made in respect of a restrictive covenant under a compromise agreement, which **reaffirms undertakings** stated in the original employment contract, or contains a provision which states that:
– the agreement is in full and final settlement of the employee's claims; and/or
– the employee agrees not to commence legal proceedings, and to discontinue any which may already be in progress.

EIM 03606 However, if the payment is **excessive**, HMRC may seek to tax it.

c. Benefits from an employer financed retirement benefit scheme

3072 s 401 ITEPA 2003

A payment will be at risk from an HMRC challenge under this provision, and therefore taxable, if the employee is at, or approaching, **retirement age** (determined either by the employment contract or the state pension age). Any payment under an arrangement could be caught, unless the package includes only benefits and no cash.

MEMO POINTS HMRC consider that an **arrangement** exists where the payment flows from any prior formal, or informal, understanding with the employee, or as a result of any system, plan, pattern or policy. Payments made in the following circumstances would be caught under this provision:
– as a result of a decision at a meeting;
– decided upon by a personnel manager who is acting under delegated authority; or
– where it is common practice for an employer to make such a payment to a particular class of employee.

d. Termination payments

Charge to tax

Payments which are validly made in connection with the termination or variation of employment are not usually taxable as earnings. However, each element of a package should be analysed to decide whether it constitutes earnings, a payment for restrictive covenants, or a retirement benefit, before taxing it as a termination payment. **3078** s 401 ITEPA 2003

Valid termination payments would include:
– redundancy payments, both statutory and non-statutory;
– non-contractual PILONs where there is no implied agreement;
– compensation for loss of office or variation of employment; and
– damages for breach of contract or wrongful dismissal.

A payment made to any of the following **in connection** with the termination of the employee's employment is deemed to have been paid to the employee: **3079**
– the spouse, civil partner, relative or any dependant of the employee; or
– the personal representatives of the employee.

MEMO POINTS 1. An employer who wishes to confirm the tax treatment of proposed termination payments should apply for **clearance** from HMRC. The written application should be accompanied with copies of relevant correspondence to employees. SP 1/94
2. An employee is dismissed by reason of **redundancy** if the dismissal is wholly or mainly attributable to the fact that: s 139 ERA 1996
a. his employer's business has either:
– completely ceased or there is an intention for this to be so; or
– ceased business in the place where the employee was so employed; or
b. the requirements of that business for employees to carry out work of a particular kind has either:
– completely ceased or diminished; or
– ceased or diminished in the place where the employee was so employed.
3. **Damages** will usually take account of the Gourley principle, which means that the amount awarded puts the employee back into the position he would have been in had he continued to work, suffering tax and NIC under PAYE. If the damages themselves are then taxable, this penalises the employee, because he is effectively charged twice on the same amount. So in practice, the award of damages is adjusted for any extra tax which falls due.

Unless an exemption applies, the payment will be taxed in the year of assessment in which it is received. **3080**

A **cash payment** is deemed to have been received on the earlier of the date on which:
– the sum is paid; or
– the recipient becomes entitled to the payment.

Benefits in kind, whether provided by the employer or a third party, are treated as received when they are used or enjoyed, and are valued at an amount equal to the cash equivalent (¶3246). The right to receive future benefits is not itself regarded as having taxable value. Where there is any potential **overlap** between the rules for benefits in kind and termination payments, the former take precedence.

The **amount of tax deducted** will not only depend on any exemptions which are available, but also on the timing of the issue of form P45 (¶4679). Where a P45 is issued before the termination payment is made, basic rate tax must be deducted from any taxable amount. Otherwise, the usual payroll procedures should be observed (¶4642), and the taxable amount included on the P45. **3082** SI 2003/2682 reg 37

Exemptions

3084 If a **payment** is validly made on termination, the following types of exemption are available:
- a basic £30,000 tax-free sum (¶3086);
- payments on death or disability (¶3089);
- payments to a registered pension scheme (¶3090); and
- certain payments relating to foreign service (¶3092).

In addition, the following **costs incurred by the employer** on behalf of the employee may be exempt from tax:
- outplacement counselling;
- retraining; and
- legal advice.

ss 411 - 412 ITEPA 2003

MEMO POINTS There are also exemptions for payments:
- received from **Commonwealth government** superannuation schemes; and
- made to members of the **armed forces**.

3086 s 403 ITEPA 2003

Tax-free amount The **maximum** exemption for each employment is £30,000. The exemption is applied first to cash payments and then benefits.

For these purposes **two or more payments** will be treated as deriving from the same employment and therefore eligible for only one £30,000 exemption where the payment is from:
- the same employer; or
- different employments with the same or associated employers (i.e. employers under common control).

If the threshold is **not used up in one tax year**, it can be carried forward and set against payments made in respect of the same employment in future tax years.

EXAMPLE Mr D's employment with E Ltd was terminated on 31 December 2010. As compensation for the loss of employment, Mr D was given a cash sum of £25,000 (payable in two equal instalments, on 31 December 2010 and 31 December 2011), and the use of his company car until 31 December 2011. The cash equivalent of the car was £3,000 for the period 1 January 2011 to 5 April 2011, and £8,000 for the remainder of 2011.
The £30,000 exemption will be applied as follows:

	£
2010/11	
Termination payment	12,500
Cash equivalent of car	3,000
	15,500
Less: Exemption (restricted)	(15,500)
	Nil
2011/12	
Termination payment	12,500
Cash equivalent of car	8,000
	20,500
Less: Balance of exemption (30,000 – 15,500)	(14,500)
Taxable car benefit	6,000

3087 s 309 ITEPA 2003

Statutory redundancy payments made under the Employment Rights Act 1996 (or under equivalent Northern Ireland legislation) are exempt from income tax. Such payments will, however, reduce the £30,000 tax-free limit.

Many employers pay amounts in **excess** of the statutory amount, and provided the whole amount is a genuine redundancy payment, it will all be treated as a termination payment.

EXAMPLE Mr F was made redundant and received £15,000 of statutory redundancy pay. He was also given his company car (cash equivalent £17,000) as compensation. Although the redundancy pay will not be subject to tax, it will reduce the amount of the exemption available with respect to the car to £15,000. (30,000 – 15,000)
The taxable amount will therefore be £2,000. (17,000 – 15,000)

Payments on death or disability Tax will not be **charged** on any payment or other benefit provided by an employer: 3089 s 406 ITEPA 2003
- in connection with the termination of employment on the death of an employee; or
- on account of injury to, or disability of, an employee.

To qualify under the latter exemption it must be established that either an injury or disability exists, and it was for this reason alone that the employer made the payment. EIM13620

This exemption must be considered at the time of the termination, as a **subsequent medical condition** cannot be cited as the reason for any payment.

MEMO POINTS 1. For these purposes, the term **disability** covers not only a condition resulting from a sudden affliction, but also continuing incapacity to perform the employment duties arising from deterioration of physical or mental health caused by chronic illness.
2. There must be medical **evidence** confirming the nature of the disability. *Horner v Hasted* [1995]

Payments to a registered pension scheme Where a lump sum is paid under the provisions of a registered occupational pension scheme, it will be **exempt** from tax and NIC if the payment is: 3090 s 407 ITEPA 2003
- compensation for either loss of employment or a decrease in earnings due to ill-health; or
- has been earned by past service.

MEMO POINTS 1. Special **employer contributions** to a registered pension scheme (personal or occupational) will be exempt from tax and NIC, if the related benefits are within the scheme rules. s 408 ITEPA 2003
2. Similarly, tax will not be charged where the employer purchases an **approved annuity** from a life office for an employee.

Defrayal of employee liabilities A payment or benefit may be exempt if it represents the reimbursement of a **deductible expense** (¶3122) of the employment. The payment or benefit must be provided during the period starting with the termination of the employment, and ending on 5 April of the sixth tax year following that in which the termination occurred. 3091 s 409 - s 410 ITEPA 2003

If the employee is deceased, a payment or benefit provided to his personal representatives is similarly exempt.

Periods of foreign service A payment may be fully or partially exempt where an employee has undertaken foreign service during his employment, and makes an appropriate claim within 5 years and 10 months following the tax year. 3092 s 413 ITEPA 2003

A period of foreign service is **defined** as a period when all duties of the employment were undertaken outside the UK; and either:
- the employee was UK domiciled but not resident and ordinarily resident (¶4152) in the UK; or
- resident and ordinarily resident in the UK, but non-UK domiciled and working for a foreign employer (¶4252).

The following table sets out the **criteria** to be satisfied for the payment to be fully exempt:

Period of service up to termination	Period of foreign service
Any duration	At least 75% of the whole period of service
More than 10 years	The last 10 years of service
More than 20 years	At least 50% of the whole period of service, including any 10 of the last 20 years

Where the employee's foreign service **does not meet the criteria** in ¶3092 above, the termination payment will be taxed as follows: 3093 s 414 ITEPA 2003

a. deduct the tax-free sum of £30,000; and

b. apply the following fraction to the remaining amount to calculate the taxable payment.

$$\frac{\text{Foreign service}}{\text{Total service}} \times \text{Amount otherwise chargeable to tax}$$

EXAMPLE Mr G has been employed by H Ltd since 1 October 2000, being in foreign service for a number of years. His employment is terminated, and he receives a lump sum of £50,000.
1. If Mr G's foreign service had commenced on 1 October 2003, and the employment terminated on 30 September 2011, the lump sum would be wholly tax exempt, because the 75% test is satisfied (8 years of foreign service from a total period of 10 years).
2. If Mr G's foreign service had commenced on 1 October 2004, and the employment terminated on 30 September 2011, the 75% test would not be satisfied (7 years of foreign service from a total period of 11 years). In this case, the payment would be taxed as follows:

	£
Total lump sum	50,000
Less: £30,000 exemption	(30,000)
	20,000
Less: Reduction for foreign service	
7 years/11 years × 20,000	(12,727)
Taxable amount	7,273

3094
s 310 ITEPA 2003

Outplacement counselling Where counselling is **provided by the employer**, the costs incurred (including related travel expenses) are not taxable on the employee, if all of the following conditions are met:
a. the employee must have been employed (either full-time or part-time) for a 2 year period ending either when the counselling begins, or when the employment ends;
b. the only or main purpose of the counselling is to enable the employee to adjust to losing his job or find some other method of earning income (including self-employment);
c. the counselling is generally available to employees or a particular class of employee; and
d. the counselling consists of the giving of advice, imparting skills, or providing normal office facilities or equipment.

MEMO POINTS 1. Any amount attributable to outplacement counselling does not use up the £30,000 **tax-free amount**.
2. There is tax relief for the costs of **retraining** provided by the employer in the event of redundancy (¶3210).

3096
s 413A ITEPA 2003

Legal costs By concession, where an **employer agrees to pay** the employee's legal costs in relation to the termination of his employment, this would normally be a taxable benefit for the employee.

However, the employee will be exempt from tax, where the dispute is settled:
a. outside Court and all of the following apply;
– the employer pays the solicitor direct;
– the fees paid only relate to the termination of employment; and
– the fees are paid under a specific term in the settlement agreement; or
b. by a **Court Order** and payment is made under such an order (even if the payment is made direct to an employee).

EIM13740

If the solicitor finds it necessary to consult with another professional, such as an accountant, whose fees are treated as **disbursements** by the solicitor, then these will also be included within the legal costs which could qualify for exemption.

e. Reporting requirements

3098
SI 2003/2682 reg 91

Employers must provide HMRC with a report including details of any payments or benefits in excess of £30,000 paid to employees on the termination (or variation of employment), unless the payment is purely in cash and form P45 has not already been issued. The report must be submitted no later than 6 July following the end of the tax year. There is no requirement to report a termination package worth less than £30,000.

3100
SI 2003/2682 reg 91(3)

The report **must state** the following:
– the total package (including estimates where necessary);
– the payments and benefits paid in the year of termination;

– any future payments and benefits to be paid; and
– the total number of years in which the package will be paid with details of any event which would reduce this period.

If an event occurs which causes the **reported payments to change**, a further report should be made no later than 6 July following the tax year in which the event occurs. SI 2003/2682 reg 92

3102 SI 2003/2682 reg 96 **Employees** must be provided with the same information as contained within the report. The employee should include the termination payment on his tax return, to ensure that the correct amount of tax is paid.

3. Payments on variation of employment duties

3104 The same **criteria** and reporting requirements apply to lump sum payments paid on the variation of an employment in connection with a change of duties, as on the cessation of employment (¶3060).

EXAMPLE As a result of a company being privatised, employees were offered the following amounts for accepting a variation to their terms and conditions of employment:
a. 30% of the amount which would have been received had the employees been made redundant by the old employer; and
b. £100 per year of service, to a maximum of £700.
It was held that **a.** was not taxable as it was compensation for giving up the right to a redundancy payment, but **b.** was taxable as it was an inducement payment to agree to the new employment conditions. *Mairs v Haughey* [1993]

SECTION 3

Expenses and benefits

3114 An employee is generally taxable on expenditure which is incurred by the employer on his behalf. A claim may be made to deduct business-related expenses from taxable earnings. Benefits in kind are also taxable on most employees (for retired employees, see ¶3667).

Expenses and benefits must be valued inclusive of VAT where it applies, and are not subject to immediate deduction of income tax through the payroll. Instead, the employer must report all relevant items to HMRC on forms P11D or P9D (¶4730), and the employee pays tax through his PAYE code (¶4618) for the next year, or through his self-assessment return (¶4476).

Classification of employees for this purpose

3116 ss 216-217 ITEPA 2003 The rules for expenses and benefits in kind depend on the type of employee, **defined** as follows:

Term	Definition	Directors (¶3120)	Summary at:
Relevant employee	An individual who earns at a rate of £8,500 or more p.a.	Included	¶3124
Lower paid	An individual earning less than £8,500 p.a.	Not included (with a limited exception)	¶3240
The threshold of £8,500 has not changed since 1979. Given the National Minimum Wage, it is now unusual for an employee to be treated as lower paid.			

3118 s 218 ITEPA 2003 To determine whether the **threshold** of £8,500 has been met or exceeded, the following items must be taken into account, on the basis of amounts earned in the tax year:
– salary;
– all benefits received, whether taxable on all employees or under the provisions relating to relevant employees (including share schemes etc), but excluding exempt income;

– any deemed earnings arising from the personal service company provisions (¶3010); and
– expenses incurred by the employee and reimbursed by the employer (other than those for which a dispensation (¶4738) is in force).

Deductions may be made for registered pension contributions, and contributions under payroll giving schemes. No deduction is made for expenses of employment.

MEMO POINTS 1. If an employee is employed for only **part of the year**, the threshold is compared to the annualised earnings.

s 220 ITEPA 2003 2. Where a person has **two or more employments** with the same employer, the total income from all employments is aggregated. If the threshold is exceeded, the employee is treated as a relevant employee for all of the employments.

s 219 ITEPA 2003 3. Where the employee is offered **a choice** of either a company car or a cash alternative then, for the purposes of the threshold calculation, the higher of the following should be included:
– the appropriate percentage of the price of the car (see ¶3294 and following) plus the fuel scale charge if applicable (¶3304); or
– the cash alternative.

4. Where the employer pays for **fuel** via a credit card or voucher, only the fuel benefit (¶3304) is taken into account.

EXAMPLE Mr A has an annual salary of £6,500, and makes a gross pension contribution of £240 in the year. His employer provides private medical insurance at a cost of £250, and the employee has a choice between a car with an assessable benefit of £2,100, or a cash alternative of £1,600 p.a.
The following calculation is required:

	£
Salary	6,500
Less: Pension contribution	(240)
Add: Private medical insurance	250
Car benefit (higher of £2,100 and £1,600)	2,100
	8,610

Mr A is a relevant employee because his earnings exceed £8,500 p.a.

Directors

3120 s 67 ITEPA 2003 As directors are in a position of control, they may be able to influence the level of benefits which they receive and are therefore identified separately.

A director is treated as a relevant employee **unless** he:
a. earns less than £8,500 per annum;
b. does not have a material interest (essentially more than 5% of the ordinary share capital of a company); and **either**
c. he is a full-time working director (devoting substantially the whole of his time to the service of the company in a managerial or technical capacity); or
d. he is a director of a non-profit making company or charitable organisation.

"Director" includes a **shadow director**: that is, anyone whose instructions the directors usually follow.

I. Expenses

A. General principles

3122 s 72 ITEPA 2003 As a general rule, where an **employer settles an expense**, the employee will be treated as having received taxable earnings. This may be relieved by a claim to deduct expenses in relation to the duties of employment, or by a dispensation (¶4738) arranged by the employer.

Less common is the situation where the employee incurs **expenses which are not reimbursed by the employer**. The employee will be at a disadvantage, having incurred expenses out of taxed income. A claim should be made to deduct business expenses from taxable income.

EXAMPLE Mr B receives an annual salary of £30,000 from C Ltd and incurs £1,500 of employment expenses in the tax year.
1. If C Ltd does not reimburse Mr B, he will have a net salary of £28,500 but, in the absence of a claim, he will still be taxed on income of £30,000.
2. If C Ltd reimburses Mr B, he will (in the absence of a claim) be treated as if he had received earnings of £31,500.
In both cases Mr B will effectively pay tax on £1,500 which he has in fact used to pay expenses.

If the relevant conditions are satisfied, he can submit a claim which will reduce earnings by the amount of the expense:

1. No reimbursement

	£
Salary	30,000
Less: Claim	(1,500)
Taxable	28,500

2. Expenses reimbursed

	£
Salary	30,000
Reimbursed expenses	1,500
	31,500
Less: Claim	(1,500)
Taxable	30,000

Summary

The **tax treatment** of expenses depends on the type of payment and of employee, as follows: 3124

Payment method	Lower paid employee	Relevant employee	¶¶
Reimbursement	Not taxable unless excessive	Taxable but may claim deduction	¶3128
No reimbursement	May claim deduction	May claim deduction	¶3130
Employer pays directly	Not taxable	Taxable but may claim deduction	¶3132

Timing

Expenses are **deemed to be incurred** in the same tax year as the earnings to which they relate. 3126 ss 327 - 328 ITEPA 2003

EXAMPLE Mr D incurred employment expenses on 15 March 2012 which were reimbursed to him on 12 April 2012. The expenses will be taxed in 2012/13.

Expenses paid by employee and reimbursed by employer

Relevant employees (¶3116) are assessed on any cash payment made to them arising from the employment. Any expenses paid to such an employee are therefore earnings. For example, an employee who is reimbursed for a train fare incurred on a business trip would be liable to tax on that amount. 3128 ss 70, 216 ITEPA 2003

Where the relevant conditions are satisfied (¶3135), a claim may be submitted which will allow the taxpayer to **deduct** a corresponding amount from his taxable income. As a result, the employee will not be taxed on genuine business expenses.

In practice, where it can be shown that specific expenses payments will always be covered by such a claim, a **dispensation** (¶4738) can be obtained which will avoid the necessity of completing a P11D and having to make an expense claim.

Employers are obliged to **declare** to HMRC all expenses payments made to employees, unless a dispensation is in place.

MEMO POINTS Expenses reimbursed to **lower paid employees** are not taxable where the reimbursement is an:
– exact repayment of expenses incurred in performing the duties of employment;
– allowance to cover expenses whilst away from home; or
– HMRC-agreed scale allowance.
Any excessive payments, however, may be taxable.

Expenses incurred by employee with no reimbursement

3130 Where the appropriate conditions are satisfied, **any employee** who incurs expenses without reimbursement may claim a deduction against his taxable earnings. HMRC will, however, often query the validity of expenses where there has been no reimbursement by the employer, because an employer would be expected to provide the tools and equipment for the employee to carry out his duties.

Expenses incurred directly by the employer

3132 For **relevant employees**, expenditure incurred directly by the employer will be taxable as earnings. A corresponding claim for a deduction can be submitted providing the conditions (¶3135) are satisfied.

For **lower paid employees**, the direct payment of bills on behalf of an employee will not be taxable unless it is the payment of a monetary liability. For example, the direct payment of a telephone bill (i.e. where the bill is addressed to the employer) is not subject to tax.

B. Claiming a deduction

3135 For an expense to **be allowable as a deduction**, an appropriate claim (known as a section 336 claim) must be submitted to HMRC. Form P87 is available for this purpose, so long as expenses do not exceed £2,500 (when a self-assessment tax return must be completed instead).

s 337 ITEPA 2003 The conditions for making a claim depend on the nature of the expense:
– qualifying **travel** expenses must have been incurred necessarily in the performance of the duties of the employment;
ss 15, 36 CAA 2001 – **capital allowances** claimed in respect of assets must relate to expenses incurred necessarily in the performance of the duties of the employment; and
s 336(1) ITEPA 2003 – all **other expenses** must have been incurred wholly, exclusively and necessarily in the performance of the employment duties.

3136 The phrase **wholly, exclusively and necessarily** is derived from the legislation but each element of it has been the subject of much case law. Even when all three elements apply, the expenses must relate specifically to the employment, rather than to the individual who holds the employment. This means that the duties of the employment must require the outlay of the expense, with any personal benefit being merely incidental. *Ricketts v Colquhoun* [1926]

Wholly and exclusively

3138 An expense may be incurred for the **purposes** of the employment but may not wholly and exclusively relate to that employment. For example, if a company decided to install a telephone in the home of an employee so that he could make business calls, the cost of the business calls would be deductible. The line rental would not, because the line can be used to make personal calls and is therefore not wholly and exclusively used for the employment.

Necessarily

The requirement for an expense to have been incurred necessarily in the performance of duties **means** that it would not be possible to perform the duties without the expense being incurred. 3140

The question of necessity can be **illustrated** by two contrasting cases, both concerning a claim for the deduction of the cost of the subscription to a club.

The claim of a bank manager, who was required to be a member of the club to further the business of his employer, was rejected on the basis that the duties of the manager's office could be performed without joining the club. *Brown v Bullock* [1961]

A claim by the director of a company based in Northern Ireland, who was required to make frequent visits to London in the course of his duties was, however, allowed on the basis that the object of joining the club was to obtain low cost accommodation and other facilities connected with the employment. Any benefit to the director resulting from the membership was held to be merely incidental. *Elwood v Utitz* [1966] HMRC's view is that this case is very unusual, and often the deductibility of expenditure in similar circumstances will be resisted.

In the performance of duties

The issue of whether an expense is incurred in the performance of duties is primarily a **question of fact**. 3142

A number of journalists were required to read certain journals and periodicals as a condition of their employment. It was held that the related cost was not deductible, and that a distinction must be drawn between expenditure incurred to put the employee in a position to perform his duties efficiently (not deductible), and expenditure incurred as part of those duties (deductible). *Smith v Abbott* [1994]

In two contrasting cases involving doctors, the key issue was **when the employment duties begin**. A general practitioner who also worked as a part-time consultant was on call and issued instructions by phone before leaving home to travel to the hospital. It was held that he commenced his employment duties when he took the phone call, and so his travel expenses were deductible. *Pook v Owen* [1969]

In another case, a doctor worked at three hospitals (including for the on-call roster), and as his duties did not commence before arriving at each particular hospital, he could not claim the travel expenses as an employment expense. *Parikh v Sleeman* [1990]

Limit on deduction

The amount of a deductible expense is limited to the amount of the earnings from which it is to be deducted. It is not possible for an allowable **loss** to be created, and surplus expenses cannot be set against other income. 3144 s 329 ITEPA 2003

EXAMPLE Mrs E has two employments. She earns £20,000 from her full-time employment, and earns £1,000 from her part-time position. She incurs travel expenses of £1,200 in relation to the part-time position which are not reimbursed.
The maximum deduction that Mrs E can claim is £1,000, as she can only make a claim up to the amount of earnings from the employment in respect of which the travel expenses were incurred.

C. Expenses subject to special rules

Summary

Some expenses in employment do not fall within the general principles outlined above because the conditions for claiming a deduction are different, or because special rules are required for calculating the amount of the expense. These expenses are covered in greater detail as follows: 3146

Expense	¶¶
Travel and subsistence	¶3148
Business entertaining	¶3182
Subscriptions	¶3184
Working at home	¶3186
Payroll giving	¶3189
Capital allowances	¶3191
Employee's liability and indemnity insurance	¶3192
Interest relief on loans	¶4363

1. Travel and subsistence

3148 s 337 ITEPA 2003 Booklet 490

Employees are taxed on travel and subsistence expenses incurred by reason of the employment and paid for or provided by the employer (or a third party), either directly or by way of reimbursement.

Where the expenses are incurred necessarily in the performance of the duties, the employee will be able to claim a deduction from his earnings.

a. Qualifying situations

3150 Whether travel and subsistence expenses (referred to for the remainder of this section as travel expenses) are incurred in the **performance of the duties** of the employment will depend in part on the nature of the journey. Broadly, a deduction will not be available if the journey represents ordinary commuting or private travel.

Qualifying travel expenses

3151 s 338 ITEPA 2003

Qualifying travelling expenses are **defined** as those incurred in the performance of the duties of the employment which are:

– necessarily incurred in travelling in the performance of those duties; or

– other travelling expenses attributable to the necessary attendance of the employee at any place of work (other than expenses connected with ordinary commuting or private travel).

Ordinary commuting is deemed to be travel between the employee's home and the permanent workplace, where the employee regularly attends to perform his duties of employment.

Private travel is deemed to be travel from the employee's home to somewhere other than a workplace. The key issue is primary purpose of the trip. For example, if an employee undertakes a journey in order to carry out employment duties, but he also visits a relative in the same town after work, the journey will not be private travel.

A journey directly from the office to a client site for a meeting will be an allowable deduction, but the following scenarios are not as clear cut:

– travel between home and workplace;

– travel between home and workplace where home is also a place of work;

– travelling between two employments; and

– travelling between two centres of the same employment.

Each of these scenarios is considered in the following paragraphs.

Travel between home and workplace

3153 As a **general rule**, the cost of travel between an employee's home and his normal place of work will not be a deductible expense. However, an **exception** allows employees to claim a deduction for qualifying travelling expenses between home and a temporary workplace.

A **temporary workplace** is a place that the employee attends in the performance of the duties of the employment for the purpose of performing a task of limited duration. 3154 s 339 ITEPA 2003

If there is no substantial effect on the journey time or expense normally incurred, travel to such a temporary workplace would still constitute ordinary commuting.

EXAMPLE Mr F normally drives the 20 miles to his employer's office. He is temporarily seconded to another office, which is only 3 miles away from his usual workplace.
This will still be treated as ordinary commuting, and hence he cannot claim a deduction in respect of his new journey.

A workplace which is attended for a **limited duration** will still be a permanent workplace if the employee attends it for practically all of the period for which he is likely to hold that employment. 3155

A workplace will **become permanent** if it is attended (or is likely to be so) for a period of continuous work of more than 24 months, during which time 40% or more of the employee's working time is spent there. It is therefore possible for an employee to have more than one permanent workplace at the same time.

Where the workplace is **expected to be temporary**, but it is then decided that the employee will actually be spending more than 24 months there, travel expenses incurred:
– up to the date when the decision is made are deductible;
– after that date relate to ordinary commuting, and no deduction can be claimed.

MEMO POINTS 1. Where the period of continuous work is 24 months or less but is likely to represent all of the employee's **remaining period of employment**, the workplace cannot be treated as temporary.
2. If the employee travels **direct from home to a temporary workplace**, he can claim the full cost as a deduction.
3. Where the employee **passes the permanent workplace** on the way to a temporary workplace, but does not stop there, he can claim a deduction for the whole journey from home to the temporary workplace.
4. For an **agency worker** (¶3004), each assignment is treated as a separate employment, and each workplace is therefore a permanent workplace. Where an agency worker **undertakes a number of different jobs on the same day** (e.g. nurses), HMRC will accept a deduction for the cost of travel between different jobs on the same day. However, there will be no deduction for the cost of travel: Booklet 490 para 3.19
– from home to the first job of the day; or
– to home from the last job of the day.

EXAMPLE Mr G lives in Town X and works 5 days a week in Town Y. He is not entitled to claim a deduction for the expense of travelling between the two towns.
Mr G's employer is setting up a new branch, and asks him to spend a proportion of his time in Town Z.
If Mr G is asked to spend:
1. 3 days a week in Town Z for a period of 18 months, he can claim a deduction for travel to Town Z, because the period is less than 24 months.
2. 1 day a week in Town Z for a period of 26 months, he can claim a deduction for travel to Town Z, because although the period exceeds 24 months, Mr G is spending less than 40% of his time there.
3. 3 days a week for a period of 26 months, he will not be entitled to a deduction as he will be deemed to have a permanent workplace in both Town Y and Town Z.
4. 3 days a week for a period of 30 months, but Mr G actually only spends 18 months in Town Z. There is still no deduction, because the initial intention was for Town Z to become a permanent workplace.
5. 3 days a week for a period of 18 months, although after 12 months, this is extended to a total of 28 months. Mr G can claim a deduction for travel to Town Z for the first year only, until the decision is made to lengthen his working period.

An **exception** to the rules on travelling expenses applies to area-based employees (such as salesmen or estate workers) who will be treated as if their permanent workplace is a specific area. 3157 s 339(8) ITEPA 2003

An **area-based employee** is one:
– whose duties are defined by reference to an area (although they may require attendance outside that area);

– who attends various places in that area in the performance of his duties; and
– where none of those places represents a permanent workplace.

Travel from home to the boundaries of the area will not be allowable as a deduction but expenses within the area will be allowable. So where the employee lives within the area, all of his travel within it will be allowable.

Home is also a workplace

3158 Expenses incurred in travelling between home and a place of work may be deductible if the employee is **genuinely** using his home as a base of operations, and there is an **objective requirement** for him to perform his employment duties at home. Where an employee works at home for reasons of convenience only, his home does not become a workplace. For household expense claims, see ¶3186.

Travelling between two employments

3160 s 340 ITEPA 2003 The cost of travelling between two different employments or between two different employers will not be a deductible expense.

By exception, expenses incurred by a employee when travelling between two companies within a group will be deductible. For this purposes, group means a company and its 51% subsidiaries (¶1520).

Travelling between two centres of employment

3162 An employee who is required to attend **more than one** place of work in the performance of his duties may claim a deduction for the expenses of travelling between two places of work (provided they are both part of the same employment).

---

b. Amount of deduction

General principles

3164 Where travel expenses qualify for relief, the amount of the deduction is the full cost with no adjustment for the saving that the employee made by not having to travel to his normal workplace.

For these purposes travelling expenses include:
– fares on a train, bus, plane etc;
– vehicle hire charges;
– costs associated with an employee's use of his private car;
– toll fees and car parking; and
– subsistence expenses where an overnight stay is required.

Where expenditure is **not attributable to the business travel** (for example the cost of private telephone calls, laundry and newspapers) it will not qualify as a deduction under these provisions. Instead, a fixed sum is allowed for incidental overnight expenses, based on the number of nights spent away from home (¶3174).

3165 In most cases the **full cost** will be the actual amount paid such as the cost of a ticket or of a hotel room. Special rules apply to determine the expense incurred by an employee who uses his own car for business journeys (¶3168).

3166 A deduction is **only available** for the expenditure actually incurred, so an employee who chooses to take a coach rather than a plane will only receive a deduction for the cost of the coach, even if the employer reimburses the cost of a plane fare. The employee will therefore be taxed on the difference.

Similarly, the fact that travel costs were not the cheapest available will not prevent a claim being allowed for the full amount of the expenditure incurred. For example, the cost of a first class ticket will be allowable even if a standard class ticket was available. However, where the cost of travel and subsistence is **unusually lavish**, HMRC may seek to tax an element of the cost, on the basis that it was provided by way of a reward. For example, if an employee, who usually travels standard class and stays in two star hotels, flies first class to New York and stays in a five star hotel, an element of the cost of the trip may be deemed to be a reward for past performance.

Use of employee's own vehicle or bicycle

There is a statutory **exemption** from tax for the following approved mileage allowance payments which are made to an employee in respect of his own vehicle (for the NIC exemption, see ¶4980). The payments must be made by the employer and are not available if the employee is a passenger in the vehicle, or if the vehicle is a company vehicle. **3168** s 230 ITEPA 2003

Vehicle	Mileage in tax year	Rate per mile
Cars and vans	Up to 10,000 miles	45p[1]
	Excess over 10,000 miles	25p
Motorcycles	No restriction	24p
Bicycles	No restriction	20p

Note
1. 40p for 2010/11.

MEMO POINTS 1. Where an employee has **two or more employments**, mileage will be aggregated where the:
– employments are for the same employer; or
– employers are controlled by the same party.
2. Certain employers have entered into **employee car ownership schemes**, which allows the employee to purchase a car on credit from a car dealer, with a sizeable discount negotiated by his employer. So the employee owns the car (thereby escaping any benefit in kind), and claims mileage payments which should cover his running costs. These schemes require HMRC approval.
3. HMRC are undertaking a review of mileage payments and car ownership schemes, and a **consultation** is ongoing. In particular, the following issues are being considered:
– whether the rates could be amended to better reflect the actual costs of different cars;
– encouraging drivers to be more environmentally aware e.g. by linking rates to CO_2 emissions; and
– the alignment of the tax and NIC mileage rates.

If an employee is entitled to, but **does not receive**, mileage allowance payments as described above, he may be able to claim a deduction from earnings, being: **3170**
– the amount of mileage allowance payments to which he would have been entitled; less
– any payments which he actually received.

If the employee receives **excess mileage payments**, he will be taxable on the excess, and only this amount should be entered on the employee's P11D and tax return. Any payments for private fuel (¶3304) are also taxable.

A driver who takes passengers with him in a car or van will not be taxable on any related payment of up to 5p per passenger per mile which is paid by his employer. The passenger must also be engaged on business travel for the employer. If no passenger allowance is payable by the employer, the employee cannot claim a deduction. **3171**

From 6 April 2011 this allowance is extended to passengers who are volunteers (persons travelling while acting for an approved voluntary organisation)

EXAMPLE Mr H uses his own car to visit his employer's clients. During the tax year, he travelled 5,000 miles on business, and took a colleague for 1,000 of those miles. He was paid 32p per mile by his employer, with no extra amount for taking a passenger.

Mr H receives £1,600, all of which is exempt from tax.	5,000 x 32p
He can claim a further deduction of £400 in relation to his business mileage, but no deduction in relation to his passenger.	5,000 × (40 – 32p

If Mr H's employer had paid (say) 3p per mile for the passenger, this would also have been exempt from tax.

Subsistence

3172 Subsistence is not defined by the legislation but is taken to be the **additional costs of living away from home**. If the employee has continuing commitments at home and is obliged to live away from home in order to carry out the duties of his employment, the additional costs will normally be allowed in full. If the employee does not have a permanent residence (e.g. he normally lives in a hotel or club) then a subsistence deduction will not be available.

3173
HMRC Brief 24/09
EIM 05231

Daily subsistence HMRC publish **benchmark scale rates** which all employers can use to make subsistence payments free of tax and NIC to employees. This affects subsistence expenses incurred while travelling on an allowable business journey during the day only, when the following **qualifying conditions** are met:
– the travel is in the performance of an employee's duties or to a temporary place of work;
– the employee is absent from his normal place of work or home for a continuous period in excess of either 5 or 10 hours; and
– the employee incurs a cost of a meal (i.e. food and drink) after starting the journey.
Employers wishing to use the benchmark system must **notify** HMRC by ticking the appropriate statement on form P11DX (¶4740) before starting to use the system.

The following **rates** (unchanged since 6 April 2009) apply:

Situation [1]	Detail	Rate (£)
Breakfast (irregular early starters only)	The employee leaves home earlier than usual (before 6 am) and pays for breakfast	5
One meal rate	The employee has been away from his home/normal place of work for a period of at least 5 hours and pays for a meal [2]	5
Two meal rate	The employee has been away from his home/normal place of work for a period of at least 10 hours and pays for meals [2]	10
Late evening meal rate (irregular late finishers only)	The employee has to work later than usual (finishing after 8 pm) having worked his normal day, and has to buy a meal which he would usually have at home [3]	15

Note:
1. A **limit** of three meal rates in a 24 hour period applies.
2. Where employees are required to **start early or finish late on a regular basis**, the 5 or 10 hour rates could be paid provided all the other qualifying rules are satisfied.
3. If the employee is **paid an allowance under the 5 or 10 hour rule**, the late meal allowance could still be paid if work finishes after 8 pm and he buys a meal that he would usually have at home, unless he regularly finishes work late.

An employer may **choose to pay higher rates**, but the excess will be liable to tax and NIC unless a specific agreement is reached with HMRC, or the employer is merely reimbursing an actual cost incurred.

3174
ss 240, 241
ITEPA 2003

Incidental overnight expenses The expenses which fall under this provision are those considered incidental to the individual's stay away from his usual abode during a qualifying absence from home. For example, this might include telephone calls home, laundry or newspapers.

A **qualifying absence** from home is any continuous period during which the individual is obliged to stay away from home for at least one night.

Personal incidental expenses are not earnings providing they are below the **de minimis limit** of £5 per night in the UK and £10 per night outside the UK. Where the de minimis limit is exceeded, the whole amount (not just the excess) will become taxable.

3175 Where the employee spends **more than one consecutive night away**, the total expense for the period is compared to the total of the de minimis amounts for the nights spent away. There is no requirement for each night to be looked at in isolation. Where the employer pays the expenses directly and the expenses for a number of employees are aggregated so that separate identification would be difficult, HMRC will accept a reasonable apportionment of the expenses.

Where the expenses of **travelling** to a particular place would **not** be **deductible**, this prohibits any claim for related accommodation expenses. For example, where a salesman makes a visit to relatives on the way to a client, the cost of travel from the office to the relatives' house will not be deductible, and neither will the cost of hotel accommodation nearby.

c. Foreign elements

Where an employee, who is resident and ordinarily resident in the UK (¶4152), performs the **duties** of his office or employment **wholly overseas**, then a deduction will be allowed for the cost of travelling from and to any place in the UK at the beginning and end of the employment. **3177** s 341 ITEPA 2003

Such an employee who performs the duties of his employment **partly overseas** can claim a deduction for an unlimited number of visits to the UK provided: s 370 ITEPA 2003

- each journey to the UK is made after carrying out duties that can only be performed outside the UK; and
- the journey outwards is undertaken in order to commence or resume such duties.

The deduction is made from taxable earnings but is restricted to the amount borne or reimbursed by the employer.

MEMO POINTS 1. If the employer is a **foreign employer**, the employee must be UK domiciled (¶4163) to claim a deduction.
2. For **non-UK domiciled** employees, see ¶4264.

Where the employee holds **two or more offices or employments**, and the duties of at least one are performed wholly or partly outside the UK, the cost of travelling from one to another will be deductible from the earnings of the destination employment. **3178** s 342 ITEPA 2003

A deduction will be available if the employer incurs the expense of certain journeys by the employee's **spouse or any child** of his, where he is absent from the UK for a continuous period of 60 days or more for the purpose of performing the duties of employment. The journeys must be made to accompany him at the beginning of the period of absence or to visit him during that period, and there is a **limit** of two return trips by the same person in any year of assessment. **3179** s 371 ITEPA 2003

MEMO POINTS 1. For these purposes, **child** includes a stepchild and an illegitimate child but does not include a person who is aged 18 or over at the beginning of the outward journey.
2. An employee's **civil partner** would be treated as a spouse for these purposes.

EXAMPLE Mr A (who has never left the UK) is employed by U Ltd, a UK employer. He is offered a secondment to the Australian parent company, where he earns £20,000, and his hotel and travel costs are reimbursed by the overseas company. The hotel costs £5,000, and travel expenses are £700.
The earnings subject to UK tax are:

	£
Salary	20,000
Hotel	5,000
Travel	700
	25,700
Less: Claim for expenses	
Hotel	(5,000)
Travel	(700)
Assessable earnings	20,000

If Mrs A travels to see Mr A, and the Australian company reimburses her travel costs of £760, Mr A will be taxable on the amount £760, but he can then claim a deduction.
If the Australian company did not bear the cost, Mr A could not claim a deduction for the cost of £760 which is privately incurred.

3180 s 376 ITEPA 2003 **Overseas subsistence allowances** Where, for the purpose of enabling the employee to perform the duties of the overseas employment, expenses are incurred on **board and lodging** outside the UK, a deduction will be allowed. Apportionment will apply where the board and lodging is only partly provided to enable the employee to perform his duties.

HMRC publish **benchmark rates** for accommodation and subsistence expenses in most foreign countries. Payments at or below the published rates are not liable to income tax or NIC, and need not be shown on a P11D. These amounts are in addition to the incidental overnight expenses of up to £10 per night outside the UK (¶3174).

The latest published rates can be found online at http://www.hmrc.gov.uk/employers/emp-income-scale-rates.htm.

s 304A ITEPA 2003 MEMO POINTS Subsistence allowances paid by certain specified EU bodies, to an employee seconded by his employer to that body as an expert, are exempt from income tax if paid for any period commencing on or after 1 January 2011.

2. Other expenses

Business entertaining

3182 ss 356, 357 ITEPA 2003 Expenses incurred in entertaining customers are considered not to be wholly, exclusively and necessarily incurred in the performance of the duties of an employment, because of the dual function of feeding the employee as well.

Often an employer will provide an employee with an **allowance** which is to be used for business entertaining purposes and is taxable. In practice, HMRC do not seek to tax reimbursed entertaining expenses, gifts or entertaining allowances on the principle that the employer will not be able to claim a trading deduction for the expenditure, and to tax the employee would create a double charge.

s 358 ITEPA 2003 **Staff entertaining** is a deductible expense, unless the entertaining of non-employees is the main purpose of the expenditure.

Subscriptions

3184 ss 343, 344 ITEPA 2003 Two types of subscriptions are **allowable as a deduction** from earnings, where the performance of the employment duties:
– requires membership of a certain organisation and it is a condition of employment; or
– is directly affected by the knowledge concerned or involves the exercise of the profession concerned.

The latter type of subscription is only eligible as a deduction if it is approved by HMRC, and a list of approved bodies, which is updated periodically, can be obtained from www.hmrc.gov.uk/list3/index.htm.

Working at home

3186 s 316A ITEPA 2003 EIM 01476 No liability to income tax arises where an **employer makes a payment** to an employee in respect of reasonable additional household expenses which the employee incurs whilst working from home. There is no wholly, exclusively and necessarily test in this case.

The annual **limit** for such payments is £156 (£3 per week). Amounts **in excess of** this figure can also be paid free of tax, provided the employer has reached prior agreement with HMRC, or he can provide supporting evidence that the payment is in respect of additional household expenses incurred by the employee.

3187 If the **employer does not pay** any homeworking allowance, a deduction will be allowed for reasonable expenses where the employee does not have a permanent office base.

Tax Bulletin 79 EIM 01472 HMRC have clarified that unreimbursed homeworking expenses are only valid as a deduction where the employee's situation fulfils all of the following **conditions**:
– the main duties of the employment are carried out at home;
– those duties require specific facilities;

– either the facilities are not available at the employer's premises, or the nature of the duties require the employee to live so far from the premises that it is unreasonable for him to travel there; and
– at no time before or after the contract is written, is the employee able to choose between working at the employer's premises and elsewhere.

In particular, HMRC have stated that no deduction can be claimed for council tax, rent, water rates, mortgage payments or insurance premiums.

However, a £3 per week deduction may be claimed where it is impossible to calculate the value of homeworking costs (which can include light and heat, and telephone), and a further amount will be allowed where evidence is retained. Alternatively, the employer can agree a different rate of average reimbursement with HMRC.

MEMO POINTS Any subsequent reliance on the capital gains tax **exemption for private residences** may be restricted (¶6166) by exclusive use of a part of the home for work purposes.

EXAMPLE

1. Mr B lives in Glasgow and is the Scottish sales area manager for a company based in London. He is required to carry out administrative duties after every client visit, and the only place available is an office in his own home.
Mr B can claim relief for the additional costs incurred because of his home working.

2. Mr C successfully applies for a job 300 miles away. The new employer is happy to pay his relocation costs, but he does not want to move because of his children's schooling. He therefore agrees with his new employer that he can work at home, and this is stipulated in his employment contract.
HMRC consider that Mr C is not eligible to claim any deductions for home working, because the contractual term is an expression of his personal choice.

3. D Ltd introduces a new home working policy so that any employee who wishes to work from home can do so. D Ltd pays £3 per week as a homeworking allowance.
The £3 per week is exempt from tax. However, any other costs incurred by the employee will not be deductible because the employee is choosing to work from home.

Payroll giving

Employees may be able to make **charitable donations** direct from their salary, where the employer operates an approved payroll deduction scheme. Under the scheme, an employee arranges for a regular amount (with no maximum limit) to be withheld from his salary by his employer, which is allowed as a tax deductible expense against his earnings. **3189** s 713 ITEPA 2003

The amounts withheld are then passed by the employer to an approved agent (or charity) for onward distribution to nominated charities.

MEMO POINTS 1. The employer must deduct the amount from earnings when calculating the **PAYE** (but not NIC) deductions. Therefore the employee obtains tax relief at source, so a donation of £100 will only cost £80 for a basic rate taxpayer, £60 for a higher rate taxpayer, and £50 for an additional rate taxpayer.
2. Employers who **second employees** to charities or educational establishments are entitled to relief for staff costs (¶181).

Capital allowances on assets other than cars

Where expenditure is incurred necessarily on **plant and machinery** (other than a car) for use in the performance of the duties of the employment, capital allowances may be claimed (for full details on capital allowances see ¶200). **3191** s 36 CAA 2001

The word **necessarily** is interpreted in the same way as for the general rules (¶3140). Thus, a vicar was not able to claim capital allowances on a slide projector because, although it was used wholly and exclusively for his employment, he was able to perform his duties without it. *White v Higginbottom* [1983]

Employee's liability and indemnity insurance

Where an employee has incurred a liability (to the employer or a third party) as a result of negligence in his capacity as an employee, he will be able to obtain a deduction for the following **types of expense**: **3192** s 346 ITEPA 2003

a. insurance premiums paid to indemnify the employee against liability for his acts or omissions whilst undertaking his employment duties;
b. payments to settle an uninsured liability for the same acts and omissions as in **a.**; and
c. payments of costs incurred which relate to the liability, such as court fees.

s 555 ITEPA 2003 An employee may also claim relief for payments made within the 6 years following the tax year in which a **previous employment** ceases. Relief is given in the year in which the payment is made, and unused relief cannot be carried forward.

s 556A ITEPA 2003 However, no deduction or relief will be due for payments where the main purpose, or one of the main purposes, is to **avoid tax**.

II. Benefits in kind

A. General principles

3196 A benefit in kind (referred to in this section as a benefit) is a payment made other than in cash to an employee or director by reason of his employment. Certain minor benefits which are available to all employees of an employer may be specifically exempted from tax.

The **general test** is whether the payment is one made in return for acting as, or being, an employee. *Hochstrasser v Mayes* [1960]

This means that payments or provisions made by an employer (other than a company) in the normal course of his **social relationships** will not constitute benefits. For example, where a sole trader owns a holiday cottage which he allows his brother to use, the fact that the brother is also an employee of the sole trader will not cause a benefit to arise.

3198 A benefit **not provided by the employer** is still taxable if it is provided by reason of the employment. For example, a car provided to a professional footballer by a car dealer would typically be a taxable benefit.

Goods and services provided to an employee by reason of his employment will not be taxable if they are for **business purposes**. Where there is an element of **private use**, or where an asset is transferred to the employee, a taxable benefit may arise.

s 721(5) ITEPA 2003 A benefit may also arise where a payment is made to a member of an employee's **family or household** by reason of the employment. "Family" is defined as the employee's spouse (¶2400), parents and children (and their spouses) and dependants. "Household" has the same definition but also includes servants and invited guests.

Comment This section identifies various benefits and explains the valuation rules applicable to each type. Exempt benefits are discussed before taxable benefits, and reference should be made first to the table at ¶3204, before consulting the table at ¶3240.

B. Non-taxable benefits

Summary

3204 The following table provides a summary of the benefits which are not taxable on any employee.

General area	Specific benefit	Basic conditions	Reference	¶¶
Subsistence	Meals and drinks	Provided to all employees on similar terms Meals made available by an employer, who is not the employee's own employer, are also exempt	s 317 ITEPA 2003 SI 2002/205	¶3206
	Small and seasonal gifts	Being made generally available to all employees on similar terms e.g. Christmas bottle of wine, flowers on birthdays etc	s 210 ITEPA 2003	
	Luncheon vouchers	Up to 15p per day	s 89 ITEPA 2003	
	Homeworking allowance	Up to £156 p.a. automatically exempt Further amounts possible	s 316A ITEPA 2003	¶3186
	Overseas	Board and lodging outside the UK may be exempt up to certain limits	s 376 ITEPA 2003	¶3180
Travel	Workplace parking space	For cars, vans, motorbikes and bicycles	s 237 ITEPA 2003	
	Mileage allowances	If within certain limits, which depend on mileage	s 229 ITEPA 2003	¶3168
	Free transport	Travel, accommodation and subsistence provided during a public transport strike	s 245 ITEPA 2003	
		Employer subsidised public bus services	s 243 ITEPA 2003	¶3219
		Work bus provided for journey between home and workplace, including minibuses with at least 9 seats	s 242 ITEPA 2003	
		Travel by taxi etc between workplace and home for occasional late night working (9pm or later, when no public transport available) if total number of late nights is less than 60 in a tax year Appropriate records must be kept	s 248 ITEPA 2003 EIM 21831	
		Provision of alternative transport when expected car sharing arrangements are not available	s 248 ITEPA 2003	
		Travel from home to workplace for disabled employees	s 246 ITEPA 2003	
	Private use of emergency vehicle	Provided only used for travel to and from home	s 248A ITEPA 2003	¶3288
	Cycling	Cycles and related safety equipment made available to all employees, and used mainly for commuting and/or certain short journeys between work and local amenities). Private or family use does not disqualify the bicycle provided it is incidental to the main purpose.	s 244 ITEPA 2003	
		Provision of breakfast to cyclists on an unlimited number of designated cycle to work days	SI 2002/205 reg 3	
	Use of a heavy goods vehicle	Exceeding 3,500 kg fully laden and mainly used for business purposes	s 238 ITEPA 2003	

General area	Specific benefit	Basic conditions	Reference	¶¶
Training and counselling	Work-related training	Includes retraining programmes on redundancy	ss 250, 251, 311, 312 ITEPA 2003	¶3208
	Scholarships	Not received by reason of employment	s 211 ITEPA 2003	¶3212
	Welfare counselling	Made available to all employees on similar terms Not relating to finance (other than debt), tax, legal issues, or leisure	SI 2000/2080	
	Pensions advice	External advice paid for by the employer up to £150 p.a.	SI 2002/205	
Provision of equipment	Any work equipment and services	Where private use is not significant	s 316 ITEPA 2003	¶3216
	Provision of single mobile phone (including a car phone)	All private use exempt unless employer pays bill in employee's name	s 319 ITEPA 2003	¶3218
Medical costs	Medical checks	Health screenings and medical check-ups	s 320B ITEPA 2003	¶3217
	Overseas medical costs	Medical insurance and treatment during foreign visits where performing employment duties	s 325 ITEPA 2003	
	Eye tests and corrective glasses	Where employee uses VDU, and provision of test and glasses is required by Health and Safety regulations	s 320A ITEPA 2003	
Miscellaneous	Childcare	Workplace facilities exempt	s 318 ITEPA 2003	¶3221
		Weekly allowance per employee per week of direct nursery payment/voucher exempt	s 318A ITEPA 2003	¶3222
	Parties and functions	Cost up to £150 per head exempt Event must be available to employees generally	s 264 ITEPA 2003	¶3224
	Removal expenses	Up to £8,000 exempt	s 271 ITEPA 2003	¶3226
	Job-related accommodation	Where necessary, or for better performance of duties, or for security reasons	ss 99, 100 ITEPA 2003	¶3254
	Personal equipment for disabled individuals	Provision of equipment and services to enable duties of employment to be performed	SI 2002/1596	
	Long service awards	For at least 20 years of service and not cash	s 323 ITEPA 2003	¶3230
	Sports facilities	Available to all employees but not to general public Facilities also made available by an employer, who is not the employee's own employer, are also exempt	s 261 ITEPA 2003 SI 2002/205	
	Staff suggestion schemes	Open to all employees on equal terms	s 321 ITEPA 2003	¶3232
	Entertaining and gifts from third parties	Cost of gift to donor is £250 or less	s 324 ITEPA 2003	¶3234
	Goods provided at a discount	Provided amount paid by employee is more than the cost of the goods incurred by the employer		
	Fees relating to monitoring schemes	Reimbursement by the employer of registration fees for the Protection of Vulnerable Groups Scheme (PVGS) in Scotland	s 326A ITEPA 2003	

Provision of meals and canteen facilities

A benefit does not arise where employees are provided with canteen facilities, even if the canteen is not on the employer's premises, or under his control. **All staff** of the employer, or all those at the particular location, must be provided with a meal. The exemption also applies where: 3206 s 317 ITEPA 2003 EIM 21670
- meals are provided on a reasonable scale; and
- the employer gives free or subsidised meal vouchers to staff for whom meals are not provided.

MEMO POINTS 1. The exemption also extends to **light refreshments** such as tea and coffee.
2. It is common for employers to provide lunch during **meetings**, which would be taxable unless all employees were to be provided with lunch.
3. Where free or subsidised canteen facilities are made available on the premises of another employer, who is not the **employee's own employer**, no benefit arises.
4. With effect from 6 April 2011, the provision of subsidised or free canteen food for workers became a taxable benefit in circumstances where:
- the availability of the canteen is linked to a salary sacrifice arrangement where the employee has given up some of their gross salary in return for food and drink; or
- there is a flexible benefits scheme in operation, so that the employee has chosen to give up some salary in return for food and drink.
The luncheon voucher scheme is unaffected by these changes, as are arrangements where the employer provides a general subsidy for canteen food, to offer food at lower prices to all employees.

Work-related training

Where an employee attends training courses **paid for by his employer** (either directly or via reimbursement), no benefit arises provided the training is related to his current employment. In certain cases, this will also be true where it relates to a position with a prospective employer. *Silva v Charnock* [2002] 3208 ss 250, 251 ITEPA 2003

In addition to the actual training course, this exemption covers any associated costs and assets provided for use by the employee during the period of training or in his employment. The exemption does not apply to entertainment and recreation costs or courses provided as an inducement or reward for services.

MEMO POINTS 1. **Associated costs** would include accommodation, examination fees and registration fees which become payable as a result of achieving a qualification.
2. If the **employee incurs the cost** of training (and is not reimbursed), the expenditure must meet the wholly, necessarily and exclusively test (¶3136 onwards) for it to be deductible. In practice, HMRC deny virtually all claims. A solution is for the employer to operate a salary sacrifice (¶3219), so that the cost is borne by the employer (and therefore becomes exempt), and the employee pays less tax on his reduced salary. EIM 32525

Certain benefits provided for employees **at a time of redundancy** are not taxable. These include training courses (plus related travel costs) of up to 2 years' duration, allowing the employee to retrain for a new career. The exemption will apply where the employee's job has already been terminated, or he ceases to be employed within 2 years of the course ending. Counselling services in connection with redundancy are also excluded from the charge to tax (¶3094). 3210 s 311 ITEPA 2003

Scholarships

Generally income from a scholarship is exempt from tax for the recipient. However, where an employee, or a member of his family or household (¶3198), receives a scholarship by reason of employment, it will be taxable on the employee (unless the employer is an individual, and the scholarship is awarded as a result of a social relationship). 3212 ss 211-213 ITEPA 2003

By **exception**, where the employer makes a scholarship available to a member of the employee's family or household, but only as a result of fortuitous circumstances (such as the employee's child winning the scholarship through a public exam), the income will be exempt, if all of the following conditions are met:
- the scholarship is not provided by reason of employment;
- the funds are provided by a trust fund or a scheme;

– the scholarship is to be held by an individual in full-time education, such as a school or university student; and
– less than 25% of the payments made by the trust are scholarship payments provided by reason of employment.

3214 SP 4/86 SI 2007/2401 EIM 06235
An employee who receives a scholarship from his employer for undertaking a **full-time educational course** is, by concession, exempt from tax and NIC up to a maximum threshold. Since the academic year 2007/08 this has been fixed at £15,480 per annum (a rate of £1,290 per month). If this limit is exceeded, the whole amount becomes taxable.

To qualify for the exemption, the employee must be enrolled in the educational establishment for at least one academic year, with an average attendance of not less than 20 weeks per year. The exemption does not apply to payments for periods spent at work (whether during college vacations or otherwise).

EXAMPLE Mr A's employer pays for him to attend college. The course starts in September and finishes at the end of the academic year, the following June. During this period he has a college vacation lasting 2 months, during which he works for his employer.
Mr A is paid at the rate of £1,200 per month until January. In February the rate is increased to £1,300 per month. He is paid the same rates whilst working for his employer.
While Mr A is at college, his monthly income up until January is less than the exempt limit of £1,290 and is not taxable. From February onwards, it is above the limit and therefore taxable in full. The increase in the rate does not affect the entitlement to exemption in the months before the increase. Income received whilst on college vacation is taxable.

Provision of equipment and services

3216 s 316 ITEPA 2003 EIM 21613
Equipment and services provided by an employer will be exempt where:
– they are **provided at** work and the employee's private use is not significant (e.g. private emails sent during lunchtime); or
– it is **intended for** home use, but the sole purpose of doing this is to enable the employee to perform his work duties, and again private use is not significant.

However, if the employer has any intention of rewarding the employee, the exemption does not apply.

Common items which could be covered by this exemption include computers, the provision of broadband, and newer PDAs which are akin to a computer. Cars, boats, aircraft and living accommodation are never covered by the exemption.

Comment HMRC decide whether private use is **not significant** by taking into account the necessity for the employee to have the equipment or services provided in order to carry out his duties. So the time spent on business or private use is of relevance but not of paramount importance.

Medical check-ups

3217 s 320B ITEPA 2003
Annual health screenings and medical check-ups provided by an employer are exempt, even if the benefit is selectively **provided** to certain employees only. The exemption is limited to one instance of each type per year per employee.

MEMO POINTS 1. **Health screenings** are assessments to identify employees who might be at particular risk of ill-health.
2. A **medical check-up** is a physical examination of an employee by a health professional in order to determining his state of health.

Mobile phones

3218 s 319 ITEPA 2003 EIM 21779
The provision of a single mobile phone (including a car phone) to an employee for his use only is not a taxable benefit, provided it is supplied under a **contract in the employer's name**. The provision of more than one phone does give rise to a benefit, although the employee can choose which phone is taxable. The provision of a voucher by the employer to facilitate the employee's use of a single mobile phone is exempt.

If the contract is in the **name of the employee**, and the employer meets the costs of the phone, any private use will be taxable. As the employer is settling a debt of the employee, the payments made should be put through the payroll, which means Class 1 NIC applies (¶4986).

When a phone is taxable, the benefit is calculated by adding together all the bills received in the tax year, and then deducting any costs for business calls. Basic contract costs are not business related for this purpose.

Comment At present BlackBerrys and other PDAs are regarded as computers (¶3216).

Childcare

Assistance provided to employees with parental responsibilities may qualify for tax relief if it takes the form of: 3219
- employer-provided childcare facilities; or
- direct payment for childcare by the employer.

If an employer offers either scheme, it must be open to all employees or to all those working at a specific site where the scheme is offered.

MEMO POINTS 1. Employers can include childcare as **part of an overall package** which offers the benefit:
a. as an addition to the existing salary;
b. as part of a flexible benefits scheme; or
c. in return for a sacrifice of salary.
2. A **salary sacrifice** is a legally-binding change in the contractual arrangements between the employer and the employee, and most commonly occurs where the employment contract is amended to reduce the employee's entitlement to cash salary in return for a non-cash benefit (such as childcare, pension contribution, or more holiday entitlement). The value of the non-cash benefit may equate to the amount of salary "sacrificed". **To be effective**, a salary sacrifice must be irrevocable and future remuneration must be given up before it is treated as received for the purposes of either NIC or income tax. Employers should ensure that the payslip shows the reduced salary only. A salary sacrifice cannot reduce an employee's remuneration below the National Minimum Wage (see *Employment Memo*). In addition, a reduction in salary may impact on other benefits, such as entitlement to state pensions and tax credits. Employers should seek legal advice when setting up sacrificial arrangements. HMRC have issued guidance about the operation of the exemptions for employer-subsidised public bus services and for bicycles, in cases where the benefit is provided through a salary sacrifice arrangement.
3. Employer-supported childcare schemes delivered through salary sacrifice or flexible remuneration arrangements attract tax and NIC relief even if the scheme is not available to certain low-paid employees (for example, because they cannot fall below the National Minimum Wage). This treatment has retrospective effect from 2005/06 onwards.

Summary 3220

Type of provision	Tax treatment	NIC treatment
Workplace nursery	Exempt	Exempt
Childcare vouchers	Exempt weekly amount: see ¶3222	Weekly amount exempt, then Class 1 due (¶4972)
Contract between employer and childcare provider	Exempt weekly amount: see ¶3222	Weekly amount exempt, then Class 1A due (¶5048)

Workplace nurseries To be excluded from taxation (and also NIC), childcare facilities must be housed in non-domestic premises that are **provided** either **by** the employer, or by a group of people including the employer. The employer must be wholly or partly responsible for managing and financing the provision of childcare facilities. Any care registration requirements for either the staff or the premises must be met. 3221 s 318 ITEPA 2003

Childcare may be **provided to** any child under 18 years of age (including a stepchild) of the employee, who either lives with the employee or is maintained fully by the employee. Children for whom he has a parental responsibility are also included, whether they live with the employee or not.

MEMO POINTS 1. HMRC have stated that the employer must make a substantial commitment to **funding** the facility, such as guaranteeing to underwrite potential losses or paying a fixed contribution for the long term. EIM 21925

EIM 21930 2. With respect to **management**, the employer must have close involvement in:
- appointing and reviewing the performance of the carers;
- the extent of care provided, and the related conditions; and
- the allocation of nursery places.

3. There are many **commercially marketed schemes** which involve an employee entering into a salary sacrifice arrangement, whereby he gives up an amount of pay equal to the cost of the nursery place that is provided. The employer pays for the nursery place for the employee's child, but also pays an additional annual fee per place. The employer appoints a scheme promoter to act as agent at meetings with the nursery management committee.

HMRC may attack these arrangements on the basis that:
- the salary sacrifice is not effective, so the full salary is taxable;
- the nursery place is in reality a contract between the employee and nursery, so the amount paid by the employer is taxable as earnings; or
- the financing and management criteria are not met because the arrangements are a sham.

3222 ss 318A, 270A ITEPA 2003 Leaflet IR115

Direct payment From 6 April 2011, the limits on tax and NIC exemption for childcare vouchers and directly-contracted childcare provided through employer-supported schemes are as follows:

Taxpayer	Maximum exemption (£ per week)
Basic rate	55
Higher (40%) rate	28
Additional (50%) rate	22

This makes the net value of the relief the same for all taxpayers at £11 per week. Employers are required to estimate the employee's likely annual earnings (including benefits, but not potential bonuses or overtime) when making payments.

These limits **do not apply** to employees who joined the childcare arrangements before 6 April 2011 and remain in the same employment after that date. For them, the former weekly limit of £55 contines to apply.

The exemption is given against the **first** earnings for the week (defined as for PAYE (¶4610)) per employee, regardless of the number of children involved. So two working basic-rate parents with one child can receive up to £110 free of tax per week.

The contract must be between the employer and the childcare provider. Alternatively the employer can provide **vouchers** (either designed in-house or supplied by a voucher provider so long as acceptable to the nursery) with a face value of up to the weekly limit which will also be exempt. Any administration costs incurred by the employer are not an assessable benefit for the employee.

For this exemption, a **qualifying child** is a child aged 15 or less, up to 1 September following the child's 15th birthday; and either he is:
- a child or stepchild of the employee who is maintained (wholly or partly) at the employee's expense; or
- resident with the employee, who has parental responsibility for him.

MEMO POINTS 1. A child for whom the employee has parental responsibility, but who **does not live with** the employee, will not qualify.
2. For **disabled children**, the age requirement is extended by a year to 16.
3. Vouchers cannot be exchanged for cash, otherwise tax and NIC become due. So any **refund** made by the nursery to the employee must be routed through the employer.
4. The provision of tax-free childcare may reduce a claim for **tax credits**, in which case HMRC should be notified (¶3729). Low paid employees who accept vouchers instead of a salary rise are particularly adversely affected, because the corresponding reduction in tax credits outweighs the value of the tax-free childcare and so they are worse off.

3223 The **types** of childcare which qualify for the exemption include registered or approved care provided by a:
- registered childminder;
- school or educational establishment;
- school or local authority in relation to pre- and after-school care; and
- registered nanny in the child's own home.

However, care provided by the employee's partner (married or unmarried), or by a relative in the child's house will not qualify unless the person registers as a childminder.

MEMO POINTS 1. There are specific **inclusions** for **qualifying childcare** in relation to England, Wales, Scotland, Northern Ireland, and outside the UK. See www.hmrc.gov.uk/childcare/index.htm for further details.
2. **Nannies** should be registered with OFSTED for their costs to qualify for this exemption.
3. The definition of **relative** includes parents, grandparents, siblings, aunts and uncles.

Parties and functions

There is an exemption which applies to an annual party or similar annual event (e.g. a summer barbecue), provided for employees where the **cost per head** does not exceed £150, and the party is either available to all: **3224** s 264 ITEPA 2003
- employees generally (including cleaners and security staff); or
- those working at a specific location, where the employer has more than one location. This can also be extended to different sections or departments providing the party is available to all staff at the site.

If the employer provides **two or more annual functions**, no charge arises in respect of the events for which the costs per head do not exceed £150 in aggregate. If the aggregate cost exceeds £150 per head, then the events within the limit are exempt (choosing the best combination), and the others are taxable.

The **cost of the function** is calculated by adding together all costs, including VAT and transport, and dividing by the number of all attendees (including non-employees). If insufficient numbers attend a function, this could make it taxable rather than exempt. However, an assessable benefit would only be calculated on the proportion of the cost represented by attendees who are employees and members of their family or household (¶3198).

Where tax arises, the employer may set up a PAYE settlement agreement (PSA) (¶4743) to relieve the employee from any liability.

EXAMPLE B Ltd holds two annual events open to all its employees in the tax year, with the costs per head being £100 and £70 respectively. The overall cost to B Ltd of each event is the same. As the total cost per head for both functions is £170, the exemption cannot cover both. Either event on its own could qualify, and so it is more beneficial for the first to be exempted.

For employees who attend:
- both events, they will be chargeable only on the benefit of £70 for the second event;
- only the first event, there will be no chargeable benefit because that event is exempt; and
- only the second event, they will be chargeable on the benefit of £70.

Removal expenses

When an individual relocates his main residence due to the needs of his employment, removal expenses **up to a maximum** of £8,000 per move may be paid by the employer without being treated as a benefit, where they consist of: **3226** s 271 ITEPA 2003
- reimbursements from his employer in respect of removal costs; or
- costs directly incurred by the employer.

For these purposes, **relocation includes** the situation where an employee moves:
- in order to take up a new employment;
- as a result of a change of duties within the organisation; or s 273 ITEPA 2003
- because the location of the current employment changes.

The relocation must be necessitated by the old residence not being within a reasonable daily travelling distance of the workplace. The new home must be within commuting distance.

MEMO POINTS 1. Where **payments exceed £8,000**, the excess will be taxed, although lower paid employees (¶3116) are only assessable on payments made to them, not on expenses directly incurred by the employer. s 287 ITEPA 2003
2. For the **NIC** treatment, see ¶4980.

3228 s 272 ITEPA 2003 The removal **costs** may include the following:
- fees in connection with selling the previous residence and acquiring the new one (including stamp taxes and legal costs);
- fees in connection with an abortive acquisition, where the intended new residence is not acquired due to circumstances outside the employee's control or other reasonable circumstances;
- costs of transporting belongings including insurance, reconnection fees etc;
- costs of replacing equipment which is not suitable for use at the new residence (e.g. replacing a gas cooker with an electric one where the new residence is not connected to the gas supply);
- travel and subsistence costs (e.g. costs incurred in going to view possible properties); and
- bridging loan expenses to the extent that the loan is used to purchase the new residence and does not exceed the proceeds from the sale of the old residence (including loans by the employer).

s 274 ITEPA 2003 Generally, qualifying removal costs must be **incurred by** the end of the tax year following that in which the employee relocated, although HMRC have discretion to extend this limit.

EXAMPLE Mr C earns £30,000 p.a. and he is required to relocate. His employer reimburses the following costs:

	£
Stamp duty land tax on new residence	4,000
Legal costs including survey fee	1,000
Selling agent's costs	2,000
Travel and subsistence when locating new residence	500
Cattery costs during the move	100
Post redirection	40
Transporting belongings	900
	8,540

Of the above costs, £8,400 potentially qualifies for the exemption (excluding the cattery and post redirection fees), so Mr C will be taxable on a benefit of £540. (8,540 – 8,000)
If Mr C moves in March 2010, the costs must be incurred by 5 April 2011. If Mr C moves in May 2010, he has until 5 April 2012 to incur the costs.

Long service awards

3230 s 323 ITEPA 2003 For service in excess of 20 years, awards **consisting of** assets or shares in the employing company with a **maximum value** of £50 for each year of service (up to 20 years) can be made to staff without a tax charge.

Where the award is made in **cash**, an assessable benefit will arise for all employees. Relevant employees (¶3116) will also be assessable where an award is made in the form of an **asset or other non-cash benefit** and the value exceeds the maximum.

Staff suggestion schemes

3232 ss 321, 322 ITEPA 2003 Awards may be made to employees under qualifying staff suggestion schemes without any tax charge. **To qualify**, a staff suggestion scheme must be open to all employees on equal terms. If the award relates to a specific suggestion, it must relate to the employer's business and be outside an employee's normal duties.

Awards are usually only made when a suggestion is **implemented** and should not exceed:
- 50% of the expected net benefit of implementation in the first year; or
- 10% of the expected net benefit over 5 years

subject to an overriding maximum award of £5,000.

Where a cash award is non-qualifying it will be assessable on all employees. However, a non-qualifying award which is made in the form of an asset is only assessable on relevant employees (¶3116).

Where a suggestion is **not implemented**, but the employer wants to encourage future suggestions, the maximum award is £25.

MEMO POINTS 1. Suggestions made during **meetings** are considered part of the employee's normal duties.
2. Where the award **exceeds** £5,000, the excess is taxable.

Third party gifts and entertaining

Goodwill gifts (such as a bottle of wine from the employer's client) can be received by an employee without an income tax charge where all of the following conditions are met: 3234 s 324 ITEPA 2003
- the cost to the donor is less than £250 (including the cumulative cost of all gifts within the same tax year);
- the gift is the goods themselves, or a voucher to acquire goods;
- the donor is not connected to the employer, or anyone connected with him (¶5570); and
- the gift is unsolicited and not given in return for the employee's service.

If these **conditions are not met**, the third party must provide the employee with information about the amount of the benefit, which the employee should then include as assessable income on his tax return. The third party may wish to enter into a taxed award scheme (¶4748) which enables him to pay the related tax instead.

Where someone other than the employer **entertains** an employee, including hospitality of any kind, there will be no taxable benefit if all of the following conditions are met: 3236 s 265 ITEPA 2003
- the entertaining was not procured by the employer, or anyone connected with him (¶5570);
- the person providing the entertainment is not connected with the employer; and
- the hospitality is not provided in return for any services of the employee.

If these **conditions are not met**, see ¶3234.

C. Taxable benefits

1. General principles

Summary of common benefits

3240

Benefit	Taxed on		Reference	¶¶
	Lower paid	Relevant (£8,500+)		
Accommodation	✓	✓	s 102 ITEPA 2003	¶3250
Ancillary expenses for accommodation	x	✓	s 315 ITEPA 2003	¶3280
Vouchers and credit cards	✓	✓	ss 73, 266 ITEPA 2003	¶3266
Permanent health benefits	✓	✓	s 660 ITEPA 2003	¶3274
Medical insurance	x	✓	s 201 ITEPA 2003	¶3244
Use of assets [1]	x	✓	s 205 ITEPA 2003	¶3276
Transfer of assets	✓ [2]	✓	s 206 ITEPA 2003	¶3278
Company cars	x	✓	s 114 ITEPA 2003	¶3286
Car fuel	x	✓	s 149 ITEPA 2003	¶3304
Company vans	x	✓	s 154 ITEPA 2003	¶3310
Cheap loans	x	✓	s 175 ITEPA 2003	¶3322
Payment of director's PAYE	x	✓	s 223 ITEPA 2003	¶3338

Note:
1. **Excluding** cars, vans, phones and accommodation.
2. See ¶3242.

Lower paid employees

3242 With the exception of living accommodation and vouchers (which have specific valuation rules), lower paid employees (¶3116) are principally assessable only on items that can readily be **converted into cash**. *Tennant v Smith* [1892]

This means that, in the absence of specific legislation, lower paid employees are only assessable on items which can be sold. For example, the right to use a car cannot be sold and therefore a lower paid employee would not be assessable. However, a gift of a car would be assessable as the employee could sell the car for cash. The cash equivalent of **an asset transferred** is the second-hand value i.e. the amount that it can be sold for. No comparison is made with its market value.

Relevant employees

3244
s 201 ITEPA 2003 Relevant employees (¶3116) are **taxed on every benefit** received by reason of employment unless a specific exemption exists (¶3204). Generally, the **time** at which the benefit becomes taxable is when it can be enjoyed by the employee, which may be later than the time when the expenditure is incurred by the employer. *Templeton v Jacobs* [1996] Where an assessable benefit arises, the cash equivalent of the benefit is included as income of the employee and taxed accordingly.

3246 The **cash equivalent** is generally calculated as follows, subject to the exception summarised in ¶3248:

	£
Full cost to provider of benefit	X
Less: Employee contribution	(X)
Cash equivalent	X

3248 Where the benefit consists of the provision of **in-house** benefits arising out of surplus capacity, the cash equivalent is usually the marginal cost incurred by the provider of the benefit. For example, in the case of a school educating the sons of teachers for reduced fees, the cost of providing education was not the expensive fees that other parents paid, but the marginal cost to the school in having one extra pupil attend (which was minimal). *Pepper v Hart* [1993]

s 109 ITEPA 2003 Where a **cash alternative** is offered in lieu of the benefit, the value of the benefit will be the amount of cash offered. The exception to this is living accommodation, where the benefit will be valued under the rules in ¶3250 if this provides a higher figure than the amount of cash offered.

2. Benefits taxable on all employees

a. Living accommodation

3250 Living accommodation is not specifically **defined** but is taken to mean all kinds of residential accommodation with the exception of overnight accommodation, a stay in a hotel room, or board and lodging.

3252
s 102 ITEPA 2003 The provision of living accommodation by reason of employment, other than job-related accommodation (¶3254), is a **taxable benefit for all employees** whether provided to the employee himself, or a member of his family or household (¶3198). Ancillary services provided with the accommodation are only taxable on relevant employees (¶3280).

s 100A ITEPA 2003 MEMO POINTS It is common for individuals to acquire holiday homes outside the UK through a company set up for that purpose (often because of foreign restrictions on the ownership of property). There is no benefit in kind charge on individuals if **overseas property** has been bought by a company:

– that is owned by individuals; and
– whose sole activity is holding that property for their occupation or letting.
The property must not have been acquired by the company at an **undervalue** from any company connected with it, or from a person connected with the director.

Job-related accommodation

The provision of living accommodation in connection with the employment will not be taxable provided it falls within one of the following exceptions: 3254 ss 99, 100 ITEPA 2003
a. where it is necessary for the **proper performance** of the employee's duties that he should occupy the accommodation e.g. a caretaker;
b. where the accommodation is provided for the **better performance** of the duties of his employment, and the employment is one where it is customary for employers to provide living accommodation for employees e.g. farm workers; or
c. where, because of a special **threat to the employee's security**, special security arrangements are in force and he resides in the accommodation as part of those arrangements e.g. the chairman of a company providing politically sensitive and therefore high risk services.

The exemptions outlined in **a**. and **b**. above will not be available to a **director** unless he is a full-time working director where either:
– he has no material interest in the company (¶3120); or
– he is a director of a non-profit making or charitable company.

MEMO POINTS A further exemption is available where a **local authority provides** accommodation for an employee on the same terms as non-employees. s 98 ITEPA 2003

Valuation of the benefit

Where taxable living accommodation is provided to an employee, the way in which the benefit is valued depends on **the cost of providing the accommodation** (typically, the cost of buying a property). 3256

All accommodation is subject to the same cash equivalent calculation, but property with a cost to the employer **in excess of £75,000** is subject to an additional charge. (If the person providing the accommodation has owned it for 6 years or more, see also ¶3262.)

MEMO POINTS 1. If a **cash alternative** is offered instead of the accommodation, this may affect the value of the taxable benefit (¶3248). s 109 ITEPA 2003
2. **Shared accommodation** is taxed by apportioning the benefit fairly between the employee occupants. s 108 ITEPA 2003
3. In the unlikely event that **more than one property** is made available to the employee, each property would be taxed separately, and so the additional charge would only be applied if one of the properties cost more than £75,000.

Basic charge for accommodation

The **cash equivalent** of the provision of living accommodation is calculated as: 3258 s 105 ITEPA 2003
– the annual value of the property (prorated where the property is provided for less than a year); less
– any rent paid by the employee.

So no benefit will arise under the basic charge where the employee's rent exceeds the annual value.

The **annual value** of the property is generally taken to be the rateable value of the property, and when this is not available, an estimated value. 3260 s 110 ITEPA 2003

The annual value is deemed to include any expenditure incurred in improving the property. Where the person providing the property to the employee pays a higher annual rent than the annual value, then the higher figure will be taken.

MEMO POINTS **Strictly**, the annual value is taken as the market value of a landlord repairing lease, where the tenant pays all rates and charges usually payable by a tenant, and the landlord incurs the costs of repairs and insurance.

EXAMPLE An employer rents a property at a cost of £700 per month which is made available for an employee to live in from 6 July. The rateable value of the property is £7,500. The employee pays rent of £250 per month.
The assessable benefit for the tax year is:

	£	£
Higher of:		
Rateable value: 7,500 x 9/12	5,625	
Rent paid by employer: 700 x 9	6,300	
		6,300
Less: Employee contribution: 250 x 9		(2,250)
Assessable benefit		4,050

3261 s 105A ITEPA 2003 If the **employer rents the accommodation**, the benefit is usually valued at the amount of the rental charge, less any amount made good by the employee. With the exception of property mainly used for a purpose other than living accommodation, any premiums for **leases of 10 years or less** entered into (or extended) on or after 22 April 2009 will be treated the same as rent, although spread over the duration of the lease. So the benefit for the employee will be valued as follows:

	£
Premium divided by number of years in lease	X
Add: Annual rent paid by employer	X
Less: Amounts paid by employee	(X)
Value of benefit	X

s 105B ITEPA 2003 Any **break clauses** are assumed to be exercised in such a way that the term of the lease is as short as possible. This prevents avoidance by entering into a lease with an artificial term of more than 10 years and inserting an earlier break clause. In the event that a break clause is not actually exercised, a notional lease is deemed to start immediately after the time at which the original lease would have ended had the break clause been exercised. The lease premium payment will be spread across the full terms of the original and notional leases.

Additional charge

3262 ESC A91 s 106 ITEPA 2003 EIM 11472 Where the annual value is taken to be the **open market rental** for the accommodation, no additional benefit will arise. **Otherwise**, if the cost of providing the accommodation is more than £75,000, a further benefit will be calculated as:

(Cost of accommodation – £75,000) × Appropriate percentage

The **cost** of accommodation is the result of the following:

	£
Purchase price of the property	X
Add: Cost of improvement expenditure incurred before the start of the tax year	X
Less: Capital contribution paid by the employee	(X)
	X

The appropriate percentage is the official rate of interest in force on the 6 April at the beginning of the relevant tax year (¶9969).

The **excess** of any rent paid by the employee over the basic accommodation benefit will be available as a deduction.

EXAMPLE An employee lives in accommodation provided by his employer. The original cost of the property was £115,000. In 2003, an extension was built at a cost of £10,000, to which the employee contributed £2,000. The annual rateable value of the house is £5,000, and the employee pays rent of £450 per month. The official rate of interest in force for 2011/12 is 4.00%.

The taxable benefit for 2011/12 is:

	£	£
Basic charge:		
Annual rateable value	5,000	
Less: Employee rent (capped at £5,000)	(5,000)	
Basic assessment		-
Additional charge:		
(115,000 + 10,000 – 2,000 – 75,000) @ 4.00%	1,920	
Less: Employee rent not already deducted: (12 x 450) – 5,000	(400)	
		1,520
Assessable benefit		1,520

Where: 3264 s 107 ITEPA 2003
- the original **costs** of purchase and subsequent improvements were **in excess** of £75,000; and
- the person providing the accommodation has **owned it for more than** 6 years before it is first occupied by the employee,

cost is substituted by the market value at the date that the property is first occupied (including any improvements made between acquisition and first occupation).

In this case, **market value** is taken as the value which the property could reasonably be expected to fetch on the basis of vacant occupation.

EXAMPLE An employer purchased a property in 1990 at a cost of £90,000. In 1995, an improvement costing £5,000 was made. The property was then made available to an employee as living accommodation in 2003, when the market value was £200,000. In 2004, an extension was built for £20,000.
For the purposes of the additional charge, the cost is deemed to be £220,000. (200,000 + 20,000)

b. Vouchers and credit cards

Vouchers and credit tokens

When any employee (or a family member (¶3198)) receives vouchers or credit tokens, an assessable benefit arises. 3266 ss 73-75 ITEPA 2003

A voucher is **defined** as any voucher, stamp or similar document, or token capable of being exchanged for money, goods or services and includes transport vouchers and cheques.

A **credit token** is something which allows the holder to obtain goods or services on presentation, without actually being surrendered at that time. A credit card is the usual example.

Vouchers giving entitlement to the following are specifically **exempt** from the benefit rules: ss 266-270A ITEPA 2003
- parking provision;
- childcare up to a weekly limit (¶3222);
- exempt transport (¶3204);
- subsidised meals;
- third party entertainment and gifts;
- cycles and associated safety equipment;
- one mobile phone;
- annual parties etc;
- sporting and recreational benefits; and
- eye tests and correctional appliances.

MEMO POINTS 1. If the voucher is used to incur expenses which are **business expenses**, a claim for a deduction can be made (¶3135).
2. PAYE must be applied if the taxable voucher can be **exchanged for** a readily convertible asset (¶4606), or the voucher can be exchanged for money. If the employee does not reimburse the employer with the amount of PAYE within 90 days, a further benefit will arise (¶3406). s694 ITEPA 2003
3. Concessions are available which allow some **employees of passenger transport undertakings**, such as railway companies, to receive non-taxable travel vouchers.

3268 Vouchers give rise to a tax liability as if the employee had received a sum equal to the **cost of providing the voucher**. Where a credit token is used, the cash equivalent is the expense incurred for the provision of the credit token. Where the token can be used on multiple occasions, the value of the benefit at each use is the additional cost to the employer. Initial or annual subscriptions are ignored, as is interest. For both vouchers and credit tokens, a deduction will be made against the taxable benefit for any sum made good by the employee.

EXAMPLE An employer provides its employees with vouchers that can be used at many high street shops. The value of the voucher is £100, but it only cost £80 to purchase.
The employees are liable to tax on the value of £80, unless the voucher can be exchanged for cash, when the face value of £100 is taxable.

3270 The **time** when the benefit is assessable depends on the type of voucher which is made available:

a. a cheque voucher is deemed to have been received in the tax year in which the voucher is exchanged for money, goods or services;
b. other types of voucher are treated as having been received in the later of the tax year in which:
– the expense of providing the voucher was incurred; and
– it was received by the employee; and
c. a credit token is taxable on every occasion that it is used.

Credit cards

3272 s 94 ITEPA 2003 **Strictly**, where a credit card is made available to any employee by reason of his employment, the employee will be taxed on any cost incurred on the card, including any subscription cost, but not any interest for late payment.

The following **exceptions** exist, however, when:
– the employer receives HMRC's approval (dispensation) that no tax liability will result from purely business use of the credit card; or
ss 266 – 268 ITEPA 2003 – the credit card is used to pay for exempt benefits, such as workplace parking, third party entertainment, incidental overnight costs or other exempt travel expenses (¶3204).

If the credit card is used to purchase **readily convertible assets** (¶4606), PAYE must be applied by the employer. If the employee does not reimburse the employer with the amount of PAYE within 90 days, a further benefit will arise (¶3406).

c. Permanent health benefits

3274 s 660 ITEPA 2003 The **right to receive sick pay** or the prospect of receiving it is not a taxable benefit. However, sick pay itself is taxable.

Where the employer pays into a permanent health insurance policy, and the employee **receives benefits** whilst suffering from ill-health, the employee will be taxed on those benefits as if they were earnings. If the policy is not funded by the employer, any benefits will be exempt.

3. Benefits taxable on relevant employees only

a. Assets made available

Use of assets

3276 s 205 ITEPA 2003 Where assets are made available (other than bicycles (¶3204), cars (¶3286) or vans (¶3310)) for a relevant employee's private use, a benefit will arise where private use is significant (¶3216). The cash equivalent of the benefit is based on the **annual value** of the asset which is calculated as 20% of the market value of the asset when first made available to the employee. Any expenses incurred in connection with the provision of the asset are added to the benefit. Where the employer pays rent or a hire charge for the asset and this is greater than the annual value calculated above, the amount paid is substituted. For an example, see ¶3278.

MEMO POINTS 1. If **two or more employees** have the use of the same asset, a fair apportionment should be made.
2. **Motorbikes** are assessed under these rules and this gives a more favourable result than the provisions for company cars.
3. **Land** is valued on the basis of the rent which might reasonably be expected to be obtained on letting. s 207 ITEPA 2003
4. HMRC have issued guidance for use in cases where the employee enters into a salary sacrifice arrangement (¶3219) in exchange for provision of a **bicycle**. EIM 21664

Computers Unless the criteria for limited private use (¶3216) apply, the loan of a computer to an employee is taxable. **3277**

If the employee only makes **business use** of the computer, this does not constitute a benefit in kind. **Mixed use** will mean that the employee is taxable on significant private use, although the employer will be liable for Class 1A NIC on the whole benefit (¶5054).

MEMO POINTS There is a limited **exemption** for arrangements entered into before 6 April 2006.

Transfer of assets

Where assets are transferred to a **lower paid employee**, the amount of benefit is the second-hand value of the asset. **3278** s 206 ITEPA 2003

Where assets (other than bicycles and some computers) are transferred to a **relevant employee**, a benefit arises which is equal to the higher of the market value at the following times:
– at the time of transfer; or
– when first made available to an employee (if the asset has already been used by the employee)
less amounts already taxed (both on the employee in question and other employees (¶3276)).

This amount is reduced by any money actually paid by the employee.

MEMO POINTS The benefit which is chargeable on the transfer of a **previously loaned bicycle** (¶3204) or a **computer** which qualified for exemption while loaned, into an employee's ownership is based on the asset's current market value only. If the employee buys the asset from the employer at this value, no benefit arises. HMRC operate a simplified procedure for valuing a bicycle transferred to an employee after the end of a loan or salary sacrifice arrangement. This avoids the difficulty of establishing a market value for the machine.

EXAMPLE On 6 October 2009, Mr D, who is a relevant employee, is provided with an audio-visual suite by his employer at a cost of £1,500. On 6 July 2010, the suite is made available to Mr E, also by reason of employment. On 6 September 2011, ownership is transferred to Mr E, when the market value is £500. Mr D and Mr E are taxed on the following employment income:

	Mr D £	Mr E £
2009/10		
Mr D		
Annual value: 1,500 @ 20% × 6/12	150	
2010/11		
Mr D		
Annual value: 1,500 @ 20%	300	
2011/12		
Mr D		
Annual value: 1,500 @ 20% × 3/12	75	
Mr E		
Annual value: 1,500 @ 20% × 9/12		225
Total	525	225

2011/12
The transfer of the suite to Mr E will be assessed on the higher of:
– the market value of £500; and
– the amount still untaxed, which is calculated as follows:

	£	£
Original cost		1,500
Assessed on Mr D		(525)
Assessed on Mr E		
Earlier years	225	
Current year: 1,500 @ 20% x 5/12	125	
		(350)
		625

So Mr E is taxed on a benefit of £625 for the transfer of ownership, and £125 for use of the suite.

b. Ancillary expenses for living accommodation

General rule

3280 Ancillary services provided in connection with living accommodation may give rise to an assessable benefit for relevant employees, and **include**:
- heating, lighting and cleaning;
- repairs, maintenance and decoration (excluding structural alterations);
- council tax; and
- furniture or other effects normal for domestic occupation.

3282 ss 203 - 205 ITEPA 2003 The **cash equivalent** of the benefit is generally the cost to the employer (e.g. if the employer provides a cleaner, the cash equivalent of the benefit will be the cleaner's wages and the cost of items such as cleaning materials). The **exception** to this rule is where the ancillary expense is in the form of an asset (e.g. a television) which is made available to the employee. In this case, the cash equivalent will be valued in accordance with the rules for assets made available for the private use of employees (¶3276).

Employee in job-related accommodation

3284 s 315 ITEPA 2003 Where the provision of living accommodation is not taxable because the employee satisfies one of the **exceptions** in ¶3254, the amount assessable in respect of ancillary services is restricted to 10% of the taxable earnings (excluding this benefit) from the employment, and then reduced by any amounts paid by the employee.

s 314 ITEPA 2003 In addition, **council tax** paid by the employer in relation to job-related accommodation is not assessable.

Taxable earnings are defined as remuneration after deducting pension contributions and deductible expenses (¶3135), including capital allowances.

EXAMPLE Job-related accommodation is made available to a factory caretaker whose only sources of income are a salary of £15,000 p.a. and bank interest of £200 (gross). He pays a gross pension contribution of £300 p.a.
The employer pays £700 for heating and lighting bills and provides furniture and other domestic equipment which originally cost £7,000. The employee pays £35 per month towards the bills.
The assessable benefit applies to the ancillary services only:

	£
Heating and lighting bills	700
Cash equivalent of furniture: 7,000 @ 20%	1,400
Total	2,100
Restricted to 10% of earnings: (15,000 – 300) @ 10%	1,470
Less: Employee's contribution: 35 × 12	(420)
Assessable benefit	1,050

c. Company cars

A benefit occurs when a car (generally referred to as a company car) is provided by reason of the employment, and is **available for private use** by a relevant employee (including a member of his family or household (¶3198)). **3286** s 114 ITEPA 2003

A car is **defined** as any mechanically propelled road vehicle, with the exception of vehicles that are unsuitable for private use, or used to convey goods or burden (other than passengers). Invalid carriages are also excluded from the definition. **3287** s 115 ITEPA 2003

The employer should **report** the provision of a car to an employee within 28 days of the end of the quarter in which the car is first made available (¶4735).

MEMO POINTS 1. Even where an employee **purchases a share** in the company car, so it is jointly owned by the employer and employee, the car benefit rules will still apply. *Vasili v Christensen* [2004]
2. A **double cab pick-up** is usually a van for income tax purposes (¶3312).
3. It has been held that a **motor home** is a car for these purposes. *Morris v HMRC* [2006]

Private use

A car is treated as being available for private use unless: **3288** s 118 ITEPA 2003
– such use is prohibited by the employer; and
– no private use actually occurs.

As an exception, the use of a **pool car** which satisfies all of the following conditions is not an assessable benefit: s 167 ITEPA 2003
– it is made available to, and actually used by, a number of employees and is not usually used by one of them to the exclusion of the others;
– it is not normally kept overnight at or near the home of any of the employees who use it; and
– any private use is incidental to its business use.

MEMO POINTS 1. No income tax charge will arise where an **emergency service worker** is required to take an emergency vehicle home at night while on call, so long as all other private use is prohibited. s 248A ITEPA 2003
2. **Test engineers** will not be treated as having private use of a car where the primary use of the car is for testing, and any private use is clearly subsidiary to that testing. EIM 23805
3. A **car salesperson or demonstrator** who takes a car home for the express purpose of calling on a prospective customer does not have private use of the car (unless it is available for their general use as well). Similarly, **servicing staff** who take a car home overnight as part of a collection and delivery arrangement with a customer, will not be treated as having private use of that car. EIM 23810

Disabled employees

A car (including the provision of fuel and other related expenses) **made available to** a disabled employee (one who holds a disabled persons badge) by an employer, will not constitute a benefit where all of the following conditions are satisfied: **3290** s 247 ITEPA 2003
– the car has been specially adapted for the employee's needs (or is an automatic car if required);
– the car is only available for business travel, home to work travel and travel to training, and any other private use is prohibited; and
– no private use actually occurs.

Where accessories are added to **convert a car** for a disabled person, the price of such accessories is not a benefit. s 125 ITEPA 2003

When calculating the benefit for an **automatic car**, the carbon dioxide emissions figure for an equivalent manual car should be used (¶3298). If the list price of the equivalent manual car is lower, that should also be used in the calculation. ss 124A, 138 ITEPA 2003

Valuation of the benefit

The **cash equivalent** of the benefit of a car made available for private use by an employee is a percentage of the list price of the car. **3292** s 120 ITEPA 2003

s 121 ITEPA 2003 Once the cash equivalent is calculated there is no separate charge on any **other costs** associated with the provision of the car (such as insurance and servicing). **Exceptions** to this rule are:
– costs relating to the provision of a chauffeur, which are assessed as a separate benefit under the normal rules (¶3244); and
– the provision of fuel for private motoring (¶3304).

List price of the car

3294 s 121(1) ITEPA 2003 The list price (or if none exists, a notional price) is reduced by any capital contributions made by the employee. The amount actually paid for the car is irrelevant.

MEMO POINTS 1. A car's **list price** is that published by the car's manufacturer, importer or distributor, as the inclusive price appropriate for a car of that kind for a single retail sale in the UK on the day immediately before its first registration. This would include the provision of standard accessories.
2. The former £80,000 limit on the list price of a car **ceased to apply** on 6 April 2011.
3. The **notional price** is the price which might reasonably be expected to be the list price if its manufacturer, importer or distributor had published one, for an equivalent car sold in the UK in a single open market sale on the day before its first registration.
s 132 ITEPA 2003 4. Where an employee makes one or more **capital contributions** to the cost of a car or accessory, the price of the car is reduced by the amount of the total contributions in that and later years, subject to a maximum of £5,000. No such deduction is made if the car's price exceeds £80,000.
EIM 23220 If the car is subsequently:
– used by another employee, no account is taken of any previous driver's capital contributions; or
– sold, the repayment of the proportion of the capital contribution represented by sale proceeds/purchase price is not taxable.
5. If the car was first **registered abroad**, it is necessary to find the price for a single UK retail sale of a car of that kind at the time of registration abroad.
s 147 ITEPA 2003 6. Where a car is at least 15 years old at the end of the tax year (i.e. a **classic car**) and the market value for the year exceeds both £15,000 and the list price, the cash equivalent is based on the market value on the last day of the tax year. If the car was withdrawn from the employee earlier in the year, the market value at that date should be used.

Accessories

3296 ss 126–127 ITEPA 2003 Accessories provided for **use in the performance of the duties** of the employment are not assessed as a benefit.

The price of **other accessories** (not supplied as standard), which are added when a car is first made available, will increase its list price. If accessories with an individual price of at least £100 are added later, their full price is included in the list price of the car for the tax year in which they are purchased, and all subsequent years.

In both cases the price of an accessory is usually taken to be its list price.

s 131 ITEPA 2003 MEMO POINTS 1. **Replacement** accessories are normally ignored unless the replacement is superior to the original. In such a case, the price of the car is increased by the difference between the price of the new accessory and that of the original.
2. **Personalised number plates** are a taxable accessory, although the actual value of the plate itself will be modest compared to the personalised number, which is an intangible right to an arrangement of letters and numbers.

Calculation of the cash equivalent

3298 s 133 ITEPA 2003 The cash equivalent is a **percentage of the price of the car**, determined by the level of the car's carbon dioxide (CO_2) emissions and the date it was first registered. There are no reductions for high business mileage.

s 139 ITEPA 2003 The following table sets out the appropriate percentage for all CO_2 emissions figures for 2011/12 to 2013/14.

CO_2 emissions figure (g/km)[1]			% of list price	
2011/12	2012/13	2013/14	Petrol	Diesel[2]
Zero[3,4]	Zero[3,4]	Zero[3,4]	0	0
1-75[3]	1-75[3]	1-75[3]	5	8
76-120[3]	76-99	76-94	10	13
	100	95	11	14
	105	100	12	15
	110	105	13	16
	115	110	14	17
125	120	115	15	18
130	125	120	16	19
135	130	125	17	20
140	135	130	18	21
145	140	135	19	22
150	145	140	20	23
155	150	145	21	24
160	155	150	22	25
165	160	155	23	26
170	165	160	24	27
175	170	165	25	28
180	175	170	26	29
185	180	175	27	30
190	185	180	28	31
195	190	185	29	32
200	195	190	30	33
205	200	195	31	34
210	205	200	32	35
215	210	205	33	35
220	215	210	34	35
≥ 225	≥ 220	≥ 215	35	35

MEMO POINTS 1. The majority of cars **registered after 31 December 1997** will have a published CO_2 emissions figure in terms of g/km driven (for dual fuel cars, see below). So for cars registered: **3300** s 140 ITEPA 2003

– between 1 January 1998 and 30 September 1999, this will be the CO_2 emissions figure shown on either the EC type approval certificate or the UK approval certificate;

– after 30 September 1999, the figure is taken from either the EC certificate of conformity or the UK approval certificate.

The level of CO_2 emissions for a car registered between 1 January 1998 and 28 February 2001 can also be found (for a fee) from the following website: www.smmt.co.uk.

If there is **no published emissions figure**, the following percentages should be used:

Engine capacity (cc)	Percentage
≤ 1400	15%
> 1400 but ≤ 2000	25%
> 2000	35%

2. Cars **registered before 1 January 1998** will not have a CO_2 emissions figure, and therefore the benefit continues to be based on the engine capacity (whether petrol or diesel), as follows. s 142 ITEPA 2003

Engine capacity (cc)	Percentage
≤ 1400	15%
> 1400 but ≤ 2000	22%
> 2000	32%

3. The applicable percentage for cars which **cannot in any circumstances emit CO_2 by being driven** is 0% for 2010/11 to 2014/15, and 9% for 2015/16 and later tax years.
4. For **vehicles not within notes 1 to 3**, the appropriate percentage is 35%.

s 137 ITEPA 2003

EXAMPLE

1. Mr F is provided with a petrol car (CO_2 emissions figure of 198g/km) which has a list price of £20,000, and further accessories of £250 are fitted. Mr F makes a capital contribution of £1,000 for the car. Assuming the car is available throughout 2011/12, the car benefit is calculated as follows:

	£
Price of the car: List price	20,000
Add: Cost of accessories	250
Less: Capital contribution	(1,000)
	19,250
CO_2 emissions are rounded down to 195g/km which is equivalent to 29%	
Car benefit: 19,250 @ 29%	5,582

Reductions in the cash equivalent

3302 s 143 ITEPA 2003 Once the cash equivalent has been calculated, it can be reduced to take account of any periods of unavailability or any employee contributions, in that order.

A **period of unavailability** will arise when the car is:
- made available or withdrawn part way through the year; or
- off the road for a period of at least 30 days (which may run into a new tax year).

s 144 ITEPA 2003 Any amount **paid by the employee** (as a condition of using the car during the tax year) reduces the cash equivalent.

MEMO POINTS 1. If the original car is unavailable for less than 30 days and the employee is provided with a **temporary replacement**, a charge could strictly be made on both cars. However, a replacement is not taxed as a benefit if it is of similar quality to the original car or it is not provided as part of an arrangement to supply a better car.

s 148 ITEPA 2003 2. Exceptionally, where a company car is **shared** between employees, the car benefit will be apportioned on a just and reasonable basis.

EIM 23815 3. It is common in the **motor manufacturing and the retail car sales industry** (both new and used) for an employee to have the contractual right to take a car home. Where there are frequent changes of car in this situation, employers may apply a simplified benefit calculation by deeming the employee to drive a single notional car powered by petrol. Full details are available at www.hmrc.gov.uk/cars/averaging.pdf.

EXAMPLE Continuing the example at ¶3300, if the car is only made available to Mr F from 6 July onwards, the benefit would be:

	£
Car benefit for whole year	5,582
Period car unavailable: 91 days (91/365 x 5,582)	(1,392)
Car benefit taking into account the period of unavailability	4,190

d. Car fuel

3304 ss 150 - 153 ITEPA 2003 If private fuel is provided for a car by reason of employment, a benefit arises unless:
- the car is a pool car (¶3288);
- the employee is disabled; or
- the fuel is electricity for an electric car, or any energy for a car which cannot in any circumstances emit CO_2 by being driven.

Where fuel is provided for a **non-company car**, the value of the benefit is the cost of providing the fuel.

Where private fuel is provided for a **company car** (¶3286), the cash equivalent of the benefit is calculated by multiplying a fixed sum of £18,800 for 2011/12 (2010/11: £18,000) by the appropriate percentage, which is calculated using the rules in ¶3298.

To **avoid creating a fuel benefit** but ensure that neither the employee nor the employer are out of pocket, either the employee must fully reimburse the employer for private fuel, or the employer can reimburse the employee for business fuel. In either case, careful records of business mileage must be kept. **Partial reimbursement** by the employee will not reduce the fuel benefit. 3306

The advisory fuel rates are reviewed by HMRC throughout the year and can rise or fall depending on the price of fuel. At the time of writing, the applicable rates for 2011/12 were as set out in the tables below. Up to date figures can be found at http://www.hmrc.gov.uk/cars/advisory_fuel_current.htm.

Journeys undertaken on or after 1 September 2011

Engine size (cc)	Petrol [1]	Diesel	LPG
Less than or equal to 1,400	15p		11p
Less than or equal to 1,600		12p	
Less than or equal to 2,000	18p	15p	12p
Greater than 2,000	26p	18p	18p

Note
1. Petrol hybrid cars are treated as petrol cars for this purpose.

Journeys undertaken from 1 June to 31 August 2011 (inclusive)

Engine size (cc)	Petrol [1]	Diesel	LPG
Less than or equal to 1,400	15p		11p
Less than or equal to 1,600		12p	
Less than or equal to 2,000	18p	15p	13p
Greater than 2,000	26p	18p	18p

Note
1. Petrol hybrid cars are treated as petrol cars for this purpose.

Journeys undertaken up to and including 31 May 2011

Engine size (cc)	Petrol [1]	Diesel	LPG
Less than or equal to 1,400	14p	13p	10p
Less than or equal to 2,000	16p	13p	12p
Greater than 2,000	23p	16p	17p

Note
1. Petrol hybrid cars are treated as petrol cars for this purpose.

MEMO POINTS HMRC have clarified the following with regard to the use of advisory fuel rates: 3307 Tax Bulletin 78
– they cannot be used by employees to claim a **deduction** where the employer reimburses business travel at lower rates;
– where employees repay the cost of **private travel**, the employer may impose the advisory rate or a higher rate. HMRC accept that the advisory rate may be used for cars where the engine size is 3 litres or less;
– they are not binding on employers, particularly where the company cars in the fleet are more efficient and a **lower rate** is paid as a result;
– an employer may pay a **higher rate**, and where it can be demonstrated that the fuel cost per mile is higher than the advised rate, no taxable or NICable profit will arise for the employee. Otherwise, any profit will be taxable and liable to Class 1 NIC, but a fuel benefit will never arise; and
– the advisory rates may also be used for VAT purposes (¶7890).

3308 s 152 ITEPA 2003 The cash equivalent of the fuel will be **reduced** where:
– the car benefit is restricted because the car is unavailable for use throughout the tax year; and
– free fuel ceases to be available to an employee from any date to the end of the tax year (although if free fuel is provided later in the same tax year, no reduction is due).

EXAMPLE Mr G is provided with a company car (with CO_2 emissions of 200g/km) and free petrol. The car is withdrawn by his employer from 1 January 2012.
The percentage used to calculate the fuel benefit for 2011/12 is 30%. The number of days that the fuel is provided is 270.
The fuel benefit is £4,172. (18,800 × 30% × 270/365)

e. Company vans

3310 s 154 ITEPA 2003 Where an employer makes a van available for the private use (other than just taking the van home overnight) of a relevant employee (or a member of his family or household (¶3198)), a taxable benefit arises.
The use of a pool van is not taxable, if the conditions of ¶3288 are satisfied.

Scope

3312 s 115 ITEPA 2003 A van is **defined** as any mechanically propelled road vehicle (not exceeding 3,500 kg fully laden) which is primarily suited to the conveyance of goods of any description.

MEMO POINTS 1. The provision of a vehicle **exceeding 3,500 kg** when fully laden is usually exempt.
2. The treatment of **double cab pick-ups** tends to follow the VAT rules, which means that a vehicle with a payload of less than a tonne is a car for tax purposes. The addition of a hard top will decrease the payload by 45 kg.

3314 s 168 ITEPA 2003 An employee who uses a **pool van** (one provided for mainly business purposes but which the employee is permitted to be take home overnight) will not be taxed on a benefit provided:
– he only uses the van for commuting; and
– any other private use is insignificant.

If private use is unrestricted, however, there will be a benefit (even where the employee makes a contribution to the costs). HMRC are unlikely to accept that a van is only used for commuting unless the employee has another vehicle available to him for private use e.g. a spouse's vehicle.

3316 MEMO POINTS 1. **Private use** includes such use by one employee, or where the private use of the van is shared between a number of employees.
EIM 22745 2. HMRC have published guidance on the interpretation of **insignificant**, which is deemed to take its dictionary meaning of "too small or unimportant to be worth consideration." Examples of insignificant use would include a call at the doctor's on the way home, or regular small detours to a newsagent on the way to work.
Examples of **significant use** would be taking the van to the supermarket every week, taking the van on holiday, or using the van for other social activities outside work.
HMRC have suggested that an employer should be able to demonstrate that business mileage is reasonable for the type of occupation involved.

Taxable amount

3318 s 155 ITEPA 2003 The cash equivalent of the van benefit is £3,000.

The amount of the cash equivalent is **reduced** where the van is either unavailable (¶3302) or is a shared van. Any payments made by the employee for private use may also be deducted from the cash equivalent.

From 6 April 2010, for a period of 5 years, a vehicle designed primarily for the carriage of goods that cannot under any circumstances produce CO_2 emissions will attract no benefit charge.

s 161 ITEPA 2003 Where **private fuel** is provided, the employee will be assessed on a benefit of £550 for 2010/11. To avoid such a benefit, but ensure both the employee and employer are not out of pocket, either the employee must fully reimburse the employer for private fuel, or the employer can reimburse the employee for business fuel. In either case, careful records of business mileage must be kept. **Partial reimbursement** by the employee will not reduce the fuel benefit.

MEMO POINTS A van is a **shared van** for any period throughout which it is **simultaneously** made available to (but not necessarily used by) more than one employee of the same employer. In this case, the van benefit (and fuel benefit if any) is reduced on a just and reasonable basis to take account of the sharing.

f. Beneficial loans

General principles

A relevant employee (including his relatives) who receives a cheap loan or credit by reason of his employment will be **liable to tax on**: 3322 s 175 ITEPA 2003
- the cash equivalent of the cheap interest rate (if this is lower than the official rate of interest (¶9969)); and
- any waiver of the loan.

MEMO POINTS 1. An employee will also be taxable on **loans obtained** in the following circumstances: s 174 ITEPA 2003
- the employer guarantees or facilitates a loan;
- low-cost alternative finance arrangements (¶2832) provided by the employer;
- a loan is provided by a shareholder in a close company as a result of the employment; or
- the employer takes over the loan from another person.

2. **Relative** includes the following for the purposes of these rules:
- employee's spouse or civil partner;
- parents, children and remoter ancestors or descendants of both spouses;
- siblings of both spouses; and
- spouses of all those mentioned above.

The following types of loan are **exempt** from these rules, and so no benefit arises if the loan: 3324

a. is an advance made by an employer to pay for necessary expenses and/or incidental overnight expenses where the amount outstanding does not exceed £1,000, and the advance is spent within 6 months of it being made; s 179 ITEPA 2003

b. is a fixed term loan with a fixed rate of interest, which, at the time the loan was made, was not less than the official rate of interest; s 177 ITEPA 2003

c. is made as a result of a personal or family relationship (¶3198); s 174 ITEPA 2003

d. would wholly qualify for tax relief if interest was charged; s 178 ITEPA 2003

e. balance is below £5,000 throughout the tax year (aggregating all loans from the employer, but ignoring any such loans qualifying for tax relief); or s 180 ITEPA 2003

f. is made on a commercial basis by an employer whose business includes the making of loans, provided a substantial proportion of loans are made to the public, and the terms received by the employee are comparable to those received by the public at arm's length; s 176 ITEPA 2003

MEMO POINTS In relation to **d.** and **e.** above, **qualifying loans** are those where related interest would qualify as a:
- trading deduction (¶120);
- deduction against property income (¶2769); or
- general deduction (¶4363).

If only **part** of the interest would **qualify as a deduction**, the loan is not exempt for these purposes.

EXAMPLE Mr H has two interest-free loans totalling £16,000 from his employer.
The £6,000 loan buys equipment which is used for his employment (a qualifying loan). He uses the other loan of £10,000 to buy a yacht.
As the £6,000 loan qualifies for tax relief, no benefit is assessable. So Mr H will only be assessed on the £10,000 loan.
If the loan to buy the yacht had only been £4,000, no benefit would be assessable, as this would have been below the limit of £5,000.

Valuation of the benefit

3326 s 181 ITEPA 2003 The **cash equivalent** of a loan is determined by calculating the difference between the interest paid by the employee and what would have been paid at the official rate of interest (¶9969), using either the **averaging method** or the **strict method**. The employee should check both methods to see which is the more beneficial for the tax year. HMRC can, however, insist that the strict method is applied.

s 191 ITEPA 2003 MEMO POINTS 1. Relief can be claimed where interest is actually **paid after the tax year**, so any assessable benefit will be recalculated to take into account the interest paid.

s 187 ITEPA 2003 2. Where the lender is a **close company** (¶2100), and the borrower is a **director**, the employer can elect (by 6 July following the tax year) to aggregate all outstanding loans in the same currency made to the director for the purposes of the calculation of the cash equivalent.

Averaging method

3328 s 182 ITEPA 2003 The cash equivalent is **normally calculated** by using the averaging method. This involves taking a simple average of the amount of the loan outstanding at the beginning and end of the tax year, and applying the official rate of interest to it. This figure is then compared to the actual amount of interest paid.

The calculation for the averaging method is as follows.

Step	Instruction	Result
1	Loan balance on 5th April preceding the tax year, or the date the loan was first made if during the tax year	A
2	Loan balance on 5th April within the tax year, or the date the loan was discharged if during the tax year	B
3	Find average balance	(A + B)/2 = C
4	Multiply step 3 by the number of whole months (beginning on 6th of the month) in the tax year during which the loan was outstanding	C × n = D
5	Divide step 4 by 12	D/12
6	Multiply step 5 by the official rate of interest	D/12 × % = E
7	Deduct any interest paid (F) by the employee	E – F

MEMO POINTS 1. If the **official rate changed** during the period, the average rate is ascertained by reference to the number of days in the period and the number of days for which each rate was in force.

2. Where the loan was **granted or discharged during a tax year**, the amount of the loan at the date of grant or discharge will be used in the average (instead of the amounts on the dates shown above) and the amount of interest will be apportioned.

EXAMPLE Before the start of the tax year, Mr A is provided with a car loan of £10,000 by his employer. Interest is paid monthly at a rate of 2% p.a. On 5 July, £2,000 of the loan was paid off. Assume the official rate of interest during the year to be as follows:

6 April to 5 January	5%
6 January to 5 April	5.5%

The assessable benefit for the year will be:

	£
Average loan outstanding:	
(10,000 + 8,000)/2	9,000
Average interest rate:	
(5 % × 275/365) + (5.5 % × 90/365)	5.123 %

	£
Assessable benefit	
Official interest (9,000 @ 5.123 %)	461
Less: Employee interest payments (9,000 @ 2%)	(180)
	281

Strict method

An alternative strict method of calculation may be used following either an **election** by the employee or the issue of a notice by HMRC (who insist on this method where the charge would be distorted by the averaging method). The calculation for the strict method is as follows. 3330 s 183 ITEPA 2003

Step	Instruction	Result
1	Find the maximum amount of the loan outstanding each day	A
2	Multiply the loan amount by the number of days in each period	A × n = B
3	Multiply step 2 by the official rate of interest in force for each period	B × % = C
4	Divide the total of step 3 by the number of days in the year	C/365 = D
5	Deduct any interest paid (E) by the employee	D – E

EXAMPLE Using the details from the example in ¶3328, the assessable benefit using the strict method would be:

	£
6 April to 5 July (10,000 @ 5% x 91)	45,500
6 July to 5 January (8,000 @ 5% × 184)	73,600
6 January to 5 April (8,000 @ 5.5% × 90)	39,600
	158,700
Divide the result by the number of days in the year (158,700/365)	435
Less: Employee payment:	
(10,000 @ 2% × 3/12) + (8,000 @ 2% × 9/12)	(170)
Assessable benefit	265

Notional interest

Where an employee has been taxed under the beneficial loan rules on a **loan** that would in the normal course of events be **eligible for tax relief** (¶4363), there are special rules which apply. The types of cheap loans that are likely to be eligible for relief are those used to purchase shares in a close company or an interest in a partnership. 3332

Where all the interest on a loan is eligible for tax relief, the loan will be exempt from the beneficial loan rules. If only **part of the interest qualifies for tax relief**, the full amount of the loan is assessable under the beneficial loan rules, and tax relief is then claimed on the notional interest which is treated as paid on the qualifying part of the loan. EIM26135

EXAMPLE Mr B is given a loan of £20,000 by his employer throughout the tax year, when the official rate of interest is 4.00%. Mr B puts £3,000 of this loan towards equipment for his employment to be used 80% for business purposes.
Mr B will be assessed as follows:

	£
Loan benefit: 20,000 @ 4.00%	800
Interest relief: 3,000 @ 4.00% x 80%	(96)
Net taxable income	704

Loan waivers

Where a loan provided by reason of employment is written off, it is **usually** taxable as regular earnings (¶3032). **Otherwise**, an assessable benefit will arise for relevant employees, and the cash equivalent is the amount of the loan written off. 3336 s 188 ITEPA 2003

A write off **after** the **death** of the employee does not lead to an assessable benefit. s 190 ITEPA 2003

g. PAYE paid on behalf of directors

3338 s 223 ITEPA 2003 Where the employer **does not deduct PAYE** from the earnings of an individual, then the PAYE itself becomes earnings (¶3406) if:
- the individual has been a director at any time during the tax year;
- the employer pays the PAYE to HMRC; and
- there is no reimbursement to the employer by the director.

For these purposes a director is defined as for a relevant employee (¶3116).

SECTION 4

Employee share schemes

3342 An employee is chargeable to income tax when, by reason of his employment, he acquires shares in the employer company at a reduced price, either immediately, or in the future via the exercise of an option.

Generally, the recipient of the shares must be resident or ordinarily resident in the UK to be chargeable to income tax under these provisions. In addition to income tax, share schemes also have implications for corporation tax (¶782), PAYE and NIC (¶3404), and capital gains tax (¶5755).

HMRC-approved schemes, involving stringent conditions, allow the employer to make shares or options available to employees with a reduced or zero tax charge. Unapproved schemes are generally subject to a higher tax charge.

MEMO POINTS The employer may choose to set up an **employee share trust** in conjunction with a share scheme, which facilitates a trading market, as well as being a vehicle in which to store shares. In addition, when the employee sells the shares to the trust, this will always be treated as a capital disposal, avoiding any possible distribution treatment (¶2080) which might apply if the company employer acquired the shares directly. However, from 6 April 2011 such arrangements are likely to fall within the rules taxing disguised remuneration (¶3039).

Terminology common to share schemes

3344 s 420 ITEPA 2003 **Shares** Although shares are most commonly involved in these schemes, **other securities** such as loan stock, are sometimes used instead. For ease of reference, the term "share" is used in the remainder of this section, being the most normal case, and this should be taken to mean any security which is involved in an incentive scheme.

3345 **By reason of employment** A person is **deemed** to acquire shares by reason of his employment, if he receives them from a current, former or prospective employer, or he receives them as a result of the employment of another person. The only exception is where shares are provided by an individual in the course of a domestic or personal relationship.

Shares which **replace** or derive from employment-related shares are also treated as employment-related. Examples would include shares resulting from bonus issues, rights issues, conversions and share for share exchanges.

Shares received under **earn-out** clauses (¶5857) in exchange for founder shares are caught by this definition, particularly where the shares are a reward for services during a performance period when the recipient is still employed.

3347 **Associated person** In general, an income tax charge will arise on disposal of employment related shares by the employee, although such a charge will not arise on a disposal to an associated person who **includes**:
- the employee himself;
- the person who initially acquired the shares by reason of employment (if not the employee);
- a person connected with the employee (¶5570); and
- a member of the employee's household (¶3198).

A subsequent **disposal** by any of the above to a **non-associated person** will be a chargeable event for income tax purposes. So in effect, it is only disposals to outside parties which result in an income tax charge.

Associated company Two companies are associated if: 3348
- one company controls another; or
- both companies are under the control of another person (company, partnership or individual).

Two companies remain associated if control existed at any time in the last year.

I. Unapproved schemes

This section outlines the tax treatment of shares and share options (¶3392) made available to employees other than through an approved scheme. 3350

Any income tax due may be payable under PAYE, and details are given at ¶3404. In addition, there are strict reporting requirements which must be complied with (¶3590). A scheme may need to be disclosed to HMRC (¶2215).

Comment This is a complex subject, and expert professional advice must always be sought.

A. Shares

Tax may be chargeable in the following **circumstances**: 3352

Circumstance	¶¶
Shares acquired for less than market value	¶3354
Shares received on a priority allocation	¶3362
Post acquisition benefits	¶3364
Shares disposed of for more than market value	¶3366

In addition, there are special rules for the following **types of share**:

Share type	¶¶
Shares with artificially depressed value	¶3368
Shares with artificially enhanced value	¶3372
Convertible shares	¶3376
Shares with restricted rights	¶3382

Many unapproved schemes will fall into more than one of the above categories.

1. Shares acquired for less than market value

If an employee acquires shares at less than market value (including where payment is delayed), he will be treated as if he had received a **loan from the employer** equal to the difference between the market value of the fully paid up shares and the amount actually paid. 3354 s 446S ITEPA 2003

MEMO POINTS 1. These notional loan rules will not displace any **other tax charges** arising under any other employment related share rules.

2. Where **restricted shares** (¶3382) are subject to **forfeiture** within 5 years, these provisions will only apply to the first chargeable event and not on acquisition.

3356 s 446R ITEPA 2003 These **rules do not apply** to shares which satisfy all of the following conditions:
a. no loan stock or other types of non-share are involved;
b. all the shares of that particular class are acquired either for no payment or a payment which is less than market value;
c. the avoidance of tax or NIC was not a main purpose of the arrangements at any time; and either
d. the company is controlled by the employees and/or directors; or
e. the majority of shares of that class have not been issued by reason of employment.

MEMO POINTS The 2008 Pre-Budget Report announced that **simplification provisions** would be included in Finance Bill 2009, but these have now been **deferred** (until at least 2011). These provisions would have meant that no tax charge arises in the following situations where the employee makes no profit on the transaction:
– when employer company shares are to be paid for in instalments, and the shares are sold before all of the instalments have been paid (although any release by the employer from the obligation to pay any outstanding instalments may still lead to a tax charge);
– on the sale by an employee of nil or partly-paid shares; and
– where a scrip issue or bonus issue is made so that the employee receives new shares in proportion to his existing holding.

Charge to tax

3358 s 446T ITEPA 2003 The charge to tax on the **notional loan** will be calculated under the beneficial loan principles (¶3322) using the official rate of interest (¶9969) to calculate the benefit to the employee. The loan is also liable to Class 1A NIC. However, no tax or NIC charge will arise where the aggregate balance of all beneficial loans given to the employee does not exceed £5,000 throughout the tax year, or tax relief would apply to any deemed interest (¶4363).

For the purposes of the beneficial loan calculation, the **amount deemed to be initially outstanding** is measured:
– for partly paid shares, as the market value of fully paid up shares of the same class at the time when the shares are acquired less any amount paid for the shares; and
– for fully paid up shares, as the difference between the market value of the shares at the time of the acquisition and the actual amount paid.

3360 The notional loan will **cease to be a benefit** to the employee when:
a. for partly paid up shares, any outstanding or contingent obligation to pay is released, transferred or adjusted;
b. the shares are adjusted or surrendered, or disposed of in another way;
c. the whole outstanding amount is paid off; or
d. the employee dies.
Where the notional loan ceases under **a**. or **b**. above, a charge to tax will arise as if the notional loan had been written off or waived.

EXAMPLE At the beginning of Year 1, Mr A is allotted 20,000 shares in his employer, and he pays £1 for each share when the market value is £2.50. He pays another £1 per share at the beginning of Year 2. The official rate of interest in both years is (say) 5%.
In Year 1, a notional loan of £1.50 per share is created, amounting to £30,000. Mr A is charged to income tax on an amount of £1,500. (30,000 @ 5%)
In Year 2, the outstanding notional loan balance is reduced to £10,000. Mr A is charged to income tax on an amount of £500. (10,000 @ 5%)

2. Other circumstances of acquisition and disposal

Priority allocation

3362 s 542 ITEPA 2003 An employee who receives a priority allocation of shares in a **public offer** will be taxed on the benefit of that priority (even where it is at the same price as the public offer) **unless**:
– a bona fide offer was made to the public at a fixed price or tender;
– the aggregate number of shares that can be issued in priority to employees does not exceed 10% of the total number of shares on offer;

– all of the persons entitled to priority allocations are entitled on similar terms; and
– the benefit of priority allocation is not restricted to employees whose remuneration exceeds a specified level.

Post-acquisition benefits

If an associated person (¶3347) receives a benefit e.g. bonus shares, which derive from employee shares acquired at any time, the **amount charged to tax** will be the value of the benefit. **3364** s 447 ITEPA 2003

This tax charge will not apply where the benefit is otherwise chargeable under another provision involving share remuneration (except in cases involving tax avoidance), or where the shares satisfy all of the conditions stated at ¶3356.

Comment It is thought by some that this provision cannot be used to tax dividends as employment income, although the strict position is unclear.

Shares disposed of for more than market value

Where an associated person disposes of shares at an **artificial profit**, an income tax charge will arise on the amount received in excess of market value less any disposal costs. **3366** s 446X ITEPA 2003

EXAMPLE Continuing the example at ¶3360, at the end of Year 3, Mr A sells his 20,000 shares to the employer's parent company for £5 per share when the market value is £4 per share.
Mr A will pay income tax on the following amounts:
– £500 under the rules of ¶3360; and
– £20,000 on the artificial profit. ((5 – 4) × 20,000)

3. Shares with artificially depressed market value

Scope of provisions

Where the market value of employment-related shares has been reduced by at least 10% by things done otherwise than for genuine commercial purposes **at any time in the previous 7 years**, an income tax charge will arise. **3368** s 446B ITEPA 2003

Examples of transactions with a non-commercial purpose are:
– an arrangement with the main purpose of avoiding tax or NIC; and
– a transaction not undertaken on an arm's length basis between members of a 51% group (¶1520), although a payment for group relief is a genuine commercial transaction for these purposes.

EXAMPLE B plc transfers an asset worth £100,000 to C Ltd, its 51% subsidiary. The consideration given by C Ltd is only £50,000. The value of B plc's shares has decreased because an asset has been disposed of for less then market value.

Tax charge

The taxable amount **on acquisition** is calculated as: **3370** s 446C ITEPA 2003

(True value) – (Artificial value)

where:
– **true value** means the market value if the non-commercial transaction had not occurred; and
– **artificial value** means the current market value at acquisition (but if the consideration paid by the employee is higher than the current market value, then the value of the consideration is substituted).

MEMO POINTS 1. When the shares are **subject to forfeit** within 5 years, there is no tax charge on acquisition. ss 446B – 446I ITEPA 2003
2. If the shares are at all **restricted** on acquisition (¶3382) and no tax avoidance is intended, the restrictions are ignored in calculating the true value, and no post-acquisition charges under the restricted shares rules will apply.
3. If the shares are **convertible** on acquisition (¶3376), the artificial value and true value ignore the value of the conversion rights.

4. The true value must be substituted for the current market value if the shares are artificially depressed when a **chargeable event** occurs in relation to the following:
– a benefit is received in respect of the share (¶3364);
– convertible shares (¶3378); and
– restricted shares which do not fall within 2. above (¶3384).

EXAMPLE B shares are currently valued at £10 per share. A non-commercial transaction occurred in the previous year, and the true value would be £12 per share.
Mr D receives B shares as part of his remuneration, and he pays £8 per share.
Mr D is assessed on a taxable amount of £2 per share under these rules, being the difference between the true value and the current market value. (He is also assessed on the underpayment of £2 under the rules in ¶3358, being the difference between the current market value and the consideration.)
If Mr D had paid £10.50 for each share, he would be assessed under these rules on a taxable amount of £1.50 per share.

4. Shares with artificially enhanced value

General principles

3372 ss 446K - 446O ITEPA 2003 Where the market value of employment-related shares (whenever acquired) has been increased by at least 10% by things done otherwise than for genuine commercial purposes, at any time **in the previous 7 years**, a tax charge will arise.
Examples of transactions with a non-commercial purpose are:
– an arrangement with the main purpose of avoiding tax or NIC;
– a transaction not undertaken on an arm's length basis between members of a 51% group (¶1520), although a payment for group relief is a genuine commercial transaction for these purposes; and
– varying the rights of shares not held by employees so the value of their employment-related shares increases.

Tax charge

3374 s 446L ITEPA 2003 Where the artificial value is at least 10% above the value which would result if the non-commercial transaction had not occurred, on the last day of each relevant period, the **taxable amount** is calculated as:

(Artificial value) – (True value)

where:
– **artificial value** means the current market value (if the consideration paid by the employee is higher than the current market value, then the amount of consideration is substituted); and
– **true value** means the market value if the non-commercial transaction had not occurred.
Relevant periods will be:
– from the date of acquisition to the following 5 April;
– every year to 5 April; until
– the last relevant period which runs from 6 April to the date the rules cease to apply (either as a result of a disposal, or where the value is no longer artificial).

EXAMPLE The EFG group undertakes transactions between them which are not commercial.
E Ltd issues shares to some of its employees on 13 March 2011. The following valuations and tax charges occur:

Date	Market value of each share	Enhanced value included	Taxable amount
	£	£	£
5 April 2011	35	5.00	5.00
5 April 2012	40	3.50	3.50

The shares are sold on 7 June 2012 when the market value is £41, including an enhanced value of £2. A further tax charge on £2 per share will arise for 2012/13.

5. Convertible shares

Definition

Broadly, a convertible share is a share which contains the right to change into another type of share at some time in the future. This type of share is often seen in management buy out situations, where conversion is dependent on the achievement of performance targets. 3376 s 436 ITEPA 2003

The following are **examples** of convertible shares:
- the holder has an immediate or conditional entitlement to convert them into other shares;
- an arrangement has been entered into which will create an entitlement to convert on the occurrence of certain events; and
- the conversion will occur on the happening of an event outside the control of the holder.

Tax charge

An **income tax charge** arises: 3378 ss 439, 443 ITEPA 2003
- on the acquisition of the shares; and subsequently
- on the occurrence of any chargeable event.

No tax charge will arise under these provisions where the conditions in ¶3356 are satisfied.

A **chargeable event** is any of the following:
- conversion of the shares whilst still owned by the employee;
- disposal of the shares for consideration while they are still convertible;
- the right to convert is extinguished in return for consideration; or
- receipt of a benefit in connection with the entitlement to convert.

The market value of convertible shares will include the value of the right to convert. Convertible shares are therefore taxed as **two separate rights**, being: 3380 s 440 ITEPA 2003
- ownership of the unconverted shares as at acquisition; and
- the future right to convert the shares.

On acquisition, only the value attributable to the unconverted part of the share is taxed (unless the shares are part of an anti-avoidance transaction, when the full value is taxed, including the right to convert).

When a **chargeable event occurs**, the following table summarises the taxable amounts:

Chargeable event	Taxable amount
Conversion	The increase in market value between the old share (as if it was not convertible) and the new share, less any consideration paid for the entitlement to convert
Disposal	Disposal proceeds less the market value of the shares (as if they were not convertible) less any consideration paid for the entitlement to convert
Right to convert extinguished	Consideration received
Receipt of benefit	Amount of money or money's worth received

EXAMPLE Mr H receives free convertible B shares worth £200 each as a result of his employment in Year 1. These shares have the right to convert into ordinary shares in Year 2, and the value of this future conversion right on acquisition of the B shares is £50.
On receipt of the B shares, Mr H will be taxed on the unconverted value of the shares of £150, under the rules for receiving shares at an undervalue (¶3354).
In Year 2, Mr H converts the B shares, when they are worth £300, into ordinary shares which are worth £400. This is a chargeable event. The amount liable to income tax on conversion is £100, being the difference between the market value of the two states of the share.

6. Restricted shares

Scope

3382 s 423 ITEPA 2003 Shares which are restricted in any way will have a lower market value than equivalent unrestricted shares. However, if an employee pays full unrestricted value for the shares on acquisition, no tax charge would arise.

Examples of restrictions include:
– forfeiture or compulsory sale if an employee leaves the employer, except in the case of misconduct;
– restricted dividend, voting or other rights;
– redeemable shares; or
– restrictions on the right to dispose of the shares excluding the usual pre-emption rights found in the Articles of Association which apply to all the company's shares, as long there is no clause which requires such shares to be sold for less than market value.

Unpaid or partly paid shares, which may be subject to forfeit if a future call is not paid, are not usually restricted shares.

s 431B ITEPA 2003 If the main purpose of a transaction involving restricted shares is the **avoidance of tax**, partly paid shares, and shares subject to forfeiture in the case of misconduct, will be liable to tax (on the unrestricted value of the shares) at the time of acquisition.

SVM109080 ERSM30520 MEMO POINTS 1. If an **option** over restricted shares is granted to an employee, the option rules (¶3392) will initially apply, and then a post-acquisition charge on restricted shares (¶3386) will occur once the option is exercised.
2. Where a **ratchet** is in place, commonly used in a management buy out situation, flowering shares will not be deemed to be restricted on acquisition if the managers pay full economic value for their shares. Further details can be found in the Memorandum of Understanding between the British Venture Capital Association and HMRC.

3384 ss 424 – 427 ITEPA 2003 Certain shares which can be **forfeited within 5 years** of acquisition are exempt from the rules for restricted shares unless an election is made (¶3388).

For **other shares**, an income tax charge will arise on acquisition and then on the happening of a chargeable event. No tax charge will arise where the restrictions applies to all shares of the same class and the conditions stated in ¶3356 apply.

A **chargeable event** is one of the following:
– the shares ceasing to be restricted shares whilst still owned by the employee (e.g. employees are commonly required to remain with an employer for a minimum time before restrictions are lifted);
– any restriction affecting the shares is varied or removed while still owned by the employee; or
– the shares are sold while still restricted.

Tax charge

3386 s 428 ITEPA 2003 **On acquisition**, the taxable amount is the restricted value received. For example, if an employee paid £20 for shares which had an initial restricted value of £30, he would be taxable on deemed earnings of £10.

The tax charge on a subsequent **chargeable event** is a proportion of the unrestricted value immediately after the event as follows:

$$\frac{\text{Unrestricted value on acquisition} - \text{Deductible amount}}{\text{Unrestricted value on acquisition}} \times \text{Unrestricted value after event}$$

where the **deductible amount** is the sum of the:
– consideration given for the shares;
– amounts already charged to income tax; and
– expenses incurred in relation to the shares.

EXAMPLE Mr A received free shares in Year 1, as a result of his employment, with the following values:

	£
Unrestricted value	20,000
Restricted value	14,000

Mr A was taxed on the restricted value of £14,000 in Year 1, leaving 30% of the unrestricted value untaxed.
The restrictions are lifted in Year 2, when the shares are worth £50,000.
The taxable income in Year 2 is £15,000. (50,000 × (20,000 – 14,000)/20,000)
When the shares are eventually sold, the total amount of £29,000 charged to income tax will be deductible in the capital gains tax calculation. (14,000 + 15,000)

Optional election

It is possible for the employee and employer to **jointly elect** for any of the following: **3388** s 431 ITEPA 2003
– to ignore outstanding restrictions and tax the receipt of the share on its unrestricted value;
– to disapply one or more restrictions, but not others, resulting in a partial disapplication of the rules; or
– to disapply the rules for shares subject to forfeit (¶3384), and so tax the shares on receipt.

An election must be **made within** 14 days of the relevant chargeable event (including acquisition) and is irrevocable. There is no requirement to submit an election to HMRC but it should be retained as it may be requested in the event of a subsequent enquiry. If the deadline for an election is missed, a minor variation of any restriction will create another 14 day window in which an election can be made. Approved forms of election are available from www.hmrc.gov.uk/shareschemes.

Comment An election can be beneficial as it fixes the income tax charge with certainty, and any subsequent growth in the value of the share will not be chargeable to income tax or NIC. However, an election also accelerates the tax charge, and with no realised value, the employee may not have the funds with which to pay the tax. If the shares do not grow in value, the employee will have paid tax unnecessarily (particularly in the case of shares which are subsequently forfeited).

EXAMPLE Taking the facts as stated in the example at ¶3386, Mr A could elect to be taxed on the unrestricted value of the shares of £20,000. He would thereafter avoid any further income tax charges under these rules.

B. Unapproved share options

Under a share option scheme, the employer grants an option to an employee, giving him a right to buy a specified number of shares in a company at a specified price during a future specified period. This is a simple but potentially expensive form of remuneration. **3392** s 471 ITEPA 2003

Options which give a **right to sell** (otherwise known as put options) are treated as securities rather than options. Any income tax arising must be paid under PAYE (¶3404 onwards).

A **tax charge** may arise on: **3393**
– the exercise of the option (¶3394);
– the release or assignment of the option (¶3396); or
– the receipt of consideration in return for not exercising the option (¶3398).

MEMO POINTS There is no income tax charge on the **grant** of an unapproved option, unless the grant is **part of a scheme to avoid tax**. In this case the income tax must be paid under PAYE (¶3404 onwards).

Exercise of an option

The exercise of an option is **taxable** if the employee was resident and ordinarily resident in the UK (¶4152) when the option was granted. The employment and residence status of the individual at the date of exercise is not relevant. **3394** s 479 ITEPA 2003

The **income tax charge** is based on the difference between:
– the market value of the shares at the date on which the option is exercised; and
– the amount paid for the shares (including the cost to the employee of receiving the option, if any).
The charge arises for the tax year in which the option is exercised.

MEMO POINTS On the **death of the grantee**, an income tax charge will not arise on the subsequent exercise of an option by the personal representative or legatee. Instead, capital gains tax will apply on the subsequent disposal of the shares, and the base cost for these purposes will be the market value of the option at the date of death plus the amount paid for the shares on exercise.

EXAMPLE Mr B exercised an option to purchase 2,000 shares in his employer, B Ltd, for £3 per share. Mr B had paid £100 for the option. Mr B's salary for the year was £45,000.
The market value of the shares at the date of the exercise was £5 per share.
Mr B's employment income is calculated as follows:

	£	£
Salary		45,000
Exercise of share option		
Market value of shares (2,000 × 5)	10,000	
Less: Cost (2,000 × 3) + 100	(6,100)	
		3,900
Total employment income		48,900

Release or assignment of an option

3396 The release or assignment of an option occurs where the holder disposes of an option by a method **other than exercise**. The most common example of release or assignment is sale.
The tax **charge** will be based on the difference between the amount received on the release or assignment and the amount paid for the option.

s 483 ITEPA 2003 MEMO POINTS If the option is released or assigned in return for the **grant of another option**, the charge to tax will arise on the exercise of that later option.

Omission to exercise an option

3398 There is an **income tax charge** when an employee, who has been granted an option in connection with his employment, receives any consideration in return for:
– the omission to exercise the option;
– an undertaking not to exercise the option; or
– the grant, by the employee, of a right to acquire the shares covered by the option or to acquire an interest in them.

s 479 ITEPA 2003 The tax charge will be **based on** the difference between the value received and the amount paid for the option.

Disposal of the shares

3400 Where, following the exercise of an option granted in connection with employment, the employee disposes of the shares, any resulting gain will be liable to capital gains tax in the normal way.

EXAMPLE Continuing the example at ¶3394, the gain on the subsequent sale of the shares for proceeds of £12,000 is calculated as follows:

	£	£
Sale proceeds		12,000
Base cost:		
Cost of shares	6,000	
Cost of option	100	
Sum assessed to income tax	3,900	
		(10,000)
Chargeable gain		2,000

C. PAYE and NIC treatment

A liability to pay income tax under PAYE will arise whenever shares are **readily convertible** 3404
s 702 ITEPA 2003
assets (¶4606) i.e. broadly exchangeable for money or money's worth. However, in this context, the definition of readily convertible assets is widened to include all unlisted shares unless those shares qualify for corporation tax relief (¶787).

Class 1 NIC, including the employer's secondary contribution, will be due whenever there is a PAYE liability. As an exception, where shares are acquired at below market value (¶3354), Class 1A NIC will be due on the deemed loan instead.

For options awarded before 6 April 1999, no NIC charge occurs on exercise.

The following decision tree is useful when **deciding** whether an event creates a PAYE liability: 3405

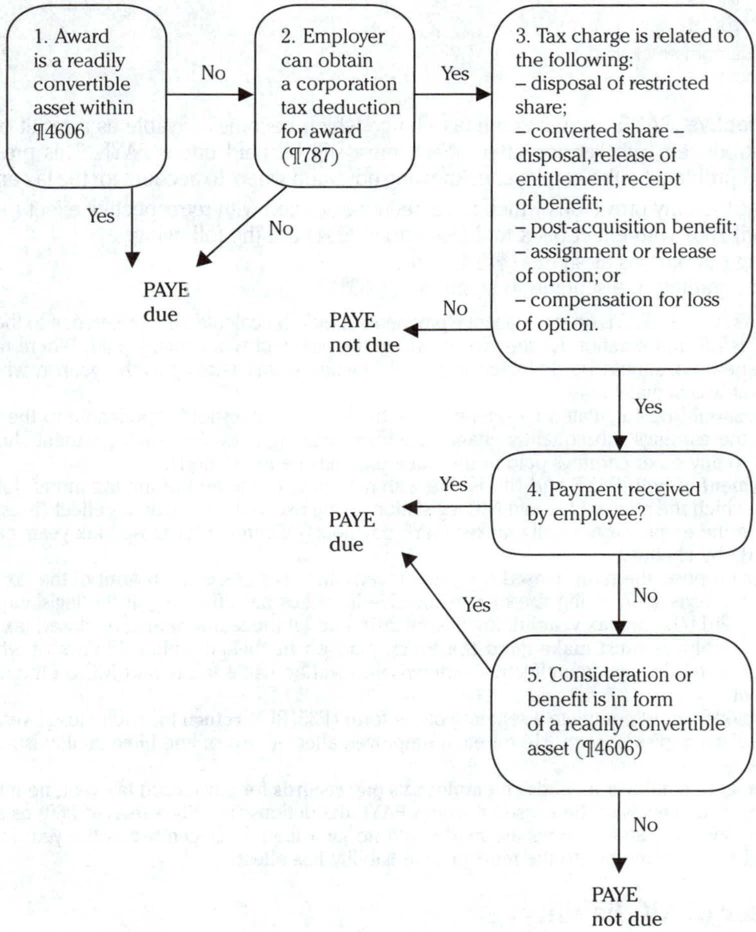

Notional payments

When an employee **receives shares** under an unapproved scheme (including options), he 3406
ss 222, 710 ITEPA 2003
will be in receipt of a notional payment which is liable to PAYE.

Where there is **insufficient income** from which to deduct the necessary PAYE for the particular pay interval (¶4608), the employer must make up the extra PAYE, and then recover it from the employee. The employee must make good the extra PAYE within 90 days of the date on which he received the notional payment. If not, additional income tax and NIC will be due on the extra PAYE paid by the employer, which itself effectively becomes income of the employee.

EXAMPLE Mr C receives shares from his employer on 1 September, and is liable to related PAYE of £5,000. His normal salary is £3,000 per month, which leaves a shortfall of £2,000.
Mr C reimburses £2,000 to his employer on 15 October, within the 90 day limit, and so no other tax charges arise.
If Mr C only reimbursed his employer on 5 December, outside the 90 day limit, the £2,000 would be deemed to be employment income, and income tax and NIC would be due as follows (assuming he is a higher rate taxpayer). He would need to declare this income on his self-assessment tax return.

	£	£
Employment income		2,000
Income tax at 40%	800	
Class 1 NIC @ 1%	20	
		820
Total due from employee		2,820

3407 s 420 ITEPA 2003 **Retrospective PAYE** Any income tax charge which becomes payable as a result of **rules** being introduced with **retrospective effect**, must still be paid under PAYE. This presents a particular problem for the employer in knowing how, and when, to account for the tax and NIC.

Currently, the only provisions which have been introduced with retrospective effect (actually on 6 April 2007 with effect back to 2 December 2004) are the following:
- treating put options as shares (¶3392); and
- options granted in a scheme to avoid tax (¶3393).

MEMO POINTS 1. PAYE on retrospective payments should be calculated by reference to the **PAYE code** (¶4618) in operation for the year in which the payment was actually paid. Where no code was issued, tax should be deducted at the higher rate of tax relating to the year in which the payment was actually paid.
2. **NIC** should be calculated by reference to the rates and thresholds applicable to the year in which the earnings subsequently chargeable were actually paid. Any such payment should be added to any other earnings paid in the same earnings period (¶4994).
3. **Payment** of both PAYE and NIC is due within 14 days of the end of the tax month following that in which the relevant tax and NIC legislation giving rise to the liability has effect (irrespective of when the employer normally makes PAYE payments). Payment for closed tax years can only be made by cheque.
For this purpose, the term "**closed tax year**" means any year preceding 6 April of the tax year in which the legislation giving rise to retrospective liabilities has effect e.g. if the legislation takes effect in 2011/12, the tax year ending 5 April 2011 and all preceding years are closed tax years.
4. The employee must **make good the PAYE** paid on his behalf within 90 days of when the retrospective rules become effective, otherwise he will be liable to tax and NIC on the notional payment.
5. Employers must complete a separate paper form (P35(RL)) **return** for each closed year along with revised copies of form P14 for each employee affected. No online filing facility is available for this.
6. Where an employer amends an **employee's pay records** for any closed tax year, he must give the employee details of the revised pay and PAYE deductions (usually a revised P60) as soon as possible after the amendments are made, and no later than 31 December in the year in which the legislation giving rise to the retrospective liability has effect.

Transfer of NIC liability

3408 SI 2001/1004 reg 69 A **joint election**, in respect of unapproved share options, convertible or restricted shares, with the approval of HMRC, can be made to:
a. transfer the liability for the employer's secondary contribution to the employee; or
b. agree that the employer can recover some or all of the secondary contribution from the employee.

However, no joint election can be made in respect of any NIC arising from the **retrospective anti-avoidance rules**, and a statement to this effect must be included on any document whenever a joint election is made.

MEMO POINTS 1. There is a facility for fast track **approval** of an election, details of which are available from www.hmrc.gov.uk/shareschemes.
2. Where the liability is transferred to the employee, the employer will not show a liability in the **company's accounts** in respect of the secondary Class 1 NIC. Quantifying the liability can be difficult due to the volatility of share prices, and so an election simplifies matters for the employer. See *Accountancy Memo* for more details of the accounting treatment.
3. **Model joint elections** have been published by HMRC, although these may not be appropriate in all circumstances.
4. The following guidance applies as to the **content** of the election, which must include:
– a clear identification of the parties, including the company's registered office and registration number, and the employee's National Insurance number;
– details of the option grant that the election refers to, along with the relevant legislation and employment income;
– the arrangements made to ensure that the employee pays the resulting liability in good time, along with a clear statement that the employee understands that he is personally liable for the secondary contribution;
– the method of disapplying the election;
– the fact that the election will continue despite any termination of the employment; and
– a declaration by both parties agreeing to be bound by the election.

Where a joint election is made, the employee can **deduct the employer's NIC** (which he has paid) from the income tax due on: **3410**
– the exercise of an unapproved share option; or
– on a chargeable event relating to convertible or restricted shares.
A deduction can only be made if the relevant NIC is paid by 5 June following the end of the tax year when the exercise or chargeable event occurred.

MEMO POINTS The amount of employer's Class 1 NIC paid by the employee does not reduce:
– the amount of employment income liable to employee's **Class 1 NIC**; or
– the corresponding relief for **corporation tax**.

EXAMPLE Mr D has a gain from an unapproved share option of £2,000, and the related employer's NIC is £256.
The amount liable to income tax is £1,744. (2,000 – 256)

Recovery of NIC

The **period** in which the employer can recover Class 1 NIC from the employee extends to the end of the tax year following that in which the employee received the share remuneration (¶5020). **3412** SI 2003/1337
Written agreements can be entered into between the employer and all employees (including employees who receive share based remuneration in the year they cease employment or the year after) enabling the employer to **withhold shares** equal to the employee's NIC liability on the share based remuneration.

II. Approved schemes

The main advantage of all the following types of approved scheme is that any profit made by the employee will be subject to capital gains tax, rather than income tax and NIC: **3416**

Type of scheme	¶¶
Approved company share option plans (ACSOP)	¶3422
Enterprise management incentives (EMI)	¶3450
Share incentive plans (SIP)	¶3510
Savings-related share option schemes (SRSOS)	¶3554

Corporation tax relief for the costs of the scheme should be available to the employer.

It should be noted that only the first two schemes tend to be appropriate for small and medium sized companies.

Conditions common to all schemes

3418 There are similar requirements for all of the schemes as follows:

Factor	Requirements
Type of share[1]	Ordinary, fully paid up, non-redeemable share in employing company or its parent
Type of company issuing shares (except EMI scheme (¶3462))	A company which is either: – quoted on a recognised stock exchange (¶9995); – controlled by a quoted company; or – not controlled by another company
Restrictions on share[2]	Minimal restrictions allowed, except those: – imposed on all shares of the same class; and – within the Articles of Association requiring disposal of the shares when the employees leave employment
Exclusion of employees with a material interest	The measure of a material interest varies according to the type of scheme, as follows: – ACSOP, 25%; – EMI, 30%; – SIP, 25%; and – SRSOS, 25%

Note:
1. **Anti-avoidance rules** may affect shares in any approved scheme. Broadly, shares are subject to the rules for unapproved schemes if the avoidance of tax or NIC was one of the main purposes of the award. These rules do not affect most approved schemes.
2. Any shares in an approved scheme which are **restricted** in any way (¶3382), will be valued on acquisition at their unrestricted value, removing any risk of a further income tax charge.

A. Approved company share option plans

3422 Approved company share option plans (ACSOPs) are discretionary, so that options may be granted to employees on a selective basis rather than to the workforce as a whole.

There will generally be no income tax charge on the grant or exercise of the options, nor on the subsequent increase in value of the shares. Capital gains tax on the eventual disposal of the shares is usually the only tax charge for the employee. The costs incurred by a company in setting up an ACSOP are allowable for corporation tax purposes (¶785).

Gaining approval

3424 Sch 4 para 28 ITEPA 2003 Once a scheme has been set up, a written **request for approval** must be made to HMRC.

Approval will be **withdrawn** where any of the conditions of the approved scheme are breached.

MEMO POINTS 1. Where HMRC have **informally approved** the draft scheme rules, formal approval will be effective from the moment that the scheme is established, provided there is no change from the draft rules.
2. If approval is not given, it is possible to **appeal** to a tribunal.

1. Eligibility

Eligible employees

An individual will only be eligible to join an ACSOP if, in relation to the company which established the scheme (or in the case of a group scheme, a participating company), he is a full-time director or any employee other than a director. **3426** Sch 4 para 8 ITEPA 2003

For these purposes, a **director** is deemed to be full-time if he normally devotes at least 25 hours per week (excluding meal breaks) to the duties of his office. In a group scheme, a director may aggregate all of the hours that he works for the participating companies.

Close companies Where the company operating the scheme is a close company (¶2100), an employee who has a material interest (at any time in the last 12 months) will not be eligible to participate. **3427** Sch 4 para 9 ITEPA 2003

A **material interest** is broadly defined as more than 25% of either the company whose shares may be acquired as part of the scheme, or a company who has control of the close company.

MEMO POINTS 1. The interests of the individual's **associates** must be taken into account (¶2105).
2. Shares held by the trustees of a **share incentive plan**, and not appropriated to the employee, are disregarded when measuring the employee's interest for these purposes.

Eligible shares

The shares which are used to form part of an ACSOP must be fully paid up, irredeemable ordinary shares **in the company** setting up the scheme or a company which controls it. The shares must be in a company that is either not controlled by another company, or is listed on a recognised stock exchange (¶9995). From 24 March 2010, shares in a company that is controlled by a listed company are not eligible. **3428** Sch 4 para 15 - 19 ITEPA 2003

The shares must not be subject to any **restrictions** other than those attaching to other shares of the same class (shares pledged as security for a loan or used to repay a loan are not restricted for this purpose).

2. Conditions for approval

The **general** conditions relating to an ACSOP are that: **3430** Sch 4 para 5, 23 ITEPA 2003
– the scheme must contain only features which are essential to the purpose of providing benefits for employees and directors in the nature of share options; and
– the rights under the scheme may not be transferred except when the participant dies, in which case the options may pass to his estate.

The extent of participation

The **aggregate market value of shares**, over which an individual may hold unexercised rights under the scheme, must not exceed £30,000. The market value is measured at the time of grant, and holdings under any other approved or savings-related share option scheme operated by the same or by an associated company (¶3348) are taken into account. **3432** Sch 4 para 6 ITEPA 2003

If an option is **granted in excess** of the aggregate market value limit, the option will be treated as unapproved (¶3392). Options which have already been exercised are left out of account.

Share price

The price at which shares may be **acquired** (the subscription price) must be specified at the time when the rights are obtained by the employee. The price must not be **manifestly less** than the market value of shares at the time when the rights are acquired (or at an earlier time that has been agreed in writing with HMRC). **3434** Sch 4 para 22 ITEPA 2003

Exercise of the option

3436 Sch 4 paras 24, 25 ITEPA 2003 Options under an ACSOP can be exercised at any **time**, so long as the scheme rules are followed (but see ¶3444).

If the participant dies before 3 years have elapsed, it is possible for the rights to be exercised within 12 months of the date of death (if they are exercised at all).

The scheme rules may allow an employee or director to exercise the options after ceasing their employment.

3. Life of the option

3438 Generally no income tax charge will arise on either the grant or exercise of an option under an ACSOP. The sale of shares will be taxable.

Grant of an option

3440 Where an ACSOP has been approved by HMRC, the grant of an option will not **usually** give rise to an income tax charge.

Any grant must be **reported** to HMRC on form 35.

3441 s 526 ITEPA 2003 **Exceptionally**, where the subscription price proves to be less than the market value of the shares on the date of the grant, an income tax charge will arise. For example, a rise in a company's share value at the time of its flotation would give rise to such a charge.

Where this provision applies, the tax charge will be levied in the tax year in which the option was granted, and will be based on the market value of the shares after deducting:
- any amount paid for the grant of the option; and
- the subscription price at which the shares may be acquired.

EXAMPLE Mr A is granted options in an ACSOP for 50p per option. The exercise price is set at £1.50 per option. As a result of the company's flotation, the market value of the shares under option is £2.50 at grant.
The amount liable to tax is calculated as follows:

	£
Market value at grant	2.50
Less: Cost of grant	(0.50)
Exercise price to be paid	(1.50)
Chargeable to income tax	0.50

3442 Where an **income tax charge has arisen** under this provision it may be:
- deducted from any income tax charge which may arise on the exercise of the option; and
- added to the cost of acquiring the shares for the purposes of calculating the capital gain on a subsequent disposal.

Exercise of an option

3444 s 524 ITEPA 2003 The **timing** of the exercise of an ACSOP option will determine its tax treatment. If exercised at least 3 but no more than 10 years after it was granted, no income tax charge will arise.

An income tax charge will also not arise:
- on **death**. If exercise occurs after death, an income tax charge will be avoided provided the exercise takes place within 10 years of the grant; or
- if the employee is a **good leaver** i.e. ceasing employment because of injury, disability, redundancy or retirement (at not less than 55), and the exercise happens within 6 months of the cessation date.

Otherwise, any shares acquired by an employee before the 3rd anniversary of the date of grant, or later than the 10th anniversary of that date, will trigger a PAYE and NIC charge (¶3404).

Sale of shares

Where the shares are eventually sold, the resulting gain or loss will be subject to capital gains tax. 3446

For these purposes, the **acquisition cost** of the shares will be taken to be the actual price (as opposed to the market value) paid for the shares by the participant. Any amount already charged to income tax, on grant or exercise, is also included as part of the acquisition cost.

EXAMPLE Continuing the example at ¶3441 Mr A exercises his option and pays the exercise price of £1.50 per share. A couple of years later, he sells his shares for £4 per share. The amount chargeable to capital gains tax is:

	£
Disposal proceeds	4.00
Less: Cost of grant	(0.50)
Exercise price paid	(1.50)
Amount charged to income tax on receipt of the option	(0.50)
Chargeable gain	1.50

B. Enterprise management incentives

The enterprise management incentive scheme (EMI) enables small higher risk trading companies to grant options (over shares with a value up to £120,000) to eligible employees without an income tax charge. Options can be granted at a discount. 3450

There are strict rules regarding eligible employees and qualifying options.

The company should receive a corporation tax deduction on the exercise of the option.

MEMO POINTS 1. The **corporation tax deduction** will be the market value of the share when the option is exercised less any amounts paid by the employee, ignoring any discount given to the employee (¶3498). For this purpose, the value would depend on whether the employee had made a restricted value election (¶3388). For further details, see ¶790. s 1010 CTA 2009
2. To provide a **market** for EMI shares, employers may wish to set up at an employee share trust (¶3342).

1. Eligible employees

An individual will be considered to be an eligible employee for EMI purposes if he is an employee of either that company or its qualifying subsidiary (¶3473) and he meets the following criteria: 3452 Sch 5 para 24 ITEPA 2003
- commitment of working time; and
- not holding a material interest.

Working time

An eligible employee's **committed time** must amount to at least 25 hours a week, or if less, 75% of his working time. 3456 Sch 5 para 27 ITEPA 2003

For these purposes, committed time is **defined** as the time that the employee is required to spend on the business of the company or, if relevant, on the business of the group. Committed time also includes any time that the employee would have been required to spend in this way but for:
- injury, ill-health or disability;
- pregnancy, childbirth, or parental leave;
- reasonable holiday entitlement; or
- not being required to work during a period of notice of termination of employment.

Material interest

3458 Sch 5 para 28 ITEPA 2003

An individual is not an employee in relation to a company if he has a material interest in that company or, where relevant, any group company.

For these purposes, a material interest is **defined** as:
- beneficial ownership of, or the ability to control, more than 30% of the ordinary share capital of the company; or
- where the company is a close company (¶2100), possession of (or a right to acquire) more than 30% of the assets that would be available for distribution on the winding up of the company.

MEMO POINTS 1. Shares that an individual **may acquire** under a qualifying option are not taken into account for the purposes of determining whether an individual has a material interest.
2. For close companies, a **right to acquire** shares is treated as a right to control them and must therefore be taken into account.
3. The interest of the trustees of a **share incentive plan** in any shares which have not been appropriated to, or acquired on behalf of, an individual will be disregarded in determining whether an individual has a material interest.

2. Qualifying options

3460

A qualifying option is a right to acquire shares, which must be granted in a **qualifying company**, for commercial reasons in order to recruit or retain a key employee, and not as part of a tax avoidance scheme.

The terms of the option must satisfy the statutory requirements, and notification must be given to HMRC.

a. Qualifying company

3462 Sch 5 para 8 ITEPA 2003

A company will be considered to be a qualifying company for EMI purposes if the following **conditions** are met:
- independence;
- gross assets;
- number of employees; and
- trading activities.

For groups, there is also a specific condition for subsidiaries to be qualifying subsidiaries (¶3473). For these purposes a company has a subsidiary if it controls another company, either on its own or with a connected person (¶5570).

Independence

3464 Sch 5 para 9 ITEPA 2003

The company must not be a 51% subsidiary (¶1520) of another company, or otherwise under the control of another company.

In addition, **arrangements** must not be in place where the company could become such a subsidiary or fall under such control.

Gross assets

3465 Sch 5 para 12 ITEPA 2003

The **maximum value** of gross assets (i.e. aggregate assets ignoring any liabilities) for a stand-alone company is £30 million.

Number of employees

3466 Sch 5 para 12A ITEPA 2003

In relation to options issued on or after 22 July 2008, there must be no more than 250 **equivalent full-time employees** working for the company. For this purpose, staff on maternity or paternity leave, and vocational students, are excluded.

MEMO POINTS 1. **Part-time** employees are counted as prorated full-time employees.
2. **Directors** are included in the number of employees.

Trading activities

A **qualifying trade** exists if it: 3467 Sch 5 paras 15 - 23 ITEPA 2003
a. is carried on through a permanent establishment in the UK (but see memo point);
b. is conducted on a commercial basis and with a view to the realisation of profits; and
c. does not consist wholly or substantially in the carrying on of any of the following **excluded** activities:
– dealing in land, commodities, futures or shares, securities or other financial instruments;
– dealing in goods other than in the course of an ordinary trade of wholesale or retail distribution;
– banking, insurance, money-lending, debt-factoring, hire-purchase financing or other financial activities;
– leasing (including letting ships on charter or other assets on hire);
– receiving royalties or licence fees, except those derived from assets created by the company itself or its subsidiary;
– providing legal or accountancy services;
– property development;
– farming or market gardening;
– holding, managing or occupying woodlands, any other forestry activities or timber production;
– operating or managing hotels or comparable establishments, or managing property used as such;
– operating or managing nursing homes or residential care homes, or managing property used as such;
– providing facilities and services to a business carrying out any of the above activities where a person (other than the parent company of the provider company) controls both the business and the provider company; and
– undertaking the activities of shipbuilding, coal or steel production (from 22 July 2008).
On request, HMRC will give **written assurance** that a company will be a qualifying company on the basis of its trade.

MEMO POINTS For options granted before 16 December 2010, the permanent establishment criterion did not apply. Instead, there was a requirement that the trade be carried on wholly or mainly in the UK.

The company must: 3468 Sch 5 para 13 ITEPA 2003
– **exist wholly for the purpose of** carrying on one or more trades (disregarding any incidental purposes); and
– **be carrying on** a qualifying trade or preparing to do so.

MEMO POINTS 1. The holding and management of **property** is not taken into account in determining whether a single company is carrying on a qualifying trade, provided the property is used by that company for carrying on one or more qualifying trades.
2. **Research and development**, which is intended to result in a qualifying trade, is treated as such. Preparing to carry on research and development is not, however, treated as preparing to carry on a qualifying trade

Parent company of a group

Gross assets The **consolidated group value** (ignoring holdings in group member's shares) must not exceed £30 million. 3469

Number of employees In relation to options issued on or after 22 July 2008, the number of **equivalent full-time employees** in the parent and all its subsidiaries must not exceed 250. 3470

3472 Sch 5 para 14 ITEPA 2003

Trading activities The trading activities requirement in the case of a parent company is that:
a. the **business of the group** does not consist wholly or substantially in the carrying on of non-qualifying activities; and
b. at least one group company exists wholly for the purpose of carrying on one or more qualifying trades (disregarding any incidental purposes) and is actually carrying it on, or preparing to do so.

The following **activities** of group companies are **disregarded** in determining the business of the group where they consist of:
– the holding of shares in (or securities of), or the making of loans to, another group company;
– the holding and managing of property used by a group company for the purposes of one or more qualifying trades carried on by a group company; or
– incidental activities of a company which meets the trading activities requirement for a single company.

3473 Sch 5 paras 10, 11 ITEPA 2003

Qualifying subsidiaries A company that has one or more subsidiaries is not a qualifying company unless they are all qualifying subsidiaries.

A qualifying subsidiary **exists** where:
a. the company (or another of its subsidiaries) owns at least 50% of the subsidiary's share capital and voting rights, and is beneficially entitled to at least 50% of both the distributable profits and the assets on a winding up;
b. no person other than the company or another of its subsidiaries has control of the subsidiary; and
c. no arrangements are in existence as a result of which the conditions above would cease to be met.

MEMO POINTS 1. For details of the factors of ownership (i.e. share capital, distributable profits and assets on winding up) see ¶1506+.
2. The subsidiary will not cease to be regarded as a qualifying subsidiary in the event of it, or another company, being **wound up** provided:
– the qualifying subsidiary conditions would be met apart from the winding up; and
– the winding up is for commercial reasons and is not part of a tax avoidance scheme.
3. A subsidiary will still be regarded as a qualifying subsidiary if arrangements are in existence for its **disposal** by the company, provided the disposal is for commercial reasons and not part of a tax avoidance scheme.
4. Where the subsidiary's main activity is to **hold land**, the rule in **a**. above is amended to require a 90% holding.

---

b. Option requirements

Type of share

3476 Sch 5 para 35 ITEPA 2003

The shares which can be acquired under the **terms** of the option must be irredeemable, fully paid up shares which form part of the ordinary share capital of the relevant company. If the employee undertakes to pay cash to the company at a later date, the shares will not be treated as fully paid up for these purposes.

Exercise period

3478 Sch 5 para 36 ITEPA 2003

The option must be **capable** of being exercised within 10 years of the date of the grant. This provision will be deemed to have been satisfied if the exercise is dependent on the fulfilment of conditions, providing the conditions may be fulfilled during the 10 year period.

Overall company limit

3480 Sch 5 para 7 ITEPA 2003

The **maximum value of shares**, in relation to which unexercised options in a relevant company may exist, is limited to £3 million. Any amount in excess of this cannot give rise to a qualifying option.

Maximum employee entitlement

An employee cannot hold **unexercised** qualifying options in respect of shares with a total unrestricted value of more than £120,000, at any given time. 3482 Sch 5 para 5 ITEPA 2003

If the limit has already been **exceeded** when a new option is issued, that option will not be a qualifying option and will be treated as unapproved (¶3392). Similarly, if the grant of a new option causes the limit to be exceeded, the excess over the limit will not be qualifying.

Once the maximum **limit has been reached**, no option granted within 3 years of the last qualifying grant can be qualifying. This rule applies regardless of whether any of the existing options have been exercised.

Where **ACSOP** options have been granted to an employee, the amount of unexercised ACSOP options count towards the limit.

EMI options with a market value of up to the maximum limit are **reported** on form 40. Options in excess of this value are reported on form 42 (¶3594).

Comment A useful ploy is to grant options just under the limit, which allows further options to be granted within the 3 year period so long as exercise occurs in the meantime.

EXAMPLE Mr B is a member of an EMI scheme operated by C Ltd. Mr B is granted (and exercises) options with the following market values:

Date of grant	Value at grant £	Date of exercise
1 Jan 2004	40,000	1 Mar 2006
1 May 2005	20,000	
1 Oct 2005	60,000	
1 May 2007	30,000	
1 Dec 2008	70,000	
2 Dec 2011	50,000	

The grant of the options will be treated as qualifying or non-qualifying as follows:

Date	Transaction	Value at grant £	Qualifying £	Non-qualifying £
1 Jan 2004	Grant	40,000	40,000	
1 May 2005	Grant	20,000	20,000	
			60,000	
1 Oct 2005	Grant	60,000	40,000	20,000
			100,000	
1 Mar 2006	Exercise	40,000	(40,000)	
			60,000	
1 May 2007	Grant	30,000		30,000
1 Dec 2008	Grant	70,000	40,000	30,000
			100,000	80,000
2 Dec 2011	Grant	50,000	20,000	30,000
			120,000	110,000

Note:
1. The grant of £40,000 on 1 October 2005 will be qualifying as this takes the value of shares up to the £100,000 limit applying at that time.
2. The grant on 1 May 2007 is not qualifying because it occurred less than 3 years after the last qualifying grant.
3. The grant of £50,000 on 2 December 2011 is partly qualifying as the limit has risen to £120,000 and it is more than 3 years after the last qualifying grant.

Person who can exercise

The **option must prohibit transfer** by the employee of any of his associated rights. The option may, however, permit the option to be exercised up to 1 year after the employee's death. 3484 Sch 5 para 38 ITEPA 2003

Company reorganisations and replacement options

3486 Sch 5 paras 39 – 43 ITEPA 2003 Where a **company acquires control** of a company whose shares are the subject of an unexercised EMI option, the acquiring company may grant equivalent rights within 6 months (known as a replacement option) to the holders of the original options. Control of the original company must be achieved as a result of a general offer to acquire the whole of the issued ordinary share capital, or all of the shares of the class to which the option relates.

The replacement option **provisions also apply** where the acquiring company obtains:
– control, as a result of an arrangement with creditors and members which is sanctioned by a court; or
– all of the shares in the original company, as a result of a qualifying exchange of shares, whereby the original company becomes a wholly owned subsidiary of the acquiring company.

c. Administration

3490 Sch 5 para 37 ITEPA 2003 There must be a **written agreement** between the person granting the option and the employee which states:
– the date on which the option was granted;
– that it is granted under the provisions of Schedule 5 of ITEPA 2003;
– the number, or maximum number, of shares that may be acquired;
– the price payable by the employee to acquire them, or the method by which that price is to be determined;
– when and how the option may be exercised;
– any conditions, such as performance criteria, affecting the terms or extent of the employee's entitlement;
– details of any restrictions attaching to the shares; and
– details of the conditions relating to any risk of forfeiture attaching to the shares.

Notification

3492 Sch 5 para 44 ITEPA 2003 Notice of an option must be given to HMRC by the employer company **within** 92 days of the date of the grant. The notice must include the written agreement and must also contain a declaration from:
– a director or the company secretary of the employer company, stating that the approval requirements have been met and that the information provided is, to the best of his knowledge, complete and correct; and
– the employee to whom the option was granted, stating that he meets the working time requirement (¶3456).

Right of enquiry

3494 Sch 5 para 46 ITEPA 2003 HMRC may issue a **notice** of enquiry in respect of the option or the employee's commitment of working time.

The notice of enquiry must normally be **issued** within 12 months of the end of the 92 day period during which notification of the option must be submitted, but may be issued at any time if HMRC discover that false or misleading information has been given. See ¶4552 for further details.

3. Life of the option

3496 s 529 ITEPA 2003 There is no income tax charge on the **grant** of an EMI option.

Exercise of the option

Special rules apply to the exercise of an option where it occurs **within 10 years** of the date of the grant, and those rules are dependent on whether the option is to acquire the shares at market value or at a discount. 3498

Where the option is exercised **more than 10 years** after the date of the grant, the option falls outside the EMI scheme and so it is treated as unapproved (¶3392).

MEMO POINTS Where a **replacement option** has been granted, references to the time of grant refer to the original option.

Exercise price	Income tax implication	Reference
Equal or above market value at grant[1]	No charge	s 530 ITEPA 2003
Less than market value at grant[2]	Charge on the difference between: – market value (at the lower of grant and exercise); and – amounts paid by the employee for both the option and shares	s 531 ITEPA 2003

Note:
1. In this case, the value of the share for income tax purposes is the unrestricted value as an election (¶3388) is deemed to have been made.
2. A restricted shares election (¶3388) should be considered.

The provisions relating to the following apply to EMI options: 3500 s 541 ITEPA 2003
– release of an option (¶3396); and
– the conversion of convertible shares (¶3378).
However, if the shares are acquired at an undervalue, there is no notional loan.

Disqualifying events

Where a disqualifying event occurs before the exercise of a qualifying option and that option is not **exercised within** 40 days of the event, the tax benefits of EMI status are lost. Examples of a disqualifying event would include: 3502 ss 532 - 539 ITEPA 2003
– ceasing to carry on a qualifying trade;
– a breach of the working time conditions;
– certain share conversions; and
– a company takeover where the options are not replaced (¶3486).
Any increase in market value between the date of the disqualifying event and exercise will be chargeable to income tax.

EXAMPLE Mr C was a member of an EMI scheme operated by D Ltd. Mr C was granted options over 1,000 shares with a market value at grant of £5 per share, and an exercise price of £2 per share. A disqualifying event occurred on 1 January when the market value was £8.

If Mr C exercised the option by 9 February (i.e. within 40 days) then, assuming the market value remained at £8 per share, he would still have benefited from the EMI provisions and the amount chargeable to tax would be the difference between the exercise price and the market value on grant i.e. the discount of £3,000. (1,000 × (5 – 2))

If Mr C exercises the option on 31 May when the market value is still £8 per share, he will be taxed on £6,000 i.e. £6 per share being the £3 discount on exercise and £3 increase in market value from grant.

If Mr C exercises the option on 31 December when the market value is £10 per share, he will be taxed on £8,000 (being the £6 per share as above plus the £2 per share increase from the date of the disqualifying event to the date of exercise).

Sale of shares

For capital gains tax purposes, the acquisition cost is taken to be the exercise price. 3505

C. Share incentive plans

General principles

3510 An approved share incentive plan (SIP) allows shares worth up to £7,500 per annum to be passed to a trust for the benefit of the employee (who is known as the **participant**) without an income tax charge. The shares are transferred to the employee once a specified period (between 3 and 5 years) has elapsed. Many of the costs incurred by a company in relation to a SIP will be allowable for corporation tax purposes (¶786).

Sch 2 para 7 ITEPA 2003

The **purpose** of a SIP must be to give employees a continuing stake in the company. A scheme with the sole purpose of making advantageous salary payments is unlikely to be approved.

Comment SIPs are only appropriate for **listed companies**, as the risks are too great for employees of smaller companies. In addition, there are substantial costs associated with the setting up and running of a SIP.

3512 Broadly, the scheme allows for four different **categories** of shares:

Category	Characteristics	¶¶
Free	Appropriated to the employee by the employer	¶3524
Partnership	Purchased by the employee through deductions from his salary	¶3530
Matching	Offered by the company if partnership shares purchased	¶3544
Dividend	Purchased with dividends reinvested on behalf of the employee	¶3546

Sch 2 para 2 ITEPA 2003

A scheme must contain free or partnership shares (or both). If partnership shares are available, the scheme may offer matching shares but there is no obligation to do so.

The scheme may offer different shares at different times. For example, a plan may specify that partnership shares will be offered only at the commencement of the scheme, and that matching shares will then be offered at specified times thereafter.

MEMO POINTS 1. Any award of shares must be **reported** to HMRC on form 39.

2. The **withdrawal of approval** of a SIP does not affect the operation of the SIP rules in relation to shares already awarded to participants.

3514 The following table summarises the main features of each type of share that may be offered:

	Free shares	Partnership shares	Matching shares	Dividend shares
¶¶	¶3524	¶3530	¶3544	¶3546
Limits on value of shares acquired	Up to £3,000 p.a.	Up to £1,500 p.a.	Up to 2 matching shares for every partnership share acquired	Up to £1,500 p.a. of dividends can be reinvested
Qualifying employment period [1]	Yes	Yes	Yes	n/a
Forfeiture on cessation of employment [2]	Possible	No	Possible	No
Performance targets [3]	Possible	No	No	No
Tax when shares acquired	None	Deduction	None	None

	Free shares	Partnership shares	Matching shares	Dividend shares
Tax if remove shares within 5 years[4]	Yes	Yes	Yes	Yes (if within 3 years)
Tax on removal after 5 years[4]	None	None	None	None

Note:
1. A **qualifying period** (if any) must not exceed:
– in the case of free shares, 18 months ending with the date of the award;
– in the case of partnership or matching shares, 18 months ending with the date of the salary deduction; and
– where relevant to partnership shares, 6 months ending with the start of the accumulation period (¶3538).
2. **Forfeiture** may be permitted for free or matching shares during a forfeiture period (which may not exceed 3 years) where the participant ceases employment, or withdraws shares from the plan (other than in certain circumstances (¶3528)). Forfeited shares are treated as having been disposed of by the participant and immediately re-acquired by the trustees at market value at the date of forfeiture.
3. A plan may specify that the award of free shares will be conditional on **performance targets** being met, which must:
– apply to all qualifying employees;
– be communicated to all employees; and
– be fair and have objective criteria.
4. Once a participant has been awarded shares, he is deemed to be absolutely entitled to them for **capital gains tax** purposes, even if they are still in the trust. Shares which **leave the plan** are treated as having been disposed of and immediately re-acquired by the participant at market value. This means that a chargeable gain will not arise if the shares are immediately sold.

1. Eligible employees

The scheme must include **all employees** who fall within the eligibility criteria, and are UK resident and ordinarily resident. Those who fail the residency test may still be included at the discretion of the employer. **3516** Sch 2 para 15 ITEPA 2003

The individual must be an employee of the company that established the plan, or of a company participating in a group scheme.

Participation must be on the **same terms** for all employees but free shares may be allocated by reference to criteria such as length of service, remuneration levels or hours worked. Performance measures may also be used to determine the allocation of free shares, and these can be revisited for future allocations where the business is suffering due to external factors. **3518** Sch 2 para 9 ITEPA 2003

The scheme must not contain features that would discourage employees (or a particular group of employees) from joining e.g. a scheme that requires employees to sacrifice other benefits in order to be eligible would be unlikely to receive approval. Sch 2 para 8 ITEPA 2003

MEMO POINTS 1. Where the company operating the scheme is a **close company** (¶2100), an employee who has a material interest (at any time in the last 12 months) will not be eligible to participate in the scheme. A material interest is broadly defined as more than 25% of either the company whose shares may be acquired as part of the scheme, or a company who has control of the close company. The interests of the individual's associates must be taken into account (¶2105). Sch 2 para 19 ITEPA 2003
2. Free, partnership or matching shares may not be allocated to an employee at the same time as when he is **already participating in another SIP** established by the same (or a connected) company (¶5572).

2. Eligible shares

The shares which are eligible for inclusion in a SIP are irredeemable, fully paid up shares which form part of the ordinary share capital of the relevant company. If there is an undertaking to pay cash to the company at a later date, the shares will not be treated as fully paid up for these purposes. **3520** Sch 2 para 28 ITEPA 2003

The shares may carry limited **voting rights** or no voting rights at all. Sch 2 para 31 ITEPA 2003

On cessation of employment, a **pre-emption** provision may require that shares awarded to an employee and held by him must be offered for sale. The provision must be applied to all employees and the shares must be offered for sale at a specified price. Sch 2 para 33 ITEPA 2003

3. Characteristics of each type of share

3522 The conditions for approval and tax treatment are different for each type of share within a SIP. The general idea is that an award of shares to an employee will not give rise to an income tax charge providing the shares are left in the plan for at least 5 years.

An **income tax charge will arise** if the shares cease to be subject to the plan too early (i.e. they are withdrawn by the employee, disposed of by the trustees, or the employment ceases), but the amount of the charge will depend on the type of share. Capital receipts may also give rise to an income tax charge.

MEMO POINTS 1. Shares are deemed to cease being subject to the plan in the **order** in which they were awarded to the participant. Where shares were awarded on the same day, the deemed order should give rise to the lowest tax charge.

ss 509, 510 ITEPA 2003 2. Where an income tax charge arises on SIP shares, and they are readily convertible assets (¶4606), the employer must normally operate **PAYE** on the amount that is likely to be subject to income tax under the SIP provisions. The employer must therefore make a reasonable estimate of this amount, although it is the trustees who are obliged to pay over a sum which will enable the employer to discharge the PAYE liability.

s 501 ITEPA 2003 3. A **capital receipt** for these purposes is defined as any money or money's worth received in respect of SIP shares other than where it:
- constitutes taxable income in the hands of the recipient;
- represents the disposal proceeds of the shares; or
- consists of new shares acquired in exchange for the original shares under a company reconstruction.

Where a capital receipt is **received within** 5 years of the acquisition date (3 years for dividend shares), a deemed employment income charge will arise on the value received. The trustees must pay the whole amount of the receipt to the employer, who then deducts PAYE before paying the balance over to the employee.

a. Free shares

3524 Sch 2 para 34-35 ITEPA 2003 Free shares are those awarded to the participant by the employer without payment. The **initial market value** (i.e. disregarding any restrictions or risk of forfeiture) of free shares awarded may not exceed £3,000 in any tax year. The number of free shares awarded may be linked to performance targets.

Holding period

3526 Sch 2 para 36 ITEPA 2003 A holding period of **between** 3 and 5 years (beginning with the date of the award) must be specified by the company during which the participant is bound by a contract with the company:
- to permit the free shares to remain in the hands of the trustees; and
- not to dispose of his beneficial interest in the shares.

s 507 ITEPA 2003 If the participant assigns, charges or otherwise **disposes** of his beneficial interest in free shares within the holding period, a tax charge will arise.

Withdrawal of shares

3528 s 498 ITEPA 2003 If free shares are withdrawn from the SIP before **5 years** have elapsed from the date of the award, an income tax charge will arise **unless** the shares cease to be subject to the plan because the relevant employment has ceased, following:
- injury or disability;
- redundancy;
- a business transfer where the new employer takes over the obligations relating to the existing employees;
- a change of control or other circumstances which mean that the company by which he is employed is no longer associated to the company operating the plan;
- retirement on or after reaching retirement age (which cannot be less than 50); or
- death.

Otherwise, the amount chargeable to tax depends on when the shares are withdrawn. s 505 ITEPA 2003

Period since shares awarded	Income tax implications
Less than 3 years	Charged on the market value of the shares when they leave the plan
More than 3 years but less than 5 years	Charged on the lower of the market value of the shares on the date: – of the award[1]; and – on which the shares leave the plan
More than 5 years	No tax

Note:
1. The tax arising is reduced by the tax payable on any capital receipts (¶3522).

EXAMPLE Mr E, Mr F and Mr G were all participants of H Ltd's SIP who were awarded 250 free shares on 1 January 2007, when each share was worth £10.
They each withdraw their shares from the scheme as follows:

	Withdrawal date	Market value
Mr E	June 2008	£12
Mr F	May 2011	£14
Mr G	August 2012	£16

Mr E, who withdraws the shares less than 3 years after the award, will be taxed on their market value at the date of withdrawal i.e. £3,000. (250 × 12)

Mr F, who withdraws the shares between 3 and 5 years after the award, will be taxed on the lower of the market value at the date of the award and the date of the withdrawal i.e. £2,500. (250 × 10)

Mr G, who withdraws the shares more than 5 years after the award, will suffer no tax.

b. Partnership shares

Partnership shares are those **acquired by employees** with sums deducted from their salary. Where a SIP provides for partnership shares, qualifying employees must enter into partnership share agreements with the company under which the: 3530 Sch 2 paras 43 – 45 ITEPA 2003
- employee authorises the company to make periodic deductions from his salary; and
- company undertakes that the deduction will be used to purchase shares under the plan.

The agreement **must specify** the amount to be deducted and at what intervals, although both may be varied with the agreement of the employee and the company.

Salary deductions

The **maximum** amount that may be deducted from an employee's salary in respect of partnership shares is £1,500 in a tax year, subject to an overriding limit of 10% of the salary for the period for which the deduction is being made (or for the accumulation period if there is one). 3532 Sch 2 paras 46, 47 ITEPA 2003

A **minimum** monthly deduction which may not exceed £10 may be specified by the plan.

MEMO POINTS 1. For these purposes, **salary** is the earnings subject to PAYE, including any bonus at the discretion of the employer, but excluding any benefits and expenses. Sch 2 para 43 ITEPA 2003
2. For **NIC purposes**, the cost of partnership shares may be deducted from earnings.
3. The amount used to fund the purchase of partnership shares is taken into account as earnings (¶3768) for the purposes of **pension contributions**.
4. Where any **deductions are repaid** to the employee (because they are surplus for example), those amounts will be taxable as employment income at the date on which the amount is refunded. Similarly, if the employee receives money or money's worth on the cancellation of the partnership share agreement, he will be taxable on the resulting employment income.

3534 Sch 2 para 49 ITEPA 2003

The **deducted amounts** are held by trustees on the employee's behalf until they are applied in acquiring partnership shares. If the money is held on an interest-bearing account, provision must be made for the trustees to account to the employee for the interest.

Sch 2 para 50 ITEPA 2003

Partnership shares must be acquired within 30 days of the deduction unless an accumulation period is provided for by the plan.

3536 Sch 2 para 53 ITEPA 2003

The SIP may specify a maximum **number of shares** to be included in an award of partnership shares providing the employees are given notice of it before the first salary deduction, or before the beginning of the accumulation period if there is one.

Where the number of shares that could be purchased with the deductions is more than the maximum, the number of shares in the award is scaled down.

Accumulation period

3538 Sch 2 para 51 ITEPA 2003

A SIP may state an accumulation period of up to 12 months (starting with the date of the first deduction), which must be the same for all participants. The **length** of the period must be specified in the partnership share agreement, and it may end on the occurrence of a particular event when deductions will be refunded to the participants.

3540

The **shares are acquired** at the lower of the market value on the:
- first day of the accumulation period; and
- acquisition date.

Any **surplus money** left over after the purchase of shares may, with the agreement of the employee, be carried forward and added to the next deduction, or repaid to him.

If the **employee leaves the employment** during the accumulation period, the deductions made from his salary will be refunded.

EXAMPLE Mr A is a member of B Ltd's SIP and agrees to a deduction of £75 per month from his salary. The plan has an accumulation period of 12 months. At the date of the first deduction from his salary the SIP shares have a market value of £5, and at the end of the accumulation period the market value is £8 per share.
At the end of the accumulation period, Mr A's fund is worth £900 which means he will be entitled to 180 shares at the lower market value of £5.

Withdrawal of shares

3542 s 506 ITEPA 2003

Where partnership shares are withdrawn from the SIP before 5 years have elapsed from the date of the award, an income tax charge will arise unless one of the exceptions in ¶3528 applies.

Period since shares acquired	Income tax implications
Less than 3 years	Charged on the market value of the shares when they leave the plan
More than 3 years but less than 5 years	Charged on the lower of the: – salary deductions used to acquire them[1]; and – market value of the shares on the withdrawal date
More than 5 years	No tax

Note:
1. The tax arising is reduced by the tax payable on any capital receipts (¶3522).

c. Matching shares

3544 Sch 2 paras 59 – 61 ITEPA 2003

Where the SIP provides for matching shares, they are given to the employee by the employer **in proportion** to the partnership shares acquired by the employee. Matching shares must be awarded to all participants on the same basis, as specified by the partnership share agreement.

The ratio of matching shares to partnership shares is always based on the number of shares as opposed to the value, and the **maximum** is two matching shares to each partnership share. The matching shares, which are awarded on the same day as the partnership shares, must be of the same class as the partnership shares and must carry the same rights.

The **holding period** provisions and consequences of **early withdrawal** are the same as for free shares.

d. Dividend shares

The terms of a SIP may provide that: 3546 Sch 2 paras 62 - 69 ITEPA 2003
- at the **direction of the company** (which is revocable at any time), all cash dividends arising from plan shares held on behalf of participants must be applied in acquiring further shares; or
- where the **participant so elects**, cash dividends arising from plan shares held on his behalf can be applied in acquiring further shares.

Dividend shares must be of the same class and carry the same rights as the shares on which the dividend was paid and must not be subject to any forfeiture provisions. Any cash dividends that are not to be reinvested must be paid over to the participant as soon as practicable.

The **maximum** amount of dividend that can be reinvested on behalf of an individual in any tax year is £1,500. This limit applies to all SIPs established by the company or its associates (¶3348).

Acquisition of shares

The shares must be acquired within 30 days of the date on which the dividend is received by the trustees on behalf of the participant. The number of shares acquired by each participant is based on the market value at the acquisition date. 3548 Sch 2 paras 66 - 68 ITEPA 2003

Any **remaining balance** of dividends can be carried forward for 3 years before repayment must be made to the participant. Where the participant ceases employment with the company, or where the plan is terminated, earlier repayment is required.

Where more than one surplus dividend is being carried forward, earlier dividends are deemed to be reinvested before later dividends.

The **holding period** provisions outlined for free shares are also applicable to dividend shares.

Tax treatment

Dividend **income reinvested** by the trustees to purchase dividend shares will not form part of the taxable income of the participant and a dividend tax credit will not be available. 3550 ss 493, 496 ITEPA 2003

The same rule applies to **surplus dividends** carried forward. If amounts are eventually repaid to the participant, he will be liable to tax (in the year in which the repayment occurs) in the usual way as if the payments were dividends.

Where dividend shares are **withdrawn** from the SIP after 3 years have elapsed since their acquisition, no tax charge arises. However, if withdrawal occurs earlier, an income tax charge will arise unless one of the exceptions in ¶3528 applies. The participant will be subject to tax on the amount of the related dividend, as if the dividend was paid in the year in which the shares ceased to be subject to the plan, and the tax credit (¶2821) is available at the rate applicable at that time. Any tax charge arising can be reduced by the tax payable on any capital receipts. Sch 2 para 80 ITEPA 2003

D. Savings-related share option schemes

A savings-related share option scheme (SRSOS) allows employees to acquire shares using the funds retained in a savings scheme (SAYE) for a period of between 3 and 7 years. Providing the scheme is approved and all of the conditions are met, the grant of the share options will be tax-free, as will the increase in value of the shares between the grant of the 3554 option and its exercise. Interest and bonuses paid in relation to the funds in the scheme are also exempt from tax.

The costs incurred by a company in setting up an SRSOS are allowable for corporation tax purposes (¶785).

The SRSOS is usually only appropriate for larger companies.

MEMO POINTS 1. Any grant must be **reported** to HMRC on form 34.
2. Simple schemes are available **off the shelf** from the major banks at no cost to the employer, so long as sufficient employee contributions are made.

1. Eligibility

Eligible employees

3556 Sch 3 paras 6 - 16 ITEPA 2003

The persons eligible to participate in the scheme **must** include every person who:
– is an employee or full-time director (¶3426) of the company which has established the scheme (or in the case of a group scheme, a participating company);
– has been employed by the company throughout the qualifying period; and
– is resident and ordinarily resident in the UK (¶4152).

The company has **discretion** to permit the following to participate under the scheme:
– part-time directors;
– employees or directors who have been employed for less than the qualifying period; and
– employees who do not satisfy the residency condition.

For close companies, the conditions at ¶3427 also apply.

3558 Sch 3 paras 6, 7 ITEPA 2003

The company may specify a **qualifying period** (of up to 5 years) throughout which the employee or director must have been employed by the company.

Those employees or directors who do participate in the scheme must do so on **similar terms** but there may be variation in the rights issued to participants based on their remuneration, length of service, or other similar factors.

Eligible shares

3560 Sch 3 paras 17- 22 ITEPA 2003

The shares which are used to form part of an SRSOS must be fully paid up, irredeemable **ordinary shares** in the company setting up the scheme, or a company which controls it. The shares must be in either a company not controlled by another company, or quoted on a recognised stock exchange (¶9995).

The shares eligible for inclusion in an SRSOS are similar to those relating to ACSOPs (¶3428). The **exception** is that SRSOS shares will be treated as subject to a restriction where the shares are pledged as security for a loan or used to repay a loan.

2. Conditions for approval

3562 Sch 3 paras 5, 29 ITEPA 2003

The general conditions relating to an SRSOS are that:
– the rights under the scheme may not be transferred, except if the participant dies, when the options may pass to his estate; and
– the scheme must not contain features that would discourage employees (or a particular group of employees) from joining.

Savings scheme

3564 Sch 3 para 24 ITEPA 2003

Shares under an SRSOS **must be acquired** out of savings (and interest) with a certified contractual savings scheme (SAYE) which is approved for this purpose by HMRC. Options under the scheme must not be **capable of being exercised** before, or more than 6 months after, the bonus date.

The **bonus date** will be 3, 5 or 7 years after the commencement of the SAYE scheme, and this period must be determined at the time when the option is granted. The rates applicable to new contracts during 2011/12 are as follows:

For new contracts from 12 August 2011		
Bonus date	Bonus rate	Annual equivalent rate
3 year	0.0% x monthly payment	0.00%
5 year	0.9% x monthly payment	0.59%
7 year	3.5% x monthly payment	1.25%

For new contracts from 27 February to 11 August 2011		
Bonus date	Bonus rate	Annual equivalent rate
3 year	0.10% x monthly payment	0.18%
5 year	1.70% x monthly payment	1.10%
7 year	4.80% x monthly payment	1.70%

For new contracts from 12 September 2010 to 26 February 2011		
Bonus date	Bonus rate	Annual equivalent rate
3 year	0.0% x monthly payment	0%
5 year	0.90% x monthly payment	0.59%
7 year	3.20% x monthly payment	1.15%

For older contracts (from 14 May 2010)		
Bonus date	Bonus rate	Annual equivalent rate
3 year	0.0% x monthly payment	0%
5 year	1.8% x monthly payment	1.16%
7 year	4.9% x monthly payment	1.74%

Contributions

The scheme rules must permit contributions **between** a minimum of £10 and a maximum of £250 per month. 3566 Sch 3 para 25 ITEPA 2003

Exercise of the option

The **general rule** is that options cannot be exercised before, or more than 6 months after, the bonus date. 3568 Sch 3 para 30 ITEPA 2003

By **exception**, an earlier exercise may be permitted:
– on the death of the participant, when the rights must be exercised within 12 months of the date of death (if they are exercised at all). If the death occurs within 6 months of the bonus date, the options may be exercised within the 12 months after the bonus date;
– for good leavers i.e. those ceasing employment because of injury, disability, redundancy or retirement (between 60 and 75) who exercise their rights within 6 months of ceasing employment; or
– following a takeover or change of control in the company.

Acquisition price

The price at which shares may be acquired (the subscription price) must be specified at the time when the rights are obtained by the participant. The price must not be **manifestly less** than 80% of the market value of shares at the time when the rights are acquired (or at an earlier time that has been agreed in writing with HMRC). 3570 Sch 3 para 28 ITEPA 2003

3. Occasions of tax charge

3572 Providing all of the conditions outlined above have been satisfied, income tax will not be chargeable on the **grant or exercise** of an option under an SRSOS.

s 519 ITEPA 2003 The exercise will be taxable as an unapproved share option (¶3392) if it takes place within 3 years of the date of grant as a result of a **takeover**, although PAYE and NIC will not apply.

3574 Where the shares acquired under an SRSOS are eventually **sold**, the resulting gain or loss will be subject to capital gains tax. For this purpose, the acquisition cost of the shares will be taken to be the actual price (as opposed to the market value) paid for the shares by the participant.

III. Administration

3590 HMRC continually monitor both approved and unapproved schemes by requiring annual reports to be submitted.

1. Reporting requirements

Responsible persons

3592 s 421J ITEPA 2003 The **obligation** to report is imposed on all of the following responsible persons:
– the employer;
– the person from whom the shares were acquired;
– the person who issued the shares; and
– any host employer (where the actual employer is abroad).

If there is more than one responsible person, the duty to report is not met until one has actually reported.

MEMO POINTS The following **forms** are relevant to each situation:
– ASCOP, form 35;
– EMI, form 40, except for any options in excess of £120,000 when form 42 applies;
– SIP, form 39;
– SRSOS, form 34; and
– any other case, form 42.

Form 42

3594 No form 42 is required for **new UK companies** on the first issue of shares, and subsequent allotments in the early life of the company.

Circumstance	When is form 42 not required
Initial shares issued to company formation agents	Acquired on incorporation
Initial subscriber shares (otherwise known as founder shares)	Where all of the following conditions apply: – all of the initial subscriber shares are acquired at nominal value; – the shares are not acquired by reason of, or in connection with, another employment; and – the shares are acquired by a director (including a prospective director) or a family member, and the acquisition opportunity is made available in the normal course of the domestic, family or personal relationship

Circumstance	When is form 42 not required
Allotment before company either commences to trade or assets are transferred to the company	Where all of the following conditions apply: – the person acquiring the shares is either a director (including a prospective director) of the company, or he has already received some of the initial subscriber shares; – the shares are acquired at nominal value; and – the reason for the allotment is not related to another employment There is no requirement for the initial subscription and subsequent allotment to be in the same tax year

Other circumstances where no report is required include: **3596** ERSM140100
– shares transferred by an individual for purely personal reasons;
– shares in flat management companies;
– members' clubs;
– share for share exchanges;
– shares acquired independently by employees or directors;
– dividend reinvestment plans (where details are provided to HMRC);
– rights issues and bonus issues; and
– scrip dividends (where details are provided to HMRC).

Events to be reported

The **general rule** is that all reportable events must be reported to HMRC before 7 July following the tax year, whether or not a return has been issued. Online reporting is encouraged. **3598**

Some companies may prefer to report events as they happen during the year, although HMRC still retain the right to issue a return.

Reportable events **include**:
– the acquisition of shares by reason of the employee's or someone else's employment;
– grant of options (a summary only);
– chargeable events in relation to restricted shares or convertible shares;
– artificially enhancing the share value;
– disposal of shares for more than market value;
– discharging a notional loan;
– receipt of a benefit which gives rise to employment income (i.e. not dividends); and
– exercise, assignment or release of a share option where a benefit is received in money or money's worth.

MEMO POINTS 1. It is important to realise that not all reportable events are actually **chargeable** to tax.
2. If a return for an unapproved scheme is **received on or after 8 June**, it must be submitted within 30 days.
3. If a person receives shares because of **another person's employment**, it is the employee's details which must be entered on the return.
4. If there are **no reportable events**, and a return has been received, a nil return should be submitted.

2. Failure to report

Failure to report will result in penalty proceedings as follows: **3600** s 98 TMA 1970
a. for **approved schemes**:
– an initial penalty of £300 per reportable event not reported; and
– once that penalty has been imposed, further penalties not exceeding £60 per day while the return remains outstanding.
b. For **unapproved schemes**:
– failure to report an event before 7 July can result in a penalty of £300 per reportable event being levied on each of the responsible persons; and

– once that penalty has been imposed, further penalties on each responsible person, not exceeding £60 per day, while the return remains outstanding.
In addition, late submission of an unapproved-scheme return attracts the same penalties as for approved schemes.

For either type of scheme, there is a penalty of up to £3,000 for fraudulently or negligently supplying incorrect information.

CHAPTER 6

State benefits and pensions

OUTLINE ¶¶

SECTION 1

Pension income and state benefits

A. Income from pensions

Pension income is **defined** as a periodical payment made by a pension provider. The terms and conditions of the pension payment are normally set out in a formal document, although it is possible for a pension to be paid informally. 3650

The pension may be **paid to** dependants, including a spouse (¶2402), instead of the individual concerned. In certain cases, the periodical payment may be called an **annuity**, but still has the characteristics of a pension payment. For the purposes of this section, the term pension includes this type of annuity, and any other income which is in the nature of a pension.

MEMO POINTS Pensioners may be entitled to an **increased personal allowance** (¶4394), and to married couples' allowance (¶4446) in certain cases.

1. State pensions

3654 State pensions are **funded** by National Insurance Contributions (NIC), and include the basic state pension, SERPs and the State Second Pension (S2P). The pensions are payable upon reaching retirement age (see below), and the amount payable is dependant on the amount of NIC paid during working life.

s 577 ITEPA 2003 The **taxable amount** is the total of the weekly entitlement for the tax year. State pensions can be paid weekly, monthly or quarterly, and are usually assessed as earned income (whether paid to a UK resident or non-resident individual). Certain special types of state pension are, however, tax free (¶3676).

MEMO POINTS 1. The Pensions Service of the Department for Work and Pensions (DWP) calculates the state pension due, and normally invites potential claimants to **claim** their entitlement a few months before reaching retirement age. Later claims can be made, although the pension will only be backdated by 12 months.
2. The **retirement age for men** is 65. The retirement age for women is rising from 60 and will reach 65 by November 2018. From December 2018 the retirement age for both sexes will rise to 66 by April 2020.
3. From April 2010, a man can obtain a pension based on his **spouse's NIC record**.

Categories

3656 There are three categories of state pension, known by the following names:
- the basic state pension (¶3657);
- SERPS, now being phased out (¶3660); and
- S2P, which replaces SERPS (¶3662).

An individual has the **option** to "contract out" of S2P, so he can make other arrangements, which can take the form of:
- an appropriate personal pension plan; or
- an occupational pension scheme.

MEMO POINTS 1. An **appropriate personal pension plan** provides protected rights (similar to the state schemes), requires a minimum level of contribution and is only available to employees.
2. The contracted out **occupational schemes** reduce the amount of NIC payable by both employees and employers, although the employer must additionally pay protected rights contributions into the scheme.
3. Contracting-out of S2P is due to cease on 5 April 2012.

Basic State Pension

3657 **Maximum entitlement** to the basic state pension relies on a full NIC record (¶4965) for 90% of working life (which starts at age 16). A full record is 30 years for both men and women.

Where an individual has an **incomplete NIC record**, the pension due will be proportionately reduced. There is no longer a minimum requirement, so that any qualifying year(s) will yield some pension. For details of maintaining the NIC record, see ¶5118.

MEMO POINTS For persons reaching **state pension age before 6 April 2010**, a full record meant 44 years' contributions for a man and 39 for a woman. A minimum of 25% of a full record was required before any pension was payable at all

Deferral option A pensioner can defer taking a pension (for a period of at least 12 months), and **choose to receive** either an increased pension (which is taxable when received), or a one-off taxable lump sum payment consisting of pension arrears and interest. The choice to defer must be made within 3 months of being appropriately notified by the authorities, although it can be changed (once only) within the subsequent 3 months. **3658** ss 7 - 10 F(N° 2)A 2005 Leaflet SPD1

The **lump sum** becomes taxable when the state pension payments resume, subject to an individual electing for it to be paid and taxed in the following tax year where this is beneficial. The applicable tax rate is the marginal tax rate applying to the taxpayer's other taxable income (ignoring the dividend and savings rates). Tax is deducted at source by the DWP. For all tax purposes, the lump sum is otherwise ignored (e.g. when calculating the age allowance).

MEMO POINTS 1. The official **notification** will state the gross income available from each option. **3659**
2. The **election to delay** payment and taxation of the lump sum must be made either at the same time as choosing to take the lump sum option or within the following month. It can be revoked at any time. Its effect is to delay payment until the first month of the following tax year, but no interest is added in the interim.
3. So that the appropriate tax is **deducted at source**, the pensioner has to declare his likely income to the DWP. If the declaration is wrong, the tax payable will be adjusted.

EXAMPLE
1. Mrs A, aged 68, chose to defer her pension from 6 April 2009, and elected to receive a lump sum of £5,000. She receives this in 2011/12, together with pensions of £32,000, gross bank interest of £4,000, and dividends of £1,000. Due to the level of her income, she receives the basic personal allowance only.
Mrs A's marginal tax rate is calculated as follows:

		£
Pension		32,000
Bank interest		4,000
Dividends		1,000
Total income		37,000
Less: Personal allowance		(7,475)
Taxable income		29,525
Tax thereon:		
Pension income	(32,000 – 7,475) @ 20%	4,905
Savings income	4,000 @ 20%	800
Dividend income	1,000 @ 10%	100
		5,805

As Mrs A is paying tax at the basic rate (ignoring the dividend rate), this is then applied to the lump sum, giving an additional tax liability of £1,000. (5,000 @ 20%)

2. Mr B, aged 67, chose to defer his pension from 6 April 2009, and elected to receive a lump sum of £5,000. He usually pays tax at the basic rate.
However, in 2010/11, Mr B had one-off other income of £50,000, which meant that the lump sum would have been taxable at 40%, and tax of £2,000 therefore payable. (5,000 @ 40%)
If he elects to delay receipt of the lump sum until 2011/12, when he is a basic rate taxpayer again, tax of only £1,000 will be suffered on the lump sum. (5,000 @ 20%)

Other pensions provision

State earnings related pension scheme (SERPS) This scheme **supplemented** the basic pension by providing an additional pension for employees only, and was based on Class 1 NIC. The accrual of benefits under SERPS ceased on 6 April 2002, although future pensions will still take account of any existing rights built up before that date. **3660**

MEMO POINTS 1. The pension is **based on** a percentage (between 20% and 25%) of earnings between the upper and employees earnings limits (¶5004).
2. Benefits can be **deferred** for 5 years, which will lead to an increase in the amount receivable.
3. In some cases, a **widow** will also be eligible for a pension based on SERPS.

3662 Leaflet PM2

State Second Pension (S2P) This scheme represents a reform of SERPS, giving **entitlement** to superior benefits for moderately paid employees, and opportunities for participation by carers and the long-term disabled.
For the NIC consequences of S2P, see ¶5004 and ¶5035.

2. Other pensions

3664 Other pension income **includes** pensions payable from the following sources:
- registered pension schemes (¶3745);
- employer financed retirement benefit schemes (unregistered schemes: ¶3900); and
- unfunded schemes.

UK source pension income

3666 s 569 ITEPA 2003

Pension income from a UK source is treated as **earned income**, but does not constitute an employment.
In addition to the usual pension payments, the following are also treated as pension income for tax purposes:
- unauthorised payments to members (¶3869);
- income withdrawals from drawdown pensions (¶3858); and
- returns of surplus contributions (¶3782).

3667 SI 2007/3537 s 393B ITEPA 2003

Unless the benefit was first provided before 6 April 1998, employers are required to report the provision of post-retirement **benefits in kind** exceeding £100 per annum (such as medical insurance) which means that the retired employee incurs a tax liability.
The following benefits are **exempt** (as long as they are provided in line with the usual rules and limits applying to working employees):

Benefit	Details
Living accommodation	Provided by a local authority employer
	Provided by an employer for the proper performance of the employee's duties [1]
	Provided by an employer because the employee's security is at risk
	Provided to family members after the employee's death [1]
	Provided to a Minister of Religion [2]
	Removal expenses
	Repairs and alterations
	Council tax
Non-cash benefits	Received in connection with the termination of an employee's employment before 6 April 1998
Welfare counselling	See ¶3204
Recreational benefits	See ¶3204
Annual parties etc	See ¶3224
Writing of wills	Provided the value does not exceed £150
Equipment for disabled employees	See ¶3204

Notes
1. The recipient must have been in continuous occupation of this or a similar property for a period of at least 5 years ending on the date of retirement.
2. The recipient must have been continuously employed as a minister for a period of at least 5 years ending on the date of retirement.

Pensions Tax Simplification Newsletter 28

MEMO POINTS Taxable non-cash benefits provided by employer financed retirement benefit schemes must be **reported** to HMRC by 7 July following the end of the relevant tax year.
If only exempt benefits are provided, these are not reportable, so where a scheme does not provide any chargeable benefits for any employee, no report is required at all.

Otherwise, the report **format** should be a list which is clearly headed with the relevant tax year and "Employer Financed Retirement Benefit Scheme – Relevant Benefits". The following information should be specified for each employee:
- name, address and NI number; and
- the nature and amount of the benefit.

The **taxable amount** is the amount to which the taxpayer is entitled in the tax year. Adjustments will generally only be required where payments are made in advance in the first year of receiving a pension, or in the tax year of death. **3668** s 571 ITEPA 2003

Arrears of pension which are paid under the scheme rules are taxable income of the member. SI 2006/614

MEMO POINTS 1. A member of a pension scheme will often receive a non-taxable **lump sum** on retirement in addition to the taxable pension income. However if the lump sum is paid in return for past service, or on loss of employment, it may be taxable.
2. In addition, an individual may make a donation through **payroll giving** (¶3189) which will reduce the amount of pension chargeable to tax.

> EXAMPLE On Mr C's retirement on 31 December 2011, his employer commenced payment of a pension of £750, payable a month in advance on the first day of each month. By 5 April 2012, Mr C had received £3,000, being 4 months of payments.
> As the payment received on 1 April 2012 relates to the month of April, only £2,250 is taxable in 2011/12.

Pension income (including income withdrawals, unauthorised payments, and retirement annuities) is **received net of tax deducted** at source under PAYE. **3669** s 683 ITEPA 2003

If the individual is **non-UK resident**, and receiving benefits from an occupational scheme, the pension will be fully exempt from UK tax when either:
- he spent the last 10 years of pensionable service abroad; or
- one half of the total pensionable service **and** at least 10 of the last 20 years were spent abroad.

Service for overseas government Where an individual is eligible for a pension payable in the UK as a result of service for an overseas government, a **deduction** of 10% will be available where all of the following conditions are satisfied: **3671** ss 615 - 617 ITEPA 2003
- the recipient is UK resident and has been employed in the service of the Crown, or in service under the government of the territory concerned (or his widow, child, relative or dependants);
- the pension is payable in the UK; and
- the territory concerned must be any country forming part of Her Majesty's dominion, a Commonwealth country other than the UK, or any territory under Her Majesty's protection.

Foreign aspects

A pension paid by a foreign source **to a person resident in the UK** will be taxable in the UK under the remittance basis (¶4200). Pension for this purpose means an amount payable to a former employee or office holder (or his widow, child, relative or dependant), by, or on behalf of, the former employer or his successors. **3672** ss 573 - 576 ITEPA 2003

MEMO POINTS Where a pension is **paid in arrears**, the taxpayer may suffer tax at a higher rate than if he had received the pension when it was originally due. In this case, he can claim for the pension to be treated as income arising in the earlier tax year. s 840 ITTOIA 2005

Where a UK pension is paid **to a non-resident individual**, the income may be taxed twice, once in the UK and once in the country where the individual is resident. **3674**

Often a double taxation agreement between the UK and the country of the individual's residence will exempt the pension from UK tax if an appropriate claim is made to HMRC.

MEMO POINTS 1. Some double taxation agreements provide that pensions paid in respect of **government service** will only be taxed in the country in which they are paid.

ss 647 - 650 ITEPA 2003

2. Where this facility is not available, certain pensions, payable to non-residents, are exempt if they arise from the **Central African Pension Fund**, **Commonwealth** government pensions or the **Overseas Superannuation** scheme.
3. Where the pension is **still liable to UK tax**, the individual may qualify for personal allowances (¶4392).

Exemption from tax

3676 The following pension payments are exempt from tax:

Type of payment	Detail	Reference
Disablement pension for work-related injury	An additional pension payable because of an injury/illness/disablement suffered in the course of the employment However, by exception, if the same amount would have been paid on ordinary ill-health grounds, the pension will not be exempt	s 644 ITEPA 2003
Voluntary pension	Paid otherwise than as result of past employment, and not paid by a past employer or his successors The payment may be subject to the termination payment rules if in excess of £30,000 (¶3078)	General law
War widow's pension (and similar pensions payable by foreign governments)	Payable in respect of death due to: – service in the armed forces; – wartime service in the merchant navy; or – war injuries	s 639 ITEPA 2003
Lump sum relevant benefits received by a non-resident [1]	From an occupational fund: – established under irrevocable trusts in connection with a trade or undertaking carried on wholly or partly outside the UK; – with the sole purpose of providing pension benefits for overseas employees; and – which is recognised by both the employer and employee	s 615(6) ICTA 1988
Lump sum relevant benefits received from an overseas employer financed retirement benefit scheme	Where the conditions for foreign service are met (¶3092)	s 554A – 554Z14 ITEPA 2003
Armed forces	Wounds and disability pensions	s 641 ITEPA 2003
	Continuing to serve and receiving payments from: – the new armed forces pensions; – armed forces compensation scheme; or – early departure payments scheme	ss 639, 640A ITEPA 2003
Nazi persecution	German and Austrian pensions for victims	s 642 ITEPA 2003
Gallantry awards	For example, the Victoria Cross or other bravery medals	s 638 ITEPA 2003

Notes
1. Rights accruing before 6 April 2011 are governed by ESC A10. Rights accruing since that date are governed by the new legislation on disguised remuneration from a third party (¶3039).

B. State benefits

3680 State benefits are mostly exempt from income tax, although those which replace an individual's main income are taxable.

Whilst the majority of state benefits are administered by the DWP, tax credits are administered by HMRC.

Summary

3682
ss 577, 660 ITEPA 2003

Category	State benefit	Taxable?
Work related	Statutory adoption pay [1]	✓
	Statutory maternity pay [1]	✓
	Maternity allowance	x
	Statutory paternity pay [1]	✓
	Statutory sick pay [1]	✓
	Employment support allowance [2]	✓
	Incapacity benefit [3,4]	✓
	Industrial injuries disablement benefit	x
	Jobseeker's allowance [4]	✓
	Income support [2]	x
	Jobfinder's grant	x
	Reduced earnings allowance	x
	Worker's compensation (supplementation) scheme	x
	Working tax credit (¶3716)	x
	Earnings top-up	x
	Back to work bonus	x
Children and dependants	Child benefit	x
	Child maintenance bonus	x
	Child's special allowance	x
	Child tax credit (¶3707)	x
	Child trust fund (¶3695)	x
	Health in pregnancy grant	x
	Education welfare benefits	x
	Guardian's allowance	x
	Lone parent's benefit run-on	x
	Widowed parents' allowance	✓
	Dependent adult's benefit	✓
Pensioners and widows	Retirement pension (¶3666)	✓
	Pension credit (¶3686)	x
	Christmas bonus	x
	War disablement pension	x
	War pensioner's mobility supplement	x
	Widow's pension and bereavement allowance [5]	✓
	Bereavement allowance	✓
	War widow's pension (¶3676)	x
	Industrial death benefit (widow's pension)	✓
Disabled and carers	Attendance allowance	x
	Constant attendance allowance	x
	Disability living allowance	x
	Severe disablement allowance [5]	x
	Motability	x
	Criminal injuries compensation	x
	Pneumoconiosis and miscellaneous disease benefits	x
	Vaccine damage	x
	Carer's allowance [5]	✓

Category	State benefit	Taxable?
Help with expenses	Council tax benefit	x
	Housing benefit	x
	Payments out of the Social Fund [6]	x

Note:
1. Further guidance can be found at ¶4750.
2. Employment support allowance replaced incapacity benefit and income support for new claimants from 27 October 2008. Contribution based (i.e. relating to the amount of NIC paid) employment support allowance is taxable. For those with insufficient contributions, income related employment support allowance is payable and this is not taxable.
3. As a general rule, the first 28 weeks of incapacity benefit are paid at a short-term lower rate, which is not taxable. Thereafter the benefit is taxable. Incapacity benefit only continues to be paid to claimants who were already receiving it on 27 October 2008.
4. Excluding non-taxable additions for children, housing and exceptional circumstances.
5. Child dependency additions paid with these benefits are not taxable.
6. These payments are made to people on low incomes and include:
- budgeting loan;
- cold weather payment;
- community care grant;
- crisis loan;
- funeral payment;
- maternity payment; and
- winter fuel payments.

3684 s 681 ITEPA 2003

Payments from a **foreign government** which correspond to the following benefits are exempt from UK income tax:
- attendance allowance;
- back to work bonus;
- bereavement payment;
- child benefit;
- child's special allowance;
- child tax credit;
- Christmas bonus;
- council tax benefit;
- disability living allowance;
- guardian's allowance;
- housing benefit;
- incapacity benefit;
- maternity allowance;
- severe disability allowance; and
- payments out of the Social Fund.

1. Pension credit

3686 SI 2002/1792

The pension credit, administered by the DWP, is aimed at poorer pensioners, and must be distinguished from tax credits despite the similarity of the name.

MEMO POINTS 1. To **obtain** the pension credit, most eligible pensioners are contacted directly by the DWP, although separate applications can be made, and approved claims can be backdated by up to 3 months. Individuals approaching retirement age are assessed for the pension credit at the same time as the basic state pension (via phone or the completion of a form). Reassessment of entitlement will then take place once every 5 years.
2. Recipients of the pension credit are **eligible for** the free installation of central heating. Other pensioners can receive a £300 discount.
3. The DWP maintains a website for Pension credit at http://www.direct.gov.uk/en/Pensionsandretirementplanning/PensionCredit/DG_10018692.

3687 DWP website

There are **two elements** to the pensions credit:
- guarantee credit; and
- savings credit.

Comment As claimants are unlikely to be told how the **award is made up**, the amounts received should be carefully checked.

Guarantee credit

Guarantee credit tops up income to a minimum amount for individuals **aged** 60 and over (the current retirement age for women). 3689 SI 2002/1792 reg 6

An individual's total entitlement is called the **appropriate amount**. There are different weekly amounts for a single person and couples (being £137.35 and £209.70 respectively from April 2011).

MEMO POINTS 1. There are also **additional amounts** available in respect of:
- mortgage payments;
- other housing costs not covered by housing benefit; and
- severely disabled individuals and their carers.

2. For details of **retirement age** see ¶3654.

Guarantee credit is payable if an individual's "qualifying income" is less than this appropriate amount. 3690 SI 2002/1792 reg 14 DWP website

Qualifying income is made up of the following:

Item	Qualifying income
Pension income (including state pensions)	✓
Housing benefit	x
Council tax benefit	x
Bereavement allowance	x
Attendance allowance	x
Disability living allowance	x
Working tax credit	✓
Most other benefits	✓
Maintenance from an ex-spouse	✓
Earnings in excess of £5 per week for an individual (£10 for couples)	✓
Savings and capital above £10,000 [1]	✓

Note:
1. For every £500 of savings above this amount, deemed income of £1 a week is included in the assessment of an individual's income. Savings includes amounts in tax exempt saving vehicles (¶2797), although the value of an individual's home is disregarded.

EXAMPLE Mrs D is a widow aged 63 with no savings. Each week she receives a state pension of £95.25 and another pension of £15, giving her a total weekly qualifying income of £110.25. The appropriate amount for Mrs D is £137.35, being the standard amount for an individual in 2011/12. As Mrs D's income is less than the appropriate amount, she is entitled to a guarantee credit of £27.10 (137.35 – 110.25).
If Mrs D had savings of £25,000, she would be deemed to have additional related income of £30 per week $\frac{(25{,}000 - 10{,}000)}{500}$, so she would not qualify for any guarantee credit.

Savings credit

Savings credit is available to individuals **aged** 65 and over, and couples of whom at least one person has reached that age. Its aim is to provide a top up, measured as 60% of the amount by which income exceeds the basic state pension (being £103.15 for a single person and £164.55 for a couple where the wife was a non-contributor, from April 2011). If **income exceeds** the appropriate amount (¶3689), the top up is tapered away at a rate of 40%. 3692 SI 2002/1792 reg 7

Qualifying income for the purposes of the savings credit is similar to that described in ¶3690, but does not include: 3693 SI 2002/1792 reg 9
- working tax credit;
- jobseeker's allowance;
- incapacity benefit; or
- severe disablement allowance; or
- maintenance payments from an ex-spouse.

If qualifying income is:
a. less than the basic state pension amount, no savings credit is due; or
b. more than the basic state pension amount, the savings credit depends on whether the individual's income is:
– up to the appropriate amount (¶3689), when Amount A is paid; or
– more than the appropriate amount, when the difference between Amount A and Amount B is paid.

MEMO POINTS 1. **Amount A** is calculated by taking 60% of the difference between the qualifying income and the basic state pension. This is subject to a **maximum** of £20.52 for a single person and £27.09 for a couple.
2. **Amount B** is calculated by taking 40% of the difference between qualifying income and the appropriate amount.

EXAMPLE Assuming Mrs D (from the example in ¶3690) is actually 65, she can also claim savings credit. The difference between her total weekly qualifying income of £110.25 and the basic state pension of £103.15 is £7.10. Amount A is therefore £4.26. (£7.10 @ 60%)
As Mrs D's income is below the appropriate amount of £137.35, she is entitled to a savings credit of the full amount of Amount A at £4.26.
Alternatively, if Mrs D had a weekly qualifying income of £140, which is more than the appropriate amount (resulting in no payment of the guarantee credit), the savings credit would be calculated as follows:

	£
Amount A: (140.00 – 103.15) × 60%	22.11
Restricted to maximum	20.52
Less: Amount B: (140 – 137.35) × 40%	(1.06)
Savings credit	19.46

2. Child trust funds

3695 ss 2, 13 Child Trust Funds Act 2004

These funds were a tax-free savings and investment account for children, sponsored by the state, which applied to all children **born between** 31 August 2002 and 31 December 2010, living in the UK, and in respect of whom child benefit was paid. A child living abroad was eligible if a parent was a Crown servant.

No new funds were opened for children born on or after 1 January 2011. The new Junior ISA (¶2812) is intended to act as a replacement.

The **tax treatment** of an existing fund is as follows:
– any income received by the fund is tax free;
– the fund is exempt from capital gains tax, including when the fund matures when the child is 18; and
– no tax relief is available for contributions into the fund.

Operating the account

3699 SI 2004/1450 reg 8

The **type of account** may be either:
– stakeholder, investing in stocks and shares; or
– non-stakeholder, effectively a deposit account with a minimum rate of interest.

There is a cap on **charges** for stakeholder accounts, broadly limiting fund management charges to 1.5% of the fund's value each year (very similar to the ISA rules).

3700 SI 2004/1450 reg 9

Contributions to the fund of up to £1,200 per annum can be made by family and friends. However, where contributions in any year are less than £1,200, the unused amount cannot be carried forward.

Any **income** arising in the fund as a result of a parental contribution is not assessed on the parents.

3702 SI 2004/1450 reg 18

Access to the funds in the account is usually prohibited until the child's 18th birthday, although there are **exceptions** for disabled children, those who are terminally ill, and on the untimely death of the child.

On reaching the age of 18, the child will be deemed to dispose and reacquire the assets in the account at market value, and there will be no restriction on how the fund is used thereafter (although subsequent income and gains will be taxable). This may be of concern to parents as it is estimated that maximum contributions could result in a capital sum on maturity of at least £30,000.

A penalty of £300 will be imposed on any person who **fraudulently**: **3703** s 20 Child Trust Funds Act 2004
- applies to open a child trust fund account;
- makes an unauthorised withdrawal; or
- secures the opening of an account by HMRC.

3. Tax credits

This section examines child tax credit and working tax credit individually, before considering the common areas of income calculation and administration. **3705** SI 2003/654 Leaflet WTC2

A claimant must be **aged** over 16 and normally living in the UK. Claims can be made by individuals or couples.

There is a 3 month **time limit** for making a claim, so for the full 2011./12 year a claim must have been made by 6 July 2011. A later claim will only be effective for the 3 months prior to the date of the claim.

MEMO POINTS 1. To qualify as **living in the UK** a claimant must be both physically present and ordinarily resident (¶4160). Short absences of 8 to 12 weeks may be ignored: see ¶3729.
2. **Same sex couples** who are living together as partners are treated in the same way as opposite sex couples, irrespective of whether a civil partnership has been formed. If a claimant begins to live with a same sex partner, HMRC must be informed when the change occurs.
3. Children aged over 16 whose families are claiming tax credits may be eligible for the **education maintenance allowance**. This is available for any academic or vocational course involving at least 12 hours of guided learning per week.
4. For applications involving any kind of disability, see ¶3726.
5. A new system of **universal credits** is expected to be phased in during 2013-18 to replace both child and working tax credits.

a. Child tax credit

Child tax credit (CTC) is a payment to support families with children, irrespective of whether there is anyone working in the family. A **claim** can be made by an individual or couple (married or unmarried, opposite sex or same sex), who has responsibility for at least one child. In 2011/12, families with income of up to £41,329 can qualify for the CTC. **3707** s 8 Tax Credits Act 2002

The CTC is **payable to** the main carer of the child, directly into a bank or building society account.

Eligibility

Eligible children **include**: **3708** SI 2002/2007 regs 3-5

a. children up to the age of 16 (see note 1);

b. students under 20 in full-time non-advanced education or a young person undertaking unwaged training (see note 2); and

c. a young person aged 16 or 17 who has left full-time education within the last 20 weeks, but does not work more than 24 hours a week and has registered with a careers service (see note 3).

MEMO POINTS 1. A child **remains eligible** for the CTC until 1 September following his 16th birthday.
2. A **gap** of up to 6 months (longer in cases of illness or disability) in education or training may be allowed without loss of entitlement.
3. The **child** cannot be:
- claiming benefits or tax credits in his own right;
- serving a custodial sentence of more than 4 months imposed by a court; or
- a fostered or adopted child where the family is in receipt of a local authority payment.

3710 SI 2002/2007 regs 7 – 8

The CTC is **made up** of a number of elements, depending on the circumstances of each claim. These elements are:

Element of CTC	2011/12 Maximum £	2010/11 Maximum £
Family element [1,2]	545	545
Child element [3]	2,555	2,300
Disabled child element [3,4]	2,800	2,715
Severely disabled child element [3,5]	1,130	1,095

Note:
1. Only one family element is available per family. In the first year of a child's life, a family is entitled to the baby addition as well as the family element.
2. The baby element formerly payable was withdrawn from 6 April 2011.
3. A family is also entitled to a child element for each child, with the various applicable elements added together.
4. An additional amount which is payable if the child:
– is eligible for disability living allowance;
– is registered blind; or
– has been taken off the blind register in the last 28 weeks before the claim.
5. An additional amount which is payable if the child is eligible for the highest rate of care component of disability living allowance.

Amount

3712 SI 2002/2008 reg 3

The amount of CTC received depends on the income of the family in the tax year, and whether working tax credit (WTC) is also being received.

If **no WTC is payable**, and family income is below the child tax credit threshold of £15,860 in 2011/12 (2010/11: £16,190), CTC is available in full.

Otherwise, the CTC (except for the family element) is gradually tapered away, at a rate of 41% of the excess income over this threshold (2010/11: 39%). The family element is not restricted until income exceeds £40,000 (2010/11: £50,000), when it too is tapered away at a rate of 41% (2010/11: 6.67%).

EXAMPLE Mr E works 14 hours per week, and earns £18,000 p.a. He has three children, one of whom has a mild disability.
The CTC payable to Mr E for 2011/12 is calculated as follows:

	£	£
Child element: (2,555 × 3)		7,665
Disabled child element		2,800
Total credits (ignoring family element)		10,465
Income	18,000	
Threshold	(15,860)	
Excess income	2,140	
At 41%		(877)
		9,588
Family element		545
Total credits due for whole year		10,133

b. Working tax credit

3716 s 10 Tax Credits Act 2002

Working tax credit (WTC) is a payment to support individuals who work but earn a relatively low wage. A **claim** can be made by an individual or couple (married or unmarried), who work a minimum number of hours per week. Payment is made by HMRC direct to the claimant.

Working hours requirement

3718 SI 2002/2005 reg 4

The claimant must usually be aged at least 25 and work a **30 hour** week.

However WTC will be payable for a **16 hour** working week where the claimant is:
– aged over 16 and responsible for a child;

- aged over 16 and disabled; or
- qualifies for the 50-plus return to work element.

WTC is payable for the 4 weeks after a person ceases to work at least 16 hours per week, which reduces the amount of any overpayment, and eases the transition back to state benefits.

A 4 week run-on also applies where either: SI 2009/1829
- a single claimant's hours fall below 30 but remain above 16; or
- in a joint claim, where one of the couple reduces hours below the 30 or 16 week thresholds. This is particularly important as the generous childcare payment requires both claimants to work at least 16 hours a week.

Elements of WTC

The WTC is **made up** of a number of elements, depending on the circumstances of each claim. These elements are: **3720** SI 2002/2005 Sch 2

Leaflet WTC5
SI 2005/769

Element of WTC	2011/12 Maximum £	2010/11 Maximum £
Basic element [1]	1,920	1,920
Additional couples and lone parent element [1, 2]	1,950	1,890
30 hour element [1,2,3]	790	790
Disability element [2,5]	2,650	2,570
Severe disability element [2,6]	1,130	1,095
50-plus return to work payment: 16 to 29 hours [2,4,7]	1,365	1,320
50-plus return to work payment: 30 or more hours [2,4]	2,030	1,965
Childcare maximum eligible cost for one child [8]	175 per week	175 per week
Childcare maximum eligible cost for any number of children	300 per week	300 per week
Percentage of eligible costs covered	70%	80%

Note:
1. One of each category per claim.
2. Paid in addition to other elements.
3. The 30-hour limit applies to a couple, provided one party works at least 16 hours. From 2012/13 the limit will fall from 30 hours to 24.
4. The 50-plus elements will be withdrawn from 2012/13.
5. Broadly payable if the claimant's disability affects his ability to work, and he is in receipt of a benefit such as disability living allowance.
6. Payable if the claimant is eligible for the highest rate care component of disability living allowance.
7. Where this element is payable, the additional couples (and lone parents) element is not paid, unless the claimant has responsibility for a child, or the disability element is also payable. This will not be paid where the claimant is eligible for the higher 50-plus return to work payment because of working in excess of 30 hours.
8. This element is payable where the claimant works at least 16 hours per week (required of both individuals where a joint claim is made) and actually pays for approved childcare. For families who employ a registered nanny, the childcare cost includes employer's Class 1 NIC (¶4974). Approved childcare cannot be provided by a relative of the child, even if the carer is registered. As an exception, where the carer runs a childcaring business, which predominantly looks after unrelated children, and the care of a related child is incidental, then the care will qualify. Payments run until 1 December following the child's 15th birthday (16th if the child is disabled).

Calculation

The **amount** of WTC received depends on the income of the whole family. If annual income is below £6,420 (unchanged since 6 April 2008), the maximum amount of WTC will be paid. Otherwise, WTC is gradually tapered away at a rate of 41% (2010/11: 39%), reducing the excess of income over this threshold. **3722** SI 2002/2008 reg 3

Where **both CTC and WTC are payable**, WTC is reduced by the tapering effect first.

EXAMPLE

1. Mr F is 26, works 35 hours per week and earns £11,000. His WTC entitlement for 2011/12 is calculated as follows:

	£	£
Basic element		1,920
30 hour element		790
		2,710
Income	11,000	
Threshold	(6,420)	
	4,580	
At 41%		(1,877)
WTC entitlement		833

2. Mr and Mrs G are married with two children. Mr G works 16 hours per week and earns £10,000 p.a. Mrs G works 35 hours per week and earns £25,000 p.a., paying childcare costs of £350 per week.
Their 2011/12 tax credit entitlement is calculated as follows:

	£	£
Working tax credit:		
Basic element		1,920
Couples element		1,950
30 hour element		790
Childcare element: (300 x 70% x 52)		10.920
Child tax credit:		
Child element per child: (2 x 2,555)		5,110
Total credits (ignoring family element)		20,690
Income: (25,000 + 10,000)	35,000	
Threshold	(6,420)	
	28,580	
At 41%		(11,717)
		8,973
Family element		545
Total credits due for full year		9,518

c. Assessable income

3724 SI 2002/2006

Income is assessed differently for the purposes of tax credits than for tax purposes, because very often the claim will relate to the income of more than one individual. The **assessment period** for income is a tax year.

The **calculation** combines incomes from all sources and all individuals involved into one claim. The basic steps are shown in the following table. For further details, see the notes which accompany form TC600.

Step	Instructions	£
1	Add together: – pension income (including state pensions, taxable lump sums and state pension lump sum); – investment (excluding tax-free income); – income from property (including any deemed income from the pre-owned assets rules); and – foreign income. If this total is less than £300, the whole amount is disregarded. If in excess of £300, the first £300 of income is ignored.	X
2	Add together all other income except for trading income.	X

Step	Instructions	£
3	Calculate the trading income (or loss) of the claimants (in joint claims losses of one claimant can be deducted from profits of the other).	X
4	Deduct the gross equivalent of pension contributions and gift aid donations paid in the year (carrying back is not allowed).	(X)
	Income for purposes of tax credits	X

MEMO POINTS Compensation payments made under the **Equitable Life Payment Scheme** (ELPS) to policy holders in Equitable Life who have suffered loss due to government maladministration are ignored for the purpose of entitlement to tax credits. SI 2011/1502

EXAMPLE Mr and Mrs H have the following income and deductions:

	Mr H £	Mrs H £
Bank interest received	200	50
Salary	15,500	
Trading result	10,000	(5,000)
Gift aid donation	100	
Pension contribution	600	

The income for the purposes of tax credits is calculated as follows:	Total £
1. Interest received of £250 is ignored as this is less than £300	-
2. Add together all other income except trading income	15,500
3. Trading profits: (10,000 – 5,000)	5,000
	20,500
4. Deduct gift aid and pension contributions: (100 + 600)	(700)
Income for tax credit purposes	19,800

d. Administration

Claims

Initial claims can only be made on a (paper) form TC600. The claim can simply be renewed for later years (¶3734). **3726** SI 2002/2014 regs 5-7

Except in certain circumstances, tax credits may only be **backdated** for 3 months from the date of the claim (1 month from 2012/13). This can lead to a loss of credits if a claim is not made in a timely manner. The initial award is estimated from the income of the previous tax year.

Due to changing circumstances and fluctuating income (particularly for the self-employed), it may be advisable to submit a **protective claim**. Even if such a claim results in a nil award initially, the amount of the award can be amended in future if necessary. This can enable a claim effectively to be backdated to the start of the tax year.

MEMO POINTS Until 2012/13, a claim may be backdated for more than 3 months in any of the following **circumstances**:
– a new claim for working tax credit is made and the applicant starts to receive qualifying sickness or disability benefits (e.g. disability living allowance);
– an existing claimant is entitled to further tax credits because of his own disability and starts to receive qualifying benefits; or
– a child, in respect of whom tax credits are already received, is disabled and disability living allowance becomes payable.
In all cases, the claim for tax credits may be backdated to the date when entitlement to benefits first arose, as long as **HMRC are notified** within 3 months of when the claimant first found out about his benefits entitlement.

3727 SI 2002/2926 SI 2002/3196

Where a claim **is successful**, an award notice will be issued, which will give brief details of the amount of tax credits which will be paid. It is possible to appeal against the amount shown on an award notice, within 30 days of HMRC's decision.

Payments can be made weekly or every 4 weeks depending on the preference of the claimant.

Change in circumstances

3729 SI 2002/2014 reg 21 Leaflet WTC7

The following changes must be **notified** within 1 month of when the change occurred, or if later, the date that the claimant first became aware of the change (e.g. if a couple split up):
- change in married status (including registering a civil partnership);
- change in co-habiting status;
- childcare costs cease, or decrease by £10 per week or more;
- the claimant or her partner leave the UK for more than 8 weeks (extended to 12 weeks where the trip is caused by illness or death);
- a decrease in working hours so that the 16 or 30 hour thresholds are not met;
- stopping work, being laid off, or being on strike for more than 10 days;
- ceasing to be responsible for a child or young person; and
- a child or young person ceasing to qualify for support, e.g. because of death, or working after the age of 16, or ceasing to be in full-time education.

If notification is **not made**, a penalty of £300 could be levied, although HMRC consider that illness and postal delays are valid excuses for a late notification.

Other changes must be notified on the finalisation of an award (¶3734), although earlier notification is advisable to avoid later adjustments to the amount of tax credits. This includes changes such as:
- the birth of a child;
- a school leaver moving into full-time education; or
- an increase of income of at least £10,000 (known as the **income disregard**).

MEMO POINTS 1. Claimants can **make notification** online, by phone, or by post.
2. **Records** must be maintained to substantiate a tax credit claim, including when circumstances change.
3. The income disregard for 2010/11 was £25,000. This figure will be used in finalising awards for that year. From 2012/13 the income disregard will be £5,000.

EXAMPLE
1. Mr A has the following income in 2009/10 to 2011/12.

	£
2009/10	11,000
2010/11	36,000
2011/12	40,000

If Mr A does not notify HMRC about his change in income during 2010/11 until September 2011, the following consequences will result:
- the tax credit entitlement for 2010/11 will be based on income of £11,000 as the increase is not above the income disregard level; but
- there will be an overpayment in relation to 2011/12, because the initial award (paid from April 2011) will be based on the 2010/11 income (which is the latest information available to HMRC).

2. Mr B had income of £18,000 in 2010/11. In early 2011/12, he believes his income will only be £14,000 and notifies HMRC. However, he receives an unexpected bonus which takes his income for 2011/12 to £25,000.
The disregard operates to ignore the rise from £18,000 to £25,000. However, the tax credits received on the basis of the estimated income of £14,000 must be repaid.

Different amount due

3730 ss 28 – 30 Tax Credits Act 2002

It is very probable that over or underpayments will arise, as the initial award is estimated from the income of the previous year, and the tax credits are not finalised until after the end of the year of payment (e.g. the 2011/12 award is based on 2010/11, and will not be finalised until 31 July 2012). In particular, current year tax credit payments made until the renewals process is complete are based on very out of date information (e.g. the 2011/12 award commenced payment in April 2011, and this was initially based on the income of 2009/10).

Underpayment As soon as an underpayment becomes apparent, HMRC will make changes to the tax credits award, which could result in a lump sum payment. **3731**

If the claimant experiences a **fall in income** which increases the tax credits award, this will lead to an increase in tax credit payments which are made subsequent to the notification of the change. Any remaining underpayment, relating to the months prior to the notification, is corrected after the end of the year, when the award is finalised.

Overpayment In some circumstances, it will be possible to **retain** an overpayment where it arose because of a mistake by HMRC or to repay would cause undue hardship. However, where it is found that there is no actual entitlement to tax credits, any overpayment must be paid back. Individuals may **dispute** whether an overpayment should be repaid by writing to HMRC, and recovery will be suspended until the dispute is resolved. **3732** COP 26

Where an overpayment is **identified within the same year**, it is possible for recovery to be made against future tax credit payments still due, although any **reduction** in tax credit payments will be **limited** to:
- 10%, where the maximum award is payable;
- 100%, where only the family element of CTC is paid; and
- 25%, in other cases.

When an award of tax credits is **finalised**, a statement of account will be sent to the individual, showing any overpayment in the year, which may be rectified by:
- reducing current tax credit payments in line with the limits above; or
- making a payment in cases where the claimant no longer receives tax credits, with a 12 month instalment option.

Renewals

The renewals **process enables** the amount of the award for the previous year to be finalised, and the award for the current year to be estimated. **3734** s 17 Tax Credits Act 2002

At the end of the tax year, tax credit payments continue uninterrupted until 30 September. Claims involving the **family element of CTC** only are automatically renewed, although the Annual Review form must be completed and returned in all cases.

For all **other claims**, both the Annual Review and Annual Declaration for each award must be completed, signed by each claimant, and returned by 31 July following the end of the tax year, otherwise the payments will cease and a penalty may arise. The tax credits award may be reinstated where the renewal is completed by 31 January, and there was good cause for missing the July deadline. Otherwise, the claimant cannot renew, and must make a fresh claim, which can only be backdated by 3 months.

As a concession, those who have made **protective claims** which result in a nil award are only required to submit an Annual Review.

MEMO POINTS 1. If a change in circumstances has occurred, **more than one** award **notice** will have been issued. Claimants may therefore need to review and complete more than one set of forms.
2. Where **information** about income is **not available** by the usual deadline, the amounts must be estimated and returned, and final figures must be submitted by 31 January following the tax year.

HMRC powers

HMRC may conduct an in-year examination at any time, which is distinct from an enquiry. **3736** s 19 Tax Credits Act 2002

A tax credits **enquiry** is not related to an enquiry for income tax purposes, although an enquiry into one area may lead to an enquiry in the other.

Subject to an appeal to the tribunal, a **penalty** of up to £3,000 (plus interest) may be levied where incorrect information is given to HMRC in relation to a tax credit claim. No penalty will Leaflet WTC7 be charged where reasonable care (¶9795) is taken to give correct information, even if a mistake is made which results in an overpayment of tax credits. The level of penalties are:

Type of inaccuracy	Maximum penalty (% of overstatement of tax credits) [1]
Mistake or misunderstanding	0
Failure to take reasonable care	15
Serious or deliberate errors	25
Deliberate and systematic overclaims	50
Note: 1. The repetition of errors made before, or serial errors, may result in a higher penalty.	

SECTION 2

Retirement provision: registered schemes

3745 s 153 FA 2004 Registered schemes have the following **tax advantages**, intended to enable efficient investment growth in order to provide funds for retirement:
– relief when funds are put into the scheme;
– exemption on income and gains derived from scheme assets; and
– exemption for a certain level of lump sum benefit paid to the member.

To obtain these tax advantages, a scheme must **register with HMRC**.

MEMO POINTS 1. This section summarises the position following the changes introduced by the Finance Act 2011. The proposals made by the previous government to restrict tax relief for pension contributions by, and impose a corresponding tax charge on, individuals with incomes exceeding £150,000 were repealed following the 2010 General Election and replaced with the current regime.
2. Compensation payments may be made under the **Equitable Life Payment Scheme** (ELPS) to pension schemes on behalf of policy holders in Equitable Life who have suffered loss due to government maladministration. These payments are tax free when passed on to the scheme member.

3746 The following table summarises the **main characteristics** of registered schemes:

Factor	Detail	¶¶
Registration	Must be registered with HMRC	¶3752
Eligibility	Individuals up to 75 An individual can be a member of both occupational and personal schemes	¶3754
Contributions	Amount which attracts tax relief is restricted by the annual allowance (£50,000 for 2011/12) Relevant earnings required if contributions are to exceed £3,600 p.a. Employer contributions deductible against taxable profits	¶3764
Size of pension fund	Limited by a lifetime allowance (£1.8m for 2011/12) Over-funding penalty of 55% of excess Transitional relief for larger funds at 6 April 2006	¶3786
Fund investments	Transactions with connected parties allowed Residential property and smaller valuable assets allowed for larger schemes only	¶3814
Retirement age	Minimum age of 55 from 2010/11 (formerly 50) No maximum age Individuals can draw pension benefits whilst working	¶3832
Lump sum	Tax free up to 25% of the value of the pension fund	¶3838

Types of registered scheme

Registered schemes fall into the following types: 3748

a. occupational schemes sponsored by an employer, and which come in two guises:
– a defined benefit (or "final salary") scheme which guarantees a pension based on the employee's final remuneration (which is usually restricted and averaged) and years of service. The employer bears the risk of making up any shortfall in the fund when the benefits are paid out; or
– a defined contribution (or "money purchase") scheme, where the scheme benefits ultimately depend on the fund amount which has accumulated, and the level of contributions paid into it. It is the employee who bears the risk of the benefits being inadequate;
b. SSASs (small self-administered schemes), a specific type of occupational scheme with a pensioneer trustee, and which must satisfy all of the following conditions:
– some or all of the income and assets are not insured;
– there are fewer than twelve members, who will normally be trustees as well; and
– at least one scheme member is connected with either another member, a scheme trustee, or the employer.

MEMO POINTS 1. A **cash balance** scheme is a type of money purchase scheme which includes a guaranteed level of growth in the fund.
2. Starting in 2012, all UK employers will become obliged to enroll all their eligible employees into a contributory pension scheme. This obligation will be phased in, starting with the biggest employers. Employers will be able to meet this obligation in any way they choose, but one way will be through a government-sponsored National Employment Savings Trust (**NEST**), a simple, low-cost scheme with very limited fund choice, and initial restrictions on transfers and contribution levels. NESTs will be operated by the NEST Corporation, a not-for-profit trustee body, and will be regulated by the Pensions Regulator.

Approved schemes

Registered pension schemes are the main type of approved pension scheme, but there are others, including: 3750

a. personal pension schemes, which cater for those not in occupational pension schemes (although it is possible for the member's employer to make contributions);
b. SIPPs (small self-administered pension plans), which are a type of one-member personal scheme which can invest in non-insured products, the choice of which can be influenced by the member;
c. stakeholder pensions, which are low-cost, government-regulated schemes available to employees, self-employed and even unemployed persons; and
d. retirement annuity contracts, which give generous benefits but ceased to be available to new members from 1988, but into which contributions can still be paid.

MEMO POINTS **Employers**, who do not provide other pension provision through either an occupational scheme or by making contributions to personal pension schemes, are **required to provide** access to a stakeholder pension scheme for those employees who earn more than the NIC lower earnings limit (¶5004). There is an **exemption** for employers with less than five employees (including directors). Further details can be found in the current edition of *Employment Memo*. Leaflet PME1

A. Establishing a scheme

Scheme registration

To obtain the tax advantages, a scheme must **register with HMRC** and submit a declaration that all the statutory rules will be met. It is possible for employers to come together and set up a scheme, even where they are not connected. 3752 s 153 FA 2004

s 157 FA 2004 MEMO POINTS 1. HMRC are able to **refuse** to register a scheme, or **withdraw registration** in cases where information is either not provided or is false, or if unauthorised payments (¶3869) are made.
2. It is possible to **establish** a new registered scheme by any of the following methods:
– setting up a trust;
– board resolution;
– contract; or
– deed poll.
A scheme must be established before it is registered, and anyone establishing a non-occupational scheme must have permission from the FSA.
3. The present regime was established on 6 April 2006. Any scheme which was already approved by HMRC on that date automatically became a registered scheme unless it opted out of the new system. For schemes which are still operating under the pre-2006 system, the earnings cap for 2010/11 was £123,600. From April 2011 this figure ceased to be published by HMRC, and schemes will be expected to compute it for themselves.

Eligibility for tax relief

3754 s 189 FA 2004 An individual **aged under 75** is eligible for tax relief on contributions to a registered scheme if he satisfies at least one of the following **criteria**:
– he was UK resident at some time during the tax year (¶4154);
– he has relevant UK earnings (¶3768) chargeable to UK income tax; or
– he was resident in the UK both at some time within the previous 5 years, and when joining the pension scheme.
An individual may belong to, and make contributions to, an unlimited number of registered schemes. The tax advantages are given on the basis of the accumulated contributions and benefits attributable to each individual across all registered schemes of which he is a member.

3756 **Overseas issues** An individual or spouse (¶2402) who has earnings from an **overseas Crown employment** which is subject to UK tax can contribute to a registered scheme, based on any earnings which are taxable in the UK.
Employees **seconded overseas** are able to remain members of an occupational scheme, even where the 10 year limit for foreign service was exceeded before 6 April 2006.
SI 2006/208 SI 2006/212 An individual **coming to work in the UK**, who is an existing member of an overseas pension (which is recognised by HMRC) is eligible for tax relief on his contributions paid whilst in the UK, so long as he was previously entitled to tax relief in the country of his residence at any time in the previous 10 years. This is known as **migrant member relief**.

MEMO POINTS Current UK legislation denies a deduction of contributions where an **overseas pensions fund** does not provide certain information to HMRC. The European Commission has formally requested that the UK amend this rule, as it is discriminatory.

B. Making contributions

1. Basic principles

3762 ss 188, 196 FA 2004 Contributions may be paid by:
– the scheme member;
– the member's employer; or
– a third party on behalf of the member.

s 195 FA 2004 MEMO POINTS 1. 1. In addition to cash, contributions may be in the **form of shares** from a Share Incentive Plan (¶3510), or Save As You Earn Scheme (¶3554).
2. 2. For the purposes of all of the pension rules, member is taken to include **former member**, and employer is taken to include **former employer**.
3. From 6 April 2011, contributions from a third party may fall under the restrictions on disguised remuneration: see ¶3039.

Limits

There is **no minimum or maximum restriction** on the amount of contributions payable either by the member or an employer, although only a limited amount will receive tax relief. This means that individuals who only receive unearned income, or who have capital to invest (for example, as a result of an inheritance), can make pension provision. In addition, grand-parents can make contributions on behalf of their grandchildren. 3764 s 190 FA 2004

HMRC contribute to personal pension schemes which have contracted out of the state system.

The **maximum aggregate contribution** on which tax relief is due for one tax year is the higher of: 3766

- £3,600; and
- the amount of relevant UK earnings (see below), up to a limit called the annual allowance (¶3771+).

In practice, most contributions will be limited by the amount of earnings.

Relevant UK earnings means income derived from: 3768 s 189 FA 2004

- employment (including directorships of non-trading companies) such as salary, bonuses, overtime, benefits and share remuneration;
- trading (either as a sole trader or in partnership);
- furnished holiday lettings;
- patent rights relating to an individual's own invention; and
- general earnings from an overseas Crown employment which are subject to UK tax.

If the annual aggregate contributions (from any source) **exceed**: 3770

- **UK relevant earnings** but not the annual allowance, no tax relief will be due on the excess over earnings; or
- the **annual allowance**, the member is liable to a higher rate tax charge (¶3777) which will be assessed via his self-assessment tax return. However, no NIC will be due on the excess.

2. The annual allowance

Amount of the allowance

Tax relief on pension contributions is limited to **£50,000** for 2011/12 (2010/11: £255,000). Excess contributions are taxed at the "appropriate rate" (effectively, the individual's marginal rate). This is called the **annual allowance charge**. 3771 ss 227 - 228 FA 2004

From 2011/12 the annual allowance charge also applies:

- in the year that benefits are drawn (for exceptions, see ¶3774); and
- to individuals with enhanced protection of pension rights as at 6 April 2006 (¶3800).

MEMO POINTS 1. The annual allowance charge arises irrespective of whether either the individual or the scheme administrator is resident, ordinarily resident or domiciled in the UK.

2. Excess contributions are not regarded as income for general tax purposes. This means that:
- other allowances, losses and reliefs cannot be set off against them; and
- they do not count as income for the purpose of double tax agreements.

Pension input periods

Strictly speaking, the annual allowance for the tax year applies to the **pension input amount** for the **pension input period** (PIP) which ends in that tax year. 3772 s 238 FA 2004

For schemes established on or after 6 April 2011, the first PIP begins when the individual's involvement in the scheme begins, and normally ends on 5 April at the end of the scheme's first tax year. Existing schemes have PIPs which normally end on the anniversary of the member's becoming involved (or on 5 April, for memberships which pre-date 6 April 2006).

If the individual belongs to more than one scheme, he may find himself with a different PIP for each one.

MEMO POINTS 1. In general, an individual's involvement begins when he first makes a contribution to the scheme. However, in a direct benefit scheme the first PIP begins when rights first accrue to the individual under the scheme.
2. It is possible to nominate a different end date for the first PIP, provided it falls before the anniversary of the individual's involvement. New end dates can also be nominated later during the time of membership (for example, to align PIPs for different schemes, or align them to the tax year). Only one change is permitted during any tax year, and retrospective changes are not accepted. Nominations are normally made by the scheme administrator, who must notify the member accordingly, but in a money purchase scheme, the individual may also nominate a change of PIP end date.

Pension input amounts

3773
s 229 FA 2004
The pension input amount means the **aggregate value of contributions** made to all registered schemes of which the individual is a member, irrespective of who makes those contributions. The way in which contributions are valued depends on the type of scheme, as follows:

Type of scheme	Measure of contributions
Money purchase	Actual amount contributed[1]
Final salary	Increase in value of the individual's fund over the PIP: see ¶3775
Personal pension schemes	Actual contributions, grossed up for basic rate tax deducted (¶3778)

Notes
1. If contributions are made under a net pay arrangement (¶3778), the effective tax relief is ignored, and the pensions input amount is the actual amount contributed.

MEMO POINTS The following **do not count** towards the annual allowance:
- NIC rebates to a contracted out scheme;
- contributions to an unregistered scheme; and
- transfers in from another registered pension scheme (which can happen without restriction).

EXAMPLE
1. Miss A earns £35,000 in 2011/12 and pays a contribution of £30,000 to her registered personal pension scheme.
The gross equivalent of this contribution is £37,500. (30,000 x 100/80)
As this exceeds Miss A's earnings, she is only able to claim tax relief in respect of a gross contribution of £35,000. This leaves an excess contribution of £2,500.
Miss A receives a refund of £2,000 from the scheme. (2,500 @ (100 % – 20%))

2. Mrs B contributes to three pension schemes in 2011/12, with the following PIPs:

	Gross contribution £	Period end
Scheme 1	20,000	5 April 2012
Scheme 2	10,000	28 February 2012
Scheme 3	15,000	31 December 2011
Total taken into account for 2011/12	45,000	

As the total contributions are less than the annual allowance of £50,000, no tax charge arises.

3774 There is **no pension input amount** for a PIP ending in the tax year:
- of the individual's death; or
- in which the individual becomes entitled to all the benefits which may be provided under the scheme; or
- in which the individual satisfies an ill-health condition.

MEMO POINTS The **ill-health condition** is satisfied if the individual:
- receives a serious ill-health lump sum from the scheme (normally paid only if the individual is not expected to live more than a year); or
- is a member of the armed forces and receives a tax-exempt wound or disability pension; or
- obtains all the benefits available under the scheme, by reason of ill health which makes him unlikely to work again before reaching pensionable age.

Final salary schemes

The individual has a pensions input amount for the PIP if his **pension entitlement** under the scheme at the end of the PIP is exceeds that at the start of the PIP by an amount greater than inflation (as measured by the CPI). 3775 ss 234-236 FA 2004

The value of the pension entitlement is the sum of:
- 16 times the pension that would be payable if the individual became entitled to it at the date of valuation; and
- the lump sum which would be payable if he became entitled to it on that date.

The scheme administrator is responsible for computing these values and notifying them to the members.

MEMO POINTS For periods before 2011/12 the valuation factor was 10 times the pension entitlement.

EXAMPLE Mr C is a member of his employer's final salary scheme. He has worked for his employer for 20 years in 2011/12. The accrued benefits which he is entitled to in 2010/11 and 2011/12 are as follows:

Tax year	Salary	Number of years service	Benefit
2010/11	£50,000	20	£16,667 (20/60 × 50,000)
2011/12	£55,000	21	£19,250 (21/60 × 55,000)

The increase in the benefit between 2010/11 and 2011/12 is £2,583. (19,250 – 16,667)
The deemed increase in the value of the fund for 2011/12 is £41,328, applying the standard multiple of 16. As this amount is well below the annual allowance, there will be no tax charge on Mr C.

Carry-forward of annual allowance

If the annual allowance for the tax year is insufficient to cover the individual's contributions, unused annual allowances can be brought forward from up to **three years** before. Allowances from earlier years are used first. 3776 s 228A FA 2004

For this purpose, the allowance for the years 2008/09 to 2010/11 is deemed to be limited to £50,000. Unused allowances for those years are computed on the basis used for 2011/12 (so, for example, in a final purchase scheme the multiplier used must be 10, not 16).

EXAMPLE Mr D has the following pension input amounts for the four years up to 6 April 2012. His inputs for 2008/09 to 2010/11 have been recalculated using the post April 2011 rules:

Tax year	Old rules £	New rules £	Unused allowances £
2008/09	31,000	34,000	16,000
2009/10	32,000	36,000	14,000
2010/11	33,000	39,000	11,000
			41,000
2011/12		100,000	50,000
			91,000

In 2011/12 Mr D will suffer an annual allowance charge (¶3777) on £9,000 (the excess of his contributions (£100,000) over the available allowances (£91,000)).
However, if Mr D had made contributions of £48,000 in 2009/10, revalued at £60,000 under the new rules, his record would look like this:

Tax year	Old rules £	New rules £	Unused allowances £
2008/09	31,000	34,000	16,000
2009/10	48,000	60,000	(10,000)
2010/11	33,000	39,000	11,000
			17,000
2011/12		100,000	50,000
			67,000

In this case, Mr E would face an annual allowance charge on £33,000 (100,000-67,000).

The annual allowance charge

3777 s 237B FA 2004

If the annual allowance charge does not exceed £2,000 it must be paid by the individual member and shown on his self-assessment tax return.

If the charge **exceeds £2,000** the member may serve a notice on the scheme administrator by 31 July following the tax year, requiring the fund to pay the charge, and reduce the individual's benefit entitlement accordingly. This is known as the **scheme pays** facility.

If the charge arose:
– entirely because of his contributions to that one scheme, the administrator must accept the charge;
– because of contributions to several schemes, no scheme is obliged to accept it, and if necessary the individual must pay it himself.

MEMO POINTS 1. For 2011/12 the deadline for serving a notice is **extended** to 31 December 2013.
2. The scheme pays facility is not available to an individual who died before 19 July 2011 (the date of Royal Assent to FA2011).

3. How tax relief is given

Individual contributions

3778 ss 192 – 194 FA 2004

All contributions, except those made by the employer, are treated as made by the member. The related tax relief is claimed by the member on his tax return.

An individual's contributions can be **paid in three ways**:
a. net of tax at the basic rate, which the scheme administrator reclaims from HMRC (this is the default option);
b. in the case of existing retirement annuity contracts, the contributions may still be paid gross if the scheme administrator agrees. Tax relief is claimed on the self-assessment tax return, or by amending a PAYE code; or
c. in relation to an occupational scheme, contributions can be paid through a net pay arrangement operated by an employer. This means that the employer deducts the employee's contribution from gross pay before applying PAYE, which effectively gives tax relief at the employee's marginal rate of tax.

s 188(3) FA 2004

MEMO POINTS **Term assurance** policies are a type of insurance which pay out on death or in the event of serious illness over a specified term. From 1 August 2007, tax relief is no longer available on an individual's contributions when they are used to fund such policies, **unless** the policy is protected i.e. either:
a. the scheme is occupational and the insurer received an application on or before 29 March 2007; or
b. for other types of scheme, either:
– the application for the policy was received by the insurer before 14 December 2006; or
– the term assurance policy was sold as part of an existing personal pension scheme, when tax relief will still apply where an application was submitted to the insurer before 13 April 2007.
Where **relief remains available**, it will be denied where the policy is amended to increase the term or amount receivable, other than when an existing option relating to the policy is exercised.

EXAMPLE Mr A, a higher rate taxpayer, receives savings and rental income of £50,000 in 2011/12. He pays a contribution of £2,880 to a personal pension scheme.
This contribution is grossed up at the basic rate to £3,600. (2,880 x 100/80)
Mr A claims higher rate tax relief on his tax return of £720. (3,600 @ (40 – 20) %)

Employer contributions

3780 s 196 FA 2004 BIM 46001

Employer contributions which are made wholly and exclusively **for the purposes of** the business are deductible against taxable profits in the period when they are paid.

In practice, a contribution will be allowable unless there is an identifiable non-trade purpose for it (for example, when the recipient or the contribution depends on some factor other than the recipient's service to the employer). Provided that employees who are controlling shareholders (or related to them) receive comparable salaries and pension contributions to other, unrelated employees, this should not provoke a challenge from HMRC.

Very **large contributions** (broadly, over £500,000) are subject to the spreading rules of ¶159. s 197 FA 2004

MEMO POINTS 1. It is possible for an employer to agree to pay a monetary contribution and then to settle this debt by way of a **transfer of an asset**. In order for the transfer to be treated as a contribution (and not an acquisition by the scheme), all of the following criteria must be met: RPSM 05102035
- there must be a clear obligation on the employer to pay a contribution of a specified monetary sum, which creates a recoverable debt obligation;
- a separate agreement must exist between the scheme trustees and employer to pass an asset to the scheme for consideration; and
- the scheme must agree for the cash contribution debt to be met by the market value of the asset. Any shortfall should be met in cash.

2. An **anti-avoidance rule** applies where an employer contributes to a registered scheme, but the related benefits will not be paid (wholly or partly) out of that scheme because some other arrangement has been made (¶3902). In this case, tax relief is limited to the proportion of contributions relating to benefits which could only be paid out of the registered scheme. s 196A FA 2004

Scheme surplus A surplus in a registered pension scheme can be **refunded** to the employer net of a tax charge at 35%. 3782 s 207 FA 2004

MEMO POINTS There is an anti-avoidance rule which operates on the **death of a member** aged over 75 who is connected to the employer, and whose benefits have been secured. In this case, any surplus should first be used to fund any dependant's benefits. Only then would any refund be made to the employer. SI 2006/574

A member is **connected to** the employer if that employer is either:
- a partnership, and he is connected to (¶5570) a partner (or a person who was a partner in the last 12 months); or
- a company, and in the past 12 months either the member, or a person connected with him (¶5570), has been a controlling director.

Early leavers Employees who leave after only **3 months** of employment have a choice of a refund, or a transfer of the contributions made to another scheme. This means that the employee can still benefit from the employer's contributions. 3784 s 205 FA 2004

Contributions are **refunded** to members net of a tax charge which is levied at:
- 20% on the first £20,000; and
- 50% on the excess.

The tax is payable by the scheme administrator.

C. Pension fund limits

Limits

There is **no upper limit** on the value of the fund, only on the tax-advantaged level of funding. 3786 ss 214-217 FA 2004

Lifetime allowance

The aggregate value of all of an individual's registered pension funds from which **tax privileged benefits** are payable on retirement or on death is limited by the lifetime allowance, which is set at £1.8 million for 2011/12 (2010/11: £1.8 million) but will fall to £1.5 million in 2012/13. 3788 ss 215, 218 FA 2004 s 218 FA 2004

If this allowance is **exceeded**, a tax charge (called the lifetime allowance charge) will apply. The rate of tax depends on whether the benefits are taken in the form of:
- a pension, when the tax charge is 25%; or
- a lump sum, when the tax charge is at an effective rate of 55%.

The charge is payable by either the member or scheme administrator on a grossed-up basis, and must be reported on the individual's tax return.

MEMO POINTS 1. The lifetime allowance is reduced if the individual retires before the statutory minimum age of 55: see ¶3833.
2. The difference in tax rates reflects the fact that the pension income is itself taxable.
3. The scheme administrator must **withhold** the tax from the benefits paid.
4. On **divorce**, where pension rights are split, the pension allocated to the former spouse (¶2402) counts against the member's lifetime allowance but not the allowance of the spouse. This would also apply to the dissolution of a civil partnership.

Valuing the fund

3790 ss 216, 276 FA 2004

For **money purchase** occupational schemes and **personal** schemes the fund is valued at the market value of its assets.

For **final salary** schemes the deemed value of the fund is 20 times the pension benefit payable, plus the value of any tax-free cash. This is a necessary simplification in order to cope with a fund which exists for a number of employees. Where a pension was already in payment at 6 April 2006, a multiplier of 25 is applied, to take account of the lump sum which has probably already been received tax free.

Applying the lifetime allowance

3792 s 216 FA 2004

Funds are only **tested** against the lifetime allowance when a **benefit crystallisation event** occurs, which is usually when the member chooses to take his benefits.

s 215 FA 2004

The **amount tested** against the allowance is the gross value of benefits received, before any possible payment of the lifetime allowance tax charge by the scheme.

MEMO POINTS 1. The full list of these **events** is as follows:
– a benefit becomes payable (for example, when a pension payment commences either in the form of an annuity or income drawdown, or a lump sum is paid on retirement or death);
– the member reaches 75 without already securing his pension (see ¶3797);
– a pension which is already being paid is increased excessively;
– the funds are transferred to an overseas scheme; or
– relief under a double taxation treaty ceases.

s 221 FA 2004

2. Where a member has been **non-resident** at any time while contributions have been paid, the allowance is enhanced to take account of the fact that the member will not have received tax relief whilst being non-resident.

Pensions Tax Simplification Newsletter 8

HMRC have stated that an **international protection** operates in both of the following situations:
– a member of a UK registered pension scheme has been an active member (i.e. pension benefits have been accruing) whilst non-UK resident; or
– funds are transferred from an overseas pension scheme to a UK registered scheme.
Any part of the fund which has not received UK tax relief will be excluded from the lifetime allowance charge.

3794 If **successive events** occur, the amount already tested is indexed to the date of the current event and deducted from the available lifetime allowance.

Comment The reduction in the lifetime allowance in 2012/13 means that some individuals who have already taken benefits may be adversely affected in later years.

EXAMPLE Mrs F retires in 2010/11, aged 60, with accrued pension rights of £1.2 million. She decides to withdraw £0.7m which leaves £500,000 in the fund. As the total rights of £1.25m are below the lifetime allowance for 2010/11 of £1.8m, no tax is charged on the fund. She has actually used up 67% of her lifetime allowance. (1.2m/1.8m x 100%)
In 2012/13, Mrs F's pension fund is worth £0.6m. The lifetime allowance is now £1.5m. As 67% of the lifetime allowance has been used up, only £500,000 remains.
Mrs F decides to take a pension of £30,000 a year. For the purpose of the lieftime allowance charge, this is valued at £600,000 (20 x 30,000).
The valuation exceeds the remaining lifetime allowance by £100,000. Mrs F will therefore be subject to a charge of £25,000 (100,000 @ 25%).
If she had taken out the remaining funds as a lump sum, the tax charge would have been £55,000 (100,000 @ 55%).

3796 The benefits which are vesting, and the relative proportion of the current lifetime allowance that they represent, must be notified to the member by the **scheme administrator**.

The **member** must certify to the administrator that he has sufficient lifetime allowance to cover the event, or inform him of the amount already used up. Failure to certify means that no lump sum can be paid, and the administrator must withhold tax on the basis that no lifetime allowance remains unused. The member enters the lifetime allowance tax charge on his self-assessment tax return, and any excess tax suffered will be repaid.

The member and scheme administrator are **jointly and severally liable** for payment of the lifetime allowance charge.

Lifetime allowance at age 75

The lifetime allowance is also tested as at the individual's 75th birthday if: **3797**
– he has funds which have not yet been used to secure a pension (known as **uncrystallised rights**); or
– he is receiving a **drawdown pension** (¶3858) which started after 6 April 2006.

Uncrystallised rights under a defined benefits (final salary) scheme are valued as if they had been used to secure a pension immediately before the individual's 75th birthday. The value of uncrystallised rights under a money purchase or a cash balance arrangement is equal to the unused funds.

A drawdown pension test depends on any increase in the value of assets remaining in the drawdown fund up to the individual's 75th birthday.

MEMO POINTS Drawdown pensions were formerly known as unsecured or alternatively secured pensions.

Fixed protection

Fixed protection offers some mitigation of the lifetime allowance charge for those who may already have built up pension savings on the expectation that the lifetime allowance would remain at the former level of £1.8 million. In effect, the individual's lifetime allowance remains fixed at that level. In return, **no further contributions** can be made into the scheme after 6 April 2012. **3798** s 237B FA 2004

To obtain protection, the individual must give notice to HMRC no later than **5 April 2012**.

Fixed protection is **not available** to those who have already secured protection for the excess value of the pension fund at 6 April 2006.

Excess pension fund at 6 April 2006

Up until 5 April 2009, those individuals who had cumulative approved pension funds in excess of the lifetime allowance before 6 April 2006, could claim to protect their accrued benefits in **two ways**: **3800** Sch 36 FA 2004
– **primary protection**, which indexes the lifetime allowance to take account of pension rights existing at 6 April 2006, and allows further contributions to be made; and
– **enhanced protection**, which allows members to retain their pension rights as they existed at 6 April 2006.

HMRC will have issued a certificate with a unique reference number, which shows the protection entitlement. When benefits are taken, the certificate should be shown to the scheme administrator to prove that protection has been claimed.

Primary protection Where the pension fund exceeded £1.5 million at 6 April 2006, the amount of the excess is recorded as a multiple of the lifetime allowance (rounded up to the nearest 2 decimal places). This can take account of generous death lump sum benefits (¶3862). **3804**

On retirement (or death), **when benefits are taken**, only the excess of the fund over the indexed lifetime allowance will attract a tax charge. Further contributions can be made, although this will increase the risk of a tax charge.

EXAMPLE On 6 April 2006, Mr H's pension fund was valued at £1.875m. This represents 1.25 times the lifetime allowance of £1.5m for 2006/07. The standard lifetime allowance for 2010/11 is £1.8m. When Mr A retires in 2010/11, his indexed lifetime allowance will be £2.25m, and only the excess fund value will be liable to tax. (1.8m × 1.25)

3806 **Enhanced protection** Alternatively, the full amount of the pension fund may be protected by enhanced protection, regardless of its value on either 6 April 2006 or the date of retirement.

SI 2006/211 For **occupational schemes**, the protected value is limited to 20 times the maximum permitted pension benefit under the approved scheme rules which applied until 6 April 2006. Any excess rights must have been surrendered for the protection to apply.

3808 Members are unable to accrue **further benefits** after 6 April 2006, which usually means no further contributions to the scheme can be made (except in the case of defined benefit and cash balance schemes). For this purpose, contracted out rebates do not count as a contribution.

If later **contributions** were to be made, protection would revert to the primary level, unless the funds were below £1.5 million at 6 April 2006, when there would be no protection at all. Where further benefits are accrued, HMRC must be notified with 90 days.

3810 Pensions Tax Simplification Newsletter 8 HMRC have clarified that for **money purchase** schemes (otherwise known as defined contribution schemes), enhanced protection will be lost if any contributions are made after 6 April 2006. For this purpose, a money purchase scheme does not include cash balance schemes, where unspecified benefits are payable from a guaranteed pot of money.

Sch 36 para 14(3) FA 2004 Individuals who are paying regular contributions to **term assurance policies**, which pay lump sum death benefits where the individual dies during the term, can continue to make contributions without giving rise to a tax charge, so long as all of the following conditions are satisfied:
- the contribution is used to pay insurance premiums for life cover;
- the insurance contract was made before 6 April 2006, and is not varied subsequently to enhance the benefits; and
- the only payment under the policy will be on the individual's death.

3812 Sch 36 para 15 FA 2004 For other types of schemes (i.e. **defined benefit** and **cash balance** schemes), protection will only be lost if the value of the benefits taken exceeds the appropriate amount, which is the higher of:

a. the result of applying the scheme rules which existed up to 6 April 2006 to the pensionable earnings at the date that the benefits are paid (i.e. length of service to 6 April 2006 and the benefit accrual rate); and

b. indexing the value of the pension rights at 5 April 2006 to the date of the benefit payment by the higher of:
- 5% interest compound;
- RPI; and
- the stated increase relating to contracted out rights.

So contributions can continue after 6 April 2006, so long as the benefits eventually received do not exceed the appropriate amount.

EXAMPLE Mr A is a member of a defined benefits scheme, and under the scheme rules the benefit accrual rate is 1/60th for each year of service. On 5 April 2006, he had 30 years of service, and his pensionable earnings were £120,000.

He retires on 1 April 2013, when his pensionable earnings are £140,000, and the lifetime allowance is £1.5m.

Using the 20 multiplier, the pension rights at 6 April 2006 are valued at £1.2m. (30/60 × 120,000 × 20)

The appropriate limit is £1.4m, which is the higher of:
- the result of applying the scheme rules to Mr A's earnings in 2012/13, which gives £1.4m. (30/60 x 140,000 x 20); and
- indexing the pension rights at 6 April 2006 by 5% or the RPI, which gives (say) £1.3m.

If Mr A's benefits in 2012/13 are (say):
– £1.45m, enhanced protection is lost because this exceeds the appropriate limit, but there is no lifetime allowance charge, because the benefits are still less than the 2012/13 lifetime allowance of £1.5m; or
– £1.6m, enhanced protection is lost, and there is a lifetime allowance charge, as this figure exceeds both the appropriate amount and the 2012/13 lifetime allowance.

D. Pension fund assets and liabilities

Investments

Any investments **existing** at 6 April 2006 can be retained. **3814** s 186 FA 2004

New investments may include residential property and works of art, although these are effectively prohibited for member-directed schemes (i.e. SIPPS and SSASs), due to the onerous tax charges which result (¶3818).

Transactions with **connected persons** (¶5570 onwards) are also permitted on a commercial basis (subject to possible anti-avoidance rules if this rule is abused). So a SIPP is able to acquire a commercial property and lease it back to the member's employer.

Investment **income** arising from scheme assets is exempt from tax, although trading income is taxable.

MEMO POINTS 1. Any investment in the **employer's shares** made after 6 April 2006 is restricted to 5% of the total value of the scheme assets (20 % if there is more than one sponsoring employer).
2. Any **use of a scheme asset** by a member (including his family or a member of his household (¶3198)), without paying an arm's length consideration, is taxable as a benefit in kind. For an occupational scheme, this will fall under the employment benefit rules and appear on the employee's P11D or P9D provided by the employer. Otherwise, it will be treated as an unauthorised payment (¶3869).

Residential property Where a member of a pension scheme is able to **occupy** a property owned wholly or partly by a pension scheme, he will be deemed to receive a benefit in kind, which is calculated under the normal employment rules (¶3250 onwards). The pension scheme is also deemed to have made an unauthorised payment (¶3869) of the same amount. **3816** SI 2006/133

Member-directed pension schemes Investments in certain assets by member-directed pension schemes (those where the member has influence in the choice of investments) is effectively prohibited in order to ensure that valuable tax relief is only available when investing to secure retirement income. This particularly **affects** SIPPS and SSASs set up since 1991. **3818** Sch 29A FA 2004

MEMO POINTS 1. For these purposes, a pension scheme is **member-directed** if it is: Sch 29A paras 1 - 2 FA 2004
– an occupational scheme and either 10% or more of the members have influence over the investment, or at least one member does and there are fewer than 50 members in the scheme; or
– non-occupational, and at least one member is able to influence the scheme's investments.
The legislation refers to these as investment-regulated schemes.
2. The **assets** concerned are: Sch 29A para 6 FA 2004
– wholly residential property wherever located, which is used or suitable for use as a dwelling;
– fine wines;
– stamp collections;
– jewellery;
– classic cars;
– boats;
– art and antiques; and
– other similar tangible property.

s 174A FA 2004 3. For this purpose, a scheme **invests** in an asset when it is acquired, improved, converted or adapted.

Sch 29A paras 16, 20 FA 2004 4. **Indirect investment**, such as the scheme acquiring a residential property through a wholly owned company, is also affected. However, scheme investment in a genuinely diverse commercial vehicle which holds residential property is permitted.

For this purpose, a **genuinely diverse commerce vehicle** should meet the following criteria:
- the scheme's investment in the vehicle is no more than 10%;
- the total value of the vehicle's assets is at least £1 million, or at least three residential properties are held;
- the residential properties do not make up more than 40% of the total value of the vehicle's assets, and no private use is allowed;
- the vehicle's main purpose is not to hold animals for sporting purposes e.g. racehorses; and
- if the vehicle is a company, it is not a close company (¶2100), or a non-resident company which would otherwise fall within the definition of a close company.

3820 s 174A FA 2004 If a scheme **invests in a prohibited investment**, the member and scheme will be subject to the unauthorised payments tax charges (¶3870). The scheme could also be deregistered.

s 185A FA 2004 In addition, any **income and gains** derived from the asset will be taxable on the scheme administrator. If the actual income is less than 10% of the asset's value, the scheme will be taxable on deemed income of this amount.

When **benefits** which relate to the asset are paid out of the scheme to the member, either as a pension or lump sum, these will not be penalised, so up to 25% of the fund will still be tax free.

Borrowings

3824 s 182 – 185 FA 2004 Scheme borrowings are restricted to a **maximum** of 50% of the value of the scheme assets.

3826 **Loans** to members (and connected persons) are prohibited and will be treated as an unauthorised payment (¶3869). This means that personal pension schemes, where there is no sponsoring employer, cannot loan monies to a member's own business.

MEMO POINTS 1. Loans **include** unpaid contributions, waivers of debt and loan guarantees.
2. **Connected persons** has the meaning given at ¶5570 onwards.

3828 Sch 30 FA 2004 Otherwise, loans made to **unconnected parties**, or by an occupational scheme to the **employer company** (and connected persons), are permitted only within the following criteria:
- loan must be secured on assets of at least equal value;
- term cannot exceed 5 years (although one rollover into another loan not extending beyond 5 years is permitted);
- value cannot exceed 50% of the total value of the fund;
- rate of interest must be at least base rate plus 1%; and
- repayments must be made by equal annual instalments.

MEMO POINTS **Pre-April 2006** loans may continue on their original terms, but any alteration will be treated as a new loan.

E. Taking benefits

General structure of benefits

3830 Pension benefits can be taken at or after the age of retirement, or on death. When taken, the benefits are said to **crystallise**, or to **vest** in the individual. The individual may continue working after the permitted retirement age and still take benefits.

At retirement, a tax free cash lump sum is available. The remaining fund is then used to produce an income which is taxable at the normal rates (¶3664). This income is created by either:
- purchasing an annuity; or
- withdrawing money from the fund itself.

This section is divided into the following subject areas:

Subject matter	¶¶
Timing of retirement	¶3832
Lump sums	¶3838
Pension income	¶3856
Benefits on death (before or after retirement)	¶3862

MEMO POINTS 1. Prior to 6 April 2011, a member's funds were permitted to remain in the scheme only until he reached the age of 75 (age 77, from 20 June 2010). At that time the remaining funds had to be used to purchase an annuity. There was a distinction between:
– secured pensions (those paid under a purchased annuity); and
– unsecured or alternatively secured pensions (those paid by drawing on scheme funds, or through a short-term annuity arrangement).
The latter were subject to special rules and limitations. For details, see *Tax Memo 2010-2011*.
2. **Inducements** paid to members of defined benefit occupational pension schemes for their agreement **to a reduction in benefits**, or to their transferring out of a defined benefit scheme into a defined contribution scheme, are liable to tax and NIC as employment income. This treatment does not apply to payments that enhance the transfer value of the pension fund, and are included in the funds transferred between schemes, as these are treated as employer contributions.

Protection of benefits

All pension benefits are protected by the Pension Protection Fund (PPF), and any related compensation paid to members in lieu of pension is taxable. 3831

MEMO POINTS 1. **Sponsoring employers** must pay levies to the PPF, which are tax deductible against trading profits. Pensions Tax Simplification Newsletter 19 SI 2006/137
4. Any payment made to a scheme member in order to compensate for the loss of his rights arising from **de-mutualisation** is not liable to tax.
2. An **insolvent occupational pension scheme** which was no longer able to meet all its pension obligations qualified for assistance from the Financial Assistance Scheme (FAS) up until 5 April 2005. As the FAS is a Government financed scheme and not a registered pension scheme, regulations will come into force at a future date to allow FAS payments (whenever made) to be given broadly the same tax treatment as if they had been made by a registered pension scheme.
3. Some **insured schemes** have received assistance from the Financial Services Compensation Scheme (FSCS), which can take the form of transferring an individual's rights to another insurer or paying compensation to the individual. Future regulations will come into force (possibly with retrospective effect) which will ensure any payments made by the FSCS are treated as if they were made by a registered pension scheme (i.e. the same tax advantages will apply as if the FSCS had not been involved).

1. Timing of retirement

Retirement benefits from registered schemes are normally only available to individual members above a **permitted retirement age** of 55 years (50 years, prior to 6 April 2010). 3832 s 165 FA 2004

Benefits may, however, become available earlier by reason of ill-health.

MEMO POINTS Ill health means that the scheme administrator has received evidence from a registered medical practitioner that the member is (and will continue to be) incapable of working because of physical or mental impairment, and the member has in fact ceased work. Sch 28 para 1 FA 2004

The lifetime allowance and early retirement

The lifetime allowance (¶3788) is applied when benefits crystallise, and tax is charged on funds in excess of the allowance. 3833

If the member retires early, the lifetime allowance is **reduced** by 2.5% for each year before the permitted retirement age.

EXAMPLE Mr B retires at 45 in May 2011. As he is 10 years younger than the normal retirement age of 55, his lifetime allowance will be reduced by 25%. (2.5 % x 10)
So Mr B's lifetime allowance will be:

	£
Standard lifetime allowance for 2011/12	1.500m
Less: 1.5m @ 25%	(0.375m)
Mr B's lifetime allowance	1.125m

3834 There are two **exceptions** from the reduction in the lifetime allowance:
- a right to retire earlier which existed at 6 April 2006; and
- being in a special occupation.

Pre-existing right to retire earlier

3835 Sch 36 para 22 FA 2004 Where a member of an occupational scheme had a pre-existing right on 10 December 2003 (which continued to 6 April 2006) to retire before the permitted age, the member will be able to retire when planned.

Members who wish to retire **before the age of 55** and then become re-employed can do so without penalty so long as they are not trying to avoid tax or NIC and either:
- the new employer is not connected (¶5570 onwards) to the member or the sponsoring employer of the pension scheme;
- the member is re-employed by his old employer, but at least 6 months have elapsed since retirement; or
- at least 1 month elapses after retirement, and the new employment with the old employer is materially different e.g. a director is re-employed as a caretaker.

MEMO POINTS 1. An **industry-wide scheme** is one where many employers in the same industry have banded together to provide one scheme for all employees.
2. Members of the **armed forces**, who are compulsorily recalled to duty after retirement, can be re-employed by their old employer with no adverse tax consequences to their pension.
SI 2006/573 3. Where a **pension scheme was transferred** between 10 December 2003 and 6 April 2006 in the following circumstances, the right to take benefits before the normal retirement age is preserved:
- a transfer of the employer undertaking occurred (e.g. a takeover or merger); or
- the sponsoring employer reorganised its pension schemes.
SI 2006/573 4. When a scheme **winds up** after 6 April 2006, any existing right to take benefits before the normal retirement age is preserved.

Special occupations

3836 Sch 36 para 23 FA 2004 A special occupation **included** activities undertaken by a:
- professional sportsperson;
- entertainer;
- fashion model;
- deep-sea diver; and
- reserve forces member.

For **new schemes** set up from **6 April 2006**, there is no reduced retirement age for these occupations.

A member of a pre-existing pension scheme (including stakeholder pensions and retirement annuity contracts) in a special occupation will still be able to retire when planned, but all benefits must then be taken in full.

Members of the **armed forces**, **police** or **fire** services will not suffer a restricted lifetime allowance if they take benefits before the age of 55.

2. Lump sums

Pension commencement lump sum

A **tax-free** cash lump sum of up to 25% of the fund value will be available when pension benefits first crystallise (usually on retirement). The amount is **calculated** at scheme level, so a member can amalgamate all potential benefits within a scheme. 3838 s 166 FA 2004 Sch 29 para 1 FA 2004

The lump sum can be paid during an 18 month period which starts 6 months before the member becomes entitled to it.

Any lump sum taken from funds which exceed the lifetime allowance will be taxed at an effective rate of 55% (¶3788). The test is applied at the date the sum is paid.

From 6 April 2011, a lump sum can also be paid in relation to pension benefits not taken until after the member has reached the age of 75. It is always tax free, but the individual may have been subject to the lifetime allowance charge at age 75 (see ¶3797).

MEMO POINTS Where a tax-free lump sum has **already been paid** before 6 April 2006, this will be taken into account when testing whether a tax charge is due on any excess lump sum. If a pension was deferred until after 6 April 2006, no further tax-free lump sum can be taken.

Other types of lump sum

Other types of lump sum benefits comprise the following: 3839 Sch 29 FA 2004
- trivial commutation;
- serious ill-health;
- winding-up;
- short service refund;
- refund of excess contributions;
- lifetime allowance excess; and
- stand-alone.

MEMO POINTS 1. A **trivial commutation lump sum** is the payment of the individual's entire entitlement in a single sum, where his pension funds are small.

2. A **serious ill health lump sum** can be paid only on medical evidence that the individual has a life expectancy of not more than one year. Any uncrystallised benefits can be taken out as a single payment.

3. A **winding-up lump sum** is the payment of the individual's entire entitlement in a single sum, where the pension fund is an occupational scheme and his funds are small.

4. A **short service refund lump sum** is the refund of contributions to an occupational scheme by an individual who was a member for less than 2 years, and provided that:
- no benefits have been taken from the scheme; and
- the payment extinguishes all his rights under the scheme (except where the scheme is required to retain liability to provide protected benefits).

5. A **refund of excess contributions lump sum** is the return of tax-relieved contributions paid in excess of the annual maximum (¶3766). Repayment must be made within six years of the end of the tax year when the contributions were paid.

6. A **lifetime allowance excess lump sum** arises when an individual has used up all of his lifetime allowance (¶3788) and the scheme pays out all (or part) of his excess funds (or commutes all (or part) of his pension entitlements) as a lump sum. Not all registered schemes permit this facility. Note that types 3, 4 and 5 above can be applied first, to obtain better tax treatment.

7. A **stand-alone lump sum** is one paid under a right that existed before 6 April 2006.

3840 For stand-alone lump sums, see ¶3842.

The tax treatment of the other types of lump sum is summarised in the following table:

Type	Age limit	Limit	Lifetime allowance applies?	Tax treatment
Trivial commutation	60 +	£18,000[1,2]	No	If no benefits have previously been taken from the scheme, 75% of the sum is taxable as income; otherwise it is all taxable[3].
Serious ill-health	None	None	Yes[4]	Tax free up to age 75[5]. Taxable at 55% if older[3].
Winding-up	None	£18,000[2,6]	No	If no benefits have previously been taken from the scheme, 75% of the sum is taxable as income; otherwise it is all taxable[3].
Short service refund	Up to 75	Total contributions paid	No	20% on the first £20,000. 50% on the balance.[7]
Refund of excess contributions	None[8]	Excess contributions paid (and not yet repaid)	No	Tax free (but any interest paid is taxable)
Lifetime allowance excess	Up to 75	None	No	55% (the lifetime allowance charge)

Notes
1. A single limit applies to the aggregate of all registered schemes to which the individual belongs.
2. The limit was formerly set at 1% of the lifetime allowance, but from 6 April 2011 it is a fixed amount.
3. Tax is deducted by the Scheme Administrator from the amount paid.
4. If paid after the age of 75, the lifetime allowance is applied as at age 75, and the age-75 test (¶3797) is ignored. The amount that can be paid is limited by the available lifetime allowance.
5. Subject to the operation of the lifetime allowance.
6. This limit applies separately to each fund.
7. Rates for 2011/12. For earlier years see *Tax Memo 2010-2011*.
8. There is no statutory limit, but since contributions are not tax-relieved at age 75+, and can only be returned within 6 tax years of payment, there is an effective limit of 81 years old.

MEMO POINTS Payments which relate to the following types of **errors** also escape a tax charge:
– a simple overpayment which was intended to be permitted by the pension rules, so long as the mistake was made in good faith. This also includes excess lump sums which relate to a miscalculation of pension rights;
– inadvertent payments made while the scheme rules were being considered by the scheme administrator, despite steps being taken to avoid making the payment; and
– a lump sum payment relating to a miscalculation in the price of a pension or annuity purchased on behalf of the member.

Stand-alone lump sums: schemes existing at 6 April 2006

3842 Sch 36 FA 2004 Before 6 April 2006 some members of occupational pension schemes had the right to receive all of their pension fund as a tax free lump sum on retirement. This right may be protected in four different ways:
– primary protection, which must have been claimed by 5 April 2009;
– enhanced protection, which also must have been claimed by 5 April 2009;
– entitlement to a greater lump sum under an occupational scheme; and
– protection if the scheme winds up.

3843 **Primary protection** mean that any lump sum in excess of £375,000, relating to the excess fund at 6 April 2006, is protected.

> EXAMPLE Mr C's lump sum entitlement was £562,500 at 6 April 2006. This represents 1.5 times the maximum lump sum entitlement of £375,000 under the lifetime allowance. (£1.5m @ 25%)
> When Mr A retires in 20- 1/12, his indexed tax-free lump sum entitlement will be £562,500. (1.5m @ 25% x 1.5)

Enhanced protection means the lump sum payable under the scheme's rules at 6 April 2006, as a proportion of uncrystallised rights, is tax free (although this cannot exceed the lifetime allowance). 3844

> EXAMPLE Mr D's lump sum entitlement was £400,000 at 6 April 2006, when his total pension rights are valued at £2m.
> The lump sum entitlement is therefore 20% of uncrystallised rights. (400,000/2m x 100%)
> If Mr D retires in 2011/12, and his uncrystallised rights are valued at (say) £2.4m, the protected lump sum will be £480,000 (£2.4m @ 20%).

For **approved occupational schemes**, where no primary or enhanced protection has been registered, and the scheme rules allowed a member to take a lump sum in excess of 25% of the fund, at retirement the member will be able to take: 3846 Sch 36 para 31 FA 2004

- the cash lump sum which was payable at 6 April 2006, increased in line with the annual allowance; and
- 25% of the capital value of the pension fund which has arisen since 6 April 2006.

Where a member is protecting the tax-free lump sum only, without protecting the value of the fund, there is no requirement to have made a claim.

If a scheme **winds up** after 5 April 2006, and benefits are secured by an annuity, any rights to take a lump sum in excess of 25% of the fund value are also preserved. 3848 SI 2006/573

Recycling lump sums

An **anti-avoidance** rule applies so that a lump sum cannot be used to fund a contribution into another registered pension scheme. This is known as recycling. 3850 Sch 29 para 3A FA 2004

The **consequence** of recycling a lump sum is that it is treated as an unauthorised payment (¶3869), on which the individual could suffer a tax charge of up to 55%. In addition, the scheme itself is subject to a charge of between 15% and 40%. Affected members must tell the scheme so that the administrator can fulfil his obligation to report the unauthorised payment.

MEMO POINTS 1. The **unauthorised payment** is the whole amount of the lump sum, irrespective of the amount actually used to fund the contribution, less any amounts that have already been taxed by the lifetime allowance charge (¶3788). It becomes taxable on the date that the lump sum is received unless the contribution is made subsequently, when the date of the contribution payment becomes the effective date.
2. Full HMRC **guidance** is given in their manual. RPSM 4104900

The **situation caught** is where all of the following occur: 3851

- an individual receives a lump sum in excess of 1% of the lifetime allowance which applies on the date of payment (including any amounts received within the last 12 months). For 2011/12, this means any lump sum in excess of £1,500;
- at least 30% of the lump sum is used to make a significantly increased contribution to a registered pension scheme; and
- these transactions were pre-planned.

If the member has **other funds** with which to fund the increased contribution, this will not avoid a recycling charge, as it is the fact that the member planned to use the lump sum as funding which is relevant. This even catches cases where the monies from the lump sum are put into savings, and the original savings are then used as the contribution.

MEMO POINTS 1. **Pre-planning** means that the individual makes a conscious decision to use the lump sum to increase a contribution, irrespective of whether it is paid before or after the lump sum is actually received.
2. The contribution could be **paid by** someone else on the individual's behalf e.g. his employer or spouse (¶2402).

3. A **significant increase** is measured as 30% above the contribution which would have been expected in a specified 5 year period, starting two tax years before the tax year in which the lump sum is received. So HMRC look at the pattern of contributions over a period of time to ascertain whether any have been significantly increased.

EXAMPLE In 2011/12, Mr E receives a lump sum of £35,000 on crystallising his pension. He previously made contributions of £10,000 p.a. in the last 6 years. As a result of the lump sum, he contributes £26,000 into another registered pension scheme. The increase in contribution of £16,000 is a "significant increase", because it exceeds 30% of the usual contribution of £10,000. The lump sum received exceeds 1% of the lifetime allowance, and more than 30% of it is used to fund the increased contribution. (16,000/35,000 = 46 %)
So Mr E is taxed on the unauthorised payment of £35,000, and the scheme administrator will be liable to a scheme sanction charge (¶3872).

3852 However, the following **increased contributions** following a lump sum payment are **excluded**, and so no adverse tax consequences result if:
- contributions are made with a view to increasing the eventual benefits, so long as the lump sum was not actually used as the means of increasing the contribution;
- the member had no intention to use a lump sum for this purpose. If he subsequently changes his mind, and uses the lump sum as a contribution, he will not be liable to any tax charge, nor will he be required to prove that his initial intention had changed. However HMRC will be entitled to consider any evidence of pre-planning;
- the individual receives an inheritance before making the contribution;
- the member always contributes a set percentage of his salary every year, and receives an extra large bonus;
- the contribution is based on profits from self-employment; or
- the individual receives a substantial windfall, such as a lottery win.

3. Pension income

3856 The **remaining fund** which is left after the payment of the lump sum must be used to provide a taxable pension which will endure to the end of the member's life. The pension must be paid at least annually, and cannot be guaranteed for a period longer than 10 years. The pension can only be assigned to another person with the agreement of HMRC, such as in the case of a pension sharing order following divorce.

Any pensions paid from funds which **exceed** the lifetime allowance will be taxed at a rate of 25%: see ¶3788.

Structure of pension benefits

3858 s 165 FA 2004 Sch 16 FA 2011

On retirement, a pension may either be:
- **secured**, usually by purchasing a lifetime annuity with scheme funds; or
- unsecured, now officially known as a **drawdown pension**.

Drawdown pensions may only be paid out of money purchase and cash balance arrangements (¶3748). In a drawdown pension, payments are made to the individual either directly out of the actual pension funds, or through the purchase of a short-term annuity.

Drawdown pensions are further divided into two types:
- **flexible** drawdown; and
- **capped** drawdown.

Amounts paid from any of the above arrangements are subject to income tax (¶3664).

MEMO POINTS 1. The former requirement that an individual secure his pension at age 77, either by purchasing an annuity, or by taking an alternatively secured pension, ceased to apply after 5 April 2011. The old rules for unsecured and alternatively secured pensions ceased to apply on that date. For details, see *Tax Memo 2010-2011*. For the transition to the current rules, see ¶3861.

Sch 28 para 2 FA 2004

2. Schemes are also permitted to provide additional pensions (known as bridging pensions) to members until they start to receive their **state pension**, where the aim is to provide the member with broadly the same amount of income throughout retirement.

3. Pensions can be paid in the case of **ill-health and incapacity** where the member has left his employment. These can be subsequently reduced at the discretion of the scheme administrator.
4. Any **reduction** in pension, caused by an insufficiency of funds on a **scheme's winding up**, will not cause the remaining pension income to become taxable unless tax avoidance is involved. SI 2009/1311

Flexible drawdown pensions

3859 Sch 28 FA 2004 Sch 16 FA 2011

In a flexible drawdown pension arrangement:
- there is **no minimum or maximum** amount of pension that has to be taken each year;
- the scheme administrator is not obliged to carry out regular calculations of the available funds.

To qualify as a flexible drawdown in any tax year (from 2011/12 onwards), the individual must be entitled to **at least £20,000 of secured income** for that tax year (the "minimum income threshold"). Sch 28 para 14A FA 2004

Secured income is officially known as "relevant income", and consists of:
- pension payments or annuity payments from a registered pension scheme;
- similar payments under an overseas pension scheme;
- state pensions; and
- payments under the financial assistance scheme (¶3831).

Capped drawdown pensions

3860 Sch 28 para 10 - 10A FA 2004

A capped drawdown pension arrangement must be based around the equivalent annuity that could be purchased with the individual's fund. This is called the **basis amount**.

The maximum amount of pension that can be paid is limited to:
- the basis amount, less
- the amount of any short-term annuity being paid from the same arrangement.

The limits are applied in relation to the individual's **pension year**. The first pension year for an arrangement runs for 12 months from the date when its funds were first designated to provide a drawdown pension, and each subsequent pension year has the same end date. Pension year dates cannot be changed until the individual reaches 75, and unused allowances cannot be carried forward to a later pension year.

The limit for each pension year is **calculated by the scheme administrator** using government-issued actuarial tables. The calculation is normally done at the start of the first pension year, and every three years thereafter until the individual reaches 75.

On arrival at the age of 75:
- the lifetime allowance test must be performed (¶3797); and
- the pension limit is recalculated at the start of each subsequent pension year.

MEMO POINTS 1. A capped drawdown pension works in much the same way as the rules for unsecured and alternatively secured pensions up to 5 April 2011. The **former age distinction**, which allowed payment of a pension of 120% of the basis amount up to age 75, and 90% thereafter, no longer applies.
2. The individual may request a new calculation before the end of any given pension year, but the scheme administrator does not have to agree. The limit must also be recalculated in the event of:
- the purchase of a lifetime annuity out of the fund;
- the use of part or all of the fund to provide a secured pension;
- the designation of additional funds for drawdown use; or
- the issuing of a pension sharing order on divorce.
3. Once the individual is over 75 he can ask the scheme administrator to change the end date of the pension year (for example, to align the dates for different schemes). This can only be done once for any scheme.

EXAMPLE On 30 September 2011 Mr Z, who has not previously drawn any benefits from his pension fund, designates £400,000 to a drawdown pension, and uses money from this fund to buy a short-term annuity. His pension years will run as follows:

Year 1	1 October 2011 to 30 September 2012
Year 2	1 October 2012 to 30 September 2013
and so on.	

At the start of Year 1, the scheme administrator calculates that the maximum drawdown pension Mr Z can receive each year is £22,000. He receives £4,500 from the short-term annuity each year. The maximum capped drawdown pension that he can take is therefore £17,500 (£22,000 – £4,500).

Transitional rules 2011

3861 Sch 28 para 85 – 100 FA 2004

An individual who received an **unsecured pension** before 6 April 2011 and was under 75 at that date can continue to take a drawdown pension at the former rate of 120% of the basis amount until the end of the reference period that was in place on 5 April 2011, or (if earlier) until the benefits are transferred to another registered pension scheme.

An individual who received an **unsecured pension** before 6 April 2011 and reached age 75 on or after 22 June 2010 will become subject to the new drawdown rules at the start of the first pension year beginning on or after 7 April 2010.

An individual who received an **alternatively secured pension** before 6 April 2011 will become subject to the new drawdown rules at the start of the first pension year beginning on or after 7 April 2010.

4. Death benefits

3862 Pension scheme rules may allow a member's remaining funds to be used to pay a lump sum or a pension to his dependants after the his death.

The tax treatment of the payment of benefits after the death of the scheme member changed considerably on 6 April 2011. For the rules applicable in previous years, see *Tax Memo 2010-2011*

Lump sum benefits on death

3863 Sch 29 FA 2004 Sch 16 FA 2011

Lump sum death benefits comprise the following types:
- defined benefits payment;
- payment out of uncrystallised funds;
- pension protection;
- annuity protection;
- payment out of a drawdown pension fund
- trivial commutation;
- winding-up; and
- charity.

The types of death benefit that may be provided by a scheme, and the persons to whom they may be paid, will depend on the scheme rules as well as on statutory restrictions.

MEMO POINTS 1. A **defined benefits payment** is made to a dependant under the terms of the scheme. A common example is the payment of a multiple of salary following death in service. However, a lump sum cannot be a defined benefits payment if it meets the conditions for a pension protection, trivial commutation or winding-up lump sum death benefit.
2. A payment out of **uncrystallised funds** can only be made from paid from a money purchase arrangement or a cash balance arrangement. It is paid from funds that have not yet been put in to payment.
3. A **pension protection** payment can only be made if the deceased was receiving a lifetime annuity or a scheme pension from a money purchase or cash balance scheme. When the pension begins or the annuity is purchased, the recipient can elect to guarantee that a set amount of pension will be provided. If he dies before that amount has been paid, the balance can be paid as a lump sum.
4. An **annuity protection** payment can only be made if the deceased was receiving a scheme pension from a defined benefits (final salary) scheme. When the pension begins, the recipient can elect to guarantee that a set amount of pension will be provided. If he dies before that amount has been paid, the balance can be paid as a lump sum.

5. A payment out of a **drawdown pension** can only be made if the deceased was receiving a drawdown pension that was not funded by a short-term annuity. The remaining funds may be paid out as a lump sum.
6. A **trivial commutation lump sum** is the payment of a dependant's entire remaining entitlement in a single sum to that dependant, where his pension funds are small.
7. A **winding-up lump sum** is the payment of a dependant's entire remaining entitlement in a single sum to that dependant, where the pension fund is being wound up.
8. A **charity** payment is a lump sum paid to a charity if an individual (or dependant) receiving a drawdown pension dies, and there are no other dependants. The charity must be chosen in advance by the deceased.

The tax treatment of the various types of lump sum is summarised in the following table. Any tax charge is normally paid by the scheme administrator by deduction from the lump sum. 3864

Type	Age limit	Limits	Lifetime allowance applies?	Tax treatment
Defined benefit Uncrystallised funds	None[1,2]	Depends on scheme rules	Yes[3]	Died at less than 75: tax free (subject to lifetime allowance) Died at 75+: 55%
Pension protection Annuity protection	None[1]	Capital value of the pension[4]	No	Died before 6 April 2011: 35% Died on or after 6 April 2011: 55%
Drawdown[5]	None[1]	Depends on scheme rules	No	Died before 6 April 2011: 35% Died on or after 6 April 2011: 55%
Trivial commutation Winding-up	None[1,6]	£18,000[7]	No	As pension income of the recipient
Charity	None[8]	Remaining funds	No	Tax free

Notes
1. If the individual died on or after 6 April 2011. If he died before that date, the payment can only be made if he was aged less than 75 when he died.
2. If the individual dies before his 75th birthday, the lump sum must be paid within two years of the date the scheme administrator first knew of his death (or, if earlier, the date the scheme administrator could reasonably have been expected to know of the death).
3. The lifetime allowance is not tested if the individual was at least 75 when he died.
4. The maximum payment is the capital value of the benefits that crystallises for lifetime allowance purposes at the time the pension entitlement initially arose.
5. Formerly known as an unsecured pension fund lump sum death benefit.
6. The former age limit applied to the member at his death.
7. This limit applies separately to each scheme of which the deceased was a member.
8. If the individual died on or after 6 April 2011. If he died before that date, the payment can only be made if he was aged at least 75 when he died.

Lump sum entitlement for schemes existing at 6 April 2006

A pre-existing lump sum entitlement on death is **eligible for** both primary protection and enhanced protection where the lump sum permitted under the old tax rules would have been greater if death had occurred before 6 April 2006. This means that the greater amount will not be liable to tax when death occurs on or after 6 April 2006. 3865

MEMO POINTS 1. For **primary protection** (¶3804), the following conditions must be satisfied: Sch 36 para 11A FA 2004
– the lifetime allowance has already been increased by primary protection;
– a lump sum death benefit is paid; and
– the recipient of the lump sum notifies HMRC that this protection is to apply.
2. For **enhanced protection** (¶3806), the recipient of the lump sum just has to notify HMRC that enhanced protection is to apply to the death benefit. Sch 36 para 15A FA 2004

Dependant's pensions

3866 s 167 FA 2004 Sch 16 FA 2011 Subject to the rules of the scheme, a dependant may be entitled to receive the following types of pension:
– a secured pension;
– an annuity; or
– a drawdown pension.

However, if the scheme is a defined benefits (final salary) type, only a secured pension can be paid.

A **dependant's drawdown pension** may be either flexible or capped, and is subject to the rules described in ¶3859 – ¶3860, except that the lifetime allowance (¶3788) is not taken into account.

MEMO POINTS 1. A **dependant** means:
– a spouse or civil partner of the scheme member when he died;
– if the scheme rules allow, a spouse or civil partner of the scheme member when he first started drawing the pension;
– a child of the scheme member who is aged less than 23, or (if older) was at the time of his death dependent on him because of physical or mental impairment; or
– some other person who was financially dependent on the scheme member at the time of his death because of physical or mental impairment.
2. **Prior to 6 April 2011**, different rules applied, according to the age of the scheme member at the date of his death. For details, see *Tax Memo 2010-2011*.

F. Compliance

3868 When deciding how to comply with the tax rules for pensions, practitioners and scheme administrators are required to self-serve. This means that the legislation and official guidance (particularly the registered pension schemes manual) should be consulted first, before requesting specific advice from HMRC staff.

All scheme **tax payments** must be made electronically.

Unauthorised payments out of a fund

3869 ss 160 - 164 FA 2004 Unauthorised payments out of a pension fund may give rise to a **tax charge** on the individual member, and in some circumstances on the scheme administrator.

Unauthorised payments may occur in any of the following **situations**:
– receiving money or money's worth from a scheme which is not authorised by the scheme rules i.e. before retirement age;
– use of a pension scheme asset with an expected life of less than 50 years e.g. cars, machinery, short leases;
– the sponsoring employer receives a payment not within the scheme rules;
– loans to a member or connected person;
– payment after death for the benefit of a connected person;
– reduction in pension payments to increase the lump sum;
– assignment of the benefits of the scheme in order to avoid a lifetime allowance charge;
– surrender of pension rights in order to avoid a lifetime allowance charge (but not where surrender is required as part of a compliance exercise or to comply with age equality legislation);
– surrender of rights to payments from a lifetime annuity, or a dependant's annuity, is subject to an unauthorised payment income charge; and
– any increase to a member's pension rights, resulting from the death of another member who was connected with him, will be taxable unless the scheme has at least 20 members and every member gains at the same rate. All such increases will be treated as an unauthori-

sed payment, with a further liability to inheritance tax where the deceased member died aged at least 77.

MEMO POINTS 1. 1. HMRC have stated that **small pension overpayments** below £250 are not to be reported, and are therefore not subject to the regime for unauthorised payments. However, overpayments relating to lump sums are not included within this concession. Pensions Tax Simplification Newsletter 19
2. Before 22 June 2010 the limiting age for an increase resulting from the death of another member was 75.
3. When an individual transfers his pension to another pension provider before reaching the age of 55, it is technically an unauthorised pension payment. However, since 6 April 2010 an individual who is at least 50 but under 55 can make such a transfer without incurring a tax charge.

Where unauthorised payments are made, the following tax charges will arise on the **member**: **3870** ss 208, 209 FA 2004
– a higher rate tax charge at 40% on the payment; and
– an additional surcharge of 15%, where the unauthorised payments in the last 12 months are 25% or more of the member's rights under the scheme.

If the **sponsoring employer** receives an unauthorised payment, the additional surcharge will apply where the total unauthorised payments within a 12 month period reaches 25% or more of the scheme value. The employer must report the payment to HMRC.

Furthermore, a higher rate tax charge (known as a **sanction charge**) on the fund value will be payable by the **scheme administrator** where a scheme: **3872** s 239 FA 2004
– makes one or more unauthorised payments in the year (excluding a benefit in kind for the use of a non-wasting asset with an expected life of at least 50 years);
– borrows more than the permitted amount; or
– is deregistered.

The amount of the unauthorised payment will be increased for any **amount withheld** by the scheme administrator to cover a sanction charge. Any excess withheld which is subsequently paid to the member is not liable to tax again. s 160(4A) FA 2004

If the member or sponsoring employer has suffered tax on the unauthorised payment, the charge on the administrator is **reduced** by the lesser of the tax paid and 25% of the unauthorised payment.

EXAMPLE Mr F has transferred an asset to a registered pension scheme and received £20,000 more than its market worth. He also uses a scheme car and the related benefit in kind is £3,000.
The total unauthorised payment is £23,000, and Mr F suffers higher rate tax of £9,200. (23,000 @ 40%)
The administrator suffers a tax charge on the £20,000 only, because the other payment is a benefit in kind on a non-wasting asset.
The charge is calculated as follows:

		£
Authorised payment at 40%	20,000 @ 40%	8,000
Less: Tax paid by member up to 25% of unauthorised payment	20,000 @ 25%	(5,000)
Tax charge on scheme		3,000

In the following cases, a tax charge may be **waived** where: **3874** s 268 FA 2004 SI 2005/3452
– the administrator acted in good faith, and it would not be just and reasonable for him to be liable to a lifetime allowance charge; or
– it would not be just and reasonable for either the member or administrator to suffer a surcharge.

A claim for waiver must be made within the following **time limits**:
– for a company claimant, 6 years; and
– for an individual, 5 years and 10 months after the tax year of charge,

unless an assessment for tax has already been received, when the relevant time limit is 2 years after the date of the assessment.

Deregistration

3876 ss 157, 242 FA 2004

HMRC may decide to deregister the scheme under any of the following **circumstances**:
- unauthorised payments exceed 25% of the fund;
- failure to provide information;
- failure to pay tax due; or
- lack of control of scheme assets which allows the employer to benefit.

At the date of deregistration, a **tax charge** at 40% is levied on the value of the scheme assets, for which the administrator is liable. If the remaining funds are paid out to members or returned to employers, this will be an unauthorised payment.

Reporting by the scheme

3878 s 250 FA 2004

A pension scheme must complete a **self-assessment tax return** by 31 January following the tax year in order to obtain a tax repayment or to report taxable income. At the moment this can only be done via a paper return.

In addition, a **pension scheme return**, which requires details about the scheme, may be issued at random.

MEMO POINTS 1. Those promoting, and in some cases using, schemes and arrangements designed to exploit the registered pension scheme rules in order to obtain a **tax advantage** are obliged to report these to HMRC (¶2215 onwards).
2. When reporting events, a letter giving details is not sufficient to satisfy the required compliance obligations. The appropriate return must be completed and submitted at the right time. It is unnecessary to complete a tax return unless the scheme has to report taxable income or claim a repayment, or if a return is issued by HMRC.

3880 s 254 FA 2004

Calendar quarter returns (also known as the "accounting for tax return") are required in the following situations:
- payment of a short service refund lump sum;
- lump sums paid on death before the age of 75;
- authorised surplus is repaid to the employer;
- exceeding the lifetime allowance; and
- on deregistration.

The due date for submission is 45 days after the end of each quarter, and the tax must be paid electronically. Nil returns are not required.

s 251 FA 2004

An **event report** will be required in many circumstances, including:
- when unauthorised payments are made;
- any change in member numbers;
- where a member receives benefits early;
- lump sum payments for serious ill-health;
- tax-free lump sums where the transitional rules have been applied;
- details of benefits taken before the normal retirement age; and
- on the scheme's winding up.

The online form APSS300 contains full details.

3882 Pensions Tax Simplification Newsletter 27

Online reporting is available for most forms, and from 16 October 2007, it is **mandatory** for pension schemes to file the following information electronically in the prescribed format:
- applications to register a pension scheme;
- pension scheme returns;
- calendar quarter returns;
- scheme administrator's declarations;
- event reports; and
- notifications of winding up and the termination of the scheme administrator's appointment.

Scheme administrators and practitioners can choose to receive automatic **notices and reminders** electronically, as long as they have registered their email address with HMRC. Otherwise, paper notices and reminders will only be received if the paper option has specifically been chosen at registration.

Penalties

The penalties for **incorrect tax returns** submitted after 1 April 2010 are the same as those for income tax returns generally: see ¶4532. 3884

Penalties for late payment of tax and late filing of returns apply from 1 April 2110: see ¶4542 and ¶4545.

In addition, the following specific penalties are levied for **non-compliance** with pension scheme reporting requirements:

Offence	Penalty	Reference (FA 2004)
Failure to provide a pension scheme return	£100 initially, with possible £60 per day for continuing failure	s 257(1)
Providing an incorrect pension scheme return	Maximum £3,000	s 257(4)
Failure to provide documents when requested in a notice	Maximum of £300 initially with possible £60 per day for continuing failure	s 259(1)
Failure to preserve documents	Maximum £3,000	s 258
Fraudulently or negligently providing false information	Maximum £3,000	s 259(4)
Failure to submit a calendar quarter return	Quarterly penalties of at least £100	s 260(1)
Providing an incorrect calendar quarter return	Difference between amount of correct tax due and amount shown on return	s 260(6)
Making a false statement in order to obtain tax relief, tax repayment or benefit from an unauthorised payment	Maximum £3,000	s 264(1)
Assisting someone to make a false statement	Maximum £3,000	s 264(2)
Deliberately winding up a scheme in order to provide lump sum benefits	Maximum £3,000 per member who receives a lump sum	s 265

SECTION 3

Unregistered pension schemes

Unapproved pension schemes are correctly referred to as **employer financed retirement benefit schemes**. There is no facility for such schemes to be registered with HMRC, and no tax advantages apply. Unregistered schemes do not count towards either the annual (¶3771) or lifetime allowances (¶3788). 3900 ss 245 - 249 FA 2004

Pre-existing rights for schemes which were established before to 6 April 2006 are protected.

MEMO POINTS There are two types of unapproved pension schemes:

1. A **funded scheme (FURBS)** is one where the employer makes arrangements for future benefits by paying into an insurance policy or by setting up a separate trust fund, thereby ringfencing assets purely for the purpose of providing pension benefits.
2. An **unfunded scheme**, where the employer promises to pay a pension or other similar benefits in the future, but makes no formal provision beforehand.

Changes made by FA2011

3901 Unregistered pension schemes will generally fall within the scope of the new rules for the taxation of disguised remuneration (¶3039). This is likely to reduce their effectiveness considerably.

RPSM 15104580 Following the decrease in the annual allowance (¶3771) for 2011/12, HMRC will look closely at any situation where it appears that contributions have been switched from a registered pension scheme to an unfunded scheme. Anti-avoidance provisions may apply.

Schemes set up after 5 April 2006

3902 s 245 FA 2004 For a **funded scheme**, the following apply:
- employer contributions (and the scheme administration costs) are only deductible from trading income when pension benefits are actually paid and taxed on the employee;
- employer contributions are not taxable on the employee nor liable to NIC;
- scheme income and gains are taxed at the rate applicable to trusts (¶7308);
- the lump sum received at retirement is fully chargeable to income tax;
- any non-cash benefits received are taxable regardless of whether they are received in conjunction with cash benefits, although there are certain exemptions (¶3667);
- lump sum death benefits are liable to both income tax and inheritance tax;
- the value of the fund (even a discretionary fund) forms part of an individual's death estate for the purposes of inheritance tax; and
- no NIC is due on benefits paid if these are within the limits which could be paid out by a registered scheme (which is unlikely).

s 246A FA 2004 MEMO POINTS Where an employer has paid contributions to a **registered scheme**, but the related benefits are reduced because benefits are paid out of an unregistered scheme instead, tax relief will be denied on any expenses associated with providing the unregistered benefits. However if the employer has already been denied relief on the contributions into the registered scheme, he will still obtain relief on the cost of the benefits.

3904 s 248 FA 2004 Where an employer guarantees benefits (whether cash or non-cash) in an **unfunded scheme**, the cost of the guarantee is assessed on the employee as a benefit in kind. The form of the guarantee could be insurance or asset backing.

Transitional protection for pre-April 2006 schemes

3906 Sch 36 FA 2004 The following protections apply to **funded schemes**:
- a proportion of the pension commencement lump sum which relates to the indexed market value of the fund at 6 April 2006 will be tax free, where either employer contributions or the fund income and gains have already been taxed on the employee. If employer contributions ceased before 6 April 2006, the lump sum will remain completely tax free;
- benefits will be exempt from NIC if they derive from contributions paid between 1999 and 2006 which were themselves subject to NIC; and
- SI 2006/210 lump sum death benefits which were provided under the scheme rules before 6 April 2006 will remain exempt from income tax and inheritance tax. Death benefits relating to post-6 April contributions and funding will be liable to both income tax and inheritance tax.

CHAPTER 7

Sundry income and anti-avoidance provisions

OUTLINE ¶¶

3945 Income not assessed under the main heading (such as employment, trade and savings) is assessable to tax as sundry income.

The tax legislation also specifically includes certain receipts within sundry income, and charges certain transactions under anti-avoidance legislation.

3947 The **main** anti-avoidance provisions deal with the following areas:

Subject	¶¶
Pre-owned assets	¶3968
Transactions in securities	¶4010
Transactions in land	¶4052
Structured finance arrangements	¶4064
Life policy gains	¶4066
Offshore funds	¶4110
Sale of future earnings	¶4132
Transfer of assets abroad	¶4137

By their nature, anti-avoidance rules are complex, and expert advice should be sought if in doubt.

MEMO POINTS **Disclosure** of tax saving schemes to HMRC is also required within a very strict time limit (¶2215).

SECTION 1

Sundry income assessments

A. General principles

3950 s 687 ITTOIA 2005 To be taxed as sundry income, receipts must have the **quality** of income, and be comparable to receipts which would otherwise be assessable as trading income or savings income. Income received on an occasional basis under an enforceable contract (such as certain commissions) is commonly taxed as sundry income. For example, if a sole trader owned a yacht which was not used for the purposes of the trade, any receipts for occasionally chartering that yacht would not form part of his trading profit, but would be taxable as sundry income.

If an item is gratuitous, such as a receipt by way of a gift or gambling winnings, it will not fall within the scope of sundry income. Income which derives from a hobby is also not taxable.

3952 Sundry income is generally taxable when received, at the non-savings income **rates** (¶4408) unless otherwise stated.

Expenses which directly relate to the receipt are allowable against sundry income. For example, where a patent right is sold, selling costs would be allowable.

3954 s 152 ITA 2007 **Losses** arising from transactions which would be taxed as miscellaneous income, if profitable, are set against the earliest arising other miscellaneous income in the same or subsequent tax years.

A claim must be made within 4 years of from the end of the year of assessment when the loss arose.

B. Specific sources of income

In addition to income arising from various anti-avoidance provisions, the following amounts are **specifically taxable**: 3956 s 30 TMA 1970

Taxable income		¶¶
Assessments to recover tax paid in error		¶4564
Receipts from intellectual property, including:		
	the sale of patent rights	¶707
	know-how	¶6030
	other income such as royalties	¶4347
Income assessed on the settlor of a trust		¶7344
Amounts received after cessation of a trade		¶2466

Commissions

In general, **ordinary retail customers** will not be liable to tax in respect of any commissions, discounts or cashbacks received by them when purchasing goods or services, including where commission is received on a life policy holder's own policy. 3958 SP 4/97 EIM 64615

Where a **trader or professional** receives commission, but passes it on to the customer, he will be taxable on the receipt, but will also be able to claim a deduction for the amount passed on (depending on the facts, this may be under the trading rules, or as sundry income). Where no commission passes through the trader's hands, it has no effect on his tax position.

See ¶74 for further details.

Compensation

The tax treatment of compensation **depends on** the cause of the claim. In certain cases, compensation is exempt from tax, as set out below. In others, the compensation will be taxable where it is in fact related to loss of income and there is a close relationship between the person's day to day activities and the payment. Examples of the latter would be certain trading receipts (¶129), and damages paid in relation to loss of employment (¶3060). 3960

Personal injury Damages will be exempt from income tax where they consist wholly or partly of **periodical payments** (including annuities), due either as a result of an order of the court or by the voluntary agreement of the defendant. 3962 ss 731 – 733 ITTOIA 2005

The exemption applies with respect to the person entitled to the compensation under the agreement or court order, and also to:
– any person receiving the payments on his behalf; or
– any trustee receiving the payments on a trust under which, during his lifetime, the person entitled to the compensation is the only beneficiary.

For the treatment of **lump sum payments**, see ¶5236.

MEMO POINTS Personal injury is **defined** for these purposes as any disease and any impairment of a person's physical or mental condition. Damages in respect of death caused by personal injury are also exempt.

Mis-sold pensions Certain capital sums received as compensation for loss (or likely loss) in relation to personal pensions is exempt from income (and capital gains) tax. The compensation must relate to **bad investment advice** given between 28 April 1988 and 30 June 1994. From 1 July 1994 new statutory safeguards were introduced to protect consumers. 3964 s 148 FA 1996

MEMO POINTS 1. Bad investment advice is **defined** for these purposes as investment advice in respect of which action has been brought (or may be brought) against the adviser for:
– negligence;

– breach of contract or fiduciary obligation; or
– a contravention of the Financial Services Act 1986, or the Financial Services and Markets Act 2000.
2. The **exemption applies** where the individual:
– joined a personal pension scheme or took out a retirement annuity contract while eligible (or reasonably likely to become eligible) to join an occupational pension scheme;
– ceased to be a member of (or ceased to pay into) an occupational pension scheme and instead joined a personal pension scheme or took out a retirement annuity contract;
– transferred accrued rights under an occupational pension scheme into a personal pension scheme; or
– ceased to be a member of an occupational pension scheme and instead entered into arrangements for securing relevant benefits by means of an annuity contract.
3. Any **interest** paid on the whole or part of the capital sum falling within the exemption will itself be exempt from income tax to the extent that it relates to a period ending on or before the earliest date on which the amount of the capital sum is first determined.

Income from domestic microgeneration

3966
ss 782A, 782B ITTOIA 2005

Income arising to an individual from:
– the **sale of electricity** generated by a microgeneration system; and
– the receipt by an individual of a **renewables obligation certificate** in connection with the generation of electricity by a microgeneration system;
are exempt from income tax, if the following conditions are met:
– the system is installed at or near domestic premises occupied by the individual; and
– the individual intends that the amount of electricity generated will not significantly exceed the amount consumed in the premises.

MEMO POINTS 1. **Microgeneration** is the production of electricity from renewable sources and which does not exceed 50 kilowatts. (The statute lists the approved sources, which include any type that results in reduced greenhouse gas emissions.)
2. Renewables obligation **certificates** are issued by Ofgen to householders who produce electricity from qualifying renewable sources.
3. A **gain on disposal** by an individual of a renewables obligation certificate which he acquired in connection with the generation of electricity by a microgeneration system is exempt from capital gains tax, if conditions **a**. and **b**. above are met (¶5232).

SECTION 2

Pre-owned assets

3968
Sch 15 FA 2004 SI 2005/724

An annual income tax charge applies to an individual who enjoys an asset (either for free or at below market value) which he either previously owned or financed, and the asset is not within the scope of inheritance tax (IHT). The aim is to charge income tax on transactions which have been arranged in order to avoid IHT.

There are detailed exemptions (discussed below) which reduce the scope of the charge. A **de minimis annual charge of £5,000** applies, which effectively excludes assets worth less than about £100,000.

An individual may elect to ignore the pre-owned assets provisions and treat the asset as chargeable to IHT instead.

3970

Deemed taxable income (like a benefit in kind) arises when **all** of the following circumstances apply (subject to the exemptions):
a. a person (the donor) has owned an asset at any time after 17 March 1986;
b. he then ceases to own the asset, or he provides funds for the acquisition of the asset which is now owned by another person (the donee);
c. the donor still derives some enjoyment (such as use or occupation) of the asset or replacement asset, either alone or with others; and

d. the asset, or the value derived from the asset, is not included in his estate for inheritance tax purposes.

MEMO POINTS **Occupation** includes: HMRC Technical Guidance 4.6
a. use for storage;
b. where only the donor can access the property and he actually uses it; or
c. a second home which is occupied on occasion by the donee and donor, except where it is:
- let to someone else;
- only occupied by the donor on his own for less than 2 weeks a year; or
- occupied by the donor with the donee for less than 1 month per year.

Examples of situations which do not constitute occupation, according to HMRC, are:
- social visits (excluding overnight stays);
- baby sitting;
- dog walking on gifted land; and
- temporary stays caused by convalescence or redecoration.

EXAMPLE In 2001 Mrs C settled £200,000 in a trust for the benefit of her children. The trust purchased a flat for £150,000 which is occupied by her after 5 April 2005.
She is enjoying the benefit of an asset which was acquired with funds originally owned by her, and the pre-owned assets rules will apply.

A. Exemptions

Types of transfer

The rules will not apply to any of the following transfers: **3972** Sch 15 para 11 FA 2004
a. transfers where the asset remains in the donor's estate and therefore **liable to IHT**, such as where the asset is:
- returned to the donor; or
- caught by the gift with reservation rules;

b. **gifts** to a UK charity, political party, housing associations, employee trusts, maintenance funds and gifts for national purposes (¶6442 onwards); and
c. transfers arising from a **deed of variation** (¶6617), or the giving of a loan guarantee for the acquisition of property by another individual.

MEMO POINTS 1. Where asset B **derives** its value from another asset (asset A), and asset B is included within the donor's estate, asset A will not be liable to the pre-owned asset rules. For example, if an individual occupies land which is owned by his personal company, the land is exempt from the pre-owned asset rules, because the company shares, which derive their value from the land, are included within the individual's estate. If asset B is worth less than 80% of asset A (e.g. land is transferred to a company when the donor only holds 40% of the shares), there will be a tax charge in relation to asset A, but it is proportionately reduced for the value which is included in asset B.
2. Where the value of an asset in an individual's estate is reduced by an **excluded liability**, the amount covered by the liability is liable to the pre-owned asset rules. An excluded liability is a debt connected to the asset as a result of an associated operation (¶6925). For example, an asset is sold but the consideration is left outstanding as a loan. If the asset and loan form part of an associated operation, the amount of the loan will be liable to the pre-owned asset rules.
3. In HMRC's view, **disclaimers** are not disposals, so the pre-owned asset rules would not apply where a beneficiary of a will disclaims his inheritance.
4. The disposal of an interest in a partnership is unlikely to give rise to a pre-owned assets charge in any circumstances.
5. In a **reversionary lease scheme**, a donor grants a long lease of a property which does not take effect until a specified future date. Such gifts made before 9 March 1999 are not gifts with reservation of benefit, and the pre-owned assets income tax charge therefore applies. If the donor acquired a freehold interest in the property more than 7 years before the gift, HMRC consider that the gifts with reservation rules do not apply. An income tax charge will therefore arise unless:
- the lease contains terms which are beneficial to the donor, for example payment of maintenance costs by the lessee; or
- the donor elects for the gift with reservation rules to apply (¶4004).

Circumstances of the donor

3974 In addition, the following situations are outside the scope of the rules, where the donor:
a. gives **full consideration** (i.e. arm's length value) in money or money's worth in return for the enjoyment of the tangible asset (land or chattels);
b. shares the asset with the donee and enjoys a negligible benefit (¶6948); or
c. reoccupies the gifted land as a result of a **change in circumstances** and all the conditions of ¶6947 are satisfied.

Foreign aspects

3976 Sch 15 para 12 FA 2004 The rules will not apply when, during the year of assessment, a person is:
– **not resident** in the UK (¶4154); or
– **domiciled abroad** (¶6380), unless the property is situated in the UK.

MEMO POINTS 1. Where a person **becomes UK domiciled**, having previously been non-UK domiciled, the rules do not apply to overseas property which was put into a trust when he was domiciled abroad. However, foreign property directly owned will be within the scope of the rules.
2. The pre-owned asset rules do not apply to **foreign trust property** where the settlor of the trust is domiciled abroad.

EXAMPLE Mr A is domiciled in Germany but UK resident, and occupies a house in Berlin which is owned by a UK incorporated company. The shares of the company are owned by a trust of which Mr A is the settlor.
The house is exempt from the pre-owned asset rules.
However, the company shares are within the scope, because they are situated in the UK.

B. Chargeable amount

3978 The calculation of the taxable amount depends on the **type of property** enjoyed by the donor, classified as follows:
– tangible assets generally (¶3982);
– land and buildings (¶3986);
– chattels (¶3992); and
– intangible assets ((¶3996)).

MEMO POINTS It is possible for **more than one charge** to be levied under these rules, and there is relief in this case.

3980 SI 2005/724 Each calculation method relies on **common terms**, which are defined in the following table.

Term	Definition
Value	Open market value
Valuation date	6 April or if later, the start of the taxable period Land and chattels are only revalued once every 5 years
Taxable period	Year of assessment, or part of the year, when the rules apply

Tangible assets

3982 Sch 15 para 10 FA 2004 SI 2005/724 reg 5 **Excluded transactions** The following cases are **excluded** from the rules applying to land and chattels:
a. transfers to one's spouse;
b. transfers to an interest in possession trust in which the spouse retains an interest (although HMRC consider that a gift into a settlor-interested trust, with a subsequent interest in possession for the spouse, does not come within this exclusion);
c. transfers for the maintenance of the family (¶6408);

d. a transfer of the whole interest in the asset (except for any rights expressly reserved by the donor, such as a right of way) made:
– at arm's length to an unconnected party; or
– between connected persons, on terms which might be expected if made at arm's length between unconnected persons;
e. a transfer of part of an interest in the asset made:
– at arm's length to an unconnected party; or
– between connected persons, on terms which might be expected if made at arm's length between unconnected persons and either the consideration was not in cash (nor in a form convertible into cash), or the disposal occurred before 7 March 2005;
f. an outright gift of money (in any currency) made at least 7 years before the donor is able to enjoy the asset acquired with the gift and in any event any cash gifted before 6 April 1998; and
g. an outright gift to an individual which is covered by the annual exemption (¶6430) or small gifts exemption (¶6432).

MEMO POINTS 1. **Spouse** includes an ex-spouse, where transfer is made under a court order. The exemption also applies after the spouse has disposed of the asset to another party.
2. The definition of a **connected person** is the one used for IHT purposes (¶6384).
3. The **exclusion** at **e**. above means that the following are not caught:
– sales to commercial providers in respect of equity release schemes;
– a child moves into the house to care for his ill parent, and is given an equitable interest in the home as consideration; and
– a father brings his son into partnership, and gives him a share in the business in return for looking after the day to day running of it.

EXAMPLE
1. Mr A sells 75% of his house to his niece for an arm's length value price on 4 April 2005. His niece moves into the house with Mr A, and she pays all of the running costs. Because Mr A did not sell his whole interest, the exemption at **d**. above will not apply. The exemption at **e**. will also not apply because the sale occurred after 7 March 2005. It may, however, be argued that a general exemption should apply because Mr A enjoys a negligible benefit (¶6948).
2. Mr D gives cash to his son in January 2002, who uses it to purchase a house. In May 2011 Mr D occupies the house, but as 9 years have elapsed since the gift, the exemption under **f**. above applies.

Reducing the taxable income If a transaction is not excluded, the taxable amount can be reduced if the donor makes a **payment** to the donee in return for his continuing enjoyment of the asset. The payment must be made: 3984
– under a legal obligation which directly relates to the use of the asset; and
– in the same tax year as the enjoyment arises.

MEMO POINTS 1. **Legal advice** must be sought in making such an arrangement.
2. Payments for **insurance and maintenance** must be made to the donee. Direct payments to service providers will not count.
3. Where the donor pays **full value** for the enjoyment of the asset, there will be no tax charge under these rules. This may be an attractive option, especially if the donee has little other income or has expenses or even losses available to offset against the income, or rent a room relief (¶2781) is relevant.

EXAMPLE On 3 April 2011, Mr B pays £1,000 in advance for the occupation of his house in 2011/12. This payment will not reduce the pre-owned asset charge in 2011/12, because it was not made in that tax year.

Land and buildings **Taxable income will arise** where land is occupied by an individual who either: 3986 Sch 15 paras 3 - 5 FA 2004
a. previously owned the land, or some other asset which was sold to finance the land (the "disposal condition"); or
b. provided the money for the purchase of the land (the "contribution condition").
The chargeable amount is the **appropriate rental value**, after deducting any payments made in return for occupation of the land. In most cases the appropriate rental value will be fixed for a period of 5 years.

MEMO POINTS 1. Where a **new interest in land is created**, such as a lease granted by the owner of a freehold, this will be treated as a part disposal of the existing interest.
2. The **contribution condition** will not be met if a lender resides in property purchased by another person using money loaned to him by the lender.

EXAMPLE

1. Mr A gave his son a painting worth £60,000 in 1993, which was sold for £150,000 in 2000. The son used these proceeds to purchase a house for Mr A, and so a charge arises if he still occupies the house after 5 April 2005, based on its value on 6 April 2005.

2. Mr B gave his daughter cash of £100,000 in 2000. She used the money to purchase a large house in 2001 which is immediately occupied by them both. Ignoring any exemptions, a charge will arise because Mr B helped to finance the purchase of the house he occupies after 5 April 2005.

3988 The appropriate rental value is calculated by using the following formula:

$$\text{Rental value for the taxable period} \times \frac{\text{Value of interest transferred}}{\text{Value of whole interest in land}}$$

The **rental value for the taxable period** is the rent which would have been payable for the period if the property had been let under a landlord's repairing lease. This is fixed for a period of 5 years.

The **value of the interest transferred** is as shown in the following table:

Land transferred	The value of the land
Donor contributes funds to donee's acquisition of land	The value which can be reasonably attributed to those funds
Proceeds of donor's property disposal are used by donee to acquire land which donor subsequently enjoys	The value which can be reasonably related to that disposal

The **value of the whole interest** in the land is the value of the interest owned by the donor before the transfer.

The values of the interest transferred, and of the whole interest, are measured at a specified valuation date (¶3980), and the valuations are fixed for 5 years.

In most cases, where the whole interest of the land is transferred, the appropriate rental value will just be the rental value for the taxable period because the fraction becomes 1.

MEMO POINTS 1. A **landlord's repairing lease** is one in which:
– the tenant undertakes to pay all taxes, rates and charges usually paid by the tenant; and
– the landlord undertakes to bear the costs of the repairs, insurance and other necessary expenses to maintain the property.

Where other expenses are also included in a market rent, such as heating, a deduction should be made to recognise this.

2. Where a **sale at undervalue** occurs between the donor and donee, the value of the interest transferred is reduced by:

$$\frac{MV - P}{MV}$$

where MV is the market value at the date of sale, and P is the price paid by the donee.

EXAMPLE

1. If Mr A owned the freehold interest and transferred his whole interest to Mr B, the interest disposed of equals the original interest held, and so the whole rental value is taken into account. However, if Mr A granted a lease to Mr B, representing 50% of the value of the freehold, only 50% of the rental value would be taken into account.

2. Mr C gave his son a painting worth £100,000 in 1994, which was sold for £300,000 in 2005. The son used these proceeds to purchase a house for Mr C, costing £400,000, and valued at £500,000 on 6 April 2011. The usual rent under a landlord's repairing lease would be £10,000, and Mr C occupies the house for 11 months in 2011/12 until February 2012. The calculation is as follows:

$$£10{,}000 \times \frac{£300{,}000}{£500{,}000} \times \frac{11}{12}$$

The chargeable amount is £5,500.

3. Mr D gave his daughter £100,000 in cash in 2001. She used the money to purchase a large house in 2002 for £300,000 which is immediately occupied by them both. Mr D occupies the house for 12 months in 2011/12, and the rent under a landlord's repairing lease would be £25,000. The house is valued at £400,000 on 6 April 2011. The calculation is:

The chargeable amount is £6,250. $$£25{,}000 \times \frac{£100{,}000}{£400{,}000}$$

If Mr D then occupies the house subsequently, the resulting annual taxable income will be £6,250 for the next 4 years.

4. Mr E sold half of his house at an undervalue of £140,000 in October 2008, when open market value was £200,000. The value of the whole house at the date of transfer was £450,000, and its value at 6 April 2011 was £475,000. The rent payable under a landlord's repairing lease would be £14,000.

The value of the interest transferred is £60,000 $$£200{,}000 \times \left(\frac{£200{,}000 - 140{,}000}{£200{,}000}\right)$$

The chargeable amount is £1,768. $$£14{,}000 \times \frac{£60{,}000}{£475{,}000}$$

Chattels A chattel is defined as any **tangible movable property**, such as a painting or statue. Taxable income will arise if either a disposal condition or a contribution condition applies (defined as in ¶3986 but reading "chattel" for "land"). **3992** Sch 15 paras 6 – 7 FA 2004

The **chargeable amount** the appropriate amount (see below), deducting any payments made in return for enjoyment of the chattel.

EXAMPLE In 2003 Mrs F gave her niece a set of statues worth £500,000. Because of the large insurance cost for removal and upkeep, the statues remain at Mrs F's house.
A pre-owned asset income charge will arise because Mrs F is still able to enjoy the statues.

The **appropriate amount** is calculated by using the following formula: **3994**

$$\text{Interest charge for the taxable period} \times \frac{\text{Value of interest transferred}}{\text{Value of whole interest in the chattel}}$$

The **interest charge** is calculated by taking the official interest rate (¶9969) in force at the valuation date and applying it to the value of the chattel at that date.

The **value of the interest transferred** is as shown in the following table:

Chattel transferred	The value of the chattel
Donor contributes funds to donee's acquisition of chattel	The value which can be reasonably attributed to those funds
Proceeds of donor's property disposal are used by donee to acquire chattel which donor subsequently enjoys	The value which can be reasonably related to that disposal

The **value of the whole interest** in the chattel is the value of the interest owned by the donor before the transfer.

Both the value of the interest transferred, and oif the whole interest, are measured at a specified valuation date (¶3980).

In most cases, where the whole interest of the chattel is transferred, the appropriate rental value will be the rental value for the taxable period because the fraction becomes 1.

MEMO POINTS 1. Where a **new interest in a chattel is created**, this will be treated as a part disposal of the existing interest.
2. Where a **sale at undervalue** occurs between the donor and donee, the following formula is used to calculate the proportion of the chattel's value to be taken into account:

$$\frac{MV - P}{MV}$$

where MV is the market value at the date of sale, and P is the price paid by the donee.

EXAMPLE The statues from the example in ¶3992 are valued at £600,000 at 6 April 2011. The prescribed rate of interest is (say) 4.75%. Mrs F pays the niece £10,000 on 6 April each year towards the insurance costs, under a legal obligation.
The chargeable amount is calculated as follows:

		£
Appropriate amount	4.75% × £600,000	28,500
Less: Payment made		(10,000)
Chargeable amount		18,500

Intangible assets

3996 Sch 15 paras 8 - 9 FA 2004

Intangible assets are **all assets other than land and chattels**, such as shares, insurance policies and cash.

Where a donor is able to benefit from such an asset, formerly owned by him, which has been **transferred into a trust** where he retains an interest (a settlor-interested trust), a charge will arise.

The asset will be **chargeable** when both of the following conditions are satisfied:
- the income from the property in the trust can be attributable to the settlor (¶7344), excluding cases where only the settlor's spouse is able to benefit from the trust assets; and
- the trust was created, or the property was added to the trust, after 18 March 1986.

MEMO POINTS 1. A **discretionary trust** used in connection with death benefits from life assurance, or pension arrangements will not be subject to the pre-owned asset rules, because the settlor cannot benefit from the trust after death.
2. Life insurance policies, taken out by **partnerships** to provide funds for the acquisition by the other partners of a deceased partner's share of the business, are not caught by these rules if there is no surrender value for the insured partner.

3998 The chargeable amount in respect of the asset is **calculated** using the following formula:

(Interest charge on asset for taxable period) less (tax already payable)

Where:

a. interest charge is calculated by taking the official interest rate (¶9969) in force at the valuation date and applying it to the value of the asset at the valuation date (which, unlike tangibles, will occur every year); and

ss 461, 624 ITTOIA 2005 ss 720 - 730 ICTA 1988 ss 77, 86 TCGA 1992

b. tax already payable is the amount of income or capital gains tax payable as a result of other existing provisions as follows:
- income attributed to the settlor where he retains an interest in the trust (¶7344);
- gains on life policies (¶4066);
- deemed income on the transfer of assets abroad (¶4137); and
- gains attributed to the settlor of a non-resident trust (¶7608).

It is irrelevant whether the donor pays for the enjoyment of the asset. Such payments will not reduce the taxable amount.

EXAMPLE Mr E transfers his share portfolio, worth £150,000 at 6 April 2011, into a discretionary trust of which he is a beneficiary. Mr E pays income tax of £1,000 under the settlor-interested trust provisions. The official rate of interest is (say) 4.75%.
The chargeable amount is £6,125 (4.75 % × £150,000) – £1,000

C. Tax charge

4000 Sch 15 para 13 FA 2004

The chargeable amount is assessable to income tax as sundry income. It is important to note that there is **no refund facility**, and the only form of redress would be to make an error or mistake claim (¶4572).

Where the aggregate chargeable amount for all pre-owned assets does not exceed the **de minimis limit** of £5,000 in a year of assessment, no charge to income tax will arise. For land and chattels, this de minimis limit is tested before any payments by the donor are set off.

Where a charge applies for only part of a year, the £5,000 exemption is not pro-rated. If the chargeable amount exceeds £5,000, the **whole amount** is liable to income tax.

EXAMPLE Taking the example at ¶3994, if the donor had paid £26,000 instead of £10,000, the chargeable amount would have been:

		£
Appropriate amount	4.75% × £600,000	28,500
Less: Payment made		(26,000)
Chargeable amount		2,500

The de minimis limit is exceeded by the appropriate amount of £28,500, and so income tax will still be levied on the chargeable amount of £2,500.

When **multiple charges** to income tax arise, these are to be dealt with as follows: 4002 Sch 15 paras 18 – 19 FA 2004

Situation	Example	Amount charged to tax
A donor is liable to the charge under the provisions for land or chattels, and also to the provisions relating to settlor-interested trusts reflecting the value of the same asset.	The donor occupies land which is owned by a company, and he is the settlor of a trust which owns the company's shares.	The higher amount resulting from the: – tangible asset calculation; and – intangible asset calculation.
A charge arises under these provisions and a charge also arises under the employment benefits regime (¶3240).	The donor occupies accommodation provided by his employer, which was originally owned by him.	The charge resulting from the employment rules takes priority. Any excess charge computed under the pre-owned asset rules will also remain chargeable.

D. Opting out

An **election** can be made (on official form IHT500) to treat the asset as property to which the **gift with reservation provisions apply** (¶6935). This takes the asset outside the scope of the pre-owned asset rules, but includes it within the person's estate for IHT purposes. The election will have effect for all subsequent tax years during which the person enjoys the use of the asset. 4004 Sch 15 paras 21 – 22 FA 2004

Alternatively, a person may choose to **dismantle** an arrangement in order to avoid a pre-owned asset charge.

MEMO POINTS 1. The election is likely to be **beneficial** when no IHT will be payable on the asset because of reliefs or exemptions, or if the donor cannot afford to pay the income tax charge. The donee should be informed when an election is made.
2. If the assets are heldin a **settlor-interested trust**, an election is only available if:
– the property remains within the trust; and
– any income arising in the trust is treated as income of the donor.
3. For **capital gains tax purposes**, it should be noted that where an election is made, there will be no automatic uplift in value of the asset on death, even though the asset is liable to IHT. Where the asset is a house principal private residence relief (¶6166) would be available if the donee occupies it after the donor's death.
4. If property is **jointly owned** by a married couple or civil partners, each partner must make an election if they both wish the income tax charge not to apply. An election can, however, be made by only one partner if the other chooses to pay the charge.

EXAMPLE Some years ago, Mr A gifted his house to Miss B, his daughter, when it was worth £300,000. He decides to make an election, and subsequently dies when the house is worth £800,000. IHT will be levied on £800,000, but Miss B's base cost for CGT purposes is only £300,000.

4006 Sch 15 para 23 FA 2004

The **time limit** for the election is 31 January following the initial year of the donor's enjoyment: that is, **the tax return filing date for the year in question**.

An election can be withdrawn or amended by a living donor at any time before the time limit, but becomes irrevocable thereafter.

4008 SI 2005/724 reg 6, SI 2005/3441

Multiple charges to IHT will not occur in relation to a **home loan scheme**, where IHT could be levied on death, and also on the potentially exempt transfer arising from the transfer of debt within the previous 7 years. Such a scheme involves the creation of a trust which acquires the settlor's asset in exchange for an IOU. The IOU is then gifted to a second trust which is outside the settlor's estate, but is a potentially exempt transfer.

If an election is made, or if the scheme is dismantled, and the donor dies within 7 years of the transfer of debt, IHT will be due on the value of the debt, or of the asset, whichever gives rise to the larger tax liability.

However, where an election is made, but the **donee predeceases** the donor, there could be an IHT charge on both deaths. In this case it would be advisable for the donee to insure against this eventuality.

In some schemes, property is sold to a trust, with the sale proceeds left outstanding on a loan to a second trust, repayable on demand. HMRC consider that there is a reservation of benefit in respect of the loan, but that the pre-owned assets charge nevertheless applies by reference to the disposal of the property.

EXAMPLE Mr A entered into an arrangement in which his house was transferred to a trust in exchange for a loan of £500,000 (the market value of the property at the time). Mr A then immediately gifted the debt to a second trust. The arrangement was later dismantled in order to avoid a pre-owned assets charge. Mr A died 4 years after making the original arrangement when the property was worth £750,000 and his other assets were valued at £500,000. Mr A utilised the annual exemption each year on small gifts. The IHT liability on death is calculated as follows:

		Calculation 1: Including loan (£)		Calculation 2: Including property (£)
Value of debt gifted		500,000		-
Value of property		-		750,000
Other estate		500,000		500,000
Total chargeable amount		1,000,000		1,250,000
Tax on debt gifted/property:				
Value of gift/property	500,000		750,000	
Less: Nil rate band at date of death	(300,000)		(300,000)	
	200,000		450,000	
IHT @ 40%	80,000		180,000	
Less: Taper relief @ 40%	(32,000)	48,000	-	180,000
Tax on other estate:				
Value of estate	500,000		500,000	
IHT @ 40%		200,000		200,000
Total liability		248,000		380,000

As calculation 2 produces the higher liability, that method must be used.

SECTION 3

Transactions in securities

4010 An individual may convert income into capital by purchasing securities just after interest has been paid, and then selling them just before the next interest payment, with the sale price reflecting the interest income. The accrued income scheme, and provisions relating to the sale and repurchase of securities, ensure that income tax is still charged.

Transactions involving securities may require a clearance from HMRC in order to be sure of the tax treatment, because of anti-avoidance legislation which may charge income tax on subsequent profits (including capital gains) from those securities.

A. Accrued income scheme

This scheme applies when a security is transferred from person to person. 4012

Interest on most securities accrues daily, but is only paid out every 6 months. The person who holds the security on a specified date (known as the **ex-div date**) receives the interest for the whole of a six-month period. The price of a security therefore normally increases before the ex-div date, to reflect the imminent payment of interest. After the ex-div date, the price will fall, as there is then no entitlement to an interest payment for another six months.

MEMO POINTS 1. The ex-div date is generally about 1 month before the actual payment date.
2. Where relevant, **foreign currency** must be converted to sterling using the London closing rate for each day.

Relevant transactions

The relevant **transfer** of a security may be by way of sale, gift, exchange or otherwise, but not: 4014 ss 619-620 ITA 2007

- a transfer on death; or
- an arrangement under which a person sells and repurchases the same security.

The accrued income scheme applies to both domiciled and non-domiciled individuals.

A **security** is any form of loan stock or similar security issued by any company, or by a government, public or local authority body. Shares issued by a building society which are treated as qualifying corporate bonds (¶5234) are also securities for these purposes.

MEMO POINTS The following are **not securities**, and are therefore outside the scope of the rules:
- shares in a company;
- units in a unit trust;
- national savings certificates;
- war savings certificates;
- certificates of deposit;
- zero coupon redeemable securities; and
- deeply discounted securities.

Exempt transfers

Transfers of securities are exempt if the **nominal value** of the individual's total holding of securities does not exceed £5,000 at any point in the tax year. In considering whether this limit has been exceeded, it is necessary to look at the year of assessment in which the end of the interest period falls, and the preceding year (see ¶4020)). 4016 ss 638-647 ITA 2007

The transferee and transferor are considered completely separately. The accrued income scheme may apply to one and not the other, depending on the particular circumstances of each.

MEMO POINTS 1. A similar provision applies to transfers made to or by:
- the personal representative of a deceased person's **estate**; or
- the trustee of a disabled person's **trust**.

In these situations, it is the nominal value of securities held in that capacity that must not exceed £5,000. Any personal holdings are not included.
2. The **interest period** is the period from the day after the payment date through to the next payment date, and cannot exceed 12 months. A longer period will be split into consecutive interest periods of 12 months with a final interest period for the remainder of the payment period.

3. Transfers made to persons who are **neither resident nor ordinarily resident** in the UK throughout the year of assessment in which the transfer takes place are exempt, unless that person is trading in the UK via a permanent establishment.
4. The following are outside the scope of accrued income scheme:
– **financial traders**, provided the profits from the transaction are included as part of their trading profits;
– **charitable trusts**, provided the interest received is exempt and is applied for charitable purposes; and
– **pension scheme trusts**, provided the interest received is exempt.

EXAMPLE A Ltd issued 7% loan stock paying interest on 7 May and 7 November.
The interest periods run as follows:
– 8 May to 7 November; and
– 8 November to 7 May.

Calculation of accrued income

4018 The treatment of accrued income depends on whether the security is transferred with the rights to accrued interest (cum-div) or without (ex-div).

If the transfer is **cum-div**, any interest accrued to the date of settlement will be received by the transferee.

A transfer **ex-div** means the transferor has retained the right to the interest even though some of it accrues after the date of transfer.

The following table summarises the position regarding when amounts are chargeable and when relief is given:

Transfer	Transferor	Transferee
Cum-div – accrued amount	Charge	Relief
Ex-div – rebate amount	Relief	Charge

4020 Accrued income is **assessed** by reference to the tax year in which the interest period ends, rather than the settlement day for the actual transfer. This means that accrued income may be assessable in the tax year after the security has been transferred.

The **settlement day** is generally shown on the contract note.

MEMO POINTS 1. For transactions **without a contract note**, the settlement day is generally the date on which the transferee agrees to pay. If, however, this falls after the next interest payment date, HMRC will determine the settlement day.
2. In other cases, for example where the transfer is a **gift**, the settlement day will be the day on which the transfer is effected.

4022
s 623 ITA 2007

Transfers with accrued interest (cum-div) The transferor of the security is assessed on the accrued interest to the settlement date, known as the accrued amount. The transferee's income from the security is correspondingly reduced.

The accrued interest is usually shown separately on the contract note. If not (for example, if a person makes a transfer by way of gift), it is necessary to calculate the accrued amount. This is done using the formula:

$$\frac{A}{B} \times C$$

where:
A is the number of days from the start of the interest period to the settlement day (inclusive);
B is the total number of days in the interest period; and
C is the interest for the interest period.

EXAMPLE Mr A transfers his holding of £8,000 7.25 % loan stock to Mr B (cum-div), with settlement taking place on 15 November. The security pays interest on 15 April and 15 October. The accrued amount is calculated as follows:

A: Number of days from the start of the interest period to the settlement day (inclusive)	
16/10 – 15/11	31
B: Total number of days in the interest period	
16/10 – 15/04	182
C: Interest for the interest period	
(8,000 @ 7.25%) × 50%	290
Accrued amount (charge for Mr A, relief for Mr B):	
$\frac{31}{182} \times 290$	£49

Transfers without accrued interest (ex-div) When a security is transferred ex-div, the income receivable by the transferor is reduced by an amount known as the **rebate amount**. This represents the interest for the period from the settlement day to the end of the interest period. The transferor obtains relief for the rebate amount, and the transferee is correspondingly assessed. 4024 s 624 ITA 2007

As with transfers cum-div, the contract note may show the amount of interest retained. Otherwise, the rebate amount is calculated using the formula:

$$\frac{B - A}{B} \times C$$

where:
A is the number of days from the start of the interest period to the settlement day (inclusive);
B is the total number of days in the interest period; and
C is the interest for the interest period.

EXAMPLE Mr A transfers his holding of £8,000 7.25 % loan stock to Mr B (ex-div) instead, with settlement taking place on 15 November. The security pays interest on 15 April and 15 October. The rebate amount is calculated as follows:

A: Number of days from the start of the interest period to the settlement day (inclusive)	
16/10 – 15/11	31
B: Total number of days in the interest period	
16/10 – 15/04	182
C: Interest for the interest period	
(8,000 @ 7.25%) × 50%	290
Rebate amount (relief for Mr A, charge for Mr B):	
$\frac{182 - 31}{182} \times 290$	£241

The general rule is that each transaction is considered separately, giving rise to a charge or relief. However, where there is **more than one transaction in the same security** during an interest period, the results are aggregated. 4028

Where the **net result** is a:
– **charge**, that amount is assessable as sundry income for the tax year in which the interest period ends. Tax on accrued income scheme charges is levied at the lower or higher rates only, not at basic rate;
– **relief**, that amount is deducted from interest received on securities during the tax year. If the relief is given in a year in which there is no actual payment of interest, the relief may be carried forward against income from securities for the following year.

MEMO POINTS 1. Any amounts assessed or relieved through the accrued income scheme must also be adjusted for when calculating any **capital gains tax** arising on a transaction. s 119 TCGA 1992
If the transfer is **cum-div**, the accrued amount is deducted from both the transferor's proceeds and the transferee's allowable expenditure.

If the transfer is **ex-div**, the rebate amount is added to both the transferor's proceeds and the transferee's allowable expenditure.
2. Special rules apply where the **proceeds** of a transaction taking place outside the UK **cannot be remitted** to the UK due to restrictions imposed by one of the following:
- the laws of the country in which the transaction occurs;
- action by government of that country; or
- the inability to obtain foreign currency in that country.

If a claim is made, the assessable amount will only become chargeable once the restriction is lifted. A claim in this respect must be made within 6 years of the end of the settlement period in which the transaction occurred.

EXAMPLE

1. Mr A held £16,000 6.5 % loan stock which pays interest on 1 March and 1 September. The stock is sold on 14 February 2012 (ex-div). He received interest on 1 September 2011 and 1 March 2012 of £520. His assessable income from this source for 2011/12 is:

Interest received	1,040
Less: Rebate amount	
A: Number of days from the start of the interest period to the settlement day (inclusive)	
2 September to 14 February	166
B: Total number of days in the interest period	
2 September to 1 March	181
C: Interest for the interest period	
(16,000 @ 6.5%) × 50%	520
Relief given for rebate amount:	
$\frac{181 - 166}{181} \times 520$	(43)
Assessable 2011/12	£997

2. Mr A subsequently purchased £9,000 7 % stock (cum-div) on 10 March 2012. Interest dates are 1 March and 1 September. He sold the stock on 12 August 2012. As both transactions fall in the same interest period (2 March to 1 September) the adjustments are aggregated:

		£
Accrued amount on acquisition		
Number of days from the start of the interest period to the settlement date (inclusive)		
2 to 10 March	9	
Total number of days in the interest period		
2 March to 1 September	184	
Rebate amount on acquisition – relief for Mr A		
9/184 × (9,000 @ 7%) × 50%		(15)
Accrued amount on disposal		
Number of days from the start of the interest period to the settlement date (inclusive)		
2 March to 12 August	164	
Accrued amount on disposal – charge for Mr A		
164/184 × (9,000 @ 7%) × 50%		280
Assessable 2012/13 (year in which interest period ends)		265

B. Tax advantage from transactions in securities

4040 These provisions **apply to income tax only** income tax (although transactions which would normally be charged to capital gains tax can be caught where an advantage is obtained by not being charged to income tax).

HMRC intervention

When a taxpayer is party to a transaction in securities, there may be a risk that HMRC will act to prevent any **income tax advantage** obtained. **4042** ss 682 - 687 ITA 2007

There is a series of tests which determine whether a transaction falls within this legislation:

Test	¶¶
Was there a transaction in securities?	¶4043
Was the transaction of a type which is caught by the legislation?	¶4044
Was the purpose of the transaction to obtain an income tax advantage?	¶4046
Was an income tax advantage actually obtained?	¶4047

Only if all these tests are positive will the transaction fall within the legislation.

MEMO POINTS This section describes the rules introduced into ITA2007 by the Finance Act 2010 and which replaced the previous rules with effect from **24 March 2010**. In general the new rules are intended to be no more than a simplified statement of the old rules.

Transaction in securities

Transaction is very widely defined, and includes almost any issue, transfer, or alteration of rights attaching to, a security. **4043** ss 684 - s 686 ITA 2007

Security means almost any share or security in a **close company** (broadly, a company under the control of 5 or fewer persons).

MEMO POINTS 1. A transaction in securities can be any of the following:
- the purchase, sale or exchange of securities;
- issuing or securing the issue of new securities;
- applying or subscribing for new securities; and
- altering or securing the alteration of the rights attached to securities.

2. A close company includes any company that would be close if it were resident in the UK.

Types of transaction caught

The purpose of the legislation is to catch transactions which would be taxable as dividends if they had not been artificially constructed as capital transactions. A transaction is caught by the legislation if: **4044** s 685 ITA 2007
- it falls into one of the specified types; and
- the individual receives "relevant consideration" as a result

and the transaction is not of a type which is specifically excluded (¶4045).

Relevant consideration means consideration which in some form represents the value of the company's assets.

Typical transactions which might be caught would include the following:

Circumstance	Details	Example
1. Receipt of an abnormally large dividend which exceeds the normal dividend payable on the securities (Type A).	The amount received is taken into account for: – any exemption from tax; – the set-off of losses; – the giving of group relief; – the calculation of franked investment income; – profits from which interest payments are made; or – deduction from interest income.	A pension scheme, which was exempt from tax, received an abnormally high dividend. *IRC v Universities Superannuation Scheme Ltd* [1996]
2. Reduction in value of securities because a dividend has been paid or some other dealing (Type A).	Resulting in a deduction of profits.	A company purchased debentures when the interest was in arrears. The interest was paid which reduced the value of the debenture when it was subsequently redeemed, thereby creating a loss. *IRC v Kleinwort Benson Ltd* [1969]

Circumstance	Details	Example
3. The other party in a transaction where a taxpayer is caught by 1. or 2. above (Type A).	An amount is received which represents assets available for distribution, future receipts of the company or trading stock in a form where it is not taxed as income.	A company knew it would make a large profit, and created new shares with the right to a very high dividend (a "forward dividend strip"). These shares were sold to a dealing company, who received the dividend, and then sold the shares at a loss. This loss could be set off against the dividend income, avoiding tax. *Greenberg v IRC* [1972]
4. No income tax charge on a distribution of profits received from a close company (Type A).	Distribution of profits is defined widely. For these purposes a close company is any company under the control of 5 persons or less, and all unquoted companies unless controlled by a quoted company.	A company sold picture frames, and one contained a valuable painting. Instead of selling the painting and distributing the proceeds, the following plan was conceived: all other stock was sold, and another company bought the shares in the framing company. So instead of a dividend, the taxpayer received a capital receipt. *IRC v Wiggins* [1979]
5. Non-taxable consideration in the form of securities received as part of a transaction involving the transfer of an asset between two close companies (Type B)	The consideration represents assets for distribution of one of the companies. If the consideration is non-redeemable shares, any tax liability resulting from HMRC counteraction is deferred until the shares are repaid.	A company owned property which was expected to be very profitable when sold. The shareholders exchanged their shares for shares in another company for a large premium. The original company then paid a dividend up to its new parent company. The shareholders took out interest-free loans from the company, which therefore avoided a tax charge. *Williams v IRC* [1980]

MEMO POINTS 1. The legislation specifies two types of transaction, Type A and Type B. It is a condition of both types that, but for the anti-avoidance legislation, the consideration would not be subject to income tax.
2. **Type A** involves obtaining consideration derived from the assets of a close company by way of:
– the distribution, transfer or realisation of assets of the company; or
– the application of assets of the company in discharge of liabilities, or
– the direct or indirect transfer of assets of one close company to another.
3. **Type B** involves obtaining consideration from the transaction in securities itself, in a case where two or more close companies are involved in the transaction.
4. The definition of relevant consideration varies according to the Type of transaction, but can include:
– the value of assets available for distribution as a dividend;
– the value of future receipts of the company;
– the value of trading stock; and
– consideration in the form of shares or securities.

4045 s 686 ITA 2007

Transactions are specifically **excluded** if:
– immediately before the transaction, the person involved (the "party") holds shares (or an interest in shares) in the company; and
– there is a fundamental change of ownership of the company.

A **fundamental change of ownership** takes place if **as a result of the transaction**, all of the following three conditions are satisfied, and continue to be satisfied for a period of two years afterwards:
– at least 75% of the ordinary share capital of the company is held beneficially by a person (or persons) not connected with the party, and who were not connected with him at any time in the two years ending with the day on which the transaction takes place;
– those shares carry an entitlement to at least 75% of the distributions which may be made by the company; and
– those shares carry an entitlement to at least 75% of the total voting rights in the company

MEMO POINTS 1. In the case of a **series of transactions**, the party must hold shares immediately before the first transaction in the series, and the three conditions must be satisfied as a result of the series.
2. This is the **main simplifying measure** in the new legislation, intended to exempt the parties to routine transactions from needing to apply for clearance.

Purposive test

A transaction is caught if: **4046** s 684 ITA 2007
– the main purpose, or one of the main purposes, of the person in being a party to the transaction is to obtain an **income tax advantage** (¶4047), and
– the person obtains an income tax advantage from the transaction (or the combined effect of a series of transactions).

MEMO POINTS This **replaces** the previous exception for transactions undertaken for genuine commercial reasons or in the ordinary course of making or managing investments, and where obtaining an income tax advantage was not the main, or one of the main objects of the transaction.

Income tax advantage

Obtaining an income tax advantage means that: **4047** s 687 ITA 2007
– the income tax which would be payable on the consideration if it were a dividend exceeds the capital gains tax actually payable on it; or
– income tax would be payable on the relevant consideration if it were a dividend, and no capital gains tax is in fact payable on it.

The **amount** of the income tax advantage is the difference between the income tax that would be payable, and the capital gains tax that is actually payable.

HMRC action

To **avoid a counteraction**, the individual must convince HMRC that one or more of the tests has produced a negative result. This will usually mean showing that either: **4048**
– the main object of the transaction is not to obtain an income tax advantage; or
– that the transaction is excluded because of a fundamental change of ownership.

MEMO POINTS 1. Under the **old rules**, it was possible to avoid a counteraction by demonstrating that the transaction was undertaken for bona fide commercial reasons. Resisting a takeover bid was held to fall within this criterion. *IRC v Brebner* [1967]
2. **Another case** involved an individual who ran his own farm. He sold shares in a private investment company to finance the purchase of a nearby farm, which he wanted to combine with his existing business. It was held that the transaction was undertaken for bona fide commercial reasons. *Clark v IRC* [1978]

If HMRC **intend to counteract** a tax advantage, a set procedure is followed whereby the taxpayer is informed how the transaction will be taxed, and given the opportunity to appeal. Counteraction may include disallowing a loss, taxing a capital receipt as income, or refusing a repayment of tax. **4049** s 695 ITA 2007

MEMO POINTS Details of the **procedure** are as follows:
a. a preliminary notice is sent to the taxpayer by HMRC;
b. the taxpayer may then assert that these rules do not apply, and give his reasons by statutory declaration within 30 days of the notice;
c. where HMRC do not agree with the taxpayer, the matter is put before a tribunal who will decide whether the counteraction is valid; and
d. where the tribunal so decides, HMRC will then serve a notice stating how the transaction will be taxed, against which the taxpayer can appeal.

Obtaining clearance

In order to obtain **certainty** on how a transaction will be taxed, it is advisable to apply for clearance (¶9896) in advance that HMRC will not counteract any tax advantage. **4050** s 701 ITA 2007

Once the written application is received, HMRC have 30 days in which to give clearance or request further information (to which the taxpayer must respond within 30 days, or the application will lapse). When refusing an application, HMRC will usually state their reasons. There is no right of appeal against a refusal.

SP 3/80

MEMO POINTS 1. The **letter requiring clearance** should contain as much information as possible about the transaction, particularly emphasising the reasons why the transaction is not being undertaken just to obtain an income tax advantage.

s 831 CTA 2009 ss 1044, 1091 - 1092 CTA 2009 ss 138, 139 TCGA 1992 s 145 ITA 2007

2. Virtually all clearances are dealt with by the same HMRC team, requiring only one letter about the transaction from the taxpayer. **Other clearances** under the following provisions may also be made at the same time as for transactions in securities:
– demergers (ss 1091 - 1092 CTA 2010);
– purchase of own shares (ss 1044 CTA 2010);
– acquisition of EIS by a new company (s 145 ITA 2007);
– share exchanges (s 138 TCGA 1992);
– reconstructions (s 139 TCGA 1992); and
– intangible fixed assets (s 831 CTA 2009).

SECTION 4

Transactions in land

General anti-avoidance

4052 ss 752 - 772 ITA 2007

Where a disposal of land situated in the UK results in a **capital gain**, the proceeds may be taxed as sundry income when any of the following conditions apply:
a. the land was acquired with the sole or main objective of making a gain on disposal;
b. development took place in order to realise a gain later on; or
c. the land was trading stock.

HMRC have stated that although the avoidance of tax does not need to be deliberate for the rules to apply, the simple purchase, improvement and subsequent sale of a property will not be caught.

s 767 ITA 2007

In addition, any disposal covered by the principal private residence exemption (¶6166) or the disposal of any other dwelling house is ignored for these purposes.

In practice, unless there are complex arrangements, only development profit is likely to be attacked under these provisions.

MEMO POINTS 1. For these purposes, **land** includes any buildings or interest in land.
2. The rules also apply to
– any disposal regardless of the **residence** of the transferor;
– an asset which **derives its value** from land, such as shares in a company which owns the land; and
– a disposal by an individual **connected** (¶5570) with the individual who acquired or developed the land..
3. In the case of a company which holds land as trading stock, and disposes of it in the normal course of trade, the rules will not apply. The disposal of shares in a holding company, which owns at least 90% of such a company, is also excluded.
4. Obtaining **planning consent** does not constitute development.

EXAMPLE Mr A purchases some land intending to make a gain. He is unlikely to be trading as this is a one-off transaction. The eventual gain will be liable to capital gains tax unless HMRC try to tax it as sundry income.

4054 s 770 ITA 2007

There is a **clearance procedure** for the first two situations in ¶4052, under which the taxpayer can write to HMRC about the transaction.

MEMO POINTS There are two cases which **illustrate** the application of these rules:
1. Trustees granted a lease to a development company, and only received a premium when the development work was finished. The amount of the premium was dependent on the eventual

sales price achieved by the company for each plot of land which was subsequently subleased. It was held that the premium should be taxed as sundry income because the trustees had entered into the arrangement in order to develop the land, and the premium was otherwise a gain of a capital nature. *Page v Lowther* [1983]; and
2. An individual entered a contract to sell land to an overseas company at undervalue, and the contract terms allowed the overseas company to sell the land on. In fact, the land was sold on three times, so that the eventual proceeds were split between the individual and three overseas companies (all of whom were not liable to UK tax on any gains). However it was held that the individual was taxable on the whole proceeds given for the land, because he provided the opportunity for the companies to make a gain by entering into this arrangement. *Sugarwhite v Budd* [1988]

The amount taxable as sundry income is the proceeds that are available for the seller to enjoy when the gain is realised, less relevant expenses. So if the seller is required to **deposit monies** (in case of refund to the purchaser on the happening of a contingency, for example), the amount of the deposit will not be taxable until it is released. **4058** s 756 ITA 2007

Where an amount is taxed as sundry income, it is excluded from any capital gains computation.

MEMO POINTS Where the transferor is **non-resident**, HMRC have the power to require the deduction of income tax at source from the sale proceeds. s 944 ITA 2007

Sale and leaseback

Where a taxpayer sells land (realising a capital gain) and then rents it back from the buyer, anti-avoidance rules apply if an **excessive rent** is paid. This prevents the taxpayer from obtaining advantageous tax relief on the rent paid. **4060** s 835 CTA 2010

In this situation, the tax deduction for the rental payments is restricted to a commercial rent, and any unrelieved expense is carried forward and set off if there are subsequent underpayments of rent.

MEMO POINTS 1. A **commercial rent** is the rent payable under a replica lease negotiated on the open market at the time the actual lease was created, with the same terms and duration.
2. The **restrictions on tax relief** for rent payments will affect property income, trading income, sundry income, and management expenses (for companies). It is very likely that some rental payments will remain unrelieved.

EXAMPLE Mr A, a printer, sells his premises to C Ltd, and leases them back for 4 years. The rent payable under the lease is £30,000 for Years 1 and 2, £1 in Year 3, and nil in Year 4. The commercial rent would be £15,000 per annum.
Mr A will be able to set off his rental payments against his trading income as follows:

Year	Unrelieved b/fwd	Rent payment	Deduction allowed	Unrelieved c/fwd
	£	£	£	£
1	Nil	30,000	15,000	15,000
2	15,000	30,000	15,000	30,000
3	30,000	1	15,000	15,001
4	Nil	Nil	Nil	Nil

Because no further rent payments are due after the end of Year 3, the unrelieved amount of £15,001 is lost.

Sale of a short lease

Where a short lease (that is, one with less than 50 years to run) is assigned or surrendered by an individual, and he then takes a **new lease** for a term of 15 years or less, part of the premium received will be taxed as income. The taxable proportion is found by using the formula: **4062** s 850 CTA 2010

$$\frac{16 - N}{15}$$

where N is the term of the new lease expressed in years.

The income will be assessed as either trading income or sundry income depending on the taxpayer's situation.

EXAMPLE Mr B surrenders the lease on his shop for £12,000. He then takes out a new 5 year lease. The amount of the premium liable to income tax will be:

$$£12{,}000 \times \frac{16-5}{15} = £8{,}800$$

SECTION 5

Structured finance arrangements

4064 ss 758 - 779 CTA 2010

A structured finance arrangement is one in which a person (including a company) transfers a stream of income (for example, rent) to another person, by transferring or refinancing the income-producing asset for an agreed period in return for a lump sum payment which includes an interest element. In the absence of specific legislation, the transferor would not be taxed on either the income transferred or the interest element of the lump sum payment.

The transferor is treated as having taken out a conventional loan, on which he receives tax relief only for the interest element. This is achieved by treating the transferred income as still arising to the transferor, and only allowing a deduction for any finance charge shown in his accounts.

These provisions also cover more complex schemes under which **partnership profit shares** are adjusted in order to transfer income.

The **disposal and reacquisition** of the asset are normally ignored for capital gains tax purposes.

The provisions **do not apply** where the whole of the lump sum would otherwise be charged to tax or brought into account for capital allowances purposes.

SECTION 6

Life policy gains

4066

A life assurance policy may be used as a medium or long term investment, to accumulate income free from tax. During the term of the policy, the taxpayer will not receive income, but depending on the type of policy, a payout will be made:

- in the event of death at any time, under a total life policy;
- on death if an individual dies during a predetermined period, under a term policy; and
- in any event under an endowment policy, whether death occurs during a certain period, or an individual survives for that period.

The individual is **potentially liable** to income tax on withdrawals, surrenders, and assignments during the life of the policy, and also on death, or when the policy matures.

ss 461 - 465 ITOIA 2005

MEMO POINTS 1. These provisions **do not apply to companies**..

2. Gains may also (less commonly) arise from **life annuities** and **capital redemption policies**, and the rules for both are broadly similar to life insurance policies. For the remainder of this section, the term "policy" will be used to refer to all three.

SI 2011/1502

3. Compensation payments made under the **Equitable Life Payment Scheme** (ELPS) to trustee policy holders in Equitable Life who have suffered loss due to government maladministration are disregarded when calculating gains on life policies and will not be included on chargeable event certificates issued by Equitable Life.

A. UK products

A UK policy is one that has been issued by a UK insurer or by an overseas insurance company who is trading in the UK. The **exception** is where a policy issued by a UK insurance company is accounted for as part of its overseas life assurance business, in which case it will be treated as a foreign life policy. For example, a policy issued by a foreign branch of a UK insurer will fall within this provision. **4068**

An income tax charge will usually only arise in respect of a policy that is not a qualifying policy. The insurance company should be consulted to ascertain the type of policy concerned.

1. Qualifying policies

Characteristics

When a qualifying policy **matures**, and it has not been varied in the meantime, the individual is not taxable on any profit made. In addition, for policies taken out before 14 March 1984 only, there is often tax relief on the premiums paid. **4070** s 269 ICTA 1988

MEMO POINTS **Tax relief on the premium** is given by allowing the individual to pay only 87.5% of the premium (up to the greater of £1,500 or one-sixth of the individual's total income), and the shortfall is claimed back by the life company from HMRC. This relief is only available if the policy was taken out before 14 March 1984, has not been varied to increase either the benefits payable or its term, and the individual must be UK resident when the premiums are paid. s 266(3)-(5) ICTA 1988

A policy will be treated as a qualifying policy provided that it: **4072** s 266(2) ICTA 1988 Sch 15 para 2 ICTA 1988
- was **taken out by** the taxpayer on his own life or that of his spouse;
- has a minimum **term** of 10 years from the commencement date to the date it is due to end, or is a whole of life policy which pays out only on death;
- involves **premiums** of even amounts, payable at regular intervals every year for at least 10 years;
- has an **assured value** which is at least 75% of the total premiums payable during the term of the policy (except if the policy is a term policy with no surrender value which ends before the individual's 75th birthday); and
- has restricted **benefits**.

MEMO POINTS 1. **Even amounts** means that the premiums payable in any year do not exceed twice the premium payable in any other year, nor one-eighth of the total due over the first 10 years. Premiums relating to exceptional risk of death or disability are ignored for this purpose.
2. The assured value condition is relaxed if the policy holder is aged at least 55 when the policy is issued.
3. Where **commission** is received, and netted off against the premiums due or invested, this will not affect the qualifying status of the policy, if the commission is paid under a separate contract.

Chargeable event

A chargeable event will only **occur** in relation to a qualifying policy if it is converted into a paid up policy, surrendered or assigned for value within: **4074** s 485 ITTOIA 2005
- 10 years from the date of inception; or, if sooner,
- three-quarters of the term for an endowment policy.

2. Non-qualifying policies

A non-qualifying policy is any policy which has never fulfilled, or no longer fulfils, all of the conditions in ¶4072. A common type of non-qualifying policy might be a single premium bond, which is a whole-of-life contract with a small amount of life cover. **4076**

When a chargeable event occurs in connection with a non-qualifying policy, any resulting gain is liable to income tax.

Chargeable events

4078 A chargeable event essentially **occurs** when money is taken out of a non-qualifying policy, or the policy comes to an end or is sold. If there is a gain (a profit from the investment), the insurance company will usually issue a chargeable event certificate which will provide details of the payment and the taxable amount.

ss 488, 497 ITTOIA 2005

No chargeable gain arises when:
– a lump sum is received as a result of a claim for critical illness benefit or disability benefit due under the policy (subject to HMRC approval);
– the policy is more than 20 years old, and the insurer stops collecting premiums because it is uneconomic; or
– a small inducement is received which does not cost the insurance company more than £30.

MEMO POINTS 1. The benefit under the policy may be paid out in a single **lump sum** or as a series of payments.

s 465 ITTOIA 2005

2. Where the taxpayer is **non-UK resident** when the chargeable event occurs, no UK tax liability will arise.

s 541A ITTOIA 2005

3. Where **commission** is paid to a policyholder or reinvested in his policy, the rules for calculating the gain arising on a chargeable event changed after 21 March 2007 (for new policies taken out on or after that date, or existing policies where benefits are increased on or after that date). The change applies where both of the following conditions are met:
– premiums exceed £100,000 in any tax year; and
– the policy or contract is surrendered, matures or is assigned for money or money's worth within 3 years of the end of the tax year in which premiums exceeded £100,000.
In such cases, the amount of any commission that is:
a. passed on by an intermediary to a policyholder, beneficiary, trustee or a connected person will be deducted from the amount of the premium that will be allowable in calculating any gain; or
b. waived by an intermediary and reinvested in the policy will be excluded from the amount of the premium that will be allowable in calculating any gain.

4080 The following chargeable events may give rise to a **chargeable event gain**:

s 484 ITTOIA 2005

– a death which gives rise to the payment of benefits;
– maturity of the policy;
– a total surrender or a partial surrender (i.e. receipt of a capital sum);
– an insurance company making a loan to the policyholder or to someone else at the policyholder's direction;
– the sale of all or part of the policy;
– the gift of part of the policy only; or
– the assignment of part or all of the policy for money or for money's worth.

Where there have been earlier withdrawals and partial surrenders which have not been taxed, those amounts are added to the surrender value to calculate the gain on maturity, death or assignment.

MEMO POINTS 1. On **maturity**, a gain may arise even in circumstances where some or all of the proceeds are retained by the insurance company and used to pay the premium of a replacement. A policy will be deemed to have matured if:
– an option to take out a new policy is exercised;
– there is a change in the life (or lives) insured under the policy; or
– changes are made to the policy by agreement between the policyholder and the insurance company.

ss 498 - 507 ITTOIA 2005

2. When **withdrawals** (i.e. a partial surrender or part assignment) are made, a taxable gain will only arise where cumulative withdrawals exceed an annual 5% allowance (calculated as 5% of the total premiums paid to date). The taxable gain is assessed at the end of the policy year. If a gain arises under this rule, a new accumulation period will start for the purposes of comparing subsequent withdrawals against the allowance.

s 487 ITTOIA 2005

3. An **assignment** is not a chargeable event if made:
– to a spouse living with the transferor; or
– for the purpose of discharging or giving security for a debt.

EXAMPLE Mr A invests £20,000 in a single premium bond on 1 January of Year 1, and withdraws £3,000 in June of Years 4, 5 and 8. The 5% allowance will build up at the rate of £1,000 per annum.

Year	Cumulative allowance	Withdrawal	Cumulative untaxed withdrawals	Taxable gain
	£	£	£	£
1	1,000	0	0	0
2	2,000	0	0	0
3	3,000	0	0	0
4	4,000	3,000	3,000	0
5	5,000	3,000	6,000	1,000
6	1,000	0	0	0
7	2,000	0	0	0
8	3,000	3,000	3,000	0
9	4,000	0	3,000	0
10	5,000	0	3,000	0

The taxable gain of £1,000 in Year 5 only arises when the cumulative withdrawal exceeds the cumulative allowance. It is deemed to occur on 31 December of Year 5, because the policy was taken out on 1 January, and so the policy year is the calendar year.
If Mr A surrenders the policy on 31 March of Year 10 for £20,100, the resulting gain, taxable on 31 March, would be:

	£
Surrender value	20,100
Add:	
Withdrawal in year 4	3,000
Withdrawal in year 5	3,000
Withdrawal in year 8	3,000
	29,100
Less:	
Premium paid	(20,000)
Withdrawals already taxed	(1,000)
Taxable gain	8,100

3. Calculation of the tax charge

A chargeable event gain is treated as **part of the total income of the individual** in the year in which the chargeable event occurs (except for withdrawals) provided that, immediately before the event, the rights under the policy were held: 4084
- by the individual as beneficial owner;
- as security for a debt owed by the individual; or
- on a trust created by the individual.

The gain is taxed as sundry income.

Deemed tax paid

An individual who makes a taxable life policy gain is deemed to have paid non-refundable tax at the basic rate on the amount of the gain. 4086 s 530 ITTOIA 2005

An individual who is not a **higher or additional rate taxpayer** will have no further tax liability. The gain is therefore effectively only subject to higher and additional rates of tax, with the availability of top slicing relief which recognises that the gain has arisen over a number of years.

Top slicing relief

Income received from chargeable event gains may have accrued over a number of years, and if the income had been taxed evenly over that period, higher rate tax may not have 4088 s 535 ITTOIA 2005 been due. As chargeable event gains are always **treated as the top slice of income**, the resulting relief is known as top slicing relief.

Relief is only available when:
– the taxable income including the chargeable event gain exceeds the total of the savings rate (if applicable) and basic rate bands (£35,000 for 2011/12); and
– the taxable income excluding the chargeable event gain is less than the total of the savings rate and basic rate bands.
For this purpose, the basic rate band is extended by contributions paid net of tax to a registered pension scheme (¶3745), but not by any Gift Aid payments (¶4420). This means that such a contribution can be very tax efficient for a higher or additional rate taxpayer.

Special rules apply (¶4092) where the taxpayer also has income from payments on retirement or removal from office or from premiums treated as rent.

4090 s 536 ITTOIA 2005

Where **only one chargeable event** occurs in the tax year, relief is given as follows.
1. Calculate the tax liability on the whole gain in the normal way.
2. Divide the gain by the number of complete years since the last chargeable event or the commencement of the policy.
3. Recalculate the tax liability by treating that proportion as the top slice of income for the year, ignoring the effect of any Gift Aid donation (¶4420) on the basic rate band.
4. Multiply the resulting figure by the same number of years used in 2.
5. The amount of the relief is the difference between the tax liability from 1. and the result of 4.

EXAMPLE In 2011/12 Mr A has employment income of £40,000 and a chargeable event gain of £21,000. The life policy commenced 3 years ago.

Step 1: Whole gain is £21,000
Calculate tax liability with whole gain included

				£
Employment income				40,000
Chargeable event gain				21,000
Income for the year				61,000
Less personal allowance				(7,475)
Taxable income				53,525
Tax thereon:				
35,000 @ 20%				7,000
18,525 @ 40%				7,410
53,525				14,410
Less tax paid on gain at 20%				(3,600)
Tax payable without top slicing relief				10,810
Steps 2 and 3: divide gain by number of years and recalculate the tax liability				£
21,000/3 years = 7,000 per year				
Tax on proportion of gain (as top slice of income)				
Balance of basic rate available after employment income:				
(35,000 – 32,525)	2,475	@ 20%	495	
	4,525	@ 40%	1,810	
	7,000			
Tax on proportion of gain (as top slice of income)				2,305
Step 4: multiply by number of years (3)			2,305 × 3	6,915
Tax charge on full gain				6,915
Step 5: amount of the relief is difference between: 10,810 and 6,915				3,895

4092 In calculating the relief, any sums relating to the following are **excluded** from total income:
– payments on retirement or removal from office (¶3060); and
– premiums treated as rent (¶2743).

EXAMPLE Mr B's employment income for 2011/12 is split between salary of £23,000 and taxable lump sum on termination of employment of £10,000. In addition he has a chargeable event gain of £18,000 from a life policy which commenced 3 years ago.
The tax payable for 2011/12 would be as follows:

	£
Employment income	23,000
Taxable lump sum on termination of employment	10,000
Chargeable event gain	18,000
	51,000
Less: Personal allowance	(7,475)
Taxable income	44,525
Tax thereon:	
35,000 @ 20%	7,000
8,525 @ 40%	3,410
43,525	
	10,410
Less: Top slicing relief (see below)	(2,400)
Lower rate tax deemed to have been paid: £18,000 @ 20%	(3,600)
Net tax payable	4,410

	£
Top slicing relief:	
Tax on full gain (after excluding taxable lump sum)	
Gain falls entirely within the basic rate band	
18,000 @ 20%	3,600
	3,600
Tax on proportion of gain (after excluding taxable lump sum)	
18,000/3 years = 6,000	
6,000 @ 20%	(1,200)
Top slicing relief	2,400

Where **more than one chargeable event gain** arises in a tax year, relief is given as follows. **4094** s 537 ITTOIA 2005

1. Calculate the tax liability on the whole gain in the normal way.
2. Divide each gain by the number of years since the last chargeable event or the commencement of the policy.
3. Recalculate the tax liability by adding together all of the apportioned gains and treating that as the top slice of income for the year, ignoring the effect of any gift aid donation on the basic rate band.
4. Multiply the resulting figure by the following formula:

$$\frac{\text{Total chargeable event gains}}{\text{Total apportioned gains}}$$

5. The amount of the relief is the difference between the tax liability from 1. and the result of 4.

EXAMPLE In 2011/12 Mr C has employment income of £34,000 and chargeable event gains as follows:

Gain	Years	Gain/years
8,000	4	2,000
10,000	2	5,000
18,000		7,000

The tax payable for 2011/12 will be as follows:

		£
Employment income		34,000
Chargeable event gains		18,000
		52,000
Less: Personal allowance		(7,475)
Taxable income		44,525
Tax thereon:		
35,000 @ 20%		7,000
9,525 @ 40%		3,810
44,525		
		10,810
Less: Top slicing relief (see below)		(1,905)
Lower rate tax deemed to have been paid: £18,000 @ 20%		(3,600)
Net tax payable		5,305
Top slicing relief:		£
Tax on full gain (as top slice of income)		
8,475 @ 20%		1,695
9,525 @ 40%		3,810
18,000		5,505
Tax on proportion of total gain of £7,000 (as top slice of income)		
Proportion falls within the basic rate band		
7,000 @ 20%	1,400	
1,400 x 18,000/7,000		(3,600)
Top slicing relief		1,905

Personal portfolio bonds

4096 ss 515-526 ITTOIA 2005

A personal portfolio bond, where the **investor can choose** the investments within the bond and the related benefits depend on property value, is taxed slightly differently.

The chargeable event gain is taken to be:

15% × (premiums paid + deemed gains from earlier years)

When the policy is totally surrendered, matures, assigned, or ends on death, the total gain already taxed will be allowed as a deduction.

EXAMPLE Mr D invests £40,000 in a personal portfolio bond in Year 1, making no subsequent withdrawals or further investment.

The taxable gain for the first 4 years of the policy will be calculated as follows:

Year	Deemed investment brought forward	Gain at 15%	Deemed investment carried forward	Taxable gain
	£	£	£	£
1	40,000	6,000	46,000	6,000
2	46,000	6,900	52,900	6,900
3	52,900	7,935	60,835	7,935
4	60,835	9,125	69,960	9,125

Deficiency relief

4098 ss 539-541 ITTOIA 2005 Tax Bulletin 82

Deficiency **relief is available** where the computation of the gain on death, maturity or surrender of the whole policy results in a **loss**, and there have been previous gains during the term of the policy. The purpose of the relief is to ensure that the total amount of taxable income is never more than the total gain made under the policy.

The relief reduces income for the purposes of calculating the charge to higher (but not to additional (50 %)) rate tax (¶4408). It operates by taking an amount of income equal to the relief due, and charging it at the basic, lower or dividend ordinary rates (depending on the type of income) instead of at the higher rate or the dividend upper rate. Relief is given against savings income in priority to non-savings income.

MEMO POINTS 1. In order to **counteract tax avoidance**, relief is limited to the amount of gains already assessed on the same person to which the losses arise, where on or after 3 March 2004:
a. benefits secured are **increased**, either by a variation of the policy or contract, or by the exercise of rights conferred by the policy or contract, including the case where the policy holder chooses to pay additional premiums; or
b. all or part of the rights conferred by the policy or contract are:
- **assigned** to another person, whether for money or money's worth; or
- are given as **security** for a debt.

2. Relief on the surrender of a policy is restricted if the main purpose of any individual who is party to the arrangements is to obtain a tax reduction greater than the tax charged on the previous gains.
3. The announcement in the March 2010 Budget that deficiency relief would also extend to the additional (50 %) rate of tax was withdrawn in the June 2010 Budget. This prevents an individual from obtaining relief at 50% for gains originally taxed only at 40%.

EXAMPLE Mr A has the following income in 2011/12:

	Gross (£)	Tax (£)
Employment income	45,000	10,000
Dividends	50,000	5,000

Mr A is entitled to deficiency relief of £30,000.
The tax payable for the year is calculated as follows:

			Non-savings £	Dividends £
Employment income			45,000	
Dividends				50,000
			45,000	
Less: Personal allowance			(7,475)	
			37,525	50,000
Tax thereon:				
Non-savings income:				
Basic rate	35,000	@ 20%		7,000
Higher rate	2,525	@ 40%		1,010
	37,525			
				8,010
Dividend income:				
Dividend higher rate	50,000 @ 32.5%			16,250
				24,260
Less: Deficiency relief (30,000 @ 22.5% (32.5 % – 10%))				(6,750)
				17,510
Less: PAYE				(10,000)
				7,510
Less: Tax credit on dividend income				(5,000)
Net tax liability				2,510

B. Foreign products

The rules relating to gains from foreign life insurance policies are very similar to those applying to UK life insurance policies. Most importantly, basic rate taxpayers will suffer tax on any gains arising from foreign policies. **4100** Sch 15 ICTA 1988

4102 s 476 ITTOIA 2005 A foreign life insurance policy is **defined** as one:
- which is part of the overseas life assurance business of a UK insurer; or
- from an insurance company resident outside the UK.

A policy from a UK trading office of a foreign insurance company is not a foreign life assurance policy for these purposes.

Non-qualifying policies

4104 Most foreign policies are not qualifying policies and gains will therefore generally be taxable.

MEMO POINTS To be considered a **qualifying policy**, the policy must have been taken out before 18 November 1983, with no changes made (for example to extend the term or to increase the benefits secured), and the other conditions in ¶4072 must also be met.

Taxation of foreign life policy gains

4106 s 528 ITTOIA 2005 Foreign life policy gains will be taxed as **foreign income**. The gain is reduced for the number of days during the whole policy when the taxpayer was non-UK resident, unless the taxpayer is a trust.

s 531 ITTOIA 2005 Unlike UK policies, no lower rate tax is **deemed to have been paid** in respect of a foreign policy, unless it is a qualifying policy, or the policy is an unchanged overseas life assurance business policy issued by a UK insurer before 17 March 1998.

Most taxpayers will therefore have a tax liability arising from a gain, although where no other income is received, the starting rate tax band may be available.

s 536(7) ITTOIA 2005 **Top slicing relief** (¶4088) may still be available in the same way as for UK policies. Where, however, the individual was not resident in the UK for any complete policy years, these will be excluded from the calculation. For example, where a taxpayer surrenders a policy after 5 years, and was non-UK resident for 2 years, the chargeable gain will be divided by 3 only.

VII. Offshore funds

4110 To prevent taxpayers avoiding UK income tax by investing in offshore funds which accrue income instead of distributing it, a gain arising on the disposal from such a fund will be liable to income tax on sundry income, instead of to capital gains tax.

This section describes the current system of tax regulations, which replaced an older regime first introduced by the Finance Act 1984. It applies to all distributions and disposals made **on or after 1 December 2009**.

MEMO POINTS **Companies** are also subject to these rules, and all references to income tax should therefore also be taken to mean corporation tax where appropriate.

A. Types of offshore fund

4112 s 354 TIOPA 2010 SI 2009/3001 When an individual **disposes of an interest in an offshore fund**, the tax treatment of the gain depends on the nature of the fund:

Type of fund	Definition	Tax treatment of disposals	¶¶
Reporting	HMRC approved. Participants are taxable on undistributed fund income.	CGT, with a deduction for undistributed amounts already taxed	¶4116
Non-reporting funds:			
Transparent	Participants are taxable on fund income by the nature of the fund (eg. a unit trust).	CGT	¶4115
Non-transparent	Other than above	Income tax	¶4117
Note: a non-reporting fund is defined as any offshore fund which is not a reporting fund.			

Offshore funds

Any fund with the following **characteristics** will be an offshore fund for this purpose: **4114** s 355 TIOPA 2010

a. a mutual fund (which includes all unit trust schemes) resident or based outside the UK;

b. that allows participants to participate in:

– the acquisition, holding, management or disposal of the property; or

– receive profits or income arising from the same activities;

c. but in which the participants do not have day to day control of the management of the property, although they might have a right to be consulted or to give directions about it; and

d. in which a reasonable investor would expect to be able to realise all or part of an investment by calculating the net asset value of the property or by using indexation.

However, a fund will not qualify if the only way to realise an investment is on liquidation or a winding up.

A fund is a **corporate fund** if it is constituted by a non-UK body corporate (though not by an LLP).

MEMO POINTS 1. The underlying funds in an umbrella fund are treated as separate funds and the overall arrangements of umbrella funds are disregarded.

2. Partnerships are specifically excluded from the definition of offshore funds.

3. Any existing fund falling within the revised definition came within the new regulations on 1 December 2009. Investors' rights in offshore funds are then treated as assets for the purposes of CGT, and investors in affected funds will have the option of making an election to backdate the effect of the new section to 2003/04 onwards. An election will be irrevocable.

Transparent funds

A transparent fund is one in which UK participants are already taxed on their share of the fund income. This applies to certain unit trusts and contractual funds. **4115** SI2009/3001 reg 11

MEMO POINTS Such a fund is deemed to be non-transparent if, at any time during the participant's membership, it held more than 5% (by value) of its assets as interests in other, non-reporting offshore funds.

Reporting funds

A reporting fund is one in which UK participants effectively agree to pay **UK income tax on the undistributed income** of the fund. The disposal of an interest in the fund is subject to capital gains tax, but any undistributed amounts already taxed are treated as part of the cost of acquisition (that is, effectively as a deduction). **4116** SI2009/3001 regs 50 – 56B

To become a reporting fund, an "eligible offshore fund" must be granted **HMRC approval**. A pre-existing offshore fund may apply for reporting fund status, and so may a fund that is still to be established.

The fund must make a **report** to its participants for each reporting period (normally, its period of account), within six months from the end of that period. The report must show:
- the amount distributed to the participants in the period, per unit investment; and
- the excess income (undistributed) of the period (if any), per unit investment.

Participants are taxed on the sum of these two amounts. The method of taxation depends on the nature of the fund:
- if the fund is a corporate fund (¶4114), the income is treated as a distribution with an attached tax credit; and
- if the fund is non-corporate (and-non transparent: ¶4115), the income is treated as miscellaneous income.

In either case, if the fund has an excess proportion of interest-bearing investments, the income is instead treated as interest received.

SI2009/3001 regs 9, 48

MEMO POINTS 1. An **eligible** offshore fund is one that is not a guaranteed return fund (broadly, an offshore fund on which the return is defined by an index).
2. To escape having the income treated as interest, the fund must pass a **qualifying assets test**. Broadly speaking, it must not hold more than 60% of its assets (by market value) in the form of interest-bearing investments.
3. If a fund changes from reporting to non-reporting status, the participant may elect to be treated for CGT purposes as making a deemed disposal and re-acquisition of his interest at market value. This would crystallise the already accrued gains within the charge to CGT, rather than to income tax.
4. If a fund changes from non-reporting to reporting status, a similar election can be made to crystallise the accrued gain within the offshore income gains regime. Subsequent gains would then be subject only to CGT. If the election is not made, any subsequent disposal will still be potentially chargeable to income tax.
5. If a fund is both transparent (¶4115) and a non-reporting fund, and has an interest in a reporting fund, the taxable income of the reporting fund is attributed directly to the participants in the transparent fund.

Non-reporting funds

4117 SI2009/3001 regs 14 - 32

Income tax is charged on a disposal of an interest in a non-reporting, non-transparent fund, if:
- an **offshore income gain** arises on that disposal; and
- the participant was **resident or ordinarily resident** in the UK at any time during the tax year of disposal.

The offshore income gain is treated as miscellaneous income of the participant, arising at the date of disposal.

MEMO POINTS 1. Certain **exceptions** apply. There is no income tax charge if the participant's interest in the fund:
- is held as trading stock, or its disposal would be taken into account in the profits of a trade; or
- consists of certain excluded indexed securities; or
- is a right arising under an insurance policy; or
- is a loan.
2. **Charities are exempt** from the income tax charge.
3. As a **transitional measure**, an interest in a fund which was acquired before 1 December 2009 does not fall within this regime if, at the time it was acquired, the fund was not within the old regime under Finance Act 1984.

Disposal

4118 SI2009/3001 reg 33

The capital gains tax **definition** of disposal (¶5500) applies for these purposes, with the following modifications:
- the death of an individual gives rise to a deemed disposal for these purposes; and
- the share re-organisation provisions (¶5794) are modified such that a disposal occurs where an interest in a non-qualifying fund is exchanged for an interest in a qualifying fund.

In either case, the shares are deemed to be disposed of at market value, and an income tax charge can arise.

B. Tax charge

Computing the offshore income gain

The offshore income gain for a non-qualifying fund is **calculated** using capital gains tax rules. If the result is a loss, the offshore income gain is nil. **4124** SI 2009/3001 regs38 – 43

An offshore income gain cannot be deferred by the action of rollover relief (¶6050) or gift relief (¶6095).

MEMO POINTS 1. Where an individual is resident or ordinarily resident in the UK, but **not UK domiciled**, he will only be taxable on the proceeds remitted to the UK. SI2009/3001 reg 19

2. It has always been understood that a **loss** could only be treated as a capital loss, but from 1 April 2007 (for companies) and 6 April 2007 (for individuals) the legislation specifically states that this is the case. s 91 CTA 2010 s 152 ITA 2007

EXAMPLE Mr A acquired 200 units in an offshore fund on 1 January 2010 for £10,000. The units are sold on 1 May 2012 for £18,000. The offshore income gain is calculated as follows:

	£
Proceeds	18,000
Less: Cost	(10,000)
Gain	8,000

Offshore profit assessable as sundry income

Interaction with capital gains tax

Where a disposal giving rise to an offshore income gain is also a disposal for capital gains tax purposes, the **disposal proceeds** for capital gains purposes are reduced by the amount of the offshore income gain. In the majority of cases, this will result in there being no capital gain. **4126** SI 2009/3001 regs 44 – 47

MEMO POINTS On a **share for share exchange** (¶5839), the new shares generally stand in the shoes of the old shares. However, this provision may be disapplied where the old holding consisted of shares in a non-qualifying offshore fund and the new holding does not. In this situation, the new shares are deemed to be acquired for consideration equal to the amount of the offshore income gain.

SECTION 8

Sale of future earnings

An individual who has high earnings could convert those earnings into capital and therefore avoid income tax. There are provisions in place to treat capital receipts from any such **arrangement** as sundry income liable to income tax when received. **4132** ss 773 – 789 ITA 2007

A likely individual may be someone working in the entertainment industry or a sportsman. A professional selling his business, and continuing to work for reduced earnings, could also fall within the scope of these rules.

MEMO POINTS These rules apply to anyone, regardless of **residence status**, where the occupation which creates the earnings is carried on wholly or partly in the UK. s 777 ITA 2007

Transactions

4134 Only an arrangement where the **main motive** is to reduce or avoid income tax is caught. In addition, the following criteria must be met:
– another party (such as a company) is able to receive income which derives from the work of another person; and
– the working person receives a capital sum, in money or money's worth.

EXAMPLE A company contracts with Miss A, an actress, that she will work for the company for a fixed allowance of £60,000 per annum, which is liable to income tax. The company is controlled by Miss A.
The company sells Miss A's services for £1.5m. The company shares are therefore very valuable, and Miss A sells her shares for £1.4m. Under these provisions, Miss A is taxed on the proceeds as sundry income.

Exception

4136 ss 784 – 785 ITA 2007 A sale of a business interest where the value received is attributable to the business as a **going concern** will be exempt from these rules. However this exemption is not available where such a value is mainly derived from the working person's activities, and he does not receive full consideration (ignoring the capital sum).

EXAMPLE Mr B is a solicitor and a sole practitioner. He sells his business as a going concern to the CAD partnership, and continues to work.
If Mr B receives:
– market value for the sale (£200,000), and then works for a commercial salary (£50,000), he will only be assessed to capital gains tax on the sale; or
– an inflated sales price (£300,000), and then works for a nominal salary, he will also be assessed to income tax on the artificial price increase of £100,000.

SECTION 9

Transfer of assets abroad

4137 ss 714 – 751 ITA 2007 If, following a transfer of assets, income becomes payable to a non-UK resident or non-UK domiciled person, the income may be deemed to be that of an individual who is ordinarily UK resident, if there was an intention to avoid UK tax. This applies whether the individual who benefits is the transferor or someone else.

MEMO POINTS For these purposes, UK taxes include income tax, corporation tax, capital gains tax, inheritance tax, VAT and National Insurance contributions.

Transferor benefits

4138 ss 716, 737 ITA 2007 This provision **applies** where:
– assets are transferred to a person resident or domiciled outside the UK;
– as a result of the transfer (either alone or as a result of a series of associated operations), income is payable to the non-resident;
– the transferor is either ordinarily resident in the UK or is not domiciled in the UK and is claiming the remittance basis; and
– the transferor (or his spouse) has the power to enjoy any income of the non-resident, or receives (or is entitled to receive) a capital sum which is in any way connected with the transfer.

The provisions will **not apply** if it can be shown that either:
a. it would not be reasonable to draw the conclusion, from all the circumstances, that the avoidance of UK tax was not the purpose, or one of the purposes, for effecting the relevant transactions; or

b. all the relevant transactions were genuine commercial transactions, and it would not be reasonable to draw the conclusion, from all the circumstances, that any one or more of those transactions was more than incidentally designed for the purpose of avoiding tax.

MEMO POINTS 1. Even where the **transferor was not ordinarily resident** in the UK at the time of the transfer, these provisions will still apply, assuming the transferor subsequently becomes ordinarily resident in the UK.
2. There is no HMRC **clearance procedure**. In the event of a challenge by HMRC, the taxpayer must be able to prove that no avoidance of tax was intended. However, aiming to achieve a tax efficient result, within the UK law, is not tax avoidance. *IRC v Willoughby* [1997]

Where the rules apply, the **income payable** to the non-resident recipient of the property will be treated as sundry income of the transferor (¶3950). **4140**

EXAMPLE A UK resident individual transferred shares in two UK companies to a Canadian company which he controlled. In return, he and his family received promissory notes and shares in the Canadian company. The company's income was assessed on the individual, because he was entitled to benefit from that income as a result of the share transfers. *Lee v IRC* [1941]

Someone else benefits

A similar provision applies where: **4142** ss 716, 732 ITA 2007
- assets are transferred to a person resident or domiciled outside the UK;
- as a result of the transfer (either alone or as a result of a series of associated operations), income is payable to a non-resident; and
- a person other than the transferor who is ordinarily resident in the UK receives a benefit out of the assets.

The **provision will not apply** if it can be shown that either **a**. or **b**. in ¶4138 apply.

MEMO POINTS If the transferor is not domiciled in the UK and is claiming the remittance basis, the income is treated as if it were his relevant foreign income.

The **value of the benefit** is treated as sundry income of the UK resident recipient. The taxable income arising in this way is restricted to the actual amount received by the non-resident in the years up to and including the year in which the benefit is received. **4144**

MEMO POINTS 1. If the **value of the benefit exceeds** the actual amount of income received by the non-resident in the year, the excess will be carried forward to subsequent years.
2. Where there are **several recipients** of a benefit under these provisions, a just and reasonable apportionment of the income received is made, based on the proportion of the whole benefit received by each recipient.

CHAPTER 8

Overseas issues

OUTLINE ¶¶

SECTION 1

Status of the taxpayer

The tax treatment of income from both within the UK and overseas sources is dependent on the status of the individual, who may be: **4150**
- UK resident; and/or
- ordinarily resident in the UK; and/or
- domiciled in the UK.

A. Link to the UK

Summary of tests used

4152 Determination of status involves tests which have been laid down by a combination of statute, case law and practice. A summary of the tests is provided in the table below.

Comment HMRC provide a summary of the taxation of overseas income and gains, residence, ordinary residence and domicile in a guide (HMRC 6). and their internal manual, "Residence, Domicile and the Remittance Basis".

Factor	Tests	¶¶
Residence	Either present in UK for at least 183 days in a tax year	¶4156
	Or regularly visits and average annual presence in UK, over a 4 year period, is at least 91 days	¶4158
Ordinary residence	Either regularly visits and has available accommodation indicating a stay of 3 years or more	¶4160
	Or regularly visits, and average annual presence in UK over a 4 year period, is at least 91 days	
Domicile	Question of fact	¶4163

MEMO POINTS Residence need not be lawful. An individual who remains in the UK for a long period without permission may become ordinarily resident, and may acquire a UK domicile of choice. *Mark v Mark* [2005]

Residence

4154 In the majority of cases the residence of an individual is a question of fact which will have a simple answer (for example, someone has lived in the UK all his life). Residence is more difficult to determine when an individual arrives in or leaves the UK. The tests use the number of days spent in the UK as the first factor to determine residence. However, since the total number of days will not be known in advance, provisional criteria are applied for individuals arriving in or leaving the UK.

An individual can be resident in **more than one country**, in which case the relevant double taxation agreement will decide in which country he is resident for tax purposes. An individual may also not be resident in any country.

In a recent case it was remarked that the test for a former UK resident to establish his non-residence is more stringent than that required for a non-resident to prove continuing non-residence. A distinct break in the pattern of residence is required. *Lyle Dicker Grace* [2011]

MEMO POINTS 1. The UK has concluded **double taxation agreements** with most countries (¶4226), which contain a tie-breaker clause for situations in which an individual would otherwise be resident in both territories. Where tax is actually suffered in both countries, double taxation relief may be available.
2. Residence and domicile are also factors which determine whether an individual is eligible for **personal allowances** in the UK (¶4390).
3. HMRC have announced that a statutory definition of residence will be introduced with effect from April 2012.

4156
s 831 ITA 2007

183 day test An individual who is physically present in the UK for 183 days or more in any tax year is resident for that tax year. Where the tax year is a leap year, the test is still 183 days. This rule applies whether the stay is for one continuous period or a succession of visits.

The **method** used to establish residence is to count the days spent in the UK. Whether a day counts towards the total of residence in the UK depends on physical presence. If an individual is present in the UK at midnight, that day counts as a day of residence. Days of departure, and days on which an individual both arrives and leaves the UK, are ignored.

MEMO POINTS 1. As an **exception**, an individual who is resident and ordinarily resident in the UK will be treated as UK resident even where he remains outside the UK for all or part of a year for the purpose only of occasional residence abroad.
2. There is little statutory guidance, and HMRC consider that other factors denoting close connection with the UK should be taken into account when deciding residence status. In particular, if someone is not in the UK for a temporary purpose, he may be considered to be UK resident. *HMRC v Grace* [2008].

There is a specific exemption for **days spent in transit** through the UK or which straddle midnight due to travel disruption or delay. The exemption applies for passengers who are in transit between two places outside the UK and either: **4157**
- the passenger stays in a restricted area, such as "airside" at an airport; or
- the mode of travel or departure point changes during the journey, such as from an airport to train station.

In addition, while in transit, the individual must not undertake **activities substantially unrelated** to his journey.

EXAMPLE
1. Mr A, a Frenchman, comes to the UK from Paris for a business meeting. He arrives in the UK in the morning and returns to Paris in the evening of the same day. This day will not count as a day of UK residence.

2. Mr B, a Belgian, arrives in the UK for a business meeting on Monday and intends to go home on the same evening. The meeting continues for longer than anticipated and Mr B has to stay until Tuesday. This counts as one day of residence in the UK. The transit exemption will not apply.

3. Mrs C, who normally lives in Spain, travels from Madrid to New York via London. She arrives at Gatwick from Madrid and intends to travel from Heathrow to New York on the same day. When she gets to Heathrow she finds that the journey to New York has been delayed and she is forced to spend the night at a Heathrow hotel. The transit exemption will apply as Mrs C has not undertaken any other activities substantially unconnected with her journey, even though she was present in the UK at midnight.

4. Mrs D, who normally lives in France, is returning from Montreal to Paris via London. Her flight is due to arrive on Monday morning and then she intends to travel by train from London to Paris, but on the same day she has arranged to see her daughter while she is in London. The flight is delayed and she arrives late. Mrs D spends Monday night with her daughter in London and leaves on Tuesday by train. Although Mrs D has been in transit through the UK, she was in the UK at midnight for one night and has undertaken activities substantially unrelated to her journey. Consequently, the transit exemption will not apply and one day will count towards UK residence.

91 day test Where an individual makes **regular visits** to the UK, he will be UK resident, although he will never be considered resident in a year in which he does not set foot in the UK. *CIR v Lysaght* [1928] **4158**

If an individual is present in the UK for an average of at least 91 days per annum over a 4 year period, the individual will become resident in the UK on the first day of the 5th tax year. The same method is used for counting days as under the 183 day test (¶4156).

The average annual number of days is taken to be:

$$\frac{\text{Total visits to the UK (in days)}}{\text{Relevant tax years (cumulative days)}} \times 365$$

MEMO POINTS 1. For the 91 day rule only, days spent in the UK in **exceptional circumstances** such as personal or family illness will be excluded. SP 2/91
2. In a recent case it was remarked that the 91-day test is an HMRC practice which has no basis in law. The number of days present in the UK is not determinative, but must be considered alongside other factors in deciding residence status. *Lyle Dicker Grace* [2011]
3. For individuals who **come to or leave** the UK see ¶4170.

EXAMPLE Mr A, a Frenchman, comes to live in the UK for a period of 4 years. He will be treated as UK resident from the day of arrival.
Mr B, a US citizen, comes to London for the first time in April and stays with relatives for 180 days in the tax year. He will not be treated as UK resident for that tax year.

Ordinary residence

4160 Ordinary residence denotes greater permanence than residence. An individual may be ordinarily resident for a year despite not setting foot in the UK during that year.

An individual may be resident for a tax year, for example where he is temporarily working in the UK, without becoming ordinarily resident. In contrast, an individual may be ordinarily resident, by virtue of living in the UK throughout his life, but not resident for a number of years because of employment abroad.

EXAMPLE Mr C, who is Australian, comes to the UK for a 9 month course in May. He will become UK resident from the day he arrives in the UK but will not be ordinarily resident for the tax year.
Mr D, who is UK domiciled, resident and ordinarily resident before his departure, goes to the USA for a tour with his band in September. The tour lasts 16 months, during which time he is no longer UK resident, but he will remain ordinarily resident throughout.

MEMO POINTS The definition of ordinary residence has been considered by the (then) Special Commissioners, who held that the term must be given its normal and natural meaning and referred to a person's abode in a particular country. The question whether an individual was ordinarily resident was one of fact, and that there was no guidance as to the minimum period required to establish that a "foreigner" had become ordinarily resident in the United Kingdom, although, in this particular case, the accepted period was 3 years. *Genovese v HMRC* [2009]

4161 If either of the following two **criteria** are satisfied, an individual will be treated as ordinarily resident:

a. he visits the UK and has available accommodation which implies a stay in the country of 3 years or more (i.e. excluding a lease for a period shorter than 3 years); or

b. his visits average 91 days or more per tax year over a 4 year period: the same test as for residence (¶4158).

EXAMPLE Mr A makes the following visits to the UK:

Tax year	Days in UK
1	86
2	0
3	146
4	143
5	92
6	0

In Tax Year 4, Mr A's average number of days in the UK is 93.69.
$$\frac{86 + 0 + 146 + 143}{366 + 365 + 365 + 365} \times 365 = 93.69 \text{ days}$$
Mr A will become resident and ordinarily resident in the UK from the beginning of Tax Year 5.

In Tax Year 5, Mr A's average number of days in the UK is 95.45.
$$\frac{0 + 146 + 143 + 92}{365 + 365 + 365 + 366} \times 366 = 95.45 \text{ days}$$
Mr A will remain resident and ordinarily resident.

In Tax Year 6, Mr A's average number of days in the UK is 95.18.
$$\frac{146 + 143 + 92 + 0}{365 + 365 + 366 + 365} \times 365 = 95.18 \text{ days}$$
As Mr A did not set foot in the UK during the year, he will not be resident in the UK for Tax Year 6, but will remain ordinarily resident.

Domicile

4163 Domicile is a concept of general law, and is more fundamental and permanent than residence or ordinary residence. Domicile is a link to a particular jurisdiction, and is not necessarily the same as nationality or place of residence. Every individual must have a domicile, but he cannot have more than one at the same time.

MEMO POINTS 1. **Deemed domicile** is an important concept for inheritance tax purposes, and this is discussed at ¶6380.
2. Strictly speaking, because there are separate jurisdictions in parts of the UK, there are three possible domiciles here: England and Wales, Scotland, or Northern Ireland.

An individual acquires a **domicile of origin** at birth. This is normally the domicile of the father at the time of birth, unless the child is born to unmarried parents, in which case it is the domicile of the mother. The domicile of origin may be abandoned in later life, or revived if a domicile of choice is no longer upheld. 4164

While the individual remains a minor, his domicile will follow the domicile of the parent from whom he acquired his domicile of origin. This is known as a **domicile of dependency**. Any changes to the parent's domicile apply to the minor. 4166

Once the individual reaches the age of 16, he may acquire a **domicile of choice**. In order to do so, the individual must physically reside in a new country, with the intention to remain there indefinitely, and must sever all ties with his former country of domicile. 4167

A domicile of choice can be lost by ceasing to live in that country, and having no intention of ever living there permanently.

If a domicile of choice is abandoned, the individual reverts to his domicile of origin until such time, if ever, that another domicile of choice is acquired.

MEMO POINTS 1. **Intention** is subjective, and the individual's conduct should support his expressed intention.
2. Before 1 January 1974, a **woman** automatically acquired her husband's domicile on marriage, as a domicile of dependency. If the husband's domicile changed, the domicile of the wife would change in accordance with his. If this circumstance applies, a wife will retain the domicile of dependency until she acquires a new domicile of choice, even if the marriage subsequently ends in divorce or on the death of the husband. The rules for the acquisition of a domicile of dependency prior to 1 January 1974 were not applicable to US domiciled women, who retain their US domicile of origin on marriage before and after that date.
3. Women who have married after 1 January 1974 determine their own domicile status which is **independent** of their husband's domicile, although marriage itself may be supporting evidence for the acquisition of a domicile of choice.

If a **foreign domiciliary** wishes to avoid becoming domiciled in the UK, he must maintain sufficient ties with another country (either his domicile of origin or his domicile of choice) and never intend to reside permanently in the UK. It is very unlikely that a foreigner would become UK domiciled immediately on arrival.

EXAMPLE Mr B had a UK domicile of origin. He moved permanently abroad to Sri Lanka and acquired a Sri Lankan domicile of choice. On retirement he left Sri Lanka permanently and returned to Europe, living in Germany, but also spending significant amounts of time in Spain and Portugal. Until Mr B acquires a new domicile of choice (which may be in Germany), his UK domicile of origin will revive.

B. Entering and leaving the UK

As an individual's residence status cannot be accurately predicted, HMRC adopt certain practices in determining whether to treat someone as resident or ordinarily resident following arrival in, or departure from, the UK. This is to enable tax to be charged in advance of a final residence position being established. If a person is treated as being resident in accordance with these practices, but subsequently proves to be non-resident, the tax position for any affected years will be recalculated. 4170

Each **individual case** is considered on its own merits, and is very dependent on the intentions of the individual. HMRC will require a form P85 to be completed shortly before departure from the UK.

Summary of status rules

The following table summarises the residence and ordinary residence status that an individual is likely to be given, based on the circumstances of his arrival in, or departure from, the UK. 4171

Situation	Accommodation available[1]	Status
Arrival in the UK		
Intention to stay in UK > 2 years	n/a	Resident from date of arrival
Intention to stay in UK > 3 years	n/a	Resident and ordinarily resident from date of arrival
No intention	✓	
No intention	X	Not resident or ordinarily resident
No intention initially, but then intention changes in tax year of arrival to stay > 3 years	X	Resident and ordinarily resident from date of arrival
No intention initially, but then intention changes after tax year of arrival to stay > 3 years	X	Resident and ordinarily resident from 6 April in tax year intention changes
No intention	Not initially, then subsequently acquired	Resident and ordinarily resident from 6 April in tax year accommodation acquired
No intention, but actually stays in UK > 3 years	X	Resident and ordinarily resident from 6 April in tax year beginning after 3 years have elapsed from date of arrival
Departure from the UK		
Full time employment abroad – contract and absence > 1 tax year	n/a	Not resident or ordinarily resident from date of departure
Evidence of intention to reside abroad permanently (or for a period of at least 3 years)	n/a	
No specific intention, or no evidence of intention to reside abroad permanently	n/a	Ordinarily resident for 3 years following departure

Note:
1. **Accommodation** refers to accommodation acquired on a basis which implies a stay in the UK of 3 years or more (i.e. not a short lease of less than 3 years).

Splitting the year of arrival or departure

4172 ESC A11 Strictly speaking, an individual's residence applies for a whole tax year. However, **by concession**, HMRC will split a tax year where an individual arrives to take up a new permanent residence, or to stay for at least 2 years, and he will be UK resident from the day of arrival.

Similarly, where a person leaves to reside permanently abroad, or to work abroad for a period spanning a whole tax year, the year of departure may be split, so that he is non-UK resident from the day after the day of departure.

MEMO POINTS 1. Where a new arrival was already **ordinarily resident** In the UK, the split year basis will not apply. Similarly, if a person remains ordinarily resident when leaving the UK, the split year basis will not apply.
2. Full **personal allowances** are available for the year of arrival or departure, on the same basis as for other UK residents, regardless of whether the concession applies..
3. If a large tax liability would arise in the event that HMRC did not apply the concessionary practice for some reason, an individual should consider accelerating or delaying an arrival or departure, to ensure that he would be non-resident for the full year in question.

Arrival

4174 For individuals arriving in the UK, the residence and ordinary residence position is initially a question of **intention**.

SP 3/81 SP 17/91 Individuals arriving in the UK who propose to live here **permanently or remain here** for 3 years or more will be treated as resident and ordinarily resident from the date of arrival.

MEMO POINTS Where an individual comes to the UK with the intention to stay for 2 years or more, he will be treated as resident from the date of arrival until the date of departure. An individual arriving with the intention to stay for less than 2 years will only be resident if caught by the 183 day rule. ESC A11

If an individual, **during the tax year of arrival**: 4176
- buys or leases (for a minimum 3 year period) accommodation for his use; or
- decides to stay in the UK for at least 3 years at any point,

he will be considered resident and ordinarily resident from the date of arrival.

In other cases, residence will be determined using the 183 and 91 day rules.

MEMO POINTS 1. Where an individual **intends to make regular visits** (satisfying the 91 day rule) when he first comes to the UK, he will be treated as resident and ordinarily resident from the start of the tax year in which the visits commence.
2. As an exception, a **student** will not be treated as ordinarily resident provided that he:
a. arrives in the UK to undertake a period of study or education lasting less than 4 years;
b. does not own or buy accommodation in the UK; and
c. will not be making regular visits (averaging 91 days or more per tax year) following his departure from the UK.

Change of circumstances If, after the tax year of arrival, an individual's **intention changes**, he will be treated as ordinarily resident from the start of the tax year in which the intention changed, but residence will only be determined using the 183 and 91 day rules. This applies if: 4178
- the proposed stay is extended during the first 3 years; or
- accommodation is bought (or leased for a minimum 3 year period) in a year other than the tax year of arrival.

Where an individual **did not initially intend** to stay in the UK for at least 3 years, he will be treated as ordinarily resident in the UK from the start of the tax year after he has been in the UK for 3 years.

Departure

On departure from the UK, the intention of the individual determines whether he remains resident and ordinarily resident. 4180

A **temporary** absence abroad of less than a year will not affect whether an individual is resident or ordinarily resident.

An individual who leaves the UK **permanently** for a settled purpose, or for a period of 3 years or more, will be treated as not resident and not ordinarily resident from the date of departure.

However, if the individual expects or intends to make **regular visits** to the UK during the period of absence, he will remain resident and ordinarily resident unless any visits during the period of absence amount to less than:
- 183 days in any tax year; and
- an average of 91 days per tax year over a period of 4 years (¶4158).

An individual who meets the 91 day test may, however, remain resident and ordinarily resident if he does not satisfy the **qualitative tests** for leaving the UK. **Evidence** of intention will normally be required to support a claim for non-residence, for example the acquisition of accommodation abroad. It is not necessary to dispose of property in the UK if the absence is for at least 3 years, and there is a valid reason for retaining the property. Where, at the time of departure, there is **insufficient evidence**, the individual will be treated as resident and ordinarily resident for the first 3 years of absence. At the end of that period the position will be reviewed and, if the individual is shown to have been not resident and not ordinarily resident, his tax position will be adjusted accordingly.

MEMO POINTS An airline pilot who moved to Cyprus and spent less than 91 days on average in the UK remained resident and ordinarily resident in the UK because:
1. he had not disposed of his UK **home**, where his wife still lived, and which he used on return visits which were more than just rest periods between flights;
2. his **UK address** continued to be the main base for administrative purposes, including correspondence with his employer, bank and HMRC; and
3. his **employment** was based in the UK, as all his duties involved flights which began or ended there. *Shepherd v HMRC* [2006]

Departing the UK for full-time employment abroad

4183 ESC A11 Where an individual takes up full-time employment abroad for at least a whole tax year, he will be treated as not resident and not ordinarily resident from the date of departure, unless he makes regular visits to the UK.

MEMO POINTS 1. For CGT purposes (¶5227) the individual will only be treated as not resident and not ordinarily resident in a tax year if his employment begins before or at the start of that year. *Gaines-Cooper v HMRC* [2010]

ESC A78 2. Where an individual goes abroad to work full time, and his spouse or civil partner accompanies him or joins him at a later date, the spouse or civil partner is treated, by concession, as being not resident and not ordinarily resident from the date of his or her departure. This concession applies so long as she would not be resident based on the normal 183 day or 91 day tests during her absence.

EXAMPLE

1. Mr A leaves the UK on 25 August 2010 to take up a full-time job in Spain. He remains there, without making regular visits to the UK, until his job ends on 30 June 2012 and he returns to the UK. Because he was absent for a whole tax year (2011/12) he is treated as not resident and not ordinarily resident for the whole period from 25 August 2010 to 30 June 2012. If his absence had not been for the purpose of full-time employment, he would be treated as non-resident only for 2011/12.

2. Mrs A remains in the UK for a short time to sell the family house, and then joins Mr A in Spain on 2 October 2010. She does not make regular visits to the UK. She returns before him, on 1 June 2012, to look for accommodation. She is treated as not resident and not ordinarily resident for the period from 2 October 2010 to 1 June 2012.

SECTION 2

UK Taxation of foreign income

4190 An individual may be taxable on various types of income from overseas. The extent of UK taxation, and the availability of reliefs, depends on the status of the individual and the source of the income.

A. Basis of UK taxation

4192 An individual may be liable to tax on his income on an **arising basis** or a **remittance basis**, depending on his circumstances. Usually income is assessed on an arising basis, but the remittance basis can be claimed where an individual is either:
– non-UK domiciled, whether or not ordinarily resident; or
– UK domiciled, but not ordinarily resident.

1. Arising basis

4194 s 830 ITTOIA 2005 The arising basis means that **income receivable is taxed on a current year basis**, regardless of whether the individual has actually received the income in the UK. An individual who is UK resident and UK domiciled is taxable on an arising basis.

MEMO POINTS A **trade** carried on abroad is taxable on the basis of its accounting period, following the rules for UK trades.

4196 ss 838 – 839 ITTOIA 2005 A **deduction** is available for:
– expenses incurred outside the UK that are related to the collection or payment of the income; and
– annuities and annual payments (excluding interest) which are payable out of the income to non-residents.

Losses can only be set against other foreign income.

Unremittable income

If the transfer of income to the UK is **restricted** by government action or foreign currency controls, the UK tax charge in respect of that income can be postponed. If and when the restrictions are lifted, the income will become taxable, although the actual assessment will relate to the tax year when the income arose. 4198 s 841 ITTOIA 2005

A **claim** for relief for unremittable income must be made within 12 months following the 31 January after the tax year when the income would otherwise be chargeable to income tax. s 842 ITTOIA 2005

2. Remittance basis

The remittance basis simply means that **income is taxed only when it is remitted to the UK**. If the money remains outside the UK, there is no UK tax liability. 4200 ss 809B - 809E ITA 2007

Claiming the remittance basis means that the personal allowances for income tax (¶4390) and the annual exemption for capital gains tax are not available, unless an exemption applies. Remitted income is taxed as non-savings income (¶4346) s 809G ITA 2007

Claiming the remittance basis involves a two-stage decision:
1. Is the individual eligible to claim the remittance basis?
2. If so, is he required to pay the remittance basis charge (¶4203)?

The diagram below illustrates how to determine **eligibility** to claim the remittance basis.

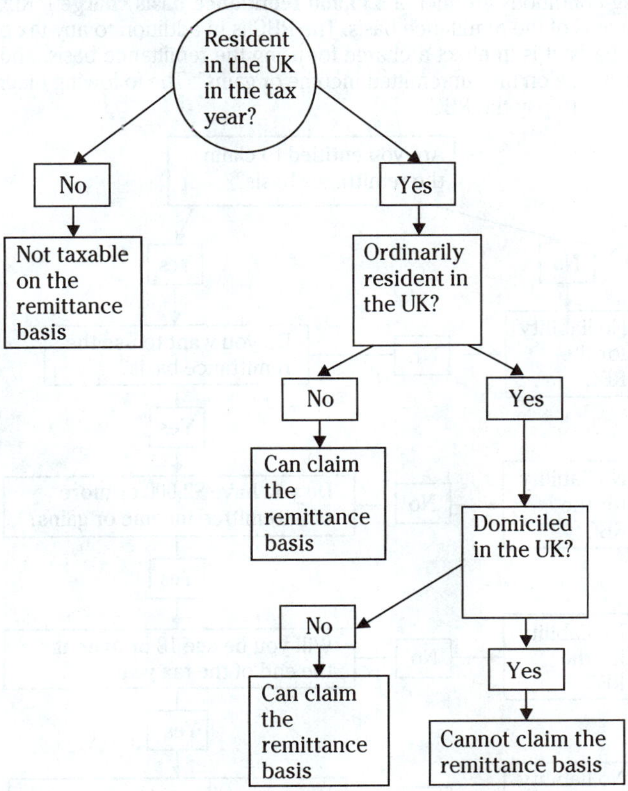

MEMO POINTS 1. Prior to 6 April 2008, the remittance basis did not apply to income which had its **source in the Republic of Ireland**: this was assessable on the arising basis. Income arising in the Republic of Ireland up to, and including, 5 April 2008 and remitted from the Republic of Ireland after 6 April 2008 should not be taxed in the UK, as it has already suffered UK taxation. s 831 ITTOIA 2005

2. An ordinarily resident individual who **becomes UK domiciled** will no longer be entitled to claim the remittance basis.
3. A **non-UK resident** is taxed on income arising in the UK only.
4. HMRC have announced that from April 2012 a non-domiciled individual will be able to remit foreign income to the UK tax free, if doing so for the purpose of making a commercial investment in a UK business.

4202 s 809B ITA 2007

An **individual** who is non-domiciled or not ordinarily resident may be eligible to claim (on a year-by-year basis) for foreign income to be assessed on a remittance basis. Without a claim for the remittance basis, generally, the arising basis will apply.

If a claim for the remittance basis has not been submitted, an **exemption** for liability to income tax for UK resident **non-domiciles only** applies where **all** of the following conditions have been met:
– income is received from an employment, the duties of which are performed wholly or partly in the United Kingdom;
– relevant foreign earnings are £10,000 or less and all are subject to a foreign tax;
– relevant foreign income from the year does not exceed £100 and all of it is subject to a foreign tax;
– there are no other foreign income or gains in the tax year;
– the individual would be otherwise liable to tax at starting rate or basic rate; and
– the individual is not required to submit a self-assessment tax return.

The remittance basis charge

4203 s 809B ITA 2007

If the qualifying conditions are met, a **£30,000 remittance basis charge** ("RBC") is applied to certain claimants of the remittance basis. The RBC is in addition to any tax payable under the remittance basis: it is in effect a charge for using the remittance basis, and is treated by HMRC as a tax charge on the "unremitted income or gains". The following diagram illustrates who may be liable to pay the RBC.

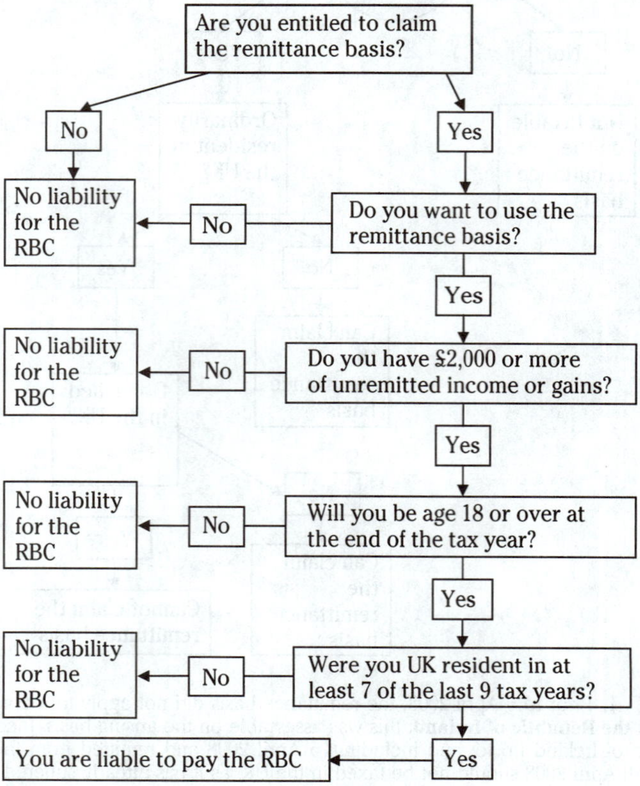

The RBC applies to non-domiciled individuals in the following circumstances: s 809H ITA 2007
1. the individual has been resident in the UK for 7 years, which do not have to be continuous, out of the previous 9 years;
2. he has more than £2,000 of unremitted foreign income or gains in the UK; and
3. he has already reached or becomes age 18 during the tax year.

The charge is **imposed** in the tenth year of residence.

There is an **exemption for payment** if an individual has less than £2,000 of unremitted foreign income and gains annually, even if the other conditions have been satisfied. In contrast, payment of the RBC is required if the other conditions have been fulfilled, but the individual is nevertheless only resident for part of the year.

MEMO POINTS 1. Where an individual has **less than £2,000** of unremitted overseas income or gains, he is not required to pay the RBC and has access to the **remittance basis by default**, without having to submit a claim. In this circumstance only, the individual will not lose either the personal allowances or the annual exemption for capital gains tax, but only those not domiciled in the UK can claim the remittance basis on capital gains. s 809D ITA 2007
2. HMRC have announced that from April 2012 the RBC will be **increased** to £50,000 for non-domiciles who have been UK resident for 12 or more years and who wish to continue to be taxed on the remittance basis. The £30,000 charge will continue for those who have been resident for at least 7 of the past 9 years, but fewer than 12 years.

Nomination of income

The individual must **nominate** income or gains to which the RBC is attributed. The nomination is to identify which of the individual's income or gains he wishes to have taxed on an arising basis, as though the remittance basis did not apply to that income or those gains. Nomination details must be entered on the individual's tax return. 4204 RDRM 32310 ss 809B, 809H, 809I, 809J ITA 2007

The nominated income should not be remitted to the UK in the same year as the nomination is made. If the nominated funds are later remitted to the UK, the tax attributed to them is treated as having already been paid.

The nomination does not have to be equal to the value of the RBC. If an individual decides to nominate a **smaller amount**, he will retain some confidentiality over his affairs, but there will not be a full tax credit available if and when funds are remitted to the UK.

If a nomination is made but is found to be **invalid**, the whole of the overseas income and gains for the year will be taxable on the arising basis, unless a new valid claim is made within the time limit.

MEMO POINTS A claim may be invalid if the individual mistakenly nominates income or gains so that the resulting tax charge exceeds £30,000.

The **general rule** is that remittances are treated as being made from un-nominated income or gains first. 4205

If remittances are made from **mixed funds**, there is a prescribed order in which remittances are treated as being made. This order means that if there are un-nominated income and gains which remain outside the UK, these are treated as remitted to the UK first, in preference to the funds which may have been nominated. The order is as follows:
1. employment income (other than relevant foreign earnings, employment income related to securities and employment income subject to a foreign tax);
2. relevant foreign earnings;
3. foreign employment income relating to securities;
4. relevant foreign income (not subject to a foreign tax);
5. foreign chargeable gains (not subject to a foreign tax);
6. employment income subject to a foreign tax;
7. relevant foreign income subject to a foreign tax;
8. foreign chargeable gains subject to a foreign tax; and
9. any other income or gains.

EXAMPLE Mrs A is non-UK domiciled and entitled to claim the remittance basis but must also pay the RBC. She decides that she does not want to inform HMRC about all her overseas income and

so nominates only £10,000 of overseas income as being on the arising basis. She is liable to pay the full RBC of £30,000 and when she brings the nominated income into the UK, she will have a tax credit of £4,000 (as a 40% taxpayer).
Mrs A remits £20,000 of income to the UK in year 2.
Mrs A claims the remittance basis in year 2, and she has to pay the following tax liabilities:
- the RBC (£30,000);
- income tax at her marginal rate on the remitted income arising in year 1 (£20,000 × 40%); and
- income tax on any UK source income.

Mrs A will be entitled to a tax credit of £4,000 for the £10,000 of nominated income from year 1 if she has no other unremitted income or gains overseas.

MEMO POINTS 1. The RBC is the equivalent of nominating £75,000 of taxable overseas income at a rate of 40% or £60,000 at 50%.
2. On 12 March 2008 HMRC published an opinion suggesting that the RBC is creditable against a tax liability in the USA. This point may be subject to interpretation by the USA taxation authorities.
3. The nomination is at the discretion of the individual and does not have to be equal to the RBC, but if the nomination is less than the RBC, the RBC will not be eligible in full for a tax foreign tax credit, if tax is due in the other jurisdiction.

EXAMPLE

1. Mr A is non-domiciled and UK resident. He is liable to pay the RBC and nominates £50,000 of his foreign income as relating to it. Mr A pays UK tax at 40%. Mr A will have to pay the RBC of £30,000 but when he brings the nominated money into the UK he will have a tax credit of £20,000.

2. Miss B is also liable to pay the RBC and decides to nominate £1 of overseas income as relating to the RBC. she is liable to pay the full £30,000 RBC despite making a low nomination. When Miss B brings her overseas money into the UK, she will be liable to pay tax on it.

Payment of tax

4206 s 809V ITA 2007

Money **to pay the RBC** can come from UK source funds or from foreign assets. If the payment is made from an overseas bank account, it will not be treated as a remittance to the UK provided it is made directly to HMRC from that overseas bank account, for example electronically or by cheque; if payment is made to a UK bank account first, it will be treated as a taxable remittance and could generate an additional tax liability. HMRC have confirmed that it is the taxpayer's obligation to prove that payment has been made directly. Payment is administered through the self-assessment system and is subject to the filing and payment regime. As the RBC has the effect of a prepayment of tax, unremitted foreign income or gains can be nominated as subject to the RBC; if the nominated funds are later remitted, there is no further tax to pay on those funds.

s 809H (1) (b) ITA 2007

MEMO POINTS 1. Residence status rules apply to **children** in the same way as to adults, but the obligation to pay the RBC only applies to adults over age 18. Minors are first liable to pay the RBC in the year in which they become 18, and only if they have also met the residence and income conditions.
2. All years of residence in the UK during the last 9 years count towards the 7 year limit. This includes split years, years spent in the UK below age 18 or years when a taxpayer is dual resident or treaty resident in another country.
3. The £2,000 exemption limit applies for the whole of the tax year even if the individual leaves the year part way through and is entitled to claim split year treatment.
4. The RBC is due in addition to any tax liability payable under the remittance basis, but unremitted foreign income and gains can be nominated as subject to the charge.
5. Unremitted income or gains are taxable when remitted to the UK, irrespective of when the income or gains arose, including in years when the former rules applied.
6. HMRC consider that the RBC is eligible for both Gift Aid relief and for double taxation relief, but it depends on the details of the relevant tax treaty as to the operation of the double taxation relief. Each situation has to be considered separately.
7. If the RBC is **paid by the employer** on behalf of an employee, this will give rise to earnings from the employment. If an employee has an employment contract which includes tax-equalisation and the RBC is paid by the employer, it should be reported as a net-of-tax benefit (together with the grossed-up tax which is payable on it) on the individual's self-assessment tax return for the year in which the RBC is paid to HMRC. This means that an RBC for the year 2009/10 which is paid by the employer on 31 January 2012 is assessable as a benefit in 2011/12 and the tax on

it is due for payment on 31 January 2013. The exemption for payment of the RBC directly to HMRC is not available.

8. If an employee is assessable on the arising basis for the tax year of payment, all of their earnings (including the grossed-up RBC) will be taxed.

9. If an employee is assessable on the remittance basis for the tax year of payment, HMRC will treat the payment of the RBC as a remittance of £30,000 of net-of-tax earnings. The cash-flow impact on the employer may be worse where the RBC is nominated to earnings that are remitted to the UK, but other remittance basis income or gains (for that or an earlier tax year from 2008/09 onwards) remain unremitted. This is due to the fact that the rules treat the unremitted income or gains as remitted before the nominated earnings that have actually been remitted (and credit will only be given for the RBC as and when the nominated earnings are assessed). This approach increases the tax liability of both the employee and the employer, and advice in this area should be sought.

EXAMPLE Mr A, who is domiciled in Italy and has money in Italian bank accounts, comes to the UK to work.

In year 1 (a split year) he is resident from the day of arrival. In year 5 he returns to work in Italy and is non-resident for the whole of that year and for year 6. He comes back to the UK in the summer of year 7 and is resident in the UK for years 7, 8 and 9. If Mr A wishes to continue to use the remittance basis, he will be liable to pay the RBC in year 10, even if he is not UK resident for the whole tax year, as he will have been resident for at least 7 out of the previous 9 years, (years 1-4 inclusive and years 7-9 inclusive). Provided Mr A sends the payment directly to HMRC, he will not trigger an additional tax liability through the payment.

Mr B, who is domiciled in France, fulfils the conditions for the RBC to apply. In year 10 of residence he sells his ski chalet in France and the capital gain, if calculated for UK tax purposes, would be £500,000. Mr B keeps the proceeds in a French bank account. This gain will be taxable when Mr B remits all or part of the funds to the UK. Mr B can nominate the RBC payment for year 10 as relating to the gain on the chalet. If Mr B later remits funds from the sale, part of the capital gains tax liability will be treated as already met by the RBC, but if he has other unremitted income or gains, not nominated, these will be treated as being remitted first.

Timing

Remittances are normally **taxable** in the tax year in which the remittance occurs, not the year in which the income arises. Income arising abroad in a year when the remittance basis is claimed is subject to tax when it is remitted to the UK. **4207** s 832A ITTOIA 2005

If an individual is a **temporary non-resident**, a tax charge may be triggered on any remittances of relevant foreign income to the UK after the year of departure, but prior to the year of return. A temporary non-resident for this purpose is someone who has been UK resident for 4 out of the 7 years prior to departure and between departure and returning to the UK, there are fewer than 5 tax years. Any remittances made during this period are treated as being remitted to the UK in the year of return. This is similar to the provisions for CGT treatment for non-residents (¶5227).

EXAMPLE Mr A was resident and ordinarily resident in the UK until October 2008 when he went to work overseas. He owns a property in Spain and continues to send the profits of this business back to the UK while he is non-resident. Mr A returns to the UK in October 2012, after 3 complete tax years since his departure have elapsed (2009/10, 2010/11 and 2011/12). He is treated as resident in the UK immediately on his return. A tax charge arises in 2012/13 on the funds that he remitted to the UK while non-resident. If Mr A had remained outside the UK until October 2014, this tax charge would not have arisen.

What constitutes a remittance

A remittance is a receipt of sums or benefits in the UK or relating to UK property. There are three situations in which overseas income or chargeable gains are treated as remitted to the UK: **4208**

1. The use by an **individual** of his own money in the UK, or the provision of benefits to, or for, a **relevant person**.

2. Qualifying property belonging to **someone who has received a gift** from the individual is
– brought to the UK and enjoyed by a relevant person; or

– used to provide a benefit or service which is enjoyed in the UK by a relevant person; or
– used outside the UK directly or indirectly in respect of a **relevant debt**.

3. In the case of a **connected operation**, property of another person, apart from a relevant person or someone who has received a gift, is:
– brought to, received in or used in the UK by a relevant person; or
– used to provide a benefit or service which is enjoyed in the UK by a relevant person; or
– used outside the UK in respect of a relevant debt.

In effect, whenever overseas income is applied with the result that **funds are received in the UK**, there is a remittance.

EXAMPLE In one case, a taxpayer used his salary from an overseas company which he controlled to subscribe for more shares. That company then made a loan to another unconnected company which in turn made a corresponding loan to the taxpayer in the UK. It was held that the loan in the UK could be traced back to the overseas salary, and therefore constituted a remittance of income.
Harmel v Wright [1974]

MEMO POINTS 1. A **relevant person** is defined as:
a. the individual, his spouse or civil partner, or anyone co-habiting as such;
b. a minor child or grandchild of those listed above;
c. a close company or an overseas company which, if resident in the UK, would be close, or a 51% subsidiary of such a company;
d. the trustees of a settlement of which any of the individuals above are beneficiaries; or
e. a body connected with such a settlement, which means any close company, a 51% subsidiary of such a company or an overseas company which would be a close company if it were resident in the UK.
The exceptions to this list are the adult children of the individual, their spouse or civil partner or anyone co-habiting as such, who are not defined as relevant persons.
2. A **relevant debt** includes:
a. overseas loans used to buy a house in the UK;
b. the use of offshore income and chargeable gains as security for the borrowing of funds overseas which are then brought into the UK; or
c. the use of offshore income and chargeable gains to pay off a foreign debt which was brought into the UK.

4209 The source of the remittance need not have existed at the beginning of the tax year. Income may have arisen in prior tax years and the source of that income closed, but such income will be taxable whenever remitted to the UK. If the source ceases part way through a tax year, income remitted at any time during that tax year is taxable.

MEMO POINTS Prior to 6 April 2008, the source of the income had to be in existence at the beginning of the tax year, or the remittance was not assessable. This means that income remitted from sources closed many years previously could be taxable if remitted now.

s 6 ITEPA 2003 The change to the source-ceasing rule applies to foreign investment income only as **earned income** has always been assessable regardless of when the employment ceased.

Assets

4210 s 809L - 809O ITA 2007 A **remittance to the UK of assets** is taxable unless one of the following exemptions applies:
1. Assets owned by an individual on 11 March 2008, even if held outside the UK at that date and later imported, but only for so long as they are retained by the same owner.
2. Assets which are remitted to the UK and kept in the UK for no more than 9 months.
3. Personal items belonging to the taxpayer, such as clothes, jewellery and watches.
4. Assets brought into the UK for the purposes of repair or restoration.
5. Assets brought into the UK for the purposes of public display or exhibition at an approved institution, for no longer than 2 years unless HMRC agree to a longer period.
6. Assets costing less than £1,000

EXAMPLE Mr B is UK resident but non-domiciled. In March 2012 he imports a painting to the UK which had originally cost him £150,000. At the time of importation, the painting is worth £120,000. Mr B will be treated as making a remittance of £150,000 unless an exemption applies.

MEMO POINTS A **statutory valuation** rule applies in circumstances where the property forms part of a set, and only part of the set is being remitted to the UK. The taxable remittance is calculated by ascertaining what the amount of the remittance would have been if the whole set had been remitted to the UK and then deciding between the part remitted and the part not, what a just and reasonable taxable remittance amount should be.

If an asset which is treated as exempt is sold while in the UK or no longer fulfils the conditions for exemption, there is a remittance at that time. In particular, if an asset is brought into the UK and drops in value or is sold in the UK at less than its value at the date of remittance, the taxable remittance will be the value of the asset when it was first remitted to the UK, not the amount of the consideration received on sale (or deemed consideration if a gift). s 809Y ITA 2007

Services

An exception applies for the provision of **UK services** in some circumstances. To qualify as an exception two conditions must be satisfied: 4211 s 809W ITA 2007
– the service must be preformed wholly or mainly in respect of non-UK property; and
– payment of the service must be made into a non-UK bank account of the service provider.
The exemption will not apply where the services are in respect of benefits arising from the transfer of assets abroad or in respect of benefits received from an overseas trust.

MEMO POINTS If a remittance basis user pays a **professional adviser** offshore for services the adviser has given in the UK, and the payment is made with funds from offshore income or gains, a remittance will be triggered.

Identification of income and capital

Whether an item is a remittance of income is a question of fact, and the onus is on the taxpayer to prove the nature of the remittance. 4212 s 832 ITTOIA 2005

It is **common practice** for individuals assessable on the remittance basis to maintain a minimum of three different overseas bank accounts, for the purpose of holding:
1. Capital.
2. Proceeds from capital gains realised offshore (which are also assessable on the remittance basis).
3. Income.

Any funds transferred to the UK should be from the capital account wherever possible.

Any **interest** earned on the accounts can be paid into a separate account.

If an individual does not maintain separate accounts and a remittance is made from a **mixed account** (i.e. one holding income and capital items), it is deemed to be income up to the maximum amount of the income in the account. 4214 s 809Q ITA 2007 RDRM35200

EXAMPLE Mr A has a foreign bank account with a balance of £32,000 comprising part capital and part income. The income element of the account is £5,000.
If Mr A makes a transfer to the UK of £6,500, £5,000 will be deemed to be a remittance of income, and the balance capital. If instead Mr A transferred £4,000, it would all be income.
If the capital and income had been held in separate accounts, Mr A could have made the full transfer from the capital account without suffering any UK tax on the remittance basis.

EXAMPLE Continuing the example at ¶4210, Mr B had purchased the painting with the sale of shares in overseas companies, triggering a gain of £50,000. The shares had, in turn, originally been purchased for £100,000 out of unremitted foreign employment income. On the importation of the painting, Mr B will be taxed on £150,000 as follows:
1. CGT on £50,000 of foreign chargeable gains, on the sale of the overseas shares; and
2. income tax on £100,000 of foreign employment income, which was used to finance the purchase of the foreign shares.

A similar provision applies where a bank account holds **mixed income**, some of which is taxable on an arising basis, and some taxable on the remittance basis (e.g. a Jersey bank 4216 account into which income from the UK and France is paid). In this situation, any amounts remitted are allocated first to amounts taxable on an arising basis (e.g. UK income).

When arranging a transaction which appears to take place entirely offshore, it is important to check that at no stage will the funds come into the UK. This may be a problem when the transaction involves overseas branches of UK banks. It should be made very clear to the bank that at no point should the funds be routed through the UK.

MEMO POINTS 1. Where a **bank error** resulted in the remittance of income to the UK from an individual's overseas income account, contrary to the account holder's wishes, which clearly stated that the remittance should be made from a capital account, it was agreed that this was not to be treated as a remittance. *Duke of Roxburghe's Executors v CIR* [1936]

2. Income held overseas cannot be **converted into capital** simply by purchasing a capital asset. Although a disposal of such an asset may produce a capital gain, the amount originally invested remains income in nature and, if brought to the UK, will be a taxable income remittance. *Walsh v Randall* [1940]

Common types of remittance

4218 The following types of remittance commonly occur:

Types of situation	Detail	Tax treatment
Dividend income	UK registered companies	Arising basis even where paid into an overseas bank account.
	Overseas companies	Remittance basis. Treated as remitted if paid via a UK paying agent or mandated directly to a UK bank account.
Gift		Depends on the legal position both in the country of origin and the country of receipt, but generally foreign law takes precedence.[1] The gift of property abroad to an individual can constitute a remittance for the donor if the gift is later remitted to the UK and the donor or his immediate family benefits from it.[2]
Credit card	UK credit card	Settling a bill using overseas income will comprise a taxable remittance.
	Overseas credit card used in UK	Depends on when debt is incurred. Generally the individual is deemed to borrow money from the credit card company at the time of the transaction, in which case there is a taxable remittance.
	Overseas credit card used overseas	Generally will not give rise to a remittance but see above for taxation of gifts. If the card was used to purchase an asset which is subsequently brought to the UK and sold, there will be a remittance if overseas income was used to settle the credit card bill. The remittance of an asset itself can be taxable unless one of the exemptions applies (¶4210).

Note:
1. A banker's draft posted in California to the individual's daughter in the UK was not a remittance of income as, under Californian law, the transfer of a banker's draft is completed at the time of posting. So the money was a gift before it reached the UK, and did not represent the mother's income. Had the gift been by way of a cheque, this would have remained the mother's property until cashed by the daughter and therefore would have constituted a remittance of income by the mother. *Carter v Sharon* [1936]
In contrast, a banker's draft drawn on an Indian account which was sent to an individual in London was deemed to constitute a remittance, as under Indian law the funds did not become the property of the recipient until presented at the bank. *Walsh v Randall* [1940]
2.See ¶4208 for the definition of immediate family. The rule which applied under the case of *Carter v Sharon* [1936] does not apply to gifts made after 11 March 2008, unless the gift is made to the adult child of the donor.

Other types of remittances

A remittance will be triggered if a mortgage on UK property is provided by an overseas lender, and the loan is paid off or varied. There are **transitional provisions** for mortgages with overseas lenders made before 12 March 2008 where the loan has been used to purchase residential property in the UK and is secured on that property. In this case, payment of interest out of relevant foreign income will not be treated as a remittance, but payment of capital will be. The provisions last until the end of the existing mortgage term or 5 April 2028, whichever is the shorter. The terms of the mortgage must not be varied, and that includes obtaining a further advance, but the exemption does extend to guarantees or an indemnity on the property. **4220** ss 809L, 809M ITA 2007

MEMO POINTS If a loan is made abroad and the money brought to the UK after any part of the loan has been satisfied, the amount brought to the UK is treated as a remittance at the date the loan was made.

B. Income liable to tax in more than one country

Foreign-source Income may be subject to tax in more than one country. However, under the terms of most double tax agreements, only one country will tax the income, and the income will be exempt from tax in the other country. **4224**

In the absence of such arrangements, foreign income commonly suffers foreign tax, either by deduction at source, or by assessment. Relief is given for the foreign tax against any UK tax liability under:
– the terms of a double tax agreement between the UK and the other country, where such an agreement exists; or
– under the unilateral double tax provisions contained in UK tax legislation.

Relief under a double tax agreement usually takes precedence.

1. Tax paid in only one country

Under the terms of a **double tax agreement**, a person who is resident in the UK will not be taxed on specified types of income arising in another country and, by reciprocal exemption, a person who is resident in that other country will not be taxed on similar income arising in the UK. A common example is income arising from property, which is usually taxable in the country where the property is located. **4226**

As it is possible for an individual to be **resident in two countries** at the same time, under the normal rules, each agreement commonly has a tie-breaker clause, which will determine the individual's residence status for the purposes of the agreement.

Some double tax agreements exempt only specific types of income, or grant only a partial exemption, and in these cases foreign tax will still be suffered.

The following table summarises the countries with which the UK currently holds a double tax treaty (excluding agreements dealing with only shipping or air transport). **4227**

MEMO POINTS The statutory reference is to the main agreement, which may then be amended by subsequent protocols.
For details of treaties currently in force, see HMRC's website at *http://www.hmrc.gov.uk/international/in_force.htm*.

Country	Reference (SI)
Anguilla [17]	
Antigua & Barbuda [5]	1947/2865
Argentina	1997/1777
Aruba [17]	
Australia	2003/3199
Austria	1970/1947
Azerbaijan	1995/762
Bangladesh	1980/708
Bahamas [4,20]	
Bahrain [4]	
Barbados	1970/952
Belarus [1]	1986/224
Belgium	1987/2053
Belize [4,22]	1947/2866
Bermuda	2008/1789
Bolivia	1995/2707
Bosnia-Herzegovina [2]	1981/1815
Botswana	2006/1925
British Virgin Islands [8]	2009/3013
Brunei	1950/1977
Bulgaria	1987/2054
Burma (Myanmar)	1952/751
Canada	1980/709
Cayman Islands [4,18]	
Chile	2003/3200
China [14]	1984/1826
Croatia [2]	1981/1815
Cyprus	1975/425
Czech Republic [3]	1991/2876
Denmark	1980/1960
Dominica [4,16]	
Egypt	1980/1091
Estonia	1994/3207
Falkland Islands	1997/2985
Faroes	2007/3469
Fiji	1976/1342
Finland	1970/153
France	2009/226
Gambia	1980/1963
Georgia	2004/3325
Germany [10]	2010/2975
Ghana	1993/1800
Gibraltar [13]	
Greece	1954/142
Grenada [4,16]	1949/361
Guernsey	1952/1215

Country	Reference (SI)
Liberia [16]	
Lesotho	1997/2986
Libya [9]	2010/243
Liechtenstein [21]	
Lithuania	2001/3925
Luxembourg [7]	1968/1100
Macedonia [2]	1981/1815
Malawi	1956/619
Malaysia	1997/2987
Malta	1995/763
Mauritius	1981/1121
Mexico [6]	1994/3212, 2010/2686
Moldova	2008/1795
Mongolia	1996/2598
Montenegro [2]	1981/1815
Montserrat	1947/2869
Morocco	1991/2881
Namibia	1967/2788
Netherlands [12]	2009/227
Netherlands Antilles [17]	
New Zealand	1984/365
Nigeria	1987/2057
Norway	2000/3247
Oman [4]	1998/2568
Pakistan	1987/2058
Papua New Guinea	1991/2882
Philippines	1978/184
Poland	1978/282
Portugal	1969/599
Qatar	2010/241
Romania	1977/57
Russia	1994/3213
St Kitts & Nevis	1947/2872
St Lucia [5]	
St Vincent [5]	
San Marino [16]	
Saudi Arabia	2008/1770
Serbia [2]	1981/1815
Sierra Leone	1947/2873
Singapore	1997/2988
Slovak Republic [3]	1991/2876
Slovenia [2]	2008/1796
Solomon Islands	1950/748
South Africa [15]	2002/3138
Spain	1976/1919
Sri Lanka	1980/713

Country	Reference (SI)	Country	Reference (SI)
Guyana	1992/3207	Sudan	1977/1719
Hong Kong [11]	2010/2974	Swaziland	1969/380
Hungary	1978/1056	Sweden	1984/366
Iceland	1991/2879	Switzerland	1978/1408 [8]
India	1993/1801	Taiwan	2002/3137
Indonesia	1994/769	Tajikistan [1]	1986/224
Ireland	1976/2151	Thailand	1981/1546
Isle of Man	1955/1205	Trinidad & Tobago	1983/1903
Israel	1963/616	Tunisia	1984/133
Italy	1990/2590	Turkey	1988/932
Ivory Coast	1987/169	Turkmenistan [1]	1986/224
Jamaica	1973/1329	Tuvalu	1950/750
Japan	2006/1924	Turks & Caicos Islands [4,19]	
Jersey	1952/1216	Uganda	1993/1802
Jordan	2001/3924	Ukraine	1993/1803
Kazakhstan	1994/3211	United States of America	2002/2848
Kenya	1977/1299	Uzbekistan	1994/770
Kiribati and Tuvalu	1950/750	Venezuela	1996/2599
Korea	1996/3168	Vietnam	1994/3216
Kuwait	1999/2036	Zambia	1972/1721
Latvia	1996/3167	Zimbabwe	1982/1842

Note:
1. Formerly part of the USSR and the convention with the USSR published in SI 1986/224 is deemed to apply.
2. Formerly part of Yugoslavia and the convention with Yugoslavia published in SI 1981/1815 is also deemed to apply.
3. Formerly part of Czechoslovakia and the convention with Czechoslovakia published in SI 1991/2876 is deemed to apply.
4. A new double taxation treaty has been recently signed and has not yet come into force.
5. New tax information exchange agreements with these members of the Organisation of East Caribbean States came into force on 19 May 2011.
6. A new protocol to the double tax treaty with Mexico took effect from 18 November 2010.
7. The third party exchange of information agreement with Luxembourg took effect from 1 and 6 April 2011 in the UK, and from 1 January 2011 in Luxembourg.
8. The new double taxation treaty with the British Virgin islands came into force on 6 April 2011.
9. The double tax agreement with Libya took effect from 1 and 6 April 2010 in the UK, and from 1 January 2011 in Libya.
10. A new double tax agreement with the Federal Republic of Germany entered into force on 30 December 2010.
11. A new double tax agreement with Hong Kong entered into force on 20 December 2010.
12. A new double tax convention with the Netherlands entered into force on 25 December 2010.
13. A tax information exchange agreement with Gibraltar came into force on 15 December 2010.
14. A new double tax agreement with the People's Republic of China has been signed but has not yet entered into force.
15. A new protocol has been signed, dealing with dividends, exchanges of information, and tax collection, but is not yet in force.
16. A tax information exchange agreement has been signed but is not yet in force.
17. Tax information exchange agreement only.
18. A tax information exchange agreement with the Cayman Islands came into force on 20 December 2010.
19. A tax information exchange agreement with the Turks & Caicos Islands came into force on 25 January 2011.
20. A tax information exchange agreement with the Bahamas came into force on 7 January 2011.
21. A tax information exchange agreement with the Liechtenstein came into force on 2 December 2010.
22. A tax information exchange agreement with Belize came into force on 1 August 2011.

2. Tax paid in more than one country

Partial DTA relief

Where a double tax agreement does not fully exempt the particular income, the amount of foreign tax eligible for relief is restricted to the minimum tax payable under the terms of the agreement. The relief is claimed as a **tax credit**, which is a form of tax reducer (¶4440), and the claimant must be UK resident for the tax year in question. **4229** s 18 TIOPA 2010

s 19 TIOPA 2010

MEMO POINTS 1. **A claim** under a double tax arrangement must be submitted:
– by the 4th anniversary of the end of the tax year in which the income or gains become subject to UK tax; or
– if later, on or before the 31 January next following the year of assessment in which the foreign tax is paid.
2. An individual who has **employment income** may claim tax credit relief even where he is not resident in the UK.

Unilateral relief

4231
s 9 TIOPA 2010

If relief is **not available under a double tax agreement**, tax paid in another country may be unilaterally allowed as a credit against UK income tax. The relief is generally only available to UK residents and may only be set against UK tax which arises from the same type of income as that on which the foreign tax was suffered.

MEMO POINTS Unilateral relief is **not available** if a double tax agreement specifically prohibits relief in particular circumstances.

4233
s 112 TIOPA 2010

In **both cases**, the taxpayer can choose whether to claim tax credit relief, or simply to deduct the foreign tax as an expense when calculating the amount of income and gains chargeable to UK tax. In most cases however, tax credit relief will be more beneficial.

a. Deducting foreign tax as an expense

4235
ss 112 - 115 TIOPA 2010

A taxpayer (including a company) may elect to treat as an expense any foreign tax suffered in respect of income assessed on the arising basis.

This will generally be beneficial when a **loss arises** under the UK rules, because tax credit relief will not be helpful. Treating the foreign tax as an expense will increase the loss which may mitigate the taxpayer's other taxable income.

EXAMPLE Mr C has UK trading losses of £50,000, and receives French investment income of £30,000, with tax deducted at source of £10,000.
He decides to expense the foreign tax suffered as follows:

	UK Trading	France Investment
	£	£
Income/(loss) from each income source	(50,000)	30,000
Deduct: foreign tax		(10,000)
Assessable income	(50,000)	20,000

The trading losses can then be relieved in the usual ways (¶2468).

b. Tax credit relief for foreign tax

4237
ss 36 - 41 TIOPA 2010
s 29(2) ITA 2007

Foreign tax suffered is deducted from the UK income tax liability. Situations where **tax credit relief is available** would include claims under a double taxation agreement, unilateral relief and the EU special withholding tax introduced by some countries from 1 July 2005 (¶4296).

The relief is **restricted** in the following ways:

a. the amount of foreign tax given relief assumes that the taxpayer has taken all reasonable steps in obtaining foreign country reliefs and allowances; and

b. the relief cannot exceed the amount of UK income tax suffered on the foreign income.

If the overseas income arises from a **trade** or a property business, relief is also restricted (¶2179).

A separate calculation is required for each source of foreign income, which must always be shown gross. Income which is taxed on a remittance basis is grossed up to include the foreign tax payable.

Apportionment of the foreign tax will be required where the basis period for the income is different in the foreign country and the UK. For example, this would occur where income in the foreign country is calculated on a calendar year basis as opposed to the fiscal year basis used in the UK. 4239

EXAMPLE Mr A, a UK resident, suffers Norwegian income tax on his foreign investments on a calendar year basis. He will therefore have to apportion a quarter of the foreign tax to the UK tax year ending on 5 April, and the remaining three quarters to the following tax year.

Full relief

Full relief for foreign tax will be given where one of the following situations applies. 4240

Type of foreign income[1]	Conditions
Non-savings income	**a.** the amount of the total non-savings income taxable at higher (or additional) rate exceeds the foreign source income for which relief is being claimed; and **b.** none of the foreign source income has been subjected to a rate of foreign tax in excess of 40% (or 50%).
Savings income (other than dividends)	**a.** the amount of the total savings income taxable at higher (or additional) rate exceeds the foreign source income for which relief is being claimed; and **b.** none of the foreign source income has been subjected to a rate of foreign tax in excess of 40% (or 50%).
Dividend income	**a.** the amount of the total dividend income taxable at higher (or additional) rate exceeds the foreign source income for which relief is being claimed; and **b.** none of the foreign source income has been subjected to a rate of foreign tax in excess of 40% (or 50%).

Note:
1. For the distinction between the different types of income, see ¶4346.

EXAMPLE Mr B is a higher rate tax payer, and has German savings income which is taxed in the UK on the remittance basis. He receives gross income of £30,000, and the German tax suffered is £10,000, leaving him with £20,000. Mr B remits an amount of £15,000 to the UK, which is 75% of the net amount. The tax credit relief will be calculated as follows:

	£
Income remitted to the UK	15,000
Add: 75% of German tax suffered	7,500
Gross income chargeable to UK tax	22,500
UK income tax @ 40%	9,000
Less: German tax	(7,500)
Remaining UK liability	1,500

Restricted relief

In **all other cases** the amount of foreign tax that can be set off in this way may not exceed the difference between: 4242

a. the amount of income tax that would be suffered by the taxpayer if he were charged to tax on his total income from all sources including foreign income; and

b. the tax suffered by the taxpayer on his total income minus the foreign income.

The **overall restriction** is that the total tax credit may not exceed the total income tax payable.

Where **more than one source of foreign income** is involved, the calculation is performed for each source separately, with the income on which relief has already been calculated being excluded from the total income figure for the next source. The taxpayer may choose the order in which each source is taken, and it will be most beneficial to take the source with the highest rate of foreign tax first. 4244

C. Specific sources of income

4248 The tax treatment of income from overseas will depend on the type of income received, and the following types are dealt with here separately:
- employment;
- trade;
- investments; and
- property.

The provisions outlined here are subject to any different treatment laid down under the terms of a double taxation agreement.

1. Employment income

4250 The taxation of employment income depends on the residence status of the employee and where the duties are performed. In general, all earnings are taxable on an individual who is resident in the UK.

There is a special treatment for a non-UK domiciled employee who works for a non-resident employer.

a. Assessment of income

Summary of tax bases

4252 The table below summarises the tax treatment of earnings, depending on the circumstances of the taxpayer, his employer, and where his duties are carried out. An employee will normally be taxed on the arising basis, unless the conditions for the remittance basis are met.

ss 15 – 27, s 721 ITEPA 2003

Status of employee		Arising basis or remittance basis [1]	Where employee's duties carried out		
			Wholly or partly in the UK		Wholly outside the UK
Residence	Domicile		In the UK	Outside the UK	
Res and ord res in UK	UK	Arising	Liable	Liable	Liable
Res and ord res in UK	Foreign	Arising	Liable	Liable	Liable
		Remittance [2]	Liable	Liable	Liable if remitted, unless for a UK resident employer, when income liable as it arises
Res but not ord res in UK	UK	Arising	Liable	Liable	Liable
		Remittance [2]	Liable	Liable if remitted	Liable if remitted
Res but not ord res in UK	Foreign	Arising	Liable	Liable	Liable
		Remittance [2]	Liable	Liable if remitted	Liable if remitted
Not res	Any	Arising	Liable	Not liable	Not liable

Note:
1. The basis depends on whether the employer is foreign. A **foreign employer** is one resident outside the UK. It is possible for a foreign employer to be considered resident outside the UK even where it has a separate permanent establishment in the UK.
2. Applies to earnings from a foreign employer.

Place where duties are carried out

Where an employee carries out his duties is a question of fact. While this is often easy to determine, an employee may sometimes carry out his duties in more than one country. In addition, certain types of occupation require the employee to travel widely, whilst having a central base of operations. In this case, the central base determines the place where duties are carried out. 4254

MEMO POINTS 1. **Crews** of ships and aircraft are treated as performing overseas duties if the journey does not begin and end in the UK. s 40 ITEPA 2003
2. **Mobile UK employees**, such as lorry and coach drivers, will remain UK resident and ordinarily resident, even though it is possible they could numerically fall within the 91 day test.

Duties performed abroad

The **remittance basis** applies to the following employees: 4256 ss 22 – 23, s 26 ITEPA 2003
– individuals who are resident but not ordinarily resident in the UK, performing duties wholly or partly abroad; and
– non-domiciled individuals performing duties wholly abroad for a foreign employer.

Incidental UK duties will be ignored for this purpose.

Earnings will be taxable when remitted, if the remittance basis applies or is claimed, even where the employment has already ceased, or the earnings relate to a previous year.

MEMO POINTS Some **foreign domiciled** employees have entered into employment contracts with both the UK employer and a foreign employer, known as dual contracts. Earnings relating to overseas duties, undertaken for the foreign employer, are only taxable in the UK if the remittance basis is claimed and the earnings are remitted. If these earnings are paid into an overseas bank account, they escape UK tax altogether. Tax bulletin 76
Whilst such contracts have always been subject to enquiry, **HMRC** are taking a harder line, as there is concern that there is often an artificial split of a single job with the motive of saving tax.

Until 5 April 2009, HMRC accepted that apportionment of income applied to an individual who was **resident but not ordinarily resident**, and performed the duties of a single employment both inside and outside the UK. 4258 SP 1/09 Tax bulletin 63 EIM 50305

The calculation was based on the number of working days spent inside and outside the UK, where the employee's rights to earnings accrued on a daily basis. It was a question of fact where the substantial duties for each working day were carried out. In some cases this basis was not appropriate, for example where the employment contract specifically allocated earnings to specific duties.

This treatment **continues to apply** from 6 April 2009, but if the employee has a mixed fund, the transfers to the UK should, strictly, be calculated separately. HMRC will continue to allow the apportionment provided that
a. the mixed fund is an account held solely by the employee; and
b. the account only contains:
– employment income from a single employment;
– interest arising or exchange gains on that account; or
– gains relating to share scheme transactions and proceeds from share scheme related transactions.

Comment It is not completely clear that HMRC will continue to apply this treatment in 2011/12. The title of SP1/09 refers only to 2009/10, but the statement itself contains no such restriction. The title of EIM40305 explicitly applies SP1/09 to 2009/10 and 2010/11.

MEMO POINTS 1. Where a fund contains more than one kind of income and capital, or income or capital of more than one year, it is known as a mixed fund. If remittances are made from such a fund, strictly, the tax liabilities are calculated for each transfer separately.
2. Where part of the income is paid in the UK, HMRC accept that a liability only arises under the remittance basis if the aggregate of the following exceeds the amount of taxable earnings for the year:
– earnings paid in the UK;
– benefits enjoyed in the UK; and
– earnings remitted to the UK.

3. Where an employee is not liable to UK tax on some of his earnings, the employer should seek a direction from HMRC that not all earnings are liable to **PAYE**.
4. Often the **overseas country** will have a similar system of PAYE, and the employer should ensure he is aware of his legal obligations.
5. In some cases, the UK employer may be **deducting both foreign and UK tax** from the employee's earnings, even though the employee will be suffering too much tax. HMRC can authorise an employer to reduce the amount of income tax paid under PAYE by the amount of foreign tax paid, which will alleviate the cashflow problem for the employee.

EXAMPLE Mr C is UK resident but not ordinarily resident in the UK for a tax year. He is paid an annual salary of £60,000 direct into an offshore bank account, for which he works 230 days in total (after taking account of holidays).
Mr C is sent to work in Spain for 50 working days, but also worked 6 Saturdays in addition to the normal working week, and he did not receive any time off in lieu. He received a £5,000 bonus in relation to his Spanish duties.
Mr C therefore spend 56 days working overseas. He worked in the UK for 180 days (230 – 50).
Mr C's earnings are allocated as follows:

		£	£
UK duties	$\frac{180}{236} \times £60,000$		45,763
Overseas duties	$\frac{56}{236} \times £60,000$	14,237	
	Bonus	5,000	
			19,237

b. Deductions

4260 s 370 ITEPA 2003 s 809G ITA 2007 Tax is charged on employment income based on the full amount of earnings from the employment after authorised deductions. The general rules outlined from ¶3122 and particularly ¶3177 apply. Special rules apply to employment income taxed on a remittance basis and to foreign earnings.

Duties performed abroad

4262 s 353(1) – (3) ITEPA 2003 Where the **remittance basis** applies, a deduction may be made for:
– expenses paid for out of those earnings;
– expenses paid on the employee's behalf and included as earnings; and
– any other expenses paid for in the UK in that year of assessment or any earlier year in which the employee was resident in the UK.

The expenses must be of a type that would be deductible if the earnings had been charged under the general rules (¶3122) for the year of assessment in which they were incurred.

Non-UK domiciled employees

4264 s 355 ITEPA 2003 An assessment in respect of **foreign earnings** may be reduced by a deduction for expenses for payments which:
– are made out of earnings subject to UK tax;
– are of a type that would normally have reduced the employee's liability to income tax; and
– would not normally fall within the scope of UK law because they were made abroad.

HMRC require **strict proof** that the payment is made out of the earnings concerned, and that the employee does not have sufficient overseas income, that is not chargeable to UK tax, from which to make the payments.

4266 s 373 ITEPA 2003 A deduction may also be allowed for **travel expenses** incurred or reimbursed by the employer (so far as it is included in the assessable earnings of the employment) for a period of 5 years beginning with the employee's date of arrival in the UK to perform the duties of the employment.

However, the deduction will **not be available unless**, on the date of his arrival in the UK to perform the duties, the employee was either:
- not resident in the UK in either of the 2 immediately preceding years of assessment; or
- not in the UK for any purpose, at any time in the 2 years ending immediately before the date of arrival.

MEMO POINTS The **allowable expenses** are those provided:
a. for any journey between the employee's place of usual abode (i.e. outside the UK) and any place in the UK, to perform the duties of the employment; or
b. where the employee is in the UK for the purposes of such an employment for a continuous period of 60 days or more, for any two outward and return journeys per person per year by the employee's spouse and/or child (¶3179), either to accompany him at the beginning of the period or to visit him during it. In practice the period of 60 days is met if the employee is:
- working in the UK for at least 2/3rds of his working days; and
- present in the UK at the beginning and end of the period.

Seafarers

Where a seafarer who is **resident and ordinarily resident** in the UK performs the duties of his employment either wholly or partly overseas during the course of a qualifying period of 365 days or more, he may claim a deduction of 100% of the earnings from the duties attributable to the period. **4268** s 378 ITEPA 2003 HMRC Brief 33/07

From 6 April 2011 this treatment also extends to seafarers resident in the EU or the European Economic Area and who pay UK tax.

The deduction is applied to earnings after capital allowances and other expenses (such as accommodation expenses and foreign travel expenses) have been deducted.

MEMO POINTS 1. For these purposes, a seafarer is **defined** as someone in an employment consisting wholly of the performance of the duties on a ship, or mainly in the performance of duties on a ship where the other duties are incidental to the ship board duties. Offshore installations such as oil rigs are specifically excluded from the definition of a ship. s 384 ITEPA 2003
2. Employment is deemed to be **performed outside the UK**, if the duties are carried out on a vessel that is engaged on a voyage which begins or ends outside the UK.
3. A **qualifying period** consists of days of absence from the UK. Visits to the UK can be included in the qualifying period providing:
- no single visit lasts more than 183 days; and
- the total number of days spent in the UK during the period is less than half of the total number of days from the first day abroad to the last day of the period spent abroad after the visit.

A period spent in the UK during a contract of employment may not be included in the qualifying period if it is not followed by a period abroad. Providing the conditions continue to be met in relation to each period of absence, successive intervening periods and periods of absence may continue to qualify.
4. Where the duties of the employment (or any associated employment) are **not performed wholly outside the UK**, the earnings eligible for the 100% deduction must be apportioned between the UK and non-UK elements. The apportionment is based on the nature of the duties, and the time devoted to the duties performed inside and outside the UK.
5. Where a claim is made in a tax return, the **names of ships** on which the employee worked must be shown in the additional information box 17 of the additional information pages of the tax return. The purpose of this requirement is to reduce the number of enquiries into tax returns where the status of a particular ship is in doubt.

2. Trading income

When a person is trading, either as a sole trader or as a partner in a partnership, it is important to determine where the trade is carried on, before considering the circumstances of the individual. **4270**

MEMO POINTS Trade is taken to include a **profession**, although the exercise of the profession is so personal that it is extremely unusual for there to be a difference in residence status between the individual and his profession.

Summary of tax treatment

4271 s 6 ITTOIA 2005 Trading profits of a UK resident are taxable wherever the trade is carried on. Profits of a non-UK resident are taxable only to the extent that they arise from a UK trade. The same rule applies to the profits of professions and vocations.

Individual's status		Trade carried on			
Domicile	Residence	Wholly in the UK	Partly in the UK and partly overseas		Wholly outside the UK
			UK part	Overseas part	
UK	Res and ord res	Liable	Liable	Liable	Liable
UK	Res but not ord res	Liable	Liable	Liable	Liable if remitted
Any	Not res	Liable	Liable	Not liable	Not liable
Not UK	Res	Liable	Liable	Liable	Liable if remitted

Location of the trade

4272 A trade is carried on where it is **managed and controlled**, not where the day to day business transactions occur, and this is a question of fact. For example, an administrative office may not have sufficient presence to be the centre of management and control. UK case law has suggested that a trade is carried on where contracts of sale are made.

MEMO POINTS 1. Under English law, the place of a **contract of sale** is the location where the acceptance of an offer is communicated. Situations involving agents can be more complicated, and the contract between the agent and his principal should be examined carefully.
2. A UK resident individual owned a trade in Canada which was actually managed by the Canadian employees. However it was held that the trade was not wholly overseas because the UK owner had the power to exert management and control, even though he did not use this power. *Ogilvie v Kitton* [1908]

4274 Where a trade is carried on:
– **wholly outside the UK**, the profits arising are assessed to UK income tax as an overseas trade (¶4278); or
– **wholly or partly within the UK**, it is assessed as an UK trade (¶2420).

Partnerships

4275 s 849 ITTOIA 2005 A trade carried on in partnership is resident where the **business** is controlled and managed, irrespective of the individual partners' residence.

If a non-resident partnership trades in the UK as well as overseas, a UK resident partner will be taxable on both the UK profits and the overseas profits. A non-resident partner will avoid UK income tax on the overseas profits.

MEMO POINTS 1. Where a partnership has an overseas trade, and a UK resident partner is **not domiciled in the UK**, he will only be liable to tax on profits from the overseas trade on a remittance basis. The usual rules will apply to profits from the UK trade.
2. Where a **partner's residence status changes** and the partnership's trade is partly carried on in the UK and overseas, the partner is treated as ceasing to be a partner at the time of the change, and then immediately becoming a partner again after the change. This enables two calculations to be made based on the residence status before and after the change.

Assessment of overseas trades

4278 s 6 ITTOIA 2005 Profits from overseas trades (including related investment income) are generally assessed on the basis of the profits **arising** for the accounts period ending in the year of assessment. So the opening year, closing year and overlap relief rules apply as for UK trades (¶2426).

s 189 ITTOIA 2005 MEMO POINTS If **trade debts** cannot be received in the UK because of restrictions by government action or foreign currency controls, then the individual can postpone the UK tax charge in respect of that income. If and when the restrictions are lifted, the income will become taxable although the actual assessment will relate to the tax year when the income actually arose.

Where an individual has made a claim to be assessed on a **remittance basis** (¶4200), only income remitted to the UK in the tax year of assessment will be liable to UK income tax. 4280

Deductions

An individual carrying on an overseas trade (either as a sole trader or in partnership) may be allowed a deduction for certain overseas **travel expenses**. The deduction is not available where the income is taxed on the remittance basis. 4282 ss 92 - 94 ITTOIA 2005

Relief is only available for expenses in connection with an absence abroad that is undertaken wholly and exclusively for the purposes of the overseas trade.

The individual may make a deduction for expenses in connection with travelling to and from the place where the trade is carried on, and the costs of board and lodging in that place.

MEMO POINTS 1. If **more than one trade** is carried on abroad, the deduction is apportioned between the trades on a reasonable basis.
2. If expenditure is incurred in **travelling between** two or more overseas trades, relief is available provided the qualifying absence is for the purposes of both those trades.
3. A deduction is also available for travel expenses of the individual's **spouse and minor children**, where a qualifying absence exceeds a period of 60 consecutive days. Relief for such expenses is restricted to a maximum of two trips per year of assessment.

Loss relief for overseas trades

Relief for losses from overseas trades is more **restricted** than loss relief for UK trades. Losses may be used in the same ways as losses from UK trades, but may only be set against: 4284 s 95 ITA 2007
- profits from overseas trades;
- earnings received by a non-domiciled employee for overseas duties from a foreign employer (¶4252); and
- certain foreign pensions (¶3671).

3. Investment income

Summary of tax treatment

The table below summarises the liability of an individual with investment income. Special rules apply to UK government securities. 4286

Individual's status		Investment income		UK Government securities
Domicile	Residence	Arising in the UK	Arising overseas	
UK	Res and ord res	Liable	Liable	Liable
UK	Res but not ord res	Liable	Liable if remitted[2]	Not liable
Any	Not res, but ord res	Liable[1]	Not liable	Liable
Any	Not res, not ord res	Liable[1]	Not liable	Not liable
Not UK	Res and ord res	Liable	Liable if remitted[2]	Liable
Not UK	Res but not ord res	Liable	Liable if remitted[2]	Not liable

Note:
1. Investment income connected to a trade carried on in the UK through a permanent establishment will be liable to tax in the normal way. The tax charge on other investment income will be limited to the amount of tax (if any) deducted at source.
2. The rules for claiming the remittance basis and paying the RBC also apply (¶4200).

4288 Investment income for these purposes **includes** the following:
- dividends and other distributions (not including those made in the course of the liquidation of an overseas company, and distributions that constitute a return of capital);
- interest; and
- benefits received (either directly or indirectly) from overseas trusts, companies and other entities.

The following are specifically **excluded** from UK income tax:
- stock dividends and scrip issues from foreign companies; and
- other distributions made by a foreign company in the form of its own shares.

MEMO POINTS A UK resident beneficiary who has an absolute right to income from a **foreign trust** is taxable on the income on an arising basis.

Interest

4290
s 852 ITA 2007
If the individual makes a declaration that he is **not ordinarily resident** in the UK, interest from UK banks and building societies can be paid gross.

ss 713 - 714 ITTOIA 2005
Similarly, interest on certain UK government securities (known as "FOTRA" securities) is not taxable for non-ordinarily resident individuals.

Tax rate

4292
ss 6 - 14 ITA 2007
The rate of tax applied to foreign investment income will follow the usual UK rules (i.e. liable to the starting, basic, higher and additional rates), **except** for income assessed on the remittance basis, which is assessed as non-savings income.

Exchange of information

4294
ss 18B - 18E TMA 1970
UK businesses and public bodies that **pay interest or collect savings income** to or for non-UK resident individuals must provide the following information to HMRC:
- details of any interest paid to the recipient; and
- details of savings income collected for the recipient.

The purpose of this information exchange is to counter cross-border tax evasion.

MEMO POINTS This information is passed onto the tax authorities of the individual's country of residence. Similarly, the tax authorities in other EU members states provide this information to HMRC in respect of UK resident individuals who receive savings income from the EU.

4296
ss 135 - 145 TIOPA 2010
Special withholding tax in the EU As an **alternative** to exchanging information about cross-border payments, Austria, Belgium and Luxembourg have imposed a special withholding tax on savings income paid to residents in other EU member states.

MEMO POINTS 1. This is **in addition** to any withholding tax usually levied under each state's domestic legislation.
2. This tax is levied at the following **rates**:
- 20% from 1 July 2008 to 30 June 2011; and
- 35% thereafter.

3. 25% of the special withholding tax is retained by the paying member states, with the remaining 75% being passed to the country of residence of the recipient. Any special withholding tax **suffered** by an individual in the UK can be credited against the individual's income and/or capital gains tax liability. Any excess credit will be repaid.
4. Any tax withheld under the paying country's **domestic laws** is credited first against any UK tax payable on the overseas income in accordance with usual double tax relief. Such tax cannot be repaid if it exceeds the UK tax liability on that income. Only after relief is given for such domestic withholding tax is special withholding tax then credited against the individual's income and/or capital gains tax liability.
5. The following countries which are **closely associated with the EU** have also imposed such a tax: Guernsey, Jersey, Isle of Man, Gibraltar, Andorra, Liechtenstein, Monaco, San Marino, Switzerland, British Virgin Islands, Netherlands Antilles and Turks & Caicos.

UK residents can **request exemption** from this withholding tax by either: 4298 s 114 TIOPA 2010
– authorising the paying agent to provide details to HMRC about the savings income payments made; or
– presenting the paying agent with a certificate drawn up by HMRC, requesting that tax is not withheld from the savings income.

MEMO POINTS The procedure for issuing a certificate takes a couple of months, and the certificate is valid for 3 years.

4. Income from property

Income from property situated outside the UK is taxed as if it were a business. If a taxpayer owns more than one foreign property, the income will be taxed as if it derived from a single business. 4300 s 269 ITTOIA 2005

Method of assessment

Income is **generally** assessed on an arising basis, unless a remittance basis election has been made (¶4200). This means that the amount assessable for a year of assessment is the full amount of income arising in that year. 4302

Where the **arising basis** applies, income from overseas property is calculated in accordance with the rules applicable to a UK property business (¶2735). Income and expenditure for all overseas properties are pooled as a separate overseas property business. Capital allowances are available in respect of overseas properties in accordance with the normal rules. Similarly, premiums received in respect of overseas properties are calculated in accordance with the UK property rules and assessable as a trade. The rules for furnished holiday lettings (¶2777) apply to properties situated in EEA countries. 4304

Where the **remittance basis** applies, the income actually received from individual overseas properties is assessable, with a deduction for any expenses which would be allowable under the rules for UK trades (¶120). 4306 ss 832 - 832B ITTOIA 2005

Loss relief on overseas properties

If a loss arises for a year of assessment, it is normally **carried forward** and set against the earliest available profits of the overseas property business for subsequent years. Losses arising from an overseas property cannot be set against profits from any UK property. For further details of the calculation of loss relief, see ¶2771. 4308 ss 118 - 120 ITA 2007

If a loss includes **capital allowances and/or allowable agricultural expenses**, it may alternatively be set against general income. See ¶2775.

SECTION 3

Foreign taxpayers and UK income

This section focuses on the tax treatment of non-resident taxpayers who receive UK income. While the main concepts have already been examined above, there are some special rules which apply to foreign taxpayers only. 4312

With the exception of rental income, the UK income tax charge relating to investment income for non-residents is limited to any tax deducted at source.

1. Limit on income tax charge

4314 ss 811 - 828 ITA 2007 The **maximum** income tax charge which can be levied on a non-resident is the sum of the following:
– tax chargeable on all income disregarding allowances (such as the personal allowance), and ignoring excluded income; and
– tax deducted at source from excluded income.

Excluded income is defined as income chargeable as:
– savings;
– dividends (including stock dividends);
– taxable social security benefits other than jobseeker's allowance and income support;
– retirement annuity contracts, and employment related pensions; and
– sundry income from transactions in deposits.

2. Dividends from UK companies

4316 s 397 ITTOIA 2005 For UK residents, dividends are received with an **associated tax credit**. However a non-UK resident is not entitled to such a tax credit unless:
– he is entitled to the personal allowance (¶4390); or
– the terms of a double tax agreement state that a tax credit is available.

s 400 ITTOIA 2005 If there is **no tax credit**, the individual is treated as having paid income tax at the dividend rate on the actual amount received (¶2825).

3. Rental income

4318 s 971 ITA 2007 SI 1995/2902 Where a non-UK resident individual owns a **property situated in the UK**, any income derived from the property will be liable to UK income tax.

Net rent

4320 The rental payable to such a landlord must be paid **net** of tax deducted at basic rate, unless the landlord joins the Non Resident Landlord Scheme. The person who is required to deduct the tax is usually the letting agent. If there is no agent involved, and the amounts paid to the landlord (including any premium) exceed £5,200 per annum, the tenant must deduct basic rate tax.

Only an agent can take into account **letting expenses** (¶2765) before calculating the income tax to deduct. Letting expenses incurred directly by the landlord are ignored for this purpose.

As the landlord's tax liability will almost certainly differ from the amount of basic rate tax suffered at source, he will either owe further tax or be due a tax repayment, which can be dealt with by submitting a tax return.

MEMO POINTS The **person deducting tax** must account for it quarterly (on a calendar year basis), submitting a return within 30 days of the quarter end. An annual return must be submitted by 5 July following the end of the March quarter. The landlord must also be given a certificate showing the amount of tax deducted.

Gross rent

4322 The **landlord** can receive rent **gross** by applying to HMRC to join the Non Resident Landlord Scheme. If the conditions for approval are met, a certificate of exemption will be issued, which can be presented to the payer of the rent. The landlord must then complete a tax return and pay income tax under the normal rules. The certificate will be withdrawn if the criteria for receiving gross payments do not continue to be satisfied.

MEMO POINTS To **apply** to receive rental payments gross, the landlord must complete form NRL1 and satisfy any of the following criteria:
– his UK tax affairs are up to date;

– he has never had any UK tax obligations; or
– he does not expect to be liable to UK tax for the year in which he is making the application.
In each case he must undertake to comply with all UK tax obligations, such as completing tax returns and paying tax on time.

4. Employment income

A non-UK resident employee is only liable to UK income tax on earnings relating to UK duties (¶4252). **4324**

Employees who are **seconded** overseas may still be liable to PAYE if they are paid by the UK employer. UK employers with overseas employees should apply for a NT code as soon as possible, which will only be issued if the employee has completed a form confirming that he has become non-resident.

If the employee is paid by the overseas company, he could still remain employed by his UK employer. If in doubt, advice should be sought on this issue.

MEMO POINTS **Tax equalisation** (¶4687) is used to ensure that an employee is no worse or better off from undertaking an overseas secondment. It works by running a dummy payroll for all non-resident employees, calculating the UK income tax which would normally be deducted if the employee was still working in the UK, and making a sure that this is deducted from the employee's pay. Where the employee is only liable to tax in the foreign country, the amounts deducted can then be used to fund the foreign tax liability.

Short stays in the UK

Whilst an employee may be non-resident applying the usual rules (¶4154), he may be deemed to be UK resident under the provisions of a **double taxation agreement**. In practice, earnings of an individual who stays in the UK for less than 60 days, and is employed by a foreign employer, will not be liable to UK income tax. **4326** Tax Bulletin 68

MEMO POINTS 1. If a short stay is actually part of a more **permanent presence**, all income will be liable to UK income tax.
2. **PAYE** should be operated after the individual has been in the UK for 60 days, including the days of arrival and departure, unless treaty relief is to be claimed.

EXAMPLE Mr A visits the UK for 35 days in June and July, then goes back to Italy for a fortnight's holiday and returns to the UK on the same contract for 40 days in August and September. The 75 days would be regarded as one period, as the gap is insignificant compared to the two periods on either side.
As the periods when Mr A is present in the UK are part of the same contract, the employer would be expected to operate PAYE from day 1.
Mrs B visits the UK for 35 days in Year 1. She then goes back to Spain, but after 7 months is unexpectedly asked to return to the UK in Year 2, and does so for 40 days.
Each period in the UK would be regarded as a separate period of less than 60 days. There was a relatively long gap between the visits, so there is no UK liability for either period and PAYE does not have to be operated.

5. Trading income

Any profits arising from a trade carried on within the UK are taxed on a non-resident trader under the usual UK trading rules. This includes profits from the UK part of a trade which is also carried on overseas, although any profits from the overseas part itself will avoid UK tax. For the location of a trade see ¶4272. **4328**

MEMO POINTS If **trade debts** cannot be received from the UK because of restrictions imposed by local government action or foreign currency controls, the individual can postpone the UK tax charge in respect of that income. If and when the restrictions are lifted, the income will become taxable, although the actual assessment will relate to the tax year when the income arose. s 189 ITTOIA 2005

Entertainers and sportsmen

4330
s 1309 CTA 2009
s 966 ITA 2007
s 13 ITTOIA 2005
SI 1987/530

Where income payments **in excess** of £1,000 per annum are made to non-resident entertainers and sportsmen in relation to activities in the UK, basic rate tax must be withheld by the payer. The obligation to deduct tax only applies when the entertainer or sportsman is non-resident when the activity is taking place, regardless of his residence status when payment is actually made.

Where the amount of tax withheld exceeds the individual's UK tax liability, a repayment will be due.

4334 The entertainer or sportsman is deemed to carry on a trade with a **basis year** congruent with the tax year. Any payments relating to the activity are assessed, even where payment is not actually made to the individual himself. In a case involving a famous tennis star, it was held that payments made by non-resident companies to a non-resident individual's personal company are liable to UK income tax, where those payments relate to the individual's activities in the UK. *Agassi v Robinson (Inspector of Taxes)* [2006]

CHAPTER 9

Computation

OUTLINE ¶¶

In order to calculate the amount of income tax payable by an individual, a computation is required showing all income assessable in the tax year, all deductions and allowances, and calculates the tax charge. **4345** s 23 ITA 2007

The basic outline of a tax computation is shown below.

Item	Reference	Computation
Total income	¶4349	X
Less: Deductions from total income	¶4358	(X)
Net income		X
Less: Allowances	¶4390	(X)
Taxable income		X
Tax charge	¶4404	X
Less: Tax reductions	¶4440	(X)
Tax borne		X
Tax deducted from annuity and patent royalty payments	¶4454	X
Tax liability		X
Less: Tax already suffered	¶4458	(X)
Tax payable		X

SECTION 1

Taxable income

Classification of income

4346 It is customary to classify all income into:
a. earned income, and
b. investment income

It is then important to identify **each type of income** as:
– non-savings income;
– savings income; or
– dividend income.

Different rules apply to each type.

Earned income is always non-savings income. The pro-forma at ¶4347 shows the categories included in savings income. Any other type of income, with the exception of dividends, is therefore also non-savings income.

4347 The following table shows typical entries in a **pro-forma computation** of UK taxable income.

	Non-savings	Savings	Dividend	Total
	£	£	£	£
Earned income				
Employment income (including pensions and taxable state benefits)	X			X
Income from trade [1]	X			X
Income from furnished holiday letting	X			X
Royalty income of an inventor	X			X
Less: Contributions to a retirement annuity contract [2]	(X)			(X)
	X			X
Investment income				
Other property income	X			X
Interest and discounts		X		X
Purchased life annuities		X		X
Other annuities and annual payments	X			X
Income from discretionary trusts	X			X
Income from other trusts [3]	X	X	X	X
Dividends			X	X
Sundry income [4]	X	X	X	X
Total income	X	X	X	X
Less: Deductions				
Trading losses	(X)	(X)	(X)	
Interest on qualifying loans	(X)			
Annuities	(X)			
Patent and copyright royalties	(X)			
Gifts of shares and land to charity	(X)			
Net income	X	X	X	X
Less: Allowances				
Personal allowance	(X)			
Blind person's allowance	(X)			
Taxable income	X	X	X	X

Note:
1. Income from trade includes income from:
- self-employment;
- the practice of a profession or vocation;
- partnerships; and
- Lloyd's underwriters.
2. This is an older type of registered pension scheme (¶3745). No new schemes of this type can be started, but existing schemes are still valid.
3. Where income is received from a non-discretionary trust, the income retains its original status. For example if the trust receives bank interest which is then distributed to the beneficiary, the distribution is taxed as if the beneficiary had received the savings income directly.
4. Type depends on source (¶3950).

Overseas income (¶4248) must be integrated into the computation (for example, income from an overseas employment forms part of employment income). Income which would normally be treated as savings income or dividend income is included as non-savings income if it is taxed on the remittance basis (¶4200). Overseas income arising from furnished holiday letting in the EU is included with income from the same activity in the UK.

A. Income

Income is assessed according to its type, and there are particular rules for each (including the set-off of reliefs and losses), which are detailed elsewhere in *Tax Memo*. Having calculated the amount of income which is taxable, specific rules determine how the figures are then used in the computation. 4349

Grossing up

The basic principle is that all income in the computation must be shown gross of any **tax deducted at source**. This is frequently the case for: 4350
- employment income, including pensions and social security benefits, which is liable to PAYE (¶4597);
- trading income received under the **Construction Industry Scheme** (¶4800);
- bank interest; and
- dividends, which are received net of a non-refundable tax credit (¶4462).

The following table shows the **rate of tax deducted** at source for common types of income, and the amount by which the income received should be grossed up before being included in the tax computation. 4352

Source of income	Rate of tax deduction or tax credit	Grossing up by
Dividends	10%	100/90
Most types of interest	20%	100/80
Purchased life annuities	20%	100/80
Other annuities	20%	100/80
Patent royalties	20%	100/80
Discretionary trust	40%	100/60
Non-discretionary trust:		
Non-savings	20%	100/80
Savings	20%	100/80
Dividend	10%	100/90

EXAMPLE Mr A receives bank interest of £800, and dividends of £540.
This income is grossed up as follows:

		£
Bank interest	$800 \times \frac{100}{80}$	1,000
Dividends	$540 \times \frac{100}{90}$	600

Couples

4354 ss 836 – 837 ITA 2007 s 1011 ITA 2007

For tax purposes, spouses or civil partners are deemed to be **living together** unless they are:
- legally separated; or
- in fact separated (and the separation is likely to be permanent).

Spouses or civil partners are usually taxed independently, even if they are living together. Some types of income are specifically required to be taxed independently, including:
- income from close company shares;
- income from furnished holiday lettings;
- employment income; and
- partnership income.

So, for example, if Mr A earns £100,000 from his employment, none of this is taxed on his wife.

The exception is income from **jointly held property** (other than those specified above). Spouses or civil partners who are living together are taxed on equal shares of the income arising, regardless of the actual beneficial interest of each spouse. This most commonly affects joint share portfolios and rental properties.

A **joint declaration** may be made by the couple, specifying an alternative split which reflects their **actual beneficial interests** in the property. The declaration takes effect from the date it is made and is irrevocable, and HMRC must be notified in writing within 60 days. The declaration lapses if the beneficial interests in the income or the property change, and the equal-shares rule will then apply unless a new declaration is made.

MEMO POINTS 1. The equal-shares rule ceases to apply on the **death of one of the couple**, or on **permanent separation**, and the income will then be taxed in accordance with each one's actual interest in the property.
2. If one spouse or civil partner owns an asset which is subsequently **transferred into joint names**, this rule (i.e. equal shares) will only apply to income arising after the transfer takes place.
3. Similarly, if property in joint names is subsequently **transferred into the sole name** of one party, this rule ceases to apply to income arising after the date of transfer.
4. The government intends to introduce legislation to prevent "income splitting", where dividends are paid to the spouse or civil partner of a main fee-earner in a family company. Legislation in this area has been postponed until at least 2011.

EXAMPLE Mr and Mrs A own 75% and 25% respectively of a cottage (not used for furnished holiday letting). During the tax year, the cottage produced income of £7,500.
For tax purposes, this is deemed to be received in equal shares of £3,750 by each spouse.
Mr and Mrs A could make a declaration specifying their actual interests in the property as being 75% and 25% respectively, in which case the income for the year would be allocated as follows:
Mr A (75 %) – £5,625
Mrs A (25 %) – £1,875
If Mr A then gave one half of his share (i.e. 37.5% of the property) to his wife, the declaration would lapse. The income would again be allocated equally, unless a new declaration is made specifying the revised interests of 37.5% (Mr A) and 62.5% (Mrs A).

B. Deductions from total income

4358 Some deductions relate to specific sources of income, such as:
- trading losses (¶2468) brought forward from earlier years, or carried back on the termination of a trade, which can be set against the income from that trade; or
- allowable expenses (¶3122), which can be set against employment income.

Other deductions are made from the individual's total income, such as current year trading losses and the other items dealt with below (¶4361). For the purposes of this section, "deductions" refers to these other items only.

Computation

Deductions from total income are **recognised** only when they are paid. The amount remaining after deductions is called **net income**. **4360** ss 23 - 25 ITA 2007

The individual can choose the order in which deductions are made, so as to minimise his net income.

If an item is given tax relief as a deduction in the computation, no other relief is available for it.

All deductions must be shown gross of tax. Deductions which are paid **net of basic rate tax** must be grossed up by 100/80 before being included in the computation. **4361**

Deduction	Paid gross	Paid net	¶¶
Interest on qualifying loans	✓		¶4363
Gifts of investments to charities	✓		¶4382
Copyright royalties	✓		
Patent royalties		✓	¶4387
Most annuities		✓	¶4387

1. Interest on qualifying loans

Interest incurred wholly and exclusively for the purposes of an indivdual's trade is allowable as a deduction against trading profits, on an accrual basis. An individual who has **rental property** can claim a deduction against rental income for any interest payable on a loan relating to the property. **4363** s 386 ITA 2007

In **any other case**, provided certain conditions are met (¶4365), an individual may claim a deduction for interest paid in respect of a loan taken out to:
- purchase plant and machinery (¶4366);
- buy an interest in, or make a loan to, a business organisation (¶4368); or
- pay an inheritance tax liability (¶4380).

A partial repayment of a **mixed use** loan is apportioned rateably between qualifying and non-qualifying parts, so the proportion of interest that is allowable remains constant.

MEMO POINTS Interest paid by certain pensioners in respect of a loan to **purchase a life annuity** is treated as a tax reduction (¶4440).

EXAMPLE Mr A takes out a loan for £10,000 in order to purchase shares in a business. He pays interest of £1,000 in the tax year. If he has non-trading income of £45,000, his taxable income will be:

	£
Other income	45,000
Less: Interest paid	(1,000)
Net income	44,000

Qualifying loans

A qualifying loan is any loan **except**: **4365** ss 383 - 385 ITA 2007
- a bank overdraft or credit card debt; or
- where the loan appears to be part of an arrangement which is likely to give a post-tax advantage to the borrower (where the risk to the borrower is minimised and the loan is likely to give rise to a profit).

s 408 ITA 2007 Where a loan replaces an existing loan, interest relief will still be available unless the new loan replaces a loan to purchase plant and machinery.

Plant and machinery

4366 ss 388-391 ITA 2007 Partners are entitled to relief for interest on a loan used to **finance the acquisition** of plant and machinery which qualifies for capital allowances. Relief is only given for interest paid during the tax year in which the loan is received and the following 3 tax years (or periods of account, for a partnership).

Employees are entitled to relief in the same way, unless the asset acquired is a car.

MEMO POINTS 1. Where the asset is only **partly used for business**, and capital allowances are restricted, the interest eligible for relief is similarly restricted.

Interests in certain business organisations

4368 s 384A, s 392 - 402 ITA 2007 Interest on loans used to **acquire an interest** in one of the following organisations may be eligible for tax relief:

Type of organisation	ITA 2007	Purpose of loan:		Other conditions
		Acquiring an interest in organisation [1]	Making a loan to organisation [2]	
Partnership [3]	s 398-399	Partnership share or capital contribution	Yes	Relief only for interest paid while individual is still a partner
Close company [4]	ss 392-395	Ordinary shares Company must be wholly or mainly trading [5]; no EIS reliefs claimed on shares (by investor or spouse)	Yes	Individual must either: – hold ordinary shares in the company, and work for the greater part of his time in the actual management or conduct of the business [6], from the time of the loan to the date interest is paid; or – hold a "material interest" [7] in the company when the interest is paid.
Employee-controlled company [8]	ss 396-397	Ordinary shares, which must be acquired either before, or within 12 months after, the company becomes employee-controlled.	No	Must be a full-time employee (or during the 12 months after the cessation of the employment. [9]
Co-operative body [10]	ss 401-402	Any shares	Yes	When interest is paid, organisation must still be a co-operative, and individual must have worked the greater part of his time as an employee [11] since the loan was made.

Type of organisation	ITA 2007	Purpose of loan:		Other conditions
		Acquiring an interest in organisation [1]	Making a loan to organisation [2]	
Film partnership	ss 398-400	Partnership share	No	Relief is for only 40% of the interest paid in the tax year [12]

Notes:
1. Relief is given only for the acquisition of the types of interest shown.
2. This column shows whether relief is available. The funds must be used wholly and exclusively for the purposes of a business carried on by:
– the organisation itself;
– a subsidiary; or
– if the organisation is a close company, a close company associated with it.
3. Limited partners, salaried partners and partners in an LLP can claim relief. Limited partners in an LLP, and any partner in an investment LLP (¶2530) cannot.
4. A close company is one controlled by 5 or fewer persons (see ¶2100). The company must be close when the investment is made, but need not be afterwards. In a **management buyout**, a new company which has been formed to take over a trade is eligible for relief. *Lord v Tustain* [1993]
5. Relief is not given for a close investment company (¶2117), or an investment company which owns a residential property occupied by the individual.
6. An individual working for an associated company (a company under common control or where one controls the other at any time within the last 12 months) will also be eligible.
7. A material interest means that the individual owns or can control more than 5% of the:
– ordinary share capital; or
– rights to the assets on a winding up.
The rights of an individual's associates (¶2105) are included in the measurement of the interest.
8. Defined as a UK resident unquoted trading company (or parent company of a trading group), in which the employees own more than 50% of both the issued ordinary share capital and the voting power. If any full-time employee owns more than 10% of the shares or votes, the excess is disregarded in determining whether this ownership criterion is satisfied.
9. The company must be employee-controlled for at least 9 months of the year in which the interest is paid (except for the year in which it first becomes employee-controlled).
10. As defined in Section 2 of the Industrial Common Ownership Act 1976.
11. Of the co-operative or a subsidiary.
12. The following conditions must also be met:
– the individual has invested in the film partnership and he, or a person connected with him, has made a separate investment in another partnership (called the investment partnership);
– the loan is secured on the activities or assets of the investment partnership; and
– the proportion of the individual's share of taxable income from the investment partnership is less than the proportion of capital contributed by him.

MEMO POINTS 1. If the **organisation changes its status** to one of the other organisations and the interest in the first organisation is exchanged for an interest in the new entity, relief may continue to be available. By concession, if a loan taken out to acquire the investment in the new entity would qualify, then interest on the existing loan can still be relieved. ss 409-410ITA 2007
2. Relief is not given for interest paid in advance of the due date.
3. Relief is not given for interest paid as part of an arrangement that is certain to allow the investor to exit with more money than was originally invested.

4371 ss 406, 407 ITA 2007

If the individual makes a **recovery of capital** from the organisation at any time after the loan is taken out, future interest relief is restricted by treating an amount of the loan, equivalent to the capital recovered, as being repaid.

MEMO POINTS A recovery of capital **includes**:
– the receipt of any consideration for the sale, exchange or assignment of an interest in the organisation;
– a repayment of the loan, or part of the loan;
– a repayment of ordinary share capital, or shares in a co-operative;
– a return of partnership capital; or
– the receipt of consideration for assigning a debt due from the organisation.
If the transaction is not by way of a bargain at arm's length, the capital recovered is deemed to be the market value rather than the actual consideration received.

EXAMPLE Mr A takes out a loan of £25,000 in order to purchase a business interest. He sells 50% of his interest 10 years later for £20,000, when the outstanding loan is still £25,000.
The amount of interest which will then be relieved is based on a loan amount of £5,000 (£25,000 – £20,000).

So if interest of £2,000 is paid on the loan of £25,000, Mr A will only be able to deduct £400 in his computation. ($\frac{5{,}000}{25{,}000} \times 2{,}000$)

4377
ss 396, 397 ITA 2007

Employee controlled companies An employee controlled company is **defined** as a UK resident unquoted trading company (or parent company of a trading group), in which the employees own more than 50% of both the issued ordinary share capital and the voting power. Full-time employees of an employee controlled company may claim interest relief on loans taken out to purchase ordinary shares in the company. The shares must be acquired either before, or within 12 months after, of the company becomes employee-controlled.

Relief is **restricted** to interest paid whilst the individual remains a full-time employee or during the 12 months after the cessation of the employment.

MEMO POINTS 1. If any full-time **employee owns more than** 10% of the shares or votes, the excess is disregarded in determining whether the ownership criteria are satisfied.
2. The company must be **employee-controlled** for at least 9 months of the year in which the interest is paid, except for the year in which the company first becomes employee-controlled.

Inheritance tax

4380
ss 403 – 405 ITA 2007

Relief is available in respect of loans made to the **personal representatives** of a deceased's estate in order to pay the inheritance tax liability before the grant of representation. Relief is only given for interest paid during the 12 months from the date on which the loan is taken out.

If the interest paid **cannot be fully relieved** in the year in which it is paid, because the personal representatives do not have sufficient income, the excess may be carried back and set against income of earlier years. Any excess still unrelieved may be carried forward and set against future income.

2. Gifts of investments to charity

4382
ss 431 – 446 ITA 2007

An individual who transfers qualifying investments to a charity, by way of either **gift or transfer at an undervalue**, may **claim** a deduction from total income for the tax year in which the transfer takes place.

s 436 ITA 2007

MEMO POINTS 1. Relief is normally based on the market value of the asset at the time of the gift. However, if the donor acquired the investments below market value as part of a tax avoidance scheme, or the market value is artificially inflated at the time of the gift, relief will be restricted to the true economic cost to the donor.

s 809ZL ITA 2007

2. The rules disallowing tax relief for tainted donations (¶7333) **do not apply** if the relief is restricted in this way.

Definition of a charity

4383
Sch 6 para 1 FA 2010

A **charity** means a body that is established for charitable purposes only, and which meets statutory conditions of jurisdiction, registration and management.

For the purposes of this relief and of Gift Aid (¶4420), a charity includes any registered Community Amateur Sports Club (CASC), and also the following tax-exempt public bodies:
– the National Heritage Memorial Fund;
– the Historic Buildings and Monuments Commission for England; and
– the National Endowment for Science, Technology and the Arts.

MEMO POINTS In brief, the statutory conditions are as follows:
– **Jurisdiction**: the charity must be subject to the law of the UK, of an EU state, or of some other territory specified by HMRC (to date only Iceland and Norway have been specified).
– **Registration**: the charity is registered under the Charities Act 1993 (or corresponding provisions in another state).
– **Management**: the charity is subject to fit and proper management throughout the period in question (eg. a tax year). HMRC have issued guidance on this requirement.

Qualifying investments are: 4384 s 432 ITA 2007
- shares and securities dealt with on a recognised stock exchange (¶9995);
- units in an authorised unit trust;
- shares in an open-ended investment company;
- interests in offshore funds; and
- freehold or leasehold UK land (where the individual has received a certificate from the charity, which specifies the date of the gift, describes the land, and contains a statement to the effect that the charity has acquired it).

The **amount** of deduction depends on the type of transfer, and on any obligations imposed on the charity as a result of the gift. The position is summarised in the following table: 4385

Type of transfer	Amount of deduction
Gift	Value of net benefit to the charity at or immediately after date of gift (whichever is less), plus incidental costs of disposal, less the value of any benefits received by the individual or a connected person as a result of the gift
At undervalue but not free	Difference between the net benefit to the charity at or immediately after date of gift (whichever is less) and the consideration received[1], less the value of any benefits received by the individual or a connected person as a result of the gift[2]

Note:
1. If the consideration which would result in a no gain/no loss disposal exceeds the actual consideration, the consideration should include the excess (or, if less, the incidental costs of disposal).
2. Often through a third party such as a trust.

3. Deductions paid net

Where deductions such as patent royalties and annuities are paid net of tax (¶2846), the payer must: 4387 ss 447 - 461 ITA 2007
- retain this tax, which will be collected as part of his self-assessment; and
- deduct the gross amount of the payment from his total income, subject to the restriction that the deductible amount cannot exceed his modified net income.

MEMO POINTS **Modified net income** is "net income" (¶4347), excluding:

a. the following types of income:
- life policy gains;
- payments from a trust which have been assessed on the settlor;
- distributions from UK resident companies on which there is no tax credit;
- stock dividends; and
- release of a loan to a participator in a close company;

b. relief for:
- payments or losses incurred, or treated as incurred, in a later year; and
- annual payments and patent royalties; and

c. adjustments in respect of:
- averaging of profits of farmers and creative artists; and
- an election to carry back post-cessation receipts.

C. Allowances

Allowances are available **only to individuals**, not to trustees or personal representatives, and treat a certain amount of income as tax-free by deduction from net income (¶4347). 4390 s 33, s 56 ITA 2007

s 278 ICTA 1988 Allowances are available to:

a. UK residents and:
– nationals of the European Economic Area; and
– Commonwealth citizens if permitted by a specific double taxation agreement.

b. any individual who:
– is resident in the Isle of Man or the Channel Islands;
– has previously resided in the United Kingdom and is resident abroad for the sake of their health, or the health of a family member;
– is a person who is or has been employed in the service of the Crown;
– is a person whose late spouse was employed in the service of the Crown;
– is employed in the service of any territory under British protection; or
– is employed in the service of a missionary society.

If the **remittance basis** (¶4200) is claimed, allowances are normally withdrawn. Allowances which exceed net income are wasted.

MEMO POINTS 1. Allowances are not available to **trustees** or **personal representatives**.
2. Allowances are usually **increased** at the beginning of every tax year to take account of inflation.
3. A **double taxation agreement** (¶4226) may extend the scope of the allowances.

1. Personal allowance

Basic allowance

4392 ss 35 - 37 ITA 2007 **All individuals** are entitled to a basic personal allowance, which is set at £7,475 for 2011/12 (2010/11: £6,475).

The personal allowance is gradually **reduced to nil** for those with adjusted net income in excess of £100,000. The reduction is at the rate of £1 for every £2 of income above £100,000. An individual with adjusted net income in excess of £114,950 receives no personal allowance at all for 2011/12.

Adjusted net income means total income (¶4349) after adding back relief for payments to trade unions or police organisations, less:
– trading losses;
– pension scheme contributions (grossed up, if paid net of tax); and
– Gift Aid donations (grossed up).

Age-related allowance

4394 An individual aged 65 or over by the end of the tax year may be able to claim an increased personal allowance called the age-related allowance. The amount of the increase depends on:

a. the individual's age, which may fall into one of two bands:
– Over 65 but less than 75, for whom the maximum allowance is £9,940 (2010/11: £9,490); and
– 75 and over, for whom the maximum allowance is £10,090 (2010/11: £9,640).

b. the level of adjusted net income (¶4392), for which the threshold is £24,000 for 2011/12 (2010/11: £22,900).

If adjusted net income is more than £24,000 but less than £100,000 the allowance is reduced by £1 for every £2 excess, until it reaches the level of the basic personal allowance.

If adjusted net income is more than £100,000 the allowance is reduced by £1 for every £2 excess, until it reaches zero.

MEMO POINTS In the **year of death**, the allowance available is dependent upon the age the individual would have been at the end of the year.

The following table summarises the allowances available for 2011/12 (see ¶9967 for earlier years): 4395

Level of Adjusted net income (£)	Age of taxpayer	
	65 to 74	75 and over
< 24,000	£9,940	£10,090
24,000 to 28,930	R1	R1
28,931 to 29,230	7,475	R1
29,231 to 100,000	7,475	7,475
100,000 to 114,950	R2	R2
> 114,950	Nil	Nil

R1 means that the allowance is reduced by 1/2 the excess of adjusted net income over £24,000.
R2 means that the allowance is reduced by 1/2 the excess of adjusted net income over £100,000.

EXAMPLE Mr A is a single man aged 70. His total income for the year 2011/12 is £28,000 and he has made a grossed-up Gift Aid donation of £2,000. His adjusted net income is therefore £26,000 (25,000 – 2,000). He will be entitled to an increased personal allowance calculated as follows:

	£
Maximum allowance (age 65 to 74)	9,9,40
Reduction for income exceeding threshold:	
(26,000 – 24,000) × 50%	(1,000)
Personal allowance due	8,940

2. Blind person's allowance

Individuals who are **registered blind** are entitled to the blind person's allowance for each year of assessment, which is set at £1,980 for 2011/12 (2010/11: £1,890). On becoming blind, the individual can also claim the allowance for the tax year prior to registering blind. 4399 ss 38 - 40 ITA 2007

If the relief is available to a married person whose total **income is insufficient** to use all the allowance, the balance may be transferred to the spouse, provided both individuals are within category **a.**, or both are within category **b.**, of ¶4390. Notification of such a transfer must be made to HMRC within 4 years from the end of the year of assessment to which it relates.

MEMO POINTS 1. In Scotland and Northern Ireland the allowance is available to any person who is unable to do work for which eyesight is essential.
2. A claim for this allowance must be made within 4 years from the end of the tax year to which it relates.

SECTION 2

Tax liability

The tax liability is calculated by following a systematic approach involving: 4404

a. different tax rates depending on the type of income, and whether there is an extension to the basic rate band;

b. adjusting the liability for top slicing relief, double taxation and tax reductions; and

c. adding back any tax deducted from payments received net.

MEMO POINTS 1. **Top slicing relief** is only available when an individual has a life policy gain. For details of the calculation, see ¶4088.
2. **Double taxation relief** may be available if an individual receives foreign income. For details of the calculation, see ¶4237.

4406 The following **pro-forma** shows the method of calculating the tax liability. Income is always taxed in the following order:
– non-savings income;
– savings income;
– dividend income; and lastly
– termination payments.

Subsequent adjustments are then made in the order shown in the pro-forma.

	Non-savings	Savings	Dividend	Total
	£	£	£	£
Taxable income	X	X	X	X
Tax calculation				
Non-savings income (excluding termination payments)				
First £35,000 (plus any extension) at basic rate[1]	X			X
Next £115,000 (plus any extension)[1] at higher rate	X			X
Balance at additional rate	X			X
Savings income				
£2,560 at starting rate for savings (if not used up)		X		X
Next £32,440 (plus any extension)[1] at basic rate (if not used up)		X		X
Next £115,000 (plus any extension)[1] at higher rate (if not used up)		X		X
Balance at additional rate		X		X
Dividend income				
First £35,000 (plus any extension)[1] at dividend rate (if not used up)			X	X
Next £115,000 (plus any extension)[1,2] at dividend higher rate (if not used up)			X	X
Balance at dividend additional rate			X	X
Termination payments				
First £35,000 (plus any extension)[1] at basic rate (if not used up)	X			X
Next £115,000 (plus any extension)[1] at higher rate (if not used up)	X			X
Balance at additional rate	X			X
Basic income tax charge	X	X	X	X
Top slicing relief				(X)
Less: Tax reductions (¶4440)				
VCT relief				(X)
EIS relief				(X)
Married couple's allowance				(X)
Double taxation relief on foreign income				(X)
Income tax borne				X
Add: Tax retained on payments made net (¶4454)				X
Income tax liability				X

Note:
1. The basic and additional rate bands may be extended by Gift Aid or the payment of contributions net of tax to a registered pension scheme (¶4435).
2. If the remittance basis is claimed, the dividend higher rate is 40% for dividends remitted from non-UK companies.

A. Rates of tax

There are a number of rates of income tax set for each year. The rates for 2011/12 are shown 4408
in the following table:

Starting rate	10%
Basic rate	20%
Higher rate	40%
Additional rate	50%
Dividend rate	10%
Higher dividend rate	32.5%
Additional dividend rate	42.5%

The applicable rate depends on the **type of income** concerned. The table below gives infor- 4409
mation for 2011/12; information for earlier years is given at ¶9966.

Type of income	Amount of taxable income (£)			
	< 2,560	2,561 to 35,000[1]	35,001 to 150,000	> 150,000
1. Non-savings income	20%	20%	40%	50%
2. Savings income	10% [2]	20%	40%	50%
3. Dividends[3]	10% [2]	10%	32.5%	42.5%

Note:
1. Taxable income up to £35,000 is usually known as "basic rate band" income, but the actual rate of tax depends on the type of income.
2. The "starting rate limit" for savings income is £2,560. If savings income exceeds the starting rate limit, the first £2,560 is taxable at 10% and the balance is taxable at the normal rates.
3. If the remittance basis of taxation is claimed, dividends remitted from non-UK companies over the higher rate threshold are taxed at 40% or 50%.

MEMO POINTS 1. The **amount of income** liable at each rate may change with each tax year. From 6 April 2010 a new 50% rate of tax, known as the **additional rate**, applies to income exceeding £150,000.

EXAMPLE Mr C has employment income of £30,000 and bank interest of £18,000 (gross). His income tax liability for 2011/12 is calculated as: 4410

				Non-savings £	**Savings** £
Employment income				30,000	
Bank interest					18,000
Less: Personal allowance				(7,475)	
				22,525	18,000
Tax thereon:					
Non-savings income:					
Basic rate	22,525		@ 20%	4,505	
					4,505
Savings income:					
Basic rate 35,000 – 22,525 =		12,475	@ 20%	2,495	
Higher rate		5,525	@ 40%	2,210	
		18,000			4,705
Income tax liability					9,210

4412 The following example illustrates the situation where a wealthy individual has **income from both savings and dividends**.

EXAMPLE Mr D received the following income in 2011/12:

	£
Income from employment	6,500
Income from property	1,000
Bank interest (net)	16,000
National savings bank interest (gross)	3,000
Dividend income (net)	135,000

His income tax liability is calculated as follows.

	Non-savings	Savings	Dividends
	£	£	£
Income from employment	6,500		
Income from property	1,000		
Bank interest (16,000 × 100/80)		20,000	
National savings bank interest		3,000	
Dividend income (135,000 x 100/90)			150,000
	7,500		
Less: Personal allowance (£nil because income exceeds £114,950)	(-)		
Taxable income	7,500	23,000	150,000

				£	£
Tax thereon:					
Earned income:					
Basic rate		7,500	@ 20%		1,500
Savings income:					
Starting rate		2,440	@ 10%	244	
Basic rate	23,000 – 2,440 =	20.560	@ 20%	4,112	
					4,536
Dividend income:					
Dividend rate	35,00 – (7,500 + 23,000)=	4,500	@ 10%	450	
Dividend higher rate 112,600 =		115,000	@ 32.5%	37,375	
Dividend additional rate 30,500 =		30,500	@ 42.5%	12,963	
		150,000			
					50,788
Income tax liability					56,824

B. Extending the basic rate band

4418 Unlike deductions, tax relief on Gift Aid donations and contributions to a registered pension scheme is given in two stages:
- payments are made net of basic rate tax, so that tax relief is given at source; and
- for higher rate and additional rate taxpayers only, the basic rate band is then extended.

1. Gift Aid

4420 ss 414 - 430 ITA 2007 Gift Aid enables a higher or additional rate taxpayer to obtain tax relief for a **qualifying donation** to a **charity** (¶4383).

The charity is treated as receiving the donation net of basic rate tax, which it can reclaim from HMRC. This **increases the value of the donation** by 25%.

MEMO POINTS 1. A donation may be **single or part of a series**. It is irrelevant whether payments are made under a covenant.
2. A basic rate taxpayer can still make a Gift Aid donation, but only the charity will benefit from it.
3. If the donor is non-resident, and has not paid sufficient UK tax to cover the repayment to the charity, the donor is obliged to make good the shortfall. The charity's position is not affected.
4. The remittance basis charge (¶4200) qualifies as a tax payment for Gift Aid purposes.

Qualifying donations

To qualify, a donation must be made in money, and not for a consideration or a benefit. 4421 s 416 ITA 2007

The following types of donation **do not qualify** for Gift Aid:
- a donation in the form of **goods or services**;
- the **waiver of a loan** owed by the charity;
- a donation made through the **payroll giving scheme** (¶3189); or
- a payment which is **otherwise tax-deductible** by the donor.

MEMO POINTS 1. A donation **in money** includes the use of cheque, credit or debit card, or standing order. A charity account can be set up with the Charities Aid Foundation, which enables individuals to donate to any charity by using vouchers or a charity card.

A donation made in return for **consideration** may not qualify for Gift Aid. This includes: 4422
- a payment which may become repayable by the charity; and
- a payment made as part of an arrangement for the charity to acquire (other than as a gift) any asset from the donor (or anyone connected with him: ¶5570).

However, Gift Aid is available when a charity agrees to sell an asset on behalf of a donor, provided the donation is voluntary. It is good practice to record the agreement in writing.

Generally, a donation does not qualify for Gift Aid if the **donor receives certain benefits** from the charity in consequence of the donation. 4423 ss 417-421 ITA 2007

However, benefits are **ignored** for any tax year in which they do not exceed the limits shown in the table below. The rules disallowing tax relief for tainted donations (¶7333) **do not apply** provided these limits are not exceeded.

Amount of the gift [1]	Limit on the benefit [2]
Up to £100	25% of donation
£100 to £1,000	£25
Over £1,000	5% of gift, up to £2,500 [3]

Note:
1. Where **more than one donation** is made **to the same charity** in a tax year, each donation is considered separately, and only the donation resulting in a breach of the limit is ineligible for relief. Subsequent donations will only be eligible for relief if no further benefit is received.
2. Where the benefit is **for a period of less than 12 months**, the annual value of the benefit must be calculated when determining whether the limit has been breached.
3. For donations before 6 April 2011 the monetary limit was £500.

Newsletters for regular donors (provided they are worth no more than 25% of the donation) are not counted as a benefit. 4424

EXAMPLE

1. Mr A makes an annual Gift Aid donation to a charity of £100 and, over a 6 month period, receives a series of booklets valued at £15. The value of the booklets for a full year is £30, calculated as follows:

$$\frac{\text{Benefit} \times 365}{\text{Number of days in the period}} = \frac{15 \times 365}{182} = £30$$

The maximum permitted benefit for a donation of £100 is £25 (i.e. 25%), so Mr A does not qualify for Gift Aid relief on his donation.

2. Mr B makes quarterly donations to a charity of £20, as a result of which he is entitled to a book which has an annual value of £15. The value of the donations for a full year is £80, calculated as follows:

$$\frac{\text{Payment} \times 365}{\text{Average number of days in the period}} = \frac{20 \times 365}{91} = £80$$

The maximum permitted benefit from a donation of £80 is £20 (i.e. 25%), so Mr B does qualify for relief on his donation.

4425 Reduced or free entry to properties or wildlife parks managed by the charity for the public benefit will generally be ignored.

A **right of admission** to view a property is not regarded as a benefit to the donor, provided the following conditions are satisfied:
a. the property is maintained or kept by the charity as part of its charitable purpose; and
b. the period during which admission is allowed is:
– at least 12 months, on the same basis as a member of the public, with unrestricted visiting (except for a maximum of 5 days in a 12-month period when events are held which are open to the public); or
– less than 12 months, but the gift is at least 10% more than the usual entry fee charged to the public.

HMRC have issued detailed guidance for charities.

Situation of the donor

4426
s 428 ITA 2007

The donor must sign a declaration to the charity stating that he has **paid sufficient tax** (income or capital gains tax) during the tax year to cover the amount of tax reclaimed by the charity.

The **declaration** can be made in writing, orally or electronically. It is usually made at the time of the donation, but it can be made in advance, or later if within 4 years from the end of the tax year in which the donation was made.

If the donor has **paid insufficient tax**, HMRC can restrict his allowances, or directly assess him, to recover the excess tax reclaimed by the charity.

MEMO POINTS 1. From April 2013 charities will be able to claim a tax repayment on donations of up to £10 without needing to obtain a Gift Aid declaration.
2. For donations made since 6 April 2010, recovery of excess tax reclaimed also applies to non-resident donors.

EXAMPLE Mr C makes a donation of £800 under Gift Aid. The grossed-up donation is £1,000 (£800 × 100/80), so the amount of tax recovered by the charity will be £200.
Suppose Mr C's only income is a pension of £6,500. His tax computation is as follows:

	£
Income	6,500
Less: Personal allowance (£7,475 restricted to £5,500)	(5,500)
	1,000
Basic rate: £1,000 @ 20%	200
Tax liability	200

Mr C's personal allowance is restricted so that enough income is left taxable to cover the basic rate tax recovered by the charity on his donation before the supplement is paid.

4427
ss 423 ITA 2007

Tax relief for the donor Gift Aid **increases the donor's basic rate band** by the grossed-up amount of the gift. A higher rate taxpayer saves tax equal to 20% of the gross gift, and an additional rate taxpayer 30%.

The grossed-up Gift Aid donations are excluded from the taxpayer's income for the purpose of calculating the personal allowance of a person aged 65 or over (¶4394).

EXAMPLE 1. Mr D, a higher rate taxpayer, makes a net donation of £1,600 to charity X. His taxable income is £50,000 in 2011/12.
The grossed-up amount of the donation is £2,000 (= £1,600 x 100/80), so Mr D's basic rate band will be extended to £37,000 (= 35,000 + 2,000). His tax computation looks like this:

			Non-savings £
Taxable income			50,000
Tax thereon:			
Non-savings income			
Basic rate	37,000	@ 20%	7,400
Higher rate	13,000	@ 40%	5,200
	50,000		
Tax payable			12,600

2. If Mr D had not made a Gift Aid donation, he would have paid further income tax of £400 (£2,000 @ 20%).

EXAMPLE If Mr D were an additional (50 %) rate taxpayer, his tax computation would look like this

			Non-savings £
Earnings (say)			200,000
Tax thereon:			
Non-savings income			
Basic rate	37,000	@ 20%	7,400
Higher rate	115,000	@ 40%	46,000
Additional rate	48,000		24,000
	200,000		
Tax payable			77,400

If Mr D had not made the Gift Aid donation, he would have paid further income tax of £600 (£2,000 @ 30%).

A **claim for tax relief** on all Gift Aid donations made in the same tax year is usually made on the donor's self-assessment return for that year. **4428** ss 426, 429 ITA 2007

A donor can also make other claims, as follows:

Type of relief	Outline	Details
Carry back of Gift Aid relief	Donation in current tax year can be treated as made in previous tax year	Only if: – the tax return for the previous year is filed by the due date (¶4484); – an election is submitted with or before that return; and – sufficient tax was paid in the previous year.
Mandating a tax repayment to a charity	Repayment shown on a submitted tax return is donated to charity	Taxpayer chooses a charity from the list on HMRC's website, and enters a corresponding code on his tax return. A maximum donation can be specified, which is important where the repayment is actually more than expected. Tax relief for the donor is claimed in the tax year when the repayment is passed to the charity, which in most cases will be the year following that of the repayment return. There is no carry back facility.

EXAMPLE

1. Mr E is completing his 2011/12 tax return in September 2012. He has made Gift Aid donations of £500 since 6 April 2012, which he can carry back and include on his 2011/12 return. Donations made after he submits the return cannot be carried back.

2. Mr F, a higher rate taxpayer, is owed a tax repayment from his 2011/12 tax return. He decides to donate this repayment to a charity under Gift Aid. He files his 2011/12 tax return in July 2012, and the repayment is passed to the charity in September 2012 (during 2012/13). Mr F will claim the related tax relief on his 2012/13 tax return.

Situation of the charity

4429 s 521 ITA 2007 s 472 CTA 2010 Sch 19 FA 2008

For the definition of a charity, see ¶4383.

The charity is treated as receiving the donation net of basic rate tax. Charitable income is not taxable, so the charity can **reclaim the tax** from HMRC by making a tax return.

MEMO POINTS 1. Following the reduction in the basic rate of income tax from 22% to 20% on 6 April 2008, a **transitional relief supplement** is being paid to protect charities' Gift Aid income until 5 April 2011. The amount paid is the difference between the donation grossed up at the basic rate for the year, and the donation grossed up at the basic rate plus 2%. It amounts to approximately 3p for every £1 donated.
2. The charity can make interim claims for repayment in advance of submitting its tax return.
3. In 2012/13 HMRC will introduce a new online system by which charities can register for Gift Aid and claim Gift Aid repayments. From April 2013 charities and CASCs will be able to claim a tax repayment on donations of up to £10 without needing to obtain a Gift Aid declaration. A charity will be able to claim repayments on up to £5,000 of such donations each year. To qualify for this treatment a charity will need to have been recognised by HMRC for Gift Aid purposes for at least 3 years, have operated Gift Aid successfully throughout that period, and have a good tax compliance record.

EXAMPLE During the tax year, a charity receives Gift Aid donations totalling £8,000. The grossed-up donations amount to £10,000 (= £8,000 x 100/80), so the tax recovered by the charity will be £2,000. The transitional supplement adds another £256.

2. Registered pension contributions

4435 A personal contribution by an individual to a registered pension scheme is made net of tax and treated in the same way as a Gift Aid donation (¶4420). The basic rate band is extended to give tax relief for higher rate and additional rate taxpayers. Allowances are restricted where insufficient tax is payable to cover the tax relief obtained when the contribution is paid. However, the individual retains the relief given at source, even if he has insufficient tax liability to cover it.

C. Tax reductions

4440 ss 26 - 29 ITA 2007

Tax reductions decrease the amount of tax charged on the individual, although they cannot reduce the tax liability below nil. Tax reductions are given in the following order:
1. Enterprise investment scheme (EIS) payments.
2. Venture capital trust (VCT) payments.
3. Community investment relief (CITR).
4. Over-75's reliefs:
– married couple's allowance;
– qualifying maintenance payable to a spouse; and
– interest on a loan to purchase a life annuity.
5. Double tax credits.

Tax reductions are usually quoted as an amount, of which a certain percentage is then treated as the tax reducer, as summarised in the following table.

Tax reducer	Reference	Annual limit	Percentage	Maximum possible tax relief	
				2011/12	2010/11
EIS	¶2861	£500,000	20%	£100,000	£100,000
VCT	¶2907	£200,000	30%	£60,000	£60,000
CITR	¶2927	No limit	25% (5 % p.a.)	No limit	No limit
Married couple's allowance (aged over 75)	¶4446	£7,295	10%	£730	£697
Maintenance	¶4452	£2,670	10%	£267	£267
Life annuity loan interest	¶4451	Depends on interest paid	23%	Variable	Variable
Double tax credits	¶4237	UK tax on same income	Foreign tax paid	Variable	Variable

EXAMPLE Mr A has a tax liability before tax reductions of £2,000. The tax reduction available is £2,200. Only £2,000 of the tax reduction will be set off. There is no relief for the remaining £200, and no tax repayment is due.

1. Reliefs available to all taxpayers

VCT and EIS reliefs

Relief is given for venture capital trust and enterprise investment scheme subscriptions by deducting a certain percentage of the subscription (subject to a maximum) from the tax liability for the year (see ¶2861 for EIS and ¶2907 for VCTs). As with all tax reductions, the relief cannot exceed the tax liability for the year, although a carry back claim may be available in respect of EIS relief. 4442

Community investment relief

An individual may claim relief equivalent to 25% of the amount invested in an enterprise located in a disadvantaged area, spread over 5 years (see ¶2927). Relief is available at no more than 5% for each of those 5 years, and sufficient income must remain to cover Gift Aid donations. 4443

2. Situations involving the over-75s

Certain tax reductions are only available to over-75s, or couples where one spouse is over 75. This may also require an individual's date of birth to be before 6 April 1935. 4445

a. Married couple's allowance

Any married couple in which at least one spouse was born before 6 April 1935 may claim a **minimum** married couple's allowance (MCA) of £2,800 for 2011/12 (2010/11: £2,670). The allowance is claimed by and given to: 4446 ss 42 - 55 ITA 2007

- the husband, if the marriage was contracted before 5 December 2005; or
- the spouse with the higher net income, if the marriage was contracted on or after that date.

To be eligible, the claimant and spouse must have lived together at some time during the tax year.

The cutoff date of 6 April 1935 means that the allowance can only be claimed for 2011/12 if one spouse is at least 76 years old.

MEMO POINTS 1. So-called **common law** marriages do not qualify.
2. In the **year of death**, the allowance available is dependent on the age the spouse would have been at the end of the year if the death had not occurred.

Amount of allowance

4447 ss 45, 46 ITA 2007 The maximum and minimum levels of MCA for 2011/12 are as follows:
- maximum £7,295 (2010/11: £6,965)
- minimum £2,800 (2010/11: £2,670).

The actual amount of MCA depends on whether the claimant's **adjusted net income** exceeds an annual threshold for 2011/12 of £24,000 (2010/11: £22,900). Adjusted net income is calculated in the same way as for the increased personal allowance (¶4392). If it does:
- first, the age-related personal allowance is reduced (¶4394) until it reaches the personal allowance; then
- any remaining excess income reduces the married couples' allowance until it reaches the minimum amount.

Note that the reduction for income in excess of £100,000 (¶4392) does not apply to MCA.

EXAMPLE Mr A is a married man aged 77, whose wife is 66. His net income for the year 2011/12 is £30,000. He will be entitled to a personal allowance and tax reduction as follows:

1. Increased personal allowance

	£	£
Maximum allowance (aged over 76)		10,090
Reduction for income exceeding threshold:		
(30,000 – 24,000) × 50%	(3,000)	
Restricted to:		(2,615)
Basic personal allowance due		7,475

2. Married couple's allowance

	£	£
Maximum allowance (aged 77)		7,295
Reduction for income exceeding threshold:		
(30,000 – 24,000) × 50%	(3,000)	
Less: Restriction in personal allowance	2,615	
		(385)
Married couple's allowance due		6,910

Transferring the allowance between spouses

4448 ss 47 - 50 ITA 2007 **Transfer of minimum allowances** The non-claimant spouse may unilaterally elect to take one half of the minimum amount (i.e. £1,400 for 2011/12).

Alternatively, the couple may make a **joint election** for the full minimum amount to be transferred to the non-claimant, provided both individuals are within category **a**., or both are within category **b**., of ¶4390.

MEMO POINTS 1. Either type of election **must be made** before the start of the first tax year for which it is to apply (except for the year of marriage, when a claim may be made in the year, effective from the date of marriage).
2. Similarly, **revocation** of an election must be made before the start of the relevant tax year.
3. On the **death** of the claimant, any election in force for that tax year is ignored, so that all available MCA is given to the claimant. Any unused allowance will be treated as normal.

4449 ss 51 - 53 ITA 2007 **Transfer of unused allowances** Where there is **excess MCA** which cannot be used because the tax liability of the spouse to whom the allowance has been allocated or transferred is insufficient, the excess amount can be transferred to the other spouse. A notice to this effect should be given to HMRC.

Year of marriage

4450 The allowance available is **restricted** in the year of marriage. The allowance is calculated as normal and then reduced by 1/12 for each tax month which had expired before the marriage took place. The minimum MCA is also pro-rated in this way.

MEMO POINTS 1. A **tax month** runs from day 6 of a month to day 5 of the next month.
2. In the **year of separation**, the allowance is given in full with no restriction.

EXAMPLE Mr A (aged 78) married Miss B (aged 68) on 7 June 2011. His net income for the year 2011/12 is £14,000. His married couple's allowance will be restricted to £6,079.

b. Interest on loan to acquire a life annuity

A person aged over 75 may claim relief at 23% for **interest** on the first £30,000 of certain secured loans taken out before 9 March 1999. **4451** s 365 ICTA 1988

To be **eligible for relief**, at least 90% of the loan must have been:
1. used to purchase an annuity which ends either with the death of the borrower, or with the last death of two or more annuitants including the borrower;
2. taken out before 9 March 1999, or replaced such a loan; and
3. secured on land used as the only or main residence of one of the annuitants immediately before 9 March 1999.

MEMO POINTS 1. If a **replacement loan** exceeds the original loan, at least 90% of the difference must also be used to purchase a qualifying life annuity.
2. Where **more than one annuitant** pays the interest on the loan, the relief is apportioned between them.

c. Maintenance payments

From 6 April 2000, payments of maintenance between divorced or separated spouses are **generally** outside the scope of the UK tax legislation. This means the payer obtains no relief for any payment made, and similarly, the recipient is not taxed on any amounts received. **4452** ss 453 - 454 ITA 2007

As an **exception**, where one of the spouses was born on or before 5 April 1935, limited tax relief is available. Qualifying maintenance payments made by one spouse to another attract tax relief at 10%, although relief is limited to payments equal to the minimum married couples' allowance of £2,800 for 2011/12 (2010/11: £2,670).

MEMO POINTS 1. The **purpose** of the payment must be to maintain the spouse or a child. This includes child support maintenance payments under the Child Support Act 1991, but payments direct to a child do not attract relief.
2. A **qualifying maintenance payment** is a payment made under a:
- court order;
- legally binding written agreement; or
- Child Support Agency assessment.
3. Payments are **not qualifying** payments if made:
- while the couple are living together; or
- after the remarriage of the recipient.

D. Tax retained on payments made net of tax

For payments which are made net of basic rate tax (¶4387), such as patent royalties and annuities, the method of computation requires that this tax is added onto the payer's tax liability. **4454**

EXAMPLE Mr A makes a payment of £400 to Mr B in respect of a patent royalty. The grossed-up charge is £500 (£400 × $\frac{100}{80}$), so the amount of tax deducted is £100.

If Mr A has trading profits of £45,000 in 2011/12, his tax computation is as follows:

	£
Non-savings income	45,000
Less: Grossed up patent royalty	(500)
Net income	44,500
Less: Personal allowance	(7,475)
	37,025
Non-savings income	
35,000 @ 20%	7,000
2,025 @ 40%	810
	7,810
Add: Tax retained on the payment	100
Tax liability	7,910

SECTION 3

Tax due

4458 Tax due is the balance left after deducting tax already suffered from the tax liability. Tax could be suffered by actual payment, deduction at source, or non-refundable tax credits on dividend income. For self-employed individuals, Class 4 NICs (¶5084) are included within tax due.

Under self-assessment, direct payments of tax are usually made in advance of the computation being prepared (¶4504). Many types of income are also received net, such as bank interest, employment income and dividends. As the gross income is always taxed in the computation, any tax already suffered is set off against the individual's total tax liability.

4460 The **order** in which tax suffered is set off is shown in the following pro-forma:

Tax payable		£	£
Income tax liability			X
Less:	**Non-refundable tax credits on dividends**		(X)
			X
Add:	Class 4 NIC (for traders only)		X
			X
Add:	Underpayments of tax brought forward from earlier years	X	
	Current year tax repayments already made	X	
			X
Less:	**UK tax deducted at source**		
	PAYE on employment income and pensions	X	
	From investment income other than dividends	X	
	Trusts, settlements and estates	X	
	Other sources [1]	X	
			(X)
			X
Less:	Overpayments brought forward from earlier years	X	
	Current year payments on account	X	
			(X)
Tax due/ (repayable)			X/(X)

Note:
1. Other sources for these purposes include property income such as wayleaves which may have had tax deducted at source.

Non-refundable tax credits

Dividends (and other income shown at ¶2819) are received net of a non-refundable tax credit, which will be available to reduce tax payable, but cannot create a tax repayment. The amount of tax credit must be shown on the dividend voucher. **4462** s397A ITTOIA 2005

As dividends are always treated as the top part of an individual's income, there should be a sufficient tax liability to **set off** the credit. However, this will be restricted if:

a. the taxpayer has a relatively low income, mostly formed of dividends; or
b. a tax reducer is claimed which is large compared to the taxpayer's other income; or
c. double taxation relief reduces the tax liability to such an extent that there is insufficient tax remaining.

The dividend tax credit system also applies to shareholdings in **non-UK resident companies**. The dividend is accompanied by a non-refundable tax credit of one ninth of the dividend paid if:

1. the company is resident in a territory with which the UK has a double tax treaty with a non-discrimination article;
2. the distribution is not part of a tax-avoidance scheme; and
3. the company is not specifically excluded (this applies to certain companies resident in Barbados, Cyprus, Jamaica, Luxembourg, Malaysia or Malta).

A distribution from an **offshore fund** is treated in the same way, provided that no more than 60% of the fund is held in interest-bearing assets. If not, the distribution is treated and taxed as interest received.

EXAMPLE Mr A has the following income in 2011/12:

Trading income	£35,000
Dividends (net)	£18,000 (tax credit £2,000)

Mr A made venture capital trust subscriptions of £35,000.
The tax payable for the year is calculated as follows:

	Non-savings £	Dividends £
Trading income	35,000	
Dividends (18,000 x 100/90)		20,000
	35,000	
Less: Personal allowance	(7,475)	
	27,525	20,000

Tax thereon:				
Non-savings income:				
Basic rate		27,525	@ 20%	5,505
		27,525		
				5,505
Dividend income:				
Dividend rate	(35,000 – 27,525) =	7,475	@ 10%	747
Dividend higher rate	(20,000 – 7,475) =	12,525	@ 32.5%	4,070
				10,322
Less: Venture capital trust subscription (35,000 @ 30%)				(10,500)
				(178)
Less: Tax credit on dividend income (restricted)				(Nil)
				Nil

All of the tax credit from the dividend is wasted because of the VCT tax reduction.

Tax deducted at source

4464 The taxpayer must be informed by the paying entity about the amount of tax deducted at source. The following table summarises the usual documentation received by the taxpayer which gives this information.

Type of income	Documentation
Employment	P60/P45
Pension	P60
Interest from banks and building societies	Certificate of interest
Interest on loan stock	Interest voucher
Purchased life annuities	Voucher from life company
Other annuities	Tax deduction certificate
Patent royalties	
Trust income	R185
Estate income	

4465 If the tax deducted at source **exceeds the individual's tax liability**, he will be due a tax repayment, which can be claimed from HMRC (¶4494).

EXAMPLE Mr A has the following income in 2011/12:

	Gross (£)	Tax (£)
Employment income	48,000	11,000
Bank interest	5,000	1,000
Dividends	8,000	800

Mr A made gross Gift Aid donations of £3,000, and an EIS subscription of £6,000.
The basic rate band is extended to £40,400 as a result of the donation.
The tax payable for the year is calculated as follows:

	Non-savings £	Savings £	Dividends £
Employment income	48,000		
Interest		5,000	
Dividends			8,000
Less: Personal allowance	(7,475)		
	40,525	5,000	8,000

Tax thereon:			
Non-savings income:			
Basic rate	38,000	@ 20%	7,600
Higher rate	2,525	@ 40%	1,010
	40,525		8,610
Savings income:			
Higher rate		5,000 @ 40%	2,000
Dividend income:			
Dividend higher rate		8,000 @ 32.5%	2,600
			13,210
Less: EIS subscription (6,000 @ 20%)			(1,200)
			12,010
Less: Tax credit on dividend income			(800)
			11,210
Less: PAYE			(11,000)
Tax deducted on interest			(1,000)
Tax repayment			(790)

CHAPTER 10

Administration

OUTLINE ¶¶

Income tax is administered through the self-assessment system, whereby each individual is responsible for the following: **4470**

Responsibility	¶¶
Notifying HMRC that he is chargeable to income tax	¶4472
Completing and filing tax returns	¶4476
Calculating and paying his tax liabilities	¶4504
Maintaining detailed records to support the entries on his tax returns	¶4528

Although the self-assessment regime has a wide scope, the term "self-assessment" simply refers to the obligation of an individual to calculate and pay his tax liability without any prompting by HMRC.

SECTION 1

Notification

4472
s 7 TMA 1970

An **individual** must notify HMRC by 5 October following the end of the tax year lin which he is chargeable to income tax (unless he has already received notification from HMRC to complete a tax return). Notification is **not required** if the individual has no chargeable gains and either:
a. does not pay higher rate tax and has received:
– income under deduction of tax; or
– distributions from UK companies; or
b. all his income falls within the following categories:
– income taxed under the PAYE system; or
– income from a source not taxable under self-assessment.

MEMO POINTS 1. **Employees** can assume that HMRC have been notified of any items reflected on a form P11D (¶4732), providing the copy P11D given to them by their employer is correct and, as far as the employee can establish, has been submitted to HMRC.
2. See ¶2215 onwards for details of **disclosure rules** in relation to certain tax schemes or arrangements that confer an income, corporation or capital gains tax advantage.

4474
s 8 TMA 1970

HMRC may notify an individual that he is required to complete a tax return by issuing either:
– a tax return (generally where a paper tax return was filed for the previous year); or
– a notice to file a return (generally where an electronic or computer-generated paper tax return was filed for the previous year).

HMRC will automatically notify an individual, requesting completion of a tax return, from one year to the next, **except** for the following taxpayers (who will be informed accordingly):
– higher rate employees with simple affairs;
– pensioners with a further tax liability which can be recovered through PAYE coding;
– individuals with claims to professional fees or expenses (up to a limit of £2,500); and
– individuals with investment income up to £10,000.

In the absence of the automatic annual notification, the responsibility falls on the taxpayer to notify HMRC if there is a change in his circumstances such that he becomes chargeable to income tax for a particular tax year.

MEMO POINTS 1. Taxpayers that are not automatically re-issued with a notice to file a return (or tax return), but have certain income or expenses (such as investment income) affecting their coding, will be sent a **Coding Review Form** (P810) in April. After HMRC receive the coding review form, any coding changes or tax repayments will be made as necessary. Thereafter, tax review forms will be sent out either on an annual or triennial basis. **Foreign dividend income** (up to £300 per annum gross) can be declared on a coding review form and an associated tax credit of 10% will be applied to the gross income. (This approach will result in a higher rate taxpayer paying up to £15 more tax than under the strict statutory liability and anyone so affected may instead request to complete a long tax return in order to accurately calculate their liability. This practice was announced following the takeover of Abbey by Banco Santander, and is to be monitored by HMRC to determine what issues arise.)
2. Where relevant, individuals will be set up on the HMRC system as **repayment** cases, and a form to claim a tax repayment will be issued annually, instead of the tax review form.
3. Where an individual who has received notification that he is no longer required to compete tax returns prefers to **continue completing tax returns**, he should contact HMRC who will act accordingly.

SECTION 2

Tax return

4476
s 8 TMA 1970
SP 4/91

The tax return provides information about the individual's tax affairs (income tax, capital gains tax etc) for the year of assessment, including details of the tax payable for the year.

Depending on the circumstances of the individual, he will complete either a **long** or **short** form tax return.

Long tax return This form comprises a number of questions. The answers to the questions determine whether additional information must be provided in the following **supplementary pages**: 4478
- employment;
- share schemes;
- self-employment;
- partnership income;
- land and property;
- foreign sources;
- trusts;
- capital gains; and
- non-residents.

If a supplementary page is required, a return is not complete unless accompanied by that page.

MEMO POINTS 1. Where supplementary pages are required, these can be obtained from HMRC by telephone or from their website.
2. If a supplementary page has been completed for the previous year, the most recent form will include the same page, unless HMRC have been informed previously that income is no longer received from that source. If a return is issued with integrated questions about supplementary income, they must be answered even if no income from that source has been received in the year.

Short tax return This form **consists of** only four pages and is issued to taxpayers with simple affairs, based on the information included in the prior year return. The short tax return does not include a facility to calculate the tax, and copies of the return will not be available generally. Where the taxpayer's circumstances have changed, the short tax return may not be appropriate and HMRC should be notified accordingly. 4480

Taxpayers who are **likely to receive** a short tax return include:
- employees (other than directors) with benefits in kind;
- self-employed individuals with a turnover of less than £30,000;
- pensioners in receipt of state retirement pension, an occupational pension or a retirement annuity;
- those who receive modest income from property; and
- those with uncomplicated investment income.

MEMO POINTS 1. Those receiving **trust income** are not permitted to use a short tax return.
2. There is **no electronic version** of the short tax return and a substitute or photocopy is prohibited.
3. Individuals with gross **foreign source dividend income** (¶4286) of no more than £300 (and no other overseas income) can still complete a short tax return.
4. There is only one **supplementary page** (a capital gains page) available with the short tax return. This can be obtained from HMRC by telephone or from their website.

Calculation When filing a **paper tax return**, the taxpayer can choose whether to calculate his liability for the year. If he wants HMRC to perform this calculation, he must file his return by the paper filing deadline (or, if later, 3 months after the date the notice or return is issued). 4482 s 9 TMA 1970

This rule is modified for long form **electronic tax returns**, as the software automatically performs the calculation whenever the return is submitted.

MEMO POINTS 1. A **taxpayer can choose** whether to file his long form tax return electronically and must register on the HMRC website for this service. If a taxpayer chooses to file a paper return, this can only be done on the form issued by HMRC and a duplicate form will not be accepted as fulfilling the filing obligations.
2. If a paper return is **submitted without a tax calculation, after the paper filing deadline**, HMRC will still carry out the calculation based on the figures in the return but will not guarantee

that the assessment will be made before the due date for payment of tax. Consequently, interest will run from the due date on any unpaid tax. (However if, due to HMRC's delay only, the assessment is issued less than 30 days before the due date for payment of tax, interest will run from 30 days from the date the assessment is issued.)

3. A **tax calculation working sheet** is provided to help the individual calculate his tax liability.

Filing date

4484 ss 8, 9 TMA 1970

The **due dates** depend on when the return is issued or notice to file given and the type of return submitted:

Return or notice to file issued	Type of return submitted	Filing date
On or before 31 October following tax year	Paper	31 October following tax year (or 3 months after date of issue if after 31 July)
	Electronic	31 January following tax year
After 31 October following end of tax year		3 months after date of issue

If the individual receives a paper return and does not wish to calculate his own tax liability, the return must be filed by 31 October following the end of the tax year (or, if later, 2 months after the date the notice or return is issued).

EXAMPLE Mr A receives a notice to file a return for 2011/12 on 10 April 2012. The return must be submitted in paper form by 31 October 2012 if he wishes HMRC to calculate his tax liability.
Mr B receives a notice to file a return for 2011/12 on 5 November 2012. The return must be submitted by 4 January 2013 if he wishes HMRC to calculate his tax liability.

4486 s 684(3A) ITEPA 2003

The basic rule is **modified** if the individual has an underpayment of less than £3,000 that he wishes to have collected through his PAYE coding (¶4512) for the following tax year:

a. electronic tax returns – the return must be filed by 30 December after the end of the tax year (or, if later, 2 months after the date the notice or return is issued); or

b. paper tax returns – the return must be filed by 31 October following the end of the tax year (or, if later, 2 months after the date the notice or return is issued).

MEMO POINTS Up to and including **19 July 2011**, the maximum amount that could be collected through coding out was £2,000.

Complete and correct return

4488

A tax return must include all the necessary information (and relevant claims and elections (¶4494)) including **accurate figures**. Where the individual can show that all reasonable steps have been taken to establish a final figure but that it has not been possible to do so, it will be acceptable to file a return containing a **best estimate**. Once it is apparent that an estimated figure is no longer the best estimate, or an accurate figure becomes available, the individual should notify HMRC as soon as possible.

A penalty may apply if the individual files an inaccurate or incomplete return: see ¶4546.

A **paper tax return** must include a signed declaration that, to the best of the individual's knowledge, the return is complete and correct. The declaration is usually signed by the person to whom the tax return relates, or in the case of a deceased person, by the executor. However, the return may be signed by someone holding a valid power of attorney if:

– the appropriate legal documents are in place;
– the attorney has full knowledge of the individual's tax affairs; and
– the taxpayer is unable to cope due to old age or infirmity.

SP 1/97

For an **electronic tax return** the following rules also apply:

– online attachments may be submitted, containing supporting information or documentation, provided the attachment is in PDF format with a file size not exceeding 5Mb;
– any supporting paper documentation will be treated as being filed when the return was filed if it is submitted to HMRC within 1 month of the date the original return was filed; and

– as it is not possible for an electronic return to contain a signed declaration, it is necessary instead to confirm on the electronic return that a hard copy of the electronic return has been printed, retained and endorsed as complete and correct by the person that would otherwise be required to sign a paper tax return.

MEMO POINTS **Figures containing pence** should be treated as follows:
– income and gains should be rounded down to the nearest pound; and
– deductions and tax credits should be rounded up to the nearest pound.

Amendments

If a **taxpayer** becomes aware that an entry on his return is incorrect, he can amend the return at any time in the 12 months after the 31 January filing due date, which applies whether or not the return was submitted electronically. If the notice to submit a return is issued after 31 October following the year in question, the 12-month window begins 3 months after the date of issue of the notice. **4490** s 9ZA TMA 1970

HMRC can also amend a return.The treatment depends on whether the return is unsatisfactory or incomplete, as follows: **4492** s 9ZB TMA 1970
a. Unsatisfactory returns are those which fail to meet the statutory requirements (e.g. unsigned, unjustified provisional figures, supplementary pages not included etc). Provided the unsatisfactory return is **filed before the due date**, HMRC will:
– send it back, with an explanatory letter to the taxpayer; and
– allow the taxpayer 14 days (or, if later, until the original statutory filing date) to amend and return the tax return.
If the unsatisfactory return is **filed after the due date**, no 14 day period of grace is given.
b. Incomplete returns are those which:
– contain obvious errors (such as arithmetical mistakes); or
– HMRC have reason to believe are incorrect in the light of other information available to them.
In these cases HMRC can issue a notice of correction. The **time limit** for such amendments is 9 months from the date of:
– submission of the return; or
– amendment by the taxpayer (if it is the amendment which has given rise to the notice of correction).
The individual may reject an amendment by HMRC within 30 days of the date of issue of the notice of correction.

If HMRC are not satisfied that the return is correct, other than for obvious correctable mistakes, they may commence an enquiry into the return (¶4552).

SECTION 3

Claims and elections

The **basic rule** is that all claims and elections must, where possible, be made on the tax return, with the **exception** of the following: **4494** s 42 TMA 1970
– claims for relief which can be given by amending the PAYE coding;
– loss carry back claims (¶2478);
– averaging of farming profits (¶2650); and
– carry back of post-cessation receipts (¶2466).

MEMO POINTS A claim that is not made on a tax return should:
– be made in writing and include a declaration that the particulars of the claim are correct to the best of the individual's information and belief; and
– quantify the amount claimed (i.e. the actual figure must be provided: a formula for calculating the relief is not acceptable).
A claim for repayment of tax must be accompanied by documentary evidence that the tax has been paid.

Time limits

4496 s 43 TMA 1970 Unless otherwise specified, a claim must be made **no later** than 4 years from the end of the tax year to which it relates.

4498 ss 43A, 43B TMA 1970 If a return is amended following an enquiry or a discovery assessment, the individual can make further **consequential claims** to reduce his tax liability at **any time** up to 12 months from the end of the tax year in which the amendment or assessment is made.

EXAMPLE Mr A files his 2011/12 tax return electronically by 31 January 2013. Following an enquiry, his return is amended on 15 January 2015. He wishes to make a further claim as a result of this amendment and will have until 5 April 2016 in which to do so.

Such claims can only be made if they affect either the period for which the assessment was made, or the following tax year, and cannot exceed the increase in the liability resulting from the assessment or amendment.

MEMO POINTS 1. If a claim would **affect the liability of any other person**, written consent must be obtained from that person before effect can be given to the claim.
2. These provisions do not apply where the increased liability results from an assessment to recover tax due to **careless or deliberate understatement**.

Amendments

4500 s 42(9) TMA 1970 An amendment to a claim can be made either by the individual or HMRC under the same time limits detailed in ¶4490 and ¶4492.

EXAMPLE Mr B files his 2011/12 tax return by 31 January 2013 and makes a claim with the return. Assuming there is no enquiry into the return, he has until 31 January 2014 to make any amendments to his return and the claim.
Mr C files his 2011/12 tax return by 31 January 2013 and makes a claim on 31 March 2013. Assuming there is no enquiry into the return, he has until 31 January 2014 to make any amendments to his return and 31 March 2014 to make any amendments to his claim.

In addition, if an individual discovers an **error in a claim**, he may amend it by making a supplementary claim at any time within the time limit for making the original claim. Once the time limit for making the original claim has expired, no further amendments can be made.

Claims affecting more than one year

4502 s 42(11A) TMA 1970 When a claim affects more than one year of assessment (e.g. a loss carry-back), the amount of relief is calculated by reference to the actual year to which the claim relates, but is actually given in the later year, thereby avoiding the need to amend previous tax returns.

SECTION 4

Payment

A. Tax liability

4504 s 59A TMA 1970 SI 1996/1654 The **general rule** is that an individual pays his income tax (and Class 4 NIC (¶5084)) liability in three instalments, as follows:
- first payment on account: by 31 January in the tax year;
- second payment on account: by 31 July following the end of the tax year; and
- final payment: by 31 January following the end of the tax year.

Payments on account **are not required** where:
– at least 80% of the tax due for the previous year was deducted at source (e.g. through PAYE); or
– the net tax liability for the previous year was less than £1000.

MEMO POINTS 1. For 2008/09 and earlier years the threshold below which payments on account were not required was £500. The first payments subject to the new limit were those due on 31 January and 31 July 2010.

The **general rule is modified** to defer the due date of the final payment where the individual gave notice of his chargeability within 6 months of the end of the tax year, but HMRC did not issue a notice to file a return until after 31 October.

In this situation, the due date for the final payment is 3 months after the issue of the notice to file a return.

Payments on account

Each payment is 50% of the net tax liability of the previous year, defined as the total amount of income tax and Class 4 NIC, as reduced by any amounts deducted at source (including amounts deducted through PAYE). 4506 s 59A TMA 1970

EXAMPLE Mr A's income tax liability for Year 1 was £4,600 and he also paid Class 4 NIC of £1,108. Of the total, £1,276 was deducted at source. His payments on account for Year 2 are calculated as follows:

	£
Income tax due – Year 1	4,600
Class 4 NIC	1,108
	5,708
Less:	
Tax deducted at source	(1,276)
Net tax liability	4,432
Each payment (50 %)	2,216

MEMO POINTS Capital gains tax is not taken into account when computing payments on account.

A claim may be made to **reduce** the payments on account (or eliminate them entirely) when an individual believes that payments based on the previous year will be too high. Such claims must be made by 31 January following the year of assessment to which the payments relate. 4508

Interest will be charged if the payments on account are reduced in error, and a **penalty** may be charged if the claim to reduce the payments was made carelessly or deliberately.

Final payment

The final payment is the balance of the tax due for the year of assessment. Where no payments on account have been made, the final payment will therefore be the net tax liability for the year. 4510 s 59B TMA 1970

EXAMPLE Continuing the previous example, Mr A's income tax liability for Year 2 is £8,100 and he must also pay Class 4 NIC of £1,640. Mr A made the payments on account as previously calculated, and suffered deduction of tax at source of £2,998. The final payment is therefore:

	£
Income tax due – Year 2	8,100
Class 4 NIC	1,640
	9,740
Less:	
Payments on account	(4,432)
Tax deducted at source	(2,998)
Final payment due	2,310

4512 s 684(3A) ITEPA 2003

Collection through PAYE An individual may opt to have an underpayment collected through his PAYE coding (¶4618) for the following year. This is generally only possible where the underpayment does not exceed £3,000 and the return is submitted or before the date required by HMRC (¶4486).

MEMO POINTS 1. The advantage of collecting via the PAYE code is that the underpayment is collected in instalments over the tax year, instead of in a single payment. Where possible, HMRC prefer to collect underpayments in this way, although the individual can specify that he does not want the underpayment to be coded out by ticking the appropriate box on the tax return.
2. Up to and including **19 July 2011**, the maximum amount that could be collected through coding out was £2,000.

Statement of account

4514 To assist the taxpayer, HMRC will issue a statement of account setting out the tax payments they believe are due, although responsibility for calculating and paying the correct amount of tax rests with the individual.

If an individual submits his tax return before 31 October and requires HMRC to calculate the tax due, he should receive a statement of account by the following 1 January, showing the amounts payable. If the statement of account is late (i.e. after 1 January), interest will only run on payments outstanding more than 30 days after the statement of account is issued.

B. Interest

4516 Interest on over- and under-payments of tax runs automatically from the date the tax is due. Interest also runs on any surcharges (¶4518) or penalties (¶4532) paid late.

To **calculate interest** it is necessary to know the date from which the interest runs, the dates of any payments made, the date and the interest rates in force. For interest on overpayments, it is also necessary to establish the date on which HMRC made any repayments.

The **rate of interest** is calculated to shadow the Bank of England rate: see ¶9782.

MEMO POINTS 1. Technically, interest on amounts outstanding up to and including 30 October 2011 is charged under s 86 TMA 1970. From 31 October 2011 the charge is made under s 101 FA 2009.
2. Where **payment is made by cheque**, the effective date of payment will be the date on which the cheque clears. Payments can also be made by credit and debit cards electronically. Each method carries a processing fee as a percentage of the amount being paid. The fee for a credit card payment is 1.25% for internet payments and 0.91% for telephone payments.

Underpayments

4518 s 101 FA 2009 s 86 TMA 1970

Interest is charged on any tax paid late. Interest runs from the **relevant date** until the day before that on which payment is actually made. The relevant date is as shown in the following table:

Type of payment	Relevant date
Payment on account (¶4506)	31 January or 31 July (see ¶4520)
Final balancing payment[2] (¶4510)	31 January following the tax year[1]
Tax arising from an amendment[3] (¶4500)	31 January following the tax year for which the payment was due
Tax charged in an assessment (¶4564)	
Tax payable after an appeal and postponement (¶4580)	
Penalty	30 days after the issue of the penalty notice

Notes
1. If the individual notifies liability (¶4472) by 5 October following the tax year, and the notice to make a tax return is not issued by the following 31 October, the relevant date is 3 months after the date of issue of the notice.
2. If the individual submits the return by 31 October and requires HMRC to calculate the tax (¶4482), the relevant date cannot be earlier than 30 days after HMRC issues the statement of account.
3. The relevant date is the same whether the amendment was made by the individual or by HMRC.

Note that the relevant date is not affected by:
- the fact that the due date for payment may be later than the relevant date; nor
- an appeal, whether or not there is an application to postpone payment of tax.

MEMO POINTS The former system of surcharges on unpaid tax ceased to have effect on 1 April 2011. For details, see *Tax Memo 2010-2011*.

EXAMPLE Mr A has a tax liability of £7,500 for Year 1, and was required to make payments on account of £1,600 and a final payment of £4,300. The actual payments made were as follows:

Date	**£**
5 February (1st payment on account)	1,600
31 July (2nd payment on account)	1,400
18 August	200
3 February (final payment)	4,300

Interest will therefore be due as follows:

Date	
31 January to 4 February	Interest on £1,600
31 July to 17 August	Interest on £200
31 January to 2 February	Interest on £4,300

Payments on account When an individual makes a claim to reduce his payments on account (¶4506) and the amount paid subsequently proves to be insufficient, special rules apply. 4520

The amount deemed to be correctly payable on account is calculated as the lower of:
- the statutory payments originally due; and
- one half of the actual net tax liability for the current year.

If the payments on account made are lower than this, interest will be charged on the difference, from the due date for the payment on account until the day before the tax was actually paid.

EXAMPLE Mr B was required to make payments on account of £4,000 for tax year 1. Mr B made a claim to reduce these payments to £3,000 each. His actual tax liability was £16,000, of which £5,500 was deducted at source. His net tax liability was therefore £10,500. All payments were made on the due dates.

Interest will be charged as though the correct payments on account were the lower of:
- the statutory payments originally due (£4,000); or
- one half of his net tax liability (£10,500 @ 50% = £5,250).

Interest will therefore run as follows:

Date	
From 31 January during tax year 1 to next 30 January	Interest on £1,000 (i.e. £4,000 – £3,000)
From 31 July after end of the tax year 1 to next 30 January	Interest on £1,000 (as above)

Overpayments

Interest on overpaid tax (referred to by HMRC as a **repayment supplement**) runs from the date on which the tax was paid until the date before that on which the repayment is made. Where tax payments were made on different dates, the repayment is deemed to be made from the latest payment first. Actual tax payments are repaid in priority to any tax deducted at source. 4522 s 102 FA 2009 s 824 ICTA 1988

Repayments of tax must be **claimed** by the individual, generally by completing the appropriate section on the tax return (or by completion of form R40). If a repayment claim is not made, any overpayments will be set against subsequent tax liabilities.

MEMO POINTS 1. Technically, interest on repayments outstanding up to and including 30 October 2011 is paid under s 824 ICTA 1988. From 31 October 2011 the payment is made under s 102 FA 2009.
2. A taxpayer may elect to donate any tax repayment to a charity under Gift Aid (¶4420).

Payments on account Interest charged on late payments on account will be refunded to the extent that each instalment exceeds 50% of the final net tax liability. 4524

SECTION 5

Record keeping

4528 An individual is required to:
s 12B TMA 1970
CH13300
– maintain detailed records and supporting documentation to enable him to complete a correct return; and
– preserve those records for future inspection.

Type of record This will vary depending on each individual's circumstances, but will generally include:
– bank or building society statements;
– details of any state benefits received;
– dividend vouchers;
– P60, P11D; and
– details of any acquisitions and disposals of capital assets.

MEMO POINTS Individuals carrying on a trade (including the receipt of rental income) are required to keep detailed records in respect of the activity of the business. This includes not only the day to day accounting records, but also the supporting documentation (for example, invoices, receipts and contracts).

4530 **Retention of records** Records **generally** must be retained until 12 months after 31 January following the end of the tax year to which they relate. **Self-employed individuals**, and those in receipt of **rental income**, must retain their records for 5 years from 31 January following the end of the tax year to which they relate.

MEMO POINTS 1. With the exception of tax vouchers, there is no requirement for records to be maintained in the original format (for example till receipts), but the information must be retained in some format (for example, a cashbook, computerised form or via digital imaging techniques).
2. HMRC do have the power to reduce the length of time for which records must be kept.
When the **return is submitted late**, records must be retained until the last day on which HMRC have the power to commence an enquiry.
When HMRC **commence an enquiry** into a return, records must be retained until the day the enquiry is completed.

SECTION 6

Penalties

4532 As self-assessment relies heavily on timely compliance with the regime, there is a range of penalties which aim to encourage taxpayers to deal promptly with their affairs.

4534 Penalties may be imposed as follows:

Misconduct	Fixed	Tax related	¶¶
Failure to notify chargeability	x	✓	¶4540
Late filing of return	✓	✓	¶4542
Late payment of tax	x	✓	¶4545
Making careless or deliberate errors in a return	x	✓	¶4546
Failure to maintain adequate records	✓	x	¶4548
Failure to comply with HMRC investigation powers	✓	✓	¶4550
Failure to notify HMRC that an assessment is understated	x	✓	¶4451

Penalty procedure Most penalties are charged by issuing an assessment. This may be combined with a tax assessment, and can be appealed (¶4580) and enforced in the same ways. 4536

Penalties must be paid within 30 days from the date that the assessment is issued. Interest (¶4516) is charged on late payment.

MEMO POINTS The former system of imposing penalties by issuing a **notice of determination** is now of very limited application. The system of appeal, and the time limit for payment, were effectively the same as those stated above.

Time limits The time limits for the imposition of a penalty are as follows: 4538

Penalty for:	Time limit	¶¶
Failure to notify chargeability	12 months from: – the end of the appeal period[1] for the assessment on the unpaid tax; or, – if there is no assessment, the date on which the amount of unpaid tax is ascertained.	¶4540
Late filing of a return	The later of: – 2 years from the due date for filing; and – 12 months from: – the end of the appeal period[1] for the assessment on the unpaid tax; or, – if there is no assessment, the date on which the amount of unpaid tax is ascertained, or the unpaid liability is determined to be nil.	¶4542
Late payment of tax	The later of: – 2 years from the due date for payment; and – 12 months from: – the end of the appeal period[1] for the assessment on the tax in question; or, – if there is no assessment, the date on which the amount of that tax is ascertained.	¶4545
Careless or deliberate error in a return	12 months from: – the end of the appeal period[1] for the decision or assessment correcting the inaccuracy; or, if there is no correcting assessment, the date on which the inaccuracy is corrected.	¶4546
Failure to maintain records	6 years from the end of the tax year concerned	¶4548
Failure to comply with HMRC investigation powers	Normally 12 months from the date on which the liability arose. For a failure relating to an information notice against which there can be an appeal, 12 months from the later of: – the end of the appeal period[1] for that notice; and – the date on which the appeal is determined or withdrawn. For a penalty for inaccuracy, there are two limits: – 12 months from HMRC first becoming aware of the inaccuracy; and – 6 years from the date of the offence.	¶4550

Penalty for:	Time limit	¶¶
Failure to notify HMRC that an assessment is understated	12 months from: – the end of the appeal period[1] for the corrected assessment; or, – if there is no correcting assessment, the date on which the understatement is corrected.	¶4451

Note
1. The appeal period for an assessment or notice is the period (normally 30 days) during which an appeal could be brought against it, or during which an existing appeal has not been determined or withdrawn. See ¶4580.

MEMO POINTS A penalty charged by a notice of determination (¶4536) could be imposed up to 6 years from the date the penalty was incurred. For tax-related penalties, the time limit was the same, or 3 years after the final determination of the amount of tax (if later).

Failure to notify chargeability

4540 If an individual fails to notify chargeability within the required time, he may be liable to a **failure to notify penalty** calculated as a percentage of the potential lost tax revenue (broadly, the late-paid tax). For details, see ¶9846.

Late filing of return

4542 Sch 55 FA 2009 A new penalty regime applies to **tax returns for 2010/11** and subsequent years:

Failure	Penalty	Notes
Return filed late by 1 or more days	£100	Applies even if no tax payable, or tax paid on time
Return outstanding 3 months from filing date	£10/day	Maximum 90 days (£900)
Return outstanding 6 months from filing date	5% of tax[1]	Subject to minimum penalty of £300
Return outstanding 12 months from filing date	5% of tax[1]	Subject to minimum penalty of £300

1. Penalty is based on the tax liability as shown in the return. If a determination is made by HMRC (because the return is outstanding), the penalty is based on the amount shown in the determination, and adjusted when the return is filed.

The minimum penalty for a return which is six months late is therefore £1,300. For further details see ¶9855+

MEMO POINTS 1. For details of the penalties for late filing of returns for 2009/10 and earlier years, see *Tax Memo 2010-2011*.
2. If an electronic filing attempt is rejected by HMRC's software and no suitable work-round can be devised, the taxpayer has to submit a paper return. This could lead to a late filing penalty if the paper return is submitted after 31 October 2009. HMRC advise that a reasonable excuse claim will be accepted in these circumstances, provided that the paper return is submitted as soon as possible, and that details of the failed electronic filing are attached.

4544 s 28C TMA 1970 If an individual fails to file his return, HMRC may issue a **determination** of the amount of tax believed to be payable. This is essentially HMRC's best estimate of the individual's tax liability based on the information available to them at that time. The deadline after which a determination cannot be issued is 3 years from the filing date for the tax return.

The **determination has effect** as though it were the individual's own self-assessment of his liability, which means that interest and penalties can be charged and payment enforced.

Once a determination has been issued, it is not possible to appeal against it. The only way the **determination can be superseded** is by the individual submitting a valid tax return and self-assessment within 12 months from the date of issue of the determination.

Late payment of tax

A new penalty regime applies to **tax payments relating to liabilities for 2010-11** and subsequent years: 4545 Sch 56 FA 2009

Tax paid:	Penalty
30 days late	5% of the tax not paid at that date
6 months late	5% of the tax still unpaid at that date
12 months late	5% of the tax still unpaid at that date

Interest will also continue to be charged on all outstanding amounts, including unpaid penalties. For further details, see ¶9857+.

Making careless or deliberate errors in a return

A **tax related penalty** may be charged where an individual carelessly or deliberately includes errors in a return leading to: 4546 Sch 24 FA 2007
– an understatement of the tax liability; or
– a false or overstated claim for a loss (including an over-inflated claim to an expense, charge or deficit); or
– a false or overstated claim for a repayment (including a claim for a tax credit).

See ¶9784+ for full details.

To comply with the European Commission on Human Rights, HMRC have stated that:
– any tax-related penalty will be charged at the same time as a related tribunal hearing, so that any appeal against it can be dealt with at the same hearing; and
– the taxpayer will be told at the start of an enquiry (and reminded when told that penalties may be sought) that he may apply to the tribunal to close the enquiry.

MEMO POINTS 1. A similar penalty may also be charged where an individual realises that the tax return is incorrect but fails to correct the error within a reasonable period. The period is not specified and each case will be looked at individually.
2. Where an individual **assists in the preparation** or delivery of any information known to be incorrect and to be (or likely to be) used for tax purposes he may be liable to a penalty of up to £3,000.
3. If the document contains more than one error, each error will incur a penalty.

Failure to maintain records

If records are not maintained or preserved, a **fixed penalty** of up to £3,000 may be charged. A penalty may not be charged if records that are not preserved relate solely to a claim or election that did not form part of the tax return for the year in question. HMRC have powers to inspect records relating to an individual's tax position at any time, whether or not a return for the period has been submitted (¶9860+). 4548 s 12B TMA 1970

Failure to comply with HMRC investigation powers

HMRC have powers to impose fixed, daily and tax-related penalties for: 4550 Sch 36 FA 2008
– failure to comply with a notice to give information;
– carelessly or deliberately providing inaccurate information in response to such a notice; or
– obstruction of an HMRC officer in an inspection of business premises approved by the tribunal.

See ¶9860+ for details.

Failure to notify underassessment

A **tax related penalty of 30%** may be charged when an individual fails to notify HMRC that an assessment (or determination) issued to him understates his liability to income tax. 4551 Sch 24 para 2 FA 2007

To avoid a penalty, the individual must take reasonable steps to notify HMRC within 30 days of the date of the assessment. The penalty is 30% of the potential lost tax, subject to reductions for disclosure or special circumstances (¶9810). The penalty is further reduced by the amount of any other penalty determined by reference to his tax liability for the same period.

MEMO POINTS The individual can also be penalized for his **agent's failure** to notify, unless he can satisfy HMRC that he took reasonable care to avoid such a failure.

SECTION 7

Enquiries

4552 An enquiry may be made by HMRC into any tax return, either selected at random, or specifically chosen because they believe the return to be inaccurate.

Commencement of an enquiry

4554 s 9A TMA 1970 HMRC must **notify** the individual of their intention to make the enquiry, and issue an enquiry notice, the scope of which may extend to anything which is, or should have been, contained in the return (including claims).

An enquiry must be started within a set **time limit** – the general rule being that HMRC have 12 months from the submission date of the return in question in which to commence an enquiry.

However, by **exception** if the return is either:
– filed late; or
– amended (including the making of a claim after the tax return has been filed),

then the deadline is extended to the quarter day following the anniversary of the date the return (or amendment) was filed, the quarter days being 31 January, 30 April, 31 July and 31 October. The details for 2011/12 are set out below:

Situation for 2011/12 Tax Returns	Enquiry window open until	Taxpayer can amend up to and until
Paper return filed on or before 31 October 2012.	12 months from date of submission.	31 January 2014
Online return filed on or before 31 January 2013.	12 months from date of submission.	31 January 2014
Paper return filed on or after 1 November 2012 but before 1 February 2013. Tax paid on or before 31 January 2013.	Up to and including the quarter day following the first anniversary of the date filed.	31 January 2014
Online return filed on or before 31 January 2013 and amendments made by taxpayer on or before 31 January 2014.	12 months from date of filing for main return. Enquiry window for amendment extended up to and including the quarter day following the first anniversary of the amendment.	31 January 2014
Notice to file issued after 31 July 2012 and on or before 31 October 2012. Paper return filed within 3 months of date of notice or online return filed by 31 January 2013.	12 months from the date the return is filed.	31 January 2014
Notice to file issued after 31 October 2012. Return filed online after 31 January 2013 but within 3 months of the date of issue of the notice.	12 months from date of filing.	15 months from the date of issue of the notice to file.

MEMO POINTS If the enquiry is raised after the date which would have been the deadline had there been no amendments to the return, the scope of the enquiry is restricted to the amendments.

During an enquiry

During the course of the enquiry the **individual may**: 4556 ss 9B, 9C, 19A, 28A TMA 1970

a. amend his tax return, but any such amendment will not take effect until the closure of the enquiry, at which point the closure notice will incorporate the amendment, or will show that it was considered by HMRC to be incorrect; and

b. apply to the tribunal to direct a closure notice if he believes an enquiry is **continuing unnecessarily**. The tribunal must give the direction unless HMRC can show that they have reasonable grounds for continuing the enquiry beyond the specified period.

HMRC may also:

a. give notice to the individual, requiring production of documents or information in connection with the enquiry. This notice may be given at the time of commencing the enquiry or during the course of the enquiry. (If the individual does not believe the documents are pertinent to the enquiry, he may appeal against the notice within 30 days of the date of issue. The tribunal will then consider each of the documents to determine whether they are reasonably required. If they confirm the notice (or part of it), the individual has 30 days in which to comply. The tribunal's decision in these matters is final); and

b. amend the individual's self-assessment and issue a notice of amendment if they believe there has been an underpayment of tax and that tax may be lost without immediate action. Where the enquiry relates solely to an amendment of the return, only the loss of tax attributable to that amendment may be charged.

Questions in connection with the subject matter of the enquiry may be **referred to the tribunal** for determination. A decision by the tribunal is binding on the parties, and HMRC must take the decision into account when ending the enquiry. An enquiry cannot be closed whilst a tribunal decision is still pending. 4558 ss 28ZA-ZE TMA 1970

End of an enquiry

Once HMRC have concluded the investigation, they will issue a **closure notice** to the individual setting out their conclusions and stating any adjustments they believe are required to the tax return or any affected claims. 4560 s 28A TMA 1970

SECTION 8

Late amendments to returns

If there is no enquiry into a return within 12 months from the filing deadline, the figures generally cannot be amended. Late amendments can, however, be made if: 4562

– a loss of tax is discovered (discovery assessment); or

– an amount of tax has been repaid to an individual or overpaid by an individual in error (error or mistake claim).

Time limits

The **time limits** for making anassessment are as follows: 4564 ss 34-36 TMA 1970

Situation	Time limit
Normal circumstances	4 years from the end of the tax year
Assessment on income received after the end of the year to which it relates	4 years from the end of the tax year in which the income is received
Tax lost due to careless misconduct (¶9795+) by the individual	6 years
Tax lost due to deliberate misconduct by the individual	20 years

MEMO POINTS 1. Misconduct includes actions on the part of the individual or a person acting on his behalf (his agent).

Discovery assessments

4566 ss 29, 30 TMA 1970 Discovery assessments **can only be made** if:
a. there is a loss of tax (or an amount over repaid) due to the taxpayer acting carelessly or deliberately; or
b. HMRC could not have been expected to be aware of the facts giving rise to an underpayment (or over-repayment), based on the information available at either:
– the date of completion of an enquiry into a return; or
– the latest date an enquiry could have commenced.

A discovery assessment **cannot be made** if the return was correctly prepared in accordance with prevailing practice.

MEMO POINTS 1. Information is deemed to be **available to HMRC** if it is contained in:
– the taxpayer's return for the current and 2 preceding years (or supporting documentation for these returns);
– a claim for the current year (or supporting documentation for the claim); or
– documents provided in the course of an enquiry.
2. There is an **underpayment** of tax is when it becomes apparent that an amount of tax has not been assessed because:
– profits which ought to have been assessed to tax have not been so assessed;
– an assessment has become insufficient; or
– a relief given has become excessive.
3. Where there has been an **over-repayment** of tax, an assessment can be made to recover tax which HMRC discover has been repaid to the individual in error. Such an assessment treats the amount repaid as sundry income of the recipient and carries interest from the date on which it was repaid until such time as the individual pays the tax on the assessment.
SP 1/06 4. HMRC have **published guidance** so that taxpayers can be more certain that if no enquiry is raised within the normal time limits, their tax affairs are settled. The general concept is that information should be entered in the Additional Information space as follows:
a. where a **valuation** is used in the Tax Return, the taxpayer should disclose:
– the fact that a valuation, carried out on an appropriate basis, has been used; and
– who carried it out, stating whether the valuer was independent and suitably qualified;
b. where an **unusual item** appears in the accounts, such as a large item in repairs, the background to it and the method of accounting (such as the allocation between revenue and capital items) should be disclosed; and
c. where a taxpayer has **adopted a different view** of the law from that published by HMRC, and this has impacted on the tax return entries, he should disclose this fact.

4568 If an individual does not agree with the amount of an assessment, he must issue a formal notice of **appeal**, in writing, within 30 days of the date of issue. If the position cannot be agreed with HMRC, the appeal will be heard by the tribunal. The appeal must be sent to HMRC prior to the application for a hearing at tribunal.

4570 **Interest** will be included in a discovery assessment, calculated from the date the tax should have been paid. See (¶4516.)

Error or mistake claim

4572 Sch 1AB TMA 1970 If an individual believes he has **overpaid tax** due to an error on a tax return, he can make a claim in writing within 4 years of the end of the relevant tax year. This claim **cannot be used** if:
– the error is not in the return (e.g. if the error is in a claim that is not required to be made on the tax return); or
– the return was prepared in accordance with prevailing practice at the time.

If HMRC decide that no repayment is due, the individual may **appeal** to the tribunal, on a point of law only, concerning the computation of profits.

MEMO POINTS Errors on claims can be corrected in accordance with the principles in ¶4490 and ¶4492.

4574 **Interest** will be payable by HMRC to the individual, in addition to any repayment of tax made following a successful claim. (See ¶4516.)

Double assessment claim

If an individual believes he has been **assessed to tax more than once** in respect of the same profits for the same tax year, he may make a claim for relief in writing. HMRC will then review the position and, if appropriate, adjust the assessment concerned or make a repayment to the individual. **4576** s 32 TMA 1970

Interest will be payable by HMRC to the individual, in addition to any repayment of tax made following a successful claim. (See ¶4516.) **4578**

SECTION 9

Appeals

If a taxpayer does not agree with a decision, he can ask HMRC to **review** their decision or lodge an appeal against it. A request for a review must be made within 30 days of receiving HMRC's decision, and they have 30 days in which to review the decision and inform the taxpayer. Instead of having a review, a taxpayer can make an appeal, but cannot ask for an appeal and request a review at the same time. **4580** ss 49A - 49I TMA 1970

The **first step** in the **appeal process** is to appeal in writing to HMRC within 30 days of the relevant decision, outlining the reason for the appeal. A late appeal may be accepted if there is a good reason for the delay.

MEMO POINTS The following information should be included in a written appeal:
- taxpayer's name, National Insurance number and HMRC reference number;
- reason for the appeal; and
- decision which the taxpayer feels should be made.

If no agreement can be reached, the **next stage** will involve a hearing at the **tribunal** (¶9920). Most hearings are heard by the first-tier tribunal. A case is allocated to a category (¶9953) and if the matter deals with complex issues or involves a significant financial sum, it is likely to be allocated to the upper tribunal. Costs are borne by each side unless the case is heard in the upper tribunal, in which case the tribunal can make an award for costs. Hearings are generally conducted in public, unless there are good reasons why they may take place in private. **4582**

At the appeal, the taxpayer should be present, with chosen representation if appropriate. The taxpayer's case should be carefully prepared before the hearing, including a full ordering of the facts, and relevant law relied on for the appeal. The tribunal will send a written decision soon after the hearing. **4584**

If the taxpayer is **dissatisfied with the decision**, he can formally appeal the decision in the upper tribunal, on a point of law only and only with permission.

MEMO POINTS For further details of the new appeals system and tax harmonisation, see ¶9896+.

PART 3

PAYE and NIC

PAYE and NIC
Summary

The numbers cross-refer to paragraphs.

CHAPTER 1 Pay as you earn

CHAPTER 2 Construction industry scheme

CHAPTER 3 National Insurance contributions

CHAPTER 1

Pay as you earn

The Pay As You Earn (PAYE) system is a method of collecting income tax at source from employment income, pensions and taxable state benefits. It is not a separate tax, although it is often mistaken for one. The mechanics of the PAYE system are also used for collecting National Insurance contributions (NIC) for employed earners. **4595**

Other topics which are closely related to PAYE earnings are benefits, expenses, and statutory payments, all of which are administered by the employer, and interact closely with PAYE cash deductions.

SECTION 1

General principles

4597 The aim of the PAYE system is to ensure that the correct amount of tax is deducted from each individual's income, according to his personal circumstances, and paid to HMRC at regular intervals. The administrative burden is placed on the employer, who has the following main obligations:
a. to calculate and deduct the correct amounts;
b. to pay the correct amounts over to HMRC by the correct day;
c. to keep detailed records for each employee, and make appropriate reports to HMRC; and
d. to provide each employee with the appropriate information so that he can check the deductions made, and complete his self-assessment tax return if relevant.

A. Persons liable

4598
SI 2003/2682 regs 10 – 12
All **employers** are automatically obliged to operate PAYE for their employees, if they have a presence in the UK. For these purposes, the term employer is deemed to include the payer of taxable pension income (such as scheme administrators) and taxable state benefits (the DWP).

The term **employee** includes:
- full and part-time employees;
- casual labour;
- pensioners;
- directors; and
- office holders (¶2980).

Special cases

4600 There are special rules in the following situations so that PAYE is not avoided.

Situation	Details	Person liable	Reference
Agency workers[1]	If: – client pays worker direct; – agency is overseas; or – client pays someone else overseas (i.e. not the worker or agency)	Client	s 688 ITEPA 2003
	Otherwise	Agency	
Intermediaries	If an employee works for, and is paid by, a person who is not the contractual employer	Intermediary[2]	s 687 ITEPA 2003
	Individual caught by personal or managed service company rules, so that deemed employment income arises (¶3010)		
Employees of a contractor	Employees work for a client whilst being employed by a contractor	Contractor, but can also be client[3]	s 691 ITEPA 2003
Tips distributed by person who is not employer[4]	Independent person, known as the troncmaster, distributes the tips Employer has no involvement in the distribution	Troncmaster	s 692 ITEPA 2003 SI 2003/2682 reg 100

Situation	Details	Person liable	Reference
Employee of overseas employer	Working for an entity which has presence in the UK (e.g. a branch) Irrelevant who pays employee's earnings	UK entity[5]	s 689 ITEPA 2003
No UK employer or intermediary	Working for an entity which has no UK presence	Employee[6]	SI 2003/2682 regs 141 - 147

Note:
1. To ascertain whether a worker is actually employed, see ¶2986 onwards.
2. Where an intermediary fails to deduct tax under PAYE, the end client becomes ultimately responsible.
3. HMRC can issue a direction to the client to make deductions under PAYE.
4. The employer must notify HMRC where a tronc commences, and the following published guidance applies:
- cash gratuities paid direct to the employee must be declared by him to HMRC and an adjustment will be made to his PAYE code. There is no entry to be made on the payroll;
- gratuities (cash, credit card or cheque) collected by the employer, and paid to the employee, should be subject to PAYE operated by the employer; and
- gratuities collected by the employer which are passed to the troncmaster must be subject to PAYE operated by the troncmaster. Alternatively the employer can operate PAYE as his agent, so long as separate records are retained by the troncmaster.

For the NIC treatment, see ¶4982.

5. Where an employee is in the UK for less than 60 days, income tax is not due, and PAYE is not required to be operated (¶4324+).
6. Under the system of direct collection, so the employee calculates his own deductions and acts as his own employer.

B. Income liable

An immediate deduction under PAYE **applies to** all taxable cash payments (including cash vouchers) received from the employment relationship, such as taxable termination payments, pensions, and statutory payments for sickness and parenting. In practice, with the exception of benefits in kind and reimbursed expenses, any items treated as employment income are earnings for this purpose. **4602** s 683 ITEPA 2003

In addition, a PAYE deduction must be operated on any round sum expense allowances. The employee may then make a claim for tax relief in respect of any qualifying expenses (¶3135).

Payments in kind

As a general rule, payments in kind are not subject to immediate deductions under the PAYE scheme (although they will be taken into account when the PAYE code for the next tax year is calculated (¶4629)). **4604** ss 694, 696, 702 ITEPA 2003

However, in a bid **to counter perceived avoidance**, immediate PAYE deductions must be made in respect of payments in the form of readily convertible assets, which are basically assets where the employer has already arranged a sale for the employee, or for which a market exists. The amount liable to PAYE is the cost to the employer of providing the employee with the asset.

In addition, **non-cash vouchers** will be liable where they can be exchanged for cash or a readily convertible asset.

MEMO POINTS An **employer can pay the tax** on behalf of the employee, but if it is not reimbursed in full within 90 days, it is treated as further taxable pay of the employee (¶3406). Where immediate PAYE deductions are made in respect of payments in kind, the employee often has little resources with which to pay the tax, because his remuneration is not in the form of cash.

The following table provides the definitions of **readily convertible assets**, and illustrates the types of items which are covered. **4606** Leaflet CWG2

Definition	Examples
Assets capable of being sold on: – a recognised investment exchange[1] – the London Bullion Market – the New York Stock Exchange	Stocks, shares, financial instruments, gold, platinum (but excluding shares or options under an HMRC approved scheme)
Right over money debt	Trade debts assigned by employer to employee
Assets subject to fiscal warehousing	Alcohol where duty has not been paid
Assets giving rise to a right to enable the employee to obtain money	Interest in trust coming to an end shortly after the assignment to the employee
Assets subject to trading arrangements (either in existence or which are likely to come into existence)	Jewellery for which employer has already either identified a purchaser or set up a disposal facility
Assets owned by the employee where the employer enhances the value of the asset	Contributions to the employee's life assurance policy
Vouchers entitling the employee to any other asset in this table	Voucher entitling employee to obtain alcohol where duty has not been paid

Note:
1. Recognised investment exchanges are those identified in the Financial Services and Markets Act 2000, for example, the London Stock Exchange or NASDAQ.

C. Taxable period

4608 As tax and NIC must be regularly deducted from earnings, the system recognises earnings on a prescribed time basis. Usually **earnings** to date in the tax year are **assessed** on a cumulative basis.

Tax year

4610 SI 2003/2682 reg 2 Most employees are paid weekly or monthly and therefore the tax year is **divided into tax weeks and months**, starting on 6 April. Tax months therefore end on the 5th day of each calendar month.

A tax year contains 52 weeks. However, as a calendar year has 52 weeks plus an extra day (or two in a leap year), it is possible for employees to be paid during tax Week 53, for which there are special rules.

Time of payment

4612 For PAYE purposes, earnings are **taxable when recognised** as employment income. There is a general rule for employees (¶3046), which is extended for directors (¶3048).

SECTION 2

PAYE deductions

4615 The employer has many obligations concerning the calculation, deduction and recording of PAYE and earnings. Every employer must run a payroll, which identifies each employee, the gross amount earned, and the deductions which are to be withheld and paid over to HMRC. For the administrative requirements applicable to benefits in kind, see ¶4728.

Setting up a new payroll

When setting up a payroll system, the employer should **notify** HMRC. The payroll will be given a unique PAYE reference which should be recorded on any correspondence. There is also substantial guidance for employers on the HMRC and Business LInk websites (www.businesslink.gov.uk/basicpayetools). 4616

A. PAYE codes

A PAYE code is issued by HMRC to tell the employer how much of an employee's salary can be paid without deduction of tax. 4618 SI 2003/2682 regs 13, 14

The code generally consists of up to 3 digits and a suffix letter (although in some circumstances the letter will be a prefix, or there may be no numbers). Examples include 503L and BR.

Two specific issues arise in relation to individuals with **income in excess of £100,000**.

Firstly, the tax code will take account of any **income-related reduction to the personal allowance**, based on an estimate of the income for the year. This will subsequently be adjusted, if necessary, following submission of the self-assessment tax return.

In addition, where an individual's **income is in excess of £150,000**, the employer will be able to deduct tax at 50 per cent on the basis of the codes issued by HMRC. The **0T code** will deduct income at the basic, higher, and additional rates, according to the level of income, whereas the **D1 code** will only deduct tax at 50%. Any adjustment required can again take place after submission of the self-assessment tax return.

1. Notification

A notice (P2) showing the calculation will be issued to the **employee**, who can object to it, or subsequently alter it where his circumstances change. 4620 SI 2003/2682 regs 16, 17

The **employer** will receive notification of the code to use (on P6), but not details of the calculation. He should continue to use the code until notified by HMRC of any amendments.

At the **start of a new tax year**, the employer should follow the guidance on notices P7X and P9X; if any other alterations are required due to Budget changes, he will be informed on notice P6(T) in respect of each affected employee.

PAYE threshold

Where an employer has **not received a PAYE code** in respect of an employee, he must notify HMRC where any payment he makes to the employee exceeds the PAYE threshold (£144 per week or £623 per month for 2011/12). 4622 SI 2003/2682 reg 9; Booklet E12

New employee

When an individual first **starts work** for an employer, the PAYE code is usually notified on form P45 (¶4676). 4624

Change of circumstances

If there is a change to the employee's circumstances **during the tax year**, a new P2 notice will be issued, and the employer will be informed via a new P6 notice. 4626

2. Number

The number usually **indicates** the amount of tax-free salary for a tax year, with the exception of K codes (¶4638). The number is calculated by adding together all the allowances to which 4628

an individual is entitled, and then reducing this for anything on which tax needs to be recovered, taking into account the employee's personal circumstances.
Once the total figure is arrived at, the last digit is dropped to give the PAYE code number.

Coding notice

4629 Booklet P2 The following **pro-forma** shows typical items which may appear in a PAYE coding notice.

	£
Personal allowances [1]	X
Add: Reliefs such as interest paid	X
Tax reducers [2]	X
Employment expenses (e.g. subscriptions paid personally)	X
	X
Less: Benefits in kind	(X)
Tax reducer restriction [2]	(X)
Unpaid tax from earlier years which has not been collected under self-assessment [3]	(X)
Basic rate restriction [4]	(X)
Higher rate tax adjustment [5]	(X)
Income with no tax deducted at source which the individual usually receives	(X)
	X

Note:
1. The effect of **allowances** in a PAYE code is to reduce the amount of salary from which tax is deducted and therefore relief is automatically given at the individual's marginal (i.e. highest) tax rate.
2. **Tax reducers** are quoted gross, but only a certain percentage is actually deducted from an individual's tax liability (¶4440) e.g if an EIS investment of £5,000 is made, this actually reduces the tax liability by £1,000 (i.e. at a rate of 20%). If an individual pays tax at 40%, the inclusion of £5,000 within the PAYE code would reduce tax by £2,000, so the tax reducer must be restricted by £1,000 to achieve the right result.
3. **Unpaid tax** must be grossed up so that the correct amount is collected based on the individual's marginal rate of tax. So for a basic rate taxpayer, the tax would be grossed up by 100/80. The maximum amount of unpaid tax that can be collected through the PAYE code for any tax year is £2,000 (it is proposed that this figure will increase to £3,000 in 2012/13).
4. Where an individual has **more than one employment**, and should pay some tax at higher rate, the basic rate band must be restricted in one employment, so that enough tax is paid.
5. Where an individual is a **higher rate taxpayer** and receives income with tax deducted at source (such as bank interest), this adjustment makes sure that the income is taxed at 40%.

4630 MEMO POINTS 1. There is a close interaction between the code and **self-assessment**, as a small income tax liability may be collected under PAYE via an adjustment to the code (¶4474). As figures used in codes are estimates, it is possible that there will be an overpayment or underpayment of tax at the end of the year. Small underpayments may be included in the code for future years to avoid the individual facing an unexpected one-off tax bill.

2. The PAYE code may include **non-PAYE income** (e.g. casual profits or property income) which is not in excess of the taxpayer's personal allowances. Its inclusion in the PAYE code means that tax is paid earlier than the formal due date (being 31 January following the tax year).
Whenever non-PAYE income is coded out for the first time, the payments on account due under self-assessment will still be based on the previous year's tax liability (¶4506), and so the taxpayer will overpay tax unless he claims to reduce these payments. A taxpayer has the right to request the removal of his non-PAYE income from the code, and HMRC should ensure it is not coded out in future tax years. However, the taxpayer would then have to complete tax returns in order to report this income.

Sch 58 FA 2009 3. HMRC may collect small debts **not exceeding** £2,000 in total by an adjustment to the PAYE code. The following **criteria** will need to be met:
– the taxpayer is in employment where PAYE applies; and
– the debt must be established and overdue i.e. the outstanding amount has been agreed and the time for appeal has either passed or the appeal has been determined.

HMRC state that if the debt has not been paid within, say, 6 months of the due date, they may issue a **notice** imposing the coding change. This will not require the taxpayer's agreement, although there will be a right of appeal. If the taxpayer does not wish to have the debts coded out, he would need to make alternative arrangements for payment.
The coding out will have the effect of stopping the **accrual of any interest** on the first day of the tax year in which the coding out is applied e.g. the effective date of payment for amounts coded

out during 2012/13 will be 6 April 2012. Outstanding interest will be calculated and collected once the debt has been fully paid.

EXAMPLE 4631

1. Mr A is a single man entitled to the personal allowance. He receives no benefits in kind and has no untaxed income. For 2011/12, the personal allowance is £7,475. The number in his PAYE code would therefore be 747.

2. Mr B is a single man and has a company car with an assessable benefit of £2,170, and other income of £300.

	£
Allowances due	7,475
Less: Benefit in kind	(2,170)
Other income	(300)
Net allowances due	5,005

The number in his PAYE code would therefore be 500.

3. Mr C is a single man and a higher rate taxpayer. His income includes bank interest of £5,000. An underpayment of £202.50 is to be collected via his PAYE code.
The bank interest is received net of tax deducted at source of £1,000 (5,000 @ 20%), but this income is actually taxable at 40%, so another £1,000 of tax must be collected. The entry in the PAYE code is grossed up to £2,500. (1,000 × 100/40)
The unpaid tax is grossed up to give £506. (202.50 × 100/40)
For 2011/12, the PAYE code would be calculated as follows:

	£
Allowances due	7,475
Less: Higher rate tax adjustment	(2,500)
Tax underpayment	(506)
Net allowances due	4,469

The number in his PAYE code would therefore be 346.

3. Letter

The letter generally **indicates** the type of personal allowance to which the employee is entitled, and is used by HMRC to make re-coding easier. 4633

Standard codes

A standard code will include one of the following letters as the **suffix**, each corresponding to a different type of personal allowance, and in some cases the expected highest rate of tax applicable. If allowances are changed, which usually happens in the Budget, HMRC can normally issue the employer with instructions on how to alter all codes with the same suffix, avoiding the need to issue revised codes for each individual employee. 4634

Letter	Meaning
L	Personal allowance
P	Maximum age related allowance for individuals under 75
Y	Maximum age related allowance for individuals aged at least 75

EXAMPLE If the personal allowance increased by £1,500, HMRC could instruct employers to increase all codes with a L suffix by 150.

As an exception, where the suffix is the **letter T**, it means that the code must be reviewed annually by HMRC and the employer cannot automatically amend it. HMRC will issue a new code to take account of any changes. 4636

MEMO POINTS 1. The letter T does not directly **correspond** to an allowance or rate of tax.
2. An individual may also **request** a T code if he feels that one of the standard codes gives too much information about his personal circumstances to his employer.

Special codes

4638 These following codes operate in a different way.

SI 2003/2682 reg 15

Letter	Meaning	Situation where normally used
0T	Tax to be deducted in the order of basic rate, higher rate, then additional rate, with no allowances	Allowances already used against other income
NT	No tax to be deducted	Employee overseas
BR	Basic rate tax to be deducted with no relief for allowances	Employee has more than one employment and is using his allowances against the other employment income
D (followed by a number)	Whole of the employee's salary to be taxed at the higher rate where the number is 0, or at the additional rate if the number is 1	For some directors, or individuals liable to higher rate tax who have more than one employment
K (followed by a number)[1]	Creates additional taxable pay because code deductions (e.g. benefits in kind) exceed allowances	Employee with sizeable benefits
E	Emergency code which gives the personal allowance only	Employee starting work with no previous code

Note:
1. A **K code** increases the amount of earnings liable to tax. The **maximum tax withheld** on any pay day is one half of the salary due on that day. Where further tax is due, the employer can usually recover this on a later pay day in the same tax year.

EXAMPLE

1. Mr D is a single man entitled to the personal allowance. He receives benefits in kind with a total value of £9,905. For 2011/12, the personal allowance is £7,475.

	£
Allowances due	7,475
Less: Benefits in kind	(9,905)
Negative allowances	(2,430)

His PAYE code would therefore be K243.

2. If Mr D's salary for July is £1,500, but the tax to deduct should actually be £900, Mr A's employer can only deduct tax of £750 on the pay day in July. The remaining £150 can be deducted on any subsequent pay day, as long as the 50% maximum is not exceeded.

4640 Individuals with **more than one employment** require separate PAYE codes for each employment. The personal allowance will generally be given in full against the earnings from one of those employments.

MEMO POINTS 1. The codes for **each further employment** will not include any allowances and may specify that tax is to be deducted at a specific rate, using the BR or D codes.
2. Where the **earnings** from any individual employment are **not sufficient to fully utilise** the personal allowances, the allowances may be split between codes, which will have the suffix T.

B. Manual calculation

4642 Many payroll systems are computerised and automatically calculate the PAYE deductions. Otherwise, there is a choice of two methods which can be used:
- PAYE tax tables; or
- the alternative method.

Recording

Whichever method is used, a separate record should be maintained of the pay and tax deductions on a cumulative basis for each employee. The official form for recording the information is the **deductions working sheet**, form P11. There is no requirement to use it (or an approved substitute) but, in all cases, the information required to complete it must be maintained in some format. The P11 has a row for each tax week during the year, and entries should be made on the row for the tax week during which the payment is made. **4643**

MEMO POINTS If the employer has agreed that the **employee is to be paid free of tax**, or a fixed amount after deductions (i.e. equalised (¶4687)), the actual payment is deemed to be the net salary and must therefore be grossed up. Special tables are provided for this purpose (Table G), and a special deductions working sheet (P11 (FOT)) must be used.

Retention

An employer is **obliged** to retain full details of the pay and benefits provided to his employees. This includes all the payroll records and other supporting documents, for example, time sheets and petty cash vouchers. These records must be retained for a minimum of 3 years from the end of the tax year to which they relate. **4644**

1. Using the PAYE code

Normally, codes operate cumulatively, giving an equal proportion of the allowances for each week of the year. **4646** SI 2003/2682 reg 22

Exceptionally, a **week 1/month 1 basis** treats each pay period as the first of the year and does not take account of any personal allowance which may have accrued earlier in the year, and which has not yet been used. This means that either week 1 or month 1 is used for each pay period. SI 2003/2682 reg 26

EXAMPLE The personal allowance for 2011/12 is £7,475. Ordinarily, this would be deemed to accrue evenly over the tax year, at a rate of £623 per month or £144 per week. By the end of week 26/month 6, allowances of approximately £3,738 would have accumulated.

For an employee first being paid during week 26/month 6 with no previous earnings, the position would be as follows:

- if code 747L is operated on cumulative basis, tax will be deducted from earnings in excess of £3,738; or
- if the emergency code 747L is operated on a week 1/month 1 basis, tax will be deducted from earnings in excess of £144 if the employee is paid weekly, or £623 if paid monthly.

2. Tax tables

HMRC publish a series of tax tables which show the cumulative deductions to be made. Before using the tables, it is important to identify the correct tax period in which the payment is made, and this will depend upon the pay interval. The calculation of the deductions is then carried out in four steps. **4648** Booklet E13

Pay intervals

Where an individual is **paid regularly**, either weekly or monthly, the tax tables for the week/month in which the pay day falls should be used. The exception is where the code is operated on a week 1/month 1 basis, in which case the week 1 or month 1 table is used regardless of the actual period in which the payment is made. **4650**

Where, however, the individual is **paid at a different interval or is paid irregularly**, the position is slightly more complicated. The following table summarises the rules:

Pay interval	Tax tables	
	Cumulative basis	**Week 1/Month 1 basis**
Fortnightly	Use table for Week 2 for first payment after 5 April. Then Week 4, Week 6, etc	Use table for Week 2
Four weekly	Use table for Week 4 for first payment after 5 April. Then Week 8, Week 12, etc	Use table for Week 4
Quarterly	Use table for Month 3 for first payment after 5 April. Then Month 6, Month 9, etc	Use table for Month 3
Half yearly	Use table for Month 6 for first payment and Month 12 for second payment	Use table for Month 6
Yearly	Use table for Month 12	Use table for Month 12
Less than 1 week	Ask HMRC for advice	Ask HMRC for advice
More than 1 week but not multiples of weeks or months	Use table for week including actual date of payment	Use table for week including actual date of payment. For subsequent payments use table for interval (e.g. if interval between pay dates is 6 weeks, use table for Week 6)
Single payment	Ask HMRC for advice	Ask HMRC for advice

4652 Leaflet CWG2 **Change in pay interval** If an employee's pay interval is changed **to a longer interval** (for example a weekly paid employee begins to be paid fortnightly), the position is straightforward and the appropriate table for the new interval can be used immediately.

If, however, the employee's pay interval changes **to a shorter interval** (for example a monthly paid employee begins to be paid weekly), the table for the new interval can only be used immediately if the employee has not already been paid in that tax month (i.e. ending on the 5th). If the employee has already been paid in the tax month of change, the monthly table should continue to be used until the first pay date in the next tax month, when the appropriate weekly table should then be used.

EXAMPLE Mr E is paid monthly on the last banking day of the month, until 1 August 2011, when he starts to be paid every Friday.
His final monthly salary payment (on 29 July) falls in tax Month 4. His first weekly payment (on 5 August) also falls in Month 4, and the table for Month 4 must continue to be used. For the next payment on 12 August, the appropriate weekly table should be used.

4654 **Change in pay day** If the employee's pay day changes but **the interval is unchanged** (for example, monthly payments are made on the 1st of the month rather than the 5th), the position will depend on whether the employee has already been paid for the tax week/month.

The tax week/month for the **first payment** after the change must be identified and if this is:
a. after the tax week/month of the previous payment, PAYE is operated as normal; or
b. the same tax week/month as for the previous payment, the free pay (¶4657) for the week/month has already been allocated and therefore the payment must be treated as an extra payment, which should be recorded on the P11, but no PAYE deduction made. This amount will then be included in taxable pay for the next pay date, and PAYE is calculated on the total figure.

Order of calculation

4656 **Step 1** is to enter, at each pay day, the **employee's pay for the period** in column 2 on the P11, and the cumulative pay to date in column 3.

4657 **Step 2** is to determine how much of each employee's earnings can be paid free of tax (known as **free pay**), using the pay adjustment tables (Tables A).

There is a separate table for each tax week and month, and it is important to make sure the correct tax week/month is used.

The free pay is recorded in column 4a on the P11. The taxable pay to date is calculated by deducting the entry in column 4a from the amount in column 3, and the result is entered in column 5.

Exceptionally, for **K codes**, the amount found will be additional taxable pay, and should be included in column 4b on the P11. The taxable pay to date is calculated by adding the entry in column 4b to the amount in column 3, and the result is entered in column 5.

MEMO POINTS 1. The **method** for using the table is to look up the employee's PAYE code in the table for the correct tax week/month and read across to obtain the free pay figure. The tables include all PAYE codes up to 500. If the code is greater than 500, it is split into multiples of 500 and the balance. The free pay for the balance is identified using the table, and the free pay for the multiples of 500 is shown at the end of each week's/month's table.
2. If the PAYE code is operated on a **week 1/month 1 basis**, the actual tax week/month during which the payment is made is ignored, and the week 1/month 1 table (or the table indicated in ¶4650) must be used.

Step 3 is to **calculate the total tax due** on the taxable pay to date, using the taxable pay tables (Tables B to D), entering it in column 6 on form P11. 4658

There is an overriding **limit** on the amount of tax which can be deducted for any period, which is 50% of the pay for that period.

The **table to use** will depend on the level of taxable pay and the PAYE code as detailed below.

Codes	Details	Table[1]
Suffix (¶4634), 0T, E, K	A chart (located at the front of the taxable pay tables) is used to identify the correct table to apply (either B, C, D or a combination)	
NT	No tax to deduct	None
BR	Tax is payable at 20% on all income	B
D	Tax is payable at 40% or 50% (¶4638). Therefore, Table D must be used on its own (i.e. without Table C[2]) The figure to look up is the total taxable pay to date, as shown in column 5	D

Note:
1. The tables reflect the highest tax rate applicable to the employee's level of earnings. **B** is the basic rate and **D** is the higher rate. If the additional rate code has been issued, tax will be deducted solely at 50%.
2. **Table C** is the maximum tax due for each tax week/month at the basic rate, and is only used in conjunction with Table D.

MEMO POINTS Whichever table is used, the **method** is similar; simply look up the taxable pay to date in the appropriate table(s) and read across to find the tax due to date. If the exact amount of pay is not shown, the actual figure should be divided into as few components as possible, rounding the total down to the nearest pound.

EXAMPLE Mr F has taxable pay to date of £137.65.
As £137.65 does not appear in the table, it should be split into components of £100 and £37, giving total taxable pay of £137.

Step 4 is to **calculate the actual PAYE deduction** to be made from the employee's pay for the period which is the total from column 6 minus the previous entry in column 6, and the appropriate entry is made in column 7. 4660

EXAMPLE Mr G has a 543L code (as he receives private medical benefit). His salary is £25,000 p.a., and he is paid through a monthly payroll. By the end of September 2011 (Month 6), he has earned £12,500, and the tax due to date is £1,956.
He receives a pay rise in October, increasing his salary to £27,500 p.a., and so he is paid salary of £2,291.67 in Month 7.
The tax-free pay up to Month 7 is £3,172.82 (taken from Tables A).
The cumulative pay that Mr G has received is £14,791.67. (12,500 + 2,291.67)
So Mr G's taxable pay up to Month 7 is £11,618.85. (14,791.67 – 3,172.82)

This is rounded down to £11,618.
Using Table B, the following amounts are found:

		£
Table B (calculates tax at 20%)		
Look up:	11,600	2,320.00
	18	3.60
Total tax to date		2,323.60
Tax already paid up to Month 6		(1,956.00)
Tax due for Month 7		367.60

Week 53 payments

4662 As the tax year is not exactly 52 weeks long, there is a possibility that a weekly paid employee may have 53 pay days during a tax year, and a similar problem can affect employees paid fortnightly or every 4 weeks.

The tax tables are prepared on the basis that payments are not made during Week 53 and so they cannot be used in the normal way for these extra payments. However, **no change is required** for an employee with one of the following codes:
– a week 1/month 1 code;
– a D code; or
– a NT code.

4663 **Suffix code** If the employee has a suffix code operating on a cumulative basis, and the pay for the year (including the Week 53 payment) is:
a. more than the total free pay to date for Week 52, the taxable pay to date is the pay for Week 53 reduced by the free pay for:
– Week 1 if paid weekly;
– Week 2 if paid fortnightly; or
– Week 4 if paid every 4 weeks; or
b. less than the total free pay to date for Week 52, no PAYE deduction is required.

4664 **K code** If the employee has a K code, the taxable pay to date is the pay for the period **plus** the additional pay (determined using the pay adjustment tables) for:
– Week 1 if paid weekly;
– Week 2 if paid fortnightly; or
– Week 4 if paid every 4 weeks.

The deduction in respect of the taxable pay is then calculated in the normal way.

3. Alternative method

4666 As an alternative to using the tax tables, the employer may decide to calculate the PAYE deductions using the actual tax rates and thresholds. The taxable pay to date must still be calculated using the pay adjustment tables (¶4657). To help employers operate the alternative method, calculator tables are available to be used with the taxable pay tables. These simply state the thresholds for each tax week/month and the rate of tax to be used.

EXAMPLE If Mr G's employer (from ¶4660 above) chose the alternative method, the calculation would proceed as follows:

	£
11,618 @ 20%	2,323.60
Total tax to date – round down to nearest £	2,323.00
Tax already paid up to Month 6	(1,956.00)
Tax due for Month 7	367.00

4. Incorrect deductions

It is the **responsibility** of the employer to ensure that the correct deductions are made from the employee's salary. The position for incorrect deductions depends on whether the mistake is discovered during the same tax year. 4668

If the mistake is **discovered after the end of the tax year**, it is not possible to correct the error and HMRC should be informed of the full circumstances of the case.

Discovered during the tax year

If the mistake is discovered during the tax year, and the mistake is that **too much tax** has been deducted, the P11 should be annotated with the correct figures as appropriate (whilst leaving the original entries legible). A refund should then be made to the employee at the next pay day. 4670 SI 2003/2682 reg 80

If, however, there has been an **underdeduction** of tax, the employer is held responsible and usually the tax is recovered from him. HMRC must be informed of the error as soon as possible, and a determination will be issued. The employer may appeal against this, but if no appeal is made, the amount stated becomes final 30 days after the issue of the notice.

Employee's liability

An employee will be **obliged** to pay further tax where HMRC accept that: 4672 SI 2003/2682 reg 72
- a genuine error occurred and that the employer took reasonable care; or
- the employee was complicit in the underdeduction, and had knowledge of it.

The payment of tax will usually be given effect by amending the PAYE code. Under no circumstances may the employer simply make an increased deduction from the employee's next earnings.

An **employer may request** in writing that an HMRC direction is made to recover underpaid PAYE from an employee. SI 2003/2682 reg 72A

MEMO POINTS 1. The **procedure** is as follows:
a. the employer must request in writing that a direction is made; and
b. if this request is:
- refused, the employer has 30 days in which to appeal; or
- authorised, a notice will be sent to the employee who then has 30 days in which to appeal.

2. The **grounds of an employee appeal** must be one of the following: SI 2003/2682 reg 72B
- the employer did not take reasonable care;
- the employer did not act in good faith; or
- the amount of the tax in the notice is incorrect.

Where an employer has **previously treated a worker as self-employed** but HMRC state that he is employed, see ¶3000 4674 SI 2003/682 reg 72E

C. New and ex-employees

New joiners

The **employee** is required to supply form P45 to his new employer, in respect of his previous employment. This automatically gives the employer sufficient information to process the payroll. 4676 SI 2003/2682 reg 40

The **employer** must complete part 3 of the form and submit it online to HMRC. SI 2003/2682 reg 42

MEMO POINTS 1. The **pay information** and the appropriate PAYE code should be entered on a new deductions working sheet (form P11), and the employer should then calculate the amount of tax due to the tax week (or month) shown on the P45 using the tables. Calculations of the deductions to be made from any subsequent pay are then completed in the normal way.

Booklet E13

2. The **appropriate PAYE code** for 2011/12 will be the one shown on the P45, unless the leaving date relating to the old job was in an earlier tax year, in which case the employer should follow the published guidance.

4677 SI 2003/2682 regs 46 - 50

If the employee **does not supply form P45**, it is usually necessary to complete form P46, unless the employee is going to work for the employer for less than a week. The employee and the employer should each complete the relevant sections of the form, which should then be submitted online to HMRC.

The following codes should be used until another is notified by HMRC.

Employee's situation	PAYE code
Has not signed form P46	0T on non-cumulative basis
First employment since the preceding 6 April, and the employee has not since received: – jobseeker's allowance or taxable employment and support allowance (previously incapacity benefit) [1]; or – a retirement pension or an occupational pension	E
Not receiving a retirement pension or an occupational pension and since the preceding 6 April has: – had another employment, but is no longer receiving any earnings from it; or – received jobseeker's allowance or taxable employment and support allowance (previously incapacity benefit) [1] but this has now ceased	E week1/month1 basis
Has another employment which is continuing or is in receipt of a retirement pension or occupational pension	BR
Note: 1. Since 27 October 2008, **employment and support allowance** has replaced incapacity benefit for new claimants.	

MEMO POINTS 1. Details of employees who are **seconded to work in the UK** whilst remaining employed by an overseas employer should be entered on form P46 (Expat).
2. For **retiring employees**, see ¶4679.

Leaving employees

4679 SI 2003/2682 reg 36

When an employee leaves the employment, the **employer must** usually:
– complete form P45; and
– annotate the deductions working sheet (form P11) with the employee's leaving date.

Where a **payment** is made to the employee **after the issue** of the P45, then from 6 April 2011 the employer must deduct PAYE from the payment on a non-cumulative basis using code 0T Before 6 April 2011, the normal procedure would have been to deduct basic rate income tax.

If the **employee retires** and the employer is paying a future pension, this is not a cessation of the employment and form P45 is not required. Instead, form P46(Pen) must be completed and submitted online to HMRC within 14 days of the change of circumstances. A copy of the form should also be given to the employee within the same period.

SI 2003/2682 regs 37, 38

MEMO POINTS 1. **Agencies** must issue a P45 to an agency worker when the worker stops doing work for the agency, or when the agency has not paid him for 3 months.
2. On the **death** of:
a. an employee, the employer must provide a P45, deduct tax at the basic rate on any payments made after the issue of the form, and submit it online to HMRC; or
b. a pensioner, pension payers should continue to deduct tax, except for payments where the P45 has been issued and the payment is made in the next tax year. In this case, basic rate tax should be deducted.
In either case, no information needs to be provided on the P45 regarding the deceased's personal representatives or subsequent payments to be made.

Form P45 shows the pay and tax details to the date of leaving, the last tax week/month for which the employee was paid and the last recorded PAYE code. 4680

The form is in 4 parts:

Part	Function
1	Old employer should submit it online to HMRC
1A	For the employee to keep
2	For the new employer to retain
3	New employer completes it and submits it online to HMRC

If **no further employment is taken up**, the form can be used to obtain a refund of tax if appropriate e.g. in respect of the personal allowances for which relief has not yet been given. Alternatively a pension payer or the unemployment office may require it. 4682 SI 2003/2682 reg 65

Failure to submit forms online

Where employers fail to send their joiner and leaver information online, **penalties** will apply as detailed at ¶4722, subject to an appeal on the grounds that either: 4683 SI 2003/2682 reg 210B
- the required return has been submitted;
- the amount of penalty is incorrect; or
- a reasonable excuse (¶4720) applies.

D. Payment

The due date for the payment of deductions to HMRC is independent of when the employee receives his pay. 4684

Amount

The amount which must be paid to HMRC is calculated as follows: 4686 SI 2003/2682 reg 68

	£
Income tax	X
Class 1 primary NIC[1]	X
Class 1 secondary NIC[1]	X
Student loan repayments (¶4782)	X
CIS deductions (¶4800)	X
	X
Less: Refunds of tax and NIC to employees[2]	(X)
Statutory parental payments (¶4770)[3]	(X)
Recoverable statutory sick pay (¶4752)[3]	(X)
PAYE due	X

Note:
1. See ¶4970.
2. Paid out of income tax deducted where possible.
3. Paid out of NIC deducted where possible. Excludes any amounts funded separately by HMRC.

Where **foreign employees** come to work in the UK, certain employers may agree to meet the UK tax bill, and provide a fixed net salary. This is known as tax equalisation. There is a system of modified PAYE which applies in this case, which allows the employer to make monthly estimated payments of PAYE, based on the grossed-up salary, by the usual due dates. Any shortfall is then payable by 31 January following the affected tax year, although 4687 Tax Bulletin 81 interest will still run from April (¶4698). The due date for the reporting of any non-cash benefits (on forms P11D and P11D(b)) is also delayed until 31 January following the affected tax year.

Electronic payments

4688 SI 2003/2682 reg 199

If the employer **has 250 or more employees**, PAYE must be paid electronically, on time and in full, otherwise interest and penalties may apply.

The **due date** for electronic payments is the 22nd day of the month (where this falls on a weekend or Bank Holiday, the payment must reach HMRC's bank account no later than the last working day before the 22nd).

Non-electronic payments

4694 SI 2003/2682 reg 69

If the employer has less than 250 employees, PAYE can be paid via cheque. The **normal due date** is 14 days after the end of the relevant tax month.

EXAMPLE A Ltd pays its 30 employees on the 21st of the month. Deductions made on 21 April fall in the tax month to 5 May and must be paid to HMRC by 19 May.

4696 SI 2003/2682 reg 70

Employers may make quarterly payments where the **average monthly PAYE is less than** £1,500 (¶4686). Payments must be made within 14 days of the end of each quarter which, for these purposes, end on 5 July, 5 October, 5 January and 5 April.

SI 2003/2682 reg 144

Deductions made using the **direct collection method** (¶4600) are also made quarterly.

Interest

4698 SI 2003/2682 regs 82, 83

Interest is automatically **charged** on any amounts outstanding on 19 April (22 April for electronic payments) following the end of the tax year. The amount outstanding is the net due after deducting any amounts recoverable from HMRC. Interest runs from the due date until the date of payment.

Interest will also be due on any amounts **overpaid**, and will run from the due date (or date of payment if later) until the date that a refund is made.

MEMO POINTS **From a date to be announced**, interest will accrue on each monthly or quarterly amount which is paid late.

Penalties for late payment

4700 Sch 56 FA 2009

Since 6 April 2010, unless a time to pay arrangement has been made (¶9857), penalties apply to late payments of PAYE as detailed at ¶9858.

There is a right of appeal against all penalties, and no penalty will be charged if a taxpayer has a reasonable excuse (¶4720) for the failure.

E. Year end routine

4702

The tax year end is a busy time for employers, because compliance for the tax year just ended is required, and the new tax year must be started.

1. Annual summaries

4704

In addition to the forms completed on an ongoing basis, the employer must consider a number of other forms at the end of the tax year. Since 6 April 2010, certain forms must be filed online by almost all employers (¶4718).

Form	Function	Due date	Electronic submission required?	¶¶
P35	Annual summary of deductions employer has made	19 May	y	¶4706
P38A	Annual summary of employees receiving pay gross	19 May	y	¶4707
P14	Employee specific summary of pay and deductions made	19 May	y	¶4709
P60	Employee's copy of P14	31 May	n/a	¶4710
P11D	Employee specific summary of benefits and expenses (£8,500 + employees)	6 July	y	¶4730
P9D	Employee's summary of benefits and expenses (lower paid employees)	6 July	y	¶4730

MEMO POINTS 1. Where a **termination payment** has been made in the tax year, the employer must report this by the following 6 July (¶3098).
2. Where any event involving **shares or options** awarded to employees has occurred in the tax year, the employer may need to make a report (¶3592).

For the employer

The employer's annual summary is known as **form P35**. This form shows the total NIC and PAYE deductions for all employees, and summarises the information from each deductions working sheet. 4706 SI 2003/2682 reg 73

The employer must sign and **submit** the form to HMRC by 19 May following the end of the tax year. HMRC now apply quality standard checks to all P35 returns, which ensure that all boxes have been completed, and that the figures add up.

If no return is due (i.e. no deductions worksheet has been completed for any employee in the tax year), HMRC should be informed.

MEMO POINTS 1. The employer must submit one P35 return in respect of **each PAYE scheme** (some larger employers may have more than one).
2. For **personal service companies** (¶3010), the usual rules relating to PAYE must be observed, including the filing of the P35 form by 19 May. HMRC allow provisional figures to be entered on the form when it is first submitted, and then subsequent amendments should be made by the self-assessment filing date to reflect the actual position.

Where **no deductions have been made** during the year for certain employees, the employer must also complete and submit form P38A by 19 May following the end of the tax year. 4707 SI 2003/2682 reg 74

The **employees concerned** are those who either:
- worked for the employer for more than a week;
- earned in excess of £100 in the tax year; or
- earned in excess of the PAYE threshold (¶4622) at any time.

For the employee

The annual summary of pay, tax and NIC for an individual employee is known as **form P14**. This should be completed for each employee who: 4709 SI 2003/2682 reg 73
- appeared on the payroll during the tax year; and
- earned more than the PAYE threshold (¶4622).

The form is in fact 3 copies of the same information prepared for the following recipients:
a. HMRC (tax copy);
b. HMRC (National Insurance copy); and
c. the employee, whose copy is called form P60.
The first two copies of form P14 must be **submitted by** 19 May following the end of the tax year.

Form P60 must be provided to each employee, who is on the payroll on the last day of the tax year, by the following 31 May. There is no requirement to provide a form P60 for any 4710 SI 2003/2682 reg 67 employees who left during the tax year, although a leaver is entitled to ask for the details in order that he may complete his tax return.

The employer is allowed to provide a **duplicate** P60 on request, as long as the copy is clearly marked as such.

Penalties

4714 Sch 55 FA 2009 **Late filing** Penalties are automatically imposed if forms P35 and P14 are **not filed** on time (¶9855).

4715 Sch 24 para 1 FA 2007 **Errors on the form** Penalties also apply to most incorrect PAYE forms (excluding P11Ds and P9Ds) (¶9784), but **no penalty will be levied unless** a taxpayer has been careless, or made a deliberate error by understating or concealing the tax due (¶9790).

2. Online filing

In-year forms

4716 Most forms can now be completed online, but it is compulsory for forms P45 and P46 to be submitted electronically.

Compulsory filing

4718 SI 2003/2682 regs 205 – 207 Subject to a few exceptions, **all employers** are required to file end of year returns online.

The following employers are **exempt** from this rule:
– those whose religious beliefs are incompatible with the use of electronic communications;
– employers who are authorised to operate the simplified deduction scheme for personal employees (i.e. who provide domestic/personal services for the employer or his family at the employer's home) and who have not received an incentive payment for filing online; and
– care and support employers (i.e. those who employ a person to provide domestic/personal services at or from the employer's home to the employer or his family, and the recipient of those services has a physical or mental disability, or is elderly or infirm), who have not received an online incentive payment in respect of any of the last 3 tax years.

MEMO POINTS 1. The online facility is **accessible** from HMRC's website, and either the employer or his agent may file.
2. It is possible to file the P35 and accompanying form P14s **in parts**, and HMRC recommend that the P35 is the last document to be filed in this instance.
3. Once the documents have been successfully **submitted online**, an on-screen message will show that the return has been accepted.

4720 SI 2003/2682 regs 209, 210 **Penalties** If the forms do not meet the Quality Standard, they will be treated as not having been submitted. Employers will face a penalty even if they try to put things right by filing return forms again online because the first item, or part of it, was not made in the right way. Failure to file correct returns on time will result in a **maximum** penalty of £3,000. Interest will be charged on penalties paid late. There is a right of appeal against the imposition of penalties.

The **amount of the penalty** depends on the number of employees for whom particulars should have been included.

MEMO POINTS 1. Employers should not send a **paper form** where they are filing online, even where they receive a form in the post. Otherwise there is a risk that the paper form is processed first, which may result in penalties for those who must file online.
2. The employer can **appeal** against penalties on the following grounds, where he:
a. has not already appealed against an e-filing notice and has religious beliefs which do not allow electronic communication;
b. did file on time;

c. had a reasonable excuse (e.g. records destroyed by fire or flood, a family death or serious illness); or

d. believes the amount of the penalty is excessive.

The following penalties apply for returns not filed online (i.e. filed on paper via the postal system): 4721 SI 2009/2029

Number of employees who should have been included on return	Penalty (£)
1 – 5	100
6 – 49	300
50 – 249	600
250 – 399	900
400 – 499	1,200
500 – 599	1,500
600 – 699	1,800
700 – 799	2,100
800 – 899	2,400
900 – 999	2,700
1,000 or more	3,000

4722

Number of items failed to supply electronically in quarter	Penalty (£)
1 – 2	0
3 – 5	100
6 – 49	100
50 – 149	300
150 – 299	600
300 – 399	900
400 – 499	1,200
500 – 599	1,500
600 – 699	1,800
700 – 799	2,100
800 – 899	2,400
900 – 999	2,700
1,000 or more	3,000

Note:
Each of the following counts as a separate item, even where they relate to the same employee:
part 1 of form P45;
part 3 of form P45;
form P46;
form P46(Expat); and
form P46(Pen).

SECTION 3

Other payments and deductions

4726 An employer often remunerates his employees by way of benefits in kind. In addition, the employer is required to make certain payments in compliance with state imposed obligations. For share schemes and retrospective PAYE, see ¶3407.

A. Benefits and expense payments

4728 An employer must make a return in respect of benefits provided to employees and expenses incurred, **unless** covered by a dispensation or PAYE settlement agreement.

1. Reporting requirements

4730 The report usually required is a form P11D, with the exception of an employee who earns at a rate of less than £8,500 per annum (¶3116), when a P9D is used instead.

The returns enable HMRC to adjust the employee's PAYE code to collect the additional tax due on any benefits, and also provide information for the employee to complete his self-assessment return where relevant.

In addition, a form P46(car) is required when a car is provided to an employee.

Forms P9D and P11D

4732
SI 2003/2682 regs 85 - 87
A form must be **completed for** each employee who received taxable benefits in kind or expenses during the tax year, including employees who have left. The employer should report the full amount of expenses incurred, ignoring any possible claim for a deduction that might be made by the employee (¶3135).

In addition, the employer must submit a **declaration** in respect of all forms P11D (form P11D(b)) confirming that the required returns have been made and submitted. All forms and the P11D(b) **must be submitted** to HMRC by 6 July following the end of the tax year.

Where **no P11Ds are due**, the declaration should still be completed and submitted by the due date (even where the P35 form has already been ticked to say no P11D(b) is due).

MEMO POINTS 1. **Details of the items** which must be disclosed on form P11D are given at ¶5052 and, in addition, if the employee has received shares in the employer during the year this must be indicated.

2. For **lower paid employees**, the P9D is a much simpler form which only requires details of expense payments, accommodation provided, benefits which are able to be realised in cash, and vouchers. There is no requirement to file a P11D(b), as the submission of a copy of each P9D is sufficient.

3. **Worksheets** are available from HMRC to help employers calculate the amounts to be entered on the forms.

4. **VAT** should be included in the amounts disclosed on the forms regardless of the employer's VAT status.

5. Where an employer **fails to report** any benefits, he will be encouraged to settle the outstanding liability on a grossed-up basis (¶4747). This avoids an unexpected tax liability for the employee.

4733
SI 2003/2682 reg 94
The employer must also **provide the employee** with a copy of the information (not necessarily a copy of the form) by 6 July.

Employees who have left may ask for return information within 3 years from the end of the tax year of leaving.

4734 **Penalties** Penalties may be charged if the **returns are filed late** (¶9855), or where an **incorrect return** is submitted (¶9784).

P46(car)

4735
SI 2003/2682 reg 90
Form P46(car) provides full details of the company car (¶3286) provided to an employee, and enables HMRC to amend his PAYE code to ensure that the correct PAYE deductions can be made.

A form must be completed in any of the following **circumstances**:
- a car is first provided to a relevant employee (¶3116);

– an additional car is provided to the employee;
– the employee ceases to have a company car; or
– a lower paid employee (¶3116), for whom a car is provided, starts to earn more than £8,500 per annum.

The P46(car) must be **submitted** within 28 days of the end of the quarter in which the circumstances change. Quarters end on 5 July, 5 October, 5 January and 5 April. There are no penalties for failing to file or filing late. However, if the form is delayed, the employee will not be paying the correct amount of tax, and so will face a tax bill at the end of the tax year.

2. Dispensations

Scope

Where HMRC are satisfied that employees provided with a particular expense payment would be entitled to a tax deduction for that amount, a dispensation may be granted to the employer. An **employee** will be **excluded** from a dispensation where it would result in his rate of earnings being reduced to below £8,500 per annum. 4738 s 65 ITEPA 2003 Leaflet P11DX

A dispensation authorises the employer not to report the specific expense, and therefore the employee is not required to submit any related claim (¶3135). This is simply a matter of administrative convenience, and does not result in a reduction of tax, merely in a reduction of forms.

Items covered by the dispensation are not subject to income tax or NIC, and commonly include business travel, subsistence, and professional subscriptions. However, taxable benefits such as a company car or medical insurance cannot be included.

Implementation

The employer should **apply** for a dispensation by completing form P11DX, setting out the items which he feels should be covered. HMRC will require evidence of the employer's control procedures and independent checks to ensure that only appropriate items are included, and where internal controls are weak, the dispensation will be restricted. 4740

MEMO POINTS 1. **Control procedures** include checks and verification by someone other than the employee incurring the expense, and where possible claims should be vouched.
2. In relation to **controlling directors**, a dispensation will only be granted where HMRC are satisfied that no additional tax is at risk. This should not deter small businesses from applying, however, as dispensations are often granted (at least in part). In particular, HMRC have confirmed that where an accountant reviews all expense reimbursements in the course of his usual work (e.g. to prepare the VAT returns), this would be considered to be an independent check.
3. The effect of a dispensation can be **backdated** to the beginning of the tax year in which the application is made.
4. **Mileage payments** made to employees for use of their own car are not covered by a dispensation. If the payments made are at, or below, the published HMRC rates (¶3168), no reporting is necessary. Higher rates should be reported on form P11D.
5. Employers have the option to use the benchmark rates for **daily subsistence payments**. There is no need to report such payments which are at, or below, the published HMRC rates (¶3173). The employer may still agree a bespoke system of payments with HMRC under a dispensation.

In force

Once a dispensation has been agreed, the employer will be sent a notice setting out the exact **terms** of the agreement, which will specify the expenses which are covered. 4741

The dispensation **remains valid** for as long as the circumstances do not change. HMRC may withdraw the dispensation by giving notice to the employer.

Comment It is important that the terms of the dispensation are **reviewed** on a regular basis (at least annually) to ensure that the employer is not vulnerable to an HMRC challenge over the treatment of employee benefits and expenses.

3. Agreements with HMRC

4742 Where it would prove **difficult or impractical** to calculate the value of certain benefits and expenses provided to employees, the employer may decide to enter into a PAYE settlement agreement (PSA). Third parties may use a taxed award scheme.

a. PAYE settlement agreements

4743 SI 2003/2682 regs 105 – 107 Under the agreement, the **employer pays** tax and Class 1B NIC (¶5064) on the items covered by the PSA, and these items are excluded from any other PAYE return.

Scope

4744 SI 2003/2682 regs 111 – 114 SP 5/96 The **types of items** which may be included in an agreement are:
- minor benefits, e.g. small gifts;
- benefits paid irregularly, such as relocation expenses in excess of £8,000;
- benefits shared between employees, e.g. an expensive staff party; or
- where it is difficult to compute the tax using the normal rules.

PSAs are **negotiated** annually with HMRC, at any time before 6 July following the relevant tax year. Once a PSA is in force, it is renewable annually provided circumstances do not change. The scope of the PSA may be amended by negotiation.

Payment

4746 SI 2003/2682 regs 109, 115 The **due date** for tax under a PSA is 19 October (22 October if paying electronically) following the end of the tax year to which it relates. Interest may be charged on any amounts unpaid at that date.

Calculation

4747 SI 2003/2682 reg 108 As the settlement of an employee's liability is a benefit in itself, the tax due is calculated on a **grossed-up basis**. Therefore, although the PSA may reduce the employer's administrative burden, there is a real tax cost which the employer suffers.

The employer must estimate the amount of the benefit liable to tax, relate this to the employees who have enjoyed the benefit, and gross it up at each employee's marginal rate of tax.

EXAMPLE C Ltd provides business lunches to employees on an irregular basis. Over the course of the tax year, it spends £2,045, and 28 members of staff benefit. As it is impossible to identify the value of the benefit to each employee, C Ltd has entered into a PSA in this respect.

Of the employees involved, ten pay tax at the basic rate (20 %), with the remainder being liable to tax at 40%.

The tax payable under the PSA would be calculated as follows:

	£	£
Value of benefits provided to basic rate employees:		
10 × (2,045/28)	730.36	
Tax due thereon @ 20%	146.07	
Grossed-up tax (146.07 × 100/80)		182.59
Value of benefits provided to higher rate employees:		
18 × (2,045/28)	1,314.64	
Tax due thereon @ 40%	525.86	
Grossed-up tax (525.86 × 100/60)		876.43
Total tax payable by C Ltd in respect of PSA		1,059.02

b. Taxed award schemes

Entities with a UK presence who provide **non-cash incentives** to either their own or another entity's employees can apply to HMRC's Incentive Award Unit to set up a taxed award scheme. As most employers prefer to use a PSA instead, these schemes are usually only entered into by third parties. 4748 EIM 11235

Under such a scheme, the third party signs a contract which ensures that tax and NIC are paid on the grossed-up value (¶4747) of the benefits provided. The third party can choose to pay **tax** at the **basic rate** only, which means that any employees who pay a higher marginal rate of tax will receive a bill for the difference.

The **third party** is required to:
- make a return of the tax deducted on the grossed-up value of the awards; and
- issue a certificate to every employee liable to higher or additional rate tax. For basic rate schemes, employees can request a certificate.

The **employee** must enter the grossed-up value of the award and related tax on any tax return.

B. State imposed payments

Payroll systems are used to administer certain state benefits. In addition to statutory sick pay, and statutory parental payments, employers are also required to make deductions in respect of student loan repayments. HMRC provide all employers with guidance on the operation of each scheme and tables to calculate the payments. 4750

Detailed commentary can be found in the latest edition of *Employment Memo*.

1. Statutory sick pay

Employers **must pay** statutory sick pay (SSP), or at least the equivalent occupational sick pay, to employees who are incapacitated and cannot work. Payments are usually made after the 4th qualifying day of incapacity. 4752 Booklet E14

Payments of SSP are subject to PAYE and NIC deductions, and must be recorded on the deductions working sheet (P11) and on the annual returns (¶4706+).

Eligible employees

SSP is only **payable** to employees whose average weekly earnings (or the monthly equivalent) for the previous 8 weeks are at least equal to the Class 1 NIC lower earnings limit (£102 per week for 2011/12). There is no need for the claimant to be liable to pay Class 1 NIC, which enables employees aged under 16 or over 65 to qualify. The length of the employee's contract is also irrelevant. 4754

SSP is **not payable** to employees who:
- have already received 28 weeks SSP for the period of absence;
- have not yet worked for the employer;
- are entitled to receive employment and support allowance; or
- are disqualified during the later stages of pregnancy, when statutory maternity pay or maternity allowance may be paid instead.

If an **employee is not entitled**, the employer should complete form SSP1 and give it to the employee. The form sets out the facts of the case and enables the employee to claim other benefits.

MEMO POINTS 1. Since October 2008, **agency workers** have been entitled to SSP even where they are working under contracts of 3 months or less. SI 2008/2776

2. For a **prospective mother**, the disqualifying period **usually starts** with the date on which she becomes entitled to statutory maternity pay or maternity allowance. It will end 39 weeks later.
If she has **no such entitlement** but is:
a. receiving SSP, her disqualifying period will start at the earlier of:
– the day after the date of birth; or
– the first day she is sick with a pregnancy-related illness on or after the start of the fourth week before the baby is due; or
b. not receiving SSP, her disqualifying period will start at the beginning of the week in which:
– the birth occurred; or, if earlier
– she is first off sick with a pregnancy-related illness (if this is on or after the start of the fourth week before the baby is due).

Incapacity to work

4756 s 151 SSCBA 1992 To qualify for SSP, an employee must be off sick with a disease or disability that renders him incapable of **performing any work** which he can reasonably be expected to do under his contract. Therefore, if an employee is able to perform contractual work other than his usual duties, he will not qualify.

SI 1982/894 reg 2 The **exception** to the rule of incapacity is when an employee is deemed incapable of work for convalescent or precautionary reasons under medical advice, or when he may carry an infectious disease which may affect other members of staff.

The employee must be **incapable** for the whole of each of the working days he is absent. Therefore, if an employee has completed even a short period of work in a working day, it will not be treated as a day of incapacity for SSP purposes.

4757 Employees must **notify** the employer of their absence from work. Employers should set out what evidence they require, and when they require it. For example, for periods lasting 4 to 7 days, employers may request form SC2 for self-certification, or use their own form.

If the absence exceeds 7 consecutive days, the employer is entitled to insist on the evidence being from a doctor or other suitably qualified person (e.g. chiropractor).

The employer may **refuse to pay** SSP if he believes the employee's incapacity for work is not genuine, and HMRC can be required to adjudicate.

Period of incapacity

4759 The employee will only qualify if the days of incapacity create a period of incapacity to work (PIW), which requires the incapacity to last for a **minimum period** of 4 consecutive calendar days. This **includes days** when the employee would not actually have been at work, for example, weekends. So if the employee is sick on Monday, the employer will need to know whether he was also sick during the weekend. However, a PIW with a former employer is ignored.

The PIW ends when the incapacity ends.

Period of entitlement

4761 ss 151-153 SSCBA 1992 The entitlement starts from the 4th qualifying day of a PIW, and is payable on all qualifying days after that for up to a **maximum** of 28 weeks. The first 3 qualifying days are called waiting days.

The entitlement to SSP **ends** on the last qualifying day in the PIW, being the earliest of when the employee:
– recovers and is able to return to work;
– reaches the maximum entitlement;
– travels outside the EEA (unless he is a mariner, airman or an employee working on the continental shelf);
– has his contract terminated (unless it was terminated by the employer in avoidance of SSP); or
– is pregnant and has reached the disqualifying period (¶4754).

MEMO POINTS 1. **Qualifying days**, which are usually the days the employee is contracted to work, may be agreed between the employee and employer, so long as there is at least 1 qualifying day per week.
2. Periods of absence may be **linked with earlier periods** of absence ending in the previous 8 weeks, but both periods must be at least 4 days. HMRC provide a table to show whether periods can be linked, and these are then treated as a single period of absence. Booklet E14

SSP is only **payable** on qualifying days. The daily rate is the fixed weekly rate (£81.60 from 6 April 2011) divided by the number of qualifying days in the week. For example, if the qualifying days are Monday to Friday, the daily rate will be the weekly rate divided by 5. If there is only 1 qualifying day in the week, then the rate for that day would be the full weekly rate. **4762** s 157 SSCBA 1992

HMRC provide a table setting out the rate for all the available combinations of qualifying days. Booklet E14

EXAMPLE Mr A is an employee who usually works Tuesday to Friday (which are his qualifying days). He is ill on the following dates:
Friday 4 May – Tuesday 8 May; and
Tuesday 19 June – Friday 29 June.
The first period of absence exceeds 4 consecutive days, and includes 2 qualifying days (Friday and Tuesday). These are both waiting days, and no SSP is actually payable.
The second period of absence is not more than 8 weeks after the first, and the two periods are therefore linked. The second period of 11 days includes 8 qualifying days (Tuesday – Friday of both weeks). Tuesday 19 June is a waiting day (bringing the total for the linked periods to 3) and therefore SSP is payable for Wednesday 20th to Friday 22nd of the first week, and Tuesday 26th to Friday 29th of the second week.
As the employee has 4 qualifying days in a week, the daily rate for the first week is 1/4 of the weekly rate, and is payable for 3 days. The second week is a full week of absence and the employee is therefore entitled to the full weekly amount.

Funding

SSP is funded by the employer and, in many cases, the payments cannot be recovered from HMRC. However, if the **SSP paid** in any tax month **exceeds** 13% of the gross Class 1 primary and secondary NIC (¶4974) payable for that month, the excess may be recovered by reducing the amount of PAYE, NIC and student loan deductions payable to HMRC. **4764**

MEMO POINTS 1. The **gross Class 1 NIC** is calculated by totalling all Class 1 payable, and deducting any contracted out rebates (¶5035). State payments (i.e. SSP and parenting payments) are not deducted.
2. If the employer runs **more than one PAYE scheme**, the total SSP and NIC is calculated by amalgamating all of the schemes.

EXAMPLE B Ltd's Class 1 NIC liability is £814 for a particular month. The SSP paid during the month was £210.
13% of the NIC liability is £105.82. (814 @ 13%)
So £104.18 can be recovered from HMRC. (210 – 105.82)

Records

Employers are **required to maintain** full records of the employee's absence from work in order that entitlement to SSP may be checked by HMRC. To aid employers, HMRC have produced an optional sick pay record sheet. **4766**

Penalties

Employers who **fail to produce** any document or record required under the SSP scheme will face an initial penalty of £300, and further penalties of £60 per day for continuing failure. **4768**

Employers who fail to, or repeatedly refuse to, **make payments** of SSP will be liable to a penalty of up to £3,000. s 11 EA 2002

s 12 EA 2002 Further, employers who **fraudulently or negligently**:
– make any incorrect payments of SSP;
– produce any incorrect document or record, provide any incorrect information, or make any incorrect return; or
– receive incorrect payments in connection with the recovery of SSP,
will be liable to a fine of up to £3,000.

Penalties may also be charged in relation to **errors on returns and documents** (¶9784).

2. Parental payments

4770 Booklet E15 Where appropriate, the following statutory payments are available to parents (which can include same-sex couples):
– statutory maternity pay (SMP) for up to 39 weeks;
– statutory adoption pay (SAP) for up to 39 weeks;
– statutory paternity pay (SPP) for up to 2 weeks; and
– additional statutory paternity pay (ASPP) for the period that the mother/main adopter would have received SMP/SAP had they not returned to work.

Statutory parental payments are liable to PAYE and NIC deductions, and also qualify as earnings for pension contributions purposes. The payments must be recorded on the deductions working sheet (P11) and on the annual returns (¶4706+).

Appropriate records must be kept for 3 years after the tax year in which the statutory payments ceased.

MEMO POINTS 1. Where a couple are **jointly adopting**, they can choose who takes adoption leave and who takes paternity leave.
2. **SPP and ASPP** are available where an individual wishes to take leave to:
– care for a newborn or newly adopted child; or
– support the child's mother or adoptive parent.
ASPP applies to parents of babies due on or after 3 April 2011, and parents who receive notification on or after 3 April 2011 that they have been matched with a child for adoption.
3. If an **employee is not entitled to SMP, SAP, SPP or ASPP**, the employer should complete form SMP1, SAP1, SPP1 or ASPP1 (as applicable) and give it to the employee. The form sets out the facts of the case and enables the employee to claim social security benefits.

Entitlement

4772 ss 164, 171ZL SSCBA 1992 To **qualify** for statutory pay, the individual must:
a. be an employed earner with average earnings of at least the lower earnings limit for Class 1 NIC (£102 for 2011/12); and
b. have been continuously employed for 26 weeks up to and including the qualifying week.

Further, to be eligible for ASPP, the mother/main adoptive parent must have at least 2 weeks of her/his SMP/SAP or maternity allowance period unexpired.

MEMO POINTS 1. The **average weekly earnings** are determined by reference to the 8 weeks up to and including the qualifying week, known as the relevant period. Earnings are defined as for Class 1 NIC (¶4978), and any earnings paid in the period (such as bonuses and pay rises), even though earned outside the period, should be included. A salary sacrifice arrangement (¶3219) could mean that the average earnings are no longer sufficient to qualify for statutory pay.
2. The **qualifying week** is for:
– SMP: the 15th week before the expected week of confinement (i.e. the week beginning with midnight between Saturday and Sunday in which it is expected that childbirth will occur);
– SAP: the week in which a match of adoption is notified; and
– SPP/ASPP: the week under the SMP or SAP rules, depending on which is relevant.
Booklet E15 3. HMRC provide a set of tables to help employers **identify** the relevant **weeks**.
4. Where SMP is not payable due to **inadequate earnings**, the employee may be entitled to maternity allowance.

4773 The employee does not lose entitlement for any week in which he/she **works**, so long as he/she does not work for more than a total of 10 days (known as keeping in touch or KIT days) during the SMP, SAP or ASPP period. KIT days must be mutually agreed between the employee and employer, including the payment to be made, and neither party is obliged to make use of them.

An employee is still entitled to statutory pay, even if he/she decides **not to return to work** after leave has ended. An employer cannot therefore require repayment of any statutory amount. However, where the employer has his own pay scheme, the contract of employment may require the repayment of any amounts exceeding the statutory entitlement.

Employees must give **notice**, 28 days before they wish their SMP, SAP and SPP to start, and 8 weeks before they wish their ASPP to start. **4774**

The following **evidence** must be provided by the employee:

a. for SMP, medical evidence of the expected week of confinement and the week of actual birth where relevant, which is usually in the form of a maternity certificate (MAT B1);

b. for SAP, evidence of the adoption (such as a matching certificate) and a declaration that he/she has elected to receive SAP and not SPP;

c. for SPP, a declaration of his/her family commitment (form SC3 or SC4); or

d. for ASPP, a declaration of his/her family commitment and a declaration by the mother/main adoptive parent.

Amounts payable

The rate at which SMP is payable in the **first 6 weeks of maternity leave** is 90% of the employee's average weekly earnings. **4775**

The weekly rate which applies for **SAP, SPP, ASPP and SMP for the remaining period of maternity leave** is the lower of 90% of the employee's normal weekly earnings and £128.73 for 2011/12.

MEMO POINTS 1. **Average weekly earnings** are always rounded up to the nearest penny, and include any pay rises.

2. Statutory pay can **start to be paid** on any day of the week, and the **weekly amount** can be divided by 7 so that the payments can be aligned with the employer's usual payroll practice.

3. In relation to **SMP**, employers should include any **pay rises** that are **awarded from** the start of the relevant period (usually the 23rd week before the expected week of confinement) **to** the end of maternity leave. This rule was introduced as a result of case law, and has retrospective effect, so a recalculation of previously paid SMP may be required. HMRC have stated that employers should consider all recalculation claims within 6 years of when the SMP was paid. If the employee has by then left the employer, any claim must be made within 6 months of leaving. As employers are only required to keep records for 3 years, HMRC consider it reasonable for the employer to request the employee to provide sufficient evidence to substantiate her claim. Any such arrears properly and reasonably calculated are recoverable from HMRC.

4. As a mother/main adopter is entitled to a longer period of leave (up to 52 weeks) than the period during which maternity/adoption pay is due (up to 39 weeks), it is possible for her/him to be, in effect, on **unpaid leave during the later stages of the maternity/adoption period**. Likewise, there is no entitlement to additional statutory paternity pay for leave which coincides with the mother's/main adopter's period of unpaid leave.

The employee will be entitled to a **refund of tax** where he/she is on a cumulative tax code (¶4646). The employer must operate PAYE on the normal pay day as if a nil payment had been made, and this will generate a tax repayment.

Employers must continue to provide any **benefits in kind** throughout the maternity/adoption/paternity leave period. Whilst most benefits are liable to Class 1A NIC (which is a liability of the employer and only applies to employees earning more than £8,500 p.a.), very occasionally there is a **liability to Class 1 NIC** (¶4986) although only where the employee is in receipt of earnings in excess of £139 per week (for 2011/12). This presents a problem when the employee is not receiving any cash earnings because the employer has nothing from which to make the necessary deduction. In this case, the employer must incur the cost of the employee's Class 1 NIC and hopefully recover it from the employee later in the same tax year (subject to the limit that any NIC deduction from the employee can only be double that which would normally be due (see the example at ¶5020)). The employer must still record the benefits and NIC liability as usual on the year end PAYE forms.

Further information can be found at: www.hmrc.gov.uk/employers/sml-sal-benefits.pdf.

Funding

4776 SI 1994/1882 regs 5, 6

Employers are required to fund the payments, but may **recover** a set amount by reducing the actual PAYE, NIC and student loan deductions paid to HMRC. The recovery rate is set annually by HMRC.

In general, employers can recover 92% of the SMP, SAP, SPP and ASPP they pay to employees.

SI 2004/698

However, **small employers** are entitled to recover 100% of the SMP, SAP, SPP and ASPP, plus an additional amount to compensate for the secondary Class 1 NIC payable (3% from 6 April 2011). A small employer is one where the total Class 1 NIC liability (i.e. primary and secondary) for the previous tax year, in respect of all PAYE schemes run by that employer, does not exceed £45,000.

Penalties

4778

Employers who **fail to produce** any document or record required under any of the schemes will face an initial penalty of £300, and further penalties of £60 per day for continuing failure.

s 11 EA 2002

Employers who fail to, or repeatedly refuse to, **make payments** will be liable to a penalty of up to £3,000.

s 12 EA 2002

Further, employers who **fraudulently or negligently**:
– make any incorrect payments;
– produce any incorrect document or record, provide any incorrect information, or make any incorrect return; or
– receive incorrect payments in connection with recovery for funding,
will be liable to a fine of up to £3,000 with regard to SMP, SAP and ASPP, and £300 with regard to SPP.

Penalties may also be charged in relation to **errors on returns and documents** (¶9784).

3. Student loan deductions

4782 SI 2000/944 reg 35 Booklet E17

Employers are also responsible for **collecting** student loan payments from employees, which are not deductible for tax or NIC purposes. The loans are only repayable once the earnings from employment exceed a certain threshold (currently £15,000). HMRC publish a special table to show the amount of the deduction required.

Student loan deductions should be made where HMRC have sent a start notification, and should cease after a stop notification. The P11 should be annotated to indicate that deductions are being made.

MEMO POINTS 1. **Earnings** are measured in the same way as for Class 1 NIC purposes (¶4978).
2. If an **employee leaves** whilst student loan deductions are being made, the P45 should be annotated accordingly.
3. If a **new employee** either:
– provides a form P45 which indicates that student loan deductions are due; or
– ticks the relevant box on a form P46,
the new employer should make the deductions without notification from HMRC.

CHAPTER 2

Construction industry scheme

OUTLINE ¶¶

SECTION 1

Scope of the scheme

The primary aim of the construction industry scheme is to prevent the evasion of tax by contractors and subcontractors working in the construction industry. Where necessary, tax is deducted at source from payments to subcontractors, in a similar manner to the operation of PAYE. A number of schemes have been employed over the years, and the current system commenced operation on 6 April 2007. **4800** s 57 FA 2004

The **scheme covers** payments by contractors to subcontractors carrying out construction operations in the UK (Great Britain and Northern Ireland) and its territorial waters.

In July 2009, HMRC issued a consultation document aimed at tackling the perceived problem of "false self-employment" in the construction industry. In HMRC's view, this occurs when workers are treated as self-employed for tax and NIC purposes, when the way in which the work is carried out might be seen as demonstrating that there is an employment relationship. The feedback from the consultation process was mixed, and the "deeming test" set out in the consultation document was seen as needing further refinement and input from concerned parties. Moreover, the recent economic downturn has been seen to have a negative effect on the construction industry, and it is intended that any change which may be introduced will only occur after further consultation with interested parties, and when the industry is in a stronger position.

Exclusions

4802 s 60 FA 2004 The scheme does not apply to:
a. payments under a **contract of employment**. The onus is on the contractor firstly to establish whether there is a contract of employment in relation to a particular job (¶2986+). If there is, then PAYE will apply, and payments will not be within the construction industry scheme; or
b. private householders having work done on their own premises (e.g. construction, extension, repair or redecoration).

1. Contractors

4806 s 57 FA 2004 There are three types of contractor:
– mainstream contractors;
– deemed contractors; and
– any subcontractor who engages other subcontractors.

Mainstream contractors

4808 A mainstream contractor is any person carrying on a business which includes construction operations.
Such persons **include**:
– construction businesses, i.e. businesses that subcontract labour to perform construction operations for third parties;
– speculative builders or property developers (excluding property investment businesses which acquire and dispose of property for capital gain and/or rental income, unless the property portfolio of the business is extensive enough for it to fall into the deemed contractor category);
– gang leaders; and
– arm's length management organisations (ALMOs) i.e. companies set up by a local authority to manage or improve its housing stock.

MEMO POINTS 1. Where a contractor negotiates and pays a **gang leader** who is then responsible for sharing out the money amongst the gang, the gang leader is the contractor for the other gang members and the original contractor only deals with him as its sole subcontractor.
2. **Labour agencies** are generally not contractors under the construction industry scheme (although they can be subcontractors), as they are usually obliged to operate PAYE.

Construction operations

4810 s 74 FA 2004 The following table indicates the scope of construction operations.

Area of operations	Included	Excluded
Buildings and structures, whether permanent or not, including site facilities, hoardings and offshore installations	Construction, alteration, repair, extension, demolition, or dismantling	Temporary structures in place for a limited time e.g. exhibition stands, film and TV sets, marquees, portacabins etc Manufacture of building or engineering components or equipment, materials, plant or machinery, or delivery of any of these things to site Extraction (whether by underground or surface working) of minerals, tunnelling or boring, or construction of underground works for this purpose Drilling for, or extraction of, oil or natural gas

Area of operations	Included	Excluded
Land and infrastructure, including walls, road works, power lines, industrial plant, telecommunication apparatus, aircraft runways, docks and harbours, railways, inland waterways, pipelines, reservoirs, water mains, wells, sewers and installations for the purposes of land drainage, coast protection and drainage	Construction, alteration, repair, extension or demolition	Repair of internally located plant and machinery Installation of separate machine tools only superficially attached to the fabric of the building Installation of light duty or moveable conveyor systems Delivery of materials, transport of spoil from site and tree felling/surgery in the course of forestry or estate management
Preparatory and finishing operations, or operations which are integral to the project	Site clearance, evacuation, laying of foundations, scaffolding, landscaping, the provision of computer and telephone networks	Installation of computer and telephone networks which do not substantially affect the fabric of the building Routine landscaping not undertaken as part of a wider project Landscaping open cast mine areas Construction of golf courses (if not associated with the construction of club houses)
Professionals	Architect acting as a developer Work involves project management or supervision other than architects and surveyors Site foremen	Work of architects, surveyors or consultants in building, engineering, interior or exterior design Planning, inspecting or testing
Painting or decorating	Internal or external surfaces of any building or structure	The making, installation and repair of artistic works (sculptures, murals and other works being wholly artistic in nature) Pesticide spraying/treatment Off-site french polishing
Fixtures and fittings	Installation of fixed furniture and fixed floor coverings included in the specifications of a building undergoing construction, alteration, extension or repair Installation of fly screens and rolling grilles	Fitting of carpet or carpet tiles Fitting of vinyl, lino, thermal insulation or soundproofing where not carried out as part of a wider construction project The installation of fixed seating, blinds, shutters and solar panels
Electrical systems	Installation of systems of heating, lighting, air conditioning, ventilation, power supply, drainage, sanitation, water supply or fire protection	Repair or maintenance of such systems Manufacture of components for such systems or delivery of any of these things to site
Security	Installation of locks on buildings where construction operations have been carried out Installation of closed circuit television for traffic management, door access systems and other security systems involving installation of special doors, gates, barriers or other structural features Installation of safes integrated into the building structure	Installation of security systems, including burglar alarms, closed circuit television, computerised locking systems, entryphone systems and public address systems

Area of operations	Included	Excluded
Cleaning	Internal cleaning of buildings and structures, so far as carried out in the course of their construction, alteration, repair, extension or restoration	External cleaning of buildings and structures/cleaning prior to sale by developer
Signs and street furniture	Installation of electrical (including neon) signs Construction of bus shelters and other similar items carrying adverts Traffic lights and road signs/markings	Sign writing and erecting, installing or repairing signboards and advertisements
Fencing	Either erected as part of a wider construction project or as part of a heavy duty structure (i.e. main supporting posts installed in concrete)	Erected as a one-off exercise that is of a light duty structure (i.e. main supporting posts simply driven into the ground)

Deemed contractors

4812 s 59 FA 2004 SI 2005/2045 regs 21 – 24

Any person or public body whose business does not include construction operations may become a deemed contractor if **average annual expenditure on construction operations exceeds** £1 million.

Some **exceptions** apply, as shown in the table below.

Deemed contractors	Exceptions
Businesses and private organisations whose average annual expenditure on construction operations in the 3 years ending with the last accounting date exceeds £1 million [1]	Expenditure on construction work on: – own premises; or – premises used for the business purposes of a company in the same group [2], unless the property is for sale, to let, or held as an investment [3]
	Expenditure by a charity [4]
The following local authorities and public bodies, where average annual expenditure on construction operations in the 3 year period to 31 March immediately preceding is in excess of £1 million: – a public office or department of the Crown; – a local authority; – a development corporation; – the Homes and Communities Agency; – the Regulator of Social Housing, housing for Wales, a housing trust/society; – Scottish Homes or the Northern Ireland Housing Executive; – any NHS trust; – Health and Social Services trusts; – the corporate officers of the House of Commons and House of Lords; and – the Scottish parliamentary corporate body	Payments which are made: – under a private finance transaction; or – by the governing body or head teacher of a school maintained by a local education authority

Note:
1. If the business has been in existence for **less than 3 years** it will be a deemed contractor if total expenditure on construction operations up to the end of the last accounting period exceeds £3 million.
2. For these purposes, two companies are in a **group** if one is at least a 75% subsidiary of the other, or if both are at least 75% subsidiaries of another company.
3. **Incidental use** of a property by another company in the same group is disregarded.
4. A **trading subsidiary of a charity** with average annual expenditure of over £1 million on construction operations would still need to apply the scheme to those payments.

A business will **continue** to be a deemed contractor **until** HMRC are satisfied that the average annual expenditure on construction operations in each of the 3 successive years beginning in or after the period of account has been less than £1 million. 4813

2. Subcontractors

A subcontractor is **defined** as any business that has agreed to carry out construction operations for a contractor or deemed contractor (whether by doing the operations itself or bringing in its own subcontractors or employees). 4815 s 58 FA 2004

Types of subcontractor **include**:
– a sole trader, partnership or company;
– a labour agency where the worker carries out construction operations under the terms of the contract he has with the agency. (However, if the worker is merely introduced to the contractor through the agency and carries out construction operations under the terms of the contract he has with the contractor, the agency will not be a subcontractor);
– a foreign business if the construction operations take place in the UK;
– a gang leader (¶4808); and
– any specified local authority or public body engaged on construction operations for someone else. Tax is not deducted from payments to these bodies, and contractors do not need to verify their status nor include details of payments in monthly returns.

MEMO POINTS The **specified local authorities or public bodies** referred to above are:
– The Post Office;
– Port of London Authority;
– Homes and Communities Agency;
– UK Atomic Energy Authority;
– Welsh Development Agency;
– Scottish Enterprise;
– Registered Housing Associations and Societies;
– British Broadcasting Corporation;
– Government Departments and Executive Agencies;
– Environment Agency;
– British Waterways Board;
– London Regional Transport; and
– Health Service bodies and NHS Trusts.

3. Payments

Broadly, all payments made by a contractor to a subcontractor will fall within the scheme (including any cash or cheque advances, travel, subsistence and accommodation payments, stage payments, retention payments etc). 4817

However the following are **excluded**:
– cost of materials (including the cost of manufacture, prefabrication and reimbursement of land costs when purchased on behalf of the contractor);
– consumable stores;
– plant hire;
– fuel (except fuel for travelling);
– Construction Industry Training Board Levy;
– VAT; and
– a payment which is a reverse premium.

Single contracts

Where a single contract relates both to **construction and non-construction** operations, all payments due under the contract are within the scheme. 4818 Booklet CIS 340 para 2.45

Small payments exemption

4820 SI 2005/2045 regs 18, 19 The scheme does not apply to contracts with a **value up to £1,000** (excluding the cost of materials) where **payments are made by** either:

a. deemed contractors with a decentralised operational function, and where local managers have the authority to commission small contracts directly; or

b. mainstream contractors, and where the work is carried out on property which the subcontractor owns, or agricultural property of which he is a tenant.

Contractors must apply to HMRC for approval to utilise the exemption.

MEMO POINTS **Agricultural property** means:
- agricultural land or pasture;
- woodland or buildings used for intensive rearing of livestock or fish, if occupied with agricultural land or pasture;
- cottages, farm buildings and farm houses of an appropriate character, and the land occupied with them; or
- land and buildings used for breeding, rearing and grazing of horses on a stud farm.

EXAMPLE A utility company lays a pipeline across some land and pays the owner of the land £750 to replace the earth afterwards.
The small payments exemption will apply.

SECTION 2

Operation of the scheme

4825 The operation of the scheme can be summarised as follows:

Aspect of scheme	Details
Registration of subcontractors	There are no registration cards or certificates, and contractors must verify the subcontractor's registration status with HMRC before making payment. Unregistered subcontractors can be paid.
Payment of subcontractors	Payment is made: – gross to subcontractors registered for gross payment; – net of a 20% tax deduction to subcontractors registered for net payment; or – net of a 30% tax deduction to unregistered subcontractors.
Administration	Contractors must submit monthly returns to HMRC and give a monthly statement to subcontractors. Payment of any tax withheld must also be made on a monthly basis.

A. Registration of contractors

4828 Booklet CIS 340 para 1.16 Contractors must register with HMRC before they engage their first subcontractor. HMRC will set up a contractor's scheme and send the contractor all necessary information.

B. Registration of subcontractors

4832 ss 63, 77 FA 2004 SI 2005/2045 reg 25 New subcontractors must register with HMRC, who will then advise contractors whether tax should be deducted from payments, and at what rate. Unregistered subcontractors may be paid, but at a higher rate of tax deduction.

MEMO POINTS Subcontractors who held a permanent registration card or certificate on 5 April 2007 are treated as registered under the new scheme. The details are as follows:

Type of card or certificate held on 5 April 2007	Status of subcontractor from 6 April 2007
CIS4(Permanent) card	Treated as registered for net payment
CIS5, CIS5(Permanent) or CIS6 certificate	Treated as registered for gross payment
CIS4(Temporary) card	No longer valid – subcontractor must register

1. Registration for net payment

Registration for net payment only enables a subcontractor to be paid net of a 20% tax deduction. No qualifying conditions need to be met, and the only requirement is proof of identity. 4834

Applying for registration

Applicants must provide such documents, records and information as HMRC may require in order to establish **proof of identity**. These may include the items set out in the following table: 4838 SI 2005/2045 reg 25

Individual applications	Company applications
Name and address National Insurance number and tax reference Birth certificate, passport and driving licence Council tax bills and utility bills	Company registration number Memorandum and Articles of Association For each director, the items required for individual applicants Where the company is a close company (¶2100), each beneficial owner of the shares must provide the same details as a director

Refusal of registration application

HMRC may refuse a subcontractor's application to register for net payment if they are not satisfied with the documents, records or information provided. 4840 s 68 FA 2004 SI 2005/2045 reg 25

A subcontractor can **appeal** against such a decision within 30 days, stating why he believes that the application should not have been refused.

Cancellation of registration

A subcontractor's registration for net payment is indefinite, but it is kept under continuous review. HMRC may cancel the registration at any time, without notice, if they have **reasonable grounds to suspect that** the subcontractor has: 4842 s 68 FA 2004 SI 2005/2045 regs 6, 26

- provided false or incorrect information;
- fraudulently made an incorrect return; or
- knowingly failed to comply with scheme rules, either as a contractor or subcontractor.

A subcontractor can **appeal** against such a decision within 30 days, stating why he believes that his registration should not have been cancelled.

If registration is cancelled, **HMRC must notify** the change of status to all contractors who have used or verified the subcontractor in the current or 2 previous tax years.

2. Registration for gross payment

Registration for gross payment enables a subcontractor to be paid without deduction of tax. 4844 ss 64, 72 FA 2004
When applying, subcontractors must provide proof of identity as in ¶4838, and qualifying

conditions must be satisfied. At least 1 month should be allowed for an application to be approved.

A **penalty** of up to £3,000 can be charged if a person knowingly or recklessly makes a false statement or submits a false document when applying for registration for gross payment.

Qualifying conditions

4848 Applicants must satisfy **three tests**, which are a business test, a turnover test and a compliance test.

4850 Sch 11 paras 2, 6, 10 FA 2004 SI 2005/2045 reg 27

Business test A business must be:
- carrying out construction work in the UK or providing labour for such work; and
- using a business bank account, with proper records, stock, equipment and other facilities appropriate for running the business in question.

4852 SI 2005/2045 regs 28 – 31 Sch 11 paras 3, 7, 11 FA 2004

Turnover test Applicants must meet the turnover test as summarised below:

Type of applicant	1 year test: minimum turnover[1] for the 12 months ending on the date of application
Individuals	£30,000
Partnerships	£30,000 multiplied by the number of individual and corporate partners[2] OR £200,000[3]
Companies	£30,000 multiplied by the number of relevant persons[4] OR £200,000[3]

Note:
1. **Turnover** means income from construction contracts excluding the direct cost of materials.
2. The **number of partners** to be included is the maximum number of partners at any one time during the 12 months ending on the application date.
3. The **fixed alternative threshold** of £200,000 applies irrespective of the number of partners or relevant persons.
4. A **relevant person** is a director of a company (or, in the case of a close company (¶2100), a beneficial owner of the shares in the company).

4854 SI 2005/2045 reg 31

If a business which **does not consist mainly of construction operations** does not meet the turnover tests, it may still qualify if HMRC are satisfied that:
- its total turnover in the 12 months ending on the date of application exceeded the relevant turnover level; and
- in the 12 months following the date of application it will receive payments for construction operations which are incidental to its main business.

4856 Sch 11 paras 4, 8, 12, 14 FA 2004

Compliance test During the **qualifying period** (the 12 months prior to the date of application), the business must have:
- completed and returned all tax returns;
- supplied any information to do with tax which has been requested;
- paid all tax/NIC due as an individual, business and employer, both in the UK and overseas; and
- paid any deductions due as a contractor under the construction industry scheme.

4858 SI 2005/2045 regs 32 – 37

It is **not sufficient** that a business brings its tax affairs up to date prior to making an application, as the following two requirements must also be satisfied:

a. it is expected that the tax affairs of the business will remain up to date **in the future**; and

b. throughout the qualifying period the business must have run its tax affairs on a timely basis. There must have been:
- no failings other than the exceptions listed in the table below, or:
- a reasonable excuse for any failure, and the failure must have been rectified without unreasonable delay after the excuse ceased.

Obligation		Permitted failings
Submission of returns	Monthly contractor returns	Submission of a return not later than 28 days after the due date, provided there have been no more than two such failures in the previous 12 months
	Annual PAYE return	Submission of a return after the due date
	Self-assessment return	
Payment of tax[1]	PAYE or tax deducted from subcontractors	Payments made not later than 14 days after the due date, provided there have been no more than two such failures in the previous 12 months
	Income tax	Payments made not later than 28 days after the due date, provided there have been no such failures in the previous 12 months
	Corporation tax	Payments made not later than 28 days after the due date, without incurring a penalty

Note:
1. The late payment of (or complete failure to pay) taxes under £100 is not a reason to refuse gross payment status.

MEMO POINTS 1. HMRC give the following examples which fall within the scope of a **reasonable excuse**: 4860 CISR 81020
– the customer is a sole trader, or director of a one man company, and has suffered a sudden and serious illness throughout the period covering the payment and filing dates;
– unavoidable and unexpected absence close to the payment and filing dates because of business commitments or domestic emergencies;
– accidental destruction of the records through fire or flood;
– exceptional postal delays because of a strike by postal workers or other civil disturbance;
– sudden disruption to a business or its records by a break in; or
– installation of a new computer system or program for the payroll or accounting which has hit unexpected teething problems.
2. Where a **sole trader** claims that for all or part of the qualifying period he was not subject to these requirements because he was **abroad, unemployed or a student**, he must provide evidence to that effect.
3. Where a **sole trader** also **has control of a company**, the company must have complied with its obligations for the accounting periods ending in the qualifying period.
Control, for these purposes, means possession of, or entitlement to acquire, over 50% of:
– share capital or issued share capital;
– voting rights;
– distributable income; or
– net assets on a winding up.

Companies must also satisfy certain Companies Act obligations such as submission of the annual return and accounts. 4862
In certain cases, HMRC may direct that **specified directors** (and, if the company is close (¶2100), beneficial shareholders) must meet the compliance test.

MEMO POINTS **Specified directors or beneficial shareholders** must meet the compliance test if the company:
– does not hold a current valid certificate or is not registered for gross payment;
– has not traded continuously in the qualifying period;
– has traded continuously in the qualifying period, but the business of the company was not at all times that of construction operations;
– was incorporated after the start of the qualifying period; or
– has been subject to a change of control.

Refusal of registration application

HMRC may refuse a subcontractor's application to register for gross payment if they are not satisfied with the documents, records or information provided. 4864 s 67 FA 2004 SI 2005/2045 reg 25(5)
A subcontractor can **appeal** against such a decision within 30 days, stating why he believes that the application should not have been refused.

Cancellation of registration

4866 ss 66, 67 FA 2004 SI 2005/2045 regs 6, 25, 26

A subcontractor's registration for gross payment is indefinite, but it is kept under continuous review, and HMRC may cancel it at any time (by giving 90 days' notice) if they have **reasonable grounds to suspect that** the subcontractor has:
- provided false or incorrect information;
- fraudulently made an incorrect return; or
- knowingly failed to comply with scheme rules, either as a contractor or subcontractor.

An **annual check** is undertaken to ensure the business has not exceeded the maximum number of compliance failures in the period (¶4858). Only those failing the check will be notified that the check has taken place, and will be advised that their gross payment status is to be withdrawn in 90 days.

A subcontractor can **appeal** against the cancellation within 30 days of the notification.

MEMO POINTS 1. If registration for gross payment is cancelled, the subcontractor must register for payment net of tax, and cannot apply to be **re-registered** for gross payment until 12 months after the date of cancellation.
2. HMRC must notify the change of status to all **contractors** who have used or verified the subcontractor in the current or 2 previous tax years.

C. Payments to subcontractors

4868 The method of payment depends on whether the subcontractor is registered for gross or net payment. The possible payment methods are summarised as follows:

Method of payment	Applies to
Gross	Subcontractors registered for gross payment
Tax deducted at 20%	Subcontractors registered for net payment
Tax deducted at 30%	Unregistered subcontractors

Before making a payment

4872 Contractors must check the subcontractor's registration status.

No action will be necessary where:
a. a contractor has already verified the subcontractor's registration status with HMRC and shown the details in a return during the current or 2 previous tax years, and HMRC have not notified him of any change; or
b. the proposed payment is under a contract acquired as part of a transfer of a business as a going concern, and:
- the previous contractor qualified under **a.** above; and
- the contractor has notified HMRC of the transfer.

4874 **If any of these circumstances apply**, the contractor can assume that there has been no change in the subcontractor's status, and can make the payment in the same way as on the previous occasion.

In all other cases the contractor must contact HMRC to verify the subcontractor's registration status.

4876 s 69 FA 2004 SI 2005/2045 reg 6

Verifying status of subcontractors A contractor who has entered into a contract, or accepted a tender for work under a contract, can contact HMRC to verify the subcontractor's registration status. For speed and convenience, verification will normally be **carried out** by telephone or online, but it can also be done by post.

The contractor should provide the following details:
– his own name, tax reference, accounts office reference and employer's reference; and
– the subcontractor's name, tax reference, National Insurance number or company registration number and, if the subcontractor is a partner, the name and tax reference of the firm.

HMRC will then check whether the subcontractor is registered for gross or net payment, inform the contractor of the rate at which any tax should be deducted, and provide a verification reference number. If more than one subcontractor is verified at the same time, they will be given the same reference number. However, where there are any unregistered subcontractors, the reference will then be followed by an identifying letter to ensure the reference is unique to that subcontractor.

MEMO POINTS **Online** verification will allow up to 100 subcontractors to be verified on each occasion.

Calculating the tax deduction

Only the subcontractor's services are liable to tax, so materials and VAT are excluded. 4878 s 61 FA 2004

EXAMPLE A Ltd incurs the following costs on work carried out by subcontractors C, D, and E:

Subcontractor	Labour	Materials	VAT		Total
			Labour	Materials	
	£	£	£	£	£
C (Registered for net payment, not VAT registered)	200				200
D (Registered for net payment, not VAT registered)	300	200		40	540
E (Registered for net payment, and VAT registered)	400	200	80	40	720

Tax is deducted as follows:

Subcontractor	Payment to subcontractor					Tax
	Labour	Materials	VAT		Total	
			Labour	Materials		
	£	£	£	£	£	£
C	160				160	40 (200 × 20%)
D	240	200		40	480	60 (300 × 20%)
E	320	200	80	40	640	80 (400 × 20%)

D. Payment to HMRC

Contractors must pay over to the Accounts Office all amounts they were liable to deduct. Payment must normally be made **monthly**, by the 19th of each month, or by the 22nd of each month if payments must be made electronically, as a large employer (¶4688). 4884 SI 2005/2045 regs 7, 8

Payments may be made **quarterly**, if the contractor has reasonable grounds for believing that over the course of a tax year his average monthly payment of PAYE, National Insurance contributions, construction industry and student loan payments will amount to less than £1,500, excluding any payments of:
– statutory maternity, paternity, sick or adoption pay; and
– (for companies only) amounts suffered by deduction under the construction industry scheme.

Failure to pay

4886 SI 2005/2045 regs 10 – 11 If a **contractor** fails to make the appropriate payments by the required date, or if HMRC are not satisfied that the full amount has been paid for the month, the contractor may be required to complete a return showing the amount that should have been paid.

Alternatively, an assessment may be raised estimating the amount of tax payable based on the contractor's past payments. If the contractor does not agree with the estimate, he may require an audit to establish the correct amount of tax due for payment.

In either case, a certificate will be issued indicating the amount of tax due, and the amount specified will be recoverable as if it were income tax charged in an assessment.

If the amount of **tax is overestimated**, the overpayment can be set against a construction industry scheme liability for a subsequent period.

Since 6 April 2010, **penalties** may also be charged in relation to late payments of tax (¶9857).

Interest

4888 SI 2005/2045 reg 14 Since April 2010, interest on **overdue tax** has accrued on each monthly or quarterly amount which is paid late. Prior to April 2010, such interest ran from the 19th April following the tax year of underpayment (or 22th April if payment was made electronically) until the date of payment.

SI 2005/2045 reg 15 Interest on **overpaid tax** is paid from the later of the end of the tax year:
- following the year to which the overpayment relates; or,
- in which the overpayment was made to HMRC.

Failure to deduct tax

4890 SI 2005/2045 reg 9 A **contractor** who fails to deduct tax can be **excused** from paying over the tax if he can show that:

a. the error was made in good faith and reasonable care was taken to comply with the regulations; or

b. the subcontractor:
- is not liable to tax on the payments; or
- has included the payments in his tax return and has paid the required tax (including any related NIC).

4892 SI 2005/2045 reg 9(10) For the purposes of determining the liability of the **subcontractor**, if a contractor correctly deducts tax under the scheme but fails to pay it over to HMRC, the amount deducted will still be treated as being paid on time.

E. Administration

1. Returns

Monthly

4898 s 70 FA 2004 SI 2005/2045 reg 4 By the 19th of each month, contractors must:
- **make** a return to HMRC, which can be sent by post or electronically; and
- **provide subcontractors with** a copy of the information relating to them which is contained in the return. This can be sent electronically, provided that the subcontractor agrees and a paper copy of the information can be produced.

Returns **must contain** the following details:

Section of return		Information
General		A declaration that: – the status of the subcontractors listed has been considered and none should be recategorised as employees[1]; – the registration status of each subcontractor was verified; and – the return contains all required information, and is complete and accurate to the best of the contractor's knowledge and belief
Contractor		Name, tax reference and Accounts Office reference
Subcontractors	All	Name, tax reference, and National Insurance/company registration number[2]
		Total payments in the month
	Registered for net payment	Total amount paid for materials in the month
		Total amount of tax deducted in the month
	Unregistered	Total amount paid for materials in the month
		Total amount of tax deducted in the month
		Verification reference for higher rate tax deducted in the month

Note:
1. See ¶2986+ for details.
2. To assist contractors, the paper returns issued by HMRC will contain these details for all subcontractors used by the contractor in the previous 3 months.

A **nil return** must be made if there were no payments in the month, unless the contractor has notified HMRC that no payments are to be made in the next 6 months. Nil returns can be made by telephone. 4900

If a contractor **fails to submit** a monthly return (including a nil return) by the due date, HMRC can: 4902 SI 2005/2045 regs 10, 11
- require the return to be made; or
- make a tax assessment.

Penalties can be charged when a failure occurs or continues. For periods after October 2011 the penalties are as set out in ¶9855. For periods before this date the charge was set at £100 for a return containing up to 50 subcontractors, plus £100 for each additional 50 (or part thereof).

An **incorrect return** attracts penalties as detailed at ¶9784. 4904

Annual

No annual scheme returns are required. **Tax deductions** under the scheme should be shown on the annual PAYE P35 form (¶4706), to enable total payments to HMRC to be reconciled. 4906 Booklet CIS 340 para 4.37

2. Record keeping

Contractors

A contractor must keep records showing payments and deductions made to subcontractors. 4908 SI 2005/2045 reg 51
HMRC have power to inspect these records in the course of an investigation or inspection, and can charge a **penalty** of up to £3,000 for failure to produce records.

Subcontractors

4910 SI 2005/2045 regs 51 – 52 A subcontractor must keep records relating to the calculation of payments and deductions made to him for contracts under which he was a subcontractor.

Companies which offset construction industry scheme deductions against other liabilities must keep records relating to the calculation of:
– the amounts that would have been payable to HMRC in the preceding 3 years for the liabilities detailed in ¶4916 (had the contractor not withheld amounts under the construction industry scheme); and
– the amounts deducted by the contractor before making payments to the subcontractor.

F. Subcontractors' use of tax deductions

4912 The treatment of tax deducted by a contractor under the construction industry scheme depends on whether the subcontractor is an individual, partnership or company.

Individuals and partnerships

4914 s 62(2) FA 2004 The tax deducted is treated as a payment in respect of the liability to income tax and Class 4 NIC on the subcontractor's profits for the year, and may therefore reduce payments on account (¶4506).

SI 2005/2045 reg 17 **During the tax year**, a **repayment** of tax may be claimed if the accounting year ends earlier than 5 April and all of the following apply:
a. vouchers for the tax deducted in the current year have been submitted to HMRC; and
b. the subcontractor's income tax and Class 4 NIC:
– for earlier years have been paid; and
– for the current year are less than the tax deductions shown on the vouchers (when including any other sums due to HMRC either as a subcontractor or as a contractor).

After the end of the tax year, a **repayment** can be claimed by submitting a self-assessment return.

Companies

4916 s 62(3) FA 2004 **During the tax year**, companies can **offset** tax deducted on payments made to them as subcontractors against their liabilities arising as employer or contractor. Any such deductions suffered will reduce the monthly PAYE, NIC and CIS payment due.

After the end of the tax year, any **excess deductions** will be repaid to the company, following the submission of the year end PAYE documentation (¶4702), provided there is no outstanding corporation tax liability. If there is an outstanding corporation tax liability, the amount required to settle this will be retained by HMRC, with the balance (if any) being repaid.

MEMO POINTS **Personal service companies** in the construction industry which are liable to PAYE on deemed payments under IR35 (¶3010), and which have also suffered a deduction of tax under CIS, can claim for the latter to be set against the PAYE due under IR35.

G. Special situations

Contractors

4918 SI 2005/2045 reg 3 **Multiple schemes** Contractors who have operations in **several locations** may find it difficult to administer one single scheme from one central location. A contractor may therefore elect to operate separate schemes for distinct divisions or parts of the business. This election must be made in writing, identify the grouping(s) concerned, and certify that payments within the construction industry scheme are only made to the subcontractor groupings which are within the election. (This is to ensure no subcontractors are left out of account).

This type of election **generally** has effect for the tax year following that in which it was made. 4920

However, where a contractor **acquires all or part of another construction business** for which such a scheme already exists, he may elect to operate the scheme on a stand-alone basis for the tax year in which the acquisition takes place.

Groups Group companies which are contractors can appoint one company as their construction industry scheme **representative**. The appointing company must notify HMRC. The representative company will operate the scheme on behalf of the appointing companies, but: 4922 SI 2005/2045 reg 5

- returns and payments must still be made in the name of each appointing company; and
- each company remains liable in relation to all of its scheme obligations.

MEMO POINTS For these purposes, **two companies are in a group** if one is at least a 75% subsidiary of the other, or if both are at least 75% subsidiaries of another company.

Transfer of a trade Where all or part of a company's trade is transferred to another company, **construction expenditure incurred by the transferring company** up to the date of transfer is apportioned to determine whether the company is a deemed contractor (¶4812) for the period prior to the transfer. 4924 s 59(4) FA 2004

Death If a contractor dies, the **responsibility for running the scheme** falls upon his personal representatives. 4926 SI 2005/2045 reg 54

Subcontractors

Reorganisations When there is a **change in the type of concern** (for example a sole trader incorporates or becomes a partnership), any existing registration status is no longer valid, and the subcontractor will need to submit a fresh application. 4928

Change in control of a subcontractor company Following a change in control of a close company (i.e. the acquisition of a majority shareholding), the **company has an obligation**, within 30 days of the change, **to notify HMRC**, who will then review the compliance history of the new shareholders to establish whether the existing registration status will still be valid. 4930 SI 2005/2045 reg 53

CHAPTER 3

National Insurance contributions

OUTLINE ¶¶

SECTION 1

General concepts

4950 The UK maintains a National Insurance fund which aims to provide subsistence level benefits to those in need. All individuals covered by the scheme are given a National Insurance number. The collection of National Insurance is administered by the National Insurance Contributions Office (NICO), which is part of HMRC.

Liability for contributions

4952 The fund is maintained, in part, by National Insurance contributions (NIC) which are payable by employees, employers, and by the self-employed. Individuals may also make voluntary contributions in certain circumstances. The types of contributions payable are set out below:

Status	Contribution	¶¶
Employee	Class 1 primary	¶4974
Employer	Class 1 secondary	¶4974
	Class 1A	¶5048
	Class 1B	¶5064
Self-employed	Class 2	¶5072
	Class 4	¶5084
Voluntary	Class 3	¶5120

4953 NIC **must be paid by** any worker who is resident or present in the UK. In addition, those who are ordinarily resident are usually required to pay NIC whilst absent from the UK. Individuals working in the UK on a short term basis, and those leaving the UK who wish to maintain their entitlement to benefits, may be able to take advantage of special rules.

New businesses in certain areas of the UK may qualify for a scheme which will reduce the amount of employer's NIC which is payable.

Voluntary contributions may be paid by anyone who is UK resident.

Condition	Basic meaning	¶¶
Present	Question of fact where individual is present	¶5162
Resident	Greater permanence, generally present in the UK for at least 183 days in a tax year An individual may be resident whilst temporarily absent from the UK	¶5165
Habitual residence	Place where individual normally lives	¶5166

Age constraints

4955 Liability for contributions **starts** once an individual reaches the age of 16.

Liability for most contributions **ceases** when an individual reaches pensionable age, except for contributions payable by the employer in respect of employees (Class 1 secondary, Class 1A and Class 1B) which remain payable even after pensionable age is reached.

4956 **Pensionable age** For **men**, pensionable age is currently 65, although it has been proposed that this will be increased to 66 for **both sexes** between 2018 and 2020.

4957 For **women**, the pensionable age is currently increasing from 60 to 65, and this affects women who were born on or after 6 April 1950.

For more details of the proposals, and for a **state pension age calculator**, see www.direct.gov.uk/en/Pensionsandretirementplanning/StatePension/DG_4017919.

Distinction between employed and self-employed workers

For National Insurance purposes, an individual is an **employed earner** if he is gainfully employed in the UK and receiving employment income. The same rules apply to decide whether an individual is an employee for NIC purposes as for income tax (¶2986), including the provisions relating to personal and managed service companies (¶3010). However, certain jobs are specifically categorised as being subject to the rules for employed earners (¶5152). **4958** s 2 SSCBA 1992

An individual is treated as **self-employed** if he is gainfully employed in the UK other than as an employed earner. This means that profitability of the self-employed activity is irrelevant, as are periods of inactivity.

Where an individual is **not sure** about his status, he should contact NICO, who will begin an enquiry to consider his circumstances. It is possible for an individual to be both employed and self-employed, and there are special rules to ensure that contributions are not overpaid in such a case (¶5110).

MEMO POINTS It is possible for the following occupations to be deemed to be an employment for NIC purposes, but not income tax purposes, therefore creating a **secondary Class 1 NIC liability** for the deemed employer: Tax Bulletin 74
- non-executive directors without a service contract;
- cleaners;
- lecturers, teachers and instructors; and
- entertainers.

Where an individual is **recategorised** (usually from self-employed to an employee), there are provisions to ensure that all NIC paid is taken into account. **4960**

On recategorisation **to an employee**, the Class 2 NIC already paid is reallocated as primary Class 1 NIC, with any excess being refunded. Any remaining amount of primary Class 1 NIC and secondary NIC are then payable by the employer. Class 4 NIC is refunded.

Where an individual is recategorised **as self-employed**, there is unlikely to be a retrospective application, so there will be no refund of Class 1 NIC already paid.

Whilst there is no time limit which applies to retrospective recategorisation, in practice any debt owed to HMRC which is more than 6 years old cannot be enforced. Limitation Act 1980

Link between contributions and benefits

The entitlement to certain benefits is linked to an individual's contributions to the fund. In addition, some benefits, known as **contributory benefits**, are paid at a higher level based on contributions. **4962** s 21 SSCBA 1992

Non-contributory benefits are generally paid from the general taxation revenues rather than from the National Insurance fund, and may be means tested.

Each class of contribution carries a different level of **entitlement to benefits**: **4963**

Class	Long term benefits	Short term benefits
1 (primary)	Earnings-related state pension [1] (¶3654) Bereavement allowance Widowed parent's allowance Bereavement payment	Incapacity benefit (replaced by employment and support allowance for new claimants from 27 October 2008) Jobseeker's allowance (contribution based) Maternity allowance
1 (secondary)	None	None
1A	None	None
1B	None	None

Class	Long term benefits	Short term benefits
2	As for Class 1 (primary)	Incapacity benefit (or employment and support allowance) Maternity allowance[2]
3	As for Class 1 (primary)	None
4	None	None

Note:
1. Employees may decide to **opt out** of the earnings-related element of the state pension scheme, and make independent arrangements. A reduced level of Class 1 primary contribution may apply (¶5035).
2. **Higher rate** Class 2 NIC is payable in the cases of share fishermen and volunteer development workers (¶5152), and this additionally gives entitlement to jobseeker's allowance (contribution based).

4965 To be entitled to the maximum rate of **long term benefits** an individual has historically been required to have a full contributions record for approximately 90% of his or her working life.

However, for individuals **reaching state pension age on or after 6 April 2010**, 30 years of contributions will be sufficient to obtain a full basic state pension. This may affect the need for, and level of, voluntary contributions (¶5120).

Entitlement to **short term benefits** is based on contributions over a short period, and each benefit has specific rules.

National Insurance number

4966 All individuals within the National Insurance scheme are given an identifying number. The National Insurance (NI) number comprises a prefix of two letters, followed by six digits and a single letter suffix, for example AB123456C.

As a rule, an individual is **issued** with an NI number shortly before the school leaving date. If an individual has not been issued with a number, he should apply for a number at the Jobcentre Plus office.

When an individual starts work for an employer, he will be asked for his NI number. If the number is not available, the employer may use a **temporary number**, which is comprised of the prefix TN followed by the employee's date of birth in 6 digit format and then a suffix of either M if male or F if female (for example TN010792M). If the employee does not provide his correct NI number within 8 weeks, the employer should apply to HMRC, either to find an existing number, or to issue a new number as appropriate.

MEMO POINTS 1. HMRC offer an NI number **tracing service**, so that an individual who has been issued with a number but has mislaid or forgotten it can trace it in the system.
2. For **employers**, HMRC offer a payroll cleansing service which ensures that all NI numbers used for the payroll are correct.

SECTION 2

Contributions for employees

4970 Various contributions may be payable in respect of the employment of an employed earner as follows:

Class 1 contributions are payable in respect of earnings by both the employer and employee.

Class 1A contributions are paid in respect of benefits in kind by the employer.

Class 1B contributions are payable by the employer where he has entered into a PAYE settlement agreement with HMRC (¶4743).

An employer can deduct employer's Class 1, Class 1A and Class 1B NIC when computing his own taxable profits (for the purpose of corporation tax or income tax).

Disclosure is required in respect of NIC saving schemes, which will mainly affect employers (¶5041).

If an individual is both employed and self-employed, see ¶5108.

A. Class 1 contributions

Earnings of an employed earner, such as salary, are liable to Class 1 NIC. Contributions are only payable if earnings reach a minimum level, and the rate of contribution depends on who is paying the contribution. For the rules specific to directors, see ¶5023. For multiple employments, see ¶5033. 4972

The amount of employer's Class 1 NIC payable can be reduced in certain circumstances under a scheme designed to **help new businesses** in many areas of the UK. The NIC Holiday scheme is available to businesses starting up between 22 June 2010 and 5 September 2013, and the areas which will benefit are Scotland, Wales, Northern Ireland, the North East, Yorkshire and the Humber, the North West, the East Midlands, the West Midlands, and the South West. 4973

New businesses (i.e. not businesses which are transferred) which start up in these areas will be entitled to apply for an **exemption from employer's Class 1 NIC** of up to £5,000 due in the first 12 months of employment. This exemption will apply in respect of each of the first 10 employees which are taken on in the first year of operation of the business.

1. Persons liable

Contributions may be payable by the primary contributor and the secondary contributor: 4974
– the **primary contributor** is the employed earner, referred to throughout as the employee; and
– the **secondary contributor** will usually be the employer, or in the case of an office holder, the body responsible for paying the earnings (referred to throughout as the employer).

Contributions are only payable by employed earners over the **age** of 16, in respect of any earnings paid after the 16th birthday, regardless of whether they were earned before that date. 4976 s 6 SSCBA 1992

Primary contributions cease being payable once the employee reaches pensionable age (¶4956+), and any earnings paid after that date are liable only to secondary contributions, for which there is no upper age limit.

2. Income liable

Contributions are payable in respect of the gross earnings of the employment. Dividend income, rent, and interest on loan accounts are therefore excluded. 4978 S 2001/1004 Sch 3 Leaflet CWG2

In the main, taxable employment income is liable to Class 1 NIC as shown in the table at ¶4984.

Variations from tax treatment

Payments from a pension scheme are taxable but will not give rise to a NIC liability (although see ¶3900 for unregistered pension schemes). 4980

The following **expenses** paid for by the employer are treated slightly differently under the NIC rules:
– removal expenses, where no Class 1 NIC is payable on any amount. However Class 1A NIC is due on expenses exceeding £8,000; and
– mileage expenses, where the NIC free rate is 40p per mile up to any level of mileage.

MEMO POINTS 1. Until 30 October 2012, **holiday pay** paid from a centralised fund in the construction industry is NIC exempt. All other holiday schemes are subject to NIC.
2. Some employers require employees to **deduct mileage**, and make a reduced claim for business travel. For example, where an employee travels direct to a client's premises from home, rather

than from the office, the employer may deduct the mileage which the employee would normally travel to the office. However, for NIC purposes, this mileage should still be included as business miles, even though not reimbursed by the employer. To be effective for NIC purposes, such a claim must be made before any further expenses are paid.

EXAMPLE Mr A drove 240 business miles in June, but his employer only reimburses him for 200 miles, at a rate of 50p per mile, and this is paid on 7 July.
The true amount liable to Class 1 NIC is calculated as:

	£
Business mileage reimbursed: 200 × 50p	100
Business mileage claimed: 240 × 40p	(96)
Amount liable to NIC	4

However, £20 will be liable to NIC if Mr A does not claim the extra 40 miles before 7 July, the date of reimbursement. (100 – (200 x 40p))

4981 The following items **are not deductible** for NIC purposes, representing a different treatment from income tax purposes:
– expenses incurred wholly, exclusively and necessarily for the duties of employment by the employee, which are not reimbursed by the employer;
– charitable donations under the payroll deduction scheme (¶3189); or
– employee contributions to registered pension schemes (including both personal and occupational schemes).

4982 **Tips and gratuities** Tips and gratuities are outside the scope of NIC, unless the employer has **control** over their distribution. This means that cash payments given directly to a waiter are not earnings, but tips included on the credit card slip, and therefore distributed by the employer, are earnings.

Booklet E24 HMRC's current view of the NIC liability of tips is shown in the following table:

Scenario		NIC applies?
No involvement of employer or tronc – tip goes direct to employee		No
Employee has contractual right to precise amount of money sourced from tips		Yes
No contractual right to tip	Employer decides who receives it and how much is received	Yes
	Employer has no such control	No

4983 Where a **tronc** is in operation, tips are exempt from NIC where both of the following conditions are satisfied:
– the troncmaster is not distributing money which was originally paid to the employer i.e. the employer is not funding the payments in any way; and
– the employer has no involvement in deciding who receives the tips. Where possible, the troncmaster should not be involved in management.

NIC will be due on any **portion** of the tips **allocated by the employer**, with the exemption covering any balance to be allocated by staff.

If any **NIC is due** on payments made by the troncmaster, it is the employer who is responsible both for calculating the amount due, and paying it to HMRC.

Tax Bulletin 71 MEMO POINTS 1. Tips and gratuities paid to an employee by a person **connected** (¶5570) with the employer are outside the scope of NIC provided the payment is made in recognition of some personal service which is not allocated by the employer, and is either:
a. similar in amount to that which an unconnected person would make; or
b. made by the person in his capacity as troncmaster.
However, payments out of a **trust** set up by the employer for the benefit of the employees will be liable to NIC.
2. **Compulsory service charges** are not tips for this purpose.

3. Whether the tips are taken into account for the purposes of the **national minimum wage** is irrelevant when determining the NIC treatment.

Items included in earnings

4984
s 3 SSCBA 1992

Remuneration	Detail	Earnings for Class 1 NIC purposes	Taxable
Wages, salary, overtime and bonuses		✓	✓
Inducement payments (¶3054)		✓	✓
Restrictive covenant payments subject to income tax (¶3068)		✓	✓
Certain employment tribunal awards	A reinstatement order or a re-engagement order An order for the continuation of the employment A protective award (NIC should be calculated on the gross amount of the award)	✓	✓
Payments in lieu of notice where contractual (¶3066)		✓	✓
Redundancy and termination payments (¶3078)		x	✓ (above £30,000)
Damages payment under contract when employee injured		✓	✓
Reimbursed expenses	All business related[1]	x	x
	Not all business related	✓	✓
Round sum allowance	Covers specific business expenses only	x	x
	Does not cover specific business expenses	✓	✓
Personal incidental expenses paid (¶3174)	Not exceeding £5 per night for UK trips and £10 per night for overseas trips	x	x
	In excess of above limits	✓[2]	✓
Tax paid on behalf of employee (¶3406)		✓	✓
Council tax for living accommodation not job related		✓	✓
Clothing allowance other than for uniform		✓	✓
Meal allowances		✓	✓
Parking fines		✓	✓
Scholarship income (¶3212)		✓	x
Luncheon vouchers	Up to 15p per day	x	x
	Excess over 15p per day	✓	✓

Remuneration	Detail	Earnings for Class 1 NIC purposes	Taxable
Non-cash vouchers	Long service awards	x	x
	Social functions which fulfil the relevant income tax conditions (¶3224)	x	x
	One mobile phone	x	x
	Eye tests and special corrective appliances	x	x
	Health screenings and medical check ups[3]	x	x
	Other vouchers	✓	✓
Childcare vouchers	Up to £55 per week[4]	x	x
	Excess over £55 per week[4]	✓	✓
Payments under the up-front childcare fund[5]		x	x
Loans written off		✓	✓
Share remuneration outside an approved scheme (¶3404)		✓	✓
Statutory pay in respect of parenthood, adoption and sickness		✓	✓

Note:
1. The **reimbursement** must be of an identifiable specific sum expended for business purposes. For example, if the employee is reimbursed for all of his home telephone costs, including line rental, and the employee makes any private calls, the full reimbursement will be subject to NIC, unless there is specific evidence of the business calls made.
2. **Unless** the employer contracted with the hotel etc when Class 1A NIC is due instead.
3. The exemption is limited to one per year. Since 6 April 2009, the benefit may be selectively provided to certain employees and still be exempt.
4. The £55 **limit** applies to the face value of the voucher (¶3222).
5. Under this scheme the Government makes payments directly to those providing childcare services to lone parents who:
– have been receiving benefits for at least 6 months;
– are participating in the New Deal for Lone Parents; and
– are moving into employment of at least 16 hours per week.
Payments from the scheme are intended to assist with registration fees, deposits and advance payments that may prove to be a barrier in returning to work.

4986 SI 2001/1004 Sch 3

Class 1 NIC is also payable on the following **payments in kind**:
a. those which can be exchanged for cash (known as readily convertible assets (¶4606)); and
b. any pecuniary liability of the employee met by the employer, where the employee enters into a contract for any goods or services and the employer pays for it by reimbursing the employee's expenditure or settling the bill directly with the provider e.g. healthcare insurance.

Recognition

4988 Contributions **become payable** on the earlier of when:
– the earnings payment is actually made (e.g. when the payment is credited to the employee's bank account); or
– the employee is absolutely entitled to be paid, even if the pay is not drawn until a later date.

Payments in respect of restrictive covenants, which were received by an employee after his contract had been terminated, were still subject to NIC. *RCI Europe v Woods* [2004]

Where earnings are received in **advance** by an employee who is not a director, the NIC treatment of a payment depends on whether: 4990
– the employee has an absolute entitlement to the income when the payment is received (when it will be liable to Class 1 NIC); or
– the payment is effectively a loan of money (which is not liable to Class 1 NIC).
An inducement payment may be liable to NIC if it relates to the employment, even where that employment has not yet started.

3. Calculation

Calculation of the NIC liability requires the application of specific rates to bands of income received in a measured period. The NIC must then be paid to HMRC. 4992

a. Earnings periods

An earnings period is simply the amount of time between payments of earnings, and is usually at least a week. 4994

Earnings periods **must begin** on the first day of the tax year (i.e. 6 April) and run consecutively. This means that weekly or monthly earnings periods will correspond with the tax weeks and months used in the operation of the PAYE system (¶4610).

MEMO POINTS 1. A **new employee's** first earnings period will be the future payment frequency, for example weekly or monthly, rather than the period between the date when the employment started and the date of first payment.
2. An **inducement payment** will have a weekly earnings period.
3. A **weekly employee** will have a short earnings period of a day at the end of the tax year (2 days in a leap year), known as Week 53.

Regular payments

Where an employee is paid at regular intervals (for example monthly), the earnings period is simply the interval at which the employee is usually paid. 4996 SI 2001/1004 reg 3

Where employees are paid at regular intervals but the actual **date of payment changes**, the earnings period is still the regular interval. 4997

EXAMPLE Mr A is an employer whose employees are all paid on the first Monday of the month. Where the normal payment day is a Bank Holiday, he pays them on the preceding working day. The employees will have a monthly earnings period.

Irregular payments

Where payments are made irregularly, and there is **no overriding regular payment** interval, the earnings period for each payment will be the period for which the earnings are paid (or 1 week if longer). 4999 SI 2001/1004 reg 4

EXAMPLE Mr B is employed as a handyman. His hours of work vary according to the jobs that need doing and he is paid on an ad hoc basis.
His earnings period will be the interval between payments, or 1 week if more than one payment is made in any week.

If an employee receives earnings on **two bases** (for example monthly salary with 6 monthly bonuses), the earnings period is the shortest interval between payments. 5000 SI 2001/1004 reg 7

EXAMPLE Mr C receives his 6 monthly bonus of £2,000 on 10 July, and his monthly salary of £1,200 on 28 July.
Mr C has a monthly earnings period, and so the NIC will be calculated on the total amount of £3,200 received in July.

SI 2001/1004 regs 3(2B), 30, 31

MEMO POINTS 1. HMRC can **direct** that a particular employee in a particular employment has a **longer earnings period** where there are:
– irregular payments;
– abnormal pay practices; or
– arrangements to avoid NIC.
2. A **leaving** employee may receive payments bundled together, which would have been received separately if the employment had continued. In this case, the normal earnings periods will still apply to each payment, as follows:
– regular payments received after ceasing employment are subject to NIC in the usual manner, as if the ex-employee was still employed; and
– one-off payments after cessation are subject to a weekly earnings period.

b. Rates

5002 The rates depend on:
– who is liable for the contribution (employee or employer); and
– whether special circumstances apply (¶5022).
The standard rate is by far the most usual case.

Standard rate

5004 The rate of **secondary** contributions is 13.8% for 2011/12, and this applies to all earnings in excess of the employer's earnings threshold (the Secondary Threshold) which is set at £136 per week (£589 per month) for 2011/12. It should be noted that the start points at which employer and employee contributions become payable are not identical in 2011/12.

The rate of **primary** contributions is 12% for earnings which fall between the employee's earnings and upper limits, and 2% on any excess earnings, as summarised in the following table.

Earnings period		Employee's NIC rate
2011/12 weekly thresholds	2011/12 monthly thresholds	
£139 to £817	£602 to £3,540	12%
Over £817	Over £3,540	2%

MEMO POINTS 1. There is also a **lower earnings limit** of £102 per week (£442 per month) for 2011/12, but no contributions are actually payable until earnings exceed the employee's earnings threshold. Weekly earnings between £102 and £139 carry entitlement to benefits, and employees who earn over £102 per week should still be included on the payroll, even where there is no NIC liability.
2. NICs must be **recorded** in the following four earnings bands for State Second Pension (S2P) purposes (¶3662):
– up to the lower earnings limit (LEL) inclusive;
– above the LEL up to the earnings threshold (ET) inclusive;
– above the ET up to the upper accrual point (UAP) inclusive; and
– above the UAP up to the upper earnings limit (inclusive).
The **upper accrual point** is a frozen limit of £770 per week (equivalent to £3,337 per month and £40,040 p.a.), when benefit entitlement stops. The gap between the UAP and upper earnings limit will therefore increase year on year, and while this will affect all employees, contracted out employees (¶5035) will notice a difference sooner.

c. Calculation methods

5006 To calculate contributions, the following methods can be used:
SI 2001/1004 reg 12
– the tables provided by HMRC; or
– the exact percentage method.

In most cases, either method may be used. However, where the **earnings period is not a multiple of a week or a month** (e.g. every 10 days) but is at least a week, the exact percentage method must be used.

A method must be used consistently for any particular employee unless the employer receives authorisation from NICO that he can change methods, or he upgrades from a manual to computerised system.

For the rules which apply to company directors, see ¶5023.

Using the NIC tables

The NIC tables are used for **manual payrolls**, and are produced annually by HMRC. **5008** Leaflet CA38

The contribution table letter should be recorded on the payroll working papers. In most cases, the employer will use Table A.

MEMO POINTS 1. The tables are **available** on the HMRC website (www.hmrc.gov.uk/employers/), or on the Business Link website (www.businesslink.gov.uk/basicpayetools). The old Employers CD-ROM is no longer being issued.
2. Where an employee is **over retirement age**, Table C should be used.
3. If the employee has a **deferment** (¶5100), Table J should be used.
4. For employees who have **contracted out** of the state pension, see ¶5035.
5. For **married women** who made a reduced rate **election**, see ¶5038.

The **method** for calculating contributions depends on whether the earnings exceed the upper earnings limit. **5009**

Earnings below upper earnings limit If earnings are below the upper earnings limit, the employer should simply find the earnings in the left-hand column of the appropriate table (i.e. weekly or monthly earnings period) and read across the row to find the contributions due. If the **exact amount** is not shown, the lower amount which is closest to the exact earnings should be used. **5011**

EXAMPLE Mr D earns £1,372.33 per month (in 2011/12). Table A applies.
The nearest lower amount is £1,370. So reading across, the following amounts are found:

Earnings	Total of employee's and employer's contributions	Employee's contributions	Employer's contributions
£	£	£	£
1,370	200.45	92.40	108.05

If the **earnings period is a multiple** of either a week or a month, the procedure is as follows: **5012**
a. divide the gross earnings by the number of weeks (or months) in the earnings period;
b. use the tables to work out the contributions due on the result of step **a.**; and
c. multiply the calculated contribution by the number of weeks (or months).

Earnings exceed the upper earnings limit The **additional gross pay table** is used to calculate the additional primary and secondary contributions which are due when earnings exceed the upper earnings limit. **5014**

The first step is to deduct the upper earnings limit from the gross earnings and round the excess down to the nearest pound. If the exact figure is not shown, it should be split into as few components as possible.

The second step is for the contributions for each component part to be added to the contributions from the main table.

MEMO POINTS The table only shows the numbers from 1 to 100, and then goes up as follows:
- multiples of 100, from 200 to 1,000;
- multiples of 1,000, from 2,000 to 10,000; and
- multiples of 10,000, from 20,000 to 100,000.

EXAMPLE Mr E earns £5,133.25 monthly. The additional gross pay table (using the 2011/12 monthly Table A) will apply as follows:

	£
Gross earnings	5,133.25
Upper earnings limit	(3,540.00)
Excess	1,593.25
Rounded to	1,593

As £1,593 does not appear in the tables, it should be split into components of £1,000, £500 and £93.

	Employee's £	Employer's £
Contributions according to Table A (for upper earnings limit)	352.56	407.23
Additional gross pay table		
1,000	20.00	138.00
500	10.00	69.00
93	1.86	12.83
Total contributions payable	384.42	627.06

Exact percentage method

5016 The exact percentage method is generally only used by **computerised payroll systems** (or for directors' earnings (¶5023)), and involves multiplying the exact amount of earnings subject to contributions for the earnings period by the appropriate rate. The earnings figure is stated in pounds and pence and the result of the calculation is rounded to the nearest penny (0.5 pence is rounded down).

EXAMPLE Mr F is an employee paid monthly and earns £1,115.55 per month. Using the exact percentage method, 2011/12 contributions will be payable as follows:

		£
Employee (primary) contributions:		
Earnings above employee's earnings threshold:	1,115.55 – 602	513.55
Contributions @ 12%	513.55 × 12%	61.626
	rounded to	61.63
Employer (secondary) contributions:		
Earnings above employer's earnings threshold:	1,115.55 – 602	513.55
Contributions @ 13.8%	513.55 × 13.8%	70.87
Total contributions payable	61.63 + 70.87	132.50

5017 SI 2001/1004 reg 11 If the **earnings period is not weekly or monthly**, the thresholds are adjusted by dividing the annual earnings threshold by 52, and multiplying the result by the number of weeks in the earnings period. The result of the calculation is rounded up to the nearest pound.

d. Payment of contributions

5019 Sch 1 para 3 SSCBA 1992 The person **liable** for the payment of both primary and secondary contributions is the employer (secondary contributor), although the primary contributions are recoverable from the employee by deduction from salary.

Class 1 contributions are generally **collected** via the PAYE system, which determines the interest and penalties which apply to contributions paid late (see ¶4698 and ¶4712 respectively).

Exceptionally, contributions may be collected via a system known as direct collection which means that the primary contributor is liable for paying contributions to HMRC. In this instance, the payment requirements and penalty provisions are the same as for contributions paid by the secondary contributor.

MEMO POINTS 1. **Direct collection** will apply in any of the following situations: SI 2001/1004 reg 84
– the employee applies to defer contributions (¶5100) which subsequently become payable;
– the secondary contributor fails to account for primary contributions due to an act or default on the part of the employee, and not due to any negligence on the part of the secondary contributor;
– the collection provisions cannot be enforced against the secondary contributor due to an international treaty or convention, and the secondary contributor is not paying primary contributions on behalf of the employee; or
– the employer is not liable to secondary contributions due to not being resident, present or having a place of business in the UK (¶5171).
2. When an **employee arrives** in the UK **from abroad**:
– who will be paid earnings in excess of the upper limit; and
– there is an employer who is liable for Class 1 secondary NIC,
the NIC liability can be paid by monthly estimates. The employer must make a special application for these rules to apply. The balance of the actual NIC due is payable by 31 March following the tax year.
3. An arrangement similar to that described in 2. above can be put in place for **employees sent to work abroad**.

Where an **underpayment** of primary contributions has been made as the result of an error in good faith, the employer can recover it by making deductions from the employee's subsequent earnings. The extra amount which can be deducted is, however, limited to the usual primary contributions due on his earnings. If recovery is not made by the end of the tax year following that in which the mistake arose, the employer must suffer any remaining shortfall. **5020**

EXAMPLE G Ltd made a mistake in good faith at the end of 2010/11 which means that Mrs H has underpaid NIC of £500.
Mrs H's normal primary contributions liability is £40 per month. The maximum further amount that G Ltd can deduct from Mrs H's salary is therefore limited to £40 per month.
As G Ltd will only be able to recover £480 of the primary contributions from Mrs H during 2011/12, G Ltd must bear the cost of the remaining £20.

MEMO POINTS 1. HMRC give the following as examples of an **error in good faith**:
– using out of date NIC rates or thresholds;
– deducting the wrong class of NIC;
– deducting the wrong category of Class 1 NIC (e.g. applying contracted out rates in error);
– arithmetical mistakes; and
– delays in implementing adjustments to the payroll, where the employee's circumstances change.
2. Where an employee's earnings from multiple employments are **aggregated** (¶5033), the primary contributions may be recovered from any part of his earnings.
3. Where an underpayment has occurred, the correct amounts actually due should be entered on the annual **payroll returns** (¶4706+).

4. Special cases

For the following types of individuals, the rules outlined above are modified: **5022**
– directors;
– employees with more than one job;
– employees who have chosen to contract out of part of the state pension; and
– married women who made an election before May 1977 to pay reduced rates of NIC.

a. Directors

Special rules apply when calculating contributions in respect of directors, because otherwise their remuneration packages could be subject to manipulation resulting in the deferral, or even avoidance, of NIC. **5023** Leaflet CA44

SI 2001/1004 reg 1 Leaflet CA44 para 4 MEMO POINTS For these purposes a director is **defined** as:
– a member of the board of directors (or similar body) which manages the company;
– a single director (or similar person) who manages the company;
– a member of the company where the company is managed by its members; or
– a shadow director, being any person in accordance with whose directions (other than in a professional capacity) the company directors are accustomed to act.

Earnings

5024 Leaflet CA44 para 30 A director's earnings will **include** all the items treated as earnings for employees, as well as any fees paid to him.

If the director is also an employee of the company, both sets of earnings should be aggregated when calculating the contributions payable.

Recognition of income

5025 Leaflet CA44 para 31 A director's remuneration is usually approved by the members of the company, and so any amounts **received in advance** of such approval cannot strictly be earnings. However the rule for NIC is that income is recognised at the earlier of:
– when payment is made; or
– when earnings are approved.

If any income is voted to a director, but subsequently waived or refunded to the company, it is still included as earnings when voted.

5026 Where the director **maintains an account with the company** to which remuneration is usually credited, amounts are included as earnings (and therefore liable to NIC) when credited to the account. Provided the account remains in credit, no further contributions are due.

If the **account becomes overdrawn** (or the overdrawn amount increases), contributions will be due if the withdrawal is in anticipation of further earnings being credited to the account. However, where the withdrawal is in anticipation of the introduction of funds from another source (for example dividends), no contributions are payable.

Rates

5028 SI 2001/1004 reg 8 **Usually**, each time a director is paid, contributions are calculated on the total earnings to date and any contributions already paid are deducted. Directors are deemed to have an annual earnings period regardless of the interval at which they are paid, so the rates are applied on an annual basis. Where a director resigns his position during the tax year, he will still have an annual earnings period for that tax year.

The only **exception** is where a director is appointed after the start of the tax year in question. In this case, the director has a pro rata annual earnings period. The pro rata period runs from the date that the director was appointed to the end of the tax year and, for these purposes, the tax year is deemed to have 52 weeks (if the director is appointed in Week 53, his earnings period will be 1 week).

2011/12 annual earnings thresholds	Employee's NIC rate	Employer's NIC rate
£7,225 to £42,475	12%	13.8%
Over £42,475	2%	13.8%

Methods of calculation

5029 Director's NIC may be **calculated** using either:
a. the **alternative** method, where:
– the director is paid at regular intervals (which is treated as the earnings period);
– the earnings exceed the lower earnings limit; and
– the director agrees to contributions being calculated in this way; or
b. the **normal** method, in any other case.

Tables or the exact percentage calculation can be used in conjunction with either method.

Normal method Although the director has an **annual earnings period**, the weekly or monthly table may be used. The earnings to date are simply divided by 52 or 12 respectively before calculating the contributions, and the result is then multiplied by 52 or 12 to give the contributions due. 5030

MEMO POINTS 1. This method will result in irregular contributions and therefore inconsistent **cash flow**.
2. If the director has a **pro rata annual earnings period**, the weekly table must be used. The earnings to date are simply divided by the number of tax weeks in the earnings period before calculating the contributions, and the result is then multiplied by the same number of weeks to give the contributions due.

EXAMPLE Mr A is a monthly paid director earning £1,000 per month payable on the 25th of the month.
He is voted a bonus on 16 June of £9,000, to be paid in his June salary.
For April and May (Months 1 and 2), Mr A's cumulative remuneration of £2,000 is less than the annual threshold of £7,225, so no NIC is due.
The bonus in June (Month 3) takes Mr A's remuneration above the employee's and employer's thresholds for the first time, and he has cumulative remuneration of £12,000 by the end of June.

Using the normal method, the NIC is calculated by dividing £12,000 by 12, to give an amount of £1,000. The monthly Table A is then used to calculate the liability.

	Employee's NIC	Employer's NIC
	£	£
Contributions according to Table A (and rounding to the nearest lower amount)	47.76	56.71
Multiply to obtain true liability	× 12	× 12
June NIC liability	573.12	680.52

Alternative method As the annual earnings period caused problems with many computerised payroll systems, an alternative was introduced, which can only be used if all of the conditions in ¶5029 are met. 5031

This method allows contributions to be calculated in accordance with the normal rules for employees throughout the tax year, with **an adjustment** when making the final earnings payment for the tax year (or the termination of the directorship, if earlier). The adjustment recalculates the NIC liability using the annual thresholds.

The alternative method should lead to a more even spread of NIC, although a large bonus soon after 6 April will result in a large amount of primary Class 1 NIC being due at the end of the year.

EXAMPLE Taking Mr A's circumstances from the example in ¶5030, the NIC due under the alternative method is:
For Months 1 and 2, Mr A's monthly remuneration is £1,000 which results in the following NIC.

	Earnings	Employee's NIC	Employer's NIC
	£	£	£
Contributions per monthly table	1,000	47.76	56.71

The bonus in Month 3 gives Mr A total remuneration of £10,000 in June.

Gross earnings	10,000
Upper earnings limit	(3,540)
Excess	6,460

As £6,460 does not appear in the tables, it should be split into components of £6,000, £400 and £60.

	Employee's NIC £	Employer's NIC £
Contributions according to Table A (for upper earnings limit)	352.56	407.23
Additional gross pay table		
6,000	120.00	828.00
400	8.00	55.20
60	1.20	8.28
Total contributions payable	481.76	1,298.71

By Month 11, Mr A will have effectively paid NIC on 10 months of £1,000, and 1 month of £10,000.

Month 11	Earnings £	Employee's NIC £	Employer's NIC £
Contributions for 10 months on earnings of £1,000	10,000	477.60	567.10
Contributions for Month 3	10,000	481.76	1,298.71
Contributions up to and including Month 11	20,000	959.36	1,865.81

In Month 12, a reassessment must be made, comparing the NIC paid with the amount due for the annual earnings period.

Month 12	Earnings £	Employee's NIC £	Employer's NIC £
Based on annual earnings period			
NIC due on £13,775 (21,000 – 7,225)	13,775	1,653.00	1,900.95
Less: Contributions already paid		(959.36)	(1,865.81)
Contributions due in Month 12		693.64	35.14

Note:
The primary contribution is very high in Month 12 because of the very large bonus which was received early in the tax year.

b. More than one employment

5033 SI 2001/1004 reg 15 Where an employee has more than one employment, each is considered separately when calculating NIC. In such cases it is **usual** to pay primary Class 1 NIC as normal in one employment, and apply for deferment (¶5100) in respect of any others. In certain circumstances, an employee may overpay contributions, and be entitled to a refund (¶5106).

As an **exception**, earnings will be combined in the following situations (unless it is too impractical):
- the employments are with the same employer;
- the two employers are carrying out business in association, sharing profits or sharing resources such as accommodation or personnel; or
- where only one employer, or some other person, is treated as the secondary contributor.

Where such **aggregation** applies, the secondary contributors must decide how to operate the deduction for primary Class 1 NIC.

c. Contracted out employees

Rates

5035 The contracted out rate **applies** to employees belonging to an occupational pension scheme which has received a contracting out certificate from HMRC. Members of such schemes are not eligible for the earnings-related element of the state pension scheme (known as S2P).

Both primary and secondary contributions are payable at a discounted rate up to the upper accrual point (¶5004), with secondary contributions depending on whether the scheme is salary related or money purchase. As is the case with the standard rate (¶5004), liability for secondary contributions begins at £136 per week (£589 per month) for 2011/12.

Earnings period		Primary contributions	Secondary contributions	
2011/12 weekly thresholds	2011/12 monthly thresholds		Salary related scheme	Money purchase scheme
£139 (secondary £136) to £770	£602 (secondary £589) to £3,337	10.4%	10.1%	12.4%
Over £770 to £817[1]	Over £3,337 to £3,540[1]	12%	13.8%	13.8%
Over £817	Over £3,540	2%	13.8%	13.8%

Note:
1. The discounted rate of NIC is only payable up to the **upper accrual point** which is a frozen amount of £770 for weekly paid employees (£3,337 for those who are paid monthly). The normal rate of employee's and employer's NIC is now payable between the UAP and upper earnings limit, which increases the overall contribution liability.

MEMO POINTS 1. A **salary related** scheme guarantees retirement benefits based on the final salary of the employee.
2. A **money purchase** scheme is a fund which provides retirement benefits based on contributions paid during the employee's working life. The reduced rates of contribution will cease on 6 April 2012 due to the proposed introduction of the Personal Account (i.e. a low cost workplace pension that employers will have to offer employees unless they provide an alternative).
3. If there is a contracted out **mixed benefit** scheme, a different rate applies to each of the salary related and money purchase elements.
4. The discounted contracted out rate also affects **low earners** (those earning between £102 and £139 a week in 2011/12), and the following rebates result (based on the earnings above £102):
– 1.6% in respect of primary contributions (maximum 59p per week), which reduce the employee's contributions to nil, and any surplus is payable to the employer;
– 3.7% in respect of secondary contributions for salary related schemes (maximum £1.37 per week), payable to the employer; and
– 1.4% in respect of secondary contributions for money purchase schemes (maximum 52p per week), also payable to the employer.
5. It is also possible for an employee to contract out using his **personal pension**, and in this case the standard rate of NIC is payable, with the difference between the standard rate and the contracted out rate paid by NICO into the personal pension fund.

If **manually** calculating the NIC liability, in most instances the employer should use Table D for salary related schemes, and Table F for money purchase schemes. **5036**

MEMO POINTS 1. Where the employee has a **deferment** and is a member of a:
– salary related scheme, Table L should be used; or
– money purchase scheme, Table S should be used.
2. Where the employee is a **married woman** who made an election before 12 May 1977, see ¶5038.

d. Married woman's election before 1977

Reduced rate contributions are **payable by** married women and widows who, before 12 May 1977, elected to pay reduced contributions, and provided that the woman's circumstances have not changed since then (e.g. she has neither divorced, nor remarried after becoming widowed). Any such change must be notified to HMRC. **5038** SI 2001/1004 reg 127

Such an election can be **revoked** at any time in writing.

The election will also **lapse** if a woman's earnings do not exceed the lower earnings limit (¶5004) for a consecutive period of 2 years.

Comment As the **employer could be liable** for any underpayment of NIC resulting from the application of the reduced rate, he should ask any affected employees to confirm annually that they still qualify.

Rates

Reduced rate contributions carry no **entitlement** to benefits and are therefore substantially lower than standard rate contributions between the employee's earnings and upper earnings limits (¶5004). The rate is 5.85% for 2011/12. For earnings in excess of the upper earnings **5039** SI 2001/1004 reg 131 limit, the standard rate of 2% applies. There is no effect on the employer's secondary contributions.

The employer should only apply the reduced rate if the employee produces a valid Certificate of Reduced Rate Liability. If manually calculating the NIC liability, the employer should normally use Table B.

MEMO POINTS Where the woman has **contracted out**, and is a member of a:
– salary related scheme, Table E should be used; or
– money purchase scheme, Table G should be used.

5. Disclosure rules

5041 SI 2007/785 SI 2010/2927 Disclosure rules, which require reporting of **NIC saving schemes**, were introduced on 1 May 2007. These basically follow the direct taxes rules (see ¶2215 onwards), although there are modifications to cope with the specific nature of NIC.

HMRC have clarified that these rules could potentially **apply to** any class of NIC, although in practice it is only Class 1 (both employer's and employee's) and Class 1A NIC which are affected.

If an arrangement is **not caught** by these rules, this does not indicate that it is approved by HMRC. Conversely, some schemes which may need to be disclosed do not constitute unacceptable avoidance.

Scope

5042 Arrangements which satisfy all of the following **criteria** must be disclosed, although no disclosure is required where the scheme is the same (or almost the same) as one which was first made available before 1 August 2006.

Criteria	Details
The scheme will allow a person to obtain a NIC advantage	– avoidance or reduction of a liability; or – deferral of payment of a liability
The obtaining of that advantage is a main benefit of the scheme	
The scheme falls within one of the stipulated hallmarks	– confidentiality (¶2217 onwards), where the person using or promoting it has reason to keep the details secret from competitors and HMRC; – premium fee (¶2222) i.e. where the fee relates to the NIC saving; and – standardised NIC products (¶2225, reading tax as NIC), which are mass marketed arrangements using standard documentation

HMRC have stated that schemes involving **salary sacrifice arrangements, childcare voucher schemes, holiday pay schemes** etc are unlikely to be notifiable because they will not fall within any of the hallmarks. Specifically they are usually not new or novel enough to merit disclosure. However, disclosure may be required where:
– there is something new, innovative or unusual about a particular scheme; or
– it seeks to use salary sacrifice differently to those schemes which were on the market before 1 August 2006.

MEMO POINTS 1. The following **transitional rules** apply, so that no disclosure is required where:
– the scheme is substantially the same as one which has already been disclosed under the direct taxes rules;
– the relevant date fell before 1 May 2007;
– the first time a promoter became aware of the scheme was before 1 May 2007; or
– for scheme users, any transaction forming part of the arrangements fell before 1 May 2007.
2. The **relevant date** is the earlier of when:
– a firm approach, or a proposal, is made available to a client; and
– arrangements begin which put a proposal into practice.

3. A **promoter** is defined as for direct taxes purposes (¶2231+), and is, briefly, someone who is responsible for the design or availability of a scheme.

How to disclose

The person who is responsible for disclosing the scheme is **usually** the promoter, although users become liable where the: 5043
- promoter is overseas;
- promoter is protected by legal professional privilege; or
- scheme is devised in-house (i.e. without the involvement of a promoter).

Where there is **no promoter**, a business will only need to disclose a scheme if it is a large enterprise, and either the confidentiality or premium fee hallmarks apply. A large enterprise is one that is not small or medium-sized (¶795).

Tight **time limits** apply, being 5 working days for promoters (¶2234), and, depending on the situation, 5 or 30 days for users (¶2237).

The **information** required is as detailed at ¶2239.

If a scheme involves both a **NIC and tax advantage**, disclosure will be required under both the NIC and direct taxes rules. However, a single form can be used for this purpose, provided that the description clearly states that both a tax and NIC advantage are being obtained.

Subsequent actions

In response to a disclosure, **HMRC** will allocate the scheme a reference number within 30 days. 5044

The **promoter** must then communicate this reference to all his client users within 30 days of the date:
- that he first became aware that the client implemented the scheme; or, if later,
- of receipt of the reference number from HMRC.

For **scheme users**, the scheme reference number should be disclosed on form AAG4, which must also state the:
- scheme reference number;
- earnings period in which an advantage is expected to be obtained; and
- employer's name, address and UTR (unique taxpayer reference).

Where the scheme user is an **employer**, the form should be submitted within the time limits applying for the relevant year end return (for Class 1 NIC see ¶4706, and for Class 1A NIC see ¶4732). Where a scheme involves both classes, the earlier time limit relating to Class 1 NIC applies.

Since 1 April 2009, a scheme user has had to provide the required information to HMRC for: SI 2009/612
- the year in which the employer first enters into the transaction which requires disclosure; and
- each subsequent year, until the advantage ceases to apply to any person.

Employees are not required to disclose where the employer has already done so.

Failing to comply

There are penalties for failing to comply with these rules, which for: 5045
- persons responsible for **making full disclosure**, are initially set at a maximum of £5,000, with a possible £600 daily penalty for continuing failure; and
- users who just need to **disclose the reference number** on the annual return, are set at £100 per scheme for the first failure. This then rises to £500 per scheme, and then £1,000 per scheme, for the second and third failures respectively within the 3 years following the date of the first failure.

No penalties will be charged where there is a **reasonable excuse** for defaulting from the rules. In this respect, HMRC state that they will consider whether the promoter (or user) has clearly followed the official guidance (at www.hmrc.gov.uk/aiu/avoidance-scheme.pdf) or has otherwise made a reasonable judgement when failing to disclose either the scheme itself, or the scheme reference number.

However, if a penalty has **already been levied** under the direct taxes disclosure rules, no penalty will be due in relation to the NIC rules.

B. Class 1A contributions

5048 Leaflet CWG5 s 10 SSCBA 1992

Contributions are payable by the secondary contributor (usually the employer), in respect of benefits in kind (¶3196) provided for relevant employees (broadly those employees earning at a rate of more than £8,500 per annum). No contributions are payable in respect of benefits provided to lower paid employees (¶3116).

Exclusions

5050 SI 2001/1004 Sch 3

The following benefits are excluded from liability:

Exemption	Details	¶¶
Earnings subject to Class 1 NIC		¶4978+
Exempt benefits for employment income purposes		¶3204
Included within a PAYE settlement		¶4743
Covered by a dispensation		¶4738
Childcare	If provided in workplace nursery, whole cost is exempt Otherwise, first £55 per week is exempt	¶3220
Shares in the employer company	Only if not readily convertible assets	¶3404
	Deemed loans are not covered by the exemption	¶3354
Tips and gratuities		¶4982
Redundancy payments	Current HMRC practice	

Common chargeable items

5052

All benefits in kind are liable unless exempt. The expenses and benefits return (form P11D) provides a useful summary of common items which are subject to Class 1A contributions (**indicated by** a brown box), including:
– assets and services made available to the employee;
– living accommodation which is not job related;
– company cars and fuel;
– private use of company vans;
– cheap loans in excess of £5,000;
– medical treatment and insurance; and
– relocation expenses in excess of £8,000.

MEMO POINTS The form P11D also contains blue boxes which indicate that **Class 1 NIC** is due. In this case, a payroll adjustment will be required (¶5056).

Mixed business and personal use

5054 Leaflet CWG5

Where benefits are provided to employees for business use and any **private use is insignificant**, no NIC will be due. There is no legal definition of insignificant, although HMRC have provided guidelines in respect of each type of benefit. This exemption does not apply to the use of cars, boats or aircraft, or the provision of an improvement or extension to living accommodation.

Where **private use is significant** and the employee does not reimburse the employer, NIC will be due on the whole taxable benefit relating to the mixed use. Unlike for tax purposes, no deduction is made for any business use. For example, Class 1A NIC will be levied on the full cost of an employer-provided chauffeur, even if he drives 50% for business purposes. Leaflet CWG5 para 13

MEMO POINTS Following a First-tier Tribunal decision in 2010, HMRC have accepted that where a benefit was provided for the tax years 2003-04 to 2005-06 and there was a **partial deduction** allowed for income tax purposes for business use, the same deduction can also be applied in calculating the Class 1A NIC due.
The legislation was amended with effect from 6 April 2007, with the result that this situation will not arise again.
Any **claims for repayment** should be sent to:
HMRC
Customer Operations PAYE Employer Office
BP4009
Chillingham House
Benton Park View
Newcastle
NE98 1ZZ
Any **claim should include**:
– why you believe there is an overpayment;
– the tax year(s) involved;
– evidence of the amount(s) paid;
– the amount of the refund(s) sought; and
– the time limit for making the claim, which is 5 April 2012 for 2004-05 and 5 April 2013 for 2005-06 (2003-04 is now out of time).

Calculation

The employer's declaration form includes a calculation of Class 1A contributions. The **method** is simply to total all the relevant benefits on the P11D (indicated by a brown 1A box) and multiply the total by the Class 1A contribution **rate**, which is set at 13.8% for 2011/12. 5056

Where payments in kind (¶4986) have been **excluded from Class 1 NIC** as a result of an oversight, under no circumstances can Class 1A NIC be paid instead. The employer must either settle the liability through a PAYE settlement, or contact HMRC for specific advice.

EXAMPLE Mr A is provided with a company car (with no private fuel) and private medical insurance by his employer. The cash equivalent of these benefits is £5,000 and £600 respectively. The Class 1A NIC liability is calculated as follows:

	£	£
Car benefit	5,000	
Medical insurance	600	
Total		5,600
Class 1A NIC @ 13.8%		772.80

Compliance

The employer's **reporting** requirements are satisfied by completion of form P11D(b) which includes a declaration by the employer that the details are fully and truly stated to the best of his knowledge (¶4732). 5058 SI 2001/1004 reg 80

The latest date that the form can be submitted is 6 July following the tax year.

MEMO POINTS 1. Employers may be liable to make **disclosure** about a scheme which reduces a Class 1A NIC liability (¶5041).
2. Entities operating **formal incentive award schemes** can pay the tax and Class 1A NIC arising on behalf of the recipients by entering into a Taxed Award Scheme (¶4748). This will usually involve any third party who provides expenses payments or benefits as incentive awards to another entity's employees.

5060 SI 2001/1004 reg 71 Contributions are **payable** in a single amount on 19 July following the tax year, unless payment is being made electronically, when the due date is 22 July. There is no compulsion to pay Class 1A NIC electronically. Interest may be charged on any amounts paid late.

When a **business ceases**, it must account for any Class 1A NIC due within 14 days of the end of the month in which cessation occurs.

C. Class 1B contributions

5064 s.10A SSCBA 1992 Where an employer has entered into a **PAYE settlement agreement** (¶4743), known as a PSA, Class 1B NIC is due on the items covered by the agreement, and is payable in a single lump sum.

The following **amounts are liable**:
- the total value of the items covered by the PSA which would otherwise give rise to a Class 1 or Class 1A NIC liability; and
- the income tax payable by the employer.

Contributions are payable at the standard **rate** for Class 1 secondary contributions (13.8 % for 2011/12).

The contribution is **payable** on the same date as the related income tax i.e. 19 October following the tax year to which it relates (extended to 22 October where payment is being made electronically).

MEMO POINTS 1. Those benefits already paid to employees **before the agreement commences** will still attract a Class 1 or Class 1A NIC liability, as appropriate, instead of Class 1B NIC.
If only Class 1B NIC is accounted for on these benefits, this will lead to either:
- an underpayment of Class 1 NIC, and interest will apply from 19 April following the tax year; or
- an interest charge on the delay in payment (as the Class 1A NIC will be the same amount as the Class 1B NIC) running from 19 July following the tax year.

2. Employers may be liable to make **disclosure** about a scheme which reduces a Class 1B NIC liability (¶5041).

EXAMPLE C Ltd provides business lunches to employees on an irregular basis. Over the course of the tax year it spends £2,045 on 28 members of staff. As it is impractical to identify the value of the benefit to each employee, C Ltd has entered into a PSA in this respect. The tax due under the PSA is £1,059.02 (for the calculation, see ¶4747).
The Class 1B NIC is calculated as follows:

	£
Value of benefits	2,045.00
Income tax payable under PSA	1,059.02
Total	3,104.02
Class 1B contributions @ 13.8%	428.35

SECTION 3

Contributions for the self-employed

5068 Self-employed individuals may be required to pay two different types of NICs, depending on the level of their earnings:
- Class 2 NIC is a flat rate charge payable by any self-employed individual earning over a certain limit; and
- Class 4 NIC is a percentage of taxable profits within certain thresholds.

Neither class is deductible against the individual's taxable profits.

There are special rules for determining the maximum contributions payable if an individual is both employed and self-employed (¶5110), and for recovering excess contributions. In addition, certain income is potentially liable to both Class 1 and Class 4 NIC (¶5150).

MEMO POINTS Exceptionally, individuals may be liable to make **disclosure** about a scheme which reduces a Class 2 or 4 NIC liability (¶5041).

Once a person is a self-employed earner in respect of a business, he will remain such until the business ceases. This does, however, imply a certain **level of involvement**. For example, a sleeping partner in a business who receives a share of profits, but who takes no part in the business, is not a self-employed earner for these purposes. 5070

A partner of a partnership is liable to pay contributions based on his share of the partnership's profits.

A. Class 2 contributions

A fixed **rate of contribution** applies, which in 2011/12 is set at £2.50 per week for most individuals. 5072 s 11 SSCBA 1992

Higher rates apply to **volunteer development workers** and **share fishermen**, which give entitlement to jobseeker's allowance (¶5152).

If the individual wishes to protect his entitlement to benefits (¶5118), contributions may be voluntarily paid, even where a liability does not arise.

Liability

Self-employed individuals between the ages of 16 and pensionable age (¶4956+) are required to pay Class 2 NIC, for each week of self-employment (including holiday periods), unless their earnings are small, or they have applied for a deferment (¶5108) because they are also employed and paying Class 1 NIC. 5074

MEMO POINTS 1. A **week of self-employment** is the period between Sunday to Saturday, where an individual is not: SI 2001/1004 regs 43, 127

a. incapacitated due to sickness;

b. receiving one of the following:

– incapacity benefit (replaced by employment and support allowance for new claimants from 27 October 2008);

– maternity allowance; or

– unemployability supplement to industrial injuries benefit or invalid care allowance;

c. imprisoned or in legal custody; or

d. a married woman or widow who made a relevant election before 12 May 1977 (¶5038).

2. The liability to pay contributions **begins** with the contribution for the week a person reaches his 16th birthday, and **ceases** with the contribution for the week prior to the week in which he attains pensionable age.

3. For voluntary payments of Class 2 NIC when **overseas**, see ¶5203.

Exception

There is an exception available for those with a low level of earnings, known as the **small earnings** exception limit. This is set at £5,315 for 2011/12, although individuals who have already earned this amount in the tax year cannot then apply for an exception. The earnings which are applicable are the actual accounting profits for the period from 6 April to 5 April, ignoring any tax adjustments. 5075 SI 2001/1004 regs 44 - 46 Leaflet CF10

Where **entitlement to state benefits** must be maintained, however, it is preferable to continue to pay Class 2 NIC rather then pay the more expensive voluntary Class 3 NIC (¶5120).

The exception must be **applied for** in writing, using form CF10. The individual must notify NICO of any change in circumstances which would invalidate the certificate, such as ceasing self-employment. Exceeding the small earnings limit automatically cancels the certificate, but no NIC payment would be sought where the certificate was applied for in good faith.

MEMO POINTS 1. An application for a certificate should be **supported by** accounts for a 12 month period ending in the relevant tax year. If anticipated earnings are below the limit, the level of expected receipts and expenses should be substantiated. NICO may attach conditions to the issue of the certificate.

SI 2001/1004 reg 47 2. Where an individual's earnings were below the small earnings exception limit, and he did not apply for a certificate, he can claim a **refund** of contributions by writing to NICO. A claim can only be made in the period between 6 April and 31 January following the end of the relevant tax year. A refund will usually result in the issue of a certificate, and the clawback of any contributory state benefits paid which relate to the overpaid Class 2 NIC. Before claiming a refund, it is therefore important to consider any effect on entitlement to state benefits.

Commencing self-employment

5077 SI 2001/1004 regs 87A - 87G

Ideally, when commencing self-employment, HMRC should be immediately informed by completing form CWF1. However, a **penalty** will only arise if notification does not occur by 31 January following the tax year in which self-employment commenced, and no reasonable excuse exists (¶9850). The amount of the penalty is a percentage of the lost contributions, depending on whether the failure is deliberate and/or concealed (¶9795+).

Payment

5079 Since April 2011, Class 2 quarterly bills have been replaced by **two statutory payment dates** of 31 January and 31 July, with the request for payment being issued approximately three months before the due date. Where a taxpayer makes payment by a monthly direct debit, the collection date of the direct debit will now be four months, rather than one month, in arrears.

5080 s 12 SSCBA 1992

There is no charge to interest on **late paid** contributions. However, late payment is an offence and, on conviction, a daily penalty will be charged until payment is made.

MEMO POINTS 1. Where contributions are **paid very late** (i.e. more than one complete tax year after they were due), the contributions may be charged at the rate for the year in which they are paid. However, voluntary contributions in respect of 2006/07 can be paid up until 5 April 2013 at the rate applying for 2006/07.
2. Contributions that are paid **more than 6 years late** may not qualify for contributory state benefits.

B. Class 4 contributions

5084 Class 4 contributions are chargeable as a **proportion** of the profits of self-employed individuals, and they are payable from the age of 16 to the end of the tax year in which the individual attains pensionable age (¶4956+).

Where an individual is **aged under 16** at the beginning of the tax year, he can apply for a certificate of exception which will last until his 16th birthday.

Exceptions

5086 SI 2001/1004 regs 91 - 94

Non-residents (¶4154) and divers (¶5143) who pay Class 1 NIC are not liable to Class 4 NIC.

Liable profits

5088 Sch 2 SSCBA 1992

Contributions are generally **based on** taxable trading profits applying to the particular accounting period (¶2420).

However, the following items represent **adjustments** which may be required to be made to obtain the NICable profits:
- no relief for tax allowances such as the personal allowance;
- pension and retirement annuity contributions are not deducted;
- deductions may be made for any interest or annual payments (¶2840) which are paid wholly and exclusively for the purposes of the trade, and have not already been deducted in arriving at the profits for tax purposes; and
- any business start-up allowance received must be added to the trading profits.

MEMO POINTS 1. Where a farmer, artist or writer has elected to **average his profits** (¶2650 and ¶2672) for income tax purposes, this will also affect the profits liable to Class 4 NIC.
2. **Furnished holiday lettings** are not usually liable, unless the taxpayer is taxed as carrying on a trade (¶2777).

Trading losses can only be set against trading income for NIC purposes. So if trading losses are set against general income (¶2478) for tax purposes, an adjustment must be made to reduce the trading profits. Excess losses which are used against general income for tax purposes are then carried forward for NIC purposes, to be used against the next available trading profits. 5090

Where losses are **carried back** against trading profits for an earlier period, contributions will be recalculated based on the reduced profits.

Comment It is vital that a separate **record** of trading losses is maintained for Class 4 NIC purposes.

EXAMPLE Mr A is a sole trader and made a loss for 2010/11 of £2,300 which was set against his other income for the year. His profit for 2011/12 is £47,000.
For 2011/12, Class 4 NIC profits would be as follows:

	£
Taxable profits	47,000
Less: Losses from 2010/11	(2,300)
Profits for NIC purposes	44,700

If Mr A subsequently incurred a trading loss for 2012/13 which was carried back against profits for 2011/12, the profits liable to Class 4 NIC would need to be recalculated again.

Partnerships

The Class 4 NIC liability of a partner trading with another individual is based on his share of the profits. If the partner also carries on a **trade outside the partnership**, then the profits from both sources are combined. 5092 Sch 2 SSCBA 1992

Members of **limited liability partnerships** are also liable to Class 4 NIC.

EXAMPLE Mr P is an active partner in the PQR partnership. The partnership has profits of £30,000, which are allocated equally to the three partners. Mr P also trades as a sole trader from which he derived profits of £14,000.
The amount of profits liable to Class 4 NIC are £24,000. (10,000 + 14,000)

Calculation

Contributions are chargeable at different rates depending on the level of profit. The following limits **apply** on a tax year basis, and there is no time apportionment if the trade commences or ceases during the tax year. 5093 s 15 SSCBA 1992

Profits assessed in the tax year (2011/12)	Rate
£7,225 to £42,475	9%
In excess of £42,475	2%

EXAMPLE Continuing the example at ¶5090, the profits liable to Class 4 NIC are calculated as follows:

	£
Profits for NIC purposes	44,700
(42,475 – 7,225) @ 9%	3,172.50
(44,700 – 42,475) @ 2%	44.50
Total Class 4 NIC liability	3,217.00

Payment of contributions

5095 s 15 SSCBA 1992 Class 4 NIC is payable in the same way and at the same time as an individual's income tax liability under self-assessment (¶4504). This means that the contribution is **initially based** on estimated profits for a year and paid in two equal instalments on 31 January in the tax year and the following 31 July. A balancing payment, where appropriate, is made on 31 January following the end of the tax year, once the liability is finalised. Relevant entries are made on the tax return to reflect the NIC liability.

Interest may be charged if contributions are paid late.

SECTION 4

Excessive contributions

5098 During a tax year, it is possible that an individual will overpay NIC where he has earnings from either:

a. more than one employment; or

b. both employment and self-employment.

The solution is either to defer contributions or to claim a refund.

Since the introduction of the additional 2% for Class 1 and Class 4 contributions, there is no overall maximum charge which applies. Instead, a strict series of steps is required for each calculation, as shown in the examples below.

Comment These provisions are not relevant in relation to any contribution suffered by the **employer**.

A. Multiple employments

Deferment

5100 Deferment is very useful where an individual's circumstances involve multiple employments (not necessarily at the same time, but within the same tax year). It is possible to defer contributions from the second and subsequent employments, paying 2% only on all earnings above the employee's earnings threshold.

The **employer** will be sent form CA2700 which authorises him to deduct primary Class 1 NIC at 2% only.

5102 Deferment should be applied for as soon as possible to reduce the amount of any overpayment. **Applications** to defer contributions must be made in writing, using form CA72A ideally before the start of the tax year to which the deferment will refer (and certainly by 14 February within the tax year). At any time, the individual must notify HMRC of any change in circumstances which may mean that deferment is no longer applicable.

If, after the end of the tax year:
- **insufficient** contributions have been paid, an assessment will be made for any shortfall, which must be paid directly by the individual within 28 days of receiving such a demand; or
- **sufficient** contributions have been paid, deferment will continue to apply for subsequent years, although a renewal form must normally be submitted.

Maximum contributions

In the absence of deferment, an individual who has multiple employments is likely to pay too much primary **Class 1 NIC**. In this case, an eight step calculation is required to ascertain the amount of NIC due. **5104** SI 2001/1004 reg 21

EXAMPLE Mr A has two employments in 2011/12, earning £46,900 from one, and £15,790 from the other.
In the absence of deferment, Mr A would have **paid the following NIC**:

		£	£
Employment 1			
Earnings between upper earnings limit and earnings threshold:	42,475 – 7,225 = 35,250		
At 12%		4,230.00	
Earnings above upper earnings limit	46,900 – 42,475 = 4,425		
At 2%		88.50	
			4,318.50
Employment 2			
Earnings above earnings threshold:	15,790 – 7,225 = 8,565		
At 12%			1,027.80
Total primary Class 1 NIC paid			5,346.30

The **maximum** primary Class 1 NIC **liability** for 2011/12 is calculated as follows:

			£	£
Step 1: Calculate the notional maximum amount liable to Class 1 NIC	53 × (817 – 139)		35,934	
Step 2: Take 12% of the figure in step 1	35,934 @ 12%			4,312.08
Step 3: Calculate the earnings which fall between the earnings threshold and the upper limit				
Employment 1	42,475 – 7,225 =	35,250		
Employment 2	15,790 – 7,225 =	8,565		
			43,815	
Step 4: Deduct the figure in step 1 from the figure in step 3	43,815 – 35,934		7,881	
Step 5: If Step 4 is positive, take 2% of that figure	7,881 @ 2%			157.62
Step 6: Calculate the earnings which exceed the upper limit in each employment	46,900 – 42,475		4,425	
Step 7: Take 2% of step 6				88.50
Step 8: Add steps 2,5 and 7, to obtain the annual maxima for Mr A				4,558.20

So £788.10 of primary Class 1 NIC has been overpaid. (5,346.30 – 4,558.20)

Refund

In any case where primary NIC is **overpaid**, because contributions have mistakenly been charged at 12% in respect of each employment, the individual can claim a refund of the excess. A claim must be made within 6 years of the end of the affected tax year. **5106** SI 2001/1004 reg 52

B. Employed and self-employed

Deferment

5108 S 2001/1004 reg 95 An individual may either be employed and self-employed at the same time, or commence self-employment after ceasing employment (or vice versa).

Where, at the beginning at the tax year, it is believed that the **Class 1 NIC maximum will be exceeded** (¶5110), an individual can apply to defer Class 4 contributions. This means that Class 4 NIC is only payable at 2% unless it is subsequently proved that the maximum was not reached. Similarly, it is possible to defer Class 2 contributions completely, where paid Class 1 NIC will be sufficient.

The same rules apply as for multiple employments (¶5100), except that form CA72B should be used for deferral of Class 2 or Class 4 contributions.

Maximum contributions

5110 SI 2001/1004 reg 100 Where **deferment has not been granted** and an individual is both employed and self-employed, it is likely that the total NIC paid under Classes 1, 2 and 4 will exceed the amount properly due. There is a maximum amount of contributions for when:
- just Classes 1 and 2 are due; or
- Classes 1, 2 and 4 are due.

5111 **Class 1 and Class 2 NIC** Where an individual earns **most of his income from employment**, but also has a small self-employment, Class 2 NIC may not be due, if sufficient Class 1 NIC has already been paid.

EXAMPLE Mr B earns £30,000 from each of two employments, and is also self-employed. The maximum Class 1 and Class 2 NIC payable by Mr B for 2011/12 is as follows:

			£	£
Step 1: Calculate the maximum amount liable to Class 1 at the main rate	53 × (817 – 139)		35,934	
Step 2: Take 12% of the figure in step 1	35,934 @ 12%			4,312.08
Step 3: Calculate the earnings which fall between the earnings threshold and the upper limit				
Employment 1	30,000 – 7,225 =	22,775		
Employment 2	30,000 – 7,225 =	22,775		
		45,550		
Step 4: Deduct the figure in step 1 from the figure in step 3	45,550 – 35,934		9,616	
Step 5: If Step 4 is positive, take 2% of that figure, otherwise the figure is taken as nil	9,616 @ 2%			192.32
Step 6: Calculate the earnings from each employment which exceed the upper limit			Nil	
Step 7: Take 2% of step 6				Nil
Step 8: Add steps 2,5 and 7, to obtain the annual maxima for Mr B				4,504.40

As Mr B will have met this liability by payment of Class 1 NIC alone, no Class 2 NIC is due.

Mr B will have paid the following Class 1 NIC:

		£
Employment 1:	(30,000 – 7,225) @ 12%	2,733.00
Employment 2:	(30,000 – 7,225) @ 12%	2,733.00
Total		5,466.00
Actually due		(4,504.40)
Overpayment of primary Class 1 NIC		961.60

Class 1, 2 and 4 NIC Where an individual has a **substantial self-employment** and he is also employed, the following example shows the steps which should be followed in order to calculate the maximum contributions due. 5112

EXAMPLE Mr C is employed and earns £36,000 (equivalent to £3,000 per month). He is also self-employed, with profits of £50,000.
In the absence of deferment, Mr C will have **paid the following NIC** in 2011/12:

		£	£
Employment – Class 1			
Earnings above earnings threshold:	36,000 – 7,225 = 28,775		
At 12%		3,453.00	
Earnings above upper earnings limit	Nil		
At 2%		Nil	
			3,453.00
Self-employment			
Class 2	52 × 2.50		130.00
Class 4			
Profits between £7,225 and £42,475	35,250		
At 9%		3,172.50	
Profits above £42,475	50,000 – 42,475 = 7,525		
At 2%		150.50	
			3,323.00
Total NIC paid			6,906.00

The **maximum NIC liability** for Mr C is calculated as follows:

		£	£
Step 1: Calculate the notional maximum amount liable to Class 4	42,475 – 7,225	35,250	
Step 2: Take 9% of the figure in step 1	35,250 @ 9%		3,172.50
Step 3: Add 53 weeks of Class 2	53 × 2.50		132.50
			3,305.00
Step 4: Calculate the amount of Class 2 paid, and the Class 1 paid at 12%:			
Class 1	(36,000 – 7,225) @ 12%	3,453.00	
Class 2	52 × 2.50	130.00	
		3,583.00	
Subtract this from step 3	3,305.00 – 3,583.00	(278.00)	
As this result is negative, this step is treated as nil			Nil
Step 5: Multiply step 4 by 100/9			Nil
Step 6: Subtract the lower profits limit from the upper profits limit, or the actual profits if this is lower:	42,475 – 7,225	35,250	
Step 7: Subtract step 5 from step 6	35,250 – Nil	35,250	
Step 8: Take 2% of the figure in step 7	35,250 @ 2%		705.00
Step 9: Calculate the amount by which the profits exceed the upper profits limit and take 2%	(50,000 – 42,475) @ 2%		150.50

Step 10: Add steps 4,8 and 9 to obtain the maximum Class 4 liability		855.50
Step 11: Add in the Class 1 and Class 2 NIC due:		
Class 4 per step 10		855.50
Class 1	12 × (3,000 – 602) @ 12%	3,453.12
Class 1 – extra 2% amount	Nil	Nil
Class 2	52 × 2.50	130.00
Total NIC liability		4,438.62

So Mr C will be due a refund of £2,467.38. (6,906.00 – 4,438.62)

Refund

5114 SI 2001/1004 reg 52A

Refunds of overpaid NIC will be made in the following **order**:
1. Class 4.
2. Class 1 at reduced rate.
3. Class 2.
4. Class 1 at standard/contracted out rate.

There is no automatic refund, so an individual must make a specific claim (using form CA5610) within 6 years of the end of the affected tax year.

SECTION 5

Maintaining the contributions record

5118 Entitlement to contributory benefits such as the earnings-related state pension requires a minimum number of years in an individual's contributions record. Where insufficient contributions have been made (for example due to an extended holiday abroad, or by applying for the exception for small earnings if self-employed), an individual may make voluntary Class 3 contributions. In certain circumstances, individuals may be given various types of credit for contributions which have not actually been paid, which reduces the number of years required for the record.

Comment It is usually **preferable** to pay Class 2 NIC, rather than claim small earnings exception and pay Class 3 contributions, because Class 2 is less expensive and also gives access to more state benefits.

A. Voluntary contributions

5120 s 13 SSCBA 1992

Class 3 NIC is a flat rate charge, set at £12.60 per week for 2011/12. Both employed and self-employed individuals may make voluntary contributions. An individual must be between the age of 16 and pensionable age (¶4956), and generally be resident in the UK throughout the year. Contributions will only be accepted if they will be beneficial, so where Class 1 or Class 2 NIC have already been paid, it may be the case that no Class 3 NIC can be paid.

1. Determining the amount payable

5122 SI 2001/1004 reg 48

Class 3 contributions may be made where an individual has either made no contributions (and received no credits (¶5128)) for a tax year, or has an incomplete record of contributions for a year.

MEMO POINTS 1. **Married women and widows** who elected to pay reduced rate NIC before 12 May 1977 (¶5038) are not eligible to pay Class 3 NIC.
2. For maintaining a contributions record whilst **overseas**, see ¶5174 and ¶5213.

No contributions

If, **at the start of a tax year**, an individual does not expect to pay (or be credited with) any contributions (of any class) for a tax year, but wishes to improve his record, he can apply to pay Class 3 NIC. A full year's contribution is required and contributions can be made throughout the year in question. If the individual begins to pay voluntary contributions but then stops, any contributions paid which do not improve his state benefits entitlement will be refunded. 5123

If, **after the end of a tax year**, it becomes clear that no contributions (of any class) have been made, an individual may apply to HMRC for a statement which will provide details of any contributions which can be made to improve the record.

Insufficient contributions

Where an individual has an incomplete contribution record for a year, he will receive a **statement** advising him of the position, usually about 20 months after the end of the year in question. The statement will also advise the amount of voluntary contributions required to complete the contributions record for that year, and provide details of the methods of payment. 5125

MEMO POINTS 1. If it is believed that an incomplete record exists for a **previous year**, an individual can request a statement (otherwise known as a deficiency notice) for that earlier period from HMRC.
2. A **state pension forecast** can be requested by completing form BR19. It should be borne in mind that where an individual is several years from retirement age, future earnings may mean that there is no need to pay contributions in respect of past incomplete years. This is especially relevant now as full entitlement to the basic state pension for individuals retiring after 5 April 2010 only requires 30 contribution years. On the other hand, rates of Class 3 NIC are likely to increase year on year, so if voluntary contributions are required in the future, these will be more expensive.

2. Payment of contributions

Since April 2011, where Class 3 payments are being made, the payments should be made on **two statutory payment dates** of 31 January and 31 July. A request for payment will normally be issued approximately three months before the due date. Where a taxpayer makes payment by a monthly direct debit, the collection date of the direct debit will now be four months, rather than one month, in arrears. 5126

As contributions are voluntary, there are no penalties or interest on late paid contributions. However, where contributions are **paid very late**, i.e. more than 2 complete tax years after they were due, the contributions may be charged at the rate for the year in which they are paid.

Contributions which are paid more than 6 years late may not qualify for benefits.

MEMO POINTS **Official error** may have removed credits (¶5128) from an individual's record. In this case, individuals can pay Class 3 NIC in respect of any affected years from **1993/94 to 2007/08**. The deadline for payment is 5 April 2014. SI 2001/1004 reg 50B

B. Credits

Where individuals have not paid sufficient contributions in a year, credits may be available, which will make the particular tax year a qualifying year for the purposes of the basic state pension and bereavement benefits. In limited circumstances, credits may also count towards 5128 SI 1975/556 employment and support allowance (which replaced incapacity benefit from 27 October 2008 for new claimants), and jobseeker's allowance.

When are credits available?

5129 Credits are only available to individuals aged 16 or over who have not reached pensionable age (¶4956), and are generally given to individuals who are unable to work, or who receive certain state benefits.

Credits are given **automatically** to individuals aged 16 to 18.

Men aged 60 or over at the end of a tax year will automatically receive credits if they are not liable to pay NIC (e.g. because of retirement before the age of 65).

Individuals who receive benefits

5131 Credits are available to individuals who receive any of the following:
- jobseeker's allowance;
- employment and support allowance (which replaced incapacity benefit for new claimants from 27 October 2008);
- maternity allowance;
- carer's allowance;
- working tax credit; or
- statutory sick pay, maternity pay, paternity pay or adoption pay.

In addition, **unemployed people** who are making a labour market declaration (signing on), and people who are not working due to **illness**, receive credits.

Other circumstances

5132 Credits are given to people on **approved training courses**, not related to their employment, who already have a contributions record. Courses must last for less than 1 year and confirmation of the availability of credits may be obtained from the DWP.

People on **jury service** (other than the self-employed) whose earnings fall below the lower earnings limit for employees (¶5004) may also receive credits.

C. Credits for parents and carers

5134 Leaflet CF411A Credits for parents and carers are available to people who **reach retirement age** after 5 April 2010, and they have replaced Home Responsibilities Protection which applied until that date.

The credits cater for people who need to take time off from their normal working lives, and will count towards future basic state pension, bereavement allowance and widowed parent's allowance.

Specifically, credits will be given to people who are:
- awarded Child Benefit for a child under 12;
- approved foster parents; or
- engaged in caring for severely disabled people for at least 20 hours per week.

Any existing Home Responsibilities Protection entitlement will be converted into credits.

Married women and widows who made a **reduced rate election** before 12 May 1977 (¶5038) were prohibited from claiming Home Responsibilities Protection, but they may apply for the credits for parents and carers.

Claiming

5137 An individual who **receives child benefit** should automatically be awarded the credits.

In **other cases**, (including where an individual who receives child benefit believes that the credits are missing from their National Insurance account) a claim is required (on form

CF411A), which should be made by the end of the tax year following that in which the caring took place.

Given that the time limit for claiming Home Responsibilities Protection was 3 years from the end of the relevant tax year, claims for entitlement for the final years of this will continue to be valid until, at the latest, 5 April 2013.

SECTION 6

Special cases

A number of occupations are subject to special rules for National Insurance purposes, generally those which involve significant duties outside the UK, or where the distinction between employment and self-employment is not clear. In some cases, the rules apply to safeguard a minimum level of state benefits. 5140

A. International transportation

Individuals working in international transportation, where the nature of the employment is such that they may not be liable to social security contributions in any country, are treated as employed earners. The rules only **apply to** individuals domiciled in (¶4163), or having a place of residence in, the UK. 5142

These rules will also be **disapplied** where a reciprocal agreement (¶5195) or EEA agreement (¶5177) results in there being a social security liability in a particular country.

MEMO POINTS Persons in these categories are treated as complying with any National Insurance **time limits** if:
- the failure to comply is as a result of being overseas; and
- the position is rectified as soon as is practical on return to the UK.

Continental shelf workers

For NIC purposes the continental shelf is treated as part of the UK. Workers **within the scope** of this provision would include oil-rig workers, divers and their supervisors, whether employed or self-employed. 5143 SI 2001/1004 reg 114

Airmen

An airman is **defined** as any person employed to carry out duties wholly or mainly whilst the aircraft is in flight. This includes pilots, navigators and cabin crew. 5145 SI 2001/1004 reg 111

If the airman is employed on a British aircraft and the secondary contributor (usually the employer) has a place of business in the UK, then UK NIC will be due.

If the aircraft is not a British aircraft, UK NIC will only be due if the employer has his principal place of business in the UK.

MEMO POINTS 1. A **British aircraft** is defined as an aircraft registered in the UK, whose owner resides in the UK, or has his principal place of business in the UK. For this purpose, the owner of a leased aircraft is the person who controls the aircraft.
2. HMRC consider the following to be a **place of business**, where:
- the employer's premises are occupied lawfully; and
- employees undertake activity at the premises, in the course of the employer's business.
3. The following are used as **indicators of premises**:
- a registered office address;
- a lease or rental agreement;

- headed paper or business cards showing the address;
- an entry in the telephone or trade directory; and
- a name plate.

Mariners

5146 SI 2001/1004 reg 115 Leaflet CA42

A mariner is **defined** as any person employed to carry out duties while a ship is at sea. This includes the captain, crew and other on board staff, such as the ship's cook.

A liability to NIC will exist if the person paying the earnings has a place of business (¶5145) in the UK and either the contract:
- refers to a British ship; or
- is entered into in the UK.

If the ship is not a British ship and the contract is entered into outside the UK, a UK liability will arise in respect of the captain and crew (but not other on board staff) if the person paying the earnings has his principal place of business in the UK.

As most mariners are employed by an offshore company, it is usual for only Class 1 primary contributions to be due.

MEMO POINTS 1. A **British ship** means a ship, hovercraft or vessel registered in the UK.

SI 2001/1004 reg 119

2. Employers who employ mariners on **foreign-going ships** pay secondary Class 1 contributions at a **rate** of 13.3% for 2011/12.

SI 2001/1004 reg 115

A foreign-going ship is one which trades beyond the UK (including the Republic of Ireland), the Channel Islands, the Isle of Man and the continent of Europe between the river Elbe and Brest inclusive. Fishing vessels proceeding beyond the following points are also foreign-going vessels:
- on the South, Latitude 48° 30'N;
- on the West, Longitude 12° W; and
- on the North, Latitude 61° N.

B. Other occupations

5150 SI 2001/1004 reg 94A

Certain occupations tend to have **both employment and self-employed elements**. In this case any income liable to Class 1 NIC is excluded from liability to Class 4 NIC.

Examples of this include:
- subpostmasters, who have a post office salary which is also included within retail profits;
- certain freelancers who include earnings in their business profits; and
- directors fees included within a professional partnership's profits.

Certain occupations have a **specific treatment**, summarised in the following table.

Summary

5152 SI 1978/1689 Sch 1 SI 2001/1004 regs 125, 150

Occupation	Details	NIC treatment
Employed by spouse/civil partner	Spouse A is employed by Spouse B for the purposes of B's own employment (or self-employment) e.g. a husband acting as his wife's book keeper	Employee of the spouse
	If spouses are in partnership	Self-employed
Agency workers	If the worker is: – supplied through a third party, gives personal service to a client; and – subject to supervision or control (by either the agent or client) Excludes entertainers, fashion, photographic and artist's models	Employee of the agent
	Where the agent merely introduces the worker to the client	Employee of the client

Occupation	Details	NIC treatment
Lloyd's underwriters	See ¶2688	Self-employed
Office cleaners	Working anywhere except a dwelling house	Employed
Ministers of religion	Remuneration is mainly a stipend or salary	Employed
Examiners	Provided the following conditions are met: – the examiner is engaged by a person responsible for administering or conducting an exam leading to a qualification; – his duties involve invigilating, moderating, examining, or setting questions or tests; and – all duties are to be performed in a period of less than 12 months	Self-employed
Teachers or instructors	Where work is undertaken in an education establishment, students are taught on site, and payments are made by the establishment	Employed
Lecturers	As for teachers. Except where lectures are open to the public, and the lecturer works less than 3 days in 3 consecutive months, when deemed to be self-employed	Usually employed
Actors and entertainers	Where remuneration includes any element of salary[1], treated as an employed earner for NIC purposes Excludes TV presenters, news reporters, and session musicians	Usually employed
Foster carers[2]	Trading profits are calculated using the income tax rules, either as: – receipts which exceed an exempt amount (¶2608); or – under normal accounting principles, with relief for expenses and capital allowances	Self-employed
	If profits treated as sundry income for income tax purposes	No liability
Share fishermen	Defined as a person employed in the fishing industry (other than under a contract of service) as a master or member of the crew of a UK registered fishing vessel, who is remunerated partly by a share of the profits or gross revenue of the boat	Self-employed, paying Class 2 NIC at a special rate (£3.15 per week for 2011/12) giving entitlement to jobseeker's allowance
Volunteer development workers	Must be: – certified as a volunteer development worker by HMRC; – ordinarily resident in the UK; and – employed overseas in a position which is not liable to Class 1 NIC	Self-employed, paying Class 2 NIC at a special rate (£5.10 for 2011/12), giving entitlement to jobseeker's allowance

Note:
1. **Salary** is defined as a payment:
- made for services rendered;
- paid under a contract for services;
- payable at specified periods (where there is more than one payment); and
- calculated by reference to the amount of time for which work has been performed.

HMRC have confirmed that musicians engaged by orchestras will not be liable to Class 1 NIC where the payments received do not amount to a salary.

2. Individuals who receive **adoption allowance** are not trading, and therefore no NIC liability arises.

SECTION 7

Overseas issues

5158 National Insurance is generally payable by anyone working in the UK. Individuals working in the UK on a short term basis, and those leaving the UK who wish to maintain their entitlement to benefits, may be able to take advantage of special rules which exist between the members of the European Economic Area (EEA). The UK has also entered into a limited number of reciprocal agreements with certain other countries.

MEMO POINTS The **term UK** includes Great Britain and Northern Ireland, because even though Northern Ireland has its own system, the same principles apply. For individuals working in international transportation, see ¶5142.

A. General principles

5160 SI 2001/1004 reg 145 The liability for NIC is **linked to** an individual's residence status and whether he is present in the UK. Special rules apply to ensure that individuals do not pay contributions in more than one country during the period in which they arrive in, or leave, the UK.

On arrival in the UK, anyone planning to work should apply for a National Insurance number (¶4966).

1. Link to UK

Presence

5162 It is usually clear whether an individual is present in the UK, as presence is simply a matter of fact.

Leaflet CA44 MEMO POINTS **Directors** of UK registered companies, if they are not resident in the EEA, or countries with which the UK has a reciprocal agreement (¶5195), may ignore certain visits to the UK to attend board meetings, where:
– no more than ten board meetings, each requiring a maximum presence of 2 days, are attended in a year; or
– if there is only one board meeting, it does not last more than 14 days.

Residence and ordinarily resident

5164 Leaflet NI38 There is no statutory **definition** for either residence or ordinarily resident for National Insurance purposes. Residence and ordinarily resident are a question of fact, and although these terms are generally given their meaning for income tax purposes (¶4154+), there are some differences as set out below.

5165 **Residence** This concept has a greater permanence than presence, and may continue even while an individual is **temporarily absent**, if the individual intends to remain resident. Where an individual leaves the UK for an unknown period of time, this will usually bring his residence status to an end.

Claiming **contributory benefits** is a strong indication that an individual is resident.

5166 Leaflet NI38 **Ordinarily resident** An individual will be ordinarily resident in a country where he normally lives, and has a settled mode of life. It can be generally concluded that it is difficult for an individual to make himself not ordinarily resident for NIC purposes, even when he is not present in the UK.

HMRC have set out **practical guidelines**, which are summarised below.

Factor	Indication of being ordinarily resident
Home retained in UK during overseas work	Strong
Home available for person's use when he returns from abroad	
Home let whilst away	Longer lease would imply person is not ordinarily resident
Person returns to the UK during a period of employment abroad	The more frequent or longer the UK visits, the stronger the indication
Person visits family who have remained in UK, including holidays at UK home	
Person returns to UK in connection with his overseas work e.g. to present a report or attend training sessions	Not an indication
Partner and/or children are with the person abroad	Probably not ordinarily resident, especially where family home is no longer retained and only occasional visits are made to the UK
Person has lived in UK for a substantial period of time before working abroad	The longer the period, the stronger the indication
Person will return to UK after employment abroad	The earlier the return, the stronger the indication
UK bank account maintained	Not particularly relevant
Still registered with UK doctor	

2. Worker's liability to UK NIC

Employment

An **employee** is liable to Class 1 primary contributions if he is either resident, present (subject to temporary absences), or ordinarily resident in the UK (¶4154+) at the time of the employment. 5168

When there is a primary contribution, there is usually is a secondary contribution. The **employer** is liable to Class 1 secondary contributions if the employer is either: 5171
- resident or present in the UK when the secondary contributions become payable; or
- has a place of business in the UK at that time.

It is unlikely that a secondary contribution would arise without a primary contribution, except where the worker is over pensionable age (¶4956+).

MEMO POINTS 1. HMRC consider the following to be a **place of business**, where: Leaflet CWG2
- the employer's premises are occupied lawfully; and
- employees undertake activity at the premises, in the course of the employer's business.

2. The following are used as **indicators of premises**:
- a registered office address;
- a lease or rental agreement;
- headed paper or business cards showing the address;
- an entry in the telephone or trade directory; and
- a name plate.

3. An **overseas company** with a UK branch will have a UK place of business, but a UK subsidiary, whilst itself having a UK presence, will not constitute a UK place of business for its overseas parent.

4. If expatriates are outside the scope of UK NIC, no **Class 1A** NIC is payable by the employer, even where P11D forms are still completed.

5. For Class 1 NIC **payment simplification**, see ¶5019.

Self-employment

5173 SI 2001/1004 reg 147 A self-employed individual is liable for **Class 2** contributions if he:
– is ordinarily resident (¶4160) in the UK for the period for which contributions are due; or
– was resident (¶4154) in the UK for at least 26 out of the preceding 52 contribution weeks.
An individual may choose to pay Class 2 contributions for any period in which he is present in the UK.
A self-employed individual will be liable for **Class 4** contributions only if resident for tax purposes in the UK.

MEMO POINTS A **contribution week** is a period of 7 days starting at midnight between Saturday and Sunday.

Voluntary contributions

5174 SI 2001/1004 reg 147 Leaflet NI38 In general, **Class 3** contributions may only be paid by individuals resident (¶4154) in the UK throughout the tax year. In certain circumstances, the cheaper Class 2 NIC may be paid instead.
HMRC can advise whether voluntary contributions are valid, on a case by case basis.

B. Application of the rules

5175 The operation of the above rules means individuals arriving in, or leaving, the UK may be liable to contributions in more than one country at the same time. Special provisions therefore apply to limit the **double charge** in some circumstances, by determining that an individual is subject to contributions in one country only. Unlike income tax, there is no set off of liabilities of one country against another.

Summary of regimes

5176 There are three different regimes which apply, depending on whether the individual is moving between the UK and:
a. an **EEA member state**;
b. a country with which the UK has a **reciprocal agreement**, which may either be full, covering both NIC and benefits, or a Double Contributions Convention (DCC) which covers NIC liability only; or
c. the **rest of the world**.

MEMO POINTS 1. The rules were amended slightly from 1 May 2010. For details of the rules applying before that date, see earlier editions of *Tax Memo*.
2. **Further information** can be found on the benefits area of the DWP's website, www.dwp.gov.uk.

5177 Details of the arrangements with EEA member states and countries with which the UK has reciprocal agreements are shown in the following table.

Country	EEA [1]	Reciprocal agreements		Reference	Leaflet
		Full	DCC		
Austria	x			EC 883/2004	SA 29
Barbados		x		SI 1992/812	SA 43
Belgium	x			EC 883/2004	SA 29
Bermuda		x		SI 1969/1686	SA 23
Bosnia Herzegovina		x		SI 1958/1263	SA 17
Canada			x	SI 1995/2699	SA 20
Croatia		x		SI 1958/1263	SA 17

Country	EEA[1]	Reciprocal agreements		Reference	Leaflet
		Full	DCC		
Cyprus	x			EC 883/2004	SA 29
Czech Republic	x			EC 883/2004	SA 29
Denmark	x			EC 883/2004	SA 29
Estonia	x			EC 883/2004	SA 29
Finland	x			EC 883/2004	SA 29
France	x			EC 883/2004	SA 29
Germany	x			EC 883/2004	SA 29
Gibraltar	x			EC 883/2004	SA 29
Greece	x			EC 883/2004	SA 29
Guernsey		x		SI 1994/2802	SA 4
Hungary	x			EC 883/2004	SA 29
Iceland	x			EC 883/2004	SA 29
Ireland	x			EC 883/2004	SA 29
Isle of Man		x		SI 1977/593	
Israel		x		SI 1957/1879	SA 14
Italy	x			EC 883/2004	SA 29
Jamaica		x		SI 1997/871	SA 27
Japan[2]			x	SI 2000/3063	
Jersey		x		SI 1994/2802	SA 4
Korea[3]			x	SI 2000/1823	
Latvia	x			EC 883/2004	SA 29
Liechtenstein	x			EC 883/2004	SA 29
Lithuania	x			EC 883/2004	SA 29
Luxembourg	x			EC 883/2004	SA 29
Macedonia		x		SI 1958/1263	SA 17
Malta	x			EC 883/2004	SA 29
Mauritius		x		SI 1981/1542	SA 38
Netherlands	x			EC 883/2004	SA 29
New Zealand		x		SI 1964/495	SA 8
Norway	x			EC 883/2004	SA 29
Philippines		x		SI 1989/2002	SA 42
Poland	x			EC 883/2004	SA 29
Portugal	x			EC 883/2004	SA 29
Romania	x			EC 883/2004	SA 29
Serbia and Montenegro		x		SI 1958/1263	SA 17
Slovak Republic	x			EC 883/2004	SA 29
Slovenia	x			EC 883/2004	SA 29
Spain	x			EC 883/2004	SA 29
Sweden	x			EC 883/2004	SA 29
Switzerland[4]	x			EC 883/2004	SA 29
Turkey		x		SI 1961/584	SA 22
USA		x		SI 1984/1817	SA 33

Note:
1. The terms of the existing bilateral treaties will continue to apply where this gives a more beneficial result (such as the agreements involving Malta, Cyprus and Slovenia).
2. Further information can be found at: www.hmrc.gov.uk/nic/japan/htm
3. Further information can be found at: www.hmrc.gov.uk/nic/korea/htm
4. Switzerland is treated as part of the EEA under the UK rules.

1. Moving within the EEA

5178 EC 883/2004 The overriding principle is that nationals of any EEA member state should only be subject to the social security legislation of one state. The rules for employees and self-employed individuals are similar. Where an individual is **both self-employed and employed** in different member states, he will be liable to contributions in the state in which he is in paid employment.

Voluntary contributions may be paid in any state, but not where they would duplicate contributions which are already payable.

Comment As local laws are often different, a worker could be treated as both self-employed and employed in the same job (e.g. company directors are treated as self-employed in many states). It is therefore vital to ascertain how the worker is treated within the particular member state when deciding on the NIC liability.

a. Employees

5180 The NIC treatment of an employee **depends on** whether he is taking on a new employment, or still working for his home employer whilst overseas. The employer in the individual's home state is referred to as his home employer.

Taking on a new contract

5181 An employee is **liable** to social security contributions **in the state** in which he works, regardless of where he lives, or where the employer's place of business is. So where an employee takes on work overseas under a contract with a new employer, he will be liable to contributions in the overseas state from day one.

Already employed in home state

5183 Where an employee remains employed by his home employer, and he is posted overseas, the NIC treatment will **depend on** the length of the assignment.

Comment It is important that employers review the situation of their employees who are working abroad at least once a year, to ensure their circumstances still merit the current social security treatment.

5184 EC 883/2004 art 12 **Short temporary assignments** For these purposes, a short assignment is one which is not expected to last **more than** 24 months. Where the employee is not replacing another employee, he will remain liable to home contributions, as long as a certificate of coverage (form E101) is obtained.

MEMO POINTS To obtain a **certificate of coverage**, the employer should apply to the social security authority in the home state with the appropriate evidence (such as the employment contract). This document satisfies the authorities in the other member state that contributions are not required.

5185 **Longer term temporary assignments** The **default treatment** is that an employee will pay contributions in the overseas state from day one.

By **exception**, it may be possible to remain liable to home contributions for a period of up to 5 years, where any of the following criteria apply:
- the employee has special skills or knowledge which are not available in the local labour market;
- the employer has specific objectives with which the employee is familiar, and for which his services are required; or
- unusually, it is shown to be in the employee's best interest (for example where the employee is nearing retirement).

MEMO POINTS 1. If one or more of the exceptions apply, an **application** should be made to the social security authorities in the home state, setting out the specific circumstances of the case. If

they agree with the application, they will seek the host state's approval to continuing home contributions. Often the host state will examine the employee's history to verify that he has an adequate contributions record in the home state, and has not just spent a minimal amount of time there in order to pay cheaper contributions.
2. Eventually, an employee may **develop stronger ties** with the host state where he is working, which means that he would need to pay contributions in that state in any event.

Working in more than one member state at the same time

Where an employee works in more than one member state at the same time (whether for the same or different employers), he will **generally be liable** to contributions in the state in which he habitually resides, provided he performs a substantial part of his duties there (or where he works for a number of employers resident in other member states). For these purposes, although the occasional business trip to another state will be ignored, an employee working a couple of days a month on a regular basis would be working in more than one state. **5187** EC 883/2004 art 13
Otherwise, the employee will be liable to contributions in the state in which his employer has its place of business or registered office (¶5171).

b. Self-employed individuals

Similar provisions apply for self-employed individuals as for employees. **5190**
In general, a self-employed individual is liable to social security contributions in the state in which he works, regardless of where he lives.

Temporary working

If a self-employed individual works temporarily in another state for a **period** of up to 24 months, he may continue to pay home contributions (i.e. contributions in the state in which he has his home). Applications to pay home contributions should be made in the same way as for employees, using form E101. **5191**
HMRC have clarified that the following **criteria** must be met before an **E101 application** can be made:
– at least 4 months of self-employment have occurred in the UK, before departure to the other member state;
– evidence is retained of the work to be performed abroad (such as contract details); and
– the conditions which enable the individual to resume work in the UK are retained (e.g. work space is still rented, registration with professional body maintained).
Any **change in circumstances** during the period covered by the E101 form must be notified to the Centre for Non-Residents.

Working in more than one state

If the individual works in more than one member state, he will **pay contributions in** whichever of those states he resides, provided that he carries out a substantial part of his activity there. Otherwise, he will be liable for contributions in the state in which he carries out his main activity. **5193**

MEMO POINTS If this rule operates in such a way that the individual is **not eligible** for the state pension scheme in any state, the authorities of the member states concerned will come to an agreement concerning the state in which contributions should be paid, in order to preserve pension entitlement.

2. Reciprocal agreement countries

The UK has entered into reciprocal agreements with a number of countries. Each agreement is unique, although they have many common features, and generally include provisions similar to those which exist between EEA member states. **5195**

Common principles

5196 The general aim of a reciprocal agreement is to ensure that an individual is only **liable to contributions** in one of the countries concerned, usually the country in which the individual is working. Most of the reciprocal agreements cover both employees and self-employed individuals.

Temporary working

5198 An individual may continue to pay home contributions (i.e. contributions in the country in which he has his home) if he works temporarily in another country. The **definition** of temporary varies according to the country concerned.

If the period of the assignment is extended due to **unforeseen circumstances**, the individual is generally permitted to continue to pay home contributions for a further period. These provisions only apply if the individual was paying contributions in the home country before the assignment.

Applications to pay home contributions should be made in the same way as for employees working in the EEA, using form E101.

MEMO POINTS The **length of temporary postings** depends on the country involved as follows:

Country	Temporary posting period
Barbados	3 years
Bermuda	12 months
Bosnia-Herzegovina	12 months
Canada	5 years
Croatia	12 months
Cyprus	3 years
Guernsey	3 years
Isle of Man	No time limit, but agreement is limited. Liability determined by place of residence.
Israel	2 years
Jamaica	3 years
Japan	5 years
Jersey	3 years
Korea	5 years
Macedonia	12 months
Malta	3 years
Mauritius	2 years
Philippines	3 years
Serbia and Montenegro	12 months
Turkey	3 years
USA	5 years

3. Other countries

5200 Where an individual moves between the UK and a country for which no special arrangements exist, liability for contributions may arise in more than one country. The rules for determining whether contributions in the UK are required are set out below.

Broadly, an **employee**:
– arriving in the UK will not be required to pay NIC for the first 52 weeks of their stay; and
– leaving the UK is required to continue paying NIC for the first 52 weeks of their absence.

For individuals other than employees, the rules are more flexible.

a. Coming to the UK

Employees

Primary and secondary Class 1 NIC are **generally payable from** the date on which an individual takes up employment in the UK. 5202 SI 2001/1004 reg 145(2)

However, an **exception** will arise where the individual is **posted temporarily** to the UK and all of the following circumstances apply:
– the employee is not ordinarily resident or employed in the UK (apart from the temporary posting);
– the posting arises in the course of an employment carried on mainly outside the UK; and
– the employer has his main place of business outside the UK.

If these criteria are met, no primary or secondary Class 1 contributions are payable from the date of last entry into the UK until the employee has been resident in the UK for a continuous period of 52 contribution weeks (¶5173).

MEMO POINTS 1. The **date of last entry** refers to the date on which the individual arrived in the UK to take up the employment. The contribution holiday requires a continuous period of residence of 52 weeks. An absence of at least 28 days is normally required to break a period of continuous residence, although the factors at ¶5166 will also be taken into account.
2. An **overseas employer** may have no place of business (¶5171) in the UK. In this case, any host employer (essentially the entity to which the employee's services are supplied) is made liable for the secondary contribution when it becomes due.
3. Where earnings need to be **apportioned** because of **duties undertaken outside the UK**, days spent performing overseas duties can be excluded from UK Class 1 NIC (apportioning earnings on the basis of 365 days) where the employee meets all of the following criteria: Tax Bulletin 79
– he is not ordinarily resident in the UK;
– he works in the UK under contract to a foreign employer;
– he returns overseas to perform foreign duties for that employer (including any holiday days which relate to the foreign employment contract); and
– a single salary is paid for both UK and overseas duties which is met by the foreign employer, and therefore incurred for the purposes of the foreign business.

Self-employed and voluntary contributions

A self-employed individual arriving in the UK is **required** to pay Class 2 NIC if he is ordinarily resident or resident for 26 weeks out of the preceding 52 weeks. 5203

Where an individual wants to maintain his contributions record, he is **entitled** to pay Class 2 or 3 NIC, if he satisfies any of the following conditions:
– he is liable to pay Class 1 or 2 contributions in respect of an earlier period during the tax year;
– he is ordinarily resident in the UK throughout the tax year, or becomes ordinarily resident during the tax year; or
– if not ordinarily resident, he arrived in the UK during the tax year (or the previous tax year) and is continuously present in the UK for 26 contribution weeks (¶5173).

An individual is able to pay Class 2 NIC for any week in which he is actually present in the UK.

Students

Students working in the UK **may be exempt** from contributions where they are: 5205 SI 2001/1004 reg 145(3)

a. pursuing a full-time course of study outside the UK, and they take up temporary employment during a vacation (not at the end of the course) which is similar to, or related to, the course of study; or

b. occupying a position comparable with that of an apprentice with someone outside the UK, and, before reaching the age of 25, they begin employment in the UK which is similar to, or related to, the apprenticeship.

b. Leaving the UK

Employees

5207 SI 2001/1004 reg 146 In such a case, the employer and employee will often have a **double charge** to NIC, both in the UK and the host country. Primary and secondary Class 1 contributions continue to be payable for 52 weeks after the employee leaves the UK if all of the following apply:
- the employee is ordinarily resident in the UK;
- the employee was resident immediately before taking up the employment overseas; and
- the employer has a place of business in the UK.

Otherwise, all liability to UK NIC ceases on the leaving date.

MEMO POINTS 1. If an individual employed abroad **changes employer**, the first employer's liability for contributions ceases with the last payment due from him. In this case, further liability for contributions will be dependent upon the three criteria above.
2. It may be beneficial for employees to retain a link with the UK NIC system, as it could be cheaper than paying local contributions. In this case, voluntary Class 2 NIC should be paid.

5208 **Temporary return to the UK** If the employee returns to the UK **before the end of the 52 week period** in any of the following situations, contributions continue to be payable until the period has expired:
- during paid leave (i.e. holiday);
- sick leave; or
- for a temporary period of employment.

5209 If the **temporary employment begins after the 52 week period** has expired, by concession, contributions are not payable for the first 6 weeks of UK duties.

If the length of the temporary assignment lasts for more than 6 weeks, UK contributions may then be payable in the normal way, unless the duties are merely incidental to the overseas employment.

5210 **Permanent return to the UK** Full **liability** to UK NIC will recommence on an individual's permanent return to the UK, and so contributions will be due on the first payment of UK earnings **unless** both of the following conditions are satisfied:
- the employee is on paid leave from the employer pending termination of that employment; and
- the 52 week contribution period had ended before the return to the UK.

In this situation, contributions are not required for the period of paid leave unless the employee takes up employment with a different employer during that period. The new employer will, of course, be required to deduct contributions in the normal way.

5211 **Further employment abroad** If, **after returning to the UK** following employment abroad, the employee takes up further employment abroad, a further 52 week period of contributions will be due if the conditions in ¶5207 are satisfied. So if the employee was not resident in the UK before taking up the new post, taking the factors at ¶5166 into consideration, no UK NIC will be due during the further employment abroad.

Voluntary contributions

5213 An individual (whether **employed or self-employed**) leaving the UK is **entitled to pay Class 2 or Class 3 NIC** if:
- he was resident in the UK for a continuous period of at least 3 years at any time before the period for which Class 3 contributions are to be paid; or
- an appropriate amount of contributions (i.e. 52 weeks at the Class 1 lower earnings limit) has been paid for each of the 3 years preceding the period for which Class 3 contributions are to be paid.

However, the individual may only **choose** to pay **Class 2 NIC** if he: 5214
- is gainfully employed (or self-employed) outside the UK but not liable to Class 1 contributions for the employment; and
- was employed or self-employed immediately before leaving.

Such contributions are paid voluntarily, for example, to maintain the contributions record (¶5118), and form CF83 should be completed. Class 2 NIC carries a greater entitlement to benefits. Individuals are not entitled to pay both contributions at the same time, but can swap between Class 2 and Class 3 at any time, providing the relevant conditions are satisfied.

PART 4

Capital gains tax

Capital gains tax
Summary

The numbers cross-refer to paragraphs.

CHAPTER 1 General principles

CHAPTER 2 Computation

CHAPTER 3 Capital gains tax losses

CHAPTER 4 Specific types of disposal

CHAPTER 5 Specific types of asset

CHAPTER 6 Reliefs

CHAPTER 7 Administration

CHAPTER 1

General principles

OUTLINE ¶¶

A. Background

To understand the concept of capital gains, particularly with respect to older assets, it is useful to examine the background to the tax. Prior to 1965, gains on the disposal of assets were not subject to UK taxation, and although an asset owned before 1965 which is sold today will be subject to capital gains tax, concessions apply which recognise that such an asset has not always been chargeable. The introduction of new rules from 6 April 2008 for individuals, trustees and personal representatives has further complicated the position, making disposals after this date considerably different to those which occurred previously. 5220

The key dates for capital gains tax can be summarised as follows.

Date	Event
6 April 1965	Introduction of capital gains tax
31 March 1982	Base date for revaluation to market value (¶1133) Introduction of indexation allowance (¶1118)
6 April 1988	Introduction of March 1982 value (¶1133) Capital gains tax aligned to income tax rates
6 April 1998	Taper relief introduced for individuals, trustees and personal representatives Indexation frozen for individuals, trustees and personal representatives
6 April 1999	Gains for individuals (except for those in excess of the basic rate band) taxed at lower rate
6 April 2008	Taper relief and indexation allowance abolished for individuals, trustees and personal representatives Flat rate of tax introduced at 18% Introduction of entrepreneurs' relief (¶6035) Compulsory rebasing to March 1982 value (¶1133)
23 June 2010	Higher rate of CGT introduced for individuals, trustees and personal representatives

5222 ss 1, 8 TCGA 1992 The basic rules for calculating chargeable gains are **common to all** persons (i.e. individuals, companies etc). This part deals with the basic principles and those rules that are specific to individuals, with the rules that apply only to companies, trustees and personal representatives being found in the respective relevant parts of *Tax Memo*. For the rules relating to disposals for individuals, trustees and personal representatives prior to 6 April 2008 see earlier editions of *Tax Memo*.

B. When will there be a chargeable gain?

1. Key concepts

5224 A chargeable gain will arise on a disposal of a capital asset by a chargeable person if the disposal proceeds exceed the allowable expenditure. A capital loss will arise where the proceeds are less than the allowable expenditure.

Other determining factors are the:
– timing of a transaction; and
– location of assets (¶5238).

2. Disposal

5225 The term disposal is not **defined** by statute, but is taken to mean more than just a transfer for consideration. A gift is therefore considered to be a disposal, as is compensation received for the loss, damage or permanent destruction of an asset. A disposal can arise where part of the asset is retained, or where an interest or right in, or over, an asset is created.

MEMO POINTS On **death** the assets comprised in an individual's estate do not constitute a disposal for capital gains purposes.

3. Chargeable person

All persons

5226 ss 2, 9 TCGA 1992 A chargeable person is essentially any person who is:
– not exempt from capital gains tax; and
– resident in the UK (¶4154).

Individuals

5227 However, the full extent of an individual's liability to capital gains tax also depends upon their **domicile** (¶4163) and residence status as follows:

Status of individual		Liable on
Resident and domiciled	Resident not domiciled	
✓		Worldwide gains
	✓	UK gains
	✓	Remitted foreign gains [1]

Note
1. For those who are not domiciled in the UK, the remittance basis is available by election (¶4202) but if no election is made all gains will be subject to tax. Where an individual makes an election for the remittance basis to apply, no annual exemption will be available to them. If the remittance basis applies due to the de minimis limit (¶4203), the annual exemption (¶6326) will continue to be available.

Individuals who, after previously being resident or ordinarily resident for 4 of the last 7 tax years, become **temporarily non-resident** for a period of less than 5 complete tax years, are treated as if they had remained resident in the UK for capital gains tax purposes. Gains and losses accruing whilst the individual was abroad are treated as if they had accrued in the year of return to the UK, unless they relate to assets acquired whilst overseas. This is also the case for non-UK domiciled individuals making remittances during a period of absence. Remittances made in the period of absence are taxed in the year of return, provided that the remittance basis applies in the year of return. s 10A TCGA 1992

MEMO POINTS Specific **anti-avoidance** provisions also apply as follows:
a. where an individual becomes non-UK resident, the terms in any relevant double tax treaty will not be able to prohibit a UK capital gains tax charge arising when a temporarily non-resident individual returns to the UK. (If it were not for this rule, it would be possible for a temporarily non-resident individual to dispose of an asset whilst outside the UK, and rely on the tax treaty to avoid a further UK capital gains tax charge on his return);

> EXAMPLE Mr A (UK resident) left the UK in February 2008 to spend 4 years in Country X. Whilst there he disposed of shares and realised a taxable gain (under UK laws) of £200,000. Country X taxes such gains at a rate of 10% and the tax treaty with the UK gives Country X exclusive taxing rights. However, Mr A will still be subject to UK tax on the gain of £200,000 on his return to the UK.

b. where an individual manipulates the residence requirements of two or more countries such that he remains resident in the UK and also resident in another country, he will be deemed to be liable to UK capital gains tax on any gains, irrespective of the terms of any double tax treaty.

> EXAMPLE Mr A spends half the year in the UK (and is therefore UK resident for capital gains tax purposes), and the rest of his time in Country X which deems an individual to be resident if he has a permanent address in the country. Under the terms of the tax treaty with the UK, Country X has exclusive taxing rights. However, this anti-avoidance rule means Mr A will be liable to UK capital gains tax on any realised gains.

Exempt bodies

The following bodies are exempt from capital gains tax: **5228**
- charities, provided that they use gains for charitable purposes;
- local authorities;
- co-operative housing associations where the gains relate to a property occupied by a tenant;
- authorised unit trusts and open ended investment companies;
- registered friendly societies;
- approved superannuation funds; and
- scientific research associations.

4. Chargeable assets

Definition

A chargeable asset is defined as any form of property (wherever situated) **including**: **5229** s 21 TCGA 1992
- options, debts and other similar property;
- any currency other than sterling (although sterling transferred to a sub-fund is chargeable (¶7434)); and
- any property which is created by the person disposing of it (e.g. patents or works of art), or which otherwise comes to be owned without having been acquired (e.g. goodwill).

MEMO POINTS A distinction is drawn between **trading assets** which are deemed to be capital in nature and those which are revenue (¶108). The distinction is important because capital assets are subject to capital gains legislation, whereas revenue assets are taxed as trading income. There is no statutory definition of either capital or revenue assets, but case law has developed a test which, in simple terms, indicates that expenditure incurred with a view to bringing an asset or advantage into existence for the enduring benefit of the trade constitutes expenditure on a capital asset. *British Insulated and Helsby Cables v Atherton* [1926]

Excluded items

5230 As the definition of a chargeable asset is very wide, certain assets, investments and receipts are, where certain conditions are met, excluded from the capital gains tax regime, and these are covered below.

5232 **Excluded assets** Subject to satisfying certain conditions, the following assets do not give rise to a chargeable gain.

Asset	Conditions	Reference
Annuity rights	Where they are granted in the ordinary course of a business (unless they are deferred annuities)	s 237 TCGA 1992
Cars	Only normal passenger vehicles (including classic cars) [1, 2]	s 263 TCGA 1992
Debts	Only if disposal is by the original creditor	s 251 TCGA 1992
Decorations for valour	Exempt unless purchased	s 268 TCGA 1992
Foreign currency	Only if held for personal use abroad	s 269 TCGA 1992
Life assurance policies	Where the disposal is made by the original beneficiary, unless purchased [3]	s 210 TCGA 1992
Non-life policies of insurance	This exemption does not apply where the insured assets are chargeable assets.	s 204 TCGA 1992
Non-marketable government securities	This includes the following securities issued under the National Loans Act 1939 and 1968 (and the corresponding Northern Ireland Acts): – savings certificates and securities; – development bonds; – defence bonds; and – premium bonds	s 121 TCGA 1992
Pension rights	Where the disposal is made by the original beneficiary. The fund in question need not be an approved scheme, but it must be established for persons employed in a trade, profession or vocation	s 237 TCGA 1992
Renewable obligation certificate (ROC) [4,5,6]	Provided that: – the individual acquired the certificate in connection with electricity generated by a microgeneration system; – the system is installed at or near the individual's domestic premises; and – the individual intends that the system will provide enough (or almost enough) electricity to run the premises concerned	s 263AZA TCGA 1992
Assets to which the structured finance arrangements apply (¶4064)	The disposal of the asset by the borrower and/or any subsequent reacquisition	s 263E TCGA 1992
Woodlands	Where managed by occupier on commercial basis	s 250 TCGA 1992

Note:
1. Excludes, for example, private number plates, racing cars, taxis, vans, commercial vehicles and motor-cycles etc.
2. Where cars are not exempt, but are privately owned and not used for a business they are exempt as wasting assets (¶5922).
3. The rights of the insurer under a policy of insurance are not considered to be an asset. However, the rights of the insured are a chargeable asset where the insured asset is itself chargeable.
4. This is a certificate issued to a householder who installs microgeneration technology in his own private home for the purposes of generating electricity for his personal use.
5. For disposals on or after 6 April 2007.
6. See ¶3966 for the income tax treatment.

Excluded investments Subject to meeting certain criteria, the following investments do not give rise to a chargeable gain. 5234

Investment	¶¶
Enterprise investment scheme shares	¶6200
Shares held in an ISA	¶2797
Shares in a venture capital trust	¶6250
Gilt edged securities	
Qualifying corporate bonds	

MEMO POINTS The definition of a **qualifying corporate bond** differs for individuals (including trustees and personal representatives) and companies: s 117 TCGA 1992
a. individuals: a QCB is broadly any security (secured or unsecured) where:
– the debt represents a normal commercial loan;
– the security is expressed in sterling; and
– there is no provision for conversion, or redemption, into any currency other than sterling.
b. companies: a QCB is broadly any asset that represents a loan relationship of the company (¶870) other than:
– a convertible security; or
– an asset linked to the value of a non-trading asset.

Excluded receipts Subject to meeting certain criteria, the following receipts do not give rise to a chargeable gain. 5236

Receipt	Reference
Compensation from foreign governments in respect of confiscated, expropriated or destroyed assets	s 268B TCGA 1992
Compensation for mis-sold pensions	s 148(2) FA 1996
Compensation for professional or personal injury	s 51 TCGA 1992
Gambling winnings	s 51 TCGA 1992
Mortgage cash backs	SP 4/97

5. Location of assets

The location of an asset for capital gains purposes is determined by legislation. As a **general rule**, an asset will be located where it is physically situated. **Special rules** apply for certain types of asset, including intangible assets whose location is harder to identify. 5238 ss 275, 275A TCGA 1992

Type of asset	Location
Rights or interests over immovable property (e.g. land)	Same country as the immovable property
Rights or interests over tangible movable property	Same country as the tangible movable property
Debts	Situated in the UK if the creditor is located here (Judgement debts are situated where the judgement was recorded)
Government issued shares and debentures	Country where issuing authority is located
Other registered shares and debentures	Country where register is kept (subject to the proviso that shares or debentures of any company incorporated in the UK are located in the UK)
Ships and aircraft	Situated in the country where the owner is resident

Type of asset	Location
Business goodwill	Situated in the country where the trade is carried on
Patents, trademarks, designs and corresponding rights	Country where they are registered. Rights or licences to use patents etc are located in the UK if they are exercisable in the UK
Copyright, design rights, franchises and corresponding rights	Located in UK if they, or any rights derived from them, are exercisable in the UK
Intangible assets	Located in the UK if created in the UK
Options/futures where the underlying subject matter is located (or treated as located) in the UK	Located in the UK
Foreign company bank account held by non-domiciled individual	Located in UK if the individual is UK resident and the account is held at a UK branch

CHAPTER 2

Computation

OUTLINE ¶¶

SECTION 1

Basic calculation

The basic computation which must be carried out for **each disposal** is as follows: 5240

	£	£
Disposal proceeds (¶5302)		xxx
Less: Incidental costs of disposal (¶5330)		(xxx)
		xxx
Less: Acquisition cost (¶5324)	xxx	
Incidental costs of acquisition (¶5330)	xxx	
Enhancement expenditure (¶5326)	xxx	
		(xxx)
Unindexed gain		xxx
Less: Indexation allowance [1]		(xxx)
Indexed gain		xxx

Note
1. Indexation allowance is only available for companies. For details on how to calculate this see ¶1118 onwards.

For individuals, trustees and personal representatives, unindexed gains and losses are then aggregated for each tax year, and finally an annual exemption (¶6326) is deducted. 5242

For companies, the indexed gains are added to the company profits for the year as if they were simply another source of income.

5244 Where allowable **losses** for a tax year exceed chargeable gains the excess may be:
– carried forward and used to offset chargeable gains in later tax years (¶5470);
– set off against other income of the same and the preceding year, to the extent that the losses relate to qualifying trading company shares (¶5486); or
– carried back in certain circumstances (¶5476).

5246 A number of **reliefs** are available to reduce the amount of gains chargeable to tax, and in some cases to extinguish the gain altogether:

Relief	¶¶
Entrepreneurs' relief	¶6035
Replacement of business assets: – depreciating assets – non-depreciating assets	 ¶6068 ¶6062
Gift relief	¶6095
Incorporation relief	¶6179
EIS and VCT relief	¶6200 and ¶6250

MEMO POINTS Any **special withholding tax** (¶4296) levied on an individual's offshore savings income can be credited against his income tax and/or capital gains tax liability. Any excess credit will be repaid.

SECTION 2

Disposal proceeds

1. Value

5302 s 38 TCGA 1992 Disposal proceeds will either be the **actual consideration** received or the **open market value** of an asset. In either case, the disposal proceeds may be reduced by incidental costs of disposal.

MEMO POINTS For the **definition** of a disposal and details of the **special rules** that apply to certain specific types of disposal (part disposals, no gain/no loss transactions, disposals between connected persons etc) see ¶5500 onwards.

2. Actual consideration

Definition

5304 Consideration is not defined for capital gains tax purposes, but the **general rule** is that where the disposal takes place at arm's length between unconnected persons, the consideration is the amount of money or money's worth which changes hands.

If the **consideration is in a foreign currency**, it must be converted to sterling at the exchange rate for the date of disposal.

s 37 TCGA 1992 MEMO POINTS 1. Consideration for capital gains tax purposes **does not include** money or money's worth:
– treated, either for income or corporation tax purposes, as the income of the person making the disposal; or
– taken into account as a receipt in computing the income, profits, gains or losses of the person making the disposal.
2. Any **VAT** charged on the disposal of the asset will be excluded from the consideration for these purposes.

Payment to third party

Payment does not have to be made to the vendor for it to be deemed to be consideration. Where a payment is made to a third party at the request of the vendor, as opposed to the sum being received by him, this is deemed to be part of the consideration. *Crusader v HMRC* [2007] **5305**

Similarly, where the purchaser made a separate payment to the vendor's company, being the subject of the sale, on the basis that the company, after completion of the transaction, would make a contribution to the vendor's pension plan, the High Court concluded that the payment should be taken into account as part of the consideration. *HMRC v Collins* [2008]

Instalment payments

Where the consideration is payable in instalments, there is a single disposal and the full amount of consideration must be brought into the computation at the date of disposal. If the instalment **period is more than 18 months**, the taxpayer may request for the related tax to be paid over a period of up to 8 years (¶6344). **5306** s 280 TCGA 1992

Ascertainable deferred consideration

If the consideration is ascertainable but is not payable until a later date, no discount will be available to take account of the risk of non-payment. If the amount concerned is subsequently deemed to be irrecoverable, a claim may be submitted for an adjustment to be made. **5308** s 48 TCGA 1992

Unascertainable deferred consideration

The disposal of an asset for future, unquantifiable or contingent consideration is a disposal of an asset and the acquisition of a new asset (i.e. the right to future consideration). *Marren v Ingles* [1980] **5310**

The **proceeds for the disposal** of the asset must therefore include an amount for the market value of the right to future consideration. This amount is also allowable expenditure for the new asset.

EXAMPLE A Ltd acquired a parcel of land in June 1996 for £20,000. The land was sold in December 2002 for £50,000 plus a right to 2% of any profit made on selling smaller parcels of the land. At the date of sale, this was estimated to be a further £15,000.
The position on the disposal of the land is as follows:

	£	£
Proceeds	50,000	
Expected future consideration	15,000	
		65,000
Less: Allowable expenditure		
Original cost	20,000	
Indexation allowance Jun 96 to Dec 02		
$\frac{178.5 - 153.0}{153.0} = 0.167 \times £20{,}000$	3,340	
		(23,340)
Chargeable gain		41,660

When **future consideration is received**, a disposal occurs. **5312**

EXAMPLE Continuing the previous example, A Ltd received further consideration of £22,000 in May 2011, once the land was sold.

	£	£
Proceeds		22,000
Less: Allowable expenditure		
Value at acquisition	15,000	
Indexation allowance Dec 02 to May 11		
$\frac{235.2 - 178.5}{178.5} = 0.318 \times £15{,}000$	4,770	
		(19,770)
Chargeable gain		2,230

If the future consideration had been only £10,000, the calculation would be as follows:

	£
Proceeds	10,000
Less: Allowable expenditure	
Value at acquisition	(15,000)
Allowable loss	5,000

Note:
For disposals by individuals, trustees and personal representatives the calculation is the same but there would be no indexation allowance.

MEMO POINTS See ¶5482 for details of **loss relief** available on the disposal of the right to future consideration.

Assumption of liability

5314 ss 48, 49 TCGA 1992 The assumption of a liability **by the vendor** in connection with the disposal of an asset will reduce the disposal consideration by the value of the liability assumed. However this provision does not apply to liabilities which are **contingent on a future event** relating to:
– the default by an assignee in relation to his obligations under a lease;
– a covenant for quiet enjoyment or any other obligation assumed as vendor of land, or of any estate or interest in land; or
– a warranty or representation made on a disposal by way of sale or lease of any property other than land.

If the liability later becomes enforceable, an adjustment may be made to the computation.

s 26(3) TCGA 1992 If a mortgage or other similar security is taken over **by the purchaser**, it will be included in the disposal consideration for the asset along with the other consideration received.

EXAMPLE Mr A acquires land from Mr B for a payment of £10,000 and also agrees to assume the outstanding obligations under Mr B's mortgage which, at the date of disposal, amount to £50,000. Mr B's disposal proceeds will be as follows:

	£
Payment received	10,000
Liabilities assumed	50,000
Disposal proceeds	60,000

3. Open market value

When is this value used?

5316 s 17 TCGA 1992 The open market value of an asset will be used as disposal proceeds **in the following circumstances**:
– the transaction was not made on arm's length terms, such as a gift, a transfer between connected persons (¶5570) or a transfer into a settlement;
– the consideration cannot be valued (such as on an exchange of assets);
– the disposal was made in connection with a loss of employment, reduction of emoluments or in recognition of past or future services;
– a claim is made for assets of negligible value (¶6025);
– assets are appropriated to or from trading stock; or
– UK permanent establishment assets are taken out of the charge to capital gains tax by a non-resident trader.

MEMO POINTS A transaction is not made on **arm's length terms** if one of the parties to the transaction does not intend to get the best deal for themselves. However, the fact that a low price has been negotiated does not mean that the transaction is not at arm's length. A transaction between connected persons (¶5570) can never be at arm's length even if the consideration is freely negotiated.

What is market value?

Market value is **defined** as the price that an asset might reasonably be expected to fetch if it was sold on the open market. 5318

The following special provisions apply for the **valuation of securities**.

Type of security	Market value	Reference
Listed shares and securities	Lower of: – one quarter up on the lower of the two quoted prices; and – the average of the highest and lowest markings at which bargains were recorded for a given date	s 272(3) TCGA 1992
Unit trusts	Lower of two prices quoted i.e. the buying price	s 272(5) TCGA 1992
Unquoted shares	Open market value on the assumption that the purchaser has all of the information that a prudent buyer would reasonably require for a purchase at arm's length	s 273(3) TCGA 1992

SECTION 3

Allowable expenditure

1. Relevant expenditure

Definition

Allowable expenditure is broadly the total cost incurred by the vendor on the acquisition and disposal of the asset and is **comprised of**: 5322 s 38 TCGA 1992
- the cost of acquiring the asset;
- enhancement expenditure;
- expenditure incurred wholly and exclusively in connection with the title to the asset; and
- incidental costs.

Some types of expenditure are specifically excluded from allowable expenditure (¶5335).

MEMO POINTS If any of the costs are incurred in **currencies other than sterling** they must be converted at the rate prevailing on the date on which they are incurred.

Acquisition cost

The acquisition cost of the asset is simply the actual or deemed consideration paid by the vendor (or on his behalf) on the initial acquisition of the asset. Where an asset is inherited on death, its base cost will be the market value at the date of death (¶7264). 5324

Enhancement expenditure

Enhancement expenditure (incurred by the owner of the asset or on his behalf) will be **included in allowable expenditure if** it is: 5326
- incurred wholly and exclusively for the purposes of enhancing the asset; and
- reflected in the state or nature of the asset at the date of disposal.

Expenditure incurred on **initial repairs** to a property (including decoration) in order to put it into a fit state for letting will be allowed as enhancement expenditure, providing it was not given as a deduction in relation to a property trade.

EXAMPLE Mr A acquired a building in Year 1 for £180,000. 4 years later, he spent £25,000 in converting the loft into a flat. The conversion was made without planning permission and he therefore had to return the top floor to its original state. Shortly thereafter, the building was sold.
The enhancement expenditure is not reflected in the property at the date of sale, and therefore does not form part of the allowable cost.

Where the enhancement expenditure was **incurred before 31 March 1982**, no deduction will be available if the gain is calculated using the market value on 31 March 1982.

Title to an asset

5328 Expenditure incurred **wholly and exclusively** for the purposes of establishing title to an asset or defending or preserving the title to an asset or rights over it will constitute allowable expenditure provided the expenditure is incurred by the owner of the asset and not on his behalf (in contrast to enhancement and acquisition expenditure).

Incidental costs

5330 The incidental costs allowable on the acquisition and disposal of an asset **consist of the following** expenditure (where it is wholly and exclusively incurred for the sale or purchase (as appropriate)):
– fees, commission or remuneration paid for the professional services of any surveyor, valuer, auctioneer, accountant, agent or legal adviser;
– costs of transfer or conveyance (including stamp duty);
– advertising to find a seller/buyer;
– costs reasonably incurred in making any valuation or apportionment required for the purposes of computing the gain or loss, including expenses incurred in ascertaining market value where this is required by the legislation. Any fees for negotiating with the Valuation Office Agency or agreeing a value with a District Valuer are not allowable.

MEMO POINTS 1. Incidental costs of disposal incurred by a shareholder on a **company takeover** (¶5839) or reconstruction (¶5854) are treated as additional consideration paid for the new shares.
2. **Indexation allowance**, where applicable, is not applied to any incidental costs of disposal (they are simply deducted from the sale proceeds).

Assets held at 31 March 1982

5332 s 35 TCGA 1992 For individuals, trustees, and personal representatives, any assets held at 31 March 1982 are deemed to have been acquired on that date for their open market value. This is the case regardless of whether this value provides a higher base cost or not.
Where enhancement expenditure was incurred before that date, the asset's value will already reflect the costs incurred. If the expenditure is incurred after 31 March 1982 the expenditure will be allowed in calculating the gain (¶5326).

2. Excluded expenditure

5335 The following expenditure is **not included** as allowable expenditure:
s 39 TCGA 1992 – expenditure which would be allowable as a deduction in calculating income or corporation tax;
– contingent liabilities;
– discounts for postponement of receipt of consideration;
s 205 TCGA 1992 – insurance premiums paid to cover the risk of damage, loss or depreciation of the asset;
s 50 TCGA 1992 – expenditure reimbursed out of public funds (such as local authority housing grants); and
s 38(3) TCGA 1992 – interest. If this is paid by a company, it is dealt with under the loan relationship provisions (¶870).

CHAPTER 3

Capital gains tax losses

OUTLINE ¶¶

SECTION 1

Utilisation of losses

When a taxpayer incurs an allowable loss on the disposal of an asset, the **most common** ways to obtain relief are as follows: 5450
- set the loss against chargeable gains of the same tax year (¶5467); or
- carry it forward to utilise against chargeable gains in later periods (¶5470).

However, in certain circumstances capital losses may be:
- carried back and used against chargeable gains of the preceding 3 tax years (¶5476); or
- set against general income of the same and/or the preceding tax year, if they arise on trading company shares (¶5486).

MEMO POINTS It is also possible for **trading losses** to be used to relieve chargeable gains of the same and/or the preceding tax year (¶1273, ¶1274, ¶2484).

SECTION 2

Allowable losses

1. When does an allowable loss arise?

Disposal

5452 An allowable loss arises where, on the disposal of a chargeable asset, the allowable expenditure exceeds the disposal proceeds.

EXAMPLE Mr A purchased shares in B Plc in Year 1 for £150,000 which he sold in Year 3 for £120,000. Incidental costs associated with the acquisition were £1,100, and with the sale £1,000.

	£	£
Disposal proceeds		120,000
Incidental disposal costs		(1,000)
		119,000
Less: Allowable expenditure:		
Acquisition cost	150,000	
Incidental acquisition costs	1,100	
		(151,100)
Allowable loss		(32,100)

5453 Allowable losses may also arise in the following circumstances where a **disposal has not taken place**:
– where the value of an asset has become negligible (¶6025); or
– when a loan or guarantee made to a trader becomes irrecoverable (¶6008).

Residency

5454 As a **general rule** a loss will only be allowable if it accrues to a person who is either resident or ordinarily resident in the UK during any part of a year of assessment.

Where a loss arises to a non-resident person on an **asset used in connection with a UK trade**, and this asset would have been chargeable on its disposal if the person had been resident, the loss will still be available for general set-off.

s 10A TCGA 1992 Where losses arise after departure from the UK for a **period of temporary non-residence**, these will be allowable if they arose on assets which belonged to the individual prior to his departure (¶5227). Such losses are treated as if they arose in the year of assessment in which UK residence was resumed.

MEMO POINTS A loss arising on the disposal of an **asset situated outside the UK** will only be allowable if the person disposing of the asset is domiciled in the UK.

Domicile

5455 ss 16ZA - 16ZD TCGA 1992 Since 6 April 2008, individuals who are resident or ordinarily resident in the UK but **not domiciled** are taxed on gains on an arising basis unless a claim is made for the remittance basis to apply (¶4200). In the first year in which the **remittance basis is claimed**, an irrevocable election can be made. If **no election is made** within the usual time limits (¶5466) then no foreign losses arising in that or any later year will be allowed against gains, unless the individual becomes domiciled in the UK.

Where **an election has been made** then losses, wherever arising, are allocated against gains in the same year as follows:

a. foreign chargeable gains arising and remitted in the tax year;

b. foreign gains arising but not remitted to the UK in that year. If the losses do not extinguish the gains in total then they are allocated to gains on a last in, first out basis. Gains on the same day have losses allocated pro rata; and

c. all other chargeable gains arising in the year. This does not, however, include gains only taxed by virtue of being remitted in the year.

The losses allocated to a. and c. are then utilised in the year to reduce those gains. The losses allocated to foreign gains which are not remitted remain allocated to such gains (in order to reduce those, should they be taxed as remittances in the future).

A gain which is remitted in a year after the one in which it arises cannot be reduced further by losses accruing in the period between the year of the disposal and the time it is remitted.

EXAMPLE An individual is resident but not domiciled in the UK and makes the following disposals in 2010/11, having already made the election the previous year:
- a gain in the UK of £30,000;
- a loss in the UK of £8,000;
- a foreign gain arising in the year of £10,000; only £4,000 of this is remitted to the UK in the year; and
- a loss on a foreign asset of £2,000.

The total losses that can be allocated amount to £10,000 (£8,000 plus £2,000). These will first be offset against the £4,000 of remitted gains, with the balance of £6,000 being allocated to the unremitted gains of £6,000. The computation of gains for the year will be:

	£
UK gains	30,000
Remitted gains	4,000
Less allowable losses	(4,000)
Total gains chargeable	30,000

The unremitted gains of £6,000 are reduced by the remaining £6,000 of losses to be utilised when they are remitted. There will be no annual exemption available as the remittance basis has been claimed.

Non-allowable losses

A loss will not be allowable when it arises: 5458
- on the disposal of exempt assets;
- on the disposal of a debt acquired from a connected person (¶5570); or
- as a result of a value shifting transaction (¶5650).

MEMO POINTS **Anti-avoidance provisions** apply to prevent a loss being an allowable capital loss if it arises on disposals made on or after 6 December 2006, and: s 16A TCGA 1992
- the loss accrues as a result of any arrangements (i.e. any agreement, understanding, scheme or transaction); and
- the main purpose of the arrangements is to secure a corporation tax, income tax or capital gains tax advantage.

These provisions are aimed at certain disclosed transactions only and it is likely that most persons will not be affected by these provisions.

2. Restriction of losses

A loss may be restricted based on the type of asset that is being disposed of, or because of the people involved in the transaction. 5460

A loss on the disposal of a chattel (¶6150) may be restricted based on the rules applying specifically to chattels.

A loss incurred on a disposal to a **connected person** (¶5570) can only be relieved against chargeable gains arising from other disposals to that person. If the two parties are no longer connected then loss relief will not be available. If the parties subsequently become connected again, the losses will then become available for offset against future connected party gains. 5462 s 18 TCGA 1992

MEMO POINTS If the disposal is of an **option** to enter into a transaction with the vendor, loss relief will not be available if the person acquiring the option makes a loss on a subsequent disposal of it, unless the subsequent disposal is on arm's length terms to a person who is not connected with him.

Remittances from foreign currency bank accounts (FCBA)

5463 s 252A, Sch 8A TCGA 1992

Due to the way that remittances from foreign currency bank accounts (FCBA) are dealt with for **those on the remittance basis**, where the same sums, or part of them, are taxed as income, an anomaly can arise which results in a capital loss where no loss is actually incurred. This is due to the adjustment made to ensure that sums taxed as income are not taxed as capital (¶4203). To counter this, specific rules apply to remittances made after 16 December 2009.

5464 **Basic position** This will apply where **all of the funds in an FCBA are withdrawn** and the **entire amount is to be taxed as income**. As outlined below, it will also apply to any elements of any withdrawal which are to be taxed as income. In such a case, no allowable loss can occur as a result of the deduction of the income element from the withdrawal.

EXAMPLE Mr A placed US$50,000, as earnings from employment, on deposit in the US. At that time, the sterling equivalent was £25,000. He then remitted these funds to the UK some years later when he claimed the remittance basis. At that time the sterling equivalent was £40,000.
The computation for this would be:

	£
Gross consideration	40,000
Less amounts taxed as income	(40,000)
Net consideration	Nil
Allowable expenditure	(25,000)
Loss	(25,000)

This loss is not considered an allowable loss as it results from the adjustment.

5465 **Part and mixed disposals** Where the **withdrawal is only part of the account**, or where the **element which is to be taxed as income only forms part of the withdrawal**, the cost of the various elements has to be ascertained. Then, where other funds are also withdrawn, the transaction is treated as consisting of 2 separate parts – one of the income and one of the balance. The apportionment of the cost is based on the amounts retained, the amount taxed as income, and the amount of other funds remitted. The income element will then be treated as in the example above with no allowable loss accruing. The amount of any other funds being remitted will be treated as a normal capital gain, and the balance remaining in the account, if any, will have its base cost reduced accordingly.

EXAMPLE Mr B has an FCBA of US$200,000 with a cost of £160,000. He remits US$120,000 of this in a year in which he elects for the remittance basis, when the sterling equivalent is £120,000. Of this amount, US$20,000 is taxed as income (sterling equivalent £20,000).
The cost of each of these elements is calculated as follows:

Income element	20,000/200,000 x £160,000	£16,000
Other funds remitted	100,000/200,000 x £160,000	£80,000
Remaining funds in the FCBA	80,000/200,000 x £160,000	£64,000

The capital gains computations will be as follows:

Income element	£
Gross consideration	20,000
Less taxed as income	(20,000)
Net consideration	Nil
Less cost as above	(16,000)
Loss	(16,000)

None of this loss is allowable as it arises from the adjustment made.

Other funds element	£
Gross consideration	100,000
Less cost as above	(80,000)
Gain	20,000

The remaining funds of US$80,000 will retain a base cost of £64,000 for future disposals.

3. Notification

Capital gains tax losses are not allowable losses unless they are notified to HMRC as if they were a claim for relief. Where possible, notification should be made on the self-assessment return (or in an amendment to it), but in other cases notification will be accepted if it is made within 4 years from the end of the relevant year. 5466 s 16(2A) TCGA 1992

SECTION 3

Current year relief

For each year of assessment the **basic rule** is that the total allowable losses are deducted from the total chargeable gains arising in the year. Where the remittance basis applies and an election has been made the situation is more complicated (¶5455). 5467

With the introduction of the **higher rate** of CGT (¶6330), losses can effectively be used at different rates. The legislation allows losses to be offset in the way that is most advantageous for the taxpayer. However, where a disposal would have attracted **entrepreneurs' relief** (¶6035) if it had resulted in a gain, the loss must be deducted from the gains eligible first. ss 4B, 169N(1) TCGA 1992

The **exception** to the basic rule is that personal losses cannot be set off against any gains attributed to a beneficiary of a non-UK resident settlement (¶7618). 5468 ss 86, 87 TCGA 1992

SECTION 4

Losses carried forward

General rules

When allowable losses exceed current year gains, the general rule is that the excess will be carried forward and set against gains in later years. There is no limit to the number of years for which a loss may be carried forward, but the loss **must be set against** the first available gains. Losses from 1996/97 and later tax years must be utilised before losses of 1995/96 and earlier tax years. (For companies, losses from accounting periods ending after 30 June 1999 must be utilised before losses relating to earlier accounting periods). 5470 s 2(2)(b) TCGA 1992; s 113 FA 1995

The **maximum** amount of brought forward losses that can be set against gains in any tax year is **restricted** to the amount required to reduce the chargeable gains to an amount equal to the annual exempt amount. 5472 s 3(5A) TCGA 1992

EXAMPLE In 2010/11 Mr A made a gain of £35,000 and an allowable loss of £7,500.
Mr A had brought forward losses from 1995/96 and before of £10,000, and from 1996/97 and later of £14,000.

The amount chargeable to capital gains tax will be:

	£
Current year gains	35,000
Less: Allowable losses	(7,500)
	27,500
Less: Brought forward losses (restricted to preserve exempt amount)	(17,400)
Gain	10,100
Less: Annual exempt amount	(10,100)
Chargeable to tax	Nil

	£
Loss memorandum:	
Loss b/fwd from 1996/97 and later	14,000
Utilised in 2010/11	(14,000)
Loss b/fwd from 1995/96 and before	10,000
Loss utilised in 2010/11	(3,400)
Loss carried forward	6,600

Attributed gains

5474 Where the taxpayer is a beneficiary of a non-UK resident settlement and has attributed gains from the settlement (¶7620) personal losses cannot reduce the attributed gains.

SECTION 5

Losses carried back

When is this possible?

5476 The only situations in which capital gains tax losses can be carried back are:
- the **death** of the taxpayer; or
- the disposal of a right to future **unascertainable consideration**.

Death of taxpayer

5478 s 62 TCGA 1992 Capital gains tax losses accruing in the year of death (but not brought forward losses) can be carried back and set against chargeable gains arising in the 3 years before the year of death. Although the legislation is not explicit on this issue, it is understood that losses carried back are deducted from chargeable gains after brought forward losses.

5480 The **maximum** amount of losses on death which can be set against gains of an earlier tax year is **restricted** to the amount required to reduce the chargeable gains to the level of the annual exempt amount. Where the chargeable gains for a year of assessment are already less than the annual exempt amount, no carried back losses may be utilised.

EXAMPLE Mr A died in 2010/11 having made an allowable loss of £15,000. Gains and losses for earlier years are as follows:
2007/08 – Gain £14,000
2008/09 – Loss £12,000
2009/10 – Gain £25,300

The loss carried back will be set against 2009/10 first:

2009/10:	£	£
Chargeable gains		25,300
Less: Losses (restricted to preserve exempt amount)		
Brought forward (from 2008/09)	12,000	
Carried back (from 2010/11)	3,200	
		(15,200)
Gain		10,100

2007/08:		£
Chargeable gains		14,000
Less: Losses carried back from 2010/11 (restricted to preserve exempt amount)		(4,800)
Gain before taper relief		9,200
Loss Memorandum:		
2008/09 Loss carried forward	12,000	
Utilised in 2009/10	(12,000)	
	Nil	
2010/11 Loss carried back	15,000	
Utilised 2009/10	(3,200)	
Utilised 2007/08	(4,800)	
Unutilised losses	7,000	

Unascertainable deferred consideration

On the disposal of a right to receive unascertainable deferred consideration (¶5310) a loss may be realised in a tax year after the disposal of the original asset. This provision is not available for companies. **5482** s 279A-D TCGA 1992

Such a loss can, after the making of an irrevocable election, be set against the chargeable gain accruing on the disposal of the original asset (after all other capital losses have been deducted from the gain). Any losses remaining are carried forward in the usual manner (¶5470), provided that: **5484**

a. the right to the unascertainable consideration was:
- not acquired second-hand;
- acquired as consideration for the disposal of another asset (the "original asset") which was disposed of in an earlier tax year (but no earlier than 1992/93);

b. a chargeable gain accrued on the disposal of the original asset. This condition will be met even if the chargeable gain is postponed by, for example, being reinvested under the Enterprise Investment Scheme (¶6200); and

c. the taxpayer is within the charge to capital gains tax in the tax year in which the loss is realised. If the taxpayer is temporarily absent from the UK (¶5227) when he disposes of the right, the loss will be treated as accruing in the tax year of his return.

EXAMPLE

1. In May 2009, A disposes of an original asset for £200,000, together with a right to receive a further cash lump sum dependent upon future events (i.e. a right to unascertainable deferred consideration) valued at £50,000. In July 2011, A disposes of this right for £40,000. The capital gains position is:

	Gain/ (loss)
2009/10:	**£**
Disposal proceeds (£200,000 plus £50,000)	250,000
Less:	
Allowable expenditure (say)	(150,000)
Capital gain	100,000
2011/12:	
Disposal proceeds	40,000
Less:	
Allowable expenditure	(50,000)
Loss	(10,000)

A elects to treat the £10,000 loss as accruing in 2009/10, reducing the capital gain for that year to £90,000. Any tax overpaid as a result of the election will be repaid.

2. B's capital gain position for 2001/02 has been agreed at:

	Gain/ (loss) £
Disposal of original asset	58,000
Less:	
Allowable current year losses	(12,000)
Allowable losses brought forward	(33,000)
	13,000
Less:	
Annual exemption	(7,500)
Net chargeable gains	5,500

In 2010/11, B disposes of a right to unascertainable consideration which he received on the disposal of the original asset in 2001/02. He realises a loss of £15,000 on this disposal and elects for the loss to be treated as accruing in 2001/02. The revised capital gain position for 2001/02 will be:

	Gain/ (loss) £
Disposal of original asset	58,000
Less:	
Allowable current year losses	(12,000)
Allowable losses brought forward	(33,000)
	13,000
Less:	
Loss carried back (restricted)	(13,000)
Net chargeable gains	Nil

The current year and brought forward losses must be set off in priority to the £15,000 loss carried back. The remaining £2,000 will be carried forward in the usual manner (¶5470).

3. C sells a piece of land in 3 tranches, receiving cash consideration and, in 2002/03, a right to unascertainable consideration. The capital gains position (ignoring indexation and taper relief) is as follows:

	Gain/ (loss) £
2001/02:	
Disposal of original asset	100,000
Less:	
Annual exemption	(7,500)
Capital gain	92,500
2002/03:	
Disposal of original asset	250,000
Less:	
Allowable current year losses	(225,000)
	25,000
Less:	
Annual exemption	(7,700)
Capital gain	17,300
2003/04:	
Disposal of original asset	75,000
Less:	
Annual exemption	(7,900)
Capital gain	67,100

In 2010/11 C disposes of the right to unascertainable consideration, realising an allowable loss of £40,000. She elects for this loss to be set against the gain realised in 2002/03. It cannot be set against the 2001/02 gain as the right was only conferred in 2002/03. The revised capital gains position is as follows:

	Gain/ (loss)
2002/03:	£
Disposal of original asset	250,000
Less:	
Allowable current year losses	(225,000)
	25,000
Less:	
Loss carried back (restricted)	(25,000)
Capital gain	Nil
2003/04:	
Disposal of original asset	75,000
Less:	
Loss carried back (balance)	(15,000)
	60,000
Less:	
Annual exemption	(7,900)
Capital gain	52,100

The loss on the disposal of the unascertainable consideration can be carried forward to a later year because:
- C had made a disposal of the original asset in 2002/03;
- C is liable to capital gains tax in 2003/04; and
- the losses brought forward will not reduce C's liability below the level of the annual exemption.

4. D disposes of an original asset in 1999/00 realising a chargeable gain of £100,000. He postpones this gain under the EIS provisions, but in 2002/03 goes abroad and ceases to be UK resident. This triggers the postponed gain and he is chargeable to capital gains tax of £100,000 in 2002/03. In 2008/09, whilst still abroad, D disposes of the right to unascertainable consideration (conferred on the disposal of the original asset in 1999/00), realising a loss of £15,000. In 2010/11, D returns to the UK. Under the rules of temporary non-residence, the 2008/09 loss is treated as accruing in 2010/11. D can therefore elect for this loss to be set against the gain which became chargeable in 2002/03.

SECTION 6

Losses on trading company shares

Offset against general income

An individual who sustains a loss on the disposal of certain shares which were acquired by **subscription**, (whether as a sole subscriber, joint owner, or nominee) may set the loss against general income (as opposed to chargeable gains) of the same or the preceding year. **5486** ss 131, 132 ITA 2007

The claim can **only be made for**:
- shares which qualify for EIS relief (¶2861); or
- ordinary shares in a qualifying trading company.

A **claim** must be submitted within 12 months from 31 January following the year of assessment in which the loss arose.

MEMO POINTS 1. The capital **loss must arise** in one of the following circumstances:
- on an arm's length sale;
- as a result of a negligible value claim (¶6025);
- as a capital distribution on a winding-up; or
- following the loss, dissolution or extinction of the asset.

2. There is no need for the shares to be acquired by **subscription** if they are transferred between spouses/civil partners. In this situation, they may be included in a loss relief claim if the spouse/civil partner acquired them by subscription.

3. HMRC historically took the view that the relief was only available where an individual personally subscribed for shares as a sole subscriber. Where a self-assessment return has been submitted but is still within the time limit for amendment, it may be amended to reflect this change of view. Moreover, where there is an open enquiry into any existing claim to the relief, such a claim can be settled in accordance with HMRC's revised opinion.
4. See ¶2132 for details of a **similar relief available to investment companies**.

Qualifying trading company

5488 ss 134, 135, 137-143 ITA 2007

A qualifying trading company is **defined** as any unquoted company which:
1. For a continuous period of 6 years, ending with the date of sale of the shares, either:
a. meets both of the following conditions:
– it exists wholly for the purposes of carrying on one or more qualifying trades (¶2873), or is a parent company of a trading group whose activities do not wholly or substantially consist of non-qualifying activities (¶2873) or non-trading activities; and
– it does not control, or have any arrangements in place to control, subsidiaries which are not qualifying subsidiaries; or
b. has ceased to meet the requirements at **a**. above not more than 3 years before the date of sale, and has not subsequently been an excluded company or an investment company; and
2. Satisfies the gross assets requirement.

MEMO POINTS 1. If a company has met the conditions in 1. above for a period which is **shorter than 6 years**, it will still qualify if it has never been an excluded company or an investment company.
2. A **trading group** is made up of a company plus its qualifying 51% and 90% subsidiaries (¶2873). For the purpose of this definition, where a subsidiary is an excluded company or is not resident in the UK, its activity is not treated as a trade.
3. An **excluded company** is:
– one whose trade consists wholly or mainly of dealing in shares, securities, land or commodity futures;
– one whose trade is not carried out on a commercial basis and in such a way that profits can reasonably be expected to be realised; or
– a holding company of a non-trading group, building society or registered industrial and provident society.
4. An **investment company** is one:
– whose business consists wholly or mainly of making investments; and
– the main part of whose income is derived from those investments.
For the purpose of these provisions a holding company of a trading group is not treated as an investment company.
5. A company satisfies the **gross assets requirement** if:
– immediately before the share issue, gross assets do not exceed £7 million; and
– immediately after the issue they do not exceed £8 million.
Gross assets are the assets of the company (or group, where appropriate, ignoring intra-group holdings and obligations) calculated as the aggregate of the assets which would be shown on a balance sheet prepared to that date, without any deduction for liabilities.

5490 s 136 ITA 2007

On a **reorganisation** of share capital, new shares may be acquired in exchange for the original holding, and the general rule for capital gains tax purposes is that a disposal will not arise in these cases.

If the **new shares are later sold**, loss relief may be available if either:
– at the date of the reorganisation the old shares met all of the conditions outlined in ¶5488; or
– the new shares were acquired for new consideration. In this case, loss relief will be restricted to the amount of that consideration used in the computation of the disposal of the new shares.

MEMO POINTS 1. This provision does not apply to shares which are eligible for **EIS relief**.
2. If the reorganisation/amalgamation takes place other than for bona fide commercial reasons and forms part of a **tax avoidance scheme**, a disposal will be deemed to arise. Any loss arising as a result will not be relievable under these provisions.

Utilisation of losses

The amount of the loss available for relief is calculated in accordance with normal capital gains tax rules. **5492** s 133 ITA 2007

Loss relief may be **claimed against** the net income (¶4360) of: **5494**
- the year of assessment in which the loss arises; and/or
- the preceding year.

The individual may choose which year to relieve the losses against first, but the income of the year which is the subject of the initial claim must be exhausted (even if the result is that personal allowances are lost) before the balance can be set against the other year.

Where **current year losses** are claimed in the same year as losses brought back from the following year, the current year losses will be relieved in priority. Similarly, losses on trading company shares will be relieved in priority to trading losses. s 133(4) ITA 2007

Relief is given by deducting the loss from the net income of the individual before personal allowances are deducted. **5496**

EXAMPLE Mr A has been trading for many years and has the following adjusted results:

Year 1	£14,000
Year 2	£18,000

His other income for the years in question was as follows:

	Salary £	Savings £
Year 1	4,500	1,500
Year 2	5,100	1,750

During Year 2 Mr A made a loss on the sale of ordinary shares in a trading company amounting to £27,500. One option for loss relief will be as follows:

	Year 1 £	Year 2 £
Income from trade	14,000	18,000
Income from employment	4,500	5,100
Earned income	18,500	23,100
Savings (gross)	1,500	1,750
Net income	20,000	24,850
Loss relief: Year 1		(24,850)
Year 2	(2,650)	
	17,350	Nil

CHAPTER 4

Specific types of disposal

OUTLINE ¶¶

SECTION 1

What is a disposal?

Definition

The term disposal is not defined by the legislation, and therefore retains its everyday meaning. The **most common** form of disposal is a change in the ownership of an asset as a result of sale, exchange or gift. **Other forms** of disposal include: 5500
a. the disposal of part of an asset;
b. capital sums received:
– as compensation for damage or destruction;

– in return for surrendering rights or refraining from exercising rights; or
– as consideration for the use or exploitation of assets;
c. the entire loss, destruction, dissipation or extinction of an asset, irrespective of whether a capital sum is received as compensation or insurance;
d. a beneficiary becoming absolutely entitled as against the trustees to settled property (¶7414); and
e. on the making of a negligible value claim (¶6025).

Date of disposal

5502 The date of disposal is **generally** taken to be the date when contracts are made, although there are a number of exceptions:

Transaction	Date of disposal
Any disposal not listed below	Date contract is made
Gifts	The date on which the donor has done everything possible to transfer the asset
Receipt of a capital sum (e.g. insurance money)	The date on which the capital sum is received
Conditional contracts	The date on which the condition is fulfilled
Hire purchase	The date on which use or enjoyment of asset is received
Value of asset becomes negligible	The date of the taxpayer claim unless an earlier time is specified
Compulsory land purchase orders	The date the compensation is agreed (or otherwise determined i.e. by arbitration)
Entire loss or destruction of an asset	The date when the loss or destruction takes place

MEMO POINTS The **disposal proceeds** used in the computation will either be the actual consideration received or the market value. See ¶5302+ for details.

SECTION 2

Part disposals

5508 A part disposal arises where:
s 21(2) TCGA 1992
– part of an asset is retained following disposal; or
– an interest or right is granted over an asset.

MEMO POINTS Special provisions apply to **small part disposals of land** (¶5682).

5510 The chargeable gain or allowable loss arising on a part disposal is **calculated** in accordance with the normal rules (¶5240 onwards) but the allowable expenditure (and 31 March 1982 value) must be apportioned between the part disposed of and the part retained.

Expenditure which relates directly to one of the parts will be allocated to that part. For example, costs relating to the part disposal itself will be allocated to the part disposed of.

Expenditure which relates to the asset as a whole will be apportioned between the two parts using the following formula:

$$\frac{A}{A + B}$$

where:
– A is the disposal proceeds of the part disposed of; and
– B is the market value of the part retained.

On a **subsequent disposal** of all or part of the remaining asset, the allowable expenditure will be reduced by the part allocated to the earlier disposal. **5512**

EXAMPLE Mr A bought a set of eight antique chairs in January 2007 for £40,000. He sold six of them in an arm's length transaction in May 2010 for £45,000 and kept the remaining two for which a value of £10,000 was agreed. The chargeable gain on the part disposal will be calculated as follows:

	£
Disposal proceeds	45,000
Less: Allowable expenditure	
$\frac{45,000}{45,000 + 10,000} \times 40,000$	(32,727)
Chargeable gain	12,273

In an unconnected transaction Mr A sells the two remaining chairs in May 2011 for £27,500. The chargeable gain on the disposal will be calculated as follows:

	£
Disposal proceeds	27,500
Less: Allowable expenditure	
(40,000 – 32,727)	(7,273)
Gain	20,227

Note:
The above calculation is the same for companies, with the exception that indexation allowance is available.

SECTION 3

Capital sums derived from assets

A. General rules

A **disposal is deemed to arise where** a capital sum (whether in money or money's worth) is received in respect of an asset: **5514** s 22(1) TCGA 1992
– as compensation for damage, loss or destruction (including payments received from insurance policies);
– under a right to receive future unquantified consideration (which was granted on the earlier disposal of the asset (¶5310));
– in return for surrendering rights over an asset or for refraining from exercising rights; or
– as consideration for the use or exploitation of assets.

The **recipient must be** the beneficial owner of the asset, and the capital sum must be derived from that ownership. It is not necessary for the person paying the capital sum to actually acquire an asset.

MEMO POINTS 1. The following types of capital sum are **excluded** from the general rules: ss 51, 249 TCGA 1992
– compensation or damages for any wrong or injury suffered by an individual in a personal or professional capacity;
– winnings from betting, lotteries, or games with prizes; and
– grants for giving up occupation of uncommercial agricultural land.
2. The date of disposal is the date on which the capital sum is received.

B. Compensation receipts

1. What type of treatment?

5516 s 24(1), (3) TCGA 1992 The treatment of compensation receipts **differs depending upon** whether the asset concerned is either:
- lost or destroyed; or
- damaged.

In both situations, **relief may be available** where:
- the capital sum is used to replace or restore the asset; or
- the amount of the capital sum received is small.

The type of relief will depend on the amount of the capital sum received and the extent to which it is used to replace or restore the asset.

2. Lost or destroyed assets

Disposal proceeds

5518 Where a capital sum such as compensation, or a payment under an insurance policy, is received for an asset which has been lost or destroyed, the capital sum received will be treated as disposal proceeds.

MEMO POINTS 1. If **compensation is not received** for the asset, the disposal proceeds will be equal to any salvage money received. The resulting loss will be allowable for offset against chargeable gains.

EXAMPLE A Ltd owned an antique desk which cost £10,000 to purchase. The desk, which was uninsured, was destroyed by fire. No salvage monies were received. An allowable loss of £10,000 arises on the deemed disposal.

2. **Land and buildings** may be treated as separate assets for these purposes. This means that if a building is completely destroyed (and therefore the subject of a deemed disposal) the related land is treated as if it were sold and immediately reacquired at market value.

Capital sum used to acquire a replacement asset

5520 s 23(4) TCGA 1992 If, within a year from receipt, the whole of the capital sum is used to acquire an asset to replace the one which was lost or destroyed, the taxpayer **may elect that a chargeable gain will not arise**.

The term replacement asset is not defined by the legislation, but HMRC are understood to interpret the term as meaning an asset which is of a similar type and function to the original asset.

5522 On submission of the appropriate claim, the **disposal proceeds** of the original asset are deemed to be such that neither a gain nor a loss arises.

The **allowable cost** of the replacement asset is then reduced to take account of the difference between:
- the capital sum received plus any residual or scrap value of the original asset; and
- the deemed disposal proceeds of the original asset.

Capital sum partly used to acquire a replacement asset

5526 s 23(5) TCGA 1992 If the capital sum received on the loss or destruction of an asset is not all used to acquire a replacement asset then relief is still available.

On submission of a claim, the amount of:
- the **gain** is restricted to the amount of the capital sum that was not used to acquire the replacement asset; and
- the **allowable cost** of the new asset is reduced by the difference between the original gain and the restricted gain.

EXAMPLE

1. Mr A bought an antique vase in December 1996 for £10,000. The vase was stolen in March 2010 and Mr A received insurance money of £18,000 in September 2010. In December 2010 Mr A bought a similar vase for £15,000.
Assuming a claim for relief was made:
- the chargeable gain will be restricted to the amount not used to acquire the replacement asset i.e. £3,000; and
- the allowable cost of the replacement asset will be:

	£	£
Actual cost		15,000
Less: Chargeable gain on original asset (see 2. below)	8,000	
Capital sum not used to acquire replacement asset	(3,000)	
		(5,000)
Allowable cost		10,000

2. Using the same facts as for 1. above, but no claim was made. The chargeable gain on receipt of the compensation is:

		£
Disposal proceeds		18,000
Less: Allowable expenditure		(10,000)
Gain		8,000

Note:
The above calculations are the same for companies, with the exception that indexation allowance is available to the date of disposal.

3. Damaged assets

Disposal proceeds

In **general**, where a capital sum is received as a result of damage to an asset, it is treated as a part disposal, provided the asset is still in existence and has not been disposed of by the taxpayer. **5528**
The chargeable gain is calculated in accordance with the normal part disposal rules (¶5508), using the following formula to calculate the allowable expenditure:

$$\frac{A}{A + B}$$

where:
- A is the capital sum received; and
- B is the market value of the asset at the date of receipt of the capital sum.

MEMO POINTS If expenditure has been incurred on **restoration of the damaged asset** before the receipt of the capital sum, it will be treated as enhancement expenditure (¶5326) and will be apportioned using the part disposal formula described above.

EXAMPLE A Ltd purchased a sculpture in June 1997 for £38,000. The sculpture was vandalised in August 2002, and in December 2002 the company incurred restoration costs of £5,000. A Ltd received compensation in March 2011 of £6,000, when the sculpture was valued at £62,000.

The chargeable gain on receipt of the compensation would be:

	£	£
Disposal proceeds		6,000
Less: Allowable expenditure		
$\frac{6,000}{6,000 + 62,000} \times 38,000$	3,352	
Indexation allowance Jun 97 to Mar 11		
$\frac{232.5 - 157.5}{157.5} = 0.476 \times 3,352$	1,596	
		(4,948)
Restoration expenditure		
$\frac{6,000}{6,000 + 62,000} \times 5,000$	441	
Indexation allowance Dec 02 to Mar 11		
$\frac{232.5 - 178.5}{178.5} = 0.303 \times 441$	134	
		(575)
Chargeable gain		477

Note:
The above calculation is the same for individuals, with the exception of the indexation allowance.

5530 The **general rule is modified** if:
a. all of the capital sum is used to restore the asset (¶5532);
b. part of the capital sum is used to restore the asset (¶5534) and the part that is not used is:
– not reasonably required for restoration; and
– small when compared to the value of the asset; or
c. the capital sum exceeds the allowable cost of the asset (¶5536).

RI 164 MEMO POINTS 1. **Small** is not defined by the legislation but for these purposes it is generally understood to mean:
– 5% or less of the value of the asset; or
– £3,000 or less (whether or not this is within the 5% limit).
2. Where the asset concerned is a **wasting asset** (¶5922), relief will only be available where the whole amount of the capital sum is used in the restoration.

Capital sum used to restore the asset

5532 s 23(1) TCGA 1992 If all of the capital sum received is used to restore the asset, then provided the **appropriate claim** is made, a part disposal will not be deemed to take place and instead the capital sum which would have been treated as disposal proceeds will be deducted from the allowable cost of the asset.

Part of capital sum used to restore the asset

5534 s 23(3) TCGA 1992 Where only part of the capital sum is applied in restoring the asset, and the **unused part** is:
– not reasonably required for restoration; and
– small when compared to the value of the asset,

the taxpayer may claim to treat the unused part as the consideration for a part disposal. In this case, the part disposal formula is applied to both cost (or 31 March 1982 value) and restoration expenses, but is amended as follows:

$$\frac{A}{A + B}$$

where:
– A is the unused part of the capital sum; and
– B is the restored value of the asset.

The part of the capital sum which is used in restoration is deducted from the allowable cost as described in ¶5532.

EXAMPLE Mr A bought a diamond necklace in March 1985 for £30,000. In October 1995 the necklace was damaged and Mr A spent £6,250 on restoration in January 1996. He received insurance money of £16,750 in March 1996 when the restored value of the necklace was £45,000. Mr A sold the necklace in May 2011 for £50,000.
The chargeable gains are calculated as follows:

Part disposal on receipt of capital sum (March 1996):	£	£
Disposal proceeds (16,750 – 6,250)		10,500
Less: Allowable expenditure		
$\frac{10,500}{10,500 + 45,000} \times 30,000$	5,675	
Indexation allowance Mar 1985 to Mar 1996		
$\frac{151.5 - 92.80}{92.80} = 0.633 \times 5,675$	3,592	
		(9,267)
Restoration expenditure		
$\frac{10,500}{10,500 + 45,000} \times 6,250$	1,182	
Indexation allowance Jan 1996 to Mar 1996		
$\frac{151.5 - 150.2}{150.2} = 0.009 \times 1,182$	11	
		(1,193)
Chargeable gain		40
Gain on subsequent disposal (May 2011):		
Disposal proceeds		50,000
Less: Allowable expenditure		
Balance of cost (30,000 – 5,675)	24,325	
Balance of restoration expenditure (6,250 – 1,182)	5,068	
	29,393	
Less: Capital sum used in restoration	(6,250)	
		(23,143)
Gain		26,857

Note:
The above calculation is the same for companies, with the exception that indexation allowance is available on the second disposal.

MEMO POINTS Where the asset concerned is a **wasting asset**, the allowable cost is restricted in accordance with the wasting asset rules (¶5922).

Capital sum exceeds allowable cost of the asset

All of capital sum used to restore asset If the capital sum received exceeds the allowable cost of the asset then relief will only be available if the entire capital sum is used in restoration (¶5532). **5536** s 23(2) TCGA 1992

Part of capital sum used to restore the asset Where part of the capital sum is used and the unused part qualifies as small, or where the capital sum itself qualifies as small (¶5530), the taxpayer may claim to treat the whole of the capital sum as disposal proceeds, and the entire allowable cost will be set against it. The allowable cost available for use against subsequent disposals will therefore be reduced to nil. **5538**

EXAMPLE Mr A bought a painting in June 1990 for £2,000. In May 1996 the painting was damaged and Mr A spent £22,500 on restoration in August 1996. He received insurance money of £25,000 in December 1996. Mr A sold the painting in July 2011 for £75,000.

The chargeable gains are calculated as follows:

	£	£
Gain on receipt of capital sum:		
Disposal proceeds		25,000
Less: Allowable expenditure:		
Original cost		(2,000)
Restoration expenditure		(22,500)
Gain		500
Gain on subsequent disposal:		
Disposal proceeds		75,000
Less: Allowable cost		-
Gain		75,000

Note:
The above calculation is the same for companies, with the exception that indexation allowance is available to the date of disposal.

MEMO POINTS This relief is **not available for wasting assets**.

SECTION 4

No gain/no loss disposals

5550 No gain/no loss disposals arise not because of the type of asset, but because of the relationship between the parties involved in the transaction. This means that although neither a chargeable gain nor allowable loss is generated in connection with the current disposal, later disposals of the same asset may be subject to capital gains tax.

The new owner of the asset will therefore be treated as if he acquired it for a consideration equal to the allowable expenditure on the asset.

EXAMPLE Asset A was acquired by Mr A in May 1995 at a cost of £10,000. A no gain/no loss disposal took place in June 2010 to Mrs A. On a subsequent disposal by Mrs A, her acquisition cost (i.e. her allowable expenditure) will be Mr A's original acquisition cost plus indexation to 5 April 1998.

	£
Mr A's acquisition cost	10,000
Indexation allowance May 1995 to Apr 1998	
$\frac{162.6 - 149.6}{149.6} = 0.087 \times 10{,}000$	870
Mrs A's allowable expenditure on a subsequent disposal	10,870

Note:
The above calculation is the same for companies, with the exception that indexation allowance is available to the date of the no gain/no loss disposal.

MEMO POINTS 1. As **indexation** was frozen for individuals, trustees and personal representatives from 6 April 1998, indexation will only be available to the earlier of the:
– date of the no gain/no loss disposal; or
– 5 April 1998.
The accrued indexation from such a transaction remains as part of the base cost for a disposal after 5 April 2008 for the transferee.
2. A person who acquires an asset **after 31 March 1982** in a no gain/no loss transaction will be treated, for rebasing purposes, as if they held the asset on 31 March 1982 providing:
– the asset was originally acquired before 31 March 1982; and
– all of the disposals of the asset between 31 March 1982 and the date of disposal were also no gain/no loss transactions.

5552 The most common example of a no gain/no loss disposal is a **transaction between spouses/civil partners** but the following would also fall under the no gain/no loss provisions:
– **deemed disposals of settled property** which revert to the settlor on the death of the person entitled;

- **changes in partnership asset sharing ratios** without adjustments through the accounts;
- a **charity** becoming absolutely entitled to settled property;
- certain **gifts** (¶5564); or
- transfers to a **harbour authority**.

MEMO POINTS A no gain/no loss transfer must not be confused with a **disposal giving rise to neither a gain nor a loss** (for example, the deemed disposal on March 1982 rebasing). In a disposal giving rise to neither a gain nor a loss, the transferor's allowable expenditure is deemed to be that which results in neither a gain nor a loss. The transferee is therefore not affected and his acquisition cost is the actual consideration.

Disposals of assets acquired as no gain/no loss transactions

For assets acquired in a way where no rebasing occurred at the time of the no gain/no loss transaction, then, for the purposes of ascertaining the allowable cost on a **disposal after 5 April 2008**, the asset will be revalued at 31 March 1982. This, together with the recalculated indexation allowance to the date the person received the asset, will form the cost on the further disposal. **5554** s 35A TCGA 1992; CGM 17402

SECTION 5

Gifts

Disposal value

The **general rule** is that where assets are disposed of by way of a gift (i.e. for little or no consideration), the disposal, and the connected acquisition, are deemed to take place for a consideration equal to the market value of the asset. Once the market value has been established, the disposal is treated like any other, and will be eligible for the usual capital gains tax exemptions and reliefs. **5560** s 17 TCGA 1992

MEMO POINTS The **donor is liable for any capital gains tax arising** on a gift, but if this is not paid within 12 months of the due date, an assessment can be made (within 2 years of the date on which the tax becomes payable) to recover the tax from the donee. The donee can subsequently recover this tax from the donor. s 282 TCGA 1992

Exempt gifts

Gifts made in contemplation of the approach of death (donatio mortis causa) are exempt from capital gains tax, and the recipient is treated as if he had acquired the asset as a legatee on the death of the donor (¶5592). **5562**

Reliefs

Certain reliefs and/or special treatments are available for the following types of gifts: **5564**

Type of gift	Relief/treatment	Reference	¶¶
Business assets	Gift holdover relief	s 165 TCGA 1992	¶6100
Unlisted shares in trading companies			¶6102
Agricultural property		Sch 7 para 1 TCGA 1992	¶6104
On which inheritance tax is chargeable		s 260 TCGA 1992	¶6106
Which is exempt from inheritance tax			¶6108
To charities	Treated as if acquired for no gain/no loss	s 257 TCGA 1992	¶5550
To employee trusts		s 239 TCGA 1992	
To housing associations		s 259 TCGA 1992	

MEMO POINTS For gifts of **land and buildings to a charity**, the charity needs to provide the donor with a certificate containing:
– a description of the qualifying interest in the land;
– the date of disposal; and
– a statement that the charity has acquired the interest in the land.
For relief from capital gains tax to be obtained, the **whole ownership of the property** must be transferred to the charity.

SECTION 6

Connected persons

Definition

5570 s 286 TCGA 1992 Many capital gains tax provisions apply special rules for disposals made to connected persons.

An **individual** is connected with:
– his spouse/civil partner;
– his relatives (brother, sister, ancestor or lineal descendant);
– a relative's spouse/civil partner (or the spouse/civil partner of a relative of his own spouse/civil partner);
– any person with whom he is in partnership;
– a partner's spouse/civil partner; and
– a partner's relatives.

MEMO POINTS 1. **Spouses/civil partners** remain connected despite the issue of a decree nisi, until such time as a decree absolute is issued.
2. If the only connection is by reason of **partnership**, bona fide commercial transactions for acquisitions or disposals of partnership assets will not be treated as being carried out by connected persons.

5571 A **trustee** is connected with:
– any individual who is a settlor of the settlement;
– any person who is connected with such an individual; and
– any company which is connected with the settlement.

The trustees of a **sub-fund settlement** (¶7206) are connected with the trustees of the principal settlement, and with the trustees of other sub-funds of that principal settlement.

5572 A **company** may be connected with either a person or another company, depending on who has control of the company.

A company is connected with any person who has control of that company.

EXAMPLE Mr A owns 100% of A Ltd. A Ltd is therefore connected with Mr A as he has control of the company.

A company is connected with a person if that person, acting alone or with persons connected with him, has control of it.

EXAMPLE Mr A owns 40% of A Ltd and his three children, B, C and D, each own 20%.
Mr A is connected with his children, and the company is therefore controlled by Mr A and persons connected with him. The company is therefore connected with Mr A and with each of his children.

A company is connected with another company if the same person controls both companies.

EXAMPLE Mr A owns 100% of the shares in A Ltd and B Ltd.
As the same person controls the companies, A Ltd and B Ltd are connected.

A company is connected with another company if one is controlled by a person and the other is controlled by persons connected with that person.

EXAMPLE Mr A owns 100% of the shares in A Ltd, and his son, Mr B owns 100% of the shares in B Ltd.
As Mr A and Mr B are connected, the companies are also connected with each other.

A company is connected with another company if one is controlled by a person who, together with persons connected with him, controls the other.

EXAMPLE Mr A owns 100% of the shares in A Ltd, and 40% of B Ltd. The remaining shares in B Ltd are owned by his three children.
As Mr A is connected with his children, he, together with persons connected with him, control both companies and therefore A Ltd and B Ltd are connected.

A company is connected with another company if the same group of persons controls both.

EXAMPLE Four friends, Mr A, Mr B, Mr C and Mr D, each own 25% of the shares in A Ltd and B Ltd.
Both companies are controlled by the same group of persons and therefore A Ltd and B Ltd are connected.

A company is connected with another company if each company is controlled by a separate group of persons but each group could be the same if the actual members were replaced by connected persons.

EXAMPLE Mr A, Mr B, Mr C and Mr D each own 25% of the shares in A Ltd.
Mrs A, B's sister, C's son and D's father each own 25% of B Ltd.
Substituting a connected person for each of the shareholders in B Ltd produces the same group as the holders of A Ltd. A Ltd and B Ltd are therefore connected.

Disposal value

In **general**, consideration for a transaction between connected persons is deemed to be the open market value. This amount will be used to calculate the chargeable gain arising on the transfer, and will represent the base cost for the subsequent sale of the asset. **5574** s 18 TCGA 1992

Where a disposal to a connected person gives rise to an **allowable loss**, that loss may only be offset against chargeable gains arising in the same or later tax years on disposals to the same connected person (¶5462).

Special rules apply for transactions between spouses/civil partners (¶5575).

MEMO POINTS There will be no liability to capital gains tax where there is a **transfer on divorce** of all or part of the rights under a: RI 267
- life assurance policy;
- life annuity contract; or
- capital redemption policy.

Spouses/civil partners

In **general**, the transfer of assets between spouses/civil partners is made on a no gain/no loss basis with both parties being treated in exactly the same way, in the following situations: **5575**
- where the spouses/civil partners are living together;
- in the part of the year following marriage; or
- in the whole of the year of separation.

The **exceptions** to this rule are as follows:
- where, until the date of disposal, the asset formed part of the **trading stock** of a trade carried on by the transferor spouse/civil partner (or was acquired for the purposes of a trade carried on by them), in which case the disposal value will be deemed to be the market value; and

– where the disposal is made in **contemplation of** of the approach of **death** (donatio mortis causa), in which case the disposal is treated as taking place at market value but any gain arising is exempt (¶5592).

Anti-avoidance

5576 ss 19, 20 TCGA 1992 As an anti-avoidance measure, where a person makes a series of **linked disposals to one or more connected persons**, the deemed proceeds of each of the disposals may be adjusted by reference to the series as a whole, if the total consideration for the assets disposed of in a series is less than it would be if the assets were sold in a single transaction.

5578 This **provision applies where** a person disposes of assets by separate transactions to connected persons and both the following occur:
– those transactions occur within a period of 6 years ending on the date of the last transaction; and
– the original market value of an individual transaction is less than a reasonable proportion of the total value of all of the assets disposed of in the series of transactions taken together.

In such a case, the value attributable to each disposal in the series will be deemed to be the relevant proportion of the total market value of all of the assets concerned.

The **most common example** of linked transactions is a **series of disposals of shares** in an unquoted company where the total value of the series of transactions may be lower than the value of a single transaction because, for example, the single shareholding constituted a majority holding and would command a higher price as a single sale.

MEMO POINTS 1. Disposals between **spouses/civil partners** which are calculated on a no gain/no loss basis may form part of a linked series for the purposes of calculating deemed value for other transactions. No adjustment will be made to the deemed consideration for the inter-spouse transaction.
2. **Intra-group transfers** (¶1600) generally do not count as transactions within a linked series.

5580 The **total market value** of all of the assets disposed of in the series of transactions is found by establishing what the market value of the assets would have been if all of the assets had been disposed of together at the time of the transaction concerned (ignoring any assets acquired after the date of the transaction in question).

MEMO POINTS The **total number of assets taken into account** is limited to the maximum number held by the transferor at any time during the period running from immediately before the first transaction until immediately before the last transaction.

SECTION 7

Death

5590 s 62(1) TCGA 1992 No chargeable gain or allowable loss will arise on the death **of an individual**. Instead, all of the assets which he was competent to dispose of will be deemed to have been acquired by his personal representatives on his death for a deemed consideration equal to the market value at the date of death. Any gain or loss accruing to the personal representatives on a subsequent disposal of the assets will be calculated by reference to the market value of the asset at the date of death.

Special rules apply to enable the carry back of losses incurred by the deceased in the year of assessment in which death occurred (¶5478).

s 62(10) TCGA 1992 MEMO POINTS The deceased will be deemed to be **competent to dispose of assets** which he could have disposed of in his will if he was of full age and capacity, and assuming:
– all the assets were located in the UK; and
– he was domiciled in the UK (or in England).

There is no disposal for capital gains tax purposes when the personal representatives **distribute the assets to the legatees**. The legatees will be deemed to acquire the assets at the market value at the date of death or, if the asset was acquired subsequent to the death, at an amount equal to the allowable expenditure incurred by the personal representatives in providing the assets. **5592**

MEMO POINTS Where a disposal is made **donatio mortis causa** (gifts of personal property made in contemplation of death) a chargeable gain will not arise, and the recipient will be treated as if he received the asset as a legatee at the date of death.

A deed of family arrangement (or similar written instrument), which **varies or disclaims** the dispositions of property does not constitute a disposal providing: **5594**
- it is made within 2 years of the date of death; and
- the instrument contains a statement to the effect that the persons do not intend the instrument to constitute a disposal.

The **exception** to this rule is where variations or disclaimers are made in return for money or money's worth, other than consideration which consists of varying or disclaiming another of the dispositions.

SECTION 8

Options

1. Grant of an option

An option, and the asset over which it is granted, are **two separate assets** for chargeable gains purposes. **5600** s 144 TCGA 1992

The grant of an option is a disposal of an asset, i.e. the option. It is not a part disposal of the underlying asset. Therefore the allowable expenditure for the grant will only be the costs associated with the grant.

EXAMPLE A Ltd owns a painting valued at £25,000 which it had acquired in May 1985 for £5,000. Several years later, A Ltd grants an option to B Ltd to acquire the painting for £50,000 in the next 5 years. B Ltd pays £6,000 for the option, and A Ltd incurs professional fees of £1,200 in connection with the grant.
A Ltd has disposed of an asset, the option, for £6,000. The allowable expenditure is £1,200 and a gain of £4,800 therefore accrues.

MEMO POINTS 1. An option with a life of 50 years or less is a **wasting asset** (¶5922).
However, note that the following options are **excluded** from the wasting asset rules:
- quoted options to subscribe for shares in a company;
- traded options;
- financial options; and
- any option where the person is intending to use the asset(s) so acquired for the purposes of a trade.

2. See ¶1195 for options and substantial shareholdings, and ¶3392 for options and share schemes.

2. Disposal of an option

Where an option is sold **without being exercised**, the gain or loss is computed in the normal manner. If the option is a wasting asset, the allowable expenditure on the option will be reduced in accordance with the wasting asset rules (¶5922). **5604**

MEMO POINTS The **abandonment** of an option is not a disposal unless the grantee of the option receives a capital sum for the abandonment.

3. Exercise of an option

Grantor

5606 When the option is exercised, the grant of the option and the disposal of the underlying asset are treated as a single transaction taking place on the date on which the option is exercised.

Any tax charged on the grant of the option will be set against any tax due on the exercise of the option.

Indexation (where relevant) will run to the date of exercise of the option.

EXAMPLE Continuing the example at ¶5600 B Ltd exercises the option in March 2011, when the painting is valued at £75,000.
A Ltd has therefore made a disposal of the painting and the chargeable gain is calculated as follows:

	£	£
Proceeds (£6,000 + £50,000)		56,000
Costs of disposal		(1,200)
Less: Allowable expenditure		
Original cost	5,000	
Indexation allowance May 1985 to March 2011		
$\frac{232.5 - 95.21}{95.21} = 1.442 \times 5,000$	7,210	
		(12,210)
Chargeable gain		42,590

Note:
1. The chargeable gain originally arising on the grant is reduced to nil, and any tax charged is repaid or set off against tax due on exercise.
2. B Ltd's acquisition cost is £56,000. On a disposal of the painting, indexation will run as follows:
– on £6,000 from the date of grant of the option to acquire the painting; and
– on £50,000 from the date of exercise (i.e. March 2011).
3. If the disposal was not by a company there would be no indexation allowance.

5608 Where the option binds the grantor to buy an asset (**a "put" option**), the consideration paid for the option is deducted from the allowable cost of the asset.

EXAMPLE On 1 March 2003, Mr A granted an option (for £5,000) to Mr B under which Mr B could sell shares in X Ltd to Mr A for £150,000.
Assuming there are no associated costs arising on the grant of the option a chargeable gain will arise to Mr A of £5,000.
In March 2011, Mr B exercised the option and sold the shares to Mr A. The chargeable gain arising on the grant is reduced to nil. Any tax charged is repaid, and the allowable expenditure relating to the shares for Mr A will be £145,000 (£150,000 – £5,000).
On a subsequent disposal, any capital gain arising to Mr A will be computed in the normal way.

MEMO POINTS An exercise of an option to acquire an asset on **non-arm's length terms** is treated as if it were a sale of the underlying asset at market value. The exercise price and any consideration given for the option will be ignored. These rules do not affect the rules applying to transactions which are on an arm's length basis, nor do they affect options granted over shares and securities by reason of an individual's employment. An exercise price will be on non-arm's length terms when:
– it is an option to buy assets and the exercise price is more than the market value of the underlying assets; or
– it is an option to sell assets and the exercise price is less than the market value of the underlying assets.

Grantee

5610 Where the option is exercised by the person to whom it is granted, there are no tax consequences for the grantee. On a subsequent sale of the asset acquired by the exercise of the option, the allowable expenditure is increased by the amount (if any) paid for the exercise of the option.

Indexation (where applicable) will be applied separately to the cost of the option and the cost of the asset itself.

EXAMPLE On 1 January 2004, Mr A granted an option to Mr B for £15,000 under which Mr B could acquire an asset for £200,000. Mr B exercised his option on 1 April 2007 and subsequently sold the asset on 1 March 2011 for £300,000.
The chargeable gain arising on sale will be computed as follows:

	£	£
Disposal proceeds		300,000
Deduct:		
Allowable expenditure	200,000	
Amount paid for option	15,000	(215,000)
Chargeable gain		85,000

MEMO POINTS 1. Where shares forming part of a **section 104 pool** (¶1203) are acquired as a result of an option, the cost of the option is added to the pool.
2. An exercise of an option to acquire an asset on **non-arm's length terms** is treated as if it were a sale of the underlying asset at market value. The exercise price and any consideration given for the option will be ignored. An exercise price will be on non-arm's length terms when:
– it is an option to buy assets and the exercise price is more than the market value of the underlying assets; or
– it is an option to sell assets and the exercise price is less than the market value of the underlying assets.

Where the option binds the grantor to buy (**a "put" option**), the cost of the option is treated as an incidental cost of the grantee on a subsequent disposal of the asset. **5612**

EXAMPLE Continuing the example above at ¶5608. Assuming Mr B had initially paid £100,000 for the shares in April 1997, he will be charged to tax as follows on the exercise of the option:

	£
Disposal proceeds	150,000
Deduct:	
Cost of the option	(5,000)
	145,000
Allowable expenditure	(100,000)
Chargeable gain	45,000

SECTION 9

Value shifting

Scope

The value shifting provisions are **anti-avoidance provisions** which aim to prevent the value being shifted out of an asset before sale, resulting in an artificial loss on disposal. The provisions effectively apply to restrict (or eliminate altogether) any loss on a disposal, if HMRC believe that value has been artificially shifted out of the asset prior to sale. **5650** ss 29-31 TCGA 1992

The provisions apply in **two distinct situations**:
– where a person exercises control over a company so that value passes out of one shareholding into another; or
– where, as part of an arrangement, value passes out of an asset and, as a consequence, a tax-free benefit arises.

Value shift in respect of share capital

5652
s 29 TCGA 1992

Where a person who has control over a company exercises that control in such a way that value passes out of shares in, or rights over, the company owned by him (or a person connected with him) into other shares in, or rights over, the company, the value shifting provisions will apply.

The **effect of the provisions** in this situation is to treat the value shift as a disposal of the shares. Where the deemed disposal gives rise to a loss, the allowable loss is restricted to the extent that it is attributable to the value shift. The adjustment applies equally to the person benefiting from the value shift.

EXAMPLE A Ltd owns B Ltd's entire issued share capital of 10,000 £1 shares which were acquired by subscription at par. Several years later, C Ltd (which is connected with A Ltd but not part of the same 75% CG group) acquired 12,000 £1 shares in B Ltd by subscription at par, when the company was worth £525,000. The market value of the new shares was £310,200.
A Ltd's interest has reduced to 45%, which has a value of £214,800, and A Ltd is deemed to make a disposal as follows:

	£
Deemed proceeds on disposal	310,200
Less: allowable cost	
$\frac{310,200}{(310,200 + 214,800)} \times £10,000$	(5,909)
Chargeable gain (before indexation)	304,291

The allowable cost of C Ltd's shares will be adjusted to reflect the market value at acquisition, i.e. £310,200.

Value shift resulting in tax-free benefit

5654
ss 30 - 31 TCGA 1992

The value shifting provisions will apply where, as part of a scheme or arrangement, the value of an asset is materially reduced and a tax-free benefit arises to:
- the person disposing of that asset;
- a person connected with the person making the disposal; or
- any other person (where one of the main reasons for the transactions was the avoidance of tax).

MEMO POINTS 1. There is no statutory definition of **material reduction** although HMRC take the view that any reduction is material unless it is negligible.
2. A **tax-free benefit** is any benefit unless it is charged to corporation tax, income tax or capital gains tax. A benefit arises where:
- a person becomes entitled to any money (or money's worth);
- the value of an asset in which he has an interest increases; or
- he is partly or wholly relieved of a liability.
3. **Special rules** apply when the asset being disposed of is shares or securities (¶5658).

5656
s 30(7) TCGA 1992

These provisions **do not apply to**:
a. transfers between spouses/civil partners;
b. transfers from personal representatives to a beneficiary;
c. ordinary payments for group relief;
d. transfers between members of the same 75% CG group of companies (¶1524), unless the asset is transferred for consideration lower than both the cost and the market value of the asset; and
e. bona fide commercial transactions which are not undertaken with the aim of avoiding tax.

EXAMPLE A Ltd owns the entire share capital of the following companies (which were acquired at par):

Company	Shares	Holding
B Ltd	Ord £1	10,000
C Ltd	Ord £1	25,000

The value of B Ltd is £250,000 which derives from an investment property it acquired for £100,000. C Ltd has no assets.

If the property is transferred from B Ltd to C Ltd for £5,000, the value of B Ltd is reduced to £5,000. The transfer is a no gain/no loss transaction.
The value shifting provisions will apply as the asset was transferred for consideration lower than both cost and market value. Therefore, when the shares in B Ltd are sold, any resulting loss will be restricted by £95,000 (i.e. the difference between the cost of the property and the value at which it was transferred).

Where the asset being disposed of is **shares or securities** in another company, the value shifting provisions are extended to include a reduction in the value of any asset (known as a relevant asset) owned by a company which is a member of the same 75% CG group of companies (¶1524). **5658**

MEMO POINTS These provisions will **only apply if** the value of the relevant asset, at the time of the disposal of the shares, would have been materially greater if the value shift had not occurred and, between the date of the value shift and the date of the share disposal, there has been neither:
- a disposal of the asset (other than an intra-group transfer); nor
- a deemed disposal on the company ceasing to be a member of the group.

The **effect of the provisions** in this situation is that the loss (or gain) arising on the disposal is calculated by substituting a just and reasonable amount for the consideration actually received. **5660**

EXAMPLE Continuing the previous example, A Ltd sets up a new subsidiary (D Ltd) which has an issued share capital of 250,000 £1 shares which are subscribed for at par.
The shares in B Ltd are then transferred to D Ltd for £250,000, again as a no gain/no loss transaction. This reduces the value of D Ltd to £5,000.
If A Ltd then sells D Ltd to an unconnected party for £5,000, A Ltd will realise a loss on disposal of £245,000.
There has been no value shift in respect of the shares in D Ltd. However, the B Ltd shares are a relevant asset, and the loss on disposal of D Ltd will therefore be calculated on a just and reasonable basis. To reflect the substance of the transactions, this would probably be considered a disposal resulting in neither a gain nor a loss.

CHAPTER 5

Specific types of asset

OUTLINE ¶¶

SECTION 1

Land and interests in land

1. General principles

Scope

5670 The general rules for the computation of chargeable gains and allowable losses apply equally to land. However, there are a number of provisions which relate specifically to land and interests in land (referred to here collectively as land). In particular, the rules relating to part disposals (¶5508) are adapted in relation to land, most notably with respect to small part disposals. In addition, the computation of chargeable gains and allowable losses on the disposal and grant of leases of land is subject to a number of specific rules arising principally from the fact that leases with 50 or fewer years to run are wasting assets.

MEMO POINTS 1. Some transactions in land are in the **nature of a trade** and as such may be taxed as trading income rather than as a capital gain. For details of the distinction between income and capital see ¶108.
2. Unless indicated otherwise the general capital gains tax principles outlined in the rest of *Tax Memo* apply to land.

Definition

5672 s 288(1) TCGA 1992 The definition of land **includes** (unless indicated otherwise under a particular provision) not only the land itself but also dwellings and other buildings or structures situated on it (whether owned or leased) and any right or interest over land. Land covered by water is also included in the definition.

s 275(1) TCGA 1992 Any interest in land is deemed to be **situated** in the same place as the land itself with the exception of a **debt secured on land**, which is located in the country in which the creditor is located.

Allowable expenditure

5675 s 39(1) TCGA 1992 Allowable expenditure for land is determined in accordance with the normal rules (¶5322). **Acquisition expenditure** will be allowable unless it is included as a deduction in the computation of income, or would have been deductible in computing trading profits if the land had been a fixed asset of that trade.

s 37(1) TCGA 1992 Similarly, **disposal consideration** received on the sale of land is reduced by any amounts which have been included as taxable income (whether as a trading receipt or miscellaneous income).

Acquisition/disposal date

5677 s 28 TCGA 1992 The acquisition/disposal date for land is **deemed to be** the date of the contract, regardless of whether the conveyance takes place at a later date. If the contract is **conditional** (for example, on the exercise of an option) the acquisition/disposal is deemed to take place when the condition is satisfied.

2. Part disposals of land

Valuation

5680 The general part disposal provisions outlined in ¶5508 also apply to disposals of land. Under these provisions the **total cost of the asset** is apportioned on the following basis:

$$\frac{A}{A+B}$$

where:
- A is the value of the part disposed of; and
- B is the value of the part remaining.

Valuation of the **remaining part of the land** can either be done by:
- the general method, involving employment of a specialist, which can be a costly exercise; or
- any fair and reasonable alternative method. The most common method is to attribute a reasonable valuation to the part disposed of at the date that it was originally acquired. The cost of the remaining land will be determined by deducting the element attributed to the part disposed of. SP D1

EXAMPLE Mr A acquires 100 acres of land for £100,000 in Year 1. In Year 6 he decides to sell 40 acres at a price of £75,000.

General method

Assuming the value of the remaining land in Year 6 is £105,000, the chargeable gain will be calculated as follows:

	£
Disposal proceeds	75,000
Cost $\frac{75,000}{(75,000 + 105,000)} \times 100,000$	(41,667)
Net gain	33,333

The cost for the remaining 60 acres is deemed to be £58,333 (£100,000 – £41,667).

Alternative method

	£
Disposal proceeds	75,000
Cost (40/100 × 100,000)	(40,000)
Net gain	35,000

The cost for the remaining 60 acres is deemed to be £60,000 (£100,000 – £40,000).
In this case the gain is higher under the alternative method but the cost of obtaining a valuation of the remaining 60 acres should also be taken into account.

Note:
The calculation is the same for disposals by companies, with the exception that indexation is added to the cost from the date of acquisition to the date of disposal.

MEMO POINTS 1. The overriding principle of any **alternative valuation method** is that the cost attributed to each part of the land must be realistic. It should be noted that HMRC may choose to apply the general rule if they are not satisfied that the apportionments are fair and reasonable.
2. Grant payments received for **giving up occupation of uncommercial agricultural units** do not constitute a part disposal. s 249 TCGA 1992

Small part disposals

Where there is a small part disposal of land, the taxpayer **may elect** that a chargeable disposal will not arise. Instead, on the later disposal of the remaining land the cost will be reduced by the net disposal proceeds arising from the earlier part disposal. **5682** s 242 TCGA 1992

MEMO POINTS The 31 March 1982 value (¶1133) will also be reduced, providing the earlier part disposal took place after that date.

In order to qualify under this provision the following **conditions must be satisfied**: **5684**

a. the consideration for the land disposed of must:
- not exceed 20% of the value of the entire holding prior to the part disposal; and
- be £20,000 or less (if more than one part disposal is made in the same tax year, the aggregate of all such proceeds must be £20,000 or less); and

b. a claim must be submitted to HMRC by the first anniversary of 31 January following the end of the tax year of the disposal (or, for companies, within 2 years after the end of the accounting period in which the disposal took place).

MEMO POINTS 1. The **£20,000 limit** does not include:
– land which is the subject of compulsory acquisition (¶5732);
– no gain/no loss transfers between spouses/civil partners (¶5550);
– transfers between group companies (¶1600); and
– an estate or interest in land which is a wasting asset such as a short lease (¶5705).
2. Where a transaction is not made for full consideration the market value is taken when comparing the proceeds to the limit.

5686 ss 243, 244 TCGA 1992

The small part disposal rules **do not apply** if:
– the allowable expenditure of the original asset is nil; or
– the consideration received for the part disposal exceeds the original allowable expenditure of the land.

In this case the individual **may elect** to calculate the gain or loss on the part disposal by deducting the total original allowable expenditure from the proceeds of the part disposal.

If this **election is made**, the allowable expenditure (and 31 March 1982 value if applicable) for the remaining land will be reduced to nil and only expenditure incurred since the part disposal will be available on any subsequent disposals.

The **election must be submitted** by the first anniversary of the 31 January following the year of assessment in which the part disposal was made (or, for companies, within 2 years after the end of the accounting period in which the disposal took place).

EXAMPLE Mr B owns land which he acquired in September 2002 for £10,000. In December 2010 when the value of the entire holding had increased to £100,000 he sells part of the land for £19,000. This was the only land transaction made in the year. Assuming that Mr B submits an election by 31 January 2013 then the chargeable gain on the part disposal will be calculated as follows:

	£
Disposal proceeds	19,000
Less: Allowable expenditure of entire holding	(10,000)
Gain	9,000

The cost available for use on the subsequent disposal of the remaining land is reduced to nil.

Note:
The calculation is the same for disposals by companies, with the exception that indexation is available from the date of acquisition to the date of disposal.

3. Leases of land

5690 The calculation of chargeable gains and allowable losses on the grant or assignment of a lease must take into account the fact that a lease with 50 or fewer years left to run (a short lease) is a wasting asset. This means that as the lease gets towards the end of its duration the value will be proportionately reduced. Conversely, a lease with more than 50 years left to run (a long lease) is not a wasting asset.

The **rules for each will depend on** whether the lease is:
– assigned (i.e. the sale of an existing interest in a lease); or
– granted (i.e. the creation of a new lease out of an existing lease or freehold).

The subject of leased land is therefore divided into four categories:
– assignment of a long lease (¶5697);
– assignment of a short lease (¶5705);
– grant of a lease out of a long lease or a freehold (¶5715); and
– grant of a sublease out of a short lease (¶5718).

Sch 8 para 10 TCGA 1992

MEMO POINTS 1. The **definition** of a lease includes underleases, subleases and any tenancy or licence and any agreements for such.
2. Where the lease relates to property which qualifies for the **principal private residence** exemption (¶6166), any gain on the lease will also qualify for the exemption.

The **duration** of a lease is typically determined by the terms of the contract. However, anti-avoidance rules apply to prevent landlords manipulating the length of the lease term so as to gain a tax advantage. Under these provisions, a lease is **deemed to expire** on: **5692** Sch 8 para 8 TCGA 1992
- the first date on which the landlord has the right to terminate the lease; or
- the date past which the terms of the lease render it unlikely that the lease will continue (because of a substantial rent increase, for example).

Note that the rules for determining the duration of a lease are different to those applying to income from property (¶2746).

MEMO POINTS The **grant of a lease to follow on from a previous lease** will be deemed to be the grant of a new lease (and therefore subject to capital gains tax) unless all of the following conditions are satisfied ESC D39
- the lease (whether or not it is between connected or unconnected persons) is made on terms which would have been made between unconnected persons who are bargaining at arm's length;
- the grant of the follow-on lease is not part of a larger scheme;
- the lessee did not receive a capital sum in respect of the transaction; and
- the property and terms of the lease (other than duration and rent) remain the same as the old lease.

Assignment of a long lease

There are no special rules for the assignment of a long lease for capital gains tax purposes. Any chargeable gain or allowable loss is therefore calculated in accordance with the normal rules (including principal private residence relief (¶6166) if applicable). **5697**

Assignment of a short lease

Short leases are wasting assets and so the original expenditure that is allowed as a deduction in the calculation of chargeable gains and allowable losses reduces each year. The reduction for leases is more complex than for other wasting assets because the value of a lease is deemed to fall by increasing amounts each year. **5705**

MEMO POINTS 1. The short lease provisions outlined here **do not apply to** land:
- used throughout the period of ownership for the purposes of a trade, profession or vocation; and
- where capital allowances have or could have been claimed in respect of the cost (¶5730).

2. Where the land disposed of has **partly qualified for capital allowances** or has only partly qualified for business use, the allowable expenditure relating to the land should be apportioned accordingly.

The **value of a short lease** is determined by a table of percentages, provided by the legislation based on the duration of the lease. Sch 8 para 1 TCGA 1992

Short lease depreciation factors					
Years	Percentage	Years	Percentage	Years	Percentage
50 (or more)	100	**33**	90.280	**16**	64.116
49	99.657	**32**	89.354	**15**	61.617
48	99.289	**31**	88.371	**14**	58.971
47	98.902	**30**	87.330	**13**	56.167
46	98.490	**29**	86.226	**12**	53.191
45	98.059	**28**	85.053	**11**	50.038
44	97.595	**27**	83.816	**10**	46.695
43	97.107	**26**	82.496	**9**	43.154
42	96.593	**25**	81.100	**8**	39.399
41	96.041	**24**	79.622	**7**	35.414
40	95.457	**23**	78.055	**6**	31.195
39	94.842	**22**	76.399	**5**	26.722
38	94.189	**21**	74.635	**4**	21.983

Short lease depreciation factors					
Years	Percentage	Years	Percentage	Years	Percentage
37	93.497	**20**	72.770	**3**	16.959
36	92.761	**19**	70.791	**2**	11.629
35	91.981	**18**	68.697	**1**	5.983
34	91.156	**17**	66.470	**0**	0

5707 To calculate the **cost allowable as a deduction** from the proceeds of the assignment of a short lease, the standard part disposal formula (¶5508) is replaced with the following formula based on the percentages from the table:

$$\text{Allowable expenditure for original lease} \times \frac{\text{\% for years left to run at assignment}}{\text{\% for years left to run from original acquisition}}$$

EXAMPLE Mr C acquired a 25 year lease on 31 March 2006 for £200,000. He assigned the lease on 31 March 2011 for £250,000. The cost available for deduction from disposal proceeds will be calculated as follows:

$$200{,}000 \times \frac{\text{\% for 20 years}}{\text{\% for 25 years}} = \frac{72.770}{81.100} = £179{,}457$$

MEMO POINTS 1. If the **lease was acquired before 31 March 1982**, the formula is amended to calculate the proportion of the 31 March 1982 value available:

$$\text{31 March 1982 value of original lease} \times \frac{\text{\% for years left to run at assignment}}{\text{\% for years left to run from 31 March 1982}}$$

2. For companies and the use of March 1982 values see ¶1133.

5710 Where the duration of the lease is **not a complete number of years** the relevant percentage is obtained by taking the whole year and adding one twelfth of the difference between the whole year and the next highest year for each extra month.

EXAMPLE Mr D acquired a 40 year lease on 31 January 2006 for £100,000. He assigned the lease on 31 March 2011 for £120,000.

	£
Disposal proceeds	120,000
Cost[1]	(96,215)
Gain	23,785

Note:

1. The period from acquisition of the lease to assignment is 5 years 2 months which is deducted from the years left to run at the date of acquisition to reach the years left to run at assignment:

$$100{,}000 \times \frac{\text{\% for 34 years 10 months}}{\text{\% for 40 years}} = \frac{91.844^*}{95.457} = 96{,}215$$

* % for	34 years		91.156
	35 years	91.981	
	34 years	(91.156)	
		0.825	
10/12 × 0.825			0.688
			91.844

The calculation is the same for disposals by companies, with the exception that indexation is available from the date of acquisition to the date of disposal.

5711 If a lease was **originally a long lease** but was assigned at a time when there were 50 years or less to run then the above provisions still apply. In this case the percentage for the number of years left to run on the lease at the original acquisition will always be 100, i.e. 50 years or more.

Where the property which is the subject of a short lease is **enhanced** before it is assigned the deductible enhancement expenditure is also restricted. For these purposes the formula is amended as follows: **5712**

$$\text{Enhancement expenditure} \times \frac{\text{\% for years left to run at assignment}}{\text{\% for years left to run from enhancement}}$$

The formula should be applied separately for each item of enhancement expenditure.

MEMO POINTS These provisions **only apply to** enhancement expenditure that is reflected in the value of the asset at sale and expenditure incurred on establishing, preserving or defending title to the lease.

A lease is not a wasting asset if at the date of assignment it is subject to an **onerous sublease**. **5713** Sch 8 para 1 TCGA 1992
An onerous sublease is one where the:
- rent payable under the sublease is less than the full annual rental value of the property; and
- value of the reversionary interest exceeds the allowable expenditure of the acquisition of the asset.

Consequently, on the assignment of such a lease, there is no wasting asset restriction applied to the cost. However, once the sublease term ends, the lease will revert back to a wasting asset and on a subsequent assignment the formula is amended as follows:

$$\text{Allowable expenditure} \times \frac{\text{\% for years left to run at assignment}}{\text{\% for years left to run from date sublease expired}}$$

EXAMPLE In Year 1 Mr E grants Mr F a lease of a property for 55 years, and 10 years later Mr F grants a sublease to Mr G for 15 years at £1,500 p.a. Mr F assigns his lease to Mr H for £30,000, 2 years after the grant of the sublease.
Mr H has acquired a 43 year lease which would (without these provisions) be a wasting asset. However, the sublease to Mr G has 13 years left to run and:
- the full annual rent would have been £3,500 p.a.
- the value of the lease is estimated to be £40,000 when the sublease expires.

Scenario 1
Mr H disposes of his lease, before the sublease has expired. Here, the wasting assets provisions would not apply.

Scenario 2
Mr H disposes of his lease for £200,000, 2 years after the sublease has expired. Here, the wasting assets (as modified) will apply, and the capital gains position is:

	£
Disposal proceeds	200,000
$30{,}000 \times \frac{\text{\% for 43 years}}{\text{\% for 30 years}} = \frac{97.107}{87.330}$	(33,359)
Gain	166,641

If a leaseholder **acquires a superior interest** in land (either a superior lease or the freehold reversion), the two leases are merged and on a subsequent assignment the following rules apply: **5714** s 43 TCGA 1992 ESC D42
- allowable expenditure will be the cost of the first lease (wasted if it is less than 50 years), together with the cost of the superior interest (again, wasted if it is a lease of less than 50 years); and
- indexation is given (for companies only) on the first lease and the superior interest from their respective dates of acquisition.

Grant of a lease out of a long lease or freehold

The grant of a lease out of a long lease or out of a freehold is deemed to be a **part disposal**. **5715** Sch 8 para 2 TCGA 1992
The chargeable gain or allowable loss will be calculated in accordance with the normal part

disposal rules (¶5508), with the allowable expenditure for the entire holding being apportioned on the following basis:

$$\frac{A}{A+B}$$

where:
– A is the value of the part disposed of (i.e. the premium received on the grant of the lease); and
– B is the value of the remainder (i.e. the market value of the remainder of the property together with the value of the right to receive rent under the lease).

MEMO POINTS If the grant of the lease is not made by way of a bargain at arm's length (between connected parties, for example) the premium is valued at market value at the time of the grant.

EXAMPLE In December 1996 Mr A acquired a property under a 99 year lease for £50,000. In March 2009 he granted a 60 year sublease for a premium of £75,000. The value of the remainder was agreed to be £30,000. The property was not his principal private residence.

	£	£
Disposal proceeds		75,000
Cost $50{,}000 \times \frac{75{,}000}{75{,}000 + 30{,}000}$		35,714
Gain		39,286

Note:
The calculation is the same for disposals by companies, with the exception that indexation is available.

5716 Where the **sublease is for 50 years or less** an adjustment is required to take account of the fact that some of the premium will be subject to income or corporation tax (¶2743). The amount of the premium included in the capital gains tax calculation will be reduced by the amount treated as income from property. However, the value of the part disposed of, included in the denominator of the part disposal fraction, will be the whole of the premium received.

EXAMPLE Carrying on from the previous example, if the sublease granted by Mr A had been 40 years in length the following would apply:

	£
Premium received	75,000
Premium taxed as income from property: 75,000 – (2 % × (40 – 1) × 75,000)	16,500
Balance for capital gains	58,500

	£	£
Disposal proceeds		58,500
Cost $50{,}000 \times \frac{58{,}500}{75{,}000 + 30{,}000}$		27,857
Gain		30,643

Note:
The calculation is the same for disposals by companies, with the exception that indexation is available.

5717 Sch 8 para 6 TCGA 1992; s 288 ITTOIA 2005

If a leaseholder charges a premium for the grant of a further sublease out of a lease, **income or corporation tax relief** is available (¶2757). For capital gains tax purposes, if the premium so charged results in a capital loss, the loss will be restricted by the amount of income tax relief already received (but not so as to turn a loss into a gain).

EXAMPLE Mr B grants a 25 year lease on a property to Mr C for rent of £10,000 p.a. and a premium of £10,000. After 2 years, Mr C sublets the property to Mr D on a 10 year lease at a premium of £4,000.

The income tax position is:
Mr B is taxable on the premium as follows:
10,000 – (10,000 × (25-1) × 2%) = £5,200

Mr C is taxable on the premium from Mr D as follows:

		£
Premium 4,000 – (4,000 × (10-1) × 2%)		3,280
Less:		
$\left(\frac{\text{Years of sublease}}{\text{Years of headlease}}\right)$ × Taxable element of headlease premium	$\frac{10}{25}$ × 5,200	(2,080)
Total charge on Mr C		1,200

The capital gains tax position is:
Mr C is taxed on the grant of the sublease to Mr D is as follows:

	£
Premium received	4,000
Less:	
$\left(\frac{\text{Years of sublease}}{\text{Years of headlease}}\right)$ × Premium paid to Mr B =	
$\left(\frac{10}{25} \times 10{,}000\right) = \frac{46.695^1}{81.100^1} \times 10{,}000$	(5,758)
	(1,758)
Less	
Relief already given for income tax (restricted)	1,758
Allowable loss	Nil

Note:
1. The value of a short lease is determined by the short lease table of percentages. See ¶5705 for details.

Grant of a sublease out of a short lease

The grant of a sublease out of a short lease is a **part disposal** and the formula applied to restrict allowable expenditure is more complex because the apportionment of allowable expenditure to the part disposed of must take account of the fact that the lease is a wasting asset. The formula used for these purposes is as follows and uses the same table of percentages (¶5705) as the assignment of a short lease: 5718

$$\text{Allowable expenditure for original lease} \times \frac{\text{\% for original lease unexpired at grant of sublease} - \text{\% for original lease unexpired at expiry of sublease}}{\text{\% for number of unexpired years at the date of acquisition of the original lease}}$$

MEMO POINTS 1. If the **lease was acquired before 31 March 1982** the formula is amended to calculate the proportion of the 31 March 1982 value available:

$$\text{31 March 1982 value of original lease} \times \frac{\text{\% for original lease unexpired at grant of sublease} - \text{\% for original lease unexpired at expiry of sublease}}{\text{\% for number of unexpired years at 31 March 1982}}$$

2. To complicate matters further, an adjustment must be made to reflect the fact that part of the **premium** received on the grant of the sublease will be subject to income tax as income from property (¶2743).
3. For companies and the use of March 1982 values see ¶1133.

The steps to calculate the chargeable gain or allowable loss on the grant of a sublease out of a short lease are as follows: 5720
1. **Calculate the taxable element of the premium** received on the grant that will be subject to income tax:
a. calculate the amount normally assessable using the formula:

$$\text{Premium received} - (2\,\% \times (n - 1) \times \text{premium received})$$

where n is the number of years in the original lease;

b. deduct a proportion of the amount taxed on the person who sold the original lease. The proportion is calculated as:

$$\text{Amount taxed on original landlord} \times \frac{\text{Number of years in sublease}}{\text{Number of years in original lease}}$$

2. **Calculate the chargeable gain**:
a. use the full amount of the premium received as the disposal proceeds;
b. apportion the cost on the basis of the formula in ¶5718;
c. calculate indexation if applicable; and,
d. deduct the element of the premium that will be taxed as income from property (1. above).

EXAMPLE On 1 April 2000 Mr E acquired a 40 year lease from Mr F for £50,000. On 1 April 2010 he granted a 20 year sublease for £75,000.

	£
Premium taxed as income from property:	
On grant of sublease (75,000 – (2 % × (20 – 1) × 75,000))	46,500
Less: Proportion of amount taxed on Mr F ((50,000 – (2 % × (40 – 1) × 50,000)) × 20/40)	(5,500)
Income from property assessment	41,000

	£	£
Capital gains tax:		
Disposal proceeds		75,000
Less: Cost [1]		21,284
		53,716
Less: Income from property assessment		(41,000)
Gain		12,716

Note:

1. $50{,}000 \times \dfrac{\text{\% for 30 yrs} - \text{\% for 10 yrs}}{\text{\% for 40 yrs}} = £21{,}284$

2. The calculation is the same for disposals by companies, with the exception that indexation is available.

5724 If the **sublease is granted at a higher rent** per year than the rent payable on the original lease, the allowable expenditure as calculated above is further reduced to take account of the fact that a higher rent is often connected with a lower premium. The allowable expenditure is therefore further reduced by the following proportion:

$$\text{Allowable expenditure as restricted} \times \frac{\text{Actual premium paid}}{\text{Notional premium that would have been payable if the rent on the sublease was the same as on the original lease}}$$

EXAMPLE Following on from the previous example, if the rent on the headlease was £2,000 p.a. and the rent on the sublease was £3,000 p.a., then it becomes necessary to calculate what the premium on the sublease would have been if the rent had been £2,000. If it is assumed that the premium would have been £80,000 the calculation would become:

	£	£
Disposal proceeds		75,000
Less: Cost (21,284 × 75,000/80,000)		(19,954)
		55,046
Less: Income from property assessment		(41,000)
Gain		14,046

Note:
The calculation is the same for disposals by companies, with the exception that indexation is available.

Where the property which is the subject of a short lease is **enhanced** before the grant of a sublease the deductible enhancement expenditure is also restricted. For these purposes the formula is amended as follows: 5725

$$\text{Enhancement expenditure} \times \frac{\begin{array}{c}\text{\% for original lease unexpired}\\ \text{at grant of sublease}\end{array} - \begin{array}{c}\text{\% for original lease unexpired}\\ \text{at expiry of sublease}\end{array}}{\begin{array}{c}\text{\% for number of unexpired years at the date}\\ \text{of enhancement expenditure}\end{array}}$$

The formula should be applied separately for each item of enhancement expenditure.

MEMO POINTS These provisions **only apply to** enhancement expenditure that is reflected in the value of the asset at sale and expenditure incurred on establishing, preserving or defending title to the lease.

4. Miscellaneous provisions relating to land

Buildings qualifying for capital allowances

Losses arising on the sale of a building may be restricted to take account of capital allowances previously given. However, a building is treated as being part of the land and, as such, the restriction for capital allowances will only arise where there is an overall loss arising on the sale of the land and building taken together. 5730 s 41 TCGA 1992

Where the restriction for capital allowances does apply, one computation is prepared for both the land and building and the allowable expenditure included for the building is reduced by the amount of capital allowances received. The effect of the computation is shown at ¶5924.

Compulsory purchase

Rollover relief This may be available where land is acquired by authorities having or exercising compulsory powers. The relief applies where: 5732 s 247 TCGA 1992

– the owner of the land **did not take any steps** to dispose of the land whether by advertising or by otherwise making his willingness to sell known to the authority; and

– the **consideration** for the disposal was applied in acquiring new land.

The general conditions for rollover relief and details of the calculation are explained in ¶6050.

MEMO POINTS 1. The rollover relief **provisions are extended** to cover gains made by a landlord following the exercise by a: CG 61940

– tenant of a statutory right to acquire the freehold reversion of a property or extend the lease; or

– crofting community body of a statutory right to acquire croft land.

Rollover relief will not be available if the new land is a **dwelling house** which qualifies for principal private residence relief (¶6166). Similarly, rollover relief previously given will be withdrawn if the new land becomes eligible for principal private residence relief within 6 years from the date of acquisition.

2. Rollover relief may be given on a **provisional basis** on:

– an exchange of contracts for the replacement land; or

– a declaration being made by the taxpayer that he intends to acquire replacement land.

3. If proceeds are reinvested into a **depreciating asset**, the gain will be held over (¶6068).

4. Any gain arising on the disposal of a qualifying asset may be rolled (or held) over into the acquisition of a qualifying replacement asset by another **group member** (¶1522). There is no requirement for both companies to be members of the group at the same time. The disposing company must be a member of the group at the time of disposal, and the acquiring company must be a member at the time at which the replacement asset is acquired. For the reliefs to apply, a joint election must be made by both companies.

Part disposal Where only part of the holding of land is acquired in a compulsory purchase then a part disposal under the normal rules will arise (¶5508). If the consideration for that part disposal includes **compensation** for severance of land (or any other injurious effect on 5735 s 245 TCGA 1992 the remaining land) a part disposal of the remaining land will also arise. For this rule to apply, both parcels of the land must have been held in the same capacity.

5737 ss 242, 243 TCGA 1992 RI 164 **Small part disposal** On a small part disposal as a result of a compulsory purchase the taxpayer **may elect** that a disposal will not arise and instead the consideration will be deducted from the allowable expenditure on the subsequent disposal of the remaining land.

MEMO POINTS 1. **Small** is not defined by the legislation but for these purposes it is generally understood to mean:
- 5% or less of the value of the asset; or
- £3,000 or less (whether or not this is within the 5% limit).

A taxpayer may suggest to HMRC that a sum higher than these limits should be considered small. HMRC will then decide, based upon the particular circumstances of the case, if a higher limit is applicable. *O'Rourke v Binks* [1992].
2. Indexation allowance on a **subsequent disposal** by a company will need to be adjusted (¶1131).
3. The claim must be **submitted by** the first anniversary of the 31 January following the year of assessment in which the part disposal occurred (or, for companies, within 2 years after the end of the accounting period in which the disposal took place).

5739 s 244 TCGA 1992 The small part disposal rules **do not apply** if:
- the allowable expenditure of the original asset is nil; or
- the consideration received for the part disposal exceeds the original allowable expenditure of the land.

In this case, a special election can be made. The rules are the same as for normal disposals of land (¶5686).

MEMO POINTS The claim must be **submitted by** the first anniversary of the 31 January following the year of assessment in which the part disposal occurred (or, for companies, within 2 years after the end of the accounting period in which the disposal took place).

Relief for exchange of joint interests

5741 In the **normal course of events**, where land which is owned jointly (whether as joint tenants or tenants in common) is partitioned between the joint owners, a disposal will be deemed to arise. Each owner will be deemed to have acquired a new interest in the part of the land allotted to him and to have disposed of the part of the land which he released to the other owner.

ss 282A-C TCGA 1992 Rollover relief (¶6050) can be claimed provided that, as a result of the exchange, each owner becomes the sole owner of part of the land that was previously owned jointly.

Land sold with right of conveyance or leaseback

5744 ss 224-226 CTA 2009; ss 284, 285 ITTOIA 2005 Special rules apply to prevent the manipulation of losses in circumstances where land is sold subject to a right to have it either:
- reconveyed back to the vendor (or a person connected with him) at a lower price; or
- leased back to the vendor a month or more after the sale.

In both cases a proportion of the excess of sale proceeds over the reconveyance (or leaseback) price will be taxed as income from property (¶2753).

In the calculation of the chargeable gain on the disposal, the disposal proceeds will be reduced by the amount already taxed as income from property.

Mineral leases

5746 s 201 TCGA 1988 Half of any royalties receivable in connection with the granting of a right to mine and work minerals in the UK are excluded from the charge to income tax and taxed as a capital gain, with no relief for any allowable expenditure.

However, a form of **relief** is available to the recipient of the royalties if a capital loss accrues to him on:
- the disposal (or deemed disposal) of the land where the mining is undertaken; or
- the lease for the mining expiring. (In this situation, there is a deemed disposal and reacquisition of the land.)

Any capital loss so arising can be either set off against mineral royalty receipts for the same tax year of disposal or carried back for offset against mineral royalty receipts in the previous 15 years (later years being relieved before earlier ones).

SECTION 2

Shares and securities

A. Background

From 6 April 2008 the rules relating to the disposal of shares and securities by individuals, trustees and personal representatives were significantly simplified. From that date all shares of a similar class in a company were pooled to create a single pot, known as the section 104 pool, that any future disposals were matched against. The only time this will not be the case is where a disposal is made and within the following 30 days shares of the same class are purchased. **5755**

MEMO POINTS 1. For capital gains tax purposes, the term **shares and securities** encompasses both quoted and unquoted shares, debentures, and loan stock, but excludes qualifying corporate bonds (QCBs) (¶5234). For the remainder of this section, the word shares will be used to refer to all types of shares and securities with the exception of QCBs.
2. The rules described in this section generally apply to **individuals, trustees and personal representatives**. The rules applying for companies can be found at ¶1188 onwards.

B. Identification rules

Before computing the chargeable gain or allowable loss on the disposal of shares, it is necessary to identify which shares are actually being disposed of. This is known as **matching**. It is important to note that matching only applies to disposals of the same class of shares. **5764** ss 105, 106A TCGA 1992

For disposals on or after 6 April 2008 by individuals, trustees and personal representatives shares are matched as follows:
- shares acquired on the day of disposal;
- shares acquired in the 30 days following the disposal; and
- shares in the section 104 pool (¶5768).

See ¶5768 for the construction of the section 104 pool and ¶1200 for the matching rules relating to **companies**.

MEMO POINTS 1. Generally, shares acquired on the same day are treated as acquired in one transaction. However, this rule can be modified for **same day acquisitions of shares by employees**, where some of the shares have been acquired as a result of exercising an option under an approved company share scheme. If an election is made, shares purchased on the day are divided into two categories – share option shares and non-share option shares. On a subsequent disposal, shares are matched with the non-share option shares in priority to the others. s 105A TCGA 1992
The election must be made on or before the first anniversary of 31 January next following the disposal of any relevant share and can only be made in respect of shares acquired on or after 6 April 2002. No election may be made for VCT shares.
2. The same day and 30 day matching rules do not apply on a **deemed disposal** and reacquisition (e.g. on the making of a negligible value claim). RI 226
3. The matching rules are modified for **EIS and VCT shares** (see ¶6206 and ¶6259 respectively).

C. The basic computation

5768 For disposals of shares by individuals, trustees and personal representatives post-5 April 2008 the calculation of the section 104 pool and of the gain on disposal is as follows.

EXAMPLE Mr A made the following acquisitions of ordinary shares in B Ltd, an unquoted company:

Date	Holding	Acquisition cost
15 October 2000	3,000	150,000
20 August 2007	500	30,000
8 September 2007	250	20,000
12 September 2007	1,250	80,000
	5,000	280,000

On 1 September 2010 Mr A sold 3,500 shares for £320,000. The shares will be matched with the s104 pool as there are no acquisitions on the same day nor any acquisitions made in the following 30 days. The total s104 pool will be as calculated above.
The chargeable gain/allowable loss will be calculated as follows:

	£	£
Disposal proceeds		320,000
Less: Acquisition cost		
(3,500 / 5,000) × 280,000		(196,000)
Net gain		124,000

D. Reorganisations

1. Scope

5794 Special rules apply on the disposal of shares that have been issued as a result of:
- bonus issues;
- rights issues;
- conversions;
- mergers and amalgamations;
- reconstructions;
- earn-outs; and
- distributions in the course of liquidations (¶1185).

2. Bonus issues

What is a bonus issue?

5797 A bonus or scrip issue arises when a company capitalises reserves and distributes additional shares to existing shareholders in proportion to their existing shareholding, or where existing shares are split to reduce the nominal value.

The treatment of a bonus issue will depend on whether the bonus shares issued are:
- of the same class;
- of a different class; or
- a scrip issue (shares issued in lieu of a dividend).

MEMO POINTS For the rules that apply to companies see ¶1215.

Bonus issue of shares of the same class

Where shares of the same class are issued without any payment from the shareholder, the bonus shares are deemed to have been acquired on the same date as the original holding. For individuals, trustees and personal representatives this means the shares will enter the section 104 pool. 5800 s 127 TCGA 1992

EXAMPLE Mr B purchased 2,000 shares for £10,000 in January 1982. These were valued at £12,000 in March 1982. He added to this with further acquisitions in June 1995 (4,000 shares for £30,000) and October 1998 (6,000 shares for £60,000). Following this a bonus issue on a 1 for 2 basis was made before he disposed of 16,000 shares in October 2010 for £200,000.
The section 104 pool will look as follows:

	Holding	Cost
Acquisition January 1982 – revalued at March 1982	2,000	12,000
Acquisition June 1995	4,000	30,000
October 1998	6,000	60,000
Total before bonus issue	12,000	102,000
Bonus issue September 1999	6,000	
Total s104 pool	18,000	102,000
Disposal October 2010	(16,000)	(90,667)
	2,000	11,333

Disposal proceeds	200,000
Cost	(90,667)
Gain	109,033

Note
1. The addition of the bonus shares no longer has to be allocated to particular acquisitions, unless the matching rules for same day acquisitions or acquisitions in the following 30 days apply (¶5764).
2. The shares held prior to March 1982 are automatically rebased to their value at that date.
3. Entrepreneurs' relief may be available on the disposal (¶6035).

Bonus issue of shares of a different class

Apportionment Where the shares received under a bonus issue are of a different class to the original holding, the original acquisition cost must be apportioned between the two classes. The **method** of apportionment will depend on whether the new shares are quoted or unquoted. 5803
Once the apportionment is made, the bonus shares are deemed to have been acquired on the same date as the original holding.

Quoted shares Where the new shares are quoted on a recognised stock exchange (¶9995) within 3 months of the issue, the original acquisition cost is apportioned on the basis of the market values of the different classes of shares on the date when the revised quotations reflecting the bonus issue are published. 5806 s 130 TCGA 1992

EXAMPLE Mr C purchased 30,000 shares for £30,000 in D plc in December 2001. In March 2007 there was a 1 for 5 bonus issue of convertible preference shares of £1 nominal value per share. On the first day after the issue, the ordinary shares had a market value of 130p and the preference shares had a value of 110p, giving a value to Mr C of £39,000 for the ordinary shares and £6,600 for the preference shares.
The acquisition cost of the shares is apportioned between the shareholdings as follows:

Cost split:
Ordinary shares:

$$\frac{39{,}000}{39{,}000 + 6{,}600} \times 30{,}000 = £25{,}658$$

Preference shares (balance of original expenditure) = £4,342.

5807 ss 128, 129 TCGA 1992 **Unquoted shares** Where the new shares are unquoted, there will be no published valuation which can be used to apportion the cost. The original and bonus shares are treated as comprising one single holding, despite being different classes of share. On each subsequent disposal of shares (of whichever class), the cost will be apportioned based on the market values at the date of disposal, using the following formula:

$$\frac{\text{No of securities sold}}{\text{No of securities of that class held}} \times \frac{\text{MV of class holding}}{\text{MV of all class holdings}} \times \text{Cost b/fwd (or indexed cost as appropriate)}$$

EXAMPLE In Year 1 Mr E acquired 1,200 ordinary shares in F Ltd at a cost of £10,000.
In Year 2, F Ltd made a bonus issue of 1 £1 preference share for every 3 £1 ordinary shares held, and Mr E received 400 £1 preference shares.
In Year 7, Mr E sold 300 ordinary £1 shares at a time when the market value of the ordinary shares was £3 per share, and the preference share £2.60 per share. The total value of the holding of ordinary shares was therefore £3,600 i.e. £3 × 1,200. Similarly, the total value of the holding of preference shares was £1,040 i.e. £2.60 × 400.

The apportioned cost of the ordinary shares will be calculated as:

$$\frac{300}{1{,}200} \times \frac{3{,}600}{4{,}640} \times 10{,}000 = \underline{\underline{£1{,}940}}$$

Scrip issue in lieu of dividends

5809 s 142 TCGA 1992 For **individuals**, shares issued in lieu of a dividend (i.e. stock dividends) are treated as a new acquisition. For **companies** they are treated as a bonus issue of shares (¶5797).

In both cases, the deemed acquisition cost of the shares will be an amount calculated by the issuing company. This will generally be equivalent to the amount of the dividend forgone.

3. Rights issues

What is a rights issue?

5812 A rights issue is a method by which companies raise additional capital through the **issue of additional shares** to existing shareholders. The shares are issued in proportion to the holdings, for a consideration which is usually below the market value.

The treatment of a rights issue will depend on whether the shares issued are:
- of the same class;
- of a different class; or
- sold nil paid.

MEMO POINTS A **warrant to subscribe** for shares is treated in a similar manner to a rights issue as it involves further payment for new shares. Frequently these are sold to enable a third party to enforce them and take up the warrant. Where this is the case they will be treated as a sale of rights nil paid (¶5821).

Rights issue of shares of the same class

5815 For individuals, trustees and personal representatives the rights issue will be treated as a new acquisition and enters the section 104 pool as such.

MEMO POINTS For companies see ¶1218.

Rights issue of shares of a different class

5818 s 130 TCGA 1992 Where the new shares received in a rights issue are of a different class to the original shares the calculation rules are the same as for bonus issues of a different class (¶5803). The acquisition cost of the rights issue shares must be added to the original cost before apportioning the cost between the classes.

Sale of rights nil paid

A sale of rights nil paid arises where the shareholder sells the rights before the new securities are actually allotted to him. The **proceeds for this disposal** are a capital distribution and the tax treatment will depend on the value of the distribution received. **5821** s 123 TCGA 1992

The **general rule** is that a disposal of this type will be treated as a part disposal (¶5508) of the holding. The amount of the acquisition cost attributable to the part disposed of is calculated using the normal part disposal formula which can be expressed as follows: **5824**

$$\frac{\text{Amount of capital distribution}}{\text{Amount of capital distribution} + \text{market value of remaining holding}} \times \text{Acquisition cost}$$

EXAMPLE In Year 1 Mr G bought 800 ordinary shares in H Ltd for £1,000. In Year 3 there was a 1: 1 rights issue of ordinary £1 shares at £1 each.
Mr G sold the rights nil paid, when they were worth £500 (and his 800 old shares were worth £3,000).
The capital gains liability is as follows:

	£
Disposal proceeds	500
Less: Allowable expenditure (500/(500 + 3,000)) × 1,000	(143)
Gain	357

There are two **exceptions** to the general rule: **5827** s 122 TCGA 1992
– where the cash received is small in relation to the value of the shares at the date of disposal; and
– where the cash received (although small) exceeds the allowable expenditure on the shares and the taxpayer elects to offset the total acquisition cost of the shares against the cash received.

Where the **cash received is small** in relation to the value of the shares at the date of disposal, the taxpayer can elect for the cash received to be simply deducted from the original cost (or March 1982 value, where appropriate). **5830**

MEMO POINTS 1. **Small** is not defined by the legislation, but for these purposes it is generally understood to mean: RI 164
– 5% or less of the value of the asset; or
– £3,000 or less (whether or not this is within the 5% limit).
A taxpayer may suggest to HMRC that a sum higher than these limits should be considered small. HMRC will then decide, based upon the particular circumstances of the case, if a higher limit is applicable. *O'Rourke v Binks* [1992].
2. Where this provision applies to shares in the 1982 pool for companies, **indexation allowance** on a subsequent disposal from the pool will need to be adjusted (¶1131).

Where the amount of the **cash received exceeds the allowable expenditure** for the entire holding (although it is small in relation to the value of the shares at the date of disposal), the shareholder may elect to calculate the gain by using the entire allowable cost. The acquisition cost for the remaining shares will therefore be reduced to nil. **5833**

4. Conversions

Where a holding of securities is subject to a conversion, the new holding is deemed to have been acquired at the same time as the original holding. For example, where a holding of convertible loan stock is converted into shares in the same company, the shares will take on the acquisition details of the loan stock. **5836** ss 132, 133 TCGA 1992

If the holder receives a premium on the conversion of the holding, the premium may give rise to a gain. The rules applying for this are the same as those for the sale of rights nil paid (¶5821).

5. Mergers and amalgamations

5839 s 135 TCGA 1992 When a company is sold, the consideration often consists wholly or partly of shares in the new company (a paper for paper transaction), issued in proportion to the shareholder's original holdings, and the new shares are deemed to have been acquired at the same time as the original holding.

5842 Where the consideration is **entirely in shares of a single class** a chargeable disposal will not arise, provided that the acquisition is for bona fide commercial purposes and the main purpose (or one of them) is not the avoidance of tax, and:
– there is a general offer for the shares which, if accepted, would give the purchaser control of the target company;
– the purchaser acquires (or already holds) more than 25% of the ordinary share capital of the target company; or
– the purchaser acquires (or already holds) the majority of the voting power of the target company.

5845 Where the consideration is **entirely in shares of more than one class**, the allowable cost is apportioned between the new classes of shares. The apportionment is calculated in the same way as bonus and rights issues of shares of different classes (¶5803).

5848 Where the consideration is **partly in shares and partly in cash**, the cash element will be a chargeable disposal. The allowable cost is apportioned between the different elements of the consideration.

MEMO POINTS Where the **consideration is in the form of QCBs** a chargeable disposal arises, the proceeds being the market value of the QCBs on acquisition. This gain only becomes chargeable when the QCB is disposed of.

5851 If the **cash element is small** in relation to the value of the shares at the date of the takeover the relief for small cash receipts will apply where relevant (¶5830).

5852 s 138 TCGA 1992 Shareholders may obtain **formal clearance** from HMRC that the transaction is for bona fide commercial reasons. Full disclosure of the facts known at the time of the application must be made. HMRC have 30 days from receipt of the application in which to grant clearance or request further details.

MEMO POINTS 1. It is **HMRC practice** to refuse clearance applications for arrangements involving loan notes which are redeemable less than 6 months from the date of issue.
2. See ¶6047 for details of an election to disapply these provisions in relation to entrepreneurs' relief.

6. Reconstructions

5854 Sch 5AA TCGA 1992 s 136 TCGA 1992 The rules for mergers and amalgamations (¶5839) also apply to a scheme of reconstruction. A scheme of reconstruction is **defined** as an arrangement whereby:
a. only shareholders of the original company receive shares in the successor company;
b. the shares so issued are in proportion to the original holdings; and either:
– substantially the whole of the business carried on by the original company is carried on by the successor company; or
– the arrangement was carried out as part of a compromise or arrangement with its members.
A reconstruction may occur, for example, where a company divides its trade and hives one trade off to a new company and, as a result, shares in the new company are issued to the existing shareholders.

7. Earn-outs

5857 s 138A TCGA 1992 On the sale of a company, it is common for part of the consideration to be **dependent upon the future results** of the company over a specified period after the sale. This right to receive future consideration is known as an earn-out and is a separate asset. Its value must therefore be included as proceeds for the disposal of the shares.

MEMO POINTS An earn-out right is expressly excluded from being a right to unascertainable consideration for capital loss purposes (¶5482).

Where the future consideration is **unascertainable** and in the form of shares (but not QCBs) in the acquiring company, they will automatically be treated as securities. Consequently the disposal will be treated as a paper for paper exchange and no gain will crystallise. An election can be made to disapply this rule (thereby crystallising a gain). This election is irrevocable and must be made within 2 years of the end of the accounting period in which the earn-out right is conferred. 5860

Any element of deferred but **ascertainable** consideration must be excluded and treated in accordance with the normal rules (¶5308).

MEMO POINTS Where the consideration is in the form of **QCBs** a chargeable disposal arises, the proceeds being the market value of the QCBs on acquisition. This gain only becomes chargeable when the QCB is disposed of.

Where the earn-out element is payable **partly in shares and partly in cash**, the elements must be treated separately. 5861

MEMO POINTS Securities issued as part of an earn-out which are intended entirely to represent sale proceeds are not subject to income tax or National Insurance Contributions on receipt. However, if an **earn-out includes an element of remuneration** (for example, the vendor may agree to stay on as an employee of the purchaser for a specified period post-completion), then securities issued will be subject to income tax and national insurance on receipt.

SECTION 3

Partnership assets

1. Assessment on partners

Where two or more persons carry on a trade or business as a partnership, any tax on chargeable gains arising from partnership assets will be assessed and charged on them separately. Any **partnership dealings** will be treated as dealings by the partners rather than the firm. These provisions also apply to members of a limited liability partnership. 5875 s 59 TCGA 1992, SP D12, SP 1/89

Partners will be **assessed** in the year of assessment (or, for companies, the accounting period), in which the gain arose and not by reference to the partnership accounts (although partnerships are required to give full details of any disposals made during the tax year on the partnership self-assessment return each year). The gains and losses arising from partnership assets will be aggregated with the partner's other gains and losses for the same tax year.

MEMO POINTS 1. A **corporate partner's** share of partnership gains/losses is computed using corporation tax principles and allocated to the partner in accordance with the relevant sharing ratio.
2. The **residence and domicile status** of the partners will determine the basis of the charge to tax, regardless of where the partnership business is carried on. Therefore, a partner who is domiciled and resident in the UK will be subject to UK capital gains tax on gains made on the disposal of partnership assets anywhere in the world.

2. Disposal of partnership assets to a third party

The chargeable gain **arising to each partner** on the disposal of partnership assets to a third party is calculated as the difference between the: 5881
- disposal consideration, pro-rated according to the asset sharing ratio at the date of disposal; and

– allowable expenditure, pro-rated according to the asset sharing ratio at the date of acquisition.

The **asset sharing ratio** will generally be the same as the capital profit sharing ratio, but where no such ratio is specified the profit sharing ratio will be used instead. The partners may specify a particular ratio with regard to a particular asset. In the absence of a written agreement or evidence of the above tests, HMRC take the view that the assets should be treated as if they were held equally.

MEMO POINTS The proportion of **allowable expenditure** may change if there has been an adjustment in the profit sharing ratio since acquisition (¶5890).

5884 The **resulting gain or loss** is then divided between the partners in accordance with the relevant ratio for that asset.

EXAMPLE ABC partnership (with three partners, A, B and C) realised a chargeable gain of £75,000. The following scenarios illustrate alternative ways of allocating the gain to the individual partners:

1. The partnership agreement states that the asset surplus ratio is 3: 2: 1 so the gain is split between the partners in that ratio, i.e.

A	37,500
B	25,000
C	12,500

2. The partners do not have a formal asset surplus ratio but the accounts show that capital was contributed in equal amounts. The gain will therefore be divided on an equal basis of £25,000 each.

3. The partners do not have a formal agreement and the accounts do not give a clear indication of capital contributed. In this case the profit sharing ratio of 2: 1: 1 will be used:

A	37,500
B	18,750
C	18,750

3. Changes in share of partnership assets

When will a capital gains tax charge arise?

5887 There are **three main situations** in which a capital gains tax charge can arise for individual partners as a result of changes in the share of partnership assets:
– an adjustment to the profit sharing ratio;
– the revaluation of an asset in the accounts; and
– payments outside the accounts.
In each case, a part disposal of partnership assets is deemed to occur but in this instance the general rules for part disposal (¶5508) do not apply.

HMRC Brief 3/08 MEMO POINTS Despite HMRC's prior interpretation the introduction of an asset into a partnership by a partner is now considered to be a part disposal by the partner owning the asset with the disposal proceeds being taken to be the market value at that time.

Adjustments to the profit sharing ratio

5890 There are three situations in which a partner will be deemed to have **disposed of all or part of his share** of partnership assets:
– retirement from the partnership;
– admission of a new partner; or
– any other reduction in the share of asset surpluses.
In each situation there will be a **corresponding acquisition** by one or more of the other partners.

EXAMPLE Mr D and Mr E have been in partnership for many years, sharing profits equally. They subsequently admit a new partner, Mr F, and the profit sharing ratio is changed to:

Mr D	45%
Mr E	35%
Mr F	20%

Mr D's share of partnership assets has therefore been reduced by 5% and Mr D's by 15%. Mr F has acquired the corresponding 20%.

Where **no adjustment is made in the partnership accounts** (for example, on a revaluation of assets (¶5902) or payments outside the partnership (¶5905)), the disposal is treated as being made for a consideration equal to the cost of the asset (i.e. no gain no loss), unless the partners are connected (¶5896). **5893**

The result of this is that the partner whose share has increased will carry forward a larger proportion of cost, and the partner whose share has reduced will carry forward a smaller proportion of cost.

EXAMPLE Following on from the previous example, assuming the partnership acquired a long lease (used in the partnership's trade) in May 1990 for a cost of £100,000, the gain/loss on the change in profit sharing ratio in June 2008 will be as follows:

Mr D's tax position:

	£	£
Deemed disposal value – cost of asset × % age change		5,000
Less: Cost		5,000
Gain		Nil

Mr D's base cost will be £45,000 i.e. 100,000 @ 45%

Mr E's tax position:

	£	£
Deemed disposal value – cost of asset × % age change		15,000
Less: Cost		15,000
Gain		Nil

Mr E's base cost will be £35,000 i.e. 100,000 @ 35%

Mr F's tax position:
Mr F will be treated as if he acquired his share of the lease at the deemed disposal values for Mr D and Mr E i.e. 5,000 + 25,000 = £20,000.

If the lease was sold after Mr F's admission to the partnership, for £200,000 the gain/loss would be calculated as follows:

	Mr D £	Mr E £	Mr F £
Disposal proceeds	90,000	70,000	40,000
Less: Cost	(45,000)	(35,000)	(20,000)
Gain	45,000	35,000	80,000

Note:
The calculation is the same for disposals by corporate partners, with the exception that indexation is available.

MEMO POINTS Where a corporate partner acquired the whole or part of an asset **after 31 March 1982** in a no gain/no loss disposal, he will be entitled to rebasing (¶1133) on a subsequent disposal of that asset if the asset had been originally acquired before 31 March 1982. In addition, the indexation allowance on such a disposal will be calculated as if he had acquired the asset on 31 March 1982. Where the disposal is made by an individual, trustee or personal representative on or after 6 April 2008 rebasing will automatically apply.

Where the partners concerned are **connected** (¶5570), market value is used for the disposal consideration. **5896**

Partners are generally considered to be connected, except when partnership is the only connection between them and the disposal is a bona fide commercial transaction.

The deemed consideration will be subject to the rules applying to payments outside the accounts (¶5905).

Revaluation of assets

5902 A revaluation does not, in itself, create a chargeable gain or loss (as an adjustment is simply made in the current or capital accounts of the individual partners of an amount equal to the fractional share of the increase of value). It will, however, have an effect on the consideration to be taken into account on a **subsequent change of profit sharing ratio**, as follows:
– if there is a reduction in a partner's profit sharing ratio after the assets have been revalued, the disposal consideration is deemed to be the partner's share of the new value of the asset multiplied by the percentage reduction in his profit sharing ratio; and
– the partner whose share of assets is correspondingly increased by the adjustment to the profit sharing ratio will have his base cost increased by the same amount.

For corporate partners, **indexation** on the eventual sale of the asset is calculated on the original value up to the date of revaluation, and on the new value from the date of revaluation to the date of sale.

EXAMPLE A Ltd, Mr B and Mr C are in partnership, sharing profits and assets in the ratio 60%, 30% and 10% respectively. In July 1994 the partnership acquired an office building used for the partnership business at a cost of £200,000. In January 2002 the office building was revalued in the balance sheet to £300,000. In October 2003 the profit sharing ratio was changed to 45%, 35% and 20% respectively. The office building was sold in April 2009 for £400,000.

Revaluation:
No tax effect

Change in profit sharing ratio:

A Ltd:
A Ltd's share of profits has reduced by 15% so the computation of its gain on the change of profit sharing ratio will be:

	£
Disposal value (300,000 @ 15%)	45,000
Less: Cost (200,000 @ 15%)	(30,000)
Indexation allowance Jul 1994 to Oct 2003 $\frac{182.6 - 144.0}{144.0} = 0.268 \times 30,000$	(8,040)
	14,196

Mr B:
Mr B's share of profit has increased by 5% so his base cost will be increased to:

200,000 @ 30%	60,000
300,000 @ 5%	15,000
	75,000

Mr C:
Mr C's share of profit has increased by 10% so his base cost will be increased to:

200,000 @ 10%	20,000
300,000 @ 10%	30,000
	50,000

Sale:

	Mr A £	Mr B £	Mr C £
Disposal proceeds	180,000	140,000	80,000
Less: Cost	(90,000)	(75,000)	(50,000)
Indexation allowance Jul 1994 to April 2009 – corporate partner only $\frac{211.5 - 144.0}{144.0} = 0.469 \times 90,000$	(42,210)		
Gain	47,790	65,000	30,000

Note:
If the corporate partner had increased its share in the partnership, indexation allowance would have been allowable on the new cost from the acquisition by the corporate partner until the disposal.

Payments outside the accounts

Where, on a **change in partnership sharing ratios**, payments are made directly between two or more partners outside the framework of the partnership accounts, the payments are treated as consideration for the disposal of the whole or part of the partner's share in the partnership assets. This consideration is in addition to that calculated under the provisions outlined above. **5905**

Where the asset concerned:

a. appears in the balance sheet of the partnership at the date on which the payment was received, the recipient may deduct the fractional amount by which his share of partnership assets has fallen from the payment;

b. does **not appear in the balance sheet** (as is commonly the case with goodwill), the recipient will be chargeable to tax on the full amount of the payment he receives less any consideration he paid on entering the partnership, or the rebased cost where applicable (¶1133 and ¶1146).

EXAMPLE Mr D and Mr E started to work in partnership in January 1995, sharing profits and assets equally. In July 1997 the partnership acquired freehold premises used for the partnership business at a cost of £250,000. In August 2001 the premises were revalued in the balance sheet to £350,000. In December 2009 Mr F entered the partnership and the profit sharing ratio was changed to 50: 30: 20. Mr F paid £10,000 to Mr E in respect of goodwill which was not shown in the balance sheet.

The gain chargeable for Mr E will be:

	£	£
Freehold premises:		
Disposal value (350,000 @ 20%)		70,000
Less: Cost (250,000 @ 20%)		(50,000)
Gain		20,000
Goodwill:		
Disposal value	10,000	
Less: Cost	-	
		10,000
Chargeable gain		30,000

The position for Mr F:
Mr F's base cost will be £70,000 (i.e. 350,000 @ 20%) for the premises and £10,000 for the goodwill.

Note:
The calculation is the same for disposals by corporate partners, with the exception that indexation is available.

MEMO POINTS If the partner is **taxed in full**, he will be able to claim a loss when he finally leaves the partnership or when his share is reduced, provided that in either case he receives, in return for his share of the asset, either:
- no consideration; or
- a lesser consideration.

4. Distribution of partnership assets to partners

Where an asset is distributed to partners rather than disposed of to a third party, the capital gains tax treatment will depend on the nature of the distribution. **5908**

If the asset is **distributed to all of the partners** in accordance with their sharing ratio, none of the partners will be treated as having made a distribution and each partner will retain the base cost that he had before the distribution.

Where the asset is **not distributed to all the partners**, or the sharing ratio is not applied, a computation is required of the gains that would be chargeable on each partner if the asset were disposed of at its current market value.

For partners who did not receive the asset, the gain will be chargeable at the time that the asset is distributed.

For partners in receipt of the asset, no charge will arise on the distribution of the asset but the base cost of the asset for each partner will be the market value of the asset at the date of the distribution, as reduced by the amount of the gain allocated to him. If the distribution results in a loss being allocated to the partner, that will be added to the base cost of the asset.

EXAMPLE Mr A, Mr B and Mr C started to work in partnership in September 1995, sharing profits and assets in the ratio 5: 3: 2. In November 1996 the partnership acquired an asset used in the partnership business at a cost of £150,000. In May 2011 when the market value of the asset was £300,000 the asset was distributed to Mr C.

The gain chargeable for Mr A will be:

	£
Disposal value (300,000 @ 50%)	150,000
Less: Cost (150,000 @ 50%)	(75,000)
Gain	75,000

The gain chargeable for Mr B will be:

	£
Disposal value (300,000 @ 30%)	90,000
Less: Cost (150,000 @ 30%)	(45,000)
Gain	45,000

The position for Mr C:
Mr C will not have a chargeable gain but his base cost carried forward will be:

	£	£
Market value of asset at date of distribution		300,000
Less: Unallocated gain		
Disposal value (300,000 @ 20%)	60,000	
Less: Cost (150,000 @ 20%)	(30,000)	
		(30,000)
Base cost carried forward		270,000

Note:
The calculation is the same for disposals by corporate partners, with the exception that indexation is available.

5. Miscellaneous rules

Mergers

5914 When two or more partnerships merge, the partners are treated as having:
- **disposed** of their interest in the assets of the old partnership; and
- **acquired** an interest in the assets of the new partnership.

The **gains and losses of the deemed disposal** are calculated in accordance with the rules outlined above where assets have been revalued or where a payment is made by the partners of one partnership to the partners of the other. If a gain arises in either case in respect of business assets, the partner may make a claim for **rollover relief** (¶6050) against the assets in the new partnership. If the consideration received for the interest in the assets of the old partnership exceeds the deemed acquisition cost of the assets in the new partnership, the gain eligible for rollover relief will be reduced by the excess.

EXAMPLE The AB partnership decided to merge with the XY partnership in June 2009. The AB partnership shared gains equally and had a property which it acquired in December 1996 for £80,000.
The XY partnership also shared gains equally and had a property which it acquired in December 1996 for £50,000.
It was agreed on the merger that:
- the properties would be revalued at £150,000 and £100,000 respectively;
- XY would pay £70,000 to the AB partners; and
- profits of the new partnership would be shared equally amongst the four partners.

The chargeable gain for Mr A and Mr B will be:

	£	£
Disposal values:		
Reduction of share in property (25 % × 150,000)	37,500	
Received from XY partnership (50 % × 70,000)	35,000	
Less:		72,500
Cost (25 % × 80,000)		(20,000)
Chargeable gain		52,500

Of this gain £25,000 (i.e. 25% of £100,000) can be rolled over into the acquisition cost of the XY partnership property.

The chargeable gain for Mr X and Mr Y will be:

	£	£
Disposal values:		
Reduction of share in property (25 % × 100,000)		25,000
Less:		
Cost (25 % × 50,000)		(12,500)
Chargeable gain		12,500

All of this gain can be rolled over into the acquisition cost of the AB partnership property and the capital payment to Mr A and Mr B, giving Mr X and Mr Y a base cost of £60,000 (i.e. £72,500 - £12,500).

Note:
The calculation is the same for disposals by corporate partners, with the exception that indexation is available.

Annuities

Where an annuity (or other annual payment) is made to a retiring partner which is in excess of an amount regarded as reasonable recognition of the partner's past service to the partnership, the **excess will be treated as** consideration for the disposal of his partnership share. 5917 SP 1/79
The deemed consideration will be subject to the rules applying to payments outside the accounts (¶5905).

The maximum amount considered to be a **reasonable annuity** is determined by applying the fractions in the following table to the average share of partnership profits (i.e. the average of the profits received by the partner in the best 3 of the last 7 years in which he was required to devote substantially all of his time to acting as a partner).

Complete years in partnership	Fraction
1 – 5	1/60 (for each year)
6	8/60
7	16/60
8	24/60
9	32/60
10 or more	40/60

Where a **lump sum** is paid in addition to an annuity, and the total of the annuity and one-ninth of the lump sum does not exceed the above fractions, then only the lump sum will be treated as disposal consideration (i.e. the capitalised value of the annuity will be excluded).

Partnership share acquired in stages

5920 The **general rule** where a partnership share is acquired in stages is that on a subsequent part disposal (such as a decrease in the partner's share of assets), the acquisitions are pooled. **However**, **for companies only**, where some or all of the stages of acquisition occurred before 6 April 1965, the subsequent disposals are to be identified with acquisitions on a first in, first out basis with the pre-6 April 1965 assets, and then on a pooled basis for post-5 April 1965 assets (although if this produces an unreasonable result when applied to temporary changes in the shares of a partnership (for example, where the dates of a partner leaving and a partner joining the partnership do not coincide), the general rule may apply instead).

MEMO POINTS This provision no longer applies to individuals, trustees and personal representatives as any assets held at 31 March 1982 would have been deemed to have been rebased at that date.

Anti-avoidance provisions

5921 s 131 FA 2004 A corporate partner will be assessed to tax as miscellaneous income, if it realises capital from untaxed profits. See ¶2588 for details.

SECTION 4

Wasting assets

5922 s 44 TCGA 1992 An asset is **defined** as a wasting asset if its predicted useful life is 50 years or less. Plant and machinery is always treated as a wasting asset, whereas freehold land is never a wasting asset.

s 46(1) TCGA 1992 The **value of a wasting asset** is deemed to diminish on a straight line basis over the course of its life. Therefore, the allowable expenditure is restricted proportionately.

If an asset has any estimated scrap value the restriction will be made to the cost after deducting the scrap value, and the scrap value will then be added back to reach the qualifying expenditure.

EXAMPLE

1. Mr A purchased a wasting asset in December 2003 for £12,000. The wasting asset had a life of 12 years from the date of purchase. In December 2010, F Ltd sold the asset for £18,000.

	£	£
Disposal proceeds		18,000
Less allowable expenditure:		
Restricted cost:		
Life at acquisition: 12 years		
Life at disposal: 5 years		
$\frac{5}{12} \times £12,000$		5,000
Chargeable gain		13,000

Note:
The calculation is the same for disposals by companies, with the exception that indexation is available.

2. An asset with an estimated useful life of 10 years and a scrap value of £1,000 is purchased in Year 1 by an individual for £11,000. It is sold in Year 8 for £20,000.

	£	£	£
Disposal proceeds			20,000
Less allowable expenditure:			
Cost	11,000		
Less: scrap value	(1,000)		
	10,000		
Restricted:			
Life at acquisition: 10 years			
Life at disposal: 2 years			
$\frac{2}{10} \times £10{,}000$		2,000	
Add: scrap value		1,000	
			3,000
Gain			17,000

MEMO POINTS Special rules apply to interests in **land** (¶5670) and **chattels** (¶6150).

SECTION 5

Assets on which capital allowances could be claimed

Where a disposal of an asset on which capital allowances could be claimed results in a: 5924 s 47 TCGA 1992
- capital **gain**, any allowances already given are clawed back by way of a balancing charge; or
- capital **loss**, special rules apply to restrict the amount of the loss that is allowable by any capital allowances given. This means in practice, that the allowable loss is restricted to any incidental costs of acquisition or disposal.

EXAMPLE

1. Mr A owns an item of machinery which it acquired in Year 1 for £10,000. The machinery is sold in Year 9 for £12,500 and the company incurred incidental costs of sale amounting to £1,200.
As the proceeds exceed the cost of the asset, all capital allowances will be withdrawn by way of a balancing charge.
The position on the disposal of the asset is therefore as follows:

	£	£
Proceeds	12,500	
Less: Incidental costs of sale	(1,200)	
		11,300
Less: Allowable expenditure		
Original cost		(10,000)
Chargeable gain		1,300

2. Taking the facts from 1. above, but the machine is sold for £8,000.
On the disposal of the machine, part of the capital allowances on the asset will be withdrawn by way of a balancing charge; however, a total of £2,000 allowances previously given will still remain.
The position on the disposal of the asset is therefore as follows:

	£	£
Proceeds	8,000	
Less: Incidental costs of sale	(1,200)	
		6,800
Less: Allowable expenditure		
Original cost	10,000	
Less: Capital allowances given	(2,000)	
		(8,000)
Allowable loss		(1,200)

SECTION 6

Debts and loans

1. Definition

5990 A debt is described as something that is owed such as money, goods or services. Debts can be divided into four distinct types for capital gains tax purposes:
- ordinary debts;
- debts on securities;
- qualifying loans to traders; and
- foreign currency bank accounts.

2. Ordinary debts

Basic rule

5993 s 251 TCGA 1992 As a **general rule**, the disposal of a debt (other than a debt on a security) will not give rise to a chargeable gain or an allowable loss.

The **exception** to this rule is where the debt is acquired from the original creditor and then disposed of. The disposal of an acquired debt will give rise to a chargeable gain or an allowable loss. For these purposes the satisfaction of a debt constitutes a disposal.

MEMO POINTS Gains and losses accruing to **companies** are taxed under the loan relationship rules (¶870). This section applies to individuals, trustees and personal representatives.

EXAMPLE In March 1995 Mr A lent £10,000 to Mr B. In December 1996 Mr A sold the debt to Mr C for £8,000. In July 2009 Mr B repaid the debt to Mr C. The tax position is as follows:

Mr A:
The disposal by Mr A does not give rise to a chargeable gain or allowable loss because he is the original creditor.

Mr C:
The satisfaction of the debt gives rise to a chargeable gain for Mr C which is calculated as follows:

	£	£
Disposal value		10,000
Less: Cost		8,000
Gain		2,000

Property received in satisfaction of a debt

5996 s 251(3) TCGA 1992 Where property is received in satisfaction of a debt, the property is treated as disposed of by the debtor and acquired by the creditor for a consideration that must not exceed the market value of the asset at the time of the disposal.

If the **original creditor** receives property in satisfaction of a debt and subsequently incurs a chargeable gain on disposal of the property, that subsequent gain will be restricted to the gain that would have accrued if he had acquired the property for a consideration equal to the debt.

EXAMPLE In June 1999 Mr D received property worth £50,000 from Mr E, in satisfaction of a debt of £60,000. In August 2009 Mr D sold the property for £70,000.

Scenario 1
If Mr D had acquired the debt in September 1997 for £55,000, the capital gains tax implications would be:

Satisfaction of debt	£
Disposal value (MV of property)	50,000
Less: Cost (amount of debt)	55,000
Allowable loss	(5,000)

Sale of property	
Disposal value	70,000
Less: Cost	(50,000)
Gain	20,000

Scenario 2

If Mr D was the original creditor, the capital gains tax implications would be:

	£
Disposal value	70,000
Less: Cost	(50,000)
Gain	20,000

As this produces a net gain, it will need to be compared to the gain that would have accrued if the property had been acquired for a consideration equal to the debt:

Disposal value	70,000
Less: Cost	(60,000)
Gain	10,000

The lower gain (£10,000) will be used.

Connected persons

Where the original creditor disposes of a debt to a connected person (¶5570), any **loss** accruing to the connected person on the subsequent satisfaction or disposal of the debt will not be allowable. The same rule does not apply to chargeable **gains** which will be taxed in full. 5999 s 251(4) TCGA 1992

3. Debts on securities

A **disposal by the original creditor** of a debt on a security can give rise to a chargeable gain or allowable loss. 6002 s 251 TCGA 1992

Securities **include** loan stock and similar securities of: s 132 TCGA 1992
- the government;
- public/local authorities; and
- companies.

Mortgages, charges or other debts in respect of which security is given are **not included** within the definition of securities.

MEMO POINTS 1. There is no requirement for the loan stock or other securities to be **UK assets**.
2. **Debentures** issued by a company after 15 March 1993 are deemed to be securities if they are issued:
- on a reorganisation;
- on a share exchange or company reorganisation where the shareholders are not treated as making a disposal; or
- in pursuance of rights attached to debentures issued in any of the above circumstances.
3. Gains and losses accruing to **companies** are taxed under the loan relationship rules (¶870). The remainder of this section applies to individuals.

There is no clear **definition** of what constitutes a debt on a security, but they are distinguished from ordinary debts by the fact that they have attributes which enable them to be realised or dealt in at a profit. 6005

The following characteristics are indicative of such a debt. No single characteristic is conclusive and each case will be judged on its own merits:
- the debt should be capable of being marketed, sold or assigned;
- the debt should be in the nature of an investment and should carry interest, thereby producing income for the creditor;
- the terms of repayment should be stated;
- the debt should be of a specified amount for a definite time;
- written documentation should be available as evidence of the debt (although a debt can still be a debt on a security without written documentation).

4. Qualifying loans to traders

Irrecoverable loans

6008
s 253 TCGA 1992

A creditor may claim relief for a loss arising when a qualifying loan to a UK resident trader becomes irrecoverable. In contrast to the general rule for debts, an original creditor may claim relief under this provision.

A **qualifying loan** is:
- one used by the borrower wholly for the purposes of a trade, profession or vocation (other than a trade consisting of or including money-lending) including money used for setting up a trade which is subsequently carried on by the borrower;
- one made to a UK resident borrower; and
- not a debt on a security.

MEMO POINTS Relief is **not available** under these provisions if the debt is one that is taken into account in an income or corporation tax computation.

6011 To claim relief, the following **conditions** must be satisfied at the time of the claim:
- any amount of the principal of the loan is irrecoverable;
- the claimant has not assigned the right to recovery of the amount;
- the claimant and the borrower are not spouses/civil partners living together; and
- the claimant and the borrower are not companies in the same group (¶1524), either when the loan was made, or on a subsequent claim.

As a general rule, the date of the disposal will be deemed to be the **time of the claim**. An earlier time may be specified, providing it is not more than 2 years before the beginning of the tax year (or accounting period) in which the claim was made and all the conditions were satisfied at that time.

s 253(12) TCGA 1992

MEMO POINTS Loss relief will **not be available** under these provisions if the loan (or part of it) becomes irrecoverable as a result of the terms of the loan or as a result of an act or omission by the lender.

Guarantees of loans

6017
s 253(4) TCGA 1992

Relief is also available when a claim is submitted by the guarantor of a qualifying loan who has made a **payment under the guarantee** to the lender or co-guarantor. To obtain the relief the guarantor must satisfy HMRC that:
- the loan is either a qualifying loan (¶6008) or a debt on a security (¶6002);
- any amount of the principal of the loan that is still outstanding has become irrecoverable from the borrower;
- the claimant has made a payment under the guarantee in respect of that amount;
- the claimant has not assigned any right to recover the amount which has accrued to him in respect of the payment; and
- the lender and borrower were not spouses/civil partners when the loan was made, when the guarantee was given or at any subsequent time.

The **effect of this provision** is that the claimant will be treated as if he made an allowable loss on the date of the payment equal to the amount of the payment. Amounts payable to the claimant by a co-guarantor will reduce the amount of loss relief available.

The **claim** must be submitted by 4 years from the end of the tax year (or relevant accounting period for companies).

MEMO POINTS Loss relief will **not be available** under these provisions if the loan (or part of it) becomes irrecoverable as a result of the terms of the loan or as a result of an act or omission by the lender or guarantor.

Clawback of relief

Where loss relief has been given for an irrecoverable loan to a trader or for the payment under a guarantee in respect of such a loan, a chargeable gain will accrue where all or any part of the outstanding **principal of the loan is recovered**. The amount of the gain will be equal to the amount of the loan recovered and the date of the charge will be the date of the recovery. 6020 s 253(5) TCGA 1992

A recovery will be deemed to take place when the taxpayer receives money or money's worth in satisfaction of the debt.

MEMO POINTS The **assignment of a right to receive money** in respect of the debt will also be deemed to be a recovery for these purposes. Where the assignment is made other than at arm's length, the taxpayer will be deemed to have received money or money's worth equal to the market value of the right at the date of the assignment.

5. Foreign currency bank accounts

In **general**, sums in a foreign currency bank account constitute chargeable assets. Therefore deposits and withdrawals are treated as separate acquisitions and disposals respectively and should be converted into sterling at the currency exchange rates prevailing at the date of the particular deposit or withdrawal. 6023 s 252 TCGA 1992

In practice, separate computations for each disposal are not required; instead, a gain computed by aggregating all the transactions within each month or tax year is sufficient. However, separate computations are required if an individual account holder, his family or dependants acquired the currency for personal expenditure outside the UK. (This includes expenditure for improving or maintaining a residence outside the UK.)

SECTION 7

Negligible value assets

Loss claim

Where an asset has become worthless, it may be difficult to find a purchaser. Therefore, provisions exist which allow the owner to treat the asset as having been sold and immediately reacquired at market value, thereby crystallising a capital loss. This is known as a negligible value claim. 6025 s 24(2) TCGA 1992

Criteria

Any asset may be subject to a negligible value claim, once its value has become negligible. 6026

When considering **buildings**, HMRC will accept a negligible value claim based solely on the value of the building becoming negligible and not the land on which it stands. However, as a building and the land are strictly a single asset, the land will be deemed to be sold separately and reacquired on the same date, which may give rise to a chargeable gain.

HMRC maintain a list of **quoted shares** which are accepted as being of negligible value. A claim is automatically accepted for any shares on this list. Claims may be made for other shares, but the owner will need to prove that the value has become negligible.

MEMO POINTS There is no statutory **definition of negligible**, although small is defined as 5% and negligible is therefore taken to be considerably less than 5%.

Time limits

6027 A negligible value claim may be **made at any time** while the value remains negligible. In this situation, the asset is deemed to be sold and immediately reacquired on the date the claim is made.

Alternatively, a claim may be made specifying a date on which the asset was of negligible value. The claim must be made within 2 years of the end of the tax year (or accounting period) in which the specified date falls, and the asset must be of negligible value on the date the claim is made and the specified date.

EXAMPLE Mr F owns shares in F Ltd, which became worthless on 1 July 2009. A negligible value claim may be made at any time while the asset is of negligible value.

If Mr F wants the loss to crystallise during the year to 5 April 2010, a claim specifying a date in 2009/10 should be made by 5 April 2012.

SECTION 8

Close non-UK resident companies

6028
s 13 TCGA 1992

Gains made by non-UK resident companies (which would be close (¶2101) if they were UK resident) are attributed to **UK resident participators**, whether or not such gains are in fact remitted back to the UK. **Non-UK domiciled individuals** will also be subject to such attribution. The gains so attributed are current year gains (as reduced by any current year losses) of the overseas company. There is no facility to carry forward losses from one year to the next for these provisions.

The following gains are specifically **excluded** from these provisions:
- those arising on the disposal of tangible assets used solely for the overseas trade; and
- foreign currency gains (where the currency is used solely for the overseas trade).

No assessment will be made unless the relevant participator's entitlement is more than 10% of the attributed gains. (In determining this, gains attributable to connected persons (¶5570) are taken into account.)

MEMO POINTS 1. **Indexation** continues to be calculated in the normal way as the gain is calculated at the company level before attribution.
2. If there is an **actual distribution** of overseas gains, any tax paid under these provisions is allowed as a credit. If the tax assessed on the attributed gains is still not fully utilised in this manner, it can be carried forward as a deduction on a chargeable gain arising on the future disposal of the overseas company shares.

s 14A TCGA 1992

3. Where a non-UK domiciled individual is attributed a gain where the asset was located outside the UK then the remittance basis will apply to the gain where it is claimed. Where the gain is remitted and taxed in a later year than the one it was attributed in then no account will be taken of the company's losses in calculating that person's apportionment.

SECTION 9

Disposal of know-how

6030
ss 176 - 179 CTA 2009
ss 193, 194 ITTOIA 2005

The tax treatment of know-how and intangible assets for companies changed for assets acquired or created on or after 1 April 2002 (¶824). Where those provisions are not applicable, the following rules apply:

Transaction	Treatment
Sale of know-how, but the trade in which know-how was previously used carries on	Disposal proceeds are treated as a trading receipt
Sale of know-how in connection with a disposal of the relevant trade	Treated as a disposal of goodwill, so the vendor will be liable to capital gains tax and the purchaser will not be able to claim capital allowances on the goodwill cost [1]

Note:
1. Alternatively, the buyer and seller may make a **joint election** to treat the consideration for the disposal as a payment for know-how. Consequently:
– the vendor will be treated as receiving a receipt taxable under Schedule D Case VI (for corporate tax purposes), or as sundry income (for income tax purposes); and
– the purchaser will be treated as having incurred capital expenditure on know-how and therefore capital allowances may be available.
Such an election must be made within 2 years of the date of disposal.

SECTION 10

Disposal of plant and machinery leased under a long funding lease

When a long funding lease (¶483 onwards) of plant or machinery **commences**, it is treated as disposed of and immediately reacquired at the date of commencement for the following values: **6032** s 25A TCGA 1992
– if the lease is a long funding operating lease, the market value of the plant and machinery at the commencement of the lease;
– if the lease is a long funding finance lease, the lessor's net investment (as would be first recognised in his accounts if they were prepared in accordance with GAAP).

On a subsequent **termination** of a long funding lease, it is treated as disposed of and immediately reacquired at the date of termination for the value of the plant and machinery at or about the time when the lease terminates.

Where the above deemed disposal and reacquisition gives rise to a capital loss, the **loss is restricted** by the following amounts: **6033** s 41A TCGA 1992
– where the plant or machinery has been leased only once, by the amount the asset has fallen in value over the term of the lease;
– where the plant or machinery has been leased more than once, by the amount the asset has fallen in value in each period it was leased.

MEMO POINTS 1. These **loss restrictions are necessary** as the normal rules that apply when capital allowances have been claimed (¶5924) do not apply to the lessor as no capital allowances will have been claimed by the lessor.
2. The **fall in value** is based on the market value at the start and end of the lease.
3. Lessors can **elect to opt into** the long funding lease regime for plant and machinery leases in certain situations (¶492).

CHAPTER 6

Reliefs

OUTLINE

¶¶

SECTION 1

Entrepreneurs' relief

6035 s 4 TCGA 1992

Entrepreneurs' relief reduces the rate of tax on qualifying business disposals to 10%. The relief is available to individuals and trusts, but not to companies.

Comment The legislation is largely modelled on the previous retirement relief provisions, with much of the same terminology being used. It is expected that case law on retirement relief will become relevant in looking at the conditions for entrepreneur's relief.

MEMO POINTS For disposals prior to 23 June 2010 the method of computation was different, although the net effect was still to charge tax at 10%. For details, see *Tax Memo 2010-2011*.

A. Qualifying business disposals

6036 Three types of disposal qualify for the relief:

Type of disposal	¶¶
A material disposal of business assets	¶6038
A disposal associated with a relevant material disposal	¶6041
A disposal of trust business assets	¶7380

s 169S(1) TCGA 1992 s 169I(8) TCGA 1992

A "**business**" is defined as a trade, profession or vocation.

Further rules extend these provisions to partners in a business and include the case where a sole trader takes on a partner, as such giving away part of his business interest. All partners in a business are treated as owning the business.

1. Material disposal of business assets

6038 s 169I TCGA 1992

To qualify, a disposal must satisfy the following two conditions:
– it is a disposal of a business asset; and
– it is considered to be material.

The interpretation of these conditions depends on the type of assets involved in the disposal, as summarised in the following table:

Type of business asset	Materiality conditions
The whole or part of a business [1]	Owned by the disposer throughout a period of at least one year ending with the date of disposal
An asset (or interest in an asset) **used for the purpose of a business** at the time the trade ceased	Two conditions [2] must be met: – the business was owned by the disposer throughout a period of at least one year ending with the date of cessation; and – the asset is disposed of on or within three years after the date of cessation [3].
Shares or securities (or an interest in the same) in a trading company [4] which continues to trade after the disposal.	Two conditions must be met: – the company was the individual's **personal company** [6]; and – the individual was an officer or employee of the company [5] These conditions must be satisfied throughout a period of at least one year ending with the date of disposal.
Shares or securities (or an interest in the same) in a trading company [4] which ceases to trade.	As above, but the conditions must also be satisfied throughout a period of one year ending with the date the trade ceased. In addition, the disposal must take place on or within three years after the date of cessation.

Note
1. Assets under this heading only qualify for relief if they are **used for the purpose of the business**, as opposed to being held as an **investment**. Goodwill specifically qualifies for relief; shares and securities specifically do not. s 169L TCGA 1992
2. This means that in winding up a business, care must be taken over the order of sale and cessation.
3. The use to which an asset is put during this three year period is irrelevant.
4. The definition of a trading company is the same as that for gift relief (¶6102).
5. The individual may be the officer or employee of the trading company itself, or of a company within a trading group
6. "Personal company" means that the individual owns at least 5% of the share capital, and this holding carries at least 5% of the voting rights.

Disposal of part of a business

Based on cases involving the former retirement relief (see ¶6035), in order for the disposal to qualify, the part involved must be identifiable as a going concern (and not be simply an asset used in the business). This may appear straightforward but has caused difficulties in the past. 6040

EXAMPLE

1. A farmer as part of his retirement process sold two portions of land in two separate transactions in a 12 month period to the same purchaser, the total amount of land amounting to 45% of the land he used to raise cattle. After this he changed the activities undertaken on the farm. On appeal the court stated that this was not sufficient to be considered to be the disposal of part of a business. In looking at the level of interference that the business suffered as a result of a disposal regard could only be taken of that particular disposal and not of any other, or of any surrounding circumstances. *Mannion v Johnston* [1988]

2. A taxpayer owned land, together with a milking parlour with yard, hay barn and cattle shed. The milking parlour and yard were sold at auction with a number of cattle sold shortly afterwards. He ceased dairy farming but continued to rear store cattle. As the dairy farming was separate from the rearing, and the sale of the parlour meant it was impossible to continue the former trade it was considered to be the disposal of part of a business. *Jarmin v Rawlings* [1994]

2. A disposal associated with a relevant material disposal

6041 s 169K TCGA 1992 Where an individual makes a **material disposal of a partnership interest** or **the sale of shares** (¶6038) that qualifies for entrepreneur's relief, further disposals may also qualify for relief if the following conditions are met:
– the disposal is made as part of the individual's withdrawal from participation in partnership business, or in the company (or a company which is a member of the trading group); and
– the assets concerned were used for the purpose of the business throughout the period of one year ending with the earlier of:
  – the date of the **material disposal**; and
  – the cessation of the business of the partnership or company.

6042 s 169P TCGA 1992 The amount of relief may be **restricted** in any of the following circumstances:

Circumstance	Amount of gain which is eligible for relief
The asset was used for the purpose of the business for only a part of the total period of its ownership	A proportion based on time of use
The asset was only partly used for the purpose of the business	A proportion based on the extent of use
The individual was only involved in the business for part of the time for which he owned the asset	A proportion based on time of involvement
Rent was charged to the business for the use of the asset	Provided the rent charged was at less than a market rate: a proportion based on the undercharge. Any rental period before 6 April 2008[1] is ignored.

Note
1. The date when the relief was introduced.

EXAMPLE

1. A partner sells his interest in the partnership. At that time he also sells property occupied by the partnership for a period of one year, but which he has owned for five years, for a gain of £100,000. Of this gain only £20,000 (1/5 × 100,000) will qualify for relief.

2. While disposing of a qualifying shareholding, an individual also sells the office that he owned and let to his company at an annual rent of £10,000. The gain on disposal of the office is £300,000. The annual market rate for the rent is estimated to have been £25,000. The amount of the gain that will qualify for relief will be restricted by £120,000 (10,000/25,000 × 300,000), leaving £180,000 eligible for relief.

B. Calculating and claiming the relief

Calculation

6043 s 169N TCGA 1992 Before calculating the relief, the **net gain** must be calculated, by aggregating the actual gains with any losses arising from disposals that would also have attracted the relief if a gain had been made on them.

There is a **maximum lifetime amount** of cumulative net gains to which the relief can apply, as shown in the following table. If the qualifying gains in a tax year cause the limit to be breached, the excess gains are subject to tax at the full rate.

Date of disposal	Maximum lifetime amount (£)
6 April 2008 to 5 April 2010	1 million
6 April 2010 to 22 June 2010	2 million
23 June 2010 to 5 April 2011	5 million
6 April 2011 onwards	10 million

EXAMPLE M disposed of his shares in his personal company in August 2010 making a gain of £7.5m. At the same time he also sold a factory which he owned and was used rent-free by the company, for a loss of £100,000. M's taxable income for 2010/11 was more than the basic rate limit.
The net gains from assets qualifying for the relief amounts to £7.4m.
Relief available:
The first £5m is taxed at 10%. The balance of £2.4m is taxed at 28% (after deducting the annual exemption).

Increases in the lifetime limit are not retrospective, and therefore cannot be used to reduce gains that arose before the limit was raised. However, any gains that exceeded the original limit, and as such did not benefit from the relief, do not count towards the new limit. 6044

EXAMPLE Continuing the above example, M disposed of his shares in another qualifying company in May 2011, making a gain of £5.2m. The new lifetime limit of £10m is in effect. His available lifetime amount is computed as follows:

	£	£
Current lifetime limit		10,000,000
Less: previous qualifying gains	7,400,000	
Reduced by: gains qualifying, but not attracting relief	(2,400,000)	
		(5,000,000)
Gain eligible for relief on second disposal		5,000,000

The excess gain of £200,000 will be subjected to tax as normal.

An individual's gains are also aggregated with gains made by a **trust** where the relief applies because he is a qualifying beneficiary (see ¶7380+). If there is a **disposal on the same day** by a trust and an individual, in applying the relief the individual's gain is deemed to be made first. While the overall level of tax will not change as a result of this, it may affect who is liable to pay it. 6045

Claiming

The relief must be claimed by the first anniversary of 31 January following the tax year of the qualifying disposal. Typically this will be done by making a claim in the tax return reporting the gain. 6046 s 169M TCGA 1992

C. Company reconstructions

Reconstructions generally

A **share for share exchange**, other than one involving qualifying corporate bonds, is usually treated as if the replacement shares were acquired at the same time as the original shares (¶5839). An election can be made to **disapply this rule** for entrepreneur's relief, and in doing so crystallise the gain (and the relief) that would otherwise have been postponed. 6047 s 169Q TCGA 1992

MEMO POINTS 1. An election would allow the initial share disposal to benefit from the availability of entrepreneurs' relief where the replacement shares may not qualify.
2. The time limit for this election is the same as for claiming the relief.
3. As the claim is for the entire gain, it is the entire gain that is added to the cumulative lifetime amount. This is the case even if only part of the gain is charged at that time.

Reconstruction involving qualifying corporate bonds

6049 s 169R TCGA 1992

For a disposal on or after **23 June 2010** an election similar to that described in ¶6047 can be made.

For **earlier disposals**, no such election was available. The gain on the disposal of the old shares was calculated, and rolled over into the new securities. Entrepreneur's relief could be claimed on this gain. At that time, the relief was given as a 4/9ths reduction in the chargeable gain. On a subsequent disposal of the replacement assets, the reduced gain becomes chargeable. If the ultimate disposal is taxable at 28%, this results in an effective tax rate of 15.55% (being 5/9 x 28%).

MEMO POINTS 1. Similar provisions apply for gains deferred into **EIS or VCT** shares.
2. Where the gain being deferred arises from a previous deferred gain being triggered, the disposal that is to be compared to the conditions for the relief will be the one giving rise to the original gain.
3. Where two or more gains are deferred in one asset each gain will be treated separately for the purposes of the relief.
4. Because of the involvement of qualifying corporate bonds, it is likely that if the election is not made in such circumstances, the ultimate disposal will not qualify for entrepreneur's relief at a later date.

SECTION 2

Rollover relief on replacement of business assets

A. Basic principles

6050

When a gain on the disposal of an asset which has been used for the purposes of a business may be possible to **defer** the payment of tax by **rolling over** the gain into the base cost of a replacement asset.

The effect is to reduce the allowable expenditure on the replacement asset, thus increasing the gain which arises on its ultimate disposal.

To be **eligible** for this relief:
- both the original and replacement assets must be qualifying assets (¶6053); and
- the replacement asset must be acquired within a set period (¶6059).

To qualify for **relief in full**, the disposal proceeds of the original asset (net of any costs of disposal) must be **fully reinvested** in a replacement asset (net of any costs of acquisition). If the proceeds are only **partially reinvested** (¶6065), the relief is restricted.

There is no requirement for the disposal to be by way of sale, nor is there a requirement for any disposal proceeds to be in the form of cash. This means that, for example, gifts of assets, or disposals in exchange for shares, may also qualify for relief.

MEMO POINTS 1. A similar relief, known as **holdover relief**, is available where the replacement asset is a depreciating asset (¶6068).
2. See ¶1630 for details of rollover relief and **groups of companies**.

B. The original asset

6053 ss 152, 157 TCGA 1992

To qualify for the relief, the original asset must be:
- used throughout the period of ownership for the purposes of a **qualifying activity**; and
- of a type which falls within one of a series of **qualifying classes**.

Qualifying activities

To qualify, the business activity must be one of the following: **6054** s 157,-158 TCGA 1992
a. a trade (including furnished holiday lettings and the management of woodlands on a commercial basis) carried on by either:
– the taxpayer; or
– the taxpayer's personal company (for example, a building owned by a shareholder and used by the company for the purposes of its trade);
b. a profession, office or employment;
c. a not-for-profit unincorporated association chargeable to corporation tax (or a company owned by it);
d. a not-for-profit professional or trade organisation;
e. share farming; or
f. discharging the responsibilities of a public authority.

MEMO POINTS 1. An individual's **personal company** is one in which he exercises not less than 5% of the voting rights. The company must be his personal company both at the time that the old asset is disposed of, and when the new asset is acquired, and the same personal company must use both the old and new assets. s 157 TCGA 1992
2. Any **non-trade use** in the period before 31 March 1982 is ignored. In limited circumstances, a restricted relief may be available for assets which are used only partly for trade purposes (¶6074).
3. A non-UK resident person trading in the UK through a **permanent establishment** will be able to claim rollover relief if the old asset and the new asset are both within the charge to UK tax.

Qualifying classes of asset

The asset must also fall within one of the following **qualifying classes**: **6055** s 155 TCGA 1992

Class	Assets
1A	Land and buildings [1,2] occupied (as well as used) for the purpose of the business
1B	Fixed plant and machinery [3]
2	Ships, aircraft and hovercraft
3	Satellites, space stations and spacecraft, including launch vehicles
4	Goodwill [4]
5	Milk quotas and potato quotas [4]
6	Ewe and suckler cow premium quotas [4]
7	Fish quotas [4]
7A	Payment to farmers under the EU single payment scheme [5]
8A	Syndicate rights of an underwriting member of Lloyd's
8B	Syndicate rights of an individual underwriting member of Lloyd's held through a Member's Pooling Arrangement

Note:
1. Buildings include:
– any part of a building; and
– any permanent or semi-permanent structures in the nature of a building.
2. Buildings used in a trade of dealing or developing land do not qualify if the profits on sale are included in trading profits.
3. Fixed is taken to mean normally in one place, and not easily moved. It is not necessary for the plant or machinery to be attached to a building. Lifts and escalators that have become part of the building are not plant and machinery.
4. These assets are removed from the list of qualifying assets for companies for acquisitions and disposals made on or after 1 April 2002. Such gains are now taxed within the intangible asset regime (¶824).
5. The single payment scheme is a subsidy scheme introduced by the EU whereby farmers receive a single payment linked to various environmental conditions. For further details, see the DEFRA website (www.defra.gov.uk).

MEMO POINTS 1. Rollover relief may be available on the grant of an **option** over land, if the underlying asset itself would have qualified for this relief. CG 61000
2. HMRC's view is that a **franchisee's rights under a franchise agreement** is a capital asset and is not automatically treated as part of goodwill. However they do accept that a franchisee may be able to generate some goodwill in a franchised business. The value of franchise rights and goodwill will depend upon the precise facts of each individual case and, in particular, the level of control exercised by the franchisor. Tax Bulletin 83

C. The replacement asset

6059 s 152 TCGA 1992 To qualify for relief the replacement asset **must**:

a. be acquired (or an unconditional contract placed) during a **qualifying period** which:
– starts one year before and
– finishes three years after
the date of disposal of the original asset;
b. be used for a **qualifying activity** (¶6053) immediately after acquisition; and
c. fall within one of the **qualifying classes** (¶6055). There is no requirement for the original and replacement asset to fall within the same class.

There is no requirement for the assets to be used for the purposes of the same trade, provided the gap between the two trades is no more than 3 years.

MEMO POINTS 1. HMRC have powers to **extend the time limit** in which a replacement asset can be acquired in limited circumstances. This is only likely to be done where the intention to acquire a replacement asset existed and can be evidenced, but circumstances beyond the individual's control prevented an acquisition taking place before the time limit expired.
2. Rollover relief is available on **deemed gains** arising, for example, on the gift of an asset, appropriation to trading stock etc.
3. Where reinvestment is made in **more than one asset** a just and reasonable apportionment is made.

6060 **By concession**, rollover relief is also available where:
a. the disposal proceeds from the old asset are used:
ESC D22 CG 60410 – for **improvements** (meaning to enhance the value of other assets, provided they are used in a trade, or will be so used once the enhancement is completed);
ESC D25 – to **acquire a further interest** in an existing asset already used in the trade (for example, by extending an existing lease);
ESC D24 CG 60810 **b.** the asset is **not brought into immediate use** because work of a capital nature is to be carried out on it (provided once this work is completed it is then brought into use); or
ESC D16 CG 60820 **c.** the **asset is sold and then reacquired for purely commercial reasons** (for example on a partnership change, resulting in a requisition of a fractional share of partnership assets).
Relief is specifically denied if a tenant acquires the freehold interest in land and immediately sells off part of it (for example, to finance the original purchase). HMRC take the view that the acquisition does not constitute expenditure on a new asset;

MEMO POINTS In practice, rollover relief is also available when assets are **exchanged or partitioned**.

D. Calculation

1. Basic calculation

Full relief

6062 s 152 TCGA 1992 To be eligible for full relief, the proceeds from the disposal (net of the costs of disposal) of the original asset must be **fully reinvested** in the replacement asset (net of the cost of acquisition). This does not mean that the specific funds must be identified, simply that expenditure of an equivalent sum must be incurred.

The **relief is determined by** calculating the gain on the original asset and reducing the allowable expenditure on the replacement asset by the same amount.

Where applicable, indexation allowance is available for both assets. For the old asset it will be calculated in accordance with the normal rules (¶1118). On the subsequent disposal of the new asset, indexation allowance will be based on the cost of the new asset after deducting the rolled over gain and will run from the date of acquisition of the new asset.

EXAMPLE Mr A bought a factory (for trade use by his personal company) on 1 December 1996 for £200,000 which he sold on 1 June 2010 for £425,000, realising a gain, after indexation of £214,400. On 31 March 2012, he acquires a freehold office building (for trade use by his personal company) at a cost of £500,000.
As all the proceeds from the disposal were reinvested, full rollover relief is available, reducing the qualifying expenditure on the replacement office building as follows:

	£
Expenditure on office building	500,000
Less: Rolled over gain	(214,400)
Qualifying expenditure	285,600

MEMO POINTS Any gain arising on a **subsequent disposal of the replacement asset** may, in its turn, qualify for rollover relief if the conditions are satisfied.

Partial relief

Where the proceeds from the sale of the original asset are only partially reinvested, so much of the gain as equals the the amount not reinvested becomes chargeable immediately, and only the balance is rolled over. **6065** s 153 TCGA 1992

Where the proceeds which are **not reinvested exceed the amount of the gain**, no rollover relief is available.

EXAMPLE Mr B bought a factory (for trade use by his personal company) on 1 December 1996 for £200,000 which he sold on 1 June 2009 for £425,000, realising a gain of £214,400. On 31 May 2011, he acquired a freehold office building (for trade use by his personal company) at a cost of £400,000.
An immediate chargeable gain arises, equal to the proceeds not reinvested (£25,000).
The balance of the gain can be rolled over, to reduce the qualifying expenditure on the replacement office building as follows:

	£
Expenditure on office building	400,000
Less: Rolled over gain (£214,400 – £25,000)	(189,400)
Qualifying expenditure	210,600

2. Depreciating assets

Temporary holdover relief

Where the replacement asset is a **depreciating asset** (broadly, one with a useful life of 60 years or less), the gain is simply held over (deferred), and **becomes chargeable** on the earliest of the following: **6068** s 154 TCGA 1992
- 10 years from the acquisition of the replacement asset;
- the disposal of the replacement asset; or
- the cessation of trading use of the replacement asset.

The amount of the gain which can be held over is calculated in exactly the same way as for non-depreciating assets.

Where a gain is held over in this way, and subsequently a qualifying **non-depreciating asset is purchased** before the gain becomes chargeable, a further claim may be made to rollover the original gain into the new asset. The qualifying expenditure on the new asset will be reduced by the held over gain in the usual way. **6071**

EXAMPLE Mr C sold fixed plant (used in his trade) in Year 1 for £500,000, realising a gain after indexation of £130,000. In Year 2, he acquired a 25 year lease on a building used for trade purposes at a cost of £550,000, and submitted a claim to hold over the gain.
In Year 9, Mr C purchased the freehold of the building also used for trade purposes at a cost of £750,000. As the leasehold building was still owned and used for trade purposes and 10 years had not elapsed since its acquisition, Mr C could claim to rollover the original gain of £130,000 against the qualifying expenditure on the new building, reducing the qualifying expenditure to £620,000.

6072 If only **part of the proceeds from the original asset are reinvested** in a non-depreciating asset in this way, the held over gain is reduced, but still becomes chargeable on the date specified in ¶6068.

EXAMPLE Mr D sold fixed plant (used in his trade) in Year 1 for £275,000, realising a gain of £50,000. In Year 2, he acquired a 25 year lease on a factory (for use in his trade) at a cost of £350,000, and submitted a claim to hold over the gain.
In Year 9, Mr D purchased the freehold of an office building also used for trade purposes at a cost of £250,000. As the factory was still owned and used for trade purposes and 10 years had not elapsed since its acquisition, Mr D could claim to rollover part of the original gain of £50,000 against the qualifying expenditure on the new building. Consequently:
– a gain equal to the proceeds not reinvested (£25,000) will become chargeable when the held over gain crystallises (¶6068); and
– the balance of the gain can be rolled over, to reduce the qualifying expenditure on the replacement office building as follows:

	£
Expenditure on building	250,000
Less: Rolled over gain (£50,000 – £25,000)	(25,000)
Qualifying expenditure	225,000

3. Partial business use

When is relief available?

6074 Assets which are only partially used for trade purposes may be eligible for relief where:
– the original asset has been used for periods of exclusive trade use and periods of exclusive non-trade use; or
– either the original or replacement asset (or both) is subject to mixed use, and the asset is a building or structure.

Exclusive periods of non-business use

6075 s 152(7) TCGA 1992 Where the original asset has been subject to periods of exclusive non-trade use, the amount of the gain eligible for rollover relief is restricted by treating the asset as two separate assets, one being a qualifying trade asset, and the other not. The proportion of the gain attributable to the trade asset is determined by the period of qualifying use as a proportion of the total period of ownership. Periods before 31 March 1982 are ignored.

EXAMPLE Mr E sold a factory (used by his personal company for trade purposes) on 31 March 2011 for £500,000, realising a chargeable gain of £75,000. The factory had been acquired 18 years ago and in that period had been let to a third party for a period of 3 years.
On 31 July 2011, he acquired another factory (for trade use by his personal company) at a cost of £600,000.
The chargeable gain is apportioned between trade and non-trade assets based on a period of ownership of 18 years, of which 15 were exclusively trade use.

	Total	Trade (15/18)	Non-trade (3/18)
	£	£	£
Total gain	75,000	62,500	12,500
Less: Rolled over gain	(62,500)	(62,500)	(0)
Chargeable gain	12,500	Nil	12,500

The qualifying expenditure on the new factory would be reduced as follows:

	£
Expenditure on factory	600,000
Less: Rolled over gain	(62,500)
Qualifying expenditure	537,500

Mixed use

Where a building or structure is used simultaneously for trade and non-trade use, it is treated for rollover relief as two separate assets, one being a qualifying asset, and the other not.. Similarly, if the replacement asset is a building or structure that is used only partly for trade purposes, it is treated as two assets and the gain on the original asset can only be rolled over into the expenditure apportioned to trade use. **6076** s 152(6) TCGA 1992

EXAMPLE Mr F sold a hotel on 31 March 2011 for £300,000, realising a chargeable gain of £100,000. The hotel had been acquired 10 years ago, and used 75% for the business, with the remainder being used as accommodation for Mr F and his family.
On 30 September 2011, Mr F acquired a new hotel at a cost of £320,000, of which 65% was used for the business.
The chargeable gain is apportioned between trade and non-trade assets based on a percentage of trade use.

	Total	Trade (75 %)	Non-trade (25 %)
	£	£	£
Total gain	100,000	75,000	25,000
Less: Rolled over gain (see below)	(58,000)	(58,000)	(0)
Chargeable gain	42,000	17,000	25,000

The proceeds of the trade element are £225,000 (being 75% of £300,000). As the expenditure on the trade element of the replacement asset is only £208,000 (being 65% of £320,000), the gain which can be rolled over is restricted by the amount not re-invested (£17,000).
The qualifying expenditure on the new asset is reduced as follows:

	Total	Trade (65 %)	Non-trade (35 %)
	£	£	£
Expenditure	320,000	208,000	112,000
Less: Rolled over gain	(58,000)	(58,000)	(0)
Qualifying expnditure	262,000	150,000	112,000

4. Relief for rebasing

Where an individual disposes of an asset with a held over gain, and the series of transactions from 31 March 1982 to the date he received the asset were all made under no gain/no loss provisions without having had the benefit of being rebased, then the "cost" for the disposal is deemed to be the market value at 31 March 1982 plus the indexation allowance accruing from 31 March 1982 to the date he received the asset (or 5 April 2008 if earlier). **6077**

MEMO POINTS Rebasing is where assets held at 31 March 1982 are treated as if they were sold and immediately reacquired on that date. For details see ¶5332.

E. Administration

Claims for relief

6080 CG 60600 Claims for rollover and depreciating-asset hold over relief are subject to the general time limits for claims. As such relief must be claimed in writing within 4 years of the relevant tax year (or, for companies, within 4 years of the end of the accounting period) to which it relates.

The **time limit** starts on the later of the end of the year of assessment (or accounting period) in which the:
- disposal takes place; or
- new assets are acquired.

MEMO POINTS 1. The claim **must specify** the following:
- identity of original asset(s);
- date of disposal;
- disposal proceeds;
- identity of replacement asset(s);
- date of acquisition;
- acquisition expenditure; and
- amount of disposal proceeds reinvested.

2. Where **more than one asset** is disposed of or acquired, the claim must also specify how the proceeds have been allocated to the replacement assets.
3. Prior to 1 April 2010 the time limit was 5 years from the 31 January following the tax year (6 years from the end of the accounting period for companies).

6083 s 153A TCGA 1992 A claim cannot be made until a replacement asset is actually acquired. However, it is possible to make a **provisional declaration** of intention to claim relief before a replacement asset is acquired. This declaration must be made on the self-assessment return for the tax year in which the disposal occurs, and the capital gains tax liability for the year can be calculated on the basis that the gain is to be rolled over. However, if a suitable replacement asset is not purchased within the time limit, the claim is invalid and the tax will be payable with interest, calculated as though no claim had been made.

MEMO POINTS The provisional declaration does not remove the requirement for a valid claim to be made once a replacement asset is acquired.

Spouses and civil partners

6084 Spouses and civil partners are treated as separate persons for rollover relief purposes. Consequently, a gain may be rolled over into a new asset acquired from a spouse or civil partner.

Partnerships

6086 Gains realised by a partnership on a disposal of qualifying assets (or on a change in a profit sharing ratio) are **assessed on** the individual partners. Such gains can be rolled over into another qualifying asset (either acquired by the individual or the partnership).

6088 For capital gains tax purposes **limited liability partnerships** (LLPs) are treated as partnerships. However, from the date of the commencement of a liquidation, an LLP is treated as a corporate entity and any gains originally rolled over into a qualifying asset within the LLP will be brought into charge.

SECTION 3

Gift relief

A. Definition

A gift is **essentially** the transfer of an asset to another person for no consideration or at less than market value. 6095 ss 165, 260 TCGA 1992

Gift relief allows the taxpayer to hold over the gain by deducting it from the deemed acquisition cost of the asset in the hands of the recipient.

MEMO POINTS See ¶5564 for details of **other reliefs** available on gifts of certain assets.

B. Assets eligible for relief

Qualifying gifts

The **following** assets qualify for relief if they are gifted to a UK resident and ordinarily resident person: 6097
- business assets;
- unlisted shares in trading companies;
- agricultural land;
- assets on which inheritance tax is chargeable; and
- certain assets which are specifically exempted from inheritance tax.

MEMO POINTS Gifts of the following will **not qualify** for gift relief:
- gifts to dual resident individuals who would not be liable to UK tax on a subsequent disposal under the terms of a tax treaty;
- gifts to companies controlled by persons connected with the donor, who would not be liable to UK tax on a subsequent disposal of their interest in the company because they are non-UK resident or ordinarily resident (either in fact or under the terms of a double tax treaty);
- certain gifts to settlor interested trusts (¶7404); and
- gifts to a company of shares and securities of any kind.

Business assets

A business asset will be eligible for gift relief if it is (or is an interest in) an **asset used in** the trade, profession or vocation of: 6100 s 165 TCGA 1992
- the taxpayer;
- his personal company; or
- a member of a trading group of which the holding company is the taxpayer's personal company.

MEMO POINTS 1. For **trustees**, gift relief will be available if the asset is used for the purposes of a trade, profession or vocation carried on by:
- the trustees; or
- a beneficiary with an interest in possession in the settled property immediately before the disposal.

2. A **personal company** means a company in which the taxpayer exercises not less than 5% of the voting rights, and a **trading group** is a group of companies the activities of which, when taken together, are wholly or mainly in the course of, or for the purposes of, a trade.

3. Assets owned by a partner but used in the trade of a **partnership** will qualify as business assets.

Unlisted shares in trading companies

6102 Shares and securities of a trading company (or the holding company of a trading group) will **qualify for gift relief where**:
– they are neither listed on a recognised stock exchange (¶9995) nor dealt in on the Unlisted Securities Market; or
– the trading company or holding company is the taxpayer's personal company (¶6100) or, in the case of trustees, the trustees hold not less than 25% of the voting rights.

MEMO POINTS 1. A **trading company** is a company that exists wholly for the purpose of carrying on one or more trades. A company will also fall within this definition if it has other purposes but those have no substantial effect on the extent of the company's activities.
2. A **holding company** is a company whose business consists wholly or mainly of holding shares in one or more companies which are its 51% subsidiaries.

Agricultural property

6104 Sch 7 para 1 TCGA 1992 Gift relief will be available for the whole value of agricultural property (whether or not that includes development value) if it falls within the **inheritance tax** definition of agricultural property, whether at 50% or 100% (¶6752).

Gifts on which inheritance tax is chargeable

6106 s 260 TCGA 1992 Gift relief will be available where the disposal constitutes a **chargeable transfer** for inheritance tax purposes (¶6530).

It is not necessary for an actual charge to inheritance tax to arise, and a transfer that falls within the nil rate band (¶6512) will therefore qualify for relief.

Gifts of certain assets which are specifically exempted from inheritance tax

6108 s 260(2) TCGA 1992 Gift relief is available if the gift is an **exempt transfer** for inheritance tax purposes and it is either a transfer:
– to a political party (¶6444);
– to a maintenance fund for historic buildings (¶6452); or
– of designated heritage property (¶6660).

MEMO POINTS For accumulation and maintenance trusts that were created **before 22 March 2006** (or for those which are transitional serial interests (¶7178)), the following rules apply:
– if there are beneficiaries who will become absolutely entitled to property after age 18, gift relief remains available, but under the provisions at ¶6106; and
– where the beneficiary is already entitled to an interest in possession and subsequently becomes absolutely entitled, gift relief will not be available.

C. Calculation

1. Basic gift relief calculation

6112 ss 165(4), 260(2) TCGA 1992 Following a gift, relief is given by **holding over** the gain against the base cost of the asset in the hands of the transferee. The effect is to reduce the allowable expenditure of the asset, thus increasing the gain which arises on its subsequent disposal.

Relief may be **clawed back** in certain situations: see ¶6128.

The amount of gain that can be held over may be **restricted** by:
– the giving of actual consideration of the asset (¶6118);
– periods of non-business use of an asset (¶6120); or
– the assets being shares in the transferor's company (¶6124).

Special rules apply when an asset which qualifies for gift relief is the subject of an **inheritance tax charge** and is later sold by the transferee: see ¶6140.

The **whole amount of the gain** is deducted from the deemed acquisition cost of the transferee when: 6114
- no consideration is given in return for a gift; or
- the actual consideration given is less than the allowable expenditure.

EXAMPLE In June 2007 Mr A gifted shares in his personal trading company worth £100,000 to Mr B. Mr A had acquired the shares in March 1997 for £25,000.
Mr B later sells the shares in July 2011 for £125,000.
The gain on the gift was held over against the base cost of the shares held by Mr B, reducing his allowable expenditure on a subsequent disposal.

The held over gain on the gift to Mr B is:

	£	£
Market value on disposal		100,000
Less: Allowable expenditure	25,000	
Indexation allowance Mar 1997 to Apr 1998		
$\frac{162.6 - 155.4}{155.4} = 0.046 \times 25,000$	1,150	
		(26,150)
Gain before taper relief		73,850

The allowable expenditure for Mr B will be:

	£
Market value on disposal	100,000
Less: Held over gain	(73,850)
Allowable expenditure	26,150

The gain to Mr B on the July 2011 disposal is:

	£
Proceeds	125,000
Less: Allowable expenditure	(26,150)
Gain	98,850

Note: The original gain will have been calculated using indexation allowance and as such affects the later disposal. However on claiming gift relief, no taper relief was given.

2. Restriction of gift relief

Consideration in excess of allowable expenditure

Where consideration received in return for a gift is in excess of its allowable expenditure, the excess will **reduce** the amount of the held over gain and will become immediately chargeable to capital gains tax. 6118 ss 165(7), 260(5) TCGA 1992

EXAMPLE In August 2011 Mr C sold a business asset worth £200,000 to Mr D for £50,000. Mr C had acquired the asset in May 1996 for £35,000.
The chargeable gain on the transfer will be:

	£	£
Market value at disposal		200,000
Less: Allowable expenditure		35,000
Gain		165,000
Less: Immediately chargeable gain (50,000 – 35,000)		(15,000)
Held over gain		150,000

The allowable expenditure for Mr D will be:

	£
Market value on disposal	200,000
Less: Held over gain	(150,000)
Allowable expenditure	50,000

Periods of non-business use

6120 Sch 7 para 5 TCGA 1992

Where gift relief is claimed for business assets (other than buildings and structures (¶6122)) the amount of the gain held over will be restricted to take account of any periods of non-business use.

The relief is restricted by the following formula:

$$\text{Gain} \times \frac{\text{Days of non-business use}}{\text{Total days of ownership}} = \text{Immediately chargeable gain}$$

Only the gain that is not immediately chargeable to capital gains tax may be held over.

EXAMPLE On 31 December 2011, Mr E gave a business asset worth £75,000 to his son. Mr E had acquired the asset 10 years ago for £45,000 and used it for business purposes for 9 years, and non-business purposes for 1 year.

The chargeable gain on the transfer will be:

	£	£
Market value at disposal		75,000
Less: Allowable expenditure		45,000
Gain		30,000
Less: Immediately chargeable gain (30,000 × 1 year/10 years)		(3,000)
Held over gain		27,000

The allowable expenditure for Mr E's son will be:

	£
Market value on disposal	75,000
Less: Held over gain	(27,000)
Allowable expenditure	48,000

MEMO POINTS The **full period of ownership** must be taken into account for this calculation, not just the period after 31 March 1982.

6122 Sch 7 para 6 TCGA 1992

Where the asset on which gift relief is claimed is a **building or structure**, part of which is used for non-business purposes for the whole or a substantial part of the period of ownership, the restriction of the held over gain is made on a just and reasonable basis.

CG 66952

MEMO POINTS Where it is necessary to **restrict the gain** held over by reference both to periods of:

a. exclusively non-business use; and

b. partial mixed use throughout the period of ownership,

the time restriction for **a**. should be applied first.

Gift of certain shares

6124 Sch 7 para 7 TCGA 1992

Where the original assets gifted are shares, any gain eligible for holdover relief may be restricted if the transferor has, in the 12 months prior to the disposal either:

- held at any time, at least 25% of the voting rights in the company; or
- the transferor is an individual and the company is his personal company (¶6054).

The gain held over is restricted by the following formula:

$$\text{Unrestricted gain} \times \frac{\text{Market value of the company's chargeable business assets}}{\text{Market value of the company's chargeable assets}}$$

where:
– chargeable business assets are assets (or interests in assets) used for the purposes of the company or any group member's trade;
– chargeable assets are assets that if sold at a profit would realise a chargeable gain (this test therefore incorporates plant and machinery and assets standing at a loss); and
– market value is taken at the date of the gift.

EXAMPLE In Year 1 Mrs AF gave her daughter shares in her personal company, F Ltd. The shares cost Mrs AF £75,000 and their current market value is £300,000. The gain realised on the shares is £215,000. The company had the following assets at the date of the gift:

Assets	Chargeable business assets	Chargeable assets	Other assets
	£	£	£
Freehold business offices	90,000	90,000	
Plant and machinery	15,000	15,000	
Shares (held as an investment)		30,000	
Trade debtors			7,000
Cash			30,000
Goodwill	50,000	50,000	
Sundry non-chargeable assets			12,000
Total	155,000	185,000	49,000

Mrs F will be able to claim gift relief as follows:

	£
Gain on the shares	215,000
Less: Heldover gain $215{,}000 \times \frac{155{,}000}{185{,}000}$	(180,135)
Chargeable to capital gains tax	34,865

3. Relief for rebasing

Where an individual disposes of an asset with a held over gain, and the series of transactions from 31 March 1982 to the date he received the asset were all made under no gain/no loss provisions without having had the benefit of being rebased then the "cost" for the disposal is deemed to be the market value at 31 March 1982 plus the indexation allowance accruing from 31 March 1982 to the date he received the asset (or 5 April 2008 if earlier). 6126

MEMO POINTS Rebasing is where assets held at 31 March 1982 are treated as if they were sold and immediately reacquired on that date. For details see ¶5332.

4. Clawback of relief

Emigration of the recipient

If the recipient of an asset on which gift relief has been claimed ceases to be resident in the UK within 6 years of the end of the tax year (or accounting period) in which the gift was made, the **relief will be clawed back**. 6128 s 168 TCGA 1992

The clawback takes the form of a deemed chargeable gain equal to the amount of the gain heldover and is treated as occurring on the date on which residence ceased.

MEMO POINTS 1. If a heldover gain is clawed back, it will no longer be used to reduce the recipient's **allowable expenditure** on a subsequent disposal.
2. If the **transferee fails to pay the tax** on a deemed chargeable gain under these provisions within 12 months of the due date (¶6340), HMRC have a right of recovery against the transferor. The transferor, in turn, then has a right of recovery against the transferee.

6130 The clawback provisions **will not apply** if:
a. the asset has previously been disposed of (other than to the spouse or civil partner of the recipient); or
b. the claimant:
– leaves the UK to take up an overseas office or employment, the duties of which are performed outside the UK and:
– within 3 years of the initial change of residence subsequently becomes resident and ordinarily resident in the UK without having disposed of the asset.

Limited liability partnerships

6134 From the date of the commencement of a liquidation, a limited liability partnership (LLP) is treated as a corporate entity for capital gains tax purposes and gains heldover under the gift relief provisions on an asset held by a member of the LLP become immediately chargeable.

MEMO POINTS **Prior to any liquidation** LLPs are treated as partnerships.

5. Administration

Claims for relief

6136 A claim for relief must **generally** be made by both parties to the transaction, **unless** the asset concerned is transferred to the trustees of a settlement in which case the claim may be made by the transferor alone.

6138 SP 8/92 CG 67130 As a general rule, the gain arising on the disposal of an asset on which gift relief is claimed should be calculated in accordance with normal rules and agreed with HMRC. HMRC have stated, however, that where the transferor and transferee both complete the second page of the claim form, a formal calculation of the gain will not be necessary. Instead they will accept:
– a joint application by the transferor and the transferee, stating that they wish SP8/92 to apply;
– provision of details concerning the asset and its history, or alternatively a calculation incorporating informally estimated valuations if necessary; and
– a statement that both parties have satisfied themselves that the value of the asset at the date of transfer was in excess of the allowable expenditure incurred.
Once a claim made on this basis has been accepted by HMRC it may not be subsequently withdrawn.

6. Interaction with inheritance tax

6140 ss 165(10), 260(7) TCGA 1992 Where a claim for gift relief is made and the disposal is also a **chargeable transfer** for inheritance tax (or the disposal becomes chargeable to inheritance tax as a result of the death of the transferor within 7 years) special rules apply.

The amount of the chargeable gain accruing to the transferee on a **subsequent disposal** of the asset will be reduced by the inheritance tax attributable to the value of the asset transferred to him. This reduction may not create a loss, so if the inheritance tax exceeds the amount of the gain, the gain will be reduced to nil.

If the inheritance tax charge is recalculated for any reason (for example on the death of the transferor) the capital gains tax charge will also need to be recalculated.

MEMO POINTS 1. The **inheritance tax attributable to the value of an asset** will depend on whether the transferee or the transferor paid the tax. If the transferee paid the inheritance tax the whole amount paid may be deducted. If the transferor paid the inheritance tax the amount that may be deducted is restricted by the formula:

$$\text{Inheritance tax paid} \times \frac{\text{Net value of transfer}}{\text{Gross value of transfer}} = \text{Amount available for deduction}$$

Full details are given at ¶6536.
2. Where only **part of an asset is subsequently sold**, any inheritance tax arising on the original transfer can be deducted in full against the part sold. There is no need to apportion the inheritance tax. Any tax remaining unrelieved is available for offset against any future disposals of the relevant asset.

SECTION 4

Chattel relief

Non-wasting chattels

Gains on the disposal of non-wasting chattels are exempt from tax where the **consideration on disposal is £6,000 or less.** 6150 s 262 TCGA 1992

MEMO POINTS 1. A chattel is **defined as tangible moveable property** and this includes items such as jewellery, paintings and antique furniture.
2. Commodities dealt with on a terminal market, and currency of any description, do not count as chattels.

If the **consideration exceeds £6,000**, the amount of any gain chargeable will be the lower of: 6154
- the computed gain; and
- 5/3 of the excess of the consideration over £6,000.

EXAMPLE Mr A sells a Regency chest of drawers for £6,950, realising a gain of £1,800.
As the consideration exceeds £6,000, the gain is chargeable.
However, the amount of the gain chargeable is restricted to a maximum of:
5/3 × (6,950 – 6,000) = £1,583.

Where a **loss arises on the disposal** of a chattel and the consideration was less than £6,000, the allowable loss may be restricted. The allowable loss is calculated using deemed consideration of £6,000. If the revised calculation produces a lower loss, that is the allowable loss. If the revised calculation produces a gain, there is neither a gain nor a loss. 6163

EXAMPLE Mr B sold an asset for £5,500, realising a loss on disposal of £1,200. The loss will be restricted as follows:

	Actual loss £	Restricted loss £
Disposal proceeds	5,500	6,000
Less:		
Costs of disposal	(200)	(200)
Acquisition cost	(6,500)	(6,500)
Net loss	1,200	700

In this situation, the allowable loss is restricted to £700. If the restricted loss calculation gives rise to a gain, the sale is deemed to realise neither a gain nor a loss.

MEMO POINTS In the case of **joint ownership**, the £6,000 limit is applied to each owner's share of the consideration.

In the case of a **part disposal** (¶5508), it is necessary to consider the disposal proceeds and the market value of the part remaining to establish whether the exemption will be available. 6164

EXAMPLE Mr C sold one third of an asset for £2,000, realising a gain of £1,200. The market value of the remaining part of the asset is £5,000. As the aggregate of the disposal proceeds and the part retained exceeds £6,000, Mr C's chargeable gain will be computed as follows:

$$\frac{2{,}000}{(2{,}000 + 5{,}000)} \times \left(\frac{5}{3} \times (7{,}000 - 6{,}000)\right) = £476$$

MEMO POINTS If assets which form part of a **set of articles** are sold on different occasions to the same person, or a connected person, the sales will be treated as a single transaction. Whether assets form part of a set of articles is a question of fact. Broadly, HMRC will treat assets as part of a set if they are essentially similar in nature and their value together is greater than the value of the parts.

Wasting chattels

6165 s 45 TCGA 1992

Where a chattel is also a wasting asset (an asset with a predicted useful life of 50 years or less), its disposal is normally exempt from capital gains tax.

However, this exemption does not apply if the asset has been **used solely for business purposes**, and could have been subject to a claim for **capital allowances**.

MEMO POINTS 1. If **capital allowances were withdrawn** on an asset before sale (because, for example, the asset was never actually used as intended), then the taxpayer is treated as if the allowances had never been made.
2. If an asset was used **partly for a trade**, any consideration and allowable expenditure is apportioned accordingly between the trade and non-trade element.
3. Where a chattel is not exempt as a wasting asset, the £6,000 **chattel exemption** may apply instead.
4. See ¶5922 for the computation of the gain on a disposal of a **wasting asset that is not a chattel**.
5. For the restriction of allowable losses when the expenditure has qualified for capital allowances see ¶5924.

SECTION 5

Principal private residence relief

1. Exempt gain

6166 ss 222 - 226B TCGA 1992

Where an individual disposes of a dwelling house (¶6167).which has been his only or main residence throughout his period of ownership, **any gain** arising on the disposal is exempt from capital gains tax and likewise any loss will not be allowable.

There is no minimum period of occupation required for the property to be considered a residence, the test being applied based on the quality of occupation.

The relief will be **restricted** where:
– the property has not been occupied as the individual's only or main residence throughout the whole period of ownership (¶6168).; or
– part of the property has been occupied exclusively for business purposes (in which case the gain will be apportioned on an appropriate basis, for example floor area).

An additional relief may be available where part of the property has been used for residential letting (¶6178).

MEMO POINTS For the interaction of **principal private residence relief and trusts** see ¶7270 and ¶7384. Note that the relief will not be available to the trustees if a holdover claim (relating to a chargeable transfer for inheritance tax) was made on the original gift into the trust.

2. What is a dwelling?

6167 CG 64230

The question of what constitutes a dwelling house has been considered in a number of cases. At a **basic level**, a house and its garden will be exempt. Caravans which are connected to mains services are also exempt, whereas mobile caravans which are simply parked (whether jacked up off the ground or not) with no connection to services are not.

The question becomes more complicated when considering **larger properties, and groups of properties**. Where a property has other buildings adjoining or in close proximity to it, for example a detached garage, these will generally be accepted as forming part of the dwelling house. This may also extend to a separate building, for example staff accommodation, where the other accommodation increases the taxpayer's enjoyment of the main house. Where buildings are separated by fences or walls, they will not generally be considered to form part of the same dwelling house. The proximity of the additional buildings to the main property will be a significant factor in determining whether they form part of the same dwelling house. There are no fixed rules in this respect, and each case will be considered separately.

The extent to which a property's **grounds** may be included within the exemption will depend on the size and nature of the property. The general rule is that grounds of up to 0.5 hectare will be included. This may be increased where it is considered appropriate. HMRC will not generally give relief for grounds which are physically separated from the main house, for example by a public road. Grounds which have a separate use, for example agricultural land, are excluded from the exemption.

Where a garden, or part of a garden, is sold separately from the dwelling house, relief will not be available, unless:
– the sale takes place before the sale of the dwelling house; and
– the vendor can demonstrate that the sale was due to financial necessity.

Any sale of a garden after the sale of the dwelling house will not qualify for relief.

3. Periods of occupation

Deemed periods of occupation

Where the property has **not been occupied throughout the period of ownership**, a measure of relief is still available, because, in addition to periods of actual occupation, the following periods of absence are deemed periods of occupation (and are therefore exempt): 6168 s 223(3) TCGA 1992

Period	Conditions
The last 36 months of ownership	
Any periods during which the owner (or spouse/civil partner) was employed abroad (with no duties being carried on in the UK)	House must be occupied as the main residence both before and after the period of absence (although there is no requirement for the occupation to be immediately before or after the period of absence).
Periods of up to 4 years, where the owner (or spouse/civil partner) was required to live elsewhere because of his employment [1]	
Periods totalling up to 3 years for any reason [1]	
The first 12 months of ownership [2, 3, 4]	Where an individual acquires a property but there is a delay in occupation because: – the house is being built on the land; – renovations or alterations are being carried out on the new property; or – a previous property is being occupied while arrangements are made to sell it.

Note:
1. The requirement for subsequent reoccupation is waived where a further period of absence because of work is required.
2. HMRC may extend this period in certain circumstances up to a maximum of 2 years.
3. As a result of these provisions an individual may have two properties which qualify for relief. In this situation a nomination (¶6172) is not required.
4. HMRC do not seek to restrict relief in the usual weeks between exchange and completion.

Any period of absence in excess of the permitted deemed periods of occupation will be split into a deemed period of occupation (which will be eligible for relief) and a period of absence (which will not be eligible for relief).

When considering periods of occupation, the period up to and including 31 March 1982 is ignored for all purposes.

EXAMPLE Mr A acquired a property on 1 January 1989 which he occupied on 30 November 1989 after renovation work had been completed. He remained in the property until 31 July 1992 when he was seconded to his employer's German headquarters for 18 months. On his return to the UK, he occupied the property for 2 months before taking up employment as a resident gamekeeper on 1 April 1994. He reoccupied the property on 1 May 2000 until 31 August 2001 when he moved into a new home with his girlfriend. The property was sold on 1 January 2012.

He has occupied the property as his only or main residence as follows:

Dates	Notes	Occupied	Chargeable
		(Months)	
01/01/89 – 30/11/89	Deemed occupation	11	
01/12/89 – 31/07/92	Actual occupation	32	
01/08/92 – 31/01/94	Deemed occupation	18	
01/02/94 – 31/03/94	Actual occupation	2	
01/04/94 – 31/03/98	Deemed occupation	48	
01/04/98 – 30/04/00	Deemed occupation	25	
01/05/00 – 31/08/01	Actual occupation	16	
01/09/01 – 31/12/08	Not occupied (no subsequent period of actual occupation)		88
01/01/09 – 31/12/11	Deemed occupation	36	
	Total	**188**	**88**

Partial business use

6170
s 224(1)TCGA 1992

Any part of a property used exclusively for business purposes cannot qualify for relief. Consequently, any gain on disposal will need to be apportioned (on a fair and reasonable basis) between the business and non-business use. This **restriction only applies if** the relevant part of the property has been exclusively used for business purposes and the test is applied throughout the entire period of ownership (including the last 36 months).

The chargeable part of the gain may be eligible for relief on replacement of business assets (¶6050).

4. Calculation

6171 Relief is calculated by multiplying the gain by the following fraction:

$$\frac{\text{Periods of actual and deemed occupation}}{\text{Period of ownership (since 31/03/82)}}$$

EXAMPLE Continuing the previous example, if Mr A realised a gain of £80,000 on the property, the chargeable gain would have been as follows:

	£
Gain	80,000
Less: Principal private residence exemption	
$80{,}000 \times \frac{188}{188 + 88}$	(54,492)
Gain	25,508

5. Special situations

More than one residence

Where an individual has more than one residence, it is possible to **nominate** one of the properties as the principal private residence. A notice must be given to HMRC within 2 years of acquiring the second residence, although the nomination may subsequently be varied when, for example, a further property is acquired, or there is a change in the owner's occupation patterns. If a nomination is not made within the 2 year period HMRC can determine, based on the facts of the case, which property is the principal residence. 6172 s 222(5) TCGA 1992

EXAMPLE Mr B bought a property on 1 April 1998 and another property on 1 October 2001. He has until 30 September 2003 in which to nominate one of the properties as his main residence. He bought another property on 1 July 2009, so he now has until 30 June 2011 in which to nominate his principal residence.

The ability to vary nominations can be a useful planning tool to reduce capital gains tax arising on the disposal of a second home.

EXAMPLE Mr C bought property one in December 1997 and property two in March 1998. He nominated property one as his main residence, but on 30 June 2009 he sold property two at a substantial gain. Mr C varied his nomination notice on 1 July 2009 to treat property two as his main residence. This nomination has effect from 1 July 2007, two years prior to the variation, and as a result the last 3 years of gain will be exempt as a deemed period of occupation (¶6168).
Mr C subsequently varies his nomination on 7 July 2009 to treat property one as his main residence again, from 7 July 2007. Therefore on the sale of property one, only 1 week of gain will be potentially chargeable.

MEMO POINTS Where spouses or civil partners **jointly own property** any election must be signed by both parties.

Spouses and civil partners

Spouses or civil partners living together can have only one principal private residence between them. 6173 s 222(6) TCGA 1992

When **couples separate** and one person moves out of the couple's home, the departing individual may continue to be treated as resident there for the purposes of this relief. This concession is only available where the departing individual's interest in the home is subsequently transferred to the remaining spouse or civil partner. This relief is not available where the departing individual nominates another residence as his principal private residence prior to disposing of his interest in the couple's home. s 225B TCGA 1992

Following a **transfer of property** between spouses or civil partners, the transferee is treated as standing in the shoes of the transferor for the purposes of principal private residence relief. Accordingly any restrictions that would have applied to the transferor will apply equally to the transferee on an eventual sale of the property. 6174

Dependent relative

Where an individual owns a property which is **occupied rent free** by a dependent relative, and has been in the same occupation since prior to 5 April 1988, a gain arising on the disposal of that property may also attract the relief. 6175 s 226 TCGA 1992

A dependent relative in relation to a taxpayer is:
- any relative who is unable to maintain themselves due to old age or infirmity; or
- a widowed, divorced or separated mother.

Where a property has been occupied for only part of the period of ownership by a dependent relative meeting the criteria, the gain will be apportioned on a time basis.

MEMO POINTS 1. An individual may claim this relief for **only one property**.
2. There is no statutory **definition of relative** for this provision, but HMRC adopt a wide definition to include foster and step parents, brothers and sisters.
3. HMRC's view is that any **losses** arising on the disposal of property occupied by a dependent relative are allowable losses.
4. The **last 36 months** (¶6168) also count towards the dependent relative's period of occupation.
5. Property will be deemed to be occupied rent free even where payments are made by the dependent relative towards such costs as **council tax, household repairs** etc.

Relocation

6176 s 225C TCGA 1992

Where an employee is relocated due to **work commitments**, HMRC may, by concession, extend the scope of the relief. This is to cover the situation where an employee sells his house, either to his employer or a relocation service, to speed up the moving process. In many cases, the employee will have a right to share in any profit made on a subsequent disposal. The relief may be extended to cover the employee's share of those profits provided that the right to share in profits has a life of 3 years or less.

Job related accommodation

6177 s 222(8) TCGA 1992

Individuals required to live in job related accommodation (for example, on site caretakers) may also own another property. The other property may be treated as the main residence of the individual provided he has the intention to occupy the property as his only or main residence in the future. Provided the intention can be demonstrated, this relief will apply even if, for whatever reason, the property is not subsequently actually occupied.

Job related accommodation can be provided under a service agreement or a tenancy. If it is the former, there is no need to make an election to treat the other property as the principal residence (¶6172), whereas with the latter an election will be required.

MEMO POINTS 1. Accommodation will be **deemed to be job related** if:
– the accommodation is necessary for the proper performance of the individual's duties;
– the accommodation is provided for the better performance of the individuals duties and it is customary in the particular trade to provide such accommodation; or
– there is a special threat to the individual's security and accommodation is provided as part of the security arrangements.
2. Accommodation (other than security accommodation) provided by a company to its **director** (or a director of an associated company) will only be deemed to be job related for these provisions if the director:
– does not have a material interest in the company; and
– is a full-time working director of the company (or the company is established for charitable purposes only).
3. For **self-employed** individuals, accommodation will be deemed to be job related if the individual is required to carry out a trade on someone else's land and live at the premises so provided. (However accommodation will not be job related if it is wholly or partly provided by a company in which he has a material interest.)
4. A **material interest** is a direct or indirect beneficial interest (either alone or with associates) in more than 5% of either the ordinary share capital of the company or, in the case of a close company, the assets available for distribution on a winding up, etc.

Residential lettings

6178 s 223(4) TCGA 1992

If during the period of ownership all of the house, or any part of it, has been let as residential accommodation, the gain attributable to the period of letting is only chargeable if it exceeds the lower of:
– £40,000; and
– the relief attributable to owner occupation.

EXAMPLE Mr D realises a gain of £95,000 on the disposal of his house. Mr D occupied the property throughout his 9 year period of ownership. Three rooms (approximately 40% of the floor area) were let as residential accommodation for 7 years.

The gain is calculated as follows:

	£	£
Gain		95,000
Gain attributable to owner occupation:		
Exclusive occupation:		
24/108 × 95,000	21,111	
Shared occupation:		
84/108 × 95,000 × 60%	44,333	
		(65,444)
Gain attributable to letting		29,556
Letting exemption[1]		(29,556)
Chargeable gain		Nil

Note:
1. The gain attributable to the period of letting is not chargeable as it does not exceed the lower of:
– £40,000; and
– the owner occupation gain (£65,444).

MEMO POINTS 1. This relief is not available where the let property either:
– qualifies for relief because it has been the residence of a **dependent relative** (¶6175); or
– forms a **separate dwelling house**. (However HMRC do allow relief if part of the house is let as a flat or series of rooms without major structural alterations.)
2. If the letting only consists of taking in a **lodger**, or letting out a room under the **rent a room scheme** (¶2781), principal residence relief will still be available in full on the eventual disposal of the property.
3. Where the property is **owned jointly** (including spouses or civil partners) each individual is entitled to the maximum relief.

SECTION 6

Incorporation relief

1. Transfer of a business

Where a person (other than a company) makes a **qualifying transfer of a business** to a company in exchange for shares in that company, the gain arising is **automatically rolled over** into the base cost of the new shares. This is known as incorporation relief or "Section 162" relief. 6179 s 162 TCGA 1992

An **election can be made for the relief not to apply**. This election must be made within the following **time limits**: s 162A TCGA 1992
– if the shares are sold in the tax year after they were acquired, the election must be made by 31 January following the tax year in which the sale took place;
– if the shares are not sold in the tax year after they were acquired, the deadline for an election is extended by a further year.

EXAMPLE If a transfer of a business to a company is made in 2009/10, and the shares are subsequently sold in 2010/11, then an election to disapply incorporation relief must be made by 31 January 2012. If, however, the shares are not sold in 2010/11, then the time limit in which to make an election is extended to 31 January 2013.

2. Qualifying transfers

A transfer is only eligible for relief if the following **conditions** are met: 6180
– the business is transferred as a going concern;
– all the business assets (or all except the cash) are transferred; and
– the consideration is wholly or partly in the form of shares in the transferee company.

6181 The relief is not available if the **transferor retains any business assets** (other than cash). If there are assets within the business which the owner wishes not to transfer to the company (for example, a freehold property), it may be possible to withdraw them prior to the transfer. Where the asset is fundamental to the operation of the business, this may prejudice the status as a going concern. It is therefore necessary to ensure that the correct legal documentation (for example a lease over the property) is in place before the transfer.

MEMO POINTS If incorporation relief is not available because, for example, the transferor is unwilling to transfer all the business assets, **gift holdover relief** on business assets (¶6100) may be available.

6182 The total consideration received is for the business as a whole. Where the **consideration is in more than one form** (for example, part in cash and part in shares), it is not possible to treat one element as being for a specific asset, and a proportion of the gain may be immediately chargeable.

MEMO POINTS HMRC will not deny relief if the **share issue is delayed**, and they cannot be issued at the time of transfer (for example, the share capital of the company may need to be increased). However, the shares must be issued promptly once the reason for the delay has been removed.

6183 ESC D32 By concession, the assumption of **business liabilities** by the company is not deemed to be part of the consideration, although it will affect the cost of the shares (¶6185).

If, however, the company assumes any **non-business liabilities** as part of the transfer, the value of the liability will be treated as consideration.

3. Calculation

Method

6185 The gain which can be deferred is calculated in **three steps**:
a. calculate the amount of the gain arising on the transfer, ignoring incorporation relief;
b. determine the value of the consideration received (being the market value of the shares at the time of issue, plus the value of any other consideration received); and
c. calculate the gain attributable to consideration in the form of shares, using the formula:

$$\frac{A}{B} \times C$$

where:
– A is the cost of the shares;
– B is the total consideration received; and
– C is the net gain arising on the transfer (i.e. total gains reduced by any losses).

MEMO POINTS 1. For step **a**. the **disposal value** of the assets is usually the market value at the date of transfer, as the person making the disposal is usually connected with the company.
2. For step **b**. where the **transferor is connected to the company** the value of the shares is the lower of:
– the market value of the shares at the time of issue; and
– the value of the assets transferred.
– For step **c**, the cost of the shares is normally their market value at the date of transfer.

6188 Part of the gain will be **chargeable immediately** if it:
– exceeds the value of the shares received, the excess being chargeable immediately, although gift holdover relief for business assets (¶6100) may be available; or
– is attributable to other consideration (unless any other relief, for example gift relief, is available).

6191 The **base cost of the new shares** for future capital gains tax purposes is the cost of the shares reduced by the amount of the gain held over. Where the consideration is in shares of more than one class, the amount of the gain attributable to each class is calculated based on the market value of each class of shares at the time of issue.

EXAMPLE Mr A runs an electrical wholesale business. He decides to transfer the business to a company, in exchange for 40,000 ordinary £5 shares (valued at par) and £43,000 cash which is left outstanding on a loan account. The assets of the business at the time of the transfer (which were all transferred) were as follows:

Asset	Value £	Gain £
Property	135,000	40,000
Goodwill	50,000	50,000
Debtors	16,500	n/a
Stock	45,250	n/a
Cash at bank	12,500	n/a
Trade creditors	(16,250)	n/a
	243,000	90,000

The gain attributable to consideration in the form of shares, which can be held over, is calculated as:

$\frac{200,000}{243,000} \times 90,000$ £74,074

The base cost of the shares for future purposes is reduced by the gain held over:

200,000 – 74,074 £125,926

The balance of the gain becoming chargeable on the transfer is:

90,000 – 74,074 £15,926

MEMO POINTS The **base cost of the assets transferred** to the company will be equal to the acquisition cost on the transfer.

Rebasing

Where an individual disposes of an asset with a held over gain, and the series of transactions from 31 March 1982 to the date he received the asset were all made under no gain/no loss provisions without having had the benefit of being rebased, then the "cost" for the disposal is deemed to be the market value at 31 March 1982 plus the indexation allowance accruing from 31 March 1982 to the date he received the asset (or 5 April 2008 if earlier). 6192 Sch 4 para 2 TCGA 1992

MEMO POINTS Rebasing is where assets held at 31 March 1982 are treated as if they were sold and immediately re-acquired on that date. For details see ¶1133.

SECTION 7

Enterprise investment scheme

A. Disposal of EIS shares

1. Qualifying shares

A gain on the disposal of shares that qualified for Enterprise Investment Scheme (EIS) income tax relief (¶2861) is **not a chargeable gain** provided that: 6200 s 150A TCGA 1992

a. the disposal is of shares on which EIS income tax relief has been given and not fully withdrawn; and

b. the shares have been held for a period of 3 years from the later of:
- the date the shares were issued; or
- the date on which the company started to trade.

The exempt gain may be restricted where the shares did not qualify in full for EIS relief, or where relief has been partially withdrawn.

There is no restriction on the availability of any **loss** on the disposal.

MEMO POINTS 1. In addition, it is possible to **defer gains on the disposal of other assets** by investing in EIS shares. This is known as EIS deferral relief: see ¶6221.
2. **Disposals between spouses or civil partners** are ignored for these purposes and, on a subsequent disposal by the receiving spouse or civil partner, the gain is calculated as though the original investor had retained the shares.

6206 s 246 ITA 2007

The normal **share identification rules** do not apply to EIS shares. Any shares sold are identified with acquisitions of shares of the same class on a first in first out basis.

Where more than one batch of shares was **purchased on the same day**, they are matched in the following order:
- shares to which neither EIS income tax relief nor deferral relief is attributable;
- shares to which deferral relief, but not EIS income tax relief, is attributable;
- shares to which EIS income tax relief, but not deferral relief is attributable; and
- shares to which both EIS income tax and deferral relief are attributable.

6209 s 150A(6) TCGA 1992

If as a result of a **company reorganisation** (¶5794) within the 3 year period, EIS shares are exchanged for shares in another company:
- there is a deemed disposal for EIS relief; and
- there is no chargeable gain on the receipt of the new shares, although the replacement shares will be chargeable on a subsequent disposal.

6210 s 150A(8A)-(8D) TCGA 1992

However these **provisions will not apply** if a company (Co A), which has issued EIS shares, takes over another company (Co B), which has also issued EIS shares provided:
- Co A has issued EIS certificates to its investors for its eligible shares; and
- the new shares issued by Co A are eligible shares (¶2869), issued outside the relevant period for Co B (¶2889).

Instead there will be no deemed disposal for EIS relief and any gain on a subsequent disposal of the replacement shares will be exempt.

MEMO POINTS 1. On a **bonus issue** in respect of EIS shares, the bonus shares are treated as acquired on the date the original shares were acquired.
2. On a **rights issue**, the share reorganisation rules (¶5812) are disapplied where either EIS income tax or deferral relief is attributable to the original holding or the new shares. The effect of this is to treat the rights issue shares as a separate acquisition.

2. Restrictions on relief

Shares not qualifying for full relief

6212 s 150A(3) TCGA 1992

Where the individual's shares did not qualify for EIS relief in full (for example, where the subscription exceeded the annual limit) the capital gains tax exemption must also be restricted. This **does not apply** where the EIS relief was restricted simply because the income tax liability was insufficient to absorb the full amount of relief.

The proportion of the gain which is exempt from capital gains tax is calculated by applying the fraction A/B, where:
- A is the EIS relief given (in terms of the reduction in the tax liability); and
- B is the tax at the lower rate on the amount subscribed (for the year of issue).

EXAMPLE Mr A acquired 3,500 shares in E Co Ltd under the EIS scheme in June 2006. He paid £275,000 for the shares and benefited from maximum EIS relief (then £200,000 @ 20%). In July 2011, the shares were sold and he realised a gain of £35,574. The chargeable gain is calculated as follows:

	£
Gain	35,574
Less: Exempt gain attributable to EIS: $\frac{200{,}000 \times 20\%}{275{,}000 \times 20\%} \times 35{,}574$	(25,872)
Chargeable gain	9,702

Return of value

The exempt gain will also be restricted where EIS relief has been withdrawn due to a return of value (¶2893). 6215 s 150B TCGA 1992

The proportion of the gain which is chargeable is calculated by applying the fraction X/Y, where:
- X is the reduction in the EIS relief given; and
- Y is the EIS relief given before the reduction.

The remaining gain will be exempt provided the other necessary conditions are met.

EXAMPLE Mr B acquired shares qualifying for EIS relief for £35,000 and received EIS relief of £7,000. Following a £10,600 return of value, relief of £2,120 was withdrawn. The shares were subsequently sold, after the minimum holding period, realising a gain of £18,550. The exempt gain is calculated as follows:

	£
Gain	18,550
Less: Chargeable gain 18,550 × (2,120/7,000)	(5,618)
Exempt gain	12,932

Where **only part of the original acquisition qualified for relief** and relief has been withdrawn following a return of value, the first step is to calculate the proportion of the gain attributable to the EIS and non-EIS shares. Then, the element of the EIS gain attributable to the return in value is calculated and added to the chargeable gain on the non-EIS shares.

EXAMPLE If, in the above example, Mr B's EIS investments has exceeded the maximum for the year, and only £25,000 had qualified for EIS relief (of £5,000), the EIS relief withdrawn would be £1,514 (25,000/35,000 × 10,600 @ 20%) and the gain would be calculated as follows:

	£
Gain	18,550
Exempt gain: 18,550 × (5,000/7,000)	(13,250)
	5,300

	Exempt £	Chargeable £
Gain (as above)	13,250	5,300
Less: Chargeable gain 13,250 × (1,514/5,000)	(4,012)	4,012
	9,238	9,312

3. Losses

Where the disposal of EIS shares gives rise to a loss, that loss is **allowable** for capital gains tax purposes, regardless of the period for which the shares were held. 6218 s 150A TCGA 1992 s 133 ITA 2007

Alternatively, a claim may be made to **set the loss against current year income**, carried forward or carried back (¶5450 onwards), unless the sale is to a connected person, in which case loss relief is restricted to gains on transactions with the same connected person.

When calculating the loss, the allowable expenditure must be reduced to take account of any EIS income tax relief given.

EXAMPLE Mr A invested £64,000 in June 2009 in qualifying EIS shares and obtained EIS relief of £12,800 (£64,000 @ 20%). If he sells the shares for £19,000 in March 2012, EIS relief would be withdrawn as they have not been held for the minimum period (¶2889). The amount of relief withdrawn is restricted to the value received for the shares at the lower rate for the year of investment, i.e. £19,000 @ 20% = £3,800.
The allowable loss on disposal is calculated as follows:

	£	£
Proceeds		19,000
Less: Cost	64,000	
EIS relief given (12,800 – 3,800)	(9,000)	
		(55,000)
Capital loss		36,000

If the shares had been held for the minimum period, no EIS relief would be withdrawn and the loss would be calculated as follows:

	£	£
Proceeds		19,000
Less: Cost	64,000	
EIS relief given	(12,800)	
		(51,200)
Capital loss		32,200

B. EIS deferral relief

1. Conditions

6221 Sch 5B TCGA 1992 A chargeable gain on any asset may be deferred where the individual makes an investment into shares that **would be eligible** for EIS income tax relief (¶2863).

6224 To qualify for deferral relief the following **conditions** must be met:
a. the investment must be a subscription in cash for **eligible shares** (¶2869);
b. the shares must be acquired within a **qualifying period** which begins 1 year before and ends 3 years after the disposal giving rise to the gain; and
c. the individual must be **resident and ordinarily resident** in the UK both at the date of disposal and the date the eligible shares are acquired.
There are two important differences from EIS income tax relief:.
– EIS deferral relief is **not denied** where the individual is **connected with the company** in which the investment is made; and
– there is **no limit on the maximum investment** in EIS shares.

MEMO POINTS 1. There is no limit on the investment because there is no requirement for EIS relief actually to have been claimed on the shares. The shares simply need to satisfy the conditions which would make them eligible for EIS relief.
2. If the original gain arises on the disposal of shares in a company, no deferral relief is available in respect of a subscription for shares in the same company, or a member of the same group of companies (¶2875).
HMRC have the power to **extend the qualifying period** in individual cases. Where the reinvestment is made during the year preceding the disposal, the new shares must continue to be held at the date of disposal.

2. Claims for relief

6227 VCM38110 Deferral relief must be **claimed in writing**. The company in which the investment is made must supply the investor with a certificate of eligibility (Form EIS 3), which must accompany the claim. A form is provided with EIS 3 on which to make the claim for deferral relief, although its use is not mandatory. Claims are often made on the individual's tax return.

The gain eligible for deferral is the gain after all reliefs have been claimed. Where a gain was deferred and taper relief was applicable this was not deducted from the original gain.

The claim must specify the amount of the gain to be deferred. The individual may choose any amount up to the maximum of the gain or the investment whichever is less. In this way, the individual may leave sufficient gain in charge to utilise losses or the annual exemption, as required.

The **time limit** for making the claim is 5 years from 31 January following the end of the year in which the disposal giving rise to the gain to be deferred occurs. A claim cannot be made until the company issuing the eligible shares has carried on a qualifying trade (¶2875) for a minimum of 4 months.

3. Crystallising the deferred gain

Trigger events

The deferred gain will crystallise at the **earliest of the following** events: 6230
- the disposal of the EIS shares, including a deemed disposal on a company reorganisation (¶6209), but excluding inter-spouse/civil partner transfers;
- the investor ceasing to be resident or ordinarily resident in the UK before the termination date (¶2865); or
- the shares ceasing to be eligible shares.

MEMO POINTS 1. A period of **residence** abroad for the purposes of employment abroad is ignored for these provisions, provided UK residence is reacquired within 3 years and before the disposal of the EIS shares.
2. Where the **shares cease to be eligible** because, for example, the company ceases to be a qualifying company, the deferred gain crystallises at the date the conditions are breached. (In particular, note that in contrast to the income tax provisions, if a return of value is received by the investor the whole of the deferred gain crystallises.)
However, if EIS relief is withdrawn before a deferral claim has been made, the shares are deemed never to have been eligible shares.
3. The **death of the investor** will not trigger the deferred gain which will therefore escape CGT.
4. Following an **inter-spouse** or **civil partner transfer**, the transferee is deemed to be the investor and the chargeable gain accrues to the individual whose actions trigger the gain.

EXAMPLE Mr A realised a gain in May 2009 of £27,600 which he deferred following an investment in eligible shares in B Ltd. In July 2011, he transferred half the B Ltd shares to his wife. In August 2011, Mrs A ceased to be resident in the UK. Mrs A therefore crystallises a chargeable gain of £13,800 (£27,600 × 50%). The remainder of the gain remains deferred until Mr A disposes of his shares, becomes non-resident or the shares cease to be eligible.

SECTION 8

Venture capital trusts

1. VCT disposal relief

In addition to the income tax reliefs available to an investor in a VCT (¶2907), capital gains arising on the disposal of VCT shares may be exempt. 6250 s 151A TCGA 1992

MEMO POINTS Historically, it was possible to defer gains arising on the disposal of any asset by reinvesting in VCT shares. This relief was withdrawn for VCT shares issued on or after 6 April 2004. (For details of the relief see earlier editions of *Tax Memo*.)

6253 Where an individual aged 18 or over disposes of shares in a VCT, any gain may be exempt from capital gains tax (and any loss arising on such a disposal is not an allowable loss).

Disposal relief is **only available where**:
- the disposal is of ordinary shares (which qualify for investment relief (¶2909)) in a company which was a VCT both when the shares were acquired and at the date of disposal;
- the shares were acquired for bona fide commercial purposes and not as part of a scheme to avoid tax; and
- the value of the VCT shares is within the permitted annual maximum (currently £200,000) for the tax year of acquisition.

MEMO POINTS 1. There is no requirement for the shares to have been acquired by subscription.
2. Relief is available regardless of the length of the **period of ownership**. If, however, the shares have been held for less than 5 years, any investment relief given will be withdrawn (¶2919).
3. Disposals between **spouses or civil partners** are ignored for these purposes.

6259 The normal **share identification rules** do not apply to VCT shares. Any shares qualifying for VCT disposal relief are identified with acquisitions of shares of the same class on a first in first out basis.

Where shares are acquired in **excess of the permitted maximum**, the shares acquired later in the year are treated as forming the excess. If shares of more than one class are acquired on the same day which takes the total over the permitted maximum, the excess is apportioned between the various classes based on the respective values of each class.

Where more than one batch of shares was **purchased on the same day**, shares in excess of the permitted maximum are deemed to be sold before shares within the maximum.

Shares acquired **before a company is approved as a VCT** are sold in priority to any shares acquired after approval was given.

6262
s 151B TCGA 1992

On a **reorganisation of share capital** (¶5794), VCT shares held are divided into the following categories:
- shares that qualify for income tax and capital gains tax relief;
- shares that qualify only for capital gains tax relief;
- shares that qualify only for income tax relief; and
- shares that do not qualify for either income tax or capital gains tax relief.

Any new shares issued in exchange for old shares must be attributed separately to each category and are treated as a new acquisition.

On a **rights issue** (where the original holding qualified for VCT disposal relief), the new shares are treated as a separate acquisition.

MEMO POINTS If ordinary VCT shares are **exchanged for non-ordinary shares**, the replacement shares will not qualify for VCT disposal relief on a subsequent disposal.

2. Withdrawal of relief

6263 If a VCT's approval is withdrawn, the VCT shares are deemed to be disposed of and reacquired at market value at the date the approval is withdrawn, (although no chargeable gain will accrue). On a subsequent disposal of the shares, any increase or decrease in value is taxed in the normal manner.

CHAPTER 7

Administration

OUTLINE ¶¶

SECTION 1

Self-assessment

Under the self-assessment regime, taxpayers are responsible for completing and filing tax returns, calculating their tax liabilities and paying tax to HMRC. They are also obliged to maintain detailed records in order that any figures used in the calculation of the tax liability may be verified. 6320

For **companies**, capital gains are charged to corporation tax, therefore the compliance requirements set out in ¶2210 onwards apply.

However, for **individuals**, although the majority of the compliance requirements for capital gains tax are identical to those for income tax (¶4470 onwards), there are a few further rules which are dealt with in this section.

SECTION 2

Disclosure rules

Disclosure rules require details of certain tax schemes or arrangements to be provided to HMRC. Responsibility for disclosure lies principally with scheme promoters (¶2231), and occasionally users (¶2236). 6321

Schemes are notifiable if they satisfy the following **conditions**:

a. they give rise to an income, corporation or capital gains tax advantage (i.e. relief or increased relief from tax, deferral of payment or advancement of repayment);

b. the obtaining of a tax advantage is the main benefit of the scheme; and

c. the scheme falls within one or more of the applicable hallmarks (¶2216) and is either:

– marketed etc by a promoter; or

– designed for use in-house by a large business (note that small and medium sized enterprises (¶795) that design in-house products are not therefore caught by the disclosure rules).

In addition, HMRC can apply to the tribunal for disclosure to be made for schemes even if they do not fall within one of the applicable hallmarks.
For further information see ¶2215 onwards.

SECTION 3

Returns

6322 ss 8 TMA 1970 As part of the tax return, an individual is required to supply details of any capital gains made in the tax year. This must be done by completing the **supplementary capital gains pages** and submitting them with the main tax return. The supplementary pages form part of the main tax return and therefore the submission deadline is the same (¶4484).

s 3A TCGA 1992 An individual is **not required** to provide full details of capital gains if:
– his total chargeable gains for the year do not exceed the current annual exemption (¶6326); and
– total proceeds from such disposals are not more than four times the current annual exemption.

However where an individual is claiming the remittance basis (¶5227) or has made an election in respect of their foreign losses (¶5455) all gains must be shown on the return.

s 2 TCGA 1992 MEMO POINTS An individual's **total chargeable gains** are his gains before loss relief.

SECTION 4

Payment requirements

A. Tax liability

1. Net taxable gain

6324 s 2 TCGA 1992 Once the capital gains and allowable losses have been calculated for all chargeable disposals during a tax year, the net taxable gain must be calculated. This is the total of all capital gains for the year, less allowable losses.

MEMO POINTS Gains accruing to **companies** are charged to corporation tax (not capital gains tax). Consequently when computing a company's tax liability in respect of capital gains, the provisions at ¶1250 onwards apply.

2. Annual exemption

6326 s 3 TCGA 1992 The net taxable gain may be reduced by the annual exemption and any losses brought forward from earlier years (¶5470).

An individual is only liable to capital gains tax for a year if his chargeable gains exceed the annual exemption:

Tax year	Annual exemption (£)
2011/12	10,600
2010/11	10,100

If an individual's gains for a tax year are below this amount, no capital gains tax is payable. Any **unused exemption** cannot be carried forward and set against future gains, nor used in any other manner.

MEMO POINTS 1. For the rules governing the interaction of the annual exemption with **capital losses** see ¶5472.
2. Following a person's death, his **personal representatives** (¶7260)are entitled to an annual exemption in respect of gains made by the estate. The exemption is only available for the year of death and the following 2 years. s 3(7) TCGA 1992
3. For the availability of an annual exemption to **trustees**, see ¶7377.

3. Rates of tax

The capital gains of **individuals** are liable to Capital Gains Tax at the following rates. The rate that applies depends on the total income and gains of the individual in the year and how this compares to the basic rate upper threshold. 6330 s 4 TCGA 1992

Rate (%)	Applies to
10	Gains subject to Entrepreneur's relief (¶6035)
18	Other gains, to the extent that total income and gains (after losses, reliefs and allowances) do not exceed the basic rate limit (¶4409)
28	The balance of other gains in excess of the basic rate limit

EXAMPLE In 2011/12, Mr A makes capital gains of £26,200 before the annual exemption. His total income for the year is £32,000.

		£
Net gains		26,200
Less: Annual exemption		(10,600)
Taxable gains		15,600

The basic rate band will be used against income as follows:

Basic rate threshold		35,000
Total income	32,000	
Less personal allowance	7,475	
Income within basic rate band		24,525
Basic rate unused		10,475

The capital gains tax due is therefore calculated as follows:

	£
£10,475@ 18%	1,885
£5,125 @ 28%	1,435
	3,320

MEMO POINTS 1. Where an individual's taxable income includes a **taxable life policy gain**, the capital gains tax liability is calculated as though only the relevant portion of the chargeable event gain was taxable in that year. The relevant portion is the total chargeable event gain divided by the complete number of years the relevant policy was held. See ¶4084 for details. s 4A(4) TCGA 1992
2. The higher rate applies to all disposals by trustees and personal representatives other than those subject to entrepreneurs' relief.

When determining the rate at which capital gains tax is payable, the following deductions are also allowed from the amount of taxable income: 6331 s 4A TCGA 1992
- deficiencies under life annuity contracts or life policies; and
- income accruing to the individual before death which is residuary income of the estate after death, and taken into account in computing the inheritance tax liability.

4. Double tax relief

Method of relief

6332 Where a capital gain liable to UK capital gains tax has also suffered **foreign tax**, double tax relief may be available either under the terms of the relevant tax treaty or unilaterally (by way of deduction or credit relief).

MEMO POINTS It is irrelevant whether the gain is taxed as income or capital in the overseas country.

Relief by deduction

6334 s 113 TIOPA 2010 Where relief is given by way of deduction, the amount of foreign tax is simply deducted from the amount of the gain before calculating the capital gains tax liability. This relief is not generally advantageous where credit relief is available, but may be advantageous, for example, where the disposal creates a loss, as the foreign tax will increase the allowable loss, and would not be available for credit relief. Relief is available by way of deduction unless credit relief has been claimed.

EXAMPLE Mr A made a capital loss on the disposal of a foreign asset of £10,000. He suffered foreign tax in respect of the disposal of £750. If relief by deduction is given, the amount of the loss allowable for capital gains tax purposes is £10,750.

Credit relief

6336 s 18 TIOPA 2010 Where credit relief is claimed, the foreign tax suffered is set against the capital gains tax payable on the gain on that asset. When computing the capital gains tax attributable to specific assets, allocation of the annual exemption is a matter of choice for the taxpayer. Where there are UK gains the most beneficial choice would be to allocate the exemption to these first.

Tax credit relief is only available where overseas tax is charged in respect of the same gain as the capital gains tax liability. Where the UK gain is deferred, for example where a claim to rollover relief on the replacement of a business asset is made, credit relief is not available as the UK capital gains tax liability crystallises in respect of a different asset. In this situation, relief by way of deduction may be given when computing the gain on the old asset that is to be rolled over into the replacement asset.

The credit relief available **is restricted** to the lower of the:
- foreign tax suffered; and
- capital gains tax payable in respect of the gain.

EXAMPLE Mr A made a capital gain of £15,000 on the disposal of a holiday home in Spain (based on UK rules), on which he suffered Spanish tax of £3,500. In Spain the gain charged was £20,000. He made other gains for the year of £20,000.
All the gains are taxable at the higher rate, due to the level of taxable income. The tax due on the foreign gain is therefore:

		£
Gain		15,000
Less: annual exemption[1]		(nil)
		15,000
Tax @ 28%		4,200
Tax credit relief available	(3,500)	
Limited to foreign tax chargeable on equivalent UK gain	$\frac{15,000}{20,000} \times 3,500$	(2,625)
		1,575

Note:
The entire annual exemption would be allocated against the UK gains first.

Any **special withholding tax** (¶4296) levied on an individual's offshore savings income can be credited against an individual's income and/or capital gains tax liability. Any excess credit will be repaid. 6338 s 108 FA 2004

B. Payment due date

General rule

The general rule is that an individual must pay his capital gains tax liability in a single payment on 31 January following the end of the year of assessment to which it relates. 6340 s 59B TMA 1970

The **general rule is modified** to defer the due date of the final payment where the:
- individual gave notice of his chargeability within 6 months of the end of the tax year; and
- HMRC issued a notice to file a return on or after 1 November after the end of the tax year.

In this situation, the due date for the final payment is 3 months after the issue of the notice to file a return.

Interest and **penalties for late payment**, as detailed in ¶4516 and ¶4545 respectively, apply equally to any capital gains tax liability that remains unpaid after the due date for payment. 6342 ss 59C, 86 TMA 1970 Sch 56 FA 2009

Payment by instalments

An individual may opt to pay capital gains tax in instalments in the following **two situations**: 6344 CG 66530

a. where any of the consideration for the disposal of an asset is received in instalments over a period in excess of 18 months from the date of disposal; or

b. where a capital gain accrues on a gift of the following assets, provided the gift does not qualify for gift holdover relief (¶6095):
- land;
- unquoted shares; or
- shares or securities which gave the transferor control of the company immediately prior to the transfer.

There is no statutory time limit for the individual to advise HMRC of his decision to opt for instalments, but HMRC expect to be notified before the date when the first instalment would be payable.

Consideration received in instalments To qualify for payment by instalments, the amount and date of each instalment must be ascertainable at the outset. Contingent consideration will not qualify. 6346 s 280 TCGA 1992 CG 14912

The number and frequency of the instalments must be agreed with HMRC. The instalment period cannot be longer than 8 years, and cannot extend beyond the date on which the final instalment of the consideration is payable.

HMRC's practice is to ask for instalments of tax equal to half of each instalment of consideration, until the total tax liability has been paid. The dates for payment of tax are as follows:
- for instalments of consideration due on or before 31 January in the tax year following that of the disposal (that is, the normal due date for tax payments), the instalments of tax are payable on that normal due date; and
- for later instalments of consideration, the instalments of tax is payable on the date that the individual is entitled to receive the consideration.

Interest will be charged on any instalment paid after its agreed date, and will run from the date the instalment was due to the date of payment.

Gift not qualifying for holdover relief To qualify for payment by instalments, it is not enough for the holdover relief simply not to be claimed: the disposal must not qualify for relief. 6348 s 281 TCGA 1992 CG 66530

The tax may be paid in ten equal instalments, starting on the date on which the liability would otherwise be payable (the original due date). **Interest** runs from the original due date until the date of each payment.

The individual may settle all outstanding instalments and interest at any time. However, the balance must be paid immediately if the original asset was gifted to a connected person (¶5570), and that person subsequently disposes of it for valuable consideration.

PART 5

Inheritance tax

Inheritance tax
Summary

The numbers cross-refer to paragraphs.

CHAPTER 1 General principles

CHAPTER 2 Lifetime transfers of value

CHAPTER 3 Transfers on death

CHAPTER 4 National heritage property

CHAPTER 5 Reliefs

CHAPTER 6 Overseas issues

CHAPTER 7 Anti-avoidance measures

CHAPTER 8 Administration

CHAPTER 1

General principles

OUTLINE ¶¶

Inheritance tax (IHT) is a tax on bequests, gifts and other transfers of property by individuals, either during lifetime or on death. It can also be charged on property held in a trust or owned by a close company. The charge to tax is determined by the nature of the transfer, the relationship between the parties, and the circumstances of the individual, trust, or company making the transfer. **6375**

SECTION 1

Overview

1. Chargeable persons

Individuals

Individuals who are **domiciled** in the UK will be subject to IHT on any chargeable transfers, regardless of whether the property transferred is located in the UK or overseas. Non-UK **6380** domiciled individuals are only subject to IHT on property located in the UK (subject to exceptions outlined in ¶6388).

s 267 IHTA 1984 MEMO POINTS The basic concept of domicile (¶4163) is **extended** for IHT purposes. An individual who is domiciled abroad will be treated, at a particular point in time, as being domiciled in the UK (known as **deemed domicile**) if he was:
- domiciled in the UK at any time during the 3 years immediately before that time; or
- resident (¶4154) in the UK for at least 17 out of the previous 20 tax years of assessment, ending with the year in question. The years of residency do not have to be consecutive.

This means that a non-UK domiciled resident should consider his potential liability to IHT before the end of the 16th year of UK residency, as, if he is resident in the UK at the start of the 17th year of residency, the deemed domicile rule will apply.

6382 An individual may make transfers during his lifetime and is deemed to make a transfer of all his estate on death.

Lifetime transfers are divided into those that are immediately chargeable to IHT and those that are potentially exempt. A potentially exempt transfer will only give rise to an IHT charge if the donor dies within 7 years of making the transfer.

Transfers on death arise in relation to the property in the estate of the deceased.

6384 s 270 IHTA 1984 For some IHT purposes it is necessary to consider **connected persons**, who are defined as follows:

Person	Connected with	Includes
Individual	Relatives	Siblings, parents, children, uncles, aunts, nephews or nieces and the spouses of each
	Spouse	Spouse's relatives and their spouses
Trustee[1]	Settlor	Persons connected with the settlor, such as a spouse, relatives, and a company controlled by the settlor
Partner	Partners	Partner's spouse and partner's relatives
Company	Another company under common control Person controlling the company	

Note:
1. Trust is **defined** as a disposition of property, however effected, where the property is:
- held in trust for individuals in succession, or for an individual subject to a contingency;
- held by trustees to accumulate the income, or to make discretionary payments out of the trust; or
- used to make an annuity payment or a similar arrangement.

MEMO POINTS In this Part, unless stated otherwise, references to:
- marriage, weddings, and married couples include civil partnership ceremonies and civil partners;
- a spouse, husband, or wife, include a civil partner;
- divorce include the dissolution of a civil partnership; and
- a widow or widower include a surviving civil partner.

Settled property

6386 Trusts are covered in detail from ¶7170 but as settled property is relevant to IHT, it is helpful to introduce some of the commonly used phrases here.

An individual is said to have an **interest in possession** in settled property if he has an immediate right to receive any income from that property, or to use or enjoy the property if he so chooses. For example, allowing a tenant to live rent free in a property owned by a trust constituted an interest in possession. *IRC v Lloyds Private Banking Limited* [1998]. However, no interest in possession exists where a tenant can only occupy a property for such period or periods as the trustees in their absolute discretion think fit. *Judge and another, personal representatives of Walden (deceased) v HMRC* [2005]

A **reversionary interest** is a future interest under a settlement, and may be either vested or contingent. For example, a settlement may be established allowing A to live in a property until he reaches the age of 18, at which time the property reverts to B. If it reverts directly to B, the property is vested in B. If the property only reverts to B if he is married by the age of 25, it is a contingent reversionary interest.

Close companies

IHT only applies to transfers made by individuals and, in certain circumstances, by trustees. As an anti-avoidance measure, however, some transactions by **close companies** are liable to IHT, because they are treated as having been made by the individuals who are the participators (¶2102) in the company. This situation is covered in detail from ¶6990 onwards. 6387

2. Location of property

There are no specific rules with regard to the location of property for IHT purposes, and the following general law provisions therefore apply: 6388

Property	Location
Leasehold and freehold land	The country in which it is situated
Tangible property	
Bank account	The branch at which the account is held
Goodwill	The country in which the business it relates to is carried on
Life policies	The country in which the proceeds are payable
Registered shares and securities	The country of registration (unless the shares are transferable in more than one country, in which case they are located in the country in which they will be dealt with in the normal course of events)
Bearer shares and securities	The country in which the certificate of title is located[1]
Debts	The country in which the debtor resides. If this does not indicate a clear country of residence, the terms of the contract may specify
Judgement debts	Where the judgement is recorded
Debt evidenced by deed	Where the deed is located
Partnership interests	The country in which the partnership business is carried on
Trust property	Follows the rules for the type of asset

1. This contrasts with the rule for capital gains tax purposes, which treats bearer shares in UK incorporated companies as situated in the UK.

3. Timing of transfers

The timing of transfers is important because IHT is a cumulative tax, and takes account of other transfers made in the 7 years immediately prior to a particular transfer. 6390

The **general rule** is that a transfer is deemed to have taken place once the value has moved from one estate to the other, which is basically when all of the legal requirements with respect to the change of ownership have been fulfilled. For most assets, a transfer will be effected by a written assignment or a declaration of trust.

The following **exceptions** apply:

– a transfer of **shares** will only be complete when it has complied with all of the requirements of the company's Articles of Association;

– a **cheque** will only be deemed to have been transferred once it has been cleared by the paying bank *Re Owen (deceased); Owen v IRC* [1949]; and

– **insurance policies** are treated as commencing once one party has notified the other party of their unconditional acceptance of an offer (or counter-offer).

SECTION 2

Transfers of value

6395 s 2 IHTA 1984 IHT is charged when a chargeable transfer, including a deemed transfer, takes place. A **chargeable transfer** is defined as any transfer of value made by an individual which is not an exempt transfer. Some transactions may appear to be a transfer of value but are deemed not to be. Some transfers of value are specifically exempted, and some property is exempt from tax because it is identified as excluded property for IHT purposes. The IHT payable is calculated on the value transferred by the chargeable transfer (¶6465).

1. Transfers within the scope of IHT

Dispositions

6398 s 3 IHTA 1984 The term disposition is not specifically defined by the legislation, and therefore takes on its **general meaning** of an act of disposing, bestowing or transferring money, goods or rights in property to another person.

A disposition **results in** the value of a person's estate immediately after the disposition being less than it was before (¶6465). The fall in value is deemed to be the value transferred.

Gifts, either to an individual or to a trust, are the most common form of disposition for IHT purposes, but the following are also relevant:
– **sale of property at an undervalue** (e.g. a mother selling shares worth £25,000 to her son for £10,000);
– **failure to exercise a right** (such as the failure to collect a debt) which results in a fall in the value of one person's estate and an increase in another person's estate, unless the omission is shown not to be deliberate;
– a **loan** for a fixed or minimum period for inadequate consideration; or
– **alteration of share capital** in a close company (¶7000).

MEMO POINTS A **failure to exercise a right** is deemed to occur on the latest date that the right could have been exercised.

Deemed dispositions

6400 Deemed dispositions include:
– transfers on death (¶6575);
– termination of an interest in possession (¶7530); and
– transfers of value made by a close company (¶6990).

6402 s 272 IHTA 1984 **Associated operations** As an anti-avoidance measure, the term disposition is also **deemed to include** a disposition effected by a series of associated operations (¶6925).

s 268 IHTA 1984 Associated operations are **defined** as any multiple operations of any kind which affect the same property, or which are effected by reference to each other. Operations can be associated whether they occur at the same or different times, and whether the same or different people carry them out. An omission can also be an operation for these purposes.

An **example** of associated operations would be giving away a set of four antique chairs in separate transfers to the same person. The value of an individual chair is likely to be less than one quarter of the value of a matching set, and these transfers will be treated as a single disposition.

Gifts with reservation A further anti-avoidance principle arises where an individual makes a gift but retains some sort of interest or benefit from the property transferred. In this case, the gift with reservation rules (¶6935) state that a transfer will arise on making the gift, and a further transfer will be deemed to occur when the reservation is lifted. **6404** s 102 FA 1986

An **example** of a gift with reservation would be giving a house to someone else, but where the donor continued to live there.

2. Dispositions which are not transfers of value

The following dispositions (explained in further detail below) do not constitute a transfer of value for IHT purposes: **6406**
- expenditure for family maintenance;
- expenditure without gratuitous intent;
- alterations in the distribution of the estate of a deceased person;
- retirement benefits;
- waiver of remuneration;
- waiver of a dividend;
- expenditure allowable for income tax or corporation tax;
- the grant of an agricultural tenancy; or
- voidable transfers.

Expenditure for family maintenance

Expenditure incurred during lifetime for the maintenance of family members does not constitute a transfer of value in any of the following circumstances: **6408** s 11 IHTA 1984

a. one **party to a marriage** pays for the maintenance of the other party, whether during the marriage or on separation or divorce;

b. where it is incurred for the purposes of a **child's** maintenance, education or training by:
- a party to a marriage in favour of a child of either party to the marriage;
- any person in favour of a child not in the care of a parent; or
- the parent of an illegitimate child in favour of that child; or

c. the provision of reasonable care and maintenance of a **dependent relative** of the donor.

A disposition which only **partially** satisfies these provisions will be split into exempt and non-exempt parts.

MEMO POINTS 1. **Child** in this case includes adopted and step-children. Expenditure relating to maintenance, education or training incurred up to 5 April following the child's 18th birthday (or after ceasing full-time education and training, if later), is not a transfer of value.
2. Where payments are made to a **child who is not cared for by a parent**, any expenditure up to the cessation of full-time education or training after the date of the child's 18th birthday will not be a transfer of value, provided the child was in the care of the donor for substantial periods.

Expenditure without gratuitous intent

In order to protect a person who merely makes a bad bargain, a disposition will not constitute a transfer of value between two **unconnected persons** where there is no intent to confer a gratuitous benefit. **6410** s 10 IHTA 1984

This will only apply to a transaction between **connected persons** if it was undertaken on a commercial arm's length basis.

These provisions will only apply to sales of **unquoted shares or securities** if it can also be shown that the price was (or was such as might have been) freely negotiated at the time of the sale.

MEMO POINTS **Partners in a partnership** are not connected persons for the purposes of transferring partnership assets from one partner to another, and so long as any arrangement has no gratuitous intent, no liability to IHT will arise.

EXAMPLE Mr B sells a painting valued at £20,000 to his daughter for only £15,000. The undervalue will not be liable to IHT if no gratuitous benefit was intended by him, and he would have sold the painting to an unconnected person for the same amount.

Alterations in the distribution of the death estate

6412 s 17 IHTA 1984 Where an individual receives property under a will or intestacy he is not obliged to accept it. In the normal course of events, to refuse property would constitute a transfer of value. To correct this inequity, the following alterations in the distribution of a deceased's estate will not constitute a transfer of value (¶6615):
- variation or disclaimer of disposition under a will or intestacy;
- alteration on the express wishes of the testator;
- election by a surviving spouse for a redemption of a life interest; or
- renunciation of a claim under the Scottish law provisions of legitim.

Retirement benefits

6414 s 12(2) IHTA 1984 **Contributions** to a registered pension scheme are not a transfer of value.

For the treatment of members' rights and benefits under pension schemes, see ¶6589.

Waiver of remuneration

6416 s 14 IHTA 1984 The waiver or repayment of remuneration will not be a transfer of value if, apart from the waiver or repayment, the remuneration would have been:
- assessed as employment income of the **recipient**; and
- allowable as a deduction in computing the profits for income tax or corporation tax purposes of the **payer**.

Waiver of a dividend

6418 s 15 IHTA 1984 A transfer of value will not arise where a person waives a dividend (of any type) **within a period** of 12 months before the date on which any right to the dividend accrued. A general waiver is only effective for 12 months, so this should be renewed annually.

Expenditure allowable for tax purposes

6420 s 12(1) IHTA 1984 A disposition will not constitute a transfer of value where the transferor could claim an allowable deduction for the transfer in calculating his profits for income tax or corporation tax purposes. An **ex gratia payment** which is not an allowable deduction will therefore be treated as a transfer of value.

MEMO POINTS If a payment is **partly allowable**, only the non-allowable part will be a transfer of value.

Grant of an agricultural tenancy

6422 s 16 IHTA 1984 The grant of a tenancy of agricultural property in the UK, the Channel Islands, or the Isle of Man is not a transfer of value, provided that the property is used for **agricultural purposes**, and the transfer is made for **full consideration** in money or money's worth.

Voidable transfers

6424 s 150 IHTA 1984 Where a transfer has been made under duress, undue influence, or is in some other way void, a claim can be made that it should be treated for IHT purposes as if it had never taken place. For example, if an individual has granted a **lasting power of attorney** (or, before 1 October 2007, an enduring power of attorney) due to reduced mental ability, the Court of Protection will need to authorise any substantial gifts, otherwise they will be void. With effect from 1 April 2011, such a claim must be made within 4 years after the claimant knew, or ought reasonably to have known, that the transfer had been set aside.

3. Exempt transfers

Exempt transfers are those which would normally constitute a transfer of value but which will never be chargeable to IHT because of specific statutory provisions. There are two types of exempt transfer: the first category apply **only** to lifetime transfers, whereas the second category **also** apply to transfers on death (¶6438). **6426**

a. Lifetime transfers only

The following are exempt lifetime transfers: **6428**
- gifts covered by the annual exemption;
- small gifts;
- normal expenditure out of income; and
- gifts in consideration of marriage.

Annual exemption

For any tax year, the first £3,000 of lifetime transfers of value (taken in date order) are exempt from IHT. Where the annual exemption is not fully utilised in one tax year it is carried forward to the next tax year only, and, if not then fully utilised, it is lost. The **current year exemption** is always used before the brought forward exemption. **6430** s 19 IHTA 1984

MEMO POINTS 1. Where several transfers are **made on the same day**, the annual exemption is pro-rated based on the value of each transfer (¶6538).
2. Where **many transfers** are made in the same tax year, the annual exemption will be allocated to whichever transfer is made first. This may result in a wasted exemption (¶6554).

EXAMPLE Mr A made chargeable transfers of £2,000 in Year 1 and of £3,750 in Year 2.

	£
Year 1	
Chargeable transfer	2,000
Less: Year 1 annual exemption	(2,000)
	Nil
Annual exemption carried forward – £1,000	
Year 2	
Chargeable transfer	3,750
Less: Year 2 annual exemption, used first	(3,000)
Year 1 annual exemption brought forward (restricted)	(750)
	Nil
Annual exemption carried forward – Nil	

Small gifts

For any tax year, small gifts to a maximum of £250 **per recipient** in that tax year are exempt transfers. There is no restriction on the number of recipients. A gift in excess of £250 does not qualify for the exemption so, for example, the whole of a gift of £255 will be a chargeable transfer of value, whereas a gift of £245 will be exempt. **6432** s 20 IHTA 1984

Normal expenditure out of income

A transfer of value will be an exempt transfer if: **6434** s 21 IHTA 1984
- taking one year with another, it is made out of **after-tax income** (as opposed to capital); and
- after taking into account all transfers of value made out of normal expenditure, the donor is left with **sufficient income** to maintain his usual standard of living.

Normal expenditure for these purposes is deemed to be the typical or habitual expenditure of the donor. Examples would include regular payments such as gifts at Christmas and birthdays, or regular premium payments to an insurance policy for another person.

The **first gift in a series** may still be treated as an exempt transfer under this provision if it can be shown that there is clear evidence of an intention to make further gifts. *Bennett v IRC* [1995]

Gifts in consideration of marriage

6436 s 22 IHTA 1984 Whether a gift is an exempt transfer depends on the **relationship** between the donor and a party to the marriage. The following table indicates the **maximum exemption** available for each relationship, which **applies to the total gift** made to the couple rather than to each of them individually. Where the amount of the gift is more than the maximum exemption, the **excess** will be subject to IHT in the normal way.

The gift **should be made** before the wedding, and should be conditional on the marriage taking place.

MEMO POINTS 1. An exempt gift may be made **after the wedding** providing it follows a binding obligation made on or before the day of the wedding.

2. A gift into a **marriage settlement** will still qualify under these provisions providing the only persons entitled to benefit from the settlement are the parties to the marriage, their children, and the spouses of their children.

Relationship to a party to the marriage	Maximum
Parent	£5,000
Grandparent or great-grandparent	£2,500
Other party to the marriage	£2,500
Any other person	£1,000

b. Both in lifetime and on death

6438 The following transfers are exempt whether made as a result of a lifetime transfer or on death:

- gifts to a spouse;
- gifts to UK charities;
- gifts to political parties;
- transfers to employee trusts;
- gifts to housing associations;
- gifts for national purposes; and
- transfers to maintenance funds for historic buildings.

All these exemptions, other than a gift to a spouse, are subject to anti-avoidance provisions (¶6454) which apply when the transfers are not true gifts.

Gifts to a spouse

6440 s 18 IHTA 1984 Any transfer of value made to a spouse, whether during the lifetime of the transferor or on death, is an exempt transfer. The only exception to this rule is where the recipient spouse is **domiciled overseas**. In this case, only the first £55,000 of transfers from a UK domiciled spouse will be exempt. The exemption is a cumulative amount, covering transfers made during lifetime and on death.

Before 22 March 2006, all transfers to **trusts** in which the spouse had an interest in possession qualified for this exemption. Transfers made on or after 22 March 2006 only qualify for the exemption where the trust is created on death, and the spouse has an immediate post-death interest (¶7178).

Where a person who was beneficially entitled to an interest in possession before 22 March 2006 dies, and a surviving spouse becomes entitled to a transitional serial interest (¶7178), the spouse exemption will apply on the death.

MEMO POINTS A **common law** husband or wife does not qualify as a spouse for these purposes. *Holland (Holland's Executor) v IRC* [2003]

Gifts to UK charities

A gift to charity is an exempt transfer provided that the **property transferred** becomes the property of the charity, or is held on trust for charitable purposes. A charity is defined using the standard income tax definition of any body of persons or trust established for charitable purposes only. **6442** s 23 IHTA 1984

Charities **registered abroad** are excluded for these purposes, although UK charities carrying on relief abroad are still eligible for the exemption. *Camille and Henry Dreyfus Foundation Inc v IRC* [1956]

Gifts to political parties

A gift to a political party is an exempt transfer providing that **at the last general election** preceding the transfer: **6444** s 24 IHTA 1984
– two members of the party were elected to the House of Commons; or
– one member of the party was elected to the House of Commons, and candidates of the party received not less than 150,000 votes.

Transfers to employee trusts

Subject to a number of conditions, a transfer of value made by an individual who is **beneficially entitled to shares** in a company will be an exempt transfer to the extent that: **6446** s 28 IHTA 1984
– the value transferred is attributable to shares in, or securities of, the company which are placed in an employee trust; and
– the beneficiaries of the trust include all or most of the employees or officers of the company.

MEMO POINTS 1. The following **conditions** must be satisfied within a year from the date of the transfer:
a. the trustees must:
– own more than 50% of the ordinary shares in the company; and
– have a majority of votes on all questions affecting the company as a whole;
b. no provisions must exist in any agreement or similar instrument affecting the company's constitution or management or its shares and securities, where the conditions in **a**. can cease to apply without the consent of the trustees; and
c. the trust must not permit any of the settled property to be applied at any time for the benefit of:
– a participator in the company (¶2102);
– a participator in a subsidiary close company (¶2101) which has provided funds to the same trust;
– any person who has been a participator in either of the above companies in the 10 years prior to the transfer; or
– any person connected to any of the above.
2. A **participator** for these purposes does not include any participator in a company who has less than a 5% interest. For a non-close company, a participator for these purposes is someone who would be a participator if the company had been a close company.

Gifts to housing associations

A gift to a registered housing association or registered social landlord is an exempt transfer to the extent that it relates to a transfer of **land situated in the UK**. **6448** s 24A IHTA 1984

Gifts for national purposes

6450
s 25 and Sch 3 IHTA 1984

Gifts made to the following **national bodies** are exempt from IHT:

National bodies
The National Gallery
The British Museum
The National Museums of Scotland
The National Museum of Wales
The Ulster Museum
Any other similar national institution which exists wholly or mainly for the purpose of preserving, for the public benefit, a collection of scientific, historic or artistic interest, and which is approved by the Treasury
Any museum or art gallery in the UK which exists wholly or mainly for that purpose and is maintained by a local authority or university in the UK
Any library whose main function is to serve the needs of teaching and research at a university in the UK
The Historic Buildings and Monuments Commission for England
The National Trust for Places of Historic Interest or Natural Beauty
The National Trust for Scotland for Places of Historic Interest or Natural Beauty
The National Art Collections Fund
The Trustees of the National Heritage Memorial Fund
The National Endowment for Science, Technology and the Arts
The Friends of the National Libraries
The Historic Churches Preservation Trust
Natural England
Scottish Natural Heritage
Countryside Council for Wales
Any local authority
Any Government department (including the National Debt Commissioners)
Any university or university college in the UK
A health service body

Maintenance funds for historic buildings

6452
s 27 and Sch 4 IHTA 1984

A transfer of property to a settlement which is **used** as a **source of funds** for the maintenance and repair of historic buildings, and in relation to which the Treasury has given a direction, is exempt.

MEMO POINTS The transfer to such a fund is eligible for gift relief from **capital gains tax** (¶6108).

Anti-avoidance provisions

6454
ss 23 – 25 IHTA 1984

Anti-avoidance provisions apply to the exempt transfers outlined above, other than transfers to a spouse (¶6440) and the conditions for the exemption to apply are:

a. the gift must not take effect **following the termination of** any interest or period after the transfer is made. For example, a gift to X for life and then to a charity would not be an exempt transfer;

b. the gift must not **be dependent on a condition** which is not satisfied within 12 months after the transfer;

c. the gift must not **be capable of being annulled or invalidated** (strictly known as a defeasible gift). For example, a gift to Y, providing he marries within 6 months, is a gift which is capable of being invalidated. The test takes place 12 months after the gift, and if it is not capable of being annulled or invalidated at that date, the exemption will apply;

d. the interest gifted must not **be less than the donor's interest** at a date 12 months after the date of the transfer;
e. the property must not be **given for a limited period**; and
f. the donor **cannot reserve or create an interest** in the property for himself, his spouse, or anyone connected with them, unless full consideration is given, or the donee's enjoyment of the property is substantially unaffected.

4. Excluded property

Excluded property is property that is outside the scope of IHT and is therefore left out of account in determining the amount transferred by a transfer of value, and in the valuation of the estate on death. **6456** s 3(2) IHTA 1984
The main types of excluded property are:
- reversionary interests;
- property abroad;
- certain government securities;
- savings owned by persons domiciled in the Isle of Man or the Channel Islands;
- dormant bank accounts of Holocaust victims; and
- decorations or awards for valour or gallantry.

Reversionary interest

A reversionary interest is excluded property **unless**: **6457** s 48(1) IHTA 1984
- it was acquired for money or money's worth (whether by the person currently entitled to it or by a person previously entitled);
- either the settlor or his spouse is, or has been, beneficially entitled; or
- it is an interest based on the anticipated termination of a lease. For example, the grant of a lease at nominal rent to X for life, with the property reverting to Y, will not be excluded property.

Property situated outside the UK

Property which is situated outside the UK is excluded property if the person making the transfer is **domiciled** outside the UK. For these purposes a double tax treaty may specify where an asset is deemed to be situated (¶6895). **6458** s 6(1) IHTA 1984

Settled property will be excluded property if the settlor was non-domiciled when the settlement was made. This does not apply where a person purchases an interest in the trust property after 4 December 2005, unless the person beneficially entitled to the property is domiciled outside the UK.

Holdings in **authorised unit trusts** and shares in **open-ended investment companies** are excluded property if the person beneficially entitled is an individual domiciled outside the UK.

Government securities

UK Government securities, such as gilts, **owned by persons** who are not ordinarily resident in the UK (¶4160) will be excluded property if: **6460** ss 6(2), 48(4) IHTA 1984
- the person owns the securities beneficially and they are not settled property;
- the person has an interest in possession (¶6468) in the securities; or
- in the case of a discretionary trust, none of the beneficiaries are ordinarily resident in the UK.

MEMO POINTS HMRC have confirmed that the **domicile** of the taxpayer is immaterial for this purpose.

Savings

6461 s 6(3) IHTA 1984

The following types of savings are excluded property when they are **beneficially owned by persons domiciled** in the Isle of Man or the Channel Islands:
– war savings certificates;
– national savings certificates (including Ulster savings certificates);
– premium savings bonds;
– deposits with the National Savings Bank or with a trustee savings bank; and
– any certified contractual savings scheme.

Holocaust victims' dormant bank accounts

6462 s 268A TCGA 1992

Where a victim of National-Socialist persecution has **died before making a compensation claim** in relation to a dormant bank account, the value of the deposit and the right to claim compensation is ignored for IHT purposes. If a **compensation claim has been made**, the value of any outstanding compensation, or of a compensation payment made to the victim or his relatives, is subject to IHT in the normal way.

Decorations and awards for valour or gallantry

6463 s 6 (1B) IHTA 1984

A decoration or award for valour or gallant conduct is treated as excluded property if it has never been transferred for consideration in money or money's worth. Decorations need not be medals, and **can include** items such as silverware or a presentation sword. The award need not have remained in the family of the original recipient, and its sale during the administration of an estate would not prevent its treatment as excluded property.

SECTION 3

Valuation

6465

The IHT charge is **based on** the fall in the value of a person's estate as the result of a transfer. The loss to the estate is measured by comparing its value before the transfer to the value after the transfer. The valuation rules depend on the nature of the asset, whether there is any related property, and whether the individual made the transfer during lifetime or on death.

The remainder of this section describes the general rules used for determining the value of transfers. The specific rules relating to the valuation of the death estate are described at ¶6584.

1. General rules

6467 s 5 IHTA 1984

A person's estate for IHT purposes comprises the aggregate of all property (other than excluded property (¶6456)) to which he is beneficially entitled, less his liabilities.

Beneficial entitlement is a question of law but is distinct from legal ownership. This is illustrated by a case where a bank account in the name of a father (and therefore legally owned by him) was held to be beneficially owned by the father and his three sons. *Anand v IRC* [1997]

Where a person has a **general power** to dispose of, or to charge money on, any property (other than settled property), he will be treated as if he were beneficially entitled to the property for the purposes of valuing his estate.

MEMO POINTS 1. The term **aggregate** used in the definition of estate is significant in that assets in the estate cannot be valued in isolation. Therefore the value of a 51% holding of shares is not 51 times the value of a 1% holding, but the value of the aggregate holding, including the increase in value relative to a majority shareholding.

2. **Property** for these purposes is defined as including all rights and interests of any description, and therefore includes tangible assets such as land, and intangible assets such as a debt owed to the owner of the estate, or a right of action for damages. s 272 IHTA 1984

6468 A person who is beneficially entitled to an **interest in possession** (¶6386) in settled property is deemed to be beneficially entitled to the settled property itself in determining the value of his estate, where the interest was created:
a. before 22 March 2006; or
b. on or after 22 March 2006, and where it is:
– an immediate post-death interest (¶7178);
– a transitional serial interest (¶7178); or
– an interest in a disabled trust (¶7190).
The **exception** to this rule is where the individual purchased the interest in possession, in which case the value for his estate will be the actual value of the interest in possession.

Loss to the estate

6470 s 160 IHTA 1984 It is a crucial concept of IHT that the value of a transfer is based on the loss to the donor's estate and not on the value to the donee.

For these purposes the open market value is used **to determine** the loss to the estate, by taking the price that the property might reasonably be expected to fetch if sold on the open market. This is based on the following assumptions:
– the property was sold in the manner that achieved the best price (for example, in small parts or as a whole); and
– any depression in the market that would arise if all of the property were sold at the same time is ignored.
The loss to the estate may exceed the value of the property in the donee's hands.

EXAMPLE A Ltd has an issued share capital of 1,000 shares. Mr B owns 750 of the shares and decides to give 300 of them to his son C. The market values per share are as follows:

10 – 30% holding	£50
31 – 49% holding	£60
50 – 74% holding	£100
75% or more	£120

	£
Value of the estate before the transfer (750 × £120)	90,000
Less: Value of the estate after the transfer (450 × £60)	(27,000)
Loss to the estate	63,000

Assuming this is C's only holding in A Ltd, the value of the shares in his estate will be £15,000 (300 × 50).

Related property

6473 s 161 IHTA 1984 The value of any property in a person's estate is found after taking into account any related property if that **produces** a higher value. Property is related to the property in a person's estate if:
a. it is part of the estate of his spouse; or
b. as a result of an exempt transfer by the person or his spouse after 15 April 1976, it is (or has been within the previous 5 years) the property of one of the following:
– a charity or charitable trust (¶6442);
– a qualifying political party (¶6444);
– a specified national body (¶6450); or
– a registered housing association (¶6448).

MEMO POINTS Property comprised in a settlement in which a person has an **interest in possession** may already be part of the estate for these purposes, depending on when the interest was created (¶6468).

6474 HMRC Brief 71/07 HMRC have published their practice relating to the valuation of land which is owned by a person and his spouse. Where IHT accounts were received by HMRC before 28 November 2007, the valuation of the land is subject to the decision of the Lands Tribunal, but if received on or after 28 November 2007, the related property rules apply to land as for any other asset. HMRC have stated that they will reconsider land valuations which were concluded between 16 July 2004 and 28 November 2007, where the related property rules were deemed to apply but now a Tribunal valuation would be preferable.

MEMO POINTS The relevant point was decided in the case by the Special Commissioner, who found that the related property rules only applied to property which had a distinct or individual existence as a unit, such as unit trusts or a set of furniture (e.g. 12 dining chairs). HMRC have since received legal advice that the related property rules can apply to fractional units, such as parcels of land, and state that they will defend the point. Arkwright and another v IRC [2004]

6476 Property is valued in accordance with the related property rules using the following formula both before and after the transfer:

$$\frac{\text{Estate property}}{\text{Estate property} + \text{Related property}} \times \text{Combined value}$$

For **shares and securities** of the same class, the apportionment should be based on the number of shares held.

For **other types of asset**, the apportionment should be based on the individual value of each asset.

EXAMPLE Mr A owns 40% of the shares in B Ltd and half of a freehold property. Mrs A owns 20% of the shares in B Ltd and the remaining half of the freehold property. Mr A decides to give 15% of his shares, and half of his share of the property, to his daughter.

The estimated values of the freehold property are:

	£
25%	45,000
50%	95,000
75%	150,000
100%	250,000

The estimated values of the shares are:

15% holding	15,000
25% holding	30,000
40% holding	50,000
45% holding	56,000
60% holding	100,000

	£	£
Value of Mr A's estate before transfer:		
Shares (40/60 × 100,000)	66,667	
Freehold (95,000/190,000 × 250,000)	125,000	
		191,667
Value of Mr A's estate after transfer:		
Shares (25/45 × 56,000)	31,111	
Freehold (45,000/(45,000 + 95,000) × 150,000)	48,214	
		(79,325)
Value of transfer		112,342

Liabilities

Liabilities reduce the value of the estate both before and after a lifetime transfer of value. This means that **in most cases** the value of the transfer will not be affected by liabilities unless the transfer in some way affects the amount or value of the liability. Liabilities are more significant to the valuation of the death estate and are therefore covered in detail in ¶6594. **6478**

Expenses

The value transferred will be **reduced by** the following expenses: **6480** ss 164, 165 IHTA 1984
– any incidental expenses (such as valuation expenses and legal fees) incurred by the donor but borne by the donee; and
– any capital gains tax arising in respect of the transfer which was borne by the donee.

In addition, the value transferred must take account of the payment of IHT on a lifetime transfer. If the donor pays the tax, the value of the transfer must be grossed up to establish the loss to the estate (¶6536). s 5 IHTA 1984

MEMO POINTS **Incidental expenses borne by the donor** do not reduce the value of a transfer.

2. Specific rules

Summary

Whilst the general rule for valuation is to use open market value, special rules exist for the valuation of the following assets. **6482**

Asset		¶¶
Land and buildings	Generally	¶6486
	Leases	¶6488
Shares and securities	Quoted	¶6490
	Unquoted	¶6492
Unit trusts		¶6494
Life policies	Assignment	¶6496
	Back-to-back arrangements	¶6500
Debts		¶6502

Restriction on freedom to dispose

Where the value of property is reduced because of a contract which excludes or restricts the right to dispose of it, the exclusion or restriction is ignored unless consideration for money or money's worth was given for it. This will apply to transfers on death. **6484** s 163 IHTA 1984

Instances where such a restriction would arise include the following:
– the grant of an option to purchase property in the future for less than market value;
– shares subject to restrictions in the company's Articles of Association; and
– partnership agreements.

MEMO POINTS The creation of the original exclusion or restriction may constitute a transfer of value, and this will be taken into account in determining the value of a subsequent transfer.

EXAMPLE Mr A grants Mr B an option to purchase a painting for its current value of £50,000 in 2 years' time. Mr B pays £10,000 for the option which is full money's worth. On the exercise of the option the painting is worth £80,000. No liability to IHT arises for Mr A as full money's worth was given for the option.

If Mr B had not paid any consideration for the grant of the option, IHT may have become chargeable on:
- the option value of £10,000; and
- the increase in value of the painting of £30,000 less the option value of £10,000.

Land and buildings

6486 The valuation of land and buildings is generally the **subject of negotiation** between the taxpayer and HMRC, who have a team of district valuers who may be utilised to arrive at a value. The taxpayer will often employ the services of a professional valuer. If agreement cannot be reached, an appeal may be made to the Lands Tribunal and from there through the courts.

The value of a half share of land held by **tenants in common** is discounted to take account of the fact that the demand for land without vacant possession is low. The appropriate discount is generally between 10% and 15%, depending on whether the co-owner has a right of occupation.

IHT Newsletter December 2004

MEMO POINTS HMRC have issued guidance in relation to **household and personal goods**, which states that these items, although sometimes small, must be valued in accordance with the general rule of open market value. It is good practice to explain how the valuation has been calculated, and how all of the goods have been accounted for.

6488 **Leases** Where **full consideration** was given for leased property on the original acquisition, the value on a subsequent chargeable transfer is the market value of the lease at that time.

Where the lessee holds the property on a **lease for life** (or for any other period determined by reference to a death), the lease may be treated as a settlement and the value of a subsequent transfer will be calculated as:
- the full value of the property; less
- the value of the lessor's interest, which is deemed to be the proportion of the value of the property given by the following fraction:

$$\text{Value of property (i.e. freehold or head lease)} \times \frac{\text{Consideration given by lessee at grant of lease}}{\text{Value of full consideration for the lease at grant of lease}}$$

This means that, if no consideration was given when the lease was originally granted, the value of the lessor's interest will be nil, and the lessee's interest will be the value of the whole property.

Shares and securities

6490 s 272 IHTA 1984

Quoted Shares and securities are deemed to be quoted for IHT purposes if they are listed on a recognised stock exchange (¶9995) or dealt in on the Unlisted Securities Market.

s 272(3) TCGA 1992

Quoted shares and securities are **valued at the lower of**:
- the lower of the two prices quoted in the Stock Exchange Daily Official List for the relevant date, plus a quarter of the difference between the two prices; and
- the average of the highest and lowest prices recorded for normal bargains on that date.

MEMO POINTS If **trading did not occur** on the day of the transfer, the value will be based on the prices for the days of trading immediately before, and after, the day of the transfer. The four prices will be compared and the lowest will form the value.

EXAMPLE Mr A owned 1,000 ordinary shares in B Plc and decided to give them to his brother Mr C. On the day in question the prices quoted by the Stock Exchange Daily Official List were 213 – 218 and the normal bargain prices for the day were recorded as 208, 210, 216 and 219.

The share valuation will be based on the lower of:
1. 213 + (1/4 × (218 – 213)) = 214.25
2. (208 + 219)/ 2 = 213.50

The shares will therefore be valued at 213.50p each, giving a total of £2,135.

Unquoted Unquoted shares and securities are **valued on the basis of** the open market value at the time of the transfer. The open market value assumes that the prospective buyer has all the information available to him that a prudent purchaser might reasonably require, if he were purchasing them from a willing vendor in a private sale at arm's length. **6492** s 168 IHTA 1984

The valuation should also take account of any restrictions on the transfer of shares found in the company's Articles of Association.

Other factors that may be important in valuing unquoted shares and securities include the following:
- the size of the shareholding;
- the state of the economy;
- the earning capacity of the business;
- the management of the business;
- the value of business assets;
- the available market for the shares;
- an estimate of future profits; and
- the potential dividend yield.

Unit trusts

Units in an approved unit trust are valued at the **lower of** the two prices published on the day of the transfer or, if that is not a business day, on the preceding business day. **6494** s 272(5) TCGA 1992

Life policies

Assignment The assignment, as a gift or at less than full value, of the benefits of a life policy constitutes a transfer of value for IHT, where the policy ceases to be part of the estate of the transferor. **6496** s 167 IHTA 1984

The value of such an assignment during the lifetime of a taxpayer is taken to be the **higher of**:

a. the market value of the policy; or

b. the total amount of premiums paid before the transfer, less any amounts received on surrender before the transfer.

MEMO POINTS 1. **Total premiums paid** include any other consideration paid at any time before the transfer of value under the policy being assigned (or any policy or contract for which it is substituted).

2. The **amounts received on surrender** include any sum that has been received at any time before the transfer of value in respect of a surrender of any right conferred by the policy (or any policy or contract for which it is substituted).

EXAMPLE Mr A assigns the benefit of a life policy on his life to Mr B. The open market value of the policy is £30,000, while the premiums paid to date amount to £34,000. No surrender has occurred. The value for IHT purposes is £34,000.

If the donor **continues to pay** premiums under the policy following the transfer, then another transfer of value occurs each time a payment is made. Regular payments made in this way may be covered by the exemption for normal expenditure out of income (¶6434). **6498**

Back-to-back arrangements The purchase of an annuity in order to produce income to pay the premiums on a life assurance policy, the benefit of which is vested in someone other than the life assured, is known as a back-to-back arrangement and is subject to **special valuation rules**. **6500**

A transfer of value arising from a back-to-back arrangement will not be eligible for the exemption for **normal expenditure out of income** (¶6434) unless it can be established that the purchase of an annuity or the making (or the variation) of a life assurance policy were not associated operations (¶6925). s 21(2) IHTA 1984

SP E4 In practice, policies and annuities are not treated as associated operations if the policy was issued on full medical evidence of the health of the insured, and it would have been issued on the same terms if the annuity had not been purchased.

If the **exemption does not apply**, the value transferred will be the lower of:

a. the aggregate of:
- the value of the consideration given for the annuity; plus
- any premium paid (or other consideration given) under the policy on or before the transfer; or

b. the value of the greatest benefit capable of being conferred by the policy at any time, calculated as if the date of the transfer was that time.

HMRC Brief 21/09 The amount of the valuation of the annuity may be subject to negotiation with HMRC. In normal situations, the life assurance company will issue a certificate stating the value of the annuity retained. HMRC may dispute this valuation where they feel the valuation is inappropriate, in particular in cases where the settlor is older than 90 next birthday (actual age or deemed age after underwriting) which could result in a higher tax liability. *HMRC v Executors of Mrs Marjorie Edna Bower (deceased)* [2008]

MEMO POINTS This case concerned the valuation of an annuity where the insured was over 90 years old. In circumstances where the insured is over 90, or is considered to be uninsurable at the time of making the gift, HMRC consider the value of the annuity entitlement to be nominal. The valuation affects the amount of tax due, should the gift be (or become) subject to IHT. Despite the issue of a valuation certificate by the insurance company, HMRC successfully argued that the annuity was worth less than the certificate stated. HMRC based their argument on the fact that no buyer would have purchased the annuity, given the age of the annuitant, and therefore it was not commercially viable.

Debts

6502
s 166 IHTA 1984 The **general rule** for the valuation of debts is to use the face value of the debt. The **exception** to this rule is where it can be shown that, through no act or omission on the part of the creditor, recovery of the debt is not reasonably practicable. In this case, a total or partial deduction may be made to the value of the debt for IHT purposes.

SECTION 4

Calculation

6510 Once the value of a transfer has been established the IHT charge can be calculated. There are four scenarios in which a tax charge will arise:
- lifetime tax on a chargeable lifetime transfer (¶6534);
- additional death tax on a chargeable lifetime transfer made within 7 years before death (¶6542);
- death tax on a potentially exempt transfer made within 7 years before death (¶6556); and
- charge to tax on the death estate (¶6600).

The basic principles of the tax calculation are the same for each of the above scenarios, although the detailed rules are given where indicated.

Basis of charge

6512 The fundamental rule is that IHT is a **cumulative tax**, which means that at the date of each transfer (or the date of death) any transfers in the previous 7 years must be taken into account. For each tax year there is a nil rate band (frozen at £325,000 until April 2015; for the limits for 2008/09 and earlier years, see ¶9981), and the excess over that amount is subject to tax at 20% for lifetime transfers and 40% for death transfers.

IHT is calculated on the total amount (including the value of previous transfers), and the proportion relating to the **current transfer** is determined on the assumption that it represents the highest part of the aggregate.

MEMO POINTS 1. See ¶6536 for details of the rates of tax used where the **donor pays the tax** on the transfer.
2. **Chargeable lifetime transfers** made within 7 years before death will be subject to an additional charge on death, but relief will be given for lifetime tax paid.
3. Where an **additional charge** arises on death, or a potentially exempt transfer becomes chargeable on death, taper relief is available (¶6565), which reduces the amount of IHT based on the number of years between the transfer and the date of death.
4. For deaths occurring on or after 9 October 2007, if a nil rate band has not been used in full on the death of a spouse, the personal representatives of the surviving spouse can claim the **percentage** of the nil rate band unused on the earlier death against the survivor's estate. See ¶6608 for details of how to calculate and claim the transferable nil rate band.

EXAMPLE In May 2011 Mr A makes a chargeable lifetime transfer of £200,000. Mr A has made no other chargeable transfers other than £170,000 (after the annual exemption) in January 2006.

			Gross	**Tax**
		£	**£**	**£**
Cumulative total brought forward			170,000	
Current transfer		200,000		
Less: Annual exemption	2011/12	(3,000)		
	2010/11	(3,000)		
			194,000	7,800
			364,000	7,800
Tax thereon:				
£325,000 covered by nil rate band for 2011/12				
(364,000 – 325,000) @ 20%		7,800		

Reliefs

There are a number of reliefs available which either reduce the amount of a transfer of value or the amount of IHT due. 6514

Relief	Effect	¶¶
Business property relief	Reduces the value of both lifetime and death transfers of relevant business property (to nil in some cases)	¶6700
Agricultural property relief	Reduces the value of both lifetime and death transfers of relevant agricultural property (to nil in some cases)	¶6750
Fall in value reliefs	Recalculates the original IHT charge where property is transferred within the 7 years before the death of the taxpayer	¶6797
	Recalculates the original IHT charge on a post-death sale	¶6814
Quick succession relief	Reduces the IHT liability on death, where IHT had already been paid (or becomes payable) on a transfer to the deceased person within the 5 years before death	¶6865

CHAPTER 2

Lifetime transfers of value

OUTLINE ¶¶

Where an individual makes a transfer of value during his lifetime which is not an exempt transfer (¶6428) or a transfer of an excluded asset (¶6456) then, depending on the recipient of the transfer, it will be either: 6525
- a chargeable lifetime transfer (CLT); or
- a potentially exempt transfer (PET).

A CLT is immediately chargeable to IHT and may be subject to an additional charge if the transferor's death occurs within 7 years of the transfer.

However, the majority of lifetime transfers are PETs, which are only chargeable if the transferor dies within 7 years of the transfer.

The death charge on both types of transfer may be mitigated by taper relief (¶6565) which reduces the IHT charge by a percentage, based on the length of time between the date of the transfer and the date of death and, since 9 October 2007, a successful claim for all or part of a transferable nil rate band (¶6608).

SECTION 1

Chargeable lifetime transfers (CLTs)

A CLT is a transfer which is neither a potentially exempt transfer nor an exempt transfer. 6530
Essentially, this means that the recipient is not an individual or exempt body. ss 2, 3 IHTA 1984

The **main examples** of a CLT are:
- transfers into chargeable trusts (¶7440);
- distributions and appointments by trustees of chargeable trusts;
- the termination of interests in possession in exempt trusts (¶7532); and
- the alteration of share capital and transfers of value by a close company.

6532 s 216 IHTA 1984 There are two **main consequences** of making a CLT:

a. the transfer will be immediately chargeable to IHT and, even if no tax is due, HMRC must be informed that the transfer has been made; and

b. the transfer forms part of the cumulative total of chargeable transfers made by the transferor.

s 260 TCGA 1992 MEMO POINTS 1. In addition, the fact that a transfer is immediately chargeable to IHT means that holdover relief may be available for **capital gains tax** purposes (¶6106).

ss 52, 53 FA 2010 2. Since 9 December 2009, where an individual **purchases an interest** in a trust, that interest forms part of the individual's estate for IHT purposes. If the **interest comes to an end** during the purchaser's lifetime, there may be an immediate charge to IHT. The same principles apply where an individual settles property on trust, and they (or their spouse) retain a future interest in it.

1. Calculation of lifetime tax

6534 s 7(2) and Sch 1 IHTA 1984 The **rate** of tax applicable to a CLT for 2011/12 is 20%, which is half of the rate applicable on death. If the transferor dies within 7 years of the transfer, additional tax may become payable (¶6542).

Each CLT is **aggregated** with all other CLTs made in the previous 7 years. If the cumulative total is less than the nil rate band for the year of the CLT (set at £325,000 for 2011/12), no IHT is payable. If the cumulative total exceeds the nil rate band for the year, tax is calculated on the assumption that the current transfer is the top slice.

EXAMPLE In June 2011 Mr A settled £150,000 into a discretionary trust. He made earlier chargeable lifetime transfers of the following amounts (after annual exemptions):

August 2003	£50,000
May 2006	£90,000
September 2007	£100,000

The trustees agreed to pay the tax, which was calculated as:

		Gross	Tax
	£	£	£
Cumulative total brought forward (90,000 + 100,000)		190,000	Nil
Transfer of value June 2011	150,000		
Annual exemption 2011/12	(3,000)		
2010/11	(3,000)		
		144,000	1,800
		334,000	1,800

Tax thereon:
£325,000 covered by nil rate band for 2011/12
334,000 – 325,000 @ 20% = £1,800

MEMO POINTS The transfer made in 2003 is not included in the cumulative total, as it was made more than 7 years before the CLT.

Transferor pays the tax

6536 The amount of IHT depends on who pays the tax.

Transfers where the **transferor pays** the tax are known as **net transfers**.

Transfers where the **recipient pays** the tax are known as **gross transfers**.

In the **absence of a specific agreement** between the parties it is assumed that the transferor will pay the tax.

IHT is charged on the amount transferred and, where the transferor pays the tax, the fall in value in his estate will include the amount of the tax paid, so it is necessary to **'gross up' net transfers** so that the amount of tax paid is included.

The tax on the grossed up amount is calculated as follows:

$$(\text{Transfer less available annual exemption}) \times 20/(100 - 20) = \text{Tax due}$$

It is the gross amount that is included in the cumulative total when calculating the tax on future transfers.

EXAMPLE Following on from the previous example, if Mr A had agreed to pay the tax on the transfer, the IHT liability would be calculated as follows:

	£	Net £	Tax £	Gross £
Cumulative total b/fwd (90,000 + 100,000)		190,000	Nil	190,000
Transfer of value June 2011	150,000			
Annual exemption 2011/12	(3,000)			
2010/11	(3,000)			
		144,000	2,250	146,250
		334,000	2,250	336,250

Tax thereon:
£325,000 covered by nil rate band for 2011/12
334,000 – 325,000 @ 20/(100 – 20) = £2,250
If Mr A made a subsequent transfer in September 2011 the cumulative total brought forward at that date would be £336,250.

Timing

The **general rule** is that transfers are dealt with in the order in which they occur, with later transfers bearing more tax than earlier transfers. **6538** s 266 IHTA 1984

The **exception** to this rule is where two or more transfers are made by the same person on the same day. In this case the transfers are deemed to have occurred at exactly the same time, and where:
- the transfers are **both gross** or **both net**, the tax liability is apportioned between them; or
- **one** of the transfers **is gross and the other is net**, the tax is calculated by dealing with the net transfer first and then the gross, to produce the lowest tax liability.

In either case, the **annual exemption** is pro-rated between the transfers. See ¶6554 for the allocation of the annual exemption between CLTs and PETs. s 19(3) IHTA 1984

EXAMPLE On 3 June 2011 Mr A settled £160,000 into discretionary trust A and £80,000 into discretionary trust B. The trustees of trust A paid the tax (a gross transfer), whilst Mr A paid the tax on the transfer to trust B (a net transfer). Mr A made an earlier chargeable lifetime transfer in January 2006 of £175,000.

The annual exemptions for 2011/12 and 2010/11 will be pro-rated on the basis of the values of £160,000 and £80,000.

June 2011 – transfer to trust B (a net transfer)	£	Net £	Tax £	Gross £
Cumulative total brought forward		175,000		175,000
Transfer of value	80,000			
Annual exemption				
2011/12	(1,000)			
2010/11	(1,000)			
		78,000	Nil	78,000
Cumulative total carried forward		253,000	Nil	253,000

The total transfer is below the nil band of £325,000.
Had any tax been due, it would have been paid by Mr A, as this was a net transfer.

June 2011 – transfer to trust A (a gross transfer)		Gross £	Tax £
Cumulative total brought forward		253,000	Nil
Transfer of value	160,000		
Annual exemption			
2011/12	(2,000)		
2010/11	(2,000)		
		156,000	16,800
		409,000	16,800

Tax thereon:
£325,000 covered by nil rate band
409,000 – 325,000 @ 20% = £16,800
This is a gross transfer, so the tax will be paid by the trustees of trust A.

Changes of tax rate

6540 The tax liability on a CLT will be based on the rate and threshold applicable on the date of the transfer. If the rate is subsequently changed, any later transfers will be taxed at the new rate, but the **cumulative total** will be based on the earlier transfers within the 7 year period as calculated at the old rates. No tax refund will ever be made for an earlier transfer as a result of a later change in tax rates.

EXAMPLE In June 2007 Mr A settled £150,000 into discretionary trust Y, for which he agreed to bear the tax, a net transfer. He made an earlier chargeable lifetime transfer in October 2001 of £200,000.
In August 2011 Mr A settled £250,000 into discretionary trust Z, for which the trustees agreed to pay the tax, a gross transfer.

		Net	Tax	Gross
June 2007 – transfer to trust Y	£	£	£	£
Cumulative total brought forward		200,000		200,000
Transfer of value	150,000			
Annual exemption				
2007/08	(3,000)			
2006/07	(3,000)			
		144,000	11,000	155,000
		344,000	11,000	355,000

Tax thereon:
£300,000 covered by nil rate band for 2007/08
344,000 – 300,000 = 44,000
44,000 @ 20/(100 – 20) = £11,000

		Gross	Tax
August 2011 – transfer to trust Z	£	£	£
Cumulative total brought forward		155,000	
Transfer of value	250,000		
Annual exemption 2011/12	(3,000)		
		247,000	15,400
		402,000	15,400

Tax thereon:
£325,000 covered by nil rate band for 2011/12
402,000 – 325,000 @ 20% = £15,400

MEMO POINTS The transfer made in 2001 is not included in the cumulative total as it was made more than 7 years before the CLT.

2. Additional tax on death

6542 The additional tax arising on death as a result of a CLT made in the 7 previous years is based on the same principles as the lifetime charge. It is calculated as the difference between:
– the IHT due on the transfer using the tax rates and nil rate band at the **date of death**; and
– the IHT (if any) paid on the transfer using the lifetime rates and nil rate band at the **date of the gift**.

Taper relief (¶6565) reduces the charge for transfers made more than 3 years before death, and relief is also available for a fall in the value of gifted property between the date of the original gift and the date of death (¶6795).

Payment of tax

6544 s 199(1)(c) IHTA 1984 Additional tax is **payable by** the transferee regardless of who paid the liability on the lifetime charge. No refund is available where the lifetime tax exceeds the liability on death, which may occur where the nil rate band has increased between the date of the gift and the date of death.

Cumulative total

It is important to note that for **each transfer** it is necessary to look back to other transfers in the previous 7 years. This means that transfers made up to 14 years before death may be taken into account when calculating the charge on death, although only those in the 7 years immediately before death will be subject to additional tax. 6546

EXAMPLE Mr A died on 1 July 2011. During his life he made the following chargeable transfers:

December 1998	£50,000	
November 2001	£150,000	
August 2006	£219,000	(after exemptions)

IHT paid: £16,800 (369,000 – 285,000) × 20%
Tax on all gifts was borne by the beneficiary.

		£	Gross £	Tax £
Additional charge on death:				
Cumulative total brought forward			150,000	
Transfer of value August 2006		225,000		
Annual exemption	2006/07	(3,000)		
	2005/06	(3,000)		
			219,000	17,600
			369,000	17,600

Tax thereon:
£325,000 covered by nil rate band for 2011/12
369,000 – 325,000 @ 40% = 17,600
Less: Lifetime tax paid (16,800)
Additional tax due 800

MEMO POINTS The transfer made in 1998 is not included in the cumulative total as it was made more than 7 years before the August 2006 CLT.

SECTION 2

Potentially exempt transfers (PETs)

A PET is a transfer made by an individual: 6550 s 3A IHTA 1984
- to another individual; or
- into a disabled trust (¶7190).

A transfer is deemed to be a PET made to another individual when:
- the value transferred is attributable to property that becomes comprised in the second individual's estate; or
- where property does not become comprised in the second individual's estate but the value of that estate is nevertheless increased.

EXAMPLE Mr and Mrs A own half of a house and Mr B owns the other half. The house is worth £200,000 but this is discounted by 20% (£40,000 in total) to reflect the difficulty of selling a half share. Therefore Mr and Mrs A's shares (under the related property rules) are worth £40,000 each and Mr B's share is worth £80,000.
If Mr B gives his share to Mrs A, Mr and Mrs A will own the whole house and there will be no need to discount the valuation. Mrs A's share is worth £150,000 and the transfer from Mr B is a PET. Mr A's share has increased to £50,000 even though no property has entered his estate. The increase in value of £10,000 also constitutes a PET.

Before 22 March 2006, the lifetime **creation** of an interest in possession trust, and a transfer into an accumulation and maintenance trust, were PETs and these transfers are still treated 6551 as PETs for the purposes of the transferor's cumulative total (¶6546), but any such transfers on or after this date are CLTs. Between 22 March 2006 and 5 October 2008 the lifetime creation of an interest in possession settlement was a PET if it was a transitional serial interest (¶7178) for a person other than the spouse of the previous life tenant. From 6 October 2008, where an interest in possession created before 22 March 2006 comes to an end and is **replaced** by another interest in possession, an IHT charge will arise.

MEMO POINTS 1. The lifetime **termination** of an interest in possession, where another individual becomes entitled to the trust property or to an interest in possession in it, is a PET if the interest was created:
– before 22 March 2006; or
– on or after 22 March 2006, and it is an immediate post-death interest (¶7178) or a transitional serial interest (¶7178) for a person other than the spouse of the previous life tenant.
2. In all other cases, the lifetime termination of an interest in possession on or after 22 March 2006 is not a transfer of value for the life tenant, because the life tenant is not considered to have the assets within his estate.
3. The termination of an immediate post-death interest in favour of ongoing trusts for a bereaved minor is also a PET.
4. The termination of an interest in possession in favour of an accumulation and maintenance trust which was created before 22 March 2006 was a PET until 5 April 2008 and remains so for the purposes of the transferor's cumulative total.
5. A **transfer to a trust** is deemed to have been a PET only if the value transferred can be attributed to property that became comprised in the trust.

Time of charge

6552 The **main consequence** of making a PET is that it will only become chargeable to IHT if the transferor dies within 7 years from the date of the transfer. During that period it is assumed that the PET will prove to be exempt, and therefore it does not form part of the transferor's cumulative total for the purposes of calculating the tax due on subsequent chargeable lifetime transfers. A PET made more than 7 years before the transferor's death will never be included in the cumulative total.

If a PET does **become chargeable** as a result of the death of the transferor, it forms part of the cumulative total for the purposes of any later transfers in order to calculate the additional tax on death.

Relief is available for a **fall in the value** of gifted property between the date of the original gift and the date of death (¶6795).

MEMO POINTS 1. **HMRC only need to be informed** that a PET has been made if it becomes chargeable. The transferor and transferee should retain details until after 7 years have expired.
2. If a PET becomes chargeable following the death of the transferor within 7 years, it will only be eligible for **holdover relief for capital gains tax** purposes if it qualifies for business (¶6700) or agricultural (¶6750) property relief, and the transfer was not to a settlor-interested trust (¶7398).

Allocation of the annual exemption

6554 s 19(3) IHTA 1984 Where the transfers in a particular year are **either all CLTs or all PETs** the annual exemption is attributed to earlier transfers first.

Where there is a **mixture of CLTs and PETs** in a particular year, the rules with respect to the allocation of the annual exemption are less clear. Broadly, the approach of HMRC is to attribute the annual exemption to earlier transfers first, whether they are CLTs or PETs. The consequence of this approach is that if the exemption is applied to a PET that never becomes chargeable, the exemption is wasted.

An alternative view is that any PETs arising in any particular year are left out of account when allocating the annual exemption. Any PETs that subsequently became chargeable are deemed to have occurred after any CLTs and therefore no adjustment is required to the lifetime tax on the CLTs.

In the absence of evidence to the contrary, HMRC's approach should be assumed to apply.

Comment For the avoidance of doubt, taxpayers may choose to arrange their affairs so that in any given year CLTs are always made before PETs.

Calculation of tax due on death

PETs made within 7 years before the date of death become liable to tax at the death **rate** (¶9981). The death charge is calculated in the same way as for CLTs, using the tax rates and nil rate band at the date of death, with the exception that no lifetime tax will have been paid. Taper relief is also available for gifts made more than 3 years before death. 6556

EXAMPLE Mr A dies on 15 November 2011. During his lifetime he made two potentially exempt transfers:

May 2003	£250,000
August 2010	£350,000

IHT will be calculated as follows:

		£	Gross £	Tax £
August 2010 transfer:				
Cumulative total brought forward			Nil	
Transfer of value		350,000		
Annual exemption	2010/11	(3,000)		
	2009/10	(3,000)		
			344,000	7,600
			344,000	7,600
Tax thereon:				
£325,000 covered by nil rate band for 2011/12				
344,000 – 325,000 @ 40%				7,600

MEMO POINTS The transfer in 2003 is not included in the calculation because it was made more than 7 years before death.

Where a PET becomes chargeable on death it may affect the cumulative brought forward figure for the additional tax on **chargeable lifetime transfers**. 6558

EXAMPLE Mr A dies on 1 December 2011. During his life he made the following transfers:

May 2006	Potentially exempt (uses exemptions from 2006/07 and 2005/06)	£180,000
July 2009	Chargeable transfer	£200,000

IHT on the chargeable lifetime transfer will be calculated as follows:

		£	Gross £	Tax £
Lifetime tax:				
Cumulative total brought forward			Nil	
Transfer of value July 2009		200,000		
Annual exemption	2009/10	(3,000)		
	2008/09	(3,000)		
			194,000	Nil
			194,000	Nil
Additional tax on death:				
Cumulative total brought forward (180,000 – 3,000 – 3,000)			174,000	
Transfer of value July 2009			194,000	17,200
			368,000	17,200
Tax thereon: £325,000 covered by nil rate band for 2011/12 368,000 – 325,000 @ 40% = £17,200				
Less: Lifetime tax paid				Nil
IHT liability				17,200

6560 A PET **becoming chargeable** as a result of death can be more costly than if the gifted amount still formed part of the death estate.

EXAMPLE Mr A dies in October 2011. During his life he made the following transfers:

November 2003	Chargeable transfer	£275,000
December 2008	Potentially exempt	£400,000

The PET becomes chargeable as it occurred within 7 years of death.

		£	Gross £	Tax £
Tax on death:				
Cumulative total brought forward			275,000	
Transfer of value December 2008		400,000		
Annual exemption	2008/09	(3,000)		
	2007/08	(3,000)		
			394,000	137,600
			669,000	137,600

Tax thereon:
£325,000 covered by nil band for 2011/12
669,000 – 325,000 @ 40% = £137,600

If the PET had not been made, and the £400,000 had formed part of the death estate, the IHT charge would have been lower:

	£
Tax on death:	
Cumulative total brought forward	Nil
Death estate	400,000
	400,000
Tax thereon:	
£325,000 covered by nil band for 2011/12	
400,000 – 325,000 @ 40%	30,000

The PET therefore resulted in further IHT of £107,600 (with a liability of £137,600 rather than £30,000).

SECTION 3

Taper relief

6565 s 7(4) IHTA 1984

For all transfers made more than 3 years before the date of death, the IHT charge on death is mitigated by taper relief. Taper relief reduces the IHT charge by a **percentage** which is determined by the time elapsed between the date of the gift and the date of death. The percentages are as follows:

Transfer between	Reduction in IHT charge
3 and 4 years before death	20%
4 and 5 years before death	40%
5 and 6 years before death	60%
6 and 7 years before death	80%

EXAMPLE Mr A died on 1 July 2011. During his life he made the following transfers:

September 2002	Chargeable transfer (after exemptions)	£65,000
November 2007	Potentially exempt (uses exemptions for 2007/08 and 2006/07)	£340,000

Tax on the PET will be calculated as follows:

	£	Gross £	Tax £
Charge on death:			
Cumulative total brought forward		65,000	
Transfer of value November 2007	340,000		
Annual exemption 2007/08	(3,000)		
2006/07	(3,000)		
		334,000	29,600
		399,000	29,600
Tax thereon:			
£325,000 covered by nil rate band for 2011/12			
399,000 – 325,000 @ 40%			29,600
Less: Taper relief @ 20%			(5,920)
(gift 3-4 years before death)			
IHT due			23,680

Limitations

Taper relief cannot result in a **repayment** of the original tax already paid during lifetime. The relief is also not helpful where a transfer is covered by the nil rate band, as the tapering effect only relates to the tax payable. **6567** s 7(5) IHTA 1984

CHAPTER 3

Transfers on death

OUTLINE ¶¶

For IHT purposes there are two main consequences of death: **6575** s 4 IHTA 1984
1. IHT will be charged on a person's death as if he made a transfer of value immediately before death; and
2. IHT may be charged on transfers of value made within the 7 years before death, as follows:
– potentially exempt transfers may become chargeable to tax; and
– chargeable lifetime transfers may become subject to additional tax.

SECTION 1

The death estate

On death, an individual is deemed to make a transfer of value of an amount equal to the value of his estate immediately before death. IHT is levied on the death estate, taking into account chargeable transfers made by the individual in the 7 years before death, and death rates of IHT apply. **6580**

Proposals have been announced which envisage a reduction in the normal rate of IHT from 40% to 36% where **10% or more** of the net estate (i.e. after deducting IHT exemptions, reliefs, and the nil rate band) is **left to charity**. If enacted, these measures would apply to **deaths occurring after 5 April 2012**.

s 4(2) IHTA 1984 Where **two or more individuals die** in circumstances which make it difficult to determine which of them died first, the law concerning the transfer of property treats them as if the eldest had died first. This could lead to a double charge to IHT. Consequently, for IHT purposes, the rule is modified and they are deemed to have died at exactly the same time. Any gift between the individuals is treated as having lapsed, and so there is no double charge to IHT, which could otherwise have arisen from the same property being taxed in each estate. The estates are, however, distributed in accordance with the individuals' wills. If, therefore, a father and son die at the same time, the son's estate for IHT purposes will not include the value of any property inherited from his father, although such property will pass to the beneficiaries of the son's estate.

MEMO POINTS HMRC accept that in England and Wales, where a married couple die at the same time having left wills, no IHT is due on either estate in respect of property left to each other, due to the combined effect of the above rule and the spouse exemption. The spouse exemption would not, however, be available in these circumstances in Scotland or Northern Ireland, where the succession laws are different, as both spouses are treated as dying at the same moment, with the result that neither can inherit from the other and the spouse exemption is therefore not available.

Exempt transfers

6582 ss 18, 23, 24, 24A, 28 IHTA 1984 Sch 3 IHTA 1984 Some transfers on death are exempt from IHT because of the type of **beneficiary** (¶6438), and so the death estate will be reduced to take account of those transfers.

The types of beneficiary include:
– the surviving spouse (total transfers limited to £55,000 where the spouse is domiciled abroad and the deceased is domiciled in the UK);
– charities;
– national bodies such as museums, galleries and libraries (see ¶6450 for a complete list of relevant bodies);
– employee trusts;
– housing associations (where the gift is of land situated in the UK); and
– political parties (where at the last general election either two members were elected or one member was elected and the party as a whole received at least 150,000 votes).

1. Valuation of the estate

6584 s 5 IHTA 1984 A person's estate is the **aggregate** of all the property to which he is beneficially entitled (except for excluded property (¶6456)), less his liabilities. It therefore includes the free estate to which the person has absolute entitlement, and it may include settled property in which he has an interest in possession, such as a life interest or an annuity.

Property in these circumstances includes rights and interests of any description, and therefore covers tangible assets such as land, buildings and money, and intangible assets such as an interest in a partnership or a right of action for damages. However, rights which are legally unenforceable are excluded.

If a person is **insolvent** at the date of death, a nil value is attributed to his free estate, and the deficiency cannot be deducted from the value of settled property in which he had an interest in possession. *St Barbe Green and another v IRC* [2005]

Settled property

6585 s 49 IHTA 1984 Since 22 March 2006, an individual's estate only includes settled property if the interest in possession was:
a. created before 22 March 2006;
b. a transitional serial interest (¶7178);
c. an immediate post-death interest (¶7178); or
d. an interest in a disabled trust (¶7190).

MEMO POINTS For deaths which occurred before 22 March 2006, an individual's estate includes settled property in which he had an interest in possession at the date of death.

For **valuation** purposes, settled property in which the individual had an interest in possession will be valued in aggregation with the property in the free estate if that results in a higher figure than a separate valuation. 6586

EXAMPLE At the date of death in July 2011, Mr A owned 40% of the shares in B Ltd and he was also beneficially entitled to an interest in possession in a trust created in 2005 which included shares in B Ltd.
The value of shares in B Ltd was as follows:

0 – 49%	£20 per share
50 – 74%	£50 per share
75% – 100%	£60 per share

If the settled property included:
1. a 5% holding, no aggregation would be necessary in valuing the death estate because valuing the shares separately would give the same result; or
2. a 15% holding, aggregation would be necessary because the shares would be valued at £50 each, as opposed to £20 using a separate valuation.

2. Specific elements of the estate

Assets

The rules for the valuation of an estate on death are the same as those applying during the lifetime of an individual (¶6465). There are also some additional rules which apply only to the death estate. 6588

Pension rights On the death of a member of a **registered pension scheme** (¶3745), the value of a pension or annuity, or the right to a pension or annuity, is **normally** left out of account in the death estate. 6589
From 5 April 2006 to 5 April 2011, IHT was due where the member died:
a. before the age of 75, having chosen not to take a pension when he was in poor health, with the result that an enhanced death benefit was payable to beneficiaries other than a spouse, financial dependant or a charity; or
b. over the age of 75, having chosen a drawdown pension (¶3858), and the residual pension funds on death:
– remained in the scheme for other members (usually the deceased's family);
– were refunded to the employer; or
– were used to provide benefits for a dependant who is not a spouse or was not financially reliant on the member.
Residual funds were **treated as** the top slice of the estate of the:
– scheme member, or
– dependant of the member, where the member died before age 75 and the dependant chose a drawdown pension.
The responsibility for **accounting for and paying** the IHT fell on the pension scheme administrator, and IHT took precedence over any income tax charge in relation to the pension rights.

The value of benefits held on discretionary trusts in employer-sponsored **unregistered schemes** (¶3900) as at 5 April 2006, together with increases in line with the retail prices index, will be left out of account in the death estate. Benefits resulting from contributions after 5 April 2006 will, however, be subject to IHT. 6590

Reversionary interests Where a person has an interest in possession in settled property, which on his death reverts to the settlor or his UK domiciled spouse (¶6457), the value of 6591 s 54 IHTA 1984

the property is left out of account in the death estate if the reversionary interest was not acquired for money or money's worth and if the interest in possession was:
a. created before 22 March 2006;
b. a transitional serial interest (¶7178);
c. an interest in a disabled trust (¶7190); or
d. an immediate post-death interest (¶7178), where:
– the interest was held by a person other than the surviving spouse;
– the person died less than 2 years after becoming entitled to the interest; and
– the surviving spouse is UK domiciled and becomes entitled to the trust property.

Where trust property is left out of account in the death estate, there may still be an effect on the valuation of other assets due to the aggregation rules (¶6586).

6592 ss 153, 157 IHTA 1984 **Other assets** Rules for other assets are summarised as follows:

Asset	Rule	¶¶
Life assurance policies assigned or taken out for the benefit of another person unless that other person predeceases the life assured	Left out of account in death estate, but may still affect the valuation of other assets in the estate because of the rules on aggregation	
Overseas pensions paid in the UK but which relate to pensions formerly due from the governments of India, Pakistan and other former colonies		
Foreign currency accounts held with a bank in the UK (or with the UK Post Office) where the individual was not domiciled, resident or ordinarily resident in the UK immediately prior to his death		
Quoted shares and securities sold, cancelled or suspended within 1 year following death	Value in estate can be adjusted if proceeds of a post-death sale are less than the value at death	¶6816
Land sold within 4 years following death		¶6836
Property which was originally valued using the related property rules sold within 3 years of death	Estate valuation on death can be adjusted so that the assets are valued separately	¶6854
Gift where donor still retained some benefit	Property will be treated as part of the donor's estate immediately before death	¶6935

Liabilities

6594 Where debts and other liabilities were incurred by the individual in his lifetime for consideration in money or money's worth, or were imposed by law (such as income tax to the date of death), they will be deducted from the chargeable assets to reach the final death estate value.

Where a liability is **not due for payment** until after the date of death it will be valued on a discounted basis.

ss 5(5), 162(1), 174 IHTA 1984 s 103 FA 1986 A liability will not be deductible from the death estate for IHT purposes where:
– it was incurred for no (or nominal) consideration (for example, a deed of covenant) and was not imposed by law;
– it has a right of reimbursement which it is reasonably likely will be paid; or
– it was owed to a person who has received property from the deceased (¶6980).

6596 Liabilities are generally **deducted** from the aggregate value of all chargeable assets, and will normally be deducted from instalment property (¶7074) in priority to non-instalment property, so that the immediate liability to IHT is not reduced.

The two **exceptions** to this rule are:
– secured liabilities reduce the value of the asset on which they are secured, for example a mortgage will reduce the value of a house on which it is secured; and
– foreign liabilities are deducted from property situated abroad.

In both cases, where the liability exceeds the value of the relevant assets, the excess will be deducted from the aggregate of chargeable assets.

EXAMPLE Mr A is domiciled in Spain and dies with the following estate:

	£	£
UK bank account	10,000	
UK home	200,000	
Mortgage secured on UK home	100,000	
UK credit card debt	3,000	
French loan	50,000	
Other foreign assets	150,000	
The UK death estate is calculated as:		
UK bank account	10,000	
UK home less mortgage (200,000 – 100,000)	100,000	
Credit card debt	(3,000)	
Total UK death estate		107,000

Expenses

Expenses in connection with the **administration of the estate** are not normally deductible for death estate purposes. There are two exceptions to this rule: **6598** ss 172, 173 IHTA 1984

a. reasonable funeral expenses, including the cost of:
- mourning clothes for the family and servants;
- a tombstone; and
- where the death occurred abroad, the cost of embalming and transporting the body; and

b. additional costs incurred in administering or realising property situated abroad up to a maximum of 5% of the value of all foreign property in the estate.

MEMO POINTS HMRC have stated that reasonable **funeral expenses** may vary from one taxpayer to another, and regard must be had to the deceased's position in life.

EXAMPLE Mr B died in the UK with an estate comprising:

	£	
Personal assets	275,000	
House in Florence	195,000	
Villa in Spain	187,000	
The personal representatives incurred the following expenses:		
Funeral (coffin, cremation etc.)		2,425
Tombstone		1,815
Legal fees		2,225
Valuation and insurance of assets		1,080
Additional costs relating to foreign property:		
House		6,255
Villa		3,500

The death estate will be calculated as follows:

	£	£
Personal assets		275,000
Foreign property (195,000 + 187,000)		382,000
		657,000
Less expenses:		
Funeral and tombstone (2,425 + 1,815)	4,240	
Foreign property (Lower of: 6,255 + 3,500 = 9,755; and (195,000 + 187,000) @ 5% = 19,100)	9,755	
		(13,995)
Value of death estate		643,005

SECTION 2

Calculation of tax on the death estate

6600 The death estate is deemed to be like any other disposition for the purposes of calculating IHT on death. This means that the cumulative total of other transfers of value (including potentially exempt transfers (PETs)) which took place in the 7 years ending with the date of death will be taken into account in determining the amount (if any) of the nil rate band that is available. The annual exemption is not available in relation to the death estate.

The chargeable transfer on death is always a gross transfer. Grossing up of gifts may be required to ensure that the burden of tax is equitable (¶6640).

EXAMPLE Mr C died on 1 June 2011 with an estate valued at £375,000. A PET of £100,000 (after annual exemption) was made in 2009. IHT on the death estate will be calculated as follows:

	£
Cumulative total brought forward	100,000
Death estate	375,000
	475,000
Tax thereon:	
£325,000 covered by nil rate band for 2011/12	
475,000 – 325,000 @ 40%	60,000

Estate which includes settled property

6602 Where the death estate contains both free and settled property, IHT is calculated on the aggregate amount and then allocated between the two sources.

EXAMPLE Mr D died on 1 September 2011 with an estate valued at £425,000 which was made up of £340,000 free estate and £85,000 settled property. A PET of £75,000 (after annual exemption) was made in 2009. IHT on the death estate will be calculated as follows:

	£
Cumulative total brought forward	75,000
Death estate	425,000
	500,000
Tax thereon:	
£325,000 covered by nil rate band for 2011/12	
500,000 – 325,000 @ 40%	70,000
Allocated:	
Free estate (70,000 × 340/425)	56,000
Settled property (70,000 × 85/425)	14,000
	70,000

Estate which includes a transferable nil rate band

6608
s 8A IHTA 1984
IHTM 43001

Since 9 October 2007 it has been possible, in certain circumstances, for the personal representatives of an individual, ("the survivor"), to claim all, or part, of a nil rate band from a pre-deceased spouse or civil partner. The allowable portion is the **transferable nil rate band** ("TNRB") and is **claimable** against the survivor's death estate. The introduction of the TNRB provisions means that on death there could potentially be up to two nil rate bands available to reduce the IHT liability.

Eligibility to claim a TNRB arises in the following circumstances:
– the survivor must have been the spouse or registered civil partner of the pre-deceased at the time of the pre-deceased's death;

- the nil rate band must have been unused in whole, or in part, at the time of the pre-deceased's death;
- the survivor's death occurs on or after 9 October 2007.

MEMO POINTS 1. Particular care should be taken when dealing with a survivor's estate where the pre-deceased died before the introduction of IHT (i.e. before 18 March 1986), as the rules for gifts to spouses and allowances available on death were different. Even if the first spouse died before the introduction of IHT, a claim may still be possible, but, in general terms, if estate duty was paid on the first death, there will be no TNRB available on the second death. For nil rate bands and estate duty allowances applying from 6 April 1980 see ¶9982. HMRC have published historic information going back to 1914, and full details can be found on their website at http://www.hmrc.gov.uk/cto/customerguide/page15.htm.
2. From 12 November 1974, unlimited exemptions were introduced for spousal and charitable bequests. Prior to 22 March 1972 there was no exemption for spouses or charitable bequests, and between 22 March 1972 and 12 November 1974 the spouse exemption was limited to £15,000 and the charitable exemption to £50,000.
3. For civil partners the first death must have occurred on or after 5 December 2005, at which date it was first possible to enter into a civil partnership in the UK. Civil partnerships also qualify for relief if they are legally registered in jurisdictions outside the UK which recognise them, and the partnership is treated in the UK as having commenced on 5 December 2005.
4. The UK marriage must be a legally recognised one; a TNRB cannot be claimed by co-habitees, former couples or civil partners, if they were not married or in a civil partnership at the date of the first death.
5. The availability of a TNRB can affect the size of a bequest (¶6611) or a trust established under a will (¶7459).

6609 s 8A(2) IHTA 1984 IHTM 43020

The **amount** of the available TNRB is calculated as the percentage, to three decimal points, of the nil rate band unused on the first death. The percentage is then multiplied by the value of the nil rate band applicable at the survivor's death. The percentage of the nil rate band unused at the first death has to be established first, before the value of the TNRB can be calculated; however, the **maximum** TNRB is an additional 100%. An estate gifted entirely to a spouse will not use up the nil rate band, which would therefore be available to claim on the survivor's death.

EXAMPLE Mr A died on 15 September 2011 with an estate valued at £500,000 and left everything to his wife. The nil rate band is not claimed and so the available nil rate band percentage for the TNRB is 100%.
When Mrs A dies her personal representatives can claim a TNRB of 100% of the value of the nil rate applicable at her death, as Mr A's nil rate band was entirely unused at his death.

It does not matter if the estate of the first to die was below or above the nil rate band threshold, only the extent to which the estate used up the nil rate band, but if the chargeable transfers on the first death **exceed** the nil rate band at that date, there is no TNRB to claim against the survivor's estate.

EXAMPLE

1. Mr A died in November 1991 with an estate valued at £50,000, when the nil rate band was £140,000. He left all of his estate to his wife and therefore the TNRB is 100%.
Mrs A dies in November 2011 with an estate valued at £1,000,000. As Mr A's nil rate band was completely unused, Mrs A's personal representatives will be able to claim a TNRB of £325,000 (100 % × £325,000, the nil rate band for 2011/12). Mrs A's estate will have a total nil rate band of £650,000 (her own nil rate band and the TNRB).

2. Mrs B died on 1 January 2003 with an estate valued at £400,000. She left £275,000 to her husband and £125,000 to her children, using 50% of the nil rate band at that time (£250,000). Mr B dies in September 2011 with an estate valued at £750,000, when the nil rate band is £325,000. As Mrs B's nil rate band was not completely used, Mr B's executors will be able to claim a TNRB of £162,500 (50 % × £325,000). Mr B's estate will therefore have a total nil rate band of £487,500 (his own nil rate band and the TNRB).

3. Mrs C died on 5 July 2005 with an estate of £100,000, when the nil rate band was £275,000. She left £27,500 (using 10% of the nil rate band) to her daughter and the rest to her husband. When her husband dies, his personal representatives will be able to claim an additional 90% of the nil rate band applicable at his death, as well as his own nil rate band.

4. Mr D died on 30 July 2006 with an estate worth £500,000. He left £200,000 to his wife and £300,000 to his children. The bequest to his children used up the nil rate band for 2006/07 in full. Mrs D does not re-marry and dies in October 2011. There will be no TNRB available for Mrs D's estate.

6610 IHTM 43030 s 8A(6) IHTA 1984

Where the survivor was bereaved, but had **remarried** or was in a civil partnership by the time of his death, the nil rate band can be claimed from the estate or estates of any previously deceased spouse, but in all circumstances the maximum TNRB is 100%.

EXAMPLE 1. Mr A was married first to Miss B who died in January 1997 leaving property worth 50% of the available nil rate band to their children and the rest of her estate to Mr A. The gift to Mr A was spouse exempt. In 1999 Mr A married Miss C.
Mr A died in October 2011 and left an estate worth £1,000,000, with a gift to his children of £450,000. Miss C is his executrix and can submit a claim for a 50% TNRB, relating to Miss B's 50% unused nil rate band. Mr A's estate will be entitled to his full nil rate band for 2011/12 of £325,000 and a TNRB of £162,500 arising from the estate of his first wife, Miss B.

If a survivor bequeaths his full estate to a subsequent spouse, that gift will be subject to the spouse exemption and the TNRB from the earlier estate could be lost.

EXAMPLE 2. The facts are as above, but, if instead of leaving a gift to his children, Mr A had left his full estate to Miss C, his estate would have qualified for a complete spouse exemption. Mr A's own nil rate band would have been unused and the 50% TNRB from Miss B would have been lost. In due course Miss C's personal representatives could make a claim for Mr A's TNRB, but cannot claim the balance from Miss B's estate, as this would exceed the maximum 100% allowance.

Where the survivor had outlived more than one spouse or civil partner, the available nil rate band can be transferred from the earlier estates but only to a limit of 100%.

EXAMPLE Mr G was first married to Miss H who died leaving 50% of the nil rate band at that time to her son and the rest of her estate to Mr G. Mr G subsequently married Miss J who died leaving 20% of the nil rate band to her daughter and the rest of her estate to Mr G. Mr G marries for a third time to Miss K and dies shortly afterwards. The executors of Mr G's estate can claim a TNRB of 50% due to Miss H's estate and a TNRB of 80% due to Miss J's estate. This would be a total of 130% but the TNRB claim will be restricted to 100%.

6611 IHTM 43021

The TNRB is set against the **cumulative estate on death**. If a PET becomes chargeable on death, or a CLT becomes subject to an additional tax charge, they will use up the TNRB first. The TNRB is not used against the tax charge on a CLT at the time of the transfer, and it is not possible to recover any tax paid during lifetime which later would not have been due. This can mean that tax relief from a TNRB is given at only 20%.

EXAMPLE 1. Mrs G died in January 2006, leaving all of her estate to her husband. In December 2008 Mr G gives his daughter a gift of £400,000 (after annual exemptions). This is a PET so no tax is due at that time. Mr G dies suddenly in September 2011 when the nil rate band is £325,000, leaving an estate of £900,000, including the PET. His personal representatives make a claim for a 100% TNRB from Mrs G's estate. The PET uses up Mr G's own personal nil rate band and £75,000 of the TNRB, (£400,000–£325,000) so there is £250,000 of the TNRB available for the rest of the estate.
2. The facts are as above, but instead of making a PET, Mr G settles a discretionary trust for his grandchildren with £400,000 in December 2008. The trustees agree to pay the tax. The lifetime tax payable is £17,600 (£312,000 covered by his nil rate band for 2008/09 and £88,000 × 20%). When Mr G dies, the trustees would be liable for additional IHT. However, on re-calculating the tax due, the transfer of £400,000 to the trust is covered by Mr G's own nil rate band (£325,000) and the TNRB (£75,000). Relief has been given at 20%, against the additional tax due on Mr G's death. £250,000 of the TNRB is available for the rest of his estate. The lifetime tax paid when the trust was created cannot be reclaimed.

It is very common for a will to include a **bequest of a pecuniary legacy** up to the value of the nil rate band applying at the time of the testator's death. This could be identified by a description in the will such as "the maximum amount that could be transferred without incurring a charge to inheritance tax". Where a TNRB could be claimed, using this type of definition would result in a bequest of up to twice the annual nil rate band and therefore could result in a bequest of a larger sum than was anticipated at the time when the will was executed. Where a will refers to a gift of property equal to the available nil rate band at the deceased's death, and a claim for a TNRB could be made, the gift will be treated as the amount of both the individual's own nil rate band and the amount of the available TNRB.

MEMO POINTS Particular care should be taken when drafting wills with this type of clause as HMRC have identified this point as an area for close attention.

EXAMPLE Mr A died in 2007 and left all his estate to his wife. Mrs A dies in July 2011 when the nil rate band is £325,000 and her executors claim a TNRB of 100%. Mrs A has left an estate worth £640,000. In her will Mrs A has left a bequest of "an amount equal the maximum sum that can be given without incurring a charge to IHT" to her son, B, and the residue to her daughter, C. As the maximum sum which can be gifted without IHT is the nil rate band and 100% TNRB, the maximum amount that B can receive is £650,000 (nil rate band of £325,000 and TNRB of 100% × £325,000). B would therefore receive the full amount of £640,000 and C would receive nothing.

The availability of a TNRB from the estate of the pre-deceased is calculated by reference to property that is potentially subject to UK IHT. For UK domiciled individuals this means the world-wide estate, but if the pre-deceased is not domiciled or deemed domiciled in the UK at the time of death, this means only UK situated property. The **domicile** of the pre-deceased particularly affects eligibility for the TNRB if the pre-deceased was UK domiciled and the survivor is not UK domiciled, but it does not matter if the pre-deceased had no property situated in the UK. **6612** IHTM 43042

EXAMPLE

1. Mr and Mrs A, who were originally domiciled in the UK, had become domiciled in Australia when Mrs A died suddenly, leaving no UK property. Mr A decided to return to the UK and his UK domicile of origin revived. When Mr A dies his personal representatives would be able to claim a TNRB of 100% from Mrs A's estate. There was no property in the UK at the time of Mrs A's death, therefore the nil rate band is available in full when Mr A dies.

2. The facts are as above, but when Mrs A dies she leaves a house in the UK to her son, using 30% of the nil rate band. On Mr A's death his executors will be able to claim a TNRB of 70%.

If the pre-deceased was UK domiciled, but the spouse was not, the spouse exemption is limited to £55,000; any gift to the non-domiciled survivor in excess of this will use up the nil rate band. If the pre-deceased was non-UK domiciled and had gifted assets to a UK domiciled spouse, there is no restriction on the spouse exemption.

EXAMPLE Mr B (UK domiciled) died in January 2003, when the nil rate band was £250,000, with an estate of £155,000. He left everything to his wife, who was French. Only £55,000 of the bequest was exempt from IHT because of the non-domiciled spouse exemption. The remaining £100,000 used up part of the nil rate band. The available proportion of the TNRB when Mrs B dies will be 60% (£250,000-£100,000/£250,000).

Who can claim a TNRB

A formal claim must be made for a TNRB and, generally, the claim is made by the personal representatives of the survivor. **6613** s 8B IHTA 1984 IHTM 43006

If no claim is submitted by the personal representatives, anyone who has to pay tax as a result of the survivor's death may submit a claim, but only when the initial period for the personal representatives to make a claim has expired.

The time limit for making the claim depends on who submits it. If the **personal representatives** make a claim, they must do so within two years from the end of the month in which the survivor died or, if it ends later, the period of three months beginning with the date on which they first act. If no claim is made within those periods, a late claim by the personal representatives may be permitted at HMRC's discretion. HMRC may only accept such a claim where:

1. it can be shown that the claim was delayed due to events beyond the claimant's control and everything possible was done to pursue matters; or

2. the claimant was unaware (and could not reasonably have been expected to be aware) that they were entitled to make the claim.

A claim may be withdrawn within one month after the end of the period concerned.

If a **person liable to pay tax** as a result of the death submits the claim, HMRC have discretion over the time limit for it to be accepted.

IHTM 43063

MEMO POINTS 1. HMRC will refuse any request to revise values of property included in the estate of the pre-deceased, while the survivor is still alive. Instead, HMRC advise that the personal representatives of the survivor should submit a claim for a TNRB when, in due course, the survivor dies.

2. It was common practice to use a discretionary trust in estate tax planning to preserve the nil rate band before the TNRB rules came into effect. A discretionary trust can be terminated as long as the first death took place less than 2 years previously. In this way, the nil rate band would be unused on the first death, making it available to the survivor's estate in due course.

EXAMPLE

1. Mrs A died in June 2009, leaving all her estate to her husband. Mr A died on 1 January 2011. Mr A's personal representatives have until 31 January 2013 to submit a claim to HMRC for Mrs A's TNRB.

2. The facts are as above, but if Mr A's personal representatives are appointed on 31 December 2012, they would have until 31 March 2013 to submit a claim. If the personal representatives do not submit a claim by this date, a beneficiary who has to pay tax as a result of Mr A's death may make a claim within a time limit allowed by HMRC. If Mr A had tried to revise the value of property within his wife's estate, HMRC would have turned down his request.

3. Mr B died on 10 October 2010. Mr B's executors have until 31 October 2012 to submit a TNRB claim.

How to claim a TNRB

6614 IHT & Trusts Newsletter December 2007 IHTM 43006

The TNRB claim is made either on form IHT 402 if made by the **personal representatives**, or on form IHT 216 if made by a **beneficiary or another person**. In every case the claim form must be accompanied by **supporting evidence**. HMRC have announced that the type of evidence they require is:

– a copy of the will of the pre-deceased, if there was one, or details of how the estate was devolved if there was no will;
– a copy of the appropriate IHT form: the IHT 400, IHT 205 or the C5 in Scotland;
– a copy of the death certificate;
– a copy of the marriage or civil partnership certificate;
– a copy of the grant of representation (confirmation in Scotland);
– a valuation of assets that passed under the will or intestacy other than to the surviving spouse or civil partner; and
– a copy of the instrument of variation or any similar document if one was executed.

HMRC may also ask for details of any specific assets which would have qualified for relief on the first death, such as business property relief or agricultural property relief and copies of any valuations obtained.

MEMO POINTS 1. Information held by HMRC about an estate is confidential and this may cause problems as regards obtaining information about an estate where the personal representatives have died.

2. If the claim is being made by the survivor's personal representatives, HMRC will release information about the first death only where there is authority to do so, through a chain of representation.

3. Where the first death takes place on or after 9 October 2007, HMRC have advised that personal representatives should provide the necessary supporting evidence to survivors in the event that a TNRB claim is later made by the survivor's own personal representatives. HMRC have advised that they will take a strict approach towards claims which do not have the full supporting evidence in these circumstances.

4. HMRC have said that where the first death was prior to 9 October 2007 and documents are now difficult to obtain, they will only expect to see copies of:
– the death certificate;
– the marriage or civil partnership certificate;

- the grant of representation;
- the will of the pre-deceased; and
- any deed of variation or disclaimer executed.

EXAMPLE Mr B died in September 2009, leaving everything to his civil partner, Mr C, so Mr B's nil rate band was unused. Mr C was also appointed executor. Mr C dies in August 2010, appointing Miss D as his executor. Miss D can make the claim for the TNRB from Mr B's estate and will be able to ask for confidential information from HMRC.
The facts are as above, but, if instead of appointing Mr C as executor, Mr B appointed someone else, that executor would have had to provide Mr C with the supporting evidence in case a TNRB claim was made later. When Mr C dies, Miss D would use that evidence to make the claim, but HMRC would not provide Miss D with information about Mr B's estate directly because of confidentiality.

If the survivor's estate exceeds the nil rate band at their death (i.e. before adding in any nil rate band from the pre-deceased's estate), a **full return (IHT400)** must be made by the survivor's personal representatives, irrespective of whether claiming the TNRB results in no tax liability.

MEMO POINTS Where the value of an asset was not formally ascertained for IHT on the first death but the asset was subsequently sold, the base cost has to be established for CGT purposes. If the survivor's personal representatives wish to consider making a TNRB claim, the asset's value when it formed part of the pre-deceased's estate will have to be ascertained for IHT. If the CGT base cost is different to the ascertained IHT value, HMRC will not replace the CGT value used. This rule only applies with claims involving the TNRB

EXAMPLE Mr G died in January 2008 leaving his half share of the matrimonial home to his son. The whole property is valued at £300,000, so the half share is worth £150,000, within the nil rate band and so is not formally ascertained. The property is sold in 2009 and the son's share is liable to CGT. The valuation for the CGT base cost has to be established and is agreed at £127,500, after a discount for joint ownership. When the surviving spouse dies in 2011, the value of the house has to be established to confirm the amount of the nil rate band available for transfer. The value of the house is agreed to have been £300,000, so for IHT the gift to the son was £150,000, which used up half of the nil rate band in January 2008. The TNRB is therefore 50% for the survivor's estate, but the CGT on the sale will not be re-calculated with the higher base cost of £150,000.

SECTION 3

Alterations of dispositions on death

Some events which occur after the death of an individual are treated for IHT purposes as if they occurred on death, and IHT is calculated accordingly. The most common of these is the disclaimer or variation of a will or intestacy. 6615

In addition, the calculation of IHT will be affected by:
- express wishes of the deceased;
- survivorship clauses;
- elections made by the surviving spouse;
- court orders; and
- distributions out of trusts which are subject to IHT.

Disclaimers and variations

An individual who is the recipient of a gift under a will or intestacy can: 6617
- accept the gift;
- disclaim the gift and refuse to accept it; or
- make a variation of the will by redirecting the gift to someone else.

If the gift is disclaimed it will **revert to** the residue of the estate unless it is a residuary gift, in which case it will pass under the intestacy rules. A disclaimer is an all or nothing event, it is not possible to disclaim part of a gift, and it must happen quickly after death, otherwise there is a risk that the gift will be treated as accepted.

6620 ss 142, 218A IHTA 1984 The disclaimer or variation of a gift is strictly a new transfer of value for IHT purposes. **Special rules** apply, however, so that the transfer will be treated as if it had been made directly by the deceased, provided that:
a. the variation or disclaimer is made by the person relinquishing some benefit within 2 years of the date of death;
b. the variation is made in a written instrument (usually a deed) that includes a statement that s142 IHTA 1984 is to apply; and
c. where the variation results in additional tax being payable, a copy of the instrument is delivered to HMRC along with notification of the extra tax due.

The **conditions will not have been satisfied** if:
– the variation or disclaimer was made in return for consideration (unless the consideration took the form of a different variation or disclaimer) *Lau v HMRC* [2009];
– the beneficiary has received a benefit from the property he wishes to disclaim; or
– the property is subject to a reservation of benefit (¶6935).

MEMO POINTS 1. If an **original beneficiary (A) of a will dies** before a variation is made, HMRC have stated that his personal representatives may enter into the variation. If the effect is to reduce the entitlements of A's own beneficiaries, evidence of their consent must also be submitted to HMRC for the variation to be effective.
2. Only **one deed of variation** may be made with respect to a particular piece of property, so if more than one is made, only the first will qualify for the special rules.
3. A variation may be set aside if the person executing it does not understand the document being signed, the need for, the effects of, and the consequences of it. *Bhatt v Bhatt* [2009]

EXAMPLE A leaves all his property to his daughter B who is already wealthy. She would prefer her youngest children (D and E) to receive A's property and so the will is varied, but her eldest child C (adult) is not included in the variation. In this way, the IHT charge will not be affected, and if B dies in the next 7 years, a second charge to IHT will be avoided.
If B dies within 2 years, and before the variation is made, B's personal representatives can still agree to the variation, so long as C consents.

Express wishes of the testator

6622 s 143 IHTA 1984 A testator may bequeath property in his will to one individual and express a wish that the property should then be **subsequently transferred** to another individual. If the property is transferred within 2 years from the date of death, it will be treated as if it were a transfer directly to the second individual for the purposes of the IHT computation.

EXAMPLE Mr A bequeaths property in his will to Mr B and expresses a wish that the property should be transferred to C when he reaches the age of 18. Providing Mr B transfers the property to C within 2 years of Mr A's death, the IHT computation will assume that the property was transferred directly to C under the will.

Survivorship clauses

6623 s 92 IHTA 1984 It is possible that a beneficiary of a death estate could die immediately after inheriting property, therefore creating another charge to IHT. Although quick succession relief (¶6865) is available in this instance, the original will should ensure that property will only pass to a beneficiary if he survives for a **stated period**. If this period does not exceed 6 months, there can only be a single charge to IHT.

EXAMPLE A's will states that £30,000 should go to B if he survives A by 5 months, otherwise the money is to go to C. Once the period of 5 months has elapsed, the beneficiary of the money will be known, and in either case, only a single charge to IHT will occur on the death of A.

Election by surviving spouse

Where a person **dies intestate**, a surviving spouse may elect that the personal representatives redeem his life interest in the residuary estate by payment of its capital value. The redemption does not constitute a transfer of value, and the surviving spouse is treated as having been entitled to that capital value instead of the life interest. **6624** s 145 IHTA 1984

Court orders

The courts may direct under the Inheritance (Provision for Family and Dependants) Act 1975 that **financial provision** be made out of the estate of the deceased for the benefit of his family or dependants. For IHT purposes the transfer is deemed to have been made directly out of the will. With effect from 1 April 2011, a claim to apply such an order must be made within 4 years of the date of the order. **6626** s 146(1) IHTA 1984

The courts also have the power to **redirect the benefit of lifetime gifts** made within 6 years before death. The IHT implications of such a direction are that: **6628**
a. IHT and interest paid in respect of the original gift may be reclaimed by the personal representatives;
b. gross cumulative transfers brought forward are reduced to take account of the cancelled gift; and
c. the redirected property together with the repaid IHT will be added to the value of the death estate.

There will be no adjustment, however, to the IHT paid on any other lifetime transfer which may have been calculated using a gross cumulative transfer brought forward which included the redirected transfer.

Distributions out of chargeable trusts

When a distribution is made out of a chargeable trust, an **exit charge** (¶7452) will arise which will generate a potential IHT liability. Where such a trust is created by a will, and a distribution is made from the trust within 2 years from the date of death, then: **6630** s 144 IHTA 1984
- no exit charge will arise on the distribution; and
- IHT will be calculated as if the distribution had been made directly by the will.

For this provision to apply, the distribution must be one that would give rise to an exit charge, so distributions made in the 3 months from the commencement of the settlement will not qualify for this treatment.

This provision is important because, for example, a payment made directly to a spouse under the terms of a will is exempt from IHT, but a distribution to a spouse from a chargeable trust gives rise to a potential IHT liability because of the exit charge.

A cash flow disadvantage will occur where property is distributed after probate is obtained, because IHT will be payable in full at that date. A refund must then be claimed.

MEMO POINTS 1. A **distribution** includes an appointment which creates a new:
- trust with an immediate post-death interest (¶7178);
- trust for bereaved minors; or
- age 18-to-25 trust.

Such trusts can normally only be created directly by the testator or under the intestacy rules.
2. It is possible to **avoid payment** of IHT where trust assets are to be appointed to a surviving spouse, although HMRC have criticised this practice. *Fitzwilliam v IRC* [1993]

An **alternative approach** is to use the will to create an immediate post-death interest (¶7178) for the spouse of the deceased, but giving the trustees a power to override the original interest. For example, this would enable them to make appointments for the children out of the property in the estate. In this way, the spouse exemption is obtained on death and any appointment made by the trustees is treated as a PET made by the spouse. Assuming the spouse survives 7 years, no IHT charge will therefore arise. The gift with reservation provisions could, however, potentially apply to an appointment out of an interest in possession on or after 22 March 2006 (¶6937). **6632**

SECTION 4

The burden of tax

6640 s 200 IHTA 1984 For IHT purposes a beneficiary can receive two types of gift under a will or intestacy:
- specific gifts e.g. £25,000 to a daughter, a house to Mr A; and
- residuary gifts which will be the whole, or a proportion, of the remainder of the estate once the specific legacies, and the costs associated with administration, have been paid out.

Specific gifts

6641 As a **general rule** the IHT associated with a specific gift will be paid out of the residue of the estate. This is known as a tax-free gift. If the will so indicates, a specific gift can be tax bearing so that the beneficiary will receive an amount net of the IHT liability.

If there are no instructions to the contrary, a specific gift of assets **situated** in the UK will be tax-free, and a specific gift of foreign assets will be tax bearing.

EXAMPLE Mr A died with an estate valued at £300,000. He made a specific bequest of £60,000 to B and left the residue of his estate to C. The nil rate band has been used in full by lifetime transfers. The amount of the residue available for transfer to C will depend on whether the bequest to B is tax-free or tax bearing:

Tax on the specific legacy:	£
60,000 @ 40%	24,000

The death estate will be divided as follows:

1. If the legacy to B is £60,000 tax-free

B	60,000
C (300,000 – 60,000 – 24,000)	216,000
	276,000

2. If the legacy to B is £60,000 tax bearing

B (60,000 – 24,000)	36,000
C (300,000 – 60,000)	240,000
	276,000

Single grossing – exempt residue

6642 Complications arise where a **tax-free** specific gift is made and the residue of the estate is exempt. The IHT on the specific gift will need to be calculated using a method known as single grossing. This calculates the size of transfer required to pay the specific gift net of tax. In simple terms, the IHT is calculated on the gift in accordance with the normal rules but the rate of tax is 40/60 rather than 40%.

EXAMPLE Mr B died on 1 June 2011 with an estate valued at £475,000. He made a specific bequest to his son of £270,000 (free of tax) and left the residue to his wife (exempt). Mr B made a chargeable lifetime transfer of £90,000 (after annual exemptions) in 2006/07.

	Gross £	Tax £	Net £
IHT on specific gift:			
Cumulative total brought forward	90,000	-	90,000
Specific gift	293,333	23,333	270,000
	383,333	23,333	360,000
Tax thereon:			
£325,000 covered by the nil rate band			
360,000 – 325,000 @ 40/60			23,333

The death estate will be divided as follows:

Son	270,000
Tax	23,333
Wife (475,000 – 270,000 – 23,333)	181,667
	475,000

Double grossing – tax-free gift and chargeable transfers

The most complex situation is where a will or intestacy is made up of tax-free specific gifts, together with tax bearing specific gifts and/or partly chargeable residue. Grossing up in this case is more difficult because the **rate for each gift** must be identified. For this reason a system known as double grossing is used. This is a complicated calculation and is shown here using a step by step explanation. The steps should be followed in order and none should be omitted. 6644

1. Gross up the tax-free legacies in accordance with the single grossing rules i.e. as if they were the only chargeable part of the estate.
2. Using the gross value from 1. to represent the tax-free legacies, calculate the value of the whole chargeable estate and work out the IHT that would be payable on this sum (include cumulative transfers to date).
3. Calculate the estate rate (ER) by dividing the tax by the value of the chargeable estate and multiplying by 100.
4. Using the following formula, gross up the tax-free legacies as in 1.:
(100/(100 – ER)) × tax-free legacies = grossed-up legacies
where ER is the estate rate from 3.
5. Repeat step 2., using the grossed-up legacies from 4. This represents the actual tax payable.
6. Allocate the burden of tax on the following basis:

Bequest	Burden of Tax
Tax-free legacies	Deducted from free estate
Tax bearing legacies	Paid net of tax
Residue	Tax on chargeable residue is borne by itself and not exempt residue

EXAMPLE Mr A died on 1 June 2011 leaving a free estate valued at £979,000. He made no lifetime transfers in the 7 years before death and had no interests in possession. Mr A left his brother a tax-free legacy of £334,000 and divided the residue equally between his wife and daughter.

Step 1: Gross up the tax-free legacy:

	Gross £	Tax £	Net £
Brought forward	-	-	-
Tax-free legacy on death	340,000	6,000	334,000
Tax thereon: (334,000 – 325,000 @ 40/60)	6,000		

Step 2: Calculate the tax on the chargeable free estate:

Total estate	979,000
Less: Grossed up legacy	(340,000)
Residue	639,000
Chargeable residue (639,000 × 1/2)	319,500
Grossed up legacy	340,000
Chargeable free estate	659,500
Tax thereon: 659,500 – 325,000 @ 40%	133,800

Step 3: Calculate the estate rate:

133,800/659,500 × 100	20.288 %

Step 4: Gross up the tax-free legacy using the estate rate:

$334{,}000 \times \frac{100}{100 - 20.288}$	419,008

Step 5: Calculate the tax on the chargeable free estate using the grossed up figure from step 4:

Total estate	979,000
Less: Grossed up legacy	(419,008)
Residue	559,992
Chargeable residue (559,992 × 1/2)	279,996
Grossed up legacy	419,008
Chargeable free estate	699,004
Tax thereon:	
699,004 – 325,000 @ 40%	149,602

Step 6: Allocate the tax to the estate:

149,602/699,004 × 100	21.4022 %
Tax is allocated:	
Grossed up legacy (419,008 @ 21.4022 %)	89,677
Chargeable residue (279,996 @ 21.4022 %)	59,925
	149,602
Residue is:	
Total estate	979,000
Less: Tax-free legacy (334,000 + 89,677)	(423,677)
	555,323
1/2 Residue chargeable – daughter	277,661
1/2 Residue exempt – wife	277,662
Division of estate	
Brother (tax-free legacy)	334,000
Residue – daughter (277,661 – 59,925)	217,736
Residue – wife	277,662
Tax to HMRC (89,677 + 59,925)	149,602
	979,000

CHAPTER 4

National heritage property

OUTLINE ¶¶

In order to encourage owners to care for heritage property, an application can be made to postpone payment of IHT on transfers of eligible property. The postponement is effected by a conditional exemption, and certain undertakings must be given with regard to the future of the property. 6660

It is possible to **defer** the charge to IHT indefinitely if the conditional exemption is satisfied on every transfer of the property. Deferred IHT can, however, become chargeable if a chargeable event occurs. 6661

MEMO POINTS Where the IHT charge is deferred by the conditional exemption, no **capital gains tax** charge will arise on the transfer (¶5564).

SECTION 1

Requirements

Qualifying property

The Board of HMRC will ultimately decide whether property is important for the national heritage, but property which falls within the definitions outlined below is likely to qualify: 6662 s 31 IHTA 1984

1. Any **pictures, prints, books, manuscripts, works of art, scientific objects** or other non-income yielding things (or any collection or group of relevant objects taken as a whole) which appear to be pre-eminent for their national, scientific, historic or artistic interest. In determining whether property falls within this definition, regard should be had for any significant association of the object, collection or group with a particular place.
2. Any **land** which is of outstanding scenic, historic or scientific interest.
3. Any **building** where special steps should be taken to preserve it, by reason of its outstanding historic or architectural interest. This definition includes any area of land which is essential for the protection of the character and amenities of such a building, and any object which is historically associated with such a building.

Qualifying transfers

6664 The conditional exemption is **not applicable** where the transfer is already exempt under the spouse exemption (¶6440) or the charitable exemption (¶6442). However, where property is the subject of an earlier conditional exemption, the undertakings should be renewed in order to retain it.

Otherwise, transfers of qualifying property **made on death** will always be eligible for the conditional exemption.

s 30(3) IHTA 1984 For **lifetime transfers of value**, the conditional exemption will only be available if either:
– the transferor and/or spouse have been beneficially entitled to the property for the 6 years ending with the transfer (so the ownership period of a husband and wife is aggregated); or
– the transferor acquired the property as a conditionally exempt transfer on the death of another person (including the termination of an interest in possession in settled property).

6665 If the transfer is **potentially exempt**, no **claim** may be made until the PET crystallises on the death of the transferor within 7 years (¶6552). In these circumstances the claim must be submitted within 2 years of the date of death, or such longer time as allowed by the Board. Otherwise the relief must usually be claimed within 2 years of the date of the transfer, or such longer time as allowed by the Board.

If there is a **subsequent transfer**, the conditional exemption can be renewed and this can continue indefinitely until a chargeable event occurs.

Agreed undertakings

6666 s 31 IHTA 1984 Certain agreed undertakings must be given to the Board before the exemption will be granted. Generally, the **person responsible** for giving the required undertakings is the transferee, but the Board may accept undertakings from any person deemed appropriate in the circumstances.

The **nature** of the undertakings required will depend on the circumstances in each case, but broadly these will encompass the preservation of property and agreed access for the public. In addition, the owners of works of art and other chattels will be required to undertake to keep the property permanently in the UK, and not to remove them other than for a temporary purpose (and period) approved by the Board.

s 31(4FA), (4FB) IHTA 1984 MEMO POINTS **Public access** may not be confined to occasions where a prior appointment has been made. In addition, individuals may be required to publicise the terms of the undertakings made, as well as any other information which might otherwise be treated as confidential, such as the tax status of the asset.

6668 Once given, the undertakings must **continue to be satisfied** until the death of the person who is beneficially entitled to the property, or the disposal of the property by sale, gift or otherwise.

s 35A IHTA 1984 The terms of the undertakings may be **varied** by agreement with the Board. If agreement cannot be reached, application for a variation can be made to the first-tier tribunal.

MEMO POINTS 1. HMRC accept that owners of eligible property may make a reasonable charge for allowing viewing or giving access. There is no cap on the amount to charge, although HMRC suggest that rates should be commensurate with those charged by locally comparable sources e.g. the National Trust. Where a visitor reports overcharging, HMRC will take a view on whether a charge is reasonable. In particular, owners are advised not to pass on the whole cost of allowing access e.g. where the item is in storage.
2. Where the property is owned by a trust and the trust has become subject to the 10 year charge regime, the trustees must obtain the conditional exemption in advance of the IHT 10 year charge becoming due, otherwise the tax charge will be payable.

SECTION 2

Loss of the conditional exemption

Chargeable events

If one of the chargeable events outlined below occurs, this will result in the loss of the conditional exemption, and will therefore give rise to an IHT liability. **6670** s 32 IHTA 1984
1. A **material failure** to observe an undertaking (e.g. restricting public access to land).
2. The **death of the person beneficially entitled** to the property unless:
– new undertakings have been given in respect of the property;
– the personal representatives sell the property to a museum or similar heritage body by private treaty within 3 years after the date of death; or
– the property is accepted by the Board in lieu of tax within 3 years after the date of death.
3. **Sale** of the property by private treaty other than to a museum or similar heritage body.
4. **Disposal other than by sale** unless a new undertaking is given in respect of the property.

MEMO POINTS **Loss or theft** is not usually a chargeable event (even if insurance monies are received) unless it can be shown that the loss or theft arose from a failure to observe the undertaking to preserve the property.

Calculation of the IHT charge

The charge on the loss of the conditional exemption will be **based on** the value of the property at the date of the chargeable event. If the chargeable event is an arm's length sale, the IHT charge will be based on the proceeds of sale after the deduction of expenses. In either case, any capital gains tax payable will be deducted in arriving at the chargeable amount. **6672** ss 33, 34 IHTA 1984

Where the disposal is a lifetime gift, the IHT charge is **payable** by the transferee. In other cases, the tax is payable by the person who would be entitled to receive the proceeds of sale if the property was sold.

The tax is calculated by reference to the personal circumstances of the **relevant person**, who is generally the person who made the last conditionally exempt transfer. Where there has been **more than one** such **transfer** in the last 30 years, HMRC may select any transferor in order to prevent the avoidance of tax. **6674**

Tax will be charged at the lifetime rate, unless the original transfer was made on death, in which case the death rate will be used. **6676**

If the **relevant person is alive** at the date of the chargeable event, tax will be calculated as if he had made a lifetime transfer of value at the date of the chargeable event, and other transfers made in the last 7 years will be taken into account.

If the **relevant person has died**, tax will be calculated as if the property was added to the value of his death estate and formed the top slice of that value.

MEMO POINTS **PETs** are ignored for the purposes of this calculation, even if they become chargeable as a result of death.

EXAMPLE In May 2006, Mr A made two conditionally exempt lifetime transfers to his sons, Mr B and Mr C. In June 2008 Mr C made a conditionally exempt transfer of the same property to his own son Mr D.
Mr A died in December 2009, at which time the value of his estate was £200,000 and the cumulative total brought forward was £87,000.

Chargeable event 1:
In September 2010 Mr B sold his property for £100,000, a chargeable event. The relevant person is Mr A, and tax will be charged at the lifetime rate as if the property formed the top slice of his estate.

	£	Gross £	Tax £
Cumulative total brought forward		87,000	
Death estate of Mr A	200,000		
Chargeable event – sale by Mr B	100,000		12,400
		300,000	
		387,000	12,400

Tax on chargeable event: £325,000 is covered by that year's (2010/11) nil rate band, so £62,000 (i.e. 387,000 – 325,000) of the chargeable event will be subject to tax:
62,000 @ 20% 12,400

Chargeable event 2:
In November 2011 Mr D sold his property for £175,000, another chargeable event. HMRC nominate Mr A as the relevant person, and tax will again be charged at the lifetime rate as if the property formed the top slice of his estate (including the previous chargeable transfer).

	£	Gross £	Tax £
Cumulative total brought forward		87,000	
Death estate of Mr A (including chargeable event 1)	300,000		
Chargeable event – sale by Mr D	175,000		35,000
		475,000	
		562,000	35,000

Tax on chargeable event:
£325,000 is covered by the nil rate band for 2011/12, so the full amount of the second chargeable event will be subject to tax:
175,000 @ 20% 35,000

Effect on the cumulative total

6678 s 34 IHTA 1984 The amount charged to tax as a result of a chargeable event arising from the loss of the conditional exemption will be added to the cumulative total of the **person who made the last conditionally exempt transfer** of the property. This person is not necessarily the relevant person on whose cumulative total the tax liability will be calculated.

EXAMPLE Mr G made a conditionally exempt transfer to his sister Mrs H in June 2006. In May 2008 Mrs H made a further conditionally exempt transfer to her son Mr K. Mr K sold the property for £200,000 in September 2010, when Mr G's cumulative total brought forward was £300,000 and Mrs H's was £75,000.
For the purposes of calculating the tax on the chargeable event arising from the sale of the property in September 2010, Mr G will be nominated as the relevant person as this will give rise to a greater tax charge, as he has the greater cumulative total brought forward. The amount charged to tax (i.e. £200,000 from Mr K's sale) will, however, be added to Mrs H's cumulative total, making the amount carried forward in her estate £275,000.

Transfers already chargeable

6680 Where the loss of the conditional exemption is **triggered by an event** which is itself a transfer of value (e.g. a gift into a discretionary trust), the tax on that transfer of value will be available as a credit against the chargeable event. The amount of tax available as a credit is restricted to the amount attributable to the conditionally exempt property. This means that any tax paid by the donor will need to be excluded.

If the trigger **does not give rise to a chargeable event**, (for example, because the transferee renews the undertakings) then, if a chargeable event arises subsequently, it is possible to carry forward the credit to the later chargeable event.

If the transfer of value that triggered the loss of the conditional exemption is a **PET**, a tax credit is also available. In this instance, however, the tax on the chargeable event is given as a credit against the PET. 6682

Subsequent potentially exempt transfer before death

Special rules apply if property is transferred as a PET which does not give rise to a chargeable event (because, for example, the undertakings are renewed). If a chargeable event then arises between the date of that PET and the death of the donor, the credit for the chargeable event can be carried forward against the PET. 6684

EXAMPLE In November 2008, Mr A made a conditionally exempt lifetime transfer to his nephew, Mr B. In February 2010 when the property was worth £120,000, Mr B gave it to his sister Miss C. Miss C did not renew the undertakings. At that time Mr A's cumulative total brought forward was £220,000. Mr B died in December 2011 when the property was worth £130,000 and his cumulative total brought forward was £250,000.
There will be two charges to IHT. The first is the chargeable event as a result of the loss of the conditional exemption and the second is the death tax on the PET from Mr B to Miss C.

1. Loss of conditional exemption – 2009/10		**Gross** £	**Tax** £
Cumulative total brought forward (Mr A)		220,000	
Chargeable event – transfer to Miss C		120,000	3,000
		340,000	3,000
Tax thereon:			
£325,000 covered by nil rate band for 2009/10			
340,000 – 325,000 @ 20%		3,000	

2. PET becomes chargeable on death – 2011/12		£	**Gross** £	**Tax** £
Cumulative total brought forward (Mr B)			250,000	
PET – February 2010		120,000		
Less: Annual exemption	2009/10	(3,000)		
	2008/09	(3,000)		
			114,000	15,600
			364,000	15,600
Tax thereon:				
£325,000 covered by nil rate band for 2011/12				
364,000 – 325,000 @ 40%			15,600	
Less: Tax paid on chargeable event			(3,000)	
Balance payable on PET			12,600	

CHAPTER 5

Reliefs

OUTLINE ¶¶

There are a number of reliefs available which either reduce the amount chargeable to IHT or reduce the amount of tax due. 6695

Business property relief and agricultural property relief can reduce the value of both lifetime and death transfers of relevant business and agricultural property (to nil in some cases).

A fall in the value of property which has been the subject of an IHT charge can give rise to two types of relief, both of which recalculate the original charge. The first arises where property is transferred within 7 years before the death of the taxpayer. The second relief relates to post-death sales.

Quick succession relief applies where IHT is paid on a transfer, and the subsequent death of the transferee results in a further IHT charge within a relatively short space of time. In this case, the later IHT liability on the second transfer is reduced.

SECTION 1

Business property relief

6700 Business property relief (BPR) reduces the value of a transfer for IHT purposes on both life and death transfers, and relief is given automatically, before other reliefs and exemptions. Any tax remaining payable after relief is likely to qualify for interest-free instalments over 10 years (¶7078).

6702
ss 105, 106, 113 IHTA 1984
IHTM 25152

To be **eligible** for relief the property must:
- be relevant business property;
- have been owned for a minimum period;
- not be subject to a binding contract for sale at the time of the transfer; and
- not be an excepted asset.

Similar conditions apply to determine whether business property relief will be **withdrawn** when the death of the transferor (within 7 years of a transfer) causes a potentially exempt transfer to become chargeable, or additional tax to become due on a chargeable lifetime transfer. An application can be made to HMRC for clearance for BPR purposes, where there is material uncertainty over whether the relief applies (¶6746).

1. Eligible property

6704
ss 103(3), 105 IHTA 1984

Relief is available at two different rates, depending on the type of property:

Type of asset	Amount of relief
Unincorporated businesses and partnership interests [1, 2, 8]	100%
Shares in any unquoted company [5,6,8]	100%
Securities of an unquoted company controlled by the transferor [3, 4, 5, 6, 8]	100%
Shares or securities of a quoted company controlled by the transferor [4, 5, 6, 8]	50%
Land, buildings, machinery or plant owned by the transferor, and used immediately prior to the transfer by a company controlled by him, or by a partnership in which he was a partner [2, 8]	50%
Land, buildings, machinery or plant in which the transferor has an interest in possession, and which is used immediately prior to the transfer wholly or mainly for the purposes of a business carried on by him [2,7,8]	50%

Note:
1. A **business** for these purposes is a business carried out in the exercise of a trade, profession or vocation but does not include a business carried on otherwise than for gain. The income or corporation tax status of a business is not relevant for business property relief.
2. This may be subject to a late claim for BPR.
3. The term **securities** is not defined by the legislation but is understood to include loan and debenture stock.
4. **Control** means control of the majority of the voting powers on all questions affecting the company as a whole. Control is tested immediately before the transfer. Related property and settled property in which the transferor (and spouse) has an interest in possession may be included for these purposes.
5. **Quoted** means listed on a recognised stock exchange (¶9995). Shares listed on the AIM are unquoted for these purposes.
6. A **company in liquidation** is not eligible for BPR unless trading is to continue after a reconstruction etc.
7. Where the property is held within an **interest in possession trust**, relief is based on the circumstances of the life tenant. For example, where the property transferred is land, buildings, machinery or plant, relief will generally be available at 50%. Following the case of *Fetherstonhaugh and others v IRC* [1984], relief will be available at 100% for the assets of a business if the business itself is transferred at the same time.
8. A **clearance application** may be appropriate in these circumstances (¶6746).

Fall in value of the estate

To be eligible for BPR, the gift must effect a reduction in the net value of the business. The test is whether there is a fall in value of the donor's estate and, if so, that fall in value must be attributable to business property, regardless of whether an actual transfer of that property takes place. **6705**

MEMO POINTS 1. The decision in *HMRC v Trustees of the Nelson Dance Family Settlement* 2009 has looked at the conditions necessary for BPR to apply. This case concerned BPR and how it applied to a lifetime transfer of an individual asset used in the business of a sole proprietor. The High Court held that 100% BPR applies where assets which form part of the net value of the business are transferred, even if the business itself or a part of the business is not transferred, provided that the fall in value of the estate leads to a reduction in the new value of the business. Although HMRC appealed against the original decision by the Special Commissioners, the High Court upheld the decision. The court held that if the net value of the business fell as a result of the transfer, then BPR was available on that transfer, as this is what it means for a transfer of value to be "attributable to" the net value of the relevant business property. *HMRC v Trustees of the Nelson Dance Family Settlement* [2009]

2. HMRC take a different approach and state that the transfer of an individual asset used in a sole proprietor's business is not eligible for BPR unless it is itself transferred. The conflict between the approaches of the court and of HMRC may make this area subject to further proceedings.

Exclusions

A business (or interest in a business, including shares and securities) will be excluded from the definition of relevant business property if the **business** itself **consists wholly or mainly** of: **6706** s 105(3) IHTA 1984

- dealing in stock, shares, securities, land or buildings; or
- making or holding investments.

The **exclusion does not apply** where: s 105(4) IHTA 1984

- the business concerned is that of a market maker or discount house carried on in the UK; or
- the shares or securities are of a company whose business consists wholly or mainly in being a holding company of one or more companies who do not themselves fall within the exclusion.

So where a **trading company holds investments** which are worth 40% of its total value, the total value of its own shares will be covered by 100% BPR. It is therefore important to ensure that the company is predominately trading.

MEMO POINTS **Wholly or mainly** is not defined, but in practice it is taken to mean 50% or more. Where a business carries on more than one type of activity, an overall view must be taken.

Letting property There have been many cases involving investment property (in particular, caravan parks). Overall, the availability of BPR will depend on the facts of the particular case. *Weston v IRC* [2000] **6708**

Where more than one relief applies, special care has to be taken to ensure that the conditions for the reliefs to apply have been met (¶6787).

MEMO POINTS The Special Commissioner considered the nature of a business which, it was claimed, qualified for BPR, on the excess value above the agricultural value (¶6766). The deceased owned land which she let to local farmers for grazing. The Commissioner held that BPR was not applicable because whilst the deceased was carrying on a business, that business was "making or holding investments" and the activities of the business were "to make available the land for other persons" in return for which payment was received. As the business did not involve the separate provision of any other substantial goods or services, the claim for BPR was denied. *PN McCall & BJA Keenan (Personal Representatives of E McClean) v HMRC* [2008]

EXAMPLE

1. The caravans in a caravan park were static, and rent was paid to the owners of the park, mainly by holidaymakers. The caravans could only be sold with the involvement of the park owners, to whom a commission was payable. Basic facilities such as toilets, showers and refuse disposal were available. Rent made up the majority of income.

It was held that the main activity was one of property rental, the commissions being ancillary, and so BPR was denied. *Hall (Executors of Hall) v IRC* [1997]

2. In another case involving a caravan park, the net profits from the sale of caravans exceeded the rental income. On this basis BPR was available. *Furness v IRC* [1999]

3. A company owned a caravan site, and carried on the following activities:
- static caravan park, including the provision of services;
- caravan sales;
- selling services (power and water) at a profit;
- providing storage of touring caravans;
- letting of a warehouse and grazing land; and
- running a country club for both residents and the public.

The static caravan park qualified as a business activity, on the basis that the level of overheads (72 % of site fees) pointed to a non-investment business. Taking an overall view, BPR was available because the investment activities generated less than 50% of the total turnover, gross profit and net profit. In addition, there was no reason why an active family business of this type should not receive BPR merely because the use of land was a necessary component of its profit-making activity. *IRC v George (Stedman Dec'd)* [2004]

2. Ownership requirements

Minimum ownership period

6712 s 106 IHTA 1984

To qualify for BPR the property must have:
- been owned by the transferor throughout the 2 years immediately prior to the transfer; or
- replaced other property which would have qualified for BPR (but for the 2 year ownership requirement), and the combined ownership periods represent at least 2 out of the 5 years immediately prior to the date of the transfer.

There is no **restriction** on the number of replacements that can take place within the 5 year period, and there is no requirement for replacements to be in the same type of business.

ss 49(1), 103(1) IHTA 1984

MEMO POINTS If the relevant business property is owned by a discretionary **trust**, the trustees must satisfy the ownership conditions unless there is an interest in possession, where the property is treated as though it forms part of the life tenant's estate, in which case the life tenant must satisfy the conditions personally.

Value of replacement assets

6714 s 107(2) IHTA 1984

Relief on replacement assets is restricted where the **replacement asset is worth more than the original asset** was worth. A strict interpretation of the legislation indicates that the amount of relief will be restricted to the value that the original asset would have had if it had still been held at the date of the transfer in question. This would involve obtaining a valuation of both assets, one of which is no longer owned. In practice, HMRC will accept the following apportionment:

$$\frac{\text{Value of original asset at date of its disposal}}{\text{Value of replacement at date of acquisition}} \times \text{Value of replacement on final transfer}$$

EXAMPLE Mr A owned Building B which had been used for many years by a company in which he had a controlling interest. In March 2008 Building B was sold for £750,000 and replaced by Building C which cost £950,000. In August 2011 Mr A gave Building C (now worth £1,000,000) to his son. Under the strict interpretation of the legislation, the amount eligible for relief would be restricted to what Building B would have been worth in August 2011.
HMRC will, however, accept the following amount as being eligible for relief:

$$\frac{750{,}000}{950{,}000} \times 1{,}000{,}000 = \underline{\underline{£789{,}474}}$$

6716 s 107(4) IHTA 1984

If the relevant business property owned by the transferor is **shares in an unquoted company**, special rules apply with respect to replacement assets. Where, immediately before the transfer, the shares would, for capital gains tax purposes, be identified with other shares previously owned by him (because of a company reconstruction, for example), the ownership period of all of the shares will be combined to establish whether the minimum period is satisfied.

This provision can be utilised on the incorporation of a business carried on by a sole trader or partnership.

Successions

Where the transferor acquired the relevant business property following the **death of another person**, the transferor's ownership period will be deemed to run from the date of that other person's death. **6718** s 108 IHTA 1984

The **exception** to this rule is where the property was acquired on the **death of a spouse**, when the transferor's ownership period will be deemed to include the ownership period of the spouse.

MEMO POINTS If the transferor acquired relevant business property from a spouse **other than on death**, the transferor's ownership period will run from the date of the transfer and will not include the spouse's ownership period.

Successive transfers

The 2 year minimum **ownership period** will be relaxed where: **6720** s 109 IHTA 1984

- the same property is the subject of two successive transfers;
- the first transfer satisfied the conditions for BPR (including the minimum ownership requirement); and
- either the first or second transfer was on death.

The subsequent transfer will be eligible for relief based on the earlier ownership period.

MEMO POINTS This provision can be contrasted to ¶6712 where an asset is acquired on the death of an individual, and relief is still available providing the two ownership periods, when combined, satisfy the requirements. To qualify under the successive transfers rule, the original transfer must have already satisfied the minimum ownership period.

EXAMPLE Mr A had owned a 40% holding in B Ltd for many years. In August 2010 Mr A gave the holding to his daughter C. The transfer qualified for 100% business property relief. C dies in November 2011 leaving the holding to her son D.
Although C has not satisfied the minimum ownership period, the transfer to D will still be eligible for 100% business property relief, given that the original transfer satisfied all of the requirements.

Binding contract for sale

Property subject to a binding contract for sale **at the time** of the transfer will not qualify for BPR. **6722** s 113 IHTA 1984

The **exception** to this rule is where the property is:

- a business or interest in a business, and the sale is to a company which will carry on the business and is made for a consideration wholly or mainly of shares in or securities of that company; or
- shares in or securities of a company, and the sale is made for the purpose of reconstruction or amalgamation.

HMRC consider that a binding contract for sale is in existence (and therefore BPR is not available) where partners and shareholder directors enter into a **buy and sell agreement**. This is an agreement whereby, in the event of death before retirement, the personal representatives are obliged to sell, and the surviving partners or directors are obliged to purchase, the deceased's business interest or shares. SP 12/80

A **solution** to this problem would be to use options, so that the personal representatives of the deceased have an option to sell, and the remaining partners/shareholders have an option to buy. As there is no agreement for a sale, BPR will still be available.

Excepted assets

Land, buildings, machinery or plant owned by the transferor and used in a company controlled by him (or by a partnership in which he was a partner) will be excepted assets, and therefore outside the scope of BPR, unless they have: **6724** s 112 IHTA 1984

- been used for business purposes throughout the 2 years immediately preceding the transfer; or

– replaced another asset so used (and the assets must have been so used for a combined period of at least 2 years out of the 5 years immediately prior to the transfer).

Other assets will be excepted assets unless they were:
– used wholly or mainly for business purposes throughout the 2 years immediately prior to the transfer (or since the date of acquisition if that is more recent); or
– required at the time of the transfer for the future use of the business.

Surplus cash in the business may be treated as an excepted asset, unless it is earmarked for future use for the purposes of the business. *Barclays Bank Trust Co Limited v IRC* [1998]

s 112(6) IHTA 1984 MEMO POINTS 1. An asset will not be deemed to have been used wholly or mainly for the purposes of the business concerned at any time when it was used for the **personal benefit** of the transferor or of a person connected with him.
2. The implications of the decision in *HMRC v Trustees of the Nelson Dance Family Settlement* [2009] (¶6705) may mean that transfers of items which previously would have been excepted, will be considered as qualifying for BPR in the future.

EXAMPLE Mr A dies leaving a business valued as follows:

	£	£
Investments	40,000	
Business assets	100,000	
Total assets		140,000
Liabilities secured on investments	10,000	
Unsecured creditors	40,000	
Total liabilities		(50,000)
Net asset value		90,000

The investments are excepted assets for the purposes of BPR. Their net value, taking account of the secured liabilities, is £30,000 (40,000 – 10,000).
The total value of assets taken into account for BPR is £130,000 (100,000 + 30,000).
The investments represent 23.077 % (30,000/130,000) of the total asset value.
So the value of the business for IHT purposes is:

	£
Net asset value represented by excepted assets: 90,000 @ 23.077 %	20,769
Net asset value represented by business assets: 90,000 – 20,769	69,231

3. Application of the relief

6726 BPR reduces the value of a transfer, and the value of the property must therefore be established before the relief can be applied. For chargeable lifetime transfers, the eligibility for relief must be addressed at the time of the transfer, and again if the transferor dies within 7 years of the transfer. For potentially exempt transfers, the relief is only relevant at death.

Valuation of business property

6728 The normal valuation rules (¶6465) apply to business property. In addition, a number of special rules are outlined below.

6730 s 110 IHTA 1984 The value of an **unincorporated business** for the purposes of BPR is deemed to be the value of all of the assets used in the business (including goodwill), less the amount of any liabilities incurred for business purposes.

Where an **interest in a partnership** is being valued, only those assets by reference to which the whole business would be valued should be taken into account. Assets owned by individual partners should be excluded, even if used for business purposes.

6732 s 111 IHTA 1984 The value of shares and securities of a **group of companies** will be reduced for BPR purposes to take account of:
– the amount attributable to any group company not carrying on a qualifying business; and
– any assets owned within the group that do not constitute relevant business property.

A group company whose business consists wholly or mainly in the holding of land or buildings will be included in the group for share valuation purposes if:
– the buildings are occupied wholly or mainly by members of the group; and
– those members carry on a qualifying business.

Calculation of tax

BPR at the appropriate percentage is deducted from the net value of the transfer. For **lifetime transfers** this means that the relief will be applied before the deduction of any exemptions, and before any grossing up in respect of the IHT payable. **6734**

For **transfers on death** the relief is simply deducted from the death estate.

There is no requirement to submit a **claim** because BPR is given automatically where it is due. In practice, relief is obtained by making a deduction in the account notifying HMRC of a transfer of value.

EXAMPLE In June 2011 Mr A died and left the whole of his estate to his daughter. The value of Mr A's estate on death included a building worth £250,000, used for many years by an unquoted company of which Mr A was a controlling shareholder. The balance of the estate was valued at £102,000. Mr A made an earlier gross chargeable transfer of £210,000 in August 2008.

	£	£
Cumulative total brought forward		210,000
Estate	352,000	
Less: 50% BPR (250,000 @ 50%)	(125,000)	
	227,000	
		227,000
		437,000
Tax thereon:		
£325,000 covered by nil rate band for 2011/12		
437,000 – 325,000 @ 40%		44,800

If there is a **change in the rate** of BPR between a lifetime transfer and the death of the transferor, the additional tax on death (¶6542) will be calculated using the new rate. **6736** s 184(6) FA 1996

MEMO POINTS 1. This rule will apply where a **chargeable lifetime transfer** of a minority holding of unquoted shares was made before 6 April 1996, and the transferor subsequently died on or after 6 April 1996. At the time of the original transfer BPR of 50% would have been available, but at the death of the transferor BPR had increased to 100%.
2. Where a change in the rate of business property relief arises after a **potentially exempt transfer**, the tax on death will be calculated in accordance with the rate applicable at the date of death.

Withdrawal of relief on lifetime transfers

Special rules apply where, because of the **death of the transferor** within 7 years of a transfer eligible for BPR: **6740**
– a potentially exempt transfer becomes chargeable; or
– additional tax becomes due on a chargeable lifetime transfer.

In order to **qualify** for BPR on the death of the transferor, the property that was the subject of the original transfer must: s 113A IHTA 1984

a. be owned by the transferee throughout the period beginning with the date of the transfer and ending with the death of the transferor;
b. not, at the time of the transferor's death, be the subject of a binding contract for sale; and
c. still qualify as relevant business property (ignoring the minimum period of ownership requirement).

MEMO POINTS 1. If the **transferee dies** before the transferor, condition **a**. should apply throughout the period up to the transferee's death.
2. Condition **c. does not apply** where, at the time of the transfer, the property was:
– quoted shares or securities;
– unquoted shares; or
– unquoted securities in a company in which the transferor had a controlling interest.

For example, if Mr A transfers a 15% holding in a quoted company to a discretionary trust, out of his total holding of 75%, this transfer will qualify for 50% BPR. If Mr A dies within 7 years, the 15% holding will still qualify for BPR.

6741 s 113A(5) IHTA 1984 If the conditions for BPR on the death of the transferor are only satisfied with regard to **part of the original property**, the restriction to BPR only applies to the part that does not satisfy the conditions.

6742 If the conditions of ¶6740 are not satisfied, the charge to tax for a **potentially exempt transfer** will be calculated without a deduction for BPR, regardless of whether the property qualified at the time of the original transfer.

If a **chargeable lifetime transfer** does not satisfy the conditions, the value transferred for the purposes of calculating the additional tax on death will be the original amount of the transfer before the deduction of BPR already given. However, the amount of the transfer as reduced by BPR will be used for the cumulative total.

EXAMPLE Mr A owned two buildings, both used for the purposes of a company in which he had a controlling interest. In October 2006 he transferred Building B to a discretionary trust at which time it was worth £600,000. The trustees agreed to pay the tax. In November 2007 he transferred Building C to his son at which time it was worth £200,000. In April 2008 both the trustees and the son sold their respective buildings and did not reinvest the proceeds. Mr A died in July 2011 having made no other lifetime transfers of value.

			£
Lifetime tax			
October 2006 transfer (chargeable lifetime transfer):			
Building B			600,000
Less: 50% BPR			(300,000)
			300,000
Less: Annual exemption –	2006/07		(3,000)
	2005/06		(3,000)
			294,000
Tax thereon:			
£285,000 covered by nil rate band for 2006/07			
294,000 – 285,000 @ 20%			1,800

The November 2007 transfer was a potentially exempt transfer and utilised the annual exemption for 2007/08.

		£	£
Death tax			
October 2006 transfer (chargeable lifetime transfer):			
Building B (BPR withdrawn)			600,000
Less: Annual exemption –	2006/07		(3,000)
	2005/06		(3,000)
			594,000
Tax thereon:			
£325,000 covered by nil rate band for 2011/12			
594,000 – 325,000 @ 40%			107,600
Less: Taper relief at 40%			(43,040)
Less: Lifetime tax paid			(1,800)
			62,760
November 2007 transfer (originally potentially exempt):			
Cumulative total brought forward			294,000
Building C (no BPR given)		200,000	
Less: Annual exemption – 2007/08		(3,000)	
			197,000
			491,000
Tax thereon:			
£325,000 covered by nil rate band for 2011/12			
491,000 – 325,000 @ 40%			66,400

Replacement property

BPR will still be available where the property which was the subject of the original transfer was replaced, provided all of the following are satisfied: 6744 s 113B IHTA 1984

- the **whole amount** of the consideration received for the disposal of any of the original property was applied in the acquisition of relevant business property (¶6704);
- the replacement property was **acquired** within 3 years (or longer as HMRC may allow) of the disposal of the original property;
- both the disposal and acquisition were **arm's length** transactions;
- throughout the **period** beginning with the date of the original transfer and **ending with the death of the transferor**, either the original property or the replacement property was **owned by** the transferee; and
- **at the death** of the transferor the replacement property **qualified** as relevant business property.

If, on the **death of the transferor**, all or part of the original property has been disposed of but the replacement property has not been acquired, the relief will still apply providing the replacement property is acquired within 3 years of the date of disposal. In this case, references to the time immediately before the date of the transferor's death are taken to be references to the time when the replacement property was acquired. 6745 s 113B(5) IHTA 1984

EXAMPLE Mr A made a potentially exempt transfer to his son Mr B of relevant business property in June 2007. In December 2009 Mr B sold the property, and in August 2010 Mr A died.
Providing Mr B replaces the property by December 2012 (and the other conditions are satisfied) BPR will be available.

Clearance applications

HMRC provide an advance clearance procedure to deal with BPR rulings. Clearances are provided to **business owners** on the availability of BPR where there is material uncertainty over the interpretation of the law. 6746

For IHT legislation older than the last four finance acts, there are further requirements that the uncertainty must relate to a commercially significant issue, and the application must identify what aspect of the law or practice is thought to be uncertain. HMRC aim to respond within 28 calendar days of the submission.

The circumstances in which an application can be made include the following:

1. to obtain HMRC's view of the tax consequences of a transfer of value;
2. which involves a change of ownership of a business; and
3. where the transfer, excluding BPR, would result in an immediate IHT charge; and
4. provided that the other conditions are met.

Clearances in cases of ownership remain valid for a limited period of 6 months. A business owner, or someone acting on his behalf, should send the application to:

HMRC Trusts and Estates Technical Team (Clearances)
Ferrers House
Castle Meadow Road
Nottingham
NG2 1BB

MEMO POINTS 1. The clearance procedure is non-statutory and may be withdrawn or amended at any time.
2. Business owners may include individuals or trustees who will become business owners as a consequence of the transaction which is the subject of the clearance application.
3. Further details, including a list of information to be supplied, are given at http://www.hmrc.gov.uk/cap/clearanceiht.htm

SECTION 2

Agricultural property relief

6750 Agricultural property relief (APR) reduces the value of a transfer for IHT purposes on both lifetime and death transfers. In order to qualify for relief, the property must fall within the definition of agricultural property and satisfy the minimum ownership requirements.

In addition there is a specific relief for woodlands (¶6790) which only defers the IHT charge.

1. Eligible property

6752 s 115 IHTA 1984

Agricultural property is broadly **defined** as agricultural land or pasture but also includes:
– woodlands and any building used in connection with the intensive rearing of livestock or fish (providing the occupation is ancillary to that of the land or pasture);
– cottages, farm buildings and farmhouses of a character appropriate to the property;
– land and buildings used for short rotation coppice; (s 154(2), (3), (5) FA 1995)
– land and buildings taken out of farming for management under a Government Habitat Scheme; (s 122 FA 2009)
– breeding, rearing and grazing of horses on a stud farm (including buildings used in connection with the activity); and
– shares in a farming company (¶6767).

To qualify for relief the property must be **situated** within the UK, the Channel Islands or the Isle of Man. Since 22 April 2009, this has been extended to include property within the EEA which is subject to the same covenants for use as agricultural land in the EEA jurisdiction.

ESC F16

MEMO POINTS 1. **Farmhouses** are unlikely to qualify for relief where the majority of the farmland has already been gifted. *Rosser v IRC* [2003]
2. By concession, a transfer of agricultural property which includes a cottage occupied by a **retired farm employee** (or their widow or widower) satisfies the conditions regarding occupation for agricultural purposes if either:
– the occupier is a statutorily protected tenant; or
– the occupation is under a lease granted to the employee for his life and that of any surviving spouse as part of his contract of employment by the landlord for agricultural purposes.
3. Land used for the growing of **energy crops** also qualifies for APR.

2. Ownership requirements

6754 s 117 IHTA 1984

To qualify for APR the transferor must have:
– **occupied** the property for the purposes of agriculture throughout the period of 2 years ending with the date of the transfer; or
– **owned** the property throughout the period of 7 years ending with the date of the transfer, and during that period it was occupied (either by him or by someone else) for the purposes of agriculture.

Occupation

6756 s 119 IHTA 1984

For the purposes of the minimum ownership requirement, occupation by a **company** which is controlled by the transferor will be treated as occupation by the transferor.

Trustees can also satisfy the ownership requirement where:
– discretionary trustees have either farmed the land themselves, or arranged for a tenant to farm the land; and
– the life tenant has farmed the land held by an interest in possession trust.

In addition, occupation by a **Scottish partnership** will be treated as occupation by the partners.

EXAMPLE Mr X owned land farmed by X Limited which is a farming company controlled by Mr X for the last 4 years. The land will satisfy the minimum ownership requirement.

Replacement property

Where the property which is transferred has **replaced** other agricultural property, then the minimum ownership periods will be satisfied if the transferor: **6758** s 118 IHTA 1984
– **occupied** the properties for the purposes of agriculture for a combined period of at least 2 years out of the 5 years before the transfer; or
– **owned** the properties for a combined period of at least 7 years out of the 10 years before the transfer, during which time the property was occupied (either by him or by someone else) for the purposes of agriculture.

Where APR is being claimed in respect of replacement property, the maximum relief which can be claimed is restricted to the lowest value of all of the properties being considered.

Successions

If the transferor became entitled to agricultural property following the **death of another individual**, he will be deemed to have acquired it on the date of death and (if he subsequently occupies the property) his occupation will be deemed to commence on the same date. **6760** s 120 IHTA 1984

The **exception** to this rule is where the transferor acquired agricultural property on the **death of a spouse**, in which case the transferor's periods of ownership and occupation are deemed to include those of the spouse.

Successive transfers

The **minimum ownership period** conditions will be **relaxed** where: **6762** s 121 IHTA 1984
– the same property is the subject of two successive transfers, one or more of which was on death;
– the first transfer satisfied the conditions for agricultural property relief (including the minimum ownership requirement); and
– the land is occupied by the transferor for agricultural purposes at the time of the current transfer.

The subsequent transfer will be eligible for relief based on the earlier ownership period.

Binding contract for sale

Agricultural property relief will not be available where the transferor has entered into a binding contract for sale **at the time** of the transfer. The exception to this rule is where the property is being sold to a company controlled by the transferor. **6763** s 124 IHTA 1984

3. Application of the relief

Rate of relief

APR is given before any other reliefs or exemptions at a rate of either 50% or 100% of the agricultural value, depending on the nature of the ownership of the property. The following table shows property which will be eligible for 100% relief. Agricultural property not shown in the table will be eligible for 50% relief. **6764**

ESC F17

Agricultural property eligible for 100% relief:
Property in which the transferor has vacant possession
Property subject to a lease granted on or after 1 September 1995
Property in which the transferor has a right to obtain vacant possession within 24 months
Property where the tenant is a company controlled by the transferor

s 116(6) IHTA 1984

MEMO POINTS 1. If the property is owned by **joint tenants or tenants in common** and all of them together carry the right of vacant possession, then that right will be treated as applying to the tenants in common or joint tenants individually.
2. Where, on the **death of the original tenant**, a tenancy passes to another person under the laws of succession, the new tenancy is deemed to begin on the death of the tenant. This means that an old lease (i.e. one granted before 1 September 1995) will cease and a new one will commence, thus entitling the transferor to 100% relief.

s 116(5A)-(5E) IHTA 1984

3. Similarly, if the existing tenant gives notice of his **retirement** from the tenancy in favour of a new tenant but dies within 30 months of giving such notice and before the change of tenants, the new tenancy is deemed to start on the death of the old tenant.

Agricultural value

6766
ss 115(3), 162(4) IHTA 1984

APR is only given in relation to the agricultural value of property, so the development value of land, for example, will not be reduced. Agricultural value for these purposes is **defined** as the value that the property would have if it were subject to a perpetual covenant prohibiting its use other than as agricultural property. The value of a farmhouse may be discounted for the purposes of the relief where the occupant is not actively engaged in farming. *Lloyds TSB Private Banking (personal representative of Rosemary Antrobus deceased) v Peter Twiddy* [2005]

Agricultural value will be **reduced by** any encumbrances such as a mortgage or other liability secured on the property.

MEMO POINTS **Excess value** relating to development potential may be covered by BPR for farmland but not a farmhouse. Liabilities will be pro-rated between the agricultural value and the developmental value. HMRC are looking at this area in more detail and are likely to challenge any claim for BPR for development value if there are no services being provided, on the basis that the business is investment rather than trading. See ¶6708.

6767
s 122 IHTA 1984

Agricultural property of companies APR also applies to property which is owned by a company **controlled by** the transferor. If the following conditions are satisfied, the value of the agricultural property can be attributed to the shares which were the subject of the transfer:
– the agricultural property must form part of the company's assets, and part of the value of the shares or securities must be attributable to the agricultural value of the land; and
– those shares or securities must give the transferor control of the company immediately before the transfer.

The legislation does not specify how to **apportion the value** of the shares between agricultural and non-agricultural value, but general practice is to apportion on an assets basis, other than secured debts, which are deducted from the burdened property.

MEMO POINTS **Control means** control of the majority of the voting rights on all questions affecting the company as a whole. Related property and settled property in which the transferor (and spouse) has an interest in possession may be included for these purposes.

EXAMPLE Mr A, a farmer, owned all of the shares in B Ltd, an agricultural company. In December, he gave 40% of the shares to his son Mr C, at which time the value of the remaining 60% was £200,000. Mr A died 18 months later, at which time the balance sheet of B Ltd contained the following entries:

	£		£
Ordinary share capital	285,000	Agricultural land (agricultural value)	275,000
Debt secured on land	40,000	Stock	20,000
Unsecured creditors	15,000	Current assets	45,000
	340,000		340,000

The agricultural value attributable to the shares gifted to Mr C will be calculated as follows:

	£	£
Agricultural value of land		275,000
Less: Secured debt	40,000	
Proportion of unsecured debt (275,000/340,000 × 15,000)	12,132	
		(52,132)
		222,868

Value of original transfer (285,000 – 200,000) = 85,000

Value of original transfer taken to be agricultural value:

$$85{,}000 \times \frac{222{,}868}{285{,}000} = £66{,}469$$

Calculation of tax

APR at the appropriate percentage is deducted from the net value of the transfer. For **lifetime transfers**, this means that the relief will be applied before the deduction of any exemptions and before any grossing up in respect of the IHT payable. For **transfers on death**, the relief is simply deducted from the death estate. 6768

There is no requirement to submit a **claim** because APR is given automatically where it is due. In practice, relief is obtained by making a deduction in the account notifying HMRC of a transfer of value.

EXAMPLE Mr A died in October 2011. His estate, which he left to his son, included a farm which Mr A had owned and occupied for farming purposes for many years. A mortgage of £50,000 was secured on the property. At the date of death the land had development value of £500,000 but the agricultural value was only £225,000. The balance of the estate was valued at £85,000. No BPR is available.
Mr A made a gross chargeable lifetime transfer of £150,000 in November 2007.
Inheritance tax on the transfer will be calculated as follows:

	£	£
Cumulative total brought forward		150,000
Estate (585,000 – 50,000)	535,000	
Less: Agricultural property relief (100 %) (225,000 – 50,000)	(175,000)	
		360,000
		510,000
Tax thereon:		
£325,000 covered by nil rate band for 2011/12		
510,000 – 325,000 @ 40%		74,000

Withdrawal of relief on lifetime transfers

Special rules apply where, because of the **death of the transferor** within 7 years: 6770 s 124A IHTA 1984
- a potentially exempt transfer becomes chargeable; or
- additional tax becomes due on a chargeable lifetime transfer.

In order to **qualify** for APR on the death of the transferor, the property that was the subject of the original transfer must:

a. be owned by the transferee throughout the period beginning with the date of the transfer and ending with the death of the transferor;

b. not, at the time of the transferor's death, be the subject of a binding contract for sale; and

c. still qualify as agricultural property immediately before the transferor's death and have been occupied (by the transferee or another) for the purposes of agriculture throughout the period.

MEMO POINTS 1. If the **transferee dies** before the transferor, requirement **a**. should apply throughout the period up to the transferee's death.
2. Where the original transfer was of **shares in an agricultural company**, the relevant agricultural property (¶6752) must have been owned by the company throughout the period and occupied (by the company or someone else) for the purposes of agriculture.

If the conditions for APR on the death of the transferor are only satisfied with regard to **part of the original property**, the restriction to APR only applies to the part that does not satisfy the conditions. 6771 s 124A(5) IHTA 1984

If the conditions outlined above are not satisfied, the charge to tax for a **potentially exempt transfer** will be calculated without a deduction for APR, regardless of whether the property qualified at the time of the original transfer. 6772

For a **chargeable lifetime transfer** which does not satisfy the conditions, the value transferred for the purposes of calculating the additional tax on death will be the original amount of the transfer before the deduction of APR already given. However, the amount of the transfer as reduced by APR will be used for the cumulative total.

EXAMPLE Mr A owns two farms, both the subject of leases granted before September 1995. In September 2007, when it was worth £700,000 (the agricultural value), he transferred Farm B to a discretionary trust, the trustees of which agreed to pay the tax. In October 2008, when it was worth £225,000 (the agricultural value), he transferred Farm C to his son. In December 2008 both the trustees and the son sold their respective buildings and did not reinvest the proceeds. Mr A died in October 2011 having made no other lifetime transfers of value.

			£
Lifetime tax			
September 2007 transfer (chargeable lifetime transfer):			
Farm B			700,000
Less: 50% APR			(350,000)
			350,000
Less: Annual exemption –	2007/08		(3,000)
	2006/07		(3,000)
			344,000
Tax thereon:			
£300,000 covered by nil rate band for 2007/08			
344,000 – 300,000 @ 20%			8,800

The October 2008 transfer was a potentially exempt transfer and utilised the annual exemption for 2008/09.

		£	£
Death tax			
September 2007 transfer (chargeable lifetime transfer):			
Farm B (APR withdrawn)			700,000
Less: Annual exemption –	2007/08		(3,000)
	2006/07		(3,000)
			694,000
Tax thereon:			
£325,000 covered by nil rate band for 2011/12			
694,000 – 325,000 @ 40%			147,600
Less: Lifetime tax paid			(8,800)
			138,800
October 2008 transfer (originally potentially exempt):			
Cumulative total brought forward			344,000
Farm C (no APR given)		225,000	
Less: Annual exemption – 2008/09		(3,000)	
			222,000
			566,000
Tax thereon:			
£325,000 covered by nil rate band for 2011/12			
566,000 – 325,000 @ 40%			96,400

Replacement property

6774 s 124B IHTA 1984

APR may still be available where the property which was the subject of the original transfer was replaced, provided all of the following are satisfied:
- the **whole amount** of the consideration received for the disposal of any of the original property was applied in the acquisition of agricultural property (¶6752);
- the replacement property was **acquired** within 3 years (or longer as HMRC may allow) of the disposal of the original property;
- both the disposal and acquisition were **arm's length** transactions;

– throughout the **period** beginning with the date of the original transfer and **ending with the disposal**, the original property was owned by the transferee and was occupied (by the transferee or another) for the purposes of agriculture;
– throughout the **period** beginning with the disposal of the original property and **ending with the death of the transferor**, the replacement property was owned by the transferee and was occupied (by the transferee or another) for the purposes of agriculture; and
– **at the death** of the transferor the replacement property **qualified** as agricultural property.

If, on the **death of the transferor**, all or part of the original property has been disposed of but the replacement property **has not been acquired**, the relief will still apply providing the replacement property is acquired within 3 years of the date of disposal. In this case, references to the time immediately before the date of the transferor's death are taken to be references to the time when the replacement property was acquired. 6775

EXAMPLE Mr A made a potentially exempt transfer to his son Mr B of agricultural property in December 2009. In June 2010 Mr B sold the property and in November 2010 Mr A died.
Providing Mr B replaces the property by June 2013 (and the other conditions are satisfied) APR will be available.

4. Interaction of BPR and APR

The scope of property qualifying for BPR is wider than APR, and so where APR is unavailable, BPR may still be useful. BPR and APR can be claimed on qualifying property situated within the EEA. 6785 s 114 IHTA 1984

MEMO POINTS Until 22 April 2009, APR was only available on **property situated** in the UK, the Channel Islands, and the Isle of Man, (¶6752), whereas BPR was not so restricted.

Where both reliefs apply

BPR and APR cannot both be used to relieve the same portion of property, and where both apply, APR is given **in priority** to BPR. 6787

For example, a farmer who owns land and farms it as part of a business would obtain 50% APR, but would still be able to claim BPR on the remaining 50%. This would be relevant where the agricultural value of property is less than the actual value (for example, because the land has **development value**). APR will apply to the agricultural value and BPR will apply to the balance. HMRC have been looking at this area in detail, and may expect services to be offered (¶6708) where BPR is claimed on agricultural land let to tenant farmers.

Another area where APR and BPR interact is when **assets are replaced**. When looking at the reliefs in isolation, there is no requirement that the replacement property has to be the same as the original property, or even part of the same business. Similarly, there is no reason why agricultural property cannot be used to replace business property and vice versa. The issue in this case would be whether the ownership requirements have been satisfied. 6788

HMRC have issued **guidelines** which state that when a farming business is replaced by non-agricultural business property, the ownership period of the original property will be relevant in applying the minimum ownership period for BPR to the replacement property. RI 95

If a farming business replaces a non-farming business, but is not owned long enough to qualify for APR, BPR may still be available based on the ownership period of the non-farming business.

5. Woodlands

Woodlands are eligible for the following reliefs, depending on the circumstances: 6790

Type of woodlands	Reliefs
Surrounding farmland	APR
Commercial woodlands	BPR
Other woodlands	Woodlands relief

Specific relief

6792 s 125 IHTA 1984 An **election** can be made within 2 years of the date of death by the personal representatives, for the value of the trees and underwood (but not the land) to be left out of account when calculating the value of the death estate.

The **deceased** must have been beneficially entitled to the woodlands for at least 5 years before his death, or have received it as a gift or inheritance (i.e. not by acquisition for consideration).

An **IHT charge** will arise if the woodlands are subsequently sold or gifted, and will be calculated as if the woodlands had been included in the death estate, but using the nil band and tax rate applying at the time of the disposal. The amount liable to IHT will be the sale proceeds, or the value at the time of the gift, less the following expenses:
- disposal costs (including felling and removal of timber); and
- replanting expenses within 3 years of the disposal.

s 122 FA 2009 The **person liable** will be the vendor or donee respectively, and the tax must be paid within 6 months of the end of the month of the disposal.

The land must be **situated** in the EEA. Prior to 22 April 2009, the requirement was that the land was situated in the UK, the Channel Islands, or the Isle of Man.

MEMO POINTS If the **disposal itself is subject to IHT**, the woodlands charge will be deducted from the value of the transfer taken into account. So if woodlands valued at £70,000 are transferred into a discretionary trust (a chargeable lifetime transfer) and the IHT on the earlier disposal is £5,000, the amount of the CLT subject to IHT will be £65,000.

EXAMPLE Mr A died in March 2008. His estate, which he left to his son, included woodlands and an election was made. At the date of death, the trees were valued at £40,000, and the land on which they stood was valued at £100,000. The balance of the estate was valued at £200,000. Mr A's son sells the woodlands in June 2011 for £50,000, incurring costs of £4,000.
Mr A made a gross chargeable lifetime transfer of £60,000 in June 2007.
Inheritance tax on the death estate will be calculated as follows:

	£
Cumulative total brought forward	60,000
Estate (200,000 + 100,000)	300,000
	360,000
Tax thereon:	
£300,000 covered by nil rate band for 2007/08	
360,000 – 300,000 @ 40%	24,000

Inheritance tax on the sale of the woodlands will be calculated as follows:

	£
Chargeable amount (50,000 – 4,000)	46,000
Value of cumulative estate	360,000
	406,000
Tax thereon:	
£325,000 covered by nil rate band for 2011/12	
406,000 – 325,000 @ 40%	32,400

SECTION 3

Reliefs for falls in value

6795 A fall in the value of property that has been the subject of an IHT charge can give rise to two types of relief. The first relief arises where a lifetime transfer is made in the 7 years before the death of the taxpayer. The second relief relates to post-death sales.

A. Relief for falls in value of lifetime transfers

1. Conditions for relief

Where a transfer of value (whether chargeable or potentially exempt) is made within the 7 years before death, an IHT liability may arise on death. 6797 s 131 IHTA 1984

In the normal course of events, the death charge on lifetime transfers of value will be based on the actual value at the date of the transfer. However, a claim may be made to calculate the tax on death based on a lower value. With effect from 1 April 2011, such a claim must be made within 4 years of the date of death.

Time to value

The lower value will either be: 6798
- the open market value at the date of the transferor's death, where the property is still owned by the transferee; or
- the proceeds from an arm's length sale to an unconnected party, which occurs before the transferor's death.

Qualifying assets

All assets potentially qualify, **except** wasting assets, which are defined as assets: 6799
- with a predictable useful life of 50 years or less; or
- which qualify as tangible movable property, such as a motor car.

MEMO POINTS **Plant and machinery** will always be regarded as a wasting asset unless it is incorporated into the structure of a building, in which case it will be immovable property. s 132(2) IHTA 1984

2. Calculation of relief

Where a claim for relief is made, the IHT arising on the death of the transferor will be calculated based on the lower value. 6800

It should be noted that the relief cannot reduce the value at the date of transfer for the purposes of the cumulative total, nor result in a tax repayment.

The fall in value is **measured** by reference to the value in the hands of the transferee, regardless of the method of valuation used to calculate the loss to the transferor's estate (¶6465).

The following pro-forma sets out the effect of the relief:

Gross chargeable transfer	X
Less: Fall in value	(X)
Reduced value	X
IHT at death rate on reduced value	X
Less: IHT paid on lifetime transfer	(X)
Additional IHT due on death	X

Where the value of the original transfer is reduced by **business or agricultural property relief**, the market value at the lower value date is reduced by the same percentage before it is deducted from the original transfer. 6802 s 131(2A) IHTA 1984

EXAMPLE In May 2007 Mr A made a potentially exempt transfer to Mr B which was valued at £215,000 (after annual exemptions). In January 2002 Mr A had made other chargeable transfers of £150,000. In August 2011, Mr A made a potentially exempt transfer to Mr C of £125,000 (after annual exemptions). Mr A died in March 2012 at which time the property given to Mr B had fallen in value to £195,000 (after annual exemptions).

	Gross £	Tax £
IHT payable on death:		
May 2007 transfer		
Cumulative total brought forward	150,000	
Transfer to Mr B	215,000	8,000
	365,000	
Less: Fall in value (215,000 – 195,000)	(20,000)	
	345,000	8,000
Tax thereon:		
£325,000 covered by nil rate band for 2011/12		
345,000 – 325,000 @ 40% = 8,000		
Less: Taper relief (4 – 5 years) (8,000 @ 40%)		(3,200)
		4,800
August 2011 transfer		
Cumulative total brought forward	215,000	
Transfer to Mr C	125,000	6,000
	340,000	6,000
Tax thereon:		
£325,000 covered by nil rate band for 2011/12		
340,000 – 325,000 @ 40% = £6,000		

No IHT taper relief is available as the transfer was made less than 3 years before the date of death.

3. Special valuation rules

6804 Special valuation rules apply for purposes of ascertaining the **market value** at the relevant date of:
- shares;
- interests in land;
- leases; and
- other property, where some change has occurred.

Shares

6806 ss 133 - 135 IHTA 1984 Where shares are received by the transferee or his spouse, and an entitlement to a **capital payment** arises before the lower value date, the amount of the payment will be added to the market value of the shares, unless the market value already reflects the right to the payment.

Where the transferee or his spouse makes the **payment of a call** on the shares transferred before the relevant date, the market value of the shares will be reduced. Similarly, the market value will be reduced where the transferee or his spouse pays consideration in return for a **reorganisation of share capital** or other similar event. The exception in both cases is again where the market value already reflects the liability.

MEMO POINTS A **capital payment** is defined as a payment in money or money's worth, and not treated as income for the purposes of income tax.

6808 s 136 IHTA 1984 **Close company** Where the property transferred is shares in a close company (¶2100), the market value will be **adjusted** when, at any time between the original transfer and the lower value date, any of the following transactions occurs:
- a transfer of value by the company; or
- an alteration of the company's share or loan capital (other than quoted shares) or in any rights attaching to unquoted shares or debentures of the company.

For example, if the market value at the date of the original transfer would have decreased because of the change, the amount of the decrease is added back to the lower value, so that the fall in value used for the computation is purely the decrease caused by market forces.

Land

The **interest in, or the state of**, the land may change between the date of the original transfer and the lower value date, e.g. through loss of planning permission. **6810** s 137 IHTA 1984

In this case the market value at the lower value date must be adjusted by the difference between:
- the market value of the interest at the time of the original transfer; and
- what the market value would have been at the date of the original transfer if the changes had prevailed at that date.

For example, if the market value at the date of the original transfer would have decreased because of the change, the amount of the decrease is added back to the lower value, so that the fall in value used for the computation is purely the decrease caused by market forces.

Compensation received as a result of the change in the interest in, or the state of, the land will be ignored when performing the recalculation, but will be added to the market value at the lower value date.

Short leases

Where the claim relates to an interest in a lease with a **period of** 50 years or less to run at the date of the original transfer, the market value is increased by an amount equal to the result of the following formula: **6812** s 138 IHTA 1984

$$\text{Market value at the relevant date} \times \frac{P(1) - P(2)}{P(1)}$$

where, using the percentage tables given at ¶5705:
- P(1) is the percentage for the duration of the lease at the date of the original transfer; and
- P(2) is the percentage for the duration of the lease at the relevant date.

EXAMPLE Mr A gifted leasehold property, worth £60,000 with 30 years left to run, to his daughter - Miss B. Mr A then died 2 years later, when the lease was worth £50,000, and had 28 years left to run.

As the lease has reduced in value, relief will be claimed as follows:

Years left to run at date of transfer	30	Appropriate percentage P(1)	87.330
Years left to run at date of death	28	Appropriate percentage P(2)	85.053
Increase		(87.330 – 85.053)/ 87.330 × £60,000	£1,564
Value chargeable is		£50,000 + £1,564	£51,564

Relief should be claimed for the fall in value from £60,000 to £51,564.

Other property

An adjustment must be made to the valuation of other property, where the **asset has changed** in some respect between the date of the original transfer and the lower value date. **6813** s 139 IHTA 1984

The market value at the lower value date must be adjusted by the difference between:
- the market value of the interest at the time of the original transfer; and
- what the market value would have been at the date of the original transfer if the changes had prevailed at that date.

For example, if the market value at the date of the original transfer would have decreased because of the change, the amount of the decrease is added back to the lower value, so that the fall in value used for the computation is purely the decrease caused by market forces.

B. Relief for falls in value on post-death sales

6814 The following types of asset qualify for relief if a loss is made as a result of an arm's length sale within a specified period after death:
- listed securities or authorised unit trusts;
- land and buildings; and
- related property.

The relief is only available to the **person responsible for paying the IHT**. In most cases this will be either:
- the personal representatives of the estate; or
- the trustees of a trust in which the deceased had an interest in possession.

The relief will not therefore be available where the asset is transferred to a beneficiary who then sells it.

Relief is given by electing to calculate the IHT liability by substituting the gross proceeds of sale for the value on death. This adjusted value for IHT is used as the base cost of the asset for capital gains tax purposes (¶7264).

ss 189, 198 IHTA 1984

MEMO POINTS The **date** on which a sale or purchase arises is taken to be the date on which a contract is entered into. Where the sale or purchase results from the exercise of an option (granted not more than 6 months earlier for the purposes of land), the date of sale or purchase is taken to be the date on which the option was granted.

1. Listed securities and unit trusts

Scope

6816 s 179 IHTA 1984

Relief is available where listed securities (including shares) or authorised unit trusts (referred to here as listed securities) are **sold within** 12 months from the date of death, for less than the amount at which they were valued in the death estate.

6818 s 186A IHTA 1984

Where listed securities held on death are **cancelled** within 12 months from the date of death, the relief is also available providing the securities:
- have not been replaced; and
- are held at the date of cancellation by the person responsible for paying the IHT on them.

For the purposes of this relief the cancelled securities will be deemed to have been sold for a nominal consideration of £1.

6820 s 186B IHTA 1984

Relief is also available for listed securities which are **suspended** at the end of the 12 months following death, and are still held by the person responsible for paying the IHT. Where the value on suspension is less than the value at death, the shares will be deemed to have been sold immediately before the anniversary of the death for the lower value.

Calculation

6822 The **basic relief** is calculated by aggregating all of the sales (whether at a gain or loss) of listed securities made by the personal representatives or trustees within the period ending 12 months from the date of death. If the net result is a loss then relief will be the amount of that loss. Relief is not given for costs associated with the sale.

EXAMPLE Mr A died leaving an estate valued at £375,000 having made no lifetime transfers of value. At the date of death the estate included the following quoted shares:

1,000 B Plc	£50,000
1,500 C Plc	£80,000
2,000 D Plc	£25,000

A year later, the personal representatives of Mr A's estate had sold the B Plc shares for £24,000 and the D Plc shares for £45,000. The allowable relief will be calculated as follows:

	£
B Plc (50,000 – 24,000)	26,000
D Plc (25,000 – 45,000)	(20,000)
Relief for fall in value	6,000

The available relief will be restricted to take account of any **purchases of listed securities** made by the personal representatives or trustees within the period commencing with the date of death, and ending 2 months after the date of the last sale in the 12 months following death. With effect from 1 April 2011, a claim for relief must be made within 4 years of the end of the above period (i.e. 50 months after the date of the last sale described above). **6824**

The restriction is calculated as follows:

$$\text{Loss} \times \frac{\text{Purchase price of new securities}}{\text{Sale proceeds of securities held on death}}$$

EXAMPLE Mr A died in August 2011 leaving an estate valued at £400,000, having made no lifetime transfers of value. At the date of death the estate included the following quoted shares:

1,750 E Plc	£65,000
3,000 F Plc	£40,000
1,000 G Plc	£15,000

The personal representatives make the following transactions:

Shares	Date	Transaction	Amount (£)
3,000 F Plc	March 2012	Sale	22,000
500 G Plc	April 2012	Sale	10,000
500 E Plc	June 2012	Purchase	20,000
750 E Plc	July 2012	Purchase	25,000

The allowable relief will be calculated as follows:

	£	£
IHT on the death estate:		
£325,000 covered by nil rate band for 2011/12		
400,000 – 325,000 @ 40%		30,000
Less relief for fall in value:		
F Plc (40,000 – 22,000)	18,000	
G Plc ((15,000/2) – 10,000)	(2,500)	
	15,500	
Less: Restriction		
$15{,}500 \times \frac{20{,}000}{(22{,}000 + 10{,}000)}$	(9,688)	
Relief for fall in value	5,812	
IHT @ 40%		(2,325)
Net IHT due		27,675

Note: The purchase price of the shares acquired in July 2012 is ignored because the purchase occurred more than 2 months after the last sale.

Where purchases are made of **securities of the same class** and in the same company as those held on death, any loss arising will be apportioned so that only the loss relating to the shares held on death will be allowed for relief. **6826** s 185 IHTA 1984

The apportionment is calculated as follows:

$$\text{Loss} \times \frac{\text{Number of shares held on death}}{\text{Total number of shares}}$$

Valuation

The sale proceeds of listed securities will be increased to take account of any **capital payments** received (whether during or after the 12 month period) in respect of the listed securities contained in the estate. For these purposes a capital payment is any money or money's worth, which does not constitute income for the purposes of income tax. For **6828** s 181 IHTA 1984 example, an amount received for the sale of rights will increase the sales proceeds to the extent that it relates to listed securities included in the estate at death.

6830 s 182 IHTA 1984 The value of listed securities on death will be increased to take account of any **calls** made (whether during or after the 12 month period) in respect of listed securities:
- comprised in the estate at the date of death; and
- sold within the 12 month period by the person responsible for paying the IHT.

However, where the inclusion of the call amount in the death estate results in a loss on sale which exceeds the value of the death estate before the call was added, the amount of the call should not be included.

6832 s 184 IHTA 1984 Where listed securities which formed part of the estate on death are **exchanged for any other property** within 12 months from the date of death, the fall in value rules are amended. For these purposes, provided that the market value of the securities at the date of exchange is greater than the value at the date of death, they are treated as having been sold at their market value at the date of the exchange.

6834 s 183 IHTA 1984 As a general rule, where a **change in the holding** of listed securities occurs within the 12 months following death, the new holding is treated the same as the old holding. The types of change that are relevant are those due to reconstruction, amalgamation, reorganisation, conversion or exchange.

However, if the new holding is sold within the 12 month period following death, the value on death for the purposes of fall in value relief will be determined by the following formula:

$$\frac{Vs\,(H - S)}{(Vs + Vr)}$$

where:
- Vs is the sale value of the securities;
- Vr is the market value at the time of the sale of any of the new holding remaining unsold;
- H is the value on death of the new holding; and
- S is the value on death of any securities which originally formed part of the new holding but which have been sold on previous occasions.

MEMO POINTS The **value on death** of the **new holding** is taken to be the same as the value on death of the original holding plus any consideration which is given (or is liable to be given) in return for the change.

EXAMPLE Mr A died in June leaving an estate which contained 5,000 shares in A Ltd which had a value on death of £50,000.
In December A Ltd is taken over by B Ltd, who issues two B Ltd shares for every A Ltd share, so the estate contains 10,000 shares in B Ltd.
A couple of months later the executors sell 3,000 B Ltd shares for £12,000 when the value of the remaining 7,000 shares is £30,000.
The executors sell a further 2,000 shares 3 months later for £10,000 when the value of the remaining 5,000 shares is £20,000.

	£	£
1. Sale of 3,000 shares		
Value on death of shares sold:		
$12{,}000 \times \frac{(50{,}000 - \text{nil})}{(12{,}000 + 30{,}000)} =$	14,286	
Sale proceeds	(12,000)	
Fall in value		2,286
2. Sale of 2,000 shares		
Value on death of shares sold:		
$10{,}000 \times \frac{(50{,}000 - 14{,}286)}{(10{,}000 + 20{,}000)} =$	11,905	
Sale proceeds	(10,000)	
Fall in value		1,905
Total fall in value available for relief		4,191

2. Land and buildings

Scope

Relief is available where an interest in land which was included in the estate of the deceased is **sold within** 3 years from the date of death for less than the amount at which it was valued in the estate, providing the sale is not made to: **6836** s 191 IHTA 1984
- any person who since the date of death was beneficially entitled to the property or to an interest in possession in it;
- the spouse, child or remoter descendant of such a person; or
- trustees of a settlement in which such a person (or that person's spouse, children or remoter descendant) has an interest in possession.

With effect from 1 April 2011, a claim for relief must be made within 7 years of the date of death (i.e. within 4 years of the end of the 3 year period during which sales are taken into account).

MEMO POINTS An interest in land is not specifically **defined** by the legislation other than to say that it does not include any estate, interest or right by way of a mortgage or other security. The general understanding is therefore that an interest in land is any interest or estate in land and any buildings or structures on it, whether situated in the UK or abroad. s 190(1) IHTA 1984

Calculation

The **basic relief** is calculated by taking all of the sales (whether at a gain or loss) made by the same person in the same capacity within the period ending 3 years from death. In addition, **sales arising** in the 4th year after death which resulted in a loss will be deemed to have been made in the 3rd year. Such sales which result in a gain are ignored for these purposes. **6838** s 197A IHTA 1984

A **de minimis limit** applies so that all sales of land are ignored where the resulting gain or loss is less than the lower of: **6839** s 191(2) IHTA 1984
- £1,000; or
- 5% of the value on death.

EXAMPLE Mr A died in August 2011. His estate was valued at £400,000 which included the following interests in land:

Land	£
B	50,000
C	75,000
D	85,000
E	90,000

The personal representatives undertake the following transactions:

Land	Date of sale	Sale proceeds (£)
B	March 2012	60,000
C	May 2013	74,500
D	October 2014	50,000
E	July 2015	100,000

The allowable relief will be calculated as follows:

		£		£
Tax on the death estate				
£325,000 covered by nil rate band for 2011/12				
400,000 – 325,000 @ 40%				30,000
Less: Relief for fall in value				
B	(50,000 – 60,000)	(10,000)		
C	(75,000 – 74,500)	–	(i)	
D	(85,000 – 50,000)	35,000		
E	(90,000 – 100,000)	–	(ii)	
Relief for fall in value		25,000		
IHT @ 40%				(10,000)
Net IHT due				20,000

Note:
(i) The fall in value of Land C is less than the de minimis limit.
(ii) The sale of Land E resulted in a gain in the 4th year from death, and so is ignored.

6840 The available relief is restricted to take account of any **purchases of land**, made by the same person in the same capacity, in the period commencing with the date of death and ending 4 months after the last sale of land in the 3 year period.

The restriction is calculated as follows:

$$\text{Loss} \times \frac{\text{Purchase price of new land}}{\text{Sale proceeds of land held on death}}$$

EXAMPLE Mr A died in December 2010. His estate was valued at £500,000 which included the following interests in land:

Land	**£**
B	45,000
C	60,000

The personal representatives undertake the following transactions:

Land	**Date of sale**	**Sale proceeds (£)**
B	March 2012	55,000
C	June 2014	35,000

In addition, the personal representatives acquire Land D in June 2012 for £50,000 and Land E in July 2014 for £70,000.
The relief for fall in value will be calculated as follows:

B	(45,000 – 55,000)	(10,000)
C	(60,000 – 35,000)	25,000
		15,000
Less: Restriction:		
$15{,}000 \times \frac{50{,}000}{(55{,}000 + 35{,}000)}$		(8,333)
Relief for fall in value		6,667

Note:
1. The purchase price of the land acquired in July 2014 is ignored because the purchase occurred more than 4 months after the last sale in the 3 year period.
2. The sale in June 2014 is not relevant in determining the date of the last sale because it occurred in the 4th year.

Valuation

6842 The **sale price** of an interest in land which has been the subject of a fall in value claim will be adjusted to take into account the following factors:
a. changes between death and sale;
b. compulsory acquisition;
c. other interests in the same or other land; and
d. transfers to beneficiaries.

In addition, short leases have special rules.

6844
s 193 IHTA 1984

Changes between death and sale Where there is a change in the interest in, or the state of, the land between the date of death and the subsequent sale, the value on death must be recalculated to take account of what it would have been if the changes had prevailed at that date. For example, where planning permission has been withdrawn, the value on death would be reduced, and so the fall in value is adjusted so that the decrease relating to the change is not taken into account.

Compensation received as a result of the change in the interest in, or the state of, the land will be ignored when recalculating the value on death but will be added to the sale price.

Compulsory acquisition Where a compulsory acquisition **notice** is served by an appropriate authority, either before death or within the 3 years after death, then, if the land is actually acquired within 6 years after death, the fall in value provisions apply as normal. **6846** s 197 IHTA 1984

Other interests Where an interest in land was **valued on death in conjunction** with other interests (whether in the same or other land), the sale price will be increased to take account of the difference between: **6848** s 195 IHTA 1984
- the original value on death; and
- what the value on death would have been if the interest had been valued independently.

Transfers to beneficiaries Once all of the other adjustments to sale price referred to above have been made, a further adjustment will be required to take account of transfers made to beneficiaries. The adjustment will be required where the personal representative (or trustee): **6850** s 196 IHTA 1984
a. transfers an interest in land (whether by sale or exchange);
b. within 3 years from the date of death (transactions in the 4th year are ignored for these purposes);
c. to a beneficiary or person connected to him as described in ¶6384; and
d. for a sale price (or, if the transfer was an exchange, the market value) in excess of the value on death.

The adjustment takes the form of an addition to the sale price of the land which is subject to the fall in value claim. Where **only one interest in land** is the subject of the claim, the excess of sale price (or market value) over the value on death will be added to the sale proceeds of that interest.

Where **more than one interest in land** is the subject of the claim, each interest is adjusted separately using the fraction:

$$\frac{A}{B}$$

where:
- A is the value on death of the individual interest in land, less the sale price of the individual interest in land as adjusted; and
- B is the aggregate of A and all the corresponding differences for all of the other interests to which the claim relates. These amounts are aggregated irrespective of whether they are positive or negative.

EXAMPLE Mr A died in July 2011 leaving an estate valued at £500,000 which included the following interests in land:

Land	**£**
B	80,000
C	85,000
D	90,000

The personal representatives undertake the following transactions:

Land	**Date of sale**	**Sale proceeds (£)**
B	August 2012	55,000
C	June 2014	95,000

In addition, the personal representatives transfer Land D to one of the beneficiaries at a cost of £102,000. The relief for fall in value will be calculated as follows:

	£	**£**
Tax on the death estate:		
£325,000 covered by nil rate band for 2011/12		
500,000 – 325,000 @ 40%		70,000

Less: Relief for fall in value

Land	**Value on death**	**Sale price**	**Difference**
B	80,000	55,000	25,000
C	85,000	95,000	(10,000)
	165,000	150,000	15,000
D	90,000	102,000	12,000

Sale prices for Land B and C must be adjusted to take account of the transfer to a beneficiary:

B 55,000 + ($\frac{25,000}{25,000 + 10,000}$ × 12,000) =		63,571
C 95,000 + ($\frac{10,000}{10,000 + 25,000}$ × 12,000) =		98,429
		162,000
Value on death		(165,000)
Relief for fall in value		(3,000)
IHT @ 40%		(1,200)
Net IHT due		68,800

6852 s 194 IHTA 1984 **Short leases** Where the claim relates to an interest in a **lease with 50 years or less left to run** at the date of death, the sale price for the purposes of a fall in value claim is increased by an amount equal to the result of the following formula:

$$\text{Value on death} \times \frac{P(1) - P(2)}{P(1)}$$

where, using the percentage tables given at ¶5705:
- P(1) is the percentage for the duration of the lease at the date of death; and
- P(2) is the percentage for the duration of the lease at the date of sale.

3. Related property

6854 s 176 IHTA 1984 Relief is available for property which was valued at the date of death using the related property rules (¶6476), but was subsequently sold separately from the property to which it was related.

Conditions

6855 The conditions for relief are that the **sale** must:
- take place within the 3 years following death;
- be to an unconnected purchaser in an arm's length transaction; and
- be for proceeds which are less than the value of the property on death under the related property rules.

A claim may also be submitted where the valuation on death was made in conjunction with other property in the estate that has not at any time since the death been vested in the vendors. An example of this would be where the free estate contained shares in an unquoted company, valued on death in conjunction with shares held in a trust in which the deceased had an interest in possession.

As an exception, relief will not be available where the property concerned is shares in (or securities of) a **close company** (¶6990) where, at any time between the date of death and the date of sale, the value of the shares or securities is reduced by more than 5% as a result of an alteration (including cancellation) of:
- the company's share or loan capital; or
- rights attaching to the shares in, or securities of, the company.

Calculation

6856 Relief is calculated by determining what the value of the property would have been on death if the related property rules had not been implemented. IHT is then recalculated using the new valuation. The **proceeds** of sale are irrelevant for this purpose.

EXAMPLE Mr A died in June 2011 leaving an estate valued at £375,000 to his son. Included within the estate were 2,000 shares in B Ltd. Mr A's wife owned 3,000 shares in the same company. At the date of death the following share values were agreed:

2,000 shares	£20,000
5,000 shares	£75,000

The personal representatives sell the 2,000 shares to an unconnected buyer in December 2011 for £15,000.
IHT will be recalculated as follows:

	£	£
Tax on the death estate:		
£325,000 covered by nil rate band for 2011/12		
375,000 – 325,000 @ 40%		20,000
Less: Related property relief		
Value at death		
($\frac{2,000}{5,000}$ × 75,000)	30,000	
Less: Unrelated value for 2,000 shares	(20,000)	
Relief for fall in value	10,000	
IHT @ 40%		(4,000)
Net IHT due		16,000

SECTION 4

Quick succession relief

Quick succession relief (QSR) is available to relieve the inequity that would arise where IHT is paid (or becomes payable) on a transfer, and the subsequent death of the transferee results in a further IHT charge within a relatively short space of time. The extent of the relief, which reduces the IHT liability on the second transfer, is dependent on the amount of time between the transfers. The benefit of the relief is spread across the estate, including settled and non-settled property. 6865

Conditions

QSR for **non-settled property** on death will be available where: 6867 s 141(1) IHTA 1984
– a chargeable transfer to the deceased was made not more than 5 years before the death; and
– a further charge arises as a result of the transfer on death.
It is not necessary for the same property to be in the estate at the time of death, as this relief relates to the increase in value of an individual's estate, rather than to a particular asset.

Relief will be available for **settled property** regardless of whether the second transfer was made on death, providing the following conditions are satisfied: 6870 s 141(2) IHTA 1984
– the transferor is entitled to an interest in possession (¶6386) in the property that is being transferred;
– both of the transfers were of the same property; and
– the first transfer occurred as a result of the creation of the settlement or a termination of an interest in possession.

EXAMPLE A life interest settlement was created in January 2006. The life interest terminated in January 2008 creating a potentially exempt transfer. The life tenant dies within 7 years. QSR is available for the January 2008 transfer.

Calculation

6872 The tax payable on the later transfer will be reduced by the following formula:

$$\text{Percentage} \times \frac{(\text{Value transferred in first transfer} - \text{Tax on first transfer})}{\text{Value transferred in first transfer}} \times \text{Tax on first transfer}$$

Depending on the period of time between the original transfer and the death of the transferee, the **percentage** will be as follows:

Period of time between transfers	Percentage
1 year or less	100%
More than 1 year but not more than 2 years	80%
More than 2 years but not more than 3 years	60%
More than 3 years but not more than 4 years	40%
More than 4 years but not more than 5 years	20%

MEMO POINTS Where the first transfer was a potentially exempt transfer (¶6550), the date on which the transfer became liable to tax (i.e. the death of the transferor within 7 years of the transfer) is not relevant.

EXAMPLE

1. **Transferor dies before transferee.**
On 1 June 2007, Mr A gave £250,000 to Mr B, who agreed to bear any tax liability. Mr A's only other chargeable transfer was £100,000 in 2006/07 although he made transfers up to the value of his annual exemption every year. He died on 10 August 2010.
Mr B died on 15 October 2011 having made no chargeable lifetime transfers. His estate, valued at £475,000, is left to his nephew Mr C.

	Gross £	Tax £
June 2007 – Mr A: first transfer:		
Cumulative total brought forward	100,000	Nil
Gift to Mr B	250,000	10,000
	350,000	10,000
Tax thereon:		
£325,000 covered by nil rate band for 2010/11		
350,000 – 325,000 @ 40% = 10,000		
Taper relief (3 – 4 years) (10,000 @ 20%)		(2,000)
IHT payable		8,000
October 2011 – Mr B: second transfer:		
Cumulative total brought forward	-	-
Value of Mr B's estate	475,000	60,000
	475,000	60,000
Tax thereon:		
£325,000 covered by nil rate band for 2011/12		
475,000 – 325,000 @ 40% = 60,000		
Quick succession relief (4 – 5 years) $20\% \times \frac{(250{,}000 - 8{,}000)}{250{,}000} \times 8{,}000$		(1,549)
IHT payable		58,451

2. **Transferee dies before transferor.**
On 1 June 2007, Mrs D gave £250,000 to Mrs E, who agreed to bear any tax liability. Mrs D's only other chargeable transfer was £100,000 in 2006/07 although she made transfers up to the value of her annual exemption every year. She died on 10 August 2011.
Mrs E died on 15 October 2010 having made no chargeable lifetime transfers. Her estate, valued at £475,000, is left to her niece Miss F.

	Gross £	Tax £
June 2007 – Mrs D: first transfer:		
Cumulative total brought forward	100,000	Nil
Gift to Mrs E	250,000	10,000
	350,000	10,000
Tax thereon: £325,000 covered by nil rate band for 2011/12 350,000 – 325,000 @ 40% = 10,000		
Taper relief (4 – 5 years) (10,000 @ 40%)		(4,000)
IHT payable		6,000
October 2010 – Mrs E: second transfer:		
Cumulative total brought forward		-
Value of Mrs E's estate	475,000	60,000
	475,000	60,000
Tax initially payable: £325,000 covered by nil rate band for 2010/11 475,000 – 325,000 @ 40% = 60,000		
Refund after Mrs D's death, in respect of quick succession relief (3 – 4 years) $40\% \times \frac{(250,000 - 6,000)}{250,000} \times 6,000$		2,342

In the unusual situation where three transfers occur as a result of **three successive deaths** in a 5 year period, special rules apply to ensure that the appropriate amount of QSR is given on the third transfer. The relief on the second transfer is calculated in the normal way but the calculation of the relief for the third transfer is based on the tax from the second transfer before any relief is given. 6874

EXAMPLE Mr A died on 1 January 2008 leaving his estate of £320,000 to his brother Mr B.
Mr B died on 1 March 2009 leaving an estate of £440,000 to his son Mr C.
Mr C died on 1 May 2011 leaving an estate of £500,000 to his cousin Miss D. None of them made any lifetime transfers of value.

	Gross £	Tax £
January 2008 – Mr A: first transfer		
Transfer on death	320,000	
Tax thereon: £300,000 covered by nil rate band for 2007/08 320,000 – 300,000 @ 40%		8,000
IHT payable		8,000
March 2009 – Mr B: second transfer		
Transfer on death	440,000	
Tax thereon: £312,000 covered by nil rate band for 2008/09 440,000 – 312,000 @ 40%		51,200
Quick succession relief (1 – 2 years) $80\% \times \frac{(320,000 - 8,000)}{320,000} \times 8,000 =$		(6,240)
IHT payable		44,960

May 2011 – Mr C: third transfer

Transfer on death	500,000	
Tax thereon:		
£325,000 covered by nil rate band for 2011/12		
500,000 – 325,000 @ 40%		70,000
Quick succession relief (2 – 3 years)		
$60\% \times \frac{(500{,}000 - 51{,}200)}{500{,}000} \times 51{,}200 =$		(27,574)
IHT payable		42,426

Settled property and multiple transfers

6876 It is possible for settled property (but not non-settled property) to be the subject of more than one later transfer. As a result, any **QSR not used up** by the first subsequent transfer can be used by any later transfer(s). An example of this situation would be where an individual is bequeathed a life interest, and he later releases a proportion of it resulting in an IHT charge. The IHT on the original bequest is apportioned in accordance with the value of the property released, before the quick succession percentage is applied.

EXAMPLE In June 2007 Mr A died and bequeathed property worth £100,000 to Mr B for life, giving rise to an IHT liability of £25,000. In August 2009 Mr B released his interest in £45,000 of the property to be held on a discretionary trust. Tax of £15,000 became due. In March 2011 Mr B released a further £20,000 to a different discretionary trust and tax of £8,000 became due. QSR will be available as follows.

	Tax £
August 2009 – Release of £45,000	
Tax due	15,000
Quick succession relief:	
$\frac{45{,}000}{100{,}000} \times \frac{100{,}000 - 25{,}000}{100{,}000} \times 25{,}000 = 8{,}438$	
Percentage for 2 – 3 years	
8,438 @ 60%	(5,063)
Adjusted liability	9,937
March 2011 – Release of £20,000	
Tax due	8,000
Quick succession relief:	
$\frac{20{,}000}{100{,}000} \times \frac{100{,}000 - 25{,}000}{100{,}000} \times 25{,}000 = 3{,}750$ (i)	
Percentage for 3 – 4 years	
3,750 @ 40%	(1,500)
Adjusted liability	6,500
Remaining tax available for relief:	
25,000 – (8,438 + 3,750)	12,812

Note:
(i) This figure would be restricted to a maximum of £20,000 – £8,438 = £11,562.

CHAPTER 6

Overseas issues

OUTLINE ¶¶

Inheritance tax (IHT) is charged on all chargeable transfers made by individuals domiciled in the UK, regardless of the location of the property. Property located overseas may therefore be exposed to a double charge to tax. In this case relief may be available in the form of: **6890**
- a double taxation agreement between the UK and the other country; or
- the UK unilateral tax relief provisions.

Further information on domicile for IHT purposes and on the location of assets is given at ¶6380 and ¶6388 respectively.

SECTION 1

Double taxation agreements

The **specific provisions** of each double taxation agreement must be studied carefully to determine the extent to which relief is given. Most agreements have been in existence for many years and therefore pre-date IHT, which came into force in 1986. For this reason, provisions in agreements relating to estate duty are extended to capital transfer tax and to IHT payable on death (but not on lifetime transfers). Similarly, provisions relating to capital transfer tax are extended to IHT payable on both chargeable lifetime transfers and on death. **6895**

Taxing rights

Under the terms of a double taxation agreement, the country in which the transferor is **domiciled** is usually entitled to tax all property owned by him. The other country usually only has the right to tax property located within its borders. The provisions of the treaty will override the general rules on the location of property, and property may be excluded property (¶6456) for UK IHT purposes. **6896**

Even where a double tax agreement is relevant, **unilateral relief** may result in a lower UK IHT liability.

Countries covered

6898 IHTM 27161 s 158 IHTA 1984 The agreements shown in the following table are currently in force:

Agreements applicable to lifetime and death transfers		Agreements applicable only to death transfers	
Country	SI	Country	SI
Eire	1978/1107	France	1963/1319[1]
South Africa	1979/576	India	1956/998
Sweden	1981/840	Italy	1968/304
USA	1979/1454	Netherlands	1980/706
		Pakistan	1957/1522
		Switzerland	1994/3214

[1] A new treaty for income tax, CGT and corporation tax has been negotiated with France, but it currently does not extend to IHT.

MEMO POINTS Not all the countries with which there are double taxation agreements will have civil partnership legislation. Consequently, civil partners may not have the same rights as spouses in those jurisdictions, which may affect a claim under the relevant agreement.

SECTION 2

Unilateral relief

6905 s 159 IHTA 1984 Unilateral relief (also known as double tax relief) takes the form of a credit for the foreign tax suffered against the UK IHT liability.

Scope

6906 Unilateral relief is given where an **overseas territory** has imposed a charge to tax payable on the value of property which has been the subject of a disposition, providing:

a. the overseas tax is:
- of a similar character to UK IHT; or
- chargeable on, or by reference to, death or lifetime gifts; and

b. UK IHT is also chargeable on the value of the property as a result of the same event.

As unilateral relief is an adjustment to the UK IHT due, the transfer is still chargeable and the gross amount must be included in the cumulative total in the normal way (¶6512).

6907 The **amount of credit** given for overseas tax suffered depends on whether the property is situated in:
- the overseas territory only;
- both the UK and the overseas territory; or
- neither the UK nor the overseas territory.

Property situated in overseas territory only

6910 Where the property is situated in the overseas territory and not the UK, credit is given for the whole amount of the overseas tax suffered subject to an **overall maximum** equal to the UK IHT liability.

EXAMPLE Mr A owned shares located in an overseas territory which he gifted to his daughter in October 2007, when the value of the transfer was £400,000 (a potentially exempt transfer). Mr A suffered £15,000 of local tax on the gift and made no other lifetime transfers of value before his death in August 2011.

The charge on death will be as follows:

		£	£
October 2007 transfer			400,000
Less: Annual exemption –	2007/08	3,000	
	2006/07	3,000	
			(6,000)
			394,000
Tax thereon:			
£325,000 covered by nil rate band for 2011/12			
394,000 – 325,000 @ 40%			27,600
Less: Taper relief at 20%			(5,520)
			22,080
Unilateral relief			(15,000)
UK IHT liability			7,080

Property situated in both the UK and the overseas territory

Where the property is treated as being situated in both the UK and the overseas territory, the credit for overseas tax is given in accordance with the following formula: 6912

$$\frac{\text{UK IHT}}{\text{UK IHT} + \text{overseas tax}} \times \text{the smaller of UK IHT or overseas tax}$$

EXAMPLE Following on from the previous example, if the shares had also been regarded as situated in the UK, the charge on death would be as follows:

	£
Chargeable transfer (as above)	394,000
Tax thereon:	
£325,000 covered by nil rate band for 2011/12	
394,000 – 325,000 @ 40%	27,600
Less: Taper relief at 20%	(5,520)
	22,080
Unilateral relief $\frac{22{,}080}{22{,}080 + 15{,}000} \times 15{,}000$	(8,932)
UK IHT liability	13,148

Where the property is treated as being situated both in the UK and **more than one overseas territory**, the formula for unilateral relief becomes: 6914

$$\frac{\text{UK IHT}}{\text{UK IHT} + \text{the aggregate of overseas taxes}} \times \text{the smaller of UK IHT or the aggregate of overseas taxes}$$

Property situated in neither the UK nor the overseas territory

The same provisions apply as for property situated in both the UK and the overseas territory. 6916

CHAPTER 7

Anti-avoidance measures

OUTLINE ¶¶

Anti-avoidance provisions seek to **prevent exploitation** of potentially exempt transfers (PETs), in particular where taxpayers give property away in a series of connected operations (known as associated operations), or where property is gifted but the transferor reserves a benefit. Since 6 April 2005, an income tax charge may also be levied where IHT is successfully avoided, and the donor still enjoys assets previously owned by him. 6920

In addition, some liabilities will not be allowed in the death estate where it can be shown that the debt is derived from property originally belonging to the transferor.

In some circumstances anti-avoidance measures are also used to 'look through' transfers of value made by close companies, by deeming them to have been made by the participators in the company.

SECTION 1

Associated operations

The principle of associated operations was introduced to prevent taxpayers splitting transfers into a series of transactions, the sum of which was less than the total value transferred. An 6925 example would be where a man, who owns a 51% shareholding which he wishes to give to his son, sells 2% to a third party before giving his son the remaining 49% (now worth significantly less than a controlling holding). After the gift the son then buys back the remaining 2% to complete the transfer. This is a series of clearly related operations with the aim of reducing the amount of IHT due.

Definition

6927 s 268 IHTA 1984 Whether a series of transactions constitutes associated operations depends on the facts of the case, but the legislation attempts to identify the **key elements**. An associated operation is therefore defined as any two or more operations of any kind which:
– affect the same property; or
– are effected by reference to one another.

MEMO POINTS 1. The term **operation** is not defined other than to say that it can include an omission.
2. The operations may be **effected by** the same or different persons and may **occur at** different times.

EXAMPLE
1. Mr A owns two statues which together are worth £80,000, but alone are worth only £30,000 each. Mr A sells one statue for £30,000 to Mr B and in a later transaction the other statue is also sold for £30,000 to Mr B.
As a result of the sale, Mr A's estate has fallen in value by £20,000, as he has received cash of only £60,000 in return for the pair of statues worth £80,000.
HMRC would be able to treat the transactions as associated and tax the £20,000 fall in value, assuming there was gratuitous intent by Mr A.

2. A taxpayer made separate transfers of shares in the same company into five different settlements over a 35 day period. HMRC contended that the five settlements should be treated as one for the purposes of calculating periodic charges. It was held, however, that the associated operations rules did not apply, because each transfer was a disposition of property into a settlement, which was separately subject to the inheritance tax settlements provisions. *Rysaffe Trustee Co (CI) v IRC* [2003]

6928 A **lease** granted at full consideration will not be associated with any operation occurring more than 3 years after the grant.

EXAMPLE Mr A grants a lease to his son at full consideration out of a freehold interest worth £300,000. As the property is now subject to a lease, the freehold value is reduced to £200,000.
If Mr A transfers the freehold to his son 2 years after the grant of the lease, the unencumbered value of the freehold of £300,000 will be chargeable to IHT as a PET.
If he transfers the freehold to his son more than 3 years after the grant of the lease, the value of the PET will be £200,000.

Operations at different times

6929 A transfer of value made by associated operations carried out at different times will be **treated** as having been made on the date of the last of them. The value of the transfer is reduced by the amount of any earlier operations which were transfers of value.

EXAMPLE Mr A owned four antique chairs worth £80,000 as a set. He made four separate transfers to his daughter of one chair a year at a value of £15,000 each.
The value transferred by the last transfer is deemed to be:
80,000 – (3 × 15,000) = £35,000

6931 The exception to this rule is where the earlier transfers of value were **exempt transfers between spouses**, in which case the earlier transfers are not deducted.

MEMO POINTS HMRC may seek to apply the associated operations rule where there is **blatant avoidance of IHT** using the spouse exemption, such as where a husband makes a transfer to his wife on condition that she makes a further transfer to others.

EXAMPLE Following on from the previous example, if Mr A had transferred two of the chairs to his wife (who then transferred them to the daughter) and then two directly to his daughter at a value of £15,000 each, the value transferred by the last transfer would be:
80,000 − 15,000 = £65,000

Where the value of an earlier transfer is reduced **by other exemptions** such as the annual exemption, the benefit is not lost if the transfers are later deemed to be associated. 6933

EXAMPLE Mr A made four annual gifts to his son each made up of 10% of his holding in B Ltd. Each individual transfer was worth £7,500 but the value of the total transfer was £40,000. Mr A made no other transfers of value. The value of each of the first three transfers would be:

	£
Transfer	7,500
Annual exemption	(3,000)
	4,500

The value transferred by the last transfer would be:
40,000 − (7,500 × 3) = £17,500

SECTION 2

Gifts with reservation

The gift with reservation rules apply where the transferor attempts to take advantage of the potential exemption for transfers to individuals, by retaining some interest or benefit in the property being transferred, with a view to surviving 7 years from the date of the transfer. For example, the transfer of a house by a parent to a child would be a potentially exempt transfer, which would be free from tax if the parent survived for 7 years. If the parent continues to live in the property, the transfer will be a gift with reservation and subject to these anti-avoidance rules. 6935

In certain cases, IHT planning may enable these rules to be circumvented, in which case an income tax charge may arise under the pre-owned asset provisions (¶3968).

Definition

A gift with reservation **arises** where an individual makes a gift of any property and either: 6937 s 102(1) FA 1986
– full possession or enjoyment is not given to the transferee at or before the relevant period; or
– the transferor is not excluded from enjoying the property, or receiving a benefit from it, at some time during the relevant period.

The rules will not apply when the taxpayer merely makes a bad bargain and has no gratuitous intent.

MEMO POINTS 1. A **gift** may be of property owned outright, or of settled property in which the individual had an interest in possession which was terminated on or after 22 March 2006 during the individual's lifetime, if the interest was created: s 102ZA FA 1986 Sch 20 paras 6(1)(c), 7 FA 1986
– before 22 March 2006; or
– on or after 22 March 2006 and was an immediate post-death interest, transitional serial interest (¶7178), or an interest in a disabled trust (¶7190).
2. A **benefit** to the transferor would include one which was obtained through a series of associated operations, one of which was the gift of the property concerned.
3. For these purposes, the **relevant period** is the period of 7 years ending on the date of the transferor's death or, if shorter, the period from the date of the gift to the date of death.
4. A gift under an **insurance policy** on the life of the transferor (or his spouse or in their joint names) will be a gift with reservation, if the benefits that may accrue to the transferee vary by reference to benefits accruing to the transferor and/or his spouse under that or another policy.

EXAMPLE

1. In May 2003, A gave B a painting which remained in A's house until March 2006. If A dies before March 2013, the gift with reservation rules will apply.

2. C takes out life policies to cover his own and his daughter's lives. The cover for the daughter is reduced for all amounts that C receives in relation to his own policy, and so C has reserved a benefit.

Transactions not subject to the rules

6940 s 102(5) FA 1986

The gift with reservation rules do not apply to a disposal by way of one of the following exempt transfers (see ¶6426 onwards):
- transfers between spouses;
- small gifts;
- gifts in consideration of marriage;
- gifts to UK charities;
- gifts to political parties;
- gifts to housing associations;
- gifts for national purposes;
- transfers to maintenance funds for historic buildings; and
- transfers to employee trusts.

6942 Sch 20 para 6(1)(a) FA 1986

The gift of land or a chattel which the transferor continues to occupy or otherwise enjoy will not be considered to be a gift with reservation where full **consideration** for its use is made in money or money's worth.

1. Specific rules for certain property

6944 Special rules apply with respect to the application of the gift with reservation provisions to land and settled property.

Land

6946 In the case of *Ingram v IRC* [1999] it was held that an **interest** (lease) retained out of gifted freehold land did not constitute a gift with reservation, because the property that was gifted, the freehold, and the leasehold that was retained, were distinct from one another.

s 102A FA 1986

Immediately after this decision, measures were introduced (effective from 8 March 1999) to ensure that the gift with reservation rules would apply to similar transactions. If the donor or his spouse enjoys a significant right or interest over gifted land, or is party to a significant arrangement in relation to the land, the interest disposed of will be treated as a gift with reservation.

MEMO POINTS 1. For these purposes a right, interest or arrangement is deemed to be **significant** if it entitles or enables the transferor to occupy all or part of the land, or to enjoy some right in relation to all or part of the land.
2. A right, interest or arrangement is **not significant** if:
– it does not, or cannot, prevent the enjoyment of the land to the entire exclusion (or virtually the entire exclusion) of the transferor;
– it does not entitle the transferor to occupy all or part of the land immediately after the gift (but would do so if it were not for the interest gifted); or
– it was granted or acquired more than 7 years before the date of the gift.

6947 Sch 20 para 6(1)(b) FA 1986

Occupation of the whole or part of a piece of land which has been the subject of a gift will not be a gift with reservation where all of the following are satisfied with respect to the occupation:
a. it results from a change of circumstances of the transferor since the time of the gift which was unforeseen, and not brought about by the transferor to take account of this provision;
b. it arises at a time when the transferor has become unable to maintain himself through age, infirmity or otherwise;

c. it represents a reasonable provision by the transferee for the care and maintenance of the transferor; and
d. the transferee is a relative of the transferor or his spouse.

The gift of an **undivided share in land** will also be treated as a gift with reservation unless either: 6948 s 102B FA 1986
- the transferor does not occupy the property;
- the transferor occupies the land to the exclusion of the transferee in return for full consideration in money or money's worth; or
- the transferor and transferee occupy the land and the transferor does not receive any benefit (other than a negligible one by or at the transferee's expense) in connection with the gift.

Settled property

Where a transferor makes a gift into a trust the application of the gift with reservation rules will depend on the nature of the reservation. 6950

Taking the strict interpretation of the legislation, the reservation of a benefit for the **transferor's spouse** is not a gift with reservation. In practical terms, however, if the transferor makes a gift of property but reserves a benefit for his spouse and then shares the enjoyment or benefit of the property without paying for it, he is likely to be deemed to have reserved a benefit for himself.

Interest in possession trusts The retention of an interest in possession in the **whole fund** is not a transfer of value for IHT purposes, and is not therefore relevant to these provisions, where the interest was created: 6951
- before 22 March 2006; or
- on or after 22 March 2006, and where it was an immediate post-death interest, transitional serial interest (¶7178), or an interest in a disabled trust (¶7190).

The retention by the transferor of an interest in possession in **part of the fund** will generally be a gift with reservation for the part retained, providing it is identifiable from the rest of the fund. However, the retention of a **reversionary interest** in the trust will not be a gift with reservation providing there is no present interest in the fund.

Similarly, where the transferor appoints himself as a **trustee**, he will not generally be treated as having reserved a benefit unless he is among the beneficiaries of the trust.

Discretionary trusts Where the transferor is a **beneficiary** of a discretionary trust, he will be treated as having reserved a benefit in the whole value of the fund, unless it can be shown that he has previously been excluded from the class of beneficiaries. 6952

2. Application of the provision

Where a transfer falls within the definition of a gift with reservation, there are IHT implications both on making the gift and on the death of the transferor within 7 years, or on the removal of the reservation. 6954

On the **date of making a gift** with reservation, a chargeable lifetime transfer or potentially exempt transfer will arise as if this were a transfer of value.

If, immediately before the **death of the transferor**, there is any property over which he has reserved a benefit, then the transferor will be deemed to be beneficially entitled to that property and it will form part of his death estate (¶6580). In this way, the value of the asset is not frozen at the time of the original transfer. 6956

If the **reservation of benefit is removed or lifted** before the death of the transferor, then a further potentially exempt transfer will arise based on the value of the property at that date, and will be subject to IHT if the transferor dies within 7 years. If the transferor survives for 7 years following the date when the reservation is removed, then no IHT liability will arise.

3. Calculation of tax

6958 SI 1987/1130 **Double charges relief** applies to ensure that the same property is only taxed once. The basis of the relief is that tax should be charged on whichever transfer would yield the greater amount of tax, and the other transfer will be ignored.

Death of the transferor

6960 On the death of the transferor, tax should be calculated for both the original transfer and the death estate, each **on the assumption** that the other transfer had not been made.

Credit will be given for any lifetime tax already charged, but for the calculation of the tax on the death estate, the tax credited may not exceed tax due on that property.

Both calculations must take account of the brought forward cumulative balance and any lifetime exemptions.

MEMO POINTS If both calculations yield the **same amount of tax**, the first calculation (i.e. the original transfer) is applied.

EXAMPLE In August 2008 Mr A gave a house to his daughter, B, but continued to live there. At the date of the transfer, the house was worth £225,000 and constituted a gift with reservation of benefit. Mr A dies in January 2012 when the house is worth £300,000. The remainder of his estate, which he leaves to his son, C, is valued at £275,000. Mr A made an earlier gross chargeable transfer of £175,000 in March 2004.

On the death of Mr A two calculations will be made:

1. **Calculation 1**: Assume house is part of death estate and ignore potentially exempt transfer.

	£
Cumulative total brought forward	–
Death estate (300,000 + 275,000)	575,000
	575,000
Tax thereon:	
£325,000 covered by nil rate band for 2011/12	
575,000 – 325,000 @ 40%	100,000

2. **Calculation 2**: Charge potentially exempt transfer separately.

		£	£	£
Lifetime transfer:				
Cumulative total brought forward			175,000	
August 2008 transfer		225,000		
Less: Annual exemption –	2008/09	(3,000)		
	2007/08	(3,000)		
			219,000	
			394,000	
Tax thereon:				
£325,000 covered by nil rate band for 2011/12				
394,000 – 325,000 @ 40%				27,600
Less: Taper relief @ 20%				(5,520)
				22,080
Death estate:				
Cumulative total brought forward			219,000	
Death estate			275,000	
			494,000	
Tax thereon:				
£325,000 covered by nil rate band for 2011/12				
494,000 – 325,000 @ 40%				67,600
Total tax due				89,680

Calculation 1. yields greater tax and will therefore be deemed to apply.

Lifting of the reservation

When a reservation of benefit is lifted before the death of the transferor, then if the **period** between the date of lifting and the date of death is: 6962
– more than 7 years, the transfer will not be chargeable to tax; or
– 7 years or less, the transfer will be deemed to be a potentially exempt transfer (regardless of the status of the original transfer), and double charges relief will apply.
Where chargeable, IHT would potentially be levied on both the original transfer and the lifting of the reservation. In this case, **each transfer** will be taxed as if the other transfer had not occurred, and the one which results in the greater amount of tax will be taken. In practice, HMRC do not reduce the deemed potentially exempt transfer by the annual exemption.

EXAMPLE In August 2006 Mr A gave a house (with a value of £300,000) to his daughter, B, but continued to live there. In September 2010 (when the house was worth £375,000) Mr A moved out. Mr A dies in March 2012. Mr A made an earlier gross chargeable transfer of £175,000 in August 2001.
Since both transfers were potentially exempt, a lifetime charge will not arise. On the death of Mr A two calculations will be made:

Calculation 1
1. Ignore the original transfer and assume the transfer to B was made when Mr A moved out:

	£
Cumulative total brought forward	–
September 2010 deemed potentially exempt transfer	375,000
	375,000
Tax thereon:	
£325,000 covered by nil rate band for 2011/12	
375,000 – 325,000 @ 40%	20,000

Calculation 2
2. Ignore the deemed transfer and assume the transfer to B was made when Mr A gifted the house:

		£	£
Cumulative total brought forward			175,000
August 2006 potentially exempt transfer		300,000	
Less: Annual exemption –	2006/07	(3,000)	
	2005/06	(3,000)	
			294,000
			469,000
Tax thereon:			
£325,000 covered by nil rate band for 2011/12			
469,000 – 325,000 @ 40%		57,600	
Less: Taper relief @ 60%		(34,560)	
			23,040

Calculation 2. yields greater tax and will therefore be deemed to apply.

4. Tracing the subject matter of a gift

Property which is the subject of a gift with reservation is charged to tax by reference to its value at the date of death, or the date on which the reservation is lifted. In normal circumstances, the value at the date when the reservation is lifted will be higher than the value at the date of the original gift. Where the property has changed in nature between the two events, or is no longer in existence, special rules are required to trace the property at the date of death (or the lifting of the reservation) back to the original property. 6964

Transferee ceases to enjoy or possess property

6966 Sch 20 para 2 FA 1986

Where the transferee ceases to have the enjoyment or possession of the property before the death of the transferor or the lifting of the reservation of benefit, any property received in substitution for the original property will be treated as if it were the original property, and subject to the same reservation.

The **exception** to this rule is where the original property gifted:
– was a sum of money in any currency; or
– was gifted to a trust.

MEMO POINTS The value of a **gift of cash** is always taken at the date of the gift. This means that strictly speaking if the cash is invested in property, the gift with reservation rules will not apply to that property. The associated operation rules would however be relevant in this case (¶6925).

6967 If the **transferee makes a gift** of the original property or otherwise disposes of it for less than its value at that time then, unless the recipient is the transferor, the transferee is treated as continuing to retain possession and enjoyment of the property.

MEMO POINTS This provision is deemed to apply where an interest in property **merges** with another interest held or acquired by the transferee in the same property.

Company shares and debentures

6968 Sch 20 para 2(6) FA 1986

Where the original gift consists of company shares or debentures, any subsequent **rights or bonus issues** which increase the transferee's holding will be treated as part of the original gift.

Any consideration given by the transferee (in money or money's worth) in return for the right to acquire shares is allowed as a deduction in valuing the original gift.

Death of the transferee

6970 Sch 20 para 4 FA 1986

If the transferee dies **before the transferor** then, for the purposes of the rules outlined in ¶6964 to ¶6968:
– the acts of his personal representatives are deemed to be his acts; and
– any property transferred under a will or intestacy is deemed to have been made as a gift at the date of death.

Settled property

6972 Sch 20 para 5 FA 1986

Different tracing rules apply to property that has become settled property following a gift with reservation. These rules also apply where the property (although not settled by the transferor's gift) has subsequently become settled on the transferee prior to the death of the transferor or the lifting of the reservation.

Where the **settlement is still in existence** on the death of the transferor or the lifting of the reservation, the property comprised in it at that time will be treated as comprised in the original gift. The amount charged to IHT is therefore the value of the fund at that date. Any property in the fund which is not the property originally comprised in the gifts, and which is neither derived from nor represents that property, will be excluded for these purposes.

If the **settlement is no longer in existence** on the death of the transferor or the lifting of the reservation, the property comprised in it immediately before it came to an end will be treated as comprised in the original gift. Property to which the transferor has become absolutely or beneficially entitled will be excluded for these purposes, but any consideration given by the transferor for any of that property will be included.

In both cases, where, in addition to the original gift, the transferor also makes a **loan to the trustees**, any property which is derived (whether directly or indirectly) from that loan is treated as property originally comprised in the gift.

SECTION 3

Deduction of liabilities

As a general rule, the liabilities of an individual will reduce the value of his estate on death (¶6580). As an anti-avoidance measure, however, a debt will not be deductible if it was owed to a person who has received property from the deceased. **6980** s 103 FA 1986

An example would be where a man gives his son money which the son then lends back to him. Without the provisions outlined below, the gift to the son would be a potentially exempt transfer (and therefore exempt if the father survives for 7 years after the transfer), and the debt owed to the son would also later reduce the value of the death estate.

Adjustment to the debt

The amount of a debt created by the deceased that can be deducted from his estate immediately before death will be **reduced by reference to** any gift relating to the debt. The value of the debt is reduced in proportion to the: **6982**

a. property derived from the deceased; or

b. consideration given by any person who was at any time entitled to any property derived from the deceased, other than if the debt has no connection to the gift, or is greater than the gifts received by the transferee.

Where a **repayment of a debt** is made that would be subject to the anti-avoidance provisions, the repayment is treated as a potentially exempt transfer.

MEMO POINTS **Property derived from the deceased** does not include dispositions without gratuitous intent.

EXAMPLE

1. A gave a statue (worth £42,000) to his brother B but then decides to buy it back for the same amount 2 years later. The amount owed to B is left outstanding as a debt until A's death in year 3.
The original gift to B is a PET, which becomes chargeable to IHT as A dies within 7 years.
The debt will not be deducted from A's death estate, as it relates to property originally owned by A.

2. If B had instead loaned £8,000 to A, which was unconnected to the statue, this debt would have been deductible in A's estate.

Calculation of tax

Where a liability is disallowed or reduced under the anti-avoidance provisions outlined above, the original transfer will be subject to IHT and, in addition, the amount of the debt will be included in the death estate and therefore taxed again. **6984**

Double charges relief is available to prevent the same property being subject to two IHT charges. The basis of the relief is that tax will be charged on whichever transaction would yield the greater amount of tax and the other transaction is then ignored. SI 1987/1130

Two calculations are required to determine the greater amount of tax:

a. the debt is set against the PET and not allowed as a deduction from the death estate; and

b. the full PET is taxed, and the debt is allowed as a deduction from the death estate.

MEMO POINTS 1. If the total **tax** chargeable **is the same** under both calculations, the first is deemed to apply.
2. Where the deceased made a **number of transfers** before death which are relevant to the abatement of the liability on death, double charges relief is applied to those transfers in reverse order.

EXAMPLE Mr B gave £250,000 to Mr C on 1 March 2007. Mr C then loaned Mr B £100,000 on 1 March 2009. Mr B dies on 1 February 2012 with a death estate valued at £300,000, having made an earlier gross chargeable transfer of £200,000 in March 2002. No annual exemptions are available.

On the death of Mr B two calculations will be made:

Calculation 1:

1. Disallow the debt and set the loan amount against the potentially exempt transfer.

	£	£	£
Lifetime transfer in March 2007:			
Cumulative total brought forward		200,000	
Potentially exempt transfer	250,000		
Less: Loan amount	(100,000)		
Net PET		150,000	
		350,000	
Tax thereon:			
£325,000 covered by nil rate band for 2011/12			
350,000 – 325,000 @ 40%			10,000
Less: Taper relief @ 40%			(4,000)
			6,000
Death estate:			
Cumulative total brought forward		150,000	
Death estate		300,000	
		450,000	
Tax thereon:			
£325,000 covered by nil rate band for 2011/12			
450,000 – 325,000 @ 40%			50,000
Total tax due			56,000

Calculation 2:

2. Allow the debt and charge the potentially exempt transfer in full.

	£	£
Lifetime transfer in March 2007:		
Cumulative total brought forward	200,000	
Potentially exempt transfer	250,000	
	450,000	
Tax thereon:		
£325,000 covered by nil rate band for 2011/12		
450,000 – 325,000 @ 40%		50,000
Less: Taper relief @ 40%		(20,000)
		30,000
Death estate:		
Cumulative total brought forward	250,000	
Death estate 300,000 – 100,000	200,000	
	450,000	
Tax thereon:		
£325,000 covered by nil rate band for 2011/12		
450,000 – 325,000 @ 40%		50,000
Total tax due		80,000

Calculation 2. yields greater tax and will therefore be deemed to apply.

SECTION 4

Close companies

6990 s 94 IHTA 1984

For IHT purposes, only individuals are chargeable on a transfer of value (¶6395) but as an anti-avoidance measure, where a close company makes one of the following transfers, it will be **deemed** to have been made by the participators:

– a transfer of value; or

– an alteration of the company's unquoted share or loan capital (or of any rights attached to them).

MEMO POINTS 1. The corporation tax **definition** of close companies (¶2101) is extended for IHT purposes to include companies resident outside the UK which would be close companies if they were resident in the UK. ss 439, 454 CTA 2010

2. Similarly the corporation tax definition of **participators** (¶2102) is modified for IHT purposes to exclude a person who is a participator by reason only of being a loan creditor. Broadly, a participator is defined as any person:
– possessing (or entitled to acquire) share capital or voting rights;
– possessing (or entitled to acquire) a right to receive distributions; or
– entitled to ensure that present or future income or assets of the company will be applied directly or indirectly for his benefit.

1. Apportionment of a transfer of value

Where a close company makes a transfer of value, the value transferred is apportioned among the participators in proportion to their respective rights and interests in the company immediately before the transfer. **6992** s 94(2) IHTA 1984

A transfer which is apportioned to participators will always be a **chargeable** lifetime transfer (¶6530) and further tax may become payable if the participator dies within 7 years.

MEMO POINTS 1. The **value transferred** by a close company is the amount by which the value of the company assets immediately after the disposition is less than it would be but for the disposition.

2. **Rights and interests** in a close company include assets of the company available for distribution on a winding up but do not include: ss 96, 97 IHTA 1984
– preference shares where a transfer of value made by the close company (or any other close company) has only a small effect on the value of the preference shares as compared to the effect on the value of other parts of the company's share capital; or
– the rights and interests of minority participators of a subsidiary company which makes a transfer (or deemed transfer) of value to another group company, where that transfer of value has only a small effect on the value of the rights and interests of the minority participators, as compared to the effect on other participators.

3. Any amount **apportioned to another close company** will be further apportioned among that company's participators and so on.

A transfer by a close company to a charity, political party, housing association or qualifying national body will be **exempt** (¶6442 onwards). **6994**

The following **transfers are not apportioned** to participators:

a. any amount which would be apportioned to a person domiciled abroad which is attributable to a transfer by the close company of property outside the UK;

b. amounts which are liable to income or corporation tax in the hands of the recipient;

c. the surrender by a close company of advance corporation tax or losses under the group relief provisions; or

d. a transfer of assets between a wholly owned subsidiary and its parent, or between wholly owned subsidiaries.

Calculation of the charge

IHT will be chargeable on the amount apportioned to participators as if each had made a net transfer of value of that same amount. This amount will then need to be grossed up at the applicable tax rate. **6996**

The following **amounts may be deducted** from the net amount of the transfer:
– the annual exemption (if unused); and
– any increase in value in the participator's estate as a result of the transfer (other than an increase in the value of his shareholding).

Where the amount apportioned to a participator is **not more than** 5% of the value transferred by the company, the amount will be disregarded in calculating the rate of tax that applies to any later transfers made by him, although the IHT charge is still levied on the company.

MEMO POINTS 1. **Business property** relief (¶6700) will be available to participators if the close company's transfer involves either part of its business, or shares in a trading subsidiary.
2. **Agricultural property** relief would also be available if the property transferred by the close company qualified (¶6752).
s 99 IHTA 1984 3. Special rules apply where amounts are apportioned to a participator who is the **trustee** of a settlement (¶7538).
s 95 IHTA 1984 4. Where a close company makes a transfer of value to another close company and an individual is a **participator in both companies**, the apportioned amount of the transfer from the transferor company can be reduced by the part of the increase in the estate of the transferee company apportioned to the individual as a result of the transfer.

EXAMPLE The participators in A Ltd, their respective holdings and their previous gross chargeable transfers (all from the 2009/10 tax year) are:

	%	£
Mr B	41	120,000
Mr C	35	75,000
Mr D	20	50,000
Mr E	4	300,000

In March 2012, A Ltd transferred shares worth £850,000 to Mr C in return for £50,000. This constituted a transfer of value of £800,000 which will be allocated to the participators as follows:

	Mr B £	Mr C £	Mr D £	Mr E £
Cumulative total brought forward	120,000	75,000	50,000	300,000
Deemed transfer	328,000	280,000	160,000	32,000
Less: Increase in Mr C's estate (850,000 – 50,000)		(800,000)		
Less: Annual exemption				
2011/12	(3,000)		(3,000)	(3,000)
2010/11	(3,000)		(3,000)	(3,000)
Chargeable	442,000	Nil	204,000	326,000
Tax thereon:				
325,000/ 204,000/325,000 @ nil	-		-	-
117,000/1,000 @ 20/80	29,250			250
	29,250		Nil	250

The total IHT is therefore £29,500. (29,250 + 250).

Collection of tax

6998 s 202 IHTA 1984 In most cases the close company will be **responsible for the payment** of any tax liability arising under these provisions.

If **payment is not made** by the due date (¶7054), HMRC can collect it from:
- the shareholders, up to the amount of the tax on the value apportioned to them; or
- the person whose estate has been increased, up to the amount of the increase.

Any participator who has less than 5% of the value apportioned to him is not liable for the IHT.

EXAMPLE Continuing the example at ¶6996, if A Ltd does not pay the tax due, HMRC will seek payment of £29,250 from Mr B, and £250 from Mr C.
Otherwise Mr C will be liable for the total IHT of £29,500, as his estate has been increased by the transfer.
Mr E escapes any liability because he owns less than 5% of the share capital.

2. Alteration of capital

7000 s 98 IHTA 1984 Where an alteration is made to the unquoted share or loan capital (or to the rights attaching to it), a **disposition** will be deemed to have been made by any of the participators whose estate has been diminished as a result. An example of this would be where shares are subscribed for at par value when the existing shares are valued at a premium.

Alterations for these purposes include extinguishments, and also a new issue of shares or securities.

A transfer that is apportioned to participators will always be a chargeable lifetime transfer (¶6530) and further tax may become payable if the participator dies within 7 years.

EXAMPLE Mr A and Mr B own C Ltd between them in the following proportions:

	Number of £1 ord shares	Value per share
Mr A	750	£200
Mr B	250	£80

In June, the company (whose shares do not qualify for business property relief) issues a further 1,000 shares to Mr B (at par) and the value per share becomes £70 for Mr A and £230 for Mr B. Mr A has already made gross chargeable transfers in excess of the nil band and has used all of his annual exemption. He is deemed to have made a disposition of the following amount:

	£
Value of original holding (750 × £200)	150,000
Value of current holding (750 × £70)	(52,500)
Deemed disposition	97,500
Tax thereon @ 20/(100 – 20)	24,375

Mr A dies in December. The additional tax due on his death is:

	£
Amount of transfer (97,500 + 24,375)	121,875
Tax thereon at 40%	48,750
Less: Lifetime tax paid	(24,375)
	24,375

CHAPTER 8

Administration

OUTLINE ¶¶

IHT is under the care and management of HMRC, and is specifically administered by the Inheritance Tax Offices. Unlike other taxes, IHT is not based on an annual process. Instead the tax will only arise when a transfer of value is made either during the lifetime of an individual or on his death. HMRC therefore rely on the individual or his representatives to inform them when, and to whom, a transfer of value has been made. As a result a number of reporting obligations exist, although the persons responsible for fulfilling them depend on the nature of the transfer. 7020

The payment of IHT is similarly based on the date of the transfer and again, the persons responsible for payment will be dependent on the nature of the transfer. Interest will accrue where IHT is paid late or where a repayment of tax is made.

The tax on some forms of property may be paid by instalments, and interest will arise if any instalment is paid late. In addition, an interest charge may be levied for using the instalment option on certain property.

Once HMRC have received the details of a transfer of value, a notice of determination will be issued to indicate the amount of IHT due. An appeal may be submitted against the notice within fixed deadlines.

HMRC have the power to request that information and documents be supplied to them but this is again subject to an appeals process.

Finally, where the IHT obligations are not met, or fraudulent or careless or deliberate errors are supplied, a system of penalties is in place. Penalties will also arise where a person fails to comply with a direction of the tribunal.

MEMO POINTS 1. IHT is subject to the recently revised rules for harmonisation of taxes (¶9775).
2. There are three separate IHT offices in the UK, in Edinburgh, Belfast and Nottingham. These handle IHT matters in Scotland, Northern Ireland, and England and Wales respectively.

SECTION 1

Delivery of accounts

7025 The accounting requirements for any chargeable transfer, and the person responsible for fulfilling them, will depend on the nature of the transfer, and whether it was made during the lifetime of the transferor or on his death.

For IHT purposes, an account is a document providing details of a transaction on which IHT may apply.

Summary of accounting requirements

7026 The following table summarises the requirements for the delivery of accounts:

Type of transfer	Person responsible for delivering account	Time limit	¶¶
Potentially exempt transfer at time of transfer	No account required	n/a	¶7032
Potentially exempt transfer becoming chargeable on death	Transferee	12 months from the end of the month in which death occurred.	¶7032
Chargeable lifetime transfer	Transferor	The later of: – 12 months from the end of the month in which the transfer took place; and – 3 months from the date on which the person delivering the account became liable.	¶7030
Death estate	Personal representatives	The later of: – 12 months from the end of the month in which the death occurs; and – 3 months from the date on which the personal representatives first act as such.	¶7034
Death estate (no personal representatives)	Persons in whom property vests under the will.	3 months from the date on which the person first had reason to believe that he would be required to deliver an account.	¶7036

Type of transfer	Person responsible for delivering account	Time limit	¶¶
Settled property	Trustees	The later of: – 12 months from the end of the month in which the transfer took place; and – 3 months from the date on which the person delivering the account became liable to tax.	¶7042

Forms

The following table summarises the principal forms that are used by HMRC for IHT purposes: 7028

Form	Used for
IHT100	The following transfers of value: – potentially exempt transfers that become chargeable; – gifts of property other than potentially exempt transfers; – terminations of interests in possession; and – other chargeable lifetime transfers.
IHT400	Application for a grant of representation on death including a claim for a transferable nil rate band
IHT205	Excepted estate of deceased who died domiciled in Northern Ireland or England and Wales
IHT207	Excepted estate of deceased who died domiciled overseas with limited assets in Northern Ireland or England and Wales
IHT217	Claim to transfer unused nil rate band for excepted estates
C5	Excepted estate of deceased who died domiciled in Scotland
C5 OUK	Excepted estate of deceased who died domiciled overseas with limited assets in Scotland

Lifetime transfers

The rules for reporting a transfer depend on whether the transfer is chargeable or potentially exempt. If a transfer is **chargeable** no account need be delivered where: 7030 SI 2008/605

a. the transfer is of cash or quoted shares or securities, and the value of the transfer and other chargeable transfers made in the preceding 7 years does not exceed the IHT threshold; or

b. the value of the transfer and other chargeable transfers made in the preceding 7 years does not exceed 80% of the IHT threshold and the value of the transfer does not exceed the net amount of the threshold available to the transferor at the time of the transfer.

Where a transfer is **immediately chargeable** to IHT (for example, a transfer to a discretionary trust) the transferor will be responsible for submitting details of the transfer. s 216(1)(a) IHTA 1984

When a lifetime transfer is made by one individual to another (i.e. a **potentially exempt transfer**), an account of the transfer is not required at the time it is made. If the transferor dies within 7 years, then the transferee is responsible for reporting details of the property which is taxable and the value of that property, but the personal representatives must make enquiries to ensure that all such transfers are accounted for in the IHT return they submit. 7032 s 216(1)(bb) IHTA 1984

Transfers on death

On the death of an individual, the **personal representatives** must deliver to HMRC an account specifying: 7034 s 216(1), (3) IHTA 1984

– all the property that formed part of the deceased's estate immediately before death; and
– details of any chargeable transfers made by the deceased within 7 years of his death.

In practice, HMRC will receive information direct from the Probate Registry for grants of probate processed after 5 April 2004. HMRC will then contact the personal representatives for more information, if required, within 35 days of the date of grant.

s 216(3A) IHTA 1984 MEMO POINTS 1. An **estimated value** may be included in the account where, despite making all reasonable enquiries, the exact value of property cannot be ascertained. An undertaking must, however, be given that a further account will be submitted as soon as an accurate value is obtained.

s 216(3) IHTA 1984 2. The personal representatives need not submit an account in respect of property which has been the subject of a **gift with reservation**. Instead it is the person who is liable for the tax on the transfer (generally the transferee of the property) who is responsible for delivering an account, and the time limit in this case is 12 months from the end of the month in which the death occurred.

7036 s 216(2) IHTA 1984 If, within 12 months from the end of the month in which the death occurred, there are **no personal representatives** because a grant of representation has not been obtained in the UK, then an account must be submitted by:

– every person in whom any of the estate property vests (or who becomes entitled to an interest in possession in estate property) on or after the deceased's death; and

– discretionary beneficiaries for whose benefit property (or income from that property) is applied.

The account must specify the property in which the individual has an interest and its value. An account will not be required where it can be shown that this will be submitted in due course by the personal representatives.

7040 SI 2004/2543 **Excepted estates** There are **three categories** of excepted estate which are not required to comply with the normal reporting requirements and these are set out in the table below. Where an estate qualifies for exception, the relevant form (IHT205 or IHT207, or form C5 in Scotland) should be submitted to the Probate Office. The form should be accompanied by a copy of form IHT217 where a claim is made to transfer a wholly unused nil rate band.

HMRC reserve the right to call for an account by issuing a notice to the personal representatives within 35 days of the issue of the grant of probate. In addition:

– an estate which includes a **drawdown pension fund** (¶6589) will not be excepted, and an account must be delivered in all such cases; and

– if there is **non-disclosure** of key information, or the estate never qualified as excepted, a liability to IHT may still arise.

Domicile at death	Property passes under	Restricted property	Chargeable lifetime transfers	Total value[1] not to exceed
UK	Will or intestacy; Nomination of asset taking effect on death; Single interest in possession settlement; Survivorship in joint tenancy.[2]	Settled property not to exceed £150,000. Property outside UK not to exceed £100,000.	Aggregate value of the following (ignoring BPR and APR) did not exceed £150,000: – cash; – personal chattels or corporeal moveable property; – quoted shares or securities; and – land (not settled property or gift with reservation of benefit).	Nil rate band
UK	As above	As above	As above	£1 million, and value remaining after deducting spouse[3] and charity exemptions, and estate liabilities, does not exceed nil rate band.

Domicile at death	Property passes under	Restricted property	Chargeable lifetime transfers	Total value [1] not to exceed
Non-UK	Will or intestacy; Survivorship in joint tenancy.	Estate situated in UK is wholly attributable to cash or quoted shares or securities, with value not exceeding £150,000.	n/a	n/a

Note:
1. Total value is the sum of the:
- gross value of the estate;
- chargeable lifetime transfers; and
- exempt transfers (where the recipient is a spouse, charity, housing association, maintenance fund or employee trust).

2. In Scotland, survivorship in a special destination.
3. For this purpose, the spouse exemption will only be available if the deceased and spouse were both born in the UK, and had their permanent home in the UK.
4. Where an estate **no longer qualifies** as an excepted estate, the personal representatives must deliver an account of the estate within 6 months of the estate no longer qualifying. HMRC will accept a Corrective Account (C4) which is accompanied by a copy of IHT205 in this case.

Settled property

Where the **trustees** of a settlement become liable to tax, an account must be delivered to HMRC specifying the property concerned and its value. 7042 s 216(1), (6) IHTA 1984

This requirement will arise on:
- transfers of value (other than potentially exempt transfers);
- the termination or disposal of an interest in possession in an exempt trust (¶7530); and
- principal (¶7446) and exit (¶7452) charges relating to a chargeable trust.

The **termination of an interest in possession** will be excepted from the reporting requirements where it is covered by an annual or marriage gift exemption, and the transferor has given notice of this to the trustees.

Corrective accounts

If, after the delivery of accounts, a **material defect** is discovered, a further account must be delivered within 6 months of the discovery to remedy the defect. Similarly, if no account was delivered because it was believed that a transfer was excepted and it is later discovered that an account is required, it must be submitted within 6 months of the discovery. 7044 s 217 IHTA 1984

SECTION 2

Payment of inheritance tax

Each type of transfer has its own rules with regard to liability and timing of payment. 7050

Liabilities in relation to certain types of property may be settled by instalments.

Interest will be due on IHT paid late. Where IHT or any related interest remains unpaid, HMRC may attach a legal charge over the property concerned.

A. Type of transfer

The persons liable and relevant time limits depend on whether the transfer is made during the transferor's lifetime, or on death. 7052

1. Lifetime transfers

Timing

7054 For **chargeable lifetime transfers** the transferor is primarily liable for the payment of IHT.

s 226 IHTA 1984 The **general due date** for payment of tax on chargeable lifetime transfers is 6 months after the end of the month in which the chargeable transfer arose. The **exception** is where the transfer was made after 5 April and before 1 October in any year, in which case the due date will be 30 April in the following year.

Tax chargeable on the ending of the conditional exemption for **national heritage property** (¶6670) will always be payable 6 months after the end of the month in which the chargeable event arose.

Liability

7056 s 199 IHTA 1984 If the **tax is not paid by the due date** the following persons will also become liable:

Person		Specific limitation of liability
Transferee	Trustee	Value of property he has received, disposed of or become liable to account to the beneficiaries for, and any other property that is, for the time being, available in his hands for the payment of tax
	Non-trustee	Amount of the property concerned
Any person in whom the property is vested	Trustee	Value of property he has received, disposed of or become liable to account to the beneficiaries for, and any other property that is, for the time being, available in his hands for the payment of tax
	Non-trustee	Amount of the property concerned
Any person who is beneficially entitled to an interest in possession in the property		Amount of the property concerned
Where the settled property becomes comprised in a settlement, any person for whose benefit the property or income is applied		The amount of property or income (as reduced by income tax borne in respect of that income) applied for his benefit by the trustee

s 203 IHTA 1984 MEMO POINTS As an anti-avoidance measure, IHT can in some circumstances be collected **from the spouse** where the tax has not been paid by the transferor. This applies where the transferor is liable for tax on a chargeable lifetime transfer and makes a separate gift to his spouse. In this case, the spouse will also be liable to tax on the chargeable lifetime transfer.
The liability of the spouse is limited to the market value of the gift at the time of the transfer, provided that the gift to the spouse is made before the chargeable lifetime transfer, it had a lower market value than the chargeable transfer, and that it is not tangible moveable property.

EXAMPLE A transfers a property worth £150,000 to his wife and then transfers £600,000 to a discretionary trust . If A fails to pay the tax arising from the transfer to the trust, his wife will become liable to IHT up to the amount of £150,000.

7058 s 204(6) IHTA 1984 Where tax has been calculated on the **grossed-up equivalent** of a net gift (¶6536), the liability of persons other than the transferor will be limited to the tax on the ungrossed amount.

EXAMPLE In October 2011 Mr A made a chargeable lifetime transfer of £425,000 to a discretionary trust and agreed to pay the tax. The gift was treated as a net gift and was therefore grossed up to calculate the tax (425,000 − 325,000 @ 20/80 = 25,000).
HMRC are unable to recover the tax and the trustees become liable. In this case the gift amount of £425,000 is treated as a gross transfer and the tax is therefore 425,000 − 325,000 @ 20% = 20,000.

If Mr A had paid £15,000 towards the tax, the trustees would have been liable on a gross gift of £440,000 (i.e. 425,000 + 15,000) on which the tax would be £23,000. The £15,000 already paid would be deducted from this to give a liability for the trustees of £8,000.

Additional charges on death

Where a lifetime transfer becomes chargeable as a result of the death of the transferor within 7 years, the following will generally be **liable** for IHT: **7062**

a. the transferee;
b. any person in whom the property is vested;
c. any person who is beneficially entitled to an interest in possession in the property; and
d. where the settled property becomes comprised in a settlement, any person for whose benefit the property or income is applied.

The limitations of liability outlined in ¶7056 also apply here.

The **due date** for payment is 6 months after the end of the month in which death occurs. s 226(3) IHTA 1984

Where the liability is not paid by any of the persons listed at ¶7056, within 12 months after the end of the month in which death occurs, the **personal representatives** will become liable for the tax. **7064** s 199(2) IHTA 1984

The liability in this case will be **limited** to the extent of assets received as a personal representative and, with respect to UK settled land, the amount at any time available in their hands for payment of tax. This includes property that would have been in the hands of the personal representatives but for their own neglect or default.

In practice, where the representatives have made all reasonable enquiries, disclosed all lifetime transfers made known to them, and received a certificate of discharge for full payment of IHT, HMRC will not pursue them for unpaid IHT on any other lifetime transfers which subsequently come to light.

2. Transfers on death

The persons liable for IHT arising as a result of transfers on the death of an individual will depend on the property transferred, as set out in the following table. The actual liability will be limited as previously described for trustees and other persons (¶7056), and personal representatives (¶7064). **7066** s 200 IHTA 1984

Property	Person liable
Non-settled property and settled land in the UK which devolves upon or vests in the personal representatives	Personal representatives
Settled property	Trustees of the settlement
Property vested in any person at any time after death, or in which any person is beneficially entitled to an interest in possession	Person in whom the property is vested, or who is beneficially entitled to an interest in possession
Property comprised in a settlement immediately before death	Any person for whose benefit any of the property or income from it (as reduced by income tax borne by him) is applied

Timing

The **due date** for the payment of IHT for transfers on death is 6 months after the end of the month in which the death occurred. **Personal representatives**, however, must pay the tax for which they are liable on the delivery of their account (¶7026) even if this is before the due date. **7068**

Funding

7070 Subject to any contrary intention in the deceased's will, any tax paid by the personal representatives in respect of unsettled property will be treated as part of the general testamentary and administrative expenses of the estate. This means that the personal representatives may **reimburse** themselves out of the share of the estate that is to bear those expenses. Personal representatives can also arrange with HMRC to make **electronic payment** direct from the deceased's bank account before probate is obtained.

Where necessary, tax will be repaid to the personal representatives by the person in whom the property is vested.

Sometimes it is necessary for a loan to be taken out in order for IHT to be paid. In this case, income tax relief is available in respect of any interest charged on the loan (¶4380).

EXAMPLE On the death of Mr A in September 2011, the personal representatives received the following property:

	£
Residence	200,000 (Left to spouse)
Freehold land	250,000 (Left to son – bears own tax)
Other property	450,000
Life interest in an exempt trust	50,000

Mr A specified a legacy of £20,000 to each of his two nephews and left the residue to his daughter.
Mr A made no lifetime transfers of value.
The value of the estate for IHT purposes is:
Estate: 250,000 + 450,000 + 50,000 = 750,000
Tax thereon:
£325,000 covered by nil rate band for 2011/12
750,000 – 325,000 @ 40% = £170,000
This is allocated as follows:

Property	Who liable	Value (£)	Tax (£)
Residence	Exempt		
Freehold land (Tax: 250,000/750,000 × 170,000)	Son	250,000	56,667
Other property (Tax: 450,000/750,000 × 170,000)	Personal representatives	450,000	102,000
Life interest in a trust (Tax: 50,000/750,000 × 170,000)	Trustees	50,000	11,333

The residue to Mr A's daughter will therefore consist of:

	£
Other property	450,000
Less: Specific bequests	(40,000)
	410,000
Less: IHT	(102,000)
	308,000

3. Interest on unpaid tax

7072
ss 101 - 104
FA 2009
SI 2009/2032 reg 13

When IHT is not paid by the due date, interest will accrue from that date to the date when the liability is finally paid. Interest is calculated using the rates shown at ¶9983. The denominator is always 365, even in a leap year.

For **personal representatives**, the due date for payment of IHT is normally the date on which delivery of accounts is required (¶7026) but, for the purposes of calculating interest, the due date is deemed to be 6 months from the end of the month in which the death occurred.

EXAMPLE Mr A made a chargeable lifetime transfer in June 2010 for which the IHT of £45,000 was due for payment on 30 April 2011. Mr A finally paid the tax on 5 September 2011 giving rise to an interest charge calculated as follows (assume a rate of interest of 3%):

1 May 2011 to 5 September 2011 – 128 days
45,000 @ 3% × 128/365 £473.42

MEMO POINTS If an interest charge is triggered, it is difficult to appeal successfully.
The Special Commissioners (now replaced by the tribunal) considered the validity of an interest charge on IHT paid late. The executor of the estate claimed that the charge was unfair on the grounds that:
– she had been misdirected by HMRC;
– the delay in dealing with the case was due to difficulties in proving the will;
– the solicitor dealing with the case had been negligent; and
– there were procedural delays in the court administration of the estate.
The Commissioners held that, irrespective of these matters, there was no power to override statute and that the interest charge was due. *Richardson v HMRC* [2009]

B. Mechanisms of payment

Depending on the circumstances, payment may be made in one lump sum, by instalments, or by giving certain property to HMRC in lieu of cash. Once payment has been made, HMRC will issue a certificate of discharge. **7073** SI 2008/2991

MEMO POINTS If payment is made online by credit card, a fee equivalent to 1.4% of the payment due will be levied.

1. Instalment payments

IHT on certain types of property (known as instalment property) may be paid in ten equal yearly instalments if an **election** is submitted to HMRC. In order to qualify for payment by instalments, the transfer must be an eligible transfer of qualifying property. **7074**

Eligible transfers

The instalment option is available in respect of IHT on the following transfers: **7076** s 227 IHTA 1984
a. all transfers on death;
b. a chargeable lifetime transfer where the transferee has agreed to pay the IHT on the transfer; or
c. a lifetime transfer that becomes chargeable (or where additional tax becomes payable) as a result of the death of the transferor within 7 years of the transfer provided that:
– the property has been owned by the transferee throughout the period between the date of the gift and the death of the transferor; or
– the property has been replaced by property qualifying for business or agricultural property relief.

The instalment option will apply to IHT charges in respect of **settled property**, provided that the property to which the charge relates continues to be comprised in the settlement, or the beneficiary who becomes entitled to the property bears the tax.

Eligible property

IHT on the following types of property will be eligible for the instalment option: **7078** ss 227(2), 228 IHTA 1984

Type of property		Restrictions
Land and buildings		None
Business or business interest – net value of business assets		Including a trade, profession or vocation, but excluding a business carried on otherwise than for gain
Shares and securities	Controlling holding of transferor immediately before death	The transferor has sufficient voting power to control all matters that affect the company. For these purposes, shares held as related property (for example by the spouse) must be included
	Unquoted (remaining unquoted throughout the period between the gift and the date of death)	**Either** the transfer is on death and the IHT payable on those and other instalment assets is at least 20% of the tax chargeable on the death
		Or HMRC are satisfied that the IHT attributable to the shares cannot be paid in one sum without undue hardship
	Unquoted shares with a value in excess of £20,000 (before BPR)	**Either** the nominal value is at least 10% of the nominal value of all of the shares of the company at the time of the transfer
		Or, for ordinary shares, the nominal value is at least 10% of the nominal value of the ordinary share capital in issue at the time of the transfer

Timing

7080 The first instalment will be payable on the date on which the whole liability would normally be due. The remaining instalments will be due on the same date in the following 9 years.

s 227(4) IHTA 1984

Where the property on which instalments are being paid is **disposed of** (by sale or a chargeable lifetime transfer) after the date of the first instalment but before the end of the instalment period, the tax outstanding at the date of the sale becomes payable immediately.

Similarly, outstanding tax will become payable immediately where:
– following an election made on a chargeable lifetime transfer on which the transferee paid the tax, the transferee makes a chargeable transfer of value of the property in question (either wholly or in part); or
– property which was settled at the time of the election subsequently leaves the settlement.

Where only **part of the property** is disposed of, an apportionment is made so that only part of the outstanding tax becomes due immediately, and the amount due in the remaining instalments is reduced.

EXAMPLE In June 2005 Mr A gave land with a value of £400,000 to his son Mr B who agreed to pay all of the IHT due. Mr A died in March 2007 and Mr B elected to pay the resulting IHT of £57,600 by instalments. The first instalment of £5,760 was due on 30 September 2007 and the remaining instalments were payable on the same date in each of the next 9 years.
Mr B sold one third of the land in December 2011 when the outstanding amount of tax was £28,800. As a result of the sale £9,600 of the tax became due immediately and the remaining six instalments were:
(28,800 – 9,600)/5 = £3,840

Interest

7082 Where IHT is payable by instalments, the calculation of the interest charge will differ depending on the type of property involved. For some types of property the instalments are interest-free, and for others the instalments are interest-bearing. The denominator in the calculation is always 365, even in a leap year.

s 234 IHTA 1984

Property		Interest-bearing	Interest-free
Business or interest in a business	All		✓
Land	Agricultural value qualifying for APR		✓
	Woodlands		✓
	Other	✓	
Shares and securities	Investment or property management company (not market makers or discount houses)	✓	
	Other		✓

Interest-free instalments An interest charge will **only arise** for interest-free instalments if payment is made after the due date, and will run from that date until the actual date of payment. If all instalments are paid on time no interest will therefore be payable. 7084

Interest-bearing instalments For interest-bearing instalments there are two potential interest charges. The **first** is a charge for using the instalment facility, and applies each year on the whole amount of the tax outstanding. 7086

The **second** interest charge arises if the instalments are not paid by the due date. Interest in this case will accrue from the due date to the date when the tax is finally paid.

EXAMPLE Mr A died in July 2009 leaving an estate on which IHT of £102,000 was due. This was allocated as follows:

	Value (£)	Tax (£)
Cash etc	102,035	17,944
Residence	316,850	55,722
Business	161,115	28,334
	580,000	102,000

The business was acquired in June 2008 and therefore did not qualify for business property relief. The due date for payment of IHT was 31 January 2010 but an election was made to pay the tax on the residence and the business by instalments. The non-instalment tax was paid on time but the first instalment of tax was paid on 14 March 2010. The second instalment was paid on 1 April 2011. The interest rate is assumed to be 3% throughout the period.

Interest is calculated as:

Interest-free instalments – Business

Instalment	Instalment amount (£)	Due date	Dates for interest	Calculation	Interest charge (£)
First	2,833	31 Jan 10	1 Feb 10 to 14 Mar 10	2,833 @ 3% × 42/365	10
Second	2,833	31 Jan 11	1 Feb 11 to 1 April 11	2,833 @ 3% × 60/365	14

Interest-bearing instalments – Residence

Instalment	Instalment amount (£)	Due date	Dates for interest	Calculation	Interest charge (£)
First	5,572	31 Jan 10	1 Feb 10 to 14 Mar 10	5,572 @ 3% × 42/365	19
Second	5,572	31 Jan 11	1 Feb 11 to 1 April 11	5,572 @ 3% × 60/365	27

The **interest charge on the capital** sum for the first year to 31 January 2011 is calculated as follows:

Capital sum outstanding at 31 January 2011:	55,722 – 5,572	£50,150
Interest at 3%	50,150 @ 3%	£1,505

2. Acceptance of property in satisfaction of tax

7088
s 230 IHTA 1984

Following an application by any person liable to pay IHT, the Board may accept the categories of property outlined below in **full or partial** satisfaction of both the tax and any related interest.

a. Land, other than:
– agricultural land (unless it is associated with a historic building); or
– buildings (unless of architectural or historic interest).

The general rule is that land or buildings will only be accepted if they can be put to a certain use, e.g. displayed as part of the national heritage.

b. Any **objects** which have been kept in any building:
– accepted in satisfaction of IHT;
– belonging to the Crown or the Duchies of Lancaster or Cornwall;
– belonging to, or used for the purposes of, a government department;
– protected under the Ancient Monuments and Archaeological Areas Act 1979 or the Historic Monuments and Archaeological Objects (Northern Ireland) Order 1995; or
– belonging to certain museums and other bodies (¶6450).

To be accepted, the Secretary of State must deem it desirable for the objects to remain with the building.

c. Any picture, book, manuscript, work of art, object of scientific interest or other thing where the Secretary of State is satisfied that it is pre-eminent on account of its **national, scientific, historic or artistic interest**.

3. Charge over property

7090
s 237 IHTA 1984

If the IHT on a transfer of value (or any interest charges accruing on it) remains unpaid, HMRC can impose a legal charge for that amount over the property concerned or, where the transfer is of settled property, over the property comprised in the settlement. The charge is subject to any prior encumbrance (such as a mortgage) which is allowable as a deduction in valuing the property.

For **transfers made on death**, a charge cannot be attached to personal or moveable property situated in the UK which was beneficially owned by the transferor immediately before his death, and which vests in his personal representatives.

Where a **potentially exempt transfer** subsequently becomes chargeable as a result of the death of the transferor within 7 years, a charge can be attached to the property which was the subject of the transfer. This rule applies even where the property has been disposed of (other than by sale) before the death of the transferor. In this case, any property which represents the original property at the date of death will be subject to the charge. If the property was sold before the death of the transferor then no charge will be possible.

Sale of the property

7092
s 238 IHTA 1984

Where property under charge is sold **for money or money's worth** (other than for a nominal consideration) it will cease to be the subject of the charge, and the charge will instead be applied to the property representing it.

The **exception** to this rule is where, at the time of completion of the sale (or for registered land, the time of registration of the disposition):

a. the charge was registered as a land charge or, for registered land, was protected by notice in the register (only applies to land in England and Wales);

b. the charge was entered as a burden in the appropriate register, or was protected by caution or inhibition, or the purchaser had notice of the facts giving rise to the charge (only applies to land in Northern Ireland);

c. the purchaser of personal property situated in the UK (other than **a**. or **b**. above) and of any property situated outside the UK had notice of the facts giving rise to the charge; or

d. a certificate of discharge had been given by HMRC, and the purchaser had notice of a fact invalidating the certificate.

Where the exception applies, the original property will remain the subject of the charge.

Where property which is the subject of a charge is **sold** in circumstances **where the charge still applies**, the charge will cease at the end of the period of 6 years beginning on the later of the dates on which either: **7094** s 238(2) IHTA 1984
– the tax became due; or
– a full and proper account of the property was first delivered to HMRC in connection with the transfer.

4. After payment made

Certificates of discharge

A certificate of discharge prevents all persons from making any further claims to tax in respect of a transfer, and will extinguish an HMRC charge (¶7090). **7096** s 239 IHTA 1984

Following an application by the person liable for IHT on the transfer of property, HMRC **may issue** a certificate of discharge if they are satisfied that the tax has been or will be paid. If the property is transferred on death, or the transferor has died within 7 years of making a lifetime transfer, HMRC **must issue** a certificate of discharge if they are satisfied that the tax has been or will be paid.

An application with respect to a **potentially exempt transfer** may not normally be made until 2 years after the transferor's death, although HMRC may allow an earlier application in some cases if it is clear that all the tax has been paid.

A certificate of discharge **will not extinguish** a charge where there has been a failure to disclose material facts, fraud, or a claim which is subsequently found to be excessive, such as a claim for a TNRB (¶6608) which is later found to be too high.

Repayment of tax

Where IHT is overpaid a repayment will automatically be made (for amounts of £25 or over) and will consist of the overpaid tax and any late payment interest on the overpaid tax. Where the repayment is an amount which is less than £25, a claim must be made. **7098** s 241 IHTA 1984

Interest will be paid on the total amount of the repayment and will run from the date of the original payment (or for late payment interest, the date on which that was paid) to the date on which the order for repayment is issued. The denominator in the calculation will always be 366. The **rate** of interest is determined by reference to that set by the Monetary Policy Committee of the Bank of England. s 235 IHTA 1984 SI 2009/2032

EXAMPLE On 15 June 2009 Mr A made a chargeable lifetime transfer of value on which IHT of £125,000 was due. The due date for payment of tax was 30 April 2010 but Mr A did not make the payment until 5 August 2010.
Late payment interest (assuming a rate of 3%) is calculated as:
125,000 @ 3% = 3,750.
3,750 × 97/365 = £996
This amount is paid on 12 September 2010.
In April 2011 Mr A is advised that the property transferred was eligible for 50% business property relief and he submits a repayment claim. On 20 May 2011 HMRC issue an order for repayment of £62,500 and half of the late payment interest. Interest on the repayment (assuming a rate of 0.5%) is calculated as:

	£
5 August 2010 to 20 May 2011 62,500 @ 0.5% × 289/366	247
12 September 2010 to 20 May 2011 (996 × 62,500/125,000) @ 0.5% × 251/366	2
Total interest repayable	249

SECTION 3

Determinations, reviews and appeals

7105 A notice of determination is issued by HMRC to indicate the amount of IHT that they believe to be due. If the person liable does not agree with the notice then, within strict time limits, a review can be requested or an appeal can be submitted.

Notice of determination

7108 s 221 IHTA 1984 A notice of determination will be issued when HMRC become aware that a transfer of value has been made. The notice will be issued in writing to any person who appears to be the transferor or the claimant, or to be liable for any of the tax chargeable on the value transferred.

The notice **will include** all or any of the following in relation to the transfer of value:
a. the date of the transfer;
b. the value transferred, and the value of any property to which the value transferred is wholly or partly attributable;
c. the name of the transferor;
d. the tax chargeable (if any) and the persons who are liable for all or part of it;
e. the amount of any payment made in excess of the tax for which a person is liable, and the date from which, and the rate at which, tax or any repayment of tax overpaid carries interest; and
f. any other matter which appears to the Board to be relevant.

The notice of determination should specify the method of appeal, and the time limit for doing so.

Subject to a review or an appeal, a determination is deemed to be **conclusive** for IHT purposes for the person against whom the notice is served.

If the notice is served on the transferor, and specifies a determination of the value transferred, then this is conclusive against any other person so far as the tax on any later transfer of value is concerned.

Reviews and appeals

7111 ARTG 8210 s 222, ss 223A-s 223I IHTA 1984 After notice of a determination has been received, a taxpayer can either appeal against the decision immediately, or ask for a review of it and then make an appeal.

An **appeal** against a determination must be submitted to HMRC within 30 days of the service of notice. For any question regarding the value of **land**, the appeal must be submitted to the Lands Tribunal. The appeal must be made in writing, and must specify the grounds on which the appeal is made.

A **review** of the decision can either be offered by HMRC, if the taxpayer disputes the liability, in which case the taxpayer has 30 days to take up the offer, or it can be requested by the taxpayer. If a review is offered, the taxpayer does not have to accept it and can, instead, submit an appeal provided it is within the 30 day appeal period. An appeal in this circumstance is submitted to the tribunal (¶9920+). However, whilst a **review is being conducted**, an appeal cannot be submitted. HMRC have 45 days (or a different period if agreed) in which to give the results of their review. The conclusion of the review will be that the decision of HMRC is to be upheld, varied or cancelled.

s 222 (3) IHTA 1984 An appeal can also be made to the tribunal, but only on a point of law where.
a. the appellant and HMRC both agree; and
b. an application is made to the tribunal by the appellant, and the tribunal is satisfied that the appeal will be substantially confined to points of law.

7114 HMRC have discretion to accept a **late appeal** where they are satisfied that there is a reasonable excuse for the delay, and the appeal was subsequently made without unreasonable delay.

Tax payment The tax which is the **subject of the appeal** is not payable at the first stage of the appeal. If there is a further appeal, the tax becomes payable, although in practice HMRC do not enforce payment. If the appeal is successful, any tax paid will be repaid with interest. 7116 s 242 IHTA 1984

SECTION 4

Disclosure of information

In order to ensure that they have all the necessary details in relation to a transfer, HMRC have the power to request information and documents, and also the right to inspect premises for the purposes of confirming a valuation for IHT (¶9882). In addition, from 6 April 2011, information relating to certain tax avoidance schemes must be disclosed to HMRC. 7120

By issuing an **information notice**, HMRC may require the supply of any information which is required for IHT purposes (¶9864+). The request may be made of the person liable to pay the IHT, or of a third party. Where the request is for information from a third party and relates to a named taxpayer, the third party does not have to comply with the notice unless the taxpayer has given permission, or the tribunal has approved the request. Such approval will only be given if it can be shown that HMRC are justified in requiring the information, and special rules apply (¶9875) where the third party is a professional adviser. Where an information notice has been issued, taxpayers and third parties have a number of responsibilities (¶9870) which must be met. 7122

HMRC may disclose information, for the purposes of taxes similar to IHT, to other **EU member states** providing the other state observes rules of confidentiality which are at least as strict as those applying in the UK. 7124

If a person is concerned with the **making of a settlement** in the course of a trade or profession carried on by him (other than as a barrister), he is obliged to make a return to HMRC if he knows, or has reason to believe, that the: 7126 s 218 IHTA 1984
- **settlor** was domiciled in the UK; and
- the **trustees** are not, or will not be, resident in the UK.

The return must be submitted within 3 months of making the settlement, and should state the names and addresses of the settlor and the trustees.

MEMO POINTS 1. Where a **settlement has been varied** immediately before the settlor's death and the variation results in additional tax payable, the relevant persons should, within 6 months after the day on which the variation was made, deliver a copy to HMRC and notify them of the amount of the additional tax. s 218A IHTA 1984
2. A return will not be required under these provisions if one has **already been submitted** by another person in relation to the settlement concerned.

Disclosure rules, which require the reporting of **IHT avoidance schemes**, were introduced on 6 April 2011. These essentially follow the similar regulations which apply to direct taxes (¶2215+), with some modifications to deal with the specific nature of IHT. 7130 SI 2011/170 SI 2011/171

The schemes which should be disclosed are where:
- property held by an individual is transferred during the individual's lifetime, as part of a scheme or arrangements which result (either at the time of transfer or at some other time) in the property becoming **relevant property** (¶7447); and
- the **IHT entry charge** which would normally apply when property is transferred into trust is avoided, reduced, or deferred.

For a scheme to be disclosable, **obtaining a tax advantage** must be one of the main benefits. HMRC take the view that it will normally be obvious whether this is the case or not.

Schemes which are the same, or substantially the same, as those which were **made available before 6 April 2011**, are exempted from the disclosure rules. HMRC have published a list (which is illustrative and not exhaustive) of such schemes.

SECTION 5

Penalties

7135 A penalty charge may arise when a person fails to meet his IHT obligations, or where he has made careless or deliberate errors in respect of IHT. The amount of the charge will depend on the nature of the failure, its duration and the degree of culpability.

For deaths occurring after 1 April 2009 and where a return for IHT purposes has to be submitted after 1 April 2010, the new system (¶9784+) applies in respect of **errors and inaccuracies** in documents.

Excepted estates fall within the scope of the penalty provisions in relation to all deaths occurring since 6 April 2004.

A penalty for failure to meet obligations will not arise where there is a reasonable excuse for the failure, unless there is an unreasonable delay between the point at which the excuse ceases to be relevant and the failure being remedied.

Failure to deliver accounts

7137 s 245 IHTA 1984 Where accounts or corrective supplementary returns are not submitted on time (¶7025) the following penalties will arise:

a. a fixed penalty of £100;
b. a further penalty of £100 if proceedings in which the failure could have been declared are not started within the 6 months from the date on which the account was due, and accounts have not been delivered by the end of that period;
c. a penalty of up to £3,000 for failure continuing more than 12 months after the due date, if IHT is due; and
d. a daily penalty of up to £60 for every day after the day on which the failure is declared by the tribunal, until the account is submitted.

The maximum penalty under **a**. and **b**. above is limited to the amount of tax due as a result of the transfer.

MEMO POINTS From a date to be announced, new penalties will apply in relation to the late filing of returns and accounts for IHT purposes and late payment of tax due (¶9855+).

Failure to supply information

7140 s 245A IHTA 1984 Failure to **submit a return** in respect of non-resident trustees or to supply information required in a written notice by HMRC (¶7128) will result in the following penalties:

a. a fixed penalty of up to £300; and
b. a daily penalty of up to £60 from the day on which the failure is declared by the tribunal, until the account is submitted.

7142 Failure to **provide documents** required by HMRC will result in the following penalties (¶9853):

a. a standard penalty of £300; and
b. a daily penalty of up to £60.

s 245A IHTA 1984 Where the failure relates to a **variation of a disposition** taking effect on death (¶6620), the following penalties will apply:

– a fixed penalty of up to £100;
– a daily penalty of up to £60 from the day on which the failure is declared by the tribunal, until the documents are submitted; and
– a penalty of up to £3,000 for failure continuing beyond 12 months after the due date.

Fraudulent or negligent supply of information

7144 s 247(3) IHTA 1984 If the information is provided by **any person not liable for the tax**, a fixed penalty of up to £3,000 will apply for either fraudulent or negligent information.

In addition, **assisting** in or inducing the supply of any information or document known to be incorrect will result in a penalty of up to £3,000. s 247(4) IHTA 1984

Where a **material error** is discovered in any information or document after it has been delivered to HMRC, it will be treated as a negligent supply of information unless it is remedied without unreasonable delay. s 248 IHTA 1984

Failure to comply with a direction of the tribunal

If the taxpayer does not comply with a procedural rule, direction or practice direction, such as 7146 ARTG 8510
- failure to attend in accordance with the summons;
- attendance but refusal to be sworn or affirm; or
- refusal to answer a lawful question;

proceedings at the tribunal will not be **automatically struck out**. However, the tribunal can take any action it thinks fit including:

a. waiving the requirement;
b. requiring the failure to be put right;
c. striking out the case; or
d. restricting the taxpayer's participation in proceedings.

The first-tier tribunal may also refer the case to the upper tribunal and ask the upper tribunal to exercise its power, which may involve a **financial penalty**, if a person does not comply with a tribunal requirement to:
- attend at any place to give evidence or make themselves available to give evidence;
- swear an oath in connection with giving evidence;
- give evidence as a witness; or
- produce a document or facilitate the inspection of a document or any other thing, including any premises.

Supply of inaccurate documents

A **careless or deliberate error** in a document supplied to HMRC (by either the taxpayer or a third party) will incur a tax-geared penalty (¶9790+). However, to attribute a penalty to a third party, HMRC have to show that the information has been deliberately withheld, or that the taxpayer has been supplied with false information so that the document supplied to HMRC is inaccurate. The penalty is increased according to the degree of culpability of the taxpayer or the third party. The penalty is also extended to cover situations where the taxpayer is under-assessed by HMRC and fails to take reasonable steps to notify them of the under-assessment. 7148 Sch 40 para 2 FA 2008 Sch 24 FA 2007

Guidance for personal representatives

The onus on personal representatives to comply with the new penalty regime has led to the publication of additional guidance for personal representatives dealing with **reporting chargeable events**. Under the new regime (¶9780+), the test for a penalty to be applied is whether the person liable has taken reasonable care. HMRC consider that the personal representatives will have taken **reasonable care** where they: 7150
- follow the guidance provided about filling in forms;
- make suitable enquiries of asset holders and other people to establish the extent of the deceased's estate;
- ensure correct instructions are given to valuers when valuing assets;
- seek advice about anything they are unsure of;
- follow up inconsistencies in information they receive from asset holders, valuers and other people; and
- identify any estimated values included on the form.

If the work is delegated to an agent, HMRC will expect the personal representatives to check the form before signing it and to question anything that does not accord with what they know about the deceased.

MEMO POINTS HMRC advise that they do not consider that simply signing the form is enough to satisfy the requirement to take reasonable care.

PART 6

Trusts, settlements and estates

Trusts, settlements and estates
Summary

The numbers cross-refer to paragraphs.

CHAPTER 1

General principles

OUTLINE ¶¶

SECTION 1

Introduction

A. Definitions

Trusts or settlements

A trust or settlement is a binding obligation on a person (known as the trustee) to hold or deal with property for the benefit of another person, or of a class of persons of which the trustee may be a member. The persons who benefit under a trust in this way are known as the beneficiaries. **7170**

A wider definition of a settlement is given where **anti-avoidance regulations** are applied to prevent the settlor benefiting under a trust (¶7344).

A settlement may be established either during the lifetime of the settlor or on death. A **lifetime** (or inter vivos) trust arises when the settlor makes a settlement passing the legal ownership of trust property to a trustee. A trust may be established by deed, but this is not a requirement when the trust arises by order of the courts. A trust may also be created where the conduct of the parties involved gives rise to the implication of a trust which is then enforced by the courts.

A trust established on **death** will generally arise as a result of the terms of a will or, in the absence of a will, by order of the courts. On the death of an individual, the property in his estate vests temporarily in his personal representatives. Special rules apply to the taxation of income and property during this period (¶7210).

MEMO POINTS In this Part, unless stated otherwise, references to:
– marriage include civil partnership;
– a spouse, husband or wife include a civil partner;
– divorce include the dissolution of a civil partnership; and
– a widow or widower include a surviving civil partner.

Settled property

7171 s 466 ITA 2007, s 68 TCGA 1992

Settled property is defined as any property held in trust, other than property held by a person:
– as nominee for another; or
– as trustee for another person who is absolutely entitled to the property, or who would be so entitled if he were not an infant or disabled.

Settlor

7172 ss 467, 470 - 473 ITA 2007, s 68A TCGA 1992

A settlor is defined as the person who has made, or is treated as having made, a settlement. A person will be **treated as having made a settlement** if:
a. he made or entered into the settlement directly or indirectly;
b. he provided or undertook to provide property directly or indirectly for the purposes of the settlement;
c. he made reciprocal arrangements with another person who has made a settlement; or
d. a settlement was created on his death, and it includes property of which he was competent to dispose immediately before his death.

Where property is **transferred from one settlement to another** other than for full consideration or at arm's length, the settlor(s) of the first settlement will be treated as the settlor(s) of the second settlement, except where the transfer is due to:
– an assignment by a beneficiary of his interest;
– the exercise of a general power of appointment; or
– a variation of a will or the intestacy provisions.

Where property becomes settled property as a result of the **variation of a will or the intestacy provisions**, the settlor will be:
a. the deceased, where property is redirected from an existing trust, or a trust created on the death of the deceased, into another settlement; or
b. the legatee, where he was beneficially entitled to the property before the variation, or would have been so entitled but for the variation.

MEMO POINTS 1. Where the trust is established on death by way of a will, the term **testator** may also be used.
2. A settlement may have **more than one settlor**, although in some cases (where the trustees are domiciled abroad, for example) the settled property will be held in separate trusts on behalf of each separate settlor.
3. An **arrangement** includes any scheme, agreement or understanding, whether or not legally enforceable.

7173 It is important to identify the settlor because:
– if the settlor is non-domiciled, the settled property may be excluded property for inheritance tax (¶6458);
– other settlements established by the same person will affect the rate of inheritance tax on chargeable trusts (¶7448); and
– settled property which reverts to the settlor may be free from tax in some circumstances (¶7426).

Trustees

7174 s 474 ITA 2007

The **powers, duties and liabilities** of trustees are governed by the terms of the trust deed and by any relevant statute.

A trustee is **not treated as an individual**. Instead, all of the trustees of a settlement are collectively regarded as a single and distinct person. The trust therefore remains unaffected by the retirement or appointment of an individual trustee.

This treatment has the following additional consequences for the trustees:
- they are not entitled to personal allowances for income tax on trust income; but
- they are not liable to higher rates of personal taxation in their capacity as trustee.

An individual will be **deemed to be a trustee** in relation to a settlement in which:
- there are no other trustees in existence; and
- either the settled property or its management is, for the time being, vested in him.

Bare trustees A bare trustee is one who holds property to which another person is absolutely entitled. Such a trustee is often called a **nominee**, particularly when the settled property consists of company shares. A common example of a bare trust is the position of a stockbroker's nominee company holding a portfolio of shares on behalf of his client. **7176** s 466 ITA 2007, s 60 TCGA 1992

The actions of bare trustees have **no tax consequences**, because they are deemed to be the actions of the beneficiary.

Beneficiaries

The principal types of interest that a beneficiary may have in a trust are as follows: **7178**

Interests	Definition	Reference
Absolute interest	Legal and beneficial entitlement to the whole property (both income and capital) – the exclusive right to direct how property should be dealt with, subject only to any right of the trustees to pay costs, taxes or other outgoings from trust funds.	s 466(5) ITA 2007
Limited interest	An interest that is less than an absolute interest and confers a right to income (but not capital) for a limited period (often the life of the beneficiary, but occasionally less).	
Interest in possession	Present right to present enjoyment of the income (if any) arising under the settlement.	*Pearson and others v IRC* [1980]
Immediate post-death interest	An interest in possession (other than in a bereaved minor's or disabled trust) which is created on the settlor's death and comes into effect immediately after that death.	s 49A(2) IHTA 1984
Transitional serial interest	An interest in possession (other than in a bereaved minor's or disabled trust) which: – was created on or after 22 March 2006 and before 6 October 2008 (or after 6 October 2008, where it is held by a surviving spouse); – is in a settlement created before 22 March 2006, in which an interest in possession existed on 21 March 2006; and – comes into effect on the termination of a previous life interest.	s 49B IHTA 1984 s 53(2A) IHTA 1984
Reversionary interest	A future or deferred interest which can be either vested or contingent.	
Vested interest	The interest will unconditionally come into the hands of the beneficiary at some later point in time.	
Contingent interest	The interest will come into the hands of the beneficiary at some later point in time providing some condition (such as age) is met.	

B. Modernisation of trust taxation

7180 In the period from 2004 to 2008 a number of significant changes were made to the taxation of trusts. Many existing trusts predate this period of change, so throughout this part, reference is necessarily made both to old and new tax regimes.

Income tax and CGT changes

7181 The following table summarises the provisions which were enacted, and the effective dates of change:

Effective date of change	Change	¶¶
6 April 2004	Introduction of trusts for vulnerable persons	¶7318, ¶7388
6 April 2005	Introduction of basic rate income tax band	¶7308
6 April 2006	New common definitions of settled property and settlor	¶7171, ¶7172
	Income of settlor-interested settlements treated as if it had arisen directly to the settlor	¶7350
	Settlor-interested trusts liable to income tax at special trust rates	¶7308
	Settlor-interested trusts for CGT purposes to include trusts where a dependent minor child can benefit	¶7404
	Introduction of sub-fund elections	¶7206, ¶7434
6 April 2007	New common test for determining residence of a trust	¶7570
6 April 2008	Taxation of non-UK domiciled beneficiaries of overseas trusts where a benefit is received in the UK	¶7618

MEMO POINTS The following further changes are proposed, although HMRC have stated that implementation is being deferred due to practical and transitional difficulties:
1. The **streaming** of income of non-interest in possession trusts. Where income is passed on to beneficiaries before 31 December after the end of the tax year, the special trust tax rate will not apply, and the beneficiaries will be taxed on the income at their own marginal rates, with a credit being given for tax paid by the trustees at the basic, lower or dividend rate;
2. The **abolition** of the tax pool (¶7312) over a transitional period, with the possibility of an election for trustees who wish to retain it.
3. Changes to the way in which **estates in administration** are charged to capital gains tax.

Inheritance tax changes

7182 Major changes to the IHT treatment of non-discretionary trusts came into effect on 22 March 2006.

New **interest in possession** trusts created during the settlor's lifetime (other than disabled trusts) are subject to the IHT regime for trusts (¶7440). The creation of such trusts is therefore a chargeable lifetime transfer, and IHT charges will arise every 10 years and when property leaves the trust.

The favoured treatment of **accumulation and maintenance** trusts (¶7485) does not apply to trusts created on or after 22 March 2006.

Two new types of trust (**bereaved minors**' and **age 18-to-25** trusts (¶7492)) were introduced to replace accumulation and maintenance trusts, but these can only be created by a parent, on death, and an IHT charge will arise unless beneficiaries become absolutely entitled to trust property on or before reaching the age of 18.

7183 Some **consequential CGT changes** arose as a result. Gift relief for CGT (¶6095) is now more widely available on transfers of assets into and from new interest in possession trusts, because these are now mostly chargeable transfers for IHT. However, there is now no tax-free uplift on the death of a life tenant (¶7426).

SECTION 2

Types of trust

The **factors** that distinguish the different types of trust are: 7185
- the powers of the trustees;
- the rights of the beneficiaries; and
- the terms of the trust.

The **main types** of trust are:

Type of trust	¶¶
Interest in possession	¶7187
Disabled and protective	¶7190
Discretionary	¶7192
Accumulation and maintenance	¶7194
Bereaved minors	¶7196
Age 18-to-25	¶7198
Charitable	¶7200
Employee	¶7202
Pension funds	¶7204

Interest in possession trusts

An interest in possession has been **defined** as a present right to the present enjoyment of the income of a trust, such as an immediate right to trust income as it arises. *Pearson and others v IRC* [1980] 7187

If the trustees have the power to withhold income, there is no interest in possession. An interest in possession trust is therefore one where the interests in the income are fixed, for example, giving the income to a widow for life and then, on her death, giving the capital to the children.

MEMO POINTS Interest in possession trustees normally have the right to **disburse administrative expenses** from the trust, which does not invalidate the interest in possession of the beneficiary.

The **rights of a beneficiary** (or life tenant) under an interest in possession trust may be defeasible, which means that they can be brought to an end, but the trust will still be an interest in possession trust until that time. A common example of this is where the income of a settlement is left to a widow for life, but ceases if she remarries. 7188

Similarly, the **trustees** of an interest in possession trust may have an overriding power of appointment or a power of revocation. The trust will however remain an interest in possession trust until such time as the power is exercised.

EXAMPLE Mr A is the beneficiary of two trusts, Trust B and Trust C.
The terms of Trust B give him the right to income for life, but the trustees may accumulate the income as they see fit.
The terms of Trust C give the trustees the right to accumulate income and also to make payments to Mr A as they see fit.
Neither trust is an interest in possession trust as the trustees can accumulate income within the terms of each trust.

Disabled and protective trusts

7190 ss 88, 89, 89A, 89B IHTA 1984

The beneficiaries of disabled and protective trusts may be treated as having an interest in possession for inheritance tax purposes.

A **disabled trust** is one where at least half of the income arising is used for the benefit of a disabled person who:
– is incapable of looking after his own affairs by reason of a recognised mental disorder; or
– receives an attendance allowance, or the middle or highest level of disability living allowance; or
– in relation to trusts created on or after 22 March 2006, is sufficiently disabled to receive one of the above allowances but does not qualify because he lives outside the UK or in paid-for accommodation.

If a **person who expects to become disabled** settles property into a trust for their own future needs on or after 22 March 2006, this will qualify as a disabled trust, provided that when the trust was created there was a reasonable expectation that the normal qualifying conditions would be met.

Disabled trusts are discretionary, but beneficiaries are deemed to have an interest in possession in an exempt trust (¶7515).

A **protective trust** is one for the benefit of any person for the period of his life, or for a shorter period if indicated. If the beneficiary becomes bankrupt or takes steps to sell, mortgage or anticipate his rights, the rights will come to an end and the trust will become a discretionary trust. The beneficiary will, however, still be treated as having an interest in possession in an exempt trust for inheritance tax purposes, where:
– the trust was created before 22 March 2006; or
– the interest in possession is an immediate post-death interest or transitional serial interest (¶7178) or an interest in a disabled trust.

Discretionary trusts

7192 s 58 IHTA 1984

A discretionary trust is a settlement without an interest in possession. As the name suggests, a discretionary trust is one where the **trustees have discretion** over the distribution of the income and capital of the trust, including the right not to appoint the income but to accumulate it instead. The powers of a discretionary trustee may extend to deciding the persons who will benefit from the trust.

The following types of trust are **excluded** from the definition of a discretionary trust:
– accumulation and maintenance trusts;
– trusts for bereaved minors;
– charitable trusts;
– most employee trusts;
– registered pension schemes; and
– trade or professional compensation funds.

Accumulation and maintenance trusts

7194 s 71 IHTA 1984

An accumulation and maintenance trust is a settlement for the benefit of a person (or persons) aged under 25. Until 5 April 2008, special inheritance tax provisions applied to such trusts which were **created before 22 March 2006**.

In the absence of contrary provisions in the trust deed, the beneficiaries of an accumulation and maintenance trust are entitled to an interest in possession once they attain the age of 18. It is not necessary for the beneficiaries to become entitled to an interest in the capital, and indeed it may remain as settled property.

MEMO POINTS 1. **Unborn** beneficiaries could be included in the class of beneficiaries provided there was at least one living beneficiary when the trust was created.
2. **Illegitimate, adopted and step-children** are treated in the same way as legitimate children of full blood.

3. Where the terms of a trust do not already provide for beneficiaries to become absolutely entitled to trust property on or before attaining the age of 18 or 25, the trustees may amend these, if they have the power to do so.

On 6 April 2008, accumulation and maintenance trusts which were created before 22 March 2006 became chargeable trusts for inheritance tax purposes unless by 5 April 2008 the trust terms provided that beneficiaries become absolutely entitled to trust property on or before attaining the age of: **7195** s 71D(3) IHTA 1984
– 18, in which case the provisions for accumulation and maintenance trusts continue to apply; or
– 25, in which case the provisions for age 18-to-25 trusts apply.

MEMO POINTS **Up to 5 April 2008**, for an accumulation and maintenance trust to be valid and enjoy the inheritance advantages, all of the following conditions had to be satisfied:
a. one or more persons must become **beneficially entitled** to the settled property, or an interest in possession in it, on attaining a specified age which may not exceed 25;
b. to the extent that the **income** arising from the settled property is not applied for the maintenance, education or benefit of a beneficiary, it must be accumulated;
c. there is no **interest in possession** in the settled property; and
d. either:
– all of the persons who are (or have been) beneficiaries are grandchildren of a common **grandparent** (or if the beneficiaries have died before attaining a vested interest, their children or spouses); or
– the **settlement ceases** or becomes an interest in possession trust not more than 25 years after its creation.

Trusts for bereaved minors

A trust for a bereaved minor is a settlement **created on** the death of a parent for the benefit of a child aged under 18. The following conditions must be satisfied: **7196** ss 71A - 71C IHTA 1984
a. the **beneficiary** must become absolutely entitled to the trust property and all related income on or before attaining age 18;
b. trust **property** may only be applied for the benefit of the beneficiary and not any other person; and
c. whilst the beneficiary is living and under the age of 18, either:
– he is entitled to all **income** which may arise from the trust; or
– such income may not be applied for the benefit of any other person.

MEMO POINTS 1. **Parent** includes a step-parent or an individual who had parental responsibility.
2. The provisions for trusts for bereaved minors **do not apply** to trust property to which the conditions for disabled persons trusts apply.
3. A trust for a bereaved minor can also be established under the Criminal Injuries Compensation Scheme.

Age 18-to-25 trusts

An age 18-to-25 trust is a settlement **created on** the death of a parent for the benefit of a child aged under 25. The following conditions must be satisfied: **7198** s 71D IHTA 1984
a. the **beneficiary** must become absolutely entitled to the trust property and all related income on or before attaining age 25;
b. trust **property** may only be applied for the benefit of the beneficiary and not any other person; and
c. whilst the beneficiary is living and under the age of 25, either:
– he is entitled to all **income** which may arise from the trust; or
– such income may not be applied for the benefit of any other person.

MEMO POINTS 1. **Parent** includes a step-parent or an individual who had parental responsibility.
2. The age 18-to-25 trust provisions **do not apply** to trust property to which the conditions for any of the following types of trust apply:
a. interest in possession trusts, where the interest in possession came into effect:
– before 22 March 2006; or
– on or after 22 March 2006, and the interest is an immediate post-death interest or a transitional serial interest;

b. accumulation and maintenance trusts;
c. trusts for bereaved minors; or
d. trusts for disabled persons.
3. An age 18-to-25 trust can also be established under the Criminal Injuries Compensation Scheme.

Charitable trusts

7200 s 519 ITA 2007 For tax purposes a charity is **defined** as any body of persons or trust established for charitable purposes only. In addition, to qualify as a charity, a charitable trust must be for the benefit of the public at large, or a sufficiently large section of the community, and exist for exclusively charitable purposes.

If, however, it can be shown that the **non-charitable purposes** are merely ancillary to the charitable purposes, then the trust will be considered charitable.

MEMO POINTS 1. **Charitable purposes** include:
– the relief of poverty;
– the advancement of religion;
– education; and
– other purposes beneficial to the community as a whole.
There is an obvious requirement that monies are not used for private benefit.

s 31 F(No.3)A 2010 2. Certain trusts for **asbestos victims** will be statutorily exempt from taxation with effect from 6 April 2006. To qualify, a trust must have been set up on or before 23 March 2010 as part of an arrangement between a company and its creditors specifically for the purpose of paying compensation to (or in respect of) victims of asbestos-related conditions.

Employee trusts

7202 ss 58, 86 IHTA 1984 A qualifying employee trust will normally be exempt from the inheritance tax charges that apply to chargeable trusts (¶7440).

An employee trust is one which **satisfies the conditions** outlined below:
a. the settled property must be held on trusts which (either indefinitely or until the end of a period) do not allow the property to be applied other than for the benefit of:
– persons employed in a particular trade or profession;
– all or most of the employees or office holders of a trade, profession or undertaking (or the trust is a share incentive plan); or
– spouses, relatives or dependants of any of the above; and
b. the settled property must be treated as comprised in one trust, and may contain an interest in possession of less than 5% of the whole.

Exemption **does not apply** to trust property in respect of which:
a. on or after 22 March 2006 an individual becomes entitled to an interest in possession other than an immediate post-death interest (¶7178), a disabled person's interest or a transitional serial interest (¶7178); or
b. a company whose business is wholly or mainly the acquisition of interests in settled property acquires an interest in possession other than an immediate post-death interest or a transitional serial interest from an individual who became entitled to the interest on or after 22 March 2006.

MEMO POINTS The settled property may **cease to be comprised** in one settlement but will be treated as if it had remained comprised in that settlement if, within 1 month, it becomes wholly comprised in another settlement which also satisfies the conditions.

Pension funds

7204 s 151 IHTA 1984 Trusts which are **registered** pension schemes (¶3745) are exempt from income tax on their investment income, and from capital gains tax, although income tax is chargeable on trading profits. Such trusts are not subject to the IHT regime for interest in possession trusts (¶7187), but in certain circumstances the value of some pension benefits can form part of a member's estate for IHT purposes (¶6589).

For information on the IHT treatment of benefits from **unregistered** schemes (¶3900), see ¶6590.

SECTION 3

Sub-fund settlements

Where trustees of a settlement (the principal settlement) earmark or allocate part of the trust's property for a particular purpose or beneficiary they can, from 6 April 2006, elect that the sub-fund be treated as a separate settlement for income tax and capital gains tax purposes. A sub-fund settlement is treated as having been created when the election takes effect, which cannot be earlier than 6 April 2006. **7206** s 477 ITA 2007, Sch 4ZA TCGA 1992

For the capital gains tax consequences of an election, see ¶7434.

Creation

The following **conditions** must be satisfied: **7207**

a. the principal settlement must not itself be a sub-fund settlement;

b. a beneficiary of the sub-fund settlement must not also be a beneficiary of the principal settlement; and

c. the sub-fund must not include:

– all of the property in the principal settlement; or

– an interest in an asset in which the principal settlement also has an interest.

The **trustees** of the sub-fund settlement may be different to those of the principal settlement. A principal settlement trustee who becomes a sub-fund settlement trustee will cease to be regarded as a trustee of the principal settlement unless he is a trustee in relation to property which remains in that settlement.

MEMO POINTS For these purposes a person is a **beneficiary** of a settlement if trust property may become payable to him or for his benefit in any circumstances, or if he enjoys a benefit deriving directly or indirectly from trust property. This extended definition does not apply where trust property would only become payable or applicable for the benefit of a person by reason of:

– marriage or civil partnership;

– the death of a beneficiary of the settlement;

– the advancement of property by the trustees; or

– the failure or determination of a protective trust.

Election

A **notice** of election for a sub-fund settlement must be given to HMRC by the trustees no later than the second 31 January following the year of assessment in which the election is to take effect. An election cannot be revoked. **7208**

The election **must contain**:

– a declaration of consent by each trustee of the principal settlement;

– a statement by the trustees of the principal settlement that the required conditions have been satisfied;

– such information as HMRC may require in relation to the principal settlement;

– a declaration by the trustees of the principal settlement that the information contained in the election is correct, to the best of their knowledge and belief; and

– such other declarations as HMRC may require.

Following an election, **HMRC** may request further information to enable them to determine whether the required conditions have been satisfied. An enquiry notice may be sent to a trustee, settlor or beneficiary of either the principal settlement or the sub-fund settlement, and it must specify a period of not less than 60 days in which the information is to be supplied.

CHAPTER 2

Taxation of estates

OUTLINE ¶¶

SECTION 1

General principles

On the death of an individual, the property in his estate does not pass directly either to the legatees or under the rules of intestacy. Instead, the property vests in the personal representatives who are responsible for collecting the property, settling any outstanding liabilities or obligations, and then distributing the residue. 7210

A distinction can therefore be drawn between an estate in the course of administration and a will trust. The former relates to the period of time between the death of an individual and the completion of the administration of the estate. The latter relates to a trust created by the will of the deceased or through the rules of intestacy.

The personal representatives are responsible for the tax liabilities arising before the death of the deceased that have not yet been settled, and for those associated with the estate while it is in administration. The remainder of this chapter deals with the income tax and capital gains tax liabilities of the personal representatives. The inheritance tax implications are covered from ¶6580. 7212

Personal representatives

A personal representative is **defined** for income tax purposes as someone who is responsible for administering the death estate, whether in the UK or elsewhere. 7214
s 989 ITA 2007

s 30AA TMA 1970 There will often be more than one personal representative, but they are treated as a single person for tax purposes.

MEMO POINTS 1. A **valid will** usually appoints executors to act as personal representatives and to obtain a grant of probate and administer the estate in accordance with the terms of the will. If the will does not appoint an executor (or appoints an executor who does not obtain a grant of probate), the court will appoint an administrator who will act as personal representative and administer the estate in accordance with the terms of the will.
2. If there is **no valid will**, the personal representative will be an administrator appointed by the court to administer the estate in accordance with the rules of intestacy.

7216 **Residence status** The residence status of the personal representatives is relevant in determining the liability to **income tax**.

s 834 ITA 2007

Residency of personal representatives	Status of deceased	Residency of estate
All UK resident or ordinarily resident	Irrelevant	UK resident
All non-resident and not ordinarily resident	Irrelevant	Non-resident [1]
At least one is UK resident, and another is non-resident	Either UK resident, or ordinarily resident, or UK domiciled	UK resident
	Non-resident, not ordinarily resident, and not UK domiciled	Non-resident [1]
Note: 1. Only taxable on UK source income.		

The **remittance basis** (¶4200 onwards) is not available to personal representatives.

7217 For **capital gains tax purposes**, the personal representatives are treated as having the same residence, ordinary residence and domicile as the deceased at the time of the death.

s 62(3) TCGA 1992

If a deceased person was not resident and not ordinarily resident in the UK at the date of death, the personal representatives will only be liable to CGT where any of the following apply:
a. the deceased had an unpaid CGT liability; or
b. the deceased was carrying on a trade, profession or vocation in the UK through a branch or agency, and:
– there are related unpaid CGT liabilities; or
– the personal representatives carry it on.

SECTION 2

Income tax

7220 An income tax charge in relation to estates may arise in the following situations:

Situation	Person liable	¶¶
Taxable income is payable in the period before death and during the administration of the estate	Personal representatives	¶7222
Payments of income are made out of the estate	Beneficiary	¶7234
A payment is made out of a foreign estate to a UK resident beneficiary	Beneficiary	¶7246

A. Personal representatives

The income tax liability of the personal representatives in respect of the estate can be divided into the following: 7222
- the tax liability of the deceased; and
- tax on any income of the estate arising during the period of administration.

The distinction between the income of the deceased and that of the personal representatives is important because the personal representatives are not entitled to a personal allowance, whereas in the year of death a full personal allowance is available to the deceased, if he would have been entitled to one while alive (¶4392).

Deceased's tax liability

The personal representatives will be **liable for payment** of: 7224 s 74 TMA 1970
- the final tax liability of the deceased up to the date of death; and
- any unassessed income tax relating to any income of the deceased arising prior to the date of death.

A tax return (¶4476) must be prepared and submitted for the period from 6 April prior to death, up to the date of death. The personal representatives may also need to complete earlier outstanding tax returns.

Income receivable **before the date of death** will be included in the final income tax computation of the deceased, regardless of whether it was actually received by that date. Income receivable **after the date of death** will be taxable on the personal representatives even if it relates to the period before death.

MEMO POINTS 1. Where the deceased's **tax liability** for earlier years **is adjusted** following death (for example, as a result of the cessation rules for trading profits (¶2452)), the relevant assessment must be issued within 3 years after the end of the year of assessment in which the death occurred.
2. A **dividend** which is declared due before death, but paid after death, will be included as income of the deceased. *Re Sebright* [1944]

EXAMPLE Mr A died on 1 June 2011. Among his sources of income were two bank accounts which paid interest as follows:

Account	Amount (£)	Due date	Received	Relating to
B	1,000	25 May 2011	15 June 2011	6 months ended 30 April 2011
C	2,000	1 July 2011	1 July 2011	12 months ended 31 May 2011

The income from Account E will be included in Mr A's final tax liability because it was receivable before the date of death. The income from Account C will be included in the liability of the personal representatives because it was receivable after the date of death.

The personal representatives will also be responsible for discharging any associated **interest and penalties**. Tax may be discharged out of the assets of the estate, and the liability of the personal representatives is therefore limited to that amount. 7226

By concession, where the taxpayer dies before the due date for the payment of tax, and the personal representatives are unable to settle the liability until the **grant of probate** or letters of administration, the due date for payment may be extended to 30 days after the date of the grant. ESC A17

MEMO POINTS Income tax is a debt of the death estate and so reduces the amount liable to **inheritance tax** (¶6594).

Income during the administration period

Income arising during the administration period (which runs from the date of death to the date when the administration of the estate is complete) is deemed to be the **income of the estate**, and the personal representatives are therefore liable to account for income tax on it. 7228 s 653 ITTOIA 2005

MEMO POINTS The date of the **completion of administration** is not defined by statute, but can be taken to be the date when the residue left in the estate has been ascertained and is ready for distribution.

7230 **Deductions** The **individual circumstances** of the personal representatives are not taken into account in the calculation of income tax of the estate.

Personal representatives may, however, claim **relief for** interest payments (other than interest charges in respect of unpaid inheritance tax) and for trading losses incurred by them in running a business.

7231 ss 403 – 405 ITA 2007 Relief may also be claimed if the personal representatives take out a **loan to pay an inheritance tax liability** (not a bank overdraft) providing the liability is payable before the grant of representation. To qualify for relief the interest must have arisen within 1 year of the date on which the loan was made. If the income in the year in which the interest is paid is not sufficient to use the relief, the excess may be carried back to previous years and then, if insufficient relief is given, against income of the following years. However, relief is only given against one loan. If it is necessary to borrow further money for the inheritance tax liability, that loan will not be eligible for relief.

7232 **Tax rates** Personal representatives pay income tax at the following **rates**:

Type of income	Rate of tax
Savings and other income[1]	20%
Dividends	10%

Note:
1. Savings income includes life policy gains (¶4066).

EXAMPLE Mr A died on 1 September 2011 and the administration of his estate was completed on 20 August 2012. During the course of the administration of the estate the personal representatives received the following income:

	Gross (£)	Tax deducted (£)	Net (£)
Income from property	16,000	-	16,000
Bank interest	10,000	2,000	8,000
Dividends	20,000	2,000	18,000

The personal representatives are liable to tax on the income as follows:

	Non-savings £	Savings £	Dividends £
Income from property	16,000		
Bank interest		10,000	
Dividends			20,000
	16,000	10,000	20,000
Tax thereon:			
16,000 @ 20%	3,200		
10,000 @ 20%		2,000	
20,000 @ 10%			2,000
Less: Tax deducted at source		(2,000)	(2,000)
Net tax liability	3,200	Nil	Nil

B. Payments to beneficiaries

7234 s 682A ITTOIA 2005 The income from the estate will retain its identity in the hands of the beneficiary and will be taxed at the rate applicable for that source.

Payments made to beneficiaries during the administration of the estate are generally detailed on a form R185 (Estate Income) issued by the personal representatives. This outlines the income and the tax treated as paid on it, which the beneficiary may use as a credit against his own tax liability. He may claim a repayment of any tax overpaid, although not in respect of the tax credits on dividends.

MEMO POINTS A beneficiary who is **not resident or ordinarily resident** in the UK (¶4152+) may claim to have his tax liability adjusted to reflect the following:
- entitlement to the personal allowance;
- relief under a double taxation agreement; and
- exemption in respect of UK government securities.

Tax deducted at source

Each source of income is **grossed up** at basic or dividend ordinary rate as appropriate. Payments are deemed to be made first out of income taxable at the basic rate, and then from dividend ordinary rate income. **7235** s 663 ITTOIA 2005

MEMO POINTS 1. The personal representatives deduct administration **expenses**, leaving a net amount available for distribution to the beneficiaries. Ideally expenses should be set against dividend income as a priority, as the associated tax credit is not repayable. s 664 ITTOIA 2005
2. The **rate** used is the one applying to the year of assessment in which the payment was made.
3. An **annuity** may be provided for in a will, and is defined as a pecuniary legacy payable in instalments (¶7296). The personal representatives must deduct tax at basic rate, and will provide the annuitant with a form R185 showing the amount of tax deducted.

Timing of payments

The property in an estate does not belong to the beneficiaries until such time as the administration is complete. The beneficiaries will not therefore be liable to income tax while the property remains in the estate. **7236**

Income distributed during the administration period will be treated as the beneficiary's income, as will payments made to the beneficiary once the administration of the estate is complete.

Type of interest in the estate

The treatment of sums paid to beneficiaries during the administration of an estate will depend on whether the beneficiary has a limited or absolute interest in the estate. **7238**

Type of interest	Description	¶¶
Limited	Entitles the beneficiary to a right to income once the administration of the estate is complete (e.g. a life tenant or immediate post-death interest).	¶7240
Absolute	Once the administration of the estate is complete, the beneficiary will be entitled to both the income and capital in his own right.	¶7242

Limited interest Payments made to a beneficiary with a limited interest will be treated as **income of the beneficiary** for the tax year in which the payment is made. **7240** s 661 ITTOIA 2005

Amounts that remain payable to the beneficiary once the administration has been completed are treated as received in the year that the completion occurred. The exception to this rule is where the limited interest **ceased** before the completion of the administration, because of the death of the beneficiary, for example. In this case the income is treated as received by the beneficiary in the year of death.

Absolute interest Payments made to a beneficiary with an absolute interest will be treated as income for the tax year in which the payment is made. The amount treated as income will, however, be **limited to** the extent of the beneficiary's entitlement to the residuary income in each tax year, up to and including the year of payment. Any excess over the entitlement to residuary income will be treated as a payment of capital. **7242** ss 660, 665 ITTOIA 2005

Where there are **excess estate expenses** compared to the residuary income, these are carried forward and deducted against the income of the following year.

MEMO POINTS 1. **Residuary income** for these purposes is defined as the aggregate of estate income excluding specific dispositions and contingent distributions, less interest (other than interest on late inheritance tax) which is charged on the residue. s 666 ITTOIA 2005

2. When the **administration of the estate ends**, any unrelieved expenses will be set against any remaining income which has not yet been paid out.

EXAMPLE Mr A died on 1 January 2008 leaving his estate to his son, Mr B, absolutely. The actual income of the estate was as follows:

	2008/09	2009/10	2010/11	2011/12
	£	£	£	£
Rental income (gross)	6,500	8,500	9,500	3,000
Other savings (gross)	4,375	4,750	5,000	2,500
	10,875	13,250	14,500	5,500

The savings income includes the tax deducted at source. Rental income will be taxed at basic rate.
The administration of the estate was completed on 1 June 2011.
The following payments were made out of the estate:

1 March 2009	£3,000
1 June 2009	£17,000
1 October 2010	£12,000

Year	Gross income	Tax	Net	Aggregated income entitlement	Payments to Mr B	Mr B's income [1,2,3]
	£	£	£	£	£	£
2008/09	10,875	2,175	8,500	8,500	3,000	3,000
2009/10	13,250	2,650	11,075	19,575	17,000	16,575
2010/11	14,500	2,900	11,600	31,175	12,000	12,175
2011/12	5,500	1,100	4,400	35,575	Nil	3,825

Note: 1. The amount deemed to be the income of Mr B in 2009/10 is restricted to the aggregate income entitlement for that year (£19,575) less the amount paid to him in 2008/09 (£3,000).
2. Similarly, the deemed income in 2010/11 is restricted to £31,175 less (£3,000 + £16,000).
3. The deemed income when the administration of the estate is complete in 2011/12 is the difference between the final aggregate income entitlement (£35,575) and the total of the amounts treated as Mr B's income to date (£3,000 + £16,575 + £12,175).

7244 Where the **income accrued** before death is included in the value of the estate for inheritance tax purposes, relief is available to the holder of an absolute interest to prevent the inclusion of the same income in the residuary estate for income tax purposes.

The relief is given by:

a. calculating the tax on the net accrued income using the average rate of inheritance tax on the estate as a whole;

b. grossing up the tax on the net accrued income at the rate applicable to the accrued income i.e. basic rate, savings rate or dividend rate; and

c. reducing the residuary income by the result.

EXAMPLE Mr A died in 2011/12 at which time his estate had residuary income of £50,000, of which £15,000 related to accrued income at the date of death. The average rate of inheritance tax applicable to the estate is (say) 25%. Mr B is the sole beneficiary of the estate.
For higher rate tax purposes, the income assessable on Mr B will be:

	£
Accrued income	15,000
Less: Basic rate tax @ 20%	(3,000)
Net accrued income	12,000
Inheritance tax on accrued income (12,000 @ 25%)	3,000
Inheritance tax on accrued income grossed up at basic rate (3,000 × 100/80)	3,750
Residuary income	50,000
Less: Relief for inheritance tax paid	(3,750)
Residuary income taxable at higher rate (40 %)	46,250

C. Foreign estates

A foreign estate is one where not all of the income is subject to UK tax or where the personal representatives are not directly assessable. An example of a foreign estate is one where the personal representatives are exempt from UK tax by reason of residence outside the UK. 7246

A UK resident beneficiary receiving income from a foreign estate will be taxed as if he had received foreign income. Credit is available for any overseas tax suffered on the income (¶4237). The rules about the date of receipt of the income from the foreign estate apply equally to both limited and absolute interests (¶7238).

UK income tax suffered

Where **part of the income** of the estate has suffered UK tax, special rules apply to determine the amount of tax payable by the beneficiary and the amount of that income which will be subject to higher rate tax. 7248

Limited interest Where the beneficiary has a limited interest and submits an **appropriate claim**, the tax chargeable will be reduced by the following formula: 7250 s 678 ITTOIA 2005

$$\frac{\text{Tax chargeable} \times \text{Net income subject to UK tax}}{\text{Net aggregate income}}$$

Where this formula has been applied, it is necessary to re-compute the beneficiary's income from the estate in order to ascertain his liability to higher rate tax. The proportion of the beneficiary's income corresponding to the net income subject to UK tax is grossed up at the rate applicable to that source of income. This amount is then added to the income that is not subject to UK tax.

EXAMPLE Mr A has a limited interest in the estate of Mr B, who died in June 2007. The administration of the estate was completed in December 2011 and the residuary income for 2011/12 was:

	Gross	Tax rate	Tax deducted	Net income
	£		£	£
Income subject to UK tax	10,000	20%	2,000	8,000
Income not subject to UK tax	16,000		-	16,000
Aggregate income	26,000		2,000	24,000

In 2011/12 Mr A received £8,000 from the personal representatives.

	£
Assessable income 8,000 @ 20%	1,600
Reduction of tax 1,600 × 8,000/24,000	(533)
Revised tax charge	1,067

For higher rate tax purposes, the amount of income deemed to have been received from the estate will be re-computed to take account of the relief given:

	£	
Net income subject to UK tax (8,000 ×,8,000/24,000) = 2,667		
Gross up 2,667 @ 100/80	3,334	
Add: Balance of income not subject to UK tax (8,000 – 2,667)	5,333	
Assessable gross income for higher rate tax	8,667	
Higher rate tax (8,667 @ (40 – 20) %)		1,733
Total tax chargeable		2,800

7252 **Absolute interest** Where the beneficiary has an absolute interest and submits an **appropriate claim**, the tax chargeable will be reduced by the following formula:

s 677 ITTOIA 2005

$$\frac{\text{Tax chargeable} \times \text{Gross income subject to UK tax}}{\text{Gross aggregate income}}$$

EXAMPLE Mr A has an absolute interest in the entire estate of Mr B, who died in October 2008. The administration of the estate was completed in July 2011 and the residuary income for 2011/12 was:

	Gross	Tax rate	Tax deducted	Net income
	£		£	£
Income subject to UK tax	15,000	20%	3,000	12,000
Income not subject to UK tax	11,000		-	11,000
Aggregate income	26,000		3,000	23,000

The income attributable to Mr A is £26,000. The assessable amount will be:

	£
Assessable income	
26,000 @ 20%	5,200
Reduction of tax	
5,200 × 15,000/26,000	(3,000)
Revised liability	2,200

The liability to higher rate tax will be calculated by reference to the attributed income i.e. £26,000.

SECTION 3

Capital gains tax

7258 Death does not constitute a disposal for capital gains tax (CGT) purposes, but a CGT charge may arise in connection with disposals:
- made by the deceased before death;
- of estate assets made by the personal representatives during the administration of the estate; and
- of estate assets by legatees.

In addition, a charge may arise where a beneficiary under an estate makes a disclaimer or variation claim.

A. Personal representatives

7260 The CGT liability of the personal representatives arises from disposals made by:
- the deceased before death (¶7262); and
- the personal representatives during the period of administration (¶7264).

1. Disposals made by the deceased before death

7262 Chargeable gains and allowable losses made by the deceased in the period between 6 April and death will be calculated in the usual manner, including a full annual exemption and any other exemptions and reliefs that may be available.

If the deceased made **allowable losses** in the tax year in which death occurred, they may be carried back and set against chargeable gains of the deceased in the 3 tax years preceding the tax year of death (¶5476). Unfortunately losses cannot be carried forward to set against gains arising from disposals made by the personal representatives.

The personal representatives are **responsible for** the payment, out of the estate, of any CGT arising as a result of disposals made by the deceased in the period before death and for any associated interest and penalties. 7263

By concession, where the taxpayer dies before the due date, and the personal representatives are unable to settle the liability until the **grant of probate** or letters of administration, the due date for payment may be extended to 30 days after the date of the grant. ESC A17

2. Disposals made by the personal representatives

At the **date of death**, those estate assets of which the deceased is competent to dispose are treated as if the personal representatives had acquired them at market value on that date. For this purpose the personal representatives are treated as having the residence, ordinary residence and domicile of the deceased at the date of his death. 7264

MEMO POINTS 1. The deceased is **competent to dispose** of assets by his will, assuming that: s 62 TCGA 1992
- he was of full age and capacity;
- all of the assets were situated in the UK; and
- he was domiciled in the UK.

2. Where **inheritance tax** is charged on the value of the estate on death and the value of a particular asset has been ascertained, that ascertained value will be used as the market value for CGT purposes.

Occasion of charge

If the personal representatives dispose of the assets of the estate to a **person other than a legatee** during the administration period, a chargeable gain or allowable loss can arise. 7265

Calculation of the gain

Annual exemption Personal representatives are treated as a single continuing body, and so many of the reliefs available to individuals will not be available to them. They are, however, entitled to an individual's **annual exemption** (¶6326) for the tax year of death and for the following 2 years (only), provided that the deceased was entitled to the annual exemption during his lifetime. 7266 s 37(7) TCGA 1992

Losses Allowable losses may only be relieved against gains made by the personal representatives in the same or a subsequent tax year. The rules for the interaction of losses and the annual exemption are the same as for individuals (¶5472). 7267

Losses made by the personal representatives cannot be set against the gains of legatees and vice versa, nor can they be carried back and set against gains made by the deceased. It is usually beneficial to transfer a loss-making asset straight to the legatee, so he can keep the loss relief.

Comment Where relief has been claimed for a **fall in value** for inheritance tax purposes (¶6814), the lower valuation will also be the market value for CGT purposes. It may be more efficient to avoid the inheritance tax relief and claim CGT loss relief instead, particularly where no repayment of inheritance tax would be due and the personal representatives have made other chargeable gains against which the CGT loss can be offset.

Entrepreneurs' relief Entrepreneurs' relief is available to personal representatives, provided there is a qualifying beneficiary for whom the qualifying assets are held (see ¶7382). 7269 s 169J TCGA 1992

7270 s 225A TCGA 1992 **Principal private residence relief** This relief (¶6166) can be claimed by the personal representatives if a house comprised in the estate has been **occupied**, before and after the deceased's death, as the only or main residence of individuals who are entitled to at least 75% of the net proceeds of the house on sale.

MEMO POINTS Where the family home **passes to the spouse**, the period of occupation by the deceased counts towards the spouse's period of occupation for the purposes of this relief.

7271 **Allowable expenditure** Allowable expenditure may be deducted in the normal way (¶5322). Personal representatives may also deduct expenditure incurred in establishing, preserving or defending **title to an asset**, which may include a proportion of the cost of obtaining probate or letters of administration.

7272 SP 2/04 **In practice**, it may be difficult to establish the appropriate proportion of expenditure relating to a particular asset, so HMRC have issued the following scales of expenses for use where death occurred on or after 6 April 2004. The personal representatives may use either the official scale rate or (if higher) the actual expenditure.

Gross value of the estate	Allowable expenditure
Up to £50,000	1.8% of the probate value of the asset
£50,001 to £90,000	Asset/Estate × £900
£90,001 to £400,000	1% of the probate value of the asset
£400,001 to £500,000	Asset/Estate × £4,000
£500,001 to £1m	0.8% of the probate value of the asset
£1m to £5m	Asset/Estate × £8,000
Over £5m	0.16% of the probate value of the asset subject to a maximum of £10,000

Corporate trustees may use the following scale to determine allowable expenditure incurred in the administration of estates. Again, the corporate trustee may choose whether to use the official scale or the actual expenses.

Nature of asset	Allowable expenditure
Transfer of assets to beneficiaries	
1. Quoted stocks and shares – one beneficiary – more than one beneficiary between whom the holding must be divided	£25 per holding £25 per holding, to be divided in equal shares between the beneficiaries
2. Unquoted shares	As for quoted shares with the addition of any exceptional expenditure
3. Other assets	
Actual disposals and acquisitions	
1. Quoted stocks and shares	The investment fee[1] as charged by the trustee
2. Unquoted shares	As for quoted shares with the addition of actual valuation costs
3. Other assets	The investment fee[1] as charged by the trustee, subject to a maximum of £75, plus actual valuation costs
Deemed disposals by trustees	
1. Quoted stocks and shares	£8 per holding
2. Unquoted shares	Actual valuation costs
3. Other assets	

Note:
1. Where a comprehensive annual management fee is charged which covers the cost of both the administration of the trust and the expenses of actual disposals and acquisitions, the investment fee will be deemed to be 0.25% of the sale or purchase money.

Tax rate The rates of CGT applicable to all chargeable gains made by personal representatives in 2011/12 are as follows. **7274** s 4 TCGA 1992

Rate (%)	Applies to
10	Gains subject to Entrepreneur's relief (¶6035)
28	All other gains

Comment Where a **legatee is exempt** from CGT, such as a UK charity, it would be preferable to transfer the asset direct to the legatee, rather than selling the asset first and then distributing the proceeds after a CGT charge.

B. Disposals made by legatees

A legatee is (broadly speaking) any beneficiary under a will or intestacy. **7276** s 64(2) TCGA 1992

When an asset is transferred to a legatee, no chargeable gain accrues to the personal representatives. The legatee is then treated as if he had acquired the asset at market value on the date of death (in the same way as the personal representatives).

Calculating the gain

The legatee's **allowable expenditure** includes any expenses incurred either by him or by the personal representatives. For example, costs incurred in transferring the title of property to the legatee will be allowable expenditure. **7277**

Disclaimer or variation

A disclaimer or variation made by a written **instrument** within 2 years from the date of death is not a chargeable disposal. The new beneficiary is treated as if he had acquired the property at market value on the death of the deceased. **7280** s 62(6) TCGA 1992

A **chargeable disposal** will, however, arise if the disclaimer or variation was made in return for consideration.

MEMO POINTS 1. The instrument must **state** that s 62(6) TCGA 1992 is to apply.
2. There is no need for the **personal representatives** to be a party to the instrument.
3. The disclaimer or variation may be effective for **inheritance tax** purposes without affecting the CGT position, and vice versa, and the instrument should be drafted accordingly.

CHAPTER 3

Income tax and trusts

OUTLINE ¶¶

Income tax in respect of settled property may be charged on: **7285**
– the trustees in respect of the income of the settlement (¶7290);
– the beneficiaries in respect of income to which they are entitled under the terms of the settlement (¶7336); or
– the settlor, when the income of the trust is treated as being his (¶7344).

SECTION 1

Income tax liability of trustees

7290 Income tax in respect of the income received by a trust will normally be the **liability of one or more of the trustees**, in their capacity as trustee. The trustees of a UK resident trust are taxable on the worldwide income of the trust. If one or more of the trustees is not resident in the UK, their liability to income tax may be affected (¶7570).

The trustees are not liable if the income is:
– paid directly to a beneficiary who is entitled to the income under the terms of the settlement;
– foreign dividends belonging and paid to a beneficiary, who is resident and domiciled abroad; or
– treated as being the income of the settlor.

7291 Trustees are required to complete an income tax self-assessment return on behalf of the trust (¶7650).

Bare trustees are not required to:
– deduct tax from payments to beneficiaries;
– complete self-assessment returns; or
– make payments on account.

Instead, the beneficiaries are liable to report trust income and gains on their own returns.

The **rate of income tax** applied to the income of a trust, and the expenses that can be deducted (if any), depend on whether the trust is an interest in possession trust or a non-interest in possession trust (such as a discretionary trust). Different sources of income may carry a tax credit at different rates.

A. General principles

7292 Trustees are subject to the general income tax rules, with the following exceptions:
– a trustee is not entitled to personal allowances, or to the 10% starting rate for savings for individuals; and
– trust income is never treated as earned income.

MEMO POINTS If a trustee **does not receive** the income of a trust (and is not entitled to receive it), he is not subject to income tax on it. This will happen, for example, when a trustee authorises the payment of income directly to a life tenant.

Rates of tax applicable to trustees

7293
s 9 ITA 2007
The general rule is that accumulated or discretionary income of the trustees (except of a trust established for charitable purposes only: ¶7200) is taxed at the following special rates:

Name	Applies to	2011/12	2010/11
The trust dividend rate	Dividends (¶2817)	42.5%	42.5%
The rate applicable to trusts	Other income	50%	50%

The rate applicable to trusts is often referred to as the **trust rate**.

See below for the specific application of these rates to different types of trust.

MEMO POINTS Income is accumulated or discretionary if by the terms of the trust it either must be accumulated, or is payable at the discretion of the trustees.

Trading income

7294 Trustees are subject to income tax on income from a trade (for example, where the trust has taken over a business on the death of the owner).

Trading income cannot be used to qualify a trustee for pension payments, but trustees can deduct trading expenses from the income, and can claim loss relief where appropriate.

Annuities

Trustees may make a **deduction** for annuities (to a particular beneficiary for example) and similar payments that are provided for in the terms of the trust. **7296** ss 900 ITA 2007

An annuity is usually expressed as a gross amount, from which the trustees must **deduct** tax at the basic rate. The trustee must provide the beneficiary with a certificate showing the amount deducted. The trustees can deduct the gross amount from the trust's taxable income, but must account to HMRC for the tax deducted.

The **beneficiary** (also known as the annuitant) must show the gross amount of the annuity on his tax return as investment income, but is entitled to a credit for the tax retained by the trustees.

EXAMPLE Trust A (an interest in possession trust) provides for an annuity of £5,000 a year to Mr B with any remaining income to be paid to Mr C. In 2011/12 the trust received income from property of £8,500. Mr B will receive £4,000 (5,000 less 20%) but will pay tax on the gross amount of £5,000 with credit for tax retained of £1,000.
The trustees will be taxed as follows:

	£
Gross income	8,500
Less: Annuity	(5,000)
Taxable income	3,500
Tax thereon:	
3,500 @ 20%	700
Add: Tax retained on annuity	1,000
Total basic rate tax payable	1,700

Alternatively, the trust may provide that an annuity should be **paid free of tax**. In this case the tax is borne by the trust, and the annuitant receives the stated amount of the annuity. The trustees must gross up a tax-free annuity to calculate the amount of tax to be retained. Any repayment of tax received by the beneficiary must be refunded to the trustee. **7297**

EXAMPLE Following on from the previous example, if the annuity to Mr B had been expressed to be free of tax, the situation would be as follows:
Mr B will receive £5,000 but will be taxed as if he received the following gross amount:
5,000 × 100/(100 – 20) = £6,250
Mr B can claim relief for tax retained of £1,250, but if any of that amount is repaid to him, he must refund it to the trust.
The trustee will be taxed as follows:

	£
Gross income	8,500
Less: Annuity	(6,250)
Taxable income	2,250
Tax thereon:	
2,250 @ 20%	450
Add: Tax retained on annuity	1,250
Total basic rate tax payable	1,700

Accrued income scheme

The accrued income scheme (¶4012) applies where the trust **purchases or sells securities**. The rules are the same as for individuals, except that the £5,000 de minimis limit is only available to disabled trusts (¶7190) and to personal representatives (¶7214). **7298** s 482 ITA 2007

If the net result for a tax year is a **charge on the trustees**, the rate of tax will always be the rate applicable to trusts (¶7293) regardless of the type of trust.

The consequences for the trustees are summarised in the following table.

Type of transaction	Treatment of dividend	Consequences for trustees
Purchase	Cum-div[1]	Relief equal to increase in price
	Ex-div[2]	Charge equal to decrease in price
Sale	Cum-div[1]	Charge equal to increase in price
	Ex-div[2]	Relief equal to decrease in price

Note:
1. Cum-div means that the price includes the right to the next interest payment.
2. Ex-div means that the security is being transferred with no right to the next interest payment.

B. Interest in possession trusts

7300 In calculating the charge to tax on the trustee of an interest in possession trust, the personal circumstances of both the trustee and the beneficiary are ignored.

Expenses

7302 s 486 ITA 2007 The income taxable is calculated using the general rules for the type of source, and expenses may be deducted as for an individual (for example, in the computation of property income).

Trust management expenses (for example, legal or accountancy expenses) arising in connection with the running of the trust are not deductible when calculating the tax liability. Such expenses must, however, be deducted before the income is paid to the beneficiaries, and are set against income in the following order:
- dividend income;
- savings income; and
- other income.

Rates of tax

7303 ss 481, 482 ITA 2007 The **normal rule** with respect to the trustees of an interest in possession trust is that they will be liable to:
- dividend rate tax on dividend income; and
- basic rate tax on all other income.

The **exception** to this rule are the following types of income which are taxable at the **trust rate** (¶7293) (50 % for 2011/12):
- receipts under the accrued income scheme;
- profit element of receipts relating to the purchase of own shares;
- life policy gains;
- profit on disposal of deeply discounted securities, where the trustees are UK resident;
- profits of a property business (e.g. lease premiums);
- profit on disposal of a future, option or deposit rights;
- profit on disposal of a foreign dividend coupon;
- chargeable events relating to employee share ownership trusts;
- offshore income gains; and
- gains arising from certain transactions in land (¶4052).

EXAMPLE Mr A is the only trustee of Trust B (an interest in possession trust) which received the following income in 2011/12:

	Gross (£)	Tax deducted (£)	Net (£)
Income from property	23,000	-	23,000
Bank interest	18,750	3,750	15,000
Dividends	12,222	1,222	11,000
		4,972	

Expenses of £2,100 were incurred in respect of the rental property, and other expenses in connection with the trust were £950.
Mr A's tax liability as a trustee will be:

	£	£
Income from property	23,000	
Less: Expenses	(2,100)	
		20,900
Bank interest		18,750
Dividends		12,222
Taxable income		51,872
Tax thereon:		
20,900 @ 20%	4,180	
18,750 @ 20%	3,750	
12,222 @ 10%	1,222	
Tax liability	9,152	
Less: Tax deducted at source (3,750 + 1,222)	(4,972)	
Tax payable	4,180	

The income available for distribution to the beneficiaries is as follows:

	£
Income from property (20,900 – 4,180)	16,720
Bank interest (18,750 – 3,750)	15,000
Dividends (12,222 – 1,222)	11,000
	42,720
Less: Other trust expenses	(950)
Available for distribution	41,770

Stock dividends

The tax treatment of stock dividends depends on whether they are treated as a receipt of **income or capital** under the terms of the trust: 7305 s 410 ITTOIA 2005
- if the dividends are **income**, they are liable to tax in the same way as individuals; and
- if the dividends are **capital**, no income tax charge arises.

MEMO POINTS 1. The rules for **individuals** are at ¶2817.
2. For **capital gains tax** purposes, the stock treated as income has a base cost of the value charged to income tax. However, the base cost for stock treated as capital is nil.

C. Non-interest in possession trusts

Rates of tax

When trust income is in excess of a **first band of £1,000**, it is taxed at the following rates: 7308 ss 479, 491 ITA 2007

Type of income	Applicable rate	Rate for 2011/12
Dividends (¶2817)	Trust dividend rate	42.5%
All other (except for items listed at ¶7310)	Trust rate	50%

If the settlor has made **more than one settlement**, the £1,000 band is divided equally between them, subject to a minimum of £200.

MEMO POINTS Income within the £1,000 band is taxable at the basic rate or the trust dividend rate, depending on the source of income. Dividend income is only covered by the £1,000 band if there is insufficient other income. Trusts with income falling entirely within the £1,000 band are not required to submit tax returns, although a return will be issued every few years, and any change in circumstances must be notified within the usual time limits (¶7652).

7310 ss 486ITA 2007

The special rates **do not apply** to the following:
- income to which general trust expenses are attributable;
- annuities and other similar payments; and
- income received and held on trust in respect of service charges or sinking funds in relation to any UK dwelling.

MEMO POINTS **General trust expenses** are set against income in the following order:
a. UK dividend income including non-qualifying distributions and stock dividends;
b. foreign dividends;
c. savings income; and
d. any other income.

EXAMPLE Trust A (a discretionary trust) received the following income in 2011/12:

	Gross (£)	Tax deducted (£)	Net (£)
Income from property	25,000	-	25,000
Bank interest	6,875	1,375	5,500
Dividends	3,500	350	3,150

Expenses for the year amounted to £2,500.
The tax liability of the trustees will be computed as follows:

		Gross £	Tax £
Income from property		25,000	
Bank interest		6,875	1,375
Dividends	3,500		350
Less: Expenses (2,500 × 100/90)	(2,778)		(278)
		722	
Taxable income		32,597	1,447
Tax thereon:			
Dividend trust rate			
722 @ 42.5%		306	
£1,000 band			
1,000 @ 20%		200	
Trust rate			
(32,597 – 722 – 1,000) = 30,875 @ 50%		15,437	
Less: Tax deducted at source		(1,447)	
		14,496	

7311 TSEM 8000

HMRC have issued detailed guidance on the tax treatment of **trust management expenses**. The guidance includes HMRC's view on whether specific types of expense are deductible in arriving at the trustees' liability to tax at the special rate, as set out in the following table. The guidance is based on HMRC's interpretation of the legislation, which differs in some respects to that of the tax profession.

MEMO POINTS The issue of management expenses was considered by the Court of Appeal in the case of *HMRC v Trustees of the Peter Clay Discretionary Settlement* [2009]. Where expenses are incurred for the benefit of the whole estate, meaning both income and capital beneficiaries, these costs should be charged against capital. It is only expenses which are incurred exclusively for the benefit of the income beneficiaries that may be charged against income. Consequently, fees charged by an executive trustee for his time spent in applying his professional judgement in relation to accountancy services (which could be apportioned between capital and income) could also be so apportioned.

Type of expense	Details	Allowable[1]	Not allowable
Accountancy or audit costs	Only the costs that relate to accounting for or auditing trust income	✓	
	Only the costs that relate to the preparation of income sections of trust tax returns (all allowable if no chargeable disposals)	✓	
Bank charges	Current account charges		✓
Depreciation			✓
Distributing income	Costs such as those in relation to posting cheques to beneficiaries		✓
Insurance	Premiums in relation to a property leased to the trustees, where: – the property is occupied by a beneficiary or generates rental income; and – the beneficiary or tenant is not legally obliged to pay the insurance	✓	
Interest	On a loan or overdraft for the benefit of the income fund, including the purchase of an income-producing asset such as shares, or the purchase of a property occupied by a beneficiary	✓	
	On a loan or overdraft for general trust administration or the purchase of a non-income producing asset		✓
	On a loan to pay inheritance tax	✓	
	On unpaid income tax, capital gains tax or inheritance tax, unless delay due to trustees' neglect	✓	
	On surcharges or interest on overdue tax		✓
Investment advice			✓
Legal costs	If exclusively in relation to a life tenant	✓	
Life insurance			✓
Personal expenses of beneficiaries			✓
Property costs	Rent or maintenance costs of a property owned by or leased to the trustees, where the property is occupied by a beneficiary who is not obliged to meet those costs	✓	
Reimbursement of expenses to trustees	If of an income nature, on general principles	✓	
Tax penalties or surcharges			✓
Travel and subsistence	If exclusively in relation to trust income	✓	
Trust running costs			✓
Trustees' fees			✓[2]

Note:
1. Any costs that are deductible in arriving at taxable trading or rental income are not again relieved as a trust management expense.
2. Any attempt to apportion the costs between income and capital is likely to be disallowed by HMRC.

The tax pool

7312
s 497 ITA 2007
Tax Bulletin 78

If a UK resident trustee makes a **discretionary payment of income** to a beneficiary, it is treated as paid net of tax at the trust rate (even if all the trust's income comes from dividends). The trustees must account to HMRC for the tax, but the liability can be covered by any tax already paid by the trustees, which is accumulated in a tax pool. If the tax pool is insufficient to cover the tax, an assessment will be raised on the trustees to cover the shortfall.

The tax pool relates to the trust as a whole rather than to individual beneficiaries, and **consists of** of the following:
- tax charged in the year at the trust rate;
- tax charged in the year at the dividend trust rate less any associated (non-repayable) tax credits; and
- the tax pool brought forward from the previous tax year.

MEMO POINTS 1. At http://www.hmrc.gov.uk/tools/trusts/index.htm, HMRC offer a trust pools calculator to help in establishing the size of the tax pool and the income available for distribution. This **cannot be used** for:
- discretionary trusts with deemed, trade or foreign income;
- discretionary trusts that are settlor-interested trusts;
- any non-discretionary trusts;
- any settlor-interested element of a discretionary trust; and
- cases where vulnerable beneficiary relief has been claimed; or
- a year earlier than 2008/09.

2. For the **beneficiary**, the payment is always treated as non-savings income.

EXAMPLE Following on from the previous example at ¶7310, the trustees of Trust A made a discretionary payment of £20,000 to beneficiary B in 2011/12. The balance brought forward on the tax pool is (say) £2,000.
Beneficiary B received £20,000, which means that the tax payable by the trustees is:
£20,000 × 50/(100 – 50) = £20,000

The liability will, in part, be covered by the tax in the tax pool:

	£	£
Tax payable		20,000
Brought forward from 2009/10	2,000	
Basic rate tax on rental income	200	
Charged at the trust rate (30,875 @ 50%)	15,437	
Charged at the dividend trust rate, less related tax credit (722 × (42.5 % – 10%))	234	
		(17,871)
Additional assessment raised on the trustees		2,129

D. Trusts for young people

7314 The tax treatment of accumulation and maintenance trusts (¶7194), trusts for bereaved minors (¶7196) and age 18-to-25 trusts (¶7198) depends on the beneficiaries' **entitlement to income**:

Entitlement to income	Tax definition of trust
None	Non-interest in possession trust
Sole beneficiary, who is entitled	Interest in possession trust[1]
Some beneficiaries entitled and some not	Mixed trust, until all beneficiaries are entitled to income

Note:
1. From the date the beneficiary becomes entitled, which is usually based on his age.

MEMO POINTS 1. If the **age** is not specified in an accumulation and maintenance trust deed, a beneficiary will be entitled to the income from the trust at the age of 18 even if he is not entitled to the capital until a later age. For example, if a beneficiary is entitled to the capital at age 30, he will still be entitled to the income at 18, and his right to capital is therefore a contingent interest, as it relies on him reaching the age of 30. s 31 Trustee Act 1925
2. A trust will **end** if the only beneficiary becomes entitled to income and capital on reaching a specified age. If there is more than one beneficiary then each beneficiary will, on reaching the specified age, receive his share of the trust capital and the trust will end when all the beneficiaries reach the specified age

Mixed trusts

Where at least one of the beneficiaries under a trust holds an interest in possession in it, and at least one does not, the income belonging to any beneficiary with an **interest in possession** must be excluded from the calculation of income tax at the trust rates. **7316**

EXAMPLE Trust B (an accumulation and maintenance trust) received the following income in 2011/12:

	Gross (£)	Tax deducted (£)	Net (£)
Income from property	18,000	Nil	18,000
Bank interest	9,000	1,800	7,200
Dividends	12,000	1,200	10,800

General expenses of £1,500 were incurred by the trust.
The terms of the trust specify that the beneficiaries will become entitled to equal shares of the capital of the trust on attaining the age of 25. The beneficiaries are:

	Age
Mr B	20
Miss C	17
Miss D	14

Mr B therefore holds an interest in possession in one third of the trust because he is over the age of 18. Tax payable by the trustees on his share is calculated as follows:

	Gross £	Tax £
Tax payable by the trustee re Mr B:		
Income from property (18,000 × 1/3)	6,000	
Bank interest (9,000 × 1/3)	3,000	600
Dividends (12,000 × 1/3)	4,000	400
Taxable income	13,000	1,000
Tax thereon:		
6,000 @ 20%	1,200	
(Bank interest and dividends covered by tax deducted at source)		
Tax payable by the trustees on the share of Miss C and Miss D:		
Income from property (18,000 × 2/3)	12,000	
Bank interest (9,000 × 2/3)	6,000	1,200
Dividends (12,000 × 2/3)	8,000	800
	26,000	2,000
Less: Expenses (1,500 × 100/90 × 2/3)	(1,111)	(111)
Taxable income	24,889	1,889
Tax thereon:		
Dividend trust rate		
8,000 – 1,111 = 6,889 @ 42.5%	2,927	
£1,000 band		
1,000 @ 20%	200	
Trust rate		
24,889 – 6,889 – 1,000 = 17,000 @ 50%	8,500	
	11,627	
Less: Tax deducted at source	(1,889)	
Tax payable by trustee	9,738	

E. Trusts for the vulnerable

7318 s 23 FA 2005 The trustees and vulnerable beneficiary of a trust can jointly and irrevocably make a **vulnerable person election** for trust income to be treated as if it were directly assessed on the beneficiary. This avoids the higher tax rates which apply to non-interest in possession trusts. The trustees remain liable for the income tax, but the beneficiary's personal circumstances are taken into account when calculating the amount payable.

ss 38 - 39 FA 2005 MEMO POINTS A vulnerable beneficiary is **defined** as a:
a. disabled person who is:
– incapable of managing his property or administering his affairs due to mental disorder; or
– entitled to receive attendance allowance or the middle or highest rate of disability living allowance (or who would be entitled but for the fact that he receives kidney treatment in hospital or is provided with certain accommodation); or
b. child under the age of 18 where at least one of his parents has died (subsequent remarriage by the surviving parent is irrelevant).

Conditions

7320 s 24 FA 2005 If a vulnerable person election is in effect at some time during the tax year, the trustees may make a claim to reduce their tax liability. The income concerned must **relate to** property held in the trust for the benefit of the vulnerable person.

The claim will **not be available** if the vulnerable beneficiary is a settlor of the trust.

ss 34 - 35 FA 2005 MEMO POINTS The definition of **qualifying trust** depends on whether the beneficiary is disabled or a minor child:
a. for a **disabled** person, the trust property must be held for his benefit during his lifetime, or until the trust terminates, if earlier. So any property applied must be for his benefit alone, and either he is entitled to all the income of the trust, or it is accumulated. The income cannot be used to benefit anyone else; and
b. for a minor **child**, the trust must be one of the following:
– a statutory trust;
– a trust established under a will of the deceased parent; or
– a trust established under the Criminal Injuries Compensation Scheme.
Unless a statutory trust, the child must become absolutely entitled to the trust property and all related income on reaching 18, any property applied must be for his benefit alone, and either he is entitled to all the income of the trust or it is accumulated. The income cannot be used to benefit anyone else.

Consequences

7321 ss 26 - 29 FA 2005 The tax liability of the **trustees** will be reduced to the amount that would be payable if the beneficiary were directly liable to tax on the trust income.

The **beneficiary's** deemed tax liability is calculated by taking his actual taxable income computed as normal and:
– adding the income received by the trust;
– excluding any payments that the beneficiary has actually received from the trustees; and
– ignoring the effect of any tax reductions (¶4440), such as EIS relief.

MEMO POINTS 1. Where only some of the trust's income qualifies for the claim, **trust management expenses** must be apportioned accordingly.
2. Where the **election is only in force** for part of the tax year, only the income arising since the election can be subject to a claim.

EXAMPLE Mr A is disabled, and a beneficiary of discretionary Trust B. An election is in force, and the trustees make a claim in relation to the rental income of £10,000 received by the trust in 2011/12.
Mr A's only gross income in 2011/12 is £8,000 of bank interest.

With a claim, the trustee's income tax liability becomes:

	Gross	Tax
	£	£
Mr A's bank interest	8,000	1,600
Trust's income from property	10,000	
	18,000	1,600
Less: Personal allowance	(7,475)	
Taxable income	10,525	
Tax thereon:		
10,525 @ 20%	2,105	
	2,305	
Less: Tax deducted at source	(1,600)	
Tax relating to rental income	705	

Without a claim, the trustees would have been liable to income tax as follows:

	£	£
Income from property		10,000
Tax thereon:		
£1,000 band: 1,000 @ 20%	200	
10,000 – 1,000 @ 50%	45,000	
	4,700	

Vulnerable person election

The election must be **made jointly** by the trustees and the beneficiary, and must specify the commencement date. Notice must be given to HMRC no later than 12 months from 31 January following the tax year in which the commencement date falls, along with any information they may require. **7323** s 37 FA 2005

The election will be **effective until** any of the following happens:
- the trust terminates;
- the trust ceases to be a qualifying trust; or
- the beneficiary ceases to be vulnerable.

Compliance

HMRC may open an **enquiry** (¶4552) to ensure that the relevant conditions are met and the election is still valid. A determination may treat the election as never having had effect, or only having effect to a certain date, although there is a right of appeal for both the trustees and the beneficiary. **7324** s 40 FA 2005

Penalties will apply to the trustees if the required information is not provided: s 43 FA 2005
- on making an election;
- during an enquiry; or
- about an event which causes the election to fail.

Failure to comply with an HMRC notice may result in a penalty of up to £300 being charged. s 98 TMA 1970

Where fraudulent or negligent information is provided, a penalty of up to £3,000 may be charged. The new penalty regime will also apply (see ¶9780+).

F. Charitable trusts

These rules only apply to charitable trusts (¶7200) established in the UK. Most income received by such trusts is exempt, as long as it is applied for charitable purposes. **7326** s 524 ITA 2007

Scope of the exemption

7328 ss 529 - 539 ITA 2007

The following types of income are exempt from income tax:
- income from land vested in the trustees;
- untaxed interest received in the UK and from abroad;
- dividend income received in the UK and from abroad;
- non-trading gains on intangible fixed assets;
- certain trading income;
- offshore income gains;
- income from estates in administration;
- public revenue dividends, to the extent that they are applied for the repair of any cathedral, college, church, chapel or other place of worship; and
- proceeds of an approved lottery.

Trading income

7329 ss 524 - 526 ITA 2007

Profits from a trade will be **generally exempt** from income tax where either of the following conditions are satisfied:
- the trade is actually exercised in the course of carrying out a primary purpose of the charity; or
- the work in connection with the trade is mainly carried out by beneficiaries of the charity.

Where **part of a charity's trade** is not carried out for the primary purpose of the charity, or by the beneficiaries of the charity, that part is treated as a separate trade so that tax relief is only lost on the profits of that part. Alternatively, relief for the whole trading profit may be available under the small trades exemption (see below).

7330 s 528 ITA 2007

Small trades exemption Subject to restrictions, where a charity has turnover within the following limits, a statutory exemption applies to its trading income:

Total gross income of charity	Maximum permitted sales turnover (£)
Under £20,000	5,000
£20,000 to £200,000	25% of charity's gross income
Over £200,000	50,000

Excess non-charitable expenditure

7332 s 539 - 540 ITA 2007

The tax-exempt income and gains of a charity are reduced by £1 for every £1 of non-charitable expenditure (which is referred to as the **non-charitable amount**). If the non-charitable expenditure exceeds the total income and gains for the year, the excess can be carried back to an earlier chargeable period within the previous 6 years.

EXAMPLE Trust A is a charitable trust with income of £14,000 and non-charitable expenditure of £1,500 in its chargeable period beginning on 1 April 2011.
The exempt amount is calculated as follows:

	£
Income	14,000
Non-charitable amount	(1,500)
Exempt amount	12,500

Tainted donations

7333 s 27 FA 2011

If a donor makes a **tainted donation** to a charity:
- the donor loses any tax relief which would otherwise have been available on the donation; and
- a tax charge may arise, if the charity is entitled to a repayment of tax through Gift Aid (¶4420) or from a donation made out of trust income.

In some circumstances the charity itself may be **jointly and severally liable** for this tax charge: see ¶7335.

These rules apply to donations made on or after 1 April 2011.

The former regime for substantial donors ceases to apply to new donors. Transactions with donors who were already substantial donors before 1 April 2011 will continue to fall under the old rules up to and including 31 March 2013. For details of the old rules, see *Tax Memo 2010-11*. s 549 ITA 2007

MEMO POINTS 1. Unlike the old rules, which penalised the charity, the new rules are aimed primarily at the donor, who is likely to be the party initiating the arrangements. The charity does not lose any entitlement to recover tax on the donation.
2. From 1 April 2011, if a pre-existing substantial donor enters into a transaction which is caught by the substantial donor rules, but is not tainted under the new rules, no tax charge arises.
3. Even after 31 March 2013, if a substantial donor enters into an arrangement before that date which would be caught under the old rules, and a transaction under that arrangement is completed after 31 March 2013, the old rules will still apply to the related donation.

For a donation (of any size) to be tainted, **three conditions**, A, B and C, must all be satisfied: **7334**

Condition		Details
A	A donation, and arrangements entered into between the donor[1] and another party in respect of the donation, are connected to each other.	"Connected" means that it is reasonable to assume from the circumstances that the donation would not have been made and the arrangements would not have been entered into independently of one another. "Arrangements" can include (for example) the sale or letting of property, the provision of services, the exchange of property, the provision of a loan or any other form of financial assistance, or making an investment in a business.
B	The main purpose, or one of the main purposes, of the arrangement is for the donor[1] to receive a financial advantage directly or indirectly from the charity.	A financial advantage is ignored if: – the person by whom it is obtained applies it for charitable purposes only; or – it is a benefit which is ignored for Gift Aid (¶4423) or charitable donations relief (¶964); or – the donation is a gift of investments (¶4382) or qualifying investments (¶966), and the advantage is a benefit the value of which is taken into account in determining the amount eligible for tax relief; or – the donation is a gift of trading stock for which tax relief would be available (¶178), and the advantage is a benefit which gives rise to a taxable profit.
C	The donor is **not** a company wholly-owned by a charity (or charities), or a relevant housing provider linked with the charity to which the donation is made.	This exemption does not apply where a person who stands to obtain a financial advantage from the arrangement was previously in control of the charity-owned company. A donor cannot take advantage of Condition C by transferring to a charity a trade or business that he (or a person connected with him) formerly carried on.

Notes
1. "Donor" includes any person connected (¶5570) with the donor during the period which begins with the earliest, and ends with the latest, of the following:
– the time when the arrangements are entered into;
– the time when the donation is made; and
– the time when the arrangements are first materially implemented.

An **income tax charge** may arise from a tainted donation if the charity is entitled to recover tax on it, either: **7335**
– under Gift Aid (¶4420); or
– because the donation was made out of trust income, either as a donation by the trustees or because the charity is entitled to the income from the trust.

The tax charge is equal to the tax recoverable by the charity, and arises even if the charity has not yet recovered the tax. If the tax has been recovered, the charity can repay it to HMRC, and the income tax charge will not then arise.

The persons who are or may be **jointly and severally liable** for the tax charge are as follows:

Persons liable	Gift Aid	Trust donation
The trustees		Yes
The donor [1]	Yes	Yes, if different from the trustees
Any person who may obtain an advantage under the arrangements	Yes	Yes
Any beneficiary who is party to the arrangements		Yes
The settlor		Yes, if the trust is settlor-interested (¶7344)
Any charity to which the donation [1] is made	Potentially [2]	Potentially [2]

Notes
1. "Donor" means the person who makes the tainted donation itself, and any other person who makes a donation in connection with the same arrangements. "Donation" is interpreted similarly.
2. A charity will only be liable if it was a party to the arrangements relating to the tainted donation, and was aware, at the time it entered into those arrangements, that the donor (or someone connected with him) was also entering (or had entered or was likely to enter) into them.

SECTION 2

The tax position of the beneficiary

7336 Trust income is usually paid to beneficiaries by the trustees of the trust (other than a bare trust), who must provide a certificate to indicate the amount of tax that they have deducted.

The rate of tax deducted by the trustees will depend on whether the payment of income is made at their discretion (¶7312).

General rules applying to income

7337 The beneficiary's taxable income is the grossed up amount of the net income, after deducting any trust expenses payable out of income.

The following **payments out of a trust** have also been held to be the income of the beneficiary for trust purposes.

Type of payment	Case
Outgoings connected with a **residence** provided for a beneficiary	*Donaldson's Executors v CIR* [1927]
Payment of **rates** for a beneficiary	*Lord Tollemache v CIR* [1926]
An annual sum towards the **upkeep** of a property occupied by a beneficiary	*Shanks v CIR* [1929]
Payments to a parent for the maintenance of a **minor child** (held to be the income of the child assessable on the parent)	*Drummond v Collins* [1915]

ss 548 - 549 CTA 2010

MEMO POINTS 1. Dividends received by shareholders from a **Real Estate Investment Trust** (REIT) are treated for income tax purposes as profits from a UK property business. There is no tax credit (¶2821), although basic rate tax may have been deducted at source (¶2846). This notional property business is separate from other businesses, so that losses from other rental activities cannot be set off against REIT distributions.

2. Compensation payments may be made under the **Equitable Life Payment Scheme** (ELPS) to trustee policy holders in Equitable Life who have suffered loss due to government maladministration. These payments are tax free to the trustees. Their tax status if passed on to **beneficiaries** is as follows:
– if the beneficiary is entitled to the income as of right (for example, in an interest in possession trust): tax free;

– if the payment is made under a power or discretion of the trustees: taxable.
3. If a payment to a beneficiary has the nature of income, the fact that it is **made out of the capital** of the trust does not affect the beneficiary's income tax liability. This would apply, for example, if the trust has insufficient income to pay an annuity, and the shortfall is made up from capital.

A. Bare trusts

The beneficiary of a bare trust (¶7176) has an absolute right to the income and capital of the trust. Income received is therefore **treated as belonging to the beneficiary**, not the trustees, and retains the nature of the original payment. 7338

Income received must be **reported** on the beneficiary's own self-assessment return pages relating to each specific source of income.

EXAMPLE Mr A is the trustee of a bare trust in favour of Mr B, whose income in 2011/12 is as follows:

	£	
Earnings	42,000	(PAYE – £14,500)
Bank interest (net)	8,000	

In the same year the trust received the following income:

	£
Rental income	10,000
Dividends (net)	9,000

Mr B will be taxed as follows:

	Gross £	Tax £
Earned income	42,000	14,500
Rental income	10,000	
Savings (8,000 × 100/80)	10,000	2,000
Dividends (9,000 × 100/90)	10,000	1,000
	72,000	
Less: Personal allowance	(7,475)	
Taxable income	64,525	17,500
Tax thereon:		
35,000 @ 20%	7,000	
19,525 @ 40%	7,810	
	14,810	
Dividend income 10,000 @ 32.5%	3,250	
	18,060	
Less: Tax deducted at source	(17,500)	
Tax payable by Mr B	560	

B. Interest in possession trusts

The beneficiary **is entitled** to the income of the trust as it arises. He is therefore liable to tax on the income in the same tax year as it is received by the trustees, whether or not he himself actually receives the income in that tax year. 7339

Each source of income retains its separate identity, and the beneficiary is taxed at the rates applicable to each source.

MEMO POINTS 1. The trustees must issue a **tax deduction certificate** (form R185) showing the net income paid to the beneficiary and any tax deducted. The beneficiary will be taxed on the gross amount, but credit will be given for the tax deducted by the trustees.

2. Where a source of income is **mandated directly to the beneficiary**, it will be taxed on him as if he owned the source himself. This income will not be included on the tax deduction certificate.

EXAMPLE Trust B (an interest in possession trust) received the following income in 2011/12:

	Gross (£)	Tax deducted (£)	Net (£)
Income from property	23,000	-	23,000
Bank interest	18,750	3,750	15,000
Dividends	12,222	1,222	11,000

Expenses of £2,100 were incurred in respect of the rental property and other expenses in connection with the trust were £950.

The income available for distribution to the beneficiary (Mr A) is as follows (see earlier example at ¶7303):

	Income	Tax	Net
Income from property	20,900	4,180	16,720
Bank interest	18,750	3,750	15,000
Dividends	12,222	1,222	11,000
			42,720
Less: Other trust expenses			(950)
Available for distribution			41,770

The tax deduction certificate will show the following:

	Gross	Tax	Net
Dividend income (11,000 – 950)	11,167	1,117 (10 %)	10,050
Savings income	18,750	3,750 (20 %)	15,000
Other income	20,900	4,180 (20 %)	16,720

Each source of income will retain its identity in the hands of the beneficiary. Mr A will pay tax on the gross amounts.

Mr A's only other income in 2011/12 was earned income of £25,000 (PAYE £5,000).

	Gross £	Tax £
Earned income	25,000	5,000
Other trust income	20,900	4,180
Savings income	18,750	3,750
Dividends	11,167	1,117
	75,817	
Less: Personal allowance	(7,475)	
Taxable income	68,342	14,047
Tax thereon:		
35,000 @ 20%	7,000	
22,175 @ 40%	8,870	
	15,870	
Dividend income 11,167 @ 32.5%	3,629	
	19,499	
Less: Tax deducted at source	(14,047)	
Tax payable by Mr A	5,452	

Reporting

Income received by the beneficiary of an interest in possession trust must be included in the trust pages of the **self-assessment return** and entered in the boxes relating to the rate of tax deducted. The exceptions are **scrip dividends**, which should be entered on the main pages, and income from **foreign sources**, which should be entered on the foreign pages. **7340**

Any income received **gross** from the trust should be entered on the relevant pages for that source of income.

C. Non-interest in possession trusts

The income received by the beneficiary of a non-interest in possession trust is **treated as** trust income, and is therefore subject to deduction of tax at the trust rate (50 % in 2011/12). Where income of a **settlor-interested trust** has already been assessed on the settlor, beneficiaries who receive payments of income have no income tax liability on the amount already assessed. The income from the trust is treated as forming the highest part of the beneficiaries' income, apart from gains from life insurance policies and payments and benefits arising on termination of employment. **7341** ss 479, 1012 ITA 2007 s 685A ITTOIA 2005

MEMO POINTS The trustees must issue a **tax deduction certificate** (form R185) showing the net income paid to the beneficiary and any tax deducted. The beneficiary will be taxed on the gross amount, but credit will be given for the tax deducted by the trustees.

EXAMPLE **Tax position of the trustees**

Trust B (a discretionary trust) received the following income in 2011/12:

	Gross (£)	Tax deducted (£)	Net (£)
Income from property	9,000	-	9,000
Bank interest	12,500	2,500	10,000
Dividends	5,000	500	4,500

General expenses of £720 were incurred. The tax liability of the trustees is calculated as follows:

		Gross £	Tax £
Income from property		9,000	
Bank interest		12,500	2,500
Dividends	5,000		500
Less: Expenses (720 × 100/90)	(800)		(80)
		4,200	
		25,700	2,920
Tax thereon:			
Dividend trust rate			
4,200 @ 42.5%		1,785	
£1,000 band			
1,000 @ 20%		200	
Trust rate			
(25,700 – 4,200 – 1,000 = 20,500) @ 50%		10,250	
Less: Tax deducted at source		(2,920)	
		9,315	

Beneficiary's tax position

The trustees made a discretionary payment of £10,000 to beneficiary C. The tax deduction certificate will show the following:

	Gross	Tax	Net
Trust income	20,000	10,000 (50 %)	10,000

C's only other income in 2011/12 was earned income of £30,000 (PAYE £5,000).

	Gross £	Tax £
Earned income	30,000	5,000
Trust income	20,000	10,000
	50,000	
Less: Personal allowance	(7,475)	
Taxable income	42,525	15,000
Tax thereon:		
35,000 @ 20%	7,000	
7,525 @ 40%	3,010	
	10,010	
Less: Tax deducted at source	(15,000)	
Tax repayable to C	(4,990)	

If the trust was settor-interested, there would be no credit for the tax suffered by the trustees and no repayment due to C in respect of the trust income. The trust income is assessed as forming the highest part of C's income without triggering an additional liability. C's tax position for the year would be:
£30,000 – personal allowance (£7,475) = £22,525 × 20%. Tax liability is £4,505. PAYE of £5,000 has been deducted, so a refund of £495 is due to C.

Overseas issues

7342 ESC B18 INTM 367700 By concession, an **exception** applies if:
– the beneficiary receives a discretionary payment from a trust; and
– if he had received the income of the trust directly, it would have been subject to an exemption or relief.

This latter occurs when the beneficiary is not subject to UK tax on all of the payment because:
– of his residence and/or ordinary residence status; or
– he was entitled to relief under a double taxation agreement (¶4226); or
– the income related to UK government securities which are free of tax for residents abroad (FOTRA securities) (¶4290).

Where the concession applies, the beneficiary is entitled to a **refund** of a part of the tax credit, based on the proportion that the non-taxable income of the trust bears to the whole.

EXAMPLE Mr A is a non-resident beneficiary of Trust B (a discretionary trust), which received the following income in 2011/12:

	Gross (£)	Tax deducted (£)	Net (£)
UK dividends	10,000	1,000	9,000
Gilt interest	7,500	1,500	6,000

The trustees make a net payment of £3,000 to Mr A in 2011/12, which is equivalent to a gross payment of £6,000 (i.e. £3,000 × 100/50) with a tax credit of £3,000.
Mr A will be entitled to a refund of part of the tax credit because if the gilt interest had been paid directly to him, it would have been free of tax.
The amount of the refund will be calculated as follows:

	£
Gross dividends	10,000
Gross gilt interest	7,500
	17,500

Tax credit refund: $\frac{7{,}500}{17{,}500} \times 3{,}000 =$ £1,285

SECTION 3

The tax position of the settlor

There are three cases in which a settlor may be liable to tax on the income of a trust as if the income were his own: **7344** s 619 ITTOIA 2005

The settlor retains an interest in the trust	¶7350
Payments are made out of (or income is accumulated in) a settlement for an unmarried minor child of the settlor	¶7356
A capital sum (including a loan or repayment of a loan) is paid to the settlor	¶7359

MEMO POINTS For these purposes, the **definition** of a settlement is widened to include any disposition, trust, covenant, agreement, arrangement or transfer of assets. However, a settlement does not include any arrangement to the extent that it consists of a loan of money made by an individual to a charity for no consideration, or for a consideration which consists only of interest. s 620 ITTOIA 2005

Income from a settlement

Settlor's status Income arising from a settlement **includes**, for these purposes: **7345** s 648 ITTOIA 2005
- any income chargeable to income tax; and
- any income which would have been chargeable if it had been received in the UK by a person domiciled, resident and ordinarily resident in the UK.

Otherwise, if the settlor is either non-domiciled, non-resident, or not ordinarily resident in the UK in a tax year, the settlement income excludes any which would not be chargeable in the UK because of his status. Such income is deemed to arise when it is actually remitted to the UK, and will then be taxable if the settlor is resident in the UK. See ¶7570+.

Gifts to charity Income used to make gifts to charity by UK resident trustees is **excluded** from the income assessable on the settlor, provided the qualifying income is: **7346** ss 628, 630 ITTOIA 2005
- donated by the trustees in the tax year in which it arises; or
- income to which a charity is entitled under the terms of the trust.

MEMO POINTS **Qualifying income**, for these purpose, is income which is:
- to be accumulated;
- payable at the discretion of the trustees or of any other person; or
- before being distributed, income of any person other than the trustees.

Tax calculation

The trust's income under these provisions is, for all tax purposes, treated as the income of the settlor, and the general rules apply with respect to the **deduction** of allowances and reliefs. Income other than dividends is taxed as sundry income, whilst dividend income is taxed as usual. **7348** s 623 ITTOIA 2005

The **charge** to tax is calculated as if the income of the settlor formed the top slice of his income after lump sum payments on loss of office (¶3078) and life policy gains (¶4066). The settlor is treated as receiving a tax credit for the tax already paid by the trustees on the trust income. Any tax suffered by the settlor in respect of the income can be reclaimed from the trustees. Similarly, any tax repaid to the settlor must be refunded to the trustees.

MEMO POINTS 1. For the income which is included in the term **dividends** for these purposes, see ¶7308.
2. Tax **suffered** by the settlor may also be reclaimed from any other person to whom income is payable under the settlement. The reverse applies to tax **repayments**.
3. The **tax credit** on the trust income received by the settlor is restricted to the actual amount of tax suffered by the trustees, to prevent the settlor obtaining a tax credit of 50% on income received by the trustees before 2010/11, when they only paid tax at 40%.
4. The settlor can require the trustees to provide a statement setting out the income which is regarded as his.

A. Settlor retains an interest

7350 s 624 ITTOIA 2005 Where a settlor retains an interest in the trust property, trust income arising during the life of the settlor is treated for all income tax purposes as the settlor's income. Tax is charged at the rates which would have applied if the income (before deduction of trustees' expenses) had arisen directly to him, and he is entitled to the same deductions and reliefs as if he had actually received the income.

Excluded income

7351 s 627 ITTOIA 2005 The settlor will not be taxed under these provisions in relation to the following **sources of income**:
- income arising under a settlement made by one party to a marriage to another after separation, divorce or annulment, where the income is payable to or applicable for the benefit of that other party;
- annual payments made by an individual for bona fide reasons in connection with his trade, profession or vocation; or
- Gift Aid payments to charity (¶4420).

Definition of a settlement

7352 s 626 ITTOIA 2005 For the purposes of this provision, a settlement does not include an outright **gift by one spouse** to the other of property from which income arises, unless:
- the gift does not carry the right to the whole of that income; or
- the property given is wholly or substantially a right to income, such as a share entitled to dividend income but which has no voting or capital rights.

MEMO POINTS An **outright gift** is one that is not subject to conditions, and could not in any circumstances become payable to the donor or be applied for his benefit.

7353 HMRC have targeted **family run businesses** under these rules, where dividend income or profits are paid to family members, by seeking to tax arrangements that are bounteous and not commercial. Legislation to prevent arrangements with family members, which HMRC consider to be settlements, has been postponed until at least 2011.

MEMO POINTS The House of Lords ruled in favour of the taxpayer in the "Arctic Systems" test case concerning dividends voted to the spouse of the main fee earner in a family company. The spouse (Mrs Jones) had subscribed for half of the share capital when the company was formed. The Lords ruled that although this constituted a settlement by the main fee earner (Mr Jones), the **exemption** for an outright gift between spouses applied, because ordinary shares were not property that was wholly or substantially a right to income. The dividends voted to Mrs Jones could not therefore be treated as Mr Jones's income. *Jones v Garnett* [2007]

Interest in property

7354 s 625 ITTOIA 2005 A settlor will be **deemed** to have an interest in property if that property could in any circumstances become payable to or applicable for the benefit of the settlor or his spouse.

An interest in property will **not arise** if the only circumstances in which it can become payable or applicable are:
- the bankruptcy of a beneficiary (including a potential beneficiary);
- an assignment of, or a charge on, the property being made or given by a beneficiary (including a potential beneficiary);
- in the case of a marriage settlement, the death of both parties to the marriage, and of all or any children of the marriage; or
- the death of a child of the settlor who had become beneficially entitled to the property at an age not exceeding 25 years.

Similarly, an interest in property will not arise where an individual under the age of 25 exists during whose life the property cannot become payable to, or applicable for the benefit of, the settlor or his spouse other than in the event of that person:
– becoming bankrupt; or
– assigning or charging his interest in the property.

MEMO POINTS 1. **Property** includes any property derived from it.
2. For these purposes a **spouse** does not include:
– a person to whom the settlor is not married but may later marry;
– a spouse from whom the settlor is separated under a court order or separation agreement, or in such circumstances that the separation is likely to become permanent; or
– the widow or widower of the settlor.
3. Where a trust has been set up for the benefit of a person who **subsequently becomes** the spouse or civil partner of the settlor, HMRC have stated that the settlement rules will only apply from the date of the change in status.
4. Trusts which **already existed on 5 December 2005** will not become settlor-interested just because the Civil Partnership Act then came into effect.

B. Payments to unmarried minor children

Income arising under a settlement (including the creation of, or addition of property to, a bare trust after 9 March 1999) will be treated as the income of the settlor where, during his life, it is paid to or for the benefit of an unmarried minor child of the settlor, except where the child is a vulnerable person and a claim has been made for the special tax treatment to apply (¶7318). **7356** s 629 ITTOIA 2005 s 28A FA 2005

A **de minimis limit** applies so that the settlor will not be taxable under this provision where the aggregate amount of the child's relevant settlement income does not exceed £100 in any year of assessment. The de minimis limit applies per parent per child.

MEMO POINTS 1. A **minor child** is a child under the age of 18, and includes illegitimate and stepchildren of the settlor, but not fostered children.
2. For these purposes, **relevant settlement income** is income paid to or for the benefit of the child which would be treated as the income of the settlor but for the de minimis provision.

Income accumulated in the trust

The settlor will not be liable to income tax under these provisions if the trustees retain or accumulate the income, or make a capital payment. **7357** s 631 ITTOIA 2005

However, if any **subsequent payment** is made to or for the benefit of the settlor's minor unmarried child, the settlor will be taxed under these provisions to the extent that there is available retained or accumulated income.

MEMO POINTS The **available retained or accumulated income** is determined by calculating the aggregate income which has arisen under the settlement since it was begun, and deducting income which has already been:
– treated as the income of the settlor or a beneficiary;
– paid (as income or capital) to or for the benefit of a beneficiary, other than an unmarried minor child of the settlor;
– treated as the income of an unmarried minor child of the settlor (i.e. under a bare trust) and subject to tax during the years 1995/96 to 1997/98; or
– applied in paying the expenses of the trustees which were properly chargeable to income.

EXAMPLE Trust A was set up by Mr B for the benefit of his children. Income may be accumulated under the terms of the trust until each child reaches the age of 18. The trust income is £5,000 for 2011/12 upon which the trustees will pay income tax of £2,500. If the income is accumulated, no further income tax is due.

If a payment of £1,500 is made to the children, it is treated as net of tax at 50% and is grossed up to £3,000. It is taxed as part of Mr B's income.
If a payment in excess of £2,500 is made to the children, the maximum taxable gross income for Mr B is £5,000, and any excess is treated as a capital advance.

C. Payments of capital

7359 s 633 ITTOIA 2005 A capital sum paid to the settlor or his spouse (or to either jointly with another person) is treated as income of the settlor if the payment falls within the amount of **income available** in the settlement:
– up to the end of the tax year in which the payment is made; or
– to the extent that the payment does not fall within that amount of income, to the end of the next and subsequent tax years, up to a maximum of 11 years after the year of the payment.

The settlor will be **treated as** receiving income equal to the amount of the payment grossed up at the trust rate (50% in 2011/12). The tax credit is not repayable, and the settlor is not entitled to a reimbursement of income tax from the trustees if his tax charge exceeds the amount paid by them.

s 640 ITTOIA 2005 MEMO POINTS Where a trust has accumulated income **before 6 April 2010**, and then a loan is made to the settlor after 5 April 2010, the trust will have suffered income tax at only 40%. The tax credit available to the settlor is limited to the amount of tax (40%) that the trustees have suffered on the accumulated income relating to the capital payment. Similarly, the tax credit available on income accumulated before 6 April 2004 is limited to 34%, that being the rate then in force.

Income available in the settlement

7360 The amount of income available in the settlement for any tax year is the **aggregate amount** of any income arising under a settlement in that and any previous year that has not been distributed, **less**:
a. any amount that has already been set against a capital payment made to the settlor;
b. any income taken into account in relation to capital sums previously paid to the settlor;
c. sums treated as the income of the settlor under other provisions; and
d. tax at the trust rate on the accumulated undistributed income (net of the amounts in **a.** to **c.** above).

s 636 ITTOIA 2005 MEMO POINTS **Undistributed income** is defined as:
Total income less (Payments out + Expenses + Net exempt charitable income)
where:
– "Payments out" means income paid to anyone by the trustees, but not including interest, sums paid to a connected company or sums paid to a trust made by the same settlor; and
– "Expenses" means amounts properly chargeable to income, and not already included in payments out.
"Net exempt charitable income" will only apply to charitable trusts (¶7326).

Capital sum

7361 s 634 ITTOIA 2005 A capital sum **includes** any payment made by way of a loan or repayment of a loan, and any sum (other than income) which is not paid in return for full consideration in money or money's worth. A payment will be treated as a capital sum paid to the settlor if it is:
– paid by the trustees to a third party at the settlor's discretion or by assignment of his right to receive it; or
– any other sum paid or applied for the settlor's benefit.

EXAMPLE On 1 June 2003 the trustees of Trust A made a loan of £30,000 to Mr B, the settlor. Mr B repaid the loan in January 2012. The undistributed income of the trust was as follows:

Date	Applicable tax rate	Undistributed income (£)
Brought forward at 5 April 2004 (say)	34%	3,500
2008/09	40%	6,000
2009/10	40%	8,000
2010/11	50%	7,500
2011/12	50%	7,000

Mr B is treated as receiving the following amounts of income:

		Income £	Tax credit £
2008/09	(3,500 × 100/66)+ (6,000 × 100/60)	15,303	5,803
2009/10	8,000 × 100/60	13,333	5,333
2010/11	7,500 × 100/50	15,000	7,500
2011/12	5,000 × 100/50 (See note)	10,000	5,000

Note: The income in 2011/12 is restricted to the amount of the loan (£30,000) less the amounts previously treated as income. (3,500 + 6,000 + 8,000 + 7,500) = 5,000.

Payments by companies

A capital sum is **deemed** to be the income of the settlor if: **7362**
- the trustees hold shares in (or are participators of) a company; and s 641 ITTOIA 2005
- the company is a close company (or would be if it were UK resident), or is controlled by a close company; and
- a capital sum is paid to the settlor by the company (or an associated company); and
- an associated payment has been made to the company (or an associated company) by the trustees.

MEMO POINTS 1. A charge could also arise under the close company provisions (¶2115) on a **loan waiver**. Where an income tax charge arises under both provisions, any amount charged under the loan waiver provisions is deducted from the deemed income for the settlor. s 639 ITTOIA 2005
2. An **associated payment** is any of the following paid to the company by the trustees within 5 years before or after the capital sum is paid to the settlor by the company:
- any capital sum; or
- any other sum paid, or asset transferred, at less than full consideration.
3. A close company (¶2100) is, broadly speaking, one that is under the control of five or fewer persons.

CHAPTER 4

Capital gains tax and trusts

OUTLINE ¶¶

A charge to CGT on UK settled property may arise in the following circumstances: **7370**

Circumstance	¶¶
The creation of a trust	¶7398
A disposal of trust assets by the trustees	¶7374
Certain events which give rise to a deemed disposal	¶7412
The **events** are: – a beneficiary becoming absolutely entitled to the property in a settlement; – termination of a life interest; – disposal of a beneficial interest; and – sub-fund elections.	

MEMO POINTS **Trust property** for CGT means property in which the trustees have different interests to the beneficiaries. Property in which the beneficiary holds an absolute interest (such as property in a bare trust (¶7176)) is not settled property for CGT.

Chargeable persons

CGT is generally **charged on the trustees**. No CGT charge occurs on a change of trustee unless it results in the trustees becoming non-UK resident. **7371**

The **exceptions** to this rule are gains accruing:
- on the creation of a trust, which will be charged on the settlor;

– to beneficiaries of a qualifying trust for the vulnerable and disabled; and
– to a non-resident trustee, which are attributed to the beneficiary (¶7618).

SECTION 1

Disposal of assets by the trustees

7374 The trustees are subject to CGT on the disposal of trust property, unless the trust is a charitable trust. Where a trust has a vulnerable beneficiary, a claim can be made for the CGT charge to be based on the beneficiary's personal circumstances: see ¶7388+.

In certain cases, the settlor will be liable for the CGT instead: see ¶7398+.

1. General calculation

7375 s 4(1AA) TCGA 1992 In the absence of provisions to the contrary, the statutory CGT tax provisions relating to individuals apply to trustees. The main exceptions are the rate of tax and the annual exemption.

Rate of tax

7376 s 4 TCGA 1992 The rate of CGT applicable to chargeable gains made by trustees in 2011/12 is 28% (except where Entrepreneur's relief applies: see ¶7380).

MEMO POINTS The rate for 2010/11 was 18% for gains arising on or before 22 June 2010, and 28% thereafter.

Annual exemption

7377 Sch 1 para 2 TCGA 1992 Sch 1 para 1 TCGA 1992 The annual exemption for most trustees is one-half of the amount for individuals.

Where property is held on trust for one of the following **disabled persons**, the annual exempt amount for the trustees will be the same as for individuals:
– a mentally disabled person; or
– a person in receipt of an attendance allowance, or the higher or middle rate of disability allowance.

Tax year	Trustees	Individuals
	£	£
2011/12	5,300	10,600
2010/11	5,050	10,100

7378 Sch 1 para 2 TCGA 1992 **More than one settlement** Where multiple settlements have been made by the **same settlor**, the annual exemption for each individual trust is the higher of:
a. the annual exemption for trustees, divided by the number of trusts; or
b. 1/10th of the annual exemption for individuals.

For these purposes, a settlement and its sub-funds (¶7206) are treated as one settlement, and the available exemption is divided between the principal settlement and its sub-funds.

EXAMPLE The trustees of Trust A made a chargeable gain of £10,000 on 5 May 2011. The settlor of Trust A is Mr B, and he has made five other settlements. The annual exempt amount available to the trustees is the higher of:
a. £5,300/6 = 883; or
b. 1/10 × 10,600 = 1,060
The trustees will therefore pay tax as follows:

	£
Chargeable gain	10,000
Less: Annual exempt amount	(1,060)
Taxable amount	8,940
Tax thereon:	
£8,940 @ 28%	£2,503.20

Entrepreneurs' relief

Entrepreneurs' relief (¶6035) reduces the rate of tax on a disposal of **trust business assets** to 10%, provided the trust has a **qualifying beneficiary** who satisfies the **relevant conditions**. Trustees have no entitlement to claim the relief in their own right: the claim must be made jointly with a beneficiary who is entitled to the relief in his personal capacity. The beneficiary effectively transfers all or part of his entitlement to the trustees, and his lifetime limit is reduced to that extent. **7380** ss 169H-169L TCGA1992

The 10% rate is applied to the net gain after calculating all disposals which would have qualified for it. The deadline for claiming the relief is the first anniversary of the 31 January following the end of the tax year in which the disposal takes place, so claims for the relief for 2011/12 disposals must be made by 31 January 2014.

MEMO POINTS For gains arising before 23 June 2010, the relief operated by reducing the aggregate gain, which was then charged at the full applicable rate to yield an effective rate of 10%. For details, see *Tax Memo 2010-2011*

Entrepreneurs' relief is **not available** for disposals: **7382**
- by trustees of discretionary trusts; or
- of trading assets included in the settled property and used by the trustees in a trade carried on by them alone; or
- of investment assets, such as rental property or shares and securities.

Trust business assets are:
- shares or securities in a trading company or the holding company of a trading group; or
- assets which have been used for the purposes of a business, including a partnership, carried on by the qualifying beneficiary.

A **qualifying beneficiary** must have an **interest in possession** in the whole of the trust's assets (or that part of the trust's assets which includes business assets) and satisfy the **relevant conditions** for the assets disposed of.

The **relevant conditions** depend on the assets disposed of:
- for the disposal of **shares or securities**, the conditions are that the qualifying beneficiary:

a. is either an employee or an office holder of the company whose shares are sold or one of the companies in the same group; and

b. personally holds at least 5% of the ordinary shares in the company with an entitlement to at least 5% of the voting rights.

- for the disposal of **assets** which have been used for the purposes of the business, the conditions are that:

a. the qualifying beneficiary carries on the business as an individual or as a member of a partnership;

b. the assets were used in the business either throughout a period of at least 1 year ending on the date of the assets' disposal or throughout the period of 1 year within the last 3 years of the assets' disposal; and

c. the qualifying beneficiary either ceases to carry on the business or leaves the partnership at the time of the assets' disposal or has done so not more than 3 years earlier.

MEMO POINTS 1. If the trust is a partner in a **partnership** in which the qualifying beneficiary is also a partner, the relief is available on the disposal of partnership assets if the asset disposal by the trustees takes place at the time when the qualifying beneficiary ceases to be a partner (or ceased to be a partner within the preceding 3 year period).

2. Where the disposal of a trust asset takes place on the **same day** as the disposal of an asset owned personally by a qualifying beneficiary, the disposal by the beneficiary is deemed to take place first. This ensures that the relief is primarily used by individuals.

Splitting the relief

7383 s 169OTCGA1992 If there is more than one qualifying beneficiary, or there are qualifying and non-qualifying beneficiaries, the relief only applies to the **relevant proportion** of the gain during the **material time**. The material time is a period of 1 year before the date of disposal. The method of computation is as follows:

1. Establish whether the conditions for an eligible beneficiary are satisfied.
2. Establish what proportion of the gain is attributable to the eligible beneficiary's entitlement to trust income. This proportion is taxable at 10%.
3. Repeat the process for any other eligible beneficiaries.
4. The balance of the gain is taxable at the trust CGT rate.

EXAMPLE The trustees of the Z trust have two beneficiaries, Mr A and Mr B. Each beneficiary has an interest in possession. Mr A is entitled to 75% of the trust's income and Mr B to 25%. Mr A has worked for a trading company for many years and owns 50% of the shares in his personal capacity. The trustees own the remaining 50% of the shares. Mr B does not work for the company.
Mr A satisfies the conditions to be an eligible beneficiary because:
1. the shares are in a trading company;
2. he is an employee of the company; and
3. he owns 50% of the company's share capital.

Mr B will not be an eligible beneficiary.
The trustees of the Z trust are offered £1.1 million for their shares. They paid £100,000 for the shares so the gain is £1 million. The gain has to be apportioned between the beneficiaries' entitlement to income, so £750,000 will be apportioned to Mr A's share and £250,000 to Mr B's share.
Mr A is entitled to claim entrepreneurs' relief on the sale of his personal shares. He also decides to make a joint claim with the trustees (effectively giving part of his lifetime allowance to them) on their gain of £750,000. This part of the gain is taxed at 10%, and the tax charge is £75,000.
The remaining gain of £250,000 is taxed at the trust's CGT rate (28 %) with no entrepreneurs' relief. The tax charge is £70,000.
The total tax payable by the trustees is £145,000 (compared with £280,000 that would have been payable at the full trust rate)..
Mr A will be able to claim the balance of his personal entrepreneurs' relief against his personal gain. If Mr A sells his shares on the same day as the trustees, the gain on Mr A's shares will be treated as arising first.

Principal private residence relief

7384 ss 226A, 226B TCGA 1992 s 260 IHTA 1984 If a trust property is **occupied by a beneficiary as his main residence**, the trustees can claim principal private residence relief (PPR) (¶6166) on its disposal. However, PPR is **not available** to the trustees if a specific type of holdover claim (relating to a chargeable transfer for inheritance tax purposes) was made on the original gift into the trust (¶7403). If the claim is revoked, PPR will become available to the trustees.

Comment This restriction is designed to affect second homes transferred into discretionary trusts by parents, where a child beneficiary then lives in the property. However, if the house is a farmhouse, which qualifies for agricultural property relief (¶6750), PPR is unaffected by these rules.

EXAMPLE On 1 March 2007 Mr B transfers a property worth £200,000, which is not his main residence, to a discretionary trust, and makes a holdover claim of £100,000. The trustees' allowable expenditure is therefore £100,000.
One of the beneficiaries occupies the property, until it is sold by the trustees on 1 October 2011 for £275,000.
The chargeable gain for the trustees is £175,000 (including the heldover gain of £100,000). No PPR is available.
If Mr B revokes his holdover relief claim, he will be assessed to a gain of £100,000 arising on 1 March 2007. The trustees will then be able to claim PPR for the remaining chargeable gain of £75,000.

There are **transitional provisions** to restrict PPR where a holdover claim was made prior to 10 December 2003, and the property was not disposed of by the trustees before that date. In this case PPR is only available on the gain up to 9 December 2003, which is calculated on a time-apportioned basis. This rule displaces the normal relief which automatically applies PPR to the last 3 years of ownership. 7385

EXAMPLE On 1 September 2002, Mr C transferred a property worth £150,000, which was not his main residence, into a discretionary trust, and held over the gain of £50,000. The trustees' allowable expenditure is £100,000.
One of the beneficiaries occupies the property from January 2003 to December 2009. The property is sold for £225,000 by the trustees in January 2012, realising a gain of £125,000 before PPR.
PPR is not available for the whole gain because the period of qualifying occupation only runs to 9 December 2003. PPR can be claimed for the period from 1 September 2002 to 9 December 2003.

2. Trusts for the vulnerable

The trustees and the vulnerable beneficiary (¶7318) of a qualifying trust can jointly and irrevocably make a **vulnerable person election** (¶7323) for trust gains to be treated as if they were directly assessed on the beneficiary, therefore taking his personal circumstances into account. In this case, the beneficiary becomes liable for the tax (unless he is non-UK resident), but will be reimbursed by the trustees. 7388

Conditions

Trustees of a qualifying trust may make a claim to reduce the CGT on gains arising in a tax year for which they are liable to UK CGT, if a vulnerable person election is in effect at some time during that tax year. The gains must **relate to** property held in the trust for the benefit of the vulnerable person and are then known as qualifying trust gains. 7390 s 30 FA 2005

A claim may be made even if the settlor has an interest in the trust.

MEMO POINTS 1. A **qualifying trust** is defined at ¶7320.
2. **Gains** includes attributed gains from non-resident close companies (¶6028).
3. To be liable to UK CGT, the trustees must be either UK resident for any part of the tax year, or ordinarily resident in the UK. The **residence of trustees** is discussed at ¶7597.

Consequences

The capital gains tax payable by the trustees in respect of qualifying trust gains is reduced by an amount equal to (A minus B), where A and B depend on the residence of the vulnerable beneficiary during the tax year. 7392 ss 31 - 32 FA 2005

Beneficiary's residence	Amount A	Amount B
Either resident in the UK for any part of the tax year, or ordinarily resident during the tax year.	CGT that would be payable by the beneficiary if the qualifying trust gains accrued to him instead of the trustees, and ignoring allowable losses.	CGT actually payable by the beneficiary.
Neither of the above.	CGT that would be payable by the beneficiary on the total of his deemed CGT taxable amount[1] plus the qualifying trust gains.	CGT that would be payable by the beneficiary on his deemed CGT taxable amount[1].

1. The beneficiary's deemed CGT taxable amount is the total of:
– the gains (net of allowable losses) on which he is actually chargeable to CGT; and
– any other net gains on which he would be chargeable to CGT if he were UK resident and domiciled throughout the year.

MEMO POINTS 1. Note that a different treatment applied for 2007/08 and earlier years.
2. On the **death** of the beneficiary, the capital gains uplift in value will still apply.
3. Where the trust assets are actually **transferred to the beneficiary**, this will not be a disposal for CGT purposes.

3. Charitable trusts

7395 s 256–256D TCGA 1992 Gains will not be taxable provided they are applied for charitable purposes only (¶7200). If the trust has non-exempt expenditure for the year, gains can be attributed to it in the same way as income, and will then become taxable: see ¶7332.

Ceasing to be a charity

7396 Where a trust ceases to be charitable, there is a **deemed** sale and re-acquisition of trust property at market value by the trustees, and any resulting gain will be taxed on the trustees under the normal rules for settlements.

The annual exemption will be restricted in accordance with rules outlined in ¶7377.

MEMO POINTS In so far as the trust property represents the **proceeds of earlier disposals**, the gains relating to those disposals will be assessable on the trustees under the normal rules for settlements.

SECTION 2

Gains assessed on the settlor

7398 The settlor will be liable to tax on gains arising from the creation of a trust. The CGT position depends on whether the trust is created on death or during the settlor's lifetime.

MEMO POINTS Before 6 April 2008 the settlor was also liable to tax on gains arising from the creation of a trust if he, his spouse or a dependent child could benefit. The definition of a settlor-interested trust continues to include such trusts.

1. On death

7400 Where a trust is created by **will or intestacy**, the trustees will be treated in the same way as for any other legatee (¶7276). The assets they receive will therefore be treated as acquired at probate value at the date of death.

2. During lifetime

7402 Where the trust is created (or added to) during the lifetime of the settlor, he will be **deemed to have made a disposal** to the trustees at market value. This rule applies regardless of whether the transfer into the trust is revocable or irrevocable, and whether or not the settlor is a trustee or a beneficiary.

Reliefs

7403 If the disposal gives rise to a chargeable gain, in certain **circumstances** the settlor may be entitled to claim holdover relief, or no gain/no loss treatment may apply, as outlined in the following table. There are, however, restrictions where the settlor has an interest in the recipient trust on creation, or subsequently becomes interested in the trust within the next 6 years.

In addition, the availability of principal private residence relief (¶7384) for the trustees may be adversely affected where the settlor makes a holdover claim on a transfer which is chargeable to inheritance tax.

Type of gift	Relief	Reference:	¶¶
Business assets	Holdover	s 165 TCGA 1992	¶6100
Unlisted shares in trading companies			¶6102
Agricultural property		Sch 7 para 1 TCGA 1992	¶6104
On which inheritance tax is chargeable		s 260 TCGA 1992	¶6106
Certain gifts which are exempt from inheritance tax			¶6108
To charities	Treated as if acquired for no gain/no loss	s 257 TCGA 1992	¶5550
To employee trusts		s 239 TCGA 1992	
To housing associations		s 259 TCGA 1992	

EXAMPLE In August 2011, Mr A transferred an asset worth £200,000 into a discretionary trust, of which he was not a beneficiary. Mr A had acquired the asset in May 1995 for £35,000.
The chargeable gain on the transfer will be:

	£	£
Market value at disposal		200,000
Less: Allowable expenditure	35,000	(35,000)
Gain before relief claimed		165,000

The allowable expenditure for the trustees will be:

	£
Market value on acquisition by trustees	200,000
Less: Heldover gain	(165,000)
Allowable expenditure	35,000

Settlor-interested trusts Holdover relief on business assets, and on transfers chargeable to inheritance tax, is **not available** on a transfer of assets into a trust from another trust or from an individual, if either: 7404 s 169B TCGA 1992

a. the settlor or his spouse has an interest in the acquiring trust, or there are arrangements (including an informal agreement) where an interest could be acquired by the settlor; or

b. a beneficiary of the acquiring trust has made a past holdover claim at any time in respect of the assets being transferred to the trust.

This restriction does not apply for transfers to trusts which benefit **disabled persons** or which provide maintenance funds for **historic buildings**. s 169D TCGA 1992

MEMO POINTS 1. A **settlor** for these purposes is an individual who originally owned the property which is transferred into the trust. s 169E TCGA 1992

2. The definition of "**settlor-interested**" is very wide. The settlor (or his spouse) could be interested in the trust by enjoying a benefit which is derived directly or indirectly from any property in the trust. This also extends to any property which derives from the trust property (such as income, or new property acquired with the proceeds from the disposal of the property originally transferred into the trust). The settlor is also treated as having an interest if his dependent child can directly or indirectly enjoy or benefit from the trust property. s 169F TCGA 1992

3. The definition of **spouse** does not include a widow or widower, or separated spouse, but does include a registered civil partner.

4. A **dependent child** is defined as a child (including a stepchild) who is:
– aged under 18; and
– unmarried and does not have a civil partner.

A settlor is not treated as having an interest, if he would not otherwise have an interest in the trust and at a time when he has no dependent child, even if the terms of a trust provide for a dependent child.

7405 s 169C TCGA 1992

Even where the trust is not originally settlor-interested, if either of conditions **a**. or **b**. in ¶7404 is satisfied within the **clawback period**, any holdover relief already claimed will be reversed. At the time of the clawback, the trustees will be treated as if they had originally acquired the asset at full market value, and a gain will be assessed on the transferor.

If the trustees have **disposed of the asset** before the trust becomes a settlor-interested trust, any chargeable gain or allowable loss is recalculated as if the holdover relief had never been claimed.

It is possible for the transferor to **revoke** a holdover claim, in which case there will be no charge under the clawback rules, although a gain will still be assessed on the transferor.

MEMO POINTS 1. The clawback period **starts** immediately after the transfer to the trust and **ends** 6 years after the end of the tax year in which the transfer was made.
2. If the **transferor dies** before either condition **a**. or **b**. is satisfied, no clawback will occur.

EXAMPLE On 1 May 2010, Mr B transferred an asset worth £500,000 to a trust, which is not settlor-interested, and claimed holdover relief of £300,000. Mr B bought the asset for £200,000 in 2003, and this becomes the base cost of the asset for the trustees.
The trustees sold the asset on 1 June 2011 for £505,000, crystallising a gain of £305,000. The trustees had capital losses of £250,000 to set against the gain, leaving them with a chargeable gain of £55,000. The related capital gains tax is paid on 31 January 2013.

Mr B becomes interested in the trust on 1 April 2013. A chargeable gain arises for Mr B in 2012/13 on the heldover gain of £300,000.
The gain arising to the trustees is recalculated, because their base cost is now £500,000. The resulting gain is only £5,000 which is covered by the capital losses. The capital gains tax paid in January 2013 is refunded, and the available capital losses to carry forward are £245,000.

Losses

7406 s 18(3), (4) TCGA 1992

Where the transfer to a settlement gives rise to an allowable loss, the **relief** available to the settlor is likely to be restricted because the settlor and the trustees are connected persons (¶5462). The loss will only be deductible from chargeable gains arising on a disposal to the same trust.

The **exception** to this rule is where the disposal is a gift into a settlement by virtue of which:
– the asset and any income from it are wholly or primarily applicable for educational, cultural or recreational purposes; and
– the benefit of the gift is limited to an association of people, most of whom are not connected with the settlor.

In this case the loss can be deducted from the settlor's other gains in the usual way (¶5450).

SECTION 3

Deemed disposals

7412 In addition to the actual sale of trust property, the trustees may be deemed to have made a disposal when:

A beneficiary becomes absolutely entitled to settled property	¶7414
A life interest terminates (depending on when the interest was created)	¶7420
A beneficiary disposes of his beneficial interest	¶7430
A sub-fund election is made	¶7434

The general principle in each case is that the trustees will be liable for CGT as if an actual disposal of trust property had taken place (¶7374).

1. Beneficiary becomes absolutely entitled

A beneficiary may become absolutely entitled (¶7178) to settled property in the following circumstances: **7414** s 71 TCGA 1992
- following the death of a beneficiary with an interest in possession for life, the remaining beneficiaries (known as the remaindermen) become entitled to the trust property outright; or
- the trustees have exercised a power of advancement of trust capital out of a discretionary trust; or
- the beneficiary of an accumulation and maintenance trust, a trust for bereaved minors or an age 18-to-25 trust becomes entitled to capital on reaching a specified age.

Liability to CGT

As a **general rule**, where the beneficiary becomes absolutely entitled to settled property, the **trustees** are deemed to have disposed of the property concerned at the market value at that date and immediately re-acquired it at the same value. The trustees are liable for any gains or losses arising on this deemed disposal, akin to an exit charge. **7415**

Gift relief (¶6095) may be claimed if the assets are business assets, or if the trust is a chargeable trust (¶7440).

At this point the CGT liability of the trust in respect of the property ends, and even if the trustees still hold the property pending transfer, the **beneficiary** becomes liable as if it were held on a bare trust. Broadly this means that, from the date of absolute entitlement, the actions of the trustees are deemed to be the actions of the beneficiary.

These rules do not apply to a **termination** of a life interest (¶7420).

MEMO POINTS 1. Where the beneficiary is **an infant** or has a **disability**, he will still be deemed to be absolutely entitled to the settled property.

2. Often a trust, such as a pre-22 March 2006 accumulation and maintenance trust, will be split up into **separate funds** with different trustees, and assets will be appropriated to these new funds. For CGT purposes the funds are treated as a single settlement if no sub-fund election is made (¶7434), resulting in:
- only a single annual exemption being available; and
- automatic set-off of losses and gains of all the sub-funds.

EXAMPLE In March 2012, beneficiary B of discretionary Trust A becomes absolutely entitled to shares worth £200,000. The shares were placed in trust in March 1994 when they were worth £75,000. The trustees of Trust A will be deemed to have disposed of the shares:

	£	£
Disposal value		200,000
Less: Acquisition cost		(75,000)
Gain on disposal		125,000

Beneficiary B will be deemed to have acquired the shares at their market value of £200,000 unless holdover relief is claimed, in which case the deemed acquisition cost will be £75,000.

Interests in land

Special rules apply where one beneficiary becomes absolutely entitled to an **undivided share** in land and the remaining beneficiaries are not absolutely entitled. In this case, the first beneficiary is really only absolutely entitled to a share in the proceeds of sale when the land is sold, and therefore no deemed disposal is required. **7416**

If the situation arises where the land is held solely for beneficiaries who can, as a group, direct the trustees how to deal with the land, then a deemed disposal will occur. *Crowe v Appleby* [1975]

Appointment or advancement from a discretionary trust

7417 Where an appointment or advancement is made from a discretionary trust, a deemed disposal will only occur if the capital leaves the settlement. Thus, if a **sub-fund** is created, the trustees will be treated as continuing to hold the property unless they elect that the sub-fund be treated as a separate settlement (¶7434).

Losses

7418 s 71(2) - (2D) TCGA 1992

A loss will be treated as **accruing to the beneficiary** rather than the trustees where:
– a beneficiary becomes absolutely entitled to trust property; and
– a loss accrues after the deemed disposal of an asset forming part of the settled property.

This provision only applies **to the extent** that the loss cannot be set against gains arising from other assets forming part of the same deemed disposal, or arising earlier in the same year of assessment. For these purposes, a loss arising in this way is treated as deductible in priority to any other allowable losses accruing to the trustee in the same year.

A loss that has accrued to a beneficiary as a result of this provision can be **carried forward** to later years of assessment, but is allowable only against gains arising from the disposal, by him, of the same asset.

MEMO POINTS If the asset is **land**, the loss can be set against any gain arising on any asset which is derived from it. The loss is deductible in priority to other losses, and when it is brought forward from earlier years it is deductible as if it were a current year loss.

EXAMPLE Mr A becomes absolutely entitled to a third of a trust fund on 1 October 2011. The assets which now belong to Mr A have lost £50,000 in value since being in the trust.
The loss realised by the trustees on the transfer of assets to Mr A can be used against other trust gains in 2011/12. Any loss not so used is then available to Mr A, who can only use the loss against gains on the future disposal of those particular assets.

2. Termination of a life interest

7420 s 72 TCGA 1992

The **implications** of the termination of a life interest depend on:
– whether the life interest ends because of the death of the person entitled to it; and
– whether another person then becomes absolutely entitled to the settled property.

7422 A **life interest** is not defined by the legislation but includes a right to the income of, or the use or occupation of, settled property for the life of a person (including the life of a person other than the one entitled).

s 72 TCGA 1992

MEMO POINTS 1. An individual who holds a life interest in **part of the income** of settled property is treated as holding an interest in the corresponding part of the settled property, provided it is one of the life interests itemised in the table at ¶7426.
2. If the interest is contingent on the exercise of a **discretion** by the trustee or some other person, it will not be considered a life interest for these purposes.

s 72(4) TCGA 1992

3. An **annuity** will generally be excluded from the rules relating to life interests unless:
– some or all of the settled property is appropriated to a separate fund out of which the annuity is payable; and
– the new fund is completely separate from the original fund, and there is no right of recourse to the property still in the original fund, or to the income from that property.
The property appropriated in this way will be subject to a new settlement. The death of the annuitant, and the related termination of his life interest, will affect only the chargeable assets in the new fund.

EXAMPLE In each of the following situations X holds a life interest.
Property is held on trust for:
a. X for life with the remainder to Y;
b. Y for life with the remainder to Z, but Y has transferred his interest to X; and
c. X for the life of Y.

Other than on death

If a life interest terminates other than on death and **another person becomes absolutely entitled** to the settled property, the trustees will be deemed to have disposed of the property and immediately re-acquired it as described in ¶7415. A chargeable gain or allowable loss will therefore arise. 7423 s 71 TCGA 1992

Gift relief (¶6095) may be claimed if the assets are business assets, or if the trust is a chargeable trust (¶7440).

If, however, **the settlement continues**, for example because another beneficiary has a life interest, there is no charge to CGT.

EXAMPLE If settled property was held for Mrs X for life or until she marries, with the remainder to Miss Y, then the marriage of Mrs X would give rise to a deemed disposal.

On death

If a life interest terminates on the death of the person entitled to it, the CGT treatment will **depend on**: 7425 s 72 TCGA 1992
- whether another person becomes absolutely entitled to the trust property;
- whether the settlement continues; and
- when the interest was created.

Special rules apply if **holdover relief** was claimed on the original transfer into the trust.

Another person becomes absolutely entitled The position depends on when the interest was created, as follows: 7426 s 73 TCGA 1992

Interest created before 22 March 2006, or is an: – immediate post-death interest or transitional serial interest (¶7178); or – interest in a bereaved minor's trust (¶7196), age 18-to-25 trust (¶7198) where the beneficiary dies before age 18, or a disabled trust (¶7190)	All other cases
The **general** rule is that the trustees will be deemed to have disposed of and immediately re-acquired the settled property at market value, but no charge to CGT will arise. The trustees will hold the settled property as nominees for the beneficiary who will therefore benefit from a tax-free uplift to the current market value. Where the settled property **reverts to the settlor**, the deemed disposal and re-acquisition are deemed to take place at the consideration that would result in neither a gain nor a loss accruing. Where the property reverts to the settlor as life tenant, a full uplift in value is given.	The trustees will be deemed to have disposed of and immediately re-acquired the settled property at market value. A charge to CGT will arise, but gift relief (¶6106) may be claimed, as the transfer is a chargeable transfer for inheritance tax purposes. The trustees will hold the settled property as nominees for the beneficiary.

MEMO POINTS Where the terminated interest was in only **part of the settled property**, a gain will arise on the deemed disposal. The gain will, however, be reduced by the proportion that the terminated part bears to the whole of the settled fund. s 73(2) TCGA 1992

EXAMPLE

1. Pre-22 March 2006 trust: In June 1991 Mr A settled property worth £300,000 in Trust B to be held for Mr C for life and then passing absolutely to Miss D. In August 2011, when the property was worth £450,000, Mr C died. The trustees are deemed to have sold the property and immediately re-acquired it for £450,000 but no CGT charge will accrue; the property is subject to IHT as part of Mr C's estate. Instead Miss D will acquire the property with a base value of £450,000.

2. Pre-22 March 2006 trust: In March 1994 Mrs W settled property worth £175,000 in Trust X to be held for Miss Y for life and then passing absolutely to Mr Z.
Mr Z died in September 1995. In December 2011, when the property was worth £325,000, Miss Y also died. In accordance with the terms of the trust the property reverted back to Mrs W.
The trustees are deemed to have sold the property and immediately re-acquired it for a value giving rise to neither a gain nor a loss.

	£	£
Deemed disposal value (balancing figure)		189,000
Less: Acquisition cost		
Market value at transfer into trust	175,000	
Enhancement expenditure by trustees	14,000	
		(189,000)
Chargeable gain/allowable loss		Nil

Mrs W is deemed to acquire the settled property with a base cost of £189,000 (as opposed to the market value of £325,000).
If the property had reverted to Mrs W on an interest in possession trust, where Mrs W was the life tenant, that trust would have acquired the property at the market value of £325,000.

3. Post-22 March 2006 trust: In October 2007 Mr E settled property worth £200,000 in Trust F to be held for Mrs G for life and then passing absolutely to Mr H. Mrs G died in March 2012 when the property was worth £250,000. The trustees are deemed to have sold the property and immediately re-acquired it for £250,000, and a CGT charge will arise on the gain of £50,000. The trustees and Mr H may, however, claim gift relief.

7427 s 72(1)(a) TCGA 1992

The settlement continues Where the settlement continues after the death of the person with a life interest, the position depends on when the interest was created, as follows:

Interest created before 22 March 2006, or is an: **– immediate post-death interest or transitional serial interest (¶7178); or** **– interest in a bereaved minor's trust (¶7196), age 18-to-25 trust (¶7198) where the beneficiary dies before age 18, or a disabled trust (¶7190)**	**All other cases**
The trustees will be deemed to have disposed of and immediately re-acquired the settled property at market value, but no charge to CGT will arise. In contrast to the rules when another person becomes absolutely entitled, on the continuation of a settlement: – it is the trustees who will benefit from a tax-free uplift to the current market value; and – there are no special rules when the property **reverts to the settlor**.	There is no deemed disposal, and accordingly no uplift to the current market value.

7428 s 74 TCGA 1992

Holdover relief If holdover relief was claimed on the **original transfer** into the trust and a deemed disposal arises when a life interest terminates on the death of the person entitled to it (regardless of whether the settlement continues), the deemed disposal is not exempt from CGT. Instead, the charge to tax is restricted to the heldover gain.

EXAMPLE In March 1999, Mr A transferred 30% of the shares in a trading company to Trust B to be held for Mr C for life and then passing absolutely to Miss D. At the date of the transfer Mr A held over the resulting gain of £35,000. In June 2011, when the shares were worth £325,000, Mr C died.
The gain chargeable on the trustees, on the termination of Mr C's life interest, will be limited to the amount of the heldover gain i.e. £35,000.

3. Disposal of a beneficial interest

7430 s 76(1) TCGA 1992

As a **general rule**, any gain accruing to a beneficiary as a result of the disposal of an interest under a settlement is exempt from the charge to CGT.

MEMO POINTS 1. For these purposes an **interest under a settlement** includes a life interest, a reversionary interest and an annuity.
2. The disposal of an interest under a **bare trust** is, however, deemed to be a disposal of the underlying asset and therefore does not qualify for the exemption.

Chargeable disposals

The disposal of an interest in a settlement will be chargeable if either of the following apply: **7431** s 76 TCGA 1992
- the owner of the interest **acquired** it (or derives his title from someone who acquired it) for a consideration in money or money's worth, other than consideration consisting of another interest under the settlement; or
- the **trustees** of the settlement were at any time neither resident nor ordinarily resident in the UK.

MEMO POINTS 1. **Consideration** in this context does not need to be adequate consideration. If the interest is acquired at an undervalue, it will not qualify for exemption from CGT.
2. Where the **predictable life** of the person which determines the duration of the trust is 50 years or less at the date of the acquisition of the interest, the interest will be treated as a wasting asset (¶5922).

Holder of the interest becomes absolutely entitled

A deemed disposal will **occur when** the owner of the beneficial interest becomes absolutely entitled to any settled property (for example, where X purchases a remainder interest from Y and the holder of the life interest dies). **7432** s 76(2) TCGA 1992

The owner will be **deemed** to have received a consideration equal to the market value of the property at the date it is received by him, less any CGT charged on the trustees.

EXAMPLE In May 2004 Mr A settled property worth £40,000 on Miss X for life with the remainder to Mr Y. In August 2004 Mr B purchased the remainder interest from Mr Y for £15,000. In July 2011 Miss X died and the property (now worth £75,000) passed to Mr B.
The CGT consequences are as follows:

Trustees:	**£**
Disposal value	75,000
Less: Acquisition cost	
Market value at transfer into trust	(40,000)
Chargeable gain	35,000
Less: Annual exemption	(5,300)
Taxable amount	29,700
Tax thereon:	
£29,700 @ 28%	8,316
Mr B:	
Market value of property received	75,000
Less: CGT paid by trustees	(8,316)
	66,684
Less: Acquisition cost paid by Mr B	(15,000)
Chargeable gain	51,684

4. Sub-fund elections

If the trustees of a settlement create a sub-fund (¶7206) and elect that it be treated as a separate settlement, there is a deemed disposal of assets which become comprised in the sub-fund. The disposal is treated as taking place when the sub-fund election takes effect. **7434** Sch 4ZA para 19 TCGA 1992

An election may be appropriate where, for example, the trustees wish to allocate losses for the benefit of a particular beneficiary.

No general **holdover relief** is available in respect of a deemed disposal to a sub-fund. Such relief can only therefore be claimed where, for example, the deemed disposal is of business assets (¶6095).

Trustees may therefore decide to create sub-funds soon after the creation of a settlement, before any significant gains have arisen.

MEMO POINTS **Assets** for these purposes include a sum of money expressed in sterling.

CHAPTER 5

Inheritance tax and trusts

OUTLINE ¶¶

SECTION 1

General principles

Inheritance tax (IHT) is a tax on inheritances, gifts and other transfers of property by individuals, either during lifetime or on death. IHT can also be charged on the value of property held in a trust. The general rules relating to IHT (including general anti-avoidance measures) begin at ¶6375. This chapter only deals with those provisions specific to trusts. **7435**

IHT may be relevant on:
– the creation and cessation either of a trust itself, or of an interest in possession in it; or
– certain events during the life of a trust.

s 43 IHTA 1984

MEMO POINTS A trust (or settlement) is **defined** for IHT purposes as a disposition of property, however effected, where the property is:
– held in trust for individuals in succession, or for an individual subject to a contingency;
– held by trustees to accumulate the income or to make discretionary payments out of the trust; or
– used to make an annuity payment or a similar arrangement.

7436 There are broadly three groups of trusts, each of which is treated differently for IHT purposes:

Type	Occasions of IHT charge	¶¶
Chargeable trusts	When property is added or leaves the trust, and every 10 years during the life of the trust	¶7440
Favoured trusts	Only on a failure to meet qualifying conditions, or a reduction in value of the trust	¶7485
Exempt trusts	Never[1]	¶7515

Notes
1. However, a person who is beneficially entitled to an interest in possession is treated as making a transfer of value when that interest in possession ends.

Changes from 22 March 2006

7437 The IHT position also depends on the date of the event in question. Significant changes to the IHT treatment of some trusts came into effect on 22 March 2006:
a. interest in possession trusts (¶7187) are chargeable, if created on or after that date during the settlor's lifetime. Exemption continues to apply to some trusts created on death;
b. accumulation and maintenance trusts (¶7194) are chargeable if created on or after that date; and
c. two **new types of trust** were introduced (trusts for bereaved minors (¶7196) and age 18-to-25 trusts (¶7198)), which replace accumulation and maintenance trusts, but with stricter conditions.

7438 There are **transitional provisions** for interest in possession and accumulation and maintenance trusts which were created before 22 March 2006. The changes for those types of trust are summarised in the following table:

Type of trust	Details	Status of trust	
		Created before 22 March 2006	Created on or after 22 March 2006
Interest in possession trust created during lifetime		Exempt until the termination of the later of: – an interest in possession in existence on 21 March 2006; or – a transitional serial interest (¶7178). Chargeable thereafter	Chargeable
	Additions of property on or after 22 March 2006	Chargeable	Chargeable
Interest in possession trust created on death		Exempt until the termination of the later of: – an interest in possession in existence on 21 March 2006; or – a transitional serial interest (¶7178). Chargeable thereafter	Exempt, provided an immediate post-death interest (¶7178) is created

Type of trust	Details	Status of trust	
		Created before 22 March 2006	Created on or after 22 March 2006
Accumulation and maintenance		Favoured accumulation and maintenance treatment applied until 5 April 2008. After which, chargeable, unless the terms were amended by that date so that beneficiaries became absolutely entitled to trust property on or before attaining the age of: – 18, in which case the favoured accumulation and maintenance treatment continues to apply; or – 25, in which case the favoured treatment for age 18-to-25 trusts (¶7198) applies	Chargeable
	Additions of property on or after 22 March 2006	Chargeable	Chargeable

SECTION 2

Chargeable trusts

7440 A chargeable trust is taxed as a **separate entity**, and the trust property does not form part of a beneficiary's estate. A person who is beneficially entitled to an interest in possession in a chargeable trust is therefore not treated as making a transfer of value when the interest in possession ends.

ss 59, 71(1A) IHTA 1984

There are three instances where a charge to IHT may arise from a chargeable trust:
- on **creation** of the trust (¶7442);
- the **principal charge** or ten-year charge (¶7446); and
- an **exit charge** when property leaves the trust (¶7452).

Special rules apply to **added property** (¶7464), agricultural and business property reliefs (¶7474) and national heritage property (¶7480).

7441 The chargeable trusts regime **applies** to the following types of trust:

Type of trust	Chargeable
Discretionary	All
Interest in possession	Trusts created during lifetime on or after 22 March 2006 (including trusts for the benefit of the settlor or the settlor's spouse), other than disabled trusts and transitional serial interests (¶7178)
	Trusts created at death on or after 22 March 2006, unless there is an immediate post-death interest (¶7178)
	Trusts created before 22 March 2006, on the termination of the later of: – an interest in possession which existed at 21 March 2006; or – a transitional serial interest (¶7178)
	Additions of property on or after 22 March 2006 to trusts created before that date
Accumulation and maintenance	From 6 April 2008, trusts created before 22 March 2006, unless by 5 April 2008 the terms provided that beneficiaries become absolutely entitled to trust property on or before attaining the age of 25
	Trusts created on or after 22 March 2006
	Additions of property on or after 22 March 2006 to trusts created before that date

A. Creation

7442 Placing property into a chargeable trust is a **chargeable lifetime transfer of value** ("CLT") by the settlor (¶6530).

The trustees must be told the settlor's cumulative lifetime total at the time the trust is created, as this amount is crucial to all calculations involving chargeable trusts.

MEMO POINTS Where the trust is a chargeable interest in possession trust, see ¶7520 for details of the valuation of the interest.

Liability for tax

7444 The **person responsible** for the payment of any IHT will depend on the terms of the transfer:
a. if the **trustees** agree to pay the tax, the chargeable amount will be the value of the gift (¶6465); and
b. if the **settlor** pays the tax, the transfer of value comprises the settled property and the tax paid on it, so the value of the gift must be grossed up (¶6536).

On the **death of the settlor** within 7 years of the creation of the trust, additional tax may become due (¶6542), payable by the trustees, although credit will be given for lifetime tax paid. Trustees should therefore be aware of this risk when making distributions from the trust and should retain sufficient funds to cover any additional IHT liability for the first 7 years of the trust.

EXAMPLE In January 2007 Mr A transferred shares worth £500,000 into a discretionary trust and agreed to pay the tax. His only other chargeable transfer was £120,000 in November 2003.
Mr A died in September 2011, at which time the value of the shares in the discretionary trust was £600,000.
IHT will be calculated as follows:

		Net	Tax	Gross
Lifetime tax:	£	£	£	£
Cumulative total brought forward		120,000		120,000
January 2007 transfer	500,000			
Less: Annual exemptions				
2006/07	(3,000)			
2005/06	(3,000)			
		494,000	82,250	576,250
		614,000	82,250	696,250
Tax thereon:				
£285,000 covered by nil rate band for 2006/07				
(614,000 – 285,000) × 20/(100 – 20)		82,250		
Tax on death:				
Cumulative total brought forward		120,000		
January 2007 transfer		576,250		
Chargeable to tax		696,250		
Tax thereon:				
£325,000 covered by nil band for 2011/12				
(696,250 – 325,000) @ 40%		148,500		
Less: IHT Taper relief (4-5 years) (148,500 @ 40%		(59,400)		
Less: Lifetime tax suffered		(82,250)		
Additional tax on death		6,850		

B. Principal charge

The principal (or periodic) charge to IHT in respect of chargeable trusts occurs on **every 10th anniversary** of the date on which the trust commenced. 7446 s 64 IHTA 1984

The charge to tax is based on the **value of any relevant property** in the trust on the anniversary date.

For the treatment of property added during the 10 year period, see ¶7466.

MEMO POINTS 1. The **date of commencement** of a trust is the date on which the property first became comprised in it. s 60 IHTA 1984
2. Where a chargeable trust is formed by the **terms of a will**, the date of death is the commencement date of the trust.

Relevant property

Relevant property for these purposes is **property held in a trust other than**: 7447 ss 58, 59 IHTA 1984 s 126 FA 1990 s 248 FA 1994
– excluded property (¶6456); and
– property held in the trusts listed in the following table:

Type of trust	Details
Exempt	Interest in possession trusts, if: – created before 22 March 2006; – an immediate post-death interest (¶7178); or – a transitional serial interest (¶7178)
	Disabled trusts
	Protective trusts, if the: – trust was created before 22 March 2006; or – interest in possession is an immediate post-death interest or a transitional serial interest
Favoured	Accumulation and maintenance trusts, if created before 22 March 2006[1]
	Bereaved minors trusts and age 18-to-25 trusts
	Charitable trusts
Trusts established for special purposes	Registered pension schemes
	Employee trusts
	Maintenance funds for historic buildings
	Trade or professional compensation funds
	Premiums trust funds of Lloyd's corporate members
	Pools payment funds for football ground improvements

Note:
1. Since 6 April 2008, property held in an accumulation and maintenance trust is relevant property unless the terms of the trust provide that beneficiaries become absolutely entitled to the property on or before attaining the age of 25.

MEMO POINTS **Income** only becomes relevant property once the trustees have made an irrevocable decision to accumulate it. SP 8/86

Calculation of tax

On each occasion of a principal charge, relevant property is taxed at a **maximum rate of 6%**. The rate is calculated as 30% of the "effective rate", which is itself determined by performing an IHT calculation based on a deemed transfer of value by a hypothetical transferor. 7448

a. The **hypothetical transferor** is treated as having a cumulative total brought forward equal to the aggregate of the value of:
– the chargeable transfers of value made by the settlor in the 7 years ending with the date of commencement of the trust; and

– any distributions made out of the trust in the 10 years before the date of the current principal charge.

b. The **deemed transfer of value** is made up of:
– the current value of any relevant property in the settlement immediately before (i.e. on the day before) the date of the charge;
– the initial value of any non-relevant property in the settlement; and
– the initial value of any property in a related settlement.

c. IHT is calculated at lifetime rates in the normal way and the **effective rate** is determined by the following formula:

$$\frac{\text{Deemed IHT charge}}{\text{Deemed transfer of value}} \times 100 = \text{Effective rate}$$

d. Once the effective rate has been calculated, the **actual rate** is calculated as:
Effective rate x 30% = Actual rate

e. The **principal charge** is then calculated by applying the actual rate to the relevant property in the trust at the date of the charge.

MEMO POINTS 1. **Normally**, only the current value of the relevant property will be involved and there will be no related settlements or non-relevant property.
2. The **initial value** is the value of the property transferred to the trust less any IHT paid on the transfer by the trustees.
3. **Business property relief** and **agricultural property relief** are both available to chargeable trusts but will only affect the amount of the property brought into charge, not the effective rate. Further details of the impact of these reliefs are given at ¶7474.
4. **Settlements are related** if they are made by the same settlor on the same day, with the exception of a settlement in which:
– a surviving spouse has an immediate post-death interest (¶7178) or an interest in a disabled trust; or
– the property is held indefinitely for charitable purposes.

EXAMPLE 1. **Simple case**: On 1 September 2001, Mr A (who had a cumulative total brought forward at that date of £325,000) settled £75,000 into a discretionary trust. The value of the trust property at 31 August 2011 is £200,000. No annual exemptions are available, and Mr A is still alive. The trustees made no capital distributions.
The principal charge is calculated as follows:

	£	£
1. Cumulative total brought forward		325,000
2. Transfer of value		
Current value of trust property		200,000
		525,000
3. Tax thereon:		
Nil rate band used up by cumulative transfer		
So the transfer of value is taxed at the lifetime rate:		
200,000 @ 20%	40,000	

Effective rate: $\frac{40,000}{200,000} \times 100 =$ 20%

4. Actual rate: 20% @ 30% = 6%

	£	£
5. Principal charge:		
Relevant property at actual rate		
200,000 @ 6%	12,000	

EXAMPLE 2. **Complex case**: On 1 September 2001 Mr B (who had a cumulative total brought forward at that date of £210,000) settled £225,000 into a discretionary trust of which £200,000 was relevant property and £25,000 was non-relevant. On the same day Mr B settled £120,000 into an interest in possession trust.
On 31 August 2011 the value of the relevant property in the discretionary trust is £400,000, and in the 10 years between 2001 and 2011 the trustees paid £40,000 out of the trust.

The principal charge will be calculated as follows:

		£	£
1. Cumulative total brought forward (210,000 + 40,000)			250,000
2. Transfer of value			
Current value of relevant property		400,000	
Initial value of non-relevant property		25,000	
Initial value of property in related settlements		120,000	
			545,000
			795,000
3. Tax thereon: £325,000 covered by the nil rate band for 2011/12 (795,000 – 325,000) @ 20%		94,000	
Effective rate: $\frac{94,000}{545,000}$ × 100 =	17.2477 %		
4. Actual rate: 17.2477 @ 30% =	5.1743 %		
5. Principal charge: Relevant property at actual rate 400,000 @ 5.1743 %		20,697	

Pro-rata charge

Where property **has not been** relevant property **for the full 10 year period**, the actual rate of tax is reduced by 1/40 for each complete quarter (3 months) of the period during which the property was not relevant property. This will apply where, for example, an accumulation and maintenance trust created before 22 March 2006 became a chargeable trust on 6 April 2008 because the terms did not provide that beneficiaries become absolutely entitled to trust property on or before attaining the age of 25. 7450

EXAMPLE On 1 October 2001 Mr C settled property into an accumulation and maintenance trust, which on the first 10 year anniversary was worth £400,000. By law, the trust became a chargeable trust on 6 April 2008.
If the effective IHT rate for the principal charge on 1 October 2011 was (say) 10%, the actual rate would be 1.05% (10 % x 30% x 14/40).
The IHT would therefore be calculated as:
400,000 @ 1.05% = £4,200.

C. Exit charge

In addition to the principal charge, a charge to tax (the exit or proportionate charge) arises whenever: 7452
– **trust property** ceases to be relevant property (¶7447) (where, for example, it is distributed or transferred into an exempt trust); or
– the **trustees** make a transfer (including an omission to exercise a right) which reduces the value of the relevant property.

For the treatment of property added during the 10 year period, see ¶7470.

MEMO POINTS 1. An exit charge will arise where a person who is entitled to an **interest in possession** in a chargeable trust becomes absolutely entitled to the trust property, as the assets will then cease to be relevant property. Conversely, no charge arises where another person becomes entitled to an interest in possession, as the assets remain relevant property. s81 IHTA 1984

2. Anti-avoidance measures apply to prevent the movement of property between settlements to take advantage of **different rates of tax**. Where IHT is calculated on a chargeable trust, any property which has been moved out of that trust into another settlement is deemed to remain in the trust, and so the transfer is ineffective.

1. Exempt transfers

7453 s 65 (4) – (8) IHTA 1984

The following transfers are exempt from the exit charge:
a. a transfer that **occurs within 3 months**, either from the date of the creation of the settlement, or from the date of a 10 year anniversary;
b. a transfer where the trustees did not intend to confer a **gratuitous benefit**, and either the transaction was at arm's length between unconnected parties or on comparable terms between connected parties (¶6384);
c. the payment of **costs or expenses** that are attributable to relevant property;
d. a payment that is (or will be) **income**, for income tax purposes, for any person. This includes a payment to a non-resident that would be income for income tax purposes if the person had been resident in the UK;
e. a change from relevant property to **excluded property**. For example, where the trustees of a settlement created by a non-domiciled settlor invest in UK government securities which are free of tax for residents abroad (FOTRA securities); and
f. property that becomes **held for**:
– charitable purposes only for an unlimited time (¶6442);
– a qualifying political party (¶6444); or
– a national body (¶6450).

2. Calculation of tax

7454 Tax is charged on the amount by which the value of the relevant property has been reduced as a result of the transfer of value, using the diminution of value principle (¶6465). The transfer will be grossed up if the trustees agree to pay the tax.

The tax rate depends on whether the exit charge arises before or after the date of the first principal charge (¶7446).

Exit charge before first principal charge

7456 s 68 IHTA 1984

Tax on an exit charge arising before the first principal charge is based on lifetime IHT rates (¶6534). The actual rate of tax is calculated by multiplying the effective rate by the appropriate fraction.

The **effective rate** is determined by performing an IHT calculation based on a deemed transfer of value by a hypothetical transferor.

The **appropriate fraction** is 1/40 for each complete quarter of a year between the date of the commencement of the settlement and the chargeable event.

7458 1. The **hypothetical transferor** is treated as having a cumulative total brought forward equal to the aggregate value of the chargeable transfers of value made by the settlor in the 7 years ending on the day on which the settlement commenced.
2. The **deemed transfer** is equal to the initial value (¶7448) of:
– all of the property (relevant or otherwise) in the settlement at the date of commencement;
– any property in a related settlement (¶7448); and
– any further property added to the settlement between the date of commencement and the date of the charge.
3. IHT is calculated at lifetime rates in the normal way and the **effective rate** is determined by the following formula:

$$\frac{\text{Deemed IHT charge}}{\text{Deemed transfer of value}} \times 100 = \text{Effective rate}$$

4. The **actual rate** is found by multiplying the effective rate by the appropriate fraction:

$$\text{Effective rate} \times 30\% \times \frac{\text{Number of complete quarter years between commencement of settlement and exit charge}}{40} = \text{Actual rate}$$

5. The actual rate is then applied to the amount of property that ceases to be relevant property. Grossing up is required if the trustees agree to pay the tax.

EXAMPLE On 1 December 2002 Mr A (who had a cumulative total brought forward at that date of £200,000) settled £200,000 into a discretionary trust. On 1 July 2011 the trustees distributed £80,000 of the trust property. The trustees agree to pay the tax.
The distribution will be liable to an exit charge which will be calculated as follows:

		£	£
1. Cumulative total brought forward			200,000
2. Transfer of value			200,000
			350,000
3. Tax thereon: £325,000 covered by the nil rate band for 2011/12 (400,000 – 325,000) @ 20%		15,000	
Effective rate: $\frac{15{,}000}{200{,}000} \times$ 100 =	7.5%		
4. There are 34 complete quarters between 1 December 2002 and 1 July 2011, so the actual rate will be:			
Actual rate: $7.5 \times 30\% \times \frac{34}{40} =$	1.9125 %		
5. Exit charge Relevant property at actual rate grossed up because the trustees are paying the tax: 80,000 @ 1.9125/(100 – 1.9125)		1,560	

7459 IHTM 43065 The introduction of the transferable nil rate band ("TNRB") on 9 October 2007(¶6608+) may affect the exit charge from a will trust before the first principal charge. The TNRB is ignored in calculating the effective rate of tax on a distribution. This could make the initial settled property greater than the value of a single nil rate band. An IHT charge will then be triggered at the time of exit.

Comment This type of will planning was very common and prior to the introduction of the TNRB, it ensured that no IHT was paid on creation of the trust or on exits within the first 10 years. Particular wording in a will may create an unexpectedly large bequest to a will trust where a TNRB can be claimed.

EXAMPLE On January 1 2008 Mr A died and in his will left property equal to an amount that would not give rise to an IHT charge on discretionary trusts. Mr A's executors claimed a TNRB of 50% and so, as this was the amount that could be settled without giving rise to a charge to IHT, property equal to £450,000 (150 % × £300,000, the nil rate band for 2007/08) was placed in the trust. There was no tax paid on the creation of the trust.
On 1 July 2011 the trustees made a distribution of £50,000 from the trust and the tax due on exit will be calculated as follows:

		£	£
1. Cumulative total brought forward		-	-
2. Transfer of value			450,000
3. Tax thereon: £350,000 covered by the nil rate band for 2011/12 (450,000 – 350,000) @ 20%		20,000	
Effective rate: $\frac{20{,}000}{450{,}000} \times 100 =$	4.4444 %		

4. There are 14 complete quarters between 1 January 2008 and 1 July 2011 so the actual rate will be:

Actual rate: 4.4444 × 30% × $\frac{14}{40}$ = 0.4666 %

5. Exit charge
Relevant property at actual rate grossed up because the trustees are going to pay the tax:

50,000 @ 0.4666/(100 – 0.4666)	234

Exit charge after the first principal charge

7460 s 69 IHTA 1984

Where settled property ceases to be relevant property after the occurrence of a principal 10 year charge, the IHT liability is based on the effective rate for that principal charge. The **actual rate** is determined by multiplying the effective rate by 1/40 for each complete quarter of a year between the date of the principal charge and the chargeable event.

EXAMPLE Continuing on from the second example in ¶7448, on 31 March 2012 the trustees paid a further £80,000 out of the trust. The beneficiary agreed to pay the tax. This is 19 months after the principal charge on 1 September 2010, so the IHT is based on the effective rate for the last principal charge.
The effective rate on the principal charge was 17.2477 % and there are six complete quarters between 1 September 2010 and 31 March 2012.
The **actual rate** will therefore be:
17.2477 × 30% × 6/40 = 0.2587 %

The charge to IHT will be:
£80,000 @ 0.7761 % = £620

7462 Sch 2 para 3 IHTA 1984

An adjustment is required if the **IHT rates or thresholds have altered** between the date of the principal charge and the date of the chargeable event. In this case, the exit charge is determined by recalculating the effective rate at the date of the principal charge as if the new IHT rates had applied at that time. (The tax on the principal charge itself is not affected by this notional recalculation.)

EXAMPLE Continuing on from the example in ¶7460, if, the nil rate band on 31 March 2012 had been £350,000, the principal charge would be recalculated using the new threshold, and the IHT calculation would proceed as follows:

	£	£
1. Cumulative total brought forward (210,000 + 40,000)		250,000
2. Transfer of value		
Current value of relevant property	400,000	
Initial value of non-relevant property	25,000	
Initial value of property in related settlements	120,000	
		545,000
		795,000
3. Tax thereon:		
£350,000 covered by the nil rate band		
(795,000 – 350,000) @ 20%	89,000	

Effective rate: $\frac{89,000}{545,000} \times 100 =$ 16.3302 %

4. There are 6 complete quarters between 1 September 2010 and 31 March 2012, so the actual rate will be:
Actual rate: 16.3302 × 30% × 6/40 = 0.7349 %
5. Exit charge:
Relevant property at actual rate

£80,000 @ 0.7349 %	588

D. Added property

The treatment of added property depends on: **7464**
- the identity of the donor;
- the type of tax charge;
- when the property was added; and
- whether it was added and distributed within the same 10 year period.

Identity of the donor

If property is added to a chargeable trust by: **7465**
- **a third party**, a new settlement is deemed to have been created on the date of the addition; ss 44(2), 67(1) IHTA 1984
- **the settlor**, and the value of the property within the trust is increased, the general rule is that the charge to IHT will only arise in respect of the period during which the property was relevant property (¶7447).

Principal charge

If property has **become relevant property during the last 10 years**, the actual rate of tax for that property is reduced by 1/40 for each complete quarter (3 months) of the period which expired before the property became (or last became) relevant property. **7466** s 66(2) IHTA 1984

This also applies to property that **has changed in nature**, for example an interest in possession in an exempt trust that reverts back to the trust.

EXAMPLE In 2001 Mr A settled property into a discretionary trust, which on the 10 year anniversary was worth £400,000. A quarter of the income of the fund was to be paid to his aunt, Miss B, for life. Miss B died in 2005, 4 years (24 quarters) into the 10 year period, and the property reverted back to the trust.
If the actual IHT rate for the principal charge in 2011 was 2.4045 %, the IHT would be calculated as:

	£
Miss B's interest i.e. £400,000 × 1/4 = £100,000 (100,000 × 2.4045 % × 24/40)	1,443
Remainder of trust i.e. £400,000 × 3/4 = £300,000 (300,000 × 2.4045 %)	7,213
Total IHT charged	8,656

Effect on cumulative total

Where property is added to the trust after its creation or where, as a result of a transaction by the settlor, the value of the property in the settlement is increased, the deemed cumulative total brought forward may be subject to adjustment. **7468** s 67 IHTA 1984

No adjustment will be made where a transfer results in an increase of not more than 5% in the value of the trust property, provided that the transfer was not primarily intended to increase the value of the property. s 67(2) IHTA 1984

Where an adjustment is necessary, a comparison will be made between the cumulative total of the hypothetical transferor based on the aggregate of the value of:
- the chargeable transfers of value made by the transferor in the 7 years ending with the date of commencement of the trust; or
- the values transferred by chargeable transfers by the settlor in the 10 years ending with the day before that on which the settlement was increased by the addition.

Whichever result is the higher will be used from that point (together with the value of any distributions made out of the trust in the 10 years before the date of the current principal charge) as the cumulative total brought forward.

EXAMPLE On 1 May 2001 Mr A transferred relevant property worth £300,000 into a discretionary trust. He added property worth £20,000 to the trust on 1 December 2005. The value of the trust property at 1 May 2011 was £470,000 of which £40,000 related to the added property. There were no related settlements.
Mr A made other chargeable transfers as follows:

	£
1 October 1995	50,000
1 June 1997	45,000
1 July 2005	70,000
1 August 2007	20,000

In April 2004 the trustees distributed £60,000.
The cumulative total brought forward for the purposes of the principal charge will be based on the higher of:
1. The transfers in the 7 years before the settlement was created:
50,000 + 45,000 = £95,000; or
2. The transfers in the 10 years to the date of the addition to the trust:
45,000 + 70,000 = £115,000
The actual cumulative total brought forward (including the distribution by the trustees) will therefore be £175,000 (115,000 + 60,000).
IHT will be calculated as follows

		£	£
1. Cumulative total (as above)			175,000
2. Transfer of value			
Current value of relevant property			470,000
			645,000
3. Tax thereon:			
£325,000 covered by the nil rate band for 2011/12			
(645,000 – 325,000) @ 20%		64,000	
Effective rate: $\frac{64,000}{470,000} \times 100 =$	13.61702 %		
4. Actual rate: 13.61702 @ 30% =	4.0851 %		
5. Principal charge:			
Original property at actual rate			
430,000 @ 4.0851 %		17,566	
Added property at actual rate limited to relevant period only.			
There are 22 quarters between December 2005 and May 2011.			
40,000 @ 4.0851 % × 22/40		899	
		18,465	

Exit charge

7470 If, **in a 10 year period**, property is added to a chargeable trust and then becomes the subject of an exit charge, the charge must be adjusted to reflect the period during which the property was not relevant. This is done by restricting the actual rate using the following formula:

$$\text{Effective rate} \times 30\% \times \frac{(A - B)}{40} = \text{Actual rate}$$

where:
– A is the number of quarters between the creation of the trust and the exit charge; and
– B is the number of quarters between the creation of the trust and the addition of property.

EXAMPLE On 1 July 2005 Mr A (who had a brought forward cumulative total at that date of £100,000) transferred relevant property worth £400,000 into a discretionary trust. He added property worth £80,000 to the trust on 1 November 2008. There were no related settlements.
In January 2012 the trustees distribute £90,000.

IHT will be calculated as follows

	£	£
1. Cumulative total brought forward		100,000
2. Transfer of value		
Initial value of original relevant property	400,000	
Initial value of added property	80,000	
		480,000
		580,000
3. Tax thereon:		
£325,000 covered by the nil rate band for 2011/12		
(580,000 – 325,000) @ 20%	51,000	

Effective rate: $\frac{51,000}{480,000} \times 100 =$ 10.625 %

4. There are 26 complete quarters between 1 July 2005 and 1 January 2012, and 13 complete quarters between 1 July 2005 and 1 November 2008. The actual rate will therefore be:
Actual rate: 10.625 × 30% × (26 – 13)/40 = 1.0359 %

5. Exit charge:
Relevant property at actual rate
90,000 @ 1.0359 % 932

If property has been added to the trust **since the last principal charge** and the date of the exit charge, a recalculation of the effective rate will be required. **7472** s 69(2) IHTA 1984

The rate is computed assuming the added property had formed part of the settlement on the date of the principal charge. This is simply a notional exercise to calculate the tax on the exit charge. The actual tax on the principal charge will not be affected.

E. Reliefs

1. Business and agricultural property

Business property relief (BPR) (¶6700) and agricultural property relief (APR) (¶6750) reduce the value transferred. **7474** s 103(1) IHTA 1984

For chargeable trusts there are two ways that the amount of tax can be affected:
– the relief can reduce the amount of the **deemed transfer of value**; and
– the **rate of tax** may be reduced if the relief was included in the deemed transfer arising on a principal or exit charge.

Creation of the trust

The fact that a **settlor** has claimed BPR or APR on the creation of a trust does not affect the initial value of the property in the trust. The initial value of the relevant property is the actual value of the property in the hands of the trustees on the date that the trust was created. Any tax paid by the trustees on the creation of the settlement is deducted from the value. **7475**

Principal charge

BPR and APR may be available to reduce the **deemed transfer of value** for the purposes of the principal charge. The charge to tax will be based on the value of the relevant property **7476** in the settlement at the date of the charge, and that value can be reduced by business and agricultural property relief where applicable.

Exit charge

7478 An exit charge arising **before the first principal charge** is based on the initial value of the settled property on the creation of the trust. **BPR and APR will not be available** to reduce the initial value so the rate of tax will not change, but the relief will reduce the amount of the value transferred giving rise to the exit charge.

An exit charge arising **after the first principal charge** is taxed at the rate used at the last 10 year anniversary, which will have been reduced by any available BPR and APR. The value transferred giving rise to the exit charge is also reduced by the relief.

2. National heritage property

7480 Property that satisfies certain conditions and is deemed to be national heritage property will be conditionally exempt, and therefore free from IHT. The subject of national heritage property is covered in full at ¶6660 and the details given here are those relating specifically to chargeable trusts.

Principal charge

7481 s 79 IHTA 1984 The **conditional exemption** for national heritage property applies to the principal charge if any of the following criteria are met:

a. the property was the subject of a conditionally exempt transfer on or before entering the trust, and has not been the subject of a chargeable event since that time; or

s 258 TCGA 1992 **b.** the property has been the subject of a disposal which was exempt from capital gains tax because it was a work of art etc which was the subject of an IHT undertaking, and no event has since occurred which will treat it as sold for these purposes; or

c. in any other case (if the property is purchased by the trustees, for example), a claim has been made for it to be designated as national heritage property and undertakings have been given by the trustees.

A **claw-back charge** will apply where relief has been given and the property is later sold at arm's length. The charge will be based on sale proceeds net of costs, and will be limited to the period for which relief was given.

MEMO POINTS If trust funds are used to acquire property, the purchase will be treated as an exit charge for the purposes of calculating the principal charge.

Exit charge

7482 ss 31, 78 IHTA 1984 The **transfer** of national heritage property out of a chargeable trust is conditionally exempt transfer from an exit charge, provided that:

- the property has been comprised in the settlement throughout the 6 years ending with the transfer;
- the property falls within the definition of national heritage property; and
- the requisite undertakings are given by a person deemed to be appropriate.

MEMO POINTS 1. The **relevant person** (¶6674) will, in all cases, be the settlor.

2. A **claim** for conditional exemption must be submitted no later than 2 years after the date of the transfer, although a later claim may be accepted in some circumstances.

7484 The events giving rise to a chargeable liability are outlined in ¶6670. If the event giving rise to a charge occurs **after the 10 year anniversary**, tax will be charged on the value of the property at the time of the event.

The **tax arising** from a chargeable event is the liability of the trustees, and of any person for whose benefit any of the property or income from it is applied at (or after) the time of the event.

The **rate** of tax is based on the aggregate of the following percentages for each complete successive quarter in the relevant period. s 79(6) IHTA 1984

Percentage	Maximum
0.25 for the first 40 quarters	10%
0.20 for the next 40 quarters	8%
0.15 for the next 40 quarters	6%
0.10 for the next 40 quarters	4%
0.05 for the next 40 quarters	2%
Maximum for 50 years (i.e. 200 quarters)	30%

MEMO POINTS 1. The **relevant period begins** on the later of when the settlement commenced or the date of the latest principal charge.
2. The **relevant period ends** on the day before the chargeable event.

SECTION 3

Favoured trusts

A. Accumulation and maintenance trusts

This section outlines the IHT provisions for accumulation and maintenance trusts (¶7194) which were created before 22 March 2006. These provisions applied to such trusts until 5 April 2008. Their application thereafter is shown by the following table: 7485

Date of creation	Beneficiaries become entitled	Tax rules applicable	¶¶
Before 22 March 2006	At or before age 18	Accumulation and maintenance	¶7486+
	At or before age 25	Age 18-to-25	¶7486+
	Neither of above	Chargeable trust	¶7440
On or after 22 March 2006	Irrelevant	Chargeable trust	¶7440
Property added on or after 22 March 2006	Irrelevant	Chargeable trust	¶7440

The IHT treatment of accumulation and maintenance trusts may be summarised as follows: ss 58(1)(b), 71 IHTA 1984
– the **creation** of a trust was a potentially exempt transfer;
– **principal charges** do not arise; and
– tax is not charged when a beneficiary **becomes entitled** to an interest in possession or an absolute interest in the settled property, or if he dies before attaining the specified age.

Occasions of charge

IHT will only be charged where: 7486 s 71(3) IHTA 1984
– trust property **ceases to meet** the qualifying conditions (¶7194), other than as a result of the death of a beneficiary; or
– the trustees make a **transfer** (including a failure to exercise a right) which reduces the value of the trust.

Value chargeable

7488 Where IHT arises, the charge is **based on** the amount by which the value of the trust property is less than it would have been but for the event giving rise to the charge (the diminution of value principle, ¶6465). That amount is grossed up where the trustees pay the tax (¶6536).

Rate of tax

7490 s 71(5) IHTA 1984

The rate of tax is determined by taking the **aggregate** of the percentages for each successive quarter (i.e. 3 months) in the relevant period, as shown in the table at ¶7484.

The **relevant period** runs from the date from which the property was first held on the accumulation and maintenance trust to the day before the chargeable event.

EXAMPLE On 31 May 1982 Mr A settled £200,000 into an accumulation and maintenance trust for the benefit of his own nephews and nieces and those of his wife. The income of the trust was to be accumulated for minor beneficiaries, who would then take a life interest at age 18.

On 1 June 2007 when the trust property was valued at £400,000, Mr A had a nephew (B) aged 26 and a niece (C) aged 17. Mrs A had a nephew (D) aged 15. At that date the trust failed because it had been in existence for more than 25 years and the beneficiaries did not have a common grandparent.

B, who is over 18, holds an interest in possession so the IHT charge is based on the remaining two-thirds of the trust property i.e. 400,000 × 2/3 = 266,667.

The aggregate rate of IHT is:

0.25% for the first 40 quarters	10%
0.20% for the next 40 quarters	8%
0.15% for the next 20 quarters	3%
	21%

IHT will be charged as follows:
266,667 @ 21% = £56,000

B. Trusts for bereaved minors and age 18-to-25 trusts

7492 ss 5(2), 53(1A), 71A, 71D IHTA 1984

Trusts for bereaved minors (¶7196) and age 18-to-25 trusts (¶7198) were introduced as replacements for accumulation and maintenance trusts, but with stricter conditions.

The IHT treatment of these trusts may be summarised as follows:
– as the trusts are **created** on death, the value of the property placed into trust forms part of the estate of the deceased parent, on which IHT may be due;
– a **principal charge** will not arise;
– an **exit or other charge** will only arise in certain circumstances; and
– **trust property** is not treated as part of the beneficiary's estate, irrespective of whether the beneficiary has an interest in possession.

Occasions of charge

7494 ss 71B (1), (2); 71E (1), (2), (5) IHTA 1984

A charge will arise where:
– trust property **ceases to meet** qualifying conditions;
– the trust **fails** other than as a result of the death of a beneficiary before attaining the age of 18;
– the trustees make a **transfer** (including a failure to exercise a right) which reduces the value of the trust; or.
– a beneficiary of an age 18-to-25 trust (only) **receives or becomes absolutely entitled** to trust property after attaining the age of 18.

Exemptions

A charge will not arise: **7496** ss 71B (3), (4), 71E (3), (4) IHTA 1984

a. where the trustees do not intend to confer a **gratuitous benefit** and the transaction is undertaken at arm's length between unconnected persons (¶6384), or on comparable terms between connected persons;

b. where the disposition by the trustees is a grant of a tenancy of **agricultural property** in the UK, Channel Islands or the Isle of Man, for use for agricultural purposes and made in return for full consideration in money and money's worth;

c. in respect of the payment of **costs or expenses** attributable to the property;

d. where any payment is (or will be) **income** for income tax purposes of any person (or would be if the person was resident in the UK); or

e. in respect of a **liability** to make a payment under **c.** or **d.**

Value chargeable

The charge is **based on** the amount by which the value of the trust property is less than it would have been, but for the event giving rise to the charge (the diminution of value principle, ¶6465). That amount is grossed up if the trustees pay the tax (¶6536). **7498**

Calculation of tax

The method of calculating tax depends on the reason for the charge. Where the charge arises due to: **7500** ss 71F, 71G IHTA 1984

a. a **beneficiary of an age 18-to-25 trust** receiving or becoming absolutely entitled to trust property after attaining the age of 18, or dying after attaining the age of 18, the charge is calculated in the same way as an exit charge for chargeable trusts. The charge will only apply from the time when the beneficiary attained the age of 18, so the rate of charge will be reduced by reference to the number of complete quarters before that time; or

b. any other reason, the charge is calculated on a quarterly basis, in the same way as for accumulation and maintenance trusts (¶7490).

EXAMPLE Mr A died on 20 September 2007. Under the terms of his will an age 18-to-25 trust was created in favour of his daughter, B, then aged 16. The trust terms provided for B to obtain absolute entitlement to the trust property on attaining the age of 21. B attained the age of 18 on 10 November 2009 and became entitled to the trust property on 10 November 2012, when the property was worth £200,000.
There are 20 complete quarters between 20 September 2007 and 10 November 2012, and 8 complete quarters between 20 September 2007 and 10 November 2009.

If the effective IHT rate was (say) 20%, the actual rate would be $(20 \times 30\% \times \frac{(20-8)}{40}) = 1.8\ \%$.

The IHT charge on B becoming entitled to the trust property would therefore be calculated as:
200,000 @ 1.8% = £3,600.

C. Charitable trusts

Settled property held in trust for charitable purposes (¶7200) is not relevant property, and is therefore not subject to principal or exit charges. **7510**

MEMO POINTS 1. Where the terms of the trust require **part of the income** of trust property to be applied for charitable purposes, a corresponding part of the trust property will be regarded as held for charitable purposes, and therefore excluded from the charge to tax. s 84 IHTA 1984

2. A charge to tax will not arise where **property ceases to be relevant property** (¶7447) and becomes property held for charitable purposes only, without any time limit. This rule also applies to property ceasing to be held on favoured accumulation and maintenance trusts, trusts for bereaved minors, age 18-to-25 trusts, employee trusts, protective trusts and disabled trusts. s 76 IHTA 1984

Property leaving temporary charitable trusts

7511 s 70 IHTA 1984

Special rules apply where property is held on a charitable trust only until the end of a specified period.

An **IHT charge will arise** when either:
– the property ceases to be held for charitable purposes; or
– the trustees make a transfer (other than for charitable purposes) which reduces the value of the settled property.

MEMO POINTS For these purposes a **transfer** includes an omission to exercise a right (unless it can be shown that the omission was not deliberate), and will be treated as being made at the latest time when the right could have been exercised.

7512 **Exemptions** The same exemptions apply as for bereaved minors' and age 18-to-25 trusts: see ¶7494

7513 **Value chargeable** The charge is **based on** the amount by which the value of the trust property is less than it would have been, but for the event giving rise to the charge (the diminution of value principle, ¶6465). That amount is grossed up if the trustees pay the tax (¶6536).

7514 s 70(6) IHTA 1984

Rate of tax The rate of tax is determined on a quarterly basis, in the same way as for national heritage trusts: see ¶7484.

EXAMPLE On 1 November 1992 Mr A settled £500,000 into a charitable trust. The trustees are given an overriding power of appointment exercisable in respect of Mr A's nephews, Mr B and Mr C. On 1 February 2012 the trustees appoint £150,000 to Mr B. Assuming £150,000 is the amount chargeable, IHT will be charged as follows:

The aggregate rate of IHT is:	
0.25% for the first 40 quarters	10.0%
0.20% for the next 37 quarters	7.4%
	17.4%

The IHT charge will therefore be:
150,000 @ 17.4% = £26,100

SECTION 4

Exempt (interest in possession) trusts

7515 ss 49 - 49D IHTA 1984

A trust **created on or after 22 March 2006** will only be exempt if it meets certain qualifying conditions. **Up to 21 March 2006**, all interest in possession trusts were exempt from IHT principal and exit charges.

Trusts **created before 22 March 2006** may remain exempt, depending on the circumstances in each case. Full details are given in the following table:

Type of trust	Exempt
Interest in possession	Trusts created before 22 March 2006 during lifetime or on death, until the termination of the later of: – the life interest as at 21 March 2006; or – a transitional serial interest (¶7178)
	Transitional serial interests (¶7178)
	Trusts created on death on or after 22 March 2006, with an immediate post-death interest (¶7178)
Disabled [1]	All

Note:
1. Although disabled trusts are discretionary trusts, beneficiaries are deemed to have an interest in possession.

A. General principles

A person who is **beneficially entitled** to an interest in possession (¶7187) in trust property is known as the life tenant. A life tenant of an exempt trust is treated as beneficially entitled to the trust property. If he **disposes** of his interest, or his interest **terminates** in some other way, he is treated for IHT purposes as if he had made a transfer of value. **7518** ss 49, 51IHTA 1984

The **annual exemption** is available to an exempt interest in possession trust if the life tenant so elects.

Valuation of an interest in possession

If the life tenant is **entitled to all of the income** from the settled property, he is treated as owning the net value of the property (to allow for the deduction of trust liabilities). If he holds an interest in possession in only part of the income of the settled property, he is treated as owning the proportion of the property that his interest bears to the whole. **7520** s 50(1) IHTA 1984

If the beneficiary is not entitled to the income of the settled property but is **entitled to use or enjoy the trust property**, he is treated as owning the whole of the property. If the beneficiary is entitled to use or enjoy the property jointly with another person or persons, his interest is in only part of that property. The interest is deemed to be that proportion of the whole property found by comparing the annual value of his interest to the aggregate annual value of all the interests. s 50(5) IHTA 1984

MEMO POINTS A beneficiary who has the right to the income of the trust for a period which is **shorter than his lifetime**, is still treated as owning the whole property in the trust during that period.

Annuities If the beneficiary is entitled to a **specified amount** of income, he is treated as owning an amount of the settled property that produces the specified amount during the period. **7522** s 50(2) IHTA 1984

To ensure that the annuity is not paid out of assets with a high income yield, there is a **restriction** on how the interest is valued. Essentially, the part of the trust capital applicable to the annuity may not be less than the capital required to yield the annuity, assuming it was invested at the current yield as specified in the FT Actuaries Index for irredeemable British Government Stock.

Similarly, special rules apply for the valuation of that part of the settled property which represents the **balance** of the income after the payment of the annuity. In this case, the part of the settled property applicable to the remainder must not be less than:
– the whole capital of the trust; less
– the capital needed to produce the annuity on the basis that the fund was currently invested at the gross dividend yield from the FT Actuaries All Share Index.

EXAMPLE Under a settlement worth £300,000, Mr A is entitled to an annuity of £10,000 and Mr B is entitled to the balance. The total income of the trust was £30,000.
If Mr A's interest terminates when the irredeemable stock yield is 15%, his interest will be valued at the greater of:

	£
a. The proportion of the assets based on the actual income of the fund: 10,000/30,000 × 300,000 =	100,000
or	
b. The proportion of the assets based on the deemed income of the fund i.e. 300,000 @ 15% = 45,000 10,000/45,000 × 300,000	66,667

If, on the other hand, Mr B's interest terminated when the All Share Index yield was 5%, his interest would be valued at the greater of:

	£
a. The total value of the fund less the value of the annuity using the actual income of the fund:	
Total value of fund	300,000
Less: 10,000/30,000 × 300,000	(100,000)
	200,000
or	
b. The total value of the fund less the value of the annuity based on the deemed income of the fund (i.e. 300,000 @ 5% = 15,000)	
Total value of fund	300,000
Less: 10,000/15,000 × 300,000	(200,000)
	100,000

7524 ss 43(3), 170 IHTA 1984

Lease for life A lease for life, or for a period ascertainable only by reference to a death (such as a lease to A to end on the death of B) will be treated as a settlement for IHT purposes unless it was **granted in return** for consideration in money or money's worth.

The value of the lessee's interest in a lease for life will be the full value of the property less the value of the lessor's interest.

The lessor's interest is valued as:

$$\frac{\text{Consideration received by lessor on grant of lease}}{\text{Full value of lease at grant}} \times \text{Value of property on termination of interest}$$

EXAMPLE In 2004 A granted B a lease for life over land worth £50,000. B did not pay any consideration for the lease. The granting of the lease was a potentially exempt transfer (PET) by A, valued at £50,000. If B had paid £10,000 for the lease, the value of the PET would have been £40,000. If the lease had been granted on or after 22 March 2006, the granting of the lease would have been a chargeable lifetime transfer (¶6530) and B would not be treated as beneficially entitled to the lease.

B. Creation

7526 The creation of an exempt interest in possession trust during the lifetime of the transferor increases the estate of the beneficiary, and is therefore a potentially exempt transfer or PET (¶6550). Note that this treatment **only applies** to the creation of disabled trusts or transitional serial interests (¶6550).

MEMO POINTS Where a settlor transfers property to an exempt interest in possession trust **for his own benefit**, a transfer of value does not arise, because there has effectively been no reduction in his estate. However, where a life tenant of an interest in possession trust existing before 22 March 2006 re-settles the trust property for his own benefit, that is a chargeable transfer of value unless it is a disabled trust or, if made prior to 6 October 2008, was a transitional serial interest.

7528 If the **transferor lives for more than 7 years** after the date of the transfer, no IHT will become due but the transfer will have used up the transferor's annual exemption if it is available (¶6554).

If the transferor **dies** within 7 years from the date of the transfer, the transfer will become chargeable to IHT like any other PET. The transfer will be taxed at death rates, using the cumulative total brought forward in the normal way. It will also form part of the cumulative total for other transfers up to the date of death. See ¶6556.

EXAMPLE Having made an earlier chargeable transfer of value of £100,000 on 31July 2004, Mr A made a transfer into an interest in possession trust of £200,000 in May 2007. He made a further PET to his son in August 2007 and died in June 2011.
IHT on the death of Mr A will be calculated as follows:

		Gross	Tax
	£	£	£
Cumulative total brought forward		100,000	
Transfer May 2007	300,000		
Less: Annual exemptions			
2007/08	(3,000)		
2006/07	(3,000)		
		294,000	27,600
		394,000	27,600
Tax thereon:			
£325,000 covered by nil rate band 2011/12			
394,000 – 325,000 @ 40%		27,600	

The cumulative total for use against the transfer in August 2007 will be £394,000. The annual exemption of £3,000 for 2007/08 is not available because it is used against the transfer to the interest in possession trust.

C. Termination

An interest in possession in settled property may be terminated either during the lifetime or on the death of the beneficiary. **7530** s 52 IHTA 1984

1. During life

Termination of an interest in possession during the lifetime of the beneficiary may arise because of the terms of the trust (for example because a spouse remarried), or as a result of a sale of the interest to a third party. For IHT purposes, the lifetime termination of a life interest in an exempt trust is treated as if the beneficiary had made a transfer of the property in which he had an interest. **7532** ss 52(1), 3A IHTA 1984

The deemed transfer of value is **potentially exempt** in 3 situations:

1. as a transitional serial interest such that:

a. another individual became entitled to the settled property; and

b. the transfer was made or the interest ended before 6 October 2008 and the other individual became entitled to an interest in possession;

2. the property is settled into a disabled trust; or

3. the property is settled into a trust for bereaved minors on the termination of an immediate post-death interest (¶7178).

The deemed transfer of value is a **chargeable lifetime transfer** if the property is settled into a chargeable trust by the beneficiary, and anti-avoidance rules may apply (¶7558).

Full termination

The actual value transferred following a lifetime termination of an interest in possession is the value of the property in which the interest in possession subsisted. This means that the loss to the transferor's estate is not relevant, and grossing up is not required. **7534**

Special rules apply to the valuation of property where a **beneficiary holds property in his own right** but also holds an interest in possession in the same property. For example, a person may own shares in a company absolutely, as well as an interest in possession in shares in the same company. On the lifetime termination of an interest in possession, the settled property must be valued in isolation, and the related property rules (¶6473) do not apply.

EXAMPLE Mr A owned 24% of the shares in B Ltd absolutely and also held an interest in possession in an exempt trust which owned 29% of the shares. The value of the different holdings is as follows:

Shareholding	Value (£)
24%	50,000
29%	60,000
53%	200,000

If Mr A's interest in possession was terminated, the value of the transfer would simply be the isolated value of the shares transferred i.e. £60,000.
Note: If Mr A had instead made a gift into a discretionary trust of his own 24% holding, the value of the transfer would be valued at the loss to his estate i.e. the value of the amount before the transfer less the value retained: 200,000 – 60,000 = £140,000.

Partial termination

7536 s 52(3) IHTA 1984

A partial termination of an interest in possession in an exempt trust will be **deemed to occur** where, as a result of a depreciatory transaction between the trustees and the beneficiary (or potential beneficiary) or any person connected with him, the value of the settled property has reduced. For example, the trustees might grant a lease to the beneficiary at less than market rent.

A commercial transaction **without gratuitous intent** (¶6410) is not caught by this provision, but for this exception to apply, the transaction must have been one that might be expected to have been made in an arm's length transaction between unconnected persons (¶6384).

Close company interests

7538 ss 99-s 101IHTA 1984

The following circumstances may give rise to IHT consequences if an interest in possession:
- was created before 22 March 2006; or
- is an immediate post-death interest, transitional serial interest or an interest in a disabled trust.

a. A transfer of value made by a close company (¶2100) may be apportioned to the participators (¶6992). Where one of the **participators** is a settlement with an interest in possession, the apportionment will be treated as a termination of the beneficiary's interest in possession to the extent of the reduction in value.
b. If there is a variation in the capital or rights of a close company, the participators will be deemed to have made a disposal. Where a settlement with an interest in possession is a participator, there will be a deemed termination of the interest in possession to the extent of the reduction in value.
c. If a close company has an interest in possession in settled property, the participators are treated as being entitled to that interest, according to their respective rights and interests in the company.

EXAMPLE A Ltd is owned equally by B Ltd, Mr C, Mr D and the trustees of the E settlement which was created in 2001. The E settlement has two beneficiaries, one of whom (Mr F) has a life interest in 50% of the trust property.
A Ltd sells an asset to B Ltd at an undervalue of £100,000.
Transfer of value apportioned to the E settlement: £25,000 (100,000/4)
Deemed partial termination of Mr F's life interest: £12,500 (25,000/2)

Reversionary interests

7544 s 55 IHTA 1984

For IHT purposes, the beneficiary of an exempt interest in possession trust is treated as having an interest in the property of the trust. The **holder** of the reversionary interest (¶7178) is ignored for IHT purposes, and no part of the trust is included in his estate.

However, if the **beneficiary** with the interest in possession **purchases** the reversionary interest, this is treated as reducing the value of the beneficiary's life interest and a PET will arise.

EXAMPLE Mr A is the life tenant of an exempt trust with property valued at £150,000. Mr A is deemed to be entitled to the whole of this value, and so £150,000 is included within his estate for IHT purposes.
Mr A purchases the reversionary interest for £50,000, which is treated as reducing the value of his life interest by the same amount. Therefore Mr A has made a PET of £50,000.

2. On death

Where an interest in possession in an exempt trust terminates on the death of the beneficiary, the property itself (rather than an interest in it) will form part of the deceased's estate. 7546 s 49 IHTA 1984

The settled property will be **valued** as part of the whole estate and the related property rules will therefore apply (¶6473). 7548

Once the IHT has been calculated, the **trustees** will be responsible for the proportion of tax that relates to the settled property, and the **personal representatives** will be responsible for the part relating to the free estate.

Comment This is a different treatment to the lifetime termination of an interest in possession, where the value of the property held by the life tenant is valued in isolation (¶7534).

EXAMPLE Mr A (who made no lifetime transfers of value) died in June 2011 leaving a free estate comprised of:
House and other assets – £350,000
Shares in B Ltd – (25 % holding)
Mr A also held an interest in possession in an exempt trust that owned a 20% holding in B Ltd.
Mrs A owned a further 10% of the shares in B Ltd. The shareholding taken into account under the related property rules is therefore 55% (25 + 20 + 10).
At the date of death shares in B Ltd were worth:

Holding	£
10%	50,000
20%	120,000
25%	155,000
55%	400,000

	£	**Gross** £	**Tax** £
Free estate:			
House and other assets	350,000		
Shares			
(25/55 × 400,000)	181,818		
		531,818	114,729
Settled property			
(20/55 × 400,000)		145,454	31,379
		677,272	146,108
Tax thereon:			
£325,000 covered by nil rate band for 2011/12			
(677,272 – 325,000) @ 40%		140,909	
Allocation of tax:			
Free estate			
(531,818/677,272) × 140,909		110,647	
Settled property			
(145,454/677,272) × 140,909		30,262	

D. Reliefs and exemptions

The available reliefs depend on whether the termination results in a lifetime charge or a charge on death. 7550

1. Lifetime events

Termination of interest in possession

7551 The lifetime charge on the termination of an interest in possession in an exempt trust is wholly or partly relieved in the following circumstances:

Relief	Details	Reference
Potentially exempt transfer of the interest in possession by the beneficiary	Exempt if beneficiary survives 7 years, otherwise partially taxable (¶6550)	s 3A IHTA 1984
Sale of interest in possession	Value transferred will be reduced to take account of any consideration received in money or money's worth	s 52(2) IHTA 1984
Person who held the interest becomes beneficially entitled to the trust property or, if the interest was created before 22 March 2006, to another interest in possession in it	Exempt, unless new interest has a lower value when a charge will arise in respect of the difference. Re-settlement must have been made before 6 October 2008 or to a trust for a disabled person	ss 53(2), 52(4)(b) IHTA 1984
Interest was created before 22 March 2006 and conditions for bereaved minors or age 18-to-25 trusts apply	Exempt	s 53(1A) IHTA 1984
Trust property reverts to the settlor	Exempt unless the settlor acquired the reversionary interest in return for money or money's worth	s 53(3), (5) IHTA 1984
Trust property reverts to the settlor's spouse who is UK domiciled on the date of the reversion	Exempt unless the settlor acquired the reversionary interest in return for money or money's worth	s 53(4), (5) IHTA 1984
Excluded property[1] in the trust	Exempt	s 53(1) IHTA 1984
Transfer of the interest in order to provide for family maintenance	Exempt	s 51(2) IHTA 1984
Disclaimer[2] of interest before it is accepted	Exempt unless made for consideration in money or money's worth	s 93 IHTA 1984
Termination of interest which represents reasonable trustee remuneration	Exempt unless unreasonable, when trustee will be taxed on the excess	s 90 IHTA 1984

Note:
1. Excluded property is discussed at ¶6456.
2. Disclaimers are discussed at ¶6617.

Termination of reversionary interest

7552 s 48(1) IHTA 1984 The termination of a reversionary interest (¶7178) is **excluded property** unless it:
– was acquired at any time (either by the person entitled to it or a person previously entitled to it) for a consideration in money or money's worth;
– is one to which either the settlor or his spouse has been entitled under a settlement; or
– is dependent on the termination of a lease that has been treated as a settlement (i.e. a lease for life at a nominal rent).

2. On death

7554 The usual IHT reliefs are available, including business property relief (¶6700) and agricultural property relief (¶6750), where the life tenant fulfilled the relevant conditions.

Related property

Relief will be available (¶6854) if the **property is sold within 3 years** from the date of death, for an amount that is less than its valuation of the property under the related property rules. 7555

On a claim by the trustees, the IHT on death will be recalculated using the unrelated value of the property.

EXAMPLE Following on from the example at ¶7548, if the trustees sold their holding of 20% of B Ltd in September 2011 for £128,000, the IHT on death would be recalculated as:

	£	£
Original IHT		30,262
IHT following claim for relief:		
Unrelated value of shares (taking 20% in isolation)	120,000	
Free estate	531,818	
	651,818	
Tax thereon:		
£325,000 covered by nil rate band for 2011/12		
651,818 – 325,000 @ 40%	130,727	
IHT allocated to settled property (120,000/651,818) × 130,727		(24,067)
Repayment to trustees		6,195

Quick succession relief

Relief is given on the same **basis** as for individuals (¶6865), provided that: 7556
- the transfer in question is of property in an exempt trust in which the transferor held an interest in possession; and
- the first transfer was either the creation of the settlement or a subsequent event.

E. Anti-avoidance measures

Provisions prevent the avoidance of tax where an exempt interest in possession settlement is created by a potentially exempt transfer, followed by the termination of the interest in possession in favour of a chargeable trust (a chargeable lifetime transfer). 7558 s 54A IHTA 1984

The purpose of such a transaction would be to avoid using the cumulative total of the settlor to calculate IHT, in favour of the cumulative total of the holder of the interest in possession.

Where an interest in possession to which the holder became entitled on or after 22 March 2006 terminates on the **death** of the holder of the interest, the provisions only apply if the interest is:
- an interest in a disabled person's trust; or
- a transitional serial interest (¶7178).

EXAMPLE Mr A (who has a cumulative total brought forward of £300,000) transfers £100,000 into an exempt interest in possession trust for the benefit of Mr B. This is a potentially exempt transfer and, if Mr A survives for 7 years, no tax will become due.

Next, Mr B (who has a cumulative total brought forward of £10,000) releases his interest in possession to a discretionary trust in favour of Miss C. This is a chargeable lifetime transfer and the IHT charge would be calculated using Mr B's cumulative total brought forward.

In the absence of the anti-avoidance provisions, Mr A has transferred £100,000 to a discretionary trust for Miss C without paying IHT.

Applicable circumstances

7560 The anti-avoidance **provisions apply** where the following five conditions are satisfied:

a. the creation of the original settlement was a potentially exempt transfer;

b. the interest in possession ends (or the life tenant dies) within 7 years from the date of the potentially exempt transfer;

c. the settlor is alive at the date of the termination of the interest in possession or the death of the life tenant;

d. on the termination or death, the property becomes held in a chargeable trust (¶7440); and

e. the property has not become held in an exempt interest in possession trust or a favoured accumulation and maintenance settlement, or become property to which an individual is beneficially entitled, within 6 months from the date of termination or death.

MEMO POINTS The application of these provisions will become progressively rarer, because an interest in possession trust can no longer be created by a PET.

Tax calculation

7561 If it produces a greater tax liability, the personal circumstances of the **original settlor** are used to determine the liability on the termination of the interest in possession.

The tax is calculated by **assuming** that a hypothetical transfer was made by a person with a cumulative total brought forward equal to that of the settlor at the time when the settlement was created (but including any other transfers caught by these provisions). The current value of the settled property is used together with the current rates of tax.

The chargeable lifetime transfer will, however, still form part of the **cumulative total** of the holder of the interest in possession.

EXAMPLE In March 2007 Mr A (who had a cumulative total brought forward of £250,000) settled property valued at £125,000 into an interest in possession trust in favour of his sister, Mrs B.
Mrs B (who had a cumulative total brought forward of £150,000) released the interest in possession in July 2011 into a discretionary trust in favour of her son, Mr C. At that time the settled property was worth £200,000.
The IHT charge will be the higher of the following:

	£	Gross £	Tax £
IHT based on Mrs B's circumstances:			
Cumulative total brought forward		150,000	
Termination of interest in possession	200,000		
Less: Annual exemption			
2011/12	(3,000)		
2010/11	(3,000)		
		194,000	6,400
		344,000	6,400
Tax thereon:			
£325,000 is covered by the nil rate band			
344,000 – 325,000 @ 20%		3,800	
IHT based on Mr A's circumstances:			
Cumulative total brought forward		250,000	
Termination of interest in possession	200,000		
Less: Annual exemption			
2011/12	(3,000)		
2010/11	(3,000)		
		194,000	26,400
		444,000	26,400
Tax thereon:			
£325,000 is covered by the nil rate band			
444,000 – 325,000 @ 20%		23,800	

The IHT charge will therefore be £23,800 based on Mr A's circumstances. His cumulative total will remain at £250,000 while Mrs B's will become £344,000.

Death

Additional tax may become due if: 7562 s 54B IHTA 1984
- the anti-avoidance provisions have been applied; and
- the circumstances of the settlor were used to calculate the liability on termination of the interest in possession.

This would happen if, for example, the settlor made PETs in the 7 years prior to his death which have become chargeable and therefore increase the cumulative total brought forward.

Similarly, if the provisions have been applied and the **beneficiary** of the interest in possession dies within 7 years, additional tax will become due on the chargeable lifetime transfer, if the IHT using the death rates results in a higher tax charge than using the settlor's circumstances under the anti-avoidance provisions.

CHAPTER 6

Overseas trusts

OUTLINE ¶¶

SECTION 1

Income tax

1. Residence of trustees

A trust's residence status is determined by the residence of its trustees. The trustees are treated as a single person for tax purposes and therefore have a **single joint residence**, which is determined by looking at the residence position of each trustee, based on his personal circumstances (¶4152). **7570** ss 474, 475 ITA 2007 TSEM 1461

For income tax purposes, the residence status of a trustee will **apply** for the whole tax year. The following table outlines the conditions for determining the residence of a trust.

Residence of trustees	Status of settlor when he provided funds to trust[1]	Residence of trust
All UK resident	(Irrelevant)	UK resident
All non-resident	(Irrelevant)	Non-resident
At least one is UK resident, and another is non-resident[2]	UK resident, or ordinarily resident, or UK domiciled	UK resident
	Non-resident, not ordinarily resident, and not UK domiciled	Non-resident

Note:
1. The test of the settlor's residence status must be **repeated** each time he adds funds to the settlement. If the trust was established on the settlor's death, the test will be based on his status at the date of death.
2. Where the trustees are of mixed residence, and the settlor has no connection with the UK, then the existence of a **single non-resident trustee** causes the trustees as a whole to be treated as non-resident.

MEMO POINTS 1. A **non-resident trustee** will be treated as UK resident at any time when he acts as trustee in the course of a business carried on in the UK through a branch, agency or permanent establishment.
2. HMRC have published guidance (at http://www.hmrc.gov.uk/cnr/trustee-res-guidance.pdf) stating their view of the factors which determine the residence of a body of trustees.

2. Income tax position of trustees

7574 The trustees of a non-resident trust are taxable on **UK source income only**, under the general rules as detailed at ¶7290.

s 487 ITA 2007 **Management expenses** of the trustees of a non-resident discretionary trust must be apportioned between the UK and non-UK income of the trust.

SI 1996/223 MEMO POINTS The trustees of a non-resident trust will be eligible to receive UK bank or building society **interest gross** if they notify the payer accordingly.

EXAMPLE Trust A is a discretionary trust resident in Guernsey. In 2011/12 the trust had the following income and management expenses:

	Gross (£)	Tax deducted (£)	Net (£)
UK dividend income	4,000	400	3,600
UK bank interest	18,000	Nil	18,000
Bank interest (Guernsey)	28,000	Nil	28,000
Expenses	2,500	Nil	2,500

UK income tax payable by the trustees will be calculated as follows:

	Gross £	**Tax £**
Dividend income	4,000	400
UK bank interest	18,000	
	22,000	
Less: Expenses		
(2,500 × 22,000/(22,000 + 28,000) = 1,100)		
1,100 × 100/90	(1,222)	(122)
	20,778	278
Tax thereon:		
Trust dividend rate: 4,000 – 1,222 = 2,778 @ 42.5%	1,180	
£1,000 band: 1,000 @ 20%	200	
20,778 – 2,778 – 1,000 = 17,000 @ 50%	8,500	
	9,880	
Less: Notional tax credit	(278)	
Income tax payable by trustees	9,602	

3. UK resident beneficiary of a non-resident trust

Interest in possession trusts

The UK resident beneficiary of a non-UK resident interest in possession trust is **treated** as if he had received the income of the trust directly, and is taxed accordingly. He can claim relief for any foreign tax borne by the trustees on non-UK income. 7576

Discretionary trusts

The UK resident beneficiary of a discretionary trust is **taxed on** the income he receives from the trust. 7578

By concession, the beneficiary is allowed **credit for UK and foreign tax** paid by the trustees. This concession is only available if the trust has submitted all of the appropriate trust returns and has paid any tax due. A claim for relief must be submitted within 4 years from the end of the tax year in which the beneficiary received the payment from the trustees. ESC B18

4. Anti-avoidance measures

Anti-avoidance measures which are relevant to offshore trusts include: 7580
- transfer of assets abroad; and
- certain transactions in land.

Transfer of assets abroad

The provisions detailed at ¶4137 may apply to UK resident settlors or beneficiaries of offshore trusts who can benefit from trust assets, including free use of trust property. 7582

EXAMPLE Mr S is ordinarily resident in the UK. He owns 80% of the shares in A Ltd, and he transfers these shares to a non-UK resident trust from which he can benefit. The anti-avoidance provisions will apply unless he had no motive to avoid tax, and his investment was a genuine commercial transaction.

Because taxable benefits are restricted to the income actually received overseas, a non-UK resident trust which accumulates income can avoid these provisions, or at least delay a charge to UK income tax, provided the **settlor and his spouse are excluded** from being beneficiaries. 7584

EXAMPLE The B trust is a non-UK resident discretionary trust which receives the following income:

Tax year	Income (£)
2009/10	10,000
2010/11	12,000
2011/12	15,000

In 2010/11, the trust pays out £8,000 each to Mr X and Mr Y, and £10,000 to Mr Z, all UK resident beneficiaries. The taxable income of the beneficiaries is calculated as follows:

Tax year	Trust income (£)	Assessed income[1, 2] (£)		
		Mr X	Mr Y	Mr Z
2009/10	10,000	Nil	Nil	Nil
2010/11	12,000	6,769	6,769	8,462
	22,000			
2011/12	15,000	1,231	1,231	1,538

Note:
1. The total benefit received by the beneficiaries is £26,000. The trust's cumulative income up to 2010/11, of £22,000, is apportioned as follows:

Mr X and Mr Y	$8,000/26,000 \times 22,000 = 6,769$
Mr Z	$10,000/26,000 \times 22,000 = 8,462$

2. The remaining benefit is taxed in 2011/12, once the trust's cumulative income exceeds the total payment to the beneficiaries of £26,000.

Transactions in land

7586 The provisions detailed at ¶4052 apply to any person (UK resident or not) if the land in question is **located in the UK**.

The capital gain arising from the disposal of any land located in the UK will be **treated as sundry income** for all tax purposes, if the land is:
- acquired with the sole or main object of realising a gain from disposing of it;
- held as trading stock; or
- developed with the sole or main object of realising a gain from disposing of it when developed.

This may be relevant where an offshore trust (or a company owned by an offshore trust) holds land in order to escape a CGT charge on its disposal (and assuming that other anti-avoidance provisions do not apply). Under this provision the gain would be taxed as sundry income, irrespective of the residence of the trust.

SECTION 2

Capital gains tax

7595 As a general rule, the trustees of a UK resident trust are subject to UK capital gains tax (CGT), whereas the trustees of a non-resident trust are not.

Special rules apply, however, where a UK resident trust becomes non-resident, or where the settlor is temporarily absent abroad. In some circumstances the trust gains may be attributed to the settlor or assessed on the beneficiaries.

A. Residence of trusts

7597 A tax year will **not be split** for a trust which changes its residence. In a tax year when a trust becomes or ceases to be UK resident, therefore, gains made while the trust is non-resident may still be taxable in the UK.

1. Determining residence

7598 The residence of a trust is determined in the same way as for income tax purposes (¶7570) and there is no exception for UK resident professional trustees.

s 69 TCGA 1992
TSEM 1461

MEMO POINTS Until 5 April 2007, a trust would be treated as non-resident if the only reason that it was UK resident was that it had a UK resident professional trustee.

EXAMPLE Trust A was established by Mr B in 2001, when he was not resident, ordinarily resident or domiciled in the UK. There are two trustees. One trustee is non-UK resident and the other is a UK resident professional trustee. Until 5 April 2007, the trust was treated as non-UK resident. Since 6 April 2007, the trust has been UK resident.

2. Trust becoming non-resident

When a trust ceases to be UK resident, the trustees are **deemed** to have disposed of the trust assets and immediately re-acquired them at the market value. **7600** s 80 TCGA 1992

MEMO POINTS 1. Special rules apply if the **death of a trustee** results in the trustees becoming non-resident. Provided the trust becomes UK resident again within 6 months of the date of death, the charge will only apply to assets disposed of during the period of non-residence. s 81 TCGA 1992
2. UK assets used by the trustees for a **trade** carried on in the UK through a permanent establishment are excluded from this charge because they remain chargeable in the UK. s 10 TCGA 1992
3. Rollover relief (¶1605C) is not available for gains realised before the emigration of the trustees if the replacement assets are acquired after emigrating. This does not apply to UK assets used by the trustees for a trade carried on in the UK through a permanent establishment. s 80(6) TCGA 1992

Unpaid tax

Where a CGT charge has arisen as a result of the emigration of a trust and the tax remains **unpaid 6 months** after the due date, HMRC can require the unpaid tax to be settled by any trustee who resigned in the 12 months before the emigration of the trust. The trustee may recover the tax from the migrating trustees. A trustee will not be liable if he can show that at the time of his resignation there was no proposal for the trust to emigrate. **7602** s 82 TCGA 1992

Disposal of an interest in a trust

The **exemption** for the disposal of a beneficial interest (¶7430) does not apply if the trustees are resident or ordinarily resident overseas. On disposing of an interest which was created or arose before the date of emigration, the person is treated as if he had sold and immediately re-acquired the interest at the market value on the date of emigration. **7604** s 85 TCGA 1992

Interaction with double tax agreements

In certain cases, a trust may be **resident and non-resident** in the same tax year, and may be subject to CGT in a country other than the UK under the terms of the relevant double tax agreement while non-resident. If the other country's CGT rate is less than that in the UK, trusts could take advantage by disposing of trust property while non-resident. **7605**

Accordingly, if the trustees are resident or ordinarily resident, or are resident in the UK at any time during the tax year, the UK retains its **taxing rights** irrespective of any double tax agreement. Double tax relief is available for tax paid abroad. s 83A TCGA 1992

Administration

Settlements with a foreign element are subject to strict **reporting requirements** which apply without notice. A return of particulars of the trust is required, and penalties will arise for failure to comply, in the following situations: **7606** Sch 5A TCGA 1992

Situation	Who responsible	Time limit
Creation of a non-resident or dual resident trust.	Settlor	Within 12 months of the date on which he became UK resident or ordinarily resident and UK domiciled, not having been so at the date of the creation of the settlement.
Trust becomes non-resident or dual resident.	Trustee	Within 12 months of the change of residence status.
Transfer of property on non-arm's length basis to non-resident trust created before 17 March 1998.	Transferor	Within 12 months of the date of the transfer.

B. Trust gains attributed to the settlor

7608 ss 86-s 86A TCGA 1992 Sch 5 para 9 TCGA 1992 CG 11030

Gains made by a non-resident trust may be attributed to the settlor if the trust was created:
- on or after 19 March 1991; or
- before 19 March 1991, and the trust is not a protected trust (¶7610).

The **conditions** for attributing gains, all of which must be satisfied, are that:

a. the trustees of the settlement are:
- neither resident nor ordinarily resident in the UK during any part of the year; or
- resident and ordinarily resident in the UK, but also resident overseas under the terms of a double tax arrangement;

b. the settlor is domiciled in the UK at some time in the tax year, and is either:
- resident in the UK during any part of the year; or
- ordinarily resident in the UK during the year;

c. the settlor has an interest in the settlement (¶7612) at any time during the tax year; and

d. none of the exceptions (¶7610) apply.

A **settlor who is non-resident** at the time a gain is been made, but who becomes UK resident again within 5 complete tax years of leaving the UK, will have the gain attributed to him in the tax year of his return.

MEMO POINTS 1. The non-domiciled settlor of an overseas trust is not subject to tax unless he is in receipt of benefits or capital payments from the trust (¶7618). The remittance basis applies where the settlor is a remittance basis user.
2. Where this provision applies, double tax agreements do not extinguish the right of the UK to tax the gain.
3. These provisions are an extension of the provisions applying to UK domiciled settlors; see ¶7636.

Exceptions to the charge

7610 Sch 5 paras 3-5 TCGA 1992

No charge arises under these provisions if the trust is a **protected trust**, or in a year of assessment in which:
- the settlor dies; or
- a defined person other than the settlor (¶7612) dies, or that person's marriage is terminated; or
- two or more defined individuals die, and their interests were deemed to make the settlor interested in the settlement.

MEMO POINTS Broadly, a **protected trust** is a trust made before 19 March 1991, where the beneficiaries are confined to the following:
- minor children of the settlor or the settlor's spouse, who were under 18 at the end of the previous tax year;
- unborn children of the settlor or his spouse;
- future spouses of any children or future children of a settlor or his spouse; and
- a future spouse of the settlor.

A trust will **cease to be protected** for the year in (and the years after which) any of the following events occur:

a. income or property is provided to the settlement other than by way of an arm's length transaction or in pursuance of any pre-19 March 1991 liability, or other than to make up a deficit between the trust income and expenses for the same year;

b. the trustees become neither resident nor ordinarily resident (or become dual resident);

c. the terms of the trust are varied to allow one of the following people to become a beneficiary or potential beneficiary for the first time:
- the settlor;
- the settlor's spouse;
- any child (or grandchild) of the settlor or his spouse;
- the spouse of any such child (or grandchild);
- a company controlled by any of the persons listed above; or
- a company associated with such a company;

d. a person from the above list enjoys a benefit from the settlement for the first time, and the person concerned is not one who (looking at the terms of the settlement immediately before 19 March 1991) would be capable of enjoying a benefit from the settlement on or after that date; or

e. the trust ceases to be a protected trust for any other reason.

Interest of the settlor

A settlor is **deemed** to have an interest in a settlement if either of the following applies: 7612 Sch 5 para 2 TCGA 1992

a. Any settlement property or income originating from him is (or may become) applicable for the benefit of:
- the settlor;
- the settlor's spouse;
- any child (or grandchild in certain situations) of the settlor or his spouse;
- the spouse of any such child (or grandchild if the settlement was created after 16 March 1998);
- a company controlled by any of the persons listed above; or
- a company associated with such a company.

b. Any such person enjoys a benefit either directly or indirectly from any settlement property or income originating from the settlor.

Benefits arising in the following situations are **ignored** for these purposes:
- on the bankruptcy of a beneficiary or a potential beneficiary;
- if the beneficiary assigns his interest or creates a charge on the property;
- in the case of a marriage settlement where both of the marriage parties die and all or any of the children die; or
- if a beneficiary dies under the age of 25 (or some lower age) who would become beneficially entitled to the property on attaining that age.

The charge to tax

The settlor is **assessed on** the net gains of the trustees, with loss relief available where appropriate. The trustees' annual exemption is not available. The gain attributed to the settlor is taxed as the top slice of his capital gains, and he can recover the tax from the trustees. For the settlor's personal losses, see ¶5452. 7614 Sch 5 para 6 TCGA 1992

C. Trust gains attributed to a beneficiary

The gains of a non-resident trust may be attributed to a beneficiary when: 7618 s 87 TCGA 1992 CG 11030
- the trustees are at no time resident and ordinarily resident in the UK; and
- the beneficiary is either resident or ordinarily resident in the UK.

MEMO POINTS Originally the provisions applied only if the settlor (or one of the settlors) was domiciled and either resident or ordinarily resident in the UK in the year of assessment, or was when he made his settlement. The provisions now apply to **all settlements**, whatever the settlor's domicile or residence status. However, the changes only take into account those chargeable gains accruing to the trustees, and capital payments made by the trustees, on or after 17 March 1998.

Where gains are **attributed to the settlor** under the rules in ¶7608 in a particular tax year, there will be no attribution of the same gains to the beneficiaries.

If a **beneficiary is non-UK domiciled** but UK resident or ordinarily resident he must claim the remittance basis (¶4200) to prevent a tax charge arising, unless the capital payment is attributed to a pre-6 April 2008 gain (¶7626).

MEMO POINTS The rules for overseas trusts and CGT changed from 6 April 2008. Where there is a non-domiciled settlor, any gains made by the trustees are immediately transferred to a trust gains pool. The gains are then available for matching against benefits made available to beneficiaries. If the remittance basis is claimed by a non-domiciled beneficiary, a gain will only be taxable if remitted to the UK, but it does reduce the amount of the gains in the trust gains pool.

Charges

7619 The gains attributed to the beneficiary are limited to the **capital payments received** from the trust. Gains attributed in this way are deemed to be made by the beneficiary in the tax year in which the attribution takes place, and are treated as the lowest slice of his gains for the year. Beneficiaries cannot set off personal losses against attributed gains (¶5468).

A **supplementary charge** (¶7628) may be made to take account of the time difference between the date of the gain and the date of the capital payment.

1. Attributed gains

Gains of the trust

7620 s 87 TCGA 1992 Sch 7 FA 2008

The gains of the trust are **deemed to be** the amount on which the trustees would be chargeable if they were resident and ordinarily resident in the UK, including any allowable losses for previous years for which relief has not been given. There is no annual exemption.

EXAMPLE A non-resident discretionary trust, with a UK domiciled and resident settlor, has gains and losses in the three years to 2011/12, which are assessed as follows:

	2009/10	2010/11	2011/12
	£	£	£
Gains	-	1,000	4,000
Allowable losses	(2,500)	(400)	-
	(2,500)	600	4,000
Losses carried forward	2,500	-	-
Losses used	-	(600)	(1,900)
Amount on which trustees are assessed	Nil	Nil	2,100

If a trust existed at **6 April 2008**, the trustees can make an irrevocable election to have the trust assets treated as being **rebased** to their value at that date. Any gain arising after 6 April 2008 will then be pro-rated so that the part of the gain accruing before that date is disregarded. Distributions made before 6 April 2008 are also disregarded.

Sch 7 para 108 FA 2008

MEMO POINTS 1. The **election** for rebasing by the trustees was introduced by Finance Act 2008 which brought non-domiciled beneficiaries into the tax charge. Rebasing does not affect the tax charge for UK domiciled beneficiaries; gains are calculated under the usual rules for these beneficiaries.

2. HMRC provide an election form, RBE1, for capital gains tax rebasing of UK assets owned by:

a. an overseas resident trust; or

b. an overseas company owned by an overseas trust.

The rebasing applies to asset values at 6 April 2008, but HMRC will only agree a valuation after an asset has been disposed of and when there are capital payments available to match against any gain on the disposal. All trustees must sign the election. It must be submitted by 31 January following the first tax year in which either a UK resident beneficiary receives a capital payment or the trustees transfer all or part of the settled property to another settlement overseas. The deadline for submission of the election for 2011/12 is 31 January 2013.

3. If the trustees **do not elect to rebase**, the gains are matched against any payment made before 12 March 2008 and then against any capital payments made on or after 6 April 2008. If there is no election for rebasing, old distributions do not become taxable, but the capital payment has to be pro-rated to match the gains made before and on or after 6 April 2008.

4. Gains, losses and capital payments made by a trust **prior to 17 March 1998** are disregarded in calculating the gains of the trust if the settlor was not UK resident or domiciled when the trust was established or when the gains were made.

Capital payment

A capital payment from a trust is **defined** as any payment which is not chargeable to income tax in the hands of the beneficiary or, if the beneficiary is neither resident nor ordinarily resident in the UK, is not received as income. A payment received in the course of an arm's length transaction is not a capital payment. **7622** s 97(1) TCGA 1992

MEMO POINTS 1. The term **payment** includes the transfer of an asset and the conferring of any other benefit. s 97(2), (4) TCGA 1992
2. The amount of a capital payment made by way of a **loan** (and of any other capital payment which is not an outright payment of money) will be taken to be equal to the benefit conferred by it.

A beneficiary is deemed to have **received** a capital payment from the trustees of a settlement if: **7624** s 97(5) TCGA 1992
- he receives it directly or indirectly from them;
- it is applied by them (either directly or indirectly) for his benefit; or
- it is received by a third person at his direction.

MEMO POINTS This includes money, other assets, benefits in kind and services.

Matching

For each year of assessment the capital payments made by the trusts are **aggregated** and then matched to the gains (after losses) on a last in/first out (LIFO) basis. **7626** ss 87A- s 87C TCGA 1992 Sch 7 para 124 FA 2008

MEMO POINTS 1. The order of matching makes it harder to distribute old gains which attract the highest rates of tax and on which the supplementary charge (¶7628) will be accumulating.
2. Gains are not matched with distributions made in the period from 12 March to 5 April 2008 inclusive. This prohibition means that distributions made during that period cannot be used to extinguish accumulated or later gains.
3. If a distribution is made to a non-domiciled beneficiary, that payment will match capital payments from the trust, but the payment will only be taxable if both the underlying gain and the capital payment arose after 5 April 2008. If the capital payment is made after 5 April 2008, but is matched with a gain made before 6 April 2008, the gain will not be taxable, whether or not the individual is a remittance basis user.

Situation in tax year	Treatment
Gains exceed capital payments	Excess gains will be carried forward and attributed to future capital payments after later gains have been matched.
Capital payments exceed gains	Excess payments will be carried forward and will be available for the attribution of gains in later years.
Gains attributed amongst different beneficiaries and excess gains	Attribution will be carried out in the proportion that the capital payments made to each individual beneficiary bear to the total capital payments for the year.

EXAMPLE Trust A is a non-resident settlement established by Mr B, who is UK resident and domiciled. In recent years the trustees have realised the following gains and made the following capital payments to beneficiaries:

	2009/10 £	2010/11 £	2011/12 £
Gains	10,000	15,000	27,000
Capital payments			
Mr C	3,000	12,000	5,000
Miss D	1,000	8,000	4,000
Mr E	2,000	10,000	1,500
	6,000	30,000	10,500

The attribution of gains to beneficiaries will be calculated as follows:

	Total £	Mr C £	Miss D £	Mr E £
2009/10				
Gains	10,000			
Capital payments		3,000	1,000	2,000
Matched to capital payments	(6,000)	(3,000)	(1,000)	(2,000)
Excess gains	4,000			
Attributed in 2010/11 (see below)	(4,000)			
	Nil			
Excess capital payments		Nil	Nil	Nil
2010/11				
Gains	15,000			
Capital payments		12,000	8,000	10,000
B/fwd gains from 2009/10 not yet matched	4,000			
	19,000			
Gains matched to capital payments: first with 2010/11 gains (12,000/30,000 × 15,000 etc)	(15,000)	(6,000)	(4,000)	(5,000)
Gains matched to capital payments: secondly with 2009/10 gains (12,000/30,000 × 4,000 etc)	(4,000)	(1,600)	(1,067)	(1,333)
	Nil			
Excess capital payments	11,000	4,400	2,933	3,667
2011/12				
Gains	27,000			
Capital payments in year matched to current gains	(10,500)	5,000	4,000	1,500
Matched to 2010/11 payments	(11,000)	4,400	2,933	3,667
Total capital payments		9,400	6,933	5,167
Matched to capital payments	(21,500)	(9,400)	(6,933)	(5,167)
Excess gains from 2011/12 c/fwd	5,500			
Excess capital payments		Nil	Nil	Nil

2. Supplementary charge

7628 s 91 TCGA 1992 When a beneficiary is charged to tax on attributed non-resident trust gains, an extra amount, known as the supplementary charge, may be payable if the capital payment was made more than one year after the end of the tax year of the gain.

Basis of calculation

7630 The charge is akin to interest but is treated as additional CGT, collected through the self-assessment system. The **period of charge** begins on 1 December in the tax year following that in which the gain arose, and ends on the 30 November in the tax year following that in which the capital payment was made.

The supplementary charge is **payable** (at an annual rate of 10%) on the tax due after the gains have been attributed to the beneficiary.

The **minimum** supplementary charge is 20% (i.e. two years) so if the gains are attributed to the beneficiaries in the year following that in which they are made, that will be the rate charged.

The **maximum** supplementary charge is 60% (i.e. six years) and, in addition, the total of tax on the attributed gain and the supplementary charge cannot exceed the amount of the capital payment.

EXAMPLE If a gain made in 2009/10 is matched with a capital payment made in 2011/12, a supplementary charge will be applied for the period 1 December 2010 to 30 November 2012. The charge amounts to 2 years at 10% = 20 %.

The attributed gain is treated as the bottom slice of the beneficiary's gains and the annual exemption may therefore have been deducted from it. **7632**

If a capital payment is **matched to more than one gain** it is deemed to do so on a LIFO basis.

D. Settlor's temporary absence abroad

Where the settlor is temporarily non-UK resident, on his return to the UK he will be chargeable in respect of any gains which would have been assessable on him if he had remained in the UK. **7636** s 10A TCGA 1992

A settlor will be **deemed** to be temporarily non-resident if:
– he was resident in the UK for at least 4 of the 7 years immediately before his departure; and
– there are fewer than 5 years of assessment between (and not including) the year of departure and the year of return.

Double charge to CGT

Special rules apply to **prevent** a double charge to CGT where the settlor of a trust becomes temporarily non-resident and: **7638** s 86A TCGA 1992
– the gains of a non-UK resident trust arising during his temporary non-residence have been taxed on him at his return; and
– gains arising in his period of non-residence have been attributed to beneficiaries receiving capital payments from the settlement.

The settlor is **only taxable** on those gains arising during his period of non-residence that have not already been taxed on the beneficiaries.

SECTION 3

Inheritance tax

Overseas trust property

For inheritance tax purposes, trust property situated outside the UK is excluded from the scope of UK IHT unless the settlor was UK domiciled when the trust was created, when the usual rules apply (¶7440). **7640**

CHAPTER 7

Administration

OUTLINE ¶¶

SECTION 1

Income tax and capital gains tax

The income, gains and losses of trusts and estates are declared to HMRC in the form of a self-assessment return. 7650

A form 41G (Trust), which can be requested from any local HMRC office or downloaded from HMRC's website, should be submitted when a new trust is created. Once received, HMRC will allocate a reference to the trust, and issue tax returns under self-assessment.

MEMO POINTS 1. For trusts with **no income**, and where no gains are likely to arise, there is no requirement to notify HMRC of the existence of the trust.
2. Where an **existing trust** is unlikely to receive income or gains, the trustees can request that returns are not issued annually. Where income is received subsequently, the rules in ¶7652 apply.
3. A trustee of a **bare trust** (¶7176) is not required to submit a return or to make payments on account as this is the responsibility of the beneficiary. A bare trustee is not however prevented from completing a return and accounting for the tax on income received gross providing the beneficiaries agree. Any capital gains or losses received by the trust (including gains on life insurance policies and life annuities) continue to be the responsibility of the beneficiary, and should not be included on a return completed by the trustees. Tax Bulletin 32

Liability to complete a return

Personal representatives complete the return for an estate, and trustees complete the trust return. 7652

Trustees who are chargeable to income tax or capital gains tax (CGT) for any year of assessment for which they do not receive a tax return or a notice to file, must **notify** HMRC of the liability to tax within 6 months from the end of the year of assessment in which the liability arises. s 7(2) TMA 1970

Personal representatives do not need to complete a formal self-assessment return where the estate being administered is: TSEM 7410
- not complex (see note below); and
- the tax arising during the administration period is less than £10,000.

HMRC will accept a simple computation of the estate's liability and will provide the personal representatives with a payslip to pay any tax due.

Sch 41 FA 2008 The penalty for failure to notify is calculated as a percentage of the potential lost revenue. The percentage rate depends on the actions of the person liable to notify HMRC (¶9848).

For the remainder of this section, references to trustees should be deemed to include personal representatives.

MEMO POINTS 1. In the year in which the **administration of an estate ends** and a trust commences, two returns will be required: one from the personal representatives and one from the trustees.
2. An **estate will be complex** if:
– the probate value exceeds £2.5 million;
– the administration of the estate has entered the 3rd income tax year; or
– the personal representatives have disposed of a capital asset and the proceeds exceed £250,000.

Details of the return

7656 A **notice** to file a return may be issued to one, some, or all of the trustees as determined by HMRC.

The **due dates** for a trust and estate self-assessment form are the same as for individuals and depend on when the return is issued and the type of return submitted:

Return issued	Type of return submitted	Filing date
On or before 31 October following tax year	Paper[1]	31 October following tax year[2] (or 3 months after date of issue if after 31 July)[3]
	Electronic	31 January following tax year
After 31 October following tax year		3 months after date of issue

Note:
1. Only original paper forms issued by HMRC will be accepted. If a substitute paper form is submitted, this will be treated as not compliant with the filing requirements.
2. Returns submitted by this date need not contain a tax calculation.
3. If a return is issued after 31 August, it need not contain a tax calculation provided it is submitted within 2 months of the date of issue.

7658 **Penalties** may be incurred if the return is not submitted by the filing date: see ¶4542.

Amendments

7660 ss 9 - 9ZB TMA 1970 Once submitted, a return can be amended by both HMRC and the trustees: see ¶4490.

7663 Sch 1AB TMA 1970 If the trustees have paid income tax or CGT under self-assessment, they may make a claim to correct an **error or mistake** in a trust return within 4 years from the end of the tax year to which the claim relates. See ¶4572.

Record keeping

7666 s 12B TMA 1970 Trustees are **required** to keep all the records necessary to enable them to make and deliver a correct return. The requirements are identical to those for individuals: see ¶4528+.

Payment

7668 **Income tax** is payable in two instalments (based on the income from the previous year) on 31 January during the tax year and 31 July following the tax year. See ¶4506 for the calculation of payments on account.

The balance of the income tax liability, together with the **CGT** liability, is payable on the 31 January following the tax year.

Interest (¶4516) and penalties (¶4545) may be payable on tax which is paid late.

Other provisions

The following self-assessment provisions for individuals apply equally to trustees, and full details are given in the sections referred to: 7672
a. interest on overdue tax (¶4516);
b. repayment of tax and repayment supplements (¶4522);
c. payment of CGT by instalments (¶6344);
d. carry back claims (¶4494);
e. discovery assessments (¶4564);
f. enquiries (¶4552); and
g. penalties (¶4532).

SECTION 2

Inheritance tax

Trustees are responsible for fulfilling the administrative requirements with respect to IHT and settlements. Details of requirements arising as a result of the death of an individual are given, along with the general IHT administration rules, at ¶7020 onwards. 7675

MEMO POINTS The penalties for the submission of IHT returns changed from 1 April 2010, under the new harmonisation rules.
If death occured in April 2009 then the IHT Return was due to be filed by 30 April 2010, and this would be covered by the new administration and penalty regime, whereas if the death was in March 2009, it would be covered by the previous regime.

Submission of accounts

The trustees must submit an account of each **chargeable transfer** by the later of: 7677 s 216 IHTA 1984
- 12 months after the end of the month in which the occasion of charge took place; or
- 3 months from the date on which tax became payable.

This requirement will arise on:
- transfers of value (other than potentially exempt transfers);
- the termination or disposal of an interest in possession in an exempt trust (¶7515); and
- the principal (¶7446) and exit (¶7452) charges on a chargeable trust.

MEMO POINTS In the case of an estate for which probate has not been issued within 12 months of death, the time limit for a particular person is three months from the date when he first became aware of his obligation to submit an account.

A trustee is liable to account to HMRC when a **potentially exempt transfer** becomes a chargeable transfer, following the death of the transferor within 7 years. The account must be submitted within 12 months from the end of the month in which the death of the transferor occurred. 7680

For this reason, it is important for trustees who receive a potentially exempt transfer to make themselves aware of other transfers (chargeable or potentially exempt) made within the 7 years before the transfer in question.

Payment

The **general due date** for payment of tax on chargeable lifetime transfers is 6 months after the end of the month in which the chargeable transfer took place. The **exception** arises if the transfer is made after 5 April and before 1 October in a tax year, when the due date is 30 April in the following year. 7682 s 226 IHTA 1984

The trustees are initially **responsible for** the payment of IHT. s 201 IHTA 1984

If the trustees default, the following persons will be liable:
– any person entitled to an interest in possession in the property;
– any person for whose benefit the settled property, or income from it, is applied; and
– the settlor, where the chargeable transfer was made during his lifetime and the trustees are not for the time being resident in the UK (¶4152).

Interest will be charged in respect of IHT paid after the due date (see ¶7072).

7685 IHT due on certain types of property may be paid in ten equal **instalments** (¶7074).

Tax may also be paid in instalments on the principal and exit charges for chargeable trusts. To qualify, either the instalment assets must continue to be comprised in the settlement, or the beneficiary must pay the tax.

Determinations and appeals

7688 ss 221-223I IHTA 1984 HMRC have the power to make a determination of the IHT due in respect of a transfer of value. Alternatively, they may offer to review their decision or the taxpayer may request that they do so. If a review does not lead to resolution of the matter, an appeal can be submitted to the tribunal. The trustees have 30 days in which to submit an **appeal** against a determination. Late appeals may be accepted if there is a reasonable excuse. The first-tier tribunal will deal with most appeals, including those relating to the valuation of shares, although the Lands Tribunal will deal with cases involving the valuation of land. Finally, subject to agreement, appeals may go directly to the upper tribunal. Further details on the appeals system is given at ¶9920+.

Information

7691 Sch 36 FA 2008 s 96 FA 2009 HMRC have extensive powers to call for information, require documents and inspect premises in relation to inheritance tax. These powers are identical to those described at ¶9322+.

PART 7

Value added tax

Value added tax
Summary

The numbers cross-refer to paragraphs.

CHAPTER 10 Administration

CHAPTER 1

First principles

OUTLINE ¶¶

The aim of this section is to cover the basic VAT issues which may arise on a day-to-day basis. For more in-depth coverage of the UK VAT system and detailed analysis of VAT rules and concepts please see *VAT Memo*. **7748**

A. What is VAT?

Scope

Value Added Tax (VAT) is an indirect tax on the supply of goods and services. The charge to VAT does not arise solely on the sale of goods and services to end-users, but is charged on the "value added" to the supply during each stage of the supply chain. **7750** s 4 VATA 1994

The VAT system is self-administered by VAT-registered businesses, which are required to calculate the correct amount of VAT on every transaction and account for the appropriate amount to HMRC.

UK VAT is **chargeable on**: **7752**
- taxable supplies made in the UK by **taxable persons** in the course of a business (¶7764);
- acquisitions of goods from other EU member states (¶8937);
- imports of goods into the UK from outside the EU (¶9037); and
- receipt of services from outside the UK (¶9108).

For VAT purposes, the UK includes the Isle of Man but not the Channel Islands or Gibraltar.

VAT is a European tax and supplies made elsewhere in the EU may be liable to VAT in another member state.

MEMO POINTS 1. The **place of supply** may not be obvious. See ¶7988.
2. For transactions between the UK and countries outside the EU and details of **cross-border** transactions with EU or non-EU countries see ¶8930.

Taxable persons

"Person" takes its legal meaning and therefore includes individuals, partnerships, companies and charities. HMRC often refer to "**traders**" or "**businesses**" instead of persons. The terms are generally interchangeable for VAT purposes. **7754** s 3 VATA 1994

A taxable person is **any person** who is **registered** for VAT, or required to be registered for VAT.

A person who makes taxable supplies which exceed a specified limit **must register** (¶7770) for VAT. All persons making taxable supplies may **choose to register** for VAT if their turnover has not reached the threshold.

MEMO POINTS 1. It is important to note that it is the person that is registered, not the business. For example, if an individual is carrying on **several unincorporated businesses**, the individual's VAT registration applies to all of his or her business activities. Thus the registration threshold applies to the person's total turnover from all his or her businesses. Note, however, that a limited company or a partnership is a separate "person". See also "Business splitting" (¶7784).

s 47 VATA 1994 2. In the normal course of events the person who has made a supply will be easy to identify. When a supply has been made through an **agent** a distinction is drawn between an agent acting in his own name, when he will be treated as the supplier, and an agent acting in the name of a principal, when the principal will be treated as the supplier. See ¶8520 for further details.

Taxable supplies

7756 The term "supply" is not defined in legislation but has wide meaning. In very **general terms**, a supply means selling or providing something in return for consideration. Anything which is not a supply of goods but is done for a consideration (including the granting, assignment or surrender of any right) is a supply of services. Traders need to consider whether they are supplying goods or services or, in limited circumstances, neither.

Once a trader has established that it is supplying goods or services each of its supplies will fall into one of the following categories:
- taxable supply;
- exempt supply; or
- outside the scope of VAT.

The default position is that supplies are taxable unless they are specifically excluded from the charge to VAT.

MEMO POINTS 1. For full details on supplies see ¶7835+.
2. There are three rates of VAT for taxable supplies (¶8030).

B. How does VAT work?

7760 On a very simple level the taxable person must charge **output tax** to his customer. He then deducts the **input tax** he has incurred on supplies made to him, and the difference is declared on a VAT return and paid to HMRC. If input tax exceeds output tax, a refund will be due from HMRC.

These terms are defined in the following table:

Term	Definition	¶¶
Input tax	VAT incurred on purchases and expenses	¶8130
Output tax	VAT charged to the customer	¶8034

There are **exceptions** for:
- traders who make exempt supplies (¶8205);
- traders who use the flat rate scheme (¶8620);
- certain farmers (¶8660);
- tour operators (¶8626); and
- traders who use the second-hand margin scheme (¶8435).

C. What is a business?

Statutory definition

The term business is not comprehensively defined by the legislation, but **includes**: 7764 s 94 VATA 1994
- any trade, profession or vocation;
- the exploitation of tangible and intangible property for the purpose of obtaining income on a continuing basis;
- services carried on by a person in his capacity as an office holder when the position is undertaken in the course of that person's trade, profession or vocation (for example, a trustee, auditor, or executor);
- use of business goods for non-business purposes (known as self-supplies);
- action in connection with the termination or intended termination of a business;
- the disposal or transfer of a business as a going concern (¶8596);
- provision of facilities to members by a club, association or organisation for consideration (for example, the use of a golf course); and
- admission to premises for compulsory consideration (requesting voluntary payments from visitors does not on its own indicate that a business is being carried on).

The **EU definition** focuses on any economic activity, regardless of the result of that activity, and is more widely drawn than the UK definition of "in the course of business". EC Directive 2006/112 art 9(1)

Case law

Due to the limited scope of the statutory definition several tests have arisen from VAT tribunal and court decisions, to help decide whether a business is being carried on. 7766

The following table summarises the **attributes that may indicate** that an activity is a business, developed from leading cases, including *Morrisons Academy Boarding Houses Association v C & E* [1978], *Lord Fisher v C & E* [1981] and *Apple and Pear Development Council v C & E* [1988].

The absence of one or more of the attributes does not necessarily mean that the activity is not a business, and each case must be considered on its own merits.

Attribute	Note
Is the activity **predominantly** concerned with the making of taxable supplies to consumers for consideration?	There must a direct link between the supply and the consideration. Consideration does not need to be monetary. If supplies are not made for consideration and there is no intention of doing so in the future, the activity is unlikely to be a business for VAT purposes.
Is the activity "a **serious undertaking** earnestly pursued" or "a serious occupation not necessarily confined to commercial or profit-making undertakings"?	Usually excludes hobbies, unless a substantial amount of value (see below) results from the activity.
Is the activity an occupation or function actively pursued with reasonable and recognisable **continuity**?	One-off or infrequent, unconnected supplies will not normally be a business activity but the nature of the activity will be relevant.
Does the activity have a certain measure of **substance** as measured by the quarterly or annual value of taxable supplies made?	Activities with a high value or goods being expensive do not, in themselves, make an activity a business.
Is the activity **conducted** in a regular manner and on **sound** and recognised **business principles**?	An activity is not required to be efficient or profitable to be considered a business.
Are the taxable supplies of a **type** which are commonly made by those who seek to profit by them?	It is not necessary for the activity to be carried on with a view to making a profit for it to be considered a business.

MEMO POINTS 1. When a person undertakes **more than one** activity, each activity must be considered in isolation. In an early case a tribunal considered the trader's activities as a whole, not just the taxable activities, to establish if there was substance to those activities. *DD Prenn* [1979]

Business Brief 2/05 2. HMRC will accept that nursery and creche facilities provided by **charities** do not constitute a business, where the aim is to break even. *St Paul's Community Project Ltd v C & E* [2004]
It remains HMRC's policy that an activity is not required to have a **profit motive** to be a business, and will only accept the St Paul's argument in specific cases. In any case, some charities may be keen for their activities to be treated as "in the course of a business" if they are incurring substantial input tax, as otherwise they would be unable to recover it.
3. The ECJ has decided that external advertising activities carried out by a publicly funded political party were not an economic activity. The case involved publicity expenses incurred on behalf of local district party groups by the provincial arm of an Austrian political party. The party partly recouped the costs from the local groups, but the ECJ held that this did not constitute an economic activity for VAT purposes. The party was not in competition with commercial advertising agencies. *SPÖ Landesorganisation Kärnten* C-267/08 [2009]

CHAPTER 2

Registering for VAT

OUTLINE ¶¶

All "persons" who are in business and make or intend to make taxable supplies (¶7756) of goods and services in the UK may be liable or entitled to register for VAT. VAT registration may be either compulsory or voluntary, and the requirement for registration may vary throughout the life of a business. 7770 Sch 1 VATA 1994

Recoverable input tax (¶8135+) can be reclaimed on all relevant expenditure from the date of registration. In addition, it is possible to reclaim input tax on certain types of expenditure incurred before becoming registered (¶8287).

SECTION 1

Registration

1. Compulsory registration

Registration for UK supplies

VAT registration is compulsory for supplies made in the UK in the following situations: 7775 Sch 1 para 1 VATA 1994

a. at the end of any month, if the value of taxable supplies in the previous 12 months exceeds the registration threshold (see ¶9987); or

b. at any time, if the value of taxable supplies in the next 30 days is expected to exceed the same threshold; and

c. where a business (or part of a business) carried on by a taxable person is transferred to another person as a going concern (¶8596) and the transferee is not already registered under VATA 1994. The transferee becomes liable to be registered from the date of transfer if:
– the value of his taxable supplies (including the value of supplies made in the previous 12 months by the business being transferred to him) in the 12 months ending at the time of the transfer has exceeded the registration threshold in **a**. above; or
– there are reasonable grounds for believing that the value of his taxable supplies in the next 30 days from the date of the transfer will exceed that limit.

It is therefore essential to maintain a cumulative record of taxable supplies to be able to identify when registration is required. For this purpose, the following must be ascertained:
– the **time** of supply (¶7900), which is usually (but not always) the invoice date;
– the **place** of supply (¶7988), as generally only supplies subject to UK VAT are taken into account; and
– the **value** of the supply.

MEMO POINTS 1. **Taxable supplies** are those which would be liable to VAT (including VAT at the zero rate) if the person was registered. An unregistered person can make taxable supplies, but must not charge VAT until he becomes registered.
2. The following can be ignored when considering whether the **threshold** has been exceeded:
– exempt supplies;
– supplies made by traders under a previous registration;
– sales of capital assets, other than supplies of interests or rights over land on which standard-rate VAT is due (¶8840+, ¶8904); and
– the last acquisition or supply of goods before removal from fiscal warehousing, or self-supply of services on removal of goods from warehousing (¶9016).
Special rules apply to the valuation of certain supplies for this purpose, including the turnover from margin schemes (¶8437) and fiscal warehousing (¶9016).
3. For details of **historic thresholds** see ¶9987.
4. When a business is transferred as a going concern (¶8596) an **election** may be made for the transferee to take over the VAT registration. This is done on form VAT 68, which must be signed by both parties. The transfer of the VAT registration will **not be allowed** if:
– the transferor's VAT registration has already been cancelled;
– the registration applies to a VAT group (¶7809);
– the transferor has been subject to civil penalties (¶9290);
– any default surcharge notices (¶9272) or centrally raised assessments remain outstanding; or
– the transferor has been subject to a direction in respect of the disaggregation of business activities (¶7788).

Other situations

7776 A requirement for registration can arise in the following overseas and cross-border situations:
– **distance selling** by a UK trader to recipients in other EU member states who will not use the goods or services received for business purposes (¶8982) – this may require the UK trader to register in another EU state; conversely an EU trader may be required to register in the UK if his distance sales to the UK exceed the UK's distance selling threshold (¶8984);
– **acquisition** of goods in the UK from other EU member states which will be used for business purposes (¶8958);
– where a UK-based trader **receives services** from other countries for business purposes (known as "reverse charge services") – registration will be required where the value of the services, alone or together with any taxable supplies made in the UK, exceeds the registration threshold (¶9110);
– **services provided electronically** to non-business customers by non-EU traders (¶9116).

Exemption from compulsory registration

7777 Sch 1para 1(3) VATA 1994

Registration may **not be required** if the trader can demonstrate to HMRC's satisfaction that supplies in the next 12 months are unlikely to exceed the deregistration threshold (see ¶9988).

Exemption from registration may also be granted where HMRC are satisfied that: Sch 1 para 14 VATA 1994
- all supplies are zero-rated (¶8052); or
- any standard-rated supplies are small in proportion to the total taxable supplies and, if registered, the input tax would normally exceed the output tax. *TK Fong* [1977]

MEMO POINTS If a request for exemption from registration, based on falling sales or zero-rated supplies, is not accepted by HMRC, registration will take effect from the day the trader first became liable to be registered.

2. Voluntary registration

7778 Sch 1 para 9 VATA 1994

Any person who is not liable to be registered is eligible for registration if:
- he can satisfy HMRC that he is carrying on a business, and that he intends to make taxable supplies in the course of that business (known as "**intending trader**" registration); or
- he satisfies HMRC that he is making taxable supplies.

In such cases HMRC must register the person from the date of his request, or an earlier date if agreed. If an earlier date is accepted the trader could, from the date of registration, **reclaim** all input tax incurred but would be **required to charge** output tax on supplies made from that date.

Voluntary registration is **beneficial** where:
- VAT on expenditure exceeds VAT on income and the trader could therefore claim a refund of VAT;
- customers are all or mainly VAT-registered and so do not mind being charged VAT, because they can recover it as their input tax;
- customers will only deal with a VAT-registered supplier; or
- having a VAT registration will enhance the image of the business.

The benefits should be weighed against the compliance burden of VAT registration, and whether charging VAT will reduce the competitiveness of the business.

3. Compulsory registration process

Where registration is compulsory, the person must notify HMRC by completing an application for VAT registration (form VAT 1) within the following time limits. 7779

Reason for registration	Time limit to notify	Date registration effective from
Past turnover	30 days following the end of the calendar month in which the registration threshold is exceeded	End of the month in which notification is required [1]
Future supplies in next 30 days [2]	30 days from when the expectation arose	Date on which the business became liable to be registered
Transfer of a going concern	Within 30 days of the transfer [3]	Date of transfer

Note:
1. This means that the supplies of the first month after the registration threshold has been exceeded are VAT-free.
2. A **one-off transaction** could create a liability to register. HMRC may accept that future supplies will be below the deregistration threshold and waive registration.
3. Notification of the transfer must be made by **both parties** to the transaction. If the new owner wishes to retain the VAT registration of the transferor, both parties must also complete form VAT 68. The business records must be transferred to the transferee but the transferor can request permission to retain the records. If a business is transferred as a going concern but the VAT registration is not transferred the business records must be retained by the transferor. Where records are retained the transferee can require the transferor to provide such information as is necessary for the transferee's VAT compliance purposes.

EXAMPLE
1. On 31 July Mr A determines that his taxable supplies for the previous 12 months have exceeded the registration threshold. Mr A is liable to be registered for VAT from 31 July and must notify HMRC by 30 August. During August, Mr A makes sales of £14,000.

HMRC will register Mr A from 1 September, unless an earlier date is mutually agreed. Mr A is not required to charge VAT on his supplies in August, thereby saving a substantial amount of VAT, which will be beneficial to his customers if they are unable to fully recover all of the VAT charged.

2. On 12 April Mr B expects his supplies in the next 30 days to exceed the registration threshold. Mr B is liable to be registered for VAT from 12 April and must notify HMRC by 12 May. The effective date of registration will be 12 April.

MEMO POINTS 1. **Registration application forms** are available to download from HMRC's website, or can be obtained by calling their National Advice Service (0845 010 9000). Alternatively it is possible in certain circumstances to register online using the Online Service pages of HMRC's website (¶9217).
2. Applications for **group** registration must include forms VAT 50 and VAT 51 (¶7810).
3. Applications for **partnership** registrations must include form VAT 2 completed by all partners (¶7821).

Consequences of failing to register

7781 There are two consequences of **failing to register** either on time or at all:
a. registration will be backdated to when it should have become effective; and
b. penalties will be due (¶9270).

MEMO POINTS If a business fails to register for VAT at the correct time, in addition to incurring a late registration penalty, it will still be liable for all VAT due on supplies made from the time that it should have been registered. This means that VAT will be due on sales from the date the business should have been registered, even though it was not charged to customers. If customers are VAT-registered, it may be possible to issue VAT invoices retrospectively, by treating the amount originally charged as net and charging output VAT. However, normally businesses which fail to register on time will have to fund the VAT that should have been charged.

After registration

7782 As soon as a person is **liable** to be registered the following consequences arise:
– VAT **records** must be kept (see ¶8305 onwards), and output VAT charged to customers in respect of supplies made from the effective date of registration onwards; and
– **invoices** raised in the period between the effective date of registration and before the issue of the VAT registration number must not show the VAT element separately and should state "this is not a tax invoice". A valid tax invoice (¶8306) identifying the VAT element must be issued within 30 days of receiving the VAT number.
After notification HMRC will issue a **certificate of registration** (VAT 4), which will show the:
- effective date of registration;
- trader's unique registration number;
- date on which the first VAT period ends; and
- length of subsequent VAT periods.

After registration has commenced HMRC must be notified of any **change in circumstances**, including:
- change of name or address;
- change of legal status, for example incorporation;
- death, incapacity, or insolvency; or
- ceasing to make taxable supplies or transferring the business.

4. Business splitting

7784 If a trader runs more than one business the sales in all of those businesses must normally be added together to determine whether or not registration is required. However, if a person runs businesses via a number of separate legal entities it may not be necessary to combine the sales of those businesses to calculate whether there is a requirement to be VAT-registered.

To avoid registration, a trader may seek to **artificially** separate his business: for example, by taking his spouse into partnership for part of the activities and retaining the other part as a sole trade. This is known as disaggregation of business activities, or business splitting.

Where HMRC consider that only one business has ever existed, a backdated **assessment** based on late registration might be issued, which could go back 20 years. Otherwise, a **notice of direction** may be issued.

Notice of direction

Where HMRC believe that business splitting has taken place, a notice of direction may be issued to the business requiring the separate legal entities to be combined under a **single VAT registration**. 7788 Sch 1 paras 1A, 2 VATA 1994

A notice can only be issued where the following **criteria** are met:
- at least two legal entities are making taxable supplies as part of a larger activity being carried on;
- there are close financial, economic and organisational links between the separated parts of the business;
- the taxable turnover of the entities, when combined, exceeds the registration threshold; and
- the separation is artificial, resulting in the avoidance of VAT.

MEMO POINTS 1. The notice of direction will **indicate the business activities** to which it relates, and the names of all persons who are to be treated as carrying on a single business under a single registration. A notice will be issued to each of the persons mentioned in it.
2. Examples of **financial, economic and organisational** links are summarised in the following table:

Financial	Economic	Organisational
Common financial support	The activities of one person benefit those of the other	Common premises and/or equipment
Common financial interest in the proceeds of the business	Supplying the same circle of customers	Common management and/or employees

3. There is no rule governing when a **separation is artificial**, although the following are circumstances which HMRC would probably wish to investigate further:
- separate entities dealing with registered and unregistered customers;
- one person controlling a number of similar type businesses in different geographical areas;
- same equipment or premises used by different entities on a regular basis, for example on different days of the week;
- splitting what is generally perceived as a single supply, for example bed and breakfast; or
- separate businesses which appear to be a single business, for example bar and catering supplies in a public house.

4. Where **self-employed** individuals are used by a business to provide a service, for example driving instructors or hairdressers, it is important to determine who is providing the end service to the customer.

EXAMPLE A café was operated by a company which was controlled by a married couple. The couple also traded as a partnership which operated a sandwich bar in the same premises. The turnover of each business was below the registration threshold but the combined turnover exceeded the threshold. HMRC raised a VAT assessment on the basis that there was in reality a single business. This was upheld by a tribunal, as was HMRC's notice of direction that the two businesses be covered by a single VAT registration. *Mr & Mrs Sterling t/a Sally's Sandwich Bar and The Corner Cafe (Tooting) Ltd* [2005]

Consequences

From the date of the notices of direction each entity that has been notified must register together as a single taxable person. The registrations of the constituent entities will be cancelled unless they genuinely have other, separate business activities. 7790

A **supplementary** notice can be issued to add further entities to the direction as appropriate.

The entities which are subject to the notices may **appeal** against the direction (¶9920+). An appeal will only be allowed where the tribunal considers that there were no reasonable grounds for HMRC making the direction.

SECTION 2

Deregistration

7796 A person must **notify HMRC** in writing within 30 days of the reason arising why deregistration should occur. A person must also notify HMRC on ceasing to be entitled to be registered for VAT (for example, where an intending trader no longer has an intention to trade). Once HMRC have been notified and are satisfied that registration is no longer required, the registration will be cancelled.

When to deregister

7798
Sch 1 para 13 VATA 1994

HMRC are required to deregister a person if any of the following apply:
– they are satisfied that the person has ceased to make taxable supplies, and is not required to be registered for any other reason;
– the business has been sold or has ceased;
– there is a change in the legal status of the business (for example, incorporation of a sole trader) unless continuation of registration is requested; or
– the conditions for compulsory registration are no longer satisfied.

A **person may opt** to deregister, with the agreement of HMRC, where either:
– HMRC are satisfied that taxable supplies in the following year will not exceed the deregistration threshold (see ¶9988); or
– input tax will regularly exceed output tax.

Until the **operative date** is officially confirmed on form VAT 35, the trader must continue VAT accounting as normal. For compulsory deregistration, the date will be that of the event causing the cancellation. For voluntary cases, the date should be mutually agreed.

MEMO POINTS 1. **Other reasons** why registration may need to continue are where the person is also:
– making distance sales (¶8982);
– acquiring goods from the EU (¶8958); or
– receiving services from outside the UK (¶9108).
2. For details of **historic thresholds** for deregistration see ¶9988.

7800 Once registration is cancelled, no further VAT **invoices** bearing the VAT number may be issued.

The requirement to prepare and maintain VAT **records** ceases when the registration is cancelled; however, records for the period of registration must be retained for a specified length of time (¶9209).

Input tax is no longer recoverable once a person deregisters. For the treatment of certain supplies and costs incurred while not registered, see ¶8285.

7802
Sch 6 para 6 VATA 1994

Final VAT return On cancellation of registration a final VAT return (VAT 193) is issued. The business is required to account for VAT on all transactions which occurred from the end of the previous return up to the date of cancellation on the final return.

The business must also use the final return to account for output VAT on the value of any **stock and business assets on hand** at the date of deregistration. This includes any tangible goods of the business but not intangibles (such as goodwill and patents). The VAT charge is **restricted** to those goods on which the business has already recovered input tax.

There is **no requirement to account for VAT** where:
– the business is transferred as a going concern;
– the business is subsequently carried on by another person in the case of death, incapacity or bankruptcy; or
– where the total output VAT due on the value of the assets would be £1,000 or less.

The VAT-exclusive **value of the goods on hand** is taken to be the amount the business would have to pay to buy identical goods, or, if this cannot be established, the price payable for similar goods. If neither of these amounts can be ascertained, the value of the goods is the cost that would have been incurred to produce them at the date of deregistration.

MEMO POINTS 1. For the recovery of **input tax** after deregistration, see ¶8295.
2. For disposals of **land and buildings** and expensive **computers**, **ships** and **aircraft** see ¶8250.

EXAMPLE Mr A is an electrical goods store owner. As his business has substantially reduced over the last year, he has decided to close the business and retire. During the period to cessation, he has managed to sell most of his stock for £3,500 plus VAT. However, at the time of deregistration, he has goods on hand valued at £1,650 (excluding VAT).
Mr A's final VAT return will therefore show actual supplies made during the period of £3,500. No deemed supply on deregistration will be included, as the VAT due on £1,650 is less than £1,000. (£1,650 x 20% = £330)

SECTION 3

Special situations

Special rules apply in relation to the VAT registration of groups of companies, companies registered in divisions and partnerships. **7805**

1. Group registration

Two or more corporate bodies can apply to be **treated as** a single taxable person for VAT purposes. Group registration is intended to ease the administrative burden of VAT. HMRC have wide powers to ensure that group registrations cannot be used to avoid VAT. **7807** s 43 VATA 1994 Notice 700/2

To be **eligible** for group treatment, members must be established in, or have a fixed establishment in, the UK and may be treated as members of a VAT group where:
– one controls the others;
– they are controlled by the same person (including another company or individual); or
– they are controlled by two or more individuals carrying on a business in partnership.
A company which is registered in **divisions** (¶7815) is not eligible to join a VAT group.

MEMO POINTS 1. The grouping provisions apply to all **corporate bodies**, including: s 43A VATA 1994
– limited liability partnerships;
– companies limited by shares, or guarantee;
– unlimited companies; and
– industrial and provident societies.
2. A company is **established in the UK** if the central management or control of the company, or its head office, is in the UK. There is no statutory definition of a **fixed establishment** but HMRC take this to mean a real and permanent trading presence, not simply a registered office address or a UK subsidiary.
3. **Control** exists for these purposes where one company is the holding company of another, its subsidiary. s 1159 CA 2006 Sch 6 CA 2006
A company is a subsidiary if another company:
– holds the majority voting rights;
– is a member of the company and has the right to appoint or remove a majority (in terms of control, not numbers) of the directors; or
– is a member and controls alone, pursuant to an agreement with other shareholders and members, the majority of voting rights.
The requirement is also satisfied where a company is a subsidiary of another company which itself is a subsidiary of the holding company, in which case they may all be included in the same VAT group.

One of the companies is appointed as the **representative member** and the VAT registration will be in the representative member's name. The representative member takes on all **responsibility** for accounting and paying VAT for the VAT group as a whole. Each member of the VAT group is, however, jointly and severally liable for any VAT liability. **7809**

All purchases and taxable supplies are deemed to be made by the representative member and any **intra-group transactions** are ignored for VAT purposes, unless the anti-avoidance rules apply.

MEMO POINTS 1. A corporate group can decide which eligible companies are to be included in the VAT group registration and the constituent **members** can be changed, subject to stringent anti-avoidance rules.
2. Care should be taken when considering which companies should be included in a VAT group registration if any of them make **exempt supplies**, as the group would become partly exempt if they were included (¶8205). This would mean that the VAT group's input tax recovery would be restricted, subject to de minimis rules (¶8218).
3. Conversely, as no VAT is chargeable on **management charges** levied between the members of a VAT group, it may be beneficial to include the company making exempt supplies in the group to stop any "VAT leakage". If management charges are made between companies not in a VAT group they are subject to VAT, which is not recoverable by the company making exempt supplies (¶8205), again subject to the de minimis rules (¶8218).

Application

7810
s 43B VATA 1994

The **representative** member must complete a VAT registration application form (VAT 1) and form VAT 50. Each **member** of the VAT group must also complete a form VAT 51.

HMRC aim to respond to an application within 15 days. If the application is successful, HMRC will register the group from the **date** on which the application was made. An earlier date may be mutually agreed, but this cannot be more than 1 month before the date of the application.

If the application is **accepted**, a new registration in the name of the representative member and a new VAT number will be issued. It is not possible to reallocate a previous VAT registration number. Even after the new registration has been accepted and a new VAT registration number has been issued, HMRC have a further 90 days to make any enquiries into the composition of the VAT group. If the application is **refused**, an appeal can be made to the tax tribunal.

s 20 FA 2004

MEMO POINTS 1. A company cannot be a member of **two group registrations** at the same time, so an application to join a new group whilst still a member of another group will be denied, as will two simultaneous applications involving the same company.
2. Any **changes to the group composition** must be notified to HMRC on form VAT 50 and accompanied by form VAT 51 for each company joining or leaving the group.
3. A **new representative member** may be appointed by completing form VAT 56. If the new representative member was not already a member of the group, forms VAT 50 and 51 must also be completed.
4. If the decision is made to **disband a group**, forms VAT 50 and 51 must be completed. The VAT registration will be cancelled and each company, if liable to register for VAT, will be required to register separately.
5. All VAT group registration applications should be sent to: HMRC, Imperial House, 77 Victoria Street, Grimsby DN31 1DB.

Anti-avoidance

7812
Sch 9A VATA 1994

Group registrations can lead to VAT advantages over and above administrative simplification. Where **HMRC** believe VAT is being avoided, they may exercise their **powers**, which include:
– removing a company from a group registration from a specified date, which can be retrospective;
– ordering that a supply between group members is to be treated as a taxable supply;
– requiring a company to become a member of the group registration (with the consequence that the company would become jointly liable for the group's VAT, even if the VAT related to a period before it became a group member); and
– identifying a company which must become the representative member.

HMRC will **issue a direction** to the company that is affected and the company has the right to request that the direction be reconsidered. An **assessment** may be issued for unpaid VAT within 1 year of the direction.

The company can also **appeal** to the tax tribunal, which will decide if HMRC have acted reasonably. HMRC may withdraw a direction at any time.

Large groups Special provisions apply in order to prevent a jointly-owned entity from joining a VAT group, where the entity is run by and for the benefit of third parties who exercise effective control of the entity. Additional eligibility conditions prevent certain suppliers from being in the same VAT group as their customers where a third party controls the suppliers and receives the main benefit of their activities. **7813** SI 2004/1931

Groups with **turnover of £10 million** or more in the last year, or expected turnover at this level in the next year (excluding intra-group supplies), are subject to additional eligibility requirements.

A **jointly-owned entity** is prevented from joining a group registration where the VAT group customer is unable to recover all of the related input tax and either the supplier is:
– run for the benefit of a third party, outside of the VAT group registration; or
– not consolidated in the group accounts of the person controlling the VAT group under generally accepted accounting practice.

MEMO POINTS 1. This rule does not apply to a supplier which is a **charity**, or **pension trustee**, or which **controls** the VAT group.
2. The **turnover threshold** includes the turnover of the supplier.
3. A supplier will be run for the **benefit of a third party** where more than 50% of the benefits of ownership accrue to a third party.

EXAMPLE S Ltd makes taxable supplies to the ABC Group, which cannot recover all of the VAT charged. S Ltd is jointly owned by A Ltd (of the ABC group) and Z Ltd, a third party. Z Ltd has the right to more than 50% of the profits from S Ltd. S Ltd is not consolidated into the group accounts of ABC Group.
S Ltd is not eligible to join the ABC Group's VAT registration.

2. Divisional registration

Where a company is organised into divisions, each with separate accounting functions, it can be administratively complex to prepare a single VAT return. To ease the compliance burden each division can register separately for VAT, although the company will remain the taxable person. **7815** s 46 VATA 1994

VAT invoices must not be issued for transactions between the divisions.

Eligibility

Divisional registration will generally only be **allowed** where the company can demonstrate that it would experience real difficulty in preparing a single VAT return within 30 days of the end of the VAT period. **7817** Notice 700/2 para 9.3

The following **criteria** must be satisfied for divisional registration to be considered:
– the company must not be partly exempt (¶8205), taking into account that the de minimis limits (¶8218) apply to the company as a whole;
– each division must be registered, irrespective of activity and scale;
– each division must operate independently and have a separate accounting function;
– the divisions must operate for different regions, supply different commodities, or carry out different functions of the business; and
– each division must have the same period end for its VAT returns.

Application

An application must be made in writing to HMRC, setting out the full circumstances of the case and the reason why a single VAT registration is not appropriate. The application must be **accompanied** by a VAT registration application form (VAT 1) for each division. **7818** Notice700/2 para 9.4

If the application is successful, each division will be registered separately, given a VAT registration number, and be responsible for filing its own VAT returns. The company as a whole remains **liable** for any VAT due from the divisions.

7819 If a division's **supplies fall below** the deregistration threshold, it can only be deregistered if the supplies will be accounted for by another division, because the company as a whole is still liable to be registered.

If a division **no longer satisfies** the conditions for divisional registration, HMRC must be informed within 30 days. A decision will then be taken by HMRC on whether the divisional registration should be allowed to continue. If the divisional registration is cancelled for the corporate body as a whole then, if it is still liable to be registered, a single VAT registration must cover all the taxable business activities of the body corporate as a whole.

3. Partnerships

7820 s 45 VATA 1994 When individuals are carrying on business in partnership, the VAT registration may be in the name of the partnership. If more than one UK partnership (excluding Scottish partnerships) has the same partners, they will be covered by a **single VAT registration**.

A partnership cannot be a partner in another partnership (except in Scotland), so if the ABC partnership joins with the DEF partnership, a wholly new partnership is created, which will have a separate registration. The original partnerships may still exist, so it is possible that three registrations would be required in this case.

MEMO POINTS 1. In **Scotland** a partnership is a distinct legal person. If separate partnership agreements exist for each business, the same group of partners may have a different registration for each business.
2. For **limited partnerships** registration is in the name of the general partners only. This means that, if the partners in a series of limited partnerships are the same, each limited partnership can have a separate VAT registration if the general partners are different in each case.
3. Limited liability partnerships (LLPs) are not partnerships for VAT purposes; instead they are corporate bodies.

Registration application

7821 All partnerships which register for VAT must complete an **application form** (VAT 1), which must be signed by one of the partners. This must be accompanied by form VAT 2, which should be signed by each partner.

Each partner is **jointly liable** for the debts of the partnership, and jointly and severally liable for the obligations of the firm. Any notice of assessment will be levied on the partners individually, and may even be directed against a single partner. That partner would then need to recover any amounts due from the other partners.

MEMO POINTS 1. In **Scotland** partners are only liable for the debts of the partnership if it becomes insolvent.
2. In the case of **limited partnerships**, only general partners must complete form VAT 2.

Changes in the composition of partnerships

7822 HMRC must be **notified** of any change in the composition of a partnership within 30 days. New partners are required to complete a supplementary form VAT 2.

There is no prescribed form for notifying HMRC when a partner leaves, although notification must be given in writing. When a **partner leaves** a partnership, he remains liable for the partnership VAT until the date on which HMRC are notified. This does not apply for Scottish partnerships.

In addition, any notices (for example, assessments) issued in relation to the VAT period in which he left, or earlier periods when he was a partner, are deemed to be served on him.

CHAPTER 3

Supplies

OUTLINE ¶¶

7830 VAT is charged on the supply of goods or services in the UK, so it is important to determine:
– whether a transaction constitutes a supply for VAT purposes;
– whether the supply is of goods or of services;
– where and when the supply occurs; and
– the value of that supply.

Once it has been established that a supply has been made, the nature of the supply will determine the rate of VAT that will apply to the transaction (i.e. standard rate, zero rate or reduced rate), or whether it is exempt from VAT.

SECTION 1

What is a supply?

7835
s 5(2) VATA 1994
EC Directive 2006/112 art 2

The term supply is **not defined** by the legislation, other than to say that anything done for no consideration is generally excluded. Anything which is not a supply of goods, but is done for a consideration, is a supply of services. Thus it is essential first to determine whether a supply has been **made for a consideration**.

Some transactions are **deemed** to be supplies (¶7849) even if there is no consideration, and are therefore within the scope of VAT.

As a general rule a supply must be either:
– a supply of goods (the passing of possession following an agreement whereby the supplier agrees to part with goods and the customer agrees to take possession); or
– a supply of services (the provision of services for a consideration to an identifiable customer).

Exclusions

7837 **Transactions** that are not supplies for VAT purposes are:
a. transactions carried out for no consideration (but see ¶7849);
b. transactions where the goods or services concerned are illegal, or banned (¶7840);
c. transactions within the same legal entity: for example, between the members of a VAT group (¶7807), or between different divisions (¶7815) of the same company;
d. transactions which are specifically excluded by VAT legislation:
– business gifts costing £50 or less (for gifts over this limit see ¶7885);
– industrial samples (¶7886); and
– transactions specifically deemed to be neither a supply of goods nor a supply of services (¶7848).

Consideration

7838 A transaction is only a supply if made for consideration, which is **any form of payment**, whether in money or in kind. In order to determine the tax due in respect of a supply, it is necessary to identify the consideration and then to calculate its value.

Consideration has a wide meaning and includes **not only money** but also anything done, given, or made in exchange for anything else. The consideration for a supply comprises everything that the supplier receives for the supply, whether from the customer or from a third party, including any payments received by a person on behalf of the supplier. However, there must be a link between the receipt and the supply for the payment to be deemed consideration.

To identify the link it is necessary to look at the arrangements made between the parties, including:

- any agreements between them, whether written or verbal; and
- the facts surrounding what was actually done by each party to the transaction.

MEMO POINTS 1. Consideration may comprise a **waiver** of a right to receive or enjoy a benefit. The grant of an extension to a lease was deemed to be consideration in respect of a supply of services by the tenant, who agreed to carry out repair work to demised premises. *Ridgeons Bulk Ltd v C&E* [1994].

2. A person who played a barrel organ in the street, and invited donations from the public, was held not to be supplying a service for a consideration, because there was no agreement between the parties and also no link between the musical service and the payment. *Tolsma v Inspecteur der Omzetbelasting Leeuwarden* [1994]

Receipts that are not consideration 7839

Type of payment	Circumstances	Reference/example
For breach of contract	Payments for allowing contracts to terminate early are, in HMRC's view, outside the scope, provided that there is a clause allowing for such a payment in the contract; where there is no such clause they consider the payment will be liable to VAT	*Financial & General Print Ltd* [1995]; VATSC 35400
Balancing payments	Made to correct the cash impact of a direct tax transfer pricing adjustment (but not if payment represents consideration for management services, etc)	(¶1732)
Security deposits	Taken to ensure the safe return of hired goods (even if the deposit is forfeited)	VATSC 53600
Dividends	Paid to holders of shares/securities	
Grants and donations	When made freely with no expectation of anything in return; mere acknowledgement of support (e.g. listing supporters' names in programmes) is not taxable; the distinction between a donation and taxable sponsorship can be difficult to determine – often sponsors will expect some return for their investment, e.g. advertising or hospitality, which will make the payment consideration for a taxable supply	VATSC 51600; VATSC 50400
Fines and penalty charges	Not usually consideration; a distinction must be drawn between genuine fines and those payments which are additional charges in respect of a supply[1]	VATSC 57600
Parking fees	VAT liability of car park fines depends on the contract terms, which either: – allow for an extension to the parking, in which case the additional consideration is subject to VAT; or – do not permit the driver to extend the original terms, as a result of which a penalty for breach of contract is payable, which is outside the scope of VAT	HMRC Brief 57/08

Type of payment	Circumstances	Reference/example
Overpayments	Made by a customer in error (for example by paying an invoice twice) do not represent consideration but if the supplier retains the amount and uses it to pay a later invoice, the amount at that point represents consideration for the later supply[2]	VATSC 63600
Tips, service charges and gratuities	If payment is **made at the customer's discretion** it is not consideration, whether in cash or included on a credit card receipt; however, where the discretion is removed – for example, the service charge is automatically added to the bill – the payment is consideration for a supply	VATSC 56400

1. A fine for the late return of a video has been held to be a payment for an extended hire period and therefore consideration for a taxable supply. *JG Leigh (t/a Moor Lane Video)* [1989]
2. A company regularly received overpayments, some of which were intended by the customers, whereas others were made in error. The company could identify the deliberate overpayments and accounted for output tax on these when the payment was received. It was held that the company was correct not to account for output tax on the unintended overpayments, as the inadvertent overpayment of a current debt is not a payment on account of a future liability. *C & E v British Telecommunications plc* [1996]

Illegal transactions

7840 A transaction will not be a supply if the goods and services concerned are illegal, or banned. This would include, for example, the supply of drugs and counterfeit money. *Witzemann v Hauptzollamt Munchen-Mitte* [1993]

Where it is the **means of supply** that is unlawful, the transaction will still be a supply for VAT purposes. For example, the sale of anabolic steroids (without a licence), counterfeit perfume and stolen cars have all been held to be supplies. *Mol v Inspecteur der Invoerrechten en Accijnzen* [1988]

Business Brief 1/06 **Missing trader fraud** (¶8186) occurs in a chain of supplies where one of the traders either goes missing or uses a hijacked VAT number, and retains the VAT he has charged on his supply, instead of paying it over to the authorities. The ECJ has stated that each transaction in a supply chain must be regarded on its own merits, and its character cannot be altered by earlier or subsequent events, even those events involving fraud. So an innocent trader caught up in a fraud of this type is still making a supply within the scope of VAT.

Grants and donations

7842 Where grants and donations are **made freely** they are not consideration for a supply. However, if the donor expects to receive something in return, the amount is consideration.

The distinction between a donation and **sponsorship** (which is a supply) is a grey area. Broadly, a sponsor will expect some return for his investment, usually in the form of advertising or hospitality. The simple acknowledgement of support (for example, inclusion in a list of supporters in a programme) is not a taxable supply.

MEMO POINTS 1. The principle that payments which are freely given are not consideration extends to **tips, service charges and gratuities**. If the payment is made at the customer's discretion, it is not consideration, whether made in cash or by asking for the amount to be included on a credit card receipt. However, where the discretion is removed, for example the service charge is automatically added to the bill, the payment is consideration for the supply.
2. A donation of £150 to a theatre in return for a plaque on a seat and **privileged** booking rights was held to be consideration for a taxable supply. Had the only benefit been the plaque on the seat, the payment would not have been consideration, as there would have been no supply. However, the privileged booking facility meant that the payment was considered more in the nature of sponsorship than a donation. *Tron Theatre Ltd v C & E* [1993]
3. **Advertising revenue** retained by a supplier who gave away free diaries to customers was held to be consideration for the supply of the diaries. *Seaton Sands Ltd and others v C & E* [1998]

HMRC have issued guidance on the interaction between gift aid (¶4420) on **charity admission charges** and VAT, which can be summarised as follows: 7844
– the addition of any amount to the admission fee does not make the entire amount a donation for VAT purposes – the admission fee will be taxable unless it qualifies for exemption (¶8042); and
– the additional amount will be a donation unless a benefit or gift is given in return by the organisation (other than a sticker or poppy which has no intrinsic value), in which case the consideration is taxable at the appropriate rate.
Further details are at: www.hmrc.gov.uk/charities/guidance-notes/chapter3/sectionf.htm.

EXAMPLE In all of the following examples, the admission fee is taxable at the standard rate, as it does not qualify for exemption.

1. A charity charges an admission fee of £10 and requests an additional payment, for which a sticker is given; any additional payment is treated as a donation, because the sticker has no intrinsic value.

2. A charity charges an admission fee of £10 to view its property and requests an additional payment, in return for which a picture of the property is given; any additional payment is also taxable at the standard rate, unless the donor refuses the gift or does not receive it for some other reason, when it is treated as a donation.

3. As for example 2, except that the charity gives a book in return for an additional payment; any additional payments are zero-rated, unless the donor refuses the gift or does not receive it for some other reason, when it is treated as a donation.

Fines and penalty charges

Fines and penalty charges are generally not consideration for a supply. A **distinction must be drawn between** genuine fines and those payments which are additional charges in respect of a supply. 7846 VATSC 57600

A fine for the late return of a video has been held to be a payment for an **extended hire** period and therefore consideration. *JG Leigh (t/a Moor Lane Video)* [1989]

Similarly, a fine for overstaying the paid period at a car park is consideration for the supply of the **parking space**. Contrast this with a fine imposed for parking on a **double yellow line**, which is a genuine fine, as there was no original supply of parking.

Neither a supply of goods nor a supply of services

Certain supplies are deemed to be neither a supply of goods nor a supply of services and are therefore **outside the scope of VAT**. The following list indicates the supplies that fall into this category. 7848

Type of supply	Reference	¶¶
Transfer of a business as a **going concern**	SI 1995/1268 reg 5	¶8596
The **issue of shares** or other securities	Business Brief 21/05	
Sales of goods to a UK recipient falling within the **second-hand margin scheme** of another member state	SI 1995/1268 reg 8	
Services in connection with the supply of second-hand goods provided by an **agent or auctioneer acting in his own name** where the consideration for the services is included in the price obtained	SI 1995/1268 reg 9	¶8538
Assignment of rights under a **hire purchase or conditional sale** agreement by the owner to a bank or other financial institution	SI 1995/1268 reg 6	
Sale of goods by a person who has **repossessed** them under the terms of a finance agreement or in settlement of an insurance claim, except where consideration for the original sale is reduced	SI 1995/1268 reg 4	

Type of supply	Reference	¶¶
Supplies by **pawn-brokers** to the person who originally pawned the goods, provided that the transaction occurs not more than 3 months after the acquisition by the pawn-broker	SI 1995/1268 reg 3	
Disposal of **cars for no consideration** where, on a previous supply, input tax on the car concerned has been blocked	SI 1992/3122 reg 4	¶8164
Making a car available for **private use**, when input tax has been blocked	SI 1992/3122 reg 4	¶8164
The letting on hire of a car for **less than full consideration**	SI 1992/3122 reg 4	
The sale of goods which have been **temporarily imported** and remain subject to the temporary importation arrangements, provided that the sale is to a person outside the EU	SI 1992/3130	¶9057
The sale by **auction** of second-hand goods temporarily imported for auction, or works of art temporarily imported for exhibition with a view to possible auction	SI 1995/958 reg 3	

Deemed supplies

7849 Even in the absence of consideration the following transactions are treated as supplies and are therefore within the scope of VAT:
- gifts of business goods (¶7885);
- self-supplies of certain goods/services (¶7888);
- private use of goods (¶7897) or services (¶7899) originally acquired for business purposes; and
- retention of business assets on deregistration (¶7895).

SECTION 2

A supply of goods or services?

7850 The distinction between a supply of goods and a supply of services is important because:
- the rules which determine the time of supply and the place of supply are different for goods and services;
- the rules relating to recovery of VAT on pre-registration expenses differ between goods and services; and
- in the case of zero-rated and exempt supplies, goods are often treated differently from supplies of services, or supplies of both goods and services.

VAT legislation provides rules to determine whether a supply is of goods or services, and in addition indicates specific supplies that are deemed to be supplies of goods or services, respectively.

A supply which has **elements of both** goods and services may be either a mixed supply (¶7882) or a composite supply (¶7880).

A. Goods

7852 The term "goods" is not defined in the legislation, therefore it takes its everyday meaning and generally covers tangible property. The supply of goods means that the seller **transfers**

all rights of ownership to the buyer, which usually involves the transfer of title and possession. If it is not clear whether the title to the goods has passed the intentions of the parties should be considered.

The following supplies are defined in the legislation as supplies of goods. **7854**

The transfer of **title** to goods and **possession** of, or control over, the goods. This means that the seller transfers all rights of ownership to the buyer. If the supplier is unable to transfer the title because he does not hold good title to the goods (if, for example, the goods are stolen), there is still a deemed supply of goods. Sch 4 para 1(1) VATA 1994

The **transfer of possession** of goods under an agreement (e.g. a hire purchase agreement) for the sale of the goods or under an agreement which expressly states that the property will pass at some time in the future. If possession of goods is transferred but title is retained (if, for example, the goods are hired out, not sold), this is a supply of services. Sch 4 para 1(2) VATA 1994

The supply of a **share in goods** is generally a supply of services (¶7866), unless there is an agreement to sell the whole property in the goods at a later date – for example, under a hire purchase agreement.

The following transactions are expressly stated in legislation to be supplies of goods: **7856**

Supply	Reference	¶¶
Grant, assignment or surrender of a major interest in land	Sch 4 para 4 VATA 1994	¶8840
Supply of any form of power, heat, refrigeration or ventilation	Sch 4 para 3 VATA 1994	
Provision of a water supply	SI 1989/1114	

Returned goods If goods are supplied to a customer and later returned to the supplier, the treatment for VAT purposes will depend on whether title to the goods has passed to the customer. So if the goods are: **7862** SI 1995/1268

– returned because they are faulty or not in accordance with the terms of the contract, the original supply to the customer may be voided and neither the original sale nor the return will constitute a supply; if replacement goods are supplied, a new supply will take place; if the goods are repaired for the customer in order to meet the terms of the original contract, the work will form part of the original supply;

– returned after title has passed to the customer, title will pass back to the supplier and this will constitute a second supply; or

– subject to repossession after the title has passed, the original supply will remain unaltered and the repossession will not be a supply.

B. Services

Anything done for a consideration that does not constitute a supply of goods is a supply of services, unless specifically treated as neither a supply of goods nor a supply of services (¶7848). VAT legislation provides that certain supplies are deemed to be supplies of services (¶7896). **7864**

A share of the property in goods

Where the title to goods is shared equally by **more than one person** (for example, part shares in a racehorse), the sale of one of the parts will not result in the transfer of the title and will therefore be treated as a supply of services. **7866** Sch 4 para 1(1) VATA 1994

If all of the shares are **sold to the same person**, title will pass to that person and the transfer will be treated as a supply of goods.

Work done on another person's goods

7868 s 30 VATA 1994 Work done on another person's goods is a supply of services whether or not the work **changes the character** of the goods or **results in new or different** goods.

If work carried out on goods results in the **production of zero-rated** goods, the supply of services can also be zero-rated.

Exchange of reconditioned goods

7872 SI 1995/1268 reg 6 If a person, in the **normal course of his trade**, supplies reconditioned goods in exchange for unserviceable goods of a similar type, a supply of services will be deemed to have arisen. **Otherwise**, the supply will be a supply of goods and will be treated as a part exchange (¶7970).

C. Single and multiple supplies

7876 When a transaction is made up of a mixture of elements, such as the supply of two or more goods or services, or a combination of goods and services, it is necessary to distinguish between:

– a composite supply (where there is **one supply** and one VAT liability); and

– a mixed supply (where the components are **separate supplies** and each has its own VAT liability).

The problem with mixed or composite supplies arises when the different elements of the supply are subject to different rates of tax (¶8030). In addition the various elements of the supply may be subject to different rules on the place (¶7988) and/or time (¶7900) of supply.

7878 The **main principles** which should be considered when deciding whether a supply is a composite or mixed supply are as follows:

– all the circumstances of the transaction should be reviewed;

– each element should normally be treated as distinct;

– a single economic supply should not be artificially split;

– one principal and one ancillary element will be determined as a single supply of the principal – for example, in the case of a tin of biscuits the biscuits are the principal element and the re-usable decorative tin is ancillary;

– the meaning of ancillary should not be strained to fit circumstances where there is in fact no subservient element, when both elements are essential to the overall supply; and

– a single, all-inclusive price is not decisive. *Card Protection Plan* [1999]

Composite or single supplies

7880 A composite supply has been described as one where a particular element is an integral part of the main supply, such as luxury packaging for food, or where it is incidental to another element, such as the supply of catering on a flight. *British Airways plc v C & E* [1990]

Where a supply is held to be a composite supply it must be considered as a whole, such that the **VAT treatment** appropriate to the main supply will apply to the whole supply.

MEMO POINTS 1. The term "**an integral part**" is used for these purposes to describe something that is intrinsically part of the whole that is being supplied. It can therefore include both essential and non-essential elements, although a necessary element will almost certainly be an integral part of the main supply.

2. An **incidental element** of a supply is something that naturally accompanies the main supply. However, any item which is at least 50% of the supply cannot be incidental.

EXAMPLE **1.** In a case involving a major retailer, a **card handling fee** was charged to customers who used debit or credit cards (when the price paid for the goods remained the same as if cash was used for the purchase). The Court of Appeal held that all of the consideration related to the normal taxable supply, rather than some of the consideration being for an exempt supply of card handling services. Use of this scheme is disclosable, as it is a tax avoidance scheme (¶9244), albeit an ineffective one. *Debenhams plc v HMRC* [2005]

2. In a case involving **distance learning**, the House of Lords held that there was a single, exempt supply of education, even though zero-rated printed matter also supplied (e.g. books) was not ancillary. The college provided the following:
- printed materials;
- face-to-face tuition;
- marking of assignments; and
- access to a virtual learning environment.

The most important factor was the purchase of a supply of education by the students. Although the printed matter was integral to the students' education, it was only one element of the overall supply. *College of Estate Management v HMRC* [2005]

3. In a case concerning the supply of food packs and associated counselling services supplied as part of a **weight loss programme**, the Court of Appeal held that there was a single, indivisible, standard-rated supply. The correct tests in deciding the issue were the economic indivisibility of each element of the supply and the perspective of the consumer. The support services offered were integral to the achievement of weight loss for the customer and therefore could not be separated from the food supplies. This decision is consistent with the judgment in the similar case of *Weight Watchers (UK) Ltd* [2008]. *David Baxendale Ltd v HMRC* [2009]

4. In a case concerning **airport parking**, a bus was provided to take motorists to the airport. The tax tribunal held that this was a single supply of standard-rated parking services and there was no separate supply of zero-rated bus transport from the car park to the airport. The tribunal distinguished airport parking from city centre "park and ride" schemes where the secure parking element would not be as significant. *Purple Parking Ltd* [2009]

5. Following the ECJ's decision in the Czech case of *RLRE Tellmer Property* [2009], HMRC have confirmed that service charges paid to landlords will generally not be paid in return for a separate, standard-rated supply of cleaning, security or similar. Generally there will be a single, exempt supply of letting, of which the services will be an incidental element. However, where the tenant has a choice whether to take the services offered by the landlord or to arrange a third party to perform the cleaning (for example) then, as in the *RLRE Tellmer Property* case, the services may be a separate supply, even where supplied by the landlord. Where the services are supplied as a condition under the lease agreement, they will be incidental and follow the VAT treatment of the lease rentals: that is, exempt, unless the landlord has opted to tax the property (¶8904).

Mixed or multiple supplies

A mixed supply will arise where the elements of the supply are separate, and clearly identifiable, so one is not an integral part of the other. The **intention** of the parties is considered in determining the existence of a mixed supply, and a clear intention to purchase two distinct services will be indicative of a mixed supply, even if one price is paid. **7882**

Where a supply is considered to be a mixed supply, each of the elements can be considered individually and, where relevant, a different **VAT treatment** can be applied to each element. When more than one treatment is applied, the value of the supply of each different element must be established; for these purposes the apportionment of the total price must be made on a fair and reasonable basis.

EXAMPLE

1. A Ltd sells a package for £225, which includes a book, DVD, and helpline.
The book and DVD can each be purchased separately for £110. Customers can separately subscribe to the helpline for £60 p.a., or subscribe to the helpline and receive either the book or DVD for £150 p.a.
The helpline and DVD are standard-rated, whereas the book is zero-rated.
The total package includes significant zero-rated and standard-rated items, so a mixed supply appears to result. In this case, the price of £225 needs to be apportioned and the VAT is found by applying the VAT fraction (see ¶8030) to the amount relating to the standard-rated supply.

Apportioning the package price based on the price of each individual element would give a VAT amount of £22.77. $\frac{1}{6} \times 225 \times \frac{60 + 110}{60 + 110 + 110}$

The package including just the book and helpline is not clear-cut. This is either a composite, zero-rated supply (with the helpline being incidental) or a mixed supply.

2. A company supplied **subscription television services** to UK customers. As part of the service a television guide was also provided. This guide was zero-rated when sold separately. The company anticipated that HMRC would argue that there was a single supply of the television service because the guide was an ancillary supply. It therefore set up a separate publications company, where:
– existing customers were notified they would in future receive television guides from the publications company;
– the contract for new customers stated that the two supplies would be received from different companies; and
– the customer still made payment to the original company.
The Court of Appeal held that there were in fact two separate supplies because:
a. existing customers **agreed to the new arrangements** and were contractually bound to the publications company, because they continued to pay for the cable television services and the magazine; and
b. there was **no authority** for the following concepts:
– principal and ancillary contracts could apply where there was more than one supplier;
– even where one supply could be said to be ancillary to another, both supplies had to share the same tax treatment; and
– two separate supplies should be treated as a single supply because the suppliers were related parties and their supplies were linked. *Telewest Communications plc and another v C & E* [2005]

3. In an Italian case referred to the ECJ two associated companies supplied leasing (standard-rated) and insurance (exempt) supplies. The arrangements were not effective to create separate standard-rated and exempt supplies, because they were held to be abusive. *Ministero dell'Economia e delle Finanze v Part Service Srl* [2008]

4. Legislation in Finance Act 2011 overturns the *Telewest* case (see example **2.**, above). Where the supply would have been a single (but not zero-rated) supply if made by a single supplier, it is now not possible to make zero-rated supplies of ancillary printed materials merely by arranging for separate supplies to be made by more than one supplier.

D. Deemed supplies

7883 A deemed **supply of goods** occurs in the following circumstances:

Transaction	Detail	Reference	¶¶
The disposal of or giving away of business assets (excluding business gifts costing less than £50) by a person carrying on a business, or putting such assets permanently into private use (whether or not for a consideration)	Certain gifts under £50 and samples are not supplies	Sch 4 para 5(1) VATA 1994	¶7884
Self-supply of specific goods when goods are taken possession of, or produced, by a person during the course of his business and then consumed by him for business purposes (applies to cars)		s 5(5) VATA 1994	¶7889

Transaction	Detail	Reference	¶¶
Fuel used for private purposes		ss 56, 57 VATA 1994	¶7890
Transfers or removals of a trader's business assets from one EU country to another		Sch 4 para 6(1) VATA 1994	¶8937
Goods sold in satisfaction of a debt	A supply of goods is deemed to be made by a taxable person when goods, which are part of the assets of his business, are sold by another person to satisfy a debt owed by the taxable person. This provision only applies where a creditor has power in law to sell the goods.	Sch 4 para 7 VATA 1994	¶7894
The retention of business assets on deregistration		Sch 4 para 7 VATA 1994	¶7895

Transfer or disposal of business assets

Where goods which are part of the assets of a business are **disposed of or given away** under the direction of the person carrying on the business, so that they no longer form part of the business assets, a supply of goods will be deemed to have taken place, whether or not consideration is received. This provision **only applies** if the person concerned or a previous owner was entitled to deduct all or part of the input tax on the goods and to the following types of transaction: 7884 Sch 4 para 5(1) VATA 1994

- assets taken into private use;
- assets given away; and
- the sale of fixed assets.

If the business assets include **land**, the grant, surrender or assignment of a major interest in land (¶8840) is a supply of goods. Any **other supply of land** is treated as a supply of services.

The supply will be deemed to take place on the date of the transfer or disposal. This rule also applies where the goods are transferred for no consideration (such as where goods are permanently taken out of the business for a non-business use). s 5(12) VATA 1994

The value on which VAT must be accounted for is the replacement cost of the goods.

EXAMPLE An old computer is given to an employee for his permanent use at home. The accumulated depreciation and maintenance costs of the computer are £1,000. The replacement cost is £600. The value of the deemed supply of goods is £600 and VAT of £120 is chargeable. (£600 x 20%)

MEMO POINTS 1. Where the cost of identical goods cannot be ascertained (for example, the range has been discontinued), the monetary consideration payable for similar goods (of the same age and condition) is acceptable.
2. If the value of identical or similar goods cannot be established, the cost of producing the goods at the time of supply may be used (that is, the cost of producing the goods at the time they are disposed of or given away, rather than the cost of the goods at the time they were themselves produced).

Gifts of business assets

For VAT purposes, a gift is made voluntarily with no conditions attached. 7885 Sch 4 para 5(2) VATA 1994

It is important to distinguish between a gift and an **inducement**. Where the donor gives something away with a reasonable expectation of some return, it is an inducement and therefore a supply.

A gift of a business asset is not a supply if the cost of the gift, together with other business gifts made to the same person **within a period of 12 months**, is less than £50.

If the total value of the gifts made to the same person **exceeds £50**, output tax is due on the total value of the gifts given in the 12-month period, not just on the excess.

MEMO POINTS A petrol manufacturer issued vouchers to petrol stations, which gave them to customers. These vouchers could be redeemed against gifts made available by the manufacturer. The company tried to argue that the customer gave consideration in return for these gifts when buying petrol. However, it was held that VAT should be accounted for as if they were true gifts for VAT purposes i.e. the customer gave no consideration. *Kuwait Petroleum (GB) Ltd v C & E* [1999]

Samples

7886 Sch 4 para 5(3) VATA 1994

Where a business gives a free sample to a customer, or prospective customer, there is no supply for VAT purposes. This rule is no longer limited to a single sample.

Where samples are provided to the general public through an intermediary (for example, through a high street retailer), there is no supply, provided that title to the goods passes direct from the manufacturer to the customer, not to the intermediary.

Self-supplies

7888 s 5(5) VATA 1994

A self-supply is deemed to take place where specified goods or services are taken possession of, or produced, by a person during the course of his business and they are then **consumed by** him for business purposes. In this case the goods or services are neither supplied to another person nor incorporated into other goods produced in the course or furtherance of the business.

The self-supply regulations **apply to** cars and certain construction services (¶8867). For example, a builder may use his own employees to carry out alterations on his business premises.

Under a **group registration**, any self-supply is deemed to be made by the representative member.

Self-supply of cars

7889 SI 1992/3122 reg 5 Notice 700/57

A car is deemed to be self-supplied where a car dealer **takes a car out of stock** for private use. In this scenario, input tax would have already been recovered, and the dealer would effectively have acquired a private asset without paying any VAT unless the self-supply charge applies. If the dealer still intends to sell the car as stock within 12 months, but just uses it as a company car in the meantime, the self-supply charge does not apply (¶8160).

s 6(11) VATA 1994

The **time of supply** for a self-supply of a car is deemed to be the time when the car is appropriated to the use which gives rise to the self-supply. The tax point is then the date when, by any positive and recorded action, the car was transferred from the new car sales stock.

Where a self-supply is deemed to have taken place, the goods are treated for VAT purposes as if they were supplied **both**:
– to the person for the purposes of the business; and
– by the person in the course or furtherance of the business.

The value of a self-supplied car will depend on whether the car is new or used.

VAT Information Sheet 8/11

Alternatively, manufacturers or dealers may opt to use a simplified method, which they must then adopt for all cars used occasionally for private purposes. This method effectively allows output tax to be accounted for on the basis of a scale charge. For further details see *VAT Memo*.

Notice 700/57 para 14 VAT Information Sheet 8/11

MEMO POINTS 1. For **manufacturers**, the value of the self-supply of a new vehicle is the full cost of manufacturing the vehicle including all related production overheads. For UK volume manufacturers, 2/3rds of the current retail list price may be used as an approximation of cost. Non-volume manufacturers may apply the 2/3rds of retail list price approximation if they are authorised to do so by their local VAT office. For **non-manufacturing traders**, the value of the self-supply of a car should include the purchase price of the car, plus any cost of incorporated parts of UK manufacture and delivery charges to the recipient's premises. Discounts received

after the time of the self-supply can be disregarded, unless the discounts were contractually agreed prior to the tax point.
2. When a self-supply of a **used vehicle** takes place, the **value** is deemed to be the current purchase price of an identical vehicle. If that price cannot be established, the current price of a similar vehicle will be used or, failing that, the current production cost, or the 2/3rds of current list price approximation of a new vehicle.

Fuel for private use

Where a business provides fuel to its proprietors and staff (including a sole trader and partners), and there is any element of private use, there is a deemed taxable supply of that fuel. Where the fuel is supplied: 7890 s 56 VATA 1994
– at or **above cost**, there is a taxable supply valued at the amount received from the employee;
– free or below cost, the fuel **scale charge** system applies.
Input tax can be recovered by the business even where it is the individual acquiring the fuel who is then reimbursed by the business (¶8182).

Fuel scale charges Scale charges depend on the type of car, and apply only to fuel supplied for use in an individual's car, or a car allocated to him at that time by reason of his office or employment, but not genuine pool cars. Fuel supplied for other vehicles, for example motorbikes and vans, is not liable to the fuel scale charge. 7891

MEMO POINTS 1. A pool car is a car that is:
– made available to more than one employee;
– not normally kept overnight by an employee; and
– not ordinarily used by one employee to the exclusion of others.
Any private use of the car must be merely incidental to the business use.
2. A business must keep records of:
– the number of cars for which fuel is supplied below cost or free;
– the CO_2 emissions figures for the cars; and
– details of any change of cars, including the date of change.

A business may avoid the fuel scale charge in the following ways: 7892
a. by agreeing not to claim a deduction for any input tax incurred on the acquisition of any road fuel, whether for business or private use; or
b. analysing the fuel costs, separating out the amount relating to business journeys, and only claiming input tax on that amount.

MEMO POINTS 1. Option **a**. is concessionary and must be agreed in advance with HMRC. Depending on the amount of the potential input tax reclaim, this option may be cheaper for the business than applying the scale charges.
2. Option **b**. requires the following records to be kept (which results in an administrative burden and as a consequence is used less often by businesses):
– mileage travelled;
– whether journey is business or private;
– rate of mileage allowance;
– CO_2 emissions figures for the car; and
– amount of input tax claimed.

EXAMPLE Mr C drives 6,000 miles in 2011, of which 4,689 are business miles. The total cost of the fuel is £575. The fuel cost relating to the business miles is: 4,689/6,000 × £575 = £449.36. The related input tax reclaim for business mileage only is 1/6 × £449.36 = £74.89.

Deemed consideration The scale charge applies to each car for which private fuel is provided during the return period. 7893 s 57 VATA 1994
The table below sets out the scale charge which should be used for VAT periods beginning on or after **1 May 2011**.
Where the CO_2 emissions figure of a vehicle is **not a multiple of 5**, the figure is rounded down to the next multiple of 5 to determine the charge.

For a **bi-fuel** vehicle with two CO_2 emissions figures, the lower figure should be used.

CO_2 band	Annual return		Quarterly return		Monthly return	
	Charge (gross) £	VAT included £	Charge (gross) £	VAT included £	Charge (gross) £	VAT included £
120 or less	630.00	105.00	157.00	26.17	52.00	8.67
125	945.00	157.50	236.00	39.33	78.00	13.00
130	1,010.00	168.33	252.00	42.00	84.00	14.00
135	1,070.00	178.33	268.00	44.67	89.00	14.83
140	1,135.00	189.17	283.00	47.17	94.00	15.67
145	1,200.00	200.00	299.00	49.83	99.00	16.50
150	1,260.00	210.00	315.00	52.50	105.00	17.50
155	1,325.00	220.83	331.00	55.17	110.00	18.33
160	1,385.00	230.83	346.00	57.67	115.00	19.17
165	1,450.00	241.67	362.00	60.83	120.00	20.00
170	1,515.00	252.50	378.00	63.00	126.00	21.00
175	1,575.00	262.50	394.00	65.67	131.00	21.83
180	1,640.00	273.33	409.00	68.17	136.00	22.67
185	1,705.00	284.17	425.00	70.83	141.00	23.50
190	1,765.00	294.17	441.00	73.50	147.00	24.50
195	1,830.00	305.00	457.00	76.17	152.00	25.33
200	1,895.00	315.00	472.00	78.67	157.00	26.17
205	1,995.00	325.83	488.00	81.33	162.00	27.00
210	2,020.00	336.67	504.00	84.00	168.00	28.00
215	2,080.00	346.67	520.00	86.67	173.00	28.83
220	2,145.00	357.50	536.00	89.33	178.00	29.67
225 or more	2,205.00	367.50	551.00	91.83	183.00	30.50

ss 56(8), 57(5) VATA 1994

MEMO POINTS 1. There is no provision allowing the scale charge to be reduced where a car is **available for only part of a period**.

2. Where a person has **two cars during a period**, the scale charge will apply to only one of the vehicles, if:
– the cars are available for different periods, i.e. not concurrently; and
– at the end of the period, one of the cars is no longer available.

If the cars fall within the same CO_2 emissions category, the fuel scale charge for that category applies. If the cars are not in the same category, the fuel scale charges for both relevant categories must be apportioned accordingly. Alternatively, the scale charge for the higher category can be used.

3. The VAT charge should be included in box 1 of the **VAT return**, while the net amount producing the VAT charge should be entered in box 6.

4. Where a business is **partly exempt** (¶8205), all fuel costs must be taken into account in the partial exemption calculation. The fuel scale charge is reduced to the same percentage as the percentage of residual input tax recoverable. This ensures that output tax is due on the same proportion of the fuel as input tax recovered. A corresponding annual adjustment (¶8220) must also be made in respect of the fuel scale charge.

EXAMPLE

1. Mr C drives a car with a CO_2 emissions figure of 192. He will show the following amounts on his quarterly VAT return:

VAT return box	Amount (£)
1	73.50
6	367 (i.e. 441 – 74)

2. A Ltd provides the following cars to two employees during the quarterly return period ended 30 September 2010:

Mr A – car with a CO_2 emissions figure of 218 available throughout period;
Mr B – car 1: CO_2 emissions figure of 173, available 1 July – 31 July;
car 2: CO_2 emissions figure of 212, available 1 August – 30 September.

The fuel scale charge in respect of Mr A's car is £520 (including VAT) and the VAT element is £86.67.
The fuel scale charge in respect of Mr B's cars is calculated as follows:

	Gross		VAT	
	£	£	£	£
Car 1: scale charge	378.00		63.00	
Available for 1 month: taking 1/3		126.00		21.00
Car 2: scale charge	504.00		84.00	
Available for 2 months: taking 2/3		336.00		56.00
Total therefore:		462.00		77.00

If A Ltd is partly exempt and able to recover 76% of its residual input tax, the gross fuel scale charge for Mr A's car would be 76% × £520, i.e. £395.20. A similar reduction would apply to the charge for Mr B's cars.

Sales in satisfaction of a debt

A supply of goods is deemed to have been made by a taxable person when goods, forming part of the **assets of a business** carried on by him, are sold by another person to satisfy a debt owed by the taxable person. This provision will not apply where a creditor has illegally repossessed property, but only where he has a power in law to sell it. **7894** Sch 4 para 7 VATA 1994

Deemed supplies on ceasing to be a taxable person

Any goods forming part of the assets of a business carried on by a person will be deemed to be supplied by him in the course of the business immediately before he ceases to be taxable, unless: **7895** Sch 4 para 8 VATA 1994
- the business is transferred as a going concern to another taxable person (¶8596); or
- from that time the business is carried on by an executor, administrator, trustee or liquidator; or
- the VAT on the deemed supply would not exceed £1,000.

The VAT on the deemed supply is accounted for on the taxable person's final VAT return.

A **deemed supply of services** occurs in the following circumstances: **7896**

Transaction	Reference	¶¶
Use of business assets for non-business purposes **where input tax has been deducted** on the goods	Sch 4 para 5(4) VATA 1994	¶7897
Private and/or non-business use of services (which have been supplied to a business) for no consideration		¶7899
Supplies of certain construction services **for no consideration**	s 5(6) VATA 1994 SI 1989/472	¶8867

Private or non-business use of business goods and services

Goods Where goods acquired for business purposes are put to temporary private or non-business use (whether or not consideration is given), a supply of services will be deemed to occur. This applies only if the person concerned or a previous owner was entitled to deduct all or part of the input tax on the goods. **7897** Sch 4 para 5(4) VATA 1994

The **time of supply** in this case is deemed to be the date when the goods are appropriated to the private or non-business use. If the services are supplied for a particular period, the time of supply is the last day of the supplier's VAT period (or of each such period) in which the goods are made available or used. Output tax is charged in each VAT period when private use occurs. The value of the supply of services is explained at ¶8146.

However, if any payment is made for private use, even if below market value, only the value of the payment is liable to output tax. For example, if an employer charges his employees in respect of private calls made on a company mobile phone, the output tax will be calculated on the amount charged. The exception is where HMRC issue a direction in respect of an employee's use of a demonstrator car (¶8160).

7899
SI 1993/1507

Services A supply of services is also deemed to be made where services are initially bought for business purposes, and then are used partly for private purposes. The deemed supply only arises if input tax was deducted on the services concerned. The value of the supply is calculated as a reasonable proportion of the cost of the supplies acquired by the business.

Business Brief 17/94

There are no set rules about the **calculation**, as long as the result is fair and reasonable, although HMRC mention the following possible method, based on the depreciation of comparable business assets:

$$\frac{\text{Cost of services} \times \text{Projected period of non-business use}}{\text{Total depreciation period of comparable assets}}$$

The trader should **stop accounting** for output tax at the earlier of when the:
– depreciated value reaches nil; or
– total output tax equals the amount of the input tax on the service as has proved not to be attributable to business use.

MEMO POINTS For further discussion of this subject see ¶8146.

SECTION 3

Time of supply

7900 The time at which a supply is treated as taking place is known as the **tax point**. Output tax must normally be accounted for in the VAT period in which the tax point occurs. Some smaller traders can opt to use the date cash is paid or received (see ¶8375). The general rules are outlined below.

In addition there are specific provisions relating to certain types of goods (¶7918+) and supplies of services (¶7932+).

Special rules apply to determine the tax point for the following types of supply:
– intra-EU supplies (¶8935);
– self-supplies by a trader (¶7888); and
– supplies of land and property (¶8842).

A. General rules

7902
s 6 VATA 1994

There are two main types of tax point: the **basic tax point** and the **actual tax point**. In general, the basic tax point is the default position, unless it is overridden by an actual tax point.

Type of supply	Basic tax point	Actual tax point
Goods	When goods are removed for despatch or made available to the customer	The earlier of these dates: **a.** the date of issue of a VAT invoice if it is either: – before the basic tax point; or – up to 14 days after the basic tax point [1]; or **b.** the date of payment (if it is before the basic tax point).
Services	When services are performed	

Note:
1. A trader can opt out of the 14-day rule or, with the approval of HMRC, extend the 14-day period (¶7910).

1. Invoices and payments

The receipt of a payment will override the basic tax point if it occurs on an **earlier date**. The issue of a VAT invoice **before** the basic tax point will also override the basic tax point. If a VAT invoice is issued up to 14 days after the basic tax point, the actual tax point created by the invoice will override the basic tax point, unless the trader elects for the basic tax point to apply. **7904** s 6(4)-(5) VATA 1994

If a supplier receives a part payment before the date that the supply takes place, the tax point becomes the date the part payment is received (assuming that no VAT invoice has been issued before this date), but only for the amount of the payment. The time of supply for the remainder will follow the normal rules and might fall into a different VAT period.

EXAMPLE Mr A supplied goods to Mr B on 15 June, which is the basic tax point. Mr B paid for the goods on 25 May, which is an earlier actual tax point.
If Mr A issued an invoice on 20 June this could be another actual tax point but is ineffective, because of the earlier payment date.
In this case, the goods are deemed to have been supplied on 25 May, the date of payment.

MEMO POINTS It is possible to extend the **14-day** time limit where there is a commercial need to do so (¶7910). s 6(6) VATA 1994

2. Issue of an invoice

Date of invoice

In order for a VAT invoice to **establish** a tax point it must be a valid VAT invoice (¶8306) and must actually be issued. The tax point is determined by the physical date of issue. **7906**

A VAT invoice cannot properly be issued for **exempt or zero-rated** supplies and an invoice does not therefore create a tax point in those cases.

MEMO POINTS 1. For **electronic data**, the physical date of issue is deemed to be the date on which the data is transmitted.
2. The issue of an **invoice for part of a larger supply** creates a tax point only for that part, not for the whole supply.
3. **Self-billing** is an arrangement where, subject to approval, the customer prepares the VAT invoice (¶8332). For the purposes of determining the time of supply, a tax point will not normally be created by a self-billed invoice. The **exception** to this rule is where the self-billed invoice is issued within 14 days after the basic tax point. In this case, the normal rules apply and the date of issue of the invoice can be used to create a tax point where appropriate. VATTOS 5225

Date of payment

The following table indicates the rules that apply for determining the date of payment for various payment methods. **7908** VATTOS 5100

Payment method	Deemed date of payment	Note
Cheque	The date on which the cheque has been presented and met by the drawer's bank (up to 5 working days after the date of presentation).	Where it is the normal commercial practice of the business to use the date of receipt of the cheque as the date of payment, that date will be used, provided that the cheque is subsequently presented and cleared without undue delay.
Credit card/charge card	The date on which the payment is received from the card company.	Where it is the normal commercial practice of the business to use the date of acceptance of the card as the date of payment, that date will be used, provided that there is no undue delay in processing the transaction. This treatment will not be allowed in cases where the card company withholds payment pending satisfactory delivery of the goods, such as in mail order transactions.
Bank transfer such as standing order, direct debit, home banking, etc	The date on which the amount in question is transferred to the recipient's bank account.	
Deposits	The date of receipt where the deposit is made in the expectation that it will eventually form part of the total payment for a supply.	Where the deposit is taken as security to ensure the safe return of goods hired out and is then refunded, the payment will not normally create a tax point. The exception is where, before the completion of the hire period, the security deposit is set against the outstanding hire charges.
Payment by book entry or adjustment to accounting records	The date on which the appropriate entries are made in the accounting records, provided that the debt is actually settled.	
Retention payments	The tax point for the retained element is delayed until the issue of an invoice or the receipt of the payment. The rest of the supply is subject to the normal rules.	A retention payment arises where a contract for the supply of goods or services provides for retention of part of the consideration pending full and satisfactory performance of the contract (or part of it) by the supplier.

EXAMPLE Mr A sells paintings in his shop. He agrees to sell a painting to a customer for £10,000 plus VAT of £2,000 and receives a deposit of £3,000 on 25 October. He delivers the painting on 10 November and the invoice is issued on 24 November.
The basic tax point is 10 November but this is superseded by the invoice date of 24 November.
The deposit creates its own tax point and therefore includes output tax of £500, which is included on the VAT return for the quarter ended 31 October. (£3,000 × 1/6)
The remaining output tax of £1,500 is included on the VAT return for the quarter ended 31 January.

3. Accommodation tax points

7910 s 6(10) VATA 1994 A taxable person may request that the time of supply is altered by either **advancing or delaying** the tax point. These are known as accommodation tax points.

Monthly invoices

Many traders issue monthly invoices covering all supplies made in the preceding month. HMRC will grant an accommodation tax point on receipt of a written application, provided that monthly invoices are part of the trader's normal commercial practice. **7912** VATTOS 6200

MEMO POINTS The **application** should state whether the accommodation tax point will be linked to the last day of the period covered by the invoice, or the date of issue of the invoice. If it is linked to the date of issue, this will not normally be permitted to exceed 14 days from the end of the commercial accounting period.

Supplies of credit

A supply of goods on credit will normally be made up of a taxable supply of goods and a **separate**, exempt supply of credit. Businesses sometimes have difficulty in identifying the element of periodical repayments attributable to the supply of credit, and the element in respect of the goods. **7916** VATTOS 6300

Accommodation tax points can be used as a single tax point for supplies of credit, provided that the nominated tax point is earlier than it would be under the normal rules. For example, the trader could identify the date of supply of the goods as the tax point.

MEMO POINTS 1. The time of supply of the **goods** will generally be determined at the outset, either by the issue of an invoice or by removal of the goods.
2. The time of supply of the **credit** is more difficult to determine and will normally occur at the time of each instalment.
3. Accommodation tax points can be used by traders making **corporate purchasing card arrangements** to overcome the problems of identifying when a VAT invoice will be issued to the customer by the card company. An accommodation tax point will allow them to treat the **date** on which details of each transaction are transmitted to the card company as the tax point for the supplies, provided that the details are keyed into the system on or before the basic tax point. Notice 701/48
4. Where a payment is made to a person other than the supplier who has acquired the right to receive the payment following the **assignment of a debt**, the supplier is still deemed to have received payment. To avoid problems connected with not being informed of the date of a payment, a trader may apply for an accommodation tax point to bring forward the time of supply to the time of assignment. VATTOS 6600

B. Specific rules for certain goods

Goods purchased by instalment

Where a customer buys goods on credit, such as in **hire purchase and conditional sales** of goods, there is a supply of the goods and a supply of exempt credit. These are dealt with separately, unless there is an application for an accommodation tax point (¶7910). **7918** VATTOS 9250

The supply of the goods will be dealt with under the normal rules for a sale where title to the goods passes at the outset. In most cases there will be only one supply of goods, but there may be two where the goods pass from the supplier to a third-party finance company, then from the finance company to the customer.

The tax point for the **credit element** of the supply is the date of payment of the interest. Where the instalments include an element attributable to the charge for credit, a tax point occurs each time that a payment is received.

Goods supplied on approval or on sale or return

Where goods are supplied on approval or on a sale or return basis, ownership of the goods remains with the supplier until they are adopted by the purchaser. The **basic tax point** in this situation is the earliest of: **7920** s 6(2)(c), (4) VATA 1994

- the date on which it becomes certain that adoption has taken place;

– 12 months after the date of removal of the goods; or
– the issue of an invoice by the supplier.

VATTOS 9550 MEMO POINTS A **supply is adopted** for these purposes when the holder of the goods indicates (either directly or by one of the example actions outlined below) that the option to return the goods is not going to be exercised, so either:
– the goods become the subject of an offer for resale by the holder;
– the holder allocates the goods to a customer;
– the goods are hired out by the holder to a customer;
– the holder uses the goods otherwise than for display purposes; or
– the goods are permanently modified or adapted by the holder or to the order of the holder.

7922 VATTOS 9550 A **payment received** by the supplier **before the basic tax point** does not, of itself, create a tax point in these circumstances, although it will often serve to indicate that the goods have been adopted, and a basic tax point may therefore be established at that time.

In some circumstances, however, it is a **condition of the agreement** that the recipient of the goods has to pay an amount to the supplier in order to receive the goods in the first place. Provided that this does not affect the unfettered right of the recipient to return the goods at a later date, the payment in these circumstances has no time of supply significance. This type of sale or return arrangement commonly exists between car manufacturers and dealers in respect of demonstrator vehicles.

Goods in the possession of the buyer

7926 SI 1995/2518 reg 88 VATTOS 9550 Special rules apply where goods are supplied under an agreement which provides that the supplier retains the property in the goods until they are appropriated (in whole or in part) by the buyer; and the whole or part of the consideration is then determined at that time. In these cases the time of supply will be **deemed** to be the earliest of the following:
– the date of appropriation by the buyer;
– when a VAT invoice is issued by the supplier; or
– when a payment is received by the supplier.

MEMO POINTS 1. If the supplier issues a **VAT invoice** in respect of goods appropriated (in whole or in part) by the buyer, the tax point will be deemed to be the date of issue of the invoice. The supplier may, however, notify HMRC in writing if he does not want this rule to apply.
2. A **retention of title clause** provides that the seller retains ownership until the goods are fully paid for, or sometimes until everything owed by the customer has been paid. This is not a sale on approval, nor a provision for future appropriation by the buyer, because there is no right of return.

Supplies of water and power

7928 SI 1995/2518 reg 86 VATTOS 9700 A supply between **unconnected parties** (see ¶5570 onwards) will be treated as taking place at the earlier of when payment is received, or the date that the supplier's VAT invoice is issued.

The following **supplies** are **affected**:
– water other than distilled water and water comprised in any of the excepted items set out in ¶8054;
– coal gas, water gas, producer gases or similar gases;
– petroleum gases, or other gaseous hydrocarbons, in a gaseous state; or
– any form of power, heat, refrigeration or ventilation.

MEMO POINTS 1. Where the whole or part of the consideration for such a supply (or a supply of electricity) is **determined or payable periodically**, each time of supply will be the earlier of when:
– part of the consideration is received by the supplier; or
– the supplier issues a VAT invoice relating to the supply.
The **exception** to this rule is when the supplier issues an **invoice** containing the following details, so that the water or power is treated as separately supplied on the earlier of when a payment becomes due or is actually received by the supplier:
– dates on which any parts of the consideration are to become due for payment in the period;
– amount payable (excluding VAT) on each date; and

– rate of VAT in force at the time of the issue of the VAT invoice and the amount of VAT chargeable on each payment.
2. If there is a **change in the rate of VAT** before any of the payment dates specified by the supplier, the invoice will cease to be treated as a VAT invoice in respect of any supplies for which payments are due after the change (and not received before the change).
3. Where water or power is **acquired from** another **EU** member state and the whole or part of any consideration is payable periodically, the goods will be treated as separately acquired on each occasion that the supplier issues an invoice in respect of the transaction.

For supplies between **connected parties**, the rules of ¶7934 apply. **7930**

C. Specific rules for certain services

Continuous supplies of services

Special rules apply where services are supplied over a period of time and under terms that provide for the consideration to be determined, or **payable, periodically or from time to time**. These are referred to as continuous supplies of services **7932** SI 1995/2518 reg 90 VATTOS 9150

Where services between **unconnected parties**, other than those in the construction industry (¶7941), are supplied over a period for a consideration which is determined or payable periodically, the services will be treated as separately **supplied at the earlier of** the time that:
– a payment in respect of the supplies is received by the supplier; or
– the supplier issues a VAT invoice relating to the supplies.

The **exception** to this rule is when the supplier issues an **advance invoice**, so that the services are treated as separately supplied on the earlier of when a payment becomes due or is actually received by the supplier. To fall within this exception, the invoice must show:
– dates on which any parts of the consideration are to become due for payment in the period;
– amount payable (excluding VAT) on each date; and
– rate of VAT in force at the time of the issue of the VAT invoice, and the amount of VAT chargeable on each payment.

MEMO POINTS 1. The **contract** does not have to be in writing, and may have been made orally or simply implied by the conduct of the parties. It must, however, exist and commit the parties to doing something during the period. An understanding that work will be undertaken should the need arise is not sufficient for this purpose.
2. The following services are **examples** of the type of supply that are usually continually supplied:
– rent;
– accountant providing ongoing advice (e.g. audit, tax returns, etc);
– the services of a trustee;
– regular or periodic maintenance work;
– services supplied by credit card companies to retailers;
– club membership;
– management services;
– agency services;
– long-term loans or secondments of staff; and
– hire, lease or rental of equipment.
3. If there is a **change in the rate of VAT** before any of the payment dates specified by the supplier, the invoice will cease to be treated as a VAT invoice in respect of any supplies for which payments are due after the change (and not received before the change).

Supplies between connected parties To prevent the avoidance of VAT by the supplier not invoicing or the recipient not paying for the supply, a **deemed tax point** occurs when taxable services are continuously supplied between connected parties, where the supplier is unable to state that the recipient is entitled to make a full input tax claim (¶8205). **Zero-rated or exempt services** are subject to the rules of ¶7932. **7934** SI 1995/2518 reg 94B VAT Information Sheet 14/03

Where such taxable supplies have been provided, and no tax point has already arisen, the time of supply is determined by whether the supply commenced:
– on or before 1 October 2003, when the date of supply will be deemed to be every following 1 October; or
– after 1 October 2003, when the date of supply will be deemed to be 12 months after it commenced and annually thereafter.

Alternatively, the tax point will be notified to the supplier by HMRC in writing.

The tax point which arises under these special rules is **overridden** if, within 6 months of the deemed date, either a payment is made or an invoice is issued.

MEMO POINTS 1. The supplier may select an **alternative period end date** with HMRC's approval.
2. HMRC may also allow another period, other than the **6-month period**, to apply.

EXAMPLE A Ltd makes a supply of heating to B Ltd, which is partly exempt. The supply is never invoiced by A Ltd, nor is payment made by B Ltd. This supply commenced before 1 October 2003. The default tax point in 2011 will be 1 October 2011, as this is the anniversary of 1 October 2003.

Services received from outside the UK

7940 SI 1995/2518 reg 82 VATTOS 9450

Under the reverse charge provisions (¶9110), services provided by a person from outside the UK to a person carrying on a business in the UK are treated as if the **customer** had supplied the services to himself in the course of his business. These are commonly known as reverse charge services.

The time of supply for these purposes is:
– for single supplies, when the service is completed or, if earlier, when it is paid for;
– in the case of **continuous supplies**, the end of each periodic billing or payment period (however, if a payment is made before the end of the period to which it relates, or before the end of the billing period, the payment date, rather than the end of the period, is treated as the tax point);
– for continuous supplies that are **not subject to billing or payment periods**, the tax point is 31 December each year, unless a payment has been made beforehand, in which case the payment creates a tax point.

Construction

7941 SI 1995/2518 reg 93 VATTOS 9350

Where supplies are made in the construction industry, the time of supply is dependent on the terms of payment.

If the terms of the contract provide for a **single payment**, the normal time of supply rules apply.

However, where the terms of the contract provide for **periodic payments** to the supplier, the time of supply is deemed to be the earlier of when:
– a payment is received by the supplier; or
– the supplier issues a VAT invoice.

Royalties and other similar payments

7942 SI 1995/2518 reg 91 VATTOS 9500

The **general rule** for royalties, repeat fees and licences is that when permanent assignment or surrender of rights occurs, there is a single supply of services which is subject to the normal rules.

Special rules apply where the consideration received by the assignor (e.g. an artist granting a licence to reproduce his artwork) is not wholly ascertainable at the time the rights are assigned.

If the use of the rights by the assignee (e.g. a gallery that purchased the licence to reproduce the artwork) gives rise to future payments to the assignor, a supply will be deemed to take place each time a payment is made, or a VAT invoice is issued, if the consideration is:
– in whole or in part determined, or payable, periodically;

– additional to the amount already paid for the supply; and
– not a payment for a continuous supply (¶7932).

EXAMPLE Mrs B is an artist who grants a licence to an art gallery to reproduce one of her paintings on postcards. On grant of the licence a VAT invoice is issued by Mrs B for £10,000 plus VAT. A condition of the licence is that Mrs B will receive a further £10,000 from the gallery for every 25,000 postcards it sells. Every time the gallery sells 25,000 postcards a supply by Mrs B to the gallery is deemed to be made and VAT will be due.

Barristers and advocates

Services supplied by a barrister (or, in Scotland, by an advocate), acting in that capacity, will be **treated as taking place** at the earliest of: **7944** SI 1995/2518 reg 92 VATTOS 8400
– when the fee in respect of those services is received by the barrister;
– when the barrister issues a VAT invoice in respect of them (which is almost always after the payment date); or
– the day when the barrister ceases to practise.

Ceasing to practise Special rules apply to allow a barrister to defer the **payment of VAT** on outstanding professional fees on ceasing to practise until such time as the fees are actually received, provided that a set procedure is followed. Any deferred fees are excluded from the VAT return. **7946** Notice 700/44 para 4

The tax point of **other supplies** is not affected by any deferral of professional fees.

When a **practising barrister dies**, the chamber clerk must inform HMRC as soon as possible. Similarly, the personal representatives (or the agent of the personal representatives) should state within 10 days of the grant of probate or order for administration whether they wish: **7947**
– to pay VAT on the barrister's outstanding professional fees straight away; or
– to defer payment.

Coin-operated machines

The **general rule** for coin-operated machines (such as vending, gaming or amusement machines) is that the tax point for such supplies is the time when the money is inserted. **7948** Notice 48 para 3.6 VATTOS 9050

As an **accounting convenience**, the operator of the machine may delay accounting for VAT until the takings are removed from the machine. The normal time of supply rules will continue to apply for all other purposes.

D. Supplies spanning a change of rate

Where there is a **change in the VAT rate** or a change in VAT liability, VAT is chargeable according to the normal tax point rules above, unless the taxpayer elects for the special change of rate provisions to apply. **7950** s 88 VATA 1994 VATTOS 7000 Notice 700 para 30.8

Under these rules, suppliers can elect to use the rate of VAT in force at the time of the basic tax point where this is different from the rate that would otherwise be applicable under the normal tax point rules.

The effect of taking this option is that, **when the VAT rate increases**, VAT may be charged at the old rate on goods removed or services performed before the date of change, even though the tax point would normally be established by the issue of a VAT invoice after the change. Similarly, **when the VAT rate goes down**, VAT may be charged at the new rate on goods removed or services performed after the date of change, even though payment has been received or a VAT invoice issued before that date

MEMO POINTS This facility **cannot be adopted** for supplies subject to self-billing arrangements, or where the supply involves goods disposed of by a third party in satisfaction of a debt.

SECTION 4

Value of supply

1. General principles

7952 s 19 VATA 1994 The value of a supply usually depends upon what is given in exchange for the supply (the consideration). If the consideration is **wholly in money**, the value of the supply will be based on that amount. If it is not in money, the value is the **monetary equivalent** of the consideration received.

The taxable value of a supply may also include other taxes which form part of the purchase price, such as stamp duty land tax. There are special rules relating to discounts, transactions between connected persons and values expressed in foreign currencies. Imports (¶9037) and acquisitions from other EU countries (¶8937) also have particular valuation rules.

Contract price

7954 Where a contract specifies the price to be:
– **inclusive of VAT**, the taxable value of the supply is calculated by applying the appropriate VAT fraction (¶8030) to the contract price; or
– **exclusive of VAT**, the taxable value is the contract price and the VAT is calculated as the appropriate percentage of that price.

Where the contract does not specify whether the price is inclusive or exclusive of VAT, the supplier should account for VAT on the basis that the price includes VAT.

EXAMPLE A Ltd sells standard-rated goods to B Ltd for £2,400.
If the contract price is stated inclusive of VAT, the VAT is 1/6 × 2,400, i.e. £400.
The taxable value of the supply is therefore £2,000.
If the contract price is stated exclusive of VAT, the taxable value of the supply is £2,400 and the VAT is an additional £480. (£2,400 x 20%)

Payments in kind

7960 s 19(3) VATA 1994 Where the consideration is in kind, the **amount taken into account** is the monetary equivalent of the consideration actually received. This is the amount the customer would have been required to pay if the consideration were wholly in money.

MEMO POINTS 1. The value of a supply of free mobile phones for non-monetary consideration comprising simply the **signing of a** line rental **agreement** and a direct debit mandate was held to be nil, therefore no VAT was payable in respect of the supply. *Thorn plc v C & E (No 2)* [1998]
2. Consideration may comprise a **waiver of a right** to receive or enjoy a benefit. The grant of an extension of a lease was deemed to be consideration in respect of the supply of services by the tenant who agreed to carry out repair work to demised premises. *Ridgeons Bulk Ltd v C & E* [1994]
3. A retailer issued **vouchers** to its customers, which could be used against future purchases in the store. It was held that these vouchers represented a future discount for customers and did not form part of the consideration, particularly as the vouchers had no value to the supplier. *Boots plc v C & E* [1990] For further details of vouchers, see ¶7974.

2. Common payment situations

Discounts

7962 Sch 6 para 4 VATA 1994 Where a supplier offers an **unconditional** discount on a supply (for example, 20% reduction on all orders in July), the value of the supply is the discounted amount.

Similarly, if the supplier offers a **prompt payment** discount, the value of the supply is the discounted amount, regardless of whether the offer is actually taken up. In this situation, the value of the supply and the VAT due cannot be simply determined by applying the VAT fraction (see ¶8030) to the amount received.

EXAMPLE A Ltd supplies standard-rated goods to B Ltd for £8,500 plus VAT. If B Ltd pays within 7 days, a 5% discount is offered, falling to 1% if the invoice is paid within 30 days.
The value of the supply is 95% of £8,500, i.e. £8,075, and the related VAT is £1,615. (£8,075 x 20%)
B Ltd pays for the goods after 14 days and is therefore entitled to a 1% discount. A Ltd will actually receive a payment of £10,030, i.e. £8,415 (99% of £8,500) plus VAT of £1,615.

If a discount is **contingent** upon another event occurring (for example, 10% discount off an order if another order is made within the next month), the value of the supply is the amount actually paid. If the discount is subsequently taken up, a credit note may be issued and the appropriate adjustments made to the VAT account (¶9205). **7964**

EXAMPLE Mr A makes a standard-rated supply to Mr B for £10,000 including VAT. If Mr B's purchases exceed £50,000 over a 3-month period, a 2.5% discount is offered on all those supplies.
At the time of the original supply, the value of the supply is £10,000 and the VAT is £2,000.
If, however, Mr B meets the discount criteria, the value of the supply will be reduced to £9,750 plus VAT of £1,950 and a credit note will be issued.

Deposits

Where a deposit is an advance payment in respect of a supply it is consideration for that supply. If a deposit is taken and the **supply is not subsequently made**, the deposit ceases to be consideration (as it cannot be linked to a supply), and any VAT already accounted for may be reclaimed. This applies whether or not the deposit is refunded to the customer. **7966** VATSC 42100

However, where the deposit is simply taken as **security** (for example, for the safe return of goods), it is not consideration in respect of a supply, even where the deposit is forfeited.

MEMO POINTS Where a supply of goods is made in a **returnable container** and a charge is made in respect of the container, it is essential to identify what the charge actually relates to. If the charge is to ensure the container is returned (i.e. a security deposit), it is not consideration. If, however, the charge is to cover costs in respect of the container (for example, the costs of cleaning after use), it is consideration for the supply.

Amounts in foreign currency

Where the consideration for a supply is specified in a foreign currency, the **general rule** is that the VAT amount must be converted into sterling at the UK market selling rate at the time of supply. The rates printed in national daily newspapers are accepted for these purposes. However, the use of forward rates, or methods deriving from forward rates, is prohibited. **7968** Sch 6 para 11 VATA 1994

Alternatively, a business may choose to use the rates of exchange published by HMRC, either for all supplies or for specific classes of supply. If a business adopts this method, it must annotate its VAT records accordingly and indicate whether it applies to all supplies or to specific classes of supplies. Once the alternative method has been used for a class of supplies, approval must be sought from HMRC before reverting to the general rates for that class.

If a business uses a different rate (or method of determining the rate) for **commercial purposes**, HMRC may permit the business to use that rate for VAT purposes.

MEMO POINTS HMRC's monthly exchange rates can be found at www.hmrc.gov.uk.

3. Special types of consideration

Part exchange

Where goods are accepted in part exchange, there are **two supplies**. The customer is making a supply to the business for consideration equal to the discount given. If the customer is **7970**

VAT-registered, VAT may be chargeable on his supply. In addition, the business is making a supply to the customer for the price which would have been charged if the part exchange had not taken place.

> EXAMPLE Mr A sells a television to Mr B (who is not VAT-registered) for a payment comprising £150 cash and Mr B's old television. Mr A normally sells the television for £175 (inclusive of VAT).
> The consideration for the supply is therefore £175 (inclusive of VAT).

7972 There are two **exceptions** to this rule:
– where the value attributed to the part exchange article is a **false value** (for example, a standard allowance is granted for any traded-in item), the sale will be treated as made for an unconditional discount, and the value of the supply is therefore the discounted value; or
– where the business values the part exchange goods, and then offers a **higher part exchange allowance** in order to get the sale, the extra may be treated as a discount.

> EXAMPLE Mr A sells a piano worth £1,500 (inclusive of VAT) and agrees to take another piano in part exchange. Mr A values the second-hand piano at £500, but offers £700 in order to clinch the sale.
> The consideration for the supply is £1,300 (inclusive of VAT), i.e. the amount which would have been paid for the goods (£1,500) reduced by the discount of £200.

Vouchers and coupons

7974 Vouchers and coupons come in various forms. The VAT position will depend on how the vouchers are issued, and the redemption conditions. For this purpose, a voucher is a document which gives value to the holder.

The most **common forms** of voucher are summarised in the following table:

Type	Category	Properties
Discount coupon		Shows a discount against the full price of certain named goods. Can either be: – restricted to use with trader himself; or – available for use at other outlets.
Face value	Retailer voucher	Voucher issued by retailer which can be used to acquire goods either from: – him; or from – elsewhere (usually part of the same retail chain), when the retailer will reimburse the vendor of the goods.
	Credit voucher	Voucher cannot be used to acquire goods from issuer. Issuer reimburses vendor of goods.
	Other	Dependent on terms of issue.

MEMO POINTS See ¶8018 for the supply of phone cards.

7978 **Money-off or discount coupons** A simple coupon may be issued in many ways, for example as part of the packaging for another item, by mailshot or in a magazine.

Where the coupon is **issued**:

a. for free, there is no VAT due on its issue; or

b. in return for consideration, VAT is due and the treatment depends on whether the coupon entitles the holder to a discount with the:
– issuer, when the applicable VAT rate follows that of the goods relating to the discount; or
– other traders, when it is a standard-rated supply of services.

When the coupon is **redeemed**, it is not treated as consideration. VAT is only due on the net amount actually paid by the customer. *Boots plc v C&E* [1990]

Where a manufacturer **reimburses a retailer** for a money-off coupon, the value of the manufacturer's taxable supply is reduced by the amount of the reimbursement.

Face value vouchers When a **retailer voucher** is sold and the trader is: 7980 Sch 10A VATA 1994
a. the issuer, any consideration given by the customer up to the face value of the voucher is not subject to VAT – any excess consideration is taxable as a supply of services; or
b. not the issuer, the full sales price is taxable.
When a **credit voucher** is sold, VAT is only due when:
– the consideration exceeds the face value of the voucher, in which case VAT is due on the excess; or
– the redeemer fails to account for VAT.
The sale of **other kinds** of face value voucher are liable to standard-rate VAT, unless it is known at the time of sale that redemption will be for goods at the zero rate or reduced rate.
Argos Distributors Ltd v C & E [1996]

On redemption, the face value of the **voucher** is included as consideration for the goods. The only exception is when cash is given in return for the voucher, which is then outside the scope of VAT, and the takings are not reduced for the amount of cash paid out. The trader may accept a **third party's voucher** in part payment for goods. In this case, only the cash received from the customer is included as consideration. The amount of any payment subsequently received from the third party in relation to the transaction is also consideration for the goods, unless the payment is a contribution to advertising or selling services. 7982

EXAMPLE

1. B Ltd sells gift vouchers at their face value, with £1 added for the card and envelope in which to put the voucher.
So if B Ltd sells a £20 voucher for £21 to Mr C, the output tax due is 1/6 of £1.
When Mr C uses the voucher to purchase clothes for £30, using £10 of his own cash, the output tax due is then 1/6 of £30.

2. If B Ltd accepts a third party's voucher in payment for the same clothes as in example 1. instead, VAT is initially only accounted for on the cash consideration of £10.
Once B Ltd receives payment from the third party, VAT is accounted for on the additional £20 of value.

Cash backs and volume bonuses

Cash backs or volume bonuses refer to payments made by a manufacturer to the customer of a wholesaler or retailer in recognition of the customer's volume of purchases. 7984 HMRC Brief 08/07

The **correct VAT treatment** is as follows:
– **manufacturers** are entitled to reduce the output tax on their sales in respect of the cash backs, provided that they charged and accounted for VAT on their original supply, and the supply is not one involving a change of VAT rate *Elida Gibbs Ltd v C & E* [1996]; and
– **customers** who are VAT-registered must reduce their input tax claim proportionately and are responsible for checking the correct position with the manufacturer.

However, **no adjustments** are required in the following situations:
– cross-border transactions;
– by wholesalers who do not get involved in the cash-back transaction; or
– where goods were supplied to the customer free of VAT.

MEMO POINTS Where the **VAT liability** of the goods **changes in the supply chain** (e.g. where a charity buys certain goods zero-rated from the wholesaler which were standard-rated for VAT when supplied by the manufacturer), the manufacturer cannot reduce its output tax in relation to the cash-back paid to the charity.

Barter transactions

In a barter transaction there is no exchange of money, simply an exchange of goods and/or services. **Each party** to the transaction is therefore making a supply. It is generally accepted that each supply may have a different value, and that value is the consideration for which the party would have made the supply. 7986 Customs manual V1-12 para 4.9

MEMO POINTS A mail order company arranged that its agents would find customers in return for gifts which were advertised in its catalogue. It was held that there were two supplies, being a supply of:
a. services by the agent to the company, which was outside the scope of VAT because the agent was unregistered; and
b. the gifts by the company to the agent. As the agent knew the value of the gifts from the catalogue, valuable consideration had been agreed.
Naturally Yours Cosmetics Ltd v C & E [1989]

EXAMPLE Mr A wishes to buy a plot of land from Mr B in order to provide access to his property. Mr B is willing to sell the land for £10,000 but instead agrees to take a field which adjoins his property from Mr A (who is short of cash). Mr A had previously obtained planning permission and the field is valued at £40,000.
Mr A was obviously prepared to pay the equivalent of £40,000 to purchase the land and therefore the consideration for the supply of his field is £40,000.
The value of the supply made by Mr B is only £10,000.

SECTION 5

Place of supply

7988 For a transaction to fall within the scope of UK VAT the place of supply must be in, or deemed to be in, the UK. It is therefore necessary to determine where the supply takes place. The rules differ for goods and for services.

As part of the "VAT Package", an EU-wide initiative which is intended to ensure that, where possible, VAT is due in the country where services are consumed (i.e. in the place where the customer is based), with a few exceptions, the **basic rule** for **business to business ("B2B")** supplies of services is that VAT is due in the place **where the customer is established**. For supplies to **non-business customers ("B2C")**, the place of supply remains **where the supplier is established**.

MEMO POINTS Changes involving **supplies to consumers**, which are among the most contentious aspects of the VAT Package, will not be introduced until 2015.

A. Goods

7990 s 7 VATA 1994 Goods situated in the UK are deemed to have been supplied in the UK if they do not leave or enter the UK during the course of the supply.

MEMO POINTS Goods that **leave and re-enter** the UK as a result of their removal from one part of the UK to another will be treated as situated in the UK. For example, the transfer of goods from Northern Ireland to England, although crossing the sea, would still be a supply in the UK.

Goods removed to the UK

7992 Goods that are brought to the UK are treated as if they were supplied in the UK when they are:
a. installed or assembled in the UK;
b. imported from outside the EU and Isle of Man by the supplier;
c. removed to the UK from another EU member state as a result of a supply made:
– to a non-taxable person;
– for a consideration; and
– by a trader who meets the conditions for compulsory registration (¶7775).
Otherwise, goods removed to the UK will be treated as supplied outside the UK.

Goods removed from the UK

Goods that are removed from the UK are treated as if they were supplied outside the UK when they are: **7994**

a. installed or assembled in the country to which they are removed;

b. first removed to the UK; or

c. removed to another EU member state by a person who is taxable in another EU state, and liable to account for the VAT on the supply in that state.

Otherwise, goods removed from the UK will be treated as supplied in the UK.

B. Services

General rule

The **general rule** for **B2B** supplies of services is that VAT is due in the place **where the customer is established**. **7996** Sch 36 FA 2009

For **B2C** supplies, the place of supply is **where the supplier is established**.

The general rule **excludes**: **7998**
– passenger transport (¶8026);
– services and ancillary services relating to cultural, artistic, sporting, scientific, educational, entertainment or similar activities, such as fairs and exhibitions, including the supply of services of the organisers of such activities (¶8010);
– restaurant and catering services, including those supplied on board ships, planes and aircraft as part of transport in the EU;
– short-term hire of means of transport; and
– services related to land (¶8794).

However, the general rule for services provided B2B **includes** the following cross-border supplies of services:
– valuation and work on goods (¶8009);
– agents' services (¶8534);
– transport of goods and ancillary transport services (¶8026);
– long-term hire of a means of transport (more than 30 days, or more than 90 days for vessels); and
– electronically supplied services by non-EU suppliers to EU business customers.

Where an overseas supplier provides any services to a UK VAT-registered customer and the place of supply of those services is the UK, the UK customer must account for VAT under the reverse charge.

Any organisation that has both **business and non-business activities** must account for VAT on a supply received from a business in another member state via the reverse charge, even if the service is received in connection with its non-business activity. However, supplies received **wholly for private purposes** will be treated as B2C supplies and no reverse charge will be necessary (although VAT will be charged as appropriate in the member state of supply).

MEMO POINTS Special place of supply rules apply where **travel, hotel, holiday** and certain other supplies of a kind enjoyed by travellers are bought in from third parties and resold as principal under the tour operators' margin scheme (see *VAT Memo* for details).

Defining business customers

Traders supplying services thus need to know whether each of their customers is in business. The legislation uses the term "relevant business person". This is a person who is: **8000** Sch 36 FA 2009

– a taxable person as defined by the VAT Directive – that is, a person carrying on an economic activity (¶7754); or
– registered for VAT in the UK, the Isle of Man, or in another member state.

In most cases a business customer in another member state will be able to **supply a valid EU VAT number** issued by its tax authority. HMRC will normally accept this as sufficient evidence of business status. If the **customer is not VAT-registered**, alternative evidence may be used. This could be in the form of a letter from a tax authority or Chamber of Commerce. If the customer cannot provide sufficient evidence to show that it is in business, or if a trader has doubts about whether any evidence provided relates to the customer, HMRC's advice is that the services should be treated as made to a non-business customer (B2C in other words). If evidence is subsequently provided, an adjustment can be made.

If customers are engaged in **both business and non-business activities** (for example, charities or government departments), supplies to those customers are treated as B2B supplies for the purposes of the place of supply rules.

Where a supplier or customer is established

8002 s 9 VATA 1994 The supplier or customer of services is deemed to belong in a country if:
a. he has a **business or fixed establishment** in that country, and no such establishment elsewhere;
b. he does not have a business or fixed establishment in that country, but has his **usual place of residence** there; or
c. he has business or fixed establishments **both in that country and elsewhere**, but the country concerned is where:
– for a supplier, the establishment most directly concerned with the supply is located; or
– for a customer, the establishment at which the services are most directly used is located.

8005 A **business establishment** means the principal place of business and is usually the head office or headquarters from which the business is run. The term would include an office, showroom or factory.

Where a supplier or customer carries on a business through a **permanent establishment** (¶22) in a particular country, he is treated as having a business establishment there.

A **fixed establishment** is an establishment (other than the business establishment) which has both the human and technical resources necessary for receiving and providing services on a permanent basis. A branch or agency may fall to be treated as a fixed establishment if these factors are present.

MEMO POINTS 1. A business may have several fixed establishments but can only have one business establishment. Where the supplier or customer has **establishments in more than one country**, the supplies made from or received at each establishment must be examined separately. Where the services are not supplied or received at a particular establishment, the place of belonging is the country where the business establishment is located.
2. **Usual place of residence** for an **individual** means the country where the individual has set up home and is in full-time work. The usual place of residence of a **corporate body** is the country in which its registered office is situated.
3. Where a supplier or customer is a member of a **VAT group** (¶7807), the group will be treated as a single entity for the purposes of the place of belonging, so that an establishment for any individual member of the group will be an establishment for the whole group.
4. The importance of establishing which fixed establishment receives the supply was illustrated in the following case. A Swiss company arranged for consultancy services to be supplied to it in relation to the installation of new software. Part of the supply was for the benefit of the UK branch of the Swiss company. HMRC argued that, as the UK fixed establishment received the benefit of the supply, the supply was made to the UK fixed establishment and therefore subject to the reverse charge. The Swiss company argued that the supply was to its head office and was therefore outside the scope of UK VAT. The Court of Appeal rejected the taxpayer's argument. The taxpayer involved was an insurance company, therefore it incurred a VAT cost which would have been avoided if the supply had been deemed to have been supplied to Switzerland. *Zurich Insurance Co v HMRC* [2007]

1. Services related to land

The place of supply of land-related services (¶8794) is where the land is situated. 8007
SI 1992/3121 reg 5

2. Valuation services and work on goods

Where the services in the following table are treated as supplied depends on the status of the customer. 8009
SI 1992/3121 reg 15

Service	Example	Place of supply
Valuation of goods[1]	– by loss adjusters or other experts in connection with an insurance claim	**B2B**: – where customer is established **B2C**: – where physically carried out
Work carried out on goods[1]	– repairs, cleaning or restoration; – processing, manufacturing or assembling; – alterations, painting, polishing, waterproofing, sharpening etc	

Note:
1. **Goods** for these purposes include all forms of tangible moveable property.

3 Cultural, artistic, educational, sporting and exhibition services

8010

Service	Examples	Place of supply
Cultural, artistic, sporting, scientific, educational or entertainment services (only where there is a live audience) and ancillary services including organising[1,2]	– an actor or singer performing live; – an interpreter at an event	**B2B**: where customer is established[1,2] **B2C**: where physically performed
Services relating to exhibitions, conferences and meetings, and services ancillary to such services including organisation[2]	– an electrician or carpenter fitting out stands at an exhibition for the organiser or exhibitors; – the provision of an undefined site for a stand at an exhibition[2]	

Note:
1. Supplies of admission to an event and services ancillary to admission are taxed where the event takes place.
2. The provision of a defined site for a **stand at an exhibition** is a service relating to land (¶8794), which is deemed to be supplied where the land is located.

4. Intangible services

The services in the table below are: 8016
Sch 4A para 16
VATA 1994

– subject to the **general rule** when supplied B2B in the EU;
– supplied where the **supplier belongs** when supplied B2C in the EU; and
– supplied where the **recipient belongs** when supplied B2C to a person who belongs outside the EU.

8018 The following table outlines the services that fall within the above provisions.

Supply	Examples	Scope
Transfers and assignments of copyright, patents, licences, trademarks and other similar intellectual property rights	Grant of a licence to use software Transfer of permission to use a logo	Covers only the supply of such rights that involve the supply of intellectual property. Other services, even if described as a "right" or "licence" (e.g. the right to a discount on an admission fee), are excluded
Acceptance of any obligation to refrain from pursuing or exercising (in whole or in part) any business activity or any intellectual property rights	A non-competition clause agreed between a vendor and a purchaser	
Advertising services	TV or radio advertising time Website advertising Devising and undertaking a promotional campaign	Includes elements supplied as part of an advertising campaign which would not otherwise amount to advertising in their own right if supplied separately (e.g. cocktail parties, seminars, etc). Simple distribution of information (e.g. leaflet drops) with no other involvement in the advertising campaign will be excluded. *Lawrence* [1995]
Services of consultants, consultancy bureaux, engineers; lawyers[1], accountants and other similar services; data processing and provision of information	Market research Intellectual advice or design Winding up of a deceased's estate Weather forecasts Engineering design The performing of mathematical and logical operations on data Tourist information, telephone helpdesks, etc	The following specific services are excluded from this provision: – services provided by engineers if they relate mainly to physical work on goods (treated as supplied where performed); and – services that consist of simple reformatting of data/delivery of another person's information (treated as supplied in accordance with the principal contract)
The supply of staff	Secondment, loan or transfer of staff by a recruitment business	Where an employer uses his staff to provide services (e.g. secretarial services) to a client, the supply is not one of staff, but of services
The letting on hire of goods other than a means of transport	Hire of computer equipment Hire of freight containers	Excludes: – land, plant and machinery installed as a fixture; and – goods which include the services of an operator This is subject to the "use and enjoyment" rule (¶8020, ¶8024)
Banking, financial and insurance services (including reinsurance but not safe deposit services)		The financial function must be the primary part of the activity, **for example**: – debt collection services; – portfolio management services; and – granting of mortgages. **Excludes** rent collection services and physical safe custody services

Supply	Examples	Scope
Telecommunication services	Telephone calls Emails Access to the Internet	This is subject to the "use and enjoyment" rule (¶8020, ¶8024)
Radio and TV broadcasting services		¶8020
Electronically provided services		¶8024
Supplies of services connected with the operation of natural gas and electricity distribution systems	Receipt of natural gas/electricity by a UK VAT-registered person in the course of a business carried on by him	

Note:
1. Legal services provided to persons who have not been given the right to stay in the UK (e.g. **asylum seekers**) are treated as being supplied in the recipient's country of origin, even if their application to stay in the UK is successful and the invoice is rendered after the right to stay has been granted. If a person is granted a right to stay in the UK but this is subsequently revoked, the legal services associated with any appeal are treated as being provided in the UK.

Radio and broadcasting

Broadcasting services are broadly supplied where the customer belongs so that any services consumed in the EU are subject to VAT and supplies to customers outside the EU are outside the scope of VAT (unless the services are used and enjoyed in the UK). **8020** SI 2003/862 SI 2003/863

It is crucial that the trader can determine:
- whether a customer is going to use the supply for business purposes; and
- where each customer is located.

The following table summarises where the place of supply occurs:

Supplier	Customer	Place of supply
UK registered	UK business	In UK, if used or enjoyed in the UK[1]
	Private customer wherever located	In UK, if used or enjoyed in the UK[1]
	EU business	Where customer belongs and customer accounts for VAT
EU registered but not UK registered	UK business	In UK, if used or enjoyed in the UK[1]
	Business in same EU state as supplier	In state of supplier – supplier accounts for VAT
	Business in different EU state from supplier	Where customer belongs and customer accounts for VAT
	UK and EU private individuals	In EU state of supplier
Non-EU	UK business	In UK, if used or enjoyed in the UK[1]
	UK and EU private individuals	Where use or enjoyment takes place[1]
	EU business	Where customer belongs and customer accounts for VAT

Note:
1. The **use and enjoyment** override means that the place of supply will be where the service is actually used. In most cases, this will be the same place as where the customer is established.

Electronically supplied services

8024 Information Sheet 1/03

From 1 July 2003 to 31 December 2014, all electronic services are usually supplied where the customer belongs so that any services consumed in the EU are subject to VAT, and supplies to customers outside the EU are outside the scope of VAT (unless the services are **used and enjoyed** in the UK).

Again, the trader must determine:

– whether a customer is going to use the supply for business purposes; and

– where each customer is located.

As these rules could lead to multiple registration requirements for non-EU traders in many EU member states, a simplified registration scheme has also been introduced (¶9116).

The following table summarises where the place of supply occurs:

Supplier	Customer	Place of supply
UK registered [1]	UK business [2]	In UK
	UK or EU private individual	In UK
	EU business	Where customer belongs and customer accounts for VAT
EU registered but not UK registered	UK business [2]	In UK (customer accounts for VAT)
	Business in same EU state as supplier	In state of supplier and supplier accounts for VAT
	Business in different EU state from supplier	Where customer belongs and customer accounts for VAT
	UK and EU private individual	In state of supplier
Non-EU	UK business [2]	In UK (customer accounts for VAT)
	UK private individual	In UK (supplier must register for VAT (¶9116))
	EU private individual	Where customer belongs and supplier must account for VAT (¶9116)
	EU business	Where customer belongs and customer accounts for VAT

Note:

1. If also providing **telecommunications and broadcasting** services, the UK business may have its accounting system set up to tax supplies where they are effectively used and enjoyed. If the business also makes supplies of electronic services to non-business customers, it can apply the used and enjoyed rule to those electronic services.

2. Where a supply would ordinarily be treated as supplied in the UK, it will be treated as supplied in the UK only to the extent that the **effective use or enjoyment** takes place in the EU. Effective use and enjoyment occurs where the customer actually uses the electronic services.

5. Transport services

Transport services

8026 SI 1992/3121 regs 6-10

The place of supply for transport services depends on the type of transport provided and the status of the customer as follows:

Transport service	Place of supply
Passenger transport and related services	
Passenger transport	The country in which the transportation takes place [1, 2]
Restaurant and catering services on board ships, planes and trains and goods or services provided on a pleasure cruise	The place of departure

Transport service	Place of supply
Freight transport and related services	
Freight transport services	**B2B**: – the general rule (¶7996) applies, so the supply is where the customer is established **B2C**: – the place where the transport takes place (or the point of departure if an intra-EU transport)
Ancillary freight transport services (loading, handling, etc)	**B2B**: – the general rule (¶7996) applies **B2C**: – where physically performed
Intermediary services of arranging freight transport	**B2B**: – the general rule (¶7996) applies **B2C**: – where the underlying principal supply takes place
Intermediary services of arranging ancillary freight transport	**B2B**: – the general rule (¶7996) applies **B2C**: – the place where the underlying supply takes place
Note: 1. Including accompanying luggage and/or motor vehicle. 2. For air and sea transport, a journey between two points in the same country is treated as taking place wholly inside the country even where it takes place partly outside, provided that the means of transport does not put in or land in another country on the way.	

SECTION 6

VAT liability

The rate of VAT chargeable on taxable supplies **depends on** the nature of the transaction. There are three rates: 8030
- the standard rate, which is currently 20%;
- the zero rate (¶8052); and
- the reduced rate (¶8060), which is currently 5%.

Where a **price** is stated as being **inclusive** of VAT (i.e. the gross amount), the VAT element is calculated by applying the appropriate VAT fraction which for:
- standard-rated transactions at 20% is 1/6; and
- reduced-rated transactions at 5% is 1/21.

For zero-rated transactions at 0% the VAT fraction is 0.

EXAMPLE
1. If a standard-rated supply has a net value of £100, the VAT charge at 20% is £20.
2. If, instead, a standard-rated supply has a gross value of £100, the VAT charge is £16.67. (£100 x 1/6)
3. For a reduced-rated supply with a net value of £100, the VAT charge is £5.00. (£100 x 5%)
4. If the reduced-rated supply had a gross value of £100, the VAT charge would be £4.76. (£100 x 1/21)

Output tax

All supplies of goods or services in the course of business are subject to VAT unless exempt, or outside the scope of VAT. VAT-registered businesses making **taxable supplies** are required to account for output tax in respect of those supplies. A supply that is liable to VAT will be standard-rated unless it is specifically zero-rated (¶8052) or reduced-rated (¶8060). 8034 s 24 VATA 1994

Output tax is the VAT due on taxable supplies made by a business. It is also due on the acquisition of goods from other EU member states (¶8937). 8036

A. Supplies on which no VAT is due

Outside the scope activities

8038 Some transactions are outside the scope of the UK VAT system. They are not taxable supplies and no VAT is charged on them. Activities which are outside the scope of VAT include:
- non-business activities, such as a hobby or private, non-business activity (for example, the sale of stamps from a private collection);
- the charging of statutory fees that are fixed by law (for example, congestion charges or vehicle MOT test fees).

No VAT is chargeable on these activities and no input VAT can be reclaimed in relation to them. Income from such activities does not count towards the registration and deregistration thresholds.

Exempt and zero-rated supplies

8040 Certain defined supplies are exempt from VAT, certain others are taxable but at the zero rate. Whilst **no VAT is charged** in either case, there are important distinctions.

MEMO POINTS 1. When determining whether a business is liable to **register** for VAT (¶7775), the value of all taxable supplies, including zero-rated supplies, must be taken into consideration. Exempt supplies are left out of the calculation.
2. A business which makes only taxable supplies, including zero-rated supplies, is entitled to recover **input tax** on its purchases (¶8135). However, a business which makes only exempt supplies is not entitled to recover any input tax incurred. A business which makes a combination of taxable and exempt supplies is partly exempt (¶8205) and able to recover a proportion of the input tax incurred, usually in line with the proportion of taxable supplies it makes.
3. A person who sells only or mainly zero-rated goods or services can apply to HMRC to be **exempted from registering** for VAT.

8041 The following tables provide a summary of the supplies which are generally either exempt or zero-rated. For full details of the rules and an in-depth analysis of the exemptions and zero-rating, please see *VAT Memo*. The supplies are ordered alphabetically.

MEMO POINTS There are special rules for **cross-border** transactions. For exports of goods to non-EU states (which may be zero-rated if certain conditions are met), see ¶9074.

Exempt supplies

8042

Supply	Further details
Admission charges to: – museums; – galleries; – art exhibitions; – zoos; – theatrical, musical or choreographic performances of a cultural nature	Charged by a public body (e.g. local authority or government department) or an eligible body. An **eligible body** is a body which: – is precluded from distributing profits; – applies any profits from exempt admission charges to the continuance or improvement of the facilities; and – is administered on an essentially voluntary basis by persons who have no direct or indirect financial interest in the results of the activities. (A person who carries out only basic tasks for remuneration will not cause the organisation to fail the last test.)
Betting and gaming	Includes: – providing facilities for placing bets or playing games of chance for prizes (free plays are not prizes for this purpose); – granting a right to take part in a lottery; and – fees for participating in bingo or games of chance. Excludes: – admission to premises; – provision of facilities to a member of a club as part of a subscription; and – provision of gaming machines.

Supply	Further details
Buildings, land and construction	Supplies relating to buildings, land and construction can be standard-rated, reduced-rated, zero-rated or exempt (¶8790).
Burial and cremation	Includes the disposal of human remains and funeral services.
Charitable fund-raising events	Admission charges for one-off events.
Education and training	See ¶8044. Includes exam services, private tuition, youth clubs and research.
Financial services	Includes: – issuing, transferring or receiving money (including foreign exchange); – making loans; – advancing credit; – provision of finance on instalment terms; – intermediary services in connection with exempt supplies of finance; – administration charges (maximum £10) in connection with provision of credit; and – debit and credit card handling charges levied by an agent on behalf of the supplier, where the service supplied by the agent includes the transmission of the card information, security information and the card issuers' authorisation codes to Girobank. Excludes: – investment, financial and taxation advice; – safe custody services; – credit checking services; – profit from hedging of own foreign exchange risk; – debt collection and credit control; – equipment leasing; – administration of estates; – trust fund management; – executor and trustee services; – portfolio management; – card handling charges provided by the supplier, or of a different nature from those listed above.
Health and welfare services	See ¶8048.
Irrecoverable input tax suffered on acquisition – subsequent onward supply	Input tax was irrecoverable because: – the VAT was incurred by a non-taxable person (i.e. before he was liable or eligible to register for VAT (¶7775)); – it related to business entertainment or cars; or – the acquisition was used to make wholly exempt supplies.
Insurance	Insurance and reinsurance provided by: – persons permitted to carry on insurance business; – persons who procure insurance cover under a block policy; – insurers who belong outside the UK; and – ECGD (the Export Credits Guarantee Department). Services of an insurance broker or agent in connection with exempt supplies of insurance.
Investment gold	
Postal services	Applies only to supplies by the Post Office. The exemption for postal services is restricted to supplies of public postal services (and incidental goods) by the universal service provider (currently Royal Mail). Postal services supplied on terms which are individually negotiated, and services not subject to price or regulatory control, are standard-rated. Unused stamps (excluding first day covers) are exempt if supplied at or below face value.

Supply	Further details
Shares and securities	Includes: – share brokerage services; – dealing system services; – nominee services; – global custody arrangements; – underwriting transactions; and – management of authorised unit trust schemes, OEICs, ITCs, VCTs. Excludes: – investment and portfolio management; – registrar services; and – safe custody fees.
Sports competitions – entry fees	Must be either: – wholly allocated towards funding prizes; or – charged by non-profit-making body.
Sports facilities	See ¶8050.
Subscriptions to: – trade unions; – professional bodies; – trade associations; – learned societies; – organisations of a political, religious, philanthropic, philosophical or patriotic nature	Body must be non-profit-making. Membership must be restricted mainly (75%) to members of the appropriate profession or trade. Services provided by those bodies to its members as a result of the membership fee are also exempt, excluding admission to premises or events.
Works of art	Disposed of by way of gift or private treaty sale to an approved body, or accepted in lieu of inheritance tax by HMRC.

Education and training

8044 Sch 9 group 6 VATA 1994

The general rule is that the provision of education and training by an eligible body is exempt. This includes related goods and services.

MEMO POINTS 1. An **eligible body** includes the following institutions:
– schools;
– universities;
– higher and further education colleges;
– government departments;
– local authorities;
– non-profit-making bodies; and
– any body teaching English as a foreign language.
2. The following types of colleges are **excluded** from being an eligible body:
– secretarial;
– tutorial; and
– correspondence course.

8046 The exemption for educational services is **extended to** the following:

Item	Notes
Examination services	Provided by an eligible body, or supplied to a person receiving education or training outside the course of a business. Includes: – setting and marking exams; – making assessments; and – setting education or training standards.
Vocational training	Provided by an eligible body, including goods or services (other than exam services) provided by the body to the trainee. Includes training and related goods and services if financed under the Employment and Training Act 1973.

Item	Notes
Private tuition	Applies to supplies made by individual teachers (independently of an employer) in subjects ordinarily taught in school or university.
Youth clubs and associations	Includes facilities provided by: – a youth club to its members; – an association of youth clubs to its members; and – an association of youth clubs to the members of a youth club which is a member of the association.

Health and welfare services

Exemption broadly applies to the provision of: **8048** Sch 9 group 7 VATA 1994 SI 2007/206

a. medical care by health professionals, including diagnosis, medical reports, treatment and home nursing; and

b. care services such as:

– the provision of hospital care (including accommodation, catering, drugs, medical and nursing services);

– the provision of drugs and medical appliances which are personally administered to a patient (and not under prescription) by a doctor in general practice, or a health professional working under the clinical supervision of a doctor;

– transportation of the sick and injured in specially designed or adapted vehicles (including air ambulances); and

c. welfare services provided by charities and state regulated private welfare institutions, such as care homes and public bodies.

MEMO POINTS 1. **Health professionals** are professionals enrolled or registered on a statutory register, including:
– doctors;
– nurses, health visitors and midwives;
– dentists;
– opticians;
– pharmacists;
– osteopaths and chiropractors; and
– supplementary professionals such as occupational therapists.

The services of therapists such as acupuncturists, hypnotherapists and others who do not have statutory registers are not exempt.

2. Examples of services which **are not "care"** and which are therefore standard-rated are: Business Brief 29/03 Notice 701/57

a. services to enable a third party to decide on a course of action, including:
– pre-employment medicals;
– medicals to assess the level of insurance premiums;
– medical reports in connection with personal injury litigation and medical negligence; and
– medical reports to assess a person's entitlement to a war pension or similar benefit;

b. services not aimed at the prevention, diagnosis, treatment or cure of a disease or health disorder, such as paternity testing and the writing of articles for journals;

c. services directly supervised by a pharmacist; and

d. general administrative services, such as countersigning passport applications and providing character references.

3. The NHS only funds the VAT-exclusive cost of **drugs dispensed by general practitioner doctors**. In order to recover any input tax incurred, affected doctors need to register for VAT (¶7775). The VAT liability of drugs depends on whether they are: Information Sheet 3/06
– personally administered or injected as part of medical treatment, which is an exempt supply;
– authorised by a private prescription, which is a standard-rated supply; or
– dispensed under a NHS prescription, which is a zero-rated supply.

If the doctor is making a mixture of exempt and taxable supplies, input tax recovery will be restricted by the partial exemption rules (¶8205).

4. The provision of medical care by **psychologists** in the fields of clinical, counselling, educational, forensic, health, occupational, and sport/exercise psychology is exempt. Certain services supplied to persons other than the patient, e.g. preparation of psychological reports for legal use, are taxable. HMRC Brief 43/09

Sporting services

8050
Sch 9 group 10
VATA 1994

Facilities which are closely related to sporting activities provided by **non-profit-making bodies** are exempt, including the following:
- use of changing rooms;
- use of equipment;
- playing facilities;
- services of judges, umpires and referees;
- coaching; and
- membership fees.

The provision of sports facilities is an exception to the usual exemption (subject to the option to tax (¶8904)) for the grant of an interest in land. However, exemption does apply if the facilities are provided for:
- a continuous period of 24 hours or more; or
- a series of 10 or more periods to a school, club or association.

If a trader has exercised his option to tax, or the hire of the sports facilities does not meet either of the above conditions, the supply will be standard-rated.

MEMO POINTS 1. The following supplies are not closely related to the supply of sports facilities:
- catering;
- residential accommodation;
- social facilities, such as a bar; and
- admission charges to spectators.

2. The First-tier Tribunal has held that UK law is wrong to exclude supplies of sporting services to non-members from VAT exemption. Where supplies to members of sporting services are exempt from VAT, supplies to non-members should be also. The Tribunal's decision limits exemption to cases where the club budgets year on year for income from non-members and that income is used to meet the club's ordinary running expenses. *The Bridport and West Dorset Golf Club Ltd* TC01214

Business Brief 22/05

3. Supplies of sporting services provided by **companies** which are not genuine non-profit-making bodies are standard-rated and do not qualify for exemption. Companies whose ability to distribute profits is restricted are not non-profit-making bodies for this purpose, because the accumulation of profit reserves is still advantageous to the shareholders. *HMRC v Messenger Leisure Developments Ltd* [2005]

Zero-rated supplies

8052

Category	Further details
Bank notes	
Books and printed matter	Includes booklets, brochures, newspapers, journals, sheet music, leaflets and pamphlets, picture books and painting books.
Caravans and houseboats	Designed for permanent residential use at the time of manufacture. Caravans are only zero-rated if the length exceeds 7 metres or the width exceeds 2.55 metres.
Charities	Includes: – sales by the charity of donated goods (whether new or second-hand); – donations of goods to a charity; – supplies to or by a charity of items used for raising money (including badges, collection boxes, advertising, etc); and – supplies to or by a charity of medicines and equipment for charitable use.
Children's items	Clothing and footwear which conform to size guidelines.
Crash helmets	For motor cycles and pedal cycles. Must meet legal standards. Protective helmets for pedal cycles must bear the European Union "CE" mark.

Category	Further details
Drugs, aids and equipment for the disabled and handicapped	Supplies to disabled persons of equipment specifically designed or adapted for their domestic or personal use. Includes supplies to charities which are then supplied to disabled persons.
Food	The **general rule** is that supplies of food are zero-rated, although there are several specific exceptions. Food does not include medicines, dietary supplements, food additives and similar products. Any supply in the course of **catering** is standard-rated. See ¶8054 for items specifically excluded from zero-rating.
Gold	Supplies of UK gold between Central Banks and members of the London Gold Market.
Maps, charts and topographical plans	Not including plans or drawings for industrial, commercial, architectural or engineering purposes.
Protective helmets and boots for industrial use	Must meet legal safety requirements. Standard-rated if supplied to a person for use by his employees.
Talking books (and related equipment) for the blind or handicapped	Supplied to a charity (including hire of equipment). Related equipment includes recording apparatus, radios, cassette players and magnetic tape.
Transport	Includes: – passenger transport (excluding taxis, pleasure flights, transport in places of entertainment or interest, airport car park transfers); – supplies of ships designed for commercial use at time of manufacture, hovercraft and aircraft (including parts and equipment); – repairs and maintenance of ships and aircraft; – charter services for ships and aircraft; – air navigation services; and – supplies to charity of lifeboats and related supplies. Excludes freight services (but see also ¶8942).
Water and sewerage	Excludes: – supplies for use in industrial activities; – deionised or distilled water; – heated water; and – drain services (cleaning, unblocking, etc).

Food specifically excluded from zero-rating

A number of food items are specifically excluded from zero-rating and are therefore standard-rated: 8054 Sch 8 group 1 VATA 1994

Food item	Standard-rated	Zero-rated
Iced products	Includes: – items eaten frozen e.g. ice cream, frozen yoghurt and sorbet; – mixes and powders; – items of a similar nature but intended to be defrosted or cooked before consumption.	
Confectionery	Includes: – chocolates; – sweets; – biscuits wholly or partly covered in chocolate; – drained, glace or crystallised fruits (but not drained cherries or candied peel); – any item of sweetened prepared food which is normally eaten with the fingers.	Includes: – Jaffa Cakes; – caramel shortbread; – marshmallow teacakes; – flapjacks; – cereal crunch cakes (i.e. cornflakes or puffed rice in chocolate).

Food item	Standard-rated	Zero-rated
Savouries	Includes: – potato snacks which are designed for human consumption without further preparation; – Pringles – roasted or salted nuts.	Includes: – breadsticks; – tortilla chips; – bagel chips; – Twiglets; – nuts held out for sale as a cooking ingredient.
Beverages	Includes – alcoholic drinks; – fruit juice; – bottled water; – carbonated drinks.	Includes: – soya and rice milk (unless sweetened or flavoured); – coconut milk; – meal replacement drinks; – tea, herbal teas and similar products; – coffee, chicory and other coffee substitutes; – milk. Preparations and extractions of these products and of meat, yeast or eggs are also zero-rated.

8056 **Catering** Supplies in the course of catering are standard-rated. Catering is not **defined** but specifically includes supplies of:
- food for consumption on the premises; and
- hot take-away food.

Catering supplied as part of hospital care is exempt from VAT. Similarly, catering supplied to school pupils, which is incidental to an exempt supply of education, is exempt.

MEMO POINTS 1. The **premises** for this purpose are the premises from which the supply of food is made. This is easy enough in a restaurant or café but not so easy where the food is supplied from a kiosk within a shopping centre or office building, when the question becomes whether the premises are the kiosk, the whole building it is within, or some limited area around the kiosk set aside for eating.

Business Brief 12/06 2. Where food is supplied at **restricted access sites** which are not open to the general public but only, for example, to employees, the retailer's premises are defined as the unit from which the sales of food have been made, rather than the larger overall premises. However, the retailer's premises will still include any facilities provided to enable the purchasers to consume the food at the unit, such as areas of seating and tables within, and adjacent to, the retail unit, whether owned by the landlord or the retailer, but clearly for the use of the food retailer's customers. This means that any supply of cold food for consumption away from the immediate premises will be zero-rated.

SI 2004/3343 3. For **hot food**, the temperature of the food when it is provided to the customer is relevant, rather than its temperature at any other time.

Business Brief 09/05 HMRC have issued guidance on the VAT liability of hot food, which should depend on the **dominant reason** for heating the food. Where the main purpose for heating is so the food can be consumed hot or warm, the supply will be standard-rated.

HMRC consider the following to be relevant in deciding on the liability of the supply:
- if an outlet is advertised as a take-away, the supply of hot food will be standard-rated;
- if food is packaged to retain heat, this would indicate a standard-rated supply, although food sold without such packaging can also be standard-rated;
- availability of utensils and sauces, which would indicate a standard-rated supply;
- heating makes food more palatable, although certain foods can be eaten whilst cold, and would still remain standard-rated;
- compliance with hygiene regulations may require food to be kept hot, although this is not usually a main purpose;
- if the food is allowed to cool naturally between heating and consumption (e.g. bread), this may indicate a zero-rated supply; and
- promotional and advertising material may also be useful indicators.

B. Reduced-rated supplies

Summary

The following supplies are liable to a reduced rate of VAT of 5%. 8060

Supply	Notes	Reference
Fuel and power	Supplies for domestic, relevant residential or charitable use qualify for reduced-rating. If the supply is used partly for charitable and partly for non-charitable use, as long as 60% is used for charitable purposes the whole supply can be zero-rated. Otherwise, an apportionment is required. Road fuel is excluded.	Sch 7A group 1 VATA 1994
Certain residential conversions, renovations and alterations of dwellings	See ¶8873 onwards.	Sch 7A groups 6, 7 VATA 1994
Installation of energy-saving materials	For use in: – residential accommodation; – a building to be used solely for charitable purposes, or as a village hall or similar. The materials must be installed to qualify, therefore the supply of goods only will be standard-rated. The up-to-date list of qualifying materials can be found on HMRC's website http://www.hmrc.gov.uk/vat/sectors/consumers/energy-saving.htm.	Sch 7A group 2 VATA 1994
Supply and installation of heating	If grant-funded by an organisation whose objectives including assisting with the provision of heating, and made to a person who is over 60 or in the receipt of one of the following: – council tax benefit; – child tax credit, other than family element; – working tax credit; – disability living allowance; – housing benefit; – jobseeker's allowance, or income support; or – disablement, or war disablement, pension.	Sch 7A group 3 VATA 1994
Installation of security products	If provided to people over the age of 60 and funded by an approved grant.	Sch 7A group 3 VATA 1994
Children's car seats	Covers any safety seat, booster seat or booster cushion designed to restrain a child in a motor vehicle and includes travel systems which are children's car seats also used as pushchairs or prams. This also applies to seat bases.	Sch 7A group 5 VATA 1994
Women's sanitary protection products	Only applies to products specifically designed for use during menstruation or following childbirth. Items designed for use as an incontinence product are not eligible for the reduced rate but in most circumstances will be zero-rated in any case. Complementary goods, such as feminine wipes and deodorants, are not eligible for the reduced rate.	Sch 7A group 4 VATA 1994

Supply	Notes	Reference
All sales of contraceptive products (including emergency contraception), whether supplied to an individual, an organisation or the NHS	Excludes: – fertility monitoring devices; – natural family planning methods; – contraceptives obtained under prescription from a medical practitioner, which are zero-rated; or – contraceptives fitted, injected or implanted by a health professional, which are exempt.	Sch 7A group 8 VATA 1994
Welfare advice and information for the elderly, disabled or children	If provided by a charity or state-regulated private institution and supply would not otherwise be exempt. Advice must not be specific to a particular individual or about his personal circumstances. Goods are unlikely to qualify unless they are supplied for the purpose of conveying the information or advice.	Sch 7A group 9 VATA 1994
Installation and supply of mobility aids for a person aged over 60 at the time of the supply	Must be one of the following for use in domestic accommodation: – grab rail; – ramp; – stair/bath lift; – built-in shower seat or shower containing built-in seat; or – walk-in bath with sealable doors.	Sch 7A group 10 VATA 1994
Smoking cessation products		Sch 7A group 11 VATA 1994

CHAPTER 4

Input tax

OUTLINE ¶¶

8130 A business will incur VAT on taxable purchases it makes from VAT-registered suppliers, acquisitions of goods from other EU countries (¶8937), imports of goods from outside the EU (¶9037) and under the reverse charge mechanism (¶9110). In general, traders can recover VAT incurred on their VAT returns, subject to specific rules. Not all VAT incurred by a business is recoverable as input tax.

SECTION 1

Input tax

What is input tax?

8135 s 24 VATA 1994 Input tax is the VAT incurred by a VAT-registered business in respect of supplies of goods and services which it uses, or intends to use, **for the purposes** of its business. Any VAT incurred on purchases for non-business purposes, or by a non-registered business, is not input tax and is usually not recoverable.

In certain circumstances, a business may be able to reclaim VAT incurred before it was registered for VAT, or after the registration has ceased (¶8285).

In order for input tax to be recoverable, it must satisfy the following conditions:
– it must have been incurred for business purposes;
– it must be wholly or partly attributable to taxable supplies (¶8205+);
– recovery must not be specifically blocked (¶8148);
– the supply must be made to the claimant;
– input tax must have been correctly charged; and
– sufficient evidence is retained (¶8188).

MEMO POINTS 1. Input tax may **also be incurred** in respect of:
– services received from overseas (¶9108); and
– goods removed from a fiscal warehouse (¶9016).

A. Business purpose

8140 The fundamental principle of VAT recovery is that goods or services must be acquired for the purpose of any business carried on, or to be carried on, by the taxable person (¶7764). Whether goods or services have been supplied for the "purposes of the business" is usually a question of fact. If there is no clear connection between the expenditure and the business purpose, it may be possible to decide the question by:
– looking at the intention of the person at the time of incurring the expenditure (this is a subjective test);
– establishing whether or not there is a clear connection between the actual or intended use of the goods or services and the business (this is an objective test of the use to which the goods or services are put).

Expenditure is not necessarily for the purposes of the business, even if it is for the benefit of the business.

Business and non-business expenditure

8142 s 24(5) VATA 1994 When a business acquires goods or services partly for business purposes, only that portion of the VAT which relates to the business can be recovered.

Where a trader incurs VAT on goods and services that are intended for both business and private purposes, he has a choice as to how to treat them for VAT purposes. The trader can either:
– apportion the VAT, and only claim the input tax relating to the business use; or
– for certain goods and services, he can claim the full amount of input tax, and account for output tax for any private use (this is known as "the Lennartz method").

MEMO POINTS 1. Lennartz accounting is **not available** for goods which are subject to input tax restriction or "block" (see ¶8148). In HMRC's view, the Lennartz mechanism is only available for services that create new goods. VAT incurred on all other services must be apportioned.
2. The Lennartz mechanism is unavailable in respect of purchases of land, property, ships and aircraft. For those assets full input tax recovery is not available on purchase; instead input tax is restricted to the business use proportion.

Apportionment Under apportionment, any VAT incurred should first be directly attributed to business and non-business supplies, or use. Any remaining amount must then be apportioned between business and non-business use and only the part that relates to business use will be potentially recoverable. **8144**

There is no defined **method**, although the result must be fair and reasonable. The traditional method is to use the ratio that business income bears to total income and apply this to the VAT to be apportioned. Other methods of apportionment would include staff time, costs, or a fixed percentage based on previous experience (particularly where the balance of activities does not fluctuate). Traders who have business activities which are exempt from VAT will need to carry out a separate partial exemption calculation to determine the proportion of business-related VAT attributable to taxable supplies (¶8213).

Lennartz method **Alternatively**, for certain **goods**, HMRC will accept that the full amount of input tax incurred may be treated as recoverable. Subsequently, when the goods are used for private purposes, there is deemed to be a supply of services and **output tax** must be accounted for. **8145** VAT Information Sheet 14/07 VAT Information Sheet 6/11

However, the Lennartz mechanism is not available in respect of purchases of land, property, ships and aircraft. For those assets full input tax recovery is not available on purchase; instead input tax is restricted to the business use proportion.

Calculation of the output tax charge under Lennartz The following **formula** should be used to calculate the taxable value in respect of private use of assets under the Lennartz method: **8146**

$$A/B \times (C \times U)$$

where:
– A is the number of months in the relevant VAT period which fall within the economic life of the asset concerned;
– B is the total number of months in the asset's economic life (60 months for all assets);
– C is the full cost of the asset; and
– U is the extent, expressed as a percentage, to which the asset is put to any private use, as compared with the total use of the asset during the VAT period.

The **full cost** should be determined by reference to the standard-rated, VAT-bearing cost of the asset, excluding VAT. Any exempt or zero-rated costs of purchase, acquisition or construction are excluded.

Where there is either **no use or no private use** during a VAT period, no deemed charge arises. However, the number of months taken into account in a subsequent VAT period where there is private use will need to include any periods since the last deemed charge arose during which there was no use of the asset at all.

If the asset is **sold**, its economic life is ended.

EXAMPLE

1. A taxable person buys a painting for £1 million (the full cost) plus £200,000 VAT. As he intends to use the painting for both business and private purposes (displaying it at business promotional functions but keeping it at his home), he decides to use the Lennartz method.
The painting is actually used for private purposes 50% of the time in the first VAT quarter.
It has an economic life for this purpose of 60 months.
Applying the formula gives a taxable value of £25,000. (3/60 x £1,000,000 x 50%)
So the output tax charge for the first VAT quarter is £5,000. (£25,000 x 20%)

2. Continuing the first example, in the second period, no use of the painting occurs, because it is being cleaned. In the third period, private use is again 50%.
So in this calculation, A is 6 months (i.e. 2 VAT quarters).
Applying the formula gives a taxable value of £50,000. (6/60 x £1,000,000 x 50%)
So the output tax charge for the third quarter is £10,000. (£50,000 x 20%)

MEMO POINTS 1. The economic life **commences on** the day of first use (for any purpose) after the supply of the goods to a person (or his predecessors, where a business has been transferred).
2. Where a trader is **partly exempt** the calculation will be more complex. Traders' partial exemption methods should be reviewed in light of the Lennartz rules to ensure they still give a fair and reasonable rate of VAT recovery.

B. Blocked input tax

8148 SI 1987/1806 reg 12 s 24(3) VATA 1994

Even when VAT incurred is attributable to a fully taxable supply, it is not possible to recover input tax in respect of:
- business entertainment (except entertainment of overseas customers);
- most cars and related supplies;
- domestic accommodation provided for a director or proprietor of a business;
- certain articles installed in new dwellings (¶8853);
- goods sold under a second-hand goods scheme (¶8435); and
- purchases to be sold under the tour operators' margin scheme (see *VAT Memo*).

1. Business entertainment

8150 SI 1992/3222 reg 5

Business entertainment is **defined** as entertainment or hospitality of any kind provided for business purposes to anyone who is not an employee. This includes:
- the provision of accommodation;
- the provision of sports or recreational facilities;
- visits to entertainment venues, such as theatres;
- meals and drinks;
- the use of capital goods, for example yachts and private jets; and
- expenses incurred when staff act as hosts.

If a taxable person is **obliged to** entertain others under a reciprocal agreement, input tax is not blocked, because this is a supply for consideration.

It is important to distinguish **promotional activities** from business entertainment, to minimise irrecoverable VAT.

MEMO POINTS 1. For these purposes an **employee** includes:
- a director of the company;
- anyone engaged in the management of the company;
- people hired casually or temporarily to work at a sporting event or similar; and
- self-employed individuals working under the direction of a single "employer", using the "employer's tools", and paid on a fixed rate basis unconnected with the profitability of the business.

Pensioners, former employees, relatives of employees, job applicants and shareholders are not employees.

2. Input tax is **not** blocked in respect of business entertainment of **overseas customers** "of a kind and on a scale which is reasonable, having regard to all the circumstances". It is expected that HMRC will interpret this latter condition strictly.

Staff entertainment

Input tax may be recovered in respect of staff entertainment where it is provided in order to maintain and improve staff relations. If provided in other circumstances, any VAT incurred is not recoverable. *Ernst & Young* [1997] 8152 Notice 700/65

Where staff are permitted to bring a **guest** to a function, the input tax incurred in relation to the entertainment of non-employees must be identified. If no charge is made for the guests, HMRC will generally expect 50% of the input tax to be disallowed. If a **fee is charged**, HMRC may accept that it is not entertainment, as a tribunal has previously ruled that a characteristic of entertainment is that it is provided free of charge. *KPMG (No 2)* [1997]

Genuine **subsistence** expenditure is not entertainment, so input tax can be recovered in full on actual expenditure. However, no input tax is recoverable if the employee is paid a **flat-rate** subsistence allowance.

EXAMPLE

1. Mr A pays for a Christmas meal for all of his employees. This is staff entertainment and he can recover all of the input tax.

2. B Ltd pays for a summer ball, to which employees can bring a guest for free. B Ltd must apportion the input tax so that no recovery is made in relation to the proportion which relates to the guests.

3. C Ltd arranges a river trip for employees and contacts and charges everyone £5. This is not entertainment, as the trip is not being provided for free. Therefore C Ltd can recover all of the related input tax. C Ltd must also account for £0.83 output VAT on each £5 charge, however. (£5 x 1/6)

Capital assets

Input tax is not recoverable in respect of capital assets (for example a yacht) **used solely for** business entertainment purposes. On the sale of such goods, VAT is only chargeable on the excess of the proceeds over the original cost. 8154

However, if a capital asset is **used partly for** business entertainment and partly for other business purposes, the input tax must be apportioned. No recovery is available in respect of the input tax relating to business entertainment. On a subsequent sale of the asset, VAT must be charged on the full selling price.

Comment If capital assets bear the company's logo, it may be possible to argue that some of the expenditure was incurred for the purpose of advertising the business.

2. Cars

The availability of an input tax deduction on the acquisition of, or hiring of, cars is very restricted. It is therefore vital to know whether a particular vehicle is a car, as defined by the VAT provisions, since input tax can be fully deducted on other types of vehicle used for taxable business purposes. 8156

Definition

A motor car is defined for VAT purposes as a **vehicle which**: 8158 SI 1992/3222 reg 2
- is normally used on public roads and has three or more wheels;
- is constructed or adapted mainly for the carriage of passengers; and
- has roofed accommodation to the rear of the driver's seat which is fitted, or could be fitted, with side windows.

MEMO POINTS The following vehicles are excluded from being cars:
– ambulances, caravans, hearses, prison vans, and other vehicles constructed for a specific purpose which does not include the carriage of people;
– single seater vehicles (i.e. those with space for only a driver);
– vehicles with capacity for twelve or more passengers;
– vehicles weighing at least three tonnes when unladen; and
– vehicles which can carry a payload of at least one tonne.

Cases where input tax is deductible

8160 SI 1992/3222 reg 7(2), (2A) Input tax is deductible on the following types of qualifying car:
– stock for resale;
– cars acquired for the purpose of a car-related trade; and
– those acquired wholly for business use.

A **qualifying car** is one which has never been purchased by a non-taxable person, or on which input tax recovery has not been blocked for a taxable person. Normally a qualifying car will be a new or a used car where the previous owners were able to recover all the VAT incurred on their purchase. This definition includes, for example, cars sold by leasing companies.

Sch 6 para 1A VATA 1994 MEMO POINTS 1. A motor manufacturer or dealer can recover input tax in respect of a **stock-in-trade car**, which must be sold within 12 months of production or acquisition.
It is common for employees (and occasionally their relatives) to have private use of such cars, often for nominal consideration, and the business must account for output tax in this case. HMRC may issue a direction, within 3 years of a **demonstrator car** being made available to an employee, so that output tax is accounted for by the employer on the open-market value of the car.
SI 1992/3222 reg 7(2F) 2. A car acquired for the following purposes will not result in blocked input tax:
– use as a **taxi** to carry passengers;
– leasing to **disabled persons**, or to a business which undertakes such leasing;
– short-term **self-drive hire**, where the hirer (or his employee) will drive the car; or
– driving instruction given by a **driving school**.

8162 HMRC will usually only accept the following situations as constituting **wholly business use**:
– valid pool cars;
– car leasing business; and
– vehicles which are unsuitable for private use, such as marked emergency cars, or those where steps have been taken to prevent private use.

If there is any element of private use, however small, no deduction is available. The input tax cannot be **apportioned** between business and private elements. If it is intended that the car be made available for private use it will not be acquired wholly for business use. Traders are assumed for this purpose to intend the likely consequences of their actions.

MEMO POINTS 1. A valid **pool car** is:
– kept at the business premises;
– never kept overnight at a private home;
– never allocated to a single employee; and
– any private use (such as lunch stops) is incidental.
2. A **leased car** is used exclusively for business purposes, unless it is:
– let on uncommercial terms not at arm's length; or
– made available for private use by the lessor and not let on hire.
Otherwise, lessors can reclaim input tax, it being irrelevant whether there is any private use of the car by the lessee.

EXAMPLE
1. A cigarette vending machine operator acquired a Lamborghini motor car for use in his business, which involved visiting night clubs. He conducted his business 7 days a week, from 8am to midnight or later and he never made personal use of the car. However, as he was unable to obtain insurance which excluded private use, it was held that he must be taken to have intended the car to be made available to him for private use, so no input tax could be recovered. *C & E v Upton (t/a Fagomatic)* [2001]

2. Contrast the above case with that involving a company which acquired a car for wholly business purposes, even though the car was driven by the company's sole employee, the director. The car's insurance cover permitted private use, but this was only because the broker had stated that it was impossible to insure a car for business use only. A Board minute noted that the company intended

to limit the use of the vehicle to business only, so if the car had been used privately, this would have constituted a breach of the employee's contract of employment. Therefore the input tax was deductible. *Elm Milk Ltd v HMRC* [2006]

All other cars

Input tax incurred on the acquisition cost of all other motor cars is **blocked**. For these purposes, hire purchase is treated as an outright acquisition. In addition, the recovery of input tax on **leased cars** is restricted to 50%. 8164

Acquisition cost The cost of the car includes delivery charges and **optional accessories** fitted by the supplier before the car is delivered, even if invoiced separately. The normal rules governing the recovery of input tax apply to accessories or modifications subsequently supplied. It is therefore advisable to acquire the car first, then fit the accessories. 8166

So as long as the car is used partly for a business purpose, and provided that the costs are paid by the business, input tax on **repairs and maintenance** can be recovered in full. There is no apportionment for business/non-business use.

Leased cars For **short hires** which do not exceed 10 days because the car is needed for a specific business trip, there is no restriction on the input tax recovery. 8168 Notice 700/64 para 4.4

Otherwise, there is a 50% reduction in the amount of input tax which can be recovered on a qualifying car (¶8160). The reduction is to take account of any private use, which is presumed to occur. Even if there is **no private use**, input tax recovery is restricted to 50%.

If the lessee is a taxi driver, car hire firm, or driving instructor, the 50% restriction does not apply.

The lessor must notify the lessee that the car is a qualifying car on any invoice.

When a **lease is terminated**, the leasing company may charge an additional payment, or may refund an amount to the customer. In either case, the leasing company may choose whether to treat the event as a taxable supply, or a supply outside the scope of VAT. 8170

If an **additional payment** is charged with VAT, the lessee may recover 100% of the VAT charged.

If a **refund** is made, the lessee must account for 50% of the VAT in respect of the rebate, provided that only 50% of the input tax was recovered in respect of the original charges.

MEMO POINTS If there is a separate charge under the leasing agreement for repairs and maintenance, 100% of the VAT incurred on this charge can be recovered.

EXAMPLE Mr D, who is VAT-registered, decides to terminate the lease of his car. The leasing company treats the termination as a taxable supply.
If a termination payment of £200 net is charged, the related input tax of £40 can be recovered by Mr D.
If the termination charge is netted against the lease payments already made, and a rebate of £100 is due to Mr D, he only needs to account for £10 of output tax, being 50% of the VAT due on £100.

3. Provision of accommodation to director

Input tax incurred on any goods or services used to provide any domestic accommodation to a director, or anyone connected with him (¶5570), is not recoverable. There is no requirement for the company to own the property and it is irrelevant whether the director pays any consideration in return for using the accommodation. 8172 s 24(3) VATA 1994

For this purpose, a director is **defined** as a: s 24(7) VATA 1994
- member of the board of directors which manages the company;
- single director who manages the company; or
- member of the company where the company is managed by its members.

s 24(5) VATA 1994 As an exception, where a director uses a part of his accommodation for **business purposes** input tax can be recovered on the business proportion of the expenses, such as repairs. Apportionment should be undertaken using an objective method, such as on a time-used or floor-area basis.

C. Deductible input tax

8176 Assuming that input tax relates to taxable business activities, in order for it to be recoverable the following criteria must be met:
- an actual supply, importation, acquisition or reverse charge must have been made;
- the supply must have been made to the claimant;
- VAT must have been correctly charged; and
- sufficient evidence must be retained.

MEMO POINTS A claim for input tax cannot be made until the evidence required to substantiate the claim is held.

Supply made

8178 s 24(1) VATA 1994 Usually it is obvious whether a supply has actually been made. However, an **aborted** supply will not result in recoverable input tax, even where the customer pays for a supply (including VAT) which he never receives.

To the claimant

8180 A business can only recover input tax incurred on supplies actually received by the business. Therefore if the supply is made to a **third party**, no recovery can be made.

This rule is relaxed in certain circumstances where the supply is made **to an employee** of the business, provided that the supply is for business purposes. In this situation, the supply is treated as being made to the business and not the employee. This would include items such as subsistence and removal expenses incurred as a result of business relocation, but not perks such as gym membership.

EXAMPLE

1. The appellant was in financial difficulties and needed to restructure its finances. In these circumstances banks and other creditors require the provision of financial information before deciding to lend. The appellant's adviser, an accountancy firm, set up an arrangement whereby the appellant was a party to the engagement with the banks. The adviser liaised with the relevant banks and other creditors and carried out a strategic review. The adviser's bills were made out to and paid by the appellant. HMRC took the view that the appellant was not entitled to recover VAT on the adviser's fees. Whilst they accepted that the appellant had benefited from the services, they considered that only the banks, as "engaging institutions", were the recipients of the adviser's supplies. The First-tier Tribunal disagreed with HMRC and allowed the appeal. This was on the basis that the appellant:
- requested the review and received a copy of the report;
- authorised the adviser to do the work, and undertook to pay;
- used the services for the purpose of the business; and
- was involved in deciding who was appointed.

However, the Upper Tribunal allowed HMRC's appeal. The accountancy services were supplied to the lending in stitutions and the appellant merely contracted to pay for the services, not to receive any services. *HMRC v Airtours Holiday Transport Ltd* [2010]

2. HMRC sought to disallow input tax on estate agent fees which were incurred by a builder. In order to incentivise prospective housebuyers, the builder agreed to pay the fees relating to the sale of the buyers' old houses.
The argument centred on whether the estate agent's services were supplied to the builder as well as to the housebuyer.

The House of Lords held that the builder had a valid claim to input tax on the agency fees because it received a supply of services, as it:
- selected and instructed the estate agent;
- agreed the selling price of the housebuyer's old home based on the agent's valuation; and
- made sure the agent was trying to sell the house as quickly as possible.

The builder therefore had control over the sale of the housebuyer's old house. In addition, the housebuyer was invited to enter into an agreement with the agent so that no other agent could be instructed. *C & E v Redrow Group plc* [1999]

Road fuel Where a **business purchases** road fuel, it has three options with regard to VAT: 8182
a. reclaim all input tax and pay a scale charge via its VAT return for any private mileage;
b. keep a mileage log and only reclaim input tax on the business miles; or
c. make no claim for input tax on any road fuel (especially if total mileage is low).

If the cost of the fuel is **reimbursed** or a **mileage allowance** is paid, this is treated as expenditure incurred for business purposes, even where some private mileage has been incurred. Again scale charges would be relevant for any fuel provided for private use. SI 1991/2306; s 56 VATA 1994

In March 2005 the ECJ concluded that the UK rules on road fuel were incompatible with the EU rules. As a result input tax can now only be **claimed** where the employer holds a valid VAT invoice (this can be a full or less detailed invoice, depending on the amount of fuel purchased). Business Brief 22/05

Receipts may cover business fuel used in more than one VAT period (particularly where fuel is purchased towards the end of the period). However, HMRC state that a claim cannot be supported by a receipt which is dated after the date of an expense claim. They advise that employees should retain all fuel invoices, so that the value of their claims are always covered by a receipt. Information Sheet 8/05

EXAMPLE Mr B is an employee who drives 1,010 miles on behalf of his employer in April 2012. His employer allows employees to claim 40p per mile, with 12p representing petrol costs.
So the amount to be reimbursed in respect of petrol is £121.20. (£1,010 × 0.12)
The employer reclaims input tax of £20.20. (£121.20 × 1/6)
Mr B retains the following invoices for April:

Date	£
4 April	46.40
14 April	15.87
18 April	45.56
25 April	35.22
Total	143.05

As Mr B only needs £121.20 to support his fuel costs, the £15.87 receipt could be lost, and there would still be sufficient receipts for the employer to reclaim input tax.

VAT correctly charged

The amount of input tax recoverable is the amount correctly chargeable in respect of the supply. Therefore where the supplier charges an **incorrect** amount of VAT, the business may only claim credit for the amount which should have been charged. For the rules for accounting for VAT on incorrect invoices, see ¶9232. 8184 s 4 VATA 1994

If a **non-registered person** incorrectly charges VAT, by concession HMRC may allow a business to recover it as input tax, provided that the business acted in good faith and did not have close knowledge of the supplier's business. The supplier must account to HMRC for the amount charged as VAT.

Missing trader fraud Input tax recovery cannot be denied if the trader has taken all reasonable steps to establish the transactions it is entering into are genuine. If it is not possible for a trader to identify fraud in a supply chain, no matter what due diligence is done, input tax should be repaid. However, where the trader knew, or ought to have known, 8186 that its transactions were connected with fraud, input tax can be denied. *HMRC v Livewire Telecom Ltd* [2009]; *Kittel v Belgium* [2006]

8187 As a fraud prevention measure, **transactions involving** mobile phones, computer chips and similar electronic goods require the customer to account for VAT under a reverse charge procedure. This also applies to supplies of emissions allowances.

MEMO POINTS 1. Carousel fraud **consists** of a chain of supplies where one of the traders either goes missing or uses a hijacked VAT number. In both cases the VAT charged on the supply is stolen, instead of being paid over to the authorities. It usually involves intra-EU trade, and the goods can go around the chain many times, hence the name carousel.

s 55A VATA 1994
HMRC Brief 24/07
Information Sheet 8/07

2. The **reverse charge** mechanism (¶9110) affects businesses which are buying and/or selling any of the following goods:
a. mobile telephones, including related accessories supplied in a single package, BlackBerrys and Pay As You Go phones, but excluding phones which are supplied with an airtime contract; and
b. computer chips, which include:
– all integrated circuits (i.e. central processing units or CPUs);
– discrete integrated circuit devices i.e. microprocessors or microprocessor units (MPUs) and microcontrollers or microcontroller units (MCUs); and
– chipsets, which are the dedicated cluster of integrated circuits which support MPUs.
The reverse charge only applies to goods with a VAT-exclusive **value** of £5,000 or more, when supplied to a VAT-registered business which will use them for business purposes. HMRC state that the normal commercial checks undertaken by traders in relation to their **customers** are sufficient when deciding whether the customer will apply the reverse charge. Where a trader takes no such action, he could be liable to pay any VAT not paid by the customer.
Reverse Charge Sales Lists are submitted online and follow the submission dates of the trader's normal VAT returns (¶9216). VAT registration numbers of customers must be obtained to complete these lists.
The supplier's **VAT invoice** must indicate that the reverse charge applies and state that the customer is required to account for the VAT.

Evidence

8188 In order to make a claim for recoverable input tax, the business must have evidence of the amount of VAT paid on acquisition, which generally takes the **form** of a valid VAT invoice (¶8306). A pro-forma invoice is not a valid invoice for these purposes.

s 24(6) VATA 1994

There is no invoice requirement for the following types of **supplies up to a value of £25** (including VAT):
– calls from public or private telephones;
– supplies through coin-operated machines;
– toll charges; and
– car parking charges (excluding charges from on-street meters which are not subject to VAT).

For **supplies at £250 or less**, a less detailed invoice may be issued by the supplier (¶8322).

MEMO POINTS 1. Where the supply was made by a **cash and carry wholesaler**, the product code list must be retained with the till roll.
2. For **non-UK supplies**, the following types of evidence are expected:
– for EU acquisitions (¶8937), the required documentation of the EU state, including a description of the goods, VAT numbers of the supplier and customer, and the VAT-exclusive price;
– for services (¶9106), an invoice from the overseas supplier; and
– for imported goods (¶9037), certificate C79.
3. In certain trade sectors, a higher level of proof is required of the genuine commercial purpose of the transaction to combat carousel fraud. The sectors affected are:
– **telephones** and related equipment, including parts and accessories, made or adapted for use in connection with telephones or telecommunication;
– **computers** and any other equipment, including parts, accessories and software, made or adapted for use in connection with computers or computer systems (this includes satellite navigation systems); and
– **electronic goods** used for leisure, amusement or entertainment.

If the invoice **is not issued in the VAT period** in which the supply is made, the business cannot claim credit for the input tax incurred until the VAT period in which the invoice is obtained. A claim for input tax cannot be made until the evidence required to substantiate the claim is held. 8190 s 29(2) VATA 1994

If a business **loses an invoice** it must obtain a duplicate from the supplier. The duplicate must be clearly marked as such because a simple photocopy of the original invoice, without any endorsement, is not acceptable.

D. Making a claim

A claim for input tax is made by deducting recoverable input tax for the VAT period from the amount of output tax due on supplies. 8192 s 25 VATA 1994 SI 1995/2518 reg 29

The amounts must be shown on the VAT return for the appropriate period.

Where the input tax incurred exceeds output tax, a refund is due (¶9260).

Timing

The **general rule** is that a claim for recoverable input tax should be made in the VAT period in which the tax point (¶7902) for the expenditure occurs. This will be shown on the purchase invoice. 8194 s 25(2) VATA 1994

MEMO POINTS 1. Smaller businesses may be eligible to account for VAT using the **cash accounting** scheme (¶8375), whereby input tax is recovered in the VAT period in which payment is made.
2. It is particularly important that **traders making any exempt supplies** claim input tax in the correct period, due to the partial exemption calculation that is required (¶8205).

If input tax is **not claimed** during the period in which credit was due, it may be claimed within the 4 years following the due date of submission of the VAT return for the period in which evidence for the claim was held. For example, if input tax should have been claimed on a return for the period ending 31 March 2007, a claim will still be valid up to 30 April 2011. 8196 SI 1995/2518 reg 29

Failure to pay supplier

If a taxable person does not pay his supplier **within** 6 months, the related input tax already recovered must be repaid to HMRC. 8198 s 26A VATA 1994

If the invoice is **subsequently paid** the input tax can be claimed again. In practice, if the invoice is paid within the VAT period when the 6-month limit expires, no repayment is necessary.

SECTION 2

Partial exemption

Input tax incurred on goods or services used in the course of making exempt supplies is not recoverable, and is known as "**exempt input tax**". Subject to the **de minimis limits** (¶8218) input tax which relates to exempt supplies cannot be recovered. A person who makes **only exempt** supplies is not able to register or recover any input tax. A person who makes **only taxable** supplies can recover all input tax incurred, subject to satisfying the relevant criteria (¶8176). A business making **both taxable and exempt** supplies and whose exempt input tax 8205 Notice 706 is over the de minimis limit is said to be **partly exempt**, and a special calculation is required to determine the proportion of input tax which is recoverable.

SI 1995/2518 reg 103

MEMO POINTS Taxable supplies include supplies of goods or services **made outside the UK** which would be taxable if made in the UK.

Calculating recoverable input tax

8207 A business making taxable and exempt supplies must go through the following process in order to calculate recoverable input tax. Step 1 is to identify input tax that can be exclusively attributed to taxable or exempt supplies. The more input tax that can be properly attributed to taxable supplies, the better, as this will increase the recovery rate overall. Step 2 is to apportion the remaining input tax between taxable and exempt, using one of the methods described below. If total input tax attributable to exempt supplies is below the de minimis limits (¶8218), it is recoverable. This procedure is undertaken for each VAT period and then reviewed again at the end of each VAT year.

Direct attribution

8208 Direct attribution of input tax is the identification of supplies of goods and services received that are used or intended to be **used exclusively** in making:
- taxable supplies; or
- exempt supplies.

Wherever possible, any input tax incurred should be attributed directly to related supplies, based on the **actual or intended use** of the goods or services when they are received. For example, a business incurring accountancy fees in respect of a property disposal should attribute the input tax incurred to the supply of the building.

However, input tax can only be directly attributed if the **whole of the supply** to which the input tax relates is used exclusively for either taxable or wholly exempt supplies, and there is a direct and immediate link. Where this is not possible, the related input tax will be treated as residual input tax.

Input tax on supplies of goods and services that are used, or to be used, exclusively in making taxable supplies or other supplies that carry the right to deduct can be recovered in full. In principle the input tax on supplies of goods and services used, or to be used, exclusively in making exempt supplies, or other supplies in respect of which input tax is non-recoverable, cannot be deducted.

VAT that **cannot be directly attributed** to either taxable supplies or to exempt supplies, because it relates to both, for example telephone bills and accountancy fees, is residual input tax. It is also known as "non-attributable" input tax.

EXAMPLE Mr A purchases a roll of carpet on which he incurs input tax of £150. He makes taxable supplies (75%) and exempt supplies (25%) from the office where the carpet is fitted.
As the carpet was acquired in a single purchase, he cannot directly attribute 75% of the input tax suffered to taxable supplies, so all of it is residual.

HMRC Brief 65/09

MEMO POINTS 1. The issue in this case was whether in-house opera production costs (such as fees for the musicians and the cost of making the set and props) had a link to taxable supplies made by the opera company (an exempt cultural body), such as sponsorship, programme sales and CD sales, or whether the costs were directly related only to exempt sales of tickets. The tribunal could see a link to taxable supplies as well as exempt supplies and decided that the VAT incurred should be apportioned. As a consequence, HMRC have revised their view on theatre production costs. HMRC accept that production costs can be residual (that is, not attributable solely to either taxable or exempt outputs) but only if they relate to specific taxable supplies as well as exempt admissions. HMRC's examples of when production costs relate to taxable supplies include where a theatre has contracted, or intends, to:
- secure sponsorship – the sponsorship must relate to an event or a clearly defined run of events over a clearly defined time and putting on the shows must be a condition of the sponsorship;
- take the production on tour; or
- record the show for later sale on CD or other media.

HMRC maintain that securing general corporate sponsorship does not make production costs residual even if the sponsorship package includes the provision of seats at performances. Similarly, catering supplies which arise as a consequence of admission do not make production costs residual. HMRC suggest that if the standard method (¶8215) is used, the inclusion of catering and refreshment supplies in the values-based apportionment formula may trigger the standard method override (¶8225) and require the theatre to carry out a use-based calculation. *Garsington Opera* [2009]
2. The tribunal has also considered the concept of the direct and immediate link between input tax and exempt activities, in a case concerning advertising costs incurred by an estate agent making taxable supplies of estate agency services, where exempt mortgage services were also offered by a company in the same VAT group. HMRC argued that all the adverts promoted the business as a whole and there was a direct link between the exempt mortgage services and the advertising material, and therefore all the input VAT incurred on advertising costs should be apportioned. The tribunal ruled that the VAT incurred in advertising houses for sale related only to the taxable supplies of estate agency services, as long as the advert did not mention that the advertiser also offered mortgage services. There was no direct link to exempt supplies in this case, therefore VAT incurred on these adverts was recoverable in full. However, input tax could not be wholly attributed to standard-rated supplies where the mortgage services were specifically referred to in advertising; in that case the input tax could only be recovered according to the partial exemption method. *Skipton Building Society* [2009]

Residual input tax

Residual input tax is the input tax incurred on goods or services which the business uses, or intends to use, in making both taxable and exempt supplies, and on general overheads. **8210** SI 1995/2518 reg 101

In many cases it will be impossible to allocate costs directly to a related supply, and residual input tax will result. For example, the annual audit of most traders is not attributable to any specific supply that they make. This input tax must be **apportioned** between exempt and taxable supplies, and the amount applicable to exempt supplies is then added to that already allocated, to give a total amount which is known as **exempt input tax**.

The result of the apportionment is **provisional** until a review is carried out at the end of the VAT year, when the calculation is undertaken on an annual basis (known as an annual adjustment). Any apportionment must be based on the facts known at the time that the input tax is incurred. In addition, an adjustment will be necessary where there is a change from the original intended use within 6 years (¶8237).

Choice of methods

There are two methods of calculating the recoverable portion of residual input tax: **8213**

a. the **standard method**, which is the default option, has fixed rules, and is relatively simple; or

b. a **bespoke special method** negotiated with HMRC.

Most businesses can use the standard method without the prior approval of HMRC, unless they are already using a special method. The standard method is commonly used by smaller businesses as it is simple to apply and is usually appropriate to their needs.

Where changes are required to the standard method to meet the needs of the business, a **special method** must be agreed. For example, this would include even simple changes to the standard method, such as allocating costs on a floor-space basis.

1. Standard method

The standard method is the calculation that **must be used** unless HMRC have given approval to use a special method. HMRC will accept use of the standard method, provided that the result it produces is fair and reasonable. Generally, its use is acceptable for most partly exempt businesses, particularly smaller ones. The standard method enables traders to calculate the proportion of residual input tax that can be attributed to taxable supplies and recovered. It works by attributing the residual input tax according to the value of taxable and exempt supplies made in the tax period in which the residual input tax is incurred. **8215** SI 1995/2518 reg 101 Information Sheet 4/09

Using the standard method, the percentage of residual input tax attributable to taxable supplies, and therefore recoverable, is **calculated** by applying the following formula:

$$\frac{\text{VAT-exclusive value of taxable supplies in period}}{\text{VAT-exclusive value of all supplies in period}} \times 100$$

The standard method **covers input tax on all supplies** except for input tax incurred in relation to investment gold. Input tax which relates to supplies:
- of financial instruments (e.g. shares and bonds); or
- which are made from overseas establishments

are included in the standard method, but instead of using the values-based calculation, input tax incurred on these supplies must be attributed based on use.

All remaining input tax is recovered by reference to the values-based calculation (unless a new partly exempt business opts to recover on the basis of use). For larger businesses with unusual circumstances, an override adjustment will be required at the end of the VAT year (¶8225).

A business which is **newly partly exempt** can opt to recover input tax on the **basis of use** rather than the value of taxable and exempt supplies. This means that input tax is attributed in accordance with the use, or intended use, of VATable costs in making taxable supplies. The use-based calculation can be applied during the period when exempt input tax was first incurred, which will be either:
- the registration period (i.e. the period running from the date of registration to the day before the start of the first VAT year);
- the first VAT year (normally the first period of 12 months commencing on 1 April, 1 May or 1 June following the end of the registration period); or
- any VAT year, as long as no exempt input tax was incurred in the previous VAT year.

Once the relevant period has expired, the business must revert to the normal values-based calculation. Where a business calculates its recovery of input tax on the basis of use, it is also required to calculate its annual adjustment (¶8220) on the basis of use to ensure consistency. A newly partly exempt business may choose to apply the normal calculation during each VAT period (i.e. using the values of taxable and exempt supplies), but then calculate a use-based annual adjustment. In any event, there is no need to notify HMRC.

8216 If the result of the values-based formula is not a whole number, it should be **rounded up** to the next whole number, except where a business has residual input tax in excess of £400,000 per month, when the percentage must be stated to 2 decimal places.

The value of the following supplies is **excluded** from the totals used in the formula:
- supplies of capital goods which have been used in the business (a capital good for this purpose has substantial durability and value compared to other items used in the day-to-day business) – the principle behind excluding such supplies is to avoid the distortion caused by one-off supplies;
- self-supplies (¶7888, ¶8830);
- incidental financial, land or property transactions;
- the value of any goods and services which are neither taxable nor exempt supplies (¶7848) (e.g. a transfer of a going concern (¶8596)); and
- the value of imported services (¶9108).

EXAMPLE Mr B is completing his VAT return for the quarter ended 30 June. From his VAT records, he has extracted the following information:

	£
Total input tax incurred	11,950
Input tax on business entertainment	150
Input tax wholly attributable to taxable supplies	4,050
Input tax wholly attributable to exempt supplies	2,500
Value of all taxable supplies (excluding VAT)	48,000
Value of exempt supplies	20,000
Value of business machine sold (excluding VAT)	2,000

The residual input tax is calculated as follows:

	£	£
Total input tax incurred		11,950
Less: Business entertainment (blocked)	150	
Attributable to taxable supplies (fully recoverable)	4,050	
Attributable to exempt supplies (irrecoverable)	2,500	
		(6,700)
		5,250

Value of taxable supplies is £46,000. (£48,000 – £2,000)
Value of all supplies is £66,000. (£48,000 + £20,000 – £2,000)
The proportion of residual input tax attributable to taxable supplies is therefore 69.69%.

$$\frac{46{,}000}{66{,}000} \times 100$$

This is rounded up to 70%
Recoverable input tax:

	£
Input tax attributable to wholly taxable supplies	4,050
Proportion of residual input tax (70% × £5,250)	3,675
	7,725

De minimis exempt input tax

8218 SI 1995/2518 reg 106

A business may be treated as fully taxable, and therefore recover all input tax incurred in a particular VAT period, where the amount of exempt input tax is below both of the following de minimis **limits**:

a. £625 per month on average (equivalent to £7,500 per annum); and
b. less than one half of the total input tax for the period.

These limits are also applicable for the annual adjustment.

MEMO POINTS 1. For this purpose, exempt input tax is the **aggregate** input tax resulting from the attribution and apportionment stages.
2. Any adjustments under the **capital goods scheme** (¶8250) are ignored when determining if the de minimis limits apply.
3. For **VAT groups**, the limits apply to the whole group.

EXAMPLE Continuing the previous example at ¶8216, the input tax attributable to exempt supplies for the period is as follows:

	£
Input tax attributable to wholly exempt supplies	2,500
Proportion of residual input tax (30% × £5,250)	1,575
	4,075

Monthly average (£4,075/3)	£1,358
One half of total input tax for period ((£11,950 – £150)/2)	£5,900

Although the exempt input tax is less than one half of the total input tax for the period, it exceeds £625 as a monthly average. The input tax attributable to exempt supplies is therefore above the de minimis limit for the period, so Mr B is unable to recover any of the input tax attributable to exempt supplies.

Businesses with exempt supplies that are less than 50% of total supplies may apply the simpler, though more stringent, tests that: 8219
- **total** input tax is less than £625 per month on average; or, if not, that
- total input tax less **input tax directly attributable to taxable supplies** is less than £625 per month on average.

If either of these tests is passed the usual de minimis tests will inevitably be passed but without such detailed calculations. If either of these tests is passed on an annual basis the trader can provisionally recover all input tax for the following year (but must still pass one of the tests for the following year on the annual basis if provisional recovery is to be made permanent), provided that input tax for the following year is not expected to exceed £1 million.

Annual adjustment

8220 SI 1995/2518 reg 107 The amount of residual input tax a business may claim for each VAT period is a provisional figure. At the **end of the VAT year** (¶8342), the position must be recalculated for the whole of that VAT year to remove any anomalies due, for example, to seasonal variations. The annual adjustment also allows the business to reconsider the use of goods or services over a longer period and to re-evaluate the position with regard to the de minimis limits.

EXAMPLE Continuing the example at ¶8216, Mr B claims the following non-attributable input tax in the VAT year ended 31 March:

Quarter ended	Recovered residual input tax £	Irrecoverable residual input tax £	Total residual input tax £
30 June	3,675	1,575	5,250
30 September	4,000	900	4,900
31 December	5,000	2,025	7,025
31 March	5,000	Nil	5,000
Total	17,675	4,500	22,175

Mr B makes the following supplies during the VAT year ended 31 March:

	£
Taxable supplies	417,000
Exempt supplies	125,000
Total	542,000

Assume Mr B has incurred exempt input tax of £10,000, which is above the de minimis limits. The recoverable input tax for the year is calculated as 77%. (417,000/542,000 rounded up)
Applying this to the residual input tax gives £17,075. (77% × £22,175)
Total input tax already recovered is £17,675 (from the table above).
Therefore £600 is owed to HMRC and should be disclosed as output tax.

However, if Mr B had initial exempt input tax of £2,000, the total exempt input tax would only be £7,100 once the exempt residual input tax is added. (£22,175 – £17,075 + £2,000)
If the amount of £7,100 satisfies both de minimis limits, Mr B can recover all of his input tax, which would lead to an annual adjustment of £6,500 in his favour. (£22,175 + £2,000 – £17,675)

MEMO POINTS A trader has the option to use his previous year's VAT recovery percentage (ignoring both the de minimis rules (¶8218) and any override calculation (¶8225)) when calculating the provisional amount of residual input tax claimable in each VAT period. The annual adjustment will then be used to calculate the amount of recoverable input tax for the whole year using actual figures for taxable and exempt supplies. There is no need to notify HMRC when using this method of calculation, although the chosen method (i.e. either using the past year's recovery rate or calculating the rate afresh for each VAT period) must be applied consistently during the VAT year.

8222 When a business **incurs exempt input tax for the first time**, the annual adjustment will be made for the period beginning with the first day of the VAT period in which exempt input tax was incurred, and ending at the end of the VAT cycle. If this is a single VAT period, no annual adjustment is required.

When a **business first registers for VAT**, a period known as the registration period must be identified. This is the period from the date of registration to the day preceding the first full VAT cycle.

If a business incurs exempt input tax during the registration period, the annual adjustment is required for the VAT period beginning on the date that exempt input tax is incurred, and ending on the last day of the registration period. However, if exempt input tax is first incurred during the VAT period ending on the last day of the registration period, no annual adjustment is required.

If a business **belatedly registers** for VAT, the first VAT return may be for a period in excess of 1 year. This period must be split, for partial exemption purposes, into a registration period and subsequent VAT cycles. A separate annual adjustment must be carried out for each of these periods.

EXAMPLE C Ltd was required to register for VAT with effect from 1 January 2011 but did not actually register until 25 January 2012. HMRC therefore backdate the registration and allocate the business a VAT year ending on 31 March.
The first VAT return will cover the period from 1 January 2011 to 31 March 2012. This period is split into the registration period (1 January 2011 to 31 March 2011) and the first VAT year (1 April 2011 to 31 March 2012).
If the company first incurs exempt input tax on 25 January 2011, no annual adjustment will be required, because this is within the last VAT period in the registration period.

The annual adjustment is normally included in the **VAT return** for the first period after the end of the VAT year. Under the standard method, a trader has the option to make the annual adjustment on the last VAT return of the VAT year, rather than the first VAT return after the end of the VAT year. If a business ceases to be registered for VAT, the annual adjustment must be made on the final VAT return. **8223**

If the recalculation shows that the value of exempt input tax was within the **de minimis limits**, any input tax not previously claimed is included on the return as underclaimed input tax.

The annual adjustment may not be used to correct **errors** in previous returns. Any genuine errors must be notified to HMRC in accordance with the usual rules (¶9222).

Override for larger businesses

The override, which is a one-off adjustment, only affects businesses with **residual input tax of at least** £50,000 per year (£25,000 for group companies outside a VAT group), and is intended to attack certain VAT avoidance schemes. **8225** SI 1995/2518 reg 107A Information Sheet 4/02

An adjustment must be made if the input tax deducted is substantially different from the amount which would have been deducted **based on use**, or intended use, in making taxable supplies during the year.

A difference is **substantial** if it is at least £25,000, and exceeds the lower of £50,000 and 50% of the residual input tax incurred. So any difference:
- below £25,000 will not cause an override adjustment;
- greater than £25,000, but less than £50,000, must be at least 50% of the residual tax to cause an adjustment.

MEMO POINTS 1. The residual input tax limits are pro-rated for **shorter periods** of less than a year.
2. **Group company** means a company which must be included in consolidated accounts, or would be but for an accounting exemption. See *Accountancy Memo* for further details.
3. See *VAT Memo* for further information on the override.

2. Special methods

Where a business believes that the standard method does not give a fair and reasonable result, it may apply to HMRC to use a special method. The method must cover all the business' activities, and be easy to apply and check. **8228** SI 1995/2518 reg 102

In general, a special method will dictate how the direct attribution is undertaken, and how apportionment is then achieved.

A business must have written approval from HMRC to use a special method, otherwise the standard method must be used.

MEMO POINTS 1. HMRC can direct that a special method must be used if the standard method does not give a fair and reasonable result. The taxpayer must still suggest the appropriate method to use.

2. Businesses may agree a **single** special input tax recovery method to take account not only of **exempt** use but also of **non-business** use.

Calculation

8230 Notice 706 para 6.7 The suitability of a special method will depend on the nature of a particular business. HMRC have given some **suggestions** of special methods they might accept:
- the ratio of the floor area of premises used for taxable supplies to the total area of the premises (unlikely to be appropriate to retailers);
- the ratio of the number of taxable transactions per year to the total number of transactions;
- separate calculations for different sectors of the business; or
- provisional claims based on the previous year's calculations, after the annual adjustment.

When using a special method, the **percentage** of residual input tax attributable to taxable supplies is calculated to at least 2 decimal places.

The **de minimis limits** (¶8218) also apply to a business using a special method.

Obtaining approval

8231 It is sometimes useful to discuss a proposed method with HMRC on an informal basis, before making a formal application.

HMRC Brief 23/07 A special method should be **proposed** in writing. A **declaration** must also accompany the application which states that the method is **fair and reasonable**. HMRC have provided a template for this purpose.

On receipt, HMRC then review the method and, unless problems are found, transpose it on to a special method letter before returning it to the business. If the business is content that the method reflects its proposal, it can adopt it as agreed without further correspondence. A special method will be rendered invalid where the business withholds relevant information.

If HMRC consider that a proposed method **cannot be approved**, they will discuss this with the business and invite a new proposal and declaration. A special method will be refused where:
- excess input tax will be recovered;
- the method cannot be checked; or
- not all input tax incurred by the business is covered.

MEMO POINTS The **declaration** must confirm that the whole method produces a fair result (both from the effective date of its application and also for the foreseeable future) based on knowledge that the person making it could reasonably be expected to have at the time.
If HMRC consider that the declaration is **incorrect** (i.e. the method is not fair, leading to an over-recovery of input tax, and the signatory could reasonably have known this at the time), they can serve an override notice (¶8233) to require the business to operate partial exemption on the basis of use. This would also affect any capital goods scheme adjustments. For methods agreed after 1 April 2007, such a notice can have effect from the method's inception. The business may appeal such a notice and also any related assessments. Interest and penalties may become due.

8232 The business must give an undertaking to keep HMRC informed of any subsequent **changes in circumstances** which will affect input tax recovery. HMRC can review the method at any time.

Control over the method

8233 As a last resort, HMRC have the power to **direct** a business to either use a particular method or to stop the current one being used. Directions are subject to appeal but there is no penal intention in their use. A directed method may be replaced by another special method proposed by the trader.

Business Brief 27/03 **Override notices** may be served by HMRC, or submitted for approval by the business, and they may be appealed. Their purpose is to make a correction because the existing special method no longer gives a fair and reasonable result, so they provide a temporary stop-gap only. The notice will expire once another method has been agreed, which could include the use of the standard method.

On receipt of a notice the business must continue to use its special method but make a subsequent adjustment based on the actual use of the expenditure to which the input tax relates, for any VAT periods beginning on or after the date stated on the notice.

3. Other adjustments

Input tax is recoverable based on the intended use of the goods or services at the time when they are received. If that intention changes, or the actual use does not reflect the initial intention, an adjustment may be required. For property and expensive computers, ships and aircraft, adjustments are required for the next 5 or 10 years, under the capital goods scheme (¶8250). The issue or receipt of credit notes can also create the need for an adjustment. However, where the VAT liability of a supply changes because the law is altered, no adjustment is required. 8235

MEMO POINTS Where goods or services are acquired in connection with intended supplies but the intended supplies are **aborted** and the goods and services are not used for alternative supplies, there is no adjustment under these provisions. *Belgium v Ghent Coal Terminal NV* [1998]

Change from original intended use

Where the intended use of an asset changes within 6 years and before the original intended use became actual use, an adjustment must be made to reflect the change in intended use. However, a change in **actual use** does not require any adjustment. 8237 SI 1995/2518 regs 108, 109

Thus where a trader acquires a machine which is **put into immediate use** for making exempt supplies, and then 3 years later the machine is used for making taxable supplies, this is a change of actual use, and no adjustment can be made.

However, where, for example, a trader intends to use some plant in the course of making an exempt supply but does not actually do so, then his **intended use** later changes to making a taxable supply, this requires an adjustment. This would also be the case where the plant was actually put into use for taxable supplies within the first 6 years, if it was not used for the original intended use.

MEMO POINTS 1. The 6-year **period starts** from the beginning of the VAT period when the original intention was formed – that is, the VAT period when the related input tax was first recognised.
2. The same partial exemption **method** as would have been used in the original attribution/apportionment must be used.

Where intended use changes, the clawback and payback provisions apply as shown in the following table: 8238

Original intention to use goods or services for	Revised intention/actual use	Provision applying
Wholly taxable supplies	Combination of taxable and exempt supplies	Clawback[1]
	Wholly exempt supplies	Clawback[1]
Combination of taxable and exempt supplies	Wholly exempt supplies	Clawback[1]
	Wholly taxable supplies	Payback[2]
Wholly exempt supplies	Combination of taxable and exempt supplies	Payback[2]
	Wholly taxable supplies	Payback[2]

Note:
1. When **clawback** applies, too much input tax has been recovered. The revised amount of input tax recoverable must be recalculated, based on the change of use, but still using the same apportionment method. The amount overclaimed is entered on the VAT return for the period in which the change of intention occurs.
2. When **payback** applies, there has been an under-recovery of input tax. In this instance, the business must write to HMRC with details of the amount repayable, calculated using the same apportionment method, but taking into account the change of use. Once this has been approved, the business can then make a corresponding entry on the next VAT return.

Credit notes

8240 PEM 4375 **Issued** If a credit note is issued in:
a. the **same VAT period** as the original supply, the partial exemption calculation should be completed with the amended value of supplies;
b. a **subsequent VAT period**, but within the same VAT year, no adjustment is made when the note is issued, as the annual adjustment will take account of the amended supply value; or
c. a **different VAT year**, the annual adjustment originally made must be recalculated to take account of the credit note, amending the value of supplies. Any necessary amendment should be included on the VAT return for the period in which the credit note is received. This amendment must be recorded separately from the VAT period's normal partial exemption calculation.

8241 PEM 4375 **Received** If a credit note is received in:
a. the **same VAT period** as the original supply, the partial exemption calculation should be made using the adjusted input tax amount, taking both the original invoice and the credit note into account;
b. a **subsequent VAT period**, but within the same VAT year, no adjustment is made when the note is received (however, the annual adjustment will take account of the reduced input tax); or
c. a **different VAT year**, the annual adjustment originally made must be recalculated to take account of the credit note, comparing to the de minimis limits where appropriate. Any necessary amendment should be included on the VAT return for the period in which the credit note is received. This amendment must be recorded separately from the VAT period's normal partial exemption calculation.

4. Special situations

Groups

8243 PEM 4300 Groups of companies may consider a group registration (¶7807) as a way of improving input tax recovery. Otherwise, inter-company charges (such as recharged salary costs) create unnecessary input tax which cannot be recovered by any recipient which is wholly or partly exempt.

A VAT group is treated as a single entity trading through its representative member, so only one **partial exemption method** can apply for the whole group (although the method can apply different calculation bases to different circumstances).

Subject to a direction from HMRC to the contrary, **supplies between group members** are disregarded for VAT purposes. When deciding whether a property or land transaction is incidental, the activities of the whole group need to be considered separately.

Transfer of a going concern

8244 Where a business is transferred as a going concern (¶8596), this is not a supply made by the transferor. Input tax incurred by the **transferor** in relation to the transfer (for example, legal fees) should be treated as an overhead. If only part of the business is being transferred, the input tax will be an overhead of the part of the business being transferred. Where that part of the business makes:
– only taxable supplies, the input tax is fully recoverable;
– only exempt supplies, the input tax is not recoverable; and
– both taxable and exempt supplies, the input tax is treated as residual, and recovered under the usual rules.

Any input tax incurred by the **transferee** in acquiring assets as part of a transfer of a going concern should be attributed to those assets. Where the assets are used for making wholly taxable supplies, the input tax is therefore recoverable. If the assets are used for making both taxable and exempt supplies, the input tax incurred must be treated as residual input tax. *C & E v UBAF Bank Ltd* [1996]

SECTION 3

Capital goods scheme

The capital goods scheme applies to businesses that make both taxable and exempt supplies, within a 5- or 10-year period depending on the type of asset acquired. It also applies to businesses that use assets partly for non-business purposes. 8250 Notice 706/2

Its aim is to ensure that input tax on computers, ships, aircraft and land interests of a certain value is recoverable in proportion to the asset's taxable use (or business use) over time. Taxable use refers to the use of the asset in making taxable supplies.

Comment Where taxable (or business) use remains consistent, the effect of the capital goods scheme on input tax recovery will be minimal.

1. General requirements

Affected assets

The capital goods scheme applies to: 8252 SI 1995/2518 reg 113
- **computer** hardware, **ships** and **aircraft** costing at least £50,000 (excluding VAT); and
- **land and property** with a value of at least £250,000 (excluding VAT), where VAT is incurred.

Where the business purchases such assets as **stock** for resale, the scheme will not apply unless the asset is actually used by the trader before being sold. If the trader's intention was to resell the asset, but this intention subsequently changes, the asset will be subject to the scheme from the date of acquisition. Adjustments are only required from the time that the asset was no longer held for resale.

Cost is the "VAT-bearing" expenditure on the asset, as opposed to the "input-tax-bearing" expenditure. This reflects the fact that from 1 January 2011 Lennartz accounting no longer applies to land, property, ships and aircraft, so there is no input tax on the non-business proportion of the expenditure.

Computer hardware The scheme will only apply where a **single item** of equipment exceeds a value of £50,000; typically this will be a mainframe computer or file server. Equipment which is manufactured by the trader himself is outside the scheme, as are software, networked personal computers, and computerised equipment (such as a telephone system or lift). 8254

Ships and aircraft With effect from 1 January 2011, the capital goods scheme applies to ships (which includes boats and other vessels) and aircraft, where the cost exceeds £50,000 (excluding VAT). For these assets, the expenditure to be taken into account includes amounts spent on: 8255
- acquisition and construction (including manufacture);
- refurbishment and fitting out; and
- alteration and (where relevant) extension.

Land and property Only property where VAT has been charged is relevant, hence zero-rated and exempt supplies are ignored. The following are also **excluded**: 8256
- property acquired for resale, or which is sold before it is used for any other purpose; and
- land acquired for a developer's land bank because of its profit potential.

Generally, buildings which are used solely for **residential or charitable** purposes are outside the scope of the scheme, although where there is a change of use from either of these purposes (¶8830 onwards), the scheme may apply.

The table shows the types of transactions which are **included** within this heading:

Situation	Criteria
Acquisition of land and buildings	Valued at more than £250,000[1]
Building constructed by owner	Taxable goods and services received are valued at £250,000 or more
Alteration, extension or annexe to a building carried out by the owner	Taxable goods and services received are valued at £250,000 or more
Self-supply (¶8830) resulting from a change of use of a residential or charitable building[2]	Valued at more than £250,000
Civil engineering work either bought in or constructed by the owner[3]	First brought into use on or after 3 July 1997; and taxable goods and services received since 3 July 1997 are valued at £250,000 or more
Refurbishment or fitting out of a building	Carried out on or after 3 July 1997; and taxable goods and services received since 3 July 1997 are valued at £250,000 or more

Note:
1. The value threshold includes the value of goods and services relating to the project. For leases, only the premium is taken into account unless the tenant is charged rent more than 12 months in advance, or is invoiced for a period exceeding a year.
2. Where the first payment of rent is zero-rated, any subsequent exempt supply is disregarded for the purposes of the scheme.
3. Civil engineering takes its everyday meaning, and includes works on bridges, roads, golf courses, and installation of pipes etc.

8257 Notice 706/2 paras 4.3 – 4.5

The value always **excludes** any zero-rated supplies, but **includes** any reduced-rated supplies and standard-rated supplies. Only capital expenditure is relevant, so for building works, directly attributable costs such as materials and labour are included in the value.

In addition, the following **professional fees** are also treated as part of the value:
- architect;
- site manager;
- surveyor;
- civil engineering contractor;
- security;
- demolition and clearing the site;
- equipment hire;
- haulage; and
- landscaping.

However, **indirect** expenses such as legal fees are excluded.

Notice 706/2 para 4.11

Goods can be included in the value of the property where they are fixed to its fabric, are generally immovable and will be sold with the building. However, items fixed to the floor for reasons of safety or security are not goods affixed for these purposes.

Private use of asset

8258 Where computer hardware is used for both business and private purposes, input tax may be treated as wholly or only partly deductible, depending on whether the apportionment method or Lennartz method is adopted (¶8142).

For the purposes of the capital goods scheme, the proportion of the asset's **value taken into account** will depend on the amount of input tax initially deductible. So for the Lennartz method, 100% of the value is taken into account. For an asset where input tax is apportioned only that proportion of the asset's value will be relevant.

Date of commencement

It is essential to identify correctly the date of acquisition, which is usually the date from which the rules of the scheme must be applied. 8260 SI 1995/2518 reg 114(4) Notice 706/2 para 5.3

For most **UK purchases** the date of acquisition is the date on the VAT invoice.

The table below sets out the date of commencement for **other types of acquisition**.

Circumstance	Date of acquisition
Imported computer hardware, ships and aircraft	Date of import entry
Assets acquired as part of a transfer of a going concern	See ¶8596
Building projects involving construction, alteration, extension or fitting out	Date of first use
Owner not registered on date of first use	Date of first use, so that the period within the capital goods scheme is reduced to that following registration, although the 5- or 10-year period runs from the date of first use

Review period

The period over which adjustments are required for change in use depends on the type of asset. 8262 SI 1995/2518 reg 114(3) Notice 706/2 para 5.2

Interval generally means the VAT year of the trader. So the first interval usually begins on the asset's acquisition and ends on 31 March, 30 April or 31 May, depending on the VAT stagger. However, the effect of the capital goods scheme does not actually start until the second interval.

Type of asset	Review period	Number of intervals	Number of adjustments
Computer hardware, ships and aircraft	5 years	5	4
Leasehold interest with less than 10 years to run when scheme starts	5 years	5	4
Other land and property	10 years	10	9

Records

Traders must keep separate records of: 8263
- the asset's description;
- its value;
- the amount of input tax recovered;
- the start and end dates of each interval;
- when adjustments are due; and
- the date and value of any disposal within the adjustment period.

It is recommended that these records are **kept for** the longer of 6 years and the length of the review period.

2. Calculation

Initial input tax recovery

The amount of input tax which may be claimed on acquisition is dependent upon the expected level of taxable (or business) use for the first VAT interval. 8265 SI 1995/2518 reg 116(1)

The level of **taxable (or business) use** is expressed as a percentage. An asset used exclusively in the making of taxable supplies has 100% taxable use, whereas an asset used exclusively in the making of exempt supplies has 0% taxable use.

The level of taxable use for assets related to both taxable and exempt supplies is calculated in accordance with the partial exemption rules (¶8205), and usually expressed to 2 decimal places. Where computer hardware is used for both business and **private purposes**, and input tax has been deducted under the Lennartz method, all of that input tax is taken account of in the scheme. Otherwise, where only a proportion of the VAT incurred is deductible as input tax, only that amount is relevant (¶8258).

Subsequent intervals where the asset retained

8267 SI 1995/2518 reg 115

No adjustments will be required when the VAT **use** of the asset **does not change** during the review period. So where an asset is continually used for exclusively taxable or exclusively exempt supplies throughout the period, the initial input tax recovery will be a fair result. The same applies to the business/non-business proportion.

The only instances where an **adjustment is required** are when the proportion of taxable or exempt use changes, or the proportion of business/non-business use changes.

8268 **Basic calculation** At the end of the second interval (and subsequent intervals), the adjustment percentage must be calculated. This is the difference between the level of taxable (or business) use for the first interval and the level of taxable (or business) use for the interval under consideration. The capital goods scheme adjustment is calculated using the following **formula**:

$$\frac{\text{Total input tax on item}}{\text{Number of intervals in review period (i.e. 5 or 10)}} \times \text{Adjustment percentage}$$

Note that the input tax to be adjusted is the input tax incurred, so a VAT rate change does not affect the calculation.

EXAMPLE A Ltd acquired a computer for £100,000 (input tax £17,500) on 1 June 2005, which had 80% taxable use during the period to 31 March 2006 (the first interval). So the initial input tax recovered was £14,000 (17,500 × 80%).

The level of taxable use increases to 90% for the year to 31 March 2007, and drops to 60% for the years to 31 March 2008, 31 March 2009 and 31 March 2010.

The capital goods scheme adjustments are calculated as follows:

Interval	Calculation	Adjustment £	Overall position £
1			14,000
2	$\frac{17,500}{5} \times (90 - 80)\%$	350	350
			14,350
3	$\frac{17,500}{5} \times (60 - 80)\%$	(700)	(700)
			13,650
4	$\frac{17,500}{5} \times (60 - 80)\%$	(700)	(700)
			12,950
5	$\frac{17,500}{5} \times (60 - 80)\%$	(700)	(700)
	Final input tax recovery		12,250

8272 **Reporting** Where the **level of taxable (or business) use** has **increased**, the business may claim additional input tax equal to the amount calculated.

Where the level of taxable (or business) use has **reduced**, the business must repay VAT to HMRC.

SI 1995/2518 reg 115(6)

Any capital goods scheme adjustments (whether positive or negative) must be recorded in the VAT account (¶9205) and included on the VAT **return** for the second VAT period after the end of the interval. This will generally be the return to 30 September, 31 October or 30 November. For businesses making monthly returns, the adjustment should be made on the VAT return to 31 May.

MEMO POINTS If a capital goods scheme adjustment is **not made** on the specified VAT return, another return may be used, subject to obtaining permission from HMRC.

Disposals

Sale Where the asset is sold during the review period, **two adjustments** are required: 8273 SI 1995/2518 reg 115(3)
a. the normal adjustment for the interval in which the sale occurs; and
b. an additional adjustment to take into account the remaining intervals after sale.
The **additional adjustment** depends on whether the sale is:
– taxable, in which case the level of taxable use is deemed to be 100%; or
– exempt, when the level of taxable use is deemed to be 0%.
In these circumstances, the amount of input tax recovered may not exceed the amount of output tax charged on the sale. However, HMRC have stated that this rule does not apply to computer equipment, and property is only affected where the anti-avoidance provisions apply (¶8274).

EXAMPLE C Ltd acquired a computer for £250,000 (input tax £50,000) which had 75% taxable use during the first interval.
The level of taxable use increased to 80% for the second interval. During the third interval, when the level of taxable use dropped to 53%, the computer was sold for £40,000 plus VAT of £8,000. As this was a taxable sale, the deemed use for the remaining intervals is 100%.
The capital goods scheme adjustments are calculated as follows:

Interval	Calculation	Additional adjustment £	Normal adjustment £	Overall position £
1	50,000 × 75%			37,500
2	$\frac{50{,}000}{5} \times (80 - 75)\%$		500	500
				38,000
3	$\frac{50{,}000}{5} \times (53 - 75)\%$		(2,200)	(2,200)
				35,800
4	$\frac{50{,}000}{5} \times (100 - 75)\%$	2,500		
5	$\frac{50{,}000}{5} \times (100 - 75)\%$	2,500		
		5,000		5,000
	Final input tax recovery			40,800

MEMO POINTS The **anti-avoidance** provisions result in input tax being **clawed back** on property where all of the following apply: 8274 Business Brief 30/97
– the total input tax recovered exceeds the output tax charged on the sale;
– there has been some exempt use of the property during the adjustment period, including the case where the onward sale is exempt;
– the transaction is not undertaken for commercial business reasons; and
– the business gains an unjustified VAT advantage as a result.
However, this does **not apply** in the case of a reduction in property value caused by market forces, such as where:
– an owner disposes of an item at a loss due to market conditions (such as a general downturn in property prices);
– the value of the item has depreciated; or
– the value of the item is reduced for other legitimate reasons (such as accepting a lower price to effect a quick sale).
It is up to the trader to decide whether he has obtained an **unfair VAT advantage**.
Where the test applies, an **adjustment** must be made to reduce the amount of input tax already recovered. To do this, the trader will need to calculate: SI 1995/2518 reg 115(3A)
– the net tax advantage; and
– how much of the net tax advantage is unjustified.
Some form of apportionment needs to be applied to work out the unjustified net tax advantage. HMRC suggest that an appropriate method may include the ratio of exempt and total supplies made.

8275 **Loss** In the event of loss, only the normal adjustment is made, treating the asset as if it had been owned for the whole interval and used in the same manner as before it was lost.

Loss for this purpose **includes** destruction or demolition, theft, and the expiry of a short-term lease.

Interaction with other taxes

8276 The scheme's adjustments affect capital allowances, research and development expenditure, and capital gains tax computations.

Where a capital goods scheme adjustment requires VAT to be paid to HMRC, this means that the cost of the asset is increased for the purposes of **capital allowances** (¶200). Conversely, where an amount of VAT is due from HMRC, this decreases the cost of the asset in the capital allowances computation. The timing of the increase/decrease to the cost of the asset occurs in the accounting period when the VAT adjustment is actually made (i.e. the last day of the VAT period of the return which includes the adjustment (¶8272)).

MEMO POINTS 1. A similar adjustment must be made for expenditure qualifying for **research and development** allowances (¶794).
2. Where **capital gains tax rollover relief** (¶6050) has been claimed, and the cost of the new asset changes because of a capital goods scheme adjustment, HMRC will not require the relief to be disturbed.

EXAMPLE D Ltd prepares accounts to 30 June but has a VAT year of 31 March. The company acquired a computer on 1 August 2010 at a cost of £100,000 plus VAT of £17,500. D Ltd makes wholly taxable supplies in interval 1 (ending 31 March 2011), but becomes partly exempt in interval 2 (ending 31 March 2012), able to recover only 80% of its input tax.
D Ltd can claim capital allowances on a reducing balance basis each year (it has used up its annual investment allowance on other assets).
The initial input tax recovered will be £17,500, so the cost of the asset for capital allowances purposes is £100,000.
In interval 2, the adjustment will be £700 due to HMRC (20% of £17,500/5), and this will be disclosed on the return for the VAT period ended 30 September 2012. This is treated as an addition to cost occurring on 30 September 2012 for capital allowances purposes.
The capital allowances computation up to 30 June 2013 will be as follows:

Year ended		Overall position (£)
30 June 2011	Acquisition	100,000
	Allowance @ 20%	(20,000)
	Value carried forward	80,000
30 June 2012	Value brought forward	80,000
	Allowance @ 18%	(14,400)
	Value carried forward	65,600
30 June 2013	Value brought forward	65,600
	Addition	700
		66,300
	Allowance @ 18%	(11,934)
	Value carried forward	54,366

3. Special situations

VAT groups

8278 SI 1995/2518 reg 114(5A) **Joining** If a VAT-registered company holds a capital asset and, during the review period, joins a VAT group (¶7807), the **company's VAT registration** will end on the day before it joins the group. An interval will also end at that date, and any capital goods scheme adjustment must be made on the final VAT return.

The responsibility for making the adjustments for the remaining intervals rests with the representative member of the VAT group. The **first interval** after the company becomes a member of the group will run for 12 months from the date of joining, and subsequent intervals will run for 12 months in the normal way.

Leaving If a company leaves a VAT group during the review period, an **interval** will end on the date of exit. The representative member must make any related adjustment on the return for the second VAT period after the end of the group's VAT year. 8279

If the company is then **registered in its own right**, the next interval runs for 12 months from the day after it leaves the group, and subsequent intervals run for 12 months in the normal way.

If, however, the company is **not required to register** for VAT, a deemed sale occurs in the interval in which the company ceases to be a member of the VAT group (¶8273).

Transfer of a going concern

Where a business is transferred as a going concern and an affected asset is transferred as part of the transaction, the new owner takes **responsibility** for any capital goods scheme adjustments. 8281 SI 1995/2518 reg 114(5A), (7)

The provisions relating to the sale of an asset under the scheme do not apply.

The **adjustment intervals** will depend on whether the VAT registration is transferred to the new owner (¶7775).

If the **VAT registration is transferred**, the transfer of the business does not cause the end of an interval. The purchaser will receive all records relating to the business, so he will have ready access to the information necessary to operate the capital goods scheme adjustments.

If, however, the **VAT registration is not transferred**, an interval will end on the day before the transfer. The **vendor** is responsible for any adjustment required for this interval. The adjustment should generally be included on the VAT return for the second VAT period after the end of the VAT year in the normal way. If, however, the vendor ceases to be VAT-registered after the transfer, the adjustment should be included on the final VAT return. The **new owner** is then responsible for any adjustments for the remaining intervals. The first interval after the transfer will run for 12 months from the date of transfer, and subsequent intervals will run for 12 months in the normal way. The seller will retain all records, so that the purchaser will need to make separate arrangements to ascertain the information necessary to operate these adjustments.

Deregistration

When a trader deregisters, an adjustment is required on the **final return**, in the same way as if the asset had been sold. In certain situations, there will be an onward supply of the asset, when output tax may be chargeable (¶7802). However, where no output tax is charged, HMRC take the view that the deemed use of the asset in the remaining intervals is exempt. 8283

SECTION 4

VAT incurred while not registered

Taxable persons are entitled to claim relief for input tax incurred. Although relief is not generally available for VAT incurred by persons who are not registered, VAT incurred by a taxable person prior to registration, or after deregistration, may be deductible. 8285

Pre-registration

8287 SI 1995/2518 reg 111

VAT incurred on goods or services before a person registers for VAT may be recoverable. If, however, the expenditure relates to future exempt supplies, there will be no recovery of the input tax incurred.

For a **partly exempt** trader, the de minimis limits (¶8218) do not apply to input tax incurred pre-registration – that is, absolutely no exempt input tax can be recovered.

8288 **Goods** VAT may be reclaimed in respect of goods **acquired no more than** 4 years before the date on which the person was required to register for VAT, where the following conditions are satisfied:

a. the goods were supplied for the purposes of a business which was carried on by the person at the time of the supply, or which he had the intention of carrying on;
b. the goods were still on hand at the date of registration;
c. the usual conditions for reclaiming input tax are satisfied (¶8135); and
d. a stock account has been prepared showing the:
– quantities purchased;
– quantities used in making other goods;
– date of purchase; and
– date, manner and quantities of any disposals.

Goods are considered to be **on hand** for these purposes if they have been consumed in the making of other goods, which themselves are still on hand at the date of registration.

8289 **Services** VAT may be reclaimed in respect of services supplied **no more than 6 months** before the date on which the person was required to register for VAT, where the following conditions are satisfied:

– the services were supplied for the purposes of a business which was carried on by the person at the time of the supply, or which he had the intention of carrying on;
– the services were not performed on goods which have since been disposed of (e.g. repairs to a machine which was sold before registration);
– the services were not performed on goods acquired more than 4 years before the date of registration;
– the usual conditions for reclaiming input tax are satisfied (¶8135); and
– a record has been maintained showing a description of the services, the date of acquisition and the date of disposal (if any).

8291 SI 1995/2518 reg 111(3), (3B)

Obtaining relief A claim for relief should strictly be made on the VAT return for the first **period** of registration. However, HMRC will generally allow a claim, provided that it is made on a return for a VAT period ending not more than 4 years after the date by which the first return should have been submitted.

MEMO POINTS If a previously unregistered company joins a **VAT group**, the representative member of the group is entitled to claim relief for pre-registration VAT where the conditions are satisfied.

Pre-incorporation

8293 SI 1995/2518 reg 111

A limited company does not exist until it is incorporated, and therefore cannot register for VAT in the meantime. However, the rules **allow input tax to be deducted** where:

– expenditure is incurred by someone who will become an officer, member or employee of the company, and is not himself a taxable person;
– the purpose of the expenditure is for the company's business; and
– that person is fully reimbursed by the company.

Otherwise the same provisions apply as for pre-registration VAT. Input tax incurred on expenditure which has a **tax point** falling after the date of incorporation cannot be recovered under these rules, although by concession, HMRC will allow it. It is therefore vital that suppliers know who to invoice.

Post-deregistration

Relief is not generally available for VAT incurred by a business after the registration has ceased. However, HMRC will allow relief for VAT incurred on supplies of **services** as long as they relate to the period during which the business was registered. **8295** SI 1995/2518 reg 111(5), (6)

A claim for relief should be made to HMRC in writing, via form VAT 427, within 4 years of the date on which the services were supplied. To be valid, the claim must be submitted with the original invoices.

Input tax can also be claimed on **goods and services** received before deregistration, where a claim was not made on a VAT return because the necessary evidence was not held. In any event, such claims must be made within 4 years of the tax point of the purchase invoice.

MEMO POINTS 1. If a company leaves a **VAT group** and is not registered in its own right, the representative member of the group is entitled to claim relief for post-deregistration VAT where the general conditions are satisfied.

2. A restaurant ceased to trade but was still committed to making lease payments (and incurring related costs) for a further 5 years. The Danish authorities challenged the deductibility of the associated input tax on the basis that no taxable activities were being carried on, and no output tax was being declared. The ECJ held that there was a direct link between the lease payments and the previous economic activity, so input tax could be deducted. *I/S Fini H v Skatteministeriet* [2005]

CHAPTER 5

Routine VAT

OUTLINE ¶¶

This chapter covers the basic VAT compliance requirements for record-keeping, as well as some of the simplification options. For further detail and analysis, see *VAT Memo*. **8300**

SECTION 1

Records

Every taxable person must keep the following records for the purposes of accounting for VAT: **8305**
– business and accounting records;

– a VAT account, showing the output tax payable and input tax reclaimable in each VAT accounting period (¶9205);
– copies of all VAT invoices issued;
– VAT invoices received;
– documentation received relating to acquisitions of any goods from other EU countries (¶8937);
– documentation issued and received relating to the transfer, despatch or transportation of goods to other EU countries (¶8968);
– documentation relating to imports and exports (¶9035);
– documentation relating to international services supplied (¶9106) and received (¶9108);
– certificates issued under provisions relating to fiscal or other warehouse regimes (¶9016);
– all credit notes, debit notes and other documents which evidence an increase or decrease in consideration (¶8355); and
– copies of any self-billing agreements entered into, including the names, addresses and VAT numbers of the suppliers (¶8332).

In addition, VAT returns must be prepared on a regular basis.

A. VAT invoices

8306 A business must prepare VAT invoices for all taxable sales. Credit notes adjust sales which have already been invoiced, and these also have specific rules. A VAT invoice **must be provided** whenever a registered trader supplies taxable goods or services to another registered trader. There is an **exception** where only zero-rated or exempt supplies are being made in the UK. There is no requirement to provide VAT invoices to non-registered customers, although it is prudent to do so unless the supplier is certain that the purchaser is not registered. Special rules apply to invoices issued to customers in other EU member states (¶8968).

VAT invoices **must not be issued** in respect of:
– supplies to customers operating a self-billing scheme (¶8332);
– gifts of goods under a promotion scheme;
– supplies under a second-hand goods scheme (¶8435); or
– supplies under the tour operators' margin scheme (see *VAT Memo* for details).

For the treatment of errors, see ¶9222.

Time limits

8307 Notice 700 para 16.2.3 Where a VAT invoice is required, the **general rule** is that it must be issued within 30 days of the tax point (¶7902).

This time limit can be **extended** if HMRC agree.

Also, it is possible to extend the time if the trader is waiting for an invoice from his supplier or subcontractor, or a newly registered person has not yet received notification of his VAT registration number. Once this has been received, invoices should be issued within the following 30 days.

1. Standard invoice

Information required

8308 SI 1995/2518 reg 14 Traders can usually recover input tax if a valid VAT invoice is held which **contains** all of the following information:
– name, address and VAT registration number of the supplier;
– purchaser's name and address;
– unique identifying number, which must be sequential;
– date of issue;
– tax point date;

- identifying description of the supply, detailing the quantity of goods or extent of services, the rate of VAT and the VAT-exclusive price;
- unit price;
- total amount payable excluding VAT;
- rate of any cash discount available;
- applicable rates of VAT; and
- total amount of VAT charged.

MEMO POINTS 1. The **unit price** for services may be an hourly rate or a standard price for that particular service. The unit price does not need to be shown where it is not normally provided in a particular business sector, and the customer does not require it.
2. Any **zero-rated or exempt items** included on the invoice must be clearly identified and totalled separately.
3. Invoices must generally be in sterling. If an invoice is supplied in a **foreign currency**, the sterling equivalent must be shown for the total and the VAT payable, using an approved exchange rate (¶7968). Invoices in euros need not show the VAT-exclusive price for each description, but all other figures must be given in sterling.
4. Invoices need not be in the English **language**, but a translation must be made available to a visiting HMRC officer within 30 days of a specific request.

VAT numbers

All registered persons are allocated a unique VAT registration number. A UK VAT number consists of nine digits. When trading within the EU, the prefix GB is also used. Each of the member states has an allocated prefix, but the format of the VAT number may be different (¶8930). 8310

Checking the validity of a VAT number The validity of a VAT number can be checked online at http://ec.europa.eu/taxation_customs/vies/vieshome.do. This check will not tell the customer whether the VAT number is being used by the correct supplier. HMRC can confirm whether a particular number is actually registered, and whether it is allocated to the supplier who is using it on his invoices. 8311

Rounding of VAT amount

As a concession, the **total VAT payable** on an invoice may be rounded down to the nearest whole penny, as long as the VAT paid by the customer is the same as the VAT paid to HMRC. 8313 Notice 700 para 17.5

Where an invoice includes **more than one supply**, the VAT on each line must either be rounded:
- down to the nearest 0.1p; or
- up or down to the nearest 1p or 0.5p.

A consistent approach must be adopted. Again, at the end of the invoice, the total amount of VAT may be rounded down to the nearest whole penny.

EXAMPLE Mr A issues an invoice showing two lines of goods. The actual values are: 97.76p and 196.64p.
He can either round:
- down to the nearest 0.1p, which gives amounts of 97.7p and 196.6p; or
- to the nearest 1p for 97.76p to give 98p, and to the nearest 0.5p for 196.64p to give 196.5p.

Typical invoice

8315 The following example shows the required **components** of a UK VAT invoice.

EXAMPLE

Issued by: A Ltd, Main Road, London W1 — VAT number: 492 6104 45

Invoice number: 123

To: B Ltd, 1 High Street, London N1

Time of supply: 1 July 2012 — Date of issue: 7 July 2012

Quantity	Description and price	Amount (excl. VAT) £	VAT Rate %
1	FC 1 Filing cabinet @ £79.99	79.99	20
4	FC 20 Hanging files @ £9.99	39.96	20
	Delivery – free	-	
		119.95	
	VAT @ 20%	23.99	
	Total	143.94	

No discount available

Format

8317 Notice 700 para 17.8

The traditional role of **paper** invoices has now been joined by paperless methods of processing. Even where paper invoices are still prepared, they may be transmitted by email or, less commonly, fax.

Customs manual V1-24A section 6 paras 6.6, 6.7

MEMO POINTS 1. To **email** invoices, no special permission is required, unless the invoice is prepared under self-billing arrangements (¶8332). If corruption occurs, HMRC expect the customer to request a fresh transmission.
2. When an invoice is **faxed** to a machine with thermal imaging, the customer should be warned that the information may not be permanent due to deterioration. If the invoice being faxed is an advance copy, this should be clearly stated, to avoid a duplicate claim for input tax by the customer.

8318 SI 1995/2518 reg 13A

Electronic invoices Businesses may produce invoices electronically. If a trader **outsources** the invoicing procedures, he remains responsible for the system's compliance.

Invoices which are transmitted electronically should be stored electronically. If the relevant conditions for transmission and storage are not satisfied, the supplier must revert to paper invoices.

Notice 700/63

MEMO POINTS 1. For electronic **transmission**, the following conditions must be satisfied:
a. both the supplier and customer must be able to verify the authenticity and integrity of the data, which therefore requires use of an approved method e.g. advance electronic signature, EDI and hosted websites;
b. the following protections should be built into the system controls:
– completeness and accuracy;
– prevention of corruption;
– timely delivery;
– prevention of duplicated processing by the customer; and
– restriction of input tax recovery by the customer to valid invoices only.
c. the invoice contents must still comply with the normal requirements (¶8308). If invoices are sent in batches, the common details may be stated only once per batch; and
d. the environment for the data and transmission must be secured using industry recognised technologies.
2. For electronic **storage**, the following criteria apply:
– the authenticity and integrity of the data must be maintained, even where it is compressed;
– the data must be in a readable format, and a recreated invoice must be available if required (containing all the information as originally transmitted);
– files must be maintained so that any past invoice can be quickly located when required by HMRC; and
– records must be retained for 6 years.

If stored outside the UK, data protection must be assured, and invoices must be accessible within a reasonable period of time. Online access would facilitate this.

2. Special situations

Retailers

For a retailer making numerous small supplies, the requirements in ¶8308 could be onerous. Retailers are therefore exempt from the **general requirement** to provide a VAT invoice for every supply. 8320

Retailers are only required to supply VAT invoices if requested by the customer. The details to be included depend on the VAT-inclusive value of the supply, unless the customer requires a full invoice.

If either of the options in ¶8322 or ¶8323 is not available, a full invoice must be supplied.

MEMO POINTS The term "retailer" is not defined but can be taken to mean a person making sales to end-consumers who are normally not VAT-registered. Retailing normally involves the supply of goods, so the supply of professional services, for example, by an accountant or solicitor, is not a retail sale.
For details of VAT accounting for retailers, see ¶8700.

If the **invoice total is £250 or less**, and there are no exempt supplies, a less detailed VAT invoice may be issued, which must show: 8322 SI 1995/2518 reg 16
- the name, address and VAT number of the supplier;
- the time of supply;
- an identifying description of the supply;
- the total VAT-inclusive amount; and
- for each rate of VAT charged, the gross amount payable including VAT, and the VAT rate.

All items must be shown in sterling (so foreign currency must be converted).

If the supply is paid for by credit card, the **credit card voucher** may be adapted to act as a less detailed VAT invoice, but it is important to remember that only one VAT invoice can be issued for each supply.

If the **invoice total is over £250**, a modified VAT invoice may be issued, with the customer's agreement. Instead of the VAT-exclusive value of each supply, the VAT-inclusive value is shown. 8323 Notice 700 para 16.6.2

At the foot of the invoice, the following totals must be shown:
- VAT-inclusive value of the standard or reduced rate supplies;
- VAT payable on those supplies shown in sterling;
- VAT-exclusive value of those supplies;
- value of any zero-rated supplies; and
- value of any exempt supplies.

In all other respects, the invoice should show all the information required for a VAT invoice (¶8308).

MEMO POINTS If a **supply of petrol or diesel oil** is valued at over £250, the VAT invoice information may be adapted to show the vehicle registration number instead of the customer's name and address. In addition, there is no requirement to show the quantity of fuel supplied, or the type of supply.

Cash and carry wholesalers

The provisions applicable to retailers are not suitable for cash and carry wholesalers, as the majority of their customers are registered for VAT. However, similar problems arise with regard to the **number of supplies**, and arrangements therefore exist whereby the till roll may be adapted to act as a VAT invoice. 8325 Notice 700 para 17.2

The **till roll** should show the same information as a VAT invoice (¶8308) with a number of modifications, and approval is not required from HMRC to take advantage of this arrangement. Full VAT invoices may be required if the conditions are not met.

8326 **Modifications** Due to limited space on a till roll, the description of each item may be replaced by a **product code**. A code may apply to a class of goods and must consist of a minimum of two digits.

A **list** of the codes must be prepared and given to each registered customer. The list must be updated and annotated with the effective date of any change. Both the customer and the supplier must retain copies of each product code list as part of their VAT records.

MEMO POINTS 1. A **class of goods** means goods of a similar nature, which are subject to the same rate of VAT and to a similar mark-up – for example, a range of bottled beers but not beers and spirits.
2. A reference number may be substituted for the **customer's name and address** where the wholesaler maintains a customer list and each customer is advised of its reference.
3. Similarly, a key may be used to indicate the **rate of VAT applicable** to an item – for example, "*" may indicate items charged at the standard rate, and " + " items charged at the zero rate.
4. Copies of till rolls and product code lists must be **kept** for at least 6 years, unless HMRC agree otherwise.

Pro-forma invoices

8328 Notice 700 para 17.3 Where a pro-forma invoice is used as an **offer to supply** goods or services, it is possible that the customer may not proceed with the order, or that the order may not actually be supplied. It is important to ensure that such an invoice is not used to recover **input tax** and the invoice must therefore bear the words "this is not a VAT invoice". Once the supply has been made, a valid VAT invoice should be issued.

Comment Pro-forma invoices are common in the construction industry and the professional services market. The advantage to suppliers of issuing pro-forma invoices is that they can demand payment using a pro-forma and issue an actual VAT invoice after payment has been received. This means that they do not have to fund VAT that remains unpaid at the end of the VAT period. Traders eligible for the cash accounting scheme (¶8375) do not need to take these steps to achieve the same beneficial result.

Corporate purchasing cards

8330 These cards allow invoicing to be carried out by the customer's card company or bank, using transaction information that has been transmitted through the purchasing card system. There are **two types** of invoice under this system:
a. detailed invoices which provide itemised information on a line-by-line basis – the date of issue is irrelevant and is not shown on the invoice – the transmission dates are shown for the purposes of the customer's input tax recovery only; and
b. simplified VAT invoices which provide a summary only – the supplier must still provide sales invoices to account for output tax where the value of a single card swipe exceeds £5,000.

Self-billing

8332 SI 1995/2518 reg 13(3) In certain circumstances, VAT-registered **customers prepare VAT invoices** for the purchases they have made. They are required to send a copy of the invoice to the supplier, together with the payment for the supply. This procedure is known as self-billing and is particularly useful where the customer, rather than the supplier, is better able to calculate the value of the supply, such as in the case of royalties.

No prior approval from HMRC is required and there are no geographical restrictions.

MEMO POINTS Self-billing should not be confused with **authenticated receipts**, which are used in the construction industry in place of VAT invoices for supplies made under contracts requiring periodic payments. Authenticated receipts are valid if they contain all the information listed in ¶8308, they are signed by the supplier, and no other invoice or self-billing document is issued for the supply.

8333 Notice 700/62 **Requirements** All of the following **conditions** must be satisfied for self-billing to take place:
– the invoice must be provided under the terms of a self-billing agreement between that customer and that supplier relating to goods or services specified in the agreement;

– the supplier must be a taxable person;
– all transactions with that supplier must be invoiced using self-billing for the duration of the agreement;
– the contents must comply with the requirements for either a full UK or EU invoice;
– each invoice must clearly state "The VAT shown is your output tax due to HMRC"; and
– an up-to-date record of all suppliers who have agreed to self-billing must be kept by the customer, to include their names, addresses and VAT registration numbers.

If any condition is **not met**, the invoice prepared by the customer is ineffective, which means he cannot reclaim the VAT as input tax and the supplier must then prepare his own invoice.

MEMO POINTS 1. The **agreement** should be in writing, either in hard copy or in electronic form, so that it has binding effect. It must be produced to HMRC on request. It should include the following **terms**:
– the supplier's agreement to receive self-billed invoices in respect of his supplies to the customer;
– the supplier's agreement that he will not raise any of his own invoices for those supplies;
– an expiry date, being the later of 12 months and the end of any contract between the parties; and
– the supplier's agreement to notify the customer if he ceases to be VAT-registered, changes his VAT number, or transfers his business.

The supplier would probably also want to know if a third party is going to prepare the invoices on the customer's behalf.

2. The **tax point** of supplies covered by self-billed invoices follows the normal rules (¶7902), except that a self-billed invoice is only effective when issued within 14 days of the basic tax point. So the tax point is normally determined by the date of despatch of goods or performance of services (basic tax point), unless this is overridden by the date of payment.
In any event, the customer must show the tax point on the invoice.

3. If the supplier **transfers his business** as a going concern and the new owner wants to continue the self-billing arrangement, a new agreement will be required.

Accounting for VAT For self-billing purposes, a **tax point is not created** if the customer issues an invoice before the goods are made available, or the services are performed. The **supplier** accounts for output tax in the VAT period when the tax point falls, which will be the later of the date the goods are made available or the services are performed, and the invoice date if it is issued within 14 days of the basic tax point. The **customer** can reclaim the input tax in the VAT period in which the tax point falls. **8334** Sch 11 para 2B VATA 1994

B. Credit and debit notes

The consideration for a supply may be adjusted after an invoice has been issued. This can occur, for example, when there is a contingent discount, or the **original invoice contained an error**. The supplier and the customer must jointly decide whether to adjust the VAT charged in respect of the original supply. It is important to note that credit notes cannot be used in respect of bad debts, as there are other procedures which must be followed (¶8350). **8335**

Where the customer is able to recover 100% of the VAT charged on the original invoice, a reduction in the VAT charge is neutral, and therefore a joint decision **not to vary** the VAT charge may be made. Where the VAT charge is not adjusted, the VAT account (¶9205) must still be adjusted to reflect the reduced value of the supply.

Where an **adjustment is made**, the standard procedure is for the supplier to raise a credit note. In some circumstances it may be preferable for the customer to raise a debit note. Both credit and debit notes are subject to the same requirements.

Time limits

8337 Notice 700 para 18.2.2 SI 1995/2518 reg 15

Where a credit note is issued as a result of a **change in the rate of VAT** (¶7950), the credit note must be issued within 14 days of the change. Credit notes issued in other circumstances are not made in accordance with any statutory provisions. Credit notes must be **issued within** 4 years of the end of the VAT period in which the original supply occurred.

Required information

8340 Where the supplier issues a credit note to a customer, he must retain a copy for his records. Similarly, if the customer issues a debit note to the supplier, the customer must retain a copy.

Both credit and debit notes must be clearly **marked** as a credit or debit note, respectively, and show the following information:
- the name, address and VAT number of the supplier;
- the purchaser's name and address;
- a unique identifying number;
- the date of issue;
- an identifying description of the supply being credited;
- for each description, the quantity of items, the amount credited and the reason for return;
- the total amount of credit given, excluding VAT;
- the rate of VAT and the amount of VAT credited; and
- the invoice number and date of issue of the original invoice.

MEMO POINTS 1. Any **zero-rated or exempt items** included on the credit note must be identified and totalled separately, and it must be clearly stated that no VAT credit has been allowed for them.

2. If a credit note is issued which **does not include a VAT adjustment**, it must be clearly endorsed with the words "This is not a credit note for VAT purposes".

3. If the credit or debit note relates to an invoice issued to a person in another **EU member state**, the note must contain all the information required to be included on an invoice (¶8977).

Accounting for credit notes

8341 An adjustment for a credit note must be made in the **VAT account** (¶9205) for the VAT period in which it is reflected in the business accounts. Both parties to the transaction should also amend their **VAT returns** accordingly.

C. VAT returns

8342 Every VAT-registered trader must submit a VAT return (form VAT 100) in respect of every VAT period, and pay any VAT due to HMRC.

VAT **returns** generally cover a 3-month period, known as a **VAT period** or **accounting period**. VAT periods usually end on the last day of a calendar month and, to spread the return cycle (known as the VAT stagger, or stagger group), different traders will have return periods ending on different dates.

HMRC may approve monthly VAT periods, VAT periods which begin and end mid-month, or 4-weekly VAT periods (usually appropriate for retailers) on request. HMRC can refuse the request for the protection of the revenue.

EXAMPLE A Ltd has a VAT period of 3 months, with the first return being due for the period to 31 January. Subsequent returns are made for the quarters ending 30 April, 31 July and 31 October. Mr B also has a VAT period of 3 months, but prepares his returns to 28 February, 31 May, 31 August and 30 November. He is in a different stagger group from A Ltd.

MEMO POINTS 1. A trader may apply to HMRC to change its stagger group to coincide with its accounting year end.

2. The length of the **first return period** may be irregular (i.e. not a whole number of months). Output tax should be charged on all taxable supplies from the date of registration. Input tax can be recovered from the date of registration and (in respect of goods) from up to 4 years before the date of registration, subject to certain conditions (¶8287).
3. **Monthly returns** can provide a cash flow advantage if the trader is in a regular VAT repayment position, as the trader will receive repayments monthly rather than quarterly.
4. Some smaller traders may choose to operate the **annual accounting** scheme (¶8405), under which they are required to submit only one VAT return each year.
5. HMRC have the power to require all **associated businesses** (for example, a corporate group) to retain the same return cycle where there is little commercial rationale for different cycles to apply. This is to prevent manipulation of tax points, where the trader incurring input tax recovers it from HMRC before the trader paying output tax has made payment to HMRC.

Returns can be completed and submitted online by using HMRC's VAT Online service (¶9217). In addition, the trader's professional agent (e.g. VAT adviser) can prepare and submit the return, and correspond with HMRC on the trader's behalf (¶9212). 8343

MEMO POINTS Traders with a turnover of more than £100,000 now have to file their VAT returns online. Traders who have registered for VAT since 1 April 2010 have to file online regardless of the value of their turnover. With effect from April 2012 all VAT returns will have to be made online.

Overview

The VAT return is a document which must cope with a wide range of trading situations. The top half of the form relates to the VAT position of the business, while the bottom half gives statistical data about sales and purchases. **Each VAT return shows** the output tax due for the period, the recoverable input tax, and the net amount payable or repayable. 8344

The return also shows the total value of supplies (whether taxable or exempt) and the total value of inputs for the period.

Further statistical information is required for transactions with other EU member states.

Content

For traders who have **no EU trade**, only boxes 1, 3, 4, 5, 6 and 7 are relevant. 8346 Notice 700/12

Basic checks should include:
- reviewing figures taken from accounting records and schedules;
- checking that figures have been entered in the correct box;
- ensuring the return is arithmetically correct;
- reconciling sales in management accounts with the figure in box 1; and
- checking whether the VAT payment position is what was expected, given the trading pattern during the VAT period, and also compared to previous returns.

MEMO POINTS 1. **Nil returns** must still be submitted, and if using:
- paper returns, all boxes should have "None" entered; or
- electronic returns, all boxes are automatically pre-filled with zeros, and the trader should confirm that he wishes to submit a nil return.

2. For paper returns, a **negative number** should be entered in brackets. For electronic returns, a minus sign should be entered before the figure.

Box	Contents	Notes
1	VAT due for the period on sales and outputs	Include: – all VAT on sales with tax point falling within VAT period; – VAT on business gifts valued at more than £50 per recipient; – reduction in respect of any credit notes issued which will reduce the box 1 figure; – errors in HMRC's favour which can be corrected on return (¶9222); – reverse charge supplies (¶9110); and – fuel scale charges (¶7893)

Box	Contents	Notes
2	VAT due on acquisitions of goods from other EU member states	If there is an entry in box 9, there should be an entry here; if the goods acquired would be taxable at the standard rate the figure to be entered here would be 20% of the box 9 figure
3	Total output tax due	Total of boxes 1 and 2
4	Input tax credit claimed for period	Include: – all VAT on purchases and expenses with tax point falling within VAT period; – bad debt relief; – credit notes received (this will reduce the box 4 figure); – errors in favour of the business which can be included on the return (¶9222); – input tax on reverse charge supplies; – input tax on goods acquired from other EU member states
5	Net VAT payable/repayable	Box 3 less box 4
6	Total value of sales and outputs excluding VAT	The VAT-exclusive, or net-of-VAT, value of sales, including items entered in box 8
7	Total value of purchases and inputs excluding VAT	The VAT-exclusive, or net-of-VAT, value of any purchases, including items entered in box 9 – if there are any purchases where it is not possible to recover the VAT, the VAT-inclusive cost of those items should be included
8	Total value of goods supplied to other EU member states (¶8968)	Include value of related services, e.g. freight and insurance
9	Total value of goods acquired from other EU member states (¶8937)	The sterling equivalent of the value of the invoice received

SECTION 2

Bad debts

8350 VAT is usually accounted for when a supply is made. If the debt in respect of a supply is not paid, the supplier may claim bad debt relief equivalent to the **output tax** paid to HMRC, provided that certain conditions are satisfied. If such a claim is made, any **input tax** recovered by the customer must be repaid to HMRC (and in any case a customer who has not paid within 6 months must repay the input tax – see ¶8366).

Retailers and suppliers using the cash accounting scheme (¶8375) are not affected by bad debts, as they account for VAT after payment has been received.

1. Suppliers

8352 Notice 700/18

A supplier may claim relief in respect of an eligible bad debt, provided that the VAT due in respect of the supply has been accounted for and paid to HMRC.

Eligible debts

8353 SI 1995/2518 reg 172

A bad debt is **eligible** for relief if it:

– has **remained unpaid** for at least 6 months from the due date for payment, or the date of supply if later;

– has been **written off** in the VAT account (¶9205) and transferred to a separate bad debt account; and
– has not been **sold or factored** under a legal arrangement.

In order to claim relief, the supplier must make an adjustment to box 4 of his VAT return for the period in which the above steps are taken. The **claim** must be made **within** 4 years and 6 months from the later of:
– the date on which the consideration was payable; or
– the date of supply.

MEMO POINTS The **due date for payment** will vary depending on the circumstances, so where:
– businesses allow customers a period of time from the invoice date to settle (for example, 30 days or 60 days) this extended date applies;
– goods are paid for in instalments (for example, hire purchase or conditional sale contracts), the due date for payment is the date of each instalment – if the customer defaults, any later payments will usually be deemed to be due at the date of the default – this date therefore becomes the due date of payment for repayment of input tax;
– suppliers simply give customers longer to pay, in order to ensure payment is eventually made, it does not alter the time at which input tax is required to be repaid by the customer or when a bad debt claim can be made by the supplier; and
– both the supplier and the customer are in dispute about a particular invoice, both parties may agree to delay settlement – provided that there is evidence to support the fact that they have agreed to delay payment, the revised payment date will be seen as the due date for payment for these purposes.

EXAMPLE Mr A issues an invoice for accountancy services supplied for the period to 31 March. The due date for payment is 30 April.
Payment is never received, so a claim for bad debt relief may be made from 30 October onwards.

Administration

The supplier must have the following **evidence** in support of the claim: **8355** SI 1995/2518 reg 167
– a copy of the original invoice provided in respect of the supply; and
– a separate bad debt account showing the consideration written off.

The following **records** must also be retained: SI 1995/2518 reg 168
a. a refunds account for bad debts, showing:
– the amount of VAT chargeable;
– the VAT period in which the output tax was accounted for and paid to HMRC;
– the date and number of any invoice; and
– any payments received in respect of the supply;
b. the amount of the debt outstanding in respect of the claim;
c. the amount of the claim; and
d. the VAT period in which the claim is made.

The evidence and records must be **retained** for a period of 4 years from the date on which the claim is made. SI 1995/2518 reg 169

MEMO POINTS 1. If the **supplier is no longer registered** for VAT, HMRC should be advised of the claim in writing and copies of the supporting evidence should be submitted.
2. If **no invoice** was issued in respect of the supply, information identifying the purchaser, the time and the nature of the supply must be retained in the refunds account for bad debts.
3. On a **transfer of a going concern**, where the VAT registration number is transferred to the purchaser, a bad debt claim may be made by the purchaser in respect of debts due to the seller.
4. A company which was a member of a **VAT group** when the debt was incurred may claim relief even if it has left the group. This is because even though the VAT was originally accounted for and paid by the representative member, the individual company funds the VAT and suffers the economic loss.
5. Where suppliers use the **annual accounting** scheme, output tax on the supply and bad debt relief can be claimed on the same return (assuming that all the other conditions are met).

Amount of the claim

Generally, the amount of bad debt relief which can be claimed is the amount of output VAT charged in respect of the supply. A change of rate (such as that from 17.5% to 20% on 4 **8357** HMRC Brief 18/09

January 2011) will not affect bad debt relief – the supplier can only claim what was charged in the first place and only insofar as the debt has not been settled.

The amount of relief will be **restricted** where the supplier owes the customer money, or where the customer has made a part payment in respect of the outstanding debt.

If the customer **stipulates the invoice(s)** to which his payment relates, the supplier must honour that allocation. So an older invoice may still be the subject of a bad debt claim, even if subsequent invoices have been paid.

Net VAT due unpaid Where a business is unable to pay the net amount due on a VAT return to HMRC, provided that an amount of input VAT in excess of the bad debt claim can be shown to be recoverable on that return, a bad debt relief claim can still be made in relation to bad debts covered by the return and will be paid. The claim will be limited to the amount by which input tax exceeds output tax payable on non-bad-debt supplies made in the period.

8358 SI 1995/2518 reg 172(3)

Mutual debts If the supplier owes the customer money, the two **VAT-inclusive amounts** must be offset before calculating the amount of bad debt relief due.

EXAMPLE Mr A wishes to claim bad debt relief in respect of an invoice for £10,000 plus VAT, issued to B Ltd in February 2011. Mr A owes B Ltd £750 (including VAT), which he has refused to pay until the bad debt is cleared.

		£
Debt due from B Ltd	10,000 plus VAT @ 20%	12,000
Debt due from A		(750)
Net debt		11,250
Bad debt relief available	VAT @ 1/6	1,875

8359 SI 1995/2518 reg 170

Part payments The amount of bad debt relief is reduced where the customer has made a part payment in respect of the debt.

Where the payment can be **matched with a specific invoice**, the payment is simply offset against the VAT-inclusive amount of the debt. The amount of VAT outstanding is then the appropriate VAT fraction (see ¶8030) of the outstanding debt.

EXAMPLE A Ltd made a supply to B Ltd on 1 June 2011, valued at £1,000 plus VAT (total £1,200). Mr B has made a payment of £500 in respect of this debt, leaving a total of £700 outstanding. The amount of VAT outstanding is therefore £116.67. (1/6 × £700)

8360 If the payment **cannot be matched** with a specific invoice (where, for example, the customer makes regular monthly payments), the payment is attributed to the earliest invoices first. Where more than one invoice was issued on the same date, the amounts of the invoices are aggregated and treated as a single supply on that date.

EXAMPLE Mr A has made the following supplies to Mr B:

Invoice	Date	Net (£)	VAT (£)	Gross (£)
1	1 June 2011	400	Exempt	400
2	1 June 2011	1,000	200	1,200
3	2 July 2011	1,200	240	1,440
4	3 Aug 2011	500	Zero-rated	500
5	3 Aug 2011	800	160	960
6	4 Sept 2011	950	190	1,140
7	5 Oct 2011	1,350	270	1,620

Mr B has made payments totalling £5,000 in respect of these invoices, including a payment of £1,140 specifically attributable to invoice 6.

The balance of the payments (£3,860) is allocated to the earliest invoices first, so:
- invoices 1, 2 and 3 are therefore settled in full (total £3,040);
- £820 is attributable to invoices 4 and 5, both issued on 3 August. These invoices must be aggregated, giving a total of £1,460 of which £160 is VAT. The total outstanding amount on these

invoices is £640, and the element of VAT outstanding is therefore £70.14 (i.e. 640/1460 × £160); and
– invoice 7 remains outstanding.
The bad debt relief which Mr A may claim is therefore £340.14. (£70.14 + £270)

VAT calculated on the profit margin If the VAT on the supply was calculated on the basis of the profit margin, the bad debt relief available is the VAT element of the outstanding profit element of the supply. 8362 SI 1995/2518 reg 172A

Traders using the second-hand margin scheme (¶8435 onwards) and undisclosed agents (¶8540) are affected by this.

EXAMPLE Mr A supplied goods to B Ltd under a margin scheme. The goods were supplied in 2011 for £1,200, of which £300 represented the profit margin.
If B Ltd pays £800 in respect of the goods, the amount of the debt is £400, which exceeds the margin. The maximum bad debt relief which can be claimed is the VAT element of the margin i.e. £50. (1/6 × £300)
If B Ltd pays £1,050 in respect of the goods, the amount of the debt is £150 and the maximum bad debt relief which can be claimed is therefore £25. (1/6 × £150)

Payment subsequently received

If, after bad debt relief has been claimed, the supplier receives a further payment from the customer, the **VAT element** of the payment must be repaid to HMRC. Such payments must be recorded in the bad debt account. 8364 SI 1995/2518 reg 171

The **amount** of VAT repayable to HMRC is calculated as follows:

$$\frac{\text{Amount of payment received}}{\text{Amount of consideration outstanding immediately before payment}} \times \begin{array}{c}\text{Bad debt relief claimed}\\\text{(or balance thereof)}\end{array}$$

The adjustment is generally **recorded on** the VAT return (in box 1) for the period in which the payment is received. If, however, the supplier has ceased to be VAT-registered, he should notify HMRC in writing of the payment.

MEMO POINTS 1. If the supplier is **insured** against non-payment of debts, any recovery under the insurance policy is ignored for bad debt relief purposes.
2. Where a debt is **assigned** to a connected party (¶5570) after a bad debt claim has been made, and the customer then pays, VAT must be repaid by the original claimant.

EXAMPLE A Ltd made a supply in 2010 valued at £5,000 (plus VAT) to B Ltd which remained unpaid. A Ltd therefore claimed bad debt relief for the full amount of VAT outstanding, £875.
Subsequently, B Ltd made a payment to A Ltd of £3,000 in respect of the debt.
A Ltd must therefore repay part of the bad debt relief claimed to HMRC. The amount repayable is calculated as £446.80. (3,000/5,875 × £875)
This leaves £428.20 of VAT unpaid.
If B Ltd were to make a further payment of £1,000, the further amount payable to HMRC would be £148.94. (1,000/2,875 × £428.20)

2. VAT-registered customers

A customer who **fails to pay** his supplier **within 6 months** of the time of the supply, or the due date of payment if later, must repay any input tax he has claimed in respect of the supply to HMRC. The customer must adjust the VAT return for the period in which the date 6 months from the tax point falls. This is done by entering a negative figure in box 4, or if other input tax is being reclaimed reducing the reclaim by the value of the "bad debt". 8366 s 26A VATA 1994 SI 1995/2518 regs 172D, 172E

If the customer **subsequently makes a payment** to the supplier in respect of the debt concerned, the input tax incurred can be reclaimed in the normal way. The amount of input tax which can be reclaimed is proportionate to the amount of the debt paid. The input tax should be reclaimed on the VAT return for the period in which the payment is made. 8368

EXAMPLE C Ltd received a supply valued at £1,000 (plus VAT of £200) from D Ltd and was unable to pay the invoice within 6 months. So input tax of £200 was repaid to HMRC.
Subsequently, C Ltd paid £900 in respect of the debt.
C Ltd can therefore reclaim input tax of £150 in respect of the original invoice. (900/1,200 × £200)

SECTION 3

Cash accounting scheme

8375 SI 1995/2518 reg 56 Notice 731 Under the cash accounting scheme a business accounts for **output tax** on the VAT return for the period in which it receives payment from its customer. **Input tax** is reclaimed on the VAT return for the period in which the supplier is paid.

The scheme is **of benefit to** a business which pays its bills promptly but whose customers do not. The scheme also gives automatic relief for bad debts.

The scheme is **unlikely to benefit** a business which normally receives VAT refunds from HMRC, as the business will not be able to reclaim the input tax incurred until it has paid its invoices.

It is possible for a business to use both the cash accounting and annual accounting (¶8405) schemes at the same time.

1. Operating the scheme

Eligibility

8377 SI 1995/2518 reg 58(1) The scheme is **available** for businesses (including groups) which have:
– annual taxable supplies (¶7775) not exceeding £1.35 million (and turnover is not expected to exceed this level in the next year); and
– a good compliance record (all VAT returns made and VAT paid in the previous 12 months).

Once operating the scheme, businesses can continue using it until annual taxable supplies reach £1.6 million.

8379 A business will be **excluded** from the scheme if, in the previous 12 months, it has:
– been convicted of a VAT offence;
– been assessed to a civil evasion penalty (¶9290);
– made a payment to settle proceedings in connection with a VAT offence; or
– been notified by HMRC that it cannot use, or must stop using, the scheme.

There is **no application process** for the scheme, and a business may start to use it from the beginning of any VAT period, provided that it satisfies the above conditions. If a business is unsure whether it may operate the scheme, it should seek advice from HMRC.

Transactions

8380 SI 1995/2518 reg 58(2), (3) If a business chooses to adopt the scheme, it **must be used for** the whole VAT-registered business, **excluding**:
– hire- or lease-purchase agreements;
– conditional sale agreements;
– credit sale agreements;
– supplies where the VAT invoice is issued and full payment is not required within 6 months of the issue of the invoice;
– supplies where the VAT invoice is issued in advance of the delivery of the goods or services (where part of the supply has been delivered at the time of issue of the VAT invoice, the VAT on that part may be accounted for under the scheme); and

– goods imported or acquired from another EU member state (including goods removed from a customs warehouse or free zone).

In these cases, VAT should be accounted for under the normal rules – that is, when the supply is made or received.

Accounting

The following table sets out when payment is made for cash accounting: 8382

Method of payment	Date of payment
Cash	Date cash received/paid
Cheque[1]	Later of: – when cheque received/sent; and – date on cheque
Credit/debit card[2]	Date on sales voucher
Bank giro/standing order/direct debit	Date bank account credited/debited

Note:
1. Where a **cheque** is not honoured, there is no need to account for VAT.
2. Where a credit or debit card payment is not honoured, there is no need to account for VAT.

When **starting** to use the scheme, the business must prepare a list of unpaid sales and purchase invoices in respect of which VAT has already been accounted for, and exclude these from the first VAT return prepared under the scheme. 8384

The business should account for VAT based on the tax points of the transactions concerned, so on a change of rate the tax points determine the VAT rate, not the date of accounting for the VAT. 8385

Records

In addition to the normal record-keeping requirements (¶9205), a business must **maintain a payment record**, providing an audit trail from payments made or received through invoices and through to the usual banking evidence (i.e. bank statements and cheque book stubs). This is usually achieved by completing a fully analysed cashbook with a separate VAT column. 8386 SI 1995/2518 reg 65 Notice 731 para 4.3

If the business makes any **payments in cash** (i.e. bank notes or coins) it must ensure that the purchase invoice is endorsed to show the amount paid, and the date of payment. Similarly if a customer pays an invoice in cash, the supplier must, if asked, endorse the sales invoice accordingly.

2. Special situations

Part payments

A part payment should be **allocated to** the earliest outstanding invoice in priority. If the invoice is for items taxable at different rates, the payment must be apportioned between the various elements to determine the amount of VAT included. 8388 Notice 731 para 4.3.3

EXAMPLE Mr A issued an invoice to Mr B on 1 December 2011, showing the following:

	£
Standard-rated supplies	2,000
Zero-rated supplies	475
VAT	400
	2,875

Mr B makes a payment of £1,800 in respect of the invoice.
The amount of VAT included in the payment is therefore £250.43. (1,800/2,875 × £400)

Deductions

8390 Notice 731 para 4.8

If a business offers a **prompt payment** discount (¶7962), the VAT element of any payment received must be identified by using the original invoice. Simply calculating the appropriate VAT fraction (see ¶8030) of the amount received will give an incorrect figure.

When a payment is **received net** of a deduction, such as a charge for commission, VAT must be calculated on the full value of the supply before such a deduction.

Outsourcing debt collection

8392 Notice 731 paras 5.2-5.4

Where the debts of a business are collected **by an agent**, VAT must be accounted for in the period in which the agent receives the payment. VAT is due on the full amount received by the agent from the customer, not any reduced amount paid by the agent to the supplier.

Where a business **sells a debt**, it must account for VAT in the period in which any debts are sold or assigned. VAT is due on the full amount of the debts sold or assigned, not the consideration for which they are transferred.

If a **debt is factored** under a **recourse** agreement (i.e. the taxpayer remains liable for the debt) the business should account for VAT when the factor collects the debt from the customer. Output tax is due on the amount collected, not what the factor pays to the supplier. If the factor is unable to collect the debt, the normal rules apply.

If a debt is factored under a **non-recourse** agreement, VAT should similarly be accounted for in the period in which the factor collects the debt from the customer. Output tax is due on the amount collected, not what the factor pays to the supplier. If the factor is unable to collect the debt, output tax must be accounted for in the period in which the factor writes off the advance made to the supplier.

If the debts are subsequently assigned back to the business under a **recourse clause** (whether in whole or in part) the business may claim bad debt relief (¶8350) in respect of any unpaid amounts, in accordance with the normal rules.

Partial exemption

8394 Notice 731 para 4.6

When carrying out a partial exemption calculation (¶8205), the business must calculate the proportion of **residual input tax** it may recover using the actual payments made and received during the period.

3. Leaving the scheme

8396 SI 1995/2518 regs 58(4), 60, 64

A business **must** leave the scheme if:
– at the end of a VAT period, the value of its taxable supplies in the previous 12 months has exceeded £1.6 million (excluding VAT);
– it cannot comply with the record-keeping requirements;
– it is convicted of a VAT offence;
– it is assessed to a civil evasion penalty; or
– it makes a payment to settle proceedings in connection with a VAT offence.

HMRC may insist that a business leaves the scheme if they believe that revenue is at risk. The business may appeal against such a decision, although it must immediately leave the scheme until the appeal is resolved.

A **business may choose** to leave the scheme at the end of any VAT period.

MEMO POINTS Where an increase in taxable turnover to a figure in excess of the limit is attributable to a **one-off transaction** – for example, the disposal of a building – HMRC may agree to allow the business to remain within the scheme if they are satisfied that taxable turnover in the next 12 months is unlikely to exceed £1.35 million.

EXAMPLE Mr A's annual taxable supplies reach £1.7 million on 20 September. His next VAT quarter ends on 30 September. Mr A must leave the scheme on 30 September. Normal VAT accounting will begin on 1 October.

Consequences

On leaving the scheme, a business must account for outstanding VAT, unless it immediately starts to use the cash-based method of the flat rate scheme. 8398
SI 1995/2518 reg 61

The outstanding VAT must be accounted for immediately, unless the business is entitled to do so over the following 6 months. Entitlement **depends on** the reason for leaving the scheme, as set out in the following table.

Reason for leaving scheme		Business may choose to account for outstanding VAT over 6 months[1]	Business must settle outstanding VAT when leaving the scheme
Business chooses to leave		✓	
Taxable supplies over £1.6 million in last 12 months	Taxable supplies during the last 3 months did not exceed £1.35m	✓	
	Taxable supplies during the last 3 months exceeded £1.35m		✓
Any other compulsory reason			✓

Note:
1. A business does not need to inform HMRC if it chooses this option.

EXAMPLE Mr B chose to leave the cash accounting scheme at the end of the period ended 30 June. Mr B has requested that he submits monthly VAT returns from 1 July. He has the following invoices in June and July.

Sales invoice – tax point date	Payment received	Output tax £	Purchase invoice – tax point date	Payment made	Input tax £
31 May	5 July	4,000	4 June	28 June	200
15 June	30 June	1,000	27 June	26 July	500
30 June	31 July	2,000	10 July	12 Aug	750
15 July	31 Aug	500			

The sales invoice issued on 15 July and the purchase invoice dated 10 July are new supplies, and the VAT should be accounted for according to the tax point date.
The invoices with tax points on or before 30 June are accounted for when payment is made or received.
The output tax to be accounted for in July will be £6,500. (£4,000 + £2,000 + £500)
The input tax to be accounted for in July will be £1,250. (£500 + £750)

Special situations

Strictly, **bad debt relief** (¶8350) can only be claimed after the VAT has been paid to HMRC. 8400
However, where a business chooses to leave the scheme or leaves because the taxable turnover exceeds the threshold, HMRC will allow a claim to bad debt relief on the final return under the scheme, provided that all other conditions for bad debt relief are satisfied. The effect is to immediately net the bad debt relief claimed against the related output tax.

A business has 2 months to submit its final VAT return after **deregistering**. On the **final VAT** 8402
return, all outstanding VAT must be accounted for, including VAT on sales invoices which remain unpaid. Bad debt relief is available for older sales invoices. VAT on purchase invoices may be reclaimed, assuming the required evidence is retained. Bad debt relief can also subsequently be claimed, even if the trader is no longer registered (¶8355).

On the **transfer of a going concern**, where the VAT registration is transferred to the 8403
purchaser, the seller must inform the purchaser that the cash accounting scheme is being used. The new owner may then continue the scheme, as if all the supplies made and

received by the seller were made by the new owner. The new owner may also choose to leave the scheme, following the procedure at ¶8398 above.

SECTION 4

Annual accounting scheme

8405 SI 1995/2518 reg 50 Notice 732 The aim of the annual accounting scheme is to assist small businesses with managing cash flow, reducing paperwork and the compliance burden generally. Under the scheme a trader need only submit one return per year.

Traders must apply to use the scheme. It cannot be used by VAT groups, or traders which have divisional registration.

Depending on the level of the VAT liability, payments may be required in a number of instalments throughout the year, with a balancing payment due on the last day for submission of the return.

It is possible for a business to use the annual accounting scheme in conjunction with the following:
– the cash accounting scheme (¶8375);
– the flat rate scheme (¶8620); or
– a retail scheme (¶8700).

Eligibility

8407 SI 1995/2518 reg 52 In order to join the annual accounting scheme a business must satisfy the following **conditions**:

a. the expected value of its taxable supplies during the 12 months following the application should be no more than £1.35 million (excluding VAT); and

b. it must not have previously operated the annual accounting scheme during the 12 months prior to the application.

A business will not generally be allowed to join the scheme if its **VAT debt is increasing**. However, if the debt is very small to start with, and arrangements are made to clear the debt, HMRC generally allow a business to join the scheme.

In addition, HMRC can refuse use of the scheme to protect tax revenues – for example, in the case of an insolvent trader.

MEMO POINTS 1. A **repayment trader** can join the scheme, and obviously no instalment payments will be required if the annual position is a VAT refund. The repayment of VAT will be delayed until the annual VAT return is submitted, therefore it is unlikely to be beneficial.
2. A **partly exempt** business (¶8205) will perform the partial exemption calculation on an annual basis only.

Application

8410 Assuming that a business satisfies the conditions, an application should be made using **form VAT 600**, identifying the month in which the business would prefer the annual period to end (the annual accounting date). Often the trader's choice aligns the annual accounting date with his financial accounting year end. For partly exempt traders, the annual accounting date must be aligned with the VAT cycle (¶8342).

The application must also specify the preferred **payment method**, from the following options:
– standing order;
– BACS/CHAPS;
– direct debit; or
– bank giro.

Starting the scheme

If accepted, the scheme will **operate from** the first day of the VAT period in which the application is made. If registering at the same time, annual accounting commences at the date of registration. **8412** SI 1995/2518 regs 50-51

The **first accounting period**, known as the transitional accounting period, will run from that date until the annual accounting date. If, however, this period is less than 3 months, there will be a 3-month period, followed by a further period of less than 12 months ending on the next annual accounting date.

If the period for which a return is required is:
- no more than 4 months, the return must be submitted by the end of the following month; or
- exceeds 4 months, the return must be submitted by the last working day of the second month following the end of the period.

> EXAMPLE A Ltd (which usually prepares VAT returns for calendar quarters) applies to join the annual accounting scheme on 1 February, retaining 31 March as the annual accounting date.
> As the first period cannot be less than 3 months, it will run from 1 February to 30 April, and the return must be submitted by 31 May. The next period will run from 1 May to the following 31 March, and the return must be submitted by 31 May.
> Subsequent periods will run for 12 months ending on 31 March annually and each return will be due on 31 May.

Payments

Businesses normally make nine **interim** payments, although HMRC may agree to three larger interim instalment payments instead. **8414** SI 1995/2518 regs 49-51

For businesses which have been registered for more than a year, these payments will be **based on** the previous year's VAT liability. Otherwise, the payments are based on the estimated turnover given on the VAT registration application.

The **balance** of the year's VAT will be due with the annual return. If the instalments exceed the actual liability, a repayment will be due.

All payments **must be made by** the last working day of the relevant month.

A business may make **voluntary interim payments** at any time, subject to the conditions that they must be a multiple of £5, and paid electronically.

The following table sets out the various rules which apply.

	Number of instalments	
	Three	Nine
Payable in months	4, 7 and 10	4 to 12
Amount payable per instalment	25% of previous year's VAT	10% of previous year's VAT
Balancing payment due	Month 14	Month 14

> EXAMPLE Mr A joined the annual accounting scheme with effect from 1 April 2010 and his annual accounting date is 31 March. HMRC have agreed to quarterly interim payments.
> During the year to 31 March 2011 he made taxable supplies of £93,000 and paid VAT of £5,500.
> For the year to 31 March 2012 he is required to make the following interim payments:
> - 31 July 2011 – £1,375
> - 31 October 2011 – £1,375
> - 31 January 2012 – £1,375.
>
> The balancing payment for the year is due on 31 May 2012.

If the current year's VAT liability **differs significantly** from the previous year, the interim payments may be revised. In general, where the **liability increases**, the business will be asked to make more frequent payments from the beginning of the next VAT period. However, **8416** where the VAT **liability is reducing**, a decrease in payments will only take place from the beginning of the next annual accounting period.

Where a business is **experiencing growth**, a revision of instalment payments will avoid a large balancing payment. HMRC must be notified immediately of any significant changes to the business which affect the amount of VAT due.

Leaving the scheme

8418 SI 1995/2518 regs 53-55

A business **must** leave the annual accounting scheme at the end of the accounting year if the value of its taxable supplies in a year exceeds £1.6 million.

If the requirements of the scheme are not met (for example, failure to make the required interim payments), a business **may be asked** to leave the scheme.

A business may **choose** to leave the scheme at any time, and must simply notify HMRC in writing and ask to return to normal VAT accounting.

On leaving, a final return must be made, and any outstanding VAT paid within 2 months of the termination date. Once a business has left the scheme, it cannot rejoin for a period of 12 months.

MEMO POINTS If a **transfer of the business** as a going concern occurs, the purchaser must make a fresh application to join the scheme if he wishes to continue using annual accounting.

CHAPTER 6

Specific situations

OUTLINE ¶¶

SECTION 1

Second-hand goods and collectors' items

VAT is usually charged by a VAT-registered trader on the full value of goods supplied. Goods supplied second-hand will already have been subject to VAT when initially sold. In certain situations (generally where a taxable trader buys goods from private individuals and then sells them on to other private individuals) VAT will not have been reclaimed on the first acquisition, and a VAT charge on the subsequent disposal would result in VAT being charged twice. To remove the double charge, goods may be sold under the **margin scheme**, in which case VAT is only charged on the profit margin i.e. the difference between the acquisition cost and the sale price. **8435** s 50A VATA 1994

In addition to the basic margin scheme, there are two modified schemes:
– the **global accounting** scheme, which is a simplified method of accounting for VAT (it is suitable for businesses if they have a large number of low-value transactions and the accounting and record-keeping requirements would otherwise be onerous); and
– the **auctioneers' scheme** which is, as its name suggests, designed specifically for use by auctioneers.

For margin schemes which apply to acquisitions and sales within the EU or other countries, see ¶9120.

A. The basic margin scheme

8437 SI 1995/1268 reg 12 Notice 718

The margin scheme may be **used for** the sale of any eligible goods, provided that no VAT was recovered, or recoverable, on the original purchase.

With limited exceptions (¶8516), the margin scheme **can only be used for** the onward sale of any goods bought:
- from a private individual or unregistered business which does not have to charge VAT; or
- from another business which is selling them under the margin scheme.

If VAT is charged on goods purchased for resale, the margin scheme cannot be used, regardless of whether the trader can reclaim the VAT. A trader using the margin scheme can reclaim input tax on overheads and repairs in the usual manner.

MEMO POINTS 1. The margin scheme is **voluntary**. Goods may be sold in accordance with the normal rules even when acquired under the margin scheme.
2. Stringent **record-keeping requirements** must be met for the margin scheme to be operated successfully.

1. Eligible goods

8440

Goods which are eligible for the margin scheme are:
- second-hand goods, including motor vehicles;
- antiques;
- collectors' items; and
- works of art.

Specifically **excluded** are precious metals, precious stones (diamonds, rubies, emeralds and sapphires) and investment gold.

SI 1995/1268 reg 2 s 21(5) VATA 1994

MEMO POINTS 1. **Second-hand goods** are broadly defined as tangible moveable property which is capable of further use, either in its present state or after repair. Special rules apply to second-hand **vehicles** (¶8466).
2. **Antiques** are any goods, other than collectors' items and works of art, which are more than 100 years old.
3. **Collectors' items** are collections and pieces of interest, such as:
- postage and revenue stamps, first-day covers and postmarks;
- items connected with the study of coins;
- historical pieces;
- archaeological artefacts;
- palaeontological items;
- items of ethnographic interest;
- anatomical specimens;
- zoological items;
- botanical specimens; or
- mineralogical pieces.

8442 s 21(6) VATA 1994

The following table sets out the conditions for specific items to be treated as **works of art**.

Item	Conditions to be treated as a work of art
Painting, drawing, collage, decorative plaque or similar picture (mounted or unmounted)	Executed by hand[1]
Original engraving, lithograph or other print	Produced from one or more plates executed entirely by hand by the artist; and either: – the only one; or – comprised in a limited edition[2]
Original sculpture or statuary	Executed entirely by the artist

Item	Conditions to be treated as a work of art
Sculpture cast	Produced by, or under the supervision of, the individual who made the mould, or who became entitled to it by succession on the death of that individual; and either: – the only cast produced from the mould; or – comprised in a limited edition (not exceeding eight items, or such number as HMRC may allow if produced before 1 January 1989)
Tapestry or other hanging	Made by hand from an original design and either: – the only one; or – comprised in a limited edition (not exceeding eight items)
Individual pieces of ceramic	Executed entirely and signed by the artist
Enamel on copper	Executed by hand; Signed either by the person who executed it or by someone on behalf of the studio where it was executed; and either: – the only one; or – comprised in a limited edition (not exceeding eight items, each numbered and signed)
Photograph (mounted or unmounted)	Printed by, or under the supervision of, the photographer and signed by him and either: – the only one; or – comprised in a limited edition (not exceeding 30 prints, each numbered and signed)

Note:
1. Specifically excluded are:
– plans, maps and drawings for architectural, engineering, industrial, commercial or topographical purposes;
– hand-decorated manufactured articles; and
– theatrical scenery.
2. Specifically excluded are items produced using a mechanical or photomechanical process.

2. Operating the scheme

Calculating the VAT due

Goods sold for more than the purchase price If the sale price exceeds the purchase price, VAT is calculated on the margin. The margin is simply the excess of the sale price (including incidental expenses directly linked to the sale) over the purchase price, and must not be reduced by any costs – for example, general business overheads or repairs. Details of the sale must be recorded in the stock book (¶8456). The margin is treated as being VAT-inclusive, so VAT should be accounted for based on the VAT fraction (¶8030). **8444**

EXAMPLE Mr A sells an antique chair for £4,000, which he purchased for £2,500.
The margin is therefore £1,500 and the VAT included is £250. (1/6 × £1,500)

Goods sold for less than the purchase price If goods are sold at a loss, there is no margin and therefore no VAT is due. **8446**

Similarly if eligible goods are disposed of by way of **gift**, the sale price is nil and therefore no VAT is chargeable.

Particular types of sale

Part exchange If the proceeds of sale of the goods include goods taken in part exchange, the sale price is the total value of the cash and goods received. **8448**

Hire purchase If goods are sold on hire purchase, they are deemed to be sold to the finance house. The sale should be treated as a cash sale and the selling price to be entered in the stock book is the cash price shown on the hire purchase agreement. No VAT is charged in respect of the **finance element**, provided that this is identified separately on the invoice. **8449**

8451 **Shared assets** If a business **sells a share in an eligible asset** but retains the remainder, no VAT is chargeable in respect of the sale and no VAT invoice can be issued. On a subsequent disposal of the whole asset, VAT must be accounted for on the value of the complete asset and not the share held. A statement should be issued to the owner of the share showing the appropriate share of the sale proceeds, excluding VAT.

8452 If an item is **purchased jointly** by two or more businesses, a set procedure must be adopted. The **procedure** is as follows:

1. **One of the purchasers** (B) is treated as the original owner of the item and must record the purchase in its stock book and retain the purchase invoice.

B should then **issue an invoice** to each of the other joint purchasers for their respective contribution towards the cost, excluding VAT. Each invoice must be endorsed with the following words (or words to the same effect): "This payment is your contribution towards the purchase of the above article. I shall be accounting for the full amount of VAT due under the scheme when it is sold."

2. B should keep copies of these sales invoices and make the appropriate entries in its **stock book**. The other joint purchasers should make no entry in their stock book.

3. If the item is **subsequently sold by B**, he must enter the details of the sale in his stock book, reflecting the full purchase price and not simply his share of the proceeds. The sales invoice must be retained and B must issue statements to the other joint purchasers showing their share of the sale proceeds. The statements should be endorsed with the following words (or words to the same effect): "This payment is your share of the proceeds of the sale of item x. I am accounting for the full amount of VAT due on the sale under the scheme."

4. If the item is subsequently **sold by another joint purchaser** (C), C must obtain the original purchase invoice from B. C should then complete his stock book showing the purchase and sale of the item as though it was made exclusively by him. C is responsible for issuing the statements to the other joint purchasers (including B). B must close the entry in his stock book, stating that the VAT has been accounted for by C, cross-referring to the statement received.

Records

8454 In addition to the normal VAT records (¶9205), a business using the margin scheme is **required to maintain** a stock book (or similar record) and retain the purchase invoice and a copy of the sales invoice for each supply. If a business finds it difficult to comply with these record-keeping requirements due to the large number of transactions, it may wish to use the global accounting scheme (¶8474), if available.

8456 The **stock book** must have separate headings for each of the following entries. Further information may be included at the option of the business.

Section	Required entries
Purchases	– stock number in numerical sequence; – date of purchase; – purchase invoice number; – name of vendor; – any unique identification number (e.g. car registration); and – description of the goods
Sales	– date of sale; – sales invoice number; and – name of buyer
Accounting	– purchase price; – selling price or method of disposal; – margin on sale (i.e. selling price less purchase price); and – VAT due

8458 Records must be **retained** for a period of 6 years.

If a business **fails to comply** with the record-keeping requirements, it is liable to account for VAT on the full value of supplies made, rather than on the margin.

Invoices

When a business **purchases goods** which it intends to resell under the margin scheme, it should obtain (or make out itself) a purchase invoice showing the following information: 8460 Information Sheet 10/07
– the vendor's name and address;
– the purchaser's name and address;
– reference to stock book numbers (in numerical order);
– reference to day book numbers (or other cross-reference to the accounts);
– the invoice number;
– the date of the transaction;
– a description of the goods including any unique identifying number;
– the total price of the goods; and
– either a reference to the relevant part of the UK or EU legislation which refers to the second-hand margin scheme, or a declaration that "This is a second-hand margin scheme supply" or "This invoice is for a second-hand margin scheme supply".

If the **vendor is registered for VAT**, he must:
– prepare the purchase invoice; and
– declare on the invoice that "input tax deduction has not been and will not be claimed by me in respect of the goods sold on this invoice".

Otherwise, the purchaser is responsible for preparing the invoice.

MEMO POINTS 1. If the invoice is for a **batch of goods** which the business intends to sell separately, the invoice must show the purchase price of the individual items.
2. If the invoice is in a **foreign currency**, it must be converted into sterling in accordance with the normal rules (¶7968). If the invoice is for a batch of goods that are to be sold individually, the total price must be converted into sterling before being apportioned between the items.
3. Where a dealer **receives a supply from another EU member state**, the supplier may include his VAT registration number on the invoice. As it may not be clear whether the supply has been zero-rated or supplied under a margin scheme, the dealer should check with the supplier before entering the goods in his stock book.

When a business **sells goods** under the margin scheme, it must provide a sales invoice to the purchaser (and retain a copy) showing the same information as listed above (see ¶8460). The invoice should also show the seller's VAT registration number, and should not identify any VAT charged separately. 8462 Information Sheet 10/07

MEMO POINTS If the invoice is issued in a **foreign currency**, the sterling equivalent must also be shown. If the invoice is for more than one item, the price for each item and the sterling equivalent should generally be shown. If, however, the items were bought as a single unit and are to be sold as a single unit, the total price (and sterling equivalent) is acceptable.

VAT return

For each VAT period, the business must include the following information on its VAT return: 8464
– any VAT due on sales of eligible goods during the period in **box 1**;
– the full selling price of eligible goods sold during the period (net of VAT) in **box 6**; and
– the full purchase price, including VAT as it is not recoverable, of any eligible goods bought during the period in **box 7**.

There is no requirement to include margin scheme purchases or sales in **boxes 8 and 9** of the VAT return.

3. Motor cars

For a car to be **treated as second-hand**, it must have been used on the road, or be appropriated to fixed assets for use in the business by a car dealer. The margin scheme cannot be used for any vehicle on which input tax was reclaimed on purchase. 8466 SI 1992/3122 reg 8 Notice 718/1

Generally, second-hand cars acquired from dealers not registered for VAT and from private individuals will qualify.

MEMO POINTS 1. **Registration and delivery mileage** are not sufficient to make a car second-hand. Demonstration cars and any cars purchased on an invoice showing VAT separately are not second-hand cars, regardless of whether the VAT was reclaimed.
2. A second-hand car which was **personally imported as new** may be sold under the margin scheme, provided that the person who imported the vehicle is not connected with the business which is buying the car (for example, as an employee, agent, or otherwise).
3. If a vehicle is **rebuilt** using parts from other vehicles, the decision as to whether it is new or second-hand depends on how it is registered with the DVLA. If the vehicle retains the registration of one of the component vehicles, it is second-hand, and the purchase price to be entered in the stock book is the purchase price for the vehicle for which the registration number is retained. If, however, the vehicle is re-registered and given a new registration number, it is considered to be a new vehicle and so cannot be sold under the terms of the scheme.

Calculation of VAT due

8468 In general, the **usual** margin scheme **rules** will apply to cars. Until April 2010 a trader who was **unable to comply** fully with the record-keeping requirements was able to use a modified calculation, under which VAT was calculated on either the price paid for the car, or one half of the selling price. That concession has now been withdrawn.

Other items sold

8470 Special rules apply to the following items that are commonly supplied with motor cars.

a. Road fund licences

– Refunds on the surrender of a road fund licence are outside the scope of VAT. Where a second-hand vehicle is purchased and the road fund licence is subsequently surrendered, no adjustment is made to the purchase price in the stock book.
– If a vehicle is sold with a road fund licence as part of the agreed sale price, the selling price for use in the margin scheme includes the road fund licence.
– If the vendor agrees to obtain the road fund licence on behalf of the purchaser and shows it separately on the invoice, the cost of the road fund licence is treated as a separate supply, provided that the conditions for treatment as a disbursement are met (¶8556). If the disbursement conditions are not met it is treated as a single supply and the selling price entered in the stock book must include the value of the road fund licence.

b. If a vehicle is sold with an **MOT**, the selling price includes the value of the MOT.

B. Global accounting

8474
Notice 718 paras 14, 15;
SI 1995/1268 reg 13

The global accounting scheme is a simplified way of accounting for VAT on sales of most margin scheme goods. It is designed for use by businesses dealing in large quantities of low-value goods, which might otherwise find the record-keeping requirements onerous.

1. Eligible goods

8476 The goods detailed at ¶8440 can be included in the scheme, provided that they cost £500 or less to buy. The following are, however, specifically **excluded**:
– aircraft;
– boats and outboard engines;
– caravans (including motorcaravans);
– horses and ponies; and
– motor vehicles, including motorcycles (except where broken up for scrap).
Any item where the VAT is shown separately on the purchase invoice must also be excluded from the scheme.

MEMO POINTS 1. For **invoices in excess of £500** which include a number of items, any individual goods costing over £500 must be identified, excluded from the scheme, and accounted for using the basic margin scheme or the normal VAT rules.
2. **Collections of items** valued at more than £500, such as stamp collections, may be split up, and the items (each worth less than £500) sold separately under the scheme. If the collection is sold in basically the same state as it was bought, and cost more than £500, it cannot be sold under the scheme.

2. Operating the scheme

Under global accounting, a business accounts for VAT on the total margin for each VAT period, not on each sale. 8480

Calculation of VAT due

The **total margin** is the excess of the total sales value for the VAT period over the total purchase value of goods for that period. If the margin is positive, the business must account for VAT based on the VAT fraction (see ¶8030). If the margin is negative (i.e. purchases exceed sales), no VAT is due and the amount of the negative margin is carried forward and included as purchases of the next VAT period. 8482

EXAMPLE During the VAT period to 31 July 2012 Mr A makes total sales under the global accounting scheme of £3,200. The total purchase value of goods during the period was £3,500 and the negative margin is therefore £300. No VAT is due for the period.
During the VAT period to 31 October 2012 Mr A makes total sales under the global accounting scheme of £4,300 and total purchases of £2,800.
The margin is therefore £1,200. (£4,300 – £2,800 – £300)
The VAT due for the period is £200. (1/6 × £1,200)

MEMO POINTS 1. The value of any goods which are **stolen or destroyed** must be deleted from the purchase record and not taken into account when calculating the VAT due.
2. If any purchases have been included in the global accounting scheme records but the **goods are sold outside the scheme** (for example, by way of a zero-rated supply), the value of purchases for that period must exclude the cost of those goods. When the purchase was part of a bulk purchase, a fair and reasonable allocation of the total cost should be made to ascertain the cost of the particular item.

Starting to use the scheme

When a business first adopts the scheme, it must decide whether to account for the value of any **goods on hand** in the first VAT period. 8484

If it decides to **take account of** the goods on hand, a stock count and valuation will be required. Where possible the actual purchase price of the goods should be identified. If the actual purchase price cannot be identified, another method of valuation may be used, provided that it is fair and reasonable. A record should be maintained of how the stock is valued. On a subsequent sale the purchase value is deductible from the sale price and the VAT fraction (see ¶8030) applied to the net figure, in order to determine the VAT due.

If **no account is taken** of the goods on hand, VAT will be accounted for on the full sale value and not on the margin.

If any goods have previously been included in the stock book for the **basic margin scheme** (¶8456), the business must decide which scheme to use. If the goods are included in the global accounting scheme, the goods must be deleted from the stock book, which should be cross-referenced to the global accounting scheme records.

Records

Under global accounting, a business is required to maintain a record of all purchases and sales, in addition to copies of all invoices. This is in addition to the standard VAT record-keeping requirements (¶9205). 8486

There is no **prescribed format** for global accounting scheme records, although the records must be maintained separately and be identified as global accounting scheme records.

The **purchase and sale summaries** should include the following:
– invoice number;
– date of purchase/sale;
– description of goods to verify correct inclusion in the scheme; and
– total price.

8488 The records must be **retained** for a period of 6 years.

If a business fails to comply with the record-keeping requirements, it is liable to account for VAT on the full value of supplies made, rather than on the margin.

Invoices

8490 On the **purchase** of goods which are to be sold under global accounting, the business must obtain a purchase invoice showing the following information:
– the buyer's name and address;
– the vendor's name and address;
– the invoice number;
– the date of the transaction;
– a description of the goods (sufficient to ensure eligibility to be in the scheme);
– the total price of the goods; and
– an endorsement stating "Global Accounting invoice".

The invoice must not show any VAT element separately.

The purchase invoice will be **prepared by** the vendor if he is registered for VAT. Otherwise the purchaser is responsible for preparing the invoice. The invoice must be certified, stating that it is not a tax invoice.

8492 When goods are **sold** under the global accounting scheme, a sales invoice must be issued (and a copy retained) in respect of any sale **to a taxable person**, showing:
– the vendor's name, address and VAT registration number;
– the buyer's name and address;
– the invoice number;
– the date of the transaction;
– a description of the goods (sufficient to ensure eligibility to be in the scheme);
– the total price of the goods, including VAT, which must not be shown separately; and
– an endorsement stating "Global Accounting invoice".

The vendor must check that the rules at ¶8490 above were applied on purchase.

MEMO POINTS 1. **If selling items for more than £500** and the vendor does not wish to disclose that he acquired the items under the global accounting scheme (i.e. that he acquired them for less than £500), he may instead include a statement on the invoice which says: "input tax deduction has not been and will not be claimed by me in respect of the goods sold on this invoice". In any event, the invoice must not separately identify any VAT charged in respect of the sale.
2. Sales **to non-taxable persons** should be recorded in the trader's usual way, for example using the till record.

VAT return

8494 For each VAT period, the business must include on its VAT return the following information:
– any VAT due on the positive margin for the period in **box 1**;
– the full selling price of eligible goods sold during the period (net of VAT) in **box 6**; and
– the full purchase price (including VAT, as it is not recoverable) of any eligible goods bought during the period in **box 7**.

A **negative margin** should not be included on the VAT return (see ¶8482).

Ceasing to use the scheme

8496 When ceasing to use the scheme, a business must make a closing adjustment to take account of **purchases already made** which have not been resold, unless the VAT due on the value of stock on hand would be no more than £1,000.

In the final VAT period of using the scheme, the sales figure must be adjusted to include the purchase value of the stock in hand.

EXAMPLE Mr A deregisters on 31 October 2012. During the VAT period to 31 October, he makes total sales under the global accounting scheme of £11,000. The total purchase value of goods during the period was £1,000 and the cost of stock on hand was £20,000. There is no negative margin carried forward from the previous VAT period.
The margin is therefore £30,000. (£11,000 + £20,000 – £1,000)
The VAT due for the period is: £5,000. (1/6 × £30,000)

C. Auctioneers' scheme

The auctioneers' scheme is a variant of the basic margin scheme, so there are many similarities. The scheme is optional and can be operated on a transaction-by-transaction basis. When an auctioneer sells **eligible goods** (¶8440) on behalf of a third party, the auctioneers' scheme may be used to calculate the VAT. **8500** Notice 718/2; SI 1995/1268 reg 10

By concession, the scheme may also be used to sell **any goods grown, made or produced** by a non-VAT-registered vendor, including livestock and bloodstock. In this situation, the vendor must confirm his non-registered status, along with his name, address and the description of the goods.

The scheme may only be used if the **vendor** is either: **8502**
- not registered for VAT;
- registered for VAT but selling the goods under the margin scheme or global accounting;
- a finance house selling repossessed, eligible margin scheme goods in the same state as they were acquired; or
- an insurance company selling eligible margin scheme goods which have been acquired as a result of an insurance claim, and sold in the same state.

Operating the scheme

VAT is **calculated** by applying the VAT fraction (see ¶8030) to the margin (i.e. the excess of the sale price over the purchase price). **8504**

Under the scheme, the **purchase price** of goods is the amount payable to the vendor by the auctioneer, i.e. the hammer price less any commission due from the vendor.

The **sale price** is the amount due from the purchaser, i.e. the hammer price plus buyer's premium (or other commission) including any incidental charges in respect of the sale.

The **following** types of charges **are excluded** from the scheme:
- disbursements which meet all the conditions in ¶8556;
- incidental expenses (packing and transport) charged on to the buyer, which are a separate supply in themselves;
- exempt supplies, such as insurance; and
- other charges which are optional and not directly related to the sale of the goods.

EXAMPLE Mr A, an auctioneer, sells an antique dining table at auction on behalf of Mr B. The hammer price is £5,500. Mr B pays 10% (plus VAT) commission, and the purchaser pays a buyer's premium of 18% (including VAT).
The auctioneer's purchase price is calculated as follows:

	£
Hammer price	5,500
Commission at 10%	(550)
VAT on commission	(110)
	4,840

The sale price is:

	£
Hammer price	5,500
Buyer's premium at 18%	990
	6,490

The margin is therefore £1,650. (£6,490 – £4,840)
The related VAT is £275. (1/6 × £1,650)

8506 If a **registered person buys goods** at auction and wishes to use either the basic margin scheme or global accounting in respect of a subsequent sale of those goods, he should inform the auctioneer after the sale. The auctioneer should then ensure that the appropriate documentation is issued.

Similarly, if a **registered person sells goods** at auction the auctioneer should be informed. After the sale, the auctioneer will provide the vendor with an account showing the hammer price, any commission due and the net amount payable. The vendor should sign and date the account, certifying that "input tax deduction has not been and will not be claimed by me in respect of the goods sold on this invoice".

MEMO POINTS The **buyer** may subsequently decide that he would prefer to pay VAT separately on the hammer price under the **normal VAT rules**, in which case the auctioneer will need to re-invoice the transaction. This can only occur if:
– the auctioneer is able to comply with all the usual VAT rules with regard to the re-invoicing;
– all the original records in respect of the transaction are still held by the auctioneer and the buyer; and
– the re-invoicing is within 4 years of the transaction.
The first entry in the accounting records should be cancelled and a cross-reference made to the new invoice. The new invoice should refer to the original transaction and should contain an instruction to the buyer to amend his VAT account.

8508 The auctioneer is deemed to both make and receive a supply, so there is a common tax point. The **time of supply** is the earlier of the transfer of the goods from the auctioneer to the buyer, or receipt of payment by the auctioneer.

Records

8510 The record-keeping requirements of the basic margin scheme must be adopted, with a number of modifications.

There is no requirement to keep a **stock book** in the strict format specified by the basic margin scheme. However, the business must retain records with the same information as required for a stock book, such as:
– sales catalogues;
– copies of lots of each day; and
– copies of sales and purchase invoices.

MEMO POINTS The records must be **retained** for a period of 6 years. HMRC can exercise their powers to vary the period for which records must be retained by specifying the period in writing, and the period may vary according to individual circumstances. If a business fails to comply with the record-keeping requirements, it is liable to account for VAT on the full value of supplies made, rather than on the margin.

8512 **Invoices** The invoices must contain the **following information** in addition to the basic margin scheme requirements:

Invoice	Information required
Purchase	– hammer price; – commission due from vendor; and – net amount due to vendor.
Sale	– hammer price; – any other charges (including buyer's premium); and – amount due from purchaser.

No VAT should be identified separately on the invoices. In relation to **commission** and similar charges, the invoice should therefore show the amount of commission including VAT with either the:
- VAT-inclusive rate of commission; or
- rate of commission and state "plus VAT at 20%".

An additional statement should be made on the invoice: "this amount includes VAT which must not be shown separately or reclaimed as input tax".

EXAMPLE Mr A charges commission at 10%. On the invoice for a sale valued at £3,000, he should show either:
a. VAT-inclusive commission at 12% i.e. £360; or
b. commission at 10% plus VAT at 20% i.e. £360.

D. Goods subject to VAT on acquisition

Goods which have been subject to VAT on acquisition are generally excluded from the second-hand goods schemes. However, the vendor may choose to use the basic margin scheme, global accounting or the auctioneers' scheme where VAT has been incurred on the following goods: 8516
- **works of art** (¶8442) obtained within the EU from the creator, or his heirs, for onward sale; or
- works of art, **antiques and collectors' pieces** (¶8440) imported by the business itself.

See ¶9120 for further details.

A business wishing to **adopt a scheme** must notify HMRC accordingly, indicating which particular scheme it is going to use. The scheme must then be **used for a period of** at least 2 years, after which the business may notify HMRC that it wishes to cease using the scheme. 8518

If a business **does not choose to adopt** one of the schemes, it must continue to account for VAT on these goods in the normal way.

SECTION 2

Agents

The **VAT treatment** of agents **depends on** a number of factors, such as whether the agent is acting in his own name or in the name of the principal, the location of the principal, and the actual nature of the service that the agent provides. 8520

1. General principles

The **term** agent is not defined in the legislation but is generally **taken to be** someone who acts for, or represents, someone else (known as the principal) in arranging the supply or acquisition of goods or services. Whether or not a person is an agent depends on the actual arrangement with the principal. Each case should be judged on its own facts, although it is crucial that both parties consent that one of them will be acting on the other's behalf. 8522

The title of agent does not necessarily create an agency relationship for VAT purposes. For example, an employment agency will usually act as a principal.

Relationship

For VAT purposes, an agent and principal relationship will be **taken to exist** where: 8524 Notice 700 para 22
a. the agent has agreed to act on behalf of the principal in relation to a particular transaction (the agreement between the parties may be written, oral or implied by the nature of the relationship and the way that business is conducted);

b. it has been clearly established between the agent and principal, and is apparent to HMRC, that the agent is arranging the transactions for the principal rather than trading on his own account;
c. the agent must not have owned any of the goods, or used any of the services which are bought or sold for the principal; and
d. the agent must not have altered the nature or value of any of the supplies made between the principal and third parties.

Transactions

8526 Notice 700 para 22.3 In most transactions the agent will be involved in two supplies:
a. the supply of services to the principal for which a fee or commission will be charged by the agent; and
b. the supply between the principal and the third party.

The **VAT liability** of the agent's supply will often follow the liability of the supply between the third party and the principal.

An agent may act in the name of the principal or in his own name.

2. Agent acting in the name of the principal

8528 Notice 700 para 22.5 Where the formal agency agreement involves a disclosed agent, the third party will be aware of the agent's involvement in the transaction. Common examples are travel agents and insurance brokers.

The main supply occurs between the principal and third party, and there is a separate supply of services between the agent and principal, for which the agent receives commission.

The agent will include only his commission on his VAT return.

EXAMPLE Mr A is a disclosed agent who arranges a sale of goods between Mr P (the principal) and Mr C (the customer). The goods are sold for £2,000 (plus VAT). Mr A charges commission at 10%. The main supply between Mr P and Mr C will occur as if no agent was involved. So the goods pass to Mr C, for which he pays £2,000 (plus VAT).
In a separate transaction, Mr A raises an invoice to Mr P for his services, and charges £200 (plus VAT).

Note:
The payment may be routed through Mr A, so that Mr P receives a net sum of £1,800 (plus VAT).

Principal's supply

8529 The VAT **liability** of the supply will depend only on the status of the third party and principal.

The **tax point** of a selling principal's supply follows the normal rules. If the agent receives monies on the principal's behalf, the principal is deemed to have received payment at the same time.

Agent's supply

8530 The VAT **liability** of the agent's supply to the principal will be standard-rated, unless it is specifically zero-rated under one of the following:
- the export of goods;
- work on goods for subsequent export; and
- certain types of transport (¶8052).

The **principal's identity** should be disclosed to customers.

8531 The **time** when the agent makes his supply depends on whether he is acting on:
- an **ongoing basis**, when he is making a continuous supply, and so the tax point is the earlier of receipt of payment or the raising of a VAT invoice; or
- a **one-off basis**, when he is making a single supply and the normal tax point rules apply (¶7902).

Place of supply

The place of supply of an agent's services when performed for a business customer is the place where the customer is established. The place of supply of an agent's services to a non-taxable person is where the agent is established. **8533**

In another EU member state When the **principal is a business** in another EU member state, the agent's supply to the principal is treated as being made in the principal's EU member state. The person who accounts for the VAT on the agent's supply depends on whether the principal is located in: **8534** SI 1992/3121 reg 14
– the same member state as the agent, when the agent accounts for the VAT; or
– in a different member state, when the principal accounts for the VAT under the reverse charge procedure (¶9110).

Most business customers will be able to provide their VAT number to the agent to show that they are in business. If the agent cannot obtain the principal's VAT number or the customer is not VAT-registered, alternative evidence may be used. If the agent cannot provide evidence that the principal is in business, the agent must account for UK VAT as if the principal were a non-business customer.

MEMO POINTS 1. If the principal is registered for VAT in **more than one EU state**, the principal should give the most appropriate VAT number to the agent.
2. The agent's invoice must quote the **principal's EU VAT number** if it has been passed to him.
3. The agent must meet the normal invoicing requirements.

EXAMPLE A UK agent arranges a supply of goods between a French seller and a German buyer who both pass on their VAT numbers to the agent. The goods are supplied in France. If the agent acts for:
a. the seller, the agent is making a supply in France, and the French seller accounts for French VAT on the commission under the reverse charge procedure;
b. the buyer, he is making a supply in Germany, because the buyer is established there and the buyer therefore accounts for German VAT on the commission under the reverse charge procedure.

Invoicing

The invoicing arrangements for supplies in the UK are as follows: **8536** Notice 700 para 23.1.1

Transaction	Supplier's VAT status	Invoicing for	
		Main supply	Agent's supply
Supply by principal	Registered	Invoiced to customer by principal, charging VAT	Invoiced to principal, charging VAT
	Unregistered	No VAT due[1]	Invoiced to principal, charging VAT
Purchase by principal	Registered	Invoiced to principal by supplier, charging VAT	Invoiced to principal, charging VAT
	Unregistered	No VAT due[1]	Invoiced to principal, charging VAT

Note:
1. The agent must retain evidence that he is arranging the supply on behalf of the principal (e.g. standing agreement or a signed declaration).

3 Agent acting in his own name

Where an agent is allowed by a principal to enter into contracts with third parties on behalf of the principal without disclosing the existence of the principal, the agent acts as an **undisclosed agent**. The customer will only deal with the agent, will only receive an invoice in the agent's name and the principal's details will not be divulged. **8538** s 47 VATA 1994 Notice 700 para 22.6

For the purposes of **VAT registration**, all supplies made by the agent in his own name (i.e. including the principal's supplies) count towards the VAT registration threshold (¶7775).

If an agent issues invoices in his own name for supplies of **goods** which he arranges for the principal, for VAT purposes he **must** treat the transaction as a supply to him and a supply by him as if he were the principal.
The same applies to **services** but only if both the agent and the supplier are registered for VAT and the services are taxable, in which case the agent **may** treat the transaction as a supply to him and a supply by him as if he were the principal.
The **VAT treatment depends on** whether or not the main supply is made wholly within the UK.

UK supplies

8539 For domestic supplies (i.e. the whole transaction occurs within the UK), an agent has a **choice** between principal treatment (which is mandatory for most international transactions) or agent treatment.

8540 **Principal treatment** The undisclosed agent is treated for VAT purposes as a principal.

8541 In this case, a **selling agent**:
- recovers input tax on the net value of the supply from the principal; and
- accounts for output tax on the supply to the customer.

There is one output and one input on the agent's VAT return, and as the time of supply for both transactions is the same, the usual procedure is to declare both on the same VAT return.
VAT incurred on other costs, such as warehousing and packing, may also be recovered by the agent.

> EXAMPLE Mr A acts as an undisclosed selling agent for Mr P, who is VAT-registered. Mr A arranges a sale of goods for £800 (net of VAT) and charges commission of 10%.
> Mr P raises an invoice for £720 plus VAT to Mr A.
> Mr A raises an invoice for £800 plus VAT to the customer.

8542 In this case, a **buying agent**:
- recovers input tax on his "purchase" from the principal's supplier; and
- accounts for output tax on his "sale" to his principal.

There is one output and one input on the agent's VAT return, and as the time of supply for both transactions is the same, the usual procedure is to declare both on the same VAT return.
VAT incurred on other costs, such as warehousing and packing, may also be recovered by the agent.

> EXAMPLE Mr A acts as an undisclosed buying agent for Mr P, who is VAT-registered. Mr A arranges a purchase of goods for £800 (net of VAT) from Mr S and charges commission of 10% to Mr P.
> Mr S raises an invoice for £800 plus VAT to Mr A.
> Mr A raises an invoice for £880 plus VAT to Mr P.

8545 Notice 700 para 23.1.2 **Agent treatment** This is only available for domestic supplies (that is, where both the principal and customer/supplier are established in the UK). A **selling agent** accounts for both the main supply and his commission as separate outputs on his VAT return, and recovers input tax on the supply from the principal. The self-billing procedure (¶8332) may be used, subject to approval from HMRC.

> EXAMPLE Mr A acts as an undisclosed selling agent for Mr P, who is VAT-registered. Mr A arranges a sale of goods for £700 (net of VAT) and charges commission of 10%.
> Mr P raises an invoice to Mr A for £700 plus VAT.
> Mr A raises two invoices:
> - £700 plus VAT to the customer; and
> - £70 plus VAT to Mr P.

A **buying agent** accounts for output tax on the value of the main supply to the principal and also on his agent's services. Both supplies can be shown on the same invoice, although the commission must be separately identified. 8546

He can also recover input tax on the value of the third party's supply.

> EXAMPLE Mr B acts as an undisclosed buying agent for Mr Q, who is VAT-registered. Mr B arranges a purchase of goods for £700 (net of VAT) and charges commission of 10%.
> The supplier raises an invoice to Mr B for £700 plus VAT.
> Mr B raises a single invoice to Mr Q showing:
> – £700 plus VAT in respect of the main supply; and
> – £70 plus VAT in respect of his commission.

International supplies

An **undisclosed agent is treated** for VAT purposes **as** a principal for international supplies (where either the actual principal or the customer/supplier is located outside the UK). The agent's own supply of agency services is subsumed within the main supply. 8548 s 47(3) VATA 1994 Notice 700 para 24

Goods The value of goods which are: 8549 s 47(1) VATA 1994
– **acquired** from a principal in another **EU member state** is the value of the principal's supply less the agent's commission (the agent accounts for output tax on the acquisition (¶8937) and is also responsible for Intrastat returns (¶9002), if relevant); or
– **imported** from outside the EU is the import value (¶9043).

Goods which are **exported** outside the EU through an agent may be zero-rated if valid evidence is retained (¶9076).

> EXAMPLE Mr P is taxable in Italy and appoints Mr A, who is taxable in the UK, as his agent. Mr P asks Mr A to sell Italian goods to a UK customer for £70,000. Mr A's commission is £7,000.
> For VAT purposes, Mr A is treated as a principal and acquires the Italian goods. The acquisition is valued net of the commission, so that he only accounts for reverse charge output tax and input tax on £63,000, which is the amount invoiced by Mr P.
> For the onward sale, Mr A charges output tax on £70,000 to the customer.

Services The VAT treatment is determined by the usual place of supply rules (¶7996) for the main supply, so if it would be **supplied where**: 8550
– the supplier is located, then as the UK agent is treated himself as a principal, the supply will be VATable in the UK; or
– the recipient is located (i.e. most business-to-business (B2B) supplies, as in the example below), the UK agent must account for the reverse charge, then charge output tax on the onward supply.

Other services which are not covered by the above rules, for example those supplied where performed, need not be accounted for as if the agent were principal.

> EXAMPLE Mr P, located in Dublin, supplies advertising services through his UK agent, Mr A, to a UK customer. Mr P invoices Mr A for £900, which takes account of Mr A's commission charge of £100.
> As B2B advertising is supplied where the customer is located, Mr P's supply is made in the UK.
> Mr A applies the reverse charge to Mr P's supply.
> So Mr A charges himself £180 of output tax, which he can also recover as input tax. (£900 x 20%)
> Mr A then sells the services on to the customer for £1,000, charging £200 of output tax. (£1,000 x 20%)

4. Disbursements

In some trades and professions, all or some of the **incidental costs** of a supply (such as travelling expenses) are charged separately on the client's invoice. 8552

The issue is whether these costs should be included in the value of the main taxable supply, or whether they can be treated as recharged expenses i.e. disbursements which are outside the scope of VAT.

Input tax recovery

8554 If costs are treated as disbursements, the **agent** cannot reclaim VAT on the cost incurred and, unless the VAT invoice for the disbursement is addressed directly to the client, the **client** is also unable to claim the input tax because he does not hold a valid invoice.

The disbursement treatment is therefore usually only advantageous where there is no VAT on the third party's supply, or where the client is not VAT-registered. It is also advantageous for traders who are partly exempt, and cannot recover VAT on expenses incurred, to have non-VATable costs treated as disbursements rather than to include them in the value of the main taxable supply.

EXAMPLE A Ltd is a bank which has agreed to lend Mr B money to build a block of flats. As part of the loan agreement the bank has appointed a surveyor to approve the stage payments to be made under the terms of the loan. The surveyor charges the bank £1,000 plus VAT of £200. The bank cannot recover this VAT, and recharges Mr B the cost of the surveyor (£1,200). Although Mr B is fully taxable and can recover any input tax incurred, he cannot recover the £200, as the service was supplied to the bank and not to him and so does not qualify as a disbursement. Also, he does not hold a valid VAT invoice.

Outside the scope of VAT

8556 Notice 700 para 25.1

The agent can treat payments to third parties as disbursements for VAT purposes, and exclude these amounts when calculating any VAT due on the main supply to the client, if all of the following **criteria** are met:

a. the agent was acting for the client when making the payment to the third party;

b. the client:

– actually received and used the goods or services provided by the third party (this condition usually prevents the agent's own travelling and subsistence expenses, telephone bills, postage and other costs from being treated as disbursements for VAT purposes);

– was responsible for paying the third party;

– authorised the agent to make the payment on his behalf;

– knew that the goods or services the agent paid for were to be provided by a third party;

c. the outlay is separately itemised when the agent invoices the client;

d. only the exact amount paid to the third party is recovered from the client; and

e. the goods or services which the agent pays for are clearly additional to the supplies which the agent makes to the client on his own account.

8558 Where a payment is treated as a disbursement, the agent must:

– retain **evidence** to show that the payment was properly treated as a disbursement, such as a copy invoice; and

– be able to show that no **input tax** on the disbursement was claimed by him.

The agent's **invoice** must carefully distinguish between true disbursements and other costs which form part of his own supply, as shown in the following pro-forma.

	£
Agent's services	X
Expenses not to be treated as disbursements	X
VATable amount	X
VAT @ 20%	X
Disbursements	X
Total	X

EXAMPLE Mr D supplies standard-rated services to Mr E for £1,000. He incurs travel costs of £200, which do not qualify as disbursements. He also incurs a postal search fee of £50, which may be treated as a disbursement.
Mr D's VAT invoice will show the following:

	£
Services	1,000
Expenses	200
Value on which VAT is charged	1,200
VAT @ 20%	240
Disbursements	50
Total	1,490

5. Agents for overseas principals

HMRC may direct any person to appoint a VAT representative to act on his behalf for VAT purposes where that person: 8560 s 48 VATA 1994
a. is either:
- a taxable person, who is required to be registered for VAT;
- a person who makes taxable supplies; or
- acquiring goods in the UK from one or more other EU member states;

b. does not have any business establishment or other fixed establishment in the UK or in any EU member state (in the case of an individual, does not have his usual place of residence in the UK); or
c. is established in a country outside the EU, with which the UK has no mutual assistance provision.

MEMO POINTS 1. A person will be **treated as having been directed** to appoint a VAT representative if HMRC have either served notice of the direction or requirement on him, or taken reasonable steps to bring the direction or requirement to his attention.
2. Where a person **fails to appoint a VAT representative** in accordance with a direction by HMRC, he may be required to provide appropriate security (¶9329) for the payment of any VAT due from him, including any future liabilities. There may also be a liability to a criminal penalty.
3. An overseas principal who satisfies **a**. and **b**. above can unilaterally **choose** to appoint a VAT representative, with the agreement of HMRC.
4. A **mutual assistance provision** is a written understanding between the authorities of two countries that information will be passed on where it is likely to be of interest to the other country.

VAT representatives

A VAT representative is **entitled to act on** the principal's behalf for all VAT purposes, and becomes: 8562 s 48(3) VATA 1994
- **responsible for** ensuring that the principal complies with and discharges all of his VAT obligations and liabilities; and
- jointly and severally **liable for** the principal's compliance with UK VAT law.

A VAT representative will **not be guilty of** any offence by virtue of the above unless:
- he consented to, or took part in, the commission of the offence by the principal;
- the commission of the offence by the principal is attributable to any neglect on the part of the VAT representative; or
- the offence consists of a contravention by the VAT representative of an obligation which is imposed both on him and on the principal.

Procedure

Where a person is appointed to be a **VAT representative** he **must notify** HMRC of his appointment. The **principal** being represented must complete forms VAT 1 (and VAT 2 if the principal or representative is in partnership). **Both the principal and representative** must complete VAT 1TR within 30 days of the date on which his appointment became effective. Evidence of the appointment must also be submitted. 8563 SI 1995/2518 reg 10

Following the appointment, the VAT representative must, within 30 days, notify HMRC in writing of:
- any changes made in the name, constitution or ownership of his business;
- his ceasing to be the principal's VAT representative; or
- any other event which may require the variation of the register.

Records

8565 The **VAT representative** is required to maintain separate VAT records for each principal that he represents, and must retain sufficient records to show how the VAT account is made up (such as VAT invoices).

The **principal**, who is making taxable supplies in the UK, must keep all of the records required under the normal regulations (¶9205).

SECTION 3

Transfer of a going concern

8596 s 49 VATA 1994 SI 1995/2518 reg 6

The **sale of a business is a taxable supply unless** it satisfies the conditions to be treated as the transfer of a going concern (TOGC), when it will be outside the scope of VAT. The sale of part of a business may be treated as a TOGC if the part is capable of being operated separately as a business.

Details about the following subjects in relation to the TOGC are covered elsewhere in *Tax Memo*, as follows:

Subject	¶¶
Transfer of VAT registration	¶7775
Recovery of input tax	¶8244
Capital goods scheme for land, computers, ships and aircraft	¶8281

MEMO POINTS Where the business consists of **property letting**, special rules apply to determine whether a transfer is a TOGC (¶8610).

Consequences

8598 Where the sale is **treated as a TOGC**, there is no supply for VAT purposes and therefore no VAT is chargeable. If VAT is charged in error, the invoice must be cancelled and a new invoice issued.

MEMO POINTS If **VAT is charged and the invoice is not cancelled**, the transferor is liable to account to HMRC for the VAT charged. Strictly, the purchaser cannot recover the amount charged as VAT in this respect, as it is not input tax.

TOGC treatment

8600 SI 1995/1268 Notice 700/9

A number of **conditions** must be satisfied for a transfer to be treated as a TOGC:

Criteria	Conditions
VAT registration	If the **vendor is registered** for VAT, the buyer must be either: – registered for VAT; – required to compulsorily register for VAT; or – accepted for voluntary registration.
	If the vendor is **not registered** for VAT, there is no requirement for the buyer to be registered. The vendor may be trading below the registration limit or making exempt supplies.

Criteria	Conditions
Business activities and trading	**At the time of the transfer**, the business must be a going concern i.e. an operating business, not necessarily commercially viable.
	The buyer must acquire **something which is capable of** being operated as a business (i.e. not just capital assets).
	There must be no significant **break in trading** either before or after the transfer. A temporary closure which does not disrupt the business is ignored (e.g. a short closure for redecorating).
	The buyer must actually **operate** the business, therefore immediately consecutive transfers do not qualify as TOGCs (e.g. Mr A transfers a business to B Ltd which immediately transfers it to C Ltd – neither transfer is a TOGC).
Assets	The assets transferred must be **intended for use** by the buyer in a similar business to that carried on by the vendor. There are special rules when land and property are transferred (¶8604).

Indicating factors

In some cases it may not be clear whether the sale is a TOGC. The substance of the transaction as a whole must be considered, and **HMRC** have a **list** of factors which they take into account when determining whether the sale should be treated as a supply. None of the factors outweigh the others, and each case must be considered on the facts. **8602** VTOGC 3500

a. The transfer of the **business name** strongly implies that the business has been transferred as a going concern.

b. The transfer of **goodwill** is a good indication of a TOGC. It is irrelevant that the contract allocates only a small percentage of the consideration to the goodwill. The transfer of items such as customer lists and records may indicate a TOGC but in isolation is unlikely to represent the transfer of a business.

c. If the transferee takes over **contracts** with suppliers and customers from the transferor and **buys work in progress**, this is a strong indication that he is taking over the business of the transferor.

d. The transfer of **premises** will imply that a business is being transferred where the premises:
– are vital to the operation of the business (for example, a swimming pool); or
– have a significant impact on the goodwill of the business (for example, the location of a restaurant can be critical to the success of the operation).

e. Restrictive covenants preventing the previous owner from carrying on a similar business will be indicative of a TOGC.

f. If the new business operates using the **same staff** as the previous business (including staff who were made redundant before the transfer), this implies a TOGC.

g. The sale of the remaining **stock** in a single transfer and the sale of **plant and equipment** required for the operation of the business are both indications that the business has been transferred as a going concern. However, where the transferee is already operating a similar business, and therefore already has stock and sufficient plant and equipment, these factors do not necessarily need to be present.

h. Publicity surrounding the sale (for example adverts showing that the business is now under new management) may also be considered.

C & E v Dearwood [1986], *H G Retail Ltd* [1998], *Grassby & Sons Ltd* [1993]

Land and property

If the sale would **normally be a taxable supply**, the buyer and vendor will need to satisfy certain conditions for the transfer to be included as part of a TOGC, as shown in the following table. **8604** SI 1995/1268 reg 5(2A)

Vendor's position	Requirements for purchaser
The vendor is transferring taxable land and buildings which: – he has opted to tax[1]; or – would normally be standard-rated (¶8847) i.e. a non-residential property under 3 years old, or civil engineering works.	By the relevant date[2] the purchaser must have notified: – HMRC of his election to opt to tax[1]; and – the vendor that the election has not been, and will not be, disapplied under the anti-avoidance rule (¶8906).
The vendor is transferring land and buildings which are zero-rated or exempt.	The purchaser does not have to opt to tax.

Note:
1. Depending on the type of property, it is possible to **opt to tax** all transactions in respect of that property which would otherwise be exempt (¶8904).
2. The **relevant date** is the time of the supply, which is normally the date of completion, but can be the date of exchange of contracts (¶8842).

8606 The **vendor** is responsible for applying the correct VAT treatment. In particular, where the purchaser must opt to tax, the vendor must be satisfied that the purchaser's option is in place by the relevant date. In addition to the requirement that the purchaser should confirm in writing that his option will not be disapplied, the vendor should obtain appropriate evidence that the purchaser has opted. Depending on what is possible due to time restraints, the vendor should, at the very least, request a copy of the purchaser's notification of his option to tax.

MEMO POINTS Where the **vendor mistakenly does not charge VAT**, because he wrongly believes the purchaser has opted to tax, he can only recover the VAT liability from the purchaser. HMRC may have discretion to treat a transaction as a TOGC where such an error has been made in good faith but this should not be relied upon.

8608 Notice 742A para 11.2

The following table **summarises** whether a TOGC exists in relation to various situations involving property:

Type of commercial building	Has the vendor opted to tax?	Has the purchaser opted to tax?	Has the purchaser's option to tax been disapplied?	TOGC?
Over 3 years old, usually exempt	y	y	y	n
	y	y	n	y
	y	n	n/a	n
	n	n	n/a	y
	n	y	y	y
	n	y	n	y
New building under 3 years old, usually standard-rated	y	y	n	y
	y	y	y	n
	y	n	n/a	n
	n	n	n/a	n
	n	y	y	n
	n	y	n	y

Rental business

8610 The conditions outlined in ¶8600 can also be applied to the transfer of a property rental business and, provided that they are satisfied, the transfer will be treated as a TOGC and therefore outside the scope of VAT.

Notice 700/9 paras 6.2, 6.3

The following **examples** illustrate where a TOGC occurs:

Example	TOGC?
Freehold property is let to a tenant and sold with the benefit of the existing lease	✓
Assignment of a lease with the benefit of a sublease	✓
Sale of a building which is let, where the sale takes place during an initial rent-free period	✓
Grant of a lease in respect of a building where the tenants are not yet in occupation	✓
Transfer of a property to a third party when the owner of the property has found a tenant but has not yet entered into a lease agreement (where the transfer takes place with the benefit of the prospective tenancy)	✓
Sale of a site as a package by a property developer which is a mixture of let and unlet, finished or unfinished properties where the sale of the site would otherwise have been standard-rated, provided that the purchaser elects to waive exemption for the whole site	✓
Property developer who has built a building and allows someone to occupy it temporarily (without any right to occupy after any proposed sale), or is actively marketing it in search of a tenant	x
Sale of a property where the lease granted is surrendered immediately before the sale	x
Sale of a property to the existing tenant, who currently leases the whole premises	x

CHAPTER 7

Special accounting methods

OUTLINE ¶¶

To reduce the administrative burden, and to facilitate VAT compliance, some simplified VAT accounting schemes are available. **8615**

SECTION 1

Flat rate scheme

The flat rate scheme removes the need to calculate and record output tax and input tax. Instead, a flat rate percentage is applied to all VAT-inclusive turnover to calculate the VAT liability due to HMRC. The flat rate percentage varies according to trade sector. The scheme is voluntary, and there is no minimum period for which a business needs to use the scheme. **8620** Notice 733 s 26E VATA 1994

Using other schemes

The flat rate scheme may be used **at the same time** as the annual accounting scheme (¶8405). If a business wishes to join both schemes, a joint application form is contained within HMRC's Notice 732, available on their website (www.hmrc.gov.uk). **8622**

Cash accounting, margin, or retail schemes **cannot be used** in conjunction with the flat rate scheme.

1. Eligibility

8624
Notice 733 para 3.1

The scheme is available for small businesses if their total taxable turnover in the next 12 months is not expected to exceed £150,000 (excluding VAT). A business may **start using the scheme from** a date determined by HMRC.

MEMO POINTS 1. **Taxable supplies** are supplies subject to VAT at any rate. For this purpose, supplies **exclude** any capital assets expected to be sold and deemed supplies under the reverse charge mechanism.
2. The **estimate of turnover** should be based on reasonable grounds, such as financial accounts or VAT returns for previous periods. The value of these supplies should be calculated in accordance with the trader's usual method of accounting for VAT on the scheme i.e. either cash received or invoices raised.
3. The **application form** (VAT600 FRS) is in HMRC's Notice 733.

Restrictions

8626
SI 1995/2518 regs 55A, 55B, 55L

An application to join the scheme will be **denied** if any of the following apply:
a. the business is not registered for VAT;
b. the business ceased to operate the flat rate scheme in the 12 months preceding the date of application;
c. in the previous 12 months the trader has been convicted of a VAT offence, or an assessment has been raised on the trader with a penalty for dishonesty;
d. the business is, or within the last 24 months has been, registered as part of a VAT group (¶7807), or as a division (¶7815);
e. the business becomes eligible for VAT group treatment or becomes associated with another person who holds a dominant influence over the business;
f. the capital goods scheme (¶8250) will apply to any of the business assets; or
g. the business is required to use the tour operators' margin scheme.

Notice 733 para 3.9

MEMO POINTS 1. A person is **regarded as associated** with another person if:
– one is able to influence the financial or operating policies of the other;
– one has the right to give directions to the other;
– in practice one habitually complies with the directions of the other; or
– they are closely bound by financial, economic and organisational links.
Persons are **not associated** by reason only of normal business relationships. If a business has been associated with another person **within the last 2 years**, and this connection has since ceased, HMRC may allow the business to join the scheme if there is no risk to revenue.
2. The **tour operators' margin scheme** must be used by any tour operator who is supplying designated travel services. For this purpose, a tour operator is either a travel agent acting as principal or undisclosed agent, or a person providing travel services which are commonly provided by such travel agents. Designated travel services are bought in and resold without any material alteration, and include accommodation, transport, etc. For further details, see *VAT Memo*.

Starting the scheme

8629
SI 1995/2518 reg 55B

A business will normally start to use the scheme at **the beginning of** the next VAT return period after HMRC process the application to join the scheme. If the start date is not the beginning of a VAT period, two separate calculations for that period will be required (¶8652).

HMRC may allow a **retrospective** start date if a person either registers for VAT late, or his VAT liability for a particular VAT year would have been lower.

MEMO POINTS It was held by a VAT tribunal that a retrospective application should be allowed back to the inception of the scheme in 2002 if the trader met the eligibility criteria at that date, as HMRC's guidance states that use of the scheme should be encouraged. *CJ Anderson* [2007]

2. Operating the scheme

To **calculate** the amount of VAT payable to HMRC, a flat rate percentage is applied to the VAT-inclusive turnover for the period. Any transactions which fall outside the scheme will be accounted for under normal VAT rules. 8632

It is important to note that **output tax** must still be shown on sales invoices as if the trader were accounting for VAT in the normal way.

MEMO POINTS 1. The fuel scale charge (¶7890), which is normally applied when **fuel is provided for private use**, is not used in conjunction with the flat rate scheme.
2. Output tax on the **acquisition of goods from the EU** must be accounted for in the normal way (¶8937), but no input tax deduction will be available, unless the goods are capital assets which meet the conditions in ¶8642.

VAT payable

Flat rate percentage The flat rate percentage **depends on** the trade sector in which the business operates. 8634

If the business falls into **more than one sector**, the lowest rate should be chosen. As it can be difficult to determine which sector is relevant, HMRC will give specific advice on an individual basis.

MEMO POINTS 1. **New businesses** should apply a 1% deduction to the relevant flat rate when using the scheme at any point during the first year of registration. If a person registers for VAT late, and HMRC allow a retrospective scheme start date, the reduced rate can only be used from the date that HMRC were notified or became aware of the requirement to register. If a person registers for VAT more than a year late, he cannot use the reduced rate. SI 1995/2518 reg 55JB
2. If the business includes supplies to **two or more trade sectors**, the percentage appropriate to the main business activity must be applied. The position should then be reviewed on each anniversary of joining the scheme, and any change made to the percentage used should be implemented from the start of the VAT period in which the anniversary date falls.

The following table shows the rates applicable to the various business sectors defined by HMRC. 8636

SI 1995/2518 reg 55K

Category of business carried on	Flat rate %
Accountancy or book-keeping	14.5
Advertising	11
Agricultural services [1]	11
Any other activity not listed elsewhere	12
Architect, civil and structural engineer or surveyor	14.5
Boarding or care of animals	12
Business services not listed elsewhere	12
Catering services, including restaurants and takeaways	12.5
Computer and IT consultancy or data processing	14.5
Computer repair services	10.5
Dealing in waste or scrap	10.5
Entertainment or journalism	12.5
Estate agency or property management services	12
Farming or agriculture that is not listed elsewhere [1]	6.5
Film, radio, TV or video production	13
Financial services	13.5
Forestry or fishing	10.5
General building or construction services [3]	9.5
Hairdressing or other beauty treatments	13
Hiring or renting goods	9.5

Category of business carried on	Flat rate %
Hotel or accommodation	10.5
Investigation or security	12
Labour-only building or construction services[3]	14.5
Laundry or dry-cleaning services	12
Lawyer or legal services	14.5
Library, archive, museum, or other cultural activity	9.5
Management consultancy	14
Manufacturing fabricated metal products	10.5
Manufacturing food	9
Manufacturing not listed elsewhere	9.5
Manufacturing yarn, textiles or clothing	9
Membership organisation	8
Mining or quarrying	10
Packaging	9
Photography	11
Post offices	5
Printing	8.5
Publishing	11
Pubs	6.5
Real estate activity not listed elsewhere	14
Repairing personal or household goods	10
Repairing vehicles	8.5
Retailing food, confectionery, tobacco, newspapers or children's clothing[2]	4
Retailing pharmaceuticals, medical goods, cosmetics or toiletries[2]	8
Retailing that is not listed elsewhere[2]	7.5
Retailing of vehicles or fuel[2]	6.5
Secretarial services	13
Social work	11
Sport or recreation	8.5
Transport or storage, including couriers, freight, removals and taxis	10
Travel agency	10.5
Veterinary medicine	11
Wholesaling agricultural products	8
Wholesaling food	7.5
Wholesaling not listed elsewhere	8.5

Note:
1. Farmers can also choose to use the agricultural flat rate scheme (¶8660).
2. Retail schemes are available to simplify VAT accounting (¶8700).
3. "Labour-only building or construction services" means building or construction services where the value of materials supplied is less than 10% of relevant turnover from such services; any other building or construction services are "General building or construction services".

EXAMPLE

1. Mr A is a vet who also owns a cattery. The veterinary business generated gross income of £60,000 and the cattery generated £12,000.
The flat rate percentage for the veterinary business (11%) is applied to the gross income of £72,000, so Mr A pays £7,920 of VAT. (£72,000 x 11%)

2. Mr B is a journalist who registered for VAT on 1 January 2011. He joined the flat rate scheme on 1 April 2011. From 1 April to 31 December, the flat rate is 11.5% (being 12.5% less the 1% deduction). From the beginning of the next calendar year, the flat rate will be 12.5%.

If, instead, Mr B's main business activity changes to publishing from 1 October 2011, the flat rate for the period from 1 October to 31 December would be 10% (being 11% less the 1% deduction), before reverting to 11% from 1 January 2012.

VAT-inclusive turnover VAT-inclusive turnover **includes**: 8638 SI 1995/2518 reg 55C
- all taxable supplies, including the VAT;
- exempt supplies;
- the full sales price of any second-hand goods;
- sales of capital goods if no input tax is claimed;
- goods despatched to other EU states; and
- excise duty.

The **time** when turnover is recognised depends on which of the three following methods is chosen: SI 1995/2518 reg 55G

a. basic method, which recognises turnover using the usual time of supply rules (¶7900);

b. cash-based method, which recognises turnover when the customer's payment is received, which will depend on the type of payment; or

c. retailers' method, which uses the daily takings (¶8714) of a retail business.

MEMO POINTS 1. The table at ¶8382 summarises the point at which **payment** is received for the cash-based method. The turnover recognised for the purposes of the scheme should ignore any deductions (such as commission) which have been netted off for the purposes of the payment. This method does not change the actual time of supply, so in the event of a change in VAT rate or insolvency, the usual tax points will apply.

2. For the retailers' method the turnover is the sum of the **daily takings** and the VAT-inclusive amount of any other income.

Input tax

Partial exemption does not apply to flat rate scheme traders, so any input tax is regarded as wholly attributable to the making of taxable supplies. 8640 SI 1995/2518 reg 55F

The usual rules still apply for recovering input tax incurred on relevant **pre-registration expenditure**, such as stock on hand (¶8287).

Capital assets Low-value capital assets are treated like any other **purchase** under the flat rate scheme; there is no separate claim for input tax. 8642 SI 1995/2518 reg 55E

However, if a capital asset with a **VAT-inclusive value** of £2,000 or more is purchased, input tax may be recovered in the normal way.

For this purpose, capital assets **exclude** assets which are acquired:
- for resale, or bought for incorporation into goods to be sold;
- to be hired out, leased or let; or
- for consumption within 12 months.

The treatment of a capital asset **sale** under the flat rate scheme depends on whether the asset was acquired: 8644

a. while under the scheme and a separate claim for input tax was:

- not made, in which case the disposal proceeds are included in the turnover to which the flat rate percentage applies; or

- made, in which case output tax must be accounted for on the sale in the normal way and the proceeds are excluded from the turnover to which the flat rate percentage applies; or

b. before joining the flat rate scheme, in which case output tax must be accounted for on the sale in the normal way.

Records

Records of the following must be kept for each VAT period: 8646 Notice 733 para 7.2
- flat rate turnover;
- flat rate percentage used; and
- VAT due under the scheme.

The **VAT liability** should be recorded in the VAT payable section of the VAT account (¶9205); this is usually the only entry. This amount may either be netted off against sales, or shown as a separate line in the profit and loss account.

Exceptionally, there also may be VAT which arises outside the flat rate scheme (for example, in relation to certain capital assets); and this should be entered in the VAT account in the normal way in addition to the flat rate liability.

The **VAT return** is completed as usual (¶8342), with the following exceptions:
– box 1 shows the liability calculated using the flat rate calculation; and
– box 6 includes the VAT-inclusive turnover to which the flat rate is applied, in addition to the VAT-exclusive value of any supplies not accounted for under the scheme.

VAT invoices must still be issued to VAT-registered customers, showing the normal VAT rate of supply (standard rate, reduced rate or zero rate) and not the flat rate percentage.

EXAMPLE Mr C is a car mechanic, therefore his relevant flat rate is 8.5% in 2011. He charges his customer £100 plus VAT for a repair, and incurs direct costs of £40 plus VAT.
The VAT-inclusive sale is £120, and this is shown as the sales price in his profit and loss account.
The VAT due to HMRC is calculated as 8.5% of gross sales, giving an amount of £10.20 (£120 x 8.5%). This can be netted against the sales figure in the accounts.
The VAT-inclusive cost is £48, and this is shown in the cost of sales in the accounts.
Overall, Mr C's gross profit is £61.80. (£120 – £10.20 – £48)
Comparing the flat rate scheme result with the normal VAT rules allows Mr C to see if he is benefiting from the scheme:

	Flat rate scheme £	Normal rules £
Gross sales	120.00	120.00
Due to HMRC	(10.20)	(20.00)
Net sales	107.80	100.00
Gross purchases	(48.00)	(48.00)
Input tax which can be recovered	0.00	8.00
Gross profit	61.80	60.00

3. Leaving

8648 In order for a trader to leave the scheme, HMRC must be notified in writing.

A business may leave the scheme **voluntarily** at any time but HMRC would expect that most businesses will leave at the end of a VAT period.

A business that has left the scheme and subsequently wishes to **rejoin** will not be able to do so until 12 months have elapsed.

Ceasing to be eligible

8650 SI 1995/2518 regs 55M-55Q Notice 733 para 12.2

A business **must** leave the scheme if any of the following occur:
a. the VAT-inclusive value of all supplies in a year exceeds £230,000;
b. there are reasonable grounds to believe turnover will exceed £230,000 in the next 30 days;
c. HMRC require the trader's removal for the protection of VAT revenue, or because a false statement was made when applying for the scheme, subject to any appeal by the trader;
d. the business becomes associated with another person (¶8626);
e. the business becomes eligible for VAT group treatment (¶7807) or divisional registration (¶7815);
f. the business intends or expects to acquire, construct or otherwise obtain an asset that is covered by the capital goods scheme (¶8250);

g. the second-hand margin scheme (¶8437) or auctioneers' scheme (¶8500) is applied for; or
h. the business becomes a tour operator (¶8626).

MEMO POINTS 1. The **£230,000 limit** includes the VAT-inclusive value of all taxable and exempt supplies, excluding supplies of capital assets and reverse charges on international services. Eligibility for the scheme is based on the level of taxable turnover, but the test of continuing eligibility for the scheme is based on all income (including exempt income).
On **each anniversary** of joining the scheme, a business must check that its income has not exceeded the limits.
2. When a business becomes ineligible because of:
– **past turnover**, the business will leave the scheme at the end of the VAT period in which the anniversary falls, unless annual accounting is being used, when the business will leave the scheme from the end of the month after it became ineligible (except where an earlier date is agreed with HMRC); or
– **future turnover** in the next 30 days, the leaving date will be the end of the 30-day period.
3. If the eligibility limits of the scheme are exceeded because of a **one-off increase in turnover**, a business may still be able to remain within the scheme with the agreement of HMRC.
4. The value of supplies should be calculated in accordance with the trader's usual method of accounting for VAT on the scheme i.e. either cash received or invoices raised.

Adjustments

Adjustments are required if a business: 8652
a. leaves the scheme **midway through a VAT period**, when the flat rate scheme is applied until the date of leaving, and the normal VAT rules apply for the remainder of the period;
b. has **stock on hand** on which no input tax claim has ever been made and remains VAT-registered, when input tax can be claimed on the increase in the stock's value between the scheme's start and end dates – the following calculation is required:
– compare the VAT-exclusive value of stock on the date of commencing to use the scheme with the value at the date of leaving the scheme;
– multiply the difference by the standard rate of VAT; and
– make a claim on the first VAT return after leaving the scheme;
c. has used the **cash-based method** for calculating turnover under the scheme and does not move immediately to cash accounting (¶8375), when VAT must be accounted for on all supplies already made but for which payment has not been received; and
d. has **recovered input tax** on capital assets, when a self-supply (¶7888) is deemed to occur on the day after the business ceases to use the scheme – so the business charges itself output tax, but can also make a corresponding input tax claim (this rule ensures that partly exempt businesses are not able to recover more input tax than they are entitled to).

SECTION 2

Agricultural flat rate scheme

An optional scheme is available for farmers under which no VAT is reclaimed on purchases, or output tax charged on sales. Instead, a **flat rate levy** is charged to VAT-registered customers and this is kept by the farmer as extra income to compensate for the non-recovery of input tax. 8660 Notice 700/46 s 54 VATA 1994

1. Eligibility

The scheme is available to farmers who are either required to be registered for VAT or are eligible for voluntary registration (¶7778). 8662

A farmer is able to join the scheme if he is **supplying** goods, or goods and services, in the course of one or more designated activities. The **supply of services alone** would not qualify. If the farmer has used the scheme in the past, see ¶8690.

If the farmer is **already registered** for VAT, one of the joining conditions requires the existing registration to be cancelled. In this instance, the usual charge for assets and goods on hand at deregistration (¶7802) does not apply.

The farmer **cannot join** the scheme where he has, in the 3 years prior to the application date:
– been convicted of a VAT offence;
– been assessed to a civil evasion penalty (¶9290); or
– accepted an offer to compound proceedings in connection with a VAT offence.

Designated activities

8664 SI 1992/3220 Notice 700/46 para 3

The various types of designated activities are set out in the following table:

Designated	Excludes	Includes
Crop production	– marketing co-operatives; – sale of peat or top soil.	– general agriculture (also viticulture); – growing fruit and vegetables, flowers and ornamental plants; – production of mushrooms, spices, seeds, and propagating materials; – nurseries.
Stock farming	– raising of animals as pets or for sport; – training of animals as a specialist activity; – providing activities involving animals, such as pony trekking.	– general stock farming; – poultry farming; – rabbit farming; – bee-keeping; – silkworm farming; – snail farming.
Forestry	– processing beyond the conversion of felled timber.	– growing and felling trees; – general husbandry of trees in a wood, copse or forest.
Fisheries		– freshwater fishing; – fish farming; – frog farming; – breeding of mussels, oysters and other molluscs and crustaceans.
Processing of products derived from the above activities	– processing of other farmers' products; – processing by someone other than the farmer (for example, a dairy co-operative or sawmill).	
Provision of services	– sale or lease of milk quotas (even if sold with the land); – grape crushing, bottling etc for other wine producers.	– hiring out of equipment for use in the activities above; – technical assistance for the activities above; – fieldwork, reaping and mowing, threshing, baling, collecting, harvesting, sowing and planting; – packing and preparing agricultural products for market; – storage of agricultural products; – stock-minding, rearing and fattening; – destruction of weeds and pests, including crop dusting and spraying; – operation of drainage and irrigation equipment; – forestry services, including lopping and tree felling.

Other activities

If non-farming turnover is **below the registration threshold** (¶7775), the farmer may still use the scheme. **8666** Notice 700/46 para 4

If the farmer has other activities which are **above the registration threshold**, the non-farming business may be registered separately, provided that it is run as a different business by persons other than the farmer (for example, by a partnership). This also means that input tax recovery for those activities is preserved.

If the other activities cannot be registered separately, the farmer cannot adopt the scheme and his whole business must be registered for VAT.

2. Joining

An **application** to join the scheme can be made to HMRC at any time, using form VAT 98. It will only be accepted where HMRC are satisfied that the farmer will not be substantially better off by more than £3,000 in the first year of using the scheme, compared to claiming input tax under the normal VAT rules. **8668** SI 1995/2518 reg 204

If the application is successful, HMRC will issue a **certificate** to the farmer, showing a unique number which must be included on any invoices issued under the scheme (¶8684). The certificate will show the effective date of certification (generally the date on which the application was received by HMRC). **8670** SI 1995/2518 reg 205

After certification the farmer must notify HMRC of any changes to the business details, including name and address.

3. Operating the scheme

Levy

Once a person has received the certificate from HMRC, a levy of 4% is **charged on** any supplies made to VAT-registered persons in the course of designated farming activities. The addition is made to all such supplies, regardless of whether the supply would be zero-rated under the normal VAT rules. **8672** SI 1992/3221

The levy is retained by the farmer and not paid to HMRC. There is no requirement to complete returns.

EXAMPLE Mr A is a farmer registered under the agricultural flat rate scheme. He supplies crops valued at £250 which he has produced on the farm. If the customer is VAT-registered, Mr A should add 4% (i.e. £10) to the invoice and retain this amount.

The levy **cannot be charged on** supplies of goods or services which are not in the course of designated activities, including: **8674**
- sales of land;
- sales of machinery; and
- maintenance and repair of buildings owned by other farmers.

The levy is not charged in respect of **supplies to unregistered persons**, including other flat rate farmers.

The **customer may** be able to **reclaim** the amount of the levy as though it were an amount of input tax, provided that he has a suitable invoice (¶8684). **8676**

Circumstances of sale

Special rules apply when a farmer sells his produce through a **farmers' group or co-operative**. In this case, the customer pays only the agreed price for the produce, with no levy added. The farmers' group will then share the sales proceeds between the various suppliers, and **8678** Notice 700/46 para 8.1

must pay the levy to any farmers operating the scheme. The farmers' group can then recover any amounts it has paid as a levy on its VAT return.

8680 Notice 700/46 para 8.2 When the farmer sells the produce **at auction**, the treatment will depend on whether the auctioneer acts as:
– the farmer's **agent**, in which case the farmer is deemed to sell the produce direct to the consumer, and therefore may charge the levy if the customer is VAT-registered; or
– a **principal**, in which case the farmer is treated as selling the produce to the auctioneer who then sells it on to the consumer. The farmer will therefore charge the levy to the auctioneer, who can recover it as his input tax. The onward sale by the auctioneer is subject to the normal VAT rules.

Records

8682 Farmers operating the scheme are not required to maintain special records. The farmer should therefore maintain normal accounting and business records, and also copies of any invoices issued under the scheme. All records must be retained for a period of 6 years.

8684 SI 1995/2518 reg 209(3) **Invoices** issued under the scheme should show the following information:
– an identifying invoice number;
– the farmer's flat rate certificate number;
– the business name and address;
– the name and address of the VAT-registered customer;
– the time of supply;
– a description of the goods or services;
– the price payable, excluding the levy; and
– the rate and amount of the levy, described as either "flat rate addition" or "FRA".

MEMO POINTS 1. A farmer operating the scheme will not normally receive an **assurance visit** (¶9324), except in exceptional circumstances.
2. It is possible for customers to **self-bill** (¶8332) using the flat rate addition but HMRC should be notified.

4. Leaving

8686 SI 1995/2518 reg 206 A farmer **must** leave the scheme if the:
– VAT registration threshold is exceeded in respect of non-designated activities;
– farmer ceases to carry on designated activities; or
– farmer is discovered to be recovering substantially more through the scheme than if he were registered and reclaiming input tax.

A farmer may **choose** to leave the scheme at any time, after having been in the scheme for at least 1 year. Applications should be made in writing to HMRC.

HMRC may also **expel** a farmer from the scheme where they believe that the VAT take is at risk, or where the business ceases to satisfy the compliance criteria (¶8662).

Consequences

8688 When a farmer leaves the scheme, the **certificate** will be cancelled and the normal VAT rules will then apply.

If subsequently registering for VAT, the farmer cannot claim any **pre-registration input tax** incurred while he was a member of the scheme. This is because the farmer has already had the benefit of the levy, which compensates for any lost input tax recovery.

Rejoining

8690 If a farmer is **not required to register** for VAT on leaving the scheme, he may apply to rejoin at any time, provided that the relevant criteria are satisfied.

Having left the scheme, a business may be required to **register for VAT**, in accordance with the normal rules. In general, such businesses may only apply to rejoin the scheme after 3 years have elapsed from the date of leaving. Exceptionally, a farmer may be readmitted after just 1 year, where the output tax due on the deemed supply of stock and fixed assets (¶7802) at the time of rejoining would be no more than £1,000. SI 1995/2518 reg 208

SECTION 3

Retail schemes

Retailers generally make a large number of low-value supplies to many customers. Such businesses can find it very difficult to account for VAT in the normal way, especially when all sales are not subject to a single VAT rate, so a retail scheme may provide a welcome solution. 8700 SI 1995/2518 reg 66 Notice 727

Under the normal rules, VAT is accounted for by calculating the VAT liability (i.e. output tax) in respect of each individual sale. Retail schemes are intended to simplify the accounting process and operate by calculating the VAT liability based on the global sales figure for each VAT period (¶8342).

1. Using a retail scheme

Retail schemes can only be used in respect of retail supplies to **non-VAT-registered customers**. Supplies to **VAT-registered customers** must be accounted for in accordance with the normal rules, except for occasional cash sales. For example, a DIY store which generally makes retail supplies to the public may include occasional cash sales to a VAT-registered builder in its chosen retail scheme. 8702

Any distance sales of goods to unregistered EU customers (¶8980) are also excluded.

MEMO POINTS Any **non-retail** sales must be accounted for using normal VAT accounting and excluded from the schemes.
The following are classed as non-retail for this purpose:
- exempt supplies, such as the receipt of rental income or the sale of National Lottery tickets;
- BT phonecards;
- sales of business assets (e.g. a company van);
- disbursements;
- fuel scale charges for private motoring; and
- savings stamps, travel cards and pools coupons.

Adoption

Choice of schemes A business may adopt one of the following **published schemes**, without prior authorisation, provided that it meets the necessary criteria: 8704
- the point of sale scheme;
- apportionment scheme 1
- apportionment scheme 2
- direct calculation scheme 1; or
- direct calculation scheme 2.

A business may not use any of the above published schemes if its annual VAT-exclusive turnover exceeds £130 million. Instead, it must agree a **bespoke scheme** with HMRC, or apply normal VAT accounting. Bespoke schemes already agreed by retailers whose annual turnover was between £100 million and £130 million (when the upper limit was £100 million) continue in operation until or unless the agreement ends.

A business which only makes taxable supplies at **one positive rate** must use the point of sale scheme. Otherwise, there is no restriction, although when charging:
- **three rates** of VAT, the direct calculation schemes become more difficult to operate;
- a higher mark-up on **zero-rated** goods, the trader will pay more output tax under apportionment scheme 1.

In addition, if the proportion of zero-rated (as compared to standard-rated) purchases increases, apportionment scheme 2 will be less beneficial.

For special rules relating to chemists, florists and caterers, see *VAT Memo*.

8706 SI 1995/2518 reg 68 **HMRC may** only **refuse** to allow a business to use a scheme where:
- the scheme does not give a fair and reasonable valuation during any period;
- they believe the scheme should not be used in order to protect tax revenues; or
- the retailer could reasonably be expected to use normal accounting methods.

The retailer can appeal against such a refusal.

8708 **Scope** A business may generally use just one of the schemes at any one time, and the scheme applies to the whole of the VAT registration.

Notice 727 para 4.1 If a **business has separate parts**, the scheme may be operated independently for different parts of the business with distinct locations (e.g. shops in different towns). Alternatively, different schemes may be appropriate for different parts of the business (including normal accounting).

The point of sale scheme and normal accounting may be used in combination with any of the other schemes. However, an apportionment scheme and a direct calculation scheme cannot be combined. Where different schemes are used it may be necessary to make adjustments for any transfers of stock between the separate parts of the business, with the agreement of HMRC.

8710 SI 1995/2518 reg 71 **Period of use** The **minimum** period of use is 12 months, starting from the beginning of the VAT period in which the retailer commenced using the scheme, unless:
- the retailer becomes ineligible for the scheme (such as through exceeding the turnover limit, or ceasing to be VAT-registered), when he must cease using it from the end of the next VAT period; or
- HMRC give specific permission for the retailer to stop using it.

It is therefore advisable to review the scheme before the anniversary date, in case the retailer wishes to change schemes.

Calculation elements

8712 A business is always required to calculate daily gross takings and, depending on the scheme used, the expected selling price of goods purchased. The business must retain appropriate evidence to support each calculation.

8714 Notice 727/3 para 5 **Daily gross takings** Daily gross takings are the total takings, as evidenced by a till roll or sales vouchers, **including**:
- all payments received from cash customers;
- the cash value of any payments in kind;
- the full VAT-inclusive value of credit sales (less any charge for credit);
- the full VAT-inclusive value of goods removed from the business for the proprietor's own use;
- the face value of any gift vouchers accepted in place of cash; and
- any other payments for retail sales.

It is the gross takings – that is, the consideration actually given by the customer – which are used; these may not be the same as the actual till contents.

8716 Notice 727/3 para 5.4 The following may **reduce** the takings, subject to appropriate evidence of the adjustment being retained:
- void transactions (which are voided at the time of the error);

– refunds to customers for faulty goods (up to a maximum of the initial amount included in the takings), or for simple overcharging (but no reduction is permitted if payment is compensatory);
– returned deposits;
– till problems, including readings from broken down tills, and the use of training tills (e.g. the till has been returned to retail use without zeroing first); and
– customer overspends using Shopacheck.

If a reduction is made in respect of an **amount which is subsequently received**, the receipt must be included in daily takings.

Expected selling price The expected selling price (ESP) has a significant effect on three of the published schemes (apportionment scheme 2, and both direct calculation schemes). All ESP **calculations must be** fair and reasonable and, once a methodology has been devised, it must be applied consistently. 8718 Notice 727/4 para 5.3.2

The most **common methods** of calculation are to:
– mark up each line of goods;
– mark up each class of goods; or
– use recommended retail prices.

The following items must be **excluded**:
– wholesale supplies;
– goods specifically bought for private use; and
– proceeds from stock sold as part of the disposal of the whole or part of the retail business.

MEMO POINTS 1. A mark-up may only be applied to a **class of goods** where it is impossible to determine the mark-up for each line of goods. The class of goods must have a commercial basis and not be constructed artificially. A mark-up cannot be applied to a class of goods where the mark-up applied to individual items within that group varies by more than 10%. All mark-ups must be reviewed quarterly.
2. **Recommended retail prices** (RRP) can only be used where the RRP can be recorded on the sales invoice and the business has documentation from the supplier:
– showing the VAT-inclusive RRP of individual lines;
– distinguishing between items taxable at the reduced, standard and zero rates; and
– showing totals for each rate of VAT.

At the **end of the VAT period**, the retailer should review the selling prices by taking into account: 8720 Notice 727/4 para 5.3.1
– price changes (particularly in respect of perishable goods which must be sold by a certain date);
– special offers and promotions which were not predicted initially;
– goods supplied from normal stock to use in business entertaining or taken for private use;
– wastage in light of actual events;
– products recalled by manufacturers;
– equipment (e.g. freezer) breakdowns;
– breakages;
– theft; and
– bad debts written off in the period.

Certain factors above may be omitted where they have **no distorting effect** on the operation of the scheme, subject to HMRC's agreement.

The most important requirement is **consistency** of calculation, both within a VAT period and throughout the scheme year.

Records

In addition to the normal VAT records (¶9205), businesses operating a retail scheme must keep a record of daily takings and, depending on the scheme used, the expected selling prices and the method of calculation. 8722

Ceasing to use a scheme

8724 SI 1995/2518 reg 72 If the business **becomes ineligible** for a scheme, it must change to another scheme or revert to normal accounting no later than the end of that VAT period.

If a business **wishes to stop** using a scheme, it should notify HMRC before the end of the last VAT period for which it is to be operated.

> EXAMPLE A Ltd ceases to be eligible for a particular published scheme during the VAT period ending 31 March. The company must adopt an alternative scheme or return to normal accounting from 1 April.

2. Published schemes

8726 Each scheme operates in a slightly different way, although the underlying principle is to identify the takings applicable to sales of standard-rated, zero-rated and reduced-rated goods so that the appropriate VAT element can be calculated. The schemes only apply to retail sales, so all other sales are subject to the normal VAT accounting requirements.

A smaller business may also take advantage of the annual and cash accounting schemes, which can be used in conjunction with a retail scheme. Cash accounting could be advantageous where the retailer makes credit sales, although input tax recovery will be delayed until suppliers are paid.

Point of sale scheme

8728 Notice 727/3 Under the point of sale (POS) scheme, **output tax is calculated** by identifying the correct VAT liability of each sale at the point of sale using, for example, an electronic till. This is potentially the most simple and accurate of the published schemes. There are **no restrictions on** the types of supply which may be included within the scheme, and there is no requirement for stocktaking or annual adjustments.

8730 **To use the scheme**, VAT-exclusive turnover must be no more than £130 million per year and the business must have adequate till facilities.

For each VAT period, the business must **calculate** the total of daily takings from standard-rated, zero-rated and reduced-rated supplies. The VAT due is then calculated by applying the appropriate VAT fraction (see ¶8030) to these totals.

A retailer may choose to treat **minor levels of zero-rated or reduced-rated supplies** as standard-rated to simplify the accounting. It should be noted that this results in VAT being payable to HMRC which is not charged to customers.

EXAMPLE Mr B runs a newsagent and general store, and he uses the POS scheme. At the end of a VAT period, his electronic till showed the following:

	£
Standard-rated sales	9,600
Reduced-rated sales	315
Zero-rated sales	2,225

The output tax due under the POS scheme is therefore:

		£
Standard-rated supplies	£9,600 × 1/6	1,600
Reduced-rated supplies	£315 × 1/21	15
Total		1,615

Apportionment scheme 1 (AP1)

8732 Notice 727/4 This scheme is relatively simple and can only be **used by** traders with an annual VAT-exclusive turnover not exceeding £1 million.

This scheme treats **all supplies** as having an equal mark-up. It may not therefore be appropriate for a business with a higher mark-up on zero-rated supplies.

To use AP1, supplies must be made at two or three VAT rates. Also, supplies of services, home-made or home-grown goods, and supplies of catering must be **excluded** from the scheme.

Calculation AP1 assumes that the proportion of goods sold at each VAT rate mirrors that of purchases (e.g. if 40% of purchases are standard-rated, 40% of takings are deemed to be standard-rated). 8734

For each VAT period the retailer must calculate the **value of purchases** for resale at each different rate of VAT. The proportion of total purchases at each rate is then determined, and the appropriate VAT fraction (see ¶8030) is applied to the same proportion of daily takings to calculate the output tax.

It is vital that **non-retail** purchases (such as overheads and fixed assets) are excluded from the calculation.

There are **seven steps** to the calculation, as shown in the following table: 8736

Step	What to do	Calculation
1	Calculate the total daily takings for the VAT period	A
2	Calculate the total VAT-inclusive cost of acquisitions for sale at the standard rate	B
3	Calculate the total VAT-inclusive cost of acquisitions for sale at the reduced rate	C
4	Calculate the total VAT-inclusive cost of acquisitions for sale at the standard, reduced and zero rates	D
5	VAT due on standard-rated supplies	A × B/D × 1/6 = E
6	VAT due on reduced-rated supplies	A × C/D × 1/21 = F
7	Output tax due	E + F

EXAMPLE C Ltd has extracted the following information from its quarterly VAT records:

	£
Total daily takings (A)	17,000
VAT-inclusive cost of acquisitions for standard-rated sales (B)	6,000
VAT-inclusive cost of acquisitions for reduced-rated sales (C)	1,050
VAT-inclusive cost of acquisitions for standard, reduced and zero-rated sales (D)	8,500

Using AP1, the output tax due is calculated as follows:

		£
Standard-rated supplies	£17,000 × 6,000/8,500 × 1/6	2,000
Reduced-rated supplies	£17,000 × 1,050/8,500 × 1/21	100
Total		2,100

Annual adjustment There is an annual adjustment to even out fluctuations during the year. 8738

In practice, it is usually **carried out** at the end of the retailer's VAT year. It must also be performed when the trader leaves the scheme.

An annual adjustment is **only required if** the scheme has been in operation for at least 12 months. The **first** annual adjustment may therefore be for a period in excess of 12 months.

The same **method** is used as for each VAT period, but using the total figures for the year under review (or longer period, as appropriate). If the annual figure is greater than the amounts already paid, this is included as VAT payable in the VAT account. If the annual figure is lower than the amounts paid, the difference is included as VAT deductible in the VAT account.

The annual adjustment will need to take account of the change in the standard rate from 17.5% to 20% on 4 January 2011 if the VAT year spans that date. The annual adjustment will therefore be two separate calculations, one for the period to 3 January 2011 and one for the period starting on 4 January 2011.

Apportionment scheme 2 (AP2)

8740 Notice 727/4 This scheme is aimed at businesses with an annual **VAT-exclusive turnover of** up to £130 million per annum. It can cope much better with the differing margins of the various goods sold.

AP2 **apportions takings on** the basis of the expected selling price (ESP) of purchases and stock. To use it, **supplies** must be made at two or three VAT rates and supplies of services and catering must be excluded from the scheme.

No adjustment is required when a business ceases to use the scheme.

8742 **Calculation** The AP2 calculation works on a rolling 12-month basis and therefore the calculation for the first year differs slightly from the ongoing calculation.

For the **first three VAT quarters** (or eleven monthly periods) the ESP of each class of stock is calculated in each VAT period, **taking into account** all goods on hand at commencement and received, made or grown for retail sale since the trader commenced using the scheme. The total takings are then **apportioned** between the different VAT rates, so that the output tax can be calculated by applying the appropriate VAT fraction.

8744

Step	What to do	Calculation
1	Calculate the total daily gross takings for the VAT period	A
2	Calculate the total VAT-inclusive ESP of acquisitions for sale at the standard rate since commencement [1]	B
3	Calculate the total VAT-inclusive ESP of acquisitions for sale at the reduced rate since commencement [1]	C
4	Calculate the total VAT-inclusive ESP of all acquisitions for sale at the standard, reduced and zero rates since commencement [1]	D
5	VAT due on standard-rated supplies	A x B/D x 1/6 = E
6	VAT due on reduced-rated supplies	A x C/D x 1/21 = F
7	Output tax due	E + F

Notes:
1. Include the ESP of stock on hand at commencement.

EXAMPLE D Ltd has opted to use AP2 and has calculated the ESP of stock on hand as follows:

	£
Goods for standard-rated sales (B)	7,000
Goods for reduced-rated sales (C)	-
Goods for standard, reduced and zero-rated sales (D)	8,500

For the first period of operating AP2, D Ltd has extracted the following information from the quarterly VAT records:

	£
Total daily takings (A)	59,000
VAT-inclusive ESP of acquisitions for standard-rated sales (B)	12,000
VAT-inclusive ESP of acquisitions for reduced-rated sales (C)	5,000
VAT-inclusive ESP of acquisitions for standard, reduced and zero-rated sales (D)	20,000

The total ESPs required for the AP2 calculation are therefore as follows:

	£	
Standard-rated sales (B)	19,000	(£7,000 + £12,000)
Reduced-rated sales (C)	5,000	(0 + £5,000)
Standard, reduced and zero-rated sales (D)	28,500	(£8,500 + £20,000)

Using AP2, the output tax due is calculated as follows:

		£
Standard-rated supplies	£59,000 × 19,000/28,500 × 1/6	6,556
Reduced-rated supplies	£59,000 × 5,000/28,500 × 1/21	493
Total		7,049

For **subsequent VAT periods** the ESP of each class of stock is calculated in each VAT period. This will take into account all goods received, made or grown for retail sale, including EU acquisitions, in the current period and the previous three periods (previous eleven periods for monthly traders). Again, total takings are then apportioned between the different VAT rates and the appropriate VAT fraction (see ¶8030) is applied to calculate the output tax. **8746**

Direct calculation scheme 1 (DC1)

DC1 **cannot be used for** supplies of catering. If a retailer makes supplies at three different VAT rates, the calculation will be complex. DC1 can only be **used by** traders with an annual VAT-exclusive turnover not exceeding £1 million. **8748** Notice 727/5

To use DC1 supplies must be made at two or three VAT rates and supplies of services taxable at the same rate(s) as minority supplies must be excluded from the scheme.

Calculation When only selling at the standard and zero rates of VAT, the calculation works by concentrating on the goods with the **VAT rate** which forms the smaller proportion of the retail sales. These are known as the **minority goods** and their expected selling price (ESP) must be identified. **8750**

The calculation then depends on whether the minority goods are:
– **zero-rated**, when the expected sales price is deducted from total takings, to identify standard-rated sales, to which the VAT fraction (see ¶8030) is then applied; or
– **standard-rated**, when the VAT fraction is just applied to the expected selling price of those goods.

The calculation is **performed** for every VAT period, using the expected selling price of the minority goods to ascertain the output tax due. Although not always necessary for the calculation, a **record of daily takings** must be maintained.

MEMO POINTS 1. If selling at **three rates of VAT**, there will be two minority goods, and the expected selling prices of both zero-rated and reduced-rated goods are deducted from takings to find the standard-rated sales. In this case, the reduced-rated sales are always treated as the second minority goods. If the calculation becomes too complex, HMRC may agree that reduced-rated sales may be accounted for outside the scheme.
2. Certain businesses, such as newsagents, may find it easier to set ESPs for the majority of goods, where there are fewer purchase records for **bulk items** such as newspapers and magazines.

There are eight steps to the calculation: **8752**

Step	What to do	Calculation
1	Calculate the total daily gross takings for the VAT period	A
2	Calculate the total VAT-inclusive ESP of acquisitions for sale at minority rate 1	B
3	Calculate the total VAT-inclusive ESP of acquisitions for sale at minority rate 2[1]	C
4	Deduct the total VAT-inclusive ESP of acquisitions for sale at minority rates from the total daily gross takings	A – B – C = D
5	VAT due on minority rate 1 supplies[2]	B × appropriate VAT fraction[3] = E
6	VAT due on minority rate 2 supplies[1,2]	C × appropriate VAT fraction[3] = F

Step	What to do	Calculation
7	VAT due on majority rate supplies[2]	D × appropriate VAT fraction[3] = G
8	Output tax due	E + F + G

Note:
1. Where supplies are **made at only two rates**, steps 3 and 6 will be omitted.
2. One of steps 5, 6 or 7 will be omitted, as it will relate to **zero-rated supplies** on which no output tax is due.
3. See ¶8030.

EXAMPLE E Ltd operates DC1. His minority supplies are zero-rated and reduced-rated. He has extracted the following information from his records for the latest VAT period:

	£
Total daily takings (A)	23,750
VAT-inclusive ESP of acquisitions for zero-rated sales (B)	5,990
VAT-inclusive ESP of acquisitions for reduced-rated sales (C)	1,260

	£
Takings	23,750
Less: ESP of minority rate 1 supplies (zero-rated)	(5,990)
ESP of minority rate 2 supplies (reduced-rated)	(1,260)
Standard-rated element of takings (D)	16,500

Using DC1, the output tax due is calculated as follows:

		£
Minority rate 2 supplies (reduced-rated) (F)	£1,260 × 1/21	60
Majority supplies (standard-rated) (G)	£16,500 × 1/6	2,750
Total		2,810

In this example step 5 has been omitted, as it relates to zero-rated supplies.

Direct calculation scheme 2 (DC2)

8754 Notice 727/5

DC2 is **fundamentally the same** calculation as DC1 but requires adjustments for stock when the annual adjustment is performed. It is aimed at larger businesses, with a VAT-exclusive turnover between £1 million and £130 million per annum.

To use DC2, **supplies** must be made at two or three rates. Supplies of catering and services taxable at the same rate(s) as minority supplies must also be excluded.

A **stocktake** is required for every annual adjustment, and also when the scheme is first adopted.

8756 **Annual adjustment** This adjustment must be **made after** the normal calculation for the fourth quarter, and any difference must be **accounted for on** the VAT return for the same quarter. On every anniversary of starting to use the scheme, the actual retail sales made in the year are compared to the amounts already accounted for every quarter, by adjusting for the goods in **stock** at the beginning and end of the year, and also for any goods disposed of other than by retail sale.

The annual adjustment will need to take account of the change in the standard rate from 17.5% to 20% on 4 January 2011 if the VAT year spans that date. The annual adjustment will therefore be two separate calculations, one for the period to 3 January 2011 and one for the period starting on 4 January 2011.

MEMO POINTS 1. HMRC may permit a business to **align** the annual adjustment **with** the end of its **financial year** to facilitate stocktaking requirements.
2. On **ceasing to use the scheme**, an annual adjustment should be completed for the quarters which have elapsed since the last adjustment was completed, excluding any goods which were initially taken into account but subsequently comprised non-retail sales. This closing adjustment still applies even if the retailer leaves the scheme within the first 12 months.

There are eight steps to the calculation: **8758**

Step	What to do	Calculation
1	Calculate the total daily gross takings for the VAT period	A
2	Calculate the adjusted VAT-inclusive ESP[1] of acquisitions for sale at minority rate 1	B
3	Calculate the adjusted VAT-inclusive ESP[1] of acquisitions for sale at minority rate 2[3]	C
4	Deduct the adjusted VAT-inclusive ESP[1] of acquisitions for sale at minority rates from the total daily gross takings	A – B – C = D
5	VAT due on minority rate 1 supplies[2]	B × appropriate VAT fraction[5] = E
6	VAT due on minority rate 2 supplies[2,3]	C × appropriate VAT fraction[5] = F
7	VAT due on majority rate supplies[2]	D × appropriate VAT fraction[5] = G
8	Output tax due[4]	E + F + G

Note:
1. The **adjusted VAT-inclusive ESP** of acquisitions for sale at a particular rate is the total ESP of goods in stock at the beginning of the year and goods acquired during the year. This is reduced by the ESP of goods in stock at the end of the year, and also by any items which have been disposed of other than by way of retail sale.
2. One of steps 5, 6 or 7 will be omitted, as it will relate to **zero-rated supplies** on which no output tax is due.
3. Where **supplies** are **made at only two rates**, steps 3 and 6 will be omitted.
4. If the **result of step 8** is:
– greater than the output tax previously accounted for under the scheme, the difference is included in the VAT payable side of the VAT account for the VAT period; or
– lower than the amounts accounted for, the difference is included as VAT deductible in the VAT account.
5. See ¶8030.

EXAMPLE F Ltd operates DC2. Its minority supplies are zero-rated and it makes no reduced-rated supplies. At the end of the first year of operating DC2, a stocktake is performed which identifies the ESP of minority goods on hand as £10,588. The opening stock ESP was £9,079. Non-retail sales with an ESP of £631 are also identified, which were included in the opening stock figure. The following information has been extracted from the records:

	£	£
Total daily takings for the year		176,313
VAT-inclusive ESP of acquisitions for zero-rated sales		58,422
Output tax accounted for under DC2:		
Quarter 1	6,096	
Quarter 2	4,113	
Quarter 3	3,744	
Quarter 4	5,907	
		19,860

	£	£
Takings (A)		176,313
Less: Adjusted ESP of minority rate 1 supplies (zero rate) (B)		
Opening stock	9,079	
Acquisition	58,422	
Closing stock	(10,588)	
Non-retail sales	(630)	
		(56,283)
Standard-rated element of takings (D)		120,030

		£
VAT due on standard rate supplies: (G)	120,030 × 1/6	20,005
Total previously accounted for		(19,860)
Annual adjustment (VAT payable)		145

3. Bespoke schemes

8760 HMRC will only agree to a business operating a bespoke scheme where the following **criteria** are met:

Notice 727/2

- the scheme reflects commercial reality;
- the scheme does not unnecessarily complicate the accounting systems; and
- the ability of HMRC to audit the VAT affairs of the business is not compromised.

Terms

8762 The terms of a bespoke scheme must be agreed in writing, and **must include** the following:

- the start date of the agreement;
- a review date;
- details of the supplies included and excluded from the scheme;
- details of the method by which different supplies will be identified (e.g. till coding);
- any specific details concerning the calculation of daily gross takings and expected selling prices;
- the name, status and signature of an HMRC officer; and
- the name, status and signature of an authorised signatory for the business.

Approval

8764 As with all retail schemes, HMRC may only **refuse** to allow a business to use a scheme where:

- it does not give a fair and reasonable result during any period;
- the tax take is at risk; or
- where the retailer could reasonably be expected to use normal accounting methods.

Once an agreement is in place, the business has an obligation to notify HMRC of any **change** to the business structure or trading patterns, or any other factor which may affect the operation of the scheme.

CHAPTER 8

Land and buildings

OUTLINE ¶¶

Transactions involving land and buildings can be extremely complex, and there are specific rules which govern when a supply is recognised and the VAT rate which applies. Supplies involving land can, depending on the circumstances, be zero-rated, reduced-rated, standard-rated, exempt, or outside the scope of VAT. Different rules apply to sales and grants of interests in land and in buildings, as opposed to supplies of construction services, and the VAT treatment of commercial buildings differs from that of domestic buildings, or those used by charities. **8790**

Summary

Many **property transactions** are exempt from VAT, which restricts the recovery of input tax on related costs (¶8205). However, freehold sales of newly constructed commercial buildings are liable to standard-rate VAT and landowners have the option to tax commercial leases. Grants of leases in new domestic property can be zero-rated. **8792**

The VAT liability of **construction services**, and supplies in the course of refurbishment, reconstruction, repair and maintenance depends on the type of building involved, and in some cases on the customer.

The following table summarises the VAT liability of common supplies:

Property involved	Type of supply	Details	VAT liability	¶¶
New buildings	Supplies in the course of construction	Commercial property (less than 3 years old to be "new")	Standard rate	¶8816
		Domestic property[1]	Zero rate	¶8818+
	Supplies involving the property	Freehold sales of commercial property which is less than 3 years old	Standard rate	¶8847
		Grant of lease or other interest in commercial property	Exempt, unless option to tax applies[2]	¶8892
		First sale or grant of long lease in domestic property[1]	Zero rate	¶8849
Land and existing buildings	Works carried out on the property	Supplies in the course of the conversion of a non-residential property to a residence	Reduced rate	¶8876
		Supplies for a residential conversion when customer is a housing association	Zero rate	¶8878
		Supplies for the refurbishment of empty premises to provide a residence	Reduced rate	¶8882
		Construction services to alter a protected residential building	Zero rate	¶8886
	Supplies involving the property	Charging for the provision of: – sleeping accommodation; – parking spaces; and – seasonal pitches for tents and caravans	Standard rate	¶8890
		Freehold sales of commercial property which is 3 years old or more	Exempt, unless option to tax applies[2]	¶8898
		Lease of commercial property	Exempt, unless option to tax applies[2]	¶8892
		Sale of freehold in domestic property[1]	Exempt	
		Lease of domestic property[1]	Exempt	
		First sale or long lease of a converted residence	Zero rate	¶8900
		First sale or long lease of a substantially reconstructed protected residence	Zero rate	¶8902

Note:
1. For this purpose, domestic property means either:
– a building designed as a dwelling; or
– a property used or intended for relevant residential use; or
– a property used or intended for use by a charity for non-business purposes.
2. It is possible to opt to tax a non-domestic property so that any future supplies relating to that property are standard-rated rather than exempt. For further details, see ¶8904.

SECTION 1

Place of supply

Services relating to land

Services in connection with land are treated as supplied in the country where the land is situated. This applies to: 8794 SI 1992/3121 reg 5

a. the **grant, assignment or surrender** of:
- any interest in or right over land;
- a personal right to call for or be granted such an interest or right; or
- a licence to occupy land or any other contractual right exercisable over (or in relation to) land;

b. any **works** of construction, demolition, conversion, reconstruction, alteration, enlargement, repair or maintenance of a building or civil engineering work; or

c. **services** closely related to land and buildings, such as those supplied by estate agents, lawyers, auctioneers, architects, surveyors, engineers and others involved in matters relating to land.

MEMO POINTS 1. For these purposes the term land **includes**:
- all forms of land and property such as buildings, walls, fences, growing crops, civil engineering works and other structures fixed permanently to the land (or sea bed); and
- machinery, plant or equipment which is an installation in its own right, such as a refinery or a gas platform.

2. Services in **c**. above will fall under this provision **only** if they relate directly to a **specific site**, as in the following examples:
- legal services such as conveyancing or dealing with planning permission applications;
- services of an architect in designing a building;
- the supply of hotel accommodation; or
- property management services such as rent collection and arranging repairs.

If the service has only an **indirect connection** with the land, or is only an **incidental part** of a more comprehensive service, the place of supply will either fall under the general rule for services or under specific rules relating to that service and not under the above rules. 8796

The following are examples of services not related to land:
- the legal administration of a deceased person's estate which includes property;
- general advice relating to land prices or property values not relating to a specific site; or
- supply of staff to a building site.

EXAMPLE A company operated a membership scheme under which owners of time-share rights in properties could exchange their rights in one property for rights in another property, in return for an "exchange fee". The ECJ has ruled that these fees, and the fees for enrolment and membership of the scheme, were consideration for the service of an exchange of property usage rights and should be taxed where the owner's property was situated (as services related to land) and not the place where the company had established its business. *RCI Europe v HMRC* [2009]

Where the land is in the UK but the **supplier belongs overseas**, then if the recipient: 8798 Notice 741 paras 6, 6.6, 6.7
- is a UK VAT-registered person, the recipient may be liable to account for the VAT under the reverse charge procedure (¶9110);
- is not registered for VAT in the UK, the overseas supplier must account for any UK VAT and may be liable to be registered (¶7770).

SECTION 2

Construction of new buildings

Construction services provided in the course of construction of a new building are standard-rated unless a specific provision reduces the VAT rate to 0%. They can never be exempt. 8800

The **disposal** of a major interest in a new building is standard-rated unless the building is used for residential or charitable purposes, when zero-rating may apply.

For short leases, see ¶8892.

Definitions

8802 Identifying whether a project qualifies as the construction of a new building, particularly when the new construction may be connected in some way to an existing building, is crucial to applying the correct VAT treatment.

A **commercial** building is treated as "new" for up to 3 years from the date of practical completion. The date of **completion** is deemed to be the earlier of the issue of a certificate of practical completion by an architect or engineer, or full occupation, or use.

If an **existing building** is demolished and is replaced, a new building will have been constructed, provided that demolition is completed before the new property is constructed.

8804 Sch 8 group 5 notes 16-18 VATA 1994

For VAT purposes, the construction of a new building **does not include**:
– the conversion, reconstruction or alteration of an existing building (for works on residential buildings see ¶8873);
– the enlargement or extension of an existing building, unless a new dwelling is created (¶8876); or
– the construction of an annexe, unless it is to be used for a relevant charitable purpose (¶8828).

A. Construction services

8808 Notice 708

It is important for both the supplier and the recipient to ensure that construction services are treated correctly for VAT purposes.

1. Time of supply

8810 Building contractors usually provide supplies of services, and the normal tax point rules (¶7902) apply for single payment contracts. For the supply of goods without services, the usual tax point rules for goods apply.

For self-billing and authenticated receipts, see ¶8332.

Retention payments

8812 SI 1995/2518 reg 89

A retention is a portion of the consideration for a contract which is retained by the customer until he is satisfied that the contract has been fully and satisfactorily performed.

Retention payments are taxable at the **earlier** of:
– the time of payment; and
– the date that an invoice relating to the retention is issued.

Stage payments

8814 SI 1995/2518 reg 93

Supplies of services and/or goods, made under a construction contract which states that **periodic payments** will be made, are treated as made at the earlier of the date that:
– each payment is received; or
– a VAT invoice (not including a self-billed invoice) is issued.

No tax point occurs on completion, unless the anti-avoidance rule applies.

Notice 708 para 24

MEMO POINTS The **anti-avoidance rule** will apply when either:
– the occupier can recover less than 80% of the VAT incurred on the construction costs; or
– the supplier (contractor or subcontractor) is connected with the occupier, and is funded by him.
In this case, the supplier must account for VAT on the full value of the contract on completion, less any amounts on which VAT has already been declared.

2. Types of building

Non-residential buildings

A commercial building is any building which **does not qualify** as a dwelling, or is not intended for relevant residential or charitable use. **8816**

The construction of a new commercial property (including services and building materials) is always standard-rated, unless there is to be some residential or charitable use of the building (termed "mixed use" (¶8832)).

For the **conversion** of a non-residential property to residential use, see ¶8876+.

Dwellings

The construction of property which is designed as a dwelling, or a number of dwellings, is zero-rated. **8818** Sch 8 group 5 item 2(a) VATA 1994

Both the main contractor and subcontractors can zero-rate their construction supplies (¶8834).

To be classed as a dwelling for VAT purposes, a building must satisfy all of the following **criteria**: Sch 8 group 5 note 2 VATA 1994
- self-contained living accommodation;
- no provision for internal access from the dwelling to any other dwelling (including a part of another dwelling);
- at the time of planning consent, the building can be separately used, let or sold, free of any restriction imposed by covenant, planning permission, etc; and
- statutory planning consent has been granted, and the dwelling's construction or conversion has been carried out in accordance with that consent.

MEMO POINTS The installation in dwellings of **mobility aids** for the elderly is reduced-rated (¶8060).

Relevant residential buildings

The construction of a property which is **intended** for use solely for a relevant residential purpose is zero-rated, provided that the customer issues a certificate confirming its intended use. Any **subsequent change of use** within 10 years of the building's completion may result in a VAT charge (¶8830+). **8820** Sch 8 group 5 item 2(a) VATA 1994

The following uses are **deemed** to qualify as a relevant residential purpose: **8822** Sch 8 group 5 note 4 VATA 1994

Type of use	Detail	Scope of zero-rating
Children's home		All areas
Residence providing personal care	For those in need by reason of old age, disablement, past or present alcohol or drug dependency, or past or present mental disorder	All areas
Hospice	Not hospitals	All areas
School or college	Residential accommodation for pupils and students (e.g. halls of residence, boarding school houses)	Residential accommodation only
Armed forces residence		Residential accommodation only
Accommodation for religious communities	Monastery, nunnery etc	All areas
An institution which is the sole or main residence for at least 90% of the residents	Excluding prisons, hotels, inns, hostels etc	All areas

8824 Notice 708 para 16 A **tax certificate** is issued by the customer i.e. the person who intends to use the building for specific purposes. Only the recipient of a **tax certificate** can zero-rate his supplies and the certificate must be received before any zero-rating can be applied.

Relevant charitable buildings

8826 Sch 8 group 5 item 2(a) VATA 1994 The construction of property which is intended for use solely for a relevant charitable purpose is zero-rated, provided that the customer issues a certificate (¶8824) confirming the intended use.

As with relevant residential use, the scope of supplies which can be zero-rated is restricted to those provided by the recipient of the certificate. Any **subsequent change of use** within 10 years of the building's completion may result in a VAT charge (¶8830+).

8828 Sch 8 group 5 note 6 VATA 1994 The following are **deemed** to qualify as use for a relevant charitable purpose:
– a property used by a charity for non-business purposes (for the meaning of business, see ¶7764) – it should be noted that business use is not just restricted to situations where a profit is made; or
– a village hall, or similar building, providing social or recreational facilities for a local community.

HMRC Brief 39/09 A building is regarded as used **solely** for a relevant charitable purpose if the relevant use is 95% or more. For this purpose any reasonable method may be used to calculate qualifying use.

Sch 8 group 5 note 17 VATA 1994 MEMO POINTS A new attached self-contained **annexe** (or part thereof) is only treated as a new building when it is to be used for a relevant charitable purpose, and:
– it is capable of functioning independently of the existing building; and
– its main or sole access is not via the existing building (and vice versa).

Self-supply charge on change of use

8830 Sch 10 para 1(4) VATA 1994 Where the **owner** or occupier of a building changes the use of the building from relevant residential or charitable use within 10 years of its completion, a self-supply will occur if the intermittent business use threshold is exceeded. The trader must charge himself output tax. The VAT charged is also potentially recoverable as input tax, subject to the normal rules on VAT recovery.

If a building is treated as a relevant charitable building under the 95% interpretation (¶8828), a self-supply will be required if the building ceases to be eligible within 10 years.

The **self-supply** is calculated by apportioning the VAT that would have been charged, had the original supply of the building been standard-rated, on a time basis.

Sch 10 para 1(6) VATA 1994 The following **formula** is used:

$$\text{VAT which would have been charged} \times \frac{(10 - \text{number of whole years of relevant use})}{10}$$

MEMO POINTS 1. The amount liable to the self-supply charge is not adjusted for any change in the building's **market value**.
2. Where the value of the original supply was **more than** £250,000 and the trader makes some exempt supplies in the 10 years following the self-supply, the input tax recovery will be subject to capital goods scheme adjustments (¶8250).

EXAMPLE On 1 September 2013 A Ltd, which is partly exempt, built a home at a cost of £750,000, which was zero-rated as it was for relevant residential use.
A Ltd then decided to occupy the home itself and used it as offices from 6 April 2017.
A Ltd will need to account for VAT as follows:

	£
VAT @ 20% on cost of £750,000	150,000
There were 4 years when the building was used for a relevant purpose, so the VAT due is:	
$150{,}000 \times (\frac{10-4}{10})$	90,000

A Ltd must charge itself VAT of £90,000 in the VAT period including 6 April 2017. As A Ltd makes some exempt supplies, not all of this VAT will be recoverable as input tax, and A Ltd must apply its usual partial exemption method and the capital goods scheme.

If a person has received a zero-rated supply of construction services, on the basis that the building would be used for residential or charitable purposes, and within 10 years of its completion there is a **grant of a lease or sale** to a **third party** who will not be using it for either type of use, VAT is chargeable. For buildings completed before 1 March 2011 the amount liable to VAT is the proportion of the disposal proceeds which relate to the part of the building which was initially zero-rated, and is now to be used for a non-relevant use. For buildings completed on or after 1 March 2011 the VAT charge is calculated in the same way as for a change of use (see ¶8830). 8831

Mixed use buildings

A builder may construct a building, part of which will be used for residential purposes, part for non-residential purposes. 8832 Sch 8 group 5 note 11 VATA 1994

In this case he must apportion his services between the zero-rated and standard-rated works, otherwise all of his charges must be standard-rated.

Any method of **apportionment** can be used but it should give a fair and reasonable result. Common methods include using cost information from a quantity surveyor, or floor space occupied for each type of use. In addition, the tax certificate should indicate which areas of the building qualify for zero-rating.

Comment No certificate is required if use will be as a dwelling.

3. Types of costs

The costs incurred when constructing a building will either be in respect of services provided by the builder and his subcontractors, or for materials used in the construction work. 8834 Notice 708 para 3.3.6

For work to be **zero-rated**, it should be carried out before completion (¶8802).

Building services

All services, **except** professional services, provided by contractors in the course of the construction of a dwelling or relevant residential or charitable building are zero-rated. In the case of **dwellings**, services provided by subcontractors can also be zero-rated, provided that those services are made in the course of construction. 8835 Sch 8 group 5 item 4 VATA 1994

Professional services include those performed by: Notice 708 para 3.4
- architects;
- accountants;
- surveyors;
- solicitors;
- consultants;
- project managers; and
- supervisors.

MEMO POINTS If professional services are included within a composite supply of building services, or under a "design and build" contract, they will also be zero-rated. Separate supplies of professional services are always standard-rated.

Typical zero-rated building services supplied in the course of construction include: 8836 Notice 708 para 3.3.4
- site clearance and demolition;
- laying of foundations;
- improving an access point to a site for deliveries;
- bricklaying, plastering, carpentry, roofing and plumbing services; and
- first-time decoration.

The following, however, will **always be standard-rated**:
– cleaning of site offices;
– transport and haulage to and from the site;
– hire of goods; and
– any private use of goods.

Building materials

8838 Sch 8 group 5 note 22 VATA 1994
Building materials and other goods **ordinarily incorporated** (or installed as fittings) into a building by a builder, who is supplying zero-rated services, are also zero-rated. Common examples include bricks, wiring and cabling, and builders' hardware.

Items that do not fall within this description will be standard-rated. For recipients of the construction services, who then sell the property after construction (i.e. developers), input tax recovery on these items is blocked (¶8853).

8839
Generally, **fixtures** will be building materials which are installed and effect a permanent and substantial improvement to the building.

However, the following items are always **standard-rated**:
– finished or prefabricated furniture (other than furniture designed to be fitted in kitchens), and materials for the construction of fitted furniture (other than kitchen furniture);
– electrical or gas appliances, except those specifically zero-rated; and
– carpets and carpeting materials (including underlay and carpet tiles), even when stuck to the floor. Other floor coverings can be zero-rated.

Notice 708 para 13.6
MEMO POINTS The following **electrical appliances** are specifically zero-rated:
– those designed to heat space or water or to provide ventilation, air cooling, air purification, or dust extraction;
– those intended for use in a building (such as a block of flats) designed as a number of dwellings (for example, a door entry system, a waste disposal unit, or a machine for compacting waste);
– burglar alarms, fire alarms, fire safety equipment and devices for summoning aid in an emergency (but not telephones); and
– lifts and hoists.

B. Freehold and leasehold disposals

8840 Notice 708 para 4
The **first-time disposal** of a major interest in certain new residential buildings and those to be used for wholly charitable purposes by the **person who constructed** them is zero-rated. Subsequent sales or grants of leases, or sales by persons who do not qualify as the constructor, will be exempt from VAT. For commercial property see ¶8847.

What is a major interest?

8841
The definition of **major interest** in land depends on its location as follows:

Location	Major interest
England or Wales	Freehold
	Lease of a term exceeding 21 years
Northern Ireland	Freehold
	Lease of a term exceeding 21 years
	Includes the estate of a person who holds land under a fee farm grant
Scotland	Estate or interest of the proprietor of the dominium utile
	In the case of land not held under feudal tenure: – estate or interest of the owner; or – lessee's interest under a lease of a term of at least 20 years

1. Time of supply

Freehold property

The sale of a freehold property is a supply of goods, so the basic tax point is the date on which it is made available to the customer. This is normally the date of the freehold conveyance (the settlement date in Scotland). **8842** Sch 4 para 4 VATA 1994

MEMO POINTS Where the **total purchase price cannot be determined** at the time when the freehold interest is transferred, the property is deemed to have been supplied in separate transactions, so for the part where the price: SI 1995/2518 reg 84(2)
a. was determinable at the time of the transfer, the normal time of supply rules apply;
b. could not be determined, the transaction occurs at the earlier of the time when:
– the remaining part of the consideration was received by the transferor; or
– the transferor issued an invoice in respect of that part.

Long leases

The supply of a lease or tenancy **exceeding 21 years** (not less than 20 years in Scotland) is deemed to be the grant of a major interest and is therefore also treated as a supply of goods. **8843** Sch 4 para 4 VATA 1994

Where all or part of the **consideration** for the grant of such a lease or tenancy is **payable periodically**, the goods are deemed to have been supplied separately at the earlier of each time that: SI 1995/2518 reg 85
– a part of the consideration is received by the supplier; or
– the supplier issues a VAT invoice relating to the grant.

The exception to this rule is where, on or around the beginning of any period of up to 12 months, the **supplier issues a VAT invoice** containing the following information:
– dates on which any parts of the consideration are to become due for payment in the period;
– amount payable (excluding VAT) on each date; and
– rate of VAT in force when the VAT invoice is issued and the amount of VAT chargeable on each payment.

In this case the goods are treated as separately supplied on the earlier of when a payment becomes due or is received by the supplier.

MEMO POINTS If there is a **change in the rate of VAT** (such as the increase from 17.5% to 20% on 4 January 2011) on or before any of the payment dates specified by the supplier, the invoice will cease to be treated as a VAT invoice in respect of any supplies for which payments are due on or after the date of change (and not received before the change).

Short leases

A lease with a term of **21 years or less** (less than 20 years in Scotland) is a continuous supply of services for VAT purposes (¶7932). **8844**

Compulsory purchases

The general rule for compulsory purchase is that the supply does not take place until a price has been agreed, so the normal time of supply rules apply (¶7902). **8845** SI 1995/2518 reg 84(1)

The **exception** is where the person from whom the land is being purchased does not know the amount of the payment that he is to receive at the normal tax point. In this case, a supply is deemed to occur each time that a payment is received for the purchase.

2. VAT liability

Commercial buildings and civil engineering works

The grant or assignment of a **freehold interest** in a commercial building or civil engineering work is standard-rated if the building/work is still under construction at the date of the grant or assignment or, if it is a building, it is still new (¶8802) and not intended for use as a qualifying building after the grant. **8847**

The grant of a **lease** in a commercial building is exempt, subject to the option to tax (¶8904).

MEMO POINTS Supplies of new freehold commercial buildings are standard-rated even if the **purchase price is determined more than 3 years after completion** of the building. This provision is intended to stop contrived transactions whereby the bulk of the consideration is paid after 3 years in order to avoid VAT on the cost of the new building.

Residential and charitable buildings

8849
Sch 8 group 5 item 1 VATA 1994
Notice 708 para 4.1

Person constructing Provided that the relevant conditions are met, the **first grant of** a major interest (¶8841) in a building which is a dwelling (or number of dwellings) or a relevant residential or charitable building (or its site) by a person qualifying as one of the following will be zero-rated:
– the developer who either constructed, or arranged for the construction of, the building on land that he owns, or has an interest in; or
– the contractor or subcontractor who provided construction services for the building.

The grant of a short lease is exempt.

Notice 708 para 16

Where there is a **subsequent change of use** within 10 years of the building's completion, see ¶8830+.

8850

Scope Zero-rating applies only to the disposal of a new:
a. dwelling (or a number of dwellings) (¶8818), unless the purchaser is prevented from residing, or not entitled to reside, in the building throughout the year; or
b. building intended for use solely for a **relevant residential** (¶8820) **or charitable** (¶8826) purpose, in which case a tax certificate is required from the purchaser.

If the building being disposed of only **partly** qualifies, the vendor must make a fair apportionment of the proceeds.

8851
Notice 708 para 4.3

Where the major interest is a **lease**, zero-rating will only apply to the premium payable on the grant. If no premium is payable, zero-rating will apply to the first rental payment due under the lease.

EXAMPLE D Ltd develops houses and grants 25-year leases to new tenants. VAT on professional fees incurred on the building and subsequent marketing amounts to £1,500. No premium is payable and the tenants are paying rent of £1,000 per month.
The first month's rent will be zero-rated and all subsequent rental payments will be exempt. D Ltd will be able to recover the input tax of £1,500, as the first rent payment is zero-rated.

8853
Notice 708 para 12

Input tax recovery Normally, all input tax incurred on costs relating to a zero-rated supply can be recovered.

However, for **developers** (¶8849), input tax recovery is blocked on any **goods incorporated into the building** which are not building materials (¶8838). Any onward supply of such goods, where input tax has been blocked, will be exempt.

Input tax can be recovered on goods which are **not incorporated** into the building, such as free-standing items. When such goods are sold with the building or as part of a design-and-build contract, a separate supply is deemed to take place and output tax will be due.

C. Special situations

DIY housebuilders

8862
s 35 VATA 1994
Notice 719

HMRC will refund any VAT chargeable on the supply, acquisition or importation of any goods used in connection with construction or conversion work where:
a. the work comprises:
– the construction of a dwelling or building (or as a part of a design-and-build contract) intended for residential or charitable use (¶8818+); or
– a residential conversion, such as a barn converted into a dwelling;

b. the work is carried out lawfully and is not in the course or furtherance of a business;
c. the work is carried out in the UK (including the Isle of Man but not the Channel Islands);
d. the goods concerned are building materials (¶8838) which are incorporated into the building or its site during the course of the works; and
e. an appropriate claim is submitted.

MEMO POINTS 1. A **residential conversion** is the conversion of a non-residential building, or a non-residential part of a building, into:
– a building designed as a dwelling or a number of dwellings;
– a building intended for use solely for a relevant residential purpose; or
– anything which would fall within either of the above if different parts of a building were treated as separate buildings.
2. If the following are **built at the same time**, and are covered by the necessary planning permission, a refund can also be claimed for the construction of:
– a domestic garage;
– a conservatory attached to the dwelling;
– a driveway and main paths on the site, but not ornamental garden features, landscaping or planting; and
– boundary and retaining walls, and boundary fences.
Buildings such as greenhouses, garden sheds and other outbuildings are not included.
3. The construction of, or conversion of a non-residential building into, a holiday home benefits from the DIY scheme.

Non-refundable costs An input tax refund will not be available for **building materials** that would be standard-rated, even when supplied with zero-rated building work (¶8838). 8864

A refund will also be unavailable for the following **services**:
– professional and supervisory services, including the fees of architects and surveyors, and any other fees for management, consultancy, design and planning;
– the purchase or hire of tools and equipment;
– consumables which are not actually incorporated in the building (for example, cleaning materials);
– transport and haulage charges, including the purchase of fuel for these;
– temporary fencing; and
– skip hire.

HMRC accept that the conversion of a building which contains **both a residential part and a non-residential part** is within the scope of the refund scheme, provided that the overall number of dwellings is increased. *C&E v Jacobs* [2005] Business Brief 22/05

A refund will be refused where a single dwelling is created by converting both the residential and non-residential parts of an existing building into a single house. *C&E v Blom-Cooper* [2003]

Making a claim Refunds may be claimed only after the work is completed. 8866 HMRC Brief 45/09

The claim **forms** can be obtained from HMRC. The completed form and supporting evidence (including original invoices) must be submitted within 3 months from the date the work was completed. If this time limit cannot be met, HMRC should be informed.

Builders using own labour

Where a builder uses his own labour to provide services and they are: 8867 Notice 708 para 25.1
– used in the course or furtherance of his business;
– made otherwise than in return for a consideration; and
– have an open-market value of at least £100,000,

there will be a deemed supply to him in the course of his business and a supply by him (known as a self-supply). **Services falling under this provision** are as follows:
– the construction of a building for use in the business which is not a dwelling, nor intended for residential or charitable use (¶8818+);
– the construction of any civil engineering work;
– works which increase the floor area by at least 10% of an existing building which is used, or to be used, in the business; and
– any demolition works carried out at the same time as, or as preparation for, any of the above.

MEMO POINTS 1. The VAT incurred in **purchasing goods and services** for such building works is treated as relating to the taxable self-supply.
2. The output tax accounted for under the self-supply charge may also be recovered as **input tax** to the extent that the person uses or intends to use the relevant building in making taxable supplies. It may be necessary to consider the capital goods scheme (¶8250).

SECTION 3

Land and existing buildings

8870 Sch 9 group 1 VATA 1994 Most supplies relating to land are exempt, including the **grant of** any of the following:
- an interest in or right over land;
- a licence to occupy land; or
- in relation to land in Scotland, any personal right to call for or be granted any such interest or right.

Notice 742 para 2.1 MEMO POINTS 1. **Land** for these purposes includes buildings and fixtures, walls, trees, plants and other structures along with natural objects in, under or over it, provided that they remain attached to it. The sale of bare land is exempt unless building work has already begun, when the VAT treatment depends on the type of construction undertaken (¶8808).
Notice 742 para 2.3 2. An **interest** in land may be in the form of legal ownership or a beneficial interest, where the holder has the right to the proceeds arising from the land's exploitation. For VAT purposes, the beneficial owner is deemed to be the grantor.
Notice 742 para 2.5 3. A **licence** to occupy land is authority given so as to avoid a trespass, where all of the following conditions are met:
a. it is granted in return for consideration;
b. the rights of occupation must relate to a specified piece of land, and must be given to the licensee;
c. the rights of the licensee are not impinged by another's person right to enter the land; and
d. the licensee is allowed either to:
- physically enjoy the land; or
- economically exploit it for the purposes of a business.

Common examples include the provision of offices and related facilities, space for advertising hoardings and the hiring out of a hall.

Exceptions

8871 The following are exceptions to this basic rule:
- building work carried out on an existing property (¶8873);
- uses of land that are specifically identified in the legislation as being standard-rated (¶8890);
- certain transactions between a landlord and tenant (¶8894+);
- certain converted, or substantially reconstructed, buildings (¶8900+); and
- transactions where an option to tax has been exercised (¶8904+).

A. Work on existing buildings

Summary

8873

Work done	VAT rating	¶¶
Residential conversions generally	Reduced rate	¶8876
Residential conversions for housing associations	Zero rate	¶8878
Refurbishment of empty residential properties	Reduced rate	¶8882
Alterations to protected buildings designed as dwellings/relevant residential or charitable use	Zero rate	¶8886
Other works	Standard rate	

Residential conversions

Construction work which **results in** the following residential conversions is liable to VAT at the reduced rate: 8876 Sch 7A group 6 VATA 1994 Notice 708 para 7.2
- a changed number of dwellings (but not less than one);
- multiple occupancy dwellings (e.g. bed-sits); and
- premises intended for a relevant residential purpose (¶8820).

Reduced-rating applies to work on the fabric of the building, and within the immediate site if the work is essential for the building to function.

Which eligible **suppliers** can reduced-rate their supplies depends on the building which is being converted. For conversions involving:
- dwellings, both the main contractor and subcontractors can reduced-rate their supplies; but
- properties to be used for a relevant residential purpose, only the main contractor can reduced-rate his work, and he must receive a tax certificate (¶8824) which states the intended use.

MEMO POINTS 1. **Work to the fabric** includes repairs and maintenance, decoration, and improvements such as an extension or the installation of double glazing. As with other types of construction, the incorporation of goods which are not building materials (¶8838) will be standard-rated.
2. Work **within the immediate site** includes the provision of:
- water and power to the building;
- access to the building;
- the means of drainage or security; and
- the means of waste disposal.
3. The installation of **mobility aids** for the elderly is also reduced-rated (¶8060).

Conversions for housing associations

A conversion undertaken on behalf of a housing association of a **non-residential building into** either dwellings (¶8818), or a building intended for use solely for a relevant residential purpose (¶8820), is zero-rated. 8878 Sch 8 group 5 item 3 VATA 1994

For this purpose the **existing building** should not have been designed or adapted for use as a dwelling or relevant residential building within the 10 years before the conversion work commences, and no part of it should have been occupied as a dwelling or residence during that time. Sch 8 group 5 note 7A VATA 1994

Where relevant, the contractor should obtain evidence of the non-occupation. It is usually possible to obtain confirmation from a local council that a property has been empty.

Only the **main contractor** can zero-rate his work and he must obtain a certificate from the housing association confirming that it is a qualifying housing association. If converting into a building for a relevant residential purpose, a further certificate of intended use from the customer must also be obtained (¶8824). 8880

The **scope of supplies** which can be zero-rated includes services (¶8835) and building materials (¶8838) supplied by the main contractor in carrying out those services.

If **only part of the work** relates to a residential conversion, the contractor must apportion his costs, otherwise all of his work must be standard-rated.

Where there is a **subsequent change of use** within 10 years of the building's completion, see ¶8830+.

Refurbishment of empty residential premises

The reduced rate of VAT applies to refurbishment of the following **residential buildings**, which must have been empty for the 2 years prior to the renovation work commencing: 8882 Sch 7A group 7 VATA 1994
- a single household dwelling, excluding a granny flat;
- a multiple occupation dwelling (e.g. bed-sits); or
- a building which, when last occupied, was used for a relevant residential purpose (¶8820), and will be solely used for this purpose after the work is done.

The **emptiness requirement** concerns the whole premises which are the subject of the renovation. So for a site which is to be used for a relevant residential purpose, all of the buildings which form part of that site must have been empty for the 2 years prior to the renovation work commencing. However, not all of the buildings on the site need to be subject to the renovation work.

MEMO POINTS For **single household dwellings**, there is an alternative test available to cover the situation where the dwelling is **occupied** while the renovation work is carried out. It requires all of the following criteria to be met:
– the occupier has acquired a major interest (¶8841);
– the dwelling was unoccupied for a period of at least 2 years;
– the subsequent occupier (for whom the renovation is done) then acquired the empty property;
– the renovation work is done for the occupier within the first year after acquisition; and
– no works were undertaken during the 2 years before the occupier's acquisition date, other than minor works to keep the dwelling dry and secure.

8884 Sch 7A group 7 note 3A, 5 VATA 1994

Supplies by the main contractor and subcontractors can be reduced-rated, except in the case of a single household dwelling where the owner is occupying it, when only the main contractor can apply the reduced rate. If renovating a building for a relevant residential purpose, a certificate of intended use must be obtained (¶8824) and only the recipient of the certificate can reduced-rate his supply.

Where applicable, reduced-rating applies to work on the fabric of the building and within the immediate site of the building. For works carried out on the site to qualify, they must be essential for the building to function (¶8876).

If only part of the work completed by the builder relates to the renovation, he must apportion his costs, otherwise all of his work must be standard-rated.

Alterations to protected buildings

8886 Sch 8 group 6 VATA 1994

Construction works for the approved alteration of a protected building are zero-rated, if they **result in** a building which is:
– designed to remain as, or become, a dwelling or number of dwellings;
– intended for use for a relevant residential purpose; or
– intended for use for a relevant charitable purpose.

Any work which **maintains or repairs** a protected property will be standard-rated.

For dwellings, both the main **contractor** and subcontractors can zero-rate their work (including building materials). For buildings to be put to a relevant residential or charitable purpose, only the recipient of the tax certificate (¶8824) can zero-rate his supply.

MEMO POINTS 1. A protected building is **defined** as a listed building or scheduled monument.

Sch 8 group 6 note 6 VATA 1994

2. An **approved alteration** requires:
– the work being done to alter the fabric of the building, excluding repairs and maintenance work and reconstructions; and
– permissions and consent, where relevant, to be obtained and complied with.

Generally, the building should be visibly improved for an alteration to have taken place. HMRC may agree in advance that works will qualify as an alteration.

3. HMRC define **repairs** as tasks undertaken to minimise the need for, and mitigate the scale and cost of, further attention to the fabric of the building. Whether the work is a one-off job is irrelevant, as is the cost. Any physical alteration resulting from repairs is excluded from zero-rating (e.g. small changes, or differences necessitated by the use of modern building materials).

8888 There is a grant scheme available for **listed buildings of worship** to cover some input tax incurred on repairs and maintenance. Further details of the scheme can be found at www.lpwscheme.org.uk.

There is a similar scheme available for the construction, renovation and maintenance of **memorials** by charities and faith groups. Further details are available at www.culture.gov.uk.

B. Exploitation and letting of property

8890 Sch 9 group 1 VATA 1994

The following table outlines the liability of common supplies made in the letting and exploitation of property.

Standard-rated supplies	Details	Exceptions	Reference
Provision of sleeping accommodation	Accommodation in an hotel, inn, boarding house or similar establishment	VAT ceases to apply to accommodation costs from the 29th day where guests stay for a continuous period of more than 4 weeks. Other supplies, such as breakfast, remain standard-rated.	Notice 709/3 paras 2, 3
Provision of holiday accommodation	Grants of an interest in (or right over or licence to occupy) accommodation, including buildings, huts, chalets, caravans, houseboats or tents	Grants of freehold interests or leases (for a premium) in existing buildings are exempt. Other lettings of houseboat accommodation, for example houseboats set aside for permanent residential use, are exempt.	Notice 709/3 para 5
Caravans and tents	Provision of seasonal pitches (and related facilities)	Supply of rented accommodation in a caravan or mobile home is exempt unless it is holiday accommodation.	Notice 701/20
Mooring and storage	For houseboats, aircraft, ships and any other vessel		Notice 742 para 3
Parking spaces	Grant or assignment of spaces for vehicles	Letting in the following circumstances will be exempt: – in conjunction with the letting of a dwelling for permanent residential use, provided that it is reasonably near the dwelling and the arrangement is between the same parties; – where references to parking a vehicle are incidental to the main use; – for the storage of the stock of a motor dealer; – for business use by a vehicle transportation firm, a vehicle distributor or a vehicle auctioneer; and – for purposes such as a car boot sale or market.	Notice 742 para 4
Sports facilities	Grant or assignment of facilities	The following facilities are exempt: – those to be used for more than 24 hours; or – which are provided as a series of at least ten shorter periods.	Notice 742 para 5
Spectator seats	Grant or assignment of any right to occupy a box, seat or any other accommodation at a sports ground, theatre, concert hall or any other place of entertainment		Notice 742 para 3.4
Gaming and fishing rights	Grant of rights	The supply will be exempt where either: – the grantor grants a freehold interest over the land over which the gaming rights are exercisable; – sporting rights forming part of a lease are no more than 10% of the value; or – an empty lake is let to someone who will stock it with fish. Shooting rights will be outside the scope of VAT when not granted in the course of a business.	Notice 742 para 6
Timber rights	Grant of rights	A supply of land which happens to contain timber will be exempt.	Notice 742 para 3

Short Leases

8892 The VAT treatment of transactions between landlord and tenant will depend on the nature of the transaction.

The **grant** of a short lease over residential property for a premium and/or rent is always exempt from VAT. The grant of a short lease over non-residential property for a premium and/or rent is exempt from VAT, unless the lessor has exercised his option to tax (¶8904).

The treatment of **subsequent supplies** under a lease depends on the nature of those supplies.

Other payments

8894
Notice 742 para 10
Business Brief 12/05

The VAT treatment of other payments which can occur between a landlord and the tenant is outlined below.

Payment	Person making supply	VAT treatment	Exceptions
The grant by the landlord of a **rent-free period**	n/a	Outside the scope	Unless the grant is in exchange for something (such as decorating) that the tenant agrees to do, in which case VAT is due on the amount of rent forgone
Inducement payments from the landlord to the tenant	n/a	Outside the scope	Unless the tenant agrees to perform specific services (such as refurbishment works, or acting as an anchor tenant), in which case VAT is due
The landlord pays the tenant for carrying out building and **refurbishment** works	Tenant	Standard-rated	
Variation of the lease e.g.: – altering the terms or length; or – extending the scope of property covered	Landlord (only if consideration received)	Outside the scope unless consideration given, in which case exempt[1]	
Lifting of a **restrictive covenant**	Landlord	Exempt[1]	
Landlord pays tenant to **surrender** the lease	Tenant	Exempt[1]	
Payment from the tenant to the landlord in return for accepting the surrender of a lease (a **reverse surrender**)	Landlord	Exempt[1]	
Assignment by an outgoing tenant, for consideration, to an incoming tenant	Outgoing tenant	Exempt[1]	
Reverse assignment (i.e. outgoing tenant pays an incoming tenant to take on the lease)	Incoming tenant	Standard-rated	
Dilapidation payments made by the tenant to the landlord at the end of the lease	n/a	Outside the scope	

Payment	Person making supply	VAT treatment	Exceptions
The payment of **statutory compensation** by a landlord to a tenant	n/a	Outside the scope	
Where the **vendor** of a lease or freehold property gives the purchaser a **guarantee** that the vendor will pay the open-market rent of the property if tenants cannot be found	n/a	Outside the scope	
Rent adjustments made between landlords on the sale of tenanted property and between tenants on the assignment of a lease	n/a	Outside the scope	

Note:
1. Subject to the option to tax (¶8904) for commercial property only, when the supply would be standard-rated.

Service charges

Where the tenant pays a service charge to the landlord for the provision of **general** services required for the upkeep of the building as a whole, the VAT liability of the service charge will follow the VAT treatment of the rent paid under the lease. An example would be services connected with the external fabric or common parts of the building, and which are levied as part of a common charge. 8896 Notice 742 para 11

Specific services paid for by the tenant may fall to be treated as:
- further payments for the lease, so that the same VAT treatment applies;
- payments for identifiable services such as telephone, office services, etc, which are usually standard-rated (although where power is provided to a domestic tenant, this qualifies for reduced-rating (¶8060)); or
- disbursements, where the landlord pays bills on behalf of the tenant, when any recharge is outside the scope of VAT (¶8552).

Comment If the **tenant cannot recover VAT**, it will be preferable for any exempt supplies included within a taxable service charge, such as insurance, to be transferred into the tenant's own name. Alternatively, the tenant could arrange its own insurance, which would be exempt, to ensure that it does not incur any avoidable irrecoverable input tax.

C. Freehold and leasehold disposals

Most sales of existing buildings and land are exempt, subject to the option to tax in certain cases (¶8904). However, there are exceptions for the first disposal of a converted building, or a substantially reconstructed protected building, where a residence has resulted from the building works undertaken and the vendor is the developer (¶8849) or contractor. 8898

1. Non-exempt sales

Converted buildings

The first sale of the freehold, or grant of a long lease, in respect of a building which has been converted from a non-residential building **into** a building designed as a dwelling or 8900 Notice 708 para 5 number of dwellings (¶8818), or intended for use solely for a relevant residential purpose (¶8820), is zero-rated.

MEMO POINTS 1. For this purpose, a **non-residential building** is one which has not been used as a residence in the 10 years immediately preceding the date of sale, or lease commencement date. It is possible to start the work before the 10-year period has elapsed, and still zero-rate the disposal, provided that the disposal date is after the 10-year period comes to an end.
2. Where **only part of a building is being converted** and the building already contains residential parts then, for zero-rating to apply, the conversion must be to a building for relevant residential use, or to create an additional dwelling or dwellings.

Protected buildings

8902 Sch 8 group 6 item 1 VATA 1994 Notice 708 para 10

The first grant of a major interest in (or in any part of) a protected building (¶8886) will be zero-rated where it is **substantially reconstructed**, and the reconstruction results in a building:

a. designed as a **dwelling** (or a number of dwellings) (¶8818), unless the acquirer is prevented from, or not entitled to, reside in the building throughout the year; or

b. intended for use solely for a **relevant residential** (¶8820) or **charitable** (¶8826) purpose, in which case a tax certificate is required.

MEMO POINTS 1. For these purposes, **substantial reconstruction** occurs where major work takes place to the building's fabric and at least one of the following conditions is fulfilled when the reconstruction is completed:
– at least 60% of the cost of the reconstruction works would qualify for zero-rating if supplied by a taxable person during an approved alteration (¶8886), and these are not excluded services; or
– the reconstructed building incorporates no more of the original building (before reconstruction began) than the external walls, together with other external features of architectural or historic interest.
2. **Excluded services** are the services of an architect, surveyor or other person acting as consultant or in a supervisory capacity (¶8835).

2. The option to tax

8904 Sch 10 para 2 VATA 1994

When a taxpayer exercises his option to tax, certain supplies which would normally be exempt will become standard-rated. **Exercising the option** to tax allows for the recovery of input tax incurred in relation to the property that would not otherwise be recoverable. Before a taxpayer opts to tax he should consider the **VAT status of tenants or potential purchasers**, to ensure that charging VAT on the letting or sale of the property does not make it unattractive to tenants/purchasers who are unable to recover all or most of the VAT they incur.

Once the taxpayer has opted to tax, all **future supplies** in connection with that particular interest in the property must be standard-rated unless the option is disapplied, or the option has been revoked.

8905 The option to tax is **personal to the taxpayer** who makes it. For example, if a landlord opts to tax a commercial property and lets it to a tenant, the landlord will charge the tenant VAT on the rent. If the tenant then sub-lets part of the property, any rent received by the tenant is not subject to VAT unless the tenant has also opted to tax the property. In this circumstance, ignoring any other activities of the relevant parties, the tenant should opt to tax, as otherwise the VAT charged by the landlord will not be recoverable, as it would relate to an exempt supply (to the sub-tenant under the sub-lease).

MEMO POINTS Options to tax can bind "relevant associates" of the opter. Relevant associates are, in general terms, the members of the same VAT group as the opter. Further details on the implications of the option to tax in relation to VAT groups can be found in *VAT Memo*.

Unaffected supplies

The option to tax has no effect on the following supplies: **8906** Notice 742A

Supply	Further information
Any supply of a dwelling or relevant residential property	
A sale of property which is treated as the **transfer of a going concern** and therefore outside the scope of VAT (¶8604), subject to certain conditions	
Any supply of a building where the intended use of the building after the transaction is as a **dwelling** or solely for a **relevant residential purpose** (¶8818+)	The purchaser must notify the vendor that his intended use is as a dwelling, or for a relevant residential purpose. Notification should be made on form VAT1614D, which must be given to the vendor before the price for the transaction is fixed. If notification is given after the price has been fixed, it is at the discretion of the supplier whether or not to accept the disapplication. If no action is taken the option to tax will apply.
Any supply of a building or part of a building where the other party informs the taxpayer that the intended use is solely for a **relevant charitable purpose** (¶8826)	Use of all or part of a building as an office does not qualify as a relevant charitable purpose, unless such use is incidental.
A supply of land (or land with buildings which will be demolished) made to a **registered housing association** which provides a certificate stating that the land is to be used by it for the construction of dwellings or relevant residential buildings	Notification by the housing association should be made on form VAT1614G and should be given to the vendor before the price for the transaction has been fixed. If the notification is given after the price has been fixed, it is at the discretion of the supplier whether or not to accept the disapplication.
A supply of **land to** an individual who will **build a dwelling** on it for his own use, other than in the course or furtherance of any business carried on by him	
The supply of a pitch for a permanent **residential caravan**	Unless occupation throughout the year is prevented by a covenant or statutory planning consent.
A mooring or berthing for a **residential houseboat**	Unless occupation throughout the year is prevented by a covenant or statutory planning consent.
Avoidance where property is to be put to non-taxable use[1]	

Note:
1. An option to tax will have no effect where:
a. the building is or will become a capital item within the **capital goods scheme** (¶8250) for either the transferor or transferee; and
b. the transferor intends or expects that the **property will be occupied** by any of the following, other than wholly or substantially wholly for taxable business purposes (up to 20% exempt use is acceptable):
– the transferor (subject to a 2% de minimis exclusion);
– a person funding the transferor (subject to a 10% de minimis exclusion); or
– a person connected with either of them (¶5570).

Scope

Usually the option is made on an individual building **basis**, although buildings which are linked internally will be treated as one unit. If land is opted, any subsequent building built on the land will be covered by that option. It is, however, possible to exclude a new building from a pre-existing option to tax made on the land on which it will be built. This is done by completing form VAT1614F. The exclusion must have effect from the earliest of: **8907** Sch 10 para 18 VATA 1994
– the first grant of any interest in the building;

– the date of first occupation of the building; or
– the date of completion of the construction works.

Traders are allowed 30 days from the effective date to notify HMRC.

If a trader opted to tax **before 1 June 2008** and his notification made it clear that it was only the building that had been opted, then if the building is subsequently demolished the trader can, if he chooses, disapply the option to tax. This would mean that the land and any future buildings on it would not be affected by the option to tax on the old building. HMRC do not have to be notified of this choice but evidence of the decision should be retained.

Notice 742A para 3.10

If the taxpayer has opted to tax a property and the option **cannot have effect for part** of it, for example a shop with a residential flat above it, the consideration received must be apportioned on a fair and reasonable basis.

MEMO POINTS It is possible to make a Real Estate Election on all of the property interests a trader has, and will have in the future. This is a complex area of VAT, and is outside the scope of *Tax Memo*; for further information please see *VAT Memo*.

Exercising the option

8908 There are two steps to exercising an option: making an election, and then notifying HMRC. In all cases, written **notification**, which can be made using form VAT 1614A, of the option must be given to HMRC within 30 days of the date of the election being made, signed by the appropriate person (e.g. the sole trader, a director, or a partner).

The option will have effect from the **date** it is made, or any later date specified in the election.

Business Brief 13/05

A **late** notification can be made and will be accepted at HMRC's discretion. They will refuse to effect the option in cases of avoidance, or where the taxpayer's previous actions indicate no original intention to elect.

8909 Notice 742A para 5 VAT Information Sheet 6/09

Exempt supplies already made Where an exempt supply of a property has already been made, an option to tax can only be exercised with the prior permission of HMRC, **unless** one of the following conditions for **automatic approval** is met:

a. the exempt supplies have been incidental to the main use of the property – for example, placing an advertising hoarding within the surrounding area of a building;

b. it is a mixed use development and the only exempt supplies made have been made in relation to the dwellings;

c. the taxpayer does not wish to recover any input tax on goods, services or acquisitions received before the option has effect and:

– the consideration for the exempt supplies has (up to the date when the option is to take effect) been solely by way of rent and

– the only input tax the taxpayer wishes to recover (after the option takes effect) is on normal overheads; or

d. the taxpayer does not intend or expect that any supply which will be taxable as a result of making the option will either:

– be made to a connected person who would be unable to recover more than 80% of the VAT (or, if so, certain additional anti-avoidance conditions will be met) (the "outputs condition"); or

– allow him to recover input tax on capital expenditure where that capital expenditure will be used in making exempt supplies (including incidental financial activities) or for non-business purposes other than use by public bodies or government departments (the "inputs condition").

The conditions applying to **d.** above are complex, and full details are outside the scope of this book. Where **automatic approval** is **unavailable**, HMRC will require a proposal from the taxpayer on how input tax will be apportioned before agreeing to the option to tax.

MEMO POINTS 1. An application for permission to opt must be made on form VAT 1614H.
2. The second inputs condition in **d.** above applies only if the trader expects to be entitled to recover input tax incurred on capital expenditure in relation to the property as a result of the option.

Input tax recovery Once a person has opted to tax, input tax recovery will **depend on** the liability of the supplies being made, in accordance with the normal rules (¶8205). 8910 Notice 742A para 9

Input tax cannot be recovered before the option to tax has been exercised, unless:
- the sale of the building is taxable in its own right – for example, the sale of a commercial building within 3 years of completion; or
- the person had a clear intention to make taxable supplies when the input tax was incurred, supported by documentary evidence.

Where a person made **exempt supplies** of land **before opting** to tax, and has incurred irrecoverable input tax as a result, HMRC may give permission for subsequent input tax recovery on these supplies.

Revocation

Cooling off period An option to tax can be revoked, using form VAT 1614, **from the date** on which it had effect, provided that: 8912 Sch 10 para 23 VATA 1994
- written consent is obtained from HMRC within 6 months of that date;
- no use has been made of the property since the option had effect, including own use of the opter;
- no VAT has become chargeable;
- no deduction for input tax has been claimed as a result of the election; and
- the property has not been sold together with a business (or part of a business) under the transfer of a going concern rules (¶8596).

6-year revocation Any option to tax which has been exercised will be **automatically** revoked if the trader has not held an interest in the property for the previous 6 years. Complex rules apply to revocations where the opter has been a member of a VAT group during the 6-year period (see *VAT Memo*). 8914 Sch 10 para 24 VATA 1994 Notice 742A para 8.2

20-year revocation Since 1 August 2009 it has been possible to revoke an option to tax which has been in operation for 20 years. 8916 Sch 10 para 25 VATA 1994 Notice 742A para 8.3

Automatic revocation will be possible when the trader (or another member of its VAT group) does not hold a relevant interest in the property at the date the option is revoked.

If a trader still holds a relevant interest in the property at the date on which it is intended to revoke the option, it can still be automatically revoked if:
- the trader held a relevant interest in the property, both when the option first had effect and more than 20 years before the date the option is revoked;
- the property is not subject to the capital goods scheme (¶8250), or, if it is, the amount of VAT repayable as a result of revocation does not exceed £10,000;
- in the 10 years before the date of the revocation the trader has not made a supply of a relevant interest at below market value, or a relevant grant; and
- there has been no prepayment by the trader which covers more than a 12-month period.

MEMO POINTS 1. A "**relevant interest**" means an interest in, right over or licence to occupy all or part of the property.
2. A "**relevant grant**" means a grant that the trader expects, or intends, will give rise to a supply made after the option is revoked for consideration which is significantly greater than any consideration for any supply arising from the same grant before revocation. An example would be a balloon payment scheduled to be paid after the date of the revocation of the option from a lessee to the landlord who is revoking the option. HMRC guidance confirms that a rent review carried out in accordance with normal commercial practice will not be treated as a relevant grant for these purposes.

Permission to revoke can be requested from HMRC if the above automatic conditions are not met. If the trader still has an interest in the property, permission to revoke will not be given unless the trader has held an interest in the property for at least 20 years. For example, if a trader opted to tax 1 High Street on 1 January 1991 but did not acquire a relevant interest in the property until 1 January 2001, he cannot revoke the option on 1 January 2011, as he 8920 did not have a relevant interest in the property more than 20 years before the date he wishes to revoke the option.

Permission must be requested on form VAT 1614J, which must contain information including:
- the trader's VAT registration details;
- address, or exact location, of the opted property and, if appropriate, the land registry number;
- date of acquisition of interest in the property;
- date of revocation;
- confirmation of which of the automatic conditions are met, and those that are not, including full details as to why the conditions are not met.

If a trader incorrectly certifies that he has met one or more of the automatic permission conditions, and it later transpires that those conditions were not met, the revocation will be invalid and supplies made will continue to be subject to VAT. HMRC have discretion to allow permission from the date requested if permission would have been granted, had it been sought, for the breached condition at the time.

MEMO POINTS 1. When reviewing which conditions have not been met, HMRC have stated that they will give particular consideration to whether the trader, or a third party, will receive a VAT benefit as a result of the trader's actions before revoking the option.
2. HMRC can **specify the day or time** from which the revocation has effect, and may do so by reference to the meeting of a condition, or the happening of an event (for example, the sale of the property).

CHAPTER 9

Cross-border transactions

OUTLINE ¶¶

8930 The VAT treatment of cross-border transactions **depends on** whether the transaction occurs within or outside the European Union (EU).

The following table shows the countries included in the EU for VAT purposes, together with the prefix codes used with VAT registration numbers and the format of the VAT numbers:

MEMO POINTS Where X appears in the specimen VAT numbers below, this could be any alpha character.

EU state	Prefix code	Includes	Excludes	Format of VAT number
Austria	AT			U12345678
Belgium	BE			123456789
Bulgaria	BG			1234567890
Cyprus	CY			12345678X
Czech Republic	CZ			12345678 or 123456789 or 1234567890
Denmark	DK		The Faroe Islands Greenland	12345678
Estonia	EE			123456789
Finland	FI		The Aland Islands	12345678
France	FR	Monaco	Martinique French Guiana Guadeloupe Reunion St. Pierre and Miquelon	12345678901 or X1123456789 or 1X123456789 or XX123456789
Germany	DE	Jungholz Mittelberg	Busingen The Isle of Heligoland	123456789
Greece	EL		Mount Athos	012345678
Hungary	HU			12345678
Italy	IT		Vatican City San Marino The communes of Livigno and Campione d'Italia The Italian waters of Lake Lugano	12345678901
The Republic of Ireland	IE			1234567X or 1X34567X
Latvia	LV			12345678901
Lithuania	LT			123456789 or 123456789012
Luxembourg	LU			12345678
Malta	MT			12345678
Netherlands	NL			123456789B01
Poland	PL			1234567890
Portugal	PT	The Azores Madeira		123456789
Romania	RO			R123456789
Slovak Republic	SK			1234567890
Slovenia	SI			12345678
Spain	ES	The Balearic Islands	The Canary Islands Ceuta Melilla Andorra	X12345678 or 12345678X or X1234567X
Sweden	SE			123456789012
UK	GB	Isle of Man	The Channel Islands Gibraltar	123456789

SECTION 1

Goods within the EU

The current system for dealing with cross-border transactions within the EU is transitional, although it has been in force since 1 January 1993. The place where a supply is deemed to take place (and therefore where it will be taxed) depends upon whether the supply is of goods or services, and the nature of the transaction. The rules to establish where a supply of services takes place are different from those for goods. **8935**

For supplies of goods in the EU, the terms "import" and "export" used for transactions outside the EU are replaced by the terms "acquisition" and "despatch". Under the **normal rules** a supplier does not need to account for VAT on the supply of goods to a VAT-registered customer in another member state. The customer instead accounts for VAT on acquisition of the goods.

Services provided to businesses (B2B) generally take place where the customer is established. Services provided to **non-business customers (B2C)** are treated as supplied where the supplier is established.

It is outside the scope of this book to cover the implications of intra-EU trading for all member states; only transactions involving UK traders are considered.

A. Acquisitions of goods

An acquisition occurs when: **8937**

- there is a supply involving the removal of goods from one EU member state to another; s 11 VATA 1994
- the acquirer is a taxable person in the country of acquisition; and
- the supplier is registered for VAT in the member state of despatch.

The following transactions are **not treated as acquisitions** for these purposes: s 11(4) VATA 1994

- a supply of second-hand goods, where VAT is accounted for by reference to the profit margin on the supply (¶8437) in accordance with the law of that member state; or
- taking possession of gold by a Central Bank, if the supplier is in another member state and the transaction involves moving the gold from that or another member state to the UK.

Special rules apply where:

- the transaction involves a supply chain of three parties, known as "triangulation" (¶8994); or
- the goods are subject to the fiscal warehousing regime (¶9016).

MEMO POINTS 1. A **supply** includes a deemed supply.
2. It is immaterial whether the removal of goods was **carried out by** or on behalf of the supplier, or by the customer or some other person.
3. A person who **transfers his own goods**, forming part of the assets of a business, to another member state will still be deemed to have made an acquisition under these provisions and will be liable to VAT in that other state. This provision applies whether or not the removal is connected with a transaction for consideration. Sch 4 para 6 VATA 1994

A transfer of a trader's **own goods** from one member state to another within the same legal entity, for example between branches of the same company, is deemed to be a supply of goods for VAT purposes. The transfer of own goods is liable to VAT in the same way as other intra-EU supplies of goods. The trader will normally be liable to account for acquisition VAT in the member state to which the goods are transferred. The business may need to be registered for VAT in the member state to which the goods are despatched in order to fulfil obligations to account for acquisition VAT and also to account for VAT if the goods are subsequently supplied there. **8938**

1. Liability to tax

When does a liability arise?

8940
s 10 VATA 1994

VAT is payable in the UK on any acquisition from another member state. The person acquiring the goods is liable for the payment, where both of the **conditions** outlined below are satisfied:
a. the acquisition takes place in the UK but does not constitute a taxable supply under the normal UK VAT rules; and
b. the acquisition is a taxable acquisition and either:
– the person who makes the acquisition is a taxable person (¶7754) – where acquisitions reach a certain level, an unregistered person must register (¶8958); or
– the goods are subject to excise duty; or
– the goods consist of a new means of transport.

s 10 VATA 1994

MEMO POINTS 1. For these purposes, a **taxable acquisition** is an acquisition (other than in relation to an exempt supply (¶8042)), where the goods are both supplied by a taxable person in another member state and acquired by the customer in the course or furtherance of any:
– business; or
– non-business activities carried on by any company, club, association, organisation or other unincorporated body.
2. Goods subject to **excise duty** are:
– beer;
– cider;
– hydrocarbon oil;
– homemade wine;
– petrol substitutes;
– power methylated spirits;
– road fuel gas;
– spirits;
– tobacco products; and
– wine.

8942
s 95 VATA 1994
Notice 728

New means of transport A new means of transport is a ship, aircraft or motorised land vehicle that is **intended for** the transport of passengers or goods, which falls within the definitions below.

Mode of transport	Definition	Excludes
Ship	Exceeding 7.5m in length	A ship which, since its first entry into service[1]: – has travelled for more than 100 hours under its own power; and – a period of more than 3 months has elapsed.
Aircraft	Take-off weight in excess of 1,550kg	An aircraft which, since its first entry into service[1]: – has travelled for more than 40 hours under its own power; and – a period of more than 3 months has elapsed.
Motorised land vehicle	Either: – engine capacity exceeds 48cc; or – constructed or adapted to be electronically propelled using more than 7.2 kilowatts.	A vehicle which, since its first entry into service[2]: – has travelled for more than 6,000km under its own power; and – a period of more than 6 months has elapsed.

Note:
1. A ship or aircraft is deemed to first enter into service at one of the following times:
a. the earlier of either the date of delivery, or the date when it was first made available to the first purchaser or owner;
b. otherwise the date when it was first taken into use for demonstration purposes by the manufacturer; or
c. if neither of the above can be established satisfactorily, the date of issue of an invoice relating to the first supply.
2. A motorised land vehicle is deemed to enter into service at one of the following times:
a. the earlier of its first registration for road use in the member state of the manufacturer, or the date when the liability to register for road use was first incurred in that state;
b. the earliest of the date:
– of its first removal by its first purchaser or owner;
– of delivery to the first purchaser or owner; or
– when it was first made available to the first purchaser or owner;
c. the date when it was first taken into use for demonstration purposes by the manufacturer; or
d. if none of the above can be established satisfactorily, the date of issue of an invoice relating to the first supply.

Identity of acquirer

As a basic rule, the person who acquires goods is the person to whom the supply is made, who may be different from the person to whom the goods are delivered. **8944**

If, however, goods are acquired by a **person who is not subject to VAT**, a taxable person may instead be treated as acquiring the goods if that taxable person: s 47(1) VATA 1994
- acts in relation to the acquisition;
- supplies the goods as agent for the person by whom they are acquired; and
- acts in his own name in relation to the supply (¶8538).

Place of acquisition

Generally, the place of supply will be determined at the time when the goods are allocated to the customer. **8946** s 13 VATA 1994 HMRC Brief 20/11

Goods will be treated as **acquired in the UK** if:
- the transaction involves their removal to the UK and does not involve their removal from the UK; and
- they are acquired by a person who, for the purposes of the transaction, makes use of a UK VAT number in circumstances where no VAT is paid in the other member state.

Where a taxpayer **pays VAT in two member states** as a result of the above provisions (for example, where he quotes a UK VAT number to a French supplier but asks for the goods to be delivered to Italy), a refund of the UK VAT (in this example) will be available, provided that the taxpayer can show that acquisition VAT has been accounted for in Italy.

Goods installed or assembled Where a supply of goods involves their installation or assembly (e.g. supplying and installing bespoke kitchen furniture), they will generally be **treated as** supplied in the member state in which they are installed. So a UK supplier who supplies goods to be assembled in another member state may need to be registered in that state. **8948** s 7(3)(a) VATA 1994 Notice 725 para 11

Alternatively, a supplier can opt for a simplified procedure whereby the customer accounts for the VAT on a taxable acquisition, if he **notifies** both the customer and HMRC of his intention to do so, no later than the date of issue of the first invoice in respect of the supply. The supplier must include "Section 14(2) VAT invoice" on his invoice. Once notified, the customer must account for acquisition VAT on each invoice received.

MEMO POINTS 1. The **simplified procedure** applies in the UK where a person belonging in another member state makes a supply of goods to a person registered for VAT in the UK and the supply involves the removal of the goods to a place in the UK where they are installed or assembled.

2. A **person is deemed to belong in another member state** if:
- his usual place of residence, including any business establishment, is not in the UK;
- he is not registered, nor required to be registered, for VAT in the UK;
- he does not have a VAT representative (¶8560+) and is not currently required to appoint one; and
- he is taxable in another member state.

EXAMPLE F SA is a French company supplying a machine to E Ltd, which requires assembly in the UK. Under the simplified procedure, E Ltd accounts for the VAT charge on the acquisition.

Time of acquisition

The time of acquisition (tax point) of goods from another member state is the earlier of the 15th day of the month following that in which the first removal of the goods occurred, and the date on which an approved invoice (¶8306) is issued in respect of the transaction. The acquirer must account for any tax due on the VAT return for the period in which the tax point occurs. **8950** s 12 VATA 1994

MEMO POINTS Where **water**, **gas**, or **any form of power, heat, refrigeration or ventilation** is acquired from another member state, this is a supply of goods and the goods are treated as separately acquired on each occasion that the supplier issues an invoice.

Taxable amount

8952 s 20(1) VATA 1994

The value of an acquisition for the purposes of calculating VAT due is usually taken to be the value of the transaction itself, although that will **depend on** whether consideration is received.

The value of a transaction made **in return for a consideration** is taken to be either the actual money received, or the monetary equivalent if the consideration is in a form other than money.

Sch 7 para 3 VATA 1994

Where goods are acquired and **no consideration is received**, the value of the transaction is taken to be the consideration that would be payable by the supplier at the time of the acquisition if:

a. he were to purchase identical goods (excluding any VAT element in the price); or

b. where **a**. cannot be established, if he were to purchase similar goods;

c. where neither **a**. nor **b**. can be established, the value is taken to be the cost of producing the goods if they were produced at that time.

In addition, the taxable amount includes excise duty charged in connection with the removal of goods from the UK, and any EU customs duty or agricultural levy on the goods.

8954 Sch 7 para 1 VATA 1994

Connected party transactions HMRC may **direct** that a transaction must be valued at its open-market value if the acquisition is made by a person connected to the supplier, where:
– the consideration is money;
– the value of the transaction is less than the open-market value; and
– the customer is not entitled to a deduction for all of the VAT on the acquisition (because, for example, he is making exempt supplies).

The direction must be issued in writing to the person making the acquisition, within 3 years of the date of the acquisition. A trader may appeal against such a direction to the tribunal (¶9318).

Rate of tax

8956 s 1(3) VATA 1994

VAT is normally charged at the rate in force **at the time** when the acquisition is treated as taking place (¶8950).

s 88(4) VATA 1994

The **exception** is where the rate of tax **changes** after the date when the goods are first removed but before the acquisition is treated as taking place. In this case the person making the acquisition can **elect** to apply the rate of tax in force at the date of the first removal. For example, if goods were removed when zero-rating applied but then the applicable rate changed to the standard rate, it might be beneficial for an election to be made.

Requirement to register

8958 Sch 3 VATA 1994

A person who is not registered for any other reason is **liable** to register for UK VAT where the value of his taxable acquisitions exceeds a certain threshold, unless exemption from registration applies. Private individuals who buy goods for **private use**, not for business purposes, are not required to register.

Registration is required where the value of relevant acquisitions:

a. from the beginning of the **calendar year** to date exceeds the registration threshold (¶9987); or

b. is expected to exceed the registration threshold in the **next 30 days**.

A person **ceases to be liable** to be registered under these provisions if:
– the value of relevant acquisitions in the previous calendar year did not exceed the registration threshold; and
– HMRC are satisfied that relevant acquisitions in the current year will not exceed the registration threshold.

MEMO POINTS 1. A non-taxable person may request **exemption** from the need to register if EU acquisitions would have been zero-rated if supplied by a hypothetical UK registered trader. The request is made during the registration application process.

2. A **relevant acquisition** is a supply of goods delivered from another EU member state where the supplier is taxable in another member state, but excluding goods which are:
- subject to excise duty;
- a new means of transport (¶8942);
- acquired to make an exempt supply; or
- installed or otherwise treated as supplied in the UK.

Acquisitions of services are ignored for the purposes of these rules.

3. A person may also request registration **voluntarily**, or under the intending trader provisions (¶7778). In this case, registration will be for a period of at least 2 years.

4. Traders should note that the deregistration threshold (¶9988) does not apply to acquisitions.

Notification Where VAT registration is **compulsory**, the person should notify HMRC of the liability to register for VAT using form VAT 1B. The time limits for notification and the effective date of registration depend on how the threshold has been exceeded. Where registration is required due to: **8960**

a. past acquisitions, a business must notify HMRC of its liability to be registered for VAT within 30 days of the end of the calendar month in which the registration threshold is exceeded – HMRC must then register the person from the day after the last day of the month following that in which the threshold was exceeded, or an earlier agreed date; or

b. expected acquisitions in the next 30 days, notification must be made within 30 days of the date the expectation arose – HMRC must register the person with effect from the beginning of the 30-day period or an earlier agreed date.

EXAMPLE

1. On 12 August Mr A determines that his taxable acquisitions since 1 January have exceeded the registration threshold. Mr A is liable to be registered for VAT from 31 August and must notify HMRC by 30 September. He will be registered from 1 October, unless an earlier date is mutually agreed.

2. On 12 April Mr B expects his acquisitions in the next 30 days to exceed the registration threshold. Mr B is liable to be registered for VAT from 12 April and must notify HMRC by 12 May. The effective date of registration will be 12 April.

2. Accounting requirements

The reporting and payment requirements arising as a result of an acquisition from another member state depend on whether or not the person who made the acquisition was a taxable person. **8962**

Taxable purchaser

If the purchaser is a taxable person (and therefore registered for VAT) the tax on acquisitions will be accounted for on his normal VAT return (¶9216). **8964**

In addition to the usual VAT routine, the purchaser must:
- maintain records of all goods acquired, including documentation such as suppliers' invoices;
- enter the amount of VAT due on EU acquisitions into box 2 of his VAT return for the period in which the acquisition occurs;
- enter the total value of EU acquisitions in boxes 7 and 9;
- treat the VAT on acquisitions as input tax and enter the VAT recoverable in box 4 of his VAT return (subject to the normal rules on input tax recovery); and
- pay the net amount of VAT due by the required date (¶9250).

Traders are liable to complete Intrastat supplementary declarations (¶9002) where cumulative acquisitions exceed £600,000 in the calendar year.

Non-taxable purchaser

Acquisitions for **private purposes** are dealt with under the distance selling rules (¶8982). EU suppliers will have to account for UK VAT if the value of their supplies to UK private customers exceeds a certain threshold. Otherwise the goods are subject to VAT in the home state of the supplier. **8966** Notice 728 Notice 725 para 15.4

A non-taxable purchaser who acquires **goods subject to excise duty** or a **new means of transport** and is going to use the acquisition for **non-private purposes** cannot account for VAT by means of a VAT return. Instead, the person making the acquisition must notify HMRC of the acquisition by the later of the time of the acquisition or the time of arrival of the goods in the UK. The VAT in this case is payable at the time of the notification. Alternatively, the purchaser may wish voluntarily to register for VAT (¶8958).

B. Supplies of goods

8968 When a person is making a supply of goods to another EU member state, it is vital to determine the place of supply (¶7990). The VAT status of the customer then determines the correct VAT treatment of the supply.

1. Taxable customer

8970 SI 1995/2518 reg 134 Notice 725 para 4

If the following **conditions are satisfied**, supplies made from the UK to another member state will be zero-rated:
– the supply is made by a taxable person;
– the supply involves the removal of goods from the UK and documentary evidence of the removal is obtained within 3 months of the time of the supply;
– the goods are acquired by a person who is registered for VAT in another member state;
– the goods are not second-hand goods, works of art, or goods on which the supplier has elected to be taxed on the profit margin (¶8437); and
– the supplier obtains, and shows on his VAT sales invoice, the customer's VAT registration number (including the two-digit country reference code).

Notice 725 para 3.4

The **time of supply** is the earlier of the invoice date and the 15th day of the month following that in which the goods are despatched. Part payments do not create a tax point in this case. When the customer receives the goods he accounts for VAT under the acquisition rules in his member state, which will follow those outlined at ¶8940+.

If the conditions are **not satisfied**, the supply will be subject to the same VAT rate as would apply in the UK and the UK rules for the time of supply will apply (¶7900).

Invalid VAT numbers

8972 Notice 725 para 4.10

If the customer's registration number **proves to be** invalid, zero-rating will normally still apply if it can be shown that the supplier took all reasonable steps to confirm the validity of the number, such as checking with HMRC. The validity of any EU VAT number can also be checked on http://ec.europa.eu/taxation_customs/vies/vieshome.do.

Where a valid number is **subsequently produced**, a credit note may be issued where VAT has already been charged on a supply to another EU member state because a valid registration number was not provided at the time that the invoice was raised.

Proof of removal

8974 Notice 703 para 5

It is immaterial whether the goods are delivered to the customer or the customer collects them but, in either case, **evidence** is required to show that goods have been removed from the UK.

MEMO POINTS 1. Where the goods are **delivered** to the customer, the supplier is required to retain normal **commercial documentation** such as purchase orders, packing lists and invoices. The supplier will also be required to retain documents such as authenticated seaway or airway bills.
2. If the **customer collects** the goods or arranges for their collection, the supplier must ensure that he is aware of how the goods are to be removed from the UK and that proof of removal will

be provided to him. In this case, in addition to the commercial documents outlined above, the supplier should **obtain** the following from the customer:
– a written order showing the name, address and VAT number of the customer, together with the delivery address; and
– a signature confirming that the goods have been collected and, if the goods are being removed by road, the registration number of the relevant vehicle.

Failure to comply

If goods are **supplied at the zero rate** under the above provisions and any of the conditions in ¶8970 are not met, or if the goods are found still to be in the UK, the supplier will have to account for VAT as if a normal UK supply had been made. **8976** Notice 725 para 5.2

Invoices to EU customers

The invoice should show all of the **information** in ¶8308, with the following modifications: **8977** SI 1995/2518 reg 14(2) Information Sheet 10/07
– the supplier should prefix GB to his VAT number;
– the customer's registration number (if relevant) must contain the alphabetical prefix of the relevant EU member state (¶8930);
– the description of each supply should state the VAT-exclusive amount in sterling, unless no UK VAT is chargeable (e.g. for zero-rated supplies);
– if the supply is a new means of transport (¶8942), the invoice should clearly identify it as such; and
– the invoice should indicate that it is an intra-EU supply, either by reference to the VAT Directive, UK legislation or any other reference. For example, stating "Zero-rated intra-EU supply" should be sufficient.

The following example shows the required **components** of an EU VAT invoice.

EXAMPLE

Issued by:	A Ltd Main Road, London W1	VAT number: GB492 6104 45
Invoice number: 123		
To:	F SA 1 Rue de Paris, Lyon	VAT number: FR12345678901
Time of supply: 1 July 2012		Date of issue: 7 July 2012

Quantity	Description and price	Amount (excl. VAT) £	VAT Rate %
1	FC 1 Filing cabinet @ £79.99	79.99	0
4	FC 20 Hanging files @ £9.99	39.96	0
	Delivery – free	0.00	
		119.95	
	VAT	0.00	
	Total	119.95	
	Zero-rated intra-EU supply		

No discount available

Note:
There is no VAT charge because the goods are despatched to a VAT-registered EU business, which is a zero-rated supply, provided that the relevant conditions are satisfied (¶8970).

EC sales lists

EC sales lists (ESLs – form VAT 101) are statements which contain details of the movement of goods between EU member states. **8978** SI 1995/2518 reg 22 Notice 725 para 17

Every taxable person who has supplied, despatched, transported or transferred goods **to a registered person in another member state** must submit an ESL to HMRC. Supplies to **non-taxable** customers, or supplies that were taxed because the VAT registration number was not known, are excluded. A nil return is not required for any quarters in which no relevant transactions are undertaken.

ESLs must be submitted within:
- 14 days of the end of the reporting period (if paper ESLs are used); or
- 21 days from the end of the reporting period for electronic submissions.

The ESL reporting period is a **calendar month**, unless:
- up to 31 December 2011, the total quarterly value of supplies of intra-EU goods (excluding VAT) does not exceed £70,000 in the current quarter, or any of the previous four quarters; or
- from 1 January 2012 onwards, if the total quarterly value of supplies of intra-EU goods (excluding VAT) does not exceed £35,000 in the current quarter, or any of the previous four quarters.

Where businesses make supplies of goods below the specified thresholds, they may continue to use a reporting period of a calendar quarter. Businesses should notify HMRC as soon as the total quarterly value of supplies of intra-EU goods exceeds the relevant threshold figure.

In addition, traders need to complete Intrastat declarations (¶9002) where EU supplies of goods exceed £250,000 in the 2011 calendar year.

MEMO POINTS The ESL regime was extended from 1 January 2010 to intra-EU supplies of services subject to a reverse charge in the customer's member state (¶9118).

8979 An ESL must contain the following **information**, unless HMRC allow otherwise:
- the business name, address and registration number (including the GB prefix);
- the last day of the period covered by the registration;
- the date of submission;
- the country prefix and VAT registration number of each customer;
- the total value of the goods (and/or services) supplied to each customer; and
- an indicator if the business is an intermediary in a triangular transaction (¶8994).

If there is any doubt about the validity of a customer's VAT number, advice should be sought from HMRC before completing the ESL. The validity of any EU VAT number can also be checked on http://ec.europa.eu/taxation_customs/vies/en/vieshome.do.

There is a facility to enable **electronic filing** of ESLs via the Internet, details of which are available from www.hmrc.gov.uk/online/index.htm.

MEMO POINTS 1. The total number of pages and lines completed must be shown on the form, and the declaration signed before submission.

2. The ESL has space for 15 lines of information. A business requiring more space must obtain a **continuation sheet** (form VAT 101A) from HMRC.

Lists may be submitted in the following **electronic** ways:
- completion of an online form;
- an upload facility for bulk files using CSV or XML formats;
- XML channel; or
- using UN-EDIFACT format.

3. **Corrections** to ESLs are made on form VAT 101B.

4. Different **branches** of the same company may apply to submit separate ESLs, as may different companies or divisions within a **group** VAT registration.

2. Non-taxable customers

8980 There are special rules which apply to the supply of goods to non-taxable customers in other member states.

Distance selling from the UK

8982 Distance selling **occurs** where a taxable person in one member state supplies and delivers goods to a non-taxable person in another member state. An example of distance selling is the supply of goods by mail order.

Distance sales made by a UK supplier to recipients in other EU member states will normally be subject to UK VAT. However, where the **value** of distance sales **exceeds** the annual threshold of the destination member state in any calendar year, the UK supplier becomes liable to register and account for VAT in that state. The customer's state becomes the place of supply and, as a consequence, any further distance sales will then be subject to VAT at the rate applicable in the customer's member state.

There are special rules when supplying excise goods (¶8988).

Distance selling to the UK

Registration An EU trader is **liable** to be registered in the UK if: 8984 Sch 2 paras 1-3 VATA 1994 SI 1995/2518 reg 98
– the value of his supplies from 1 January in each calendar year exceeds the threshold (currently 100,000 euros or £70,000);
– he has exercised an option in his home state to treat relevant supplies as taking place outside that state; or
– he makes supplies to the UK of goods subject to excise duty.

MEMO POINTS 1. For these purposes a **distance sale** is a supply of goods (other than exempt goods, those subject to excise duty, or a new means of transport) that are:
– removed to the UK without needing to be installed or assembled in the UK;
– received by a non-taxable person; and
– supplied in the course of a business.
2. A **non-taxable person** would include private individuals as well as businesses, public bodies and charities whose turnover is below the registration threshold, or whose activities are entirely exempt.
3. Each member state has a choice of whether to apply a distance selling **threshold** of 35,000 euros or 100,000 euros. While most states have chosen the 35,000 euro threshold, the following states have chosen the 100,000 euro threshold:
– Austria;
– France;
– Germany;
– Luxembourg;
– Netherlands; and
– the UK.
4. A distance seller may appoint a **tax representative** in the other EU state to manage his VAT affairs (see ¶8560+ for the equivalent in the UK).

A person **ceases to be liable** to be registered under these provisions if the value of relevant supplies in the previous calendar year did not exceed the limit, and HMRC are satisfied that relevant supplies in the current year will not exceed the limit.

MEMO POINTS 1. An **EU person** who has **opted** to treat all distance sales as taking place outside his home state will be liable to register for UK VAT where:
– a distance sale is made in the UK while the option is in force;
– the option covers the removal of goods from the home state; and
– without the option, the goods would have been treated as supplied in the home state.
The registration has effect from the date of the first distance sale made following exercise, or an earlier agreed date, usually for a minimum period of 2 years. HMRC must be informed at least 30 days before the first UK sale, and written evidence of the option must be available. If the option is subsequently revoked, HMRC must be notified within 30 days.
2. A **UK trader** may **choose** to voluntarily register in the EU destination member state, and therefore make it the place of supply, before reaching the distance selling threshold. If he does so he must:
– at least 30 days before the first supply, notify HMRC in writing, giving the name of the state or states involved; and
– within 30 days of making the first supply, provide documentary evidence to HMRC showing that he has notified the tax authority in the other state that he intends to account for VAT there.
3. Where a business supplies a **new means of transport** (¶8942) to a non-taxable customer in another member state, the business will be able to zero-rate the supply where:
– the new means of transport is removed from the UK to the other member state within 2 months of the date of supply; and
– the supplier and customer make a joint declaration on form VAT 411.
Otherwise, UK VAT must be charged by the supplier.

EXAMPLE On 16 August Mr A determines that he has sold goods with a value of 36,000 euros to his Spanish private customers since 1 January. Up to now he has been charging UK VAT on his supplies.
Because the threshold of 35,000 euros has been exceeded, he must now register for VAT in Spain and start charging Spanish VAT.

8986 **Reporting requirements** The following table summarises the reporting requirements in relation to distance selling:

Notice 725 para 6.17

Type of supply	VAT accounting	UK VAT return entries
Distance sales to EU state which are below that state's registration threshold	UK VAT charged as if domestic supply	Box 1: output tax Box 6: value of supply
Distance sales to EU state which are above that state's registration threshold	EU VAT charged in state where customer located	Box 6: value of supply Box 8: value of supply
Distance sales to UK which are above UK's registration threshold, or where supplier chooses to register in UK	UK VAT charged	Box 1: output tax Box 6: value of supply

Goods subject to excise duty

8988 Where any excise goods are supplied and delivered to a non-registered UK person by an EU supplier in the course of his business, the EU supplier is liable to register for UK VAT under the distance selling rules. Where a UK supplier makes such a supply to an EU customer, the supplier must similarly register in the other member state.

Sch 2 para 1 (3) VATA 1994

If the customer is going to use the goods for **business purposes**, the supply may be zero-rated, provided that certain criteria are met. In this case, the customer accounts for VAT under the acquisition rules (¶8940).

SI 1995/2518 reg 135

MEMO POINTS For **UK** suppliers, the **criteria** for zero-rating a supply to be used for business purposes are as follows:
a. the supplier is registered for VAT;
b. the goods are removed from the UK;
c. the goods must not be second-hand goods or works of art in relation to which the supplier uses a margin scheme (¶8437);
d. all excisable goods travel with an accompanying administrative document (AAD) to indicate their status;
e. within 15 days of the end of the month in which the goods were moved, the supplier obtains and keeps copy 1 of the AAD, and a receipted copy 3 of the AAD certified by the customer or the fiscal authority of the destination member state; and
f. the movement of the goods and the issue of the receipt are completed within 4 months of the date of the supply.

Tax-free shopping

8990 Goods sold from shops at UK ports or airports will be subject to UK VAT at the rate applicable for general retail sales of the same goods.

Sales **on board** trains, aircraft or ships (other than on cruises) will be subject to the rate applicable in the country of departure (i.e. the first passenger point of embarkation in the EU). However, goods sold for **consumption** on board the ship, aircraft or trains (such as food, drink and tobacco) are free from VAT.

MEMO POINTS 1. Purchases of goods for consumption on board **cruises** are free from VAT and excise duty, provided that the quantity is such that passengers are unlikely to take them away at the end of a cruise. Where a cruise starts and ends in the UK but stops at a non-EU country, passengers are allowed to purchase VAT-free goods, provided that they have an opportunity to disembark and make purchases in that country.

2. HMRC have clarified that most sales from an **on-board bar or restaurant** are treated as being for immediate consumption. Food, confectionery and soft drinks sold on a ship or aircraft are treated as consumed on board, provided that they are not more suited to becoming gifts or for consumption at home.

C. Special situations involving goods

Special rules apply in relation to: 8992
a. triangulation, where there is a chain of supplies involving an intermediate supplier;
b. Intrastat declarations – a statistical reporting procedure for cumulative EU transactions of a certain value; and
c. fiscal warehousing, which allows VAT-free trading of certain goods until they are removed from the warehouse.

1. Triangulation

The term triangulation applies to the situation where there is a **supply chain** involving three parties, in which goods pass directly from the first to the last person in the chain, rather than passing to and from the intermediate supplier. 8994 Notice 725 para 13

Under the **normal rules** the intermediate supplier may potentially be liable to register for VAT in the country of destination of the goods, and to account for VAT both on his acquisition and onward supply of the goods.

To avoid the imposition of this burden, the EU member states have agreed to adopt a **simplified procedure**. The effect of the simplified procedure will depend on whether the end customer or the intermediate supplier is registered in the UK.

Simplified procedure

The simplified procedure **may be used if**: 8996 s 14(1) VATA 1994 Notice 725 para 13.6
– the customer belongs in another member state and is VAT-registered there;
– the supply involves the removal of goods from one member state to another; and
– the intermediate supplier is not registered for VAT in the member state to which the goods are delivered but is registered somewhere in the EU.

End customer registered in the UK

Under the simplified procedure the **original supply** made to the intermediary is disregarded. 8998

Instead the **subsequent supply** by the intermediary to the customer is treated as the removal of goods from another EU state to the UK. The customer therefore accounts for the VAT on the supply i.e. the supply from the intermediate supplier is zero-rated.

The simplified procedure may only be applied if the **intermediate supplier** gives both: s 14(3) VATA 1994 Notice 725 para 13.9
a. a **written notification** to the customer and HMRC no later than the date of issue of the first invoice, such notification to include:
– the name, address and VAT registration number of the intermediate supplier;
– the customer's name, address and VAT number; and
– the date of the intended delivery of the goods to the customer; and
b. an **invoice** which complies with the requirements of the member state in which the intermediate supplier was registered and which has been issued within 15 days of the date on which the supply would otherwise have been taking place.

EXAMPLE E Ltd, a UK company, orders goods from F SA, a French supplier. F SA arranges for the goods to be sent directly from B SA, its own supplier, which is located in Belgium.

Under the simplified procedure B SA zero-rates its supply to F SA, assuming F SA gives B SA its VAT registration number. F SA then issues an invoice complying with **b**. above and also zero-rates its supply. E Ltd then accounts for UK VAT on the supply as an EU acquisition.

Intermediate supplier registered in the UK

9000 SI 1995/2518 reg 11 Notice 725 para 13.7

If the intermediate supplier is registered in the UK and the **goods are removed** to another member state, the simplified procedure will have effect for UK VAT purposes by disregarding both the supply to the intermediate supplier and the onward supply by him to the customer.

If the intermediate supplier chooses to take advantage of the simplified procedure, he must issue the customer with an invoice which contains all the details normally required for intra-EU supplies. The intermediary must also provide his VAT number to his supplier to enable the supplier to zero-rate the despatch of the goods.

EXAMPLE C Ltd, a UK company, is an intermediate supplier which receives an order from F SA, a company located in France. To fulfil this order C Ltd arranges for goods to be supplied direct from S SA, a company located in Spain.
C Ltd gives S SA its VAT registration number. This enables S SA to zero-rate its supply. C Ltd then issues a tax invoice to F SA, which contains the required information as stated at ¶8998, and zero-rates the supply. F SA accounts for the VAT in France as an EU acquisition.

2. Intrastat

9002 Notice 60

Intrastat is the name given to the method of collecting information and producing statistics on the movement of goods between member states. This is in addition to the general information about EU trade which is disclosed on the VAT return in boxes 8 and 9 (¶8346). Further information on Intrastat is available from HMRC at https://www.uktradeinfo.com.

For Intrastat purposes, supplies of services are ignored, except those integral to the supply of goods, such as freight charges.

Exclusions

9004

Intrastat does not apply to:
- businesses which are **not registered** for VAT, or have been exempted from registration because they make **zero-rated** supplies only (¶7777);
- any intermediate supplier in the case of **triangulation** (¶8994) – only the ultimate supplier and the ultimate customer record the movement of the goods;
- sales to **unregistered customers** if these are below the distance selling threshold (¶8982) in the customer's member state;
- **temporary movements** (goods to be returned within 2 years to the same ownership);
- goods **in transit** through the UK; and
- commercial **samples**.

Terminology

9006

For the purposes of Intrastat, a **supply** to an EU customer is called a "despatch".
An **acquisition** from an EU supplier is called an "arrival".

Scope

9009

All businesses must monitor arrivals and despatches and if either **exceeds an annual threshold**, the business must submit **Supplementary Declarations (SDs)**. Note that arrivals and despatches are different requirements, so a business may be required to submit SDs in relation to either arrivals or despatches only, depending on the circumstances. For 2009 the threshold for both arrivals and despatches was £270,000. However, for 2010 the despatches threshold was reduced to £250,000 and the arrivals threshold increased to £600,000. The same limits apply in 2011.

SDs must be completed with sterling **values** (rounded up to the nearest £), translated using the same exchange rates as for VAT purposes (¶7968). The value includes any freight or insurance costs.

The **liability to submit** SDs for arrivals and/or despatches ceases once the level of arrivals and/or despatches falls below the relevant threshold. **9010**

For a **continuing business**, the rules can be summarised as follows (taking despatches as the example – the same applies for arrivals, apart from the different threshold):
a. if the business was submitting despatches SDs in 2010 and:
– despatches fell below £250,000 in 2010, there is no need to submit despatches SDs in 2011, until the start of the month in which despatches exceed £250,000; or
– the despatches threshold of £250,000 was exceeded in 2010, the business must continue to submit despatches SDs in 2011; or
b. if despatches exceeded £250,000 by 31 December 2010 (whether SDs were submitted or not), the business must submit despatches SDs for the whole of 2011.

MEMO POINTS 1. Where a business exceeds the Intrastat threshold due to a **one-off transaction**, HMRC will, as a concession, input nil returns on behalf of the business if it is not expected to have further trade with EU member states.
2. HMRC are seeking to relieve smaller businesses from the need to be involved in the Intrastat system, which is one reason why the arrivals threshold was increased so significantly in 2010.

Recognition of transactions

The **reference date** for the movement of goods is slightly different from the time of supply under the general VAT rules, being the earlier of: **9011**
– the date of issue of the invoice; or
– the 15th day of the month following despatch.
The **reference period** for an SD is normally a calendar month, although a business may use another period if that is more convenient.

Information

The SD must include information about the following **movements of goods**, being those: **9012** Notice 60 para 4
– bought and sold;
– transferred within the same legal entity;
– sent for process or repair;
– supplied as part of a contract for services;
– to be installed or used in construction;
– supplied free of charge; and
– on long-term hire.
Every arrival or despatch must be correctly **coded** using the Intrastat Classification Nomenclature, available from HMRC (www.uktradeinfo.com).

Administration

The **due date** for submitting SDs is 1 month after the end of the reference period. **9014** Notice 60 para 3

If a transaction is **omitted** from a particular month's SD, a declaration should be made as early as possible on an additional SD.

If an **error** is made on an SD, a copy of it should be submitted marked "Amendment Only" at the top and the correction made above the original error, both completed in red ink.

Defaults, such as persistently late or inaccurate SDs, are dealt with under criminal law, although in practice HMRC normally offer a fine in lieu of criminal proceedings.

A business must **retain** all SDs submitted and all supporting documentation for 6 years.

MEMO POINTS From April 2012 the due date is 21 days after the end of the reference period. Mandatory electronic submission of SDs is effective from April 2012 also.

3. Fiscal warehousing

9016 s 18 VATA 1994 Notice 702/8

Fiscal warehousing allows VAT-free trading of certain goods within the EU. Basically, no VAT is payable when goods are placed into a fiscal warehouse, nor when goods are acquired or supplied within the warehouse regime. In addition, there is relief for associated services.

VAT only becomes chargeable when goods are removed from the warehouse.

The regime **applies to eligible goods** which are kept in a fiscal warehouse or are transferred between fiscal warehouses. Non-eligible goods may be stored in a fiscal warehouse but with no VAT advantage.

s 18B(6) VATA 1994

MEMO POINTS 1. **Eligible goods** are goods falling within the following list, on which any import duties, taxes and levies have been either paid or deferred:
- aluminium, copper, iridium, lead, nickel, platinum, palladium, rhodium, silver, tin and zinc;
- cereals;
- chemicals in bulk;
- cocoa beans, whole or broken, raw or roasted;
- coconuts, brazil nuts, cashew nuts and other nuts;
- coffee, not roasted;
- grains and seeds (including soya beans);
- mineral oils (including propane and butane; also including crude petroleum oils);
- oil seeds and oleaginous fruit;
- olives;
- potatoes;
- raw sugar;
- rubber, in primary forms or in plates, sheets or strip;
- tea;
- vegetable oils and fats and their fractions, whether or not refined, but not chemically modified; and
- wool.

SI 1995/2231

2. To combat an **avoidance scheme** in the retail trade, the fiscal warehousing regime does not apply where retail goods are sold to, or are to be sold by, non-taxable persons (i.e. those who are not registered for VAT).

In the warehouse

9018 s 18A VATA 1994

A fiscal warehouse is **defined** as any place in the UK in the occupation or under the control of a fiscal warehouse-keeper (other than retail premises), in respect of which the warehouse-keeper gives written notification to HMRC.

A place will **remain** a fiscal warehouse until such time as HMRC:
- receive written notification that the place is to cease being a fiscal warehouse; or
- withdraw fiscal warehousing status from the premises.

MEMO POINTS 1. A **fiscal warehouse-keeper** is any person approved as such by the HMRC and, in addition to the following criteria, each case will be judged on its own merits:

a. the applicant must be registered for VAT in the UK;

b. all business revenue records such as VAT returns and payments must be of a high standard and up to date;

c. if authorised to operate any similar schemes in the UK, the applicant must have a satisfactory record in that respect;

d. the applicant must be able to comply with the current and any future conditions of authorisation;

e. the administration and organisation of the business must be sound and subject to strict management;

f. a list of addresses of all storage sites which are to form part of the fiscal warehouse must be provided, together with the addresses of any premises where documents are to be kept; and

g. accounts and stock control records must be capable of meeting the requirements and, in particular, must be able to distinguish between fiscally warehoused goods and other stock.

2. A person will **remain** a fiscal warehouse-keeper until such time as he ceases to be registered for VAT, or HMRC:
- receive written notification that the person is going to cease being a fiscal warehouse-keeper; or
- withdraw approval of the person as a fiscal warehouse-keeper.

Acquisitions An acquisition is treated as taking place **outside the UK** (and therefore not subject to UK VAT) where: 9020 s 18B(1) VATA 1994
a. there is an acquisition of eligible goods from another member state;
b. the acquirer prepares (beforehand, or at the time of acquisition) a certificate that the goods are subject to the fiscal warehousing regime, which is retained; and
c. either:
– the acquisition takes place while the goods are subject to the fiscal warehousing regime; or
– the goods are placed in a fiscal warehousing regime after the acquisition but before any subsequent supply.

Supplies A supply is treated as taking place **outside the UK** (and therefore not subject to UK VAT) where: 9021 s 18B(2) VATA 1994
a. there is a supply of eligible goods (other than a retail transaction); and
b. either:
– the supply takes place while the goods are subject to the fiscal warehousing regime; or
– the goods are placed in a fiscal warehousing regime after the first supply but before any subsequent supply, and the buyer gives a certificate to the supplier (beforehand, or at the time of acquisition), stating that he intends to enter the goods into a fiscal warehousing regime.

Associated services Services provided in connection with a fiscal warehouse may be **relieved** from VAT at the time of supply. VAT may become due, however, when the goods in question are subsequently removed from the fiscal warehouse. 9022 Notice 702/8 para 2.16

A supply of specified services which is performed on, or in relation to, goods in the fiscal warehousing regime will be zero-rated if it would otherwise be taxable. The **recipient** of the services must provide the supplier with a certificate stating that the relevant services are fiscal warehousing services and that the supply is eligible for zero-rating. On receipt of the certificate the supplier has 30 days from the supply of the services to give the recipient a VAT invoice.

MEMO POINTS 1. **Specified services** are:
a. storage charges; and
b. the normal forms of handling that may be carried out in a warehouse, such as:
– preparing goods for distribution or resale;
– operations to ensure the preservation of goods in good condition during storage; and
– operations to improve the presentation or marketability of the goods.
2. Relief can also be claimed for **services other than those specified**, if written authority from HMRC is obtained.

Removal from the warehouse

Goods A charge to VAT will arise where eligible goods are removed from the fiscal warehousing regime, unless one of the following **exemptions** applies: 9024
a. removal for use in the UK of:
– zero-rated goods; or
– the taxpayer's own goods which he entered into fiscal warehousing but which have not been used within the fiscal warehousing regime;
b. goods exported outside the EU;
c. goods removed in the course of an intra-EU supply;
d. transfer to another UK fiscal warehouse;
e. transfer to a corresponding fiscal warehouse regime in another EU member state;
f. temporary removal for repair, processing, treatment or other operations; and
g. small quantities of goods with a negligible commercial value removed for sampling.

Otherwise, the **amount of VAT** that becomes payable is: 9026 s 18B(5) VATA 1994
– the amount that would have been due on the transaction as a result of which the goods were entered into the fiscal warehouse; and

– if the goods were supplied within the warehouse, the amount which would have been due in respect of the last supply.
The **person liable** for the VAT is the person who caused the goods to cease to be covered by the regime. The charge is payable at the **time** of removal.

9028 **Associated services** Services that have **previously been zero-rated** at the time of supply will become taxable when the related goods are removed from the fiscal warehouse **unless**:
– the service has created new goods;
– the goods themselves have been the subject of a supply (while still in the fiscal warehouse) after the service was provided;
– the goods are exported under duty suspension arrangements directly from the warehouse to a non-EU country; or
– the goods are sent under duty suspension arrangements to a customs or fiscal warehouse in another EU member state.
The **taxable amount** is the same as the previously zero-rated supply, and the person removing the goods is responsible for ensuring that the correct amount of VAT is paid.

SECTION 2

Goods outside the EU

9035 This section only applies to transactions which do not take place wholly within the EU. Special rules apply where goods are imported to the UK from a country outside the EU or exported from the UK to a country outside the EU. There are also special rules for the supply of international services (¶9106).

A. Imports

9037 VAT is chargeable on goods imported into the UK at the same rate as if the goods had been supplied in the UK. It is immaterial whether the person importing the goods is **registered** for VAT.
A number of reliefs and suspensions of liability are available (¶9047).

MEMO POINTS 1. For these purposes the **UK includes** the waters within 12 nautical miles of the coastline.
2. **Import duty** is separate from import VAT and is also levied on imported goods. Further information is available from HMRC's website.

1. Scope

Imports into the UK

9039 Goods are **treated as imported** from outside the EU where they:
s 15 VATA 1994
Notice 702 para 1.5
a. enter the UK for use here, having been removed directly from a territory outside the EU; or
b. have been placed (either in the UK or another EU state) in one of the customs suspension arrangements with a view to removal for use in the UK (¶9059).
For goods purchased over the **Internet**, import VAT is only payable where the value of goods is at least £18 (£15 from 1 November 2011).

Liable person

The person who is deemed to be the **importer** of goods is the person who would be liable for discharging a VAT debt in respect of those goods. 9041

Between the importation of the goods and the time of delivery the importer includes **any person** who, at that time, either owns, is in possession of, or has a beneficial interest in those goods. An importer may therefore be different from the person who ordered or paid for the goods.

Where the importer is registered for VAT, he may claim a deduction for the input tax incurred.

2. Import value

Value for import VAT

The value of goods imported into the UK **includes** all of the following: 9043 s 21 VATA 1994 Notice 702 para 3.1
– the price paid for the goods (strictly the value determined by the EU customs rules);
– taxes, duties and other charges; and
– incidental expenses incurred up to the date of the arrival at the first destination in the UK (and any further destination within the EU which is known at the time of importation).
A deduction will be made to take account of any **discount** given for prompt payment.

MEMO POINTS **Incidental expenses** include commission, packing, handling, storage, transport and insurance costs. The importer can choose between including actual costs within the taxable amount, applying internationally agreed rates, or reaching an individual agreement with HMRC.

Rate of VAT

At importation, VAT is charged at the rate that would be applicable if the goods were supplied in the UK. 9045 Notice 702 para 2.1

3. Reliefs

There are three types of relief from import VAT: 9047
a. absolute reliefs;
b. temporary import reliefs; and
c. suspension of the charge.

Absolute reliefs

The following goods may be imported into the UK **without a VAT charge**: 9049 SI 1984/746 s 36A VATA 1994 Notice 702 para 5.1
– capital goods or equipment imported for the purposes of a business which has ceased to be carried on abroad;
– scientific instruments and donated medical equipment;
– goods used in the promotion of a trade;
– goods for testing and samples of minimal value;
– items such as human blood and tissue, or biological or chemical substances used for non-commercial medical or scientific purposes;
– goods for charities and disabled people;
– printed matter;
– works of art, antiques, decorations and awards;
– fuel and lubricants used in a vehicle or special container transporting goods to the UK;
– goods for use in the construction, upkeep or ornamentation of war graves; and
– coffins and urns containing human remains or ashes and flowers, wreaths and other ornamental objects accompanying them.

9051 s 37(1) VATA 1994

Low-value supplies A small, non-commercial consignment of goods will be exempt from import VAT, provided that it does not form part of a larger consignment and the value for customs purposes (¶9043) is **less than** £40.

A consignment is deemed to be **non-commercial** for these purposes if:
– it is consigned from one private individual to another;
– the importation is not in return for consideration in money or money's worth; and
– it is consigned solely for personal use by the recipient or his family.

9052 VAT-free importation of the following **products** is **limited** to the amounts stated.

Tobacco	– 200 cigarettes; – 100 cigarillos; – 50 cigars; – 250 g of smoking tobacco; or – a pro-rated proportion of more than one of the above (for example, 100 cigarettes plus 50 cigarillos)
Alcohol and alcoholic drinks	– 1 litre of spirits or strong liqueurs over 22% volume; – 2 litres of fortified or sparkling wines or other alcoholic drink up to 22% volume; or – a pro-rated proportion of both the above; and – 16 litres of beer; and – 4 litres of still wine
All other goods	– £390 (if travelling by commercial sea or air transport); or – £270 (if travelling by other means, including private plane or boat)

9054 SI 1995/2518 reg 121D

Re-imported goods Re-imported goods do not give rise to a VAT charge where the importer is the person who previously exported the goods. The relief is **reduced** for any unpaid VAT which is still due on an earlier importation.

Anti-avoidance rules disapply this relief where the importer seeks to abuse it by bringing goods into the UK without paying VAT.

9055 SI 1995/2518 reg 126 Notice 702/9 para 7

Goods which are re-imported **after process or repair** are subject to a reduced charge where:
– the goods were temporarily exported;
– it was intended that re-importation would occur;
– ownership was not transferred; and
– a declaration is made at the time of re-importation.

The **taxable amount** is the total of the price paid for the repair or process (including parts), including freight charges and any customs or excise duties.

Temporary import reliefs

9057 Notice 702/9 para 3

The goods outlined below may be imported temporarily into the UK (for a period of between 6 weeks and 2 years, depending on the goods) without an import charge:
a. goods for removal to another EU member state;
b. commercial vehicles and aircraft;
c. containers and pallets; and
d. goods imported from outside the EU without being released into free circulation and intended for re-export without undergoing any change.

A VAT liability may arise, however, if the goods **remain** in the UK beyond the specified time, or if any of the conditions are otherwise breached.

Suspension of charge

9059 Notice 702/9

The VAT charge on importation will be suspended while goods are in one of the suspension **regimes** outlined below:
– free zones;
– customs warehousing;
– temporary storage;

– inward processing relief (the duty suspension system);
– Community Transit arrangements, where goods enter more than one EU member state after importation;
– for the fuelling and provisioning of drilling or production platforms; and
– goods admitted into territorial waters in order to be incorporated into drilling or production platforms.

A VAT **liability** will crystallise (and become payable) when the goods are removed from the regime and entered into free circulation in the UK.

Importation into a free zone A free zone is a designated area in which non-EU goods are treated as if they are outside the customs territory of the EU and stored without payment of import duties and import VAT. Goods **supplied within** the free zone are treated as a UK supply and subject to the normal VAT rules. **9061** SI 1984/1177 Notice 702/9 para 5

By concession, the supply of free zone goods which were **originally imported** into the UK may be zero-rated if both the customer and supplier agree that the customer will:
– take responsibility for the import VAT; and
– clear the goods for removal from the free zone for use in the UK.

Where a supply is made within a free zone to a **non-taxable person**, the amount of VAT payable on the removal of goods from the free zone is reduced by the VAT already due on the supply (otherwise both import VAT and output VAT would be paid). Notice 702/9 para 5.3

MEMO POINTS Five **sites** in the UK are currently designated as free zones and these are located in:
– Liverpool;
– Tilbury;
– Prestwick;
– Sheerness; and
– Southampton.

The Isle of Man is also a free zone.

Importation into a customs warehouse A warehouse is, for these purposes, a place **approved** by HMRC as a place of security for depositing, keeping and securing specific dutiable goods without payment of duty. **9062** Notice 702/9 para 4

Sales which take place **within** the warehouse are ignored for VAT purposes, and goods can be re-exported without any VAT becoming payable.

Import VAT will be payable once the goods are **removed** from the warehouse and placed in free circulation in the UK.

4. Payment

Goods may not be delivered or removed from HMRC's charge until such time as any VAT chargeable has been paid. Import VAT is due for payment at the time of importation, unless the importer or his agent has been approved for deferment. **9064** s 38 VATA 1994

If import VAT is **overpaid**, a claim for payment to be adjusted must be made on the trader's VAT return (not, as previously, on form C285 or C&E 1179). Notice 702 para 2.6

Time of importation

The time of importation **depends on** the method by which the goods arrive into the UK. **9065** s 5 CEMA 1979

Method of import	Time of importation
By sea	When the ship comes within the limits of a port.
By air	The earlier of the time when: – the aircraft lands in the UK; or – the goods are unloaded in the UK.
By land	When the goods cross the boundary into Northern Ireland.

Method of import	Time of importation
By the Channel Tunnel	When the goods cross the frontier or: – for goods intended to be carried in a shuttle train, the time when they are taken into a control zone in France within the tunnel system; or – for goods carried in a through train carrying passengers on a journey intended to end at a place in Great Britain other than London, while the train constitutes a control zone in either France or Belgium, the time when authorised officers begin to carry out controls.
By pipeline	When the goods are brought within the limits of a port or cross the boundary into Northern Ireland.

Deferment

9066 SI 1976/1223 Notice 101

Under the deferment scheme, the payment of VAT can be deferred until the 15th day of the month following the importation or, if that is not a working day, the next working day after it. Payment is made in sterling by direct debit.

HMRC must give their **approval**, by issuing a certificate, before the scheme can be operated and the importer or his agent must provide suitable security to cover the deferrable charge.

MEMO POINTS 1. **Suitable security** will be in the form of a bank or insurance company guarantee on form C1201. The guarantee should agree to cover every liability for a calendar month up to an overall maximum. A guarantee can be replaced with one of a greater or lesser amount and a supplementary guarantee can be given to cover unusually high levels of imports.
2. A certificate of approval can cover a **group** of companies where all are members of the same group VAT registration (¶7807).

9067 Notice 101 para 5.8

Simplified Import VAT Accounting (SIVA) Importers can also apply to join the SIVA scheme using form SIVA1, which removes the requirement for a bank guarantee in relation to import VAT.

HMRC will approve a **current deferment account holder** who satisfies all of the following conditions:
- registered for at least 3 years;
- good VAT compliance history and no serious VAT offences in the past;
- good payment history (with regard to VAT and other taxes);
- good duty deferment compliance record; and
- sufficient financial means to meet any amount deferred under the scheme.

An applicant who **does not currently hold a deferment account** is also required to have:
- a 12-month record of international trade operations; and
- a good compliance record for international trade.

5. Administration

9068 Notice 702 paras 3.2, 8.1

Subject to the rules for postal imports, all goods imported into the UK must be **declared to HMRC** and may be subject to examination and documentary checks to ensure that:
- all of the required VAT documentation is present;
- the value of the goods for VAT purposes and the amount of VAT due are correct;
- the rate of VAT applied has been correctly stated; and
- the importer is eligible for any relief claimed.

MEMO POINTS 1. The required **VAT documentation** consists of:
- the Single Administrative Document (SAD form C88A); and
- a declaration of value form (C105A, C105B or C109A).

Each document should state the Trader Unique Reference Number (TURN), which is the trader's normal VAT registration number with a 3-digit suffix.
2. To **recover import VAT as input tax**, form C79 is required, which HMRC issue monthly to every VAT-registered trader who has made a declaration of import.

3. Even low-value imports which exceed 10 euros must be declared on an SAD where any **relief** is to be claimed.
4. Subject to the approval of HMRC, a single entry (known as a **bulked entry**) may be made when goods are consigned to several importers. An agent who makes a bulked entry must pay the VAT or use his own deferment account (¶9066).
5. A similar provision applies where a single importer receives goods **imported from several suppliers** in the same vessel or aircraft. Prior approval is not required in this case.

Postal imports

Different rules apply for the following postal imports: 9070 SI 1995/2518 reg 122 Notice 702 para 4.3

Value	Type of import	Procedure
Up to £2,000	Datapost packets	Post Office requires payment of the VAT when the packet is delivered. The charge label attached to the packet should be retained to support any input tax claim.
	Other consignments[1]	Not required to pay VAT immediately if HMRC declaration shows the importer's VAT number, and the nature, quantity and value of the goods. Instead, entries made in boxes 1 and 3 of VAT return for the VAT period in which import occurred.
Over £2,000	All consignments	SAD must be completed where declared for home use or free circulation, and a declaration made to show receipt of the consignment. VAT and other import charges are payable immediately (unless the deferment scheme applies (¶9066)). Once the VAT has been paid, HMRC will send the importer a copy of the declaration to support a claim for input tax.

Note:
1. Taxable amount excludes postage if importing a private gift.

B. Exports

An export is defined for VAT purposes as the sending of goods from the UK to a destination outside the EU. 9074 Notice 703

Most exports are a taxable supply, except for the following: Notice 703 para 2.14
– the supply and export of goods which are to be installed for the customer outside the EU;
– the transfer of the supplier's own goods to a place outside the EU;
– the temporary export of goods to a place outside the EU for exhibition; and
– goods exported outside the EU on a sale-or-return basis.
Even where no VAT is due, proof of export must still be retained.

1. Zero-rating

The export of goods can be zero-rated, provided that the exporter complies with all of the following **conditions**: 9076 s 30(6) VATA 1994 Notice 703 paras 2, 3
– the export must not constitute the supply of goods to a UK VAT-registered trader;
– goods must be exported within 3 months of the time of supply;
– goods must not be delivered or posted to (or collected by) a UK customer or other UK person at a UK address, even for subsequent export, although goods may be delivered to (or collected by) an overseas person in the UK;

– the exporter must not allow the goods to be used in the UK in the period between supply and export;
– the exporter must obtain within 3 months of the time of supply and keep valid evidence of the export; and
– records of the export must be maintained by the exporter.

MEMO POINTS 1. An **exporter** is the person who supplies the goods to an overseas person or, where there is no supply, the person who owns the exported goods.
2. An **indirect export** is one where the goods are delivered to or collected by an overseas person who then arranges the export of the goods outside the EU – for these purposes, an overseas person is one who is:
– not resident in the UK;
– a trader who has no business establishment in the UK from which taxable supplies are made; or
– an overseas authority.
3. The **time of supply** for these purposes is the earlier of when:
– goods are sent to or removed by the customer; or
– full payment is received for the goods.
4. If an export is made up of a **series of transactions**, only the final supply can be zero-rated.
Notice 703 para 6 5. The required **evidence** usually takes the form of a Single Administrative Document from HMRC, or commercial evidence (¶8974).

Failure to comply

9078 Notice 703 para 11.2 If exported goods have been zero-rated and are **found still to be in the UK** after the alleged date of exportation, or the **other conditions** are later shown not to have been complied with, the goods are liable to forfeiture.

The VAT payable is that which would have been due but for the zero-rating. The person liable is the supplier.

Use of agents

9080 Notice 703 para 2.5 Both the **exporter and the overseas recipient** may appoint an agent (such as a freight forwarder, airline, shipping company or other person) to act on their behalf by handling the export transaction and producing the necessary declarations to HMRC. The agent must be provided with full information on the goods so that he can complete the appropriate documentation, and he must then take reasonable steps to ensure that all of the export formalities are complied with.

If the agent **fails to comply** with his obligations, the exporter is responsible for paying any VAT charges that arise as a result.

2. Particular supplies

Summary

9082 **Additional conditions** apply for the zero-rating of the following categories of exports:

Type of export	¶¶
Work carried out on goods	¶9086
Supplies to persons departing from the EU	¶9088
Motor vehicles	¶9092
Freight containers	¶9096
Tools for the manufacture of goods for export	¶9098
Stores for ships, aircraft, etc	¶9100
Exports by charities	¶9102
Sailaway boats	¶9104

Type of export	¶¶
Racehorses	
Supplies at tax-free shops [1]	
Supplies intended for continental shelf installations	
Supplies to the Foreign and Commonwealth Office and other government departments	
Supplies to regimental shops	
Supplies in connection with the manufacture of defence projects	

Note:
1. Persons leaving on flights to destinations outside the EU may purchase goods from a **tax-free shop** at the zero rate, provided that the shop is approved by HMRC and satisfactory evidence of export is retained. In this case the supplier is deemed to be an exporter.

Work carried out on goods

Work carried out on goods for export outside the EU can be zero-rated if the following conditions are met: **9086** Notice 741 para 7.6
– the goods on which the work is to be carried out must have been obtained, acquired within, or imported into the EU for the purposes of being worked on;
– the goods must not be used in the UK between the time of leaving the supplier's premises and exportation; and
– on completion of the work, the goods are intended to be and are exported from the EU, either by the exporter or the supplier of the service (or someone acting on his behalf), or by the customer who belongs outside the EU (or someone acting on the customer's behalf).

Supplies to persons departing from the EU

Supplies to persons departing from the EU may be zero-rated under the **retail export scheme**. **9088** SI 1995/2518 reg 130 Notice 704
Under the scheme, a registered trader can eventually zero-rate eligible goods supplied to overseas visitors, provided that:
– the purchase is made in person;
– the goods are exported from the UK within 3 months of the end of the month of purchase; and
– the customer sends evidence of the export to the retailer (certified by a UK or other EU customs official) on an approved VAT refund document, which must be retained by the retailer.

MEMO POINTS 1. **Eligible goods** are any standard-rated goods, **excluding**: SI 1995/2518 reg 117(7A), (7B)
– motor vehicles;
– goods with a value in excess of £600 exported for the purposes of the customer's business;
– goods for consumption in the EU;
– goods exported as freight;
– goods purchased by mail order;
– goods (other than antiques) requiring an export licence;
– sailaway boats;
– unmounted gemstones; and
– bullion over 125g.
2. An **overseas visitor** is defined as a traveller whose domicile or habitual residence is outside the EU. Evidence must be provided (e.g. a passport, or ID card).
3. **Students and migrant workers** can only use the scheme if they intend to remain outside the EU for at least 12 months.
4. The retail export scheme can also be applied to:
– **any person who has been resident in the EU for a period of at least 365 days** in the 2 years before the purchase, and who is going to a destination outside the EU for a continuous period of at least 12 months; and
– **a member of a ship or aircraft crew** who is an overseas visitor and who is departing from the UK (or Isle of Man) to an immediate destination outside the EU.

9090 Notice 704 para 3 **Procedure** Under the scheme the retailer charges the usual rate of VAT and **issues** a VAT refund document to the customer, who can then use the document to claim a refund of the VAT after the goods have been exported. The **customer** must arrange for the document to be certified by HMRC and then send it back to the retailer, who will then forward a refund to him.

The retailer must keep a **record** of all sales under the retail export scheme (special rules apply for retailers operating retail schemes and the second-hand goods scheme).

MEMO POINTS 1. The **VAT refund document** can be either a form VAT 407 (or an approved version of it), or a sales invoice approved by HMRC for the purposes of the retail export scheme. A full description of the goods must appear on the form.
Normally VAT 407 is completed at the time of purchase. However, the form can be completed on the production of past receipts, as a concession, provided that the retailer's system is adequate to prevent abuse.
2. An **administrative or handling charge** may be deducted from the refund and the amount of the charge and the net refund must be shown on the VAT refund document.
3. If the customer is **departing directly to a destination outside the EU**, the VAT refund document must be presented to HMRC at the port or airport of departure. The relevant goods must be available for inspection at the same time. If satisfactory, the certified document will be returned to the customer, who must then send it back to the retailer or refund company.
4. Similar rules apply if the customer **departs from the EU via another EU member state**. In this case the refund documents and goods should be presented to the customs authority in the final EU member state of departure.

Motor vehicles

9092 **Generally**, the supply of a motor vehicle may be zero-rated if it is exported outside the EU. This provision applies to both new and second-hand vehicles.

However, the **indirect** export (i.e. where someone else other than the supplier undertakes the export) of a motor vehicle to a place outside the EU can be zero-rated if both of the following conditions are satisfied:
– a separate record is maintained of each transaction, including evidence that the buyer was an overseas customer; and
– the vehicle is not subsequently hired or used other than for the trip to the place of departure from the EU.

9094 Notice 705 **Personal export scheme** Under this scheme, a **new** motor vehicle can be purchased free of VAT, provided that the following conditions are satisfied:
a. the vehicle is purchased from a VAT-registered trader who operates the scheme;
b. the purchaser must take delivery of the vehicle personally and must sign a receipt for the vehicle;
c. the purchaser must export the vehicle from the EU within 12 months of delivery for overseas visitors (in other cases, the time limit is 6 months);
d. prior to exportation the vehicle may only be used in the UK by the purchaser or another person approved by HMRC who is leaving the EU and has the purchaser's permission to use the vehicle;
e. the purchaser must remain outside the EU with the vehicle for at least 6 consecutive months from the date of export of the vehicle;
f. the purchaser must not dispose, or attempt to dispose, of the vehicle in the UK; and
g. HMRC must be notified immediately if the purchaser changes his plans before the vehicle is removed from the UK.

If any of the **conditions are not met**, the vehicle will be liable to forfeiture and may be seized, and VAT will be payable on the value of the vehicle when new.

MEMO POINTS 1. For these purposes an **overseas visitor** is a person who has been in the EU for:
– 365 days or less in the 2 years immediately preceding the date of the application; or
– less than 1,096 days in the 6 years immediately before that date.
2. VAT will be payable if the vehicle cannot be exported, even if for unavoidable reasons such as **accident or theft**.

Freight containers

The export of a freight container may be zero-rated if the general conditions are satisfied (¶9076). However, the **indirect** export of a freight container may only be zero-rated if the supplier obtains a written undertaking from the customer that: **9096** Notice 703/1
a. the container will be exported from the EU;
b. the container will not be used within the EU except for:
– a single domestic journey (on which inland freight may be carried) before the export of the container on a reasonably direct route from the point of supply to the place where it is to be loaded with the export cargo or exported; or
– international movements of goods, which may include a journey within the UK for the purpose of loading or unloading the goods; and
c. records which account for the use of the container will be maintained.
If the container is **subsequently used in the UK**, other than within the terms of the undertaking, it may be seized by HMRC. In this case the VAT that would have been charged if the supply had been standard-rated will immediately become payable by the customer, or any other person now in possession of the container.

Tools for the manufacture of goods for export

The supply of jigs, patterns, templates, dies, moulds, punches and similar machine tools solely for the manufacture of goods which are to be exported will be zero-rated when made to an overseas trader, body or authority. **9098** Notice 701/22

Stores for ships, aircraft etc

Stores for use in ships and aircraft are usually fuel, goods for carrying out maintenance and repairs, and goods for use on board by the crew. Goods for retail sale to passengers on voyages or flights also come within this category. **9100** Notice 703 para 10
VAT-registered shipping companies and airlines can **choose** either:
a. to pay VAT at the standard rate on the stores and then deduct input tax in the normal way; or
b. to arrange for the stores to be supplied directly to foreign-going craft, which can then be zero-rated, provided that certain conditions are met.

MEMO POINTS The **conditions for zero-rating** to apply in **b**. above are:
1. a written declaration is made by the person to whom the goods are to be supplied that the goods are for use as stores on a voyage or flight which is to be made for a non-private purpose;
2. the supplier obtains a written confirmation from the master or authorised agent, which contains a declaration that the goods are solely for use as stores;
3. the goods must be sent direct to the ship or aircraft, or through freight forwarders, or delivered to the vessel care of the shipping line or agent;
4. a receipt confirming delivery of the goods on board must be signed by the master or responsible officer and retained by the supplier; and
5. where supplies are made direct from a customs warehouse not operated or owned by the supplier, the supplier must obtain a certificate of export from the warehouse-keeper.

Charities

Where **proof** of export is obtained, the export of any goods by a charity may be zero-rated. The export will be treated as a supply by the charity in the UK in the course or furtherance of a business carried on by it. **9102** s 30(5) VATA 1994
The charity is therefore able to **reclaim** any VAT paid on the purchase of goods and any expenses incurred in exporting them (including registration for VAT in order to do so) in situations where VAT would not otherwise be recoverable.

Sailaway boats

A sailaway boat is one that is to be removed under its own power. Under certain conditions the supply of such a boat can be zero-rated, once satisfactory evidence of the export has been received. **9104** Notice 703/02

MEMO POINTS 1. The **conditions** for making a zero-rated supply of a sailaway boat are that the supplier must:
a. ensure that the customer intends to export the boat under its own power within 6 months of the date of delivery for non-EU residents (for EU residents, this time limit is reduced to 2 months);
b. ensure that the customer is aware that he must not dispose (or attempt to dispose) of the boat in the UK or any other EU state;
c. maintain a separate record of the sale;
d. ensure that form VAT 436 is fully completed by the customer and complete the supplier's declaration when the boat is delivered to the customer;
e. agree how any VAT refund is to be paid; and
f. where the customer is an EU resident, ensure that he intends to keep the boat outside the EU for a continuous period of at least 12 months. (However, this is by concession and from 1 January 2012 zero-rating will no longer apply to a supply of a sailaway boat to a UK resident who intends to keep it outside the EU.)
2. The **satisfactory evidence** must be received within a certain time limit from the date of delivery (i.e. when the boat leaves the supplier's premises):
– for non-EU residents, within 6 months; and
– for EU residents, 2 months.

SECTION 3

Supplies of services

9105 The liability of a supply of international services depends on the rules for the **place of supply** of services (¶7996). These are considered in more detail in chapter 3. Where the place of supply is deemed to be outside the UK, the services are **outside the scope of UK VAT**. Where the place of supply is deemed to be in the UK, the services are subject to the normal UK provisions. There are limited specific categories of services to which zero-rating applies.

A. Supplies of international services by UK traders

9106 The **general rule** for services provided to businesses (B2B), whether inside or outside the EU, is that they take place where the **customer is established**. Business customers are defined as "**relevant business persons**" (¶8000).

Services provided to **non-business customers** (B2C) are treated as supplied where the supplier is established. However, this rule is subject to a number of specific rules for certain types of supply (including land (¶8007), intra-EU transport (¶8026) and electronically supplied services (¶8024)).

9107 In the case of services which are deemed to be supplied **where the customer belongs** (¶8016), the EU business customer accounts for the VAT under the reverse charge procedure (¶9110).

However, where:
– it is not possible to ascertain where the customer is located; or
– the customer is not in business, or is not using the service for a business purpose,

the place of supply reverts to being where the supplier is located, and the supplier must account for the VAT.

The place of supply for work on goods when supplied B2B is where the customer is established. For B2C supplies, the place of supply is where the work is physically carried out.

B. International services received by UK persons

Scope

Where an overseas supplier provides any services to a UK VAT-registered customer and the place of supply of those services is the UK, the UK customer must account for VAT under the reverse charge procedure. 9108

The reverse charge procedure

The reverse charge only **applies to** services which are taxable at a positive rate, and so does not apply to services which are either zero-rated or exempt. 9110 s 8 VATA 1994 Notice 741

The value of such services received must be taken into account in determining whether the registration threshold (¶7775) is reached.

MEMO POINTS The reverse charge **also applies to** certain supplies of mobile phones, computer chips and emissions allowances. See ¶8186+.

Operating the charge Under the reverse charge procedure, the customer (that is, in this context, the UK person) is treated as though he had supplied the services to himself and must therefore, if registered for VAT, account for output tax on the supply. Input tax may be claimed, depending on the supplies made by the UK person (¶8205). 9112

The **VAT return** for the period in which the services are supplied must include the output tax due in respect of the supply and, where eligible, a claim for input tax in respect of the supply.

MEMO POINTS 1. For single supplies, the tax point occurs when the service is completed or when it is paid for, whichever is the earlier. In the case of **continuous supplies**, the tax point is the end of each periodic billing or payment period. For example, if leasing charges are billed monthly or the customer is required to pay a monthly amount, the tax point will be the end of the month to which the bill or payment relates. If a payment is made before the end of the period to which it relates or before the end of the billing period, that payment date will be treated as the tax point.
2. The **value of the supply** is the consideration paid, including any taxes levied abroad, but excluding VAT.

EXAMPLE A Ltd prepares VAT returns quarterly, to 31 March, 30 June, etc. On 25 June 2012 the company purchases relevant services from B SA (a company registered in France) and pays £6,000 on 15 July 2012. The services are supplied in the UK.
On its VAT return for the VAT period ended 30 September 2012 A Ltd must account for VAT of £1,200. (£6,000 x 20%)
If A Ltd uses the services wholly to make taxable supplies, it can also claim a deduction for input tax of £1,200.

Consequences Where the business is able to attribute the services wholly to taxable supplies, the effect of the reverse charge is to put the business in exactly the same position as if the supply had been made by a UK supplier. 9114

If the **input tax** is not fully recoverable, the business has incurred a VAT charge which would only have been avoided if the supply had been made by a non-registered UK supplier.

Electronically provided services

Electronically provided services (¶8024) supplied by non-EU businesses to private individuals and non-business organisations in the EU are taxed in the country where the customer belongs. This means that non-EU businesses providing such services are normally required to **register** and account for VAT in every EU member state where they make supplies. 9116 Information Sheet 7/03

However, an **optional simplified special scheme** (expected to run until 31 December 2014) allows such businesses to electronically:
– register in a single member state of their choice; and
– declare the EU tax due on a single VAT return to the member state of registration.

The member state of registration then distributes the VAT due to the other appropriate member states.

To **register in the UK**, traders should visit https://secure.hmce.gov.uk/ecom/voes.

EC sales lists for services

9118 Businesses in the EU which supply services where the reverse charge applies (¶8016) are required to submit EC sales lists (ESLs). The information which must be provided is the same as is currently required for the cross-border movement of goods (¶8979). ESLs are **not required** from businesses which are providing the following:
– supplies exempt in the member state where the supply takes place;
– B2B supplies made to recipients who are not VAT-registered;
– B2C supplies where the customer is purchasing the services for non-business purposes.

The **due date** for submission of ESLs is one month after the end of the reporting period.

MEMO POINTS The ESL reporting period for services is a **calendar quarter**, although businesses may instead choose a reporting period of a calendar month. It is possible to submit ESLs electronically or on paper, using form VAT 101.

SECTION 4

Special rules relating to second-hand goods

9120 Special rules apply to second-hand goods which are involved in overseas transactions. For the general rules relating to these goods, see ¶8435+.

A. Transactions within the EU

9122 Both the margin scheme and the global accounting scheme are available across the EU. Under the schemes, goods acquired from other EU member states are taxable in the state of origin, rather than the state of destination.

Acquisitions

9124 The treatment of acquisitions depends on the status of the supplier.
Notice 718 para 15.1

Goods purchased:
a. from a **private individual** will not be subject to VAT when they are brought into the UK – assuming that all of the conditions for operating the schemes are satisfied, the global or margin accounting schemes can be used for the resale of the goods;
b. from a **registered business** will be liable to tax on acquisition – the purchaser will be able to reclaim this tax under the normal rules but if he does so, the margin and global accounting schemes are not available for the resale of the goods; and
c. under the margin scheme, **global accounting, or the auctioneers' scheme** will not be liable to tax on acquisition and may be resold under those schemes – before entering goods into the UK margin scheme, it is important to check that the goods are being supplied under a margin scheme (which should be declared on the supplier's invoice).

Second-hand cars A second-hand car (as defined at ¶8466 but not including a new means of transport (¶8942)) purchased **from a private individual** in another member state, or from a **registered dealer under the margin scheme**, will not be subject to VAT when it is brought into the UK. The margin scheme may be used for the onward sale of the car. 9126 Notice 718 para 19.1

If, however, a second-hand car is purchased **outside the margin scheme** from a registered dealer in another member state, acquisition VAT at the standard rate will be due when the car is brought into the UK.

Sales

Sales made **under the margin scheme or global accounting** to another EU member state should be treated in the same way as sales within the UK. As the place of supply is the UK, sales made in this way cannot be zero-rated and tax on the margin will be due in the UK. However, no further tax will be due from the buyer when the goods are taken into the other member state. Distance selling arrangements do not apply to goods sold under the schemes. 9128 Notice 718 para 15.2

Alternatively, the supplier may prefer not to sell the goods under either of the schemes, in which case the sale can be zero-rated under the normal EU supply rules (¶8968), and completion of an EC sales list (¶8978) is therefore appropriate. However, if the eventual buyer of the goods is a registered dealer, he will not be able to resell the goods under either of the schemes.

B. Transactions outside the EU

The import and export of second-hand goods outside the EU is subject to special rules and in most cases the second-hand goods schemes do not apply. 9130

1. Imports

VAT is **usually** chargeable on the importation of second-hand goods and the margin scheme cannot be used when the goods are resold. Instead, VAT must be charged on the full selling price, although the VAT paid at importation will be deductible under the normal rules. 9132

The **exceptions** to this rule are:
- second-hand cars; and
- works of art, antiques and collectors' pieces.

Second-hand cars

Cars on which the input tax on importation is irrecoverable may be **resold** under the margin scheme, but not global accounting. 9134 Notice 718/2

Import VAT is due at the standard rate, unless the car meets the criteria for returned goods relief (¶9054) or can be classified as a collectors' piece.

If the car qualifies as a **collectors' piece or an antique**, the margin scheme can be applied on resale.

Works of art, collectors' items and antiques

Imported works of art, antiques and collectors' pieces which fall within the category of eligible goods (¶8440) are liable to VAT at the **effective rate** of 5%. 9135 Notice 702 para 3.4

MEMO POINTS The **calculation** works by taking 25% of the item's value and applying the standard rate (20%) of VAT.

A business may opt to use the margin scheme (¶8437) or auctioneers' scheme (¶8500) when **reselling** the following assets: 9136

– imported works of art, collectors' items or antiques (¶8440); and
– works of art obtained from the creator (or his heirs) by supply in the UK, or acquisition from another EU state.
Alternatively, the business may choose to account for VAT in the normal way.

9138 **Using a margin scheme** If the business opts to use the margin scheme or the auctioneers' scheme, imports at both the standard rate and the effective rate of 5% will be covered.

Notice 718 para 18.3

MEMO POINTS 1. If a business opts to use either the margin scheme or auctioneers' scheme, the following **conditions** must be satisfied:
– HMRC must be notified in writing that the option will be taken up, specifying the date from which it will be applied;
– the option is exercised for a period of at least 2 years and thereafter HMRC are notified in writing when it is to cease;
– if a scheme is used, it must be applied to all transactions and goods referred to above, not just in respect of certain categories of transactions or certain categories of goods; and
– if, having exercised the option, the business decides to sell (outside a scheme) any goods covered by the option, it is not entitled to recover any input tax on those goods until the period in which VAT on their sale is accounted for.
2. When the business opts to use the margin scheme under these provisions **global accounting** may be used, provided that the general conditions (¶8474) are met.
The business must not, however, enter eligible taxed goods into global accounting until it has the documentation which would have allowed it to reclaim input tax (or acquisition/import VAT if applicable) had it not taken up the option.

9139 Notice 718 para 18.4

The **purchase cost** to be entered in the records depends on the type of scheme used:
– for the margin scheme, the cost is the value for VAT at import, plus the import VAT; and
– for the auctioneers' scheme, the cost is to be calculated according to the normal rules.
Under either scheme, **VAT is calculated** on the margin at the standard rate, using the VAT fraction (see ¶8030). and the import VAT cannot be recovered as input tax.

MEMO POINTS **Auctioneers' fees** (including buyer's premium) are always subject to standard-rate VAT, even when the goods being sold are subject to the effective rate of 5%.

EXAMPLE Mr A imports a statue which is valued for import purposes at £2,000. He sells it for £2,700. The VAT due under the margin scheme is calculated as follows:

	£
Value for import purposes	2,000
Import VAT @ 5%	100
Purchase price for margin scheme	2,100
Sales price	2,700
Margin	600
VAT @ 1/6	100

9140 Notice 718 para 18.2

Works obtained from the creator When either the margin scheme or the auctioneers' scheme is used for works of art obtained from the creator (or his heirs), any VAT charged cannot be recovered.

The **acquisition cost** to be entered in the records is:
– for the margin scheme, the total price of the work of art inclusive of any VAT; and
– for the auctioneers' scheme, the purchase price, as calculated under the normal rules of the scheme. If the vendor is VAT-registered, this amount will also be the vendor's VAT-inclusive selling price.

2. Exports

9142 Notice 718 para 17.2

The direct export of eligible goods (¶8440) will be zero-rated, provided that appropriate evidence of export is obtained.

In addition, second-hand goods that are **indirectly** exported (¶9076) may only be zero-rated if the agent or dealer (who is acting in his own name) is located outside the EU.

Second-hand **vehicles** supplied to an overseas person for export may be zero-rated where the vehicle is only used in the UK to make the trip to the place of departure from the EU (¶9092).

SECTION 5

Repayment of overseas VAT

UK traders who are not registered for VAT in other EU member states may incur EU VAT, which would be a cost unless special rules applied. For example, a trader may attend a trade fair in Germany, incurring German VAT which would be irrecoverable if refund provisions did not exist. This VAT can be recovered via a claim made to the overseas tax authority. Claims are made online via HMRC. 9145

VAT incurred in the UK by **non-UK traders** is also refundable under similar provisions.

A. Repayments to EU traders

A separate claim must be made to recover VAT incurred in another EU member state, as there is no mechanism for this claim to be made on a VAT return. These claims are usually referred to as 8th Directive claims. Claims are made by the trader online via HMRC to the member state where the VAT was incurred, known as the member state of refund (MSR). 9146 s 39 VATA 1994

Eligible persons

A claim may be made by a trader carrying on a business in another member state if he satisfies all of the following **criteria**: 9148 Notice 723 para 2.2

- he is not, and is not required to be, registered for VAT in the MSR;
- he has no business establishment in the MSR;
- his usual place of residence is not in the MSR; and
- he has not made any supplies in the MSR.

Eligible supplies

A claim for a refund may be submitted in respect of **VAT incurred on**: 9150 SI 1995/2518 reg 175

- supplies made to the trader in the MSR; and
- goods imported to the MSR by the trader from a place outside the EU in respect of which no other relief is available.

The supplies received in the UK must not be **used** by the trader in making his own supplies in the MSR. Where goods are purchased in the MSR they must be consumed there and not taken out of the MSR.

In the UK the following **cannot be claimed**: SI 1995/2518 reg 177 Notice 723A para 4.5

- VAT incorrectly invoiced, or VAT charged on the despatch of goods to another member state or the export of goods outside the EU;
- VAT on the purchase of a car;
- VAT incurred in relation to business entertainment, or non-business activities.

In addition, only 50% of VAT incurred on charges for hiring or leasing a motor car may be claimed.

Period of claim

9152 SI 1995/2518 reg 179 Claims are made by **reference to** the calendar year.

The period covered by the claim must be between 3 months and a year, unless the claim period starts on or after 1 October, when a shorter period is allowed.

Amount of the claim

9154 SI 1995/2518 reg 179 The tax available for refund will be **restricted** to the tax that would be available for deduction as input tax by taxable persons in the UK.

The **minimum** limit is £130, except for claims commencing on or after 1 October, when the minimum is £16.

Administration in the UK

9156 SI 1995/2518 reg 178 On **1 January 2010** a new electronic VAT refund system for traders incurring VAT in other EU countries was introduced to replace the previous paper-based system.

9158 Under the electronic system:
- the claim is sent to the MSR via the business' own tax authority, so there is no need for a VAT certificate of status;
- the time limit for making claims is **extended by 3 months** to 9 months from the end of the calendar year in which the VAT was incurred (and because some member states were slow to implement the new electronic procedures, for the first year of operation the deadline was extended from 30 September 2010 to 31 March 2011);
- tax authorities only have **4 rather than 6 months** to make repayments;
- businesses have the **right of appeal** against non-payment; and
- member states have to pay **interest** where they fail to meet the deadline for repayment.

MEMO POINTS A UK business that wishes to make claims for recovering VAT incurred in another EU member state must register on the UK government portal via the Government Gateway.

B. Repayments to non-EU traders

9160 s 39 VATA 1994 Where a non-EU trader incurs UK VAT, he may be able to recover it if his own country provides a similar relief for UK traders. Eligible supplies are those defined at ¶9150. Such claims are commonly referred to as 13th Directive claims.

Eligible traders

9162 SI 1995/2518 reg 188 The trader must be **registered** for business purposes in another country and satisfy all of the following criteria:
- he is not, and is not required to be, registered for VAT in the UK;
- he has no business establishment anywhere in the EU; and
- he has not made any supplies in the UK.

Period of claim

9164 SI 1995/2518 reg 185 Claims are made by **reference to** the year ended 30 June.

The period covered by the claim must be between 3 months and a year, unless the claim period starts on or after 1 April, when a shorter period is allowed.

Amount of the claim

9166 SI 1995/2518 reg 192 The tax available for refund will be **restricted** to the tax that would be available for deduction as input tax by taxable persons in the UK.

The **minimum** limit is £130, except for claims commencing on or after 1 April, when the minimum is £16.

Administration

Claims must be **submitted** in English on form VAT 65A by 31 December. **9168** SI 1995/2518 reg 191

The following **documents** (originals not photocopies) must be attached to the claim:
a. a certificate of status such as form VAT 66A (or its foreign equivalent); and
b. invoices, import documents or warehouse documents relating to the supplies or imports for which the claim is made, showing:
- an identifying number and the date of supply;
- the supplier's name, address and VAT registration number;
- the applicant's name and address;
- the cost of the goods or services (excluding VAT), in sterling; and
- the rate and amount of VAT charged (in sterling).

MEMO POINTS Where the normal practice is to issue **invoices in the name of employees**, HMRC do not insist on claims being supported by valid VAT invoices in the name of the business. However, alternative evidence may be required and HMRC retain the right to delay repayment or even refuse claims. In particular, this affects input tax recovery on hotel expenses. HMRC have stated that there is no legal barrier to a hotel issuing an invoice which includes the name of the employee's company. Information Sheet 2/05

A **repayment** is due within 6 months of HMRC receiving satisfactory evidence. The payment will be in the currency of the payee and is transferred to the payee's bank account direct. False claims will result in recovery proceedings and possibly penalties. **9170**

If a repayment is **refused**, the trader can appeal to the tribunal.

C. Anti-avoidance

Traders who are not established in the UK are required to register for UK VAT if they **intend to make taxable supplies** of goods (including capital assets) in the UK, on which VAT has previously been recovered under the refund rules. **9172** Sch 3A VATA 1994

There is no registration threshold for this purpose. Traders who intend to make only zero-rated supplies can apply for an exemption from this requirement.

HMRC must be **notified** within 30 days of the date on which the business expects to make such supplies; registration will be effective from the date on which the business first becomes liable. **9174**

Once a business has registered, it will be subject to all of the usual UK VAT rules and can no longer claim refunds under the provisions outlined in ¶9146 to ¶9170.

A trader can **deregister** once he ceases making supplies which use goods on which a refund was previously claimed.

CHAPTER 10

Administration

OUTLINE ¶¶

9200 A taxable person is required to maintain certain records, which must be available for HMRC to inspect. He must account for and pay VAT on a regular basis. Interest may be charged if VAT is paid late and HMRC may raise an assessment to recover any VAT they believe is payable.

Penalties may be charged for any breach of the administrative requirements, including failure to disclose use of a scheme which results in a tax advantage. A taxable person may appeal to the tribunal on many VAT matters. HMRC also have various legal powers to enable them to monitor and enforce VAT compliance.

9202 Following the merger of HMRC in 2005 the department began a programme to simplify compliance and harmonise procedures across all taxes under its management. The first of the simplification measures, introduced by Finance Act 2007, covered penalties for VAT errors in returns or documents and came into force on 1 April 2008, with effect for returns or documents filed after 1 April 2009. In Finance Act 2008 the new penalty framework was **extended** to cover:
- penalties for failure to notify a liability to register and other notification requirements;
- penalties for unauthorised issue of VAT invoices;
- new penalties for offences caused by third parties;
- new information gathering powers, including a new compliance visit framework;
- new record-keeping requirements; and
- new time limits for assessments.

In addition, a new appeals and tribunal regime for all taxes was introduced on 1 April 2009.

It is important to note that the new penalties apply only in relation to inaccuracies in documents, specific failures to notify under VAT obligations, and the unauthorised issue of VAT invoices. All other pre-existing VAT penalties continue to apply. For details of the **harmonised penalties, powers and tribunals**, and details of future changes, please see *Harmonisation of tax administration* from ¶9775.

SECTION 1

Records

VAT account

9205 SI 1995/2518 reg 32 Notice 700/21 Taxable persons must maintain a VAT account for each VAT period (¶8342). The VAT account must be split into sections for VAT payable and VAT deductible and show the following **information**:
- total output tax due (including that relating to acquisitions from other EU member states);
- details of every correction or adjustment in respect of output tax;
- total input tax recoverable; and
- details of every correction or adjustment in respect of input tax.

The amounts calculated in the VAT account are then **transferred to** the VAT return.

Notice 700 para 19.14 The account may be kept in any **form**, although HMRC give the following pro-forma as a guide.

MEMO POINTS 1. Usually VAT is added up at convenient **intervals**, such as months.
2. **Estimates** may be allowed where approved.
3. Any VAT **adjustments notified by HMRC** should be excluded from the VAT account, unless the trader is specifically told to include them.

VAT period ended April

Deductible VAT – Input tax	**£**	**Payable VAT – Output tax**	**£**
VAT on purchases:		VAT on sales:	
Feb	X	Feb	X
Mar	X	Mar	X
April	X	April	X
	X		X
VAT on EU acquisitions[1]	X	VAT on EU acquisitions[1]	X
Net over-claim of input tax on prior VAT returns	(X)	Net underdeclaration of output tax on prior VAT returns	X
Bad debt relief[2]	X	Adjustments for special schemes[3]	X
Adjustments from special schemes[3]	X		
	X		X
VAT on credit notes received from suppliers	(X)	VAT on credit notes issued to customers	(X)
Total deductible VAT	**X**	**Total VAT payable**	**X**
		Less: Total deductible VAT	(X)
		Net amount due to/from HMRC	X

Note:
1. See ¶8937 for further details.
2. See ¶8350 for further details.
3. These would include:
- partial exemption methods (¶8213);
- capital goods scheme (¶8272);
- retail schemes (¶8700); and
- use of TOMS by tour operators (see *VAT Memo* for details).

Other records

In addition to the VAT account, all traders must maintain the following records: 9207 SI 1995/2518 reg 31
- general business and accounting records;
- copies of all VAT invoices issued and received;
- a record of any exempt supplies;
- details of self-supplies;
- credit and debit notes;
- a refund of bad debts account;
- documentation regarding any imports or exports;
- documentation issued or received relating to the transfer, despatch or transportation of goods to or from other EU member states or services subject to the reverse charge;
- certificates relating to supplies of goods and services or supplies involving fiscal warehousing; and
- any self-billing agreement to which they are a party and the name, address and VAT registration number of each supplier with whom they have entered into any self-billing agreement.

Users of **special VAT schemes** may be required to keep additional records.

MEMO POINTS 1. **Business and accounting records** should reflect the size and complexity of the business. They include the annual accounts, a list of all branches, orders, delivery notes, cash and other accounting books, purchase and sales books, records of daily takings, business correspondence, bank statements, and paying-in books. Evidence of the volume of trade outside the accounting records is also extremely useful.
It is important that the records are kept up to date and are sufficiently detailed so that the trader can calculate accurate amounts to enter on VAT returns, which can then be easily checked by HMRC.
2. **Copies of invoices** may be on paper, computer or other media.
3. A business **temporarily moving goods** between member states must maintain a log of any such movements. The record must show the date of both arriving in and leaving the UK. Goods are moved temporarily if they are returned to the original location within 2 years. SI 1995/2518 reg 33
4. HMRC have the power to issue a **direction** to individual businesses which requires specified **additional records** to be maintained (e.g. IMEI numbers for mobile phones). A direction can only be issued where HMRC believe that additional records may help to identify supplies in Sch 11 para 6A VATA 1994

relation to which VAT might not be paid. The **affected goods** are likely to be those which have systematically been used as part of missing trader intra-community (carousel) fraud (¶9332), such as mobile phones and computer equipment.

s 69B VATA 1994 Failure to comply with a direction will result in a penalty of £200 per day, up to a maximum of £6,000. Both a direction and any penalty may be appealed to the tribunal.

9209 Sch 11 para 6 VATA 1994 All records must be **retained** for a period of 6 years, unless HMRC agree to a shorter period (usually because the business has storage problems or is incurring undue expense).

There is no requirement to maintain the records in their original **format**, although HMRC should approve a change to an alternative medium (e.g. paper to computer records). No prior approval is required for records which are produced on a computer but then stored on paper.

HMRC have a right to **access** records, irrespective of format and location, and also to request assistance to gain access (e.g. to operate a computer system).

MEMO POINTS 1. If records are kept at an **accountant's premises**, HMRC may agree to check the records there. If any records are officially removed, the accountant should ask for a receipt.
2. For **buildings** which are items covered by the capital goods scheme (¶8263), or where an option to tax has been exercised (¶8904), the record-keeping requirements are extended.
3. A **business which is no longer VAT-registered** is still required to maintain records until 6 years have elapsed from the date of deregistration, except where a VAT registration number is transferred on the transfer of a business as a going concern, in which case the transferee is responsible for maintaining and holding the records (¶7779).

SECTION 2

Reporting

9210 Most VAT information is reported on VAT returns, although there are additional requirements when trading with EU businesses.

When errors occur, there is a set procedure to be followed. In addition, disclosure of certain VAT-saving schemes is required.

Authorised agents

9212 HMRC will only release **confidential information** about a business to an agent, such as an accountant or business adviser, if appropriate authorisation is sent to HMRC.

MEMO POINTS 1. A trader who wishes to authorise an agent must complete form 64-8 and send it to HMRC. If the trader is authorising an agent for other taxes as well, this can be done on the same 64-8.
2. It is possible for agents to register to submit their clients' VAT returns **online** (¶9217).

Senior accounting officers

9213 HMRC Brief 37/09 Special rules apply to **larger companies and their senior accounting officers** personally. The "senior accounting officer" is defined as "the director or officer of the company who has overall responsibility for the company's financial accounting arrangements". Senior accounting officers are required to:
– take reasonable steps to establish and monitor accounting systems to ensure they are adequate for the purposes of tax reporting; and
– certify annually that the systems are adequate or specify the nature of the inadequacies.

The company must also advise HMRC of the identity of the senior accounting officer for the company. Penalties of £5,000 can be levied on the senior accounting officer for each of the following:
– failure to maintain, and monitor that the company has, appropriate tax accounting arrangements; and
– failure to provide a certificate, or provision of a certificate that contains a careless or deliberate inaccuracy.

See also ¶2360.

MEMO POINTS The provisions apply to companies with either, or both:
- annual turnover in excess of £200m;
- balance sheet assets of £2 billion.

1. VAT returns

In addition to VAT returns, traders may also be required to submit EC sales lists for supplies of goods and services to a registered person in another EU member state (¶8978); and/or Intrastat supplementary declarations, which are required where the EU trade in goods exceeds certain thresholds (¶9002). 9214

Filing requirements

Paper returns A VAT return (form VAT 100) is required for each VAT period (¶8342). A special return (form VAT 193) is required for the final period before deregistration. The information required for completion of the VAT return broadly corresponds to the information recorded in the VAT account (¶9205), plus total VAT-exclusive sales and purchases. 9216 S 1995/2518 reg 25

A return must usually be **submitted** within 1 calendar month of the end of the VAT period to which it relates. For the avoidance of doubt, the due date is always printed on the front of the return form. **Late** returns mean the trader may become liable to a default surcharge (¶9272).

The return includes a **declaration** that the return is true and complete. The declaration must be signed by an authorised person and must not be qualified in any way, otherwise the return is not correctly made.

Failing to submit a return will result in an assessment for the amount of VAT estimated as due by HMRC. This assessment cannot be appealed until the return itself has been submitted. In practice, the assessment will be cancelled if the return is submitted and the related VAT paid.

MEMO POINTS The submission deadline is extended to 2 months in the case of a business using the **annual accounting scheme** (¶8405).

Electronic filing VAT returns and EC sales lists may be submitted **electronically** on HMRC's website (www.hmrc.gov.uk) via the VAT Online service. Traders must register for online services and any VAT liability must be paid by bank transfer (e.g. BACS, or CHAPS). In this case the **submission deadline**, and due date for payment, is extended by 7 calendar days, unless payments on account (¶9255) are being made. 9217

If VAT returns are filed online no paper copy of the VAT return will be issued. If the trader provides HMRC with an email address he should receive a reminder that his VAT return is due to be filed shortly after the end of the VAT return period.

MEMO POINTS 1. **Compulsory online filing** is currently being phased in:
- traders who registered on or after 1 April 2010 are required to file online;
- traders with a turnover of more than £100,000 must file VAT returns online for accounting periods that started on or after 1 April 2010; and
- all traders must file online from April 2012.

2. There is also a service which is directed solely at **agents**, who can declare and submit clients' returns online without the need for signatures. For this purpose, an agent is a third party authorised to submit online returns on behalf of a VAT-registered client.

Estimates

If a business is **unable to include the exact amount** of input or output tax on the VAT return, agreement should be sought from HMRC to include an estimate. Permission will be given, provided that an adjustment is made for the estimate in the next VAT period or, if the exact amount is still not known then, in the next but one VAT period. 9218 SI 1995/2518 regs 28, 29(3)

Where permission is granted before the due date of the return, the business will not be liable to **penalties** (¶9272), provided that the return is submitted and VAT is paid by the due date. If, however, permission is sought retrospectively, any default recorded will stand.

Disputed transactions

9220 Notice 700/45 para 8

HMRC's position is that VAT returns should be completed in line with their guidance, even if the taxpayer disputes their interpretation. This position is maintained even if an appeal has been lodged. If a trader **ignores HMRC's guidance**, an assessment for any VAT HMRC deem to be due will normally be issued. If the matter is settled in HMRC's favour, the assessment will be payable. In addition, interest and penalties may be due (¶9270).

An appeal can only be heard if the VAT in dispute has been paid, unless the tribunal decides, or HMRC agrees, that payment would cause hardship to the appellant.

Comment The **safest option** is to complete the VAT return in line with HMRC's guidance but to lodge a claim in respect of the dispute (¶9224) so that the business is not at a disadvantage should the appeal be won.

2. Errors

9222 SI 1995/2518 regs 34, 35 Notice 700/45

If a business discovers an error after having submitted a VAT return the value of the error, and when and by whom it is discovered, will affect how the business should correct the error.

Time limits

9224 s 80 VATA 1994 s 77 VATA 1994

Taxpayers may only correct errors within 4 years of the relevant date.

The only **exceptions** are tax point errors (i.e. where the tax point has been incorrectly identified and an amount of VAT has been included on the VAT return immediately preceding or following the correct one).

The 4-year time limit for making corrections starts from the following **dates**, depending on the circumstances:

Circumstance	Date
Over-declaring output tax	End of VAT period of return
Under-claiming input tax	Due date of submission of return
Disclosure of error	End of VAT period in which disclosure made
Assessment	End of VAT period in which assessment made
Duplicate payment	Date of overpayment

MEMO POINTS 1. If the taxpayer has **subsequently deregistered**, the time limits apply as if he were still registered.

9225 **Retrospective VAT claims** HMRC issued **guidance** in May 2009 for their staff on the handling of historic VAT claims by traders following *Fleming t/a Bodycraft v HMRC* [2008] and *Conde Naste v HMRC* [2008]. The guidance (http://www.hmrc.gov.uk/thelibrary/fleming-claims.htm) includes information on how HMRC will deal with claims by assignees and transferees after the Court of Appeal in *Midlands Cooperative Society Ltd v HMRC* [2008] held that the right to claim for overpaid VAT can be assigned, transferred or sold. The guidance also covers HMRC's policy on verifying claims, set-off, and claims for compound interest.

Overpaid VAT

9226 s 80 VATA 1994

If a business has overpaid VAT, HMRC may make a repayment.

Valid claims for **input tax** and refunds of **duplicated VAT** will always be repaid. Amounts included as VAT, which were not VAT, will also always be repaid.

However, in relation to **output tax** declared in error, a repayment will not be made if the business would thereby be unjustly enriched.

Unjust enrichment occurs where the customer has borne the VAT cost and the business is unable, or unwilling, to pass the refunded VAT back to the customer. 9227 SI 1995/2518 reg 43A

Separate claims must be made for:
a. the overpaid VAT; and
b. any balance due to the taxpayer to actually be repaid.

HMRC can refuse to recognise any overpaid VAT where they believe that the taxpayer will be unjustly enriched. In response to such a challenge, the trader should provide evidence of his direct monetary loss.

Even if the overpayment is recognised, it will be **set off** against other VAT liabilities before any repayment is made. Interest (¶9264) will only apply on the balance left remaining to the taxpayer.

To obtain a **VAT repayment**, a claimant must give an undertaking that he will reimburse any amounts of VAT which have actually been suffered by his customers within 90 days. The trader must also notify HMRC of any amounts which are not reimbursed, and make a payment back to them within the 14 days after the 90-day period has expired. SI 2005/2231

EXAMPLE The ECJ has held that member states can only rely on unjust enrichment when refusing to repay over-declared output tax if **all traders in similar circumstances** are treated the same. This does not mean that traders have to be in direct competition, and there must be an objective justification for different treatment. In UK legislation prior to 26 May 2005 the unjust enrichment defence could only be used against payment traders, and not repayment traders. The ECJ held that unjust enrichment could not be used in this case to refuse repayment of overpaid VAT. Furthermore the fact the trader had passed on the VAT to their customers did not necessarily correlate to them not suffering any loss, as their sales may have decreased.
The ECJ stated that it was for the national courts to decide whether repaying the overpaid VAT would remedy the infringement of equal treatment, even if this meant that the trader would be unjustly enriched, but that, in principle, repayment should be made to compensate the trader for the discrimination unless national law has another method of compensation.
Marks and Spencer plc v HMRC [2008]

Advice from HMRC

The taxpayer can ask for **advice from** HMRC in relation to any VAT issue. Where they provide advice that is incorrect in law they will be bound by it if it is clear, unequivocal and explicit, and: 9228 Notice 700/6
- taxpayers can demonstrate that they reasonably relied on the advice;
- where appropriate, they made full disclosure of all the relevant facts; and
- the application of the statute would result in financial detriment.

Where HMRC have given incorrect information or advice, their primary duty is to collect the correct amount of tax required by the law. Therefore there will be some occasions when they will **not be bound** by their advice. If they provide taxpayers with incorrect advice that is binding on them, and subsequently notify the taxpayer that it is incorrect, taxpayers will only be required to start accounting for tax on the correct basis from the date of notification. All cases will be subject to any statutory time limits. HMRC Brief 15/09

Changes in practice

HMRC usually announce changes in their policy or their interpretation of the law in advance. Whilst changes in policy are given a future **implementation date**, a change in interpretation of the law will mean that the law should always have been applied in a certain way, so the change is retrospective. 9230 HMRC Brief 24/11

On this basis, HMRC have stated that they:
- will not require a correction of past errors, based on the old interpretation of the law, so the new interpretation can be applied from a current or future date;

– will accept a correction of past errors if the business will not be better off, and HMRC no worse off than if the correction was not made; and
– may exercise their discretion not to collect outstanding VAT where the business has been misdirected by an HMRC officer (who gave a clear ruling when in possession of all the facts).

VAT invoices

9232 Notice 700 para 19.10 **VAT account** If a business **issues** a VAT invoice showing an incorrect amount of VAT, the entry in the records depends on whether VAT is:
– overstated, in which case the amount of VAT shown on the invoice is to be accounted for; or
– understated, in which case the business must record and account for the correct amount of VAT.
If a business **receives** a VAT invoice showing an incorrect amount of VAT, the position is reversed, so if VAT has been:
– overstated, the business must record and account for the correct amount of VAT; or
– understated, it must record and account for only the amount of VAT shown on the invoice.

9234 **Paperwork** In a case where an incorrect amount of VAT has been shown on an invoice, if **both the supplier and the customer agree**, it is possible to:
– cancel the original invoice and issue a replacement showing the correct amount of VAT; or
– issue a credit or debit note, or a supplementary invoice, cross-referenced to the original invoice, to correct the position.
Both parties must adjust their VAT accounts accordingly and ensure that the adjustments flow through to their VAT returns.

VAT returns

9236 Notice 700 para 19.11 If a **business discovers** an error in a VAT return, it should be corrected or notified as soon as possible.
If the **net error** is:
a. less than the higher of £10,000, or 1% of turnover (up to a maximum of £50,000), the business may adjust its VAT account for the period in which the error occurred and include the value of the adjustment on its next VAT return; no interest will be charged for errors corrected in this way; alternatively, the business may choose to notify HMRC in writing, as below; or
b. greater than or equal to the above limit, it must be disclosed to HMRC in writing, generally using form VAT 652. No adjustment should be made to the VAT account or return. HMRC will issue an assessment to collect the VAT. Interest will be charged in respect of errors notified in this way from the due date of the return to the date of the notification.

Under the new harmonised penalty regime for errors, an error notification will not necessarily protect taxpayers from a penalty. See ¶9835 for details of the new tests to establish whether a penalty is due.

9238 **Failing to disclose an error** If a business identifies an error but fails to disclose it to HMRC, a civil **penalty** may be charged for evasion of VAT (¶9290). In more serious cases, a criminal penalty may be imposed (¶9304).

If an error made on a return or other document is **deliberate and concealed**, a penalty of up to 100% of the tax lost will be imposed (¶9798+).

3. Disclosure of VAT-saving schemes

9240 Sch 11A VATA 1994 Notice 700/8 To combat VAT avoidance, traders with annual turnover exceeding £600,000 (or £10 million in certain circumstances), or their advisers, are required to notify HMRC of VAT-saving schemes which are in use. The disclosure requirements apply to schemes used in VAT periods starting on or after 1 August 2004 (including schemes that started before that date). Disclosure is an information-gathering exercise for the authorities, so that they become aware of the extent of the use of known schemes, and it also serves as an early warning of new schemes. Failing to disclose may result in a penalty.

Notification does not undermine the legality of the scheme itself, provided that it is in accordance with UK and EU law. Disclosure may provoke future regulation to control or even outlaw such schemes.

MEMO POINTS 1. **Turnover** is defined as the trader's total taxable and exempt supplies, measured over both the:
- year ending immediately prior to the VAT return affected by use of a scheme; and
- VAT return period immediately prior to the affected return (with the limits being appropriately apportioned).

Income which is outside the scope of VAT, such as grants and donations, is ignored for this purpose.
2. For a **quarterly VAT period**, the limits are divided by four.
3. For a **monthly VAT period**, the limits are divided by twelve.
4. The turnover limits apply to a whole **group of companies**. For this purpose, a group is **defined** as all companies included in the consolidated accounts plus other UK subsidiaries.
5. If a business has been **artificially split** (¶7784), HMRC can direct that the resulting entities should be treated as one for the purposes of these rules.

Scope

The following schemes must be disclosed: 9242 Sch 11A para 7 VATA 1994
- **listed schemes**, which are specifically identified devices already known by HMRC; and
- **hallmarked schemes**, which use certain features which are regularly associated with avoidance. A promoter (¶9246) may choose to disclose this type of scheme on behalf of all his clients who are using it (¶9249).

There are different **criteria** for disclosing each type of scheme, the most important of which is the size of the business, as determined by turnover.

MEMO POINTS The following are **not regarded as schemes** for this purpose:
- merely claiming recoverable input tax (perhaps by engaging a VAT specialist to undertake a review);
- using a published concession;
- using the grouping provisions and making changes to the group members; or
- agreeing a new partial exemption special method with HMRC.

Annual turnover[1]	Disclosure requirement
< £600,000	None
£600,000 – £10m	Listed schemes only
> £10m	Listed schemes and hallmarked schemes

Note:
1. Businesses with turnover close to the limits will need to monitor their turnover levels every quarter to check whether the rules apply to them.

EXAMPLE Mr A has been using a listed scheme which first affects his return for the quarter ending 30 September.
To see if he must disclose the scheme, he must check whether his turnover in the:
- year to 30 June is greater than £600,000; and
- quarter to 30 June is greater than £150,000.

Listed schemes

A return or claim is **affected** if the scheme results in a beneficial change in the amount of VAT payable or repayable i.e. it either reduces output tax due or increases an input tax reclaim. Where the business has exempt supplies or non-business activities, any reduction in the amount of irrecoverable input tax is also potentially notifiable. There is no motive test under these rules, so the VAT benefit does not have to be intentional. 9244 SI 2004/1933 Sch 1 Notice 700/8 para 6

A **penalty** of 15% of the VAT saving is levied, unless the business notifies HMRC of the use of any of the following listed schemes.

Scheme number	Title	Details
1	First grant of a major interest in a building	Interest in a dwelling, or property intended for relevant residential or charitable use, is granted to a connected person[1]. The grantor recovers input tax in relation to a service charge or repairs and similar expenditure.
2	Credit card or cash handling services charged by a retailer	Price for the goods remains the same as when cash is paid. The scheme relies on the payment handling charge being an exempt supply, but it has been held that all of the price charged in this situation relates to a standard-rated supply. *HMRC v Debenhams Retail plc* [2005]
3	Value shifting	A retailer sells a bundle of goods and services at a single price, including add-ons which are either zero-rated or exempt – for example insurance. The customer enters into a separate agreement for the add-on when he hands over payment. However, the price charged is the same whether the customer agrees to receive it or not.
4	Leaseback of goods	Excludes land transactions and any transactions between unconnected parties. Scheme enables partly exempt businesses to access a full input tax refund up front and repay the VAT over a period of time. In all cases, 90% of the acquisition cost of the goods is financed by the partly exempt business. Scheme comes in two guises, either: – a taxable connected person[1] acquires the goods and then leases them to a partly exempt trader, which uses the goods in the course of its business; or – a partly exempt trader sells or leases goods to a taxable connected party[1], which then leases them back to the trader.
5	Extended approval period	Where a retailer has received payment but the tax point is delayed until the end of the approval period.
6	Partly exempt groups bringing a supplier of outsourced services into the group	In order to minimise the input tax cost of supplies, a group may wish to bring a supplier within the VAT group. Scheme is notifiable if the supplier is either: – run for the benefit of a third party (i.e. where more than 50% of the benefits of ownership accrue to a third party); or – not consolidated within the group accounts of the person controlling the VAT group under generally accepted accounting practice.
7	An eligible body (¶8044) makes exempt supplies of education and profits are diverted to a non-eligible body	Educational services provided by eligible bodies are exempt. A normal company which provides education sets up a connected non-profit-making entity, which qualifies as an eligible body. The education is then provided through this new entity, so that the supply becomes exempt. The entity is charged for certain services[2] by the company so that the profits from the education business are diverted to the company. In this way the company still enjoys the profits but at a much lower VAT cost.
8	A non-eligible body makes taxable supplies of education and gifts the profits to an eligible body (¶8044)	Scheme increases the input tax recovery for an eligible body, which is supplying education to bodies which can recover VAT e.g. taxable businesses. The eligible body sets up another connected entity which is fully taxable and can distribute its profits. The new entity now provides the education which becomes a taxable supply, so input tax can be recovered. The eligible body makes supplies of certain services[2] to the entity which make up at least of 20% of the cost of making the educational supplies. The entity gifts or distributes its profits back to the eligible body.

Scheme number	Title	Details
9	Use of face value vouchers	Only applies to the supply of telecommunications, broadcasting or electronically supplied services (¶8024). A UK business makes a supply of these services to a connected[1] EU trader, which then makes a retail supply of those same services to an unregistered UK customer. The UK customer pays for the services using a face value voucher issued from outside the UK (but within the EU). The EU trader does not account for VAT on his supply anywhere in the EU or in the UK, because of the special place of supply rules which apply to these types of services.
10	Lease surrender and subsequent grant	This affects partly exempt tenants who incur VAT on their rent because their landlord has opted to tax the premises, where the building is subject to the capital goods scheme – that is, if the value is at least £250,000. The occupier of a leasehold building surrenders the opted lease but he remains in the building, because of the grant of a new lease. Under the new lease terms, he has the right to occupy at least 80% of the original area. However, this new lease is not subject to an option to tax, so the occupier ceases to incur VAT on his rental payments. Disclosure must be made where the amount of his VAT payable is reduced by at least 50% because of the regrant.

Note:
1. Persons are **connected** if they are either:
– members of the same group, including partnerships and unincorporated associations carrying on a trade; or
– connected to the same trust – that is, either a settlor, beneficiary or trustee – or hold shares in a company under the terms of the trust. A connected person would also be someone on whose behalf such shares are held.
2. **Certain services** means the supply of:
– a capital item to be used in the education business;
– staff;
– management services;
– administration services; or
– accountancy services.

Hallmarked schemes

There are more general reporting requirements for larger businesses, where a transaction is undertaken with the main purpose of gaining a tax advantage and includes any of the hallmarks listed below. **9246** SI 2004/1933 Sch 2 Notice 700/8 para 10

Failure to disclose will result in a fixed penalty of £5,000.

MEMO POINTS 1. **Tax avoidance** is defined as obtaining a VAT advantage, for example:
– VAT payable is less than it would have been;
– VAT repayable is more than it would have been;
– the difference in timing between when the customer accounts for input tax and when the supplier accounts for output tax is greater than it would have been; or
– the amount of irrecoverable input tax is reduced, where there are exempt supplies or non-business activities.
2. In general, where the arrangements would not have been implemented at all, or would have been carried out differently, if the tax advantage did not exist, it is likely that their **main purpose** is to obtain a tax advantage. However, where there are multiple ways of achieving a genuine commercial objective and the choice was made for reasons other than the VAT saving but a tax advantage is still obtained, it is unlikely that the main purpose test is met.

Hallmark	Details
Confidentiality condition	Condition prevents or limits the disclosure of how a scheme gives rise to a tax advantage. However, general confidentiality conditions relating to all advice given by a practitioner do not cause that advice to be treated as a disclosable scheme.
Sharing of tax advantage	Sharing the advantage with a promoter of the scheme[1] or another party to the scheme.

Hallmark	Details
Contingency fee payable on success of scheme	Payable to the promoter[1]. Employing an outsider to review previous input tax claims, where the fee is contingent on the amount of input tax refunded, is not obtaining a tax advantage.
Prepayments between connected persons[2]	Payments before the basic tax point (¶7902), or payments received before a continuous supply of goods or services is provided. The amount and timing of the prepayment is irrelevant.
Funding between connected persons[2]	By share subscriptions, the issue of securities or loans.
Offshore loops	Offshore routing of certain services[3] which are then used by the recipient to make a subsequent supply to a UK person, which is then either zero-rated, exempt, or treated as supplied outside the UK, so VAT is avoided in the UK.
Construction services between connected persons[2]	A business, which makes both taxable and exempt supplies, grants an interest in property, other than the first grant of an interest in either a dwelling, a building used for relevant residential or charitable purposes (¶8849), or a protected building (¶8902).
Use of face value vouchers with low redemption rates	Only where: – the issuer does not expect that at least 75% of the face value will be redeemed within 3 years of issue; or – the issuer and recipient are connected[2] (but not including members of the same VAT group (¶7807)).

Note:
1. A **promoter** is defined as a person who is in business supplying taxation services and:
– is responsible for the design of the scheme; or
– invites others to enter into contracts for the implementation of the scheme.
2. Persons are **connected** if they are either:
– members of the same group, including partnerships and unincorporated associations carrying on a trade; or
– connected to the same trust – that is, either a settlor, beneficiary or trustee – or hold shares in a company under the terms of the trust. A connected person would also be someone on whose behalf such shares are held.
3. The **affected services** are
a. the following:
– supplies made outside the UK that would be taxable if they were made within the UK;
– finance and insurance supplies made by a UK business to a customer who belongs outside the EU; and
– supplies of investment gold; or
b. services treated as supplied in the place where the recipient belongs (¶8016).

Notification

9248 Notice 700/8 paras 5, 8

The **deadline** for reporting details of a scheme is 30 days after the due date for filing the relevant VAT return (or the date of the relevant claim where a claim is made for the repayment of output tax, or an increased credit for input tax). For example, a person preparing a VAT return to 30 November will need to report by the next following 30 January.

There is no requirement for a business to state the **amount of tax advantage** obtained from using a scheme.

To report use of a **listed scheme**, a business should write to HMRC, stating the following:
- business name;
- business address;
- VAT registration number; and
- scheme number used.

The disclosure must be headed "Disclosure of use of listed scheme – Notification under paragraph 6(2) of Sch 11A to VATA 1994".

MEMO POINTS 1. The **postal address** where notifications should be sent is:
VAT Avoidance Disclosures Unit
Anti-Avoidance Group (Intelligence)
HMRC
1st Floor, 22 Kingsway
London
WC2B 6NR
Notifications sent elsewhere are invalid.
2. Notifications can be **emailed** to: vat.avoidance.disclosures.bst@hmrc.gsi.gov.uk

Larger businesses reporting **hallmarked** schemes must include the following information: 9249 Notice 700/8 para 8.3
a. which hallmark is involved;
b. how the scheme gives rise to a tax advantage, including:
– a description of the transaction;
– the sequence and timing involved; and
– the goods or services involved;
c. how the involvement of any party to the scheme helps to obtain the tax advantage; and
d. the VAT law relied upon for the tax advantage.

The disclosure must be headed "Disclosure of use of hallmarked scheme – Notification under paragraph 6(3) of Sch 11A to VATA 1994".

There is no need to report a scheme which already has a reference number, or which has already been notified.

Practitioners may voluntarily report schemes which they are involved in, by giving the same information as above. HMRC will then assign a reference number to that scheme. Any business subsequently using the scheme is not required to make any separate disclosure. Notice 700/8 para 9

SECTION 3

Payment of VAT

The VAT payment requirements **depend on** the size of a trader's annual VAT liability. For businesses with an annual **VAT liability of less than £2.3 million**, payment of tax due is usually made concurrently with the submission of the return. If the **annual VAT liability exceeds £2.3 million**, payments on account are required. 9250

Normal businesses

If submitting **paper returns**, payment may be made by the following methods: 9252 Notice 700 para 21
– electronically (e.g. Internet, telephone banking, BACS, CHAPS or bank giro transfer);
– cheque;
– postal order; or
– debit or credit card over the Internet (BillPay).

If the return is submitted **electronically**, payment must be made electronically. In this case payment may also be made by direct debit via the VAT Online service.

Traders can choose to pay by different methods in every quarter, without notifying HMRC of any change.

MEMO POINTS 1. **Compulsory electronic payment and filing** has now been introduced. All VAT-registered traders with a turnover of £100,000 or more, plus any traders newly registered since 1 April 2010, must submit their returns online and pay electronically. With effect from April 2012 all traders must both file and pay electronically.
2. It is possible to make payment in **euros**, although the return must still be completed in sterling, and not all banks offer every payment method in euros. The sterling amount received in HMRC's bank account will be calculated using the exchange rate ruling at the date of clearance. Hence there will inevitably be unders and overs every time. However, HMRC do not pass on any costs of conversion to the trader.
3. **Cheques refused** by the bank because of insufficient funds in the trader's bank account will not be presented by HMRC again. The trader must therefore cancel the old cheque and send a new one, and it is likely that the payment will be late.
4. **Incomplete payments** are allocated to the oldest VAT debt first.
5. If a business makes a **duplicate payment**, this will always be repaid, provided that the refund is claimed within 4 years of the date of the overpayment.
6. HMRC will **impose a fee**, equivalent to 1.4% of the payment due, when the taxpayer chooses to use a credit card over the Internet to discharge a VAT debt.
7. Cheque payments by post are treated by HMRC as received on the date when cleared funds reach HMRC's bank account.

9254 The **due date** for paying a VAT liability shown on a return is the same as the due date for submitting the return i.e. the end of the month following the last day of the VAT period.

If paying **electronically**, the due date is automatically extended by an extra 7 days, unless the trader is using the annual accounting scheme (¶8405), or is a large business (¶9255) and not submitting monthly returns. This extension only applies to payments which relate to returns.

If payment is made **late**, default interest (¶9258) will be charged and the trader may also be liable to a default surcharge penalty (¶9272).

If the trader is **unable to pay** all of the VAT due, he should contact HMRC immediately to explain the reason why. HMRC have discretion to agree a period in which payment can be made. The use of a post-dated cheque will automatically lead to a default (¶9272).

MEMO POINTS To encourage businesses to pay their VAT liability by direct debit, the 7-day extension applies as with other forms of electronic payment. However, there is an added **cash flow advantage** of paying by direct debit, as payment is not taken from the taxpayer's bank account until 3 days after the due date by which the return must be received. For example, A Ltd files its VAT return electronically for the period ended 31 July on 7 August. A Ltd is due to pay VAT of £10,000. The company pays its liability by direct debit, meaning payment is not collected by HMRC until 10 August. If A Ltd paid by BACS or any other electronic means, payment would have to reach HMRC by 7 August.

Large businesses

9255 SI 1995/2518 regs 45-48 Notice 700/60

Payments on account For businesses with an annual VAT liability in excess of £2.3 million, VAT payments must usually be made on account, in advance, via estimated monthly instalments, as notified by HMRC.

However, instead of paying on account, there are two **alternative** monthly payment mechanisms, as follows:
- paying the actual VAT due for each month (so February's VAT will be due on 31 March); or
- filing monthly VAT returns.

A business may **apply to be removed** from the payment on account regime at any time if its VAT liability for the year to the latest quarter end falls below £1.8 million.

MEMO POINTS 1. For this purpose, the **annual VAT liability** includes VAT arising from the following:
- returns;
- assessments;
- voluntary disclosures;
- imports; and
- goods transferred from a fiscal or customs warehouse.

The VAT liability is measured over the **basis period**, which is either:
- any year ending at any quarter end, which is relevant when determining when payments on account should commence or cease; or
- the reference year, which is used for calculating the payments during each VAT cycle on a continuing basis.

2. The **reference year** is a period of 12 months ending 6 months before the VAT cycle begins. The VAT cycle generally begins with the first VAT period beginning after 31 March in a calendar year, although a business may agree a different VAT cycle to coincide with its financial year.
3. Where a business opts to pay the **actual monthly amount due**, it must continue to pay on this basis for at least a year. Where a refund is shown as due for a particular month, no repayment will be made, as HMRC will only make any necessary repayment at the end of the VAT period. Opting to file monthly returns would avoid this problem.
4. If choosing to submit **monthly returns**, this must also continue for at least 12 months. The 7-day extension for paying electronically will apply as for smaller businesses (¶9254).

EXAMPLE

1. **12-month test** A Ltd, which submits returns for quarters ending 30 April, 31 July etc, had a VAT liability for the year ended 31 October 2010 of £1.8 million. However, the VAT liability for the year to 30 April 2011 is £2.4 million, which makes B Ltd a "very large business".

2. **Reference year test** B Ltd is a very large business and had a VAT liability of £2.5 million for the year ended 30 September. This liability will be used to calculate the payments on account for the following VAT cycle beginning on the 1 April following the year end.

Operation The **amount** of each payment on account is determined by HMRC, and is generally 1/24th of the annual VAT liability (excluding VAT on imports and warehoused goods) for the reference year. 9256

When the business **becomes very large**, the annual VAT liability will be measured in the basis period. The payments then remain the same until that particular VAT cycle ends.

For the **first quarter** in which a business falls within the scheme, an interim payment must be made by the end of the third month of the return period, with the balance of the VAT for that quarter being due on the normal date (i.e. the end of the month following the return period). For subsequent quarters, interim payments are due at the end of the second and third months of the quarter, with the balance being payable on the normal due date.

For **subsequent VAT cycles**, the liability in the previous reference year is used to calculate the payments on account. If the VAT liability in the last 12 months (measured to any quarter end) varies by at least 20% from that of the basis period, the payments will be adjusted. However, the business must wait to be notified by HMRC before making any changes to the amounts paid.

Return periods	Reference year ending	Determines instalments for VAT cycle beginning
June/September/December/March	30 September	Following 1 April
July/October/January/April	31 October	Following 1 May
August/November/February/May	30 November	Following 1 June

EXAMPLE A Ltd has been notified by HMRC that, with effect from 1 April, it must start paying VAT in instalments.
For the VAT period to 30 June, an instalment is required by 30 June, with the balance of the period's liability being due by 31 July.
For the VAT period to 30 September, instalments are required by 31 August and 30 September, with the balance of the period's liability being due by 31 October.
Monthly payments are required thereafter: two instalment payments followed by the balancing payment for the quarter, continuing until the company is no longer required to pay by instalments.

Payment method Payments must be **made by** electronic transfer or standing order and instalment payments must **clear by** the last working day of the month for which they are due. If the business has non-standard return periods, the payments must clear by the last working day before the due date. 9257

A business which **fails to pay** any instalment or balancing payment by the due date is in default and may be subject to a default surcharge (¶9272); HMRC may also require monthly returns.

Default interest

Default interest **will be charged when** any of the following has occurred: 9258 s 74 VATA 1994 Notice 700/43
- an underdeclaration of output tax or over-claim of input tax has been made on a VAT return;
- a trader fails to submit a return, resulting in an assessment which is too low; or
- a trader discloses an error in excess of the error correction threshold (¶9236).

If there is **no overall loss of VAT**, there may be no charge, as interest should only represent commercial restitution. For example, where output tax has not been declared but input tax could have been claimed by a third party but it has not been, interest may not be levied.

The **rates** of interest are shown at ¶9989.

Repayments

If a repayment is due for a VAT period (i.e. input tax exceeds output tax), HMRC will usually refund it to the business, provided that no other VAT debt is due and the amount exceeds £1. Repayments are generally made within 10 days of the submission of the return. 9260 s 33 VATA 1994

VAT repayments relating to **errors** are subject to special rules (¶9226).

HMRC may **withhold** the repayment if:
– VAT returns for previous periods are outstanding;
– the trader fails, when requested, to produce evidence supporting the input tax claimed; or
– the business fails to provide security (¶9329) which HMRC believe is required for the protection of the revenue.

MEMO POINTS 1. If HMRC make a repayment **in error**, an assessment may be issued to recover the excess repayment. Any VAT assessed in this way carries interest. If the over-repayment arose due to dishonesty by the business, civil penalties may also be due. See ¶9316 for details of the time limits that apply to assessments by HMRC.
2. If a repayment relates to a **disputed point of law**, HMRC may issue an assessment to negate the claim (¶9316). If out of time to make such an assessment, monies will only be repaid to the trader if he signs an undertaking to return any payment if it turns out (usually once case law is resolved) that the repayment was not actually due.

9262
s 79 VATA 1994
Notice 700 para 21.6

Repayment supplement Where a repayment due to a trader is **delayed**, HMRC will pay a repayment supplement, provided that certain criteria are satisfied.

The **amount** of supplement payable is the greater of £50 or 5% of the VAT payable.

However, supplement is **never due** in relation to refunds arising from:
– bad debt relief claims (¶8350);
– claims related to services received after deregistration;
– amounts notified by HMRC as overdeclared (perhaps in response to a voluntary disclosure);
– the DIY housebuilders' scheme (¶8862); or
– refunds paid to EU traders (¶9146).

However, in these cases statutory interest may be payable instead.

MEMO POINTS The **criteria** for supplement to become payable are as follows:
– the return was submitted by the due date;
– the repayment is made more than 30 days after the date on which VAT for that return period would have been due (or the date the return was submitted, if later); and
– the amount shown in the tax return is not overstated by more than £250 or 2% of the amount due.
The 30-day clock may be stopped while HMRC make reasonable enquiries into the trader's claim.

9264
s 78 VATA 1994

Statutory interest Statutory interest is intended to give commercial restitution to the trader, who would otherwise have had use of the money he has mistakenly paid to HMRC.

It is **only payable** when repayment supplement is not due, where an error by HMRC (even one made in good faith) has caused a trader to either:
– account for output tax which was not due;
– fail to claim eligible input tax;
– pay any other VAT due (e.g. import VAT); or
– suffer delay in receiving a repayment.

A written claim must be made within 4 years.

MEMO POINTS 1. In the direct tax case of *Sempra Metals Ltd v HMRC* [2007] it was held that the taxpayer was entitled to **compound interest** on tax paid early. The rationale behind the decision was that a compound interest calculation fairly reflected the commercial reality of how interest would have been calculated.
2. In a case concerning the availability of compound interest on claims for overpaid VAT, the High Court has held that businesses are in principle entitled to compound interest, rather than simple interest, on overpaid VAT. However, this applies only if the overpayments were caused by a breach of a provision of EU law which has direct effect in the UK. *F J Chalke Ltd and another v HMRC* [2009]
3. The issue has now been referred to the CJEU, so may not finally be settled for some considerable time. *Littlewoods Retail Ltd and others v HMRC* [2010]

SECTION 4

Penalties

Failure to comply with any of its administrative obligations will render a business liable to a fiscal penalty. The most common penalty is default surcharge, which is imposed for late rendering of returns or late payment of VAT due. 9270

Where an offence could give rise to multiple civil penalties, only one such penalty may be charged, generally the higher one.

However, if HMRC decide to instigate a criminal prosecution (¶9304) civil penalties (other than the default surcharge) will not be levied.

There is now one **harmonised penalty system** across the main taxes (see ¶9780), including VAT, which applies to:
- inaccuracies in returns or other documents;
- deliberately supplying false information to, or withholding information from, another person; and
- failing to notify HMRC of an under-assessment of tax.

The amounts levied will be a percentage of the potential lost tax revenue, on a scale according to the seriousness of the offence.

The inaccuracy penalties therefore replace the VAT misdeclaration penalty (see previous issues of *Tax Memo*) and, in some cases, may replace the civil evasion penalty (¶9290).

MEMO POINTS For periods beginning on or after 1 April 2010, Finance Act 2008 introduced new harmonised penalties for **failure to notify** a relevant obligation, such as a requirement to register, or notify a change in trading activity, and for the **issue of unauthorised VAT invoices**. The most frequent circumstance when the failure to notify penalty will apply is where a business exceeds the VAT threshold and does not inform HMRC at the right time.

Naming of tax defaulters

Finance Act 2009 provides the power to HMRC to **publish the names** of both corporate and individual taxpayers who: 9271 s 94 FA 2009
- are penalised for deliberately understating tax due, or overstating claims or losses of more than £25,000;
- deliberately fail to notify HMRC when required to do so, leading to a loss of tax of more than £25,000; or
- are penalised for deliberately committing certain VAT offences, leading to a loss of tax of more than £25,000.

Names will not be published of those who make a full unprompted disclosure or a full prompted disclosure within the required time. Details will be published quarterly within 1 year of the penalty becoming final and will remain on HMRC's website for 12 months.

1. Default surcharge

A business is in default if it fails to submit its VAT return or pay its VAT liability by the due date. Even where HMRC's prior agreement has been obtained to delay a VAT payment, this will still be a default. 9272 s 59 VATA 1994 Notice 700/50

The **first** default by a business will result in the issue of a surcharge liability notice. The notice is valid for a period of 12 months, starting from the day of the notice (the default period).

A **further** default during the period of the surcharge liability notice will result in the issue of a surcharge liability notice extension and possibly a surcharge assessment. The surcharge period will be extended until 12 months after the end of the latest default period.

MEMO POINTS 1. For **new businesses** with annual turnover of up to £150,000, no notice is issued in respect of the first default Instead, help and support are offered. Notice 700/50 para 3.2

2. From a date to be announced, new regimes will apply separately to failures to file returns on time and to make payment on time. These penalties are described at ¶9855 and ¶9857.

Amount

9274 Notice 700/50 para 3.3

After the issue of a surcharge liability notice, a surcharge assessment will be issued in respect of any subsequent default occurring during the default period.

The surcharge is the **greater of** £30 or a percentage of the VAT outstanding at the due date, as follows:
- first late payment during surcharge period – 2%;
- second late payment – 5%;
- third late payment – 10%; and
- fourth and subsequent late payments – 15%.

Notice 700/50 para 3.5

A surcharge assessment **will not be issued** where:
a. the return shows nil VAT due, or a repayment;
b. the return is late but the VAT is paid on time; or
c. the amount of surcharge due at 2% or 5% is less than £400.

In **a**. and **b**. above, a default will be recorded and the surcharge period extended, although the rate of surcharge will not be increased.

s 59A VATA 1994

MEMO POINTS Where the business is required to make **payments on account** of its VAT liability (¶9255), the late payment of any interim or balancing payment is a default. A surcharge assessment will only be issued after the balancing payment is due, and will be calculated on the total amount of late VAT for each payment, subject to a maximum of the VAT due as shown on the return.

s 108 FA 2009

Where a taxpayer is in default but before the date he becomes liable to a surcharge he has requested and been granted **permission to defer** the tax, he will not be liable to a penalty. This is subject to the taxpayer complying with any conditions of the deferral agreement, including paying any tax due by the end of the deferral period.

EXAMPLE A Ltd has a poor compliance record. The following table summarises its compliance history since it first registered for VAT on 1 April 2009. All VAT payments are made by cheque.

VAT period end	Due date	Return submitted	VAT paid	Default?	Action	Surcharge
30 June 09	31 July 09	4 Aug 09	£2,000 4 Aug 09	Yes	Issue surcharge liability notice to 30 June 10	n/a
30 Sept 09	31 Oct 09	31 Oct 09	£1,200 31 Oct 09	No		n/a
31 Dec 09	31 Jan 10	31 Jan 10	£6,000 3 Feb 10	Yes	Surcharge – 2% Extend surcharge period to 31 Dec 10	£120 – not collected as below £400
31 Mar 10	30 Apr 10	5 May 10	£3,225 30 Apr 10	Yes	Extend surcharge period to 31 Mar 11	£0 VAT paid by due date
30 June 10	31 July 10	30 July 10	£10,000 10 Aug 10	Yes	Surcharge – 5% Extend surcharge period to 30 June 11	£500
30 Sept 10	31 Oct 10	1 Nov 10	£250 1 Nov 10	Yes	Surcharge – 10% Extend surcharge period to 30 Sept 11	£30 (minimum)
31 Dec 10	31 Jan 11	30 Jan 11	£500 30 Jan 11	No		n/a
31 Mar 11	30 Apr 11	28 Apr 11	£1,000 2 May 11	Yes	Surcharge – 15% Extend surcharge period to 31 Mar 12	£150
30 June 11	31 July 11	8 Aug 11	£4,000 8 Aug 11	Yes	Surcharge – 15% Extend surcharge period to 30 June 12	£600

Appeals

A business may appeal (¶9920) against a surcharge assessment within 30 days on any of the following **grounds**: 9276 Notice 700/50 para 5
- it has evidence that the return and payment were sent in sufficient time to arrive by the due date;
- it believes the surcharge is at the wrong rate;
- it believes part payments have not been taken into account correctly;
- it has a reasonable excuse for the default;
- no surcharge liability notice was received;
- the surcharge liability notice was incorrect; or
- there are exceptional circumstances.

MEMO POINTS The concept of a **reasonable excuse** has been tested at VAT tribunals on numerous occasions, but each case is different and the decisions of tribunals are not binding for future cases.

HMRC have given the following **examples** of where a business may have a reasonable excuse: Notice 700/50 para 4
- sudden illness of the person responsible for completion of the VAT returns where there is no other person capable of completing the return;
- computer breakdown just before or during the preparation of the VAT return;
- an unforeseen crisis (for example, the unexpected withdrawal or reduction of an overdraft facility, or a burglary); or
- the loss of a key member of staff at short notice.

Whatever the situation, HMRC expect a business to take all possible steps to **make alternative arrangements** for the completion of the VAT return and payment of the VAT liability as soon as possible.

By law, a simple lack of funds, or reliance on another person who fails to perform a task accurately or without delay, cannot be a reasonable excuse for late filing or payment.

2. Dishonest conduct

If a business evades VAT through dishonest conduct, a civil **evasion** penalty may be charged. 9290 s 60 VATA 1994
The penalty provisions for giving HMRC an inaccurate document (e.g. a return, statement or declaration) which leads to an understatement of liability or an overstatement of entitlement to a repayment are covered by the harmonised penalty for inaccuracies (¶9784). The penalty provisions for dishonest conduct contained in VATA 1994 ss 60 and 61 are, however, retained in respect of conduct involving dishonesty which does not relate to an inaccuracy in a document.

In cases of fraud and cases where the business does not cooperate with HMRC, criminal proceedings may be taken as an alternative (¶9304).

Otherwise, the **maximum penalty** which may be charged under ss 60 and 61 is 100% of the VAT evaded (i.e. the arrears).

MEMO POINTS If a company is liable to a penalty for the dishonest evasion of VAT due wholly or partly to the **dishonesty of a director** or managing officer, HMRC may issue a notice specifying that all or part of the penalty will be payable by the named officer. s 61 VATA 1994

3 Other civil penalties

Circumstances

The following table summarises the other civil penalties which may arise. Whilst several of these are no longer current, penalties tend to attach to historic events discovered later, so they are listed here in case readers encounter them in respect of past periods. 9292

Offence	Penalty	Reference
Failure to notify liability to register	£50 or the following % of VAT for period by which registration was delayed: – 9 months or less, 5%; – over 9 and up to 18 months, 10%; or – over 18 months, 15%. For periods from 1 April 2010, see ¶9846.	s 67 VATA 1994
Unauthorised issue of invoices	Greater of £50 or 15% of VAT shown on invoices. For offences on or after 1 April 2010, see ¶9846.	s 67 VATA 1994
Failure to: – notify cessation of liability to be registered; – maintain the required records; or – produce records	For offences after issue of warning notice, penalty of £50, or daily penalty (max 100 days) if greater, based on number of failures in previous 2 years: – no previous failures, £5 per day; – one previous failure, £10 per day; – two or more previous failures, £15 per day.	s 69 VATA 1994
Failure to preserve records for the prescribed period	£500	s 69 VATA 1994
Issue of incorrect tax certificate relating to transactions which are zero-rated or reduced-rated (e.g. for certain property transactions)	Difference between tax charged and tax due	s 62(1) VATA 1994
Preparation of incorrect zero-rating certificate re goods acquired from other EU member states	VAT actually chargeable on acquisition	s 62(1A) VATA 1994
Failure by non-taxable person to notify acquisition of a new means of transport or goods subject to excise duty	£50 or the following % of VAT due on acquisition for period by which registration was delayed: – 9 months or less, 5%; – over 9 and up to 18 months, 10%; – over 18 months, 15%. For offences on or after 1 April 2010, see ¶9846.	s 67 VATA 1994
Breach of walking possession agreement (not in Scotland)	50% of VAT in respect of which agreement issued	s 68 VATA 1994
Breaches of regulatory provisions involving failure to file VAT return or pay VAT by due date	For offences after issue of warning notice, penalty of £50, or daily penalty (max 100 days) if greater, based on number of failures in previous 2 years: – no previous failures, £5 per day or 1/6% of VAT due; – one previous failure, £10 per day or 1/3% of VAT due; – two or more previous failures, £15 per day or 1/2% of VAT due	s 69 VATA 1994
Other breaches of regulatory provisions	For offences after issue of warning notice, penalty of £50, or daily penalty (max 100 days) if greater, based on number of failures in previous 2 years: – no previous failures, £5 per day; – one previous failure, £10 per day; – two or more previous failures, £15 per day	s 69 VATA 1994

Mitigation

HMRC have the power to mitigate a penalty and will usually do so unless a business fails to cooperate. 9294 s 70 VATA 1994 Notice 700/41

The penalties which **cannot** be mitigated are the:
- default surcharge;
- regulatory penalties;
- penalty for providing incorrect tax certificates;
- penalties in relation to sales lists; and
- penalty for breach of a walking possession agreement.

In most cases the **maximum reduction** will be 80%, unless there are exceptional circumstances, such as a full and unprompted voluntary disclosure.

The following **factors** are taken into account:
- how the offence occurred, and whether there are any compassionate grounds, or unforeseen events which explain the failure;
- the complexity and frequency of the transaction compared to the size of business; and
- the extent of cooperation, such as providing an early and truthful explanation of why the arrears arose and their true extent, and accepting and meeting responsibilities by supplying information promptly, including full written disclosure, attending meetings and answering questions.

From 1 April 2010 the above mitigation provisions no longer apply to penalties imposed for:
- failure to notify a liability to register;
- errors or inaccuracies on returns or other documents; and
- issue of unauthorised VAT invoices.

For details of how taxpayers can reduce these penalties, see ¶9810+.

Taxpayers' rights

Civil evasion penalties must be issued no later than 20 years after the conduct giving rise to the penalty has ceased. 9296

Appeals against penalty notices can be made within 45 days from the date the notice was given. HMRC will then have a further 45 days to confirm, withdraw or vary their decision. Subsequent appeals can be made to the tribunal (¶9920).

MEMO POINTS When considering whether to confirm, withdraw or **vary their decision**, HMRC or the tribunal will not take into account:
- insufficiency of funds;
- the fact that there has been no significant loss of VAT/duty; or
- the fact that the person acted in good faith.

4. Overseas issues

EC sales lists (ESLs)

Failure to submit If a business fails to submit an ESL (¶8978, ¶9118) within the required time, HMRC will issue a notice of default. If the position is not rectified within 14 days of the date of issue of the notice, the business is liable to a penalty. 9298 s 66 VATA 1994

A further penalty may be issued without notice if the business fails to submit an ESL within 12 months of a previous default.

A business is **not in default** if it can prove that the ESL was submitted in circumstances where it was reasonable to expect that it would be received by HMRC by the appropriate date. In addition, a business having a reasonable excuse (¶9276) is not in default.

The **amount** of the penalty is as follows:
- initial default which is rectified within 14 days, no penalty;
- 1st subsequent default, the greater of £50 or £5 per day (maximum £500);

– 2nd subsequent default, the greater of £50 or £10 per day (maximum £1,000); and
– 3rd and subsequent defaults, the greater of £50 or £15 per day (maximum £1,500).

9299 s 65 VATA 1994 **Inaccurate information** The three **main types** of inaccuracy are:
– details which are not valid, such as an incorrect VAT registration number;
– factual inaccuracies; and
– missing data.

HMRC may issue a **written warning** if a business submits an inaccurate ESL.

If, **within 2 years** of the warning, a further inaccurate ESL is submitted, a notice will be issued identifying the inaccurate return and advising that penalties may be charged in future.

A penalty of £100 may be charged if the business submits a **second inaccurate** ESL within 2 years of the receipt of the notice, or of an earlier penalty in this respect.

The penalty will **not be charged** if the business can show a reasonable excuse (¶9276), or if the business is convicted of a criminal offence in this respect.

Import and export duties

9300 HMRC can impose civil penalties if a trader either:
– fraudulently evades VAT/duty on import or export (civil evasion penalty); or
– contravenes any duty, obligation, requirement or condition in relation to import or export (civil non-evasion penalty).

9301 s 25 FA 2003 If a trader **fraudulently evades**:
– customs duty;
– customs export/import duty;
– import VAT; or
– customs duty of a preferential tariff country,

HMRC can impose a **maximum** civil evasion penalty up to the amount of VAT/duty evaded.

However, a civil evasion penalty **cannot be levied** if:
– criminal proceedings and/or penalties have already been instigated; or
– a non-evasion penalty has already been issued.

A civil evasion penalty can be issued to an individual director/managing officer of a company, if HMRC feel the individual has acted dishonestly. The company would only then be liable for the balance (if any) of the amount specified in the penalty notice.

9302 s 26 FA 2003 If a trader **contravenes any duty**, obligation, requirement or condition in relation to:
– customs duty;
– customs export/import duty;
– import VAT; or
– customs duty of a preferential tariff country,

HMRC can impose a civil non-evasion penalty up to a **maximum** of £2,500.

However, a civil non-evasion penalty **cannot be imposed** if:
– criminal proceedings and/or penalties have already been instigated;
– a penalty has been issued under a different legal provision; or
– the individual has a reasonable excuse (¶9276) for not meeting his obligations.

5. Criminal penalties

9304 s 72 VATA 1994 Generally, a criminal prosecution is only instigated in serious fraud cases. Whether a case is serious or not may depend on the amount of VAT involved, the identities of the persons involved, or the nature of the offence. The involvement of a business adviser (for example, an accountant or a lawyer) in evasion is likely to make it a serious offence, as is evasion of VAT totalling more than £75,000 in a 3-year period.

Criminal proceedings may be instigated against a business where one of the following **offences** has been committed:
- fraudulent evasion of VAT;
- production or use of false documents and statements;
- being a party to a transaction in the knowledge that evasion of VAT is intended;
- bribery and obstruction of HMRC officer(s);
- failure to provide security where required; or
- any conduct which must have involved one of the above offences, although the particulars of the offence are not known.

Summary

The amount of the penalty charged as a result of criminal proceedings will **depend on** 9306
whether the case is dealt with by summary conviction (i.e. in the magistrates' court) or by indictment (i.e. at crown court).

<table>
<tr><th>Offence</th><th>Summary conviction</th><th>Conviction on indictment</th></tr>
<tr><td>Fraudulent evasion of VAT</td><td rowspan="3">Penalty equal to the greater of £5,000 or three times the VAT; and/or prison sentence of up to 6 months.</td><td rowspan="3">Penalty of any amount; and/or prison sentence up to 7 years.</td></tr>
<tr><td>Production of false documentation or making false declarations</td></tr>
<tr><td>Conduct which must have involved an offence</td></tr>
<tr><td>Bribery and obstruction of officers</td><td>Penalty of £2,500; and/or prison sentence of up to 6 months.</td><td>Penalty of any amount; and/or prison sentence of up to 7 years.</td></tr>
<tr><td>Being a party to a transaction in the knowledge that evasion of VAT is intended</td><td>Penalty equal to the greater of £5,000 or three times the VAT.</td><td>n/a</td></tr>
<tr><td>Failure to provide security where required</td><td>Penalty equal to the greater of £5,000 or three times the VAT.</td><td>n/a</td></tr>
</table>

SECTION 5

HMRC's powers

The following paragraphs summarise the existing powers HMRC have in relation to VAT. For 9308
details of the additional powers which came into force on 1 April 2009 under the harmonisation of HMRC powers, see ¶9860.

1. Assessments

HMRC have power to assess VAT which they believe to be due from taxable persons, non- 9310
taxable persons and fiscal warehouse-keepers. Generally assessments are issued in relation to:
- the amount of VAT due;
- notification of interest and penalties (including default surcharge); or
- overpaid interest and/or repayments.

There are two types of assessment: central assessments, which are automatically generated by the central VAT computer system when a VAT return is not rendered; and officer assessments, which are raised manually by VAT officers.

Details of assessments to recover VAT in special situations can be found in *VAT Memo*.

Time limits

9311 An assessment must normally be made **not later** than 2 years after the end of the VAT period to which it relates. However, an assessment can be made later if it is made within 1 year of evidence of facts which HMRC consider sufficient to justify making the assessment coming to their knowledge. The 2-year time limit is then **extended** to:
a. 4 years; or
b. 20 years, where a person:
– or a person acting on that person's behalf, has deliberately brought about a tax loss, or failed to notify HMRC of the person's liability to register or account for VAT;
– knowingly participated in a transaction intended to bring about a tax loss;
– issued invoices whilst unauthorised;
– failed to comply with a notification obligation;
– dishonestly evaded VAT; or
– has been convicted of fraud.

Assessment for VAT due

9312 s 73(1) VATA 1994 This type of assessment commonly arises when an incorrect or no return is submitted, or as a result of a visit from HMRC. The amount on the assessment will stand as a Crown debt unless the assessment is withdrawn or reduced.

Additional assessments can also arise from the **receipt of information**, resulting from internal liaison within HMRC, or voluntary disclosure.

Assessment of interest and penalties

9314 s 76(1) VATA 1994 An assessment which notifies interest and penalties may be combined with an assessment showing the amount of VAT due.

Where interest is shown as accruing on a daily basis, the assessment must show the date to which interest has been calculated.

Excess repayments of VAT

9316 s 73(2) VATA 1994 Excess repayments or overpayments are dealt with by the issue of an assessment for the amount due to HMRC.

Where a trader makes a claim for **overstated output tax** which has been repaid by HMRC, but was not due to be repaid, an assessment can be raised within the time limits described at ¶9311.

Where a taxpayer has made a claim for **input tax** which is later discovered to have been erroneous, an assessment can be raised within the same time limits.

Business Brief 25/04 MEMO POINTS 1. In relation to this type of assessment:
a. an assessment will not be issued which relies on a court judgment as evidence of facts;
b. where a past recovery assessment relied on a court judgment, the recovery of VAT was properly due because a mistake of law was being rectified, so the assessment stands, subject to an appeals process;
c. where an assessment is made which is technically flawed (such as being for the wrong VAT period or out of time), it will not be withdrawn and no repayment will be made.
2. The **prescribed accounting period** for these purposes only will be the VAT accounting period of the taxpayer in which the repayment is made by HMRC to the taxpayer.

EXAMPLE A Ltd submits a VAT return for the period ended 31 March 2010. A Ltd is due a repayment of £15,000 which HMRC pays on 15 May 2010. During a control visit on 20 May 2011 it is discovered that A Ltd was not entitled to recover £10,000 of the input tax it had claimed. HMRC have until the later of 1 year of being in full possession of the facts (20 May 2012), or 2 years from the end of the prescribed accounting period to raise an assessment. The prescribed accounting period is the period ended 30 June 2010, as this was the period in which the repayment was made. HMRC therefore have until 30 June 2012 to make the assessment.

Procedure

The **usual practice** is for HMRC to write to the taxpayer in advance of issuing an assessment, detailing the reasons for and the calculation of the assessment. Correspondence which occurs between the local VAT office and the taxpayer can sometimes resolve the situation to the satisfaction of both sides. 9317

Comment On receipt of an assessment it is important that the business checks its **validity**, including all manual entries, dates, the VAT registration number, and the name and address of the person who is the subject of the assessment. HMRC are required to make assessments to the best of their judgment which, being necessarily subjective, often leads to disagreement with the taxpayer.

Appeals

The **main areas** on which an appeal can be heard include: 9318 ss 82-85 VATA 1994
- registration and cancellation of registration, including directions against business splitting;
- the quantum and timing of assessments;
- the VAT liability of a supply;
- input tax claims and bad debt claims;
- refusal to allow use of a retail scheme, cash accounting scheme or flat rate scheme;
- penalties, interest, and security;
- claims for repayment; and
- refusal of an application for, or change to, a group registration.

For further details of the appeal system see ¶9920.

2. Other powers

Summary

HMRC have extensive powers in relation to VAT to require the provision of information, records and to inspect premises. From 1 April 2009 Finance Act 2008 brought their inspection powers with respect to other taxes into line with those which already existed for VAT, and consolidated a range of existing information powers. For details of the new powers of inspection, which came into force on 1 April 2009, see ¶9862. 9322

Action	¶¶
Assurance visits	¶9324
Access to information	¶9327
Provision of security	¶9329
Distress proceedings	¶9331
Joint and several liability	¶9332

Assurance visits

As VAT is a self-assessed tax, HMRC check taxpayers' compliance by carrying out assurance visits. 9324 Sch 36 para 10 FA 2008

The **frequency** with which a particular business will receive an assurance visit will depend on the nature and size of the business, as well as its VAT compliance record. A business with a good compliance history will generally receive fewer visits than a business with a bad track record.

During a visit HMRC will expect to be able to inspect the VAT records and other business records, and ask questions of the person responsible for the VAT. If the business has any queries about VAT issues, there is an opportunity for the position to be explained and any problems resolved. 9325

A visit will usually be arranged in advance with a proposed agenda and 24 hours' notice will be given. However, in some circumstances HMRC may visit unannounced.

If any **errors** come to light as a result of the visit, HMRC will explain why any adjustments are required and seek agreement from the business. If the business does not agree with the proposed adjustment and the position cannot be resolved with the visiting officer, the local VAT office should be notified in writing.

Access to information

9327 CH 20250 Sch 36 FA 2008

HMRC's powers include the following, to monitor and control VAT compliance.

a. The right to **enter and inspect business premises**, including an individual's private residence, if it is used wholly or partly for business purposes. A warrant may be obtained to enter premises by force, if necessary, where an offence involving fraud is suspected.

HMRC also have the right to:
– **mark** any goods inspected with an official stamp; and
– record details of goods by any means (including **electronic scanning** of barcodes).

Although this last provision is really aimed at combating missing trader fraud (¶8186), traders may be required to unpack goods, etc, which may lead to increased costs.

Sch 36 FA 2008 **b.** The power to require persons to **produce documents and information** in connection with any business activities and also copy or remove any documents required in connection with the trader's VAT position. HMRC specifically have the right to order the production of documents as a condition for making a repayment of VAT or allowing a credit.

Sch 36 FA 2008 **c.** The power to issue legal notices requiring persons, including third parties, to provide information or produce documents.

Sch 11 para 11 VATA 1994 **d.** The power to inspect any **computer** used in the production of a document required for VAT purposes. An order may be obtained to allow access to any recorded information (e.g. computer disks, tapes, etc) where it is suspected that an offence has been, or is being, committed. Under an order HMRC can take copies of, make extracts from, or remove such information.

Sch 11 para 8 VATA 1994 **e.** Where **fraud is suspected**, HMRC may take samples of goods in order to ascertain how they are to be treated for VAT purposes. Such samples must be returned in good condition and within a reasonable time, otherwise HMRC must pay compensation.

MEMO POINTS 1. In relation to **d.**, **samples** may only be taken from:
– a person who supplies goods to, or acquires goods from, another EU member state; or
– a fiscal warehouse-keeper (¶9018).

2. **Gaming machines** may be required to be opened in order to identify the value of taxable supplies.

Provision of security

9329 Sch 11 para 4 VATA 1994

Where HMRC perceive **a threat to the collection of VAT**, they may require a person to provide security.

The **amount** of security required will generally be equivalent to 6 months' VAT (or 4 months' if monthly returns are made) but may be higher. The security must be lodged with HMRC in the form of a banker's draft, cash or a guarantee from an approved financial institution. These provisions are trader-specific and limit action to current and future VAT liabilities of a specific business.

HMRC are also able to demand security from businesses which, despite warnings, **continue to trade** with other businesses or individuals that habitually evade VAT (by, for example, using VAT registration numbers of other businesses, going "missing", or becoming insolvent owing VAT). Under these provisions HMRC can demand security proportionate to the total VAT at risk in the supply chain. They cannot, however, require security from a person for payment of VAT by another party with whom that person is not jointly and severally liable.

Distress proceedings

The levy of distress (also known as distraint) is the process by which HMRC take possession of a trader's goods or chattels, sell them and set the receipts against his outstanding VAT liability. **9331** SI 1997/1431

Distraint is often the first type of formal recovery **action** taken by HMRC, as it is quick, cost-efficient and effective. In many cases the threat of distraint results in traders paying the outstanding VAT, to avoid the inconvenience, embarrassment or cost which distraint might cause. There are rules governing the **items** which may be removed.

A similar provision, known as diligence, applies under Scottish law. This allows recovery by means of an earnings arrestment.

Joint and several liability

This is a power which enables HMRC to collect VAT from any trader involved in a fraudulent supply chain, in relation to affected goods, where one of the traders in the chain has disappeared without accounting for VAT (known as missing trader fraud). The ECJ has ruled that this measure is supported in European law. *HMRC v Federation of Technological Industries and others* [2006] **9332** s 77A VATA 1994 Notice 726

However, the following situations are **excluded**, where: Notice 726 para 4.9
- VAT is unpaid because of a genuine bad debt or business failure; or
- the business purchases the goods for its own use and not for resale.

MEMO POINTS The **affected goods** are:
- phones, computer equipment, or similar goods; and
- satellite navigation systems and electronic goods used for leisure, amusement or entertainment.

Where a trader receives a supply of affected goods and he either knew or had reasonable grounds to suspect that some or all of the VAT payable in respect of that supply (or an earlier or subsequent supply of those goods) would go unpaid, HMRC can serve notice on him stating that he is jointly and severally liable with the supplier for an amount of unpaid VAT. This unpaid VAT will be subject to recovery proceedings. **9333**

There is a presumption that the trader had knowledge or grounds for suspicion where the **price** he paid for the goods was less than:
- the lowest open market price; or
- the price payable on any previous supply of those goods.

MEMO POINTS 1. The **amount of VAT payable** is the lesser of: Notice 726 para 2.2
- the VAT chargeable on the supply; and
- the amount of VAT due from the supplier taking into account any input tax deduction and repayments due from HMRC.

2. Before the notice of liability is served, a **notification letter** is sent giving the trader 21 days to explain why the price paid for the goods is legitimately low.
3. The trader can ask for reconsideration and lodge an **appeal** against a notice.
4. For the **input tax implications** of being involved in this type of supply chain, see ¶8192 and ¶8194.
5. HMRC can extend the circumstances in which a person is presumed to have reasonable grounds for suspecting that VAT will go unpaid elsewhere in the supply chain.

The only **protection** that a trader can invoke is that he has completed burdensome due diligence procedures, or that there is a legitimate reason for the low price which is unconnected with fraud. **9334**

MEMO POINTS The **due diligence** requires the trader to have reviewed all of the following issues: Notice 726 para 8
a. undertaking reasonable commercial checks to consider the legitimacy of customers or suppliers e.g. the supplier's trading history;
b. undertaking reasonable checks to ensure the commercial viability of the transaction e.g. considering whether there is a market for this type of goods;
c. undertaking reasonable checks to ensure the goods will be as described by the supplier;
d. checking the validity of the supplier e.g. verifying VAT registration details with HMRC and obtaining some form of trade or credit reference; and
e. retaining additional paperwork, such as purchase orders, delivery notes, airway bills and inspection reports.

PART 8

Stamp taxes

Stamp taxes
Summary

The numbers cross-refer to paragraphs.

CHAPTER 1 Stamp duty land tax

CHAPTER 2 Stamp duty

CHAPTER 3 Stamp duty reserve tax

CHAPTER 4 Specific business issues

CHAPTER 1

Stamp duty land tax

OUTLINE ¶¶

9340 s 42 FA 2003 **Stamp duty land tax** (SDLT) is charged as a percentage of the amount paid when land or property is bought or transferred. It applies to transactions involving land situated in the UK. The **regime applies** regardless of where the transaction is executed, where the parties are located or whether the transfer is effected by a legal document or otherwise.

This chapter deals with SDLT issues in general. For specific situations involving partnerships, groups and special reliefs, see ¶9720+.

Errors on land transaction returns which were due to be filed on or after 1 April 2010, where the return relates to a tax period beginning on or after 1 April 2009, are subject to the harmonised error penalties regime (¶9784). Provisions in Finance Act 2009 extended HMRC's powers in relation to information and inspection (¶9862+) to the administration of SDLT, and also provided for a new system of penalties for late payment and late filing of returns (¶9855+). Implementation of the new penalties for late filing and late payment is to be staged over a number of years, starting from April 2010, but a commencement date for SDLT has not yet been announced. For details of the harmonised provisions, see ¶9775+.

SECTION 1

General principles

9345 SDLT is a self-assessed tax. The **obligations** of the tax fall on the purchaser (¶9371); these include notifying HMRC that a transfer has taken place and submitting a self-assessment of the tax liability (known as a "land transaction return"). In practice most people use a solicitor or conveyancer to do this on their behalf. The purchaser is also liable to pay any SDLT due.

Scope

9347 s 43 FA 2003 **A land transaction is** defined as any acquisition of a chargeable interest together with any relevant interest or right.

s 48 FA 2003 The following are **exempt** interests which do not attract a charge:
– any security interest, such as a mortgage;
– a licence to use or occupy land; and
– tenancies at will.

The SDLT regime applies regardless of how the acquisition is effected. It therefore includes transfers made as a result of a court order, or by operation of the law.

MEMO POINTS 1. **Land** includes buildings, structures, land covered by water and anything annexed to the land, such as fixtures and fittings. Chattels which can be removed from the property without damage are excluded. Goodwill which is inherent to the land is also chargeable to SDLT.

2. **Chattels**, which are free from SDLT, include:
– carpets;
– curtains and blinds;
– free-standing furniture;
– kitchen white goods;
– moveable electric and gas fires; and
– light shades and fittings (unless recessed).

3. **Acquisition** includes the creation, surrender, release or variation of a chargeable interest.

4. A **chargeable interest** is any estate, interest, right or power in or over land in the UK. It includes the benefit of any obligation, restriction or condition that affects the value of that estate, interest, right or power, such as a restrictive covenant.

5. A **licence** is a personal right which neither gives exclusive occupation nor any right to an estate or interest in land. The distinction between a licence and lease is often difficult to determine, but the intention of the parties, and the legal effect of the transaction, are paramount (¶9383).

6. An SDLT **charge will not be incurred** if property is purchased through a Real Estate Investment Trust (see *Corporation Tax Memo* for details).

1. Exempt transactions

The following transactions are exempt from SDLT and so do not need to be notified on a return: 9348 s 49, Sch 3 FA 2003

Exempt situation	Details
No chargeable consideration	Except for: – a gift of land to a connected company (¶9369); or – land subject to a mortgage for which the transferee takes responsibility (¶9363)
Transaction between spouses/civil partners on separation, divorce or annulment	As a result of a court order, or by virtue of an agreement in the course of the annulment, separation or divorce
Appropriation of assets by personal representatives	To beneficiaries of a will or on intestacy unless the beneficiary gives consideration
Variation or disposition of will	Within 2 years of the death of the owner, provided that it is not for consideration, other than the making of another variation in return
Registered social landlord	Grant of lease for an indefinite term, or terminable by notice of 1 month or less.
Note: It is not necessary for the purchaser to self-certify that the transaction is exempt in order for the transaction to be registered at the Land Registry.	

2. Time of charge

The general rule for SDLT is that a **transaction is deemed to take place** on completion of a contract. This is known as the effective date. As an anti-avoidance measure, if a contract is substantially performed before it is fully completed, the effective date will be the time of substantial performance. 9350 s 44 FA 2003

MEMO POINTS 1. **Substantial** is not defined in the legislation, but substantial performance is broadly either payment of most of the consideration, or taking possession of the property. This includes an entitlement to receive rents or profits, so where rental income is the only consideration, receipt of the first rent payment is substantial performance of the contract. The provision applies even if the contract is conditional, although if the condition is not satisfied, any SDLT paid can be reclaimed. SDLT will also be repaid if the contract is subsequently rescinded or annulled.
2. HMRC have stated that they treat a contract as substantially performed where 90% or more of the **consideration due** under the contract has been paid. However, each case will be considered on its own merits.
3. Where substantial performance **occurs before completion** of the contract, both events are notifiable transactions (¶9430).
4. A **deed of rectification** will normally give rise to a further transfer of land, where the original deed does not correctly reflect the intention of the parties. In respect of leases, such a deed might be a variation to the lease, or a supplemental lease.

Transfer to a third party

Where two parties enter into a contract and, before completion of the contract, a third party becomes entitled to acquire all or part of the land **at completion**, there is a transfer of rights. This may arise as a result of a sub-sale, assignment or other transaction. 9351 s 45 FA 2003

Under the general rules, both the original contract and the transfer of rights would be treated as chargeable transactions. However, where the **original contract** is substantially performed or completed at the same time as the second contract, there is only one charge to SDLT. The charge is on completion of the contract with the third party, and it is the third party who is responsible for paying the SDLT.

Similarly, where a longer **series** of sub-sales or transfers arises, provided that they are all substantially performed or completed at the same time, only the final purchaser will be liable to SDLT.

s 45A FA 2003 MEMO POINTS 1. Where there is a transfer of rights relating to **only part** of the original contract, there will be deemed to be two separate original contracts for the purposes of SDLT as follows:
– one contract for the part transferred to the third party; and
– another contract for the remaining part not transferred.
2. With effect from 24 March 2011 sub-sale relief no longer has effect in combination with any of the reliefs for **alternative finance transactions** (see ¶9404) intended to place Islamic mortgage products on an equal footing with other property financing structures.

EXAMPLE Mr A enters into a contract to sell land to Mr B for consideration of £250,000. Mr B transfers his rights under the contract to Mr C for £50,000. On completion, Mr A will transfer the land directly to Mr C.
This represents a transfer of rights. Provided that both contracts are substantially performed or completed at the same time, Mr C will be chargeable on £300,000, being the £50,000 that he paid Mr B and the £250,000 that Mr B owes Mr A. Mr B will not be liable to SDLT.

Options

9353 s 46 FA 2003 Acquisition of options, or rights of first refusal, over land are transactions subject to SDLT. Once the option or right is **exercised**, the resulting transaction is also chargeable to SDLT in its own right. The grant and exercise of an option may be a linked transaction (¶9378).

3. Chargeable consideration

9354 Sch 4 FA 2003 Chargeable consideration is broadly anything given directly or indirectly for a transaction by the purchaser or a connected party – that is, money or money's worth.

Chargeable consideration does not include:
– a **reverse premium** on the grant or surrender of a lease;
– a **replacement lease** granted on the surrender of an existing lease, where the new lease is for the same premises, on the same terms and with the same unexpired period as the existing lease;
– **indemnities** given by the purchaser to the vendor for ongoing liabilities in relation to the land; or
– a gift of land where the transferee agrees to pay any related **inheritance tax** or **capital gains tax**.

MEMO POINTS 1. **Non-monetary** consideration is taken at its market value.
2. If payment is made in a **foreign currency**, it will be converted into sterling at the London closing exchange rate on the effective date of the transaction, unless the parties agree that a different rate should be used.
3. Consideration should be apportioned on a just and reasonable basis where:
– the consideration relates to a land transaction and **other items** (e.g. chattels); or
– there are **multiple land transactions**.
Professional valuations may be required to substantiate the apportionment.
4. Where land is transferred **between pension schemes**, the assumption by the recipient scheme of the liability to pay future pension benefits is not consideration in money or money's worth.
5. A covenant by an **agricultural tenant** to assign entitlement to the Single Farm Payment to the landlord on termination of the tenancy is not chargeable consideration.
6. Where a beneficiary has given consent to the **reallocation of trust property** on or after 19 July 2006, typically on the creation of a sub-fund, this does not constitute chargeable consideration for the purposes of SDLT.

VAT

9356 Any VAT **due on a transaction** is included as chargeable consideration.

The exception to this rule is where the vendor has exercised an option to tax (¶8904) after the date on which the transaction becomes effective. In this case, any VAT that subsequently becomes payable as a result of the option is not included as chargeable consideration.

Future payments

9357 Where some or all of the consideration is to be **postponed**, the chargeable consideration will be the total amount that is payable for the transaction. There is no reduction or discount for any subsequent delay in payment (except for rent, see ¶9388).

If the consideration is in the form of an **annuity**, the chargeable consideration is deemed to be a one-off payment made up of 12 years' payments. Where the payments vary, and this is not due to inflation, the twelve highest payments will be taken into account. s 52 FA 2003

Contingent consideration Where the consideration for a transaction is contingent on an event, such as the grant of planning permission, the chargeable amount is based on the assumption that the amount relating to the contingency will be paid. Note that this amount is not discounted to reflect the delay in actual payment. 9359 s 51 FA 2003

If the consideration is **uncertain or unascertained**, the chargeable consideration will be based on a reasonable estimate of the amount that will be paid. There are special rules for leases (¶9392).

Once the amount of consideration is **actually established**, an adjustment must be made. If tax has been overpaid, a claim may be submitted for repayment and interest. If more tax is payable, a return must be submitted within 30 days of the time when the actual consideration is established, together with payment. Note that the original purchaser remains liable for any SDLT debt under these provisions, even where he has since sold the land. s 80 FA 2003

Alternatively, where some or all of the contingent, unascertainable or uncertain consideration is **payable** more than 6 months **after the effective date** of the transaction, the purchaser may make a deferral application to HMRC (¶9454). This provision **does not apply to** rental payments. 9360 s 90 FA 2003 SI 2003/2837

Work done

Where **construction** work, improvements or repairs to a property are carried out by the **purchaser** as a condition of the contract, the market value of the work will form part of the consideration. 9362 Sch 4 para 10 FA 2003

Where all or part of the consideration consists of the **provision of services**, the open-market value of those services will be deemed to be chargeable consideration.

If it is agreed that the **vendor** will carry out construction works, such as constructing a building on a plot of land, after the vendor has sold the plot to the purchaser, the consideration for the building works will not form part of the chargeable consideration. To meet this condition the land must be conveyed to the purchaser before construction begins and neither the purchaser nor the vendor can be entitled to unwind the contract, should there be a problem with construction. *Prudential Assurance Co Ltd v HMRC* [1992]

MEMO POINTS 1. The **property** on which the purchaser carries out the work does not have to be the property which is the subject of the transaction. It could be on another property held by the purchaser or a connected party (¶5570).
2. If the transaction is **substantially performed** before completion and the construction works are carried out between performance and completion without being a condition of the transaction, their value will not form part of the consideration.

EXAMPLE C Ltd, a builder, enters into a contract to acquire land from Mr D for £750,000. Under the contract, C Ltd will also construct a new building for Mr D in another location and the associated cost will be £1.5 million.
The consideration for the land transaction is £2.25 million. (£750,000 + £1.5 million)

Debt

The **release or assumption** of a debt (other than a mortgage to secure the property) is chargeable consideration for SDLT purposes. However, if the amount of the debt exceeds the market value of the property, the chargeable consideration will be restricted to the market value. 9363 Sch 4 para 8 FA 2003

MEMO POINTS 1. Where a **gift is made to a family member**, the donee will often take over responsibility for any mortgage, which means a charge to SDLT will arise. If possible, the donor should retain responsibility for the debt in this situation, which will therefore exempt the gift from SDLT.
2. Where a person **already owns part of a property in joint ownership** which is subject to debt, and he increases his ownership, the amount liable to SDLT will not take into account the propor-

tion of debt already owned. For example, if A and B own a property subject to a debt equally, and A gives 30% of the property to B, B is treated as assuming debt on 30% of the property only.
3. **On marriage** or entering a civil partnership, if a property is transferred into joint ownership, half of any outstanding mortgage will constitute chargeable consideration along with any cash payment given by the acquiring spouse/partner.
4. If a **beneficiary** receives land under the terms of a **will** or under **intestacy**, the assumption of a debt is not chargeable consideration for SDLT purposes.

Land exchanges

9365
s 47 FA 2003

Exchanges of land are **treated as** two separate transactions for the purposes of SDLT. The consideration for each acquisition is the market value of the land concerned (or what the chargeable consideration would be under the normal rules for consideration, if greater), together with any rent if the transaction relates to a new lease.

Where the interests in land being exchanged are **not major interests** (¶9430), such as the lifting of restrictive covenants, the value of the interests being exchanged are disregarded and only other consideration will be chargeable to SDLT.

If the exchange takes place **between connected persons** (¶5570), the transaction would normally be treated as linked (¶9378), which would mean the values would be aggregated, creating a higher SDLT charge. However, for transactions with an effective date on or after 19 July 2007, this rule has been disapplied, so that the SDLT charge is based on the isolated market value of each piece of land.

9366 Where a transaction in land results in the **partition or division** of a chargeable interest held jointly, the share held by the purchaser immediately before the transaction is not counted as consideration.

EXAMPLE E and F are brothers who inherited the family farm some years ago. They now wish to own half of the farm each, with E taking all of the arable land and F occupying the farmhouse and owning the dairy buildings.
As the arable land is worth £400,000 less than the remainder of the farm, F pays E £200,000 as compensation. This payment is chargeable to SDLT.

Particular parties involved

9367 For partnerships, see ¶9491 and ¶9766+.

For trustees, see ¶9492.

9368
Sch 4 para 12 FA 2003

Employee Where a land transaction is entered into for the purposes of employment and is one that is treated as a **taxable benefit under the income tax provisions** for living accommodation provided by an employer (¶3250), the consideration is deemed to be the higher of the market-value rent or the amount treated as employment income.

If the accommodation is **exempt from the income tax charge**, the chargeable consideration for SDLT purposes will be the actual amount (if any) paid by the employee.

There is a relief for the acquisition of property by employers (¶9407).

9369
s 53 FA 2003

Connected company Where the purchaser is a company, the chargeable **consideration** will be **deemed** to be the market value of the land at the effective date if either the vendor is connected with that company (¶5572), or some or all of the consideration consists of the issue or transfer of shares in any company with which the vendor is connected.

s 54 FA 2003

As an **exception** to this rule, only the actual consideration paid for the transaction will be chargeable where:
a. the transaction relates to a **distribution of the assets** of the vendor company; or
b. the purchaser holds the land as a **trustee** and either he is not connected with the vendor (other than as a trustee of a settlement which is connected to the company) or he holds it in the course of a trust management business.
On **incorporation** of a business (¶9729) any transfer of land will result in a charge to SDLT.

4. Responsible person

In any transaction the **purchaser** is obliged to fulfil the reporting requirements and pay any tax due. For joint purchasers, see ¶9490. 9371 s 85 FA 2003

A person cannot be a purchaser unless he has given consideration, or is a party to the transaction (except in a sub-sale situation).

The following table illustrates the **person deemed** to be the purchaser for various transactions.

Transaction	Purchaser
Conveyance or assignment	Transferee or assignee
Grant of a lease	Lessee or tenant
Grant of rights including an easement, servitude or profit à prendre	Person who becomes entitled to the right
Surrender of a lease	Landlord
Variation of a lease	Person whose estate, interest or right is affected
Making or release of a covenant or condition	Person whose estate, interest or right is affected

SECTION 2

Calculation of the charge

In general, the calculation is determined by the use made of the property i.e. residential or commercial. 9375

Special rules apply for:
- linked transactions (¶9378);
- a series of transactions which effect a reduced SDLT charge (¶9380); and
- transactions where the consideration includes rent – that is, leases (¶9383).

A. Sale and purchase

Rates of tax

The charge to SDLT is based on the **slab system**. This provides that when a rate threshold is exceeded, the higher rate applies to the whole consideration. 9376 s 55 FA 2003

The rates **depend on** whether the land consists entirely of residential property or includes property that is not residential.

Residential property		Non-residential or mixed property	
Relevant consideration	%	Relevant consideration	%
up to £125,000	0	up to £150,000	0
£125,001 to £250,000	1	£150,001 to £250,000	1
£250,001 to £500,000	3	£250,001 to £500,000	3
£500,001 to £1 million	4	More than £500,000	4
More than £1 million	5		
Until 24 March 2012 **first-time buyers** who intend to live in the property as their only or main home pay **no SDLT** on purchases with a value up to £250,000. The buyer must intend to live in the property and it must be the buyer's only or main home. The buyer must not previously have owned property or land either in the UK or anywhere else in the world, including property bought with anyone else.			

EXAMPLE Mr A buys two residential properties, B and C. B costs £110,000 and C costs £450,000.
There is no SDLT charge on B, as the consideration is below £125,000.
The SDLT charge on C is £13,500, being 3% of £450,000.

MEMO POINTS 1. The status of the building on **purchase**, rather than its intended use, is the critical factor in classifying the building for SDLT purposes.
2. Where a **building is not in use**, the use for which it is most suitable will override any other.
s 116 FA 2003 3. For SDLT purposes, **residential property** is defined as:
– a building that is used as, or is suitable for use as, a dwelling; and
– land that forms part of the garden or grounds, and any outbuildings.
3. Residential accommodation for school pupils, members of the armed forces and students (excluding halls of residence) is specifically included in the definition of dwellings. It also includes accommodation which is an institution that is the **sole or main residence** of at least 90% of its residents and does not fall within the excluded list below.
The following properties are specifically **excluded** from the definition of a dwelling:
– children's homes;
– residential institutions for the care of persons who are old, disabled, have a drug or alcohol dependency, or have a past or present mental disorder;
– hospitals or hospices;
– prisons;
– hotels, inns or similar establishments;
– student halls of residence.

Linked transactions

9378 s 55(4) FA 2003 s 108 FA 2003 Transactions are linked if they form part of a single scheme, arrangement or series of transactions between the same vendor and purchaser, or persons connected with them (¶5570).

Where transactions are linked, the **rate of tax** will be determined on the basis of the aggregate chargeable consideration.

In addition, at the option of the purchaser, linked transactions with the **same effective date** can be reported on the same land transaction return.

ss 74, 75 FA 2003 Transactions involving **leaseholders** banding together to buy the freehold (or head lease) of a block of flats, or a **crofting community** exercising its right to buy, are not linked. In this case, the rate of tax is calculated by aggregating the consideration given by all the tenants and dividing it by the number of properties involved.

A **new relief** now applies where the land transaction involves interests in more than one dwelling. For so-called "bulk purchases" of dwellings, the SDLT rate is determined on the basis of the average, not aggregate, value of the dwellings, subject to a minimum rate of 1%. Accordingly, purchases of more than five dwellings are no longer treated as transactions involving non-residential property.

Comment It is possible that transactions undertaken between the same parties are not linked. If so, it is necessary to keep evidence of the separate negotiations, to support the disclosure made to HMRC.

EXAMPLE E and his brother F want to purchase a block of flats with spacious communal grounds.
The total market value of the property is £900,000.
They wish to reduce the SDLT liability, so they split the transaction up: E buying the flats for £700,000 and F buying the land for £200,000.
As these transactions are linked, SDLT of £36,000 is still due on the aggregate consideration of £900,000. (£900,000 x 4%)

9379 s 46 FA 2003 **Options** The grant and exercise of an option may be a linked transaction; in this case HMRC have stated that the following calculations are required:
a. on grant, SDLT is calculated on the consideration for the grant; and
b. on exercise, SDLT is calculated on the aggregated consideration for grant and exercise as if there was only one transaction, with credit given for the previous SDLT paid on grant.

EXAMPLE On 1 January Mr F is granted an option by Mrs G to buy her house for £730,000 on or before 31 December. Mr F paid £230,000 for the grant of the option and exercised it on 5 November.
The grant of the option is a land transaction which occurs on 1 January. A return must be made to HMRC and the SDLT of £2,300 (1% of £230,000) must be paid.
The exercise of the option is another land transaction, for which a separate return must be submitted. The SDLT liability is calculated as follows:

	£	£
Consideration at grant	230,000	
Consideration at exercise	730,000	
Total consideration		960,000
SDLT at 4% of £960,000		38,400
Less: SDLT paid on grant		(2,300)
SDLT liability on exercise		36,100

Anti-avoidance

Where one person disposes of a chargeable interest to another person using a **series of transactions** (excluding incidental transactions) resulting in a **reduced SDLT charge**, the purchaser is taxed as if only a single transaction had occurred. This single transaction is called the **notional land transaction**. The actual transactions are ignored for SDLT purposes. 9380 s 75A FA 2003 SDLT Technical News Issue 4

Unlike many other anti-avoidance provisions, there is no **motive test** and the scope of these provisions is very wide. However, it is not the intention of the legislation to catch legitimate transactions.

MEMO POINTS 1. **Transactions** which could form part of a string for this purpose include:
- a non-land transaction;
- an agreement, offer or undertaking not to take specified action;
- any kind of arrangement, whether or not it could be described as a transaction;
- a transaction which takes place subsequent to the acquisition of the land interest; or
- a transfer involving a land investment partnership.

2. Subject to transitional provisions, from 24 March 2010 where anti-avoidance rules charge SDLT on a "notional land transaction" in the context of a series of transactions resulting in a reduced SDLT charge – that is, in the context of this anti-avoidance rule – the preferential rules enjoyed by **partnerships** no longer apply.
3. In view of this rule it would be prudent to seek **expert advice** when undertaking anything other than the most basic type of transaction.

The following commercial situations are **expressly excluded** from the above provision: 9381
- consideration that is attributable to a construction contract which is therefore not part of the consideration for a land transaction;
- repairs or other works carried out which relate to a land purchase, where the work is undertaken by someone who is neither the vendor nor connected to him (¶5570);
- the purchase of assets along with land where consideration is apportioned between the two elements;
- a transfer of shares in a company or units in a unit trust, where there is a subsequent land transaction (although where a land transaction precedes the transfer of shares/units, this would be caught);
- a loan to fund a land acquisition from a person who is not a party to the land transaction, nor connected to any party;
- the issue of shares where a land transaction qualifies for acquisition relief (¶9739) or reconstruction relief (¶9738);
- the acquisition of land and a subsequent lease, where the lessee is not connected to the purchaser; and
- acquisitions of separate parcels of land.

Where the rule does apply, the **chargeable consideration** is the largest amount (or aggregate amount) given or received by any person in respect of any of the transactions (excluding any consideration given for incidental transactions, when a just and reasonable apportionment of 9382 the total consideration is allowed). The effective date is the earlier of the last date of completion and substantial performance.

The usual **SDLT reliefs** are still available to mitigate any resulting charge.

HMRC have issued guidance, including example situations, where they consider s 75A will and will not apply. This can be found at www.hmrc.gov.uk/so/advice75a.htm.

B. Leases

9383 Sch 17A FA 2003 A lease is a document that gives exclusive possession of a property, or part of a property, to a person ("the lessee") for a term. Such a document refers to a legal estate in specific property, which may be land, a property, or a right over land, such as fishing rights, or a right of way.

In contrast, a licence grants permission to do something, but does not give exclusive possession of property or grant an interest in land.

For SDLT purposes, the **legal effect** of a document is more important than the specific terminology which is used.

Where a **series of transactions** involves a lease, and a reduced SDLT charge results, the anti-avoidance rule at ¶9380 may apply.

1. Lease term

9384 The amount of SDLT will be determined by the term of the lease, which is the **shorter of** the contractual period specified in the lease and the period from the date of grant to the end of the contractual term.

Break clauses and renewal clauses are ignored for this purpose.

MEMO POINTS 1. Where a lease continues **beyond its fixed term**, say for an extra 6 months, the term of the lease for SDLT purposes becomes the fixed term plus 1 year. (If the lease continued for an extra 13 months, the term would become the fixed term plus 2 years.) The continuation of a lease beyond its fixed term may cause the transaction to become notifiable (¶9430).
2. Leases for an **indefinite term** are deemed to have a fixed term of 1 year, until this period elapses, when the rules in 1. above will apply.

2. Consideration

9385 The consideration for a lease is usually in the **form** of a premium and rent, each of which requires a separate SDLT calculation.

A peppercorn (trivial amount) is not liable to SDLT, as either a premium or rent.

The following do **not constitute** consideration for these purposes:
– service charges;
– a tenant's obligation to maintain or insure;
– guarantees of payment;
– extra amounts which become due on any breach of the lease conditions; and
– the payment of a landlord's reasonable costs on the grant, variation or termination of a lease.

Premium

9386 Premiums are liable to the SDLT rates shown at ¶9376.

In order to stop a lease being structured to obtain double use of the zero-rate band, there is **no zero rate** for a premium if the annual rent of a **non-residential** property is £1,000 or more.

This rule does not apply to properties which are wholly used for **residential** purposes. Any premiums paid, regardless of the rent, are taxable in line with the rate bands at ¶9376.

If there is mixed use of a property, provided that the rent which can be apportioned, on a just and reasonable basis, to the non-residential part of the building is less than £1,000, the zero rate will still apply. If the rent applicable to the non-residential part exceeds £1,000, an apportionment of the premium must be made between the residential and non-residential elements.

MEMO POINTS 1. **Rent received before** the formal grant of a lease is taxed as if it were a premium.
2. A **reverse premium** (a payment from the landlord to the tenant) is not chargeable consideration.

EXAMPLE H Ltd takes on a 3-year lease on a property, paying a premium of £100,000 and annual rent of £9,000. The property's floor space is 80% residential and 20% commercial, and HMRC accept that this is a just and reasonable method for H Ltd to apportion the rent it is paying.

The rent apportioned to the non-residential part of the building is £9,000 × $\frac{20}{100}$ = £1,800. As the annual rent applicable to the non-residential part of the building exceeds £1,000, there is no zero-rate band for the premium relating to the non-residential part.

The premium needs to be apportioned between the two elements, as if two separate premiums had been paid. H Ltd again uses floor area, calculating that:
- £80,000 of the premium relates to the residential part of the building (£100,000 × 80%); and
- £20,000 of the premium relates to the non-residential part of the building.

No SDLT is payable on the £80,000, as this is below the zero-rate threshold for residential properties. SDLT is levied at 1% on the £20,000 which is attributable to the non-residential part, as no zero-rate band is available.

Rent

Rent payable under a lease is subject to SDLT. SDLT is chargeable on the "relevant rental value" of the lease, which is the "net present value" of all rental payments due under the lease agreement. 9388 Sch 5 FA 2003

The **net present value** is calculated by applying the temporal discount rate (currently set at 3.5% by the Treasury) to the rent payable in respect of each year during the term of the lease, and can be best demonstrated by example. 9389

EXAMPLE A Ltd takes on a commercial 3-year lease with rent of £100,000 p.a.
The net present value is calculated using a discount rate of 3.5% as follows:

Year	1	2	3	Total £
Discount factor	1/1.035 = 0.96618	$1/(1.035)^2$ = 0.93351	$1/(1.035)^3$ = 0.90194	
Rent	100,000	100,000	100,000	
Discounted rent	96,618	93,351	90,194	280,163

So the net present value of the rental payments is £280,163.

MEMO POINTS 1. Where a **rent review** occurs just before the end of the 5th year, any increase is ignored for the purposes of the net present value calculation.
2. Where two or more leases form a **linked transaction**, the net present value will take account of all the leases as if there was only one transaction.

If VAT is payable on the rent it should be included in the NPV calculation. When calculating the VAT on rental payments for the NPV, the relevant date (tax point) is the earlier of when a VAT invoice is issued or a payment is received. This will be of significance in the case of a VAT rate change, such as the increase in the standard rate from 17.5% to 20% on 4 January 2011.

Since a potential future change in VAT rate can never be discounted, all affected **rents are variable or uncertain** for the purposes of SDLT (¶9391).

When the **amount of rent payable for the first 5 years** of the lease's term becomes certain, the purchaser can submit an SDLT return to HMRC.

The following **rates** are then applied. In this instance only, the slab system does not operate, so the zero rate is akin to a nil-rate band. 9390

Residential property		Non-residential or mixed property	
Relevant consideration	**%**	**Relevant consideration**	**%**
Not more than £125,000	0	Not more than £150,000	0
More than £125,000	1	More than £150,000	1

EXAMPLE The commercial lease from the example in ¶9389 above has a net present value of £280,163.
The SDLT liability is £1,301. ((£280,163 – £150,000) x 1%, rounded down to the nearest £1)

9391 Sch 17A para 7 FA 2003 **Changeable rent** It is not unusual for rental payments to be variable or uncertain. In this situation the following rules apply for the **first 5 years** of the lease only:
– if the amount of rent is **contingent on an event**, the chargeable consideration is based on the assumption that the amount relating to the contingency will be paid; and
– where the rent is **uncertain or unascertained**, the chargeable consideration will be based on a reasonable estimate of the amount that will be paid. If a VAT rate change is only a possibility – that is, a rate change has not been announced – it is reasonable to assume that the rate will not change.
It is not possible to defer payment of SDLT on a lease payment on the basis that it is uncertain or contingent on a particular event.
If the **contingency or uncertainty ceases** within the first 5 years, an adjustment is required. The **taxpayer must** complete a return (¶9427) and pay any additional SDLT due within 30 days of the contingency or uncertainty ceasing. Taxpayers who have overpaid SDLT will be entitled to a refund.

MEMO POINTS Rent payable under **agricultural tenancies** governed by any of the following legislation is treated as being uncertain or unascertained:
– Agricultural Holdings Act 1986, ss 12, 13 or 33;
– Agricultural Tenancies Act 1995, Part 2;
– Agricultural Holdings (Scotland) Act 1991, ss 13, 14, 15 or 31; or
– Agricultural Holdings (Scotland) Act 2003, ss 9, 10 or 11.

9392 If the uncertainty or contingency persists **beyond 5 years**, an additional SDLT calculation is required at the 5-year point. This should include the actual rent paid in the first 5 years and any further rent payable, estimated at the level of the highest rent payable in any 12-month period in the first 5 years. See also ¶9396.

EXAMPLE Mr A is granted a 20-year lease and the rent remains uncertain until Year 8. He has paid the following rent in the first 5 years:

Year	Rent £
1	16,500
2	17,400
3	18,000
4	19,000
5	18,800
Total paid	89,700

At the end of Year 5, an adjustment to the SDLT is required, which will take the following amounts into account:

	£	£	
Rent paid in first 5 years		89,700	(as above)
Rent estimated to be paid in Years 6 to 20:			
Highest rent in first 5 years (Year 4)	19,000		
19,000 for 15 years		285,000	
Total rent to be taken into account when calculating the NPV		374,700	

9393 Sch 17A para 18A FA 2003 Often a lessee or assignee must make a **loan** or pay a **deposit** when taking on the lease, such that any repayment is contingent on his actions (e.g. whether any damage to the property occurs). The amount of the loan or deposit is the chargeable consideration, except where it does not exceed twice the highest rent payable in any 12-month period in the first 5 years of the lease. Where the amount is liable to SDLT, the zero-rate band will be available. No repayment of SDLT will be due when the loan or deposit is repaid.

3. Specific transactions

Agreement for lease

An agreement for a lease is **treated as** a lease for the purposes of SDLT once substantial performance has occurred. **9394** Sch 17A para 12A FA 2003 SDLT Technical News Issue 4

Following substantial performance of an agreement for lease, any **subsequent grant** of the lease will always be treated as a separate transaction (i.e. not linked). However, overlap relief (¶9418) reduces the rent liable to SDLT on the grant of the lease, usually to nil.

Assignment

The assignment of a lease is **treated in the same way as** the transfer of rights under a sale and purchase agreement for a freehold property (¶9351). Any amount payable by the assignor to the assignee is not chargeable consideration. **9395**

An assignment of an **agreement for lease** will be treated as an assignment of a lease.

Variation

Where a lease is varied, an SDLT charge may arise. **9396** Sch 17A paras 13-15 FA 2003

If the **rent** is:

– **reduced**, the variation is treated as an acquisition of a chargeable interest in the land by the tenant; or

– **increased** within the first 5 years, and is outside the terms of the existing lease, this will be treated as the grant of a new lease.

If the **term** is:

– **reduced**, the variation is treated as an acquisition of a chargeable interest by the landlord; or

– **increased**, this will usually be treated as a surrender and re-grant of the lease. See ¶9354 for details of when this will not be treated as chargeable consideration.

Any form of **consideration given by the tenant**, such as a variation to include a restrictive covenant, is treated as chargeable consideration.

MEMO POINTS There is an **anti-avoidance** rule which applies to leases granted on or after 1 December 2003. If the **level of rent**, after the first 5 years of the lease, **rises** by more than 20% per year on average. a new lease is deemed to have been granted for the purposes of SDLT. This rule applies for any increase in rent which first had effect after 19 July 2006. Sch 17A para 15 FA 2003

Surrender

Where a **landlord pays** the tenant to surrender the lease, the landlord will be liable to pay SDLT on the payment. **9397**

Where the **tenant pays** the landlord, known as a **reverse surrender**, no SDLT liability arises.

On the **surrender and re-grant** of a lease between the same parties, the grant of the new lease is not treated as chargeable consideration for the surrender. Also, the surrender is not treated as chargeable consideration for the grant of the new lease. Both "legs" of this transaction are therefore exempt from SDLT. Sch 17A para 16 FA 2003

Sale and leaseback

On a sale and leaseback, where a property is sold and then leased back by the vendor, the **leaseback element** is exempt from SDLT when granted out of the major interest, if the following conditions are met: **9399** s 57A FA 2003

1. the sale is entered into wholly, or partly, in consideration of the leaseback;

2. the only other consideration for the sale is cash, or the assumption of debt – there does not have to be any other consideration for the conditions to be met;
3. the sale is not a sub-sale, assignment or other transfer of rights to a third party; and
4. the vendor and the purchaser must not be members of the same group for SDLT group relief purposes (¶9751).

The **sale element** will be subject to SDLT under the normal rules.

C. Reliefs

Summary

9401 The following reliefs apply to SDLT:

Relief	¶¶
Compulsory purchase	¶9402
Compliance with planning obligations	¶9403
Alternative property finance	¶9404
Disadvantaged areas	¶9406
Employee relocation	¶9407
Housebuilding companies	¶9408
Property traders	¶9409
Zero-carbon dwellings	¶9410
Right to buy	¶9412
Shared ownership	¶9413
Social landlords	¶9415
Charities and national bodies	¶9416
Leasehold enfranchisement	¶9417
Overlap relief	¶9418
Transfer to a limited liability partnership	¶9731
Corporate reconstructions	¶9738
Corporate groups	¶9751

Compulsory purchase

9402 s 60 FA 2003 A compulsory purchase made by a local planning authority (or similar organisation) **to facilitate development** will be exempt from SDLT. The subsequent transfer to a developer will be subject to SDLT in the usual way. For these purposes, the entity making the compulsory purchase and the developer must be separate persons.

MEMO POINTS The above also applies to vesting orders in Northern Ireland.

Compliance with planning obligations

9403 s 61 FA 2003 An exemption is available where a transaction is entered into in order to comply with planning obligations (or their modification), and all of the following **conditions** are satisfied:
– the planning obligation is enforceable against the vendor;
– the purchaser is a public authority; and
– the transaction occurs within 5 years from the date on which the planning obligation (or modification) was entered into.

In practice, this provision prevents a **double charge** where, in order to comply with a planning obligation, a developer acquires land (subject to SDLT) for a public facility and then disposes of the land to the public authority that will manage it.

Comment This type of planning obligation is commonly referred to as a "section 106" obligation in England and Wales.

Alternative property finance

Where a transaction involves an alternative property financing structure, such as an **Islamic mortgage**, there is an SDLT relief which applies to put the transaction on a level footing with a conventional mortgage arrangement. 9404 ss 71A and 72A FA 2003

The **structure** of alternative property finance involves a financial institution purchasing a major interest, or an undivided share of a major interest, in a property and granting a lease or sublease to the other person involved in the transaction. As part of the agreement the other person has the right to require that the financial institution transfers the whole interest in the property to him at the end of the lease.

For both the initial purchase by the financial institution and the subsequent lease to the person involved to benefit from the exemption, the following **conditions** must be met:

– the financial institution acquires land from either the other party to the transaction, or another financial institution which has previously entered into a similar agreement with the other party;

– the land is then **leased** to the other party on a long lease; and

– at the end of the term of the lease, the title of the property is transferred to the other party.

The institution and person can be beneficial **tenants in common** and the beneficial ownership can transfer to the person during the arrangement.

The relief also applies where: s 73 FA 2003

– a financial institution acquires a major interest in land from the other party to the agreement, or another financial institution which acquired its interest under a similar agreement between it and the other party to the contract;

– the land is **sold** to the other party for a consideration that is paid in instalments; and

– that person grants the institution a legal mortgage over the land.

Relief from a charge to SDLT which arises on the **transfer and return of land** assets by and to persons seeking to obtain finance under alternative finance investment arrangements with bond-issuers is also available. The legislation ensures that no charge to SDLT arises on the bond-holders. s 123 FA 2009

Relief from SDLT applies under arrangements where a person (A) transfers a major interest in land to another person (B), where: Sch 61 FA 2009

– B issues an **alternative finance investment bond** to A, who holds the land throughout the life of the bond as a bond asset;

– within 30 days of the transfer, B grants A a sublease under a leaseback arrangement to generate income for the bond;

– over the life of the bond, B receives payments of capital of at least 60% of the value of the interest in land at the time of the first transfer of the interest;

– a charge in favour of HMRC must be registered with the land registry against the title of the land (to include the amount of SDLT that would be due on the market value of the transfer of the interest at the date of transfer);

– B must provide prescribed evidence that a satisfactory legal charge has been entered on the Land Register; and

– on termination of the bond, the interest is transferred to A by B, and this takes place no later than 10 years after the first transaction.

Regulations specify the documents required to be provided to HMRC as evidence of the legal charge. SI 2009/2052

MEMO POINTS 1. For these purposes, **person** includes an individual, a partner, a trustee and a company.

2. It is no longer possible to qualify as a **financial institution** for the purposes of the alternative finance reliefs, merely by holding a Consumer Credit Licence.

9405 **Restrictions on relief** The reliefs do not apply where either **group** (¶9751) or **corporate reconstruction** (¶9738) relief is claimed in respect of the first transaction.

Sub-sale relief (¶9351) does not have effect in combination with alternative finance relief.

s 73AB FA 2003 Relief is not available where a financial institution sets up a **subsidiary company** to purchase a property under an alternative property finance arrangement if the **arrangements include** arrangements whereby another person can acquire control of the subsidiary.

Sch 61 FA 2009 The relief from SDLT which applies to alternative finance investment bonds is **not available** where a bond-holder, or a group of connected bond-holders, acquires control of the underlying asset.

Disadvantaged areas

9406 Sch 6 FA 2003 Certain acquisitions of **residential property** (¶9376) in areas designated as being disadvantaged are exempt from SDLT. Relief is usually claimed on a land transaction return (¶9428), although, exceptionally, a stand-alone claim can be made.

The exemption applies if **chargeable consideration** does not exceed £150,000. Where the consideration:
– consists entirely of rent, the exemption applies if the rental value does not exceed £150,000; or
– includes both rent and a premium, the relief will apply to both, provided that the premium does not exceed £150,000.

MEMO POINTS 1. There are approximately 2,000 disadvantaged **areas** and it is advisable to undertake a postcode search on HMRC's website at www.hmrc.gov.uk/so/dar/dar-search.htm, to check if a proposed transaction might qualify for this relief.
2. Where land is situated **only partly in a disadvantaged area**, the consideration for each part is determined on a just and reasonable basis.
3. Where land has **both residential and non-residential use**, the consideration attributable to each is determined on a just and reasonable basis, such as percentage areas as shown on a planning application.

Employee relocation

9407 Sch 6A para 5 FA 2003 Where an **employer or relocation company** acquires a dwelling in connection with the relocation of an individual's employment, then, subject to the conditions outlined below, the chargeable consideration will be deemed to be zero.

The **conditions** for relief are that:
– the employee must have occupied the property as his only or main residence at some point during the 2 years ending with the transaction;
– the consideration must not exceed the market value of the dwelling; and
– the land acquired must not exceed the permitted area (¶9408).

MEMO POINTS 1. A change of residence is deemed to **result from a relocation of employment** if it is made wholly or partly to allow the individual to live within a reasonable travelling distance of the new place of employment.
2. **Relocation of employment** means a change in the individual's place of employment as a result of:
– becoming an employee of the employer;
– an alteration of duties; or
– a change in the place where duties are normally performed.

Housebuilding companies

9408 Sch 6A para 1 FA 2003 A housebuilding company is a company that, in the course of its trade, constructs or adapts buildings to be used as dwellings. There is an exemption from SDLT for housebuilding companies in the following circumstances:
– the company acquires a dwelling (¶9376) in **part exchange** for a newly constructed dwelling; and
– both the old and new dwellings are the only or main residences of the individual(s) acquiring the new dwelling.

This relief is available where the land acquired by the company does not exceed the **permitted area** of 0.5 hectares.

The relief will still apply if the site purchased is bigger than 0.5 hectares and, after taking into account the size and character of the dwelling, the land is required for reasonable enjoyment of the dwelling.

If the land being purchased with the dwelling is **greater than the permitted area**, the chargeable consideration for the acquisition of the old dwelling is the market value of that property as a whole, less the market value of the permitted area.

Property traders

A property trader for these purposes is either a company, LLP or partnership (whose members are all companies or LLPs) which carries on the business of buying and selling dwellings. 9409 Sch 6A para 2 FA 2003

For the purchase **to qualify for relief** the individual selling the property must be buying a new dwelling from a housebuilding company, and must have occupied the old dwelling as his only or main residence and intend to occupy the new dwelling as his only or main residence.

In addition the following **conditions** must be met by the property trader:
- it does not intend to spend more than the permitted amount on refurbishing the old dwelling;
- it does not intend to grant a lease or licence of the old dwelling, apart from a lease or licence to the individual from whom it is buying the property for a period of no more than 6 months;
- it will not allow any principals or employees to occupy the dwelling; and
- the area of land acquired with the dwelling does not exceed the permitted area. The conditions relating to the permitted area are as at ¶9408.

MEMO POINTS Similar relief is available when:
a. a property trader purchases a dwelling from **personal representatives**; or
b. a property trader acquires a dwelling from an individual and all of the following conditions are satisfied (**chain-breaking relief**):
- arrangements have been made by the individual to sell the old property;
- those arrangements fail; and
- the property trader acquires the old property to enable the acquisition of the new property to proceed.

Zero-carbon dwellings

Until at least 30 September 2012, the first acquisition of a new dwelling **valued** at up to £500,000 which satisfies the zero-carbon criteria will be relieved from SDLT. Dwellings in excess of this value will be liable to SDLT but with a discount of £15,000. No relief will apply to second or subsequent sales. 9410 s 58B FA 2003 SI 2007/3437

Where **more than one home is acquired** as part of a linked transaction, the relief will still be available to each qualifying home.

Property will be subject to a certification **process** and homebuyers must receive a certificate from the vendor before the relief can apply.

MEMO POINTS 1. Originally the relief only applied to single dwellings but not flats. Finance Act 2008 amended the legislation to include flats, or any part of a building which has been constructed for use as a single dwelling. Certificates for zero-carbon flats built between 1 October 2007 and 21 July 2008 must still be issued for any SDLT paid during that period to be reclaimed.
2. The **first acquisition** of a dwelling means that the dwelling has not previously been occupied.
3. The zero-carbon **certificate** must state:
- the date of issue;
- the address and post code;
- that the dwelling satisfies the criteria;
- the accredited assessor's full name, including that of his employer or his trading name if he is self-employed; and
- for English and Welsh dwellings, the unique energy performance certificate number if relevant, and the accreditation scheme to which the assessor belongs (if applicable).

4. An **accredited assessor** is permitted to charge a reasonable fee in respect of his verification services. It may be that this charge needs to be borne by the purchaser but more likely the builder will absorb this cost.
5. HMRC have the **power to refuse** the relief (even where a zero-carbon certificate has been issued) where they think that a dwelling does not qualify.

9411 For a dwelling to be deemed to be zero-carbon, the following criteria must be met:

Criteria	Detail
Heat loss parameter must not exceed 0.8 Watts per square metre Kelvin	Heat loss per unit of temperature difference per unit floor area determined by the: – internal dimensions of surfaces bounding the dwelling; – thermal performance of the materials used in construction; and – air permeability of the dwelling envelope
Carbon dioxide emission rate over the period of a year must be no more than 0 kg/m²	Annual emissions per unit floor area for: – space heating; – water heating; and – ventilation and lighting, less the emissions saved by energy generation in or on the dwelling
Net carbon dioxide emissions must not exceed 0 kg/m²	As above, less emissions saved by additional allowable electricity i.e. electricity generated by a wind, light or hydro-electric power source which is designed to serve the dwelling

SDLT Technical News Issue 6

MEMO POINTS New homes may still qualify for the zero-carbon relief even if they are **connected to mains** gas and electricity. If they are connected to the mains, then provided that they produce sufficient additional renewable energy to cover the average annual consumption of a dwelling, the new dwelling may qualify (subject to the above conditions). HMRC's guidance does not provide details of what the "average annual consumption" of a dwelling is.

Right to buy

9412 Sch 9 FA 2003

A right to buy transaction is **defined** as the sale of a dwelling at a discount by a relevant public sector body.

Where a transaction involves a right to buy, the contingent consideration provisions (¶9359) are disregarded.

MEMO POINTS A **public sector body** includes an organisation under the control of any of the following:
– the government;
– local government;
– social housing;
– new town and development corporations; or
– police.

Shared ownership

9413 Sch 9 FA 2003

A shared ownership or **equity sharing scheme** is an arrangement under which a tenant buys a dwelling gradually from a housing association or similar entity by initially paying less than the full value of the property. The housing association generally grants a long lease with a premium representing the value of the share acquired, and rent is payable for the remaining portion.

SDLT on shared ownership homes is not required to be paid until the tenant owns at least 80% of the equity in his home.

Alternatively, an irrevocable election may be made for SDLT to be calculated by reference to the market value of the dwelling, or on the maximum share which can ever be purchased, meaning that SDLT is due when the first instalment is paid. Once such an election has been made, no further SDLT charge will arise on rental payments or the future acquisition of an additional share of the property.

EXAMPLE Mr A enters into a shared ownership agreement on 1 August and will initially purchase a 50% interest in the property. The market value of the property is £320,000.
The initial premium is £160,000 (representing 50% of the market value of the property). The annual rent payable on the other 50% of the property is £2,000.
No SDLT is payable on the initial premium.
Mr A subsequently purchases another 25% of the property for a premium of £80,000. As he still owns less than 80% of the property, no SDLT is payable on this second staircasing payment. Shortly afterwards Mr A purchases another 10% of the property for £32,000. As he now owns more than 80% of the property, SDLT is payable at 1% on the £32,000 (£32,000 × 1% = £320).
Should Mr A make any further staircasing payments they will be liable to SDLT, as he has more than an 80% share in the property.

Rent to shared ownership (known as "Rent to Homebuy") is a scheme under which the grant of a shared ownership lease (or the declaration of a shared ownership trust) is preceded by the grant of an assured shorthold tenancy at a subsidised rent in order to allow the tenant to occupy the property while saving for a deposit. A charge arises only on the shared ownership lease when it is **granted**, or on the shared ownership trust when it is **declared**. This treatment applies where the grant of shared ownership lease or the declaration of shared ownership trust was made on or after 22 April 2009.

This relief also applies to **shared ownership trusts** for English and Welsh transactions. Under such an arrangement, a dwelling is held in commonhold between the trustees (who will be a housing association or similar entity) and the purchaser. The trustees own the dwelling but the purchaser retains a beneficial share of the equity and has the exclusive right to occupy the property as his main residence. The purchaser must make an initial capital payment to the trustees followed by regular rent payments and he must be given the choice to purchase a further equity interest in the property from the trustees at some later date. **9414**

This favourable SDLT treatment **extends** to purchasers under shared ownership schemes operated by profit-making Registered Providers of Social Housing, where the scheme is funded by public subsidy.

Social landlords

No SDLT is payable on the transfer of land or leases to a registered social landlord where the transfer is **made by** the tenants or qualifying transferors, or funded by public subsidy. **9415** s 71 FA 2003

Qualifying transferors include:
- registered social landlords;
- housing action trusts; and
- various specified councils.

The SDLT relief for social landlords also **extends** to purchases by profit-making Registered Providers of Social Housing, where the purchase is funded by public subsidy.

Charities and national bodies

Where the **purchaser** is a charity, the transaction will be exempt from SDLT if: **9416** Sch 8 FA 2003
- following the purchase, the land is held for qualifying charitable purposes; and
- the charity is not entering into the purchase for the purposes of avoiding SDLT.

Partial relief is also available if the charity intends to **hold the majority**, but not necessarily all, of the property for qualifying charitable purposes.

Relief will be **withdrawn** if charity relief is claimed in respect of a purchase and the purchaser ceases to be a charity, or the land is used for non-charitable purposes within 3 years of the transaction (or after that date if arrangements were made during the 3-year period).

MEMO POINTS 1. "Charity" includes a **charitable trust**, defined as a trust of which all the beneficiaries are charities, or a unit trust scheme in which all the unit holders are charities.
2. **Qualifying charitable purposes** means:
- for use in furthering a charity's purposes; or
- to be held as an investment, the profits of which are used for charitable purposes.

s 69 FA 2003

3. Acquisitions by the following national **bodies** are also exempt from SDLT:
- Historic Buildings and Monuments Commission for England;
- National Endowment for Science, Technology and the Arts;
- Trustees of the British Museum;
- Trustees of the National Heritage Memorial Fund; and
- Trustees of the Natural History Museum.

Leasehold enfranchisement

9417 s 74 FA 2003

Relief from SDLT applies to a nominee or appointee who acquires the freehold of a block of flats on behalf of leaseholders under a statutory right of leasehold enfranchisement.

Overlap relief

9418 Sch 17A para 9 FA 2003

Overlap relief is available where one **lease** is replaced or followed by another. Both leases must be for substantially the same property and the respective lease periods must overlap. The relief works by reducing the net present value (NPV) (¶9389) for the new lease by any rent payable under the new lease which has already been included in the SDLT calculation for the initial lease. This is intended to prevent double taxation.

The relief is **only available if** the initial lease was subject to SDLT and no exemption applied to the first lease.

The **overlap period** is the period from the date the new lease is granted to the date the old lease would have ceased, which is common to both the old and new leases. This includes any extension to lease terms.

EXAMPLE A lease is granted on 1 April 2004 for 25 years (the old lease);
- the date of expiry is 31 March 2029;
- rent of £144,000 per annum is payable under this old lease;
- the NPV of the old lease is £2,373,337;
- SDLT of £22,233 is payable on the rent.

The old lease is surrendered and a new lease is granted on 1 April 2008 for 150 years. The annual rent under the new lease is £110,000.

The overlap period runs from 1 April 2008 to 31 March 2029 (21 years). As the old rent was more than the new rent the NPV for the first 21 years of the new lease is nil. Therefore no SDLT is payable on that part of the new lease. The NPV can never be a negative figure, so the relief is restricted to the value of the rental payments under the new lease.

For years 22 to 150 the annual rent of £110,000 is used to calculate the NPV and SDLT will be payable in line with the normal calculation.

Sch 17A para 9A FA 2003

MEMO POINTS If a tenant **continues in occupation after the termination** of an earlier lease (which was chargeable to SDLT) and he is granted a new lease for basically the same premises, the term of the second lease will be deemed to begin immediately after the termination date. This applies even if the second lease is granted from a later date. Any rent for the period prior to the grant of the second lease, which was taken into account when calculating the SDLT charge on the first lease, is ignored when taxing the second lease.

SECTION 3

Administration

9420 Errors on land transaction returns which were due to be filed on or after 1 April 2010, where the return relates to a tax period beginning on or after 1 April 2009, are subject to the harmonised error penalties regime (¶9784). Provisions in Finance Act 2009 extended HMRC's powers in relation to information and inspection (¶9862+) to the administration of SDLT, and also provided for a new system of penalties for late payment and late filing of returns (¶9855+). Implementation of the new penalties for late filing and late payment is to be staged over a number of years, starting from April 2010, but a commencement date for SDLT has not yet been announced. For details of the harmonised provisions, see ¶9775+.

Certain SDLT schemes are required to be disclosed to HMRC.

A. Disclosure rules

Schemes involving: 9422 SI 2005/1868
– any wholly **non-residential property** with a market value of at least £5 million;
– wholly **residential property** with a market value of at least £1 million;
– **mixed** non-residential and residential property where either the residential property has a market value of at least £1 million or the value of the property as a whole is at least £5 million; or
– where the value of the property is unknown

must be disclosed unless an exemption applies. Only schemes which are expected to provide an SDLT advantage as a main benefit are affected.

Disclosure will usually be by the scheme promoter. The user of the scheme must make the notification where the scheme is devised "in-house", where the promoter is outside the UK and no promoter notifies, or where the information is covered by legal professional privilege.

HMRC have stated that these rules are not intended to affect advisers or promoters who merely assist their clients to understand the tax system and plan transactions appropriately.

The penalty for **failing to comply** can be up to £5,000. If, after the penalty has been imposed, the person does not comply with the disclosure rules, he can face further penalties of up to £600 per day. s 315 FA 2004

MEMO POINTS 1. For these purposes, **market value** is measured by taking all chargeable interests held by the same person or connected persons (¶5570) into account.

2. A **promoter** is the person who designed the scheme, but excludes professionals who have only advised on technical points without being involved in the design as a whole.

3. If the promoter is unsure:
– what **type of property** is involved in the transaction, he is to assume that the property is non-residential; and
– whether the **value** limit (whether £5 million or £1 million) has been exceeded, he is to assume that it has.

Exemptions

The following situations require **no disclosure unless** two or more of the circumstances in the second column apply (any combination, or two or more instances of the same circumstance). If another step or circumstance is involved, upon which the SDLT advantage relies, the scheme must be disclosed. 9423 SI 2005/1868 reg 2(3B)

No disclosure required	Circumstances requiring disclosure
A. Statutory relief claimed [1, 2]	When two of the following are present, or more than one instance of any of the following: 1. acquisition of the land by a special purpose vehicle (SPV) [3]; 2. sale of shares in an SPV which holds the land and is to a third party not connected with the SPV or the vendor; 3. not opting to tax (¶8904)
B. Transfer of a business as a going concern (¶8596)	
C. Undertaking a joint venture partnership which receives the land	

Note:
1. The following **reliefs** are relevant for this purpose:
– all those mentioned at ¶9401, excluding overlap relief;
– sale and leaseback (¶9399);
– collective acquisition by leaseholders (¶9378); and
– croft community right to buy (¶9373).
2. Claims for **multiple reliefs** require no disclosure (except for combinations involving corporate reconstruction, acquisition or group reliefs). **Multiple claims** to the same relief do require disclosure.
3. A **special purpose vehicle** is defined as a company specifically created for the purposes of the transaction.

How to disclose

9424 The rules are **similar to** those for direct taxes (¶2215+), with the following **exceptions**:
– the hallmarks have no relevance for SDLT disclosure;
– a reference number will only be issued by HMRC so that the scheme can be identified internally by the promoter; and
– the time limit applying to disclosure where the promoter is protected by legal professional privilege is different.

Promoters must disclose within 5 working days of the relevant date.

MEMO POINTS 1. The **relevant date** is the earlier of the date on which:
– the promoter makes the scheme available for implementation; or
– he first becomes aware of any transaction forming part of arrangements which must be disclosed.
2. Once a scheme has **been disclosed**, there is no need to either disclose it again, nor disclose a scheme which is substantially the same as that already notified.
3. There is no requirement for the **reference number** to be communicated to users of the scheme.
4. HMRC can apply to the Upper Tribunal for disclosure to be made where they **suspect a notifiable scheme is being used** (¶9920+). Further, a pre-disclosure enquiry can be commenced (¶2234).

9425 In most cases **users** (¶2236) of the scheme will not be required to make any notification, except where:
– the scheme promoter is offshore;
– the promoter is a lawyer who is prohibited from making disclosure because of legal professional privilege (unless the client has waived that right); or
– the user has devised the scheme in-house, so there is no promoter.

Schemes must be disclosed by users within the following timescales:

Type of scheme/arrangement	Timescale
User of product from overseas promoter	Within 5 working days of entering into the first transaction forming part of the scheme
User where promoter is protected by legal professional privilege	Within 30 working days of entering into the first transaction forming part of the scheme
All other users	

9426 The **information** to be disclosed is summarised below (there is no requirement for documents, such as sale agreements, to be submitted):
– name of the promoter, if relevant;
– details of the legal provisions which make the scheme notifiable (that is, within SI 2005/1868);
– summary of the proposals or arrangements, and the name by which they are known;
– explanation of the elements of the scheme, and how the expected tax advantage arises; and
– the law on which the tax advantage is based.

B. Returns

9427 There are strict rules on notifying land transactions.

1. Land transaction returns

9428 Every notifiable transaction must be entered on a land transaction return (form SDLT 1), which must include a self-assessment of liability. The return can be completed manually or online.

A new return form was introduced in April 2001. Use of this has been compulsory from 4 July 2011. A unique reference is now required for the lead purchaser: a National Insurance number for individuals, its UTR (unique taxpayer reference) or VAT registration number for a company or partnership. If no such reference is available, the lead purchaser may use a tax reference number from abroad, stating the name of the country or place of issue. If no tax reference is available, the lead purchaser may use another unique reference, such as a passport number or driving licence number stating the country or place of issue. A lead purchaser who does not have any of the above unique identifiers should contact the Stamp Taxes helpline (0845 603 0135 or, from abroad, +44 1726 209 042) to obtain a reference.
It is vital to retain a copy of the return.

MEMO POINTS 1. Before the return is filed, the purchaser can apply to the Stamp Office for a **post-transaction ruling** on how SDLT applies to the transaction. If the transaction has not yet occurred, it is also possible to apply for guidance in advance (¶9896+). COP 10
2. To **file online**, a purchaser must use a registration process which is similar to that for corporation tax. Practitioners can also register, and must obtain a Stamp Taxes Online Reference Number. Returns can then be filed online on behalf of their clients. Electronic payment is recommended but not compulsory.
Further information is available from www.hmrc.gov.uk/so/online/menu.htm.

Notifiable transactions

The table shows all transactions which are notifiable. 9430 s 77 FA 2003

Type of transaction	Exclusions
Transfer of any major interest[1] in UK land	Exempt transactions (¶9348); and non-leasehold agreements where the consideration is less than £40,000[2]
Lease	Grant of a lease for a term of 7 years or more, in return for a chargeable consideration other than rent of less than £40,000, with annual rent of less than £1,000
	Grant of a lease for a term of less than 7 years where the chargeable consideration does not exceed the zero-rate threshold[3]
	Assignment or surrender of a lease which was originally granted for a term of 7 years or more, and the chargeable consideration is less than £40,000
	Assignment or surrender of a lease which was originally granted for a term of less than 7 years where the chargeable consideration is below the zero-rate threshold[3]
A notional transaction under the anti-avoidance provisions (¶9380)	
Any other transfer	Chargeable consideration is below the zero-rate threshold before any reliefs are applied

Note:
1. A **major interest** is defined as:
– any freehold or leasehold estate whether legal or equitable, in England, Wales and Northern Ireland; or
– the interest of a landowner, or tenant's rights under a lease, in Scotland.
2. Any **linked transactions** must be taken into account when considering the threshold.
3. If a transaction is below the zero-rate threshold because of a specific relief from SDLT (¶9401+), the purchaser needs to consider whether the chargeable consideration **before the relief** was more than the zero-rate threshold to decide whether the transaction is notifiable or not.

Completing the return

HMRC have noted the following in relation to the administration of returns: 9431
– the **amount of SDLT** due should be rounded down to the nearest pound;
– **other documents** should not be enclosed with the SDLT 1 (but see ¶9473); and
– **photocopies** of any supplementary forms will be rejected.

MEMO POINTS 1. Strictly, a separate return is required for every **postal address** involved in a transaction, although HMRC will agree to a list of addresses submitted on a spreadsheet.
2. In addition, where the **same persons** are involved in multiple transactions (i.e. at least six), it is possible to reduce the number of returns required with the agreement of HMRC Complex Transactions Unit (Birmingham Stamp Office, 9th Floor, City Centre House, 30 Union Street, Birmingham B2 4AR; tel: 0845 603 0135).

9433 Sch 10 para 1A FA 2003

Signatories Normally the return will be signed by the purchaser. For joint purchasers, see ¶9490.

A **practitioner** can sign a land transaction return on behalf of a purchaser, provided that the purchaser has declared that all information on the return, with the exception of the effective date, is correct and complete to the best of his knowledge. The purchaser remains responsible for the entries on the return.

Filing date

9434 s 76 FA 2003

The return must be delivered to HMRC within 30 days of the effective date (¶9350).

A return may be filed **later** if the purchaser has a reasonable excuse and submits the return without delay. Examples of a reasonable excuse include postal delays and the serious illness or death of an adviser.

HMRC can serve a **notice** for the taxpayer to submit a return, where they become aware of a transaction and no return has been received.

Amendments

9435 Sch 10 paras 6, 7 FA 2003

Any **incomplete or incorrect** land transaction returns will not be processed by HMRC. The taxpayer will either receive an SDLT 8 letter or phone call, which will indicate why the return is not acceptable. The return will be logged by HMRC until the required information is provided by the taxpayer. This should all occur within the 30-day filing period for the return, otherwise a late filing penalty will be levied.

The **purchaser** may amend a return by notice to HMRC within 12 months of the filing date. **HMRC** may also correct obvious errors and omissions in the return, by issuing a notice within 9 months from either the date on which the return was delivered or the date of amendment by the purchaser. The purchaser can reject the correction by amending the return within 3 months of the notice.

Records

9437 Sch 10 para 9 FA 2003

A **purchaser** who is required to deliver a land transaction return is **obliged to keep** sufficient records to enable him to deliver a complete and correct return. These records must be **preserved** for 6 years from the effective date of the land transaction or the end of any enquiry, although HMRC may specify a different period. Records must be retained even if the land is sold within the 6-year (or specified) period.

Sch 10 para 11 FA 2003

A **penalty** of up to £3,000 may be imposed for failure to preserve records.

Penalties

9438

Errors and inaccuracies on land transaction returns are subject to penalties under the harmonised penalties regime (see ¶9780). Penalties are **notified by** a formal HMRC notice and may be appealed against to the tax tribunal (¶9920).

9439 Sch 10 para 3 FA 2003 SDLTM 86460

Failure to file return If a purchaser fails to submit a land transaction return by the filing date, the flat-rate penalty of £100 will **initially** be charged. If the return is filed **more than 3 months** after the filing date, the flat-rate penalty will be £200.

Sch 10 para 4 FA 2003

If the return is still outstanding **12 months** after the filing date, a **tax-related penalty** is payable, which will not exceed the tax due. In addition, a daily penalty of up to £60 per day may be imposed if the purchaser fails to respond to a notice demanding submission of a return.

MEMO POINTS 1. Finance Act 2009 introduced **new penalties for late filing and payment**. For SDLT, the changes will have effect from a date yet to be announced. See ¶9858 for further details.
2. Contrary to HMRC's view stated in the Stamp Duty Land Tax Manual, the First-tier Tribunal has held that it is a reasonable excuse for failure to make a SDLT return on time (within 30 days of the effective date of the transaction) that the return was lost in the post. *C Runham and C Naramore* TC00933 [2011]

Senior accounting officers Special responsibilities to larger companies and their senior accounting officers personally. The "senior accounting officer" is defined as "the director or officer of the company who has overall responsibility for the company's financial accounting arrangements". Senior accounting officers are required to: 9440 Sch 46 FA 2009 HMRC Brief37/09
– take reasonable steps to establish and monitor accounting systems to ensure they are adequate for the purposes of tax reporting; and
– certify annually that the systems are adequate or specify the nature of the inadequacies.

The company must also advise HMRC of the identity of the senior accounting officer for the company. Penalties of up to £5,000 can be levied on the senior accounting officer for failure to comply with the regime. For further details, see ¶2360.

Incorrect return Errors on land transaction returns are subject to the harmonised error penalties regime (see ¶9784). 9441

Determinations

If a land transaction **return has not been submitted by the filing date**, HMRC may, within 4 years of the effective date of the transaction, make a determination of the amount of tax chargeable. Notice of the determination must be issued to the purchaser. The determination will have the same effect as a self-assessment for the purpose of penalties. 9443 Sch 10 para 25 FA 2003

The determination is **superseded** by any subsequent self-assessment submitted within 4 years from the day on which the power to make the determination first became exercisable or, if later, 12 months after the date of the determination.

MEMO POINTS Prior to 1 April 2011 the limit was 6 years. However, in a case where a loss of tax is brought about deliberately, or where there is a failure to disclose a tax avoidance scheme, the period is extended to 20 years. Sch 51 FA 2009

2. Registration of land transactions

The **Land Registry** is usually prohibited from registering a transaction unless an appropriate certificate, confirming compliance with the SDLT provisions, has been issued by HMRC, evidencing the submission of a land transaction return. 9445 s 79 FA 2003

The **exceptions** to this rule are:

a. a contract for a land transaction under which the transaction is to be completed by a conveyance, or a transfer of rights (¶9351) under such a contract; and

b. the transaction was not a notifiable transaction (¶9430).

MEMO POINTS 1. HMRC no longer issue a paper certificate (SDLT 5) if the SDLT return is submitted online. Instead, an electronic certificate is available after the return has been successfully submitted online. It is important that a copy of this certificate is made to enable the purchaser to provide the appropriate information to the Land Registry. It should be noted that the e-certificates are automatically deleted from HMRC's website 30 days after the submission of the return.
2. In **Scotland** HMRC respond to returns within 16 calendar days, because of the tighter registration deadlines involved. The optional Automated Registration to Title of Land (ARTL) system is available. All Scottish practitioners may apply for a licence. The ARTL is used for whole registered titles, so first registrations, part registrations and leases are excluded.
ARTL provides an integrated service enabling:
– online registration of a title to land;
– electronic payment of registration fees;
– electronic processing of land transaction returns; and
– collection of SDLT by HMRC through direct debits.

3. At a future date, **electronic conveyancing** will be introduced for the whole of the UK, and the SDLT rules will be integrated with the new process. In particular:
– information currently contained on the return will be delivered to the land registrar first;
– the effective date of a transaction may only occur once the electronic registration process is complete; and
– the registrar will be given various administration powers currently undertaken by HMRC.

Self-certification

9447 Sch 11 FA 2003 Prior to 12 March 2008 a purchaser who did not have an SDLT liability, and therefore was not required to complete an SDLT return, had to self-certify that no SDLT was payable before the Land Registry would register the transaction.

The Land Registry has confirmed that, by concession, any transactions where the registration was being held over because of an outstanding SDLT 60 (a self-certification form) will now be registered, even if the effective date was before 12 March 2008.

9450 Sch 11 para 3 FA 2003 A tax-related **penalty** (which cannot exceed the amount of tax due) will be imposed if a purchaser:
– discovers that a transaction is a chargeable transaction and does not remedy the error without unreasonable delay; or
– fraudulently or negligently claims that no SDLT is due.

Sch 11 para 6 FA 2003 Failing to keep and preserve **records** which supported self-certification made for a transaction entered into before 12 March 2008 can result in a penalty of up to £3,000.

C. Payment of tax

9451 The purchaser is **liable** for the payment of SDLT in respect of a chargeable transaction. **Special rules** apply where purchasers act jointly (¶9490).

Due date

9453 s 86 FA 2003 SDLT Technical News Issue 4 Payment of SDLT must be made by the due date of the return (i.e. 30 days after the effective date of the transaction).

Where a **further return** is submitted (¶9464), the resulting tax must be paid by the return's filing due date.

Where a **return is amended**:
– before the filing date, any additional tax arising as a result is due on the filing date;
– after the filing date, the additional tax is due on the date of the amendment.

If additional tax becomes payable as a result of an HMRC **determination or assessment** (¶9443), it must be paid within 30 days of its issue.

MEMO POINTS Finance Act 2009 introduced **new penalties for late filing and payment**. For SDLT, the changes will have effect for returns from a date yet to be announced. See ¶9858 for further details.

9454 s 90 FA 2003 **Uncertain consideration** An application to **defer payment of tax** may be submitted by the purchaser of the **freehold** within the usual filing date for a return (¶9434) where the amount of tax payable depends on consideration that:
– is contingent or uncertain (¶9359); and
– falls to be paid on one or more future dates of which at least one may be more than 6 months after the effective date of the transaction.

There is no deferment provision if the consideration for a **lease** is uncertain (¶9392).

The application will not affect the **purchaser's obligations** as regards SDLT on chargeable consideration that has already been paid, or is not contingent and is ascertained or ascertainable.

Method

Payment may be made by: 9456
- cheque;
- bank giro;
- BACs;
- CHAPs;
- billpay (using a debit card);
- telephone/internet banking;
- attending the Post Office; or
- using a credit card over the Internet.

A **receipt** will only be issued on request.

MEMO POINTS HMRC will impose a **fee**, equivalent to 1.4% of the payment due, when the taxpayer chooses to use a **credit card** over the Internet to discharge a tax debt.

Interest

Underpayments Interest on unpaid tax will be levied from 30 days after the relevant date, to the date on which the tax is paid. For the rates of interest, see ¶9974. 9458 ss 87, 88 FA 2003

The **relevant date** is generally 30 days after the effective date of the transaction. However:
a. on the withdrawal of certain reliefs (housebuilding, charities, and corporate reliefs for groups, acquisitions and re-organisations), it is the date of the disqualifying event; and
b. where an application is made to defer payment on the basis of contingent or uncertain consideration (¶9454), the relevant date is that on which the deferred payment is due.

Interest will also be levied on unpaid **penalties** from the date of determination to the date of payment.

MEMO POINTS Harmonised interest rates now apply across the taxes. Details are given at ¶9782.

Overpayments Interest will be paid by HMRC on any repayments of tax or penalties from the relevant time to the date of repayment. For the rates of interest, see ¶9974. 9459 s 89 FA 2003

The **relevant time** is the date on which the payment of tax or penalty is made.

D. Subsequent actions

Once the land transaction return has been filed, and possibly amended, the SDLT liability is final, subject to: 9461
- a subsequent claim by the taxpayer in the event of a mistake or error;
- a further return required because of a withdrawal of relief, a linked transaction or contingent consideration;
- an enquiry into the return which amends the amount shown as due; or
- a discovery assessment.

In addition, HMRC have powers to access information in order to enforce full compliance, and there is a penal code which applies if the taxpayer fails to fulfil his obligations.

1. By the taxpayer

Error or mistake claim

If the purchaser believes that **too much tax** has been paid as a result of a mistake on the return, he may submit a freestanding claim for relief within 6 years of the effective date of the transaction (to be reduced to 4 years from a date to be announced). 9463 Sch 10 para 34 FA 2003

Legislation effective from 1 April 2011 removes the requirement that the overpayment was caused by a mistake in a return and that it must have been subject to an assessment. The rules also confirm that HMRC are not liable to repay any amount except as provided for in legislation.

Relief is not available where the return was made in accordance with prevailing practice, or where the error related to a claim or election contained within the return.

Further returns

9464 s 81 FA 2003

A further return must be submitted within 30 days of a disqualifying event where one of the following **reliefs** has been withdrawn:
- group relief (¶9751);
- reconstruction or acquisition relief (¶9738);
- charities relief (¶9416); or
- housebuilding relief (¶9408).

A further return will **also be required** in the event of a linked transaction (¶9378), on the cessation of a contingency, or when an uncertainty is resolved (¶9359).

2. By HMRC

Enquiries

9466 Sch 10 para 12 FA 2003

HMRC may initiate an enquiry into a land transaction return **within** 9 months of:
- the due date for filing, if the return was submitted by this date;
- the date of submission, if the return was filed late; or
- the date that any amendment was made by the purchaser.

The enquiry can **relate to** either the amount of tax chargeable or whether tax is chargeable at all.

MEMO POINTS 1. An enquiry can also be raised into a **self-certificate** (¶9447).
2. If an enquiry is initiated with respect to a **return amended** after the enquiry period is ended, the scope of the enquiry is limited to the amendments.
3. Where an initial return is followed by a **further return** relating to the same transaction (e.g. in the case of a linked transaction or contingent consideration), HMRC are able to raise an enquiry into the earlier return, even where it would normally be out of time.
4. HMRC's harmonised powers in relation to inspection and information **extend to SDLT**. See ¶9862.

9467 **Request for information** HMRC's harmonised powers in relation to inspection and information **extend to SDLT**. See ¶9862.

9469 Sch 10 paras 19 and 21 FA 2003

Appeal to the tribunal During the enquiry, any question in connection with the subject matter of the enquiry may be referred for **determination** by the tax tribunal. While proceedings with respect to the referral are in progress, the enquiry cannot be closed. For details of the appeal process, see ¶9938.

9470 **Changes to tax liability** HMRC may amend the assessment of tax due if, during the course of the enquiry, it is established that the self-assessment of the amount of tax payable is insufficient.

The **purchaser** may also amend the return during the course of the enquiry.

Leaflet SD8

MEMO POINTS When an enquiry is completed and an **amendment** is found to be required to the submitted return, HMRC will either write to the taxpayer or request a meeting. In addition, **penalties** will be due in cases of fraudulent or negligent conduct, although mitigation is available for disclosure and co-operation.
The taxpayer is expected to make a **formal** written **offer** to pay one sum in respect of the tax, interest and penalties, and, if accepted, HMRC will issue a letter of acceptance. This arrangement constitutes a legal contract. In certain cases payments by instalments will be accepted.

If the taxpayer **does not make such an offer**, HMRC will issue a closure notice which will state the changes made, and the tax, interest and penalties which are due.
There is a **right of appeal** against any amendments or any penalties levied.

Completion The enquiry is complete when HMRC issue a **notice** informing the purchaser that they have completed their enquiries, and stating their conclusion. 9471

Discovery assessments

HMRC may **issue** a discovery assessment where they establish that: 9473 Sch 10 para 28 FA 2003
- an amount of tax that should have been assessed has not been;
- an assessment to tax is insufficient; or
- excessive relief has been given.

Similarly, they may also issue an assessment to recover an excessive repayment of tax. This assessment will be treated as if it referred to unpaid tax.

In both cases, if the purchaser **has submitted a land transaction return**, an assessment may only be issued where:
- the situation is attributable to fraudulent or negligent conduct on the part of the purchaser or someone acting on his behalf; or
- HMRC could not reasonably have been expected, on the basis of the information available to them, to be aware of the situation.

An assessment may **not be made** if the situation is attributable to a mistake on the return as to the basis of the tax liability, and the return was completed in accordance with prevailing practice.

HMRC have stated that a **taxpayer can protect himself** from a discovery assessment by taking note of the guidance already issued in respect of income tax (¶4566). Briefly, this requires taxpayers to disclose anything which might be relevant to the interpretation of entries on a tax return. However, HMRC believe that it would be unusual for any disclosure to be necessary. For example, no additional disclosure is required when apportioning consideration between chattels and land, or on the sale of a business. If a taxpayer does wish to make a disclosure, he should write to the Complex Transactions Unit (¶9431) at or before the time that the land transaction return is submitted. SDLT Technical News Issue 4

The **time limit** for an assessment is 4 years from the effective date of the transaction, unless it relates to fraudulent or negligent conduct on the part of the purchaser or someone acting on his behalf, in which case the assessment may be made up to 20 years from the effective date. 9474

The purchaser may **appeal** against an assessment within 30 days of the date of issue.

MEMO POINTS Prior to 1 April 2011 the limit was 6 years.

Provision of information

HMRC's harmonised powers in relation to inspection and information **extend to SDLT**. See ¶9862. 9476

Provided that consent is given by an appropriate judicial authority, a tax accountant may be required to provide papers to HMRC, but only where the accountant has been **convicted of** an offence in relation to tax or has been **penalised** for assisting in the preparation of an incorrect return. Where the tax accountant has submitted an appeal, a notice under this provision cannot be issued for 12 months from the date of the conviction. 9477

MEMO POINTS 1. An **appropriate judicial authority** is a Circuit Judge in England, a Sheriff in Scotland or a County Court Judge in Northern Ireland.

In response to evasion

A person who is **knowingly involved in the fraudulent evasion of SDLT**, either on his own or someone else's behalf, may, on summary conviction, be sentenced to up to 6 months in 9484 s 95 FA 2003 prison, a fine, or both. On conviction on indictment, the maximum sentence is 7 years in prison, a fine, or both.

9486 s 96 FA 2003 A person who **knowingly assists in the preparation of an incorrect return**, information or other document may be subject to a penalty of up to £3,000.

Reconsiderations and appeals

9487 A taxpayer can appeal **penalties** by giving written notice to HMRC within 30 days of the penalty notice, stating the grounds for the appeal. If the appeal is based on reasonable excuse, which is accepted by HMRC, the penalty will be waived. If it is not possible to reach an agreement, the taxpayer has the option to:
– appeal to the tax tribunal; or
– request that HMRC carry out an internal review of the decision, by following the direct tax procedure as set out in ¶9930.

To avoid interest, the taxpayer should pay the penalty within 30 days of the notice. If the appeal is successful, the penalty will be repaid with interest.

E. Joint purchasers

9490 s 103 FA 2003 The **general rule** for joint purchasers is that they have joint and several liability to comply with the requirements of the SDLT regime. However, **compliance obligations** – such as the submission of a land transaction return – may be discharged by any purchaser on behalf of the others. **Interest and penalties** imposed as a result of a failure to submit a land transaction return, or pay the requisite tax, can be recovered from all or any of the joint purchasers. **Special rules** apply where the joint purchasers are partners or trustees.

Partnerships

9491 Sch 15 FA 2003 For the purposes of SDLT, the **assets** of a partnership are treated as held by the partners. Only partners who occupy that position at the effective date of the transaction are jointly and severally liable for complying with the obligations of SDLT. A person who subsequently becomes a partner is not liable to the tax, penalty or any related interest.

All of the partners must **sign** the return. Alternatively, the majority of partners can nominate a "**responsible partner**", who can sign on their behalf, to act as a representative of the partnership.

Trusts and trustees

9492 Sch 16 FA 2003 The position of trustees in relation to a land transaction depends on the type of trust involved. Any trustee may **sign** the return.

MEMO POINTS Any **interests in a partnership** (¶9766) held or acquired by trustees are treated as a chargeable interest.

9494 Where a chargeable interest in land is acquired by **bare trustees or nominees**, it is treated as an acquisition by the person for whom they act. However, where a bare trustee grants a **lease to the beneficiary**, he will be treated as a separate person.

Where the **trustees of a non-bare trust** acquire a chargeable interest, the trustees are treated as the purchaser. In this case, responsible trustees are **jointly and severally liable** for complying with the obligations of SDLT, even where the effective date of a transaction falls before a person became a trustee. However, new trustees will not be liable to interest or penalties which predate their appointment. Land transaction returns may be submitted by one or more of the trustees, known as "**relevant trustees**", on behalf of the others.

CHAPTER 2

Stamp duty

OUTLINE ¶¶

SECTION 1

General principles

Stamp duty now only applies to instruments relating to stock or marketable securities and to certain transfers of interests in partnerships. 9540 Sch 13 FA 1999

With the exception of specified electronic transfers, a company may only register a **transfer** of shares if a proper instrument of transfer is effected. As most transfers of shares are effected within the CREST electronic settlement system, no stamp duty is payable in respect of such transfers, although SDRT will be charged (¶9645).

No stamp duty is chargeable in respect of the **issue** of shares and on the initial transfer of shares into the CREST system. s 186 FA 1996

MEMO POINTS 1. Stamp duty is also applicable when transferring a **partnership interest** when the partnership has stock investments (¶9773). Between 1 December 2003 and 22 July 2004, stamp duty also applied to transfers of land in and out of **partnerships**, and the acquisition of a partnership interest where the partnership held land.
2. Before 1 December 2003, stamp duty applied to **land** and leases, and full details were included in earlier editions of *Tax Memo*.

Scope

Stamp duty **applies to** any instrument used to transfer stock and marketable securities executed in the UK, or applying to property located in the UK, wherever executed. 9542 s 125 FA 2003

There are specific rules for bearer instruments, depositary receipts and clearance services.

Rate

9543 Sch 13 FA 1999 s 112 FA 1999 s 97 FA 2008 Stamp duty is generally **payable by** the transferee, for example the purchaser, and the rate payable depends on the instrument.

If the transfer is by way of **sale**, the instrument is subject to ad valorem duty at a rate of 0.5% (except for bearer instruments), and the charge is rounded up to the nearest multiple of £5.

1. Instruments

9545 s 122 SA 1891 An instrument is not **defined** but includes every written document, although not a receipt, because this is not generally the means of transfer.

A document that is to be stamped must be written so that the stamp may be placed on the face of the document and cannot be used for any other document. The most common example would be a stock transfer form.

MEMO POINTS 1. Where **more than one instrument** is written on the same paper, each instrument must be stamped separately.

s 5 SA 1891 2. The instrument must set out all the **facts and circumstances** affecting the liability to stamp duty. If a person fraudulently executes or prepares a document which does not comply with this requirement, he is liable to a penalty of up to £3,000.

2. Exemptions

9546 Sch 32 FA 2008 Instruments which do not give effect to a sale for consideration are **generally** exempt from the charge to stamp duty.

Certain instruments executed, other than by way of sale, before 13 March 2008, and stamped before 19 March 2008, were subject to a **fixed duty** of £5. Prior to 13 March 2008, where the transaction was certified (¶9552), it would have become fully exempt. This included shares given by way of gift, on marriage and on death.

The following transactions were also subject to a fixed rate of £5 until 13 March 2008:
- surrender of property;
- written declaration of trust;
- duplicate or counterpart;
- partition or division of property; and
- release or renunciation other than on sale.

Low-value transactions

9547 s 98 FA 2008 If the **value of a transfer** is less than £1,000, no stamp duty is payable. This **applies** for instruments executed after 13 March 2008 and not stamped before 19 March 2008. It will need to be certified that the value of the instrument is less than £1,000 and that the transaction does not form part of a larger transaction, or series of transactions.

The certificate is on the reverse of the stock transfer form and does not need to be presented to HMRC for stamping.

If the transaction is part of a series of transaction where the total value will be more than £1,000 the instrument will be chargeable to stamp duty and must be submitted to HMRC for stamping.

For details of self-certification prior to 13 March 2008, see ¶9552.

Specific exempt instruments

9548 Sch 13 para 24(a) FA 1999 s 50 FA 1987 s 57 FA 1947 s 126 FA 1984 The following are specifically exempt:

a. government stocks;
b. warrants to purchase government stocks;
c. treasury guaranteed stocks;
d. stocks of designated international organisations; and
e. some loan capital and debentures.

Certain transactions on the following exchanges are exempt from stamp duty and SDRT (see ¶9658): 9549 s 116 FA 1991
- Eurex Clearing AG;
- European Central Counterparty Ltd;
- European Multilateral Clearing Facility NV;
- LCH.Clearnet Ltd; and
- SIX X-CLEAR AG.

Loan capital includes any debenture stock, corporation stock or funded debt issued by a body corporate, regardless of what it is called. The definition also includes any capital raised which has the character of borrowed money. Stock or marketable securities issued by the government of any country or territory outside the UK are also loan capital for these purposes. 9550 s 78 FA 1986

Loan capital is **not exempt** from stamp duty if it is equity-related.

MEMO POINTS 1. Loan capital will be **equity-related** if either: s 79 FA 1986
a. at the time of execution, the instrument carries a right of conversion into shares or securities, or to acquire further shares or securities including loan stock of the same description; or
b. the instrument carries or has carried, a right to interest:
- at a rate exceeding a normal commercial rate of return;
- determined by the results of the business (although exemption is available where the amount of interest has an inverse relationship with the business results or the value of its assets – that is, as the results improve the amount of interest payable falls); or
- on repayment to an amount exceeding the nominal value of the stock that is not reasonably comparable with the capital return on loan stock quoted on the Stock Exchange.
Capital market instruments are not excluded from the exemption from stamp duty just because they carry a right, or have carried a right, to interest which ceases or reduces because the issuer has insufficient funds to meet the interest payment after meeting other liabilities under the capital market arrangement.
2. Sukuk, which is an **Islamic investment bond**, is treated as loan capital and is therefore exempt.

Anti-avoidance provisions A deemed sale, subject to ad valorem stamp duty, will occur where **marketable securities** are transferred in return for non-chargeable securities. This applies, for example, where exempt gilts are transferred in exchange for shares. 9551 s 122 FA 2000

MEMO POINTS 1. The **consideration for the transfer** is the market value of the marketable securities immediately before the transfer, if less than the consideration for the sale.
2. **Non-chargeable securities** means any stock, securities and debts due which are not chargeable to stamp duty.

Self-certification With effect **from 13 March 2008**, self-certification is no longer required, except for instruments relating to land transactions and low-value transactions (¶9547). 9552 SI 1987/516

Divorce and dissolution of civil partnership No stamp duty is payable in respect of the transfer or sale of any property transferred from one party to a marriage or partnership to the other party, where the instrument is **executed as a result of**: 9555 s 83 FA 1985
a. an agreement between the parties in connection with:
- the dissolution or annulment of their marriage/partnership;
- their judicial separation; or
- a separation order in respect of them; or
b. a court order made:
- on the granting of a divorce, annulment or judicial separation;
- in connection with the dissolution, annulment of a marriage/partnership or a judicial separation, made at any time after the relevant event; or
- under sections 22A, 23A or 24A of the Matrimonial Causes Act 1973.

Exempt transferees No ad valorem stamp duty is payable in respect of the transfer of any property to: 9558 s 129 FA 1982
- a charity (evidence of charitable status should be verified by checking the entry on the online register of the Charity Commission or the Office of the Scottish Charity Regulator);

– the Trustees of the National Heritage Memorial Fund;
– the Historic Buildings and Monuments Commission for England; or
– the National Endowment for Science, Technology and the Arts.

Such transfers are only exempt from ad valorem stamp duty if **subjected to** the adjudication process (¶9578).

The exemption does not extend to **transfers made by** the above bodies.

3. Time of charge

9560 The liability to stamp duty arises at the time an instrument is executed.

Incomplete documents do not require stamping and therefore the liability becomes due when the document is completed.

MEMO POINTS 1. A document is **complete** when it has been executed by the last person required to make it an effective document.
2. If a transfer requires **registering**, it is not complete until executed by all parties required for registration.

4. Consideration

9562 s 6 SA 1891 Ad valorem duty will be charged on the consideration for a transfer (including VAT where appropriate).

Where the consideration is in **cash**, the value will be self-evident, unless payments are made over a period of time (¶9568).

Consideration may also be in non-monetary form (i.e. stock or marketable securities, or debts and other liabilities), in which case the market value of that consideration is used. HMRC should be told how the amount has been ascertained.

Where the consideration is expressed in a **foreign currency**, it should be converted to sterling at the exchange rate on the date of execution.

Shares and securities

9564 s 272(3) TCGA 1992 **Quoted** shares and securities are valued at the lower of:
– the lower of the two prices quoted in the Stock Exchange Daily Official List for the relevant date plus a quarter of the difference between the two prices; and
– the average of the highest and lowest prices recorded for normal bargains on that date.

EXAMPLE As consideration for a chargeable transfer, Mr B receives 1,000 ordinary shares in A Plc. On the day in question the prices quoted by the Stock Exchange Daily Official List were 213 – 218 and the normal bargain prices for the day were recorded as 208, 210, 216 and 219.
The share valuation will be based on the lower of:
– 213 + (1/4 × (218 – 213)) = 214.25; and
– (208 + 219)/ 2 = 213.50.
The shares will therefore be valued at 213.5p each, giving a total consideration of £2,135.

9565 **Unquoted** shares and securities are valued on the basis of the open-market value at the time of the transfer. The open-market value in this case is based on the assumption that the prospective buyer has all the information available to him that a prudent purchaser might reasonably require, if he was purchasing them from a willing vendor in a private sale at arm's length.

s 55 SA 1891 The valuation should also take account of **restrictions** on the transfer of shares found in the company's Articles of Association. However, the possibility of future issues of stock – that is, the right to acquire future shares – is not relevant when determining the value of the consideration.

MEMO POINTS When **registering a transfer** of shares on a sale (other than transfers processed within the CREST settlement system), the company must ensure that the instrument has been adequately stamped. The consideration for the transfer is shown on the top left of the stock transfer form and, if the company believes this is not the market value of the shares, it may request the person to increase the consideration or submit the instrument to the adjudication process.

Debts and liabilities

Where the consideration is in the **form** of: 9567 s 57 SA 1891
– debts and other liabilities, the amount of consideration is the amount of the debt; or
– a debt due to the transferee, the chargeable consideration is limited to the value of the property transferred, irrespective of whether the debt exceeds this amount, provided that the document is subject to adjudication (¶9578). s 102 FA 1980

Future payments

Where the consideration is in the form of **periodic payments**, the general rule is that the consideration is the total value of payments expected to be made in the 20 years following execution of the instrument. This is reduced to 12 years where the payments are to be made periodically through someone's life, or more than 1 person's life. 9568 s 56 SA 1891

Where the consideration **is contingent on a future event and unascertainable** at the date of execution, the following rules generally apply: 9570

a. if the maximum consideration payable can be ascertained, that is the consideration for stamp duty purposes (e.g. 10% of the profits for the first 4 years subject to a maximum of £1 million, so £1 million is the consideration) – this is particularly useful where the consideration is unknown but a maximum figure can be used for the transfer documents;
b. if the maximum is unascertainable but the minimum consideration can be ascertained, that minimum is the consideration (e.g. £50,000 plus an increase for inflation for the first 18 months, when £50,000 is taken into account); or
c. where neither the minimum nor maximum can be ascertained but a basic figure is stated, which may be reduced or increased depending on circumstances, that basic figure is deemed to be the consideration (e.g. basic £300,000 plus 5% of profits or minus 5% of losses for the first 12 months, when £300,000 is taken into account).

Documents can be **provisionally stamped** using the initial consideration or an estimate. However, HMRC must receive an undertaking (either from the purchaser, or from an agent acting on his behalf) to resubmit the documents, with any additional duty, when the final figure is known.

EXAMPLE Mr C sells his shares in D Ltd to E Ltd for consideration of £100,000 plus 10% of the profits for the first year.
The consideration for stamp duty purposes is £100,000 and ad valorem duty of £500 is due.

SECTION 2

Administration

1. Stamping of documents

The payment of stamp duty is generally reflected on a document by the presence of an impressed duty-paid stamp, which is obtained by posting the document to the Birmingham Stamp Office (¶9431). The stamp simply shows that duty has been paid, but does not indicate that the correct amount has been paid. HMRC aim to return stamped documents within 5 working days. 9575

To be certain that the **correct duty is paid**, a document must be submitted for adjudication.

Original document unavailable

9576 s 12A SDMA 1891 Where a stamped document has been lost or spoiled and a **replacement document** prepared, an allowance may be claimed in respect of the stamp duty originally paid.

If the original document has been:

a. lost, the holder of the document must agree that should the original be subsequently found, it must be surrendered to HMRC for destruction (a claim for relief can be made at any time); or

b. spoiled, a claim for relief must be made within 2 years of the date of the document, or the date that the document was executed if it is undated. HMRC have the power to extend this time limit. A claim can only be made if:

– no legal proceedings have been started in which the document would be, or has been, offered in evidence; and

– the original document is handed to HMRC for destruction.

If a **valid claim** for relief is made, no duty is actually charged in respect of the replacement document, although it is stamped with the duty which would otherwise be chargeable. If duty has already been paid in respect of the replacement document, a repayment will be made of the duty and any interest and penalties paid.

2. Adjudication

9578 As mentioned above, the stamping of a document is not evidence that the correct amount of duty has been paid. This confirmation can only be given if a document is subject to the adjudication process, in which case an adjudication stamp (either "Adjudged not chargeable to duty" or "Adjudged duly stamped") will be fixed to the document.

A person may **request** adjudication in respect of any transfer.

For certain transfers, adjudication is **compulsory**. This is generally for transfers where an exemption is claimed, including those:

– to charities and national bodies (¶9558);

– where the exemption for company reorganisations (¶9743) or associated companies (¶9758) is claimed; and

– for consideration comprising a debt due to the transferee (¶9567).

MEMO POINTS 1. Adjudication may be requested in respect of a **document which has already been stamped** and where an exemption is now claimed. However, a repayment of overpaid duty can only be made if the request is made within 2 years of the date of the document, or (if undated) the date of execution.

2. Adjudication can be particularly important when a **third party** is involved – for example, a company takeover situation – as the process gives certainty to the amount of a stamp duty liability.

Procedure

9579 s 12 SA 1891 If a document is to be adjudicated, it should be **posted to** the Birmingham Stamp Office, **accompanied by** a copy of the document and a statement giving full disclosure of the facts which may affect the liability to duty. The person submitting the document may also make representations concerning duty he believes to be payable but HMRC will determine the amount payable.

a. If **no duty is payable**, the document will be stamped "Adjudged not chargeable to duty".

b. If **duty is payable**, HMRC will issue an informal statement of duty. If the person submitting the document is satisfied with the amount of duty adjudicated, the duty can be paid and the document stamped "Adjudged duly stamped".

9580 ss 13, 13B SA 1891 If the person is **not satisfied** that the amount of duty is correct, he should raise the matter with HMRC and attempt to reach an agreement. Penalties will not be charged where stamp duty is paid following informal adjudication.

If agreement cannot be reached informally, HMRC will issue a **formal notice** of decision of adjudication, against which the person can appeal within 30 days of the date of issue.

Once the amount of duty has been formally adjudged, the **stamp duty must be paid within** 30 days to avoid a penalty. s 12A(2) SA 1891

MEMO POINTS For an **appeal** to be heard, the full amount of the adjudged duty must be paid beforehand. Once the appeal application has been made and the duty adjudged, HMRC will then state the case and the matter will be referred to the High Court, which will determine the amount of duty due. In exceptional cases, an appeal may be made against the decision of the High Court. Once the appeal has been determined and the correct amount of duty, interest and penalties (if any) have been paid, the document will be stamped "Adjudged duly stamped".

3. Payment of duty

Due date

In general, chargeable documents should be **presented for stamping** at the Birmingham Stamp Office no later than 30 days after the document is executed. Duty is payable at the same time. 9582 s 15 SA 1891

If **SDRT** has already been paid, this will be refunded (¶9664).

If an instrument is **executed outside the UK**, it must be stamped within 30 days of execution. If stamping is delayed, interest will run in the normal way. ss 15A, 15B SA 1891

A document cannot be stamped until the duty and any applicable interest and penalties have been paid. However, if a transaction involves contingent or uncertain consideration, see ¶9570.

MEMO POINTS HMRC impose a **fee** equivalent to 1.4% of the payment due if the taxpayer chooses to pay by credit card over the Internet.

Interest

Interest charges are mandatory and HMRC have no power to mitigate any charge. However, interest is only charged where the amount due is at least £25. Any charge is rounded down to the nearest multiple of £5. 9584 s 15A SA 1891

Interest runs from 30 days after the execution of the document to the actual date of payment. For the applicable interest rates, see ¶9974. Where the amount of stamp duty payable cannot be ascertained within this period, a payment may be lodged with HMRC on account to minimise the interest charge.

Repayments

A repayment of duty may occur where the amount of duty paid in respect of a document subsequently proves excessive: for example, where a document is subject to adjudication and the adjudged duty is less than the payment on account. 9585 s 110 FA 1999

A repayment may also be made where a stamp is spoiled or misused (¶9576).

Repayments of stamp duty **of at least £25** carry interest from the date of payment (or 30 days from the execution of the document, if later) to the date that the repayment is made. Repayments of **amounts paid on account** of a stamp duty liability will only carry interest if the document is actually stamped. If the document is withdrawn unstamped, no interest is due.

4. Failure to comply

If a person fails to stamp a document, the consequences depend on whether the document is required for legal purposes (such as proving legal title to shares). If, to rectify the position, 9587 a document is stamped late, penalties may be charged. Penalties may also be charged in respect of other administrative failures.

Consequences of failing to stamp a document

9589 ss 14(4), 17 SA 1891

Failure to stamp an instrument is not an offence in its own right. However, to encourage stamping, an unstamped document is **inadmissible** in the Courts of Law (with the exception of criminal cases). In addition, such a document is ineffective for the purposes of registration. For example, a company must refuse to reflect unstamped transactions in its share register.

HMRC will not accept an unstamped instrument as **evidence** of a transaction. Should the instrument be required as evidence, it will therefore be necessary to submit the instrument to HMRC for stamping and to pay the stamp duty, any interest and the penalty for late stamping.

Penalties

9590 Penalties may be levied in respect of a failure to comply with any of the administrative obligations. Penalties are **rounded down** to the nearest multiple of £5.

HMRC may **mitigate** a penalty, depending on the circumstances. In particular, late fixed duty cases will not be liable to a penalty, provided that the document is presented for stamping within 12 months.

No penalty is payable where there is a **reasonable excuse** for the delay. Reasonable excuse is not defined but the defence is generally only accepted where the delay was due to an exceptional, unforeseeable event.

9592 s 15B SA 1891

Late stamping of a document If a document is presented for stamping outside the 30-day time limit, a penalty is due as follows, so if the delay is:
- **less than 12 months**, the penalty is the lower of £300 or the stamp duty payable; or
- **more than 12 months**, the penalty is the greater of £300 or the stamp duty payable.

s 13A SA 1891

A person may **appeal** against a penalty within 30 days of notification of the penalty. This will be heard by the tax tribunal.

9593 **Other penalties** The following table summarises other penalties which may be levied.

Offence	Penalty
Failure to stamp a document following formal notification of adjudication	£300
Registration of incorrectly stamped document	£300
Failure to allow inspection of documents	£300
Failure to set out true facts in a document affecting the liability to duty	£3,000
Fraudulent acts	£3,000

SECTION 3

Special situations

9595 Specific rules apply to the following types of instruments and circumstances:
- bearer instruments;
- depositary receipts (affecting banks only);
- clearance services;
- transactions involving intermediaries; and
- repurchases and stock lending.

A. Bearer instruments

A bearer instrument is a document which constitutes the rights of the holder to the securities represented by that document. The rights can therefore be transferred by delivery – that is, simply handing over the bearer instrument, so there is no stampable document in respect of a transfer. **Stamp duty** is therefore **imposed** at the time the bearer instrument is issued and, in limited circumstances, on a subsequent transfer. 9596

1. Scope

Stamp duty is chargeable in respect of the **issue** of bearer instruments in the UK, and instruments issued outside the UK by, or on behalf of, a UK company. SDRT may also be charged in respect of certain agreements to transfer bearer instruments (¶9657). 9597

Stamp duty is charged on the **transfer** of the stock constituted by the bearer instrument in the UK if no duty was charged on the issue of the bearer instrument and either:
– duty would be chargeable as a conveyance or transfer on sale if the instrument was not a bearer instrument; or
– the underlying stock is units in a unit trust scheme.

MEMO POINTS For these purposes, a UK company does not include a **Societas Europea** (¶2193+) which has transferred its registered office outside the UK.

Value liable to duty

Issue If duty is charged on the issue of a bearer instrument, the market value is determined in accordance with the following rules: 9598 Sch 15 para 7 FA 1999
a. if the stock was offered for **public subscription** in the 12 months preceding the issue of the bearer instrument, the market value is the amount subscribed; and
b. in **other circumstances**, the market value will depend on whether the stock is traded on the UK stock exchange:
– within 1 month of the issue of the bearer instrument, when the market value is the value on the first day of trading; or
– after 1 month, when the market value is the value immediately after the issue of the bearer instrument.

Transfer Where duty is charged on the transfer of the instrument, the market value on **sale** is the value of the stock on the date that the contract is made (generally the contract price). 9599 Sch 15 para 8 FA 1999
Otherwise, the market value is the value of the stock on the day immediately before the document is stamped or, if not stamped, the value on the day of transfer.

Rate

The **general rule** is that stamp duty is charged at a rate of 1.5% of the market value of the underlying stock. 9600 Sch 15 paras 4-5 FA 1999

The **exception** is where the instrument represents stock in a single non-UK company, with the rate then being 0.2%.

2. Exemptions

Stamp duty is not chargeable in respect of a bearer instrument which represents stock which is exempt from all stamp taxes (¶9548). 9602 s 79(2) FA 1986 Sch 15 paras 13-20 FA 1999

No duty is charged where an **amendment** is made to a previously stamped instrument which reflects a change in the original terms or conditions.

Type of bearer instrument	Circumstances for exemption to apply
Relates to loan capital	Any
Renounceable letter of allotment	Only if rights can be renounced no later than 6 months after the issue of the instrument
Stock denominated in a foreign currency	Including units which are defined by reference to more than one currency (whether or not this includes sterling)
Foreign currency loan	Only if instrument is not offered for subscription: – in the UK; or – with a view to an offer for sale of the securities in the UK

3. Administration

9604 The general administrative rules (¶9575) are **modified** slightly when applied to bearer instruments.

Procedure

9605 Before its issue, an instrument issuing a bearer instrument **must be produced** by the transferee to HMRC, accompanied by form B1.1. The instrument will be stamped with the bearer instrument denoting stamp which indicates that it is validly stamped.

Sch 15 paras 21, 22 FA 1999

Within 6 weeks of the instrument's issue, form B1.2 must be submitted, with a written statement giving the particulars of the issue, and the duty must be paid.

Failure to comply

9606 Failing to **provide** the instrument and submit the relevant forms will result in a penalty not exceeding the aggregate of £300 plus the duty charged.

Sch 15 para 23 FA 1999

If stock is transferred by way of an instrument which is **not correctly stamped**, the person effecting the transfer is liable to a penalty not exceeding the aggregate of £300 plus the duty chargeable. That person is also liable for the duty and any interest due.

Sch 15 para 25 FA 1999

If a person makes a **false statement** in connection with a bearer instrument, a penalty may be charged which does not exceed the aggregate of £300 plus twice the difference between the correct amount of duty and the duty paid.

B. Depositary receipts

9608 Depositary receipts are issued by banks and backed by shares held by the bank's nominee. A depositary receipt acknowledges the rights of the holder to the underlying shares and any related dividends and rights issues, and may be issued in either registered or bearer form. For the charge to SDRT in respect of depositary receipts, see ¶9666 onwards.

Scope

9610 Stamp duty is charged in respect of an instrument which transfers relevant securities **to a person**:

a. whose business consists exclusively of holding relevant securities as nominee or agent for a person whose business is (or includes) the issue of depositary receipts for relevant securities; or

b. who is specified by statutory instrument and whose business either includes:
– the issue of depositary receipts for relevant securities; or
– holding relevant securities as nominee or agent for a person whose business is (or includes) issuing depositary receipts for relevant securities.

MEMO POINTS **Relevant securities** are shares, stock or marketable securities of any company, regardless of where the company is incorporated.

Notification

A person **issuing** depositary receipts **or holding** relevant securities as nominee for the issuer is required to notify HMRC within 1 month of first doing so, otherwise a penalty of £1,000 may be charged. 9611 s 68 FA 1986

A **UK incorporated company** is required to notify HMRC if it becomes aware that its shares are held by an issuer of depositary receipts, or his nominee. Again, notification must be made within 1 month of becoming aware of the fact, and a penalty of £100 may be charged for failing to do so.

Rate

Stamp duty on transfers of depositary receipts is **usually** charged at the special rate of 1.5% regardless of how the transfer is effected. Where the transfer is other than by way of sale, the consideration is the market value of the securities on the date that the instrument is executed. 9613 ss 67, 72A FA 1986

There are two **exceptions** to the charge:

a. transfer of relevant securities of a company incorporated in the UK between corporate nominees, whose businesses consist exclusively of holding relevant securities as the nominee for the issuer of depositary receipts; and

b. transfer between a depositary receipt system and a clearance service.

C. Clearance services

A clearance service is a system for holding securities and settling transactions by way of book entry. For the charge to SDRT in respect of clearance services, see ¶9673 onwards. 9615

Stamp duty does not apply to clearance services where the alternative arrangements for SDRT have been adopted (¶9680). However, the standard 0.5% charge continues to apply to transfers on sale into a clearance service. s 97A FA 1986

Scope

Stamp duty is charged in respect of an instrument which transfers relevant securities **to a person**: 9616 s 70 FA 1986

a. whose business consists exclusively of holding relevant securities as nominee or agent for a person whose business is (or includes) the provision of clearance services for relevant securities; or

b. who is specified by statutory instrument and whose business either includes:
– the provision of clearance services for relevant securities; or
– holding relevant securities as nominee or agent for a person whose business is (or includes) the provision of clearance services for relevant securities.

MEMO POINTS **Relevant securities** are shares, stock or marketable securities of any company, regardless of where the company is incorporated.

Notification

A person **providing** clearance services **or holding** relevant securities as nominee for the clearer is required to notify HMRC within 1 month of first doing so, otherwise a penalty of £1,000 may be charged. 9617 s 71 FA 1986

A **UK incorporated company** is required to notify HMRC if it becomes aware that its shares are held by a clearer or his nominee. Notification must be made within 1 month of becoming aware of the fact, and a penalty of £100 may be charged for failing to do so.

Rate

9618 ss 70, 72A FA 1986 Stamp duty on relevant transfers is **usually** charged at the special rate of 1.5% regardless of whether the transfer is by way of sale or otherwise. Where the transfer is other than by way of sale, the consideration is the market value of the securities on the date that the instrument is executed.

There are two **exceptions** to the charge:

a. transfers of relevant securities of a company incorporated in the UK between corporate nominees, whose businesses consist exclusively of holding relevant securities as the nominee for a clearer; and

b. transfers between a clearance service and a depositary receipt system.

D. Transactions carried out by professionals

9620 Relief is available for certain transactions carried out by professionals, provided that the document is presented for stamping. There are equivalent reliefs for SDRT (¶9652 and ¶9654).

Intermediaries

9621 s 80A FA 1986 Relief is available for stock transfers to a member of a regulated market, multilateral trading facility, or recognised foreign exchange on which stock of that kind is regularly traded, or an intermediary who is recognised as such by the market, facility or exchange.

MEMO POINTS 1. For this purpose, an **intermediary is defined** as a person who carries on a bona fide business of dealing in stock and does not carry on an excluded business.

2. An **excluded** business:
– consists mainly of making or managing investments; or
– provides services to persons who are connected (¶5570) with the person carrying on the business; or
– is an insurance business; or
– manages, or acts as a trustee in relation to, a pension scheme; or
– operates, or acts as a trustee in relation to, a collective investment scheme.

Repurchases and stock lending

9623 ss 80C and 80D FA 1986 Repurchases or stock lending **occur** where a person (A) has entered into an arrangement with another person (B) under which:
– B is to transfer stock of a particular kind to A (or his nominee); and
– A (or his nominee) is to transfer stock of the same kind and amount to B (or his nominee).

Repurchases and stock lending transactions are **exempt** from stamp duty where:
– the agreement is between investment firms which have EEA authorisation (under the Markets in Financial Instruments Directive), provided that the stock is regularly traded on a regulated market; or
– the stock involved is regularly traded on a multilateral trading facility or a recognised foreign exchange, provided that the transaction is effected on that facility or exchange.

Sch 37 FA 2009 When a stock lending or repurchase arrangement terminates **owing to the insolvency** of one of the parties to the arrangement, there is exemption from a charge to stamp duty and SDRT. In addition, if the lender or seller buys securities to replace those lost due to the insolvency of the borrower or purchaser, the purchase will also be relieved from stamp duty and SDRT. Replacement of lost collateral securities by a borrower under a stock loan arrangement is also relieved of stamp duty and SDRT.

CHAPTER 3

Stamp duty reserve tax

OUTLINE

¶¶

Stamp duty reserve tax (SDRT) was introduced to tax transactions in shares where no instrument of transfer was executed and which were therefore outside the scope of stamp duty. It is a transaction-based tax, charged on "agreements to transfer chargeable securities", unlike stamp duty, which is charged upon documents. SDRT therefore ensures that every stage of a chain of share transactions is taxed. Often SDRT is superseded by a stamp duty charge (¶9540) and SDRT is then repaid. **9640**

SDRT has become more significant as the number of share transfers processed electronically has increased. Most UK registered securities are now held within the CREST electronic settlement service. Special regulations govern the administration of SDRT in relation to transactions using CREST, which are outside the scope of this book.

For other transactions, only those involved in the financial markets are likely to be affected by SDRT.

SECTION 1

The principal charge

An SDRT charge arises where a person (A) agrees with another person (B) to transfer chargeable securities (whether or not to B) for consideration in money or money's worth, unless an exemption (¶9651) applies. The issue of securities is not subject to an SDRT charge. **9645** s87 FA 1986

There is no requirement for the transfer agreement to be in written form, or made in the UK, or for the transfer to take place within the UK. A conditional agreement will only be liable to SDRT when the condition is satisfied.

Special SDRT charges apply to depositary receipts, clearance services and unit trusts.

Consideration

9647 s 87(7) FA 1986 If the consideration for the transfer is in:
- **cash**, SDRT is calculated on that amount;
- **money's worth**, the value of the consideration is the market value at the time that the agreement is made; or
- **foreign currency**, it should be converted to sterling before calculating the SDRT due, using the foreign exchange rate ruling at the time the agreement is made, as published in the *Financial Times* on the following day. Where the transfer is made using CREST (the UK's electronic registration and settlement system for equity share trading), the previous day's closing rate may be used, provided that it is applied consistently.

Chargeable securities

9648 s 99 FA 1986 Chargeable securities **include**:
- stocks, shares or loan capital;
- interests in, or dividends or other rights arising out of, stocks, shares or loan capital;
- rights to allotments of (or to subscribe for), or options to acquire, stocks, shares or loan capital; and
- units in a unit trust (¶9682).

This includes securities in a company **incorporated outside the UK**, provided that:
- the securities are registered in the UK; or
- the shares are paired with shares issued by a UK company (for example, French shares in Eurotunnel are paired with UK shares).

Securities which are **exempt** for all **stamp duty** purposes (¶9548), such as government stocks, are similarly exempt from SDRT.

MEMO POINTS 1. **Depositary receipts** are excluded from the definition of chargeable securities but do not escape SDRT, as they are brought into charge under a special regime (¶9666).
2. In relation to a **Societas Europea** (¶2193+), securities are chargeable to SDRT at the time that the SE has its registered office in the UK, if ever. Otherwise the securities are exempt.

A. Exemptions

Charities and other institutions

9651 s 90(7) FA 1986 SDRT does not apply to agreements **transferring** chargeable securities **to**:
- a body established only for charitable purposes (evidence of charitable status should be verified by checking the entry on the online registers of the Charity Commission or the Office of the Scottish Charity Regulator);
- the trustees of a charitable trust;
- the trustees of the National Heritage Memorial Fund;
- the Historic Buildings and Monuments Commission for England; or
- the National Endowment for Science, Technology and the Arts.

In practice, the exemption for charities purchasing securities is **claimed by** the exchange member or qualified dealer (i.e. the accountable person) who is purchasing the shares:
- on behalf of the charity; or
- as instructed by a fund/investment manager with an underlying client who is a charity.

An **accountable person** must be able to demonstrate that:
a. instructions to purchase shares have been received from a client which is a bona fide charity; or
b. he is acting for and on behalf of an underlying client which is a bona fide charity; and
c. checks have been undertaken to verify that the charity is, and continues to be, a registered charity and eligible for exemption from SDRT.

A **fund/investment manager** may not be willing to divulge details of his client to the accountable person, either for client confidentiality or other commercial reasons. In this case a specific prior arrangement can be made with HMRC Stamp Taxes whereby the fund/investment manager, rather than the accountable person, agrees to retain records regarding the charity client and its purchase instructions.

Intermediaries

Certain transactions undertaken by intermediaries are **exempt** from the principal SDRT charge, provided that certain conditions are met. 9652 s 88A FA 1986

Relief is available for stock transfers to a member of a regulated market, multilateral trading facility, or recognised foreign exchange on which stock of that kind is regularly traded, or an intermediary who is recognised as such by the market, facility or exchange.

MEMO POINTS 1. For this purpose, an **intermediary is defined** as a person who carries on a bona fide business of dealing in stock and does not carry on an excluded business.
2. An **excluded** business:
– consists mainly of making or managing investments; or
– provides services to persons who are connected (¶5570) with the person carrying on the business; or
– is an insurance business; or
– manages, or acts as a trustee in relation to, a pension scheme; or
– operates, or acts as a trustee in relation to, a collective investment scheme.

Repurchases and stock lending

Repurchases or stock lending **occurs** where a person (A) has entered into an arrangement with another person (B) under which: 9654 s 89AA FA 1986
– B is to transfer stock of a particular kind to A (or his nominee); and
– A (or his nominee) is to transfer stock of the same kind and amount to B (or his nominee).

Repurchases and stock lending transactions are exempt from principal SDRT charge where:
– the agreement is between investment firms which have EEA authorisation (under the Markets in Financial Instruments Directive), provided that the stock is regularly traded on a regulated market; or
– the stock involved is regularly traded on a multilateral trading facility or a recognised foreign exchange, provided that the transaction is effected on that facility or exchange.

The exemption from the principal SDRT charge applies only if, in pursuance of the arrangement, stock is transferred in both directions. SI 2008/3236

When a stock lending or repurchase arrangement **terminates** owing to the **insolvency** of one of the parties to the arrangement, there is exemption from a charge to stamp duty and SDRT. In addition, if the lender or seller buys securities to replace those lost due to the insolvency of the borrower or purchaser, the purchase will also be relieved from stamp duty and SDRT. Replacement of lost collateral securities by a borrower under a stock loan arrangement is also relieved of stamp duty and SDRT. Sch 37 FA 2009

Public issues

SDRT is not charged when an **issuing house** acts as principal in one of the following transactions: 9655 s 89A FA 1986

a. the purchase of existing registered shares or fully paid renounceable letters of allotment as part of an offer for sale (where the applicant is able to renounce the shares in favour of subsequent purchasers); or

b. the issue of renounceable letters of acceptance to applicants in an offer for the sale of either new shares or existing registered shares.

In each case, the placing must involve an offer to the public and be conditional on the admission of the shares to the Official List of the London Stock Exchange.

Bearer instruments

9657 s 90 FA 1986 SDRT does not apply to an agreement involving a **non-UK** bearer instrument – that is, an instrument issued by or on behalf of a company or body of persons formed or established outside the UK.

Transfers of **UK** bearer instruments are exempt from SDRT, **subject to** three exceptions:

a. letters of allotment which are renounceable within 6 months of the date of issue are subject to SDRT;

b. agreements to transfer **foreign currency** bearer instruments issued by a UK-incorporated body remain chargeable to SDRT, **unless**:
– the securities are listed on a recognised stock exchange; and
– the agreement for transfer was not made in connection with the takeover of the issuing body; and

c. agreements to transfer **bearer loan capital** (¶9549) are subject to SDRT **unless**:
– the securities are listed on a recognised stock exchange;
– the agreement for transfer was not made in connection with the takeover of the issuing body; and
– the securities do not carry rights to conversion into, or to the acquisition of, shares which are not listed on a recognised stock exchange.

MEMO POINTS For these purposes, a **UK-incorporated company** does not include a Societas Europea (¶2193+) which has transferred its registered office outside the UK.

Exchanges

9658 s 117 FA 1991 Certain transactions on the following exchanges are exempt from SDRT and stamp duty (see ¶9549):
– Eurex Clearing AG;
– European Central Counterparty Ltd;
– European Multilateral Clearing Facility NV;
– LCH.Clearnet Ltd; and
– SIX X-CLEAR AG.

B. Liability

Chargeable person

9660 s 91 FA 1986 The person liable for SDRT is best illustrated by example:

One person (A) agrees with another person (B) that A will transfer chargeable securities for consideration. B is liable to pay any SDRT due, and to notify HMRC, regardless of whether the shares are transferred to B, or another person.

9661 SI 1986/1711 reg 2 As an alternative, notification and payment requirements can be met by **intermediaries** involved in the transaction, where one of the parties to the agreement is a member of an exchange or a registered dealer.

The accountable person will be determined in the following order:
1. if both parties are members of an exchange, B;
2. if one party is a member of an exchange, that party;
3. if both parties are qualified dealers, B;
4. if one party is a qualified dealer, that party; or
5. if neither is a member of an exchange nor a qualified dealer, B.

This means that a **private individual** will generally only be responsible for the administration of SDRT where he is involved in a private sale of shares without a document.

MEMO POINTS 1. References to a **party** to the transaction include a person acting as his agent, who may be accountable if he meets the criteria.
2. In a **sub-sale** situation, where A transfers securities to B, who then transfers them to C, SDRT will be payable by B on the transfer from A, but the stamp duty charge (¶9664) will be payable by C on the transfer from A to C.
3. If the **accountable person is not B**, he may make a claim to be relieved of his obligation to account for and pay the tax, if he can satisfy HMRC that he has taken all reasonable steps to recover the SDRT from B. Action will then be taken to recover the SDRT from B directly. SI 1986/1711 reg 7

Calculation

The basic charge is 0.5% of the consideration and no rounding up applies. **9663**

EXAMPLE A Ltd transfers shares for £1,500 to B Ltd without using a stampable instrument. B Ltd must pay SDRT of £7.50 on the transfer.

Interaction with stamp duty

Transactions on which stamp duty is paid are not generally liable to SDRT. However, it is possible that SDRT will become payable before the stamp duty is paid. **9664** s 92 FA 1986

The SDRT charge is **cancelled** if, within 6 years of the SDRT charge arising, an instrument is:
- executed to transfer all the securities to which the agreement relates; and
- duly stamped in accordance with the stamp duty rules.

The charge will **not be cancelled** where the instrument is exempt from stamp duty: for example, renounceable letters of allotment (¶9602) and transfers to the stock exchange nominee (¶9621). s 88 FA 1986

If the **SDRT has already been paid**, a repayment may be claimed, although related interest and penalties may not be cancelled (¶9701).

SECTION 2

Other charges

Special rules apply to depositary receipts, clearance services and unit trusts. **9665**

1. Depositary receipts

Shares can be deposited with a custodian such as a bank. A depositary receipt is then issued by the bank and backed by the shares held by the bank's nominee. A depositary receipt acknowledges the rights of the holder to the underlying shares and any related dividends and rights issues, and may be issued in either registered or bearer form. Depositary receipts are not chargeable securities for SDRT and therefore dealings in them are not subject to SDRT. An entry charge is thus made when shares are transferred into a depositary receipt scheme. **9666** s 93 FA 1986

Chargeable event

A charge to SDRT will arise where chargeable securities are issued, transferred or appropriated: **9668**
- **by** a person whose business is, or includes, issuing depositary receipts for chargeable securities;
- **to** a person who holds such securities as nominee or agent for an issuer of depositary receipts as part of an arrangement for the issuer to issue depositary receipts.

Exceptions

9669 There is no charge in any of the following situations:

s 95 FA 1986 **a.** where the transfer is between **corporate nominees** whose businesses consist exclusively of holding relevant securities as the nominee for the issuer of depositary receipts;

b. the issue, transfer or appropriation of UK **bearer instruments**, although the following are chargeable:

– renounceable letters of allotment where the rights are renounceable within 6 months of issue; and

– non-sterling instruments which do not raise new capital;

c. the issue of securities in a company, A, **in exchange** for shares in another company, B, where company A has control over company B and B's shares are held in a depositary receipt scheme;

s 95A FA 1986 **d.** the transfer, issue or appropriation of **replacement securities** in place of existing securities under a depositary receipt to the extent that the value of the new securities does not exceed the value of the old securities;

s 119 FA 1999 **e.** transfers of UK depositary interests in **foreign securities**; and

s 97B FA 1986 **f.** transfers between a depositary receipt system and a **clearance service** which have been subject to stamp duty (¶9608+).

An overseas **Exchange Traded Fund** which satisfies the following conditions can list its shares in London but still remain exempt from SDRT:

– the central management and control is outside the UK; and

– its share register is kept outside the UK.

s 97C FA 1986 The European Court of Justice ruled in October 2009 that the UK is not entitled to apply a stamp duty or SDRT charge when new shares are first issued to an EU clearance service or depositary receipt system. The various relevant exemptions in place to prevent double taxation are therefore no longer necessary. Legislation taking effect from 1 October 2009 thus removes the exemptions for transfers where companies and issuers of depositary receipts arrange for shares to be issued to an EU clearance service or depositary receipt system (free of stamp duty or SDRT) and the shares are subsequently transferred to a depositary receipt system or clearance service outside the EU. *HSBC Holdings plc and Vidacos Nominees Ltd v HMRC* [2009]

Person

9670 The general rule is that the **person liable** for SDRT is the issuer of the depositary receipt. However, where the issuer is non-UK-resident and has no permanent establishment in the UK, the transferee is liable for the SDRT.

Amount of charge

9671 SDRT is charged at a **rate** of 1.5% of the relevant value.

s 93 FA 1986 The SDRT charge is cancelled to the extent that ad valorem stamp duty (¶9540) is payable in respect of an instrument of transfer.

s 93(4) FA 1986 MEMO POINTS The **relevant value** is determined as follows:

– where the securities are issued, it is the issue price;

– where the securities are transferred, the relevant value is the consideration received, or the value of that consideration if in non-monetary form; and

– in any other case, the relevant value is just stated to be the value of the securities.

2. Clearance services

9673 A clearance service is a system for holding securities and settling transactions by way of book entry. Securities are held indefinitely in the name of a nominee company acting for the clearance service. Transfers of securities within a clearance service are not liable to SDRT; a special entry charge is therefore made when securities enter the clearance service.

Chargeable event

A **charge to SDRT** will arise where: 9674 s 96 FA 1986
– a person (the clearer), whose business is, or includes, the provision of clearance services for the purchase and sale of chargeable securities, enters into an agreement to provide such services to another person; and
– in pursuance of the agreement, chargeable securities are transferred or issued to the clearer (or his nominee).

Exceptions

There is no charge in the following situations: 9676 s 97 FA 1986
a. where the transfer is between **corporate nominees** whose businesses consist exclusively of holding relevant securities as the nominee for a clearer;
b. the issue or transfer of UK **bearer instruments**, although the following are chargeable:
– renounceable letters of allotment where the rights are renounceable within 6 months of issue; and
– non-sterling instruments which do not raise new capital;
c. the issue of securities in a company, A, **in exchange** for shares in another company, B, where company A has control over company B and B's shares are held in a clearance service;
d. the transfer or issue of **replacement securities** in place of existing securities under a clearance service scheme to the extent that the value of the new securities does not exceed the value of the old securities; and s 97AA FA 1986
e. transfers between a **depositary receipt system** and a clearance service which have been subject to stamp duty (¶9608+). s 97B FA 1986

Person

The general rule is that the **person liable** for SDRT is the clearer. However, if the clearer is non-UK-resident and has no permanent establishment in the UK, the transferee is liable for the SDRT. 9677

Calculation

SDRT is charged at a **rate** of 1.5% of the relevant value, unless an election is made to use the alternative system. 9679 s 96 FA 1986

The SDRT charge is cancelled to the extent that ad valorem stamp duty is payable in respect of an instrument of transfer.

MEMO POINTS The **relevant value** is determined as follows: s 96(2) FA 1986
– where the securities are issued, it is the issue price;
– where the securities are transferred, the relevant value is the consideration received, or the value of that consideration if in non-monetary form; and
– in any other case, the relevant value is stated to be the value of the securities.

Alternative system of charge

As an alternative to the 1.5% charge, the clearer may elect to use a system where SDRT is chargeable at 0.5% on any transfers of chargeable securities held within the clearance system. Stamp duty is also chargeable in respect of certain transfers under the alternative system (¶9615). 9680 s 97A FA 1986

An **election** in this respect must be made in writing to HMRC and comes into force on a specified date when approval is granted.

Once the system has been adopted, the clearer must enter into special arrangements with HMRC for the **collection and payment** of SDRT.

The alternative system continues to apply until it is **terminated**, either by the clearer or by HMRC. At this point, an exit charge arises, equal to 1.5% of the value of the securities held within the clearance system immediately before the termination.

MEMO POINTS The clearer must give **written notice** 30 days before he stops using the system. HMRC may give notice to the clearer to terminate use of the system where the clearer is in breach of any of the conditions.

3. Unit trusts and open-ended investment companies (OEICs)

9682
s 122 FA 1999

A charge to SDRT arises where a unit holder **surrenders** units to the scheme managers or trustees, whether in the UK or otherwise. However, the issue of units is outside the scope of SDRT.

The **charge** is 0.5% of the market value of the unit at the time of transfer. For this purpose, the market value is taken as the higher of:
– the price the unit might be expected to realise on an open-market sale; and
– the cancellation price (or redemption price if redeemed).

The **persons liable** to SDRT are the trustees of the unit trust.

Third-party transfers

9683
Sch 19 para 6 FA 1999

A third-party transfer is one where a person, A, transfers units to another person, B, and the transfer is handled by the unit trust manager or trustee, who amends the register. Third-party transfers are **exempt** from SDRT under this regime where either:
a. no consideration in money, or money's worth, is given in return for the transfer;
b. the transferee is a charity or other institution (as set out in ¶9651); or
c. the transfer would, if a written instrument were effected, be exempt from stamp duty as an exempt instrument (¶9548) or under the group relief provisions (¶9758).

SDRT Customer Newsletter 10

Investors in collective investment schemes often make their investment through an intermediary. Intermediaries may deal with the fund managers by sending aggregated sell and aggregated buy instructions separately (known as "gross dealing") or intermediaries may net off buy and sell instructions for each fund and thus send only one net buy or sell instruction to each fund manager. This is known as "net dealing". Fund managers should only include in their Schedule 19 calculations transactions for which they have received instructions.

HMRC previously took the view that net dealing would not generally give rise to any principal SDRT charges. HMRC's advice is that net dealing, depending on the facts of each case, gives rise to **two principal SDRT charges** in respect of the transactions which have been netted off: one on the intermediary; and one on the ultimate purchaser of the investment. HMRC will not pursue any such charges that arose on or before 14 July 2009.

MEMO POINTS HMRC issued guidance in early 2004 (see www.hmrc.gov.uk/so/sdlt_news7.htm) stating that the following situations would not be liable to SDRT:
– a unit trust amalgamating with another unit trust;
– an OEIC merging with another OEIC;
– sub-funds of one or more unit trusts or OEICs merging; and
– partitions and reconstructions involving unit trusts and OEICs (including sub-funds of either type of fund).

Reductions to the charge

9685
Sch 19 para 4 FA 1999

In a monetary transaction, if the number of units **surrendered exceeds** the number of units issued in the relevant 2-week period, the SDRT liability is reduced by applying the following fraction:

$$\frac{\text{Number of units issued}}{\text{Number of units surrendered}}$$

This fraction is applied to the total SDRT liability for surrenders in a week – that is, the liability for week 1 is reduced by a fraction based on the total number of issues and surrenders in weeks 1 and 2.

Only surrenders and issues for consideration wholly in money and of the same class of units are taken into account.

The effect of this reduction is to levy a charge only where a unit is resold, not where it is merely surrendered. In this way SDRT is only charged when ownership changes.

MEMO POINTS 1. A **week** is a period of 7 days beginning on a Sunday.
2. The **relevant 2-week period** is the period from the beginning of the week in which the surrender occurs (the liability week) to the end of the following week.
3. When **cancelled and altered deals** are included as amendments to surrenders and issues, this can result in negative figures which give rise to a negative SDRT liability. HMRC have issued the following guidance (see www.hmrc.gov.uk/so/sdrt-news6.htm):
– where a cumulative net negative figure results, this should be treated as zero;
– excess cancelled or altered issues over the actual number of issues in the charging period are to be carried forward and set against the actual number of issues in the next charging period;
– the same treatment is to be applied to excess surrenders as for excess issues; and
– where the value of surrenders in the period is negative, this should be treated as nil for the purposes of the SDRT calculation.

EXAMPLE

	Value of surrenders £	SDRT @ 0.5% £	Units surrendered	Units issued
Week 1				
Monday	50,000	250	5,000	
Tuesday	80,000	400	7,950	3,600
	130,000	650		
Week 2				
Monday			10,000	
Wednesday			2,000	8,000
			24,950	11,600

SDRT liability for Week 1: $650 \times \frac{11,600}{24,950} = £302$

The SDRT liability is further reduced if the trust property is invested in both **exempt and non-exempt investments**, by applying the following fraction: 9686 Sch 19 para 5 FA 1999

$$\frac{N}{N+E}$$

where:
– N is the average market value of non-exempt investments over the relevant 2-week period; and
– E is the average market value of exempt investments over the relevant 2-week period.

MEMO POINTS 1. An **exempt investment** is broadly an investment which is not a chargeable security and which would not be subject to ad valorem stamp duty on a transfer. This includes derivatives where the whole of the underlying investment is exempt. s 99(5B) FA 1986
Invested funds which are for the day-to-day management of the unit trust scheme are not considered to be investments for these purposes.
2. There is no charge to SDRT where, immediately before surrender, the unit is held in an **individual pension account**. Sch 19 para 6A FA 1999

In specie redemptions

SDRT is not charged in respect of **pro-rata** in specie redemptions – that is, where the unit holder receives a share of each underlying asset which is proportionate (or as near as possible) to the unit holder's share. 9688

However, where the redemption is **not pro-rata**, SDRT is due. In this situation a reduction may be made based on the proportion of exempt investments held by the trust. (No reduction based on the number of units issued and surrendered during the relevant 2-week period is allowed, because a reduction only applies where the consideration is wholly monetary.)

Procedural aspects

9690 SI 1999/3264 If the unit trust does not have a manager, the compliance obligations fall upon the trustees of the trust. Each month the managers of the unit trust scheme must deliver a **return** to HMRC for all funds, setting out details of all the surrenders and the calculation of the tax due (including nil returns). The return must be submitted 14 days after the end of the month to which it relates and must include details for all relevant 2-week periods ending in that month. A separate calculation must be shown for each liability week. The SDRT payable, as shown on the return, **must be paid** within 14 days of the end of the month to which the return relates. A receipt will be issued to the person forwarding payment. HMRC will undertake a **random review** of returns received and where requested, fund managers will be required to provide necessary supporting material to the return.

MEMO POINTS 1. When assets and liabilities are transferred between **pension schemes**, there is no charge to SDRT, where the only consideration given is the liability to pay future pension benefits.
2. Where a change in ownership of unit trusts or OEICs needs to be recorded, the fund manager will need to report the units or shares surrendered on the monthly return as a third-party exemption.

SECTION 3

Administration

9695 In the majority of cases, SDRT will be calculated, collected and accounted for by a member of a stock exchange or a registered dealer. Private individuals are only required to account for SDRT personally for transactions which are undertaken without the involvement of such professionals.

This chapter covers the law in force at the date of publication. As part of the harmonisation of tax administration, **errors or inaccuracies** on SDRT documents made after 1 April 2010, and where the return relates to a tax period beginning on or after 1 April 2009, are subject to the harmonised error penalties regime (¶9784). Further provisions in Finance Act 2009 extend HMRC's powers in relation to information and inspection for other taxes to the administration of SDRT and provide for a new system of penalties for late payment and late filing (from a date still to be announced). For details of the harmonised provisions see ¶9775+.

Payment

9696 Where the transaction is processed using the **CREST settlement system**, SDRT will automatically be calculated, deducted and paid to HMRC by CREST. There is no need for any action by the individual.

SI 1986/1711 regs 2-4 If the transaction is **not processed through CREST**, the accountable person (¶9660) must, within 7 days of the end of the month in which the charge arises:
- give written notice of the transaction; and
- pay the SDRT to HMRC.

By concession, where stamp duty is paid within 60 days of the transaction, SDRT is not required to be notified or paid.

For **conditional agreements**, SDRT is payable within 7 days of the end of the month in which the condition is satisfied.

s 86 TMA 1970 **Interest** will be charged if the SDRT is paid late, and runs from the due date of payment to the actual date of payment. For the rates of interest, see ¶9974.

SI2008/2991 MEMO POINTS HMRC impose a fee, equivalent to 1.4% of the payment due, when the taxpayer chooses to use a credit card over the Internet to discharge a tax debt.

Repayment

Where SDRT is overpaid, a repayment may be **claimed** within 4 years of the date that the liability arises, or the date of payment if later. HMRC will usually refund the tax immediately on receiving a claim. In some cases further verification will be undertaken (usually within 60 days), requiring additional information from the taxpayer before a refund can be made. 9698 SI 1986/1711 reg 14

Prior to 1 April 2011 the limit was 6 years.

Repayments of SDRT carry **interest** from the date of payment (or the due date if later) to the date of repayment, provided that the SDRT repaid is at least £25. Such interest is exempt from income tax. For the rates of interest see ¶9974. 9699 SI 1986/1711 reg 11 s 92(4A) FA 1986

Interest is similarly payable on a repayment of SDRT following the payment of stamp duty. s 92(2) TMA 1970

Paying stamp duty

Often **SDRT is left unpaid** to preserve cash flow where the purchaser knows that stamp duty will be paid which will reduce the SDRT liability to nil. However, HMRC obviously prefer the SDRT liability to be paid up front. 9701

Where stamp duty is paid on shares held outside CREST, HMRC will not seek **interest** on the unpaid SDRT liability if a properly stamped instrument is produced within 60 days after the agreement is made. Otherwise, interest will strictly apply from the original due date for SDRT.

Comment **In practice**, the purchaser should make a payment on account of the estimated stamp duty liability, which is also treated as a payment on account for SDRT purposes, thereby avoiding interest charges.

Determinations

HMRC can only **enforce payment** of SDRT by issuing a determination of the amount payable at any time within 4 years from the later of the date on which: 9702 SI 1986/1711 regs 6, 8 13
- the SDRT charge arises; or
- any SDRT was paid in respect of the transaction.

The recipient may **appeal** to the tax tribunal against a notice of determination within 30 days of the date of issue, if he believes it to be incorrect.

Once a determination has been issued, HMRC may take **legal action** to enforce payment of the SDRT due. Legal action may not be taken whilst the matter is under appeal.

Prior to 1 April 2011 the limit was 6 years.

If it becomes apparent that a **repayment** of SDRT has been **made in error**, HMRC may issue a determination for the amount. The time limit for issuing the determination is 4 years from the date on which the amount was repaid in error, unless the repayment is brought about carelessly, in which case the time limit is extended to 6 years, or deliberately, in which case the time limit is extended to 20 years. 9704 SI 1986/1711 reg 18

Prior to 1 April 2011 the 4-year limit was 6 years.

Provision of information

HMRC's powers to obtain information and inspect businesses extend to matters concerning SDRT. See ¶9862+. 9706

Notification penalties

A penalty may be charged if notice of the transaction is given late. 9708 s 93(2), (5) TMA 1970

If notice is given **within 12 months** of the due date, the penalty is £100. However, the penalty will not generally exceed the amount of SDRT due in respect of the transaction.

If the notice is still outstanding **more than 12 months** after the due date, a penalty equal to 100% of the SDRT outstanding may also be levied.

s 95 TMA 1970 If an **incorrect notice** is submitted, either fraudulently or negligently, a penalty equal to the amount of SDRT understated could be charged.

MEMO POINTS From a date yet to be announced, new penalties for late filing and payment of SDRT will be imposed under the new harmonised penalties regime. See ¶9775+.

Senior accounting officers

9710 Sch 46 FA 2009 HMRC Brief 37/09 For SDRT returns, as with other tax reporting, special rules apply to large companies and their senior accounting officers personally. The "senior accounting officer" is defined as "the director or officer of the company who has overall responsibility for the company's financial accounting arrangements". Senior accounting officers are required to:
– take reasonable steps to establish and monitor accounting systems to ensure they are adequate for the purposes of tax reporting; and
– certify annually that the systems are adequate or specify the nature of the inadequacies and confirm that these have been notified to the company's auditors.

The company must also advise HMRC of the identity of the senior accounting officer for the company. Penalties of up to £5,000 can be levied on the senior accounting officer for failure to comply with the regime. For further details, see ¶2360.

CHAPTER 4

Specific business issues

OUTLINE ¶¶

The application of stamp taxes to business transactions depends on the type of transaction, its timing and the type of entities involved. In particular, SDLT is an important consideration when a business is sold, and is a complex issue for partnerships. 9720

A. Sale or transfer of a business

Sale of shares

If the transfer is a sale of shares, ad valorem stamp duty at a rate of 0.5% is payable (¶9540). 9726

Sale of trade

If the transfer is a sale of trade, it will probably involve the following **assets**: 9728
- land and premises;
- tangible assets (stock, furniture, etc); and
- intangible assets (moveable goodwill, debts, etc).

Stamp duty land tax (SDLT) applies to transfers of **land** regardless of whether an instrument has been executed (¶9345).

Transfers of **tangible** and **intangible assets** are outside the scope of both SDLT and stamp duty, unless those assets comprise:
- securities which are liable to ad valorem stamp duty (¶9540);
- goodwill inherent to land or property which is liable to SDLT (¶9347); or
- fixtures and fittings attached to property which are also liable to SDLT (¶9347).

Incorporation

The incorporation of a business is effectively the same as the sale of the assets, and the principles outlined in ¶9728 above therefore apply. 9729

9731 s 65 FA 2003 When a business is transferred from a partnership to a **limited liability partnership** (LLP), the transfer will be exempt from SDLT where all of the following conditions are satisfied:
1. the transfer occurs within 1 year of incorporation of the LLP;
2. the transferring partnership includes all current and future members of the limited liability partnership; and
3. there is a mirror image in the proportional interests of the partners before and after the transfer, or any small difference is not due to the avoidance of tax.

B. Purchase of own shares

9735 s 66 FA 1986 A company purchasing its own shares (¶2080) is required to file a return (form 169) with the Registrar of Companies, giving details of the purchase. This return is deemed to be an instrument effecting a **transfer on sale**, and is therefore subject to ad valorem stamp duty (¶9545). A stock transfer form does not need to be completed.

MEMO POINTS 1. The **redemption** of the company's own redeemable shares is not a purchase of own shares.
2. **Treasury shares** are shares registered in the name of the company itself.
If shares are **purchased** by the company to hold in treasury, form 169(1B) must be submitted to the registrar, and ad valorem stamp duty is due.
If the shares are **cancelled** or **transferred** to a **share scheme** for the benefit of employees, form 169A(2) must be submitted to the registrar.
3. HMRC have announced a change of policy where companies buy back their own shares held on **overseas branch registers**. HMRC's former view was that the returns companies are required to send to Companies House were chargeable with stamp duty at the rate of 0.5%. HMRC have taken legal advice and they now consider that a company's purchase of its own shares held on an overseas branch register is relieved from stamp duty by s 133, Companies Act 2006.

C. Company reorganisations

9737 There are reliefs from both SDLT and stamp duty when a reorganisation occurs.

1. Reliefs from SDLT

Reconstruction relief

9738 Sch 7 para 7 FA 2003 If a transfer of **land or property** is made under a scheme of reconstruction **in exchange for shares**, it will be exempt from SDLT if all of the following criteria are met:
a. the consideration for the transaction consists wholly or partly of the issue of non-redeemable shares in the acquiring company, either to the target company or any of the target company's shareholders;
b. after the acquisition has been made, the shareholders of each company are shareholders of the other in the same, or nearly the same, proportions; and
c. the acquisition takes place for bona fide commercial reasons and does not form part of a scheme to avoid tax.

MEMO POINTS 1. For the purposes of **c**. above, **tax** includes SDLT, stamp duty, income tax, corporation tax and capital gains tax.
Condition **c**. will be satisfied if any direct tax clearances have been given (¶4048 and ¶5852).
2. If the **consideration consists only partly of non-redeemable shares**, the relief will only be available if the rest of the consideration consists wholly of the assumption or discharge by the acquiring company of the liabilities of the target company.

3. Any **treasury shares** (shares held by the target company in itself) are deemed to be cancelled before the transaction occurs. This means that the acquirer does not need to take these into account when issuing shares to the target's shareholders.

Acquisition relief

Where **land** forms part of an undertaking **acquired for consideration** of which at least 90% is shares, the rate of SDLT is reduced to 0.5%, provided that the following conditions are met: 9739 Sch 7 para 8 FA 2003

a. the undertaking is a trade (excluding property dealing);

b. the consideration for the transaction consists wholly or partly of the issue of non-redeemable shares in the acquiring company to the target company, or any of the target company's shareholders;

c. the acquiring company is not associated with another company that is party to arrangements with the target company relating to shares of the acquiring company; and

d. the acquisition takes place for bona fide commercial reasons and does not form part of a scheme to avoid tax.

MEMO POINTS 1. For the purposes of **d**. above, **tax** includes SDLT, stamp duty, income tax, corporation tax and capital gains tax.
Condition **d**. will be satisfied if any direct tax clearances have been given (¶4048 and ¶5852).
2. If the consideration consists only **partly of the issue of non-redeemable shares**, the relief will still be available if the rest of the consideration consists wholly of:
- cash not exceeding 10% of the nominal value of the non-redeemable shares issued; and/or
- the assumption or discharge by the acquiring company of the liabilities of the target company.

Withdrawal of reliefs

Both reconstruction and acquisition reliefs will be withdrawn where **control of the acquiring company changes** either within 3 years of the date of the transaction, or as a result of arrangements made during the 3 years following the transaction. 9741 Sch 7 para 9 FA 2003

The **exception** to this rule is where control changes as a result of one of the following transactions: Sch 7 para 10 FA 2003

a. a share transaction in connection with divorce;

b. a share transaction that varies a disposition following death;

c. a loan creditor who is treated as gaining or ceasing to have control;

d. an exempt intra-group transfer of shares when associated companies relief applies (¶9758); or

e. a transfer to another company when share acquisition relief applies (¶9746).

Where relief is withdrawn, the SDLT **charge is based on** the amount which would have been chargeable had the relief not been claimed originally (that is, market value). If the resulting tax is not paid within 6 months, HMRC can recover the unpaid tax from the vendor, another group company, or a controlling director. Sch 7 para 12 FA 2003

MEMO POINTS 1. Where the group transaction was a **grant of a lease**, the amount of rent will be taken into account when calculating the consideration upon which the SDLT is charged on withdrawal of relief.
2. Where **relief was not withdrawn** because of **d**. or **e**. above, a **subsequent transfer** which changes the control of the acquiring company will cause the relief to be withdrawn. Sch 7 para 11 FA 2003

2. Reliefs from stamp duty

A number of reliefs apply to allow the reorganisation of companies to be effected without giving rise to a charge to stamp duty, or to apply a reduced rate of duty. The reliefs must be claimed and the instruments presented for adjudication. 9743

Companies resident anywhere in the world can use the reliefs.

The reliefs **only apply where shares are** issued – that is, allotted and registered. The issue of a renounceable letter of allotment is not sufficient for the exemptions to apply. *National Westminster Bank plc and another v CIR* [1994]

Acquisition of trade – exemption

9744 s 75 FA 1986 Where, as part of a scheme of reconstruction, a company (A Ltd) acquires the whole, or part, of the business of another company (B Ltd), the document giving effect to the transfer is exempt from stamp duty, provided that a number of conditions are satisfied and the document is presented for adjudication (¶9578).

The **conditions** are as follows.

a. The **consideration** for the transfer must consist of non-redeemable shares in A Ltd which are issued to the shareholders of B Ltd in such a way that each of the shareholders holds the same (or nearly the same) proportion of shares in A Ltd as they previously held in B Ltd. This means that the share structure of A Ltd should mirror as closely as possible that of B Ltd. In addition to shares, the only other permissible consideration is the assumption or discharge of liabilities.

b. The transfer must be effected for **bona fide commercial reasons** and not as part of any scheme or arrangement which has as its main purpose, or one of them, the avoidance of tax. If any direct tax clearances have been given, this condition will be satisfied (see ¶4048 and ¶5852).

MEMO POINTS Any **treasury shares** (shares held by the target company in itself) are deemed to be cancelled before the transaction occurs. This means that the acquirer avoids having to issue shares to the target company.

Acquisition of company

9746 s 77 FA 1986 An instrument giving effect to the acquisition by a company (A Ltd) of the **entire issued share capital** of another company (B Ltd) is exempt from stamp duty, provided that certain conditions are satisfied. The instrument must be presented for adjudication (¶9578).

The **conditions** are as follows.

a. The **consideration** for the transfer must consist only of shares in A Ltd and the share capital of A Ltd must consist of the same classes of shares in the same proportion as the share capital of B Ltd. After the acquisition, each of the shareholders that held shares in B Ltd must hold the same (or nearly the same) proportion of shares of the same class in A Ltd. This means that the share structure of both companies must be either be identical, or as identical as is practically possible.

b. The transfer must be effected for **bona fide commercial reasons** and not as part of any scheme or arrangement which has tax avoidance as its main purpose, or one of them. If any direct tax clearances have been given, this condition will be satisfied (see ¶4048 and ¶5852).

MEMO POINTS Any **treasury shares** (shares held by the target company in itself) can be ignored, as these are deemed to be cancelled before the transaction occurs. This means that the acquirer avoids having to issue shares to the target company.

D. Transfers between group companies

9750 Group relief applies for both SDLT and stamp duty to enable asset transfers to be made within a group without incurring a tax charge.

1. SDLT group relief

9751 Sch 7 para 1 FA 2003 Intra-group transfers of property, including the sale of a freehold or the grant of a lease, will be exempt from SDLT. Group relief **does not apply unless** the transaction has been entered into for bona fide commercial reasons and does not form part of a scheme to avoid liability to tax.

Group relief should be claimed when completing the land transaction return.

For these purposes, companies are members of the same group if one is the 75% subsidiary of the other or both are 75% subsidiaries of a third company (¶9759). It does not matter where the companies are incorporated or resident.

MEMO POINTS 1. For this purpose tax includes SDLT, stamp duty, income tax, corporation tax and capital gains tax.
2. For group relief to apply the group relationship must apply at the date of completion, or the date the contract is substantially performed.
3. HMRC now accept that, for the purposes of SDLT group relief, a "body corporate" does include an LLP. An LLP can therefore be the parent in a group structure. However, as an LLP does not itself have issued ordinary share capital it cannot be the subsidiary of other companies. This also means that any subsidiaries of the LLP cannot be grouped with the companies that are the corporate members of the LLP.

Scope

HMRC have indicated that group relief will always be available where a **freehold** is transferred, or a **lease is assigned**, to a group company in any of the following situations: 9752 SDLTM 23040
a. there is a **possibility** at the time of the transfer that shares in that company might be sold:
– more than 3 years after the date of transfer; or
– within 3 years of the date of transfer, in order that any increase in the value of the property after the intra-group transfer might be sheltered from SDLT;
b. the transfer occurs before the **sale of** shares in the **transferor** company, in order that the property should not pass to the purchaser of the shares (¶9755);
c. the reason for the transfer is to **match** commercially generated rental **income** with commercially generated losses (¶782), or chargeable **gains** with commercially generated allowable losses (¶1110);
d. the transfer is part of a normal commercial **securitisation**;
e. the property is transferred to a **non-resident** group company in the knowledge that future appreciation or depreciation in value will be outside the scope of UK corporation tax;
f. the freehold reversion in a property is transferred to the group lessee in order to **merge** the freehold and leasehold interests, which avoids the lease being subject to the wasting assets rules (¶5922).
Group relief will also be retained when arrangements are entered into with a view to effecting an **acquisition qualifying for stamp duty relief** (¶9744); or
g. the transfer of property to a group company in order that interest payable on borrowings from a commercial lender on ordinary commercial terms, may be set against commercially generated income.

Comment Care should be taken when relying on the above, as they are only indicators given by HMRC. Any changes in the law, such as at ¶9755, should be taken into account.

Relief denied Relief will be denied where **arrangements** are in place at the effective date of the transaction as a result of which any of the following apply: 9753 Sch 7 para 2 FA 2003
a. a person has, or could obtain, control of the purchaser but not the vendor;
b. the consideration is to be provided or received (directly or indirectly) by a person other than a group company;
c. the vendor and purchaser are to cease being members of the same group because the purchaser ceases to meet the 75% test; or
d. there is a transfer of rights (¶9351) under a contract to another group member.

Comment "Arrangements are in place" is not restricted to legally binding documents and care should be taken that no arrangements have been reached during any negotiations taking place before the effective date of the transaction.

EXAMPLE A Ltd wants to sell a property worth £750,000 to T Ltd but tries to avoid SDLT by transferring the property to B Ltd, its 100% subsidiary. The consideration is left outstanding on loan account, so B Ltd is worth only £1,000, the value of its subscribed share capital. B Ltd is then sold to T Ltd for £1,000. T Ltd lends B Ltd £750,000 to repay A Ltd.

As T Ltd is indirectly providing the consideration for the property, an SDLT charge will arise on the consideration of £750,000.

Withdrawal of relief

9754 Sch 7 para 3 FA 2003 **Purchaser leaves group** Relief will be withdrawn where the purchaser ceases to be a member of the same group as the vendor either **within 3 years** of the transaction, or as a result of arrangements made during the 3 years following the transaction.

Sch 7 para 4 FA 2003 The **exception** to this rule is that relief will not be withdrawn where the purchaser ceases to be a member of the same group as the vendor:
– by reason of anything done in the course of winding up the vendor; or
– where there is an acquisition of shares in the purchaser by another company in relation to which stamp duty acquisition relief (¶9746) applies, and the purchaser leaves the group as a result.

9755 Sch 7 para 4ZA FA 2003 **Vendor leaves group** **Relief is available** if the vendor leaves the group by being sold, or if another company, above the vendor in the group, is sold.

Relief is **withdrawn** if, after the vendor has left the group, there is a change in control of the purchaser. A **change in control** includes:
– the person controlling the purchaser ceases to do so;
– a new person obtains control of the purchaser; or
– the purchaser is wound up.

MEMO POINTS 1. For the definition of **control** for these purposes, see ¶2104.
2. A person (A) does not control, and cannot obtain control of, another person (B) if B is under the control of another (C).
3. A company (D) is **above the vendor** in the group if the vendor, or another company above the vendor, is a 75% subsidiary of D.

9756 Sch 7 para 4A FA 2003 **Chain of transactions** An **anti-avoidance** rule is in operation in relation to chains of transactions. This means that all previous transfers which have occurred in the 3 years before the change of control of the transferee leaving the group are taken into account. Transfers where no relief (that is, group, reconstruction or acquisition) has been claimed are ignored for this purpose.

EXAMPLE In Year 1, A Ltd transfers Unit 1 to B Ltd.
In Year 2, B Ltd transfers Unit 1 to C Ltd.
In Year 3, C Ltd transfers Unit 1 to D Ltd.
In Year 4, D Ltd transfers Unit 1 to E Ltd.
There is a change of control of E Ltd 6 months later but, under the normal provisions, no group relief is withdrawn.

All of the above transfers were exempted from charge by group relief.
As the transfer in Year 1 happened more than 3 years ago, it is ignored.
The relevant transfer is the one between B Ltd and C Ltd in Year 2. If E Ltd has ceased to be in the same group as B Ltd, group relief will be withdrawn.

9757 Sch 7 para 5 FA 2003 Where relief is withdrawn, the SDLT **charge is based on** the amount which would have been chargeable had the relief not been claimed originally (that is, based on the market value at that time). If the resulting tax is not paid within 6 months, HMRC can recover the unpaid tax from the vendor, another group company, or a controlling director.

Where the group transaction was a **grant of a lease**, the amount of rent will be taken into account when calculating the chargeable consideration.

2. Stamp duty group relief

9758 s 42 FA 1930 Relief from ad valorem stamp duty is available where an instrument transfers a beneficial interest in the asset from one company to another and the companies are associated at the time that the instrument is executed.

This relief is only relevant for the transfer of shares and securities between associated companies.

The relief must be claimed and the instrument adjudicated (¶9578) to confirm that no stamp duty is payable. The adjudication request must be accompanied by a **statutory declaration** setting out the grounds for claiming relief and giving assurance that there has been no breach of the statutory provisions.

Eligible groups

Two companies are **associated** for these purposes if one is the parent of the other, or a third company is the parent of both. 9759

MEMO POINTS 1. A company is a **parent** if it satisfies all of the following criteria: s 42(2B) FA 1930
- it is the beneficial owner (¶9761) of at least 75% of the ordinary share capital of the other company;
- it is beneficially entitled to at least 75% of the profits available for distribution to equity holders; and
- it is beneficially entitled to at least 75% of the assets on a winding up.

A company is not a parent if there are arrangements in existence for any person to obtain control of the transferor but not the transferee.

There are no restrictions on the residence status of the companies.

2. **Ordinary share capital** is defined as all the share capital of a company, other than capital that entitles the holder to a fixed-rate dividend with no other right to share in the profits of the company. The name given to the capital is irrelevant, as it is the nature of the capital that is important. It is not necessary for capital to carry voting entitlement for it to be ordinary share capital. s 42(4) FA 1930

Where there is a **series of holdings**, the holding is calculated by multiplying out the fractional entitlements. 9760

EXAMPLE A Ltd owns 95% of B Ltd, which in turn owns 78% of C Ltd.
A Ltd therefore owns (95% × 78%) = 74.1% of C Ltd.
A Ltd is therefore associated with B Ltd but not with C Ltd. B Ltd and C Ltd are associated.

A company is considered to own share capital of another company if it has **beneficial ownership**. This means that where a company cannot actually take the benefit of the shares it owns, it ceases to have beneficial ownership, such as where another person has a specifically enforceable right to acquire the shares. 9761

The passing of a resolution or making an order for the **winding up** of one of the companies will result in the companies ceasing to be associated.

Beneficial ownership does not cease where the company has granted an option over shares which may or may not be taken up.

Relief unavailable

The relief is denied if the transfer is made in connection with an **arrangement** whereby: 9763 s 27(3) FA 1967
- the consideration is provided or received, directly or indirectly, by a person outside the group;
- the interest being transferred was previously transferred by a person outside the group; or
- the transferee or transferor are no longer to be part of the same group.

"Group" in this context is used to refer to the associated companies and any other companies which are associated with one or other of those companies.

The **effect** of these provisions is, broadly, that the relief is denied where the property, or an economic interest in it, passes out of the group.

E. Partnerships

The term partnership takes its usual legal meaning and includes limited partnerships and limited liability partnerships. Partnerships are only liable to SDLT where land is involved, and to stamp duty where shares or securities are held. 9765

1. SDLT

Scope

9766 Sch 15 para 1 FA 2003 A transfer is transparent for SDLT purposes, so a land transaction is treated as being undertaken by the partnership on behalf of all the partners. For land transfers **to or from an unconnected third party**, SDLT applies in the usual way, including any applicable reliefs.

For transfers of land **between the partnership and any partner** (including anyone connected with him), and also a transfer of an interest in a **land investing/dealing partnership**, there are special rules.

MEMO POINTS 1. A document **creating** a partnership that simply reflects the pooling of assets is not liable to SDLT. Although, according to HMRC, if a partner agrees that land owned by him is to become available for the partnership's use, there will be an SDLT charge (¶9767).
2. A partnership is treated as **continuing**, provided that at least one partner remains the same before and after any change in partners.

Transfer into the partnership

9767 Sch 15 para 10 FA 2003 There is a charge to SDLT when an interest in UK land (including the granting of a lease) is transferred into a partnership by any of the following **persons**:
– a partner;
– an incoming partner (who transfers land in return for a partnership interest); or
– a person who is connected (¶5570) with either an existing partner or incoming partner.

SDLT Technical News Issue 5 A chargeable interest is held by a partnership if it is held by either the partnership, or all of the partners, for the purposes of the partnership's business. If the business of the partnership is carried on in a property owned by one or more of the partners, this does not make it a partnership asset.

9768 The **value subject to SDLT** is calculated as follows, and is best illustrated by example:
1. calculate the percentage interest of each relevant owner;
2. establish who the corresponding partners of each relevant owner are;
3. apportion the percentage interest calculated under **1**. between the relevant owner and any other corresponding partners;
4. find the lower percentage for each corresponding partner (including the relevant owners) of:
– the proportion of the chargeable interest attributable to each partner; or
– the partner's partnership share immediately after the transaction;
5. add together all of the lower percentages for the corresponding partners (including relevant owners);
6. deduct the cumulative lower percentages from 100% and multiply by the market value of the property to establish the chargeable amount.

The proportion of the land's value attributable to partners which are not individuals is always chargeable to SDLT. So where the partners are all connected with the transferor and are individuals, there will be no SDLT charge.

MEMO POINTS 1. **Relevant owners** are persons who have a chargeable interest in the property immediately before the transaction and are partners immediately after the transaction, or are connected with a partner.
2. **Corresponding partners** are persons who immediately after the transfer are partners and are relevant owners before the transaction. **Individuals** connected with relevant owners who are also partners in the partnership are corresponding partners. There is no set way of apportioning the relevant owner's interest between the corresponding partners, so it can be split in such a way as gives the best result for the partnership.
Corporate partners connected with relevant owners are ignored for the purposes of establishing corresponding partners.
3. The **partner's partnership share** is the share of the income profits to which the partner is entitled. Income profits are the entire profits of the partnership derived from income, irrespective of whether that income has to be allocated in specific ways or whether certain partners have prior allocation of profits from various sources.

4. **Corporate partners**:
– which are **members of the same group** as the transferor can claim a relief which means that their share of the land's market value is ignored when calculating the chargeable amount;
– which hold property as **trustees** and are only connected to the transferor because he is also a trustee, are deemed to be individuals, so their share of the land's market value is also ignored.

EXAMPLE

1. Mr A, Mr B, Mrs C and Mr D are in partnership. Mrs C transfers a building valued at £500,000 into the ABCD partnership. Following the transfer of the property, the partners share income profits in the proportion 25/25/25/25. Mrs C is married to Mr D, therefore they are connected.
1. Mrs C is the only relevant owner. Her interest is 100%.
2. Mrs C and Mr D are the corresponding partners.
3. Mrs C's relevant interest can be apportioned between Mrs C and Mr D in the most advantageous way.
Initially, the split is calculated on a 50:50 basis.
4. For Mrs C and Mr D the lowest percentage is the lower of the apportioned interest under step **3**. (50%), or their partnership share after the transaction (25%).
5. The cumulative lower percentage under step **4**. is 50% (25 + 25).
6. The value chargeable to SDLT is 100-50% × £500,000 = £250,000.
The charge to SDLT represents the percentage of the property in which Mrs C and her connected parties no longer have an interest. In this circumstance, it would make no difference how the relevant interest was split under step **3**.

2. The ABCD partnership consists of four company partners, who share income profits in the proportions of 40:35:15:10.
A Ltd and B Ltd are members of the same group, which is owned by Mr X. C Ltd is also owned by Mr X but is not grouped with A Ltd and B Ltd. D Ltd is unconnected.
A Ltd transfers property into the partnership.
60% of the land's market value is subject to SDLT. However, group relief can be claimed in respect of B Ltd's 35% interest, which takes the chargeable amount down to 25% of the property's value.

An SDLT charge is also levied where the transferor subsequently **takes money out** of the partnership within 3 years (**other than** income profit). **9769** Sch 15 para 17A FA 2003

This rule is widely drawn, such that an SDLT charge will arise on the value of any of the following:
– a direct withdrawal of cash by the transferor;
– the withdrawal of money by a connected person (¶5570) who has made a loan to the partnership; or
– the partnership repaying a loan made by either the transferor or a connected person.

The **maximum chargeable consideration** is the market value of the land originally transferred into the partnership (as reduced for any value previously charged to SDLT).

For any transaction which is **liable to a double charge** (that is, on the transfer of the land into the partnership (¶9767) and also on the withdrawal of funds), the SDLT payable on the transfer is deducted from the SDLT charge relating to the withdrawn funds.

Transfer of a property investment partnership interest

Only transfers **involving** partnerships **whose main activity** is investing in, dealing or developing land are within the scope of the following rules. **9770** Sch 15 para 14 FA 2003

A **charge** to SDLT **arises** on the transfer of a partnership interest (that is, a new partner is taken on, or a partner increases his existing right to income profits) when the partnership holds any chargeable interest in land. The charge to SDLT depends on how the transfer is effected:

If the transfer is **effected for consideration** ("Type A transfers") SDLT will be payable on the proportion of the income profit entitlement of the interest transferred by reference to the market value of the property held by the partnership immediately before the transaction.

All other transfers of partnership interests ("Type B transfers") will be subject to SDLT on the market value of every chargeable interest held by the partnership immediately after the transaction. The following interests are disregarded:
– property transferred to the partnership on or before 23 July 2004;

– property acquired from a vendor who was not a relevant owner, or a person connected with a relevant owner (¶9767);
– a chargeable interest not attributed to the interest of the partnership that is transferred;
– property where an election has been made to disapply the charging provisions where property is transferred to a partnership by a relevant owner, or connected party.

The SDLT charge will be levied on the person who increases his partnership interest or becomes a new partner.

EXAMPLE

1. **Type A transfer**
Mr X is a partner in the XYZ partnership whose principal activity is buying and selling plots of land for development.
The partnership's income-sharing proportions are as follows:
- Mr X = 10%
- Mrs Y = 40%
- Mrs Z = 40%
- Mr A = 10%

Mr X decides to sell his 10% income share in the partnership for £1 million to Mrs V. At the date of the transfer XYZ owns the following property:

Plot	Market value	Date acquired	Further information
Plot C	£100,000	1 February 2008	Election made to disapply charging provisions
Plot D	£500,000	1 May 2008	Election made to disapply charging provisions
Plot E	£1,000,000	1 April 1999	Acquired for £100,000
Plot F	£2,000,000	20 July 2007	Acquired from Mr A in exchange for 10% share. Market value at date of acquisition was £1 million
Total	£3,600,000		

Mrs V is due to pay SDLT on £360,000. (3.6 million × 10%)

2. **Type B transfer**
Continuing the above example, Mrs Y decides to retire from the partnership and gifts her share to her son, Mr W. Using the above figures as an example, the market value taken into account for the purposes of calculating the charge to SDLT is:

Total market value of properties after transfer has taken place	£3.6 million
less:	
Plot C, as an election was made	£100,000
Plot D, again as an election was made	£500,000
Plot E, as it was acquired before 22 July 2004	£1 million
Market value of chargeable interests subject to charge	**£2 million**

Mr W will be liable to pay SDLT on £800,000. (£2 million × 40%)

Transfer out of or between partnerships

9772 Sch 15 paras 18-23 FA 2003

A charge to SDLT will arise on the transfer of UK land out of a partnership when the **transferee** is a present or previous partner (including a connected party (¶5570)).

An SDLT charge will be levied on the person acquiring the land.

The **chargeable amount** is a proportion of the land's market value, based on the share of the partnership's income profits which are not held by the transferee (or anyone connected with him) after the transaction has occurred.

The proportion of the land's value attributable to partners which are not individuals is always chargeable to SDLT (irrespective of whether the corporate partners and the transferee are in the same group). If the transferee is connected with all the continuing partners, and they are individuals, there will be no SDLT charge under these rules. There are complicated provisions which apply if the income profit shares have changed over time.

MEMO POINTS 1. **Corporate partners** who hold property **as trustees**, and are only connected to the transferor because he is also a trustee, are deemed to be individuals for the purposes of calculating the chargeable amount.

2. If a partnership has made an election to disapply the special charging provisions, SDLT is chargeable on the full market value.

EXAMPLE Mr X transferred land worth £150,000 to the XYZ partnership when he became a partner many years ago. Mr X is not connected to Mr Y or Mrs Z. Income profits have always been shared equally between all three partners.
Mr X then retires, and pays £150,000 for the return of the land to his sole ownership. The land is now worth £1.5m.
The amount liable to SDLT is £1m. (£1.5m x 66.67%)

Where land is transferred between **two partnerships** which have at least one partner in common, or are otherwise connected, a single charge to SDLT will arise, based on the highest possible charge (given that a charge will arise on both the transfer of land out of one partnership and on the transfer of land into the other). Sch 15 para 23 FA 2003

2. Stamp duty

Scope

Unless the partnership property includes stock or marketable securities, no stamp duty will be due. 9773 Sch 15 para 33 FA 2003

MEMO POINTS 1. A document **admitting** a new partner to an existing partnership is not chargeable unless the terms represent a sale of an interest in the existing partnership's assets to the new partner.
2. A **contribution of capital** which is credited to the new partner's capital account does not indicate a sale unless there is a corresponding withdrawal by an existing partner, so there is no stamp duty charge.
3. On the **incorporation of a partnership**, the document giving effect to the transfer to the company is charged to ad valorem stamp duty as a transfer on sale.
4. Where there is a **division or partition** of the partnership (¶9546), exemption from stamp duty will apply, unless there is a sale of assets, when ad valorem duty is chargeable.

Transfer of partnership interest

When the partnership asset-sharing ratios change (usually on the joining or leaving of a partner), the **chargeable amount** is a proportion of the net market value of the stock and securities. 9774

The proportion is measured by the interest of the partner before and after the transfer.

The net market value is the market value less any liability secured solely on those securities.

It is important to note that the **rate of stamp duty** follows that of the SDLT thresholds for residential property (¶9992), so where the deemed consideration does not exceed £125,000, no stamp duty charge will arise. Sch 13 para 4 FA 1999

EXAMPLE Mr A transfers his 20% interest in the ABC partnership to Mr D.
The ABC partnership holds shares with a net market value of £1m.
The value chargeable to stamp duty will be £200,000. (£1m x 20%)
So a stamp duty charge of £2,000 will arise. (£200,000 x 1%)

PART 9

Harmonisation of tax administration

Harmonisation of tax administration
Summary

The numbers cross-refer to paragraphs.

CHAPTER 1

Scope of harmonisation

OUTLINE ¶¶

When the Inland Revenue and Customs and Excise merged in 2005 one of the stated aims was to **simplify procedures** for businesses by streamlining them. The "Review of HMRC powers, deterrents and safeguards" was launched with the aim of **aligning and modernising** their powers. The review represents the largest change to the tax system since the implementation of self-assessment in 1997. 9775

The following chapters deal with the areas which have been, and will be, affected by the review as well as other "cross-cutting" changes. Where the new rules are not yet in force, or where separate systems are maintained, the specific rules for each tax are covered within the Administration chapter of each Part of *Tax Memo*.

What are the key areas?

The main areas covered in the following chapters are: 9776
- penalties for compliance failures;
- compliance checks and information-gathering powers;
- tribunals reform;
- requesting clearances; and
- rights of set-off.

In addition the time limits for taxpayers making amendments to returns and the time limits for HMRC to raise assessments are being amended across all taxes.

Implementation

The implementation of the changes to the compliance system is an **ongoing process**, and it is crucial for businesses to be aware of whether the old or new rules are in force when dealing with HMRC. The following table indicates when the new rules first have effect, and where to find further information: 9777

Area of harmonisation	Date of first implementation	¶¶	Reference
Penalties	1 April 2008	¶9780	Sch 24 FA 2007
Information powers	1 April 2009	¶9862	Sch 36 FA 2008 Sch 47 FA 2009
Record-keeping requirements	1 April 2009	¶9892	Sch 37 FA 2008
Requesting clearances	New procedure for businesses – 1 May 2008	¶9896	HMRC Brief 25/08, COP 10, VAT Notice 706

Area of harmonisation	Date of first implementation	¶¶	Reference
Rights of set-off	25 June 2008	¶9894	ss 130 – 133 FA 2008
Tribunals reform, and requesting reviews of decisions	1 April 2009	¶9920	Tribunals, Courts and Enforcement Act 2007
Time limits	1 April 2009	¶9778	Sch 39 FA 2008

MEMO POINTS **Taxpayers' safeguards** have also been considered in the reform process. HMRC have announced that they will consider taxpayers' needs when considering specific legislation to ensure it is fair, clear and coherent.

Time limits

9778 Sch 39 FA 2008; SI 2009/403; CH 56100-56300

Commencing with VAT on 1 April 2009, HMRC's time limits for **raising assessments** have been aligned across all of the major taxes. The new time limits for corporation tax, income tax, CGT and PAYE took effect from 1 April 2010. The changes can be summarised as follows, and further detail can be found in each Part of *Tax Memo*.

Tax	Mistake	Discovery	Failure to take reasonable care	Loss of tax brought about carelessly or deliberately
VAT [1]	4 years	N/A	4 years	20 years
IT & CGT	N/A	4 years	6 years	20 years
Corporation tax	N/A	4 years	6 years	20 years
PAYE	4 years	N/A	6 years	20 years

Notes:
1. The new time limit applies to VAT claims for repayments and assessments from 1 April 2009.

MEMO POINTS A transitional provision applies in limited circumstances. From 1 April 2012, the new time limits will be applied to income tax and CGT where tax has been overpaid and the taxpayer was not issued with a notice to file a tax return within 1 year of the end of the tax year. The delayed introduction of the new time limits, in this situation only, gives additional time to taxpayers who would be entitled to make a claim for repayment of tax, but have not made the claim thus far.

In addition to the above, the taxpayer's time limit for **amending returns** is now 4 years. The affected areas have been highlighted in the relevant Parts of *Tax Memo*.

9779 Sch 51 FA 2009; SI 2010/867

Time limits were also amended for the following taxes from 1 April 2011.

Tax	Mistake	Discovery	Failure to take reasonable care	Loss of tax brought about carelessly or deliberately
IHT [1]	4 years	4 years	6 years	20 years
SDLT	4 years	4 years	6 years	20 years

Notes:
1. Where personal representatives are required to submit income tax and CGT returns for a deceased, the returns submitted come under the new time limits for those taxes.

CHAPTER 2

Penalties

OUTLINE ¶¶

As part of the **harmonisation** of HMRC's powers the penalties regime is being amended across all taxes. These changes have been implemented over a period and as such it is important to check which taxes and penalties apply from which dates. **9780**

Finance Act 2007 contained **provisions** for the harmonisation of the penalties regime for incorrect returns, and other documents submitted to HMRC. Finance Act 2008 contained provisions to extend the new system to errors attributable to a person other than the taxpayer and the penalties were extended further by Finance Act 2009. **9782** Sch 24 FA 2007

Finance Act 2008 also included provisions to align the penalties applicable across a range of taxes for failure to notify HMRC of, broadly, liability to tax. Sch 41 FA 2008

Further provisions in Finance Act 2009 provide for a new system of penalties for **late payment** of tax, and **late filing** of returns and other supporting documents, for income tax, capital gains tax, corporation tax, PAYE, NIC, the construction industry scheme (CIS), stamp duty land tax, stamp duty reserve tax, inheritance tax and pension schemes. In a further development, provisions have been made for the names of **tax defaulters** (¶9857) to be published. Sch 55 - 56 FA 2009

MEMO POINTS New provisions have been brought in to harmonise the **rates of interest** charged and paid on tax either paid late or overpaid by taxpayers. The interest rate applied by HMRC shadows that set by the monetary policy committee of the Bank of England, with two exceptions:
- the rate for interest **charged** on late paid tax will never drop below 1.5%; and
- the rate for interest **paid on** overpaid tax will never drop below 0.5%.

Both of these rates apply irrespective of how low the rate set by the Bank of England drops. Interest rates change 13 days after the announcement of a rate change by the Bank.

SECTION 1

Incorrect returns and documents

9784 As the legislation is being implemented over a number of years, the **commencement date** of the new regime is not the same for all taxes. The following table summarises the implementation date for each tax:

Tax[1]	Periods commencing on or after[2]	Documents due to be submitted on or after	Further information
Income tax and corporation tax	1 April 2008	1 April 2009	¶9786
VAT	1 April 2008	1 April 2009	Any VAT return, other return or written claim
PAYE (including CIS)	1 April 2008	1 April 2009	Any returns submitted under the PAYE (¶4595) and CIS (¶4800) regulations
NIC	1 April 2008	1 April 2009	
SDLT	1 April 2009[3] (effective date)	1 April 2010	Errors on land transaction returns
SDRT	1 April 2009 (effective date)	1 April 2010	Notice of charge to tax
Inheritance tax (IHT)	1 April 2009[4] (effective date)	1 April 2010	¶9788

Note:
1. Finance Act 2008 also extended the regime for penalties for errors to most other taxes and duties, which are outside the scope of *Tax Memo*.
2. A period for these purposes is a tax year, an accounting period or any other period for which tax is charged or due.
3. For SDLT the new rules have effect where the effective date (¶9350) was on or after 2 March 2010, as the due date for submission of the SDLT return is thirty days after the effective date of the transaction.
4. For IHT purposes the new regime has effect for deaths on or after 1 April 2009, as the relevant returns were due for submission on 30 April 2010.

A. Documents affected

9786 Sch 24 para 1 FA 2007 Any errors on an income tax (including CGT) or corporation tax **self-assessment return** or a VAT return, are subject to the new rules from 1 April 2008 where a document was due to be filed on or after 1 April 2009. IHT returns and accounts, returns for stamp duties and pension schemes also come under these rules for periods starting on or after 1 April 2009 where a document was to be filed on or after 1 April 2010.

Income tax self-assessment returns include individual returns, trustee returns, partnership returns and income tax returns due from companies.

Corporation tax returns, or any document or return used to claim an allowance or relief, are subject to the new provisions. Any error in accounts submitted as part of the return which have been used to calculate the tax liability are also covered by the new rules. This also includes any claim for repayable tax credits.

VAT returns and other returns, statements or declarations in connection with a claim are subject to the new provisions. This includes documents submitted under VAT return adjustment or error notification arrangements.

IHT returns include accounts, statements or declarations in connection with a deduction, exemption or relief.

Stamp duties includes returns for stamp duty land tax and stamp duty reserve tax.

Pension scheme returns are within the regime from 1 April 2009 for returns due to be filed after 1 April 2010.

MEMO POINTS Errors on income tax returns include errors calculating a **capital gains tax** liability.

The following documents associated with **IHT** are subject to the new provisions: 9788

a. main IHT return and associated documents, including errors in notifying:
- failed potentially exempt transfers;
- chargeable lifetime transfers;
- transfers on death; or
- settled property;

b. any return or information submitted under the excepted estates rules (¶7040); and

c. any other statement or declaration claiming a relief, deduction or exemption from IHT.

Document

While the word document has its ordinary meaning it is also extended in this situation to include any means of communicating information to HMRC, including: 9789 Sch 24 para 28(h) FA 2007
- post;
- fax;
- email; or
- telephone.

Comment The inclusion of a telephone call in this list is presumably to ensure that amendments to documents, or claims, made by telephone are covered by the new penalty regime.

B. When will a penalty be imposed?

Taxpayer inaccuracies: Two **conditions** need to be satisfied before HMRC can charge a penalty: 9790

1. the document submitted must contain an inaccuracy that leads to either:
- an **understatement** of the tax liability, including an overstatement of a VAT credit;
- a **false**, or **inflated** statement of **loss**, including an over-inflated claim to an expense, charge or deficit; or
- a **false**, or **inflated** claim to a **repayment**, including a claim to a tax credit; and

2. the inaccuracy must be careless, deliberate or deliberate and concealed.

This means that **simple mistakes** will not attract penalties where they are corrected by the taxpayer.

MEMO POINTS For documents filed on or after 1 April 2010 a penalty may be imposed where an error in a taxpayer's document is attributable to the actions of a third party (see ¶9845).

HMRC's under-assessment: If a taxpayer has been issued with a return, or is required to file a return and has not done so, HMRC will issue an assessment. If an assessment is issued which understates the tax liability and the taxpayer fails, within 30 days of the assessment, to take reasonable steps to advise HMRC of the under-assessment, he may be liable to a penalty. 9792 Sch 24 para 2(1) FA 2007

1. Calculation of the penalty

Carelessness

A taxpayer will not be deemed to have been careless if he has taken **reasonable care**. There is **no statutory definition** of reasonable care, and HMRC have stated that the **test** will be 9795 HMRC Brief 19/08 applied subjectively. While this makes it difficult to quantify, HMRC have provided guidance on their interpretation.

CH81120 The **guidance** states that the level of care a taxpayer must show in order to avoid a penalty for carelessness will depend on the **status of the taxpayer**. For example, the test for reasonableness will not be the same for sole traders and large corporates. The guidance also states that a higher level of care will be expected for one-off transactions compared with day-to-day compliance.

HMRC have also likened carelessness to the previous standard of negligence. Negligence has previously been defined as the omission to do something that a reasonable man would do taking into account all the circumstances at the time, or doing something a reasonable man would not have done. *Blyth v Birmingham Waterworks Co* [1856]

9796 CH81130 HMRC have advised that the following situations will **not be treated as careless**:
– where advice has been taken from a competent adviser, who was presented with the full facts, and it transpires that the advice provided was wrong;
– where an arithmetical error or transposition occurs which is not large in absolute terms, or relative terms, and is something that a reasonable quality check would identify;
– if they are presented with the accurate facts, advice from HMRC which is wrong; or
– a reasonably held view of the law is argued.

Reasonable care will have been seen to have been taken where:
– there are systems in place that, if followed, would be expected to produce an accurate basis for calculations;
– despite these systems an inaccuracy arises due to a processing or coding error; and
– the inaccuracy in the tax liability is not significant compared to that taxpayer's overall liability for that period.

CH84540 MEMO POINTS HMRC's guidance states that an **adviser** is **competent** if he is "trained and competent for the task in hand". It is not clear how HMRC will establish whether an agent is "trained and competent". This may lead to taxpayers using fully qualified advisers, rather than those qualified by experience, to ensure they are seen to be taking reasonable care.

Deliberate error

9798 A deliberate error will be **deemed** to have been made on a return, or any other document, if the taxpayer is aware that the action he is taking is not correct, or that the statement he has made is incorrect.

CH81150 HMRC have given the following **examples** of when they deem an action to be deliberate:
– systematically paying wages without accounting for or operating PAYE/NIC;
– knowingly failing to record all sales, especially where there is a pattern to the under-recording, such as omitting all transactions with a particular customer or at a particular time of the week, month or year;
– describing transactions inaccurately, or in a way likely to mislead;
– giving a VAT return to HMRC that includes a figure of net VAT due that is too low because the person does not have the cash at that time to pay the full amount, and later telling HMRC the true figure when he has the funds to pay;
– claiming a deduction for personal expenses of such a size or frequency that the inaccuracy must have been known;
– withdrawing money for personal use from an incorporated business and not making any attempt to ensure correct treatment for tax purposes.

HMRC can also refer deliberate actions to underpay tax to their criminal investigations team.

9800 CH81160 If a taxpayer has taken **deliberate steps** to underpay, or over-claim tax, he will be liable to a penalty. Penalties are higher if **concealment** of a tax liability has taken place.

HMRC give the following **examples** of when they believe a taxpayer is concealing his actions:
– creating false invoices to support inaccurate figures in the return;
– backdating or post-dating contracts or invoices;
– creating false minutes of meetings or minutes of fictitious meetings;
– destroying books and records;

– systematically diverting takings into undisclosed bank accounts and covering the traces;
– invoice routing – for example, the purported sale or purchase of goods through a tax haven company (with no activity undertaken by that company even though contracts exist showing the contrary), leaving profits untaxed in that company;
– creating sales records that deliberately understate the value of the goods sold, the balance of the full price being paid separately to the person;
– describing expenditure in the business records in such a way as to make it appear to be business related when it is in fact private (possibly with the supplier agreeing to change the description on the relevant invoices); and
– alteration of genuine purchase invoices to inflate their value.

2. Level of penalties

9802 The amount of the penalty levied is a **percentage of** the potential lost tax revenue. This is **calculated** depending on the seriousness of the offence, and whether the taxpayer has co-operated with HMRC.

Type of inaccuracy	Maximum penalty (% of potential lost tax revenue)	Minimum penalty following a disclosure (% of potential lost tax revenue)	
		Unprompted disclosure	Prompted disclosure
Carelessness	30	0	15
Deliberate but not concealed	70	20	35
Deliberate and concealed	100	30	50
Under-assessment not corrected	30		

Notes:
If an inaccuracy, which was neither careless nor deliberate, is discovered by the taxpayer but the taxpayer then takes no steps to advise HMRC of the error, the omission to advise will be treated as careless.

Overseas issues

9803 Sch 10 FA 2010 SI 2011/976 From 6 April 2011 the penalties above are altered, for **income tax and capital gains tax only**, where the error involves an overseas tax matter. Overseas territories are split into **three categories**. Categorisation is based on whether the territory shares information with the UK and whether such information is freely volunteered, or has to be requested. Penalties in relation to Category 1 territories (those sharing information freely) are the same as those relating to UK tax matters, as outlined above. Penalties in relation to Category 2 and 3 territories are as shown below.

Type of inaccuracy	Category 2			Category 3		
	Maximum penalty (% of potential lost tax revenue)	Minimum % for unprompted disclosure	Minimum % for prompted disclosure	Maximum penalty (% of potential lost tax revenue)	Minimum % for unprompted disclosure	Minimum % for prompted disclosure
Carelessness	45	0	22.5	60	0	30
Deliberate but not concealed	105	30	52.5	140	40	70
Deliberate and concealed	150	45	75	200	60	100
Under-assessment not corrected	30					

a. Calculation of potential lost tax revenue

9804 Sch 24 para 5 FA 2007 HMRC Brief 15/11

The **basic rule** is that the potential lost tax revenue (PLR) is the additional amount due or payable once the error or under-assessment has been corrected. This includes amounts of tax incorrectly repaid by HMRC, or amounts that would have been incorrectly repaid.

There are **special rules** where the error involves group relief (¶9832), or the error results in losses (¶9826).

The PLR is reduced where the error is **automatically reversed** in a subsequent period. This is a way of acknowledging that the tax revenue is only lost temporarily. HMRC have not in the past applied this reduction where they have discovered the error before it has automatically been reversed but say they will do so from 2011.

EXAMPLE HMRC guidance confirms that a penalty can be levied under the new system where a **claim for repayment** has been made, but the tax has yet to be repaid.
Mr A, a company director, submitted his 2009-10 return claiming a repayment of tax deducted at source of £15,000. Following a compliance check in advance of the repayment being made, it was agreed that no repayment was due and that Mr A owed income tax of £2,000.
The PLR is £17,000. (£15,000 + £2,000)

More than one inaccuracy

9806 Sch 24 para 6 FA 2007

Where it is discovered that a document or return has more than one error, strictly each error should be considered separately. To **simplify the process**, HMRC have advised that their officers can treat more than one inaccuracy in a document as a single inaccuracy, if the underlying reason for the error is the same. However, if the taxpayer so wishes he can have each error treated separately.

If **more than one document** has been submitted in one tax period, each document must be treated separately for the purposes of calculating any penalty due.

9808

Calculating a multiple penalty Where there has been more than one error and they are different classes of errors, there is a set order in which the penalties are dealt with:
– if a taxpayer is subject to **tax at different rates** the PLR for the most serious penalty is treated as occurring in the highest rate band;
– if there is also an **overstatement of tax**, either in the same return or document or in the same period, it is set off against the least serious offence first; and
– if the overall effect of over and understatements is that the **taxpayer is due a repayment** there is no PLR, therefore there will be no penalty. If a penalty has been raised, and it is later discovered that the taxpayer made an error on the same document resulting in an overpayment, it is possible for a taxpayer to have the penalty reduced if he submits a claim within the ordinary time limits for amending the assessment.

EXAMPLE Mr A submits his VAT return for the period ended 30 September. HMRC carry out a routine visit, and establish that Mr A has under-declared output VAT totalling £100,000. During the visit HMRC also discover that Mr A has incorrectly under-claimed input tax on the same VAT return totalling £50,000.
The errors have been categorised, and the under-claimed input VAT is offset in the following order:

Nature of inaccuracy	Amount	Under-claimed input VAT allocated
Inaccuracy despite taking reasonable care	£25,000	(£25,000)
Careless inaccuracy	£5,000	(£5,000)
Deliberate	£50,000	(£20,000)
Deliberate and concealed	£20,000	(£0)
Total	**£100,000**	**(£50,000)**

The net understatement on the return is £50,000 PLR. Mr A will be liable to penalties (subject to any reductions) as follows:
Deliberate error penalty @ 70%: (£50,000 – £20,000) × 70% = £21,000.
Deliberate and concealed penalty @ 100%: £20,000 × 100% = £20,000. This means that the effective rate of the penalty is 82% of the net under-declaration of £50,000.

b. Reduction for disclosure

Under the new rules, reduction for disclosure of errors may be given. This **replaces the concepts of** abatement and mitigation which existed under the previous procedures. 9810

The **level of reduction** depends on whether the disclosure is unprompted or prompted and the quality of the disclosure. The **quality of the disclosure** is measured against three tests:
- telling;
- helping; and
- giving access to information.

Prompted or unprompted?

A disclosure by a taxpayer of an error is unprompted if the error has not been discovered by HMRC, or is not about to be discovered. In all other cases disclosures are treated as prompted. 9812

HMRC's guidance states that the measure of whether a disclosure is unprompted is an **objective test**, and that it is unlikely a disclosure after a taxpayer has been notified of a compliance visit, or one made during the visit will be treated as unprompted.

MEMO POINTS The guidance states that a **national awareness campaign** will not be treated as prompting a disclosure.

Once it is established whether a penalty is prompted or unprompted, HMRC consider the **quality of the disclosure**. 9814

MEMO POINTS This is similar to the procedure of mitigation of penalties under the former VAT regime.

Telling The **maximum reduction** available for disclosing the error to HMRC is 20% of the penalty due. 9815

HMRC's guidance states that telling **includes**:
- admitting the document was inaccurate;
- disclosing the inaccuracy in full; and
- explaining how the inaccuracy arose.

If there is only a **partial disclosure** of the above, the full 20% reduction will not be due.

Helping The **maximum reduction** available for assisting HMRC with correcting the error is 40%. 9816 CH82450

HMRC's guidance states that in order to receive the full reduction of 40% the taxpayer must actively help with quantifying the error, and volunteer any information relevant to the disclosure.

Giving access The **maximum reduction** available for giving HMRC access to information relevant to the error is 30%. To receive the full 30% reduction the taxpayer must freely provide access to the information when requested, and provide the information at a convenient location, with copies made available. 9818

Comment The guidance on this point has been drafted in line with the information powers included in Finance Act 2008 (¶9862). The guidance states that if HMRC are required to use their **information powers** the full reduction, and perhaps any reduction, will not be given.

HMRC also have powers to reduce penalties further in certain **special circumstances**, but their internal guidance suggests that this will be rare. 9820 CH82480

3. Suspension of a penalty

As part of the drive to encourage compliance and full disclosure, HMRC have a new power enabling them to suspend penalties for a **period of** up to 2 years. Suspension is **dependent on** the taxpayer meeting certain conditions, and if the conditions are met the penalty will be cancelled at the end of the agreed period. 9822

When will suspension be possible?

9824 It may be possible to agree with HMRC that a penalty should be suspended if the penalty is for a **careless error**. Suspension will not be available for penalties involving deliberate inaccuracies.

HMRC will consider the **quality of the disclosure** (¶9814+) when deciding whether the taxpayer is a suitable candidate for suspension. Taxpayers who have made a full disclosure, whether prompted or otherwise and have a good compliance record, are likely to be considered for suspension.

Conversely, if HMRC feel the taxpayer has **not co-operated** with them regarding the error, or the error is one of a series of errors, they are unlikely to offer to suspend the penalty.

9825 Penalties **will not be suspended** in the following circumstances:
– it is not possible to set conditions for avoidance of repetition of the error;
– the penalty has arisen as a result of the use of an avoidance scheme;
– past compliance behaviour is poor, in particular the penalty has arisen within 3 years of a previous suspended penalty; and
– the penalty is the second within the penalty period.

Comment Penalty suspension has now been recognised to reward those who commit systematic errors (which can be eradicated by systematic improvement) at the expense of those who commit one-off errors (which are by definition not susceptible to systematic improvement but may in some circumstances be less reprehensible than systematic errors).

C. Specific situations

1. Losses

9826 Sch 24 para 7 FA 2007 As the method for calculating penalties is based on potential lost tax revenue (PLR), there is special regime for losses, depending on whether they have been used or not. Under the general rules there could have been an argument that overstating a loss, in certain circumstances, does not create any PLR – especially where the loss may not be used for some reason.

Losses wholly used to reduce tax payable

9828 In these circumstances the artificial loss is **treated as** PLR and any penalty due is calculated under the general rules.

EXAMPLE Mrs B is self-employed. She has calculated that she generated a loss for the year ended 5 April of £10,000. Mrs B claims the loss on her tax return and offsets the trading loss against her other income for the year:

Other income	£25,000
Loss from self-employment	(£10,000)
Taxable income	£15,000

HMRC enquire into Mrs B's tax return and discover that the trading loss has been overstated, as Mrs B forgot to include income of £5,000 from one of her clients. Mrs B has therefore understated her tax liability by £1,000 (£5,000 x 20%, ignoring personal allowances). This is the PLR and any penalty will be based on this amount.

Unused losses

9830 If **all or part** of a loss claimed in error has not been used, the taxpayer may still be liable to a penalty, even though there has been no tax loss at the time the error is discovered.

The penalty is **calculated** on 10% of the unused loss.

MEMO POINTS If there is **no prospect of using the loss** in the future – for example, because the trade has ceased – the PLR will be nil. Again, the test of whether there is a reasonable prospect of using the loss is subjective and unless there is a legal reason why the loss cannot be used, the taxpayer has to make representations to HMRC detailing why the overstated loss would never have been used.

2. Groups of companies

HMRC will **ignore group relief** (¶1540) when calculating the PLR (¶9802). There are two **exceptions** to this rule: 9832 CH82282
– an inaccurate claim to group relief has been made; or
– group relief has been claimed which has the effect of creating an aggregate loss for a group of companies.

9834

EXAMPLE HMRC give the following examples of how to calculate PLR where groups are involved.

1. Inaccurate claim to relief

A, B and C are a group of companies.
Their returned results are

Company A profits	50,000	less Group Relief 50,000
Company B loss	(75,000)	
Company C profits	60,000	less Group Relief 25,000
Aggregate profit	35,000	

Company B's return is carelessly inaccurate. Company B's true loss is 40,000, so the group relief surrenders must be reduced.
Company B must withdraw its surrenders of 50,000 to Company A and 25,000 to Company C.
Company B then surrenders 40,000 to Company A.
The group relief claims by both Company A and Company C are inaccurate. It is only necessary for the claims originally made by Company A and Company C to have been inaccurate, not carelessly inaccurate, as the error by Company B was careless.
Assuming liability at the small companies' rate, the additional tax due and payable as a result of putting right the inaccuracy is:

A Ltd	**Correct**	**Original**	**Additional**
Trading income	50,000	50,000	0
Less Group Relief	40,000	50,000	-10,000
Profits chargeable to CT	10,000	0	10,000
Tax at small companies' rate (say 20%)	2,000		2,000

C Ltd	**Correct**	**Original**	**Additional**
Trading income	60,000	60,000	0
Less Group Relief	0	25,000	-25,000
Profits chargeable to CT	60,000	35,000	25,000
Tax at small companies' rate (say 20%)	12,000	7,000	5,000

The PLR for Company B's penalty is:

PLR on Company A's inaccurate Group Relief claim	2,000
PLR on Company C's inaccurate Group Relief claim	5,000
Total PLR	7,000

2. Ignoring group relief

A, B and C are a group of companies.
Their returned results are:

Company A profits	50,000	less Group Relief 50,000
Company B loss	(75,000)	
Company C profits	60,000	less Group Relief 25,000
Aggregate profit	35,000	

Company A's return is found to contain a careless inaccuracy which is corrected to produce a true profit of £85,000. Company B can, and does, withdraw its surrenders of £50,000 to Company A and £25,000 to Company C and replaces them with a surrender of £75,000 to Company A. Company A amends its Group Relief claim to £75,000.
The inaccuracy did not have the affect of creating or increasing an aggregate loss recorded for the group.
Assuming liability at the normal CT rate, the additional tax due and payable as a result of putting right the inaccuracy is:

A Ltd	**Correct**	**Original**	**Additional**
Trading income	85,000	50,000	35,000
Less Group Relief	75,000	50,000	25,000
Profits chargeable to CT	10,000	0	10,000
Tax at small companies' rate (say 20%)	2,000		2,000

C Ltd	**Correct**	**Original**	**Additional**
Trading income	60,000	60,000	0
Less Group Relief	0	25,000	-25,000
Profits chargeable to CT	60,000	35,000	25,000
Tax at small companies' rate (say 20%)	12,000	7,000	5,000

However the PLR for Company A's penalty is calculated ignoring group relief

A Ltd	**Correct**	**Original**	**Additional**
Trading income	85,000	50,000	35,000
Less Group Relief	75,000	50,000	0[1]
Profits chargeable to CT	10,000	0	35,000
Tax at small companies' rate (say 20%)	2,000		7,000

Notes:
1. Ignore £25,000

C Ltd	**Correct**	**Original**	**Additional**
Trading income	60,000	60,000	0
Less Group Relief	0	25,000	0[1]
Profits chargeable to CT	60,000	35,000	0
Tax at small companies' rate (say 20%)	12,000	7,000	0

Notes:
1. Ignore £25,000

Total PLR = £7,000 + 0 = £7,000

3. Aggregate loss for the group

Company D, E, F and G are a group of companies.
Their returned results are:

D profits	110,000	Less Group Relief 110,000 (110,000 surrendered by Company F)
E profits	160,000	Less Group Relief 160,000 (90,000 surrendered by Company F + 70,000 by Company G)
F loss	(200,000)	
G loss	(85,000)	
Aggregate loss	(15,000)	

Company D's return is found to contain a careless inaccuracy of £40,000. Its actual profit is £150,000.
Company F withdraws its group relief surrenders to Companies D and F and makes new surrenders of £150,000 to Company D and £50,000 to Company E.
Company G can and does withdraw its surrender to Company E and makes a new surrender to Company E of £85,000.
The inaccuracy has the effect of creating the aggregate loss recorded for the group, so the PLR is calculated using the rules for losses.
The losses rules apply to the amount of Company D's understated profit and the PLR for the inaccuracy is calculated in the context of the aggregate loss position of the group.
Under the normal rules for calculating PLR, Company D's PLR, assuming liability at the small companies' rate, would be £40,000 × 20% = £8,000. Instead, the inaccuracy is considered in the context of the aggregate loss for the group. The PLR for company D's penalty is:

Normal rule

	£		£
Correct amount due or payable by D	150,000 profit		
Less	150,000 group relief		
Tax due	0 × 20%	=	0
Returned amount due or payable by D	110,000 profit		
Less	110,000 group relief		
	0 × 20%	=	0
PLR in respect of D			0
Correct amount due or payable by E	160,000		
Less	135,000 group relief		
Tax due	25,000 × 20%	=	5,000
Returned amount due or payable by E	160,000		
less	160,000 group relief		
	0 ×20 %	=	0
PLR in respect of E			5,000

Unused loss rule

£15,000 x 10% =	1,500

Total PLR for Company D's penalty = 0 + £5,000 + £1,500 = £6,500.

Only £25,000 of the inaccuracy has reduced group tax liability for the period. The balance has created the group's aggregate loss for the period.

In this example, at the time that the penalty is to be imposed, G has not made use of the surplus loss of £15,000 in a later or earlier period, so the PLR in respect of the £15,000 is calculated under the unused loss rule.

If Company G had used the surplus loss to reduce tax liability in another period, the PLR would be the additional tax due and payable.

3. VAT error correction

If a taxpayer makes an error on a VAT return and that error is below the limit set (¶9236) the error can be corrected on a later return without any interest being charged. **9835** CH81142

HMRC have advised that if an **error** is not careless or deliberate, and is **below the threshold**, a taxpayer will be deemed to have taken reasonable steps to inform HMRC by amending a later return. In this case no further action is required.

If the error is **careless or deliberate** but below the threshold, HMRC have advised that they require a **separate disclosure** of the error to be made in order for the correction of the error to be treated as unprompted.

EXAMPLE Mrs C submits her VAT return for the period ended 31 January. She has not completed the return correctly, as she has not processed all of the invoices for the sales made over the busy Christmas period. In March Mrs C catches up on her administration and calculates that invoices with a VAT-exclusive value of £9,000 had not been included on the previous return. Mrs C's turnover in the quarter ended 30 April is £90,000. The voluntary disclosure threshold for Mrs C is therefore £10,000 (the higher of £10,000 or 1% of turnover up to £50,000).

Mrs C completes her April return and includes the £9,000-worth of invoices relating to December on the return and she thinks she need take no further action.

HMRC carry out a control visit in June and note that some December invoices were included on the April return. They take the view that the error on the January return was careless and that Mrs C has not taken reasonable steps to notify them of the error. A penalty may then be levied.

If there is an inaccuracy in a VAT return which **cannot be amended in a later VAT return** a taxpayer must make a separate disclosure of the error. **9836**

Under the new rules, a penalty will not be levied on errors above the threshold if they are not careless or deliberate. However, if the error is neither careless nor deliberate at the time the original return was submitted but the taxpayer **does not take reasonable steps** to notify HMRC of the error, that omission to notify HMRC will then be treated as careless.

If the taxpayer adjusts a future return for an error totalling more than the threshold, rather than submitting an error notification, HMRC will treat the error, at the least, as careless and a penalty will be levied.

EXAMPLE D Ltd has submitted its VAT return for the period ended 31 March. During a review of the return in May it is identified that a claim was made for 100% of the input VAT on leased cars in error. Only 50% of the input VAT should have been recovered and the total, net of VAT, error was £51,000. D Ltd's threshold for making corrections by way of later returns is £50,000.
The error was an innocent mistake and a one-off therefore the error was not careless. D Ltd decides that as the error is only £1,000 over its threshold, the £51,000 will be included on the 30 June VAT return. HMRC carry out a review of the June VAT return and notice the £51,000 adjustment relating to the March period. As D Ltd had not taken reasonable steps to notify HMRC of the error a penalty may be levied in respect of the earlier return.

4. Employees and officers of a company

9838 If an **error** in a document is as a **result of the action of** an agent, employee, officer of a company or a third party there are special rules regarding the calculation of the penalty.

9840 CH84530 Generally, an **employee** is not acting as the agent of his or her employer. However, it is the **responsibility of the employer** to ensure that, if an employee has prepared a document, it does not contain any inaccuracies. The reasonable steps that a business must take to ensure that no inaccuracies have been made will depend on the size of the business, but they must have reasonable checks and systems in place to make sure errors do not occur. If a business does not take reasonable care it will be liable to a penalty for carelessness.

If an error in a document is the result of an action of an employee, and the **employer has taken reasonable care**, a penalty should not be levied. HMRC give the example of the perpetration of a sophisticated fraud by the employee which no reasonable employer in the same situation could reasonably be expected to spot.

9842 CH84610 HMRC have the power to raise a penalty, or part of a penalty, against an officer or **officers of a company** if:
- they have deliberately made an error, or deliberately taken action to understate the company's tax liability; or
- the company is insolvent, or it is reasonably expected to become insolvent.

MEMO POINTS 1. The **penalty** levied on the company and the officers of the company **cannot exceed** 100% of the penalty which would be applicable if assessed solely on the company.
2. HMRC's guidance states that they will consider whether officers of a company have **personally gained** from any deliberate action when deciding whether to levy the penalty on them.
3. **Signing a document** does not in itself make an officer personally responsible for the error.
4. If it is found that more than one officer is responsible for the deliberate error, **each officer** should be assessed on a fair and reasonable basis. HMRC cannot demand payment of an officer's share of the penalty from another officer of the company. For example, if officers A and B are both found to have carried out a deliberate action in understating the tax liability of the company, and have each been assessed 50% of the total penalty, HMRC must pursue both A and B for payment, and they cannot request that either A or B pays 100% of the penalty.
5. In Finance Act 2009, specific obligations were announced for the **senior accounting officers** of large companies (see ¶2360).

5. Partnerships

9844 s 12AA TMA 1970; CH84700 If there is an error in a partnership tax return no penalty is levied on the partnership, because there is no potential lost revenue, since the partnership does not pay tax. Instead each partner will receive a **partners' penalty** on the basis that he has made an error on his personal tax return. The error, and therefore the amount chargeable to a penalty, will be divided between the partners based on how they shared the profits for the tax return in question.

EXAMPLE Partnership ABC prepares its accounts for the year ending 5 April showing a profit of £40,000. The profits are shared as follows:

Partner	%	Profit share (£)
A	50%	£20,000
B	25%	£10,000
C	25%	£10,000

HMRC enquire into the partnership, and partners' tax returns for the above period, and discover a careless error, resulting in an under-declaration of £10,000.
All of the partners are basic rate taxpayers. Ignoring personal allowances the potential lost tax for each partner is:

Partner	Potential lost revenue (£)
A	(10,000 × 50%) × (20% + 9%) = 1,450
B	(10,000 × 25%) × (20% + 9%) = 725
C	(10,000 × 25%) × (20% + 9%) = 725

20% = basic rate tax
9% = class 4 NIC

6. Errors attributable to third parties

Third parties who either **deliberately supply** false information used by a taxpayer to complete his return, or **withhold information** which a taxpayer requires to complete his return, may be liable to a penalty. The third party must intend to cause the taxpayer to supply an inaccurate document to HMRC. 9845 Sch 24 para 1A FA 2007

The penalty applies where the inaccuracy is contained in a **return or other document** which was due to be filed on or after 1 April 2010, and the return or other document relates to a tax period beginning on or after 1 April 2009.

The penalty can be levied on a third party, even if the **taxpayer** is also **subject to a penalty**.

SECTION 2

Failure to notify and unauthorised VAT invoices

From 1 April 2009, the new penalties regime was extended to include failure to notify HMRC of coming within a charge to tax, failure to register where a relevant obligation exists, and unauthorised issue of VAT invoices. The new failure to notify regime applies to failures occurring **on or after 1 April 2010**. Thus, for example, if a liability to register for VAT arose in March 2010 the relevant penalty will be the old late registration penalty (¶9292), even though the failure is discovered on or after 1 April 2010. 9846 Sch 41 FA 2008

The following table summarises the effect of the new changes on the taxes covered by *Tax Memo*.

Tax	Circumstances	Statutory reference
Income tax and CGT	Failure to notify liability	s 7 TMA 1970
Corporation tax	Failure to notify coming within the charge to tax	Sch 18 para 2 FA 1998
VAT	Failure to notify liability to register arising on or after 1 April 2010	Schs 1-3A VATA 1994
	Failure to notify on or after 1 April 2010 a change in nature of supplies if person has previously been exempted from registration	
	Unauthorised issue of VAT invoices on or after 1 April 2010	s 67 VATA 1994

A. Calculation of the penalty

9847 Under the new regime the level of the penalty is calculated with reference to the **potential lost tax revenue (PLR)**. The penalties are calculated on a percentage of PLR, with the percentage applicable dependant on the actions of the taxpayer.

Reason for failure	Maximum penalty (%)	Minimum penalty (%)	Further detail
Deliberate action of taxpayer	70%	30%	
Concealment of a deliberate action	100%	20%	
Any other situation	30%	0%	If the disclosure is not within 12 months of the date the tax was first due the penalty will be a minimum of 10%

MEMO POINTS From 6 April 2011 these penalties apply in a similar way to that outlined at ¶9803 for income tax and capital gains tax where the failure to notify involves an overseas tax matter. The penalty levels will be the same for deliberate or concealed and deliberate failures as shown above but are more complex for careless failures. For **careless** failures the following percentages apply:

Category	Standard %	HMRC become aware within 12 months of due date of tax		HMRC become aware 12 months or more after due date of tax	
		Minimum % for unprompted disclosure	Minimum % for prompted disclosure	Minimum % for unprompted disclosure	Minimum % for prompted disclosure
1	30	0	10	10	20
2	45	0	15	15	30
3	60	0	20	20	40

9848 As with penalties for errors, the possibility to **reduce** the maximum penalty is available for failure to notify. The amount of the **reduction depends on** the quality of the disclosure given. **Quality is defined** in the legislation as having the attributes of timing, nature and extent of the disclosure and reductions are given for **telling** HMRC of the error, **giving** the relevant information to allow them to quantify the error, and **allowing (helping)** them access to records to check how much was unpaid.

No reduction is available where the disclosure has been prompted by HMRC. See ¶9812 for what HMRC believe a prompted disclosure is.

9849 The legislation gives HMRC powers to offer **special reductions** as well as the above. It is possible for HMRC to stay a penalty, and the procedure follows the penalties for errors procedure (¶9822+).

MEMO POINTS The special reductions rules specifically include the following **exclusions**:
- no reduction will be given solely on the basis that the taxpayer does not have the ability to settle the liability; and
- special reduction will not be available on the ground that there has been no loss to the public revenue, because the liability due from the taxpayer who has failed to notify has been offset with another taxpayer.

B. Reasonable excuse

If a taxpayer has a reasonable excuse he may be able to have the penalty cancelled. 9850

The legislation does not **define** what a reasonable excuse is and each case is judged on the facts. It is expected that the large body of case law which has developed over time for income tax, corporation tax and VAT, will continue to apply.

MEMO POINTS The following are specifically excluded from being reasonable excuses under the new rules:
- insufficiency of funds;
- unreasonable delay in bringing affairs up to date after a reasonable excuse has ceased;
- relying on another person, unless reasonable care to avoid the failure has been taken. A penalty may be levied if the taxpayer relies on an agent but can be avoided if the taxpayer can show that he took reasonable care that the agent would carry out his instructions.

SECTION 3

Penalties under the information powers

Since 1 April 2009 HMRC have had new powers of inspection and for information gathering (¶9862). 9852 Sch 36 FA 2008; Sch 48 FA 2009

Under the new rules, it is possible for HMRC to levy the following penalties where there is a failure to comply with requests made under these powers:
- standard penalties;
- daily default penalties; and
- tax-related penalties.

MEMO POINTS The powers apply across all taxes and to third parties as well as the taxpayer.

A **standard penalty** of £300 will be levied if a taxpayer **fails to comply** with an information notice (¶9865), or **deliberately obstructs** an officer of HMRC who is attempting to carry out an inspection that has been approved by the First-tier Tribunal. 9853

Failure to comply with an information notice includes the **concealment, destruction or disposal** of information requested in the notice.

A standard penalty will not be levied under these provisions for failure to meet the time limit specified in the notice, unless the delay continues beyond further time which an officer of HMRC has allowed. This is also the case where a reasonable excuse can be shown.

A **daily default** penalty for a continuing failure or obstruction can be levied in addition to the standard penalty. The daily penalty cannot exceed £60 per day.

In either case HMRC must assess the penalty and issue notification of it to the taxpayer within 12 months of the later of the date:
- the taxpayer became liable to the penalty;
- on which the right to appeal has expired; or
- when the appeal is determined or withdrawn.

MEMO POINTS There is a **right of appeal** against either of these penalties to the First-tier Tribunal. Such an appeal must be lodged within 30 days in writing to HMRC. The tribunal is able to substitute any penalty that HMRC could have imposed under the circumstances.

If obstruction or failure to comply with an information notice continues and HMRC believe that the tax paid is significantly less than it otherwise would be, they can apply to the tribunal (¶9922) to apply a **tax-related penalty**. 9854

HMRC have 12 months to apply for tax-related penalties. The time limit runs from the date the taxpayer became liable to the penalty or, if the taxpayer appeals against the notice, the later of 30 days after the notice was given to the taxpayer or the date of the determination of the appeal.

SECTION 4

Penalties for late filing and payment

A. Failure to file on time

9855 Sch 55 FA 2009; F(no 3)A 2010 Sch 10

From various dates, not all yet announced, a late filing penalty will be imposed when a return or other document is submitted after the filing date. The affected taxes and documents are set out below:

<table>
<tr><th>Tax (and commencement date, if known)</th><th>Documents</th><th>Penalties within initial 12 months</th><th>Additional penalties after 12 months</th></tr>
<tr><td>Income tax and CGT (April 2011)</td><td>Tax returns, including any statements or documents in support of the returns, accounts, pension scheme returns</td><td rowspan="6">Initial penalty of £100
Where failure continues beyond 3 month period, daily penalty of £10 to a maximum of £900.
Where failure continues beyond 6 months, penalty is greater of:
5% of any tax which would have been shown in the return and £300.</td><td rowspan="6">Tax geared and depends on the actions of the taxpayer.
Basic penalty is greater of:
5% of any tax liability which would have been shown on the return and £300.
Where withholding of information is deliberate but not concealed, the penalty is the greater of:
70% of the tax liability which would have been shown on the return and £300.
Where withholding of information is deliberate and concealed, the penalty is the greater of:
100% of the tax liability which would have been shown on the return and £300.</td></tr>
<tr><td>Corporation tax</td><td>Returns, accounts including any statements or documents in support of the return</td></tr>
<tr><td>IHT</td><td>IHT 400 and any return or document required to report a transaction see (¶9788)</td></tr>
<tr><td>PAYE and NICs (April 2010)</td><td>P14, P9D, P35, P38, P38A, P11D(b)</td></tr>
<tr><td>SDLT</td><td>Land transaction return</td></tr>
<tr><td>SDRT</td><td>Notice of a charge to tax</td></tr>
<tr><td>CIS (October 2011)</td><td>Monthly returns[1]</td><td>Initial penalty of £100 increasing to £200 if return not submitted within 2 months
Where failure continues beyond 6 months from the date of submission, the penalty is greater of:
5% of the tax liability which would have been shown on the return and £300</td><td>Tax geared and depends on the actions of the taxpayer.
Basic penalty is greater of:
5% of any tax liability which would have been shown on the return and £300.
Where withholding of information is deliberate but not concealed, the penalty is the greater of:
70% of the tax liability which would have been shown on the return and £1,500
Where withholding of information is deliberate and concealed, the penalty is the greater of:
100% of the tax liability which would have been shown on the return and £3,000.</td></tr>
</table>

Tax (and commencement date, if known)	Documents	Penalties within initial 12 months	Additional penalties after 12 months
VAT	Quarterly returns	Initial penalty of £100 and further failures within a 12 month period will result in an increase in the penalty by £100 and an extension of the penalty period. Maximum penalty will be £400 per failure. Where failure continues **beyond 6 months** from the date of submission, the penalty is 5% of the tax liability which would have been shown on the return.	Tax geared and depends on the actions of the taxpayer. **Basic penalty** is 5% of any tax liability which would have been shown on the return Where withholding of information is **deliberate** to ensure an accurate assessment cannot be made the maximum penalty is 100% of the tax liability which would have been shown on the return.
	Monthly returns	As quarterly returns but the first 6 failures in a penalty period will only attract a £100 penalty, the maximum penalty being capped at £200.	

Notes:
1. Where a return is still outstanding beyond 12 months and relates only to those receiving payments without deduction of tax there is a further penalty of £3,000 or £1,500 depending on whether the information is concealed or not.
2. From 6 April 2011 the percentages, not the fixed monetary sums, for penalties for failures exceeding 12 months match those outlined at ¶9803 where the failure involves either income tax or capital gains tax and relates to an offshore matter. This does not apply to PAYE or CIS returns.

MEMO POINTS The rules mean that there is an automatic late filing penalty of £100 for tax returns, irrespective of the amount of the tax liability or whether it has been paid on time.

A penalty **may be reduced** where the taxpayer makes a disclosure to HMRC of the information which has been withheld by a failure to make a return. The **disclosure** can be made by telling HMRC about it, giving them reasonable help in quantifying any tax unpaid by reason of its having been withheld and allowing them access to records for the purposes of checking the amount of tax unpaid. The size of the reduction depends on whether the disclosure was prompted or unprompted and the reduced percentages are the same as those in (¶9802). The taxpayer can also appeal against the imposition of a penalty.

A penalty **may be mitigated** where, on appeal to the tribunal or to HMRC, the taxpayer is able to prove that he had a **reasonable excuse** for the failure. However, the following will not be accepted as being a reasonable excuse:
- an insufficiency of funds, unless attributable to events outside the taxpayer's control; and
- reliance on any other person to do anything, unless the taxpayer took reasonable care to avoid the failure.

Where the taxpayer had a reasonable excuse for the failure but the **excuse has ceased**, it will be treated as having continued to exist if the failure is remedied without unreasonable delay after the excuse ceases.

MEMO POINTS 1. The penalty does not have to be paid before the appeal is made.
2. The taxpayer cannot be assessed twice for the same penalty.

On an **appeal to the tribunal**, the imposition of the penalty may be affirmed or another penalty within HMRC's power may be substituted for that penalty. This also enables the tribunal to apply or increase a mitigation percentage.

B. Failure to pay on time and tax defaulters

9857 DMBM 800020; Sch 56 FA 2009; F(no 3)A 2010 Sch 11

Finance Act 2009 introduced new penalties for failure to pay tax on time. The commencement date for PAYE, CIS. NIC and pension schemes is 6 April 2010; for income tax self-assessment it is 6 April 2011. Penalties for late payment of tax are **in addition to** any interest charge arising from the late payment. A penalty cannot be charged if a taxpayer has a reasonable excuse for his failure to pay (¶9850).

If a late payment penalty could apply under more than one provision, the taxpayer is liable for a penalty under each one.

If a taxpayer realises that he will be likely to pay a tax liability late, he can make an agreement with HMRC in certain cases. This provision is limited and is considered on an individual basis, but HMRC advise that taxpayers in such situations should contact them immediately to discuss any liabilities.

Where a taxpayer enters into a time to pay arrangement or **managed payment plan** with HMRC, any late payment penalties that he would otherwise become liable to after the agreement is reached will be suspended, provided that the taxpayer meets the terms of the agreement.

In addition, where a taxpayer has entered into an agreement with HMRC to **defer** payment, he is not liable to surcharges or penalties that would otherwise be due because of late payment. However, if the terms of the deferral agreement are **not observed**, HMRC have the power to re-impose the surcharge or penalty. The details of the taxes affected by the penalty regime and the deferral and managed payment plans are set out in the following table:

Tax	Subject to late payment penalty regime	Penalties suspended with deferral arrangement[1]	Managed payment plan available[2]
Income tax	✓	✓	✓
Capital gains tax	✓	✓	✓
VAT[3]	✓	✓	x
Corporation tax	✓	x	✓
PAYE	✓	x	x
NICs	✓	x	x
CIS	✓	x	x
SDLT	✓	x	x
SDRT	✓	x	x
IHT	✓	x	x
Pension schemes	✓	x	x

Notes:
1. This change became effective for deferral agreements reached on or after 24 November 2008.
2. The time to pay arrangements are agreed on a case by case basis and are not the same as the statutory right to pay some tax liabilities by instalments, such as inheritance tax due on instalment option property (¶7073).
3. Failure to pay VAT on time is currently subject to default surcharge (¶9272).

Comment HMRC advise that they consider the taxpayer's current ability to pay, whether the proposals are reasonable, the future payment and compliance history and the enforcement options available to them. HMRC also advise that their approach to time to pay arrangements at the present time is with the intention to support businesses and individuals who are experiencing short-term difficulties.

Calculation of the penalty

The penalties due and the date on which they become payable are outlined below for taxes due on returns. 9858

Tax	Payment	Penalty
Income tax and capital gains tax	Balancing payment of tax for the year	5% 31 days after the due date of payment 5% on outstanding balances at 5 and 11 months later
Income tax	PAYE – where the return period is over 6 months	5% on day after due date of payment 5% on outstanding balances at 5 and 11 months later
	PAYE – return period 6 months or less	Based on number of defaults in the year – see below
Income tax	Payment by pension scheme administrators	5% 31 days after the due date of payment 5% on outstanding balances at 5 and 11 months later
Corporation tax	Payments shown due on return	5% the day after the due date of filing 5% on outstanding balances at 3 and 9 months later
CIS deductions	Where the return period is over 6 months	5% the day after the due date of payment 5% on outstanding balances at 5 and 11 months later
	Where the return period is 6 months or less	Based on number of defaults in the year – see below
National Insurance Contributions	PAYE – where the return period is over 6 months ie class 1A and 1B	5% 31 days after the due date of payment 5% on outstanding balances at 5 and 11 months later
	PAYE – return period 6 months or less	Same as PAYE
Inheritance tax	All payments	5% on day after due date of return. Where the tax is being paid by instalments second and subsequent payments will be penalised from 31 days after they are due. 5% on outstanding balances at 5 and 11 months later
Stamp duty land tax	All payments	5% on day after due date of payment 5% on outstanding balances at 5 and 11 months later
Stamp duty reserve tax	All payments	5% 31 days after due date of payment 5% on outstanding balances at 5 and 11 months later

Where the **late payment of PAYE (including NIC) or CIS** is for a period of 6 months or less there is a sliding scale based on the number of late payments in the tax year:
– the first late payment is not considered to be a default and attracts no penalty unless the PAYE remains unpaid after 6 months;
– where there are 2, 3 or 4 defaults in a year the penalty is 1%;
– where there are 5, 6 or 7 the penalty is 2%;

– where there are 8, 9 or 10 the penalty is 3%; and
– where there are more than 10 defaults the penalty is 5%.

The percentage is applied to the total of the late payments throughout the year, ignoring the first one. If the payment is still outstanding 6 months after it is due a penalty of 5% is charged. This also applies to the first default in the year. A similar penalty is charged where it is 12 months late. These are both in addition to the penalties listed above.

For **quarterly VAT payments** the first failure to pay on time will attract no penalty but will commence a penalty period lasting a year. Further failures continue to extend the penalty period and the following percentages are charged:
– the second failure: 2%
– the third failure: 3%: and
– further failures: 4%.

If the tax remains **outstanding after 6 months** 5% of the unpaid tax is charged, with the same percentage payable again at 12 months.

For **monthly payments** failures 2, 3 and 4 are liable to a penalty at 2%, and failures 5, 6 and 7 attract a 3% penalty. Any further failures in the penalty period remain at 4%.

Tax defaulters

9859 s 94 FA 2009 In an attempt to discourage tax defaulters, or those who do not provide accurate information, from 1 April 2010 HMRC have the power to make public the names of defaulters.

Publication of the details of a tax defaulter is only allowed in limited circumstances.

It must arise as a **consequence of an investigation** conducted by HMRC where one or more relevant tax penalties has been incurred by the taxpayer and the potential lost revenue arising from that penalty or penalties in total exceeds £25,000.

A "**relevant tax penalty**" is a:
– penalty arising from an inaccuracy, or a deliberate inaccuracy;
– a penalty arising from an inaccuracy in a taxpayer's document attributable to a deliberate supply of false information or deliberate withholding of information by a person; or
– a penalty for a deliberate failure to notify (¶9846) by a person; or
– a penalty for issuing an unauthorised VAT invoice.

The **information that may be published** is:
– the person's name (including any trading name, previous name or pseudonym);
– the person's address or registered office;
– the nature of any business carried on by the person;
– the amount of the penalty or penalties and the potential lost revenue in relation to them;
– the periods or times to which the inaccuracy, failure or action giving rise to the penalty or penalties relates, and
– any such other information as HMRC consider it appropriate to publish in order to make clear the person's identity.

Before publishing any information HMRC must inform the person that they are considering doing so, and allow the person reasonable opportunity to make representations about whether the information should be published.

No information may be published before the day when the penalty becomes final or the latest day when any of the penalties become final.

No information may be published for the first time more than one year after the penalty becomes final. In addition, no information may be published if the amount of the penalty is reduced under the reductions for disclosure rules.

Comment These are controversial rules and HMRC have indicated that this power will only be used as last resort and deterrent for frequent tax defaulters. The right of HMRC to put a name on a published list for up to a year may be subject to challenge over the taxpayer's right to confidentiality.

CHAPTER 3

Powers and procedures

OUTLINE ¶¶

Finance Act 2008 contained provisions to align the powers of HMRC to request information and inspect business records and premises. The **new rules** came **into force on** 1 April 2009 and 1 April 2010. All taxes are now covered. 9860

SECTION 1

Information and inspection powers

The long-standing powers of HMRC to request information relating to returns, or documents submitted, have been extended under the new regime. The old powers to request information were, generally, "after the fact" provisions which allowed HMRC to request information to support tax, or VAT, returns which had been submitted. These powers have, generally, remained and the procedure for direct tax enquiries and VAT inspections are dealt with in the relevant *Administration* sections of *Tax Memo*. The old stamp duty land tax inspection powers were repealed with effect from 1 April 2010. 9862 Sch 36 FA 2008

What distinguishes the new powers is that HMRC are able to carry out **real-time checks** on taxpayers. The powers and penalties open to them mean that businesses have an increased **compliance burden** through their annual cycle.

A. Power to obtain information and documents

9864 Schs 47-48 FA 2009 SI 2009/1916 Sch 36 FA 2008

HMRC are able to obtain information and documents relating to a taxpayer's affairs from the taxpayer or a third party. The powers also allow HMRC, in certain circumstances, to request information relating to an unknown taxpayer or group of taxpayers.

From the taxpayer

9865 Sch 48 FA 2009 Sch 36 para 1 FA 2008 Sch 18 para 27 FA 1988 ss 19A, 20 TMA 1970

HMRC may request any information or documents from the taxpayer which they believe are reasonably required to check the taxpayer's tax position. The request must be **in writing** and is referred to as an **information notice** or **taxpayer notice**. Previously HMRC had the power to request documents supporting returns already submitted by taxpayers. They may now request information for the current tax position as well.

Comment "**Tax position**" is defined in the legislation as any past, present or future liability. The generally held view is that this is **not limited to** self-assessments, or claims submitted to HMRC. Whether a taxpayer can have a "tax position" when either contemplating a transaction, or before submitting a self-assessment, is not clear.
The extension of the power to request supporting information could mean that HMRC may expect to be provided with meeting minutes to explain why decisions have been made where no such minutes may exist. If information is requested in real time, before a transaction is finalised or included in a self-assessment, this may enable HMRC to close loopholes in the legislation before they can be widely exploited.

Third-party requests

9866 Sch 36 paras 2, 61A FA 2008

HMRC have the power to request documents from third parties or, in certain cases, an involved third party, relating to either a named taxpayer, or, in defined circumstances, a taxpayer whose identity is unknown.

HMRC Brief 54/09

Where the request is for information relating to a **named taxpayer**, the third party does not have to comply with the notice unless the taxpayer has given permission or the tribunal has approved the request.

The information requested must be reasonably required to check the tax position of the named taxpayer, whose name must be included on the notice, unless the tribunal disapplies this requirement.

If the taxpayer refuses to give permission for the request to be made, the HMRC officer may apply to the tribunal (¶9922) to give approval for issuing the notice. The tribunal cannot give its approval unless:
- a written application has been made by an authorised officer of HMRC;
- there is justification for making the application;
- the information has been requested from the taxpayer and the taxpayer has had time to make reasonable representations to HMRC as to why the information is not required; and
- if the taxpayer has made representations they have been presented to the tribunal.

HMRC cannot request information and documents which are subject to **professional privilege**. A dispute over the scope of professional privilege may be referred to the tribunal (¶9880).

MEMO POINTS 1. An **authorised officer** is an officer of HMRC authorised by the Board of HMRC to carry out the relevant action.
2. The tribunal has the option of ignoring the above conditions for granting approval of a third-party notice if it believes that by following the conditions the collection, or assessment, of tax revenue will be prejudiced.
3. The taxpayer is not permitted to attend the hearing and there is no right of appeal against a decision of the tribunal in this respect.
4. The definition of an **involved** third party has been included with amendments to the original legislation. It is very widely drawn and includes references to a charity, a plan manager for

individual investment plans, a child trust fund account provider, a Lloyd's agent, an insurance broker or an accountable person for stamp duty reserve tax.
5. Records held solely for the purposes of IHT are not subject to inspection.

HMRC may also request information from third parties relating to **unknown taxpayers**, or groups of taxpayers. HMRC must first obtain **approval from** the tribunal, which must be satisfied that the unknown person, or class of persons, has failed to comply with his or its **UK tax obligations** and that HMRC cannot obtain the information from another source. **9868** Sch 36 para 5 FA 2008

B. Complying with requests for information

Taxpayers, or third parties, have certain **responsibilities** to meet when they are issued with an information notice. **9870** Sch 36 para 7 FA 2008

The **information** requested has to be **supplied**:
– within a period of time which is reasonably specified;
– in the form specified by HMRC; and
– at a place agreed with HMRC. If no agreement can be reached HMRC can specify where they wish the information to be provided.

It is sufficient for **copies of documents** to be provided, unless the information notice specifically requests originals, or HMRC subsequently request originals. HMRC have the power to take copies, or extracts from documents.

MEMO POINTS 1. HMRC cannot specify that the documents should be produced at a place used solely as a **dwelling**. If a business is run from an individual's dwelling this will not be excluded, as it is not solely used as a dwelling.

Comment The power allowing HMRC to take copies of documents further strengthens their ability to perform "real time" analysis of transactions or tax planning schemes.

Taxpayers and third parties are only required to produce information where it is within their possession, or they have power to obtain it. **9872** Sch 36 paras 18-20, para 22 FA 2008

Further, the recipient of an **information notice** does **not have to provide**:
– information or documents relating to a pending appeal;
– journalistic material;
– documents which were wholly originated more than 6 years before the date of the notice, unless an authorised officer believes fraud has taken place (using the new terminology, it may be that this power is exercised when an authorised officer believes a deliberate and concealed action has taken place); or
– information held in personal records.

An information notice cannot be issued to check the tax position of a **deceased taxpayer** more than 4 years after the taxpayer has died.

What if a tax return has been submitted?

If a taxpayer notice is issued requesting **specific information** which relates to a chargeable period for which the taxpayer has already submitted a self-assessment tax return (or any other return), the taxpayer does not have to comply with the notice. **9874** Sch 36 para 21 FA 2008

The following situations are **excluded** (in these circumstances the taxpayer must comply with the notice):
– a notice of enquiry (¶2330, ¶4552) has been issued to the taxpayer relating to a chargeable period for which a return has been submitted and that enquiry is not yet complete;
– an officer of HMRC has reason to suspect that:
a. an amount ought to have been charged to tax for the period and it has not been;
b. an assessment has been raised which charges an insufficient amount of tax; or
c. a taxpayer has claimed excessive relief from tax; or

– the notice was issued to allow HMRC to check the taxpayer's VAT or PAYE position and during those checks it comes to light that an underdeclaration of tax has been made.

Comment The restriction on requests for information after submission of a tax return limits HMRC's powers so that they are unable to request information without opening a formal enquiry.

Third-party compliance

9875 There are some **safeguards** built into the new rules for certain third parties. After lobbying from various bodies there are special rules for solicitors and barristers, and tax advisers and auditors.

9876 Sch 36 paras 23-25 FA 2008

Third-party adviser	Documents outside the scope of an information notice
Tax adviser	– any information held relating to relevant communication between the adviser and his client, or another adviser of his client; and – documents containing relevant information which are held as the property of the taxpayer
Auditor	– information held for the purposes of his appointment; and – documents created during the course of the audit which remain the property of the auditor
Solicitor or barrister	– any document or information which is subject to legal professional privilege

9878 Sch 36 para 26 FA 2008 There is a specific **exclusion** from the above for **auditors and tax advisers**. HMRC have the power to request information, or a document containing information, which explains any document or information a taxpayer has provided to HMRC, from the taxpayer's "tax accountant".

Comment This provision puts accountants and tax advisers at a commercial disadvantage to providers who are protected by legal professional privilege. A solicitor could, for instance, help a client prepare a trust tax return and any information or documents relating to that form would then be outside the scope of an information notice, whereas if the client appointed a firm of accountants to assist with the preparation of the same form the information could legitimately be requested.

9880 SI 2009/1916 HMRC Brief 54/09 If there is any dispute as to whether a document or information is subject to **legal professional privilege** the matter can be referred to the tribunal. A list of disputed documents has to be produced for consideration by the tribunal and for the tribunal to issue directions.

MEMO POINTS 1. If disputes arise **during the course of an inspection of premises**, protection is given to individuals removing documents in advance of the tribunal's decision as to whether the documents are covered by professional privilege. HMRC are protected by the requirement that the agreed documents are not changed.
The tribunal may either direct that the whole of a document is covered by privilege or that part of it is so covered. The tribunal must also direct which part or parts of a document (if any) may be disclosed.
The parties involved may agree the list of documents without the direction of the tribunal at any time.
2. HMRC have published guidance about whether a document can be withheld from inspection on the grounds of professional privilege. Where there is a dispute over whether documents qualify for professional privilege the taxpayer, or his agent, should submit a list to HMRC specifying each disputed document for identification purposes. The list should be reviewed by HMRC and, if they do not agree that a document is privileged, they will advise the taxpayer accordingly. Following receipt of that letter, if the taxpayer does not wish to make the documents available to HMRC, he can make an application to the tribunal for directions, which must be submitted within 20 days of the letter from HMRC. The tribunal will then make a decision on the matter. When a request for documents is given at an inspection of premises, the disputed documents should be put in a sealed container for review by the tribunal and its decision on the matter.

C. Inspection of business premises

HMRC have **powers to enter** and **inspect** business premises. Under the old powers given to the former HM Customs & Excise, officers had the powers to enter and inspect premises of VAT-registered traders. This power has been extended to cover all other taxes. In a further extension of their powers, HMRC can enter the premises of involved third parties for the purposes of inspecting the premises or business assets which are on the premises. In addition, HMRC can enter a property for valuation purposes if it is necessary to check a person's tax position. **9882** Sch 36 paras 10-14 FA 2008; SI 2009/404; Sch 47 FA 2009

MEMO POINTS The term "**business**" **specifically includes** the letting of property, activities of a charity and activities of local authorities and government departments. "**Premises**" includes any building or structure and any land, and "**assets**" includes any means of transport. This gives HMRC the power to enter and inspect vehicles which are used for business purposes, such as lorries and cars.

Notification of visit

HMRC **must give** the taxpayer 7 days' notice of its officer's intended visit, **unless**: **9884**
- an earlier time is agreed with the occupier; or
- the inspection is carried out, or authorised, by an authorised officer of HMRC.

If the inspection is being carried out under the authority of an authorised officer a notice must be provided to the **occupier** if present, or the person who appears to be in charge at the time of the visit. If **no-one** is **present** the notice will be left for the occupier. The notice should state the consequences of obstruction, and whether the notice has been approved by the tribunal.

If the **notice** has been **approved by the** tribunal it cannot be appealed.

MEMO POINTS Notice can be given either in writing or verbally.

During the visit

Once an inspection has been notified, or approved by an authorised officer, HMRC have the power to enter the business premises of the taxpayer. If the taxpayer **attempts to obstruct** entry he may be liable to a penalty. **9886**

HMRC cannot enter premises that are solely used as a **dwelling** but they can enter part of dwelling if it is used for business purposes.

Once the officer has gained **entry to the premises** he is **entitled to** inspect business assets and any documents relating to carrying on the business, or which form part of the statutory records, if to do so is reasonably required for the officer to check the taxpayer's tax position. **9888**

MEMO POINTS 1. The legislation defines "**tax position**" as any past, present or future liability to pay any tax. Also included with the definition of tax position are penalties payable and any claims, elections, applications or notices given to HMRC.

2. HMRC cannot inspect documents which are excluded from information notices by virtue of legal professional privilege, or excluded documents and information of tax advisers and auditors (¶9876).

3. The power is an inspection power, not a search power. For **VAT** purposes this curtails the right of search (compared to the old search power) but it is permissible for an officer to take copies of documents and to mark them as having been examined.

HMRC have the power to inspect **computers** and associated equipment used to produce documents. An authorised person, who may include a specialist, rather than, or as well as, an officer from HMRC, can access and inspect any such equipment; **taxpayers** are **obliged** to provide the necessary assistance to allow HMRC to use and check the computer. Assistance must be provided in a reasonable amount of time. If it is not, a penalty of £300 may be levied. **9890** s 114 FA 2008 Sch 37 FA 2008

MEMO POINTS The same restrictions which apply for records on paper also apply for those stored in electronic formats. The penalty for failure to comply is now a civil matter.

SECTION 2

Record-keeping requirements

9892 Sch 37 FA 2008 Records should be kept for 6 years, although HMRC do now have power to agree a shorter period.

The **new powers** also confer a right on HMRC to specify in secondary or tertiary legislation what supporting documents and information taxpayers should keep.

Comment The legislative changes appear to give some welcome **flexibility** in the system, as taxpayers should be able to agree less burdensome record-keeping formats and periods. It is essential to keep records if an enquiry has been opened by HMRC. Once an enquiry is taking place, records must be kept until the enquiry is completed, or at least while the enquiry window is still open.

SECTION 3

Power to obtain contact details of debtors

9893 Sch 49 FA 2009 New powers have been granted to HMRC to obtain **from certain third parties** the contact details of persons who have a tax debt owing to HMRC, where those details are necessary for the settlement of that debt.

HMRC must have reasonable grounds to believe that the third party has the details.

The **third party must be** a company, a local authority or a local authority association, or HMRC must have reasonable grounds to believe that the third party obtained the details in the course of carrying on a business.

Details obtained by a charity in the course of providing services free of charge, or obtained by a company for a charity where the recipient has received services free of charge, are not included.

Comment This allows confidentiality to individuals who are struggling to pay tax liabilities and who seek advice from debt advisory charities.

HMRC must issue a **written notice** to the third party, naming the debtor. The third party is required to provide the details within a specified period but can appeal to the tribunal against the notice on the ground that compliance with it would be unduly onerous. However, the **penalty** for failure to comply with the notice is £300.

MEMO POINTS It has been made clear that the requirements do not apply to employees of a company.

SECTION 4

Right of set-off

9894 ss 130-133 FA 2008 HMRC have a **statutory power** to set off any tax owed to a taxpayer against any tax owed by that taxpayer. This is a cross-cutting measure meaning that if a taxpayer has, for example, a VAT credit but owes HMRC unpaid corporation tax, the two may be offset.

MEMO POINTS 1. If a taxpayer has elected that his income tax repayment be donated to a charity, HMRC will not offset the amount being donated against any other liability.
2. HMRC cannot offset a post-insolvency credit against a pre-insolvency debt.

In a Court of Appeal decision it was held that if a **right to repayment** of VAT was **assigned** from one party to another, there was no provision under the VAT legislation to refuse repayment to the assignee. HMRC argued that the only person capable of making a claim for repayment of overpaid VAT was the person who actually paid the VAT to HMRC. The court unanimously rejected this argument and held that the term "person" **included** successors and agents of the taxpayer. **9895** s 133 FA 2008

HMRC also argued that if it was possible to assign credits this would make establishing **unjust enrichment** very difficult, and on that basis assignees should not be able to make a claim. Again, the court rejected this, as there was nothing in the VAT legislation which excluded assignees from making a claim. *Midlands Co-operative Society Ltd v HMRC* [2008]

In response to this decision provisions have been made which effectively put the assignee (referred to as the "current creditor") into the shoes of the assignor (the "original creditor"). This means that if the current creditor makes a claim for overpaid or over-declared tax, the claim will be restricted if the original creditor also owes a debt to HMRC.

The power also includes provision whereby if the original creditor would have been unjustly enriched by making the claim, the same restriction will apply to the current creditor.

The rules **apply** to any assignment of rights **on or after** 25 June 2008 and cover **all taxes**.

Comment The legislation has been drafted to close a "potential avoidance opportunity". It would appear from the legislation that the above provisions will cover every assignment, not just those carried out with the purpose of avoiding tax. This provision affects the drafting of tax warranties and covenants, so purchasers should take care to ensure they do not fund any underpayment of tax by the assignor. HMRC have stated that the current creditor will not be liable for the debts of the original creditor. However, if the original creditor owes tax to HMRC, this will be taken into account when calculating the current creditor's repayment. The original creditor will also then be released from his obligation to pay the tax.

CHAPTER 4

Other reforms

OUTLINE ¶¶

SECTION 1

Requesting clearances

Since 1 April 2008 a **new non-statutory clearance procedure** for all businesses has replaced code of practice 10 (COP 10). Non-business taxpayers should continue to use the procedure as set out in COP 10 when requesting ruling on direct tax issues, and VAT Notice 706 when requesting rulings on VAT issues. 9896

MEMO POINTS 1. In addition to the non-statutory procedure, there are also **statutory clearances** which can be applied for relating to:
- company reconstructions (¶5852);
- purchase of own shares (¶2090);
- CFC exemptions (¶2154); and
- transactions in securities (¶4048).

2. Contact details and a list of clearances which are handled on an integrated basis, where only a single application is necessary, can be found at www.hmrc.gov.uk/cap/index.htm.

A. Businesses

Businesses can request clearance from HMRC using the new clearance procedure. The procedure covers all **taxes**, **including**: 9898 HMRC Brief 25/08
- corporation tax;

- PAYE and NIC;
- capital gains tax;
- business income tax;
- VAT; and
- SDLT.

HMRC aim to provide **clearances** on transactions **within** 28 days in the **following circumstances**:
- on areas of material uncertainty arising within four Finance Acts of the introduction of new legislation; and
- on legislation older than the last four Finance Acts where there is material uncertainty on the tax outcome of a transaction of commercial significance to a business.

HMRC will accept **applications** from any business, or its advisers, as long as they can demonstrate uncertainty. HMRC have stated that this process **will not be used** for personal taxation issues, or for product endorsement. Also, the process is not intended to replace HMRC's existing guidance, or public notices. These should be considered before using the clearance procedure.

HMRC will provide clearances both **before** and **after** transactions. For clearance to be given **pre-transaction** the business will need to demonstrate that the transaction is being genuinely contemplated.

The guidance goes on to state that full **details** of the taxpayer, including commercial background, and full details of the transaction must be provided, along with the taxpayer's understanding of the legislation. A checklist of information HMRC require to enable them to give a ruling is available on their website (see www.hmrc.gov.uk/cap/index.htm).

MEMO POINTS 1. Clearances can only be **relied on** by the applicant for the transaction that was the subject of the application. Tax advisers cannot rely on rulings for other clients, even if the facts are similar.
2. Where clearance is requested for **business property relief** (¶6700) for IHT purposes, the request should be sent to Trusts and Estates Technical Team (Clearances), Ferrers House, Castle Meadow Road, Nottingham, NG2 1BB. The existing rules are broadly the same as for requesting any other clearance, and clearance can be requested either by the current owner (or his agent), or the proposed new owner.

9900 Once HMRC are in full possession of the information they require they will **respond in writing in one of the following ways**:
- accepting the application for clearance and accepting the taxpayer's interpretation of the legislation;
- accepting the application for clearance but rejecting the taxpayer's interpretation of the legislation;
- accepting the application for clearance but requesting further information;
- rejecting the application and referring the taxpayer to the relevant public guidance; or
- rejecting the application and stating clearly why non-statutory clearance cannot be given.

MEMO POINTS 1. If HMRC **give an incorrect statement** they are bound by their statement as long as it is clear, unequivocal and explicit and the taxpayer relied on HMRC's advice and would suffer loss if the correct law were applied. Once HMRC **notify the taxpayer** that the advice they gave is incorrect the taxpayer need only start accounting for tax on the correct basis from the date of notification.
2. HMRC are **only bound by a correct statement if** the facts presented by the taxpayer do not change and materially alter the transaction, or if the taxpayer presented the full facts.
3. Should a court change the **interpretation of the law**, subject to legitimate expectation, HMRC will not be bound by their guidance if the transaction has not taken place or there is still an opportunity to amend the return on which the transaction was declared.
4. If **statutory law is changed**, HMRC will not be bound by any ruling if the law has retrospective effect. If the law is to come into force at a later date, HMRC's ruling cannot be relied upon once the law has changed.
5. Clearance **applications** should either be **sent to** taxpayer's Customer Relationship Manager (CRM) if the taxpayer is a large business, or to HMRC Clearances Team, Alexander House, 21 Victoria Avenue, Southend-on-Sea, SS99 1BD.

HMRC **will not accept applications for** non-statutory clearances in the following circumstances: 9902
– when a taxpayer has asked HMRC for, or to comment on, tax planning advice;
– when an application has been previously refused and it is resubmitted with a minor variation – this does not include the situation where the facts of a transaction under consideration have changed;
– when HMRC take the view that the motive behind the transaction is to gain a tax advantage rather than being commercially motivated;
– when HMRC have already opened an enquiry or audit into the transaction, or when an enquiry or audit has been opened into the self-assessment return on which the transaction was, or should have been, included – also, if the time limit for opening an audit or enquiry into a return has passed HMRC will not give a ruling;
– when asset valuation, or clearance of transfer pricing method, is requested;
– whether a project qualifies for research and development tax incentives – in this circumstance the taxpayer should contact the HMRC R&D Specialist Unit; or
– in relation to the tax consequences of executing trust deeds, or settlements.

B. Non-business clearances

Non-business taxpayers are not covered by the new rules. Non-business taxpayers who are unsure of their tax position can request clearances in the following circumstances. **COP 10** will be used for all personal tax and inheritance tax issues (excluding business property relief (¶9898)). **VAT Notice 700/6** provides the procedure for VAT matters. In due course these will be replaced by a single guidance document **CAP 1**. 9904

MEMO POINTS **Non-business taxpayers include**:
– individuals who are not trading;
– personal representatives; and
– taxpayers who are not in business for VAT purposes.

1. Direct taxes

A taxpayer can request a ruling on the application of tax law to a specific transaction after the transaction has taken place. A ruling will **only be provided if**: 9905 COP 10
– the issues involve genuine points of doubt or difficulty over the interpretation of tax law;
– the transaction covers income tax, capital gains tax, corporation tax or petroleum revenue tax (inheritance tax is excluded); and
– HMRC feel the issue can be resolved before the filing date for the relevant return.

A **post-transaction ruling will not be given**:
– for executing non-charitable trust deeds or settlements;
– after an enquiry into the return is opened (or after the time limit has passed to begin an enquiry); or
– where the period in question is the subject of any other HMRC enquiry.

Clearance can be provided without time limit for transactions involving **stamp duty land tax**.

MEMO POINTS When applying for a ruling the following **information must be provided**:
– an explanation of the transaction concerned (including a full technical analysis) and details of the particular aspect(s) of the transaction that a ruling is required for;
– name and tax reference number;
– copies of all relevant documents, with the relevant parts or passages identified; and
– the taxpayer's opinion of the tax consequences of the particular transaction (and why), including relevant case law, legislation, extra-statutory concessions or statements of practice relied upon.

In addition the taxpayer must provide a formal statement that, to the best of his knowledge and belief, the facts given are correct and all relevant facts have been disclosed.

9906 The **aim of the ruling** is to help the taxpayer complete his return and know how much tax will be due.

Once a ruling is given, HMRC will be bound by their decision, unless it comes to light that the information originally supplied on which the decision was based was incorrect or incomplete, or the relevant legislation is subsequently changed. A ruling will not be withdrawn if the interpretation of the relevant law is discovered to be incorrect – for example, following a court decision.

MEMO POINTS 1. HMRC **aim to respond** to post-transaction ruling requests within 28 days. However, where difficult or complicated issues are involved, this may not be possible, in which case they will acknowledge receipt and provide a timescale for a reply.
2. There is no **right of appeal** against a post-transaction ruling but it does not have to be followed if the taxpayer disagrees with the ruling. The fact that a ruling was given and has not been complied with must be disclosed on the return.
3. If a post-transaction ruling has been applied for but not given before the **normal filing date**, the tax return must be filed by the normal due date, based on the taxpayer's understanding of the law. The return can be subsequently amended subject to the normal time limits.

9908 A taxpayer can request information and guidance from HMRC on **any transaction**, provided that the query is actuated by genuine uncertainty about the meaning of the law and it relates either to:
– the interpretation of legislation passed in the last four Finance Acts;
– the application of double taxation agreements;
– whether someone is employed or self-employed;
– statements of practice and extra-statutory concessions; or
– other areas concerning matters of major public interest in an industry or in the financial sector.

MEMO POINTS When applying for a ruling, in addition to the **information** detailed at ¶9898, a taxpayer will need to:
– provide full details, including tax reference numbers, of any other parties involved; and
– make it clear that he is seeking considered guidance and for what use (for example for publication).

9910 Once a **ruling is given**, HMRC will be bound by its decision, unless it comes to light that the information originally supplied on which the decision was based was incorrect or incomplete.

A ruling will not be binding if, before the transaction is entered into, there is a change in either:
– the law (either by legislation or court decision); or
– HMRC's interpretation of the law (provided that such a change has been made public).

MEMO POINTS HMRC **aim to respond** to pre-transaction ruling requests within 28 days. However, where difficult or complicated issues are involved, this may not be possible, in which case they will acknowledge receipt and provide a timescale for a reply.

2. VAT

9912
Notice 700/6
Non-business taxpayers who are unsure of a **major issue** relating to their VAT affairs must apply to HMRC under a **separate procedure**.

HMRC aim to give a **ruling within** 15 days of the request. If the matter is complicated the ruling will take longer to obtain. **In practice**, it is likely that HMRC will reply soon after receiving the clearance application but will advise that they require further time to assess the information. At this stage an estimate of the time required will be given.

Comment It is not clear from HMRC's guidance what category of taxpayers they expect to use this procedure, as most taxpayers with VAT queries will be business taxpayers. It is assumed that this procedure has been retained for **individuals** who are unsure whether they can recover VAT charged to them (such as on alterations and repairs to a listed building), and **charities** that are unsure of the nature of their supplies, or whether, for example, they are using a building for business purposes.

In addition to the information required under the procedure for businesses (¶9898), taxpayers must also provide an **estimate of the monetary value** of the transaction. 9914

Comment HMRC state that the estimate of monetary value is required to enable them to "target resources appropriately". This would appear to mean that they will scrutinise requests relating to large amounts more closely, or in more depth than requests that may still have significant points of law but be for smaller amounts. This might be viewed as inequitable. Notice 700/6 para 2.4

VAT **rulings** under this procedure will **not be given** if: 9916
- the situation is hypothetical;
- the transaction relates to a tax planning scheme, or is for the purpose of tax avoidance; or
- the answer to the query is included in public guidance.

Only the **taxpayer who requests** the ruling can rely on it, unless:
- the ruling has been requested by a trade body; or
- the application states that the request is for additional taxpayers, or a group of taxpayers.

If, in the future, an **associated organisation**, in the same situation as the original taxpayer, requires a ruling it can apply under the simplification procedure. It should send a copy of the original ruling and confirm that it will operate in the same way, although if there are any differences, the associate should highlight these when requesting its ruling.

If a **taxpayer disagrees** with the ruling, it can be appealed if it is one of the appealable matters (details can be found in *VAT Memo*). 9918

Taxpayers are **not bound** by rulings given by HMRC and if they disagree with HMRC's opinion they can treat the transaction differently if they wish. In these circumstances it is likely that HMRC will take further action against the taxpayer.

MEMO POINTS For details of the circumstances in which HMRC are bound, or otherwise, by their rulings see ¶9900.

SECTION 2

Reviews and appeals

A new system of appeals to tribunals and thence to the courts, which **covers all taxes**, has been implemented for appeals made since 1 April 2009. There are also procedures for requesting an internal review (similar to the former non-statutory reconsideration for VAT purposes) by HMRC if the taxpayer does not wish to go directly to appeal. 9920 Tribunals, Courts and Enforcement Act 2007

MEMO POINTS 1. Some offences did not come under the **new penalty regime** until 1 April 2010, but any appeals against a decision made by HMRC since 1 April 2009 have had to be made under the **new appeals process**. For details of the penalty regime see ¶9780+.
2. Appeals which had commenced under the **previous procedure** were automatically transferred to the new system.
3. New guidance on the procedures has been issued by HMRC and is contained in a new manual, the Appeals, Reviews and Tribunal Guidance Manual ("ARTG").

Structure of the appeal and tribunal system

The new tribunal system is under the control of the Ministry of Justice. There is a First-tier Tribunal, appeals from which are made to the Upper Tribunal. Each Tribunal is divided into chambers responsible for matters across legislation formerly dealt with in separate tribunals. Direct and indirect tax matters are dealt with in the Tax Chamber, whereas tax credits are 9922 dealt with in the Social Entitlement Chamber and appeals concerning land valuations must be made to the Lands Chamber.

The **First-tier Tribunal** hears most appeals in the first instance but the Tribunal President can determine whether the initial appeal should be heard by the **Upper Tribunal** because of its complexity.

The Upper Tribunal hears appeals on points of law from decisions made by the First-tier Tribunal. Appeals against a decision made in the Upper Tribunal are heard by the Court of Appeal but consent must be given by the Upper Tribunal or, if it is withheld, directly by the Court of Appeal to hear the case. Appeals from the Court of Appeal are made to the Supreme Court (formerly the House of Lords).

A. Transitional rules

9924 If an **appeal** was **pending under the previous system** on 1 April 2009, special transitional provisions apply.

9926 If an appeal had been **notified** to one of the previous tribunals **before** 1 April 2009 the matter will be dealt with by the First-tier Tribunal under the new rules but subject to the tribunal's ability to apply any of the rules in force before commencement of the new system.

B. Direct tax model

9930 A **taxpayer has** 30 days from the date of a tax assessment, or the date he is notified that his self-assessment tax return has been amended, to notify HMRC that he does not agree with the assessment, or amendment.

If it is possible to **reach an agreement** with HMRC at this stage, no further action is required. If it is **not possible** to reach an agreement, the taxpayer will have the following options:
1. **appeal** to the tribunal; or
2. **request** that HMRC carry out an internal review of the decision.

HMRC also have the **power to offer** an internal review of the decision.

If a **taxpayer does not want** HMRC to carry out a review, he can appeal to the tax tribunal at the same time as notifying HMRC that he does not agree with their decision.

Internal review

9932 An internal review of the case for **direct and indirect taxes** is conducted by an officer from HMRC who is unconnected with the case. The officer independently reviews the facts to reach his own conclusions as to whether he agrees with the original decision.

The reviews are subjective and the extent of the review of each case takes into account the level of disagreement (see ¶9944).

9934 If a **taxpayer requests** an internal review, or **accepts the offer of** a review, HMRC have 45 days from the date of the request to carry out the review, unless a longer period is agreed.

The taxpayer **cannot appeal** to the tax tribunal **during** the 45-day period of the review. It is only possible to appeal to the tribunal once the 45-day period has elapsed or, if earlier, once the review has been completed. In this circumstance any **appeal** to the tribunal must be **within** 30 days of the date of the notification of the review findings, or the expiry of the 45-day period.

MEMO POINTS Taxpayers should be aware that if **HMRC do not notify** the taxpayer of the outcome of the review within the agreed time limit, the original decision is treated as being the outcome of the review. The 30-day time limit for appealing to the tax tribunal therefore runs from the day when the time limit for the completion of the internal review expires. Taxpayers and advisers need to keep the time limits under review to ensure that the deadline for appealing to the tax tribunal is not missed because of a lack of response on the part of HMRC.

Comment Guidance provided by HMRC states that the nature and extent of the review will depend on the circumstances in each case. The guidance states that the review officer will consider what level of scrutiny the original decision received and the input from specialised departments before it was notified to the taxpayer. This would seem to suggest that the more scrutiny and time spent on the first decision, the less detailed the review at the second stage will be.

The review **procedure covers** all matters which are appealable and which are capable of further review. 9936

Sch 19A TMA 1970
para 27 Sch 18 FA 1998
Sch 36 FA 2008

Appealing to the tribunal

An appeal may be made by the person who is the subject of the decision, or his personal representative or trustee. In certain cases other interested parties may also be able to appeal. It is possible to appeal to the tribunal at various stages through the negotiation process, including: 9938

SI 2009/273 rule 20
ARTG 8210

– at any time **after** sending HMRC an objection to their initial decision, as long as it is before the taxpayer has requested, or accepted, the offer of a review; or
– **within** 30 days of the notification of the conclusion of the review, or the expiry of the review period.

It is also possible to appeal to the tribunal once the statutory **time limits** have **expired**. The taxpayer must request permission from the tribunal to grant leave to appeal out of time.

MEMO POINTS 1. Any appeal to the tribunal must be made in writing.
2. The taxpayer's representative can appeal on his behalf.
3. The appeal must be sent first to HMRC by the taxpayer
4. HMRC cannot ask for a direct tax appeal to be considered by the tribunal. They must first offer a review.

Payment of tax A taxpayer can apply to HMRC to **postpone** the payment of the tax which is the subject of the dispute. If **HMRC refuse** to postpone payment of the tax they claim is due, they will notify the taxpayer, who then has 30 days to appeal to the tribunal for a postponement (¶9952). 9940

If the matter is subject to a **further appeal**, to the Upper Tribunal or beyond, any tax due, or due to be repaid, should be paid based on the decision of the first hearing. 9942

If, after the appeal, the result is that too much tax has been paid by the taxpayer, the overpayment will be repaid with interest. If too little tax has been paid, the excess becomes payable 30 days after HMRC issue a notice of the total amount payable.

C. Indirect tax model

The indirect tax model **broadly follows** the direct tax model. 9944

When HMRC notify a taxpayer of a decision which can be appealed, they also notify the right to appeal and offer a review of the decision. The taxpayer has 30 days following notification to appeal to the tribunal, or accept the offer of a review. The taxpayer cannot do both at the same time.

MEMO POINTS The time limit for HMRC to notify the taxpayer of their decision is the same as under the direct tax model (¶9934). The rules for late appeals are also in line with the direct tax model (¶9938).

9946 Under the indirect tax model it is **no longer required** that all returns and payments of outstanding VAT are made before an appeal can be heard by the tribunal. The taxpayer has to pay the VAT which is in dispute before the tribunal hearing, unless he can successfully show that paying the VAT will lead to undue hardship.

There are exceptions to the above, which are primarily aimed at preventing **missing trader fraud** (¶8186), including:
- where the trader is involved in acquisitions from other member states (¶8937);
- where security has been requested by HMRC (¶9329);
- where joint and several liability has been established in the supply chain;
- where a penalty has been levied under the information powers (¶9862); and
- where an assessment has been raised (¶9310).

9948 Under previous practice HMRC did not normally seek **costs** when responding to an appeal at the VAT tribunal, unless they felt that the appeal was frivolous, or that they were protecting the public revenue. Under the new system this is no longer the case and it is likely that HMRC will seek costs from taxpayers when successful. However, that assumes that costs can be awarded in the first place. The general rule is that no costs are awarded by the First-tier Tribunal but further details are given at ¶9959.

9950 If a taxpayer loses an appeal in the First-tier Tribunal but is **granted leave to appeal** to the Upper Tribunal, he must pay the tax determined by HMRC as a result of the tribunal decision. Payment is due within 30 days of HMRC notifying the taxpayer of the amount of tax and interest due. If the taxpayer is successful at a later appeal the tax he has paid will be repaid, with interest.

If HMRC lose an appeal in the First-tier Tribunal, they are required to repay the taxpayer any tax which has been withheld. As an exception to this rule HMRC can request permission from the tribunal not to pay the tax, subject to a later appeal, on the grounds of revenue protection, or if security would be required.

SECTION 3

Tribunal procedure

9951 SI 2009/273 rules 2, 3 The rules for dealing with an appeal include an **overriding objective** for the tribunal to deal with cases fairly and justly. This means the tribunal must avoid unnecessary formality and delays (as far as possible), must consider the complexity of the issues and resources of the parties, and use any special expertise effectively. There is an **obligation on the parties** to help the tribunal in achieving the overriding objective and to cooperate with the tribunal generally. The tribunal should encourage the parties to use alternative dispute resolution methods if that would resolve the matter more quickly and cheaply than pursuing the dispute through the tribunal system.

Comment The rules and procedures, as a result of the overriding objective, delegate substantial powers to the tribunal to reduce time and costs and in the administration of the case. The procedures outlined here are in respect of First-tier Tribunal appeals. Further specialist advice is recommended depending on individual circumstances, or if dealing with a matter in the Upper Tribunal or courts.

A. Before the hearing

The law allows taxpayers a right of appeal against particular decisions of HMRC, including 9952 SI 2009/273, rules 18, 20-22 ARTG 2140, 3000
- assessments;
- decisions to refuse or reduce claims;
- credits or refunds;
- penalties and decisions not to suspend a penalty; and
- certain rulings and directions and information notices.

Indirect tax proceedings are started by **notification** of the appeal (¶9938) by the taxpayer to the tribunal. HMRC will also be informed by the Tribunals Service that an appeal has been lodged. The distinction between direct and indirect taxes at the appeal level must be carefully observed.

The appeal **must be submitted** to the central processing centre, which is at the following address:
Tribunals Service Tax
2nd Floor 54 Hagley Road
Birmingham
B16 8PE

A taxpayer must send a written appeal to HMRC before notifying a direct tax appeal to the tribunal.

The appeal notification must state the following:
1. the name and address of the appellant;
2. the name and address of any representative;
3. an address for delivery of documents; and
4. details of the decision being appealed against, the result the appellant is seeking and grounds for making the appeal.

Comment If an appeal on an indirect tax matter is sent to HMRC instead of to the Tribunals Service, it should be forwarded to the Tribunals Service but HMRC may contact the taxpayer to advise that the appeal has been sent to the wrong place. An appeal for direct tax purposes is sent to HMRC first anyway. An appeal form can be requested by telephone.

The appeal is then considered by the Tribunals Service, allocated to an appeal category (see ¶9953) and HMRC are formally notified about it. The central processing centre will also allocate the case to be heard at a particular tribunal venue. An appellant can also enclose a **hardship application**, in cases where the tax must be paid before the appeal can proceed, unless HMRC or the tribunal consent to the appeal proceeding without payment. In this circumstance the appellant must include the following with the notice of appeal:
1. a statement as to whether the amount of tax has been paid;
2. a statement as to whether HMRC have consented to the appeal proceeding; and if they have not
3. an application to the tribunal for consent to the appeal proceeding, together with reasons for the application and any documents in support of it.

If there are two or more cases which have been started with the tribunal and they deal with common or related issues of fact or law, the tribunal may decide to specify one as a **lead case**. This means that the decision from that case will be binding on each of the parties. However, before doing so, the tribunal must give notice to the other parties, who have 28 days in which to apply in writing to the tribunal that the decision should not be binding on them.

Allocation of cases to categories

On receipt of the appeal, the tribunal must allocate it to one of the appeal categories. The allocation will depend on the type of dispute and the level of complexity involved. The categories are: 9953 SI 2009/273 rule 23

1. **default paper** – the most straightforward cases which usually will not require a hearing;
2. **basic** – will require a hearing but with only a small exchange of documents in advance of the hearing;
3. **standard** – subject to more detailed case management and will require a hearing; and
4. **complex** – subject to a full hearing and cases in this category will:
– require lengthy or complex evidence or a lengthy hearing;
– involve a complex or important principle or issue; or
– involve a large financial sum.

Guidance has been issued as to which **types of cases** should be allocated to each category as follows:
– default paper cases are those involving penalties for: late income tax and corporation tax self-assessment returns, late employer end of year returns, late CIS returns, late NIC Class 2 notifications and appeals against fixed percentage surcharges for late payment of income tax;
– basic cases are those involving **appeals against** penalties for deliberate action (whether concealed or not), appeals for indirect assessments on the basis of reasonable care, CIS penalties and against information notices to provide information in connection with a case;
– in addition, basic cases include **applications for** permission to make a late appeal, permission for the postponement of the payment of tax, including applications under the Stamp Duty Land Tax Regulations 2003 and inheritance tax regulations, and applications for a direction that HMRC close an enquiry;
– if a case is not allocated to the complex category or is not one of the matters listed above, it will be categorised as a standard case.

MEMO POINTS A case allocated to the complex category can be transferred immediately to the Upper Tribunal for hearing and is subject to special provisions for costs (¶9959).

B. At the hearing

9955 SI 2009/273 rules 11-13 SI 2009/1916

After a case has been allocated to a category, the procedure adopted by the tribunal depends on the category of the appeal.

Category of case	Procedure
Paper	Statement of case must be received within 42 days of notification of the appeal[1]
Basic	Case proceeds directly to hearing unless HMRC intend to raise grounds at the hearing which have not already been communicated to the taxpayer
Standard and complex	Statement of case must be received within 60 days of notification of the appeal[1,2]

Notes:
1. Copies of the statement of case in response to an appeal must be given to the tribunal, the taxpayer and any other person involved.
2. Each party must submit a list of documents to be sent to the tribunal and all parties involved, within 42 days of HMRC sending their statement of case in response to the appeal. This list must comprise all the documents intended to be used or relied upon in the hearing and which are in the party's possession, or to which the party has access.

Where the taxpayer or a third party disputes that a document is open to inspection, a list of documents must be sent to HMRC for them to specify which documents are in dispute. This procedure is intended to reduce the number of documents which the tribunal will have to consider. The list is then sent to the tribunal for directions.

MEMO POINTS If disputes arise during the course of an inspection of premises, protection is given to individuals removing documents in advance of the tribunal's decision as to whether the documents are covered by professional privilege. HMRC are protected by the requirement that the agreed documents are not changed. The tribunal may either direct that the whole of a document is covered by privilege or that part of it is so covered. The tribunal must also direct which part or parts of a document (if any) may be disclosed. The parties involved may agree the list of documents for disclosure without the direction of the tribunal at any time.

Evidence and proceedings

Notice of the date of the hearing must be given at least 14 days in advance, unless the parties agree to a shorter period. 9956 SI 2009/273 rules14-16, 29-33

If any party **fails to appear** the tribunal may proceed if it is satisfied that notice of the hearing has been given, or that reasonable steps have been taken to notify the party of the hearing and the tribunal considers that it is in the interests of justice to proceed with the hearing.

The taxpayer may appoint a **representative**, who does not have to be legally qualified, to represent his case in the proceedings. He may also have a person to accompany him to the tribunal hearing. However, the tribunal can refuse to permit a person to act as a representative if it believes that there are good reasons for doing so.

The tribunal may hear evidence from third parties and where a case proceeds to a **full hearing**, in general it will be conducted in public. A hearing may take place in private where it is in the interests of public order, or national security, to preserve a right to private and family life, to maintain confidentiality for sensitive information, or for the purposes of public interest to avoid prejudicing the interests of justice. The tribunal can also give directions that documents or information relating to proceedings should be kept confidential where their disclosure or publication could lead to the identification of a party and the tribunal considers that he should not be identified.

The tribunal can give directions as to the issues on which it requires evidence or submissions and the nature of the evidence or submissions it requires. The tribunal may also decide on the number of **witnesses** which may give evidence and whether it will accept evidence from expert witnesses. Witnesses may be summoned to appear at the tribunal and to answer questions or produce documents; evidence may be delivered orally or by a witness statement. The tribunal may also make an order that a witness's expenses are paid and by whom.

An appeal **can be struck out** by the tribunal where the appellant fails to comply with a direction which stated that failure could result in a strike-out or the appellant has failed to co-operate with the tribunal, or the appellant has no reasonable chance of success. An appeal **must be struck out** where the appellant fails to comply with a direction which stated that failure would result in striking out or if the tribunal has no jurisdiction to hear the appeal.

The same sanction does not apply to HMRC. HMRC can only be prevented from taking further part in the proceedings and so the appeal can still fail, albeit in HMRC's absence.

C. Tribunal decisions and further appeals

A tribunal decision may be given orally at the hearing. However, the tribunal must give each party a **decision notice** within 28 days of the hearing which finally disposes of the matter. 9958 SI 2009/273 rules 34-42
The notice:
- must state the decision; and
- may include a **summary** of the findings of fact; or
- may be accompanied by **full written** findings of fact and the reasons for the decision.

If the decision notice is accompanied by a summary only, a party can **apply for full written reasons**, provided that the party does so within 28 days of the decision being issued. In this case the tribunal has 28 days in which to provide the full reasons. If a party wants to appeal the decision, the party must first apply for the full written findings (if not provided) before the party can apply for permission to appeal.

If a party wants to take the case for a **further appeal**, the party must apply to the tribunal within 56 days after receiving the tribunal's full written decision, or amended reasons, whichever is later.

An appeal can be made from the First-tier Tribunal to the Upper Tribunal **on a point of law only** and only if permission is given by the First-tier Tribunal. If permission is refused, it can be sought from the Upper Tribunal.

The procedure is that on receipt of an application for permission to appeal the First-tier Tribunal must decide whether to **review** (change) its decision. It can review a decision only if there has been an error of law. If it decides not to review the decision it then decides whether to give permission to appeal.

Awarding costs

9959 SI 2009/273 rule 10

The treatment of costs under the new system is the **same for direct and indirect cases**. The tribunal can make an order for costs if it:

– considers that the party has acted unreasonably in bringing, defending or conducting the proceedings; or

– the case has been allocated to the complex category and the appellant has not given notice to the tribunal that he does not want to participate in the costs regime.

Without an order for costs, each party is responsible for its own expenses and costs. This is the same practice as applied for direct tax cases prior to the new tribunal system, but is new for indirect tax cases. With a costs order, the tribunal may make a party liable for both sets of costs.

MEMO POINTS The rules for costs in the Upper Tribunal are not the same as those in the First-tier Tribunal. Costs can be awarded on an appeal from the First-tier Tribunal, in proceedings transferred to the Upper Tribunal to hear in the first instance (which will be complex cases) and where a party has acted unreasonably in bringing, defending or conducting proceedings. An application for costs in the Upper Tribunal can be made at any time during the proceedings, or up to a month after the decision notice has been issued.

General information

OUTLINE ¶¶

Appendix

OUTLINE ¶¶

Finance Acts

9960

Year	Budget	Royal Assent
2011	23 March 2011	19 July 2011
2010 (No.3)	22 June 2010	16 December 2010
2010 (No.2)	22 June 2010	27 July 2010
2010	24 March 2010	8 April 2010
2009	22 April 2009	21 July 2009
2008	12 March 2008	21 July 2008
2007	21 March 2007	19 July 2007
2006	22 March 2006	19 July 2006
2005 (No.2)	16 March 2005	20 July 2005
2005	16 March 2005	7 April 2005
2004	17 March 2004	22 July 2004
2003	9 April 2003	10 July 2003
2002	17 April 2002	24 July 2002
2001	7 March 2001	11 May 2001
2000	21 March 2000	28 July 2000
1999	9 March 1999	27 July 1999
1998	17 March 1998	31 July 1998
1997 (No.2)	2 July 1997	31 July 1997
1997	26 November 1996	19 March 1997
1996	28 November 1995	29 April 1996
1995	29 November 1994	1 May 1995
1994	30 November 1993	3 May 1994
1993	16 March 1993	27 July 1993
1992 (No.2)	10 March 1992	16 July 1992
1992	10 March 1992	16 March 1992
1991	19 March 1991	26 July 1991
1990	20 March 1990	26 July 1990
1989	14 March 1989	27 July 1989
1988	15 March 1988	29 July 1988

Corporation tax rates

9962

Financial year	Full rate %	Small companies' rate %	Profit limit for small companies' rate (lower limit)	Profit limit for small companies' marginal relief (upper limit)	Marginal relief fraction for small companies	Starting rate % [1]	Profit limit for starting rate (lower limit)	Profit limit for starting rate marginal relief (upper limit)	Marginal relief fraction for starting rate
2011	26	20	300,000	1,500,000	3/200	n/a	n/a	n/a	n/a
2010	28	21	300,000	1,500,000	7/400	n/a	n/a	n/a	n/a
2009	28	21	300,000	1,500,000	7/400	n/a	n/a	n/a	n/a
2008	28	21	300,000	1,500,000	7/400	n/a	n/a	n/a	n/a
2007	30	20	300,000	1,500,000	1/40	n/a	n/a	n/a	n/a
2006	30	19	300,000	1,500,000	11/400	n/a	n/a	n/a	n/a
2005	30	19	300,000	1,500,000	11/400	0	10,000	50,000	19/400
2004	30	19	300,000	1,500,000	11/400	0	10,000	50,000	19/400
2003	30	19	300,000	1,500,000	11/400	0	10,000	50,000	19/400

Note :
1. Small companies were subject to the non-corporate distribution rate of tax of 19 % if profits were distributed to non-corporate entities between 1 April 2004 and 31 March 2006 (¶1820).

Rates of interest on unpaid/overpaid corporation tax

9964

Unpaid tax

Rates of interest on unpaid corporation tax for accounting periods ending after 30 June 1999 for payments **other than instalment** payments.

Period of application	Rate %
From 29 September 2009	3.00
24 March 2009 to 28 September 2009	2.50
27 January 2009 to 23 March 2009	3.50
6 January 2009 to 26 January 2009	4.50
6 December 2008 to 5 January 2009	5.50
6 November 2008 to 5 December 2008	6.50
6 January 2008 to 5 November 2008	7.50
6 August 2007 to 5 January 2008	8.50
6 September 2006 to 5 August 2007	7.50
6 September 2005 to 5 September 2006	6.50
6 September 2004 to 5 September 2005	7.50
6 December 2003 to 5 September 2004	6.50
6 August 2003 to 5 December 2003	5.50
6 November 2001 to 5 August 2003	6.50
6 May 2001 to 5 November 2001	7.50
6 February 2000 to 5 May 2001	8.50

Rates of interest on unpaid **corporation tax instalments** for accounting periods ending after 30 June 1999.

Period of application	Rate %
From 16 March 2009	1.50
16 February 2009 to 15 March 2009	2.00
19 January 2009 to 15 February 2009	2.50
15 December 2008 to 18 January 2009	3.00
17 November 2008 to 14 December 2008	4.00
20 October 2008 to 16 November 2008	5.50
21 April 2008 to 19 October 2008	6.00
18 February 2008 to 20 April 2008	6.25
17 December 2007 to 17 February 2008	6.50
16 July 2007 to 16 December 2007	6.75
21 May 2007 to 15 July 2007	6.50
22 January 2007 to 20 May 2007	6.25
20 November 2006 to 21 January 2007	6.00
14 August 2006 to 19 November 2006	5.75
15 August 2005 to 13 August 2006	5.50
16 August 2004 to 14 August 2005	5.75
21 June 2004 to 15 August 2004	5.50
17 May 2004 to 20 June 2004	5.25
16 February 2004 to 16 May 2004	5.00
17 November 2003 to 15 February 2004	4.75
21 July 2003 to 16 November 2003	4.50
17 February 2003 to 20 July 2003	4.75
19 November 2001 to 16 February 2003	5.00
15 October 2001 to 18 November 2001	5.50
1 October 2001 to 14 October 2001	5.75
13 August 2001 to 30 September 2001	6.00
21 May 2001 to 12 August 2001	6.25
16 April 2001 to 20 May 2001	6.50
19 February 2001 to 15 April 2001	6.75
20 April 2000 to 18 February 2001	7.00
21 February 2000 to 19 April 2000	8.00
24 January 2000 to 20 February 2000	7.75

Overpaid tax

Rates of interest on overpaid corporation tax for accounting periods ending after 30 June 1999 for payments **other than instalment** payments (interest runs from normal due date).

Period of application	Rate %
From 29 September 2009	0.5
27 January 2009 to 28 September 2009	0
6 January 2009 to 26 January 2009	1
6 December 2008 to 5 January 2009	2
6 November 2008 to 5 December 2008	3
6 January 2008 to 5 November 2008	4
6 August 2007 to 5 January 2008	5
6 September 2006 to 5 August 2007	4
6 September 2005 to 5 September 2006	3
6 September 2004 to 5 September 2005	4
6 December 2003 to 5 September 2004	3
6 August 2003 to 5 December 2003	2
6 November 2001 to 5 August 2003	3
6 May 2001 to 5 November 2001	4
6 February 2000 to 5 May 2001	5

Rates of interest on overpaid corporation tax for accounting periods ending after 30 June 1999 for **instalment** payments **and** on corporation **tax paid early** (interest period runs until normal due date).

Period of application	Rate %
From 21 September 2009	0.5
16 March 2009 to 20 September 2009	0.25
16 February 2009 to 15 March 2009	0.75
19 January 2009 to 15 February 2009	1.25
15 December 2008 to 18 January 2009	1.75
17 November 2008 to 14 December 2008	2.75
20 October 2008 to 16 November 2008	4.25
21 April 2008 to 19 October 2008	4.75
18 February 2008 to 20 April 2008	5.00
17 December 2007 to 17 February 2008	5.25
16 July 2007 to 16 December 2007	5.50
21 May 2007 to 15 July 2007	5.25
22 January 2007 to 20 May 2007	5.00
20 November 2006 to 21 January 2007	4.75
14 August 2006 to 19 November 2006	4.50
15 August 2005 to 13 August 2006	4.25
16 August 2004 to 14 August 2005	4.50
21 June 2004 to 15 August 2004	4.25
17 May 2004 to 20 June 2004	4.00
16 February 2004 to 16 May 2004	3.75
17 November 2003 to 15 February 2004	3.50
21 July 2003 to 16 November 2003	3.25
17 February 2003 to 20 July 2003	3.50

Period of application	Rate %
19 November 2001 to 16 February 2003	3.75
15 October 2001 to 18 November 2001	4.25
1 October 2001 to 14 October 2001	4.50
13 August 2001 to 30 September 2001	4.75
21 May 2001 to 12 August 2001	5.00
16 April 2001 to 20 May 2001	5.25
19 February 2001 to 15 April 2001	5.50
21 February 2000 to 18 February 2001	5.75
24 January 2000 to 20 February 2000	5.50

Income tax rates

9966

Year	Taxable income band		Tax rate [1, 2] %	Tax on band £
	Individuals £	Trusts £		
2011/12	0 – 35,000 [1,2]		20	7,000
	35,001 – 150,000		40	46,000
	Over 150,000		50	-
		0 – 1,000 [3]	20	200
		Over 1,000 [2,3,4]	50	-
2010/11	0 – 37,400 [1, 2]		20	7,480
	37,401 – 150,000		40	45,040
	Over 150,000		50	-
		0 – 1,000 [2,3]	20	200
		Over 1,000 [2,3,4]	50	-
2009/10	0 – 37,400 [1, 2]		20	7,480
	Over 37,400		40	-
		0 – 1,000 [2,3]	20	200
		Over 1,000 [2,3,4]	40	-
2008/09	0 – 34,800 [1, 2]		20	6,960
	Over 34,800		40	-
		0 – 1,000 [2,3]	20	200
		Over 1,000 [2,3,4]	40	-
2007/08	0 – 2,230		10	223.00
	2,231 – 34,600		22	7,121.40
	Over 34,600		40	-
		0 – 1,000 [2,3]	22	220.00
		Over 1,000 [2,3,4]	40	-
2006/07	0 – 2,150		10	215.00
	2,151 – 33,300		22	6,853.00
	Over 33,300		40	-
		0 – 1,000 [2,3]	22	220.00
		Over 1,000 [2,3,4]	40	-

Year	Taxable income band		Tax rate [1, 2] %	Tax on band £
	Individuals £	Trusts £		
2005/06	0 – 2,090		10	209.00
	2,091 – 32,400		22	6,668.20
	Over 32,400		40	-
		0 – 500 [2,3]	22	110.00
		Over 500 [2,3,4]	40	-
2004/05	0 – 2,020		10	202.00
	2,021 – 31,400		22	6,463.60
	Over 31,400		40	-
	Rate applicable to trusts [4]		40	-
2003/04	0 – 1,960		10	196.00
	1,961 – 30,500		22	6,278.80
	Over 30,500		40	-
	Rate applicable to trusts [4]		34	-
2002/03	0 – 1,920		10	192.00
	1,921 – 29,900		22	6,155.60
	Over 29,900		40	-
	Rate applicable to trusts [4]		34	-

Note :
1. Prior to 5 April 2008, savings income was subject to a tax rate of 10 % in the starting rate band, 20 % in the basic rate band, and 40 % in the higher rate band. From 6 April 2008, a new starting rate for savings income only applies. For 2011-12, the band is £2,560 (2010-11 : £2,440). Where both savings and non-savings income is received up to, and not exceeding, the band, savings are taxed at 10 %. Where income from non-savings exceeds the band, the 10 % does not apply.
2. Dividend income is subject to a tax rate of 10 % in the starting and basic rate bands, 32.5 % in the higher rate band, and 42.5 % in the additional rate band or for the dividend income of non-interest in possession trusts.
3. The band is applicable to non-interest in possession trusts.
4. The rate is applicable to non-interest in possession trusts (¶7308) for all income other than dividends.

Personal reliefs

9967

Type of relief	2011/12 £	2010/11 £	2009/10 £	2008/09 £	2007/08 £	2006/07 £
Personal allowance [1]						
Age under 65	7,475	6,475	6,475	6,035	5,225	5,035
Age 65-74 [2]	9,940	9,490	9,490	9,030	7,550	7,280
Age 75 & over [2]	10,090	9,640	9,640	9,180	7,690	7,420
Married couple's allowance [3, 4]						
Age 65-74		6,865	6,865	6,535	6,285	6,065
Age 75 & over	7,295	6,965	6,965	6,625	6,365	6,135
Minimum amount	2,800	2,670	2,670	2,540	2,440	2,350
Monthly reduction in year of marriage						
Age 65-74	n/a	n/a	n/a	544.58	523.75	505.42
Age 75 and over				552.08	530.41	511.25

Type of relief	2011/12 £	2010/11 £	2009/10 £	2008/09 £	2007/08 £	2006/07 £
Maximum income before abatement of relief for taxpayers aged 65 and over						
Abatement income ceiling [5]	24,000	22,900	22,900	21,800	20,900	20,100
Personal						
No extra allowance if income exceeds :						
Age 65-74	28,930	28,930	28,930	27,790	25,550	24,590
Age 75 & over	29,230	29,230	29,230	28,090	25,830	24,870
Married						
– Husband under 65 (Eldest spouse under 75)	n/a	n/a	n/a	29,790	28,590	27,530
– Husband 65-74 (Eldest spouse under 75)	n/a	n/a	n/a	36,980	33,240	32,020
– Husband 75 or over	38,220	37,820	37,820	36,260	33,680	32,440
– Spouse 75 or over (Husband 65-74)	37,920	37,320	37,320	35,780	33,400	32,160
– Spouse 75 or over (Husband under 65)	38,220	37,820	37,820	27,790	28,750	27,670
Blind person's allowance	1,980	1,890	1,890	1,800	1,730	1,660
"Rent a room" limit [6]	4,250	4,250	4,250	4,250	4,250	4,250

Note :

1. For 2010-11 and later years the personal allowance is gradually reduced to nil for individuals with net income (generally, after losses, pension relief and charitable donations) in excess of £100,000. The reduction is at the rate of £1 for every £2 of income above £100,000.
2. A claimant is entitled to the appropriate age personal allowance if he/she is aged at least 65-75 at any time in the tax year ; the allowance is restricted according to his/her income only.
3. Relief for married couple's allowance, and other reliefs linked to it, is restricted to 10 %.
4. Married couples are only entitled to the married couple's allowance if either spouse was born before 6 April 1935. The allowance is usually restricted by the husband's income (¶4446), although for marriages which occur on or after 5 December 2005, the highest income of either spouse is taken into account.
5. Relief is abated by 1/2 total income over the maximum income limit subject to the abatement income ceiling.
6. Gross annual rents from furnished letting of rooms in only or main residence exempt for owner occupiers up to specified limit. If more than one person is in receipt of income from furnished residential accommodation in the residence, the exempt limit is halved.

9968

Approved fuel and mileage rates

Using own vehicle

These mileage rates are the statutory maximum amounts which can be paid to employees for using their own vehicles for business purposes without having to pay tax or NIC.

From 6 April 2011	Rate per mile	
	Income tax	NIC
Cars and vans		
On the first 10,000 miles in the tax year	45p	45p
On each additional mile over 10,000 miles	25p	45p
Each passenger making the same business trip	5p	5p
Motorcycles	24p	24p
Bicycles	20p	-

Fuel for company cars

Where private fuel is provided for a company car (¶3304), a taxable benefit can be avoided if either the employee fully reimburses the employer for private fuel, or the employer reimburses the employee for business fuel.

The following table sets out the advisory fuel rates which should be used in either case.

Dates	Engine size (cc)	Petrol	Diesel	LPG
From 1 June 2011	≤ 1400	15p		11p
	≤ 1600		12p	
	Greater than above but ≤ 2000	18p	15p	13p
	> 2000	26p	18p	18p
1 March to 31 May 2011	≤ 1400	14p	13p	10p
	> 1400 but ≤ 2000	16p	13p	12p
	> 2000	23p	16p	17p
1 December 2010 to 28 February 2011	≤ 1400	13p	12p	9p
	> 1400 but ≤ 2000	15p	12p	10p
	> 2000	21p	15p	15p
1 June to 30 November 2010	≤ 1400	12p	11p	8p
	> 1400 but ≤ 2000	15p	11p	10p
	> 2000	21p	16p	14p
From 1 December 2009 to 31 May 2010	≤ 1400	11p	11p	7p
	> 1400 but ≤ 2000	14p	11p	8p
	> 2000	20p	14p	12p
1 July 2009 to 30 November 2009	≤ 1400	10p	10p	7p
	> 1400 but ≤ 2000	12p	10p	8p
	> 2000	18p	13p	12p
1 January 2009 to 30 June 2009	≤ 1400	10p	11p	7p
	> 1400 but ≤ 2000	12p	11p	9p
	> 2000	17p	14p	12p
1 July 2008 to 31 December 2008	≤ 1400	12p	13p	7p
	> 1400 but ≤ 2000	15p	13p	9p
	> 2000	21p	17p	13p
1 January to 30 June 2008	≤ 1400	11p	11p	7p
	> 1400 but ≤ 2000	13p	11p	8p
	> 2000	19p	14p	11p
1 August to 31 December 2007	≤ 1400	10p	10p	6p
	> 1400 but ≤ 2000	13p	10p	8p
	> 2000	18p	13p	10p
1 February to 31 July 2007	≤ 1400	9p	9p	6p
	> 1400 but ≤ 2000	11p	9p	7p
	> 2000	16p	12p	10p
1 July 2006 to 31 January 2007	≤ 1400	11p	10p	7p
	> 1400 but ≤ 2000	13p	10p	8p
	> 2000	18p	14p	11p
1 July 2005 to 30 June 2006	≤ 1400	10p	9p	7p
	> 1400 but ≤ 2000	12p	9p	8p
	> 2000	16p	13p	10p

Official rate of interest

9969 The official rate of interest relating to beneficial loan arrangements is that rate prescribed from time to time by Treasury order. The official rate for such loans has been set as follows :

Date	Rate %	Reference
From 6 April 2010	4.00	SI 2010/415
1 March 2009 to 5 April 2010	4.75	SI 2009/199
6 April 2007 to 28 February 2009	6.25	SI 2007/684
6 January 2002 to 5 April 2007	5.00	SI 2001/3860
6 March 1999 to 5 January 2002	6.25	SI 1999/419

Official rate of interest on foreign currency loans

9970

Loans in Swiss francs	
Date	Rate %
From 6 July 1994	5.5

Loans in Japanese yen	
Date	Rate %
From 6 June 1994	3.9

Tax credits

9971

Child tax credit

The CTC is made up of a number of elements which may be applicable, depending on the circumstances of each claim.

Element of CTC	2011/12 Maximum £	2010/11 Maximum £	2009/10 Maximum £	2008/09 Maximum £
Family element [1]	545	545	545	545
Family element – baby addition [1,2]	n/a	545	545	545
Child element [3]	2,555	2,300	2,235	2,085
Disabled child element [3, 4]	2,800	2,715	2,670	2,540
Severely disabled child element [3, 5]	1,130	1,095	1,075	1,020
Income threshold for whole of CTC to be received	15,860	16,190	16,040	15,575

Note :
1. Only one family element is available per family. In the first year of a child's life, a family is entitled to the baby addition as well as the family element.
2. The baby element was withdrawn with effect from 6 April 2011.
3. A family is also entitled to a child element for each child, with the various applicable elements added together.
4. An additional amount which is payable if the child is eligible for disability living allowance, is registered blind, or has been taken off the blind register in the last 28 weeks before the claim.
5. An additional amount which is payable if the child is eligible for the highest rate of care component of disability living allowance.

Working tax credit

The WTC is made up of a number of elements which may be applicable, depending on the circumstances of each claim.

Element of WTC	2011/12 Maximum £	2010/11 Maximum £	2009/10 Maximum £	2008/09 Maximum £
Basic element[1]	1,920	1,920	1,890	1,800
Additional couples and lone parent element[1]	1,950	1,890	1,860	1,770
30 hour element[1, 2]	790	790	775	735
Disability element[2, 3]	2,650	2,570	2,530	2,405
Severe disability element[2, 4]	1,130	1,095	1,075	1,020
50 plus return to work payment : 16 to 29 hours[2, 5, 7]	1,365	1,320	1,300	1,235
50 plus return to work payment : 30 or more hours[2, 7]	2,030	1,965	1,935	1,840
Childcare maximum eligible cost for one child[6]	175 per week	175 per week	175 per week	175 per week
Childcare maximum eligible cost for any number of children	300 per week	300 per week	300 per week	300 per week
Percentage of eligible costs covered	70 %	80 %	80 %	80 %

Note :
1. One element of each category per claim.
2. Paid in addition to other elements.
3. Broadly payable if the claimant is disabled, this affects his ability to work, and he is in receipt of a benefit such as disability living allowance.
4. Payable if the claimant is eligible for the highest rate care component of disability living allowance.
5. Where this element is payable, the additional couples (and lone parents) element is not paid, unless the claimant has responsibility for a child, or the disability element is also payable. This will not be paid where the claimant is working 30 hours or more and he is eligible for the higher 50 plus return to work payment.
6. This element is payable where the claimant works at least 16 hours per week (required of both individuals where a joint claim is made) and pays for approved childcare. For families who employ a registered nanny, the childcare cost includes employer's NIC. Approved childcare cannot be provided by a relative of the child, even if the carer is registered. As an exception, where the carer runs a childcaring business, which predominantly looks after unrelated children, and the care of a related child is incidental, then the care will qualify.
7. This element will be withdrawn from 2012/13.

Registered pension schemes

The maximum aggregate **contribution** on which tax relief is due is the higher of £3,600 per tax year and 100 % of earnings as restricted by the annual allowance. 9972

Tax year	Annual allowance (£)
2011/12	50,000
2010/11	255,000
2009/10	245,000
2008/09	235,000
2007/08	225,000
2006/07	215,000

The aggregate value of all registered pension **funds,** from which tax privileged benefits are payable on retirement or on death, is limited by the lifetime allowance.

Tax year	Lifetime allowance (£million)
2012/13	1.50
2011/12	1.80
2010/11	1.80
2009/10	1.75
2008/09	1.65
2007/08	1.60
2006/07	1.50

Rates of interest on unpaid/overpaid tax

9974 These rates apply to :
– income tax ;
– Class 1, 1A, 1B (from 6 April 1999) and Class 4 NIC ;
– capital gains tax ; and
– SDLT (from 26 September 2005), stamp duty, and SDRT (from 1 October 1999).

For corporation tax, inheritance tax and VAT see respectively ¶9964, ¶9983, ¶9989, and ¶9990.

Period of application	Rate %	
	Unpaid tax	Overpaid tax [1]
From 29 September 2009	3.00	0.5
24 March 2009 to 28 September 2009	2.50	Nil
27 January 2009 to 23 March 2009	3.50	Nil
6 January 2009 to 26 January 2009	4.50	0.75
6 December 2008 to 5 January 2009	5.50	1.50
6 November 2008 to 5 December 2008	6.50	2.25
6 January 2008 to 5 November 2008	7.50	3.00
6 August 2007 to 5 January 2008	8.50	4.00
6 September 2006 to 5 August 2007	7.50	3.00
6 September 2005 to 5 September 2006	6.50	2.25
6 September 2004 to 5 September 2005	7.50	3.00
6 December 2003 to 5 September 2004	6.50	2.25
6 August 2003 to 5 December 2003	5.50	1.50
6 November 2001 to 5 August 2003	6.50	2.25
6 May 2001 to 5 November 2001	7.50	3.00
6 February 2000 to 5 May 2001	8.50	4.00

Note :
1. The rates of interest applying to overpaid tax from 6 May 2001 onwards were retrospectively reduced in September 2005.

NIC thresholds and rates

9976

Class of NIC	Threshold	2011/12	2010/11	2009/10	2008/09	2007/08	2006/07
1	Lower earnings limit (per week)	£102	£97	£95	£90	£87	£84
	Earnings threshold (per week) – employees	£139	£110	£110	£105	£100	£97
	Earnings threshold (per week) – employers	£136	£110	£110	£105	£100	£97
	Upper earnings limit (per week)	£817	£844	£844	£770	£670	£645
	Employee's rate between employee's earnings threshold and upper earnings limits [1]	12 %	11 %	11 %	11 %	11 %	11 %
	Employee's rate above the upper earnings limit	2 %	1 %	1 %	1 %	1 %	1 %
	Employer's rate (on all earnings, including those above the upper earnings limit) [1]	13.8 %	12.8 %	12.8 %	12.8 %	12.8 %	12.8 %
1A and 1B	Rate	13.8 %	12.8 %	12.8 %	12.8 %	12.8 %	12.8 %
2	Standard rate [2] (per week)	£2.50	£2.40	£2.40	£2.30	£2.20	£2.10
	Small earnings exception (per year)	£5,315	£5,075	£5,075	£4,825	£4,635	£4,465
3	Rate (per week)	£12.60	£12.05	£12.05	£8.10	£7.80	£7.55
4	Lower profits limit (per year)	£7,225	£5,715	£5,715	£5,435	£5,225	£5,035
	Upper profits limit (per year)	£42,475	£43,875	£43,875	£40,040	£34,840	£33,540
	Rate between lower and upper profits limits	9 %	8 %	8 %	8 %	8 %	8 %
	Rate above upper profits limits	2 %	1 %	1 %	1 %	1 %	1 %

Note :
1. For the rates which apply when the employer's occupational pension scheme has **contracted out** see ¶5035.
2. For the rates which apply to **share fishermen** and **volunteer development workers,** see ¶5152.

Capital gains tax thresholds and rates

9978

Tax year	Annual exempt amount		Chattel exemption (max sale proceeds) [1]	Rate	
	Individuals, personal representatives [2], trusts for mentally disabled [3]	Other trusts [3]		Individuals [4,5]	Trustees and personal representatives [6]
	£	£	£	%	%
2011/12	10,600	5,300	6,000	10/18/28	28
2010/11	10,100	5,050	6,000	18/28	18/28
2009/10	10,100	5,050	6,000	18	18
2008/09	9,600	4,800	6,000	18	18
2007/08	9,200	4,600	6,000	10/20/40	40
2006/07	8,800	4,400	6,000	10/20/40	40
2005/06	8,500	4,250	6,000	10/20/40	40
2004/05	8,200	4,100	6,000	10/20/40	40

Note :

1. Where disposal proceeds exceed the exemption limit, marginal relief restricts any chargeable gain to 5/3 of the excess. Where there is a loss and the proceeds are less than £6,000, the proceeds are deemed to be £6,000.
2. For year of death and next 2 years.
3. If multiple trusts are created by the same settlor, each attracts relief equal to the annual amount divided by the number of such trusts (subject to a minimum of 10 % of the full annual amount).
4. Prior to 6 April 2008, gains were taxed as the top slice of income, 10 % to starting rate limit, 20 % to basic rate limit, and 40 % above, subject to tapering in certain cases. From 6 April 2008, taper relief was abolished and CGT was charged at 18 % on all chargeable gains after reliefs and exemptions, up until 23 June 2010. For gains arising on or after 23 June 2010 the rate charged will depend on the level of other income and gains. See ¶6330 for full details.
5. In 2011/12 the 10 % rate applies only to gains subject to entrepreneur's relief (¶6035).
6. Applicable to trustees of discretionary trusts and subject to a joint election with a vulnerable beneficiary (¶7388).

Retail prices index

9979

	Jan	Feb	Mar	Apr	May	June	July	Aug	Sept	Oct	Nov	Dec
1965	14.47	14.47	14.52	14.80	14.85	14.90	14.90	14.93	14.93	14.96	15.01	15.08
1966	15.11	15.11	15.13	15.34	15.44	15.49	15.41	15.51	15.49	15.51	15.61	15.64
1967	15.67	15.67	15.67	15.79	15.79	15.84	15.74	15.72	15.69	15.86	15.92	16.02
1968	16.07	16.15	16.20	16.50	16.50	16.58	16.58	16.60	16.63	16.70	16.76	16.96
1969	17.06	17.16	17.21	17.41	17.39	17.47	17.47	17.41	17.47	17.59	17.64	17.77
1970	17.90	18.00	18.10	18.38	18.43	18.48	18.63	18.61	18.71	18.91	19.04	19.16
1971	19.42	19.54	19.70	20.13	20.25	20.38	20.51	20.53	20.56	20.66	20.79	20.89
1972	21.01	21.12	21.19	21.39	21.50	21.62	21.70	21.88	22.00	22.31	22.38	22.48
1973	22.64	22.79	22.92	23.35	23.52	23.65	23.75	23.83	24.03	24.51	24.69	24.87
1974	25.35	25.78	26.01	26.89	27.28	27.55	27.81	27.83	28.14	28.69	29.20	29.63
1975	30.39	30.90	31.51	32.72	34.09	34.75	35.11	35.31	35.61	36.12	36.55	37.01
1976	37.49	37.97	38.17	38.91	39.34	39.54	39.62	40.18	40.71	41.44	42.03	42.59
1977	43.70	44.24	44.53	45.70	46.06	46.54	46.59	46.82	47.07	47.28	47.50	47.76
1978	48.04	48.31	48.62	49.33	49.61	49.99	50.22	50.54	50.75	50.98	51.33	51.76
1979	52.52	52.95	53.38	54.30	54.73	55.67	58.07	58.53	59.11	59.72	60.25	60.68
1980	62.18	63.07	63.93	66.11	66.72	67.35	67.91	68.06	68.49	68.92	69.48	69.86
1981	70.29	70.93	71.99	74.07	74.55	74.98	75.31	75.87	76.30	76.98	77.78	78.28
1982	78.73	78.76	79.44	81.04	81.62	81.85	81.88	81.90	81.85	82.26	82.66	82.51
1983	82.61	82.97	83.12	84.28	84.64	84.84	85.30	85.68	86.06	86.36	86.67	86.89
1984	86.84	87.20	87.48	88.64	88.97	89.20	89.10	89.94	90.11	90.67	90.95	90.87
1985	91.20	91.94	92.80	94.78	95.21	95.41	95.23	95.49	95.44	95.59	95.92	96.05
1986	96.25	96.60	96.73	97.67	97.85	97.79	97.52	97.82	98.30	98.45	99.29	99.62
1987	100.00	100.40	100.60	101.80	101.90	101.90	101.80	102.10	102.40	102.90	103.40	103.30
1988	103.30	103.70	104.10	105.80	106.20	106.60	106.70	107.90	108.40	109.50	110.00	110.30
1989	111.00	111.80	112.30	114.30	115.00	115.40	115.50	115.80	116.60	117.50	118.50	118.80
1990	119.50	120.20	121.40	125.10	126.20	126.70	126.80	128.10	129.30	130.30	130.00	129.90
1991	130.20	130.90	131.40	133.10	133.50	134.10	133.80	134.10	134.60	135.10	135.60	135.70
1992	135.60	136.30	136.70	138.80	139.30	139.30	138.80	138.90	139.40	139.90	139.70	139.20
1993	137.90	138.80	139.30	140.60	141.10	141.00	140.70	141.30	141.90	141.80	141.60	141.90
1994	141.30	142.10	142.50	144.20	144.70	144.70	144.00	144.70	145.00	145.20	145.30	146.00
1995	146.00	146.90	147.50	149.00	149.60	149.80	149.10	149.90	150.60	149.80	149.80	150.70
1996	150.20	150.90	151.50	152.60	152.90	153.00	152.40	153.10	153.80	153.80	153.90	154.40
1997	154.40	155.00	155.40	156.30	156.90	157.50	157.50	158.50	159.30	159.50	159.60	160.00
1998	159.50	160.30	160.80	162.60	163.50	163.40	163.00	163.70	164.40	164.50	164.40	164.40
1999	163.40	163.70	164.10	165.20	165.60	165.60	165.10	165.50	166.20	166.50	166.70	167.30
2000	166.60	167.50	168.40	170.10	170.70	171.10	170.50	170.50	171.70	171.60	172.10	172.20
2001	171.10	172.00	172.20	173.10	174.20	174.40	173.30	174.00	174.60	174.30	173.60	173.40
2002	173.30	173.80	174.50	175.70	176.20	176.20	175.90	176.40	177.60	177.90	178.20	178.50
2003	178.40	179.30	179.90	181.20	181.50	181.30	181.30	181.60	182.50	182.60	182.70	183.50
2004	183.10	183.80	184.60	185.70	186.50	186.80	186.80	187.40	188.10	188.60	189.00	189.90
2005	188.90	189.60	190.50	191.60	192.00	192.20	192.20	192.60	193.10	193.30	193.60	194.10
2006	193.40	194.20	195.00	196.50	197.70	198.50	198.50	199.20	200.10	200.40	201.10	202.70
2007	201.60	203.10	204.40	205.40	206.20	207.30	206.10	207.30	208.00	208.90	209.70	210.90
2008	209.80	211.40	212.10	214.00	215.10	216.80	216.50	218.40	217.20	217.70	216.00	212.90
2009	210.10	211.40	211.30	211.50	212.80	213.40	213.40	214.40	215.30	216.00	216.60	218.00
2010	218.00	219.20	220.70	222.80	223.60	224.10	223.60	224.50	225.30	225.80	226.80	228.40
2011	229.00	231.30	232.50	234.40	235.20	235.20						

Inheritance tax rates

9981

Tax years	Lifetime transfers				Death rates			
	Lower limit £	Rate of tax %	Upper limit £	Rate of tax %	Lower limit £	Rate of tax %	Upper limit £	Rate of tax %
2011/12	0-325,000	Nil	> 325,000	20	0-325,000	Nil	> 325,000	40
2010/11	0-325,000	Nil	> 325,000	20	0-325,000	Nil	> 325,000	40
2009/10	0-325,000	Nil	> 325,000	20	0-325,000	Nil	> 325,000	40
2008/09	0-312,000	Nil	> 312,000	20	0-312,000	Nil	> 312,000	40
2007/08	0-300,000	Nil	> 300,000	20	0-300,000	Nil	> 300,000	40
2006/07	0-285,000	Nil	> 285,000	20	0-285,000	Nil	> 285,000	40
2005/06	0-275,000	Nil	> 275,000	20	0-275,000	Nil	> 275,000	40
2004/05	0-263,000	Nil	> 263,000	20	0-263,000	Nil	> 263,000	40
2003/04	0-255,000	Nil	> 255,000	20	0-255,000	Nil	> 255,000	40
2002/03	0-250,000	Nil	> 250,000	20	0-250,000	Nil	> 250,000	40

Inheritance tax nil rate bands

9982

Tax year	Nil rate band (£)
2001/02	242,000
2000/01	234,000
1999/2000	231,000
1998/99	223,000
1997/98	215,000
1996/97	200,000
1995/96	154,000
1994/95	150,000
1993/94	150,000
1992/93	150,000
From 10 March 1992 to 5 April 1992	150,000
From 6 April 1991 to 9 March 1992	140,000
1990/91	128,000
1989/90	118,000
1988/89	110,000
From 15 March 1988 to 5 April 1988	110,000
From 17 March 1987 to 14 March 1988	90,000
From 18 March 1986 to 16 March 1987	71,000
From 6 April 1985 to 17 March 1986[1]	67,000
1984/85[1]	64,000
1983/84[1]	60,000
1982/83[1]	55,000
1981/82[1]	50,000
1980/81[1, 2]	50,000

Note :

1. Capital transfer tax applied in these years and the nil rate band is the appropriate threshold before any tax became due.

2. For deaths prior to 6 April 1980, HMRC publish the historic rates at http://www.hmrc.gov.uk/cto/customerguide/-page15.htm

Inheritance tax interest rates

Up to 28 September 2009, interest on **both overdue and overpaid** inheritance tax is applied at the rates shown below. Since 29 September 2009, the rate of interest on **overpaid** inheritance tax has been **reduced** to 0.5 %. 9983

Dates at which rates applicable	Chargeable transfers made on death or during life %	Days
From 29 September 2009	3	
From 24 March 2009 to 28 September 2009	0	189
27 January 2009 to 23 March 2009	1	56
6 January 2009 to 26 January 2009	2	21
6 November 2008 to 5 January 2009	3	61
6 January 2008 to 5 November 2008	4	304
6 August 2007 to 5 January 2008	5	153
6 September 2006 to 5 August 2007	4	334
6 September 2005 to 5 September 2006	3	365
6 September 2004 to 5 September 2005	4	365
6 December 2003 to 5 September 2004	3	275
6 August 2003 to 5 December 2003	2	122
6 November 2001 to 5 August 2003	3	638
6 May 2001 to 5 November 2001	4	184
6 February 2000 to 5 May 2001	5	455

Inheritance tax due dates of payment

9984

Month of death	Due date for payment of IHT	Interest starts from
January	31 July	1 August
February	31 August	1 September
March	30 September	1 October
April	31 October	1 November
May	30 November	1 December
June	31 December	1 January
July	31 January	1 February
August	28/29 February	1 March
September	31 March	1 April
October	30 April	1 May
November	31 May	1 June
December	30 June	1 July

VAT rates

9986

Period of application	Standard rate %	VAT fraction	Reduced rate %	VAT fraction
From 4 January 2011	20.0	1/6	5.0	1/21
From 1 January 2010 to 3 January 2011	17.5	7/47	5.0	1/21
1 December 2008 to 31 December 2009	15.0	3/23	5.0	1/21
1 April 1997 to 30 November 2008	17.5	7/47	5.0	1/21

VAT registration limits

9987

Taxable supplies

Past turnover			Future turnover [2] (£)
Period of application [1]	1 year (£)	Unless turnover for next year will not exceed (£)	30 days [3]
From 1 April 2011	73,000	71,000	73,000
From 1 April 2010	70,000	68,000	70,000
1 May 2009 to 31 March 2010	68,000	66,000	68,000
1 April 2008 to 30 April 2009	67,000	65,000	67,000
1 April 2007 to 31 March 2008	64,000	62,000	64,000
1 April 2006 to 31 March 2007	61,000	59,000	61,000
1 April 2005 to 31 March 2006	60,000	58,000	60,000
1 April 2004 to 31 March 2005	58,000	56,000	58,000
10 April 2003 to 31 March 2004	56,000	54,000	56,000
25 April 2002 to 9 April 2003	55,000	53,000	55,000
1 April 2001 to 24 April 2002	54,000	52,000	54,000

Note :
1. The period of application works so that if the trader exceeds the relevant threshold at any time within the relevant dates, he must register.
2. The value of taxable supplies at the zero rate and all positive rates are included.
3. A person is liable to register if there are reasonable grounds for believing that the value of his taxable supplies in the period of the next 30 days will exceed this limit.

Supplies from other member states – distance selling

Period of application	Cumulative relevant supplies in calendar year (£)
From 1 January 1993	70,000

Acquisitions from other member states

Period of application	Cumulative relevant acquisitions in calendar year (£)
From 1 April 2011	73,000
From 1 April 2010	70,000
1 May 2009 to 31 March 2010	68,000
1 April 2008 to 30 April 2009	67,000
1 April 2007 to 31 March 2008	64,000
1 April 2006 to 31 March 2007	61,000
1 April 2005 to 31 March 2006	60,000
1 April 2004 to 31 March 2005	58,000
10 April 2003 to 31 March 2004	56,000
25 April 2002 to 9 April 2003	55,000

VAT deregistration limits 9988

Taxable supplies

Period of application [1]	Future annual turnover [2] (£)
From 1 April 2011	71,000
From 1 April 2010	68,000
1 May 2009 to 31 March 2010	66,000
1 April 2008 to 30 April 2009	65,000
1 April 2007 to 31 March 2008	62,000
1 April 2006 to 31 March 2007	59,000
1 April 2005 to 31 March 2006	58,000
1 April 2004 to 31 March 2005	56,000
10 April 2003 to 31 March 2004	54,000
25 April 2002 to 9 April 2003	53,000
1 April 2001 to 24 April 2002	52,000

Note :
1.The period of application works so that if the trader does not exceed the relevant threshold at any time within relevant dates, he can deregister.
2. Where HMRC are satisfied this limit will not be exceeded in the period.

Supplies from other member states

Period of application	Past relevant supplies in last year to 31 December (£)	Future relevant supplies in immediately following year [1] (£)
From 1 January 1993	70,000	70,000

Note :
1. Where HMRC are satisfied this limit will not be exceeded in the period.

Acquisitions from other member states

Period of application	Past relevant acquisitions in last year to 31 December (£)	Future relevant acquisitions in immediately following year [1] (£)
From 1 April 2011	73,000	73,000
From 1 April 2010	70,000	70,000
1 May 2009 to 31 March 2010	68,000	68,000
1 April 2008 to 30 April 2009	67,000	67,000
1 April 2007 to 31 March 2008	64,000	64,000
1 April 2006 to 31 March 2007	61,000	61,000
1 April 2005 to 31 March 2006	60,000	60,000
1 April 2004 to 31 March 2005	58,000	58,000
10 April 2003 to 31 March 2004	56,000	56,000
25 April 2002 to 9 April 2003	55,000	55,000
1 April 2001 to 24 April 2002	54,000	54,000

Note :
1. Where HMRC are satisfied this limit will not be exceeded in the period.

VAT and indirect taxes default interest

9989

Period of application	Rate %
From 29 September 2009	3.0
24 March 2009 to 28 September 2009	2.5
27 January 2009 to 23 March 2009	3.5
6 January 2009 to 26 January 2009	4.5
6 December 2008 to 5 January 2009	5.5
6 November 2008 to 5 December 2008	6.5
6 January 2008 to 5 November 2008	7.5
6 August 2007 to 5 January 2008	8.5
6 September 2006 to 5 August 2007	7.5
6 September 2005 to 5 September 2006	6.5
6 September 2004 to 5 September 2005	7.5
6 December 2003 to 5 September 2004	6.5
6 August 2003 to 5 December 2003 [1]	5.5
6 November 2001 to 5 August 2003	6.5
6 May 2001 to 5 November 2001	7.5
6 February 2000 to 5 May 2001	8.5

Note :
1. The rate of interest applying to the period from 6 August 2003 to 5 December 2003 was retrospectively reduced in September 2005.

Interest on overpaid VAT and indirect taxes

9990

Period of application	Rate %
From 29 September 2009	0.5
27 January 2009 to 28 September 2009	0
6 January 2009 to 26 January 2009	1
6 December 2008 to 5 January 2009	2
6 November 2008 to 5 December 2008	3
6 January 2008 to 5 November 2008	4
6 August 2007 to 5 January 2008	5
6 September 2006 to 5 August 2007	4
6 September 2005 to 5 September 2006	3
6 September 2004 to 5 September 2005	4
6 December 2003 to 5 September 2004	3
6 August 2003 to 5 December 2003[1]	2
6 November 2001 to 5 August 2003	3
6 May 2001 to 5 November 2001	4
6 February 2000 to 5 May 2001	5

Note :
1. The rate of interest applying to the period from 6 August 2003 to 5 December 2003 was retrospectively reduced in September 2005.

Stamp duty land tax

Stamp duty land tax (SDLT) replaced ad valorem stamp duty for all land transactions with effect from 1 December 2003 (with the exception of certain partnership transactions until 22 July 2004). 9992

Rates of tax

The charge to SDLT is based on the slab system which provides that when the chargeable consideration exceeds a rate threshold, the higher rate applies to the whole consideration. Different rates apply depending on whether the land consists entirely of residential property, or includes land that is not residential property.

Residential property		Non-residential or mixed property	
Relevant consideration	**%**	**Relevant consideration**	**%**
Up to £125,000	0	Up to £150,000[1]	0
£125,001 to £250,000	1	£150,001 to £250,000	1
£250,001 to £500,000	3	£250,001 to £500,000	3
£500,001 to £1 million	4	More than £500,000	4
More than £1 million	5		

Note :
1. For transactions between 25 March 2010 and 24 March 2012 first-time buyers will not pay tax on properties under £250,000 (see ¶9376 for details).

Residential transactions with an effective date on or after 3rd September 2008 and before 3rd September 2009 were exempt from SDLT.

Leases

The consideration for a lease is usually in the form of a premium and rent, each of which requires separate SDLT calculations.

A **premium** is liable to the SDLT rates as shown above. There is no zero rate for a premium where the annual rent for the lease exceeds £600.

Rent requires a net present value calculation (¶9389) to be undertaken of all rental payments due under the lease agreement

To calculate the SDLT due, the following rates are then applied to the net present value, with the zero rate treated as a nil rate band.

Residential property		Non-residential or mixed property	
Relevant consideration	**%**	**Relevant consideration**	**%**
Not more than £125,000	0	Not more than £150,000	0
More than £125,000	1	More than £150,000	1

Stamp duty and SDRT

9993 From 1 December 2003, stamp duty only applies to stock transfers. (In addition, partnership land transactions were subject to stamp duty until 22 July 2004).

Stamp duty is rounded up to the nearest £5.

Rates of stamp duty

Stock transfers

Type of transfer	Rate of tax %
Agreements to transfer chargeable securities	0.5
Bearer instruments	1.5
Depositary receipts	1.5
Clearance services	1.5

SDRT

SDRT applies to transfers of stock and securities.

Type of transfer	Rate of tax %
Agreements to transfer chargeable securities	0.5
Depositary receipts	1.5
Clearance services	1.5
Unit trusts and open ended investment companies	0.5

Recognised stock exchanges

A recognised stock exchange for tax purposes is one which has been so designated by HMRC. 9995

The only recognised **UK exchange** is the London Stock Exchange.

The following is a list of countries with exchanges that have been designated as recognised stock exchanges. Unless otherwise specified, any stock exchange (or options exchange) in a country listed below is a recognised stock exchange for these purposes, provided it is recognised under the law of the country concerned relating to stock exchanges.

Country	Effective date
Australia	
Australian Stock Exchange and its stock exchange subsidiaries	22 September 1988
Austria [1]	22 October 1970
Bahamas	19 April 2010
Belgium [1]	22 October 1970
Bermuda	4 December 2007
Brazil	
Rio De Janeiro Stock Exchange	17 August 1995
Sao Paulo Stock Exchange	11 December 1995
Canada	
Any stock exchange prescribed for the purposes of the Canadian Income Tax Act	22 October 1970
Cayman Islands	4 March 2004
China	
Hong Kong – Any stock exchange recognised under Section 2A(1) of the Hong Kong Companies Ordinance	26 February 1971
Cyprus	22 June 2009
Denmark	
Copenhagen Stock Exchange	22 October 1970
Estonia	5 May 2010
Finland	
Helsinki Stock Exchange	22 October 1970
France [1]	22 October 1970
Germany [1]	5 August 1971
Greece	
Athens Stock Exchange	14 June 1993
Guernsey [1]	10 December 2002
Iceland	31 March 2006
Irish Republic [1]	22 October 1970
Italy [1]	3 May 1972
Japan [1]	22 October 1970
Korea	10 October 1994
Luxembourg [1]	21 February 1972
Malaysia	
Kuala Lumpur Stock Exchange	10 October 1994
Malta	29 December 2005
Mauritius	31 January 2011

Country	Effective date
Mexico	10 October 1994
Netherlands [1]	22 October 1970
New Zealand	22 September 1988
Norway [1]	22 October 1970
Poland	25 February 2010
Portugal [1]	21 February 1972
Russia	
Moscow Interbank Currency Exchange (MICEX)	5 January 2011
Singapore	30 June 1977
South Africa	
Johannesburg Stock Exchange	22 October 1970
The Bond Exchange of South Africa	16 April 2008
Spain [1]	5 August 1971
Sri Lanka	
Colombo Stock Exchange	21 February 1972
Sweden	
Stockholm Stock Exchange	16 July 1985
Switzerland	
Swiss Stock Exchange	12 May 1997
Thailand	10 October 1994
UK	6 April 1965
AIM	19 July 2007
United States	
Any stock exchange registered with the Securities and Exchange Commission as a national securities exchange [2]	22 October 1970
Nasdaq Stock Market [3]	10 March 1992

Note :
1. Any stock exchange that is a stock exchange within the meaning of the law of the country concerned relating to stock exchanges.
2. The term 'national securities exchange' does not include any local exchanges registered with the Securities and Exchange Commission.
3. As maintained through the facilities of the National Association of Securities Dealers Inc and its subsidiaries.

Recognised futures exchanges

The following is a list of exchanges that have been designated as recognised futures exchanges under s 288(6) TCGA 1992. 9996

Country	From tax year
Australia	
Sydney Futures Exchange	1988-89
Canada	
Montreal Exchange	1987-88
China	
Hong Kong Futures Exchange	1987-88
Sweden	
OM Stockholm	1991-92
United Kingdom	
International Petroleum Exchange of London	1985-86
London Gold Market	1985-86
London International Financial Futures and Options Exchange (LIFFE)	1991-92
London Metal Exchange	1985-86
London Silver Market	1985-86
OM London	1991-92
United States	
Chicago Board of Trade	1987-88
Chicago Mercantile Exchange	1986-87
Commodity Exchange (COMEX)	1988-89
Mid America Commodity Exchange	1987-88
New York Board of Trade [1]	[1]
New York Mercantile Exchange	1986-87
Philadelphia Board of Trade	1986-87

Note :
1. Formed by the merger of
- Citrus Associates of New York Cotton Exchange (1988-89) ;
- Coffee, Sugar and Cocoa Exchange, New York (1987-88) ; and
- New York Cotton Exchange (1988-89).

Alternative Finance Stock Exchanges

The following stock exchanges are designated as recognised stock exchanges for the purposes of alternative finance arrangements only. For alternative finance investment bonds to be treated as qualifying alternative finance arrangements, they must be listed on one of these exchanges. These stock exchanges are not designated as recognised stock exchanges for any other tax purposes.

Country	Exchange
United Arab Emirates	Abu Dhabi Stock Exchange
Bahrain	Bahrain Stock Exchange
United Arab Emirates	Dubai Financial Market
United Arab Emirates	Dubai International Financial Exchange
Malaysia	Labuan International Financial Exchange
Saudi Arabia	Saudi Stock Exchange (Tadawul)
Indonesia	Surabaya Stock Exchange

Official information

9997 The latest version of all official publications can be obtained from the following website addresses :

Source	Website address
HMRC	http://www.hmrc.gov.uk/leaflets/
DWP	www.dwp.gov.uk/publications/specialist-guides/
Pension Service	www.direct.gov.uk/en/Pensionsandretirementplanning/index.htm

The address to which an appeal must be sent is :
The Tribunals Service
Tax
2nd floor
54 Hagley Road
Birmingham
B16 8PE

Table of cases

A list of cases mentioned in *Tax Memo* is detailed below, in **alphabetical order,** together 9999
with the year of the case, the VTD number (if applicable) and the paragraph where the case appears in *Tax Memo*.

Case name	Year	VTD Number	¶¶
Agassi v Robinson	2006		¶4334
Anand v IRC	1997		¶6467
Ansell Computer Services Ltd v Richardson	2004		¶2996
Apple and Pear Development Council v C & E	1988		¶7766
Argos Distributors Ltd v C & E	1996		¶7980
Arkwright and another v IRC	2004		¶6474
Associated Restaurants Ltd v Warland	1988		¶281
Atherton v British Insulated and Helsby Cables Ltd	1925		¶117
Ball v Johnson	1971		¶3038
Barclays Bank Trust Co Ltd v IRC	1998		¶6724
Barnett v Brabyn	1996		¶2992
Beauty Consultants v HMIT	2002		¶186
Belgium v Ghent Coal Terminal NV	1998		¶8235
Ben-Odeco Ltd v Powlson	1978		¶214
Bennett v IRC	1995		¶6434
Bhatt v Bhatt	2009		¶6620
Bird v Martland	1982		¶3038
Birmingham and District Cattle By-Products Ltd v CIR	1919		¶2440
Blyth v Birmingham Waterworks Co	1856		¶9795
Boots plc v C & E	1990		¶7960, ¶7978
Bridport and West Dorset Golf Club Ltd	2011	TC01214	¶8050
British Airways plc v C & E	1990		¶7880
British Insulated and Helsby Cables v Atherton	1926		¶5229
Brown v Bullock	1961		¶3140
Brown v Burnley Football and Athletic Co Ltd	1980		¶150
BUPA Hospitals Ltd and Goldsborough Developments Ltd v HMRC	2006		¶7904
Burdge v Pyne	1968		¶78
Burmah Steamship Co Ltd v CIR	1931		¶131
C & E v Blom-Cooper	2003		¶7891
C & E v British Telecommunications plc	1996		¶7839
C & E v Dearwood	1986		¶8602
C & E v Jacobs	2005		¶8864
C & E v Redrow Group plc	1999		¶8180
C & E v UBAF Bank Ltd	1996		¶8244
C & E v Upton (t/a Fagomatic)	2001		¶8162
C J Anderson	2007	20255	¶8629

Case name	Year	VTD Number	¶¶¶¶
Cable & Wireless v Muscat	2006		¶3017
Calvert v Wainwright	1947		¶3038
Camille and Henry Dreyfus Foundation Inc v IRC	1956		¶6442
Card Protection Plan	1999		¶7878
Carlisle and Silloth Golf Club v Smith	1913		¶68
Carter v Sharon	1936		¶4218
Castle Construction (Chesterfield) Ltd v HMRC	2008		¶2991
Cerberus Software Ltd v Rowley	2001		¶3067
CIR v Barclay, Curle & Co Ltd	1969		¶283
CIR v Lysaght	1928		¶4158
Clark v IRC	1978		¶4048
College of Estate Management v HMRC	2005		¶7880
Collins v HMRC	2008		¶5304
Conde Naste v HMRC	2008		¶9225
Conservative & Unionist Central Office v Burrell	1982		¶14
Cooke v Beach Station Caravans Ltd	1974		¶281
Crompton v Reynolds and Gibson	1952		¶112
Crowe v Appleby	1975		¶7416
Crusader v HMRC	2007		¶5304
Dacas v Brook Street Bureau (UK) Ltd	2004		¶3008
Danfoss A/S and another v Skatteministeriet	2008		¶8150
David Baxendale Ltd v HMRC	2009		¶7880
DD Prenn	1979		¶7766
Debenhams plc v HMRC	2005		¶7880, ¶9244
Donaldson's Executors v CIR	1927		¶7335
Donnelly v Williamson	1982		¶3038
Dragonfly Consulting Ltd v HMRC	2008		¶3017
Drummond v Collins	1915		¶7335
Duke of Roxburghe's Executors v CIR	1936		¶4216
Edwards v Clinch	1981		¶2980
Elida Gibbs Ltd v C & E	1996		¶7984
Elm Milk Ltd v HMRC	2006		¶8162
Elson v Johnston (James G) Ltd	1965		¶132
Elwood v Utitz	1966		¶3140
EMI Group Electronics Ltd v Coldicott	1999		¶3067
Ernst & Young	1997	15100	¶8152
Fall v Hitchin	1972		¶2990
Family Golf Centres Ltd v Thorne	1998		¶283
Fetherstonhaugh and others v IRC	1984		¶6704
Financial & General Print Ltd	1995	13795	¶7839
Fitzwilliam v IRC	1993		¶6630
FJ Chalke Ltd & Anor v HMRC	2009		¶9264
Fleming t/a Bodycraft v HMRC	2008		¶9225
Furness v IRC	1999		¶6708
Garsington Opera	2009	TC00045	¶8208
Genovese v HMRC	2009		¶4160
Glantre Engineering v Goodhand	1983		¶3056
Glenboig Union Fireclay Ltd v CIR	1921		¶131

Case name	Year	VTD Number	¶¶¶¶
Graham v Green	1925		¶78
Grassby & Sons Ltd	1993	11423	¶8602
Great Western Rly Co v Bater	1920		¶2980
Green v Craven's Railway Carriage and Wagon Co Ltd	1951		¶116
Greenberg v IRC	1972		¶4044
Greycon Ltd v Klaentschi	2003		¶186
H G Retail Ltd	1998	15557	¶8602
Halifax and others v HMRC	2006		¶8135
Hall (Executors of Hall) v IRC	1997		¶6708
Hall v Lorimer	1994		¶2988, ¶2995
Hamblett v Godfrey	1987		¶3034
Hampton v Fortes Autogrill Ltd	1980		¶281
Harmel v Wright	1974		¶4208
Heaton v Bell	1969		¶3042
Henriksen v Grafton Hotel Ltd	1942		¶117
HMRC v Airtours Holiday Transport Ltd	2010		¶8180
HMRC v Debenhams Retail plc	2005		¶9244
HMRC v Grace	2008		¶4156
HMRC v IDT Card Services Ireland	2006		¶8018
HMRC v Livewire Telecom Ltd	2009		¶8186
HMRC v Messenger Leisure Developments Ltd	2005		¶8050
HMRC v Executors of Mrs Marjorie Edna Bower (Deceased)	2009		¶6500
HMRC v Taylor & Haimendorf	2010		¶2082
HMRC v Trustees of the Nelson Dance Family Settlement	2009		¶6705, ¶6724
HMRC v Trustees of the Peter Clay Discretionary Settlement	2009		¶7311
HMRC v William Grant and Sons Distillers Ltd	2007		¶157
Hochstrasser v Mayes	1960		¶3034, ¶3196
Holland (Holland's Executor) v IRC	2003		¶6440
Horner v Hasted	1995		¶3089
Hunt v Henry Quick	1992		¶281
HSBC Holdings plc and Vidacos Nominees Ltd v HMRC	2009		¶9669
Ingram v IRC	1999		¶6946
IRC v Aken	1990		¶76
IRC v Anchor International Ltd	2004		¶283
IRC v Brebner	1967		¶4048
IRC v George (Stedman Dec'd)	2004		¶6708
IRC v Kleinwort Benson Ltd	1969		¶4044
IRC v Lloyds Private Banking Ltd	1998		¶6386
IRC v Scottish and Newcastle Breweries	1982		¶281
IRC v Universities Superannuation Scheme Ltd	1996		¶4044
IRC v Wiggins	1979		¶4044
IRC v Willoughby	1997		¶4138
I/S Fini H v Skatteministeriet	2005		¶8295
J D Wetherspoon plc v HMRC	2007		¶214, ¶281

Case name	Year	VTD Number	¶¶¶¶
Jarmin v Rawlings	1994		¶6040
Jarrold v John Good & Sons Ltd	1962		¶281
JG Leigh (t/a Moor Lane Video)	1989	5098	¶7839, ¶7846
Jones v Garnett	2007		¶7353
Judge and another, personal representatives of Walden (deceased) v HMRC	2005		¶6386
King v Brindisco	1992		¶281
Kittel v Belgium	2006		¶8186
KPMG (No 2)	1997	14962	¶8152
Kuwait Petroleum (GB) Ltd v C & E	1999		¶7885
Ladler v Perry	1966		¶3038
Lady Foley v Fletcher	1858		¶2835
Lau v HMRC	2009		¶6620
Law Shipping Co Ltd v CIR	1923		¶146
Lawrence	[1995]	13092	¶8018
Lee v IRC	1941		¶4140
Leeds Permanent Building Society v Proctor	1982		¶281
Littlewoods Retail Ltd and others v HMRC	2010		¶9264
Liverpool Corn Trade Association Ltd v Monks	1926		¶68
Lloyds TSB Private Banking (personal representative of Rosemary Antrobus deceased) v Peter Twiddy	2005		¶6766
Lord Fisher v C & E	1981		¶7766
Lord Tollemache v CIR	1926		¶7335
Lord v Tustain	1993		¶4368
Lyle Dicker Grace	2011		¶4183, ¶4158
Mairs v Haughey	1993		¶3104
Mannion v Johnston	1988		¶6040
Mansworth v Jelley	2003		¶3400
Mark v Mark	2005		¶4152
Market Investigations Ltd v Minister of Social Security	1969		¶2993
Marks and Spencer plc v HMRC	2007		¶1569
Marks and Spencer plc v HMRC	2008		¶9227
Marren v Ingles	1980		¶5310
Marson v Morton	1986		¶56
McKnight v Sheppard	1999		¶126
McMeechan v Secretary of State for Employment	1997		¶3005
Midlands Co-operative Society Ltd v HMRC	2008		¶9895, ¶9264
Ministero dell'Economia e delle Finanze v Part Service Srl	2008		¶7882
Mol v Inspecteur der Invoerrechten en Accijnzen	1988		¶7840
Moore v Griffiths	1972		¶3038
Moorhouse v Dooland	1954		¶3038
Morris v HMRC	2006		¶3287
Morrisons Academy Boarding Houses Association v C & E	1978		¶7766
Mr & Mrs Sterling t/a Sally's Sandwich Bar and The Corner Cafe (Tooting) Ltd	2005		¶7788
National Westminster Bank plc and another v CIR	1994		¶9743

Case name	Year	VTD Number	¶¶¶¶
Naturally Yours Cosmetics Ltd v C & E	1989		¶7986
Odeon Associated Theatres Ltd v Jones	1971		¶146
Ogilvie v Kitton	1908		¶4272
O'Rourke v Binks	1992		¶5737 , ¶5830
Ounsworth v Vickers Ltd	1915		¶116
Owen v IRC	1949		¶6390
Page v Lowther	1983		¶4054
Parikh v Sleeman	1990		¶3142
Pearson and others v IRC	1980		¶7178, ¶7187
Pepper v Hart	1993		¶3248
Pertemps Recruitment Partnership Ltd v HMRC	2011		¶104
PN McCall & BJA Keenan (Personal Representatives of E McClean) v HMRC	2008		¶6708
Pook v Owen	1969		¶3142
Pritchard v Arundale	1971		¶3056
Prudential Assurance Co Ltd v HMRC	1992		¶9362
Purple Parking Ltd	2009	TC00118	¶7880
R (on the application of Federation of Technological Industries and others) v HMRC	2006		¶9332
R Gaines-Cooper v HMRC	2010		¶4183
Raja's Commercial College v Gian Singh	1976		¶2741
RCI Europe v Woods	2004		¶4988
RCI Europe v HMRC	2009		¶8796
Re Owen (deceased)	1949		¶6390
Re Sebright	1944		¶7224
Ready Mixed Concrete (South East) Ltd v Minister of Pensions and National Insurance	1968		¶2991
Richardson v Delaney	2001		¶3067
Richardson v HMRC	2009		¶7072
Ricketts v Colquhoun	1926		¶3136
Ridgeons Bulk Ltd v C & E	1994		¶7960
RLRE Tellmer Property	2009		¶7880
Rosser v IRC	2003		¶6752
Runham and Naramore	2011	TC00933	¶9439
Rutledge v CIR	1929		¶61
Rysaffe Trustee Co (CI) v IRC	2003		¶6927
Sabine v Lookers Ltd	1958		¶132
Samuel Jones and Co (Devonvale) Ltd v CIR	1951		¶150
SCA Packaging Ltd v HMRC	2007		¶3067
Schofield v R & H Hall Ltd	1974		¶283
Seaton Sands Ltd and others v C & E	1998		¶7842
Sempra Metals Ltd v HMRC	2007		¶9264
Shanks v CIR	1929		¶7335
Sharkey v Wernher	1955		¶2422
Shepherd v HMRC	2006		¶4180
Shilton v Wilmshurst	1991		¶3034, ¶3038
Shove v Dura Manufacturing Co Ltd	1941		¶116
Silva v Charnock	2002		¶3208

Case name	Year	VTD Number	¶¶¶¶
Skipton Building Society	2009	TC00146	¶8208
Smith v Abbott	1994		¶3142
Southwell v Savill Bros Ltd	1901		¶108
SPÖ Landesorganisation Kärnten	2009		¶7766
St Barbe Green and another v IRC	2005		¶6584
St Paul's Community Project Ltd v C & E	2004		¶7766
Staatssecretaris van Financiën v Arthur Anderson & Co	2005		¶8042
Sugarwhite v Budd	1988		¶4054
Taylor v Haimendorf	2010		¶2867
Telewest Communications plc and another v C & E	2005		¶7882
Templeton v Jacobs	1996		¶3244
Tennant v Smith	1892		¶3242
Thorn plc v C & E (No 2)	1998		¶7960
TK Fong	1977		¶7777
Tolsma v Inspecteur der Omzetbelasting Leeuwarden	1994		¶7838
Tron Theatre Ltd v C & E	1993		¶7842
Trustees of the Peter Clay Discretionary Settlement v HMRC	2009		¶7311
Tucker v Granada Motorway Services Ltd	1979		¶117
Usetech Ltd v Young	2004		¶3017
Van Arkadie v Sterling Coated Materials Ltd	1983		¶214
Vasili v Christensen	2004		¶3287
Walls v Livesey	1995		¶2470
Walsh v Randall	1940		¶4216, ¶4218
Weston v IRC	2000		¶6708
White v Higginbottom	1983		¶3191
Whitechapel Art Gallery	2008	20720	¶8145
Wilcock v Eve	1995		¶3038
Wilkins v Rogerson	1960		¶3038
Williams v IRC	1980		¶4044
Wilson v Clayton	2004		¶3065
Wimpey International Ltd v Warland	1988		¶281
Witzemann v Hauptzollamt Munchen-Mitte	1993		¶7900
Wood v Holden	2006		¶20
Zurich Insurance Company v HMRC	2007		¶8005

Index

Using the index

The numbers cross-refer to paragraphs. A list of abbreviations is given below.

ACT	Advance corporation tax
ANG	Application Note G
APD	Air passenger duty
CFC	Controlled foreign company
CGT	Capital gains tax
CITR	Community investment tax relief
CTSA	Corporation tax self assessment
EIS	Enterprise investment scheme
EMI	Enterprise management incentive scheme
IHT	Inheritance tax
LFT	Landfill tax
NIC	National Insurance contributions
OECD	Organisation for Economic Co-operation and Development
PAYE	Pay as you earn
PE	Permanent establishment
R & D	Research and development
SAYE	Save as you earn
SDLT	Stamp duty land tax
SDRT	Stamp duty reserve tax
VAT	Value added tax
VCT	Venture capital trust
WDA	Writing down allowance
WIP	Work in progress

B

E

F

M

N

Q

S

V

W

Y

Z

Composition réalisée par NORD COMPO

Achevé d'imprimer en septembre 2011
sur le presses de L.E.G.O. S.p.A., Lavis (TN)